BLUE PAGES
USA

New York London Toronto Sydney Tokyo Singapore

First Edition

Copyright © 1991 by General Information, Inc.
All rights reserved
including the right of reproduction
in whole or in part in any form

Prentice Hall General Reference
15 Columbus Circle
New York, NY 10023

An Arco Book

Prentice Hall and colophons are
registered trademarks of Simon & Schuster, Inc.

Manufactured in the United States of America

1 2 3 4 5 6 7 8 9 10

LC Number 91-28762

ISBN 0-13-094830-6

TABLE OF CONTENTS

HOW TO USE THIS DIRECTORY

WHAT KIND OF INFORMATION IS PROVIDED IN BLUE PAGES USA?

Blue Pages USA lists the most important organizations, institutions and government offices in the United States.

Each listing in *Blue Pages USA* consists of the official name, a telephone number, fax information (when available), street or mailing address, city, state and zip code. (Nine-digit zip codes have been provided when possible. Four zeros have been inserted at the end of a five-digit zip code if the nine-digit zip was unavailable. The four zeros should not be used for mailing.)

Approximately 14,000 fax numbers are included in the Alphabetical Section. Fax listings include an organization's direct facsimile number or extension, or instructions to call the organization's switchboard ("Call company operator") when special arrangements are needed in order to transmit a facsimile message.

This first edition of *Blue Pages USA* contains more than 20,000 unique listings appearing in both the alphabetical and classified sections of the book. Classified sections include:

ASSOCIATIONS AND ORGANIZATIONS:
- Chambers of commerce for each of the fifty states.
- Important government and military organizations.
- Major political parties and influential political action committees (PACs).
- Democratic and Republican party headquarters for each state.
- Important consumer affairs and social services organizations.

COLLEGES AND UNIVERSITIES:
- Every institution offering a four-year educational degree and many offering two-year degrees.
- Major graduate schools for selected disciplines.

GOVERNMENT:
- Toll-free phone numbers for every Federal Information Center.
- Important national and regional offices in the executive, judicial and legislative branches of the US federal government.
- Every US Senator and Representative in the 102nd Congress.
- Military installations selected by number of personnel.
- City government offices for the nation's largest cities (selected on basis of population).
- Every county, parish and independent city in the US.
- Important state government departments and offices for every state.

INTERNATIONAL:
- Major foreign chambers of commerce in the US.
- Every embassy and selected consulates in the US.
- Selected United Nations offices and agencies as well as every foreign mission to the UN.
- Selected agencies that foster international trade.

LIBRARIES AND MUSEUMS:
- Important state, local and university libraries and library system headquarters.
- Prestigious national, state and local museums.

TOLL-FREE NUMBERS:
- Useful toll-free phone numbers for many government and social services.

TRAVEL:
- Selected national and state agencies offering information on popular travel destinations.

Special features—such as Profiles of Top US Cities, the Area Code and Zip Code Guide, a Time Zone and Area Code Map, etc.—have been created to make *Blue Pages USA* even more useful.

We have also included a subject index at the end of the book to assist you in using *Blue Pages USA*.

HOW TO USE THIS DIRECTORY

HOW ACCURATE IS THE INFORMATION?

General Information, Inc.'s telephone research staff verified every listing in *Blue Pages USA* by phoning the main telephone number and confirming all the information for each listing. Names, addresses, phone numbers and fax numbers were updated during this process.

HOW DO I FIND WHAT I'M LOOKING FOR?

Blue Pages USA is arranged in two main sections: the Alphabetical Section and the Classified Section.

- The Alphabetical Section lists nearly every entity in the directory in alphabetical order, allowing you to easily find information on a specific organization, institution or government office.

- The Classified Section is organized by subject. This section allows you to identify numerous organizations in a specific category.

Listings in both the alphabetical and classified sections of *Blue Pages USA* are alphabetized on a word-by-word basis. A space between two words functions as a "letter" before the letter "a." Therefore, a listing for "San Saba County" will be listed before "Sanborn County." In this example, the space between "San" and "Saba" alphabetizes before the "b" in "Sanborn."

Listings composed of a first name (or initial) and surname—e.g., "Susan Molinari"—are listed last name first: "Molinari Susan." The customary rendering has been retained when "last-name-first" would be awkward or less useful, such as "George Washington University."

Footnotes at the bottom of some pages help explain how the listings in that section are organized. In some cases the data is alphabetized according to name, but grouped by state and city also, so you can locate organizations regionally.

On the title pages of the Alphabetical and Classified Sections, you will find additional information on the organization of listings in each section.

A comprehensive Table of Contents appears on page iii and a mini table of contents appears on the title page for each subsection of the Classified Section.

ABBREVIATIONS USED IN BLUE PAGES USA

Associates	Assoc	Lane	Ln
Association	Assn	Limited	Ltd
Avenue	Ave	Limited Partnership	LP
Avenues	Aves	Manufacturing	Mfg
Boulevard	Blvd	Mount	Mt
Building	Bldg	North	N
Causeway	Cswy	Northeast	NE
Center	Ctr	Northwest	NW
Circle	Cir	Park	Pk
Companies	Cos	Parkway	Pkwy
Company	Co	Place	Pl
Cooperative	Co-op	Road	Rd
Corporation	Corp	Roads	Rds
Court	Ct	Room	Rm
Department	Dept	Route	Rt
Division	Div	Routes	Rts
Doing business as	DBA	Rural Delivery	RD
Drive	Dr	Rural Route	RR
East	E	Saint	St
Expressway	Expy	South	S
Extension	Ext	Southeast	SE
Facsimile	Fax	Southwest	SW
Farm to Market Road	FM	Square	Sq
Floor	Fl	State Route	SR
Freeway	Fwy	Station	Stn
Freeways	Fwys	Street	St
Highway	Hwy	Streets	Sts
Highways	Hwys	Terrace	Terr
Incorporated	Inc	Turnpike	Tpke
Interstate	I-	West	W
Interstate Highway	IH-		

TIME ZONES & ABBREVIATIONS

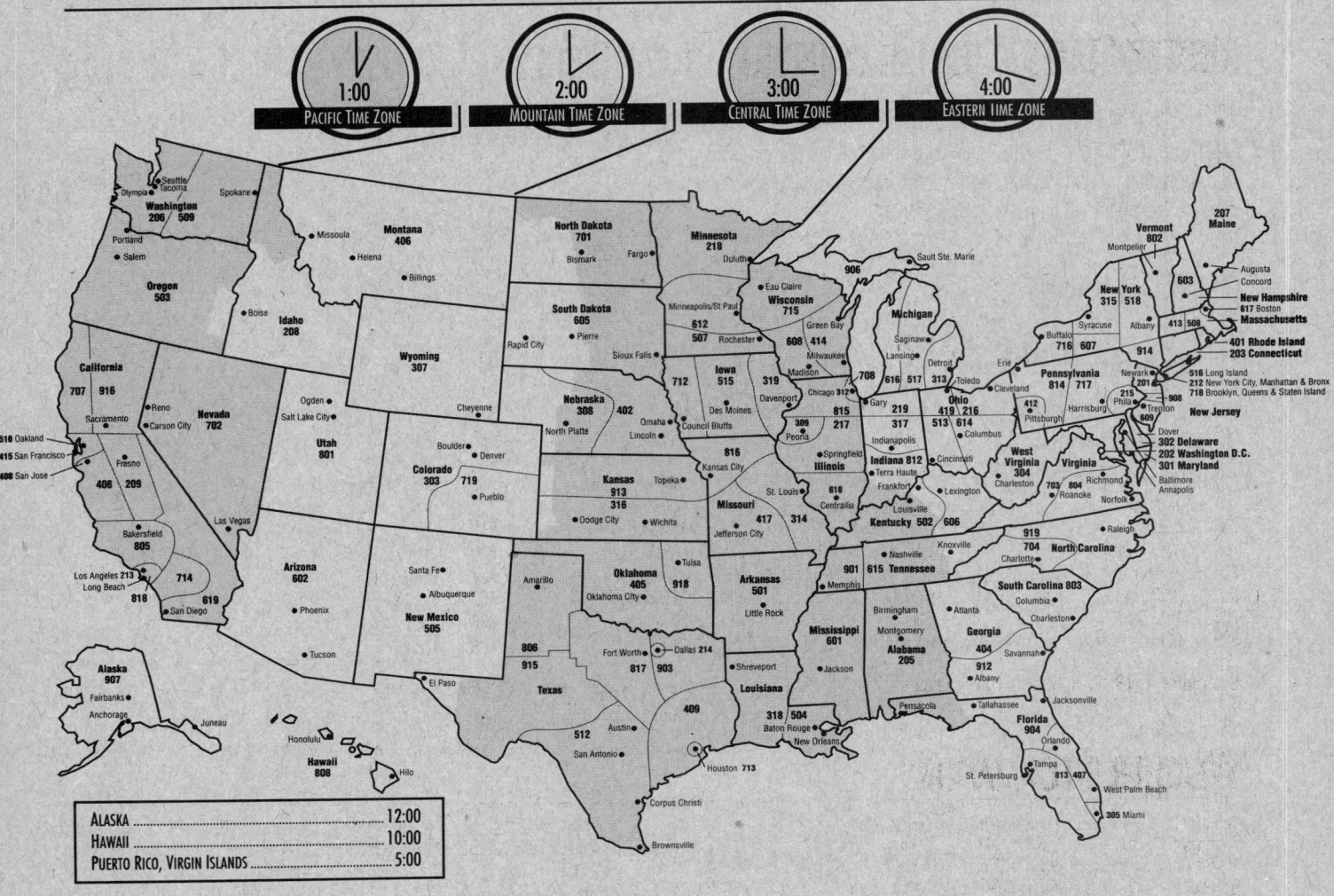

	1:00	2:00	3:00	4:00
	PACIFIC TIME ZONE	MOUNTAIN TIME ZONE	CENTRAL TIME ZONE	EASTERN TIME ZONE

ALASKA		12:00
HAWAII		10:00
PUERTO RICO, VIRGIN ISLANDS		5:00

TWO-LETTER STATE, POSSESSION AND PROVINCE ABBREVIATIONS

						Canadian
Alabama	AL	Kentucky	KY	Ohio	OH	**Province Abbreviations**
Alaska	AK	Louisiana	LA	Oklahoma	OK	
Arizona	AZ	Maine	ME	Oregon	OR	Alberta .... AB
Arkansas	AR	Maryland	MD	Pennsylvania	PA	British Columbia .... BC
California	CA	Massachusetts	MA	Puerto Rico	PR	Manitoba .... MB
Colorado	CO	Michigan	MI	Rhode Island	RI	New Brunswick .... NB
Connecticut	CT	Minnesota	MN	South Carolina	SC	Newfoundland .... NF
Delaware	DE	Mississippi	MS	South Dakota	SD	NW Territories .... NT
District of Columbia	DC	Missouri	MO	Tennessee	TN	Nova Scotia .... NS
Florida	FL	Montana	MT	Texas	TX	Ontario .... ON
Georgia	GA	Nebraska	NE	Utah	UT	Prince Edward Island .... PE
Guam	GU	Nevada	NV	Vermont	VT	Quebec .... PQ
Hawaii	HI	New Hampshire	NH	Virginia	VA	Saskatchewan .... SK
Idaho	ID	New Jersey	NJ	Virgin Islands	VI	Yukon Territory .... YT
Illinois	IL	New Mexico	NM	Washington	WA	
Indiana	IN	New York	NY	West Virginia	WV	
Iowa	IA	North Carolina	NC	Wisconsin	WI	
Kansas	KS	North Dakota	ND	Wyoming	WY	

AREA CODES & WEATHER

UNITED STATES AREA CODES IN NUMERICAL ORDER

201 ...... New Jersey	310 ..... California	502 ..... Kentucky	615 ..... Tennessee	805 ..... California
202 ..... District of Columbia	312 ..... Illinois	503 ..... Oregon	616 ..... Michigan	806 ..... Texas
203 ...... Connecticut	313 ..... Michigan	504 ..... Louisiana	617 ..... Massachusetts	808 ..... Hawaii
205 ..... Alabama	314 ..... Missouri	505 ..... New Mexico	618 ..... Illinois	809 ..... Puerto Rico & Virgin Isls
206 ...... Washington	315 ..... New York	507 ..... Minnesota	619 ..... California	812 ..... Indiana
207 ...... Maine	316 ..... Kansas	508 ..... Massachusetts	701 ..... North Dakota	813 ..... Florida
208 ..... Idaho	317 ..... Indiana	509 ..... Washington	702 ..... Nevada	814 ..... Pennsylvania
209 ...... California	318 ..... Louisiana	510 ..... California	703 ..... Virginia	815 ..... Illinois
212 ..... New York	319 ..... Iowa	512 ..... Texas	704 ..... North Carolina	816 ...... Missouri
213 ..... California	401 ..... Rhode Island	513 ..... Ohio	707 ..... California	817 ..... Texas
214 ..... Texas	402 ..... Nebraska	515 ..... Iowa	708 ...... Illinois	818 ..... California
215 ..... Pennsylvania	404 ..... Georgia	516 ..... New York	712 ..... Iowa	901 ..... Tennessee
216 ..... Ohio	405 ..... Oklahoma	517 ..... Michigan	713 ..... Texas	903 ..... Texas
217 ..... Illinois	406 ..... Montana	518 ..... New York	714 ..... California	904 ..... Florida
218 ..... Minnesota	407 ..... Florida	601 ..... Mississippi	715 ..... Wisconsin	906 ..... Michigan
219 ..... Indiana	408 ..... California	602 ..... Arizona	716 ..... New York	907 ..... Alaska
301 ..... Maryland	409 ..... Texas	603 ..... New Hampshire	717 ..... Pennsylvania	908 ..... New Jersey
302 ..... Delaware	412 ..... Pennsylvania	605 ..... South Dakota	718 ..... New York	912 ..... Georgia
303 ..... Colorado	413 ..... Massachusetts	606 ..... Kentucky	719 ..... Colorado	913 ..... Kansas
304 ..... West Virginia	414 ..... Wisconsin	607 ..... New York	800 ..... Toll-free: all states	914 ..... New York
305 ..... Florida	415 ..... California	608 ..... Wisconsin	801 ..... Utah	915 ..... Texas
307 ..... Wyoming	417 ..... Missouri	609 ..... New Jersey	802 ..... Vermont	916 ..... California
308 ..... Nebraska	419 ..... Ohio	612 ..... Minnesota	803 ..... South Carolina	918 ..... Oklahoma
309 ..... Illinois	501 ..... Arkansas	614 ..... Ohio	804 ..... Virginia	919 ..... North Carolina

On October 7, 1991 area code 510 will become effective in the San Francisco area. In November 1991 area code 310 will become effective in the Los Angeles area.

WEATHER INFORMATION

Akron, OH 216 869-8686	Concord, NH 603 225-3161	Long Beach, CA 213 554-1212	Reno, NV 702 793-1300
Albuquerque, NM 505 821-1111	Corpus Christi, TX 512 289-1861	Los Angeles, CA 213 554-1212	Richmond, VA 804 226-4423
Amarillo, TX 806 358-7755	Dallas, TX 214 787-1111	Louisville, KY 502 363-9655	Rochester, NY 716 235-0240
Anchorage, AK 907 936-2525	Dayton, OH 513 258-2000	Lubbock, TX 806 762-0141	Sacramento, CA 916 646-2000
Arlington, TX 817 787-1111	Denver, CO 303 398-3964	Madison, WI 608 249-6645	Saint Louis, MO 314 321-2222
Atlanta, GA 404 762-6151	Des Moines, IA 515 285-6906	Memphis, TN 901 756-4141	Saint Paul, MN 612 452-2323
Aurora, CO 303 337-2500	Detroit, MI 313 941-7192	Mesa, AZ 602 957-8700	Salt Lake City, UT 801 575-7669
Austin, TX 512 476-7736	El Paso, TX 915 778-9343	Miami, FL 305 661-5065	San Antonio, TX 512 828-0683
Baltimore, MD 301 936-1212	Fort Wayne, IN 219 747-0576	Milwaukee, WI 414 936-1212	San Diego, CA 619 289-1212
Baton Rouge, LA 504 355-0368	Fort Worth, TX 817 787-1700	Minneapolis, MN 612 452-2323	San Francisco, CA 415 936-1212
Birmingham, AL 205 945-7000	Fresno, CA 209 442-1212	Mobile, AL 205 478-6666	San Jose, CA 415 364-7974
Bismarck, ND 701 223-3700	Grand Rapids, MI 616 776-1234	Montgomery, AL 205 262-6800	Seattle, WA 206 526-6087
Boise, ID 208 342-8303	Great Falls, MT 406 453-5469	Nashville, TN 615 244-9393	Shreveport, LA 318 635-7575
Boston, MA 617 567-4670	Hartford, CT 203 936-1212	New Orleans, LA 504 465-9212	Sioux Falls, SD 605 330-4444
Buffalo, NY 716 634-1615	Houston, TX 713 228-8703	New York, NY 212 976-1212	Spokane, WA 509 624-8905
Burlington, VT 802 862-2475	Huntington Beach, CA 714 536-9303	Newark, NJ 201 624-8118	Stockton, CA 209 982-1793
Charleston, WV 304 345-2121	Indianapolis, IN 317 222-2362	Norfolk, VA 804 666-1212	Syracuse, NY 315 457-9000
Charlotte, NC 704 359-8466	Jackson, MS 601 936-2121	Oakland, CA 415 936-1212	Tampa, FL 813 645-2506
Chattanooga, TN 615 855-6490	Jacksonville, FL 904 741-4110	Oklahoma City, OK 405 360-8106	Tucson, AZ 602 881-3333
Cheyenne, WY 307 635-9901	Jersey City, NJ 201 624-8118	Omaha, NE 402 392-1111	Tulsa, OK 918 743-3311
Chicago, IL 708 298-1413	Kansas City, KS 913 384-6600	Philadelphia, PA 215 936-1212	Washington, DC 202 936-1212
Cincinnati, OH 513 241-1010	Kansas City, MO 816 531-4444	Phoenix, AZ 602 957-8700	Wichita, KS 316 942-3102
Cleveland, OH 216 931-1212	Knoxville, TN 615 970-2417	Pittsburgh, PA 412 936-1212	Wilmington, DE 302 429-9000
Colorado Springs, CO 719 596-1116	Las Vegas, NV 702 734-2010	Portland, ME 207 775-7781	Worcester, MA 508 752-1046
Columbia, SC 803 822-8135	Lexington, KY 606 233-1541	Portland, OR 503 236-7575	
Columbus, GA 205 298-0000	Lincoln, NE 402 477-6005	Providence, RI 401 738-1211	
Columbus, OH 614 841-2222	Little Rock, AR 501 371-7777	Raleigh, NC 919 860-1234	

PROFILES OF TOP U.S. CITIES

Albuquerque
NEW MEXICO   505

Important Phone Numbers

AAA	505 291-6611	Emergency	911
American Express	505 255-5558	Poison Control Center	505 843-2551
Better Business Bureau	505 884-0500	Time/Temp	505 247-1611
City Hall	505 768-2000	Weather	505 821-1111

■ Travel Information

505 764-3700 **Chamber of Commerce** 401 2nd St NW .... Albuquerque NM 87102-2203
505 243-3696 **Convention & Visitors Bureau** 625 Silver Ave SW .... Albuquerque NM 87102-3123

Travel

■ Airport

505 842-4366 **Albuquerque International Airport** 5 miles N of downtown (approx 10 minutes)

■ Airport Transportation

505 982-4311 **Shuttlejack** $20 fare to downtown
505 843-9200 **Sun Tran Bus Service** $.60 fare to downtown
              Taxi $7-9 fare to downtown

■ Scheduled Airlines

America West	505 247-0737	Southwest	505 831-1221
American	505 242-9464	TWA	505 842-4010
Continental	505 842-8220	United	800 241-6522
Delta	505 243-2794	USAir	505 243-8461
Mesa	505 326-3338		

■ Charter Airlines

Cutter Flying Service Inc	505 842-4184	Seven Bar Flying Services	505 842-4949
Mesa	505 326-3338		

■ Car Rentals

Alamo	505 842-4057	Hertz	505 842-4235
American International	505 243-1899	National	505 842-4222
Avis	505 842-4080	Rent-A-Wreck	505 256-9693
Budget	505 884-2666	Rich Ford Rent-A-Car	505 247-9255
Enterprise	505 764-9100	Thrifty	505 842-8733

■ Limo/Taxi

Albuquerque Cab	505 883-4888	Dream Limousine	505 884-6464
At Last the Past	505 298-9944	Yellow Cab	505 247-8888

■ Mass Transit

505 843-9200 **Sun Tran Bus Service** $.60 Base fare .... Albuquerque NM 87106-0000

■ Rail/Bus

505 842-9650 **Albuquerque Station** 314 1st St SW .... Albuquerque NM 87102-3405
505 243-4435 **Greyhound/Trailways Bus Station** 300 2nd St SW .... Albuquerque NM 87102-3394

Hotels

505 247-3344 **Albuquerque Doubletree Hotel** 201 Marquette Ave NW ...... Albuquerque NM 87102-2248
505 884-2500 **Albuquerque Hilton Inn** 1901 University Blvd NE .... Albuquerque NM 87102-1713
505 843-7000 **Amfac Hotel** 2910 Yale Blvd SE .... Albuquerque NM 87106-4231
505 255-5566 **Barcelona Court All-Suite Hotel** 900 Louisiana Blvd NE ..... Albuquerque NM 87110-7009
505 883-5252 **Best Western Winrock Inn** 18 Winrock Ctr .... Albuquerque NM 87110-0000
505 888-3311 **Clarion Four Seasons Hotel** 2500 Carlisle Blvd NE .... Albuquerque NM 87110-3808
505 247-1501 **El Centro Plaza Hotel** 717 Central Ave NW .... Albuquerque NM 87102-3007
505 821-3333 **Holiday Inn Pyramid** 5151 San Francisco Rd NE .... Albuquerque NM 87109-4641
505 821-9451 **Howard Johnson Plaza Hotel**
              6000 Pan American East Fwy NE .... Albuquerque NM 87109-3431
505 884-0250 **Le Baron Inn & Suites** 2120 Menaul Blvd NE .... Albuquerque NM 87107-1713
505 881-6800 **Marriott Hotel** 2101 Louisiana Blvd NE .... Albuquerque NM 87110-5478
505 247-0512 **Radisson Inn Albuquerque Airport**
              1901 University Blvd SE .... Albuquerque NM 87106-3928
505 881-0000 **Ramada Hotel** 6815 Menaul Blvd NE .... Albuquerque NM 87110-3623
505 265-3585 **Royal Motor Hotel** 4119 Central Ave NE .... Albuquerque NM 87108-1160

Restaurants

505 296-8822 **County Line of Albuquerque**
              (American) 9600 Tramway Blvd NE .... Albuquerque NM 87122-0000
505 292-3473 **Firehouse Restaurant**
              (Seafood/Steak) 10 Tramway Loop NE .... Albuquerque NM 87122-2017
505 843-7270 **Indian Pueblo Cultural Center**
              (American Indian) 2401 12th St NW .... Albuquerque NM 87102-0000
505 884-8937 **Japanese Kitchen** (Japanese) 12 Winrock Ctr .... Albuquerque NM 87110-0000
505 821-6279 **Le Marmiton** (French) 5415 Academy Rd NE .... Albuquerque NM 87109-3301

505 242-3900 **Maria Teresa Restaurant**
              (Mexican/American) 618 Rio Grande Blvd NW .... Albuquerque NM 87104-2004
505 255-2424 **Monte Vista Restaurant**
              (Nouvelle American) 3201 Central Ave NE .... Albuquerque NM 87106-0000
505 897-3131 **Rancho de Corrales** (Mexican) 4895 Corrales Rd .... Corrales NM 87048-0000
505 243-6111 **Rio Grande Yacht Club** (Continental) 2500 Yale Blvd SE ..... Albuquerque NM 87106-4274
505 821-0020 **Seagull Street Restaurant**
              (Seafood) 5410 Academy Rd NE .... Albuquerque NM 87109-3302
505 242-9996 **Smiroll's International Cuisine**
              (Continental) 108 Rio Grande Blvd NW .... Albuquerque NM 87104-1445
505 764-9665 **Wool Warehouse Theatre Restaurant**
              (Continental) 518 1st St NW .... Albuquerque NM 87102-2304

Goods & Services

■ Department Stores

505 881-4600 **Coronado Center** 1100 Coronado Ctr NE .... Albuquerque NM 87110-0000
505 265-6931 **Kistler-Collister** 1100 San Mateo Blvd NE .... Albuquerque NM 87110-6473

■ Banks

505 765-4000 **First National Bank in Albuquerque** 3rd & Tijeras NW .... Albuquerque NM 87103-0000
505 765-2211 **Sunwest Bank of Albuquerque NA** 303 Roma Ave NW ..... Albuquerque NM 87102-2263
505 765-5000 **United New Mexico Bank at Albuquerque**
              200 Lomas Blvd NW .... Albuquerque NM 87102-2258

■ Messenger/Postal

Federal Express	800 238-5355	UPS	505 344-1100
Mail & Parcel Express	505 242-8181	Vince's Delivery Service	505 266-1515
Paper Taker	505 296-6242		

■ Secretarial/Temp Services

505 884-4557 **Accountemps** 2155 Louisiana NE Suite 8200 .... Albuquerque NM 87110-0000
505 888-4545 **ADIA–The Employment People**
              2900 Louisiana NE Suite G1 .... Albuquerque NM 87110-0000
505 265-5881 **Kelly Temporary Services Inc**
              1128 Pennsylvania St NE Suite 220 .... Albuquerque NM 87110-7417
505 888-4700 **Manpower Temporary Services** 3655 Carlisle NE .... Albuquerque NM 87110-1644

Media

■ Newspapers/Magazines

505 823-7777 **Albuquerque Journal** 7777 Jefferson St NE .... Albuquerque NM 87109-4360
505 255-4648 **Albuquerque Monthly** 7911 Mountain Rd NE .... Albuquerque NM 87110-7804
505 823-7777 **Albuquerque Tribune** 7777 Jefferson St NE .... Albuquerque NM 87109-4361

■ Television

505 243-2285 **KGGM-TV Ch 13 (CBS)** 13 Broadcast Plaza SW .... Albuquerque NM 87104-1056
505 836-6585 **KNAT-TV Ch 23** 1510 Coors Blvd NW .... Albuquerque NM 87121-1152
505 277-2121 **KNME-TV Ch 5 (PBS)** 1130 University Blvd NE .... Albuquerque NM 87102-1702
505 884-7777 **KOAT-TV Ch 7 (ABC)** 3801 Carlisle Blvd NE .... Albuquerque NM 87107-4530
505 243-4411 **KOB-TV Ch 4 (NBC)** 1430 Coal Ave SW .... Albuquerque NM 87104-1005

■ Radio

505 243-1744 **KABQ-AM 1350 kHz (Span)**
              1400 Central Ave SE Suite 2200 .... Albuquerque NM 87106-0000
505 828-1600 **KFMG-FM 107.9 MHz (AOR-ABC)**
              5700 Harper Dr NE Suite 290 .... Albuquerque NM 87109-3584
505 262-2631 **KHFM-FM 96.3 MHz (Clas)** 5900 Domingo Rd NE .... Albuquerque NM 87108-1721
505 243-4411 **KKOB-AM 770 kHz (AC-ABC)** 77 Broadcast Plaza SW ...... Albuquerque NM 87104-1056
505 243-4411 **KKOB-FM 93.3 MHz (AC-ABC)** 1430 Coal Ave SW .... Albuquerque NM 87104-1005
505 884-5778 **KRST-FM 92.3 MHz (Ctry)** 2400 Monroe St NE .... Albuquerque NM 87110-4063
505 277-4806 **KUNM-FM 89.9 MHz (Misc-NPR)**
              Onate Hall University of New Mexico .... Albuquerque NM 87131-0001

Local Attractions & Special Events

■ Sports

505 243-1791 **Albuquerque Dukes** 1601 Stadium Blvd SE .... Albuquerque NM 87106-3930

■ Special Events

505 243-3696 **Albuquerque International Balloon Fiesta** (October 5-13)

■ Local Attractions

505 867-5351 **Coronado State Monument** SR-44 .... Albuquerque NM 87004-0000
505 843-7270 **Indian Pueblo Cultural Center** 2401 12th St NW .... Albuquerque NM 87102-0000
505 845-6670 **National Atomic Museum**
              Kirtland Air Force Base Bldg 20358 .... Albuquerque NM 87115-0000
505 841-8837 **New Mexico Museum of Natural History**
              1801 Mountain Rd NW .... Albuquerque NM 87104-1375
505 842-9566 **Old Town** 323 Romero NW .... Albuquerque NM 87104-0000
505 897-8814 **Petroglyph City Park** 6900 Unscer Dr NW .... Albuquerque NM 87124-0000
505 344-7240 **Rio Grande Nature Center** 2901 Candelaria Rd NE .... Albuquerque NM 87107-0000
505 298-8518 **Sandia Peak Tramway** Tramway Rd .... Albuquerque NM 87124-0000
505 281-5233 **Turquoise Trail** N SR-14 & Hwy 536 .... Sandia Park NM 87047-0000

Atlanta

GEORGIA 404

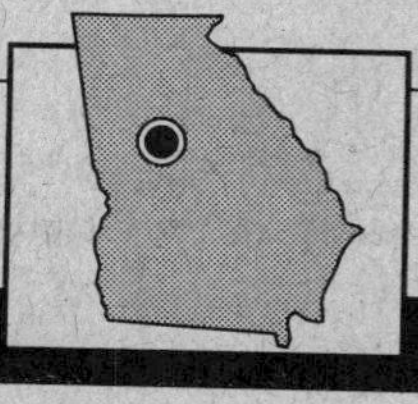

Important Phone Numbers

AAA	404 843-4500
American Express	404 262-7561
Better Business Bureau	404 688-4910
City Hall	404 330-6000
Emergency	911
Poison Control Center	404 589-4400
Time	404 455-7141
Weather	404 762-6151

■ Travel Information

404 880-9000	**Chamber of Commerce** 235 International Blvd NW	Atlanta	GA	30303-2718
404 521-6600	**Convention & Visitors Bureau** 233 Peachtree St NE Suite 2000	Atlanta	GA	30303-1508

Travel

■ Airport

404 530-6600 **Hartsfield Atlanta International Airport** 10 miles S of city (approx 20 minutes)

■ Airport Transportation

404 525-2177 **Airport Shuttle** $7 fare to downtown
404 455-1600 **Northside Airport Express** Fare varies with destination
Taxi $13.50 fare to downtown

■ Scheduled Airlines

Air Jamaica	800 523-5585
American	404 521-2655
British Airways	800 247-9297
Cayman	800 422-9626
Delta	404 765-5000
Eastern	404 435-1111
Japan	404 521-1616
KLM	800 777-5553
Lufthansa	800 645-3880
Midwest Express	800 452-2022
Northwest	800 225-2525
Pan Am	800 221-1111
Sabena	800 955-2000
SwissAir	404 859-1400
TWA	404 522-5738
United	800 241-6522
USAir	404 681-3100

■ Charter Airlines

Epps Air Service Inc	404 458-9851
Flight Services	404 455-3456

■ Car Rentals

Alamo	404 763-5205
Automate	404 231-1650
Avis	404 530-2700
Budget	404 530-3000
Capital Automobile Co	404 952-2277
Enterprise	404 261-7337
General	404 763-2035
Hertz	404 530-2925
National	404 530-2800
Thrifty	404 761-5286

■ Limo/Taxi

A-1 Limousine Service	404 299-2388
Carey Limousine	404 681-3366
Checker Cab	404 351-1111
Yellow Cab	404 521-0200

■ Mass Transit

404 848-4711	**MARTA** $.85 Base fare	Atlanta	GA	30324-0000

■ Rail/Bus

404 881-3060	**Brookwood Station** 1688 Peachtree St NW	Atlanta	GA	30309-2411
404 522-6300	**Greyhound/Trailways Bus Station** 81 International Blvd	Atlanta	GA	30303-0000

Hotels

404 767-7451	**Atlanta Airport North Hotel** 1200 Virginia Ave	Atlanta	GA	30344-5212
404 659-2000	**Atlanta Hilton & Towers Hotel** 255 Courtland St NE	Atlanta	GA	30303-1214
404 521-0000	**Atlanta Marriott Marquis** 265 Peachtree Center Ave NE	Atlanta	GA	30303-1208
404 892-6000	**Colony Square Hotel** 188 14th St NE	Atlanta	GA	30361-0001
404 523-1144	**Days Inn Downtown** 300 Spring St NW	Atlanta	GA	30308-3000
404 762-5141	**Harley Hotel Atlanta** 3601 N Desert Dr	Atlanta	GA	30344-5789
404 659-2727	**Holiday Inn Downtown** 175 Piedmont Ave NE	Atlanta	GA	30303-1708
404 659-2660	**Howard Johnson Plaza** 70 Houston St NE	Atlanta	GA	30303-2430
404 577-1234	**Hyatt Regency Atlanta** 265 Peachtree St NE	Atlanta	GA	30303-1204
404 395-1234	**Hyatt Regency Ravinia** 4355 Ashford-Dunwoody Rd NE	Atlanta	GA	30346-1521
404 577-6970	**Inn at the Peachtree** 330 W Peachtree St NW	Atlanta	GA	30308-3517
404 955-3838	**Marriott Courtyard at Windy Hill** 2045 S Park Pl NW	Atlanta	GA	30339-2014
404 659-0000	**Omni Hotel at CNN Center** 100 CNN Ctr	Atlanta	GA	30335-0001
404 659-6500	**Radisson Hotel Atlanta** 165 Courtland St NE	Atlanta	GA	30303-1750
404 659-0400	**Ritz-Carlton Atlanta** 181 Peachtree St NE	Atlanta	GA	30303-1744
404 237-2700	**Ritz-Carlton Buckhead** 3434 Peachtree Rd NE	Atlanta	GA	30326-1114
404 261-9250	**Terrace Garden Inn** 3405 Lenox Rd NE	Atlanta	GA	30326-1389
404 659-1400	**Westin Peachtree Plaza Hotel** 210 Peachtree St NW	Atlanta	GA	30303-1745

Restaurants

404 233-5993	**103 West Restaurant** (Continental) 103 W Paces Ferry Rd	Atlanta	GA	30305-1393
404 876-8532	**Abbey** (Continental) 163 Ponce De Leon Ave NE	Atlanta	GA	30308-1941
404 261-8186	**Abruzzi** (Italian) 2355 Peachtree Rd	Atlanta	GA	30305-0000
404 262-7379	**Anthony's** (Continental) 3109 Piedmont Rd NE	Atlanta	GA	30305-2531
404 436-5218	**Aunt Fanny's Cabin** (Southern) 2155 Campbell Rd	Smyrna	GA	30080-3814
404 237-9939	**Azalea** (American) 3167 Peachtree Rd	Atlanta	GA	30305-0000
404 237-2663	**Bone's Steak & Seafood** (American) 3130 Piedmont Rd NE	Atlanta	GA	30305-2508
404 262-3336	**Buckhead Diner** (American) 3073 Piedmont Rd NE	Atlanta	GA	30305-2625
404 262-2675	**Chops** (Steak/Seafood) 70 W Paces Ferry Rd	Atlanta	GA	30305-0000
404 872-6666	**Coach & Six Restaurant** (Steak/Seafood) 1776 Peachtree St NW	Atlanta	GA	30309-2304
404 457-6788	**First China** (Chinese) 5295 Buford Hwy NE	Doraville	GA	30340-1106
404 458-0558	**Gojinka** (Japanese) 5269 Buford Hwy NE	Doraville	GA	30340-0000
404 233-7673	**Hedgerose Heights Inn** (Continental) 490 E Paces Ferry Rd NE	Atlanta	GA	30305-3301
404 231-1368	**La Grotta** (Northern Italian) 2637 Peachtree Rd NE	Atlanta	GA	30305-3607
404 266-1799	**Le Crocodile** (Nouvelle) 2974 Grandview Ave NE	Atlanta	GA	30305-3214
404 659-2000	**Nikolai's Roof** (Continental/Russian) 255 Courtland St NE	Atlanta	GA	30303-1214
404 435-4215	**Old South Bar-B-Que** (American) 601 Burbank Cir	Smyrna	GA	30080-1819
404 261-3662	**Pano's & Paul's** (Continental) 1232 W Paces Ferry Rd NW	Atlanta	GA	30327-2319
404 525-8228	**Pittypat's Porch** (Southern) 25 International Blvd	Atlanta	GA	30303-0000
404 875-8424	**Veni-Vidi-Vici** (Italian) 41 14th St	Atlanta	GA	30309-0000

Goods & Services

■ Department Stores

404 221-7221	**Macy's** 180 Peachtree St NW	Atlanta	GA	30303-1725
404 266-8200	**Neiman-Marcus** 3393 Peachtree Rd NE	Atlanta	GA	30326-1178
404 586-4200	**Rich's** 45 Broad St SW	Atlanta	GA	30303-3162

■ Banks

404 529-4111	**Bank South NA** 55 Marietta St NW	Atlanta	GA	30303-2807
404 332-5000	**First National Bank of Atlanta** 2 Peachtree St	Atlanta	GA	30383-0001
404 588-7711	**Trust Co Bank** 25 Park Pl NE	Atlanta	GA	30303-2900

■ Messenger/Postal

Any Time Service	404 763-0142
Central Delivery Service	404 892-1350
Courier Dispatch of Georgia	404 767-7930
Dependable Courier Service	404 763-1100
Executive Courier	404 249-9000
Federal Express	404 321-7566
Georgia Messenger Service	404 681-3278
MLQ Express	404 350-3000
Sonic Delivery	404 763-3400
UPS	404 432-9494

■ Secretarial/Temp Services

404 659-2476	**Kelly Services Inc** 229 Peachtree St NE Suite 604	Atlanta	GA	30303-1601
404 659-3565	**Manpower Temporary Services Inc** 260 Peachtree St NE Suite 900	Atlanta	GA	30303-0000
404 659-6111	**Olsten Temporary Services** 229 Peachtree St NE Suite 901	Atlanta	GA	30303-1605

Media

■ Newspapers/Magazines

404 526-5151	**Atlanta Constitution** 72 Marietta St NW	Atlanta	GA	30303-2804
404 526-5151	**Atlanta Journal** 72 Marietta St NW	Atlanta	GA	30303-2804
404 872-3100	**Atlanta Magazine** 1360 Peachtree St NE Suite 1800	Atlanta	GA	30309-3214

■ Television

404 875-5551	**WAGA-TV Ch 5 (CBS)** PO Box 4207	Atlanta	GA	30302-4207
404 827-8900	**WPBA-TV Ch 30 (PBS)** 740 Bismark Rd NE	Atlanta	GA	30324-4136
404 897-7000	**WSB-TV Ch 2 (ABC)** 1601 W Peachtree St NE	Atlanta	GA	30309-2641
404 892-1611	**WXIA-TV Ch 11 (NBC)** 1611 W Peachtree St NE	Atlanta	GA	30309-2664

■ Radio

404 827-8900	**WABE-FM 90.1 MHz (Clas)** 740 Bismark Rd NE	Atlanta	GA	30324-4136
404 955-0101	**WKHX-AM 590 kHz (Ctry-ABC)** 360 Interstate North Pkwy NW Suite 101	Atlanta	GA	30339-2204
404 325-0960	**WKLS-FM 96.1 MHz (AOR-ABC)** 1800 Century Blvd NE	Atlanta	GA	30345-3201
404 261-9500	**WPCH-FM 95 MHz (B/EZ-CBS)** 550 Pharr Rd NE Suite 400	Atlanta	GA	30363-0001
404 897-7500	**WSB-FM 98.5 MHz (AC-ABC)** 1601 W Peachtree St NE	Atlanta	GA	30309-2641
404 898-8900	**WVEE-FM 103.3 MHz (UC)** 120 Ralph McGill Blvd Suite 1000	Atlanta	GA	30365-0001

Local Attractions & Special Events

■ Sports

404 522-7630	**Atlanta Braves** 521 Capitol Ave SW Fulton County Stadium	Atlanta	GA	30312-2896
404 261-5400	**Atlanta Falcons** 521 Capitol Ave SW Atlanta-Fulton County Stadium	Atlanta	GA	30312-2896
404 827-3865	**Atlanta Hawks** Omni Coliseum	Atlanta	GA	30303-0000
404 946-4211	**Atlanta International Raceway Inc** Hwys 19 & 41	Hampton	GA	30228-0000

■ Local Attractions

404 658-7625	**Atlanta Cyclorama** 800 Cherokee Ave SE	Atlanta	GA	30315-1440
404 892-2414	**Atlanta Memorial Arts Center** 1280 Peachtree St NE Symphony Hall	Atlanta	GA	30309-0000
404 892-3600	**High Museum of Art** 1280 Peachtree St NE	Atlanta	GA	30309-3549
404 524-1956	**Martin Luther King Jr Center for Nonviolent Social Change** 449 Auburn Ave NE	Atlanta	GA	30312-1503
404 656-0769	**New Georgia Railroad** 1 Martin Luther King Jr Dr SW	Atlanta	GA	30334-9004
404 948-9290	**Six Flags Over Georgia** 7561 Six Flags Pkwy	Mapleton	GA	30059-0000
404 498-5630	**Stone Mountain Park** US Hwy 78	Stone Mountain	GA	30086-0000
404 252-8960	**Theater of the Stars** 660 Peachtree St	Atlanta	GA	30365-0000

Austin

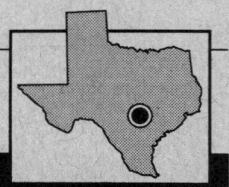

TEXAS   512

Important Phone Numbers

AAA	512 345-1727	Emergency	911
American Express	512 452-8166	Poison Control Center	409 765-1420
Better Business Bureau	512 476-6943	Time/Temp	512 973-3555
City Hall	512 499-2000	Weather	512 476-7736

■ Travel Information

512 478-9383 **Chamber of Commerce** 111 Congress Ave Suite P-10 .... Austin TX 78701-4043
512 474-5171 **Convention & Visitors Bureau** 900 Congress Ave Suite 300 .... Austin TX 78701-2432

Travel

■ Airport

512 472-5439 **Robert Mueller Municipal Airport** 4 miles NE of city (approx 15 minutes)

■ Airport Transportation

512 474-1200 **Capital Metropolitan Transit Authority** $.50 fare to downtown
Taxi $8 fare to downtown

■ Scheduled Airlines

America West	512 477-4856	Pan Am	512 476-7511
American	512 476-7611	Southwest	512 476-6354
Conquest Airlines'	800 722-0860	TWA	800 221-2000
Continental	512 477-6716	United	800 241-6522
Delta	512 477-5911	USAir	800 428-4322
Northwest	800 225-2525		

■ Charter Airlines

Austin Jet	512 472-8739	Berry Aviation	512 251-4103

■ Car Rentals

Agency	512 462-9696	Dollar	512 480-0048
Alamo	512 474-9916	Hertz	512 478-9321
Avis	512 476-6137	National	512 476-6189
Budget	512 478-6437	Thrifty	512 476-6802

■ Limo/Taxi

Ace Taxi	512 244-1133	Harlem Cab	512 472-2404
American Cab	512 452-9999	Roy's Taxi	512 482-0000
Carey Limousine	512 448-3492	Yellow Cab	512 472-1111
Dav-El Limousines	512 345-6789		

■ Mass Transit

512 474-1200 **Capitol Metropolitan Transit Authority** $.50 Base fare .... Austin TX 78702-0000

■ Rail/Bus

512 476-5684 **Austin Station** 250 N Lamar Blvd .... Austin TX 78703-4624
512 458-3823 **Greyhound/Trailways Bus Station** 916 E Koenig Ln .... Austin TX 78751-0000

Hotels

512 451-5757 **Austin Airport Hilton & Towers** 6000 Middle Fiskville Rd .... Austin TX 78752-4399
512 478-9611 **Crest Hotel** 111 E 1st St .... Austin TX 78701-4001
512 454-3737 **Doubletree Hotel** 6505 IH-35 N .... Austin TX 78752-4346
512 474-5911 **Driskill Hotel** 604 Brazos St .... Austin TX 78701-3247
512 469-9000 **Embassy Suites Downtown** 300 S Congress Ave .... Austin TX 78704-1279
512 454-8004 **Embassy Suites North** 5901 N IH-35 .... Austin TX 78723-1799
512 478-4500 **Four Seasons Hotel** 98 San Jacinto Blvd .... Austin TX 78701-4085
512 459-3335 **Hawthorn Suites Central Hotel** 935 La Posada Dr .... Austin TX 78752-3813
512 459-4251 **Holiday Inn Airport** 6911 N IH-35 .... Austin TX 78752-3237
512 472-8211 **Holiday Inn Town Lake** 20 N IH-35 .... Austin TX 78701-4396
512 477-1234 **Hyatt Regency Austin** 208 Barton Springs Rd .... Austin TX 78704-1284
512 443-1774 **La Quinta Ben White** 4200 S IH-35 .... Austin TX 78745-1252
512 261-6600 **Lakeway Resort & Conference Center** 101 Lakeway Dr .... Austin TX 78734-0000
512 476-3700 **Radisson Plaza Hotel** 700 San Jacinto Blvd .... Austin TX 78701-3294
512 448-2222 **Wyndham Hotel Southpark** 4140 Governors Row .... Austin TX 78744-1891

Restaurants

512 473-2413 **Chez Nous** (French) 510 Neches St .... Austin TX 78701-3710
512 459-4121 **Fonda San Miguel** (Mexican) 2330 W North Loop Blvd .... Austin TX 78756-2327
512 477-5584 **Jeffery's Restaurant** (Continental) 1204 W Lynn St .... Austin TX 78703-3969
512 472-6770 **Mezzaluna** (Italian) 310 Colorado St .... Austin TX 78701-0000
512 478-1661 **Night Hawk** (American) 336 S Congress Ave .... Austin TX 78704-1221
512 858-4959 **Salt Lick** (Barbecue) FM 1826 .... Austin TX 78619-0000
512 451-5440 **Threadgill's** (American) 6416 N Lamar Blvd .... Austin TX 78752-4008

Goods & Services

■ Department Stores

512 444-4711 **Beall's** 2415 S Congress St .... Austin TX 78704-5598
512 327-6100 **Dillard's** 2901 S Capital of Texas Hwy .... Austin TX 78746-8196
512 327-6000 **Scarbroughs** 2901 S Capitol of Texas Hwy .... Austin TX 78746-8112

■ Banks

512 479-5400 **Bank One Texas** 221 W 6th St .... Austin TX 78701-3403
512 473-4343 **First City Texas** 823 Congress Ave .... Austin TX 78701-2435
512 397-2200 **NCNB Texas National Bank** 503 Congress Ave .... Austin TX 78701-3501

■ Messenger/Postal

Austin Delivery Service	512 389-2292	Post Office	512 929-1252
Federal Express	800 238-5355	UPS	800 292-7129
Pony Express Courier Corp	512 929-7380	Vianet Inc	512 832-5300

■ Secretarial/Temp Services

512 345-2999 **Kelly Services** 4030 W Breaker Ln Suite 400 .... Austin TX 78759-5329
512 343-2141 **Manpower Temporary Services** 8303 Mopac Expy Suite 220 ...... Austin TX 78759-0000
512 345-3327 **Olsten Temporary Services** 8140 Mopac Expy Bldg 1 Suite 150 ... Austin TX 78759-8858

Media

■ Newspapers/Magazines

512 445-3500 **Austin American-Statesman** PO Box 670 .... Austin TX 78767-0670
512 250-9023 **Austin Magazine** 12416 Hymeadow Dr .... Austin TX 78750-1849

■ Television

512 471-4811 **KLRU-TV Ch 18 (PBS)** 2504-B Whitis Ave .... Austin TX 78705-0000
512 476-7777 **KTBC-TV Ch 7 (CBS)** 119 E 10th St .... Austin TX 78701-2495
512 459-6521 **KVUE-TV Ch 24 (ABC)** 3201 Steck Ave .... Austin TX 78758-0000
512 476-3636 **KXAN-TV Ch 36 (NBC)** 908 W Martin Luther King Jr Blvd .... Austin TX 78701-1093

■ Radio

512 495-1300 **KASE-FM 100.7 MHz (Ctry)** 705 N Lamar Blvd .... Austin TX 78703-5415
512 328-1035 **KEYI-AM 1490 kHz (Gold)** 1250 Capital of Texas Hwy .... Austin TX 78746-0000
512 474-9233 **KHFI-FM 98.3 MHz (CHR)** 1219 W 6th St .... Austin TX 78703-5208
512 323-9595 **KKMJ-FM 95.5 MHz (AC)** 3108 N Lamar Blvd .... Austin TX 78705-2013
512 832-4000 **KLBJ-AM 590 kHz (N/T-CBS)** 8309 N IH-35 .... Austin TX 78753-5771
512 832-4000 **KLBJ-FM 93.7 MHz (AOR-CBS)** 8309 N IH-35 .... Austin TX 78753-5720
512 471-1631 **KUT-FM 90.5 MHz (Jazz)**
             University of Texas Communications Bldg B .... Austin TX 78712-0000
512 495-1300 **KVET-AM 1300 kHz (Ctry-ABC)** 705 N Lamar Blvd .... Austin TX 78703-5415

Local Attractions & Special Events

■ Sports

512 272-5851 **Manor Downs** 101 Hill Ln .... Manor TX 78653-0000

■ Special Events

512 472-7142 **Diez y Seis de Septiembre** Mexican Independence Day Festival (mid-September)

■ Local Attractions

512 472-8180 **French Legation** 802 San Marcos .... Austin TX 78702-2647
512 471-7324 **Huntington Archer M Art Gallery**
             23rd & San Jacinto Sts University of Texas ....Austin TX 78712-0000
512 482-5137 **Johnson Lyndon Baines Presidential Library & Museum**
             2313 Red River St .... Austin TX 78705-0000
512 472-1903 **O Henry Home & Museum** 409 E 5th St .... Austin TX 78701-3705

Baltimore

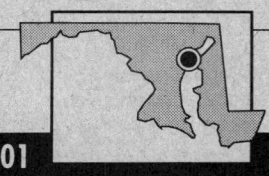

MARYLAND 301

Important Phone Numbers

AAA	301 462-4000	Emergency	911
American Express	301 539-7300	Poison Control Center	301 528-7701
Better Business Bureau	301 347-3990	Time	301 844-1212
City Hall	301 396-3100	Weather	301 936-1212

■ Travel Information

301 727-2820 **Chamber of Commerce** 111 S Calvert St Suite 1500 .... Baltimore MD 21202-6180
301 659-7300 **Convention & Visitors Assn** 1 E Pratt St Plaza Level Suite 14 ... Baltimore MD 21202-0000

Travel

■ Airport

301 859-7111 **Baltimore-Washington International Airport** 8 miles SW of city (approx 35 minutes)

■ Airport Transportation

301 859-0800 **Airport Commuter Limo Service** $5.75 fare to downtown
301 859-1100 **Airport Taxi** $12-13 fare to downtown
301 539-2112 **Amtrak** $6 fare to downtown

■ Scheduled Airlines

Air Jamaica	800 523-5585	Mexicana	800 531-7921
American	301 850-5800	Northwest	800 225-2525
American Eagle	301 850-5800	Pan Am	800 221-1111
Continental	800 525-0280	TWA	301 859-2511
Delta	301 768-9000	United	301 850-4557
Eastern	301 768-3100	USAir	301 727-0825

■ Charter Airlines

Butler Aviation	301 859-4000	US Jet Aviation	703 892-6200

■ Car Rentals

Agency	301 760-8100	Hertz	301 850-7400
Avis	301 859-1680	National	301 859-8860
Budget	301 859-0851	Thrifty	301 768-4900
Dollar	301 684-2020		

■ Limo/Taxi

Airport Taxi	301 859-1100	Maryland Limousine Service	301 850-4100
Arrow Cab	301 358-9696	Royal Cab	301 327-0330
Carey International Limousine	301 837-1234	Sun Cab	301 235-0300
Diamond Cabs	301 947-3333	Yellow Cab	301 685-1212
Harford Limousines	301 426-7780		

■ Mass Transit

301 539-5000 **Mass Transit** $1 Base fare .... Baltimore MD 21201-0000

■ Rail/Bus

301 674-1167 **BWI Airport Rail Station** Amtrak Way .... Baltimore MD 21240-0000
301 744-9311 **Greyhound/Trailways Bus Station** 210 W Fayette St ...... Baltimore MD 21201-3471
301 291-4261 **Pennsylvania Station** 1500 N Charles St .... Baltimore MD 21201-5820

Hotels

301 522-7377 **Admiral Fell Inn** 888 S Broadway .... Baltimore MD 21231-3486
301 653-1100 **Baltimore Hilton Inn** 1726 Reisterstown Rd .... Pikesville MD 21208-2984
301 962-0202 **Baltimore Marriott Inner Harbor** 110 Eutaw St .... Baltimore MD 21201-0000
301 332-1000 **Belvedere Hotel** 1 E Chase St .... Baltimore MD 21202-2586
301 576-8400 **Comfort Inn** 24 W Franklin St .... Baltimore MD 21201-5090
301 882-0900 **Days Inn** 8801 Loch Raven Blvd .... Towson MD 21204-6271
301 859-8400 **Holiday Inn Airport** 890 Elkridge Landing Rd .... Linthicum Heights MD 21090-2978
301 823-4410 **Holiday Inn Towson** 1100 Cromwell Bridge Rd .... Baltimore MD 21204-0001
301 528-1234 **Hyatt Regency Baltimore** 300 Light St .... Baltimore MD 21202-1092
301 675-6800 **Johns Hopkins Inn** 400 N Broadway .... Baltimore MD 21231-1199
301 752-1100 **Omni Inner Harbor Hotel** 101 W Fayette St .... Baltimore MD 21201-3798
301 727-7101 **Peabody Court** 612 Cathedral St .... Baltimore MD 21201-5180
301 725-5100 **Quality Inn Colony Seven** I-295 & Rt 32 .... Baltimore MD 20701-0000
301 539-8400 **Radisson Plaza Lord Baltimore Hotel** 20-30 W Baltimore St ... Baltimore MD 21223-1558
301 788-3900 **Red Carpet Inn** 6422 Baltimore National Pike .... Baltimore MD 21228-3903
301 962-8300 **Sheraton Inner Harbor Hotel** 300 S Charles St .... Baltimore MD 21201-2497
301 859-3300 **Sheraton International Hotel** 7032 Elm Rd .... Baltimore MD 21240-0000
301 576-1200 **Tremont Plaza Hotel** 8 E Pleasant St .... Baltimore MD 21202-2160

Restaurants

301 327-5795 **Bertha's Dining Room** (Seafood) 734 S Broadway ...... Baltimore MD 21231-3494
301 547-8480 **Brass Elephant** (Northern Italian) 924 N Charles St ...... Baltimore MD 21201-5346
301 732-4080 **Bud Paolino's Restaurant** (Seafood) 3919 E Lombard St ...... Baltimore MD 21224-2443
301 752-8030 **Chez Fernand** (French) 805 E Fayette St .... Baltimore MD 21202-4726
301 727-7101 **Conservatory** (Continental) 612 Cathedral St .... Baltimore MD 21201-5102
301 539-1393 **Danny's** (Continental) 1201 N Charles St .... Baltimore MD 21201-5582
301 752-4515 **Germano's Trattoria Petrucci** (Italian) 300 S High St ...... Baltimore MD 21202-4353
301 354-0085 **Gunnings Crab House** (Seafood) 3901 S Hanover St ...... Baltimore MD 21225-1710
301 327-8365 **Haussner's** (German) 3244 Eastern Ave .... Baltimore MD 21224-4085
301 752-0311 **Helmand The** (Afghan) 806 N Charles St .... Baltimore MD 21201-0000
301 727-9522 **Marconi Restaurant** (French/Italian) 106 W Saratoga St ...... Baltimore MD 21201-3509
301 732-6399 **Obrycki's Crab House** (Seafood) 1727 E Pratt St .... Baltimore MD 21231-1817
301 685-6600 **Phillips Harborplace** (Seafood) 301 Light Street Pavillion ...... Baltimore MD 21202-0000
301 539-4675 **Tio Pepe** (Spanish) 10 E Franklin St .... Baltimore MD 21202-2294

Goods & Services

■ Department Stores

301 752-1951 **Convention Center Mall** 100 S Charles St .... Baltimore MD
301 625-1445 **Epsteins** 201 W Lexington St .... Baltimore MD 21201-3493

■ Banks

301 244-4000 **First National Bank of Maryland** PO Box 1596 .... Baltimore MD 21203-0000
301 334-9471 **First United National Bank & Trust Co** 19 S 2nd St ...... Oakland MD 21550-1517
301 547-4000 **Maryland National Bank** 100 S Charles St .... Baltimore MD 21201-2791
301 244-5000 **Maryland National Bank** 10 Light St .... Baltimore MD 21202-1435

■ Messenger/Postal

Acme Delivery & Messenger	301 945-3900	Global Messenger	301 889-1777
Allied Delivery & Messenger	301 243-1230	Magic Messengers Inc	301 625-2600
Apache Couriers Co	301 687-3432	Maryland Messenger Service	301 837-5550
Carl Messenger Service Inc	301 685-8700	Post Office	301 347-4425
Expressway Couriers Service	301 889-0880	UPS	800 346-0106
Federal Express	301 792-8200		

■ Secretarial/Temp Services

301 685-0697 **Manpower Temporary Services Inc** 120 E Baltimore St .... Baltimore MD 21202-1674
301 685-7955 **Olsten Temporary Services** 200 E Lexington St Suite 100 ...... Baltimore MD 21202-3524

Media

■ Newspapers/Magazines

301 332-6000 **Baltimore Evening Sun** 501 N Calvert St .... Baltimore MD 21278-0001
301 752-1300 **Baltimore Magazine** 16 S Calvert St Suite 1000 .... Baltimore MD 21202-1385
301 332-6000 **Baltimore Sun** 501 N Calvert St .... Baltimore MD 21278-0001

■ Television

301 467-3000 **WBAL-TV Ch 11 (CBS)** 3800 Hooper Ave .... Baltimore MD 21211-1397
301 466-0013 **WJZ-TV Ch 13 (ABC)** 3725 Malden Ave .... Baltimore MD 21211-1392
301 377-2222 **WMAR-TV Ch 2 (NBC)** 6400 York Rd .... Baltimore MD 21212-2198
301 356-5600 **WMPB-TV Ch 67 (PBS)** 11767 Bonita Ave .... Owings Mills MD 21117-1414

■ Radio

301 467-3000 **WBAL-AM 1090 kHz (N/T-CBS)** 3800 Hooper Ave ...... Baltimore MD 21211-1313
301 466-9272 **WBSB-FM 104.3 MHz (CHR-ABC)** 3701 Malden Ave ...... Baltimore MD 21211-1322
301 444-3564 **WEAA-FM 88.9 MHz (Jazz-NPR)** Cold Spring Ln & Hillen Rd ... Baltimore MD 21239-0000
301 823-1570 **WLIF-FM 101.9 MHz (B/EZ-ABC)** 1570 Hart Rd .... Towson MD 21204-1699
301 366-3693 **WPOC-FM 93.1 MHz (Ctry-ABC)** 711 W 40th St .... Baltimore MD 21211-2163
301 653-2200 **WXYV-FM 102.7 MHz (UC)** 1829 Reisterstown Rd Suite 420 ... Baltimore MD 21208-6301

Local Attractions & Special Events

■ Sports

301 528-0100 **Baltimore Blast** 201 W Baltimore St Baltimore Arena ...... Baltimore MD 21201-2589
301 243-9800 **Baltimore Orioles** Memorial Stadium .... Baltimore MD 21218-0000
301 727-0703 **Baltimore Skipjacks** 201 W Baltimore St Baltimore Arena ...... Baltimore MD 21201-2576
301 542-9400 **Pimlico Race Course** Hayward & Winner Aves .... Baltimore MD 21215-5178

■ Special Events

301 837-3030 **Preakness Celebration Week** (May 10-18)

■ Local Attractions

301 752-2461 **B & O Railroad Museum** 901 W Pratt St .... Baltimore MD 21223-0000
301 727-1539 **Babe Ruth Birthplace**
216 Emory St Maryland Baseball Hall of Fame Museum .... Baltimore MD 21230-0000
301 396-7100 **Baltimore Museum of Art** 10 Art Museum Dr .... Baltimore MD 21218-3801
301 396-7932 **Edgar Allan Poe House** 203 N Amity St .... Baltimore MD 21223-0000
301 962-4290 **Fort McHenry National Monument & Historic Shrine**
Fort Ave .... Baltimore MD 21230-0000
301 332-4191 **Harborplace & The Gallery** 200 E Pratt St .... Baltimore MD 21202-6117
301 342-7561 **Lloyd Street Synagogue** Lloyd & E Baltimore Sts ...... Baltimore MD 21201-0000
301 783-8110 **Meyerhoff Symphony Hall** 1212 Cathedral St .... Baltimore MD 21201-0000
301 576-3810 **National Aquarium** 501 E Pratt St Pier 3 .... Baltimore MD 21202-0000

Baton Rouge

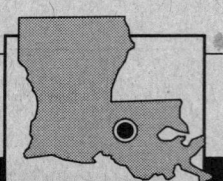

LOUISIANA   **504**

Important Phone Numbers

AAA	504 927-1200	Emergency	911
American Express	504 927-6002	Time/Temp	504 387-5411
Better Business Bureau	504 926-3010	Weather	504 355-0368
City Hall	504 389-3000		

■ Travel Information

504 381-7125   **Chamber of Commerce** 564 Laurel St .... Baton Rouge LA 70801-1808
504 383-1825   **Convention & Visitors Bureau** 730 North Blvd .... Baton Rouge LA 70802-5726

Travel

■ Airport

504 355-0333   **Baton Rouge Metropolitan Airport** 8 miles N of city (approx 20 minutes)

■ Airport Transportation

Limo $8 fare to downtown
Taxi $11-12 fare to downtown

■ Scheduled Airlines

American	504 387-1497	Delta	504 356-4361
Continental	504 387-4911	Northwest	800 225-2525

■ Charter Airlines

Baton Rouge Aircraft	504 357-6471	Louisiana Aircraft	504 356-1401

■ Car Rentals

Audubon	504 292-1047	Hertz	504 357-5992
Avis	504 355-4721	Thrifty	504 356-2576
Budget	504 355-0312		

■ Limo/Taxi

MRS Express	504 664-3222	Yellow Cab	504 926-6400
Riverside Limousine	504 928-5466		

■ Mass Transit

504 343-8331   **Capitol Transportation** $.75 Base fare .... Baton Rouge LA 70805-0000

■ Rail/Bus

504 345-6264   **Amtrak Passenger Station** NW Railroad Ave .... Hammond LA 70401-0000
504 383-3124   **Greyhound/Trailways Bus Station** 1253 Florida St .... Baton Rouge LA 70802-4699

Hotels

504 924-5000   **Baton Rouge Hilton Hotel** 5500 Hilton Ave .... Baton Rouge LA 70808-2522
504 357-8612   **Bellemont Hotel** 7370 Airline Hwy .... Baton Rouge LA 70805-5595
504 924-6566   **Embassy Suites Hotel Baton Rouge**
     4914 Constitution Ave .... Baton Rouge LA 70808-3352
504 926-9990   **Hampton Inn** 4646 Constitution Ave .... Baton Rouge LA 70808-3205
504 293-6880   **Holiday Inn East** 10455 Rieger Rd .... Baton Rouge LA 70809-4599
504 925-2244   **Sheraton Baton Rouge Hotel** 4728 Constitution Ave .... Baton Rouge LA 70808-3298

Restaurants

504 927-6040   **Chalet Brandt** (Continental) 7655 Old Hammond Hwy .... Baton Rouge LA 70809-1296
504 343-1702   **Chez Paris** (French) 3723 Government St .... Baton Rouge LA 70806-0000
504 275-3755   **Maison Lacour** (French) 11025 N Harrell's Ferry Rd .... Baton Rouge LA 70816-0000
504 767-4794   **Mulate's** (Cajun/Seafood) 8322 Bluebonnet Rd .... Baton Rouge LA 70810-2825
504 924-5069   **Place** (Steak/Seafood) 5255 Florida Blvd .... Baton Rouge LA 70806-4128
504 356-2361   **Ralph & Kacoos Seafood** (Cajun) 7110 Airline Hwy .... Baton Rouge LA 70805-5598

Goods & Services

■ Department Stores

504 923-1712   **Dillard's** 9301 Cortana Pl .... Baton Rouge LA 70815-8694
504 389-7000   **Maison Blanche** 1500 Main St .... Baton Rouge LA 70802-3759

■ Banks

504 387-2151   **City National Bank** 445 North Blvd .... Baton Rouge LA 70802-5709
504 924-8015   **First National Banker's Bank**
     5551 Corporate Blvd Suite 3-R .... Baton Rouge LA 70808-2512
504 927-1220   **Sunburst Bank** 8440 Jefferson Hwy .... Baton Rouge LA 70809-1626

■ Messenger/Postal

Action Enterprises Inc	504 927-7972	Post Office	504 381-0362
Express Courier Services Inc	504 924-9990	UPS	504 733-7250
Federal Express	800 238-5355		

■ Secretarial/Temp Services

504 926-7050   **Kelly Temporary Services**
     4815 Jamestown Ave Suite 101 .... Baton Rouge LA 70808-3225
504 924-4281   **Manpower Temporary Services Inc** 677 S Foster Dr .... Baton Rouge LA 70806-5904
504 924-0200   **Olsten Temporary Services**
     5615 Corporate Blvd Suite 1-H .... Baton Rouge LA 70808-2515

Media

■ Newspapers/Magazines

504 456-2220   **Louisiana Life** 4200 S I-10 Service Rd Suite 220 .... Metairie LA 70004-0000
504 383-1111   **Morning Advocate** 525 Lafayette St .... Baton Rouge LA 70802-5494
504 383-1111   **State Times** 525 Lafayette St .... Baton Rouge LA 70802-5494

■ Television

504 383-9999   **WAFB-TV Ch 9 (CBS)** 844 Government St .... Baton Rouge LA 70802-6030
504 387-2222   **WBRZ-TV Ch 2 (ABC)** 1650 Highland Rd .... Baton Rouge LA 70802-7000
504 767-5660   **WLTB-TV Ch 27 (PBS)** 7860 Anselmo Ln .... Baton Rouge LA 70810-1101
504 766-3233   **WVLA-TV Ch 33 (NBC)** 5220 Essen Ln .... Baton Rouge LA 70809-3595

■ Radio

504 926-1106   **KQXL-FM 106.5 MHz (CHR)** 7707 Waco Ave .... Baton Rouge LA 70806-1440
504 383-5271   **WFMF-FM 102.5 MHz (CHR)** 444 Florida St .... Baton Rouge LA 70801-1722
504 926-3050   **WRKF-FM 89.3 MHz (Clas-NPR)** 3050 Valley Creek Dr ...... Baton Rouge LA 70808-3145
504 927-7060   **WXOK-AM 1460 kHz (UC-ABC)** 6819 Cezanne Ave .... Baton Rouge LA 70806-2185
504 343-8348   **WYNK-AM 1380 kHz (Ctry)** 842 Main St .... Baton Rouge LA 70802-5528

Local Attractions & Special Events

■ Sports

318 896-7223   **Evangeline Downs Race Track** Hwy 167 N .... Carencro LA 70520-0000

■ Special Events

504 383-1825   **Cajun Bastille Day** (mid-July)

■ Local Attractions

504 381-9606   **Clemens Samuel Riverboat** Foot of France St .... Baton Rouge LA 70802-0000
504 344-9463   **Louisiana Arts & Science Center** 100 S River Rd .... Baton Rouge LA 70801-0000
504 342-1942   **Louisiana Naval War Memorial** 305 S River Rd .... Baton Rouge LA 70802-6220
504 765-2437   **LSU Rural Life Museum** Essen Ln .... Baton Rouge LA 70803-0000
504 343-4955   **Magnolia Mound** 2161 Nicholson Dr .... Baton Rouge LA 70802-8105
504 766-8600   **Mount Hope Plantation** 8151 Highland Rd .... Baton Rouge LA 70801-0000
504 346-8263   **Nattoway Plantation Home** River Rd .... White Castle LA 70788-0000
504 342-8211   **Old State Capitol** 150 North Blvd .... Baton Rouge LA 70801-0000

Boston

MASSACHUSETTS 617

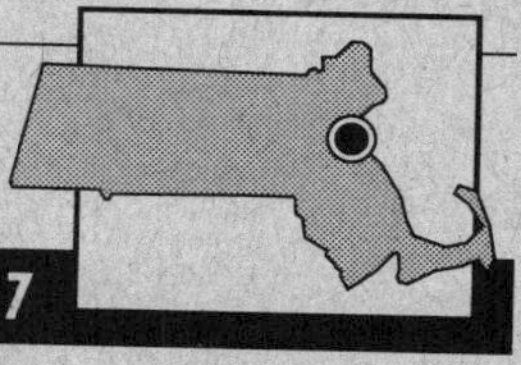

Important Phone Numbers

AAA ... 617 723-9666
American Express ... 617 723-8400
Better Business Bureau ... 617 482-9151
City Hall ... 617 725-4000
Emergency ... 911
Poison Control Center ... 617 232-2120
Time/Temp ... 617 637-1234
Weather ... 617 567-4670

■ Travel Information

617 227-4500 **Chamber of Commerce** 600 Atlantic Ave 13th Fl ... Boston MA 02210-2200
617 536-4100 **Convention & Visitors Bureau** Prudential Center Plaza ... Boston MA 02199-8102

Travel

■ Airport

617 561-1818 **Logan International Airport** 3 miles NE of downtown (approx 10 minutes)

■ Airport Transportation

617 267-2981 **Airway Transportation** $6.50 fare to downtown
617 561-1800 **Massport Shuttle Bus** $6.50 fare to downtown
617 722-3200 **MBTA** $.75 fare to downtown
Taxi $10-12 fare to downtown

■ Scheduled Airlines

Aer Lingus ... 617 742-7120
Air Atlantic ... 800 246-7000
Air Canada ... 800 776-3000
Air France ... 800 237-2747
Alitalia ... 800 223-5737
American ... 617 542-6700
American Eagle ... 617 542-6700
British Airways ... 800 247-9297
Canadian ... 800 426-7000
Continental ... 800 525-0280
Delta ... 617 567-4100
Eastern ... 617 262-3700
El Al ... 800 223-6700
First Air ... 800 776-3000
Lufthansa ... 800 645-3880
Midway ... 800 621-5700
Mohawk Airlines ... 800 252-2144
Northwest ... 617 267-4885
Pan Am ... 800 221-1111
Piedmont ... 617 523-1100
Sabena ... 800 955-2000
Swissair ... 800 221-4750
TAP Portugal ... 800 221-7370
TWA ... 617 367-2800
United ... 800 241-6522
USAir ... 617 482-3160

■ Charter Airlines

Diamond Air ... 617 274-6626
Flight Time Corp ... 617 965-7060
Jet Aviation ... 617 274-0030
North Atlantic Air ... 508 774-2070
Wiggins EW Airways Inc ... 617 762-5690

■ Car Rentals

Agency ... 617 289-1683
American International ... 617 569-3550
Avis ... 617 424-0800
Budget ... 617 561-2362
Dollar ... 800 421-6868
Hertz ... 617 569-7272
National ... 800 227-7368
Thrifty ... 617 569-6500

■ Limo/Taxi

A & A Limo Renting ... 617 623-8700
Boston Cab ... 617 536-5010
Cleveland Cab ... 617 277-8700
Commonwealth Limousine ... 617 787-5575
Coopers of Boston Limo Service ... 617 482-1000
Hub Limousine ... 617 567-1459
Independent Taxi ... 617 426-8700
Red Cab ... 617 734-5000
Town Cab ... 617 536-5000

■ Mass Transit

617 722-5000 **MBTA Bus** $.50 Base fare ... Boston MA 02116-4628
617 722-5000 **MBTA Train** $.75 Base fare ... Boston MA 02116-0000

■ Rail/Bus

617 423-5810 **Greyhound Bus Station** 10 St James Ave ... Boston MA 02116-3899
617 439-3720 **South Station** Atlantic Ave & Summer St ... Boston MA 02210-0000

Hotels

617 236-1100 **Back Bay Hilton Hotel** 40 Dalton St ... Boston MA 02115-3123
617 236-5800 **Boston Marriott Copley Place** 110 Huntington Ave ... Boston MA 02116-5706
617 426-2000 **Boston Park Plaza Hotel & Towers** 64 Arlington St ... Boston MA 02117-0000
617 424-7000 **Colonnade Hotel** 120 Huntington Ave ... Boston MA 02116-5782
617 267-5300 **Copley Plaza Hotel** 138 St James Ave ... Boston MA 02116-5071
617 267-1607 **Eliot Hotel** 370 Commonwealth Ave ... Boston MA 02115-0000
617 338-4400 **Four Seasons Hotel Boston** 200 Boylston St ... Boston MA 02116-3999
617 864-5200 **Harvard Manor House** 110 Mt Auburn St ... Cambridge MA 02138-5794
617 492-1234 **Hyatt Regency Cambridge** 575 Memorial Dr ... Cambridge MA 02139-4896
617 451-2600 **Lafayette Hotel** 1 Ave de Lafayette ... Boston MA 02111-1725
617 536-5300 **Lenox Hotel** 710 Boylston St ... Boston MA 02116-2602
617 227-0800 **Marriott Hotel Long Wharf** 296 State St ... Boston MA 02109-2606
617 451-1900 **Meridien Hotel** 250 Franklin St ... Boston MA 02110-2897
617 262-1000 **Midtown Hotel** 220 Huntington Ave ... Boston MA 02115-4798
617 426-6220 **Milner Hotel** 78 Charles St S ... Boston MA 02116-5430
617 227-8600 **Omni Parker House** 60 School St ... Boston MA 02108-4198
617 569-5250 **Ramada Hotel International Airport** 225 McClellan Hwy ... East Boston MA 02128-0000
617 536-5700 **Ritz-Carlton Hotel** 15 Arlington St ... Boston MA 02116-3400
617 236-2000 **Sheraton Boston Hotel & Towers** 39 Dalton St ... Boston MA 02199-3999
617 426-1400 **Tremont House** 275 Tremont St ... Boston MA 02116-5615
617 262-9600 **Westin Hotel Copley Place** 10 Huntington Ave ... Boston MA 02116-5798

Restaurants

617 367-0880 **Another Season** (Continental) 97 Mt Vernon St ... Boston MA 02108-121
617 482-6262 **Anthony's Pier 4** (Seafood) 140 Northern Ave ... Boston MA 02210-189
617 242-9600 **Barrett's on Boston Harbor** (American) 2 Constitution Plaza ... Charlestown MA 02129-209
617 723-1666 **Bay Tower Room** (American) 60 State St ... Boston MA 02109-180
617 266-3537 **Boodle's** (Steak) 40 Dalton St ... Boston MA 02115-312
617 734-3388 **Cafe Budapest** (Hungarian/Continental) 90 Exeter St ... Boston MA 02116-350
617 227-1576 **Chart House** (Steak/Seafood) 60 Long Wharf ... Boston MA 02110-360
617 894-3339 **Chateau Restaurant** (Italian/American) 195 School St ... Waltham MA 02154-459
617 262-4810 **Davio's** (Italian) 269 Newbury St ... Boston MA 02116-247
617 566-7000 **Dover Sea Grille** (Seafood) 1223 Beacon St ... Brookline MA 02146-533
617 227-2038 **Durgin-Park** (American) 30 N Market St ... Boston MA 02109-162
617 542-2255 **Grill 23 & Bar** (Steak/Seafood) 161 Berkeley St ... Boston MA 02116-510
617 227-9600 **Hampshire House** (American/Seafood) 84 Beacon St ... Boston MA 02108-349
617 492-1115 **Harvest** (Continental) 44 Brattle St ... Cambridge MA 02138-373
617 231-2300 **Hilltop Steak House** (American) 855 Broadway ... Saugus MA 01906-329
617 233-9719 **Kowloon** (Oriental) 948 Broadway ... Saugus MA 01906-3299
617 262-3023 **L'Espalier** (French) 30 Gloucester St ... Boston MA 02116-0000
617 451-2600 **Le Marquis de Lafayette** (French) 1 Ave de Lafayette ... Boston MA 02111-1725
617 426-4444 **Legal Seafoods** (Seafood) 35 Columbus Ave ... Boston MA 02116-3907
617 542-1340 **Locke-Ober** (Continental) 3 Winter Pl ... Boston MA 02108-4733
617 338-7539 **No Name Restaurant** (Seafood) 17 Fish Pier ... Boston MA 02110-0000
617 439-7000 **Rowes Wharf** (American) 70 Rowes Wharf ... Boston MA 02110-3330
617 227-4545 **Sally Ling's Cafe** (Chinese) 256 Commercial St ... Boston MA 02109-1125
617 523-4119 **Seasons** (American) Faneuil Hall Market Pl ... Boston MA 02109-0000
617 227-2750 **Union Oyster House** (Seafood) 41 Union St ... Boston MA 02108-2494
617 864-1933 **Upstairs at the Pudding** (Continental) 10 Holyoke St ... Cambridge MA 02138-5014

Goods & Services

■ Department Stores

617 965-1400 **Bloomingdale's** 175 Boylston St ... Chestnut Hill MA 02167-1691
617 357-2978 **Filene's** 426 Washington St ... Boston MA 02108-0000
617 492-1000 **Harvard Co-op Society** 1400 Massachusetts Ave ... Cambridge MA 02138-3833
617 357-3000 **Jordan Marsh** 450 Washington St ... Boston MA 02205-0000

■ Banks

617 434-2200 **Bank of Boston** 100 Federal St ... Boston MA 02110-1898
617 742-4000 **Bank of New England NA** 28 State St ... Boston MA 02109-1784
617 556-6305 **BayBank Boston NA** 175 Federal St ... Boston MA 02110-2204
617 292-2000 **Shawmut Bank NA** 1 Federal St ... Boston MA 02211-0001

■ Messenger/Postal

Archer Services of Massachusetts ... 617 426-9293
Boston Bicycle Couriers ... 617 426-7575
Central Delivery Service ... 617 391-7300
Choice Courier Systems Inc ... 617 787-2020
Courier Dispatch Group Inc ... 617 442-2770
Courier Express ... 617 889-5353
Federal Express ... 617 391-4760
Marathon Messenger Co Inc ... 617 266-8990
Middlesex Courier Service ... 617 272-0000
Post Office ... 617 654-5083
Sullivan's Express ... 617 269-2000
UPS ... 617 461-5700

■ Secretarial/Temp Services

617 951-4000 **Accountemps** 101 Arch St ... Boston MA 02201-0001
617 482-8833 **Kelly Services** 60 Temple Pl ... Boston MA 02111-1328
617 723-7350 **Manpower Temporary Services** 1 State St Suite 950 ... Boston MA 02109-3507
617 426-3910 **Olsten Temporary Services** 1 Bromfield St ... Boston MA 02108-5193

Media

■ Newspapers/Magazines

617 929-2000 **Boston Globe** 135 Morrissey Blvd ... Boston MA 02125-3338
617 262-9700 **Boston Magazine** 300 Massachusetts Ave ... Boston MA 02115-4598
617 536-5390 **Boston Phoenix** 126 Brookline Ave ... Boston MA 02215-3900

■ Television

617 787-7000 **WBZ-TV Ch 4 (NBC)** 1170 Soldiers Field Rd ... Boston MA 02134-1092
617 449-0400 **WCVB-TV Ch 5 (ABC)** 5 TV Pl ... Needham MA 02192-0000
617 492-2777 **WGBH-TV Ch 2 (PBS)** 125 Western Ave ... Boston MA 02134-1098
617 725-0777 **WHDH-TV Ch 7 (CBS)** 7 Bulfinch Pl ... Boston MA 02114-2913

■ Radio

617 266-1111 **WBCN-FM 104.1 MHz (AOR)** 1265 Boylston St ... Boston MA 02215-3480
617 353-2790 **WBUR-FM 90.9 MHz (Clas-NPR)** 630 Commonwealth Ave ... Boston MA 02215-2422
617 787-7000 **WBZ-AM 1030 kHz (AC-ABC)** 1170 Soldiers Field Rd ... Boston MA 02134-1092
617 523-6611 **WJIB-FM 96.9 MHz (B/EZ)** 68 Commercial Wharf ... Boston MA 02110-3894
617 236-6800 **WRKO-AM 680 kHz (N/T)** 3 Fenway Plaza ... Boston MA 02215-0000
617 396-1430 **WXKS-FM 107.9 MHz (CHR)** 99 Revere Beach Pkwy ... Medford MA 02155-5183

Local Attractions & Special Events

■ Sports

617 227-3200 **Boston Bruins** 150 Causeway St Boston Garden ... Boston MA 02114-1389
617 523-3030 **Boston Celtics** 150 Causeway St Boston Garden ... Boston MA 02114-0000
617 267-9440 **Boston Red Sox** 24 Yawkey Way Fenway Pk ... Boston MA 02215-0000
508 543-7911 **New England Patriots** Rt 1 Sullivan Stadium ... Foxboro MA 02035-0000

■ Special Events

617 227-1528 **Boston Harborfest** (July 2-7)
617 236-1652 **Boston Marathon** (April 15)

■ Local Attractions

617 954-2096 **Boston Common** Charles St ... Boston MA 02116-0000
617 267-9300 **Boston Museum of Fine Arts** 465 Huntington Ave ... Boston MA 02115-5519
617 266-1492 **Boston Pops** 301 Massachusetts Ave (May-July) ... Boston MA 02115-4511
617 338-1773 **Boston Tea Party Ship Museum** Congress St Bridge ... Boston MA 02210-0000
617 426-2800 **Computer Museum** 300 Congress St ... Boston MA 02210-0000
617 523-1300 **Faneuil Hall & Quincy Market** 4 S Market St ... Boston MA 02109-1626
617 495-9400 **Fogg Art Museum** 32 Quincy St Harvard University ... Cambridge MA 02138-3883
617 536-4100 **Freedom Trail** ... Boston MA
617 566-1401 **Gardner Isabella Stewart Museum** 280 The Fenway ... Boston MA 02115-5809
617 227-2155 **King's Chapel** 58 Tremont St ... Boston MA 02108-3289
617 523-6676 **Old North Church** 193 Salem St ... Boston MA 02113-1198
617 523-1676 **Paul Revere House** 19 North Sq ... Boston MA 02113-2406
617 266-1492 **Symphony Hall** 301 Massachusetts Ave ... Boston MA 02115-4511

Buffalo

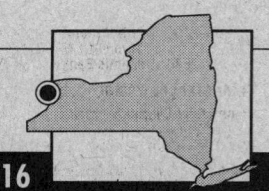

NEW YORK · 716

Important Phone Numbers

AAA	716 634-7900	Emergency	911
American Express	716 856-7373	Poison Control Center	716 878-7654
Better Business Bureau	716 856-7180	Time/Temp	716 844-1717
City Hall	716 851-4200		

■ Travel Information

716 852-7100 **Chamber of Commerce** 107 Delaware Ave .... Buffalo NY 14202-2810
716 852-0511 **Convention & Visitors Bureau** 107 Delaware Ave .... Buffalo NY 14202-2810

Travel

■ Airport

716 632-3115 **Greater Buffalo International Airport** 9 miles E of downtown (approx 35 minutes)

■ Airport Transportation

716 633-8294 **Airport Taxi** $14 fare to downtown
716 855-7211 **NFTA Metrobus** $1.20 fare to downtown

■ Scheduled Airlines

American	716 856-7050	Northwest	800 225-2525
Continental	716 852-1233	United	800 241-6522
Eastern	716 852-3170	USAir	716 632-3000

■ Charter Airlines

Prior Aviation Service Inc 716 633-1000

■ Car Rentals

Agency	716 681-2100	Hertz	716 632-4772
American International	716 633-8500	National	716 632-0203
Avis	716 632-1808	Thrifty	716 634-5992
Budget	716 632-4662		

■ Limo/Taxi

Broadway Cab	716 896-4600	Kenmore Cab	716 876-3030
Buffalo Limousine	716 835-4997	Liberty Cab	716 877-7111

■ Mass Transit

716 855-7211 **Niagara Frontier Transit Metro System** $1 Base fare .... Buffalo NY 14201-0000

■ Rail/Bus

716 856-2075 **Exchange Street Railroad Station** 75 Exchange St .... Buffalo NY 14203-2918
716 855-7522 **Greyhound/Trailways Bus Station** 181 Ellicott St .... Buffalo NY 14203-2221

Hotels

716 845-5100 **Buffalo Hilton Waterfront** 120 Church St .... Buffalo NY 14202-3961
716 631-0800 **Days Inn Buffalo Airport** 4345 Genesee St .... Buffalo NY 14225-1930
716 634-6969 **Holiday Inn Airport** 4600 Genesee St .... Cheektowaga NY 14225-2492
716 773-1111 **Holiday Inn Grand Island** 100 Whitehaven Rd .... Grand Island NY 14072-1999
716 856-1234 **Hyatt Regency Buffalo** 2 Fountain Plaza .... Buffalo NY 14202-2290
716 681-2400 **Sheraton Inn Buffalo Airport** 2040 Walden Ave .... Buffalo NY 14225-5186

Restaurants

716 886-8920 **Anchor Bar & Restaurant** (Italian/American) 1047 Main St .... Buffalo NY 14209-2397
716 856-9187 **Chef's** (Italian) 291 Seneca St .... Buffalo NY 14204-0000
716 856-1234 **EB Green's** (Continental) 2 Fountain Plaza .... Buffalo NY 14202-2220
716 877-8788 **Hourglass** (Continental) 981 Kenmore Ave .... Kenmore NY 14217-2995
716 881-1888 **Just Pasta** (Pasta) 307 Bryant St .... Buffalo NY 14222-1941
716 886-2220 **Lord Chumley's** (Continental) 481 Delaware Ave .... Buffalo NY 14202-0000
716 852-4416 **Rue Franklin** (French) 341 Franklin St .... Buffalo NY 14202-1702
716 683-7990 **Salvatore's Italian Gardens** (Italian) 6461 Transit Rd .... Depew NY 14043-1089

Goods & Services

■ Department Stores

716 853-4020 **Adam Meldrum & Anderson** 389 Main St .... Buffalo NY 14203-2147
716 856-5300 **LL Berger's** 514 Main St .... Buffalo NY 14202-2598

■ Banks

716 842-5287 **Manufacturers & Traders Trust Co** 1 M & T Plaza 1st Fl .... Buffalo NY 14203-2399
716 841-2424 **Marine Midland Bank NA** 237 Main St .... Buffalo NY 14203-2702
716 847-7200 **Norstar Bank** 10 Fountain Plaza .... Buffalo NY 14202-2288

■ Messenger/Postal

Federal Express	716 823-1335	Town Express	716 882-1035
Mail Delivery Service Inc	716 893-8204	U-Need-A-Parcel Delivered	716 875-5918
Post Office	716 846-2434	UPS	716 685-1700

■ Secretarial/Temp Services

716 833-5322 **Accountemps** 4053 Maple Rd .... Amherst NY 14202-0000
716 853-7411 **Kelly Services** 1904 Liberty Bldg .... Buffalo NY 14202-3681
716 854-4000 **Manpower Temporary Services** 135 Delaware Ave .... Buffalo NY 14202-2489
716 854-4020 **Olsten Temporary Services** 43 Court St .... Buffalo NY 14202-3183

Media

■ Newspapers/Magazines

716 849-3434 **Buffalo News** 1 News Plaza .... Buffalo NY 14203-2994
716 839-3405 **Buffalo Spree Magazine** 4511 Harlem Rd .... Buffalo NY 14226-3859

■ Television

716 856-1414 **WGRZ-TV Ch 2 (NBC)** 259 Delaware Ave .... Buffalo NY 14202-2055
716 874-4410 **WIVB-TV Ch 4 (CBS)** 2077 Elmwood Ave .... Buffalo NY 14207-1975
716 845-6100 **WKBW-TV Ch 7 (ABC)** 7 Broadcast Plaza .... Buffalo NY 14202-2699
716 881-5000 **WNED-TV Ch 17 (PBS)** 184 Barton St .... Buffalo NY 14213-1536

■ Radio

716 876-0930 **WBEN-AM 930 kHz (AC-CBS)** 2077 Elmwood Ave .... Buffalo NY 14207-1903
716 831-2555 **WBFO-FM 88.7 MHz (Jazz-NPR)** 3435 Main St .... Buffalo NY 14214-3000
716 882-4300 **WBUF-FM 92.9 MHz (AC-AP)** 715 Delaware Ave .... Buffalo NY 14209-2212
716 854-1120 **WHTT-AM 1120 kHz (Gold)** Church & Terrace Sts .... Buffalo NY 14202-0000
716 854-1120 **WHTT-FM 104.1 MHz (Gold)** Church & Terrace Sts .... Buffalo NY 14202-0000
716 856-3550 **WJYE-FM 96.1 MHz (AC)** 1700 Rand Bldg .... Buffalo NY 14203-0000
716 884-5101 **WKSE-FM 98.5 MHz (CHR-ABC)** 695 Delaware Ave .... Buffalo NY 14209-2201
716 852-7444 **WYRK-FM 106.5 MHz (Ctry)** 500 Rand Bldg .... Buffalo NY 14203-0000

Local Attractions & Special Events

■ Sports

716 649-0015 **Buffalo Bills** Abbott Rd & US Hwy 20 Rich Stadium .... Orchard Park NY 14127-0000
716 856-7300 **Buffalo Sabres** 140 Main St Memorial Auditorium .... Buffalo NY 14202-4190

■ Local Attractions

716 882-8700 **Albright-Knox Art Gallery** 1285 Elmwood Ave .... Buffalo NY 14222-1096
716 896-5200 **Buffalo Museum of Science** 1020 Humboldt Pkwy .... Buffalo NY 14211-1208
716 885-5000 **Buffalo Philharmonic Orchestra**
370 Pennsylvania St Kleinhans Music Hall .... Buffalo NY 14201-1298
716 652-8854 **Millard Fillmore Landmark House & Museum**
24 Shearer Ave .... East Aurora NY 14052-0000
716 884-0095 **Theodore Roosevelt Inaugural National Historical Site**
641 Delaware Ave Wilcox Mansion .... Buffalo NY 14202-0000

Charlotte
NORTH CAROLINA 704

Important Phone Numbers

AAA	704 377-3600	Poison Control Center	704 379-5827
American Express	704 364-3373	Time/Temp	704 375-6711
City Hall	704 336-2040	Weather	704 359-8466
Emergency	911		

■ Travel Information
704 377-6911 **Chamber of Commerce** 129 W Trade St .... Charlotte NC 28202-2172
704 371-8700 **Convention & Visitors Bureau** 229 N Church St .... Charlotte NC 28202-2103

Travel

■ Airport
704 359-4000 **Charlotte/Douglas International Airport** 5 miles W of city (approx 15 minutes)

■ Airport Transportation
704 567-1335 **LATCO** $4 fare to downtown
Taxi $12 fare to downtown

■ Scheduled Airlines
American	704 333-0130	TWA	800 221-2000
Delta	704 372-3000	United	800 241-6522
Eastern	704 366-6131	USAir	704 376-0235
Pan Am	800 221-1111		

■ Charter Airlines
Butler Aviation	704 359-8415	Thurston Aviation	704 359-8670
Southeast Airmotive Corp	704 359-8403		

■ Car Rentals
Ace	704 394-0151	Dollar	704 359-4700
Agency	704 537-7272	Hertz	704 359-0114
Alamo	704 392-8020	National	704 359-0215
Avis	704 359-4580	Payless	704 359-4640
Budget	704 359-5000	Thrifty	704 394-6588

■ Limo/Taxi
Bush Limo Service	704 394-0131	Circle Cab Co	704 375-2561
Charlotte Checker Cab	704 333-1111	Rose Limousine	704 522-8258
Checker Cab	704 334-2875	Yellow Cab Co	704 332-6161

■ Mass Transit
704 336-3366 **Charlotte Transit System** $.70 Base fare .... Charlotte NC 28206-3368

■ Rail/Bus
704 376-4416 **Charlotte Station** 1914 N Tryon St .... Charlotte NC 28206-2734
704 375-9536 **Greyhound/Trailways Bus Terminal** 601 W Trade St .... Charlotte NC 28202-1335

Hotels

704 372-4100 **Adam's Mark Hotel** 555 S McDowell St .... Charlotte NC 28204-2678
704 596-7020 **Carriage Inn** 4330 N I-85 .... Charlotte NC 28206-0000
704 527-9650 **Charlotte Marriott Executive Park** 5700 W Park Dr .... Charlotte NC 28217-0000
704 377-1501 **Coliseum Inn** 3000 E Independence Blvd .... Charlotte NC 28205-7037
704 364-2400 **Guest Quarters Suite Hotel** 6300 Morrison Blvd .... Charlotte NC 28211-3501
704 525-0747 **Hampton Inn** 440 Griffith Rd .... Charlotte NC 28217-3569
704 547-7444 **Hilton Hotel at University Place** 8629 JM Keynes Dr .... Charlotte NC 28213-8426
704 394-4301 **Holiday Inn Airport** 2707 Little Rock Rd .... Charlotte NC 28214-3069
704 377-4441 **Holiday Inn North** 3815 N Tryon St .... Charlotte NC 28206-2000
704 333-9000 **Marriott City Center** 100 W Trade St .... Charlotte NC 28202-2144
704 364-8220 **Park Hotel** 2200 Rexford Rd .... Charlotte NC 28211-3455
704 377-0400 **Radisson Plaza Hotel** 2 NCNB Plaza .... Charlotte NC 28280-0001
704 527-3000 **Ramada Inn Airport** 515 Clanton Rd .... Charlotte NC 28217-1354
704 537-1010 **Ramada Inn Independence** 3501 E Independence Blvd .... Charlotte NC 28205-7261
704 525-4441 **Registry Hotel** 321 W Woodlawn Rd .... Charlotte NC 28217-2057
704 392-1200 **Sheraton Airport Plaza Hotel** 3315 S I-85 .... Charlotte NC 28208-0000
704 525-5454 **Sterling Inn** 242 E Woodlawn Rd .... Charlotte NC 28217-2224

Restaurants

704 541-3026 **Alfredo's Italian Restaurant**
(Italian) 9101 Pineville Matthews Rd .... Pineville NC 28226-0000
704 332-3224 **Chez Daniel** (French) 1742 Lombardy Cir .... Charlotte NC 28203-5842
704 375-0756 **Eli's on East** (American/French) 311 East Blvd .... Charlotte NC 28203-4721
704 377-4529 **Epicurean** (Continental) 1324 East Blvd .... Charlotte NC 28203-5899
704 365-0883 **Fishmarket** (Seafood) 6631 Morrison Blvd .... Charlotte NC 28211-3535
704 332-3663 **Jonathon's Uptown** (Regional) 330 N Tryon St .... Charlotte NC 28202-2139
704 372-5343 **Lamplighter** (Continental) 1065 E Morehead St .... Charlotte NC 28203-0000
704 596-8014 **Old Hickory House Restaurant** (Barbecue) 6538 N Tryon St .... Charlotte NC 28213-5519
704 377-0400 **Reflections** (Continental) 2 NCNB Plaza Radisson Plaza Hotel .... Charlotte NC 28280-0001
704 556-0914 **Si** (Italian) 8418 Park Rd .... Charlotte NC 28210-0000
704 372-2258 **Tio Montero** (Spanish) 1801 Scott Ave .... Charlotte NC 28203-0000
704 335-1546 **Townhouse The** (American) 1011 Providence Rd .... Charlotte NC 28207-0000

Goods & Services

■ Department Stores
704 364-4251 **Belk** 4400 Sharon Rd .... Charlotte NC 28211-3592

■ Banks
704 374-6161 **First Union National Bank of North Carolina** 301 S Tryon St .... Charlotte NC 28288-0001

---

704 374-5000 **NCNB National Bank of North Carolina**
S Tryon St 1 NCNB Plaza .... Charlotte NC 28255-0001
704 377-2676 **Republic Bank & Trust Co** 101 S Kings Dr .... Charlotte NC 28204-2619

■ Messenger/Postal
Commercial Courier Express	704 359-8290	Post Office	704 393-4495
Federal Express	800 238-5355	Quick as a Wink Delivery Service	704 536-8375
Pony Express Courier Corp	704 359-8473	UPS	704 372-3490

■ Secretarial/Temp Services
704 372-3440 **Kelly Services** 901 W Trade St Suite 150 .... Charlotte NC 28202-1100
704 377-4102 **Manpower Temporary Services** 301 S College St Suite 2020 ... Charlotte NC 28202-6016
704 527-6691 **Olsten Temporary Services** 756 Tyvola Rd Suite 160 .... Charlotte NC 28217-3535

Media

■ Newspapers/Magazines
704 332-0148 **Charlotte Magazine** 307 E Tremont Ave .... Charlotte NC 28203-0000
704 379-6371 **Charlotte Observer** 200 S Tryon St .... Charlotte NC 28202-3214

■ Television
704 374-3500 **WBTV-TV Ch 3 (CBS)** 1 Julian Price Pl .... Charlotte NC 28208-5211
704 536-3636 **WNC-TV Ch 36 (NBC)** 8036 Hood Rd .... Charlotte NC 28215-8701
704 335-4999 **WSOC-TV Ch 9 (ABC)** 1901 N Tryon St .... Charlotte NC 28206-2700
704 372-2442 **WTVI-TV Ch 42 (PBS)** 42 Coliseum Dr .... Charlotte NC 28205-7094

■ Radio
704 374-3500 **WBT-AM 1110 kHz (AC-NBC)** 1 Julian Price Pl .... Charlotte NC 28208-5211
704 549-9323 **WFAE-FM 90.7 MHz (Misc-NPR)** 1 University Pl Suite 91 ...Charlotte NC 28213-0000
704 342-2644 **WGIV-AM 1600 kHz (UC)** PO Box 128 .... Concord NC 28026-0128
704 570-9739 **WRFX-FM 99.7 MHz (AOR)** 915 E 4th St .... Charlotte NC 28204-2270
704 392-6191 **WROQ-AM 610 kHz (AOR)** 400 Radio Rd .... Charlotte NC 28216-1630
704 335-4800 **WSOC-FM 103.7 MHz (Ctry-MBS)** 1901 N Tryon St .... Charlotte NC 28206-2700
704 570-9700 **WTDR-FM 96.9 MHz (Ctry)** 301 S McDowell St Suite 210 .... Charlotte NC 28204-0000

Local Attractions & Special Events

■ Sports
704 376-6430 **Charlotte Hornets** 2 First Union Ctr .... Charlotte NC 28282-0001
803 548-8051 **Charlotte Knights** 2280 Deerfield Dr .... Fort Mill SC 29715-0000
704 455-3200 **Charlotte Motor Speedway** Hwy 29 N .... Concord NC 28026-0000

■ Local Attractions
704 372-6261 **Discovery Place** 301 N Tryon St .... Charlotte NC 28202-2179
704 358-2100 **Federal Reserve** 530 E Trade St .... Charlotte NC 28202-0000
704 889-7145 **James K Polk Memorial** US Hwy 521 .... Pineville NC 28134-0000
704 337-2000 **Mint Museum of Art** 2730 Randolph Rd .... Charlotte NC 28207-2031
704 376-8883 **Spirit Square** 345 N College St .... Charlotte NC 28202-2140

Chicago

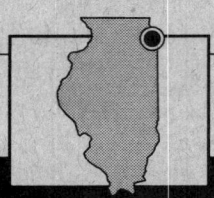

ILLINOIS   312

Important Phone Numbers

AAA	312 372-1818	Emergency	911
American Express	312 902-1343	Poison Control Center	800 942-5969
Better Business Bureau	312 346-3313	Time	708 976-1616
City Hall	312 744-4000	Weather	708 298-1413

■ Travel Information

312 580-6900	**Chamber of Commerce** 200 N La Salle St	Chicago IL 60601-1014
312 567-8500	**Convention & Visitors Bureau** McCormack Pl	Chicago IL 60616-0000
312 645-1836	**International Visitor's Center** 520 N Michigan Ave	Chicago IL 60611-3702
312 280-5748	**Tourism Council** 163 E Pearson St	Chicago IL 60611-2126

Travel

■ Airport: O'Hare

312 686-2200 **O'Hare International Airport** 21 miles NW of city (approx 45-60 minutes)

■ Airport Transportation: O'Hare

312 664-7200 **Chicago Transit Authority** $1 fare to downtown
312 454-7800 **Continental Air Transport** $12 fare to downtown
Taxi $18-20 fare to downtown

■ Scheduled Airlines: O'Hare

Aer Lingus	800 223-6537	Northwest	800 225-2525
Air Canada	800 776-3000	Pan Am	800 221-1111
Air France	800 237-2747	Philippine	800 435-9725
Alitalia	800 223-5730	Qantas	800 227-4500
America West	312 372-2402	Royal Jordanian	800 223-0470
American	312 372-8000	Sabena	800 955-2000
British Airways	800 247-9297	SAS	800 221-2350
Britt Airways	800 525-0280	Southwest	312 922-1221
Continental	800 525-0280	SwissAir	312 641-8830
Delta	800 221-1212	Trans North Aviation	715 479-6777
Eastern	800 327-8376	Trans World Express	312 558-7000
El Al	800 223-6700	TWA	312 938-9000
Great Lakes	800 554-5111	United	312 569-3000
Japan	312 565-7000	United Express	312 569-3000
KLM	800 777-5553	USAir	312 726-1201
Lufthansa	800 645-3880	Yugoslav Airlines	312 782-1322
Mexicana	800 531-7921		

■ Charter Airlines: O'Hare

American Transair	312 686-6552	Priester Aviation Service Inc	708 537-1200
Emery Air Charter Service	815 968-8287	Sunstream Aircraft Inc	708 584-8250
Midwest Helicopter Airways Inc	708 325-7860		

■ Airport: Midway

312 767-0500 **Midway Airport** 15 miles SW of downtown (approx 40 minutes)

■ Airport Transportation: Midway

312 664-7200 **Chicago Transit Authority** $1.25 fare to downtown
312 454-7800 **Continental Air Transport** $12 fare to downtown
Taxi $10 fare to downtown

■ Scheduled Airlines: Midway

America West	800 247-5692	Southwest	312 922-1221
Continental	312 686-6500	TWA	312 938-9000
Midway	312 767-3400	United	800 241-6522
Northwest	312 346-4900		

■ Charter Airlines: Midway

Aero Services	312 582-5721	Executive Flight Management	312 735-6906

■ Car Rentals

Ace	708 827-6082	Hertz	312 686-7272
Agency	708 298-0200	National	312 694-4640
Airways	708 675-7300	Payless	708 635-6140
Alamo	708 671-7662	Rent-A-Wreck	312 585-7300
Avis	312 694-5600	Sears	312 686-4951
Budget	708 968-6661	Snappy	708 671-2600
Dollar	312 694-5100	Thrifty	708 298-3383

■ Limo/Taxi

Checker Taxi Co Inc	312 421-1300	Metropolitan Dav-el Limousines	312 808-8000
Chicago Limousine	312 726-1035	Phoenix Charter Transportation	312 666-3309
CW Airport Service	312 493-2700	Ribaldo Limousines	312 332-1221
Delaware Cars & Limousines	312 337-2800	Yellow Cab Co Inc	312 225-7440
Flash Cab	312 878-8500		

■ Mass Transit

312 664-7200	**Chicago Transit Authority** $1.25 Base fare	Chicago IL 60654-0000
312 836-7000	**L-Train** $1.25 Base fare	Chicago IL 60602-0000

▣ Rail/Bus

312 408-5971	**Greyhound/Trailways Bus Station** 630 W Harrison St	Chicago IL 60607-3611
312 930-4303	**Union Station** 225 S Canal St	Chicago IL 60606-5715

Hotels

312 440-1500	**Allerton Hotel** 701 N Michigan Ave	Chicago IL	60611-2522
312 787-6000	**Barclay Chicago** 166 E Superior St	Chicago IL	60611-2924
312 236-0123	**Bismarck Hotel** 171 W Randolph St	Chicago IL	60601-3199
312 427-4300	**Blackstone Hotel** 636 S Michigan Ave	Chicago IL	60605-1902
312 922-4400	**Chicago Hilton Inn & Towers** 720 S Michigan Ave	Chicago IL	60605-2116
708 635-1300	**Comfort Inn O'Hare** 2175 E Touhy Ave	Des Plaines IL	60018-3637
312 427-3800	**Congress Hotel** 520 S Michigan Ave	Chicago IL	60605-1626
312 787-2200	**Drake Hotel** 140 E Walton St	Chicago IL	60611-1545
708 574-5700	**Drake Oak Brook Hotel** 2301 York Rd	Oak Brook IL	60521-2381
708 699-6300	**Embassy Suites O'Hare** 6501 N Mannheim Rd	Rosemont IL	60018-3681
312 939-2800	**Essex Inn** 800 S Michigan Ave	Chicago IL	60605-2115
312 346-7100	**Executive House Hotel** 71 E Wacker Dr	Chicago IL	60601-3786
312 565-8000	**Fairmont Hotel at Illinois Center** 200 N Columbus Dr	Chicago IL	60601-0000
312 922-2900	**Grant Park Hotel** 1100 S Michigan	Chicago IL	60605-0000
312 744-1900	**Hotel Nikko Chicago** 320 N Dearborn	Chicago IL	60610-4810
312 565-1234	**Hyatt Regency Chicago** 151 E Wacker Dr	Chicago IL	60601-3709
708 696-1234	**Hyatt Regency O'Hare** 9300 Bryn Mawr Ave	Rosemont IL	60018-5238
312 751-8100	**Knickerbocker Chicago Hotel** 163 E Walton St	Chicago IL	60611-1527
312 836-0100	**Marriott Hotel Downtown** 540 N Michigan Ave	Chicago IL	60611-3822
312 787-8500	**Mayfair Regent Hotel** 181 E Lake Shore Dr	Chicago IL	60611-1337
312 791-1900	**McCormick Center Hotel** 451 E 23rd Dr	Chicago IL	60616-1496
312 332-1200	**Midland Hotel** 172 W Adams St	Chicago IL	60603-3604
312 693-4444	**O'Hare Marriott Hotel** 8535 W Higgins Rd	Chicago IL	60631-2872
312 787-7200	**Omni Ambassador East Hotel** 1301 N State Pkwy	Chicago IL	60610-2147
312 346-6585	**Oxford House** 225 N Wabash Ave	Chicago IL	60601-2490
312 726-7500	**Palmer House** 17 E Monroe St	Chicago IL	60603-5605
312 280-2222	**Park Hyatt Hotel** 800 N Michigan Ave	Chicago IL	60611-2123
312 943-5000	**Raphael Hotel** 201 E Delaware Pl	Chicago IL	60611-1746
312 787-3580	**Richmont Hotel** 162 E Ontario St	Chicago IL	60611-2849
312 266-1000	**Ritz-Carlton Hotel** 160 E Pearson St	Chicago IL	60611-2124
312 787-2900	**Sheraton Plaza Hotel** 160 E Huron St	Chicago IL	60611-2918
312 944-4970	**Talbott Hotel** 20 E Delaware Pl	Chicago IL	60606-0000
312 751-1900	**Tremont Hotel** 100 E Chestnut St	Chicago IL	60611-2054
312 943-7200	**Westin Hotel Chicago** 909 N Michigan Ave	Chicago IL	60611-1531
708 698-6000	**Westin Hotel O'Hare** 6100 N River Rd	Rosemont IL	60018-5197
312 944-6300	**Whitehall Hotel** 105 E Delaware Pl	Chicago IL	60611-1441

Restaurants

312 787-9596	**95th The** (American) 172 E Chestnut St	Chicago IL	60611-0000
312 472-5959	**Ambria** (Nouvelle/French) 2300 N Lincoln Pk W	Chicago IL	60614-0000
312 266-4800	**Arnie's** (Continental) 1030 N State St	Chicago IL	60610-2844
312 427-3170	**Berghoff** (German/American) 17 W Adams St	Chicago IL	60603-5502
708 520-3633	**Bob Chinn's Crab House** (Steak/Seafood) 393 S Milwaukee Ave	Wheeling IL	60090-5002
708 827-7818	**Cafe La Cave** (French/Continental) 2733 Manheim Rd	Des Plaines IL	60018-3687
312 787-2200	**Cape Cod Room** (Seafood) 140 E Walton Pl	Chicago IL	60611-1545
708 432-0770	**Carlos'** (French) 429 Temple Ave	Highland Park IL	60035-1428
312 280-9200	**Carson's the Place for Ribs** (Barbecue) 612 N Wells St	Chicago IL	60610-3715
312 527-3100	**Charley & Pasquale's** (Steak/Seafood) 405 N Wabash Ave	Chicago IL	60611-3579
312 248-6228	**Charlie Trotter's** (Nouvelle French) 816 W Armitage Ave	Chicago IL	60614-0000
312 280-2720	**Chestnut Street Grill** (Seafood) 845 N Michigan Water Tower Pl Mezzanine Level	Chicago IL	60611-0000
312 944-6680	**Chez Paul** (French) 660 N Rush	Chicago IL	60611-2747
312 421-5222	**Como Inn** (Italian) 546 N Milwaukee Ave	Chicago IL	60622-5994
312 280-2100	**Cricket's** (Continental) 100 E Chestnut St	Chicago IL	60611-2054
312 280-1790	**Ditka's City Lights** (Steak/Seafood) 223 W Ontario St	Chicago IL	60610-3604
312 642-1393	**Eli's the Place for Steak** (Steak/Continental) 215 E Chicago Ave	Chicago IL	60611-2610
312 663-8920	**Everest Room** (French) 440 S LaSalle St	Chicago IL	60605-0000
312 661-1434	**Frontera Grill** (Mexican) 445 N Clark St	Chicago IL	60610-0000
312 527-3718	**Gene & Georgetti** (Steak) 500 N Franklin St	Chicago IL	60610-4169
312 644-2290	**George's** (Seafood) 230 W Kinzie St	Chicago IL	60610-4408
312 467-9780	**Gordon** (Nouvelle American) 500 N Clark St	Chicago IL	60610-4202
312 943-2252	**Hard Rock Cafe** (American) 63 W Ontario St	Chicago IL	60610-3808
312 280-8287	**Hatsuhana** (Japanese) 160 E Ontario St	Chicago IL	60611-2809
312 539-2999	**Jimmy's Place** (French) 3420 N Elston	Chicago IL	60618-5608
708 299-0011	**Knickers** (Steaks) 1050 Oakton St	Des Plaines IL	60018-2094
312 280-2230	**La Tour** (French) 800 N Michigan Ave	Chicago IL	60611-2123
312 787-5000	**Lawry's Prime Rib** (American) 100 E Ontario St	Chicago IL	60611-2806
708 541-7470	**Le Francais** (French) 269 S Milwaukee Ave	Wheeling IL	60090-5097
312 944-7990	**Le Perroquet** (Nouvelle French) 70 E Walton	Chicago IL	60611-1427
708 506-0222	**Le Titi de Paris** (French) 1015 W Dundee Rd	Arlington Heights IL	60004-1419
312 327-8861	**Leona's** (Italian) 3215 N Sheffield St	Chicago IL	60657-2210
312 951-6441	**Mirador** (French) 1400 N Wells St	Chicago IL	60610-0000
312 266-4820	**Morton's of Chicago** (Steak) 1050 N State St	Chicago IL	60610-2855
312 621-0200	**Nick's Fishmarket** (Seafood) 1 First National Plaza	Chicago IL	60603-0000
708 296-7777	**Omega Pancake House** (American) 9100 Gulf Rd	Niles IL	60016-1906
312 944-0135	**Palm The** (Steak/Seafood) 181 E Lake Shore Dr	Chicago IL	60611-1337
708 848-4250	**Philander's** (Seafood) 1120 Pleasant St	Oak Park IL	60302-3010
312 266-0360	**Pump Room** (Continental) 1301 N State Pkwy	Chicago IL	60610-2117
312 227-5866	**Ritz-Carlton Dining Room** (Nouvelle French) 160 E Pearson St	Chicago IL	60611-2124
312 880-7878	**Rust Belt Cafe** (American) 2747 N Lincoln Ave	Chicago IL	60614-0000
312 527-2722	**Shaw's Crab House** (Seafood) 21 E Hubbard St	Chicago IL	60610-0000
312 280-2750	**Spiaggia** (Italian) 980 N Michigan Ave	Chicago IL	60611-9739
312 943-4041	**Su Casa** (Mexican) 49 E Ontario	Chicago IL	60611-2727
312 661-1434	**Topolobampo** (Mexican) 445 N Clark St	Chicago IL	60610-0000
312 944-6300	**Whitehall Club** (Continental) 105 E Delaware Pl	Chicago IL	60611-1441

Goods & Services

■ Department Stores

312 641-8000	**Carson Pirie Scott** 1 S State St	Chicago IL	60603-2895
312 751-0500	**I Magnin** 830 N Michigan Ave	Chicago IL	60611-2194
312 787-7400	**Lord & Taylor** 835 N Michigan Ave	Chicago IL	60611-2293
312 781-1000	**Marshall Field's** 111 N State St	Chicago IL	60602-1658
312 642-5900	**Neiman-Marcus** 737 N Michigan Ave	Chicago IL	60611-2657
312 944-6500	**Saks Fifth Avenue** 669 N Michigan	Chicago IL	60611-2884

■ Banks

312 661-5000	**American National Bank & Trust Co of Chicago** 33 N La Salle St	Chicago IL	60678-0001
312 781-8000	**Exchange National Bank** 120 S La Salle St	Chicago IL	60603-3499
312 732-4000	**First National Bank of Chicago** 1 First National Plaza	Chicago IL	60670-0001
312 461-2121	**Harris Trust & Savings Bank** 111 W Monroe St	Chicago IL	60603-0000
312 693-5555	**Northern Trust Bank/O'Hare NA** 8501 W Higgins Rd	Chicago IL	60631-2881

■ Messenger/Postal

Agency Expediting	312 642-8040	Federal Express	800 238-5355
Archer Services of Chicago Inc	312 939-5656	Post Office	312 765-3210
Arrow Messenger Service Inc	312 489-6688	Quicksilver Messenger Service	312 726-3736
Cannonball Messenger Service	312 829-1234	Reli On Inc	312 726-2585
Cheetah Messenger Service	312 235-9146	SEKO-Rocket Bonded Delivery Svc	312 527-0100
Chicago Messenger Service	312 666-6800	UPS	708 990-2900
Comet Messenger Service Inc	312 786-2288		

■ Secretarial/Temp Services

312 616-8367	Accountemps 9205 N Michigan Ave	Chicago IL	60601-2191
312 853-3434	Kelly Temporary Services 55 W Monroe St Suite 690	Chicago IL	60603-5041
312 263-5144	Manpower Temporary Services 55 E Monroe St	Chicago IL	60603-5702
312 782-1014	Olsten Temporary Services 123 W Madison St	Chicago IL	60602-4511

Media

■ Newspapers/Magazines

312 222-8999	Chicago Magazine 414 N Orleans St Suite 800	Chicago IL	60610-4497
312 321-3000	Chicago Sun-Times 401 N Wabash Ave	Chicago IL	60611-3593
312 222-3232	Chicago Tribune 435 N Michigan Ave	Chicago IL	60611-4022

■ Television

312 944-6000	WBBM-TV Ch 2 (CBS) 630 N McClurg Ct	Chicago IL	60611-3074
312 528-2311	WGN-TV Ch 9 2501 W Bradley Pl	Chicago IL	60618-4767
312 750-7777	WLS-TV Ch 7 (ABC) 190 N State St	Chicago IL	60601-3379
312 836-5555	WMAQ-TV Ch 5 (NBC) 454 N Columbus Dr NBC Towers	Chicago IL	60611-0000
312 583-5000	WTTW-TV Ch 11 (PBS) 5400 N St Louis Ave	Chicago IL	60625-4698

■ Radio

312 944-6000	WBBM-AM 780 kHz (CHR-CBS) 630 N McClurg Ct	Chicago IL	60611-3074
312 890-8225	WBEZ-FM 91.5 MHz (Misc-NPR) 1819 W Pershing Rd	Chicago IL	60609-2317
312 427-4800	WGCI-FM 107.5 MHz (UC) 332 S Michigan Ave Suite 600	Chicago IL	60604-4390
312 222-4700	WGN-AM 720 kHz (N/T) 435 N Michigan Ave	Chicago IL	60611-4001
312 440-5270	WLUP-FM 97.9 MHz (AOR) 875 N Michigan Ave Suite 3750	Chicago IL	60611-1901
312 440-3100	WXEZ-FM 100 MHz (B/EZ-MBS) 875 N Michigan Ave Suite 3201	Chicago IL	60611-1890

Local Attractions & Special Events

■ Sports

312 663-5100	Chicago Bears 425 McFetridge Pl Soldier Field	Chicago IL	60616-0000
312 733-5300	Chicago Blackhawks 1800 W Madison St Chicago Stadium	Chicago IL	60612-2698
312 943-5800	Chicago Bulls 980 N Michigan Ave	Chicago IL	60611-4502
312 404-2827	Chicago Cubs 1060 W Addison St Wrigley Field	Chicago IL	60613-4397
312 924-1000	Chicago White Sox 324 W 35th St	Chicago IL	60616-3696

■ Special Events

312 744-3315	Chicago Blues Festival (June 14-16)
312 744-3370	Chicago Jazz Festival (August 29-September 1)

■ Local Attractions

312 443-3600	Art Institute of Chicago Michigan Ave & Adams St	Chicago IL	60603-6494
708 485-0263	Brookfield Zoo 31st St & 1st Ave	Brookfield IL	60513-1099
312 871-2668	Chicago Academy of Sciences 2001 N Clark St	Chicago IL	60601-0000
312 435-8122	Chicago Symphony Orchestra 220 S Michigan Ave	Chicago IL	60604-2559
312 947-0600	Dusable Museum of African-American History 740 E 56th Pl	Chicago IL	60637-1495
312 922-9410	Field Museum of Natural History Roosevelt Rd & Lake Shore Dr	Chicago IL	60605-0000
708 848-1978	Frank Lloyd Wright Home & Studio 951 Chicago Ave	Oak Park IL	60302-2007
312 443-3800	Goodman Theatre 200 S Columbus Dr	Chicago IL	60603-6491
312 939-2438	John G Shedd Aquarium 1200 S Lake Shore Dr	Chicago IL	60601-0000
708 634-0200	Marriott's Lincolnshire Theatre 10 Marriott Dr	Lincolnshire IL	60069-3702
312 684-1414	Museum of Science & Industry 57th St & Lake Shore Dr	Chicago IL	60637-0000
312 440-8840	North Pier 455 E Illinois St	Chicago IL	60611-4305
312 782-6171	Old Saint Patrick's Church 718 W Adams St	Chicago IL	60606-3512
312 875-9696	Sears Tower 233 S Wacker Dr	Chicago IL	60684-0000
312 337-3992	Second City ETC 1608 N Wells St	Chicago IL	60614-6002
312 440-3165	Water Tower Place 835 N Michigan Ave	Chicago IL	60611-2265

Cincinnati

OHIO 513

Important Phone Numbers

AAA	513 762-3100	Emergency	911
American Express	513 241-1300	Poison Control Center	513 558-5111
Better Business Bureau	513 421-3015	Time/Temp	513 721-1700
City Hall	513 352-3000	Weather	513 241-1010

■ Travel Information

513 579-3100 **Chamber of Commerce** 441 Vine St Carew Tower Suite 300 .... Cincinnati OH 45202-0000
513 621-2142 **Convention & Visitors Bureau** 300 W 6th St .... Cincinnati OH 45202-2361

Travel

■ Airport

606 283-3151 **Greater Cincinnati International Airport** 12 miles SW of downtown (approx 15 minutes)

■ Airport Transportation

606 283-3260 **Airport Taxi Service** $18 fare to downtown
Taxi $20 fare to downtown

■ Scheduled Airlines

American	513 621-6200	Pan Am	800 221-1111
Comair	800 354-9822	TWA	513 381-1600
Delta	513 721-7000	United	800 241-6522
Enterprise	606 283-3280	USAir	513 621-9220
Northwest	800 225-2525		

■ Charter Airlines

Corp Flight	606 283-3500	Sunbird Air Services	513 322-2711
Executive Jet Management Inc	513 871-2004		

■ Car Rentals

Alamo	606 586-8050	Dollar	513 721-8885
Budget	606 283-1166	Hertz	606 283-3535
Burnett	513 271-0300	National	606 283-3655

■ Limo/Taxi

Barrs Ltd Limo	513 531-7321	Washington Limo	513 221-0074
Checker Cab	513 621-3600	Yellow Cab	513 241-2100
VIP Transportation Services	513 281-0285		

■ Mass Transit

513 621-9450 **Queen City Metro** $.50 Base fare .... Cincinnati OH 45202-0000

■ Rail/Bus

800 872-7245 **Cincinnati Station** 1901 River Rd .... Cincinnati OH 45204-1333
513 352-6012 **Greyhound/Trailways Bus Station** 1005 Gilbert Ave .... Cincinnati OH 45202-1491

Hotels

513 821-5110 **Carrousel Inn** 8001 Reading Rd .... Cincinnati OH 45237-1477
513 352-2100 **Clarion Hotel** 141 W 6th St .... Cincinnati OH 45202-2393
606 341-2800 **Drawbridge Inn & Convention Center**
I-75 & Buttermilk Pike .... Fort Mitchell KY 41017-0000
513 771-3400 **Howard Johnson Plaza Hotel** 11440 Chester Rd .... Cincinnati OH 45246-4005
513 579-1234 **Hyatt Regency Cincinnati** 151 W 5th St .... Cincinnati OH 45202-2716
513 574-6000 **Imperial House West** 5510 Rybolt Rd .... Cincinnati OH 45248-1099
513 772-1720 **Marriott Hotel** 11320 Chester Rd .... Cincinnati OH 45246-4090
513 421-9100 **Omni Netherland Plaza** 35 W 5th St .... Cincinnati OH 45202-2899
513 381-4000 **Terrace Hilton** 15 W 6th St .... Cincinnati OH 45202-2301
513 281-3300 **Vernon Manor Hotel** 400 Oak St .... Cincinnati OH 45219-2538
513 621-7700 **Westin Hotel** 5th & Vine Sts .... Cincinnati OH 45202-3160

Restaurants

513 771-1440 **Burbank's Real Barbecue** (Barbecue) 11167 Dowlin Dr .... Cincinnati OH 45215-0000
513 241-4455 **Celestial** (Continental) 1071 Celestial St .... Cincinnati OH 45202-1661
606 431-6700 **Coach & Four Restaurant** (Nouvelle American) 214 Scott St ... Covington KY 41011-1524
513 241-3663 **Del's**
(Nouvelle American) Westin Hotel Fountain Square Plaza .... Cincinnati OH 45202-0000
513 932-5065 **Golden Lamb** (Continental) 27 S Broadway .... Lebanon OH 45036-1705
513 721-2761 **La Normandie Grill** (Steak) 114 E 6th St .... Cincinnati OH 45202-3202
513 721-2260 **Maisonette** (French) 114 E 6th St .... Cincinnati OH 45202-3299
606 261-4212 **Mike Fink** (Steaks/Seafood) Foot of Greenup St .... Covington KY 41011-0000
513 791-3482 **Montgomery Inn Ribs King**
(Barbecue) 9440 Montgomery Ave .... Montgomery OH 45242-7603
513 321-5454 **Precinct The** (Steak) 311 Delta Ave .... Cincinnati OH 45226-2135
513 251-6467 **Primavista** (Italian) 810 Matson Pl .... Cincinnati OH 45204-0000
513 871-7427 **Ribbobbies Grill** (Barbecue) 2038 Madison Rd .... Cincinnati OH 45208-0000
513 381-4000 **Terrace Gardens** (French) 15 W 6th St .... Cincinnati OH 45202-2301
606 581-1414 **Waterfront** (Steak/Seafood) 14 Pete Rose Pier .... Covington KY 41011-1267

Goods & Services

■ Department Stores

513 369-7000 **Lazarus** 699 Race St .... Cincinnati OH 45202-2395
513 352-4400 **McAlpin's** 13 W 4th St .... Cincinnati OH 45202-3697
513 421-6800 **Saks Fifth Avenue** 5th & Race St .... Cincinnati OH 45202-0000

■ Banks

513 651-8896 **Central Trust Co** 201 E 5th St .... Cincinnati OH 45202-4117
513 579-5300 **Fifth Third Bank** 38 Fountain Square Plaza .... Cincinnati OH 45263-0001
513 632-4000 **Star Bank** 425 Walnut St .... Cincinnati OH 45264-0001

■ Messenger/Postal

Cincinnati Express Inc	513 542-1900	Post Office	513 684-5664
City Dash Delivery Service Inc	513 641-2000	Priority Dispatch	513 421-8800
Corporate Express Delivery	513 793-9991	Rapid Delivery Service	513 733-0500
Federal Express	513 530-5660	UPS	513 241-5161
Parcel Shipping Center Inc	513 793-3744	Western Union Errands Msgr Svc	513 621-4321

■ Secretarial/Temp Services

513 241-3161 **Kelly Services** 120 E 4th St Suite 520 .... Cincinnati OH 45202-4018
513 621-7250 **Manpower Temporary Services** 895 Central Ave Suite 101 ..... Cincinnati OH 45202-0000
513 621-1177 **Olsten Temporary Services** 36 E 4th St Suite 600 .... Cincinnati OH 45202-3839

Media

■ Newspapers/Magazines

513 721-2700 **Cincinnati Enquirer** 617 Vine St .... Cincinnati OH 45202-2410
513 421-4300 **Cincinnati Magazine** 409 Broadway .... Cincinnati OH 45202-3340
513 352-2000 **Cincinnati Post** 125 E Court St .... Cincinnati OH 45202-1214

■ Television

513 381-4033 **WCET-TV Ch 48 (PBS)** 1223 Central Pkwy .... Cincinnati OH 45214-2890
513 721-9900 **WCPO-TV Ch 9 (CBS)** 500 Central Ave .... Cincinnati OH 45202-2376
513 763-5500 **WKRC-TV Ch 12 (ABC)** 1906 Highland Ave .... Cincinnati OH 45219-3161
513 352-5000 **WLWT-TV Ch 5 (NBC)** 140 W 9th St .... Cincinnati OH 45202-1975

■ Radio

513 241-6565 **WCKY-AM 1530 kHz (N/T-CBS)** 219 McFarland St .... Cincinnati OH 45202-2614
513 621-9326 **WEBN-FM 102.7 MHz (AOR)** 1111 St Gregory St .... Cincinnati OH 45202-1723
513 556-4444 **WGUC-FM 90.9 MHz (Clas-NPR)** 1223 Central Pkwy .... Cincinnati OH 45214-2889
513 763-5500 **WKRQ-FM 101.9 MHz (CHR-ABC)** 1906 Highland Ave .... Cincinnati OH 45219-3161
513 241-9597 **WLW-AM 700 kHz (N/T-ABC)** 1111 St Gregory St .... Cincinnati OH 45202-1723
513 721-5678 **WWEZ-FM 92.5 MHz (B/EZ)** 219 McFarland St .... Cincinnati OH 45202-2696

Local Attractions & Special Events

■ Sports

513 621-3550 **Cincinnati Bengals** 200 Riverfront Stadium .... Cincinnati OH 45202-3589
513 421-4510 **Cincinnati Reds** 100 Riverfront Stadium .... Cincinnati OH 45202-3590

■ Special Events

513 871-3900 **Riverfront Stadium Festival** (July 26-27)

■ Local Attractions

513 721-5204 **Cincinnati Art Museum** 958 Eden Park Dr .... Cincinnati OH 45202-0000
513 398-5410 **College Football Hall of Fame** 5440 Kings Island Dr .... Kings Island OH 45034-0000
513 632-5120 **Harriet Beecher Stowe House** 2950 Gilbert Ave .... Cincinnati OH 45206-0000
513 398-5600 **Kings Island** 6300 Kings Island Dr .... Kings Island OH 45034-0000
513 352-4086 **Krohn Conservatory** Eden Park Dr .... Cincinnati OH 45202-0000
513 891-2900 **Meier's Wine Cellars Inc** 6955 Plainfield Rd .... Cincinnati OH 45236-3793
513 621-3889 **Museum of Natural History & Planetarium** 1720 Gilbert Ave ... Cincinnati OH 45202-0000
513 721-8222 **Music Hall** 1241 Elm St .... Cincinnati OH 45201-0000
513 241-0343 **Taft Museum** 316 Pike St .... Cincinnati OH 45202-4293
513 684-3262 **William Howard Taft National Historical Site**
2038 Auburn Ave .... Cincinnati OH 45219-0000

Cleveland

OHIO   216

Important Phone Numbers

AAA	216 361-6000	Emergency	911
American Express	216 241-4575	Poison Control Center	216 231-4455
Better Business Bureau	216 241-7678	Time	216 931-1212
City Hall	216 664-2000	Weather	216 931-1212

■ Travel Information

216 621-3300   **Chamber of Commerce** 690 Huntington Bldg .... Cleveland OH 44115-0000
216 621-4110   **Convention & Visitors Bureau** 3100 Tower City Ctr .... Cleveland OH 44113-0000

Travel

■ Airport

216 265-6000   **Cleveland Hopkins International Airport** 12 miles SW of downtown (approx 20 minutes)

■ Airport Transportation

216 621-9500   **Regional Transit Authority (RTA)** $1 fare to downtown
                 Taxi $12-15 fare to downtown

■ Scheduled Airlines

Air Canada	800 776-3000	Northwest	800 225-2525
American	216 881-4341	Pan Am	800 221-1111
Continental	216 771-8419	TWA	216 781-2700
Delta	216 781-8800	United	216 356-1311
Eastern	216 861-7300	USAir	216 696-8050

■ Charter Airlines

Corporate Wings Inc	216 261-3500	Jet Aviation Business Jets	216 234-9700
Five Key	216 267-7032		

■ Car Rentals

American Excell	216 944-7333	Hertz	800 654-3131
Avis	216 265-3700	National	800 227-7368
Budget	216 433-4433	Thrifty	216 267-6811
Dollar	216 267-3133		

■ Limo/Taxi

Americab Taxi	216 881-1111	Touch of Class Limousine	216 225-5382
American Limousine	216 221-9330	Yellow Cab	216 623-1500
Elegant Limousine	216 582-1555	Zone Cab	216 623-1550

■ Mass Transit

216 621-9500   **Regional Transit Authority (RTA)** $1 Base fare .... Cleveland OH 44113-0000

■ Rail/Bus

216 781-0520   **Greyhound Bus Station** 1465 Chester Ave .... Cleveland OH 44114-3676
216 696-5115   **Lakefront Station** 200 Cleveland Memorial Shoreway NE .... Cleveland OH 44114-1007

Hotels

216 252-5333   **Cleveland Airport Marriott** 4277 W 150th St .... Cleveland OH 44135-1310
216 447-1300   **Cleveland Hilton South** 6200 Quarry Ln .... Independence OH 44131-2218
216 791-1900   **Clinic Center Hotel** 2065 E 96th St .... Cleveland OH 44106-2916
216 734-4477   **Hampton Inn Airport** 25105 Country Club Blvd .... North Olmsted OH 44070-5312
216 241-5100   **Holiday Inn Lakeside** 1111 Lakeside Ave E ....Cleveland OH 44114-1174
216 238-8800   **Holiday Inn Strongsville** 15471 Royalton Rd .... Strongsville OH 44136-5498
216 771-7600   **Sheraton Cleveland City Center Hotel** 777 St Clair Ave NE ..... Cleveland OH 44114-1791
216 267-1500   **Sheraton Hopkins Airport Hotel** 5300 Riverside Dr .... Cleveland OH 44135-3196
216 696-5600   **Stouffer Tower City Plaza Hotel** 24 Public Sq .... Cleveland OH 44113-2222

Restaurants

216 831-6626   **Chez Voisin** (French) 25540 Miles Rd .... Bedford Heights OH 44146-1324
216 791-1300   **Classics** (Continental) 2065 E 96th St .... Cleveland OH 44106-2916
216 696-5600   **French Connection** (French) 24 Public Sq .... Cleveland OH 44113-2201
216 835-5010   **Glass Garden at the Atrium**
                 (Swiss/Italian/French) 30400 Detroit Rd .... Westlake OH 44145-1893
216 356-2559   **Heck's Cafe** (Continental) 19300 Detroit Rd .... Rocky River OH 44116-1846
216 371-7611   **Lopez Gonzalez** (Mexican) 2066 Lee Rd .... Cleveland Heights OH 44118-2539
216 696-2323   **Massimo da Milano** (Northern Italian) 1400 W 25th St .... Cleveland OH 44113-0000
216 881-0700   **Parker's** (French) 6802 St Clair Ave .... Cleveland OH 44103-0000
216 831-8625   **Ristorante Giovanni's**
                 (Northern Italian) 25550 Chagrin Blvd .... Beachwood OH 44122-5628
216 523-5560   **Sammy's** (American) 1400 W 10th St .... Cleveland OH 44113-1209
216 464-7575   **Samurai Japanese Steak House**
                 (Japanese) 23611 Chagrin Blvd .... Beachwood OH 44122-5540
216 321-0210   **Shujiro's** (Japanese) 2206 Lee Rd .... Cleveland Heights OH 44118-2902
216 376-7171   **Tangier** (Continental) 532 W Market St .... Akron OH 44303-1893
216 831-5800   **Watership Down** (Continental) 34105 Chagrin Blvd .... Moreland Hills OH 44022-1028
216 991-1580   **Z Contemporary Cuisine**
                 (Nouvelle) 20600 Chagrin Blvd .... Shaker Heights OH 44122-5334

Goods & Services

■ Department Stores

216 579-2580   **Higbee's** 100 Public Sq .... Cleveland OH 44113-2227
216 664-6000   **May Co** 158 Euclid Ave .... Cleveland OH 44114-2299
216 292-5500   **Saks Fifth Avenue** 26100 Cedar Rd .... Beachwood OH 44122-1188

■ Banks

216 737-5000   **Ameritrust Co** 900 Euclid Ave .... Cleveland OH 44115-1461
216 575-2000   **National City Bank Cleveland** 1900 E 9th St .... Cleveland OH 44114-3484
216 689-3000   **Society National Bank** 800 Superior Ave E .... Cleveland OH 44114-2692

■ Messenger/Postal

A-Best Way Delivery Co Inc	216 641-5556	Federal Express	800 238-5355
Bonnie Speed Delivery Inc	216 696-6033	In Town Delivery Service Inc	216 781-3318
City Express Delivery	216 781-6500	J & L Kwik Delivery Service Inc	216 431-1310
Delivery Service Inc	216 267-8113	Post Office	216 443-4100
EMS Courier Inc	216 676-8200	Star Express Delivery Service	216 241-2410
Executive Delivery Systems Inc	216 861-4560	UPS	614 272-8500

■ Secretarial/Temp Services

216 771-2800   **Kelly Temporary Services** 1111 Superior St .... Cleveland OH 44114-2507
216 771-5474   **Manpower Temporary Services** 1375 E 9th St ....Cleveland OH 44114-1724
216 861-1900   **Olsten Temporary Services** 2000 E 9th St .... Cleveland OH 44115-1364

Media

■ Newspapers/Magazines

216 771-2833   **Cleveland Magazine** 1422 Euclid Ave .... Cleveland OH 44115-2000
216 344-4500   **Plain Dealer** 1801 Superior Ave E .... Cleveland OH 44114-2198

■ Television

216 431-5555   **WEWS-TV Ch 5 (ABC)** 3001 Euclid Ave .... Cleveland OH 44115-2579
216 431-8888   **WJW-TV Ch 8 (CBS)** 5800 S Marginal Dr .... Cleveland OH 44103-1086
216 344-3333   **WKYC-TV Ch 3 (NBC)** 1403 E 6th St .... Cleveland OH 44114-1669
216 398-2800   **WVIZ-TV Ch 25 (PBS)** 4300 Brookpark Rd .... Cleveland OH 44134-1191

■ Radio

216 432-3700   **WCPN-FM 90.3 MHz (Jazz-NPR)** 3100 Chester Ave .... Cleveland OH 44114-4617
216 391-1260   **WMJI-FM 105.7 MHz (AC)** 3940 Euclid Ave .... Cleveland OH 44115-2506
216 781-9667   **WMMS-FM 100.7 MHz (CHR-NBC)**
                 1200 Statler Office Tower .... Cleveland OH 44115-0000
216 696-6666   **WQAL-FM 104.1 MHz (B/EZ)** 1621 Euclid Ave Suite 1800 .... Cleveland OH 44115-2138
216 861-0228   **WWWE-AM 1100 kHz (N/T-CBS)** 1 Radio Ln .... Cleveland OH 44114-4016

Local Attractions & Special Events

■ Sports

216 696-3800   **Cleveland Browns** Cleveland Municipal Stadium
216 659-9100   **Cleveland Cavaliers** 2923 W Streetsboro Rd Coliseum .... Richfield OH 44286-9632
216 861-1200   **Cleveland Indians** Cleveland Municipal Stadium ....Cleveland OH 44114-0000

■ Special Events

216 781-0747   **National Air Show** (August 31-September 2)

■ Local Attractions

216 834-4012   **Century Village** 14653 E Park St .... Burton OH 44021-0000
216 421-7340   **Cleveland Museum of Art** 11150 East Blvd .... Cleveland OH 44106-1797
216 231-1111   **Cleveland Orchestra** 11001 Euclid Ave .... Cleveland OH 44106-1796
216 433-2001   **NASA Lewis Research Center** 21000 Brookpark Rd .... Cleveland OH 44135-0000
216 621-8500   **Old Arcade** 401 Euclid Ave .... Cleveland OH 44114-2402
216 562-8101   **Sea World of Ohio** 1100 Sea World Dr .... Aurora OH 44202-8700
216 621-4110   **The Flats** Superior Ave & W 10th .... Cleveland OH 44113-0000

Columbus

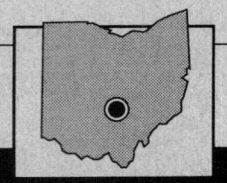

OHIO 614

Important Phone Numbers

AAA	614 431-7800	Emergency	911
American Express	614 228-6666	Poison Control Center	614 228-1323
Better Business Bureau	614 221-6336	Time/Temp	614 281-1111
City Hall	614 645-8100	Weather	614 841-2222

■ Travel Information

614 221-1321 **Chamber of Commerce** 37 N High St .... Columbus OH 43215-3065
614 221-6623 **Convention & Visitors Center** 10 W Broad St Suite 1300 .... Columbus OH 43215-3418

Travel

■ Airport

614 239-4000 **Port Columbus International Airport** 8 miles NE of downtown (approx 15 minutes)

■ Airport Transportation

Taxi $12-14 fare to downtown
614 221-3800 **United Transportation** $12 fare to downtown

■ Scheduled Airlines

Air Canada	800 776-3000	Enterprise	800 343-7300
American	614 228-3211	Jet Stream	614 221-3015
Christman	800 999-8359	Midway	800 621-5700
Comair	800 354-9822	Northwest	800 225-2525
Continental	614 224-3152	TWA	614 221-6411
Delta	614 228-6000	United	614 228-4751
Eastern	614 228-2061	USAir	614 228-4564

■ Charter Airlines

Central Skyport Inc	614 237-6578	Lane Aviation	614 237-3747
Executive Jet Aviation Inc	614 239-5500		

■ Car Rentals

Agency	614 885-8824	National	614 237-0333
Avis	614 235-3477	Sears	800 527-0770
Budget	614 471-2434	Snappy	614 239-1010
Dollar	614 231-1814	Thrifty	614 237-5800
Hertz	614 239-1084		

■ Limo/Taxi

A Cab	614 443-1100	Columbus Limousine	614 228-5466
Airport Taxi	614 299-6400	Yellow Cab	614 224-4141

■ Mass Transit

614 228-1776 **Central Ohio Transit Authority (COTA)** $.75 Base fare .... Columbus OH 43222-0000

■ Rail/Bus

614 221-5311 **Greyhound/Trailways Bus Station** 111 E Town St .... Columbus OH 43215-5151

Hotels

614 861-7220 **Columbus East Hotel** 2124 S Hamilton Rd .... Columbus OH 43232-4181
614 885-1885 **Columbus Marriott North** 6500 Doubletree Ave .... Columbus OH 43229-0000
614 888-4300 **Harley Hotel** 1000 E Granville Rd .... Columbus OH 43229-0000
614 868-1380 **Hilton East** 4560 Hilton Corporate Dr .... Columbus OH 43232-4159
614 436-0700 **Hilton Inn North** 7007 N High St .... Worthington OH 43085-2352
614 228-1234 **Hyatt on Capitol Square** 75 E State St .... Columbus OH 43215-4299
614 463-1234 **Hyatt Regency of Columbus at Ohio Center** 350 N High St ..... Columbus OH 43215-2058
614 228-4600 **Pickett Suite Hotel** 50 S Front St .... Columbus OH 43215-4129
614 221-3281 **Quality Hotel City Center** 175 E Town St .... Columbus OH 43215-4654
614 846-0300 **Radisson Hotel Columbus North** 4900 Sinclair Rd .... Columbus OH 43229-5498

Restaurants

614 235-3950 **Cafe Martinique** (French) 2894 E Main St .... Columbus OH 43209-2613
614 228-3800 **Chutney's Cafe** (American) 310 S High St .... Columbus OH 43215-4508
614 443-1125 **Clarmont The** (Seafood/Steak) 684 S High St .... Columbus OH 43215-5646
614 443-4877 **Engine House #5** (Seafood) 121 Thurman Ave .... Columbus OH 43206-2699
614 228-5555 **Fifty Five on the Blvd** (Seafood) 55 Nationwide Blvd .... Columbus OH 43215-0000
614 299-1844 **Firdou's Deli & Cafe** (Middle East) 1538 N High St .... Columbus OH 43201-0000
614 459-3933 **Hunan Lion** (Chinese) 2000 Bethel Rd Crown Point Plaza .... Columbus OH 43235-0000
614 488-0605 **Jotham's Riverside** (French) 3140 Riverside Dr .... Columbus OH 43221-2545
614 228-4343 **Lindey's** (Continental/American) 169 E Beck St .... Columbus OH 43206-0000
614 444-0131 **Old Swiss House** (German/Swiss) 961 S High St .... Columbus OH 43206-2525
614 431-3333 **Otani** (Japanese) 5900 Roche Dr .... Columbus OH 43229-3232
614 451-9774 **Refectory** (French/Continental) 1092 Bethel Rd .... Columbus OH 43220-0000
614 461-7888 **Rigsby's Cuisine Volatile** (International) 698 N High St .... Columbus OH 43215-1548
614 444-6808 **Schmidt's Sausage Haus** (German) 240 E Kossuth St .... Columbus OH 43206-2188
614 224-8669 **Tony's Italian Ristorante** (Italian) 16 W Beck St .... Columbus OH 43211-0000
614 885-7700 **Worthington Inn The** (American) 649 High St .... Worthington OH 43085-4144

Goods & Services

■ Department Stores

614 463-2121 **Lazarus** 141 S High St .... Columbus OH 43215-3470
614 221-4325 **Madison's** 72 N High St .... Columbus OH 43215-3085
614 471-4711 **Schottenstein** 3251 Westerville Rd .... Columbus OH 43224-3790

■ Banks

614 463-7100 **BancOhio National Bank** 155 E Broad St .... Columbus OH 43251-0001
614 248-5800 **Bank One Columbus NA** 100 E Broad St .... Columbus OH 43271-0001
614 476-8300 **Huntington National Bank** 17 S High St .... Columbus OH 43215-3456

■ Messenger/Postal

Federal Express	800 238-5355	Seidel Delivery Service	614 276-6000
Local Mail & Freight	614 231-7165	United Transportation Inc	614 221-1313
Mail Service Inc	614 878-5854	UPS	614 272-8500
Post Office	614 469-4223	US Cargo & Courier Service Inc	614 491-8608
Priority Dispatch Inc	614 464-4545	Yellow Courier	614 444-4444

■ Secretarial/Temp Services

614 221-9300 **Accountemps** 88 E Broad St .... Columbus OH 43201-0000
614 221-6775 **Kelly Services Inc** 175 S 3rd St Suite 175 .... Columbus OH 43215-5147
614 228-3322 **Manpower Temporary Services Inc**
175 S 3rd St Penthouse 1 .... Columbus OH 43215-5134
614 228-8114 **Olsten Temporary Services** 88 E Broad St Suite 630 .... Columbus OH 43215-3527

Media

■ Newspapers/Magazines

614 461-5000 **Columbus Dispatch** 34 S 3rd St .... Columbus OH 43215-4241
614 464-4567 **Columbus Monthly** 171 E Livingston Ave .... Columbus OH 43215-5786

■ Television

614 460-3700 **WBNS-TV Ch 10 (CBS)** 770 Twin Rivers Dr .... Columbus OH 43215-1159
614 263-4444 **WCMH-TV Ch 4 (NBC)** 3165 Olentangy River Rd .... Columbus OH 43202-1518
614 292-9678 **WOSU-TV Ch 34 (PBS)** 2400 Olentangy River Rd .... Columbus OH 43210-1027
614 481-6666 **WSYX-TV Ch 6 (ABC)** 1261 Dublin Rd .... Columbus OH 43215-7000

■ Radio

614 365-5555 **WCBE-FM 90.5 MHz (Clas-NPR)** 270 E State St .... Columbus OH 43215-4312
614 481-7800 **WMNI-AM 920 kHz (Ctry-MBS)** 1458 Dublin Rd .... Columbus OH 43215-1010
614 224-9624 **WNCI-FM 97.9 MHz (CHR)** 1 Nationwide Plaza 2nd Fl ...... Columbus OH 43215-2240
614 821-9769 **WSNY-FM 94.7 MHz (AC)** 4401 Carriage Hill Ln .... Columbus OH 43220-3837
614 486-6101 **WTVN-AM 610 kHz (AC)** 1301 Dublin Rd .... Columbus OH 43215-1008

Local Attractions & Special Events

■ Sports

614 462-5250 **Columbus Clippers** 1155 W Mound St .... Columbus OH 43223-2298
614 587-1005 **National Trail Raceway** 120 Linden Pl .... Granville OH 43023-1373
614 491-2515 **Scioto Downs** 6000 S High St .... Columbus OH 43207-0000

■ Special Events

614 889-6700 **Memorial Tournament at Muirfield** PGA Golf (May 13-19)

■ Local Attractions

614 847-6270 **Anheuser-Busch Brewery** 700 Schrock Rd .... Columbus OH 43229-1159
614 228-2674 **Center of Science & Industry** 280 E Broad St .... Columbus OH 43215-3773
614 221-8888 **German Village** 624 S Third St .... Columbus OH 43206-0000
614 297-2300 **Ohio Historical Center** 1982 Velma Ave .... Columbus OH 43211-2497
614 469-1331 **Palace Theatre** 34 W Broad St .... Columbus OH 43215-0000
614 622-9310 **Roscoe Village** 381 Hill St .... Coshocton OH 43812-1098
614 833-1880 **Slate Run Living Historical Farm** 9130 Marcy Rd .... Ashville OH 43103-9758
614 464-1032 **Thurber House** 77 Jefferson Ave .... Columbus OH 43215-0000

Dallas

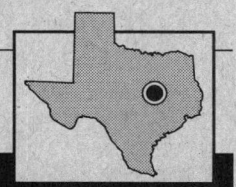

TEXAS   214

Important Phone Numbers

AAA 214 526-7911
American Express 214 749-4078
Better Business Bureau 214 220-2000
City Hall 214 670-3011

Emergency 911
Poison Control Center 214 590-5000
Time/Temp 214 844-6611
Weather 214 787-1111

■ Travel Information

214 746-6600   **Chamber of Commerce** 1201 Elm St Suite 2000 .... Dallas TX 75270-2099
214 658-7000   **Convention & Visitors Center** 650 S Griffin St .... Dallas TX 75202-5098

Travel

■ Airport

214 574-8888   **Dallas-Fort Worth International Airport** 18 miles W of downtown (approx 30 minutes)

■ Airport Transportation

817 329-2000   **Link** $10-12 fare to downtown
              Taxi $21-24 fare to downtown
817 267-5150   **TBS** $8 fare to downtown

■ Scheduled Airlines

American 817 267-1151
American Eagle 214 267-1151
British Airways 800 247-9297
Continental 817 268-2300
Delta 214 630-3200
Exec Express II 800 877-3932
Lufthansa 800 645-3880
Mexicana 800 531-7921

Midway 800 621-5700
Midwest Express 800 452-2022
Northwest 800 225-2525
Southwest 214 263-1717
Thai 800 426-5204
TWA 800 221-2000
United 214 988-1004
USAir 214 647-8823

■ Charter Airlines

Alpha Aviation 214 352-4801
Jet East Inc 214 350-8523
Jet Fleet Corp 214 350-4061

Kitty Hawk Airways Inc 214 574-7474
Million Air 214 248-1600

■ Car Rentals

Advantage 214 350-8961
Agency 214 233-2300
Airways 800 952-9200
Avis 214 574-4100
Budget 214 574-4800

Dollar 214 256-4576
Hertz 214 456-0885
Holiday-Payless 214 357-8888
National 214 574-3400
Thrifty 214 929-1320

■ Limo/Taxi

American Limousine & Coach 214 905-9999
Carey Limousine 214 638-4828
Limousines Unlimited 214 824-2424
Republic Taxi Service 214 631-5544

Terminal Cab 214 350-4445
VIP Limousine Service 214 490-6305
West End Cab Co 214 631-4700
Yellow Cab 214 426-6262

■ Mass Transit

214 979-1111   **Dallas Area Rapid Transit (DART)** $.75 Base fare .... Dallas TX 75202-0000

■ Rail/Bus

214 653-1101   **Dallas Union Station** 400 S Houston St .... Dallas TX 75202-4802
214 655-7084   **Greyhound/Trailways Bus Station** 205 S Lamar St .... Dallas TX 75202-4497

Hotels

214 742-8200   **Adolphus Hotel** 1321 Commerce St .... Dallas TX 75202-4294
214 630-7000   **Clarion Hotel** 1241 W Mockingbird Ln .... Dallas TX 75247-4999
214 871-3200   **Crescent Court Hotel** 400 Crescent Ct .... Dallas TX 75201-1842
214 827-4100   **Dallas Hilton Inn** 5600 N Central Expy .... Dallas TX 75206-5191
214 747-7000   **Dallas Park Plaza** 1914 Commerce St .... Dallas TX 75201-5205
214 661-3600   **Dallas Parkway Hilton** 4801 LBJ Fwy .... Dallas TX 75244-6002
214 934-8400   **Doubletree Hotel** 5410 LBJ Fwy .... Dallas TX 75240-6276
214 691-8700   **Doubletree Inn Campbell Center** 8250 N Central Expy .... Dallas TX 75206-1888
214 720-2020   **Fairmont Hotel** 1717 N Akard St .... Dallas TX 75201-2399
214 717-0700   **Four Seasons Resort & Club** 4150 N MacArthur Blvd .... Irving TX 75038-6499
214 651-1234   **Hyatt Regency Dallas** 300 E Reunion Blvd .... Dallas TX 75207-4498
214 634-8550   **LeBaron Best Western Hotel** 1055 Regal Row .... Dallas TX 75247-4404
214 748-1200   **Loews Anatole Hotel** 2201 Stemmons Fwy .... Dallas TX 75207-2899
214 559-2100   **Mansion on Turtle Creek** 2821 Turtle Creek Blvd .... Dallas TX 75219-4802
214 556-0800   **Marriott Mandalay Las Colinas** 221 E Las Colinas Blvd .... Irving TX 75039-5590
214 233-4421   **Marriott Park Central** 7750 LBJ Fwy .... Dallas TX 75251-1297
214 661-2800   **Marriott Quorum Hotel** 14901 Dallas Pkwy .... Dallas TX 75240-7573
214 979-9000   **Plaza of the Americas Hotel** 650 N Pearl St .... Dallas TX 75201-2877
214 922-8000   **Sheraton Dallas Hotel** 400 N Olive St .... Dallas TX 75201-4007
214 385-3000   **Sheraton Park Central Hotel & Towers** 12720 Merit Dr .... Dallas TX 75251-1290
214 631-2222   **Stouffer Dallas Hotel** 2222 N Stemmons Fwy .... Dallas TX 75207-2802
214 243-3363   **Summit Hotel** 2645 LBJ Fwy .... Dallas TX 75234-7394
214 934-9494   **Westin Hotel Dallas** 13340 Dallas Pkwy .... Dallas TX 75240-6698
214 978-4400   **Wyndham Hotel** 2001 Ross Ave .... Dallas TX 75201-2965

Restaurants

214 361-8833   **Arthur's** (Steak/Seafood) 8350 N Central Expy Suite M-1000 .... Dallas TX 75206-0000
214 385-7227   **August Moon** (Chinese) 15030 Preston Rd .... Dallas TX 75240-7814
214 520-1985   **Cafe Margaux** (Cajun) 4216 Oak Lawn Ave .... Dallas TX 75219-2312
214 871-3242   **Conservatory The** (American) 400 Crescent Ct .... Dallas TX 75201-0000
214 556-0800   **Enjolie** (French Nouvelle) 221 E Las Colinas Blvd .... Irving TX 75039-5504
214 742-8200   **French Room** (French) 1321 Commerce St .... Dallas TX 75202-4294
214 559-2680   **Hoffbrau Steaks** (Steak) 3205 Knox St .... Dallas TX 75205-4031
214 528-6010   **Jennivine's** (Continental) 3605 McKenney Ave .... Dallas TX 75204-0000
214 747-0322   **Lombardi's** (Italian) 311 Market St .... Dallas TX 75202-0000

214 526-2121   **Mansion on Turtle Creek**
            (Southwest American) 2821 Turtle Creek Blvd .... Dallas TX 75219-4802
214 556-0796   **Mercado Juarez** (Mexican) 1901 W Northwest Hwy .... Dallas TX 75220-0000
214 528-0032   **Old Warsaw** (French) 2610 Maple Ave .... Dallas TX 75201-1924
214 720-2020   **Pyramid Room** (French) 1717 N Akard St .... Dallas TX 75201-2399
214 871-7161   **Routh Street Cafe** (Southwestern American) 3005 Routh St .... Dallas TX 75201-1307
214 902-8080   **Ruth's Chris Steak House** (Steak) 5922 Cedar Springs Rd .... Dallas TX 75235-6894
214 357-7120   **Sonny Bryan's Smokehouse** (Barbecue) 2202 Inwood Rd .... Dallas TX 75235-7321
214 357-3862   **Trail Dust Steak House** (Steak) 10841 Composite Dr .... Dallas TX 75220-1209

Goods & Services

■ Department Stores

214 851-1000   **Marshall Field's** 13550 Dallas Pkwy .... Dallas TX 75240-6696
214 741-6911   **Neiman-Marcus** 1618 Main St .... Dallas TX 75201-4704
214 458-7000   **Saks Fifth Avenue** 13250 Dallas Pkwy .... Dallas TX 75240-6699

■ Banks

214 290-2000   **Bank One Texas** 1717 Main St .... Dallas TX 75201-4689
214 521-0721   **Mario's Chiquita** (Mexican) 4514 Travis St .... Dallas TX 75205-0000
214 988-6262   **NCNB Texas National Bank** 1401 Elm St .... Dallas TX 75202-2988
214 922-2300   **Texas Commerce Bank Dallas NA** 2200 Ross Ave .... Dallas TX 75201-2780

■ Messenger/Postal

City Wide Delivery 214 827-5555
Federal Express 214 358-5271
One Hour Delivery Service Inc 214 352-1732
Post Office–Dallas 214 741-5508

United Messengers Inc 214 528-4211
UPS 800 762-4188
Wingtip Couriers 214 222-0222

■ Secretarial/Temp Services

214 363-3300   **Accountemps** 3 North Park E Suite 200 .... Dallas TX 75231-0000
214 740-3666   **Kelly Services Inc** 500 N Akard St Suite 230 .... Dallas TX 75201-3320
214 954-0085   **Manpower Temporary Services** 500 N Akard St Suite 2880 .... Dallas TX 75201-3372
214 979-0099   **Olsten Temporary Services** 2001 Bryan St .... Dallas TX 75201-3094

Media

■ Newspapers/Magazines

214 827-5000   **D Magazine** 3988 N Central Expy Suite 1200 .... Dallas TX 75204-3005
214 977-8222   **Dallas Morning News** 508 Young St .... Dallas TX 75202-4808
214 720-6111   **Dallas Times Herald** 1101 Pacific Ave .... Dallas TX 75202-1902

■ Television

214 720-4444   **KDFW-TV Ch 4 (CBS)** 400 N Griffin St .... Dallas TX 75202-1996
214 871-1390   **KERA-TV Ch 13 (PBS)** 3000 Harry Hines Blvd .... Dallas TX 75201-1012
817 429-1550   **KXAS-TV Ch 5 (NBC)** 3900 Barnett St .... Fort Worth TX 76103-1499
214 748-9631   **WFAA-TV Ch 8 (ABC)** 606 Young St Communications Ctr .... Dallas TX 75202-0000

■ Radio

214 871-1390   **KERA-FM 90.1 MHz (Clas)** 3000 Harry Hines Blvd .... Dallas TX 75201-1098
214 556-8100   **KJMZ-FM 100.3 MHz (UC)** 545 E John W Carpenter Fwy 17th Fl ... Irving TX 75062-0000
214 263-9911   **KKDA-AM 730 kHz (Gold)** 621 NW 6th St .... Grand Prairie TX 75050-5555
214 526-2400   **KPLX-FM 99.5 MHz (Ctry-AP)** 3500 Maple Ave Suite 1600 .... Dallas TX 75219-0000
214 634-1080   **KRLD-AM 1080 kHz (N/T-CBS)** 1080 Metro Media Pl .... Dallas TX 75247-4797
214 826-7900   **KVIL-AM 1150 kHz (AC)** 5307 E Mockingbird Ln Suite 500 .... Dallas TX 75206-5184
214 826-7900   **KVIL-FM 103.7 MHz (AC)** 5307 E Mockingbird Ln Suite 500 .... Dallas TX 75206-5118

Local Attractions & Special Events

■ Sports

214 556-2500   **Dallas Cowboys** 1 Cowboy Pkwy Texas Stadium .... Irving TX 75063-4999
214 658-7068   **Dallas Mavericks** 777 Sports Pl Reunion Arena .... Dallas TX 75207-4499
214 361-5425   **Dallas Sidekicks** 6116 N Central Expy Reunion Arena .... Dallas TX 75206-0000
817 273-5100   **Texas Rangers** 1700 Copeland Rd Arlington Stadium .... Arlington TX 76011-0000

■ Special Events

214 638-2695   **Cotton Bowl** (New Year's Weekend)

■ Local Attractions

214 922-1200   **Dallas Museum of Art** 1717 N Harwood St .... Dallas TX 75201-2398
214 369-8966   **Dallas Repertory Theater** 150 N Park Ctr .... Dallas TX 75225-0000
214 428-8351   **Dallas Science Place Two** 1620 1st Ave .... Dallas TX 75210-0000
214 692-0203   **Dallas Symphony Orchestra** 2301 Flora St .... Dallas TX 75201-0000
214 565-1116   **Music Hall** 1st Ave & Perry St .... Dallas TX 75226-0000
817 640-8900   **Six Flags Over Texas** 2201 Road to Six Flags .... Arlington TX 76010-0000
214 653-6666   **Sixth Floor Kennedy Exhibit** 411 Elm St .... Dallas TX 75202-3317
214 442-6536   **Southfork Ranch** Parker Rd & FM 2551 .... Parker TX 75002-0000
214 954-4350   **West End Marketplace** 603 Munger Ave .... Dallas TX 75202-1847

Denver

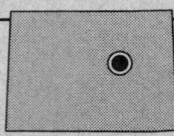

COLORADO 303

Important Phone Numbers

AAA	303 753-8800	Emergency	911
American Express	303 298-7100	Poison Control Center	303 629-1123
Better Business Bureau	303 758-8200	Time/Temp	303 976-1311
City Hall	303 575-2613	Weather	303 398-3964

■ Travel Information

303 894-8500 **Chamber of Commerce** 1600 Sherman St .... Denver CO 80203-1604
303 892-1112 **Convention & Visitors Center** 225 W Colfax Ave .... Denver CO 80202-5304

Travel

■ Airport

303 398-3844 **Stapleton International Airport** 7 miles NE of downtown (approx 15 minutes)

■ Airport Transportation

303 778-6000 **Regional Transportation District Bus** $1 fare to downtown
Taxi $8 fare to downtown

■ Scheduled Airlines

Air Midwest	800 835-2953	Mesa	800 637-2247
America West	303 571-0738	Mexicana	303 398-2241
American	303 595-9304	Midway	800 621-5700
Aspen	303 398-4141	Midwest Express	800 452-2022
Continental	303 398-3000	Northwest	800 225-2525
Delta	303 696-1322	TWA	303 534-8505
Eastern	303 398-3333	United	303 398-4141
GP Express	303 398-2194	USAir	303 893-3567

■ Charter Airlines

Hoffman Pilot Center	303 469-3333	Richmor Aviation	303 398-5678
Mayo Aviation Inc	303 398-5445		

■ Car Rentals

A-Courtesy	303 333-5155	Enterprise	303 320-1121
Agency	303 340-2121	General	303 320-1244
Alamo	303 321-1176	National	303 321-7990
Avis	303 839-1280	Payless	303 399-2608
Budget	303 399-0444	Thrifty	303 388-4634
Dollar	303 398-2323	USA	303 399-5020

■ Limo/Taxi

Airport Express	303 482-0505	Skiers Connection	303 343-6000
Colorado Transit Authority	303 830-0085	Yellow Cab	303 777-7777
Keywest Limousines Ltd	303 293-9378	Zone Cabs	303 861-2323
Lights Luxury Limosine	303 333-9999		

■ Mass Transit

303 628-9000 **RTD** $.50 Base fare .... Denver CO 80202-1399

■ Rail/Bus

303 292-6111 **Greyhound/Trailways Bus Station** 1055 19th St .... Denver CO 80202-1807
800 872-7245 **Union Station** 1701 Wynkoop St .... Denver CO 80202-1047

Hotels

303 297-3111 **Brown Palace Hotel** 321 17th St .... Denver CO 80202-4099
303 831-1252 **Cambridge Club & Hotel** 1560 Sherman St .... Denver CO 80203-1703
303 837-1261 **Colburn Hotel** 980 Grant St .... Denver CO 80203-2907
303 373-5730 **Denver Airport Hilton** 4411 Peoria St .... Denver CO 80239-4896
303 297-1300 **Denver Marriott City Center** 1701 California St .... Denver CO 80202-3402
303 758-7000 **Denver Marriott Hotel Southeast** 6363 E Hampden Ave .... Denver CO 80222-7677
303 331-9106 **Franklin House** 1620 Franklin St .... Denver CO 80218-1627
303 321-9975 **Holiday Chalet Hotel** 1820 E Colfax Ave .... Denver CO 80218-2605
303 573-1450 **Holiday Inn Denver Downtown** 1450 Glenarm Pl .... Denver CO 80202-5039
303 295-1200 **Hyatt Regency** 1750 Welton St .... Denver CO 80202-3999
303 782-9300 **Loews Giorgio Hotel** 4150 E Mississippi Ave .... Denver CO 80222-3045
303 628-5400 **Oxford Alexis Hotel** 1600 17th St .... Denver CO 80202-1204
303 893-3333 **Radisson Hotel** 1550 Court Pl .... Denver CO 80202-5199
303 458-0808 **Regency Hotel** 3900 Elati St .... Denver CO 80216-4800
303 779-1100 **Sheraton Denver Tech Center** 4900 DTC Pkwy .... Denver CO 80237-2799
303 534-3231 **Standish Hotel** 1530 California St .... Denver CO 80202-4215
303 321-3500 **Stapleton Plaza Hotel** 3333 Quebec St .... Denver CO 80207-2396
303 861-2000 **Warwick Hotel** 1776 Grant St .... Denver CO 80203-0000
303 756-8877 **Writers' Manor Hotel** 1730 S Colorado Blvd .... Denver CO 80222-4099

Restaurants

303 573-8900 **Adirondacks** (Californian/French) 901 Larimer St Tifoli Bldg .... Denver CO 80204-2076
303 292-5065 **Broker Restaurant** (Continental) 821 17th St .... Denver CO 80202-3004
303 534-9505 **Buckhorn Exchange** (American) 1000 Osage St .... Denver CO 80204-3918
303 825-6555 **Cafe Giovanni** (Continental) 1515 Market St .... Denver CO 80202-1607
303 770-6660 **Chateau Pyrenees** (French) 6538 S Yosemite Cir .... Englewood CO 80111-4902
303 355-2323 **Chez Thoa** (Vietnamese/French) 158 Fillmore St .... Denver CO 80206-4914
303 722-3800 **Chives** (Nouvelle) 1120 E 6th Ave .... Denver CO 80218-3413
303 697-4771 **Fort The** (Steak) 19192 Hwy 8 .... Morrison CO 80465-8731
303 321-3311 **Normandy French** (French) 1515 Madison St .... Denver CO 80206-1821
303 297-3111 **Palace Arms**
(French/Continental) 321 17th St Brown Palace Hotel .... Denver CO 80202-4003
303 321-4700 **Sfuzzi** (Italian) 3000 E 1st Ave .... Denver CO 80206-0000

Goods & Services

■ Department Stores

303 534-0441 **Joslin's** 934 16th St .... Denver CO 80202-2902
303 629-1111 **Mantaldo's** 1630 Stout St .... Denver CO 80202-3196
303 620-7500 **May D & F** 16th & Tremont Pl .... Denver CO 80202-0000

■ Banks

303 893-1862 **Colorado National Bank of Denver** 918 17th St .... Denver CO 80202-2827
303 293-2211 **First Interstate Bank of Denver NA** 633 17th St .... Denver CO 80270-0001
303 861-8811 **United Bank of Denver**
1700 Broadway St First United Bank Plaza .... Denver CO 80274-0001

■ Messenger/Postal

Apollo Courier Systems Inc	303 573-0303	Post Office	303 297-6016
City Express	303 377-5222	Speedy Messenger Service	303 292-6000
Concorde Express Messenger Svc	303 771-7288	UPS	303 429-3340
Express Messenger Systems Inc	303 936-0200		

■ Secretarial/Temp Services

303 623-6262 **Kelly Services Inc** 1625 Broadway .... Denver CO 80202-4731
303 297-9802 **Manpower Temporary Service Inc** 1401 17th St Suite 560 .... Denver CO 80202-5913
303 534-4357 **Olsten Temporary Services**
600 17th St Dominion Towers Suite 1110 S .... Denver CO 80202-0000

Media

■ Newspapers/Magazines

303 322-6400 **Denver Magazine** 100 Garfield St .... Denver CO 80206-5550
303 820-1010 **Denver Post** 1560 Broadway .... Denver CO 80202-5177
303 892-5000 **Rocky Mountain News** 400 W Colfax Ave .... Denver CO 80204-2694

■ Television

303 861-4444 **KCNC-TV Ch 4 (NBC)** 1044 Lincoln St .... Denver CO 80203-2714
303 832-7777 **KMGH-TV Ch 7 (CBS)** 123 E Speer Blvd .... Denver CO 80203-3417
303 892-6666 **KRMA-TV Ch 6 (PBS)** 1261 Glenarm Pl .... Denver CO 80204-2100
303 893-9000 **KUSA-TV Ch 9 (ABC)** 1089 Bannock St .... Denver CO 80204-4036

■ Radio

303 572-6200 **KBPI-FM 105.9 MHz (AOR)** 1200 17th St Suite 2300 .... Denver CO 80202-5835
303 871-9191 **KCFR-FM 90.1 MHz (N/T-NPR)** 2249 S Josephine St .... Denver CO 80210-4805
303 893-8500 **KOA-AM 850 kHz (N/T-CBS)** 1380 Lawrence St Suite 1300 ...... Denver CO 80204-2060
303 696-1714 **KOSI-FM 101.1 MHz (B/EZ)** 10200 E Girard Ave Suite B131 .... Denver CO 80231-5071
303 989-1075 **KRXY-AM 1600 kHz (CHR)** 7075 W Hampden Ave .... Denver CO 80227-5303
303 989-1075 **KRXY-FM 107.5 MHz (CHR)** 7075 W Hampden Ave .... Denver CO 80227-5303

Local Attractions & Special Events

■ Sports

303 433-7466 **Denver Broncos** 1900 Elliot St Mile High Stadium .... Denver CO 80204-0000
303 893-3865 **Denver Nuggets** 1635 Clay McNichols Arena .... Denver CO 80204-0000
303 433-8645 **Denver Zephyrs** 2850 W 20th Ave .... Denver CO 80211-5103

■ Local Attractions

303 526-0747 **Buffalo Bill's Grave & Museum** Lookout Mountain Rd .... Golden CO 80401-0000
303 575-2295 **Denver Art Museum** 100 W 14th Ave Pkwy .... Denver CO 80204-2788
303 292-6683 **Denver Symphony Orchestra**
621 17th St First Interstate Tower S Suite 810 .... Denver CO 80293-0000
303 399-1859 **Four-Mile Historic Park** 715 S Forestry St .... Denver CO 80222-0000
303 534-2367 **Larimer Square** 14th & Larimer Sts .... Denver CO 80202-1610
303 832-4092 **Molly Brown House Museum** 1340 Pennsylvania St .... Denver CO 80203-2417
303 296-1880 **Museum of Western Art** 1727 Tremont Pl .... Denver CO 80202-4028
303 640-2637 **Red Rocks Amphitheater** Red Rocks Pk .... Morrison CO 80401-0000
303 844-3332 **US Mint** 320 W Colfax Ave .... Denver CO 80204-2693

Detroit

MICHIGAN 313

Important Phone Numbers

AAA	313 336-1234	**Emergency**	911
American Express	313 259-5030	**Poison Control Center**	313 745-5711
Better Business Bureau	313 962-7566	**Time**	313 472-1212
City Hall	313 224-2989	**Weather**	313 941-7192

■ Travel Information

313 964-4000	**Chamber of Commerce** 600 W Lafayette Blvd	Detroit	MI	48226-3193
313 259-4333	**Convention & Visitors Bureau** 100 Renaissance Ctr Suite 1950	Detroit	MI	48243-1009
313 567-1170	**Visitor Information Center** 2 E Jefferson Ave	Detroit	MI	48226-4328

Travel

■ Airport: Detroit Metropolitan

313 942-3550 **Detroit Metropolitan Airport** 20 miles E of downtown (35 minutes)

■ Airport Transportation: Detroit Metropolitan

313 941-3252 **Commuter Transportation** $12 fare to downtown
Taxi $25 fare to downtown

■ Scheduled Airlines: Detroit Metropolitan

American	313 965-1000	**Northwest**	313 962-2002
British Airways	800 247-9297	**Pan Am**	800 221-1111
Delta	313 355-3200	**TWA**	313 962-8650
Eastern	313 965-8200	**United**	313 336-9000
JAT Yugoslavian	313 355-2299	**USAir**	313 963-8340
Midway	800 621-5700		

■ Charter Airlines: Detroit Metropolitan

Aviation Group Inc	313 666-3630	**Martin Air**	800 366-4655

■ Airport: Detroit City

313 267-6400 **Detroit City Airport** 6 miles E of downtown (20 minutes)

■ Airport Transportation: Detroit City

313 372-0690 **Commuter Transportation** $5 fare to downtown
Taxi $25-30 fare to downtown

■ Scheduled Airlines: Detroit City

Sky Craft Air Transport	313 527-3095	**Southwest Airlines**	313 562-1221

■ Charter Airlines: Detroit City

Olsen Flight Service	313 526-9022

■ Car Rentals

American International	313 729-3355	**Hertz**	313 729-5200
Avis	313 942-3450	**McDonald Ford**	313 341-4800
Budget	313 355-7900	**National**	313 941-7000
Fairlane	313 565-5900	**Thrifty**	313 946-7830

■ Limo/Taxi

Blue Eagle Cab	313 934-2000	**Detroit Metro Airport Taxicab**	313 942-4690
Dearborn Limousines	313 582-6900	**Metropolitan Cadillac Limousine**	313 895-3555

■ Mass Transit

313 274-6300	**Dearborn Trolley** $.50 Base fare	Detroit	MI	48201-0000
313 224-2160	**Detroit People Mover** $.50 Base fare	Detroit	MI	48201-0000
313 962-5515	**Southeast Michigan Transit Authority** $1 Base fare	Detroit	MI	48231-0000

■ Rail/Bus

313 964-5335	**Detroit Station** 2601 Rose St	Detroit	MI	48216-1581
313 961-8562	**Greyhound/Trailways Bus Station** 1000 W Lafayette St	Detroit	MI	48226-4399

Hotels

313 356-4333	**Berkshire Hotel** 26111 Telegraph Rd	Southfield	MI	48034-5362
313 462-2000	**Courtyard by Marriott** 17200 N Laurel Park Dr	Livonia	MI	48152-2651
313 557-4800	**Days Hotel** 17017 W Nine-Mile Rd	Southfield	MI	48075-0000
313 271-2700	**Dearborn Inn & Marriot Hotel** 20301 Oakwood Blvd	Dearborn	MI	48124-4099
313 292-3400	**Detroit Airport Hilton Inn** 31500 Wick Rd	Romulus	MI	48174-1989
313 350-2000	**Embassy Suites Hotel of Southfield** 28100 Franklin Rd	Southfield	MI	48034-5514
313 294-0400	**Georgian Inn** 31327 Gratiot Ave	Roseville	MI	48066-4595
313 278-4800	**Holiday Inn Dearborn** 22900 Michigan Ave	Dearborn	MI	48124-2071
313 873-3000	**Hotel Saint Regis New Center Area** 3071 W Grand Blvd	Detroit	MI	48202-3092
313 593-1234	**Hyatt Regency Dearborn** Fairlane Town Ctr	Dearborn	MI	48126-2793
313 644-1400	**Kingsley Inn Hotel** 1475 N Woodward Ave	Bloomfield Hills	MI	48304-2868
313 963-3950	**Milner Hotel** 1538 Centre St	Detroit	MI	48226-2119
313 965-0200	**Radisson Hotel Pontchartrain** 2 Washington Blvd	Detroit	MI	48226-4416
313 827-4000	**Radisson Plaza Hotel at Town Center** 1500 Town Ctr	Southfield	MI	48075-1140
313 729-6300	**Ramada Inn Metro Airport** 8270 Wickham Rd	Romulus	MI	48174-1990
313 441-2000	**Ritz-Carlton Dearborn** 300 Town Center Dr	Dearborn	MI	48126-2705
313 728-7900	**Sheraton Inn Detroit Airport** 8600 Merriman Rd	Romulus	MI	48174-1918
313 643-7800	**Somerset Inn Troy** 2601 W Big Beaver Rd	Troy	MI	48084-3390
313 642-7900	**Townsend Hotel** 100 Townsend	Birmingham	MI	48009-0000
313 568-8000	**Westin Hotel** Renaissance Ctr	Detroit	MI	48243-1598

Restaurants

313 833-0700	**Carl's Chop House** (Steak/Seafood) 3020 Grand River	Detroit	MI	48201-2996
313 965-4970	**Caucus Club** (American) 150 W Congress St	Detroit	MI	48226-3208
313 879-2060	**Charley's Crab** (Steak/Seafood) 5498 Crooks Rd	Troy	MI	48098-2867
313 994-0211	**Earle The** (French/Italian) 121 W Washington St	Ann Arbor	MI	48104-1300
517 652-9941	**Frankenmuth Bavarian Inn** (German) 713 S Main St	Frankenmuth	MI	48734-1621
313 559-4230	**Golden Mushroom** (Continental) 18100 W Ten-Mile Rd	Southfield	MI	48075-0000
313 567-1088	**Joe Muer's Seafood** (Seafood) 2000 Gratiot Ave	Detroit	MI	48207-2797
313 661-4466	**Lark Restaurant** (European) 6430 Farmington Rd	West Bloomfield	MI	48322-2209
313 544-2887	**Les Auteurs** (American/Californian) 222 Sherman Dr Washington Sq Plaza	Royal Oak	MI	48067-0000
313 962-0277	**London Chop House** (American) 155 W Congress St	Detroit	MI	48226-3292
313 626-4200	**Machus Red Fox** (Continental) 6676 Telegraph Rd	Birmingham	MI	48010-0000
313 963-8888	**New Parthenon** (Greek) 547 Monroe St	Detroit	MI	48226-0000
313 288-3210	**Nippon Kai** (Japanese) 511 W 14-Mile Rd	Clawson	MI	48017-1929
313 961-7766	**Opus One** (French American) 565 E Larned	Detroit	MI	48226-4316
313 963-1785	**Pontchartrain Wine Cellars** (French/American) 234 W Larned St	Detroit	MI	48226-0000
313 567-4400	**Rattlesnake Club** (Nouvelle American) 300 Riverplace	Detroit	MI	48207-0000
313 568-8600	**Summit Steak House** (Steak) Renaissance Ctr Westin Hotel	Detroit	MI	48243-0000
313 348-5555	**Too Chez** (Multi-Ethnic) 27155 Sheraton Dr	Novi	MI	48377-0000
313 964-4144	**Tres Vite** (American) 2203 Woodward Ave	Detroit	MI	48201-0000
313 821-2620	**Van Dyke Place** (French) 649 Van Dyke St	Detroit	MI	48214-2621
313 832-5701	**Whitney The** (American) 4421 Woodward Ave	Detroit	MI	48201-1821

Goods & Services

■ Department Stores

313 962-2400	**Crowley's** 2301 W Lafeyette Blvd	Detroit	MI	48216-0000
313 336-3100	**Lord & Taylor** 18900 Michigan Ave	Dearborn	MI	48126-3998
313 336-3070	**Saks Fifth Avenue** Fairlane Towncenter	Dearborn	MI	48126-0000

■ Banks

313 222-3300	**Comerica Bank Detroit** 211 W Fort St	Detroit	MI	48275-0001
313 596-8000	**First of America Bank Detroit NA** PO Box 2659	Detroit	MI	48231-2659
313 225-1000	**National Bank of Detroit** 611 Woodward Ave	Detroit	MI	48226-3497

■ Messenger/Postal

EDS Express Package Co	313 349-0640	**PDQ Courier**	313 965-9600
Expeditors of Michigan	313 535-9797	**Post Office**	313 226-8675
Federal Express	313 961-8771	**Professional Delivery**	313 964-6645
MGS Instant Couriers Inc	313 843-9547	**UPS**	313 261-8500

■ Secretarial/Temp Services

313 259-1400	**Kelly Services Inc** 100 Renaissance Ctr Suite 1650	Detroit	MI	48243-1077
313 965-7000	**Manpower Temporary Services** 660 Plaza Dr Suite 250	Detroit	MI	48226-1206
313 962-9650	**Olsten Temporary Services** 155 W Congress St Suite 324	Detroit	MI	48226-3212

Media

■ Newspapers/Magazines

313 222-6400	**Detroit Free Press** 321 W Lafayette Blvd	Detroit	MI	48226-2706
313 222-2095	**Detroit News** 615 W Lafayette Blvd	Detroit	MI	48226-3197
313 336-1211	**Michigan Living** 1 Auto Club Dr	Dearborn	MI	48126-2607

■ Television

313 222-0444	**WDIV-TV Ch 4 (NBC)** 550 W Lafayette Blvd	Detroit	MI	48231-0000
313 557-2000	**WJBK-TV Ch 2 (CBS)** 16550 W Nine-Mile Rd	Southfield	MI	48075-0000
313 873-7200	**WTVS-TV Ch 56 (PBS)** 7441 2nd Ave	Detroit	MI	48202-2796
313 827-7777	**WXYZ-TV Ch 7 (ABC)** 20777 W Ten-Mile Rd	Southfield	MI	48037-0000

■ Radio

313 577-4146	**WDET-FM 101.9 MHz (Misc-NPR)** 60001 Cass Ave	Detroit	MI	48202-0000
313 965-2000	**WJLB-FM 97.9 MHz (UC)** 645 Griswold St Suite 633	Detroit	MI	48226-4108
313 423-3697	**WJOI-FM 97.1 MHz (B/EZ-CBS)** 16550 W Nine-Mile Rd	Southfield	MI	48086-0000
313 875-4440	**WJR-AM 760 kHz (N/T-ABC)** 3011 W Grand Blvd Suite 2100	Detroit	MI	48202-3047
313 855-5100	**WLLZ-FM 98.7 MHz (AOR)** 31555 W 14-Mile Rd	Farmington Hills	MI	48334-1239
313 423-3300	**WWJ-AM 950 kHz (N/T)** 16550 W Nine-Mile Rd	Southfield	MI	48086-0000

Local Attractions & Special Events

■ Sports

313 335-4151	**Detroit Lions** 1200 Featherstone Rd Silverdome	Pontiac	MI	48342-1938
313 377-0100	**Detroit Pistons** 1 Championship Dr The Palace	Auburn Hills	MI	48326-1753
313 567-6000	**Detroit Red Wings** 600 Civic Center Dr Joe Louis Arena	Detroit	MI	48226-4419
313 962-4000	**Detroit Tigers** 2121 Trumbull St	Detroit	MI	48216-1343

■ Special Events

313 259-5400 **Detroit/Windsor International Freedom Festival** (June 21-July 4)
313 259-5400 **Miller Lite Montreux-Detroit Jazz Festival** (August 29-September 2)
313 259-5400 **Valvoline Detroit Grand Prix** (June 14-16)

■ Local Attractions

313 843-8800	**Boblo Island** 4401 W Jefferson St	Detroit	MI	48209-0000
313 833-7900	**Detroit Institute of Arts** 5200 Woodward Ave	Detroit	MI	48202-4094
313 567-1400	**Detroit Symphony Orchestra** 20 E Jefferson St	Detroit	MI	48226-4385
313 267-6440	**Dossin Great Lakes Museum** 100 Strand Dr Belle Isle	Detroit	MI	48207-0000
313 271-1620	**Henry Ford Museum** 20900 Oakwood Blvd	Dearborn	MI	48121-0000
313 867-0991	**Motown Museum** 2648 W Grand Blvd	Detroit	MI	48208-1237

El Paso

TEXAS 915

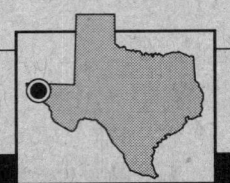

Important Phone Numbers

AAA 915 778-9521
American Express 915 779-7311
Better Business Bureau 915 545-1212
City Hall 915 541-4000
Emergency 911
Poison Control Center 915 533-1244
Time/Temp 915 532-9911
Weather 915 778-9343

■ **Travel Information**

915 534-0500 **Chamber of Commerce** 10 Civic Center Plaza .... El Paso TX 79901-1188
915 534-0696 **Tourist & Convention Bureau** 1 Civic Center Plaza .... El Paso TX 79901-1153

Travel

■ **Airport**

915 772-4271 **El Paso International Airport** 8 miles NE of downtown (approx 15 minutes)

■ **Airport Transportation**

915 833-8282 **Airport Shuttle** $12 fare to downtown
              Taxi $15 fare to downtown

■ **Scheduled Airlines**

America West 915 532-0955
American 915 433-7300
Continental 800 525-0280
Delta 915 779-2288
Southwest 915 859-1221

■ **Charter Airlines**

Aero Freight Inc 915 772-3273
Air Transport 915 772-1448

■ **Car Rentals**

Avis 915 779-2700
Budget 915 778-5287
Dollar 915 778-5445
Hertz 915 772-4255
National 915 778-9417
Thrifty 915 778-9236

■ **Limo/Taxi**

Border Cab 915 533-4245
Checker Cab 915 532-2626
La Calesa Limousine Service 915 533-3492
Western Coach Limousine Service 915 751-5466
Yellow Cab 915 533-3433

■ **Mass Transit**

915 533-1220 **El Paso Public Transit** $.75 Base fare .... El Paso TX 79901-0000

■ **Rail/Bus**

915 545-2248 **El Paso Union Depot** 700 San Francisco Ave .... El Paso TX 79901-1060
915 544-7200 **Greyhound/Trailways Bus Station** 111 San Francisco St .... El Paso TX 79901-1192

Hotels

915 533-8241 **Clarion Hotel** 325 N Kansas St .... El Paso TX 79901-1434
915 778-4241 **El Paso Airport Hilton** 2027 Airway Blvd .... El Paso TX 79925-1030
915 779-6222 **El Paso Embassy Suites** 6100 Gateway Blvd E .... El Paso TX 79905-2087
915 779-3300 **El Paso Marriott Hotel** 1600 Airway Blvd .... El Paso TX 79925-0000
915 533-6801 **Exec-U-Lodge** 4501 N Mesa St .... El Paso TX 79912-6101
915 532-8981 **Executive Inn** 500 Executive Center Blvd .... El Paso TX 79902-1075
915 852-9141 **Horizon Lodge** 13781 Horizon Blvd .... El Paso TX 79927-8373
915 544-3300 **Ramada Inn Central** 113 W Missouri Ave .... El Paso TX 79901-1129
915 544-3333 **TraveLodge City Center** 409 E Missouri Ave .... El Paso TX 79901-1288
915 534-3000 **Westin Paso del Norte Hotel** 101 S El Paso St .... El Paso TX 79901-1157

Restaurants

915 584-3321 **Bella Napoli** (Italian) 6331 N Mesa St .... El Paso TX 79912-4521
915 833-1151 **Casa Jurado** (Mexican) 4772 Doniphan Dr .... El Paso TX 79922-1008
915 544-3200 **Cattleman's Steakhouse** (Steak) Indian Cliff's Ranch .... Fabens TX 79838-9999
915 772-0066 **Forti's Mexican Elder** (Mexican) 321 Chelsea St .... El Paso TX 79905-1705
915 751-5300 **Great American Land & Cattle Co** (Steak) 7600 Alabama St ...... El Paso TX 79904-3134
915 598-3451 **Griggs** (Mexican) 9007 Montana Ave .... El Paso TX 79935-5003
915 592-1084 **Gunther's Edelweiss** (German) 11055 Gateway Blvd W .... El Paso TX 79935-5003
915 779-6222 **Isabella's** (Continental) 6100 Gateway Blvd E .... El Paso TX 79905-0000
915 778-9696 **Jackson's Headquarters**
              (Mexican/American) 1135 Airway Blvd .... El Paso TX 79925-0000
915 544-1188 **Jaxon's** (Southwestern) 4799 N Mesa St .... El Paso TX 79912-6105
505 524-3524 **La Posta** (Mexican) Mesilla Plaza .... Mesilla NM 88046-9999
915 859-3916 **Wings**
              (American Indian) 122 S Old Pueblo Dr Tigua Reservation .... El Paso TX 79907-6625

Goods & Services

■ **Department Stores**

915 779-6969 **Dillard's** 8401 Gateway Blvd W .... El Paso TX 79925-5650
915 532-7755 **Popular Dry Goods Co** 301 E San Antonio Ave .... El Paso TX 79922-2333
915 778-5411 **White House** Bassett Ctr .... El Paso TX 79925-3490

■ **Banks**

915 546-5700 **First City Texas** PO Box 1572 .... El Paso TX 79948-1572
915 532-9922 **MBank El Paso** 221 N Kansas St .... El Paso TX 79901-1440
915 546-6500 **Texas Commerce Bank El Paso NA** 201 E Main Dr .... El Paso TX 79901-1333

■ **Messenger/Postal**

Federal Express 800 238-5355
Miracle Delivery Armored Service 915 532-6959
Post Office 915 775-7502
Rush Delivery 915 581-2340
UPS 800 222-8333

■ **Secretarial/Temp Services**

915 544-6699 **Accountemps** 4100 Rio Bravo Blvd Suite 201 .... El Paso TX 79902-1010
915 772-8811 **Kelly Services** 6028 Surety Dr Suite 100 .... El Paso TX 79905-0000
915 778-6321 **Manpower Temporary Services** 8201 Lockheed Dr Suite 214 .... El Paso TX 79925-0000
915 592-5400 **Olsten Temporary Services** 1200 Golden Key Cir .... El Paso TX 79925-5820

Media

■ **Newspapers/Magazines**

915 546-6100 **El Paso Herald Post** 401 E Mills Ave .... El Paso TX 79901-1446
915 546-6100 **El Paso Times** 401 E Mills Ave .... El Paso TX 79901-1446

■ **Television**

915 533-1414 **KCIK-TV Ch 14** 3100 N Stanton St .... El Paso TX 79902-2310
915 747-6500 **KCOS-TV Ch 13 (PBS)** Education Bldg University of Texas ...... El Paso TX 79902-0000
915 532-6551 **KDBC-TV Ch 4 (CBS)** 2201 Wyoming Ave .... El Paso TX 79903-3806
915 532-5421 **KTSM-TV Ch 9 (NBC)** 801 N Oregon St .... El Paso TX 79902-4001
915 532-7777 **KVIA-TV Ch 7 (ABC)** 4140 Rio Bravo St .... El Paso TX 79902-1084

■ **Radio**

915 544-7600 **KAMA-AM 750 kHz (Span)** 4150 Pinnacle St Suite 120 .... El Paso TX 79902-1019
915 533-9400 **KEZB-FM 93.9 MHz (AC)** 2501 N Mesa St .... El Paso TX 79902-3129
915 565-9927 **KHEY-FM 96.3 MHz (Ctry-ABC)** 2419 N Piedras St .... El Paso TX 79930-3403
915 544-8864 **KLAQ-FM 95.5 MHz (AOR)** 4141 Pinnacle St Suite 120 .... El Paso TX 79902-0000
915 532-4979 **KLTO-FM 94.7 MHz (AC)** 4180 N Mesa St .... El Paso TX 79902-1420
915 747-5152 **KTEP-FM 88.5 MHz (Clas-NPR)**
              University of Texas El Paso 500 W University Ave .... El Paso TX 79968-0001
915 595-6700 **XEROK-AM 80 kHz (Span)** 2100 Trawood Dr .... El Paso TX 79935-3301

Local Attractions & Special Events

■ **Sports**

915 755-2000 **El Paso Diablos** 9700 Gateway Blvd N .... El Paso TX 79924-6000
915 542-1942 **Juarez Mexico Race Track** 123 Pioneer Plaza .... El Paso TX 79901-1341

■ **Special Events**

915 544-2582 **World Championship Finals Rodeo** (November 2-9)

■ **Local Attractions**

915 568-2121 **Fort Bliss** .... El Paso TX 79916-0001
915 851-2333 **San Elizario Presidio of El Paso** 1540 San Elizario Rd .... El Paso TX 79849-0000
915 859-7718 **Socorro Mission** 328 S Nevarez .... El Paso TX 79927-9510
915 859-3916 **Tigua Indian Reservation** 122 S Old Pueblo Rd .... El Paso TX 79907-6636
915 859-9848 **Ysleta Mission** 131 S Zaragosa .... El Paso TX 79907-6523

Fort Worth

TEXAS   **817**

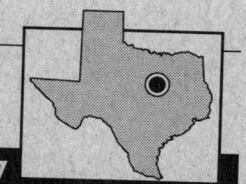

Important Phone Numbers

AAA 817 335-4871	Emergency 911
American Express 817 738-5441	Time/Temp 214 844-6611
Better Business Bureau 817 332-7585	Weather 817 787-1700
City Hall 817 870-6000	

■ Travel Information

817 336-2491   **Chamber of Commerce** 777 Taylor St Suite 900 .... Fort Worth TX 76102-4997
817 336-8791   **Convention & Visitors Bureau** 100 E 15th St Suite 400 .... Fort Worth TX 76102-6500

Travel

■ Airport

214 574-8888   **Dallas-Fort Worth International Airport** 17 miles NE of city (approx 25 minutes)

■ Airport Transportation

817 870-6230   **Fort Worth Airporter** $7 fare to downtown
817 329-2020   **Super Shuttle** $10-15 fare to downtown
              Taxi $25 fare to downtown

■ Scheduled Airlines

American 817 267-1151	Midwest Express 800 452-2022
British Airways 800 247-9297	Northwest 800 225-2525
Continental 817 268-2300	Pan Am 800 221-1111
Delta 214 630-3200	Thai 800 426-5204
Exec Express II 800 877-3932	TWA 800 221-2000
Lufthansa 800 645-3880	United 214 988-1004
Mexicana 800 531-7921	USAir 214 647-8823
Midway 800 621-5700	

■ Charter Airlines

Alpha Aviation 214 352-4801	Kitty Hawk Airways Inc 214 574-7474
Jet East Inc 214 350-8523	Million Air 214 248-1600
Jet Fleet Corp 214 350-4061	

■ Car Rentals

Agency 817 589-0471	Hertz 817 332-5205
Avis 817 335-3211	Payless 214 790-9522
Budget 817 336-6600	Thrifty 214 929-1320
Dollar 214 256-4576	

■ Limo/Taxi

American Cab 817 332-1919	Texas Limousine 214 426-1111
Fort Worth Limousine 817 870-9783	Yellow Cab 817 534-5555

■ Mass Transit

817 870-6200   **The T** Fort Worth Transportation Authority .75 Base fare .... Fort Worth TX 76102-0000

■ Rail/Bus

817 332-2931   **Amtrak Station** 1501 Jones St .... Fort Worth TX 76102-6516
817 429-3089   **Greyhound/Trailways Bus Station** 901 Commerce St .... Fort Worth TX 76102-6492

Hotels

817 335-7000   **Fort Worth Hilton** 1701 Commerce St .... Fort Worth TX 76102-6511
817 738-7311   **Green Oaks Inn & Conference Center** 6901 West Fwy .... Fort Worth TX 76116-1725
817 625-9911   **Holiday Inn North & Conference Center**
              2540 Meacham Blvd .... Fort Worth TX 76106-2398
817 870-1234   **Hyatt Regency Hotel** 815 Main St .... Fort Worth TX 76102-5493
817 870-1011   **Marriott Residence Inn** 1701 S University Dr .... Fort Worth TX 76107-6544
817 336-2011   **Park Central Hotel** 1010 Houston St .... Fort Worth TX 76102-6415
817 534-4801   **Plaza Hotel** 2000 Beach St .... Fort Worth TX 76103-2399
817 625-6427   **Stockyards Hotel** 109 E Exchange Ave .... Fort Worth TX 76106-8211
817 870-1000   **Worthington Hotel** 200 Main St .... Fort Worth TX 76102-3073

Restaurants

817 332-0357   **Angelo's BBQ** (Barbecue) 2533 White Settlement Rd .... Fort Worth TX 76107-1452
817 625-6427   **Booger Red's** (Steak) 109 E Exchange St Stockyards Hotel .... Fort Worth TX 76106-0000
817 624-3945   **Cattlemen's Steak House** (Steak) 2458 N Main St .... Fort Worth TX 76106-8500
817 924-2426   **Ciao** (Italian) 2455 Forest Pk .... Fort Worth TX 76110-0000
817 921-4567   **City Park Cafe**
              (Steak/Seafood/Pasta) 2418 Forest Park Blvd .... Fort Worth TX 76110-1702
817 626-4356   **Joe T Garcia's** (Mexican) 2201 N Commerce St .... Fort Worth TX 76164-0000
817 926-5622   **Le Chardonnay** (French) 2443 Forest Park Blvd .... Fort Worth TX 76110-0000
817 877-1531   **Old Swiss House** (Continental) 1541 Merrimac Cir .... Fort Worth TX 76107-6512
817 335-2041   **Paris Coffee Shop** (American) 700 W Magnolia .... Fort Worth TX 76104-4609
817 737-2781   **Saint Emilion** (French) 3617 W 7th St .... Fort Worth TX 76107-2533
817 763-8787   **Seterry's** (Continental) 4930 Camp Bowie Blvd .... Fort Worth TX 76107-0000

Goods & Services

■ Department Stores

817 390-1411   **Dillard's** 200 Two Tandy Ctr .... Fort Worth TX 76102-0000
817 738-3581   **Neiman-Marcus** 2100 Green Oaks Rd .... Fort Worth TX 76116-1778
817 738-7361   **Stripling & Cox** 6370 Camp Bowie Blvd .... Fort Worth TX 76116-5498

■ Banks

817 334-9000   **Bank One Texas** 777 Main St .... Fort Worth TX 76102-5358
817 390-6161   **NCNB Texas National Bank** 500 W 7th St .... Fort Worth TX 76102-4700
817 884-4000   **Team Bank** 500 Throckmorton St .... Fort Worth TX 76102-3708

■ Messenger/Postal

Express 60 Minutes Delivery 817 336-5333	Quick Way Courier Inc 817 83
Federal Express 800 238-5355	Security Couriers Corp 817 83
Metrocall Messengers Inc 817 572-4303	UPS 214 35
Post Office 817 332-3260	

■ Secretarial/Temp Services

817 332-7807   **Kelly Services Inc** 801 Cherry St .... Fort Worth TX 7610
817 877-1212   **Manpower Temporary Services** 777 Main St Suite 1515 .... Fort Worth TX 7610.
817 336-9401   **Olsten Temporary Services** 100 E 15th St Suite 215 .... Fort Worth TX 7610*

Media

■ Newspapers/Magazines

817 332-8236   **Fort Worth Magazine** 777 Taylor St .... Fort Worth TX 76102
817 390-7400   **Fort Worth Star-Telegram** 400 W 7th St .... Fort Worth TX 76102

■ Television

214 720-4444   **KDFW-TV Ch 4 (CBS)** 400 N Griffin St .... Dallas TX 75202
214 871-1390   **KERA-TV Ch 13 (PBS)** 3000 Harry Hines Blvd .... Dallas TX 75201
817 429-1550   **KXAS-TV Ch 5 (NBC)** 3900 Barnett St .... Fort Worth TX 76103
214 748-9631   **WFAA-TV Ch 8 (ABC)** 606 Young St Communications Ctr .... Dallas TX 75202

■ Radio

214 871-1390   **KERA-FM 90.1 MHz (Clas)** 3000 Harry Hines Blvd .... Dallas TX 75201
817 336-7175   **KFJZ-AM 870 kHz (Span)** 2214 E 4th St .... Fort Worth TX 76102
214 263-9911   **KKDA-AM 730 kHz (Gold)** 621 NW 6th St .... Grand Prairie TX 75050
817 429-2330   **KSCS-FM 96.3 MHz (Ctry-ABC)** 1 Broadcast Hill St .... Fort Worth TX 76103
214 826-7900   **KVIL-FM 103.7 MHz (AC)** 5307 E Mockingbird Ln Suite 500 .... Dallas TX 75206-

Local Attractions & Special Events

■ Sports

817 273-5100   **Texas Rangers** 1700 Copeland Rd Arlington Stadium .... Arlington TX 76011-

■ Special Events

817 624-2727   **Fort Worth Air Show** (October 12-13)

■ Local Attractions

817 738-1933   **Carter Amon Museum** 3501 Camp Bowie Blvd .... Fort Worth TX 76107-
817 332-7064   **Cattleman's Museum** 1301 W 7th St .... Fort Worth TX 76107-
817 732-1631   **Fort Worth Museum of Science & History**
              1501 Montgomery St .... Fort Worth TX 76102-*
817 640-8900   **Six Flags Over Texas** 2201 Road to Six Flags .... Arlington TX 76010-
817 624-4741   **Stockyards Area** 123-A E Exchange St .... Fort Worth TX 76106-
817 870-8150   **Will Rogers Memorial Center** 3401 W Lancaster St .... Fort Worth TX 76107-

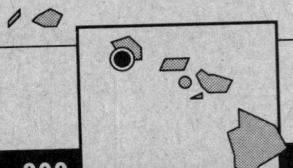

Honolulu

HAWAII | 808

Important Phone Numbers

AAA	808 528-2600	Emergency	911
American Express	808 946-7741	Poison Control Center	808 941-4411
Better Business Bureau	808 942-2355	Time	808 983-3211
City Hall	808 523-4385	Weather	808 836-2102

■ Travel Information

808 522-8800 **Chamber of Commerce** 735 Bishop St Suite 220 .... Honolulu HI 96813-4897
808 923-1811 **Visitors Bureau** .... Honolulu HI 96815-2568

Travel

■ Airport

808 836-6413 **Honolulu International Airport** 5 miles SW of city (approx 15 minutes)

■ Airport Transportation

808 949-5249 **Airport Express** $5 fare to downtown
808 926-4747 **Airport Motorcoach** $5 fare to downtown
808 834-1033 **Gray Line Limo** $8 fare to downtown
808 531-1611 **Public Transit** $.60 fare to downtown
Taxi $10 fare to downtown

■ Scheduled Airlines

Air Molokai	808 521-0090	Korean	808 923-7302
Air New Zealand	800 262-1234	Northwest	808 955-2255
Aloha	808 836-1111	Pan Am	800 221-1111
Aloha Islandair	808 833-3219	Panorama Air	808 836-2122
American	808 526-0044	Philippine	800 435-9725
China Airlines	808 536-6951	Qantas	808 922-5341
Continental	808 523-0000	Singapore	808 524-6063
Delta	800 221-1212	TWA	800 221-2000
Hawaiian	808 537-5100	United	808 547-2211
Japan	808 521-1441		

■ Charter Airlines

Kenai Helicopters 808 836-2071

■ Car Rentals

Alamo	808 833-4585	National	808 831-3800
Avis	808 834-5536	Payless	808 877-5600
Budget	808 922-3600	Thrifty	808 836-2388
Dollar	808 944-1544	Tropical	808 957-0800
Hertz	808 836-2691	United	808 922-4605
Honolulu Rent A Car	808 941-9099	Waikiki Rent A Car	808 946-2181
Maxi Car Rentals	808 923-7381		

■ Limo/Taxi

Aloha State Cab	808 847-3566	Elite Limousine Service	808 735-2431
Americabs	808 531-9999	Executive Limousine Service	808 941-1999
Big Island Limousine Service	808 325-1088		

■ Mass Transit

808 531-1611 **MTL** $.60 Base fare .... Honolulu HI 96813-0000

■ Rail/Bus

808 732-0909 **Greyhound** 550 Payea St .... Honolulu HI 96819-1837

Hotels

808 926-6400 **Aston Waikiki Beach Tower** 2470 Kalakaua Ave .... Honolulu HI 96815-3265
808 923-5751 **Colony Surf Hotel** 2895 Kalakaua Ave .... Honolulu HI 96815-4093
808 923-2311 **Halekulani Hotel** 2199 Kalia Rd .... Honolulu HI 96815-1988
808 922-6611 **Hawaiian Regent Hotel** 2552 Kalakaua Ave .... Honolulu HI 96815-3699
808 949-4321 **Hilton Hawaiian Village** 2005 Kalia Rd .... Honolulu HI 96815-1999
808 836-0661 **Holiday Inn Honolulu Airport** 3401 N Nimitz Hwy .... Honolulu HI 96819-1964
808 922-2511 **Holiday Inn Waikiki Beach** 2570 Kalakaua Ave .... Honolulu HI 96815-3698
808 923-1234 **Hyatt Regency Waikiki** 2424 Kalakaua Ave .... Honolulu HI 96815-3289
808 949-3811 **Ilikai Hotel** 1777 Ala Moana Blvd .... Honolulu HI 96815-1606
808 734-2211 **Kahala Hilton Hotel** 5000 Kahala Ave .... Honolulu HI 96816-5498
808 923-1555 **New Otani Kaimana Beach Hotel** 2863 Kalakaua Ave .... Honolulu HI 96815-4095
808 922-0811 **Outrigger Prince Kuhio Hotel** 2500 Kuhio Ave .... Honolulu HI 96815-3696
808 923-3111 **Outrigger Reef Hotel** 2169 Kalia Rd .... Honolulu HI 96815-1989
808 922-1233 **Pacific Beach Hotel** 2490 Kalakaua Ave .... Honolulu HI 96815-3286
808 923-7311 **Royal Hawaiian Hotel** 2259 Kalakaua Ave .... Honolulu HI 96815-2578
808 922-3111 **Sheraton Moana Surfrider** 2365 Kalakaua Ave .... Honolulu HI 96815-2943
808 922-5811 **Sheraton Princess Kaiulani** 120 Kaiulani Ave .... Honolulu HI 96815-3227
808 922-4422 **Sheraton Waikiki Hotel** 2255 Kalakaua Ave .... Honolulu HI 96815-2579

Restaurants

808 923-1234 **Bagwells 2424** (Continental/Seafood) 2424 Kalakaua Ave .... Honolulu HI 96815-3236
808 942-3837 **Bon Appetit** (French) 1778 Ala Moana Blvd .... Honolulu HI 96815-1605
808 949-8855 **Byron II Steak House** (Steak/Seafood) 1259 Ala Moana Ctr .... Honolulu HI 96814-4205
808 955-7866 **Chez Michel** (French) 444 Hobron Ln Eaton Sq .... Honolulu HI 96815-0000
808 737-5558 **Gonbei** (Japanese) 1018 Kapahulu Ave .... Honolulu HI 96816-1309
808 943-0052 **Greek Island Taverna** (Greek) 2370 S Beretania St .... Honolulu HI 96826-1513
808 923-2311 **La Mer** (French) 2199 Kalia Rd Halekulani Hotel .... Honolulu HI 96815-0000
808 667-2288 **Longhi's** (Northern Italian) 888 Front St .... Lahaina HI 96761-1636
808 923-6552 **Michel's** (French/Continental) 2895 Kalakaua Ave Colony Surf Hotel .... Honolulu HI 96815-0000
808 955-4466 **Nicholas Nickolas** (Steak/Seafood) 410 Atkinson Dr Suite 300 .... Honolulu HI 96814-4722

808 396-7697 **Roy's Restaurant** (Nouvelle Eurasian) 6600 Kalanianaole Hwy .... Honolulu HI 96825-0000
808 922-2887 **Shorebird Beach Broiler** (Seafood) 2169 Kalia Rd Reef Hotel ... Honolulu HI 96815-1936

Goods & Services

■ Department Stores

808 941-2345 **Liberty House of Hawaii** 1450 Ala Moana Blvd .... Honolulu HI 96814-4685
808 483-2343 **Ritz** 123 Pearl Ridge Ctr .... Aiea HI 96701-0000
808 941-9111 **Shirokiya** 2250 Ala Moana Ctr .... Honolulu HI 96814-0000

■ Banks

808 537-8111 **Bank of Hawaii** 111 S King St .... Honolulu HI 96813-3597
808 525-7000 **First Hawaiian Bank** 165 S King St .... Honolulu HI 96813-3594

■ Messenger/Postal

ADDS Messenger Service .... 808 946-1565   Rabbit Transit 808 524-4273
Elite .... 808 533-3182   UPS 808 839-1907
Post Office 808 423-3930

■ Secretarial/Temp Services

808 536-9343 **Kelly Temporary Services Inc** 1100 Ward Ave Suite 1020 .... Honolulu HI 96814-1617
808 524-3630 **Manpower Temporary Services** 737 Bishop St Suite 1880 .... Honolulu HI 96813-3209

Media

■ Newspapers/Magazines

808 523-9871 **Aloha** 49 S Hotel St Suite 309 .... Honolulu HI 96813-3108
808 525-8000 **Honolulu Advertiser** 605 Kapiolani Blvd .... Honolulu HI 96813-5129
808 525-8000 **Honolulu Star-Bulletin** 605 Kapiolani Blvd .... Honolulu HI 96813-5129

■ Television

808 944-5200 **KGMB-TV Ch 9 (CBS)** 1534 Kapiolani Blvd .... Honolulu HI 96814-3799
808 955-7878 **KHET-TV Ch 11 (PBS)** 2350 Dole St .... Honolulu HI 96822-2410
808 847-3246 **KHNL-TV Ch 13 (Fox)** 150-B Puuhale Rd .... Honolulu HI 96819-2233
808 531-8585 **KHON-TV Ch 2 (NBC)** 1116 Auahi St .... Honolulu HI 96814-4917
808 545-4444 **KITV-TV Ch 4 (ABC)** 1290 Ala Moana Blvd .... Honolulu HI 96814-4299

■ Radio

808 536-2728 **KCCN-AM 1420 kHz (Misc)** 900 Fort St Suite 400 .... Honolulu HI 96813-3704
808 955-8821 **KHPR-FM 88.1 MHz (Misc-NPR)** 738 Kaheka St .... Honolulu HI 96814-3726
808 531-4602 **KIKI-AM 830 kHz (CHR)** 345 Queen St Suite 601 .... Honolulu HI 96813-4793
808 524-7100 **KPOI-FM 97.5 MHz (AOR)** 741 Bishop St .... Honolulu HI 96813-5282
808 539-9369 **KQMQ-AM 690 kHz (CHR)** 711 Kapiolani Blvd Suite 1193 ...... Honolulu HI 96813-5282
808 539-9369 **KQMQ-FM 93.1 MHz (CHR)** 711 Kapiolani Blvd Suite 1193 ...... Honolulu HI 96817-4822
808 841-8300 **KSSK-AM 590 kHz (AC)** 1505 Dillingham Blvd Suite 208 ...... Honolulu HI 96817-5063
808 531-4511 **KUMU-AM 1500 kHz (B/EZ)** 441 N Nimitz Hwy .... Honolulu HI 96817-5063
808 531-4511 **KUMU-FM 94.7 MHz (B/EZ)** 441 N Nimitz Hwy .... Honolulu HI 96817-5063

Local Attractions & Special Events

■ Special Events

808 548-4512 **King Kamehameha Celebration** (June 8)
808 923-1811 **Lei Day** (May 1)
808 638-7266 **Triple Crown of Surfing** (November 18-December 17)

■ Local Attractions

808 946-2811 **Ala Moana Hawaii's Center** 1450 Ala Moana Blvd Suite 3200 ... Honolulu HI 96814-4602
808 848-4129 **Bishop Museum** 1525 Bernice St .... Honolulu HI 96801-0000
808 537-6191 **Honolulu Symphony Society** 1441 Kapiolani Blvd Suite 1515 ... Honolulu HI 96814-4495
808 538-1471 **Iolani Palace** King & Richards Sts .... Honolulu HI 96801-0000
808 423-1341 **Pacific Submarine Museum** 11 Arizona Memorial Rd .... Honolulu HI 96818-3145
808 293-3000 **Polynesian Cultural Center** 55-370 Kamehameha Hwy .... Laie HI 96762-0000
808 422-2771 **USS Arizona Memorial (Pearl Harbor)** 1 Arizona Memorial Rd .... Honolulu HI 96818-3145
808 923-1811 **Waikiki Beach** .... Honolulu HI 96815-0000

Houston

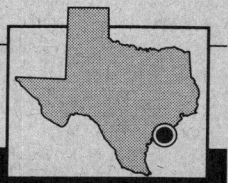

TEXAS — 713

713 875-2222 **Wyndham Greenspoint Hotel** 12400 Greenspoint Dr .... Houston TX 77060-190
713 526-1991 **Wyndham Warwick Hotel** 5701 Main St .... Houston TX 77005-189

Important Phone Numbers

AAA	713 524-1851	Emergency	911
American Express	713 658-1114	Poison Control Center	713 654-1701
Better Business Bureau	713 868-9500	Time	713 976-8463
City Hall	713 247-1000	Weather	713 228-8703

■ Travel Information
713 651-1313 **Chamber of Commerce** 1100 Milam St 25th Fl .... Houston TX 77002-5566
713 523-5050 **Convention & Visitors Bureau** 3300 Main St .... Houston TX 77002-9319

Travel

■ Airport: Houston Intercontinental
713 230-3000 **Houston Intercontinental Airport** 18 miles N of city (approx 60 minutes)

■ Airport Transportation: Houston Intercontinental
713 523-8888 **Airport Express** $8.50 fare to downtown
Taxi $50-60 fare to downtown
713 523-5694 **Texas Bus Lines** $8.50 fare to downtown

■ Scheduled Airlines: Houston Intercontinental
AeroMexico	713 939-0077	Northwest	800 225-2525
Air France	800 237-2747	Sasha	713 667-6611
American	713 222-9873	Southwest	713 237-1221
Aviateca	713 821-0451	TACA International	713 965-0507
British Airways	800 247-9297	TWA	800 221-2000
Cayman	800 422-9626	United	713 650-1055
Continental	713 821-2100	USAir	713 757-9707
Delta	713 448-3000	Viasa	713 877-8223
KLM	713 658-9741		

■ Charter Airlines: Houston Intercontinental
Aviation Charter International	713 644-4111	Million Air	713 649-2888
Aviex Jet Inc	713 641-1576	Omega Helicopters	713 370-3133
JBH Air Charter	713 644-8429		

■ Airport: Hobby
713 643-4597 **William P Hobby Airport** 8 miles SE of downtown (approx 25 minutes)

■ Airport Transportation: Hobby
713 644-8359 **Hobby Airport Limousine** $4.35 fare to downtown
713 635-4000 **Metropolitan Transit** $.70 fare to downtown
Taxi $35-40 fare to downtown

■ Scheduled Airlines: Hobby
American	713 222-9873	Pan Am	713 847-2777
Continental	713 821-2100	Southwest	713 237-1221
Delta	713 448-3000	TWA	800 221-2000
Northwest	800 225-2525	United	713 650-1055

■ Charter Airlines: Hobby
Septor Services International 713 484-9100

■ Car Rentals
Advantage	713 644-4343	Freedom	713 691-0485
Agency	713 820-8972	General	713 446-4070
Alamo	713 590-5100	Hertz	713 443-0800
Ashbaugh Auto Rental	713 659-8555	Holiday-Payless	713 590-4636
Avis	713 443-5800	National	713 443-8850
Budget	713 449-0145	Snappy	713 432-0766
Dollar	713 449-0161	Thrifty	713 449-0126

■ Limo/Taxi
Concorde Limousine	713 461-8323	Limousines of Houston	713 699-1444
Fiesta Cab	713 225-2666	United Cab Co	713 699-0000
Liberty Cab Co	713 695-6700	Yellow Cab	713 236-1111
Limousine VIP Service	713 522-0861		

■ Mass Transit
713 635-4000 **Metropolitan Transit** $.70 Base fare .... Houston TX 77002-0000

■ Rail/Bus
713 759-6581 **Greyhound/Trailways Bus Terminal** 2121 Main St .... Houston TX 77002-8896
713 224-1577 **Houston Station** 902 Washington Ave .... Houston TX 77002-1541

Hotels

713 978-7400 **Adam's Mark Hotel Houston** 2900 Briarpark Dr .... Houston TX 77042-3777
713 688-0100 **Brookhollow Marriott Hotel** 3000 North Loop W .... Houston TX 77092-0000
713 442-8000 **Doubletree Hotel Airport** 15747 John F Kennedy Blvd .... Houston TX 77032-2399
713 650-1300 **Four Seasons Hotel** 1300 Lamar St .... Houston TX 77010-3098
713 871-8181 **Four Seasons Inn on the Park** 4 Riverway .... Houston TX 77056-1999
713 228-9500 **Lancaster Hotel** 701 Texas St .... Houston TX 77002-2794
713 443-2310 **Marriott Hotel Airport** 18700 John F Kennedy Blvd .... Houston TX 77032-5099
713 961-1500 **Marriott JW Houston Galleria** 5150 Westheimer Rd .... Houston TX 77056-5506
713 960-0111 **Marriott West Loop Hotel by Galleria** 1750 Roy St .... Houston TX 77007-2238
713 682-1611 **Ramada Hotel Galleria West** 7787 Katy Fwy .... Houston TX 77024-2093
713 840-7600 **Ritz-Carlton Hotel Houston** 1919 Briar Oaks Ln .... Houston TX 77027-3491
713 629-1200 **Stouffer President Hotel** 6 E Greenway Plaza .... Houston TX 77046-0602
713 974-1000 **Westchase Hilton Hotel & Towers** 9999 Westheimer Rd .... Houston TX 77042-3899
713 960-8100 **Westin Galleria Plaza Hotel** 5060 W Alabama St .... Houston TX 77056-5898
713 623-4300 **Westin Oaks** 5011 Westheimer Rd .... Houston TX 77056-5602

Restaurants

713 524-3354 **Bertolotti** (Italian) 2300 Richton St .... Houston TX 77098-322
713 522-9711 **Brennan's of Houston** (Southwestern/Creole) 3300 Smith St ..... Houston TX 77006-669
713 840-1111 **Cafe Annie** (Southwestern) 1728 Post Oak Blvd .... Houston TX 77056-380
713 224-4438 **Charley's 517** (American/Continental) 517 Louisiana St .... Houston TX 77002-169
713 789-2333 **Chris Ruth's Steak House** (Steak) 6213 Richmond Ave .... Houston TX 77057-000
713 783-1566 **Cite Grill** (French/Californian) 5860 Westheimer .... Houston TX 77057-000
713 893-3339 **Del Frisco's Steakhouse**
(Steak/Continental) 14641 Gladebrook Dr .... Houston TX 77068-280
713 759-0202 **Dover** (Southwestern) 400 Dallas St .... Houston TX 77002-470
713 789-9055 **Fuji** (Japanese) 11124 Westheimer Rd .... Houston TX 77042-329
713 650-1980 **Harry's Kenya** (Continental) 1160 Smith St .... Houston TX 77002-520
713 931-7654 **Jimmy G's** (Cajun) 307 N Belt Dr .... Houston TX 77060-240
713 524-7999 **La Colombe D'Or** (French) 3410 Montrose Blvd .... Houston TX 77006-000
713 871-8181 **La Reserve** (Continental) 4 Riverway .... Houston TX 77056-191
713 228-9500 **Lancaster Grille** (Southwestern) 701 Texas St .... Houston TX 77002-279
713 623-4666 **Le Francais** (French) 5016 Westheimer .... Houston TX 77056-000
713 840-0303 **Ma Maison** (French) 1515 S Post Oak Ln .... Houston TX 77056-280
713 228-1175 **Ninfa's Navigation** (Mexican) 2704 Navigation Rd .... Houston TX 77003-151
713 840-7600 **Ritz-Carlton** (American) 1919 Briar Oaks Ln .... Houston TX 77027-349
713 524-3839 **Ruggles Grill** (American) 903 Westheimer .... Houston TX 77006-000
713 622-6778 **Tony's** (Continental) 1801 Post Oak Blvd .... Houston TX 77056-380
713 960-8000 **Uncle Tai's Hunan Yuan** (Chinese) 1980 Post Oak Blvd .... Houston TX 77056-386

Goods & Services

■ Department Stores
713 622-1200 **Dillard's** 4925 Westheimer Rd .... Houston TX 77056-5776
713 651-7038 **Foley's** 1110 Main St .... Houston TX 77002-6303
713 621-7100 **Neiman-Marcus** 2600 S Post Oak Rd .... Houston TX 77056-5777

■ Banks
713 224-6611 **First Interstate Bank of Texas NA** 1000 Louisiana St .... Houston TX 77002-5081
713 247-6000 **NCNB Texas National Bank** 700 Louisiana St .... Houston TX 77002-2725
713 236-4865 **Texas Commerce Bank Houston NA** 712 Main St .... Houston TX 77002-3206

■ Messenger/Postal
Central Delivery Service	713 931-4710	Red Hot Documentation	713 863-8080
Eagle Messenger Services Inc	713 963-8840	Runners Group Corp	713 939-0900
Federal Express	713 667-2500	Southwest Transferal Systems	713 354-7460
Houston Delivery Service	713 225-2222	UPS	713 820-1880
Post Office	713 227-1474		

■ Secretarial/Temp Services
713 623-8367 **Accountemps** 1360 Post Oak Blvd .... Houston TX 77056-3020
713 785-5359 **Kelly Services Inc** 5718 Westheimer Rd Suite 1720 .... Houston TX 77057-5733
713 228-3131 **Manpower Temporary Services** 440 Louisiana St .... Houston TX 77002-1634
713 658-1150 **Olsten Temporary Services** 801 Travis St Suite 1610 .... Houston TX 77002-5733

Media

■ Newspapers/Magazines
713 220-7171 **Houston Chronicle** 801 Texas St .... Houston TX 77002-2907
713 777-4636 **Houston Living Magazine** 6700 West Loop S Suite 100 .... Bel Air TX 77401-0000
713 840-5600 **Houston Post** 4747 Southwest Fwy .... Houston TX 77027-6901

■ Television
713 526-1111 **KHOU-TV Ch 11 (CBS)** 1945 Allen Pkwy .... Houston TX 77019-0000
713 771-4631 **KPRC-TV Ch 2 (NBC)** 8181 Southwest Fwy .... Houston TX 77074-1791
713 666-0713 **KTRK-TV Ch 13 (ABC)** 3310 Bissonnet St .... Houston TX 77005-2195
713 748-8888 **KUHT-TV Ch 8 (PBS)** 4513 Cullen Blvd .... Houston TX 77004-0000

■ Radio
713 772-4433 **KIKK-FM 95.7 MHz (Ctry)** 6306 Gulfton St .... Houston TX 77081-1108
713 526-6855 **KLOL-FM 101.1 MHz (AOR-NBC)** 510 Lovett Blvd .... Houston TX 77006-0000
713 623-0102 **KMJQ-FM 102.1 MHz (UC)** 24 E Greenway Plaza Suite 1508 .... Houston TX 77046-2402
713 266-1000 **KRBE-FM 104.1 MHz (CHR)** 9801 Westheimer Rd Suite 700 .... Houston TX 77042-3993
713 526-5874 **KTRH-AM 740 kHz (N/T-ABC)** 510 Lovett Blvd .... Houston TX 77006-0000
713 749-7188 **KUHF-FM 88.7 MHz (Clas-NPR)**
4800 Calhoun University of Houston .... Houston TX 77204-0001

Local Attractions & Special Events

■ Sports
713 799-9555 **Houston Astros** 8400 Kirby Dr Astrodome .... Houston TX 77054-1504
713 797-9111 **Houston Oilers** 8400 Kirby Dr Astrodome .... Houston TX 77054-1504
713 627-9470 **Houston Rockets** 10 Greenway Plaza The Summit .... Houston TX 77046-1099

■ Local Attractions
713 799-9500 **Astrodome** 8400 Kirby Dr .... Houston TX 77054-0000
713 479-2411 **Battleship Texas** 3527 Battleground Rd .... La Porte TX 77571-9773
713 224-4240 **Houston Symphony Orchestra** 615 Louisiana St .... Houston TX 77002-2798
713 483-4321 **Lyndon B Johnson Space Center (NASA)** 2101 Nasa Rd .... Houston TX 77052-0000
713 526-1361 **Museum of Fine Arts** 1001 Bissonnet St .... Houston TX 77005-1896
713 524-9839 **Rothko Chapel** 3900 Yupon .... Houston TX 77006-0000
713 655-1912 **Sam Houston Park** 1100 Bagby .... Houston TX 77002-0000
713 479-2431 **San Jacinto Battleground** 3523 Hwy 134 .... La Porte TX 77571-9773

Indianapolis

INDIANA   **317**

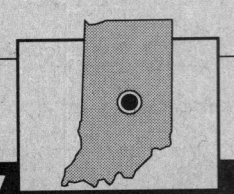

Important Phone Numbers

AAA	317 923-3311	Emergency	911
American Express	317 237-2230	Poison Control Center	317 929-2323
Better Business Bureau	317 637-0849	Time/Temp	317 632-1511
City Hall	317 236-3200	Weather	317 222-2362

■ Travel Information

317 464-2200 **Chamber of Commerce** 320 N Meridian St Suite 928 .... Indianapolis IN 46204-1777
317 639-4282 **Convention & Visitors Assn**
200 S Capitol Ave 1 Hoosier Dome Suite 100 ....Indianapolis IN 46225-0000
317 237-5200 **Indianapolis City Center** 201 S Capitol Ave Pan Am Plaza .... Indianapolis IN 46225-0000

Travel

■ Airport

317 248-9594 **Indianapolis International Airport** 7 miles SW of city (approx 12 minutes)

■ Airport Transportation

317 247-7301 **AAA Shuttle Express** $5 fare to downtown
317 635-3344 **Metro Bus** $1 fare to downtown
Taxi $10-12 fare to downtown

■ Scheduled Airlines

Air Canada	800 776-3000	Midway	800 621-5700
American	317 262-1054	Northwest	800 225-2525
American Trans Air	317 243-4561	Pan Am	800 221-1111
Comair	800 354-9822	Southwest	317 637-1717
Continental	317 635-0290	TWA	317 635-4381
Delta	317 634-3200	United	317 638-6363
Eastern	317 639-6611	USAir	317 248-1211

■ Charter Airlines

Aviation Charter Service	317 244-7200	Roto-Whirl	317 241-2484

■ Car Rentals

Ace	317 243-6336	Hertz	317 243-9321
Avis	317 244-3307	National	317 243-7501
Budget	317 248-1100	Snappy	317 247-0333
Dollar	317 241-8206	Thrifty	317 243-2282

■ Limo/Taxi

Airport Limousine Service	317 247-7301	Metro Taxi	317 634-1112
Indianapolis Yellow Cab	317 637-5421	Touch of Class Limousine Service	317 846-4743

■ Mass Transit

317 632-1900 **Metro** $.75 Base fare .... Indianapolis IN 46204-0000

■ Rail/Bus

317 635-4501 **Greyhound/Trailways Bus Station** 127 N Capitol Ave .... Indianapolis IN 46204-2299
317 263-0550 **Indianapolis Station** 350 S Illinois St .... Indianapolis IN 46225-1198

Hotels

317 248-2481 **Adam's Mark Hotel** 2544 Executive Dr .... Indianapolis IN 46241-5096
317 634-3000 **Canterbury Hotel** 123 S Illinois St .... Indianapolis IN 46225-1056
317 248-0621 **Days Inn Airport** 5860 Fortune Cir W .... Indianapolis IN 46241-5597
317 236-1800 **Embassy Suites Downtown** 110 W Washington St .... Indianapolis IN 46204-3423
317 872-7700 **Embassy Suites North** 3912 W Vincennes Rd .... Indianapolis IN 46268-3024
317 635-2000 **Hilton Hotel at the Circle** 31 W Ohio St .... Indianapolis IN 46204-1916
317 244-6861 **Holiday Inn Airport** 2501 S High School Rd .... Indianapolis IN 46241-4991
317 631-2221 **Holiday Inn Union Station** 123 W Louisiana St .... Indianapolis IN 46206-0000
317 632-1234 **Hyatt Regency Indianapolis** 1 S Capitol Ave .... Indianapolis IN 46204-3495
317 352-1231 **Marriott Hotel Indianapolis** 7202 E 21st St .... Indianapolis IN 46219-1798
317 846-2700 **Radisson Hotel** 8787 Keystone Crossing .... Indianapolis IN 46240-4604
317 787-3344 **Ramada Inn South** 4514 S Emerson Ave .... Indianapolis IN 46204-5991
317 897-4000 **Sheraton Northeast** 7701 E 42nd St .... Indianapolis IN 46226-5296
317 299-6165 **Signature Inn West** 3850 Eagle View Dr .... Indianapolis IN 46254-4660

Restaurants

317 634-3000 **Canterbury Hotel Beaulieu Restaurant**
(Nouvelle American) 123 S Illinois St .... Indianapolis IN 46225-1056
317 243-1040 **Chanteclair** (French) 2501 S High School Rd .... Indianapolis IN 46241-4919
317 831-0870 **Chez Jean Restaurant Francais** (French) 9027 S SR-67 .... Camby IN 46113-9722
317 257-1872 **Dodd's Town House** (Steak/Seafood) 5694 N Meridian St .... Indianapolis IN 46208-1503
317 632-2500 **Fletcher's American Grill & Cafe**
(Nouvelle American) 107 S Pennsylvania St .... Indianapolis IN 46204-3643
317 844-0921 **Glass Chimney** (French) 12901 N Old Meridian St .... Carmel IN 46032-0000
317 638-5588 **King Cole** (Continental) 7 N Meridian St .... Indianapolis IN 46204-3026
317 637-9333 **Peter's** (Midwest/Regional) 936 Virginia Ave .... Indianapolis IN 46203-1706
317 637-1811 **Saint Elmo Steak House** (Steak) 127 S Illinois St .... Indianapolis IN 46225-1079
317 631-4041 **Shapiro's** (German/Hungarian) 808 S Meridian St .... Indianapolis IN 46225-0000

Goods & Services

■ Department Stores

317 262-4411 **Ayres LS & Co** 1 W Washington St .... Indianapolis IN 46204-3483
317 631-8511 **Lazarus** 50 N Illinois St .... Indianapolis IN 46204-2804

■ Banks

317 321-3000 **Bank One Indianapolis NA** 111 Monument Cir .... Indianapolis IN 46277-0001
317 266-6000 **Indiana National Bank** 1 Indiana Sq .... Indianapolis IN 46266-0001
317 267-7000 **Merchants National Bank & Trust Co of Indiana**
1 Merchants Plaza ....Indianapolis IN 46255-0001

■ Messenger/Postal

AD Com Express	317 486-0038	Now Courier Messenger Service	317 638-6066
Cycle Dispatch	317 351-7757	Post Office	317 464-6000
Federal Express	317 636-4845	UPS	317 875-0060

■ Secretarial/Temp Services

317 634-3600 **Kelly Services Inc** 1099 N Meridian St Suite 160 .... Indianapolis IN 46204-1036
317 635-1001 **Manpower Temporary Services Inc** 205 E New York St ...... Indianapolis IN 46204-2100
317 237-7990 **Olsten Temporary Services** 95 N Meridian St Suite 960 ...... Indianapolis IN 46204-3002

Media

■ Newspapers/Magazines

317 259-8222 **Indianapolis Monthly** 8425 Keystone Crossing Suite 225 .... Indianapolis IN 46240-4377
317 633-1240 **Indianapolis News** 307 N Pennsylvania St ....Indianapolis IN 46204-1811
317 633-1240 **Indianapolis Star** 307 N Pennsylvania St .... Indianapolis IN 46204-1811

■ Television

317 636-2020 **WFYI-TV Ch 20 (PBS)** 1401 N Meridian St .... Indianapolis IN 46202-2304
317 923-8888 **WISH-TV Ch 8 (CBS)** 1950 N Meridian St .... Indianapolis IN 46202-1304
317 635-9788 **WRTV-TV Ch 6 (ABC)** 1330 N Meridian St .... Indianapolis IN 46202-2364
317 636-1313 **WTHR-TV Ch 13 (NBC)** 1000 N Meridian St .... Indianapolis IN 46204-1076

■ Radio

317 926-9252 **WAJC-FM 104.5 MHz (Jazz)** 2835 N Illinois St .... Indianapolis IN 46208-4705
317 266-9700 **WENS-FM 97.1 MHz (AC)** 1099 N Meridian St Suite 1197 .... Indianapolis IN 46204-1065
317 257-7565 **WFBQ-FM 94.7 MHz (AOR-NBC)** 6161 Fall Creek Rd .... Indianapolis IN 46220-5032
317 842-9550 **WFMS-FM 95.5 MHz (Ctry)** 8120 Knue Rd .... Indianapolis IN 46250-1932
317 844-7200 **WIBC-AM 1070 kHz (AC)** 9292 N Meridian St .... Indianapolis IN 46260-1804
317 844-7200 **WKLR-FM 93.1 MHz (Gold)** 9292 N Meridian St .... Indianapolis IN 46260-1804
317 637-8000 **WZPL-FM 99.5 MHz (CHR)** 1440 N Meridian St .... Indianapolis IN 46202-2305

Local Attractions & Special Events

■ Sports

317 263-2100 **Indiana Pacers** 300 E Market St .... Indianapolis IN 46204-2603
317 632-5371 **Indianapolis Indians** 1501 W 16th St .... Indianapolis IN 46202-2003

■ Special Events

317 241-2500 **Indianapolis 500** (May 26)

■ Local Attractions

317 636-9378 **Eiteljorg Museum of American Indian & Western Art**
500 W Washington St .... Indianapolis IN 46204-2707
317 635-5277 **Indiana Repertory Theatre** 140 W Washington St .... Indianapolis IN 46204-0000
317 241-2501 **Indianapolis Motor Speedway & Hall of Fame Museum**
4790 W 16th St .... Speedway IN 46224-0000
317 923-1331 **Indianapolis Museum of Art** 1200 W 38th St .... Indianapolis IN 46208-4196
317 635-6355 **Indianapolis Symphony Orchestra** 45 Monument Cir .... Indianapolis IN 46204-0000
317 261-0483 **National Track & Field Hall of Fame**
200 S Capitol Ave Suite 140 .... Indianapolis IN 46204-0000
317 267-0701 **Union Station** 39 W Jackson Pl .... Indianapolis IN 46225-1050

Jacksonville

FLORIDA 904

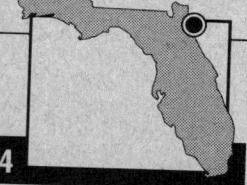

Important Phone Numbers

AAA 904 398-0564
American Express 904 565-6000
Better Business Bureau 904 721-2288
City Hall 904 630-1178

Emergency 911
Poison Control Center 904 387-7500
Time 904 358-1212
Weather 904 741-4110

■ Travel Information

904 353-0300   Chamber of Commerce 3 Independent Dr .... Jacksonville FL 32202-5092
904 353-9736   Convention & Visitors Bureau 6 Eastbay St Suite 200 .... Jacksonville FL 32202-0000

Travel

■ Airport

904 741-2000   Jacksonville International Airport 20 miles N of downtown (approx 20 minutes)

■ Airport Transportation

Taxi $18 fare to downtown

■ Scheduled Airlines

American 904 354-2593
Continental 904 354-3452
Delta 904 398-3011
Eastern 904 355-7392

Midway 800 621-5700
Pan Am 800 221-1111
TWA 800 221-2000
USAir 904 353-7065

■ Charter Airlines

Corporate Airways 904 721-2275
Craig Air Center 904 641-0542

Holiday Air 904 741-4222

■ Car Rentals

Avis 904 741-2327
Budget 904 741-4555
Hertz 904 741-2151

Holiday-Payless 904 353-5333
National 904 741-4580
Thrifty 800 367-2277

■ Limo/Taxi

AAA Limousine 904 751-4800
ABC Checker Cab 904 764-2472
Bob's Limo 904 241-1013

Gator City Taxi 904 355-8294
Greater Jacksonville Trans 904 356-8888
People's Cab 904 642-4200

■ Mass Transit

904 630-3100   Jacksonville Transit Authority $.60 Base fare .... Jacksonville FL 32204-0000

■ Rail/Bus

904 766-5110   Clifford Lane Station 3570 Clifford Ln .... Jacksonville FL 32209-2123
904 737-7011   Greyhound/Trailways Bus Station 8030 Phillips Hwy .... Jacksonville FL 32217-2324

Hotels

904 751-0351   Admiral Benbow Inn 820 Dunn Ave .... Jacksonville FL 32218-4803
904 757-0990   Days Inn 1057 Broward Rd .... Jacksonville FL 32218-5307
904 741-4980   Hampton Inn Airport 1170 Airport Entrance Rd ..... Jacksonville FL 32218-0000
904 741-4404   Holiday Inn Airport 14670 Duval Rd .... Jacksonville FL 32218-2460
904 724-3410   Holiday Inn East 5865 Arlington Expy .... Jacksonville FL 32211-5669
904 355-3744   Hospitality Inn 901 N Main St .... Jacksonville FL 32202-3093
904 741-4747   Jacksonville Airport Plaza Hotel 14000 Dixie Clipper Rd ..... Jacksonville FL 32218-0000
904 398-8800   Jacksonville Hotel 565 S Main St .... Jacksonville FL 32207-9059
904 396-5100   Marina Hotel at Saint John's Place 1515 Prudential Dr ..... Jacksonville FL 32207-8153
904 296-2222   Marriott Jacksonville 4670 Salisbury Rd .... Jacksonville FL 32256-0978
904 355-6664   Omni Jacksonville Hotel 245 Water St .... Jacksonville FL 32202-4403
904 731-3555   Park Suites Hotel 9300 Baymeadows Rd .... Jacksonville FL 32256-7710
904 725-5093   Ramada Inn East 6237 Arlington Expy .... Jacksonville FL 32211-5798
904 268-8080   Ramada Inn Mandarin Conference Center
3130 Hartley Rd .... Jacksonville FL 32257-0000
904 249-7402   Sea Turtle Inn 1 Ocean Blvd .... Jacksonville FL 32233-5295
904 731-7317   TraveLodge at Baymeadows 8765 Baymeadows Rd .... Jacksonville FL 32256-7425

Restaurants

904 448-2424   24 Miramar (American/Continental) 4446 Hendricks Ave ..... Jacksonville FL 32207-0000
904 641-1212   Alhambra Dinner Theatre (American) 12000 Beach Blvd ..... Jacksonville FL 32216-6799
904 285-5073   American Bounty Cafe (American) 244 Solano Rd .... Ponte Vedra Beach FL 32082-0000
904 398-3353   Chart House (Steak/Seafood) 601 Hendricks Ave ..... Jacksonville FL 32207-9001
904 396-3546   Crawdaddy's (Steak/Seafood) 1643 Prudential Dr ..... Jacksonville FL 32207-8178
904 824-8897   Fiddlers Green (Seafood) 2750 Anahma Dr ..... Saint Augustine FL 32095-2901
904 824-8244   Gypsy Cab Co (Continental) 828 Anastasia Blvd ..... Saint Augustine FL 32084-4660
904 269-5738   La Pasta Fresca (Italian) 502 Wells Rd ..... Orange Park FL 32073-2924
904 826-0781   Old City House Inn & Restaurant
(American) 115 Cordova St
904 725-1662   Patti's (Italian) 7300 Beach Blvd ..... Saint Augustine FL 32084-0000
904 241-7877   Ragtime Tavern Seafood & Grill
(Seafood) 207 Atlantic Blvd ..... Jacksonville FL 32216-2946
904 829-5953   Raintree (Continental) 102 San Marco Ave ..... Atlantic Beach FL 32233-0000
904 398-7918   South Bank Marina (Seafood) 835 Gulf Life Dr ..... Saint Augustine FL 32084-3223
904 387-0700   Sterling's Flamingo Cafe
(Continental) 3551 St John's Ave ..... Jacksonville FL 32207-9003
904 398-8989   Wine Cellar (Continental) 1314 Prudential Dr ..... Jacksonville FL 32205-8465
.... Jacksonville FL 32207-8199

Goods & Services

■ Department Stores

904 721-9166   Dillards 9501 Arlington Expy .... Jacksonville FL 32225-8243
904 642-5000   Jacobson's 9911 Old Baymeadows Rd .... Jacksonville FL 32256-0000
904 725-7744   Maison Blanche 9501 Arlington Expy .... Jacksonville FL 32201-0000

■ Banks

904 791-7500   Barnett Bank of Jacksonville NA 50 N Laura St ..... Jacksonville FL 32202-3638
904 361-2265   First Union National Bank of Florida 225 Water St ..... Jacksonville FL 32202-0000
904 359-5111   First Union National Bank of Jacksonville 225 Water St ..... Jacksonville FL 32202-0000

■ Messenger/Postal

Federal Express 904 358-3334
General Delivery Systems 904 448-1993
Metro Parcel 904 387-4942

Post Office
Reliable Express Service Inc 904 355-7311
UPS 904 396-5588
.... 904 398-5272

■ Secretarial/Temp Services

904 725-5574   Associated Temporary Staffing 6440 Atlantic Blvd ..... Jacksonville FL 32211-8724
904 399-0883   Kelly Services Inc 1965 Beachway Rd Suite 3 ..... Jacksonville FL 32207-2340
904 737-2400   Olsten Temporary Services
8386 Baymeadows Rd Suite 1 .... Jacksonville FL 32256-7438

Media

■ Newspapers/Magazines

904 359-4111   Florida Times-Union 1 Riverside Ave .... Jacksonville FL 32202-4904
904 396-8666   Jacksonville Today 1325 San Marco Blvd Suite 900 ..... Jacksonville FL 32207-8549

■ Television

904 642-3030   WAWS-TV Ch 30 (Fox) 8675 Hogan Rd .... Jacksonville FL 32216-0401
904 353-7770   WJCT-TV Ch 7 (PBS) 100 Festival Park Ave ..... Jacksonville FL 32202-1309
904 641-1700   WJKS-TV Ch 17 (ABC) 9117 Hogan Rd .... Jacksonville FL 32216-0400
904 399-4000   WJXT-TV Ch 4 (CBS) 1851 Southampton Rd ..... Jacksonville FL 32207-8648
904 725-4700   WNFT-TV Ch 47 2117 University Blvd S .... Jacksonville FL 32216-8936
904 354-1212   WTLV-TV Ch 12 (NBC) 1070 E Adams St ..... Jacksonville FL 32202-1998

■ Radio

904 725-9273   WAPE-FM 95.1 MHz (CHR-ABC)
9487 Regency Square Blvd Suite 95 ..... Jacksonville FL 32225-8149
904 636-0507   WCRJ-FM 107.3 MHz (Ctry-NBC)
8386 Baymeadows Rd Suite 107 ..... Jacksonville FL 32256-7481
904 642-1055   WFYV-FM 104.5 MHz (AOR-ABC) 9090 Hogan Rd ..... Jacksonville FL 32216-4648
904 721-9111   WIVY-FM 102.9 MHz (AC)
3101 University Blvd S Suite 200 ..... Jacksonville FL 32216-4291
904 743-2400   WJAX-AM 1220 kHz (B/EZ) 5353 Arlington Expy ..... Jacksonville FL 32211-5540
904 359-9090   WJCT-FM 89.9 MHz (Clas-NPR) 100 Festival Park Ave ..... Jacksonville FL 32202-1309
904 783-3711   WKQL-FM 96.9 MHz (Gold) 6869 Lenox Ave ..... Jacksonville FL 32205-6149
904 743-2400   WKTZ-FM 90.9 MHz (B/EZ-MBS) 5353 Arlington Expy ..... Jacksonville FL 32211-5587
904 354-7121   WPDQ AM 690 kHz (Gold) PO Box 486 ..... Orange Park FL 32067-0486
904 388-7711   WQIK-AM 1320 kHz (Ctry-ABC) 5555 Radio Ln ..... Jacksonville FL 32205-6899
904 388-7711   WQIK-FM 99.1 MHz (Ctry-ABC) 5555 Radio Ln ..... Jacksonville FL 32205-6899
904 743-6970   WVOJ-AM 970 kHz (CC) 2427 University Blvd N ..... Jacksonville FL 32211-3229
904 389-1111   WZAZ-AM 1400 kHz (UC-SBN) 2611 WERD Radio Dr ..... Jacksonville FL 32204-1751
904 389-1111   WZAZ-FM 92.7 MHz (UC-MBS) 2611 WERD Radio Dr ..... Jacksonville FL 32204-1751

Local Attractions & Special Events

■ Sports

904 646-0001   Greyhound Racing Information 1440 N McDuff Ave ..... Jacksonville FL 32205-2036
904 358-2846   Jacksonville Expos 1201 E Duval St .... Jacksonville FL 32202-0000

■ Special Events

904 285-7888   Tournament Player's Championship (March 25-31)

■ Local Attractions

904 261-7378   Amelia Island Museum of History 233 S 3rd St ..... Fernandina Beach FL 32034-0000
904 398-8336   Jacksonville Art Museum 4160 Boulevard Center Dr ..... Jacksonville FL 32207-2805
904 353-1188   Jacksonville Landing 2 Independent Dr .... Jacksonville FL 32202-0000
904 354-5479   Jacksonville Symphony Orchestra
33 S Hogan St Suite 400 ..... Jacksonville FL 32202-0000
904 251-3122   Kingsley Plantation 11676 Palmetto Ave .... Jacksonville FL 32226-0000
912 496-3331   Okefenokee Swamp 45 miles N of Jacksonville ..... Folkston GA 31357-0000
904 396-4900   Riverwalk Prudential Dr .... Jacksonville FL 32202-0000

Kansas City
MISSOURI   816

Important Phone Numbers

AAA	816 931-5252	Emergency	911
American Express	816 531-9114	Poison Control Center	816 234-3434
Better Business Bureau	816 421-7800	Time/Temp	816 844-4444
City Hall	816 274-2000	Weather	816 531-4444

■ Travel Information
816 221-2424 Chamber of Commerce 920 Main St .... Kansas City MO 64105-2049
816 221-5242 Convention & Visitors Bureau 1100 Main St Suite 2550 ... Kansas City MO 64105-2195

Travel

■ Airport
816 243-5259 Kansas City International Airport 18 miles NW of city (approx 30 minutes)

■ Airport Transportation
816 243-5950 KCI Airport Express $9 fare to downtown
Taxi $20-25 fare to downtown

■ Scheduled Airlines
Air Midwest	800 835-2953	Northwest	800 225-2525
American	816 221-7767	Southwest	816 474-1221
Continental	816 471-3700	TWA	816 842-4000
Delta	816 471-1828	United	816 471-6060
Eastern	816 471-4353	USAir	800 428-4322
Midway	800 621-5700		

■ Charter Airlines
Executive Beachcraft	816 842-8484	Ralph Aviation	816 221-3192

■ Car Rentals
Avis	816 243-5760	National	816 243-5770
Budget	816 471-3953	Snappy	913 649-5277
Dollar	816 243-5600	Thrifty	816 464-5670
Hertz	816 243-5765		

■ Limo/Taxi
American Cab Co	816 421-5553	Community Cab	816 474-7474
American Limousine Service	816 471-6050	Yellow Cab	816 471-5000
Batesway Taxi	816 231-3000		

■ Mass Transit
816 221-0660 Metro Bus System $.75 Base fare .... Kansas City MO 64108-0000

■ Rail/Bus
816 698-0080 Greyhound/Trailways Bus Station 1101 Troost St ... Kansas City MO 64106-2678
816 421-3622 Kansas City Station 2200 Main St .... Kansas City MO 64108-4312

Hotels
816 737-0200 Adam's Mark Hotel Kansas City 9103 E 39th St ... Kansas City MO 64133-1196
816 421-6800 Allis Plaza Hotel 200 W 12th St .... Kansas City MO 64105-1637
816 753-7400 Hilton Plaza Inn 1 E 45th St .... Kansas City MO 64111-1883
816 891-8900 Hilton Plaza Inn Airport 8801 NW 112th St ... Kansas City MO 64195-0000
816 421-1234 Hyatt Regency Crown Center 2345 McGee St ... Kansas City MO 64108-2695
816 531-3000 Kansas City Marriott Plaza 4445 Main St ... Kansas City MO 64111-1811
816 464-2200 Marriott Hotel Airport 775 Brasilia Ave ... Kansas City MO 64153-0000
816 483-9900 Park Place Hotel 1601 N Universal Ave ... Kansas City MO 64120-1396
816 741-9500 Ramada Inn Kansas City Airport
 7301 NW Tiffany Springs Rd .... Kansas City MO 64153-1830
816 756-3800 Raphael Hotel 325 Ward Pkwy .... Kansas City MO 64112-2162
816 756-1500 Ritz-Carlton Hotel 401 Ward Pkwy .... Kansas City MO 64112-2199
816 474-4400 Westin Crown Center 1 Pershing Rd .... Kansas City MO 64108-2599

Restaurants
816 426-1133 American Restaurant (American) 2450 Grand Ave ... Kansas City MO 64108-2530
816 231-1123 Arthur Bryant Barbeque (Barbecue) 1727 Brooklyn Ave ... Kansas City MO 64127-2590
816 842-6984 Boulevard Cafe
 (Spanish/Middle Eastern) 703 Southwest Blvd ... Kansas City MO 64112-1896
816 756-0606 Bristol Bar & Grill (Seafood) 4740 Jefferson St ... Kansas City MO 64111-4401
816 561-3663 Cafe Allegro (Nouvelle American) 1815 W 39th St ... Kansas City MO 64111-0000
816 531-7878 Californos (Grilled American) 4124 Pennsylvania Ave ... Kansas City MO 64154-9532
816 436-8700 Dinner Horn Country Inn (Regional) 2820 NW Barry Rd ... Kansas City MO 64112-1606
816 561-6565 Fedora Cafe & Bar (Nouvelle American) 210 W 47th St ... Kansas City MO 64110-0000
816 921-0409 Gates Barbque (Barbecue) 1411 Swope Pkwy
816 842-2866 Golden Ox Restaurant & Lounge
 (Steak) 1600 Gennessee St .... Kansas City MO 64102-1039
816 756-1500 Grill The (Continental) 401 Ward Pkwy .... Kansas City MO 64112-2199
816 842-1080 Herford House (Steak) 2 E 20th St .... Kansas City MO 64108-1991
816 363-3003 Jasper's (Continental/Italian) 405 W 75th St ... Kansas City MO 64114-1534
816 561-2916 La Mediterranee (French) 4742 Pennsylvania St ... Kansas City MO 64112-2091
816 931-4849 Margarita's (Mexican) 2829 Southwest Blvd ... Kansas City MO 64111-0000
816 753-1550 Metropolis American Grill (American) 303 Westport Rd ... Kansas City MO 64111-0000
816 842-3890 Savoy Grill & Restaurant (Seafood) 9th & Central Sts ... Kansas City MO 64105-0000
816 373-5400 Stephenson's Old Apple Farm Restaurant
 (American) 16401 E 40 Hwy .... Kansas City MO 64136-0000
816 561-3311 Venue (American) 4532 Main St .... Kansas City MO 64111-0000

Goods & Services

■ Department Stores
816 363-8800 Dillard's 8800 Ward Pkwy .... Kansas City MO 64114-2699
816 274-8111 Hall's 200 E 25th St .... Kansas City MO 64108-2598
816 391-7000 Jones Store 1201 Main St .... Kansas City MO 64105-2183

■ Banks
816 221-2800 Boatmen's First National Bank of Kansas City
 14 W 10th St .... Kansas City MO 64105-1702
816 234-2000 Commerce Bank of Kansas City NA 922 Walnut St ... Kansas City MO 64106-1871
816 556-7000 United Missouri Bank of Kansas City NA 1010 Grand Ave ... Kansas City MO 64106-2220

■ Messenger/Postal
AB Express Inc	816 931-3880	Flexfleet Couriers Inc ... 816 756-3505
Central Delivery Svc of Kansas City	913 384-6055	Post Office ... 816 374-9275
Direct Messenger Service	913 631-7515	Sun Courier Service ... 816 436-2801
Federal Express	913 661-0255	UPS ... 913 281-1000

■ Secretarial/Temp Services
816 474-4583 Accountemps 127 W 10th St Suite 956 ... Kansas City MO 64105-1716
913 661-0402 Kelly Temporary Services
 9200 Indian Creek Pkwy Bldg 9 Suite 510 ... Overland Park KS 66210-0000
816 561-3358 Manpower Temporary Services Inc
 3100 Broadway Suite 224 .... Kansas City MO 64111-2437

Media

■ Newspapers/Magazines
816 234-4141 Kansas City Star 1729 Grand Ave ... Kansas City MO 64108-1413

■ Television
816 756-3580 KCPT-TV Ch 19 (PBS) 125 E 31st St ... Kansas City MO 64108-3216
913 677-5555 KCTV-TV Ch 5 (CBS) 4500 Shawnee Mission Pkwy ... Fairway KS 66205-2509
816 221-9999 KMBC-TV Ch 9 (ABC) 1049 Central St ... Kansas City MO 64105-0000
816 753-4567 WDAF-TV Ch 4 (NBC) 3030 Summit St ... Kansas City MO 64108-3312

■ Radio
816 276-1551 KCUR-FM 89.3 MHz (N/T-NPR) 4825 Troost St Suite 202 ... Kansas City MO 64110-2030
913 236-9800 KMBZ-AM 980 kHz (N/T-NBC) 4935 Belinder Rd ... Shawnee Mission KS 66205-1937
913 342-1266 KNHN-AM 1340 kHz (N/T) 4121 Minnesota Ave ... Kansas City KS 66102-0000
816 471-2100 KPRS-FM 103.3 MHz (UC-ABC)
 2440 Pershing Rd Suite 118 .... Kansas City MO 64108-2558
816 561-9102 KYYS-FM 102.1 MHz (AOR-NBC) 3020 Summit St ... Kansas City MO 64108-3312
816 931-6100 WDAF-AM 610 kHz (Ctry-ABC) 3020 Summit St ... Kansas City MO 64108-3312

Local Attractions & Special Events

■ Sports
816 924-9400 Kansas City Chiefs 1 Arrowhead Dr Arrowhead Stadium ... Kansas City MO 64129-1651
816 421-7770 Kansas City Comets 1800 Genessee St Kemper Arena ... Kansas City MO 64102-1083
816 921-8000 Kansas City Royals Royals Stadium .... Kansas City MO 64102-1083

■ Special Events
816 221-9800 American Royal Livestock Horse Show & Rodeo (November 8-23)

■ Local Attractions
816 761-5055 Benjamin Ranch on the Santa Fe Trail 6401 E 87th ... Kansas City MO 64138-0000
816 753-0100 Country Club Plaza 4625 Wornall .... Kansas City MO 64112-0000
816 274-3613 Hallmark Visitors Center
 Pershing & Grand Ave Crown Center Complex ... Kansas City MO 64141-0000
816 254-9929 Harry S Truman Home 223 N Main St ... Independence MO 64050-2804
816 833-1400 Harry S Truman Library 1200 N McCoy ... Independence MO 64050-1798
816 483-8300 Kansas City Museum 3218 Gladstone Blvd ... Kansas City MO 64123-1199
816 471-1100 Kansas City Symphony 1020 Central Ave ... Kansas City MO 64105-1619
816 561-4000 Nelson-Atkins Museum of Art 4525 Oak St ... Kansas City MO 64111-1818
816 931-3440 Westport Market Place 4149 Pennsylvania ... Kansas City MO 64111-2294

Las Vegas

NEVADA 702

702 796-3300 **Pegasus** (French) 375 E Harmon Ave .... Las Vegas NV 89109-7081
702 794-8240 **Saint Thomas Seafood Grotto**
(Seafood) 3120 S Las Vegas Blvd .... Las Vegas NV 89109-0000
702 731-4036 **Tillerman** (Steak/Seafood) 2245 E Flamingo .... Las Vegas NV 89119-5109

Goods & Services

■ Department Stores

702 734-2111 **Dillard's** 3588 Maryland Pkwy Boulevard Mall .... Las Vegas NV 89109-0000
702 731-3636 **Neiman-Marcus** 3200 Las Vegas Blvd S .... Las Vegas NV 89109-2699
702 733-8300 **Saks Fifth Avenue** 3200 Las Vegas Blvd S .... Las Vegas NV 89109-2698

■ Banks

702 385-8321 **First Interstate Bank** 300 Carson Ave .... Las Vegas NV 89101-5997
702 383-4111 **Nevada State Bank** 201 S 4th St .... Las Vegas NV 89101-5716
702 386-1000 **Valley Bank of Nevada** 300 S 4th St .... Las Vegas NV 89101-6014

■ Messenger/Postal

Armored Transport .... 702 457-3934   **Mac's Delivery Service Inc** 702 367-0252
Courier Express Inc .... 702 871-8112   **Post Office** 702 361-9212
Federal Express .... 800 238-5355   **UPS** 702 385-3636
Legal Wings 702 384-0305

■ Secretarial/Temp Services

702 739-9797 **Accountemps** 3800 Howard Hughes Pkwy Suite 540 .... Las Vegas NV 89109-0905
702 796-0203 **Kelly Services Inc** 3900 Paradise Rd Suite 231 .... Las Vegas NV 89109-0933
702 386-2626 **Manpower Temporary Services Inc** 314 Las Vegas Blvd N .... Las Vegas NV 89101-2990

Media

■ Newspapers/Magazines

702 383-0211 **Las Vegas Review-Journal** 1111 W Bonanza Rd .... Las Vegas NV 89106-3545
702 385-3111 **Las Vegas Sun** 121 S Martin Luther King Blvd .... Las Vegas NV 89106-4339
702 687-5416 **Nevada Magazine** 1800 Hwy 50 E .... Carson City NV 89710-0001

■ Television

702 733-8850 **KLAS-TV Ch 8 (CBS)** 3228 Channel Eight Dr .... Las Vegas NV 89109-9097
702 737-1010 **KLVX-TV Ch 10 (PBS)** 4210 Channel Ten Dr .... Las Vegas NV 89119-5454
702 876-1313 **KTNV-TV Ch 13 (ABC)** 3355 S Valley View Blvd .... Las Vegas NV 89102-8298
702 642-3333 **KVBC-TV Ch 3 (NBC)** 1500 Foremaster Ln .... Las Vegas NV 89101-1103

■ Radio

702 385-7212 **KDWN-AM 720 kHz (N/T)** 1 Main St .... Las Vegas NV 89101-6312
702 876-1460 **KENO-AM 1460 kHz (Gold)** 4660 S Decatur Blvd .... Las Vegas NV 89103-5209
702 732-7753 **KFMS-FM 102 MHz (Ctry)**
101 Convention Center Dr Suite P-120 .... Las Vegas NV 89109-2001
702 739-9383 **KLUC-AM 1140 kHz (CHR)** 3510 W Hacienda Ave .... Las Vegas NV 89118-1763
702 739-9383 **KLUC-FM 98.5 MHz (CHR)** 3510 W Hacienda Ave .... Las Vegas NV 89118-1763
702 456-6695 **KNPR-FM 89.5 MHz (Clas-NPR)** 5151 Boulder Hwy .... Las Vegas NV 89122-6001
702 876-1460 **KOMP-FM 92.3 MHz (AOR)** 4660 S Decatur Blvd .... Las Vegas NV 89103-5209
702 731-9797 **KORK-AM 920 kHz (BBnd-ABC)** 101 Convention Center Dr ..... Las Vegas NV 89109-2001
702 564-6066 **KXTZ-FM 94.1 MHz (B/EZ)** 307 S Water St .... Henderson NV 89015-7310
702 731-9797 **KYRK-FM 97.1 MHz (CHR)** 101 Convention Center Dr .... Las Vegas NV 89109-2001

Local Attractions & Special Events

■ Sports

702 386-7200 **Las Vegas Stars** 850 Las Vegas Blvd N .... Las Vegas NV 89101-2062

■ Local Attractions

702 293-1081 **Hoover Dam & Lake Mead** 753 Nevada Hwy .... Boulder City NV 89005-0000
702 798-5595 **Liberace Museum** 1775 E Tropicana Ave .... Las Vegas NV 89119-0000
702 486-5205 **Nevada State Museum & Historical Society**
700 Twin Lakes Dr .... Las Vegas NV 89107-0000
702 386-6510 **Old Las Vegas Fort** Las Vegas Blvd & Washington St .... Las Vegas NV 89125-0000
702 875-4191 **Old Nevada** 1 Gunfighter Ln Bonnie Springs Ranch .... Old Nevada NV 89004-9999
702 735-8153 **Studio 96** 3890 S Swensen St .... Las Vegas NV 89119-7408

Important Phone Numbers

AAA 702 878-1822
American Express 702 876-1410
Better Business Bureau 702 731-9877
City Hall 702 386-6011
Emergency 911
Poison Control Center 702 732-4989
Time/Temp 118
Weather 702 734-2010

■ Travel Information

702 457-4664 **Chamber of Commerce** 2301 E Sahara Ave .... Las Vegas NV 89104-4198
702 733-2323 **Convention & Visitors Center** 3150 Paradise Rd .... Las Vegas NV 89109-9096

Travel

■ Airport

702 739-5211 **McCarran International Airport** 7 miles S of city (approx 15 minutes)

■ Airport Transportation

Airport Limo $4.25 fare to downtown
702 384-1234 **Gray Line Airport Express** $4.25 fare to downtown
702 384-3540 **Las Vegas Transit** $.95 fare to downtown
Taxi $6-14 fare to downtown

■ Scheduled Airlines

Air Nevada 702 736-8900
America West 702 736-1737
American 702 385-3781
Continental 702 383-8291
Delta 702 731-3111
Hawaiian 702 796-9696
Midway 800 621-5700
Northwest 800 225-2525
Scenic Airlines 702 739-1900
Sierra Nevada Airways 702 736-6770
Sky West 800 453-9417
Southwest 702 382-1221
TWA 702 385-1000
United 702 385-3222
USAir 702 382-1905

■ Charter Airlines

Action Helicopters 702 739-9444
Air Nevada 702 736-2702
Air Vegas 702 736-3599
Bauer Helicopters 702 293-4022
Charter Airlines Inc 702 878-2264
Helicop-Tours 702 736-0606
Lake Mead Air 702 293-1848
Scenic Airlines Inc 702 739-5611

■ Car Rentals

Agency 702 871-8508
Alamo 702 737-1562
Avis 702 739-5595
Budget 702 736-1212
Dollar 702 739-8400
General 702 739-1954
Hertz 702 736-4900
National 702 739-5391
Payless 702 739-8488
Sears Budget 702 736-8006
Snappy 702 739-0200
Thrifty 702 736-4706
Valley Car Rental 702 732-1991
Value 702 733-8886

■ Limo/Taxi

ABC Union Cab Co 702 736-8383
Bell Trans Limo 702 382-7060
Desert Cab 702 736-1702
Henderson Taxi 702 384-2322
Western Cab 702 736-8000
Yellow Checker Star Cab Co 702 873-2227

■ Mass Transit

702 384-3540 **Las Vegas Transit** $1.10 Base fare .... Las Vegas NV 89102-0000

■ Rail/Bus

702 386-6896 **Amtrak Las Vegas** 1 S Main St .... Las Vegas NV 89101-6320
702 382-2640 **Greyhound/Trailways Bus Station** 200 S Main St .... Las Vegas NV 89101-6357

Hotels

702 736-0111 **Aladdin Hotel** 3667 Las Vegas Blvd S .... Las Vegas NV 89109-4306
702 739-4111 **Bally's Casino Resort** 3645 Las Vegas Blvd S .... Las Vegas NV 89109-4307
702 731-7110 **Caesars Palace Hotel** 3570 Las Vegas Blvd S .... Las Vegas NV 89109-8933
702 734-0410 **Circus Circus Hotel** 2880 Las Vegas Blvd S .... Las Vegas NV 89109-1120
702 733-4444 **Desert Inn Hotel Casino & Country Club**
3145 Las Vegas Blvd S .... Las Vegas NV 89109-1916
702 737-4110 **Dunes Hotel & Country Club** 3650 Las Vegas Blvd S .... Las Vegas NV 89109-4305
702 733-3111 **Flamingo Hilton & Tower** 3555 Las Vegas Blvd S .... Las Vegas NV 89109-8934
702 385-4011 **Four Queens Hotel & Casino** 202 E Fremont St .... Las Vegas NV 89101-5673
702 385-7111 **Golden Nugget Hotel & Casino** 129 Fremont St .... Las Vegas NV 89101-5677
702 739-8911 **Hacienda Hotel & Casino Resort** 3950 Las Vegas Blvd S ..... Las Vegas NV 89119-1096
702 382-1600 **Horseshoe Inn** 128 E Fremont St .... Las Vegas NV 89101-5676
702 732-5111 **Las Vegas Hilton Hotel** 3000 Paradise Rd .... Las Vegas NV 89109-1283
702 737-2111 **Sahara Hotel** 2535 Las Vegas Blvd S .... Las Vegas NV 89109-1123
702 733-5000 **Sands Hotel & Casino** 3355 Las Vegas Blvd S .... Las Vegas NV 89109-8931
702 386-2110 **Union Plaza Hotel & Casino** 1 S Main St .... Las Vegas NV 89101-6320

Restaurants

702 731-7519 **Ah-So Japanese Steakhouse**
(Japanese) 3570 Las Vegas Blvd .... Las Vegas NV 89109-8920
702 734-6888 **Alpine Village Inn & Rathskeller**
(German/Swiss) 3003 Paradise Rd .... Las Vegas NV 89109-1299
702 385-5016 **Andre's** (French) 401 S 6th St .... Las Vegas NV 89101-6915
702 795-3236 **Carluccio's Tivoli Gardens** (Italian) 1775 E Tropicana Ave ..... Las Vegas NV 89119-6529
702 733-8899 **Chin's** (Chinese) 3200 Las Vegas Blvd S .... Las Vegas NV 89109-2612
702 737-4110 **Dome of the Sea** (Seafood) 3650 Las Vegas Blvd S .... Las Vegas NV 89109-4312
702 385-7111 **Elaine's** (Continental) 129 Fremont St .... Las Vegas NV 89101-5603
702 384-4470 **Golden Steer Steak House** (Steak) 308 W Sahara Ave .... Las Vegas NV 89102-5010
702 792-3772 **Jerome's** (Continental) 4503 Paradise Rd .... Las Vegas NV 89109-0000
702 739-8000 **Kiefer's** (American/Continental) 105 E Harmon Ave .... Las Vegas NV 89109-0000
702 732-5111 **Le Montrachet** (French) 3000 Paradise Rd .... Las Vegas NV 89109-0000
702 731-7547 **Palace Court** (French) 3570 Las Vegas Blvd S .... Las Vegas NV 89109-8933

Long Beach
CALIFORNIA 213

Important Phone Numbers

AAA	213 428-6461	Emergency-Police	213 435-6711
American Express	213 542-8631	Poison Control Center	213 484-5151
Better Business Bureau	714 527-0680	Time/Temp	213 554-1212
City Hall	213 590-6555	Weather	213 554-1212
Emergency-Fire	213 436-8211		

■ Travel Information

213 436-1251 **Chamber of Commerce** 1 World Trade Ctr Suite 350 .... Long Beach CA 90831-0350
213 436-3645 **Convention & Visitors Council**
1 World Trade Ctr Suite 300 .... Long Beach CA 90831-0300

Travel

■ Airport: Long Beach International

213 421-8293 **Long Beach International Airport** 22 miles SE of downtown (approx 20 minutes)

■ Airport Transportation: Long Beach International

213 777-8000 **SuperShuttle** $15 fare to downtown
Taxi $12 fare to downtown

■ Scheduled Airlines: Long Beach International

Alaska	800 426-0333	Island Express	213 491-5550
American	213 935-6045	TWA	800 221-2000
American Eagle	213 924-3313	United	213 772-2121
American Eagle	800 433-7300	United Express	800 241-6522
Delta	800 221-1212	USAir	213 637-6767

■ Charter Airlines: Long Beach International

Atlantic Jet Aviation	213 426-5500	Helitrans	714 546-6016

■ Airport: John Wayne Airport

714 755-6500 **John Wayne Airport (Orange County)** 15 miles SE of downtown (approx 40 minutes)

■ Scheduled Airlines: John Wayne Airport

Alaska	800 426-0333	Delta	714 534-8468
America West	213 637-9858	Sky West	800 453-9417
American	714 750-4090	United	714 973-2121
Continental	714 751-0250	United Express	714 973-2121

■ Charter Airlines: John Wayne Airport

Helistream	714 662-3163	Martin Aviation Inc	714 852-8300

■ Car Rentals

Alamo	213 649-2245	Hertz	213 420-2322
Avis	213 421-3767	Kott Don Extra Car	213 435-0783
Budget	213 597-3354	National	213 421-8877
Dollar	213 421-8841		

■ Limo/Taxi

Checker Cab	213 421-7180	Versaille Limo	213 498-0844
Harry Hamilton Limousine	213 421-9100	Yellow Cab	213 435-6111

■ Mass Transit

213 591-2301 **Long Beach Transit** $.60 Base fare .... Long Beach CA 90813-0000

■ Rail/Bus

213 428-7777 **Greyhound/Trailways Bus Station** 6601 Atlantic Ave .... Long Beach CA 90805-1409
800 872-7245 **Long Beach Station** 355 E 1st St .... Long Beach CA 90802-2462

Hotels

213 548-1080 **Best Western Sunrise** 525 S Harbor Blvd .... San Pedro CA 90731-3335
213 596-1631 **Golden Sails Hotel** 6285 E Pacific Coast Hwy .... Long Beach CA 90803-4893
213 597-4401 **Holiday Inn** 2640 N Lakewood Blvd .... Long Beach CA 90815-1795
213 435-3511 **Hotel Queen Mary** 1126 Queens Hwy .... Long Beach CA 90801-6900
213 434-8451 **Hyatt Edgewater** 6400 E Pacific Coast Hwy .... Long Beach CA 90803-4291
213 491-1234 **Hyatt Regency** 200 S Pine Ave .... Long Beach CA 90802-4553
213 425-5210 **Long Beach Airport Marriott** 4700 Airport Plaza Dr .... Long Beach CA 90815-1252
213 437-5900 **Ramada Renaissance Hotel** 111 E Ocean Blvd .... Long Beach CA 90802-4794
213 436-3000 **Sheraton Long Beach at Shoreline Square**
333 E Ocean Blvd .... Long Beach CA 90802-4800

Restaurants

213 437-0626 **555 East** (Continental/American) 555 E Ocean Blvd .... Long Beach CA 90802-5003
213 491-1234 **Beacon** (Seafood) 200 S Pine Ave .... Long Beach CA 90802-4553
213 438-2881 **Caffe Gazelle** (Italian) 5325 E 2nd St .... Long Beach CA 90803-5335
213 437-5900 **Floreale** (Italian) 111 E Ocean Blvd .... Long Beach CA 90802-4714
213 548-1240 **Grand Cottages** (Mediterranean) 809 S Grand Ave .... San Pedro CA 90731-3127
213 433-4983 **Kelly's** (American) 5716 E 2nd St .... Long Beach CA 90803-5046
213 437-2119 **La Grotte** (French/Continental) 300 Oceangate Suite 150 ..... Long Beach CA 90802-6802
714 497-5434 **Las Brisas** (Mexican/Seafood) 361 Cliff Dr .... Laguna Beach CA 92651-1623
213 925-6551 **Magdalena's** (California French) 17818 Bellflower Blvd .... Bellflower CA 90706-6614
213 531-1412 **Mandarin Palace** (Chinese) 4074 Hardwick St .... Lakewood CA 90712-2349
213 422-6090 **Mustard Seed** (American/Continental) 5624 Atlantic Ave ..... Long Beach CA 90805-4711
213 427-1003 **Nino's** (Italian) 3853 Atlantic Ave .... Long Beach CA 90807-3505
714 720-1800 **Ritz The** (Continental) 880 Newport Center Dr .... Newport Beach CA 92660-6387
213 434-3469 **Shenandoah Cafe** (American/Regional) 4722 E 2nd St .... Long Beach CA 90803-5309

Goods & Services

■ Department Stores

818 790-6801 **Buffums** 663 Foothill Blvd .... La Canada CA 91011-3403
213 924-0940 **Nordstrom** 600 Los Cerritos Mall .... Cerritos CA 90701-5467
213 860-8555 **Robinson's** 300 Los Cerritos Mall .... Cerritos CA 90701-5491

■ Banks

213 437-0011 **Farmers & Merchants Bank** 302 Pine Ave .... Long Beach CA 90802-2326
213 499-1500 **First Interstate Bank** 200 Pine Ave .... Long Beach CA 90802-3041
213 595-5281 **National Bank of Long Beach** 4150 N Long Beach Blvd .... Long Beach CA 90807-2676

■ Messenger/Postal

Air & Surface Systems	714 832-1212	Magic Messenger	213 436-2494
ASAP Courier Service Inc	213 426-8899	Modern Messengers Inc	213 597-7020
Federal Express	213 687-9767	Post Office	213 983-3056
Genni Courier Systems	213 434-1288	UPS	213 626-1551

■ Secretarial/Temp Services

213 595-6781 **Kelly Services** 3780 Kilroy Airport Way Suite 410 .... Long Beach CA 90806-0000
213 432-8582 **Manpower Temporary Services**
1 World Trade Ctr Suite 208 .... Long Beach CA 90802-4307

Media

■ Newspapers/Magazines

213 435-1161 **Press-Telegram** 604 Pine Ave .... Long Beach CA 90844-0001

■ Television

213 557-7777 **KABC-TV Ch 7 (ABC)** 4151 Prospect Ave .... Los Angeles CA 90027-4524
213 460-3000 **KCBS-TV Ch 2 (CBS)** 6121 W Sunset Blvd .... Hollywood CA 90028-6455
213 666-6500 **KCET-TV Ch 28 (PBS)** 4401 Sunset Blvd .... Los Angeles CA 90027-6017
818 840-4444 **KNBC-TV Ch 4 (NBC)** 3000 W Alameda Ave .... Burbank CA 91523-0001

■ Radio

213 840-4900 **KABC-AM 790 kHz (N/T-ABC)** 3321 S La Cienega Blvd ..... Los Angeles CA 90016-3114
213 466-8381 **KIIS-FM 102.7 MHz (CHR)** 6255 W Sunset Blvd .... Los Angeles CA 90028-8703
213 874-4664 **KPWR-FM 105.9 MHz (CHR)** 2600 W Olive St .... Burbank CA 91505-4549

Local Attractions & Special Events

■ Special Events

213 548-7562 **Grunion Run** (Dates vary)

■ Local Attractions

213 510-1520 **Catalina Island Information** 1 Pleasure Pier .... Avalon CA 90704-0000
213 433-9595 **Gondola Getaway Cruises** 5437 E Ocean Blvd .... Long Beach CA 90803-4405
213 439-2119 **Long Beach Art Museum** 2300 E Ocean Blvd .... Long Beach CA 90803-2442
213 435-3511 **Queen Mary & Spruce Goose Attractions**
1126 Queens Hwy .... Long Beach CA 90801-0000
213 431-3541 **Rancho Los Alamitos** 6400 Bixby Hill Rd .... Long Beach CA 90815-4706
213 424-9423 **Rancho Los Cerritos** 4600 Virginia Rd .... Long Beach CA 90807-1916
213 590-8427 **Shoreline Village** 407 Shoreline Village Dr Suite S .... Long Beach CA 90802-4540

Los Angeles

CALIFORNIA 213

Important Phone Numbers

AAA	213 747-6800
American Express	213 783-6900
Better Business Bureau	714 527-0680
City Hall	213 485-2121
Emergency-Fire	213 384-3131
Emergency-Police	213 625-3311
Poison Control Center	213 484-5151
Time/Temp	213 554-1212
Weather	213 554-1212

■ Travel Information

213 629-0602 **Chamber of Commerce** 404 S Bixel St .... Los Angeles CA 90017-1487
021 624-7300 **Visitors & Convention Bureau** 515 S Figueroa St 11th Fl ..... Los Angeles CA 90071-3304

Travel

■ Airport: Los Angeles International

213 646-5252 **Los Angeles International Airport** 17 miles SW of downtown (approx 45 minutes)

■ Airport Transportation: Los Angeles International

213 936-2974 **Celebrity Line** $10 fare to downtown
213 971-8265 **Flight Line** $12 fare to downtown
818 991-9611 **Great American Stage Lines** $9-19 fare to downtown
213 301-8099 **LA Express** $10 fare to downtown
213 558-1606 **Prime Time Shuttle** $10 fare to downtown
213 626-4455 **RTD** $1.10 fare to downtown
213 451-5445 **Santa Monica City Bus** $.80 fare to downtown

■ Scheduled Airlines: Los Angeles International

Aerolineas Argentinas	800 333-0276	Iberia	305 381-9360
Air Canada	800 776-3000	Island Express	213 491-5550
Air France	213 646-8006	Japan	213 322-3999
Air Jamaica	800 523-5585	KLM	713 658-9741
Air LA	213 641-1114	Korean	800 421-8200
Air New Zealand	800 262-1234	LACSA	213 385-2272
Alaska	800 426-0333	LTU International	213 216-7623
Alitalia	800 223-5730	Lufthansa	800 645-3880
America West	213 746-6400	Malaysia Airlines	213 642-0849
American	213 935-6045	Mexicana	800 531-7923
American Eagle	800 433-7300	Northwest	213 380-1511
ANA-All Nippon Airways	213 646-1116	Pan Am	800 221-1111
Avianca	213 626-5656	Philippine	800 435-9725
British Airways	213 646-7844	Qantas	800 227-4500
CAAC	213 384-2703	SAS	800 221-2350
Canadian	800 426-7000	Singapore	213 655-9270
China Airlines	213 641-8888	Sky West	800 453-9417
Condor	213 646-4900	Southwest	213 485-1221
Continental	800 525-0280	Stateswest	800 428-4322
Delta	213 386-5510	TACA International	213 385-9425
Eastern	800 327-8376	TWA	213 484-2244
Ecuatoriana	213 627-0615	United	213 772-2121
El Al	800 223-6700	United Express	800 241-6522
Finnair	213 646-1257	USAir	213 935-5005
Garuda Indonesian Airways	213 387-3323	Varig	213 646-2190
Hawaiian	213 215-1866		

■ Charter Airlines: Los Angeles International

Air LA	213 641-1114	Martin Air	800 366-4655
Condor	213 646-4900	Newport Executive Air	714 241-9200
Gunnell Aviation	213 391-6354	West Coast Air Charter Inc	714 983-3322

■ Airport: Burbank

818 840-8847 **Burbank Airport** 15 miles NW of downtown (approx 45 minutes)

■ Airport Transportation: Burbank

213 558-1606 **Prime Time Shuttle** $10 fare to downtown
213 626-4455 **RTD** $1.10 fare to downtown
818 244-2700 **Super Shuttle** $15 fare to downtown

■ Scheduled Airlines: Burbank

America West	818 843-3200	Sky West	800 453-9417
American	213 604-8451	Stateswest	800 428-4322
American Eagle	800 433-7300	United	800 241-6522
Continental	800 525-0280	United Express	800 241-6522
Delta	213 386-5510		

■ Charter Airlines: Burbank

Martin Aviation Inc 714 852-8300

■ Airport: Ontario

714 988-2716 **Ontario International Airport** 52 miles E of downtown (approx 45 minutes)

■ Airport Transportation: Ontario

213 827-8000 **LA Express** $45 fare to downtown
213 626-4455 **RTD** $3.70 fare to downtown
818 244-2700 **Super Shuttle** $12-27 fare to downtown
Taxi $26 fare to downtown

■ Scheduled Airlines: Ontario

America West	818 843-3200	TWA	213 603-8770
American	213 935-6045	United	213 417-2621
Continental	800 525-0280	United Express	800 241-6522
Delta	213 386-5510	USAir	800 428-4322
Sky West	800 453-9417	West Air	800 241-6522
Southwest	213 485-1221		

■ Car Rentals

Agency	213 494-1499	Hertz	213 646
Alamo	213 649-2245	National	213 670
Avis	213 646-5600	Payless	213 641
Budget	213 645-4500	Thrifty	213 645
Dollar	213 645-9333		

■ Limo/Taxi

Affordable Class Limousine	213 470-6111	LA Taxi	213 627-
Carey Limousine	213 275-4153	RMP Services	213 650-
Checker Cab	213 204-4833	United	213 653-
Independent Cab	213 385-8294	Yellow Cab	213 413-

■ Mass Transit

213 626-4455 **RTD** $1.10 Base fare .... Los Angeles CA 90013-

■ Rail/Bus

213 620-1200 **Greyhound/Trailways Bus Station** 208 E 6th St .... Los Angeles CA 90014-
213 624-0171 **Union Passenger Terminal** 800 N Alameda St .... Los Angeles CA 90012-

Hotels

213 276-2251 **Beverly Hills Hotel** 9641 Sunset Blvd .... Beverly Hills CA 90210-
213 274-7777 **Beverly Hilton** 9876 Wilshire Blvd .... Beverly Hills CA 90210-
213 624-1011 **Biltmore Hotel** 506 S Grand Ave .... Los Angeles CA 90071-
213 277-2000 **Century Plaza Hotel & Towers** 2025 Ave of the Stars ..... Los Angeles CA 90067-
714 739-5600 **Embassy Suites Buena Park** 7762 Beach Blvd ...... Buena Park CA 90620-
213 748-4141 **Hilton Hotel University** 3540 S Figueroa St .... Los Angeles CA
213 472-1211 **Hotel Bel-Air** 701 Stone Canyon Rd .... Los Angeles CA 90007-4
213 670-9000 **Hyatt Regency Airport** 6225 W Century Blvd ...... Los Angeles CA 90077-2
213 683-1234 **Hyatt Regency Los Angeles** 711 S Hope St .... Los Angeles CA 90045-
213 381-7411 **Hyatt Regency Wilshire** 3515 Wilshire Blvd .... Los Angeles CA 90017-3
213 278-3344 **L'Ermitage Hotel** 9291 Burton Way .... Beverly Hills CA 90210-3
213 854-1111 **Le Bel Age Hotel** 1020 N San Vicente Blvd ...... West Hollywood CA 90069-3
213 410-4000 **Los Angeles Airport Hilton Towers** 5711 W Century Blvd ..... Los Angeles CA 90045-5
213 641-5700 **Los Angeles Airport Marriott** 5855 W Century Blvd ...... Los Angeles CA 90045-5
213 629-1200 **New Otani Hotel & Garden** 120 S Los Angeles St .... Los Angeles CA 90045-
213 476-6571 **Radisson Bel Air Summit Hotel** 11461 W Sunset Blvd ...... Los Angeles CA 90012-3
213 275-5200 **Regent Beverly Wilshire Hotel** 9500 Wilshire Blvd ...... Los Angeles CA 90049-2
213 617-1133 **Sheraton Grande Hotel** 333 S Figueroa St .... Beverly Hills CA 90212-2
213 642-1111 **Sheraton Plaza La Reina** 6101 W Century Blvd .... Los Angeles CA 90071-1
213 382-7171 **Sheraton Town House** 2961 Wilshire Blvd .... Los Angeles CA 90045-5
213 216-5858 **Stouffer Concourse Hotel** 5400 W Century Blvd ...... Los Angeles CA 90010-1
818 506-2500 **Universal City Hilton Hotel** 555 Universal Terrace Pkwy .... Universal City CA 90045-5
213 624-1000 **Westin Hotel Bonaventure** 404 S Figueroa St ...... Los Angeles CA 91608-1
213 208-8765 **Westwood Marquis Hotel & Garden** 930 Hilgard Ave ...... Los Angeles CA 90024-3

Restaurants

213 612-1580 **Bernard's** (French) 506 S Grand Ave .... Los Angeles CA 90071-26
213 550-3900 **Bistro Garden** (Continental) 176 N Cannon Dr ...... Beverly Hills CA 90210-26
213 938-1447 **Campanile** (Italian) 624 S La Brea Ave .... Los Angeles CA 90036-00
213 271-2168 **Chasen's** (American/Continental) 9039 Beverly Blvd ...... West Hollywood CA 90048-24
213 306-3344 **Cheesecake Factory** (American) 4142 Via Marina ...... Marina del Rey CA 90292-53
213 392-9025 **Chinois on Main** (French/Chinese) 2709 Main St ...... Santa Monica CA 90405-40
714 673-0100 **Crab Cooker** (Seafood) 2200 Newport Blvd ...... Newport Beach CA 92663-43
213 734-2773 **El Cholo** (Mexican) 1121 S Western Ave .... Los Angeles CA 90006-23
213 447-8000 **Eureka** (International) 1845 S Bundy Dr .... Los Angeles CA 90025-00
213 457-1519 **Geoffrey's** (California) 27400 Pacific Coast Hwy ...... Malibu CA 90265-43
213 277-2333 **Harry's Bar & American Grill**
(Italian/American) 2020 Ave of the Stars .... Los Angeles CA 90067-47
213 275-5444 **Il Giardino** (Italian) 9235 W 3rd St .... Beverly Hills CA 90210-37
213 475-5771 **Junior's** (Deli) 2379 Westwood Blvd .... Westwood CA 90064-219
213 665-1891 **Katsu** (Japanese) 1972 Hillhurst Ave .... Los Angeles CA 90027-27
213 652-5840 **L'Ermitage Restaurant** (French) 730 N La Cienega Blvd ...... Los Angeles CA 90069-528
213 652-9770 **L'Orangerie** (French) 903 N La Cienega Blvd ...... Los Angeles CA 90069-479
213 277-2000 **La Chaumiere** (French) 2025 Ave of the Stars 5th Fl ...... Los Angeles CA 90067-470
213 275-0579 **La Scala** (Italian) 410 N Canon Dr .... Beverly Hills CA 90210-482
213 656-7515 **La Toque** (French) 8171 W Sunset Blvd .... Los Angeles CA 90046-241
213 652-2827 **Lawry's The Prime Rib** (American) 55 N La Cienega Blvd ...... Beverly Hills CA 90211-229
213 651-5553 **Le Restaurant** (French) 8475 Melrose Pl .... Los Angeles CA 90069-538
213 489-4900 **Little Joe's** (Italian American) 900 N Broadway ...... Los Angeles CA 90012-178
213 282-8870 **Lunaria** (French Bistro) 10351 Santa Monica Blvd ...... Los Angeles CA 90025-000
213 274-9800 **Maple Drive** (Californian) 345 N Maple Dr .... Beverly Hills CA 90210-000
213 451-0843 **Michael's** (French/American) 1147 3rd St .... Santa Monica CA 90403-501
213 278-9911 **Mr Chow** (Mandarin Chinese) 344 N Camden Dr ...... Beverly Hills CA 90210-511
213 934-4400 **Muse** (California-American) 7360 Beverly Blvd ...... Los Angeles CA 90036-250
213 483-6000 **Pacific Dining Car** (Seafood/Prime Rib) 1310 W 6th St ...... Los Angeles CA 90017-120
213 550-8811 **Palm The** (Continental) 9001 Santa Monica Blvd ...... Los Angeles CA 90069-551
213 545-1334 **Saint Estephe**
(Modern Southwest) 2640 N Sepulveda Blvd .... Manhattan Beach CA 90266-272
213 652-4025 **Spago** (Nouvelle American) 1114 Horn Ave .... Los Angeles CA 90069-2102
213 855-1480 **Trumps** (Nouvelle American) 8764 Melrose Ave ...... West Hollywood CA 90069-507
213 829-4313 **Valentino** (Italian) 3115 Pico Blvd .... Santa Monica CA 90405-209

Goods & Services

■ Department Stores

213 612-5000 **Bullock's** 800 S Hope St .... Los Angeles CA 90017-4684
818 765-6622 **Harris & Frank Inc** 13451 Sherman Way ...... North Hollywood CA 91605-4416
213 382-6161 **I Magnin** 3050 Wilshire Blvd .... Los Angeles CA 90010-1375
213 683-1144 **May Co** 920 W 7th St .... Los Angeles CA 90017-2502
213 488-5522 **Robinson's** 600 W 7th St .... Los Angeles CA 90017-3870

■ Banks

213 239-4000 **First Interstate Bank of California** 707 Wilshire Blvd ...... Los Angeles CA 90017-3500
213 557-1211 **First Los Angeles Bank** 2029 Century Pk E ...... Los Angeles CA 90067-1901
213 277-2265 **Mercantile National Bank** 1840 Century Pk E ...... Los Angeles CA 90067-2122
213 345-6211 **Security Pacific National Bank** 333 S Hope St ...... Los Angeles CA 90071-2701
213 236-5000 **Union Bank** 445 S Figueroa St .... Los Angeles CA 90071-1602

■ **Messenger/Postal**

Century City Messenger Service Inc	213 556-1883
Federal Express	213 687-9767
LA Courier Service	213 628-3904
Marathon Express Messenger Svc	213 291-8898
Messenger Express Inc	213 659-3660
NOW Courier Service	213 671-1200
Post Office	213 586-1467
UPS	213 626-1551
US Courier Corp	213 975-1000

■ **Secretarial/Temp Services**

213 965-2950 **Kelly Services Inc** 4600 Wilshire Blvd Suite 100 .... Los Angeles CA 90010-0000
213 930-0530 **Olsten Temporary Services** 5750 Wilshire Blvd .... Los Angeles CA 90036-3697

Media

■ **Newspapers/Magazines**

213 467-4244 **LA Style** 6834 Hollywood Blvd Suite 400 .... Hollywood CA 90028-6175
213 557-7592 **Los Angeles Magazine** 1888 Century Pk E Suite 920 .... Los Angeles CA 90067-1792
213 237-5000 **Los Angeles Times** Times Mirror Sq .... Los Angeles CA 90012-3816

■ **Television**

213 557-7777 **KABC-TV Ch 7 (ABC)** 4151 Prospect Ave .... Los Angeles CA 90027-4524
213 460-3000 **KCBS-TV Ch 2 (CBS)** 6121 W Sunset Blvd .... Hollywood CA 90028-6455
213 666-6500 **KCET-TV Ch 28 (PBS)** 4401 Sunset Blvd .... Los Angeles CA 90027-6017
818 840-4444 **KNBC-TV Ch 4 (NBC)** 3000 W Alameda Ave .... Burbank CA 91523-0001

■ **Radio**

213 840-4900 **KABC-AM 790 kHz (N/T-ABC)** 3321 S La Cienega Blvd .... Los Angeles CA 90016-3114
213 466-8381 **KIIS-FM 102.7 MHz (CHR)** 6255 W Sunset Blvd .... Los Angeles CA 90028-8703
818 578-7231 **KPCC-FM 89.3 MHz (BBnd-NPR)** 1570 E Colorado Blvd .... Pasadena CA 91106-2003
213 874-4664 **KPWR-FM 105.9 MHz (CHR)** 2600 W Olive St .... Burbank CA 91505-4549
818 955-7000 **KXEZ-FM 98.7 MHz (B/EZ)** 3500 W Olive Ave Suite 250 .... Burbank CA 91505-4628

Local Attractions & Special Events

■ **Sports**

714 937-6700 **California Angels**
2000 S State College Blvd Anaheim Stadium .... Anaheim CA 92806-6116
213 748-0500 **Los Angeles Clippers**
3939 S Figueroa St Los Angeles Sports Arena .... Los Angeles CA 90037-0000
213 224-1400 **Los Angeles Dodgers** 1750 Stadium Way Dodger Stadium .. Los Angeles CA 90012-0000
213 480-3232 **Los Angeles Kings**
3900 W Manchester Blvd Great Western Forum .... Inglewood CA 90306-0000
213 419-3100 **Los Angeles Lakers**
3900 W Manchester Blvd Great Western Forum .... Inglewood CA 90305-2200
213 322-5901 **Los Angeles Raiders** 332 Center St Coliseum .... El Segundo CA 90245-4098
714 937-6767 **Los Angeles Rams** 1900 State College Blvd Anaheim Stadium .. Anaheim CA 92806-6135

■ **Special Events**

213 681-3724 **Tournament of Roses Parade & Rose Bowl Game** (January 1)

■ **Local Attractions**

213 557-4396 **ABC Studio** 4151 Prospect Ave .... Hollywood CA 90027-4524
213 744-7400 **California State Museum of Science & Industry**
700 State Dr .... Los Angeles CA 90037-1210
213 852-2345 **CBS Studio** 7800 Beverly Blvd .... Los Angeles CA 90001-0000
714 999-4565 **Disneyland** 1313 Harbor Blvd .... Anaheim CA 92803-0000
213 936-2230 **George C Page Museum of La Brea Discoveries**
5801 Wilshire Blvd .... Los Angeles CA 90036-0000
213 850-2000 **Hollywood Bowl** 3701 Wilshire Blvd .... Los Angeles CA 90001-0000
213 458-2003 **J Paul Getty Museum** 17985 Pacific Coast Hwy .... Malibu CA 90265-5799
714 827-1776 **Knott's Berry Farm** 8039 Beach Blvd .... Buena Park CA 90620-3225
213 857-6111 **Los Angeles County Museum of Art** 5905 Wilshire Blvd ...... Los Angeles CA 90036-4504
213 972-7211 **Los Angeles Philharmonic** 135 N Grand Ave .... Los Angeles CA 90012-3042
213 464-8111 **Mann's Chinese Theatre** 6925 Hollywood Blvd .... Hollywood CA 90027-0000
818 840-4444 **NBC Studio** 3000 W Alameda Ave .... Burbank CA 91523-0001
213 687-4344 **Olvera Street Information** .... Los Angeles CA 90012-0000
213 276-4723 **Rodeo Drive Information** Rodeo Dr .... Beverly Hills CA 90212-0000
818 508-9600 **Universal Studios** 3900 Lankershim Blvd .... Studio City CA 90001-0000

Louisville

KENTUCKY   502

Important Phone Numbers

AAA 502 582-2222	Emergency 911
American Express 502 585-2368	Poison Control Center 502 589-8222
Better Business Bureau 502 583-6546	Time/Temp 502 585-5961
City Hall 502 625-3131	Weather 502 363-9655

■ Travel Information

502 566-5000 **Chamber of Commerce** 1 Riverfront Plaza .... Louisville KY 40202-2974
502 582-3732 **Convention & Visitors Bureau** 1st & Liberty Sts .... Louisville KY 40202-0000

Travel

■ Airport

502 367-4636 **Standiford Field** 5 miles S of city (approx 5 minutes)

■ Airport Transportation

502 585-1234 **TARC** $.60 fare to downtown
　　　　　　　 Taxi $10 fare to downtown
502 636-5511 **Yellow Cab Limo** $4.50 fare to downtown

■ Scheduled Airlines

Air Canada 800 776-3000	Northwest 800 225-2525
American 502 589-3730	TWA 502 584-8101
Comair 800 354-9822	United 800 241-6522
Delta 502 584-6151	USAir 502 584-0354
Eastern 502 587-7551	

■ Charter Airlines

Falcon Aviation 502 459-5045	Stevens Aviation 502 451-2800

■ Car Rentals

Agency 502 895-0915	Hertz 502 361-0181
Avis 502 368-5851	National 502 361-2515
Budget 502 363-3194	Snappy 502 895-2782
Dollar 502 366-6944	Thrifty 502 367-0231

■ Limo/Taxi

Checker Cab 502 583-6561	Yellow Cab 502 636-3471
Supreme Limousine Service 502 772-0200	

■ Mass Transit

502 585-1234 **TARC (Transit Authority of River City)** $.35 Base fare .... Louisville KY 40203-0000

■ Rail/Bus

502 561-2802 **Greyhound/Trailways Bus Station**
　　　　　　　 720 W Muhammad Ali Blvd .... Louisville KY 40203-1999

Hotels

502 456-5050 **Breckinridge Inn** 2800 Breckinridge Ln .... Louisville KY 40220-1498
502 583-1234 **Brown Hotel** 335 W Broadway .... Louisville KY 40202-2105
502 367-6161 **Executive Inn** 978 Phillips Ln .... Louisville KY 40213-1692
502 367-2251 **Executive West Motor Hotel** 830 Phillips Ln .... Louisville KY 40209-1387
502 589-3300 **Galt House East** 441 N 4th Ave .... Louisville KY 40202-4217
502 589-5200 **Galt House Hotel** 140 N 4th Ave .... Louisville KY 40202-4217
502 582-2241 **Holiday Inn Louisville Downtown** 120 W Broadway .... Louisville KY 40202-2136
502 964-3311 **Holiday Inn South Airport** 3317 Fern Valley Rd .... Louisville KY 40213-3595
502 587-3434 **Hyatt Regency Louisville** 320 W Jefferson St .... Louisville KY 40202-2997
502 499-6220 **Radisson East** 1903 Embassy Square Blvd .... Louisville KY 40299-1859
502 585-3200 **Seelbach Hotel** 500 S 4th Ave .... Louisville KY 40202-2518

Restaurants

502 458-4830 **Cafe Metro** (Continental) 1700 Bardstown Rd .... Louisville KY 40205-1273
502 584-4377 **Casa Grisanti** (Italian) 1000 E Liberty St .... Louisville KY 40204-1099
502 581-9129 **Ditto's Food & Drink** (American) 1114 Bardstown Rd .... Louisville KY 40204-0000
502 583-1234 **English Grill** (American) 335 W Broadway .... Louisville KY 40202-2105
502 585-5555 **Kunz's** (Continental) 115 S 4th Ave .... Louisville KY 40202-2999
502 897-5804 **Maharaja** (Indian) 2901 Brownsboro Rd .... Louisville KY 40206-0000
502 426-1577 **New Orleans East** (Seafood) 9424 Shelbyville Rd .... Louisville KY 40222-8567
502 896-9234 **Pat's Steak House** (Steak) 2437 Brownsboro Rd .... Louisville KY 40206-2300
502 499-1515 **Rib Tavern** (Barbecue) 4157 Bardstown Rd .... Louisville KY 40218-3244

Goods & Services

■ Department Stores

502 456-4000 **Bacon's** 3600 Bardstown Rd .... Louisville KY 40218-2253
502 426-2400 **Hess's** 7900 Shelbyville Rd .... Louisville KY 40222-5439
502 423-3212 **Lazarus** 7900 Shelbyville Rd .... Louisville KY 40222-5492

■ Banks

502 581-2100 **Citizens Fidelity Bank & Trust Co** 500 W Jefferson St .... Louisville KY 40296-0001
502 566-2000 **Liberty National Bank & Trust Co** 416 W Jefferson St .... Louisville KY 40202-3244

■ Messenger/Postal

Federal Express 800 238-5355	UPS 502 363-3511
Post Office 502 454-1650	Zip Express 502 587-3487

■ Secretarial/Temp Services

502 585-2171 **Kelly Temporary Services** 515 W Market St .... Louisville KY 40202-3333
502 583-1674 **Manpower Temporary Services Inc** 755 Meidinger Tower .... Louisville KY 40202-3443
502 499-2442 **Olsten Temporary Services** 9420 Bunsen Pkwy Suite 110 .... Louisville KY 40220-4203

Media

■ Newspapers/Magazines

502 582-4011 **Courier-Journal** 525 W Broadway St .... Louisville KY 40202-2137
502 566-5050 **Louisville Magazine** 1 Riverfront Plaza Suite 604 .... Louisville KY 40202-2936

■ Television

502 585-2201 **WAVE-TV Ch 3 (NBC)** 725 S Floyd St .... Louisville KY 40203-2391
502 582-7840 **WHAS-TV Ch 11 (ABC)** 520 W Chestnut St .... Louisville KY 40202-2200
606 233-3000 **WKLE-TV Ch 46 (PBS)** 600 Cooper Dr .... Lexington KY 40502-2296
502 893-3671 **WLKY-TV Ch 32 (CBS)** 1918 Mellwood Ave .... Louisville KY 40206-1030

■ Radio

502 589-4800 **WDJX-FM 99.7 MHz (AC-AP)** 612 4th Ave Suite 100 .... Louisville KY 40202-2505
502 561-8640 **WFPK-FM 91.9 MHz (Clas-NPR)** 301 York St .... Louisville KY 40203-2205
502 582-7840 **WHAS-AM 840 kHz (AC-ABC)** 520 W Chestnut St .... Louisville KY 40202-2200
502 636-3535 **WLOU-AM 1350 kHz (UC-SBN)** 2549 S 3rd St .... Louisville KY 40208-1407
502 896-4400 **WQMF-FM 95.7 MHz (AOR)** 4010 Dupont Cir .... Louisville KY 40207-4802

Local Attractions & Special Events

■ Sports

502 367-9121 **Louisville Redbirds**
　　　　　　　 Freedom Way & Phillips Ln Cardinal Stadium .... Louisville KY 40213-0000

■ Special Events

502 585-1362 **Bluegrass Music Festival** (August 30-September 2)
502 637-1111 **Kentucky Derby** (May 4)

■ Local Attractions

502 637-1111 **Churchill Downs/Kentucky Derby Museum** 704 Central Ave .... Louisville KY 40208-0000
502 635-5083 **Filson Club** 1310 S 3rd St .... Louisville KY 40208-0000
502 581-1986 **Louisville Falls Fountain** 500 4th Ave .... Louisville KY 40202-0000
502 561-6103 **Museum of History & Science** 727 W Main St .... Louisville KY 40202-2681
502 635-5244 **Old Louisville Historic District** W Main St .... Louisville KY 40201-0000

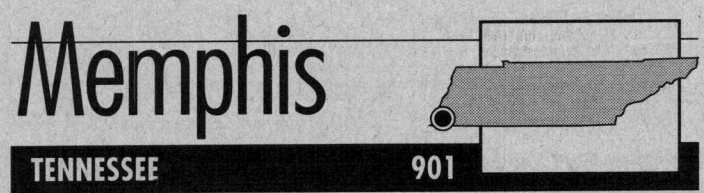

Memphis
TENNESSEE 901

Important Phone Numbers

AAA	901 761-5371	Emergency	911
American Express	901 525-0151	Poison Control Center	901 528-6048
Better Business Bureau	901 795-8771	Time/Temp	901 526-5261
City Hall	901 576-6000	Weather	901 756-4141

■ **Travel Information**

901 575-3500	Chamber of Commerce 22 N Front St Suite 200	Memphis TN	38103-2109
901 576-8181	Convention & Visitors Bureau 50 N Front St Suite 450	Memphis TN	38103-1104
901 526-4881	Visitor's Center 207 Beale St	Memphis TN	38103-3133

Travel

■ **Airport**

901 922-8000 Memphis International Airport 10 miles SE of city (approx 20 minutes)

■ **Airport Transportation**

901 577-7700 **Limo** $6 fare to downtown
901 274-6282 **Memphis Area Mass Transit** $.85 fare to downtown
             Taxi $14 fare to downtown

■ **Scheduled Airlines**

American	901 526-8861	TWA	800 221-2000
Delta	800 221-1212	United	800 241-6522
Northwest	901 525-7681	USAir	901 526-7691
Northwest Airlink	901 525-7681		

■ **Charter Airlines**

AMR Charter	901 345-4720	Transarrow	901 345-2376
Richards Aviation	901 332-7239		

■ **Car Rentals**

Alamo	901 332-8412	Dollar	901 345-3890
American International	901 345-2440	Hertz	901 345-5680
Avis	901 345-2847	National	901 345-0070
Budget	901 332-2222	Thrifty	901 345-0170

■ **Limo/Taxi**

Classic Rolls Royce Limo Service	901 332-6880	United Cab Co	901 525-0521
Memphis Executive Limousine	901 396-7733	Yellow Cab	901 526-2121

■ **Mass Transit**

901 274-6282 Memphis Area Mass Transit $.85 Base fare Memphis TN 38108-0000

■ **Rail/Bus**

901 523-9253	Greyhound/Trailways Bus Station 203 Union Ave	Memphis TN	38103-5298
901 526-0052	Memphis Station 545 S Main St	Memphis TN	38103-4809

Hotels
---

901 525-2511	Brownstone Hotel 300 N 2nd St	Memphis TN	38105-2614
901 767-6300	Days Inn International 5877 Poplar Ave	Memphis TN	38119-3949
901 728-4000	French Quarter Inn 2144 Madison Ave	Memphis TN	38104-6523
901 767-6666	Garden Plaza Hotel 5069 Sanderlin Ave	Memphis TN	38117-4331
901 278-4100	Holiday Inn Overton Square Midtown 1837 Union Ave	Memphis TN	38104-3972
901 366-9333	Lexington Hotel Suites 4300 American Way	Memphis TN	38118-0000
901 332-1130	Memphis Airport Hilton 2240 Democrat Rd	Memphis TN	38132-1803
901 362-6200	Memphis Marriott 2625 Thousand Oaks	Memphis TN	38118-2415
901 684-6664	Omni Memphis Hotel 939 Ridge Lake Blvd	Memphis TN	38103-2696
901 529-4000	Peabody Hotel 149 Union Ave	Memphis TN	38103-2619
901 528-1800	Radisson Hotel Downtown 185 Union Ave	Memphis TN	38103-2618
901 525-5491	Ramada Hotel Convention Center 160 Union Ave	Memphis TN	38103-2618
901 332-2370	Sheraton Airport Memphis 2411 Winchester Rd	Memphis TN	38116-3864

Restaurants
---

901 521-8213	Ben's Restaurant (French) 110 Wagner Pl	Memphis TN	38103-0000
901 527-7300	Chervil's (French) 250 N Main St	Memphis TN	38103-1624
901 529-4188	Chez Philippe (French) 149 Union Ave	Memphis TN	38103-2617
901 529-4199	Dux (Nouvelle American) 149 Union Ave	Memphis TN	38103-2617
901 761-9462	Frank Grisanti's (Northern Italian) 1022 Shady Grove	Memphis TN	38119-4119
901 763-0272	Genghis Khan (Chinese) 5100 Poplar Ave	Memphis TN	38137-0000
901 757-8323	Hemmings Restaurant & Bar		
	(Southwestern) 7615 W Farmington Blvd	Germantown TN	38138-0000
901 274-8000	John Will's Barbecue Pit (Barbecue) 5101 Sanderlin St	Memphis TN	38117-0000
901 527-9973	Justine's (French) 919 Coward Pl	Memphis TN	38104-4499
901 725-6797	La Chardonnay (Continental) 2100-2 Overton Square Ln	Memphis TN	38104-0000
901 767-0069	La Patisserie (French Bistro) 5689 Quince Rd	Memphis TN	38119-0000
901 726-5771	La Tourelle (French Provincial) 2146 Monroe Ave	Memphis TN	38104-0000
901 522-8800	Marmalade (Southern) 153 E Calhoun Ave	Memphis TN	38103-4507
901 726-5128	Paulette's (Continental) 2110 Madison Ave	Memphis TN	38104-6502
901 726-4040	Public Eye (Barbecue) 17 S Cooper St	Memphis TN	38104-4244
901 523-2746	Rendezvous (Barbecue) 52 S 2nd St	Memphis TN	38103-2628

Goods & Services

■ **Department Stores**

901 363-0063	Dillard's 4430 American Way	Memphis TN	38118-8404
901 766-2323	Goldsmith's 4545 Poplar Ave	Memphis TN	38117-0000

■ **Banks**

901 523-4883	First Tennessee Bank 165 Madison Ave	Memphis TN	38103-2723
901 523-3434	National Bank of Commerce 1 Commerce Sq	Memphis TN	38150-0001
901 523-6000	Union Planters National Bank 67 Madison Ave	Memphis TN	38103-2147

■ **Messenger/Postal**

Above Average Express	901 763-3306	Southland Courier Service	901 324-3339
Emery Worldwide	901 365-7180	Sunbelt Couriers Inc	901 522-8485
Federal Express	901 369-3600	UPS	615 889-5700
Post Office	901 521-2140	VIP Express	901 375-4200

■ **Secretarial/Temp Services**

901 375-4251	Kelly Services 4045 American Way Suite 202	Memphis TN	38118-0000
901 761-3232	Manpower Temporary Services 4938 Poplar Ave	Memphis TN	38117-0000
901 761-1060	Olsten Temporary Services 5050 Poplar Ave Suite 517	Memphis TN	38157-0505

Media

■ **Newspapers/Magazines**

901 529-2345	Commercial Appeal 495 Union Ave	Memphis TN	38103-3221
901 521-9000	Memphis Magazine 460 Tennessee St	Memphis TN	38103-4400

■ **Television**

901 320-1313	WHBQ-TV Ch 13 (ABC) 485 S Highland St	Memphis TN	38111-4391
901 458-2521	WKNO-TV Ch 10 (PBS) 900 Getwell Rd	Memphis TN	38111-7494
901 726-0555	WMC-TV Ch 5 (NBC) 1960 Union Ave	Memphis TN	38104-4069
901 577-0100	WREG-TV Ch 3 (CBS) 803 Channel Three Dr	Memphis TN	38103-4699

■ **Radio**

901 323-0101	KHUL-FM 101.1 MHz (UC) 80 N Tillman St	Memphis TN	38111-2727
901 767-6532	WGKX-FM 106 MHz (Ctry) 5900 Poplar Ave	Memphis TN	38119-3999
901 458-8255	WHBQ-AM 560 kHz (Gold) 483 S Highland St	Memphis TN	38111-4301
901 529-4397	WHRK-FM 97.1 MHz (UC-NBC) 112 Union Ave	Memphis TN	38103-5126
901 323-9566	WKNO-FM 91.1 MHz (Clas-NPR) 900 Getwell Rd	Memphis TN	38111-7494
901 726-0555	WMC-FM 100 MHz (AC-ABC) 1960 Union Ave	Memphis TN	38104-4031

Local Attractions & Special Events

■ **Sports**

901 272-1687	Memphis Chicks 800 Home Run Ln	Memphis TN	38104-5987
901 358-7223	Memphis International Motorsports Park		
	5500 Taylor Forge Rd	Millington TN	38053-8320
501 735-3670	Southland Greyhound Park 1550 N Ingram Blvd	West Memphis AR	72301-2299

■ **Local Attractions**

901 525-8979	Beale Street Between 2nd & 4th St	Memphis TN	38103-0000
901 785-3160	Chucalissa Indian Village 1987 Indian Village Dr	Memphis TN	38109-0000
901 332-3322	Graceland (Elvis Presley Mansion) 3764 Elvis Presley Blvd	Memphis TN	38116-0000
901 320-6320	Memphis Pink Palace Museum & Planetarium		
	3050 Central Ave	Memphis TN	38111-3399
901 527-5694	Mississippi River Excursions Monroe Ave & Riverside Dr	Memphis TN	38173-0000
901 576-7241	Mud Island 125 Front St	Memphis TN	38103-0000

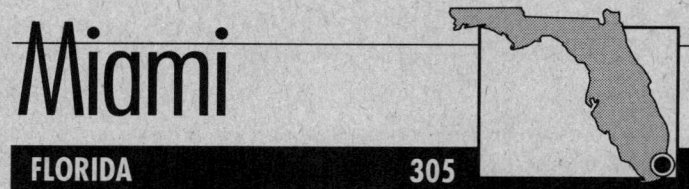

Miami

FLORIDA　　　305

Important Phone Numbers

AAA 305 573-6911
American Express 305 865-5959
Better Business Bureau 305 625-0307
City Hall 305 579-6093

Emergency 911
Poison Control Center 800 585-7378
Time 305 324-8811
Weather 305 661-5065

■ Travel Information

305 350-7700　**Chamber of Commerce** 1601 Biscayne Blvd Ballroom Level .... Miami FL　33132-0000
305 539-3000　**Convention & Visitors Bureau** 701 Brickell Ave Suite 2700 .... Miami FL　33131-0000

Travel

■ Airport

305 876-7515　**Miami International Airport** 7 miles NW of city (approx 20 minutes)

■ Airport Transportation

305 638-6700　**Metro Transit Buses** $1 fare to downtown
305 871-2000　**SuperShuttle** $5-7 fare to downtown
　　　　　　　Taxi $2-12 fare to downtown

■ Scheduled Airlines

Aero Coach Aviation International Inc　305 359-1600
Aerolineas Argentinas 305 371-4800
Aerolineas El Salvador 305 526-5758
AeroMexico 305 871-8307
AeroPeru 305 594-0022
Air Canada 800 776-3000
Air France 305 526-6210
Air Jamaica 305 358-3222
ALM-Antillean 305 477-0955
American 305 358-6800
Avensa 305 381-8001
Avianca 305 883-5151
Aviateca 305 871-1587
Bahamasair 305 593-1910
British Airways 305 347-6300
BWIA 305 371-2942
Cayman 305 446-8696
Chalk's & Paradise Island Airline .. 305 524-0333
Continental 305 871-1400
Delta 305 448-7000
Dominicana 305 590-2500
Eastern 305 873-3000
Ecuatoriana 305 592-0200
El Al 305 532-5441
Faucett Peruvian Airlines 305 591-0610

Guyana 305 871-8480
Haiti Air 305 871-5814
Iberia 305 381-9360
LACSA 305 593-0967
Ladeco 305 371-2794
Lan Chile 305 526-5226
LAP Lineas Aereas Paraguayas 305 591-1900
Lloyd Aero Boliviano Airlines 305 374-4600
Lufthansa 800 645-3880
Mexicana 800 531-7921
Midway 800 621-5700
Northwest 800 225-2525
Pan Am 305 874-5000
Royal Jordanian 305 599-0800
Sabena 800 955-2000
Saeta 305 477-2104
Surinam 305 262-9792
TACA International 305 358-0066
Tan-Sahsa Honduras Airline 305 526-4300
TWA 305 371-7471
United 800 241-6522
USAir 305 358-3396
Varig 800 468-2744
Viasa 305 374-5000
Virgin Atlantic Airways 305 445-9940

■ Charter Airlines

Action Cargo Service Inc 305 883-3286
Aerolineas El Salvador SA 305 526-5320
Air Ambulance Network Inc 305 387-1708
Airlift International Inc 305 526-6133
Amerijet International Inc 305 522-1555

Creative Charters 305 445-7318
Imperial Aviation Inc 407 683-3576
Miami Helicopter 305 685-8223
Personal Jet Charter Service 305 776-4515
Trans-Brazil 305 591-8322

■ Car Rentals

Ajax 305 871-5050
Alamo 305 525-4713
Avis 305 637-4900
Avon 305 445-8787
Budget 305 871-2722
Dollar 305 887-6000
General 305 926-1700

Hertz 305 871-0300
Holiday-Payless 305 871-3540
National 305 638-1026
Sears 305 871-1444
Snappy 305 884-8808
Thrifty 305 871-2277
Value 305 871-6760

■ Limo/Taxi

Ambassador Limousines 305 931-3111
Broward Limousine & Airport Service　305 791-3000
Central Cab 305 532-5555
Club Limousine 305 893-9850

Limousines of South Florida 305 940-5252
Metro Taxi 305 888-8888
Yellow Cab 305 444-4444

■ Mass Transit

305 638-6700　**Metrobus/Metrorail** $1 Base fare .... Miami FL　33142-0000

■ Rail/Bus

305 374-7222　**Greyhound/Trailways Bus Station** 99 NE 4th St .... Miami FL　33132-2111
305 835-1222　**Miami Station** 8303 NW 37th Ave .... Miami FL　33147-3975

Hotels

305 262-1000　**Airport Hilton & Marina** 5101 Blue Lagoon Dr .... Miami FL　33126-2021
305 865-6500　**Alexander Hotel** 5225 Collins Ave .... Miami Beach FL　33140-2598
305 534-2135　**Art Deco Hotel** 1320 Ocean Dr .... Miami Beach FL　33139-4210
305 445-1926　**Biltmore Hotel** 1200 Anastasia Ave .... Coral Gables FL　33134-6300
305 374-3900　**Biscayne Bay Marriott** 1633 N Bayshore Dr .... Miami FL　33132-1261
305 532-3600　**Doral Ocean Beach Resort** 4833 Collins Ave .... Miami Beach FL　33140-2751
305 592-2000　**Doral Resort & Country Club** 4400 NW 87th Ave .... Miami FL　33178-2192
305 531-0000　**Eden Roc Hotel Miami Beach** 4525 Collins Ave .... Miami FL　33140-3286
305 858-9600　**Grand Bay Hotel** 2669 S Bayshore Dr .... Coconut Grove FL　33133-5497
305 446-9000　**Holiday Inn Le Jeune Center** 950 NW Le Jeune Rd ...... Miami FL　33126-3695
305 358-1234　**Hyatt Regency Miami** 400 SE 2nd Ave .... Miami FL　33131-2197
305 577-1000　**Inter-Continental Hotel Miami** 100 Chopin Plaza .... Miami FL　33131-4323
305 441-0000　**Mayfair House Hotel** 3000 Florida Ave .... Coconut Grove FL　33133-5297
305 649-5000　**Miami Airport Marriott Hotel** 1201 NW 42nd Ave .... Miami FL　33126-2656
305 374-0000　**Omni International Hotel** 1601 Biscayne Blvd .... Miami FL　33132-1240

305 932-1100　**Radisson Pan American Hotel** 17875 Collins Ave .... Miami Beach FL　33160-2741
305 871-3800　**Sheraton River House** 3900 NW 21st St .... Miami FL　33142-6791
305 531-7684　**Waldorf Towers Hotel** 860 Ocean Dr .... Miami Beach FL　33139-5897

Restaurants

305 763-2777　**15th Street Fisheries** (Seafood) 1900 SE 15th St .... Fort Lauderdale FL　33316-3006
305 866-2768　**Benihana of Tokyo**
　　　　　　　(Japanese) 1665 NE 79th Street Cswy .... North Bay Village FL　33141-4163
305 642-2452　**Casa Juancho** (Spanish) 24th Ave & 8th St .... Miami FL　33135-0000
305 935-2900　**Chef Allen's**
　　　　　　　(Regional American) 19088 NE 29th Ave .... North Miami Beach FL　33180-2802
305 446-1400　**Christy's** (Steak) 3101 Ponce de Leon Blvd .... Coral Gables FL　33134-6816
305 861-5252　**Dominique's** (French) 5225 Collins Ave .... Miami FL　33140-2514
305 642-3144　**El Cid** (Spanish) 117 NW 42nd Ave .... Miami FL　33126-0000
305 893-4811　**El Tulipano** (Italian) 11052 Biscayne Blvd .... Miami FL　33161-7462
305 538-8533　**Forge The** (American/Continental) 432 Arthur Godfrey Rd .. Miami Beach FL　33140-3504
305 565-2929　**Gibby's Steaks & Seafood**
　　　　　　　(Steak/Seafood) 2900 NE 12th Terr .... Fort Lauderdale FL　33334-4498
305 858-0009　**Grand Cafe** (Continental) 2669 S Bayshore Dr .... Miami FL　33133-5423
305 673-0365　**Joe's Stone Crab** (Seafood) 227 Biscayne St .... Miami Beach FL　33139-7395
305 444-7501　**La Carreta** (Cuban) 3632 SW 8th St .... Miami FL　33135-0000
305 563-3272　**Mai Kai** (Cantonese/American) 3599 N Federal Hwy .... Fort Lauderdale FL　33308-6222
305 947-4581　**Rascal House** (American/Jewish) 17190 Collins Ave .... Miami Beach FL　33160-3691
305 584-1637　**Rustic Inn Crabhouse**
　　　　　　　(Seafood) 4331 Ravenswood Rd .... Fort Lauderdale FL　33312-0000
305 361-3818　**Rusty Pelican** (Seafood) 3201 Rickenbacker Cswy .... Miami FL　33149-1015
305 781-2200　**Sea Watch Restaurant** (Seafood) 6002 N Ocean Blvd .... Fort Lauderdale FL　33308-2320
305 566-2855　**Shooters On The Water** (American) 3033 NE 32nd Ave .... Fort Lauderdale FL　33308-0000
305 561-4400　**Yesterday's**
　　　　　　　(American/Continental) 3001 E Oakland Park Blvd .... Fort Lauderdale FL　33306-1817

Goods & Services

■ Department Stores

305 835-5151　**Burdine's** 22 E Flagler St .... Miami FL　33131-1018
305 620-3000　**Byrons Inc** 15600 NW 15th Ave .... Miami FL　33169-5684
305 377-1911　**Jordan Marsh** 1501 Biscayne Blvd .... Miami FL　33132-1499

■ Banks

305 442-2660　**Ocean Bank of Miami** 780 NW 42nd Ave .... Miami FL　33126-5597
305 375-7500　**Southeast Bank NA** 200 S Biscayne Blvd .... Miami FL　33131-2390
305 577-5115　**SunBank Miami NA** 777 Brickell Ave .... Miami FL　33131-2865

■ Messenger/Postal

Choice Courier System 305 949-0909
Courier Dispatch Group Inc 305 592-0474
Executive Express Couriers 305 854-0565
Federal Express 800 238-5355
Legal Couriers 305 379-0011
Miami Messenger Service 305 821-6000

Post Office 305 470-0450
Star Messenger Service 305 594-1981
Sunshine State Messenger Co 305 944-6363
UPS 305 238-0134
Zoom International Courier Inc 305 592-1050

■ Secretarial/Temp Services

305 447-1757　**Accountemps** 2655 Le Jeune Rd Suite 814 .... Coral Gables FL　33134-5873
305 371-8743　**Kelly Temporary Services** 310 SE 1st St .... Miami FL　33131-2002
305 374-3892　**Manpower Temporary Services** 150 SE 2nd Ave Suite 504 .... Miami FL　33131-1570

Media

■ Newspapers/Magazines

305 350-2111　**Miami Herald** 1 Herald Plaza .... Miami FL　33132-1693
305 374-5011　**Miami/South Florida** 600 Brickell Ave Suite 207 .... Miami FL　33131-2539

■ Television

305 593-0606　**WCIX-TV Ch 6 (CBS)** 8900 NW 18th Terr .... Miami FL　33172-0000
305 949-8321　**WPBT-TV Ch 2 (PBS)** 14901 NE 20th Ave .... Miami FL　33181-1121
305 576-1010　**WPLG-TV Ch 10 (ABC)** 3900 Biscayne Blvd .... Miami FL　33137-3786
305 379-4444　**WTVJ-TV Ch 4 (NBC)** 316 N Miami Ave .... Miami FL　33128-1800

■ Radio

305 623-7711　**WEDR-FM 99.1 MHz (UC)** 3790 NW 167th St .... Opa Locka FL　33054-0000
305 925-7117　**WHYI-FM 100.7 MHz (CHR)** 2741 N 29th Ave Suite 300 ..... Hollywood FL　33020-1594
305 624-6101　**WINZ-AM 940 kHz (N/T-CBS)** 4330 NW 207th Dr .... Miami FL　33055-1250
305 995-2220　**WLRN-FM 91.3 MHz (Jazz-NPR)** 172 NE 15th St .... Miami FL　33132-1349
305 653-8811　**WLYF-FM 101.5 MHz (B/EZ)** 20450 NW 2nd Ave .... Miami FL　33169-2505
305 447-1140　**WQBA-AM 1140 kHz (Span)** 2828 Coral Way .... Miami FL　33145-3226

Local Attractions & Special Events

■ Sports

305 885-8000　**Hialeah Race Course** 2200 E 4th St .... Miami FL　33101-0000
305 620-5000　**Miami Dolphins** 2269 NW 199th St Joe Robbie Stadium ..... Miami FL　33056-0000
305 577-4328　**Miami Heat** 721 NW 1st Ave Miami Arena .... Miami FL　33136-0000
305 633-6400　**Miami Jai-Alai Fronton** 3500 NW 37th Ave .... Miami FL　33142-4997

■ Special Events

305 644-8888　**Carnival Miami** (March 1-10)

■ Local Attractions

305 866-0311　**Bal Harbour Shops** 9700 Collins Ave .... Bal Harbour FL　33154-0000
305 247-2400　**Biscayne National Park Tourboats** SW 328th St .... Homestead FL　33030-0000
813 695-2800　**Eden of the Everglades** Dupont Rd .... Everglades City FL　33929-9999
305 247-6211　**Everglades National Park** .... Homestead FL　33030-0000
305 642-3870　**Little Havana Information Number** SW 8th St .... Miami FL　33135-2299
305 361-5703　**Miami Seaquarium** Rickenbacker Cswy .... Miami FL　33101-0000
305 854-4247　**Museum of Science** 3280 S Miami Ave .... Miami FL　33129-2899
305 666-7834　**Parrot Jungle & Gardens** 11000 SW 57th Ave .... Miami FL　33156-0000
305 579-2813　**Vizcaya** 3251 S Miami Ave .... Miami FL　33101-0000

Milwaukee
WISCONSIN 414

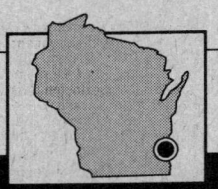

Important Phone Numbers

AAA	414 464-1212	Emergency	911
American Express	414 271-1250	Poison Control Center	414 266-2222
Better Business Bureau	414 273-1600	Time	414 844-1414
City Hall	414 278-3200	Weather	414 936-1212

■ Travel Information

414 273-3000 **Chamber of Commerce** 756 N Milwaukee St .... Milwaukee WI 53202-3719
414 273-3950 **Convention & Visitors Bureau** 756 N Milwaukee St .... Milwaukee WI 53202-3719

Travel

■ Airport

414 747-5300 **General Mitchell International Airport** 11 miles SE of downtown (approx 15 minutes)

■ Airport Transportation

414 272-1955 **AAA Limo** $6.50 fare to downtown
414 344-6711 **Milwaukee Transit System** $1 fare to downtown
Taxi $13 fare to downtown

■ Scheduled Airlines

American	414 344-6700	Midway	800 621-5700
American Eagle	800 433-7300	Midwest	414 747-4646
Apex	414 786-9300	Northwest	414 272-8920
Comair	800 354-9822	TWA	414 933-8292
Continental	414 342-3099	United	414 273-8400
Eastern	414 344-7910	USAir	414 747-4714
Enterprise	800 343-7300		

■ Charter Airlines

Grand Air	414 461-3222	Scott Air Charter	414 744-1300
Mitchell Aeronautical	414 747-5707	Wisconsin Aviation Inc	414 261-4567

■ Car Rentals

Agency	414 769-9800	Budget	414 481-2409
Alamo	414 481-6600	Dollar	414 747-0066
American International	414 481-8750	Hertz	414 747-5335
Avis	414 744-2266	National	414 483-9800

■ Limo/Taxi

Carey Limousine	414 271-5466	Limousines of Abbey Town Cars	414 445-2030
City Veteran Taxicab	414 643-1212	Yellow Cab	414 271-1800

■ Mass Transit

414 344-4550 **Milwaukee County Transit System** $1 Base fare .... Milwaukee WI 53205-0000

■ Rail/Bus

414 272-6688 **Greyhound Bus Station** 606 N 7th St .... Milwaukee WI 53233-0000
414 271-0840 **Milwaukee Station** 433 W St Paul Ave .... Milwaukee WI 53203-3007
800 472-6723 **Trailways** 433 W St Paul Ave .... Milwaukee WI 53203-3007

Hotels

414 271-4220 **Astor Hotel** 924 E Juneau Ave .... Milwaukee WI 53202-2748
414 242-9680 **Bed & Breakfast of Milwaukee** 1916 W Donges Bay Rd .... Mequon WI 53092-5510
414 769-2100 **Best Western Midway Motor Lodge** 5105 S Howell Ave ...... Milwaukee WI 53207-6109
414 782-2900 **Embassy Suites Hotel** 1200 S Moorland Rd .... Brookfield WI 53005-6959
414 481-8000 **Grand Milwaukee Hotel** 4747 S Howell Ave .... Milwaukee WI 53207-5913
414 271-4900 **Hotel Wisconsin** 720 N 3rd St .... Milwaukee WI 53203-2204
414 276-1234 **Hyatt Regency Milwaukee** 333 W Kilbourn Ave .... Milwaukee WI 53203-1507
414 276-8500 **Knickerbocker on the Lake** 1028 E Juneau Ave .... Milwaukee WI 53202-2886
414 271-7250 **Marc Plaza Hotel** 509 W Wisconsin Ave .... Milwaukee WI 53203-2006
414 786-1100 **Milwaukee Marriott Hotel** 375 S Moorland Rd .... Brookfield WI 53005-4250
414 962-6040 **Milwaukee River Hilton Inn** 4700 N Port Washington Rd ...... Milwaukee WI 53212-1045
414 276-8800 **Park East Hotel** 916 E State St .... Milwaukee WI 53202-3451
414 273-8222 **Pfister Hotel & Tower** 424 E Wisconsin Ave .... Milwaukee WI 53202-4406
414 764-5300 **Ramada Inn Airport South** 6401 S 13th St .... Milwaukee WI 53221-5299
414 257-3400 **Sheraton Mayfair Inn** 2303 N Mayfair Rd .... Milwaukee WI 53226-1505
414 355-8585 **Sheraton Milwaukee North** 8900 N Kildeer Ct .... Brown Deer WI 53209-1219

Restaurants

414 321-6365 **Antonino's** (Italian) 8412 W Morgan Ave .... Milwaukee WI 53228-1518
414 273-8222 **English Room** (Continental) 424 E Wisconsin Ave .... Milwaukee WI 53202-4406
414 628-1111 **Fox & Hounds** (American) 1298 Friess Lake Rd .... Hubertus WI 53033-9751
414 276-0747 **Grenadier's** (Continental) 747 N Broadway .... Milwaukee WI 53202-4302
414 291-5220 **John Byron's** (Nouvelle American) 777 E Michigan St .... Milwaukee WI 53202-5303
414 273-1878 **John Ernst Restaurant** (German) 600 E Ogden Ave .... Milwaukee WI 53202-2699
414 276-2720 **Karl Ratzsch's Old World Restaurant**
(German) 320 E Mason St .... Milwaukee WI 53202-3656
414 271-7111 **Koto Japanese Sushi Restaurant**
(Japanese) 1854 E Kenilworth Pl .... Milwaukee WI 53202-1120
414 271-7250 **Le Bistro** (Continental) 509 W Wisconsin Ave .... Milwaukee WI 53203-2006
414 271-3377 **Mader's German Restaurant**
(German) 1037 N Old World 3rd St .... Milwaukee WI 53203-1389
414 643-0072 **Mike & Anna's** (French) 1978 S 8th St .... Milwaukee WI 53204-3850
414 271-0597 **Pieces of Eight** (Steak/Seafood) 550 N Harbor Dr .... Milwaukee WI 53202-0000
414 354-1995 **River Lane Inn** (Seafood) 4313 W River Ln .... Brown Deer WI 53223-2425
414 272-5363 **Sally's Steak House** (Steak) 1028 E Juneau Ave .... Milwaukee WI 53202-2850
414 271-5166 **Toy's China Town** (Chinese/American) 830 N 3rd St .... Milwaukee WI 53203-1795

Goods & Services

■ Department Stores

414 347-4141 **Boston Store** 331 W Wisconsin Ave .... Milwaukee WI 53203-2295
414 276-7050 **Marshall Field's** 101 W Wisconsin Ave .... Milwaukee WI 53260-0001

■ Banks

414 765-3000 **Bank One Milwaukee** 111 E Wisconsin Ave .... Milwaukee WI 53202-4865
414 765-4321 **First Wisconsin National Bank** 777 E Wisconsin Ave .... Milwaukee WI 53202-5371
414 765-7700 **M & I Marshall & Ilsley Bank** 770 N Water St .... Milwaukee WI 53202-3529

■ Messenger/Postal

Action Express Inc	414 549-3300	Federal Express	800 238-5355
Bonded Messenger Service Inc	414 933-4500	Post Office	414 291-2544
City Veterans Package Delivery	414 643-1100	UPS	414 786-2800
Dispatch 10 Ltd Messenger Service	414 761-1010		

■ Secretarial/Temp Services

414 277-9900 **Kelly Services Inc** 310 W Wisconsin Ave Suite 1204 .... Milwaukee WI 53203-2211
414 272-8500 **Manpower Temporary Services**
111 E Kilbourn Ave Suite 100 .... Milwaukee WI 53202-6611
414 278-7900 **Olsten Temporary Services** 411 E Wisconsin Ave .... Milwaukee WI 53202-4400

Media

■ Newspapers/Magazines

414 224-2000 **Milwaukee Journal** 333 W State St .... Milwaukee WI 53203-1309
414 273-1101 **Milwaukee Magazine** 312 E Buffalo St .... Milwaukee WI 53202-5828
414 224-2000 **Milwaukee Sentinel** 918 N 4th St .... Milwaukee WI 53203-1500

■ Television

414 342-8812 **WISN-TV Ch 12 (ABC)** 759 N 19th St .... Milwaukee WI 53233-2715
414 355-6666 **WITI-TV Ch 6 (CBS)** 9001 N Green Bay Rd .... Milwaukee WI 53209-1297
414 271-1036 **WMVS-TV Ch 10 (PBS)** 1036 N 8th St .... Milwaukee WI 53233-1409
414 332-9611 **WTMJ-TV Ch 4 (NBC)** 720 E Capitol Dr .... Milwaukee WI 53212-1308

■ Radio

414 272-1040 **WEZW-FM 103.7 MHz (AC)**
735 W Wisconsin Ave Suite 401 .... Milwaukee WI 53233-2464
414 271-5511 **WKLH-FM 96.5 MHz (Gold)**
735 W Wisconsin Ave Suite 700 .... Milwaukee WI 53233-2413
414 332-9611 **WKTI-FM 94 MHz (CHR-NBC)** 720 E Capitol Dr .... Milwaukee WI 53212-1308
414 332-9611 **WTMJ-AM 620 kHz (N/T-NBC)** 720 E Capitol Dr .... Milwaukee WI 53212-1308
414 229-4664 **WUWM-FM 89.7 MHz (N/T-NPR)** 3203 N Downer Ave .... Milwaukee WI 53211-3153

Local Attractions & Special Events

■ Sports

414 494-2345 **Green Bay Packers** 1265 Lombardi Ave Lambeau Field .... Green Bay WI 54303-0000
414 933-1818 **Milwaukee Brewers** 201 S 46th St County Stadium .... Milwaukee WI 53214-0000
414 227-0500 **Milwaukee Bucks** 1001 N 4th St Bradley Ctr .... Milwaukee WI 53203-0000

■ Special Events

414 273-3950 **Circus Parade** (July 14th)
414 273-2680 **Summerfest** (June 27-July 7)

■ Local Attractions

414 288-7039 **Joan of Arc Chapel** 601 N 14th St .... Milwaukee WI 53201-0000
414 782-8074 **Kettle Moraine Scenic Steam Train** (June-October)
Hwy 83 .... North Lake WI 53064-0000
414 931-2153 **Miller Brewing Co** 4251 W State St .... Milwaukee WI 53201-0000
414 649-9830 **Mitchell Park Domes** 524 S Layton Blvd .... Milwaukee WI 53215-1295
414 276-9100 **Old World Third Street** 1030 N Old World Third St .... Milwaukee WI 53203-0000
414 594-2116 **Old World Wisconsin** S 103 West 37890 Hwy 67 .... Eagle WI 53119-0000

Minn/St Paul

MINNESOTA   **612**

Important Phone Numbers

AAA	612 927-2727	Emergency	911
American Express	612 343-5500	Poison Control Center	612 347-3141
Better Business Bureau	612 699-1111	Time	612 546-8463
City Hall–Minneapolis	612 673-2735	Weather	612 452-2323
City Hall–Saint Paul	612 298-4012		

■ Travel Information

612 370-9132 **Chamber of Commerce–Minneapolis**
81 S 9th St Suite 200 .... Minneapolis MN 55402-3225
612 222-5561 **Chamber of Commerce–Saint Paul**
445 Minnesota St NCL Tower Suite 600 .... Saint Paul MN 55101-2165
612 348-4313 **Convention & Visitors Assn–Minneapolis**
1219 Marquette Ave Suite 300 .... Minneapolis MN 55403-2486
612 297-6985 **Convention & Visitors Bureau–Saint Paul**
445 Minnesota St Suite 600 .... Saint Paul MN 55101-2108

Travel

■ Airport

612 726-5555 **Minneapolis-Saint Paul International Airport** 10 miles SE of Minneapolis (approx 20 minutes)

■ Airport Transportation

612 827-7777 **Airport Express** $7.50 fare to downtown
612 827-7733 **Minneapolis Transit Bus Service** $.75-$1.00 fare to downtown
Taxi $15-20 fare to downtown

■ Scheduled Airlines

American	612 332-4168	Northwest	612 726-1234
Canadian	800 426-7000	Pan Am	800 221-1111
Continental	612 332-1471	TWA	612 333-6543
Delta	612 339-7477	United	612 339-3671
Eastern	612 339-9520	USAir	612 338-5841
Midway	800 621-5700		

■ Charter Airlines

Charter Flight Services	612 726-5491	Sun Country Airlines Inc	612 726-1427
Great Western Aviation	612 688-0759		

■ Car Rentals

American International	612 866-4918	Holiday-Payless	612 854-5115
Avis	612 726-5220	IRA	612 854-3003
Budget	612 726-5622	National	612 726-5600
Dollar	612 726-9494	Snappy	612 854-2226
Hertz	612 726-1600	Thrifty	612 854-8080

■ Limo/Taxi

Blue & White Taxi	612 333-3331	Red & White Taxi	612 871-1600
Carey Limousine	612 824-7665	Town Taxi	612 331-8294
Johnson-Williams Auto Livery	612 646-1013	Yellow Taxi Service	612 824-4444

■ Mass Transit

612 827-7733 **Metropolitan Transit Commission** $.50 Base fare .... Minneapolis MN 55411-0000

■ Rail/Bus

612 371-3325 **Greyhound/Trailways Bus Station** 29 N 9th St .... Minneapolis MN 55403-1397
612 222-0509 **Greyhound/Trailways Bus Station** 25 W 7th St .... Saint Paul MN 55102-1103
612 644-1127 **Midway Station** 730 Transfer Rd .... Saint Paul MN 55114-1404

Hotels

612 370-1400 **Best Western Normandy Inn** 405 S 8th St .... Minneapolis MN 55404-1026
612 854-1000 **Embassy Suites Airport** 7901 34th Ave S .... Bloomington MN 55425-1604
612 731-2220 **Holiday Inn Saint Paul Center** 2201 Burns Ave .... Saint Paul MN 55119-0000
612 636-4123 **Howard Johnson's Hotel** 1201 W County Rd E .... Saint Paul MN 55110-5139
612 370-1234 **Hyatt Regency Hotel** 1300 Nicollet Mall .... Minneapolis MN 55403-2693
612 332-2351 **Marquette Hotel** 710 Marquette Ave .... Minneapolis MN 55402-0000
612 349-4000 **Minneapolis Marriott City Center Hotel** 30 S 7th St .... Minneapolis MN 55402-1601
612 331-1900 **Minneapolis Metrodome Hilton** 1330 Industrial Blvd NE ..... Minneapolis MN 55413-1703
612 331-1800 **Nicollet Island Inn** 95 Merriam St .... Minneapolis MN 55401-1524
612 338-2288 **Omni Northstar** 618 2nd Ave S .... Minneapolis MN 55402-1900
612 633-6333 **Paul's Place Inn** 2965 Snelling Ave N .... Saint Paul MN 55113-1498
612 553-1600 **Plymouth Place Hotel** 2705 Annapolis Ln N .... Plymouth MN 55441-3612
612 292-1900 **Radisson Hotel Saint Paul** 11 Kellogg Blvd E .... Saint Paul MN 55101-1065
612 379-8888 **Radisson University Hotel** 615 Washington Ave SE .... Minneapolis MN 55414-2931
612 735-2330 **Ramada Hotel** 1870 Old Hudson Rd .... Saint Paul MN 55119-4377
612 292-9292 **Saint Paul Hotel** 350 Market St .... Saint Paul MN 55102-1484
612 339-9300 **Whitney Hotel** 150 Portland Ave .... Minneapolis MN 55401-2594

Restaurants

612 874-6440 **510 The** (French) 510 Groveland Ave .... Minneapolis MN 55403-3224
612 339-8000 **Atrium International Cafe** (Italian) 275 Market St .... Minneapolis MN 55405-1619
612 342-2500 **Azur** (French) 651 Nicollet Mall .... Minneapolis MN 55402-0000
612 872-0812 **Black Forest Inn** (German) 1 E 26th St .... Minneapolis MN 55404-4399
612 645-8101 **Blue Horse** (Continental) 1355 University Ave .... Saint Paul MN 55104-4096
612 222-8499 **Boca Chica** (Mexican) 11 Concord St .... Saint Paul MN 55107-0000
612 861-3333 **Champs Sports Cafe** (Italian/American) 790 W 66th St ..... Richfield MN 55423-2203
612 544-4014 **Cocolezzone** (Italian) 5410 Wayzata Blvd .... Minneapolis MN 55416-1322
612 338-2401 **D'Amico Cucina** (Italian) 100 N 6th St .... Minneapolis MN 55403-0000
612 854-4056 **Eddie Webster's** (American) 1501 E 78th St .... Bloomington MN 55425-1116
612 332-3515 **Faegre's** (Nouvelle) 430 1st Ave N .... Minneapolis MN 55401-1713
612 349-4022 **Fifth Season** (American) 30 S 7th St .... Minneapolis MN 55402-1601

612 332-4800 **Goodfellow's** (Regional) 800 Nicollet Mall .... Minneapolis MN 55402-0000
612 339-0540 **Ichiban Japanese Steak House**
(Japanese) 1333 Nicollett Mall .... Minneapolis MN 55403-2696
612 789-7298 **Jax Cafe** (Continental) 1928 University Ave NE .... Minneapolis MN 55418-4397
612 222-5878 **Lexington** (American) 1096 Grand Ave .... Saint Paul MN 55105-3001
612 439-1100 **Lowell Inn** (American) 102 N 2nd St .... Stillwater MN 55082-5099
612 339-0909 **Murray's** (Steak) 26 S 6th St .... Minneapolis MN 55402-1571
612 338-3790 **New French Cafe** (French) 128 N 4th St .... Minneapolis MN 55401-1708
612 871-8969 **Rudolph's Bar-B-Que** (Barbecue) 1933 Lyndale Ave S ...... Minneapolis MN 55403-3104
612 544-4993 **Rupert's American Cafe & Nightclub**
(American) 5410 Wayzata Blvd .... Minneapolis MN 55416-1322
612 929-1010 **Tour D'France** (International) 4924 France Ave S .... Edina MN 55410-0000
612 331-9041 **Village Wok** (Chinese) 610 Washington Ave SE .... Minneapolis MN 55414-0000

Goods & Services

■ Department Stores

612 347-7611 **Carson Pirie Scott** 600 Nicollet Ave .... Minneapolis MN 55402-1697
612 375-2200 **Dayton's** 700 Nicollet Mall .... Minneapolis MN 55402-2065

■ Banks

612 298-6000 **American National Bank & Trust Co** 101 5th St E .... Saint Paul MN 55101-1860
612 370-4141 **First Bank Minneapolis** 120 S 6th St .... Minneapolis MN 55480-0000
612 291-5000 **First Bank National Assn** 332 Minnesota St .... Saint Paul MN 55101-1314
612 341-5600 **Marquette Bank Minneapolis NA** 6th St & Marquette Ave ... Minneapolis MN 55480-0000
612 646-2661 **Midway National Bank of Saint Paul** 1578 University Ave W ... Saint Paul MN 55104-3948
612 667-1234 **Norwest Bank Minnesota NA** 6th & Marquette Sts .... Minneapolis MN 55479-0000

■ Messenger/Postal

Action Messenger Inc	612 881-5100	Federal Express	612 340-0887
Adcom Express	612 829-7990	Post Office	612 349-4704
Bicycle Express Inc	612 340-0059	Road Runner Parcel Service	612 644-8444
Courier Dispatch Group Inc	612 338-6300	Skywalkers Courier Service	612 371-8778
Dependable Courier Inc	612 338-5088	UPS	612 378-0700
Express Messenger Services Inc	612 623-5900		

■ Secretarial/Temp Services

612 339-5521 **Accountemps** 2800 Norwest Ctr .... Minneapolis MN 55402-0000
612 339-7154 **Kelly Services** 200 S 6th St Suite 145 .... Minneapolis MN 55402-0000
612 375-9200 **Manpower Temporary Services** 150 S 5th St Suite 336 ...... Minneapolis MN 55402-4203
612 339-7981 **Olsten Temporary Services** 733 Marquette Ave Suite 241 ... Minneapolis MN 55402-2315

Media

■ Newspapers/Magazines

612 339-7571 **Minneapolis/Saint Paul Magazine** 12 S 6th St Suite 400 .... Minneapolis MN 55402-1509
612 222-5011 **Saint Paul Pioneer Press** 345 Cedar St .... Saint Paul MN 55101-1057
612 372-4141 **Star Tribune** 425 Portland Ave S .... Minneapolis MN 55488-0001

■ Television

612 546-1111 **KARE-TV Ch 11** (NBC) 8811 Olson Memorial Hwy .... Minneapolis MN 55427-4754
612 646-5555 **KSTP-TV Ch 5** (ABC) 3415 University Ave W .... Saint Paul MN 55114-1019
612 222-1717 **KTCA-TV Ch 2** (PBS) 172 E 4th St .... Saint Paul MN 55101-1400
612 330-2400 **WCCO-TV Ch 4** (CBS) 90 S 11th St .... Minneapolis MN 55403-2450

■ Radio

612 645-7757 **KEEY-FM 102.1 MHz** (Ctry-MBS) 611 Frontenac Pl .... Saint Paul MN 55104-4947
612 545-5601 **KQRS-AM 1440 kHz** (AOR-ABC) 917 Lilac Dr N .... Minneapolis MN 55422-4688
612 545-5601 **KQRS-FM 92.5 MHz** (AOR-ABC) 917 Lilac Dr N .... Minneapolis MN 55422-4688
612 642-4141 **KSTP-FM 94.5 MHz** (AC-ABC) 3415 University Ave SE .... Minneapolis MN 55414-3327
612 625-3500 **KUOM-AM 770 kHz** (N/T) 330 21st Ave S .... Minneapolis MN 55455-0415
612 370-0611 **WCCO-AM 830 kHz** (N/T-CBS) 625 2nd Ave S .... Minneapolis MN 55402-1912

Local Attractions & Special Events

■ Sports

612 853-9300 **Minnesota North Stars** 7901 Cedar Ave Met Ctr .... Bloomington MN 55425-0000
612 337-3865 **Minnesota Timberwolves**
501 Chicago Ave S HHH Metrodome .... Minneapolis MN 55415-1596
612 375-7444 **Minnesota Twins** 501 Chicago Ave S HHH Metrodome ...... Minneapolis MN 55415-1596
612 828-6500 **Minnesota Vikings** 501 Chicago Ave S HHH Metrodome ..... Minneapolis MN 55415-1596

■ Special Events

612 377-4621 **Aquatennial** (July 12-21)
612 297-6953 **Saint Paul Winter Carnival** (January 23-February 3)

■ Local Attractions

612 726-9430 **Fort Snelling State Park** Hwys 5 & 55 .... Minneapolis MN 55150-0000
612 348-2142 **Minnehaha Falls** 50th St & Minnehaha Ave .... Minneapolis MN 55417-0000
612 292-4355 **Minnesota Museum of Art** 5th & Market .... Saint Paul MN 55102-0000
612 431-9200 **Minnesota Zoo** 13000 Zoo Blvd .... Apple Valley MN 55124-0000
612 340-9122 **Nicollet Mall** 81 S 9th St .... Minneapolis MN 55402-0000
612 378-1969 **Riverplace** 1 Main St SE .... Minneapolis MN 55414-0000
612 228-1766 **Saint Paul's Cathedral** 239 Selby Ave .... Saint Paul MN 55102-1811
612 377-4621 **Science Museum of Minnesota** 10th & Wabesha .... Saint Paul MN 55101-0000
612 375-7600 **Walker Art Center** Vineland Pl .... Minneapolis MN 55403-1195

Nashville
TENNESSEE   615

Important Phone Numbers

AAA	615 244-8889	Emergency	911
American Express	615 256-0745	Poison Control Center	615 322-6435
Better Business Bureau	615 254-5873	Time/Temp	615 259-2222
City Hall	615 259-5620	Weather	615 244-9393

■ Travel Information

615 259-4755 **Chamber of Commerce** 161 4th Ave N .... Nashville TN 37219-2485
615 259-4747 **Tourist Information Center** 300 Main St .... Nashville TN 37213-1007

Travel

■ Airport

615 275-1600 **Metropolitan Nashville Airport** 8 miles SE of city (approx 12 minutes)

■ Airport Transportation

615 242-4433 **Metropolitan Transit Authority** $.75 fare to downtown
Taxi $15 fare to downtown

■ Scheduled Airlines

American	615 244-5500	Pan Am	800 221-1111
American Eagle	615 244-5500	Southwest	615 255-1221
Comair	800 354-9822	TWA	615 244-9010
Delta	615 244-9860	United	800 241-6522
Eastern	615 244-3780	USAir	615 361-4030
Northwest	800 225-2525		

■ Charter Airlines

Corporate Air Fleet Inc	615 367-3405	Tennessee Valley Airways	615 361-3293
Nashville Jet Center	615 361-3000	Van Dusen Airport Services	615 361-8070

■ Car Rentals

Alamo	615 367-1844	Dollar	615 275-1111
American International	615 361-8896	Hertz	615 361-3131
Avis	615 361-1212	National	615 361-7467
Budget	615 366-0800	Thrifty	615 361-6050

■ Limo/Taxi

Checker Cab	615 254-5031	Nashville Cab	615 242-7070
Imperial Limousines	615 361-3055	Yellow Cab	615 256-0101
Music City Cab	615 262-0451		

■ Mass Transit

615 242-4433 **Metropolitan Transit Authority** $.75 Base fare .... Nashville TN 37210-0000

■ Rail/Bus

615 255-3556 **Greyhound/Trailways Bus Station** 200 8th Ave S .... Nashville TN 37203-3992

Hotels

615 244-6050 **Budget Host Inn** 10 Interstate Dr .... Nashville TN 37213-1003
615 259-4343 **Clarion Maxwell House** 2025 Metrocenter Blvd .... Nashville TN 37228-1599
615 244-8200 **Doubletree Hotel** 2 Commerce Pl .... Nashville TN 37219-1693
615 244-3121 **Hermitage Nashville All Suite Hotel** 231 6th Ave N .... Nashville TN 37219-1986
615 327-4707 **Holiday Inn Vanderbilt** 2613 West End Ave .... Nashville TN 37219-1776
615 259-1234 **Hyatt Regency Nashville** 623 Union St .... Nashville TN 37210-0000
615 889-9300 **Nashville Marriott Hotel** 1 Marriott Dr .... Nashville TN 37214-1297
615 889-1000 **Opryland Hotel** 2800 Opryland Dr .... Nashville TN 37214-1297
615 871-0033 **Park Suites Hotel** 10 Century Blvd .... Nashville TN 37214-3675
615 361-7666 **Quality Inn Airport** 1 International Plaza .... Nashville TN 37217-2079
615 885-2200 **Sheraton Music City Hotel** 777 McGavock Pike .... Nashville TN 37214-3175
615 255-8400 **Stouffer Hotel** 611 Commerce St .... Nashville TN 37203-3725

Restaurants

615 255-1494 **Arthur's** (Continental) 1001 Broadway .... Nashville TN 37203-3148
615 320-1700 **Chancellor's** (American) 2100 West End Ave .... Nashville TN 37203-5207
615 352-8121 **Dalts Grill** (American/Mexican) 38 White Bridge Rd .... Nashville TN 37205-1411
615 244-3121 **Hermitage The** (Continental) 231 6th Ave N .... Nashville TN 37219-1986
615 329-4349 **Jim Kelly's** (Steak) 217 Louise Ave .... Nashville TN 37203-1811
615 327-2412 **Julian's** (French) 2412 West End Ave .... Nashville TN 37203-1798
615 646-9700 **Loveless Motel & Restaurant** (Southern) RR 5 .... Nashville TN 37221-9805
615 327-3232 **Mario's** (Northern Italian) 2005 Broadway .... Nashville TN 37203-0000
615 320-0163 **Ruth's Chris Steak House** (Steak) 204 21st Ave S .... Nashville TN 37203-2401
615 256-0760 **Satsuma** (Southern) 417 Union St .... Nashville TN 37219-1726
615 356-6206 **Sportsman's Grille** (American) 5405 Harding Rd .... Nashville TN 37205-0000
615 255-6464 **Stockyard** (Steak) 901 2nd Ave N .... Nashville TN 37201-1000
615 327-2233 **Third Coast** (American) 913 20th Ave S .... Nashville TN 37212-2100

Goods & Services

■ Department Stores

615 256-6411 **Castner-Knott Co** 618 Church St .... Nashville TN 37219-2393
615 297-0971 **Dillard's** 3855 Greenhills Village Dr .... Nashville TN 37215-2621

■ Banks

615 748-2000 **First American National Bank of Nashville** 300 Union St .... Nashville TN 37237-0001
615 749-3333 **Sovran Bank Central South** 1 Commerce Pl .... Nashville TN 37219-1697
615 748-4000 **Third National Bank** PO Box 305110 .... Nashville TN 37230-5110

■ Messenger/Postal

AA Dispatch	615 329-4297	Rapid Messenger Service	615 254-0807
Accelerated Inc	615 367-0949	UPS	615 889-5700
Federal Express	800 238-5355	Wells Fargo Armored Service	615 256-3112
Post Office	615 885-1005		

■ Secretarial/Temp Services

615 367-1960 **Kelly Services Inc** 404 BNA Dr Suite 200 .... Nashville TN 37217-2527
615 248-3144 **Manpower Temporary Services** 424 Church St Suite 1504 ..... Nashville TN 37219-2363
615 872-9600 **Olsten Temporary Services** 616 Marriott Dr Suite 110 .... Nashville TN 37210-4024

Media

■ Newspapers/Magazines

615 259-8800 **Nashville Banner** 1100 Broadway .... Nashville TN 37203-3116
615 259-8000 **Tennessean** 1100 Broadway .... Nashville TN 37203-3116

■ Television

615 259-9325 **WDCN-TV Ch 8 (PBS)** 161 Rains Ave .... Nashville TN 37203-5330
615 259-2200 **WKRN-TV Ch 2 (ABC)** 441 Murfreesboro Rd .... Nashville TN 37210-2878
615 749-2244 **WSMV-TV Ch 4 (NBC)** 5700 Knob Rd .... Nashville TN 37209-4596
615 244-5000 **WTVF-TV Ch 5 (CBS)** 474 James Robertson Pkwy .... Nashville TN 37219-1298

■ Radio

615 244-9533 **WKDF-FM 103.3 MHz (AOR-ABC)** 506 2nd Ave S .... Nashville TN 37210-2002
615 256-0555 **WLAC-AM 1510 kHz (N/T-CBS)** 10 Music Cir E .... Nashville TN 37203-4338
615 259-6004 **WPLN-FM 90.3 MHz (Clas-NPR)** 222 8th Ave N .... Nashville TN 37203-3502
615 664-2400 **WSIX-FM 97.9 MHz (Ctry)** 21 Music Sq W .... Nashville TN 37203-3203
615 256-6556 **WYHY-FM 107 MHz (CHR)** 810 Division St .... Nashville TN 37203-4109
615 259-9393 **WZEZ-FM 92.9 MHz (AC)** 504 Rosedale Ave .... Nashville TN 37211-2028

Local Attractions & Special Events

■ Sports

615 726-1818 **Nashville Motor Raceway** Wedgewood Ave .... Nashville TN 37204-0000
615 242-4371 **Nashville Sounds** 534 Chestnut St Herschel Greer Stadium ..... Nashville TN 37203-4800

■ Special Events

615 889-7503 **International Country Music Fan Fair** (June 10-16)

■ Local Attractions

615 356-0501 **Belle Meade Mansion** Harding Rd & Leake Ave .... Nashville TN 37205-9998
615 256-1639 **Country Music Hall of Fame & Museum** 4 Music Sq E .... Nashville TN 37203-4398
615 889-3060 **Grand Ole Opry** 2808 Opryland Dr .... Nashville TN 37214-1209
615 889-2941 **Hermitage** 4580 Rachel's Ln .... Hermitage TN 37076-1344
615 889-6611 **Opryland USA** 2802 Opryland Dr .... Nashville TN 37214-1296

New Orleans

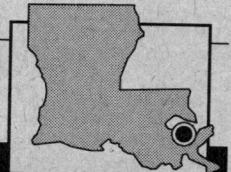

LOUISIANA   **504**

Important Phone Numbers

AAA	504 838-7500
American Express	504 586-8201
Better Business Bureau	504 581-6222
City Hall	504 586-4311
Emergency	911
Time	504 529-6111
Weather	504 465-9212

■ Travel Information

504 527-6900   **Chamber of Commerce** 301 Camp St .... New Orleans LA   70130-2865
504 566-5011   **Tourist & Convention Commission** 1520 Sugar Bowl Dr .... New Orleans LA   70112-1255
504 566-5031   **Visitor Information** 529 Saint Ann St .... New Orleans LA   70116-3318

Travel

■ Airport

504 464-0831   **New Orleans International Airport** 14 miles NW of city (approx 20 minutes)

■ Airport Transportation

504 737-9611   **Louisiana Transit Co** $1.10 fare to downtown
504 469-4555   **Rhodes Transportation Service** $7 fare to downtown
           Taxi $18 fare to downtown

■ Scheduled Airlines

American	504 523-2188	Pan Am	800 221-1111
Aviateca	504 522-1010	Southwest	504 523-5683
Continental	504 581-2965	TACA International	504 466-6913
Delta	504 529-2431	Tan-Sahsa Honduras Airlines	504 464-1212
Eastern	504 524-4211	TWA	504 529-2585
LACSA	504 464-0182	United	800 241-6522
Midway	800 621-5700	USAir	504 566-7554
Northwest	800 225-2525		

■ Car Rentals

Alamo	504 469-0532	National	504 466-4335
Avis	504 464-9511	Payless	504 466-3977
Budget	504 467-2277	Thrifty	504 467-8796
Dollar	504 468-3643	Value	504 469-2688
Hertz	504 468-3695		

■ Limo/Taxi

A Touch of Class Limousine Service	504 522-7565	United Cab	504 522-9771
Carey Limousine	504 523-5466	White Fleet Cabs	504 948-6605
Orleans Limousine	504 529-5226	Yellow Checker Cab	504 525-3311

■ Mass Transit

504 569-2700   **Mass Transit RTA** $.60 Base fare .... New Orleans LA   70112-0000

■ Rail/Bus

504 525-6075   **Greyhound/Trailways Bus Station** 1001 Loyola Ave .... New Orleans LA   70113-1929
504 528-1631   **Union Passenger Terminal** 1001 Loyola Ave .... New Orleans LA   70113-1929

Hotels

504 523-2222   **Bourbon Orleans Hotel** 717 Orleans Ave .... New Orleans LA   70116-3189
504 529-7111   **Fairmont Hotel at University Place** 123 Baronne St ...... New Orleans LA   70140-1018
504 522-1331   **Grenoble House** 329 Dauphine St .... New Orleans LA   70112-3129
504 525-5566   **Hotel Inter-Continental** 444 St Charles Ave .... New Orleans LA   70130-3171
504 561-1234   **Hyatt Regency Hotel** 500 Poydras Plaza .... New Orleans LA   70140-1012
504 581-3111   **Le Pavillon Hotel** 833 Poydras St .... New Orleans LA   70140-1019
504 561-5858   **Maison de Ville & the Audubon Cottages**
           727 Toulouse St .... New Orleans LA   70130-2188
504 586-8000   **Maison Dupuy** 1001 Toulouse St .... New Orleans LA   70112-3494
504 581-1000   **Marriott Hotel** 555 Canal St .... New Orleans LA   70140-1008
504 523-3341   **Monteleone Hotel** 214 Royal St .... New Orleans LA   70140-1011
504 561-0500   **New Orleans Hilton Riverside & Towers Hotel**
           2 Poydras St .... New Orleans LA   70140-0000
504 529-5333   **Omni Hotel** 621 Saint Louis St .... New Orleans LA   70130-2119
504 524-0581   **Pontchartrain Hotel** 2031 St Charles Ave .... New Orleans LA   70140-1009
504 586-0300   **Royal Sonesta Hotel** 300 Bourbon St .... New Orleans LA   70140-1014
504 525-2500   **Sheraton New Orleans Hotel** 500 Canal St .... New Orleans LA   70130-2396
504 523-6000   **Windsor Court Hotel** 300 Gravier St .... New Orleans LA   70140-1035

Restaurants

504 834-8583   **Andrea's** (Northern Italian) 3100 19th St .... Metairie LA   70002-0000
504 581-4422   **Antoine's** (French/Creole) 713 Saint Louis St .... New Orleans LA   70130-2182
504 523-5433   **Arnaud's** (French/Creole) 813 Bienville St .... New Orleans LA   70112-3191
504 524-3386   **Bon Ton Cafe** (Cajun) 401 Magazine St .... New Orleans LA   70130-2426
504 525-9711   **Brennan's Restaurant** (Creole) 417 Royal St .... New Orleans LA   70130-2191
504 581-3866   **Broussard's Restaurant & Picturesque Patio**
           (French/Creole) 819 Conti St .... New Orleans LA   70112-3497
504 482-4924   **Christian's** (French/Creole) 3835 Iberville St .... New Orleans LA   70119-5294
504 899-8221   **Commander's Palace** (Creole) 1403 Washington Ave .... New Orleans LA   70130-5798
504 522-7273   **Court of Two Sisters** (Creole) 613 Royal St .... New Orleans LA   70130-2181
504 833-8108   **Crozier's** (French) 3216 W Esplanade .... Metairie LA   70002-0000
504 528-9393   **Emeril's** (Creole) 800 Tchoupitoulas St .... New Orleans LA   70130-0000
504 525-2021   **Galatoire's** (French/Creole) 209 Bourbon St .... New Orleans LA   70130-2298
504 899-7397   **Gautreau's** (American) 1728 Soniat St .... New Orleans LA   70115-4919
504 523-6000   **Grill Room** (Nouvelle American) 300 Gravier St .... New Orleans LA   70130-2417
504 525-6500   **Henri** (French) 614 Canal St .... New Orleans LA   70130-2308
504 942-7500   **K-Paul's Louisiana Kitchen** (Cajun) 416 Chartres St ..... New Orleans LA   70130-2102
504 626-7662   **La Provence** (French) Hwy 190 .... Lacombe LA   70445-0000
504 362-4914   **Le Ruth's** (French) 636 Franklin St .... Gretna LA   70053-2198

504 523-9814   **Old New Orleans Creole & Cajun Cuisine**
           (Creole/Cajun) 611 Decatur St .... New Orleans LA   70130-1029
504 895-4877   **Pascal's Manale Restaurant** (Italian) 1838 Napoleon Ave ... New Orleans LA   70115-5540
504 486-0810   **Ruth's Chris Steak House** (Steak) 711 N Broad .... New Orleans LA   70119-4294
504 891-9822   **Upperline** (Creole) 1413 Upperline St .... New Orleans LA   70115-4037
504 524-2535   **Versailles** (Continental) 2100 St Charles Ave .... New Orleans LA   70130-5383

Goods & Services

■ Department Stores

504 831-6111   **Dillard's** 3301 Veterans Blvd .... Metairie LA   70002-0001
504 523-3311   **Krauss Department Store** 1201 Canal St .... New Orleans LA   70112-2629
504 592-5985   **Macy's** 1400 Poydras St .... New Orleans LA   70112-5100
504 524-2200   **Saks Fifth Avenue** 301 Canal St .... New Orleans LA   70130-1103

■ Banks

504 561-1371   **First National Bank of Commerce** 210 Baronne St ...... New Orleans LA   70112-1722
504 586-5552   **Hibernia National Bank** 313 Carondelet St .... New Orleans LA   70130-3178
504 586-7272   **Whitney National Bank** 228 St Charles Ave .... New Orleans LA   70130-2615

■ Messenger/Postal

Ace Delivery Service Inc	504 522-7810	Post Office	504 589-1111
Choice Courier	504 466-3111	Reliable Ron Courier Service	504 525-9269
Federal Express	800 238-5355	UPS	504 733-7250
New Orleans Messenger Service	504 586-0036	World Courier Inc	504 586-1416

■ Secretarial/Temp Services

504 529-1451   **Kelly Temporary Services Inc**
           1515 Poydras St Suite 2280 .... New Orleans LA   70112-0000
504 523-6381   **Manpower Temporary Services Inc**
           650 Poydras St Suite 1815 .... New Orleans LA   70130-6115
504 581-9401   **Olsten Temporary Services** 1515 Poydras St Suite 2060 .... New Orleans LA   70112-3741

Media

■ Newspapers/Magazines

504 831-3731   **New Orleans Magazine** 111 Veterans Blvd Suite 1810 .... Metairie LA   70005-0000
504 826-3279   **Times-Picayune** 3800 Howard Ave .... New Orleans LA   70140-1097

■ Television

504 527-0666   **WDSU-TV Ch 6 (NBC)** 520 Royal St .... New Orleans LA   70130-2114
504 486-6161   **WVUE-TV Ch 8 (ABC)** 1025 S Jefferson Davis Pkwy .... New Orleans LA   70125-1298
504 529-4444   **WWL-TV Ch 4 (CBS)** 1024 N Rampart St .... New Orleans LA   70116-2487
504 486-5511   **WYES-TV Ch 12** 916 Navarre Ave .... New Orleans LA   70124-2793

■ Radio

504 581-7002   **WEZB-FM 97.1 MHz (CHR)** 601 Loyola Ave .... New Orleans LA   70113-7115
504 581-1280   **WQUE-AM 1280 kHz (UC)** 1440 Canal St .... New Orleans LA   70112-2711
504 581-1280   **WQUE-FM 93 MHz (UC)** 1440 Canal St .... New Orleans LA   70112-2711
504 529-6376   **WWL-AM 870 kHz (N/T-CBS)** 1024 N Rampart St .... New Orleans LA   70116-2406
504 286-7000   **WWNO-FM 89.9 MHz (Misc-NPR)**
           University of New Orleans Lake Front Campus .... New Orleans LA   70148-0001
504 822-1945   **WYLD-AM 940 kHz (Rel)** 2228 Gravier St .... New Orleans LA   70119-7522

Local Attractions & Special Events

■ Sports

504 522-2600   **New Orleans Saints**
           1500 Poydras St Louisiana Superdome .... New Orleans LA   70115-0000

■ Special Events

504 566-5011   **Mardi Gras** French Quarter (February 12)

■ Local Attractions

504 523-4522   **Confederate Museum** 929 Camp St .... New Orleans LA   70130-0000
504 566-5011   **French Market** French Quarter .... New Orleans LA   70116-0000
504 588-9357   **Lafayette Cemetery** 1400 Washington Ave .... New Orleans LA   70130-0000
504 488-5488   **Longue Vue House & Garden** 7 Bamboo Rd .... New Orleans LA   70124-1007
504 568-6968   **Louisiana State Museum** 751 Chartres St .... New Orleans LA   70116-3289
504 566-5011   **Mississippi River Cruises** Canal & Toulouse St Wharfs ..... New Orleans LA   70130-0000
504 522-2841   **Preservation Hall** 726 Peter St .... New Orleans LA   70116-0000
504 522-1555   **Riverwalk** 1 Poydras St .... New Orleans LA   70130-1694
504 525-9585   **Saint Louis Cathedral** 615 Pere Antoine Alley Jackson Sq .. New Orleans LA   70116-3234

New York

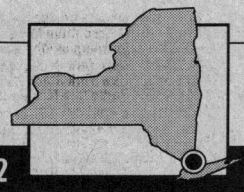

NEW YORK   **212**

Important Phone Numbers

AAA	212 586-1166	Emergency	911
American Express	212 687-3700	Poison Control Center	212 764-7667
Better Business Bureau	212 533-6200	Time	212 976-1616
City Hall	212 566-5700	Weather	212 976-1212

■ Travel Information

212 561-2020 **Chamber of Commerce** 200 Madison Ave 3rd Fl .... New York NY 10016-3901
212 397-8222 **Convention & Visitors Center** 2 Columbus Cir .... New York NY 10019-1890

Travel

■ Airport: Kennedy

718 656-4520 **John F Kennedy International Airport** 15 miles SE of city (approx 60 minutes)

■ Airport Transportation: Kennedy

718 632-0500 **Carey Airport Express** $9.50 fare to downtown
212 757-6840 **Grey Line Air Shuttle** $11 fare to downtown
516 228-8300 **New York Helicopter** $65 fare to downtown
             Taxi $20-30 fare to downtown

■ Scheduled Airlines: Kennedy

Aer Lingus	212 557-1110	Kuwait Airways	212 308-5454
Aerolineas Argentinas	800 333-0276	Lan Chile	800 735-5526
AeroMexico	718 686-6177	LOT Polish	212 869-1074
Air France	212 247-0100	LTU International	212 922-9033
Air India	212 751-6200	Lufthansa	718 895-1277
Air Jamaica	718 830-0303	Martinair Holland	516 627-8711
Alitalia	212 582-8900	Mexicana	800 531-7921
ALM-Antillean	212 545-8455	Nigeria	212 935-2700
American	212 431-1132	Northwest	212 563-7200
American Eagle	800 433-7300	Olympic	212 838-3600
Avianca	212 246-5241	Pakistan	212 370-9158
British Airways	800 247-9297	Pan Am	212 687-2600
BWIA	212 581-3200	Pan Am Express	800 221-1111
CAAC	212 371-9898	Qantas	212 764-0200
Cayman	800 422-9626	Royal Air Maroc	212 750-6071
China Airlines	800 227-5118	Royal Jordanian	212 949-0050
CSA Czechoslovak	212 682-5833	Sabena	212 247-8880
Delta	212 239-0700	SAS	800 221-2350
Dominicana	718 275-7676	Saudi Arabian	212 758-4727
Ecuatoriana	213 627-0615	SwissAir	718 995-8400
Egypt Air	718 997-7700	TAP Portugal	800 221-7370
El Al	212 768-9200	Tower Air	718 917-8500
Finnair	212 689-9300	TWA	212 290-2121
Iberia	305 381-9360	United	800 241-6522
Icelandair	212 967-8888	USAir	212 489-1460
Japan	212 838-4400	USAir Express	800 428-4253
JAT Yugoslavian	212 246-6401	Varig	212 682-3100
KLM	212 759-3600	Viasa	800 327-5454
Korean	212 326-5001		

■ Charter Airlines: Kennedy

Air Taxi Charter	201 751-1111	Jet Aviation EAF Charter	201 288-8400
Atlantic Jet Charter	201 288-7660	Northeast Airway	201 267-2450
Island Helicopter	718 895-1626	United Air Fleet World Jet Corp	516 585-0600

■ Airport: La Guardia

718 476-5000 **La Guardia Airport** 8 miles NE of city (approx 45 minutes)

■ Airport Transportation: La Guardia

718 632-0500 **Carey Airport Express** $7.50 fare to downtown
212 757-6840 **Giraldo Limousine Service** $11 fare to downtown
             Taxi $15-25 fare to downtown
718 335-1000 **Triboro Coach** $1.15 fare to downtown

■ Scheduled Airlines: La Guardia

Air Canada	212 869-1900	Mohawk Airlines	315 470-4400
American	212 431-1132	Northwest	718 767-6868
American Eagle	800 433-7300	Pan Am	212 687-2600
Continental	718 565-1100	Pan Am Express	800 221-1111
Delta	212 239-0700	TWA	212 290-2121
East Hampton Air	718 476-0334	United	800 241-6522
Eastern Express	212 986-5000	USAir	212 489-1460
Midway	800 621-5700	USAir Express	800 428-4253
Midwest Express	800 452-2022		

■ Charter Airlines: La Guardia

Air Taxi Charter	201 751-1111	Jet Aviation EAF Charter	201 288-8400
Atlantic Jet Charter	201 288-7660	Northeast Airway	201 267-2450

■ Airport: Newark

201 961-2000 **Newark International Airport** 16 miles SW of city (approx 45 minutes)

■ Airport Transportation: Newark

201 460-8444 **Airlink** $4 fare to downtown
201 460-8444 **New Jersey Transit Express Bus** $7 fare to downtown
212 964-6233 **Olympia Trails Airport Express** $7 fare to Grand Central Stn or Penn Stn
             Taxi Fare varies with destination

■ Scheduled Airlines: Newark

American	201 643-0340	TWA	201 623-0422
Continental	201 596-6000	United	201 624-1500
Delta	201 622-2111	USAir	201 624-8311
Midwest Express	800 452-2022	Virgin Atlantic	212 242-1330
Northwest	201 643-8555		

■ Charter Airlines: Newark

Air Taxi Charter	201 751-1111	Jet Aviation EAF Charter	201 288-8400
Atlantic Jet Charter	201 288-7660	Northeast Airway	201 267-2450

■ Car Rentals

Alamo	212 832-1228	Hertz	212 486-5935
Avis	212 977-3300	National	800 328-4567
Budget	718 656-6010	Thrifty	718 656-4600
Dollar	718 656-2400	Value	718 779-3300

■ Limo/Taxi

All City Radio Cabs	212 402-4747	Carey Limousine	212 599-1122
Bell Taxi	212 691-9191	Carmel Car & Limousine	212 662-9300
Bermuda Limousines	212 249-8400	Fugazy Limousine	212 661-0100

■ Mass Transit

718 330-1234 **New York City Transit Authority** $1 Base fare .... Brooklyn NY 11201-0000

■ Rail/Bus

212 560-7360 **Grand Central Terminal** 89 E 42nd St .... New York NY 10017-5503
212 560-7373 **Pennsylvania Station** 7th Ave & 32nd St .... New York NY 10001-0000
212 564-8484 **Port Authority Bus Terminal** 825 8th Ave .... New York NY 10019-7416

Hotels

212 840-6800	Algonquin Hotel 59 W 44th St	New York NY	10036-6638
212 247-7300	Dorset Hotel Downtown 30 W 54th St	New York NY	10019-5487
212 421-0900	Drake Swissotel 440 Park Ave	New York NY	10022-2684
212 883-1234	Grand Hyatt New York Park Ave & E 42nd St	New York NY	10017-0000
212 755-4000	Halloran House 525 Lexington Ave	New York NY	10017-1226
212 888-7000	Helmsley Palace Hotel 455 Madison Ave	New York NY	10022-6829
212 371-4000	Helmsley Park Lane Hotel 36 Central Pk S	New York NY	10019-1600
212 744-1600	Hotel Carlyle 35 E 76th St	New York NY	10021-1826
212 755-5900	Hotel Inter-Continental New York 111 E 48th St	New York NY	10017-1297
212 247-2200	Hotel Peninsula 700 5th Ave	New York NY	10019-0000
212 734-9100	Hotel Plaza Athenee 37 E 64th St	New York NY	10021-7023
212 581-4100	Howard Johnson's Hotel 851 8th Ave	New York NY	10019-6289
718 565-8900	La Guardia Marriott 102-05 Ditmars Blvd	East Elmhurst NY	11369-0000
212 752-7000	Loews Summit Hotel 569 Lexington Ave	New York NY	10022-0000
212 288-0800	Mayfair Regent Hotel 610 Park Ave	New York NY	10021-0000
212 686-0300	Morgan's 237 Madison Ave	New York NY	10016-2850
212 490-8900	New York Helmsley Hotel 212 E 42nd St	New York NY	10017-5857
212 586-7000	New York Hilton 1335 Ave of the Americas	New York NY	10019-6078
212 398-1900	New York Marriott Marquis Hotel 1535 Broadway	New York NY	10036-4017
212 247-0300	Nikko Essex House 160 Central Pk S	New York NY	10019-1502
212 753-5800	Omni Berkshire Place 21 E 52nd St	New York NY	10022-5389
212 765-1900	Park 51 Hotel 152 W 51st St	New York NY	10019-6890
212 245-5000	Parker Meridien Hotel 119 W 56th St	New York NY	10019-3802
212 355-0300	Pickwick Arms Hotel 230 E 51st St	New York NY	10022-6597
212 838-8000	Pierre Hotel 2 E 61st St	New York NY	10021-8402
212 759-3000	Plaza Hotel 768 5th Ave	New York NY	10019-1603
212 759-4100	Regency Hotel 540 Park Ave	New York NY	10021-7385
212 757-1900	Ritz-Carlton Hotel 112 Central Pk S	New York NY	10019-1564
212 755-5800	Saint Moritz on the Park 50 Central Pk S	New York NY	10019-1613
212 581-1000	Sheraton Centre Hotel & Towers 811 7th Ave	New York NY	10019-6002
212 685-7676	Sheraton Park Avenue Hotel 45 Park Ave	New York NY	10016-3495
212 355-2800	Sherry-Netherland Hotel 781 5th Ave	New York NY	10022-1046
212 288-5800	Stanhope 995 5th Ave	New York NY	10028-0125
212 355-3400	United Nations Plaza Hotel 1 United Nations Plaza	New York NY	10017-3575
212 938-9100	Vista International Hotel 3 World Trade Ctr	New York NY	10048-1001
212 355-3000	Waldorf-Astoria Hotel 301 Park Ave	New York NY	10022-6897
212 247-2700	Warwick Hotel 65 W 54th St	New York NY	10019-5488
212 535-2000	Westbury Hotel 15 E 69th St	New York NY	10021-4997

Restaurants

212 582-7200	21 Club (American) 21 W 52nd St	New York NY	10019-6181
212 684-2122	American Place (American) 2 Park Ave & 32nd St	New York NY	10016-0000
212 223-2900	Arcadia (American) 21 E 62nd St	New York NY	10021-7222
212 319-1660	Aureole (American/French) 34 E 61st St	New York NY	10021-0000
212 692-9292	Aurora (French) 60 E 49th St	New York NY	10017-1173
212 265-7770	Bellini (Italian) 777 7th Ave	New York NY	10019-6806
212 581-8888	Ben Benson's Steakhouse (Steak) 123 W 52nd St	New York NY	10019-6003
212 688-1999	Bice (Italian) 7 E 54th St	New York NY	10022-3106
212 758-8320	Box Tree (Continental) 250 E 49th St	New York NY	10017-1502
212 877-3500	Cafe des Artistes (Continental) 1 W 67th St	New York NY	10023-6200
212 940-8185	Cafe Pierre (French/Continental) 2 E 61st St	New York NY	10021-0000
212 938-1100	Cellar in the Sky (Continental) 1 World Trade Ctr 107th Fl	New York NY	10048-0202
212 697-2479	Christ Cella (Continental/Seafood) 160 E 46th	New York NY	10017-2697
212 758-1479	Felidia (Northern Italian) 243 E 58th St	New York NY	10022-1220
212 754-9494	Four Seasons (Continental) 99 E 52nd St	New York NY	10023-0000
212 245-5336	Gallagher's Steak House (American) 228 W 52nd St	New York NY	10019-5897
212 399-2358	Ginger Man (Continental) 51 W 64th St	New York NY	10023-6731
212 620-4020	Gotham Bar & Grill (American) 12 E 12th St	New York NY	10003-4428
212 490-6650	Grand Central Station Oyster Bar & Restaurant (Seafood) Grand Central Stn Lower Level	New York NY	10017-9998
212 459-9320	Hard Rock Cafe (American) 221 W 57th St	New York NY	10019-2181
212 355-3345	Hatsuhana (Japanese) 17 E 48th St	New York NY	10017-1065
212 753-8450	Il Nido (Italian) 251 E 53rd St	New York NY	10022-4801
212 832-9221	Il Vagabondo (Italian) 351 E 62nd St	New York NY	10021-8251
212 243-1680	John's (Pizza) 278 Bleecker St	New York NY	10014-4104
212 586-4252	La Caravelle (French) 33 W 55th St	New York NY	10019-4902
212 688-6525	La Cote Basque (French) 5 E 55th St	New York NY	10022-3198
212 752-1495	La Grenouille (French) 3 E 52nd St	New York NY	10022-5335
212 489-1515	Le Bernardin (French/Seafood) 155 W 51st St	New York NY	10019-6019
212 751-2931	Le Chantilly (French) 106 E 57th St	New York NY	10022-2601
212 794-9292	Le Cirque (French) 58 E 65th St	New York NY	10021-7087
212 755-6244	Le Perigord (French) 405 E 52nd St	New York NY	10022-6401
212 752-2225	Lutece (French) 249 E 50th St	New York NY	10022-7791
212 586-5151	Mamma Leone's (Italian) 261 W 44th St	New York NY	10036-3907
212 371-7777	Manhattan Ocean Club (Seafood) 57 W 58th St	New York NY	10019-1630
201 731-2360	Manor The (Continental) 111 Prospect Ave	West Orange NJ	07052-4202
212 751-5111	Maxim's (French) 680 Madison Ave	New York NY	10021-7246

212 355-9020	**Nippon** (Japanese) 155 E 52nd St	New York NY	10022-6029
212 242-9040	**Old Homestead** (Steak) 56 9th Ave	New York NY	10011-4994
212 245-4850	**Palio** (Italian) 151 W 51st St	New York NY	10019-6024
212 687-2953	**Palm** (Steak/Seafood) 837 2nd Ave	New York NY	10017-4303
212 288-2391	**Parioli Romanissimo** (Italian) 24 E 81st St	New York NY	10028-0226
212 682-8660	**Pen & Pencil** (Continental/Seafood/Steak) 205 E 45th St	New York NY	10017-3301
212 675-6777	**Prix Fixe** (American) 18 W 18th St	New York NY	10011-0000
212 593-1221	**Quilted Giraffe** (Nouvelle American) 550 Madison Ave	New York NY	10022-3211
212 832-1565	**Restaurant Lafayette** (French) 65 E 56 St	New York NY	10022-2509
212 265-0947	**Russian Tea Room** (Russian/Continental) 150 W 57th St	New York NY	10019-3377
212 371-8844	**Shun Lee Palace** (Chinese) 155 E 55th St	New York NY	10022-4038
212 861-8080	**Sign of the Dove** (American) 1110 3rd Ave	New York NY	10021-6693
212 753-1530	**Smith & Wollensky** (Steak/Seafood) 201 E 49th St	New York NY	10017-1501
212 873-3200	**Tavern on the Green** (Steak/Seafood) 67th St & Central Pk W	New York NY	10023-6093
212 683-3333	**Water Club** (Seafood) 500 E 30th St	New York NY	10016-0000
212 938-1111	**Windows on the World** (International) 1 World Trade Ctr 107th Fl	New York NY	10048-0202

212 877-1800	**Lincoln Center for the Performing Arts** 140 W 65th St	New York NY	10023-6969
212 535-7710	**Metropolitan Museum of Art** 5th Ave & 82nd St	New York NY	10028-0113
212 708-9400	**Museum of Modern Art** 11 W 53rd St	New York NY	10019-5498
212 221-7676	**New York Public Library** 5th Ave & 42nd St	New York NY	10018-0000
212 656-5167	**New York Stock Exchange** 20 Broad St	New York NY	10005-2601
212 247-4777	**Radio City Music Hall** 1260 Ave of the Americas	New York NY	10020-1797
212 753-2261	**Saint Patrick's Cathedral** 5th Ave & 50th St	New York NY	10022-0000
212 360-3500	**Solomon R Guggenheim Museum** 1071 5th Ave	New York NY	10128-0173
212 669-9400	**South Street Seaport** 207 Front St	New York NY	10038-2198
212 363-3200	**Statue of Liberty National Monument** Liberty Island	New York NY	10004-1467
212 397-8222	**Times Square/Broadway Information**	New York NY	
212 963-1234	**United Nations** 1st Ave & 42nd St UN Headquarters	New York NY	10017-0000
212 570-3600	**Whitney Museum of American Art** 945 Madison Ave	New York NY	10021-2790
212 466-7377	**World Trade Center** West & Church Sts Tower 2	New York NY	10048-0000

Goods & Services

■ Department Stores

212 753-7300	**Bergdorf Goodman** 754 5th Ave	New York NY	10019-2581
212 705-2000	**Bloomingdale's** 1000 3rd Ave	New York NY	10022-1299
212 836-4867	**Bonwit Teller** 1633 Broadway 40th Fl	New York NY	10019-6708
212 543-6420	**Loehmann's** Broadway & W 236th St	Riverdale NY	10463-0000
212 391-3344	**Lord & Taylor** 424 5th Ave	New York NY	10018-2771
212 695-4400	**Macy's** 151 W 34th St	New York NY	10001-2101
212 753-4000	**Saks Fifth Avenue** 611 5th Ave	New York NY	10022-6899

■ Banks

212 635-1111	**Bank of New York** 1 Wall St	New York NY	10015-0000
212 250-2500	**Bankers Trust Co** 280 Park Ave	New York NY	10017-1270
212 552-2222	**Chase Manhattan Bank NA** 1 Chase Manhattan Plaza	New York NY	10081-0001
212 310-6161	**Chemical Bank** 277 Park Ave	New York NY	10172-0087
212 559-1000	**Citibank NA** 399 Park Ave	New York NY	10043-0001
212 286-6000	**Manufacturers Hanover Trust Co** 270 Park Ave	New York NY	10017-0000
212 483-2323	**Morgan Guaranty Trust Co of New York** 23 Wall St	New York NY	10005-1915
212 978-5000	**Security Pacific National Trust** 2 Rector St 9th Fl	New York NY	10006-1897

■ Messenger/Postal

AAA Couriers International	718 361-9468	
Airline Delivery Services Corp	212 687-5145	
ARC Trucking & Messenger Corp	212 741-1400	
Archer Services Inc	212 563-8800	
Bullit Courier	212 952-8500	
Choice Courier Systems Inc	212 683-6411	
Columbus Messenger Service Inc	212 532-8440	
Cycle Service	212 925-5900	
Federal Express	800 238-5355	
Good Rush Messenger Service	212 840-6300	
Immediate Service Systems Inc	212 989-5600	
Metro Express	212 765-2720	
Minute Men Messenger Svc Inc	212 354-6555	
National Messenger Service	212 599-1010	
Post Office	212 967-8585	
Rapid Couriers Ltd	212 594-0900	
Service Messenger	212 391-1900	
Speedmore Messenger Service	212 947-2662	
UPS	212 560-6029	

■ Secretarial/Temp Services

212 221-6500	**Accountemps** 522 5th Ave	New York NY	10036-7601
212 949-8555	**Kelly Services Inc** 420 Lexington Ave Suite 204	New York NY	10170-0197
212 557-9110	**Manpower Temporary Services Inc** 100 E 42nd St 17th Fl	New York NY	10017-5613

Media

■ Newspapers/Magazines

212 880-0700	**New York Magazine** 755 2nd Ave	New York NY	10017-5998
212 815-8000	**New York Post** 210 South St	New York NY	10002-7889
212 556-1234	**New York Times** 229 W 43rd St	New York NY	10036-3959
212 416-2000	**Wall Street Journal** 200 Liberty St	New York NY	10281-1099

■ Television

212 456-7777	**WABC-TV Ch 7 (ABC)** 77 W 66th St	New York NY	10019-0000
212 975-4321	**WCBS-TV Ch 2 (CBS)** 51 W 52nd St	New York NY	10019-6101
212 664-4444	**WNBC-TV Ch 4 (NBC)** 30 Rockefeller Plaza	New York NY	10112-0035
212 560-2000	**WNET-TV Ch 13 (PBS)** 356 W 58th St	New York NY	10019-1896

■ Radio

201 867-5000	**WHTZ-FM 100.3 MHz (CHR)** 333 Meadowlands Pkwy	Secaucus NJ	07094-1801
212 397-1010	**WINS-AM 1010 kHz (N/T-ABC)** 888 7th Ave	New York NY	10106-0201
212 669-7800	**WNYC-FM 93.9 MHz (Clas-NPR)** 1 Centre St	New York NY	10007-2304
212 642-4500	**WOR-AM 710 kHz (N/T)** 1440 Broadway	New York NY	10018-2390
201 345-9300	**WPAT-FM 93.1 MHz (B/EZ)** 1396 Broad St	Clifton NJ	07013-4222
212 642-4300	**WRKS-FM 98.7 MHz (UC)** 1440 Broadway	New York NY	10018-2301

Local Attractions & Special Events

■ Sports

201 935-8222	**New York Giants** Giants Stadium	East Rutherford NJ	07073-0000
516 794-4100	**New York Islanders** Nassau Coliseum	Uniondale NY	11553-0000
212 421-6600	**New York Jets** Giants Stadium		
212 563-8300	**New York Knicks** 7th Ave & 32nd St Madison Square Garden	New York NY	10001-0000
718 507-8499	**New York Mets** Roosevelt Ave Shea Stadium	New York NY	11368-0000
212 563-8300	**New York Rangers** 7th Ave & 32nd St Madison Square Garden	New York NY	10001-0000
212 293-6000	**New York Yankees** Yankee Stadium	Bronx NY	10451-0000

■ Special Events

212 695-4400	**Macy's Thanksgiving Day Parade** (November 28)
212 860-4455	**New York Marathon** (November 3)

■ Local Attractions

212 769-5000	**American Museum of Natural History** Central Pk W & 79th St	New York NY	10024-5192
212 367-1010	**Bronx Zoo**	Bronx NY	10460-0000
212 247-7800	**Carnegie Hall** 154 W 57th St	New York NY	10019-3321
212 397-3156	**Central Park**	New York NY	10001-0000
212 860-6868	**Cooper-Hewitt Museum (Smithsonian Institution)** 2 E 91st St	New York NY	10128-0669
212 736-3100	**Empire State Building** 5th Ave & 34th St	New York NY	10118-0000
212 666-1640	**General Grant National Memorial** Riverside Dr & 122nd St	New York NY	10027-0000
212 397-8222	**Greenwich Village/Soho Information**	New York NY	10019-0000

Norfolk

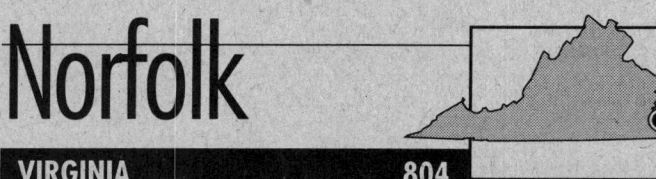

VIRGINIA   804

Important Phone Numbers

AAA	804 622-5634	Emergency	911
American Express	804 622-6691	Poison Control Center	804 489-5288
Better Business Bureau	804 627-5651	Time	804 622-9311
City Hall	804 441-2000	Weather	804 666-1212

■ Travel Information

804 622-2312 **Chamber of Commerce** 420 Bank St .... Norfolk VA 23510-2421
804 441-5266 **Convention & Visitor Bureau** 236 E Plume St .... Norfolk VA 23510-1787

Travel

■ Airport

804 857-3351 **Norfolk International Airport** 9 miles NE of city (approx 15 minutes)

■ Airport Transportation

804 857-1231 **Airport Limousine** $7.50 fare to downtown
                   Taxi $10 fare to downtown

■ Scheduled Airlines

American	804 622-2643	Pan Am	800 221-1111
Delta	800 221-1212	TWA	804 461-6116
Eastern	804 625-0316	United	804 627-7411
Northwest	800 225-2525	USAir	804 622-4350

■ Charter Airlines

Nasworthy Aviation	804 460-2219	Piedmont Aviation	804 857-3309

■ Car Rentals

Ace	804 855-1922	Hertz	804 857-1261
Avis	804 855-1944	Holiday-Payless	804 853-6277
Budget	804 855-1038	National	804 857-5385
Dollar	804 855-1988	Thrifty	804 857-0111

■ Limo/Taxi

Black & White Taxi	804 489-7777	Norfolk Checker	804 855-6611
Celebrity Limousine	804 853-5466	Yellow Cab	804 622-3232
Elite Limousine	804 424-6646		

■ Mass Transit

804 623-3222 **Tidewater Regional Transit** $.80 Base fare .... Norfolk VA 23510-0000

■ Rail/Bus

804 627-5641 **Greyhound/Trailways Carolina Coach** 701 Monticello Ave .... Norfolk VA 23510-2508
804 422-0444 **Norfolk Station (Holiday Inn)** 700 Monticello Ave .... Norfolk VA 23510-0000

Hotels

804 623-5700 **Comfort Inn Town Point** 930 E Virginia Beach Blvd .... Norfolk VA 23504-3226
804 622-6682 **Days Hotel Waterside** 345 Granby St .... Norfolk VA 23510-1926
804 826-4500 **Holiday Inn Newport News** 6128 Jefferson Ave .... Newport News VA 23605-1592
804 583-2621 **Holiday Sands Motel** 1330 E Ocean View Ave .... Norfolk VA 23503-2208
804 466-8000 **Norfolk Airport Hilton** 1500 N Military Hwy .... Norfolk VA 23502-1813
804 622-6664 **Omni International Hotel** 777 Waterside Dr .... Norfolk VA 23510-2102
804 461-1081 **Ramada Inn Newtown** 6360 Newtown Rd .... Norfolk VA 23502-4883

Restaurants

804 496-3348 **Coastal Grill** (Bistro) 1427 N Great Neck Rd .... Virginia Beach VA 23454-0000
804 623-3663 **Dumbwaiter The** (Bistro) 128 College Pl .... Norfolk VA 23510-0000
804 622-3966 **Freemason Abbey Restaurant**
                   (American) 209 W Freemason St .... Norfolk VA 23510-1213
804 422-2323 **Ice House** (Continental) 604 Norfolk Ave .... Virginia Beach VA 23451-4419
804 422-6464 **Il Giardino** (Italian) 910 Atlantic Ave .... Virginia Beach VA 23451-3530
804 623-7202 **Le Charlieu** (French) 112 College Pl .... Norfolk VA 23510-0000
804 428-9851 **Lighthouse The** (Steak/Seafood) 1st St & Atlantic Ave ..... Virginia Beach VA 23451-0000
804 481-0003 **Lynnhaven Fish House** (Seafood) 2350 Starfish Rd .... Virginia Beach VA 23451-1216
804 627-6600 **Phillips** (Seafood) 333 Waterside Dr .... Norfolk VA 23510-3200
804 623-0778 **Shine Shine Palace** (Chinese) 333 Waterside Dr .... Norfolk VA 23510-3202
804 583-4659 **Ships Cabin** (Seafood) 4110 E Ocean View Ave .... Norfolk VA 23518-1616
804 623-3872 **Stripes** (American) 210 York St .... Norfolk VA 23510-1514
804 627-6130 **Szechuan Garden** (Chinese) 123 W Charlotte St .... Norfolk VA 62410-0000
804 422-1511 **Westley's** (American) 500 Pinewood Dr .... Virginia Beach VA 23451-4425

Goods & Services

■ Department Stores

804 622-2317 **Altschul's** 427 Granby St .... Norfolk VA 23510-1928
804 459-2000 **Smith & Welton** 880 N Military Hwy .... Norfolk VA 23502-3705

■ Banks

804 628-0400 **Dominion Bank** 999 Waterside Dr .... Norfolk VA 23510-3312
804 628-6600 **First Virginia Bank of Tidewater** 555 Main St .... Norfolk VA 23510-0000
804 441-4000 **Sovran Bank** 1 Commercial Pl .... Norfolk VA 23510-2103

■ Messenger/Postal

Commercial Courier Express	804 855-6562	Post Office	804 629-2194
Federal Express	800 238-5355	UPS	800 552-3908
Metro Courier Inc	804 625-1311		

■ Secretarial/Temp Services

804 461-5435 **Kelly Services** 6160 Kempsville Cir Suite 303B .... Norfolk VA 23502-4103
804 490-0904 **Olsten Temporary Services**
                   4452 Corporation Ln Suite, 123 .... Virginia Beach VA 23462-3173

Media

■ Newspapers/Magazines

804 446-2000 **Ledger-Star** 150 W Brambleton Ave .... Norfolk VA 23510-2018
804 422-5577 **Virginian** 508 N Birdneck Rd Suite A .... Virginia Beach VA 23458-0000
804 446-2000 **Virginian-Pilot** 150 W Brambleton Ave .... Norfolk VA 23510-2075

■ Television

804 393-1010 **WAVY-TV Ch 10 (NBC)** 300 Wavy St .... Portsmouth VA 23704-5200
804 489-9476 **WHRO-TV Ch 15 (PBS)** 5200 Hampton Blvd .... Norfolk VA 23508-1598
804 446-1000 **WTKR-TV Ch 3 (CBS)** 720 Boush St .... Norfolk VA 23510-1583
804 625-1313 **WVEC-TV Ch 13 (ABC)** 613 Woodis Ave .... Norfolk VA 23510-1017

■ Radio

804 424-1050 **WCMS-FM 100.5 MHz (Ctry-ABC)**
                   900 Commonwealth Pl .... Virginia Beach VA 23464-4517
804 622-6771 **WFOG-FM 92.9 MHz (B/EZ)** 215 Brooke Ave .... Norfolk VA 23510-1234
804 489-9484 **WHRO-FM 89.5 MHz (Clas-NPR)** 5200 Hampton Blvd .... Norfolk VA 23508-1598
804 623-9667 **WNOR-AM 1230 kHz (AOR)** 801 Boush St .... Norfolk VA 23510-1510
804 623-9667 **WNOR-FM 98.7 MHz (AOR)** 801 Boush St .... Norfolk VA 23510-1510
804 497-1067 **WNVZ-FM 104.5 MHz (CHR)** 5555 Greenwich Rd .... Virginia Beach VA 23462-6542

Local Attractions & Special Events

■ Sports

804 461-5600 **Tidewater Tides** 6000 Northampton Blvd .... Norfolk VA 23502-5509

■ Special Events

804 627-5329 **Harborfest** (June 7-9)

■ Local Attractions

804 622-1211 **Chrysler Museum** Olney Rd & Mowbray Arch .... Norfolk VA 23510-1587
804 441-2965 **General Douglas MacArthur Memorial**
                   City Hall Ave & Bank St MacArthur Sq .... Norfolk VA 23510-0000
804 423-2052 **Hermitage Foundation Museum** 7637 North Shore Rd .... Norfolk VA 23505-0000
804 622-1211 **Moses Myers Home** Freemason & Bank Sts .... Norfolk VA 23510-0000
804 441-5385 **Norfolk Botanical Gardens** Airport Rd .... Norfolk VA 23518-5802
804 444-7955 **Norfolk Naval Station** 9809 Hampton Blvd .... Norfolk VA 23511-0000
804 425-7511 **Virginia Beach Tourist Information** 19th & Pacific Ave .... Virginia Beach VA 23451-3362
804 627-3300 **Waterside Market** 333 Waterside Dr .... Norfolk VA 23510-3202

Oakland
CALIFORNIA　　415

Important Phone Numbers

AAA	415 654-8454	Emergency	911
American Express	415 452-3044	Poison Control Center	415 476-6600
Better Business Bureau	415 839-5900	Time/Temp	415 936-1212
City Hall	415 444-2489	Weather	415 936-1212

■ Travel Information
415 874-4800　**Chamber of Commerce** 475 14th St .... Oakland CA 94612-1903
415 839-9000　**Convention & Visitors Bureau** 1000 Broadway Suite 200 .... Oakland CA 94607-4040

Travel

■ Airport
415 577-4000　**Oakland International Airport** 10 miles SE of city (approx 20 minutes)

■ Airport Transportation
415 839-2882　**AC Transit** $.75 fare to downtown
415 632-5506　**Air-BART Shuttle Express** $1 Fare to Oakland Coliseum
415 465-2278　**Bay Area Rapid Transit (BART)** $.80 fare to downtown
　　　　　　　Taxi $16-17 fare to downtown

■ Scheduled Airlines
Alaska	415 839-5686	Sunworld	800 722-4222
America West	800 247-5692	United	415 891-9497
American	415 836-6164	United Express	415 891-9497
Delta	415 626-9313	USAir	415 444-7363

■ Charter Airlines
Helicopters Unlimited	415 632-9422	KaiserAir	415 569-9622

■ Car Rentals
Avis	415 562-9000	Hertz	415 568-1177
Budget	415 875-7540	National	415 632-2225
Dollar	415 638-2750	Thrifty	415 568-1220

■ Limo/Taxi
Friendly Cab	415 536-3000	Taxi Taxi	415 444-1177
Goodwill Cab	415 836-1234		

■ Mass Transit
415 839-2882　**AC Transit** $.75 Base fare .... Oakland CA 94612-0000
415 465-2278　**Bay Area Rapid Transit (BART)** $.80 Base fare .... Oakland CA 94607-0000

■ Rail/Bus
415 834-3070　**Greyhound/Trailways Bus Station** 2103 San Pablo Ave .... Oakland CA 94612-1308
800 872-7245　**Oakland Railroad Station** 1701 Wood St .... Oakland CA 94607-0000

Hotels
415 436-0103　**Apple Inn** 1801 Embarcadero .... Oakland CA 94606-5224
415 843-3000　**Claremont Resort Hotel** 41 Tunnel Rd .... Berkeley CA 94705-2429
415 568-1880　**Days Inn Oakland Airport** 8350 Edes Ave .... Oakland CA 94621-1363
415 658-9300　**Holiday Inn Bay Bridge** 1800 Powell St .... Emeryville CA 94608-1898
415 562-5311　**Holiday Inn Oakland Airport** 500 Hegenberger Rd .... Oakland CA 94621-1394
415 562-6100　**Hyatt Oakland International** 455 Hegenberger Rd .... Oakland CA 94621-1499
415 893-1234　**Hyatt Regency** 1001 Broadway .... Oakland CA 94607-4077
415 635-5000　**Oakland Airport Hilton** 1 Hegenberger Rd .... Oakland CA 94621-1405
415 635-5300　**Park Plaza Hotel** 150 Hegenberger Rd .... Oakland CA 94621-1422

Restaurants
415 849-0526　**4th Street Grill** (Continental) 1820 4th St .... Berkeley CA 94710-1911
415 655-6004　**Bay Wolf Restaurant** (Mediterranean) 3853 Piedmont Ave .... Oakland CA 94611-5351
415 652-4442　**Broadway Terrace Cafe** (California) 5891 Broadway Terr .... Oakland CA 94618-2001
415 444-7373　**Gingerbread House** (Cajun) 741 5th St .... Oakland CA 94607-3019
415 839-6950　**Gulf Coast Oyster Bar**
　　　　　　　(Cajun/Creole/Seafood) 736 Washington St .... Oakland CA 94607-3925
415 465-2188　**Il Piscatore** (Italian/Seafood) 57 Jack London Sq .... Oakland CA 94607-3728
415 893-6206　**La Brasserie** (French) 542 Grand Ave .... Oakland CA 94610-3515
415 836-2519　**Oyster Reef** (Seafood/Thai) 1000 Embarcadero .... Oakland CA 94606-5133
415 444-3456　**Scott's Seafood Grill & Bar** (Seafood) 73 Jack London Sq .... Oakland CA 94607-3728
415 763-1310　**Seafood Conspiracy** (Seafood) 365 19th St .... Oakland CA 94612-3424
415 652-9200　**Yoshi's Japanese Restaurant**
　　　　　　　(Japanese) 6030 Claremont Ave .... Oakland CA 94618-1223

Goods & Services

■ Department Stores
415 891-5000　**Emporium** Broadway & 20th St .... Oakland CA 94612-0000
415 444-7722　**I Magnin** Broadway & 20th St .... Oakland CA 94612-0000

■ Banks
415 763-8486　**Bank of Oakland** 360 14th St .... Oakland CA 94612-3211
415 464-1830　**Wells Fargo Bank** 3450 Fruitvale Ave .... Oakland CA 94602-2376

■ Messenger/Postal
Aero Special Delivery	415 982-1303	Post Office	415 874-8723
ASAP Inc	415 839-4225	Same Day Attorney Service	415 420-6981
Capitol Courier Services	415 839-9255	United Couriers Inc	415 569-1717
Federal Express	415 568-2380	UPS	916 383-1119
PDQ	415 834-7900		

■ Secretarial/Temp Services
415 444-8964　**Kelly Temporary Services Inc** 300 Lakeside Dr Suite 106 .... Oakland CA 94612-3534
415 465-3131　**Manpower Temporary Services** 1820 Franklin St .... Oakland CA 94612-3410
415 540-0550　**Olsten Temporary Services** 2150 Shattuck Ave Suite 204 .... Berkeley CA 94704-0000

Media

■ Newspapers/Magazines
415 420-1091　**Lifestyle** 421 W MacArthur Blvd .... Oakland CA 94609-2808
415 645-2000　**Tribune** 409 13th St .... Oakland CA 94612-2637

■ Television
415 954-7777　**KGO-TV Ch 7 (ABC)** 900 Front St .... San Francisco CA 94111-1427
408 298-3636　**KICU-TV Ch 36** 1585 Schallenberger Rd .... San Jose CA 95131-2434
415 362-5550　**KPIX-TV Ch 5 (CBS)** 855 Battery St .... San Francisco CA 94111-1597
415 864-2000　**KQED-TV Ch 9 (PBS)** 500 8th St .... San Francisco CA 94103-4492
415 441-4444　**KRON-TV Ch 4 (NBC)** 1001 Van Ness Ave .... San Francisco CA 94109-6982
415 834-1212　**KTVU-TV Ch 2 (Fox)** 2 Jack London Sq .... Oakland CA 94607-3727

■ Radio
415 788-5225　**KABL-FM 98.1 MHz (AC)** 1025 Battery St .... San Francisco CA 94111-1277
415 648-1177　**KALW-FM 91.7 MHz (Jazz-NPR)** 2905 21st St .... San Francisco CA 94110-2718
415 954-8100　**KGO-AM 810 kHz (N/T-ABC)** 900 Front St .... San Francisco CA 94111-1427
415 391-1061　**KMEL-FM 106.1 MHz (CHR)** 55 Francisco St Suite 400 ..... San Francisco CA 94133-2122
415 765-4000　**KRQR-FM 97.3 MHz (AOR)** 1 Embarcadero Ctr 32nd Fl ..... San Francisco CA 94111-3607

Local Attractions & Special Events

■ Sports
415 638-6000　**Golden State Warriors**
　　　　　　　Oakland Alameda County Coliseum Arena .... Oakland CA 94621-1996
415 638-4900　**Oakland Athletics** Oakland Alameda Coliseum Complex .... Oakland CA 94621-0000

■ Local Attractions
415 562-0328　**Dunsmuir House & Gardens** 2960 Peralta Oaks Ct .... Oakland CA 94605-5320
415 893-7884　**Jack London's Waterfront** Embarcadero & Webster Sts .... Oakland CA 94607-3761
415 444-3807　**Lake Merritt** 1520 Lakeside Dr .... Oakland CA 94612-4521
707 644-4000　**Marine World Africa USA** Marine World Pkwy .... Vallejo CA 94589-0000
415 834-2413　**Oakland Museum Complex** 10th & Oak St .... Oakland CA 94607-4892
415 893-2300　**Paramount Theatre of the Arts** 2025 Broadway .... Oakland CA 94612-2303

Oklahoma City
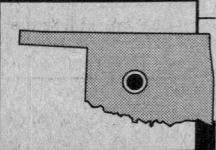

OKLAHOMA · 405

——— Important Phone Numbers ———

AAA	405 943-9922	Emergency-Police	405 231-2121
American Express	405 842-7636	Poison Control Center	405 271-5454
Better Business Bureau	405 235-5954	Time/Temp	405 599-1234
City Hall	405 297-2011	Weather	405 360-8106
Emergency-Fire	405 235-1313		

■ Travel Information

405 278-8900 **Chamber of Commerce** 1 Santa Fe Plaza .... Oklahoma City OK 73102-9083
405 278-8912 **Convention & Tourism Bureau** 4 Santa Fe Plaza .... Oklahoma City OK 73102-9027

——— Travel ———

■ Airport

405 681-5311 **Will Rogers World Airport** 10 miles SW of city (approx 20 minutes)

■ Airport Transportation

405 681-3311 **Airport Express** $9 fare to downtown
Taxi $12 fare to downtown

■ Scheduled Airlines

American	405 235-2471	Southwest	405 235-1221
Continental	800 525-0280	TWA	405 232-3511
Delta	405 235-3374	United	800 241-6522
Northwest	800 225-2525		

■ Charter Airlines

Oklahoma Executive Jet 405 681-3000

■ Car Rentals

Agency	405 681-2923	Hertz	405 681-2341
Avis	405 685-7781	National	405 685-7726
Budget	405 681-4671	Snappy	405 942-6105
Dollar	405 681-0151	Thrifty	405 682-5433

■ Limo/Taxi

ABC Cab	405 232-2402	Regency Limousine Service	405 722-1312
King Limousine	405 787-9475	Royal Coach Ltd	405 685-5466
Northside Cab	405 525-5526	Yellow Cab	405 232-6161

■ Mass Transit

405 235-7433 **Masstrans** $.75 Base fare .... Oklahoma City OK 73104-0000

■ Rail/Bus

405 235-6425 **Union Bus Station** 427 W Sheridan Ave .... Oklahoma City OK 73102-5098

——— Hotels ———

405 677-0521 **Days Inn** 2616 S I-35 .... Oklahoma City OK 73129-0000
405 946-0741 **Days Inn Northwest** 2801 NW 39th St .... Oklahoma City OK 73112-3703
405 682-6000 **Embassy Suites Hotel** 1815 S Meridian Ave .... Oklahoma City OK 73108-1796
405 947-7681 **Hilton Inn West** 401 S Meridian Ave .... Oklahoma City OK 73108-1099
405 942-8511 **Holiday Inn Airport West** 801 S Meridian Ave .... Oklahoma City OK 73108-1670
405 528-2741 **Lincoln Plaza Inn** 4445 N Lincoln Blvd .... Oklahoma City OK 73105-5109
405 672-2341 **Plaza Inn** 3200 S Prospect Ave .... Oklahoma City OK 73129-6699
405 631-3321 **Ramada Inn Airport South** 6800 S I-35 .... Oklahoma City OK 73149-0000
405 235-2780 **Sheraton Century Center** 1 N Broadway Ave .... Oklahoma City OK 73102-9201
405 848-4782 **Waterford Hotel** 6300 Waterford Blvd .... Oklahoma City OK 73118-1123

——— Restaurants ———

405 686-0288 **Aloha Garden** (Chinese/American) 2219 SW 74th St .... Oklahoma City OK 73159-3931
405 947-8484 **Applewoods Restaurant** (Regional) 4301 SW 3rd .... Oklahoma City OK 73108-1023
405 236-0416 **Cattlemans Cafe** (Steak/American) 1309 S Agnew Ave .... Oklahoma City OK 73108-2499
405 495-3444 **City Bites** (Deli/Bakery) 7603 NW 23rd .... Bethany OK 73008-0000
405 840-5655 **Eagle's Nest** (Steak/Seafood) 5900 Mosteller Dr .... Oklahoma City OK 73112-4628
405 787-2944 **Eddy's of Oklahoma City**
(Steak/Seafood) 4227 N Meridian Ave .... Oklahoma City OK 73112-2456
405 843-6233 **Hu-Nan** (Chinese) 9211 N 10th Pl .... Oklahoma City OK 73120-0000
405 478-4955 **Oklahoma County Line** (Barbecue) 1226 NE 63rd St .... Oklahoma City OK 73111-7806
405 848-4660 **Pepporoni Grill**
(Italian/American) 1901 Northwest Expy Suite 1001 .... Oklahoma City OK 73118-0000
405 424-1614 **Sleepy Hollow** (American) 1101 NE 50th St .... Oklahoma City OK 73111-6627
405 943-5740 **Sullivan's** (Steaks) 4401 W Reno Ave .... Oklahoma City OK 73107-6594

——— Goods & Services ———

■ Department Stores

405 235-3711 **Anthony's** 701 N Broadway .... Oklahoma City OK 73102-6091
405 634-6569 **Dillard's** 7000 Crossroads Blvd .... Oklahoma City OK 73149-4298

■ Banks

405 272-4000 **First Interstate Bank of Oklahoma** 120 N Robinson Ave ... Oklahoma City OK 73102-7407
405 751-9520 **Founders Bank & Trust Co** 5613 N May Ave .... Oklahoma City OK 73112-4201
405 231-6000 **Liberty National Bank & Trust Co** 100 N Broadway Ave ... Oklahoma City OK 73102-8625

■ Messenger/Postal

Dispatch Delivery Inc	405 236-8674	Post Office	405 278-6219
Federal Express	800 238-5355	Speedy Delivery Service Inc	405 728-8700
One Hour Express Inc	405 631-4687	UPS	405 947-5631

■ Secretarial/Temp Services

405 478-0730 **Kelly Temporary Services Inc**
9400 N Broadway Suite 540 .... Oklahoma City OK 73114-0000
405 942-5111 **Manpower Temporary Services Inc**
3030 Northwest Expy Suite 702 .... Oklahoma City OK 73112-0000
405 840-3456 **Olsten Temporary Services** 5101 N Classen Suite 104 .... Oklahoma City OK 73118-0000

——— Media ———

■ Newspapers/Magazines

405 232-3311 **Daily Oklahoman** 500 N Broadway Ave .... Oklahoma City OK 73102-6210

■ Television

405 848-8501 **KETA-TV Ch 13 (PBS)** 7403 N Kelley Ave .... Oklahoma City OK 73111-8420
405 478-1212 **KFOR-TV Ch 4 (NBC)** 500 E Britton Rd .... Oklahoma City OK 73114-7701
405 478-3000 **KOCO-TV Ch 5 (ABC)** 1300 E Britton Rd .... Oklahoma City OK 73131-2007
405 843-6641 **KWTV-TV Ch 9 (CBS)** 7401 N Kelley Ave .... Oklahoma City OK 73111-8420

■ Radio

405 848-0100 **KATT-FM 100.5 MHz (AOR)** 4045 NW 64th St .... Oklahoma City OK 73116-1693
405 325-3388 **KGOU-FM 106.3 MHz (Clas-NPR)** 780 Van Vleet Oval .... Norman OK 73019-0001
405 840-5271 **KJYO-FM 102.7 MHz (CHR)** 50 Penn Pl .... Oklahoma City OK 73118-1807
405 525-5595 **KKNG-FM 92.5 MHz (AC)** 110 NE 48th St .... Oklahoma City OK 73105-2021
405 840-5271 **KTOK-AM 1000 kHz (N/T-ABC)** 50 Penn Pl .... Oklahoma City OK 73118-1802
405 528-5543 **KXXY-FM 96.1 MHz (Ctry)** 101 NE 28th St .... Oklahoma City OK 73105-2720

——— Local Attractions & Special Events ———

■ Sports

405 946-8989 **Oklahoma City 89ers** All Sports Stadium .... Oklahoma City OK 73107-0000

■ Local Attractions

405 235-4058 **Horn Homestead & 1889er Museum** 313 NE 16th .... Oklahoma City OK 73104-0000
405 427-5461 **Kirkpatrick Center Museum Complex** 2100 NE 52nd St ... Oklahoma City OK 73111-7107
405 478-2251 **National Cowboy Hall of Fame & Western Heritage Center**
1700 NE 63rd St .... Oklahoma City OK 73111-7906
405 424-5266 **National Softball Hall of Fame** 2801 NE 50th St .... Oklahoma City OK 73111-0000
405 424-5545 **Omniplex Science & Art Museum** 2100 NE 52nd St .... Oklahoma City OK 73111-7198
405 424-1000 **Remington Park** 1 Remington Pl .... Oklahoma City OK 73111-0000
405 235-8675 **Stockyards & Cowtown** 2501 Exchange Ave .... Oklahoma City OK 73108-0000

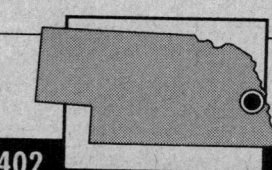

Omaha

NEBRASKA 402

Important Phone Numbers

AAA 402 390-1000
American Express 402 333-7878
Better Business Bureau 402 346-3033
City Hall 402 444-5001

Emergency 911
Poison Control Center 402 390-5555
Time/Temp 402 342-8463
Weather 402 392-1111

■ Travel Information

402 346-5000 **Chamber of Commerce** 1301 Harney St .... Omaha NE 68102-1804
402 444-4660 **Convention & Visitors Bureau** 1819 Farnam St Suite 1200 .... Omaha NE 68183-0001

Travel

■ Airport

402 422-6800 **Eppley Airfield** 5 miles NE of city (approx 10 minutes)

■ Airport Transportation

Taxi $6 fare to downtown

■ Scheduled Airlines

America West 402 341-1230
American 402 345-5559
Continental 402 422-6170
Delta 800 221-1212

Midway 800 621-5700
Northwest 800 225-2525
TWA 402 422-0170
United 800 241-6522

■ Charter Airlines

Duncan Aviation Inc 402 475-2611
Elliot Beechcraft 402 422-6789

Sky Harbor 402 422-6633
Werner Aviation Inc 402 895-3500

■ Car Rentals

Agency 402 592-5744
Avis 402 422-6480
Budget 402 348-0455
Dollar 402 341-5577

Hertz 402 422-6870
National 402 422-6565
Thrifty 402 345-1040

■ Limo/Taxi

Accent Limousine Service 402 399-9300
Checker Cab 402 342-8000
Happy Cab 402 339-0110
Old Market Limousine 402 346-5512

Private Coach Limousine Service . 402 346-3779
Safeway Cabs Inc 402 342-7474
Yellow Cab 402 341-9000

■ Mass Transit

402 341-0800 **Metro Area Transit (MAT)** $.75 Base fare .... Omaha NE 68102-0000

■ Rail/Bus

402 342-7500 **Greyhound Bus Station** 1601 Jackson St .... Omaha NE 68102-3144
402 342-1501 **Omaha Station** 1003 S 9th St .... Omaha NE 68108-3238

Hotels

402 339-7400 **Best Western Omaha Inn** 4706 S 108th St .... Omaha NE 68137-2392
402 397-5141 **Embassy Suites Hotel** 7270 Cedar St .... Omaha NE 68124-2347
402 393-3950 **Holiday Inn Central** 3321 S 72nd St .... Omaha NE 68124-3587
402 397-7137 **Oak Creek Inn** 2808 S 72nd St .... Omaha NE 68124-3501
402 399-9000 **Omaha Marriott Hotel** 10220 Regency Cir .... Omaha NE 68114-3749
402 331-8220 **Quality Inn West Sunset Inn** 10909 M St .... Omaha NE 68137-2391
402 342-5100 **Ramada Inn Airport** 2002 E Locust St .... Omaha NE 68110-2689
402 397-7030 **Ramada Inn Central** 7007 Grover St .... Omaha NE 68106-3500
402 346-7600 **Red Lion Hotel Omaha** 1616 Dodge St .... Omaha NE 68102-1503
402 553-8898 **Residence Inn Omaha Central** 6990 Dodge St .... Omaha NE 68132-0000
402 391-5757 **Rodeway Inn** 7101 Grover St .... Omaha NE 68106-3599
402 895-1000 **Sheraton Inn Southwest** 4888 S 118th St .... Omaha NE 68137-2299

Restaurants

402 399-8405 **Bercima Cafe** (Mediterranean) 10311 Pacific St ...... Omaha NE 68114-0000
402 342-6700 **Chez Chong** (Chinese) 415 S 11th St .... Omaha NE 68102-2805
402 341-3547 **French Cafe** (Continental) 1017 Howard St .... Omaha NE 68102-2833
402 393-1421 **Gallaghers** (International) 10730 Pacific St .... Omaha NE 68114-4761
402 731-4774 **Johnny's Cafe** (Steak) 4702 S 27th St .... Omaha NE 68107-2732
402 333-8048 **La Fonda de Acebo** (Mexican) 2820 S 123rd Ct .... Omaha NE 68144-3952
402 397-8389 **La Strada 72** (Italian) 3125 S 72nd St .... Omaha NE 68106-0000
402 341-2063 **Neon Goose** (Continental) 1012 S 10th St .... Omaha NE 68108-3210
402 393-2030 **Ross Steak House** (Italian/Steak) 909 S 72nd St ..... Omaha NE 68114-4633
402 345-8980 **V Mertz Restaurant** (Continental) 1022 Howard St .. Omaha NE 68102-2815

Goods & Services

■ Department Stores

402 392-0333 **Dillard's** 7400 Dodge St .... Omaha NE 68114-3616
402 345-4000 **Younkers** 1930 S 41st St .... Omaha NE 68105-2949

■ Banks

402 341-0500 **First National Bank of Omaha** 1620 Dodge St .... Omaha NE 68102-0000
402 348-6000 **FirsTier Bank NA Omaha** 17th & Farnam Sts .... Omaha NE 68102-2107

■ Messenger/Postal

Express Messenger Systems Inc 402 734-4650
Federal Express 800 238-5355
Intercity Courier Systems Inc 402 734-6626

Post Office 402 348-2861
UPS 402 734-6700

■ Secretarial/Temp Services

402 393-5000 **Kelly Services Inc** 9140 W Dodge Rd .... Omaha NE 68114-3340
402 397-5455 **Manpower Temporary Services Inc** 8701 W Dodge Rd .... Omaha NE 68114-3429

Media

■ Newspapers/Magazines

402 444-1000 **Omaha World-Herald** 14th & Dodge Sts .... Omaha NE 68102-0000

■ Television

402 345-7777 **KETV-TV Ch 7 (ABC)** 27th & Douglas Sts .... Omaha NE 68131-0000
402 592-3333 **KMTV-TV Ch 3 (CBS)** 10714 Mockingbird Dr .... Omaha NE 68127-1999
402 558-4200 **KPTM-TV Ch 42** 4625 Farnam St .... Omaha NE 68132-3242
402 554-2516 **KYNE-TV Ch 26 (PBS)** 60th & Dodge Sts Rm 200 ... Omaha NE 68182-0001
402 346-6666 **WOWT-TV Ch 6 (NBC)** 3501 Farnam St .... Omaha NE 68131-3356

■ Radio

402 556-6700 **KESY-AM 1420 kHz (B/EZ-ABC)** 4807 Dodge St ..... Omaha NE 68132-3123
402 556-6700 **KESY-FM 104.5 MHz (B/EZ-ABC)** 4807 Dodge St .... Omaha NE 68132-3123
402 592-3500 **KEZO-FM 92.3 MHz (AOR)** 11128 John Galt Blvd ... Omaha NE 68137-0000
402 556-8000 **KFAB-AM 1110 kHz (N/T-NBC)** 5010 Underwood Ave ... Omaha NE 68132-0000
402 556-2323 **KGOR-FM 99.9 MHz (Gold-NBC)** 5010 Underwood Ave ... Omaha NE 68132-0000
402 554-6444 **KIOS-FM 91.5 MHz (Misc-NPR)** 3230 Burt St .... Omaha NE 68131-2014
402 345-2526 **KOIL-AM 1290 kHz (Gold-CBS)** 1108 Douglas St Suite 100 .... Omaha NE 68102-1814
402 342-2000 **KQKQ-FM 98.5 MHz (CHR)** 1001 Farnam St .... Omaha NE 68102-0000

Local Attractions & Special Events

■ Sports

402 556-2305 **Ak-Sar-Ben Racetrack** Ak-Sar-Ben Field .... Omaha NE 68106-0000
402 734-2550 **Omaha Royals** 1202 Bert Murphy Ave .... Omaha NE 68107-2253

■ Local Attractions

402 498-1111 **Boys Town** 136th & W Dodge Rd .... Omaha NE 68010-0000
402 731-3140 **Fontenelle Forest** 1111 Bellevue Blvd N .... Bellevue NE 68005-4008
402 444-5900 **Gerald R Ford Birth Site** 32nd & Woolworth Ave ... Omaha NE 68105-0000
402 342-3300 **Joslyn Art Museum** 2200 Dodge St .... Omaha NE 68102-1294
402 731-4980 **Omaha Livestock Market**
              29th & 'O' Sts Livestock Exchange Bldg Rm 126 .... Omaha NE 68107-0000
402 271-3530 **Union Pacific Museum** 1416 Dodge St .... Omaha NE 68108-0000

Philadelphia

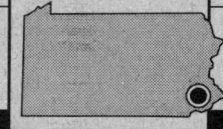

PENNSYLVANIA 215

Important Phone Numbers

AAA	215 864-5000	Emergency	911
American Express	215 592-9211	Poison Control Center	215 922-5523
Better Business Bureau	215 496-1000	Time	215 846-1212
City Hall	215 686-1776	Weather	215 936-1212

■ Travel Information

215 545-1234 **Chamber of Commerce** 1346 Chestnut St Suite 800 .... Philadelphia PA 19107-4608
215 636-1666 **Convention & Visitors Bureau**
16th & John F Kennedy Blvd .... Philadelphia PA 19102-0000

Travel

■ Airport

215 492-3181 **Philadelphia International Airport** 7 miles SW of city (approx 30 minutes)

■ Airport Transportation

215 551-6772 **Econoline Limousine** $9 fare to downtown
215 580-7800 **SEPTA Airport Rail Line** $4.50 fare to downtown
Taxi $20-25 fare to downtown

■ Scheduled Airlines

Air France	215 492-4534	Lufthansa	800 645-3880
Air Jamaica	800 523-5585	Mexicana	800 531-7921
American	215 365-4000	Midway	800 621-5700
American Eagle	800 433-7300	Northwest	800 225-2525
British Airways	800 247-9297	Pan Am Express	800 221-1111
ComAir/Delta Connection	215 928-1700	TWA	215 923-2000
Continental	800 525-0280	United	215 568-2800
Continental Express	800 525-0280	USAir	215 563-8055
Delta	215 928-1700	USAir Express	800 428-4253
Eastern	215 923-3500	Wings Airways	215 646-4446
Eastern Express	212 986-5000		

■ Charter Airlines

Basco	215 327-0200	Flight Dept	609 784-2799
Cole	215 266-0990	Sterling Helicopters	215 271-2510
Fleet Helicopter	215 282-4100	Wings Airways	215 646-4446

■ Car Rentals

Agency	215 492-5022	Hertz	215 492-7200
American International	215 492-1750	Holiday-Payless	215 365-2100
Avis	215 492-0900	National	215 567-1760
Budget	215 492-9442	Snappy	215 492-9114
Dollar	215 365-2700	Thrifty	215 365-3900
Enterprise	215 521-3700	Ugly Duckling	215 336-8459

■ Limo/Taxi

Ali Baba Limousine	215 842-0328	United Cab	215 625-2881
Dav-El Limousines	215 334-7900	Yellow Cab	215 922-8400
JM Steffen Limousine	215 476-8100	Yellow Cab	215 551-6640
Quaker City Cab	215 728-8000	Yellow Cab	215 829-4222

■ Mass Transit

609 772-6900 **Port Authority Transit Corp** $.75 Base fare .... Lindenwold NJ 08021-0000
215 580-4000 **SEPTA** $1.25 Base fare .... Philadelphia PA 19107-0000

■ Rail/Bus

215 895-7123 **30th Street Station** 30th & Market Sts .... Philadelphia PA 19104-2813
215 931-4000 **Greyhound/Trailways Bus Station** 1001 Filbert St .... Philadelphia PA 19107-3001

Hotels

215 581-5000 **Adam's Mark Hotel Philadelphia**
City Line & Monument Rd .... Philadelphia PA 19131-0000
215 755-9500 **Airport Hilton Inn Philadelphia** 10th St & Packer Ave .... Philadelphia PA 19148-0000
215 545-0300 **Barclay Hotel Center City** 237 S 18th St .... Philadelphia PA 19103-6164
215 963-1500 **Four Seasons Hotel** 1 Logan Sq .... Philadelphia PA 19103-6933
215 365-6600 **Guest Quarters Hotel at the Airport** 1 Gateway Ctr .... Philadelphia PA 19153-3226
215 893-1600 **Hershey Philadelphia Hotel** Broad & Locust Sts .... Philadelphia PA 19107-5686
215 893-1776 **Hotel Atop Bellevue** Broad & Walnut Sts .... Philadelphia PA 19106-0000
215 563-7474 **Latham Hotel Center City** 135 S 17th St .... Philadelphia PA 19103-5460
215 387-8333 **Penn Towers Hotel** 34th & Civic Center Blvd .... Philadelphia PA 19104-4385
215 365-4150 **Philadelphia Airport Marriott** 4509 Island Ave .... Philadelphia PA 19153-0000
215 963-2222 **Radisson Suite Hotel** 18th St & Ben Franklin Pkwy .... Philadelphia PA 19103-0000
215 238-6000 **Sheraton Society Hill Hotel** 2nd & Walnut Sts .... Philadelphia PA 19106-0000
215 735-6000 **Warwick Hotel Downtown** 1701 Locust St .... Philadelphia PA 19103-6107
215 448-2000 **Wyndham Franklin Plaza Hotel** 17th & Race St .... Philadelphia PA 19103-0000

Restaurants

215 546-4424 **A'Propros** (Nouvelle American) 211 S Broad St .... Philadelphia PA 19107-5324
215 629-1126 **Alouette** (French/Asian) 334 Bainbridge St .... Philadelphia PA 19147-1544
215 545-1137 **Bookbinders Seafood House** (Seafood) 215 S 15th St .... Philadelphia PA 19102-3895
215 627-2590 **Cafe Nola** (Cajun) 328 South St .... Philadelphia PA 19147-1536
215 923-6059 **City Tavern** (American) 2nd & Walnut Sts .... Philadelphia PA 19148-0000
215 851-6262 **Cutter's Grand Cafe & Bar**
(Contemporary) 2005 Market St .... Philadelphia PA 19103-0000
215 546-1190 **Deja Vu** (French) 1609 Pine St .... Philadelphia PA 19103-6751
215 546-2000 **Dilullo Centro** (Italian) 1407 Locust St .... Philadelphia PA 19102-3807
215 629-0525 **Downey's** (Continental) 526 S Front St .... Philadelphia PA 19147-1797
215 963-1500 **Fountain The** (French/Continental) 1 Logan Sq .... Philadelphia PA 19103-6933
215 546-4455 **Garden The** (Continental) 1617 Spruce St .... Philadelphia PA 19103-6306

215 985-4659 **Girasole** (Contemporary Italian) 1305 Locust St .... Philadelphia PA 19107-0000
215 561-5757 **Harry's Bar & Grill** (Continental) 22 S 18th St .... Philadelphia PA 19103-3720
215 928-1911 **Jim's Steaks** (Steak) 400 South St .... Philadelphia PA 19147-0000
215 567-1000 **Le Bec-Fin** (French) 1523 Walnut St .... Philadelphia PA 19102-3067
215 467-6644 **Melrose Diner** (American) 1501 Snyder Ave .... Philadelphia PA 19145-3031
215 925-7027 **Old Original Bookbinder's** (Seafood) 125 Walnut St .... Philadelphia PA 19106-3085
215 546-8065 **Ristorante II Gallo Nero** (Italian) 254 S 15th St .... Philadelphia PA 19102-5036
215 545-2666 **Susanna Foo** (Chinese) 1512 Walnut St .... Philadelphia PA 19102-3603

Goods & Services

■ Department Stores

215 922-3399 **Stern's** 937 Market St .... Philadelphia PA 19107-0000
215 629-6000 **Strawbridge & Clothier** 8th & Market Sts .... Philadelphia PA 19107-0000
215 422-2000 **Wanamaker's** 1300 Market St .... Philadelphia PA 19101-0000

■ Banks

215 786-5000 **CoreStates First Pennsylvania Bank** 1500 Market St .... Philadelphia PA 19102-0000
215 553-4405 **Mellon Bank East** Broad & Chestnut Sts .... Philadelphia PA 19110-1024
215 973-8400 **Philadelphia National Bank** 5th & Market Sts .... Philadelphia PA 19110-0001

■ Messenger/Postal

American Eagle Express	215 569-3330	Post Office	215 895-8000
Federal Express	215 923-3085	Quick Courier Service	215 592-9933
Kangaroo Couriers	215 561-5132	Rapid Delivery Service	215 496-9600
Philadelphia Express Courier Inc	215 627-6700	UPS	215 463-7300

■ Secretarial/Temp Services

215 568-4580 **Accountemps** 2000 Market St 18th Fl .... Philadelphia PA 19103-3218
215 564-3110 **Kelly Services** 1635 Market St 7 Penn Ctr Suite 1220 .... Philadelphia PA 19103-7241
215 568-4050 **Manpower Temporary Services** 1801 Market St .... Philadelphia PA 19103-1639
215 568-7795 **Olsten Temporary Services** 1617 JFK Blvd Suite 1160 .... Philadelphia PA 19103-1811

Media

■ Newspapers/Magazines

215 854-2000 **Philadelphia Daily News** 400 N Broad St .... Philadelphia PA 19130-4015
215 854-2000 **Philadelphia Inquirer** 400 N Broad St .... Philadelphia PA 19130-4099
215 545-3500 **Philadelphia Magazine** 1500 Walnut St .... Philadelphia PA 19102-3584

■ Television

215 238-4700 **KYW-TV Ch 3 (NBC)** Independence Mall E .... Philadelphia PA 19106-0000
215 668-5510 **WCAU-TV Ch 10 (CBS)** City Ave & Monument Rd .... Philadelphia PA 19131-1007
215 351-1200 **WHYY-TV Ch 12 (PBS)** 150 N 6th St .... Philadelphia PA 19106-1589
215 878-9700 **WPVI-TV Ch 6 (ABC)** 4100 City Line Ave .... Philadelphia PA 19131-1610

■ Radio

215 238-4700 **KYW-AM 1060 kHz (N/T-NBC)** Independence Mall E .... Philadelphia PA 19106-0000
215 667-8400 **WEAZ-FM 101.1 MHz (AC)** 10 Presidential Blvd .... Bala-Cynwyd PA 19004-1107
215 667-3939 **WEGX-FM 106.1 MHz (CHR)** 3 Bala Plaza Suite 580E .... Bala-Cynwyd PA 19004-3481
215 351-1200 **WHYY-FM 91 MHz (Clas-NPR)** 150 N 6th St .... Philadelphia PA 19106-1508
215 561-0933 **WMMR-FM 93.3 MHz (AOR-NBC)** 19th & Walnut Sts .... Philadelphia PA 19103-0000
215 483-8900 **WUSL-FM 98.9 MHz (CHR-ABC)** 440 Domino Ln .... Philadelphia PA 19128-4395

Local Attractions & Special Events

■ Sports

215 339-7676 **Philadelphia 76ers** Spectrum .... Philadelphia PA 19147-0000
215 463-5500 **Philadelphia Eagles**
Broad St & Pattison Ave Veterans Stadium .... Philadelphia PA 19148-0000
215 755-9700 **Philadelphia Flyers** Spectrum .... Philadelphia PA 19148-0000
215 463-6000 **Philadelphia Phillies**
Broad St & Pattison Ave Veterans Stadium .... Philadelphia PA 19148-0000

■ Local Attractions

215 627-5343 **Betsy Ross House** 239 Arch St .... Philadelphia PA 19106-0000
215 574-0560 **Elfreth's Alley Museum** 126 Elfreth's Alley .... Philadelphia PA 19106-0000
215 597-2761 **Franklin Court** 322 Market St .... Philadelphia PA 19106-9996
215 448-1200 **Franklin Institute Science Museum & Planetarium**
20th St & Benjamin Franklin Pkwy .... Philadelphia PA 19103-0000
215 862-5880 **Historic New Hope** 1 W Mechanic St .... New Hope PA 18938-0000
215 597-8974 **Independence Hall & Congress Hall** 6th & Chestnut Sts .... Philadelphia PA 19106-0000
215 922-5792 **Italian Market** 1019 S 9th St .... Philadelphia PA 19147-4706
215 597-8974 **Liberty Bell Pavilion** Market & 5th Sts .... Philadelphia PA 19104-0000
215 388-6741 **Longwood Gardens** US Rt 1 S .... Kennett Square PA 19348-0000
215 923-8181 **Penn's Landing** Delaware Ave & Walnut St .... Philadelphia PA
215 763-8100 **Philadelphia Museum of Art**
26th & Benjamin Franklin Pkwy .... Philadelphia PA 19130-2399
215 787-5476 **Rodin Museum** 22nd & Benjamin Franklin Pkwy .... Philadelphia PA 19130-0000
215 597-7350 **US Mint** 5th & Arch Sts .... Philadelphia PA 19106-0000
215 783-7700 **Valley Forge National Historical Park**
SR-23 & N Gulph Rd .... Valley Forge PA 19481-0000

Phoenix

ARIZONA　　602

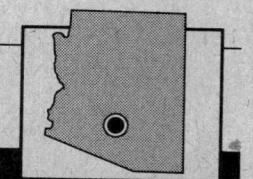

Important Phone Numbers

AAA 602 274-1116
American Express 602 954-1000
Better Business Bureau 602 264-1721
City Hall 602 262-6011
Emergency 911
Poison Control Center 602 253-3334
Time/Temp 602 976-5555
Weather 602 957-8700

■ Travel Information

602 254-5521　Chamber of Commerce 34 W Monroe St Suite 900 .... Phoenix AZ　85003-1796
602 254-6500　Convention & Visitors Bureau 505 N 2nd St Suite 300 .... Phoenix AZ　85004-3905

Travel

■ Airport

602 273-3455　Sky Harbor International Airport 3 miles SE of city (approx 15 minutes)

■ Airport Transportation

602 257-8426　Phoenix Transit System $.75 fare to downtown
602 253-5200　Super Shuttle $5 fare to downtown
　　　　　　　Taxi $5-6 fare to downtown
602 275-8501　Yellow Cab Special Services $8 fare to downtown

■ Scheduled Airlines

Alaska 602 921-3100
America West 602 894-0737
American 602 258-6300
Canadian Holidays 800 237-0314
Continental 800 525-0280
Delta 602 258-5930
Eastern 602 271-0878
Mesa 602 225-5155
Midway 800 621-5700
Northwest 800 225-2525
Sky West 800 453-9417
Southwest 602 273-1221
Stateswest 602 220-0070
TWA 602 252-7711
United 602 273-3131
USAir 602 258-7355

■ Charter Airlines

Corporate Air Charter 602 991-1014
Corporate Jets Inc 602 948-2400
Grand Canyon Helicopters 602 967-6150
Sawyer Aviation 602 273-3770
Scottsdale Aviation Center 602 951-4100
Sky Cab Inc 602 998-1778

■ Car Rentals

Alamo 602 244-0897
American International 602 273-6181
Avis 602 273-3222
Budget 602 267-4000
Dollar 602 275-7588
Elite 602 244-1148
Hertz 602 267-8822
National 602 275-4771
Payless 602 275-5701
Snappy 602 841-1292
Thrifty 602 244-0311

■ Limo/Taxi

Air Courier Cab 602 232-2222
Arizona Limousines 602 267-7097
Carey Limousine 602 996-1955
LA Limousine Service 602 242-3094
Scottsdale Cab 602 994-1616
Valley Limousines 602 254-1955
Yellow Cab 602 252-5252

■ Mass Transit

602 257-8426　Phoenix Transit System $.75 Base fare .... Phoenix AZ　85004-0000

■ Rail/Bus

602 248-4040　Greyhound/Trailways Bus Station 525 E Washington St .... Phoenix AZ　85004-2370
602 253-0121　Phoenix Amtrak Station 401 W Harrison St .... Phoenix AZ　85003-2433

Hotels

602 955-6600　Arizona Biltmore Resort 24th St & Missouri Ave .... Phoenix AZ　85016-0000
602 244-8800　Embassy Suites Camelhead 1515 N 44th St .... Phoenix AZ　85008-5656
602 279-3211　Embassy Suites West Side 3210 Grand Ave .... Phoenix AZ　85017-4597
602 375-1777　Fountains Suite Hotel 2577 W Greenway Rd .... Phoenix AZ　85023-4288
602 997-5900　Hotel Westcourt 10220 N Metro Pkwy E .... Phoenix AZ　85051-1516
602 252-1234　Hyatt Regency 122 N 2nd St .... Phoenix AZ　85004-9954
602 279-9811　La Mancha Athletic Club & Resort Hotel
　　　　　　　100 W Clarendon Ave .... Phoenix AZ　85013-3503
602 948-1700　Marriott Camelback Inn 5402 E Lincoln Dr .... Scottsdale AZ　85253-4190
602 997-2626　Pointe at Squaw Peak Resort 7677 N 16th St .... Phoenix AZ　85020-4495
602 866-7500　Pointe at Tapatio Cliff 11111 N 7th St .... Phoenix AZ　85020-1199
602 438-9000　Pointe on South Mountain 7777 S Pointe Pkwy W .... Phoenix AZ　85044-5497
602 993-0800　Sheraton Greenway Inn 2510 W Greenway Rd .... Phoenix AZ　85023-4298
602 257-1525　Sheraton Phoenix 111 N Central Ave .... Phoenix AZ　85004-2308

Restaurants

602 944-1286　Aunt Chilada's (Mexican) 7330 N Dreamy Draw Dr .... Phoenix AZ　85020-5212
602 956-0900　Avanti's (Italian) 2728 E Thomas Rd .... Phoenix AZ　85016-8298
602 957-3214　Bistro The (Contemporary French) 2398 E Camelback Rd .... Phoenix AZ　85016-0000
602 998-5591　Bobby McGee's (Nouvelle American) 7000 E Shea Blvd .... Scottsdale AZ　85254-5261
602 948-1700　Chaparral Room (Continental) 5402 E Lincoln Dr .... Scottsdale AZ　85253-4118
602 957-3214　Christopher's (French) 2398 E Camelback Rd .... Phoenix AZ　85016-0000
602 863-0912　Etienne's Different Pointe of View (French) 11111 N 7th St .... Phoenix AZ　85020-1176
602 234-0245　French Corner (French) 50 E Camelback Rd .... Phoenix AZ　85012-1621
602 945-1647　Garcia's del Este (Mexican) 7633 E Indian School Rd .... Scottsdale AZ　85251-3607
602 257-7700　Golden Eagle (American Southwest) 201 N Central Ave .... Phoenix AZ　85073-0001
602 488-4141　Ianuzzi's (Italian) 34505 N Scottsdale Rd .... Scottsdale AZ　85255-0000
602 946-5115　La Chaumiere (French) 6910 E Main St .... Scottsdale AZ　85251-4312
602 955-1213　La Fontanella (Italian) 4231 E Indian School Rd .... Phoenix AZ　85018-5343
602 263-8000　Mr Louie's (Continental) 645 E Missouri Ave .... Phoenix AZ　85014-0000
602 954-2507　Orangerie (Continental) 24th St & Missouri Ave .... Phoenix AZ　85016-0000
602 956-5705　Oscar Taylor (American) 2420 E Camelback Rd .... Phoenix AZ　85016-4202
602 274-2795　Pasta Segio's (Italian) 1904 E Camelback Rd .... Phoenix AZ　85016-4110
602 866-7500　Pointe in Tyme (Steak/Seafood) 11111 N 7th St .... Phoenix AZ　85020-1176
602 953-3264　Shogun (Japanese) 12615 N Tatum Blvd .... Phoenix AZ　85032-7710
602 273-7378　Stockyards The (Steak) 5001 E Washington St .... Phoenix AZ　85034-2010
602 276-0945　T-Bone Steak House (Steak) 10037 N 19th Ave .... Phoenix AZ　85021-1907
602 224-0225　Vincent's (Nouvelle) 3930 E Camelback Rd .... Phoenix AZ　85018-2617

Goods & Services

■ Department Stores

602 994-3111　Bullock's 6900 E Camelback Rd .... Scottsdale AZ　85251-2489
602 849-0100　Dillard's 7621 W Thomas Rd .... Phoenix AZ　85033-5490
602 955-8000　Saks Fifth Avenue 2500 E Camelback Rd .... Phoenix AZ　85106-0000

■ Banks

602 528-6000　First Interstate Bank of Arizona NA 100 W Washington St .... Phoenix AZ　85003-1869
602 262-2000　Security Pacific Bank Arizona 101 N 1st Ave .... Phoenix AZ　85003-1999
602 261-2900　Valley National Bank 241 N Central Ave .... Phoenix AZ　85004-2268

■ Messenger/Postal

Courier Express 602 254-3237
Dependable Messenger 602 955-3899
Dial-A-Messenger 602 954-6060
Federal Express 602 254-4662
Hawkins & Campbell Inc 602 254-6147
Hop to It Messenger 602 252-3971
Moody's Quick Inc 602 861-2121
Post Office 602 225-3434
UPS 602 272-5555

■ Secretarial/Temp Services

602 264-6488　Accountemps 100 W Clarendon Suite 1150 .... Phoenix AZ　85013-3518
602 264-0717　Kelly Services Inc 3030 N 3rd St Suite 1040 .... Phoenix AZ　85012-3039
602 955-5026　Olsten Temporary Services 2207 E Camelback Rd Suite 103 ... Phoenix AZ　85016-9000

Media

■ Newspapers/Magazines

602 271-8000　Arizona Republic 120 E Van Buren St .... Phoenix AZ　85004-2227
602 271-8000　Phoenix Gazette 120 E Van Buren St .... Phoenix AZ　85004-2227
602 248-8900　Phoenix Magazine 4707 N 12th St .... Phoenix AZ　85014-4009

■ Television

602 965-3506　KAET-TV Ch 8 (PBS) Arizona State University .... Tempe AZ　85287-0001
602 257-1212　KPNX-TV Ch 12 (NBC) 1101 N Central Ave .... Phoenix AZ　85004-1853
602 257-1234　KTSP-TV Ch 10 (CBS) 511 W Adams St .... Phoenix AZ　85003-1638
602 266-5691　KTVK-TV Ch 3 (ABC) 3435 N 16th St .... Phoenix AZ　85016-7185

■ Radio

602 834-5627　KJZZ-FM 91.5 MHz (Jazz-NPR) 1435 S Dobson Rd .... Mesa AZ　85202-4772
602 279-5577　KMEO-FM 96.9 MHz (AC) 3719 N 32nd Ave .... Phoenix AZ　85017-4501
602 966-6236　KNIX-FM 102.5 MHz (Ctry) 600 E Gilbert Dr .... Tempe AZ　85281-2021
602 274-6200　KTAR-AM 620 kHz (N/T-ABC) 301 W Osborn Rd 4th Fl ...... Phoenix AZ　85013-3921
602 838-0400　KUPD-FM 97.9 MHz (AOR) 1900 W Carmen St .... Tempe AZ　85283-2596

Local Attractions & Special Events

■ Sports

602 967-1402　Phoenix Cardinals Sun Devil Stadium .... Tempe AZ　85282-0000
602 263-7867　Phoenix Suns 1826 W McDowell Rd .... Phoenix AZ　85007-1612

■ Local Attractions

602 941-1225　Desert Botanical Garden 1201 N Galvin Pkwy .... Phoenix AZ　85008-3490
602 495-0333　Encanto 1 & 2 2705 N 15th Ave .... Phoenix AZ　85026-0000
602 860-2700　Frank Lloyd Wright/Taliesin West 13201 N 108th St .... Scottsdale AZ　85259-0000
602 252-8848　Heard Museum of Anthropology & Primitive Arts
　　　　　　　22 E Monte Vista Rd .... Phoenix AZ　85026-0000
602 257-1222　Phoenix Art Museum 1625 N Central Ave .... Phoenix AZ　85004-1686
602 495-0900　Pueblo Grande Museum 4619 E Washington St .... Phoenix AZ　85034-1909

Pittsburgh

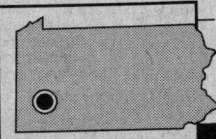

PENNSYLVANIA　412

Important Phone Numbers

AAA	412 362-3300	Emergency	911
American Express	412 391-3202	Poison Control Center	412 681-6669
Better Business Bureau	412 456-2700	Time/Temp	412 391-9500
City Hall	412 255-2100	Weather	412 936-1212

■ Travel Information

412 392-4500　Chamber of Commerce 3 Gateway Ctr .... Pittsburgh PA 15222-1006
412 281-7711　Convention & Visitors Bureau 4 Gateway Ctr Suite 514 .... Pittsburgh PA 15222-1207

Travel

■ Airport

412 778-2525　Greater Pittsburgh International Airport 16 miles W of city (approx 25 minutes)

■ Airport Transportation

412 471-8900　Airlines Transportation Co $8 fare to downtown
Taxi $35 fare to downtown

■ Scheduled Airlines

American	412 771-4437	Midway	800 621-5700
British Airways	412 262-4651	Northwest	800 447-4747
Canadian Air International	412 391-6351	Pan Am	412 391-6907
Christman	412 225-4000	TWA	412 391-3600
Continental	412 391-6910	United	800 241-6522
Delta	412 566-2100	USAir	412 922-7500
Eastern	412 471-7100	USAir Express	800 428-4253

■ Charter Airlines

Beaver Aviation Services Inc	412 843-8600	Corporate Wings	412 469-6800
Corporate Jets Inc	412 466-2500		

■ Car Rentals

Agency	412 741-5188	Hertz	412 262-1705
Alamo	412 264-6204	National	412 262-2312
Avis	412 262-5160	Payless	412 521-5700
Budget	412 262-1500	Snappy	412 655-0121
Dollar	412 262-1300	Thrifty	412 264-1775

■ Limo/Taxi

Airlines Transportation	412 471-8900	Limo Center	412 923-1650
Allegheny Limousines	412 731-8671	Peoples Cab	412 681-3131
Carriage Limousine Services	412 488-7000	Riemer's Limousine	412 661-6054
Colonial Taxi	412 833-3300	Yellow Cab	412 665-8100

■ Mass Transit

412 231-5707　Port Authority Transit $1.10 Base fare .... Pittsburgh PA 15233-0000

■ Rail/Bus

412 392-6527　Greyhound/Trailways 11th & Liberty Ave .... Pittsburgh PA 15222-4286
800 872-7245　Pittsburgh Amtrak Station Liberty & Grant Sts .... Pittsburgh PA 15212-0000

Hotels

412 922-8400　Green Tree Marriott 101 Marriott Dr .... Pittsburgh PA 15205-4334
412 244-1600　Harley Hotel Pittsburgh 699 Rodi Rd .... Pittsburgh PA 15235-4588
412 262-3600　Holiday Inn Airport 1406 Beers School Rd .... Coraopolis PA 15108-2591
412 963-0600　Holiday Inn Allegheny Valley-RIDC Park 180 Gamma Dr ...... Pittsburgh PA 15238-2978
412 471-1234　Hyatt Pittsburgh Chatham Center 112 Washington Pl .... Pittsburgh PA 15219-3419
412 391-4600　Pittsburgh Hilton Hotel & Towers 600 Commonwealth Pl ...... Pittsburgh PA 15222-1075
412 231-3338　Priory The 614 Pressley St .... Pittsburgh PA 15212-5616
412 343-4600　Sheraton Inn South Hills 164 Fort Couch Rd .... Pittsburgh PA 15241-1090
412 261-2000　Sheraton Inn Station Square 7 Station Sq .... Pittsburgh PA 15219-1124
412 281-3700　Vista International Hotel 1000 Penn Ave .... Pittsburgh PA 15222-3873
412 281-7100　Westin William Penn Hotel 530 William Penn Pl .... Pittsburgh PA 15230-0000

Restaurants

412 381-4500　Christopher's Restaurant
　　　　　　　(Continental) 1411 Grandview Ave .... Pittsburgh PA 15211-1199
412 431-6996　Cliffside (Continental) 1208 Grandview Ave .... Pittsburgh PA 15211-1239
412 561-2060　Colony The (Steak) Greentree & Cochran Rds .... Pittsburgh PA 15220-0000
412 765-3598　Emilia Romagna Ristorante (Italian) 942 Penn Ave .... Pittsburgh PA 15222-3706
412 261-1717　Grand Concourse (Steak/Seafood) 1 Station Sq .... Pittsburgh PA 15219-1183
412 488-8100　Hunan Gourmet (Oriental) 1211 E Carson St .... Pittsburgh PA 15203-0000
412 264-3116　Hyeholde (Continental) 190 Hyeholde Dr .... Coraopolis PA 15108-2932
412 338-0900　Jake's Above the Square (American) 430 Market St .... Pittsburgh PA 15222-0000
412 431-3100　Le Mont (Continental) 1114 Grandview Ave .... Mount Washington PA 15211-1399
412 621-9000　Le Petit Cafe (Nouvelle) 809 Bellefonte St .... Pittsburgh PA 15232-2213
412 481-1118　Louis Tambellini's Restaurant (Seafood/Italian) Rt 51 ...... Pittsburgh PA 15226-0000
412 521-6400　Poli's (Seafood) 2607 Murray Ave .... Squirrel Hill PA 15217-0000
412 264-7004　Season's Cafe (American) 1100 5th Ave .... Coraopolis PA 15108-0000

Goods & Services

■ Department Stores

412 553-8000　Joseph Horne 501 Penn Ave .... Pittsburgh PA 15222-0000
412 232-2000　Kaufmann's 400 5th Ave .... Pittsburgh PA 15281-0001

■ Banks

412 234-5000　Mellon Bank 3 Mellon Bank Ctr .... Pittsburgh PA 15259-0001
412 762-2000　Pittsburgh National Bank 5th Ave & Wood St .... Pittsburgh PA 15274-0001
412 644-8111　Union National Bank of Pittsburgh 300 4th Ave .... Pittsburgh PA 15278-0001

■ Messenger/Postal

Courier Express	412 481-7300	Mercury	412 391-2016
Federal Express	800 238-5355	Post Office	412 359-7600
Fleet Feet	412 281-2460	UPS	412 323-1500

■ Secretarial/Temp Services

412 471-5946　Accountemps 2 Gateway Ctr .... Pittsburgh PA 15222-0000
412 391-3222　Kelly Services Inc 625 Liberty Ave 2nd Fl .... Pittsburgh PA 15222-3111
412 391-7030　Manpower Temporary Services Inc
　　　　　　　1 Oliver Plaza Suite 3510 .... Pittsburgh PA 15222-2602

Media

■ Newspapers/Magazines

412 622-1360　Pittsburgh Magazine 4802 5th Ave .... Pittsburgh PA 15213-2918
412 263-1100　Pittsburgh Post-Gazette 50 Blvd of the Allies .... Pittsburgh PA 15222-1208
412 263-1100　Pittsburgh Press 34 Blvd of the Allies .... Pittsburgh PA 15222-1200

■ Television

412 392-2200　KDKA-TV Ch 2 (CBS) 1 Gateway Ctr .... Pittsburgh PA 15222-1416
412 237-1100　WPXI-TV Ch 11 (NBC) 11 Television Hill .... Pittsburgh PA 15214-4014
412 622-1300　WQED-TV Ch 13 (PBS) 4802 5th Ave .... Pittsburgh PA 15213-2956
412 242-4300　WTAE-TV Ch 4 (ABC) 400 Ardmore Blvd .... Pittsburgh PA 15221-3090

■ Radio

412 392-2200　KDKA-AM 1020 kHz (AC-NBC) 1 Gateway Ctr .... Pittsburgh PA 15222-0000
412 471-2181　WAMO-FM 105.9 MHz (UC-SBN) 411 7th Ave Suite 1500 ...... Pittsburgh PA 15219-1905
412 381-8100　WBZZ-FM 93.7 MHz (CHR) 1715 Grandview Ave .... Pittsburgh PA 15211-1015
412 434-6030　WDUQ-FM 90.5 MHz (Jazz-NPR)
　　　　　　　Duquesne University Des Places Communication Ctr .... Pittsburgh PA 15282-0001
412 531-9500　WSHH-FM 99.7 MHz (B/EZ) Broadcast Plaza .... Pittsburgh PA 15220-0000
412 731-1250　WTAE-AM 1250 kHz (N/T-ABC) 400 Ardmore Blvd .... Pittsburgh PA 15221-3090

Local Attractions & Special Events

■ Sports

412 642-1800　Pittsburgh Penguins 300 Auditorium Pl Civic Arena .... Pittsburgh PA 15219-0000
412 323-1919　Pittsburgh Pirates 600 Stadium Cir Three Rivers Stadium .... Pittsburgh PA 15212-5740
412 323-1200　Pittsburgh Steelers 300 Stadium Cir Three Rivers Stadium ... Pittsburgh PA 15212-5721

■ Local Attractions

412 237-3310　Buhl Science Center Allegheny Sq .... Pittsburgh PA 15219-0000
412 622-3131　Carnegie Museums & Libraries 4400 Forbes Ave .... Pittsburgh PA 15213-4080
412 381-1665　Duquesne Incline 1220 Grandview Ave .... Pittsburgh PA 15211-1204
412 281-9284　Fort Pitt Museum 101 Commonwealth Pl .... Pittsburgh PA 15222-0000
412 371-0600　Frick Art Museum 7227 Reynolds St .... Pittsburgh PA 15208-2923
412 624-4157　Heinz Memorial Chapel 5th & Bellefield Aves .... Pittsburgh PA 15260-0000
412 266-1803　Old Economy Village 14th & Church Sts .... Ambridge PA 15003-0000
412 392-4800　Pittsburgh Symphony Orchestra 600 Penn Ave .... Pittsburgh PA 15222-3259
412 471-5808　Station Square 450 Landmark Bldg .... Pittsburgh PA 15219-0000
412 624-4100　Stephen Foster Memorial Forbes St .... Pittsburgh PA 15260-0000

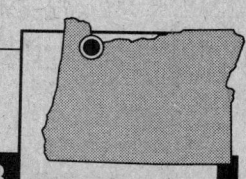

Portland

OREGON   503

Important Phone Numbers

AAA 503 222-6734
American Express 503 226-2961
Better Business Bureau 503 226-3981
City Hall 503 226-3161
Emergency 911
Poison Control Center 503 225-8968
Time/Temp 503 282-2222
Weather 503 236-7575

■ Travel Information

503 228-9411 **Chamber of Commerce** 221 NW 2nd Ave .... Portland OR 97209-3958
503 222-2223 **Visitors Assn** 26 SW Salmon St .... Portland OR 97204-3299

Travel

■ Airport

503 249-4744 **Portland International Airport** 20 miles NE of city (approx 20 minutes)

■ Airport Transportation

503 246-4676 **Raz Tranz** $5 fare to downtown
              Taxi $20 fare to downtown
503 239-6465 **Tri-Met** $.85 fare to downtown

■ Scheduled Airlines

Alaska 503 224-2547
America West 800 247-5692
American 503 241-9145
Continental 503 224-4560
Delta 503 228-2128
Eastern 503 224-7550
Horizon 503 249-4114
Northwest 800 225-2525
TWA 800 221-2000
United 503 226-7211
United Express 503 249-4717
USAir 503 284-5193

■ Charter Airlines

Eagle Flight Center Inc 503 648-7151
Evans Aviation 503 640-4520
Flightcraft 503 281-3300

■ Car Rentals

Agency 503 256-0873
Alamo 503 252-7039
American International 503 255-7711
Avis 503 249-4955
Budget 503 249-4556
Dollar 503 249-4790
General 503 257-3451
Hertz 503 249-8216
National 503 249-4900
Payless 503 249-0630
Snappy 503 626-3032
Thrifty 503 254-6565

■ Limo/Taxi

Broadway Deluxe Cab 503 227-1234
Classic Chauffeur 503 238-8880
New Rose City Cab 503 282-7707
Portland Taxi 503 256-5400
Radio Cab 503 227-1212

■ Mass Transit

503 233-3511 **Tri County Metropolitan District (Tri-Met)** $.85 Base fare .... Portland OR 97202-0000

■ Rail/Bus

503 243-2323 **Greyhound/Trailways Bus Station** 550 NW 6th Ave .... Portland OR 97209-3798
503 273-4871 **Portland Station** 800 NW 6th Ave .... Portland OR 97209-3715

Hotels

503 228-9611 **Benson Hotel on Broadway** 309 SW Broadway .... Portland OR 97205-3794
503 256-4111 **Chumaree Inn** 8247 NE Sandy Blvd .... Portland OR 97220-4990
503 241-4100 **Heathman Hotel** 1009 SW Broadway .... Portland OR 97205-3096
503 226-1611 **Hilton Hotel** 921 SW 6th Ave .... Portland OR 97204-1296
503 256-5000 **Holiday Inn Airport** 8439 NE Columbia Blvd .... Portland OR 97220-1382
503 226-7600 **Marriott Hotel** 1401 SW Front Ave .... Portland OR 97201-5192
503 297-2551 **Nendel's Motor Inn** 9900 SW Canyon Rd .... Portland OR 97225-2996
503 281-6111 **Red Lion Hotel Lloyd Center** 1000 NE Multnomah St .... Portland OR 97232-2111
503 228-3233 **Riverplace Alexis Hotel** 1510 SW Harbor Way .... Portland OR 97201-5105
503 281-2500 **Sheraton Airport Hotel** 8235 NE Airport Way .... Portland OR 97220-1398

Restaurants

503 275-3600 **Atwaters** (Continental) 111 SW 5th Ave .... Portland OR 97204-3604
503 223-5048 **Cisco & Pancho's** (Mexican) 107 NW 5th St .... Portland OR 97209-3820
503 223-6173 **Couch Street Fish House** (Seafood) NW 3rd & Couch St .... Portland OR 97209-0000
503 234-7909 **Esparza's Tex-Mex Cafe** (Mexican) 2725 SE Ankeny .... Portland OR 97214-0000
503 241-4100 **Heathman Restaurant**
              (Nouvelle American) 1009 SW Broadway .... Portland OR 97205-3096
503 226-1419 **Jake's Famous Crawfish** (Seafood) 401 SW 12th Ave ... Portland OR 97205-2397
503 223-3302 **L'Auberge** (French) 2601 NW Vaughn St .... Portland OR 97210-2223
503 295-4110 **London Grill** (Continental) 309 SW Broadway .... Portland OR 97205-3725
503 232-1801 **Polo Club** (American) 718 NE 12th Ave .... Portland OR 97232-2274
503 223-5033 **Regions** (International) 53 NW 1st Ave .... Portland OR 97209-0000
503 223-1513 **Ringside West** (Steak) 2165 W Burnside St .... Portland OR 97210-3598
503 228-8633 **River Queen Restaurant** (Seafood) 1300 NW Front Ave .... Portland OR 97209-0000
503 249-8486 **Winterbourne** (Seafood) 3520 NE 42nd Ave .... Portland OR 97213-1002
503 287-3698 **Yer Ha** (Vietnamese) 6820 NE Sandy Blvd .... Portland OR 97213-0000

Goods & Services

■ Department Stores

503 223-0512 **Meier & Frank** 621 SW 5th Ave .... Portland OR 97204-1499
503 224-6666 **Nordstrom** 701 SW Broadway .... Portland OR 97205-3398

■ Banks

503 225-2111 **First Interstate Bank of Oregon NA** 1300 SW 5th Ave .... Portland OR 97201-5699
503 243-7100 **Security Pacific Bank Oregon** 1001 SW 5th Ave .... Portland OR 97204-1176
503 275-6111 **US Bank** 111 SW 5th Ave .... Portland OR 97204-3604

■ Messenger/Postal

American Messenger Service 503 243-2275
Blue Max Express 503 256-5232
Federal Express 800 238-5355
Post Office 503 294-2424
Pronto Select Messenger Co 503 239-7666
UPS 503 283-7750

■ Secretarial/Temp Services

503 223-8369 **Accountemps** 1 SW Columbia Suite 650 .... Portland OR 97258-2007
503 243-2444 **Barrett Business Services** 2828 SW Kelly Ave .... Portland OR 97201-4854
503 224-5500 **Express Personnel Service** 621 SW Morrison St Suite 500 ... Portland OR 97205-3808
503 227-3850 **Kelly Services Inc** 1020 SW Taylor St Suite 240 .... Portland OR 97205-2556
503 226-6281 **Manpower Temporary Services Inc**
              1211 SW 5th Ave Suite 550 .... Portland OR 97204-3791
503 222-3511 **Olsten Temporary Services** 421 SW 6th Ave Suite 802 .... Portland OR 97204-1617

Media

■ Newspapers/Magazines

503 221-8327 **Oregonian** 1320 SW Broadway .... Portland OR 97201-3499
503 274-7640 **Portland Life & Business Magazine** 816 SW 1st Ave .... Portland OR 97204-3308

■ Television

503 231-4222 **KATU-TV Ch 2 (ABC)** 2153 NE Sandy Blvd .... Portland OR 97232-2819
503 226-5000 **KGW-TV Ch 8 (NBC)** 1501 SW Jefferson St .... Portland OR 97201-2549
503 464-0600 **KOIN-TV Ch 6 (CBS)** 222 SW Columbia St .... Portland OR 97201-6600
503 244-9900 **KOPB-TV Ch 10 (PBS)** 7140 SW Macadam Ave .... Portland OR 97219-3013

■ Radio

503 280-5828 **KBPS-AM 1450 kHz (Misc-NPR)** 546 NE 12th Ave .... Portland OR 97232-2719
503 643-5103 **KKCW-FM 103.3 MHz (AC)** 12655 Southwest Ctr Suite 500 .... Beaverton OR 97005-0000
503 226-0100 **KKRZ-FM 100.3 MHz (CHR-ABC)** 4949 SW Macadam Ave .... Portland OR 97201-3987
503 297-3311 **KUPL-AM 1330 kHz (Ctry)** 6400 SW Canyon Ct .... Portland OR 97221-1486
503 231-0750 **KXL-AM 750 kHz (N/T-NBC)** 1415 SE Ankeny St .... Portland OR 97214-1471
503 231-0750 **KXL-FM 95.5 MHz (B/EZ-NBC)** 1415 SE Ankeny St .... Portland OR 97214-1471

Local Attractions & Special Events

■ Sports

503 223-2837 **Portland Beavers** Civic Stadium .... Portland OR 97205-0000
503 234-9291 **Portland Trail Blazers** 700 NE Multnomah St .... Portland OR 97232-2172
503 238-6366 **Portland Winter Hawks** Memorial Coliseum .... Portland OR 97208-0000

■ Special Events

503 227-2681 **Portland Rose Festival** (May 31-June 23)

■ Local Attractions

503 622-3017 **Columbia River Gorge** .... Portland OR
503 228-8732 **Hoyt Arboretum** 4000 SW Fairview Blvd .... Portland OR 97221-2706
503 282-2511 **Lloyd Center** NE 9th Ave & NE Multnomah .... Portland OR 97232-1277
503 226-2811 **Oregon Art Institute** 1219 SW Park Ave .... Portland OR 97205-2486
503 222-2828 **Oregon Museum of Science & Industry** 4015 SW Canyon Rd .... Portland OR 97221-2705
503 228-4294 **Oregon Symphony Orchestra** 711 SW Alder St .... Portland OR 97205-3170
503 222-6072 **Saturday Market** Between 1st & Front Sts .... Portland OR 97209-0000

Saint Louis
MISSOURI 314

Important Phone Numbers

AAA	314 576-7373	Emergency	911
American Express	314 863-9595	Poison Control Center	314 772-5200
Better Business Bureau	314 531-3300	Time/Temp	314 321-2522
City Hall	314 622-4000	Weather	314 321-2222

■ Travel Information

314 421-1023 **Convention & Visitors Commission**
10 S Broadway Suite 300 .... Saint Louis MO 63102-1779
314 231-5555 **Saint Louis Regional Commerce & Growth Assn**
100 S 4th St Suite 500 .... Saint Louis MO 63102-1807
314 421-2100 **Tourist Information** .... Saint Louis MO 63101-0000

Travel

■ Airport

314 426-8000 **Saint Louis International Airport** 10 miles NW of city (approx 20 minutes)

■ Airport Transportation

314 429-4940 **Airport Limousine Service** $6 fare to downtown
314 231-2345 **Bi-State Transportation** $.85 fare to downtown
Taxi $22 fare to downtown

■ Scheduled Airlines

American	314 231-9505	Southwest	314 421-1221
Continental	314 241-7205	TWA	314 291-7500
Delta	314 421-2600	United	314 454-0088
Eastern	314 621-8900	USAir	314 421-1018
Northwest	800 225-2525		

■ Charter Airlines

Archway Aviation	314 576-5499	Saint Louis Helicopter Airways Inc	314 532-1177
Roederer Aviation Inc	314 532-4150	Spirit Jet Center	314 532-5100

■ Car Rentals

American International	314 423-1200	Hertz	314 426-7555
Avis	314 426-7766	National	314 426-6272
Budget	314 423-3000	Payless	314 429-5657
Dollar	314 423-4004	Thrifty	314 423-3737

■ Limo/Taxi

Admiral Limousine Service	314 991-5466	Laclede Cab	314 535-1162
Airflight Cab	314 837-3218	Show Me Limousine Service	314 522-0888
Airport Cab	314 843-3571	Yellow Cab	314 361-2345
JED Limousine Service	314 991-0767		

■ Mass Transit

314 231-2345 **Bi-State Transportation** $.85 Base fare .... Saint Louis MO 63102-0000

■ Rail/Bus

314 231-7800 **Greyhound/Trailways Bus Station** 809 N Broadway .... Saint Louis MO 63102-2176
314 331-3300 **Saint Louis Station** 550 S 16th St .... Saint Louis MO 63103-2611

Hotels

314 241-7403 **Adam's Mark Hotel** 4th & Chestnut .... Saint Louis MO 63102-0000
314 993-1100 **Breckenridge Frontenac Hotel & Conference Center**
1335 S Lindbergh Blvd .... Saint Louis MO 63131-2983
314 427-7600 **Breckenridge Lambert Hotel** 9600 Natural Bridge Rd .... Saint Louis MO 63134-3198
314 647-7300 **Cheshire Inn & Lodge** 6300 Clayton Rd .... Saint Louis MO 63117-2500
314 241-9500 **Clarion Hotel Saint Louis** 200 S 4th St .... Saint Louis MO 63102-1896
314 532-5000 **Doubletree Hotel & Conference Center**
16625 Swingley Ridge Rd .... Chesterfield MO 63017-1798
314 731-3040 **Henry VIII Hotel & Conference Center**
4690 N Lindbergh Blvd .... Saint Louis MO 63044-0000
314 731-2100 **Holiday Inn Airport North** 4545 N Lindbergh Blvd .... Bridgeton MO 63044-2274
314 421-4000 **Holiday Inn Convention Center** 811 N 9th St .... Saint Louis MO 63101-1096
314 621-8200 **Holiday Inn Riverfront** 200 N 4th St .... Saint Louis MO 63102-1977
314 436-2355 **Hotel Majestic** 1019 Pine St .... Saint Louis MO 63101-2014
314 241-6664 **Hyatt Regency Saint Louis** 1820 Market St .... Saint Louis MO 63103-2208
314 421-1776 **Marriott Pavilion Hotel** 1 S Broadway .... Saint Louis MO 63102-1772
314 426-5500 **Saint Louis Airport Hilton** 10330 Natural Bridge Rd .... Saint Louis MO 63134-3303
314 423-9700 **Saint Louis Airport Marriott Hotel** I-70 .... Saint Louis MO 63134-0000
314 434-5010 **Sheraton Plaza Hotel Westport** 900 Westport Plaza .... Saint Louis MO 63146-3104
314 231-5100 **Sheraton Saint Louis Hotel** 910 N 7th St .... Saint Louis MO 63101-1095

Restaurants

314 863-8878 **Al Baker's Restaurant** (Italian/Seafood) 8101 Clayton Rd ..... Saint Louis MO 63117-1185
314 421-6399 **Al's** (Continental) 1200 N Main St .... Saint Louis MO 63102-0000
314 231-2434 **Anthony's** (Continental) 10 S Broadway .... Saint Louis MO 63102-1700
314 361-8085 **Balaban's** (Continental) 405 N Euclid Ave .... Saint Louis MO 63108-1698
314 647-7300 **Cheshire Inn** (Steak/Seafood) 7036 Clayton Ave .... Saint Louis MO 63117-2500
314 421-1772 **Dierdorf & Hart's Steak House** (Steak) 1820 Market St .... Saint Louis MO 63103-0000
314 771-1632 **Dominic's Restaurant** (Italian) 5101 Wilson Ave .... Saint Louis MO 63110-3196
314 863-6866 **Fio's La Fourchette** (French) 1153 St Louis Galleria .... Saint Louis MO 63117-1169
314 772-5958 **Giovanni's** (Italian) 5201 Shaw Ave .... Saint Louis MO 63110-3074
314 227-7230 **Giovanni's Little Place** (Italian) 14560 Manchester Rd .... Ballwin MO 63011-3933
314 721-0100 **L'Auberge Bretonne** (French) 200 S Brentwood Blvd .... Clayton MO 63105-1601
314 427-8070 **Mandarin House** (Chinese) 9150 Oberland Plaza .... Saint Louis MO 63114-6123
314 426-5500 **Posh's** (Nouvelle American) 10330 Natural Bridge Rd .... Saint Louis MO 63134-3303
314 436-2355 **Richard Perry** (New American) 1019 Pine St .... Saint Louis MO 63101-2014

314 241-6664 **Station Grill The** (Steak/Seafood) 1820 Market St .... Saint Louis MO 63103-2208
314 231-7007 **Tony's** (Italian/Continental) 826 N Broadway .... Saint Louis MO 63102-2109

Goods & Services

■ Department Stores

314 231-5080 **Dillard's** 601 Washington Ave .... Saint Louis MO 63101-1207
314 444-3111 **Famous-Barr** 601 Olive St .... Saint Louis MO 63101-1767
314 567-9811 **Neiman-Marcus** 100 Plaza Frontenac .... Saint Louis MO 63131-3587

■ Banks

314 554-6000 **Boatmen's National Bank of Saint Louis** 800 Market St .... Saint Louis MO 63101-2506
314 425-2525 **Mercantile Bank NA** 721 Locust St .... Saint Louis MO 63101-1602

■ Messenger/Postal

Adcom Express	314 521-0020	Post Office	314 436-4417
All Around Town Express Inc	314 241-3220	Saint Louis Metro Delivery Inc	314 423-0002
Associated Couriers Inc	314 739-0400	Special Dispatch Inc	314 739-7720
Corporate Transit Inc	314 739-8282	UPS	314 291-7900
Federal Express	314 367-8278		

■ Secretarial/Temp Services

314 621-8367 **Accountemps** .... Saint Louis MO 63102-0000
314 421-4111 **Kelly Services Inc** 200 N Broadway Suite 1730 .... Saint Louis MO 63102-2730
314 241-1356 **Manpower** 200 N Broadway Suite 1450 .... Saint Louis MO 63102-0000
314 421-3858 **Olsten Temporary Services** 901 N 10th St .... Saint Louis MO 63101-2911

Media

■ Newspapers/Magazines

314 231-7200 **Saint Louis Magazine** 612 N 2nd St .... Saint Louis MO 63102-2553
314 622-7000 **Saint Louis Post-Dispatch** 900 N Tucker Blvd .... Saint Louis MO 63101-1099
314 968-4940 **Where Magazine** 1750 S Brentwood Blvd Suite 311 .... Saint Louis MO 63144-1315

■ Television

314 725-2460 **KETC-TV Ch 9 (PBS)** 6996 Millbrook Blvd .... Saint Louis MO 63130-0000
314 621-4444 **KMOV-TV Ch 4 (CBS)** 3102 Memorial Dr .... Saint Louis MO 63102-0000
314 421-5055 **KSDK-TV Ch 5 (NBC)** 1000 Market St .... Saint Louis MO 63101-2060
314 647-2222 **KTVI-TV Ch 2 (ABC)** 5915 Berthold Ave .... Saint Louis MO 63110-0000

■ Radio

314 727-2160 **KEZK-FM 102.5 MHz (B/EZ)** 7711 Carondelet Ave .... Saint Louis MO 63105-3313
314 361-1108 **KMJM-FM 107.7 MHz (UC)** 532 De Baliviere Ave .... Saint Louis MO 63112-1906
314 621-2345 **KMOX-AM 1120 kHz (N/T-CBS)** 1 Memorial Dr .... Saint Louis MO 63102-0000
314 621-0095 **KSHE-FM 94.7 MHz (AOR)**
700 St Louis Union Stn Suite 101 .... Saint Louis MO 63103-2240
314 553-5968 **KWMU-FM 90.7 MHz (Clas-NPR)** 8001 Natural Bridge Rd .... Saint Louis MO 63121-0000
314 436-1600 **WIL-FM 92.3 MHz (Ctry)** 300 N Tucker Blvd .... Saint Louis MO 63101-1914

Local Attractions & Special Events

■ Sports

314 781-5300 **Saint Louis Blues** 5700 Oakland Ave Arena .... Saint Louis MO 63110-1397
314 421-3060 **Saint Louis Cardinals**
250 Stadium Plaza Busch Memorial Stadium .... Saint Louis MO 63102-0000

■ Special Events

314 535-3247 **Veiled Prophet Fair** (August 31-September 2)

■ Local Attractions

314 577-2626 **Anheuser-Busch Brewery** 13th & Lynch .... Saint Louis MO 63118-0000
314 771-5828 **Chatillon-DeMenil Mansion** 3352 DeMenil Pl .... Saint Louis MO 63118-3294
314 843-1700 **Grant's Farm** 10501 Gravois Rd .... Saint Louis MO 63123-1899
314 425-4465 **Jefferson National Expansion Memorial (Gateway Arch)**
11 N 4th St .... Saint Louis MO 63102-1882
314 231-5860 **Laclede's Landing Merchants' Assn** 801 N 2nd St .... Saint Louis MO 63102-0000
314 577-5100 **Missouri Botanical Garden** 4344 Shaw Blvd .... Saint Louis MO 63110-2291
314 231-6340 **National Bowling Hall of Fame** 111 Stadium Plaza .... Saint Louis MO 63102-0000
314 425-4465 **Old Courthouse** 11 N 4th St .... Saint Louis MO 63102-1810
314 721-0067 **Saint Louis Art Museum** 1 Fine Arts Dr Forest Pk .... Saint Louis MO 63110-1380
314 421-6655 **Saint Louis Union Station** 1820 Market St .... Saint Louis MO 63103-2208

San Antonio

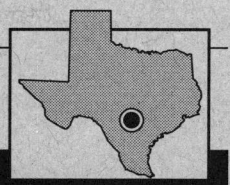

TEXAS — 512

Important Phone Numbers

AAA 512 736-1665
American Express 512 828-4809
Better Business Bureau 512 828-9441
City Hall 512 299-7011
Emergency 911
Poison Control Center 713 654-1701
Time/Temp 512 226-3232
Weather 512 828-0683

■ Travel Information

512 229-2100 **Chamber of Commerce** 602 E Commerce St .... San Antonio TX 78205-2699
512 270-8700 **Convention & Visitors Bureau** 121 Alamo Plaza .... San Antonio TX 78205-2601
512 299-8155 **Visitor Information** 317 Alamo Plaza .... San Antonio TX 78205-2667

Travel

■ Airport

512 821-3411 **San Antonio International Airport** 8 miles N of city (approx 20 minutes)

■ Airport Transportation

512 344-7433 **Super Van Shuttle** $7 fare to downtown
    Taxi $12-14 fare to downtown
512 227-2020 **VIA Metropolitan Transit** $.75 fare to downtown

■ Scheduled Airlines

American 512 222-0121
Conquest Airlines 800 722-0860
Continental 512 828-8381
Delta 512 222-2354
Mexicana 512 525-9191
Northwest 800 225-2525
Pan Am 512 227-8196
Southwest 512 696-1221
TWA 512 226-0626
United 800 241-6522
USAir 800 428-4322

■ Charter Airlines

Gunn Air Charter 512 824-8960

■ Car Rentals

Agency 512 349-4555
Alamo 512 828-7967
Avis 512 826-6332
Budget 512 828-5693
Dollar 512 826-0363
National 512 824-1841
Thrifty 512 341-4677

■ Limo/Taxi

Checker Cab 512 222-2151
Limo Unlimited 512 222-2222
Yellow Cab 512 226-4242

■ Mass Transit

512 227-2020 **VIA Metropolitan Transit** $.40 Base fare .... San Antonio TX 78212-4295

■ Rail/Bus

512 270-5800 **Greyhound/Trailways Bus Station** 500 N Saint Marys .... San Antonio TX 78205-1799
512 223-3226 **San Antonio Station** 1174 E Commerce St .... San Antonio TX 78205-3313

Hotels

512 225-6500 **Crockett Hotel** 320 Bonham St .... San Antonio TX 78205-2083
512 224-8800 **Fairmont Hotel** 401 S Alamo .... San Antonio TX 78205-3200
512 366-2424 **Fountain Plaza Hotel** 37 NE Loop 410 .... San Antonio TX 78212-4230
512 222-1400 **Hilton Palacio del Rio** 200 S Alamo St .... San Antonio TX 78205-3299
512 349-9900 **Holiday Inn Airport** 77 NE Loop 410 .... San Antonio TX 78216-0000
512 222-1234 **Hyatt Regency San Antonio** 123 Losoya St .... San Antonio TX 78205-2688
512 225-2581 **La Mansion Del Rio** 112 College St .... San Antonio TX 78205-1844
512 224-4555 **Marriott Hotel Riverwalk** 711 E Riverwalk .... San Antonio TX 78205-0000
512 229-1000 **Plaza San Antonio Hotel** 555 S Alamo St .... San Antonio TX 78205-3298
512 692-9600 **Residence Inn North** 4041 Bluemel Rd .... San Antonio TX 78240-1095
512 227-4392 **Saint Anthony Hotel** 300 E Travis St .... San Antonio TX 78205-1898
512 824-5371 **Seven Oaks Hotel & Conference Center** 1400 Austin Hwy ... San Antonio TX 78209-4300

Restaurants

512 224-8484 **Boudro's Restaurant** (Steak/Seafood) 421 E Commerce ...... San Antonio TX 78205-2657
512 223-2281 **Cocula** (Mexican) 329 Alamo Plaza .... San Antonio TX 78205-2667
512 821-5454 **Crumpets** (French) 5800 Broadway .... San Antonio TX 78209-5294
512 828-1111 **EZ's** (American) 6498 N New Brunfels .... San Antonio TX 78209-0000
512 695-8301 **Grey Moss Inn** (Steak) 19010 Scenic Loop Rd .... San Antonio TX 78238-0000
512 340-1384 **La Fogata** (Mexican) 2427 Vance Jackson Rd .... San Antonio TX 78213-4000
512 225-7984 **La Louisiane Restaurant** (French/Creole) 2632 Broadway ... San Antonio TX 78215-1021
512 225-0722 **La Provence** (French) 206 E Locust St .... San Antonio TX 78212-3954
512 225-1262 **Mi Tierra Cafe & Bakery** (Tex/Mex) 218 Produce Row .... San Antonio TX 78230-0000
512 342-2321 **Old San Francisco Steak House**
    (Steak/Seafood) 10223 Sahara St .... San Antonio TX 78216-3993
512 698-0003 **Romano's Macaroni Grill** (Italian) RR 26 Box 570 .... San Antonio TX 78249-0000
512 641-6100 **Ruffino's** (Italian) 9802 Colonnade Blvd .... San Antonio TX 78230-2202
512 650-0097 **Vienna Wein Stube** (German) 1006 Holbrook Rd .... San Antonio TX 78218-3325
512 734-3283 **Zinfandeli's** (Nouvelle American) 741 W Ashby Pl .... San Antonio TX 78212-0000

Goods & Services

■ Department Stores

512 821-7611 **Dillard's** 9315 Broadway St .... San Antonio TX 78217-5900
512 340-4320 **Foley's** 200 North Star Mall .... San Antonio TX 78216-5398

■ Banks

512 220-4011 **Frost National Bank** 100 W Houston St .... San Antonio TX 78205-1498
512 270-5555 **NCNB Texas National Bank** 300 Convent St .... San Antonio TX 78205-3701

■ Messenger/Postal

Bexar Delivery Service 512 650-3110
Consolidated Parcel Service 512 654-4547
Federal Express 800 238-5355
Flash Carrier Service Inc 512 646-9944
Go-fer Couriers Corp 512 340-0691
Post Office 512 657-8300
UPS 800 292-7129

■ Secretarial/Temp Services

512 680-1000 **Kelly Services Inc** 4801 NW Loop 410 Suite 120 .... San Antonio TX 78229-0000
512 342-2100 **Manpower Temporary Services Inc** 7550 Hwy 10 W .... San Antonio TX 78229-0000
512 349-9911 **Olsten Temporary Services** 40 Loop St Suite 545 .... San Antonio TX 78212-4231

Media

■ Newspapers/Magazines

512 225-7411 **San Antonio Express-News** Ave E & 3rd St .... San Antonio TX 78205-2082
512 271-2700 **San Antonio Light** 420 Broadway St .... San Antonio TX 78205-1987
512 491-0461 **San Antonio Monthly** 13750 N San Pedro Ave Suite 790 ..... San Antonio TX 78232-4358

■ Television

512 366-5000 **KENS-TV Ch 5 (CBS)** 5400 Fredericksburg Rd .... San Antonio TX 78229-3504
512 270-9000 **KLRN-TV Ch 9 (PBS)** 801 S Bowie St .... San Antonio TX 78205-3209
512 226-4251 **KMOL-TV Ch 4 (NBC)** 1031 Navarro St .... San Antonio TX 78205-3800
512 351-1200 **KSAT-TV Ch 12 (ABC)** 1408 N Saint Marys St .... San Antonio TX 78215-1739

■ Radio

512 225-2751 **KCOR-AM 1350 kHz (Span)** 1115 W Martin St .... San Antonio TX 78207-3058
512 342-4999 **KISS-FM 99.5 MHz (AOR)** 8023 Vantage Dr Suite 1200 .... San Antonio TX 78230-0000
512 225-5111 **KITY-FM 92.9 MHz (CHR)** 317 Arden Grove St .... San Antonio TX 78215-1744
512 220-3100 **KQXT-FM 101.9 MHz (AC)** 1115 W Martin St .... San Antonio TX 78207-3058
512 655-5500 **KTFM-FM 102.7 MHz (CHR)** 4050 Eisenhauer Rd .... San Antonio TX 78218-3409
512 734-7301 **WOAI-AM 1200 kHz (N/T-CBS)** 6222 NW IH-10 .... San Antonio TX 78201-2097

Local Attractions & Special Events

■ Sports

512 434-9311 **San Antonio Missions**
    NW 36th & Culebra St VJ Keefe Field .... San Antonio TX 78228-0000
512 554-7787 **San Antonio Spurs**
    600 E Market St Convention Center Arena .... San Antonio TX 78205-0000

■ Local Attractions

512 222-1693 **Alamo** Alamo Plaza & E Houston .... San Antonio TX 78299-0000
512 821-3120 **Brackenridge Park** 3000 Saint Mary's St .... San Antonio TX 78212-3533
512 299-8600 **El Mercado** 514 W Commerce St .... San Antonio TX 78205-0000
512 299-8480 **Hemisfair Urban Water Park** 200 S Alamo .... San Antonio TX 78205-0000
512 299-8610 **La Villita** 418 Villita St .... San Antonio TX 78205-0000
512 824-2537 **Pioneer Museum** 3805 Broadway .... San Antonio TX 78209-0000
512 299-8480 **River Walk City Park** Downtown .... San Antonio TX 78205-0000
512 821-5115 **San Antonio Botanical Center** 555 Funston Pl .... San Antonio TX 78209-6631
512 229-5701 **San Antonio Missions National Historic Park**
    2202 Roosevelt Ave .... San Antonio TX 78210-4919
512 223-5591 **San Antonio Symphony Orchestra**
    109 Lexington Ave Suite 203 .... San Antonio TX 78205-1312
512 224-0601 **Spanish Governor's Palace** 105 Military Plaza .... San Antonio TX 78205-0000

San Diego

CALIFORNIA   619

Important Phone Numbers

AAA	619 668-0250	Emergency	911
American Express	619 297-8101	Poison Control Center	619 543-6000
Better Business Bureau	619 281-6422	Time	619 853-1212
City Hall	619 236-6047	Weather	619 289-1212

■ Travel Information

619 232-0124 **Chamber of Commerce** 110 W 'C' St Suite 1600 .... San Diego CA 92101-3900
619 232-3101 **Convention & Visitors Bureau** 1200 3rd Ave Suite 824 .... San Diego CA 92101-4190

Travel

■ Airport

619 291-3900 **San Diego International Airport** 3 miles NE of city (approx 10 minutes)

■ Airport Transportation

619 233-3004 **San Diego Transit** $1 fare to downtown
Taxi $8-10 fare to downtown

■ Scheduled Airlines

Air Resorts Airlines	619 438-3600	National	800 227-7368
Alaska	800 426-0333	Northwest	800 225-2525
America West	619 560-0727	Pan Am	800 221-1111
American	619 232-4051	Sky West	800 453-9417
American Eagle	800 433-7300	Southwest	619 232-1221
British Airways	800 247-9297	TWA	619 295-7009
Continental	619 232-9155	United	619 234-7171
Delta	619 235-4344	USAir	800 428-4322

■ Charter Airlines

Cinema Air Jet Center	619 438-0877	Jimsair Aviation Services	619 298-7704

■ Car Rentals

Agency	619 295-9226	Enterprise	800 325-8007
Alamo	800 279-9633	Hertz	619 231-7000
Avis	800 331-1212	National	800 227-7368
Budget	619 279-2900	Payless	800 729-5377
Dollar	619 234-3388	Thrifty	619 239-2281

■ Limo/Taxi

American Cab	619 292-1111	Old English Livery Service	800 468-6066
Co-op Cab	619 280-5555	Orange Cab	619 291-3337
Coast Cab Co	619 226-8294	Touch of Class Limousines	619 265-1995
Kelly's Limousine	619 480-6020	Yellow Cab	619 234-6161

■ Mass Transit

619 233-3004 **San Diego Transit** $1 Base fare .... San Diego CA 92101-0000

■ Rail/Bus

619 239-3266 **Greyhound/Trailways Bus Station** 120 W Broadway .... San Diego CA 92101-3811
619 239-9021 **San Diego Station** 1050 Kettner Blvd .... San Diego CA 92101-3305

Hotels

619 488-0551 **Bahia Resort Hotel** 998 W Mission Bay Dr .... San Diego CA 92109-7895
619 224-8888 **Bay Club Hotel & Marina** 2131 Shelter Island Dr .... San Diego CA 92106-3106
619 272-3812 **Beach Haven Inn** 4740 Mission Blvd .... San Diego CA 92109-2539
619 454-3001 **Empress Hotel** 7766 Fay Ave .... La Jolla CA 92037-4309
619 298-0511 **Handlery Stardust Hotel** 950 Hotel Cir N .... San Diego CA 92108-2995
619 239-6171 **Holiday Inn Harbor View** 1617 1st Ave .... San Diego CA 92101-3093
619 435-6611 **Hotel Del Coronado** 1500 Orange Ave .... Coronado CA 92118-2986
619 224-1234 **Hyatt Islandia Hotel** 1441 Quivira Rd .... San Diego CA 92109-7898
619 232-6141 **Kingston Hotel** 1055 1st Ave .... San Diego CA 92101-4890
619 239-2200 **Omni San Diego Hotel** 910 Broadway Cir .... San Diego CA 92101-6114
619 487-1611 **Rancho Bernardo Inn** 17550 Bernardo Oaks Dr .... San Diego CA 92128-2198
619 276-4010 **San Diego Hilton Hotel** 1775 E Mission Bay Dr .... San Diego CA 92109-6895
619 234-1500 **San Diego Marriott Hotel & Marina** 333 W Harbor Dr .... San Diego CA 92101-7709
619 692-3800 **San Diego Marriott Mission Valley** 8757 Rio San Diego Dr ... San Diego CA 92108-1688
619 291-6400 **Sheraton Grand on Harbor Island** 1590 Harbor Island Dr .... San Diego CA 92101-1063
619 291-2900 **Sheraton on Harbor Island** 1380 Harbor Island Dr .... San Diego CA 92101-1092
619 291-7131 **Town & Country Hotel** 500 Hotel Cir N .... San Diego CA 92108-3091
619 232-3121 **US Grant Hotel** 326 Broadway .... San Diego CA 92101-4800
619 238-1818 **Westgate Hotel** 1055 2nd Ave .... San Diego CA 92101-4811

Restaurants

619 291-4779 **Abbey The** (Regional) 2825 5th Ave .... San Diego CA 92103-6326
619 232-7408 **Anthony's Star of the Sea Room**
(Seafood) 1360 N Harbor Dr .... San Diego CA 92101-3396
619 224-2884 **Bungalow The**
(Continental/American) 4996 W Point Loma Blvd .... San Diego CA 92107-1311
619 233-7391 **Chart House The** (Steak/Seafood) 525 E Harbor Dr .... San Diego CA 92101-5995
619 231-6771 **Dobson's** (French) 956 Broadway Cir .... San Diego CA 92101-6114
619 233-5687 **Falco** (Continental) 835 5th Ave .... San Diego CA 92101-0000
619 234-3467 **Fio's** (Italian) 801 5th Ave .... San Diego CA 92101-0000
619 232-3474 **Fish Market** (Seafood) 750 N Harbor Dr .... San Diego CA 92101-0000
619 454-4244 **George's at the Cove** (California) 1250 Prospect St .... La Jolla CA 92037-3618
619 585-3017 **La Fonda Roberto's** (Mexican) 300 3rd Ave .... Chula Vista CA 92010-2701
619 238-1818 **Le Fontainbleau** (French) 1055 2nd Ave Westgate Hotel .... San Diego CA 92101-0000
619 232-5129 **Lubach's** (Continental) 2101 N Harbor Dr .... San Diego CA 92101-1078
619 756-3085 **Mille Fleur** (French) 6009 Paseo Delicias .... Rancho Santa Fe CA 92067-9999
619 696-9226 **Pacifica Grill** (Seafood/Pasta) 1202 Kettner Blvd .... San Diego CA 92101-3338
619 232-7581 **Papagayo** (Seafood) 861 W Harbor Dr .... San Diego CA 92101-7702

---

619 223-1109 **Point Loma Seafoods** (Seafood) 2805 Emerson St .... San Diego CA 92106-0000
619 233-5757 **Rainwater's** (Steak/Seafood) 1202 Kettner Blvd .... San Diego CA 92101-3338
619 292-0141 **Tengu** (Japanese) 8690 Aero Dr .... San Diego CA 92123-1734
619 944-1771 **When in Rome** (Italian) 828 N Hwy 101 .... Leucadia CA 92024-2055

Goods & Services

■ Department Stores

619 231-4747 **Broadway** 160 Horton Plaza .... San Diego CA 92101-6199
619 698-6422 **Bullock's** 5500 Grossmont Center Dr .... La Mesa CA 92042-3009
619 297-2511 **May Co** 1702 Camino del Rio N .... San Diego CA 92108-1580
619 239-1700 **Nordstrom** 103 Horton Plaza .... San Diego CA 92101-6144

■ Banks

619 699-3058 **First Interstate Bank** 401 B St .... San Diego CA 92101-4270
619 557-2200 **San Diego Trust & Savings Bank** 530 Broadway .... San Diego CA 92101-5209
619 238-5118 **Security Pacific Bank** 1200 3rd Ave .... San Diego CA 92101-4198

■ Messenger/Postal

Federal Express	619 295-5545	Pacific Messengers Service Inc	619 232-3141
Great Delivery Machine	619 280-7340	Post Office	619 574-0477
Hesco Courier	619 571-7395	Top Priority	619 278-7070
Knox Professional Court Msgr Svc	619 233-9700	UPS	619 565-1551
Marathon Messenger	619 270-6300	US Courier Corp	619 560-1212
Marrob Courier & Mail Service	619 283-6125		

■ Secretarial/Temp Services

619 260-2100 **Eastridge Temporary Services** 824 Camino del Rio N .... San Diego CA 92108-3291
619 298-6600 **Kelly Services Inc** 1450 Frazee Rd Suite 305 .... San Diego CA 92108-4392
619 234-6433 **Manpower Temporary Services** 401 W 'A' St Suite 610 .... San Diego CA 92101-7903
619 268-4444 **Olsten Temporary Services**
5205 Kearny Villa Way Suite 105 .... San Diego CA 92123-1420

Media

■ Newspapers/Magazines

619 225-8953 **San Diego Magazine** 4206 W Point Loma Blvd .... San Diego CA 92110-5696
619 299-3131 **San Diego Tribune** 350 Camino de la Reina .... San Diego CA 92108-3003
619 299-3131 **San Diego Union** 350 Camino de la Reina .... San Diego CA 92108-3003

■ Television

619 571-8888 **KFMB-TV Ch 8 (CBS)** 7677 Engineer Rd .... San Diego CA 92111-1582
619 237-1010 **KGTV-TV Ch 10 (ABC)** 4600 Air Way .... San Diego CA 92102-0000
619 279-3939 **KNSD-TV Ch 39 (NBC)** 8330 Engineer Rd .... San Diego CA 92171-0000
619 594-1515 **KPBS-TV Ch 15 (PBS)**
5164 College Ave San Diego State University .... San Diego CA 92182-0001

■ Radio

619 292-1360 **KGB-FM 101.5 MHz (AOR)** 7150 Engineer Rd .... San Diego CA 92111-1422
619 238-1037 **KJQY-FM 103.7 MHz (B/EZ)** 625 Broadway Suite 1200 .... San Diego CA 92101-5419
619 565-6006 **KKLQ-FM 106.5 MHz (CHR)** 8525 Gibbs Dr Suite 204 .... San Diego CA 92123-1737
619 265-6431 **KPBS-FM 89.5 MHz (N/T-NPR)** San Diego State University .... San Diego CA 92182-0001
619 278-1130 **KSDO-AM 1130 kHz (N/T-ABC)** 5050 Murphy Canyon Rd .... San Diego CA 92123-4356
619 299-1240 **KSON-AM 1240 kHz (Ctry)**
1615 Murray Canyon Rd Suite 710 .... San Diego CA 92108-4321

Local Attractions & Special Events

■ Sports

619 280-2111 **San Diego Chargers** 9449 Friars Rd Jack Murphy Stadium ..... San Diego CA 92108-0000
619 283-4494 **San Diego Padres** 9449 Friars Rd Jack Murphy Stadium ...... San Diego CA 92108-0000
619 224-4625 **San Diego Sockers**
3500 Sports Arena Blvd San Diego Sports Arena .... San Diego CA 92110-4973

■ Special Events

619 236-1212 **Sand Castle Days** (1st weekend in August)

■ Local Attractions

619 239-0512 **Balboa Park** .... San Diego CA
619 557-5450 **Cabrillo National Monument** 1800 Cabrillo Memorial Way ..... San Diego CA 92106-0000
619 233-5227 **Gaslamp Quarter** 410 Island Ave .... San Diego CA 92101-6925
619 298-4105 **Mexican Tourist Information** .... San Diego CA 92101-0000
619 281-8449 **Mission Basilica San Diego de Alacala**
10818 San Diego Mission Rd .... San Diego CA 92108-0000
619 237-6770 **Old Town** 4002 Wallace Ave .... San Diego CA 92110-0000
619 234-3153 **San Diego Zoo** 2920 Zoo Dr .... San Diego CA 92101-1693
619 534-4086 **Scripps Aquarium** 8602 La Jolla Shores Dr .... La Jolla CA 92093-0207
619 226-3901 **Sea World** 1720 S Shores Rd .... San Diego CA 92101-0000
619 235-4013 **Seaport Village** 849 W Harbor Dr .... San Diego CA 92101-7796
619 239-2211 **Villa Montezuma** 1925 K St .... San Diego CA 92102-0000

San Francisco

CALIFORNIA 415

Important Phone Numbers

AAA	415 863-3432	Emergency	911
American Express	415 788-4367	Poison Control Center	415 476-2845
Better Business Bureau	415 243-9999	Time/Temp	415 936-1212
City Hall	415 554-4000	Weather	415 936-1212

■ Travel Information

415 392-4511 **Chamber of Commerce** 465 California St ... San Francisco CA 94104-1872
415 974-6900 **Convention & Visitors Bureau** 900 Market Dr Holiday Plaza 1st Fl ... San Francisco CA 94103-0000

Travel

■ Airport

415 761-0800 **San Francisco International Airport** 15 miles S of city (approx 25 minutes)

■ Airport Transportation

415 885-2666 **Airport Connection** $8 fare to downtown
415 761-7000 **SAMTRANS** $1.25 fare to downtown
415 673-2433 **SFO Airporter** $6 fare to downtown
415 558-8500 **Super Shuttle** $10 fare to downtown
Taxi $24 fare to downtown

■ Scheduled Airlines

Air Canada	800 776-3000	Mexicana	800 531-7921
Air China	415 392-2156	Northwest	800 225-2525
Alaska	415 931-8888	Pan Am	800 221-1111
American	415 398-4434	Philippine	415 391-0470
British Airways	800 247-9297	Qantas	415 761-8000
Canadian	800 426-7000	Singapore	800 742-3333
Cathay Pacific Airways	415 982-3242	Southwest	415 885-1221
China Airlines	415 391-3950	TACA International	415 421-5850
Continental	415 397-8818	TWA	415 864-5731
Delta	415 552-5700	United	415 397-2100
Eastern	415 474-5858	United Express	415 891-9497
Japan	800 525-3663	USAir	415 956-8636
Lufthansa	800 645-3880		

■ Charter Airlines

Air Share	415 856-3858	KaiserAir	415 569-9622
Commodore Helicopters	415 332-4482		

■ Car Rentals

Agency	415 952-9100	Enterprise	415 441-3369
Alamo	415 347-9911	Hertz	415 877-1600
Avis	415 877-6780	National	415 877-4745
Budget	415 875-7540	Payless	415 872-6565
Dollar	415 692-1204	Thrifty	415 392-4444

■ Limo/Taxi

City Cab	415 468-7200	Luxury Limousine Service	415 824-6767
Ishi Limousine Service	415 586-6000	Veterans Taxicab	415 552-1300
Luxor Cabs	415 282-4141	Yellow Cab	415 626-2345

■ Mass Transit

415 788-2278 **Bay Area Rapid Transit (BART)** $.80 Base fare ... Oakland CA 94607-0000
415 673-6864 **Municipal Railway (MUNI Bus/Cable Cars)** $.85 Base fare ... San Francisco CA 94115-0000

■ Rail/Bus

415 558-6789 **Greyhound/Trailways Bus Station** 50 7th St ... San Francisco CA 94103-1508
415 495-4546 **Southern Pacific Station** 4th & Townsend ... San Francisco CA 94107-0000

Hotels

415 563-7872 **Archbishop's Mansion Inn** 1000 Fulton St ... San Francisco CA 94117-1608
415 781-5555 **Campton Place Hotel** 340 Stockton St ... San Francisco CA 94108-4691
415 776-8200 **Cathedral Hill Hotel** 1101 Van Ness Ave ... San Francisco CA 94109-6986
415 441-7100 **Donatello Hotel** 501 Post St ... San Francisco CA 94102-1228
415 772-5000 **Fairmont Hotel & Tower** 950 Mason St ... San Francisco CA 94108-2098
415 775-4700 **Four Seasons Clift Hotel** 495 Geary St ... San Francisco CA 94102-1280
415 589-0770 **Hilton Airport** San Francisco Yacht Harbor ... San Francisco CA 94123-1062
415 771-1400 **Hilton Hotel & Tower** 1 Hilton Sq ... San Francisco CA 94102-2116
415 771-9000 **Holiday Inn Fishermen's Wharf** 1300 Columbus Ave ... San Francisco CA 94133-1397
415 474-5400 **Huntington Hotel** 1075 California St ... San Francisco CA 94108-2282
415 398-1234 **Hyatt Grand Regency on Union Square** 345 Stockton St ... San Francisco CA 94108-4694
415 788-1234 **Hyatt Regency** 5 Embarcadero Ctr ... San Francisco CA 94111-4856
415 974-6400 **LeMeridien Hotel** 50 3rd St ... San Francisco CA 94103-3198
415 885-0999 **Mandarin Oriental Hotel** 222 Sansome ... San Francisco CA 94104-2792
415 392-3434 **Mark Hopkins Inter-Continental** 1 Nob Hill ... San Francisco CA 94108-2287
415 771-8600 **Pan Pacific Hotel** 500 Post St ... San Francisco CA 94102-1240
415 441-2828 **Queen Anne Hotel** 1590 Sutter St ... San Francisco CA 94109-5395
415 986-2000 **Raphael Hotel** 386 Geary St ... San Francisco CA 94102-1890
415 362-5500 **Sheraton Fishermen's Wharf** 2500 Mason St ... San Francisco CA 94133-1499
415 392-8600 **Sheraton Palace Hotel** 2 New Montgomery St ... San Francisco CA 94105-3402
415 563-3600 **Sherman House** 2160 Green St ... San Francisco CA 94123-4708
415 392-7755 **Sir Francis Drake Hotel** 450 Powell St ... San Francisco CA 94102-1591
415 989-3500 **Stanford Court Hotel** 905 California St ... San Francisco CA 94108-2289
415 397-7000 **Westin Saint Francis** 335 Powell St ... San Francisco CA 94102-1897

Restaurants

415 771-6775 **A Sabella's** (Seafood/Italian) 2766 Taylor St ... San Francisco CA 94133-1288
415 397-4339 **Amelio's** (French) 1630 Powell St ... San Francisco CA 94133-2814
707 963-1211 **Auberge du Soleil** (French) 180 Rutherford Hill Rd ... Rutherford CA 94573-9999
415 981-1177 **Blue Fox** (Italian) 659 Merchant St ... San Francisco CA 94111-2571
415 391-8480 **Cafe Mozart** (French) 708 Bush St ... San Francisco CA 94108-3403
415 981-1251 **Caffe Sport** (Seafood & Pasta) 574 Green St ... San Francisco CA 94133-3920
415 781-5155 **Campton Place** (Nouvelle American) 340 Stockton St ... San Francisco CA 94108-4691
415 548-5525 **Chez Panisse** (French/Italian) 1517 Shattuck Ave ... Berkeley CA 94709-1598
415 982-9500 **Ciao Ristorante** (Italian) 230 Jackson St ... San Francisco CA 94111-1806
415 386-3330 **Cliff House** (Continental/Seafood) 1090 Point Lobos Ave ... San Francisco CA 94121-1496
415 441-7182 **Donatello** (Italian) 501 Post St ... San Francisco CA 94102-1228
415 434-1345 **Empress of China** (Chinese) 838 Grant Ave ... San Francisco CA 94108-1738
415 397-5969 **Ernie's** (French) 847 Montgomery St ... San Francisco CA 94133-5108
415 673-7779 **Fleur de Lys** (French) 777 Sutter St ... San Francisco CA 94109-6416
415 989-1910 **Fournou's Ovens** (Nouvelle American) 905 California St ... San Francisco CA 94133-0000
415 771-6222 **Greens** (Vegetarian) Fort Mason Ctr Bldg A ... San Francisco CA 94123-0000
415 991-9067 **Jil's** (International) 11 Colma Blvd ... Colma CA 94104-0000
415 752-5652 **Kabuto** (Japanese) 5116 Geary Blvd ... San Francisco CA 94118-2816
415 982-2388 **Kan's** (Chinese) 708 Grant Ave ... San Francisco CA 94108-2114
415 433-4343 **Little Joe's** (Italian) 523 Broadway St ... San Francisco CA 94133-4506
415 673-8812 **Mandarin The** (Chinese) 900 N Point St ... San Francisco CA 94109-1112
415 989-7154 **Masa's** (French) 648 Bush St ... San Francisco CA 94108-3509
415 392-1587 **North Beach Restaurant** (Italian) 1512 Stockton St ... San Francisco CA 94133-3306
415 776-7825 **Postrio** (Chinese/Italian) 545 Post St ... San Francisco CA 94102-0000
415 362-7115 **Pung Fong** (Dim Sum) 808 Pacific Ave ... San Francisco CA 94133-4302
415 421-0594 **Sam's** (Seafood) 374 Bush St ... San Francisco CA 94104-2805
415 841-4740 **Santa Fe Bar & Grill** (Southwest) 1310 University Ave ... Berkeley CA 94702-1711
415 771-4383 **Scoma's** (Seafood) Fishermans Wharf Pier 47 ... San Francisco CA 94133-0000
707 963-3970 **Showley's at Miramonte** (Ecclectic) 1327 Railroad Ave ... Saint Helena CA 94574-1192
415 788-1110 **Square One** (International/Mediterranean) 190 Pacific Ave ... San Francisco CA 94111-1905
415 861-7827 **Stars** (Nouvelle American) 150 Redwood St ... San Francisco CA 94102-3222
415 391-2373 **Tadich Grill** (American) 240 California St ... San Francisco CA 94111-4322
415 982-8123 **Washington Square Bar & Grill** (Italian) 1707 Powell St ... San Francisco CA 94133-2808
415 982-6020 **Yuet Lee Seafood** (Seafood/Chinese) 1300 Stockton St ... San Francisco CA 94133-3807

Goods & Services

■ Department Stores

415 764-2222 **Emporium-Capwell** 835 Market St ... San Francisco CA 94103-1872
415 362-2100 **I Magnin** 135 Stockton St ... San Francisco CA 94108-5892
415 362-3900 **Neiman-Marcus** 150 Stockton St ... San Francisco CA 94108-4680
415 243-8500 **Nordstrom** 865 Market St ... San Francisco CA 94103-1950

■ Banks

415 622-3456 **Bank of America National Trust & Savings Assn** 555 California St ... San Francisco CA 94104-1590
415 765-0400 **Bank of California** 400 California St ... San Francisco CA 94104-1382
415 772-8200 **Sanwa Bank of California** 444 Market St ... San Francisco CA 94111-5381
415 445-4000 **Security Pacific National Bank** 201 California St ... San Francisco CA 94111-5083
415 477-7093 **Wells Fargo Bank NA** 55 Sansome St ... San Francisco CA 94104-4497

■ Messenger/Postal

Aero Special Delivery	415 982-1303	Special T Msgr Delivery Svc Inc	415 861-2225
Federal Express	415 877-9000	Specialized Messenger Services	415 861-2129
Now Courier Service	415 543-2212	Speedway Msgr & Delivery Svc	415 243-8600
PDQ Delivery	415 346-4229	UPS	415 952-5200
Post Office	415 550-6500	Western Messenger Service	415 864-4100

■ Secretarial/Temp Services

415 788-7030 **Accountemps** 388 Market St Suite 1400 ... San Francisco CA 94111-5682
415 982-2200 **Kelly Services Inc** 1 Post St Suite 2150 ... San Francisco CA 94104-5290
415 781-7171 **Manpower Temporary Services Inc** 50 California St Suite 440 ... San Francisco CA 94111-4605
415 433-1110 **Olsten Temporary Services** 120 Montgomery St Suite 700 ... San Francisco CA 94104-4310

Media

■ Newspapers/Magazines

415 777-1111 **San Francisco Chronicle** 901 Mission St ... San Francisco CA 94103-2905
415 777-2424 **San Francisco Examiner** 110 5th St ... San Francisco CA 94103-2918
415 553-2800 **San Francisco Focus** 680 8th St ... San Francisco CA 94103-4989

■ Television

415 954-7777 **KGO-TV Ch 7 (ABC)** 900 Front St ... San Francisco CA 94111-1427
415 362-5550 **KPIX-TV Ch 5 (CBS)** 855 Battery St ... San Francisco CA 94111-1597
415 864-2000 **KQED-TV Ch 9 (PBS)** 500 8th St ... San Francisco CA 94103-4492
415 441-4444 **KRON-TV Ch 4 (NBC)** 1001 Van Ness Ave ... San Francisco CA 94109-6982

■ Radio

415 788-5225 **KABL-FM 98.1 MHz (AC)** 1025 Battery St ... San Francisco CA 94111-1277
415 648-1177 **KALW-FM 91.7 MHz (Jazz-NPR)** 2905 21st St ... San Francisco CA 94110-2718
415 765-4000 **KCBS-AM 740 kHz (N/T-CBS)** 1 Embarcadero Ctr 32nd Fl ... San Francisco CA 94111-3607
415 954-8100 **KGO-AM 810 kHz (N/T-ABC)** 900 Front St ... San Francisco CA 94111-1427
415 391-1061 **KMEL-FM 106.1 MHz (CHR)** 55 Francisco St Suite 400 ... San Francisco CA 94133-2122
415 765-4000 **KRQR-FM 97.3 MHz (AOR)** 1 Embarcadero Ctr 32nd Fl ... San Francisco CA 94111-3607
415 341-8777 **KSOL-FM 107.7 MHz (UC)** 1730 S Amphlett Blvd Suite 327 ... San Mateo CA 94402-2714

Local Attractions & Special Events

■ Sports

415 468-2249 **San Francisco 49ers** Candlestick Pk ... San Francisco CA 94124-3902
415 330-2490 **San Francisco Giants** Candlestick Pk ... San Francisco CA 94124-3902

■ Special Events

415 974-6900 **Chinese New Year Celebration** (February 15)

■ Local Attractions

415 546-2805 **Alcatraz Island** Pier 41 Red & White Fleet ... San Francisco CA 94101-0000
415 668-8921 **Asian Art Museum** Golden Gate Pk ... San Francisco CA 94101-0000
415 474-1887 **Cable Car Barn & Museum** 1201 Mason St ... San Francisco CA 94108-1010

415 974-6900	**Chinatown** Grant & Bush Sts	San Francisco	CA	94101-0000
415 274-0203	**Coit Tower** 1 Telegraph Hill Blvd	San Francisco	CA	94133-3106
415 772-0500	**Embarcadero Information Center**	San Francisco	CA	94111-0000
415 626-7070	**Fisherman's Wharf** 1873 Market St	San Francisco	CA	94103-1100
415 775-5500	**Ghirardelli Square** 900 N Point St	San Francisco	CA	94101-0000
415 666-7200	**Golden Gate Park** McLaren Lodge	San Francisco	CA	94117-0000
415 621-8203	**Mission Dolores** 3321 16th St	San Francisco	CA	94114-0000
415 388-2595	**Muir Woods National Monument**	Mill Valley	CA	94941-0000
415 744-6830	**Old Mint** 88 5th St	San Francisco	CA	94103-0000
415 563-6504	**Palace of Fine Arts** 3601 Lyon St	San Francisco	CA	94123-1019
415 981-7437	**Pier 39** Beach & Embarcadero	San Francisco	CA	94133-0000
415 556-6706	**San Francisco Mint** 155 Hermann St	San Francisco	CA	94102-0000
415 332-0505	**Sausalito Information** 333 Calidonia	San Francisco	CA	94965-0000
415 561-2211	**The Presidio**	San Francisco	CA	94129-0000

San Jose

CALIFORNIA   **408**

Important Phone Numbers

AAA	408 246-5811	Emergency	911
American Express	408 244-1015	Poison Control Center	408 299-5112
Better Business Bureau	408 978-8700	Time	408 767-8900
City Hall	408 277-4000	Weather	415 364-7974

■ Travel Information

408 998-7000 **Chamber of Commerce** 180 S Market St .... San Jose CA 95113-2307
408 295-9600 **Convention & Visitors Bureau**
               333 W San Carlos St Suite 1000 .... San Jose CA 95110-2711

Travel

■ Airport

408 277-5366 **San Jose International Airport** 3 miles NW of city (approx 15 minutes)

■ Airport Transportation

415 872-2552 **Airport Connection** $17 fare to downtown
415 467-1800 **Bay Porter Express** $16-20 fare to downtown
408 287-4210 **Santa Clara County Transit** $.75 fare to downtown
               Taxi $8-11 fare to downtown

■ Scheduled Airlines

Alaska	408 279-8866	Sky West	800 453-9417
America West	800 247-5692	TWA	408 298-6600
American	408 298-8220	United	408 984-5400
Continental	800 525-0280	USAir	408 971-8000
Delta	408 287-1313		

■ Charter Airlines

Aris Helicopters	408 998-3266	Jet Center	408 297-7552
Barbary Coast Charters	408 297-9000	Silicon Valley Express	408 292-0677
Gateway Charters	408 971-4283		

■ Car Rentals

Alamo	408 453-8180	Hertz	408 437-5700
Avis	408 993-2224	National	408 920-2266
Budget	415 342-7573	Thrifty	408 727-4567
Dollar	408 280-1111		

■ Limo/Taxi

Alpha Cab	408 295-9500	Elegance Unlimited Limousine	408 723-3414
Associated Limousines	408 435-1999	South Bay Cab	408 296-1700
Champagne Limousine	408 866-1700	United Cab	408 243-2220
Corinthian Coach Limousine Service	408 395-5466	Yellow Checker Cab	408 293-1234
Courtesy Limousine Service	408 988-0445		

■ Mass Transit

408 287-4210 **Santa Clara County Transit** $.75 Base fare .... San Jose CA 95112-0000

■ Rail/Bus

408 295-1644 **Greyhound/Trailways Bus Terminal** 70 S Almaden Ave .... San Jose CA 95113-2199
408 287-7462 **San Jose Station** 65 Cahill St .... San Jose CA 95110-2501

Hotels

408 986-0700 **Doubletree Hotel** 5101 Great America Pkwy .... Santa Clara CA 95054-1132
408 998-1900 **Fairmont Hotel** 170 S Market St .... San Jose CA 95113-2395
408 435-8800 **Gateway Inn** 2585 Seaboard Ave .... San Jose CA 95131-1006
408 453-5340 **Holiday Inn Airport** 1355 N 4th St .... San Jose CA 95112-4783
408 993-1234 **Hyatt San Jose** 1740 N 1st St .... San Jose CA 95112-4584
408 453-6200 **Le Baron Hotel** 1350 N 1st St .... San Jose CA 95112-4789
408 298-0100 **Radisson Plaza Hotel** 1471 N 4th St .... San Jose CA 95112-4716
408 453-4000 **Red Lion Hotel** 2050 Gateway Pl .... San Jose CA 95110-1047
408 293-9361 **San Jose Inn** 1860 The Alameda .... San Jose CA 95126-1781
408 295-0159 **TraveLodge Downtown** 1041 The Alameda .... San Jose CA 95126-3142
408 453-8822 **Vagabond Inn** 1488 N 1st St .... San Jose CA 95112-4818

Restaurants

408 867-3110 **Adriatic** (Continental) 14583 Big Basin Way .... Saratoga CA 95070-6072
408 998-2883 **C'est Bon** (French) 71 N San Pedro St .... San Jose CA 95110-0000
408 289-1960 **Emil's** (French) 545 S 2nd St .... San Jose CA 95112-5708
408 294-6785 **Gordon Biersch Brewery Restaurant**
               (American) 33 E San Fernando St .... San Jose CA 95112-0000
408 295-5414 **Henry's Hi-life** (Barbecue/Steak) 301 W Saint John St .... San Jose CA 95110-2345
408 453-8148 **House of Cathay** (Chinese) 1339 N 1st St .... San Jose CA 95112-4710
408 379-3000 **Komatsu** (Japanese) 300 Orchard City Dr .... Campbell CA 95008-2932
408 997-3458 **La Foret** (Continental) 21747 Bertram Rd .... San Jose CA 95120-4329
408 867-5272 **La Mere Michelle** (Continental) 14467 Big Basin Way .... Saratoga CA 95070-6008
408 867-7017 **Le Mouton Noir** (French) 14560 Big Basin Way .... Saratoga CA 95070-6014
408 262-2563 **Marina Seafood Grotto** (Seafood) 995 Elizabeth St .... Alviso CA 95002-9999
408 252-5311 **Pacific Fresh** (Seafood) 21255 Stevens Creek Blvd .... Cupertino CA 95014-0000
408 294-2558 **Paolo's** (Italian) 520 E Santa Clara .... San Jose CA 95112-0000
408 279-3110 **Pathaya Cuisine** (Thai) 40 N Market St .... San Jose CA 95113-1206
408 971-1700 **Scott's Seafood Grill & Bar** (Seafood/Steak) 185 Park Ave ...... San Jose CA 95113-2224
408 286-1770 **Victoria Garden Restaurant** (Italian/Continental) 476 S 1st St ... San Jose CA 95113-2815

Goods & Services

■ Department Stores

408 296-1111 **Emporium-Capwell** 3051 Stevens Creek Blvd .... Santa Clara CA 95050-6793
408 244-4100 **I Magnin** 3047 Stevens Creek Blvd .... Santa Clara CA 95050-6791
408 248-3333 **Macy's** 2801 Stevens Creek Blvd .... Santa Clara CA 95050-6796

■ Banks

408 244-1700 **Pacific Western Bank** 1245 S Winchester Blvd .... San Jose CA 95128-3955
408 294-8940 **Plaza Bank of Commerce** 55 Almaden Blvd .... San Jose CA 95113-1693
408 947-7562 **San Jose National Bank** 1 N Market St .... San Jose CA 95113-1269

■ Messenger/Postal

Blue Ribbon Express	408 945-0312	Post Office	408 452-0660
Express Messenger Systems Inc	415 956-5800	Specialized Messenger Services	408 946-6670
Federal Express	408 279-8870	UPS	415 952-5200

■ Secretarial/Temp Services

408 286-4912 **Accountemps** 10 Almaden Blvd Suite 530 .... San Jose CA 95113-0000
408 267-9650 **Kelly Services Inc** 3315 Almaden Expy Suite 37 .... San Jose CA 95118-1557
408 241-4900 **Manpower Temporary Services Inc** 2960 Stevens Creek Blvd .. San Jose CA 95128-2022

Media

■ Newspapers/Magazines

408 298-8000 **Metro** 410 S 1st St .... San Jose CA 95113-2815
408 920-5000 **San Jose Mercury News** 750 Ridder Park Dr .... San Jose CA 95190-0001

■ Television

408 286-1111 **KNTV-TV Ch 11 (ABC)** 645 Park Ave .... San Jose CA 95110-2613
415 362-5550 **KPIX-TV Ch 5 (CBS)** 855 Battery St .... San Francisco CA 94111-1597
415 441-4444 **KRON-TV Ch 4 (NBC)** 1001 Van Ness Ave .... San Francisco CA 94109-6982
408 437-5454 **KTEH-TV Ch 54 (PBS)** 100 Skyport Dr .... San Jose CA 95110-1301

■ Radio

408 370-7377 **KBAY-FM 100.3 MHz (B/EZ)** 399 N 3rd St .... Campbell CA 95008-1210
415 954-8100 **KGO-AM 810 kHz (N/T-ABC)** 900 Front St .... San Francisco CA 94111-1427
408 943-0770 **KHQT-FM 97.7 MHz (CHR)** 2860 Zanker Rd Suite 201 .... San Jose CA 95134-2120
408 985-9800 **KOME-FM 98.5 MHz (AOR)** 3031 Tisch Way Suite 3 .... San Jose CA 95128-2530
408 459-4036 **KZSC-FM 88.1 MHz (AC-NPR)** University of California ....Santa Cruz CA 95064-0000

Local Attractions & Special Events

■ Sports

415 574-7223 **Bay Meadows Race Course** 2600 S Delaware St .... San Mateo CA 94403-1904
408 297-1435 **San Jose Giants** S 10th & E Alma Sts Municipal Stadium .... San Jose CA 95112-0000

■ Local Attractions

408 288-5057 **J Lohr Winery** 1000 Lenzen Ave .... San Jose CA 95126-0000
408 274-5061 **Lick Observatory** Mt Hamilton .... San Jose CA 95101-0000
408 274-4000 **Mirassou Vineyards** 3000 Aborn Rd .... San Jose CA 95135-1799
408 287-2290 **Peralta Adobe** 184 W Saint John St .... San Jose CA 95110-0000
408 287-9171 **Rosicrucian Egyptian Museum** Park & Naglee Aves .... San Jose CA 95191-0001
408 279-7150 **Technology Center of Silicon Valley**
               95 S Market St Suite 650 .... San Jose CA 95113-2306
408 247-2000 **Winchester Mystery House** 525 S Winchester Blvd ....San Jose CA 95128-2588

Seattle
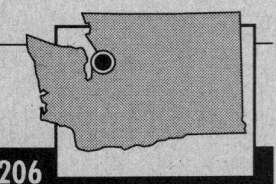

WASHINGTON   206

Important Phone Numbers

AAA 206 448-5353
American Express 206 441-8622
Better Business Bureau 206 448-8888
City Hall 206 386-1234
Emergency 911
Poison Control Center 206 526-2121
Time/Temp 206 526-7777
Weather 206 526-6087

■ Travel Information

206 461-7200 **Chamber of Commerce** 600 University St Suite 1200 .... Seattle WA 98101-0000
206 461-5800 **Convention & Visitors Bureau** 520 Pike St Suite 1300 .... Seattle WA 98101-4001
206 461-5840 **Visitor Information** 800 Convention Pl .... Seattle WA 98101-0000

Travel

■ Airport

206 433-5217 **Seattle-Tacoma International Airport** 13 miles S of city (approx 25 minutes)

■ Airport Transportation

206 624-5077 **Gray Line Downtown Airporter** $6 fare to downtown
206 447-4800 **Metro** $.75-$1 fare to downtown
206 622-1424 **ShuttleExpress** $12 fare to downtown
Taxi $20-24 fare to downtown

■ Scheduled Airlines

Alaska 206 433-3100
America West 206 433-5704
American 206 241-0920
British Airways 800 247-9297
Canadian 800 426-7000
Continental 206 624-1740
Delta 206 241-2300
Eastern 206 622-1881
Harbor 206 675-6666
Horizon 206 762-3646
Japan Air Lines 206 624-3133
Kenmore Air 206 486-1257
Mexicana 800 531-7921
Northwest 206 433-3500
Pan Am 800 221-1111
SAS 800 221-3300
TWA 206 447-9400
United 206 441-3700
USAir 206 587-6229

■ Charter Airlines

Air Gemini Inc 206 851-2381
Flightcraft 206 764-6100
Galvin Flying Service 206 763-0350
Lake Union Air Service 206 284-0300
Snohomish Flying Service Inc ... 206 568-1541

■ Car Rentals

Alamo 206 433-0182
Allstar 206 431-3368
Avis 206 433-5231
Budget 206 433-5243
Dollar 206 433-5825
Hertz 206 433-5262
National 206 433-5501
Payless 206 243-1497
Practical 206 241-4645
Thrifty 206 246-7565

■ Limo/Taxi

Elegance Limousine 206 682-3839
Far West Cab 206 622-1717
Graytop Cab 206 782-8294
London Limousine 206 622-0444
Star Limousine 206 824-1124
Yellow Cab 206 622-6500

■ Mass Transit

206 447-4800 **Metro Transit** $.55 Base fare .... Seattle WA 98104-0000
206 464-6400 **Washington State Ferry System** Fare varies with destination ...... Seattle WA

■ Rail/Bus

206 383-4615 **Cascade Trailways** 2209 Pacific Ave .... Tacoma WA 98402-3005
206 624-3456 **Greyhound/Trailways Bus Station** 8th Ave & Stewart St .... Seattle WA 98101-1396
206 382-4125 **King Street Station** 303 S Jackson St .... Seattle WA 98104-0000

Hotels

206 624-4844 **Alexis Hotel** 1007 1st Ave .... Seattle WA 98104-1007
206 878-1814 **Best Western Airport Executel** 20717 Pacific Hwy S .... Seattle WA 98198-5808
206 284-1900 **Best Western Continental Plaza** 2500 Aurora Ave N .... Seattle WA 98109-2206
206 246-8220 **Doubletree Inn** 205 Strander Blvd .... Seattle WA 98188-2869
206 728-7000 **Edgewater Inn** 2411 Alaskan Way .... Seattle WA 98121-1398
206 621-1700 **Four Seasons Olympic Hotel** 411 University St .... Seattle WA 98101-2559
206 244-4800 **Hilton Inn Airport** 17620 Pacific Hwy S .... Seattle WA 98188-4001
206 464-1980 **Holiday Inn Crowne Plaza** 1113 6th Ave .... Seattle WA 98101-3048
206 462-1234 **Hyatt Regency** 900 Bellevue Way NE .... Bellevue WA 98004-0000
206 443-3600 **Inn at the Market** 86 Pine St .... Seattle WA 98101-1571
206 623-8700 **Mayflower Park Hotel** 4th & Olive Way .... Seattle WA 98101-1149
206 634-2000 **Meany Tower Hotel** 4507 Brooklyn Ave NE .... Seattle WA 98105-4508
206 244-6000 **Radisson Hotel Seattle Airport** 17001 Pacific Hwy S .... Seattle WA 98188-3593
206 455-1300 **Red Lion Hotel Bellevue** 300 112th Ave SE .... Bellevue WA 98004-6400
206 246-8600 **Red Lion Inn Sea-Tac** 18740 Pacific Hwy S .... Seattle WA 98188-4271
206 226-5500 **Residence Inn Seattle South** 16201 W Valley Hwy .... Seattle WA 98188-5529
206 621-9000 **Sheraton Hotel & Towers** 1400 6th Ave .... Seattle WA 98101-2398
206 622-6400 **Sorrento Hotel** 900 Madison St .... Seattle WA 98104-1297
206 583-0300 **Stouffer Madison Hotel** 515 Madison St .... Seattle WA 98104-1119
206 728-1000 **Westin Hotel** 1900 5th Ave .... Seattle WA 98101-1281
206 822-3700 **Woodmark Hotel** 1200 Carillon Point .... Kirkland WA 98033-0000

Restaurants

206 285-5000 **Adriatica** (Mediterranean) 1107 Dexter Ave N .... Seattle WA 98109-3517
206 622-7688 **Al Boccalino** (Italian) 1 Yesler Way .... Seattle WA 98104-0000
206 443-6000 **Cafe Sport** (Northwest American) 2020 Western Ave .... Seattle WA 98121-2109
206 283-3313 **Canlis Restaurant** (American) 2576 Aurora Ave N .... Seattle WA 98109-2299
206 467-9990 **Chez Shea** (Northwest/French) 94 Pike St .... Seattle WA 98101-2066
206 682-4142 **Dahlia Lounge** (International) 1904 4th Ave .... Seattle WA 98101-0000
206 329-6620 **Dominique's Place** (French) 1927 43rd Ave E .... Seattle WA 98112-3234

---

206 451-0426 **Fountain Court** (French) 22 103rd Ave NE .... Bellevue WA 98004-5619
206 447-5544 **Fuller's** (Continental/American) 1400 6th Ave .... Seattle WA 98101-2318
206 621-7889 **Georgian Room** (American) 411 University St .... Seattle WA 98101-0000
206 329-8063 **Henry's Off Broadway** (Northwest) 1705 E Olive Way .... Seattle WA 98102-5684
206 784-2222 **Herb Farm**
(Nouvelle American) 32804 SE Issaquah-Fall City Rd .... Fall City WA 98024-5704
206 624-6852 **Ivar's Acres of Clams** (Seafood) 1000 Alaskan Way Pier 54 .... Seattle WA 98104-0000
206 441-4805 **Kasper's by the Bay** (American) 2701 1st Ave .... Seattle WA 98121-0000
206 441-8899 **La Buznick** (Czechoslovakian/Continental) 1924 1st Ave .... Seattle WA 98101-0000
206 283-0991 **Le Tastevin** (French) 19 W Harrison Ave .... Seattle WA 98119-4109
206 624-3287 **Metropolitan Grill** (American) 818 2nd Ave .... Seattle WA 98104-0000
206 624-4550 **Mirabeau** (Northwestern) 1001 4th Ave 46th Fl .... Seattle WA 98154-0000
206 322-4641 **Nikko** (Japanese) 1306 S King St .... Seattle WA 98144-2027
206 623-7340 **Other Place The** (Northwest) 96 Union St .... Seattle WA 98101-2026
206 728-1000 **Palm Court The** (Continental/Northwest) 1900 5th Ave .... Seattle WA 98101-0000
206 789-3770 **Ray's Boathouse** (Seafood) 6049 Seaview Ave NW .... Seattle WA 98107-2690
206 325-7442 **Rover's** (Nouvelle American) 2808 E Madison .... Seattle WA 98112-4862
206 524-4044 **Saleh al Lago** (Italian) 6804 East Green Lake Way N .... Seattle WA 98115-5417
206 623-2100 **Sea Garden Restaurant** (Chinese/Seafood) 509 7th Ave S .... Seattle WA 98104-2905
206 323-7772 **Settebello** (Italian) 1525 E Olive Way .... Seattle WA 98122-2129

Goods & Services

■ Department Stores

206 344-2121 **Bon Marche** 1601 3rd Ave .... Seattle WA 98181-0001
206 682-5500 **Frederick & Nelson** 5th Ave & Pine St .... Seattle WA 98101-0000
206 628-2111 **Nordstrom** 1501 5th Ave .... Seattle WA 98101-1603

■ Banks

206 447-5700 **Puget Sound Bank** 815 2nd Ave .... Seattle WA 98104-1594
206 358-0800 **SeaFirst Bank** 1001 4th Ave .... Seattle WA 98154-9998
206 621-4111 **Security Pacific Bank Washington** 1301 5th Ave .... Seattle WA 98101-2678
206 344-2300 **US Bank of Washington NA** 1414 4th Ave .... Seattle WA 98101-2282

■ Messenger/Postal

ABC Legal Messengers Inc 206 623-8771
American Messenger Services 206 441-4555
Bucky's Messenger Service 206 448-9280
Dependable Messenger Service 206 728-4066
Eastside Expediters 206 483-4555
Elliott Bay Messenger Co 206 728-8505
ENA Couriers 206 624-3200
Federal Express 206 282-9766
Fleetfoot Messenger Service 206 728-7700
Post Office 206 442-6340
UPS 206 767-9700

■ Secretarial/Temp Services

206 282-9000 **Della Street Office Support** 5 W Harrison St .... Seattle WA 98119-4181
206 382-7171 **Kelly Services Inc** 999 3rd Ave Suite 2580 .... Seattle WA 98104-4001
206 583-0880 **Manpower Temporary Services Inc** 1420 5th Ave Suite 1850 ..... Seattle WA 98101-0000
206 441-2962 **Olsten Temporary Services** 2033 6th Ave Suite 910 .... Seattle WA 98121-2526

Media

■ Newspapers/Magazines

206 682-2704 **Pacific Northwest Magazine** 222 Dexter Ave N .... Seattle WA 98109-5197
206 448-8000 **Seattle Post-Intelligencer** 101 Elliott Ave W .... Seattle WA 98119-4295
206 464-2111 **Seattle Times** 1120 John St .... Seattle WA 98109-5321

■ Television

206 728-6463 **KCTS-TV Ch 9 (PBS)** 401 Mercer St .... Seattle WA 98109-4640
206 448-5555 **KING-TV Ch 5 (NBC)** 333 Dexter Ave N .... Seattle WA 98109-5107
206 728-7777 **KIRO-TV Ch 7 (CBS)** 2807 3rd Ave .... Seattle WA 98121-0000
206 443-4000 **KOMO-TV Ch 4 (ABC)** 100 4th Ave N .... Seattle WA 98109-4997

■ Radio

206 728-7777 **KIRO-AM 710 kHz (N/T-CBS)** 2807 3rd Ave .... Seattle WA 98121-0000
206 285-7625 **KISW-FM 99.9 MHz (AOR-AP)** 712 Aurora Ave N .... Seattle WA 98109-4314
206 443-4010 **KOMO-AM 1000 kHz (AC-ABC)** 100 4th Ave N .... Seattle WA 98109-4997
206 223-5703 **KPLZ-FM 101.5 MHz (CHR-UPI)** 7th & Olive .... Seattle WA 98101-0000
206 728-5732 **KSEA-FM 100.7 MHz (AC)** 2807 3rd Ave .... Seattle WA 98121-0000
206 322-1622 **KUBE-FM 93.3 MHz (CHR)** 120 Lakeside Ave Suite 310 .... Seattle WA 98122-6542
206 543-2710 **KUOW-FM 94.9 MHz (Misc-NPR)**
University of Washington DS-50 .... Seattle WA 98195-0001

Local Attractions & Special Events

■ Sports

206 296-3111 **Seattle Mariners** 100 S King St Kingdome .... Seattle WA 98104-0000
206 827-9766 **Seattle Seahawks** 100 S King St Kingdome .... Seattle WA 98104-0000
206 281-5850 **Seattle SuperSonics** 190 Queen Anne Ave N Coliseum .... Seattle WA 98109-4926

■ Special Events

206 684-7337 **Bumbershoot Festival** (August 30-September 2)
206 728-0123 **Seafair** (July 12-August 4)

■ Local Attractions

206 783-7001 **Chittenden Locks** 3015 NW 54th .... Seattle WA 98107-3530
206 764-5700 **Museum of Flight** 9404 E Marginal Way S .... Seattle WA 98108-4097
206 443-2001 **Pacific Science Center** 200 2nd Ave N .... Seattle WA 98109-4895
206 682-7453 **Pike Place Market** 85 Pike St .... Seattle WA 98101-2045
206 624-1164 **Pioneer Square** 1st Ave & James St .... Seattle WA 98104-0000
206 746-4025 **Puget Sound & Snoqualmie Valley Railroad** 109 King St .... Snoqualmie WA 98065-0000
206 386-4300 **Seattle Aquarium** Pier 59 .... Seattle WA 98104-0000
206 684-7200 **Seattle Center** 305 Harrison St .... Seattle WA 98109-4695
206 684-7200 **Seattle Opera House/Playhouse** Mercer St & 3rd Ave N .... Seattle WA 98101-0000
206 443-2100 **Space Needle** Seattle Center .... Seattle WA 98109-0000
206 461-5840 **Waterfront Park** .... Seattle WA 98104-0000
206 467-1600 **Westlake Center** 1601 5th Ave .... Seattle WA 98101-0000

Tampa/St Pete
FLORIDA 813

Important Phone Numbers

AAA	813 289-5000	Emergency	911
American Express	813 273-0310	Poison Control Center	813 253-4444
Better Business Bureau	813 875-6200	Time/Temp	813 622-1212
City Hall	813 223-8131	Weather	813 645-2506

■ Travel Information
813 228-7777 **Chamber of Commerce** 801 E Kennedy Blvd .... Tampa FL 33602-4195
813 223-1111 **Convention & Visitors Assn** 111 E Madison St .... Tampa FL 33602-4705

Travel

■ Airport
813 870-8700 **Tampa International Airport** PO Box 22287

■ Airport Transportation
813 254-4278 **HARTline** $.75 fare to downtown
Taxi $10 fare to downtown

■ Scheduled Airlines
Air Canada	800 776-3000	Northwest	813 885-7811
American	813 221-5831	Pan Am	800 221-1111
British Airways	800 247-9297	TWA	813 229-7961
Continental	813 874-7151	United	800 241-6522
Delta	813 286-1800	USAir	813 223-1890
Eastern	813 877-8811		

■ Charter Airlines
Air New Orleans	800 535-2643	Tampa Flying Service Inc	813 251-1752

■ Car Rentals
Alamo	813 289-4323	Hertz	813 874-3232
American International	813 289-4443	Holiday-Payless	813 289-6554
Avis	813 276-3500	National	813 276-3782
Budget	813 877-6051	Thrifty	813 289-4006
Dollar	813 276-3640		

■ Limo/Taxi
Alpha Limousine	813 247-6190	United Cab	813 253-2424
Central Florida Limousines	813 276-3730	Yellow Cab	813 253-0121
Tampa Bay Cab	813 251-5555		

■ Mass Transit
813 254-4278 **HARTline** $.75 Base fare .... Tampa FL 33605-2311

■ Rail/Bus
813 221-7600 **Amtrak Passenger Station** 601 N Nebraska Ave .... Tampa FL 33602-3555
813 229-1831 **Trailways Bus Terminal** 610 E Polk St .... Tampa FL 33602-3909

Hotels

813 289-1750 **Admiral Benbow Inn** 1200 N Westshore Blvd .... Tampa FL 33607-4697
813 879-4800 **Holiday Inn Airport** 4500 W Cypress St .... Tampa FL 33607-4084
813 225-1234 **Hyatt Regency Tampa Downtown** 211 N Tampa St .... Tampa FL 33602-5127
813 874-1234 **Hyatt Regency Westshore** 6200 W Courtney Campbell Cswy ...... Tampa FL 33607-5916
813 223-2222 **Riverside Hotel** 200 N Ashley Dr .... Tampa FL 33602-5138
813 988-9191 **Safari Resort Inn** 4139 E Busch Blvd .... Tampa FL 33617-5935
813 360-1811 **Saint Petersburg Beach Hilton Inn**
5250 Gulf Blvd .... Saint Petersburg Beach FL 33706-2408
813 894-5000 **Saint Petersburg Hilton & Towers** 333 1st St S .... Saint Petersburg FL 33701-4342
813 360-5551 **Sandpiper Resorts** 6000 Gulf Blvd .... Saint Petersburg Beach FL 33706-3799
813 286-4400 **Sheraton Grand Hotel** 4860 W Kennedy Blvd .... Tampa FL 33609-2591
813 879-5151 **Tampa Airport Marriott Hotel** Tampa International Airport .... Tampa FL 33607-5934
813 877-6688 **Tampa Hilton at Metrocenter** 2225 N Lois Ave .... Tampa FL 33607-2395
813 287-2555 **Tampa Marriott Hotel Westshore** 1001 N Westshore Blvd .... Tampa FL 33607-4796
813 229-5000 **Wyndham Harbour Island Hotel** 725 S Harbour Island Blvd .... Tampa FL 33602-5707

Restaurants

813 894-7880 **Basta's** (Northern Italian) 1625 4th St S .... Saint Petersburg FL 33701-5808
813 251-2421 **Bern's Steak House** (Steak) 1208 S Howard Ave .... Tampa FL 33606-3197
813 248-4961 **Columbia Restaurant** (Spanish) 2117 E 7th Ave .... Ybor City FL 33605-3999
813 973-1111 **Cypress Room** (Continental) 100 Saddlebrook Way .... Wesley Chapel FL 33543-4411
813 875-6660 **Donatello** (Italian) 232 N Dale Mabry Hwy .... Tampa FL 33609-1237
813 726-4734 **Kapok Tree** (Continental) 923 McMullen Booth Rd .... Clearwater FL 34619-3499
813 391-8592 **Lobster Pot** (Seafood) 17814 Gulf Blvd .... Redington Shores FL 33708-1165
813 366-0007 **Michael's On East** (Continental/American) 1212 East Ave S .... Sarasota FL 33579-0000
813 254-5373 **Misc En Place** (American) 1815 W Platt St .... Tampa FL 33606-0000
813 821-3773 **Pepin** (Spanish/American) 4125 4th St N .... Saint Petersburg FL 33703-5799
813 794-1235 **Seafood Shack Restaurant** (Steak/Seafood) 4110 127th St W ...... Cortez FL 34215-2502
813 889-8800 **Villa Nova by Lauro** (Italian) 4010 W Waters Ave .... Tampa FL 33614-1952

Goods & Services

■ Department Stores
813 895-7525 **Maas Brothers/Jordan Marsh** 101 3rd St N .... Saint Petersburg FL 33701-0000
813 223-7525 **Maas Brothers/Jordan Marsh** 610 N Franklin St .... Tampa FL 33602-4497
813 344-4611 **Maison Blanche** 6901 22nd Ave N .... Saint Petersburg FL 33710-0000
813 977-8080 **Maison Blanche** 2200 E Fowler Ave .... Tampa FL 33612-5508

■ Banks
813 225-8111 **Barnett Bank of Tampa** 101 E Kennedy Blvd .... Tampa FL 33602-5133
813 224-5805 **NCNB National Bank of Florida** 400 N Ashley Dr .... Tampa FL 33602-4325

■ Messenger/Postal
Corporate Courier Inc	813 837-9198	Pace Messenger Service 813 223-3232
Crosstowne Express Delivery	813 286-3085	Post Office–Saint Petersburg 813 323-6570
Express-It Messenger Service	813 968-5757	Post Office–Tampa 813 877-0666
Federal Express	800 238-5355	UPS 800 222-8333

■ Secretarial/Temp Services
813 327-8689 **Alpha Personnel** 3530 1st Ave N .... Saint Petersburg FL 33713-0000
813 289-9452 **Kelly Services Inc** 4890 W Kennedy Blvd Suite 130 .... Tampa FL 33609-2524
813 286-0010 **Olsten Temporary Services** 4950 W Kennedy Blvd Suite 101 ...... Tampa FL 33609-1853

Media

■ Newspapers/Magazines
813 893-8111 **Saint Petersburg Times** 490 1st Ave S .... Saint Petersburg FL 33701-4204
813 791-4800 **Tampa Bay Magazine** 2531 Landmark Dr Suite 101 .... Clearwater FL 34621-3928
813 272-7711 **Tampa Tribune** 202 S Parker St .... Tampa FL 33606-2395

■ Television
813 253-2736 **WEDU-TV Ch 3 (PBS)** 1300 North Blvd .... Tampa FL 33607-0000
813 228-8888 **WFLA-TV Ch 8 (NBC)** 905 E Jackson St .... Tampa FL 33602-4193
813 224-9877 **WTSP-TV Ch 10 (ABC)** 11450 Gandy Blvd N .... Saint Petersburg FL 33702-1998
813 876-1313 **WTVT-TV Ch 13 (CBS)** 3213 W Kennedy Blvd .... Tampa FL 33609-3092

■ Radio
813 576-6055 **WQYK-FM 99.5 MHz (Ctry)**
9450 Koger Blvd N Suite 103 .... Saint Petersburg FL 33702-2432
813 287-1047 **WRBQ-AM 1380 kHz (CHR-ABC)** 5510 W Gray St Suite 130 ...... Tampa FL 33609-1016
813 287-1047 **WRBQ-FM 104.7 MHz (CHR-ABC)** 5510 W Gray St Suite 130 ...... Tampa FL 33609-1016
813 974-4890 **WUSF-FM 89.7 MHz (Clas-NPR)** 4202 E Fowler Ave .... Tampa FL 33620-0001
813 229-8650 **WWRM-FM 107.3 MHz (AC)**
877 Executive Center Dr W Suite 300 .... Saint Petersburg FL 33702-2474

Local Attractions & Special Events

■ Sports
813 872-7977 **Tampa Bay Buccaneers** 4201 N Dale Mabry Hwy .... Tampa FL 33607-6103
813 831-1411 **Tampa Jai-Alai Fronton** 5125 S Dale Mabry Hwy .... Tampa FL 33611-3505

■ Local Attractions
813 971-8282 **Busch Gardens** Busch Blvd & 40th St .... Tampa FL 33601-0000
813 228-7807 **Market on Harbour Island** .... Tampa FL 33602-0000
813 985-5531 **Museum of Science & Industry** 4801 E Fowler Ave .... Tampa FL 33617-2099
813 823-3767 **Salvador Dali Museum** 1000 3rd St S .... Saint Petersburg FL 33701-4901
813 391-6211 **Suncoast Seabird Sanctuary** 18328 Gulf Blvd .... Indian Shores FL 34635-0000
813 896-3186 **Sunken Gardens** 1825 4th St N .... Saint Petersburg FL 33704-4397
813 223-8130 **Tampa Museum of Art** 601 Doyle Carlton Dr .... Tampa FL 33601-0000
813 821-6164 **The Pier** 800 2nd Ave NE .... Saint Petersburg FL 33701-0000
407 824-4321 **Walt Disney World** 100 miles E of Tampa .... Orlando FL
813 247-4497 **Ybor Square** 1901 13th St .... Tampa FL 33605-3612

Toledo

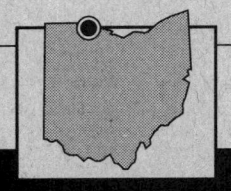

OHIO   419

Important Phone Numbers

AAA	419 241-0115	Emergency	911
American Express	419 244-3322	Poison Control Center	419 381-3897
Better Business Bureau	419 241-6276	Time/Temp	419 936-1212
City Hall	419 245-1000		

■ Travel Information

419 243-8191	Chamber of Commerce 218 N Huron St	Toledo OH 43604-1150
419 321-6404	Office of Tourism & Conventions 218 N Huron St	Toledo OH 43604-1109

Travel

■ Airport

419 865-2351 Toledo Express Airport 20 miles SW of city (approx 35 minutes)

■ Airport Transportation

419 865-8825 Airport Limousine Service
Limo $13 fare to downtown
Taxi $20-25 fare to downtown

■ Scheduled Airlines

American Eagle	800 433-7300	Northwest	800 225-2525
ComAir/Delta Connection	419 241-4156	United Express	800 241-6522
Continental	800 525-0280	USAir	419 243-8211

■ Charter Airlines

Bluffton Flying Service Inc 419 358-7045

■ Car Rentals

Agency	419 531-6044	Hertz	419 866-3400
Avis	419 865-5541	National	419 865-5513
Budget	419 535-5610	Snappy	419 867-0100

■ Limo/Taxi

Black & White Cab	419 478-8300	Sylvania Limousines	419 475-7358
Checker Cab	419 243-2537	Town & Country Limousines	419 841-8092
Jetport Express	419 470-5600	VIP Limousines	419 476-6643

■ Mass Transit

419 243-7433 TARTA $.75 Base fare ... Toledo OH 43610-0000

■ Rail/Bus

419 244-6639	Central Union Terminal 415 Emerald Ave	Toledo OH 43602-1817
419 248-1498	Greyhound/Trailways Bus Station 811 Jefferson Ave	Toledo OH 43624-1919

Hotels

419 666-5120	Econo Lodge 1800 Miami St	Toledo OH 43605-3318
419 874-3111	Holiday Inn French Quarter 10630 Fremont Pike	Perrysburg OH 43551-3354
419 666-2600	Northwood Motor Lodge 2426 Oregon Rd	Northwood OH 43619-1123
419 241-1987	Radisson Hotel Toledo 101 N Summit St	Toledo OH 43604-1096
419 865-1361	Ramada Inn Southwyck 2340 S Reynolds Rd	Toledo OH 43614-1468
419 866-5512	Red Roof Inn 1214 Corporate Dr	Holland OH 43528-9591
419 243-8860	Riverview Inn 141 N Summit St	Toledo OH 43604-1033
419 535-7070	Sheraton Westgate Hotel 3536 Secor Rd	Toledo OH 43606-1597
419 381-6800	Toledo Hilton 3100 Glendale Ave	Toledo OH 43614-2500
419 241-1411	Toledo Marriott Portside 2 Seagate	Toledo OH 43604-1580

Restaurants

419 241-1411	Ashley's(Continental) 2 Seagate	Toledo OH 43604-1580
419 243-1607	Dyer's Chop House (Seafood) 216 N Superior St	Toledo OH 43604-1296
419 385-2904	Frank Unkle's (Steak/Seafood) 2605 Broadway	Toledo OH 43609-3118
419 872-9400	Josephine's (Mexican/American) 27511 Holiday Ln	Perrysburg OH 43551-0000
419 476-4154	Mancy's (Steak/Seafood) 953 Phillips Ave	Toledo OH 43612-0000
419 729-3791	Northwood Villa (Continental) 6630 Gixie Hwy	Erie MI 48133-0000
419 536-5486	Thai Guy (Thai) 3550 Executive Pkwy	Toledo OH 43606-0000
419 242-8312	Theo's Taverna (Greek) 823 Summit St	Toledo OH 43604-0000
419 691-6054	Tony Packo's (Hungarian) 1902 Front St	Toledo OH 43605-0000

Goods & Services

■ Department Stores

419 531-2451	Elder Beerman Westgate 3311 Secor Rd	Toledo OH 43606-1535
419 479-2300	Hudson's 5001 Monroe St Franklin Park Mall	Toledo OH 43623-0000
419 535-9500	Lion Store 300 Southwych Mall	Toledo OH 43614-0000

■ Banks

419 243-2400	AmeriTrust Co National Assn 420 Madison Ave	Toledo OH 43604-1225
419 259-7890	Fifth Third Bank of Toledo 606 Madison Ave	Toledo OH 43604-1102
419 259-7700	Ohio Citizens Bank 405 Madison Ave	Toledo OH 43604-1263

■ Messenger/Postal

Colonial Courier Service	419 891-0922	Senior Cartage Inc	419 248-3527
Federal Express	800 238-5355	Tri-State Expedited Services Inc	419 874-2251
Post Office	419 245-6811	UPS	800 621-5621
Roco Mail Car Service	419 666-4896	US Cargo & Courier Service Inc	419 893-2245

■ Secretarial/Temp Services

419 247-5151	Kelly Temporary Services Inc 1 Seagate Suite 780	Toledo OH 43604-1555
419 247-1212	Manpower Temporary Services 1 Seagate	Toledo OH 43604-1550

Media

■ Newspapers/Magazines

419 245-6000	Blade 541 N Superior St	Toledo OH 43660-0001
614 461-5083	Ohio Magazine 62 E Broad St	Columbus OH 43215-4272

■ Television

419 243-3091	WGTE-TV Ch 30 (PBS) 136 N Huron St	Toledo OH 43604-1008
419 535-0024	WNWO-TV Ch 24 (ABC) 300 S Byrne Rd	Toledo OH 43615-6298
419 248-1111	WTOL-TV Ch 11 (CBS) 730 N Summit St	Toledo OH 43604-1808
419 531-1313	WTVG-TV Ch 13 (NBC) 4247 Dorr St	Toledo OH 43607-2199
419 244-3600	WUPW-TV Ch 36 (Fox) 4 Seagate	Toledo OH 43604-1553

■ Radio

419 248-2627	WCWA-AM 1230 kHz (Gold-MBS) 124 N Summit St Suite 400	Toledo OH 43604-1034
419 243-3091	WGTE-FM 91.3 MHz (Clas-NPR) 136 N Huron St	Toledo OH 43604-1008
419 243-3377	WIOT-FM 104.7 MHz (AOR-NBC) 124 N Summit St Suite 400	Toledo OH 43604-1064
419 385-2536	WKKO-FM 99.9 MHz (Ctry-ABC) 3225 Arlington Ave	Toledo OH 43614-5803
419 244-8321	WLQR-FM 101.5 MHz (AC-NBC) 125 S Superior St	Toledo OH 43602-1790
419 255-1470	WOHO-AM 1470 kHz (Ctry) 2965 Pickle Rd	Toledo OH 43616-4020
419 385-2507	WTOD-AM 1560 kHz (Ctry-ABC) 3225 Arlington Ave	Toledo OH 43614-2495
419 531-1681	WVKS-FM 92.5 MHz (CHR) 4665 W Bancroft St	Toledo OH 43615-3945
419 255-1470	WWWM-FM 105.5 MHz (AC) 2965 Pickle Rd	Toledo OH 43616-4020

Local Attractions & Special Events

■ Sports

419 893-9483	Toledo Mudhens 2901 Key St	Maumee OH 43537-2401
419 476-7751	Toledo Raceway Park 5700 Telegraph Rd	Toledo OH 43612-3691
419 729-1634	Toledo Speedway 5639 Benore Rd	Toledo OH 43612-3803

■ Local Attractions

419 874-4121	Fort Meigs Rt 65	Toledo OH 43551-0000
419 321-6404	Historic Old West End	Toledo OH 43606-0000
419 244-7000	Portside Festival Market 5 Seagate St	Toledo OH 43604-1551
419 536-8365	Toledo Botanical Gardens 5403 Elmer Dr	Toledo OH 43615-2803
419 255-8000	Toledo Museum of Art 2445 Monroe St	Toledo OH 43620-1517

Tucson
ARIZONA   602

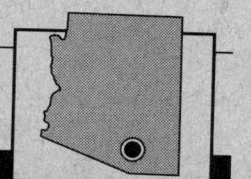

Important Phone Numbers

AAA 602 296-7461	Emergency 911
American Express 602 795-8400	Poison Control Center 602 626-6016
Better Business Bureau .. 602 622-7651	Time/Temp 602 676-1676
City Hall 602 791-4326	Weather 602 881-3333

■ Travel Information
602 792-1212   Chamber of Commerce 465 W St Marys Rd .... Tucson AZ 85701-8299
602 624-1889   Convention & Visitors Bureau 130 S Scott Ave .... Tucson AZ 85701-1922

Travel

■ Airport
602 573-8000   Tucson International Airport 12 miles S of city (approx 20 minutes)

■ Airport Transportation
Suntran $.60 fare to downtown
Taxi $12-15 fare to downtown

■ Scheduled Airlines
AeroMexico 602 573-8316	Delta 800 221-1212
Alaska 800 426-0333	Northwest 800 447-4747
America West 602 623-8917	TWA 602 624-2771
American 602 882-0331	United 602 622-1214
Continental 800 525-0280	USAir 602 623-3428

■ Charter Airlines
Ratliff Aero 602 746-1411

■ Car Rentals
Alamo 602 746-0196	Enterprise 602 747-9700
Avis 602 294-1494	Hertz 602 294-7616
Budget 602 889-8800	National 602 573-8050
Dollar 602 573-1100	Thrifty 602 889-5761

■ Limo/Taxi
A & A Limousine 602 622-6441	All-State Limousines 602 325-5588
ABC Cab 602 623-7979	Yellow Cab 602 624-6611

■ Mass Transit
602 623-4301   Suntran $.60 Base fare .... Tucson AZ 85714-0000

■ Rail/Bus
602 882-4386   Greyhound/Trailways 2 S 4th Ave .... Tucson AZ 85701-1891
602 623-4442   Tucson Station 400 E Toole Ave .... Tucson AZ 85701-1815

Hotels

602 325-1541	Arizona Inn 2200 E Elm St .... Tucson AZ 85719-4395
602 622-8871	Best Western Royal Sun Hotel & Suites 1015 N Stone Ave .. Tucson AZ 85705-7748
602 881-4200	Doubletree Hotel at Randolph Park 445 S Alvernon Way .... Tucson AZ 85711-4198
602 573-0700	Embassy Suites Hotel 7051 S Tuscon Blvd .... Tucson AZ 85706-6932
602 745-2700	Embassy Suites Tucson 5335 E Broadway Blvd ...... Tucson AZ 85711-3772
602 624-8711	Holiday Inn Broadway 181 W Broadway .... Tucson AZ 85701-1616
602 299-2020	Loews Ventana Canyon Resort 7000 N Resort Dr .... Tucson AZ 85715-1345
602 721-0991	Marriott Residence Inn 6477 E Speedway Blvd .... Tucson AZ 85710-1115
602 327-7341	Plaza Hotel 1900 E Speedway Blvd .... Tucson AZ 85719-4694
602 721-7100	Radisson Suite Hotel Tucson 6555 E Speedway Blvd .... Tucson AZ 85710-1146
602 742-7000	Sheraton Tucson El Conquistador Resort 10000 N Oracle Rd .... Tucson AZ 85737-7696
602 296-6275	Tanque Verde Guest Ranch 14301 E Speedway Blvd .... Tucson AZ 85748-7100
602 297-2271	Tucson National Resort 2727 W Club Dr .... Tucson AZ 85741-9766
602 742-6000	Westin La Paloma Resort 3800 E Sunrise Dr .... Tucson AZ 85718-3399
602 297-1151	Westward Look Resort 245 E Ina Rd .... Tucson AZ 85704-6296

Restaurants

602 571-9070	Bit of Budapest (Hungarian) 5754 E 22nd St .... Tucson AZ 85711-0000
602 577-9309	Boccata (Northern Italian) 5605 E River Rd .... Tucson AZ 85715-0000
602 296-7173	Charles (Continental) 6400 E El Dorado Cir .... Tucson AZ 85715-0000
602 742-3200	Daniel's (Continental) 2930 N Swan Rd Suite 209 .... Tucson AZ 85715-4626
602 791-7458	El Adobe (Mexican) 40 W Broadway Blvd .... Tucson AZ 85712-1255
602 622-5465	El Charro (Mexican) 311 N Court Ave .... Tucson AZ 85701-1606
602 884-9426	Janos (Southwest) 150 N Main Ave .... Tucson AZ 85701-1016
602 721-0311	Jerome's (Cajun) 6958 E Tanque Verde Rd .... Tucson AZ 85701-8281
602 622-5081	Mia Nidito (Mexican) 1813 S 4th Ave .... Tucson AZ 85715-5308
602 293-0375	Mountain View (Czech) 1220 E Prince Rd .... Tucson AZ 85713-0000
602 795-5561	Palomino The (Continental) 2959 N Swan Rd .... Tucson AZ 85719-1835
602 624-8946	Scordato's (Italian) 4405 W Speedway Blvd .... Tucson AZ 85712-1297
602 722-2800	Tack Room (American/Continental) 2800 N Sabino Canyon Rd .... Tucson AZ 85745-9647 / 85715-3298

Goods & Services

■ Department Stores
602 322-2100   Broadway Southwest 5850 E Broadway Blvd Tucson Park Mall ... Tucson AZ 85711-3998
602 742-2171   Dillard's 1616 Priest St .... Tempe AZ 85281-0000
602 882-3111   Foley's 3435 E Broadway Blvd .... Tucson AZ 85716-5468

■ Banks
602 620-3400   Citibank 1 S Church Ave .... Tucson AZ 85701-1612
602 792-5000   First Interstate Bank of Arizona NA 150 N Stone Ave ... Tucson AZ 85701-1525
602 792-7818   Security Pacific Bank Arizona 33 N Stone Ave .... Tucson AZ 85701-1404

■ Messenger/Postal
Arizona Messenger 602 325-1234	Federal Express 800 238-5355
Cherrybell Post Office 602 620-5142	UPS 602 882-4000
E-Z Messenger Attorney Service Inc ..602 623-8436	

■ Secretarial/Temp Services
602 323-8778   A & M Temporaries Services Ltd 1661 N Swan Rd Suite 134 ..... Tucson AZ 85712-4051
602 748-2681   Kelly Services Inc 432 S Williams Blvd Suite 100 .... Tucson AZ 85711-4405
602 886-8816   Manpower Temporary Services Inc 6365 E Tanque Verde Rd .... Tucson AZ 85715-3830
602 748-9041   Olsten Temporary Services 6245 E Broadway Suite 540 .... Tucson AZ 85711-4019

Media

■ Newspapers/Magazines
602 573-4111   Arizona Daily Star 4850 S Park Ave .... Tucson AZ 85714-3395
602 573-4560   Tucson Citizen 4850 S Park Ave .... Tucson AZ 85714-3395
602 721-2929   Tucson Lifestyle 7000 E Tanque Verde Suite 30 .... Tucson AZ 85715-5319

■ Television
602 722-5486   KGUN-TV Ch 9 (ABC) 7280 E Rosewood St .... Tucson AZ 85710-1350
602 624-2511   KOLD-TV Ch 13 (CBS) 115 W Drachman St .... Tucson AZ 85705-7388
602 621-5828   KUAT-TV Ch 6 (PBS) University of Arizona .... Tucson AZ 85721-0001
602 792-2270   KVOA-TV Ch 4 (NBC) 209 W Elm St .... Tucson AZ 85705-6592

■ Radio
602 887-1000   KCUB-AM 1290 kHz (Ctry) 575 W Roger Rd .... Tucson AZ 85705-2616
602 795-1490   KKLD-FM 94.9 MHz (AC) 3438 N Country Club .... Tucson AZ 85716-1247
602 622-6711   KLPX-FM 96.1 MHz (CHR) 1920 W Copper St .... Tucson AZ 85745-1158
602 323-9400   KNST-AM 940 kHz (N/T-ABC) 4400 E Broadway Blvd Suite 200 ... Tucson AZ 85711-3521
602 323-9400   KRQQ-FM 93.7 MHz (CHR) 4400 E Broadway Blvd Suite 200 ... Tucson AZ 85711-3521
602 622-6711   KTKT-AM 990 kHz (N/T) 1920 W Copper St .... Tucson AZ 85745-1158
602 621-7548   KUAT-AM 1550 kHz (Jazz-NPR)
     Modern Languages Bldg University of Arizona Rm 222 .... Tucson AZ 85721-0001
602 623-7556   KWFM-FM 92.9 MHz (Gold) 2100 N Silverbell Rd .... Tucson AZ 85745-1126

Local Attractions & Special Events

■ Sports
602 884-7576   Tucson Greyhound Park 2601 S 3rd Ave .... Tucson AZ 85713-4899

■ Special Events
602 741-2233   La Fiesta de los Vaqueros Rodeo (February 21-24)

■ Local Attractions
602 883-1380   Arizona-Sonora Desert Museum 2021 N Kinney Rd .... Tucson AZ 85743-9719
602 620-5350   Kitt Peak National Observatory Rt 386 .... Tucson AZ 85701-0000
602 883-0100   Old Tucson 201 S Kinney Rd .... Tucson AZ 85746-9322
602 574-0462   Pima Air Museum 6000 E Valencia Rd .... Tucson AZ 85706-9403
602 296-8576   Saguaro National Monument 3693 S Old Spanish Trail .... Tucson AZ 85730-5601
602 294-2624   San Xavier Del Bac Mission Mission & San Xavier Rds .... Tucson AZ 85746-0000

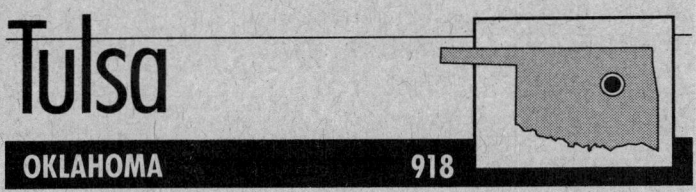

Tulsa
OKLAHOMA 918

Important Phone Numbers

AAA 918 748-1000
American Express 918 743-8856
Better Business Bureau 918 492-1266
City Hall 918 596-7777

Emergency 911
Poison Control Center 800 522-4611
Time/Temp 918 477-1000
Weather 918 743-3311

■ Travel Information

918 585-1201 **Chamber of Commerce** 616 S Boston Ave .... Tulsa OK 74119-1289
918 596-7177 **Convention Center of Tulsa** 100 Civic Ctr .... Tulsa OK 74103-3828

Travel

■ Airport

918 838-5000 **Tulsa International Airport** 9 miles NE of city (approx 10 minutes)

■ Airport Transportation

Taxi $12 fare to downtown

■ Scheduled Airlines

American 918 834-7490
Delta 800 843-9378
Northwest 800 225-2525

Southwest 918 583-1221
TWA 918 584-3471
United 800 241-6522

■ Charter Airlines

Butler Aviation 918 836-3731

■ Car Rentals

Alamo 918 836-0775
Avis 918 664-4600
Budget 918 836-3761
Dollar 918 838-5236

Enterprise 918 583-4880
Hertz 918 838-1999
National 918 838-5270
Thrifty 918 838-3333

■ Limo/Taxi

Franklin Limousine Service 918 585-5466
Royal Coachman Limousine 918 437-3975

Tulsa City Cab 918 425-5584
Yellow & Checker Cab 918 587-6611

■ Mass Transit

918 584-6421 **Metropolitan Tulsa Transit Authority** $.60 Base fare .... Tulsa OK 74120-0000

■ Rail/Bus

918 584-4428 **Greyhound/Trailways Bus Station** 317 S Detroit Ave .... Tulsa OK 74120-2424

Hotels

918 747-8811 **Camelot Hotel** 4956 S Peoria St .... Tulsa OK 74105-4698
918 495-1000 **Doubletree Hotel at Warren Place** 6110 S Yale Ave .... Tulsa OK 74136-1904
918 587-8000 **Doubletree Hotel Downtown** 616 W 7th St .... Tulsa OK 74127-8983
918 627-5000 **Marriott Hotel** 10918 E 41st St .... Tulsa OK 74146-2799
918 622-7000 **Park Plaza Hotel** 5000 E Skelly Dr .... Tulsa OK 74135-7013
918 835-9911 **Sheraton Inn Tulsa Airport** 2201 N 77th East Ave .... Tulsa OK 74115-3799
918 493-7000 **Sheraton Kensington Hotel** 1902 E 71st St .... Tulsa OK 74136-5477
918 582-9000 **Westin Hotel Williams Center** 10 E 2nd St .... Tulsa OK 74103-3202

Restaurants

918 583-0571 **15th Street Grill** (American) 1542 E 15th St .... Tulsa OK 74120-6041
918 584-4111 **15th Street Wok** (Chinese) 1335 E 15th St .... Tulsa OK 74120-5833
918 587-4411 **Chimi's** (Mexican) 1413 E 15th St .... Tulsa OK 74120-5807
918 481-3338 **Green Onion** (Continental) 4532 E 51st St .... Tulsa OK 74135-3705
918 742-9097 **Jamil's** (American/Lebanese) 2833 E 51st St .... Tulsa OK 74105-1701
918 664-4004 **Joseph's Steak & Seafood** (American) 4933 E 44st St .... Tulsa OK 74135-0000
918 299-1902 **La Cuisine** (American) 8178A S Louis St .... Tulsa OK 74137-0000
918 744-9463 **Montrachet** (French) 3509 S Peoria Ave .... Tulsa OK 74105-0000
918 496-7638 **Rile's** (Vietnamese) 7140 S Lewis Ave .... Tulsa OK 74136-5454
918 665-1939 **Ti Amo** (Italian) 8151 E 21st St .... Tulsa OK 74112-0000

Goods & Services

■ Department Stores

918 252-0211 **Dillard's** 6919 S Memorial Dr .... Tulsa OK 74133-2027
918 628-1800 **Vandever's** 5985 E 41st St .... Tulsa OK 74135-6509

■ Banks

918 588-6000 **Bank of Oklahoma NA Tulsa** 1 William Ctr .... Tulsa OK 74103-0000
918 586-1000 **First National Bank & Trust Co of Tulsa** 15 E 5th St .... Tulsa OK 74103-4367
918 581-0400 **Fourth National Bank** 515 S Boulder Ave .... Tulsa OK 74103-4207

■ Messenger/Postal

A'La Carte Courier Service Inc 918 627-8387
Darrell's Messenger Service Inc 918 583-8216
Federal Express 800 238-5355

Post Office 918 599-6800
Services Delivery Inc 918 836-0487
UPS 800 222-8333

■ Secretarial/Temp Services

918 585-1700 **Accountemps** 1 W 3rd St Suite 1120 .... Tulsa OK 74103-3515
918 250-5355 **Kelly Services** 7666 E 61st St Suite 140 .... Tulsa OK 74133-1192
918 492-3131 **Manpower Temporary Services Inc**
                5314 S Yale Ave Park Towers Suite 150 .... Tulsa OK 74135-0000
918 254-6800 **Olsten Temporary Services** 6126 S Memorial .... Tulsa OK 74146-0000

Media

■ Newspapers/Magazines

918 622-3730 **Tulsa Magazine** 4129 S 72nd East Ave .... Tulsa OK 74145-4608
918 581-8400 **Tulsa Tribune** 318 S Main St .... Tulsa OK 74103-3673
918 583-2161 **Tulsa World** 315 S Boulder Ave .... Tulsa OK 74103-3423

■ Television

405 848-8501 **KETA-TV Ch 13 (PBS)** 7403 N Kelley Ave .... Oklahoma City OK 73111-8420
918 743-2222 **KJRH-TV Ch 2 (NBC)** 3701 S Peoria Ave .... Tulsa OK 74105-3269
918 663-6880 **KOKI-TV Ch 23 (Fox)** 7422 E 46th Pl .... Tulsa OK 74145-6306
918 582-6666 **KOTV-TV Ch 6 (CBS)** 302 S Frankfort Ave .... Tulsa OK 74120-2495
918 446-3351 **KTUL-TV Ch 8 (ABC)** Lookout Mountain .... Tulsa OK 74107-0000

■ Radio

918 496-9336 **KBEZ-FM 92.9 MHz (B/EZ)** 5314 S Yale Ave Suite 400 .... Tulsa OK 74135-6271
918 445-1186 **KCFO-AM 970 kHz (Rel)** 3737 S 37th West Ave .... Tulsa OK 74107-5125
918 664-2810 **KMOD-FM 97.5 MHz (AOR)** 5801 E 41st St Suite 900 .... Tulsa OK 74135-5631
918 585-5555 **KRAV-FM 96.5 MHz (AC)** 1638 S Carson Ave 11th Fl .... Tulsa OK 74119-4242
918 493-7400 **KRMG-AM 740 kHz (AC)** 7136 S Yale Ave Suite 500 .... Tulsa OK 74136-6359
918 836-5512 **KTFX-FM 103.3 MHz (Ctry-ABC)** 8107 E Admiral Pl .... Tulsa OK 74115-8116
918 494-9500 **KWEN-FM 95.5 MHz (Ctry-AP)** 7136 S Yale Ave Suite 500 ... Tulsa OK 74136-6315
918 631-2577 **KWGS-FM 89.5 MHz (N/T-NPR)** 600 S College Ave .... Tulsa OK 74104-3135

Local Attractions & Special Events

■ Sports

918 744-5901 **Tulsa Drillers** 4802 E 15th St Drillers Stadium .... Tulsa OK 74112-0000
918 665-6111 **Tulsa Fast Breakers** Expo Square Pavilion .... Tulsa OK 74112-0000
918 425-7551 **Tulsa Speedway** Hwy 75 N & 66th St N .... Tulsa OK 74054-0000

■ Special Events

918 596-7877 **Annual Tulsa Powwow** (August 9-11)

■ Local Attractions

918 582-3122 **Gilcrease Thomas Institute of American History & Art**
                1400 Gilcrease Museum Rd .... Tulsa OK 74127-2100
918 749-7941 **Philbrook Museum of Art** 2727 S Rockford Rd .... Tulsa OK 74114-4104
918 749-6401 **Tulsa Garden Center** 2435 S Peoria Ave .... Tulsa OK 74114-1350
918 341-0719 **Will Rogers Memorial** 1760 W Will Rogers Blvd .... Tulsa OK 74018-0000

Washington

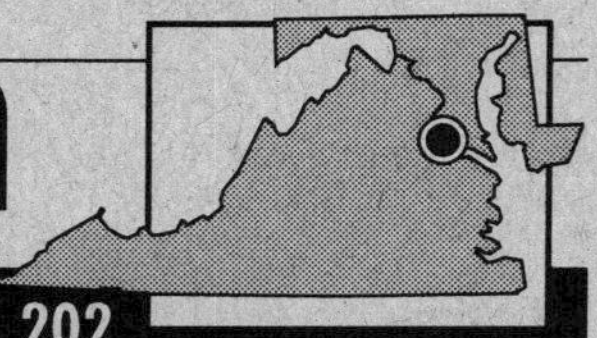

DISTRICT OF COLUMBIA 202

Important Phone Numbers

AAA	703 222-6000	**Emergency**	911
American Express	202 457-1300	**Poison Control Center**	202 625-3333
Better Business Bureau	202 393-8000	**Time/Temp**	202 844-2525
City Hall	202 724-8000	**Weather**	202 936-1212

■ Travel Information

202 347-7201	**Chamber of Commerce** 1411 K St NW Suite 500	Washington	DC	20005-3412
202 789-7000	**Convention & Visitors Assn** 1212 New York Ave NW Suite 600	Washington	DC	20005-3987

Travel

■ Airport: Dulles

703 471-4322 **Dulles International Airport** 31 miles W of city (approx 35 minutes)

■ Airport Transportation: Dulles

Taxi $30-35 fare to downtown
703 685-1400 **Washington Flyer** $12 fare to downtown

■ Scheduled Airlines: Dulles

Aeroflot	202 429-4922	**Lufthansa**	800 645-3880
Air France	800 237-2747	**Northwest**	202 737-7333
American	202 393-2345	**Pan Am**	800 221-1111
ANA-All Nippon Airways	800 235-9262	**Saudi Arabian**	202 333-3800
Bahamasair	800 222-4262	**TWA**	202 737-7400
British Airways	800 247-9297	**United**	202 742-4600
Continental	202 478-9700	**USAir**	202 783-4500
Delta	202 468-2282		

■ Charter Airlines: Dulles

Fairway Corp	703 260-0601	**US Jet Aviation**	703 892-6200
Page Flight	202 478-5990		

■ Airport Transportation: National

202 637-7000 **Metrorail** $1.05 fare to downtown
Taxi $7 fare to downtown
703 685-1400 **Washington Flyer** $12 fare to downtown

■ Scheduled Airlines: National

American	202 393-2345	**Midwest Express**	800 452-2022
Business Express	800 345-3400	**Northwest**	202 737-7333
Continental	202 478-9700	**Pan Am**	202 845-8000
Continental Express	800 525-0280	**Pan Am Express**	800 221-1111
Delta	202 468-2282	**TWA**	202 737-7400
Eastern	202 393-4000	**United**	703 742-4600
Midway	800 621-5700	**USAir**	202 783-4500

■ Charter Airlines: National

Bet Jet	703 685-1313	**US Jet Aviation**	703 892-6200
Page Flight	202 478-5990		

■ Car Rentals

Alamo	703 478-9597	**Hertz**	800 654-3131
America West	800 247-5692	**Jiffy**	202 526-5632
Avis	800 331-1212	**National**	800 227-7368
Bargin Buggies	703 841-0000	**Sterling Buggies**	703 478-0045
Budget	800 448-3957	**Thrifty**	703 548-1600
Dollar	703 661-8577		

■ Limo/Taxi

A-1 Quality Limousines	202 575-2040	**Manhattan/DC Executive Trans**	202 775-1888
Checker Cab	202 636-1600	**Red Top Cab**	703 522-3333
DC Express Cab	202 526-5656	**Yellow Cab**	202 544-1212

■ Mass Transit

202 637-7000	**Metrorail/Metrobus** $.85 Base fare	Washington	DC	20001-0000

■ Rail/Bus

202 289-5155	**Greyhound/Trailways Bus Terminal** 1005 1st St NE	Washington	DC	20002-4283
202 484-7540	**Union Station Railroad Terminal** 50 Massachusetts Ave NE	Washington	DC	20002-4296

Hotels

202 393-1000	**Capital Hilton Hotel** 1001 16th St NW	Washington	DC	20036-5794
202 265-1600	**Embassy Row Hotel** 2015 Massachusetts Ave NW	Washington	DC	20036-1075
202 342-0444	**Four Seasons Hotel** 2800 Pennsylvania Ave NW	Washington	DC	20007-3758
202 429-0100	**Grand Hotel** 2350 M St NW	Washington	DC	20037-1490
202 338-4600	**Holiday Inn Georgetown** 2101 Wisconsin Ave NW	Washington	DC	20007-2293
703 684-7200	**Howard Johnson National Airport** 2650 Jefferson Davis Hwy	Arlington	VA	22202-4092
202 737-1234	**Hyatt Regency Washington** 400 New Jersey Ave NW	Washington	DC	20001-2097
202 347-2200	**Jefferson Hotel** 1200 16th St NW	Washington	DC	20036-3295
202 393-2000	**JW Marriott Hotel** 1331 Pennsylvania Ave NW	Washington	DC	20004-1796
202 484-1000	**Loews L'Enfant Plaza** 480 L'Enfant Plaza SW	Washington	DC	20024-2197
202 862-1600	**Madison Hotel** 1177 15th St NW	Washington	DC	20005-1705
202 347-3000	**Mayflower Stouffer Hotel** 1127 Connecticut Ave NW	Washington	DC	20036-4393
202 234-0700	**Omni Shoreham Hotel** 2500 Calvert St NW	Washington	DC	20008-2648
202 332-9300	**Quality Hotel Central** 1900 Connecticut Ave NW	Washington	DC	20009-5787
202 293-2100	**Ritz-Carlton Hotel** 2100 Massachusetts Ave NW	Washington	DC	20008-2863
202 337-7600	**River Inn** 924 25th St NW	Washington	DC	20037-2126
202 638-2626	**Sheraton Carlton** 923 16th St NW	Washington	DC	20006-1797
202 328-2000	**Sheraton Washington Hotel** 2660 Woodley Rd NW	Washington	DC	20008-0000
202 628-2100	**Washington Court Hotel** 525 New Jersey Ave NW	Washington	DC	20001-2098
703 471-9500	**Washington Dulles Airport Marriott** 333 W Service Rd	Chantilly	VA	22021-0000
202 483-3000	**Washington Hilton Hotel & Towers** 1919 Connecticut Ave NW	Washington	DC	20009-5788
202 872-1500	**Washington Marriott Hotel** 1221 22nd St NW	Washington	DC	20037-1294
202 965-2300	**Watergate Hotel** 2650 Virginia Ave NW	Washington	DC	20037-1969
202 429-2400	**Westin Hotel** 2401 M St NW	Washington	DC	20037-1489
202 628-9100	**Willard Inter-Continental Hotel** 1401 Pennsylvania Ave NW	Washington	DC	20004-1010

Restaurants

202 342-0810	**Aux Beaux Champs** (French) 2800 Pennsylvania Ave NW	Washington	DC	20007-3721
202 785-0734	**Bacchus** (Lebanese) 1827 Jefferson Pl NW	Washington	DC	20036-2504
202 659-1830	**Cantina D'Italia** (Northern Italian) 1214-A 18th St NW	Washington	DC	20036-2502
202 393-3000	**Chaucer's** (Continental) 1733 'N' St NW	Washington	DC	20036-2896
202 483-6700	**Childe Harold** (Traditional American) 1610 20th St NW	Washington	DC	20009-1001
202 466-3730	**Duke Ziebert's** (Steak/Seafood) 1050 Connecticut Ave NW	Washington	DC	20036-0000
202 338-3121	**El Caribe** (Spanish/South American) 3288 M St NW	Washington	DC	20007-3624
202 338-7772	**Enriqueta's** (Mexican) 2811 M St NW	Washington	DC	20007-3712
202 293-7191	**Galileo** (Italian) 1110 21st St	Washington	DC	20037-0000
202 463-6470	**Gary's** (Steak/Seafood) 1800 M St NW	Washington	DC	20036-5802
202 484-6300	**Hogate's** (Seafood) 9th St & Maine Ave SW	Washington	DC	20024-0000
202 298-4488	**Jean-Louis at Watergate** (French) 2650 Virginia Ave NW	Washington	DC	20037-1935
202 659-8000	**Jockey Club** (French/Continental) 2100 Massachusetts Ave NW	Washington	DC	22008-0000
202 546-6066	**La Brasserie** (French) 239 Massachusetts Ave NE	Washington	DC	20002-4913
202 338-1784	**La Chaumiere** (Seafood) 2813 M St NW	Washington	DC	20007-3712
202 737-0400	**La Colline** (French/Seafood) 400 N Capitol St NW	Washington	DC	20001-1511
202 296-7972	**Le Lion d'Or** (French) 1150 Connecticut Ave NW Entrance loc on 18th St	Washington	DC	20036-4169
202 833-3846	**Le Pavillion** (French) 1050 Connecticut Ave NW Terrace Level	Washington	DC	20036-5303
202 842-0070	**Maison Blanche** (French) 1725 F St NW	Washington	DC	20006-5203
202 862-1712	**Montpelier Restaurant** (French/Continental) 1177 15th St NW Madison Hotel	Washington	DC	20005-0000
202 331-8868	**Mr K's** (Chinese) 2121 K St NW	Washington	DC	20037-1801
202 462-5143	**Nora** (Nouvelle American) 2132 Florida Ave NW	Washington	DC	20008-1925
202 783-1475	**Occidental** (American) 1475 Pennsylvania Ave NW	Washington	DC	20004-1076
202 347-4800	**Old Ebbitt Grill** (American) 675 15th St NW	Washington	DC	20005-5702
202 293-9091	**Palm The** (American) 1225 19th St NW	Washington	DC	20036-2411
202 244-7774	**Rossini's Ristorante D'Italia** (Italian) 5507 Connecticut Ave NW	Washington	DC	20015-2601
202 387-8876	**Thai Taste** (Thai) 2606 Connecticut Ave NW	Washington	DC	20008-1521
202 452-1915	**Tiberio** (Italian) 1915 K St NW	Washington	DC	20006-1101

Goods & Services

■ Department Stores

202 628-7730	**Garfinckel's** 1401 F St NW	Washington	DC	20004-1093
202 628-6661	**Hecht's Co** 1201 G St NW	Washington	DC	20005-0000
202 347-5300	**Woodward & Lothrop** 1025 F St NW	Washington	DC	20004-1414

■ Banks

202 624-4000	**American Security Bank NA** 1501 Pennsylvania Ave NW	Washington	DC	20005-1066
202 879-6000	**Crestar Bank** 1445 New York Ave NW	Washington	DC	20005-2191
202 637-6100	**First American Bank of Washington** 740 15th St NW	Washington	DC	20005-1088
202 537-2000	**National Bank of Washington** 619 14th St NW	Washington	DC	20005-2052
202 835-6000	**Riggs National Bank of Washington DC** 1503 Pennsylvania Ave NW	Washington	DC	20005-1016

■ Messenger/Postal

A-1 Courier Services	202 332-4900	**Metropolitan Msgr & Delivery Svc**	202 387-8200
Choice Courier	202 783-9400	**Post Office**	202 268-2000
Congressional Record Delivery	202 667-5100	**Quick Messenger Service**	202 783-3600
Dependable Courier Service	202 638-0114	**UPS**	301 595-9090
Federal Express	301 953-3333		

■ Secretarial/Temp Services

202 463-4500	**Accounting Temporary** 1625 K St NW Suite 735	Washington	DC	20006-0000
202 296-2424	**Kelly Services** 1801 K St NW	Washington	DC	20006-1389
202 331-8300	**Manpower Temporary Services Inc** 1130 Connecticut Ave NW Suite 530	Washington	DC	20036-3904
202 296-5066	**Olsten Temporary Services** 1730 K St NW	Washington	DC	20006-3876
202 463-4500	**Temporary Help Experts** 1625 K St NW Suite 735	Washington	DC	20006-0000

Media

■ Newspapers/Magazines

202 334-6000	**Washington Post** 1150 15th St NW	Washington	DC	20071-0001
202 636-3000	**Washington Times** 3600 New York Ave NE	Washington	DC	20002-1996
202 296-3600	**Washingtonian** 1828 L St NW Suite 200	Washington	DC	20036-5169

■ Television

703 998-2600	**WETA-TV Ch 26 (PBS)** 3700 S Four-Mile Run Dr	Arlington	VA	22206-0000
202 364-7777	**WJLA-TV Ch 7 (ABC)** 3007 Tilden St NW	Washington	DC	20008-3021
202 885-4000	**WRC-TV Ch 4 (NBC)** 4001 Nebraska Ave NW	Washington	DC	20016-2733
202 364-3900	**WUSA-TV Ch 9 (CBS)** 4001 Brandywine St NW	Washington	DC	20016-1864

■ Radio

202 885-1030	**WAMU-FM 88.5 MHz (N/T-NPR)** American University Broadcast Ctr	Washington	DC	20016-0000
301 587-4900	**WGAY-FM 99.5 MHz (B/EZ)** 8121 Georgia Ave	Silver Spring	MD	20910-4933
202 686-9300	**WKYS-FM 93.9 MHz (UC)** 4001 Nebraska Ave NW	Washington	DC	20016-2733
202 686-3100	**WMAL-AM 630 kHz (N/T-ABC)** 4400 Jenifer St NW	Washington	DC	20015-2113
202 362-8330	**WMZQ-FM 98.7 MHz (Ctry)** 5513 Connecticut Ave NW	Washington	DC	20015-2601

Local Attractions & Special Events

■ Sports

301 350-3400	**Washington Bullets** 1 Harry S Truman Dr Capital Centre	Landover	MD	20785-4798
301 350-3400	**Washington Capitals** 1 Harry S Truman Dr Capital Centre	Landover	MD	20785-4798
202 546-2222	**Washington Redskins** RFK Stadium	Washington	DC	20015-2697

■ **Special Events**

202 737-2599 **National Cherry Blossom Festival** (March 31-April 7)

■ **Local Attractions**

202 692-0931	**Arlington National Cemetery** ....Arlington	VA	22211-5003
202 447-0193	**Bureau of Engraving & Printing** 14th & C Sts SW .... Washington	DC	20228-0000
202 324-3447	**FBI Headquarters** 9th St & Pennsylvania Ave NW .... Washington	DC	20535-0000
202 347-4833	**Ford's Theatre** 511 10th St NW .... Washington	DC	20001-0000
202 426-5960	**Frederick Douglass Home** 1411 W St SE .... Washington	DC	20020-0000
202 426-6841	**Jefferson Memorial** 900 Ohio Dr SW W Potomac Pk .... Washington	DC	20001-0000
202 707-5000	**Library of Congress** 101 Independence Ave SE .... Washington	DC	20540-0001
202 426-6841	**Lincoln Memorial** 23rd St NW & W Potomac Pk .... Washington	DC	20001-0000
703 780-2000	**Mount Vernon** George Washington Memorial Pkwy ....Mount Vernon	VA	22121-9999
202 523-3616	**National Archives & Records Administration**		
	8th St & Pennsylvania Ave NW .... Washington	DC	20408-0001
202 737-4215	**National Gallery of Art** 4th St & Constitution Ave NW .... Washington	DC	20565-0001
703 695-1776	**Pentagon The** .... Arlington	VA	20301-0000
202 285-2598	**Roosevelt Memorial** .... McClean	VA	22101-0000
202 357-2700	**Smithsonian Institution** 1000 Jefferson Dr SW .... Washington	DC	20560-0001
202 225-6827	**US Capitol** 1st St & Independence Ave .... Washington	DC	20510-0000
202 479-3011	**US Supreme Court** 1 1st St NE .... Washington	DC	20543-0001
202 634-1568	**Vietnam Veterans Memorial** 23rd & Constitution Ave .... Washington	DC	20020-0000
202 426-6841	**Washington Monument** 15th St NW & W Potomac Pk .... Washington	DC	20001-0000
202 456-1414	**White House** 1600 Pennsylvania Ave NW .... Washington	DC	20500-0001

ALPHABETICAL SECTION

WHAT DOES THE ALPHABETICAL SECTION CONTAIN?

Each listing in the Alphabetical Section consists of a telephone number, fax information (when available), official name, street or mailing address, city, state and zip code. (Nine-digit zip codes have been provided when possible. Four zeros have been inserted at the end of a five-digit zip code if the nine-digit zip was unavailable. The four zeros should not be used for mailing.)

HOW DO I FIND WHAT I'M LOOKING FOR?

Listings in both the alphabetical and classified sections of *Blue Pages USA* are alphabetized on a word-by-word basis. A space between two words functions as a "letter" before the letter "a." Therefore, a listing for "San Saba County" will be listed before "Sanborn County." In this example, the space between "San" and "Saba" alphabetizes before the "b" in "Sanborn."

Listings composed of a first name (or initial) and surname—e.g., "Susan Molinari"—are listed last name first: "Molinari Susan." The customary rendering has been retained when "last-name-first" would be awkward or less useful, such as "George Washington University."

Listings for foreign diplomatic offices in the US are in the order: embassy (if one exists), followed by the country's mission to the UN, followed by its consulate(s).

When several offices of a federal government agency or department are listed, the national offices are listed first, followed by the regional locations.

US Senators and Representatives are listed last name first, followed by their title (*Sen*=Senator and *Rep*=Representative), party affiliation (*D*=Democrat and *R*=Republican) and state represented - all in parentheses. For instance, the listing "Foley Thomas S (Rep - D - Washington)" signifies "Representative Thomas S. Foley, Democrat from Washington State."

When several listings with identical names appear (like "Douglas County"), they are further alphabetized by state. In these cases, you can easily find the specific listing you seek by scanning down the state column.

Alphabetical Section

For your convenience, the Alphabetical Section lists nearly all of the organizations, institutions and government offices appearing in the directory. For information on alphabetization, see the title page of this section.

If an organization cannot receive mail at its street address, the post office box is listed. When available, facsimile numbers have been included - for a total of approximately 14,000 fax numbers.

A

207 288-3519 **Abbe Museum** PO Box 286 .... Bar Harbor ME 04609-0286
803 459-5074 **Abbeville County** PO Box 99 .... Abbeville SC 29620-0099
804 220-7671 **Abbey Rockefeller Folk Art Center** 307 S England St .... Williamsburg VA 23185-0000
202 225-2726 **Abercrombie Neil (Rep - D - Hawaii)**
1440 Longworth Bldg .... Washington DC 20515-0001
Fax: 202 225-4580
915 674-2000 **Abilene Christian University** 1600 Campus Ct .... Abilene TX 79699-0001
Fax: 915 674-2202 Library
915 674-2296 *Journalism & Mass Communications Div* ACU Stn .... Abilene TX 79699-0001
915 677-2474 **Abilene Public Library** 202 Cedar St .... Abilene TX 79601-5793
912 386-3236 **Abraham Baldwin Agricultural College** PO Box 3 ABAC Stn .... Tifton GA 31793-0003
Fax: 912 386-7006
415 673-4200 **Academy of Art College** 540 Powell St .... San Francisco CA 94108-3893
215 299-1000 **Academy of Natural Sciences Museum**
19th & Ben Franklin Pkwy .... Philadelphia PA 19103-0000
Fax: 215 299-1028
215 947-4200 **Academy of the New Church College**
2815 Huntingdon Pike .... Bryn Athyn PA 19009-9999
Fax: Unlisted
318 788-8881 **Acadia Parish** PO Box 922 .... Crowley LA 70527-0922
804 787-5776 **Accomack County** County Courthouse .... Accomac VA 23301-0000
202 371-6710 **Accuracy in Media Inc** 1275 K St NW Suite 1150 .... Washington DC 20005-4090
Fax: 202 371-9054
202 225-2601 **Ackerman Gary L (Rep - D - New York)** 238 Cannon Bldg ... Washington DC 20515-0001
Fax: Unlisted
202 634-9282 **Action** 1100 Vermont Ave NW .... Washington DC 20525-0001
Fax: 202 634-9190 Acctg
617 565-7000 *Region 1* 10 Causeway St Rm 473 .... Boston MA 02222-1039
Fax: 617 565-7011
212 466-3481 *Region 2* 6 World Trade Ctr Rm 758 .... New York NY 10048-0084
Fax: 212 466-4195
215 597-9972 *Region 3* 2nd & Chestnut Sts Rm 108 .... Philadelphia PA 19106-0000
Fax: 215 597-4933
404 331-2859 *Region 4* 101 Marietta St NW Suite 1003 .... Atlanta GA 30323-0001
Fax: 404 331-2438
312 353-5107 *Region 5* 10 W Jackson Blvd 6th Fl .... Chicago IL 60604-3909
Fax: 312 353-5343
214 767-9494 *Region 6* 1100 Commerce St Rm 6B11 .... Dallas TX 75242-1001
Fax: 214 767-5465
303 844-2671 *Region 8* 1405 Curtis St Suite 2930 .... Denver CO 80202-2358
Fax: 303 844-2217
415 744-3013 *Region 9* 211 Main St Rm 530 .... San Francisco CA 94105-1974
Fax: 415 744-3046
206 442-1558 *Region 10* 909 1st Ave Suite 3039 .... Seattle WA 98174-1101
Fax: 206 399-4415
617 876-6620 **Action for Children's Television** 20 University Rd .... Cambridge MA 02138-5756
202 223-3111 **Active Ballot Club** 1775 K St NW .... Washington DC 20006-1502
Fax: 202 466-1562
208 383-4417 **Ada County** 650 Main St .... Boise ID 83702-5986
Fax: 208 383-4400
515 743-2445 **Adair County** PO Box L .... Greenfield IA 50849-1290
502 384-2801 **Adair County** 500 Public Sq .... Columbia KY 42728-1451
816 665-3350 **Adair County** County Courthouse .... Kirksville MO 63501-0000
918 696-7198 **Adair County** PO Box 169 .... Stilwell OK 74960-0169
907 592-8251 **Adak Naval Air Station** .... Adak AK 98111-0002
202 224-2621 **Adams Brock (Sen - D - Washington)** 513 Hart Bldg .... Washington DC 20510-0001
Fax: 202 224-0238
303 659-2120 **Adams County** 450 S 4th Ave .... Brighton CO 80601-3196
Fax: 303 659-0577
515 322-4711 **Adams County** Davis & 9th .... Corning IA 50841-0000
208 253-4561 **Adams County** PO Box 48 .... Council ID 83612-0048
Fax: 208 253-4258
217 223-6300 **Adams County** 521 Vermont St .... Quincy IL 62301-2934
219 724-2600 **Adams County** 112 S 2nd St .... Decatur IN 46733-1694
601 446-6684 **Adams County** 1 Court St .... Natchez MS 39120-2011
701 567-2460 **Adams County** County Courthouse .... Hettinger ND 58639-0000
402 461-7107 **Adams County** 4th & Denver Sts .... Hastings NE 68901-0000
513 544-2344 **Adams County** 110 W Main St .... West Union OH 45693-1347
717 334-6781 **Adams County** 111 Baltimore St .... Gettysburg PA 17325-2312
Fax: 717 334-2091
509 659-0090 **Adams County** 210 W Broadway Ave .... Ritzville WA 99169-1860
Fax: 509 659-0118
608 339-4200 **Adams County** PO Box 278 .... Friendship WI 53934-0278
Fax: 608 339-6414
303 288-2001 **Adams County Public Library** 8992 N Washington St .... Thornton CO 80229-4537
719 589-7121 **Adams State College** .... Alamosa CO 81102-0001
Fax: 719 589-7522
802 388-4237 **Addison County** 5 Court St .... Middlebury VT 05753-1405
508 475-7515 **Addison Gallery of American Art** Main St .... Andover MA 01810-0000
516 294-8700 **Adelphi University** 1 South Ave .... Garden City NY 11530-4299
Fax: 516 294-6182
516 663-1177 *Graduate School for Business* South Ave Rm 107 .... Garden City NY 11530-4299
518 793-4491 **Adirondack Community College** 440 Bay Rd .... Queensbury NY 12804-5816
Fax: Ext 416
312 322-0304 **Adler Planetarium** 1300 S Lake Shore Dr .... Chicago IL 60605-2489
Fax: 312 322-2257
202 254-7020 **Administrative Conference of the US**
2120 L St NW Suite 500 .... Washington DC 20037-1568
Fax: 202 254-3077
202 633-6097 **Administrative Office of the US Courts**
811 Vermont Ave NW Rm 655 .... Washington DC 20544-0001
Fax: 202 786-6018
517 265-5161 **Adrian College** 110 S Madison St .... Adrian MI 49221-2575
Fax: 517 264-3331
202 732-2270 **Adult Education Div (US Dept of Education)**
400 Maryland Ave SW Rm 4428 .... Washington DC 20202-0001
Fax: 202 732-1132
202 653-5640 **Advisory Commission on Intergovernmental Relations**
1111 20th St NW Suite 2000 .... Washington DC 20575-0001
Fax: 202 653-5429
202 786-0503 **Advisory Council on Historic Preservation**
1100 Pennsylvania Ave NW Rm 809 .... Washington DC 20004-2501

312 408-0101 **Aero-Space Institute** 161 W Harrison St .... Chicago IL 60605-1025
Afghanistan: Democratic Republic of Afghanistan
202 234-3770 *Embassy* 2341 Wyoming Ave NW .... Washington DC 20008-1642
Fax: 202 328-3516
212 754-1191 *Mission to the UN* 866 UN Plaza Rm 520 .... New York NY 10017-1890
202 647-7371 **African Affairs Bureau (US Dept of State)**
2201 C St NW Rm 3509 .... Washington DC 20520-0001
Fax: 202 647-6367
212 949-4242 **AFS International Intercultural Programs** 313 E 43rd St .... New York NY 10017-4809
Fax: 212 949-9379
671 344-8103 **Agana Naval Air Station** .... Agana GU 96637-1250
213 384-1882 **Agape Bible College** 920 S Grandview St .... Los Angeles CA 90006-0000
Fax: Unlisted
202 663-1451 **Agency for International Development** 2401 E St NW .... Washington DC 20523-0001
202 647-9620 **Agency for International Development**
320 21st St NW Rm 6226 .... Washington DC 20523-0001
Fax: 202 647-8511
404 371-6000 **Agnes Scott College** 141 E College Ave .... Decatur GA 30030-3797
Fax: 404 371-6177
202 447-5115 **Agricultural Marketing Service (US Dept of Agriculture)**
14th St & Independence Ave SW Rm 3071 .... Washington DC 20250-0001
Fax: 202 447-2104
202 225-2171 **Agriculture Committee (US House of Representatives)**
1301 Longworth Bldg .... Washington DC 20515-0001
Fax: 202 225-8510
202 224-2035 **Agriculture Nutrition & Forestry Committee (US Senate)**
328-A Russell Bldg .... Washington DC 20510-0001
Fax: 202 224-2001
216 264-3911 **Agriculture Technical Institution** 1328 Dover Rd .... Wooster OH 44691-8905
Fax: 216 262-7634
803 642-2013 **Aiken County** 828 Richland Ave W .... Aiken SC 29801-3834
Fax: 803 642-2124
803 593-9231 **Aiken Technical College** PO Box 696 .... Graniteville SC 29802-0600
Fax: 803 593-6641 Admin
803 642-7575 **Aiken-Bamberg-Barnwell-Edgefield Regional Library System**
314 Chesterfield St SW .... Aiken SC 29801-3850
303 330-8008 **Aims Community College** 5401 W 20th St .... Greeley CO 80634-3000
Fax: 303 330-5705
412 232-3444 **Air & Waste Management Assn** Gateway 3 4 West .... Pittsburgh PA 15222-0000
Fax: 412 232-3450
703 247-5800 **Air Force Assn** 1501 Lee Hwy .... Arlington VA 22209-1198
Fax: 703 247-5855
301 899-3500 **Air Force Sergeants Assn** 5211 Auth Rd .... Suitland MD 20746-4396
Fax: Unlisted
202 797-4033 **Air Line Pilots Assn PAC** 1625 Massachusetts Ave NW .... Washington DC 20036-2283
Fax: 202 797-4052
301 695-2000 **Aircraft Owners & Pilots Assn PAC** 421 Aviation Way .... Frederick MD 21701-4756
Fax: 301 695-2375
218 927-2102 **Aitkin County** 209 2nd St NW .... Aitkin MN 56431-1297
202 224-6361 **Akaka Daniel K (Sen - D - Hawaii)** 109 Hart Bldg .... Washington DC 20510-0001
Fax: 202 224-2126
216 376-9185 **Akron Art Museum** 70 E Market St .... Akron OH 44308-2084
216 762-7621 **Akron-Summit County Public Library** 55 S Main St .... Akron OH 44326-0001
Fax: 216 762-6623
205 851-5000 **Alabama A & M University** .... Normal AL 35762-0000
205 851-5425 *Department of Community Planning & Urban Studies*
Carver Complex S Rm 218 .... Normal AL 35762-0000
205 774-5113 **Alabama Aviation & Technical College** PO Box 1209 .... Ozark AL 36361-1209
205 242-4169 **Alabama Bureau of Tourism & Travel** 532 S Perry St .... Montgomery AL 36104-4616
Fax: 205 264-7060
205 595-9090 **Alabama Democratic State Committee** 4120 3rd Ave S .... Birmingham AL 35222-1919
Fax: 205 591-8020
205 277-7330 **Alabama Public Library Service** 6030 Monticello Dr .... Montgomery AL 36130-0001
Fax: 205 272-9419
205 324-1990 **Alabama Republican Party** 2940 Clairmont Ave S .... Birmingham AL 35205-1000
Fax: 205 324-0682
205 837-3400 **Alabama Space & Rocket Center** 1 Tranquility Base .... Huntsville AL 35807-0000
Fax: 205 837-6137
Alabama State Government
205 261-2500 *Information* 501 Dexter Ave .... Montgomery AL 36130-0001
205 261-7305 *Attorney General* 11 S Union St .... Montgomery AL 36130-0001
Fax: 205 261-7458
205 242-8700 *Board of Pardons & Paroles*
50 North Ripley St Gordon Persons Bldg Plaza Level .... Montgomery AL 36130-0001
205 261-5033 *Bureau of Vital Statistics* 434 Monroe St Rm 215 .... Montgomery AL 36130-0001
205 269-2700 *Commission on Higher Education* 1 Court Sq Suite 221 Montgomery AL 36197-0000
Fax: 205 263-3335
205 261-2650 *Department of Agriculture & Industries* PO Box 3336 .... Montgomery AL 36193-0000
Fax: 205 240-3135
205 261-3486 *Department of Conservation & Natural Resources*
64 N Union St Rm 702 .... Montgomery AL 36130-0001
Fax: 205 240-3009
205 242-9400 *Department of Corrections*
50 Ripley St Gordon Persons Bldg 3rd Fl .... Montgomery AL 36130-0001
Fax: 205 242-9399
205 242-8672 *Department of Economics & Community Affairs*
3465 Norman Bridge Rd .... Montgomery AL 36105-2310
Fax: 205 284-8670
205 242-9700 *Department of Education* 50 N Ripley St .... Montgomery AL 36130-0001
Fax: 205 242-9708
205 271-7700 *Department of Environmental Management*
1751 Congressman WL Dickinson Dr .... Montgomery AL 36130-0001
Fax: 205 271-7950
205 261-7160 *Department of Finance* 11 S Union St Rm 207 .... Montgomery AL 36130-0001
Fax: 205 240-3164
205 261-3460 *Department of Labor* 64 N Union St Rm 651 .... Montgomery AL 36130-0001
205 261-5052 *Department of Public Health* 434 Monroe St .... Montgomery AL 36130-0001
Fax: 205 240-3097
205 242-4371 *Department of Public Safety* PO Box 1511 .... Montgomery AL 36102-1511
Fax: 205 261-4385
205 242-1175 *Department of Revenue* 50 N Ripley St .... Montgomery AL 36132-0001
Fax: 205 242-8915
205 242-7334 *Division of Consumer Protection* 11 S Union St Rm 429 . Montgomery AL 36130-0001
Fax: 205 242-7345
205 261-7250 *Division of Purchasing* 11 S Union St Rm 200 .... Montgomery AL 36130-0001
Fax: 205 240-3174
205 254-1275 *Division of Safety & Inspection* PO Box 10444 .... Birmingham AL 35202-0444
205 567-2221 *Draper Correctional Center* PO Box 1107 .... Elmore AL 36025-0000
205 261-3318 *Emergency Management Agency* 520 S Court St .... Montgomery AL 36130-0001
Fax: 205 240-3118
205 349-2852 *Geological Survey* 420 Hackberry Ln .... Tuscaloosa AL 35486-0000
Fax: Ext 294
205 261-7100 *Governor* 11 S Union St Rm 217 .... Montgomery AL 36130-0001
Fax: 205 240-3151
205 261-6311 *Highway Dept* 1409 Coliseum Blvd .... Montgomery AL 36130-0001
Fax: 205 262-8041

205 261-4361 *History & Archives* 624 Washington Ave ... Montgomery AL 36130-0001
Fax: 205 240-3109
205 269-3550 *Insurance Dept* 135 S Union St ... Montgomery AL 36130-0001
Fax: 205 240-3194
205 242-5891 *Law Enforcement Planning Agency*
3465 Norman Bridge Rd ... Montgomery AL 36105-2310
Fax: 205 284-8670
205 261-7900 *Lieutenant Governor* 11 S Union St Rm 725 ... Montgomery AL 36130-0001
205 261-5218 *Public Service Commission* PO Box 991 ... Montgomery AL 36101-0991
Fax: 205 240-3134
205 261-5544 *Real Estate Commission* 4121 Carmichael Rd Suite 401 . Montgomery AL 36106-0000
205 832-4140 *Retirement Systems* 135 S Union St ... Montgomery AL 36130-0001
Fax: 205 240-3032
205 467-6112 *Saint Clair Correctional Facilities* 1000 St Clair Rd ... Springville AL 35146-9790
Fax: 205 467-6111
205 284-8952 *Science Technology & Energy Div*
3465 Norman Bridge Rd ... Montgomery AL 36105-2399
Fax: 205 284-8670
205 261-7200 *Secretary of State* 11 S Union St Rm 208 ... Montgomery AL 36130-0001
Fax: 205 242-4707
205 261-2984 *Securities Commission* 166 Commerce St 2nd Fl ... Montgomery AL 36130-0001
Fax: 205 265-4033
205 261-4076 *State Council on the Arts* 1 Dexter Ave ... Montgomery AL 36130-0001
205 261-4609 *Supreme Court* 445 Dexter Ave ... Montgomery AL 36130-0001
Fax: 205 242-4483
205 261-7500 *Treasury Dept* 11 S Union St Rm 240 ... Montgomery AL 36130-0001
Fax: 205 240-3172
205 242-8025 *Unemployment Compensation Div* 649 Monroe St ... Montgomery AL 36130-0001
Fax: 205 240-3070
205 261-2868 *Workmen's Compensation Div* Industrial Relations Bldg . Montgomery AL 36130-0001
205 293-4100 **Alabama State University** 915 S Jackson St ... Montgomery AL 36101-0000
904 374-5210 **Alachua County** 21 E University Ave ... Gainesville FL 32601-5348
Fax: 904 338-7363
904 371-2665 **Alachua Library District** 222 E University Ave ... Gainesville FL 32601-5456
Fax: 904 375-1659
919 578-2002 **Alamance Community College** Jimmy Kerr Rd & I-85 ... Haw River NC 27258-0000
Fax: 919 578-1987 Mail Rm
919 228-1312 **Alamance County** 124 W Elm St ... Graham NC 27253-2802
Fax: 919 227-0439
415 437-3171 **Alameda Coast Guard Support Center** Coast Guard Island ... Alameda CA 94501-5100
Fax: 415 437-3670
415 272-6790 **Alameda County** 1225 Fallon St ... Oakland CA 94612-4218
Fax: Unlisted
415 745-1500 **Alameda County Libraries** 2450 Stevenson Blvd ... Fremont CA 94538-0000
Fax: 415 783-2987
415 263-3079 **Alameda Naval Air Station** ... Alameda CA 94501-5000
Fax: 415 263-3039
719 589-5887 **Alamosa County** 402 Edison Ave ... Alamosa CO 81101-2560
Fax: 719 589-6118
907 822-3201 **Alaska Bible College** PO Box 289 ... Glennallen AK 99588-0289
Fax: 907 822-3290
907 258-3050 **Alaska Democratic Party**
1443 W Northern Lights Blvd Suite S ... Anchorage AK 99503-2307
907 465-2010 **Alaska Div of Tourism** 333 Willoughby Ave ... Juneau AK 99811-0001
Fax: 907 586-8399
907 561-1266 **Alaska Pacific University** 4101 University Dr ... Anchorage AK 99508-4672
Fax: 907 562-4276
907 586-7405 **Alaska Power Administration (US Dept of Energy)**
PO Box 020050 ... Juneau AK 99802-0050
Fax: 907 586-7270
907 586-2323 **Alaska State Chamber of Commerce** 217 2nd St Suite 201 ... Juneau AK 99801-1267
Fax: 907 463-5515
Alaska State Government
907 465-2111 *Information* 333 Willoughby Ave 8th Fl ... Juneau AK 99811-0001
Fax: 907 463-5661
907 561-7877 *Alaska Energy Authority* PO Box 190869 ... Anchorage AK 99519-0869
Fax: 907 561-8584
907 465-3384 *Alaska State Board of Parole* PO Box T ... Juneau AK 99811-2000
Fax: 907 465-2006
907 465-2270 *Archives & Records Management* 141 Willoughby Ave ... Juneau AK 99801-1720
Fax: 907 465-2465
907 465-3600 *Attorney General* PO Box K ... Juneau AK 99811-0000
Fax: 907 463-5295
907 465-3393 *Bureau of Vital Records* PO Box H ... Juneau AK 99822-0675
907 465-2500 *Commerce & Economic Development*
333 Willoughby Ave 9th Fl ... Juneau AK 99801-0000
Fax: 907 463-3841
907 465-2854 *Commission of Postsecondary Education*
400 Willoughby Ave 1st Fl ... Juneau AK 99811-0001
Fax: 907 586-4002
907 465-3376 *Department of Corrections* PO Box T ... Juneau AK 99811-0000
Fax: 907 465-2006
907 465-2800 *Department of Education* PO Box F ... Juneau AK 99811-0001
Fax: 907 463-5279
907 465-2600 *Department of Environmental Conservation* PO Box O ... Juneau AK 99811-0001
Fax: 907 586-1391
907 465-2700 *Department of Labor* 1111 W 8th St ... Juneau AK 99801-1894
Fax: 907 465-2784
907 465-2400 *Department of Natural Resources* 400 Willoughby Ave ... Juneau AK 99801-1796
Fax: 907 586-2754
907 465-4322 *Department of Public Safety* PO Box N ... Juneau AK 99811-0001
Fax: 907 465-4362
907 465-2300 *Department of Revenue* 333 Willoughby Ave ... Juneau AK 99811-0001
Fax: 907 465-2389
907 465-3900 *Department of Transportation & Public Facilities* PO Box Z ... Juneau AK 99811-0001
Fax: 907 586-8365
907 745-7200 *Division of Agriculture* 915 S Bailey St ... Palmer AK 99645-6923
Fax: 907 745-7112
907 465-2521 *Division of Banking Securities & Corps*
333 Willoughby Ave 9th Fl ... Juneau AK 99801-0000
Fax: Unlisted
907 376-3061 *Division of Emergency Services* 3501 E Bogard Rd ... Wasilla AK 99687-8998
Fax: 907 376-0219
907 465-3082 *Division of Finance* PO Box H-02 ... Juneau AK 99811-0000
Fax: 907 465-3068
907 465-2250 *Division of General Services & Supply*
333 Willoughby Ave 7th Fl ... Juneau AK 99811-0001
Fax: 907 465-2189
907 465-2515 *Division of Insurance* 333 Willoughby Ave ... Juneau AK 99801-0000
Fax: 907 465-2974
907 762-2518 *Division of Mining* PO Box 107016 ... Anchorage AK 99510-7016
Fax: 907 563-1853
907 465-2534 *Division of Occupational Licensing* 333 Willoughby Ave ... Juneau AK 99801-0001
Fax: 907 465-2974
907 465-3573 *Division of Policy* 4th & Main Sts Diamond Court Bldg 4th Fl .. Juneau AK 99811-0000
Fax: 907 465-2079
907 465-3090 *Division of Public Health* 350 Main St Rm 503 ... Juneau AK 99801-0000
Fax: 907 586-1877
907 465-4460 *Division of Retirement & Benefits* PO Box CR-0203 ... Juneau AK 99811-0001
Fax: 907 465-3086
907 269-5641 *Division of State Troopers* 5700 E Tudor Rd ... Anchorage AK 99507-1225
Fax: 907 337-2059
907 465-2790 *Division of Workers' Compensation* 1111 W 8th St ... Juneau AK 99801-1802
Fax: 907 465-2784
907 465-2712 *Employment Security Div* 1111 W 8th St ... Juneau AK 99801-1802
Fax: 907 465-4537
907 452-3125 *Fairbanks Correctional Center* PO Box 70317 ... Fairbanks AK 99707-0317
Fax: Ext 132
907 465-3500 *Governor* PO Box A ... Juneau AK 99811-0001
Fax: 907 463-3454
907 694-9511 *Highland Mountain Correctional Center* PO Box 600 ... Eagle River AK 99577-0600
Fax: 907 694-4507
907 465-3520 *Lieutenant Governor* PO Box AA ... Juneau AK 99811-0001
Fax: 907 463-5364
907 465-4855 *Occupational Safety & Health Section* 1111 W 8th St ... Juneau AK 99801-1802
Fax: 907 465-2784
907 279-7541 *Public Defender Agency* 900 W 5th St Suite 200 ... Anchorage AK 99501-2090
Fax: 907 269-5476
907 276-6222 *Public Utilities Commission* 1016 W 6th Ave Suite 400 ... Anchorage AK 99501-1963
Fax: 907 276-0160
907 563-2169 *Real Estate Commission* 3601 C St Suite 722 ... Anchorage AK 99503-5934
Fax: 907 562-5781
907 279-1558 *State Council on the Arts* 619 Warehouse Ave Suite 220 ... Anchorage AK 99501-1665
Fax: 907 279-4330
907 264-0607 *Supreme Court* 303 K St ... Anchorage AK 99501-2013
Fax: 907 276-5808
907 465-2712 *Unemployment Insurance* 1111 W 8th St ... Juneau AK 99801-1802
Fax: 907 465-4537
907 465-2910 **Alaska State Library** PO Box G ... Juneau AK 99811-0000
Fax: 907 465-2665
907 465-2901 **Alaska State Museum** 395 Whittier St ... Juneau AK 99801-1718
Fax: 907 465-2976
212 249-2059 **Albania: People's Socialist Republic of Albania Mission to the UN**
320 E 79th St ... New York NY 10021-0904
518 445-7211 **Albany College of Pharmacy** 106 New Scotland Ave ... Albany NY 12208-3492
Fax: 518 445-7202
518 445-7644 **Albany County** 16 Eagle St ... Albany NY 12207-1019
Fax: 518 426-4104
307 721-2541 **Albany County** County Courthouse ... Laramie WY 82070-0000
518 449-3380 **Albany Public Library** 161 Washington Ave ... Albany NY 12210-2398
912 430-4600 **Albany State College** 504 College Dr ... Albany GA 31705-2797
Fax: Unlisted
804 296-5841 **Albemarle County** 401 McIntire Rd ... Charlottesville VA 22901-4579
203 773-8550 **Albertus Magnus College** 700 Prospect St ... New Haven CT 06511-1189
Fax: 203 773-9539
517 629-1000 **Albion College** 611 E Porter St ... Albion MI 49224-1899
Fax: 517 629-0509
215 921-2381 **Albright College** 13th & Exeter St ... Reading PA 19612-0000
Fax: 215 921-7530
716 882-8700 **Albright-Knox Art Gallery** 1285 Elmwood Ave ... Buffalo NY 14222-1096
Fax: 716 882-1958
505 768-2000 **Albuquerque City Hall** 400 Marquette Ave ... Albuquerque NM 87103-0000
505 243-7255 **Albuquerque Museum** 2000 Mountain Rd NW ... Albuquerque NM 87104-1459
Fax: 505 764-6546
505 768-5140 **Albuquerque Public Library** 501 Copper Ave NW ... Albuquerque NM 87102-3129
Fax: 505 768-5182
517 724-5374 **Alcona County** 106 5th St ... Harrisville MI 48740-0000
Fax: 517 724-5684
601 286-7700 **Alcorn County** PO Box 112 ... Corinth MS 38834-0112
601 877-6100 **Alcorn State University** Hwy 552 ... Lorman MS 39096-0000
Fax: 601 877-2975
304 457-1700 **Alderson-Broaddus College** College Hill ... Philippi WV 26416-1051
Fax: Call company operator
202 225-4076 **Alexander Bill (Rep - D - Arkansas)** 233 Cannon Bldg ... Washington DC 20515-0001
Fax: 202 225-6182
618 734-3947 **Alexander County** 2000 Washington Ave ... Cairo IL 62914-1717
704 632-2215 **Alexander County** 100 1st St SW ... Taylorsville NC 28681-2592
703 838-4550 **Alexandria (Independent City)** 301 King St ... Alexandria VA 22314-3211
Fax: 703 838-4948
703 838-4555 **Alexandria Library** 717 Queen St ... Alexandria VA 22314-2471
612 762-0221 **Alexandria Technical College** 1601 Jefferson St ... Alexandria MN 56308-3799
Fax: 612 762-4501
405 596-2392 **Alfalfa County** 300 S Grand Ave County Courthouse ... Cherokee OK 73728-0000
607 871-2111 **Alfred University** 2 Main St ... Alfred NY 14802-0000
Fax: 607 871-2339
607 871-2141 *Graduate School of Engineering* PO Box 1155 ... Alfred NY 14802-0155
Fax: 607 871-2114
906 387-2076 **Alger County** 101 Court St ... Munising MI 49862-1196
Algeria: Democratic & Popular Republic of Algeria
202 265-2800 *Embassy* 2137 Wyoming Ave NW ... Washington DC 20008-3905
212 750-1960 *Mission to the UN* 15 E 47th St ... New York NY 10017-1982
606 368-2101 **Alice Lloyd College** Purpose Rd ... Pippa Passes KY 41844-0000
Fax: 606 368-2125
319 568-3318 **Allamakee County** PO Box 248 ... Waukon IA 52172-0248
805 922-6966 **Allan Hancock College** 800 S College Dr ... Santa Maria CA 93454-6368
Fax: 805 928-7905
202 225-4676 **Allard Wayne (Rep - R - Colorado)** 513 Cannon Bldg ... Washington DC 20515-0001
Fax: 202 225-8630
616 673-8471 **Allegan County** 113 Chestnut St ... Allegan MI 49010-1362
Fax: 616 673-6094
301 724-7700 **Allegany Community College** Willow Brook Rd ... Cumberland MD 21502-0000
Fax: 301 724-1349
301 777-5911 **Allegany County** 3 Pershing St ... Cumberland MD 21502-3043
716 268-7612 **Allegany County** Court St ... Belmont NY 14813-0000
Fax: 716 268-9446
919 372-8949 **Alleghany County** Main St ... Sparta NC 28675-0000
Fax: 919 372-2061
703 962-3906 **Alleghany County** 266 W Main St ... Covington VA 24426-1550
814 332-3100 **Allegheny College** 520 N Main St ... Meadville PA 16335-3902
Fax: 814 333-8180
412 355-5313 **Allegheny County** 436 Grant St ... Pittsburgh PA 15219-2403
216 337-6403 **Allegheny Wesleyan College** 2161 Woodsdale Rd ... Salem OH 44460-9504
219 428-7124 **Allen County** 1 E Main St ... Fort Wayne IN 46802-1887
316 365-7491 **Allen County** 1 N Washington St ... Iola KS 66749-2841
502 237-3706 **Allen County** PO Box 336 ... Scottsville KY 42164-0336
419 228-3700 **Allen County** 301 N Main St ... Lima OH 45801-4456
316 365-5116 **Allen County Community College** 1801 N Cottonwood St ... Iola KS 66749-1698
219 424-7241 **Allen County Public Library** 900 Webster St ... Fort Wayne IN 46802-3699
Fax: 219 422-9688
318 639-4396 **Allen Parish** PO Box G ... Oberlin LA 70655-2007
803 254-9735 **Allen University** 1530 Harden St ... Columbia SC 29204-1085
803 584-2737 **Allendale County** PO Box 126 ... Allendale SC 29810-0126

Allentown / Anniston

Phone	Name / Address	City	State	ZIP
215 282-1100	**Allentown College of Saint Francis DeSales** Station Ave *Fax:* 215 282-2342	Center Valley	PA	18034-0000
215 820-2400	**Allentown Public Library** 1210 Hamilton St *Fax:* 215 820-0640	Allentown	PA	18102-4371
517 463-7111	**Alma College** 614 W Superior St *Fax:* 517 463-7277	Alma	MI	48801-1599
517 356-9021	**Alpena Community College** 666 Johnson St *Fax:* Unlisted	Alpena	MI	49707-1495
517 356-0115	**Alpena County** 720 W Chisholm St	Alpena	MI	49707-2453
916 694-2281	**Alpine County** PO Box 158 *Fax:* 916 694-2491	Markleeville	CA	96120-0158
814 946-0417	**Altoona Area Public Library** 1600 5th Ave *Fax:* 814 946-3230	Altoona	PA	16602-3621
405 482-8100	**Altus Air Force Base** *Fax:* Unlisted	Altus	OK	73523-0000
215 777-5411	**Alvernia College** 400 Saint Bernadine St *Fax:* 215 777-6632	Reading	PA	19607-1799
414 382-6000	**Alverno College** 3401 S 39th St *Fax:* 414 382-6354	Milwaukee	WI	53215-4093
713 331-6111	**Alvin Community College** 3110 Mustang Rd	Alvin	TX	77511-4895
209 223-6463	**Amador County** 108 Court St	Jackson	CA	95642-2379
806 371-5000	**Amarillo College** 2201 S Washington St *Fax:* 806 371-5370	Amarillo	TX	79178-0001
806 378-3054	**Amarillo Public Library** 413 E 4th St *Fax:* 806 378-4245	Amarillo	TX	79101-1523
818 304-6000	**Ambassador College** 300 W Green St *Fax:* 818 356-0552	Pasadena	CA	91129-0001
804 561-3039	**Amelia County** PO Box A	Amelia Court House	VA	23002-0066
818 798-0777	**American Academy of Dramatic Arts** 2550 Paloma St *Fax:* Unlisted	Pasadena	CA	91107-2697
212 686-9244	**American Academy of Dramatic Arts** 120 Madison Ave	New York	NY	10016-7089
714 593-0432	**American Armenian International College** 1950 3rd St *Fax:* 714 593-0879	La Verne	CA	91750-0000
703 823-9800	**American Assn for Counseling & Development** 5999 Stevenson Ave *Fax:* 703 823-0252	Alexandria	VA	22304-3398
202 429-1825	**American Assn for Marriage & Family Therapy** 1717 K St NW Suite 407 *Fax:* 202 331-0699	Washington	DC	20006-1504
202 728-4300	**American Assn of Retired Persons** 1909 K St NW *Fax:* 202 785-8526	Washington	DC	20049-0001
615 262-3433	**American Baptist College of American Baptist Theology** 1800 White's Creek Pike	Nashville	TN	37207-4994
415 841-1905	**American Baptist Seminary of the West** 2606 Dwight Way	Berkeley	CA	94704-3029
318 396-6000	**American Christian Schools of Religion** 3201 N 7th St *Fax:* 318 396-6327	West Monroe	LA	71291-2229
212 944-9800	**American Civil Liberties Union** 132 W 43rd St *Fax:* 212 730-4652	New York	NY	10036-6599
203 583-6070	**American Clock & Watch Museum** 100 Maple St	Bristol	CT	06010-5034
213 470-2000	**American College for the Applied Arts** 1651 Westwood Blvd	Los Angeles	CA	90024-5603
404 231-9000	**American College for the Applied Arts** 3330 Peachtree Rd NE *Fax:* 404 231-1062	Atlanta	GA	30326-1016
202 546-6555	**American Conservative Union** 38 Ivy St SE *Fax:* 202 546-7370	Washington	DC	20003-4097
312 263-4161	**American Conservatory of Music** 16 N Wabash Ave Suite 1850 *Fax:* 312 263-8419	Chicago	IL	60602-4792
212 956-3535	**American Craft Museum** 40 W 53rd St *Fax:* 212 956-3699	New York	NY	10019-6112
703 522-1820	**American Defense Preparedness Assn** 2101 Wilson Blvd Suite 400 *Fax:* 703 522-1885	Arlington	VA	22201-9803
202 898-2424	**American Dental PAC** 1111 14th St NW Suite 1100 *Fax:* 202 898-2437	Washington	DC	20005-5683
202 862-5800	**American Enterprise Institute for Public Policy Research** 1150 17th St NW Suite 1200 *Fax:* 202 862-7178	Washington	DC	20036-4670
305 891-1700	**American Federation of Police** 1100 NE 125th St Suite 100 *Fax:* 305 891-1884	North Miami	FL	33161-5083
202 452-4800	**American Federation of State County & Municipal Employees** 1625 L St NW *Fax:* 202 429-1293	Washington	DC	20036-5601
213 856-7628	**American Film Institute** 2021 N Western Ave *Fax:* 213 467-4578	Los Angeles	CA	90027-1625
703 274-4839	**American Forces Information Service (US Dept of Defense)** 601 N Fairfax St Suite 311 *Fax:* 703 274-4865	Alexandria	VA	22314-2060
215 241-7000	**American Friends Service Committee** 1501 Cherry St *Fax:* 215 864-0104	Philadelphia	PA	19102-1477
303 695-0811	**American Humane Assn** 623 Inverness Dr E *Fax:* Call company operator	Englewood	CO	80112-0000
203 868-0518	**American Indian Archaeological Institute** 38 Curtis Rd	Washington Green	CT	06793-1701
602 944-3335	**American Indian Bible College** 10020 N 15th Ave *Fax:* 602 943-8299	Phoenix	AZ	85021-2199
413 737-7000	**American International College** 1000 State St *Fax:* 413 737-2803	Springfield	MA	01109-3189
312 281-4700	**American Islamic College** 640 W Irving Park Rd	Chicago	IL	60613-3106
202 466-2520	**American Logistic Assn** 1133 15th St NW Suite 640 *Fax:* 202 296-4419	Washington	DC	20005-2710
202 789-7400	**American Medical Assn PAC** 1101 Vermont Ave NW Suite 1200 *Fax:* 202 898-0026	Washington	DC	20005-3583
212 769-5000	**American Museum of Natural History** Central Pk W & 79th St	New York	NY	10024-5192
615 576-3200	**American Museum of Science & Energy** 300 S Tulane Ave *Fax:* 615 576-6024	Oak Ridge	TN	37830-6726
212 234-3130	**American Numismatic Society Museum** Broadway & 155th St *Fax:* 212 234-3381	New York	NY	10032-7598
212 677-4400	**American ORT Federation** 817 Broadway *Fax:* 212 979-9545	New York	NY	10003-4756
202 872-0611	**American Planning Assn** 1776 Massachusetts Ave NW Suite 704 *Fax:* 202 872-0643	Washington	DC	20036-1997
502 895-2405	**American Printing House for the Blind (US Dept of Education)** 1839 Frankfort Ave *Fax:* Call company operator	Louisville	KY	40206-3152
202 682-0100	**American Public Welfare Assn** 810 1st St NE Suite 500 *Fax:* 202 289-6555	Washington	DC	20002-4227
312 667-2200	**American Public Works Assn** 1313 E 60th St 3rd Fl *Fax:* 312 667-2304	Chicago	IL	60637-2882
202 737-8300	**American Red Cross** 430 17th St NW *Fax:* 202 639-3791 Admin	Washington	DC	20006-0000
916 484-8011	**American River College** 4700 College Oak Dr *Fax:* 916 484-8674	Sacramento	CA	95841-4286
202 393-7878	**American Society for Public Administration** 1120 G St NW Suite 500 *Fax:* 202 638-4952	Washington	DC	20005-3885
212 876-7700	**American Society for the Prevention of Cruelty to Animals** 441 E 92nd St *Fax:* 212 348-3031	New York	NY	10128-6803
215 540-2295	**American Society of International Executives** 18 Sentry Pkwy Suite 1 *Fax:* 215 540-2290	Blue Bell	PA	19422-2339
703 836-6727	**American Society of Naval Engineers** 1452 Duke St *Fax:* 703 836-7491	Alexandria	VA	22314-3403
415 543-2617	**American Society on Aging** 833 Market St Suite 512 *Fax:* 415 882-4280	San Francisco	CA	94103-1824
213 641-0030	**American Tourist Bureau** 6045 W Century Blvd Suite 720 *Fax:* 213 641-0182	Los Angeles	CA	90045-5309
301 925-8811	**American Trauma Society** 1400 Mercantile Ln Suite 188 *Fax:* 301 925-8815	Landover	MD	20785-5365
202 686-2000	**American University** 4400 Massachusetts Ave NW *Fax:* 202 885-2013	Washington	DC	20016-8002
202 885-2060	*School of Communication* 4400 Massachusetts Ave NW	Washington	DC	20016-8099
202 885-2944	*School of Public Affairs* 4400 Massachusetts Ave NW Ward Circle Bldg Rm 104 *Fax:* 202 885-2353	Washington	DC	20016-8002
202 885-2605	*Washington College of Law* 4400 Massachusetts Ave NW *Fax:* 202 885-3601	Washington	DC	20016-8002
212 687-4505	**American-Indonesian Chamber of Commerce** 711 3rd Ave 17th Fl *Fax:* 212 867-9882	New York	NY	10017-4014
312 641-2937	**American-Israel Chamber of Commerce & Industry** 180 N Michigan Ave Suite 911 *Fax:* 312 641-2941	Chicago	IL	60601-7453
212 971-0310	**American-Israel Chamber of Commerce & Industry** 350 5th Ave Suite 1919 *Fax:* 212 971-0331	New York	NY	10118-0110
216 267-1200	**American-Israel Chamber of Commerce & Industry** 10800 Brookpark Rd *Fax:* 216 267-3925	Cleveland	OH	44130-1119
212 986-7229	**American-Mideast Business Association** 80 Park Ave Suite 17N *Fax:* Unlisted	New York	NY	10016-2540
202 638-6447	**Americans for Democratic Action** 1511 K St NW Suite 941 *Fax:* 202 638-2962	Washington	DC	20005-1401
413 542-2000	**Amherst College** Stn 2 *Fax:* 413 542-2309 Mail Rm	Amherst	MA	01002-0000
804 929-9321	**Amherst County** 100 E Court St	Amherst	VA	24521-2702
601 657-8022	**Amite County** PO Box 680	Liberty	MS	39645-0000
212 807-8400	**Amnesty International of the USA** 322 8th Ave *Fax:* 212 627-1451	New York	NY	10001-4808
312 856-6317	**Amoco PAC** 200 E Randolph St *Fax:* 312 856-2454	Chicago	IL	60601-7125
202 906-3000	**Amtrak** 60 Massachusetts Ave NE *Fax:* 202 906-3865	Washington	DC	20002-4225
202 287-3306	**Anacostia Museum (Smithsonian Institution)** 1901 Fort Pl SE *Fax:* 202 287-3183	Washington	DC	20020-3298
714 999-1880	**Anaheim Public Library** 500 W Broadway *Fax:* Unlisted	Anaheim	CA	92805-3699
907 261-2975	**Anchorage Municipal Libraries** 3600 Denali St *Fax:* 907 562-1244	Anchorage	AK	99503-6055
907 343-4326	**Anchorage Museum of History & Art** 121 W 7th Ave *Fax:* 907 343-6149	Anchorage	AK	99501-3611
219 936-8898	**Ancilla College** Union Rd *Fax:* 219 935-1785	Donaldson	IN	46513-9999
913 448-6841	**Anderson County** 100 E 4th Ave	Garnett	KS	66032-1595
502 839-3041	**Anderson County** 151 S Main St	Lawrenceburg	KY	40342-1192
803 260-4053	**Anderson County** PO Box 1656	Anderson	SC	29622-1656
615 457-5400	**Anderson County** 100 N Main St	Clinton	TN	37716-3615
903 723-7432	**Anderson County** 500 N Church St	Palestine	TX	75801-3024
803 260-4500	**Anderson County Library** 202 E Greenville St	Anderson	SC	29621-5595
804 367-1522	**Anderson Gallery** 907 1/2 W Franklin St Virginia Commonwealth University	Richmond	VA	23284-0001
202 225-6676	**Anderson Glenn M (Rep - D - California)** 2329 Rayburn Bldg *Fax:* 202 225-1597	Washington	DC	20515-0001
317 649-9071	**Anderson University** 1100 E 5th St *Fax:* Unlisted	Anderson	IN	46012-3495
912 732-2171	**Andrew College** 413 College St	Cuthbert	GA	31740-1395
816 324-3624	**Andrew County** PO Box 206	Savannah	MO	64485-0206
301 981-4511	**Andrews Air Force Base** *Fax:* 301 981-4246 PR	Camp Springs	MD	20331-0001
915 524-1426	**Andrews County** PO Box 727	Andrews	TX	79714-0727
202 225-7508	**Andrews Michael A (Rep - D - Texas)** 303 Cannon Bldg *Fax:* 202 225-4210	Washington	DC	20515-0001
202 225-6501	**Andrews Robert E (Rep - D - New Jersey)** 1005 Longworth Bldg *Fax:* 202 225-6583	Washington	DC	20515-0001
202 225-6116	**Andrews Thomas H (Rep - D - Maine)** 1724 Longworth Bldg *Fax:* 202 225-9065	Washington	DC	20515-0001
616 471-7771	**Andrews University** US 31 N *Fax:* 616 471-9751	Berrien Springs	MI	49104-0001
207 784-8390	**Androscoggin County** 2 Turner St	Auburn	ME	04210-5978
409 639-1301	**Angelina Community College** PO Box 1768 *Fax:* 409 639-4299	Lufkin	TX	75901-0000
409 634-8339	**Angelina County** 215 E Lufkin Ave	Lufkin	TX	75901-3047
915 942-2041	**Angelo State University** 2601 West Ave N *Fax:* 915 942-2038 Admin	San Angelo	TX	76909-0001
212 861-5656	**Angola: People's Republic of Angola Mission to the UN** 135 E 73rd St *Fax:* 212 832-8191	New York	NY	10021-0000
202 447-2511	**Animal & Plant Health Inspection Service (US Dept of Agriculture)** 14th St & Independence Ave SW *Fax:* 202 447-3982	Washington	DC	20250-0001
313 994-2333	**Ann Arbor Public Library** 343 S 5th Ave	Ann Arbor	MI	48104-2293
508 757-4586	**Anna Maria College** 50 Sunset Ln *Fax:* 508 756-2970	Paxton	MA	01612-1198
508 757-4586	*Graduate School of Public Administration* Trinity Hall *Fax:* 508 756-2970	Paxton	MA	01612-1198
301 647-7100	**Anne Arundel Community College** 101 College Pkwy *Fax:* 301 541-2489	Arnold	MD	21012-1895
301 222-1821	**Anne Arundel County** 44 Calvert St	Annapolis	MD	21401-1986
205 237-6766	**Anniston Museum of Natural History** PO Box 1587	Anniston	AL	36202-1587

202 225-6661 **Annunzio Frank (Rep - D - Illinois)** 2303 Rayburn Bldg ...... Washington DC 20515-0001
612 421-4760 **Anoka County** 325 E Main St .... Anoka MN 55303-2479
612 780-1463 **Anoka County Library** 707 Hwy 10 NE .... Blaine MN 55434-2398
    Fax: 612 784-3233
612 427-2600 **Anoka-Ramsey Community College**
    11200 Mississippi Blvd NW .... Coon Rapids MN 55433-3499
    Fax: 612 422-3341
704 826-8333 **Anson Community College** Hwy 52 .... Ansonville NC 28007-9999
    Fax: 704 826-8633
704 694-2796 **Anson County** N Green St .... Wadesboro NC 28170-0000
402 887-4410 **Antelope County** 501 Main St .... Neligh NE 68756-1424
805 943-3241 **Antelope Valley College** 3041 W Ave 'K' .... Lancaster CA 93536-5426
    Fax: 805 943-5573
202 225-3772 **Anthony Beryl Jr (Rep - D - Arkansas)**
    1212 Longworth Bldg .... Washington DC 20515-0001
    Fax: 202 225-3646
212 490-2525 **Anti-Defamation League** 823 United Nations Plaza .... New York NY 10017-3560
    Fax: 212 867-0779
Antigua & Barbuda
202 362-5122   *Embassy* 3400 International Dr NW Suite 4-M .... Washington DC 20008-3006
    Fax: 202 362-5225
212 541-4117   *Mission to the UN* 610 5th Ave Suite 311 .... New York NY 10020-2403
    Fax: 212 757-1607
513 767-7331 **Antioch College** 795 Livermore St .... Yellow Springs OH 45387-1697
    Fax: 513 767-1891
206 441-5352 **Antioch University** 2607 2nd Ave .... Seattle WA 98121-1211
    Fax: 206 441-3307
202 633-2401 **Antitrust Div (US Dept of Justice)**
    10th St & Constitution Ave NW Rm 3107 .... Washington DC 20530-0001
    Fax: 202 633-1023
404 331-7100   *Atlanta Office* 75 Spring St SW Suite 1394 .... Atlanta GA 30303-3308
    Fax: 404 331-7110
312 353-7530   *Chicago Office* 230 S Dearborn St Suite 3820 .... Chicago IL 60604-1662
    Fax: 312 353-1046
216 522-4070   *Cleveland Office* 1240 E 9th St Rm 995 .... Cleveland OH 44199-2063
    Fax: 216 522-7214
214 767-8051   *Dallas Office* 1100 Commerce St Rm 8C6 .... Dallas TX 75242-1003
    Fax: 214 767-1007
212 264-0390   *New York Office* 26 Federal Plaza Rm 3630 .... New York NY 10278-0004
    Fax: 212 264-0678
215 597-7405   *Philadelphia Office*
    7th & Walnut Sts Curtis Ctr Suite 650 W .... Philadelphia PA 19106-0000
    Fax: 215 597-8148
415 556-6300   *San Francisco Office* 450 Golden Gate Ave .... San Francisco CA 94102-3478
    Fax: 415 556-9041
616 533-8607 **Antrim County** PO Box 520 .... Bellaire MI 49615-0520
    Fax: 616 533-8392
602 337-4364 **Apache County** PO Box 428 .... Saint Johns AZ 85936-0428
    Fax: 602 337-2003
612 739-7686 **Apostolic Bible Institute Inc** 6944 Hudson Blvd N ...... Saint Paul MN 55128-0000
304 877-6428 **Appalachian Bible College** PO Box ABC .... Bradley WV 25818-1353
606 986-9341 **Appalachian Museum** PO Box CPO2298 .... Berea KY 40404-0001
202 673-7968 **Appalachian Regional Commission**
    1666 Connecticut Ave NW .... Washington DC 20235-0001
    Fax: 202 673-7930
919 838-2818 **Appalachian Regional Library** 913 C St .... North Wilkesboro NC 28659-4119
704 262-2000 **Appalachian State University** .... Boone NC 28608-0001
    Fax: 704 262-3001 Library
515 856-6101 **Appanoose County** County Courthouse .... Centerville IA 52544-0000
202 225-6265 **Applegate Douglas (Rep - D - Ohio)** 2183 Rayburn Bldg .... Washington DC 20515-0001
    Fax: Unlisted
912 367-8100 **Appling County** 100 N Oak St .... Baxley GA 31513-2097
804 352-5275 **Appomattox County** PO Box 672 .... Appomattox VA 24522-0000
202 225-2771 **Appropriations Committee (US House of Representatives)**
    Capitol Bldg Suite H-218 .... Washington DC 20515-0001
202 224-3471 **Appropriations Committee (US Senate)**
    Capitol Bldg Rm S-128 .... Washington DC 20510-0001
    Fax: 202 224-8553
616 459-8281 **Aquinas College** 1607 Robinson Rd SE .... Grand Rapids MI 49506-1799
    Fax: 616 459-2563
617 696-3100 **Aquinas College at Milton** 303 Adams St .... Milton MA 02186-4296
615 297-7545 **Aquinas Junior College** 4210 Harding Rd .... Nashville TN 37205-2086
    Fax: 615 297-7557
512 729-7430 **Aransas County** 301 N Liveoak St .... Rockport TX 78382-2744
303 794-1550 **Arapahoe Community College** 2500 W College Dr .... Littleton CO 80120-1955
    Fax: 303 797-5935
303 795-4630 **Arapahoe County** 5334 S Prince St .... Littleton CO 80166-0001
    Fax: 303 730-2508
303 798-2444 **Arapahoe Library District** 2305 E Arapahoe Rd .... Littleton CO 80122-1522
    Fax: Unlisted
202 225-2571 **Archer Bill (Rep - R - Texas)** 1236 Longworth Bldg .... Washington DC 20515-0001
    Fax: 202 225-4381
817 574-4615 **Archer County** PO Box 815 .... Archer City TX 76351-0815
303 264-2536 **Archuleta County** PO Box 1507 .... Pagosa Springs CO 81147-1507
    Fax: 303 264-4896
517 846-4626 **Arenac County** PO Box 747 .... Standish MI 48658-0747
Argentina: Argentine Republic
202 939-6400   *Embassy* 1600 New Hampshire Ave NW .... Washington DC 20009-2512
    Fax: 202 332-3171
212 688-6300   *Mission to the UN* 1 UN Plaza 25th Fl .... New York NY 10017-0000
    Fax: 212 980-8395
312 263-7435   *Chicago Consulate* 20 N Clark St Suite 602 .... Chicago IL 60602-4183
    Fax: 312 263-0674
213 739-5959   *Los Angeles Consulate* 3550 Wilshire Blvd Suite 1450 .... Los Angeles CA 90010-2415
    Fax: 213 487-1491
212 603-0400   *New York Consulate General* 12 W 56th St .... New York NY 10019-3890
    Fax: 212 397-3523
212 564-3855 **Argentine-American Chamber of Commerce**
    50 W 34th St 6th Fl Suite C2 .... New York NY 10001-0000
708 972-2000 **Argonne National Laboratories (US Dept of Energy)**
    9700 Cass Ave .... Argonne IL 60439-4803
    Fax: 708 972-2206
602 248-9172 **Arizona Chamber of Commerce** 1221 E Osborn Rd .... Phoenix AZ 85014-5539
    Fax: 602 265-1262
602 995-2670 **Arizona College of the Bible** 2045 W Northern Ave .... Phoenix AZ 85021-5197
602 257-9136 **Arizona Democratic State Party** 1509 N Central Ave Suite 100 .. Phoenix AZ 85004-1621
    Fax: 602 952-9198
602 255-4470 **Arizona Historical Society** 1242 N Central Ave .... Phoenix AZ 85004-1887
    Fax: 602 255-5289
602 255-3791 **Arizona Mineral Museum** State Fairgrounds Mineral Bldg .. Phoenix AZ 85007-0000
    Fax: 602 255-3793
602 253-2734 **Arizona Museum** PO Box 926 .... Phoenix AZ 85001-0926
602 542-3618 **Arizona Office of Tourism** 1100 W Washington St .... Phoenix AZ 85007-2939
    Fax: 602 542-4068
602 957-7770 **Arizona Republican State Committee** 3501 N 24th St .... Phoenix AZ 85016-6691
    Fax: 602 224-0932

602 542-4581 **Arizona State Capitol Museum** 1700 W Washington Ave .... Phoenix AZ 85007-2810
Arizona State Government
602 542-4900   *Information* 1700 W Washington St .... Phoenix AZ 85007-2812
    Fax: 602 542-3998
602 868-4011   *Arizona State Prison* E Butte .... Florence AZ 85232-0000
    Fax: 602 868-5333
602 574-0024   *Arizona State Prison–Tucson* 10000 S Wilmot Rd .... Tucson AZ 85777-0001
    Fax: 602 574-2213 Admin
602 542-5025   *Attorney General* 1275 W Washington St .... Phoenix AZ 85007-2926
    Fax: 602 542-1275
602 542-5656   *Board of Pardons & Paroles* 1645 W Jefferson St Suite 326 .. Phoenix AZ 85007-3009
    Fax: 602 542-5680
602 255-3109   *Commission for Postsecondary Education*
    3030 N Central Ave Suite 1407 .... Phoenix AZ 85012-2720
    Fax: 602 255-4099
602 542-4373   *Commission of Agriculture & Horticulture*
    1688 W Adams St Rm 421 .... Phoenix AZ 85007-2621
    Fax: 602 542-5420
602 255-5882   *Commission on the Arts* 417 W Roosevelt St .... Phoenix AZ 85003-1326
602 255-2114   *Consumer Affairs* 3030 N 3rd St Suite 1100 .... Phoenix AZ 85012-3049
    Fax: 602 255-4722
602 280-1300   *Department of Commerce* 3800 N Central Ave Suite 1400 .... Phoenix AZ 85012-1908
    Fax: 602 280-1305
602 542-5536   *Department of Corrections* 1601 W Jefferson St .... Phoenix AZ 85007-3056
    Fax: 602 542-1728
602 542-4791   *Department of Economic Security* 1717 W Jefferson St .... Phoenix AZ 85007-3295
    Fax: 602 340-8532
602 542-4271   *Department of Education* 1535 W Jefferson St .... Phoenix AZ 85007-3280
    Fax: 602 542-1849
602 542-1024   *Department of Health Services* 1740 W Adams St Rm 407 .... Phoenix AZ 85007-0000
    Fax: 602 542-1062
602 542-4035   *Department of Library Archives & Public Record*
    1700 W Washington St Rm 200 .... Phoenix AZ 85007-2877
    Fax: 602 256-6372
602 255-3791   *Department of Mines & Mineral Resources*
    State Fairgrounds Mineral Bldg .... Phoenix AZ 85007-0000
    Fax: 602 255-3793
602 223-2000   *Department of Public Safety* 2102 W Encanto Blvd .... Phoenix AZ 85009-0000
    Fax: 602 223-2347
602 255-4345   *Department of Real Estate* 202 E Earll Dr Suite 400 .... Phoenix AZ 85012-2633
602 255-3381   *Department of Revenue* 1600 W Monroe St .... Phoenix AZ 85007-2650
    Fax: 602 542-4772
602 255-7226   *Department of Transportation* 206 S 17th Ave .... Phoenix AZ 85007-3213
    Fax: 602 271-4214
602 542-1554   *Department of Water Resources* 15 S 15th Ave .... Phoenix AZ 85007-3226
    Fax: 602 256-0506
602 244-0504   *Division of Emergency Services* 5636 E McDowell Rd .... Phoenix AZ 85008-0000
    Fax: 602 231-6231
602 542-4886   *Division of Finance* 1700 W Washington St Rm 210 .... Phoenix AZ 85007-2803
    Fax: 602 542-4082
602 255-7437   *Division of Highways* 206 S 17th Ave Room 102-A .... Phoenix AZ 85007-3213
    Fax: 602 255-6538
602 542-5795   *Division of Occupational Safety & Health*
    800 W Washington St Rm 202 .... Phoenix AZ 85007-2934
    Fax: 602 542-3104
602 542-4331   *Division of Planning & Policy Development*
    1700 W Washington St .... Phoenix AZ 85007-2810
    Fax: 602 254-7601
602 280-1300   *Energy Commission* 3800 N Central Ave Suite 1400 .... Phoenix AZ 85012-0000
    Fax: 602 280-1305
602 542-4331   *Governor* 1700 W Washington St .... Phoenix AZ 85007-2883
    Fax: 602 254-7601
602 255-5400   *Insurance Dept* 3030 N 3rd St Suite 1100 .... Phoenix AZ 85012-3039
    Fax: 602 255-4722
602 542-4515   *Labor Dept* 800 W Washington St Rm 102 .... Phoenix AZ 85007-2934
    Fax: 602 542-3104 Mail Rm
602 542-4625   *Natural Resources Div* 1616 W Adams St .... Phoenix AZ 85007-2606
    Fax: 602 542-2590
602 257-2277   *Office of Air Quality* 2005 N Central Ave Suite 603 .... Phoenix AZ 85004-1546
    Fax: 602 257-6948
602 542-1084   *Office of Vital Records* PO Box 3887 .... Phoenix AZ 85030-0000
    Fax: 602 542-1100
602 255-5161   *Oil & Gas Conservation Commission*
    5150 N 16th St Suite B-141 .... Phoenix AZ 85016-0000
602 542-4285   *Secretary of State* 1700 W Washington St 7th Fl .... Phoenix AZ 85007-2888
    Fax: 602 542-6172
602 542-4242   *Securities Div* 1200 W Washington St .... Phoenix AZ 85007-2927
    Fax: 602 542-4111
602 631-2000   *State Compensation Fund* 3031 N 2nd St .... Phoenix AZ 85012-3009
    Fax: 602 631-2213
602 542-5482   *State Personnel Dept of Administration* 1831 W Jefferson St . Phoenix AZ 85007-3293
    Fax: 602 542-4507
602 542-1463   *State Treasurer* 1700 W Washington St .... Phoenix AZ 85007-2867
    Fax: 602 258-6627
602 542-4536   *Supreme Court* State Capitol Bldg 201 W Wing .... Phoenix AZ 85007-0000
    Fax: 602 542-5819
602 542-3667   *Unemployment Insurance Administration*
    1300 W Washington .... Phoenix AZ 85007-2929
    Fax: 602 542-6474
602 542-4251   *Utilities Div* 1200 W Washington St .... Phoenix AZ 85007-2927
    Fax: 602 542-2129
602 621-6281 **Arizona State Museum** University of Arizona Bldg 26 .... Tucson AZ 85721-0001
    Fax: 602 621-2976
602 965-9011 **Arizona State University** .... Tempe AZ 85287-0001
    Fax: 602 965-2012
602 965-3536   *College of Architecture & Environmental Design*
    University St & Forrest St .... Tempe AZ 85287-0001
    Fax: 602 965-1594
602 965-6181   *College of Law* Armstrong Hall .... Tempe AZ 85287-0001
    Fax: 602 965-2427
602 965-3244   *College of Nursing* .... Tempe AZ 85287-0001
    Fax: 602 965-2012 Mail Rm
602 965-5081   *Graduate School of Geology* Physical Science Bldg .... Tempe AZ 85287-0001
    Fax: 602 965-8102
602 965-3926   *Graduate School of Public Affairs* Wilson Hall .... Tempe AZ 85287-0001
    Fax: 602 965-9248 Communications
602 965-6164   *Library* Hayden Library .... Tempe AZ 85287-0000
    Fax: 602 965-9169
602 965-5011   *Walter Cronkite School of Journalism & Telecommunications*
    Forrest Mall Stauffer Hall .... Tempe AZ 85287-0001
    Fax: 602 965-2012
602 726-1000 **Arizona Western College** Hwy 95 & Araby Rd .... Yuma AZ 85366-0000
    Fax: Unlisted
602 252-6448 **Arizona-Mexico Chamber of Commerce** PO Box 626 .... Phoenix AZ 85001-0000
602 883-1380 **Arizona-Sonora Desert Museum** 2021 N Kinney Rd .... Tucson AZ 85743-9719
501 374-7856 **Arkansas Baptist College** 1600 Bishop St .... Little Rock AR 72202-6099

501 793-9813 **Arkansas College** 2300 Highland Rd — Batesville AR 72501-3699
Fax: 501 698-4622
501 673-7311 **Arkansas County** PO Box 719 — Stuttgart AR 72160-0719
501 682-7777 **Arkansas Div of Parks & Tourism** 1 Capitol Mall — Little Rock AR 72201-1087
Fax: 501 682-1364
501 371-3521 **Arkansas Museum of Science & History** MacArthur Pk — Little Rock AR 72202-0000
Fax: Unlisted
501 229-4418 **Arkansas River Valley Regional Library** 501 N Front St — Dardanelle AR 72834-0000
501 374-9225 **Arkansas State Chamber of Commerce** 410 Cross St — Little Rock AR 72201-0000
Fax: 501 372-2722
Arkansas State Government
501 682-3000 *Information* 1 State Capitol Mall — Little Rock AR 72201-1090
501 371-2539 *Arts Council* 225 E Markham St Suite 200 — Little Rock AR 72201-1647
501 682-2007 *Attorney General* 323 Center St Tower Bldg Suite 200 — Little Rock AR 72201-0000
Fax: 501 682-8084
501 682-5193 *Community Assistance Div* 1 State Capitol Mall Rm 4B-210 — Little Rock AR 72201-1012
Fax: 501 682-7341
501 682-2341 *Consumer Advocacy Div* 323 Center St Tower Bldg Suite 200 — Little Rock AR 72201-0000
Fax: 501 682-8084
501 247-1800 *Department of Corrections* RR 8 Box 65 — Pine Bluff AR 71602-9401
Fax: 501 247-3700
501 682-4475 *Department of Education* 4 State Capitol Mall — Little Rock AR 72201-1011
Fax: 501 682-4466
501 682-2242 *Department of Finance & Administration* 1509 W 7th St Rm 401 — Little Rock AR 72201-3933
Fax: 501 682-1086
501 371-1441 *Department of Higher Education* 1220 W 3rd St — Little Rock AR 72201-1933
Fax: 501 371-1445
501 682-4500 *Department of Labor* 10421 W Markham St — Little Rock AR 72205-2193
501 562-7444 *Department of Pollution Control & Ecology* 8001 National Dr — Little Rock AR 72209-4800
Fax: 501 562-4632
501 247-1800 *Division of Parole Services* Rt 8 Box 65 — Pine Bluff AR 71602-9401
Fax: 501 247-3700
501 682-7000 *Division of Revenues* PO Box 1272 — Little Rock AR 72203-1272
Fax: 501 682-7158
501 661-2134 *Division of Vital Records* 4815 W Markham St — Little Rock AR 72205-3866
501 682-2121 *Employment Security Div* 2 State Capitol Mall — Little Rock AR 72201-1011
Fax: 501 682-3713
501 682-1370 *Energy Office* 1 State Capitol Mall Rm 4B-215 — Little Rock AR 72201-1012
Fax: 501 682-7341
501 682-2345 *Governor* 250 State Capitol — Little Rock AR 72201-1091
Fax: 501 682-1382
501 661-2509 *Health Services Agency* 4815 W Markham St — Little Rock AR 72205-3866
Fax: 501 661-2468
501 682-6900 *History Commission* 1 State Capitol Mall — Little Rock AR 72201-1014
501 682-1121 *Industrial Development Commission* 1 State Capitol Mall — Little Rock AR 72201-1012
Fax: 501 682-7341
501 371-1325 *Insurance Dept* 400 University Tower Bldg — Little Rock AR 72204-0000
Fax: 501 371-5723
501 682-2144 *Lieutenant Governor* 270 State Capitol Bldg — Little Rock AR 72201-0000
Fax: 501 682-2894
501 783-2103 *Mine Inspection Div* 616 Garrison Ave Rm 205 — Fort Smith AR 72901-2521
501 329-5601 *Office of Emergency Services* PO Box 758 — Conway AR 72032-0758
Fax: 501 327-8047
501 371-2336 *Office of State Purchasing* PO Box 2940 — Little Rock AR 72203-2940
Fax: 501 682-1086
501 862-4965 *Oil & Gas Commission* PO Box 1472 — El Dorado AR 71731-1472
501 682-1453 *Public Service Commission* 1000 Center St — Little Rock AR 72202-3800
Fax: 501 682-5731
501 371-1247 *Real Estate Commission* 1 Riverfront Pl Suite 660 — North Little Rock AR 72114-5646
Fax: 501 372-4904
501 569-2235 *Safety Div* 10324 I-30 — Little Rock AR 72203-0000
501 682-1010 *Secretary of State* 256 State Capitol Bldg — Little Rock AR 72201-0000
Fax: 501 682-1284
501 371-1011 *Securities Dept* 201 E Markham St Suite 300 — Little Rock AR 72201-1692
Fax: 800 221-7790
501 682-1611 *Soil & Water Conservation Commission* 1 Capitol Mall Suite 2D — Little Rock AR 72201-1012
Fax: 501 682-3991
501 562-7444 *Solid Waste Div* 8001 National Dr — Little Rock AR 72209-4800
Fax: 501 562-4632
501 569-2000 *State Hwy & Transportation Dept* 10324 I-30 — Little Rock AR 72209-0000
Fax: 501 569-2400
501 224-4111 *State Police* PO Box 5901 — Little Rock AR 72215-5901
Fax: 501 224-4722
501 682-6849 *Supreme Court* 625 Marshall St — Little Rock AR 72201-1079
501 682-5888 *Treasurer* State Capitol Bldg Rm 220 — Little Rock AR 72201-0000
Fax: 501 682-3820
501 842-2519 *Tucker Unit Correctional Facility* Star Rt Box 228 — Tucker AR 72168-9999
501 372-3930 *Worker's Compensation Commission* 625 Marshall St Justice Bldg — Little Rock AR 72201-0000
Fax: 501 682-2777
501 682-1527 **Arkansas State Library** 1 Capitol Mall — Little Rock AR 72201-1081
Fax: Unlisted
501 882-6452 **Arkansas State University** N Palm & Iowa Sts — Beebe AR 72012-0000
Fax: 501 882-6209
501 972-2100 **Arkansas State University** — State University AR 72467-9999
Fax: 501 972-3843 Admissions
501 972-2468 *College of Communications* PO Box 540 — State University AR 72467-0024
501 972-2074 *Museum* PO Box 490 — Jonesboro AR 72403-0490
Fax: 501 972-5706
501 968-0389 **Arkansas Tech University** — Russellville AR 72801-0000
Fax: 501 968-0633 Purchasing
817 461-8741 **Arlington Baptist College** 3001 W Division — Arlington TX 76012-3497
703 358-3000 **Arlington County** 2100 Clarendon Blvd — Arlington VA 22201-5445
Fax: 703 358-3903
817 459-6900 **Arlington Public Library** 101 E Abram — Arlington TX 76010-1183
703 358-5990 **Arlington Public Library** 1015 N Quincy St — Arlington VA 22201-4603
Fax: Call company operator
703 631-6100 **Armed Forces Communications & Electronics Assn** 4400 Fair Lakes Ct — Fairfax VA 22033-3899
Fax: 703 631-4693
804 444-5231 **Armed Forces Staff College (US Dept of Defense)** 7800 Hampton Blvd — Norfolk VA 23511-1739
703 756-8500 **Armed Services Board of Contract Appeals (US Dept of Defense)** 5109 Leesburg Pike Skyline 6 7th Fl — Falls Church VA 22041-0000
Fax: Unlisted
202 225-4151 **Armed Services Committee (US House of Representatives)** 2120 Rayburn Bldg — Washington DC 20515-0001
Fax: 202 225-9077
202 224-3871 **Armed Services Committee (US Senate)** 228 Russell Bldg — Washington DC 20510-0001
Fax: 202 224-9231

202 225-7772 **Armey Richard K (Rep - R - Texas)** 130 Cannon Bldg — Washington DC 20515-0001
Fax: 202 225-7614
202 647-8715 **Arms Control & Disarmament Agency** 320 21st St NW Rm 5843 — Washington DC 20451-0001
Fax: 202 647-6928
202 797-4626 **Arms Control Assn** 11 Dupont Cir NW Suite 250 — Washington DC 20036-1207
Fax: 202 797-4611
415 848-2500 **Armstrong College** 2222 Harold Way — Berkeley CA 94704-1489
Fax: 415 848-9438
412 543-2500 **Armstrong County** Market St — Kittanning PA 16201-0000
Fax: Unlisted
806 226-2081 **Armstrong County** PO Box 189 — Claude TX 79019-0000
912 927-5275 **Armstrong State College** 11935 Abercorn St — Savannah GA 31419-1988
202 541-0101 **Army Distaff Foundation** 6200 Oregon Ave NW — Washington DC 20015-1543
Fax: 202 364-2856
207 532-7317 **Aroostook County** PO Box 803 — Houlton ME 04730-0787
Fax: 207 532-7319
608 755-2490 **Arrowhead Library System** 20 E Milwaukee Suite 204 — Janesville WI 53545-0000
513 721-5205 **Art Academy of Cincinnati** Eden Park Dr — Cincinnati OH 45202-1597
818 584-5000 **Art Center College of Design** 1700 Lida St — Pasadena CA 91103-1999
Fax: 818 405-9104
312 443-3600 **Art Institute of Chicago** Michigan Ave & Adams St — Chicago IL 60603-6494
Fax: 312 443-0849
714 497-3309 **Art Institute of Southern California** 2222 Laguna Canyon Rd — Laguna Beach CA 92651-1136
Fax: 714 497-4399
512 884-3844 **Art Museum of South Texas** 1902 N Shoreline Rd — Corpus Christi TX 78401-1164
308 764-2203 **Arthur County** Main St — Arthur NE 69121-0000
606 858-3511 **Asbury College** 201 N Lexington Ave — Wilmore KY 40390-1198
Fax: Ext 135
504 473-9866 **Ascension Parish** Houmas St — Donaldsonville LA 70346-0000
919 246-8841 **Ashe County** Court St — Jefferson NC 28640-0000
704 253-3227 **Asheville Art Museum** Asheville Civic Ctr — Asheville NC 28801-4556
704 255-5203 **Asheville-Buncombe Library System** 67 Haywood St — Asheville NC 28801-2834
Fax: 704 255-5213
704 254-1921 **Asheville-Buncombe Technical Community College** 340 Victoria Rd — Asheville NC 28801-4816
Fax: 704 251-6355
606 329-2999 **Ashland Community College** 1400 College Dr — Ashland KY 41101-3683
Fax: 606 325-8124
419 289-0000 **Ashland County** 110 W 2nd St — Ashland OH 44805-2101
715 682-7000 **Ashland County** 201 2nd St W — Ashland WI 54806-1652
419 289-4142 **Ashland University** 401 College Ave — Ashland OH 44805-3702
Fax: 419 289-5333
501 853-5144 **Ashley County** 215 E Jefferson Ave — Hamburg AR 71646-3007
216 576-9090 **Ashtabula County** 25 W Jefferson St — Jefferson OH 44047-1092
Fax: 216 576-2344
415 668-8922 **Asian Art Museum of San Francisco** Golden Gate Pk — San Francisco CA 94118-4598
Fax: 415 668-8928
203 745-1603 **Asnuntuck Community College** 170 Elm St — Enfield CT 06082-3800
Fax: 203 253-9310 Library
509 243-4181 **Asotin County** PO Box 159 — Asotin WA 99402-0159
Fax: 509 243-4978
301 827-7168 **Aspen Institute** Carmichael Rd — Queenstown MD 21658-0000
Fax: 301 827-9182
303 925-4000 **Aspen Reservations Inc** 517 E Hopkins Ave Suite 203 — Aspen CO 81611-2951
Fax: 303 925-1255
303 925-9500 **Aspen Ski Tours** 300 S Spring St — Aspen CO 81611-2085
Fax: 303 925-8505
202 225-3031 **Aspin Les (Rep - D - Wisconsin)** 2336 Rayburn Bldg — Washington DC 20515-0001
Fax: Unlisted
212 741-0100 **Association for Children with Retarded Mental Development** 162 5th Ave 11th Fl — New York NY 10010-5902
Fax: 212 627-8318
718 523-2222 **Association for the Advancement of the Blind & Retarded** 164-09 Hillside Ave — Jamaica NY 11432-4140
Fax: 718 739-4750
202 463-5485 **Association of American Chambers of Commerce in Latin America** 1615 H St NW 6th Fl — Washington DC 20062-0001
Fax: 202 463-3114
505 842-0644 **Association of Commerce & Industry of New Mexico** 2309 Renard Pl SE Suite 402 — Albuquerque NM 87106-4259
Fax: 505 842-0734
703 549-1600 **Association of Old Crows** 1000 N Payne St — Alexandria VA 22314-1696
Fax: 703 549-2589
703 841-4300 **Association of the US Army** 2425 Wilson Blvd — Arlington VA 22201-3326
Fax: 703 525-9039
202 544-5150 **Association to Unite the Democracies** 1506 Pennsylvania Ave SE — Washington DC 20003-3116
Fax: Unlisted
508 752-5615 **Assumption College** 500 Salisbury St — Worcester MA 01609-1296
Fax: 508 756-1780
201 543-6528 **Assumption College for Sisters** Mallinckrodt Convent Hilltop Rd — Mendham NJ 07945-0000
Fax: 201 543-9459
504 369-7435 **Assumption Parish** Martin Luther King Dr & Hwy 1 — Napoleonville LA 70390-0000
503 861-0105 **Astoria Coast Guard Air Station** 2185 SE Airport Rd — Warrenton OR 97146-9694
Fax: 503 861-0119
512 769-2511 **Atascosa County** Circle Dr — Jourdanton TX 78026-0000
913 367-1653 **Atchison County** 5th & Parallel — Atchison KS 66002-0000
816 744-2707 **Atchison County** PO Box J — Rock Port MO 64482-0410
513 231-2223 **Athenaeum of Ohio** 6616 Beechmont Ave — Cincinnati OH 45230-2000
Fax: 513 231-3254
614 592-3242 **Athens County** Court & Washington Sts — Athens OH 45701-0000
404 354-2620 **Athens Regional Library** 120 W Dougherty St — Athens GA 30601-2653
205 233-8100 **Athens State College** 300 N Beaty St — Athens AL 35611-1999
Fax: 205 233-8164
202 225-3411 **Atkins Chester G (Rep - D - Massachusetts)** 123 Cannon Bldg — Washington DC 20515-0001
Fax: Unlisted
912 422-3391 **Atkinson County** PO Box 518 — Pearson GA 31642-0518
404 330-6000 **Atlanta City Hall** 55 Trinity Ave SW — Atlanta GA 30335-0001
Fax: 404 658-7673
404 761-8861 **Atlanta Christian College** 2605 Ben Hill Rd — East Point GA 30344-1999
Fax: 404 669-2024
404 898-1164 **Atlanta College of Art** 1280 Peachtree St NE — Atlanta GA 30309-3582
Fax: 404 898-9577
404 756-4358 **Atlanta Metropolitan College** 1630 Stewart Ave SW — Atlanta GA 30310-4498
404 872-8233 **Atlanta Museum** 537-39 Peachtree St NE — Atlanta GA 30308-0000
404 730-1700 **Atlanta-Fulton Public Library** 1 Margaret Mitchell Sq NW — Atlanta GA 30303-1089
Fax: 404 730-1990
919 237-3161 **Atlantic Christian College** 400 Atlantic Christian College Dr NE ACC Stn — Wilson NC 27893-2575
Fax: 919 237-4957
609 625-1111 **Atlantic Community College** Black Horse Pike — Mays Landing NJ 08330-9115
Fax: 609 343-4917

For information on alphabetization, see the Alphabetical Section title page.

609 625-4011 **Atlantic County** 2 Main St W .... Mays Landing NJ 08330-1800
609 646-8699 **Atlantic County Library-Mays Landing** 2 S Farragut Ave .. Mays Landing NJ 08330-1750
Fax: 609 625-8143
508 365-4561 **Atlantic Union College** 338 Main St .... South Lancaster MA 01561-0000
Fax: 508 368-2015
405 889-2643 **Atoka County** 201 E Court St .... Atoka OK 74525-2056
601 289-2921 **Attala County** W Washington St .... Kosciusko MS 39090-0000
202 633-2001 **Attorney General of the US**
10th St & Constitution Ave NW Rm 5111 .... Washington DC 20530-0001
Fax: 202 633-4371
215 922-3031 **Atwater Kent Museum-History Museum of Philadelphia**
15 S 7th St .... Philadelphia PA 19106-2313
205 844-4000 **Auburn University** .... Auburn AL 36849-0000
Fax: 205 844-6436 Admissions
205 844-4326 *College of Engineering* Ramsay Hall Rm 108 .... Auburn AL 36849-0000
Fax: 205 844-2672 Admin
205 244-3000 *Montgomery Campus* 7300 University Dr .... Montgomery AL 36117-3596
Fax: 205 244-3762
205 844-2345 *School of Agriculture* Comer Hall Rm 107 .... Auburn AL 36849-0000
205 844-4740 *School of Pharmacy* Pharmacy Bldg .... Auburn AL 36849-0000
Fax: 205 844-8353
202 225-0855 **AuCoin Les (Rep - D - Oregon)** 2159 Rayburn Bldg .... Washington DC 20515-0001
Fax: 202 225-2707
703 756-6121 **Audit Div (US Dept of Justice)**
5113 Leesburg Pike Suite 701 .... Falls Church VA 22041-3204
Fax: 703 756-6299
404 331-5928 *Atlanta Office* 101 Marietta Tower Suite 2322 .... Atlanta GA 30323-0001
Fax: 404 331-5046
307 261-5776 *Casper Office* 100 E 'B' St .... Casper WY 82601-0000
312 353-1203 *Chicago Office* 175 W Jackson Blvd Rm A-1335 .... Chicago IL 60604-0000
Fax: 312 886-0513
214 939-6625 *Dallas Office* 207 S Houston St Rm 334 .... Dallas TX 75202-0000
303 844-3638 *Denver Office* 1244 Steer Blvd Suite 640 .... Denver CO 80204-0000
Fax: 303 844-2780
703 756-6121 *District of Columbia Office*
5113 Leesburg Pike Suite 701 .... Falls Church VA 22041-3204
Fax: 703 756-6299
415 744-6567 *San Francisco Office* 525 Market St Suite 3522 .... San Francisco CA 94105-2743
Fax: 415 744-6566
918 581-6430 *Tulsa Office* 5100 E Skelly Dr .... Tulsa OK 74135-0000
202 697-9108 **Audit Service (US Dept of Defense)**
400 Army-Navy Dr Rm 808 .... Arlington VA 22202-2885
Fax: 202 693-0496
314 581-8211 **Audrain County** County Courthouse .... Mexico MO 65265-0000
Fax: 314 581-2380
712 563-4275 **Audubon County** County Courthouse .... Audubon IA 50025-0000
502 827-1893 **Audubon John James Museum** PO Box 576 .... Henderson KY 42420-0576
419 738-7896 **Auglaize County** 36 E Auglaize St .... Wapakoneta OH 45895-1505
612 330-1000 **Augsburg College** 731 21st Ave S .... Minneapolis MN 55454-1398
Fax: 612 330-1695
404 737-1400 **Augusta College** 2500 Walton Way .... Augusta GA 30910-0001
Fax: 404 737-1773
703 885-8931 **Augusta County** 6 E Johnson St .... Staunton VA 24401-4303
Fax: 703 886-2523
404 722-8454 **Augusta Richmond County Museum** 540 Telfair St .... Augusta GA 30901-2396
309 794-7000 **Augustana College** 638 38th St .... Rock Island IL 61201-0000
Fax: 309 794-7422 Admin
605 336-0770 **Augustana College** 29th & S Summit Ave .... Sioux Falls SD 57197-0001
Fax: 605 336-5490
303 556-2400 **Auraria Higher Education Center** 1250 7th St .... Denver CO 80204-4440
Fax: 303 556-4596 Admin
605 942-7165 **Aurora County** PO Box 366 .... Plankinton SD 57368-0366
303 340-2240 **Aurora Public Library** 14949 E Alameda Dr .... Aurora CO 80012-1500
Fax: 303 340-2299
708 892-6431 **Aurora University** 347 S Gladstone Ave .... Aurora IL 60506-4892
Fax: 708 892-9286 Library
512 499-2000 **Austin City Hall** 124 W 8th St .... Austin TX 78701-2300
Fax: 512 499-3000
903 813-2000 **Austin College** 900 N Grand Ave .... Sherman TX 75090-4440
Fax: 903 813-3199
507 433-0505 **Austin Community College** 1600 8th Ave NW .... Austin MN 55912-1400
Fax: 507 433-0515
512 483-7000 **Austin Community College** PO Box 140526 .... Austin TX 78714-0526
Fax: 512 483-7786
409 865-5911 **Austin County** 1 E Main St .... Bellville TX 77418-1598
615 648-7011 **Austin Peay State University** 601 College St .... Clarksville TN 37044-0001
Fax: 615 648-7475
512 499-7300 **Austin Public Library** 800 Guadalupe St .... Austin TX 78701-2314
Australia: Commonwealth of Australia
202 797-3000 *Embassy* 1601 Massachusetts Ave NW .... Washington DC 20036-2209
Fax: 202 797-3168
212 421-6910 *Mission to the UN* 885 2nd Ave 16th Fl .... New York NY 10017-2201
Fax: 212 371-5843
312 645-9440 *Chicago Consulate General* 321 N Clark Suite 2930 .... Chicago IL 60610-4794
Fax: 312 645-1940
213 469-4300 *Los Angeles Consulate General* 611 N Larchmount Blvd .... Hollywood CA 90004-1321
Fax: 213 469-9176
212 245-4000 *New York Consulate General*
636 5th Ave Rockefeller Ctr 4th Fl .... New York NY 10111-0000
Fax: 212 265-1917
415 362-6160 *San Francisco Consulate General* 360 Post St .... San Francisco CA 94108-4979
Fax: 415 986-5440
212 687-6300 **Australian Tourist Commission** 489 5th Ave .... New York NY 10017-6182
Fax: 212 661-3340
Austria: Republic of Austria
202 483-4474 *Embassy* 2343 Massachusetts Ave NW .... Washington DC 20008-2803
Fax: 202 483-2743
212 949-1840 *Mission to the UN* 809 UN Plaza 7th Fl .... New York NY 10017-0000
Fax: 212 953-1302
312 222-1515 *Chicago Consulate General* 400 N Michigan Ave Suite 707 .... Chicago IL 60611-4102
Fax: 312 222-4113
213 444-9310 *Los Angeles Consulate General*
11859 Wilshire Blvd Suite 501 .... Los Angeles CA 90025-6601
Fax: 213 477-9897
212 737-6400 *New York Consulate General* 31 E 69th St .... New York NY 10021-4976
Fax: 212 772-8926
212 944-6880 **Austrian National Tourist Office** 500 5th Ave .... New York NY 10110-0199
Fax: 212 730-4568
205 365-2281 **Autauga County** 4th & Court Sts .... Prattville AL 36067-0000
617 237-5200 **Automobile Legal Assn** 888 Worcester St .... Wellesley MA 02181-3717
Fax: 617 237-2763
804 791-5600 **Averett College** 420 W Main St .... Danville VA 24541-3692
704 733-5186 **Avery County** Main St .... Newland NC 28657-0000
816 942-8400 **Avila College** 11901 Wornall Rd .... Kansas City MO 64145-1698
Fax: 816 942-3362
318 253-7523 **Avoyelles Parish** 301 N Main St .... Marksville LA 71351-2493
818 969-3434 **Azusa Pacific University** 921 E Alosta Ave .... Azusa CA 91702-2769
Fax: 818 969-7180

B

202 857-6600 **B'nai B'rith International** 1640 Rhode Island Ave NW .... Washington DC 20036-3279
Fax: 202 857-1099
202 857-6583 **B'nai B'rith Klutznick Museum**
1640 Rhode Island Ave NW .... Washington DC 20036-3287
Fax: 202 857-1099
617 235-1200 **Babson College** Babson Pk .... Wellesley MA 02157-0310
Fax: 617 239-5614
719 523-4372 **Baca County** 741 Main St .... Springfield CO 81073-1548
Fax: 719 523-4735
202 225-3671 **Bacchus Jim (Rep - D - Florida)** 431 Cannon Bldg .... Washington DC 20515-0001
Fax: 202 225-9039
912 632-5214 **Bacon County** 502 W 12th St .... Alma GA 31510-1957
918 683-4581 **Bacone College** 99 Bacone Rd .... Muskogee OK 74403-1597
Bahamas: Commonwealth of the Bahamas
202 944-3390 *Embassy* 600 New Hampshire Ave NW Suite 865 .... Washington DC 20037-2403
Fax: 202 333-7487
212 421-6925 *Mission to the UN* 767 3rd Ave 9th Fl .... New York NY 10017-2076
Fax: 212 759-2135
305 373-6295 *Miami Consulate General* 25 SE 2nd Ave .... Miami FL 33131-1506
Fax: 305 373-6312
212 421-6420 *New York Consulate General* 767 3rd Ave .... New York NY 10017-2023
Fax: 212 759-2135
Bahrain: State of Bahrain
202 342-0741 *Embassy* 3502 International Dr NW .... Washington DC 20008-3035
Fax: 202 362-2192
212 223-6200 *Mission to the UN* 2 UN Plaza 25th Fl .... New York NY 10017-0000
Fax: 212 319-0687
806 272-3044 **Bailey County** 300 S 1st St .... Muleshoe TX 79347-3621
912 248-2500 **Bainbridge College** US Hwy 84-E .... Bainbridge GA 31717-0000
Fax: 912 248-2589 Library
313 767-7600 **Baker College** G1050 W Bristol Rd .... Flint MI 48507-0000
Fax: 313 766-4049
616 726-4904 **Baker College of Muskegon** 141 Hartford St .... Muskegon MI 49442-3497
Fax: 616 728-1417
904 259-3613 **Baker County** 55 N 3rd St .... Macclenny FL 32063-2100
Fax: 904 259-2799
912 734-3004 **Baker County** Courthouse Way .... Newton GA 31770-0000
503 523-6414 **Baker County** 1995 3rd St .... Baker OR 97814-3399
517 723-5251 **Baker Junior College** 1020 S Washington St .... Owosso MI 48867-4400
Fax: 517 723-3355
202 225-3901 **Baker Richard H (Rep - R - Louisiana)** 404 Cannon Bldg .... Washington DC 20515-0001
Fax: 202 225-7313
913 594-6451 **Baker University** 8th & Grove St .... Baldwin City KS 66006-0000
Fax: 913 594-6721
805 395-4011 **Bakersfield College** 1801 Panorama Dr .... Bakersfield CA 93305-1299
Fax: 805 395-4241
205 937-0347 **Baldwin County** PO Box 639 .... Bay Minette AL 36507-0639
912 453-4007 **Baldwin County** 201 W Hancock St .... Milledgeville GA 31061-3346
216 826-2900 **Baldwin-Wallace College** 275 Eastland Rd .... Berea OH 44017-2088
Fax: 216 826-2329
317 289-1797 **Ball State University** .... Muncie IN 47306-0001
Fax: 317 285-1797
317 285-8200 *Department of Journalism* W Quad 308 .... Muncie IN 47306-0001
Fax: 317 285-7997
502 335-5168 **Ballard County** PO Box 145 .... Wickliffe KY 42087-0145
202 225-2576 **Ballenger Cass (Rep - R - North Carolina)**
328 Cannon Bldg .... Washington DC 20515-0001
Fax: 202 225-0316
301 396-3100 **Baltimore City Hall** 100 N Holliday St .... Baltimore MD 21202-3417
Fax: 301 396-9568
301 887-3196 **Baltimore County** 400 Washington Ave .... Towson MD 21204-4606
301 887-6100 **Baltimore County Public Library** 320 York Rd .... Towson MD 21204-5179
Fax: 301 296-3139
301 578-6900 **Baltimore Hebrew University** 5800 Park Heights Ave .... Baltimore MD 21215-3996
Fax: 301 578-6940
301 396-7100 **Baltimore Museum of Art** 10 Art Museum Dr .... Baltimore MD 21218-3801
Fax: 301 396-6562
803 245-3025 **Bamberg County** PO Box 150 .... Bamberg SC 29003-0150
Fax: Unlisted
512 796-3332 **Bandera County** 500 Main St .... Bandera TX 78003-0000
Bangladesh: People's Republic of Bangladesh
202 342-8372 *Embassy* 2201 Wisconsin Ave NW Suite 300 .... Washington DC 20007-4105
Fax: 202 333-4971
212 867-3434 *Mission to the UN* 821 UN Plaza 8th Fl .... New York NY 10017-0000
Fax: 212 972-4038
202 225-4247 **Banking Finance & Urban Affairs Committee (US House of Representatives)**
2129 Rayburn Bldg .... Washington DC 20515-0001
Fax: 202 225-6580
202 224-7391 **Banking Housing & Urban Affairs Committee (US Senate)**
534 Dirksen Bldg .... Washington DC 20510-0001
Fax: 202 224-5137
404 677-2320 **Banks County** PO Box 130 .... Homer GA 30547-0130
308 436-5265 **Banner County** State St .... Harrisburg NE 69345-0000
208 236-7210 **Bannock County** 624 E Center St .... Pocatello ID 83201-6274
Fax: 208 236-7013
417 869-9811 **Baptist Bible College** 628 E Kearney St .... Springfield MO 65803-3498
Fax: 417 831-8029
717 587-1172 **Baptist Bible College of Pennsylvania** 538 Venard Rd ... Clarks Summit PA 18411-1297
Fax: 717 586-2400
318 631-8875 **Baptist Christian College** 3031 Hollywood Ave .... Shreveport LA 71108-0000
803 797-4011 **Baptist College at Charleston** 9200 University Blvd .... Charleston SC 29418-9121
Fax: 803 764-3867
205 288-2100 **Baptist Medical Center** 2105 E South Blvd .... Montgomery AL 36116-2498
Fax: Unlisted
906 524-6183 **Baraga County** 12 S 3rd St .... L'Anse MI 49946-1090
907 486-5920 **Baranov Museum** 101 Marine Way Erskine House .... Kodiak AK 99615-0000
708 234-3000 **Barat College** 700 E Westleigh Rd .... Lake Forest IL 60045-3297
Fax: 708 615-5000
Barbados
202 939-9200 *Embassy* 2144 Wyoming Ave NW .... Washington DC 20008-3995
Fax: 202 332-7467
212 867-8431 *Mission to the UN* 800 2nd Ave 18th Fl .... New York NY 10017-4790
Fax: 212 682-5496
213 380-2198 *Los Angeles Consulate* 3440 Wilshire Blvd Suite 1215 .... Los Angeles CA 90010-2113
Fax: 213 384-2763
212 867-8435 *New York Consulate General* 800 2nd Ave 18th Fl .... New York NY 10017-4709
Fax: 212 986-1030
316 886-3961 **Barber County** 120 E Washington Ave .... Medicine Lodge KS 67104-1421

704 786-5171 **Barber-Scotia College** 145 Cabarrus Ave W .... Concord NC 28025-5187
Fax: 704 784-3817
808 682-2614 **Barbers Point Coast Guard Air Station** .... Barbers Point HI 96862-0001
Fax: 808 682-2681
808 684-3176 **Barbers Point Naval Air Station** .... Ewa Beach HI 96862-0001
Fax: 808 684-7350
205 775-3203 **Barbour County** PO Box 398 .... Clayton AL 36016-0398
304 457-2232 **Barbour County** PO Box 310 .... Philippi WV 26416-0310
316 862-5252 **Barclay College** 607 N Kingman St .... Haviland KS 67059-0000
914 758-6822 **Bard College** .... Annandale-on-Hudson NY 12504-0000
Fax: 914 758-9654
318 456-2252 **Barksdale Air Force Base** .... Bossier City LA 71110-5000
Fax: 318 456-2250
212 854-5262 **Barnard College** 3009 Broadway .... New York NY 10027-6598
Fax: Call company operator
202 225-4101 **Barnard Doug Jr (Rep - D - Georgia)** 2227 Rayburn Bldg .... Washington DC 20515-0001
Fax: 202 225-1873
701 845-8512 **Barnes County** PO Box 774 .... Valley City ND 58072-0774
508 362-2511 **Barnstable County** Rt 6-A .... Barnstable MA 02630-0000
803 259-3485 **Barnwell County** PO Box 723 .... Barnwell SC 29812-0723
502 651-3783 **Barren County** County Courthouse 1st Fl .... Glasgow KY 42141-2812
202 225-6435 **Barrett Bill (Rep - R - Nebraska)** 1607 Longworth Bldg ..... Washington DC 20515-0001
Fax: 202 225-0207
702 739-3381 **Barrick Marjorie Museum of Natural History**
4505 S Maryland Pkwy UNLV .... Las Vegas NV 89154-0001
Fax: 702 739-3094
715 537-6200 **Barron County** 330 E La Salle Ave .... Barron WI 54812-1591
Fax: 715 537-6277
404 867-7581 **Barrow County** 310 S Broad St .... Winder GA 30680-1973
616 948-4810 **Barry County** 220 W State St .... Hastings MI 49058-1849
417 847-2561 **Barry County** County Courthouse .... Cassville MO 65625-0000
305 758-3392 **Barry University** 11300 NE 2nd Ave .... Miami Shores FL 33161-6690
Fax: 305 899-3104 Admissions
619 252-2411 **Barstow College** 2700 Barstow Rd .... Barstow CA 92311-6699
Fax: 619 252-1875
812 379-1600 **Bartholomew County** PO Box 924 .... Columbus IN 47202-0924
918 333-6151 **Bartlesville Wesleyan College** 2201 Silver Lake Rd .... Bartlesville OK 74006-6299
202 225-4201 **Bartlett Steve (Rep - R - Texas)** 1113 Longworth Bldg ...... Washington DC 20515-0001
Fax: Unlisted
316 792-7391 **Barton County** PO Box 1089 .... Great Bend KS 67530-1089
417 682-3529 **Barton County** County Courthouse .... Lamar MO 64759-0000
202 225-2002 **Barton Joe (Rep - R - Texas)** 1225 Longworth Bldg .... Washington DC 20515-0001
Fax: 202 225-3052
404 382-4766 **Bartow County** PO Box 543 .... Cartersville GA 30120-0543
305 673-7530 **Bass Museum of Art** 2121 Park Ave .... Miami Beach FL 33139-1756
503 228-6528 **Bassist College** 2000 SW 5th Ave .... Portland OR 97201-4907
512 321-4443 **Bastrop County** 803 Pine St .... Bastrop TX 78602-3841
202 225-4261 **Bateman Herbert H (Rep - R - Virginia)**
1030 Longworth Bldg .... Washington DC 20515-0001
Fax: 202 225-4382
207 786-6255 **Bates College** Andrews Rd Lane Hall .... Lewiston ME 04240-0000
Fax: 207 786-6123
816 679-3371 **Bates County** County Courthouse .... Butler MO 64730-0000
606 674-2613 **Bath County** Main St .... Owingsville KY 40360-0000
703 839-2361 **Bath County** PO Box 180 .... Warm Springs VA 24484-0180
504 389-3000 **Baton Rouge City Hall** 222 Saint Louis St .... Baton Rouge LA 70802-5817
Fax: 504 389-3127
202 224-2651 **Baucus Max (Sen - D - Montana)** 706 Hart Bldg .... Washington DC 20510-0001
Fax: Call company operator
305 491-7171 **Bauder Fashion College** 4801 N Dixie Hwy .... Fort Lauderdale FL 33334-3971
501 425-3475 **Baxter County** County Courthouse .... Mountain Home AR 72653-0000
904 763-9061 **Bay County** 300 E 4th St .... Panama City FL 32401-3073
Fax: Unlisted
517 892-3528 **Bay County** 515 Center Ave .... Bay City MI 48708-5941
Fax: 517 893-3266
517 894-2837 **Bay County Library System** 307 Lafayette Ave .... Bay City MI 48708-7796
Fax: 517 894-2021
906 786-5802 **Bay de Noc Community College** 2001 N Lincoln Rd .... Escanaba MI 49829-2511
Fax: Ext 244
413 567-0621 **Bay Path College** 588 Longmeadow St .... Longmeadow MA 01106-2292
Fax: 413 567-9324
715 373-6100 **Bayfield County** 117 E 5th St .... Washburn WI 54891-9464
713 798-4841 **Baylor College of Medicine** 1 Baylor Plaza .... Houston TX 77030-3498
817 888-3322 **Baylor County** PO Box 689 .... Seymour TX 76380-0689
817 755-1011 **Baylor University** 500 Speight St .... Waco TX 76798-0001
Fax: 817 755-3843 Admin
817 755-2911 *Biology Dept* BU Box 7388 .... Waco TX 76798-0001
Fax: 817 752-5332 Library
214 828-8100 *College of Dentistry* 3302 Gaston Ave .... Dallas TX 75246-2098
Fax: 214 828-8346
817 755-3261 *Department of Journalism* Castellaw Bldg BU-Box 7353 .... Waco TX 76798-0001
Fax: 817 755-1321
512 221-6443 *Graduate School of Health Administration*
Stanley Rd .... Fort Sam Houston TX 78234-0000
Fax: 512 221-6901
817 755-1911 *School of Law* BU Box 7288 .... Waco TX 76798-0001
Fax: 817 755-2294
605 353-7165 **Beadle County** 450 3rd St SW .... Huron SD 57350-1814
207 947-4591 **Beal College** 629 Main St .... Bangor ME 04401-6896
916 634-3000 **Beale Air Force Base** .... Marysville CA 95903-0000
Fax: Call company operator
208 945-2212 **Bear Lake County** 7 E Center St .... Paris ID 83261-0000
Fax: 208 945-2780
919 946-7721 **Beaufort County** 112 W 2nd St .... Washington NC 27889-4940
803 525-7307 **Beaufort County** PO Box 1128 .... Beaufort SC 29901-1228
919 946-6194 **Beaufort County Community College** Hwy 264 E .... Washington NC 27889-0000
Fax: 919 946-0271
803 522-7100 **Beaufort Marine Corps Air Station** .... Beaufort SC 29902-0000
Fax: 803 522-7032
409 838-6606 **Beaumont Public Library System** 801 Pearl St .... Beaumont TX 77704-0000
318 463-7019 **Beauregard Parish** PO Box 310 .... De Ridder LA 70634-0310
Fax: 318 462-2567
215 572-2900 **Beaver College** Easton & Church Rds .... Glenside PA 19038-0000
Fax: 215 572-0240 Library
405 625-3151 **Beaver County** 111 W 2nd St .... Beaver OK 73932-0000
Fax: 405 625-3430
412 728-5700 **Beaver County** 3rd & Turnpike St .... Beaver PA 15009-0000
Fax: 412 728-4133 Library
801 438-2352 **Beaver County** PO Box 392 .... Beaver UT 84713-0392
406 683-5245 **Beaverhead County** 2 S Pacific Cluster 3 .... Dillon MT 59725-0000
218 847-7659 **Becker County** PO Box 787 .... Detroit Lakes MN 56501-0787
508 791-9241 **Becker Junior College** 61 Sever St .... Worcester MA 01609-2195
Fax: 508 831-7505
405 928-2457 **Beckham County** PO Box 67 .... Sayre OK 73662-0067
304 253-7351 **Beckley College** 609 S Kanawha St .... Beckley WV 25801-5624
Fax: 304 253-0789

703 586-7102 **Bedford (Independent City)** 215 E Main St .... Bedford VA 24523-2012
Fax: 703 586-7198
814 623-4836 **Bedford County** 230 S Juliana St .... Bedford PA 15522-1716
Fax: 814 623-7478
615 684-1921 **Bedford County** 1 Public Sq .... Shelbyville TN 37160-3953
703 586-7601 **Bedford County** 129 E Main St .... Bedford VA 24523-2034
Fax: 703 586-0406
512 358-3664 **Bee County** 105 W Corpus Christi St .... Beeville TX 78102-5684
512 358-3130 **Bee County College** 3800 Charco Rd .... Beeville TX 78102-2197
Fax: 512 358-3971
202 225-5911 **Beilenson Anthony C (Rep - D - California)**
1025 Longworth Bldg .... Washington DC 20515-0001
Fax: Unlisted
212 967-9898 **Belgian-American Chamber of Commerce in US**
350 5th Ave Suite 703 .... New York NY 10118-0110
Fax: 212 629-0349
Belgium: Kingdom of Belgium
202 333-6900 *Embassy* 3330 Garfield St NW .... Washington DC 20008-3515
Fax: 202 333-3079
212 599-5250 *Mission to the UN* 809 UN Plaza 2nd Fl .... New York NY 10017-0000
Fax: 212 599-6843
312 263-6624 *Chicago Consulate General* 333 N Michigan Ave .... Chicago IL 60601-4186
Fax: 312 263-4805
213 857-1244 *Los Angeles Consulate General*
6100 Wilshire Blvd Suite 1200 .... Los Angeles CA 90048-5119
Fax: 213 936-2564
212 586-5110 *New York Consulate General*
50 Rockefeller Plaza Rm 1120 .... New York NY 10020-1605
Fax: 212 582-9657
601 968-5940 **Belhaven College** 1500 Peachtree St .... Jackson MS 39202-1789
Belize
202 363-4505 *Embassy* 3400 International Dr NW Suite 2J .... Washington DC 20008-3006
Fax: 202 362-7468
212 599-0233 *Mission to the UN* 820 2nd Ave Suite 922 .... New York NY 10017-4504
Fax: 212 599-3391
603 524-3570 **Belknap County** 64 Court St .... Laconia NH 03246-3679
606 337-6143 **Bell County** County Courthouse .... Pineville KY 40977-0000
Fax: 606 337-6144
817 939-3521 **Bell County** Main & Central Sts .... Belton TX 76513-0000
Fax: 817 939-0202 Legal
502 452-8211 **Bellarmine College** 2001 Newburg Rd .... Louisville KY 40205-1877
Fax: 502 451-3766 Admin
504 393-3011 **Belle Chasse Naval Air Station** .... New Orleans LA 70143-0001
Fax: 504 363-2244
303 427-5461 **Belleview College** 3455 W 83rd Ave .... Westminster CO 80030-4098
618 235-2700 **Belleville Area College** 2500 Carlyle Rd .... Belleville IL 62221-5899
Fax: 618 235-1578
402 291-8100 **Bellevue College** Galvin Rd & Harvell Dr .... Bellevue NE 68005-0000
Fax: 402 293-3819
206 641-0111 **Bellevue Community College** 3000 Landerholm Cir SE .... Bellevue WA 98007-0000
Fax: 206 641-0246
414 433-3560 **Bellin College of Nursing** 929 Cass St .... Green Bay WI 54301-3510
704 825-6700 **Belmont Abbey College** 100 Belmont-Mt Holly Rd .... Belmont NC 28012-2795
Fax: 704 825-6743
615 383-7001 **Belmont College** 1900 Belmont Blvd .... Nashville TN 37212-3757
Fax: 615 385-6446
614 695-2121 **Belmont County** 100 W Main St .... Saint Clairsville OH 43950-1225
614 695-9500 **Belmont Technical College** 120 Fox Shannon Pl .... Saint Clairsville OH 43950-9766
Fax: Call company operator
608 365-3391 **Beloit College** 700 College St .... Beloit WI 53511-5595
Fax: 608 365-0806
218 759-4109 **Beltrami County** 619 Beltrami Ave NW .... Bemidji MN 56601-3041
218 755-2000 **Bemidji State University** 1500 Birchmont Dr NE .... Bemidji MN 56601-2699
Fax: 218 755-4048
912 423-2455 **Ben Hill County** 401 E Central Ave .... Fitzgerald GA 31750-2596
803 256-4220 **Benedict College** 1600 Harden St .... Columbia SC 29204-1086
Fax: 803 253-5065
913 367-5340 **Benedictine College** 1020 N 2nd St .... Atchison KS 66002-1499
Fax: 913 367-6102 Library
208 245-2234 **Benewah County** 7th & College Aves .... Saint Maries ID 83861-0000
Fax: 208 245-3046
Benin: People's Republic of Benin
202 232-6656 *Embassy* 2737 Cathedral Ave NW .... Washington DC 20008-4119
212 249-6014 *Mission to the UN* 4 E 73rd St .... New York NY 10021-4135
Fax: 212 734-4735
202 225-2501 **Bennett Charles E (Rep - D - Florida)** 2107 Rayburn Bldg ... Washington DC 20515-0001
Fax: 202 225-9635
919 273-4431 **Bennett College** 900 E Washington St .... Greensboro NC 27401-3298
Fax: 919 378-0511
605 685-6969 **Bennett County** PO Box 281 .... Martin SD 57551-0281
802 442-5401 **Bennington College** Rt 67 A .... Bennington VT 05201-0000
802 447-2700 **Bennington County** 207 South St .... Bennington VT 05201-2247
802 447-1571 **Bennington Museum** W Main St .... Bennington VT 05201-2194
701 473-5340 **Benson County** 311 B Ave S .... Minnewaukan ND 58351-0000
719 456-2009 **Bent County** PO Box 350 .... Las Animas CO 81054-0350
617 891-2000 **Bentley College** 175 Forest St .... Waltham MA 02154-4705
Fax: 617 891-2569
202 225-3061 **Bentley Helen Delich (Rep - R - Maryland)**
1610 Longworth Bldg .... Washington DC 20515-0001
Fax: 202 225-4251
501 271-1015 **Benton County** PO Box 699 .... Bentonville AR 72712-0699
319 472-2766 **Benton County** 100 E 4th St .... Vinton IA 52349-1771
317 884-0930 **Benton County** 700 E 5th St .... Fowler IN 47944-1556
612 968-6254 **Benton County** 531 Dewey St .... Foley MN 56329-0000
816 438-7326 **Benton County** PO Box 1238 .... Warsaw MO 65355-1238
601 224-6611 **Benton County** Main St .... Ashland MS 38603-0000
503 757-6800 **Benton County** 180 NW 5th St .... Corvallis OR 97330-4777
Fax: 503 757-6897
901 584-6053 **Benton County** Court Sq .... Camden TN 38320-0000
509 786-5600 **Benton County** PO Box 190 .... Prosser WA 99350-0190
Fax: 509 786-5560
202 224-5922 **Bentsen Lloyd (Sen - D - Texas)** 703 Hart Bldg .... Washington DC 20510-0001
Fax: Unlisted
616 882-9671 **Benzie County** 224 Court Pl .... Beulah MI 49617-0000
606 986-9341 **Berea College** Chestnut St .... Berea KY 40404-0001
Fax: 606 986-4506
417 862-2781 **Berean College** 1445 Boonville Ave .... Springfield MO 65802-1805
Fax: 417 862-8558
202 225-4806 **Bereuter Doug (Rep - R - Nebraska)** 2348 Rayburn Bldg .... Washington DC 20515-0001
Fax: 202 226-1148
201 447-7200 **Bergen Community College** 400 Paramus Rd .... Paramus NJ 07652-1595
Fax: 201 444-7036
201 646-2500 **Bergen County** 21 Main St .... Hackensack NJ 07601-7000
Fax: 201 646-3101
512 479-4100 **Bergstrom Air Force Base** .... Austin TX 78743-0001
Fax: 512 369-3960

803 761-8210 **Berkeley County** 223 N Live Oak Dr .... Moncks Corner SC 29461-3707
Fax: 803 761-8251
304 267-3000 **Berkeley County** 119 W King St .... Martinsburg WV 25401-3209
803 761-8082 **Berkeley County Library** 100 Library St .... Moncks Corner SC 29461-2355
415 644-6095 **Berkeley Public Library** 2090 Kittredge St .... Berkeley CA 94704-1491
Fax: 415 845-7598
617 266-1400 **Berklee College of Music** 1140 Boylston St .... Boston MA 02215-3693
Fax: 617 247-6878
215 378-8000 **Berks County** 33 N 6th St .... Reading PA 19601-3540
Fax: 215 378-8913
413 499-4660 **Berkshire Community College** 1350 West St .... Pittsfield MA 01201-5786
Fax: 413 448-2700
413 448-8424 **Berkshire County** 76 East St .... Pittsfield MA 01201-5304
Fax: 413 443-6407
413 442-1793 **Berkshire County Historical Society** 780 Holmes Rd .... Pittsfield MA 01201-7199
202 225-4695 **Berman Howard L (Rep - D - California)** 137 Cannon Bldg .. Washington DC 20515-0001
Fax: Unlisted
505 768-4000 **Bernalillo County** 1 Civic Plaza 10th Fl .... Albuquerque NM 87102-0000
912 686-5421 **Berrien County** 105 E Washington Ave .... Nashville GA 31639-2256
616 983-7111 **Berrien County** 811 Port St .... Saint Joseph MI 49085-1114
Fax: 616 982-8642
404 232-5374 **Berry College** 2277 Martha Berry Blvd NE .... Rome GA 30149-0000
Fax: 404 236-2248
919 794-5300 **Bertie County** 106 W Dundee St .... Windsor NC 27983-1208
Fax: 919 794-5327
205 428-6391 **Bessemer State Technical College** PO Box 308 .... Bessemer AL 35021-0308
Fax: 205 424-8575
719 475-5170 **Beth El College of Nursing** 10 N Farragut Ave .... Colorado Springs CO 80909-0000
408 438-3800 **Bethany Bible College** 800 Bethany Dr .... Scotts Valley CA 95066-2896
Fax: 408 438-1621
913 227-3311 **Bethany College** 421 N 1st St .... Lindsborg KS 67456-1897
Fax: Unlisted
304 829-7000 **Bethany College** Main St .... Bethany WV 26032-0000
Fax: 304 829-7108
507 625-2977 **Bethany Lutheran College** 734 Marsh St .... Mankato MN 56001-4490
Fax: 507 625-1849
219 259-8511 **Bethel College** 1001 W McKinley Ave .... Mishawaka IN 46545-5591
Fax: Ext 435
316 283-2500 **Bethel College** 300 E 27th St .... North Newton KS 67117-0000
Fax: 316 283-2505 Ext 286
901 352-5321 **Bethel College** 212 Cherry St .... McKenzie TN 38201-0000
Fax: 901 352-3683
612 638-6400 **Bethel College & Seminary** 3900 Bethel Dr .... Saint Paul MN 55112-6999
Fax: 612 638-6001
215 867-3761 **Bethlehem Area Public Library** 11 W Church St .... Bethlehem PA 18018-5804
Fax: 215 865-2551
904 255-1401 **Bethune-Cookman College** 640 2nd Ave .... Daytona Beach FL 32114-3099
Fax: Unlisted
202 225-4876 **Bevill Tom (Rep - D - Alabama)** 2302 Rayburn Bldg .... Washington DC 20515-0001
Fax: 202 225-1604
512 220-2011 **Bexar County** 100 Dolorosa St Rm 1120-A .... San Antonio TX 78205-3002
614 231-2793 **Bexley Public Library** 2411 E Main St .... Columbus OH 43209-2498
212 826-1919 **Bhutan: Kingdom of Bhutan Mission to the UN**
2 UN Plaza 27th Fl .... New York NY 10017-0000
Fax: 212 826-2998
205 926-4745 **Bibb County** Court Sq .... Centreville AL 35042-1244
912 749-6527 **Bibb County** 601 Mulberry St .... Macon GA 31201-2672
202 224-5042 **Biden Joseph R Jr (Sen - D - Delaware)** 221 Russell Bldg .. Washington DC 20510-0001
Fax: 202 224-0139
318 263-2123 **Bienville Parish** 300 Courthouse Sq .... Arcadia LA 71001-0000
509 762-5351 **Big Bend Community College** 28th Ave & Chanute St .... Moses Lake WA 98837-0000
Fax: 509 762-6329 Admin
215 567-7000 **Big Brothers/Big Sisters of America** 230 N 13th St .... Philadelphia PA 19107-1551
Fax: 215 567-0394
406 665-3520 **Big Horn County** 121 3rd St W .... Hardin MT 59034-1905
Fax: 406 665-1608
307 568-2357 **Big Horn County** PO Box 31 .... Basin WY 82410-0031
612 839-2537 **Big Stone County** 20 2nd St SE .... Ortonville MN 56278-1544
202 225-5965 **Bilbray James H (Rep - D - Nevada)** 319 Cannon Bldg .... Washington DC 20515-0001
Fax: 202 225-8808
202 225-5755 **Bilirakis Michael (Rep - R - Florida)** 2432 Rayburn Bldg .... Washington DC 20515-0001
Fax: 202 225-4085
701 623-4491 **Billings County** PO Box 138 .... Medora ND 58645-0138
202 224-5521 **Bingaman Jeff (Sen - D - New Mexico)** 524 Hart Bldg .... Washington DC 20510-0001
Fax: 202 224-1810
208 785-5005 **Bingham County** 501 N Maple St .... Blackfoot ID 83221-1700
Fax: 208 785-5199
213 944-0351 **Biola University** 13800 Biola Ave .... La Mirada CA 90639-0001
Fax: 213 903-4748
205 254-2565 **Birmingham Museum of Art** 2000 8th Ave N .... Birmingham AL 35203-2278
Fax: 205 254-2714
205 226-3600 **Birmingham Public & Jefferson County Free Library**
2100 Park Pl .... Birmingham AL 35203-2744
205 226-4600 **Birmingham-Southern College** 900 Arkadelphia Rd .... Birmingham AL 35254-0001
Fax: 205 226-4931
402 559-3100 **Bishop Clarkson College** 333 S 44th St .... Omaha NE 68131-3703
Fax: 402 559-3177
808 847-3511 **Bishop Museum** 1525 Bernice St .... Honolulu HI 96817-2704
Fax: 808 841-8968
205 690-6412 **Bishop State Community College** 351 N Broad St .... Mobile AL 36603-5898
Fax: Unlisted
202 343-5951 **Black Colleges & Job Corps (US Dept of the Interior)**
1849 C St NW Rm 2759 .... Washington DC 20240-0001
Fax: 202 343-5048
Black Hawk College
309 852-5671 *East Campus* PO Box 489 .... Kewanee IL 61443-0489
Fax: 309 856-6005
309 796-1311 *Quad Cities Campus* 6600 34th Ave .... Moline IL 61265-5899
Fax: 309 792-5976 Communications
319 291-2500 **Black Hawk County** 316 E 5th St .... Waterloo IA 50703-4712
605 642-6011 **Black Hills State University** 1200 University St .... Spearfish SD 57799-0001
Fax: 605 642-6400
217 854-3231 **Blackburn College** 700 College Ave .... Carlinville IL 62626-1498
Fax: 217 854-8564
406 338-5441 **Blackfeet Community College** PO Box 819 .... Browning MT 59417-0819
Fax: 406 338-7808
317 348-3213 **Blackford County** 110 W Washington St .... Hartford City IN 47348-2251
608 756-4121 **Blackhawk Technical College** 6004 Prairie Rd .... Janesville WI 53546-9528
Fax: 608 757-7740
919 862-3438 **Bladen County** Courthouse Dr .... Elizabethtown NC 28337-0000
208 788-4290 **Blaine County** PO Box 400 .... Hailey ID 83333-0400
406 357-3250 **Blaine County** PO Box 278 .... Chinook MT 59523-0278
Fax: 406 357-2932
308 547-2222 **Blaine County** Lincoln Ave .... Brewster NE 68821-0000
405 623-5890 **Blaine County** 212 N Weigle Ave .... Watonga OK 73772-3893

814 695-5541 **Blair County** 423 Allegheny St .... Hollidaysburg PA 16648-2022
Fax: 814 696-9214
512 868-7357 **Blanco County** PO Box 65 .... Johnson City TX 78636-0117
703 688-4562 **Bland County** PO Box 295 .... Bland VA 24315-0295
202 225-1188 **Blaz Ben (Rep - R - Guam)** 1130 Longworth Bldg .... Washington DC 20515-0001
Fax: 202 225-0086
912 934-3200 **Bleckley County** 306 2nd St SE .... Cochran GA 31014-1633
Fax: 912 934-3205
615 447-2137 **Bledsoe County** PO Box 212 .... Pikeville TN 37367-0212
202 225-2815 **Bliley Thomas J Jr (Rep - R - Virginia)**
2241 Rayburn Bldg .... Washington DC 20515-0001
Fax: Unlisted
409 830-4150 **Blinn College** 902 College Ave .... Brenham TX 77833-4049
Fax: 409 830-4116
201 748-9000 **Bloomfield College** 467 Franklin St .... Bloomfield NJ 07003-4895
Fax: 201 743-3998
717 389-4316 **Bloomsburg University of Pennsylvania** .... Bloomsburg PA 17815-1301
Fax: 717 389-4001
205 274-9111 **Blount County** 220 2nd Ave E .... Oneonta AL 35121-1716
615 982-4391 **Blount County** 301 Court St .... Maryville TN 37801-4997
Fax: 615 977-1276
507 625-3031 **Blue Earth County** 204 S 5th St .... Mankato MN 56001-4585
Fax: 507 388-7916
615 388-9282 **Blue Grass Regional Library** 104 E 6th St .... Columbia TN 38401-3359
Fax: 615 388-1762
601 685-4771 **Blue Mountain College** PO Box 338 .... Blue Mountain MS 38610-0338
Fax: 601 685-4776
503 276-1260 **Blue Mountain Community College** 2411 NW Carden Ave ..... Pendleton OR 97801-1166
Fax: 503 276-6119
704 692-3572 **Blue Ridge Community College** RR 2 Box 133-A .... Flat Rock NC 28731-9802
Fax: 704 692-2441
703 234-9261 **Blue Ridge Community College** PO Box 80 .... Weyers Cave VA 24486-0080
Fax: 703 234-9006
703 326-3682 **Bluefield College** 3000 College Dr .... Bluefield VA 24605-1799
Fax: Ext 75
304 327-4065 **Bluefield State College** 219 Rock St .... Bluefield WV 24701-2198
Fax: 304 325-7747
419 358-8015 **Bluffton College** 280 W College Ave .... Bluffton OH 45817-1198
Fax: 419 358-3330
202 254-8040 **Board for International Broadcasting**
1201 Connecticut Ave NW Suite 400 .... Washington DC 20036-2605
Fax: 202 254-3929
202 366-4305 **Board of Contract Appeals (US Dept of Transportation)**
400 7th St SW Rm 5101 .... Washington DC 20590-0000
803 242-5100 **Bob Jones University** 1700 Wade Hampton Blvd .... Greenville SC 29614-0001
Fax: Ext 3015
803 242-5100 **Bob Jones University Collection of Sacred Art**
1700 Wade Hampton .... Greenville SC 29614-0001
Fax: Ext 3015
305 292-2107 **Boca Chica Naval Air Station** .... Key West FL 33040-0000
202 225-3665 **Boehlert Sherwood L (Rep - R - New York)**
1127 Longworth Bldg .... Washington DC 20515-0001
Fax: 202 225-1891
202 225-6205 **Boehner John A (Rep - R - Ohio)** 1020 Longworth Bldg ..... Washington DC 20515-0001
Fax: 202 225-0704
208 344-5515 **Boise Area Chamber of Commerce** 300 N 6th St .... Boise ID 83701-0000
Fax: 208 344-5849
208 376-7731 **Boise Bible College** 8695 Marigold St .... Boise ID 83714-1220
208 392-4431 **Boise County** PO Box 157 .... Idaho City ID 83631-0157
Fax: 208 392-4473
208 384-4466 **Boise Public Library & Information Center** 715 S Capitol Blvd ..... Boise ID 83702-7195
Fax: 208 384-4025
208 385-1011 **Boise State University** 1910 University Dr .... Boise ID 83725-0001
Fax: 208 385-1778
208 385-3301 *Library* 1910 University Dr .... Boise ID 83725-0001
Fax: 208 385-1394
601 843-2071 **Bolivar County** 401 S Court St .... Cleveland MS 38732-2696
Bolivia: Republic of Bolivia
202 483-4410 *Embassy* 3014 Massachusetts Ave NW .... Washington DC 20008-3603
Fax: 202 328-3712
212 682-8132 *Mission to the UN* 211 E 43rd St Rm 802 .... New York NY 10017-4707
Fax: 212 687-4642
202 545-6700 **Bolling Air Force Base** .... Washington DC 20332-0001
Fax: 202 767-3835 Library
314 238-2126 **Bollinger County** PO Box 46 .... Marble Hill MO 63764-0046
605 589-3382 **Bon Homme County** PO Box 6 .... Tyndall SD 57066-0006
202 224-5721 **Bond Christopher (Sen - R - Missouri)** 293 Russell Bldg .... Washington DC 20510-0001
Fax: 202 224-8149
618 664-0449 **Bond County** PO Box 407 .... Greenville IL 62246-0407
202 225-2106 **Bonior David E (Rep - D - Michigan)** 2242 Rayburn Bldg .... Washington DC 20515-0001
Fax: 202 226-1169
208 263-6841 **Bonner County** 215 S 1st Ave .... Sandpoint ID 83864-1392
Fax: 208 263-0896
208 529-1350 **Bonneville County** 605 N Capital Ave .... Idaho Falls ID 83402-3582
503 230-5101 **Bonneville Power Administration (US Dept of Energy)**
905 NE 11th Ave .... Portland OR 97232-4170
Fax: 503 230-5211
501 741-8428 **Boone County** PO Box 846 .... Harrison AR 72602-0846
515 432-6291 **Boone County** County Courthouse .... Boone IA 50036-0000
815 544-3103 **Boone County** 601 N Main St .... Belvidere IL 61008-2600
317 482-3510 **Boone County** 1 Courthouse Sq Rm 212 .... Lebanon IN 46052-2150
606 334-2108 **Boone County** 2950 E Washington Sq .... Burlington KY 41005-0000
314 874-7574 **Boone County** 8th & Walnut .... Columbia MO 65201-0000
402 395-2055 **Boone County** 222 S 4th St .... Albion NE 68620-1247
304 369-3925 **Boone County** 200 State St .... Madison WV 25130-1152
316 227-8188 **Boot Hill Museum** Front St .... Dodge City KS 67801-0000
915 856-4312 **Borden County** 101 Main St .... Gail TX 79738-0000
202 224-4721 **Boren David L (Sen - D - Oklahoma)** 453 Russell Bldg .... Washington DC 20510-0001
Fax: 202 224-2290
212 694-1000 **Boricua College** 3755 Broadway .... New York NY 10032-1599
809 882-3513 **Borinquen Coast Guard Air Station** .... Aguadilla PR 00604-0000
216 585-5900 **Borromeo College of Ohio** 28700 Euclid Ave .... Wickliffe OH 44092-2585
202 225-8251 **Borski Robert A (Rep - D - Pennsylvania)**
407 Cannon Bldg .... Washington DC 20515-0001
Fax: 202 225-4628
817 435-2201 **Bosque County** Morgan & Main Sts .... Meridian TX 76665-0000
318 965-2336 **Bossier Parish** PO Box 369 .... Benton LA 71006-0369
Boston City Government
617 725-4600 *City Clerk* 1 City Hall Plaza Rm 601 .... Boston MA 02201-0000
617 725-4000 *City Hall* 1 City Hall Plaza .... Boston MA 02201-0001
Fax: 617 523-6966
617 725-4488 *Department of Transportation* 1 City Hall Plaza Rm 721 .... Boston MA 02201-0000
Fax: 617 523-4475
617 725-3550 *Fire Dept* 115 Southampton St .... Boston MA 02118-0000
617 725-3562 *Human Rights Commission* 1 City Hall Plaza Rm 716 .... Boston MA 02201-0000
617 725-4500 *Mayor's Office* 1 City Hall Plaza 5th Fl .... Boston MA 02201-0000

617 247-4500 *Police Dept* 154 Berkeley St ... Boston MA 12116-0000
617 725-4352 *Public Facilities* 26 Court St ... Boston MA 02108-0000
617 725-4900 *Public Works* 1 City Hall Plaza Rm 714 ... Boston MA 02201-0000
Fax: 617 723-7290
617 722-4300 *Redevelopment Authority* 1 City Hall Sq 9th Fl ... Boston MA 02201-0000
Fax: 617 472-8904
617 725-4138 *Treasurer* 1 City Hall Plaza Rm M-5 ... Boston MA 02201-0000
617 223-3257 **Boston Coast Guard Support Center** 427 Commercial St ... Boston MA 02109-1096
Fax: 617 223-3166
617 552-8000 **Boston College** 140 Commonwealth Ave ... Chestnut Hill MA 02167-9991
Fax: 617 552-8828
617 552-4250 *Graduate School of Nursing* 140 Commonwealth Ave ... Chestnut Hill MA 02167-9991
617 552-8550 *Law School* 885 Centre St ... Newton MA 02159-1100
Fax: 617 552-2615
617 536-6340 **Boston Conservatory of Music & Dance** 8 Fenway ... Boston MA 02215-4099
617 267-9300 **Boston Museum of Fine Arts** 465 Huntington Ave ... Boston MA 02115-5519
Fax: 617 267-0280
617 536-5400 **Boston Public Library** 666 Boylston St ... Boston MA 02117-0000
617 353-2000 **Boston University** 775 Commonwealth Ave ... Boston MA 02215-9991
Fax: 617 353-2053
617 353-9760 *College of Engineering* 705 Commonwealth Ave Rm 112 ... Boston MA 02215-1401
Fax: 617 353-6322
617 638-4700 *Henry Goldman School of Graduate Dentistry*
100 E Newton St ... Boston MA 02118-2392
Fax: Call company operator
617 353-3112 *School of Law* 765 Commonwealth Ave ... Boston MA 02215-1401
Fax: 617 353-5995
617 638-4630 *School of Medicine* 80 E Concord St ... Boston MA 02118-2394
Fax: Unlisted
617 638-5052 *School of Public Health* 80 E Concord St Bldg A 4th Fl ... Boston MA 02118-2394
Fax: 617 638-5374
703 473-8220 **Botetourt County** 1 W Main St Box 1 ... Fincastle VA 24090-3006
Fax: 703 473-8207
Botswana: Republic of Botswana
202 244-4990 *Embassy*
8400 International Dr NW Intelfat Bldg Suite 7-M ... Washington DC 20008-0000
Fax: 202 244-4164
212 889-2277 *Mission to the UN* 103 E 37th St ... New York NY 10016-3002
Fax: 212 725-5061
701 228-3983 **Bottineau County** 315 W 5th St ... Bottineau ND 58318-1214
202 225-3861 **Boucher Rick (Rep - D - Virginia)** 405 Cannon Bldg ... Washington DC 20515-0001
Fax: 202 225-0442
303 441-3131 **Boulder County** PO Box 471 ... Boulder CO 80306-0471
Fax: 303 441-4525
303 441-3100 **Boulder Public Library** 1000 Canyon Blvd ... Boulder CO 80302-5120
Fax: 303 442-1808
208 267-2242 **Boundary County** 315 Kootnai St ... Bonners Ferry ID 83805-0000
Fax: 208 267-7814
316 223-3800 **Bourbon County** 210 S National Ave ... Fort Scott KS 66701-1328
606 987-2430 **Bourbon County** Main St ... Paris KY 40361-0000
Fax: 606 987-4083
207 725-3000 **Bowdoin College** ... Brunswick ME 04011-0000
Fax: 207 725-3123
207 725-3275 **Bowdoin College Museum of Art** Walker Art Bldg ... Brunswick ME 04011-2599
Fax: 207 725-3123
903 628-2571 **Bowie County** PO Box 248 ... New Boston TX 75570-0248
Fax: 903 628-2426
301 464-3000 **Bowie State University** 14000 Jericho Park Rd ... Bowie MD 20715-3318
Fax: 301 464-9350
419 372-2531 **Bowling Green State University** ... Bowling Green OH 43403-0001
Fax: 419 372-2300
419 433-5560 *Firelands College* 901 Rye Beach Rd ... Huron OH 44839-9791
Fax: Call company operator
419 372-2076 *School of Journalism* 319 West Hall ... Bowling Green OH 43403-0001
701 523-3450 **Bowman County** 104 W 1st ... Bowman ND 58623-0000
308 762-6565 **Box Butte County** 5th & Box Butte Sts ... Alliance NE 69301-0000
801 734-2031 **Box Elder County** 1 S Main St ... Brigham City UT 84302-2599
Fax: 801 734-2038
202 225-5161 **Boxer Barbara (Rep - D - California)** 307 Cannon Bldg ... Washington DC 20515-0001
Fax: 202 226-1004
606 739-5116 **Boyd County** 2800 Louisa St ... Catlettsburg KY 41129-1610
Fax: 606 739-6357
402 775-2391 **Boyd County** County Courthouse ... Butte NE 68722-0000
606 238-1100 **Boyle County** Main St ... Danville KY 40422-0000
606 735-2952 **Bracken County** Locus St ... Brooksville KY 41004-0000
505 667-4444 **Bradbury Science Museum** Diamond Dr MS-M897 ... Los Alamos NM 87545-0001
Fax: 505 667-3669
508 372-7161 **Bradford College** 320 S Main St ... Bradford MA 01835-7393
Fax: 508 521-0480
904 964-6280 **Bradford County** PO Box B ... Starke FL 32091-1286
717 265-5700 **Bradford County** 301 Main St ... Towanda PA 18848-1884
Fax: 717 265-4610
202 224-3224 **Bradley Bill (Sen - D - New Jersey)** 731 Hart Bldg ... Washington DC 20510-0001
Fax: 202 224-8567
501 226-3853 **Bradley County** County Courthouse ... Warren AR 71671-0000
615 479-9654 **Bradley County** PO Box 46 ... Cleveland TN 37364-0046
309 676-7611 **Bradley University** 1501 W Bradley Ave ... Peoria IL 61625-0001
Fax: Unlisted
213 663-1111 **Braille Institute of America Inc** 741 N Vermont Ave ... Los Angeles CA 90029-3594
Fax: 213 666-5881
213 660-3880 **Braille Institute of America Library** 4205 Melrose Ave ... Los Angeles CA 90029-3508
218 828-2525 **Brainerd Community College** 501 W College Dr ... Brainerd MN 56401-3900
Fax: 218 828-2710
517 279-8411 **Branch County** 31 Division St ... Coldwater MI 49036-1904
617 736-2000 **Brandeis University** 415 South St ... Waltham MA 02154-2700
Fax: 617 736-4724 Library
617 736-2300 *Graduate School of Biochemistry* 415 South St ... Waltham MA 02254-2700
Fax: 617 736-2349
617 736-3100 *Graduate School of Biology*
415 South St Bassine Bldg Rm 235 ... Waltham MA 02254-0000
Fax: 617 736-3107
617 736-3410 *Graduate School of Chemistry* 415 South St ... Waltham MA 02254-0000
617 736-2803 *Graduate School of Physics*
415 South St Bass Bldg Rm 210 ... Waltham MA 02254-9110
Fax: 617 736-2915
302 478-3000 **Brandywine College** 4601 Concord Pike ... Wilmington DE 19803-1435
505 526-1047 **Branigan Thomas Memorial Library** 200 E Picacho Ave ... Las Cruces NM 88001-3499
912 462-5256 **Brantley County** PO Box 398 ... Nahunta GA 31553-0398
Fax: 912 462-5538
304 765-2833 **Braxton County** PO Box 486 ... Sutton WV 26601-0486
212 286-9600 **Brazil Tourism** 551 5th Ave Suite 915 ... New York NY 10176-0000
Fax: 212 490-9294
202 463-5485 **Brazil-US Business Council** 1615 H St NW 6th Fl ... Washington DC 20062-0001
Fax: 202 463-3114

Brazil: Federative Republic of Brazil
202 745-2700 *Embassy* 3006 Massachusetts Ave NW ... Washington DC 20008-3603
Fax: 202 745-2827
212 832-6868 *Mission to the UN* 747 3rd Ave 9th Fl ... New York NY 10017-2803
Fax: 212 371-5716
312 372-2177 *Chicago Consulate General* 20 N Wacker Dr Suite 1010 ... Chicago IL 60606-2901
Fax: 312 372-1806
213 382-3133 *Los Angeles Consulate General*
3810 Wilshire Blvd Suite 1500 ... Los Angeles CA 90010-4014
Fax: 213 487-4341
212 757-3080 *New York Consulate General* 630 5th Ave Suite 2720 ... New York NY 10111-0252
212 575-9030 **Brazilian-American Chamber of Commerce**
22 W 48th St Rm 404 ... New York NY 10036-1803
Fax: 212 921-1078
409 849-5711 **Brazoria County** 111 E Locust St ... Angleton TX 77515-4622
Fax: Call company operator
409 849-5711 **Brazoria County Library System** 401 E Cedar St ... Angleton TX 77515-0000
Fax: Ext 1273
409 775-7400 **Brazos County** 300 E 26th St ... Bryan TX 77803-5359
409 265-6131 **Brazosport College** 500 College Dr ... Lake Jackson TX 77566-3199
Fax: 409 265-2944
202 269-0200 **Bread for the World** 802 Rhode Island Ave NE ... Washington DC 20018-1763
Fax: 202 529-8546
606 666-3810 **Breathitt County** 1127 Main St ... Jackson KY 41339-1194
202 224-4623 **Breaux John B (Sen - D - Louisiana)** 516 Hart Bldg ... Washington DC 20510-0001
Fax: 202 224-2435
502 756-2269 **Breckinridge County** PO Box 227 ... Hardinsburg KY 40143-0227
Fax: 502 756-5444
319 352-5040 **Bremer County** 415 E Bremer Ave ... Waverly IA 50677-3536
404 534-6299 **Brenau College** 204 Boulevard St ... Gainesville GA 30501-3697
Fax: 404 534-6114
516 273-7883 **Brentwood Public Library** 2nd Ave & 4th St ... Brentwood NY 11717-4676
Fax: 516 273-7896
502 685-3131 **Brescia College** 717 Frederica St ... Owensboro KY 42301-2298
Fax: 502 686-4213
704 883-8292 **Brevard College** 400 N Broad St ... Brevard NC 28712-9904
Fax: 704 884-3790
407 632-1111 **Brevard Community College** 1519 Clearlake Rd ... Cocoa FL 32922-6597
407 269-8011 **Brevard County** 700 S Park Ave ... Titusville FL 32780-4001
205 932-3221 **Brewer State Junior College** 2631 Temple Ave N ... Fayette AL 35555-1198
Fax: 205 932-6974
202 225-4565 **Brewster Bill (Rep - D - Oklahoma)** 1407 Longworth Bldg .. Washington DC 20515-0001
Fax: 202 225-9029
915 837-3366 **Brewster County** 201 W Ave ... Alpine TX 79830-0000
912 583-2241 **Brewton-Parker College** Hwy 280 ... Mount Vernon GA 30445-0000
Fax: 912 583-4498
712 279-5321 **Briar Cliff College** 3303 Rebecca St ... Sioux City IA 51104-2340
Fax: 712 279-5992 Admissions
207 985-4802 **Brick Store Museum** PO Box 177 ... Kennebunk ME 04043-0177
203 255-2623 **Bridgeport Engineering Institute** 785 Unquowa Rd ... Fairfield CT 06430-5002
Fax: 203 359-9372
203 576-7777 **Bridgeport Public Library** 925 Broad St ... Bridgeport CT 06604-4871
Fax: 203 576-8255
703 828-2501 **Bridgewater College** 402 E College St ... Bridgewater VA 22812-1599
Fax: Unlisted
508 697-1200 **Bridgewater State College** ... Bridgewater MA 02325-0001
Fax: 508 697-1705
801 378-1211 **Brigham Young University** Administration Bldg ... Provo UT 84602-0000
Fax: 801 378-5278 Admin
801 378-4144 *College of Nursing* Spencer W Kimball Tower Suite 500 ... Provo UT 84602-0000
801 378-2077 *Department of Communications* E-509 Harris Fine Arts Ctr ... Provo UT 84602-0000
Fax: 801 378-2959
808 293-3211 *Hawaii Campus* 55-220 Kulanui St ... Laie HI 96762-1294
Fax: 808 293-3645
801 378-4274 *J Reuben Clark Law School* 348 J Reuben Clark Bldg ... Provo UT 84602-0000
Fax: 801 378-3595
806 823-2131 **Briscoe County** 415 Main St ... Silverton TX 79257-0000
703 466-2221 **Bristol (Independent City)** 497 Cumberland St ... Bristol VA 24201-4394
907 246-4224 **Bristol Bay Borough** PO Box 189 ... Naknek AK 99633-0189
508 678-2811 **Bristol Community College** 777 Elsbree St ... Fall River MA 02720-7395
Fax: Ext 470
508 823-6588 **Bristol County** 9 Court St ... Taunton MA 02780-3223
401 245-7977 **Bristol County** 516 Main St ... Warren RI 02885-4369
212 581-4708 **British Tourist Authority** 40 W 57th St Suite 320 ... New York NY 10019-4096
Fax: 212 265-0649
212 889-0680 **British-American Chamber of Commerce**
275 Madison Ave Suite 1714 ... New York NY 10016-1101
Fax: 212 683-0621
406 266-3443 **Broadwater County** PO Box 489 ... Townsend MT 59644-0489
212 590-3644 **Bronx County** 851 Grand Concourse Rm 118 ... Bronx NY 10451-2937
908 842-1900 **Brookdale Community College** 765 Newman Springs Rd ... Lincroft NJ 07738-1597
304 737-3661 **Brooke County** Main & 7th Sts ... Wellsburg WV 26070-0000
214 620-4803 **Brookhaven Community College** 3939 Valley View Ln ... Farmers Branch TX 75244-4997
Fax: 214 620-4897
605 688-4208 **Brookings County** 314 6th Ave ... Brookings SD 57006-2041
202 797-6000 **Brookings Institution** 1775 Massachusetts Ave NW ... Washington DC 20036-2188
Fax: 202 797-6004
718 615-2420 **Brooklyn Coast Guard Air Station** Floyd Bennett Field ... Brooklyn NY 11234-7097
Fax: 718 615-2411
718 625-2200 **Brooklyn Law School** 250 Joralemon St ... Brooklyn NY 11201-3798
Fax: 718 797-1403
718 638-5000 **Brooklyn Museum** 200 Eastern Pkwy ... Brooklyn NY 11238-6052
Fax: 718 638-3731
718 780-7700 **Brooklyn Public Library** Grand Army Plaza ... Brooklyn NY 11238-5698
Fax: 718 783-1770
512 536-1110 **Brooks Air Force Base** ... San Antonio TX 78235-0000
Fax: 512 536-2935
912 263-5561 **Brooks County** Hwy 76 & Hwy 33 ... Quitman GA 31643-0000
512 325-5604 **Brooks County** County Courthouse ... Falfurrias TX 78355-0000
805 966-3888 **Brooks Institute of Photography** 801 Alston Rd ... Santa Barbara CA 93108-2399
Fax: 805 564-1475
202 225-6565 **Brooks Jack (Rep - D - Texas)** 2449 Rayburn Bldg ... Washington DC 20515-0001
Fax: 202 225-1584
607 771-5000 **Broome Community College** PO Box 1017 ... Binghamton NY 13902-1017
Fax: Call company operator
607 778-2451 **Broome County** 44 Hawley St ... Binghamton NY 13901-3722
607 723-6457 **Broome County Public Library** 78 Exchange St ... Binghamton NY 13901-3489
202 225-6135 **Broomfield William S (Rep - R - Michigan)**
2306 Rayburn Bldg ... Washington DC 20515-0001
Fax: 202 225-1807
305 475-6500 **Broward Community College** 225 E Las Olas Blvd ... Fort Lauderdale FL 33301-2298
305 357-7283 **Broward County** PO Box 14668 ... Fort Lauderdale FL 33302-0000
305 357-7444 **Broward County Library System** 100 S Andrews Ave ... Fort Lauderdale FL 33301-1830
Fax: 305 357-7399 Admin

202 225-3261 **Browder Glenn (Rep - D - Alabama)**
1221 Longworth Bldg .... Washington DC 20515-0000
Fax: 202 225-9020
217 773-3421 **Brown County** 21 W Court St .... Mount Sterling IL 62353-1241
812 988-4796 **Brown County** Van Buren & Main Sts .... Nashville IN 47448-0000
913 742-2581 **Brown County** Courthouse Sq .... Hiawatha KS 66434-0000
Fax: 913 742-3255
507 359-7900 **Brown County** Center & State Sts .... New Ulm MN 56073-0000
Fax: 507 359-9562
402 387-2705 **Brown County** 148 W 4th St .... Ainsworth NE 69210-1696
513 378-3100 **Brown County** Danny L Pride Courthouse .... Georgetown OH 45121-0000
Fax: 513 378-3956
605 622-2451 **Brown County** 101 1st Ave SE .... Aberdeen SD 57401-4203
915 643-2594 **Brown County** 200 S Broadway St .... Brownwood TX 76801-3136
414 436-3250 **Brown County** PO Box 1600 .... Green Bay WI 54305-5600
414 497-3452 **Brown County Library** 515 Pine St .... Green Bay WI 54301-5194
Fax: 414 497-4344
202 225-6161 **Brown George E (Rep - D - California)** 2188 Rayburn Bldg .. Washington DC 20515-0001
Fax: 202 225-8671
202 224-5941 **Brown Hank (Sen - R - Colorado)** 902-B Hart Bldg .... Washington DC 20510-0001
Fax: Unlisted
401 863-1000 **Brown University** .... Providence RI 02912-0001
Fax: 401 863-3700 Communications
401 863-2256 *Department of Chemistry* 324 Brook St .... Providence RI 02912-0001
Fax: 401 863-2594
401 863-7600 *Department of Computer Science* 115 Waterman St .... Providence RI 02906-1101
Fax: 401 863-7657
401 863-3357 *Department of Geological Sciences* PO Box 1846 .... Providence RI 02912-0001
Fax: 401 863-2058
401 863-1661 *Graduate School of Cellular/Molecular Biology* PO Box G .. Providence RI 02912-0000
Fax: 401 863-1201
401 863-2378 *Graduate School of Physics* 42 Charlesfield St .... Providence RI 02912-0001
401 863-2149 *Program in Medicine* 97 Waterman St G-A212 .... Providence RI 02912-0001
203 869-0376 **Bruce Museum** 1 Museum Dr .... Greenwich CT 06830-7100
202 225-5001 **Bruce Terry L (Rep - D - Illinois)** 419 Cannon Bldg .... Washington DC 20515-0001
Fax: 202 225-9810
605 734-5443 **Brule County** 300 S Courtland St .... Chamberlain SD 57325-1599
Brunei: Sultanate of Brunei Darussalam
202 342-0159 *Embassy* 2600 Virginia Ave NW Suite 300 .... Washington DC 20037-1905
Fax: 202 342-0158
212 838-1600 *Mission to the UN* 866 United Nations Plaza Rm 248 .... New York NY 10017-1811
912 264-7253 **Brunswick College** Altama & 4th St .... Brunswick GA 31523-0001
Fax: 912 264-7274
919 253-4331 **Brunswick County** PO Box 249 .... Bolivia NC 28422-0249
Fax: 919 253-6029
804 848-3107 **Brunswick County** 102 Tobacco St .... Lawrenceville VA 23868-1824
207 921-1110 **Brunswick Naval Air Station** .... Brunswick ME 04011-2494
Fax: Unlisted
912 267-1212 **Brunswick-Glynn County Regional Library**
208 Gloucester St .... Brunswick GA 31523-0901
Fax: Unlisted
615 775-2041 **Bryan College** Bryan Hill St Box 7000 .... Dayton TN 37321-0000
Fax: 615 775-7330
912 653-4912 **Bryan County** 401 S College St .... Pembroke GA 31321-0000
405 924-2201 **Bryan County** 402 W Evergreen St .... Durant OK 74701-4703
409 779-1736 **Bryan Public Library** 201 E 26th St .... Bryan TX 77803-5389
202 224-6244 **Bryan Richard H (Sen - D - Nevada)** 364 Russell Bldg .... Washington DC 20510-0001
Fax: 202 224-1867
401 232-6000 **Bryant College** 450 Douglas Pike .... Smithfield RI 02917-1284
Fax: 401 232-6319
401 232-6231 *Graduate School* 1150 Douglas Pike .... Smithfield RI 02917-0000
Fax: 401 232-6319
202 225-2231 **Bryant John (Rep - D - Texas)** 208 Cannon Bldg .... Washington DC 20515-0001
Fax: 202 225-9721
215 526-5000 **Bryn Mawr College** .... Bryn Mawr PA 19010-0000
319 334-2196 **Buchanan County** 210 5th Ave NE .... Independence IA 50644-1959
816 271-1411 **Buchanan County** 5th & Jules Sts .... Saint Joseph MO 64501-0000
703 935-6500 **Buchanan County** PO Box 950 .... Grundy VA 24614-0950
Fax: 703 935-4479
804 969-4242 **Buckingham County** PO Box 252 .... Buckingham VA 23921-0252
717 523-1271 **Bucknell University** .... Lewisburg PA 17837-0000
215 348-6000 **Bucks County** Main & Court Sts .... Doylestown PA 18901-0000
Fax: 215 348-6379
215 348-0332 **Bucks County Free Library** 150 S Pine St .... Doylestown PA 18901-4626
Fax: 215 348-4760
202 226-7200 **Budget Committee (US House of Representatives)**
House Annex 1 Rm 214 .... Washington DC 20515-0001
Fax: Unlisted
202 224-0642 **Budget Committee (US Senate)** 621 Dirksen Bldg .... Washington DC 20510-0001
Fax: 202 224-4835
703 261-6121 **Buena Vista (Independent City)** 2039 Sycamore Ave .... Buena Vista VA 24416-3133
515 576-4881 **Buena Vista College** 330 Ave M Library Bldg Rm 104 .... Fort Dodge IA 50501-0000
712 749-2105 **Buena Vista College** 610 W 4th St .... Storm Lake IA 50588-1798
Fax: 712 749-2037
712 749-2546 **Buena Vista County** PO Box 1186 .... Storm Lake IA 50588-1186
716 873-9644 **Buffalo & Erie County Historical Society** 25 Nottingham Ct .... Buffalo NY 14216-3119
716 858-8900 **Buffalo & Erie County Public Library** Lafayette Sq .... Buffalo NY 14203-0000
716 851-4200 **Buffalo City Hall** 65 Niagara Sq .... Buffalo NY 14202-3331
Fax: 716 851-4031 Acctg
307 587-4771 **Buffalo Bill Historical Center** 720 Sheridan Ave .... Cody WY 82414-3428
Fax: 307 587-5714
308 236-1226 **Buffalo County** 16th & Central Ave .... Kearney NE 68848-0000
605 293-3234 **Buffalo County** PO Box 148 .... Gann Valley SD 57341-0148
608 685-4940 **Buffalo County** 407 N 2nd St .... Alma WI 54610-9673
716 896-5200 **Buffalo Museum of Science** 1020 Humboldt Pkwy .... Buffalo NY 14211-1208
202 822-0200 **Build PAC of the National Assn of Home Builders**
1201 15th St NW .... Washington DC 20005-2802
Fax: 202 822-0559
Bulgaria: Republic of Bulgaria
202 387-7969 *Embassy* 1621 22nd St NW .... Washington DC 20008-1921
Fax: 202 234-7973
212 737-4790 *Mission to the UN* 11 E 84th St .... New York NY 10028-0407
502 543-2262 **Bullitt County** Buckman St .... Shepherdsville KY 40165-0000
912 764-9009 **Bulloch County** N Main St .... Statesboro GA 30458-0000
205 738-2280 **Bullock County** PO Box 230 .... Union Springs AL 36089-0230
Fax: 205 738-2282
202 224-4843 **Bumpers Dale (Sen - D - Arkansas)** 229 Dirksen Bldg .... Washington DC 20510-0001
Fax: 202 224-6435
704 251-6007 **Buncombe County** 60 Courthouse Plaza .... Asheville NC 28801-3519
617 241-8600 **Bunker Hill Community College** New Rutherford Ave .... Boston MA 02129-0000
Fax: Ext 402
202 225-3465 **Bunning Jim (Rep - R - Kentucky)** 116 Cannon Bldg .... Washington DC 20515-0001
Fax: 202 225-0003
202 224-2551 **Burdick Quentin N (Sen - D - North Dakota)** 511 Hart Bldg .. Washington DC 20510-0001
Fax: 202 224-1193

815 875-2014 **Bureau County** County Courthouse .... Princeton IL 61356-0000
Fax: 815 872-0027
202 647-4440 **Bureau of African Affairs (US Dept of State)**
2201 C St NW Rm 6234-A .... Washington DC 20520-3430
Fax: 202 647-6301
202 566-7135 **Bureau of Alcohol Tobacco & Firearms**
1200 Pennsylvania Ave NW Rm 4402 .... Washington DC 20226-0001
Fax: 202 566-7442
312 353-3778 *Midwest Region* 230 S Dearborn St 15th Fl .... Chicago IL 60604-1502
Fax: 312 353-3779
212 264-2328 *North Atlantic Region* 6 World Trade Ctr Rm 620 .... New York NY 10048-0206
Fax: 212 264-7878
404 986-6040 *Southeast Region* 3835 Presidential Pkwy .... Atlanta GA 30340-3792
Fax: 404 986-6071
214 767-2277 *Southwest Region* 1114 Commerce St .... Dallas TX 75242-1001
Fax: 214 767-3009
415 744-7013 *Western Region* 221 Main St 11th Fl .... San Francisco CA 94105-1906
Fax: 415 974-9661
202 647-7971 **Bureau of Economic & Business Affairs (US Dept of State)**
2201 C St NW Rm 6828 .... Washington DC 20520-0001
Fax: 202 647-5713
202 523-0693 **Bureau of Economic Analysis (US Dept of Commerce)**
1401 K St NW Tower Bldg Rm 705 .... Washington DC 20230-0001
Fax: 202 523-7538
202 447-0917 **Bureau of Engraving & Printing (US Dept of the Treasury)**
14th & C Sts SW .... Washington DC 20228-0001
Fax: 202 447-0109
202 377-5491 **Bureau of Export Administration (US Dept of Commerce)**
14th St & Constitution Ave NW Rm 3886C .... Washington DC 20230-0001
Fax: 202 377-2387
202 208-5116 **Bureau of Indian Affairs** 1849 C St NW .... Washington DC 20245-0001
Fax: 202 343-4097
605 226-7343 *Aberdeen Area* 115 4th Ave SE .... Aberdeen SD 57401-4382
Fax: Ext 446
505 766-3170 *Albuquerque Area* 615 1st St NW .... Albuquerque NM 87102-2305
Fax: 505 766-2666
405 247-6673 *Anadarko Area* PO Box 368 .... Anadarko OK 73005-0000
Fax: Ext 233
406 657-6315 *Billings Area* 316 N 26th St Rm 4430 .... Billings MT 59101-1397
Fax: 406 585-6559
703 235-2571 *Eastern Area* 3701 N Fairfax Dr .... Arlington VA 22203-0000
Fax: 703 235-8610
907 586-7177 *Juneau Area* PO Box 3-8000 .... Juneau AK 99802-1219
Fax: 907 586-7169
612 349-3631 *Minneapolis Area* 15 S 5th St .... Minneapolis MN 55402-1020
Fax: 612 349-3365
918 687-2295 *Muskogee Area* 5th & W Okmulgee .... Muskogee OK 74401-0000
Fax: 918 736-2571
602 871-5151 *Navajo Area* PO Box M .... Window Rock AZ 86515-0714
Fax: Ext 5122
602 379-6600 *Phoenix Area* PO Box 10 .... Phoenix AZ 85001-0010
Fax: 602 379-4413
503 231-6702 *Portland Area* 1002 NE Holladay St .... Portland OR 97232-4182
Fax: 503 231-6731
916 978-4691 *Sacramento Area* 2800 Cottage Way .... Sacramento CA 95825-1884
Fax: 916 978-5447
202 523-6043 **Bureau of International Labor Affairs (US Dept of Labor)**
200 Constitution Ave NW Rm S2235 .... Washington DC 20210-0001
Fax: 202 523-9880
202 523-1913 **Bureau of Labor Statistics** 441 G St NW .... Washington DC 20212-0001
202 523-1180 *Employment & Unemployment Statistics*
441 G St NW Rm 2919 .... Washington DC 20212-0001
Fax: 202 523-4558
202 523-1382 *Office of Compensation & Working Conditions*
441 G St NW Rm 2021 .... Washington DC 20212-0001
Fax: 202 523-6830
202 272-5381 *Office of Employment Projections* 600 E St NW Rm 9216 Washington DC 20212-0001
Fax: 202 504-2086
404 347-4418 *Atlanta Office* 1371 Peachtree St NE Suite 540 .... Atlanta GA 30367-0001
Fax: 404 347-2447
617 565-2327 *Boston Office* JFK Federal Bldg Government Ctr Rm 1603 .... Boston MA 02203-0000
Fax: 617 565-3847
312 353-7226 *Chicago Office* 230 S Dearborn St 9th Fl .... Chicago IL 60604-1502
Fax: 312 353-1886
214 767-6953 *Dallas Office* 525 Griffin St Federal Bldg Rm 221 .... Dallas TX 75202-0000
Fax: 214 767-3720
816 426-2378 *Kansas City Office* 911 Walnut St Rm 1604 .... Kansas City MO 64106-2009
Fax: 816 426-6537
212 337-2400 *New York Office* 201 Varick St Rm 808 .... New York NY 10014-4800
Fax: 212 337-2532
215 596-1154 *Philadelphia Office* PO Box 13309 .... Philadelphia PA 19101-3309
Fax: 215 596-4263
415 744-6600 *San Francisco Office* 71 Stevenson St .... San Francisco CA 94105-2934
Fax: 415 744-7138
202 208-3801 **Bureau of Land Management** 1849 C St NW Rm 5600 .... Washington DC 20240-0001
Fax: 202 343-4152 PR
907 271-5076 *Anchorage Office* 222 W 7th Ave Box 13 .... Anchorage AK 99513-7504
Fax: 907 271-5425
208 334-1401 *Boise Office* 3380 Americana Terr .... Boise ID 83706-2544
Fax: 208 334-1800
307 772-2326 *Cheyenne Office* 2515 Warren Ave .... Cheyenne WY 82001-3198
Fax: 307 772-2053
303 236-2100 *Denver Office* 2850 Youngfield St .... Lakewood CO 80215-7093
Fax: 303 238-2537
703 461-1400 *Eastern States Office* 350 S Pickett St .... Alexandria VA 22304-4714
Fax: 703 461-1376
406 255-2904 *Montana Office* 222 N 32nd St .... Billings MT 59101-1911
Fax: 406 255-2762
602 640-5547 *Phoenix Office* PO Box 16563 .... Phoenix AZ 85011-6563
Fax: 602 640-5556
503 280-7026 *Portland Office* 825 NE Multnomah St .... Portland OR 97232-2162
Fax: 503 231-6246
702 328-6202 *Reno Office* 850 Harvard Way .... Reno NV 89502-2055
Fax: 702 784-5460
916 978-4743 *Sacramento Office* 2800 Cottage Way Rm E-2841 .... Sacramento CA 95825-0000
Fax: 916 978-4715
801 539-4010 *Salt Lake City Office* 324 S State St Suite 301 .... Salt Lake City UT 84111-2397
Fax: 801 539-4183
505 988-6030 *Santa Fe Office* 120 S Federal Pl Suite 304 .... Santa Fe NM 87501-1902
Fax: 505 988-6530
202 634-1001 **Bureau of Mines (US Dept of the Interior)**
2401 E St NW MS-1040 .... Washington DC 20241-0001
202 647-7209 **Bureau of Near Eastern & South Asian Affairs (US Dept of State)**
2201 C St NW Rm 6242 .... Washington DC 20520-0001
Fax: 202 647-7720

202 307-3198 **Bureau of Prisons (US Dept of Justice)**
320 1st St NW Suite 640 Washington DC 20534-0001
Fax: 202 272-6775
913 682-8700 *US Penitentiary–Leavenworth* 1300 Metropolitan Leavenworth KS 66048-1254
Fax: 913 682-3617
717 523-1251 *US Penitentiary–Lewisburg* Lewisburg PA 17837-0000
805 735-2771 *US Penitentiary–Lompoc* 3901 Klein Blvd Lompoc CA 93436-2706
Fax: 805 736-6959
618 964-1441 *US Penitentiary–Marion* PO Box 2000 Marion IL 62959-0901
Fax: 618 564-1695
301 317-7000 *Mid-Atlantic Region*
10010 Junction Dr Junction Business Park Suite 100-N Annapolis JunctionMD20701-0000
Fax: 301 317-7004
816 891-7007 *North Central Region*
10920 NW Ambassador Dr Suite 200 Kansas City MO 64153-1270
Fax: 816 891-1349
215 597-6317 *Northeastern Region*
2nd & Chestnut Sts US Customs House 7th Fl Philadelphia PA 19106-0000
Fax: 215 597-6315
214 767-9700 *South Central Region* 4211 Cedar Springs Rd Suite 300 Dallas TX 75219-2690
Fax: 903 729-9724
404 624-5202 *Southeastern Region* 523 McDonough Blvd SE Atlanta GA 30315-4215
Fax: 404 624-5225
415 595-8160 *Western Region* 1301 Shoreway Rd 4th Fl Belmont CA 94002-4106
Fax: 415 593-0153
202 208-4157 **Bureau of Reclamation** 1849 C St NW Rm 7644 Washington DC 20240-0001
Fax: 202 343-3484
406 657-6214 *Great Plains Region* PO Box 36900 Billings MT 59107-6900
Fax: 406 657-6418
702 293-8000 *Lower Colorado Region* PO Box 427 Boulder City NV 89005-0427
Fax: 702 293-8416
916 978-5135 *Mid-Pacific Region* 2800 Cottage Way Rm 1105 Sacramento CA 95825-1897
Fax: 916 978-5284
208 334-1908 *Pacific Northwest Region* 550 W Fort St Boise ID 83724-0001
Fax: 208 334-1341
801 524-5566 *Upper Colorado Region* 125 S State St Rm 6224 Salt Lake City UT 84138-1102
Fax: 801 524-5499
301 763-4040 **Bureau of the Census** 8903 Presidential Pkwy Bldg 3 Suitland MD 20746-0000
Fax: 301 763-7322
404 347-2274 *Atlanta Region* 1365 Peachtree St NE Atlanta GA 30309-3147
Fax: 404 347-5224
617 565-7200 *Boston Region* 10 Causeway St Rm 553 Boston MA 02222-1047
Fax: 617 565-7108
704 371-6142 *Charlotte Region* 222 S Church St Suite 505 Charlotte NC 28202-3213
Fax: 704 371-6515
312 353-6251 *Chicago Region* 175 W Jackson Blvd Suite 557 Chicago IL 60604-2689
Fax: 312 353-3824
214 767-0621 *Dallas Region* 1100 Commerce St Rm 3C54 Dallas TX 75242-1003
Fax: 214 767-0359
301 763-4040 *Data Requests/Information* 8903 Presidential Pkwy Bldg 3 Suitland MD 20772-2656
Fax: 301 763-4794
303 969-6750 *Denver Region* 7655 W Mississippi Ave Denver CO 80226-4332
Fax: 303 969-6777
313 226-7742 *Detroit Region* 231 W Lafayette Blvd Rm 565 Detroit MI 48226-2769
Fax: 313 226-6068
913 236-3728 *Kansas City Region*
4th & State Sts 1 Gateway Ctr Suite 500 Kansas City KS 66101-0000
213 253-1200 *Los Angeles Region* 262 Los Angeles St 3rd Fl Los Angeles CA 90012-0000
212 264-3860 *New York Region*
Jacob Javitz Bldg 26 Federal Plaza Rm 37-130 New York NY 10278-0000
Fax: 212 264-3862
215 597-4920 *Philadelphia Region* 105 S 7th St 1st Fl Philadelphia PA 19106-3395
Fax: 215 597-7507
206 728-5500 *Seattle Region* 101 Stewart St Rm 500 Seattle WA 98101-1048
Fax: 206 442-5563
202 287-4113 **Bureau of the Public Debt (US Dept of the Treasury)**
1300 C St SW Washington DC 20239-0001
Fax: Call company operator
404 554-2324 **Burke County** 6th & Liberty St Waynesboro GA 30830-0000
Fax: 404 554-0350
704 438-5540 **Burke County** PO Box 796 Morganton NC 28655-0000
701 377-2718 **Burke County** PO Box 219 Bowbells ND 58721-0219
206 543-5590 **Burke Thomas Memorial Museum**
University of Washington DB-10 Seattle WA 98195-0001
Fax: 206 543-9285
Burkina Faso
202 332-5577 *Embassy* 2340 Massachusetts Ave NW Washington DC 20008-2801
212 288-7515 *Mission to the UN* 115 E 73rd St New York NY 10021-3575
701 222-6702 **Burleigh County** 514 E Thayer Ave Bismarck ND 58501-4413
409 567-4326 **Burleson County** 205 W Buck St Caldwell TX 77836-1798
802 862-9616 **Burlington College** 95 North Ave Burlington VT 05401-2998
609 265-5000 **Burlington County** 49 Rancocas Rd Mount Holly NJ 08060-1384
Fax: Unlisted
609 894-9311 **Burlington County College** Rt 530 Pemberton NJ 08068-0000
Fax: 609 894-0183 Admin
609 267-9660 **Burlington County Library** W Woodlane Rd Mount Holly NJ 08060-0000
Fax: 609 267-4091
512 756-5420 **Burnet County** 220 S Pierce St Burnet TX 78611-3136
715 349-2147 **Burnett County** 7410 County Rd K Box 115 Siren WI 54872-9043
202 224-2644 **Burns Conrad (Sen - R - Montana)** 183 Dirksen Bldg Washington DC 20510-0001
Fax: 202 224-8594
205 536-2882 **Burritt Museum & Park** 3101 Burritt Dr Huntsville AL 35801-1142
402 374-1955 **Burt County** 111 N 13th St Tekamah NE 68061-1043
202 225-2276 **Burton Dan (Rep - R - Indiana)** 120 Cannon Bldg Washington DC 20515-0001
Fax: 202 225-0016
Burundi: Republic of Burundi
202 342-2574 *Embassy* 2233 Wisconsin Ave NW Suite 212 Washington DC 20007-4104
Fax: 202 342-2578
212 687-1180 *Mission to the UN* 201 E 42nd St 28th Fl New York NY 10017-5704
Fax: Unlisted
617 495-2317 **Busch-Reisinger Museum** 32 Quincy St Harvard University Cambridge MA 02138-3804
Fax: 617 495-9936
205 834-6000 **Business Council of Alabama** 468 S Perry St Montgomery AL 36104-4236
Fax: 205 262-7371
404 223-2264 **Business Council of Georgia** 233 Peachtree St Suite 200 Atlanta GA 30303-0000
Fax: 404 223-2290
202 833-1880 **Business Industry PAC**
1747 Pennsylvania Ave NW Suite 250 Washington DC 20006-4604
Fax: 202 833-2338
202 225-4511 **Bustamante Albert G (Rep - D - Texas)**
1116 Longworth Bldg Washington DC 20515-0001
Fax: Unlisted
205 382-3612 **Butler County** PO Box 756 Greenville AL 36037-0756
319 267-2487 **Butler County** PO Box 325 Allison IA 50602-0307
316 321-1960 **Butler County** 200 W Central Ave El Dorado KS 67042-2101
Fax: 316 321-1011
502 526-5676 **Butler County** PO Box 448 Morgantown KY 42261-0448
314 785-8201 **Butler County** County Courthouse Poplar Bluff MO 63901-0000
Fax: 314 785-8404
402 367-3091 **Butler County** 451 5th St David City NE 68632-0000
513 887-3000 **Butler County** 130 High St Hamilton OH 45011-2756
Fax: 513 887-3568
412 285-4731 **Butler County** Main St Butler PA 16001-0000
Fax: Unlisted
316 321-5083 **Butler County Community College** 901 S Haverhill Rd El Dorado KS 67042-3280
412 287-8711 **Butler County Community College** PO Box 1203 Butler PA 16003-1203
Fax: 412 285-6047
216 743-1711 **Butler Institute of American Art** 524 Wick Ave Youngstown OH 44502-1213
Fax: 216 743-9567
317 283-8000 **Butler University** 4600 Sunset Ave Indianapolis IN 46208-3485
Fax: 317 283-9930 Library
317 283-9322 *College of Pharmacy* 4600 Sunset Ave Indianapolis IN 46208-3485
Fax: 317 283-9519
916 895-2361 **Butte College** 3536 Butte Campus Dr Oroville CA 95965-8399
Fax: 916 895-2345
916 538-7551 **Butte County** 25 County Center Dr Oroville CA 95965-3316
208 527-3021 **Butte County** PO Box 737 Arco ID 83213-0737
Fax: 208 527-3916
605 892-4485 **Butte County** 839 5th Ave Belle Fourche SD 57717-1799
916 538-7642 **Butte County Library** 1820 Mitchell Ave Oroville CA 95966-5387
Fax: 916 538-7235
404 775-8215 **Butts County** PO Box 320 Jackson GA 30233-0320
212 535-3420 **Byelorussian Soviet Socialist Republic Mission to the UN**
136 E 67th St New York NY 10021-6137
Fax: 212 734-4810
202 224-3954 **Byrd Robert C (Sen - D - West Virginia)** 311 Hart Bldg Washington DC 20510-0001
Fax: Unlisted
202 225-2721 **Byron Beverly B (Rep - D - Maryland)** 2430 Rayburn Bldg Washington DC 20515-0001
Fax: 202 225-6159

C

704 786-4137 **Cabarrus County** PO Box 70 Concord NC 28026-0070
304 526-8625 **Cabell County** 8th St & 4th Ave Huntington WV 25701-0000
304 523-9451 **Cabell County Public Library** 455 9th Street Plaza Huntington WV 25701-1482
Fax: 304 522-4721
408 479-6100 **Cabrillo College** 6500 Soquel Dr Aptos CA 95003-3198
215 971-8100 **Cabrini College** 610 King of Prussia Rd Radnor PA 19087-3698
Fax: 215 971-8539
801 752-3542 **Cache County** 170 N Main St Logan UT 84321-4541
405 247-3105 **Caddo County** PO Box 1427 Anadarko OK 73005-1427
318 226-6911 **Caddo Parish** 501 Texas St Shreveport LA 71101-5476
209 754-6310 **Calaveras County** 891 Mountain Ranch Rd San Andreas CA 95249-9713
318 437-3550 **Calcasieu Parish** PO Box 1030 Lake Charles LA 70602-1030
318 437-3485 **Calcasieu Parish Public Library System** 411 Pujo St Lake Charles LA 70601-4254
201 228-4424 **Caldwell College** 9 Ryerson Ave Caldwell NJ 07006-6195
Fax: 201 226-3851 Library
704 726-2200 **Caldwell Community College & Technical Institute**
1000 Hickory Blvd Hudson NC 28638-2397
502 365-6754 **Caldwell County** 100 E Market St Rm 3 Princeton KY 42445-1675
816 586-2571 **Caldwell County** PO Box 67 Kingston MO 64650-0067
704 758-0161 **Caldwell County** PO Box 1376 Lenoir NC 28645-0000
512 398-2428 **Caldwell County** Main St Lockhart TX 78644-0000
318 649-2681 **Caldwell Parish** Main St Columbia LA 71418-0000
802 748-6600 **Caledonia County** PO Box 404 Saint Johnsbury VT 05819-0404
205 236-3521 **Calhoun County** 1702 Noble St Suite 103 Anniston AL 36201-3889
Fax: 205 237-6956
501 798-2517 **Calhoun County** Main St Hampton AR 71744-0000
904 674-4545 **Calhoun County** 425 E Central Ave Blountstown FL 32424-2242
Fax: 904 674-5553
912 849-4835 **Calhoun County** Courthouse Sq Morgan GA 31766-0000
712 297-8122 **Calhoun County** PO Box 273 Rockwell City IA 50579-0273
618 576-2351 **Calhoun County** County Rd Hardin IL 62047-0000
616 781-0700 **Calhoun County** 315 W Green St Marshall MI 49068-1585
Fax: 616 781-3007
601 983-3117 **Calhoun County** PO Box 8 Pittsboro MS 38951-0008
803 874-3524 **Calhoun County** 302 S Railroad Ave Saint Matthews SC 29135-1452
512 553-4411 **Calhoun County** 211 S Ann St Port Lavaca TX 77979-4249
304 354-6725 **Calhoun County** Main St Grantsville WV 26147-0000
415 221-5100 **California Academy of Sciences** Golden Gate Pk San Francisco CA 94118-4599
Fax: 415 750-7346
714 689-5771 **California Baptist College** 8432 Magnolia Ave Riverside CA 92504-3297
Fax: 714 351-1808
916 444-6670 **California Chamber of Commerce** 1201 K St 12th Fl Sacramento CA 95814-0000
Fax: 916 444-6685
209 251-4215 **California Christian College** 4881 E University Ave Fresno CA 93703-3533
714 639-3961 **California Christian Institute** 1744 W Katella Suite 26 Orange CA 92667-3432
415 653-8118 **California College of Arts & Crafts** 5212 Broadway Oakland CA 94618-1426
Fax: 415 547-1623
415 896-5503 **California Democratic Party** 329 Bryant St Suite 3-C San Francisco CA 94107-1406
Fax: 415 896-1952
818 356-6811 **California Institute of Technology** 1201 E California Blvd Pasadena CA 91125-0001
Fax: 818 795-1547
818 356-6842 *Department of Computer Science*
1201 E California Blvd Jorgensen Bldg MS 256-80 Pasadena CA 91125-0001
Fax: 818 795-1547
818 356-4585 *Division of Physics Math & Astronomy*
Jorgensen Bldg MS 103-33 Pasadena CA 91125-0001
Fax: 818 795-1547
818 356-6444 *Graduate School of Cellular/Molecular Biology*
1201 E California Blvd MS 147-75 Pasadena CA 91125-0000
Fax: 818 449-0756
818 356-6110 *Graduate School of Chemistry*
1201 E California Blvd Jorgensen Bldg MS 164-30 Pasadena CA 91125-0001
Fax: 818 568-8824
818 356-6367 *Graduate School of Engineering* 1201 E California Blvd Pasadena CA 91125-0001
Fax: 818 577-9246
818 356-6346 *Graduate School of Geoscience* 1201 E California Blvd Pasadena CA 91125-0001
805 255-1050 **California Institute of the Arts** 24700 McBean Pkwy Valencia CA 91355-2397
Fax: 805 254-8352 Admin
213 381-3719 **California International University** 2706 Wilshire Blvd Los Angeles CA 90057-3202
Fax: 213 381-6990
805 492-2411 **California Lutheran University** 60 W Olsen Rd Thousand Oaks CA 91360-2787
Fax: 805 493-3513
707 648-4200 **California Maritime Academy** 200 Maritime Academy Dr Vallejo CA 94590-8181
Fax: 707 648-4204
213 925-4082 **California Missionary Baptist Institute** 9246 Rosser St Bellflower CA 90706-2932
213 744-2160 **California Museum of Science & Industry**
700 State Dr Exposition Pk Los Angeles CA 90037-1210
Fax: 213 744-2034

916 322-2881 **California Office of Tourism** 1121 L St Suite 103 .... Sacramento CA 95814-3926
Fax: 916 322-3402
619 695-3292 **California Pacific University** 10650 Treena St Rm 203 .... San Diego CA 92131-2436
Fax: Unlisted
805 756-1111 **California Polytech State University** 1 Grand Ave .... San Luis Obispo CA 93407-0001
Fax: 805 756-1279
805 756-2132 *School of Engineering* .... San Luis Obispo CA 93407-0001
Fax: 805 756-6503
213 739-8200 **California Real Estate PAC** 525 S Virgil Ave .... Los Angeles CA 90020-1431
Fax: 213 480-7724
818 841-5210 **California Republican Party** 1903 W Magnolia Blvd .... Burbank CA 91506-1797
Fax: 818 841-6668
California State Government
916 322-9900 *Information (Northern)* 601 Sequoia Pacific Blvd .... Sacramento CA 95814-0000
Fax: 916 323-3722
213 620-3030 *Information (Southern)* .... Sacramento CA 95814-0000
916 445-4383 *Air Resources Board* 1102 Q St .... Sacramento CA 95814-6511
Fax: 916 322-6003
916 322-8911 *Arts Council* 1901 Broadway Suite A .... Sacramento CA 95818-2492
Fax: 916 327-1867
916 445-9555 *Attorney General* 1515 K St Suite 511 .... Sacramento CA 95814-4030
Fax: 916 324-5205
916 445-3956 *Board of Equalization* 1020 N St .... Sacramento CA 95814-5691
Fax: 916 324-3984
916 322-3330 *California Integrated Waste Management Board*
1020 9th St Suite 300 .... Sacramento CA 95814-3515
Fax: 916 323-3725
707 448-6841 *California Medical Facility* 1600 California Dr .... Vacaville CA 95696-0000
Fax: 707 447-8098
805 543-2700 *California Men's Colony* Hwy 1 .... San Luis Obispo CA 93409-0001
Fax: 805 544-6254
916 985-2561 *California State Prison–Old Folsom* PO Box W .... Represa CA 95671-7100
415 454-1460 *California State Prison–San Quentin* 100 Main St .... San Quentin CA 94974-0000
Fax: 415 454-6228
916 445-3028 *Controller's Office* PO Box 942850 .... Sacramento CA 94250-0001
Fax: 916 445-6379
916 322-3241 *Department of Commerce* 1121 L St Suite 600 .... Sacramento CA 95814-3981
Fax: 916 322-3524
916 445-4465 *Department of Consumer Affairs* 1020 N St .... Sacramento CA 95814-5624
Fax: 916 443-1601
916 445-7688 *Department of Corrections* 1515 S St Rm 351-N .... Sacramento CA 95814-7243
Fax: 916 322-2877
916 322-2940 *Department of Economic Opportunity* 700 N Pent .... Sacramento CA 95814-6422
Fax: 916 327-3153
916 445-2700 *Department of Education* 721 Capitol Mall Rm 524 .... Sacramento CA 95814-4785
Fax: 916 327-1146
916 445-4141 *Department of Finance* State Capitol Rm 1145 .... Sacramento CA 95814-4998
Fax: 916 324-7311
916 445-7126 *Department of Food & Agriculture* 1220 N St .... Sacramento CA 95814-5621
Fax: 916 324-1681
916 445-1248 *Department of Health Services* 714 P St .... Sacramento CA 95814-6414
Fax: 916 327-4521
415 557-3356 *Department of Industrial Relations*
525 Golden Gate Ave .... San Francisco CA 94102-3284
Fax: 415 557-8964
213 736-2551 *Department of Insurance* 3450 Wilshire Blvd .... Los Angeles CA 90010-2208
Fax: 213 736-4891
916 739-3600 *Department of Real Estate* PO Box 187000 .... Sacramento CA 95818-7000
Fax: 916 739-3595
916 445-2201 *Department of Transportation* 1120 N St .... Sacramento CA 95814-5620
Fax: 916 324-9673
916 445-9248 *Department of Water Resources* 1416 9th St .... Sacramento CA 95814-5511
Fax: 916 445-8122
415 737-2618 *Division of Industrial Accidents*
395 Oyster Point Blvd 5th Fl Wing B .... South San Francisco CA 94080-0000
Fax: 415 737-2977
916 445-1825 *Division of Mines & Geology* 1416 9th St Rm 1341 .... Sacramento CA 95814-5511
Fax: 916 445-5718
916 324-3331 *Energy Commission* 1516 9th St .... Sacramento CA 95814-5504
Fax: 916 327-4620
916 322-4203 *Environmental Affairs Agency* 1102 Q St .... Sacramento CA 95814-6511
Fax: 916 445-6401
916 445-2841 *Governor* State Capitol 1st Fl .... Sacramento CA 95814-4991
Fax: 916 445-4633
916 445-1719 *Health Data & Statistics Branch* 410 N St .... Sacramento CA 95814-4381
Fax: 916 327-8417
916 445-8994 *Lieutenant Governor* State Capitol Rm 1114 .... Sacramento CA 95814-4905
Fax: 916 323-4998
916 322-3640 *Oaccupational Safety & Health Standards Board*
1006 4th St 3rd Fl .... Sacramento CA 95814-3314
Fax: 916 445-5939
916 324-9100 *Office of Criminal Justice Planning* 1130 K St Suite 300 .. Sacramento CA 95814-3927
Fax: 916 324-9167
916 427-4201 *Office of Emergency Services* 2800 Meadowview Rd ...... Sacramento CA 95832-1441
Fax: 916 427-4215
916 322-8515 *Office of Planning & Research* 1400 10th St Rm 108 ...... Sacramento CA 95814-5502
Fax: 916 323-3018
916 445-6942 *Office of Procurement* 1823 14th St .... Sacramento CA 95814-7131
Fax: 916 323-4609
916 322-5639 *Office of Tourism* 1121 L St Suite 103 .... Sacramento CA 95814-0000
Fax: 916 322-3402
916 445-6200 *Parole & Community Services Div* 1615 S St Rm 212N ... Sacramento CA 95814-0000
Fax: 916 322-6985
916 445-1000 *Postsecondary Education Commission*
1020 12th St 3rd Fl .... Sacramento CA 95814-3985
Fax: 916 327-4417
415 557-1600 *Public Defender* 1390 Market St Suite 425 .... San Francisco CA 94102-5470
Fax: 415 557-0958
415 557-1487 *Public Utilities Commission* 505 Van Ness Ave .... San Francisco CA 94102-3214
Fax: 415 557-1923
916 445-5656 *Resources Agency* 1416 9th St Rm 1311 .... Sacramento CA 95814-5569
Fax: 916 323-1972
916 445-6371 *Secretary of State* 1230 J St .... Sacramento CA 95814-2974
Fax: 916 324-4573
916 445-4293 *State Archives* 1020 'O' St Rm 130 .... Sacramento CA 95814-5777
916 445-1150 *State Police* 815 S St .... Sacramento CA 95814-7040
Fax: 916 444-6433
415 557-0587 *Supreme Court* 455 Golden Gate Ave .... San Francisco CA 94102-3674
Fax: 415 557-2709
916 445-6562 *Treasurer* 915 Capitol Mall Rm 110 .... Sacramento CA 95814-4810
Fax: 916 327-4215
916 445-2585 **California State Library** 914 Capitol Mall .... Sacramento CA 95814-4877
Fax: 916 324-8120
714 869-7659 **California State Polytechnic University** 3801 W Temple Ave .... Pomona CA 91768-2557
Fax: 714 869-2292
714 869-2688 *Department Urban & Regional Planning* 3801 W Temple Ave Pomona CA 91768-2557

213 590-5506 **California State University (System)** 400 Golden Shore St .. Long Beach CA 90802-4275
Fax: 213 590-5749
California State University
805 664-2011 *Bakersfield Campus* 9001 Stockdale Hwy .... Bakersfield CA 93311-1022
Fax: 805 664-3194
916 898-6116 *Chico Campus* .... Chico CA 95929-0001
Fax: Unlisted
213 516-3300 *Dominguez Hills Campus* 1000 E Victoria St .... Carson CA 90747-0001
Fax: 213 516-3449
209 278-4240 *Fresno Campus* 5241 N Maple .... Fresno CA 93740-0001
Fax: 209 278-4660
714 773-2011 *Fullerton Campus* 800 N State College Blvd .... Fullerton CA 92631-3547
Fax: 714 773-3990
415 881-3000 *Hayward Campus* .... Hayward CA 94542-0000
Fax: 415 881-7484
213 985-4111 *Long Beach Campus* 1250 Bellflower Blvd .... Long Beach CA 90840-0001
Fax: 213 985-8887
213 343-3000 *Los Angeles Campus* 5151 State University Dr .... Los Angeles CA 90032-8000
Fax: 213 343-2670
818 885-1200 *Northridge Campus* 18111 Nordhoff St .... Northridge CA 91330-0001
Fax: 818 885-4545
916 278-6011 *Sacramento Campus* 6000 J St .... Sacramento CA 95819-6000
Fax: 916 278-6664
714 880-5000 *San Bernardino Campus* 5500 University Pkwy .... San Bernardino CA 92407-2393
Fax: 714 880-5902 Computer Ctr
209 667-3122 *Stanislaus Campus* 801 W Monte Vista Ave .... Turlock CA 95380-0256
Fax: 209 667-3333
California State University Fresno
209 278-2087 *Department of Journalism* Cedar & Shaw Aves .... Fresno CA 93740-0001
209 278-2041 *Department of Nursing* MS-25 .... Fresno CA 93740-0001
714 773-3517 **California State University Fullerton Department of Communications**
800 N State College Blvd .... Fullerton CA 92631-3547
213 985-5761 **California State University Long Beach Art Museum**
1250 Bellflower Blvd CSULB .... Long Beach CA 90840-0001
Fax: 213 985-7602
213 343-4730 **California State University Los Angeles Department of Nursing**
5151 State University Dr .... Los Angeles CA 90032-8000
Fax: 213 343-2670
818 885-3135 **California State University Northridge Department of Journalism**
18111 Nordhoff St .... Northridge CA 91330-0001
Fax: 818 885-4545 Admin
412 938-4000 **California University of Pennsylvania** 3rd St .... California PA 15419-0000
Fax: 412 938-4138
619 239-0391 **California Western School of Law** 350 Cedar St .... San Diego CA 92101-3196
Fax: 619 696-9999
915 854-1217 **Callahan County** 400 Market St .... Baird TX 79504-5305
202 225-4931 **Callahan Sonny (Rep - R - Alabama)**
1330 Longworth Bldg .... Washington DC 20515-0001
Fax: 202 225-0562
314 642-0730 **Callaway County** 5 E 5th St .... Fulton MO 65251-1700
502 753-2920 **Calloway County** 101 S 5th St .... Murray KY 42071-2583
219 473-7770 **Calumet College of Saint Joseph** 2400 New York Ave .... Whiting IN 46394-2195
414 849-2361 **Calumet County** 206 Court St .... Chilton WI 53014-1198
816 322-0110 **Calvary Bible College** 15800 Calvary Rd .... Kansas City MO 64147-1341
301 535-1600 **Calvert County** 175 Main St .... Prince Frederick MD 20678-9302
301 326-2042 **Calvert Marine Museum** 14130 Solomons Island Rd .... Solomons MD 20688-0000
616 957-6000 **Calvin College** 3201 Burton St SE .... Grand Rapids MI 49546-4388
Fax: 616 957-8551
208 764-2242 **Camas County** PO Box 430 .... Fairfield ID 83327-0430
Fax: 208 764-2349
212 888-6646 **Cambodia Mission to the UN** 747 3rd Ave 8th Fl .... New York NY 10017-2803
814 472-5440 **Cambria County** 200 S Center St .... Ebensburg PA 15931-1936
Fax: 814 472-4661
814 536-5131 **Cambria County Library System** 248 Main St .... Johnstown PA 15901-1677
Fax: 814 536-6905
617 498-9080 **Cambridge Public Library** 449 Broadway .... Cambridge MA 02138-4191
Fax: 617 868-2938
912 576-5601 **Camden County** 4th St .... Woodbine GA 31569-0000
Fax: 912 576-5647
314 346-4440 **Camden County** 1 Court Cir .... Camdenton MO 65020-0000
Fax: 314 346-5181
919 338-0066 **Camden County** Hwy 343 .... Camden NC 27921-0000
609 757-8457 **Camden County** 5th & Mickle Blvd .... Camden NJ 08103-4000
Fax: 609 541-6198
609 227-7200 **Camden County College** Little Gloucester Rd .... Blackwood NJ 08012-3398
Fax: 609 227-3629
609 772-1636 **Camden County Free Library** Laurel Rd Echelon Urban Ctr ..... Voorhees NJ 08043-2378
Fax: Unlisted
814 486-2315 **Cameron County** 20 E 5th St .... Emporium PA 15834-1469
512 544-0815 **Cameron County** 964 E Harrison St .... Brownsville TX 78520-7123
318 775-5316 **Cameron Parish** PO Box 549 .... Cameron LA 70631-0549
405 581-2255 **Cameron University** 2800 W Gore Blvd .... Lawton OK 73505-6377
Fax: Unlisted
Cameroon: Republic of Cameroon
202 265-8790 *Embassy* 2349 Massachusetts Ave NW .... Washington DC 20008-2803
Fax: 202 387-3826
212 794-2295 *Mission to the UN* 22 E 73rd St .... New York NY 10021-4138
903 856-2731 **Camp County** 126 Church St .... Pittsburg TX 75686-0000
202 225-3561 **Camp Dave (Rep - D - Michigan)** 511 Cannon Bldg .... Washington DC 20515-0001
Fax: 202 225-9679
919 451-1113 **Camp Lejeune Marine Corps Base** .... Camp Lejeune NC 28542-0000
Fax: 919 451-2415
619 725-4111 **Camp Pendleton Marine Corps Base** .... Camp Pendleton CA 92055-9998
Fax: 619 725-5147 PR
808 477-5052 **Camp Smith HM Marine Corps Base** .... Oahu HI 96861-0001
202 543-5016 **Campaign America** 511 Capitol Ct NE Suite 100 .... Washington DC 20002-4937
Fax: 202 543-4104
202 225-4761 **Campbell Ben Nighthorse (Rep - D - Colorado)**
1530 Longworth Bldg .... Washington DC 20515-0001
Fax: 202 225-0228
606 292-3838 **Campbell County** PO Box 340 .... Newport KY 41071-0000
Fax: 606 292-3888
605 955-3366 **Campbell County** PO Box 37 .... Mound City SD 57646-0000
615 562-4985 **Campbell County** PO Box 13 .... Jacksboro TN 37757-0013
804 332-5161 **Campbell County** PO Box 7 .... Rustburg VA 24588-0007
Fax: 804 332-7872
307 682-7285 **Campbell County** 500 S Gillette Ave Suite 220 .... Gillette WY 82716-4208
Fax: 307 686-1947 Legal
202 225-5411 **Campbell Tom (Rep - R - California)** 313 Cannon Bldg ...... Washington DC 20515-0001
Fax: 202 225-5944
919 893-4111 **Campbell University** PO Box 66 .... Buies Creek NC 27506-0066
919 893-2773 *School of Law* Kivett Hall .... Buies Creek NC 27506-0000
Fax: 919 893-9850
919 893-4111 *School of Pharmacy* PO Box 1090 .... Buies Creek NC 27506-1090
Fax: 919 893-9850

502 465-8158 **Campbellsville College** 200 W College St ... Campbellsville KY 42718-2799
Fax: Ext 6333
Canada
202 682-1740 *Embassy* 501 Pennsylvania Ave NW ... Washington DC 20001-2111
Fax: 202 682-7726
212 751-5600 *Mission to the UN* 866 UN Plaza Suite 250 ... New York NY 10017-0000
Fax: 212 486-1295
312 427-1031 *Chicago Consulate General* 310 S Michigan Ave Suite 1200 .. Chicago IL 60604-4295
Fax: 312 922-0637
213 687-7432 *Los Angeles Consulate General* 300 S Grand Ave 10th Fl . Los Angeles CA 90071-3100
Fax: 213 620-8827
212 768-2400 *New York Consulate General* 1251 Ave of the Americas ... New York NY 10020-1194
Fax: 212 768-2440
415 495-6021 *San Francisco Consulate General*
50 Fremont St Suite 2100 ... San Francisco CA 94105-2277
Fax: 415 541-7708
206 443-1777 *Seattle Consulate General*
6th & Stewart Sts Plaza 600 Rm 412 ... Seattle WA 98101-0000
Fax: 206 443-1782
415 364-1212 **Canada College** 4200 Farm Hill Blvd ... Redwood City CA 94061-1099
405 262-1070 **Canadian County** 301 N Choctaw Ave ... El Reno OK 73036-2407
212 221-3300 **Cancer Care Inc** 1180 Ave of the Americas ... New York NY 10036-8401
Fax: 212 719-0263
912 685-2835 **Candler County** Courthouse Sq ... Metter GA 30439-0000
Fax: 912 685-2296
716 883-7000 **Canisius College** 2001 Main St ... Buffalo NY 14208-1098
Fax: 716 888-2525
505 784-3311 **Cannon Air Force Base** ... Clovis NM 88103-0000
Fax: 505 681-4684
615 563-4278 **Cannon County** County Courthouse ... Woodbury TN 37190-0000
208 454-7300 **Canyon County** 1115 Albany St ... Caldwell ID 83605-3542
Fax: 208 454-7525
508 968-5300 **Cape Cod Coast Guard Air Station**
Otis Air National Guard Base ... Buzzards Bay MA 02542-0000
Fax: 508 968-5321
508 362-2131 **Cape Cod Community College** 2240 Rt 132 ... West Barnstable MA 02668-1599
Fax: 508 362-8741 Admin
919 343-0481 **Cape Fear Community College** 411 N Front St ... Wilmington NC 28401-3993
Fax: Call company operator
314 243-3547 **Cape Girardeau County** 1 Barton Sq ... Jackson MO 63755-1866
Fax: 314 243-4474
609 884-3491 **Cape May Coast Guard Air Station** ... Cape May NJ 08204-0000
Fax: 609 884-6705
609 465-7111 **Cape May County** 7 N Main St ... Cape May Court House NJ 08210-2117
Fax: 609 463-8625
Cape Verde: Republic of Cape Verde
202 965-6820 *Embassy* 3415 Massachusetts Ave NW ... Washington DC 20007-1446
Fax: 202 965-1207
212 472-0333 *Mission to the UN* 27 E 69th St ... New York NY 10021-4917
Fax: 212 794-1398
614 236-6011 **Capital University** 2199 E Main St ... Columbus OH 43209-2394
Fax: 614 236-6490
614 445-8836 *Law School* 665 S High St ... Columbus OH 43215-5683
Fax: 614 445-7125
301 953-0060 **Capitol College** 11301 Springfield Rd ... Laurel MD 20708-9758
Fax: 301 953-3876 Mail Rm
202 452-1270 **Capitol Reservations**
1730 Rhode Island Ave NW Suite 302 ... Washington DC 20036-3101
Fax: 202 452-8217
406 446-1595 **Carbon County** PO Box 887 ... Red Lodge MT 59068-0887
Fax: 406 446-2640
717 325-3611 **Carbon County** Broadway Lock Box 129 ... Jim Thorpe PA 18229-0129
Fax: 717 325-3622
801 637-4700 **Carbon County** 120 E Main St ... Price UT 84501-3057
Fax: 801 637-5767
307 328-2668 **Carbon County** PO Box 6 ... Rawlins WY 82301-0006
Fax: 307 328-2669
202 225-4016 **Cardin Benjamin L (Rep - D - Maryland)**
117 Cannon Bldg ... Washington DC 20515-0001
Fax: 202 225-9219
414 352-5400 **Cardinal Stritch College** 6801 N Yates Rd ... Milwaukee WI 53217-3985
Fax: 414 351-7516
212 686-3110 **CARE** 660 1st Ave ... New York NY 10016-3295
Fax: 212 696-4005
202 466-7464 **Caribbean Central American Action**
1211 Connecticut Ave NW Suite 510 ... Washington DC 20036-2701
Fax: 202 822-0075
708 699-7570 **Caribbean Information Office** 3166 S River Rd Suite 33 ... Des Plaines IL 60018-4204
Fax: 708 699-7583
208 547-4324 **Caribou County** PO Box 775 ... Soda Springs ID 83276-0775
Fax: 208 547-4759
309 344-2518 **Carl Sandburg College** 2232 S Lake Storey Rd ... Galesburg IL 61401-9576
Fax: 309 344-3526 Library
507 663-4000 **Carleton College** 1 N College St ... Northfield MN 55057-4015
Fax: 507 663-4204
502 628-5451 **Carlisle County** Court St ... Bardwell KY 42023-0000
412 578-6000 **Carlow College** 3333 5th Ave ... Pittsburgh PA 15213-3165
Fax: 412 578-6019
218 384-4281 **Carlton County** 30 Maple St ... Carlton MN 55718-0000
Fax: Unlisted
412 622-3100 **Carnegie Library of Pittsburgh** 4400 Forbes Ave ... Pittsburgh PA 15213-4080
Fax: 412 621-1267
412 268-2000 **Carnegie Mellon University** 5000 Forbes Ave ... Pittsburgh PA 15213-3890
Fax: 412 268-5249 Computer Ctr
412 268-2477 *Carnegie Institute of Technology* 101 Scaife Hall ... Pittsburgh PA 15261-2001
Fax: 412 268-6421
412 268-2355 *Department of Architecture* Schenley Pk CFA 201 ... Pittsburgh PA 15213-0000
Fax: 412 268-7819
412 268-2734 *Department of Physics* Wean Hall Rm 7325 ... Pittsburgh PA 15213-0000
Fax: 412 681-0688
412 268-3125 *Graduate School of Chemistry*
4400 5th Ave Mellon Institute ... Pittsburgh PA 15213-0000
Fax: 412 268-7129
412 268-2265 *Graduate School of Industrial Administration*
Frew & Tech Sts ... Pittsburgh PA 15213-0000
Fax: 412 268-6837
412 268-2592 *School of Computer Science* Wean Hall ... Pittsburgh PA 15213-0000
Fax: 412 268-5016
412 268-2159 *School of Urban & PR* Hamburg Hall Rm 1104 ... Pittsburgh PA 15213-0000
Fax: 412 268-7036
412 622-3200 **Carnegie Museum of Art** 4400 Forbes Ave ... Pittsburgh PA 15213-4080
Fax: 412 622-3112
412 622-3243 **Carnegie Museum of Natural History** 4400 Forbes Ave ... Pittsburgh PA 15213-4080
Fax: 412 622-8837
301 479-0660 **Caroline County** PO Box 207 ... Denton MD 21629-0207
804 633-5800 **Caroline County** PO Box 309 ... Bowling Green VA 22427-0309

202 546-6206 **Carpenter's Legislative Improvement Committee**
101 Constitution Ave NW ... Washington DC 20001-2133
Fax: 202 543-5724
202 225-4165 **Carper Thomas R (Rep - D - Delaware)** 131 Cannon Bldg ... Washington DC 20515-0001
Fax: 202 225-1912
202 225-4872 **Carr Bob (Rep - D - Michigan)** 2439 Rayburn Bldg ... Washington DC 20515-0001
Fax: 202 225-1260
406 442-3450 **Carroll College** 1400 N Benton Ave ... Helena MT 59625-0002
Fax: 406 442-9291 Admin
414 547-1211 **Carroll College** 100 N East Ave ... Waukesha WI 53186-5593
Fax: 414 524-7139
501 423-2022 **Carroll County** 210 W Church Ave ... Berryville AR 72616-4233
404 834-0064 **Carroll County** 311 Newnan St ... Carrollton GA 30117-3124
712 792-4327 **Carroll County** PO Box 867 ... Carroll IA 51401-0867
815 244-9171 **Carroll County** Rt 78 & Rapp Rd ... Mount Carroll IL 61053-0000
Fax: 815 244-2784
317 564-4485 **Carroll County** County Courthouse ... Delphi IN 46923-0000
502 732-2446 **Carroll County** Court St County Courthouse ... Carrollton KY 41008-0000
301 876-2085 **Carroll County** 225 N Center St ... Westminster MD 21157-5194
Fax: 301 848-0003
816 542-0615 **Carroll County** County Courthouse ... Carrollton MO 64633-0000
601 237-9283 **Carroll County** PO Box 291 ... Carrollton MS 38917-0291
603 539-7751 **Carroll County** Rt 171 ... Ossipee NH 03864-0000
216 627-2250 **Carroll County** 119 Public Sq ... Carrollton OH 44615-1448
901 986-8237 **Carroll County** PO Box 110 ... Huntingdon TN 38344-0000
703 728-3331 **Carroll County** PO Box 515 ... Hillsville VA 24343-0515
Fax: 703 728-4938
702 887-2100 **Carson City (Independent City)** 2621 Northgate Ln ... Carson City NV 89706-1619
806 537-3873 **Carson County** 501 Main St ... Panhandle TX 79068-0000
Fax: 806 537-5395
615 475-9061 **Carson-Newman College** S Russell Ave ... Jefferson City TN 37760-0000
Fax: 615 475-7956
817 782-5000 **Carswell Air Force Base** ... Fort Worth TX 76127-0000
Fax: 817 782-7457
817 738-1933 **Carter Amon Museum** 3501 Camp Bowie Blvd ... Fort Worth TX 76107-2695
Fax: Unlisted
606 474-5188 **Carter County** Courthouse Rm 232 ... Grayson KY 41143-0000
314 323-4527 **Carter County** PO Box 517 ... Van Buren MO 63965-0517
406 775-8749 **Carter County** Courthouse Park St ... Ekalaka MT 59324-0000
405 223-8162 **Carter County** 1st & B St SW ... Ardmore OK 73401-0000
615 542-1814 **Carter County** Main St County Courthouse ... Elizabethton TN 37643-0000
919 728-8500 **Carteret County** Courthouse Sq ... Beaufort NC 28516-0000
Fax: 919 728-2092
414 551-8500 **Carthage College** 2001 Alford Dr ... Kenosha WI 53140-1994
Fax: 414 551-7920
404 527-4520 **Carver Bible Institute & College** 437 Nelson St SW ... Atlanta GA 30313-0000
612 448-3435 **Carver County** 600 E 4th St ... Chaska MN 55318-2183
406 761-6700 **Cascade County** 415 2nd Ave N ... Great Falls MT 59401-2536
216 368-2000 **Case Western Reserve University** 10900 Euclid Ave ... Cleveland OH 44106-1724
Fax: 216 368-4335
216 368-2540 *Francis Payne Bolton School of Nursing* 2121 Abington Rd . Cleveland OH 44106-2333
Fax: 216 368-3813
216 368-3344 *Graduate School of Biochemistry* 2119 Abington Rd ... Cleveland OH 44106-2333
Fax: 216 368-4544
216 368-3200 *School of Dentistry* 2123 Abington Rd ... Cleveland OH 44106-2333
Fax: 216 368-3204
216 368-3280 *School of Law* 11075 E Blvd ... Cleveland OH 44106-0000
Fax: 216 368-6144
216 368-2820 *School of Medicine* 2107 Adelbert Rd Rm T-106 ... Cleveland OH 44106-2624
Fax: Unlisted
606 787-6471 **Casey County** PO Box 310 ... Liberty KY 42539-0310
307 268-2110 **Casper College** 125 College Dr ... Casper WY 82601-4699
Fax: 307 268-2682
712 243-2105 **Cass County** 7th St Courthouse ... Atlantic IA 50022-0000
217 452-7217 **Cass County** County Courthouse ... Virginia IL 62691-0000
219 753-7700 **Cass County** 200 Court Pk ... Logansport IN 46947-3114
616 445-8621 **Cass County** 120 N Broadway St ... Cassopolis MI 49031-1302
Fax: 616 445-8978
218 547-3300 **Cass County** Hwy 371 ... Walker MN 56484-0000
816 884-5100 **Cass County** County Courthouse ... Harrisonville MO 64701-0000
701 241-5660 **Cass County** 207 9th St S ... Fargo ND 58103-1833
402 296-2164 **Cass County** 4th & Main Sts ... Plattsmouth NE 68048-0000
903 756-5071 **Cass County** PO Box 468 ... Linden TX 75563-0468
208 678-7302 **Cassia County** County Courthouse ... Burley ID 83318-0000
Fax: 208 678-9747
209 726-2011 **Castle Air Force Base** ... Merced CA 95342-0001
Fax: 209 726-2549
802 468-5611 **Castleton State College** Seminary St ... Castleton VT 05735-0000
Fax: 802 468-2421 Library
806 647-3338 **Castro County** 100 E Bedford St ... Dimmitt TX 79027-2643
919 694-4193 **Caswell County** E Church St & North Ave ... Yanceyville NC 27379-0000
318 744-5497 **Catahoula Parish** PO Box 198 ... Harrisonburg LA 71340-0198
202 707-6100 **Cataloging Distribution Service (Library of Congress)**
101 Independence Ave SE JA 3014W ... Washington DC 20541-0000
704 637-4111 **Catawba College** 2300 W Innes St ... Salisbury NC 28144-2488
Fax: 704 637-4304
704 464-7880 **Catawba County** PO Box 389 ... Newton NC 28658-0389
Fax: 704 465-8392
704 464-2421 **Catawba County Library** 115 W 'C' St ... Newton NC 28658-3397
704 327-9124 **Catawba Valley Community College** RR 3 Box 283 ... Hickory NC 28602-9803
Fax: 704 327-7000 Ext 301
619 745-0505 **Cathedral Bible College** 927 Idaho Ave ... Escondido CA 92025-6399
Fax: Unlisted
202 319-5000 **Catholic University of America** 620 Michigan Ave NE ... Washington DC 20064-0001
Fax: Unlisted
202 319-5144 *Columbus School of Law* 620 Michigan Ave NE ... Washington DC 20064-0001
Fax: 202 319-4498
202 319-5400 *School of Nursing* 620 Michigan Ave NE Gowan Hall ... Washington DC 20064-0001
Fax: 202 319-6485
301 455-6050 **Catonsville Community College** 800 S Rolling Rd ... Catonsville MD 21228-5384
Fax: 301 455-4411
404 935-2500 **Catoosa County** 206 E Nashville St ... Ringgold GA 30736-1799
505 533-6423 **Catron County** PO Box 507 ... Reserve NM 87830-0507
716 938-9111 **Cattaraugus County** 303 Court St ... Little Valley NY 14755-1028
701 256-2124 **Cavalier County** 901 3rd St ... Langdon ND 58249-2457
315 253-1011 **Cayuga County** 160 Genesee St ... Auburn NY 13021-3421
Fax: 315 253-1586
315 255-1743 **Cayuga County Community College** 197 Franklin St ... Auburn NY 13021-3099
Fax: 315 255-2050
315 655-8283 **Cazenovia College** ... Cazenovia NY 13035-1084
Fax: 315 655-2190
301 287-6060 **Cecil Community College** 1000 N East Rd ... North East MD 21901-1999
Fax: 301 287-1026
301 398-0200 **Cecil County** E Main St ... Elkton MD 21921-0000
Fax: 301 398-2819
904 778-6052 **Cecil Field Naval Air Station** ... Cecil Field FL 32215-9998

319 886-2101 **Cedar County** 400 Cedar St ... Tipton IA 52772-1752
417 276-3514 **Cedar County** PO Box 126 ... Stockton MO 65785-0126
402 254-7411 **Cedar County** 101 S Broadway Ave ... Hartington NE 68739-0000
215 437-4471 **Cedar Crest College** 100 College Dr ... Allentown PA 18104-6196
Fax: 215 437-5955
319 366-7503 **Cedar Rapids Museum of Art** 410 3rd Ave SE ... Cedar Rapids IA 52401-1606
Fax: 319 366-4111
319 398-5123 **Cedar Rapids Public Library** 500 1st St SE ... Cedar Rapids IA 52401-2002
513 766-2211 **Cedarville College** 251 S Main St ... Cedarville OH 45314-9725
Fax: 513 766-2760
318 869-5011 **Centenary College** 2911 Centenary Blvd ... Shreveport LA 71104-3396
Fax: 318 869-5026
908 852-1400 **Centenary College** 400 Jefferson St ... Hackettstown NJ 07840-2100
Fax: Unlisted
202 328-7700 **Center for Auto Safety** 2001 S St NW Suite 410 ... Washington DC 20009-1160
Fax: 202 387-0140
313 872-3118 **Center for Creative Studies** 201 E Kirby St ... Detroit MI 48202-4034
Fax: 313 872-8377
202 332-9110 **Center for Science in the Public Interest**
1501 16th St NW ... Washington DC 20036-1499
Fax: 202 265-4954
202 463-5482 **Central & Eastern Europe Trade & Technical Assistance Center**
1615 H St NW 6th Fl ... Washington DC 20062-0001
Fax: 202 463-3114
Central African Republic
202 483-7800 *Embassy* 1618 22nd St NW ... Washington DC 20008-1920
212 689-6195 *Mission to the UN* 386 Park Ave S Suite 1614 ... New York NY 10016-8851
205 234-6346 **Central Alabama Community College** PO Box 699 ... Alexander City AL 35010-0699
Fax: Ext 201
205 378-5576 **Central Alabama Community College** PO Box 389 ... Childersburg AL 35044-0389
Fax: Call company operator
602 723-4141 **Central Arizona College** 8470 N Overfield Rd ... Coolidge AZ 85228-9030
Fax: 602 426-4284
501 370-5954 **Central Arkansas Library System** 700 Louisiana St ... Little Rock AR 72201-4698
Fax: 501 375-7451
501 329-6872 **Central Baptist College** CBC Stn ... Conway AR 72032-6470
417 833-2551 **Central Bible College** 3000 N Grant Ave ... Springfield MO 65803-1096
Fax: 417 833-5141
919 775-5401 **Central Carolina Community College** 1105 Kelly Dr ... Sanford NC 27330-9000
Fax: 919 775-1221
816 263-3900 **Central Christian College of the Bible** 911 E Urbandale Dr ... Moberly MO 65270-1997
316 241-0723 **Central College** 1200 S Main St ... McPherson KS 67460-5799
402 463-9811 **Central Community College** E Hwy 6 ... Hastings NE 68901-0000
Fax: 402 461-2454
402 564-7132 *Platte Campus* 4500 63rd St ... Columbus NE 68601-8031
Fax: Ext 201
203 827-7000 **Central Connecticut State University** 1615 Stanley St ... New Britain CT 06053-2490
Fax: 203 827-7200
904 237-2111 **Central Florida Community College** 3001 SW College Rd ... Ocala FL 32674-4478
Fax: 904 237-0510 Purchasing
904 629-8551 **Central Florida Regional Library** 15 SE Osceola Ave ... Ocala FL 32671-2150
202 482-1100 **Central Intelligence Agency** ... Washington DC 20505-0001
515 277-0220 **Central Iowa Regional Library System** 4715 Grand Ave ... Des Moines IA 50312-2001
Fax: 515 277-4085
207 795-2840 **Central Maine Medical Center School of Nursing**
300 Main St ... Lewiston ME 04240-0305
207 784-2385 **Central Maine Vocational College** 1250 Turner St ... Auburn ME 04210-6436
Fax: Ext 271
508 799-1654 **Central Massachusetts Regional Library System** Salem Sq .. Worcester MA 01608-2015
Fax: 508 799-1728
816 248-3391 **Central Methodist College** 411 Central Methodist Sq ... Fayette MO 65248-1129
Fax: 816 248-2287
517 774-4000 **Central Michigan University** ... Mount Pleasant MI 48859-0001
Fax: 517 774-3537
816 429-4111 **Central Missouri State University** ... Warrensburg MO 64093-5000
Fax: 816 747-7813 Library
816 429-4840 *Department of Communication* Martin Bldg ... Warrensburg MO 64093-0000
Fax: 816 747-1651
919 227-2096 **Central North Carolina Regional Library** 342 S Spring St ... Burlington NC 27215-5863
Fax: 919 222-8835
614 366-1351 **Central Ohio Technical College** University Dr ... Newark OH 43055-0000
Fax: 614 366-5047
503 382-6112 **Central Oregon Community College** 2600 NW College Way ... Bend OR 97701-5998
Fax: 503 385-5978
717 732-0702 **Central Pennsylvania Business School** College Hill Rd ... Summerdale PA 17093-9999
704 342-6633 **Central Piedmont Community College** PO Box 35009 ... Charlotte NC 28235-6099
Fax: 704 342-6214
202 377-3271 **Central Reference & Records Inspection Facility (US Dept of Commerce)**
14th St & Constitution Ave NW Rm 6622 ... Washington DC 20230-0001
Fax: 202 377-5270
513 376-6011 **Central State University** 1400 Rush Row Rd ... Wilberforce OH 45384-9999
Fax: 513 376-6530
405 341-2980 **Central State University** 100 N University Dr ... Edmond OK 73034-5209
Fax: 405 341-4964
817 526-1211 **Central Texas College** American Educational Complex Hwy 190 .. Killeen TX 76540-0000
Fax: 817 526-0817
515 628-4151 **Central University of Iowa** 812 University St ... Pella IA 50219-1902
Fax: 515 628-5316
804 386-4500 **Central Virginia Commmunity College** 3506 Wards Rd ... Lynchburg VA 24502-2498
Fax: 804 386-4681
509 963-1111 **Central Washington University** ... Ellensburg WA 98926-0000
Fax: 509 963-1241
803 639-2453 **Central Wesleyan College** 1 Wesleyan Dr ... Central SC 29630-0000
Fax: 803 639-0826
307 856-9291 **Central Wyoming College** 2660 Peck St ... Riverton WY 82501-2273
Fax: Ext 191
606 236-5211 **Centre College of Kentucky** 600 W Walnut St ... Danville KY 40422-1394
Fax: 606 236-9610
814 355-6700 **Centre County** County Courthouse ... Bellefonte PA 16823-3005
Fax: 814 355-6707
213 860-2451 **Cerritos Community College** 11110 Alondra Blvd ... Norwalk CA 90650-6296
Fax: 213 860-9680
619 375-5001 **Cerro Coso Community College** 3000 College Heights Blvd ... Ridgecrest CA 93555-9571
Fax: Ext 252
515 421-3074 **Cerro Gordo County** 220 N Washington Ave ... Mason City IA 50401-3254
415 786-6600 **Chabot College** 25555 Hesperian Blvd ... Hayward CA 94545-2447
Fax: Unlisted
Chad: Republic of Chad
202 462-4009 *Embassy* 2002 R St NW ... Washington DC 20009-1012
212 490-2072 *Mission to the UN* 211 E 43rd St Rm 1703 ... New York NY 10017-4707
308 432-4451 **Chadron State College** 10th & Main Sts ... Chadron NE 69337-0000
Fax: 308 432-6204 Admin
202 224-2921 **Chafee John H (Sen - R - Rhode Island)** 567 Dirksen Bldg .. Washington DC 20510-0001
Fax: Unlisted
719 539-4004 **Chaffee County** 132 Crestone Ave ... Salida CO 81201-1566
714 987-1737 **Chaffey Community College** 5885 S Haven Ave ... Alta Loma CA 91701-3002
Fax: 714 941-2783
202 659-6000 **Chamber of Commerce of the US** 1615 H St NW ... Washington DC 20062-0001
Fax: 202 463-5836
205 864-8823 **Chambers County** County Courthouse ... Lafayette AL 36862-0000
409 267-3471 **Chambers County** 404 Washington ... Anahuac TX 77514-0000
808 735-4711 **Chaminade University of Honolulu** 3140 Waialae Ave ... Honolulu HI 96816-1578
Fax: 808 735-4870
217 384-3720 **Champaign County** 204 E Elm St ... Urbana IL 61801-3324
513 653-5896 **Champaign County** Main & Court St ... Urbana OH 43078-0000
802 658-0800 **Champlain College** 163 S Willard St ... Burlington VT 05401-3950
Fax: 802 860-2750
202 225-7761 **Chandler Rod (Rep - R - Washington)** 223 Cannon Bldg ... Washington DC 20515-0001
Fax: 202 225-7762
217 495-1110 **Chanute Air Force Base** ... Rantoul IL 61868-0000
Fax: Unlisted
714 997-6815 **Chapman College** 333 N Glassell St ... Orange CA 92666-1099
Fax: 714 532-6048
202 225-3035 **Chapman Jim (Rep - D - Texas)** 236 Cannon Bldg ... Washington DC 20515-0001
Fax: Unlisted
816 288-3273 **Chariton County** County Courthouse ... Keytesville MO 65261-0000
804 829-2401 **Charles City County** PO Box 128 ... Charles City VA 23030-0128
Fax: 804 829-5819
301 645-0550 **Charles County** PO Box B ... La Plata MD 20646-0167
Fax: 301 645-0543
301 934-2251 **Charles County Community College** Mitchell Rd ... La Plata MD 20646-0000
Fax: 301 934-5255 Admin
605 487-7131 **Charles Mix County** PO Box 640 ... Lake Andes SD 57356-0640
313 762-0200 **Charles Stewart Mott Community College** 1401 E Court St ... Flint MI 48503-6208
Fax: 313 762-0257 Admin
803 554-0230 **Charleston Air Force Base** ... Charleston SC 29404-0000
Fax: 803 566-5604 PR
803 724-7600 **Charleston Coast Guard Base** 196 Tradd St ... Charleston SC 29401-1899
Fax: 803 724-7652
803 723-6724 **Charleston County** PO Box 70219 ... North Charleston SC 29415-0000
803 723-1645 **Charleston County Library** 404 King St ... Charleston SC 29403-6466
Fax: 803 722-0429
803 722-2996 **Charleston Museum** 360 Meeting St ... Charleston SC 29403-6297
803 743-4111 **Charleston Naval Base** ... Charleston SC 29408-0000
Fax: 803 743-2651
616 547-7200 **Charlevoix County** 301 State St County Bldg ... Charlevoix MI 49720-0000
704 336-2040 **Charlotte City Hall** 600 E 4th St ... Charlotte NC 28202-2870
Fax: 704 336-3497
813 637-2279 **Charlotte County** 116 W Olympia Ave ... Punta Gorda FL 33950-4431
Fax: 813 637-2171
804 542-5147 **Charlotte County** PO Box 38 ... Charlotte Court House VA 23923-0038
804 971-3101 **Charlottesville (Independent City)** 605 E Main St ... Charlottesville VA 22901-5397
Fax: 804 293-3166
912 496-2549 **Charlton County** 100 3rd St ... Folkston GA 31537-0000
316 273-6423 **Chase County** PO Box 547 ... Cottonwood Falls KS 66845-0547
308 882-5266 **Chase County** 921 Broadway ... Imperial NE 69033-0000
512 354-5119 **Chase Field Naval Air Station** ... Beeville TX 78103-0001
513 875-3344 **Chatfield College** 20918 SR-251 ... Saint Martin OH 45118-0000
412 365-1100 **Chatham College** Woodland Rd ... Pittsburgh PA 15232-2826
Fax: 412 365-1505
912 944-4984 **Chatham County** 133 Montgomery St ... Savannah GA 31401-3230
919 542-3240 **Chatham County** Courthouse Sq ... Pittsboro NC 27312-0000
912 234-5127 **Chatham-Effingham-Liberty Regional Library** 2002 Bull St ... Savannah GA 31499-0001
Fax: 912 232-7037
404 989-3602 **Chattahoochee County** PO Box 299 ... Cusseta GA 31805-0000
205 291-4900 **Chattahoochee Valley Community College**
2602 College Dr ... Phenix City AL 36867-0000
Fax: 205 291-4980
404 327-0211 **Chattahoochee Valley Regional Library** 1120 Bradley Dr ... Columbus GA 31906-0000
615 697-4400 **Chattanooga State Technical Community College**
4501 Amnicola Hwy ... Chattanooga TN 37406-1018
Fax: Unlisted
615 757-5310 **Chattanooga-Hamilton County Bicentennial Library**
1001 Broad St ... Chattanooga TN 37402-2620
Fax: Unlisted
404 857-4796 **Chattooga County** PO Box 211 ... Summerville GA 30747-0211
Fax: 404 857-7130
316 725-3370 **Chautauqua County** 215 N Chautauqua St ... Sedan KS 67361-1397
716 753-4211 **Chautauqua County** Gerace Office Bldg ... Mayville NY 14757-0000
Fax: 716 753-4756
716 484-7135 **Chautauqua-Cattaraugus Library System** PO Box 730 ... Jamestown NY 14702-0730
505 624-6614 **Chaves County** 401 N Main St ... Roswell NM 88201-4726
205 463-7125 **Cheaha Regional Library** 111 W Coleman St ... Heflin AL 36264-0000
Fax: Call company operator
615 792-5179 **Cheatham County** 100 Public Sq ... Ashland City TN 37015-1711
616 627-8808 **Cheboygan County** 870 S Main St ... Cheboygan MI 49721-2220
716 892-8089 **Cheektowaga Public Library** 2580 Harlem Rd ... Cheektowaga NY 14225-4606
509 664-5380 **Chelan County** PO Box 3025 ... Wenatchee WA 98807-3025
503 399-5006 **Chemeketa Community College** 4000 Lancaster Dr NE ... Salem OR 97305-1453
Fax: 503 399-3918
607 737-2811 **Chemung County** 425 Pennsylvania Ave ... Elmira NY 14904-1762
607 733-9173 **Chemung-Southern Tier Library System/Steele Memorial Library**
1 Library Plaza ... Elmira NY 14901-2739
607 335-4500 **Chenango County** 5 Court St ... Norwich NY 13815-1676
205 927-3079 **Cherokee County** Courthouse Annex Rm 303 ... Centre AL 35960-0000
404 479-1953 **Cherokee County** 100 North St ... Canton GA 30114-2794
712 225-2706 **Cherokee County** PO Box F ... Cherokee IA 51012-0000
316 429-2042 **Cherokee County** PO Box 14 ... Columbus KS 66725-0014
704 837-5527 **Cherokee County** 201 Peachtree St ... Murphy NC 28906-2994
918 456-3171 **Cherokee County** 213 W Delaware St ... Tahlequah OK 74464-3639
803 487-2562 **Cherokee County** PO Box 866 ... Gaffney SC 29342-0866
Fax: 803 487-2594
903 683-2350 **Cherokee County** 6th St ... Rusk TX 75785-0000
402 376-2771 **Cherry County** PO Box 120 ... Valentine NE 69201-0120
919 466-2811 **Cherry Point Marine Corps Air Station** ... Cherry Point NC 28533-5000
Fax: 919 466-3635
804 547-6166 **Chesapeake (Independent City)** 306 Cedar Rd ... Chesapeake VA 23320-5514
Fax: 804 547-6507
301 745-2916 **Chesapeake Bay Maritime Museum** PO Box 636 ... Saint Michaels MD 21663-0636
301 758-1537 **Chesapeake College** PO Box 8 ... Wye Mills MD 21679-0008
Fax: 301 827-9466
804 547-6579 **Chesapeake Public Library** 298 Cedar Rd ... Chesapeake VA 23320-5514
Fax: 804 547-8971
603 352-0056 **Cheshire County** 33 West St ... Keene NH 03431-3355
215 344-6000 **Chester County** Market & High Sts ... West Chester PA 19380-0000
803 385-2605 **Chester County** Main St ... Chester SC 29706-0000
901 989-2233 **Chester County** PO Box 205 ... Henderson TN 38340-0205
215 363-0884 **Chester County Library** 400 Exton Square Pkwy ... Exton PA 19341-2496
Fax: 215 524-1326
803 623-2574 **Chesterfield County** 200 W Main St ... Chesterfield SC 29709-1527

804 748-1200 **Chesterfield County** 9901 Lori Rd .... Chesterfield VA 23832-6626
Fax: 804 748-1006
804 748-1601 **Chesterfield County Public Library** 9501 Lori Rd .... Chesterfield VA 23832-6631
Fax: 804 751-4679
803 537-5286 **Chesterfield-Marlboro Technical College** PO Box 1007 .... Cheraw SC 29520-1007
Fax: 803 537-6148
215 248-7000 **Chestnut Hill College** Northwestern & Germantown Aves ... Philadelphia PA 19118-0000
Fax: 215 248-7056 Library
719 767-5685 **Cheyenne County** PO Box 67 .... Cheyenne Wells CO 80810-0067
913 332-2401 **Cheyenne County** PO Box 985 .... Saint Francis KS 67756-0985
Fax: Unlisted
308 254-2141 **Cheyenne County** 1000 10th Ave .... Sidney NE 69162-1612
215 399-2299 **Cheyney University of Pennsylvania** Cheyney & Creek Rds ..... Cheyney PA 19319-0000
Fax: 215 399-2415
Chicago City Government
312 744-6878 *City Clerk* 121 N La Salle St Rm 107 .... Chicago IL 60601-0000
312 408-7485 *Department of Economic Development* 24 E Congress Pkwy . Chicago IL 60605-1226
Fax: 312 408-7499
312 744-3400 *Department of Inspectional Services*
121 N La Salle St Suite 900 .... Chicago IL 60602-1202
Fax: 312 744-0682
312 646-4400 *Illinois International Port* 3600 E 95th St .... Chicago IL 60617-0000
Fax: 312 221-7678
312 744-5000 *Mayor's Office* 121 N La Salle St Rm 507 .... Chicago IL 60602-1207
Fax: 312 744-3300
312 744-5000 *Mayor's Office of Inquiry & Information* 121 N La Salle St .... Chicago IL 60602-1201
312 744-4471 *Planning Dept* 121 N La Salle St 10th Fl .... Chicago IL 60602-1202
Fax: 312 744-6550
312 744-6230 *Police Dept* 1121 S State St .... Chicago IL 60605-2398
312 744-3674 *Public Works* 121 N La Salle St .... Chicago IL 60602-1202
Fax: 312 744-1200
312 744-3360 *Treasurer* 121 N La Salle St Rm 204 .... Chicago IL 60602-1204
Fax: 312 744-3220
312 641-2595 **Chicago Citywide College** 226 W Jackson Blvd .... Chicago IL 60606-6997
Fax: 312 368-6030
708 657-2145 **Chicago Coast Guard Air Station** .... Glenview IL 60026-0000
Fax: 708 657-2147
312 642-4600 **Chicago Historical Society Museum** Clark St & North Ave .... Chicago IL 60614-6099
Fax: 312 266-2077
312 269-2800 **Chicago Public Library** 400 N Franklin St .... Chicago IL 60610-4481
Fax: 312 222-9625
312 995-2000 **Chicago State University** 9500 S King Dr .... Chicago IL 60628-1502
Fax: 312 995-3762
515 394-2106 **Chickasaw County** Prospect St .... New Hampton IA 50659-0000
601 456-2513 **Chickasaw County** County Courthouse .... Houston MS 38851-0000
501 265-2208 **Chicot County** County Courthouse .... Lake Village AR 71653-0000
202 638-2952 **Child Welfare League of America**
440 1st St NW Suite 310 .... Washington DC 20001-2085
Fax: 202 638-4004
317 924-5431 **Children's Museum** 3000 N Meridian St .... Indianapolis IN 46208-4716
Fax: 317 921-4019
617 426-6500 **Children's Museum** 300 Congress St Museum Wharf .... Boston MA 02210-1034
313 494-1210 **Children's Museum** 67 E Kirby St .... Detroit MI 48202-4001
817 937-6143 **Childress County** 100 Ave 'E' NW .... Childress TX 79201-3755
Chile: Republic of Chile
202 785-1746 *Embassy* 1732 Massachusetts Ave NW .... Washington DC 20036-1903
Fax: 202 887-5579
212 687-7547 *Mission to the UN* 809 UN Plaza 4th Fl .... New York NY 10017-0000
Fax: 212 972-9875
205 755-1551 **Chilton County** PO Box 557 .... Clanton AL 35045-0557
Fax: 205 755-8921
China: People's Republic of China
202 328-2500 *Embassy* 2300 Connecticut Ave NW .... Washington DC 20008-1724
Fax: 202 234-4055
212 787-3838 *Mission to the UN* 155 W 66th St .... New York NY 10023-6501
Fax: 212 787-1173
312 346-0287 *Chicago Consulate General* 104 S Michigan Ave Suite 500 .... Chicago IL 60603-5907
Fax: 312 580-2570
212 868-7752 *New York Consulate General* 520 12th Ave .... New York NY 10036-1007
Fax: 212 629-2698
415 563-4885 *San Francisco Consulate General* 1450 Laguna St .... San Francisco CA 94115-3717
Fax: 415 563-0494
415 982-3000 **Chinese Chamber of Commerce of San Francisco**
730 Sacramento St .... San Francisco CA 94108-2571
Fax: 415 982-4720
904 526-2761 **Chipola Junior College** 1200 College St .... Marianna FL 32446-2000
Fax: 904 526-4153
906 635-6300 **Chippewa County** 319 Court St .... Sault Sainte Marie MI 49783-2183
Fax: 906 635-6325
612 269-7774 **Chippewa County** 11th St & Hwy 7 .... Montevideo MN 56265-0000
Fax: 612 269-7733
715 723-1831 **Chippewa County** 711 N Bridge St .... Chippewa Falls WI 54729-1876
715 833-6200 **Chippewa Valley Technical College** 620 W Clairemont Ave ... Eau Claire WI 54701-6162
612 257-1300 **Chisago County** County Courthouse .... Center City MN 55012-0000
802 863-3467 **Chittenden County** 175 Main St .... Burlington VT 05401-8310
205 459-2155 **Choctaw County** 117 S Mulberry Ave .... Butler AL 36904-2557
601 285-6329 **Choctaw County** 112 Quinn St .... Ackerman MS 39735-0000
405 326-5331 **Choctaw County** County Courthouse .... Hugo OK 74743-0000
205 774-3112 **Choctawhatchee Regional Library System** 320 James St .... Ozark AL 36360-2015
Fax: Unlisted
406 622-5151 **Chouteau County** 1308 Franklin .... Fort Benton MT 59442-0000
Fax: 406 622-3631
919 398-4101 **Chowan College** 200 Jones Dr .... Murfreesboro NC 27855-1844
Fax: 919 398-8225
919 482-2323 **Chowan County** S Broad St .... Edenton NC 27932-0000
714 854-8002 **Christ College Irvine** 1530 Concordia Dr .... Irvine CA 92715-3299
Fax: 714 854-6854
814 539-8086 **Christ the Saviour Seminary** 225 Chandler Ave .... Johnstown PA 15906-2103
703 636-2908 **Christendom College** 2101 Shenandoah Shores Rd .... Front Royal VA 22630-5149
901 722-0200 **Christian Brothers University** 650 East Pkwy S .... Memphis TN 38104-5581
Fax: 901 722-0494
804 644-4654 **Christian Children's Fund Inc** 203 E Cary St .... Richmond VA 23219-6107
Fax: 804 225-8385
217 824-4969 **Christian County** 600 N Main St .... Taylorville IL 62568-1599
502 887-4105 **Christian County** 511 S Main St .... Hopkinsville KY 42240-2300
417 485-6360 **Christian County** PO Box 549 .... Ozark MO 65721-0549
619 440-3043 **Christian Heritage College** 2100 Greenfield Dr .... El Cajon CA 92019-1157
Fax: 619 440-0209
708 259-1840 **Christian Life College** 400 E Gregory St .... Mount Prospect IL 60056-0000
Fax: 708 259-3888
804 594-7000 **Christopher Newport College** 50 Shoe Ln .... Newport News VA 23606-2998
Fax: 804 594-7464 Purchasing
804 622-1211 **Chrysler Museum** Olney Rd & Mowbray Arch .... Norfolk VA 23510-1587
Fax: 804 623-5282
619 691-5168 **Chula Vista Public Library** 365 F St .... Chula Vista CA 92010-2697
702 423-6028 **Churchill County** 10 W Williams Ave .... Fallon NV 89406-2940

702 423-3677 **Churchill County Museum & Archives** 1050 S Maine St .... Fallon NV 89406-8925
505 287-9431 **Cibola County** 515 W High Ave .... Grants NM 87020-2526
405 544-2251 **Cimarron County** PO Box 145 .... Boise City OK 73933-0145
513 352-3000 **Cincinnati City Hall** 801 Plum St .... Cincinnati OH 45202-1927
513 721-5204 **Cincinnati Art Museum** 958 Eden Park Dr .... Cincinnati OH 45202-0000
Fax: 513 721-0129
513 244-8100 **Cincinnati Bible College & Seminary** 2700 Glenway Ave ...... Cincinnati OH 45204-1799
Fax: 513 244-8140
513 287-7000 **Cincinnati Museum of Natural History**
1301 Western Ave Museum Ctr .... Cincinnati OH 45203-0000
513 569-1500 **Cincinnati Technical College** 3520 Central Pkwy .... Cincinnati OH 45223-2612
Fax: 513 559-0040
614 474-8896 **Circleville Bible College** 1476 Lancaster Pike .... Circleville OH 43113-9487
608 356-8341 **Circus World Museum** 426 Water St .... Baraboo WI 53913-2597
Fax: Unlisted
817 442-2567 **Cisco Junior College** RR 3 Box 3 .... Cisco TX 76437-9321
Fax: 817 442-2546
803 792-5000 **Citadel The** Moultrie St .... Charleston SC 29409-0001
Fax: 803 792-7084
213 451-8548 **Citizens for the Republic** 233 Wilshire Blvd Suite 275 ...... Santa Monica CA 90401-1207
Fax: 213 451-3471
818 963-0323 **Citrus Community College** 1000 W Foothill Blvd .... Glendora CA 91740-1899
Fax: 818 335-3159 Admissions
904 726-2881 **Citrus County** 110 N Apopka Ave .... Inverness FL 32650-4245
Fax: 904 344-4259
415 239-3000 **City College of San Francisco** 50 Phelan Ave .... San Francisco CA 94112-1821
Fax: 415 239-3936
213 412-5397 **City of Inglewood Public Library** 101 W Manchester Blvd ..... Inglewood CA 90301-1753
Fax: 213 671-2162
408 970-9966 **City University** 3333 Bowers Ave Suite 155 .... Santa Clara CA 95054-2912
Fax: 408 748-1826
206 624-1688 **City University** 16661 Northrup Way .... Bellevue WA 98008-0000
Fax: 206 746-2567
213 382-3801 **City University Los Angeles** 3960 Wilshire Blvd Suite 501 .. Los Angeles CA 90010-3306
Fax: 213 382-8481
415 499-6051 **Civic Center Library** Administration Bldg .... San Rafael CA 94903-9992
202 633-3301 **Civil Div (US Dept of Justice)**
10th St & Constitution Ave NW Rm 3143 .... Washington DC 20530-0001
Fax: 202 633-1071
202 633-2151 **Civil Rights Div (US Dept of Justice)**
10th St & Constitution Ave NW Rm 5643 .... Washington DC 20530-0001
Fax: 202 786-3905
202 586-6850 **Civilian Radioactive Waste Management (US Dept of Energy)**
1000 Independence Ave SW Rm 5A-085 .... Washington DC 20585-0001
Fax: 202 586-5049
503 657-8400 **Clackamas Community College** 19600 S Molalla Ave .... Oregon City OR 97045-9049
Fax: 503 655-5153
503 655-8581 **Clackamas County** 906 Main St .... Oregon City OR 97045-1881
Fax: 503 650-8944
503 655-8543 **Clackamas County Library** 16201 SE McLoughlin Blvd .... Oak Grove OR 97267-4653
803 534-2710 **Claflin College** 400 College St NE .... Orangeburg SC 29115-4498
Fax: 803 531-2860
601-437-5841 **Claiborne County** PO Box 449 .... Port Gibson MS 39150-0449
615 626-3283 **Claiborne County** PO Box 173 .... Tazewell TN 37879-0173
318 927-9601 **Claiborne Parish** Courthouse Sq .... Homer LA 71040-0000
206 452-7831 **Clallam County** 223 E 4th St .... Port Angeles WA 98362-3025
Fax: 206 452-6260
517 539-7131 **Clare County** PO Box 438 .... Harrison MI 48625-0438
Fax: 517 539-5721
714 621-8000 **Claremont McKenna College** 500 E 9th St Bauer Ctr .... Claremont CA 91711-0000
Fax: 714 621-8249
714 621-8026 **Claremont University Center (System)** 150 E 10th St .... Claremont CA 91711-6160
Fax: 714 621-8390
806 874-3571 **Clarendon College** PO Box 968 .... Clarendon TX 79226-0968
Fax: 806 874-3201
803 435-4444 **Clarendon County** PO Box E .... Manning SC 29102-0136
Fax: 803 435-8258
814 226-4000 **Clarion County** 421 Main St .... Clarion PA 16214-1028
814 226-6340 **Clarion District Library Assn** 663 Main St .... Clarion PA 16214-1292
Fax: 814 226-6750
814 226-2000 **Clarion University of Pennsylvania** 836 Wood St .... Clarion PA 16214-1240
Fax: 814 226-1826 Admin
814 676-6591 *Venango Campus* 1801 W 1st St .... Oil City PA 16301-3254
Fax: 814 676-1348
206 694-6521 **Clark College** 1800 E McLoughlin Blvd .... Vancouver WA 98663-3598
Fax: 206 690-7149
501 246-4491 **Clark County** County Courthouse Sq .... Arkadelphia AR 71923-0000
208 374-5304 **Clark County** PO Box 205 .... Dubois ID 83423-0205
217 826-8311 **Clark County** 501 Archer Ave .... Marshall IL 62441-1275
812 285-6200 **Clark County** City Court Bldg 501 E Court Ave .... Jeffersonville IN 47130-0000
316 635-2813 **Clark County** PO Box 886 .... Ashland KS 67831-0886
606 745-0200 **Clark County** 34 S Main St Rm 103 .... Winchester KY 40391-2600
816 727-3283 **Clark County** 111 E Court St .... Kahoka MO 63445-1268
702 455-3156 **Clark County** 200 S 3rd St .... Las Vegas NV 89155-0001
513 328-2458 **Clark County** 101 N Limestone St .... Springfield OH 45502-1123
605 532-5851 **Clark County** PO Box 294 .... Clark SD 57225-0000
206 699-2292 **Clark County** PO Box 5000 .... Vancouver WA 98668-0000
715 743-3241 **Clark County** 517 Court St .... Neillsville WI 54456-1992
702 643-6060 **Clark County Community College**
3200 E Cheyenne Ave .... North Las Vegas NV 89030-4228
Fax: 702 643-6427
702 455-7955 **Clark County Heritage Museum** 1830 S Boulder Hwy .... Henderson NV 89015-8502
702 737-7031 **Clark County Republican Central Committee**
6116 W Charleston Blvd .... Las Vegas NV 89102-0000
513 325-0691 **Clark Technical College** 570 E Leffel Ln .... Springfield OH 45505-4795
Fax: 513 328-6133
508 793-7711 **Clark University** 950 Main St .... Worcester MA 01610-1477
Fax: 508 793-7780
404 880-8000 **Clark-Atlanta University** James P Brawley Dr & Fair St SW .... Atlanta GA 30314-4389
Fax: 404 880-8222
319 588-6300 **Clarke College** 1550 Clarke Dr .... Dubuque IA 52001-3198
Fax: 319 588-6789
601 683-2061 **Clarke College** College St .... Newton MS 39345-0000
205 275-3507 **Clarke County** 117 Court St .... Grove Hill AL 36451-0000
404 354-2660 **Clarke County** 325 E Washington St .... Athens GA 30601-2750
Fax: 404 354-2669
515 342-2213 **Clarke County** 117 1/2 S Main St .... Osceola IA 50213-1299
601 776-2126 **Clarke County** PO Box M .... Quitman MS 39355-1013
703 955-1309 **Clarke County** 102 N Church St .... Berryville VA 22611-1110
707 443-1947 **Clarke Memorial Museum** 240 E St .... Eureka CA 95501-0433
315 268-6400 **Clarkson University** Pierrepontt Ave Snell Hall .... Potsdam NY 13699-0001
Fax: 315 268-4475
315 268-6446 *School of Engineering* 126 Old Main St .... Potsdam NY 13699-0001
Fax: 315 268-6438
503 325-0910 **Clatsop Community College** 1653 Jerome Ave .... Astoria OR 97103-3698
Fax: 503 325-5738

Phone	Name / Address	City	State	ZIP
503 325-1000	**Clatsop County** PO Box 179	Astoria	OR	97103-0179
	Fax: 503 325-8606			
501 598-2813	**Clay County** 2nd St	Piggott	AR	72454-0000
904 284-6300	**Clay County** PO Box 698	Green Cove Springs	FL	32043-0698
	Fax: 904 284-6390			
912 768-2631	**Clay County** PO Box 550	Fort Gaines	GA	31751-0550
712 262-4335	**Clay County** 215 W 4th St	Spencer	IA	51301-3822
618 665-3626	**Clay County** County Courthouse	Louisville	IL	62858-0000
812 448-8727	**Clay County** 1206 E National Ave	Brazil	IN	47834-2797
913 632-2552	**Clay County** PO Box 98	Clay Center	KS	67432-0098
606 598-3663	**Clay County** PO Box 463	Manchester	KY	40962-0463
218 299-5002	**Clay County** 807 11th St N	Moorhead	MN	56560-1500
	Fax: 218 299-5195			
816 792-7733	**Clay County** Administration Bldg Courthouse Sq	Liberty	MO	64068-0000
	Fax: 816 792-7777			
601 494-3124	**Clay County** PO Box 815	West Point	MS	39773-0815
704 389-6301	**Clay County** PO Box 118	Hayesville	NC	28904-0118
402 762-3463	**Clay County** 111 W Fairfield St	Clay Center	NE	68933-1436
605 624-2281	**Clay County** 211 W Main St	Vermillion	SD	57069-2097
615 243-2249	**Clay County** PO Box 218	Celina	TN	38551-0218
817 538-4631	**Clay County** 100 N Bridge St	Henrietta	TX	76365-2858
304 587-4259	**Clay County** Main St	Clay	WV	25043-0000
202 225-2406	**Clay William (Rep - D - Missouri)** 2470 Rayburn Bldg	Washington	DC	20515-0001
	Fax: 202 225-1725			
404 478-9911	**Clayton County** 121 S McDonough St	Jonesboro	GA	30236-3694
319 245-2204	**Clayton County** 111 High St	Elkader	IA	52043-0000
404 961-3400	**Clayton State College** 5900 N Lee St	Morrow	GA	30260-0000
	Fax: 404 961-3700			
606 337-3196	**Clear Creek Baptist Bible College** 300 Clear Creek Rd	Pineville	KY	40977-9752
303 534-5777	**Clear Creek County** PO Box 2000	Georgetown	CO	80444-2000
	Fax: Ext 314			
814 765-2641	**Clearfield County** N 2nd & Market Sts	Clearfield	PA	16830-0000
	Fax: 814 765-6089			
813 726-1153	**Clearwater Christian College** 3400 Gulf To Bay Blvd	Clearwater	FL	34619-4514
	Fax: 813 726-8597			
813 535-1437	**Clearwater Coast Guard Air Station**	Clearwater	FL	34622-2990
208 476-3615	**Clearwater County** PO Box 586	Orofino	ID	83544-0586
218 694-6520	**Clearwater County** 213 N Main Ave	Bagley	MN	56621-0000
313 483-4400	**Cleary College** 2170 Washtenaw Ave	Ypsilanti	MI	48197-1788
	Fax: 313 483-0090			
205 463-2651	**Cleburne County** Vickery St	Heflin	AL	36264-0000
501 362-8141	**Cleburne County** 301 W Main St	Heber Springs	AR	72543-3016
202 225-4311	**Clement Bob (Rep - D - Tennessee)** 325 Cannon Bldg	Washington	DC	20515-0001
	Fax: 202 226-1035			
803 656-3311	**Clemson University**	Clemson	SC	29634-0001
	Fax: 803 656-0333			
803 656-3201	*College of Engineering* Riggs Hall Rm 109	Clemson	SC	29634-0001
	Fax: 803 656-2698			
803 656-3926	*Department of Planning Studies* Lee Hall Rm 125	Clemson	SC	29634-0001
	Fax: 803 656-0204			
803 656-3013	*Graduate School of Agriculture* 102 Barr Hall Rm 102	Clemson	SC	29634-0001
	Fax: 803 656-3608			
513 732-7300	**Clermont County** 76 S Riverside Dr	Batavia	OH	45103-2635
	Fax: 513 732-7826			
513 732-2736	**Clermont County Public Library** 326 Broadway St	Batavia	OH	45103-2806
216 664-2000	**Cleveland City Hall** 601 Lakeside Ave E	Cleveland	OH	44114-1078
704 484-4000	**Cleveland Community College** 137 S Post Rd	Shelby	NC	28150-6296
	Fax: 704 484-4036			
501 325-6521	**Cleveland County** Main & Magnolia Sts	Rison	AR	71665-0000
704 484-4800	**Cleveland County** PO Box 1210	Shelby	NC	28150-0000
	Fax: 704 484-4895			
405 366-0201	**Cleveland County** 201 S Jones Ave	Norman	OK	73069-6046
	Fax: 405 366-8401			
216 231-5010	**Cleveland Health Education Museum** 8911 Euclid Ave	Cleveland	OH	44106-2039
216 932-3600	**Cleveland Heights-University Heights Public Library** 2345 Lee Rd	Cleveland Heights	OH	44118-3434
	Fax: 216 932-0932			
216 421-4322	**Cleveland Institute of Art** 11141 East Blvd	Cleveland	OH	44106-1700
	Fax: 216 421-7438			
216 791-5000	**Cleveland Institute of Music** 11021 East Blvd	Cleveland	OH	44106-1705
	Fax: 216 791-3063			
216 421-7340	**Cleveland Museum of Art** 11150 East Blvd	Cleveland	OH	44106-1797
	Fax: 216 421-0411			
216 231-4600	**Cleveland Museum of Natural History** Wade Oval University Cir	Cleveland	OH	44106-1797
	Fax: 216 231-5919			
216 623-2800	**Cleveland Public Library** 325 Superior Ave	Cleveland	OH	44114-1271
	Fax: 216 623-6987 Admin			
615 472-7141	**Cleveland State Community College** 3570 Adkisson Dr NW	Cleveland	TN	37312-2858
	Fax: 615 478-6255			
216 687-2000	**Cleveland State University** 1802 E 25th St	Cleveland	OH	44114-4420
	Fax: 216 687-9366			
216 687-2344	*Marshall College of Law* 1801 Euclid Ave	Cleveland	OH	44115-2223
	Fax: 216 687-6881			
703 863-5091	**Clifton Forge (Independent City)** PO Box 631	Clifton Forge	VA	24422-0631
912 487-2667	**Clinch County** 100 Court Sq	Homerville	GA	31634-1400
703 328-0100	**Clinch Valley College of the University of Virginia** College Ave	Wise	VA	24293-0000
	Fax: 703 328-0115			
202 225-5121	**Clinger William F Jr (Rep - R - Pennsylvania)** 2160 Rayburn Bldg	Washington	DC	20515-0001
	Fax: 202 225-4681			
319 242-6841	**Clinton Community College** 1000 Lincoln Blvd	Clinton	IA	52732-6299
	Fax: 319 242-7868 Library			
518 561-6650	**Clinton Community College** Rt 9 S	Plattsburgh	NY	12901-0000
319 243-6210	**Clinton County** PO Box 157	Clinton	IA	52732-0157
618 594-2464	**Clinton County** 850 Fairfax County Courthouse	Carlyle	IL	62231-0000
317 659-1891	**Clinton County** 50 N Jackson St	Frankfort	IN	46041-1993
606 387-5234	**Clinton County** County Courthouse	Albany	KY	42602-0000
517 224-5100	**Clinton County** 100 E State St	Saint Johns	MI	48879-1571
	Fax: 517 224-5254			
816 539-3713	**Clinton County** PO Box 245	Plattsburg	MO	64477-0245
518 565-4700	**Clinton County** 137 Margaret St	Plattsburgh	NY	12901-2933
513 382-2103	**Clinton County** 46 S South St	Wilmington	OH	45177-2214
	Fax: 513 382-7530			
717 893-4000	**Clinton County** County Courthouse	Lock Haven	PA	17745-0000
	Fax: 717 893-4028			
518 563-5190	**Clinton-Essex-Franklin Library System** 17 Oak St	Plattsburgh	NY	12901-2810
913 243-4319	**Cloud County** 811 Washington St	Concordia	KS	66901-3415
	Fax: 913 243-2239			
913 243-1435	**Cloud County Community College** 2221 Campus Dr	Concordia	KS	66901-5305
	Fax: 913 243-1459			
406 727-8787	**CM Russell Museum** 400 13th St N	Great Falls	MT	59401-1498
601 624-3001	**Coahoma County** 115 1st St	Clarksdale	MS	38614-4227
405 927-3122	**Coal County** 3 N Main St	Coalgate	OK	74538-2832
202 296-6107	**Coalition for Employment Through Exports Inc** 1801 K St NW 8th Fl	Washington	DC	20006-1301
202 544-7190	**Coalition to Stop Gun Violence** 100 Maryland Ave NE	Washington	DC	20002-5625
	Fax: 202 544-7213			
714 432-5898	**Coast Community College (System)** 1370 Adams Ave	Costa Mesa	CA	92626-5429
	Fax: 714 432-5177			
716 846-4184	**Coast Guard Group at Buffalo** 1 Fuhrmann Blvd	Buffalo	NY	14203-0000
	Fax: Call company operator			
305 292-8800	**Coast Guard Group at Key West**	Key West	FL	33040-0005
	Fax: 305 292-8739			
408 647-7300	**Coast Guard Group at Monterey** 100 Lighthouse Ave	Monterey	CA	93940-1497
	Fax: 408 647-7307			
813 893-3454	**Coast Guard Group at Saint Petersburg** 600 8th Ave SE	Saint Petersburg	FL	33701-5030
	Fax: 813 826-3480			
919 455-1221	**Coastal Carolina Community College** 444 Western Blvd	Jacksonville	NC	28546-6899
	Fax: 919 455-7027			
714 546-7600	**Coastline Community College** 11460 Warner Ave	Fountain Valley	CA	92708-2597
	Fax: 714 241-6248			
202 224-5623	**Coats Dan (Sen - R - Indiana)** 407 Russell Bldg	Washington	DC	20510-1403
	Fax: 202 224-8964			
404 429-3210	**Cobb County** 10 E Park Sq	Marietta	GA	30090-0001
	Fax: 404 429-3301			
404 528-2320	**Cobb County Public Library System** 266 Roswell St	Marietta	GA	30060-1975
	Fax: 404 528-2367			
202 225-3065	**Coble Howard (Rep - R - North Carolina)** 430 Cannon Bldg	Washington	DC	20515-0001
	Fax: 202 225-8611			
704 254-7162	**Coburn Memorial Mineral Museum** Asheville Civic Ctr	Asheville	NC	28801-0000
602 364-7943	**Cochise College** RR 1 Box 100	Douglas	AZ	85607-9724
	Fax: 602 364-0320 Library			
602 432-5471	**Cochise County** PO Box CK	Bisbee	AZ	85603-0000
602 432-2950	**Cochise County Library System** Old Bisbee High School	Bisbee	AZ	85603-0000
	Fax: 602 432-5016			
806 266-5450	**Cochran County** 100 N Main St	Morton	TX	79346-2558
202 224-5054	**Cochran Thad (Sen - R - Mississippi)** 326 Russell Bldg	Washington	DC	20510-0001
	Fax: Unlisted			
615 623-6176	**Cocke County** Court Ave	Newport	TN	37821-0000
602 779-6806	**Coconino County** 100 E Birch Ave Flagstaff Justice Ct	Flagstaff	AZ	86001-4696
605 886-8497	**Codington County** 14 1st Ave SE	Watertown	SD	57201-3611
	Fax: 605 886-3019			
319 399-8000	**Coe College** 1220 1st Ave NE	Cedar Rapids	IA	52402-5092
	Fax: 319 399-8748			
205 897-2954	**Coffee County** PO Box 402	Elba	AL	36323-0402
912 384-4799	**Coffee County** 210 S Coffee Ave	Douglas	GA	31533-3815
615 728-3024	**Coffee County** 300 Hillsboro Blvd Box 8	Manchester	TN	37355-2702
316 364-2191	**Coffey County** 6th & Neosho	Burlington	KS	66839-0000
316 251-7700	**Coffeyville Community College** 11th & Willow	Coffeyville	KS	67337-5064
	Fax: 316 251-7798			
206 822-3137	**Cogswell College North** 10626 NE 37th Cir	Kirkland	WA	98033-7921
	Fax: 206 822-1006			
408 252-5550	**Cogswell Polytechnical College** 10420 Bubb Rd	Cupertino	CA	95014-4150
	Fax: 408 253-2413			
202 224-2523	**Cohen William S (Sen - R - Maine)** 322 Hart Bldg	Washington	DC	20510-0001
	Fax: 202 224-2693			
915 453-2631	**Coke County** 13 E 7th St	Robert Lee	TX	76945-0000
803 383-8000	**Coker College** 300 E College Ave	Hartsville	SC	29550-3797
205 386-8500	**Colbert County** 201 N Main St	Tuscumbia	AL	35674-2060
207 872-3000	**Colby College** 150 Mayflower Hill Dr	Waterville	ME	04901-4799
	Fax: 207 872-3555			
207 872-3228	**Colby College Museum of Art** Mayflower Hill	Waterville	ME	04901-4799
	Fax: 207 872-3555			
913 462-3984	**Colby Community College** 1255 S Range Ave	Colby	KS	67701-4099
	Fax: 913 462-8315			
603 526-2010	**Colby-Sawyer College** 100 Main St	New London	NH	03257-4648
	Fax: 603 526-2135			
314 634-9110	**Cole County** 301 E High St	Jefferson City	MO	65101-3212
	Fax: 314 635-0796			
619 465-3990	**Coleman College** 7380 Parkway Dr	La Mesa	CA	92042-1500
	Fax: 619 463-0162			
915 625-2889	**Coleman County** PO Box 591	Coleman	TX	76834-0591
202 225-7041	**Coleman E Thomas (Rep - R - Missouri)** 2468 Rayburn Bldg	Washington	DC	20515-0001
	Fax: 202 225-4799			
202 225-4831	**Coleman Ronald D (Rep - D - Texas)** 440 Cannon Bldg	Washington	DC	20515-0001
	Fax: Unlisted			
217 348-0501	**Coles County** PO Box 207	Charleston	IL	61920-0207
402 352-3434	**Colfax County** 411 E 11th St	Schuyler	NE	68661-1940
505 445-9661	**Colfax County** PO Box 1498	Raton	NM	87740-1498
315 824-1000	**Colgate University** 13 Oak Dr	Hamilton	NY	13346-1386
	Fax: Ext 292			
213 852-1321	**College for Developmental Studies** 563 N Alfred St	West Hollywood	CA	90048-2512
	Fax: 213 651-0860			
212 989-2002	**College for Human Services** 345 Hudson St 14th Fl	New York	NY	10014-4598
717 675-2181	**College Misericordia** Lake St	Dallas	PA	18612-0000
	Fax: 717 675-2441			
718 429-6600	**College of Aeronautics** 86th St & 23rd Ave La Guardia Airport	Flushing	NY	11371-0000
	Fax: 718 429-0256			
415 522-7221	**College of Alameda** 555 Atlantic Ave	Alameda	CA	94501-2109
	Fax: 415 769-6019			
407 994-0770	**College of Boca Raton** 3601 N Military Trail	Boca Raton	FL	33431-5598
	Fax: 407 994-5827			
803 792-5507	**College of Charleston** 66 George St	Charleston	SC	29424-0001
	Fax: 803 792-5505			
708 858-2800	**College of DuPage** 22nd St & Lambert Rd	Glen Ellyn	IL	60137-6599
	Fax: 708 858-8671			
801 637-2120	**College of Eastern Utah** 451 E 400 North	Price	UT	84501-2699
	Fax: 801 637-4102			
406 761-8210	**College of Great Falls** 1301 20th St S	Great Falls	MT	59405-4996
	Fax: Ext 700			
208 459-5011	**College of Idaho** 2112 Cleveland Blvd	Caldwell	ID	83605-4494
	Fax: 208 459-5665			
212 962-4111	**College of Insurance** 101 Murray St	New York	NY	10007-2132
	Fax: 212 964-3381			
708 223-6601	**College of Lake County** 19351 W Washington St	Grayslake	IL	60030-1198
	Fax: 708 223-9371			
415 457-8811	**College of Marin** 835 College Ave	Kentfield	CA	94904-2590
	Fax: 415 456-7770			
415 883-2211	*Indian Valley Campus* 1800 Ignacio Blvd	Novato	CA	94949-4912
513 244-4200	**College of Mount Saint Joseph on the Ohio** 5701 Delhi Rd	Mount Saint Joseph	OH	45051-0001
	Fax: 513 244-4222			
212 549-8000	**College of Mount Saint Vincent** Riverdale & 263rd Sts	Riverdale	NY	10471-0000
	Fax: Unlisted			
914 632-5300	**College of New Rochelle** 29 Castle Pl	New Rochelle	NY	10805-2308
	Fax: 914 654-5554			
415 593-1601	**College of Notre Dame** 1500 Ralston Ave	Belmont	CA	94002-1997
	Fax: 415 441-3307			

301 435-0100 **College of Notre Dame of Maryland** 4701 N Charles St ... Baltimore MD 21210-2476
Fax: 301 435-5937
413 594-2761 **College of Our Lady of the Elms** 291 Springfield St ... Chicopee MA 01013-2837
Fax: 413 592-4871
612 363-5011 **College of Saint Benedict** 37 College Ave S ... Saint Joseph MN 56374-2001
Fax: 612 363-6099
612 690-6000 **College of Saint Catherine** 2004 Randolph Ave ... Saint Paul MN 55105-1750
Fax: 612 690-6024
201 292-6300 **College of Saint Elizabeth** 2 Convent Rd ... Convent Station NJ 07960-6989
815 740-3360 **College of Saint Francis** 500 Wilcox St ... Joliet IL 60435-6188
Fax: 815 740-4285
815 740-3478 *Graduate Program in Health Services Administration*
500 Wilcox St ... Joliet IL 60435-6188
Fax: 815 740-4285
802 773-5900 **College of Saint Joseph in Vermont** 71 Clement Rd ... Rutland VT 05701-3899
402 399-2400 **College of Saint Mary** 1901 S 72nd St ... Omaha NE 68124-2377
Fax: 402 399-2686 Library
518 454-5111 **College of Saint Rose** 432 Western Ave ... Albany NY 12203-1419
218 723-6000 **College of Saint Scholastica** 1200 Kenwood Ave ... Duluth MN 55811-4199
Fax: 218 723-6278
415 574-6161 **College of San Mateo** 1700 W Hillsdale Blvd ... San Mateo CA 94402-3784
505 473-6011 **College of Santa Fe** 1600 St Michaels Dr ... Santa Fe NM 87501-5634
Fax: 505 473-6504
208 733-9554 **College of Southern Idaho** 315 Falls Ave ... Twin Falls ID 83301-3367
Fax: 208 734-2362
919 335-0821 **College of the Albemarle** Hwy 17 N ... Elizabeth City NC 27909-0000
Fax: 919 335-2011
207 288-5015 **College of the Atlantic** 105 Eden St ... Bar Harbor ME 04609-1198
Fax: 207 288-2328
805 259-7800 **College of the Canyons** 26455 N Rockwell Canyon Rd ... Valencia CA 91355-1899
Fax: 805 259-8302
619 346-8041 **College of the Desert** 43500 Monterey Ave ... Palm Desert CA 92260-2499
Fax: 619 341-8678
508 793-2011 **College of the Holy Cross** 1 College St ... Worcester MA 01610-2322
Fax: 508 793-2336
409 938-1211 **College of the Mainland** 1200 N Amburn Rd ... Texas City TX 77591-2499
Fax: 409 938-7073
707 445-6700 **College of the Redwoods** 7351 Tompkins Hill Rd ... Eureka CA 95501-9300
Fax: 707 445-6990
502 451-4144 **College of the Scriptures** 4601 Old Shepherdsville Rd ... Louisville KY 40218-3440
209 733-2050 **College of the Sequoias** 915 S Mooney Blvd ... Visalia CA 93277-2234
Fax: 209 627-1705
505 392-6561 **College of the Southwest** 6610 N Lovington Hwy ... Hobbs NM 88240-9129
Fax: 505 392-6006
508 997-7831 **College of Visual & Performing Arts** 1213 Purchase St ... New Bedford MA 02740-6636
804 221-4000 **College of William & Mary** ... Williamsburg VA 23185-0000
804 221-3800 *Marshall-Wythe School of Law* S Henry St ... Williamsburg VA 23185-0000
Fax: 804 221-3261
216 263-2000 **College of Wooster** ... Wooster OH 44691-0000
Fax: 216 263-2427
803 549-5791 **Colleton County** PO Box 620 ... Walterboro SC 29488-0620
813 774-8999 **Collier County** 3301 Tamiami Trail E ... Naples FL 33962-4902
813 262-4130 **Collier County Public Library** 650 Central Ave ... Naples FL 33940-6087
Fax: 813 649-1293 Admin
214 548-4100 **Collin County** 210 S McDonald St ... McKinney TX 75069-5655
Fax: 214 548-7221
806 447-2408 **Collingsworth County** County Courthouse ... Wellington TX 79095-0000
202 225-2261 **Collins Barbara-Rose (Rep - D - Michigan)**
1541 Longworth Bldg ... Washington DC 20515-0001
Fax: Unlisted
202 225-5006 **Collins Cardiss (Rep - D - Illinois)** 2264 Rayburn Bldg ... Washington DC 20515-0001
Fax: 202 225-8396
Colombia: Republic of Colombia
202 387-8338 *Embassy* 2118 Leroy Pl NW ... Washington DC 20008-1847
Fax: 202 232-8643
212 355-7776 *Mission to the UN* 140 E 57th St 5th Fl ... New York NY 10022-2706
Fax: 212 371-2813
212 233-7776 **Colombian-American Assn** 150 Nassau St Rm 2015 ... New York NY 10038-1516
Fax: 212 233-7779
804 520-9265 **Colonial Heights (Independent City)** 1507 Boulevard ... Colonial Heights VA 23834-3049
Fax: 804 520-9338
804 229-1000 **Colonial Williamsburg Foundation** PO Box C ... Williamsburg VA 23187-3707
Fax: 804 220-7685
804 253-2277 **Colonial Williamsburg Reservation Center**
102 Visitors Center Dr ... Williamsburg VA 23187-0000
Fax: 804 220-7729
303 831-7411 **Colorado Assn of Commerce & Industry**
1776 Lincoln St Suite 1200 ... Denver CO 80203-0000
Fax: 303 860-1439
303 238-5386 **Colorado Christian University** 180 S Garrison St ... Denver CO 80226-7499
719 473-2233 **Colorado College** 14 E Cache La Poudre St ... Colorado Springs CO 80903-3294
Fax: 719 634-4180
409 732-2155 **Colorado County** 400 Spring St ... Columbus TX 78934-2456
303 830-8989 **Colorado Democratic State Committee**
1600 Downing St 6th Fl ... Denver CO 80218-1532
Fax: 303 830-7675
303 866-3682 **Colorado History Museum** 1300 Broadway ... Denver CO 80203-2104
Fax: 303 866-5739
303 945-8691 **Colorado Mountain College (System)** 215 9th St ... Glenwood Springs CO 81601-3307
Fax: 303 945-7279
Colorado Mountain College
303 945-7481 *Spring Valley Campus* 3000 County Rd 114 ... Glenwood Springs CO 81601-9394
Fax: 303 945-1227
719 486-2015 *Timberline Campus* ... Leadville CO 80461-0000
Fax: 719 486-3212
303 675-2261 **Colorado Northwestern Community College** 500 Kennedy Dr ... Rangely CO 81648-3502
Fax: 303 675-3330
303 893-1776 **Colorado Republican Party** 1275 Tremont Pl ... Denver CO 80204-2118
Fax: 303 629-0459
303 273-3000 **Colorado School of Mines** 1500 Illinois St ... Golden CO 80401-1887
Fax: 303 273-3278
Colorado State Government
303 866-5000 *Information* 1525 Sherman St ... Denver CO 80203-1712
Fax: 303 866-2763
303 866-3281 *Accounts & Control Div* 1525 Sherman St 7th Fl ... Denver CO 80203-1712
Fax: 303 866-4161
303 331-8500 *Air Quality Commission* 4210 E 11th Ave ... Denver CO 80220-3700
Fax: 303 320-4079
719 267-3520 *Arkansas Valley Correctional Facility* 12750 Ln 13 ... Crowley CO 81034-0001
Fax: Unlisted
303 866-3611 *Attorney General* 1525 Sherman St 3rd Fl ... Denver CO 80203-1760
Fax: 303 866-5001
719 395-2404 *Buena Vista Correctional Facility* PO Box 2017 ... Buena Vista CO 81211-2017
Fax: 719 395-8200
303 866-2723 *Commission on Higher Education* 1300 Broadway 2nd Fl ... Denver CO 80203-2104
Fax: 303 860-9750
303 866-5167 *Consumer Protection Unit* 1525 Sherman St Rm 215 ... Denver CO 80203-1717
Fax: 303 866-5001
303 894-2617 *Council on the Arts & Humanities* 750 Pennsylvania St ... Denver CO 80203-3699
303 866-2811 *Department of Agriculture* 1525 Sherman St 4th Fl ... Denver CO 80203-1712
Fax: 303 866-4073
719 579-9580 *Department of Corrections*
2862 S Circle Dr Suite 400 ... Colorado Springs CO 80906-4195
Fax: 719 540-2145
303 866-6806 *Department of Education* 201 E Colfax Ave ... Denver CO 80203-1799
Fax: 303 830-0793
303 320-8333 *Department of Health* 4210 E 11th Ave ... Denver CO 80220-3783
Fax: 303 322-9076
303 866-3311 *Department of Natural Resources* 1313 Sherman St Rm 718 ... Denver CO 80203-2239
Fax: 303 866-2115
303 866-3304 *Department of Regulatory Agencies*
1525 Sherman St Rm 110 ... Denver CO 80203-1749
Fax: 303 866-2018
303 534-1208 *Department of Revenue* 1375 Sherman St ... Denver CO 80261-0001
Fax: 303 620-4487
303 866-2442 *Department of the Treasury* 200 E Colfax Ave Rm 140 ... Denver CO 80203-1716
Fax: 303 866-2123
303 892-3840 *Division of Commerce & Development*
1625 Broadway Suite 1710 ... Denver CO 80202-4729
Fax: 303 892-3848
303 239-4442 *Division of Criminal Justice* 700 Kipling St Suite 3000 ... Denver CO 80215-5865
Fax: 303 239-4485
303 273-1624 *Division of Disaster Emergency Services* Camp George W ... Golden CO 80401-0000
Fax: 303 273-1795
303 764-2913 *Division of Labor* 1120 Lincoln Chancery Bldg 14th Fl ... Denver CO 80203-0000
Fax: 303 764-2973
303 866-3401 *Division of Mines* 1313 Sherman St Rm 215 ... Denver CO 80203-2243
Fax: 303 832-8106
303 620-4441 *Division of Purchasing* 303 W Colfax Ave Suite 600 ... Denver CO 80204-2623
Fax: 303 620-4434
303 894-2320 *Division of Securities* 1580 Lincoln St Suite 420 ... Denver CO 80203-0000
Fax: Unlisted
303 866-2055 *Division of State Archives & Public Records*
1313 Sherman St Rm 1B-20 ... Denver CO 80203-2236
303 866-3581 *Division of Water Resources* 1313 Sherman St Rm 818 ... Denver CO 80203-2238
Fax: 303 866-3589
303 866-2471 *Governor* 136 State Capitol ... Denver CO 80203-0000
Fax: 303 894-8243
303 331-4902 *Health & Statistics Div* 4210 E 11th Ave ... Denver CO 80220-3700
303 757-9011 *Highways Dept* 4201 E Arkansas Ave ... Denver CO 80222-3406
Fax: 303 757-9149 Mail Rm
303 620-4300 *Insurance Div* 303 W Colfax Ave Suite 500 ... Denver CO 80204-2623
303 866-2087 *Lieutenant Governor* 130 State Capitol ... Denver CO 80203-0000
Fax: 303 894-8243
303 894-2144 *Office of Energy Conservation* 112 E 14th Ave ... Denver CO 80203-2129
Fax: 303 832-3148
303 866-3386 *Office of State Planning & Budgeting* 111 State Capitol ... Denver CO 80203-0000
Fax: 303 894-8243
303 894-2100 *Oil & Gas Conservation Commission*
1580 Logan St Suite 380 ... Denver CO 80203-1940
Fax: 303 894-2109
303 620-4888 *Public Defender* 110 16th St Suite 800 ... Denver CO 80202-5210
303 894-2001 *Public Utilities Commission* 1580 Logan St 2nd Fl ... Denver CO 80203-1939
Fax: 303 894-2065
303 894-2166 *Real Estate Commission* 1776 Logan St 4th Fl ... Denver CO 80203-1248
303 894-2200 *Secretary of State* 1560 Broadway Suite 200 ... Denver CO 80202-5169
Fax: 303 894-2242
303 866-5700 *Social Services Dept* 1575 Sherman St ... Denver CO 80203-1714
Fax: 303 866-4214
303 894-2465 *State Board of Parole* 1580 Lincoln St Suite 920 ... Denver CO 80203-1511
Fax: 303 894-2473
303 620-4451 *State Buildings Div* 303 W Colfax Ave Suite 1450 ... Denver CO 80204-2600
Fax: 303 620-4833
303 239-4403 *State Patrol* 700 Kipling St Suite 3000 ... Denver CO 80215-5885
Fax: 303 239-4485
303 861-1111 *Supreme Court* 1301 Pennsylvania Ave ... Denver CO 80203-2116
Fax: 303 831-1814
303 866-6357 *Unemployment Insurance Section* 251 E 12th Ave ... Denver CO 80203-2272
303 331-4830 *Waste Management Div* 4210 E 11th Ave ... Denver CO 80220-3700
Fax: 303 322-9076
303 866-6900 **Colorado State Library** 201 E Colfax Ave ... Denver CO 80203-1704
Fax: 303 830-0793
303 491-1101 **Colorado State University** ... Fort Collins CO 80523-0001
Fax: 303 491-0520
303 491-6273 *College of Agricultural Sciences*
Shepardson Bldg Rm 121 ... Fort Collins CO 80523-0001
Fax: 303 491-4895
303 491-6603 *College of Engineering* Engineering Bldg Rm 111 ... Fort Collins CO 80523-0001
Fax: 303 491-2249
303 491-7051 *College of Veterinary Medicine & Biomedical Science*
Anatomy Bldg Rm W-102 ... Fort Collins CO 80523-0001
Fax: 303 491-2250
303 491-6381 *Department of Chemistry* Chemistry Bldg Rm B101 ... Fort Collins CO 80523-0001
Fax: 303 491-1801
719 598-0200 **Colorado Technical College** 4435 N Chestnut St ... Colorado Springs CO 80907-3895
Fax: 719 598-3740
303 592-5410 **Colorado Tourism Board** 1625 Broadway Suite 1700 ... Denver CO 80202-4734
Fax: 303 592-5406
912 985-1324 **Colquitt County** Main St ... Moultrie GA 31776-0000
509 547-0511 **Columbia Basin College** 2600 N 20th Ave ... Pasco WA 99301-3397
Fax: Ext 260
803 754-4100 **Columbia Bible College & Seminary** PO Box 3122 ... Columbia SC 29230-3122
Fax: Unlisted
503 255-7060 **Columbia Christian College** 9101 E Burnside St ... Portland OR 97216-1599
209 533-5100 **Columbia College** PO Box 1849 ... Columbia CA 95310-1849
Fax: 209 533-5104
312 663-1600 **Columbia College** 600 S Michigan Ave ... Chicago IL 60605-1996
Fax: 312 663-1707
314 875-8700 **Columbia College** 10001 Rogers St ... Columbia MO 65216-0001
Fax: 314 875-8765 Admin
803 786-3012 **Columbia College** 1301 Columbia College Dr ... Columbia SC 29203-5998
Fax: 803 786-3647
414 961-4202 **Columbia College** 2121 E Newport Ave ... Milwaukee WI 53211-2952
Fax: 414 961-8712
213 851-0550 **Columbia College-Hollywood** 925 N La Brea Ave ... Hollywood CA 90038-2392
Fax: 213 851-6401
501 234-2542 **Columbia County** 1 Court Sq ... Magnolia AR 71753-3527
904 755-4100 **Columbia County** 35 N Hernando St ... Lake City FL 32055-4008
Fax: 904 752-7125
404 541-1139 **Columbia County** PO Box 100 ... Appling GA 30802-0100
518 828-3339 **Columbia County** Allen & Union Sts ... Hudson NY 12534-0000

503 397-4322 **Columbia County** County Courthouse .... Saint Helens OR 97051-0000
Fax: 503 397-2760

717 784-1991 **Columbia County** PO Box 380 .... Bloomsburg PA 17815-0380
Fax: 717 784-0257

509 382-4542 **Columbia County** 341 E Main St .... Dayton WA 99328-1361

608 742-2191 **Columbia County** PO Box 177 .... Portage WI 53901-0177

803 799-2810 **Columbia Museum of Art** 1112 Bull St .... Columbia SC 29201-3703
Fax: 803 343-2150

415 459-1650 **Columbia Pacific University** 1415 3rd St .... San Rafael CA 94901-2860
Fax: 415 459-5856

503 325-2323 **Columbia River Maritime Museum** 1792 Marine Dr .... Astoria OR 97103-3525
Fax: 503 325-2331

615 388-0120 **Columbia State Community College** Hwy 99 W .... Columbia TN 38402-0000

301 270-9200 **Columbia Union College** 7600 Flower Ave .... Takoma Park MD 20912-7796
Fax: 301 270-1618

212 854-1754 **Columbia University** E 116th St & Broadway .... New York NY 10029-1728
Fax: 212 749-0397

212 305-3592 *College of Physicians & Surgeons* 630 W 168th St .... New York NY 10032-3702
Fax: Unlisted

212 305-3451 *Department of Anatomy & Cell Biology* 630 W 168th St .... New York NY 10032-3702
Fax: 212 305-3970

212 854-3414 *Graduate School of Architecture*
Broadway & W 116th St Avery Hall Rm 400 .... New York NY 10027-0000
Fax: 212 864-0410

212 854-3513 *Graduate School of Architecture Planning & Preservation*
Avery Hall Rm 400 .... New York NY 10027-0000
Fax: 212 864-0410

212 854-4737 *Graduate School of Arts & Science*
107 Low Memorial Library .... New York NY 10027-0000

212 305-3882 *Graduate School of Biochemistry* 630 W 168th St .... New York NY 10032-3702
Fax: 212 305-6279

212 854-2747 *Graduate School of Business*
Broadway & W 116th St Uris Hall Rm 810 .... New York NY 10027-0000
Fax: 212 678-0825

212 854-2433 *Graduate School of Chemistry* Havemeyer Hall Rm 344 .... New York NY 10027-0000
Fax: 212 932-1289

212 854-4150 *Graduate School of Journalism*
Broadway & W 116th St 7th Fl .... New York NY 10027-0000
Fax: 212 854-7837

212 854-3366 *Graduate School of Physics* 538 W 120th St .... New York NY 10027-6601
Fax: 212 316-9504

212 854-2241 *Library* Butler Library .... New York NY 10027-0000

212 305-3478 *School of Dental & Oral Surgery* 630 W 168th St .... New York NY 10032-3702
Fax: 212 305-8119

212 854-2931 *School of Engineering & Applied Science*
500 W 120th St Mudd Bldg Rm 530 .... New York NY 10027-0000
Fax: 212 932-9420

212 854-2993 *School of Engineering & Applied Science*
500 W 120th St Mudd Bldg Rm 510 .... New York NY 10027-0000

212 854-2640 *School of Law* 435 W 116th St .... New York NY 10027-7201
Fax: 212 854-1915

212 854-2294 *School of Library Service* 516 Butler Library .... New York NY 10027-0000

212 305-5756 *School of Nursing* 617 W 168th St .... New York NY 10032-3703
Fax: 212 305-1116

212 305-4122 *School of Public Health* 600 W 168th St .... New York NY 10032-3702
Fax: 212 305-6832

518 828-4181 **Columbia-Greene Community College** Rt 23 .... Hudson NY 12534-0000
Fax: 518 828-8543

216 424-9511 **Columbiana County** 105 S Market St .... Lisbon OH 44432-1255

614 645-8100 **Columbus City Hall** 90 W Broad St .... Columbus OH 43215-4144
Fax: 614 645-7051 Purchasing

601 434-7322 **Columbus Air Force Base** .... Columbus MS 39701-0000

404 568-2001 **Columbus College** .... Columbus GA 31993-0001
Fax: 404 568-2084

614 224-9101 **Columbus College of Art & Design** 107 N 9th St .... Columbus OH 43215-1758

919 642-5700 **Columbus County** 111 Washington St .... Whiteville NC 28472-3323
Fax: 919 642-1876

614 645-2800 **Columbus Metropolitan Library** 28 S Hamilton Rd .... Columbus OH 43213-2013
Fax: 614 645-2080

404 322-0400 **Columbus Museum** 1251 Wynnton Rd .... Columbus GA 31906-2810

614 221-6801 **Columbus Museum of Art** 480 E Broad St .... Columbus OH 43215-3886

614 227-2400 **Columbus State Community College** 550 E Spring St .... Columbus OH 43215-1786
Fax: 614 227-5117

916 458-5146 **Colusa County** 546 Jay St .... Colusa CA 95932-2443

512 620-5501 **Comal County** 100 Main Plaza .... New Braunfels TX 78130-5140
Fax: 512 620-5592

316 582-2361 **Comanche County** PO Box 397 .... Coldwater KS 67029-0397

405 353-3717 **Comanche County** PO Box 9026 .... Lawton OK 73501-0000

915 356-2655 **Comanche County** County Courthouse .... Comanche TX 76442-0000

202 225-4005 **Combest Larry (Rep - R - Texas)** 1527 Longworth Bldg .... Washington DC 20515-0001
Fax: 202 225-9615

215 665-0445 **Combs College of Music** 1811 Spring Garden St .... Philadelphia PA 19130-3916

202 224-5115 **Commerce Science & Transportation Committee (US Senate)**
508 Dirksen Bldg .... Washington DC 20510-0001
Fax: Unlisted

202 366-2937 **Commercial Space Transportation (US Dept of Transportation)**
400 7th St SW Rm 10401 .... Washington DC 20590-0000
Fax: 202 426-0755

216 736-2161 **Commission for Racial Justice** 700 Prospect Ave E .... Cleveland OH 44115-1131
Fax: 216 736-2171

202 504-2200 **Commission of Fine Arts**
401 F St NW Tension Bldg Suite 312 .... Washington DC 20001-0000
Fax: 202 504-2195

202 376-8364 **Commission on Civil Rights** 1121 Vermont Ave NW .... Washington DC 20425-0001
Fax: 202 376-1163

816 426-5253 *Central Region* 911 Walnut St .... Kansas City MO 64106-2009
Fax: 816 426-2233

202 523-5264 *Eastern Region* 1121 Vermont Ave NW .... Washington DC 20425-0001
Fax: 202 376-1163

213 894-3437 *Western Region* 3660 Wilshire Blvd Suite 810 .... Los Angeles CA 90010-2714
Fax: 213 894-0508

212 688-2063 **Committee for Economic Development**
477 Madison Ave 6th Fl .... New York NY 10022-5893
Fax: 212 758-9068

703 557-1145 **Committee for Purchase from the Blind & Other Severely Handicapped**
1755 Jefferson Davis Hwy Suite 1107 .... Arlington VA 22202-3509
Fax: 703 521-7713

512 340-9100 **Committee for Thorough Agricultural Political Education**
6609 Blanco Rd .... San Antonio TX 78216-6131
Fax: 512 340-9158

202 393-4695 **Committee on Letter Carriers Political Education**
100 Indiana Ave NW .... Washington DC 20001-2144
Fax: 202 737-1540

202 447-4785 **Commodity Credit Corp (US Dept of Agriculture)**
14th St & Independence Ave SW Rm 5714-S .... Washington DC 20250-0001

202 254-8630 **Commodity Futures Trading Commission** 2033 K St NW .... Washington DC 20581-0001
Fax: 202 254-6265

312 353-6642 *Central Region* 233 S Wacker Dr Suite 4600 .... Chicago IL 60606-6397
Fax: 312 886-8470

212 466-2071 *Eastern Region* 1 World Trade Ctr Suite 4747 .... New York NY 10048-0471
Fax: 212 466-5723

816 374-6602 *Southwestern Region* 4900 Main St Suite 721 .... Kansas City MO 64112-2644
Fax: 816 374-6595

213 209-6783 *Western Region* 10880 Wilshire Blvd Suite 1005 .... Los Angeles CA 90024-4111
Fax: 213 470-6397

202 833-1200 **Common Cause** 2030 M St NW .... Washington DC 20036-3380
Fax: 202 659-3716

202 728-2465 **Communications Workers of America COPE Political Contributions Committee**
1925 K St NW Suite 211 .... Washington DC 20006-1153
Fax: 202 659-1094

212 989-4994 **Communist Party USA** 235 W 23rd St 7th Fl .... New York NY 10011-2383
Fax: 212 645-5436

703 548-8600 **Community Assns Institute** 1423 Powhatan St Suite 7 .... Alexandria VA 22314-1343
Fax: 703 684-1581

Community College of Allegheny County

412 237-2525 *Allegheny Campus* 808 Ridge Ave .... Pittsburgh PA 15212-6097

412 371-8651 *Boyce Campus* 595 Beatty Rd .... Monroeville PA 15146-1348

412 366-7000 *North Campus* 1130 Perry Hwy .... Pittsburgh PA 15237-2174
Fax: 412 369-3624

412 469-1100 *South Campus* 1750 Carton Rd .... West Mifflin PA 15122-0000
Fax: 412 469-6370

301 396-0203 **Community College of Baltimore** 2901 Liberty Heights Ave .... Baltimore MD 21215-7807
Fax: 301 728-4079

412 775-8561 **Community College of Beaver County** 1 Campus Dr .... Monaca PA 15061-2588

303 556-2600 **Community College of Denver** PO Box 173363 .... Denver CO 80217-3363
Fax: 303 556-8555

215 751-8000 **Community College of Philadelphia**
1700 Spring Garden St .... Philadelphia PA 19130-3991
Fax: 215 751-8762 Library

Community College of Rhode Island

401 333-7000 *Flanagan Campus* 1762 Louisquissett Pike .... Lincoln RI 02865-4585
Fax: 401 333-7111

401 825-1000 *Knight Campus* 400 East Ave .... Warwick RI 02886-1807
Fax: 401 825-2418

205 293-7064 **Community College of the Air Force** CCAF-RR Bldg 836 .... Maxwell AFB AL 36112-0000

716 394-3500 **Community College of the Finger Lakes** Lincoln Hill Rd .... Canandaigua NY 14424-0000
Fax: 716 394-5005 Library

802 241-3535 **Community College of Vermont** PO Box 120 .... Waterbury VT 05676-0120
Fax: 802 244-5400

202 755-6270 **Community Planning & Development Program (US Dept of Housing & Urban Development)**
451 7th St SW Rm 7100 .... Washington DC 20410-0001
Fax: 202 755-0299

301 492-5929 **Community Relations Service (US Dept of Justice)**
5550 Friendship Blvd Rm 330 .... Chevy Chase MD 20815-7287
Fax: 301 492-5984

617 565-6830 *Region 1* 10 Causeway St Rm 1192 .... Boston MA 02222-1047
Fax: 617 565-6840

212 264-0700 *Region 2* 26 Federal Plaza Suite 3402 .... New York NY 10278-0140
Fax: 212 264-2143

215 597-2344 *Region 3* 2nd & Chestnut Sts Rm 309 .... Philadelphia PA 19106-0000
Fax: 215 597-9148

404 331-6883 *Region 4* 75 Piedmont Ave NE Suite 900 .... Atlanta GA 30303-2588
Fax: 404 331-4471

312 353-4391 *Region 5* 175 W Jackson Blvd Suite 1113 .... Chicago IL 60604-2701
Fax: 312 353-4390

214 767-0824 *Region 6* 1100 Commerce St Suite 13B37 .... Dallas TX 75242-1003
Fax: 214 767-8731

816 426-2022 *Region 7* 911 Walnut St Suite 2411 .... Kansas City MO 64106-2009
Fax: 816 426-7512

303 844-2973 *Region 8* 1244 N Speer Blvd Suite 650 .... Denver CO 80204-3584
Fax: 303 564-2907

415 744-6565 *Region 9* 211 Main St Suite 1040 .... San Francisco CA 94105-1924
Fax: 415 744-6590

206 442-4465 *Region 10* 915 2nd Ave Rm 1898 .... Seattle WA 98174-1001
Fax: 206 442-4905

212 972-8010 **Comoros: Islamic Federal Republic of the Comoros Mission to the UN**
336 E 45th St 2nd Fl .... New York NY 10017-3401

719 594-9900 **Compassion International** 3955 Cragwood Dr .... Colorado Springs CO 80918-7860
Fax: 719 594-6271

213 637-2660 **Compton Community College** 1111 E Artesia Blvd .... Compton CA 90221-5393
Fax: 213 608-3721

202 447-1750 **Comptroller of the Currency (US Dept of the Treasury)**
490 L'Enfant Plaza SW .... Washington DC 20219-0001
Fax: 202 447-1957

Comptroller of the Currency

312 663-8000 *Central District* 440 S La Salle St .... Chicago IL 60605-1073
Fax: 312 663-8102

816 556-1800 *Midwestern District* 2345 Grand Ave Suite 700 .... Kansas City MO 64108-2600
Fax: Unlisted

212 819-9860 *Northeastern District* 1114 Ave of the Americas Suite 3900 . New York NY 10036-7703
Fax: 212 790-4098

404 659-8855 *Southeastern District*
245 Peachtree Center Ave NE 1 Marquis Tower Suite 600 .... Atlanta GA 30303-1246
Fax: 404 588-4532

214 720-0656 *Southwestern District* 500 N Akard St Suite 1600 .... Dallas TX 75201-3342
Fax: 214 720-7098

415 545-5900 *Western District* 50 Fremont St Suite 3900 .... San Francisco CA 94105-2240
Fax: 415 545-5925

617 426-2800 **Computer Museum** 300 Congress St .... Boston MA 02210-0000
Fax: 617 426-2943

816 944-2218 **Conception Seminary College** Conception Abbey .... Conception MO 64433-0000
Fax: Unlisted

915 732-4322 **Concho County** PO Box 98 .... Paint Rock TX 76866-0098

304 384-3115 **Concord College** Vermillion St .... Athens WV 24712-0000
Fax: 304 384-9044

205 874-5700 **Concordia College** 1804 Green St .... Selma AL 36701-3323
Fax: 205 822-8307

708 771-8300 **Concordia College** 7400 Augusta St .... River Forest IL 60305-1499
Fax: 708 209-3176

313 995-7300 **Concordia College** 4090 Geddes Rd .... Ann Arbor MI 48105-2797
Fax: 313 995-7405

914 337-9300 **Concordia College** 171 White Plains Rd .... Bronxville NY 10708-1998
Fax: 914 395-4500

503 288-9371 **Concordia College** 2811 NE Holman St .... Portland OR 97211-6099
Fax: 503 280-8518

414 243-5700 **Concordia College** 12800 N Lake Shore Dr .... Mequon WI 53092-7699
Fax: 414 243-4351

218 299-4321 **Concordia College at Moorhead** 901 S 8th St .... Moorhead MN 56562-0001
Fax: 218 299-3947

612 641-8278 **Concordia College at Saint Paul** 275 Syndicate St N .... Saint Paul MN 55104-5494
Fax: 612 659-0207

512 452-7661 **Concordia Lutheran College** 3400 N IH-35 .... Austin TX 78705-2799
  Fax: 512 459-8517
318 336-4204 **Concordia Parish** PO Box 790 .... Vidalia LA 71373-0790
402 643-3651 **Concordia Teachers College** 800 N Columbia Ave .... Seward NE 68434-1594
  Fax: 402 643-4073
202 225-6131 **Condit Gary (Rep - D - California)** 1529 Longworth Bldg .... Washington DC 20515-0001
  Fax: 202 225-0819
205 578-2095 **Conecuh County** PO Box 347 .... Evergreen AL 36401-0347
719 376-5772 **Conejos County** PO Box 157 .... Conejos CO 81129-0157
Congo: People's Republic of the Congo
202 726-5500 *Embassy* 4891 Colorado Ave NW .... Washington DC 20011-3731
212 744-7840 *Mission to the UN* 14 E 65th St .... New York NY 10021-7005
718 434-3580 **Congress of Racial Equality** 1457 Flatbush Ave .... Brooklyn NY 11210-2428
  Fax: 718 434-6273
202 586-5450 **Congressional & Intergovernmental Affairs Office (US Dept of Energy)**
  1000 Independence Ave SW Rm 7B-138 .... Washington DC 20585-0001
  Fax: 202 586-4891
202 343-7693 **Congressional & Legislative Affairs Office (US Dept of the Interior)**
  1849 C St NW MS-6246 .... Washington DC 20240-0001
  Fax: 202 343-7619
202 226-2621 **Congressional Budget Office** 2nd & D Sts SW .... Washington DC 20515-0001
  Fax: 202 226-2601
202 332-1155 **Congressional Club** 2001 New Hampshire Ave NW .... Washington DC 20009-3484
202 447-7095 **Congressional Relations Office (US Dept of Agriculture)**
  14th St & Independence Ave SW Rm 205-E .... Washington DC 20250-0001
  Fax: 202 447-8077
202 707-5700 **Congressional Research Service**
  101 Independence Ave SE LM 213 .... Washington DC 20540-0000
203 547-1661 **Connecticut Business & Industry Assn** 370 Asylum St 5th Fl .... Hartford CT 06103-2022
  Fax: 203 278-8562
203 447-1911 **Connecticut College** 270 Mohegan Ave .... New London CT 06320-4196
  Fax: 203 447-7809
203 278-6080 **Connecticut Democratic State Central Committee**
  634 Asylum Ave .... Hartford CT 06105-3836
  Fax: 203 278-5879
203 236-5621 **Connecticut Historical Society Museum** 1 Elizabeth St ...... Hartford CT 06105-2292
  Fax: 203 236-2664
203 547-0589 **Connecticut Republican Party** 78 Oak St .... Hartford CT 06106-1514
  Fax: 203 278-8563
Connecticut State Government
203 566-2750 *Information* 165 Capitol Ave .... Hartford CT 06106-1630
203 566-4667 *Agriculture Dept* 165 Capitol Ave .... Hartford CT 06106-1630
  Fax: 203 566-6094
203 566-3690 *Archives Dept* 231 Capitol Ave .... Hartford CT 06106-1537
203 566-7098 *Attorney General* 55 Elm St 4th Fl .... Hartford CT 06106-1774
  Fax: 203 566-1704
203 566-4030 *Bureau of Air Management* 165 Capitol Ave Rm 144 .... Hartford CT 06106-1630
  Fax: 203 566-6144
203 566-3854 *Bureau of Highways* 24 Wolcott Hill Rd .... Wethersfield CT 06109-1154
  Fax: 203 566-5824 Personnel
203 566-7177 *Bureau of Licensing & Regulation* 165 Capitol Ave .... Hartford CT 06106-1630
  Fax: 203 566-7630
203 566-3360 *Bureau of Public Works* 165 Capitol Ave .... Hartford CT 06106-1630
  Fax: 203 566-1934
203 638-3267 *Bureau of Purchases* 460 Silver St .... Middletown CT 06457-0000
  Fax: 203 638-3329
203 566-5328 *Chief Public Defender Services Commission*
  1 Hartford Sq W Suite 201 .... Hartford CT 06106-5114
203 566-4770 *Commission on the Arts* 227 Lawrence St .... Hartford CT 06106-1430
203 566-4298 *Comprehensive Planning Div Office of Policy & Management*
  80 Washington St .... Hartford CT 06106-4417
  Fax: 203 566-6295
203 749-8391 *Connecticut Correctional Institution* PO Box 100 .... Somers CT 06071-0100
203 566-7528 *Department of Administrative Services* 165 Capitol Ave ...... Hartford CT 06106-1630
  Fax: 203 566-3678
203 566-4999 *Department of Consumer Protection* 165 Capitol Ave .... Hartford CT 06106-1630
  Fax: 203 566-7630
203 566-4457 *Department of Corrections* 340 Capitol Ave .... Hartford CT 06106-1494
  Fax: 203 566-1741
203 258-4244 *Department of Economic Development* 865 Brook St .... Rocky Hill CT 06067-3405
  Fax: 203 721-7650
203 566-5061 *Department of Education* 165 Capitol Ave .... Hartford CT 06106-1630
  Fax: 203 566-1625
203 566-2110 *Department of Environmental Protection* 165 Capitol Ave ..... Hartford CT 06106-1600
  Fax: 203 566-7932
203 566-2038 *Department of Health Services* 150 Washington St .... Hartford CT 06106-4476
  Fax: 203 566-3302
203 566-3913 *Department of Higher Education* 61 Woodland St .... Hartford CT 06105-2326
  Fax: 203 566-7865
203 566-4384 *Department of Labor* 200 Folly Brook Blvd .... Wethersfield CT 06109-1109
  Fax: 203 566-1520
203 827-1553 *Department of Public Utility Control* 1 Central Park Plaza .. New Britain CT 06051-2291
  Fax: 203 827-2613
203 566-8520 *Department of Revenue Services* 92 Farmington Ave .... Hartford CT 06105-3712
  Fax: 203 297-5797
203 566-3477 *Department of Transportation* 24 Wolcott Hill Rd .... Wethersfield CT 06109-1100
  Fax: 203 566-4904
203 566-4550 *Division of Occupational Safety & Health*
  200 Folly Brook Blvd .... Wethersfield CT 06109-1109
  Fax: Unlisted
203 566-4560 *Division of Securities & Business Investments*
  44 Capitol Ave .... Hartford CT 06106-1706
  Fax: 203 566-8382
203 566-3200 *Division of State Police* 100 Washington St .... Hartford CT 06106-4419
  Fax: 203 566-8453
203 240-3256 *Economic Development Branch of Commerce*
  450 Main St Rm 519 .... Hartford CT 06106-0000
203 566-4280 *Employment Security Div* 200 Folly Brook Blvd .... Wethersfield CT 06109-1113
  Fax: 203 566-1520
203 566-2800 *Energy Div* 80 Washington St .... Hartford CT 06106-4417
  Fax: 203 566-6295
203 566-4840 *Governor* 210 Capitol Ave .... Hartford CT 06106-1568
  Fax: 203 566-4677
203 297-3800 *Insurance Dept* 165 Capitol Ave .... Hartford CT 06106-1630
  Fax: 203 566-7410
203 566-2614 *Lieutenant Governor* 210 Capitol Ave .... Hartford CT 06106-1501
203 566-3020 *Management & Justice Planning Div* 80 Washington St .... Hartford CT 06106-4417
  Fax: 203 566-6295
203 566-8350 *Office of Adult Probation* 643 Maple Ave .... Hartford CT 06114-1888
203 566-3180 *Office of Emergency Management* 360 Broad St .... Hartford CT 06105-3713
  Fax: 203 247-0664
203 566-8070 *Office of Policy & Management* 80 Washington St .... Hartford CT 06106-4458
  Fax: 203 566-6295
203 566-5131 *Real Estate Commission* 165 Capitol Ave .... Hartford CT 06106-1630
  Fax: 203 566-7630

203 566-2668 *Secretary of State* State Capitol Bldg Rm 104 .... Hartford CT 06106-0000
  Fax: 203 566-6318
203 566-3672 *Solid Waste Management Unit* 1820 Trinity St .... Hartford CT 06106-0000
203 566-8160 *Supreme Court* PO Box Z Stn A .... Hartford CT 06106-0977
203 566-5050 *Treasurer* 55 Elm St .... Hartford CT 06106-1773
  Fax: 203 566-3442
203 566-5790 *Unemployment Compensation Div* 90 Washington St .... Hartford CT 06103-1085
203 566-1188 *Vital Records & Statistics* 150 Washington St .... Hartford CT 06106-4405
  Fax: 203 566-3302
203 566-7220 *Water Resources Unit* 165 Capitol Ave .... Hartford CT 06106-1630
  Fax: 203 566-5587
203 789-7783 *Worker's Compensation Commission* 1890 Dixwell Ave ...... Hamden CT 06514-3182
  Fax: 203 789-7375
203 566-4301 **Connecticut State Library** 231 Capitol Ave .... Hartford CT 06106-1537
203 486-4460 **Connecticut State Museum of Natural History**
  75 N Eagleville Rd University of Connecticut U-23 .... Storrs CT 06269-0001
203 258-4286 **Connecticut Tourism Div** 865 Brook St .... Rocky Hill CT 06067-3405
  Fax: 203 563-4877
413 732-3080 **Connecticut Valley Historical Museum** 194 State St .... Springfield MA 01103-1715
317 776-6000 **Conner Prairie Museum** 13400 Allisonville Rd .... Noblesville IN 46060-4499
  Fax: 317 776-6014
918 463-2931 **Connors State College** RR 1 Box 1000 .... Warner OK 74469-9700
  Fax: 918 463-2233
202 224-2043 **Conrad Kent (Sen - D - North Dakota)** 361 Dirksen Bldg ..... Washington DC 20510-0001
  Fax: 202 224-7776
800 523-2929 **Conservation & Renewal Energy Hotline (US Dept of Energy)**
  200 N 15th St S Suite 407 .... Arlington VA 22202-3304
  Fax: Unlisted
703 522-2104 **Conservative National Committee**
  2030 Clarendon Blvd Suite 305 .... Arlington VA 22201-2915
  Fax: 703 528-8724
718 921-2158 **Conservative Party** 486 78th St .... Brooklyn NY 11209-3404
  Fax: 718 921-5268
202 647-1488 **Consular Affairs Bureau (US Dept of State)**
  2201 C St NW Rm 5807 CA-PA .... Washington DC 20520-0001
  Fax: 202 647-0341
202 387-6121 **Consumer Federation of America**
  1424 16th St NW Suite 604 .... Washington DC 20036-2211
301 492-6800 **Consumer Product Safety Commission** 5401 Westbard Ave .... Bethesda MD 20816-0000
  Fax: 301 492-6924
404 347-2231 *Atlanta Region* 730 Peachtree St NE Suite 871 .... Atlanta GA 30365-0001
  Fax: 404 347-3649
312 353-8260 *Chicago Region* 230 S Dearborn St Rm 2944 .... Chicago IL 60604-1671
  Fax: 312 353-5013
212 264-1125 *New York Region* 6 World Trade Ctr Suite 301 .... New York NY 10048-0950
  Fax: 212 264-1372
415 705-1816 *San Francisco Region* 555 Battery St Suite 415 .... San Francisco CA 94111-2390
  Fax: 415 556-8832
202 785-4835 **Consumers for World Trade** 1726 M St NW Suite 900 ...... Washington DC 20036-4502
  Fax: 202 833-1577
202 225-5335 **Conte Silvio O (Rep - R - Massachusetts)**
  2300 Rayburn Bldg .... Washington DC 20515-0001
  Fax: 202 226-1224
713 526-0773 **Contemporary Arts Museum** 5216 Montrose Blvd .... Houston TX 77006-6598
  Fax: 713 526-6749
415 229-1000 **Contra Costa Community College (System)** 500 Court St .... Martinez CA 94553-1278
  Fax: 415 370-6517
415 235-7800 **Contra Costa Community College San Pablo Campus**
  2600 Mission Bell Dr .... San Pablo CA 94806-3195
  Fax: 415 236-6768
415 646-2950 **Contra Costa County** 725 Court St .... Martinez CA 94553-1233
415 646-6423 **Contra Costa County Library** 1750 Oak Park Blvd .... Pleasant Hill CA 94523-4412
803 585-6421 **Converse College** 580 E Main St .... Spartanburg SC 29302-0006
  Fax: 803 596-9158
307 358-2061 **Converse County** PO Box 990 .... Douglas WY 82633-0990
501 354-9621 **Conway County** Moose & Church Sts .... Morrilton AR 72110-0000
202 225-5126 **Conyers John Jr (Rep - D - Michigan)** 2426 Rayburn Bldg .. Washington DC 20515-0001
  Fax: 202 225-0072
912 896-2266 **Cook County** 212 N Hutchinson Ave .... Adel GA 31620-2400
312 443-6398 **Cook County** 118 N Clark St Suite 567 .... Chicago IL 60602-1311
218 387-2524 **Cook County** PO Box 1048 .... Grand Marais MN 55604-0117
817 668-5420 **Cooke County** Dixon St County Courthouse .... Gainesville TX 76240-0000
  Fax: 817 668-5499 Legal
817 668-7731 **Cooke County College** 1525 W California St .... Gainesville TX 76240-4699
  Fax: 817 668-6049
816 882-2114 **Cooper County** PO Box 123 .... Boonville MO 65233-0123
202 225-6831 **Cooper Jim (Rep - D - Tennessee)** 125 Cannon Bldg .... Washington DC 20515-0001
  Fax: 202 225-4520
212 254-6300 **Cooper Union College** E 7th St 41 Cooper Sq .... New York NY 10003-0000
  Fax: 212 353-4327 PR
212 860-6868 **Cooper-Hewitt Museum (Smithsonian Institution)**
  2 E 91st St .... New York NY 10128-0669
  Fax: 212 860-6909
212 870-3000 **Coordination in Development** 475 Riverside Dr Rm 1842 ...... New York NY 10115-0122
  Fax: 212 870-3545
603 788-4900 **Coos County** PO Box 309 .... Lancaster NH 03584-0309
503 396-3121 **Coos County** 250 N Baxter St .... Coquille OR 97423-1894
  Fax: 503 396-4861
205 377-2420 **Coosa County** PO Box 218 .... Rockford AL 35136-0218
601 894-3021 **Copiah County** PO Box 507 .... Hazlehurst MS 39083-0507
601 643-5101 **Copiah-Lincoln Community College** PO Box 457 .... Wesson MS 39191-0457
  Fax: 601 643-2366
301 333-5990 **Coppin State College** 2500 W North Ave .... Baltimore MD 21216-3698
202 479-0700 **Copyright Office** 101 Independence Ave SE .... Washington DC 20559-0001
  Fax: 202 707-8366
202 653-5175 **Copyright Royalty Tribunal** 1111 20th St NW Suite 450 ...... Washington DC 20036-3477
202 638-3211 **Corcoran Gallery of Art** 17th St & New York Ave NW .... Washington DC 20006-0000
  Fax: 202 737-2664
202 628-9484 **Corcoran School of Art** 17th St & New York Ave NW .... Washington DC 20006-0000
  Fax: 202 737-2664
309 452-4485 **Corn Belt Library System** 1809 Hovey Ave .... Normal IL 61761-4395
  Fax: 309 454-8716
319 895-4000 **Cornell College** 600 1st St W .... Mount Vernon IA 52314-1098
  Fax: 319 895-5237
607 255-2000 **Cornell University** .... Ithaca NY 14853-0001
  Fax: 607 255-3803 Admin
607 255-2241 *College of Agriculture & Life Sciences* Roberts Hall Rm 260 .... Ithaca NY 14853-0001
  Fax: 607 255-3803
607 255-4326 *College of Engineering* 242 Carpenter Hall .... Ithaca NY 14853-0001
  Fax: 607 255-9606
607 255-8593 *Computer Science Program* Upson Hall Rm 4126 .... Ithaca NY 14853-0001
  Fax: 607 255-4428
607 255-2203 *Department of Biochemistry Molecular & Cell Biology*
  Biotechnology Bldg .... Ithaca NY 14853-0001
  Fax: 607 255-2428

607 255-6848 *Department of City & Regional Planning* W Sibley Hall .... Ithaca NY 14853-0001
Fax: 607 255-1900
607 255-5267 *Department of Geological Science* Snee Hall Rm 4122 .... Ithaca NY 14853-0001
Fax: 607 254-4780
607 255-2376 *Division of Biological Sciences* Biotechnology Bldg Rm 169 .... Ithaca NY 14853-0001
Fax: 607 255-2428
607 255-4884 *Graduate School of Physics* 117 Clark Hall .... Ithaca NY 14853-0001
Fax: 607 255-6428
607 255-5036 *Johnson Graduate School of Management* Malott Hall .... Ithaca NY 14853-0001
Fax: 607 254-4590
607 255-3626 *Law School* Myron Taylor Hall .... Ithaca NY 14853-0001
Fax: 607 255-7193
607 255-4144 *Library* Olin Library .... Ithaca NY 14850-0000
Fax: 607 255-9091
212 746-5454 *Medical College* 1300 York Ave .... New York NY 10021-4896
Fax: 212 746-0931
607 253-3000 *New York State College of Veterinary Medicine* Tower Rd .... Ithaca NY 14853-0001
Fax: 607 253-3708
607 255-4139 *School of Chemistry* Baker Laboratory .... Ithaca NY 14853-0001
Fax: 607 255-4137
719 593-7887 **Cornerstone Baptist Bible College** 3615 Vickers Dr .... Colorado Springs CO 80918-0000
607 962-9011 **Corning Community College** Spencer Hill Rd .... Corning NY 14830-0000
Fax: 607 962-9456 Admin
607 937-5371 **Corning Museum of Glass** 1 Museum Way .... Corning NY 14830-2253
Fax: 607 937-3352
206 323-1400 **Cornish College of the Arts** 710 E Roy St .... Seattle WA 98102-4696
Fax: 206 323-1574
202 879-9600 **Corporation for Public Broadcasting** 901 E St NW .... Washington DC 20004-0000
Fax: 202 783-1019
512 939-2070 **Corpus Christi Coast Guard Air Station**
US Coast Guard Group Hangar 41 .... Corpus Christi TX 78419-5500
Fax: Ext 325
512 939-2674 **Corpus Christi Naval Air Station** .... Corpus Christi TX 78418-0000
Fax: 512 939-2913
512 880-7000 **Corpus Christi Public Libraries** 805 Comanche St .... Corpus Christi TX 78401-2715
512 991-6810 **Corpus Christi State University** 6300 Ocean Dr .... Corpus Christi TX 78412-5599
Fax: 512 993-4204
605 273-4201 **Corson County** PO Box 175 .... McIntosh SD 57641-0175
607 753-5052 **Cortland County** 60 Central Ave .... Cortland NY 13045-2718
Fax: 607 753-5392
817 865-5016 **Coryell County** PO Box 237 .... Gatesville TX 76528-0237
614 622-1753 **Coshocton County** 349 1/2 Main St .... Coshocton OH 43812-1510
Fax: 614 622-4487
Costa Rica: Republic of Costa Rica
202 234-2945 *Embassy* 1825 Connecticut Ave NW Suite 211 .... Washington DC 20009-5708
Fax: 202 234-8653
212 986-6373 *Mission to the UN* 211 E 43rd St Suite 903 .... New York NY 10017-4707
Fax: 212 986-6842
202 225-5661 **Costello Jerry (Rep - D - Illinois)** 119 Cannon Bldg .... Washington DC 20515-0001
Fax: 202 225-0285
719 672-3962 **Costilla County** PO Box 100 .... San Luis CO 81152-0100
417 667-8181 **Cottey College** 1000 W Austin St .... Nevada MO 64772-2700
Fax: 417 667-8103
806 492-3823 **Cottle County** PO Box 717 .... Paducah TX 79248-0717
405 875-3026 **Cotton County** 301 N Broadway St .... Walters OK 73572-1271
507 831-1905 **Cottonwood County** 900 3rd Ave .... Windom MN 56101-1699
602 634-7559 **Cottonwood Public Library** 401 E Mingus Ave .... Cottonwood AZ 86326-0000
Fax: 602 634-0253
202 225-6111 **Coughlin Lawrence (Rep - R - Pennsylvania)**
2309 Rayburn Bldg .... Washington DC 20515-0001
Fax: 202 226-1238
617 542-2282 **Council for a Livable World** 20 Park Plaza Suite 603 .... Boston MA 02116-4303
Fax: 617 542-6695
202 395-5108 **Council of Economic Advisers**
17th St & Pennsylvania Ave .... Washington DC 20500-0001
Fax: 202 395-6947
606 252-2291 **Council of State Governments** Iron Works Pike .... Lexington KY 40578-0000
Fax: 606 231-1858
202 624-5386 **Council of State Policy & Planning Agencies**
400 N Capitol St NW Suite 285 .... Washington DC 20001-1511
Fax: 202 624-7846
212 628-3200 **Council of the Americas** 680 Park Ave .... New York NY 10021-5009
Fax: 212 517-6247
202 395-5750 **Council on Environmental Quality** 722 Jackson Pl NW .... Washington DC 20503-0001
Fax: 202 395-3744
202 466-6512 **Council on Foundations** 1828 L St NW Suite 300 .... Washington DC 20036-5168
Fax: 202 785-3926
201 361-5000 **County College of Morris** Rt 10 & Center Grove Rd .... Randolph NJ 07869-0000
Fax: 201 328-1282
804 222-1643 **County of Henrico Public Library** 1001 N Laburnum Ave .... Richmond VA 23223-2705
Fax: 804 222-5566
404 820-1560 **Covenant College** Scenic Hwy .... Lookout Mountain GA 30750-0000
Fax: 404 820-0672
907 766-2992 **Covenant Life College** 26th Mile Hanines Hwy .... Haines AK 99827-0000
401 822-9100 **Coventry Public Library** 1672 Flat River Rd .... Coventry RI 02816-0000
703 965-6300 **Covington (Independent City)** 158 N Court Ave .... Covington VA 24426-1534
Fax: 703 962-7874
205 222-4313 **Covington County** County Courthouse .... Andalusia AL 36420-0000
601 765-4242 **Covington County** PO Box 1679 .... Collins MS 39428-1679
404 254-2600 **Coweta County** PO Box 945 .... Newnan GA 30264-0945
Fax: 404 253-1658
509 456-3931 **Cowles Cheney Museum** W 2316 1st Ave .... Spokane WA 99204-1099
316 221-4066 **Cowley County** 311 E 9th Ave .... Winfield KS 67156-2864
316 442-0430 **Cowley County Community College** 125 S 2nd St .... Arkansas City KS 67005-2662
Fax: 316 442-0713
206 577-3016 **Cowlitz County** 312 SW 1st Ave .... Kelso WA 98626-1798
202 225-5611 **Cox Christopher (Rep - R - California)** 412 Cannon Bldg .... Washington DC 20515-0001
Fax: 202 225-9177
202 225-5676 **Cox John W Jr (Rep - D - Illinois)** 501 Cannon Bldg .... Washington DC 20515-0001
Fax: Unlisted
202 225-2301 **Coyne William J (Rep - D - Pennsylvania)**
2455 Rayburn Bldg .... Washington DC 20515-0001
Fax: Unlisted
304 325-3943 **Craft Memorial Library** 600 Commerce St .... Bluefield WV 24701-3107
714 794-2161 **Crafton Hills College** 11711 Sand Canyon Rd .... Yucaipa CA 92399-1799
Fax: 714 794-0423
918 256-2507 **Craig County** 301 W Canadian Ave .... Vinita OK 74301-3640
703 864-6141 **Craig County** PO Box 185 .... New Castle VA 24127-0185
202 224-2752 **Craig Larry E (Sen - R - Idaho)** 708 Hart Bldg .... Washington DC 20510-0001
Fax: Unlisted
501 933-4500 **Craighead County** 511 S Main St .... Jonesboro AR 72401-2849
202 225-4801 **Cramer Bud (Rep - D - Alabama)** 1431 Longworth Bldg .... Washington DC 20515-0001
Fax: 202 225-4392
313 645-3323 **Cranbrook Academy of Art Museum** 500 Lone Pine Rd .. Bloomfield Hills MI 48013-0000
Fax: 313 646-0046
313 645-3230 **Cranbrook Institute of Science** PO Box 801 .... Bloomfield Hills MI 48304-0000
Fax: 313 645-6545
915 558-3581 **Crane County** PO Box 578 .... Crane TX 79731-0578
202 225-3711 **Crane Philip M (Rep - R - Illinois)** 1035 Longworth Bldg .... Washington DC 20515-0001
Fax: Unlisted
202 224-3553 **Cranston Alan (Sen - D - California)** 112 Hart Bldg .... Washington DC 20510-0001
Fax: 202 224-8128
919 638-4131 **Craven Community College** 800 College Ct .... New Bern NC 28562-5184
Fax: 919 638-4232
919 633-3126 **Craven County** 302 Broad St .... New Bern NC 28560-4903
919 638-2127 **Craven-Pamlico-Carteret Regional Library** 400 Johnson St ... New Bern NC 28560-4048
501 474-1511 **Crawford County** 3rd & Main Sts .... Van Buren AR 72956-0000
912 836-3782 **Crawford County** PO Box 389 .... Knoxville GA 31050-0389
712 263-2242 **Crawford County** PO Box 546 .... Denison IA 51442-0546
618 546-1212 **Crawford County** Douglas St .... Robinson IL 62454-2146
812 338-2565 **Crawford County** PO Box 375 .... English IN 47118-0375
316 724-6115 **Crawford County** County Courthouse .... Girard KS 66743-0000
Fax: 316 724-8823
517 348-2841 **Crawford County** 200 W Michigan Ave .... Grayling MI 49738-1745
Fax: 517 348-7582
314 775-2376 **Crawford County** 201 Main St .... Steelville MO 65565-0000
419 562-5876 **Crawford County** 112 E Mansfield St .... Bucyrus OH 44820-2389
814 336-1151 **Crawford County** 360 Center St .... Meadville PA 16335-0000
608 326-0200 **Crawford County** 220 N Beaumont Rd .... Prairie du Chien WI 53821-1405
Fax: Call company operator
918 224-0278 **Creek County** PO Box 129 .... Sapulpa OK 74067-0129
402 280-2700 **Creighton University** 2400 California St .... Omaha NE 68178-0001
Fax: 402 280-2211
402 280-5060 *Graduate School of Dentistry* 2500 California St .... Omaha NE 68178-0001
Fax: 402 280-5004
402 280-2875 *School of Law* 2133 California St .... Omaha NE 68178-0001
Fax: 402 280-2244
402 280-2900 *School of Medicine* 24th & California Sts .... Omaha NE 68178-0001
Fax: 402 280-2334
402 280-2950 *School of Pharmacy & Allied Health Professions*
24th & California Sts .... Omaha NE 68178-0001
Fax: 402 280-2334
205 335-6568 **Crenshaw County** PO Box 227 .... Luverne AL 36049-0227
901 367-9800 **Crichton College** PO Box 757830 .... Memphis TN 38175-7830
202 633-2601 **Criminal Div (US Dept of Justice)**
10th St & Constitution Ave NW Rm 2107 .... Washington DC 20530-0001
Fax: 202 786-4029
912 276-2672 **Crisp County** 210 7th St S .... Cordele GA 31015-4295
Fax: 912 273-4209
501 739-4434 **Crittenden County** County Courthouse .... Marion AR 72364-0000
502 965-5251 **Crittenden County** 107 S Main St .... Marion KY 42064-1500
916 449-5423 **Crocker Art Museum** 216 'O' St .... Sacramento CA 95814-5399
901 696-5452 **Crockett County** County Courthouse .... Alamo TN 38001-0000
915 392-2022 **Crockett County** 907 Ave D .... Ozona TX 76943-0000
503 447-6555 **Crook County** 300 E 3rd St .... Prineville OR 97754-1949
307 283-1323 **Crook County** PO Box 37 .... Sundance WY 82729-0037
Fax: 307 283-2990
806 675-2334 **Crosby County** PO Box 218 .... Crosbyton TX 79322-0218
501 238-3373 **Cross County** 705 E Union Ave .... Wynne AR 72396-3039
205 493-9526 **Cross Trails Regional Library Service** PO Box 717 .... Opp AL 36467-0717
Fax: Unlisted
218 828-3970 **Crow Wing County** 326 Laurel St .... Brainerd MN 56401-3523
417 451-3223 **Crowder College** 601 Laclede Ave .... Neosho MO 64850-9160
Fax: 417 451-4280
719 267-4643 **Crowley County** 6th & Main St .... Ordway CO 81063-0000
501 935-5133 **Crowley Ridge Regional Library** 315 W Oak St .... Jonesboro AR 72401-3594
Fax: 501 935-7987
212 689-7215 **Cuba: Republic of Cuba Mission to the UN**
315 Lexington Ave .... New York NY 10016-2606
805 546-3100 **Cuesta Community College** Hwy 1 .... San Luis Obispo CA 93401-0000
Fax: 805 546-3904
915 283-2058 **Culberson County** PO Box 158 .... Van Horn TX 79855-0158
914 452-9600 **Culinary Institute of America** 433 Albany Post Rd .... Hyde Park NY 12538-1499
Fax: 914 452-8629
205 739-3530 **Cullman County** 500 2nd Ave SW .... Cullman AL 35055-4155
Fax: 205 737-0876
703 825-3035 **Culpeper County** 135 W Cameron St .... Culpeper VA 22701-0000
Fax: 703 825-1677
314 288-5221 **Culver-Stockton College** .... Canton MO 63435-0000
Fax: 314 288-3984
606 549-2200 **Cumberland College** CC Stn .... Williamsburg KY 40769-0000
Fax: Ext 4490
217 849-2631 **Cumberland County** Courthouse Sq .... Toledo IL 62468-0000
502 864-3726 **Cumberland County** PO Box 275 .... Burkesville KY 42717-0275
207 871-8380 **Cumberland County** 142 Federal St .... Portland ME 04101-4151
919 486-1351 **Cumberland County** 113 Dick St .... Fayetteville NC 28301-5725
609 451-8000 **Cumberland County** Broad & Fayette St .... Bridgeton NJ 08302-2552
717 240-6100 **Cumberland County** Hanover & High Sts .... Carlisle PA 17013-0000
Fax: 717 240-6415
615 484-8212 **Cumberland County** Main St .... Crossville TN 38555-0000
Fax: 615 484-5374
804 492-4280 **Cumberland County** County Courthouse .... Cumberland VA 23040-0000
Fax: 804 492-9224
609 691-8600 **Cumberland County College** Orchard & Sherman Ave .... Vineland NJ 08360-0000
609 453-2210 **Cumberland County Library** 800 E Commerce St .... Bridgeton NJ 08302-2295
Fax: 609 451-1940
919 483-1580 **Cumberland County Public Library** 300 Maiden Ln .... Fayetteville NC 28301-5000
Fax: 919 483-8644
615 444-2562 **Cumberland University** 220 S Greenwood St .... Lebanon TN 37087-3554
402 372-2144 **Cuming County** PO Box 290 .... West Point NE 68788-0290
904 356-6857 **Cummer Gallery of Art** 829 Riverside Ave .... Jacksonville FL 32204-3386
202 225-5452 **Cunningham Randy (Rep - R - California)**
1017 Longworth Bldg .... Washington DC 20515-0001
Fax: 202 225-2558
212 794-5555 **CUNY (System) City University of New York** 535 E 80th St .... New York NY 10021-0795
Fax: 212 794-5397
CUNY
212 447-3000 *Bernard M Baruch College* 155 E 24th St .... New York NY 10010-3727
Fax: 212 447-3705
212 618-1000 *Borough of Manhattan Community College*
199 Chambers St .... New York NY 10007-1006
Fax: 212 618-1010
212 220-6450 *Bronx Community College* W 181st & University Ave .... Bronx NY 10453-2805
Fax: 212 295-2643
718 780-5485 *Brooklyn College* Bedford Ave & Ave H .... Brooklyn NY 11210-0000
Fax: 718 780-3835 Library
212 650-7000 *City College* 138th St & Convent Ave Administration Bldg ... New York NY 10031-0000
Fax: 212 650-5299
718 390-7733 *College of Staten Island* 715 Ocean Terr .... Staten Island NY 10301-4547
Fax: 718 981-2546 Admin

212 960-8000 *Herbert H Lehman College* 250 Bedford Park Blvd W .... Bronx NY 10468-1527
    Fax: 212 584-1765

212 960-1114 *Hostos Community College* 475 Grand Concourse .... Bronx NY 10451-5307
    Fax: 212 960-1120

212 772-4000 *Hunter College* 695 Park Ave .... New York NY 10021-5085
    Fax: 212 772-4724

212 237-8000 *John Jay College of Criminal Justice* 445 W 59th St .... New York NY 10019-1199
    Fax: 212 237-8901

718 368-5000 *Kingsborough Community College* 2001 Oriental Blvd .... Brooklyn NY 11235-2336
    Fax: 718 934-5357

718 482-5000 *La Guardia Community College* 31-10 Thomson Ave . Long Island City NY 11101-3071
    Fax: 718 482-5599

718 270-4900 *Medgar Evers College* 1650 Bedford Ave .... Brooklyn NY 11225-2017
    Fax: 718 270-6496 Admin

212 241-7335 *Mount Sinai School of Medicine* 1 Gustave L Levy Pl .... New York NY 10029-6504
    Fax: 212 996-9764

718 643-4900 *New York City Technical College* 300 Jay St ....Brooklyn NY 11201-2902
    Fax: 718 855-2933

718 520-7000 *Queens College* 65-30 Kissena Blvd ....Flushing NY 11367-1597
718 631-6262 *Queensborough Community College* 222-05 56th Ave .... Bayside NY 11364-1432
718 262-2000 *York College* 94-20 Guy R Brewer Blvd .... Jamaica NY 11451-0001
    Fax: 718 262-2730

212 690-5439 **CUNY City College School of Engineering**
    Convent Ave & W 140th St Steinman Hall ....New York NY 10031-0000

718 390-7994 **CUNY College of Staten Island Graduate School of Environmental Sciences**
    50 Bay St ....Staten Island NY 10301-2511

212 772-5517 **CUNY Hunter College Graduate Program in Urban Affairs & Planning**
    695 Park Ave ....New York NY 10021-5085

212 481-4312 **CUNY Hunter-Bellevue College School of Nursing**
    425 E 25th St ....New York NY 10010-2547
    Fax: 212 418-5078

603 669-6144 **Currier Gallery of Art** 192 Orange St .... Manchester NH 03104-4393
919 232-2075 **Currituck County** PO Box 39 .... Currituck NC 27929-0039
    Fax: 919 232-3026

617 333-0500 **Curry College** 1071 Blue Hill Ave .... Milton MA 02186-2395
    Fax: 617 333-0309

505 763-5591 **Curry County** 700 N Main St ....Clovis NM 88101-6664
503 247-7011 **Curry County** PO Box 746 .... Gold Beach OR 97444-0746
    Fax: 503 247-2718

215 893-5252 **Curtis Institute of Music** 1726 Locust St .... Philadelphia PA 19103-6187
    Fax: 215 893-0194

719 783-2441 **Custer County** 205 S 6th St .... Westcliffe CO 81252-9504
    Fax: 719 783-9085

208 879-2325 **Custer County** PO Box 597 .... Challis ID 83226-0000
406 232-7800 **Custer County** 1010 Main St .... Miles City MT 59301-3419
    Fax: 406 232-7477

308 872-5701 **Custer County** 431 S 10th Ave .... Broken Bow NE 68822-2099
405 323-4420 **Custer County** 675 W 'B' St .... Arapaho OK 73620-0000
605 673-4816 **Custer County** 420 Mt Rushmore Rd .... Custer SD 57730-1998
216 987-4000 **Cuyahoga Community College** 700 Carnegie Ave .... Cleveland OH 44115-2878
    Fax: 216 987-4758 Acctg

216 443-7950 **Cuyahoga County** 1200 Ontario St .... Cleveland OH 44113-1604
216 398-1800 **Cuyahoga County Public Library** 4510 Memphis Ave ...... Cleveland OH 44144-1999
    Fax: 216 398-6104

619 670-1980 **Cuyamaca College** 2950 Jamacha Rd .... El Cajon CA 92019-4304
    Fax: 619 670-7204

301 396-0180 **Cylburn Arboretum** 4915 Greenspring Ave .... Baltimore MD 21209-4698
714 826-2220 **Cypress College** 9200 Valley View St ....Cypress CA 90630-5897
    Fax: 714 527-8238
Cyprus: Republic of Cyprus
202 462-5772 *Embassy* 2211 R St NW .... Washington DC 20008-4017
    Fax: 202 483-6710

212 481-6023 *Mission to the UN* 13 E 40th St .... New York NY 10016-0110
    Fax: 212 685-7316

202 463-5482 **Czechoslovak-US Economic Council** 1615 H St NW 6th Fl .. Washington DC 20062-0001
    Fax: 202 463-3114
Czechoslovakia: Czechoslovak Federal Republic
202 363-6315 *Embassy* 3900 Linnean Ave NW ....Washington DC 20008-3803
    Fax: 202 966-8540

212 535-8814 *Mission to the UN* 1109-11 Madison Ave .... New York NY 10028-0000
    Fax: 212 772-0586

D

202 224-6542 **D'Amato Alfonse M (Sen - R - New York)** 520 Hart Bldg ..... Washington DC 20510-0001
    Fax: 202 224-5871

313 882-5522 **D'Etre University** 377 Fisher Rd ....Grosse Pointe MI 48230-1602
    Fax: 313 882-4723

716 881-3200 **D'Youville College** 320 Porter Ave ....Buffalo NY 14201-1084
    Fax: 716 881-7790

916 758-0470 **D-Q University** PO Box 409 ....Davis CA 95617-0409
    Fax: 916 758-4891

703 862-4246 **Dabney S Lancaster Community College** PO Box 1000 .....Clifton Forge VA 24422-1000
    Fax: 703 862-2398

305 375-5124 **Dade County** 111 NW 1st Ave Suite 220 .... Miami FL 33128-1895
404 657-4778 **Dade County** PO Box 417 ....Trenton GA 30752-0000
417 637-2724 **Dade County** County Courthouse .... Greenfield MO 65661-0000
716 839-3600 **Daemen College** 4380 Main St .... Amherst NY 14226-3591
    Fax: 716 839-5231

801 784-3154 **Daggett County** PO Box 218 .... Manila UT 84046-0218
612 438-4295 **Dakota County** 1560 Hwy 55 W .... Hastings MN 55033-2392
    Fax: 612 438-4347

402 987-2126 **Dakota County** PO Box 38 .... Dakota City NE 68731-0038
612 452-9600 **Dakota County Library System** 1340 Wescott Rd .... Eagan MN 55123-1099
    Fax: 612 452-2208

605 256-5139 **Dakota State College** 820 N Washington Ave .... Madison SD 57042-1799
    Fax: 605 256-5316

605 995-2600 **Dakota Wesleyan University** 1200 W University Ave ...... Mitchell SD 57301-4398
    Fax: 605 995-2699

205 774-6025 **Dale County** PO Box 246 .... Ozark AL 36361-0246
806 249-4751 **Dallam County** 101 E 5th St .... Dalhart TX 79022-2728
214 331-8311 **Dallas Baptist University** 7777 W Kiest Blvd .... Dallas TX 75211-9800
    Fax: 214 333-5323

214 241-3371 **Dallas Christian College** 2700 Christian Pkwy .... Dallas TX 75234-7299
Dallas City Government
214 670-3536 *City Controller* 1500 Marilla St .... Dallas TX 75201-0000
214 670-4050 *City Council* 1500 Marilla St .... Dallas TX 75201-0000
214 670-3011 *City Hall* 1500 Marilla St .... Dallas TX 75201-6320
    Fax: 214 670-3764 Personnel
214 670-3302 *City Manager* 1500 Marilla St Rm 4E-N .... Dallas TX 75201-0000
214 670-3738 *City Secretary* 1500 Marilla St .... Dallas TX 75201-0000
214 670-4026 *Department of Transportation* 1500 Marilla St .... Dallas TX 75201-0000
214 670-4048 *Mayor's Office* 1500 Marilla St Rm 5E-N .... Dallas TX 75201-0000
214 670-4127 *Planning Dept* 1500 Marilla St .... Dallas TX 75201-0000

214 670-4403 *Police Dept* 2014 Main St Rm 504 .... Dallas TX 75201-0000
214 948-4200 *Public Works* 320 E Jefferson St .... Dallas TX 75203-0000
205 875-4401 **Dallas County** PO Box 997 .... Selma AL 36702-0997
501 352-3371 **Dallas County** 3rd & Oak Sts .... Fordyce AR 71742-0000
515 993-4789 **Dallas County** 801 Court St .... Adel IA 50003-1478
417 345-2632 **Dallas County** PO Box 436 .... Buffalo MO 65622-0436
214 653-7131 **Dallas County** 500 Main St .... Dallas TX 75202-3513
214 746-2125 **Dallas County Community College (System)** 701 Elm St .... Dallas TX 75202-3299
    Fax: 214 746-2475

214 922-1200 **Dallas Museum of Art** 1717 N Harwood St .... Dallas TX 75201-2398
    Fax: 214 954-0174

214 670-8460 **Dallas Museum of Natural History** PO Box 26193 ....Dallas TX 75226-0193
    Fax: 214 428-4356

214 266-6111 **Dallas Naval Air Station** .... Dallas TX 75211-0000
404 278-3113 **Dalton College** 213 N College Dr .... Dalton GA 30720-3797
    Fax: 404 272-4588

404 278-4507 **Dalton Regional Library** 310 Cappes St .... Dalton GA 30720-4123
    Fax: 404 278-7519 Admin

402 426-4101 **Dana College** 2848 College Dr .... Blair NE 68008-1099
    Fax: 402 426-7332 Library

608 266-4121 **Dane County** 210 Martin Luther King Jr Blvd Rm 12 .... Madison WI 53709-0001
    Fax: 608 266-1242

202 224-6154 **Danforth John C (Sen - R - Missouri)** 249 Russell Bldg ...... Washington DC 20510-0001
    Fax: Call company operator

314 443-3161 **Daniel Boone Regional Library** 100 W Broadway St ...... Columbia MO 65203-3302
    Fax: 314 443-3281

603 883-3556 **Daniel Webster College** 20 University Dr .... Nashua NH 03063-1300
    Fax: 603 882-8505

406 487-5561 **Daniels County** PO Box 247 .... Scobey MT 59263-0247
202 225-4111 **Dannemeyer William E (Rep - R - California)**
    2351 Rayburn Bldg ....Washington DC 20515-0001
    Fax: 202 225-1755

804 799-5171 **Danville (Independent City)** 212 Lynn St .... Danville VA 24541-1208
217 443-1811 **Danville Area Community College** 2000 E Main St .... Danville IL 61832-5199
    Fax: 217 443-8560

804 797-3553 **Danville Community College** 1008 S Main St .... Danville VA 24541-4004
    Fax: 804 792-6810

202 225-2931 **Darden George (Rep - D - Georgia)** 228 Cannon Bldg ......Washington DC 20515-0001
    Fax: Unlisted

919 473-1101 **Dare County** Budleigh St .... Manteo NC 27954-0000
    Fax: Unlisted

513 547-7370 **Darke County** 4th & Broadway .... Greenville OH 45331-0000
    Fax: 513 548-9235

803 393-3836 **Darlington County** Courthouse Public Sq .... Darlington SC 29532-0000
603 646-1110 **Dartmouth College** .... Hanover NH 03755-0000
    Fax: Unlisted

603 646-2460 *Amos Tuck School of Business* .... Hanover NH 03755-0000
    Fax: 603 646-1308

603 646-2359 *Graduate School of Physics* Wilder Hall .... Hanover NH 03755-1477
    Fax: Unlisted

603 646-7480 *Medical School* Remsen Bldg Rm 300 ....Hanover NH 03756-0000
    Fax: 603 646-8828

202 224-2321 **Daschle Thomas A (Sen - D - South Dakota)**
    317 Hart Bldg .... Washington DC 20510-0001
    Fax: 202 224-2047

717 255-2741 **Dauphin County** Front & Market Sts .... Harrisburg PA 17101-2012
    Fax: 717 257-1604

717 234-4961 **Dauphin County Library System** 101 Walnut St .... Harrisburg PA 17101-1696
    Fax: Unlisted

616 451-3511 **Davenport College** 415 E Fulton St ....Grand Rapids MI 49503-4498
    Fax: 616 451-2450

319 326-7804 **Davenport Museum of Art** 1737 W 12th St .... Davenport IA 52804-3596
    Fax: 319 326-7739

319 326-7832 **Davenport Public Library** 321 Main St .... Davenport IA 52801-1490
    Fax: 319 326-7809

615 269-1000 **David Lipscomb University** 3901 Granny White Pike .... Nashville TN 37204-3951
    Fax: 615 269-1796

704 892-2000 **Davidson College** Concord Rd .... Davidson NC 28036-0000
    Fax: 704 892-2625

704 249-7011 **Davidson County** PO Box 1067 .... Lexington NC 27292-0000
    Fax: 704 246-4122

615 244-1000 **Davidson County** 700 2nd Ave S .... Nashville TN 37210-2006
704 249-8186 **Davidson County Community College** PO Box 1287 .... Lexington NC 27293-1287
    Fax: 704 249-0379

704 634-5513 **Davie County** 123 S Main St .... Mocksville NC 27028-2424
812 254-1090 **Daviess County** County Courthouse .... Washington IN 47501-0000
502 685-8434 **Daviess County** PO Box 389 .... Owensboro KY 42302-0389
    Fax: 502 686-7111

816 663-2641 **Daviess County** County Courthouse .... Gallatin MO 64640-0000
304 636-1900 **Davis & Elkins College** 100 Sycamore St .... Elkins WV 26241-3996
    Fax: 304 636-8624

515 664-2011 **Davis County** Courthouse Sq .... Bloomfield IA 52537-1600
801 451-3214 **Davis County** PO Box 618 .... Farmington UT 84025-0618
801 451-2322 **Davis County Library** 38 S 100 East .... Farmington UT 84025-0000
202 225-4735 **Davis Robert W (Rep - R - Michigan)** 2417 Rayburn Bldg ... Washington DC 20515-0001
    Fax: 202 225-3588

602 750-3900 **Davis-Monthan Air Force Base** .... Tucson AZ 85707-5000
    Fax: 602 750-4744 Admin

605 996-7727 **Davison County** 200 E 4th Ave .... Mitchell SD 57301-2692
308 432-2863 **Dawes County** 451 Main St .... Chadron NE 69337-2649
406 365-3396 **Dawson Community College** 300 College Dr .... Glendive MT 59330-1405
    Fax: 406 365-5928

404 265-3164 **Dawson County** PO Box 192 .... Dawsonville GA 30534-0192
406 365-3562 **Dawson County** 207 W Bell St .... Glendive MT 59330-1694
    Fax: 406 365-4568

308 324-2127 **Dawson County** 7th & Washington Sts .... Lexington NE 68850-0000
806 872-3778 **Dawson County** N 1st & Main Sts .... Lamesa TX 79331-0000
605 345-3771 **Day County** 710 W 1st St .... Webster SD 57274-1391
513 227-9500 **Dayton & Montgomery County Public Library** 215 E 3rd St ... Dayton OH 45402-2135
    Fax: 513 227-9539

513 223-5277 **Dayton Art Institute** Forest & Riverview Aves .... Dayton OH 45405-0000
513 275-7431 **Dayton Museum of Natural History** 2629 Ridge Ave .... Dayton OH 45414-5499
904 255-8131 **Daytona Beach Community College** 1200 Volusia Ave ... Daytona Beach FL 32114-2817
    Fax: 904 254-3044

505 355-2601 **De Baca County** PO Box 347 .... Fort Sumner NM 88119-0347
219 925-2362 **De Kalb County** 100 Main St .... Auburn IN 46706-0000
816 449-5402 **De Kalb County** PO Box 248 .... Maysville MO 64469-0248
    Fax: 816 449-2440

404 294-6641 **De Kalb County Public Library** 3560 Kensington Rd .... Decatur GA 30032-1328
    Fax: 404 299-6030

202 225-2531 **De la Garza E (Rep - D - Texas)** 1401 Longworth Bldg .... Washington DC 20515-0001
    Fax: 202 225-2533

202 225-1790 **De Lugo Ron (Rep - D - Virgin Islands)**
    2238 Rayburn Bldg ....Washington DC 20515-0001
    Fax: 202 225-9392

813 494-3773 **De Soto County** 201 E Oak St .... Arcadia FL 33821-4425

601 429-5011 **De Soto County** 2535 Hwy 51 S Courthouse Sq ... Hernando MS 38632-2134
Fax: 601 429-1311
217 935-2119 **De Witt County** 201 W Washington St ... Clinton IL 61727-1639
Fax: 217 935-4227
314 768-3044 **Deaconess College of Nursing** 6150 Oakland Ave ... Saint Louis MO 63139-3297
Fax: Unlisted
806 364-1746 **Deaf Smith County** 243 E 3rd County Courthouse ... Hereford TX 79045-0000
703 821-7000 **Dealers Election Action Committee of the National Automobile Dealers Assn**
8400 Westpark Dr 10th Fl ... McLean VA 22102-3522
Fax: 703 821-7075
508 528-9100 **Dean Junior College** 99 Main St ... Franklin MA 02038-1994
Fax: 508 528-7846
812 537-1040 **Dearborn County** 215-B W High St ... Lawrenceburg IN 47025-1909
313 943-2330 **Dearborn Department of Libraries** 16301 Michigan Ave ... Dearborn MI 48126-2792
Fax: 313 943-2853
619 786-2331 **Death Valley Museum** Death Valley National Monument ... Death Valley CA 92328-0000
912 248-3031 **Decatur County** 122 W Water St ... Bainbridge GA 31717-3664
Fax: 912 246-2062
515 446-4331 **Decatur County** 207 N Main St ... Leon IA 50144-1647
812 663-2546 **Decatur County** 150 Courthouse Sq Suite 5 ... Greensburg IN 47240-2091
913 475-2132 **Decatur County** 194 S Penn Ave ... Oberlin KS 67749-2243
901 852-3417 **Decatur County** PO Box 488 ... Decaturville TN 38329-0488
202 224-4521 **DeConcini Dennis (Sen - D - Arizona)** 328 Hart Bldg ... Washington DC 20510-0001
Fax: 202 224-3464
406 563-8421 **Deer Lodge County** 800 S Main St ... Anaconda MT 59711-2999
Fax: 406 563-2069
202 225-6416 **DeFazio Peter A (Rep - D - Oregon)** 1233 Longworth Bldg ... Washington DC 20515-0001
Fax: Unlisted
703 694-3007 **Defense Advanced Research Projects Agency (US Dept of Defense)**
1400 Wilson Blvd ... Arlington VA 22209-2300
Fax: 703 694-5004
703 692-0018 **Defense Communications Agency (US Dept of Defense)**
8th & S Courthouse Rd ... Arlington VA 22204-0000
Fax: 703 692-2045
703 274-6785 **Defense Contract Audit Agency (US Dept of Defense)**
Cameron Stn Rm 4C-346 ... Alexandria VA 22304-0000
Fax: 703 274-7567
703 693-5080 **Defense Hotline (US Dept of Defense)** Pentagon ... Washington DC 20301-1900
Fax: 703 694-9501
202 697-5128 **Defense Intelligence Agency (US Dept of Defense)**
Pentagon Rm 3E-258 ... Washington DC 20340-0001
703 285-9144 **Defense Mapping Agency (US Dept of Defense)** 8613 Lee Hwy ... Fairfax VA 22031-2137
Fax: 703 285-9374
703 325-7328 **Defense Nuclear Agency (US Dept of Defense)**
6801 Telegraph Rd ... Alexandria VA 22310-3398
Fax: 703 325-2500
312 944-0575 **Defense Research Institute** 750 N Lake Shore Dr Suite 500 ... Chicago IL 60611-4490
Fax: 312 944-2003
419 784-4010 **Defiance College** 701 N Clinton St ... Defiance OH 43512-1695
Fax: 419 783-2309
419 782-4761 **Defiance County** 500 Court St ... Defiance OH 43512-2157
602 299-9191 **DeGrazia Art & Cultural Foundation** 6300 N Swan Rd ... Tucson AZ 85718-3697
205 845-0404 **Dekalb County** 300 Grand Ave SW ... Fort Payne AL 35967-1863
404 371-2000 **DeKalb County** 556 N McDonough St ... Decatur GA 30030-3356
Fax: 404 371-7054 Legal
815 895-9161 **DeKalb County** 110 E Sycamore St ... Sycamore IL 60178-1497
Fax: 815 895-7129
615 597-5177 **DeKalb County** County Courthouse Rm 205 ... Smithville TN 37166-0000
512 886-1200 **Del Mar College** 101 Baldwin Blvd ... Corpus Christi TX 78404-3894
Fax: 512 886-1561 Purchasing
707 464-7205 **Del Norte County** 625 6th St ... Crescent City CA 95531-0000
Fax: 707 465-1470
202 225-3661 **DeLauro Rosa L (Rep - D - Connecticut)** 327 Cannon Bldg ... Washington DC 20515-0001
Fax: Unlisted
302 571-9590 **Delaware Art Museum** 2301 Kentmere Pkwy ... Wilmington DE 19806-2096
Fax: Unlisted
319 927-4942 **Delaware County** PO Box 527 ... Manchester IA 52057-0527
317 747-7726 **Delaware County** PO Box 1089 ... Muncie IN 47308-1089
607 746-2123 **Delaware County** 4 Court St ... Delhi NY 13753-1081
614 369-8761 **Delaware County** 91 N Sandusky St ... Delaware OH 43015-1797
918 253-4432 **Delaware County** Krouse St ... Jay OK 74346-0000
215 891-4000 **Delaware County** W Front St ... Media PA 19063-0000
Fax: Unlisted
215 359-5000 **Delaware County Community College** Rt 252 & Medialine Rd ... Media PA 19063-0000
Fax: 215 359-5343 Library
302 739-4748 **Delaware Div of Libraries** 43 S Dupont Hwy ... Dover DE 19901-7430
Fax: 302 739-6787
302 658-9111 **Delaware Museum of Natural History** PO Box 3937 ... Wilmington DE 19807-0937
302 651-0260 **Delaware Republican Party** 2 Mill Rd ... Wilmington DE 19806-2114
Fax: 302 651-0270
302 655-7221 **Delaware State Chamber of Commerce**
1 Commerce Ctr Suite 200 ... Wilmington DE 19801-5401
Fax: 302 654-0691
302 736-4917 **Delaware State College** 1200 N Dupont Hwy ... Dover DE 19901-2277
Fax: 302 736-5203 Admin
302 996-9458 **Delaware State Democratic Committee**
609 W Newport Pike Graystone Plaza ... Wilmington DE 19804-0000
Fax: 302 998-9080
Delaware State Government
302 736-4000 *Information* 604 Otis Dr ... Dover DE 19901-0000
302 571-3838 *Attorney General* 820 N French St 8th Fl ... Wilmington DE 19801-3509
Fax: 302 571-3090
302 571-3452 *Board of Parole* 820 N French St ... Wilmington DE 19801-3509
302 736-5318 *Bureau of Archives & Records Management* Hall of Records ... Dover DE 19901-0000
Fax: 302 735-6710
302 571-4169 *Commerce Dept* 800 N French St 9th Fl ... Wilmington DE 19801-3590
Fax: 302 571-4454
302 571-3250 *Consumer Affairs* 820 N French St 4th Fl ... Wilmington DE 19801-3509
Fax: 302 571-3862
302 571-3430 *Criminal Justice Council* 820 N French St ... Wilmington DE 19801-3509
Fax: 302 571-3862
302 653-9261 *Delaware Correctional Center* PO Box 500 ... Smyrna DE 19977-0000
302 736-3611 *Department of Administrative Services*
Federal St Townsend Bldg 3rd Fl ... Dover DE 19901-0000
302 736-4811 *Department of Agriculture* 2320 S DuPont Hwy ... Dover DE 19901-5501
Fax: 302 697-6287
302 736-5601 *Department of Corrections* 80 Monrovia Ave ... Smyrna DE 19977-1597
Fax: 302 735-6740
302 736-4201 *Department of Finance* 540 S DuPont Hwy ... Dover DE 19901-4516
Fax: 302 736-5661
302 571-2710 *Department of Labor* 820 N French St 6th Fl ... Wilmington DE 19801-3534
Fax: 302 571-2735
302 736-4629 *Department of Public Instruction* Lockerman & Federal Sts ... Dover DE 19901-7421
Fax: 302 736-4654
302 739-4306 *Department of Transportation* Rt 113 ... Dover DE 19901-0000
Fax: 302 736-4329
302 736-4271 *Development Office* 99 Kings Hwy ... Dover DE 19901-3816
Fax: 302 736-5749
302 834-4531 *Division of Emergency Planning & Operations*
PO Box 527 ... Delaware City DE 19706-0527
Fax: 302 834-7495
302 739-4301 *Division of Highways* Rt 113 ... Dover DE 19903-0000
Fax: 302 736-4329
302 736-4522 *Division of Professional Regulation* Federal St ... Dover DE 19901-0000
Fax: 302 735-6148
302 736-4701 *Division of Public Health* PO Box 637 ... Dover DE 19903-0637
Fax: 302 736-3008
302 834-7081 *Division of Purchasing* PO Box 299 ... Delaware City DE 19706-0299
Fax: Ext 142
302 571-3302 *Division of Revenue* 820 N French St ... Wilmington DE 19801-3530
302 571-2515 *Division of Securities* 820 N French St 8th Fl ... Wilmington DE 19801-3530
Fax: 302 655-0576
302 736-4411 *Division of Soil & Water Conservation* 89 Kings Hwy 2nd Fl ... Dover DE 19903-0000
302 736-5911 *Division of State Police* PO Box 430 ... Dover DE 19903-0430
Fax: 302 736-5966
302 571-3540 *Division of the Arts/State Arts Council* 820 N French St ... Wilmington DE 19801-3530
302 368-6730 *Division of Unemployment Insurance* Rt 273 & Chapman Rd ... Newark DE 19714-0000
Fax: 302 368-6748
302 736-4101 *Governor* Legislative Ave Legislative Hall ... Dover DE 19901-0000
Fax: 302 736-2775
302 571-3594 *Industrial Accident Board* 820 N French St ... Wilmington DE 19801-3533
302 736-4251 *Insurance Dept* 841 Silver Lake Blvd ... Dover DE 19901-2407
Fax: 302 736-5280
302 736-4151 *Lieutenant Governor* 820 N French St 11th Fl ... Wilmington DE 19801-3509
Fax: 302 571-3019
302 736-4403 *Natural Resources & Environmental Control Dept*
89 Kings Hwy ... Dover DE 19901-3816
Fax: 302 735-6242
302 571-3908 *Occupational Safety & Health* 820 N French St ... Wilmington DE 19801-3509
302 736-4208 *Office of Pensions* 540 S DuPont Hwy ... Dover DE 19901-4516
Fax: 302 736-6219
302 736-4721 *Office of Vital Statistics*
Federal & Water Sts Jessie Cooper Bldg ... Dover DE 19901-0000
Fax: 302 736-3008
302 571-3240 *Postsecondary Education Commission*
820 N French St 4th Fl ... Wilmington DE 19801-3561
Fax: 302 571-3862
302 571-3230 *Public Defender's Office* 820 N French St 5th Fl ... Wilmington DE 19801-3509
Fax: 302 571-3973
302 736-4247 *Public Service Commission* 1560 S DuPont Hwy ... Dover DE 19901-4906
Fax: 302 736-4849
302 736-4186 *Real Estate Commission* Federal St O'Neil Bldg Box 1401 ... Dover DE 19903-0000
Fax: 302 735-6148
302 736-4111 *Secretary of State* Federal & Duke of York Sts Townsend Bldg ... Dover DE 19903-0000
Fax: 302 736-3811
302 736-5361 *Solid Waste Authority* PO Box 455 ... Dover DE 19903-0455
Fax: 302 736-4287
302 571-2427 *Supreme Court* 820 N French St ... Wilmington DE 19801-3509
302 856-5548 *Sussex Correctional Institution* Rt 1 Box 500 ... Georgetown DE 19947-9780
302 736-3382 *Treasurer* PO Box 1401 ... Dover DE 19903-1401
Fax: 302 736-5635
302 739-3260 **Delaware State Museum Meeting House Gallery**
316 S Governor's Ave ... Dover DE 19901-6706
Delaware Technical & Community College
302 856-5400 *Southern Campus* Rt 18 ... Georgetown DE 19947-0000
Fax: 302 856-5395
302 454-3900 *Stanton Campus* 400 Stanton-Christiana Rd ... Newark DE 19713-2111
Fax: 302 368-6620
302 736-5414 *Terry Campus* 1832 N Dupont Hwy ... Dover DE 19901-2221
Fax: 302 735-6169
302 739-4271 **Delaware Tourism Office** 99 Kings Hwy ... Dover DE 19901-3816
Fax: 302 639-5749
215 345-1500 **Delaware Valley College of Science & Agriculture**
Route 202 ... Doylestown PA 18901-0000
Fax: 215 345-1711 Library
202 225-5951 **DeLay Tom (Rep - R - Texas)** 308 Cannon Bldg ... Washington DC 20515-0001
Fax: Unlisted
504 483-4114 **Delgado Community College** 501 City Park Ave ... New Orleans LA 70119-4324
Fax: 504 483-4386
202 225-2661 **Dellums Ronald V (Rep - D - California)**
2136 Rayburn Bldg ... Washington DC 20515-0001
Fax: 202 225-9817
517 686-9000 **Delta College** ... University Center MI 48710-0001
Fax: 517 686-8736
303 874-7595 **Delta County** 501 Palmer St ... Delta CO 81416-1753
906 786-1763 **Delta County** 310 Ludington St ... Escanaba MI 49829-4057
903 395-4110 **Delta County** PO Box 455 ... Cooper TX 75432-0455
601 846-3000 **Delta State University** Hwy 8W ... Cleveland MS 38733-0000
Fax: 601 846-4016 Admissions
612 293-1200 **Democratic Farmer Labor Party of Minnesota**
525 Park St Suite 100 ... Saint Paul MN 55103-2106
202 863-8000 **Democratic National Committee** 430 S Capitol St SE ... Washington DC 20003-4095
Fax: 202 863-8081
501 374-2361 **Democratic Party of Arkansas** 1300 W Capitol Ave ... Little Rock AR 72201-2900
Fax: 501 376-8409
404 872-1992 **Democratic Party of Georgia** 1100 Spring St Suite 350 ... Atlanta GA 30367-0001
Fax: 404 873-4396
808 536-2258 **Democratic Party of Hawaii**
50 S Beretania St KuKui Plaza Suite C101B ... Honolulu HI 96813-5105
503 370-8200 **Democratic Party of Oregon** PO Box 15057 ... Salem OR 97309-2057
Fax: 503 370-6215
601 969-2913 **Democratic Party of the State of Mississipi**
832 N Congress St ... Jackson MS 39202-2551
Fax: 601 354-1599
608 255-5172 **Democratic Party of Wisconsin** 126 S Franklin St ... Madison WI 53703-3494
Fax: 608 255-8919
202 624-8743 **Democratic Republican Independent Voter Education Committee**
25 Louisiana Ave NW ... Washington DC 20001-2130
Fax: 202 624-6918
202 338-9092 **Democrats for the 90s** 3032 N St NW ... Washington DC 20007-3404
Fax: Unlisted
614 587-0810 **Denison University** Main St ... Granville OH 43023-0000
Fax: 614 587-6417
803 793-3301 **Denmark Technical College** PO Box 327 ... Denmark SC 29042-0327
Fax: 803 793-5942
Denmark: Kingdom of Denmark
202 234-4300 *Embassy* 3200 White Haven St NW ... Washington DC 20008-0000
Fax: 202 328-1470
212 308-7009 *Mission to the UN* 2 UN Plaza 26th Fl ... New York NY 10017-0000
Fax: 212 308-3384

312 787-8780 *Chicago Consulate General*
875 N Michigan Ave John Hancock Ctr Suite 3430 Chicago IL 60611-0000
Fax: 312 787-8740
213 387-4277 *Los Angeles Consulate General*
3440 Wilshire Blvd Suite 904 Los Angeles CA 90010-2110
Fax: 213 387-9456
212 223-4545 *New York Consulate General* 825 3rd Ave 32nd Fl New York NY 10022-7519
Fax: 212 754-1904
314 729-4144 **Dent County** County Courthouse Salem MO 65560-0000
817 565-8500 **Denton County** 401 W Hickory St Denton TX 76201-9030
303 575-5555 **Denver City Hall** 14th & Bannock Denver CO 80202-0000
Fax: 303 892-0523
303 575-2295 **Denver Art Museum** 100 W 14th Ave Pkwy Denver CO 80204-2788
303 761-2482 **Denver Conservative Baptist Seminary**
3401 S University Blvd Englewood CO 80110-3198
Fax: 303 761-8060
303 575-2721 **Denver County** City-County Bldg Rm 350 Denver CO 80202-0000
Fax: 303 575-2329
303 370-6347 **Denver Museum of Natural History** 2001 Colorado Blvd Denver CO 80205-5798
Fax: 303 331-6492
303 571-2000 **Denver Public Library** 1357 Broadway Denver CO 80203-2165
Fax: 303 595-3034
303 329-3000 **Denver Technical College** 925 S Niagara Denver CO 80224-1658
Fax: 303 321-3412
505 646-3007 **Department of Agriculture** PO Box 30005 Dept 3189
Fax: 505 646-3303
312 362-8000 **DePaul University** 25 E Jackson Blvd Chicago IL 60604-2287
Fax: 312 362-5322
312 341-8701 *College of Law* 25 E Jackson Blvd Chicago IL 60604-2287
Fax: 312 341-6908
312 362-8150 *Department of Nursing* 2323 N Seminary Ave Chicago IL 60614-3298
317 658-4800 **DePauw University** 313 S Locus St Greencastle IN 46135-0000
Fax: 317 658-4177
202 633-2101 **Deputy Attorney General of the US**
10th St & Constitution Ave NW Rm 4111 Washington DC 20530-0001
Fax: 202 786-4109
202 447-6158 **Deputy Secretary of Agriculture (US Dept of Agriculture)**
14th St & Independence Ave SW Rm 200-A Washington DC 20250-0001
Fax: 202 447-2166
202 377-4625 **Deputy Secretary of Commerce (US Dept of Commerce)**
14th St & Constitution Ave NW Rm 5838 Washington DC 20230-0001
Fax: 202 377-8610
202 695-6352 **Deputy Secretary of Defense (US Dept of Defense)**
Pentagon Rm 3E-944 Washington DC 20301-1000
Fax: 202 697-9080
202 586-5500 **Deputy Secretary of Energy (US Dept of Energy)**
1000 Independence Ave SW Rm 7B-252 Washington DC 20585-0001
Fax: 202 586-7644
202 523-6151 **Deputy Secretary of Labor (US Dept of Labor)**
200 Constitution Ave NW Rm S-2018 Washington DC 20210-0001
Fax: 202 523-6161
202 647-9640 **Deputy Secretary of State (US Dept of State)**
2201 C St NW Rm D-7220 Washington DC 20520-7512
Fax: 202 647-5372
202 566-2801 **Deputy Secretary of the Treasury (US Dept of the Treasury)**
1500 Pennsylvania Ave NW Rm 3326 Washington DC 20220-0001
Fax: 202 535-3659
202 366-2222 **Deputy Secretary of Transportation (US Dept of Transportation)**
400 7th St SW Rm 10200 Washington DC 20590-0001
Fax: 202 366-3918
202 233-5515 **Deputy Secretary of Veterans Affairs (US Dept of Veterans Affairs)**
810 Vermont Ave NW Rm 1001 Washington DC 20420-0001
Fax: 202 233-4786
202 732-5404 **Deputy Under Secretary of Education (US Dept of Education)**
400 Maryland Ave SW Rm 3073 Washington DC 20202-0001
Fax: 202 732-1971
202 225-5301 **Derrick Butler Jr (Rep - D - South Carolina)**
201 Cannon Bldg Washington DC 20515-0001
Fax: 202 225-5383
515 964-6200 **Des Moines Area Community College** 2006 S Ankeny Blvd Ankeny IA 50021-3993
Fax: 515 964-6206
515 277-4405 **Des Moines Art Center** 4700 Grand Ave Des Moines IA 50312-2099
319 753-8272 **Des Moines County** PO Box 158 Burlington IA 52601-0158
503 388-6570 **Deschutes County** 1130 NW Harriman St Bend OR 97701-1947
501 877-2426 **Desha County** PO Box 188 Arkansas City AR 71630-0188
318 872-0738 **DeSoto Parish** Parish Courthouse Mansfield LA 71052-0000
Detroit City Government
313 224-3260 *City Clerk* 2 Woodward St Rm 1304 Detroit MI 48226-0000
313 224-3270 *City Hall* 2 Woodward St Detroit MI 48226-3400
313 224-3252 *Department of Buildings & Safety* 2 Woodward St Rm 401 Detroit MI 48226-0000
313 833-7670 *Department of Transportation* 1301 E Warren Ave Detroit MI 48207-0000
Fax: 313 833-5523
313 596-2900 *Fire Dept* 250 W Larned St Detroit MI 48226-0000
313 224-3400 *Mayor's Office* 2 Woodward St Rm 1126 Detroit MI 48226-0000
Fax: 313 224-7157
313 224-6380 *Planning Dept* 2300 Cadillac Tower Detroit MI 48226-0000
313 596-2200 *Police Dept* 1300 Beaubien St Detroit MI 48226-0000
Fax: Unlisted
313 224-3901 *Public Works* 2 Woodward St City County Bldg Rm 513 Detroit MI 48226-0000
313 224-3540 *Treasurer* 2 Woodward St Rm 650 Detroit MI 48226-0000
313 224-4800 *Water Dept* 735 Randolph St Detroit MI 48226-0000
313 466-4745 **Detroit Coast Guard Air Station**
Selfridge Air National Guard Base Bldg 1401 Mount Clemens MI 48045-0000
Fax: Call company operator
313 331-3110 **Detroit Coast Guard Base** Bell Isle Detroit MI 48207-4345
313 581-4400 **Detroit College of Business** 4801 Oakman Blvd Dearborn MI 48126-3799
Fax: 313 581-1985 Admin
313 239-1443 *Flint Campus* 3115 Lawndale Ave Flint MI 48504-2699
Fax: 313 239-1294
313 558-8700 *Warren Campus* 27500 Dequindre Rd Warren MI 48092-5209
Fax: 313 558-7868
313 965-0150 **Detroit College of Law** 130 E Elizabeth St Detroit MI 48201-3454
Fax: 313 965-5097
313 833-1805 **Detroit Historical Museum** 5401 Woodward Ave Detroit MI 48202-4097
Fax: 313 833-5342
313 833-7900 **Detroit Institute of Arts** 5200 Woodward Ave Detroit MI 48202-4094
Fax: 313 833-2357
313 833-1000 **Detroit Public Library** 5201 Woodward Ave Detroit MI 48202-4093
Fax: 313 832-0877
313 577-8400 **Detroit Science Center** 5020 John R St Detroit MI 48202-4045
Fax: 313 832-1623
308 874-3308 **Deuel County** 3rd & Vincent Chappell NE 69129-0000
605 874-2120 **Deuel County** PO Box 125 Clear Lake SD 57226-0000
602 870-9222 **DeVry Institute of Technology** 2149 W Dunlap Ave Phoenix AZ 85021-2995
Fax: 602 870-1209
213 699-9927 **DeVry Institute of Technology**
12801 Crossroads Pkwy S City of Industry CA 91746-3595
Fax: 213 692-6272
404 292-7900 **DeVry Institute of Technology** 250 N Arcadia Ave Decatur GA 30030-2198
Fax: 404 292-2321 Admin
312 929-8500 **DeVry Institute of Technology** 3300 N Campbell Ave Chicago IL 60618-5994
Fax: 312 348-1780 Admin
708 953-1300 **DeVry Institute of Technology** 2000 S Finley Rd Lombard IL 60148-4892
Fax: 708 953-1236 Admin
816 941-0430 **DeVry Institute of Technology** 11224 Holmes St Kansas City MO 64131-3698
Fax: Unlisted
614 253-7291 **DeVry Institute of Technology** 1350 Alum Creek Dr Columbus OH 43209-2764
Fax: 614 252-4108
214 258-6767 **DeVry Institute of Technology** 4250 N Belt Line Rd Irving TX 75038-4299
Fax: 214 659-1748
405 328-5390 **Dewey County** PO Box 368 Taloga OK 73667-0368
605 865-3672 **Dewey County** County Courthouse Timber Lake SD 57656-0000
512 275-3724 **DeWitt County** 307 N Gonzales St Cuero TX 77954-2970
415 685-1230 **Diablo Valley College** 321 Golf Club Rd Pleasant Hill CA 94523-1576
Fax: 415 685-1551
806 623-5531 **Dickens County** PO Box 120 Dickens TX 79229-0120
703 926-1616 **Dickenson County** PO Box 190 Clintwood VA 24228-0190
701 349-3560 **Dickey County** 309 N 2nd St Ellendale ND 58436-0000
717 245-1231 **Dickinson College** PO Box 1773 Carlisle PA 17013-2896
Fax: 717 245-1899
712 336-1138 **Dickinson County** 18th & Hill County Courthouse Spirit Lake IA 51360-0000
913 263-3774 **Dickinson County** PO Box 248 Abilene KS 67410-0248
906 774-0988 **Dickinson County** PO Box 609 Iron Mountain MI 49801-0609
717 243-4611 **Dickinson School of Law** 150 S College St Carlisle PA 17013-2877
Fax: 717 243-4443
701 227-2507 **Dickinson State University** May Hall Dickinson ND 58601-0000
Fax: 701 227-2006
202 225-2901 **Dickinson William L (Rep - R - Alabama)**
2406 Rayburn Bldg Washington DC 20515-0001
Fax: Unlisted
202 225-5916 **Dicks Norman D (Rep - D - Washington)**
2429 Rayburn Bldg Washington DC 20515-0001
Fax: Unlisted
615 789-4171 **Dickson County** Court Sq Charlotte TN 37036-4935
504 283-8822 **Dillard University** 2601 Gentilly Blvd New Orleans LA 70122-3097
803 774-1400 **Dillon County** PO Box 449 Dillon SC 29536-0449
512 876-3569 **Dimmit County** 103 N 5th St Carrizo Springs TX 78834-3198
202 225-4071 **Dingell John D (Rep - D - Michigan)** 2328 Rayburn Bldg Washington DC 20515-0001
Fax: 202 225-7426
804 469-4533 **Dinwiddie County** PO Box 280 Dinwiddie VA 23841-0280
805 687-3694 **Direct Relief International** 21 N Salsipuedes St Santa Barbara CA 93103-0000
Fax: 805 687-2318
414 765-9966 **Discovery World Museum of Science Economics & Technology**
818 W Wisconsin Ave Milwaukee WI 53233-2309
Fax: 414 765-0311
202 426-3500 **Discrimination Complaint Hotline (US Dept of Housing & Urban Development)**
451 7th St SW Washington DC 20410-0001
Fax: 202 755-0299
202 879-1010 **District of Columbia** 500 Indiana Ave NW Washington DC 20001-2131
202 225-4457 **District of Columbia Committee (US House of Representatives)**
1310 Longworth Bldg Washington DC 20515-0001
Fax: Unlisted
202 727-1101 **District of Columbia Public Library** 901 G St NW Washington DC 20001-4531
Fax: 202 727-1129
202 662-1382 **District of Columbia Republican State Committee**
440 1st St NW Suite 300 Washington DC 20001-2028
Fax: 202 628-6492
202 727-5225 **District of Columbia School of Law** 719 13th St NW Washington DC 20005-3997
Fax: 202 727-9608
216 368-3648 **Dittrick Museum of Medical History** 11000 Euclid Ave Cleveland OH 44106-1714
701 965-6351 **Divide County** 300 N Main St Crosby ND 58730-0000
319 876-3353 **Divine Word College** S Center Ave Epworth IA 52045-0000
801 673-4811 **Dixie College** 225 S 700 East Saint George UT 84770-3876
Fax: 801 673-8552
904 498-7021 **Dixie County** PO Box 1206 Cross City FL 32628-1206
202 224-2854 **Dixon Alan J (Sen - D - Illinois)** 331 Hart Bldg Washington DC 20510-0001
Fax: Unlisted
402 755-2881 **Dixon County** 302 3rd St Ponca NE 68770-0000
202 225-7084 **Dixon Julian C (Rep - D - California)** 2400 Rayburn Bldg Washington DC 20515-0001
Fax: 202 225-4091
Djibouti: Republic of Djibouti
202 331-0270 *Embassy* 1156 15th St NW Suite 515 Washington DC 20005-1704
Fax: 202 331-0302
212 753-3163 *Mission to the UN* 866 UN Plaza Suite 4011 New York NY 10017-1811
402 826-2161 **Doane College** 1014 Boswell Ave Crete NE 68333-2495
Fax: 402 826-8600
202 224-2823 **Dodd Christopher J (Sen - D - Connecticut)**
444 Russell Bldg Washington DC 20510-0001
Fax: Unlisted
304 873-2631 **Doddridge County** 118 E Court St West Union WV 26456-1262
316 225-1321 **Dodge City Community College** 2501 N 14th Ave Dodge City KS 67801-2399
Fax: 316 225-0918
912 374-4361 **Dodge County** PO Box 818 Eastman GA 31023-0818
507 635-6230 **Dodge County** PO Box 38 Mantorville MN 55955-0038
Fax: 507 635-6265
402 727-2765 **Dodge County** 435 N Park Ave Fremont NE 68025-4967
414 386-4411 **Dodge County** County Courthouse Juneau WI 53039-0000
202 224-6521 **Dole Robert (Sen - R - Kansas)** 141 Hart Bldg Washington DC 20510-0001
Fax: Unlisted
303 677-2383 **Dolores County** 4th & Main Sts Dove Creek CO 81324-0000
202 224-6621 **Domenici Pete V (Sen - R - New Mexico)**
434 Dirksen Bldg Washington DC 20510-0001
Fax: 202 224-7371
202 566-2103 **Domestic Finance Office (US Dept of the Treasury)**
1500 Pennsylvania Ave NW Rm 2326 Washington DC 20220-0001
Fax: 202 786-8450
914 359-7800 **Dominican College** 10 N Western Hwy Orangeburg NY 10962-1299
Fax: 914 359-2313
415 457-4440 **Dominican College of San Rafael** 50 Acacia Ave San Rafael CA 94901-2230
Fax: 415 485-3205
Dominican Republic
202 332-6280 *Embassy* 1715 22nd St NW Washington DC 20008-1902
Fax: 202 265-8057
212 867-0833 *Mission to the UN* 144 E 44th St 4th Fl New York NY 10017-4053
212 432-9498 **Dominican Republic Export Promotion Center**
1 World Trade Ctr Rm 2441 New York NY 10048-0577
Fax: 212 432-9376
415 849-2030 **Dominican School of Philosophy & Theology** 2401 Ridge Rd Berkeley CA 94709-1211
818 280-0451 **Don Bosco Technical Institute** 1151 San Gabriel Blvd Rosemead CA 91770-4299
Fax: 818 280-9316
505 525-6659 **Dona Ana County** 251 W Amador Ave Las Cruces NM 88005-2800

913 985-3513 **Doniphan County** Main St .... Troy KS 66087-0000
806 874-3436 **Donley County** PO Box U .... Clarendon TX 79226-2020
202 225-3215 **Donnelly Brian J (Rep - D - Massachusetts)**
2229 Rayburn Bldg .... Washington DC 20515-0001
Fax: Unlisted
913 621-6070 **Donnelly College** 608 N 18th St .... Kansas City KS 66102-4298
Fax: 913 621-0354
202 225-3341 **Dooley Calvin (Rep - D - California)**
1022 Longworth Bldg .... Washington DC 20515-0001
Fax: 202 225-9308
202 225-2511 **Doolittle John T (Rep - R - California)**
1223 Longworth Bldg .... Washington DC 20515-0001
Fax: 202 225-5444
912 268-4228 **Dooly County** PO Box 322 .... Vienna GA 31092-0322
414 743-5511 **Door County** 138 S 4th Ave .... Sturgeon Bay WI 54235-2204
301 228-1700 **Dorchester County** PO Box 26 .... Cambridge MD 21613-0026
803 563-2331 **Dorchester County** PO Box 613 .... Saint George SC 29477-0000
712 722-3771 **Dordt College** 498 4th Ave NE .... Sioux Center IA 51250-1697
Fax: Unlisted
202 225-2611 **Dorgan Byron L (Rep - D - North Dakota)**
203 Cannon Bldg .... Washington DC 20515-0001
Fax: 202 225-9436
202 225-2965 **Dornan Robert K (Rep - R - California)** 301 Cannon Bldg ... Washington DC 20515-0001
Fax: 202 225-3694
912 431-2198 **Dougherty County** PO Box 1827 .... Albany GA 31703-5301
912 431-2900 **Dougherty County Public Library** 300 Pine Ave .... Albany GA 31701-2533
Fax: 912 430-4020
303 688-6260 **Douglas County** 301 Wilcox St .... Castle Rock CO 80104-2454
Fax: 303 688-1293 Admin
404 949-2000 **Douglas County** 6754 Broad St .... Douglasville GA 30134-4501
Fax: 404 489-9614
217 253-2411 **Douglas County** 401 S Center St .... Tuscola IL 61953-1603
913 841-7700 **Douglas County** 111 E 11th St .... Lawrence KS 66044-2990
612 762-2381 **Douglas County** 305 8th Ave W .... Alexandria MN 56308-1758
Fax: 612 762-2389
417 683-4714 **Douglas County** 203 SE 2nd Ave .... Ava MO 65608-0000
402 444-7000 **Douglas County** 1819 Farnam St .... Omaha NE 68183-0001
702 782-9821 **Douglas County** PO Box 218 .... Minden NV 89423-0218
Fax: 702 782-9007
503 672-3311 **Douglas County** 1036 SE Douglas Ave .... Roseburg OR 97470-3396
Fax: 503 440-4408
605 724-2585 **Douglas County** PO Box 36 .... Armour SD 57313-0000
509 745-8529 **Douglas County** PO Box 516 .... Waterville WA 98858-0516
Fax: 509 745-8027
715 394-0341 **Douglas County** 1313 Belknap St .... Superior WI 54880-2769
Fax: 715 394-3858
205 493-3573 **Douglas MacArthur State Technical College** PO Box 649 .... Opp AL 36467-0649
302 677-3000 **Dover Air Force Base** .... Dover DE 19902-0000
Fax: 302 678-6883
516 589-6100 **Dowling College** 150 Idle Hour Blvd .... Oakdale NY 11769-1999
Fax: 516 563-7831 Admin
202 225-3335 **Downey Thomas J (Rep - D - New York)**
2232 Rayburn Bldg .... Washington DC 20515-0001
Fax: 202 226-1275
515 271-2011 **Drake University** 25th St & University Ave .... Des Moines IA 50311-0000
Fax: 515 271-3977
515 271-2172 *College of Pharmacy & Health Sciences* Fitch Hall .... Des Moines IA 50311-0000
515 271-2824 *Law School* 27th St & Carpenter .... Des Moines IA 50311-0000
Fax: 515 271-2530
515 271-3194 *School of Journalism & Mass Communication*
Meredith Hall Rm 118 .... Des Moines IA 50311-0000
Fax: Unlisted
615 282-3320 **Draughon Junior College** 2220 College Rd .... Johnson City TN 37601-1744
Fax: 615 282-6742
202 225-2305 **Dreier David (Rep - R - California)** 411 Cannon Bldg .... Washington DC 20515-0001
Fax: 202 225-4745
501 367-3574 **Drew County** 210 S Main St .... Monticello AR 71655-4796
201 408-3000 **Drew University** 36 Madison Ave .... Madison NJ 07940-1493
Fax: 201 408-3939 Admin
215 895-2000 **Drexel University** 32nd & Chestnut Sts .... Philadelphia PA 19104-0000
Fax: 215 895-1414
215 895-2474 *College of Information Studies* Rush Bldg Rm 306 .... Philadelphia PA 19104-0000
Fax: 215 895-2494
215 895-2424 *Museum* 32nd & Chestnut Sts .... Philadelphia PA 19104-2884
202 307-1000 **Drug Enforcement Administration** 700 Army Navy Dr .... Arlington VA 20537-0001
Fax: 202 307-7965
404 331-7308 *Atlanta Office* 75 Spring St SW Rm 740 .... Atlanta GA 30303-3307
Fax: 404 331-7340
617 565-2800 *Boston Office* 50 Staniford St Suite 200 .... Boston MA 02114-2503
Fax: 617 565-2831
312 353-7875 *Chicago Office* 219 S Dearborn St Rm 500 .... Chicago IL 60604-1792
Fax: 312 886-8439
214 767-7151 *Dallas Office* 1880 Regal Row .... Dallas TX 75235-2392
Fax: 214 767-7139
303 844-3951 *Denver Office* PO Box 1860 .... Denver CO 80201-1860
Fax: 303 564-4195
313 226-7290 *Detroit Office* 231 W Lafayette St Federal Bldg Rm 357 .... Detroit MI 48226-2793
Fax: 313 226-6145
713 681-1771 *Houston Office* 333 West Loop N Suite 300 .... Houston TX 77024-7794
Fax: Ext 213
213 894-2650 *Los Angeles Office* 350 S Figueroa St .... Los Angeles CA 90071-1101
Fax: 213 894-4244
305 591-4870 *Miami Office* 8400 NW 53rd St .... Miami FL 33166-4580
Fax: 305 536-4200
504 589-3894 *New Orleans Office* 1661 Canal St Suite 2200 .... New Orleans LA 70112-2888
Fax: 504 589-3989
212 399-5151 *New York Office* 555 W 57th St Suite 1900 .... New York NY 10019-2925
Fax: 212 662-2927
201 645-6060 *Newark Office* 970 Broad St Rm 806 .... Newark NJ 07102-2580
Fax: 201 645-2317
215 597-9530 *Philadelphia Office* 600 Arch St Suite 10224 .... Philadelphia PA 19106-1650
Fax: 215 597-6063
602 640-5700 *Phoenix Office* 3010 N 2nd Street Suite 301 .... Phoenix AZ 85012-0000
Fax: 602 261-5714
314 425-3241 *Saint Louis Office* 7911 Forsyth Suite 500 .... Saint Louis MO 63105-3860
Fax: 314 279-3245
619 585-4200 *San Diego Office* 402 W 35th St .... National City CA 92050-7963
Fax: 619 894-6224
415 556-6771 *San Francisco Office* 450 Golden Gate Ave .... San Francisco CA 94102-3584
Fax: 415 556-8764
206 442-5443 *Seattle Office* 220 W Mercer St .... Seattle WA 98119-3964
Fax: 206 442-1576
202 724-7834 *Washington Office* 400 6th St SW Rm 2558 .... Washington DC 20024-2780
Fax: 202 724-7861
215 628-2288 **Drug Information Assn** PO Box 3113 .... Maple Glen PA 19002-0713
Fax: 215 641-1229

417 865-8731 **Drury College** 900 N Benton Ave .... Springfield MO 65802-3791
Fax: 417 865-3138 Library
708 682-7035 **Du Page County** 421 N County Farm Rd .... Wheaton IL 60187-3978
302 888-4600 **Du Pont Henry Francis Winterthur Museum & Garden** .... Winterthur DE 19735-0001
Fax: 302 888-4849
812 482-1633 **Dubois County** Main St .... Jasper IN 47546-0000
319 589-4418 **Dubuque County** 720 Central Ave .... Dubuque IA 52001-7079
801 738-2435 **Duchesne County** PO Box 270 .... Duchesne UT 84021-0270
Fax: 801 738-5522
919 684-8111 **Duke University** .... Durham NC 27706-0000
Fax: 919 684-3200 Communications
919 684-3048 *Computer Science Dept* 202 North Bldg .... Durham NC 27706-0000
Fax: 919 660-6519
919 684-2495 *Fuqua School of Business* Towerview Dr .... Durham NC 27706-0000
Fax: 919 684-2818
919 684-3913 *Graduate School of Biochemistry*
321 Nanaline Duke Box 3711 .... Durham NC 27706-0000
Fax: 919 684-3200 Admin
919 684-6204 *Graduate School of Chemistry*
Towerview Dr Gross Chemistry Lab Rm 328 .... Durham NC 27706-0000
Fax: 919 684-3628
919 684-5138 *Graduate School of Microbiology* PO Box 3020 .... Durham NC 27710-0001
Fax: 919 684-8735
919 684-8140 *Graduate School of Physics* Physics Bldg Rm 107 .... Durham NC 27706-0000
Fax: 919 684-8101
919 684-5135 *Museum of Art* College Stn .... Durham NC 27708-0000
919 684-2834 *School of Law* Towerview Dr & Science Dr .... Durham NC 27706-0000
Fax: 919 684-3417
919 684-2498 *School of Medicine* PO Box 3005 .... Durham NC 27710-0000
Fax: 919 684-2593
508 627-5535 **Dukes County** PO Box 190 .... Edgartown MA 02539-0000
Fax: 508 627-7571
218 723-3800 **Duluth Public Library** 520 W Superior St .... Duluth MN 55802-1578
Fax: 218 723-7835
202 342-3200 **Dumbarton Oaks Collection** 1703 32nd NW .... Washington DC 20007-2961
202 225-5435 **Duncan John J (Rep - R - Tennessee)** 115 Cannon Bldg .... Washington DC 20515-0001
Fax: 202 225-6440
301 282-6700 **Dundalk Community College** 7200 Sollers Point Rd .... Baltimore MD 21222-4694
Fax: 301 285-9903
308 423-2058 **Dundy County** Chief St .... Benkelman NE 69021-0000
314 888-2796 **Dunklin County** PO Box 188 .... Kennett MO 63857-0188
701 573-4447 **Dunn County** County Courthouse .... Manning ND 58642-0000
715 232-1677 **Dunn County** 800 Wilson Ave .... Menomonie WI 54751-2785
708 232-8457 **DuPage Library System** PO Box 268 .... Geneva IL 60134-0268
Fax: 708 232-1584
919 296-1240 **Duplin County** Courthouse Plaza .... Kenansville NC 28349-0000
Fax: 919 296-0251
412 434-6000 **Duquesne University** 600 Forbes Ave .... Pittsburgh PA 15282-0001
Fax: 412 642-9055
412 434-6300 *School of Law* 900 Locust St .... Pittsburgh PA 15282-0001
Fax: 412 434-6294
412 434-6380 *School of Pharmacy* 410 Mellon Hall .... Pittsburgh PA 15282-0001
Fax: Unlisted
202 225-5271 **Durbin Richard J (Rep - D - Illinois)** 129 Cannon Bldg .... Washington DC 20515-0001
Fax: 202 225-0170
202 224-3244 **Durenberger Dave (Sen - R - Minnesota)**
154 Russell Bldg .... Washington DC 20510-0001
Fax: Unlisted
919 560-0025 **Durham County** 201 E Main St .... Durham NC 27701-3641
Fax: 919 560-7008
919 560-0220 **Durham County Library** 300 N Roxboro St .... Durham NC 27701-3414
Fax: 919 560-0106
919 598-9222 **Durham Technical Institute** 1637 E Lawson St .... Durham NC 27703-5023
Fax: 919 598-9412
914 471-4500 **Dutchess Community College** 53 Pendell Rd .... Poughkeepsie NY 12601-1595
Fax: 914 471-8467
914 431-2020 **Dutchess County** 22 Market St .... Poughkeepsie NY 12601-3233
Fax: 914 431-1876
904 630-2028 **Duval County** 330 E Bay St .... Jacksonville FL 32202-2997
512 279-3322 **Duval County** 400 E Gravis St .... San Diego TX 78384-1816
202 225-6301 **Dwyer Bernard J (Rep - D - New Jersey)**
2428 Rayburn Bldg .... Washington DC 20515-0001
Fax: 202 225-1553
901 286-7814 **Dyer County** PO Box 1360 .... Dyersburg TN 38025-1360
Fax: 901 286-6462
901 286-3200 **Dyersburg State Community College** 1510 Nichols Ave .... Dyersburg TN 38024-2450
Fax: 901 286-5333
915 696-0212 **Dyess Air Force Base** .... Abilene TX 79607-0000
216 696-9000 **Dyke College** 112 Prospect Ave E .... Cleveland OH 44115-1096
Fax: 216 696-6430 Library
202 225-5425 **Dymally Mervyn M (Rep - D - California)**
1717 Longworth Bldg .... Washington DC 20515-0001
Fax: 202 225-6847

E

303 328-7311 **Eagle County** PO Box 850 .... Eagle CO 81631-0850
501 762-7000 **Eaker Air Force Base** .... Blytheville AR 72315-0000
317 983-1200 **Earlham College** 701 National Rd W .... Richmond IN 47374-4000
Fax: 317 983-1304
912 723-3033 **Early County** 105 Courthouse Sq .... Blakely GA 31723-1890
202 225-6101 **Early Joseph D (Rep - D - Massachusetts)**
2349 Rayburn Bldg .... Washington DC 20515-0001
Fax: 202 225-3181
501 633-4480 **East Arkansas Community College** Newcastle Rd .... Forrest City AR 72335-0000
Fax: 501 633-7222
202 647-4835 **East Asian & Pacific Affairs Bureau (US Dept of State)**
2201 C St NW Rm 6205 .... Washington DC 20520-0001
Fax: 202 647-7350
504 389-3000 **East Baton Rouge Parish** 222 Saint Louis St .... Baton Rouge LA 70802-5817
504 389-3360 **East Baton Rouge Parish Library** 7711 Goodwood Blvd .... Baton Rouge LA 70806-7625
919 757-6131 **East Carolina University** 1000 E 5th St .... Greenville NC 27858-2598
Fax: 919 757-4155 Admin
919 551-2201 *School of Medicine*
Brody Medical Sciences Bldg Rm 1N-12 .... Greenville NC 27858-0000
Fax: Unlisted
318 559-2256 **East Carroll Parish** 400 1st St .... Lake Providence LA 71254-2616
314 583-5193 **East Central College** PO Box 529 .... Union MO 63084-0529
601 635-2126 **East Central Community College** Broad St .... Decatur MS 39327-0000
Fax: 601 635-2150 Library
404 821-2600 **East Central Georgia Regional Library** 902 Greene St .... Augusta GA 30901-2232
319 365-0521 **East Central Regional Library** 625 Guarantee Bldg .... Cedar Rapids IA 52401-0000
612 689-1901 **East Central Regional Library** 244 S Birch St .... Cambridge MN 55008-1588

405 332-8000	**East Central University**	Ada	OK	74820-0000
	Fax: 405 436-4064			
704 394-2307	**East Coast Bible College** 6900 Wilkinson Blvd	Charlotte	NC	28214-3152
504 683-5145	**East Feliciana Parish** PO Box 595	Clinton	LA	70722-0595
912 237-7831	**East Georgia College** 237 Thigpen Dr	Swainsboro	GA	30401-2699
	Fax: 912 237-5161			
213 265-8650	**East Los Angeles College** 1301 W Brooklyn Ave	Monterey Park	CA	91754-6099
	Fax: Unlisted			
601 476-8442	**East Mississippi Community College** Kemper St	Scooba	MS	39358-0000
717 424-3542	**East Stroudsburg University**	East Stroudsburg	PA	18301-0000
615 929-4112	**East Tennessee State University** Boundry Rd	Johnson City	TN	37614-0000
	Fax: 615 929-5770			
615 929-6219	*School of Medicine* PO Box 19900A	Johnson City	TN	37614-1000
903 935-7963	**East Texas Baptist University** 1209 N Grove St	Marshall	TX	75670-1498
	Fax: 903 935-3447			
903 886-5014	**East Texas State University** East Texas Stn	Commerce	TX	75428-9998
	Fax: 903 886-5010 Admin			
903 886-5239	*Department of Journalism & Graphic Arts* University Dr	Commerce	TX	75428-0000
	Fax: 903 886-5723 Library			
903 838-6514	*Texarkana Campus* 2600 N Robison Rd	Texarkana	TX	75501-3098
	Fax: 903 832-8890			
312 939-0111	**East-West University** 816 S Michigan Ave	Chicago	IL	60605-2103
	Fax: 312 939-0083			
602 428-1133	**Eastern Arizona College** 600 Church St	Thatcher	AZ	85552-0000
	Fax: 602 428-7462			
301 879-9300	**Eastern Christian College** PO Box 629	Bel Air	MD	21014-0629
215 341-5800	**Eastern College** 10 Fairview Dr	Saint Davids	PA	19087-3696
	Fax: 215 341-1375			
203 456-2231	**Eastern Connecticut State University** 83 Windham St	Willimantic	CT	06226-2295
	Fax: 203 456-5508			
217 581-5000	**Eastern Illinois University**	Charleston	IL	61920-0000
	Fax: 217 581-6371			
319 322-5015	**Eastern Iowa Community College District (System)**			
	306 W River Dr	Davenport	IA	52801-1221
	Fax: 319 322-3956			
606 622-1000	**Eastern Kentucky University** 521 Lancaster Ave	Richmond	KY	40475-3101
	Fax: 606 622-2301 PR			
207 941-4600	**Eastern Maine Vocational College** 354 Hogan Rd	Bangor	ME	04401-4206
	Fax: 207 941-4608 Admin			
703 433-2771	**Eastern Mennonite College** 1200 Park Rd	Harrisonburg	VA	22801-2462
	Fax: 703 432-4444			
313 487-1849	**Eastern Michigan University**	Ypsilanti	MI	48197-0000
	Fax: 313 487-0366			
406 657-2011	**Eastern Montana College** 1500 N 30th St	Billings	MT	59101-0298
	Fax: 406 657-2051			
617 773-6350	**Eastern Nazarene College** 23 E Elm Ave	Quincy	MA	02170-2999
	Fax: 617 773-6324 Admin			
505 562-2121	**Eastern New Mexico University**	Portales	NM	88130-0000
	Fax: 505 562-2409			
918 683-2846	**Eastern Oklahoma District Library System**			
	801 W Okmulgee Ave	Muskogee	OK	74401-6840
918 465-2361	**Eastern Oklahoma State College** 1301 W Main St	Wilburton	OK	74578-4999
503 963-2171	**Eastern Oregon State College** 1410 L Ave	La Grande	OR	97850-2899
	Fax: 503 963-1335			
804 787-5900	**Eastern Shore Community College** RR 1 Box 6	Melfa	VA	23410-9755
	Fax: 804 787-5919			
509 359-6200	**Eastern Washington University**	Cheney	WA	99004-0000
	Fax: Unlisted			
509 359-2288	*Department of Urban & Regional Planning* 201 Isle Hall	Cheney	WA	99004-0000
	Fax: 509 359-6927			
307 532-7111	**Eastern Wyoming College** 3200 W 'C' St	Torrington	WY	82240-1699
	Fax: 307 532-2668			
214 324-7694	**Eastfield College** 3737 Motley Dr	Mesquite	TX	75150-2099
	Fax: 214 324-7183			
817 629-8622	**Eastland County** PO Box 110	Eastland	TX	76448-0110
	Fax: Unlisted			
517 543-7500	**Eaton County** 1045 Independence Dr	Charlotte	MI	48813-1095
715 839-5106	**Eau Claire County** 721 Oxford Ave	Eau Claire	WI	54703-5481
912 559-6538	**Echols County** PO Box 190	Statenville	GA	31648-0190
202 225-6331	**Eckart Dennis E (Rep - D - Ohio)** 1111 Longworth Bldg	Washington	DC	20515-0001
	Fax: Unlisted			
813 867-1166	**Eckerd College** 4200 54th Ave S	Saint Petersburg	FL	33711-4744
	Fax: 813 866-2304			
202 647-1942	**Economic & Business Affairs Bureau (US Dept of State)**			
	2201 C St NW Rm 6822	Washington	DC	20520-0001
	Fax: 202 647-5713			
202 377-2235	**Economic Affairs Office (US Dept of Commerce)**			
	14th St & Constitution Ave NW Rm 4855	Washington	DC	20230-0001
	Fax: 202 377-0432			
202 377-5081	**Economic Development Administration**			
	14th St & Constitution Ave NW Rm 7804	Washington	DC	20230-0001
	Fax: 202 377-0995			
404 347-7401	*Atlanta Region* 1365 Peachtree St NE Suite 750	Atlanta	GA	30309-3146
	Fax: 404 257-3524			
512 482-5461	*Austin Region* 611 E 6th St Suite 201	Austin	TX	78701-3748
	Fax: 512 482-5613			
312 353-7706	*Chicago Region* 175 W Jackson Blvd Suite A-1630	Chicago	IL	60604-0000
	Fax: 312 353-8575			
303 844-4714	*Denver Region* 1244 N Speer Blvd Suite 670	Denver	CO	80204-3584
	Fax: 303 844-3968			
215 597-4603	*Philadelphia Region* 105 S 7th St 1st Fl	Philadelphia	PA	19106-3324
	Fax: 215 597-6669			
206 442-0596	*Seattle Region* 915 2nd Ave Rm 1856	Seattle	WA	98174-1001
	Fax: 206 442-1459			
202 586-6781	**Economic Regulatory Administration (US Dept of Energy)**			
	1000 Independence Ave SW Rm 5B-148	Washington	DC	20585-0001
	Fax: 202 586-2931			
214 655-6900	*Dallas Office* Frito-Lay Tower Suite 225-B	Dallas	TX	75235-0000
	Fax: 214 655-6930			
713 653-3089	*Houston Office* 1919 Smith St Suite 450	Houston	TX	77002-8050
	Fax: 713 653-3093			
915 335-3045	**Ector County** 300 N Grant Ave	Odessa	TX	79761-5162
	Ecuador: Republic of Ecuador			
202 234-7200	*Embassy* 2535 15th St NW	Washington	DC	20009-4102
	Fax: 202 667-3482			
212 935-1680	*Mission to the UN*			
	5th Ave & 48th St 866 UN Plaza Suite 516	New York	NY	10017-0000
	Fax: 212 935-1835			
212 233-7776	**Ecuadorean-American Assn** 150 Nassau St Rm 2015	New York	NY	10038-1516
	Fax: 212 233-7779			
701 947-2434	**Eddy County** 524 Central Ave	New Rockford	ND	58356-1698
505 887-9511	**Eddy County** PO Box 1139	Carlsbad	NM	88221-1139
217 465-4151	**Edgar County** County Courthouse	Paris	IL	61944-0000
919 823-5166	**Edgecombe Community College** 20009 W Wilson St	Tarboro	NC	27886-0000
	Fax: 919 823-6817			
919 823-6161	**Edgecombe County** 301 Saint Andrews St	Tarboro	NC	27886-5111
803 637-5781	**Edgefield County** PO Box 663	Edgefield	SC	29824-0663
608 257-4861	**Edgewood College** 855 Woodrow St	Madison	WI	53711-1997
814 732-2000	**Edinboro University of Pennsylvania**	Edinboro	PA	16444-0001
	Fax: 814 732-2693 Acctg			
813 489-9300	**Edison Community College** 8099 College Pkwy SW	Fort Myers	FL	33919-5598
	Fax: 813 489-9399			
513 778-8600	**Edison State Community College** 1973 Edison Dr	Piqua	OH	45356-9253
	Fax: 513 778-1920			
206 771-1545	**Edmonds Community College** 20000 68th Ave W	Lynnwood	WA	98036-5999
	Fax: 206 594-7024			
502 597-2819	**Edmonson County** Main & Cross St	Brownsville	KY	42210-0000
605 426-6671	**Edmunds County** 2nd St	Ipswich	SD	57451-0000
202 225-4527	**Education & Labor Committee (US House of Representatives)**			
	2181 Rayburn Bldg	Washington	DC	20515-0001
	Fax: 202 225-9070			
904 355-3030	**Edward Waters College** 1658 Kings Rd	Jacksonville	FL	32209-6199
201 692-2675	**Edward Williams College** 150 Kotte Pl	Hackensack	NJ	07601-6199
805 277-1110	**Edwards Air Force Base**	Edwards AFB	CA	93523-0000
	Fax: 805 277-5931			
202 225-6105	**Edwards Chet (Rep - D - Texas)** 425 Cannon Bldg	Washington	DC	20515-0001
	Fax: 202 225-0350			
618 445-2115	**Edwards County** 50 E Main St	Albion	IL	62806-1262
316 659-3121	**Edwards County** 312 Massachusetts Ave	Kinsley	KS	67547-1099
512 683-2235	**Edwards County** PO Box 184	Rocksprings	TX	78880-0184
202 225-3072	**Edwards Don (Rep - D - California)** 2307 Rayburn Bldg	Washington	DC	20515-0001
	Fax: 202 225-9460			
202 225-2132	**Edwards Mickey (Rep - R - Oklahoma)**			
	2330 Rayburn Bldg	Washington	DC	20515-0001
	Fax: Unlisted			
912 754-6071	**Effingham County** 901 N Pine St	Springfield	GA	31329-0000
217 342-6535	**Effingham County** PO Box 628	Effingham	IL	62401-0628
904 882-1110	**Eglin Air Force Base**	Eglin AFB	FL	32542-7000
	Egypt: Arab Republic of Egypt			
202 232-5400	*Embassy* 2310 Decatur Pl NW	Washington	DC	20008-4010
	Fax: 202 332-7894			
212 879-6300	*Mission to the UN* 36 E 67th St	New York	NY	10021-6120
	Fax: Call company operator			
312 443-1190	*Chicago Consulate General* 30 S Michigan Ave 7th Fl	Chicago	IL	60603-3201
	Fax: 312 443-1463			
212 759-7120	*New York Consulate General* 1110 2nd Ave Rm 201	New York	NY	10022-2021
	Fax: 212 308-7643			
415 346-9700	*San Francisco Consulate General* 3001 Pacific Ave	San Francisco	CA	94115-1013
	Fax: 415 346-9480			
907 377-1178	**Eielson Air Force Base**	Eielson AFB	AK	99702-0000
	Fax: 907 377-2389			
213 532-3670	**El Camino College** 16007 S Crenshaw Blvd	Torrance	CA	90506-0001
	Fax: 213 715-7794 Personnel			
214 746-2200	**El Centro College** Main & Lamar	Dallas	TX	75204-0000
	Fax: 214 746-2335			
916 621-6426	**El Dorado County** 495 Main St	Placerville	CA	95667-5699
915 541-4000	**El Paso City Hall** 2 Civic Center Plaza	El Paso	TX	79901-1124
	Fax: 915 541-4501			
915 594-2000	**El Paso Community College** PO Box 20500	El Paso	TX	79998-0500
	Fax: 915 594-2157			
719 630-2800	**El Paso County** 20 E Vermijo Ave	Colorado Springs	CO	80903-2214
915 546-2071	**El Paso County** 500 E San Antonio Ave	El Paso	TX	79901-2421
915 541-4040	**El Paso Museum of Art** 1211 Montana Ave	El Paso	TX	79902-5588
915 543-5433	**El Paso Public Library** 501 N Oregon St	El Paso	TX	79901-1195
405 262-2552	**El Reno Junior College** PO Box 370	El Reno	OK	73036-0370
	El Salvador: Republic of El Salvador			
202 331-4032	*Embassy* 2308 California St NW	Washington	DC	20008-1637
	Fax: 202 332-5103			
212 679-1616	*Mission to the UN* 46 Park Ave 3rd Fl	New York	NY	10016-3407
	Fax: 212 725-7831			
714 726-2100	**El Toro Marine Corps Air Station** Trabuco Rd	Santa Ana	CA	92709-0000
303 621-2080	**Elbert County** PO Box 37	Kiowa	CO	80117-0037
404 283-4702	**Elbert County** 14 N Oliver St	Elberton	GA	30635-1498
202 732-5113	**Elementary & Secondary Education Div (US Dept of Education)**			
	400 Maryland Ave SW Rm 2189	Washington	DC	20202-0001
	Fax: 202 732-5112			
708 697-1000	**Elgin Community College** 1700 Spartan Dr	Elgin	IL	60123-7193
919 335-6360	**Elizabeth City Coast Guard Air Station**	Elizabeth City	NC	27909-0000
	Fax: 919 931-6430			
919 335-3400	**Elizabeth City State University** 1001 Parkview Dr	Elizabeth City	NC	27909-6426
	Fax: 919 335-7408			
908 354-6060	**Elizabeth Public Library** 11 S Broad St	Elizabeth	NJ	07202-3486
717 367-1151	**Elizabethtown College** 1 Alpha Dr	Elizabethtown	PA	17022-2699
	Fax: 717 367-7567 Library			
502 769-2371	**Elizabethtown Community College** College Street Rd	Elizabethtown	KY	42701-0000
	Fax: 502 769-1618			
316 374-2490	**Elk County** PO Box 606	Howard	KS	67349-0606
814 776-1161	**Elk County** Main St	Ridgway	PA	15853-0000
	Fax: 814 772-1697			
219 534-3541	**Elkhart County** 117 N 2nd St	Goshen	IN	46526-3297
702 738-5398	**Elko County** 571 Idaho St	Elko	NV	89801-3787
	Fax: 702 753-8535			
205 221-2568	**Elliott Carl Regional Library** 20 E 18th St	Jasper	AL	35501-5402
	Fax: Unlisted			
606 738-5421	**Elliott County** PO Box 225	Sandy Hook	KY	41171-0225
913 625-6558	**Ellis County** 1204 Fort St	Hays	KS	67601-3899
	Fax: 913 625-4218			
405 885-7301	**Ellis County** 100 S Washington Courthouse Sq	Arnett	OK	73832-0000
214 937-8620	**Ellis County** PO Box 250	Waxahachie	TX	75165-0250
605 385-1000	**Ellsworth Air Force Base**	Rapid City	SD	57706-0000
	Fax: 605 385-1374			
515 648-4611	**Ellsworth Community College** 1100 College Ave	Iowa Falls	IA	50126-1199
	Fax: 515 648-3128			
913 472-4161	**Ellsworth County** PO Box 396	Ellsworth	KS	67439-0396
907 552-1110	**Elmendorf Air Force Base**	Anchorage	AK	99506-0000
	Fax: Unlisted			
708 279-4100	**Elmhurst College** 190 Prospect Ave	Elmhurst	IL	60126-3296
	Fax: 708 617-3332			
607 734-3911	**Elmira College** McGrow Bldg	Elmira	NY	14901-0000
	Fax: 607 737-0911			
205 567-2571	**Elmore County** PO Box 338	Wetumpka	AL	36092-0338
	Fax: 205 567-1109			
208 587-2129	**Elmore County** 150 S 4th East St	Mountain Home	ID	83647-3028
	Fax: 208 587-2159			
919 584-9711	**Elon College** 101 W Haggard Ave	Elon College	NC	27244-9344
	Fax: 919 584-2575			
608 263-2246	**Elvehjem Museum of Art**			
	800 University Ave University of Wisconsin	Madison	WI	53706-0001
	Fax: 608 262-2150			
912 237-3881	**Emanuel County** 101 N Main St	Swainsboro	GA	30401-2042
	Fax: 912 237-2593			

602 776-3728 **Embry-Riddle Aeronautical University** 3200 Willow Creek Rd .. Prescott AZ 86301-8662
Fax: 602 445-3184
904 239-6000 **Embry-Riddle Aeronautical University**
600 S Clyde Morris Blvd .... Daytona Beach FL 32114-3900
Fax: 904 239-6459
202 659-5147 **Emergency Committee for American Trade**
1211 Connecticut Ave Suite 801 .... Washington DC 20036-2701
Fax: 202 659-1347
202 225-4404 **Emerson Bill (Rep - R - Missouri)** 438 Cannon Bldg .. Washington DC 20515-0001
Fax: 202 225-9621
617 578-8500 **Emerson College** 100 Beacon St .... Boston MA 02116-1596
Fax: 617 578-8511
801 381-2465 **Emery County** PO Box 907 .... Castle Dale UT 84513-0907
404 245-7226 **Emmanuel College** 212 Spring St .... Franklin Springs GA 30639-9999
617 277-9340 **Emmanuel College** 400 The Fenway .... Boston MA 02115-5798
Fax: Unlisted
319 588-8000 **Emmaus Bible College** 2570 Asbury Rd .... Dubuque IA 52001-3096
Fax: 319 588-1216
712 362-3325 **Emmet County** 609 1st Ave N .... Estherville IA 51334-0000
616 348-1744 **Emmet County** 200 Division St .... Petoskey MI 49770-2444
701 254-4701 **Emmons County** PO Box 87 .... Linton ND 58552-0087
703 944-3121 **Emory & Henry College** Hillman Hwy .... Emory VA 24327-9999
Fax: 703 944-4438
404 727-6123 **Emory University** .... Atlanta GA 30322-1100
Fax: 404 727-0251 Communications
404 727-4282 *Museum of Art & Archaeology* 571 S Kilgo Cir Carlos Hall ..... Atlanta GA 30322-0000
Fax: 404 727-4292
404 727-6802 *School of Law* Gambrell Hall .... Atlanta GA 30322-0000
Fax: 404 727-6820
404 727-5660 *School of Medicine* 1440 Clifton Rd NE ...... Atlanta GA 30307-1053
Fax: 404 727-0473
202 857-0857 **Employee Relocation Council** 1720 'N' St NW .... Washington DC 20036-2900
Fax: 202 467-4012
202 523-6871 **Employment & Training Administration (US Dept of Labor)**
200 Constitution Ave NW Rm S2307 .... Washington DC 20210-0001
Fax: 202 523-6827
Employment & Training Administration
617 565-2240 *Region 1* JFK Federal Bldg Rm 1703 .... Boston MA 02203-0000
Fax: 617 565-2023
212 337-2139 *Region 2* 201 Varick St Rm 755 .... New York NY 10014-4800
Fax: 212 337-2305
215 596-6336 *Region 3* 3535 Market St Gateway Bldg Rm 13300 .... Philadelphia PA 19104-0000
Fax: 215 596-6455
404 347-4411 *Region 4* 1371 Peachtree St NE Rm 400 .... Atlanta GA 30367-0001
Fax: 404 347-3341
312 353-0313 *Region 5* 230 S Dearborn St 6th Fl ....Chicago IL 60604-1591
Fax: 312 353-0127
214 767-2154 *Region 6* 525 Griffin St Federal Bldg Rm 317 .... Dallas TX 75202-0000
Fax: 214 767-4681
816 426-3796 *Region 7* 911 Walnut St Rm 700 ....Kansas City MO 64106-2009
Fax: 816 426-7157
303 844-4477 *Region 8* 1961 Stout St 16th Fl .... Denver CO 80294-0101
Fax: 303 844-6323
415 744-6650 *Region 9* 71 Stevenson St .... San Francisco CA 94105-2934
206 442-7700 *Region 10* 1111 3rd Ave Suite 900 .... Seattle WA 98101-3207
Fax: 206 442-1917
202 523-8743 **Employment Standards Administration**
200 Constitution Ave NW Rm C4331 .... Washington DC 20210-0001
Fax: 202 523-8457
617 565-2066 *Region 1* JFK Federal Bldg Rm 1612-C .... Boston MA 02203-0000
Fax: 617 565-2023
212 337-2000 *Region 2* 201 Varick St Rm 750 .... New York NY 10014-4800
Fax: 212 337-2023
215 596-1185 *Region 3* 3535 Market St Rm 15230 .... Philadelphia PA 19104-3309
404 347-2818 *Region 4* 1375 Peachtree St NE Rm 664 .... Atlanta GA 30367-0001
312 353-7280 *Region 5* 230 S Dearborn St Rm 820 .... Chicago IL 60604-1503
214 767-6894 *Region 6* 525 S Griffin St Federal Bldg Suite 800 .... Dallas TX 75202-0000
Fax: 214 767-2730
816 426-5381 *Region 7* 911 Walnut St Rm 2000 .... Kansas City MO 64106-2009
Fax: 816 426-3482
303 844-5903 *Region 8* 1961 Stout St Rm 1490 .... Denver CO 80294-0101
Fax: 303 844-6323
415 744-6620 *Region 9* 211 Main St Rm 341 .... San Francisco CA 94105-1910
206 442-1536 *Region 10* 1111 3rd Ave Suite 600 .... Seattle WA 98101-3207
Fax: 206 399-1663
804 634-3332 **Emporia (Independent City)** 201 N Main St .... Emporia VA 23847-1605
316 343-1200 **Emporia State University** 12th & Commercial St ...... Emporia KS 66801-0000
Fax: 316 343-5073 Admin
508 927-0585 **Endicott College** 376 Hale St .... Beverly MA 01915-2096
Fax: 508 927-0084
202 225-2927 **Energy & Commerce Committee (US House of Representatives)**
2125 Rayburn Bldg .... Washington DC 20515-0001
Fax: 202 225-2525
202 224-4971 **Energy & Natural Resources Committee (US Senate)**
364 Dirksen Bldg .... Washington DC 20510-0001
Fax: Unlisted
202 208-0000 **Energy Regulatory Commission**
825 N Capitol St NE 2nd Fl .... Washington DC 20426-0000
Fax: 202 357-8147
404 347-4134 *Atlanta Region* 730 Peachtree St NE Rm 800 .... Atlanta GA 30308-1212
Fax: 404 347-3510
312 353-6173 *Chicago Region* 230 S Dearborn St Rm 3130 .... Chicago IL 60604-1670
Fax: 312 353-0109
212 337-2609 *New York Region* 201 Varick St Rm 664 .... New York NY 10014-4811
Fax: 212 337-2624
503 326-5840 *Portland Region* 1120 SW 5th Ave Suite 1340 .... Portland OR 97204-1933
Fax: 503 326-5857
415 744-3075 *San Francisco Region* 901 Market St Suite 350 .... San Francisco CA 94103-1778
Fax: 415 974-7169
202 586-5430 **Energy Research Program (US Dept of Energy)**
1000 Independence Ave SW Rm 7B-058 .... Washington DC 20585-0001
Fax: 202 586-4120
202 225-2464 **Engel Eliot L (Rep - D - New York)** 1213 Longworth Bldg ... Washington DC 20515-0001
Fax: Unlisted
318 448-2100 **England Air Force Base** .... Alexandria LA 71311-0001
Fax: 318 448-5325
202 225-5565 **English Glenn (Rep - D - Oklahoma)** 2206 Rayburn Bldg .... Washington DC 20515-0001
Fax: 202 225-8698
301 396-5430 **Enoch Pratt Free Library** 400 Cathedral St ...... Baltimore MD 21201-4484
Fax: 301 396-5856 Admin
205 347-2623 **Enterprise State Junior College** 600 Plaza Dr ...... Enterprise AL 36330-0000
Fax: Ext 306
202 224-6176 **Environment & Public Works Committee (US Senate)**
458 Dirksen Bldg .... Washington DC 20510-0001
Fax: 202 224-1273

202 586-6151 **Environment Safety & Health Office (US Dept of Energy)**
1000 Independence Ave SW Rm 7A-097 .... Washington DC 20585-0001
Fax: 202 586-2268
Environmental Project Review (US Dept of the Interior)
404 331-4524 *Atlanta Region* 75 Spring St SW Suite 1320 .... Atlanta GA 30303-3308
Fax: 404 331-6315
303 236-6900 *Denver Region* PO Box 25007 .... Denver CO 80225-0007
Fax: 303 776-6763
415 556-8200 *San Francisco Region*
450 Golden Gate Ave Box 36098 Rm 14448 .... San Francisco CA 94102-3506
Fax: 415 556-2793
202 382-2090 **Environmental Protection Agency** 401 M St SW .... Washington DC 20460-0001
Fax: 202 382-7884
617 565-3715 *Region 1* JFK Federal Bldg Rm 2203 ....Boston MA 02203-0000
Fax: 617 565-3468
212 264-2525 *Region 2* 26 Federal Plaza Rm 906 .... New York NY 10278-0012
Fax: 212 264-8100
215 597-9800 *Region 3* 841 Chestnut St .... Philadelphia PA 19107-4431
Fax: 215 597-7906
404 347-4727 *Region 4* 345 Courtland St NE .... Atlanta GA 30365-0001
Fax: 404 347-4702
312 353-2000 *Region 5* 230 S Dearborn St .... Chicago IL 60604-1586
Fax: 312 886-9096
214 655-2100 *Region 6* 1445 Ross Ave Suite 1200 .... Dallas TX 75202-2733
Fax: 214 655-2142
913 551-7006 *Region 7* 726 Minnesota Ave .... Kansas City KS 66101-2798
Fax: 913 551-7467
303 293-1603 *Region 8* 999 18th St Suite 500 .... Denver CO 80202-2405
Fax: 303 293-1647
415 556-6322 *Region 9* 215 Fremont St .... San Francisco CA 94105-2350
Fax: 415 556-6874
206 442-1200 *Region 10* 1200 6th Ave .... Seattle WA 98101-1128
Fax: 206 442-4672
805 648-2715 **EP Foster Library** 651 E Main St .... Ventura CA 93001-2814
202 663-4264 **Equal Employment Opportunity Commission**
1801 L St NW .... Washington DC 20507-0001
Fax: 202 663-4912
404 331-6531 *Atlanta District* 75 Piedmont Ave Suite 1150 .... Atlanta GA 30335-0001
Fax: 404 331-4220
301 962-3932 *Baltimore District* 111 Market Pl Suite 4000 .... Baltimore MD 21202-4012
Fax: 301 922-4270
205 731-1166 *Birmingham District* 1900 3rd Ave N .... Birmingham AL 35203-3502
Fax: Unlisted
704 563-2501 *Charlotte District* 5500 Central Ave .... Charlotte NC 28212-2708
Fax: 704 628-7192
312 353-8550 *Chicago District* 536 S Clark St Suite 900 ....Chicago IL 60605-1526
Fax: 312 767-7059
216 522-2001 *Cleveland District* 1375 Euclid Ave Rm 600 ....Cleveland OH 44115-1808
Fax: 216 522-7395
214 767-7015 *Dallas District* 8303 Elmbrook Dr .... Dallas TX 75247-4014
Fax: 214 767-7959
303 866-1300 *Denver District* 1845 Sherman St Rm 201 ....Denver CO 80203-1166
Fax: 303 564-1085
313 226-7639 *Detroit District* 477 Michigan Ave Rm 1540 ....Detroit MI 48226-2519
Fax: 313 226-2778
713 653-3320 *Houston District* 1919 Smith St 6th Fl .... Houston TX 77002-8049
Fax: 713 653-3381
317 226-7210 *Indianapolis District* 46 E Ohio St .... Indianapolis IN 46204-1903
Fax: 317 226-7953
213 251-7278 *Los Angeles District* 3660 Wilshire Blvd Suite 500 . Los Angeles CA 90010-2782
Fax: 213 252-7800
901 722-2540 *Memphis District* 1407 Union Ave Suite 621 .... Memphis TN 38104-3629
Fax: 901 722-2602
305 536-4491 *Miami District* 1 NE 1st St Metro Mall 6th Fl .... Miami FL 33132-0000
Fax: 305 536-4011
414 297-1111 *Milwaukee District* 310 W Wisconsin Ave Suite 800 .... Milwaukee WI 53203-2292
Fax: 414 297-4133
504 589-3842 *New Orleans District* 701 Loyola Ave Suite 600 .... New Orleans LA 70113-1931
Fax: 504 682-6861
212 264-3332 *New York District* 90 Church St Rm 1501 .... New York NY 10007-2967
Fax: 212 264-3135
215 597-7784 *Philadelphia District* 1421 Cherry St 10th Fl .... Philadelphia PA 19102-1428
Fax: 215 597-4073
602 640-5000 *Phoenix District* 4520 N Central Ave Suite 300 .... Phoenix AZ 85012-1833
314 425-6585 *Saint Louis District* 625 N Euclid Ave 5th Fl .... Saint Louis MO 63108-1660
Fax: 314 425-6105
512 229-4810 *San Antonio District* 5410 Fredrickburg Rd Suite 200 ..... San Antonio TX 78229-3550
Fax: 512 229-4806
415 744-6500 *San Francisco District* 901 Market St Suite 500 ..... San Francisco CA 94103-1735
Fax: 415 484-7423
206 442-0968 *Seattle District* 2815 2nd Ave Suite 500 .... Seattle WA 98121-1261
Fax: 206 442-1308
817 965-1482 **Erath County** County Courthouse Sq .... Stephenville TX 76401-4219
202 225-4921 **Erdreich Ben (Rep - D - Alabama)** 439 Cannon Bldg ... Washington DC 20515-0001
Fax: 202 225-1751
Erie Community College
716 842-2770 *City Campus* 121 Ellicott St .... Buffalo NY 14203-2698
Fax: 716 842-1972
716 634-0800 *North Campus* Main St & Youngs Rd .... Williamsville NY 14221-7095
Fax: 716 634-3802
716 648-5400 *South Campus* 4140 Southwestern Blvd .... Orchard Park NY 14127-2199
Fax: 716 648-9953
716 858-6392 **Erie County** 95 Franklin St .... Buffalo NY 14202-3968
Fax: 716 858-8072
419 627-7705 **Erie County** 323 Columbus Ave .... Sandusky OH 44870-2695
814 451-6000 **Erie County** 140 W 6th St .... Erie PA 16501-1002
Fax: 814 451-6323
814 451-6900 **Erie County Library System** 3 S Perry Sq .... Erie PA 16501-1102
Fax: 814 451-6907
803 379-2131 **Erskine College** PO Box 338 .... Due West SC 29639-0338
Fax: 803 379-8759
205 867-6261 **Escambia County** PO Box 848 .... Brewton AL 36427-0848
904 436-5783 **Escambia County** 223 S Palafox Pl .... Pensacola FL 32501-5845
Fax: 904 436-5802
702 485-6367 **Esmeralda County** PO Box 547 .... Goldfield NV 89013-0547
Fax: 702 485-3524
202 225-5876 **Espy Mike (Rep - D - Mississippi)** 216 Cannon Bldg .... Washington DC 20515-0001
Fax: 202 225-5898
508 774-0050 **Essex Agricultural & Technical Institute** 562 Maple St .... Hathorne MA 01937-9999
301 682-6000 **Essex Community College** 7201 Rossville Blvd .... Baltimore MD 21237-3898
Fax: 301 574-2172
508 741-0200 **Essex County** 36 Federal St .... Salem MA 01970-3437
201 621-4916 **Essex County** 469 King Blvd .... Newark NJ 07102-0000
518 873-6301 **Essex County** Court St .... Elizabethtown NY 12932-0000
Fax: 518 873-6826

804 443-3541 **Essex County** PO Box 445 ... Tappahannock VA 22560-0000
Fax: Unlisted
802 676-3910 **Essex County** PO Box 75 ... Guildhall VT 05905-0075
201 877-3000 **Essex County College** 303 University Ave ... Newark NJ 07102-1798
Fax: 201 877-3044
606 723-5156 **Estill County** 130 Main St ... Irvine KY 40336-1098
212 247-1450 **Estonia Embassy** 9 Rockefeller Plaza Suite 1421 ... New York NY 10020-2081
Ethiopia: People's Democratic Republic of Ethiopia
202 234-2281 *Embassy* 2134 Kalorama Rd NW ... Washington DC 20008-1618
Fax: 202 328-7950
212 421-1830 *Mission to the UN* 866 UN Plaza Rm 560 ... New York NY 10017-0000
Fax: 212 754-0360
216 391-9696 **ETI Technical College** 4300 Euclid Ave ... Cleveland OH 44103-3752
205 549-5313 **Etowah County** 800 Forrest Ave ... Gadsden AL 35901-3641
213 291-7821 **Eubanks Conservatory of Music & Arts**
4928 S Crenshaw Blvd ... Los Angeles CA 90043-1896
503 485-1780 **Eugene Bible College** 2155 Bailey Hill Rd ... Eugene OR 97405-1194
212 741-5665 **Eugene Lang College** 65 W 11th St ... New York NY 10011-8601
503 687-5450 **Eugene Public Library** 100 W 13th Ave ... Eugene OR 97401-3484
309 467-3721 **Eureka College** 300 E College Ave ... Eureka IL 61530-1562
Fax: 309 467-6325 Admin
702 237-5262 **Eureka County** PO Box 677 ... Eureka NV 89316-0677
Fax: 702 237-5707
202 647-9626 **European & Canadian Affairs Bureau (US Dept of State)**
2201 C St NW Rm 6228 ... Washington DC 20520-0001
Fax: 202 647-0967
202 862-9500 **European Economic Community Embassy**
2100 M St NW Suite 707 ... Washington DC 20037-1292
Fax: 202 429-1766
417 865-2811 **Evangel College** 1111 N Glenstone Ave ... Springfield MO 65802-2191
318 363-5651 **Evangeline Parish** Court St 2nd Fl ... Ville Platte LA 70586-0000
912 739-1141 **Evans County** 3 Freeman St ... Claxton GA 30417-0000
202 225-5905 **Evans Lane (Rep - D - Illinois)** 1121 Longworth Bldg ... Washington DC 20515-0001
Fax: 202 225-5396
812 425-2406 **Evansville Museum of Arts & Sciences** 411 SE Riverside Dr ... Evansville IN 47713-1098
Fax: 812 421-7507
812 428-8200 **Evansville-Vanderburgh County Public Library** 22 SE 5th St ... Evansville IN 47708-1604
Fax: 812 428-8215
206 259-7151 **Everett Community College** 801 Wetmore Ave ... Everett WA 98201-1390
Fax: 206 339-9121
206 866-6000 **Evergreen State College** 2700 Evergreen Pkwy NW ... Olympia WA 98505-0001
Fax: 206 866-6823 Admin
408 274-7900 **Evergreen Valley College** 3095 Yerba Buena Rd ... San Jose CA 95135-1598
Fax: 408 223-9291
315 474-6064 **Everson Museum of Art** 401 Harrison St ... Syracuse NY 13202-3091
202 633-2121 **Executive Office for US Attorneys (US Dept of Justice)**
10th St & Constitution Ave NW Rm 1619 ... Washington DC 20530-0001
Fax: 202 786-3938
202 724-8391 **Executive Office of US Trustees (US Dept of Justice)**
320 1st St NW Rm 812 ... Washington DC 23530-0001
Fax: 202 724-7659
202 224-4224 **Exon J James (Sen - D - Nebraska)** 330 Hart Bldg ... Washington DC 20510-0001
Fax: Unlisted
202 566-8990 **Export-Import Bank of the US** 811 Vermont Ave NW ... Washington DC 20571-0001
Fax: 202 566-7524

F

202 755-7252 **Fair Housing & Equal Opportunity Program (US Dept of Housing & Urban Development)**
451 7th St SW Rm 5100 ... Washington DC 20410-0001
802 748-2372 **Fairbanks Museum of Natural Science & Planetarium**
Main St ... Saint Johnsbury VT 05819-2295
907 452-5177 **Fairbanks North Star Borough Public Library & Regional Center**
1215 Cowles St ... Fairbanks AK 99701-4313
Fax: 907 456-3057
509 247-1212 **Fairchild Air Force Base** ... Fairchild AFB WA 99011-0000
Fax: 509 247-5938
703 385-7855 **Fairfax (Independent City)** 10455 Armstrong St ... Fairfax VA 22030-3630
Fax: 703 385-7811
703 246-2000 **Fairfax County** 4110 Chain Bridge Rd ... Fairfax VA 22030-4041
703 222-3155 **Fairfax County Public Library**
13135 Lee Jackson Memorial Hwy Suite 301 ... Fairfax VA 22033-0000
Fax: 703 222-3193
614 687-7030 **Fairfield County** 224 E Main St ... Lancaster OH 43130-3842
803 635-1415 **Fairfield County** 115 S Congress St Drawer 60 ... Winnsboro SC 29180-0060
Fax: 803 635-5969
614 653-2745 **Fairfield County District Library** 219 N Broad St ... Lancaster OH 43130-3098
Fax: 614 653-6745
203 579-6527 **Fairfield Judicial District** 1061 Main St ... Bridgeport CT 06601-0000
203 254-4000 **Fairfield University** 1073 N Benson Rd ... Fairfield CT 06430-5195
Fax: 203 254-4112
201 460-5000 **Fairleigh Dickinson University** 223 Montross Ave ... Rutherford NJ 07070-1977
Fax: 201 460-5017
201 593-8500 *Florham-Madison Campus* 285 Madison Ave ... Madison NJ 07940-1099
Fax: 201 593-8510
201 692-2000 *Teaneck-Hackensack Campus* 1000 River Rd ... Teaneck NJ 07666-1996
Fax: 201 692-0185 Admin
304 367-4000 **Fairmont State College** 1201 Locust Ave ... Fairmont WV 26554-2491
Fax: 304 366-4870 Admin
515 964-0601 **Faith Baptist Bible College & Theological Seminary**
1900 NW 4th St ... Ankeny IA 50021-2198
Fax: Ext 217 Admin
202 225-8577 **Faleomavaega Eni (Rep - D - American Samoa)**
413 Cannon Bldg ... Washington DC 20515-0001
Fax: 202 225-8757
605 745-5132 **Fall River County** 906 N River St ... Hot Springs SD 57747-1387
406 778-2883 **Fallon County** 10 W Fallon Ave ... Baker MT 59313-0000
702 426-2880 **Fallon Naval Air Station** ... Fallon NV 89406-5099
Fax: 702 426-2848 Admin
703 241-5014 **Falls Church (Independent City)** 300 Park Ave ... Falls Church VA 22046-3332
Fax: 703 241-5144
817 883-2061 **Falls County** PO Box 458 ... Marlin TX 76661-0458
414 359-1040 **Family Service America** 11700 W Lake Park Dr ... Milwaukee WI 53224-3099
Fax: 414 359-2115
202 252-4500 **Family Support Administration (US Dept of Health & Human Services)**
370 L'Enfant Promenade SW 6th Fl ... Washington DC 20447-0001
Fax: 202 252-4683
404 632-2203 **Fannin County** PO Box 487 ... Blue Ridge GA 30513-0487
903 583-7486 **Fannin County** County Courthouse ... Bonham TX 75418-0000
701 241-1490 **Fargo Public Library** 102 N 3rd St ... Fargo ND 58102-4899
507 526-5145 **Faribault County** N Main St ... Blue Earth MN 56013-0000
Fax: 507 526-3566

703 883-4000 **Farm Credit Administration** 1501 Farm Credit Dr ... McLean VA 22102-5090
Fax: 703 734-5784
314 966-5070 *Central Region* 13537 Barrett Parkway Dr Suite 300 ... Ballwin MO 63021-5866
Fax: 314 966-2092
703 883-4251 *Eastern Region* 1501 Farm Credit Dr ... McLean VA 22102-0000
303 696-9737 *Western Region* 3131 S Vaughn Way Suite 227 ... Aurora CO 80014-0000
202 447-7967 **Farmers Home Administration (US Dept of Agriculture)**
14th St & Independence Ave SW Rm 5014 ... Washington DC 20250-0001
Fax: 202 382-9719
207 596-6457 **Farnsworth William A Library & Art Museum** PO Box 466 ... Rockland ME 04841-0466
202 225-4506 **Fascell Dante B (Rep - D - Florida)** 2354 Rayburn Bldg ... Washington DC 20515-0001
Fax: 202 225-0724
213 624-1200 **Fashion Institute of Design & Merchandising**
919 S Grand Ave ... Los Angeles CA 90015-1426
Fax: 213 624-4777
212 760-7660 **Fashion Institute of Technology** 227 W 27th St ... New York NY 10001-5902
Fax: 212 594-9206
605 598-6224 **Faulk County** PO Box 309 ... Faulkton SD 57438-0309
501 450-4900 **Faulkner County** 801 Locust St ... Conway AR 72032-5360
205 272-5820 **Faulkner University** 5345 Atlanta Hwy ... Montgomery AL 36193-4601
Fax: Unlisted
703 347-8600 **Fauquier County** 40 Culpeper St ... Warrenton VA 22186-3298
202 225-3515 **Fawell Harris W (Rep - R - Illinois)** 435 Cannon Bldg ... Washington DC 20515-0001
Fax: 202 225-9420
205 932-4510 **Fayette County** PO Box 819 ... Fayette AL 35555-0819
404 461-6041 **Fayette County** 200 Courthouse Sq ... Fayetteville GA 30214-2198
Fax: 404 460-9412
319 422-6061 **Fayette County** Vine St ... West Union IA 52175-0000
618 283-5000 **Fayette County** 221 S 7th St ... Vandalia IL 62471-2755
317 825-1813 **Fayette County** 401 N Central Ave ... Connersville IN 47331-1997
606 253-3344 **Fayette County** 162 E Main St ... Lexington KY 40507-1363
Fax: 606 231-9619
614 335-0720 **Fayette County** 110 E Court St ... Washington Court House OH 43160-1355
Fax: 614 335-0762
412 430-1201 **Fayette County** 61 E Main St ... Uniontown PA 15401-3514
901 465-5213 **Fayette County** Court Sq County Courthouse ... Somerville TN 38068-0000
409 968-3251 **Fayette County** 151 N Washington St ... La Grange TX 78945-2657
304 574-1200 **Fayette County** Court St ... Fayetteville WV 25840-1298
919 486-1111 **Fayetteville State University** 1200 Murchison Rd ... Fayetteville NC 28301-4298
Fax: 919 486-1780
919 323-1961 **Fayetteville Technical Community College** 2201 Hull Rd ... Fayetteville NC 28303-4761
Fax: 919 484-6600
302 225-5716 **Fazio Vic (Rep - D - California)** 2113 Rayburn Bldg ... Washington DC 20515-0001
Fax: 202 225-0354
916 283-0202 **Feather River College** PO Box 11110 ... Quincy CA 95971-0000
Fax: 916 283-3757
202 267-3484 **Federal Aviation Administration**
800 Independence Ave SW Rm 600E ... Washington DC 20591-0001
Fax: 202 755-4161
202 267-8781 *Air Traffic Evaluations & Analysis*
800 Independence Ave SW Rm 400E ... Washington DC 20591-0000
Fax: 202 267-8129
202 267-3053 *Airport Standards* 800 Independence Ave SW Rm 600E ... Washington DC 20591-0001
Fax: 202 267-5383
202 267-9613 *Aviation Safety Office*
800 Independence Ave SW Rm 1000E ... Washington DC 20591-0000
Fax: 202 267-5496
405 680-3011 *Aviation Standards* 6500 S MacArthur Blvd Rm 116 ... Oklahoma City OK 73169-6969
Fax: 405 680-3548
202 267-8237 *Flight Standards* 800 Independence Ave SW Rm 302 ... Washington DC 20591-0000
Fax: 202 267-5230
202 267-3213 *International Aviation*
800 Independence Ave SW Rm 1027 ... Washington DC 20591-0000
Fax: 202 267-5306
405 680-3011 *Monroney Aeronautical Center*
6500 S MacArthur Blvd ... Oklahoma City OK 73169-6969
Fax: 405 680-3548
202 267-3557 *Research & Development*
800 Independence Ave SW Rm 508 ... Washington DC 20591-0000
907 271-5645 *Alaska Region* 222 W 7th Ave ... Anchorage AK 99513-7540
Fax: 907 276-7261
816 426-5626 *Central Region* 601 E 12th St Rm 1501B ... Kansas City MO 64106-2808
Fax: 816 426-2798
718 917-1005 *Eastern Region* Fitzgerald Bldg JFK International Airport ... Jamaica NY 11430-0000
Fax: 718 917-0058
312 694-7294 *Great Lakes Region* 2300 E Devon Ave Rm 401 ... Des Plaines IL 60018-4686
Fax: 312 694-7310
617 273-7244 *New England Region* 12 New England Executive Pk ... Burlington MA 01803-5299
Fax: 617 273-7269
206 431-2001 *Northwestern Region* PO Box C68966 ... Seattle WA 98168-0000
Fax: 206 431-2071 Admin
404 763-7527 *Southern Region* 3400 Norman Berry Dr ... East Point GA 30344-5198
817 624-5000 *Southwestern Region* 4400 Blue Mound Rd ... Fort Worth TX 76193-0001
Fax: 817 624-5029
213 297-1427 *Western Pacific Region*
PO Box 92007 World Way Postal Ctr ... Los Angeles CA 90009-2007
Fax: 213 643-8724
202 324-3000 **Federal Bureau of Investigation**
9th St & Pennsylvania Ave NW ... Washington DC 20535-0001
Fax: 202 324-4705
202 633-6550 **Federal Circuit Court** 717 Madison Pl NW Rm 401 ... Washington DC 20439-0001
Fax: 202 523-0072
202 632-7000 **Federal Communications Commission** 1919 M St NW ... Washington DC 20554-0001
Fax: 202 653-5402
404 347-2631 *Atlanta Region* 1365 Peachtree St NE Rm 440 ... Atlanta GA 30309-3152
617 770-4023 *Boston Region* 1 Batterymarch Pk ... Quincy MA 02169-7495
708 298-5171 *Chicago Region* 1550 Northwest Hwy Rm 306 ... Park Ridge IL 60068-0000
Fax: Unlisted
816 926-5179 *Kansas City Region* 8800 E 63rd St Rm 320 ... Kansas City MO 64133-4895
415 744-2722 *San Francisco Region* 211 Main St Rm 537 ... San Francisco CA 94105-1914
Fax: 415 744-2721
206 764-3324 *Seattle Region* 3605 132nd Ave SE Rm 414 ... Bellevue WA 98006-1333
202 619-2451 **Federal Council on the Aging**
330 Independence Ave SW Rm 4280 ... Washington DC 20201-0001
Fax: 202 245-6699
202 447-6795 **Federal Crop Insurance Corp**
14th St & Independence Ave SW Rm 4096 ... Washington DC 20250-0001
Fax: 202 447-4990
314 875-2909 *Claims Office* Parkade Ctr Rm 128 ... Columbia MO 65203-0000
605 353-1882 *Claims Office* 200 4th St SW Rm 317 ... Huron SD 57350-2476
509 353-2319 *AK ID OR UT WA* W 601 1st Ave Suite 507 ... Spokane WA 99204-0000
Fax: 509 439-2325
601 965-4328 *AL LA MS* 100 W Capitol St Suite 1201 ... Jackson MS 39269-0001
Fax: 601 965-4621
916 551-1717 *AZ HI CA NV* 1303 J St Suite 470 ... Sacramento CA 95814-2941
Fax: 916 442-8488

913 537-4980 *CO KS* 2601 Anderson Ave ... Manhattan KS 66502-2898
Fax: 913 539-5072

717 782-4803 *CT DE ME MD MA NH NJ NY PA RI VT*
1 Credit Union Pl Suite 310 ... Harrisburg PA 17110-2995
Fax: 717 782-4829

803 765-5766 *FL GA SC* 1835 Assembly St Rm 1222 ... Columbia SC 29201-2430
Fax: 803 253-3905

515 284-4316 *IA MO* 210 Walnut St Federal Bldg Rm 509 ... Des Moines IA 50309-2174
Fax: 515 284-4917

217 492-4280 *IL* 2305 W Monroe St Suite 2 ... Springfield IL 62704-1401
Fax: 217 492-4075

317 290-3050 *IN MI OH* 5969 Lakeside Blvd Suite B ... Indianapolis IN 46278-1996
Fax: 317 290-3065

615 736-5591 *KY TN AR* 8th & Broad Sts US Courthouse Rm 301 ... Nashville TN 37203-0000
Fax: 615 736-7223

612 290-3871 *MN WI* 375 Jackson St Rm 300 ... Saint Paul MN 55101-1810
Fax: 612 290-4023

406 657-6196 *MT WY* 2110 Overland Ave Suite 108 ... Billings MT 59102-7496
Fax: 406 657-6573

919 856-4470 *NC VA WV* 4407 Bland Rd Suite 280 ... Raleigh NC 27609-6296
Fax: 919 790-2800

701 250-4271 *ND* 309 N Mandan St ... Bismarck ND 58501-3859
Fax: 701 222-2242

402 437-5531 *NE SD* 100 Centennial Mall N Rm 259 ... Lincoln NE 68508-3886
Fax: 402 437-5142

409 260-9391 *NM OK TX* 7607 E Mark Dr Suite 240 ... College Station TX 77840-0000
Fax: 409 260-9463

202 393-8400 **Federal Deposit Insurance Corp** 550 17th St NW ... Washington DC 20429-0001
Fax: 202 347-2775

404 525-0308 *Atlanta Region* 245 Peachtree Center Ave NE Suite 1200 ... Atlanta GA 30303-1225
Fax: 404 225-5012

617 449-9080 *Boston Region* 160 Gould St ... Needham MA 02194-2300
Fax: 617 455-0295

312 207-0210 *Chicago Region* 30 S Wacker Dr Suite 3100 ... Chicago IL 60606-7406
Fax: 312 207-0195

214 220-3342 *Dallas Region* 1910 Pacific Ave Suite 1700 ... Dallas TX 75201-4522
Fax: 214 220-3370

816 234-8000 *Kansas City Region* 2345 Grand Ave Suite 1500 ... Kansas City MO 64108-2679
Fax: 816 234-8182

901 685-1603 *Memphis Region* 5100 Poplar Ave Suite 1900 ... Memphis TN 38137-1901
Fax: 901 685-1846

212 704-1200 *New York Region* 452 5th Ave ... New York NY 10018-2796
Fax: 212 768-1058

415 546-0160 *San Francisco Region* 25 Ecker Pl ... San Francisco CA 94105-2780
Fax: 415 543-2624

202 376-5140 **Federal Election Commission** 999 E St NW ... Washington DC 20463-0001
Fax: 202 376-5280

202 646-2500 **Federal Emergency Management Agency** 500 C St SW ... Washington DC 20472-0001
Fax: 202 646-2464

617 223-9540 *Region 1* JW McCormack POCH Rm 442 ... Boston MA 02109-0000
Fax: 617 223-9519

212 238-8200 *Region 2* 26 Federal Plaza ... New York NY 10278-0183
Fax: 212 238-8245

215 931-5500 *Region 3* 105 S 7th St ... Philadelphia PA 19106-3324
Fax: 215 489-5513

404 853-4200 *Region 4* 1371 Peachtree St NE Suite 700 ... Atlanta GA 30309-3166
Fax: 404 853-4230

312 408-5500 *Region 5* 175 W Jackson Blvd 4th Fl ... Chicago IL 60604-2607
Fax: 312 408-5521

817 898-9399 *Region 6* 800 N Loop 288 ... Denton TX 76201-0000
Fax: 817 898-9290

816 283-7063 *Region 7* 911 Walnut St Rm 200 ... Kansas City MO 64106-2009
Fax: 816 759-7504

303 235-4800 *Region 8* PO Box 25267 ... Denver CO 80225-0267
Fax: 303 235-4976

415 923-7120 *Region 9* 940 Presidio Ave Bldg 105 ... San Francisco CA 94129-0000
Fax: 415 923-7157

206 481-8800 *Region 10* 130 228th St SW ... Bothell WA 98021-8627
Fax: 206 390-4707

202 566-2468 **Federal Financing Bank**
1500 Pennsylvania Ave NW Rm 3054-MT ... Washington DC 20220-0001
Fax: 202 343-0287

202 366-0660 **Federal Highway Administration** 400 7th St SW Rm 4210 ... Washington DC 20590-0001
Fax: 202 366-7239

703 285-0000 *Eastern District* 21400 Ridgetop Cir ... Sterling VA 22170-6511
Fax: 703 285-0011

202 366-2045 *Environmental Policy* 400 7th St SW Rm 3232 ... Washington DC 20590-0000
Fax: 202 366-3409

202 366-1153 *Highway Safety* 400 7th St SW Rm 3401 ... Washington DC 20590-0000
Fax: 202 366-2249

703 285-2770 *National Highway Institute* 6300 Georgetown Pike ... McLean VA 22101-0000
Fax: 703 285-2791

202 366-0342 *Office of Right-Of-Way* 400 7th St SW Rm 3221 ... Washington DC 20590-0000
Fax: 202 366-3049

518 472-6476 *Regions 1 & 2*
Clinton Ave & N Pearl St Leo O'Brien Federal Bldg Rm 719 ... Albany NY 12207-0000
Fax: 518 472-4242

301 962-2773 *Region 3* 31 Hopkins Plaza Rm 1621 ... Baltimore MD 21201-2822
Fax: 301 962-3418

404 347-4078 *Region 4* 1720 Peachtree Rd NW Suite 200 ... Atlanta GA 30367-0001
Fax: 404 347-2125

708 799-6300 *Region 5* 18209 Dixie Hwy ... Homewood IL 60430-2294
Fax: Ext 202

817 334-3232 *Region 6* 819 Taylor St Rm 8A00 ... Fort Worth TX 76102-6114
Fax: 817 334-4144

816 926-7563 *Region 7* 6301 Rockhill Rd 2nd Fl ... Kansas City MO 64131-1117
303 969-6704 *Region 8* 555 Zang St Rm 400 ... Lakewood CO 80228-1097
Fax: 303 969-6727

415 744-3100 *Region 9* 211 Main St Rm 1100 ... San Francisco CA 94105-1926
Fax: 415 744-2620

503 326-2053 *Region 10* 708 SW 3rd Ave Rm 312 ... Portland OR 97204-2489
Fax: 503 326-3928

202 906-6000 **Federal Home Loan Bank Board** 1700 G St NW ... Washington DC 20552-0001
Fax: 202 789-2670

617 542-0150 *Region 1* 1 Financial Ctr 20th Fl ... Boston MA 02111-2664
Fax: 617 292-9645

212 912-4600 *Region 2* 1 World Trade Ctr 103rd Fl ... New York NY 10048-0610
Fax: 212 912-4623

412 288-3400 *Region 3* 20 Stanwix St ... Pittsburgh PA 15222-4893
Fax: 412 288-0117

404 888-8000 *Region 4* 1475 Peachtree St NE ... Atlanta GA 30309-3037
Fax: 800 225-1626

513 852-7500 *Region 5* 221 E 4th St 2000 Atrium II ... Cincinnati OH 45202-0000
Fax: 513 852-7655

317 465-0200 *Region 6* 8250 Woodfield Crossing Ln ... Indianapolis IN 46240-2480
Fax: 317 465-0397

312 565-5700 *Region 7* 111 E Wacker Dr Suite 800 ... Chicago IL 60601-4360
Fax: 312 565-5823

515 243-4211 *Region 8* 907 Walnut St ... Des Moines IA 50309-3500
Fax: 515 281-1022

214 541-8500 *Region 9* 500 E John W Carpenter Fwy ... Irving TX 75062-3997
Fax: 214 541-8603

913 233-0507 *Region 10* 200 E 6th St 2 Townsite Plaza ... Topeka KS 66603-0000
Fax: 913 234-1797

415 393-1000 *Region 11* PO Box 7948 ... San Francisco CA 94120-7948
Fax: 415 393-0752

206 340-2300 *Region 12* 1501 4th Ave 19th Fl ... Seattle WA 98101-1693
Fax: 206 340-2485

202 759-8000 **Federal Home Loan Mortgage Corp** 1776 G St NW ... Washington DC 20006-4705

202 755-6600 **Federal Housing Commissioner (US Dept of Housing & Urban Development)**
451 7th St SW Rm 9100 ... Washington DC 20410-0001
Fax: 202 755-2580

202 633-6347 **Federal Judicial Center** 1520 H St NW ... Washington DC 20005-1081
Fax: 202 786-6389

202 382-0711 **Federal Labor Relations Authority** 500 C St SW ... Washington DC 20424-0001
Fax: 202 382-0729

617 565-7280 *Region 1* 10 Causeway St Rm 1017 ... Boston MA 02222-1046
Fax: 617 565-5538

212 264-4934 *Region 2* 26 Federal Plaza Rm 3700 ... New York NY 10278-0179
Fax: 212 264-8038

202 653-8500 *Region 3* PO Box 33758 ... Washington DC 20033-0758
Fax: 202 653-5091

404 347-2324 *Region 4* 1371 Peachtree St NE Suite 736 ... Atlanta GA 30367-0001
Fax: 404 347-1032

312 353-6306 *Region 5* 175 W Jackson Blvd Suite A-1359 ... Chicago IL 60604-0000
Fax: 312 886-5977

214 767-4996 *Region 6* 525 Griffin St Suite 926 LB 107 ... Dallas TX 75202-0000
Fax: 214 767-0156

303 844-5224 *Region 7* 535 16th St Suite 310 ... Denver CO 80202-4238
Fax: Unlisted

213 894-3805 *Region 8* 350 S Figueroa St Suite 370 ... Los Angeles CA 90071-1395
Fax: 213 894-6202

415 744-4000 *Region 9* 901 Market St Suite 220 ... San Francisco CA 94103-1791
Fax: 415 744-4117

912 267-2100 **Federal Law Enforcement Training Center (US Dept of the Treasury)**
Hwy 303 ... Brunswick GA 31524-0001
Fax: 912 230-2217 Admin

202 523-5725 **Federal Maritime Commission** 1100 L St NW ... Washington DC 20573-0001
Fax: 202 523-3782

202 523-5860 *Bureau of Investigations* 1100 L St NW ... Washington DC 20573-0001
Fax: 202 523-3725

213 514-6127 *Los Angeles Office* PO Box 3184 ... Terminal Island CA 90731-0000
Fax: 213 514-6129

305 536-6963 *Miami Office* 1001 North American Way ... Miami FL 33132-2060
Fax: 305 536-4668

504 589-6662 *New Orleans Office*
2 Canal St World Trade Ctr Suite 440 ... New Orleans LA 70130-0000
Fax: 504 589-2000

212 264-1430 *New York Office* 6 World Trade Ctr Suite 614 ... New York NY 10048-0949
Fax: 212 264-7465

809 766-5581 *Puerto Rico Office* Federal Office Bldg Rm 762 ... Hato Rey PR 00918-0000
415 744-7016 *San Francisco Office* 525 Market St Rm 3510 ... San Francisco CA 94105-2743
Fax: 415 744-7020

202 653-5290 **Federal Mediation & Conciliation Service** 2100 K St NW ... Washington DC 20427-0001
Fax: 202 653-5247
404 347-2473 *Atlanta District* 1720 Peachtree St NW ... Atlanta GA 30309-0000
213 965-3814 *Los Angeles District* 4221 Wilshire Blvd Suite 210 ... Los Angeles CA 90010-0000
708 887-4750 *Hinsdale District* 908 N Elm St Elm Plaza Suite 203 ... Hinsdale IL 60521-0000
612 670-3300 *Minneapolis District* 1300 Godward St Suite 3950 ... Minneapolis MN 55413-0000
212 399-5038 *New York District* 1633 Broadway 2nd Fl ... New York NY 10019-0000
215 597-7690 *Philadelphia District* 600 Arch St Federal Bldg Rm 3456 ... Philadelphia PA 19106-0000
314 576-3922 *Saint Louis District* 12140 Woodcrest Executive Dr ... Saint Louis MO 63141-0000
206 442-5800 *Seattle District* 2001 6th Ave Westin Bldg Rm 310 ... Seattle WA 98121-0000
202 653-5390 *Washington District* 2100 K St NW ... Washington DC 20427-0000

216 522-4800 **Federal Mediation & Concilidation Service Broadview Heights District**
3505 East Royalton Rd Suite 200 ... Broadview Heights OH 44147-0000

202 653-5633 **Federal Mine Safety & Health Review Commission**
1730 K St NW Suite 600 ... Washington DC 20006-3868

202 752-7000 **Federal National Mortgage Assn** 3900 Wisconsin Ave NW ... Washington DC 20016-2896
Fax: 202 537-6099 Admin

312 641-0740 *Midwestern Region* 1 S Wacker Dr Suite 3100 ... Chicago IL 60606-4667
Fax: 312 368-6350

215 574-1400 *Northeastern Region* 510 Walnut St 16th Fl ... Philadelphia PA 19106-3696
Fax: 215 574-1781

404 365-6000 *Southeastern Region* 950 E Paces Ferry Rd NE Suite 1800 ... Atlanta GA 30326-1161
Fax: 404 365-6238

214 991-7771 *Southwestern Region*
13455 Noel Rd 2 Galleria Tower Suite 600 ... Dallas TX 75240-0000
Fax: 214 770-7606

818 568-5000 *Western Region* 135 N Los Robles Ave Suite 300 ... Pasadena CA 91101-1758
Fax: 818 568-5481

202 366-0881 **Federal Railroad Administration** 400 7th St SW ... Washington DC 20590-0001
Fax: 202 366-7099

202 366-9657 *Freight Services* 400 7th St SW Rm 8128 ... Washington DC 20590-0000
Fax: 202 366-3055

202 366-9332 *Passenger Services* 400 7th St SW Rm 5407 ... Washington DC 20590-0000
Fax: 202 366-0646

202 366-9252 *Safety Enforcement* 400 7th St SW Rm 8326 ... Washington DC 20590-0000
Fax: 202 366-7136

312 353-6203 *Central Region* 165 N Canal St Rm 1400SA ... Chicago IL 60606-1510
Fax: 312 886-9634

215 597-0750 *Eastern Region* 841 Chestnut St Rm 712 ... Philadelphia PA 19107-4433
Fax: 215 597-0089

816 426-2497 *Midwest Region* 911 Walnut St Rm 1806 ... Kansas City MO 64106-2095
Fax: 816 426-2010

617 494-2302 *Northeastern Region* 55 Broadway 10th Fl ... Cambridge MA 02142-1003
Fax: 617 494-2967

503 326-3011 *Northwest Region* 1500 SW 1st Ave Suite 250 ... Portland OR 97201-5871
Fax: 503 423-4832

404 347-2751 *Southern Region* 1720 Peachtree Rd NW Suite 440-N ... Atlanta GA 30309-2469
Fax: 404 347-5295

817 334-3601 *Southwest Region* 819 Taylor St Rm 7A35 ... Fort Worth TX 76102-6114
Fax: 817 334-3034

415 744-3092 *Western Region* 211 Main St Rm 1085 ... San Francisco CA 94105-1924
Fax: 415 744-2672

202 452-3000 **Federal Reserve System** 20th & C Sts NW ... Washington DC 20551-0001
Fax: 202 452-3819

202 326-2000 **Federal Trade Commission**
Pennsylvania Ave & 6th St NW ... Washington DC 20580-0001
Fax: 202 326-2222

404 347-4836 *Atlanta Region* 1718 Peachtree St NW Rm 1000 ... Atlanta GA 30367-0001
Fax: 404 347-4725

617 565-7240 *Boston Region* 10 Causeway St Rm 1184 ... Boston MA 02222-1073
Fax: 617 723-6344
312 353-4423 *Chicago Region* 55 E Monroe St Suite 1437 ... Chicago IL 60603-5793
Fax: 312 353-4438
216 522-4207 *Cleveland Region* 668 Euclid Ave Suite 520-A ... Cleveland OH 44114-3006
Fax: 216 522-7239
214 767-5501 *Dallas Region* 100 N Central Expy Suite 500 ... Dallas TX 75201-4329
Fax: Unlisted
303 844-2271 *Denver Region* 5353 16th St Suite 310 ... Denver CO 80202-0000
Fax: 303 844-2774
213 209-7575 *Los Angeles Region* 11000 Wilshire Blvd Suite 13209 ... Los Angeles CA 90024-3679
212 264-1207 *New York Region* 150 William St 13th Fl ... New York NY 10038-2688
Fax: 212 264-0459
415 744-7920 *San Francisco Region* 901 Market St Suite 570 ... San Francisco CA 94103-1768
Fax: 415 744-7940
206 442-4655 *Seattle Region* 915 2nd Ave Federal Bldg Rm 2806 ... Seattle WA 98174-0000
Fax: 206 442-2699
202 225-5731 **Feighan Edward F (Rep - D - Ohio)** 1124 Longworth Bldg ... Washington DC 20515-0001
Fax: 202 226-1230
201 778-1190 **Felician College** 260 S Main St ... Lodi NJ 07644-2198
Fax: 201 778-4111
316 292-5594 **Fellow-Reeve Museum of History & Science**
2100 University St ... Wichita KS 67213-3379
Fax: 316 263-1092
615 879-8014 **Fentress County** PO Box C ... Jamestown TN 38556-0200
406 538-5119 **Fergus County** 712 W Main St ... Lewistown MT 59457-2562
218 739-7500 **Fergus Falls Community College** 1414 College Way ... Fergus Falls MN 56537-1009
Fax: 218 739-7475
203 964-1000 **Ferguson Library** 1 Public Library Plaza ... Stamford CT 06904-0000
Fax: Unlisted
404 378-4311 **Fernbank Science Center** 156 Heaton Park Dr NE ... Atlanta GA 30307-1398
616 592-2000 **Ferris State University** 901 S State St ... Big Rapids MI 49307-2295
Fax: 616 592-2990
616 592-3700 *College of Optometry* 901 S State St ... Big Rapids MI 49307-2295
Fax: 616 592-3551 Admin
616 592-3780 *School of Pharmacy* 901 S State St ... Big Rapids MI 49307-2295
Fax: 616 592-3829
703 365-2121 **Ferrum College** Rt 40 ... Ferrum VA 24088-0000
Fax: 703 365-4203
509 775-3161 **Ferry County** PO Box 302 ... Republic WA 99166-0302
Fax: 509 775-2492
312 922-9410 **Field Museum of Natural History**
Roosevelt Rd & Lake Shore Dr ... Chicago IL 60605-0000
Fax: 312 427-7269
202 225-4901 **Fields Jack (Rep - R - Texas)** 108 Cannon Bldg ... Washington DC 20515-0001
Fax: Unlisted
Fiji
202 337-8320 *Embassy* 2233 Wisconsin Ave NW Suite 240 ... Washington DC 20007-4104
Fax: 202 337-1996
212 355-7316 *Mission to the UN* 1 UN Plaza 26th Fl ... New York NY 10017-0000
Fax: 212 319-1896
507 765-2144 **Fillmore County** Fillmore St ... Preston MN 55965-0000
402 759-4931 **Fillmore County** 900 G St ... Geneva NE 68361-2005
202 224-4515 **Finance Committee (US Senate)** 205 Dirksen Bldg ... Washington DC 20510-0001
Fax: 202 228-5568
205 343-2667 **Fine Arts Museum of the South at Mobile**
4850 Museum Dr Langan Pk ... Mobile AL 36608-0000
Fax: 205 434-7552
415 750-3600 **Fine Arts Museums of San Francisco** Golden Gate Pk ... San Francisco CA 94118-0000
Fax: 415 750-7692
607 273-4074 **Finger Lakes Library System** 314 N Cayuga St ... Ithaca NY 14850-4279
Finland
202 363-2430 *Embassy* 3216 New Mexico Ave NW ... Washington DC 20016-2745
Fax: 202 363-8233
312 670-4700 *Chicago Consulate General* 321 N Clark St Suite 2880 ... Chicago IL 60610-4717
Fax: 312 670-4777
213 203-9903 *Los Angeles Consulate General*
1900 Ave of the Stars Suite 1025 ... Los Angeles CA 90067-4401
Fax: 213 203-0301
212 573-6007 *New York Consulate General* 380 Madison Ave 24th Fl ... New York NY 10017-0000
Fax: 212 573-6310
212 355-2100 **Finland: Republic of Finland Mission to the UN**
866 UN Plaza Rm 222 ... New York NY 10017-0000
Fax: 212 759-6156
816 523-6030 **Finlay Engineering College** 7 E 79th Terr ... Kansas City MO 64114-2599
316 276-3051 **Finney County** PO Box M ... Garden City KS 67846-0450
212 832-2588 **Finnish-American Chamber of Commerce**
380 Madison Ave 24th Fl ... New York NY 10017-0000
Fax: 212 370-2863
312 670-4700 **Finnish-American Chamber of Commerce of the Midwest**
321 N Clark St Suite 2880 ... Chicago IL 60610-4717
Fax: 312 670-4777
601 429-4439 **First Regional Library** 370 W Commerce St ... Hernando MS 38632-2130
202 225-5441 **Fish Hamilton Jr (Rep - R - New York)**
2269 Rayburn Bldg ... Washington DC 20515-0001
Fax: 202 225-0962
915 776-2401 **Fisher County** PO Box 368 ... Roby TX 79543-0368
213 743-2799 **Fisher Gallery** University of Southern California ... Los Angeles CA 90089-0292
Fax: Unlisted
617 262-3240 **Fisher Junior College** 118 Beacon St ... Boston MA 02116-1500
Fax: 617 236-8858
615 329-8500 **Fisk University** 1000 17th Ave N ... Nashville TN 37208-3045
Fax: 615 329-8715
508 345-2151 **Fitchburg State College** 160 Pearl St ... Fitchburg MA 01420-2631
918 683-1701 **Five Civilized Tribes Museum** Honor Heights Dr ... Muskogee OK 74401-0000
904 829-6481 **Flagler College** 74 King St ... Saint Augustine FL 32085-1027
904 437-2218 **Flagler County** 200 E Moody Blvd ... Bunnell FL 32110-0000
Fax: 904 437-4259
407 655-2833 **Flagler Henry M Museum** PO Box 969 ... Palm Beach FL 33480-0969
Fax: 407 655-2826
602 779-7670 **Flagstaff City-Coconino County Public Library System**
300 W Aspen Ave ... Flagstaff AZ 86001-5304
Fax: 602 774-9573
202 225-3461 **Flake Floyd H (Rep - D - New York)** 1034 Longworth Bldg ... Washington DC 20515-0001
Fax: 202 226-4169
406 752-5300 **Flathead County** 800 S Main St ... Kalispell MT 59901-5400
406 752-5222 **Flathead Valley Community College** 1 1st St E ... Kalispell MT 59901-4599
Fax: 406 755-4044 Library
202 785-2768 **Fleet Reserve Assn** 1303 New Hampshire Ave NW ... Washington DC 20036-1598
Fax: 202 429-0516
606 845-7571 **Fleming County** Court Sq ... Flemingsburg KY 41041-1399
802 656-0750 **Fleming Robert Hull Museum**
Colchester Ave University of Vermont ... Burlington VT 05405-0001
313 232-7111 **Flint Public Library** 1026 E Kearsley St ... Flint MI 48502-0000
Fax: 313 767-6740
404 227-2756 **Flint River Regional Library** 800 Memorial Dr ... Griffin GA 30223-4443

803 665-3031 **Florence County** 180 N Irby St ... Florence SC 29501-3456
715 528-3201 **Florence County** PO Box 410 ... Florence WI 54121-0410
803 662-8424 **Florence County Library** 319 S Irby St ... Florence SC 29501-4795
803 661-8324 **Florence-Darlington Technical College** PO Box F8000 ... Florence SC 29501-0057
Fax: 803 661-8011
904 599-3000 **Florida A & M University** Martin Luther King Jr Blvd ... Tallahassee FL 32307-0001
Fax: 904 599-3347
904 599-3593 *College of Pharmacy* Pharmacy Bldg Rm 201 ... Tallahassee FL 32307-0001
Fax: 904 599-3347
407 367-3000 **Florida Atlantic University** 500 NW 20th St ... Boca Raton FL 33431-6498
Fax: 407 338-3863 Library
904 263-3261 **Florida Baptist Theological College** 1306 College Dr ... Graceville FL 32440-1833
Fax: Call company operator
813 531-4498 **Florida Beacon Bible College** 6900 142nd Ave N ... Largo FL 34641-0000
Fax: 813 531-6580
407 933-4500 **Florida Bible College** 1701 Poinciana Blvd ... Kissimmee FL 34758-2096
407 847-8966 **Florida Christian College Inc** 1011 Osceola Blvd ... Kissimmee FL 34744-8614
813 988-5131 **Florida College** 119 N Glen Arven Ave ... Temple Terrace FL 33617-5527
Fax: 813 985-9654
904 632-3000 **Florida Community College of Jacksonville**
501 W State St ... Jacksonville FL 32202-4097
Fax: 904 632-3393
904 222-3411 **Florida Democratic Party** PO Box 1758 ... Tallahassee FL 32302-1758
Fax: 904 222-0916
904 487-0162 **Florida Div of Tourism** 107 W Gaines St Rm 505 ... Tallahassee FL 32399-2000
Fax: 904 487-0132
407 768-8000 **Florida Institute of Technology** 150 W University Blvd ... Melbourne FL 32901-0000
Fax: 407 984-8461
305 554-2000 **Florida International University** Tamiami Trail ... Miami FL 33199-0001
Fax: 305 559-7251
305 940-5895 *Department of Health Services Administration*
North Miami Campus Bldg AC1 Rm 225 ... North Miami FL 33181-0000
Fax: 305 940-5980
305 296-9081 **Florida Keys Community College** 5901 W Junior College Rd ... Key West FL 33040-4397
Fax: 305 296-7707 Library
305 625-4141 **Florida Memorial College** 15800 NW 42nd Ave ... Opa Locka FL 33054-6198
Fax: 305 623-4123
904 392-1721 **Florida Museum of Natural History**
Museum Rd University of Florida ... Gainesville FL 32611-2035
Fax: 904 392-8783
813 680-4100 **Florida Southern College** 111 Lake Hollingsworth Dr ... Lakeland FL 33801-5607
Fax: 813 680-4126
904 222-2831 **Florida State Chamber of Commerce** 136 S Bronough St ... Tallahassee FL 32302-0000
Fax: 904 222-5520
Florida State Government
904 488-1234 *Information*
Koger Executive Ctr 2737 Center Knight Bldg Suite 110 ... Tallahassee FL 32399-0950
904 487-1963 *Attorney General* Capitol Bldg ... Tallahassee FL 32399-0000
Fax: 904 487-2564
904 488-0090 *Bureau of Public Safety Management*
2740 Centerview Dr ... Tallahassee FL 32399-6558
Fax: 904 487-4414
904 488-6971 *Department of Agriculture & Consumer Services*
407 S Calhoun St ... Tallahassee FL 32399-0800
Fax: 904 488-8087
904 488-0520 *Department of Banking & Finance* State Capitol ... Tallahassee FL 32399-0350
Fax: 904 488-9818
904 488-3104 *Department of Commerce*
107 W Gaines St Collins Bldg Suite 510-C ... Tallahassee FL 32399-0000
Fax: 904 488-9804
904 488-5021 *Department of Corrections* 1311 Winewood Blvd ... Tallahassee FL 32399-2500
Fax: Unlisted
904 487-1785 *Department of Education*
325 W Gaines St Florida Education Center Suite 101 ... Tallahassee FL 32399-0400
Fax: 904 488-1492
904 488-4805 *Department of Environmental Regulation*
2600 Blair Stone Rd ... Tallahassee FL 32399-2400
Fax: 904 487-4938
904 488-2786 *Department of General Services*
2737 Centerview Dr Knight Bldg Suite 307 ... Tallahassee FL 32399-0000
Fax: 904 922-6312
904 488-4115 *Department of Health & Rehabilitative Services*
1323 Winewood Blvd Bldg 1 Rm 115 ... Tallahassee FL 32399-0700
Fax: 904 488-2112
904 488-3440 *Department of Insurance* 200 E Gaines St ... Tallahassee FL 32399-0300
Fax: 904 488-6581
904 488-8771 *Department of Law Enforcement* 208 W Carolina St ... Tallahassee FL 32301-1128
Fax: 904 487-1030
904 488-1554 *Department of Natural Resources*
3900 Commonwealth Blvd ... Tallahassee FL 32399-3000
Fax: 904 487-1469
904 487-2252 *Department of Professional Regulation*
1940 N Monroe St ... Tallahassee FL 32399-0750
Fax: 904 487-9622
904 488-5050 *Department of Revenue* 501 S Calhoun St Rm 104 ... Tallahassee FL 32399-0100
Fax: 904 488-0024
904 488-6721 *Department of Transportation* 605 Suwannee Burns Bldg . Tallahassee FL 32399-0000
Fax: 904 487-3403
904 488-1344 *Division of Air Resources Management*
2600 Blair Stone Rd ... Tallahassee FL 32399-6564
Fax: 904 487-4938
904 488-2774 *Division of Building Construction*
2737 Centerview Dr Knight Bldg Suite 300 ... Tallahassee FL 32399-0950
Fax: 904 487-9947
904 488-2226 *Division of Consumer Services* 508 Mayo Bldg ... Tallahassee FL 32399-0000
Fax: 904 487-4177
904 488-1083 *Division of Cultural Affairs* State Capitol ... Tallahassee FL 32399-0000
904 488-6300 *Division of Economic Development*
107 W Gaines St Collins Bldg Suite 501-B ... Tallahassee FL 32399-2000
Fax: 904 488-9804
904 487-4918 *Division of Emergency Management* 2740 Centerview Dr . Tallahassee FL 32399-6558
Fax: 904 488-6250
904 488-7228 *Division of Labor Employment & Training*
1320 Executive Center Dr Suite 300 ... Tallahassee FL 32399-6511
Fax: 904 487-1753
904 487-2651 *Division of Library & Information Services*
500 S Bronough St RA Gray Bldg ... Tallahassee FL 32399-6519
Fax: 904 488-2746
904 488-1194 *Division of Purchasing*
2737 Centerview Dr Night Bldg Suite 110 ... Tallahassee FL 32399-0950
Fax: 904 488-5498
407 423-6053 *Division of Real Estate* 400 W Robinson St ... Orlando FL 32801-1736
904 488-5541 *Division of Retirement* 2639 N Monroe St ... Tallahassee FL 32399-1560
904 488-6093 *Division of Unemployment Compensation*
107 E Madison St ... Tallahassee FL 32399-6545
Fax: 904 487-0402

904 488-2514 *Division of Worker's Compensation* 2728 Centerview Dr .. Tallahassee FL 32399-0680
Fax: 904 922-5167
904 488-6764 *Energy Office* 214 S Bronough St .... Tallahassee FL 32301-1705
Fax: 904 487-0801
904 964-8125 *Florida State Prison* PO Box 747 .... Starke FL 32091-0747
Fax: Unlisted
904 488-4441 *Governor* Capitol Bldg .... Tallahassee FL 32399-0001
Fax: 904 487-0801
904 488-4711 *Lieutenant Governor* Capitol Bldg Plaza Level 5 .... Tallahassee FL 32399-0000
Fax: 904 487-0801
407 597-3705 *Martin Correctional Institution* 1150 SW Allapattah Rd ..... Indiantown FL 34956-4397
904 488-7810 *Office of Planning & Budgeting* Carlton Bldg Rm 415 ...... Tallahassee FL 32399-0001
Fax: 904 487-0526
904 359-6971 *Office of Vital Statistics* 1217 Pearl St .... Jacksonville FL 32202-3926
Fax: 904 359-6697
904 488-1653 *Parole Commission* 1309 Winewood Blvd .... Tallahassee FL 32399-6568
904 488-7181 *Public Service Commission* 101 E Gaines St .... Tallahassee FL 32399-0850
Fax: 904 487-0509
904 488-3680 *Secretary of State* State Capitol Plaza Level Rm 2 .... Tallahassee FL 32399-0000
Fax: 904 487-2214
904 488-4234 *State University System of Florida* 325 W Gaines St .... Tallahassee FL 32399-6557
Fax: 904 487-4568
904 488-0125 *Supreme Court* 500 S Duval St .... Tallahassee FL 32399-1900
Fax: Unlisted
904 644-2525 **Florida State University** College Ave .... Tallahassee FL 32306-1096
Fax: 904 644-4702 Library
904 644-3400 *College of Law* 425 W Jefferson St Rm 210 .... Tallahassee FL 32306-0001
Fax: 904 644-5487
904 644-3525 *Department of Public Administration*
Bellamy Bldg Rm 614 .... Tallahassee FL 32306-0001
Fax: 904 644-7617
904 644-4510 *Department of Urban & Regional Planning*
Bellamy Bldg Rm 355 .... Tallahassee FL 32306-0001
Fax: Unlisted
904 644-3023 *Graduate School of Cellular/Molecular Biology*
204 Conradi Bldg .... Tallahassee FL 32306-2043
Fax: 904 644-9829
904 644-3810 *Graduate School of Chemistry*
Hoffman Teaching Laboratory .... Tallahassee FL 32306-1096
Fax: 904 644-8281
904 644-4473 *Graduate School of Physics* 307 Keen Bldg .... Tallahassee FL 22306-0000
Fax: 904 644-6735 Admin
904 644-5775 *School of Library & Information Studies*
101 Lewis Schores Bldg .... Tallahassee FL 32306-2048
Fax: 904 644-9763
404 295-6339 **Floyd College** PO Box 1864 .... Rome GA 30162-1864
Fax: 404 295-6610
404 291-5110 **Floyd County** PO Box 946 .... Rome GA 30162-0946
515 228-7111 **Floyd County** 101 S Main St .... Charles City IA 50616-2756
812 948-5411 **Floyd County** 211 W 1st St .... New Albany IN 47150-3501
606 886-9193 **Floyd County** 3rd Ave .... Prestonsburg KY 41653-0000
Fax: 606 886-1083
806 983-3236 **Floyd County** 100 Main St .... Floydada TX 79235-0000
703 745-4158 **Floyd County** 100 E Main St Rm 200 .... Floyd VA 24091-2100
804 589-3138 **Fluvanna County** PO Box 299 .... Palmyra VA 22963-0000
817 684-1365 **Foard County** PO Box 539 .... Crowell TX 79227-0539
617 495-9400 **Fogg Art Museum** 32 Quincy St Harvard University .... Cambridge MA 02138-3883
Fax: 617 495-9936
202 225-4731 **Foglietta Thomas M (Rep - D - Pennsylvania)**
231 Cannon Bldg .... Washington DC 20515-0001
Fax: 202 225-0088
202 225-2006 **Foley Thomas S (Rep - D - Washington)**
1201 Longworth Bldg .... Washington DC 20515-0001
Fax: Unlisted
704 298-7928 **Folk Art Center** PO Box 9545 .... Asheville NC 28815-0545
414 929-3000 **Fond du Lac County** 160 S Macy St .... Fond du Lac WI 54935-4241
314 862-3456 **Fontbonne College** 6800 Wydown Blvd .... Saint Louis MO 63105-3098
Fax: Unlisted
301 443-2410 **Food & Drug Administration** 5600 Fishers Ln Rm 14-71 .... Rockville MD 20852-0000
Fax: 301 443-1863
301 443-3170 *Consumer Affairs* 5600 Fishers Ln Rm 16-63 .... Rockville MD 20857-0001
404 347-7355 *Atlanta Office* 60 8th St NE .... Atlanta GA 30309-3959
Fax: 404 257-4206
301 962-3731 *Baltimore Office* 900 Madison Ave .... Baltimore MD 21201-2199
Fax: 301 962-2307
617 565-4701 *Boston Office* 1 Montvale Ave 4th Fl .... Stoneham MA 02180-3500
Fax: 617 835-4709
716 846-4483 *Buffalo Office* 599 Delaware Ave .... Buffalo NY 14202-1291
Fax: 716 846-4470
312 353-7126 *Chicago Office* 433 W Van Buren Rm 1222 .... Chicago IL 60607-3926
Fax: 312 886-3280
513 684-3501 *Cincinnati Office* 1141 Central Pkwy .... Cincinnati OH 45202-1097
Fax: 513 621-6014
214 655-5315 *Dallas Office* 1200 Main Tower Bldg Rm 2100 .... Dallas TX 75202-0000
Fax: 214 255-5331
303 236-3000 *Denver Office*
6th & Kipling Sts Denver Federal Center Bldg 20 .... Denver CO 80225-0087
Fax: 303 236-3099
313 226-6274 *Detroit Office* 1560 E Jefferson Ave .... Detroit MI 48207-3179
Fax: 313 226-3076
713 220-2322 *Houston Office* 1445 North Loop W Suite 420 .... Houston TX 77008-0000
Fax: Unlisted
317 226-6500 *Indianapolis Office* 101 W Ohio St Suite 1300 .... Indianapolis IN 46204-1586
Fax: 317 226-6506
816 374-6371 *Kansas City Office* 1009 Cherry St .... Kansas City MO 64106-2694
Fax: 816 374-6369
213 252-7597 *Los Angeles Office* 1521 W Pico Blvd .... Los Angeles CA 90015-2486
Fax: 213 252-7701
612 334-4100 *Minneapolis Office* 240 Hennepin Ave .... Minneapolis MN 55401-1999
Fax: 612 334-4134
615 736-2088 *Nashville Office* 297 Plus Park Blvd .... Nashville TN 37217-1088
Fax: 615 736-5435
504 589-2420 *New Orleans Office* 4298 Elysian Fields Ave .... New Orleans LA 70122-3896
Fax: 504 589-6360
718 965-5043 *New York Office* 850 3rd Ave 7th Fl .... Brooklyn NY 11232-1593
Fax: 718 965-5117
402 331-8536 *Omaha Office* 11061 "I" St .... Omaha NE 68137-0000
Fax: Unlisted
407 855-0900 *Orlando Office* 7200 Lake Ellenor Dr Suite 120 .... Orlando FL 32809-5797
Fax: Unlisted
215 597-4390 *Philadelphia Office*
2nd & Chestnut Sts US Custom House Rm 900 .... Philadelphia PA 19106-2973
Fax: 215 597-6649
809 729-6852 *Puerto Rico Office* PO Box 5719 .... San Juan PR 00906-5719
Fax: 809 729-6809

314 425-5021 *Saint Louis Office* 808 N Collins Alley .... Saint Louis MO 63102-2140
Fax: 314 425-4896
512 229-6737 *San Antonio Office* 727 E Durango Rm B-406 .... San Antonio TX 78206-0001
Fax: 512 229-4115
415 556-1457 *San Francisco Office* 50 United Nations Plaza Rm 526 .. San Francisco CA 94102-4980
Fax: 415 556-2524
206 483-4999 *Seattle Office* 22201 23rd Dr SE .... Bothell WA 98021-4421
Fax: 206 486-8788
201 645-3265 *West Orange Office* 61 Main St .... West Orange NJ 07052-5390
Fax: 201 645-3848
703 756-3276 **Food & Nutrition Service (US Dept of Agriculture)**
3101 Park Center Dr .... Alexandria VA 22302-1509
Fax: 703 756-3895
602 998-3100 **Food for the Hungry Inc** 7729 E Greenway Rd .... Scottsdale AZ 85260-1795
Fax: 602 443-1420
202 447-7943 **Food Safety & Inspection Service (US Dept of Agriculture)**
14th St & Independence Ave SW .... Washington DC 20250-0001
Fax: 202 447-2682
415 949-7777 **Foothill College** 12345 El Monte Rd .... Los Altos Hills CA 94022-4599
217 379-2721 **Ford County** 200 W State St Rm 101 .... Paxton IL 60957-1145
Fax: 217 379-3258
316 227-3184 **Ford County** Central & Spruce Sts .... Dodge City KS 67801-4482
202 225-3265 **Ford Harold E (Rep - D - Tennessee)** 2305 Rayburn Bldg ... Washington DC 20515-0001
Fax: 202 225-9215
202 224-4343 **Ford Wendell H (Sen - D - Kentucky)** 173-A Russell Bldg ... Washington DC 20510-0001
Fax: Unlisted
202 225-6261 **Ford William D (Rep - D - Michigan)** 2371 Rayburn Bldg ... Washington DC 20515-0001
Fax: Unlisted
212 579-2000 **Fordham University** 441 E Fordham Rd .... Bronx NY 10458-5149
212 841-5100 *College at Lincoln Center* 113 W 60th St .... New York NY 10023-7484
Fax: 212 581-1284
202 225-5021 **Foreign Affairs Committee (US House of Representatives)**
2170 Rayburn Bldg .... Washington DC 20515-0001
Fax: Unlisted
202 447-7115 **Foreign Agricultural Service Information (US Dept of Agriculture)**
14th St & Independence Ave SW Rm 5074 .... Washington DC 20250-0001
Fax: 202 382-1727
202 653-5883 **Foreign Claims Settlement Commission (US Dept of Justice)**
1111 20th St NW Rm 400 .... Washington DC 20579-0001
Fax: 202 653-6009
212 306-5000 **Foreign Credit Insurance Assn** 40 Rector St 11th Fl .... New York NY 10006-1778
Fax: 212 513-4704
212 947-5368 **Foreign Credit Interchange Bureau National Assn of Credit Management**
520 8th Ave .... New York NY 10018-0000
Fax: 212 465-8360
202 224-4651 **Foreign Relations Committee (US Senate)**
446 Dirksen Bldg .... Washington DC 20510-0001
Fax: 202 224-5011
703 875-5370 **Foreign Service Institute (US Dept of State)** 1400 Key Blvd .... Arlington VA 22209-1518
Fax: 703 875-5398
202 377-2862 **Foreign-Trade Zones Board**
14th St & Constitution Ave NW Rm 2835 .... Washington DC 20230-0001
Fax: 202 377-0002
814 755-3537 **Forest County** 526 Elm St .... Tionesta PA 16353-0000
715 478-2422 **Forest County** County Courthouse .... Crandon WI 54520-0000
205 536-9088 **Forest Institute of Professional Psychology**
2611 Leeman Ferry Rd .... Huntsville AL 35801-5611
Fax: 205 533-7405
601 582-3213 **Forrest County** 629 Main St .... Hattiesburg MS 39401-3453
404 781-2100 **Forsyth County** PO Box 128 .... Cumming GA 30130-0128
Fax: 404 791-2199
919 727-2071 **Forsyth County** Hall of Justice Rm 700 .... Winston-Salem NC 27101-0000
Fax: 919 727-8045 Finance
919 727-2556 **Forsyth County Public Library** 660 W 5th St .... Winston-Salem NC 27101-2705
Fax: 919 727-2549 Admin
919 723-0371 **Forsyth Technical Community College**
2100 Silas Creek Pkwy .... Winston-Salem NC 27103-5150
Fax: 919 761-2399
703 664-6071 **Fort Belvoir** .... Fort Belvoir VA 22060-0000
713 342-3411 **Fort Bend County** PO Box 520 .... Richmond TX 77469-0000
713 342-4455 **Fort Bend County Library System** 1001 Golfview St .... Richmond TX 77469-5141
Fax: 713 341-9538
317 546-9211 **Fort Benjamin Harrison** .... Fort Benjamin Harrison IN 46216-0000
Fax: 317 542-4171
404 544-1011 **Fort Benning** .... Fort Benning GA 31905-0000
Fax: 404 545-7415
915 568-2121 **Fort Bliss** .... El Paso TX 79916-0001
Fax: 915 568-1777
919 396-0011 **Fort Bragg** .... Fort Bragg NC 28307-5000
809 793-0370 **Fort Buchanan** .... Fort Buchanan PR 00934-0000
502 798-2151 **Fort Campbell** .... Fort Campbell KY 42223-5000
719 579-5811 **Fort Carson** .... Fort Carson CO 80913-2505
501 484-2141 **Fort Chaffee** .... Fort Chaffee AR 72905-5000
808 438-1834 **Fort DeRussy** .... Honolulu HI 96815-0000
Fax: 808 438-1860
301 663-8000 **Fort Detrick** .... Fort Detrick MD 21701-0000
508 796-3911 **Fort Devens** .... Fort Devens MA 01433-1241
609 562-1011 **Fort Dix** .... Fort Dix NJ 08640-0000
Fax: 609 944-5855
801 524-4155 **Fort Douglas** .... Fort Douglas UT 84113-5007
315 772-6900 **Fort Drum** .... Fort Drum NY 13602-0001
Fax: 315 772-5809 PR
804 878-5251 **Fort Eustis** .... Fort Eustis VA 23604-0000
404 363-5000 **Fort Gillem** .... Forest Park GA 30050-0000
Fax: 404 363-5133
404 791-0110 **Fort Gordon** .... Fort Gordon GA 30905-0000
Fax: 404 791-2061
907 873-1121 **Fort Greely** .... Fort Greely AK 98733-5000
Fax: 907 873-4603 Communications
718 630-4101 **Fort Hamilton** .... Fort Hamilton NY 11252-0001
913 628-4000 **Fort Hays State University** 600 Park St .... Hays KS 67601-4009
Fax: 913 628-4096 Library
804 633-5041 **Fort Hill AP** .... Bowling Green VA 22427-0000
Fax: 804 633-8442 Mail Rm
817 287-1110 **Fort Hood** .... Fort Hood TX 76544-0000
Fax: 817 287-6509
512 221-1211 **Fort Houston Sam** .... San Antonio TX 78234-5000
602 538-7111 **Fort Huachuca** .... Fort Huachuca AZ 85613-0000
Fax: 602 538-6602 Communications
717 865-5444 **Fort Indiantown Gap** .... Annville PA 17003-0000
Fax: Ext 2710
619 386-1111 **Fort Irwin** .... Fort Irwin CA 92310-0000
Fax: 619 470-3734
803 751-7601 **Fort Jackson** .... Fort Jackson SC 29207-0000
Fax: 803 751-7124

32 ALPHABETICAL SECTION
Fort / Freestone

Phone	Name / Address	City	State	ZIP
502 624-1181	**Fort Knox**	Fort Knox	KY	40121-0000
	Fax: 502 624-2945			
305 462-3761	**Fort Lauderdale College** 100 E Broward Blvd	Fort Lauderdale	FL	33301-3595
	Fax: 305 524-1645			
913 684-4021	**Fort Leavenworth**	Fort Leavenworth	KS	66027-0000
804 734-1011	**Fort Lee** Bldg 8045	Fort Lee	VA	23801-0000
	Fax: 804 734-1397			
206 967-3158	**Fort Lewis**	Fort Lewis	WA	98433-9998
	Fax: 206 967-5520			
303 247-7010	**Fort Lewis College** College Heights	Durango	CO	81301-3999
	Fax: Call company operator			
919 247-4598	**Fort Macon Coast Guard Base** Fort Macon Road	Atlantic Beach	NC	28512-9999
	Fax: 919 247-4579			
205 848-4611	**Fort McClellan**	Fort McClellan	AL	36205-0000
	Fax: 205 848-4212			
608 388-2222	**Fort McCoy**	Fort McCoy	WI	54656-5000
	Fax: 608 388-4237			
202 545-6700	**Fort McNair Leslie J**	Fort McNair	DC	20319-0001
	Fax: 202 475-1199 Mail Rm			
404 752-3113	**Fort McPherson** Bldg 65	Fort McPherson	GA	30330-5000
	Fax: 404 752-3153			
301 677-6261	**Fort Meade George G** Bldg 4215-A	Fort Meade	MD	20755-0000
	Fax: 301 923-5568			
908 532-9000	**Fort Monmouth**	Fort Monmouth	NJ	07703-0000
804 727-2111	**Fort Monroe**	Fort Monroe	VA	23651-9998
	Fax: 804 727-3614			
202 696-3189	**Fort Myer**	Fort Myer	VA	22211-5000
408 242-2211	**Fort Ord**	Fort Ord	CA	93941-5000
	Fax: 408 242-3100			
804 292-8621	**Fort Pickett**	Blackstone	VA	23824-5000
	Fax: 804 292-2409			
412 281-9284	**Fort Pitt Museum** 101 Commonwealth Pl	Pittsburgh	PA	15222-0000
318 535-2911	**Fort Polk**	Fort Polk	LA	71459-0000
	Fax: 318 535-2217			
907 864-0113	**Fort Richardson**	Fort Richardson	AK	99505-0000
913 239-3911	**Fort Riley**	Fort Riley	KS	66442-0000
301 733-7100	**Fort Ritchie**	Fort Ritchie	MD	21719-0000
	Fax: 301 878-5025 PR			
205 255-6181	**Fort Rucker**	Fort Rucker	AL	36362-0000
	Fax: 205 255-2210			
316 223-2700	**Fort Scott Community College** 2108 Horton St	Fort Scott	KS	66701-3199
	Fax: 316 223-6530			
808 438-1175	**Fort Shafter**	Fort Shafter	HI	96858-0001
	Fax: 808 438-6350 PR			
708 926-4111	**Fort Sheridan**	Fort Sheridan	IL	60037-0000
	Fax: 708 926-2507			
405 351-8111	**Fort Sill**	Fort Sill	OK	73503-0000
501 783-0229	**Fort Smith Public Library** 61 S 8th St	Fort Smith	AR	72901-2415
	Fax: 501 782-8571			
912 767-1110	**Fort Stewart**	Fort Stewart	GA	31314-0000
	Fax: 912 767-7939			
804 422-7102	**Fort Story**	Fort Story	VA	23459-5066
912 825-6211	**Fort Valley State College** 1005 State College Dr	Fort Valley	GA	31030-3298
	Fax: 912 825-6394 PR			
206 695-1561	**Fort Vancouver Regional Library** 1007 E Mill Plain Blvd	Vancouver	WA	98663-3504
	Fax: 206 693-2681			
907 353-6113	**Fort Wainwright**	Fort Wainwright	AK	99703-0000
	Fax: 907 353-6211			
219 422-6467	**Fort Wayne Museum of Art** 311 E Main St	Fort Wayne	IN	46802-1997
314 596-0131	**Fort Wood Leonard**	Fort Wood	MO	65473-0000
	Fax: 314 563-5131			
817 870-6000	**Fort Worth City Hall** 1000 Throckmorton St	Fort Worth	TX	76102-6311
	Fax: 817 870-6134			
817 732-1631	**Fort Worth Museum of Science & History** 1501 Montgomery St	Fort Worth	TX	76107-3017
	Fax: 817 732-7635			
817 870-7700	**Fort Worth Public Library** 3rd & Taylor St	Fort Worth	TX	76102-7333
202 586-4695	**Fossil Energy Program (US Dept of Energy)** 1000 Independence Ave SW Rm 4G-084	Washington	DC	20585-0001
	Fax: 202 586-5146			
701 652-2491	**Foster County** 1000 5th St N	Carrington	ND	58421-1113
202 634-9353	**Foster Grandparents Program** 1100 Vermont Ave NW Rm 6100	Washington	DC	20525-0001
	Fax: 202 634-9421			
401 826-2500	**Foster Parents Plan International** 804 Quaker Ln	East Greenwich	RI	02818-1667
	Fax: 401 826-2680			
317 793-2192	**Fountain County** County Courthouse	Covington	IN	47932-1293
708 759-2102	**Fountaindale Public Library** 300 W Briarcliffe Rd	Bolingbrook	IL	60440-0000
	Fax: 708 759-9519			
607 723-8236	**Four County Library System** 304 Clubhouse Rd	Binghamton	NY	13903-1296
213 825-4361	**Fowler Museum of Cultural History** Haines Hall UCLA	Los Angeles	CA	90024-0000
202 224-3643	**Fowler Wyche Jr (Sen - D - Georgia)** 204 Russell Bldg	Washington	DC	20510-0001
	Fax: 202 224-8227			
414 735-5600	**Fox Valley Technical College** 1825 N Bluemound Dr	Appleton	WI	54913-0000
	Fax: 414 735-2582			
508 620-1220	**Framingham State College** 100 State St	Framingham	MA	01701-2460
	Fax: 508 626-4592 Admin			
	France: French Republic			
202 944-6000	*Embassy* 4101 Reservoir Rd	Washington	DC	20007-2186
	Fax: 202 944-6116			
212 308-5700	*Mission to the UN* 245 E 47th St	New York	NY	10017-2201
	Fax: 212 355-2763			
312 787-5359	*Chicago Consulate General* 737 N Michigan Ave Suite 2020	Chicago	IL	60611-2694
	Fax: 312 664-4196			
213 653-3120	*Los Angeles Consulate General* 8350 Wilshire Blvd	Beverly Hills	CA	90211-2327
212 606-3600	*New York Consulate General* 934 5th Ave	New York	NY	10021-2697
	Fax: 212 606-3688 Admin			
415 397-4330	*San Francisco Consulate General* 540 Bush St	San Francisco	CA	94108-3604
	Fax: 415 433-8357			
803 661-1362	**Francis Marion College** 301 N & Marion Hwy	Florence	SC	29501-0000
	Fax: 803 661-1165 Purchasing			
415 848-5232	**Franciscan School of Theology** 1712 Euclid Ave	Berkeley	CA	94709-1294
614 283-3771	**Franciscan University of Steubenville** Franciscan Way	Steubenville	OH	43952-0000
	Fax: 614 283-6442			
202 225-5931	**Frank Barney (Rep - D - Massachusetts)** 2404 Rayburn Bldg	Washington	DC	20515-0001
	Fax: 202 225-0182			
806 274-5311	**Frank Phillips College** 1301 Roosevelt St	Borger	TX	79007-4427
	Fax: 806 274-8635			
717 291-3911	**Franklin & Marshall College** PO Box 3003	Lancaster	PA	17604-3003
	Fax: 717 291-4143			
804 562-8500	**Franklin (Independent City)** 207 2nd Ave W	Franklin	VA	23851-1713
317 736-8441	**Franklin College of Indiana** 501 E Monroe St	Franklin	IN	46131-2597
	Fax: 317 736-6030			
205 332-1210	**Franklin County** 410 N Jackson St	Russellville	AL	35653-0000
501 667-3607	**Franklin County** Commercial St	Ozark	AR	72949-0000
904 653-8861	**Franklin County** Market St	Apalachicola	FL	32320-0000
404 384-2514	**Franklin County** Courthouse Sq	Carnesville	GA	30521-0000
515 456-5626	**Franklin County** 12 1st Ave NW	Hampton	IA	50441-0000
	Fax: 515 456-2216			
208 852-1091	**Franklin County** 39 W Oneida St	Preston	ID	83263-1234
	Fax: 208 852-2926			
618 438-3221	**Franklin County** Public Sq	Benton	IL	62812-2264
317 647-5111	**Franklin County** 459 Main St	Brookville	IN	47012-1405
913 242-1471	**Franklin County** 3rd & Main Sts	Ottawa	KS	66067-0000
502 875-8702	**Franklin County** PO Box 338	Frankfort	KY	40602-0338
413 774-4015	**Franklin County** 425 Main St	Greenfield	MA	01301-3313
207 778-6614	**Franklin County** 38 Main St	Farmington	ME	04938-1818
	Fax: 207 778-5899			
314 583-6355	**Franklin County** PO Box 311	Union	MO	63084-0311
601 384-2330	**Franklin County** PO Box 297	Meadville	MS	39653-0297
919 496-5994	**Franklin County** 215 E Nash St	Louisburg	NC	27549-2545
308 425-6202	**Franklin County** 405 15th Ave	Franklin	NE	68939-1309
518 483-6767	**Franklin County** 63 W Main St	Malone	NY	12953-1817
	Fax: 518 483-0141			
614 462-3322	**Franklin County** 410 S High St	Columbus	OH	43215-0000
	Fax: 614 462-3144			
717 264-4125	**Franklin County** 157 Lincoln Way E	Chambersburg	PA	17201-2211
	Fax: 717 267-3894			
615 967-2541	**Franklin County** Public Sq	Winchester	TN	37398-0000
903 537-4252	**Franklin County** Dallas & Kaufman Sts	Mount Vernon	TX	75457-0000
703 483-3065	**Franklin County** Main St	Rocky Mount	VA	24151-1392
802 524-3863	**Franklin County** PO Box 808	Saint Albans	VT	05478-0808
509 545-3525	**Franklin County** 1016 N 4th Ave	Pasco	WA	99301-3706
	Fax: 509 545-2243			
617 423-4630	**Franklin Institute of Boston** 41 Berkeley St	Boston	MA	02116-6296
	Fax: 617 482-3706			
215 448-1200	**Franklin Institute Science Museum & Planetarium** 20th St & Benjamin Franklin Pkwy	Philadelphia	PA	19103-0000
	Fax: 215 448-1235			
318 435-9429	**Franklin Parish** 210 Main St	Winnsboro	LA	71295-2750
	Franklin Pierce College			
603 749-5587	*Dover Campus* 7 1/2 Summersworth Rd	Dover	NH	03820-2202
603 357-0079	*Keene Campus* 43 Arch St	Keene	NH	03431-2232
603 889-4143	*Nashua Campus* 20 Cotton Rd	Nashua	NH	03063-1204
	Fax: 603 889-3795			
603 899-5111	*Rindge Campus* College Rd	Rindge	NH	03461-0000
	Fax: Unlisted			
603 898-1263	*Salem Campus* 91 Stiles Rd	Salem	NH	03079-4830
603 228-1541	**Franklin Pierce Law Center** 2 White St	Concord	NH	03301-4197
	Fax: 603 224-3342			
614 224-6237	**Franklin University** 201 S Grant Ave	Columbus	OH	43215-5301
	Fax: 614 461-0957			
202 225-3822	**Franks Gary A (Rep - R - Connecticut)** 1609 Longworth Bldg	Washington	DC	20515-0001
	Fax: 202 225-5085			
202 472-1388	**Fraud Hotline (US Dept of Agriculture)** PO Box 23399	Washington	DC	20026-3399
	Fax: 202 447-4683			
800 424-5197	**Fraud Hotline (US Dept of Commerce)** Office of Inspector General	Washington	DC	20044-0000
800 424-9098	**Fraud Hotline (US Dept of Energy)** Pentagon	Washington	DC	20301-1900
	Fax: 202 694-9501			
800 424-5081	**Fraud Hotline (US Dept of the Interior)**	Washington	DC	20240-0001
202 233-5394	**Fraud Hotline (US Dept of Veterans Affairs)**	Washington	DC	20420-0001
301 694-5240	**Frederick Community College** 7932 Opossumtown Pike	Frederick	MD	21702-0000
	Fax: 301 694-1298			
301 694-1100	**Frederick County** 12 E Church St	Frederick	MD	21701-5402
703 665-5666	**Frederick County** 9 Court Sq	Winchester	VA	22601-4736
	Fax: 703 667-0370			
301 694-1613	**Frederick County Public Library** 110 E Patrick St	Frederick	MD	21701-5630
703 372-1010	**Fredericksburg (Independent City)** PO Box 7447	Fredericksburg	VA	22404-7447
	Fax: 703 372-1121			
202 546-3004	**Free Congress Foundation PAC** 717 2nd St NE	Washington	DC	20002-4368
	Fax: 202 546-7689			
215 686-5322	**Free Library of Philadelphia** Logan Sq	Philadelphia	PA	19103-0000
	Fax: 215 563-3628			
609 392-7188	**Free Public Library of the City of Trenton** 120 Academy St	Trenton	NJ	08608-1302
	Fax: 609 396-7655			
908 634-4450	**Free Public Library of Woodbridge** George Frederick Plaza	Woodbridge	NJ	07095-0000
	Fax: 908 634-7610			
615 383-1340	**Free Will Baptist Bible College** 3606 West End Ave	Nashville	TN	37205-2498
507 377-5153	**Freeborn County** 411 S Broadway Ave	Albert Lea	MN	56007-4506
	Fax: 507 377-5160			
901 989-6000	**Freed-Hardeman College** 158 E Main St	Henderson	TN	38340-2398
	Fax: 901 989-6065			
314 882-4856	**Freedom of Information Center** 20 Walter Williams Hall	Columbia	MO	65211-0000
	Fax: 314 882-9002			
202 785-3704	**Freedom of Information Clearinghouse (US Dept of the Interior)** 2000 P St NW Suite 700	Washington	DC	20036-5915
	Fax: 202 452-8658			
202 447-8164	**Freedom of Information Office (US Dept of Agriculture)** 14th St & Independence Ave SW Rm 536A	Washington	DC	20250-0001
	Fax: 202 475-5396			
202 377-3271	**Freedom of Information Office (US Dept of Commerce)** 14th St & Constitution Ave NW Rm 6622	Washington	DC	20230-0001
	Fax: 202 377-5270			
202 697-1180	**Freedom of Information Office (US Dept of Defense)** Pentagon Rm 2C-757	Washington	DC	20301-0001
202 732-4568	**Freedom of Information Office (US Dept of Education)** 400 Maryland Ave SW Rm 2089	Washington	DC	20202-0001
	Fax: 202 732-3130			
202 586-5955	**Freedom of Information Office (US Dept of Energy)** 1000 Independence Ave SW Rm 1G-051	Washington	DC	20585-0001
	Fax: 202 586-6783			
202 755-6420	**Freedom of Information Office (US Dept of Housing & Urban Development)** 451 7th St SW Rm 8141	Washington	DC	20410-0001
	Fax: 202 755-6749			
202 633-3642	**Freedom of Information Office (US Dept of Justice)** 10th St & Constitution Ave NW Rm 7238	Washington	DC	20530-0001
	Fax: 202 633-2424			
202 523-8088	**Freedom of Information Office (US Dept of Labor)** 200 Constitution Ave NW Rm N2428	Washington	DC	20210-0001
	Fax: 202 523-9255			
202 647-7740	**Freedom of Information Office (US Dept of State)** 2201 C St NW Rm 1239	Washington	DC	20520-0001
	Fax: 202 647-7897			
202 566-2789	**Freedom of Information Office (US Dept of the Treasury)** 1500 Pennsylvania Ave NW Rm 1054	Washington	DC	20220-0000
202 366-4542	**Freedom of Information Office (US Dept of Transportation)** 400 7th St SW Suite 5432	Washington	DC	20590-0001
903 389-2635	**Freestone County** Main & Mount Sts	Fairfield	TX	75840-1594

For information on alphabetization, see the Alphabetical Section title page.

719 275-7521 **Fremont County** 615 Macon Rm 100 .... Canon City CO 81212-0000
712 374-2232 **Fremont County** Courthouse Sq .... Sidney IA 51652-0549
208 624-7332 **Fremont County** 151 W 1st North .... Saint Anthony ID 83445-1403
Fax: 208 624-4485
307 332-2405 **Fremont County** PO Box CC .... Lander WY 82520-0900
Fax: 307 332-5318
307 332-4137 **Fremont County Pioneer Museum** 630 Lincoln St .... Lander WY 82520-2732
212 757-1125 **French Government Tourist Office** 610 5th Ave .... New York NY 10020-2493
Fax: 212 247-6468
212 371-4466 **French-American Chamber of Commerce in the US**
509 Madison Ave Suite 1900 .... New York NY 10022-5599
Fax: 212 371-5623
209 485-4810 **Fresno Arts Museum** 2233 N 1st St .... Fresno CA 93703-2364
209 442-4600 **Fresno City College** 1101 E University Ave .... Fresno CA 93741-0001
Fax: 209 485-3367
209 488-3531 **Fresno County** 2281 Tulare St Rm 300 .... Fresno CA 93721-2105
209 488-3191 **Fresno County Free Library** 2420 Mariposa St .... Fresno CA 93721-2204
Fax: 209 488-1971
209 251-7194 **Fresno Pacific College** 1717 S Chestnut Ave .... Fresno CA 93702-4798
Fax: 209 453-2007
412 371-0600 **Frick Art Museum** 7227 Reynolds St .... Pittsburgh PA 15208-2923
Fax: 412 241-5393
212 288-0700 **Frick Collection** 1 E 70th St .... New York NY 10021-4907
Fax: 212 861-7347
212 247-8077 **Friends of Animals Inc** 1841 Broadway Suite 212 .... New York NY 10023-7999
Fax: 212 582-4482
316 261-5800 **Friends University** 2100 University St .... Wichita KS 67213-3397
Fax: 316 263-1092 Library
516 549-5000 **Friends World College** 14 Plover Ln .... Huntington NY 11743-1098
Fax: 516 549-5346
512 334-2214 **Frio County** PO Box X .... Pearsall TX 78061-1423
Fax: 512 334-4881
303 466-8811 **Front Range Community College** 3645 W 112th Ave .... Westminster CO 80030-2199
Fax: 303 466-1623 Acctg
618 842-3711 **Frontier Community College** Frontier Dr Lot 2 .... Fairfield IL 62837-9801
Fax: Ext 4496
308 367-8641 **Frontier County** 1 Wellington St .... Stockville NE 69042-0040
202 225-3605 **Frost Martin (Rep - D - Texas)** 2459 Rayburn Bldg .... Washington DC 20515-0001
Fax: Unlisted
301 689-4000 **Frostburg State University** .... Frostburg MD 21532-0000
Fax: Unlisted
206 622-9250 **Frye Charles & Emma Art Museum** PO Box 3005 .... Seattle WA 98114-3005
508 588-6000 **Fuller Museum of Art** 455 Oak St .... Brockton MA 02401-1340
818 584-5200 **Fuller Theological Seminary** 135 N Oakland Ave .... Pasadena CA 91182-0001
Fax: 818 584-5369
714 992-7000 **Fullerton Community College** 321 E Chapman Ave .... Fullerton CA 92632-2095
Fax: 714 447-4097
714 738-6380 **Fullerton Public Library** 353 W Commonwealth Ave .... Fullerton CA 92632-1796
Fax: 714 447-3280
501 895-3341 **Fulton County** PO Box 278 .... Salem AR 72576-0278
404 730-4000 **Fulton County** 160 Pryor St Rm 208 .... Atlanta GA 30303-3405
309 547-3041 **Fulton County** 100 N Main St .... Lewistown IL 61542-1445
219 223-2911 **Fulton County** 815 Main St .... Rochester IN 46975-1546
502 236-2727 **Fulton County** Moulton & Wellington Sts .... Hickman KY 42050-0000
Fax: 502 236-3933
518 762-0540 **Fulton County** 223 W Main St .... Johnstown NY 12095-2309
Fax: 518 762-2042
419 337-9255 **Fulton County** 210 S Fulton St Rm B-10 .... Wauseon OH 43567-1355
717 485-4212 **Fulton County** N 2nd St .... McConnellsburg PA 17233-0000
518 762-4651 **Fulton-Montgomery Community College** Rt 67 .... Johnstown NY 12095-0000
Fax: Ext 374
305 923-2808 **Fun in the Sun Yacht Charters** 320 N Federal Hwy .... Dania FL 33004-2808
212 758-3007 **Fund for Multinational Management Education**
40 E 49th St Suite 501 .... New York NY 10017-1110
Fax: 212 371-7420
212 661-5900 **Fund for Peace** 345 E 46th St Suite 712 .... New York NY 10017-3518
Fax: 212 661-5904
803 294-2000 **Furman University** Poinsett Hwy .... Greenville SC 29613-0001
Fax: 803 294-3001
308 268-4145 **Furnas County** PO Box 387 .... Beaver City NE 68926-0387
202 225-2615 **Fuster Jaime B (Rep - D - Puerto Rico)** 427 Cannon Bldg .... Washington DC 20515-0001
Fax: 202 225-1959

G

Gabon: Gabonese Republic
202 797-1000 *Embassy* 2034 20th St NW .... Washington DC 20009-5001
Fax: 202 332-0668
212 686-9720 *Mission to the UN* 18 E 41st St 6th Fl .... New York NY 10017-6222
904 875-4700 **Gadsden County** 10 E Jefferson St .... Quincy FL 32351-2406
Fax: 904 627-6526
205 546-0484 **Gadsden State Community College** 1001 George Wallace Dr .... Gadsden AL 35903-2269
Fax: 205 546-6048
205 549-4699 **Gadsden-Etowah County Library** 254 College St .... Gadsden AL 35999-0000
402 228-3355 **Gage County** PO Box 429 .... Beatrice NE 68310-0429
915 758-3521 **Gaines County** 100 S Main St .... Seminole TX 79360-4342
Fax: 915 758-9258
404 535-6239 **Gainesville College** 3820 Mundy Mill Rd .... Gainesville GA 30501-8299
Fax: 404 535-6359
703 236-3441 **Galax (Independent City)** 123 Main St N .... Galax VA 24333-2907
618 269-3025 **Gallatin County** PO Box K .... Shawneetown IL 62984-0550
606 567-5411 **Gallatin County** PO Box 616 .... Warsaw KY 41095-0616
406 585-1430 **Gallatin County** 311 W Main St Rm 204 .... Bozeman MT 59715-4576
202 651-5000 **Gallaudet University** 800 Florida Ave NE .... Washington DC 20002-3660
Fax: 202 651-5463
202 651-5100 *TTY Line* 800 Florida Ave NE .... Washington DC 20002-3660
202 225-5811 **Gallegly Elton (Rep - R - California)** 107 Cannon Bldg .... Washington DC 20515-0000
Fax: 202 225-0713
614 446-4374 **Gallia County** 18 Locust St .... Gallipolis OH 45631-1251
Fax: 614 446-4804
504 523-6722 **Gallier House Museum** 1118-32 Royal St .... New Orleans LA 70116-0000
202 225-5034 **Gallo Dean A (Rep - R - New Jersey)**
1318 Longworth Bldg .... Washington DC 20515-0001
Fax: 202 225-0658
409 766-5601 **Galveston Coast Guard Base** PO Box 1912 .... Galveston TX 77553-0000
Fax: 409 766-5628
409 763-6551 **Galveston College** 4015 Ave Q .... Galveston TX 77550-7496
Fax: 409 762-9367
409 766-2210 **Galveston County** 722 Moody Ave .... Galveston TX 77550-2317
Fax: 409 766-2661 Mail Rm
Gambia: Republic of Gambia
202 842-1356 *Embassy* 1030 15th St Suite 720 .... Washington DC 20005-1503
Fax: 202 842-2073

212 949-6640 *Mission to the UN* 820 2nd Ave Suite 900-C .... New York NY 10017-4504
Fax: 212 808-4975
814 871-7000 **Gannon University** 109 W 6th St University Sq .... Erie PA 16541-0001
Fax: 814 459-0996 Library
316 276-7611 **Garden City Community College** 801 Campus Dr .... Garden City KS 67846-6399
Fax: 316 276-9630
308 772-3924 **Garden County** Main St .... Oshkosh NE 69154-0000
617 566-1401 **Gardner Isabella Stewart Museum** 280 The Fenway .... Boston MA 02115-5809
Fax: 617 232-8039
704 434-2361 **Gardner-Webb College** PO Box 997 .... Boiling Springs NC 28017-0997
Fax: 704 434-6246
303 945-2377 **Garfield County** 109 8th St Suite 200 .... Glenwood Springs CO 81601-3362
406 557-2760 **Garfield County** PO Box 7 .... Jordan MT 59337-0007
308 346-4161 **Garfield County** PO Box 218 .... Burwell NE 68823-0218
405 237-0227 **Garfield County** County Courthouse Rm 101 .... Enid OK 73701-0000
801 676-8826 **Garfield County** PO Box 77 .... Panguitch UT 84759-0077
Fax: 801 676-8239
509 843-3731 **Garfield County** PO Box 915 .... Pomeroy WA 99347-0915
Fax: 509 843-1224
501 321-2819 **Garland County** 501 Ouachita Ave .... Hot Springs AR 71901-5154
501 767-9371 **Garland County Community College** 1 College Dr .... Hot Springs AR 71913-9120
Fax: 501 767-3427
202 224-5444 **Garn Jake (Sen - R - Utah)** 505 Dirksen Bldg .... Washington DC 20510-0001
Fax: Unlisted
606 792-3531 **Garrard County** Public Sq .... Lancaster KY 40444-0000
301 387-6666 **Garrett Community College** Mosser Rd .... McHenry MD 21541-0000
Fax: 301 387-7469
301 334-8970 **Garrett County** 203 S 4th St .... Oakland MD 21550-1535
Fax: 301 334-5000
405 238-2685 **Garvin County** Walnut & Grant .... Pauls Valley OK 73075-3290
219 886-2484 **Gary Public Library** 220 W 5th Ave .... Gary IN 46402-1270
Fax: 219 882-9528
806 495-3535 **Garza County** County Courthouse .... Post TX 79356-3241
314 486-5427 **Gasconade County** PO Box 295 .... Hermann MO 65041-0295
704 922-6200 **Gaston Community College** 201 Hwy 321-S .... Dallas NC 28034-1499
Fax: 704 922-6440
704 868-5800 **Gaston County** 151 South St .... Gastonia NC 28052-4128
704 868-2164 **Gaston County Public Library** 1555 E Garrison Blvd .... Gastonia NC 28054-4556
Fax: 704 853-0609
919 357-1240 **Gates County** PO Box 141 .... Gatesville NC 27938-0141
602 275-8500 **Gateway Community College** 108 N 40th St .... Phoenix AZ 85034-1795
Fax: 602 392-5329
414 656-6900 **Gateway Technical College** 3520 30th Ave .... Kenosha WI 53144-0000
Fax: 414 656-7209
408 847-1400 **Gavilan College** 5055 Santa Teresa Blvd .... Gilroy CA 95020-9599
Fax: 408 848-4801
202 225-4631 **Gaydos Joseph M (Rep - D - Pennsylvania)**
2186 Rayburn Bldg .... Washington DC 20515-0001
Fax: Unlisted
913 238-3912 **Geary County** 8th & Franklin .... Junction City KS 66441-0000
216 285-2222 **Geauga County** 231 Main St .... Chardon OH 44024-1243
Fax: Unlisted
202 225-2076 **Gejdenson Sam (Rep - D - Connecticut)**
2416 Rayburn Bldg .... Washington DC 20515-0001
Fax: 202 225-4977
202 225-4315 **Gekas George W (Rep - R - Pennsylvania)**
1519 Longworth Bldg .... Washington DC 20515-0001
Fax: 202 225-8440
208 365-4561 **Gem County** 415 E Main St .... Emmett ID 83617-3049
Fax: 208 365-6172
202 275-5067 **General Accounting Office** 441 G St NW .... Washington DC 20548-0001
Fax: 202 275-1410
202 272-5557 *Fraud Hotline* 600 E St NW Rm 1000 .... Washington DC 20548-0001
202 707-5522 **General Reading Rooms Div (Library of Congress)**
101 Independence Ave SE .... Washington DC 20540-0000
202 501-1231 **General Services Administration**
18th & F Sts NW Rm 6010 .... Washington DC 20405-0001
Fax: 202 501-0735
202 472-1100 *National Capitol Region* 7th & D Sts SW .... Washington DC 20407-0001
Fax: 202 755-1966
202 501-1780 *Fraud Hotline* 18th & F Sts NW .... Washington DC 20405-0001
Fax: 202 501-4119
617 565-8121 *Region 1* 10 Causeway St .... Boston MA 02222-1047
212 264-2600 *Region 2* 26 Federal Plaza .... New York NY 10278-0022
Fax: 212 264-3998
215 597-1237 *Region 3* 9th & Market Sts .... Philadelphia PA 19107-4278
Fax: 215 597-6771
404 331-6891 *Region 4* 75 Spring St SW .... Atlanta GA 30303-3309
312 353-5395 *Region 5* 230 S Dearborn St .... Chicago IL 60604-1505
Fax: 312 886-9893
816 926-7201 *Region 6* 1500 E Bannister Rd .... Kansas City MO 64131-3009
Fax: Unlisted
817 334-3284 *Region 7* 819 Taylor St .... Fort Worth TX 76102-6181
Fax: 817 334-4609
303 236-7329 *Region 8* PO Box 25006 .... Denver CO 80225-0006
Fax: 303 236-7280 Admin
415 724-5246 *Region 9* 525 Market St .... San Francisco CA 94102-3464
206 931-7000 *Region 10* 15th & C Sts SW .... Auburn WA 98001-6599
Fax: 206 939-7932
716 343-0055 **Genesee Community College** 1 College Rd .... Batavia NY 14020-0000
Fax: Call company operator
313 257-3283 **Genesee County** 900 S Saginaw St Rm 202 .... Flint MI 48502-0000
716 344-2550 **Genesee County** Main & Court Sts .... Batavia NY 14020-3199
313 732-0110 **Genesee District Library** G-4195 W Pasadena Ave .... Flint MI 48504-0000
Fax: 313 732-1715
412 846-5100 **Geneva College** 3200 College Ave .... Beaver Falls PA 15010-3599
Fax: Unlisted
205 684-2275 **Geneva County** PO Box 430 .... Geneva AL 36340-0430
816 726-3618 **Gentry County** County Courthouse .... Albany MO 64402-1499
307 766-4218 **Geological Museum** University of Wyoming .... Laramie WY 82070-3404
619 269-1110 **George Air Force Base** .... Adelanto CA 92394-0000
Fax: 619 269-3339
George C Wallace State Community College
205 983-3521 *Dothan Campus* .... Dothan AL 36303-0000
Fax: 205 983-4255
205 352-6403 *Hanceville Campus* 801 Main St NW .... Hanceville AL 35077-0000
205 875-2634 *Selma Campus* 3000 Rangeline Rd .... Selma AL 36701-0000
Fax: 205 874-7116
601 947-7506 **George County** Courthouse Sq .... Lucedale MS 39452-0000
Fax: 601 947-4811
503 538-8383 **George Fox College** 414 N Meridian St .... Newberg OR 97132-2625
Fax: 503 538-7234 Admissions
703 323-2000 **George Mason University** 4400 University Dr .... Fairfax VA 22030-4443
Fax: 703 323-3849
703 841-2600 *School of Law* 3401 N Fairfax Dr .... Arlington VA 22201-4411
Fax: 703 841-7112

202 994-1000 **George Washington University** 2121 'I' St NW .... Washington DC 20052-0001
Fax: 202 994-0458 Communications
202 994-6295 *Department of Public Administration*
2115 G St NW Monroe Hall Rm 302 .... Washington DC 20052-0001
Fax: 202 994-4930
202 994-6584 *Graduate School of Business & Public Management*
710 21st St NW Rm 208 .... Washington DC 20052-0001
Fax: 202 994-4930
202 994-6260 *National Law Center* 720 20th St NW .... Washington DC 20052-0001
Fax: 202 994-9446
202 994-3506 *School of Medicine & Health Sciences*
2300 'I' St NW Ross Hall Rm 615 .... Washington DC 20037-0000
502 863-8011 **Georgetown College** 400 E College St .... Georgetown KY 40324-1620
Fax: Unlisted
803 546-5011 **Georgetown County** 715 Prince St .... Georgetown SC 29440-3631
202 687-1000 **Georgetown University** 37th & 'O' Sts NW .... Washington DC 20057-0001
202 662-9000 *Law Center* 600 New Jersey Ave NW .... Washington DC 20001-2075
Fax: 202 662-9444
202 687-7452 *Library* 37th & N St .... Washington DC 20057-0001
202 687-1164 *School of Medicine* 3900 Reservoir Rd NW .... Washington DC 20007-2187
Fax: 202 687-7660
404 761-8343 **Georgia Baptist College** 4140 Stacks Rd .... College Park GA 30349-2839
912 453-5350 **Georgia College** 231 W Hancock St .... Milledgeville GA 31061-0000
Fax: 912 453-6847
404 656-3553 **Georgia Dept of Industry Trade & Tourism**
285 Peachtree Ctr Ave NE Marquis Tower II Suite 1000 .... Atlanta GA 30303-1505
Fax: 404 651-9063
404 894-2000 **Georgia Institute of Technology** 225 North Ave NW .... Atlanta GA 30332-0001
Fax: 404 894-3120
404 894-3880 *College of Architecture* 247 4th St .... Atlanta GA 30332-0155
404 894-3152 *College of Computing* 801 Atlantic Dr .... Atlanta GA 30332-0280
Fax: 404 853-9378
404 894-3350 *College of Engineering* 225 North Ave .... Atlanta GA 30332-0001
Fax: 404 853-0168
404 894-2351 *Graduate Program in City Planning*
Old Architecture Bldg Rm 217 .... Atlanta GA 30332-0155
Fax: 404 894-3874
404 894-8227 *School of Chemistry* Boggs Bldg Rm 156 .... Atlanta GA 30332-0001
Fax: 404 894-7452
912 453-3481 **Georgia Military College** 201 Green St .... Milledgeville GA 31061-3398
404 542-3255 **Georgia Museum of Art** Jackson St North Campus .... Athens GA 30602-0000
404 365-7700 **Georgia Republican Party** 3091 Maple Dr Suite 315 .... Atlanta GA 30305-2620
Fax: 404 365-7718
912 681-5531 **Georgia Southern University** Landrum St .... Statesboro GA 30460-0001
Fax: 912 681-0081
912 928-1279 **Georgia Southwestern College** 800 Wheatley St .... Americus GA 31709-4635
Fax: 912 928-1630
Georgia State Government
404 656-2000 *Information* 330 Capitol Ave SW .... Atlanta GA 30334-9002
404 656-6900 *Air Protection Branch* 205 Butler St SE East Tower Rm 1162 .. Atlanta GA 30334-0000
Fax: 404 651-9425
404 656-4586 *Attorney General* 132 State Judicial Bldg .... Atlanta GA 30334-0000
Fax: 404 651-9148
404 656-5651 *Board of Pardons & Paroles* 2 Martin Luther King Jr Dr SE .... Atlanta GA 30334-9008
Fax: 404 651-8502
404 656-2202 *Board of Regents* 244 Washington St SW .... Atlanta GA 30334-5809
Fax: 404 651-9301
404 656-3250 *Building Authority* 1 Martin Luther King Jr Dr SW .... Atlanta GA 30334-9004
Fax: 404 651-9614
404 656-2190 *Business Services & Regulation*
2 Martin Luther King Jr Dr West Tower Suite 315 .... Atlanta GA 30334-9008
Fax: 404 651-9059
404 656-2056 *Commissioner of Insurance*
2 Martin Luther King Jr Dr SW 716 West Tower .... Atlanta GA 30334-9008
404 656-3790 *Consumer Affairs* 2 Martin Luther King Jr Dr SW Suite 356 .... Atlanta GA 30334-9008
Fax: 404 651-9018
404 493-5780 *Council for the Arts* 2082 E Exchange Pl Suite 100 .... Tucker GA 30084-5334
404 656-1721 *Criminal Justice Coordinating Council*
10 Park Place S Suite 200 .... Atlanta GA 30303-0000
404 656-3608 *Department of Agriculture* 19 Martin Luther King Jr Dr SW .... Atlanta GA 30334-9900
Fax: 404 656-9380
404 656-2358 *Department of Archives & History* 330 Capitol Ave SE .... Atlanta GA 30334-0000
Fax: 404 651-9270
404 986-1633 *Department of Banking & Finance*
2990 Brandywine Rd Suite 200 .... Atlanta GA 30341-0000
Fax: 404 986-1654
404 656-4605 *Department of Corrections*
2 Martin Luther King Jr Dr SW East Tower 7th Fl .... Atlanta GA 30334-9008
Fax: 404 656-6694
404 624-7000 *Department of Defense* 935 E Confederate Ave SE .... Atlanta GA 30316-2531
Fax: 404 624-7205
404 656-2534 *Department of Education* 205 Butler St SE .... Atlanta GA 30334-4909
Fax: 404 651-9416
404 656-5542 *Department of Human Resources* 47 Trinity Ave .... Atlanta GA 30334-0000
Fax: 404 656-0709
404 656-3545 *Department of Industry & Trade*
285 Peachtree Center Ave NE Suite 1100 .... Atlanta GA 30303-1232
Fax: 404 656-3567
404 656-3011 *Department of Labor* 148 International Blvd NE .... Atlanta GA 30303-1752
Fax: 404 656-3113
404 894-7505 *Division of Public Health* 878 Peachtree St NE Suite 201 .... Atlanta GA 30309-3917
Fax: 404 894-7799
404 656-3240 *Division of Purchasing & Surplus Property*
200 Piedmont Ave NE Suite 1302 .... Atlanta GA 30303-1702
Fax: 404 651-9477
404 656-4713 *Environmental Protection Div*
205 Butler St East Tower Suite 1152 .... Atlanta GA 30334-9001
Fax: 404 651-2369
404 656-3900 *Examining Boards Div* 166 Pryor St SW .... Atlanta GA 30303-3422
Fax: 404 651-9532
404 775-3161 *Georgia Diagnostic & Classification Center* PO Box 3877 ..... Jackson GA 30233-0877
Fax: Ext 292
404 778-2273 *Georgia Industrial Institute* PO Box 709 .... Alto GA 30510-0709
Fax: 404 776-4710
404 656-1776 *Governor* 203 State Capitol .... Atlanta GA 30334-0000
Fax: 404 656-2612
404 656-5030 *Lieutenant Governor* 240 State Capitol SW .... Atlanta GA 30334-1600
Fax: 404 656-6739
404 656-3530 *Natural Resources Dept* 205 Butler St SE .... Atlanta GA 30334-4100
Fax: 404 656-2285
404 656-5176 *Office of Energy Resources* 270 Washington St SW Suite 615 . Atlanta GA 30334-9009
Fax: 404 651-9513
404 656-3820 *Office of Planning & Budget* 270 Washington St SW Rm 611 .. Atlanta GA 30334-9009
Fax: 404 651-9513
404 656-4501 *Public Service Commission* 244 Washington St SW .... Atlanta GA 30334-5700
Fax: 404 656-2341
404 656-3916 *Real Estate Commission* 148 International Blvd NE Suite 500 .. Atlanta GA 30303-1734
404 656-4015 *Revenue Dept* 410 Trinity Washington Bldg .... Atlanta GA 30334-0000
Fax: 404 651-9490
404 656-2881 *Secretary of State* 214 State Capitol SW .... Atlanta GA 30334-1600
Fax: 404 651-9531
404 624-6077 *State Patrol* 959 E Confederate Ave SE .... Atlanta GA 30371-0001
404 656-3470 *Supreme Court* 244 Washington St SW .... Atlanta GA 30334-9007
Fax: Unlisted
404 656-5206 *Transportation Dept* 2 Capitol Sq SW .... Atlanta GA 30334-9003
Fax: 404 656-3507
404 656-2168 *Treasurer* PO Box 38918 .... Atlanta GA 30334-0000
Fax: Unlisted
404 656-3050 *Unemployment Insurance Div*
148 International Blvd Sussex Bldg .... Atlanta GA 30303-0000
Fax: 404 656-7361
404 656-4750 *Vital Records Service* 47 Trinity Ave SW Rm 217-H .... Atlanta GA 30334-9006
Fax: 404 651-9427
404 656-2034 *Worker's Compensation Board* 1 CNN Ctr S Tower Suite 1000 . Atlanta GA 30303-2788
Fax: 404 651-9467
404 656-2846 **Georgia State Museum of Science & Industry**
State Capitol Bldg Rm 432 .... Atlanta GA 30334-0000
404 656-2461 **Georgia State Public Library Services Div Dept of Education**
156 Trinity Ave SW 1st Fl .... Atlanta GA 30303-3600
Fax: 404 656-7297
404 651-2000 **Georgia State University** University Plaza .... Atlanta GA 30303-3044
404 651-2048 *College of Law* PO Box 4037 .... Atlanta GA 30302-4037
Fax: 404 651-2092
908 364-2200 **Georgian Court College** Lakewood Ave .... Lakewood NJ 08701-0000
202 225-2671 **Gephardt Richard A (Rep - D - Missouri)**
1432 Longworth Bldg .... Washington DC 20515-0001
Fax: 202 225-7452
202 225-5071 **Geren Pete (Rep - D - Texas)** 1730 Longworth Bldg .... Washington DC 20515-0001
Fax: 202 225-2786
212 308-3300 **German National Tourist Office** 747 3rd Ave .... New York NY 10017-2852
Fax: 212 688-1322
212 974-8830 **German-American Chamber of Commerce Inc**
666 5th Ave 21st Fl .... New York NY 10103-0166
Fax: 212 974-8867
312 782-8557 **German-American Chamber of Commerce of Chicago**
104 S Michigan St Suite 600 .... Chicago IL 60603-5978
Fax: 312 782-3892
213 381-2236 **German-American Chamber of Commerce of Los Angeles**
3250 Wilshire Blvd Suite 1612 .... Los Angeles CA 90010-1676
Fax: 213 381-3449
415 392-2262 **German-American Chamber of Commerce of the Pacific Coast**
465 California St Suite 910 .... San Francisco CA 94104-1822
Fax: 415 392-1314
703 399-1333 **Germanna Community College** PO Box 339 .... Locust Grove VA 22508-0339
Fax: 703 399-1009
Germany: Federal Republic of Germany
202 298-4000 *Embassy* 4645 Reservoir Rd NW .... Washington DC 20007-1918
Fax: 202 298-4249
212 949-9200 *Mission to the UN* 600 3rd Ave 41st Fl .... New York NY 10016-1902
Fax: 212 490-0857
312 263-0850 *Chicago Consulate General* 104 S Michigan Ave .... Chicago IL 60603-5902
Fax: 312 853-1940
213 930-2703 *Los Angeles Consulate General*
6222 Wilshire Blvd Suite 500 .... Los Angeles CA 90048-5123
Fax: Unlisted
212 308-8700 *New York Consulate General* 460 Park Ave .... New York NY 10022-1906
Fax: 212 308-3422
213 459-7611 **Getty J Paul Museum** 17985 Pacific Coast Hwy .... Malibu CA 90265-5799
Fax: 213 459-9413
717 337-6000 **Gettysburg College** .... Gettysburg PA 17325-0000
Fax: 717 337-6251
Ghana: Republic of Ghana
202 686-4520 *Embassy* 3512 International Dr NW .... Washington DC 20008-3035
Fax: 202 686-4527
212 832-1300 *Mission to the UN* 19 E 47th St .... New York NY 10017-1984
Fax: 212 751-6743
803 722-2706 **Gibbes Museum of Art** 135 Meeting St .... Charleston SC 29401-2217
202 225-3376 **Gibbons Sam (Rep - D - Florida)** 2204 Rayburn Bldg .... Washington DC 20515-0001
Fax: Unlisted
812 385-8260 **Gibson County** Courthouse Sq .... Princeton IN 47670-1542
Fax: 812 385-3428
901 855-7642 **Gibson County** County Courthouse .... Trenton TN 38382-0000
602 425-3231 **Gila County** 1400 E Ash St .... Globe AZ 85501-1414
Fax: 602 425-0319
202 225-5311 **Gilchrest Wayne T (Rep - D - Maryland)** 502 Cannon Bldg .. Washington DC 20515-0001
Fax: 202 225-0254
904 463-2345 **Gilchrist County** 112 S Main St .... Trenton FL 32693-0000
Fax: 904 463-6534
918 582-3122 **Gilcrease Thomas Institute of American History & Art**
1400 Gilcrease Museum Rd .... Tulsa OK 74127-2100
615 363-1509 **Giles County** PO Box 678 .... Pulaski TN 38478-0678
703 921-1722 **Giles County** PO Box 502 .... Pearisburg VA 24134-0502
512 997-6515 **Gillespie County** PO Box 351 .... Fredericksburg TX 78624-0000
503 384-2311 **Gilliam County** 221 S Oregon St .... Condon OR 97823-0000
202 225-6405 **Gillmor Paul E (Rep - R - Ohio)** 1203 Longworth Bldg .... Washington DC 20515-0001
Fax: Unlisted
202 225-3776 **Gilman Benjamin A (Rep - R - New York)**
2185 Rayburn Bldg .... Washington DC 20515-0001
Fax: Unlisted
404 635-4361 **Gilmer County** 1 Westside Sq .... Ellijay GA 30540-0000
Fax: 404 635-4359
304 462-7641 **Gilmer County** 10 Howard St .... Glenville WV 26351-1246
303 572-0567 **Gilpin County** PO Box 366 .... Central City CO 80427-0366
202 225-4501 **Gingrich Newt (Rep - R - Georgia)** 2438 Rayburn Bldg .... Washington DC 20515-0001
Fax: 202 225-4656
406 873-5063 **Glacier County** 502 E Main St .... Cut Bank MT 59427-3025
813 946-0949 **Glades County** PO Box 10 .... Moore Haven FL 33471-0010
Fax: 813 946-0560
517 426-7351 **Gladwin County** 401 W Cedar Ave .... Gladwin MI 48624-2023
404 598-2084 **Glascock County** PO Box 231 .... Gibson GA 30810-0231
609 863-5000 **Glassboro State College** .... Glassboro NJ 08028-0000
Fax: 609 863-6553
915 354-2371 **Glasscock County** PO Box 190 .... Garden City TX 79739-0190
616 467-9945 **Glen Oaks Community College** 62249 Shimmel Rd .... Centreville MI 49032-9719
Fax: 616 467-4114
602 435-3000 **Glendale Community College** 6000 W Olive Ave .... Glendale AZ 85302-3006
Fax: 602 435-3329
818 240-1000 **Glendale Community College** 1500 N Verdugo Rd .... Glendale CA 91208-2809
Fax: 818 549-9436
602 435-4953 **Glendale Public Library** 5959 W Brown St .... Glendale AZ 85302-1248
Fax: 602 931-5662

818 956-2020 **Glendale Public Library** 222 E Harvard St .... Glendale CA 91205-1075
Fax: 818 241-5082
916 934-3834 **Glenn County** 526 W Sycamore .... Willows CA 95988-2746
202 224-3353 **Glenn John (Sen - D - Ohio)** 503 Hart Bldg .... Washington DC 20510-0001
Fax: Unlisted
708 657-2107 **Glenview Naval Air Station** .... Glenview IL 60026-0000
Fax: 708 657-2173
304 462-7361 **Glenville State College** 200 High St .... Glenville WV 26351-1200
Fax: 304 462-7610 Admin
202 225-6216 **Glickman Dan (Rep - D - Kansas)** 2311 Rayburn Bldg .... Washington DC 20515-0001
Fax: 202 225-5398
803 665-4654 **Gloryland Bible College** PO Box 3966 .... Florence SC 29502-3966
609 853-3237 **Gloucester County** 1 N Broad St .... Woodbury NJ 08096-4611
Fax: 609 853-2770
804 693-4042 **Gloucester County** PO Box 329 .... Gloucester VA 23061-0329
609 468-5000 **Gloucester County College** Tanyard Rd .... Sewell NJ 08080-9191
Fax: 609 468-9462
609 589-2000 **Gloucester County Library** 200 Holly Dell Dr .... Sewell NJ 08080-9191
Fax: 609 589-8710
912 267-5600 **Glynn County** 701 G St .... Brunswick GA 31520-6750
Fax: 912 267-5691
313 762-9500 **GMI Engineering & Management Institute** 1700 W 3rd Ave .... Flint MI 48504-4890
Fax: 313 762-9807
802 454-8311 **Goddard College** 2 Pitkin Pl .... Plainfield VT 05667-0000
906 932-4231 **Gogebic Community College** E 4946 Jackson Rd .... Ironwood MI 49938-0000
Fax: 906 932-0868
906 663-4518 **Gogebic County** 200 N Moore St .... Bessemer MI 49911-1052
213 623-6000 **Golden Gate University** 919 S Grand Ave Suite 250 .... Los Angeles CA 90015-0000
Fax: 213 624-4777
415 442-7000 **Golden Gate University** 536 Mission St .... San Francisco CA 94105-2968
Fax: 415 495-2671
415 442-7225 *College of Business Administration* 536 Mission St ... San Francisco CA 94105-2967
Fax: 415 495-2671
415 442-7870 *Graduate School of Public Administration*
536 Mission St .... San Francisco CA 94105-2967
Fax: 415 495-2671
415 442-7216 *School of Health Services Management*
536 Mission St .... San Francisco CA 94105-2967
Fax: 415 495-2671
415 442-7250 *School of Law* 536 Mission St .... San Francisco CA 94105-2967
Fax: 415 495-2671
406 568-2231 **Golden Valley County** PO Box 10 .... Ryegate MT 59074-0010
701 872-4352 **Golden Valley County** PO Box 596 .... Beach ND 58621-0596
714 892-7711 **Golden West College** 15744 Golden West St .... Huntington Beach CA 92647-0000
Fax: 714 895-8243
302 998-8814 **Goldey Beacom College** 4701 Limestone Rd .... Wilmington DE 19808-1999
Fax: 302 998-3467
512 645-3294 **Goliad County** PO Box 5 .... Goliad TX 77963-0005
509 328-4220 **Gonzaga University** E 502 Boone Ave .... Spokane WA 99258-0001
Fax: 509 484-2804
509 484-6481 *School of Law* E 601 Sharp .... Spokane WA 99220-0000
Fax: 509 484-2833 Library
512 672-2801 **Gonzales County** 414 Saint Joseph St .... Gonzales TX 78629-4069
202 225-3236 **Gonzalez Henry B (Rep - D - Texas)** 2413 Rayburn Bldg ..... Washington DC 20515-0001
Fax: 202 225-1915
804 556-5300 **Goochland County** 2938 River Rd W .... Goochland VA 23063-3229
Fax: 804 556-4617
915 654-3231 **Goodfellow Air Force Base** .... San Angelo TX 76908-0001
Fax: 915 654-5400
612 388-8261 **Goodhue County** 509 5th St W Rm 310 .... Red Wing MN 55066-2525
Fax: Ext 144
208 934-4221 **Gooding County** PO Box 417 .... Gooding ID 83330-0417
Fax: 208 934-4408
202 225-5836 **Goodling William F (Rep - R - Pennsylvania)**
2263 Rayburn Bldg .... Washington DC 20515-0001
Fax: Unlisted
301 530-6500 **Goodwill Industries of America Inc** 9200 Wisconsin Ave .... Bethesda MD 20814-3814
Fax: 301 530-1516
202 225-4231 **Gordon Bart (Rep - D - Tennessee)** 103 Cannon Bldg .... Washington DC 20515-0001
Fax: 202 225-6887
404 358-5000 **Gordon College** 103 College Dr .... Barnesville GA 30204-1799
Fax: 404 358-3031
508 927-2300 **Gordon College** 255 Grapevine Rd .... Wenham MA 01984-1899
Fax: 508 927-4527
404 629-3795 **Gordon County** 100 S Wall St Annex 1 .... Calhoun GA 30701-2244
Fax: Call company operator
202 224-4944 **Gore Albert Jr (Sen - D - Tennessee)** 393 Russell Bldg ...... Washington DC 20510-0001
Fax: Unlisted
202 224-3441 **Gorton Slade (Sen - R - Washington)** 730 Hart Bldg .... Washington DC 20510-0001
Fax: 202 224-9393
219 535-7000 **Goshen College** 1700 S Main St .... Goshen IN 46526-4724
Fax: 219 535-7660
307 532-4051 **Goshen County** PO Box 160 .... Torrington WY 82240-0160
308 785-2611 **Gosper County** PO Box 136 .... Elwood NE 68937-0136
202 225-2536 **Goss Porter J (Rep - R - Florida)** 224 Cannon Bldg .... Washington DC 20515-0001
Fax: 202 225-6820
301 337-6000 **Goucher College** Dulaney Valley Rd .... Towson MD 21204-2794
Fax: 301 337-6123
913 938-2300 **Gove County** PO Box 128 .... Gove KS 67736-0128
202 755-5926 **Government National Mortgage Assn**
451 7th St SW Suite 6100 .... Washington DC 20410-0001
202 225-5051 **Government Operations Committee (US House of Representatives)**
2157 Rayburn Bldg .... Washington DC 20515-0001
Fax: 202 225-4784
202 275-2091 **Government Printing Office** 710 N Capitol St NW .... Washington DC 20042-0001
Fax: 202 275-2717
205 731-1056 *Birmingham Bookstore* 2021 3rd Ave N .... Birmingham AL 35203-3301
617 565-6680 *Boston Bookstore* 10 Causeway St Rm 179 .... Boston MA 02222-0000
312 353-5133 *Chicago Bookstore* 219 S Dearborn St Rm 1365 .... Chicago IL 60604-1705
216 522-4922 *Cleveland Bookstore* 1240 E 9th St Rm 1653 .... Cleveland OH 44199-2002
614 469-6956 *Columbus Bookstore* 200 N High St .... Columbus OH 43215-2493
Fax: 614 469-2103
214 767-0076 *Dallas Bookstore* 1100 Commerce St Rm 1C46 .... Dallas TX 75242-1001
303 844-3964 *Denver Bookstore* 1961 Stout St .... Denver CO 80294-0101
313 226-7816 *Detroit Bookstore* 477 Michigan Ave Rm 160 .... Detroit MI 48226-2518
713 653-3100 *Houston Bookstore* 801 Travis Suite 120 .... Houston TX 77002-5727
904 791-3801 *Jacksonville Bookstore* PO Box 35089 .... Jacksonville FL 32202-0089
816 765-2256 *Kansas City Bookstore*
5600 E Bannister Rd 120 Bannister Mall .... Kansas City MO 64137-0000
Fax: Unlisted
301 953-7974 *Laurel Bookstore* 8660 Cherry Ln .... Laurel MD 20707-4989
213 239-9844 *Los Angeles Bookstore* 505 S Flower St Level C .... Los Angeles CA 90071-0000
414 297-1304 *Milwaukee Bookstore* 517 E Wisconsin Ave Rm 190 .... Milwaukee WI 53202-4504
212 264-3825 *New York Bookstore* 26 Federal Plaza Rm 110 .... New York NY 10278-0022
215 597-0677 *Philadelphia Bookstore* 100 N 17th St 1st Fl .... Philadelphia PA 19103-2737
412 644-2721 *Pittsburgh Bookstore* 1000 Liberty Ave Rm 118 .... Pittsburgh PA 15222-4004

719 544-3142 *Pueblo Bookstore* 720 N Main St .... Pueblo CO 81003-3020
415 556-0643 *San Francisco Bookstore* 450 Golden Gate Ave .... San Francisco CA 94102-3400
206 442-4270 *Seattle Bookstore* 915 2nd Ave Rm 194 .... Seattle WA 98174-1009
202 224-4751 **Governmental Affairs Committee (US Senate)**
340 Dirksen Bldg .... Washington DC 20510-0001
Fax: 202 224-9682
212 668-7354 **Governor's Island Coast Guard Support Center**
Governor's Island Bldg 110 .... New York NY 10004-0000
Fax: 212 668-7792
708 534-5000 **Governors State University**
Governors Hwy & University Pkwy .... University Park IL 60466-0000
Fax: 708 534-0054 Library
616 538-2330 **Grace Bible College** 1011 Aldon St SW .... Grand Rapids MI 49509-1921
219 372-5100 **Grace College & Seminary** 200 Seminary Dr .... Winona Lake IN 46590-1224
Fax: 219 372-5265
402 449-2800 **Grace College of the Bible** 1515 S 10th St .... Omaha NE 68108-3600
515 784-5000 **Graceland College** 700 College Ave .... Lamoni IA 50140-1611
Fax: 515 784-5480 Admin
816 833-0524 **Graceland College** 9900 E Winner Rd .... Independence MO 64052-2150
Fax: Unlisted
202 225-3164 **Gradison Willis D Jr (Rep - R - Ohio)** 1125 Rayburn Bldg ... Washington DC 20515-0001
Fax: Unlisted
912 377-1512 **Grady County** 250 N Broad St .... Cairo GA 31728-4101
405 224-5211 **Grady County** PO Box 459 .... Chickasha OK 73023-0459
603 787-6941 **Grafton County** PO Box 108 .... Woodsville NH 03785-0108
615 968-4201 **Graham Bible College** 2690 Volunteer Pkwy .... Bristol TN 37620-6924
202 224-3041 **Graham Bob (Sen - D - Florida)** 241 Dirksen Bldg ...... Washington DC 20510-0001
Fax: Unlisted
602 428-3250 **Graham County** 800 Main St .... Safford AZ 85546-2829
Fax: 602 428-5951
913 674-3453 **Graham County** 410 N Pomeroy St .... Hill City KS 67642-1645
704 479-3361 **Graham County** PO Box 575 .... Robbinsville NC 28771-0575
615 828-3511 **Grainger County** County Courthouse .... Rutledge TN 37861-0000
318 274-2435 **Grambling State University** 100 Main St .... Grambling LA 71245-0000
202 224-2934 **Gramm Phil (Sen - R - Texas)** 370 Russell Bldg ...... Washington DC 20510-0001
602 638-7769 **Grand Canyon National Park Museum**
Grand Canyon Village South Rim .... Grand Canyon AZ 86023-9999
Fax: 602 638-7797
602 249-3300 **Grand Canyon University** 3300 W Camelback Rd .... Phoenix AZ 85017-3030
Fax: 602 589-2895 Library
303 725-3347 **Grand County** 308 Byers Ave .... Hot Sulphur Springs CO 80451-9999
Fax: 303 725-3227
801 259-5645 **Grand County** 125 E Center St .... Moab UT 84532-2449
Fax: 801 259-2959
701 747-3000 **Grand Forks Air Force Base** .... Grand Forks ND 58205-0000
Fax: Call company operator
701 780-8238 **Grand Forks County** PO Box 1477 .... Grand Forks ND 58206-1477
802 372-8350 **Grand Isle County** Rt 2 .... North Hero VT 05474-0000
616 459-4677 **Grand Rapids Art Museum** 155 Division N .... Grand Rapids MI 49503-3154
Fax: 616 459-8491
616 949-5300 **Grand Rapids Baptist College & Seminary**
1001 E Beltline Ave NE .... Grand Rapids MI 49505-5803
616 456-4899 **Grand Rapids Junior College** 143 Bostwick Ave NE .... Grand Rapids MI 49503-3295
616 456-3600 **Grand Rapids Public Library** 60 Library Plaza NE .... Grand Rapids MI 49503-3093
616 922-4700 **Grand Traverse County** 400 Boardman Ave .... Traverse City MI 49684-2577
Fax: 616 922-4598
616 895-6611 **Grand Valley State University** .... Allendale MI 49401-9523
Fax: 616 895-3506
515 263-2800 **Grand View College** 1200 Grandview Ave .... Des Moines IA 50316-1599
Fax: 515 263-2998
202 225-5476 **Grandy Fred (Rep - R - Iowa)** 418 Cannon Bldg .... Washington DC 20515-0001
Fax: Unlisted
406 859-3771 **Granite County** Sampson & Kearney Sts .... Philipsburg MT 59858-0000
501 942-2631 **Grant County** Main & Center Sts .... Sheridan AR 72150-0000
317 668-8121 **Grant County** County Courthouse .... Marion IN 46952-0000
316 356-1335 **Grant County** 108 S Glenn St .... Ulysses KS 67880-2551
Fax: 316 356-5379
606 824-3321 **Grant County** PO Box 469 .... Williamstown KY 41097-0469
218 685-4520 **Grant County** County Courthouse .... Elbow Lake MN 56531-0000
701 622-3615 **Grant County** County Courthouse .... Carson ND 58529-0000
308 458-2488 **Grant County** PO Box 139 .... Hyannis NE 69350-0139
505 538-9581 **Grant County** PO Box 898 .... Silver City NM 88062-0898
405 395-2214 **Grant County** County Courthouse Rm 104 .... Medford OK 73759-1244
503 575-0059 **Grant County** 200 S Canyon Blvd .... Canyon City OR 97820-0000
Fax: 503 575-0193
605 432-6711 **Grant County** 210 E 5th Ave .... Milbank SD 57252-2433
509 754-2011 **Grant County** PO Box 37 .... Ephrata WA 98823-0037
Fax: 509 754-3639
608 723-2675 **Grant County** 130 W Maple St .... Lancaster WI 53813-1625
304 257-4422 **Grant County** 5 Highland Ave .... Petersburg WV 26847-1705
318 627-3157 **Grant Parish** Main St .... Colfax LA 71417-0000
919 693-5240 **Granville County** 141 Williamsboro St .... Oxford NC 27565-3318
202 224-3744 **Grassley Charles E (Sen - R - Iowa)** 135 Hart Bldg ...... Washington DC 20510-0001
Fax: 202 224-0473
517 875-5215 **Gratiot County** 214 E Center St .... Ithaca MI 48847-1446
215 635-7300 **Gratz College** Old York Rd & Melrose Ave .... Melrose Park PA 19126-1297
Fax: 215 635-7320
502 247-3626 **Graves County** Courthouse .... Mayfield KY 42066-0000
316 855-3618 **Gray County** PO Box 487 .... Cimarron KS 67835-0487
Fax: 316 855-3107
806 669-8004 **Gray County** 205 N Russell St .... Pampa TX 79065-6441
202 225-4001 **Gray William H III (Rep - D - Pennsylvania)**
2454 Rayburn Bldg .... Washington DC 20515-0001
Fax: 202 225-2995
206 249-3842 **Grays Harbor County** PO Box 711 .... Montesano WA 98563-0590
502 259-3201 **Grayson County** 100 Court Sq .... Leitchfield KY 42754-0000
903 868-9515 **Grayson County** Houston & Lamar Sts .... Sherman TX 75090-0000
703 773-2231 **Grayson County** 129 Davis St .... Independence VA 24348-0000
Fax: 703 773-3338
903 465-6030 **Grayson County College** 6101 Grayson Dr .... Denison TX 75020-8238
Fax: 903 463-5284
Great Britain
202 462-1340 *Embassy* 3100 Massachusetts Ave NW .... Washington DC 20008-3605
Fax: 202 898-4255
212 752-8400 *Mission to the UN* 845 3rd Ave 10th Fl .... New York NY 10022-6601
Fax: 212 306-0316
617 248-9555 *Boston Consulate General*
600 Atlantic Ave Federal Reserve Plaza 25th Fl .... Boston MA 02210-0000
Fax: 617 248-9578
312 346-1810 *Chicago Consulate General* 33 N Dearborn St .... Chicago IL 60602-3102
Fax: 312 346-7021
713 659-6270 *Houston Consulate General* 601 Jefferson Suite 2250 .... Houston TX 77002-7910
Fax: 713 659-7094
213 385-7381 *Los Angeles Consulate General*
3701 Wilshire Blvd Suite 312 .... Los Angeles CA 90010-2810
Fax: 213 381-5450

212 752-8400 *New York Consulate General* 845 3rd Ave .... New York NY 10022-6601

Fax: 212 754-3062

415 981-3030 *San Francisco Consulate General*

1 Sansome St Suite 850 .... San Francisco CA 94104-4429

Fax: 415 434-2018

406 453-0349 **Great Falls Public Library** 301 2nd Ave N .... Great Falls MT 59401-2593

Fax: 406 453-0181

517 321-0242 **Great Lakes Bible College** 6211 W Willow Hwy .... Lansing MI 48917-1231

Fax: 517 321-5902

708 688-3300 **Great Lakes Naval Training Center** .... Great Lakes IL 60088-0000

612 251-7282 **Great River Regional Library** 405 St Germain .... Saint Cloud MN 56301-3667

307 638-3388 **Greater Cheyenne Chamber of Commerce** 301 W 16th St .... Cheyenne WY 82001-4437

203 520-7800 **Greater Hartford Community College** 61 Woodland St .... Hartford CT 06105-2354

Fax: 203 520-7906

701 237-9461 **Greater North Dakota Assn** 808 3rd Ave S .... Fargo ND 58108-0000

Fax: 701 237-9463

401 521-5000 **Greater Providence Chamber of Commerce**

30 Exchange Terr .... Providence RI 02903-1022

Fax: 401 751-2434

206 389-7200 **Greater Seattle Chamber of Commerce**

600 University St Suite 1200 .... Seattle WA 98101-1129

Fax: 206 389-7288

Greece: Hellenic Republic

202 667-3168 *Embassy* 2221 Massachusetts Ave NW .... Washington DC 20008-2813

Fax: 202 939-5824

212 490-6060 *Mission to the UN* 733 3rd Ave 23rd Fl .... New York NY 10017-3296

Fax: 212 490-5894

312 372-5356 *Chicago Consulate General* 168 N Michigan Ave .... Chicago IL 60601-7509

Fax: 312 372-6272

212 988-5500 *New York Consulate General* 69 E 79th St .... New York NY 10021-0291

Fax: 212 734-8492

415 775-2102 *San Francisco Consulate General* 2441 Gough St .... San Francisco CA 94123-5010

Fax: 415 776-6815

316 376-4256 **Greeley County** PO Box 277 .... Tribune KS 67879-0277

308 428-3625 **Greeley County** 28th & Kildare Sts .... Greeley NE 68842-0000

202 225-2436 **Green Bill (Rep - R - New York)** 2301 Rayburn Bldg .... Washington DC 20515-0001

Fax: 202 225-0840

502 932-4024 **Green County** 203 W Court St .... Greensburg KY 42743-1522

608 328-9430 **Green County** County Courthouse .... Monroe WI 53566-2098

Fax: 608 328-2835

414 294-4060 **Green Lake County** 570 South St .... Green Lake WI 54941-9720

Fax: 414 294-4066

802 287-9313 **Green Mountain College** College St .... Poultney VT 05764-1199

Fax: Ext 340

206 833-9111 **Green River Community College** 12401 SE 320th St .... Auburn WA 98002-3699

Fax: 206 939-5135

304 645-2373 **Greenbrier County** PO Box 506 .... Lewisburg WV 24901-0506

205 372-3349 **Greene County** PO Box 656 .... Eutaw AL 35462-0656

501 239-4097 **Greene County** PO Box 364 .... Paragould AR 72451-0364

404 453-7716 **Greene County** 201 N Main St .... Greensboro GA 30642-1109

Fax: 404 453-3353

515 386-2516 **Greene County** County Courthouse .... Jefferson IA 50129-2294

217 942-5443 **Greene County** 519 N Main St .... Carrollton IL 62016-1033

812 384-8532 **Greene County** Main & Washington Sts .... Bloomfield IN 47424-0000

417 868-4055 **Greene County** 940 Boonville Ave .... Springfield MO 65802-0000

Fax: 417 868-4050

601 394-2377 **Greene County** PO Box 610 .... Leakesville MS 39451-0610

919 747-3505 **Greene County** 2nd & Greene .... Snow Hill NC 28580-0675

518 943-2050 **Greene County** Main St .... Catskill NY 12414-1396

513 376-5000 **Greene County** 45 N Detroit St .... Xenia OH 45385-3199

Fax: 513 376-5309

412 852-1171 **Greene County** 93 E High St County Office Bldg .... Waynesburg PA 15370-1888

615 639-5321 **Greene County** 101 S Main St .... Greeneville TN 37743-4932

804 985-5299 **Greene County** Court Sq .... Stanardsville VA 22973-0000

513 376-2995 **Greene County District Library** 76 E Market St .... Xenia OH 45385-3100

Fax: 513 372-4673

413 774-3131 **Greenfield Community College** 1 College Dr .... Greenfield MA 01301-9700

Fax: 413 774-3056

602 865-4242 **Greenlee County** PO Box 1027 .... Clifton AZ 85533-1027

Fax: 602 865-4465

919 272-7102 **Greensboro College** 815 W Market St .... Greensboro NC 27420-6050

Fax: 919 271-2237

919 373-2043 **Greensboro Historical Museum** 130 Summit Ave .... Greensboro NC 27401-3016

919 373-2474 **Greensboro Public Library** 201 N Greene St .... Greensboro NC 27401-2410

Fax: 919 333-6781

804 348-4215 **Greensville County** 337 S Main St .... Emporia VA 23847-2027

606 473-7455 **Greenup County** 301 Main St .... Greenup KY 41144-1055

618 664-1840 **Greenville College** 315 E College Ave .... Greenville IL 62246-1199

Fax: 618 664-1748

803 240-7105 **Greenville County** 301 University Ridge Suite 100 .... Greenville SC 29601-3665

803 242-5000 **Greenville County Library** 300 College St .... Greenville SC 29601-2086

Fax: 803 235-8375

803 271-7570 **Greenville County Museum of Art** 420 College St .... Greenville SC 29601-2017

919 758-1946 **Greenville Museum of Art** 802 S Evans St .... Greenville NC 27834-3268

803 250-8000 **Greenville Technical College** PO Box 5616 .... Greenville SC 29606-5616

Fax: 803 239-3056

316 583-7421 **Greenwood County** 311 N Main St .... Eureka KS 67045-1321

803 229-6622 **Greenwood County** 528 Monument St .... Greenwood SC 29646-0000

803 223-4515 **Greenwood-Abbeville Regional Library** 106 N Main St .... Greenwood SC 29646-2240

405 782-2329 **Greer County** Courthouse Sq .... Mangum OK 73554-4260

903 758-6181 **Gregg County** PO Box 3049 .... Longview TX 75606-3049

605 775-2665 **Gregory County** PO Box 430 .... Burke SD 57523-0430

202 265-2561 **Grenada Embassy** 1701 New Hampshire Ave NW .... Washington DC 20009-2501

Fax: 202 265-2468

601 226-1821 **Grenada County** PO Box 1208 .... Grenada MS 38901-1208

206 728-6800 **Griffin College** 2025 2nd Ave .... Seattle WA 98121-2205

Fax: 206 441-3039

315 330-1110 **Griffiss Air Force Base** .... Rome NY 13441-0000

Fax: 315 330-7537

701 797-2772 **Griggs County** PO Box 326 .... Cooperstown ND 58425-0326

409 873-2662 **Grimes County** Main St .... Anderson TX 77830-0000

515 269-4000 **Grinnell College** PO Box 805 .... Grinnell IA 50112-0810

Fax: 515 269-3408

317 688-5211 **Grissom Air Force Base** .... Bunker Hill IN 46971-0000

Fax: 317 688-2522

619 465-1700 **Grossmont College** 8800 Grossmont College Dr .... El Cajon CA 92020-1765

Fax: 619 461-3396 Admin

412 458-2000 **Grove City College** .... Grove City PA 16127-0000

Fax: 412 458-2190

319 824-5229 **Grundy County** 700 G Ave .... Grundy Center IA 50638-1440

815 942-9024 **Grundy County** 111 E Washington St .... Morris IL 60450-2268

Fax: Call company operator

816 359-6305 **Grundy County** 700 Main St .... Trenton MO 64683-2063

615 692-3622 **Grundy County** PO Box 215 .... Altamont TN 37301-0215

202 472-1804 **GSA Business Service Center** 7th & D Sts SW Rm 1050 .... Washington DC 20407-0001

617 565-8100 *Region 1* 10 Causeway St Rm 290 .... Boston MA 02222-1047

212 264-1234 *Region 2* 26 Federal Plaza Rm 112 .... New York NY 10278-0022

215 597-9613 *Region 3* 9th & Market Sts Rm 5151 .... Philadelphia PA 19107-0000

404 331-5103 *Region 4* 75 Spring St SW .... Atlanta GA 30303-3309

312 353-5383 *Region 5* 230 S Dearborn St Rm 3714 .... Chicago IL 60604-1602

816 926-7203 *Region 6* 1500 E Bannister Rd .... Kansas City MO 64131-3009

Fax: 816 926-7513

817 334-3284 *Region 7* 819 Taylor St Rm 11A05 .... Fort Worth TX 76102-6114

Fax: 817 334-4609

303 236-7408 *Region 8* Denver Federal Ctr Bldg 41 Rm 145 .... Denver CO 80225-0006

Fax: 303 776-0455

415 744-5050 *Region 9* 525 Market St .... San Francisco CA 94105-2799

206 931-7956 *Region 10* 15th & C Sts SW Rm 2413 .... Auburn WA 98001-0000

505 472-3791 **Guadalupe County** 420 Park Ave .... Santa Rosa NM 88435-0000

512 379-4188 **Guadalupe County** 101 E Court St .... Seguin TX 78155-5700

202 225-2765 **Guarini Frank J (Rep - D - New Jersey)**

2458 Rayburn Bldg .... Washington DC 20515-0001

Fax: 202 225-7023

Guatemala: Republic of Guatemala

202 745-4952 *Embassy* 2220 R St NW .... Washington DC 20008-4018

Fax: 202 745-1908

212 679-4760 *Mission to the UN* 57 Park Ave 2nd Fl .... New York NY 10016-3006

Fax: 212 685-8741

614 432-2505 **Guernsey County** 836 Steubenville Ave .... Cambridge OH 43725-2335

Fax: 614 432-2643

919 292-5511 **Guilford College** 5800 W Friendly Ave .... Greensboro NC 27410-4173

Fax: Unlisted

919 373-3778 **Guilford County** 301 Market St .... Greensboro NC 27402-0000

919 334-4822 **Guilford Technical Community College** High Point Rd .... Jamestown NC 27282-0000

Fax: 919 841-2158

Guinea-Bissau: Republic of Guinea-Bissau

212 661-3977 *Embassy* 211 E 43rd St Suite 604 .... New York NY 10017-4793

Fax: 212 983-2794

212 661-3977 *Mission to the UN* 211 E 43rd St .... New York NY 10017-4793

Guinea: Republic of Guinea

202 483-9420 *Embassy* 2112 Leroy Pl NW .... Washington DC 20008-1847

212 687-8115 *Mission to the UN* 140 E 39th St 29th Fl .... New York NY 10016-0000

904 769-1551 **Gulf Coast Community College** 5230 W Hwy 98 .... Panama City FL 32401-1041

Fax: 904 872-3836

904 229-6113 **Gulf County** 1000 5th St .... Port Saint Joe FL 32456-1648

Fax: 904 229-6174

202 225-5506 **Gunderson Steve (Rep - R - Wisconsin)**

2235 Rayburn Bldg .... Washington DC 20515-0001

Fax: 202 225-6195

919 694-6241 **Gunn Memorial Public Library** 317 E Main St .... Yanceyville NC 27379-0000

303 641-0248 **Gunnison County** 200 E Virginia Ave .... Gunnison CO 81230-2297

507 931-8000 **Gustavus Adolphus College** College Ave .... Saint Peter MN 56082-0000

Fax: Ext 7041

515 747-3415 **Guthrie County** 200 N 5th St .... Guthrie Center IA 50115-1331

Guyana: Cooperative Republic of Guyana

202 265-6900 *Embassy* 2490 Tracy Pl NW .... Washington DC 20008-1627

Fax: 202 232-1297

212 527-3232 *Mission to the UN* 866 UN Plaza Suite 555 .... New York NY 10017-0000

Fax: 212 935-7548

404 822-8000 **Gwinnett County** 75 Langley Dr .... Lawrenceville GA 30245-6935

Fax: 404 822-8014

215 646-7300 **Gwynedd Mercy College** Sumneytown Pike .... Gwynedd Valley PA 19437-9999

Fax: 215 641-5596

H

605 859-2627 **Haakon County** PO Box 70 .... Philip SD 57567-0070

404 754-6264 **Habersham County** PO Box 227 .... Clarkesville GA 30523-0227

Fax: 404 754-1014

401 253-8388 **Haffenreffer Museum of Anthropology**

Mt Hope Grant Brown University .... Bristol RI 02809-0000

301 790-2800 **Hagerstown Junior College** 751 Robinwood Dr .... Hagerstown MD 21740-6590

Fax: Ext 386 Admin

302 658-2400 **Hagley Museum & Library** 298 Buck Rd E .... Wilmington DE 19807-0000

Fax: 302 658-0568

215 448-7000 **Hahnemann University** Broad & Vine Sts .... Philadelphia PA 19102-1192

Fax: 215 448-8109

215 448-7604 *School of Medicine* Broad & Vine Sts MS-440 .... Philadelphia PA 19102-1192

Fax: 215 448-8654

907 766-2711 **Haines Borough** PO Box 1209 .... Haines AK 99827-1209

Haiti: Republic of Haiti

202 332-4090 *Embassy* 2311 Massachusetts Ave NW .... Washington DC 20008-2802

Fax: 202 745-7215

212 370-4840 *Mission to the UN* 801 2nd Ave Rm 300 .... New York NY 10017-4706

Fax: 212 661-8698

205 624-4257 **Hale County** 1001 Main St .... Greensboro AL 36744-1510

806 293-8481 **Hale County** 500 Broadway .... Plainview TX 79072-0000

919 536-2551 **Halifax Community College** Hwy 158 W .... Weldon NC 27890-0000

Fax: 919 536-4144

919 583-1131 **Halifax County** King St .... Halifax NC 27839-0000

804 476-2141 **Halifax County** Main St Courthouse Sq .... Halifax VA 24558-0786

404 531-7000 **Hall County** 116 Spring St E .... Gainesville GA 30501-3765

Fax: 404 536-0702

308 381-5080 **Hall County** 121 S Pine St .... Grand Island NE 68801-0000

806 259-2511 **Hall County** County Courthouse .... Memphis TX 79245-3343

202 225-6673 **Hall Ralph M (Rep - D - Texas)** 2236 Rayburn Bldg .... Washington DC 20515-0001

Fax: 202 225-3332

202 225-6465 **Hall Tony P (Rep - D - Ohio)** 2162 Rayburn Bldg .... Washington DC 20515-0001

Fax: 202 225-6766

615 586-1993 **Hamblen County** 511 W 2nd North St .... Morristown TN 37814-3964

315 859-4011 **Hamilton College** College Hill Rd .... Clinton NY 13323-0000

Fax: 315 859-4648 Communications

904 792-1288 **Hamilton County** 207 NE 1st St .... Jasper FL 32052-0000

Fax: 904 792-1272

515 832-1771 **Hamilton County** County Courthouse .... Webster City IA 50595-3158

Fax: 515 832-3568

618 643-2721 **Hamilton County** Public Sq .... McLeansboro IL 62859-1489

317 773-6110 **Hamilton County** Public Sq .... Noblesville IN 46060-1697

316 384-5629 **Hamilton County** N Main St .... Syracuse KS 67878-0000

Fax: 316 384-5835

402 694-3443 **Hamilton County** County Courthouse .... Aurora NE 68818-2097

518 548-7111 **Hamilton County** Rt 8 .... Lake Pleasant NY 12108-0000

513 632-6500 **Hamilton County** 1000 Main St .... Cincinnati OH 45202-1217

Fax: 513 241-7985 Admin

615 757-2185 **Hamilton County** County Courthouse .... Chattanooga TN 37402-0000

817 386-3518 **Hamilton County** County Courthouse .... Hamilton TX 76531-1859

202 225-5315 **Hamilton Lee H (Rep - D - Indiana)** 2187 Rayburn Bldg ..... Washington DC 20515-0001

Fax: Unlisted

605 783-3751 **Hamlin County** PO Box 256 .... Hayti SD 57241-0256

612 641-2800 **Hamline University** 1536 Hewitt Ave ... Saint Paul MN 55104-1284
Fax: 612 641-2956
612 641-2400 *School of Law* 1536 Hewitt Ave ... Saint Paul MN 55104-1284
Fax: 612 641-2956
202 225-4301 **Hammerschmidt John Paul (Rep - R - Arkansas)**
2110 Rayburn Bldg ... Washington DC 20515-0000
Fax: 202 225-7492
413 781-8100 **Hampden County** 50 State St ... Springfield MA 01103-2002
804 223-4381 **Hampden Sydney College** College Rd ... Hampden Sydney VA 23943-0000
Fax: 804 223-7629
413 549-4600 **Hampshire College** 893 West St ... Amherst MA 01002-3328
Fax: 413 549-0707
413 584-0557 **Hampshire County** 99 Main St ... Northampton MA 01060-3119
304 822-5112 **Hampshire County** Main St ... Romney WV 26757-1696
804 727-6000 **Hampton (Independent City)** 22 Lincoln St ... Hampton VA 23669-0000
803 943-3668 **Hampton County** PO Box 7 ... Hampton SC 29924-0007
804 727-1154 **Hampton Public Library** 4207 Victoria Blvd ... Hampton VA 23669-4243
804 727-5000 **Hampton University** E Queen St ... Hampton VA 23668-0000
404 444-5746 **Hancock County** Courthouse Sq ... Sparta GA 31087-0000
Fax: 404 444-6231
515 923-2532 **Hancock County** 855 State St ... Garner IA 50438-1645
217 357-3911 **Hancock County** Courthouse Sq ... Carthage IL 62321-1359
317 462-1106 **Hancock County** 9 E Main St ... Greenfield IN 46140-2320
502 927-6117 **Hancock County** County Administration Bldg ... Hawesville KY 42348-0000
207 667-9542 **Hancock County** 60 State St ... Ellsworth ME 04605-1926
Fax: 207 667-7516
601 467-5404 **Hancock County** 242 Main St ... Bay Saint Louis MS 39520-3595
419 424-7037 **Hancock County** 300 S Main St ... Findlay OH 45840-3345
615 733-4341 **Hancock County** Main St ... Sneedville TN 37869-9501
Fax: 615 733-4348
304 564-3311 **Hancock County** PO Box 367 ... New Cumberland WV 26047-0367
202 225-6536 **Hancock Melton D (Rep - R - Missouri)** 318 Cannon Bldg ... Washington DC 20515-0001
Fax: 202 225-7700
605 853-3337 **Hand County** 415 W 1st Ave ... Miller SD 57362-1346
202 898-0792 **Handgun Control Inc** 1225 Eye St NW Suite 1100 ... Washington DC 20005-0000
Fax: 202 371-9615
314 221-3675 **Hannibal-LaGrange College** 2800 Palmyra Rd ... Hannibal MO 63401-1999
Fax: 314 221-6594
812 866-7000 **Hanover College** ... Hanover IN 47243-0000
Fax: 812 866-2164
804 537-6000 **Hanover County** PO Box 470 ... Hanover VA 23069-0470
617 377-4441 **Hanscom Air Force Base** ... Bedford MA 01731-0001
Fax: 617 377-5077 PR
202 225-0453 **Hansen James V (Rep - R - Utah)** 2421 Rayburn Bldg ... Washington DC 20515-0001
Fax: 202 225-5857
806 659-2666 **Hansford County** 1 NW Court ... Spearman TX 79081-3499
Fax: 806 659-2025
605 239-4446 **Hanson County** PO Box 127 ... Alexandria SD 57311-0127
404 646-2002 **Haralson County** PO Box 488 ... Buchanan GA 30113-0488
Fax: Unlisted
215 525-4100 **Harcum Junior College** Morris & Montgomery Aves ... Bryn Mawr PA 19010-3505
Fax: 215 526-6086 Library
813 773-6952 **Hardee County** 412 W Orange St ... Wauchula FL 33873-2831
Fax: 813 773-0958
901 658-3541 **Hardeman County** 100 N Main St ... Bolivar TN 38008-2322
817 663-2901 **Hardeman County** PO Box 30 ... Quanah TX 79252-0030
515 858-3461 **Hardin County** Edgington Ave ... Eldora IA 50627-1741
618 287-2251 **Hardin County** Main St ... Elizabethtown IL 62931-0000
502 765-2171 **Hardin County** 14 Public Sq ... Elizabethtown KY 42701-1437
Fax: 502 765-6762
419 674-2205 **Hardin County** Public Sq ... Kenton OH 43326-9700
901 925-3921 **Hardin County** 601 Main St ... Savannah TN 38372-2061
409 246-5185 **Hardin County** Hwy 326 & Courthouse Sq ... Kountze TX 77625-0000
915 670-1000 **Hardin-Simmons University** 2200 Hickory St ... Abilene TX 79698-0001
Fax: 915 677-8351 Library
505 673-2301 **Harding County** PO Box 1002 ... Mosquero NM 87733-1002
605 375-3351 **Harding County** 901 Ramsland St ... Buffalo SD 57720-0000
501 279-4000 **Harding University** 900 E Center Ave ... Searcy AR 72143-5608
Fax: 501 279-4407 Admissions
304 538-2929 **Hardy County** Washington St ... Moorefield WV 26836-0000
301 879-8920 **Harford Community College** 401 Thomas Run Rd ... Bel Air MD 21014-1698
Fax: 301 836-4198
301 838-6000 **Harford County** 220 S Main St ... Bel Air MD 21014-3833
301 838-7484 **Harford County Library** 100 Pennsylvania Ave ... Bel Air MD 21014-3799
Fax: 301 838-7527
202 224-3254 **Harkin Tom (Sen - D - Iowa)** 316 Hart Bldg ... Washington DC 20510-0001
Fax: 202 224-7431
606 573-2600 **Harlan County** PO Box 956 ... Harlan KY 40831-0956
308 928-2173 **Harlan County** PO Box 379 ... Alma NE 68920-0379
Fax: 308 928-2592
405 688-3658 **Harmon County** 114 W Hollis County Courthouse ... Hollis OK 73550-0000
919 893-7500 **Harnett County** 729 S Main St ... Lillington NC 27546-0000
Fax: 919 893-4992
503 573-6641 **Harney County** 450 N Buena Vista St ... Burns OR 97720-1565
Fax: 503 573-5207
316 842-5555 **Harper County** County Courthouse ... Anthony KS 67003-2799
405 735-2012 **Harper County** 311 SE 1st ... Buffalo OK 73834-0000
312 939-4975 **Harrington Institute of Interior Design** 410 S Michigan Ave ... Chicago IL 60605-1496
202 225-2665 **Harris Claude (Rep - D - Alabama)** 1009 Longworth Bldg ... Washington DC 20515-0001
Fax: 202 225-0175
404 628-4944 **Harris County** PO Box 528 ... Hamilton GA 31811-0528
713 221-5000 **Harris County** 1001 Preston St ... Houston TX 77002-1816
713 221-5350 **Harris County Public Library System**
49 San Jacinto Suite 200 ... Houston TX 77002-1214
314 533-3366 **Harris-Stowe State College** 3026 Laclede Ave ... Saint Louis MO 63103-2199
Fax: 314 533-0916
717 780-2300 **Harrisburg Area Community College** 3300 Cameron St ... Harrisburg PA 17110-2902
Fax: 717 236-0709
712 644-2665 **Harrison County** 113 N 2nd Ave ... Logan IA 51546-1331
812 738-8241 **Harrison County** 300 N Capitol Ave ... Corydon IN 47112-1139
606 234-2232 **Harrison County** 190 W Pike St ... Cynthiana KY 41031-1426
816 425-6424 **Harrison County** PO Box 27 ... Bethany MO 64424-0027
601 865-4001 **Harrison County** 1801 23rd Ave ... Gulfport MS 39501-2983
Fax: 601 865-4087
614 942-8861 **Harrison County** 100 W Market St ... Cadiz OH 43907-1132
Fax: 614 942-4693
903 935-4858 **Harrison County** Houston & Wellington Sts ... Marshall TX 75670-0000
304 624-8611 **Harrison County** 301 W Main St ... Clarksburg WV 26301-2909
601 868-1383 **Harrison County Library System** 14th St & 21st Ave ... Gulfport MS 39501-2092
703 434-6776 **Harrisonburg (Independent City)** 345 S Main St ... Harrisonburg VA 22801-3638
Fax: 703 434-0634
205 831-4540 **Harry M Ayers State Technical College** 1801 Coleman Rd ... Anniston AL 36201-6858
312 878-1700 **Harry S Truman College** 1145 W Wilson Ave ... Chicago IL 60640-5691
Fax: 312 989-6135
404 376-2024 **Hart County** PO Box 279 ... Hartwell GA 30643-0279
502 524-2751 **Hart County** PO Box 277 ... Munfordville KY 42765-0000

203 236-1215 **Hartford College for Women** 1265 Asylum Ave ... Hartford CT 06105-2299
Fax: 203 232-3402
203 566-3170 **Hartford Judicial District** 95 Washington St ... Hartford CT 06106-4406
203 293-6000 **Hartford Public Library** 500 Main St ... Hartford CT 06103-3075
203 232-4451 **Hartford Seminary** 77 Sherman St ... Hartford CT 06105-2260
203 527-4111 **Hartford State Technical College** 401 Flatbush Ave ... Hartford CT 06106-3757
Fax: Ext 171
806 235-3582 **Hartley County** PO Box T ... Channing TX 79018-0400
408 755-6700 **Hartnell College** 156 Homestead Ave ... Salinas CA 93901-1698
Fax: 408 755-6751
607 432-4200 **Hartwick College** ... Oneonta NY 13820-0000
Fax: 607 431-4457
617 495-1000 **Harvard University** 1350 Massachusetts Ave Holyoke Ctr ... Cambridge MA 02138-3800
Fax: 617 495-0500
617 495-2591 *Department of Architecture* 48 Quincy St Gund Hall ... Cambridge MA 02138-0000
Fax: 617 495-8916
617 495-4106 *Department of Biochemistry* 7 Divinity Ave ... Cambridge MA 02138-2019
Fax: 617 495-8308
617 495-2351 *Department of Earth & Planetary Sciences*
20 Oxford St Hoffman Laboratory ... Cambridge MA 02138-2902
Fax: 617 495-8839
617 495-2872 *Department of Physics* Jefferson Physical Laboratory ... Cambridge MA 02138-0000
Fax: 617 495-0416
617 495-6550 *Graduate School of Business Administration* Soldiers Field ... Boston MA 02163-0000
Fax: 617 495-6001
617 495-4076 *Graduate School of Chemistry* 12 Oxford St ... Cambridge MA 02138-2902
Fax: 617 495-1792
617 495-1105 *John F Kennedy School of Government*
79 John F Kennedy St ... Cambridge MA 02138-5801
Fax: 617 495-1972
617 495-3100 *Law School* Griswold Hall ... Cambridge MA 02138-3800
Fax: 617 495-1110
617 495-2411 *Library* Wadsworth House ... Cambridge MA 02138-0000
Fax: 617 495-3650
617 432-1580 *Medical School* 25 Shattuck St ... Boston MA 02115-6092
Fax: 617 432-2651
617 432-1000 *School of Dental Medicine* 188 Longwood Ave ... Boston MA 02115-5888
Fax: 617 432-4266
617 432-1035 *School of Public Health* 677 Huntington Ave ... Boston MA 02115-0000
Fax: 617 734-8869
316 283-6900 **Harvey County** PO Box 687 ... Newton KS 67114-0687
714 621-8011 **Harvey Mudd College** 301 E 12th St ... Claremont CA 91711-5990
Fax: 714 621-8360
316 675-2263 **Haskell County** PO Box 518 ... Sublette KS 67877-0518
Fax: 316 675-8142
918 967-4352 **Haskell County** 202 E Main St ... Stigler OK 74462-2439
817 864-2451 **Haskell County** PO Box 725 ... Haskell TX 79521-0725
202 225-2976 **Hastert J Dennis (Rep - R - Illinois)** 515 Cannon Bldg ... Washington DC 20515-0001
Fax: 202 225-0697
402 463-2402 **Hastings College** 7th & Turner Ave ... Hastings NE 68901-7696
Fax: 402 463-3002 Library
402 461-2399 **Hastings Museum** 1330 N Burlington ... Hastings NE 68901-3099
202 224-5251 **Hatch Orrin G (Sen - R - Utah)** 135 Russell Bldg ... Washington DC 20510-0001
Fax: 202 224-6331
202 225-3631 **Hatcher Charles (Rep - D - Georgia)** 2434 Rayburn Bldg ... Washington DC 20515-0001
Fax: 202 225-1117
202 224-3753 **Hatfield Mark O (Sen - R - Oregon)** 711 Hart Bldg ... Washington DC 20510-0001
Fax: Unlisted
215 896-1000 **Haverford College** 370 Lancaster Ave ... Haverford PA 19041-1392
Fax: 215 896-1224
808 522-8800 **Hawaii Chamber of Commerce** 735 Bishop St Suite 220 ... Honolulu HI 96813-4897
Fax: 808 522-8836
808 961-8255 **Hawaii County** 25 Aupuni St ... Hilo HI 96720-4252
Fax: 808 969-7138
808 548-7700 **Hawaii Dept of Business Economic Development & Tourism**
737 Bishop St Grosvenor Center Mauka Tower Suite 1900 ... Honolulu HI 96813-0000
Fax: 808 523-8637
808 235-3641 **Hawaii Loa College** 45-045 Kamehameha Hwy ... Kaneohe HI 96744-5297
Fax: 808 247-8166
808 544-0200 **Hawaii Pacific University** 1166 Fort St ... Honolulu HI 96813-2717
Fax: 808 544-1144
Hawaii State Government
808 548-2211 *Information* 415 S Beretania St ... Honolulu HI 96813-2407
808 548-4511 *Accounting & General Services Dept* 1151 Punchbowl St ... Honolulu HI 96813-3007
Fax: Unlisted
808 548-2355 *Archives Div* Iolani Palace Grounds ... Honolulu HI 96813-0000
Fax: 808 586-0330
808 548-4740 *Attorney General* 415 S Beretania St Rm 405 ... Honolulu HI 96813-2407
Fax: 808 548-1900
808 956-8213 *Board of Regents*
University of Hawaii Bachman Hall Rm 209 ... Honolulu HI 96822-2394
Fax: 808 956-5156
808 548-2560 *Consumer Protection Office*
828 Fort Street Mall Suite 600-B ... Honolulu HI 96813-4321
Fax: 808 548-6062
808 847-4491 *Corrections Div* 2199 Kam Hwy ... Honolulu HI 96819-0000
Fax: 808 548-3600
808 548-7101 *Department of Agriculture* 1428 S King St ... Honolulu HI 96814-2512
Fax: 808 548-6100
808 548-2325 *Department of Budget & Finance* 415 S Beretania St ... Honolulu HI 96813-2407
Fax: 808 548-5575
808 548-7505 *Department of Commerce & Consumer Affairs*
1010 Richards St 2nd Fl ... Honolulu HI 96813-2920
808 734-2195 *Department of Defense* 3949 Diamond Head Rd ... Honolulu HI 96816-4413
Fax: 808 732-8810 Personnel
808 586-3310 *Department of Education* 1390 Miller St ... Honolulu HI 96813-2418
Fax: 808 586-3234
808 548-6505 *Department of Health* PO Box 3378 ... Honolulu HI 96801-3378
Fax: 808 548-3263
808 548-3150 *Department of Labor & Industrial Relations*
830 Punchbowl St Rm 321 ... Honolulu HI 96813-5045
Fax: 808 548-3285
808 548-3205 *Department of Transportation* 869 Punchbowl St ... Honolulu HI 96813-5036
Fax: 808 548-3235
808 548-5414 *Disability Compensation Div* 830 Punchbowl St ... Honolulu HI 96813-5045
808 548-6590 *Division of Consumer Advocacy* PO Box 541 ... Honolulu HI 96809-0541
Fax: 808 548-2028
808 548-7510 *Division of Occupational Safety & Health* 830 Punchbowl St ... Honolulu HI 96813-5045
Fax: 808 548-3285
808 548-4560 *Division of Public Works* 1151 Punchbowl St ... Honolulu HI 96813-3024
Fax: 808 548-2129
808 548-4080 *Energy Div* 335 Merchant St Rm 110 ... Honolulu HI 96813-2921
Fax: 808 531-5243
808 548-4145 *Foundation on Culture & Art* 335 Merchant St Rm 202 ... Honolulu HI 96813-2921
Fax: 808 548-5428

808 548-5420 *Governor* State Capitol Bldg 5th Fl .... Honolulu HI 96813-0000
    Fax: 808 548-1559
808 486-2600 **Halawa Correctional Facility** 99-902 Moanalua Hwy .... Aiea HI 96701-3252
808 548-5710 *Highways Div* 869 Punchbowl St .... Honolulu HI 96813-5036
    Fax: 808 548-7608
808 548-6522 *Insurance Div* 250 S King St 5th Fl .... Honolulu HI 96813-2920
    Fax: 808 543-2721
808 548-6550 *Land & Natural Resources Dept*
    1151 Punchbowl St Rm 130 .... Honolulu HI 96813-3007
    Fax: 808 548-6461
808 548-2544 *Lieutenant Governor* 415 S Beretania St .... Honolulu HI 96813-2407
    Fax: 808 548-3844
808 847-4491 *Oahu Community Correctional Center* 2199 Kam Hwy .... Honolulu HI 96819-2307
808 548-6915 *Office of Environmental Quality Control*
    465 S King St Rm 104 .... Honolulu HI 96813-2910
808 548-6454 *Office of Health Status Monitoring* 1250 Punchbowl St .... Honolulu HI 96813-2428
    Fax: 808 548-1793
808 548-2530 *Paroling Authority* 250 S King St Rm 400 .... Honolulu HI 96813-4521
808 548-6520 *Professional & Vocational Licensing Div* 1010 Richards St .. Honolulu HI 96813-2920
    Fax: 808 548-8113
808 548-6273 *Public Defender* 1130 N Nimitz Hwy Suite A135 .... Honolulu HI 96817-4580
    Fax: 808 524-9227
808 548-3990 *Public Utility Commission* 465 S King St Rm 103 .... Honolulu HI 96813-2910
    Fax: 808 548-4376
808 548-4057 *Purchasing & Supply Div* 1151 Punchbowl St .... Honolulu HI 96813-3024
    Fax: Unlisted
808 548-7464 *Real Estate Commission* PO Box 3469 .... Honolulu HI 96801-3469
808 548-3800 *Resource Coordination Div* 425 Queen St Rm 221 .... Honolulu HI 96813-2904
    Fax: 808-586-1373
808 548-3120 *Sheriff's Dept* 111 Alakea St .... Honolulu HI 96813-0000
808 548-7431 *Supreme Court* 417 S King St .... Honolulu HI 96813-2912
    Fax: 808 543-2706
808 548-7650 *Taxation Dept* 830 Punchbowl St .... Honolulu HI 96813-5045
808 548-6951 *Unemployment Insurance Div* 830 Punchbowl St Rm 325 ... Honolulu HI 96813-5045
    Fax: 808 548-3285
808 548-5596 **Hawaii State Public Library System** 465 S King St Rm B-1 ..... Honolulu HI 96813-0000
    Fax: 808 548-5588
319 296-2320 **Hawkeye Institute of Technology** 1501 E Orange Rd .... Waterloo IA 50701-9298
    Fax: 319 296-2874
615 272-7002 **Hawkins County** Main St .... Rogersville TN 37857-3390
202 225-4372 **Hayes Charles A (Rep - D - Illinois)** 1131 Longworth Bldg .. Washington DC 20515-0001
    Fax: 202 225-7571
308 286-3413 **Hayes County** Troth St .... Hayes Center NE 69032-0000
202 225-2031 **Hayes James A (Rep - D - Louisiana)** 503 Cannon Bldg .... Washington DC 20515-0001
    Fax: 202 225-8976
512 396-2601 **Hays County** County Courthouse .... San Marcos TX 78666-0000
415 784-8688 **Hayward Public Library** 835 C St .... Hayward CA 94541-5120
    Fax: Unlisted
704 627-2821 **Haywood Community College** 1 Freedlander Dr .... Clyde NC 28721-9454
    Fax: 704 627-3606
704 452-6625 **Haywood County** County Courthouse Annex .... Waynesville NC 28786-0000
901 772-2362 **Haywood County** 1 N Washington St .... Brownsville TN 38012-2561
606 436-5721 **Hazard Community College** 1 Community College Dr .... Hazard KY 41701-2403
    Fax: Ext 305
606 255-6653 **Headley-Whitney Museum** 4435 Old Frankfort Pike .... Lexington KY 40510-9623
415 228-9000 **Heald Institute of Technology** 2860 Howe Rd .... Martinez CA 94553-0000
    Fax: 415 229-3792
415 441-5555 **Heald Institute of Technology** 150 4th St .... San Francisco CA 94103-3048
    Fax: 415 543-9530
301 966-3000 **Health Care Financing Administration**
    6325 Security Blvd Rm 700 .... Baltimore MD 21207-5161
    Fax: 301 966-5267
617 565-1232 *Region 1* JFK Federal Bldg Government Ctr Suite 1301 .... Boston MA 02203-0000
    Fax: 617 835-1339
212 264-4488 *Region 2* 26 Federal Plaza Rm 3811 .... New York NY 10278-0022
    Fax: 212 264-2580
215 596-1351 *Region 3* 3535 Market St Rm 3100 .... Philadelphia PA 19104-3309
    Fax: 215 596-5084
404 331-2329 *Region 4* 101 Marietta Tower Suite 701 .... Atlanta GA 30323-0001
    Fax: 404 331-0102
312 353-7180 *Region 5* 105 W Adams St 15th Fl .... Chicago IL 60603-6201
    Fax: 312 353-0252
214 767-6427 *Region 6* 1200 Main Tower Bldg Rm 2000 .... Dallas TX 75202-0000
    Fax: 214 767-0323
816 426-5233 *Region 7* 601 E 12th St Rm 235 .... Kansas City MO 64106-2808
    Fax: 816 426-3548
303 844-2111 *Region 8* 1961 Stout St Rm 1185 .... Denver CO 80294-0101
    Fax: 303 844-3753
415 744-3501 *Region 9* 50 United Nations Plaza 4th Fl ..... San Francisco CA 94105-3901
    Fax: 415 744-3517
206 442-0425 *Region 10* 2201 6th Ave .... Seattle WA 98121-1832
    Fax: Unlisted
404 675-3821 **Heard County** PO Box 40 .... Franklin GA 30217-0040
    Fax: 404 675-6795
602 252-8840 **Heard Museum** 22 E Montevista Rd .... Phoenix AZ 85004-1480
    Fax: 602 252-9757
617 232-8710 **Hebrew College** 43 Hawes St .... Brookline MA 02146-5495
    Fax: 617 734-9769
312 267-9800 **Hebrew Theological College** 7135 N Carpenter Rd .... Skokie IL 60077-3263
212 674-5300 **Hebrew Union College** 1 W 4th St .... New York NY 10012-1186
    Fax: 212 533-0129
213 749-3424 **Hebrew Union College California Branch**
    3077 University Ave .... Los Angeles CA 90007-3796
    Fax: 213 747-6128
202 225-4422 **Hefley Joel (Rep - R - Colorado)** 222 Cannon Bldg ...... Washington DC 20515-0001
    Fax: 202 225-1942
202 224-4124 **Heflin Howell (Sen - D - Alabama)** 728 Hart Bldg .... Washington DC 20510-0001
    Fax: 202 224-3149
202 225-3715 **Hefner WG (Rep - D - North Carolina)** 2161 Rayburn Bldg .. Washington DC 20515-0001
    Fax: 202 225-4036
419 448-2000 **Heidelberg College** 310 E Market St .... Tiffin OH 44883-2434
    Fax: 419 448-2124
202 224-6324 **Heinz John (Sen - R - Pennsylvania)** 277 Russell Bldg ...... Washington DC 20510-0001
    Fax: 202 224-7763
212 807-5800 **Helen Keller International** 15 W 16th St .... New York NY 10011-6301
    Fax: 212 463-9341
617 731-3500 **Hellenic College** 50 Goddard Ave .... Brookline MA 02146-7496
212 629-6380 **Hellenic-American Chamber of Commerce**
    960 Ave of the Americas Suite 1204 .... New York NY 10001-2112
202 224-6342 **Helms Jesse (Sen - R - North Carolina)** 403 Dirksen Bldg .. Washington DC 20510-0001
    Fax: Unlisted
806 323-6212 **Hemphill County** PO Box 867 .... Canadian TX 79014-0867
501 777-6164 **Hempstead County** PO Box 1420 .... Hope AR 71801-1420
502 827-1867 **Henderson Community College** 2660 S Green St .... Henderson KY 42420-4623
    Fax: 502 827-8635
309 867-2911 **Henderson County** PO Box 308 .... Oquawka IL 61469-0308

502 827-5671 **Henderson County** 232 1st St .... Henderson KY 42420-3146
    Fax: 502 826-1974
704 697-4808 **Henderson County** 100 N King St .... Hendersonville NC 28792-5053
    Fax: 704 697-4976
901 968-2856 **Henderson County** Church & Main Sts .... Lexington TN 38351-0000
903 675-6140 **Henderson County** Courthouse Sq .... Athens TX 75751-0000
501 246-5511 **Henderson State University** 12th & Henderson .... Arkadelphia AR 71923-4899
    Fax: 501 246-3199
317 745-9207 **Hendricks County** County Courthouse .... Danville IN 46122-1993
501 329-6811 **Hendrix College** 1601 Harkrider St .... Conway AR 72032-0000
    Fax: 501 450-1200
813 675-5217 **Hendry County** Hwys 80 & 29 .... La Belle FL 33935-1760
612 348-7574 **Hennepin County** 300 S 6th St .... Minneapolis MN 55487-0001
612 541-8530 **Hennepin County Library** 12601 Ridgedale Dr .... Minnetonka MN 55343-5638
    Fax: Unlisted
804 672-4000 **Henrico County** 4301 E Parham Rd .... Richmond VA 23229-0000
206 543-2280 **Henry Art Gallery** University of Washington DE-15 .... Seattle WA 98195-0001
    Fax: 206 685-3123
205 585-2753 **Henry County** Court Sq .... Abbeville AL 36310-2135
404 954-2400 **Henry County** 345 Phillips Dr .... McDonough GA 30253-3425
    Fax: 404 954-2418
319 385-8480 **Henry County** 100 E Washington St .... Mount Pleasant IA 52641-1931
309 937-2426 **Henry County** 100 S Main .... Cambridge IL 61238-0000
    Fax: 309 937-5936
317 529-4705 **Henry County** Broad St .... New Castle IN 47362-0000
502 845-2891 **Henry County** PO Box 202 .... New Castle KY 40050-0202
816 885-6963 **Henry County** Main & Franklin Sts .... Clinton MO 64735-2199
419 592-4876 **Henry County** PO Box 546 .... Napoleon OH 43545-0546
901 642-2412 **Henry County** County Courthouse .... Paris TN 38242-0024
703 638-3961 **Henry County** PO Box 1049 .... Martinsville VA 24114-1049
313 271-2750 **Henry Ford Community College** 5101 Evergreen Rd .... Dearborn MI 48128-1495
    Fax: 313 845-9658
202 225-3831 **Henry Paul B (Rep - R - Michigan)** 215 Cannon Bldg ...... Washington DC 20515-0001
    Fax: Unlisted
202 225-3076 **Herger Wally (Rep - R - California)** 1108 Longworth Bldg .. Washington DC 20515-0001
    Fax: Unlisted
919 892-4268 **Heritage Bible College** PO Box 1628 .... Dunn NC 28334-1628
509 865-2244 **Heritage College** 3540 Fort Rd .... Toppenish WA 98948-0000
    Fax: 509 865-4469
315 867-1002 **Herkimer County** 109 Mary St .... Herkimer NY 13350-1921
315 866-0300 **Herkimer County Community College** Reservoir Rd .... Herkimer NY 13350-0000
    Fax: 315 866-7253
904 754-4000 **Hernando County** 20 N Main St .... Brooksville FL 34601-0000
    Fax: 904 799-3659
208 733-9554 **Herrett Museum** 315 Falls Ave College of Southern Idaho ...... Twin Falls ID 83303-1238
    Fax: 208 734-2362
202 225-6276 **Hertel Dennis M (Rep - D - Michigan)** 2442 Rayburn Bldg .. Washington DC 20515-0001
    Fax: 202 225-6209
919 358-7845 **Hertford County** King St .... Winton NC 27986-0000
316 327-4221 **Hesston College** PO Box 3000 .... Hesston KS 67062-9989
701 824-2545 **Hettinger County** 336 Pacific Ave .... Mott ND 58646-0000
212 674-6800 **HIAS (Hebrew Immigrant Aid Society)**
    200 Park Ave S 2nd Fl .... New York NY 10003-1503
    Fax: Unlisted
218 262-6700 **Hibbing Community College** 1515 E 25th St .... Hibbing MN 55746-3354
    Fax: 218 262-6717
808 449-2490 **Hickam Air Force Base** .... Honolulu HI 96853-0001
502 653-4369 **Hickman County** Courthouse Sq .... Clinton KY 42031-1295
615 729-2621 **Hickman County** Public Sq Rm 8 .... Centerville TN 37033-0000
417 745-6450 **Hickory County** Main & Polk Sts .... Hermitage MO 65668-0000
505 542-9213 **Hidalgo County** 300 S Shakespeare St .... Lordsburg NM 88045-1939
512 383-2751 **Hidalgo County** 100 N Closner St .... Edinburg TX 78539-3563
404 892-3600 **High Museum of Art** 1280 Peachtree St NE .... Atlanta GA 30309-3549
    Fax: 404 898-9578
303 356-4357 **High Plains Regional Library Service System**
    800 8th Ave Suite 341 .... Greeley CO 80631-1100
919 841-9000 **High Point College** PO Box HP-2 .... High Point NC 27261-1949
    Fax: 919 841-5123
815 235-6121 **Highland Community College** 2998 W Pearl City Rd .... Freeport IL 61032-9341
    Fax: 815 235-6130
913 442-3238 **Highland Community College** Hwy 36 W .... Highland KS 66035-0000
    Fax: 913 442-3599
513 393-1911 **Highland County** 114 Governor Foraker Pl .... Hillsboro OH 45133-1055
703 468-2447 **Highland County** Main St .... Monterey VA 24465-0000
313 252-0475 **Highland Park Community College** Glendale & 3rd Sts ... Highland Park MI 48203-3190
    Fax: 313 252-0397 Personnel
615 893-3380 **Highland Rim Regional Library Center**
    2102 Mercury Blvd .... Murfreesboro TN 37130-4098
    Fax: 615 895-6727
813 385-2581 **Highlands County** 430 S Commerce Ave .... Sebring FL 33870-3705
206 878-3710 **Highline Community College** PO Box 98000 .... Des Moines WA 98198-9800
    Fax: Call company operator
404 236-4600 **Hightower Sara Regional Library** 205 Riverside Pkwy .... Rome GA 30161-2913
    Fax: 404 236-4605
202 857-1200 **Highway Users Federation for Safety & Mobility**
    1776 Massachusetts Ave NW 5th Fl .... Washington DC 20036-1904
    Fax: 202 857-1220
716 649-7900 **Hilbert College** 5200 S Park Ave .... Hamburg NY 14075-1597
    Fax: 716 649-0702
801 777-7221 **Hill Air Force Base** .... Ogden UT 84056-0000
    Fax: 801 777-3358
406 265-5481 **Hill County** 315 4th St County Courthouse .... Havre MT 59501-3999
    Fax: 406 265-5487
817 582-2161 **Hill County** PO Box 398 .... Hillsboro TX 76645-0398
203 677-4787 **Hill-Stead Museum** 35 Mountain Rd .... Farmington CT 06032-2304
813 253-7000 **Hillsborough Community College** PO Box 31127 .... Tampa FL 33631-3127
    Fax: 813 253-7136
813 272-5000 **Hillsborough County** 419 N Pierce St .... Tampa FL 33602-4022
603 882-9471 **Hillsborough County** 19 Temple St .... Nashua NH 03060-3472
517 437-7341 **Hillsdale College** 33 E College St .... Hillsdale MI 49242-1298
    Fax: 517 437-3923
517 437-3391 **Hillsdale County** 29 N Howell St County Courthousee .... Hillsdale MI 49242-1865
405 794-6661 **Hillsdale Free Will Baptist College** PO Box 7208 .... Moore OK 73153-1208
803 785-9050 **Hilton Head Central Reservations** 3 Towne Ctr .... Hilton Head Island SC 29928-0000
601 857-5261 **Hinds Community College** Main St .... Raymond MS 39154-9778
    Fax: 601 857-3392
601 354-2327 *Utica Campus* Hwy 18 W .... Utica MS 39175-0000
    Fax: 601 885-6026
601 968-6501 **Hinds County** PO Box 686 .... Jackson MS 39205-0686
303 944-2225 **Hinsdale County** PO Box 277 .... Lake City CO 81235-0277
216 569-3211 **Hiram College** .... Hiram OH 44234-0000
    Fax: 216 569-5291
202 357-3091 **Hirshhorn Museum & Sculpture Garden (Smithsonian Institution)**
    Independence Ave & 8th St SW .... Washington DC 20560-0001
    Fax: 202 786-2682
504 523-4662 **Historic New Orleans Collection** 533 Royal St .... New Orleans LA 70130-2179

305 375-1492 **Historical Museum of Southern Florida** 101 W Flagler St ... Miami FL 33130-1538
Fax: 305 375-1609

314 361-1424 **History Museum** Jefferson Memorial Bldg Forest Pk ... Saint Louis MO 63112-1099

308 334-5646 **Hitchcock County** 229 E 'D' St ... Trenton NE 69044-0000

615 442-2001 **Hiwassee College** Hiwassee Rd ... Madisonville TN 37354-0000
Fax: 615 442-3520 Chapel

202 225-4155 **Hoagland Peter (Rep - D - Nebraska)**
1709 Longworth Bldg ... Washington DC 20515-0001
Fax: 202 225-4684

315 789-5500 **Hobart & William Smith Colleges** 337 Pulteney St ... Geneva NY 14456-0000
Fax: 315 781-3560 Library

407 546-5534 **Hobe Sound Bible College** PO Box 1065 ... Hobe Sound FL 33475-1065

202 225-4324 **Hobson David L (Rep - R - Ohio)** 1338 Longworth Bldg ... Washington DC 20515-0001
Fax: 202 225-1984

202 225-3826 **Hochbrueckner George J (Rep - D - New York)**
124 Cannon Bldg ... Washington DC 20515-0001
Fax: 202 225-0776

614 385-5195 **Hocking County** 1 E Main St ... Logan OH 43138-1207
Fax: Call company operator

614 753-3591 **Hocking Technical College** 3301 Hocking Pkwy ... Nelsonville OH 45764-9588
Fax: 614 753-4097

806 894-3185 **Hockley County** 800 Houston St Courthouse Box 13 ... Levelland TX 79336-0000

316 357-6421 **Hodgeman County** PO Box 247 ... Jetmore KS 67854-0247

516 560-6600 **Hofstra University** 1000 Fulton Ave ... Hempstead NY 11550-1009
Fax: 516 564-4296

516 560-5916 *School of Law* California Ave ... Hempstead NY 11550-0000
Fax: 516 560-7676

919 875-8751 **Hoke County** 227 N Main St ... Raeford NC 28376-0266
Fax: 919 875-2207 Library

202 224-6121 **Hollings Ernest F (Sen - D - South Carolina)**
125 Russell Bldg ... Washington DC 20510-0001
Fax: Unlisted

703 362-6000 **Hollins College** 7916 Williamson Rd ... Roanoke VA 24020-4410
Fax: 703 362-6642

505 479-7510 **Holloman Air Force Base** ... Alamogordo NM 88330-5000
Fax: 505 479-5908 PR

202 225-4926 **Holloway Clyde C (Rep - R - Louisiana)**
1206 Longworth Bldg ... Washington DC 20515-0001
Fax: 202 225-6252

601 472-2312 **Holmes Community College** PO Box 369 ... Goodman MS 39079-0369
Fax: 601 472-2566 Admin

904 547-2835 **Holmes County** 201 N Oklahoma St ... Bonifay FL 32425-2243
Fax: 904 547-4013

601 834-2508 **Holmes County** PO Box 239 ... Lexington MS 39095-0239

216 674-0286 **Holmes County** E Jackson St ... Millersburg OH 44654-1349

816 446-3303 **Holt County** 102 Nodaway St ... Oregon MO 64473-9643

402 336-1762 **Holt County** PO Box 329 ... O'Neill NE 68763-0329

203 635-5311 **Holy Apostles College & Seminary** 33 Prospect Hill Rd ... Cromwell CT 06416-2005

215 637-7700 **Holy Family College** Grant & Frankford Aves ... Philadelphia PA 19114-2094

415 436-1000 **Holy Names College** 3500 Mountain Blvd ... Oakland CA 94619-1627
Fax: 415 436-1199

Holy See: State of the Vatican City

202 333-7121 *Embassy* 3339 Massachusetts Ave NW ... Washington DC 20008-3610
Fax: 202 337-4036

212 734-2900 *Mission to the UN* 20 E 72nd St ... New York NY 10021-4106
Fax: 212 988-3633

413 538-7000 **Holyoke Community College** 303 Homestead Ave ... Holyoke MA 01040-1091
Fax: 413 534-8975

305 257-7113 **Homestead Air Force Base** ... Homestead FL 33039-5000
Fax: 305 257-6120

Honduras: Republic of Honduras

202 966-7702 *Embassy* 3007 Tilden St NW Pod 4M ... Washington DC 20008-0000
Fax: 202 966-9751

212 752-3370 *Mission to the UN* 866 UN Plaza Suite 417 ... New York NY 10017-0000
Fax: 212 223-0498

808 523-4385 **Honolulu City Hall** 530 S King St ... Honolulu HI 96813-3014
Fax: 808 523-4666 Admin

808 538-3693 **Honolulu Academy of Arts** 900 S Beretania St ... Honolulu HI 96814-1495
Fax: 808 521-6591

808 541-2481 **Honolulu Coast Guard Base** Sand Island Access Rd ... Honolulu HI 96819-0000

808 523-4141 **Honolulu County** 530 S King St ... Honolulu HI 96813-3014
Fax: Unlisted

808 949-5531 **Honolulu-Japanese Chamber of Commerce**
2454 S Beretania St ... Honolulu HI 96826-1502
Fax: 808 949-3020

301 663-3131 **Hood College** Rosemont Ave ... Frederick MD 21701-8599
Fax: 301 694-7653

817 579-3222 **Hood County** 101 Pearl St ... Granbury TX 76048-2498

603 646-2808 **Hood Museum of Art** Dartmouth College Wheelock St ... Hanover NH 03755-1812
Fax: 603 646-1400

503 386-3970 **Hood River County** 309 State St ... Hood River OR 97031-2037

308 546-2244 **Hooker County** PO Box 184 ... Mullen NE 69152-0184

616 392-5111 **Hope College** 141 E 12th St ... Holland MI 49423-0000
Fax: Unlisted

804 541-2243 **Hopewell (Independent City)** 300 N Main St ... Hopewell VA 23860-2740
Fax: 804 541-2318

502 821-8294 **Hopkins County** Main & Center ... Madisonville KY 42431-2064

903 885-3929 **Hopkins County** PO Box 288 ... Sulphur Springs TX 75482-0288

202 225-4706 **Hopkins Larry J (Rep - R - Kentucky)** 2437 Rayburn Bldg ... Washington DC 20515-0001
Fax: 202 225-1413

502 886-3921 **Hopkinsville Community College** PO Box 2100 ... Hopkinsville KY 42241-0000
Fax: 502 886-0237

202 225-2561 **Horn Joan Kelly (Rep - D - Missouri)**
1008 Longworth Bldg ... Washington DC 20515-0001
Fax: 202 225-1378

803 248-1200 **Horry County** PO Box 677 ... Conway SC 29526-0677

803 248-4898 **Horry County Memorial Library** 1008 5th Ave ... Conway SC 29526-5196

803 347-3186 **Horry-Georgetown Technical College** PO Box 1966 ... Conway SC 29526-1966
Fax: 803 347-4207

205 825-9232 **Horseshoe Bend Regional Library** 203 West St ... Dadeville AL 36853-1301
Fax: Unlisted

202 225-4916 **Horton Frank (Rep - R - New York)** 2108 Rayburn Bldg ... Washington DC 20515-0001
Fax: 202 225-5909

501 332-2261 **Hot Spring County** 3rd & Locust St ... Malvern AR 72104-0000

307 864-3515 **Hot Springs County** Arapahoe St ... Thermopolis WY 82443-2299
Fax: 307 864-5116

501 321-2277 **Hot Springs Tourist Information** 134 Convention Blvd ... Hot Springs AR 71901-4135

202 225-3161 **Houghton Amo (Rep - R - New York)**
1217 Longworth Bldg ... Washington DC 20515-0001
Fax: 202 225-5574

716 567-2211 **Houghton College** 1 Willard Ave ... Houghton NY 14744-0000
Fax: 716 567-9570

716 674-6363 *Buffalo Campus* 910 Union Rd ... West Seneca NY 14224-3499
Fax: Unlisted

906 482-1150 **Houghton County** 401 E Houghton Ave ... Houghton MI 49931-2016
Fax: 906 482-7238

203 579-6400 **Housatonic Community College** 510 Barnum Ave ... Bridgeport CT 06608-2408
Fax: 203 579-6993

202 225-2061 **House Administration Committee (US House of Representatives)**
Capitol Bldg Rm H-326 ... Washington DC 20515-0001
Fax: 202 225-4345

713 774-7661 **Houston Baptist University** 7502 Fondren Rd ... Houston TX 77074-3298
Fax: 713 995-3489

Houston City Government

713 247-1000 *City Hall* 901 Bagby St ... Houston TX 77002-2526
Fax: 713 247-2355

713 247-1840 *City Secretary* PO Box 1562 ... Houston TX 77251-0000

713 247-2087 *Department of Finance & Administration* 901 Bagby St ... Houston TX 77002-0000
Fax: 713 247-1860

713 658-4340 *Department of Traffic & Transportation*
500 Jefferson Suite 1600 ... Houston TX 77002-0000
Fax: 713 658-4382

713 247-2200 *Mayor's Office* 901 Bagby St ... Houston TX 77002-0000

713 247-5420 *Police Dept* 61 Riesner St ... Houston TX 77002-0000

713 247-2033 *Public Works Dept* 901 Bagby St ... Houston TX 77002-0000

713 481-0025 **Houston Coast Guard Air Station** 1178 Ellington Field ... Houston TX 77209-0001
Fax: 713 481-9628

713 869-5021 **Houston Community College** PO Box 7849 ... Houston TX 77270-7849
Fax: 713 869-5319

713 523-5050 **Houston Convention & Visitors Bureau** 3300 Main St ... Houston TX 77002-9319
Fax: 713 524-5376

205 677-4800 **Houston County** PO Box 6406 ... Dothan AL 36302-6406
Fax: 205 794-6633

912 922-4471 **Houston County** 200 Carl Vinson Pkwy ... Warner Robins GA 31088-5808
Fax: 912 923-5697

507 724-5211 **Houston County** 304 S Marshall St ... Caledonia MN 55921-1324
Fax: 507 724-5550

615 289-3141 **Houston County** PO Box 388 ... Erin TN 37061-0388

409 544-3256 **Houston County** PO Box 370 ... Crockett TX 75835-0370

713 639-4600 **Houston Museum of Natural Science** 1 Hermann Circle Dr ... Houston TX 77030-1799
Fax: 713 639-4635

713 236-1313 **Houston Public Library** 500 McKinney Ave ... Houston TX 77002-2534

301 992-4800 **Howard Community College** 10901 Little Patuxent Pkwy ... Columbia MD 21044-3197
Fax: 301 992-4803

501 845-5916 **Howard County** 421 N Main St ... Nashville AR 71852-2008

319 547-2661 **Howard County** 218 N Elm St ... Cresco IA 52136-1522

317 456-2204 **Howard County** Main & Sycamore ... Kokomo IN 46901-4543

301 992-2025 **Howard County** 3430 Courthouse Dr ... Ellicott City MD 21043-4300
Fax: 301 992-2125

816 248-2284 **Howard County** PO Box 551 ... Fayette MO 65248-0551

308 754-4343 **Howard County** 612 Indian St ... Saint Paul NE 68873-1642

915 263-7247 **Howard County** 300 Main St ... Big Spring TX 79720-2521

301 997-8000 **Howard County Central Library** 10375 Little Patuxent Pkwy ... Columbia MD 21044-3499
Fax: 301 997-4135

915 264-5000 **Howard County Junior College District** 1001 Birdwell Ln ... Big Spring TX 79720-3702
Fax: 915 264-5082

915 646-2502 **Howard Payne University** 1000 Fisk Ave ... Brownwood TX 76801-2715
Fax: 915 643-7835

202 636-6100 **Howard University** 2400 6th St NW ... Washington DC 20059-0001
Fax: 202 636-5960 Communications

202 806-6270 *College of Medicine* 520 W St NW ... Washington DC 20059-0001
Fax: 202 806-7934

202 806-6530 *College of Pharmacy & Pharmacal Sciences*
2300 4th St NW ... Washington DC 20059-0001

202 806-0100 *School of Dentistry* 600 W St NW ... Washington DC 20059-0001
Fax: 202 806-0354 Communications

202 806-8000 *School of Law*
2900 Van Ness St NW Houston Hall Rm 106 ... Washington DC 20008-1196
Fax: 202 806-8090

417 256-2591 **Howell County** County Courthouse Sq ... West Plains MO 65775-0000

202 225-4131 **Hoyer Steny H (Rep - D - Maryland)**
1214 Longworth Bldg ... Washington DC 20515-0001
Fax: 202 225-4300

202 225-3115 **Hubbard Carroll Jr (Rep - D - Kentucky)**
2267 Rayburn Bldg ... Washington DC 20515-0001
Fax: 202 225-1622

218 732-3196 **Hubbard County** 301 Court St ... Park Rapids MN 56470-1421

202 225-2376 **Huckaby Jerry (Rep - D - Louisiana)** 2182 Rayburn Bldg ... Washington DC 20515-0001
Fax: 202 225-2387

201 795-6000 **Hudson County** 595 Newark Ave ... Jersey City NJ 07306-2301
Fax: Call company operator

201 656-2020 **Hudson County Community College** 168 Sip Ave ... Jersey City NJ 07306-3009
Fax: 201 656-8961 Admin

317 545-1000 **Hudson Institute** 5395 Emerson Way ... Indianapolis IN 46226-1415
Fax: 317 545-9639

518 283-1100 **Hudson Valley Community College** 80 Vandenburgh Ave ... Troy NY 12180-6096
Fax: 518 270-7542

915 369-2301 **Hudspeth County** PO Box A ... Sierra Blanca TX 79851-0058

719 738-2370 **Huerfano County** 400 Main St ... Walsenburg CO 81089-2034

405 379-2746 **Hughes County** PO Box 914 ... Holdenville OK 74848-0914

605 773-3713 **Hughes County** 104 E Capitol Ave ... Pierre SD 57501-2563

202 225-6572 **Hughes William J (Rep - D - New Jersey)**
341 Cannon Bldg ... Washington DC 20515-0001
Fax: 202 226-1108

516 747-5400 **Human Resources Center** 201 IU Willetts Rd W ... Albertson NY 11507-1599
Fax: 516 746-3298

202 628-4160 **Human Rights Campaign Fund** 1012 14th St NW 6th Fl ... Washington DC 20005-3495
Fax: 202 347-5323

707 839-6115 **Humboldt Bay Coast Guard Air Station** ... McKenleyville CA 95521-9309

707 445-7258 **Humboldt County** 825 5th St ... Eureka CA 95501-1153

515 332-1806 **Humboldt County** County Courthouse ... Dakota City IA 50529-9999

702 623-6343 **Humboldt County** Bridge & 5th Sts ... Winnemucca NV 89445-3199

707 445-7284 **Humboldt County Library** 636 F St ... Eureka CA 95501-1012
Fax: Unlisted

707 826-3011 **Humboldt State University** Plaza Ave ... Arcata CA 95521-0000
Fax: 707 826-5555

209 478-0800 **Humphreys College** 6650 Inglewood Ave ... Stockton CA 95207-3896
Fax: 209 478-8721

601 247-1740 **Humphreys County** PO Box 547 ... Belzoni MS 39038-0547

615 296-7671 **Humphreys County** 102 Thompson St ... Waverly TN 37185-0000

202 463-5482 **Hungarian-US Business Council** 1615 H St NW 6th Fl ... Washington DC 20062-0001
Fax: 202 463-3114

Hungary: Republic of Hungary

202 362-6730 *Embassy* 3910 Shoemaker St NW ... Washington DC 20008-3811
Fax: 202 966-8135

212 535-8660 *Mission to the UN* 10 E 75th St ... New York NY 10021-2687
Fax: 212 734-6036

903 455-6460 **Hunt County** 2500 Lee St ... Greenville TX 75401-4246

202 225-5672 **Hunter Duncan (Rep - R - California)** 133 Cannon Bldg ... Washington DC 20515-0000
Fax: 202 225-0235

615 267-0968 **Hunter Museum of Art** 10 Bluff View ... Chattanooga TN 37403-1197

908 782-4300 **Hunterdon County** 71 Main St ....Flemington NJ 08822-1412
Fax: 908 782-4068
205 265-0511 **Huntingdon College** 1500 E Fairview Ave ....Montgomery AL 36194-6201
814 643-3091 **Huntingdon County** 223 Penn St ....Huntingdon PA 16652-1443
Fax: 814 643-8152
512 471-7324 **Huntington Archer M Art Gallery**
23rd & San Jacinto Sts University of Texas ....Austin TX 78712-0000
714 842-4481 **Huntington Beach Library** 7111 Talbert Ave ....Huntington Beach CA 92648-1296
Fax: 714 848-6783
219 356-6000 **Huntington College** 2303 College Ave ....Huntington IN 46750-1299
Fax: 219 356-9448
219 356-3122 **Huntington County** N Jefferson St ....Huntington IN 46750-0000
304 529-2701 **Huntington Museum of Art** 2033 McCoy Rd ....Huntington WV 25701-4999
205 535-4350 **Huntsville Museum of Art** 700 Monroe St SW ....Huntsville AL 35801-5523
205 532-5940 **Huntsville-Madison County Public Library** 915 Monroe St .... Huntsville AL 35801-5007
Fax: 205 532-5994
517 269-9942 **Huron County** 250 E Huron Ave ....Bad Axe MI 48413-1317
419 668-3092 **Huron County** 2 E Main St ....Norwalk OH 44857-0000
605 352-8721 **Huron University** 333 9th St SW ....Huron SD 57350-2798
Fax: 605 352-7421
207 947-1121 **Husson College** 1 College Cir ....Bangor ME 04401-2999
Fax: 207 947-6024
512 476-7421 **Huston-Tillotson College** 1820 E 8th St ....Austin TX 78702-2762
Fax: 512 474-0762
316 665-3500 **Hutchinson Community College** 1300 N Plum St ....Hutchinson KS 67501-5894
Fax: 316 665-3310
605 387-5335 **Hutchinson County** PO Box 7 ....Olivet SD 57052-0007
806 878-2829 **Hutchinson County** PO Box F ....Stinnett TX 79083-0526
202 225-4136 **Hutto Earl (Rep - D - Florida)** 2435 Rayburn Bldg ....Washington DC 20515-0001
Fax: 202 225-5785
518 792-1761 **Hyde Collection** 161 Warren St ....Glens Falls NY 12801-4520
919 926-5711 **Hyde County** 264 Business Hwy ....Swan Quarter NC 27885-0000
Fax: 919 926-2040
605 852-2512 **Hyde County** PO Box 306 ....Highmore SD 57345-0306
202 225-4561 **Hyde Henry J (Rep - R - Illinois)** 2262 Rayburn Bldg ....Washington DC 20515-0001
Fax: 202 226-1240

I

318 365-8246 **Iberia Parish** 300 Iberia St Suite 400 ....New Iberia LA 70560-4543
504 687-5160 **Iberville Parish** PO Box 423 ....Plaquemine LA 70765-0423
Iceland: Republic of Iceland
202 265-6653 *Embassy* 2022 Connecticut Ave NW ....Washington DC 20008-6131
Fax: 202 265-6656
212 686-4100 *Mission to the UN* 370 Lexington Ave Suite 505 ....New York NY 10017-6503
Fax: 212 532-4138
712 364-2628 **Ida County** 401 Moorehead St ....Ida Grove IA 51445-1429
208 983-2751 **Idaho County** 320 W Main St ....Grangeville ID 83530-1948
Fax: 208 983-2376
208 236-3168 **Idaho Museum of Natural History** Idaho State University ....Pocatello ID 83209-0001
Fax: 208 236-4000
208 343-6405 **Idaho Republican State Committee** 612 W Hays St ....Boise ID 83702-5511
Fax: 208 343-6414
208 336-1815 **Idaho State Democratic Party** 1020 W Franklin St ....Boise ID 83702-5466
Idaho State Government
208 334-2411 *Information* 650 W State St Rm 100 ....Boise ID 83720-0001
Fax: 208 334-5315
208 334-3356 *Archives & Records* 610 N Julia Davis Dr ....Boise ID 83702-7646
208 334-2400 *Attorney General* State Capitol Rm 210 ....Boise ID 83720-0001
Fax: 208 334-2530
208 334-5898 *Bureau of Air Quality* 1410 N Hilton ....Boise ID 83706-0000
Fax: 208 334-0417
208 334-3460 *Bureau of Disaster Services* 650 W State St ....Boise ID 83720-0000
Fax: Call company operator
208 334-3233 *Bureau of Occupational Licenses* 2417 Bank Dr Rm 312 ....Boise ID 83705-2578
208 334-5976 *Bureau of Vital Statistics Standards & Local Health Services*
450 W State St ....Boise ID 83720-0001
208 334-2318 *Commission for Pardons & Paroles*
1075 Park Blvd State House Mail ....Boise ID 83720-0001
Fax: 208 334-2443
208 334-2119 *Commission on the Arts* 304 W State St ....Boise ID 83720-0001
208 334-2424 *Consumer Protection Unit* State Capitol Bldg Rm 210 ....Boise ID 83720-0001
Fax: 208 334-2530
208 334-3240 *Department of Agriculture* 2270 Old Penitentiary Rd ....Boise ID 83712-8298
Fax: 208 334-2170
208 334-2470 *Department of Commerce* 700 W State St 2nd Fl ....Boise ID 83720-0001
Fax: 208 334-2631
208 334-2318 *Department of Corrections* 1075 Park Blvd ....Boise ID 83720-0001
Fax: 208 334-2443
208 334-3301 *Department of Education* 650 W State St ....Boise ID 83720-0001
Fax: 208 334-2228
208 334-6200 *Department of Employment* 317 Main St ....Boise ID 83735-0000
Fax: 208 334-6430
208 334-3313 *Department of Finance* 700 W State St ....Boise ID 83720-0001
Fax: 208 334-2216
208 334-5500 *Department of Health & Welfare* 450 W State St ....Boise ID 83720-0000
Fax: 208 334-5694
208 334-2250 *Department of Insurance* 500 S 10th St ....Boise ID 83720-0001
Fax: 208 334-2298
208 334-2327 *Department of Labor & Industrial Services* 277 N 6th St ....Boise ID 83720-0001
208 334-3284 *Department of Lands* State Capitol Bldg Rm 121 ....Boise ID 83720-0001
Fax: 208 334-2339
208 334-3560 *Department of Revenue & Taxation* 700 W State St ....Boise ID 83702-5822
Fax: 208 334-7844
208 327-7900 *Department of Water Resources* 1301 N Orchard ....Boise ID 83720-0000
Fax: 208 327-7666
208 334-5839 *Division of Environmental Quality* 1410 N Hilton St ....Boise ID 83706-1255
Fax: 208 334-0417
208 334-8300 *Division of Highways* PO Box 8028 ....Boise ID 83707-2028
Fax: 208 334-8321
208 334-3453 *Division of Public Works* 502 N 4th St ....Boise ID 83720-0001
Fax: 208 334-4031
208 334-2465 *Division of Purchasing* 801 Reserve St ....Boise ID 83720-0001
Fax: 208 334-5320
208 334-2100 *Governor* 700 W Jefferson State House ....Boise ID 83720-0001
Fax: 208 334-2175
208 336-0740 *Idaho State Correctional Institution* PO Box 14 ....Boise ID 83707-0014
208 334-6000 *Industrial Commission* 317 Main St ....Boise ID 83720-0001
Fax: 208 334-2321
208 334-2200 *Lieutenant Governor* Jefferson & Capitol Blvd State House ....Boise ID 83720-0001
208 334-0300 *Public Utilities Commission* 472 W Washington St ....Boise ID 83702-5983
Fax: 208 334-3762
208 334-3285 *Real Estate Commission* 633 N 4th St ....Boise ID 83702-4500

208 334-2300 *Secretary of State* State House Rm 203 ....Boise ID 83720-0001
Fax: 208 334-2282
208 334-3684 *Securities Bureau* 700 W State St ....Boise ID 83720-0001
Fax: 208 343-2216
208 334-2270 *State Board of Education* 650 W State St Rm 307 ....Boise ID 83720-0001
Fax: 208 334-2632
208 334-5731 *State Economic Opportunity Office* 450 W State St ....Boise ID 83720-0001
Fax: 208 334-5817
208 334-2503 *State Police* PO Box 55 ....Boise ID 83707-0055
Fax: 208 334-2585
208 334-2210 *Supreme Court* 451 W State St ....Boise ID 83720-0001
Fax: 208 334-2616
208 334-8000 *Transportation Dept* 3311 W State St ....Boise ID 83703-5881
Fax: 208 334-3858
208 334-3200 *Treasurer* State Capitol Bldg Rm 102 ....Boise ID 83720-0001
Fax: Unlisted
208 334-2120 **Idaho State Historical Museum** 610 N Julia Davis Dr ....Boise ID 83702-7695
208 334-2150 **Idaho State Library** 325 W State St ....Boise ID 83702-6055
Fax: 208 334-4016
208 236-0211 **Idaho State University** 741 S 7th St ....Pocatello ID 83209-0001
Fax: 208 236-4000
208 236-2175 *College of Pharmacy* Campus Box 8288 ....Pocatello ID 83209-0001
Fax: 208 236-4482
208 334-2017 **Idaho Tourism Div** 700 W State St 2nd Fl ....Boise ID 83720-0001
Fax: 208 334-2631
213 470-2293 **IHC Center** 10951 W Pico Blvd ....Los Angeles CA 90064-2126
Fax: 213 441-9244
708 960-1500 **Illinois Benedictine College** 5700 College Rd ....Lisle IL 60532-2851
Fax: 708 960-1126 Library
309 694-5011 **Illinois Central College East Campus** 1 College Dr ....Peoria IL 61635-0001
Fax: 309 694-5473
217 245-3000 **Illinois College** 1101 W College Ave ....Jacksonville IL 62650-2299
Fax: 217 245-3034
312 225-1700 **Illinois College of Optometry** 3241 S Michigan Ave ....Chicago IL 60616-3816
Fax: 312 225-1724
312 464-1900 **Illinois Democratic Party** 13126 Merchandise Mart ....Chicago IL 60654-0000
Fax: 312 464-1907
618 393-2982 **Illinois Eastern Community College (System)** 233 E Chestnut St .. Olney IL 62450-2227
Fax: 618 392-4816
312 567-3000 **Illinois Institute of Technology** 3300 S Federal St ....Chicago IL 60616-3732
Fax: 312 567-8828
312 567-3900 *West Campus* 600 S Lambert Rd ....Glen Ellyn IL 60137-6598
Fax: 708 790-1826 Admin
309 745-8927 **Illinois Missionary Baptist Institute** 209 Vohland St ....Washington IL 61571-1933
217 525-0011 **Illinois State Central Republican Party** 223 S 3rd St ....Springfield IL 62701-1144
Fax: 217 753-4712
312 372-7373 **Illinois State Chamber of Commerce** 20 N Wacker Dr ....Chicago IL 60606-3084
Fax: 312 372-7382
Illinois State Government
217 782-2000 *Information* 501 S 2nd St Rm 176 ....Springfield IL 62706-0001
217 782-2172 *Agriculture Dept* 8th & Sangamon St State Fairgrounds ....Springfield IL 62794-0000
Fax: 217 785-4505
312 814-6750 *Arts Council* 100 W Randolph St Suite 10-500 ....Chicago IL 60601-3220
217 782-1090 *Attorney General* 500 S 2nd St ....Springfield IL 62706-0001
Fax: 217 782-7046
217 782-2551 *Board of Higher Education* 4 W Old State Capitol Plaza .....Springfield IL 62701-1214
217 782-8725 *Capital Development Board*
401 S Spring St William G Stratton Bldg 3rd Fl ....Springfield IL 62706-0001
Fax: 217 782-8625
217 782-9011 *Consumer Protection Div* 500 S 2nd St ....Springfield IL 62706-0001
Fax: 217 782-7046
312 793-8550 *Criminal Justice Authority* 120 S Riverside Plaza Suite 1016 .. Chicago IL 60606-3910
Fax: 312 793-8422
217 782-2141 *Department of Central Management Services*
715 William G Stratton Bldg 7th Fl ....Springfield IL 62706-0001
Fax: 217 782-0781
217 782-7500 *Department of Commerce & Community Affairs*
620 E Adams St ....Springfield IL 62701-1615
Fax: 217 785-6454
217 522-2666 *Department of Corrections* 1301 Concordia Ct ....Springfield IL 62702-5699
Fax: 217 522-5089
312 793-5700 *Department of Employment Security* 401 S State St ....Chicago IL 60605-0000
Fax: 312 793-9306
217 785-2800 *Department of Energy & Natural Resources*
325 W Adams St 3rd Fl ....Springfield IL 62704-0000
Fax: 217 785-2618
217 782-4515 *Department of Insurance* 320 W Washington St ....Springfield IL 62767-0001
Fax: 217 782-5020
217 782-6206 *Department of Labor* 1 W Old State Capitol Plaza 3rd Fl .... Springfield IL 62701-1217
Fax: 217 782-0596
217 782-6791 *Department of Mines & Minerals*
300 W Jefferson St Suite 300 ....Springfield IL 62791-0000
Fax: 217 524-4819
217 785-9900 *Department of Nuclear Safety* 1035 Outer Park Dr ....Springfield IL 62704-0000
Fax: 217 782-9762
217 785-0800 *Department of Professional Regulation*
320 W Washington St 3rd Fl ....Springfield IL 62786-0001
Fax: 217 782-7645
217 782-4977 *Department of Public Health* 535 W Jefferson St ....Springfield IL 62761-0000
Fax: 217 782-3987
217 785-2602 *Department of Revenue* 101 W Jefferson St ....Springfield IL 62702-5145
Fax: 217 782-4217
217 785-4941 *Department of Securities* 900 S Spring St ....Springfield IL 62704-2725
217 782-2841 *Department of State Police* 103 Armory Bldg ....Springfield IL 62706-0001
Fax: 217 785-2821
217 782-5597 *Department of Transportation* 2300 S Dirksen Pkwy ....Springfield IL 62764-0001
Fax: 217 782-1927
217 782-7326 *Division of Air Pollution Control* 1340 N 9th St ....Springfield IL 62702-0000
Fax: 217 782-2465
217 782-2151 *Division of Highways* 2300 S Dirksen Pkwy ....Springfield IL 62764-0001
Fax: 217 782-6828
217 782-7756 *Division of Oil & Gas* 300 W Jefferson St Suite 300 ....Springfield IL 62791-0000
Fax: 217 524-4819
312 793-4240 *Division of Unemployment Insurance* 401 S State St ....Chicago IL 60605-1225
Fax: 312 793-9306
217 782-6553 *Division of Vital Records* 605 W Jefferson St ....Springfield IL 62702-5035
Fax: Unlisted
217 782-2152 *Division of Water Resources* 2300 S Dirksen Pkwy ....Springfield IL 62764-0001
Fax: 217 785-5014
217 782-7860 *Emergency Services & Disaster Agency* 110 E Adams St .. Springfield IL 62706-0001
Fax: 217 782-2589
217 782-3397 *Environmental Protection Agency* 2200 Churchill Rd ....Springfield IL 62702-3406
Fax: 217 782-9039
217 782-6830 *Governor* 207 State House ....Springfield IL 62706-0001
Fax: 217 782-3560
312 814-6500 *Industrial Commission* 100 W Randolph St ....Chicago IL 60601-3275

217 782-7884 *Lieutenant Governor* 214 State House .... Springfield IL 62706-0001
   Fax: 217 524-6262
618 826-5071 *Menard Correctional Center* Kaskaskia St .... Menard IL 62259-9999
   Fax: Ext 245
217 782-2654 *Office of Planning* 107 Stratton Bldg .... Springfield IL 62706-0001
   Fax: 217 782-6620
217 782-7273 *Prisoner Review Board* 319 E Madison St Suite A .... Springfield IL 62701-1096
217 782-4705 *Procurement Services Div* 801 Stratton Office Bldg .... Springfield IL 62706-0001
   Fax: 217 782-5187
217 782-7892 *Public Utility Div* 527 E Capitol Ave 3rd Fl .... Springfield IL 62701-1827
   Fax: 217 782-1042
217 785-0800 *Real Estate Commission* 320 W Washington St .... Springfield IL 62786-0001
   Fax: 217 782-7645
217 782-2201 *Secretary of State* 213 State House Capitol Bldg Rm 213 .. Springfield IL 62756-0001
   Fax: 217 785-0358
217 782-7203 *State Appellate Defender's Office* PO Box 5780 .... Springfield IL 62705-0000
   Fax: 217 782-5385
217 782-4682 *State Archives* Archives Bldg .... Springfield IL 62756-0001
217 782-2221 *State Board of Education* 100 N 1st St .... Springfield IL 62777-0001
   Fax: 217 782-0679
815 727-3607 *Stateville Correctional Center* PO Box 112 .... Joliet IL 60434-0112
   Fax: Call company operator
217 782-2035 *Supreme Court* Supreme Court Bldg .... Springfield IL 62706-0001
   Fax: 217 782-3520
217 782-2211 *Treasurer* State Capitol Rm 219 .... Springfield IL 62706-0001
   Fax: 217 785-2777
217 782-2994 **Illinois State Library** 300 S 2nd St .... Springfield IL 62701-0000
   Fax: 217 785-4326
217 782-7386 **Illinois State Museum** Spring & Edwards Sts .... Springfield IL 62706-0001
   Fax: 217 782-1254
309 438-2111 **Illinois State University** .... Normal IL 61761-6901
   Fax: 309 438-5748
309 438-8800 *Museum* Illinois State University .... Normal IL 61761-6901
312 793-2094 **Illinois Tourist Informational Center** 310 S Michigan .... Chicago IL 60604-4287
   Fax: 312 793-1601
815 224-2720 **Illinois Valley Community College** 2578 E 350th Rd .... Oglesby IL 61348-1074
   Fax: 815 224-3033
309 556-3131 **Illinois Wesleyan University** PO Box 2900 .... Bloomington IL 61702-2900
   Fax: 309 556-3411
215 647-4400 **Immaculata College** .... Immaculata PA 19345-9999
715 834-3301 **Immanuel Lutheran College** 501 Grover Rd .... Eau Claire WI 54701-7199
202 514-4316 **Immigration & Naturalization Service**
   425 I St NW Rm 7016 .... Washington DC 20536-0001
   Fax: 202 633-3296
202 633-1689 *US Border Patrol* 425 I St NW Rm 6023 .... Washington DC 20536-0001
   Fax: 202 633-3296
802 951-6223 *Eastern Region* Elmwood Ave Federal Bldg .... Burlington VT 05401-0000
612 725-3850 *Northern Region* Fort Snelling Federal Bldg .... Twin Cities MN 55111-0000
214 767-7010 *Southern Region* 311 N Stemmons Fwy .... Dallas TX 75207-4324
   Fax: 903 729-7491
714 643-4775 *Western Region* 24000 Avila Rd .... Laguna Niguel CA 92607-0000
318 439-3797 **Imperial Calcasieu Museum** 204 W Sallier St .... Lake Charles LA 70601-5844
619 339-4256 **Imperial County** 852 Broadway .... El Centro CA 92243-2312
   Fax: 619 352-7876
619 352-8320 **Imperial Valley College** PO Box 158 .... Imperial CA 92251-0158
   Fax: 619 355-2663
512 828-1261 **Incarnate Word College** 4301 Broadway .... San Antonio TX 78209-6398
   Fax: 512 829-1220
316 331-4100 **Independence Community College**
   Brookside Dr & College Ave .... Independence KS 67301-3791
   Fax: 316 331-5344
501 793-8800 **Independence County** 192 E Main St .... Batesville AR 72501-5510
   Fax: Unlisted
202 628-4321 **Independent Action Inc** 1511 K St NW Suite 619 .... Washington DC 20005-1401
   Fax: 202 628-3367
214 337-3144 **Independent Baptist College** 3940 Blue Ridge .... Dallas TX 78233-0000
202 223-8100 **Independent Sector** 1828 L St NW Suite 1200 .... Washington DC 20036-5107
   Fax: 202 457-0609
India: Republic of India
202 939-7000 *Embassy* 2107 Massachusetts Ave NW .... Washington DC 20008-2811
   Fax: 202 939-7027
212 751-0900 *Mission to the UN* 866 UN Plaza Suite 505 .... New York NY 10017-0000
   Fax: 212 751-1393
312 781-6280 *Chicago Consulate General* 150 N Michigan Ave Suite 1100 .. Chicago IL 60601-7524
   Fax: 312 781-6269
212 879-7800 *New York Consulate General* 3 E 64th St .... New York NY 10021-7097
   Fax: 212 988-6423
415 668-0662 *San Francisco Consulate General* 540 Arguello Blvd .... San Francisco CA 94118-3203
   Fax: 415 668-2073
515 856-2143 **Indian Hills Community College** 721 N 1st St .... Centerville IA 52544-0000
   Fax: Unlisted
407 468-4700 **Indian River Community College** 3209 Virginia Ave .... Fort Pierce FL 34981-5599
407 567-8000 **Indian River County** 1840 25th St .... Vero Beach FL 32960-3416
   Fax: 407 567-9323
904 243-6521 **Indian Temple Mound Museum**
   139 Miraclestrip Pkwy SE .... Fort Walton Beach FL 32548-5817
412 465-3800 **Indiana County** 825 Philadelphia St .... Indiana PA 15701-3934
317 231-7100 **Indiana Democratic State Committee** 1 N Capitol .... Indianapolis IN 46206-0000
   Fax: 317 231-7129
317 232-8860 **Indiana Dept of Commerce Tourism & Film Development Div**
   1 N Capitol Ave Suite 700 .... Indianapolis IN 46204-2026
   Fax: 317 232-4146
219 422-5561 **Indiana Institute of Technology** 1600 E Washington Blvd .... Fort Wayne IN 46803-1297
   Fax: 219 422-7696
317 635-7561 **Indiana Republican Center** 200 S Meridian St Suite 400 ... Indianapolis IN 46225-0000
   Fax: 317 632-8510
317 634-6407 **Indiana State Chamber of Commerce**
   1 N Capitol Suite 200 .... Indianapolis IN 46204-2248
   Fax: 317 264-6855
Indiana State Government
317 232-1000 *Information* 100 N Senate Ave .... Indianapolis IN 46204-2208
317 232-8770 *Agriculture Div* 1 N Capitol Ave Suite 600 .... Indianapolis IN 46204-2026
   Fax: 317 232-8766
317 232-3661 *Archives Div Commission on Public Records*
   100 N Senate Ave Rm 117 .... Indianapolis IN 46204-0000
317 232-1286 *Arts Commission* 47 S Pennsylvania St 6th Fl .... Indianapolis IN 46204-3663
317 232-6201 *Attorney General* 219 State House .... Indianapolis IN 46204-0000
   Fax: 317 232-7979
317 232-5610 *Budget Agency* 100 N Senate St State House Rm 212 .. Indianapolis IN 46204-0000
812 254-1040 *Bureau of Mines & Mining Safety* 6 NE 21st St .... Washington IN 47501-3134
317 232-1900 *Commission for Higher Education*
   101 W Ohio St Suite 550 .... Indianapolis IN 46204-1971
   Fax: 317 232-1899
317 232-6201 *Consumer Protection Div* 219 State House .... Indianapolis IN 46204-0000
   Fax: 317 232-7979

317 232-3114 *Department of Administration* 100 N Senate Ave Rm 508 Indianapolis IN 46204-2215
   Fax: 317 232-7132
317 232-8801 *Department of Commerce* 1 N Capitol Ave Suite 700 ...... Indianapolis IN 46204-2026
   Fax: 317 232-4146
317 232-5766 *Department of Corrections*
   100 N Senate Ave State Office Bldg Suite 804 ... Indianapolis IN 46204-0000
   Fax: 317 232-6798
317 232-6610 *Department of Education* 229 State House .... Indianapolis IN 46204-2798
   Fax: 317 232-8004
317 232-7670 *Department of Employment & Training Services*
   100 N Senate Ave .... Indianapolis IN 46204-2201
   Fax: 317 232-6950
317 232-3210 *Department of Environmental Management*
   105 S Meridian St .... Indianapolis IN 46225-0000
   Fax: 317 232-3403
317 232-2385 *Department of Insurance*
   311 W Washington St Suite 300 .... Indianapolis IN 46204-2720
   Fax: 317 237-4949
317 232-2663 *Department of Labor*
   100 N Senate Ave State Office Bldg Rm 1013 .... Indianapolis IN 46204-0000
317 232-4020 *Department of Natural Resources*
   State Office Bldg Rm 608 .... Indianapolis IN 46204-0000
   Fax: 317 232-8036
317 232-2101 *Department of Revenue* 100 N Senate Ave .... Indianapolis IN 46204-2253
   Fax: 317 232-1021
317 232-5115 *Department of Transportation* 100 N Senate Ave .... Indianapolis IN 46204-2208
   Fax: 317 232-0238
317 232-8940 *Division of Energy Policy* 1 N Capitol St .... Indianapolis IN 46204-2026
   Fax: 317 232-8995
317 633-0147 *Division of Industrial Hygiene & Radiological Health*
   1330 W Michigan St .... Indianapolis IN 46206-0000
   Fax: 317 633-0776
317 232-4055 *Division of Oil & Gas*
   309 W Washington St Old Trails Bldg Suite 601 .... Indianapolis IN 46204-2721
317 232-4161 *Division of Water* 2475 Directors Row .... Indianapolis IN 46241-4938
   Fax: 317 241-8771
317 232-3830 *Emergency Management Agency*
   100 N Senate Ave Rm 90B .... Indianapolis IN 46204-2252
   Fax: 317 232-4987
317 232-4567 *Governor* 206 State House .... Indianapolis IN 46204-0000
   Fax: 317 232-3443
219 874-7258 *Indiana State Prison* PO Box 41 .... Michigan City IN 46360-0440
   Fax: Call company operator
317 232-4545 *Lieutenant Governor* 333 State House .... Indianapolis IN 46201-0000
   Fax: 317 232-4788
317 232-8222 *Office of Air Management* 105 S Meridian St Rm 201 .... Indianapolis IN 46225-1016
   Fax: 317 233-3257
317 232-4454 *Office of Solid & Hazardous Waste Management*
   105 S Meridian St .... Indianapolis IN 46225-0000
   Fax: 317 232-3403
317 232-5726 *Parole Services Section*
   100 N Senate Ave State Office Bldg Suite 804 .... Indianapolis IN 46204-2218
   Fax: 317 232-5728
317 232-3032 *Procurement Div* 100 N Senate Ave .... Indianapolis IN 46204-2208
317 232-2980 *Professional Licensing Agency* 100 N Senate Ave .... Indianapolis IN 46204-2208
   Fax: 317 232-2312
317 232-2490 *Public Defender Council* 309 W Washington St Suite 401 Indianapolis IN 46204-2700
   Fax: 317 232-5524
317 633-8512 *Public Health Statistics* 1330 W Michigan St Rm 332 ..... Indianapolis IN 46206-0000
   Fax: 317 633-0776
317 232-3000 *Public Works Div* 100 N Senate Ave Rm 510 .... Indianapolis IN 46204-2215
   Fax: 317 232-0748
317 232-6531 *Secretary of State* 201 State House .... Indianapolis IN 46204-0000
   Fax: 317 637-8270
317 232-6681 *Securities Div* 1 N Capitol St Suite 560 .... Indianapolis IN 46204-2227
   Fax: 317 637-8270
317 633-8400 *State Board of Health* 1330 W Michigan St .... Indianapolis IN 46202-2874
   Fax: 317 633-0779
317 232-8241 *State Police* 100 N Senate Ave Rm 301 .... Indianapolis IN 46204-2259
   Fax: 317 232-5682
317 232-1930 *Supreme Court* 217 State House .... Indianapolis IN 46204-0000
   Fax: 317 232-8365
317 232-6386 *Treasurer* 242 State House .... Indianapolis IN 46204-0000
   Fax: 317 232-5656
317 232-8087 *Unemployment Insurance* 10 N Senate Ave .... Indianapolis IN 46204-2277
   Fax: 317 232-6950
317 232-2700 *Utility Regulatory Commission* 913 State Office Bldg ..... Indianapolis IN 46204-0000
   Fax: 317 232-6758
219 785-2511 *Westville Correctional Center* 1100 W County Rd .... Westville IN 46391-0000
   Fax: Ext 472
317 232-3675 **Indiana State Library** 140 N Senate Ave .... Indianapolis IN 46204-2207
   Fax: 317 232-3728
317 232-1637 **Indiana State Museum** 202 N Alabama St .... Indianapolis IN 46204-2185
812 237-6311 **Indiana State University** 217 N 6th St .... Terre Haute IN 47809-0001
   Fax: 812 237-4292 Admin
812 332-0211 **Indiana University** 813 E 3rd St .... Bloomington IN 47405-0001
   Fax: 812 855-5678
812 855-5445 *Art Museum* 7th St Fine Arts Plaza .... Bloomington IN 47405-0001
   Fax: 812 855-5678
812 855-9343 *Department of Microbiology* Jordan Hall Rm 127 .... Bloomington IN 47405-0001
   Fax: 812 855-6705
812 855-3973 *Department of Physics* Swain W Rm 132 .... Bloomington IN 47405-0001
317 966-8261 *East Campus* 2325 Chester Blvd .... Richmond IN 47374-1289
   Fax: 317 973-8315
812 855-7323 *Graduate School of Biology* Jordan Hall Rm 142 .... Bloomington IN 47405-0001
   Fax: 812 855-6705
812 855-8006 *Graduate School of Business* 10th & Feelane St .... Bloomington IN 47405-0000
   Fax: 812 855-8679
812 855-2068 *Graduate School of Chemistry*
   Department of Chemistry Chemistry Bldg .... Bloomington IN 47405-0001
   Fax: 812 855-8300
317 453-2000 *Kokomo Campus* 2300 S Washington St .... Kokomo IN 46904-0000
   Fax: 317 455-9276
812 855-8028 *Libraries* 10th & Jordan Sts .... Bloomington IN 47405-0000
219 980-6500 *Northwest Campus* 3400 Broadway .... Gary IN 46408-1197
   Fax: 219 980-6670 Admin
317 274-8191 *School of Dentistry* 1121 W Michigan St .... Indianapolis IN 46202-5211
   Fax: 317 274-2419
812 855-9247 *School of Journalism* Ernie Pyle Hall Rm 200 .... Bloomington IN 47405-0001
   Fax: 812 855-3393
317 274-8157 *School of Medicine* 1120 South Dr .... Indianapolis IN 46202-5135
   Fax: 317 274-5276
812 855-4447 *School of Optometry* 800 E Atwater Ave .... Bloomington IN 47405-3680
   Fax: 812 855-6616

317 274-4656 *School of Public & Environmental Affairs*
801 W Michigan BS-3027 .... Indianapolis IN 46202-5152
Fax: 317 274-3753

219 237-4111 *South Bend Campus* 1700 Mishawaka Ave .... South Bend IN 46634-0000
Fax: 219 237-4599 Admin

812 945-2731 *Southeast Campus* 4201 Grant Line Rd .... New Albany IN 47150-6405
Fax: Ext 693 Purchasing

Indiana University Bloomington
812 855-5582 *Department of Geology* 1005 E 10th St Rm 129 .... Bloomington IN 47405-0001
Fax: 812 855-7899

812 855-7995 *School of Law* 3rd St & Indiana Ave .... Bloomington IN 47405-0000
Fax: 812 855-0555 Dean

317 274-8523 **Indiana University Indianapolis School of Law**
735 W New York St .... Indianapolis IN 46202-5222
Fax: 317 274-8825

412 357-2230 **Indiana University of Pennsylvania** 216B Pratt Hall .... Indiana PA 15705-0001
Fax: 412 357-2685 Personnel

219 481-6100 **Indiana University-Purdue University at Fort Wayne**
2101 E Coliseum Blvd .... Fort Wayne IN 46805-1445
Fax: 219 481-6880

317 274-5555 **Indiana University-Purdue University at Indianapolis**
425 University Blvd .... Indianapolis IN 46202-5148
Fax: 317 274-4615

Indiana Vocational Technical College
317 921-4882 *Central Indiana Campus* 1 W 26th St .... Indianapolis IN 46208-4777
Fax: 317 921-4753

812 372-9925 *Columbus Campus* 4475 Central Ave .... Columbus IN 47203-1868
Fax: Ext 21

317 289-2291 *East Central Campus* 4301 S Cowan Rd .... Muncie IN 47302-9448
Fax: Call company operator

317 459-0561 *Kokomo Campus* 1815 E Morgan St .... Kokomo IN 46901-2548
Fax: Ext 19 Admin

317 477-7401 *Lafayette Campus* 3208 Ross Rd .... Lafayette IN 47905-5217
Fax: Ext 204 Admin

219 289-7001 *North Central Campus* 1534 W Sample St .... South Bend IN 46619-3837
Fax: Ext 295

219 482-9171 *Northeast Campus* 3800 N Anthony Blvd .... Fort Wayne IN 46805-1489
Fax: 219 480-4177

219 981-1111 *Northwest Campus* 1440 E 35th Ave .... Gary IN 46409-1499
Fax: Ext 212

812 246-3301 *South Central Campus* 8204 Hwy 311 .... Sellersburg IN 47172-1829
Fax: 812 246-9905

812 265-2579 *Southeast Campus* Ivy Tech Dr & Hwy 62 .... Madison IN 47250-0000
Fax: 812 265-2580

812 426-2865 *Southwest Campus* 3501 N 1st Ave .... Evansville IN 47710-3319
Fax: 812 429-1483

812 299-1121 *Wabash Valley Campus* 7377 S Dixie Bee Rd .... Terre Haute IN 47802-4845
Fax: Ext 325

317 966-2656 *Whitewater Campus* 2325 Chester Blvd .... Richmond IN 47374-1289
Fax: Call company operator

317 674-6901 **Indiana Wesleyan University** 4201 S Washington St .... Marion IN 46953-4999
Fax: 317 677-2499

317 236-3200 **Indianapolis City Hall** 200 E Washington St .... Indianapolis IN 46204-3307
Fax: 317 236-3980

317 923-1331 **Indianapolis Museum of Art** 1200 W 38th St .... Indianapolis IN 46208-4196
Fax: 317 926-8931

317 269-1700 **Indianapolis-Marion County Public Library** PO Box 211 .... Indianapolis IN 46206-0211
Fax: 317 269-1768

715 839-5082 **Indianhead Federated Library System** 3301 Golf Rd .... Eau Claire WI 54701-8017

312 621-1200 **Indo-American Chamber of Commerce**
19 S La Salle St Suite 200 .... Chicago IL 60603-1402
Fax: 312 621-0740

Indonesia: Republic of Indonesia
202 775-5200 *Embassy* 2020 Massachusetts Ave NW .... Washington DC 20036-1083
Fax: 202 775-5365

212 972-8333 *Mission to the UN* 325 E 38th St .... New York NY 10016-2745
Fax: 212 972-9780

202 475-1716 **Industrial College of the Armed Forces (US Dept of Defense)**
4th & P Sts SW Fort McNair .... Washington DC 20319-0001
Fax: 202 475-0724

312 782-6730 **Industrial Engineering College** 316 N Michigan Ave .... Chicago IL 60601-3707
605 224-6161 **Industry & Commerce Assn of South Dakota** 108 N Euclid Ave .... Pierre SD 57501-2521
202 523-9711 **Information & Public Affairs Office (US Dept of Labor)**
200 Constitution Ave NW Rm S1032 .... Washington DC 20210-0001
Fax: 202 523-8699

517 676-0240 **Ingham County** PO Box 179 .... Mason MI 48854-0179
517 676-8440 **Ingham County Library** 407 N Cedar St .... Mason MI 48854-1012
Fax: 517 676-9646

202 225-2211 **Inhofe James M (Rep - R - Oklahoma)** 408 Cannon Bldg .... Washington DC 20515-0001
Fax: 202 225-9187

202 224-3934 **Inouye Daniel K (Sen - D - Hawaii)** 722 Hart Bldg .... Washington DC 20510-0001
Fax: 202 224-6747

202 647-9567 **Inspector General (US Dept of State)**
2201 C St NW Rm 6817 .... Washington DC 20520-0001
Fax: 202 647-7660

202 357-0227 **Inspector General Fraud Hotline (US Dept of Labor)**
200 Constitution Ave NW Rm S5512 .... Washington DC 20210-0001

512 477-5701 **Institute for Christian Studies** 1909 University Ave .... Austin TX 78705-5610
505 988-6493 **Institute of American Indian Arts** St Michaels Dr .... Santa Fe NM 87501-0000
Fax: 505 988-6446

203 226-6347 **Insurance Crime Prevention Institute** 15 Franklin St .... Westport CT 06880-5985
Fax: 203 227-4663

703 247-1500 **Insurance Institute for Highway Safety**
1005 N Glebe Rd Suite 800 .... Arlington VA 22201-5723
Fax: 703 247-1678

202 647-9673 **Intelligence & Research Office (US Dept of State)**
2201 C St NW 8th Fl .... Washington DC 20520-0001

202 647-9210 **Inter-American Affairs Bureau (US Dept of State)**
2201 C St NW Rm 6263 .... Washington DC 20520-0001
Fax: 202 647-0791

202 623-1000 **Inter-American Development Bank (US Dept of the Treasury)**
1300 New York Ave NW .... Washington DC 20577-0001
Fax: 202 623-3096

703 841-3800 **Inter-American Foundation** 1515 Wilson Blvd .... Rosslyn VA 22209-2402
Fax: 703 841-0973

202 225-2761 **Interior & Insular Affairs Committee (US House of Representatives)**
1324 Longworth Bldg .... Washington DC 20515-0001

202 566-4743 **Internal Revenue Service** 1111 Constitution Ave NW .... Washington DC 20224-0001
Fax: 202 566-6105

202 233-1580 *Corporation Statistics* 1201 East St NW Rm 406 .... Washington DC 20224-0001
Fax: 202 233-1620

313 226-3562 *Detroit Computing Center* 1300 John C Lodge Dr .... Detroit MI 48226-2414
Fax: 313 226-2970

202 233-1658 *Individual Statistics Branch* 500 N Capitol St NW 5th Fl ... Washington DC 20001-0000
Fax: 202 233-1620

304 267-2911 *National Computer Center* Rt 9 & Needy Rd .... Martinsburg WV 25401-9809
Fax: Ext 221

202 233-1741 *Statistics & Income Div* 500 N Capitol St NW 5th Fl .... Washington DC 20224-0001
Fax: 202 233-1620

513 684-3613 *Central Region* 550 Main St Rm 7112 .... Cincinnati OH 45202-3212
Fax: 513 684-2330

215 597-2040 *Mid-Atlantic Region* 841 Chestnut St .... Philadelphia PA 19107-4414
Fax: 215 597-9394

312 886-5600 *Midwest Region* 1 N Wacker Dr .... Chicago IL 60606-3303
Fax: 312 886-5655

212 264-7061 *North Atlantic Region* 90 Church St Rm 1128 .... New York NY 10007-2919
Fax: 212 264-2333

404 522-0050 *Southeast Region* 401 W Peachtree St .... Atlanta GA 30365-0000
214 308-7000 *Southwest Region* 4050 Alpha Rd .... Dallas TX 75244-4203
Fax: 214 308-7148

415 556-3009 *Western Region* 1650 Mission St .... San Francisco CA 94103-0000
312 820-0422 **International Academy of Merchandising** 350 N Orleans ...... Chicago IL 60654-1587
Fax: 312 828-9405

202 586-5800 **International Affairs & Energy Emergencies Program (US Dept of Energy)**
1000 Independence Ave SW Rm 7C-016 .... Washington DC 20585-0001
Fax: 202 586-3047

202 566-2269 **International Affairs (US Dept of the Treasury)**
1500 Pennsylvania Ave NW Rm 3430 .... Washington DC 20220-0001
Fax: 202 566-8066

202 566-2773 *Foreign Exchange* 1500 Pennsylvania Ave NW Rm 5037 .. Washington DC 20220-0001
Fax: 202 786-8446

202 566-5628 *International Banking*
1500 Pennsylvania Ave NW Rm 5323 .... Washington DC 20220-0001
Fax: 202 566-8066

202 566-5081 *International Monetary Policy*
1500 Pennsylvania Ave NW Rm 5050 .... Washington DC 20220-0001
Fax: 202 786-8446

214 404-9980 **International Airline Passengers Assn** PO Box 870188 .... Dallas TX 75287-0188
Fax: 214 526-4888

312 947-2064 **International Assn of Assessing Officers** 1313 E 60th St .... Chicago IL 60637-2830
Fax: 312 363-2246

703 243-6500 **International Assn of Chiefs of Police**
1110 N Glebe Rd Suite 200 .... Arlington VA 22201-5718
Fax: 703 243-0684

202 783-5880 **International Assn of Sheet Metal Workers Political Action League**
1750 New York Ave NW 6th Fl .... Washington DC 20006-5386
Fax: 202 737-2424

212 963-6011 **International Atomic Energy Agency**
1 UN Plaza Rm DC1-1155 .... New York NY 10017-0000
Fax: 212 751-4117

202 477-1234 **International Bank for Reconstruction & Development**
1818 H St NW .... Washington DC 20433-0001
Fax: 202 477-6391

205 766-6610 **International Bible College** 3625 Pelton Dr .... Florence AL 35630-0000
213 939-7179 **International Bible College** 1218 S Fairfax Ave .... Los Angeles CA 90019-0000
512 434-5541 **International Bible College** 2369 Benrus Blvd .... San Antonio TX 78228-2353
212 425-2750 **International Cargo Gear Bureau** 17 Battery Pl Suite 1726 ..... New York NY 10004-1102
Fax: 212 269-9469

202 626-4600 **International City Management Assn**
777 N Capitol St NE Suite 500 .... Washington DC 20002-4239
Fax: 202 962-3500

808 595-8377 **International College & Graduate School of Theology**
20 Dowsett Ave .... Honolulu HI 96817-1105

813 774-4700 **International College of Naples** 2654 Tamiami Trail E .... Naples FL 33962-0000
Fax: 813 774-4593

202 647-5727 **International Communications & Information Policy (US Dept of State)**
2201 C St NW Rm 6317 .... Washington DC 20520-0001
Fax: 202 647-5957

213 699-0541 **International Conference of Building Officials**
5360 S Workman Mill Rd .... Whittier CA 90601-2299
Fax: 213 692-3853 Orders

717 342-7701 **International Correspondence School Center for Degree Studies**
925 Oak St .... Scranton PA 18515-0001
Fax: 717 347-9072

202 477-1234 **International Development Assn** 1818 H St NW .... Washington DC 20433-0001
Fax: 202 477-6391

203 967-6000 **International Executives Service Corps** 8 Stamford Forum ..... Stamford CT 06904-2005
Fax: 203 324-2531

202 477-1234 **International Finance Corp** 1818 H St NW .... Washington DC 20433-0001
Fax: 202 477-6391

305 373-4684 **International Fine Arts College** 1737 N Bayshore Dr .... Miami FL 33132-1121
Fax: 305 374-5933

202 462-6644 **International Institute of Interior Design** 2225 R St NW ..... Washington DC 20008-4017
212 697-0150 **International Labor Organization (ILO)** 820 2nd Ave 18th Fl ... New York NY 10017-0000
Fax: 212 883-0844

202 628-4546 **International Longshoremen's Assn Committee on Political Education**
815 16th St NW .... Washington DC 20006-4104
Fax: 202 628-4187

202 623-7000 **International Monetary Fund (IMF) (US Dept of the Treasury)**
700 19th St NW .... Washington DC 20431-0001
Fax: 202 623-4661

202 647-7399 **International Narcotics Matters (US Dept of State)**
2201 C St NW Rm 7333 .... Washington DC 20520-0001
Fax: 202 647-4912

202 647-9600 **International Organization Affairs Bureau (US Dept of State)**
2201 C St NW Rm 6323 .... Washington DC 20520-0001
Fax: 202 647-6510

202 862-1826 **International Organization for Migration**
1750 K St NW Suite 1110 .... Washington DC 23406-0000
Fax: 202 862-1879

213 538-0233 **International Right of Way Assn** 13650 S Gramercy Pl .... Gardena CA 90249-2465
Fax: 213 538-1471

508 881-5800 **International Society of Fire Service Instructors** 30 Main St ...... Ashland MA 01721-1101
Fax: 508 881-6829

202 566-2748 **International Trade & Investment Policy (US Dept of the Treasury)**
1500 Pennsylvania Ave NW Rm 3208 .... Washington DC 20220-0001
Fax: 202 566-8066

202 377-5087 **International Trade Administration**
14th St & Constitution Ave NW Rm 3414 .... Washington DC 20230-0001
Fax: 202 377-5819

202 377-1780 *Import Administration*
14th St & Constitution Ave NW Rm 3099B .... Washington DC 20230-0001
Fax: 202 377-0947

202 377-3022 *International Economic Policy*
14th St & Constitution Ave NW Rm 3864 .... Washington DC 20230-0001
Fax: 202 377-5444

202 377-1461 *Trade Development Office*
14th St & Constitution Ave NW Rm 3832 .... Washington DC 20230-0001
Fax: 202 377-5697

505 766-2070 *Albuquerque Office* 625 Silver SW Rm 320 .... Albuquerque NM 87102-3123

907 271-5041 *Anchorage Office* 222 W 7th Ave Box 32 — Anchorage AK 99513-7504
Fax: 907 271-5173
404 347-4872 *Atlanta Office* 1365 Peachtree St NE Suite 504 — Atlanta GA 30309-3120
Fax: 404 347-0108
301 962-3560 *Baltimore Office* 40 S Gay St Rm 413 — Baltimore MD 21202-4022
Fax: 301 962-7813
205 731-1331 *Birmingham Office* 2015 2nd Ave N Suite 302 — Birmingham AL 35203-3711
Fax: 205 731-0076
617 565-8576 *Boston Office* World Trade Ctr Suite 307 — Boston MA 02210-1595
Fax: 617 565-8530
716 846-4191 *Buffalo Office* 111 W Huron St Rm 1312 — Buffalo NY 14202-2301
Fax: 716 846-5290
304 347-5123 *Charleston Office* 500 Quarrier St Rm 3402 — Charleston WV 25301-2130
Fax: 304 347-5408
312 353-4450 *Chicago Office* 55 E Monroe St Rm 1406 — Chicago IL 60603-5704
Fax: 312 886-8025
513 684-2944 *Cincinnati Office* 550 Main St Rm 9504 — Cincinnati OH 45202-3222
Fax: 513 684-3200
216 522-4750 *Cleveland Office* 668 Euclid Ave Suite 600 — Cleveland OH 44114-3002
Fax: 216 522-2235
803 765-5345 *Columbia Office* 1835 Assembly St Suite 172 — Columbia SC 29201-2430
Fax: 803 253-3614
214 767-0542 *Dallas Office* 1100 Commerce St Suite 7A5 — Dallas TX 75242-1001
Fax: 214 767-8240
303 844-3246 *Denver Office* 1625 Broadway Suite 680 — Denver CO 80202-4706
Fax: 303 844-5651
515 284-4222 *Des Moines Office* 210 Walnut St Rm 817 — Des Moines IA 50309-2105
Fax: 515 284-4021
313 226-3650 *Detroit Office* 477 Michigan Ave McNamara Bldg Suite 1140 — Detroit MI 48226-2518
Fax: 313 226-3657
202 377-3181 *District of Columbia Office*
14th St & Constitution Ave NW Rm 1066 — Washington DC 20230-0001
Fax: 202 377-5270
203 240-3530 *Hartford Office* 450 Main St Rm 610-B — Hartford CT 06103-3002
Fax: 203 240-3473
808 541-1782 *Honolulu Office* 300 Ala Moana Blvd Rm 4106 — Honolulu HI 96850-0001
Fax: 808 541-3435
713 229-2578 *Houston Office* 515 Rusk Ave Rm 2625 — Houston TX 77002-2603
Fax: 713 229-2203
317 226-6214 *Indianapolis Office* 1 N Capitol St Suite 520 — Indianapolis IN 46204-2227
Fax: 317 226-6139
601 965-4388 *Jackson Office* 300 W Woodrow Wilson Dr Suite 328 — Jackson MS 39213-7649
816 426-3141 *Kansas City Office* 601 E 12th St Rm 635 — Kansas City MO 64106-2855
Fax: 816 426-3140
501 378-5794 *Little Rock Office* 320 W Capitol Ave Suite 811 — Little Rock AR 72201-3520
Fax: 501 378-7380
502 582-5066 *Louisville Office* 601 W Broadway Rm 636-B — Louisville KY 40202-0000
901 521-4137 *Memphis Office* 22 N Front St Suite 200 — Memphis TN 38103-2109
Fax: 901 575-3510
305 536-5267 *Miami Office* 51 SW 1st Ave Suite 224 — Miami FL 33130-1623
Fax: 305 536-4765
414 297-3473 *Milwaukee Office* 517 E Wisconsin Ave Rm 606 — Milwaukee WI 53202-4507
Fax: 414 291-3470
612 348-1638 *Minneapolis Office* 110 S 4th St Rm 108 — Minneapolis MN 55401-2227
Fax: 612 348-1650
615 736-5161 *Nashville Office* 404 James Robertson Pkwy Suite 1114 — Nashville TN 37219-1505
Fax: 615 736-2454
504 589-6546 *New Orleans Office*
2 Canal St World Trade Ctr Suite 432 — New Orleans LA 70130-1408
Fax: 504 589-2337
212 264-0634 *New York Office* 26 Federal Plaza Rm 3718 — New York NY 10278-0022
Fax: 212 264-1356
405 231-5302 *Oklahoma City Office* 6601 N Broadway Ext Suite 200 — Oklahoma City OK 73116-8214
Fax: 405 841-5199
402 221-3665 *Omaha Office* 11133 'O' St — Omaha NE 68137-2337
Fax: 402 221-3668
602 379-3285 *Phoenix Office* 230 N 1st Ave Rm 3412 — Phoenix AZ 85025-0001
Fax: 602 379-4324
412 644-2850 *Pittsburgh Office* 1000 Liberty Ave Rm 2002 — Pittsburgh PA 15222-4004
Fax: 412 644-4875
503 326-3001 *Portland Office*
121 SW Salmon St 1 World Trade Ctr Suite 242 — Portland OR 97204-0000
Fax: 503 221-6351
809 766-5555 *Puerto Rico Office* Federal Bldg Rm G55 — Hato Rey PR 00918-0000
702 784-5203 *Reno Office* 1755 E Plumb Ln Suite 152 — Reno NV 89502-3600
Fax: 702 784-5343
804 771-2246 *Richmond Office* 400 N 8th St Suite 8010 — Richmond VA 23240-1001
Fax: 804 771-2390
314 425-3302 *Saint Louis Office* 7911 Forsyth Blvd Suite 610 — Saint Louis MO 63105-3860
Fax: 314 425-3381
801 524-5116 *Salt Lake City Office* 324 S State St Suite 105 — Salt Lake City UT 84101-2106
Fax: 801 524-5886
619 557-5395 *San Diego Office* 6363 Greenwich Dr — San Diego CA 92122-3939
Fax: 619 557-6176
415 556-5860 *San Francisco Office* 450 Golden Gate Ave — San Francisco CA 94102-3400
Fax: 415 556-2121
714 836-2461 *Santa Ana Office* 116-A W 4th St Suite 1 — Santa Ana CA 92701-0000
Fax: 714 836-2332
912 944-4204 *Savannah Office* 120 Barnard St Rm A-107 — Savannah GA 31401-3641
Fax: 912 944-4241
206 442-5615 *Seattle Office* 3131 Elliott Ave Suite 290 — Seattle WA 98121-1047
Fax: 206 442-7253
609 989-2100 *Trenton Office* 3131 Princeton Pike Bldg 6 Suite 100 — Trenton NJ 08648-2207
Fax: 609 989-2395
202 566-5305 **International Trade Office** 15th St & Pennsylvania Ave — Washington DC 20220-0001
Fax: 202 566-8066
202 275-7252 **Interstate Commerce Commission**
12th St & Constitution Ave NW — Washington DC 20423-0001
Fax: 202 275-9237
312 353-6204 *Central Region* 219 S Dearborn St Rm 1304 — Chicago IL 60604-1705
215 596-4040 *Eastern Region* 3535 Market St Rm 16400 — Philadelphia PA 19104-3309
415 744-6527 *Western Region* 211 Main St Suite 500 — San Francisco CA 94105-1914
Fax: 415 744-6547
612 450-8501 **Inver Hills Community College**
8445 College Trail E — Inver Grove Heights MN 55076-0000
703 693-0044 **Investigative Service (US Dept of Defense)**
400 Army-Navy Dr Rm 901-E — Arlington VA 22202-2885
Fax: 703 694-9501
619 878-2411 **Inyo County** 168 N Edwards St — Independence CA 93526-0000
Fax: 619 878-2542
914 633-2000 **Iona College** 715 North Ave — New Rochelle NY 10801-1890
Fax: 914 633-2020 Finance
914 969-4000 **Iona College Elizabeth Seton School** 1061 N Broadway — Yonkers NY 10701-1105
Fax: 914 969-4106
616 527-5322 **Ionia County** Main St — Ionia MI 48846-0000
517 362-3497 **Iosco County** PO Box 838 — Tawas City MI 48764-0838

319 642-3914 **Iowa County** Court Ave — Marengo IA 52301-0000
608 935-5445 **Iowa County** 222 N Iowa St — Dodgeville WI 53533-1557
515 244-7292 **Iowa Democratic Party** 2116 Grand Ave — Des Moines IA 50312-5304
Fax: 515 244-5051
515 281-3251 **Iowa Dept of Economic Development** 200 E Grand Ave — Des Moines IA 50309-1827
Fax: 515 281-7276
515 281-3100 **Iowa Div of Tourism** 200 E Grand Ave — Des Moines IA 50309-1827
Fax: 515 281-7276
712 362-2604 **Iowa Lakes Community College** 300 S 18th St — Estherville IA 51334-2721
Fax: 712 362-7649
Iowa State Government
515 281-5011 *Information* E 10th & Grand Ave — Des Moines IA 50319-0001
515 281-4451 *Arts Council* 1223 E Court Ave State Capitol Complex — Des Moines IA 50319-0001
515 281-5164 *Attorney General* 1300 E Walnut St — Des Moines IA 50319-0001
Fax: 515 281-4209
515 281-4817 *Board of Parole* 523 E 12th St Capitol Annex Basement — Des Moines IA 50319-0001
Fax: 515 281-7620
515 281-5526 *Bureau of Job Insurance* 1000 E Grand Ave — Des Moines IA 50319-0001
Fax: 515 242-6301
515 281-3007 *Bureau of Library/Archives* 600 E Locust St — Des Moines IA 50319-0001
Fax: 515 282-0502
515 281-5926 *Consumer Protection Div* 1300 E Walnut St — Des Moines IA 50319-0001
Fax: 515 281-4209
515 281-5321 *Department of Agriculture & Land Stewardship*
E 9th & Grand Ave — Des Moines IA 50319-0001
Fax: 515 281-6236
515 281-7400 *Department of Commerce* 1918 SE Hulsizer Ave — Ankeny IA 50021-3941
Fax: 515 281-7372
515 281-4811 *Department of Corrections* 523 E 12th St Capitol Annex — Des Moines IA 50319-0001
Fax: 515 281-7345
515 281-7636 *Department of Economic Development* 200 E Grand Ave — Des Moines IA 50309-0000
Fax: 515 281-7276
515 281-5294 *Department of Education* Grimes State Office Bldg — Des Moines IA 50319-0001
Fax: 515 242-5988
515 281-5361 *Department of Employment Services* 1000 E Grand Ave — Des Moines IA 50319-0000
Fax: Unlisted
515 281-3322 *Department of Management*
1070 E Grand Ave State Capitol Bldg Rm 12 — Des Moines IA 50319-0001
Fax: 515 252-5897
515 281-5145 *Department of Natural Resources* 900 E Grand Ave — Des Moines IA 50319-0001
Fax: 515 281-8895
515 281-8852 *Air Quality & Solid Waste* 900 E Grand Ave — Des Moines IA 50319-0001
Fax: 515 281-8895
515 281-8681 *Energy Bureau* 900 E Grand Ave Wallis State Office Bldg — Des Moines IA 50319-0001
Fax: 515 281-8895
515 281-5605 *Department of Public Health* 321 E 12th St — Des Moines IA 50319-0001
Fax: 515 281-4958
515 281-3112 *Department of Revenue & Finance* 1300 E Walnut St — Des Moines IA 50319-0001
Fax: 515 242-6040
515 239-1101 *Department of Transportation* 800 Lincoln Way — Ames IA 50010-6915
Fax: 515 239-1639
515 281-3231 *Disaster Services Div* 1300 E Walnut St — Des Moines IA 50319-0001
Fax: 515 282-7539
515 281-5934 *Division of Industrial Services* 1000 E Grand Ave — Des Moines IA 50319-0001
Fax: 515 281-6501
515 281-3606 *Division of Labor* 1000 E Grand Ave — Des Moines IA 50319-0001
Fax: 515 242-6301
515 281-4159 *Employment Appeal Board*
Lucas State Office Bldg 2nd Fl — Des Moines IA 50319-0001
515 281-6284 *Environmental Protection Div* 900 E Grand Ave — Des Moines IA 50319-0001
Fax: 515 281-8895
515 281-5856 *General Services Dept* 1305 E Walnut St Hoover Bldg — Des Moines IA 50319-0001
Fax: 515 242-5974
515 281-5211 *Governor* State Capitol — Des Moines IA 50319-0001
Fax: 515 281-6611
515 239-1124 *Highway Div* 800 Lincoln Way — Ames IA 50010-6915
Fax: 515 239-1639
515 281-5705 *Insurance Div* E 12th & Walnut Sts 6th Fl — Des Moines IA 50319-0001
Fax: 515 281-3059
319 372-5432 *Iowa State Penitentiary* PO Box 316 — Fort Madison IA 52627-0316
Fax: 319 372-6967
515 281-3421 *Lieutenant Governor* State Capitol — Des Moines IA 50319-0001
Fax: 515 242-6108
319 462-3504 *Men's Reformatory* PO Box B — Anamosa IA 52205-0010
515 281-4126 *Professional Licensing & Regulation* 1918 SE Hulsizer Ave — Ankeny IA 50021-0000
Fax: 515 281-7372
515 281-5981 *Purchasing Div* 1305 E Walnut St Hoover Bldg Level A — Des Moines IA 50319-0001
Fax: 515 242-5974
515 281-3183 *Real Estate Commission* 1918 SE Hulsizer Ave — Ankeny IA 50021-0000
Fax: 515 281-7372
515 281-5864 *Secretary of State* State House — Des Moines IA 50319-0001
Fax: 515 242-5952
515 281-4441 *Securities Bureau* Lucas State Office Bldg 2nd Fl — Des Moines IA 50319-0001
Fax: 515 246-8520
515 281-3934 *State Board of Regents*
E 12th & Grand Sts Old Historical Bldg — Des Moines IA 50319-0001
Fax: 515 281-6420
515 281-5824 *State Patrol* E 9th & Grand Ave — Des Moines IA 50319-0001
515 281-5911 *Supreme Court* State Capitol Ground Fl — Des Moines IA 50319-0001
Fax: Unlisted
515 281-5366 *Treasurer* Hoover State Office Bldg 1st Fl — Des Moines IA 50319-0001
Fax: 515 281-6962
515 281-5256 *Utilities Board* E 12th & Walnut Sts Lucas Bldg 5th Fl — Des Moines IA 50319-0001
Fax: 515 281-5329
515 281-4944 *Vital Records Section* 321 E 12th St — Des Moines IA 50319-0001
Fax: 515 281-4958
515 294-4111 **Iowa State University** — Ames IA 50011-0001
Fax: 515 294-6060 Finance
515 294-5933 *College of Engineering* 104 Marston Hall — Ames IA 50011-0001
Fax: 515 294-9273
515 294-1242 *College of Veterinary Medicine* — Ames IA 50011-0001
Fax: 515 294-8341
515 294-5836 *Department of Biochemistry* Gilman Hall Rm 397 — Ames IA 50011-0001
Fax: 515 294-0453
515 294-7810 *Department of Chemistry* Gilman Hall Rm A111F — Ames IA 50011-0001
Fax: 515 294-0105
515 294-8958 *Department of Community & Regional Planning*
College of Design Rm 126 — Ames IA 50011-0001
Fax: 515 294-9755
515 294-4340 *Department of Journalism & Mass Communication*
Hamilton Hall Rm 114 — Ames IA 50011-1180
Fax: 515 294-0907
515 294-5440 *Department of Physics* Physics Bldg Rm 12 — Ames IA 50011-0001
Fax: 515 294-0689
515 294-4531 *Graduate School* 207 Beardshear — Ames IA 50011-0001

319 385-8021 **Iowa Wesleyan College** 601 N Main St .... Mount Pleasant IA 52641-1398
Fax: 319 385-6296 Admin
Iowa Western Community College
712 542-5117 *Clarinda Campus* 923 E Washington St .... Clarinda IA 51632-1958
712 325-3200 *Council Bluffs Campus* 2700 College Rd .... Council Bluffs IA 51503-0567
Fax: 712 325-3424
212 687-2020 **Iran: Islamic Republic of Iran Mission to the UN**
622 3rd Ave 34th Fl .... New York NY 10017-6707
Fax: 212 867-7086
Iraq: Republic of Iraq
202 483-7500 *Embassy* 1801 P St NW .... Washington DC 20236-0000
Fax: 202 462-5066
212 737-4433 *Mission to the UN* 14 E 79th St .... New York NY 10021-0106
Fax: Unlisted
704 878-3000 **Iredell County** PO Box 788 .... Statesville NC 28677-0788
Fax: Unlisted
202 225-5015 **Ireland Andy (Rep - R - Florida)** 2466 Rayburn Bldg .... Washington DC 20515-0001
Fax: 202 225-6944
212 751-2660 **Ireland-US Council** 460 Park Ave 22nd Fl ....New York NY 10022-1906
Fax: 212 751-8951
Ireland: Republic of Ireland
202 462-3939 *Embassy* 2234 Massachusetts Ave NW .... Washington DC 20008-2812
Fax: 202 232-5993
212 421-6934 *Mission to the UN* 885 2nd Ave 19th Fl .... New York NY 10017-2201
Fax: 212 223-0926
617 267-9330 *Boston Consulate General* 535 Boylston St .... Boston MA 02116-3720
Fax: 617 267-6375
312 337-1868 *Chicago Consulate General* 400 N Michigan Ave Rm 911 ...... Chicago IL 60611-4102
Fax: Unlisted
212 319-2555 *New York Consulate General* 515 Madison Ave .... New York NY 10022-5403
Fax: 212 980-9475
415 392-4214 *San Francisco Consulate General*
655 Montgomery St 9th Fl .... San Francisco CA 94111-2635
Fax: Unlisted
915 835-2421 **Irion County** County Courthouse .... Mertzon TX 76941-0000
212 418-0800 **Irish Tourist Board** 757 3rd Ave .... New York NY 10017-2082
Fax: 212 371-9052
906 875-3221 **Iron County** 2 S 6th St .... Crystal Falls MI 49920-1413
Fax: 906 875-6775
314 546-2912 **Iron County** 250 S Main St .... Ironton MO 63650-1308
801 477-3375 **Iron County** PO Box 429 .... Parowan UT 84761-0429
Fax: 801 477-8847
715 561-3375 **Iron County** 300 Taconite St .... Hurley WI 54534-1546
815 432-6960 **Iroquois County** 550 S 10th .... Watseka IL 60970-1810
202 566-4743 **IRS (US Dept of the Treasury)** 1111 Constitution Ave NW ... Washington DC 20224-0001
Fax: 202 566-6105
714 559-9300 **Irvine Valley College** 5500 Irvine Center Dr .... Irvine CA 92720-4399
Fax: 714 559-3270
214 721-2639 **Irving Public Library System** 801 W Irving Blvd ....Irving TX 75060-2845
Fax: 214 259-1171
912 468-9441 **Irwin County** S Irwin Ave .... Ocilla GA 31774-1098
517 772-0911 **Isabella County** 200 N Main St .... Mount Pleasant MI 48858-2321
Fax: 517 773-7431
612 689-3859 **Isanti County** 237 2nd Ave SW .... Cambridge MN 55008-1536
206 679-7359 **Island County** PO Box 5000 .... Coupeville WA 98239-5000
804 357-3191 **Isle of Wight County** Hwy 258 County Courthouse .... Isle of Wight VA 23397-9999
704 286-3636 **Isothermal Community College** PO Box 804 .... Spindale NC 28160-0804
Fax: 704 286-1120
Israel: State of Israel
202 364-5500 *Embassy* 3514 International Dr NW .... Washington DC 20008-3035
Fax: 202 363-4156
212 351-5200 *Mission to the UN* 800 2nd Ave .... New York NY 10017-4755
Fax: 212 953-0317
312 565-3300 *Chicago Consulate General* 111 E Wacker Dr Suite 1308 ...... Chicago IL 60601-4402
Fax: 312 565-2063
213 651-5700 *Los Angeles Consulate General*
6380 Wilshire Blvd Suite 1700 .... Los Angeles CA 90048-5019
Fax: 213 651-3123
305 358-8111 *Miami Consulate General* 330 Biscayne Blvd Suite 510 .... Miami FL 33132-2229
Fax: 305 371-5034
212 351-5200 *New York Consulate General* 800 2nd Ave .... New York NY 10017-4755
Fax: Unlisted
415 398-8885 *San Francisco Consulate General*
220 Bush St Suite 550 .... San Francisco CA 94104-3507
Fax: 415 398-8589
601 873-2761 **Issaquena County** PO Box 27 .... Mayersville MS 39113-0027
212 245-4822 **Italian Government Travel Office** 630 5th Ave 15th Fl .... New York NY 10111-0100
Fax: 212 245-5869
312 661-1336 **Italian-American Chamber of Commerce of Chicago**
126 W Grand Ave .... Chicago IL 60610-4206
212 279-5520 **Italy-America Chamber of Commerce**
350 5th Ave Suite 3015 .... New York NY 10118-0110
Fax: 212 279-5839
Italy: Italian Republic
202 328-5500 *Embassy* 1601 Fuller St NW .... Washington DC 20009-5601
Fax: 202 238-5542
212 486-9191 *Mission to the UN* 2 UN Plaza 24th Fl .... New York NY 10017-0000
Fax: 212 486-1036
312 467-1550 *Chicago Consulate General* 500 N Michigan Ave ....Chicago IL 60611-3771
213 820-0622 *Los Angeles Consulate General*
12400 Wilshire Blvd Suite 300 .... Los Angeles CA 90025-1022
212 737-9100 *New York Consulate General* 690 Park Ave .... New York NY 10022-6815
Fax: 212 832-5914
218 327-4461 **Itasca Community College** 1851 E Hwy 169 ....Grand Rapids MN 55744-3361
Fax: 218 327-4269
218 327-2941 **Itasca County** Courthouse .... Grand Rapids MN 55744-2600
Fax: 218 327-2848
601 862-3101 **Itawamba Community College** 602 W Hill St .... Fulton MS 38843-1099
601 862-3421 **Itawamba County** 201 W Main St .... Fulton MS 38843-1153
607 274-3011 **Ithaca College** Danby Rd .... Ithaca NY 14850-5815
Fax: 607 274-3474
818 960-8681 **ITT Technical Institute of West Covina**
1530 W Cameron Ave .... West Covina CA 91790-2711
Ivory Coast: Republic of the Ivory Coast
202 483-2400 *Embassy* 2424 Massachusetts Ave NW .... Washington DC 20008-2804
Fax: 202 483-8482
212 371-7036 *Mission to the UN* 866 UN Plaza Rm 580 .... New York NY 10017-0000
Fax: 212 935-5347
501 368-4316 **Izard County** PO Box 95 .... Melbourne AR 72556-0095

J

804 371-3000 **J Sargeant Reynolds Community College** PO Box C-32040 ... Richmond VA 23261-2040
Fax: 804 371-3386

817 567-2111 **Jack County** 100 N Main St .... Jacksboro TX 76056-1746
601 981-1611 **Jackson College of Ministries** 1555 Beasley Rd ....Jackson MS 39206-2099
517 787-0800 **Jackson Community College** 2111 Emmons Rd .... Jackson MI 49201-8399
Fax: 517 789-1623
205 574-9320 **Jackson County** PO Box 397 .... Scottsboro AL 35768-0397
501 523-6152 **Jackson County** Main St .... Newport AR 72112-0000
303 723-4334 **Jackson County** PO Box 337 .... Walden CO 80480-0337
904 482-9552 **Jackson County** PO Box 510 .... Marianna FL 32446-0510
Fax: 904 482-7849
404 367-1199 **Jackson County** PO Box 68 .... Jefferson GA 30549-0068
319 652-4946 **Jackson County** 201 W Platt St .... Maquoketa IA 52060-2243
618 684-2151 **Jackson County** 1001 Walnut St .... Murphysboro IL 62966-2177
812 358-6116 **Jackson County** PO Box 122 .... Brownstown IN 47220-0122
913 364-2891 **Jackson County** Courthouse Sq .... Holton KS 66436-1791
606 287-7800 **Jackson County** PO Box 700 .... McKee KY 40447-0000
517 788-4265 **Jackson County** 120 W Michigan Ave .... Jackson MI 49201-1315
507 847-4400 **Jackson County** 413 4th St .... Jackson MN 56143-1529
Fax: 507 847-5433
816 881-3333 **Jackson County** 415 E 12th St .... Kansas City MO 64106-2706
Fax: 816 881-3398
601 769-3131 **Jackson County** 3109 Canty St .... Pascagoula MS 39567-4209
Fax: 601 769-3291
704 586-4312 **Jackson County** 50 Keener St Suite 102 .... Sylva NC 28779-0000
Fax: 704 586-6879
614 286-3301 **Jackson County** 226 Main St .... Jackson OH 45640-0000
Fax: 614 286-4560
405 482-4420 **Jackson County** 101 W Broadway .... Altus OK 73521-3898
503 776-7231 **Jackson County** 10 S Oakdale .... Medford OR 97501-2952
Fax: 503 776-7278
605 837-2121 **Jackson County** 1 Main St .... Kadoka SD 57543-0000
615 268-9212 **Jackson County** PO Box 346 .... Gainesboro TN 38562-0346
512 782-3563 **Jackson County** 115 W Main St .... Edna TX 77957-2733
715 284-0208 **Jackson County** 307 Main St .... Black River Falls WI 54615-1756
304 372-2011 **Jackson County** Court St .... Ripley WV 25271-0000
503 776-7281 **Jackson County Library System** 413 W Main St ....Medford OR 97501-2730
Fax: 503 776-7290
517 788-4087 **Jackson District Library** 244 W Michigan Ave .... Jackson MI 49201-2275
Fax: 517 782-8635
318 259-2424 **Jackson Parish** PO Box 737 .... Jonesboro LA 71251-0737
907 747-8981 **Jackson Sheldon Museum** 104 College Dr .... Sitka AK 99835-7657
Fax: 907 747-3004
901 424-3520 **Jackson State Community College** 2046 North Pkwy ....Jackson TN 38301-3797
Fax: 901 425-2647
601 968-2121 **Jackson State University** 1400 John R Lynch St .... Jackson MS 39217-0001
Fax: 601 968-2358 Library
601 769-3060 **Jackson-George Regional Library System**
3214 Pascagoula St .... Pascagoula MS 39567-4217
Fax: 601 769-3113
601 968-5811 **Jackson/Hinds Library System** 300 N State St .... Jackson MS 39201-1799
904 630-1919 **Jacksonville City Hall** 220 E Bay St .... Jacksonville FL 32202-3418
Fax: 904 630-2910
904 398-8336 **Jacksonville Art Museum** 4160 Boulevard Center Dr ....Jacksonville FL 32207-2805
903 586-2518 **Jacksonville College** 500 W Pine St .... Jacksonville TX 75766-4746
904 772-2345 **Jacksonville Naval Air Station** .... Jacksonville FL 32212-0000
Fax: 904 779-3400
904 630-1994 **Jacksonville Public Library System** 122 N Ocean St .... Jacksonville FL 32202-3314
Fax: Unlisted
205 782-5781 **Jacksonville State University** 817 Pelham Rd S .... Jacksonville AL 36265-2796
Fax: 205 782-5291
904 744-3950 **Jacksonville University** 2800 University Blvd N .... Jacksonville FL 32211-3396
Fax: 904 744-0101
202 225-4011 **Jacobs Andrew Jr (Rep - D - Indiana)** 2313 Rayburn Bldg . Washington DC 20515-0001
Fax: 202 226-4093
Jamaica
202 452-0660 *Embassy* 1850 K St NW International Sq Bldg Suite 355 .. Washington DC 20006-0000
Fax: 202 452-0081
212 688-7040 *Mission to the UN* 866 2nd Ave 15th Fl .... New York NY 10017-2998
Fax: 212 308-3730
305 374-8431 *Miami Consulate General* 25 SE 2nd Ave Suite 842 .... Miami FL 33131-1680
Fax: 305 577-4970
212 935-9000 *New York Consulate General* 866 2nd Ave ....New York NY 10017-2993
Fax: 212 832-0411
305 667-1774 **Jamaica Reservation Service Inc** 1320 S Dixie Hwy Suite 1102 .. Miami FL 33146-2903
Fax: 305 665-3163
804 229-2552 **James City County** 321-45 Court St W ....Williamsburg VA 23185-0000
202 225-4035 **James Craig T (Rep - R - Florida)** 1408 Longworth Bldg .... Washington DC 20515-0001
Fax: 202 225-1727
205 937-9581 **James H Faulkner State Junior College**
1900 US Hwy 31 S .... Bay Minette AL 36507-0000
Fax: 205 937-3404
703 568-6211 **James Madison University** .... Harrisonburg VA 22807-0001
Fax: 703 568-6920
919 296-1341 **James Sprunt Technical College** Hwy 11 S .... Kenansville NC 28349-0000
Fax: 919 296-1636
717 326-0536 **James V Brown Library of Williamsport & Lycoming County**
19 E 4th St .... Williamsport PA 17701-6390
Fax: Call company operator
701 252-3467 **Jamestown College** .... Jamestown ND 58401-3456
Fax: 701 253-2318
716 665-5220 **Jamestown Community College** 525 Falconer St ....Jamestown NY 14701-0000
Fax: 716 665-3498 Admin
608 755-2800 **Janesville Public Library** 316 S Main St ....Janesville WI 53545-3912
Fax: Unlisted
Japan
202 234-2266 *Embassy* 2520 Massachusetts Ave NW .... Washington DC 20008-2822
Fax: 202 328-2187
212 223-4300 *Mission to the UN* 866 UN Plaza Suite 230 .... New York NY 10017-0000
Fax: 212 751-1966
213 624-8305 *Los Angeles Consulate General* 250 E 1st St Suite 1507 .. Los Angeles CA 90012-3831
Fax: 213 625-2231
212 371-8222 *New York Consulate General* 299 Park Ave ....New York NY 10171-0102
Fax: 212 319-6357
415 777-3533 *San Francisco Consulate General*
50 Fremont St 23rd Fl .... San Francisco CA 94105-2230
Fax: 415 974-3660
213 485-0160 **Japan Business Assn of Southern California**
345 S Figueroa St Suite 206 .... Los Angeles CA 90071-1002
Fax: 213 626-5526
415 921-5225 **Japanese American Citizens League** 1765 Sutter St .... San Francisco CA 94115-3297
Fax: 415 931-4671
212 935-0303 **Japanese Chamber of Commerce** 115 E 57th St 6th Fl ... New York NY 10022-2049
Fax: 212 935-0908
312 332-6199 **Japanese Chamber of Commerce & Industry of Chicago**
401 N Michigan Ave Suite 602 .... Chicago IL 60611-4205
Fax: 312 822-9773

415 543-8522 **Japanese Chamber of Commerce of Northern California**
685 Market St Suite 820 ... San Francisco CA 94105-4212
Fax: 415 543-8799
213 626-3067 **Japanese Chamber of Commerce of Southern California**
244 S San Pedro St Suite 504 ... Los Angeles CA 90012-3888
Fax: 213 626-3070
212 757-5640 **Japanese National Tourist Organization**
630 5th Ave Suite 2101 ... New York NY 10111-0007
Fax: 212 307-6754
903 769-2174 **Jarvis Christian College** Hwy 80-E ... Hawkins TX 75765-0000
Fax: 903 769-4842
404 468-2812 **Jasper County** County Courthouse ... Monticello GA 31064-0000
515 792-3255 **Jasper County** 100 1st St ... Newton IA 50208-0000
618 783-3124 **Jasper County** 100 W Jourdan St ... Newton IL 62448-1973
219 866-4933 **Jasper County** Courthouse Sq ... Rensselaer IN 47978-0000
417 358-0416 **Jasper County** County Courthouse ... Carthage MO 64836-1696
Fax: Ext 104
601 764-3368 **Jasper County** Court St ... Bay Springs MS 39422-0000
803 726-8832 **Jasper County** PO Box 248 ... Ridgeland SC 29936-0248
409 384-2632 **Jasper County** Main & Lamar St ... Jasper TX 75951-0000
219 726-4951 **Jay County** Court St ... Portland IN 47371-0000
912 375-6611 **Jeff Davis County** Jeff Davis St ... Hazlehurst GA 31539-0000
915 426-3251 **Jeff Davis County** PO Box 398 ... Fort Davis TX 79734-0398
314 789-3951 **Jefferson College** Hwy 21 ... Hillsboro MO 63050-0000
Fax: 314 789-4012
502 584-0181 **Jefferson Community College** 109 E Broadway ... Louisville KY 40202-2000
Fax: Ext 111
315 782-5250 **Jefferson Community College** Outer Coffeen St ... Watertown NY 13601-1899
205 325-5300 **Jefferson County** 716 N 21st St ... Birmingham AL 35263-0001
501 541-5322 **Jefferson County** PO Box 6317 ... Pine Bluff AR 71611-6317
303 279-6511 **Jefferson County** 1700 Arapahoe St ... Golden CO 80419-0001
904 997-3596 **Jefferson County** US Hwys 90 & 19 County Courthouse ... Monticello FL 32344-1498
Fax: 904 997-1904
912 625-3332 **Jefferson County** 202 E Broad St ... Louisville GA 30434-1622
515 472-3454 **Jefferson County** PO Box 984 ... Fairfield IA 52556-0984
208 745-9222 **Jefferson County** 134 N Clark St ... Rigby ID 83442-1437
618 244-8020 **Jefferson County** County Courthouse Rm 105 ... Mount Vernon IL 62864-4086
812 265-8900 **Jefferson County** 300 E Main St ... Madison IN 47250-3537
913 863-2272 **Jefferson County** PO Box 321 ... Oskaloosa KS 66066-0321
502 625-5000 **Jefferson County** 527 W Jefferson St ... Louisville KY 40202-2814
Fax: 502 625-6605
314 789-3911 **Jefferson County** PO Box 100 ... Hillsboro MO 63050-0100
Fax: 314 789-5506
601 786-3021 **Jefferson County** 307 Main St ... Fayette MS 39069-0000
406 225-4251 **Jefferson County** PO Box H ... Boulder MT 59632-0249
402 729-2323 **Jefferson County** 411 4th St ... Fairbury NE 68352-2536
315 785-3090 **Jefferson County** 175 Arsenal St ... Watertown NY 13601-2522
614 283-4111 **Jefferson County** 301 Market St ... Steubenville OH 43952-2149
405 228-2241 **Jefferson County** 220 N Main St Rm 101 ... Waurika OK 73573-2235
503 475-2449 **Jefferson County** 657 C St ... Madras OR 97741-1709
Fax: 503 475-6063
814 849-8031 **Jefferson County** 200 Main St ... Brookville PA 15825-1236
615 397-2935 **Jefferson County** PO Box 710 ... Dandridge TN 37725-0710
409 835-8475 **Jefferson County** 1149 Pearl St ... Beaumont TX 77701-3619
206 385-9125 **Jefferson County** PO Box 1220 ... Port Townsend WA 98368-0920
414 674-2500 **Jefferson County** 320 S Main St ... Jefferson WI 53549-1718
304 725-9761 **Jefferson County** George & Washington Sts ... Charles Town WV 25414-0000
315 782-3491 **Jefferson County Historical Society** 228 Washington St ... Watertown NY 13601-3379
303 232-7114 **Jefferson County Public Library** 10200 W 20th Ave ... Lakewood CO 80215-1402
Fax: 303 233-5729
601 792-4204 **Jefferson Davis County** PO Box 1137 ... Prentiss MS 39474-1137
318 824-4792 **Jefferson Davis Parish** PO Box 1409 ... Jennings LA 70546-1409
205 867-4832 **Jefferson Davis State Junior College** Alco Dr ... Brewton AL 36426-0000
Fax: 205 867-7339
504 364-2800 **Jefferson Parish** 2nd & Derbigny ... Gretna LA 70053-3299
Fax: 504 364-3849
504 834-5850 **Jefferson Parish Library Dept** 3420 N Causeway Blvd ... Metairie LA 70002-3509
Fax: 504 838-1110
205 853-1200 **Jefferson State Community College** 2601 Carson Rd ... Birmingham AL 35215-3007
Fax: 205 853-0340
614 264-5591 **Jefferson Technical College** 4000 Sunset Blvd ... Steubenville OH 43952-3512
Fax: 614 264-1338
202 225-6636 **Jefferson William J (Rep - D - Louisiana)**
506 Cannon Bldg ... Washington DC 20515-0001
Fax: 202 226-1239
804 979-7151 **Jefferson-Madison Regional Library** 201 E Market St ... Charlottesville VA 22901-5287
Fax: 804 571-7035
202 224-5141 **Jeffords James M (Sen - R - Vermont)** 530 Dirksen Bldg ... Washington DC 20510-0001
Fax: 202 224-1507
912 982-2563 **Jenkins County** PO Box 797 ... Millen GA 30442-0797
202 225-5211 **Jenkins Ed (Rep - D - Georgia)** 2427 Rayburn Bldg ... Washington DC 20515-0001
Fax: Unlisted
812 346-5977 **Jennings County** County Courthouse ... Vernon IN 47282-0000
605 539-1202 **Jerauld County** PO Box 435 ... Wessington Springs SD 57382-0435
208 324-8811 **Jerome County** 300 N Lincoln Ave ... Jerome ID 83338-2344
Fax: 208 324-2719
201 547-4500 **Jersey City Public Library** 472 Jersey Ave ... Jersey City NJ 07302-3499
Fax: 201 547-4584
201 547-6000 **Jersey City State College** 2039 John F Kennedy Blvd ... Jersey City NJ 07305-1527
Fax: 201 547-2072
618 498-5571 **Jersey County** 201 W Pearl St ... Jerseyville IL 62052-1675
606 885-4161 **Jessamine County** PO Box 38 ... Nicholasville KY 40356-0036
415 841-8804 **Jesuit School of Theology** 1735 Leroy Ave ... Berkeley CA 94709-1193
Fax: 415 841-8536
913 378-3121 **Jewell County** 307 N Commercial St ... Mankato KS 66956-2025
Fax: 913 378-3053
212 860-1889 **Jewish Museum** 1109 5th Ave ... New York NY 10128-0118
Fax: 212 410-3855
212 678-8000 **Jewish Theological Seminary of America** 3080 Broadway ... New York NY 10027-4650
Fax: 212 678-8947
205 539-8161 **JF Drake State Technical College** 3421 Meridian St N ... Huntsville AL 35811-1544
512 527-4031 **Jim Hogg County** PO Box 729 ... Hebbronville TX 78361-0729
Fax: 512 527-4611
512 668-5702 **Jim Wells County** PO Box 1459 ... Alice TX 78333-1459
815 777-0161 **Jo Daviess County** 330 N Bench St ... Galena IL 61036-1828
Fax: 815 777-3688
615 327-3927 **John A Gupton College** 2507 West End Ave ... Nashville TN 37203-1494
618 985-3741 **John A Logan College** ... Carterville IL 62918-0000
Fax: 618 985-2248
501 524-3131 **John Brown University** ... Siloam Springs AR 72761-2121
Fax: 501 524-4196 Admissions
205 353-3102 **John C Calhoun State Community College** Hwy 31 N ... Decatur AL 35609-0000
Fax: 205 350-1379

216 397-1886 **John Carroll University** 20700 N Park Blvd ... University Heights OH 44118-4581
Fax: 216 397-4256
205 288-1080 **John M Patterson State Technical College**
3920 Troy Hwy ... Montgomery AL 36116-2612
312 427-2737 **John Marshall Law School** 315 S Plymouth Ct ... Chicago IL 60604-3968
Fax: 312 427-8307
804 796-4000 **John Tyler Community College** 13101 Jefferson Davis Hwy ... Chester VA 23831-5316
Fax: 804 796-4163
217 224-6500 **John Wood Community College** 150 S 48th St ... Quincy IL 62301-9147
Fax: 217 224-4208
301 955-5000 **Johns Hopkins Medical Institutions School of Medicine**
720 Rutland Ave ... Baltimore MD 21205-2109
Fax: 301 955-3182 Admissions
301 338-8000 **Johns Hopkins University** 3400 N Charles St ... Baltimore MD 21218-2608
Fax: 301 338-5200 Communications
301 338-7034 *Department of Earth & Planetary Science*
3400 N Charles St Olin Hall ... Baltimore MD 21218-0000
Fax: 301 338-7933
301 955-3671 *Graduate School of Biochemistry* 615 N Wolfe St ... Baltimore MD 21205-2103
Fax: 301 955-7407
301 955-3204 *Graduate School of Cell Biology & Anatomy*
725 N Wolfe St ... Baltimore MD 21205-2105
Fax: 301 955-4129
301 338-7429 *Graduate School of Chemistry*
3400 N Charles St Remsen Hall ... Baltimore MD 21218-0000
Fax: 301 338-8420
301 338-7347 *Graduate School of Physics*
3400 N Charles St Bloomberg Ctr Rm 366-K ... Baltimore MD 21218-0000
Fax: 301 338-8260
301 338-8350 *GWC Whiting School of Engineering*
3400 N Charles St New Engineering Bldg Rm 120 ... Baltimore MD 21218-0000
Fax: 301 338-8627
301 955-3543 *School of Hygiene & Public Health* 615 N Wolfe St ... Baltimore MD 21205-2103
Fax: 301 955-7407
401 456-1000 **Johnson & Wales University** 8 Abbott Park Pl ... Providence RI 02903-3775
Fax: 401 421-9598
615 573-4517 **Johnson Bible College** 7900 Johnson Dr ... Knoxville TN 37998-0001
Fax: 615 579-2337
704 378-1000 **Johnson C Smith University** 100 Beatties Ford Rd ... Charlotte NC 28216-5398
Fax: 704 333-7854
501 754-2175 **Johnson County** PO Box 278 ... Clarksville AR 72830-0278
912 864-3388 **Johnson County** PO Box 269 ... Wrightsville GA 31096-0269
319 356-6060 **Johnson County** 417 S Clinton St ... Iowa City IA 52240-4108
618 658-3611 **Johnson County** PO Box 96 ... Vienna IL 62995-0096
317 736-5000 **Johnson County** 5 E Jefferson St ... Franklin IN 46131-0000
913 782-5000 **Johnson County** Santa Fe & Kansas Aves ... Olathe KS 66061-3195
Fax: 913 791-5000
606 789-2550 **Johnson County** Court St ... Paintsville KY 41240-0000
816 747-6161 **Johnson County** County Courthouse ... Warrensburg MO 64093-1794
402 335-3246 **Johnson County** PO Box 416 ... Tecumseh NE 68450-0416
615 727-9633 **Johnson County** 222 Main St ... Mountain City TN 37683-0000
Fax: 615 727-9486
817 641-4421 **Johnson County** PO Box 662 ... Cleburne TX 76033-0662
307 684-7272 **Johnson County** 76 N Main St ... Buffalo WY 82834-1847
Fax: 307 684-9598
913 469-8500 **Johnson County Community College**
12345 College & Quivira ... Overland Park KS 66210-0000
Fax: 913 469-4409
913 831-1550 **Johnson County Library** 8700 W 63rd St ... Shawnee Mission KS 66202-2892
Fax: 913 831-0601
607 255-6464 **Johnson Herbert F Museum of Art** Cornell University ... Ithaca NY 14853-0001
214 670-1400 **Johnson J Eric Public Library** 1515 Young St ... Dallas TX 75201-5499
202 225-4476 **Johnson Nancy L (Rep - R - Connecticut)**
227 Cannon Bldg ... Washington DC 20515-0001
Fax: 202 225-4488
802 635-2356 **Johnson State College** College Hill ... Johnson VT 05656-0000
Fax: 802 635-7615 Library
202 225-2801 **Johnson Tim (Rep - D - South Dakota)** 428 Cannon Bldg ... Washington DC 20515-0001
Fax: 202 225-2427
919 989-5100 **Johnston County** 207 E Johnston St ... Smithfield NC 27577-4515
Fax: 919 989-5179
405 371-3058 **Johnston County** PO Box 338 ... Tishomingo OK 73460-0338
202 225-3001 **Johnston Harry A (Rep - D - Florida)**
1028 Longworth Bldg ... Washington DC 20515-0001
Fax: 202 225-8791
202 224-5824 **Johnston J Bennett (Sen - D - Louisiana)** 136 Hart Bldg ... Washington DC 20510-0001
Fax: Unlisted
919 934-3051 **Johnston Technical Institute** Hwy 70 E ... Smithfield NC 27577-0000
Fax: 919 934-2823
202 697-4272 **Joint Chiefs of Staff (Chairman)** Pentagon Rm 2E-857 ... Washington DC 20318-0001
Fax: 202 697-8758
202 697-9225 *Air Force Chief of Staff* Pentagon Rm 4E-924 ... Washington DC 20330-0001
Fax: 202 693-7553
202 695-2077 *Army Chief of Staff* Pentagon Rm 3E-668 ... Washington DC 20310-0001
Fax: 202 695-9439
202 695-6007 *Chief of Naval Operations* Pentagon Rm 4E-658 ... Washington DC 20350-0001
Fax: 202 697-6290
202 694-2500 *Office of the Commandant of the Marine Corps*
Headquarters US Marine Corps ... Washington DC 20380-0001
Fax: 202 695-5035
202 224-5241 **Joint Committee on Printing** 818 Hart Bldg ... Washington DC 20510-0001
Fax: 202 224-1176
202 225-3621 **Joint Committee on Taxation** 1015 Longworth Bldg ... Washington DC 20515-0001
Fax: 202 225-0832
202 226-7633 **Joint Committee on the Library** House Annex 1 Rm 103 ... Washington DC 20510-0001
202 224-5171 **Joint Economic Committee** G-01 Dirksen Bldg ... Washington DC 20510-0001
Fax: 202 224-0240
815 729-9020 **Joliet Junior College** 1216 Houbolt Ave ... Joliet IL 60436-9352
Fax: 815 744-5507
202 225-4272 **Jones Ben (Rep - D - Georgia)** 514 Cannon Bldg ... Washington DC 20515-0001
Fax: 202 225-8675
904 743-1122 **Jones College at Jacksonville** 5353 Arlington Expy ... Jacksonville FL 32211-5588
Fax: Call company operator
912 986-6405 **Jones County** PO Box 1359 ... Gray GA 31032-1359
319 462-4341 **Jones County** High St ... Anamosa IA 52205-0000
601 428-0527 **Jones County** PO Box 1468 ... Laurel MS 39441-1468
919 448-7571 **Jones County** PO Box 266 ... Trenton NC 28585-0266
Fax: 919 448-1072
605 669-2361 **Jones County** PO Box 448 ... Murdo SD 57559-0448
915 823-3762 **Jones County** PO Box 552 ... Anson TX 79501-0552
601 477-9311 **Jones County Junior College** College Dr ... Ellisville MS 39437-3901
Fax: 601 477-2600
202 225-3101 **Jones Walter B (Rep - D - North Carolina)**
241 Cannon Bldg ... Washington DC 20515-0001
Fax: Unlisted

202 225-5037 **Jontz James (Rep - D - Indiana)** 1317 Longworth Bldg ...... Washington DC 20515-0001
Fax: 202 225-5870
616 696-1180 **Jordan College (System)** 360 W Pine St .... Cedar Springs MI 49319-9686
Fax: 616 696-3790
Jordan: Hashemite Kingdom of Jordan
202 966-2664 *Embassy* 3504 International Dr NW .... Washington DC 20008-3035
Fax: 202 966-3110
212 752-0135 *Mission to the UN* 866 UN Plaza Rm 552 .... New York NY 10017-0000
Fax: Unlisted
503 474-5221 **Josephine County** County Courthouse .... Grants Pass OR 97526-0000
Fax: 503 474-5101
402 342-3300 **Joslyn Art Museum** 2200 Dodge St .... Omaha NE 68102-1294
Fax: 402 342-2376
801 623-0271 **Juab County** 160 N Main St .... Nephi UT 84648-1412
Fax: 801 623-1507
202 225-3951 **Judiciary Committee (US House of Representatives)**
2138 Rayburn Bldg .... Washington DC 20515-0001
Fax: 202 225-1958
202 224-5225 **Judiciary Committee (US Senate)** 224 Dirksen Bldg .... Washington DC 20510-0001
Fax: 202 224-9516
406 566-2250 **Judith Basin County** Courthouse .... Stanford MT 59479-0000
205 683-6161 **Judson College** Bibb St .... Marion AL 36756-0120
708 695-2500 **Judson College** 1151 N State St .... Elgin IL 60123-1404
Fax: 708 695-0407
212 799-5000 **Juilliard School** 144 W 66th St .... New York NY 10023-6502
Fax: 212 724-0263
907 586-3300 **Juneau Borough** 155 S Seward St .... Juneau AK 99801-1332
Fax: 907 463-4808
608 847-9300 **Juneau County** 220 E State St .... Mauston WI 53948-1345
Fax: 608 847-9369
907 586-3572 **Juneau Douglas City Museum** 115 S Seward St .... Juneau AK 99801-1332
814 643-4310 **Juniata College** 1700 Moore St .... Huntingdon PA 16652-2119
Fax: 814 643-3620 Library
717 436-8991 **Juniata County** PO Box 68 .... Mifflintown PA 17059-0068
305 446-7608 **Junior Chamber International** 400 University Dr .... Coral Gables FL 33134-7186
Fax: 305 442-0041
619 297-3258 **Junipero Serra Museum** PO Box 81825 .... San Diego CA 92138-1825

K

616 383-8400 **Kalamazoo College** 1200 Academy St .... Kalamazoo MI 49007-3295
Fax: 616 383-5688
616 383-8840 **Kalamazoo County** 201 W Kalamazoo Ave .... Kalamazoo MI 49007-0000
616 342-9837 **Kalamazoo Public Library** 315 S Rose St .... Kalamazoo MI 49007-5270
Fax: 616 342-0414
616 372-5000 **Kalamazoo Valley Community College** 6767 W 'O' Ave .... Kalamazoo MI 49009-9606
Fax: Unlisted
616 258-3300 **Kalkaska County** 605 N Birch St .... Kalkaska MI 49646-0000
612 679-1022 **Kanabec County** 18 Vine St N .... Mora MN 55051-1351
304 357-0101 **Kanawha County** PO Box 3627 .... Charleston WV 25336-0000
304 343-4646 **Kanawha County Public Library** 123 Capitol St .... Charleston WV 25301-2686
612 231-6202 **Kandiyohi County** 515 Becker Ave SW .... Willmar MN 56201-3281
Fax: 612 231-6276
708 232-3400 **Kane County** 100 S 3rd St .... Geneva IL 60134-2722
Fax: 708 232-0375
801 644-2551 **Kane County** 76 N Main St .... Kanab UT 84741-3219
808 257-2170 **Kaneohe Bay Marine Corps Air Station** .... Kaneohe Bay HI 96863-0001
202 225-6511 **Kanjorski Paul E (Rep - D - Pennsylvania)**
424 Cannon Bldg .... Washington DC 20515-0001
Fax: 202 225-9024
815 933-0345 **Kankakee Community College** River Rd .... Kankakee IL 60901-0000
Fax: 815 933-0217
815 937-2990 **Kankakee County** 450 E Court St .... Kankakee IL 60901-3997
913 357-6321 **Kansas Chamber of Commerce & Industry** 500 Bank IV Tower .. Topeka KS 66603-3406
Fax: 913 357-4732
816 274-2000 **Kansas City City Hall** 414 E 12th St .... Kansas City MO 64106-2705
816 561-4852 **Kansas City Art Institute** 4415 Warwick Blvd .... Kansas City MO 64111-1874
Fax: 816 561-6404
913 334-1100 **Kansas City Kansas Community College** 7250 State Ave .... Kansas City KS 66112-3003
Fax: 913 596-9606
913 621-3073 **Kansas City Kansas Public Library System**
625 Minnesota Ave .... Kansas City KS 66101-2899
Fax: 913 621-0963
816 483-8300 **Kansas City Museum** 3218 Gladstone Blvd .... Kansas City MO 64123-1199
Fax: Ext 232
816 221-2685 **Kansas City Public Library** 311 E 12th St .... Kansas City MO 64106-2412
Fax: 816 842-6839
913 825-0275 **Kansas College of Technology** 2409 Scanlan Ave .... Salina KS 67401-8196
Fax: 913 835-8475
913 234-0425 **Kansas Democratic State Committee**
700 SW Jackson St Suite 305 .... Topeka KS 66603-3738
Fax: 913 234-8420
913 296-2009 **Kansas Div of Travel & Tourism** 400 SW 8th St 5th Fl .... Topeka KS 66603-0000
Fax: 913 296-5055
913 272-8681 **Kansas Museum of History** 6425 SW 6th St .... Topeka KS 66615-1099
316 942-4291 **Kansas Newman College** 3100 McCormick St .... Wichita KS 67213-2008
Fax: 316 942-4483
913 234-3416 **Kansas Republican Party** 214 SW 6th Ave .... Topeka KS 66603-3719
Fax: 913 234-3436
Kansas State Government
913 296-0111 *Information* 915 SW Harrison St .... Topeka KS 66612-1505
Fax: 913 296-6729
913 296-3251 *Archives & Records* 120 W 10th St .... Topeka KS 66612-0000
Fax: 913 296-1005
913 296-3335 *Arts Commission* 700 SW Jackson St Suite 1004 .... Topeka KS 66603-3742
913 296-2215 *Attorney General* 301 W 10th St 2nd Fl .... Topeka KS 66612-0000
Fax: 913 296-6296
913 296-3558 *Board of Agriculture* 109 SW 9th St .... Topeka KS 66612-1215
Fax: 913 296-2217
913 296-3421 *Board of Regents* 400 SW 8th St .... Topeka KS 66603-3958
Fax: 913 296-0983
913 296-1540 *Bureau of Air Quality & Radiation Control*
Forbes Field Bldg 740 .... Topeka KS 66620-0001
Fax: 913 296-6247
913 296-1593 *Bureau of Waste Management* Forbes Field Bldg 740 .... Topeka KS 66620-0001
Fax: 913 296-6247
913 296-3751 *Consumer Protection Div* 301 W 10th St .... Topeka KS 66612-0000
Fax: 913 296-6296
913 296-3011 *Department of Administration*
9th & Jackson Sts State Capitol Rm 263-E .... Topeka KS 66612-0000
Fax: 913 296-7973
913 296-3317 *Department of Corrections*
900 SW Jackson St Landon State Office Bldg 4th Fl .... Topeka KS 66612-1284
Fax: 913 296-0014
913 296-3201 *Department of Education* 120 E 10th St .... Topeka KS 66612-0000
Fax: 913 296-7933
913 296-5076 *Department of Human Resources* 401 Topeka Blvd .... Topeka KS 66603-0000
Fax: 913 296-0179
913 296-3041 *Department of Revenue* State Office Bldg 2nd Fl .... Topeka KS 66612-0000
Fax: 913 296-7928
913 296-3461 *Department of Transportation*
Docking State Office Bldg 7th Fl .... Topeka KS 66612-0000
Fax: 913 296-0287
913 266-1000 *Division of Emergency Preparedness* 2800 Topeka Ave .... Topeka KS 66601-0000
Fax: 913 266-1129
913 296-1535 *Division of Environment* Forbes Field Bldg 740 .... Topeka KS 66620-0001
Fax: 913 296-6247
913 296-7475 *Division of Labor-Management Relations & Employment Standards*
1430 SW Topeka Blvd .... Topeka KS 66612-1853
Fax: 913 296-4065
913 296-2376 *Division of Purchasing* 900 SW Jackson St Rm 102 N .... Topeka KS 66612-1220
Fax: 913 296-7240
913 296-3441 *Division of Worker's Compensation*
800 S W Jackson St Merchants Bank Tower Suite 600 .... Topeka KS 66612-1227
913 271-3170 *Energy Programs Div Kansas Corporation Commission*
1500 SW Arrowhead Rd .... Topeka KS 66604-0000
Fax: 913 271-3354
913 296-3232 *Governor* 9th & Jackson Sts State Capitol 2nd Fl .... Topeka KS 66612-1590
Fax: 913 296-7973
913 296-6800 *Highway Patrol* 122 SW 7th St .... Topeka KS 66603-3847
Fax: 913 296-5956
913 296-4505 *Indigents' Defense Services* 900 SW Jackson St Rm 506 N .... Topeka KS 66612-1255
913 296-3483 *Industrial Development Div Kansas Dept of Commerce*
400 SW 8th St Suite 500 .... Topeka KS 66603-0000
Fax: 913 296-5055
913 296-4386 *Industrial Safety & Health Section* 512 W 6th St .... Topeka KS 66603-0000
Fax: 913 296-4789
913 296-3071 *Insurance Dept* 420 SW 9th St .... Topeka KS 66612-1678
Fax: 913 296-2283
316 662-2321 *Kansas State Industrial Reformatory* PO Box 1568 .... Hutchinson KS 67504-1568
Fax: 316 662-8662
913 727-3235 *Kansas State Penitentiary* Kansas Ave .... Lansing KS 66043-0002
Fax: Call company operator
913 296-2213 *Lieutenant Governor* State Capitol Rm 222-S .... Topeka KS 66612-0000
913 296-1400 *Office of Vital Statistics* 900 SW Jackson St .... Topeka KS 66612-1290
913 296-3469 *Parole Board* 900 SW Jackson St 4th Fl .... Topeka KS 66612-1236
Fax: 913 296-0014
913 296-3411 *Real Estate Commission* 900 SW Jackson St Rm 501 .... Topeka KS 66612-1226
913 296-2236 *Secretary of State* State Capitol 2nd Fl .... Topeka KS 66612-0000
Fax: 913 296-3659
913 296-3307 *Securities Commissioner* 618 S Kansas Ave 2nd Fl .... Topeka KS 66603-3804
Fax: 913 296-6872
913 296-3289 *State Historical Society* 120 W 10th St .... Topeka KS 66612-1291
Fax: 913 296-1005
913 296-3229 *Supreme Court* 301 SW 10th St .... Topeka KS 66612-1599
913 296-3171 *Treasurer* 900 Jackson St Suite 201 .... Topeka KS 66612-1235
Fax: 913 296-7950
913 296-1796 *Unemployment Insurance Program* 1431 Topeka Ave .... Topeka KS 66612-0000
913 296-4191 *Utilities Div* Docking State Office Bldg 4th Fl .... Topeka KS 66612-0000
Fax: 913 296-3596
913 296-3185 *Water Office* 109 SW 9th St Suite 200 .... Topeka KS 66612-1249
Fax: 913 296-2247
913 296-3296 **Kansas State Library** State Capitol 3rd Fl .... Topeka KS 66612-0000
Fax: 913 296-6650
913 532-6011 **Kansas State University** .... Manhattan KS 66506-0001
Fax: 913 532-5632 Admissions
913 532-6890 *AQ Miller School of Journalism & Mass Communication*
Kedzie Hall Rm 104 .... Manhattan KS 66506-0001
Fax: 913 532-7309
913 532-6147 *College of Agriculture* Waters Hall Rm 117 .... Manhattan KS 66506-0001
Fax: 913 532-6563
913 532-5660 *College of Veterinary Medicine* Trotter Hall Rm 101 .... Manhattan KS 66506-0001
Fax: 913 532-5884
913 532-5958 *Department of Regional & Community Planning*
Seaton Hall Rm 302 .... Manhattan KS 66506-0001
Fax: 913 532-6722
913 827-5541 **Kansas Wesleyan University** 100 E Claflin Ave .... Salina KS 67401-6196
Fax: 913 827-0927
808 734-9111 **Kapiolani Community College** 4303 Diamond Head Rd .... Honolulu HI 96816-4416
Fax: 808 734-9287 Library
202 225-4146 **Kaptur Marcy (Rep - D - Ohio)** 1228 Longworth Bldg .... Washington DC 20515-0001
Fax: 202 225-7711
512 780-3938 **Karnes County** 101 N Panna Maria St .... Karnes City TX 78118-2959
202 225-5355 **Kasich John R (Rep - R - Ohio)** 1133 Longworth Bldg .... Washington DC 20515-0001
Fax: Unlisted
618 532-1981 **Kaskaskia College** Shattuc Rd .... Centralia IL 62801-0000
Fax: Ext 263
202 224-4774 **Kassebaum Nancy Landon (Sen - R - Kansas)**
302 Russell Bldg .... Washington DC 20510-0001
Fax: 202 224-3514
202 224-5323 **Kasten Robert W Jr (Sen - R - Wisconsin)** 110 Hart Bldg ... Washington DC 20510-0001
Fax: 202 224-2548
808 245-8311 **Kauai Community College** 3-1901 Kaumualii Hwy .... Lihue HI 96766-9591
Fax: 808 245-8288
808 245-4785 **Kauai County** 4396 Rice St .... Lihue HI 96766-1337
214 932-4331 **Kaufman County** Washington St .... Kaufman TX 75142-0000
405 362-3116 **Kay County** PO Box 450 .... Newkirk OK 74647-0450
908 527-2000 **Kean College of New Jersey** 1000 Morris Ave .... Union NJ 07083-7133
Fax: 908 527-2243
308 832-1155 **Kearney County** PO Box 339 .... Minden NE 68959-0339
308 236-8441 **Kearney State College** 905 W 25th St .... Kearney NE 68849-0001
Fax: 308 234-8665 Admin
316 355-6422 **Kearny County** 305 N Main St .... Lakin KS 67860-0000
603 352-1909 **Keene State College** 229 Main St .... Keene NH 03431-4183
Fax: Ext 272
601 377-1110 **Keesler Air Force Base** .... Biloxi MS 39534-0000
Fax: 601 377-3750
308 284-4726 **Keith County** PO Box 149 .... Ogallala NE 69153-0149
Fax: 308 284-6951
616 965-3931 **Kellogg Community College** 450 North Ave .... Battle Creek MI 49017-3397
Fax: Call company operator
512 925-1110 **Kelly Air Force Base** .... San Antonio TX 78241-5000
313 763-3559 **Kelsey Museum of Ancient & Medieval Archaeology**
434 S State St University of Michigan .... Ann Arbor MI 48109-1390
Fax: 313 764-2697
601 743-2460 **Kemper County** PO Box 188 .... De Kalb MS 39328-0188
816 882-5623 **Kemper Military School & College** 701 3rd St .... Boonville MO 65233-1670
Fax: 816 882-3332
907 262-4441 **Kenai Peninsula Borough** 144 N Binkley .... Soldotna AK 99669-7520
Fax: 907 262-1892

907 262-5801 **Kenai Peninsula College** 34820 College Dr ... Soldotna AK 99669-9732
Fax: 907 262-9280
708 866-1300 **Kendall College** 2408 Orrington Ave ... Evanston IL 60201-2899
Fax: 708 866-1320
616 451-2787 **Kendall College of Art & Design** 111 N Division Ave ... Grand Rapids MI 49503-3102
Fax: 616 451-9867
708 553-4104 **Kendall County** 110 W Ridge St ... Yorkville IL 60560-1432
Fax: 708 553-4214
512 249-9343 **Kendall County** 204 E San Antonio St ... Boerne TX 78006-2050
617 784-5642 **Kendall Whaling Museum** 27 Everett St ... Sharon MA 02067-1018
512 294-5220 **Kenedy County** PO Box 7 ... Sarita TX 78385-0007
207 622-0971 **Kennebec County** 95 State St ... Augusta ME 04330-5611
202 224-4543 **Kennedy Edward M (Sen - D - Massachusetts)**
315 Russell Bldg ... Washington DC 20510-0001
Fax: 202 224-2417
305 821-2700 **Kennedy John F Library** 190 W 49th St ... Hialeah FL 33012-3712
202 225-5111 **Kennedy Joseph P II (Rep - D - Massachusetts)**
1208 Longworth Bldg ... Washington DC 20515-0001
Fax: 202 225-9322
312 962-3200 **Kennedy-King College** 6800 S Wentworth Ave ... Chicago IL 60621-3798
Fax: Ext 505
202 225-2265 **Kennelly Barbara B (Rep - D - Connecticut)**
204 Cannon Bldg ... Washington DC 20515-0001
Fax: 202 225-1031
404 423-6000 **Kennesaw State College** 3455 Frey Lake Rd ... Kennesaw GA 30144-3031
Fax: 404 423-6433
414 656-6400 **Kenosha County** 912 56th St ... Kenosha WI 53140-3747
Fax: 414 665-6708
414 656-8026 **Kenosha Public Museum** 5608 10th Ave ... Kenosha WI 53140-4091
818 240-9166 **Kensington University** 124 S Isabel St ... Glendale CA 91205-4911
Fax: 818 240-1707
302 736-2040 **Kent County** 414 Federal St ... Dover DE 19901-3615
Fax: 302 736-2244
301 778-4600 **Kent County** 230 N Cross St ... Chestertown MD 21620-1512
616 774-3548 **Kent County** 300 Monroe Ave NW ... Grand Rapids MI 49503-0000
401 822-1311 **Kent County** 222 Quaker Ln ... West Warwick RI 02893-2144
806 237-3881 **Kent County** Main St ... Jayton TX 79528-0000
616 774-3250 **Kent County Library System** 775 Ball Ave NE ... Grand Rapids MI 49503-1397
Fax: 616 242-6981
216 672-2121 **Kent State University** ... Kent OH 44242-0001
Fax: 216 672-2190 Admin
216 964-3322 *Ashtabula Campus* 3325 W 13th St ... Ashtabula OH 44004-2299
Fax: 216 964-2237
216 385-3805 *East Liverpool Campus* 400 E 4th St ... East Liverpool OH 43920-3497
Fax: 216 385-6348
216 332-0361 *Salem Campus* 2491 SR-45 S ... Salem OH 44460-9412
Fax: 216 332-9256
216 672-2572 *School of Journalism & Mass Communications* 130 Taylor Hall .. Kent OH 44242-0001
216 499-9600 *Stark Campus* 6000 Frank Ave NW ... Canton OH 44720-7599
Fax: 216 494-6121
216 847-0571 *Trumbull Campus* 4314 Mahoning Ave NW ... Warren OH 44483-1998
Fax: 216 847-6172 Admin
216 339-3391 *Tuscarawas Campus* University Dr NE ... New Philadelphia OH 44663-9422
Fax: 216 339-3321
606 491-0702 **Kenton County** 3rd & Court St 1st Fl ... Covington KY 41012-0000
606 491-7610 **Kenton County Public Library** 502 Scott St ... Covington KY 41011-1590
502 695-4700 **Kentucky Chamber of Commerce** 452 Versailles Rd ... Frankfort KY 40602-0000
Fax: 502 695-6824
606 474-6613 **Kentucky Christian College** 617 N Carol Malone Blvd ... Grayson KY 41143-1199
Fax: 606 474-3502
502 695-4828 **Kentucky Democratic State Committee** PO Box 694 ... Frankfort KY 40602-0694
502 875-7000 **Kentucky Department for Libraries & Archives**
300 Coffee Tree Rd ... Frankfort KY 40601-0000
Fax: 502 564-5773
502 564-4930 **Kentucky Dept of Travel Development**
Capital Plaza Tower 22nd Fl ... Frankfort KY 40601-0000
Fax: 502 564-5695
502 745-2592 **Kentucky Museum**
Western Kentucky University College Heights ... Bowling Green KY 42101-3576
Kentucky State Government
502 564-2500 *Information* State Capitol Annex Rm 52 ... Frankfort KY 40601-3410
502 564-7600 *Attorney General* Capitol Ave Rm 116 ... Frankfort KY 40601-0000
Fax: 502 564-2894
502 564-4726 *Corrections Cabinet*
Holmes & High Sts State Office Bldg 5th Fl ... Frankfort KY 40601-0000
Fax: 502 564-5229
502 564-3553 *Council on Higher Education* 1050 US Hwy 127 S ... Frankfort KY 40601-4326
Fax: 502 564-2063
502 564-5331 *Department for Employment Services* 275 E Main St ... Frankfort KY 40621-0001
Fax: 502 564-7452
502 564-3970 *Department for Health Services* 275 E Main St ... Frankfort KY 40621-0001
Fax: 502 564-4537
502 875-7000 *Department for Libraries & Archives* 300 Coffee Tree Rd ... Frankfort KY 40601-0000
Fax: 502 564-5773
502 564-4696 *Department of Agriculture* 500 Capitol Plaza Towers 7th Fl .. Frankfort KY 40601-1970
Fax: 502 564-6527
502 564-4770 *Department of Education* Capitol Plaza Tower 1st Fl ... Frankfort KY 40601-1972
Fax: 502 564-6771
502 564-2150 *Department of Environmental Protection* 18 Reilly Rd ... Frankfort KY 40601-1139
Fax: 502 564-4245
502 564-4890 *Department of Highways* Clinton & High Sts ... Frankfort KY 40622-0001
Fax: 502 564-4809
502 564-3630 *Department of Insurance* 229 W Main St ... Frankfort KY 40601-0000
Fax: 502 564-6090
606 254-0367 *Department of Mines & Minerals* 3572 Iron Works Pike ... Lexington KY 40511-0000
502 564-5213 *Department of Public Advocacy*
1264 Louisville Rd Perimeter Pk W ... Frankfort KY 40601-0000
502 695-6300 *Department of State Police* 919 Versailles Rd ... Frankfort KY 40601-4740
Fax: 502 564-6615
502 564-8076 *Department of the Arts* Berry Hill Mansion ... Frankfort KY 40601-0000
Fax: 502 564-7588
502 564-5550 *Department of Workers' Claims* 1270 Louisville Rd Bldg C .. Frankfort KY 40601-0000
502 564-3382 *Division of Air Pollution Control* 316 St Clair Mall ... Frankfort KY 40601-1189
Fax: 502 564-3787
502 564-2200 *Division of Consumer Protection* 209 Saint Clair St ... Frankfort KY 40601-1855
502 564-8682 *Division of Disaster & Emergency Services*
Boone National Guard Ctr ... Frankfort KY 40601-1189
Fax: 502 564-8614
502 564-2980 *Division of Engineering* State Capitol Annex Rm 128 ... Frankfort KY 40601-0000
Fax: 502 564-3649
502 564-3296 *Division of Occupational & Professional Licensing*
PO Box 456 ... Frankfort KY 40602-0456
Fax: 502 564-4818
502 564-4510 *Division of Purchases* State Capitol Annex Rm 348 ... Frankfort KY 40601-0000
Fax: 502 564-7209
502 564-2180 *Division of Securities* 911 Leawood Dr ... Frankfort KY 40601-3319
Fax: 502 564-8787
502 564-2900 *Division of Unemployment Insurance*
275 E Main St 2nd Fl E ... Frankfort KY 40621-0001
Fax: 502 564-7452
502 564-6716 *Division of Waste Management* 18 Reilly Rd ... Frankfort KY 40601-1189
Fax: 502 564-4245
502 564-3410 *Division of Water* 18 Reilly Rd ... Frankfort KY 40601-1189
Fax: 502 564-4246
502 564-4240 *Finance & Administration Cabinet*
State Capitol Annex Rm 301 ... Frankfort KY 40601-0000
Fax: 502 564-6785
502 564-2611 *Governor* State Capitol Rm 100 ... Frankfort KY 40601-3492
Fax: 502 564-2735
502 564-7300 *Governors Office for Policy & Management*
State Capitol Annex Rm 209 ... Frankfort KY 40601-0000
Fax: 502 564-6684
502 388-2211 *Kentucky State Penitentiary* Rt 2 & Old Eddyville Rd ... Eddyville KY 42038-9802
Fax: Unlisted
502 222-9441 *Kentucky State Reformatory* 3001 W Hwy 146 ... La Grange KY 40032-0001
502 564-3070 *Labor Cabinet* 1049 US Hwy 127 S ... Frankfort KY 40601-0000
Fax: 502 564-6103
502 564-7562 *Lieutenant Governor* State Capitol Rm 142 ... Frankfort KY 40601-0000
Fax: 502 875-5954
502 564-6892 *Occupational Safety & Health Review Commission*
Rt 3 & Millville Rd Suite 4 ... Frankfort KY 40601-9803
606 252-5535 *Office for Coal & Energy Policy* PO Box 11888 ... Lexington KY 40578-1916
Fax: 606 255-4457
502 564-4212 *Office of Vital Statistics* 275 E Main St 1st Fl ... Frankfort KY 40621-0001
606 254-0367 *Oil & Gas Div Dept of Mines & Minerals*
3572 Iron Works Pike ... Lexington KY 40511-8410
502 564-4221 *Probation & Parole Div*
Holmes & High Sts State Office Bldg Rm 514 ... Frankfort KY 40601-0000
Fax: 502 564-5229
502 564-3940 *Public Services Commission* 730 Schenkel Ln ... Frankfort KY 40601-1402
Fax: 502 564-7279
502 425-4273 *Real Estate Commission* 10200 Linn Station Rd Suite 201 .. Louisville KY 40223-0000
502 564-4646 *Retirement Systems* 1260 Louisville Rd ... Frankfort KY 40601-6157
Fax: 502 564-7289
502 564-3226 *Revenue Cabinet* State Capitol Annex Rm 401 ... Frankfort KY 40601-0000
Fax: 502 564-3875
502 564-3490 *Secretary of State* State Capitol Rm 150 ... Frankfort KY 40601-0000
Fax: 502 564-4075
502 564-4720 *Supreme Court* State Capitol Rm 209 ... Frankfort KY 40601-0000
Fax: 502 564-5491
502 564-4890 *Transportation Cabinet* Clinton & High Sts 10th Fl ... Frankfort KY 40622-0001
Fax: 502 564-4809
502 564-4722 *Treasury Dept* State Capitol Annex Rm 129 ... Frankfort KY 40601-0000
Fax: 502 564-6545
502 227-6000 **Kentucky State University** 400 E Main St ... Frankfort KY 40601-2355
Fax: 502 227-6412 Admin
502 926-3111 **Kentucky Wesleyan College** 3000 Frederica St ... Owensboro KY 42301-6057
Fax: 502 926-3196
Kenya: Republic of Kenya
202 387-6101 *Embassy* 2249 R St NW ... Washington DC 20008-4017
Fax: 202 462-3829
212 421-4740 *Mission to the UN* 866 UN Plaza Rm 486 ... New York NY 10017-0000
614 427-5000 **Kenyon College** ... Gambier OH 43020-0000
Fax: 614 427-3077
515 622-2210 **Keokuk County** Courthouse Sq ... Sigourney IA 52591-1499
805 861-2111 **Kern County** 1415 Truxtun Ave ... Bakersfield CA 93301-5222
805 861-2130 **Kern County Library** 701 Truxten Ave ... Bakersfield CA 93301-4800
805 861-2132 **Kern County Museum** 3801 Chester Ave ... Bakersfield CA 93301-1345
512 257-6181 **Kerr County** 700 Main St ... Kerrville TX 78028-5323
202 224-6551 **Kerrey Bob (Sen - D - Nebraska)** 302 Hart Bldg ... Washington DC 20510-0001
Fax: 202 224-7645
202 224-2742 **Kerry John F (Sen - D - Massachusetts)** 421 Russell Bldg .. Washington DC 20510-0001
Fax: 202 224-8525
803 425-1527 **Kershaw County** 1121 Broad St ... Camden SC 29020-3638
Fax: 803 425-1502
907 225-6151 **Ketchikan Borough** 344 Front St ... Ketchikan AK 99901-6494
907 228-0220 **Ketchikan Coast Guard Base** ... Ketchikan AK 99901-0000
513 296-7201 **Kettering College of Medical Arts** 3737 Southern Blvd ... Kettering OH 45429-1299
Fax: 513 296-4226
315 536-4411 **Keuka College** Keuka Park Rd ... Keuka Park NY 14478-0000
Fax: Ext 216
414 388-4410 **Kewaunee County** 613 Dodge St ... Kewaunee WI 54216-0000
Fax: Ext 102
906 337-2229 **Keweenaw County** 4th St County Courthouse ... Eagle River MI 49924-9999
402 497-3791 **Keya Paha County** PO Box 349 ... Springview NE 68778-0349
717 945-5141 **Keystone Junior College** PO Box 50 ... La Plume PA 18440-0200
Fax: Call company operator
701 475-2672 **Kidder County** PO Box 110 ... Steele ND 58482-0110
202 225-3611 **Kildee Dale E (Rep - D - Michigan)** 2239 Rayburn Bldg ... Washington DC 20515-0001
Fax: Unlisted
903 984-8531 **Kilgore College** 1100 Broadway ... Kilgore TX 75662-0000
Fax: 903 983-8600
817 332-8451 **Kimball Art Museum** 3333 Camp Bowie Blvd ... Fort Worth TX 76107-2792
Fax: 817 877-1264
308 235-2241 **Kimball County** 114 E 3rd St ... Kimball NE 69145-1456
915 446-3353 **Kimble County** 501 Main St ... Junction TX 76849-4763
804 785-2460 **King & Queen County** County Courthouse ... King & Queen Courthouse VA 23085-0000
615 968-1187 **King College** 1350 King College Rd ... Bristol TN 37620-2632
Fax: 615 968-4456
806 596-4412 **King County** County Courthouse ... Guthrie TX 79236-9999
Fax: 806 596-4413
206 344-4040 **King County** 516 3rd Ave ... Seattle WA 98104-0000
Fax: 209 206-0194
206 684-6600 **King County Library System** 300 8th Ave N ... Seattle WA 98109-5191
Fax: 206 464-7481
703 775-3322 **King George County** PO Box 105 ... King George VA 22485-0105
804 769-4927 **King William County** PO Box 215 ... King William VA 23086-0215
Fax: 804 769-4964
914 941-7200 **King's College** 150 Lodge Rd ... Briarcliff Manor NY 10510-1200
Fax: 914 944-5636
717 826-5900 **King's College** 133 Darrow St ... Wilkes-Barre PA 18711-0000
Fax: 717 825-9049
405 375-3808 **Kingfisher County** PO Box 118 ... Kingfisher OK 73750-0118
316 532-2521 **Kingman County** 130 N Spruce St ... Kingman KS 67068-1647
616 965-5117 **Kingman Museum of Natural History**
W Michigan Ave & 20th St ... Battle Creek MI 49017-0000
209 582-3211 **Kings County** 1400 W Lacey Blvd ... Hanford CA 93230-5925
718 643-5771 **Kings County** 360 Adams St ... Brooklyn NY 11201-3712
209 638-3641 **Kings River Community College** 995 N Reed Ave ... Reedley CA 93654-2099
Fax: 209 638-5040
605 854-3811 **Kingsbury County** 101 2nd St SE ... De Smet SD 57231-0000

512 595-6146 **Kingsville Naval Air Station** .... Kingsville TX 78363-5000
512 563-2521 **Kinney County** Ann & James Sts .... Brackettville TX 78832-0000
719 438-5421 **Kiowa County** 1305 Goff St .... Eads CO 81036-0000
316 723-3366 **Kiowa County** 211 E Florida Ave .... Greensburg KS 67054-2294
405 726-5125 **Kiowa County** County Courthouse .... Hobart OK 73651-0000
405 427-5461 **Kirkpatrick Center Museum Complex** 2100 NE 52nd St .. Oklahoma City OK 73111-7107
Fax: 405 424-1407
319 398-5411 **Kirkwood Community College** 6301 Kirkwood Blvd SW .... Cedar Rapids IA 52404-5260
Fax: 319 398-5492
505 844-0011 **Kirtland Air Force Base** .... Albuquerque NM 87117-0001
Fax: 505 846-5700
517 275-5121 **Kirtland Community College** 10775 N St Helen Rd .. Roscommon MI 48653-9699
Fax: 517 275-8510
815 825-2086 **Kishwaukee College** Malta Rd & Hwy 38 .... Malta IL 60150-0000
Fax: 815 825-2072
407 847-5000 **Kissimmee Convention & Visitors Bureau** 1925 E 192 Hwy ..Kissimmee FL 34744-0000
719 346-8638 **Kit Carson County** PO Box 249 .... Burlington CO 80807-0249
206 876-7164 **Kitsap County** 614 Division St .... Port Orchard WA 98366-4676
206 377-7601 **Kitsap Regional Library** 1301 Sylvan Way .... Bremerton WA 98310-3498
Fax: 206 479-6149
509 962-7531 **Kittitas County** 205 W 5th Ave .... Ellensburg WA 98926-2887
218 843-3632 **Kittson County** 410 S 5th St .... Hallock MN 56728-0000
Fax: 218 843-2020
503 883-5134 **Klamath County** 316 Main St .... Klamath Falls OR 97601-6385
Fax: 503 882-6953
503 883-4208 **Klamath County Museum** 1451 Main St ...... Klamath Falls OR 97601-5989
512 592-6448 **Kleberg County** PO Box 1327 .... Kingsville TX 78364-1327
202 225-4572 **Kleczka Gerald D (Rep - D - Wisconsin)** 226 Cannon Bldg .. Washington DC 20515-0001
Fax: 202 225-0719
509 773-5744 **Klickitat County** 205 S Columbus Ave Rm 204 .... Goldendale WA 98620-9294
Fax: Unlisted
202 225-2906 **Klug Scott L (Rep - R - Wisconsin)** 1224 Longworth Bldg .. Washington DC 20515-0001
Fax: Unlisted
606 785-5651 **Knott County** PO Box 446 .... Hindman KY 41822-0446
309 343-0112 **Knox College** 2 E South St .... Galesburg IL 61401-4999
Fax: 309 343-8921
309 343-3121 **Knox County** 200 S Cherry St .... Galesburg IL 61401-4991
812 885-2521 **Knox County** 7th & Broadway .... Vincennes IN 47591-0000
606 546-3568 **Knox County** PO Box 105 .... Barbourville KY 40906-0105
Fax: 606 546-3589
207 594-0420 **Knox County** PO Box 885 .... Rockland ME 04841-0885
Fax: 207 594-0433
816 397-2184 **Knox County** 305 E Lafayette St .... Edina MO 63537-0000
402 288-4282 **Knox County** Main St .... Center NE 68724-0000
614 397-2727 **Knox County** 106 E High St .... Mount Vernon OH 43050-3453
Fax: 614 392-3533
615 521-2385 **Knox County** 300 W Main Ave .... Knoxville TN 37902-1805
817 454-2441 **Knox County** PO Box 196 .... Benjamin TX 79505-0196
615 544-5750 **Knox County Public Library System** 500 W Church Ave ...... Knoxville TN 37902-2505
Fax: Unlisted
615 524-6500 **Knoxville College** 901 College St NW .... Knoxville TN 37921-4799
Fax: 615 523-6917
615 586-5262 _Morristown Branch_ 417 N James St .... Morristown TN 37814-4470
907 486-5736 **Kodiak Borough** 710 Mill Bay Rd .... Kodiak AK 99615-6398
Fax: 907 486-2886
907 487-5733 **Kodiak Coast Guard Air Station** PO Box 33 .... Kodiak AK 99619-0001
907 487-5920 **Kodiak Coast Guard Support Center** PO Box 14 ...... Kodiak AK 99619-5000
907 486-4161 **Kodiak College** 117 Benny Benson Dr .... Kodiak AK 99615-6998
Fax: 907 486-4166
202 224-5653 **Kohl Herbert H (Sen - D - Wisconsin)** 702 Hart Bldg .... Washington DC 20510-0001
Fax: Unlisted
202 225-2542 **Kolbe Jim (Rep - R - Arizona)** 410 Cannon Bldg .... Washington DC 20515-0001
Fax: 202 225-0378
202 225-2565 **Kolter Joe (Rep - D - Pennsylvania)** 212 Cannon Bldg .... Washington DC 20515-0001
Fax: 202 225-0526
218 283-6261 **Koochiching County** 4th St & 6th Ave .... International Falls MN 56649-0000
Fax: 218 283-6262
208 769-4400 **Kootenai County** 501 N Government Way .... Coeur d'Alene ID 83814-2990
202 225-5711 **Kopetski Mike (Rep - D - Oregon)** 1520 Longworth Bldg .... Washington DC 20515-0001
Fax: 202 225-9477
Korea: Republic of Korea
202 939-5600 _Embassy_ 2370 Massachusetts Ave NW .... Washington DC 20008-2801
Fax: 202 797-0595
212 371-1280 _Mission to the UN_ 866 United Nations Plaza Suite 300 ...... New York NY 10017-1811
312 822-9485 _Chicago Consulate General_ 500 N Michigan Ave Suite 900 .... Chicago IL 60611-3701
213 385-9300 _Los Angeles Consulate General_
3243 Wilshire Blvd 2nd Fl .... Los Angeles CA 90010-1303
Fax: 213 385-1849
212 752-1700 _New York Consulate General_ 460 Park Ave .... New York NY 10022-1906
Fax: 212 348-1756
219 267-4444 **Kosciusko County** 100 W Center St .... Warsaw IN 46580-2846
515 295-3240 **Kossuth County** 114 W State St .... Algona IA 50511-2613
202 225-4276 **Kostmayer Peter H (Rep - D - Pennsylvania)**
2436 Rayburn Bldg .... Washington DC 20515-0001
Fax: 202 225-5060
217 333-1860 **Krannert Art Museum**
500 E Peabody Dr University of Illinios .... Champaign IL 61820-6986
Fax: 217 333-0883
907 543-4500 **Kuskokwim College** PO Box 368 .... Bethel AK 99559-0368
Fax: 907 543-4527
215 683-4000 **Kutztown University** .... Kutztown PA 19530-0000
Fax: 215 683-4010 Personnel
Kuwait: State of Kuwait
202 966-0702 _Embassy_ 2940 Tilden St NW .... Washington DC 20008-1193
Fax: 202 966-0517
212 973-4300 _Mission to the UN_ 321 E 44th St .... New York NY 10017-4401
Fax: 212 370-1733
202 225-3361 **Kyl Jon L (Rep - R - Arizona)** 336 Cannon Bldg .... Washington DC 20515-0001
Fax: 202 225-1143

L

608 785-9581 **La Crosse County** 400 4th St N .... La Crosse WI 54601-3200
404 882-2911 **La Grange College** 601 Broad St .... La Grange GA 30240-2999
619 293-3760 **La Jolla University** 5005 Texas St .... San Diego CA 92108-0000
Fax: 619 293-3737
701 883-5193 **La Moure County** 202 4th Ave NE .... La Moure ND 58458-0000
602 669-6131 **La Paz County** 1713 Kofa Suite C .... Parker AZ 85344-6477
303 259-4000 **La Plata County** 1060 E 2nd Ave .... Durango CO 81301-5157
Fax: Call company operator
219 326-6808 **La Porte County** Courthouse Sq .... La Porte IN 46350-0000
Fax: 219 326-5615
412 367-9300 **La Roche College** 9000 Babcock Blvd .... Pittsburgh PA 15237-5898
Fax: 412 367-9277 Library

215 951-1000 **La Salle University** 20th & Olney Ave .... Philadelphia PA 19141-0000
316 421-6700 **Labette Community College** 200 S 14th St .... Parsons KS 67357-4299
316 795-2138 **Labette County** PO Box 387 .... Oswego KS 67356-0387
Fax: 316 795-2928
202 224-5375 **Labor & Human Resources Committee (US Senate)**
428 Dirksen Bldg .... Washington DC 20510-0001
Fax: 202 224-5128
202 523-9674 **Labor Management Standards (US Dept of Labor)**
200 Constitution Ave NW Rm S2203 .... Washington DC 20210-0001
404 347-4237 _Atlanta Office_ 1371 Peachtree St NE Suite 300 .... Atlanta GA 30367-0001
Fax: 404 347-4634
205 731-0239 _Birmingham Office_ 1800 5th Ave N Rm 420 .... Birmingham AL 35203-2114
617 223-9990 _Boston Office_ JW McCormack POCH Rm 801 .... Boston MA 02109-0000
312 353-7264 _Chicago Office_ 230 S Dearborn St Rm 774 .... Chicago IL 60604-1503
Fax: 312 353-6263
216 522-3855 _Cleveland Office_ 1240 E 9th St Rm 831 .... Cleveland OH 44199-2002
214 767-6834 _Dallas Office_ 525 Griffin St Federal Bldg Rm 300 .... Dallas TX 75202-0000
Fax: 214 767-6874
313 226-6200 _Detroit Office_ 231 W Lafayette Rm 630 .... Detroit MI 48226-2799
616 456-2335 _Grand Rapids Office_ 148 Federal Bldg .... Grand Rapids MI 49503-0000
808 541-2705 _Honolulu Office_ 300 Ala Moana Blvd Rm 5115 .... Honolulu HI 96850-0001
816 426-2547 _Kansas City Office_ 911 Walnut St Suite 1606 .... Kansas City MO 64106-2009
Fax: 816 426-2550
213 252-7508 _Los Angeles Office_ 3660 Wilshire Blvd Suite 708 .... Los Angeles CA 90010-2713
212 337-2580 _New York Office_ 201 Varick St Rm 878 .... New York NY 10014-4811
215 597-4960 _Philadelphia Office_ 600 Arch St Rm 9452 .... Philadelphia PA 19106-1611
412 644-2925 _Pittsburgh Office_ 1000 Liberty Ave Rm 804 .... Pittsburgh PA 15222-4004
619 557-6153 _San Diego Office_ 880 Front St Rm 5N-37A .... San Diego CA 92188-1003
415 974-0544 _San Francisco Office_ 71 Stevenson St Suite 725 .... San Francisco CA 94105-2936
202 254-6510 _Washington DC Office_
1730 K St NW Riddell Bldg Suite 558 .... Washington DC 20006-0000
202 632-4950 **Labor Relations Board** 1717 Pennsylvania Ave NW .... Washington DC 20570-0001
Fax: 202 634-4832
212 752-1530 **Laboratory Institute of Merchandising** 12 E 53rd St .... New York NY 10022-5208
Fax: 212 832-6708
617 296-8300 **Laboure College** 2120 Dorchester Ave .... Boston MA 02124-5698
612 598-3536 **Lac qui Parle County** 600 6th St .... Madison MN 56256-1233
Fax: 612 598-3915
717 963-6723 **Lackawanna County** PO Box 133 .... Scranton PA 18503-0000
717 961-7810 **Lackawanna Junior College** 901 Prospect Ave .... Scranton PA 18505-1870
Fax: 717 961-7858
512 671-1110 **Lackland Air Force Base** .... San Antonio TX 78236-5000
417 532-5471 **Laclede County** 2nd & Adam Sts .... Lebanon MO 65536-0000
202 225-3231 **LaFalce John J (Rep - D - New York)** 2367 Rayburn Bldg ... Washington DC 20515-0001
Fax: 202 225-8693
215 250-5000 **Lafayette College** High St .... Easton PA 18042-0000
501 921-4858 **Lafayette County** PO Box 754 .... Lewisville AR 71845-0754
904 294-1600 **Lafayette County** Main St .... Mayo FL 32066-0000
Fax: 904 294-2846
816 259-4315 **Lafayette County** Main St .... Lexington MO 64067-0000
601 234-7563 **Lafayette County** PO Box 1240 .... Oxford MS 38655-1240
608 776-4850 **Lafayette County** 626 Main St .... Darlington WI 53530-1396
Fax: 608 776-4808
318 234-2208 **Lafayette Museum** 1122 Lafayette St .... Lafayette LA 70501-6838
318 268-5544 **Lafayette Natural History Museum & Planetarium**
637 Girard Park Dr .... Lafayette LA 70503-2803
Fax: 318 261-8041
318 233-6220 **Lafayette Parish** PO Box 4508 .... Lafayette LA 70502-4508
318 261-5775 **Lafayette Parish Public Library** 301 W Congress St ...... Lafayette LA 70502-0000
504 446-8427 **Lafourche Parish** 209 Green St .... Thibodaux LA 70301-3021
202 225-3601 **Lagomarsino Robert J (Rep - R - California)**
2332 Rayburn Bldg .... Washington DC 20515-0001
Fax: 202 225-3096
219 463-2183 **Lagrange County** 114 W Michigan St .... Lagrange IN 46761-1853
218 233-3757 **Lake Agassiz Regional Library** 118 S 5th St .... Moorhead MN 56560-2713
Fax: 218 233-7556
904 752-1822 **Lake City Community College** RR 3 Box 7 .... Lake City FL 32055-8703
Fax: 904 755-1521
707 263-2372 **Lake County** 255 N Forbes St .... Lakeport CA 95453-4747
Fax: 707 263-2207
719 486-1410 **Lake County** PO Box 917 .... Leadville CO 80461-0917
904 343-9850 **Lake County** 315 W Main St .... Tavares FL 32778-3878
Fax: 904 343-9638
708 360-6600 **Lake County** 18 N County St .... Waukegan IL 60085-4339
Fax: 708 360-1538
219 755-3440 **Lake County** 2293 N Main St .... Crown Point IN 46307-1896
Fax: 219 755-3820
616 745-4641 **Lake County** 800 10th St .... Baldwin MI 49304-0000
Fax: 616 745-2241
218 834-8300 **Lake County** 601 3rd Ave .... Two Harbors MN 55616-0000
406 883-6211 **Lake County** 106 4th Ave E .... Polson MT 59860-2125
Fax: 406 883-2720
216 357-2500 **Lake County** 105 Main St .... Painesville OH 44077-3414
Fax: 216 357-2672
503 947-6006 **Lake County** 513 Center St .... Lakeview OR 97630-1579
Fax: 503 947-3724
605 256-5644 **Lake County** 200 E Center County Courthouse .... Madison SD 57042-0000
901 253-7582 **Lake County** 229 Church St .... Tiptonville TN 38079-1162
219 769-3541 **Lake County Public Library** 1919 W 81st Ave .... Merrillville IN 46410-5382
Fax: 219 769-0690
216 352-3361 **Lake Erie College** 391 W Washington St .... Painesville OH 44077-3309
708 234-3100 **Lake Forest College** College & Sheridan Rds .... Lake Forest IL 60045-0000
Fax: 708 234-7170 Library
217 235-3131 **Lake Land College** SR-45 .... Mattoon IL 61938-0000
Fax: 217 258-6459
616 927-3571 **Lake Michigan College** 2755 E Napier Ave .... Benton Harbor MI 49022-1899
Fax: 616 927-4491
218 634-2836 **Lake of the Woods County** 206 SE 8th Ave .... Baudette MN 56623-0000
Fax: 218 634-2509
518 523-2445 **Lake Placid Commerce & Visitor's Bureau** Olympic Ctr ...... Lake Placid NY 12946-0000
Fax: 518 523-2605
218 727-0687 **Lake Superior Museum of Transportation** 506 W Michigan St ...... Duluth MN 55802-1505
906 632-6841 **Lake Superior State University** 1000 College Dr .... Sault Sainte Marie MI 49783-0000
Fax: 906 635-2111 Admin
916 541-4660 **Lake Tahoe Community College** PO Box 14445 .... South Lake Tahoe CA 95702-4445
Fax: 916 541-7852
916 544-5050 **Lake Tahoe Visitors Authority** PO Box 16299 .... South Lake Tahoe CA 95706-0299
Fax: 916 544-2386
904 787-3747 **Lake-Sumter Community College** 9501 S US Hwy 441 ...... Leesburg FL 34788-8751
Fax: 904 365-3501
414 565-2111 **Lakeland College** RR 4 .... Plymouth WI 53073-9804
Fax: 414 565-1206
216 953-7000 **Lakeland Community College** SR-306 & I-90 .... Mentor OH 44060-0000
Fax: 216 953-9710
414 458-4183 **Lakeshore Technical College** 1290 North Ave .... Cleveland WI 53015-0000
Fax: 414 457-6211

Phone	Name / Address	City	State	ZIP
414 636-9211	**Lakeshores Library System** 730 Wisconsin Ave	Racine	WI	53403-1238
309 686-7000	**Lakeview Museum of Arts & Sciences** 1125 W Lake Ave	Peoria	IL	61614-5985
719 336-2248	**Lamar Community College** 2401 S Main St	Lamar	CO	81052-3999
	Fax: 719 336-2448			
205 695-7333	**Lamar County** Pond St	Vernon	AL	35592-0000
	Fax: 205 695-9253			
404 358-0150	**Lamar County** 327 Thomaston St	Barnesville	GA	30204-1616
601 794-8504	**Lamar County** PO Box 247	Purvis	MS	39475-0247
	Fax: 601 794-1049			
903 737-2420	**Lamar County** 119 N Main St	Paris	TX	75460-4265
409 880-7011	**Lamar University** 4400 M L King Pkwy	Beaumont	TX	77710-0000
	Fax: 409 880-2309			
806 385-5173	**Lamb County** 100 6th St	Littlefield	TX	79339-3367
901 425-2500	**Lambuth College** 705 Lambuth Blvd	Jackson	TN	38301-5296
	Fax: 901 423-1990			
802 888-2207	**Lamoille County** PO Box 303	Hyde Park	VT	05655-0303
512 556-8271	**Lampasas County** PO Box 231	Lampasas	TX	76550-0231
717 569-7071	**Lancaster Bible College** 901 Eden Rd	Lancaster	PA	17601-5036
402 471-7481	**Lancaster County** 555 S 10th St	Lincoln	NE	68508-2803
717 299-8300	**Lancaster County** 50 N Duke St	Lancaster	PA	17602-2805
803 285-1581	**Lancaster County** PO Box 1809	Lancaster	SC	29720-1411
804 462-5611	**Lancaster County** PO Box 125	Lancaster	VA	22503-0125
717 394-2651	**Lancaster County Library** 125 N Duke St	Lancaster	PA	17602-2883
	Fax: 717 299-9645			
202 225-3415	**Lancaster H Martin (Rep - D - North Carolina)** 1417 Longworth Bldg	Washington	DC	20515-0001
	Fax: 202 225-0666			
202 633-2701	**Land & Natural Resources Div (US Dept of Justice)** 10th St & Constitution Ave NW Room 2143	Washington	DC	20530-0001
	Fax: 202 786-4215			
803 229-8300	**Lander College** 320 Stanley Ave	Greenwood	SC	29649-2099
702 635-5738	**Lander County** 315 S Humboldt	Battle Mountain	NV	89820-1982
	Fax: 702 635-0604			
901 424-4600	**Lane College** 545 Lane Ave	Jackson	TN	38301-4598
	Fax: Unlisted			
503 747-4501	**Lane Community College** 4000 E 30th Ave	Eugene	OR	97405-0640
	Fax: 503 747-1229			
316 397-5356	**Lane County** 144 South Ln	Dighton	KS	67839-0000
	Fax: 316 397-5937			
503 687-4203	**Lane County** 125 E 8th Ave	Eugene	OR	97401-2926
	Fax: 503 687-3803			
513 894-7156	**Lane Public Library** 300 N 3rd & Buckeye St	Hamilton	OH	45011-1692
415 834-5740	**Laney College** 900 Fallon St	Oakland	CA	94607-4893
	Fax: 415 464-3418 Admin			
715 627-6200	**Langlade County** 800 Clermont St	Antigo	WI	54409-1985
804 764-9990	**Langley Air Force Base**	Hampton	VA	23665-0000
	Fax: 804 764-7843			
405 466-2231	**Langston University**	Langston	OK	73050-9999
	Fax: 405 466-2381			
912 482-2088	**Lanier County** 100 W Main St	Lakeland	GA	31635-1191
517 483-1957	**Lansing Community College** 422 Washington Sq N	Lansing	MI	48901-0000
	Fax: 517 483-1854			
517 374-4600	**Lansing Public Library** 401 S Capitol Ave	Lansing	MI	48933-2003
	Fax: 517 374-4192			
202 225-3531	**Lantos Tom (Rep - D - California)** 1526 Longworth Bldg	Washington	DC	20515-0001
	Fax: 202 225-3127			
	Laos: Lao People's Democratic Republic			
202 332-6416	*Embassy* 2222 S St NW	Washington	DC	20008-4014
212 986-0227	*Mission to the UN* 820 2nd Ave Suite 1200	New York	NY	10017-0000
313 667-0356	**Lapeer County** 255 Clay St	Lapeer	MI	48446-2298
	Fax: 313 667-0340			
307 638-4296	**Laramie County** 19th St & Cary Ave	Cheyenne	WY	82001-0000
307 634-5853	**Laramie County Community College** 1400 E College Dr	Cheyenne	WY	82007-3204
	Fax: 307 638-1581 Library			
307 742-4448	**Laramie Plains Museum** 603 Ivinson St	Laramie	WY	82070-3243
512 722-0521	**Laredo Junior College** Washington St	Laredo	TX	78040-4396
	Fax: 512 721-5122			
512 722-8001	**Laredo State University** Washington St	Laredo	TX	78040-4398
	Fax: 512 726-3405 Admin			
303 221-7000	**Larimer County** PO Box 1190	Fort Collins	CO	80522-1190
202 225-6611	**LaRocco Larry (Rep - D - Idaho)** 1117 Longworth Bldg	Washington	DC	20515-0001
	Fax: 202 226-1213			
502 358-3544	**Larue County** County Courthouse	Hodgenville	KY	42748-0000
719 846-3481	**Las Animas County** 1st & Maple Sts	Trinidad	CO	81082-0000
	Fax: 719 846-7061			
702 386-6011	**Las Vegas City Hall** 400 E Stewart Ave	Las Vegas	NV	89101-2986
	Fax: 702 388-1807			
702 733-7810	**Las Vegas-Clark County Library District** 1401 E Flamingo Rd	Las Vegas	NV	89119-5256
	Fax: 702 369-1137			
815 434-8202	**LaSalle County** 707 E Etna Rd	Ottawa	IL	61350-1033
	Fax: 815 434-8319			
512 879-2421	**LaSalle County** PO Box 340	Cotulla	TX	78014-0340
318 992-2101	**LaSalle Parish** PO Box 57	Jena	LA	71342-0057
617 243-2000	**Lasell Junior College** 1844 Commonwealth Ave	Auburndale	MA	02166-2716
	Fax: 617 243-2389			
916 257-6181	**Lassen College** PO Box 3000	Susanville	CA	96130-3000
	Fax: 916 257-8964			
916 257-8311	**Lassen County** 220 S Lassen St	Susanville	CA	96130-4324
	Fax: 916 257-8115			
208 882-8580	**Latah County** 522 S Adams St	Moscow	ID	83843-2963
	Fax: 208 883-4338			
918 465-2021	**Latimer County** 109 N Central St	Wilburton	OK	74578-2440
801 363-2765	**Latter Day Saints Business College** 411 E South Temple	Salt Lake City	UT	84111-1302
	Fax: 801 359-1304			
202 726-8213	**Latvia Embassy** 4325 17th St NW	Washington	DC	20011-4203
	Fax: Unlisted			
205 760-5700	**Lauderdale County** PO Box 1059	Florence	AL	35631-1059
601 482-9714	**Lauderdale County** 500 Constitution Ave	Meridian	MS	39301-5160
	Fax: 601 482-1587			
901 635-2561	**Lauderdale County** County Courthouse	Ripley	TN	38063-0000
512 298-3511	**Laughlin Air Force Base**	Del Rio	TX	78843-0001
	Fax: 512 298-4179			
202 225-2831	**Laughlin Greg (Rep - D - Texas)** 218 Cannon Bldg	Washington	DC	20515-0001
	Fax: 202 225-1108			
606 864-5158	**Laurel County** County Courthouse	London	KY	40741-0000
	Fax: 606 864-7369			
912 272-4755	**Laurens County** 101 N Jefferson St	Dublin	GA	31021-6198
803 984-5214	**Laurens County** PO Box 445	Laurens	SC	29360-0445
202 224-4744	**Lautenberg Frank R (Sen - D - New Jersey)** 717 Hart Bldg	Washington	DC	20510-0001
	Fax: 202 224-9707			
512 798-3612	**Lavaca County** PO Box 326	Hallettsville	TX	77964-0326
	Fax: 512 797-2816			
313 421-6600	**Lavonia Public Library** 32901 Plymouth Rd	Livonia	MI	48150-1717
	Fax: Unlisted			
205 974-0663	**Lawrence County** 750 Main St	Moulton	AL	35650-1553
501 886-2167	**Lawrence County** PO Box 553	Walnut Ridge	AR	72476-0553
618 943-2346	**Lawrence County** County Courthouse	Lawrenceville	IL	62439-0000
812 275-7543	**Lawrence County** Bedford Sq	Bedford	IN	47421-0000
606 638-4108	**Lawrence County** 122 S Main Cross St	Louisa	KY	41230-1393
417 466-2638	**Lawrence County** PO Box 309	Mount Vernon	MO	65712-0309
601 587-7162	**Lawrence County** PO Box 40	Monticello	MS	39654-0040
614 533-4355	**Lawrence County** 5th & Park Ave	Ironton	OH	45638-0000
412 658-2541	**Lawrence County** 433 Court St	New Castle	PA	16101-3599
605 578-1941	**Lawrence County**	Deadwood	SD	57732-0000
615 762-7700	**Lawrence County** PO Box NBU 2	Lawrenceburg	TN	38464-0000
313 356-0200	**Lawrence Technological University** 21000 W Ten-Mile Rd	Southfield	MI	48075-1058
	Fax: Ext 3005			
414 832-7000	**Lawrence University** 115 S Drew St	Appleton	WI	54911-5798
	Fax: 414 735-6606			
205 925-2515	**Lawson State Community College** 3060 Wilson Rd SW	Birmingham	AL	35221-1717
405 581-3450	**Lawton Public Library** 110 SW 4th St	Lawton	OK	73501-4034
	Fax: 405 248-0243			
918 647-2527	**Le Flore County** PO Box 607	Poteau	OK	74953-0607
315 445-4100	**Le Moyne College**	Syracuse	NY	13214-1301
	Fax: 315 445-4540			
612 357-2251	**Le Sueur County** 88 South Pk	Le Center	MN	56057-0000
505 396-8521	**Lea County** PO Box 4C	Lovington	NM	88260-0000
	Fax: 505 396-5684			
202 225-6576	**Leach Jim (Rep - R - Iowa)** 1514 Longworth Bldg	Washington	DC	20515-0001
	Fax: 202 226-1278			
202 785-8683	**League of Conservation Voters** 1150 Connecticut Ave NW Suite 201	Washington	DC	20036-4104
	Fax: 202 835-0491			
202 429-1965	**League of Women Voters of the United States** 1730 M St NW	Washington	DC	20036-4587
	Fax: 202 429-0854			
202 224-4242	**Leahy Patrick J (Sen - D - Vermont)** 433 Russell Bldg	Washington	DC	20510-0001
	Fax: Unlisted			
601 267-7372	**Leake County** Court Sq	Carthage	MS	39051-0000
913 682-7611	**Leavenworth County** S 4th & Walnut St	Leavenworth	KS	66048-2781
717 273-7624	**Lebanon Community Library** 125 N 7th St	Lebanon	PA	17042-5000
717 274-2801	**Lebanon County** 400 S 8th St	Lebanon	PA	17042-6794
717 867-6100	**Lebanon Valley College** 101 N College Ave	Annville	PA	17003-1400
	Fax: 717 867-4454			
	Lebanon: Republic of Lebanon			
202 939-6300	*Embassy* 2560 28th St NW	Washington	DC	20008-2744
	Fax: Unlisted			
212 355-5460	*Mission to the UN* 866 UN Plaza Rm 531	New York	NY	10017-0000
	Fax: 212 838-2819			
615 472-2111	**Lee College** 1120 N Ocoee St	Cleveland	TN	37311-4475
	Fax: 615 478-7041			
713 427-5611	**Lee College** 511 S Whiting St	Baytown	TX	77520-4796
	Fax: 713 425-6555 Admin			
205 745-9767	**Lee County** 215 S 9th St	Opelika	AL	36801-4919
501 295-2339	**Lee County** 15 E Chestnut St	Marianna	AR	72360-2330
813 335-2259	**Lee County** 2115 2nd St	Fort Myers	FL	33901-3053
912 759-6000	**Lee County** PO Box 56	Leesburg	GA	31763-0056
319 372-3523	**Lee County** PO Box 1443	Fort Madison	IA	52627-1443
815 288-3309	**Lee County** Galena & 3rd Sts	Dixon	IL	61021-0000
606 464-2596	**Lee County** PO Box 551	Beattyville	KY	41311-0000
601 841-9100	**Lee County** 300 W Main St	Tupelo	MS	38801-3920
919 774-8403	**Lee County** PO Box 1968	Sanford	NC	27331-1968
	Fax: 919 774-8407			
803 484-5341	**Lee County** PO Box 309	Bishopville	SC	29010-0000
	Fax: 803 484-5043			
409 542-3684	**Lee County** Main & Hempstead Sts	Giddings	TX	78942-0000
703 346-7763	**Lee County** PO Box 326	Jonesville	VA	24263-0326
813 334-3221	**Lee County Library System** 2050 Lee St	Fort Myers	FL	33901-3989
	Fax: 813 334-4369			
616 256-9824	**Leelanau County** PO Box 467	Leland	MI	49654-0467
	Fax: 616 256-7850			
606 666-7521	**Lees College** 601 Jefferson Ave	Jackson	KY	41339-1196
	Fax: 606 666-8910			
704 898-5241	**Lees-McRae College** College Dr	Banner Elk	NC	28604-0000
808 455-0217	**Leeward Community College** 96-045 Ala Ike St	Pearl City	HI	96782-3393
601 453-1041	**Leflore County** 315 W Market St	Greenwood	MS	38930-4330
	Fax: 601 453-7460			
202 863-1820	**Legal Services Corp** 400 Virginia Ave SW	Washington	DC	20024-2730
	Fax: 202 863-1859			
215 820-3000	**Lehigh County** 455 Hamilton St	Allentown	PA	18101-1614
	Fax: 215 820-2013			
215 799-2121	**Lehigh County Community College** 2370 Main St	Schnecksville	PA	18078-9329
	Fax: 215 799-1159 Library			
215 758-3000	**Lehigh University**	Bethlehem	PA	18015-0000
	Fax: 215 758-5423 Library			
215 758-4025	*College of Engineering & Applied Science* 308 Packard Laboratory	Bethlehem	PA	18015-0000
	Fax: Unlisted			
202 225-4540	**Lehman Richard H (Rep - D - California)** 1319 Longworth Bldg	Washington	DC	20515-0001
	Fax: Unlisted			
202 225-4211	**Lehman William (Rep - D - Florida)** 2347 Rayburn Bldg	Washington	DC	20515-0001
	Fax: 202 225-6208			
208 756-2815	**Lemhi County** 206 Courthouse Dr	Salmon	ID	83467-3992
	Fax: 208 756-4673			
209 998-2211	**LeMoore Naval Air Station**	LeMoore	CA	93246-5001
901 774-9090	**LeMoyne-Owen College** 807 Walker Ave	Memphis	TN	38126-6595
	Fax: 901 942-3572			
517 263-8831	**Lenawee County** 425 N Main St	Adrian	MI	49221-2198
	Fax: 517 265-5721			
919 527-6223	**Lenoir Community College** Hwy 70 E	Kinston	NC	28502-0000
	Fax: Ext 323			
919 523-2417	**Lenoir County** PO Box 3289	Kinston	NC	28502-3289
704 328-1741	**Lenoir-Rhyne College** 7th Ave & 8th St NE	Hickory	NC	28603-0000
	Fax: 704 328-7338			
202 225-7896	**Lent Norman (Rep - R - New York)** 2408 Rayburn Bldg	Washington	DC	20515-0001
	Fax: 202 225-0357			
904 488-4710	**Leon County** 301 S Monroe St	Tallahassee	FL	32301-1856
	Fax: 904 488-1670			
903 536-2352	**Leon County** PO Box 98	Centerville	TX	75833-0098
904 487-2665	**Leon County Public Library System** 1940 N Monroe St Suite 26	Tallahassee	FL	32303-4797
617 868-9600	**Lesley College** 29 Everett St	Cambridge	MA	02138-2790
	Fax: 617 661-8788			
617 868-9600	*Graduate School of Management* 29 Everett St	Cambridge	MA	02138-2790
	Fax: 617 661-8788			
606 672-2193	**Leslie County** PO Box 916	Hyden	KY	41749-0000
	Lesotho: Kingdom of Lesotho			
202 797-5533	*Embassy* 2511 Massachusetts Ave NW	Washington	DC	20008-2823
	Fax: 202 234-6815			

212 661-1690 *Mission to the UN* 204 E 39th St New York NY 10016-0911
Fax: 212 682-4388
606 633-2432 **Letcher County** PO Box 58 Whitesburg KY 41858-0058
903 753-0231 **LeTourneau University** 2100 S Mobberly Ave Longview TX 75602-3524
Fax: 903 237-2730
202 224-6221 **Levin Carl (Sen - D - Michigan)** 459 Russell Bldg Washington DC 20510-0001
Fax: Unlisted
202 225-4961 **Levin Sander M (Rep - D - Michigan)** 323 Cannon Bldg Washington DC 20515-0001
Fax: 202 226-1033
202 225-6451 **Levine Mel (Rep - D - California)** 2443 Rayburn Bldg Washington DC 20515-0001
Fax: 202 225-6975
904 486-4311 **Levy County** PO Box 610 Bronson FL 32621-0610
Fax: 904 486-7052
302 645-0458 **Lewes Historical Society** 119 W 3rd St Lewes DE 19958-1315
503 244-6161 **Lewis & Clark College** 615 SW Palatine Hill Rd Portland OR 97219-7898
Fax: 503 768-7805
503 244-1181 *Northwestern School of Law* 10015 SW Terwilliger Blvd Portland OR 97219-7768
Fax: 503 246-8542
618 466-3411 **Lewis & Clark Community College** 5800 Godfrey Rd Godfrey IL 62035-2466
Fax: 618 466-2798
406 443-1010 **Lewis & Clark County** 316 N Park Ave Helena MT 59624-0000
313 862-6300 **Lewis College of Business** 17370 Meyers Rd Detroit MI 48235-1498
Fax: 313 862-1027
208 937-2661 **Lewis County** 510 Oak St Nezperce ID 83543-0000
Fax: 208 937-2459
606 796-3062 **Lewis County** 2nd St Vanceburg KY 41179-0000
314 767-5205 **Lewis County** 100 E Lafayette St Monticello MO 63457-0000
315 376-5333 **Lewis County** 7660 N State St Lowville NY 13367-1328
615 796-3378 **Lewis County** County Courthouse Hohenwald TN 38462-0000
206 748-9121 **Lewis County** 351 NW North St Chehalis WA 98532-1926
304 269-8215 **Lewis County** 110 Center Ave Weston WV 26452-0000
202 225-5861 **Lewis Jerry (Rep - R - California)** 2312 Rayburn Bldg Washington DC 20515-0001
Fax: 202 225-6498
202 225-3801 **Lewis John (Rep - D - Georgia)** 329 Cannon Bldg Washington DC 20515-0001
Fax: 202 225-0351
202 225-5792 **Lewis Tom (Rep - R - Florida)** 1216 Longworth Bldg Washington DC 20515-0001
Fax: 202 225-1860
815 838-0500 **Lewis University** Rt 53 Romeoville IL 60441-0000
Fax: 815 838-9456 Library
208 799-5272 **Lewis-Clark State College** 8th Ave & 6th St Lewiston ID 83501-0000
Fax: 208 746-7354
703 463-7133 **Lexington (Independent City)** PO Box 922 Lexington VA 24450-0922
606 252-1130 **Lexington Baptist College** 147 Walton Ave Lexington KY 40508-0000
606 257-4871 **Lexington Community College** Cooper Dr Oswald Bldg Lexington KY 40506-0001
803 359-8212 **Lexington County** 139 E Main St Lexington SC 29072-3456
803 532-9223 **Lexington County Circulating Library** 203 Armory St Batesburg SC 29006-0000
606 231-5504 **Lexington Public Library** 140 E Main St Lexington KY 40507-1376
Fax: 606 231-5598
Liberia: Republic of Liberia
202 723-0437 *Embassy* 5201 16th St NW Washington DC 20011-3615
212 687-1033 *Mission to the UN* 300 E 44th St 4th Fl New York NY 10017-4403
202 543-1988 **Libertarian Party** 1528 Pennsylvania Ave SE Washington DC 20003-3116
Fax: 202 546-6094
904 453-3451 **Liberty Bible College** 8600 Hwy 98 W Pensacola FL 32506-0000
904 643-5404 **Liberty County** Hwy 20 Bristol FL 32321-0000
912 876-2164 **Liberty County** Courthouse Sq Hinesville GA 31313-3240
Fax: 912 369-5463
406 759-5365 **Liberty County** 101 1st St E Chester MT 59522-0000
409 336-8071 **Liberty County** 1923 Sam Houston St Liberty TX 77575-4899
202 546-5611 **Liberty Lobby** 300 Independence Ave SE Washington DC 20003-1081
Fax: Unlisted
804 582-2000 **Liberty University** 3765 Candlers Mountain Rd Lynchburg VA 24502-2213
202 755-6420 **Library & Information Services (US Dept of Housing & Urban Development)**
451 7th St SW Rm 8141 Washington DC 20410-0001
602 542-4035 **Library of Archives & Public Records**
1700 W Washington St Rm 200 Phoenix AZ 85007-2877
Fax: 602 256-6372
202 707-5000 **Library of Congress** 101 Independence Ave SE Washington DC 20540-0001
Fax: 202 287-5844
202 707-2905 **Library of Congress Public Affairs Office**
101 Independence Ave SE LM 105 Washington DC 20540-0000
Fax: 202 707-9199
212 752-5775 **Libya: Socialist People's Libyan Arab Jamahiriya Mission to the UN**
309 E 48th St New York NY 10017-1746
Fax: 212 593-4787
614 349-6000 **Licking County** 20 S 2nd St Newark OH 43055-5663
202 224-4041 **Lieberman Joseph (Sen - D - Connecticut)** 502 Hart Bldg Washington DC 20510-0001
Fax: 202 224-9750
714 599-5433 **Life Bible College** 1100 Covina Blvd San Dimas CA 91773-0000
703 382-7100 **Life Bible College East** Rt 3 Box 12 Christiansburg VA 24073-9407
202 225-3806 **Lightfoot Jim (Rep - R - Iowa)** 1222 Longworth Bldg Washington DC 20515-0001
Fax: 202 225-6973
419 228-5113 **Lima Public Library** 650 W Market St Lima OH 45801-4678
Fax: 419 228-0955
419 222-8324 **Lima Technical College** 4240 Campus Dr Lima OH 45804-3597
Fax: 419 221-0450
803 489-7151 **Limestone College** 1115 College Dr Gaffney SC 29340-3798
205 233-6400 **Limestone County** 310 W Washington St Athens AL 35611-2597
817 729-5504 **Limestone County** PO Box 350 Groesbeck TX 76642-0350
Fax: 817 729-5626
217 732-3168 **Lincoln Christian College & Seminary** 100 Campus View Dr Lincoln IL 62656-2111
402 471-8500 **Lincoln City Libraries** 136 S 14th St Lincoln NE 68508-1899
501 628-4147 **Lincoln County** Drew & Wiley Sts Star City AR 71667-0000
719 743-2444 **Lincoln County** 718 3rd Ave Hugo CO 80821-0000
Fax: 719 743-2392
404 359-4444 **Lincoln County** Humphrey St Lincolnton GA 30817-0000
208 886-7641 **Lincoln County** 111 W 'B' St Shoshone ID 83352-0000
Fax: 208 886-2581
913 524-4757 **Lincoln County** 216 E Lincoln Ave Lincoln KS 67455-2097
606 365-2601 **Lincoln County** County Courthouse Stanford KY 40484-0000
207 882-6311 **Lincoln County** High St County Courthouse Wiscasset ME 04578-0000
Fax: 207 882-7550
507 694-1529 **Lincoln County** N Rebecca Ivanhoe MN 56142-0000
314 528-4415 **Lincoln County** 201 Main St Troy MO 63379-1194
601 835-3411 **Lincoln County** 300 S 1st St Brookhaven MS 39601-3321
406 293-7781 **Lincoln County** 512 California Ave Libby MT 59923-0000
Fax: 406 293-9816
704 732-3361 **Lincoln County** 115 W Main St Lincolnton NC 28092-2643
308 534-4350 **Lincoln County** County Sq North Platte NE 69101-0000
505 648-2331 **Lincoln County** 300 Central Ave Carrizozo NM 88301-0000
702 962-5390 **Lincoln County** 1 Main St Pioche NV 89043-0000
Fax: 702 962-5497
405 258-1264 **Lincoln County** PO Box 126 Chandler OK 74834-0126
503 265-6611 **Lincoln County** 225 W Olive St Newport OR 97365-3811
Fax: 503 265-5466
605 987-2581 **Lincoln County** 100 E 5th St Canton SD 57013-1732

615 433-2454 **Lincoln County** PO Box 577 Fayetteville TN 37334-0577
509 725-1401 **Lincoln County** PO Box 369 Davenport WA 99122-0369
Fax: 509 725-1150
715 536-0312 **Lincoln County** 1110 E Main St Merrill WI 54452-2554
304 824-3336 **Lincoln County** 8000 Court Ave Hamlin WV 25523-1419
307 877-9056 **Lincoln County** PO Box 670 Kemmerer WY 83101-0670
Fax: 307 877-3101
405 258-2425 **Lincoln County Historical Society Museum of Pioneer History**
PO Box 458 Chandler OK 74834-0458
217 732-3155 **Lincoln Junior College** 300 Keokuk St Lincoln IL 62656-1699
Fax: 217 732-8859
217 786-2200 **Lincoln Land Community College** Shepherd Rd Springfield IL 62792-0000
Fax: 217 786-2251
217 753-4900 **Lincoln Library** 326 S 7th St Springfield IL 62701-1691
Fax: Unlisted
615 869-3611 **Lincoln Memorial University** Cumberland Pkwy Harrogate TN 37752-0000
Fax: 615 869-4875
219 427-3864 **Lincoln Museum** PO Box 1110 Fort Wayne IN 46801-1110
Fax: 219 427-2301
318 255-3663 **Lincoln Parish** 100 W Texas Ave Ruston LA 71270-4463
618 544-8657 **Lincoln Trail College** RR 3 Robinson IL 62454-9803
Fax: Ext 1161
217 352-0047 **Lincoln Trail Libraries System** 1704 W Interstate Dr Champaign IL 61821-1088
Fax: 217 352-7153
415 221-1212 **Lincoln University** 281 Masonic Ave San Francisco CA 94118-4498
Fax: 415 751-0947
314 681-5000 **Lincoln University** 820 Chestnut St Jefferson City MO 65101-3500
Fax: 314 681-5511 Library
215 932-8300 **Lincoln University** Lincoln University PA 19352-0000
314 949-2000 **Lindenwood College** 209 S Kingshighway St Saint Charles MO 63301-1695
Fax: Ext 211
502 384-2126 **Lindsey Wilson College** 210 Lindsey Wilson St Columbia KY 42728-1298
503 472-4121 **Linfield College** 900 S Baker St McMinnville OR 97128-6894
Fax: Unlisted
319 398-3411 **Linn County** 50 3rd Ave Bridge Cedar Rapids IA 52401-1704
913 795-2660 **Linn County** PO Box B Mound City KS 66056-0601
816 895-5417 **Linn County** County Courthouse Linneus MO 64653-0000
503 967-3825 **Linn County** PO Box 100 Albany OR 97321-0031
Fax: 503 926-8228
503 928-2361 **Linn-Benton Community College** 6500 Pacific Blvd SW Albany OR 97321-3774
Fax: 503 967-6550
202 225-5701 **Lipinski William O (Rep - D - Illinois)**
1501 Longworth Bldg Washington DC 20515-0001
Fax: 202 225-1012
806 862-3091 **Lipscomb County** PO Box 175 Lipscomb TX 79056-0175
203 567-0885 **Litchfield Judicial District** 20 West St Litchfield CT 06759-3500
Fax: 203 567-4779
202 234-5860 **Lithuania Embassy** 2622 16th St NW Washington DC 20009-4292
Fax: Unlisted
501 898-5021 **Little River County** 351 N 2nd St Ashdown AR 71822-2753
501 988-3131 **Little Rock Air Force Base** Jacksonville AR 72099-0001
Fax: 501 988-3717
512 449-2733 **Live Oak County** PO Box 280 George West TX 78022-0280
202 225-3015 **Livingston Bob (Rep - R - Louisiana)** 2368 Rayburn Bldg Washington DC 20515-0001
Fax: 202 225-0739
815 844-5166 **Livingston County** 112 W Madison St Pontiac IL 61764-1871
502 928-2162 **Livingston County** PO Box 400 Smithland KY 42081-0400
517 546-0500 **Livingston County** 200 E Grand River Ave Howell MI 48843-2267
816 646-2293 **Livingston County** County Courthouse Chillicothe MO 64601-0000
716 243-2500 **Livingston County** 2 Court St Geneseo NY 14454-0000
504 686-2266 **Livingston Parish** PO Box 427 Livingston LA 70754-0427
205 652-9661 **Livingston University** College St Livingston AL 35470-0000
Fax: Ext 482
704 638-5500 **Livingstone College** 701 W Monroe St Salisbury NC 28144-5298
915 247-4455 **Llano County** 801 Ford St Llano TX 78643-1997
202 225-3271 **Lloyd Marilyn (Rep - D - Tennessee)** 2266 Rayburn Bldg Washington DC 20515-0001
Fax: 202 225-6974
717 893-2002 **Lock Haven University** Lock Haven PA 17745-0000
Fax: 717 893-2432 Admin
501 675-2951 **Logan County** Broadway St Booneville AR 72927-0000
303 522-0888 **Logan County** 315 Main St Sterling CO 80751-4349
217 732-4148 **Logan County** 601 Broadway St Lincoln IL 62656-2732
Fax: 217 732-6064
913 672-4244 **Logan County** 710 W 2nd St Oakley KS 67748-1233
502 726-6061 **Logan County** 426 E 4th St Russellville KY 42276-1897
701 754-2504 **Logan County** 301 Main St Napoleon ND 58561-0000
308 636-2311 **Logan County** PO Box 8 Stapleton NE 69163-0008
513 599-7275 **Logan County** Main & E Columbus 2nd Fl Bellefontaine OH 43311-0000
Fax: 513 592-4327
405 282-2124 **Logan County** 301 E Harrison Ave Guthrie OK 73044-4939
304 752-2000 **Logan County** Main & Stratton Sts Logan WV 25601-0000
703 274-6135 **Logistics Agency (US Dept of Defense)** Cameron Stn Alexandria VA 22304-0000
Fax: 703 274-4618
714 824-4508 **Loma Linda University** 11139 Anderson St Loma Linda CA 92350-0001
Fax: 714 824-4019
714 796-0141 *School of Dentistry* 24777 University Ave Loma Linda CA 92350-0001
Fax: 714 824-4211
714 824-4463 *School of Medicine* 11234 Anderson St Loma Linda CA 92350-0001
Fax: 714 824-4146
903 586-2471 **Lon Morris College** 800 College Ave Jacksonville TX 75766-2900
703 328-8061 **Lonesome Pine Regional Library** PO Box 1379 Wise VA 24293-1379
Fax: 703 328-1739
213 590-6101 **Long Beach City Hall** 333 W Ocean Blvd Long Beach CA 90802-4604
213 420-4111 **Long Beach Community College** 4901 E Carson St Long Beach CA 90808-1780
Fax: 213 420-4118
213 547-6721 **Long Beach Naval Station** Long Beach CA 90822-0000
Fax: 213 547-6636
213 437-2949 **Long Beach Public Library & Information Center**
101 Pacific Ave Long Beach CA 90802-0000
912 545-2143 **Long County** McDonald St Ludowici GA 31316-0000
516 299-0200 **Long Island University (System)** Northern Blvd Greenvale NY 11548-0000
Fax: 516 626-1086
Long Island University
718 403-1105 *Arnold & Marie Schwartz College of Pharmacy & Health Sciences*
75 DeKalb Ave Brooklyn NY 11201-5423
Fax: 718 625-6068
516 273-5112 *Brentwood Campus* 100 2nd Ave Brentwood NY 11717-5307
Fax: 516 273-5198
718 834-6000 *Brooklyn Campus* 1 University Plaza Brooklyn NY 11201-5372
Fax: 718 403-1088
718 403-1060 *College of Pharmacy* 75 Dekalb Ave Brooklyn NY 11201-5423
Fax: 718 643-9687
516 299-0200 *CW Post Campus* Northern Blvd Greenvale NY 11548-0000
914 359-7200 *Rockland Campus* Rt 340 Orangeburg NY 10962-2219
Fax: 914 359-7248

516 283-4000 *Southampton Campus* 239 Montauk Hwy ... Southampton NY 11968-0000
Fax: 516 283-4081
Long Island University CW Post Campus
516 299-2716 *Graduate School of Public Adminstration*
Roth Hall Rm 302 ... Brookville NY 11548-0000
Fax: 516 299-2587
516 299-2771 *Program in Health Administration* Roth Hall Rm 100 ... Brookville NY 11548-0000
202 225-4436 **Long Jill L (Rep - D - Indiana)** 1513 Longworth Bldg ... Washington DC 20515-0000
816 763-7777 **Longview Community College** 500 SW Longview Rd ... Lees Summit MO 64081-2100
Fax: 816 761-4457
804 395-2000 **Longwood College** 201 High St ... Farmville VA 23901-1899
Fax: 804 395-2635
501 676-6403 **Lonoke County** PO Box 431 ... Lonoke AR 72086-0431
216 329-5536 **Lorain County** PO Box 749 ... Elyria OH 44036-0749
216 365-4191 **Lorain County Community College** 1005 N Abbe Rd ... Elyria OH 44035-1691
Fax: 216 365-6519
216 244-1192 **Lorain Public Library** 351 6th St ... Lorain OH 44052-1770
Fax: 216 244-1733
319 588-7100 **Loras College** 1450 Alta Vista St ... Dubuque IA 52001-4399
Fax: 319 588-7964
703 869-1120 **Lord Fairfax Community College** Rt 11 ... Middletown VA 22645-0000
Fax: 703 869-7881
207 999-1110 **Loring Air Force Base** ... Limestone ME 04751-5000
Fax: 207 493-3245
505 662-8010 **Los Alamos County** 2300 Trinity Dr ... Los Alamos NM 87544-3051
505 662-6272 **Los Alamos Historical Museum** 1921 Juniper St 3rd Fl ... Los Alamos NM 87544-3026
213 669-4000 **Los Angeles City College** 855 N Vermont Ave ... Los Angeles CA 90029-3588
Los Angeles City Government
213 485-5705 *City Clerk* 200 N Spring St Rm 395 ... Los Angeles CA 90012-4801
213 485-2121 *City Hall* 200 N Spring St ... Los Angeles CA 90012-4800
Fax: 213 680-3435
213 485-7826 *City Planning Dept* 200 N Spring St Rm 460 ... Los Angeles CA 90012-4806
Fax: 213 237-0552
213 519-3400 *Harbor Dept* 425 S Palos Verdes St ... San Pedro CA 90731-3309
Fax: 213 831-0439
213 485-3311 *Mayor's Office* 200 N Spring St Rm 305 ... Los Angeles CA 90012-4805
Fax: 213 628-0389
213 626-5273 *Police Dept* 150 N Los Angeles St ... Los Angeles CA 90012-3392
213 485-3719 *Public Works Dept* 200 N Spring St Rm 373 ... Los Angeles CA 90012-4805
Fax: 213 237-1445
213 485-2496 *Treasurer* 200 N Spring St Rm 295 ... Los Angeles CA 90012-4804
Fax: 213 628-6467
213 215-2204 **Los Angeles Coast Guard Air Station** 7159 World Way W ... Los Angeles CA 90045-5824
Fax: 213 215-2460
213 891-2000 **Los Angeles Community College (System)** 617 W 7th St ... Los Angeles CA 90017-3895
Fax: 213 891-2393
213 974-5401 **Los Angeles County** 111 N Hill St ... Los Angeles CA 90012-3117
213 857-6111 **Los Angeles County Museum of Art** 5905 Wilshire Blvd ... Los Angeles CA 90036-4504
Fax: 213 931-7347
213 940-8462 **Los Angeles County Public Library Headquarters**
7400 E Imperial Hwy ... Downey CA 90242-3375
Fax: 213 803-3032
213 518-1000 **Los Angeles Harbor College** 1111 Figueroa Pl ... Wilmington CA 90744-2311
Fax: 213 834-1882
818 365-8271 **Los Angeles Mission College** 1320 San Fernando Rd ... San Fernando CA 91340-3214
Fax: 818 365-3623
818 347-0551 **Los Angeles Pierce College** 6201 Winnetka Ave ... Woodland Hills CA 91371-0000
Fax: 818 710-9844
213 612-3200 **Los Angeles Public Library System** 630 W 5th St ... Los Angeles CA 90071-2097
Fax: 213 612-0536
213 777-2225 **Los Angeles Southwest College** 1600 W Imperial Hwy ... Los Angeles CA 90047-4899
Fax: 213 777-1851
213 744-9500 **Los Angeles Trade-Technical College**
400 W Washington Blvd ... Los Angeles CA 90015-4180
Fax: 213 748-7334
818 781-1200 **Los Angeles Valley College** 5800 Fulton Ave ... Van Nuys CA 91401-4062
Fax: 818 785-4672
415 439-2181 **Los Medanos College** 2700 E Leland Rd ... Pittsburg CA 94565-5197
Fax: 415 427-1599
702 397-2193 **Lost City Museum** 721 S Hwy 169 ... Overton NV 89040-0000
202 224-6253 **Lott Trent (Sen - R - Mississippi)** 487 Russell Bldg ... Washington DC 20510-0001
Fax: 202 224-2262
615 458-3314 **Loudon County** Grove St ... Loudon TN 37774-0000
703 777-0200 **Loudoun County** 18 N King St ... Leesburg VA 22075-2818
Fax: 703 777-0325
319 523-4541 **Louisa County** 117 S Main St ... Wapello IA 52653-1547
703 967-0401 **Louisa County** PO Box 160 ... Louisa VA 23093-0160
Fax: 703 967-9531
919 496-2521 **Louisburg College** 501 N Main St ... Louisburg NC 27549-2399
Fax: 919 496-1788
415 974-6666 **Louise Salinger Academy of Fashion** 101 Jessie St ... San Francisco CA 94105-3507
504 344-9463 **Louisiana Arts & Science Center** 100 S River Rd ... Baton Rouge LA 70801-0000
504 928-5388 **Louisiana Assn of Business & Industry**
3113 Valley Creek Dr ... Baton Rouge LA 70898-0000
Fax: 504 929-6054
318 487-7776 **Louisiana College** 1140 College Dr ... Pineville LA 71359-0001
Fax: 318 487-7191
504 927-7895 **Louisiana Democratic Party** 3114 College Dr Suite J ... Baton Rouge LA 70808-3119
Fax: 504 927-9327
504 342-8119 **Louisiana Office of Tourism** 900 Riverside St N ... Baton Rouge LA 70802-5236
Fax: 504 342-3207
504 383-7234 **Louisiana Republican Party** 650 N 6th St ... Baton Rouge LA 70802-5319
Fax: 504 383-8334
Louisiana State Government
504 342-6600 *Information* 150 Riverside Mall ... Baton Rouge LA 70801-1303
Fax: 504 342-7757
504 342-1206 *Air Quality Div* PO Box 44096 ... Baton Rouge LA 70804-4096
Fax: 504 342-9048
504 342-7013 *Attorney General* PO Box 94005 ... Baton Rouge LA 70804-9005
Fax: 504 342-7335
504 342-4253 *Board of Regents* 150 Riverside Mall ... Baton Rouge LA 70801-1303
Fax: 504 342-9318
504 342-7071 *Budget Office* State Capitol Annex ... Baton Rouge LA 70804-0401
Fax: 504 342-1057
504 342-7013 *Consumer Protection Section* State Capitol ... Baton Rouge LA 70804-0401
Fax: 504 342-7335
504 922-1234 *Department of Agriculture & Forestry* 5825 Florida Blvd . Baton Rouge LA 70806-4248
Fax: 504 922-1289
504 342-5359 *Department of Economic Development*
101 France St Suite 124 ... Baton Rouge LA 70802-6250
Fax: 504 342-5389
504 342-3602 *Department of Education* 626 N 4th St ... Baton Rouge LA 70802-5321
Fax: 504 342-7316
504 295-8900 *Department of Environmental Quality* 11720 Airline Hwy Baton Rouge LA 70817-4401
Fax: 504 295-8587

504 342-9500 *Department of Health & Hospitals*
1201 Capitol Access Rd ... Baton Rouge LA 70802-4438
Fax: 504 342-4419
504 342-5900 *Department of Insurance* 950 N 5th St ... Baton Rouge LA 70802-5213
Fax: 504 342-3078
504 342-3111 *Department of Labor* 1001 N 23rd St ... Baton Rouge LA 70802-3338
Fax: 504 342-3021
504 342-4503 *Department of Natural Resources* 625 N 4th St ... Baton Rouge LA 70802-5364
Fax: 504 342-2707
504 342-6740 *Department of Public Safety & Corrections*
504 Mayflower St ... Baton Rouge LA 70802-6419
Fax: 504 342-6593
504 925-7680 *Department of Revenue & Taxation*
330 N Ardenwood Dr ... Baton Rouge LA 70806-2650
Fax: 504 925-7494
504 379-1200 *Department of Transportation & Development*
1201 Capitol Access Rd ... Baton Rouge LA 70802-4438
Fax: 504 379-1851
504 342-7410 *Division of Administration* PO Box 94095 ... Baton Rouge LA 70804-9095
Fax: 504 342-1057
504 342-6448 *Division of Health Standards*
1201 Capital Access Rd 6th Fl ... Baton Rouge LA 70801-1807
504 342-6609 *Division of Probation & Parole* 504 Mayflower St ... Baton Rouge LA 70802-6419
Fax: 504 342-6593
504 342-8180 *Division of the Arts* 900 Riverside St N Rm 420 ... Baton Rouge LA 70802-5236
Fax: 504 342-3207
504 342-1399 *Energy Div* 625 N 4th St ... Baton Rouge LA 70802-5364
Fax: 504 342-2707
504 379-1220 *Flood Control & Water Management Div*
1201 Capitol Access Rd Rm 211 ... Baton Rouge LA 70802-4438
Fax: 504 379-1394
504 342-7015 *Governor* State Capitol Bldg 4th Fl ... Baton Rouge LA 70804-0402
Fax: 504 342-0909
504 642-3306 *Hunt Correctional Center* PO Box 174 ... Saint Gabriel LA 70776-0174
Fax: Ext 216
504 342-7009 *Lieutenant Governor* State Capitol ... Baton Rouge LA 70804-0401
Fax: 504 342-3207
504 655-4411 *Louisiana State Penitentiary* General Delivery ... Angola LA 70712-9999
504 925-4518 *Nuclear Energy Div* 8955 Whitehall Dr ... Baton Rouge LA 70808-3225
Fax: 504 926-1903
504 342-3126 *Occupational Safety & Health Survey* 1001 N 23rd St ... Baton Rouge LA 70805-0000
Fax: 504 342-9193
504 922-1200 *Office of Archives Records Management & History*
3851 Essen Ln ... Baton Rouge LA 70809-2137
504 342-5470 *Office of Emergency Preparedness* 625 N 4th St ... Baton Rouge LA 70802-5364
Fax: 504 342-5471
504 342-3124 *Office of Employment Security* 1001 N 23rd St ... Baton Rouge LA 70802-3338
Fax: 504 342-3021
504 379-1208 *Office of Highways* 1201 Capitol Access Rd ... Baton Rouge LA 70804-0000
504 342-4615 *Office of Mineral Resources* 625 N 4th St ... Baton Rouge LA 70802-0000
Fax: 504 342-2707
504 342-1216 *Office of Solid & Hazardous Waste Management*
438 Main ... Baton Rouge LA 70802-0000
Fax: 504 342-0871
504 342-6363 *Office of Water Resources* PO Box 44091 ... Baton Rouge LA 70804-4091
Fax: 504 342-8929
504 342-4404 *Public Service Dept* PO Box 91154 ... Baton Rouge LA 70821-9154
504 342-8010 *Purchasing Section* 950 N 5th St ... Baton Rouge LA 70802-5213
Fax: 504 342-8688
504 925-4800 *Real Estate Commission* 9071 Interline Ave ... Baton Rouge LA 70809-1904
Fax: 504 925-4431
504 342-4479 *Secretary of State* 900 Riverside St N 20th Fl ... Baton Rouge LA 70802-5236
Fax: 504 342-2066
504 925-6117 *State Police* PO Box 66614 ... Baton Rouge LA 70896-6614
Fax: 504 925-3742
504 568-5707 *Supreme Court* 301 Loyola Ave ... New Orleans LA 70112-1841
Fax: Unlisted
504 342-0010 *Treasurer* PO Box 44154 ... Baton Rouge LA 70804-4154
Fax: 504 342-0046
504 342-3017 *Unemployment Insurance Services* 1001 N 23rd St ... Baton Rouge LA 70802-3338
Fax: 504 342-3021
504 568-8353 *Vital Records Section* 325 Loyola Ave ... New Orleans LA 70112-1829
Fax: 504 568-2543
504 342-7558 *Worker's Compensation Administration* 1001 N 23rd St . Baton Rouge LA 70802-0000
Fax: 504 342-3021
504 342-4922 **Louisiana State Library** 760 Riverside St N ... Baton Rouge LA 70802-5232
Fax: 504 342-3207
504 568-6968 **Louisiana State Museum** 751 Chartres St ... New Orleans LA 70116-3289
318 632-2020 **Louisiana State Museum-Shreveport** 3015 Greenwood Rd .. Shreveport LA 71109-4640
Fax: Unlisted
504 388-6935 **Louisiana State University (System)**
99 University Lakeshore Dr ... Baton Rouge LA 70803-0001
Fax: 504 388-5524
Louisiana State University
504 388-6935 *A & M College* 99 University Lakeshore Dr ... Baton Rouge LA 70803-0001
Fax: 504 388-5524
318 445-3672 *Alexandria Campus* 8100 US Hwy 71 S ... Alexandria LA 71302-9119
Fax: 318 473-6418
504 388-3202 *Baton Rouge Campus* Tower Dr ... Baton Rouge LA 70803-0001
Fax: 504 388-5911 Admissions
504 388-2311 *College of Agriculture*
124 Agriculture Administration Bldg ... Baton Rouge LA 70803-0001
Fax: 504 388-2526
318 457-7311 *Eunice Campus* PO Box 1129 ... Eunice LA 70535-1129
Fax: 318 546-6620
504 388-8875 *Library* ... Baton Rouge LA 70803-0001
Fax: 504 388-6992
504 388-2336 *Manship School of Journalism*
Journalism Bldg Rm 222 ... Baton Rouge LA 70803-0001
Fax: 504 388-6447
504 568-4808 *Medical Center* 4330 Bolizar St ... New Orleans LA 70112-0000
504 388-2934 *Museum of Geoscience*
109 Howe-Russell Geoscience Bldg ... Baton Rouge LA 70803-0001
504 388-8491 *Paul M Hebert Law Center*
Paul M Hebert Law Ctr Rm 210 ... Baton Rouge LA 70803-0001
Fax: 504 388-8202
504 947-9961 *School of Dentistry* 1100 Florida Ave Rm 2103 ... New Orleans LA 70119-2714
Fax: 504 942-8340 Admin
504 568-4006 *School of Medicine* 1542 Tulane Ave ... New Orleans LA 70112-2865
Fax: 504 568-4843
504 346-3100 *School of Veterinary Medicine* S Stadium Dr ... Baton Rouge LA 70803-0001
Fax: 504 346-3295
318 797-5000 *Shreveport Campus* 1 University Pl ... Shreveport LA 71115-2301
Fax: 318 797-5156 Library

Louisiana / Maine

504 568-4101 **Louisiana State University Medical Center School of Nursing**
1900 Gravier St ... New Orleans LA 70112-2262
Fax: 504 568-5859
318 674-5000 **Louisiana State University Shreveport Medical Center**
1501 Kings Hwy ... Shreveport LA 71103-4228
Fax: 318 674-5442
318 257-0211 **Louisiana Tech University** 700 W California ... Ruston LA 71272-0001
Fax: 318 257-4041
318 257-4647 *College of Engineering* Arizona Ave Bogart Hall ... Ruston LA 71272-0001
Fax: 318 257-2562
502 625-3131 **Louisville City Hall** 601 E Jefferson St ... Louisville KY 40202-1184
Fax: 502 625-2551
502 637-8663 **Louisville Bible College** PO Box 91046 ... Louisville KY 40291-0000
502 561-8600 **Louisville Free Public Library** 301 York St ... Louisville KY 40203-2257
Fax: 502 561-8657
308 942-3135 **Loup County** 4th St ... Taylor NE 68879-0000
419 885-3211 **Lourdes College** 6832 Convent Blvd ... Sylvania OH 43560-2898
405 276-3059 **Love County** 405 W Main St ... Marietta OK 73448-2837
915 377-2441 **Loving County** Hwy 302 ... Mentone TX 79754-9999
Fax: 915 377-2541
305 284-3536 **Lowe Art Museum** 1301 Stanford Dr University of Miami ... Coral Gables FL 33124-6310
Fax: 305 284-2024
202 225-3201 **Lowery Bill (Rep - R - California)** 2433 Rayburn Bldg ... Washington DC 20515-0001
Fax: Unlisted
202 225-6506 **Lowey Nita M (Rep - D - New York)** 1313 Longworth Bldg .. Washington DC 20515-0001
Fax: 202 225-0456
415 642-3681 **Lowie Museum of Anthropology**
University of California 103 Kroeber Hall ... Berkeley CA 94720-0001
205 548-2331 **Lowndes County** PO Box 65 ... Hayneville AL 36040-0065
912 333-5117 **Lowndes County** PO Box 1349 ... Valdosta GA 31603-0000
601 329-5880 **Lowndes County** PO Box 1364 ... Columbus MS 39703-1364
Fax: 601 327-9624
303 370-1110 **Lowry Air Force Base** ... Denver CO 80230-0000
Fax: Unlisted
301 323-1010 **Loyola College** 4501 N Charles St ... Baltimore MD 21210-2699
Fax: 301 323-2768
213 338-2700 **Loyola Marymount University** 7101 W 80th St ... Los Angeles CA 90045-2699
Fax: 213 338-2702
504 865-2011 **Loyola University** 6363 St Charles Ave ... New Orleans LA 70118-6195
Fax: 504 865-2149
708 216-4200 **Loyola University Dental School** 2160 S 1st Ave ... Maywood IL 60153-5589
Fax: 708 409-5857
213 736-1000 **Loyola University Law School** 1441 W Olympic Blvd ... Los Angeles CA 90015-3980
Fax: 213 380-3769
312 915-6000 **Loyola University of Chicago** 820 N Michigan Ave ... Chicago IL 60611-2196
Fax: 312 670-3217
312 915-7120 *School of Law* 1 E Pearson St ... Chicago IL 60611-2001
Fax: 312 337-5797 Library
312 508-3249 *School of Nursing* 6525 N Sheridan Rd ... Chicago IL 60626-5385
504 861-5575 **Loyola University School of Law** 7214 St Charles Ave ... New Orleans LA 70118-3538
Fax: Unlisted
708 531-3000 **Loyola University Stritch School of Medicine**
2160 S 1st Ave ... Maywood IL 60153-5589
Fax: 708 216-6772 Library
806 792-3221 **Lubbock Christian University** 5601 19th St ... Lubbock TX 79407-2099
Fax: 806 796-8917
806 762-6411 **Lubbock City-County Library** 1306 9th St ... Lubbock TX 79401-2708
806 741-8089 **Lubbock County** 904 Broadway St ... Lubbock TX 79401-3420
515 774-4421 **Lucas County** County Courthouse ... Chariton IA 50049-0000
906 293-5521 **Luce County** E Court St ... Newberry MI 49868-0000
419 245-4000 **Lucus County** 1 Government Ctr Suite 800 ... Toledo OH 43604-2202
202 224-4814 **Lugar Richard G (Sen - R - Indiana)** 306 Hart Bldg ... Washington DC 20510-0001
Fax: Unlisted
602 856-7411 **Luke Air Force Base** ... Litchfield Park AZ 85309-0000
Fax: 602 856-3738
202 225-2216 **Luken Charles (Rep - D - Ohio)** 1632 Longworth Bldg ... Washington DC 20515-0001
Fax: 202 225-2293
404 864-3742 **Lumpkin County** 280 Courthouse Cir NE ... Dahlonega GA 30533-1167
505 546-6501 **Luna County** 700 S Silver Ave ... Deming NM 88030-4173
208 743-2535 **Luna House Museum** 3rd & C Sts ... Lewiston ID 83501-0000
804 696-2230 **Lunenburg County** County Courthouse ... Lunenburg VA 23952-0000
205 222-6591 **Lurleen B Wallace State Junior College** PO Box 1418 ... Andalusia AL 36420-1418
Fax: 205 222-6567
319 387-2000 **Luther College** 700 College Dr ... Decorah IA 52101-1043
Fax: 319 387-1657
904 724-4722 **Luther Rice Seminary** 7565 Beach Blvd ... Jacksonville FL 32216-3085
Fax: 904 724-3197
206 392-0400 **Lutheran Bible Institute of Seattle**
4221 228th Ave SE Suite 7 ... Issaquah WA 98027-9299
Luxembourg: Grand Duchy of Luxembourg
202 265-4171 *Embassy* 2200 Massachusetts Ave NW ... Washington DC 20008-2812
Fax: 202 328-8270
212 370-9850 *Mission to the UN* 801 2nd Ave 13th Fl ... New York NY 10017-0000
Fax: 212 697-5529
415 788-0816 *Consulate General* 1 Sansome St Suite 830 ... San Francisco CA 94104-4429
Fax: 415 788-0985
717 825-1500 **Luzerne County** 211 N River St ... Wilkes-Barre PA 18704-5038
717 829-7300 **Luzerne County Community College**
S Prospect St & Middle Rd ... Nanticoke PA 18634-3814
Fax: Call company operator
717 321-4000 **Lycoming College** 700 College Pl ... Williamsport PA 17701-5192
Fax: 717 321-4337
717 327-2200 **Lycoming County** 48 W 3rd St ... Williamsport PA 17701-6536
203 443-2545 **Lyman Allyn Art Museum** 625 Williams St ... New London CT 06320-4199
605 869-2247 **Lyman County** County Courthouse ... Kennebec SD 57544-0000
808 935-5021 **Lyman House Memorial Museum** 276 Haili St ... Hilo HI 96720-2978
804 847-1443 **Lynchburg (Independent City)** 900 Church St ... Lynchburg VA 24504-1620
Fax: 804 845-4304
804 522-8100 **Lynchburg College** 1501 Lakeside Dr ... Lynchburg VA 24501-3199
Fax: 804 522-0658 Admin
802 626-9371 **Lyndon State College** Vail Hill ... Lyndonville VT 05851-0000
Fax: 802 626-9770
806 998-4750 **Lynn County** PO Box 937 ... Tahoka TX 79373-0937
712 472-2623 **Lyon County** 206 S 2nd Ave ... Rock Rapids IA 51246-1597
316 342-4950 **Lyon County** 402 Commercial St ... Emporia KS 66801-4000
Fax: 316 342-2652
502 388-2331 **Lyon County** PO Box 350 ... Eddyville KY 42038-0350
507 537-6727 **Lyon County** 607 Main St W ... Marshall MN 56258-3021
702 463-3341 **Lyon County** 31 S Main St ... Yerington NV 89447-2532

M

612 696-6000 **Macalester College** 1600 Grand Ave ... Saint Paul MN 55105-1899
Fax: 612 696-6689
312 922-1884 **MacCormac Junior College** 327 S La Salle St ... Chicago IL 60604-3395
813 830-1110 **MacDill Air Force Base** ... Tampa FL 33608-0000
202 857-5295 **Machinists Non-Partisan League**
1300 Connecticut Ave NW Suite 404 ... Washington DC 20036-1703
Fax: 202 296-1638
202 225-4911 **Machtley Ronald K (Rep - R - Rhode Island)**
132 Cannon Bldg ... Washington DC 20515-0001
Fax: 202 225-4417
718 331-6613 **Machzikei Hadath Rabbinical College** PO Box 799 ... Brooklyn NY 11219-0799
Fax: 718 331-4451
202 224-5274 **Mack Connie (Sen - R - Florida)** 517 Hart Bldg ... Washington DC 20510-0001
Fax: Unlisted
702 784-6988 **Mackay School of Mines Museum** University of Nevada ... Reno NV 89557-0001
Fax: 702 784-1766
906 643-7300 **Mackinac County** 100 Marley St ... Saint Ignace MI 49781-0000
Fax: 906 643-7320
217 245-6151 **MacMurray College** 447 E College Ave ... Jacksonville IL 62650-2590
Fax: 217 245-5214
313 286-2000 **Macomb Community College** 44575 Garfield Rd ... Mount Clemens MI 48044-1498
Fax: 313 286-2211
313 445-7000 *South Campus* 14500 E 12-Mile Rd ... Warren MI 48093-0000
Fax: 313 445-7157
313 469-5100 **Macomb County** 40 N Gratiot Ave ... Mount Clemens MI 48043-5688
313 286-6660 **Macomb County Library** 16480 Hall Rd ... Mount Clemens MI 48044-3198
Fax: 313 286-7187
912 471-2700 **Macon College** College Station Dr ... Macon GA 31297-0001
Fax: 912 471-2846
205 727-5120 **Macon County** 210 N Elm St ... Tuskegee AL 36083-1757
912 472-7021 **Macon County** Sumter St ... Oglethorpe GA 31068-0000
217 424-1305 **Macon County** 253 E Wood St Rm 52 ... Decatur IL 62523-1488
816 385-2913 **Macon County** PO Box 96 ... Macon MO 63552-0096
704 524-6421 **Macon County** 5 W Main St ... Franklin NC 28734-3005
615 666-2333 **Macon County** Public Sq Courthouse ... Lafayette TN 37083-0000
217 854-3214 **Macoupin County** County Courthouse ... Carlinville IL 62626-0000
Madagascar: Democratic Republic of Madagascar
202 265-5525 *Embassy* 2374 Massachusetts Ave NW ... Washington DC 20008-2801
Fax: 202 483-7603
212 986-9491 *Mission to the UN* 801 2nd Ave Rm 404 ... New York NY 10017-4759
Fax: 212 986-6271
209 675-7721 **Madera County** 209 W Yosemite Ave ... Madera CA 93637-3534
202 225-2371 **Madigan Edward R (Rep - R - Illinois)** 2109 Rayburn Bldg .. Washington DC 20515-0001
Fax: 202 225-8071
205 532-3300 **Madison County** 100 Courthouse Sq SE ... Huntsville AL 35801-4820
Fax: 205 532-6977
501 738-6721 **Madison County** PO Box 37 ... Huntsville AR 72740-0037
904 973-4176 **Madison County** PO Box 237 ... Madison FL 32340-0237
Fax: 904 973-3780
404 795-3351 **Madison County** PO Box 147 ... Danielsville GA 30633-0147
515 462-4451 **Madison County** PO Box 152 ... Winterset IA 50273-0152
208 356-3662 **Madison County** PO Box 389 ... Rexburg ID 83440-0389
618 692-6290 **Madison County** 155 N Main St ... Edwardsville IL 62025-1999
317 641-9480 **Madison County** 16 E 9th St ... Anderson IN 46016-1576
606 624-4703 **Madison County** 101 W Main St ... Richmond KY 40475-1415
314 783-2176 **Madison County** 1 Courthouse Sq ... Fredericktown MO 63645-1137
601 859-1177 **Madison County** PO Box 404 ... Canton MS 39046-0404
406 843-5392 **Madison County** 110 W Wallace St ... Virginia City MT 59755-0000
704 649-2531 **Madison County** PO Box 684 ... Marshall NC 28753-0684
402 454-3311 **Madison County** PO Box 290 ... Madison NE 68748-0290
315 366-2011 **Madison County** N Court St ... Wampsville NY 13163-9999
614 852-2972 **Madison County** County Courthouse ... London OH 43140-0000
901 423-6022 **Madison County** County Courthouse Rm 105 ... Jackson TN 38301-0000
409 348-2639 **Madison County** 101 W Main St ... Madisonville TX 77864-1901
703 948-6102 **Madison County** PO Box 220 ... Madison VA 22727-0220
318 574-0655 **Madison Parish** 100 N Cedar St ... Tallulah LA 71282-3840
608 266-6300 **Madison Public Library** 201 W Mifflin St ... Madison WI 53703-2597
Fax: 608 266-4338
502 821-2250 **Madisonville Community College** 2000 College Dr ... Madisonville KY 42431-9185
Fax: 502 825-8553
313 591-5000 **Madonna College** 36600 Schoolcraft Rd ... Livonia MI 48150-1173
Fax: 313 591-0156
603 669-7735 **Magdalen College** 270 Daniel Webster Hwy S ... Bedford NH 03102-6170
Fax: Unlisted
415 849-2710 **Magnes Judah L Memorial Museum** 2911 Russell St ... Berkeley CA 94705-2333
Fax: 415 849-3650
601 289-2896 **Magnolia Bible College** 820 S Huntington ... Kosciusko MS 39090-0000
606 349-2216 **Magoffin County** Court St ... Salyersville KY 41465-0000
515 472-5031 **Maharishi International University** 1000 N 4th St ... Fairfield IA 52556-2046
Fax: 515 472-1189
515 673-7786 **Mahaska County** PO Box 30 ... Oskaloosa IA 52577-0030
218 935-5669 **Mahnomen County** PO Box 379 ... Mahnomen MN 56557-0379
Fax: 218 935-5946
216 740-2104 **Mahoning County** 120 Market St ... Youngstown OH 44503-1710
207 623-4568 **Maine Chamber of Commerce & Industry** 126 Sewall St ... Augusta ME 04330-6822
Fax: Unlisted
207 622-6233 **Maine Democratic State Committee** 51 Sewall St ... Augusta ME 04330-7313
207 289-5710 **Maine Div of Tourism** 189 State St ... Augusta ME 04333-0001
Fax: 207 289-2861
207 326-4311 **Maine Maritime Academy** C-3 ... Castine ME 04420-0001
Fax: 207 326-9703
207 443-1316 **Maine Maritime Museum** 243 Washington St ... Bath ME 04530-1638
207 622-6247 **Maine Republican Party** 24 Stone St ... Augusta ME 04330-5209
Fax: 207 623-5322
Maine State Government
207 289-1110 *Information* State St ... Augusta ME 04333-0001
207 289-2724 *Arts Commission* 55 Capitol St Stn 25 ... Augusta ME 04333-0001
Fax: 207 289-2861
207 289-3661 *Attorney General* State House Stn 6 ... Augusta ME 04333-0001
Fax: 207 289-3145
207 289-2437 *Bureau of Air Quality Control* Hospital St ... Augusta ME 04333-0001
Fax: 207 289-7641
207 582-8718 *Bureau of Consumer Credit Protection* State House Stn 35 ... Augusta ME 04333-0001
Fax: 207 582-5415
207 289-3201 *Bureau of Health* 151 Capitol St ... Augusta ME 04333-0001
Fax: 207 289-4172
207 582-8707 *Bureau of Insurance* 124 Northern Ave ... Gardiner ME 04344-2809
Fax: 207 582-8716
207 289-3881 *Bureau of Public Improvements*
State Office Bldg Stn 77 Rm 211 ... Augusta ME 04333-0001
Fax: 207 289-4008
207 289-3521 *Bureau of Purchases* Capitol St State House Stn 9 ... Augusta ME 04333-0001
Fax: 207 289-3597
207 289-2950 *Bureau of State Police* 36 Hospital St ... Augusta ME 04333-0001
Fax: 207 289-2098
207 289-2076 *Bureau of Taxation* Capitol St State House Stn 24 ... Augusta ME 04330-0000
Fax: 207 289-4028

207 289-3871 *Department of Agriculture* Blossom Ln State House Stn 28 ... Augusta ME 04333-0001
Fax: 207 289-7548
207 289-2711 *Department of Corrections* State House Stn 111 Rm 400 ..... Augusta ME 04333-0001
Fax: 207 289-4340
207 289-2183 *Department of Educational & Cultural Services*
State House Stn 119 ... Augusta ME 04333-0001
207 289-7688 *Department of Environmental Protection* State House Stn 17 . Augusta ME 04333-0001
Fax: 207 289-7826
207 289-3446 *Department of Finance* State Office Bldg Rm 317 ... Augusta ME 04333-0000
207 289-3788 *Department of Labor* 20 Union St State House Stn 54 ... Augusta ME 04333-0001
Fax: 207 289-5292
207 289-2316 *Bureau of Employment Security* 20 Union St ... Augusta ME 04330-0000
Fax: 207 289-5292
207 289-2551 *Department of Transportation* Child St State House Stn 16 ... Augusta ME 04333-0001
Fax: 207 289-2896
207 582-8723 *Division of Licensing & Enforcement* State House Stn 35 ..... Augusta ME 04333-0001
Fax: 207 582-5414
207 289-6460 *Division of Safety* State House Stn 82 ... Augusta ME 04333-0000
Fax: 207 289-6449
207 289-4080 *Emergency Management Agency* State Office Bldg Stn 72 .... Augusta ME 04333-0000
Fax: 207 289-4079
207 289-6000 *Energy Divison Department of Economic & Community Development*
State House Stn 53 ... Augusta ME 04333-0001
207 289-3531 *Governor* State House Stn 1 ... Augusta ME 04333-0001
Fax: 207 289-1034
207 892-6716 *Maine Correctional Center* 17 Mallison Falls Rd ... Windham ME 04062-4135
Fax: Ext 279
207 354-2535 *Maine State Prison* PO Box A ... Thomaston ME 04861-0500
Fax: 207 354-6901
207 289-3001 *Office of Data Research & Vital Statistics*
32 Winthrop St State House Stn 11 ... Augusta ME 04333-0011
207 289-3261 *Planning Office* 184 State St State House Stn 38 ... Augusta ME 04333-0000
Fax: 207 289-5756
207 289-3831 *Public Utilities Commission* 242 State St State House Stn 18 . Augusta ME 04333-0001
Fax: 207 289-1039
207 582-8727 *Real Estate Commission* State House Stn 35 ... Augusta ME 04333-0001
Fax: 207 582-5415
207 289-1090 *Secretary of State* State House Stn 148 ... Augusta ME 04333-0001
Fax: 207 289-8598
207 289-5790 *State Archives* State House Stn 84 ... Augusta ME 04333-0001
207 879-4765 *Supreme Judicial Court* 142 Federal St ... Portland ME 04101-4161
207 289-2771 *Treasury Dept* State Office Bldg Rm 318 ... Augusta ME 04333-0001
Fax: Unlisted
207 289-3831 *Water & Gas Div* 242 State St State House Stn 18 ... Augusta ME 04333-0001
Fax: 207 289-1039
207 289-3751 *Worker's Compensation Commission*
Deering Bldg AMHI Grounds Stn 27 ... Augusta ME 04333-0001
Fax: 207 289-7198
207 289-5600 **Maine State Library** LMA Bldg State House Stn 64 ... Augusta ME 04333-0001
Fax: 207 622-0933
207 289-2301 **Maine State Museum** State House Complex ... Augusta ME 04333-0001
405 227-4732 **Major County** PO Box 379 ... Fairview OK 73737-0379
212 949-0180 **Malawi: Republic of Malawi Mission to the UN**
600 3rd Ave 30th Fl ... New York NY 10016-0000
Fax: 212 599-5021
Malaysia
202 328-2700 *Embassy* 2401 Massachusetts Ave NW ... Washington DC 20008-2805
Fax: 202 483-7661
212 986-6310 *Mission to the UN* 140 E 45th St 43rd Fl ... New York NY 10017-3144
Fax: 212 490-8576
312 942-3000 **Malcolm X College** 1900 W Van Buren St ... Chicago IL 60612-3197
Fax: 312 738-5851
212 599-6195 **Maldives: Republic of Maldives Mission to the UN**
820 2nd Ave Suite 800C ... New York NY 10017-0000
Fax: 212 972-3970
503 473-5151 **Malheur County** PO Box 4 ... Vale OR 97918-0004
Fax: 503 473-5136
Mali: Republic of Mali
202 332-2249 *Embassy* 2130 R St NW ... Washington DC 20008-1907
212 737-4150 *Mission to the UN* 111 E 69th St ... New York NY 10021-5004
Fax: 212 472-3778
708 256-1094 **Mallinckrodt College of the North Shore** 1041 Ridge Rd ... Wilmette IL 60091-1591
406 731-1110 **Malmstrom Air Force Base** ... Great Falls MT 59402-0000
216 489-0800 **Malone College** 515 25th St NW ... Canton OH 44709-3897
Fax: Unlisted
Malta: Republic of Malta
202 462-3611 *Embassy* 2017 Connecticut Ave NW ... Washington DC 20008-6132
Fax: 202 387-5470
212 725-2345 *Mission to the UN* 249 E 35th St ... New York NY 10016-4259
Fax: 212 779-7097
703 335-8800 **Manassas Park (Independent City)** 1 Park Center Pl ..... Manassas Park VA 22111-1800
Fax: 703 335-0053
813 755-1511 **Manatee Community College** 5840 26th St W ... Bradenton FL 34207-3596
Fax: Ext 4331
813 749-1800 **Manatee County** PO Box 1000 ... Bradenton FL 34206-1000
813 748-5555 **Manatee County Public Library System**
1301 Barcarrota Blvd W ... Bradenton FL 34205-7599
603 624-6550 **Manchester City Library** 405 Pine St ... Manchester NH 03104-6199
219 982-2141 **Manchester College** 604 E College Ave ... North Manchester IN 46962-1225
Fax: 219 982-6868
203 646-4900 **Manchester Community College** 60 Bidwell St ... Manchester CT 06040-6497
Fax: 203 647-6238 Library
913 539-3571 **Manhattan Christian College** 1415 Anderson Ave ... Manhattan KS 66502-4081
212 920-0100 **Manhattan College** 4513 Manhattan College Pkwy ... Bronx NY 10471-4099
212 749-2802 **Manhattan School of Music** 120 Claremont Ave ... New York NY 10027-4698
914 694-2200 **Manhattanville College** 125 Purchase St ... Purchase NY 10577-2400
Fax: 914 694-1732 Admin
616 723-3331 **Manistee County** 415 3rd St ... Manistee MI 49660-1606
616 723-5531 **Manistee County Historical Museum** 425 River St ... Manistee MI 49660-1522
414 683-4000 **Manitowoc County** 1010 S 8th St ... Manitowoc WI 54220-5392
Fax: 414 683-4499
414 683-4863 **Manitowoc-Calumet Library System** 808 Hamilton St ... Manitowoc WI 54220-5390
507 389-2463 **Mankato State University** Ellis Ave & South Rd ... Mankato MN 56001-0000
Fax: 507 389-1812 Admin
215 843-3600 **Manna Bible Institute** 700 E Church Ln ... Philadelphia PA 19144-1496
212 580-0210 **Mannes College of Music** 150 W 85th St ... New York NY 10024-4499
Fax: 212 580-1738
215 885-2360 **Manor Junior College** Fox Chase Rd & Forest Ave ... Jenkintown PA 19046-0000
717 662-4000 **Mansfield University** ... Mansfield PA 16933-0000
Fax: 717 662-4995
419 524-1041 **Mansfield-Richland County Public Library** 43 W 3rd ... Mansfield OH 44902-1295
Fax: 419 525-4750
202 225-3965 **Manton Thomas J (Rep - D - New York)** 331 Cannon Bldg .. Washington DC 20515-0001
Fax: Unlisted

816 436-6500 **Maple Woods Community College** 2601 NE Barry Rd ... Kansas City MO 64156-1254
Fax: 816 734-2963
414 261-9300 **Maranatha Baptist Bible College Inc** 745 W Main St ... Watertown WI 53094-7638
Fax: 414 261-9109
715 847-5500 **Marathon County** 500 Forest St ... Wausau WI 54401-5568
Fax: 715 848-9210
715 847-5400 **Marathon County Public Library** 400 1st St ... Wausau WI 54401-5445
Fax: 715 848-3578
714 655-1110 **March Air Force Base** ... Riverside CA 92518-0000
Fax: 714 655-4113
205 295-2200 **Marengo County** 101 E Coats Ave ... Linden AL 36748-1546
518 438-3111 **Maria College** 700 New Scotland Ave ... Albany NY 12208-1798
317 929-0123 **Marian College** 3200 Cold Spring Rd ... Indianapolis IN 46222-1997
Fax: 317 929-0263
414 923-7600 **Marian College of Fond du Lac** 45 S National Ave ... Fond du Lac WI 54935-4699
Fax: 414 923-7154
602 262-3011 **Maricopa County** 111 S 3rd Ave ... Phoenix AZ 85003-2225
602 269-2535 **Maricopa County Library District** 3375 W Durango ... Phoenix AZ 85009-6298
Fax: 602 269-4689
314 422-3388 **Maries County** PO Box 167 ... Vienna MO 65582-0167
614 373-4643 **Marietta College** ... Marietta OH 45750-0000
Fax: 614 374-4896
415 499-6407 **Marin County** 1501 Civic Center Dr ... San Rafael CA 94903-0000
207 288-3395 **Marine Atlantic** 121 Eden St ... Bar Harbor ME 04609-1137
202 347-8585 **Marine Engineers Beneficial Assn Political Action Fund**
444 N Capitol St NW Suite 800 ... Washington DC 20001-1512
Fax: 202 347-4724
804 595-0368 **Mariners' Museum** 100 Museum Dr ... Newport News VA 23606-3757
Fax: Unlisted
715 735-3371 **Marinette County** 1926 Hall Ave ... Marinette WI 54143-1728
Fax: 715 735-9297
205 921-7451 **Marion County** PO Box 1595 ... Hamilton AL 35570-1595
501 449-6231 **Marion County** Courthouse Sq ... Yellville AR 72687-0000
904 622-0305 **Marion County** 601 SE 25th Ave ... Ocala FL 32671-2690
Fax: 904 368-2322
912 649-2603 **Marion County** Courthouse Sq ... Buena Vista GA 31803-0000
515 828-2207 **Marion County** PO Box 497 ... Knoxville IA 50138-0497
618 548-3400 **Marion County** Broadway & Main St ... Salem IL 62881-0000
317 236-3200 **Marion County** 200 E Washington St ... Indianapolis IN 46204-3353
Fax: 317 236-3980
316 382-2185 **Marion County** S 3rd St Courthouse Sq ... Marion KS 66861-0000
502 692-2651 **Marion County** Main St ... Lebanon KY 40033-0000
314 769-2549 **Marion County** County Courthouse ... Palmyra MO 63461-0000
601 736-2691 **Marion County** 502 Broad St Suite 2 ... Columbia MS 39429-3037
614 387-5871 **Marion County** 114 N Main St ... Marion OH 43302-3030
Fax: 614 383-1190
503 588-5212 **Marion County** 100 High St NE ... Salem OR 97301-3665
Fax: 503 588-5237
803 423-3904 **Marion County** PO Box 183 ... Marion SC 29571-0183
Fax: 803 423-8252
615 942-2515 **Marion County** County Courthouse Sq ... Jasper TN 37347-0000
903 665-3971 **Marion County** PO Box F ... Jefferson TX 75657-0420
304 367-5440 **Marion County** 211 Adams St ... Fairmont WV 26554-2876
205 683-6172 **Marion Military Institute** PO Box 420 ... Marion AL 36756-0420
Fax: Ext 565
614 389-4636 **Marion Technical College** 1465 Mt Vernon Ave ... Marion OH 43302-5628
209 966-2005 **Mariposa County** PO Box 247 ... Mariposa CA 95338-0247
914 471-3240 **Marist College** 290 North Rd ... Poughkeepsie NY 12601-1387
Fax: 914 471-0466
202 366-5807 **Maritime Administration** 400 7th St SW Rm 7219 ... Washington DC 20590-0001
Fax: 202 366-3889
202 366-5123 *Domestic Shipping* 400 7th St SW Rm 7301 ... Washington DC 20590-0001
Fax: 202 366-3889
202 366-5773 *International Activities* 400 7th St SW Rm 7119 ... Washington DC 20590-0001
Fax: 202 366-3746
202 366-5517 *Market Development* 400 7th St SW Rm 7209 ... Washington DC 20590-0001
Fax: 202 366-5522
202 366-2323 *Ship Operating Assistance* 400 7th St SW Rm 8114 ... Washington DC 20590-0001
Fax: 202 426-1575
202 366-1875 *Ship Operations* 400 7th St SW Rm 2122 ... Washington DC 20590-0001
Fax: 202 366-3954
516 773-5000 *US Merchant Marine Academy* Steamboat Rd ... Kings Point NY 11024-0000
Fax: 516 773-5774
504 589-6556 *Central Region* 365 Canal St Suite 2590 ... New Orleans LA 70130-1137
Fax: 504 589-6559
708 298-4535 *Great Lakes Region* 2300 E Devon Ave Suite 366 ... Des Plaines IL 60018-4608
Fax: 708 298-4537
212 264-1300 *North Atlantic Region* 26 Federal Plaza Rm 3737 ... New York NY 10278-0004
Fax: 212 264-1958
804 441-6393 *South Atlantic Region* 7737 Hampton Blvd Bldg 4D Rm 211 ... Norfolk VA 23505-0000
Fax: 804 440-0812
415 744-3125 *Western Region* 211 Main St Rm 1112 ... San Francisco CA 94105-1926
Fax: 415 744-2591
202 225-2836 **Markey Edward J (Rep - D - Massachusetts)**
2133 Rayburn Bldg ... Washington DC 20515-0001
Fax: 202 225-8689
802 257-4333 **Marlboro College** College Rd ... Marlboro VT 05344-9999
803 479-5613 **Marlboro County** PO Box 996 ... Bennettsville SC 29512-0996
202 225-1555 **Marlenee Ron (Rep - R - Montana)** 2465 Rayburn Bldg ..... Washington DC 20515-0001
Fax: 202 225-1558
906 228-1501 **Marquette County** 234 W Baraga Ave ... Marquette MI 49855-4751
Fax: 906 228-1500
608 297-9114 **Marquette County** 77 W Park St ... Montello WI 53949-0000
Fax: 608 297-7606
414 224-7700 **Marquette University** 1217 W Wisconsin Ave ... Milwaukee WI 53233-2290
Fax: 414 288-3300
414 288-7132 *College of Communications Journalism & Performing Arts*
1131 W Wisconsin Ave ... Milwaukee WI 53233-2382
Fax: 414 288-7074
414 288-3811 *College of Nursing*
530 N 16th St Emory T Clark Hall Rm 265 ... Milwaukee WI 53233-0000
414 288-7090 *Law School* 1103 W Wisconsin Ave ... Milwaukee WI 53233-2381
Fax: 414 288-5914
414 288-3532 *School of Dentistry* 604 N 16th St Rm 304 ... Milwaukee WI 53233-2188
Fax: Unlisted
704 689-1111 **Mars Hill College** ... Mars Hill NC 28754-0000
Fax: 704 689-1474 Library
205 571-7701 **Marshall County** 540 Ringo St ... Guntersville AL 35976-0000
Fax: 205 571-7899
515 754-6373 **Marshall County** 17 E Main St ... Marshalltown IA 50158-4906
309 246-6325 **Marshall County** 122 N Prairie St ... Lacon IL 61540-1216
219 936-8922 **Marshall County** 211 W Madison St ... Plymouth IN 46563-1762
913 562-5361 **Marshall County** 1201 Broadway ... Marysville KS 66508-1844
Fax: 913 562-3226
502 527-3323 **Marshall County** 1101 Main St ... Benton KY 42025-1498

218 745-4851 **Marshall County** 208 E Colbin Ave .... Warren MN 56762-0000
Fax: 218 745-4343
601 252-4431 **Marshall County** PO Box 219 .... Holly Springs MS 38635-0219
405 795-3165 **Marshall County** County Courthouse .... Madill OK 73446-2261
605 448-5213 **Marshall County** County Courthouse .... Britton SD 57430-0000
615 359-1072 **Marshall County** Public Sq .... Lewisburg TN 37091-0000
304 845-1220 **Marshall County** 7th St .... Moundsville WV 26041-0000
304 696-3170 **Marshall University** 400 Hal Greer Blvd .... Huntington WV 25755-0001
Fax: 304 696-6565
304 696-7000 *School of Medicine* 1801 6th Ave .... Huntington WV 25755-0001
Fax: 304 696-7297
304 696-2360 *W Page Pitt School of Journalism* Smith Hall Rm 321 .... Huntington WV 25701-0000
Fax: 304 696-6565
515 752-7106 **Marshalltown Community College** 3700 S Center St .... Marshalltown IA 50158-4760
Fax: 515 752-8149
317 543-3235 **Martin Center College** 2171 Avondale Pl .... Indianapolis IN 46218-3867
Fax: Unlisted
919 792-1521 **Martin Community College** Kehukee Park Rd .... Williamston NC 27892-0000
Fax: 919 792-4425
407 288-5400 **Martin County** 2401 SE Monterey Rd .... Stuart FL 34996-3397
812 247-3651 **Martin County** PO Box 170 .... Shoals IN 47581-0170
606 298-2810 **Martin County** Main St .... Inez KY 41224-0000
507 238-3214 **Martin County** 201 Lake Ave .... Fairmont MN 56031-1845
919 792-1901 **Martin County** PO Box 668 .... Williamston NC 27892-0668
915 756-3412 **Martin County** PO Box 906 .... Stanton TX 79782-0906
202 225-4611 **Martin David (Rep - R - New York)** 442 Cannon Bldg .... Washington DC 20515-0001
Fax: Unlisted
507 354-8221 **Martin Luther College** 1884 College Heights .... New Ulm MN 56073-3300
408 277-4822 **Martin Luther King Jr Library** 180 W San Carlos St .... San Jose CA 95113-2096
Fax: 408 277-3187
717 846-5300 **Martin Memorial Library** 159 E Market St .... York PA 17401-1269
Fax: Unlisted
615 363-7456 **Martin Methodist College** 433 W Madison St .... Pulaski TN 38478-2799
202 225-5464 **Martinez Matthew G (Rep - D - California)**
2446 Rayburn Bldg .... Washington DC 20515-0001
Fax: 202 225-5467
703 638-3971 **Martinsville (Independent City)** PO Box 1112 .... Martinsville VA 24114-1112
Fax: 703 638-3158
703 887-7000 **Mary Baldwin College** .... Staunton VA 24401-0000
Fax: 703 885-2011
601 494-6820 **Mary Holmes College** Hwy 50 W .... West Point MS 39773-0000
703 899-4100 **Mary Washington College** .... Fredericksburg VA 22401-0000
Fax: 703 899-4373
319 326-9512 **Marycrest College** 1607 W 12th St .... Davenport IA 52804-4096
Fax: 319 326-9250
313 862-8000 **Marygrove College** 8425 W McNichols Rd .... Detroit MI 48221-2599
Fax: Call company operator
301 685-2370 **Maryland Academy of Sciences** 601 Light St .... Baltimore MD 21230-3812
Fax: 301 837-8840
301 269-0642 **Maryland Chamber of Commerce** 275 West St Suite 400 .... Annapolis MD 21401-3400
Fax: 301 269-5247
301 280-2300 **Maryland Democratic State Committee** 224 Main St .... Annapolis MD 21401-2009
Fax: 301 974-8356
301 669-9200 **Maryland Institute College of Art** 1300 W Mt Royal Ave .... Baltimore MD 21217-4191
Fax: 301 669-9206
301 333-2113 **Maryland Library Development & Services Div Dept of Education**
200 W Baltimore St .... Baltimore MD 21201-2500
Fax: 301 333-2507
301 333-6611 **Maryland Office of Tourist Development**
217 E Redwood St 9th Fl .... Baltimore MD 21202-3316
Fax: 301 333-6643
301 269-0113 **Maryland Republican Party** 1623 Forest Dr Suite 400 .... Annapolis MD 21403-1020
Fax: 301 269-5937
Maryland State Government
301 974-3431 *Information* 80 Calvert St Rm 105 .... Annapolis MD 21401-1931
301 631-3255 *Air Management Administration* 2500 Broening Hwy .... Baltimore MD 21224-6612
Fax: 301 631-3202
301 333-8232 *Arts Council* 15 W Mulberry St .... Baltimore MD 21201-4479
Fax: 301 333-1062
301 576-6300 *Attorney General* 200 St Paul Pl 2nd Fl .... Baltimore MD 21202-2004
Fax: 301 576-6404
301 974-3443 *Board of Public Works* Goldstein Treasury Bldg Rm 213 .... Annapolis MD 21404-0000
Fax: 301 974-2585
301 689-4136 *Bureau of Mines* 69 Hill St .... Frostburg MD 21532-2299
Fax: 301 689-4756
301 528-8662 *Consumer Protection Div* 200 St Paul Pl .... Baltimore MD 21202-2022
Fax: 301 576-6404
301 841-5880 *Department of Agriculture* 50 Harry S Truman Pkwy .... Annapolis MD 21401-7080
Fax: 301 841-5914
301 333-2000 *Department of Education* 200 W Baltimore St .... Baltimore MD 21201-2595
Fax: 301 333-2226
301 225-6500 *Department of Health & Mental Hygiene* 201 W Preston St .... Baltimore MD 21201-2323
Fax: Call company operator
301 974-2700 *Department of Housing & Community Development*
45 Calvert St .... Annapolis MD 21401-1940
Fax: 301 974-3932
301 974-3041 *Department of Natural Resources* 580 Taylor Ave .... Annapolis MD 21401-0000
Fax: 301 974-5206
301 859-7397 *Department of Transportation* BWI Airport .... Baltimore MD 21201-0000
Fax: 301 859-7615
301 764-4100 *Division of Corrections* 6776 Reisterstown Rd Suite 309 .... Baltimore MD 21215-2311
Fax: 301 764-4182
301 333-4195 *Division of Labor & Industry* 501 St Paul Pl 3rd Fl .... Baltimore MD 21202-2235
Fax: 301 333-1229
301 764-4276 *Division of Parole & Probation*
6776 Reisterstown Rd Suite 305 .... Baltimore MD 21215-2311
Fax: Call company operator
301 576-6360 *Division of Securities* 200 St Paul Pl 20th Fl .... Baltimore MD 21202-1958
Fax: 301 576-6404
301 764-3034 *Division of Vital Records* 4201 Patterson Ave .... Baltimore MD 21215-0000
Fax: 301 764-5918
301 651-9000 *Eastern Correctional Institution* RR 1 Box 500 .... Westover MD 21871-9799
Fax: 301 651-2412
301 261-8596 *Environmental Service* 2020 Industrial Dr .... Annapolis MD 21401-2995
Fax: 301 974-7267
301 554-5500 *Geological Survey* 2300 Saint Paul St .... Baltimore MD 21218-5210
Fax: 301 554-5502
301 974-3901 *Governor* State House .... Annapolis MD 21401-0000
Fax: 301 974-3275
301 321-3521 *Governor's Office of Justice Assistants*
300 E Joppa Rd Suite 1105 .... Towson MD 21204-3016
301 333-1111 *Highway Administration* 707 N Calvert St .... Baltimore MD 21202-3615
Fax: 301 333-1586
301 974-3441 *Income Tax Div* 110 Carroll St .... Annapolis MD 21411-0001
Fax: 301 974-3456
301 333-6300 *Insurance Div* 501 St Paul Pl 7th Fl .... Baltimore MD 21202-2235
Fax: 301 333-1229
301 974-2804 *Lieutenant Governor* State House 2nd Fl .... Annapolis MD 21401-0000
Fax: 301 974-5252
301 791-7200 *Maryland Correctional Training Center*
18800 Rocksbury Rd .... Hagerstown MD 21744-0000
Fax: 301 739-1458
301 225-4500 *Office of Planning* 301 W Preston St Rm 1101 .... Baltimore MD 21201-2305
Fax: 301 225-4480
301 974-2261 *Power Plant & Environmental Review Div* 580 Taylor Ave .... Annapolis MD 21401-0000
Fax: 301 974-3770
301 333-4826 *Public Defender System* 201 Saint Paul Pl .... Baltimore MD 21202-2001
Fax: 301 333-4864
301 333-6000 *Public Service Commission* 231 E Baltimore St 14th Fl .... Baltimore MD 21202-3486
Fax: 301 333-6495
301 225-4620 *Purchasing Bureau* 301 W Preston St Rm M2 .... Baltimore MD 21201-2367
Fax: 301 333-5482
301 333-6230 *Real Estate Commission* 501 St Paul Pl .... Baltimore MD 21202-2269
Fax: 301 333-1229
301 974-5521 *Secretary of State* 16 Francis St .... Annapolis MD 21401-1733
Fax: 301 974-5190
301 974-3915 *State Archives* 350 Rowe Blvd .... Annapolis MD 21401-1685
Fax: 301 974-3895
301 974-2971 *State Board for Higher Education* 16 Francis St .... Annapolis MD 21401-1781
Fax: 301 974-5376
301 974-3341 *State Court of Appeals* 361 Rowe Blvd 4th Fl .... Annapolis MD 21401-1698
301 653-4219 *State Police* 1201 Reisterstown Rd .... Pikesville MD 21208-3898
Fax: 301 653-4269
301 974-3533 *Treasurer* 80 Calvert St Rm 109 .... Annapolis MD 21401-1931
Fax: 301 974-3530
301 333-5309 *Unemployment Insurance Div* 1100 N Eutaw St Rm 501 .... Baltimore MD 21201-2206
Fax: 301 333-7003
301 974-3846 *Water Resources Administration* 580 Taylor Ave .... Annapolis MD 21401-2397
Fax: 301 974-2618
301 333-4775 *Workers' Compensation Commission* 6 N Liberty St 9th Fl .... Baltimore MD 21201-3785
Fax: 301 333-8122
503 224-5828 **Marylhurst College** US Hwy 43 .... Marylhurst OR 97036-9999
Fax: 503 636-9526
914 631-3200 **Marymount College** 100 Marymount Ave .... Tarrytown NY 10591-3796
Fax: 914 631-8586
213 377-5501 **Marymount College Palos Verdes**
30800 Palos Verdes Dr E .... Rancho Palos Verdes CA 90274-6299
Fax: 213 377-6223
212 517-0400 **Marymount Manhattan College** 221 E 71st St .... New York NY 10021-4597
Fax: 212 879-0921
703 522-5600 **Marymount University** 2807 N Glebe Rd .... Arlington VA 22207-4299
Fax: 703 284-1693
314 576-9300 **Maryville College** 13550 Conway Rd .... Saint Louis MO 63141-7299
Fax: 314 542-9085
615 982-6412 **Maryville College** .... Maryville TN 37801-0000
Fax: 615 983-0581
314 576-9317 *Management Div* 13550 Conway Rd .... Saint Louis MO 63141-7299
Fax: 314 542-9085
717 348-6211 **Marywood College** 2300 Adams Ave .... Scranton PA 18509-1598
Fax: 717 348-1817
309 543-6661 **Mason County** County Courthouse .... Havana IL 62644-0000
606 564-3341 **Mason County** PO Box 234 .... Maysville KY 41056-0234
616 843-8202 **Mason County** 300 E Ludington Ave .... Ludington MI 49431-2121
915 347-5253 **Mason County** Westmoreland St & Post Hill .... Mason TX 76856-0000
206 427-9670 **Mason County** PO Box 186 .... Shelton WA 98584-0186
304 675-1997 **Mason County** 6th & Main St .... Point Pleasant WV 25550-0000
618 524-5213 **Massac County** PO Box 429 .... Metropolis IL 62960-0429
617 237-1100 **Massachusetts Bay Community College** 50 Oakland St .... Wellesley Hills MA 02181-5359
Fax: 617 239-1047
617 267-9400 **Massachusetts Board of Library Commissioners**
648 Beacon St .... Boston MA 02215-2002
Fax: 617 421-9833
617 232-1555 **Massachusetts College of Art** 621 Huntington Ave .... Boston MA 02115-5882
Fax: 617 232-0050
617 732-2800 **Massachusetts College of Pharmacy & Allied Health Sciences**
179 Longwood Ave .... Boston MA 02115-5804
Fax: 617 732-2801
617 426-4760 **Massachusetts Democratic State Committee**
45 Bromfield St 7th Fl .... Boston MA 02108-4116
Fax: 617 426-0567
617 253-1000 **Massachusetts Institute of Technology**
77 Massachusetts Ave .... Cambridge MA 02139-4307
Fax: 617 253-8000
617 253-3730 *Alfred P Sloan School of Management*
50 Memorial Dr Rm E52-112 .... Cambridge MA 02139-0000
Fax: 617 253-5719
617 253-7791 *Department of Architecture*
77 Massachusetts Ave Rm 7-303 .... Cambridge MA 02139-4307
Fax: 617 253-8993
617 253-4791 *Department of Biology* 77 Massachusetts Ave .... Cambridge MA 02139-0000
Fax: 617 253-8699
617 253-3381 *Department of Earth & Planetary Science*
77 Massachusetts Ave Bldg 54 Rm 913 .... Cambridge MA 02139-4307
Fax: 617 253-6208
617 253-2022 *Department of Urban Studies & Planning*
77 Massachusetts Ave Bldg 7 Rm 338 .... Cambridge MA 02139-4307
Fax: Unlisted
617 253-4603 *Electrical Engineering & Computer Science Dept*
50 Vassar St Bldg 38 Rm 444 .... Cambridge MA 02139-4309
617 253-4738 *Graduate School of Biology*
77 Massachusetts Ave Bldg 56-524 .... Cambridge MA 02139-4307
Fax: 617 253-8699
617 253-1845 *Graduate School of Chemistry* Dreyfus Bldg Rm 18392 .... Cambridge MA 02139-0000
617 253-4851 *Graduate School of Physics*
77 Massachusetts Ave Bldg 6-107 .... Cambridge MA 02139-4307
Fax: 617 253-4803
617 253-3291 *School of Engineering* 77 Massachusetts Ave .... Cambridge MA 02139-4307
Fax: 617 253-8549
617 253-4444 **Massachusetts Institute of Technology Museum**
265 Massachusetts Ave .... Cambridge MA 02139-4109
Fax: 617 253-8994
508 759-5761 **Massachusetts Maritime Academy** Pierless Point .... Buzzards Bay MA 02532-0000
Fax: 508 759-4116
617 727-3206 **Massachusetts Office of Business Development**
100 Cambridge St 13th Fl .... Boston MA 02202-0000
617 727-3205 **Massachusetts Office of Travel & Tourism**
100 Cambridge St 13th Fl .... Boston MA 02202-0001
Fax: 617 727-6525
617 924-8683 **Massachusetts Republican State Committee**
9 Galen St Suite 320 .... Watertown MA 02172-4520
Fax: 617 924-7860

Massachusetts State Government
617 727-7030 *Information* 1 Ashburton Pl — Boston MA 02108-1518
617 727-2816 *Archives Div* 220 Morrissey Blvd — Boston MA 02125-0000
Fax: Ext 257
617 727-2200 *Attorney General* 1 Ashburton Pl — Boston MA 02108-1698
Fax: 617 727-3251
617 727-8872 *Board of Regents of Higher Education*
1 Ashburton Pl Rm 1401 — Boston MA 02108-1518
Fax: 617 727-6397
617 727-7376 *Board of Registration of Real Estate*
100 Cambridge St Rm 1518 — Boston MA 02202-0001
508 820-2000 *Civil Defense Agency* 400 Worcester Rd — Framingham MA 01701-0000
Fax: 508 820-2030
617 482-6212 *Committee for Public Counsel Services*
80 Boylston St Suite 600 — Boston MA 02116-4802
Fax: 617 695-0930
617 727-6300 *Committee on Criminal Justice* 100 Cambridge St — Boston MA 02202-0001
Fax: 617 727-5077
617 727-8400 *Consumer Protection Div* 131 Tremont St — Boston MA 02111-1317
Fax: 617 727-1047
617 727-3301 *Department of Corrections* 100 Cambridge St — Boston MA 02202-0001
Fax: 617 727-7403
617 770-7300 *Department of Education* 1385 Hancock St — Quincy MA 02169-5183
Fax: 617 770-7332
617 727-6600 *Department of Employment & Training* 19 Staniford St — Boston MA 02114-2526
Fax: 617 727-0315
617 727-3159 *Department of Environmental Management* 100 Cambridge St — Boston MA 02202-0001
Fax: 617 723-3096
617 292-5961 *Department of Environmental Protection* 1 Winter St 4th Fl — Boston MA 02108-4703
Fax: 617 556-1049
617 727-3000 *Department of Food & Agriculture* 100 Cambridge St — Boston MA 02202-0001
Fax: 617 727-7235
617 727-3454 *Department of Labor & Industries* 100 Cambridge St 11th Fl — Boston MA 02202-0001
617 727-2882 *Department of Procurement & General Services*
1 Ashburton Pl Rm 1017 — Boston MA 02108-1518
Fax: 617 727-4527
617 727-0201 *Department of Public Health* 150 Tremont St — Boston MA 02111-1197
Fax: 617 727-6496
617 566-4500 *Department of Public Safety* 1010 Commonwealth Ave — Boston MA 02215-1200
Fax: 617 566-6945
617 727-3500 *Department of Public Utilities* 100 Cambridge St 12th Fl — Boston MA 02202-0001
Fax: 617 723-8812
617 973-7800 *Department of Public Works* 10 Park Plaza — Boston MA 02116-3973
Fax: 617 973-8031
617 727-4201 *Department of Revenue* 100 Cambridge St — Boston MA 02204-0000
Fax: 617 727-5109
617 292-5593 *Division of Air Quality Control* 1 Winter St 8th Fl — Boston MA 02108-4703
Fax: 617 556-1049
617 727-3333 *Division of Insurance* 280 Friend St — Boston MA 02114-1808
617 727-3246 *Division of Neighborhoods & Economic Opportunity*
100 Cambridge St Rm 1103 — Boston MA 02202-0001
617 727-3074 *Division of Registration* 100 Cambridge St Rm 1520 — Boston MA 02202-0001
Fax: 617 727-7378
617 727-3267 *Division of Water Resources* 100 Cambridge St Rm 1304 — Boston MA 02202-0001
Fax: 617 723-3096
617 727-1136 *Energy Facilities Siting Council* 100 Cambridge St Suite 2109 — Boston MA 02202-0001
Fax: 617 727-0030
617 727-2040 *Executive Office for Administration & Finance*
State House Rm 373 — Boston MA 02133-0000
Fax: 617 727-1024
617 727-4732 *Executive Office of Energy Resources*
100 Cambridge St Rm 1500 — Boston MA 02202-0001
Fax: 617 727-0030
617 727-9800 *Executive Office of Environmental Affairs*
100 Cambridge St 20th Fl — Boston MA 02202-0001
Fax: 617 727-2754
617 727-3600 *Governor* State House Executive Office — Boston MA 02113-0000
Fax: 617 523-7984
617 727-4900 *Industrial Accident Board* 600 Washington St 7th Fl — Boston MA 02111-1704
617 727-7200 *Lieutenant Governor* State House Rm 259 — Boston MA 02133-0000
Fax: 617 727-8136
617 727-1480 *Massachusetts Correctional Institution* 2 Clark St — Norfolk MA 02056-0000
Fax: 617 727-7168
617 727-3668 *Massachusetts Cultural Council* 80 Boylston St 10th Fl — Boston MA 02116-4802
617 727-1686 *Massachusetts State Prison* 2405 N Main St — South Walpole MA 02071-0000
617 727-3281 *Parole Board* 27-43 Wormwood St 3rd Fl — Boston MA 02210-0000
Fax: 617 727-2753
617 727-5300 *Probation Office of the Commissioner*
1 Ashburton Pl Rm 405 — Boston MA 02108-1518
Fax: 617 727-5006
617 727-0036 *Registry of Vital Records & Statistics* 150 Tremont St — Boston MA 02111-1126
617 727-7030 *Secretary of State* State House Rm 337 — Boston MA 02133-1003
617 727-3548 *Securities Div* 1 Ashburton Pl Rm 1701 — Boston MA 02108-1552
617 367-7770 *State Board of Retirement* 1 Ashburton Pl Rm 1219 — Boston MA 02108-1506
Fax: 617 723-1438
617 725-8055 *Supreme Court* 1412 Pemberton Sq — Boston MA 02108-0000
617 973-7031 *Transportation Dept* 10 Park Plaza — Boston MA 02116-3933
Fax: 617 523-6454
617 367-6900 *Treasurer* State House Rm 227 — Boston MA 02133-0000
Fax: 617 722-2879
508 588-9100 **Massasoit Community College** 1 Massasoit Blvd — Brockton MA 02402-3996
Fax: 508 588-9641
805 259-3540 **Master's College** 21726 W Placerita Canyon Rd — Newhall CA 91321-1200
Fax: 805 254-7609
409 244-7680 **Matagorda County** 1700 7th St — Bay City TX 77414-5034
907 745-4801 **Matanuska-Susitna Borough** PO Box 1608 — Palmer AK 99645-1608
907 745-4255 **Matanuska-Susitna College** Mile 2 Trunk Rd — Palmer AK 99645-0000
Fax: 907 745-9711
315 393-5930 **Mater Dei College** Riverside Dr — Ogdensburg NY 13669-0000
Fax: Call company operator
916 364-1110 **Mather Air Force Base** — Mather CA 95655-0000
Fax: 916 364-4248
812 855-6873 **Mathers Museum** 601 E 8th St Indiana University — Bloomington IN 47405-0001
804 725-2550 **Mathews County** PO Box 463 — Mathews VA 23109-0463
202 225-7163 **Matsui Robert T (Rep - D - California)** 2353 Rayburn Bldg — Washington DC 20515-0001
Fax: 202 225-0566
203 575-0328 **Mattatuck Community College** 750 Chase Pkwy — Waterbury CT 06708-3000
Fax: 203 575-8228
203 753-0381 **Mattatuck Museum** 144 W Main St — Waterbury CT 06702-1298
808 243-7825 **Maui County** 200 S High St — Wailuku HI 96793-2134
Mauritania: Islamic Republic of Mauritania
202 232-5700 *Embassy* 2129 Leroy Pl NW — Washington DC 20008-1848
212 737-7780 *Mission to the UN* 9 E 77th St — New York NY 10021-1703
Fax: 212 472-3314

Mauritius
202 244-1491 *Embassy* 4301 Connecticut Ave NW Suite 134 — Washington DC 20008-2304
Fax: 202 966-0983
212 949-0190 *Mission to the UN* 211 E 43rd St 15th Fl — New York NY 10017-4707
Fax: 212 697-3829
615 381-3690 **Maury County** PO Box 1615 — Columbia TN 38402-1615
512 773-2829 **Maverick County** PO Box 4050 — Eagle Pass TX 78853-4050
202 225-8020 **Mavroules Nicholas (Rep - D - Massachusetts)**
2334 Rayburn Bldg — Washington DC 20515-0001
Fax: 202 225-8023
205 293-1110 **Maxwell Air Force Base** — Montgomery AL 36112-9799
Fax: 205 293-5140
505 277-4404 **Maxwell Museum of Anthropology**
University of New Mexico — Albuquerque NM 87131-0001
918 825-0639 **Mayes County** PO Box 95 — Pryor OK 74362-0095
704 765-7351 **Mayland Community College** Hwy 19 E — Spruce Pine NC 28777-0000
Fax: 704 765-0728
507 284-3671 **Mayo Medical School** 200 1st St SW — Rochester MN 55905-0001
Fax: 507 284-0532
904 247-7301 **Mayport Coast Guard Base** 4200 Ocean St — Mayport FL 32267-0385
Fax: 904 247-7371
904 246-5226 **Mayport Naval Station** — Mayport FL 32228-0000
Fax: 904 246-5329
606 759-7141 **Maysville Community College** RR 2 — Maysville KY 41056-9807
Fax: 606 759-7176
701 786-2301 **Mayville State University** 330 3rd St NE — Mayville ND 58257-1299
Fax: Unlisted
202 225-5401 **Mazzoli Romano L (Rep - D - Kentucky)**
2246 Rayburn Bldg — Washington DC 20515-0001
Fax: Unlisted
202 224-2235 **McCain John (Sen - R - Arizona)** 111 Russell Bldg — Washington DC 20510-0001
Fax: 202 224-8938
202 225-5330 **McCandless Alfred A (Rep - R - California)**
2422 Rayburn Bldg — Washington DC 20515-0001
Fax: 202 226-1040
206 984-2521 **McChord Air Force Base** — Tacoma WA 98438-0001
Fax: 206 976-3115
405 527-3117 **McClain County** PO Box 629 — Purcell OK 73080-0629
916 643-2111 **McClellan Air Force Base** — Sacramento CA 95652-0000
Fax: 916 643-2670
202 225-4636 **McCloskey Frank (Rep - D - Indiana)** 127 Cannon Bldg — Washington DC 20515-0001
Fax: 202 225-4688
615 974-2144 **McClung Frank H Museum**
1327 Circle Park Dr University of Tennessee — Knoxville TN 37996-0001
202 225-2176 **McCollum Bill (Rep - R - Florida)** 2453 Rayburn Bldg — Washington DC 20515-0001
Fax: 202 225-0999
406 485-3505 **McCone County** 206 2nd Ave — Circle MT 59215-0000
316 652-6100 **McConnell Air Force Base** — Wichita KS 67221-0000
Fax: 316 652-5418
202 224-2541 **McConnell Mitch (Sen - R - Kentucky)** 120 Russell Bldg — Washington DC 20510-0001
Fax: 202 224-2499
308 345-6303 **McCook Community College** 1205 E 3rd St — McCook NE 69001-2631
605 425-2781 **McCook County** 130 W Essex Ave — Salem SD 57058-8901
803 465-2195 **McCormick County** PO Box 86 — McCormick SC 29835-0086
708 491-5220 **McCormick School of Engineering Technological Institute**
2145 Sheridan Rd Rm 2390 — Evanston IL 60208-0001
Fax: 708 491-4133 Mail Rm
502 444-4700 **McCracken County** Washington & 7th Sts — Paducah KY 42003-0000
Fax: 502 444-4704
606 376-2411 **McCreary County** Main St — Whitley City KY 42653-0000
Fax: 606 376-3398
202 225-2777 **McCrery Jim (Rep - R - Louisiana)** 429 Cannon Bldg — Washington DC 20515-0001
Fax: 202 225-8039
915 597-2355 **McCulloch County** County Courthouse — Brady TX 76825-0000
202 225-6165 **McCurdy Dave (Rep - D - Oklahoma)** 2344 Rayburn Bldg — Washington DC 20515-0001
Fax: 202 225-9746
405 286-7428 **McCurtain County** 108 N Central Ave — Idabel OK 74745-3835
202 225-3731 **McDade Joseph M (Rep - R - Pennsylvania)**
2370 Rayburn Bldg — Washington DC 20515-0001
Fax: 202 225-9594
202 225-3106 **McDermott James A (Rep - D - Washington)**
1707 Longworth Bldg — Washington DC 20515-0001
Fax: 202 225-9212
417 223-4717 **McDonald County** PO Box 665 — Pineville MO 64856-0665
309 833-2474 **McDonough County** County Courthouse — Macomb IL 61455-0000
704 652-7121 **McDowell County** 10 E Court St — Marion NC 28752-4041
304 436-6587 **McDowell County** PO Box 447 — Welch WV 24801-0447
704 652-6021 **McDowell Technical Community College** RR 1 Box 170 — Marion NC 28752-9725
404 595-3982 **McDuffie County** PO Box 28 — Thomson GA 30824-0028
Fax: 404 595-4710
202 225-5705 **McEwen Bob (Rep - R - Ohio)** 2431 Rayburn Bldg — Washington DC 20515-0001
Fax: 202 225-0224
202 225-5516 **McGrath Raymond J (Rep - R - New York)**
205 Cannon Bldg — Washington DC 20515-0001
Fax: 202 225-3626
609 724-1100 **McGuire Air Force Base** — Wrightstown NJ 08641-7999
815 338-2040 **McHenry County** 2200 N Seminary Ave — Woodstock IL 60098-2621
Fax: 815 338-9612
701 537-5729 **McHenry County** 407 Main St S — Towner ND 58788-0000
815 455-3700 **McHenry County College** RR 14 & Lucas Rd — Crystal Lake IL 60012-0000
Fax: 815 455-3999
202 225-6335 **McHugh Matthew F (Rep - D - New York)**
2335 Rayburn Bldg — Washington DC 20515-0001
Fax: Unlisted
912 437-6671 **McIntosh County** PO Box 584 — Darien GA 31305-0584
701 288-3450 **McIntosh County** 112 NE 1st St — Ashley ND 58413-0000
918 689-2362 **McIntosh County** 110 N 1st St — Eufaula OK 74432-2449
814 887-5571 **McKean County** 500 W Main St — Smethport PA 16749-1144
618 537-4481 **McKendree College** 701 College Rd — Lebanon IL 62254-1299
Fax: 618 537-6259
701 842-3451 **McKenzie County** PO Box 523 — Watford City ND 58854-0523
505 722-3869 **McKinley County** 200 W Hill Ave — Gallup NM 87301-6309
Fax: 505 722-9380
803 777-7251 **McKissick Museum** University of South Carolina — Columbia SC 29208-0001
Fax: 803 777-3697
309 888-5001 **McLean County** 104 W Front St — Bloomington IL 61701-5091
502 273-3082 **McLean County** PO Box 57 — Calhoun KY 42327-0057
701 462-8541 **McLean County** 712 5th Ave — Washburn ND 58577-0000
817 756-6551 **McLennan Community College** 1400 College Dr — Waco TX 76708-1498
Fax: 817 756-0934
817 757-5000 **McLennan County** 5th & Washington New Records Bldg — Waco TX 76701-0000
612 864-5551 **McLeod County** 830 11th St E — Glencoe MN 55336-2216
Fax: 612 864-3410
202 225-1976 **McMillan J Alex (Rep - R - North Carolina)**
401 Cannon Bldg — Washington DC 20515-0001
Fax: 202 225-8995

202 225-8090 **McMillen C Thomas (Rep - D - Maryland)**
420 Cannon Bldg ... Washington DC 20515-0001
Fax: 202 225-8099
615 745-1281 **McMinn County** 6 E Madison Ave ... Athens TN 37303-3659
512 274-3215 **McMullen County** River & Elm Sts ... Tilden TX 78072-0000
915 691-6200 **McMurry University** 14th & Sayles St ... Abilene TX 79697-0001
Fax: 915 691-6599
901 645-3511 **McNairy County** County Courthouse ... Selmer TN 38375-0000
512 824-5368 **McNay Marion Koogler Art Museum**
6000 N New Braunfels ... San Antonio TX 78209-4618
318 475-5000 **McNeese State University** ... Lake Charles LA 70609-0000
Fax: 318 475-5082 Purchasing
202 225-5076 **McNulty Michael R (Rep - D - New York)**
414 Cannon Bldg ... Washington DC 20515-0001
Fax: 202 225-5077
316 241-0731 **McPherson College** 1600 E Euclid St ... McPherson KS 67460-3899
316 241-3656 **McPherson County** Kansas & Maple Sts ... McPherson KS 67460-0000
308 587-2363 **McPherson County** PO Box 122 ... Tryon NE 69167-0122
605 439-3316 **McPherson County** County Courthouse ... Leola SD 57456-0000
414 459-3400 **Mead Public Library** 710 Plaza 8 ... Sheboygan WI 53081-0000
Fax: Unlisted
316 873-2581 **Meade County** 200 N Fowler St ... Meade KS 67864-0000
502 422-2152 **Meade County** PO Box 614 ... Brandenburg KY 40108-0614
605 347-4411 **Meade County** PO Box 939 ... Sturgis SD 57785-0939
214 692-2516 **Meadows Museum**
Owen Fine Arts Ctr Southern Methodist University ... Dallas TX 75275-0001
Fax: 214 692-3272
318 869-5169 **Meadows Museum of Art of Centenary College**
2911 Centenary Blvd ... Shreveport LA 71104-3335
406 547-3612 **Meagher County** 15 W Main St ... White Sulphur Springs MT 59645-0000
704 336-2040 **Mecklenburg County** 600 E 4th St ... Charlotte NC 28202-2835
804 738-6191 **Mecklenburg County** Washington St ... Boydton VA 23917-0000
616 592-0783 **Mecosta County** 400 Elm St ... Big Rapids MI 49307-1849
Fax: 616 796-5577
716 884-3281 **Medaille College** 18 Agassiz Cir ... Buffalo NY 14214-2695
Fax: 716 884-0291
404 721-0211 **Medical College of Georgia** 1120 15th St ... Augusta GA 30912-0001
Fax: 404 721-4012
404 721-2117 *School of Dentistry* 15th St & Laney-Walker Blvd Rm AD109 . Augusta GA 30912-0001
404 721-2231 *School of Medicine* 1459 Laney-Walker Blvd ... Augusta GA 30912-0001
404 721-3771 *School of Nursing* 1446 Harper St ... Augusta GA 30912-0001
Fax: 404 721-6258
804 446-5600 **Medical College of Hampton Roads East Virginia Medical School**
PO Box 1980 ... Norfolk VA 23501-1980
Fax: 804 446-5135 Admin
419 381-4107 **Medical College of Ohio** PO Box 10008 ... Toledo OH 43699-0008
Fax: 419 385-6351
215 842-4166 **Medical College of Pennsylvania** 3200 Henry Ave ... Philadelphia PA 19129-1137
803 792-2300 **Medical University of South Carolina** 171 Ashley Ave ... Charleston SC 29425-0001
Fax: 803 792-8950
803 792-3116 *College of Pharmacy* 171 Ashley Ave ... Charleston SC 29425-0001
Fax: 803 792-0529
216 723-3641 **Medina County** 93 Public Sq ... Medina OH 44256-2292
512 426-5381 **Medina County** County Courthouse ... Hondo TX 78861-0000
216 725-0588 **Medina County District Library** 210 S Broadway ... Medina OH 44256-2602
Fax: 216 725-2053
612 693-2458 **Meeker County** 325 N Sibley Ave ... Litchfield MN 55355-2155
615 327-6000 **Meharry Medical College** 1005 Dr DB Todd Jr Blvd ... Nashville TN 37208-3599
Fax: 615 327-6448 Library
615 327-6207 *School of Dentistry* 1005 Dr DB Todd Jr Blvd ... Nashville TN 37208-3599
Fax: Unlisted
614 992-2895 **Meigs County** 2nd St ... Pomeroy OH 45769-0000
Fax: 614 992-2270
615 334-5747 **Meigs County** Main St ... Decatur TN 37322-0000
605 259-3230 **Mellette County** S 1st St ... White River SD 57579-0000
716 473-7720 **Memorial Art Gallery**
500 University Ave University of Rochester ... Rochester NY 14607-1415
901 576-6500 **Memphis City Hall** 125 N Main St ... Memphis TN 38103-2017
Fax: 901 576-6193
901 722-3525 **Memphis Brooks Museum of Art** Overton Pk ... Memphis TN 38112-5497
Fax: 901 722-3522
901 726-4085 **Memphis College of Art** 1930 Overton Park Ave ... Memphis TN 38112-5498
Fax: Unlisted
901 873-5111 **Memphis Naval Air Station** ... Millington TN 38054-0000
901 320-6320 **Memphis Pink Palace Museum & Planetarium**
3050 Central Ave ... Memphis TN 38111-3399
Fax: 901 454-5620
901 678-2040 **Memphis State University** ... Memphis TN 38152-0001
Fax: 901 678-3299
901 678-2421 *Cecil C Humphreys School of Law* Central Ave Rm 207 ... Memphis TN 38152-0001
Fax: 901 678-3299
901 678-2401 *Department of Journalism*
3711 Veterans St Meeman Journalism Bldg Rm 300 ... Memphis TN 38152-0001
Fax: 901 678-3299
901 678-2161 *Graduate Program in City & Regional Planning*
226 Johnson Hall ... Memphis TN 38152-0001
Fax: 901 678-3299
901 678-2431 *Sogelman College of Business & Economics* ... Memphis TN 38152-0001
Fax: 901 678-3759
901 725-8855 **Memphis/Shelby County Public Library & Information Center**
1850 Peabody Ave ... Memphis TN 38104-4025
Fax: 901 725-8883
217 632-2415 **Menard County** PO Box 456 ... Petersburg IL 62675-0456
915 396-4682 **Menard County** PO Box 1028 ... Menard TX 76859-1028
707 463-4379 **Mendocino County** State & Perkins ... Ukiah CA 95482-0000
606 768-3512 **Menifee County** County Courthouse ... Frenchburg KY 40322-0000
415 323-6141 **Menlo School & College** 1000 El Camino Real ... Atherton CA 94027-4301
Fax: 415 324-4937
906 863-9968 **Menominee County** 839 10th Ave ... Menominee MI 49858-3000
715 799-3311 **Menominee County** County Courthouse ... Keshena WI 54135-0000
209 384-6000 **Merced College** 3600 M St ... Merced CA 95348-2898
209 385-7434 **Merced County** 2222 M St ... Merced CA 95340-3780
209 385-7484 **Merced County Library** 2100 'O' St ... Merced CA 95340-3637
Fax: 209 726-7912
309 582-7021 **Mercer County** College Ave & SW 3rd St ... Aledo IL 61231-0000
606 734-6310 **Mercer County** 224 S Main St ... Harrodsburg KY 40330-1696
816 748-3425 **Mercer County** County Courthouse ... Princeton MO 64673-0000
701 745-3262 **Mercer County** PO Box 39 ... Stanton ND 58571-0039
609 989-6517 **Mercer County** PO Box 8068 ... Trenton NJ 08650-0068
Fax: 609 695-5124
419 586-3178 **Mercer County** 101 N Main St ... Celina OH 45822-1794
Fax: Unlisted
412 662-3800 **Mercer County** 138 S Diamond St ... Mercer PA 16137-1284
304 425-9571 **Mercer County** County Courthouse Sq ... Princeton WV 24740-0000
609 586-4800 **Mercer County Community College** PO Box B ... Trenton NJ 08690-0182
Fax: 609 890-6338

609 989-6916 **Mercer County Library** 2751 Brunswick Pike ... Lawrenceville NJ 08648-4132
912 752-2700 **Mercer University** 1400 Coleman Ave ... Macon GA 31207-0001
Fax: 912 752-4125 Purchasing
404 986-3000 *Atlanta Campus* 3001 Mercer University Dr ... Atlanta GA 30341-4155
Fax: 404 986-3150
912 752-2524 *School of Medicine* 1550 College St ... Macon GA 31207-0001
Fax: 912 752-2051
404 653-8800 *Southern School of Pharmacy* 345 Boulevard NE ... Atlanta GA 30312-1252
Fax: 404 653-8856
912 752-2601 *Walter F George School of Law* 1021 Georgia Ave ... Macon GA 31207-0001
Fax: 912 752-2101
202 225-4047 **Merchant Marine & Fisheries Committee (US House of Representatives)**
1334 Longworth Bldg ... Washington DC 20515-0001
Fax: 202 225-7094
914 693-4500 **Mercy College** 555 Broadway ... Dobbs Ferry NY 10522-1189
Fax: 914 693-9455
212 518-7710 *Bronx Branch Campus* 50 Antin Pl ... Bronx NY 10462-3003
Fax: 212 518-7879
914 948-3666 *White Plains Branch Campus* 277 Martine Ave ... White Plains NY 10601-3494
Fax: 914 686-7403
914 245-6100 *Yorktown Heights Branch Campus*
2651 Strang Blvd ... Yorktown Heights NY 10598-2997
Fax: 914 962-0931
814 825-0238 **Mercyhurst College** 501 E 38th St ... Erie PA 16546-0001
Fax: 814 825-0438
919 833-6461 **Meredith College** 3800 Hillsborough St ... Raleigh NC 27607-5298
Fax: 919 829-2828
601 483-8241 **Meridian Community College** 910 Hwy 19 N ... Meridian MS 39307-5890
Fax: 601 482-5803
601 679-2318 **Meridian Naval Air Station** ... Meridian MS 39309-0001
Fax: 601 679-2160
404 672-1314 **Meriwether County** PO Box 428 ... Greenville GA 30222-0428
308 946-2881 **Merrick County** PO Box 27 ... Central City NE 68826-0027
508 683-7111 **Merrimack College** 315 Turnpike St ... North Andover MA 01845-5800
Fax: 508 975-8541
603 228-0331 **Merrimack County** 163 N Main St ... Concord NH 03301-5001
415 531-4911 **Merritt College** 12500 Campus Dr ... Oakland CA 94619-3196
Fax: 415 436-2405
602 461-7000 **Mesa Community College** 1833 W Southern Ave ... Mesa AZ 85202-4866
Fax: 602 461-7804 Admin
303 244-1670 **Mesa County** PO Box 20000 ... Grand Junction CO 81502-0000
602 644-2702 **Mesa Public Library** 64 E 1st St ... Mesa AZ 85201-6768
303 248-1020 **Mesa State College** PO Box 2647 ... Grand Junction CO 81502-0000
Fax: 303 248-1903
218 749-7700 **Mesabi Community College** 9th Ave & W Chestnut St ... Virginia MN 55792-0000
Fax: 218 749-7753
717 766-2511 **Messiah College** ... Grantham PA 17027-9999
Fax: 717 691-6042
502 432-4821 **Metcalfe County** PO Box 850 ... Edmonton KY 42129-0000
919 488-7110 **Methodist College** 5400 Ramsey St ... Fayetteville NC 28311-1498
Fax: 919 822-1289
405 235-0571 **Metropolitan Library System of Oklahoma County**
131 Dean A McGee Ave ... Oklahoma City OK 73102-6499
Fax: 405 236-5219
212 879-5500 **Metropolitan Museum of Art** 1000 5th Ave ... New York NY 10028-0198
Fax: 212 570-3879
303 556-2400 **Metropolitan State College** PO Box 173362 ... Denver CO 80217-3362
Fax: 303 556-4429
612 296-3875 **Metropolitan State University** 121 Metro Sq ... Saint Paul MN 55101-0000
Fax: 612 297-2193
402 449-8400 **Metropolitan Technical Community College** PO Box 3777 ... Omaha NE 68103-0777
Fax: 402 449-8332
202 224-2315 **Metzenbaum Howard M (Sen - D - Ohio)**
140 Russell Bldg ... Washington DC 20510-0001
Fax: 202 224-8906
213 688-7330 **Mexican Chamber of Commerce of the County of Los Angeles**
125 Paseo de la Plaza Rm 404 ... Los Angeles CA 90012-2922
Fax: 213 688-7562
Mexico: United Mexican States
202 293-1710 *Embassy* 1019 19th St NW ... Washington DC 20036-5105
Fax: 202 775-4552
212 752-0220 *Mission to the UN* 2 UN Plaza 28th Fl ... New York NY 10017-0000
Fax: 212 688-8862
512 478-2866 *Austin Consulate* 200 E 6th St Suite 200 ... Austin TX 78701-3648
Fax: 512 478-8008
312 855-1380 *Chicago Consulate General* 300 N Michigan Ave 2nd Fl ... Chicago IL 60601-3702
214 630-7341 *Dallas Consulate General* 1349 Empire Central Suite 100 ... Dallas TX 75247-4029
Fax: 214 630-3511
602 242-7398 *Phoenix Consulate* 1990 W Camelback ... Phoenix AZ 85015-0000
415 392-5554 *San Francisco Consulate General*
870 Market St Suite 528 ... San Francisco CA 94102-3012
Fax: 415 392-3233
206 448-3526 *Seattle Consulate* 2132 3rd Ave ... Seattle WA 98121-0000
202 225-2865 **Meyers Jan (Rep - R - Kansas)** 1230 Longworth Bldg ... Washington DC 20515-0001
Fax: 202 225-0554
202 225-4741 **Mfume Kweisi (Rep - D - Maryland)** 217 Cannon Bldg ... Washington DC 20515-0001
Fax: 202 225-3178
305 579-6065 **Miami City Hall** 3500 Pan American Dr ... Miami FL 33133-5504
Fax: 305 858-1610
305 953-1122 **Miami Christian College** 2300 NW 135th St ... Miami FL 33167-1398
Fax: 305 953-1117
305 953-2100 **Miami Coast Guard Air Station** Opa Locka Airport ... Opa Locka FL 33054-2397
Fax: 305 953-2231
305 535-4300 **Miami Coast Guard Base** 100 MacArthur Cswy ... Miami Beach FL 33139-5101
Fax: 305 535-4493
317 472-3901 **Miami County** 21 Court St ... Peru IN 46970-2266
913 294-3976 **Miami County** 120 S Pearl St ... Paola KS 66071-1774
513 332-6800 **Miami County** 201 W Main St ... Troy OH 45373-3263
Fax: 513 332-7019
513 529-1809 **Miami University (System)** 500 E High St ... Oxford OH 45056-1618
Fax: 513 529-3841
Miami University
513 863-8833 *Hamilton Campus* 1601 Peck Blvd ... Hamilton OH 45011-3399
Fax: 513 863-1655
513 424-4444 *Middletown Campus* 4200 E University Blvd ... Middletown OH 45042-3497
Fax: 513 424-4632
513 529-1809 *Oxford Campus* 500 E High St ... Oxford OH 45056-1618
Fax: 513 529-3841
Miami-Dade Community College
305 347-1000 *North Campus* 11380 NW 27th Ave ... Miami FL 33167-3495
Fax: 305 347-1663
305 347-2000 *South Campus* 11011 SW 104th St ... Miami FL 33176-3393
Fax: 305 347-2924
305 375-2665 **Miami-Dade Public Library System** 101 W Flagler St ... Miami FL 33130-1504
Fax: 305 374-1573

202 225-6201 **Michel Robert H (Rep - R - Illinois)** 2112 Rayburn Bldg ..... Washington DC 20515-0001
Fax: 202 225-9249

313 651-5800 **Michigan Christian College** 800 W Avon Rd .... Rochester Hills MI 48307-2764

517 371-5410 **Michigan Democratic State Committee** 606 Townsend St .... Lansing MI 48933-2384
Fax: 517 371-2056

517 487-5413 **Michigan Republican State Committee**
2121 E Grand River Ave .... Lansing MI 48912-3299
Fax: 517 487-0090

517 371-2100 **Michigan State Chamber of Commerce** 600 S Walnut St .... Lansing MI 48933-2262
Fax: 517 371-7224

Michigan State Government

517 373-1837 *Information* PO Box 30026 .... Lansing MI 48909-7526
Fax: Unlisted

517 373-7023 *Air Quality Div Dept of Natural Resources* PO Box 30028 ...... Lansing MI 48909-7528
Fax: 517 373-1265

517 373-1110 *Attorney General* 525 W Ottawa St .... Lansing MI 48913-0001
Fax: 517 335-4213

517 335-9218 *Bureau of Environmental & Occupational Health*
3423 N Logan St .... Lansing MI 48906-0000
Fax: 517 335-8298

517 373-0510 *Bureau of History* 717 W Allegan Ave .... Lansing MI 48918-0001
Fax: 517 373-0851

517 322-6215 *Bureau of Retirement Systems* PO Box 30171 .... Lansing MI 48909-7671
Fax: 517 322-6269

517 373-3196 *Bureau of Revenue* Allegan St Treasury Bldg 1st Fl .... Lansing MI 48922-0001
Fax: 517 373-4023

313 876-5465 *Bureau of Unemployment Insurance*
7310 Woodward Ave Rm 506 .... Detroit MI 48202-3152
Fax: 313 876-5072

517 373-3490 *Bureau of Workers' Disability Compensation*
201 N Washington St 2nd Fl .... Lansing MI 48933-0000
Fax: 517 335-5829

517 335-8676 *Center for Health Statistics* 3423 N Logan St .... Lansing MI 48906-2934
Fax: Unlisted

517 373-0947 *Consumers Council* 106 W Allegan St .... Lansing MI 48933-1793

517 334-6206 *Corporation & Securities Bureau* 6546 Mercantile Way .... Lansing MI 48909-0000
Fax: 517 334-6155

313 475-1358 *Corrections Camp Program* 6000 Maute Rd .... Grass Lake MI 49240-9225
Fax: Ext 170

313 256-3735 *Council for the Arts* 1200 6th St 11th Fl .... Detroit MI 48226-2418
Fax: 313 256-3781

517 373-1050 *Department of Agriculture* PO Box 30017 .... Lansing MI 48909-7517
Fax: 517 335-0628

517 373-7230 *Department of Commerce* 525 W Ottawa St 4th Fl .... Lansing MI 48933-1067
Fax: 517 373-3872

517 373-0720 *Department of Corrections* PO Box 30003 .... Lansing MI 48909-7503
Fax: 517 373-2628

517 373-3354 *Department of Education* 608 W Allegan St .... Lansing MI 48909-0000
Fax: 517 373-2537

517 373-9600 *Department of Labor*
Victor Bldg 201 N Washington 5th Floor .... Lansing MI 48933-0000
Fax: 517 373-3728

517 373-1870 *Department of Licensing & Regulation* 611 W Ottawa St ...... Lansing MI 48909-0000
Fax: 517 335-4978

517 373-1220 *Department of Natural Resources* PO Box 30028 .... Lansing MI 48909-7528
Fax: 517 335-4242 Admin

517 373-3200 *Department of the Treasury*
430 W Allegan St Treasury Building .... Lansing MI 48922-0001
Fax: 517 373-4968

517 373-2090 *Department of Transportation* 425 W Ottawa St 4th Fl .... Lansing MI 48933-1532
Fax: 517 373-0167

517 335-4933 *Division of Postsecondary Education* 608 W Allegan St .... Lansing MI 48933-0000
Fax: 517 335-4565

517 373-6271 *Emergency Management Div*
300 S Washington Sq Suite 300 .... Lansing MI 48913-0001
Fax: 517 482-7914

313 876-5500 *Employment Security Commission* 7310 Woodward Ave .... Detroit MI 48202-3152
Fax: 313 876-5072

517 334-6951 *Geological Survey Div* PO Box 30028 .... Lansing MI 48909-0000
Fax: 517 334-6919

517 373-3400 *Governor* State Capitol Bldg 2nd Fl .... Lansing MI 48913-0001
Fax: 517 373-1769

517 373-9273 *Insurance Bureau* PO Box 30220 .... Lansing MI 48909-7720
Fax: 517 335-4978

517 373-6800 *Lieutenant Governor* State Capitol Bldg Rm 128 .... Lansing MI 48913-0001
Fax: 517 335-0088

517 373-6655 *Office of Criminal Justice* 320 S Walnut St .... Lansing MI 48933-2014
Fax: 517 373-7268

517 373-0330 *Office of Purchasing* PO Box 30026 .... Lansing MI 48909-7526
Fax: 517 335-0046

517 373-0270 *Parole Board* Grandview Plaza 2nd Fl .... Lansing MI 48909-0000
Fax: 517 335-3840

517 335-8000 *Public Health* 3500 N Logan .... Lansing MI 48906-2933
Fax: 517 335-8560

517 334-6424 *Public Service Commission* 6545 Mercantile Way .... Lansing MI 48909-0000
Fax: 517 882-5170

517 373-2510 *Secretary of State* Treasury Bldg 1st Fl .... Lansing MI 48918-0001
Fax: 517 373-0727

517 332-2521 *State Police* 714 S Harrison Rd .... East Lansing MI 48823-5196
Fax: 517 337-6257

517 788-7560 *State Prison of Southern Michigan* 4000 Cooper St .... Jackson MI 49201-9503
Fax: 517 788-7492

517 373-0120 *Supreme Court* PO Box 30052 .... Lansing MI 48909-7552
Fax: Unlisted

517 373-1949 *Surface Water Quality Div* PO Box 30028 .... Lansing MI 48909-7528
Fax: 517 373-9958

517 355-1855 **Michigan State University** John A Hanna Bldg .... East Lansing MI 48824-0001
Fax: 517 353-9724

517 355-0234 *College of Agriculture & Natural Resources*
121 Agriculture Hall .... East Lansing MI 48824-0001
Fax: Unlisted

517 353-1730 *College of Human Medicine* E Fee Hall Rm A-118 .... East Lansing MI 48824-0001
Fax: 517 355-0342

517 355-6509 *College of Veterinary Medicine* A-133 E Fee Hall .... East Lansing MI 48824-0001
Fax: 517 336-1037

517 355-1600 *Department of Biochemistry* Biochemistry Bldg Rm 212 . East Lansing MI 48824-0001
Fax: 517 353-9334

517 355-9717 *Graduate School of Chemistry* 320 W Shaw Ln .... East Lansing MI 48824-0001
Fax: 517 353-1793

517 353-6430 *Graduate School of Journalism*
305 Communication Art Bldg .... East Lansing MI 48824-0001
Fax: 517 336-1244

517 355-6498 *Graduate School of Microbiology* Giltner Hall Rm 152 ... East Lansing MI 48824-0001
Fax: 517 353-8957

517 355-9666 *Graduate School of Physics*
Physics-Astronomy Bldg Rm 106 .... East Lansing MI 48824-0001
Fax: 517 355-6661

517 355-2370 *Museum* W Circle Dr .... East Lansing MI 48824-0001

517 353-9055 *Urban Planning Program*
Urban Planning & Landscape Architecture Bldg Rm 201 . East Lansing MI 48824-0001
Fax: 517 355-1912

906 487-1885 **Michigan Tech University** 1400 Townsend Dr .... Houghton MI 49931-1295
Fax: 906 487-2398

517 373-0670 **Michigan Travel Bureau** 333 S Capitol Ave Suite F .... Lansing MI 48933-2022
Fax: 517 373-0059

517 386-7792 **Mid Michigan Community College** 1375 S Clare Ave .... Harrison MI 48625-9447
Fax: 517 386-2411

308 532-8740 **Mid Plains Community College Voc-Tech Campus**
RR 4 Box 1 .... North Platte NE 69101-9499

405 691-3800 **Mid-America Bible College** 3500 SW 119th St .... Oklahoma City OK 73170-9704
Fax: 405 691-3961

502 247-8521 **Mid-Continent Baptist Bible College** PO Box 7010 .... Mayfield KY 42066-7010

816 836-5200 **Mid-Continent Public Library** 15616 E 24 Hwy .... Independence MO 64050-0000
Fax: Ext 253

914 471-6060 **Mid-Hudson Library System** 103 Market St .... Poughkeepsie NY 12601-4098
Fax: 914 454-5940

414 921-3670 **Mid-Wisconsin Federated Library System**
32 Sheboygan St .... Fond du Lac WI 54935-4220

315 735-8328 **Mid-York Library System** 1600 Lincoln Ave .... Utica NY 13502-5395

913 782-3750 **MidAmerica Nazarene College** 2030 E Collegeway St .... Olathe KS 66062-1899
Fax: 913 791-3290

312 782-4654 **MidAmerica-Arab Chamber of Commerce**
135 S La Salle St Suite 1020 .... Chicago IL 60603-4202
Fax: 312 782-4871

912 934-6221 **Middle Georgia College** Sarah St .... Cochran GA 31014-0000
Fax: 912 934-3199

912 744-0800 **Middle Georgia Regional Library** 1180 Washington Ave .... Macon GA 31201-1762
Fax: 912 742-3161

615 898-2300 **Middle Tennessee State University** .... Murfreesboro TN 37132-0001
Fax: 615 898-5538

802 388-3711 **Middlebury College** Old Chapel .... Middlebury VT 05753-0000
Fax: 802 388-6436 PR

203 344-3011 **Middlesex Community College** 100 Training Hill Rd .... Middletown CT 06457-4889
Fax: 203 344-7488 Library

617 275-8910 **Middlesex Community College** 202 Springs Rd .... Bedford MA 01730-1197
Fax: 617 275-2590 Admin

617 494-4003 **Middlesex County** 40 Thorndike St .... East Cambridge MA 02141-1755

908 745-3000 **Middlesex County** 1 John F Kennedy Sq .... New Brunswick NJ 08901-2149

804 758-5317 **Middlesex County** Rts 17 & 33 .... Saluda VA 23149-0000

908 548-6000 **Middlesex County College** 155 Mill Rd Box 3050 .... Edison NJ 08837-3675
Fax: 908 494-8244

203 344-2966 **Middlesex Judicial District** 265 DeKoven Dr .... Middletown CT 06457-3460

513 424-1251 **Middletown Public Library** 125 S Broad St .... Middletown OH 45044-4004

517 832-6739 **Midland County** 220 W Ellsworth St .... Midland MI 48640-5180
Fax: 517 832-6608

915 688-1000 **Midland County** 200 W Wall St .... Midland TX 79701-4512

915 683-2708 **Midland County Public Library** 301 W Missouri St .... Midland TX 79701-5108

402 721-5480 **Midland Lutheran College** 900 N Clarkson St .... Fremont NE 68025-4254
Fax: 402 727-6223

803 738-1400 **Midlands Technical College** 316 S Beltline Blvd .... Columbia SC 29205-4204
Fax: Call company operator

309 673-6365 **Midstate College** 244 SW Jefferson Ave .... Peoria IL 61602-1489
Fax: 309 673-5814

606 846-4421 **Midway College** 512 E Stephens St .... Midway KY 40347-1120
Fax: 606 846-5349

817 692-6611 **Midwestern State University** 3400 Taft Blvd .... Wichita Falls TX 76308-2036
Fax: Unlisted

717 248-6733 **Mifflin County** 20 N Wayne St .... Lewistown PA 17044-1770

202 224-4654 **Mikulski Barbara A (Sen - D - Maryland)** 320 Hart Bldg ..... Washington DC 20510-0001
Fax: 202 224-8858

817 697-6596 **Milam County** 100 S Fannin Ave .... Cameron TX 76520-4216

205 923-2771 **Miles College** 5500 Myron Massey Blvd .... Fairfield AL 35064-2697
Fax: 205 923-9292

406 232-3031 **Miles Community College** 2715 Dickinson St .... Miles City MT 59301-4799
Fax: 406 232-5705

501 253-8961 **Miles Musical Museum** PO Box 488 .... Eureka Springs AR 72632-0488

801 743-6223 **Millard County** PO Box 226 .... Fillmore UT 84631-0226

612 983-2561 **Mille Lacs County** 635 2nd St SE .... Milaca MN 56353-1305
Fax: Ext 306

202 225-5131 **Miller Clarence E (Rep - R - Ohio)** 2308 Rayburn Bldg ...... Washington DC 20515-0001
Fax: 202 225-5132

501 774-1500 **Miller County** 4 Laurel St .... Texarkana AR 75502-0000

912 758-4104 **Miller County** 155 S 1st St Suite 2 .... Colquitt GA 31737-1284

314 369-2731 **Miller County** Courthouse Sq .... Tuscumbia MO 65082-0000

202 225-2095 **Miller George (Rep - D - California)** 2228 Rayburn Bldg .... Washington DC 20515-0001
Fax: 202 225-5609

202 225-6311 **Miller John R (Rep - R - Washington)** 322 Cannon Bldg ..... Washington DC 20515-0001
Fax: Unlisted

717 872-3011 **Millersville University of Pennsylvania** .... Millersville PA 17551-0000
Fax: 717 872-3846 Admin

615 929-0116 **Milligan College** .... Milligan College TN 37682-0000

217 424-6211 **Millikin University** 1184 W Main St .... Decatur IL 62522-2084
Fax: 217 424-3993

415 430-2255 **Mills College** 5000 MacArthur Blvd .... Oakland CA 94613-1301
Fax: 415 430-3314

712 527-4880 **Mills County** 418 Sharp St .... Glenwood IA 51534-1756

915 648-2711 **Mills County** PO Box 646 .... Goldthwaite TX 76844-0646

601 354-5201 **Millsaps College** .... Jackson MS 39210-0001
Fax: Ext 406

414 278-3200 **Milwaukee City Hall** 200 E Wells St .... Milwaukee WI 53202-3515

414 278-6600 **Milwaukee Area Technical College** 700 W State St .... Milwaukee WI 53233-1419
Fax: 414 271-2195

414 271-9508 **Milwaukee Art Museum** 750 N Lincoln Memorial Dr .... Milwaukee WI 53202-4077
Fax: 414 271-7588

414 747-7170 **Milwaukee Coast Guard Base** 2420 S Lincoln Memorial Dr ... Milwaukee WI 53207-1902
Fax: 414 362-1882

414 278-4067 **Milwaukee County** 901 N 9th St .... Milwaukee WI 53233-1417

414 273-8288 **Milwaukee County Historical Society Museum**
910 N Old World 3rd St .... Milwaukee WI 53203-1501

414 276-7889 **Milwaukee Institute of Art & Design** 342 N Water St .... Milwaukee WI 53202-5700

414 278-3000 **Milwaukee Public Library** 814 W Wisconsin Ave .... Milwaukee WI 53233-2385
Fax: 414 278-2137

414 278-2702 **Milwaukee Public Museum** 800 W Wells St .... Milwaukee WI 53233-1478
Fax: 414 223-1396

414 277-7300 **Milwaukee School of Engineering** 1025 N Milwaukee St ...... Milwaukee WI 53202-3182
Fax: 414 277-7186

703 235-1452 **Mine Safety & Health Administration** 4015 Wilson Blvd .... Arlington VA 22203-1984
Fax: 703 235-1563

304 547-0400 *Approval & Certification Center* Industrial Park Rd .... Triadelphia WV 26059-0000
Fax: Call company operator

703 235-1140 *Coal Mine Safety & Health* 4015 Wilson Blvd ... Arlington VA 22203-1984
Fax: 703 235-1563
703 235-8480 *Metal & Non-Metal Mine Safety & Health* 4015 Wilson Blvd . Arlington VA 22203-1984
Fax: 703 235-1563
303 231-5449 *Mining Information Systems* PO Box 25367 ... Denver CO 80225-0367
Fax: 303 776-2848
304 255-0451 *National Mine Health & Safety Academy* PO Box 1166 ... Beckley WV 25802-1166
Fax: 304 256-3299
605 772-4612 **Miner County** N Main St ... Howard SD 57349-0000
314 431-4593 **Mineral Area College** ... Flat River MO 63601-0000
Fax: 314 431-6807
719 658-2440 **Mineral County** Creede Ave ... Creede CO 81130-0000
Fax: 719 658-2764
406 822-4541 **Mineral County** 300 River St ... Superior MT 59872-0000
702 945-2446 **Mineral County** PO Box 1450 ... Hawthorne NV 89415-1450
304 788-3924 **Mineral County** 150 Armstrong St ... Keyser WV 26726-3505
202 343-3983 **Minerals Management Service (US Dept of the Interior)**
1849 C St Rm 4245 ... Washington DC 20240-0001
Fax: 202 343-3918
202 225-2631 **Mineta Norman Y (Rep - D - California)**
2350 Rayburn Bldg ... Washington DC 20515-0001
Fax: Unlisted
304 235-1638 **Mingo County** PO Box 1197 ... Williamson WV 25661-1197
208 436-9511 **Minidoka County** 715 G St ... Rupert ID 83350-0000
Fax: 208 436-9561 Communications
202 225-4906 **Mink Patsy (Rep - D - Hawaii)** 2135 Rayburn Bldg ... Washington DC 20515-0001
Fax: 202 225-4987
612 673-3000 **Minneapolis City Hall** 350 S 5th St ... Minneapolis MN 55415-1318
Fax: 612 673-2555 Communications
612 341-7000 **Minneapolis Community College** 1501 Hennepin Ave ... Minneapolis MN 55403-1710
Fax: 612 341-7075
612 372-6500 **Minneapolis Public Library & Information Center**
300 Nicollet Mall ... Minneapolis MN 55401-1992
Fax: 612 372-6546
605 339-6418 **Minnehaha County** 415 N Dakota Ave ... Sioux Falls SD 57102-0136
507 288-4563 **Minnesota Bible College** 920 Mayowood Rd SW ... Rochester MN 55902-2382
612 292-4650 **Minnesota Chamber of Commerce** 480 Cedar St Suite 500 ... Saint Paul MN 55101-2240
Fax: 612 292-4656
612 296-3990 **Minnesota Community College (System)**
550 Cedar St 2nd Fl ... Saint Paul MN 55101-2233
Fax: 612 297-7024
612 854-1446 **Minnesota Independent Republicans**
8030 Cedar Ave Suite 202 ... Minneapolis MN 55425-1215
Fax: 612 854-8488
612 292-4355 **Minnesota Museum of Art** 5th & Market ... Saint Paul MN 55102-0000
612 296-5029 **Minnesota Office of Tourism** 375 Jackson St Suite 250 ... Saint Paul MN 55101-1810
Minnesota State Government
612 296-6013 *Information* 50 Sherburne Ave Rm G18B ... Saint Paul MN 55155-0001
Fax: 612 296-7654
612 297-2603 *Arts Board* 432 Summit Ave ... Saint Paul MN 55102-2624
Fax: 612 297-4304
612 296-6196 *Attorney General* 102 State Capitol Bldg ... Saint Paul MN 55155-0001
Fax: 612 297-4193
612 296-4645 *Building Construction Div* 50 Sherburne Ave Rm G10 ... Saint Paul MN 55155-0001
Fax: 612 296-7654
612 296-3353 *Consumer Div* 117 University Ave Ford Bldg Rm 124 ... Saint Paul MN 55155-0001
Fax: 612 297-4348
612 297-3219 *Department of Agriculture* 90 Plato Blvd W ... Saint Paul MN 55107-2094
Fax: 612 297-5522
612 296-4026 *Department of Commerce* 133 E 7th St ... Saint Paul MN 55101-0000
Fax: 612 296-4328
612 642-0282 *Department of Corrections* 450 Syndicate St N Suite 300 ... Saint Paul MN 55104-4107
Fax: 612 642-0223
612 297-2436 *Department of Criminal Justice*
658 Cedar St Centennial Bldg Suite 300 ... Saint Paul MN 55155-0001
Fax: 612 296-3698
612 296-2358 *Department of Education* 550 Cedar St ... Saint Paul MN 55101-2270
Fax: 612 297-7201
612 296-2438 *Department of Finance* 658 Cedar St 400 Centennial Bldg .. Saint Paul MN 55155-0001
Fax: 612 296-8685
612 296-6107 *Department of Labor & Industry* 443 Lafayette Rd ... Saint Paul MN 55155-0001
Fax: 612 297-1329
612 296-2549 *Department of Natural Resources* 500 Lafayette Rd ... Saint Paul MN 55155-0001
Fax: 612 296-3500
612 296-7107 *Department of Public Service* 150 Kellogg Blvd E ... Saint Paul MN 55101-1421
Fax: 612 297-1959
612 296-3401 *Department of Revenue* 10 River Park Plaza ... Saint Paul MN 55146-0001
Fax: 612 297-5309
612 297-1291 *Department of Trade & Economic Development*
150 E Kellog Blvd 900 ... Saint Paul MN 55101-1495
Fax: 612 296-1290
612 296-7331 *Division of Air Quality* 520 Lafayette Rd ... Saint Paul MN 55155-0001
Fax: 612 297-1456
612 296-2233 *Division of Emergency Management*
Aurora Ave & Park St State Capitol Rm B-5 ... Saint Paul MN 55155-0000
Fax: 612 296-0459
612 296-4807 *Division of Minerals* 500 Lafayette Rd ... Saint Paul MN 55155-0001
Fax: 612 296-5939
612 643-3403 *Division of Solid & Hazardous Waste* 520 Lafayette Rd ... Saint Paul MN 55155-0001
Fax: 612 297-1456
612 296-4810 *Division of Water* 500 Lafayette Rd ... Saint Paul MN 55155-0001
Fax: 612 296-0445
612 296-4657 *Economic Opportunity Office* 150 E Kellogg Blvd Rm 670 .. Saint Paul MN 55101-1421
Fax: 612 297-5820
612 297-4685 *Energy Div Dept of Public Service*
150 Kellogg Blvd E Suite 900 ... Saint Paul MN 55101-1421
Fax: 612 297-1959
612 296-2603 *Environmental Quality Board*
658 Cedar St Centennial Bldg Suite 300 ... Saint Paul MN 55155-0001
Fax: 612 296-3698
612 296-3391 *Governor* 130 State Capitol Bldg ... Saint Paul MN 55155-0001
Fax: 612 296-2089
612 623-5000 *Health Dept* 717 Delaware St SE ... Minneapolis MN 55440-0000
Fax: 612 623-5043
612 296-9665 *Higher Education Coordinating Board*
550 Cedar St Capitol Square Bldg Rm 400 ... Saint Paul MN 55101-2233
Fax: 612 296-3272
612 296-2374 *Lieutenant Governor* State Capitol Bldg Rm 121 ... Saint Paul MN 55155-0001
Fax: 612 296-0491
612 296-6152 *Materials Management Div* 50 Sherburne Ave Rm 112 ... Saint Paul MN 55155-0001
Fax: 612 297-3996
612 255-5000 *Minnesota Correctional Facility Saint Cloud* PO Box B ... Saint Cloud MN 56302-1000
Fax: 612 255-5082
612 779-2700 *Minnesota Correctional Facility Stillwater*
5500 Pickett Ave N ... Stillwater MN 55082-0000
Fax: 612 779-2711
612 642-0270 *Office of Adult & Juvenile Release*
450 Syndicate St N Bigelow Bldg Rm 300 ... Saint Paul MN 55104-0000
Fax: 612 642-0223
612 297-2325 *Planning Agency* 658 Cedar St Centennial Bldg Suite 300 ... Saint Paul MN 55155-0001
Fax: 612 296-3698
612 296-2878 *Power Plant Siting Section*
658 Cedar St Centennial Office Bldg Suite 300 ... Saint Paul MN 55155-0001
Fax: 612 296-3698
612 625-5008 *Public Defender* University of Minnesota 95 Law Ctr ... Minneapolis MN 55455-0000
Fax: 612 626-0241
612 296-3266 *Secretary of State* 180 State Office Bldg ... Saint Paul MN 55155-0001
Fax: 612 297-5844
612 296-4520 *Securities Registration Unit* 133 E 7th St ... Saint Paul MN 55101-0000
Fax: 612 296-4328
612 296-6980 *State Archives* 1500 Mississippi St ... Saint Paul MN 55101-3101
Fax: 612 296-9961
612 296-3080 *State Patrol Div* Transportation Bldg Rm 107 ... Saint Paul MN 55155-0001
Fax: 612 296-5937
612 296-2581 *Supreme Court* 230 State Capitol Bldg ... Saint Paul MN 55155-0001
Fax: Unlisted
612 296-7091 *Treasurer* 50 Sherburne Ave Rm 303 ... Saint Paul MN 55155-0001
Fax: 612 296-8615
612 623-5121 *Vital Records & Statistics* PO Box 9441 ... Minneapolis MN 55440-9441
Fax: Unlisted
612 296-6490 *Worker's Compensation Div* 443 Lafayette Rd ... Saint Paul MN 55155-0000
Fax: 612 296-9634
612 296-2821 **Minnesota State Library Agency** 550 Cedar St Rm 440 ... Saint Paul MN 55101-2233
Fax: 612 296-3272
612 296-2844 **Minnesota State University (System)** 555 Park St Suite 230 .. Saint Paul MN 55103-2111
Fax: 612 296-3214
202 377-2414 **Minority Business Development Agency**
14th St & Constitution Ave NW Rm 5099 ... Washington DC 20230-0001
Fax: 202 377-5117
404 347-4091 *Atlanta Region* 1371 Peachtree St NE Suite 505 ... Atlanta GA 30367-7101
Fax: 404 257-5030
312 353-0182 *Chicago Region* 55 E Monroe St Suite 1440 ... Chicago IL 60603-5760
Fax: 312 353-0191
214 767-8001 *Dallas Region* 1100 Commerce St Suite 7B-23 ... Dallas TX 75242-0790
Fax: 214 767-0613
212 264-3262 *New York Region* 26 Federal Plaza Rm 3720 ... New York NY 10278-0004
Fax: 212 264-0725
415 744-3001 *San Francisco Region* 221 Main St Suite 1280 ... San Francisco CA 94105-1929
Fax: 415 744-3061
202 377-8275 *Washington DC Region*
14th St & Constitution Ave NW Rm 6723 ... Washington DC 20230-0001
Fax: 202 377-5117
701 723-1110 **Minot Air Force Base** ... Minot ND 58705-0001
Fax: Unlisted
701 857-3000 **Minot State University** 500 University Ave W ... Minot ND 58701-2215
Fax: 701 839-6933
704 337-2000 **Mint Museum of Art** 2730 Randolph Rd ... Charlotte NC 28207-2031
Fax: 704 337-2101
619 757-2121 **Mira Costa College** 1 Barnard Dr ... Oceanside CA 92056-3899
Fax: 619 757-2601
304 845-6911 **Miracle Valley Regional Library System** 700 5th St ... Moundsville WV 26041-1906
619 537-1011 **Miramar Naval Air Station** ... San Diego CA 92145-0001
Fax: 619 537-4126 Admin
616 839-4967 **Missaukee County** PO Box J ... Lake City MI 49651-0000
408 988-2200 **Mission College** 3000 Mission College Blvd ... Santa Clara CA 95054-1897
Fax: Unlisted
808 531-0481 **Mission Houses Museum** 553 S King St ... Honolulu HI 96813-3002
501 455-4588 **Missionary Baptist Seminary & Institute**
5224 Stagecoach Rd ... Little Rock AR 72204-8599
601 925-3000 **Mississippi College** College St ... Clinton MS 39058-0001
601 944-1950 *School of Law* 151 E Griffith St ... Jackson MS 39201-1302
Fax: 601 353-7111
501 763-3212 **Mississippi County** Walnut & 2nd Sts ... Blytheville AR 72315-0000
314 683-2146 **Mississippi County** PO Box 304 ... Charleston MO 63834-0304
501 762-1020 **Mississippi County Community College** S Hwy 61 ... Blytheville AR 72316-0000
Fax: 501 763-0948
601 246-5631 **Mississippi Delta Community College** PO Box 668 ... Moorhead MS 38761-0668
Fax: 601 246-8627 Library
601 969-0022 **Mississippi Economic Council** PO Box 23276 ... Jackson MS 39225-3276
Fax: 601 353-0247
601 928-5211 **Mississippi Gulf Coast Community College** Hwy 49 S ... Perkinston MS 39573-0000
Fax: Ext 386
601 359-1036 **Mississippi Library Commission** 1221 Ellis Ave ... Jackson MS 39289-0700
Fax: 601 354-4181
601 354-7303 **Mississippi Museum of Natural Science** 111 N Jefferson St ... Jackson MS 30202-2897
Fax: Call company operator
601 948-5191 **Mississippi Republican Party** 555 Tombigbee St ... Jackson MS 39201-4806
Fax: 601 354-0972
Mississippi State Government
601 359-1000 *Information* 239 N Lamar St ... Jackson MS 39201-1311
Fax: 601 359-1500
601 359-6030 *Arts Commission* 239 N Lamar St Suite 207 ... Jackson MS 39201-1393
601 359-3680 *Attorney General* 450 High St Gartin Bldg ... Jackson MS 39201-1081
Fax: 601 359-3796
601 961-5171 *Bureau of Pollution Control* 2380 Hwy 80 W ... Jackson MS 39204-2312
Fax: 601 961-5190
601 359-3409 *Bureau of Purchasing* 1504 Walter Sillers Bldg ... Jackson MS 39201-1113
601 354-6018 *Consumer Protection Div* 802 N State St ... Jackson MS 39202-2605
Fax: 601 354-6295
601 359-6850 *Department of Archives & History* 100 S State St ... Jackson MS 39201-2812
Fax: 601 359-6905
601 354-6454 *Department of Corrections* 723 N President St ... Jackson MS 39202-3097
Fax: Ext 308
601 359-3449 *Department of Economic Development*
550 High St Suite 1400 ... Jackson MS 39201-1113
Fax: 601 359-2832
601 359-3513 *Department of Education* PO Box 771 ... Jackson MS 39205-0771
Fax: 601 359-2326
601 961-5000 *Department of Enviromental Quality* PO Box 20305 ... Jackson MS 39289-1305
Fax: 601 961-5190
601 359-3402 *Department of Finance & Administration*
550 High St Suite 906 ... Jackson MS 39201-1113
Fax: 601 359-2405
601 960-7635 *Department of Health* 2423 N State St ... Jackson MS 39216-0000
Fax: 601 960-7948
601 359-3569 *Department of Insurance*
550 High St Walter Sillers Bldg Suite 1804 ... Jackson MS 39205-0000
Fax: 601 359-2474
601 961-5062 *Division of Hazardous Waste Management* 2380 Hwy 80 W .. Jackson MS 39204-2312
Fax: 601 961-5190
601 949-2225 *Division of Public Safety Planning* 301 W Pearl St ... Jackson MS 39203-3039
Fax: 601 960-4263

601 352-9100 *Emergency Management Agency* 1410 Riverside Dr .... Jackson MS 39202-1237
    Fax: 601 352-8314
601 354-8711 *Employment Security Commission* 1520 W Capitol St ...... Jackson MS 39203-1601
    Fax: 601 961-7405
601 961-4733 *Energy & Transportation Div* 510 George St Suite 101 ... Jackson MS 39202-0000
    Fax: 601 969-7300
601 359-3150 *Governor* PO Box 139 .... Jackson MS 39205-0139
    Fax: 601 359-2917
601 359-1209 *Highway Dept* 500 N West St 1004 Woolfolk Bldg ... Jackson MS 39201-0000
    Fax: 601 359-2233
601 987-1212 *Highway Safety Patrol* 1900 E Woodrow Wilson Dr ... Jackson MS 39216-5118
    Fax: 601 987-1480
601 982-6611 *Institutions of Higher Learning* 3825 Ridgewood Rd .... Jackson MS 39211-6463
    Fax: 601 982-6610
601 359-3200 *Lieutenant Governor* PO Box 1018 .... Jackson MS 39215-1018
    Fax: 601 359-3935
601 354-6228 *Mining & Reclamation Div* 2525 N West St .... Jackson MS 39216-3840
    Fax: 601 354-6327
601 745-6611 *Mississippi State Penitentiary* .... Parchman MS 38738-0000
601 987-3981 *Occupational Safety & Health Branch* 305 W Lorenz Blvd ..... Jackson MS 39213-7034
601 359-3621 *Office of Building Ground & Real Property Management*
    Walter Sillers Bldg 15th Fl .... Jackson MS 39201-0000
    Fax: 601 359-2470
601 960-7960 *Office of Public Health Statistics* 2423 N State St Rm 110 .... Jackson MS 39216-4504
    Fax: 601 960-7948
601 354-7142 *Oil & Gas Board* 500 Greymont Ave Suite E .... Jackson MS 39202-3446
601 354-6454 *Parole Board* 723 N President St .... Jackson MS 39202-3029
    Fax: Ext 308
601 961-5400 *Public Service Commission* 550 High St Walter Sillers Bldg .. Jackson MS 39201-1182
    Fax: 601 961-5469
601 932-2880 *Rankin County Correctional Facility* PO Box 88550 .... Pearl MS 39288-8550
    Fax: Ext 324
601 987-3969 *Real Estate Commission* 1920 Dunbarton Dr .... Jackson MS 39216-5087
    Fax: 601 987-4984
601 359-3598 *Research Planning Policy & Development Dept of Education*
    Walter Sillers Bldg Rm 306 .... Jackson MS 39201-0000
    Fax: 601 359-2326
601 359-1350 *Secretary of State* 401 Mississippi St .... Jackson MS 39201-1012
    Fax: 601 354-6243
601 359-1350 *Security Div* 401 Mississippi St .... Jackson MS 39201-1012
    Fax: 601 354-6243
601 359-3694 *Supreme Court* 450 High St Gartin Bldg 3rd Fl .... Jackson MS 39201-0000
    Fax: 601 359-2407
601 359-1098 *Tax Commission* PO Box 1033 .... Jackson MS 39215-1033
    Fax: 601 359-1255
601 359-3531 *Treasury Dept* 550 High St Rm 404 .... Jackson MS 39201-1192
    Fax: 601 359-2001
601 961-7700 *Unemployment Insurance Div* 1520 W Capitol St .... Jackson MS 39203-1601
    Fax: 601 961-7405
601 987-4200 *Workers' Compensation Commission* 1428 Lakeland Dr ...... Jackson MS 39216-4788
601 359-6920 **Mississippi State Historical Museum** PO Box 571 .... Jackson MS 39205-0571
601 325-2323 **Mississippi State University** .... Starkville MS 39762-9999
    Fax: 601 325-3299
601 325-2110 *College of Agriculture & Home Economics*
    130 Lloyd Ricks Bldg .... Mississippi State MS 39762-9999
    Fax: 601 325-8580
601 325-7667 *Library* Hardy Rd .... Starkville MS 39762-9999
    Fax: 601 325-3560
601 359-3297 **Mississippi Tourism Div** 550 High St Suite 1200 .... Jackson MS 39201-1113
    Fax: 601 359-2832
601 329-4750 **Mississippi University for Women** 1224 College St .... Columbus MS 39701-9984
    Fax: 601 329-7297
601 254-9041 **Mississippi Valley State University** Hwy 82 W .... Itta Bena MS 38941-0000
    Fax: 601 254-6704 Library
406 721-5700 **Missoula County** 200 W Broadway St .... Missoula MT 59802-4292
    Fax: 406 721-4043
406 721-2665 **Missoula Public Library** 301 E Main .... Missoula MT 59802-4799
    Fax: 406 728-5900
406 542-6811 **Missoula Vocational Technical Center** 909 South Ave W ...... Missoula MT 59801-7910
314 434-1115 **Missouri Baptist College** 12542 Conway Rd .... Saint Louis MO 63141-8698
314 636-5241 **Missouri Democratic State Committee** PO Box 719 ... Jefferson City MO 65102-0719
    Fax: 314 634-8176
314 751-4133 **Missouri Div of Tourism** 301 W High St .... Jefferson City MO 65102-0000
    Fax: 314 751-5160
314 636-3146 **Missouri Republican Party** 204 E Dunklin St .... Jefferson City MO 65101-3127
    Fax: 314 636-3273
417 625-9300 **Missouri Southern State College** 3950 Newman Rd .... Joplin MO 64801-1512
    Fax: 417 625-9744 Admin
314 634-3511 **Missouri State Chamber of Commerce**
    428 E Capitol Ave .... Jefferson City MO 65101-3069
    Fax: 314 634-8855
Missouri State Government
314 751-2000 *Information* 301 W High St .... Jefferson City MO 65101-1580
    Fax: 314 751-3299
314 751-4817 *Air Pollution Control Program* 205 Jefferson St .... Jefferson City MO 65101-2982
    Fax: 314 751-2706
314 751-3321 *Attorney General* Supreme Court Bldg 1st Fl .... Jefferson City MO 65101-0000
    Fax: 314 751-0774
314 751-2389 *Board of Probation & Parole* PO Box 267 .... Jefferson City MO 65102-0267
    Fax: 314 751-4099
314 751-6383 *Bureau of Vital Records* 1730 E Elm St .... Jefferson City MO 65101-4130
    Fax: 314 751-6010
314 751-3359 *Department of Agriculture* 1616 Missouri Blvd .... Jefferson City MO 65109-1764
    Fax: 314 751-1784
314 751-2389 *Department of Corrections* 2729 Plaza Dr .... Jefferson City MO 65109-4406
    Fax: 314 751-4099
314 751-4241 *Department of Economic Development* 301 W High St ..Jefferson City MO 65101-1580
    Fax: 314 634-5472
314 751-3503 *Department of Elementary & Secondary Education*
    PO Box 480 .... Jefferson City MO 65102-0480
    Fax: 314 751-1179
314 751-6001 *Department of Health* 1730 E Elm St .... Jefferson City MO 65101-4130
    Fax: 314 751-6010
314 751-2361 *Department of Higher Education* 101 Adams St .... Jefferson City MO 65101-3000
    Fax: 314 751-6635
314 751-4091 *Department of Labor & Industrial Relations*
    PO Box 504 .... Jefferson City MO 65102-3138
    Fax: Unlisted
314 751-4422 *Department of Natural Resources* 205 Jefferson St ..... Jefferson City MO 65101-2981
    Fax: 314 751-9277
314 751-4905 *Department of Public Safety*
    301 W High St Truman Bldg .... Jefferson City MO 65101-1580
    Fax: 314 635-2808
314 751-4450 *Department of Revenue* 301 W High St Truman Bldg .. Jefferson City MO 65101-0000
314 751-2345 *Division of Budget & Planning* PO Box 809 .... Jefferson City MO 65102-0809
    Fax: 314 751-4173

314 751-3339 *Division of Design & Construction*
    301 W High St Truman Bldg Rm 730 .... Jefferson City MO 65102-0000
    Fax: 314 751-7277
314 751-3215 *Division of Employment Security* 421 E Dunklin St ...... Jefferson City MO 65104-0001
    Fax: Unlisted
314 751-4000 *Division of Energy* 205 Jefferson St .... Jefferson City MO 65102-0000
    Fax: 314 751-6860
314 751-4810 *Division of Environmental Quality* PO Box 176 .... Jefferson City MO 65102-0176
    Fax: 314 751-9277
314 751-3242 *Division of Finance* Truman State Office Bldg Rm 630 .. Jefferson City MO 65102-0000
    Fax: 314 751-9192
314 751-4126 *Division of Insurance* 301 W High St Truman Bldg ...... Jefferson City MO 65101-1580
    Fax: 314 751-1165
314 751-0293 *Division of Professional Registration*
    3523 N Ten-Mile Dr .... Jefferson City MO 65109-0000
    Fax: 314 751-4176
314 751-2387 *Division of Purchasing*
    301 W High St Truman Bldg Rm 580 .... Jefferson City MO 65101-1580
    Fax: Unlisted
314 751-4231 *Division of Worker's Compensation*
    3315 W Truman Blvd .... Jefferson City MO 65109-5711
314 751-9571 *Emergency Management Agency* 1717 Industrial Dr .... Jefferson City MO 65109-1403
    Fax: 314 634-7966
314 751-3222 *Governor* 216 State Capitol .... Jefferson City MO 65101-1556
    Fax: 314 751-2128
314 751-2551 *Highway Dept* Capitol Ave & Jefferson St .... Jefferson City MO 65101-2983
    Fax: 314 751-6555
314 751-3313 *Highway Patrol* 1510 E Elm St .... Jefferson City MO 65101-4118
    Fax: 314 751-9419
314 751-3000 *Lieutenant Governor* PO Box 563 .... Jefferson City MO 65102-0563
    Fax: 314 751-9422
314 751-3224 *Missouri State Penitentiary for Men* 631 State St ... Jefferson City MO 65101-3026
816 263-3778 *Missouri Training Center for Men* PO Box 7 .... Moberly MO 65270-0007
    Fax: Call company operator
417 887-9800 *Public Defender Commission* Plaza Towers Suite 811 ...... Springfield MO 65804-1686
    Fax: 417 887-4101
314 751-3234 *Public Service Commission* 301 W High St Suite 530 ... Jefferson City MO 65101-1580
    Fax: 314 751-1847
314 751-2628 *Real Estate Commission* 3523 N Ten-Mile Dr .... Jefferson City MO 65101-0000
314 751-4717 *Records Management & Archives* 1001 Industrial Dr ... Jefferson City MO 65109-1459
314 751-3318 *Secretary of State*
    301 W High St Truman Bldg Rm 208 .... Jefferson City MO 65101-0000
    Fax: 314 751-5841
314 751-4136 *Security Div* 301 W High St Truman Bldg Rm 830 .... Jefferson City MO 65102-0000
314 751-4932 *Soil & Water Conservation Program* 205 Jefferson St ...Jefferson City MO 65101-2982
314 444-6845 *State Council on the Arts* 111 N 7th St Suite 105 .... Saint Louis MO 63101-2134
314 751-4144 *Supreme Court* PO Box 150 .... Jefferson City MO 65102-0150
    Fax: 314 751-2573
314 751-5333 *Trade Offense Div* Supreme Court Bldg .... Jefferson City MO 65101-0000
    Fax: 314 751-0774
314 751-4123 *Treasurer* PO Box 210 .... Jefferson City MO 65102-0210
    Fax: 314 751-9443
314 751-3643 *Unemployment Insurance Operations* 421 E Dunklin St .Jefferson City MO 65101-0000
    Fax: 314 751-7973
314 751-3176 *Waste Management Program* 205 Jefferson St .... Jefferson City MO 65101-2982
    Fax: 314 751-7869
314 751-3615 **Missouri State Library** PO Box 387 .... Jefferson City MO 65102-0387
    Fax: Unlisted
816 886-6924 **Missouri Valley College** 500 E College St ....Marshall MO 65340-3197
    Fax: 816 886-9818
816 271-4200 **Missouri Western State College** 4525 Downs Dr ..... Saint Joseph MO 64507-2246
    Fax: 816 271-4571
617 253-1000 **MIT (Massachusetts Institute of Technology)**
    77 Massachusetts Ave .... Cambridge MA 02139-4307
    Fax: 617 253-8000
203 443-2811 **Mitchell College** 437 Pequot Ave ....New London CT 06320-4498
    Fax: 203 437-0632
704 878-3200 **Mitchell Community College** 500 W Broad St .... Statesville NC 28677-5293
    Fax: 704 878-0872
912 336-2000 **Mitchell County** 12 Broad St .... Camilla GA 31730-0000
515 732-3726 **Mitchell County** County Courthouse .... Osage IA 50461-0000
913 738-3652 **Mitchell County** PO Box 190 .... Beloit KS 67420-0190
704 688-2434 **Mitchell County** Crimson Laurel Way Administration Bldg .... Bakersville NC 28705-0000
915 728-3481 **Mitchell County** 301 Oak St .... Colorado City TX 79512-6225
    Fax: 915 728-8319
202 224-5344 **Mitchell George J (Sen - D - Maine)** 176 Russell Bldg .... Washington DC 20510-0001
    Fax: Unlisted
612 227-9171 **Mitchell William College of Law** 875 Summit Ave .... Saint Paul MN 55105-3076
    Fax: 612 290-6414
202 225-8273 **Moakley Joe (Rep - D - Massachusetts)** 221 Cannon Bldg .. Washington DC 20515-0001
    Fax: 202 225-7804
816 263-4110 **Moberly Area Junior College** College & Rollins Sts .... Moberly MO 65270-0000
    Fax: 816 263-6252
205 690-2217 **Mobile Coast Guard Base** S Broad St .... Mobile AL 36615-1390
    Fax: 205 690-2216
205 675-5990 **Mobile College** 5735 College Pkwy .... Mobile AL 36613-2842
    Fax: 205 675-3404 Library
205 690-8615 **Mobile County** 109 Government St .... Mobile AL 36602-3108
    Fax: 205 690-4770
205 434-7073 **Mobile Public Library** 701 Government St .... Mobile AL 36602-1499
817 738-9215 **Modern Art Museum of Fort Worth** 1309 Montgomery St ..... Fort Worth TX 76107-3080
    Fax: 817 735-1161
209 575-6498 **Modesto Junior College** 435 College Ave .... Modesto CA 95350-5800
    Fax: 209 575-6516
916 233-3939 **Modoc County** PO Box 131 .... Alturas CA 96101-0131
303 824-5517 **Moffat County** 221 W Victory Way .... Craig CO 81625-2716
    Fax: 303 824-3542
415 966-5976 **Moffett Field Naval Air Station** .... Moffett Field CA 94035-5000
    Fax: 415 966-5533
602 757-4331 **Mohave Community College** 1971 Jagerson Ave .... Kingman AZ 86401-1299
    Fax: 602 757-0896
602 753-9141 **Mohave County** 401 E Spring St .... Kingman AZ 86401-5878
315 792-5400 **Mohawk Valley Community College** 1101 Sherman Dr ...... Utica NY 13501-5308
    Fax: 315 792-5666
203 886-1931 **Mohegan Community College** 21 Mahan Dr .... Norwich CT 06360-2497
    Fax: 203 886-0691
202 225-3371 **Molinari Susan (Rep - R - New York)** 315 Cannon Bldg ..... Washington DC 20515-0001
    Fax: 202 226-1272
202 225-4172 **Mollohan Alan B (Rep - D - West Virginia)**
    229 Cannon Bldg .... Washington DC 20515-0001
    Fax: 202 225-7564
516 678-5000 **Molloy College** 1000 Hempstead Ave .... Rockville Centre NY 11570-1199
    Fax: 516 678-7295
212 759-5227 **Monaco: Principality of Monaco Mission to the UN**
    845 3rd Ave 19th Fl .... New York NY 10022-6601
    Fax: 212 754-9320

412 684-4750 **Monessen Public Library & District Center** 326 Donner Ave .. Monessen PA 15062-1182
Fax: 412 684-7077
212 861-9460 **Mongolia: Mongolian People's Republic Mission to the UN**
6 E 77th St ... New York NY 10021-1791
Fax: 212 861-9464
314 796-4661 **Moniteau County** 200 E Main St ... California MO 65018-1675
309 457-2311 **Monmouth College** 700 E Broadway Ave ... Monmouth IL 61462-1998
Fax: 309 457-2141
908 222-6600 **Monmouth College** 400 Cedar Ave ... West Long Branch NJ 07764-1890
Fax: 908 571-3570
908 431-7387 **Monmouth County** Main St Hall of Records ... Freehold NJ 07728-0000
Fax: 908 409-4820
619 932-7911 **Mono County** PO Box 537 ... Bridgeport CA 93517-0537
Fax: 619 932-7520
712 423-2491 **Monona County** 610 Iowa Ave ... Onawa IA 51040-1699
304 291-7230 **Monongalia County** 243 High St ... Morgantown WV 26505-5434
Fax: 304 291-7273
716 424-5200 **Monroe Community College** 1000 E Henrietta Rd ... Rochester NY 14623-5780
Fax: 716 427-2749
205 743-3782 **Monroe County** S Mount Plaza Ave ... Monroeville AL 36461-0000
Fax: 205 743-4107
501 747-3921 **Monroe County** 123 Madison St ... Clarendon AR 72029-2794
305 294-4641 **Monroe County** 500 Whitehead St ... Key West FL 33040-6581
912 994-7000 **Monroe County** PO Box 189 ... Forsyth GA 31029-0189
Fax: 912 994-7012
515 932-5212 **Monroe County** County Courthouse ... Albia IA 52531-0000
618 939-8681 **Monroe County** 100 S Main St ... Waterloo IL 62298-1399
812 333-3600 **Monroe County** PO Box 547 ... Bloomington IN 47402-0547
502 487-5471 **Monroe County** PO Box 335 ... Tompkinsville KY 42167-0335
313 243-7081 **Monroe County** 106 E 1st St ... Monroe MI 48161-2143
816 327-5817 **Monroe County** 300 N Main St ... Paris MO 65275-1399
Fax: 816 327-4865
601 369-8143 **Monroe County** PO Box 578 ... Aberdeen MS 39730-0578
716 428-5151 **Monroe County** 39 W Main St ... Rochester NY 14614-1408
614 472-5181 **Monroe County** PO Box 574 ... Woodsfield OH 43793-0574
717 424-5100 **Monroe County** County Courthouse Sq ... Stroudsburg PA 18360-0000
615 442-3981 **Monroe County** 105 College St ... Madisonville TN 37354-1451
608 269-8705 **Monroe County** 112 S Court St ... Sparta WI 54656-1764
Fax: 608 269-8889
304 772-3096 **Monroe County** Main St ... Union WV 24983-0000
313 242-7300 **Monroe County Community College** 1555 S Raisinville Rd ... Monroe MI 48161-9746
Fax: 313 242-9711
313 243-7137 **Monroe County Historical Museum** 126 S Monroe St ... Monroe MI 48161-2275
313 241-5277 **Monroe County Library System** 3700 S Custer Rd ... Monroe MI 48161-9732
Fax: 313 241-4722
812 339-2271 **Monroe County Public Library** 303 E Kirkwood Ave ... Bloomington IN 47408-3592
Fax: Unlisted
817 894-2461 **Montague County** PO Box 77 ... Montague TX 76251-0077
406 442-2405 **Montana Chamber of Commerce** 2030 11th Ave ... Helena MT 59601-0000
Fax: 406 442-2409
406 496-4101 **Montana College of Mineral Science & Technology** W Park St .... Butte MT 59701-0000
Fax: 406 496-4133 Library
406 442-9520 **Montana Democratic State Central Committee** 616 Helena Ave .. Helena MT 59601-3654
406 444-2654 **Montana Promotion Div** 1424 9th Ave ... Helena MT 59601-4503
Fax: 406 444-2808
406 442-6469 **Montana Republican State Committee** 1425 Helena Ave ... Helena MT 59601-3024
Fax: 406 442-3293
Montana State Government
406 444-2511 *Information* Mitchell Bldg Rm 219 ... Helena MT 59620-0000
Fax: 406 444-5545
406 444-3454 *Air Quality Bureau* 1400 Broadway Cogswell Bldg ... Helena MT 59620-0000
Fax: 406 444-2606
406 444-3104 *Architecture & Engineering Div* 1520 E 6th Ave ... Helena MT 59620-0103
Fax: 406 444-3399
406 444-2681 *Archives & Library Div* 225 N Roberts St ... Helena MT 59620-0000
406 444-6430 *Arts Council* 48 N Last Chance Gulch St ... Helena MT 59601-4122
Fax: 406 442-6179
406 444-2026 *Attorney General* 215 N Sanders St Justice Bldg 3rd Fl ... Helena MT 59620-0000
Fax: 406 444-3549
406 444-2961 *Board of Realty Regulation* 1424 9th Ave ... Helena MT 59620-0000
Fax: 406 444-2903
406 496-4180 *Bureau of Mines & Geology* W Park St ... Butte MT 59701-0000
Fax: 406 496-4133
406 444-4912 *Community Corrections Bureau (Probation & Parole)*
1539 11th Ave ... Helena MT 59620-0000
Fax: 406 444-4920
406 444-4312 *Consumer Affairs Unit* 1424 9th Ave ... Helena MT 59601-4503
406 444-3604 *Crime Control Div* 303 N Roberts St 4th Fl ... Helena MT 59620-0000
Fax: 406 444-4722
406 444-3144 *Department of Agriculture*
Agriculture/Livestock Bldg Capitol Stn ... Helena MT 59620-0000
Fax: 406 444-5409
406 444-3494 *Department of Commerce* 1424 9th Ave ... Helena MT 59601-4503
Fax: 406 444-2903
406 444-2544 *Department of Health & Environmental Sciences*
1400 Broadway Cogswell Bldg Rm C108 ... Helena MT 59620-0000
Fax: 406 444-2606
406 444-6201 *Department of Highways* 2701 Prospect Ave ... Helena MT 59620-0000
Fax: 406 444-6363
406 444-5671 *Department of Institutions* 1539 11th Ave ... Helena MT 59601-4599
Fax: 406 444-4920
406 444-3555 *Department of Labor & Industry* PO Box 1728 ... Helena MT 59624-1728
Fax: 406 444-2699
406 444-6699 *Department of Natural Resources & Conservation*
1520 E 6th Ave ... Helena MT 59601-4541
Fax: 406 444-6721
406 444-2460 *Department of Revenue*
205 Roberts Sam W Mitchell Bldg Rm 455 ... Helena MT 59620-0000
Fax: 406 444-3696
406 444-6911 *Disaster & Emergency Services Div* 1100 N Main St ... Helena MT 59601-0000
Fax: 406 444-6965
406 444-6754 *Energy Div* 1520 E 6th Ave ... Helena MT 59620-0000
Fax: 406 444-6721
406 444-3948 *Environmental Sciences Div*
Lockey Ave & Roberts St Cogswell Bldg ... Helena MT 59620-0000
Fax: 406 444-2606
406 444-3111 *Governor* State Capitol ... Helena MT 59620-0001
Fax: 406 444-5529
406 444-3780 *Highway Patrol* 303 N Roberts ... Helena MT 59620-0000
Fax: 406 444-4169
406 444-3111 *Lieutenant Governor* State Capitol ... Helena MT 59620-1901
Fax: 406 444-5529
406 846-1320 *Montana State Prison* 400 Conley Lake Rd ... Deer Lodge MT 59722-9755
Fax: Ext 2345
406 444-6570 *Montana University (System)* 33 S Last Chance Gulch St ... Helena MT 59601-4132
Fax: 406 444-7729
406 444-3671 *Occupational Health Bureau*
1400 Broadway Cogswell Bldg Rm A113 ... Helena MT 59620-0000
Fax: 406 444-2606
406 444-3616 *Office of Budget & Program Planning* State Capitol Rm 220 ... Helena MT 59620-0000
Fax: 406 444-5529
406 444-3095 *Office of Public Instruction* Capitol Stn ... Helena MT 59620-0000
Fax: 406 444-3924
406 444-6675 *Oil & Gas Conservation Div* 1520 E 6th Ave ... Helena MT 59620-0000
Fax: 406 444-6721
406 444-3737 *Professional & Occupational Licensing* 1424 9th Ave ... Helena MT 59620-0000
Fax: 406 444-2808
406 444-6199 *Public Service Commission* 2701 Prospect Ave ... Helena MT 59601-9726
Fax: 406 444-7618
406 444-2575 *Purchasing Div* 205 Robert St Mitchell Bldg Rm 165 ... Helena MT 59620-0000
Fax: 406 444-2529
406 444-2034 *Secretary of State* State Capitol Rm 225 ... Helena MT 59620-0000
Fax: 406 444-3976
406 444-2821 *Solid & Hazardous Waste Bureau* Cogswell Bldg ... Helena MT 59620-0000
Fax: 406 444-1499
406 444-2040 *State Auditor Office Insurance Dept*
126 N Sanders St Mitchell Bldg Rm 270 ... Helena MT 59620-0000
Fax: 406 444-3497
406 444-6518 *State Compensation Mutual Insurance* 5 S Last Chance Gulch . Helena MT 59601-4132
Fax: 406 444-5963
406 444-3858 *Supreme Court* 215 N Sanders St Justice Bldg Rm 323 ... Helena MT 59620-0000
406 444-6190 *Transportation Div* 2701 Prospect Ave ... Helena MT 59601-9726
Fax: 406 444-7618
406 444-2032 *Treasurer* 205 Robert St Rm 175 ... Helena MT 59620-0000
Fax: 406 444-2812
406 444-2723 *Unemployment Insurance Div* PO Box 1728 ... Helena MT 59624-1728
Fax: 406 444-2699
406 444-2614 *Vital Records & Statistics Bureau*
1400 Broadway Cogswell Bldg Rm C118 ... Helena MT 59620-0000
Fax: 406 444-2606
406 444-6601 *Water Resources Div* 1520 E 6th Ave ... Helena MT 59620-2301
Fax: 406 444-6721
406 444-3115 **Montana State Library** 1515 E 6th Ave ... Helena MT 59620-0000
Fax: 406 444-5612
406 994-0211 **Montana State University** ... Bozeman MT 59717-0001
Fax: 406 994-2893
406 994-3171 *Library* Renne Library ... Bozeman MT 59717-0001
Fax: 406 994-4117
312 539-1919 **Montay College** 3750 W Peterson Ave ... Chicago IL 60659-3115
Fax: 312 539-1913
517 328-2111 **Montcalm Community College** 2800 College Dr ... Sidney MI 48885-9746
Fax: 517 328-2950
517 831-5226 **Montcalm County** 211 W Main St ... Stanton MI 48888-0000
Fax: 517 831-8863
201 893-4000 **Montclair State College** Normal Ave & Valley Rd ... Upper Montclair NJ 07043-0000
Fax: 201 893-5455
408 755-5030 **Monterey County** PO Box 1819 ... Salinas CA 93902-1819
408 424-3244 **Monterey County Free Library** 26 Central Ave ... Salinas CA 93901-2628
Fax: 408 755-5839
408 646-4000 **Monterey Peninsula College** 980 Fremont St ... Monterey CA 93940-4799
Fax: 408 655-2627
408 372-7591 **Monterey Peninsula Museum of Art** 559 Pacific St ... Monterey CA 93940-2880
303 565-8317 **Montezuma County** 109 W Main St Suite 302 ... Cortez CO 81321-3154
205 284-7920 **Montgomery City-County Public Library**
135 Norman Dale Arcade ... Montgomery AL 36111-0000
Montgomery College
301 353-7700 *Germantown Campus* 20200 Observation Dr ... Germantown MD 20876-4098
Fax: 301 353-7719
301 279-5000 *Rockville Campus* 51 Mannakee St ... Rockville MD 20850-1195
Fax: 301 251-7134
919 572-3691 **Montgomery Community College** Old Biscoe Rd ... Troy NC 27371-0000
Fax: 919 576-2176
205 832-4950 **Montgomery County** PO Box 1667 ... Montgomery AL 36192-0000
501 867-3114 **Montgomery County** PO Box 717 ... Mount Ida AR 71957-0717
912 583-2363 **Montgomery County** Railroad Ave ... Mount Vernon GA 30445-0000
712 623-4986 **Montgomery County** 105 Coolbaugh St ... Red Oak IA 51566-0000
217 532-9530 **Montgomery County** 1 Courthouse Sq ... Hillsboro IL 62049-1137
Fax: Unlisted
317 364-6400 **Montgomery County** 100 E Main St ... Crawfordsville IN 47933-1715
316 331-4840 **Montgomery County** PO Box 446 ... Independence KS 67301-0446
Fax: 316 331-1686
606 498-8700 **Montgomery County** Court St ... Mount Sterling KY 40353-0000
Fax: 606 498-8729
301 217-1000 **Montgomery County** 100 Maryland Ave Courthouse 2nd Fl ... Rockville MD 20850-0000
314 564-3357 **Montgomery County** 211 E 3rd St ... Montgomery City MO 63361-1956
601 283-2333 **Montgomery County** PO Box 71 ... Winona MS 38967-0071
Fax: 601 283-2233
919 572-2575 **Montgomery County** PO Box 637 ... Troy NC 27371-0637
518 853-3431 **Montgomery County** Broadway ... Fonda NY 12068-0000
Fax: 518 853-4714
513 225-4000 **Montgomery County** 451 W 3rd St ... Dayton OH 45422-0002
Fax: 513 225-4774
215 278-3000 **Montgomery County** Swede & Airy Sts ... Norristown PA 19404-0000
615 648-5711 **Montgomery County** PO Box 687 ... Clarksville TN 37041-0687
Fax: 615 553-5150
409 539-7885 **Montgomery County** 300 N Main St ... Conroe TX 77301-2898
703 382-5700 **Montgomery County** 1 E Main St ... Christiansburg VA 24073-3027
Fax: 703 382-6943
215 641-6300 **Montgomery County Community College** 340 DeKalb Pike ... Blue Bell PA 19422-1400
Fax: 215 653-0585 Library
301 217-3850 **Montgomery County Dept of Public Libraries**
99 Maryland Ave ... Rockville MD 20850-2372
Fax: 301 217-3895
215 278-5100 **Montgomery County-Norristown Public Library**
Swede & Elm Sts ... Norristown PA 19401-0000
Fax: 215 278-5110
202 225-5031 **Montgomery GV (Rep - D - Mississippi)**
2184 Rayburn Bldg ... Washington DC 20515-0001
Fax: 202 225-3375
517 785-4794 **Montmorency County** County Courthouse ... Atlanta MI 49709-0000
717 271-3012 **Montour County** 29 Mill St ... Danville PA 17821-1945
704 669-8011 **Montreat-Anderson College** 310 Gaither Cir ... Montreat NC 28757-9999
Fax: 704 669-9554
303 249-7755 **Montrose County** PO Box 1289 ... Montrose CO 81402-1289
508 922-8222 **Montserrat College of Art** PO Box 26 ... Beverly MA 01915-0001
912 333-4211 **Moody Air Force Base** Bemis Rd ... Valdosta GA 31699-0001
Fax: 912 333-3078
312 329-4000 **Moody Bible Institute** 820 N La Salle St ... Chicago IL 60610-3276
Fax: 312 329-2033
605 997-3181 **Moody County** 101 E Pipestone Ave ... Flandreau SD 57028-1730
202 225-3571 **Moody Jim (Rep - D - Wisconsin)** 1019 Longworth Bldg ... Washington DC 20515-0001
Fax: 202 225-1396

215 568-4515 **Moore College of Art & Design** 20th & Race St .... Philadelphia PA 19103-0000
Fax: 215 568-8017
919 947-2396 **Moore County** PO Box 936 .... Carthage NC 28327-0936
615 759-7346 **Moore County** County Courthouse .... Lynchburg TN 37352-0000
806 935-6164 **Moore County** PO Box 396 .... Dumas TX 79029-0396
202 225-4176 **Moorhead Carlos J (Rep - R - California)**
2346 Rayburn Bldg .... Washington DC 20515-0001
Fax: Unlisted
218 236-2011 **Moorhead State University** 1104 7th Ave S .... Moorhead MN 56563-0001
Fax: 218 236-2168
805 529-2321 **Moorpark College** 7075 Campus Rd .... Moorpark CA 93021-1695
Fax: 805 378-1499
505 387-5279 **Mora County** Hwy 518 .... Mora NM 87732-0000
414 922-8611 **Moraine Park Technical College** 235 N National Ave .... Fond du Lac WI 54935-2897
Fax: 414 929-2471
708 974-4300 **Moraine Valley Community College** 10900 S 88th Ave .... Palos Hills IL 60465-0937
Fax: 708 974-1184 Library
202 225-4376 **Moran James P Jr (Rep - D - Virginia)**
1523 Longworth Bldg .... Washington DC 20515-0001
Fax: 202 225-0017
215 861-1300 **Moravian College** 1210 Main St .... Bethlehem PA 18018-6650
Fax: 215 861-1577
606 783-2221 **Morehead State University** 100 University Blvd .... Morehead KY 40351-1680
Fax: 606 783-2678
404 681-2800 **Morehouse College** 830 Westview Dr SW .... Atlanta GA 30310-1427
Fax: Ext 411 Admin
318 281-4132 **Morehouse Parish** 125 E Madison St .... Bastrop LA 71221-0000
404 752-1500 **Morehouse School of Medicine** 720 Westview Dr SW .... Atlanta GA 30310-1495
Fax: 404 755-7318 Library
202 225-5341 **Morella Constance A (Rep - R - Maryland)**
1024 Longworth Bldg .... Washington DC 20515-0001
Fax: 202 225-1389
303 867-3081 **Morgan Community College** 17800 County Rd 20 .... Fort Morgan CO 80701-4399
Fax: Ext 333
205 351-4600 **Morgan County** 302 Lee St NE .... Decatur AL 35601-1999
303 867-8202 **Morgan County** 231 Ensign St .... Fort Morgan CO 80701-2307
Fax: 303 867-6448
404 342-0725 **Morgan County** PO Box 168 .... Madison GA 30650-0168
217 245-4619 **Morgan County** 300 W State St .... Jacksonville IL 62650-2063
317 342-1025 **Morgan County** PO Box 1556 .... Martinsville IN 46151-0556
606 743-3897 **Morgan County** 505 Prestonsburg St .... West Liberty KY 41472-1162
Fax: Unlisted
314 378-5436 **Morgan County** 100 E Newton St .... Versailles MO 65084-1298
614 962-4752 **Morgan County** 19 E Main St .... McConnelsville OH 43756-1198
615 346-3480 **Morgan County** Main St .... Wartburg TN 37887-0000
801 829-6811 **Morgan County** 48th W Young St .... Morgan UT 84050-0000
304 258-2774 **Morgan County** 202 Fairfax St .... Berkeley Springs WV 25411-1501
301 444-3333 **Morgan State University** Hillen Rd & Cold Spring Ln .... Baltimore MD 21239-0000
Fax: 301 444-1013
301 444-3225 *City & Regional Planning Program*
Cold Spring Ln & Hillen Rd .... Baltimore MD 21239-4098
Fax: 301 444-3698
304 291-7425 **Morgantown Public Library** 373 Spruce St .... Morgantown WV 26505-5564
712 274-5000 **Morningside College** 1501 Morningside Ave .... Sioux City IA 51106-1751
Fax: 712 274-5101
Morocco: Kingdom of Morocco
202 462-7979 *Embassy* 1601 21st St NW .... Washington DC 20009-1002
Fax: 202 265-0161
212 421-1580 *Mission to the UN* 767 3rd Ave 30th Fl .... New York NY 10017-2023
Fax: Unlisted
308 262-0860 **Morrill County** PO Box 610 .... Bridgeport NE 69336-0610
404 525-7831 **Morris Brown College** 643 Martin Luther King Jr Dr NW .... Atlanta GA 30314-4140
Fax: 404 525-3952
803 775-9371 **Morris College** N Main St .... Sumter SC 29150-0000
Fax: 803 773-3687
316 767-5518 **Morris County** 501 W Main St .... Council Grove KS 66846-1701
201 285-6040 **Morris County** PO Box 900 .... Morristown NJ 07963-0900
Fax: 201 539-6466
903 645-3911 **Morris County** 500 Broadnax St .... Daingerfield TX 75638-1315
201 285-6930 **Morris County Free Library** 30 E Hanover Ave .... Whippany NJ 07981-1853
201 538-0454 **Morris Museum** 6 Normandy Heights Rd .... Morristown NJ 07960-4627
Fax: 201 538-0154
612 632-2941 **Morrison County** County Courthouse .... Little Falls MN 56345-0000
Fax: Ext 129
202 225-5816 **Morrison Sid (Rep - R - Washington)**
1434 Longworth Bldg .... Washington DC 20515-0001
Fax: 202 225-9293
419 947-2085 **Morrow County** 48 E High St .... Mount Gilead OH 43338-1430
Fax: 419 947-1860
503 676-9061 **Morrow County** PO Box 338 .... Heppner OR 97836-0338
Fax: 503 676-5577
407 644-3686 **Morse Charles Hosmer Museum of American Art**
131 E Welbourne Ave .... Winter Park FL 32789-4337
708 656-8000 **Morton College** 3801 S Central Ave .... Cicero IL 60650-4398
Fax: 708 656-3297
316 697-2157 **Morton County** PO Box 1116 .... Elkhart KS 67950-1116
Fax: 316 697-2159
701 667-3355 **Morton County** 210 2nd Ave NW .... Mandan ND 58554-3158
806 347-2621 **Motley County** Main St .... Matador TX 79244-0000
615 455-8511 **Motlow State Community College** Lynchburg Hwy .... Tullahoma TN 37388-0000
Fax: 615 454-0059
714 727-3227 **Motorcycle Safety Foundation** 2 Jenner St Suite 150 .... Irvine CA 92718-3806
Fax: 714 727-4217
217 728-4389 **Moultrie County** Courthouse .... Sullivan IL 61951-0000
814 886-4131 **Mount Aloysius Junior College** William Penn Hwy .... Cresson PA 16630-0000
Fax: 814 886-5061
503 845-3951 **Mount Angel Seminary** .... Saint Benedict OR 97373-9999
Fax: 503 845-3594
413 538-2000 **Mount Holyoke College** College St .... South Hadley MA 01075-1415
Fax: 413 538-2391
503 667-6422 **Mount Hood Community College** 26000 SE Stark St .... Gresham OR 97030-3300
Fax: 503 667-7389
617 969-7000 **Mount Ida College** 777 Dedham St .... Newton Center MA 02159-3310
Fax: 617 969-6993
605 668-1011 **Mount Marty College** 1105 W 8th St .... Yankton SD 57078-3724
Fax: Unlisted
414 258-4810 **Mount Mary College** 2900 N Menomonee River Pkwy .... Milwaukee WI 53222-4597
Fax: 414 258-7505 Library
319 363-8213 **Mount Mercy College** 1330 Elmhurst Dr NE .... Cedar Rapids IA 52402-4797
Fax: 319 363-5270
919 658-2502 **Mount Olive College** 209 N Breazeale Ave .... Mount Olive NC 28365-1699
319 242-4023 **Mount Saint Clare College** 400 N Bluff Blvd .... Clinton IA 52732-3997
Fax: 319 242-2003
914 561-0800 **Mount Saint Mary College** 330 Powell Ave .... Newburgh NY 12550-3494
213 476-2237 **Mount Saint Mary's College** 12001 Chalon Rd .... Los Angeles CA 90049-1597
Fax: 213 476-9296 Library
301 447-6122 **Mount Saint Mary's College** 16300 Old Emmitsburg Rd .... Emmitsburg MD 21727-7799
Fax: 301 447-5755
213 746-0450 *Doheny Campus* 10 Chester Pl .... Los Angeles CA 90007-2598
714 594-5611 **Mount San Antonio College** 1100 N Grand Ave .... Walnut CA 91789-1399
Fax: 714 594-8060
714 654-8011 **Mount San Jacinto College** 1499 N State St .... San Jacinto CA 92383-2399
Fax: 714 654-6236
715 532-5511 **Mount Senario College** 1500 College Ave W .... Ladysmith WI 54848-2196
Fax: 715 532-7690
216 821-5320 **Mount Union College** 1972 Clark Ave .... Alliance OH 44601-3993
Fax: 216 821-0425
202 331-0400 **Mount Vernon College** 2100 Foxhall Rd NW .... Washington DC 20007-1199
Fax: 202 337-0255
614 397-1244 **Mount Vernon Nazarene College** 800 Martinsburg Rd .... Mount Vernon OH 43050-9500
Fax: 614 397-2769
508 632-6600 **Mount Wachusett Community College** 444 Green St .... Gardner MA 01440-1337
Fax: 508 632-6155
703 523-2400 **Mountain Empire Community College** PO Box 700 .... Big Stone Gap VA 24219-0700
Fax: 703 523-4130
208 828-2111 **Mountain Home Air Force Base** .... Mountain Home ID 83648-0000
Fax: 208 828-6648
406 761-0308 **Mountain States Baptist College** 824 3rd Ave N .... Great Falls MT 59401-1504
214 333-8600 **Mountain View College** 4849 W Illinois Ave .... Dallas TX 75211-6599
Fax: 214 333-8708
701 628-2915 **Mountrail County** PO Box 69 .... Stanley ND 58784-0069
507 437-9535 **Mower County** 201 1st St NE .... Austin MN 55912-3475
Fax: 507 437-9471
202 224-4451 **Moynihan Daniel Patrick (Sen - D - New York)**
464 Russell Bldg .... Washington DC 20510-0001
Fax: 202 224-9293
Mozambique: People's Republic of Mozambique
202 293-7146 *Embassy* 1990 M St NW Suite 570 .... Washington DC 20036-3404
Fax: 202 835-0245
212 517-4550 *Mission to the UN* 70 E 79th St .... New York NY 10021-0299
202 225-5956 **Mrazek Robert J (Rep - D - New York)** 306 Cannon Bldg .... Washington DC 20515-0001
Fax: Unlisted
215 821-3100 **Muhlenberg College** 2400 W Chew St .... Allentown PA 18104-5586
Fax: 215 821-3234
502 338-1441 **Muhlenberg County** PO Box 272 .... Greenville KY 42345-0272
503 248-3511 **Multnomah County** 1021 SW 4th Ave .... Portland OR 97204-1123
Fax: 503 248-5009
503 223-7201 **Multnomah County Library** 801 SW 10th Ave .... Portland OR 97205-2597
Fax: 503 221-7723
503 255-0332 **Multnomah School of the Bible** 8435 NE Glisan St .... Portland OR 97220-5898
Fax: 503 254-1268
312 262-8100 **Mundelein College** 6363 N Sheridan Rd .... Chicago IL 60660-1793
Fax: 312 262-0059
907 343-4311 **Municipality of Anchorage** PO Box 196650 .... Anchorage AK 99519-6650
202 224-6665 **Murkowski Frank H (Sen - R - Alaska)** 709 Hart Bldg .... Washington DC 20510-0001
Fax: 202 224-5301
202 225-4665 **Murphy Austin J (Rep - D - Pennsylvania)**
2210 Rayburn Bldg .... Washington DC 20515-0001
Fax: 202 225-4772
404 695-2932 **Murray County** 3rd Ave .... Chatsworth GA 30705-0000
507 836-6148 **Murray County** 2500 28th St .... Slayton MN 56172-0000
Fax: 507 836-6019
405 622-3777 **Murray County** PO Box 240 .... Sulphur OK 73086-0240
405 371-2371 **Murray State College** Byrd St .... Tishomingo OK 73460-0000
502 762-3011 **Murray State University** University Stn .... Murray KY 42071-0000
502 762-2387 *Department of Journalism & Radio-TV* University Stn .... Murray KY 42071-3311
202 225-2065 **Murtha John P (Rep - D - Pennsylvania)**
2423 Rayburn Bldg .... Washington DC 20515-0001
Fax: 202 225-5709
804 221-2700 **Muscarelle Museum of Art** College of William & Mary .... Williamsburg VA 23185-0000
Fax: Unlisted
319 263-8250 **Muscatine Community College** 152 Colorado St .... Muscatine IA 52761-5396
Fax: Unlisted
319 263-6511 **Muscatine County** PO Box 327 .... Muscatine IA 52761-0327
205 764-6563 **Muscle Shoals Regional Library System** 218 N Wood Ave .... Florence AL 35630-4793
Fax: 205 764-6629
404 571-4860 **Muscogee County** 100 10th St .... Columbus GA 31901-2736
314 882-3764 **Museum of Anthropology**
104 Swallow Hall University of Missouri .... Columbia MO 65211-0001
919 759-5282 **Museum of Anthropology** Wake Forest University .... Winston-Salem NC 27109-0000
305 525-5500 **Museum of Art** 1 E Los Olas Blvd .... Fort Lauderdale FL 33301-1845
Fax: 305 524-6011
314 882-3591 **Museum of Art & Archaeology**
Pickard Hall University of Missouri .... Columbia MO 65211-0001
Fax: 314 882-6957
203 372-3521 **Museum of Art Science & Industry Inc** 4450 Park Ave .... Bridgeport CT 06604-1098
Fax: 203 374-1929
401 331-3511 **Museum of Art-Rhode Island School of Design**
224 Benefit St .... Providence RI 02903-2711
904 255-0285 **Museum of Arts & Sciences** 1040 Museum Blvd .... Daytona Beach FL 32114-4597
912 477-3232 **Museum of Arts & Sciences** 4182 Forsyth Rd .... Macon GA 31210-4806
617 495-2463 **Museum of Comparative Zoology**
26 Oxford St Harvard University .... Cambridge MA 02138-2902
Fax: 617 495-5667
213 621-2766 **Museum of Contemporary Art** 250 S Grand Ave .... Los Angeles CA 90012-3007
Fax: 213 620-8674
312 280-2660 **Museum of Contemporary Art** 237 E Ontario St .... Chicago IL 60611-3236
Fax: 312 280-2687
312 663-5554 **Museum of Contemporary Photography**
600 S Michigan Ave Columbia College .... Chicago IL 60605-1996
413 732-6092 **Museum of Fine Arts** 49 Chestnut St .... Springfield MA 01103-1788
713 526-1361 **Museum of Fine Arts** 1001 Bissonnet St .... Houston TX 77005-1896
Fax: 713 639-7399
904 488-1484 **Museum of Florida History** 500 S Bronough St .... Tallahassee FL 32399-6519
Fax: 904 488-3353
605 394-2467 **Museum of Geology**
501 E Saint Joseph St South Dakota School of Mines .... Rapid City SD 57701-3901
206 324-1125 **Museum of History & Industry** 2700 24th Ave E .... Seattle WA 98112-2099
Fax: 206 324-1346
502 561-6103 **Museum of History & Science** 727 W Main St .... Louisville KY 40202-2681
Fax: 502 561-6145
505 827-8350 **Museum of International Folk Art** PO Box 2087 .... Santa Fe NM 87504-2087
Fax: 505 827-8349
212 708-9400 **Museum of Modern Art** 11 W 53rd St .... New York NY 10019-5498
Fax: 212 708-9889
504 388-2855 **Museum of Natural Science**
119 Foster Hall Louisiana State University .... Baton Rouge LA 70803-0001
Fax: 504 388-6400
213 617-0274 **Museum of Neon Art** 704 Traction Ave .... Los Angeles CA 90013-1814
Fax: 213 620-8904
505 827-6450 **Museum of New Mexico** PO Box 2087 .... Santa Fe NM 87504-2087
Fax: 505 827-6427

208 664-3448 **Museum of North Idaho** PO Box 812 .... Coeur d'Alene ID 83814-0812

602 774-5211 **Museum of Northern Arizona** RR 4 Box 720 Fort Valley Rd ...... Flagstaff AZ 86001-9302

617 861-6559 **Museum of Our National Heritage** 33 Marrett Rd .... Lexington MA 02173-5703
Fax: 617 863-1833

305 854-4247 **Museum of Science** 3280 S Miami Ave .... Miami FL 33129-2899
Fax: 305 285-5801

617 589-0100 **Museum of Science** Science Pk .... Boston MA 02114-1099
Fax: 617 742-2246

904 396-7062 **Museum of Science & History** 1025 Gulf Life Dr .... Jacksonville FL 32207-9053

813 985-5531 **Museum of Science & Industry** 4801 E Fowler Ave .... Tampa FL 33617-2099
Fax: 813 985-5535 Ext 55

312 684-1414 **Museum of Science & Industry** 57th St & Lake Shore Dr .... Chicago IL 60637-0000
Fax: 312 684-7141

704 497-3481 **Museum of the Cherokee Indian** PO Box 1599 .... Cherokee NC 28719-0000
Fax: 704 497-4985

312 549-0607 **Museum of the Chicago Academy of Sciences**
2001 N Clark St .... Chicago IL 60614-4712
Fax: 312 549-5199

212 534-1672 **Museum of the City of New York** 5th Ave & 103rd St .... New York NY 10029-0000
Fax: 212 534-5974

804 649-1861 **Museum of the Confederacy** 1201 E Clay St .... Richmond VA 23219-1615

406 338-2230 **Museum of the Plains Indians & Crafts Center** PO Box 400 ... Browning MT 59417-0400

406 994-2251 **Museum of the Rockies** Montana State University .... Bozeman MT 59717-0001
Fax: 406 994-2682

303 296-1880 **Museum of Western Art** 1727 Tremont Pl .... Denver CO 80202-4028

607 432-4200 **Museums at Hartwick** Hartwick College .... Oneonta NY 13820-1764

516 751-0066 **Museums at Stony Brook** 1208 Rt 25A .... Stony Brook NY 11790-1992

205 434-7620 **Museums of the City of Mobile** 355 Government St .... Mobile AL 36602-2315

616 773-9131 **Muskegon Community College** 221 S Quarterline Rd .... Muskegon MI 49442-1493
Fax: 616 777-0255

616 724-6221 **Muskegon County** 990 Terrace St .... Muskegon MI 49442-3398
Fax: 616 724-6673

616 724-6248 **Muskegon County Library System** 635 Ottawa St .... Muskegon MI 49442-1094

614 454-2501 **Muskingum Area Technical College** 1555 Newark Rd .... Zanesville OH 43701-2694
Fax: 614 454-0035

614 826-8211 **Muskingum College** Montgomery .... New Concord OH 43762-0000
Fax: 614 826-8404

614 455-7104 **Muskingum County** PO Box 268 .... Zanesville OH 43702-0268

614 453-0391 **Muskingum County Library System** 220 N 5th St .... Zanesville OH 43701-3508
Fax: 614 455-6357

918 682-9601 **Muskogee County** PO Box 2307 .... Muskogee OK 74402-2307

406 323-1104 **Musselshell County** 506 Main St .... Roundup MT 59072-2498

Myanmar: Union of Myanmar
202 332-9044 *Embassy* 2300 S St NW .... Washington DC 20008-4016
Fax: 202 332-9046
212 535-1310 *Mission to the UN* 10 E 77th St .... New York NY 10021-1704
Fax: 212 737-2421

202 225-5805 **Myers John T (Rep - R - Indiana)** 2372 Rayburn Bldg .... Washington DC 20515-0001
Fax: 202 225-1649

803 238-7211 **Myrtle Beach Air Force Base** .... Myrtle Beach SC 29579-0001
Fax: 803 238-6175

203 572-0711 **Mystic Seaport Museum** 50 Greenmanville Ave .... Mystic CT 06355-1935
Fax: 203 572-8693

N

301 358-8900 **NAACP** 4805 Mt Hope Dr .... Baltimore MD 21215-3206
Fax: 301 358-2332

409 560-7733 **Nacogdoches County** 101 W Main St .... Nacogdoches TX 75961-5119

312 761-5000 **NAES College** 2838 W Peterson Ave .... Chicago IL 60659-3813
Fax: 312 761-3808

202 225-3301 **Nagle David R (Rep - D - Iowa)** 214 Cannon Bldg .... Washington DC 20515-0001
Fax: 202 225-9104

308 536-2331 **Nance County** PO Box 338 .... Fullerton NE 68638-0338

508 228-7229 **Nantucket County** Town & County Bldg .... Nantucket MA 02554-0000
Fax: 508 228-3725

707 253-4241 **Napa City-County Library** 1150 Division St .... Napa CA 94559-3334
Fax: 707 253-4615

707 253-4481 **Napa County** PO Box 880 .... Napa CA 94559-0880
Fax: 707 253-4229

707 253-3000 **Napa Valley College** .... Napa CA 94558-6236
Fax: 707 253-3015

303 444-0202 **Naropa Institute** 2130 Arapahoe Ave .... Boulder CO 80302-6697

202 453-1000 **NASA** 600 Independence Ave SW .... Washington DC 20546-0001
Fax: 202 755-9234

713 483-4241 **NASA Lyndon B Johnson Space Center** 2101 NASA Rd 1 .... Houston TX 77058-0000
Fax: 713 483-4876 PR

919 443-4011 **Nash Community College** Old Carriage Rd .... Rocky Mount NC 27804-0000
Fax: 919 443-0828

603 883-4141 **Nashua Public Library** 2 Court St .... Nashua NH 03060-3475
Fax: 603 883-9824

615 259-5620 **Nashville City Hall** 110 Public Sq .... Nashville TN 37201-0000
Fax: 615 862-6040

615 259-4755 **Nashville Area Chamber of Commerce** 161 4th Ave N .... Nashville TN 37219-2411
Fax: 615 256-3074

615 353-3333 **Nashville State Technical Institute** 120 White Bridge Rd .... Nashville TN 37209-4515
Fax: 615 353-3499

516 222-7355 **Nassau Community College** Stewart Ave .... Garden City NY 11530-2200

904 261-6127 **Nassau County** 416 Centre St .... Fernandina Beach FL 32034-4243
Fax: 904 879-1029

516 535-2663 **Nassau County** 240 Old Country Rd .... Mineola NY 11501-4248

516 292-8920 **Nassau Library System** 900 Jerusalem Ave .... Uniondale NY 11553-3097
Fax: 516 481-4777

207 324-5340 **Nasson College** 7 Bradeen St .... Springvale ME 04083-1901
Fax: 207 324-1855

202 225-3501 **Natcher William H (Rep - D - Kentucky)**
2333 Rayburn Bldg .... Washington DC 20515-0001

318 352-2714 **Natchitoches Parish** PO Box 799 .... Natchitoches LA 71458-0799

202 408-4600 **National Abortion Rights Action League**
1101 14th St NW 5th Fl .... Washington DC 20005-5601
Fax: 202 408-4698

202 334-2000 **National Academy of Sciences** 2101 Constitution Ave NW .. Washington DC 20418-0001
Fax: 202 334-1597

202 566-5227 **National Advisory Council on International Monetary & Financial Policies**
15th St & Pennsylvania Ave NW .... Washington DC 20220-0001
Fax: 202 566-8066 Communications

202 453-1000 **National Aeronautics & Space Administration**
600 Independence Ave SW .... Washington DC 20546-0001
Fax: 202 755-9234

301 344-3778 **National Agricultural Library (US Dept of Agriculture)**
10301 Baltimore Blvd .... Beltsville MD 20705-2351
Fax: 301 344-5472

202 447-3638 **National Agricultural Statistics Service State Statistical Div**
14th St & Independence Ave SW 4143 South Bldg .... Washington DC 20250-0001
Fax: 202 382-0507

202 357-1400 **National Air & Space Museum (Smithsonian Institution)**
Independence Ave & 6th St SW .... Washington DC 20560-0001

703 578-4200 **National Alcoholic Beverage Control Assn** 4216 King St ...... Alexandria VA 22302-1507
Fax: 703 820-3551

703 528-4380 **National Alliance of Senior Citizens** 2525 Wilson Blvd .... Arlington VA 22201-3835
Fax: 703 528-2763

202 523-3616 **National Archives & Records Administration**
8th St & Pennsylvania Ave NW .... Washington DC 20408-0001
Fax: 202 523-4357

301 263-0991 **National Assn for Senior Living Industries**
184 Duke of Gloucester St .... Annapolis MD 21401-2515
Fax: 301 263-1262

301 358-8900 **National Assn for the Advancement of Colored People**
4805 Mt Hope Dr .... Baltimore MD 21215-3206
Fax: 301 358-2332

202 547-6223 **National Assn of Conservation Districts**
509 Capitol Court NE .... Washington DC 20002-4937
Fax: 202 547-6450

202 393-6226 **National Assn of Counties** 440 1st St NW 8th Fl .... Washington DC 20001-2080
Fax: 202 393-2630

202 429-2960 **National Assn of Housing & Redevelopment Officials**
1320 18th St NW .... Washington DC 20036-1811
Fax: 202 429-9684

816 842-3600 **National Assn of Insurance Commissioners**
120 W 12th St Suite 1100 .... Kansas City MO 64105-1917
Fax: 816 471-7004

202 347-1444 **National Assn of Life Underwriters PAC** 1922 F St NW ...... Washington DC 20006-4305
Fax: 202 331-2179

202 637-3000 **National Assn of Manufacturers**
1331 Pennsylvania Ave NW Suite 1500N .... Washington DC 20004-1703
Fax: 202 637-3182

202 898-2200 **National Assn of Regulatory Utility Commissioners**
12th & Constitution Ave NW ICC Bldg Rm 1102 .... Washington DC 20423-0001
Fax: 202 898-2213

703 648-9300 **National Assn of Rehabilitation Facilities**
1910 Association Dr Suite 200 .... Reston VA 22091-1502
Fax: 703 648-0346

202 234-0832 **National Assn of Retired Federal Employees PAC**
1533 New Hampshire Ave NW .... Washington DC 20036-1279
Fax: 202 797-9697

202 624-5411 **National Assn of State Development Agencies**
444 N Capitol NW Suite 611 .... Washington DC 20001-1512
Fax: 202 624-5417

215 649-7055 **National Assn of Town Watch**
7 Wynnewood Rd Suite 215 .... Wynnewood PA 19096-1923
Fax: 215 649-5456

505 845-6670 **National Atomic Museum**
Kirtland Air Force Base Bldg 20358 .... Albuquerque NM 87115-0000
Fax: 505 846-8206

708 430-2430 **National Automobile Theft Bureau**
10330 S Roberts Rd Suite 3A .... Palos Hills IL 60465-1997
Fax: 708 430-2446

202 829-5900 **National Business League** 4324 Georgia Ave NW .... Washington DC 20011-7197
Fax: 202 726-6141

202 724-0174 **National Capital Planning Commission**
1325 G St NW 10th Fl .... Washington DC 20576-0001
Fax: 202 724-0195

212 571-5000 **National Cargo Bureau Inc** 30 Vesey St 6th Fl .... New York NY 10007-2914
Fax: 212 571-5005

202 637-8400 **National Caucus & Center on Black Aged Inc**
1424 K St NW Suite 500 .... Washington DC 20005-2410
Fax: 202 347-0895

301 436-8500 **National Center for Health Statistics**
6525 Belcrest Rd Rm 1100 .... Hyattsville MD 20782-0000
Fax: Unlisted

202 331-1103 **National Center for Neighborhood Enterprise**
1367 Connecticut Ave NW 3rd Fl .... Washington DC 20036-0000
Fax: 202 296-1541

816 753-4554 **National College** 600 W 39th St .... Kansas City KS 64111-0000
Fax: 816 753-5707

605 394-4800 **National College** 321 Kansas City St .... Rapid City SD 57701-3692
Fax: 605 394-4871
505 265-7517 *Albuquerque Branch* 1202 Pennsylvania NE .... Albuquerque NM 87110-0000
Fax: 505 265-7542
719 471-4205 *Colorado Springs Branch* 2577 N Chelton St .... Colorado Springs CO 80909-1345
303 758-6700 *Denver Branch* 1325 S Colorado Blvd Suite 100 .... Denver CO 80222-3308
Fax: 303 758-6810
719 545-8763 *Pueblo Branch* 330 Lake Ave .... Pueblo CO 81004-2330
Fax: 719 546-0924
612 644-1265 *Saint Paul Branch* 1380 Energy Ln .... Saint Paul MN 55108-5271
Fax: 612 644-0690
605 334-5430 *Sioux Falls Branch* 3201 S Kiwanis .... Sioux Falls SD 57105-4293
Fax: 605 334-1575

301 283-2113 **National Colonial Farm of Accokeek Foundation**
3400 Bryan Point Rd .... Accokeek MD 20607-9654
Fax: 301 283-2049

202 254-3100 **National Commission on Libraries & Information Science**
1111 18th St NW Suite 310 .... Washington DC 20036-3810
Fax: 202 254-3111

202 547-1151 **National Committee for an Effective Congress**
507 Capitol Ct NE .... Washington DC 20002-4937
Fax: 202 547-3191

202 822-9459 **National Committee to Preserve Social Security & Medicare**
2000 K St NW Suite 800 .... Washington DC 20006-1809
Fax: 202 822-9612

303 623-7800 **National Conference of State Legislatures**
1050 17th St Suite 2100 .... Denver CO 80265-2101
Fax: 303 893-0705

202 546-9404 **National Congress of American Indians**
900 Pennsylvania Ave SE .... Washington DC 20003-0000
Fax: 202 546-3741

919 850-0399 **National Congressional Club**
4505 Falls of Neuse Rd Suite 600 .... Raleigh NC 27609-6265
Fax: 919 850-0046

703 684-1800 **National Conservative PAC** 618 S Alfred St .... Alexandria VA 22314-4002
Fax: 703 836-2413

202 659-0006 **National Council of Negro Women Inc**
1211 Connecticut Ave NW Suite 702 .... Washington DC 20036-2701
Fax: 202 785-8733

202 347-8800 **National Council of Senior Citizens** 925 15th St NW .... Washington DC 20005-2385
Fax: 202 624-9595

202 624-7710 **National Council of State Housing Agencies**
444 N Capitol St NW Suite 118 .... Washington DC 20001-1512
Fax: 202 624-7719
212 697-1278 **National Council of Women of the US** 777 UN Plaza 7th Fl ..... New York NY 10017-0000
Fax: 212 972-0164
415 896-6223 **National Council on Crime & Delinquency**
685 Market St 4th Fl Suite 620 .... San Francisco CA 94105-0000
Fax: 415 896-5109
202 479-1200 **National Council on the Aging**
600 Maryland Ave SW Suite 100W .... Washington DC 20024-2571
Fax: 202 479-0735
202 682-9600 **National Credit Union Administration**
1776 G St NW 6th Fl .... Washington DC 20456-0001
Fax: 202 682-9620
518 472-4554 *Region 1* 9 Washington Sq Washington Ave Ext .... Albany NY 12205-5576
Fax: 518 869-1788
202 682-1900 *Region 2* 1776 G St NW Suite 800 .... Washington DC 20006-4791
Fax: 202 789-2043
404 396-4042 *Region 3* 7000 Central Pkwy NE Suite 1600 .... Atlanta GA 30328-4598
Fax: 404 698-8211
708 250-6000 *Region 4* 300 Park Blvd Suite 155 .... Itasca IL 60143-2652
Fax: 312 886-9707
512 482-4500 *Region 5* 4807 Spicewood Springs Rd Suite 5200 .... Austin TX 78759-8490
Fax: 512 482-4511
415 825-6125 *Region 6* 2300 Clayton Rd Suite 1350 .... Concord CA 94520-2407
202 466-6272 **National Crime Prevention Council** 1700 K St NW 2nd Fl ... Washington DC 20006-3817
Fax: 202 296-1356
212 432-0050 **National Customs Brokers & Forwarders Assn of America**
1 World Trade Ctr Suite 1153 .... New York NY 10048-0202
Fax: 212 432-5709
202 475-1966 **National Defense University (US Dept of Defense)**
4th & P Sts SW Fort McNair Bldg 59 .... Washington DC 20319-0001
Fax: 202 475-0724
202 833-4000 **National Education Assn** 1201 16th St NW .... Washington DC 20036-3290
Fax: 202 822-7292
813 238-0455 **National Education Center**
3920 E Hillsborough Ave Tampa Technical Institute Campus .... Tampa FL 33610-4595
Fax: 813 239-2163
202 682-5400 **National Endowment for the Arts**
1100 Pennsylvania Ave NW Rm 803 .... Washington DC 20506-0001
Fax: 202 682-5798
202 786-0438 **National Endowment for the Humanities**
1100 Pennsylvania Ave NW Rm 406 .... Washington DC 20506-0001
Fax: 202 786-0240
202 586-8800 **National Energy Information Center (US Dept of Energy)**
1000 Independence Ave SW Rm 1F-048 .... Washington DC 20585-0001
212 697-5895 **National Export Traffic League** 234 5th Ave Rm 301 .... New York NY 10001-7607
Fax: 212 213-6737
301 589-5600 **National Foundation for Consumer Credit**
8701 Georgia Ave Suite 507 .... Silver Spring MD 20910-3713
Fax: 301 495-5623
202 737-4215 **National Gallery of Art** 4th St & Constitution Ave NW .... Washington DC 20565-0001
Fax: 202 842-2356
202 332-6483 **National Gay/Lesbian Task Force** 1517 U St NW .... Washington DC 20009-3911
Fax: 202 332-0207
202 624-5300 **National Governors' Assn** 444 N Capitol St NW Suite 250 ... Washington DC 20001-1512
Fax: 202 624-5313
301 565-4167 **National Health Information Center (US Dept of Health & Human Services)**
1010 Wayne Ave Suite 300 .... Silver Spring MD 20910-5600
Fax: 301 565-5112
202 366-9550 **National Highway Traffic Safety Administration**
400 7th St SW Rm 5232 .... Washington DC 20590-0001
Fax: 202 366-5962
202 366-9588 *Alcohol & State Programs* 400 7th St SW Rm 5130 .... Washington DC 20590-0000
Fax: 202 366-2766
202 366-1503 *Center for Statistics & Analysis* 400 7th St SW Rm 6125 . Washington DC 20590-0000
Fax: 202 366-7078
202 366-2850 *Defects Investigation* 400 7th St SW Rm 5326 .... Washington DC 20590-0001
Fax: 202 366-1767
513 666-4511 *Vehicle Research & Test Center* Hwy 33 .... East Liberty OH 43319-0000
Fax: Ext 205
202 366-2832 *Vehicle Safety Compliance* 400 7th St SW Rm 6111 ...... Washington DC 20590-0001
Fax: 202 366-1024
202 366-0842 *Vehicle Safety Standards* 400 7th St SW Rm 5320 .... Washington DC 20590-0000
Fax: 202 366-4329
617 494-3427 *Region 1* 55 Broadway .... Cambridge MA 02142-1003
Fax: 617 494-3646
914 683-9690 *Region 2* 222 Mamaroneck Ave Suite 204 .... White Plains NY 10605-1316
Fax: 914 328-7925
301 768-7111 *Region 3* 7526 Connelley Dr Suite L .... Hanover MD 21076-1600
404 347-4537 *Region 4* 1720 Peachtree Rd NW Suite 501 .... Atlanta GA 30309-2486
Fax: 404 347-0097
708 799-6067 *Region 5* 18209 Dixie Hwy Suite A .... Homewood IL 60430-2205
Fax: 708 799-2658
817 334-3653 *Region 6* 819 Taylor St Rm 8A38 .... Fort Worth TX 76102-6114
Fax: 817 334-8339
816 926-7887 *Region 7* 6301 Rockhill Rd Rm 106 .... Kansas City MO 64131-1117
Fax: 816 926-7884
303 969-6917 *Region 8* 555 Zang St 4th Fl .... Denver CO 80228-1000
Fax: 303 969-6294
415 744-3089 *Region 9* 211 Main St Suite 1000 .... San Francisco CA 94105-1924
Fax: 415 744-2532
206 442-5934 *Region 10* 915 2nd Ave Rm 3140 .... Seattle WA 98174-1001
Fax: 206 442-0480
415 451-0511 **National Hispanic University** 255 E 14th St .... Oakland CA 94606-2235
Fax: 415 451-4648
201 595-9200 **National Industries for the Blind** 524 Hamburg Tpke .... Wayne NJ 07470-2092
Fax: 201 595-9122
202 289-7800 **National Institute of Building Sciences**
1201 L St NW Suite 400 .... Washington DC 20005-4024
Fax: 202 289-1092
301 443-1124 **National Institute of Drug Abuse** 5600 Fishers Ln .... Rockville MD 20857-0001
Fax: 301 443-7397
301 975-3058 **National Institute of Standards & Technology (US Dept of Commerce)**
Quince Orchard Rd .... Gaithersburg MD 20899-0001
Fax: 301 975-2128
404 353-1331 **National Interfaith Coalition on Aging Inc** PO Box 1924 .... Athens GA 30603-1924
202 254-9200 **National Labor Relations Board**
1717 Pennsylvania Ave NW .... Washington DC 20570-0001
Fax: 202 634-4832 Mail Rm
617 565-6700 *Region 1* 10 Causeway St Rm 601 .... Boston MA 02222-1072
Fax: 617 565-6725
212 264-0330 *Region 2* 26 Federal Plaza Rm 3614 .... New York NY 10278-0179
Fax: 212 264-8427
716 846-4931 *Region 3* 111 W Huron St Rm 901 .... Buffalo NY 14202-2387
Fax: 716 846-4972
215 597-7608 *Region 4* 1 Independence Mall 7th Fl .... Philadelphia PA 19106-0000
Fax: 215 597-7658
301 962-2737 *Region 5* 109 Market Pl 4th Fl .... Baltimore MD 21202-4035
Fax: 301 962-2198
412 644-2977 *Region 6* 1000 Liberty Ave Rm 1501 .... Pittsburgh PA 15222-4173
Fax: 412 644-5986
313 226-3210 *Region 7* 477 Michigan Ave Rm 300 .... Detroit MI 48226-2569
Fax: 313 226-2090
216 522-3715 *Region 8* 1240 E 9th St Suite 1695 .... Cleveland OH 44199-2086
Fax: 216 522-2418
513 684-3686 *Region 9* 550 Main St Rm 3003 .... Cincinnati OH 45202-3271
Fax: 513 684-3946
404 331-2896 *Region 10* 101 Marietta St NW Marietta Tower Suite 2400 ..... Atlanta GA 30323-0001
Fax: 404 331-2858
919 631-5201 *Region 11* 251 N Main St Federal Bldg Rm 447 .... Winston-Salem NC 27101-0000
Fax: 919 631-5210
813 228-2641 *Region 12* 700 Twiggs St Suite 511 .... Tampa FL 33602-4018
Fax: 813 228-2874
312 353-7574 *Region 13* 200 W Adams St Suite 800 .... Chicago IL 60606-5208
Fax: 312 886-1341
314 425-4142 *Region 14* 210 N Tucker Blvd .... Saint Louis MO 63101-1947
Fax: 314 425-4179
504 589-6361 *Region 15* 1515 Poydras St Suite 610 .... New Orleans LA 70112-3723
Fax: Unlisted
817 334-2938 *Region 16* 819 Taylor St Rm 8A24 .... Fort Worth TX 76102-6114
Fax: Unlisted
913 236-2777 *Region 17* 5799 Broadmoor St Suite 500 .... Mission KS 66202-2408
Fax: Unlisted
612 348-1757 *Region 18* 110 S 4th St Rm 316 .... Minneapolis MN 55401-2291
Fax: 612 348-1785
206 442-4532 *Region 19* 915 2nd Ave Rm 2948 .... Seattle WA 98174-1078
Fax: 206 442-8022
415 744-6810 *Region 20* 901 Market St Suite 400 .... San Francisco CA 94103-1797
Fax: 415 744-7828
213 894-5254 *Region 21* 615 S Flower St 11th Fl .... Los Angeles CA 90017-2803
Fax: 213 894-2778
201 645-2100 *Region 22* 970 Broad St Rm 1600 .... Newark NJ 07102-2570
Fax: 201 645-3852
809 766-5225 *Region 24* Federal Office Bldg Rm 591 .... Hato Rey PR 00918-0000
Fax: 809 766-5478
317 226-7401 *Region 25* 575 N Pennsylvania St Suite 238 .... Indianapolis IN 46204-1577
Fax: 317 226-5103
901 722-2707 *Region 26* 1407 Union Ave Suite 800 .... Memphis TN 38104-3642
Fax: 901 722-2657
303 844-3551 *Region 27* 600 17th St Suite 300S .... Denver CO 80202-5459
Fax: 303 844-6249
602 379-3361 *Region 28* 234 N Central Ave Suite 440 .... Phoenix AZ 85004-2212
Fax: 602 379-4982
718 330-7713 *Region 29* 75 Clinton St 8th Fl .... Brooklyn NY 11201-4201
Fax: 718 330-7579
414 297-3870 *Region 30* 310 W Wisconsin Ave Suite 700 .... Milwaukee WI 53203-2283
Fax: 414 297-3880
213 209-7371 *Region 31* 11000 Wilshire Blvd 12th Fl .... Los Angeles CA 90024-3602
Fax: Unlisted
415 273-4285 *Region 32* PO Box 12983 .... Oakland CA 94604-2983
Fax: 415 273-7969
309 671-7080 *Region 33* 411 Hamilton Blvd 16th Fl .... Peoria IL 61602-1104
Fax: 309 671-7095
202 626-3000 **National League of Cities**
1301 Pennsylvania Ave NW Suite 600 .... Washington DC 20004-1763
Fax: 202 626-3043
301 496-6308 **National Library of Medicine (US Dept of Health & Human Services)**
8600 Rockville Pike Rm 2F-10 .... Bethesda MD 20894-0001
Fax: 301 496-4450
202 707-5100 **National Library Service for the Blind & Physically Handicapped**
1291 Taylor St NW .... Washington DC 20542-0000
Fax: 202 707-0712
301 427-2239 **National Marine Fisheries Service** 1335 East-West Hwy ... Silver Spring MD 20910-0000
Fax: 301 427-2258
907 586-7221 *Alaska Region* PO Box 21668 .... Juneau AK 99802-1668
Fax: 907 586-7131
508 281-9300 *Northeastern Region* 1 Blackburn Dr .... Gloucester MA 01930-2298
Fax: 508 281-9333
206 526-6150 *Northwestern Region* 7600 Sand Point Way NE .... Seattle WA 98115-6349
Fax: 206 526-6426
813 893-3141 *Southeastern Region* 9450 Koger Blvd N .... Saint Petersburg FL 33702-2496
Fax: 813 893-3111
213 514-6196 *Southwestern Region* 300 Ferry St Suite 2005 .... Terminal Island CA 90731-7495
Fax: 213 514-6194
202 523-5920 **National Mediation Board** 1425 K St NW Suite 910 .... Washington DC 20572-0001
Fax: 202 523-1494
202 357-4600 **National Museum of African Art (Smithsonian Institution)**
950 Independence Ave SW .... Washington DC 20560-0001
Fax: 202 357-4879
202 357-1959 **National Museum of American Art (Smithsonian Institution)**
8th & G Sts NW .... Washington DC 20560-0001
Fax: 202 786-2607
202 357-1300 **National Museum of American History (Smithsonian Institution)**
12th St & Constitution Ave NW .... Washington DC 20560-0001
Fax: Call company operator
202 357-2664 **National Museum of Natural History (Smithsonian Institution)**
10th St & Constitution Ave NW .... Washington DC 20560-0001
Fax: 202 357-4779
212 283-2420 **National Museum of the American Indian**
Broadway & 155th St .... New York NY 10032-0000
Fax: 212 491-9302
314 965-6885 **National Museum of Transport** 3015 Barrett Station Rd ...... Saint Louis MO 63122-3303
202 377-4190 **National Oceanic & Atmospheric Administration**
14th St & Constitution Ave NW Rm 5805 .... Washington DC 20230-0001
Fax: 202 377-8203
202 763-7190 *Environmental Satellite Data Service* Federal Bldg 4 .... Washington DC 20233-0001
Fax: 301 763-4011
301 443-8910 *Oceanic & Atmospheric Research* 6010 Executive Blvd ...... Rockville MD 20852-3809
Fax: 301 443-8850
703 549-9040 **National Office Products Assn** 301 N Fairfax St .... Alexandria VA 22314-2696
Fax: 703 683-7552
202 879-7710 **National PAC** 555 New Jersey Ave NW Suite 718 .... Washington DC 20001-2029
Fax: 202 879-7728
202 785-4500 **National Park Foundation** 1850 K St NW Suite 210 .... Washington DC 20006-2213
202 343-7394 **National Park Service** 1849 C St NW Rm 3424 .... Washington DC 20240-0001
Fax: 202 343-7520
202 426-6650 *US Park Police* 1100 Ohio Dr SW .... Washington DC 20242-0001
Fax: 202 755-5910
907 271-2737 *Alaska Region* 2525 Gambell St .... Anchorage AK 99503-2892
Fax: 907 257-2510

215 597-7018 *Mid-Atlantic Region* 143 S 3rd St .... Philadelphia PA 19106-2878
Fax: 215 597-1085
402 221-3431 *Midwest Region* 1709 Jackson St .... Omaha NE 68102-2571
Fax: 402 864-3461
202 426-6612 *National Capitol Region* 1100 Ohio Dr SW Rm 336 .... Washington DC 20242-0001
Fax: 202 485-9691
617 223-5200 *North Atlantic Region* 15 State St .... Boston MA 02109-3572
Fax: 617 223-5022
206 442-5565 *Pacific Northwest Region* 83 S King St Suite 212 .... Seattle WA 98104-2887
Fax: 206 442-4896
303 969-2000 *Rocky Mountain Region* 12795 W Alameda Pkwy .... Denver CO 80228-2849
Fax: 303 969-2717
404 331-5187 *Southeast Region* 75 Spring St SW .... Atlanta GA 30303-3378
Fax: 404 331-5848
505 988-6388 *Southwest Region* PO Box 728 .... Santa Fe NM 87504-0728
Fax: 505 988-6694
415 556-4196 *Western Region* 450 Golden Gate Ave .... San Francisco CA 94102-3491
Fax: 415 556-2793
202 265-7685 **National Planning Assn** 1424 16th St NW Suite 700 .... Washington DC 20036-2211
Fax: 202 797-5516
202 357-1300 **National Portrait Gallery (Smithsonian Institution)**
F St & 8th NW .... Washington DC 20560-0001
202 383-3000 **National Railroad Passenger Corp (Amtrak)**
400 N Capitol St NW .... Washington DC 20001-1511
Fax: 202 906-3175 Personnel
202 828-6000 **National Rifle Assn of America**
1600 Rhode Island Ave NW .... Washington DC 20036-3240
Fax: 202 861-0306
202 626-8800 **National Right to Life Committee Inc**
419 7th St NW Suite 500 .... Washington DC 20004-2293
Fax: 202 737-9189
312 527-4800 **National Safety Council** 444 N Michigan Ave .... Chicago IL 60611-3991
Fax: 312 527-9381
301 688-6524 **National Security Agency (US Dept of Defense)**
9800 Savage Rd .... Fort Meade MD 20755-0000
Fax: Unlisted
202 395-4974 **National Security Council** 17th & Pennsylvania Ave .... Washington DC 20500-0001
Fax: Unlisted
202 775-1440 **National Security Industrial Assn**
1025 Connecticut Ave NW Suite 300 .... Washington DC 20036-5405
Fax: 202 775-1309
703 836-7827 **National Sheriffs' Assn** 1450 Duke St .... Alexandria VA 22314-3490
Fax: 703 683-6541
703 684-2810 **National Society of Professional Engineers** 1420 King St .... Alexandria VA 22314-2794
Fax: 703 836-4875
708 843-2020 **National Society to Prevent Blindness**
500 E Remington Rd .... Schaumburg IL 60173-5624
Fax: 708 843-8458
202 543-1300 **National Taxpayers Union** 325 Pennsylvania Ave SE .... Washington DC 20003-1100
Fax: 202 546-2086
716 475-6400 **National Technical Institute for the Deaf**
1 Lomb Memorial Dr .... Rochester NY 14623-5603
Fax: 716 475-6500
303 484-6050 **National Technological University** 700 Centre Ave .... Fort Collins CO 80526-0000
Fax: 303 484-0668
202 377-1840 **National Telecommunication Information Administration**
14th St & Constitution Ave NW Rm 4898 .... Washington DC 20230-0001
Fax: 202 377-1635
608 257-7712 **National Telemedia Council** 120 E Wilson St .... Madison WI 53703-3423
202 382-6735 **National Transportation Safety Board**
800 Independence Ave SW .... Washington DC 20594-0001
619 563-7100 **National University** University Pk .... San Diego CA 92108-0000
Fax: 619 563-7392 Library
301 495-4999 **National Urban Coalition** 8601 Georgia Ave Suite 500 .... Silver Spring MD 20910-3439
Fax: 301 587-0868
212 310-9000 **National Urban League Inc** 500 E 62nd St .... New York NY 10021-8393
Fax: 212 593-8250
202 475-1776 **National War College (US Dept of Defense)**
4th & P Sts SW Fort McNair Bldg 61 .... Washington DC 20319-0001
Fax: 202 475-1745
703 524-1544 **National Water Resources Assn** 3800 N Fairfax Dr Suite 4 .... Arlington VA 22203-0000
Fax: 703 524-1548
301 427-7689 **National Weather Service** 1325 East-West Hwy .... Silver Spring MD 20912-0000
Fax: 301 427-2610
907 271-5136 *Alaska Region* 222 W 7th Ave .... Anchorage AK 99513-7575
Fax: 907 271-3711
816 426-5400 *Central Region* 601 E 12th St Rm 1835 .... Kansas City MO 64106-2808
Fax: 816 426-3270
516 244-0100 *Eastern Region* 630 Johnson Ave .... Bohemia NY 11716-2640
Fax: 516 244-0167
808 541-1641 *Pacific Region* PO Box 50027 .... Honolulu HI 96850-0001
Fax: 808 541-1678
817 334-2668 *Southern Region* 819 Taylor St Rm 10-A26 .... Fort Worth TX 76102-6114
Fax: 817 334-2022
801 524-5122 *Western Region* 125 S State St Rm 1215 .... Salt Lake City UT 84138-1102
Fax: 801 524-5246
202 898-1100 **National Women's Political Caucus**
1275 K St NW Suite 750 .... Washington DC 20005-4051
Fax: 202 898-0458
708 256-5150 **National-Louis University** 2840 Sheridan Rd .... Evanston IL 60201-1730
Fax: 708 256-1057 Library
312 621-9650 *Urban Campus* 18 S Michigan Ave .... Chicago IL 60603-3301
Fax: 312 621-1205
307 235-9206 **Natrona County** 200 N Center St Rm 157 .... Casper WY 82601-1991
619 232-3821 **Natural History Museum** 1788 El Prado .... San Diego CA 92112-0000
213 744-3414 **Natural History Museum of Los Angeles County**
900 Exposition Blvd .... Los Angeles CA 90007-4057
704 372-6261 **Nature Museum** 1658 Sterling Rd .... Charlotte NC 28209-1599
Fax: 704 337-2670
919 767-6730 **Nature Science Center** Museum Dr .... Winston-Salem NC 27105-0000
602 724-3311 **Navajo Community College** .... Tsaile AZ 86556-0000
Fax: 602 724-3327
602 524-6161 **Navajo County** PO Box 668 .... Holbrook AZ 86025-0668
Fax: 602 524-2201
903 874-6501 **Navarro College** 3200 W Hwy 31 .... Corsicana TX 75110-9796
Fax: 903 874-4636
903 654-3035 **Navarro County** 300 W 3rd Ave .... Corsicana TX 75110-4694
703 528-1775 **Navy League of the US** 2300 Wilson Blvd .... Arlington VA 22201-3308
Fax: 703 528-2333
505 877-0240 **Nazarene Indian Bible College** 2315 Markham Rd SW .... Albuquerque NM 87105-7028
616 349-4200 **Nazareth College** 3333 Gull Rd .... Kalamazoo MI 49001-1282
716 586-2525 **Nazareth College of Rochester** 4245 East Ave .... Rochester NY 14618-3790
Fax: 716 586-2452
212 925-1400 **NCITD-International Trade Facilitation Council**
350 Broadway Suite 205 .... New York NY 10013-3982
Fax: 212 941-0371

202 225-5601 **Neal Richard E (Rep - D - Massachusetts)**
437 Cannon Bldg .... Washington DC 20515-0001
Fax: 202 225-8112
202 225-2071 **Neal Stephen L (Rep - D - North Carolina)**
2463 Rayburn Bldg .... Washington DC 20515-0001
Fax: 202 225-4060
202 647-7207 **Near Eastern & South Asian Affairs Bureau (US Dept of State)**
2201 C St NW Rm 6242 .... Washington DC 20520-0001
402 474-4422 **Nebraska Chamber of Commerce & Industry**
1320 Lincoln Mall .... Lincoln NE 68508-0000
Fax: 402 474-2510
402 371-5960 **Nebraska Christian College** 1800 Syracuse .... Norfolk NE 68701-2400
308 367-4124 **Nebraska College of Technical Agriculture** 404 E 7th St .... Curtis NE 69025-0000
Fax: 308 367-5203
402 475-4584 **Nebraska Democratic State Committee** 715 S 14th St .... Lincoln NE 68508-3701
Fax: 402 475-4639
402 475-2122 **Nebraska Republican Party** 421 S 9th St Suite 233 .... Lincoln NE 68508-2245
Fax: Unlisted
Nebraska State Government
402 471-2311 *Information* 301 Centennial Mall .... Lincoln NE 68509-0000
Fax: 402 471-4867
402 471-2189 *Air Quality Div* PO Box 98922 .... Lincoln NE 68509-8922
Fax: 402 471-2909
402 595-2122 *Arts Council* 1313 Farnam on the Mall .... Omaha NE 68102-1873
Fax: 402 595-2217
402 471-2682 *Attorney General* PO Box 98920 .... Lincoln NE 68509-8920
Fax: 402 471-3297
402 471-3445 *Bureau of Securities* 301 Centennial Mall S .... Lincoln NE 68508-2529
Fax: 800 221-7791
402 471-2871 *Bureau of Vital Statistics* 301 Centennial Mall S .... Lincoln NE 68509-0000
402 473-1430 *Civil Defense Agency* 1300 Military Rd .... Lincoln NE 68508-1051
Fax: 402 473-1433
402 471-2194 *Commission on Law Enforcement & Criminal Justice*
PO Box 94946 .... Lincoln NE 68509-4946
Fax: 402 471-2837
402 471-4723 *Consumer Fraud Div* 2115 State Capitol .... Lincoln NE 68509-0000
Fax: 402 471-3591
402 471-2847 *Coordinating Commission for Postsecondary Education*
PO Box 95005 .... Lincoln NE 68509-5005
402 471-2526 *Department of Administrative Services Budget Dept*
1445 K St Rm 1322 .... Lincoln NE 68508-2731
402 471-2341 *Department of Agriculture* 301 Centennial Mall S .... Lincoln NE 68508-2529
Fax: 402 471-3252
402 471-2654 *Department of Corrections* 801 W Van Dorn St Bldg 15 .... Lincoln NE 68522-1970
Fax: 402 479-5663
402 471-3111 *Department of Economic Development* 301 Centennial Mall S .... Lincoln NE 68508-2529
Fax: 402 471-3778
402 471-2465 *Department of Education* 301 Centennial Mall S .... Lincoln NE 68509-0000
Fax: 402 471-2701
402 471-2186 *Department of Environmental Control* PO Box 98922 .... Lincoln NE 68509-8922
Fax: 402 471-2909
402 471-2133 *Department of Health* 301 Centennial Mall S .... Lincoln NE 68508-2529
Fax: 402 471-0383
402 471-2201 *Department of Insurance* 941 'O' St Suite 400 .... Lincoln NE 68508-3626
Fax: 402 471-4610
402 475-8451 *Department of Labor* 550 S 16th St .... Lincoln NE 68508-1829
Fax: 402 471-2318
402 471-2971 *Department of Revenue* 301 Centennial Mall S .... Lincoln NE 68508-2529
Fax: 402 471-5608
402 471-4567 *Department of Roads* 1500 SR-2 .... Lincoln NE 68502-0000
Fax: 402 479-4325
402 471-2363 *Department of Water Resources* 301 Centennial Mall S .... Lincoln NE 68508-2529
Fax: Unlisted
402 471-4771 *Division of Archives/Library* 1500 R St .... Lincoln NE 68508-1651
Fax: 402 471-3100
402 471-2239 *Division of Safety* PO Box 95024 .... Lincoln NE 68509-5024
402 471-2867 *Energy Office* 1445 K St .... Lincoln NE 68509-0000
Fax: 402 471-2063
402 471-2244 *Governor* 2316 State Capitol .... Lincoln NE 68509-0000
Fax: 402 471-4867
402 471-2256 *Lieutenant Governor* State Capitol Rm 2315 .... Lincoln NE 68509-0000
402 471-2861 *Lincoln Correctional Center* PO Box 2800 .... Lincoln NE 68502-0800
Fax: 402 471-4327
402 471-2081 *Natural Resources Commission* 301 Centennial Mall S .... Lincoln NE 68508-2529
Fax: 402 471-3232
402 471-3161 *Nebraska State Penitentiary* 14th & Pioneer Blvd .... Lincoln NE 68502-0000
308 254-4595 *Oil & Gas Conservation Commission* PO Box 399 .... Sidney NE 69162-0399
402 471-2654 *Parole Administration* 801 W Van Dorn St .... Lincoln NE 68509-0000
Fax: 402 479-5119
402 471-3101 *Public Service Commission* 1200 N St Suite 300 .... Lincoln NE 68508-2006
Fax: 402 471-0254
402 471-2401 *Purchasing Div* 301 Centennial Mall S 1st Fl .... Lincoln NE 68508-2529
Fax: 402 471-2089
402 471-2004 *Real Estate Commission* 301 Centennial Mall S .... Lincoln NE 68508-2529
Fax: 402 471-4492
402 471-2554 *Secretary of State* 2300 State Capitol .... Lincoln NE 68509-0000
Fax: 402 471-4429
402 471-3191 *State Building Div* 1445 K St .... Lincoln NE 68509-0000
Fax: 402 471-0421
402 471-4545 *State Patrol* PO Box 94907 .... Lincoln NE 68509-4907
Fax: 402 471-4002
402 471-3731 *Supreme Court* 2413 State Capitol .... Lincoln NE 68509-0000
402 471-2455 *Treasurer* PO Box 94788 .... Lincoln NE 68509-4788
Fax: 402 471-4390
402 475-8451 *Unemployment Insurance Div* 550 S 16th St .... Lincoln NE 68509-0000
Fax: 402 471-2318
402 471-2568 *Worker's Compensation Court* 1445 K St .... Lincoln NE 68508-2731
402 471-3189 **Nebraska State Library** State Capitol 3rd Fl S .... Lincoln NE 68509-0000
402 471-3794 **Nebraska Travel & Tourism Div Department Economic Development**
301 Centennial Mall S .... Lincoln NE 68508-2529
Fax: 402 471-3778
402 466-2371 **Nebraska Wesleyan University** 50th & St Paul Sts .... Lincoln NE 68504-0000
Fax: 402 465-2179
702 652-1110 **Nellis Air Force Base** .... Las Vegas NV 89191-5000
Fax: 702 652-3283
502 348-1800 **Nelson County** 113 E Stephen Foster Ave .... Bardstown KY 40004-1546
701 247-2462 **Nelson County** PO Box 565 .... Lakota ND 58344-0565
804 263-4245 **Nelson County** PO Box 55 .... Lovingston VA 22949-0055
816 561-4000 **Nelson-Atkins Museum of Art** 4525 Oak St .... Kansas City MO 64111-1818
913 336-2146 **Nemaha County** 607 Nemaha St .... Seneca KS 66538-1761
Fax: 913 336-3373
402 274-4213 **Nemaha County** 1824 N St .... Auburn NE 68305-2341
718 291-6900 **Nemet Motors International Assn** 153-12 Hillside Ave .... Jamaica NY 11432-3322
Fax: 718 739-0310
316 244-3293 **Neosho County** PO Box 138 .... Erie KS 66733-0237

316 431-2820 **Neosho County Community College** 1000 S Allen Ave .... Chanute KS 66720-2699
Fax: Ext 146
Nepal: Kingdom of Nepal
202 667-4550 *Embassy* 2131 Leroy Pl NW .... Washington DC 20008-1848
Fax: 202 667-5534
212 370-4188 *Mission to the UN* 820 2nd Ave Rm 202 .... New York NY 10017-4504
Fax: 212 953-2038
301 484-7200 **Ner Israel Rabbinical College** 400 Mt Wilson Ln .... Baltimore MD 21208-1198
Fax: 301 484-3060
601 656-3581 **Neshoba County** PO Box 67 .... Philadelphia MS 39350-0067
913 798-2401 **Ness County** 202 W Sycamore St .... Ness City KS 67560-1558
212 370-7367 **Netherlands Board of Tourism** 355 Lexington Ave 21st Fl ...... New York NY 10017-6603
Fax: 212 370-9507
212 265-6460 **Netherlands Chamber of Commerce in the US**
1 Rockefeller Plaza 11th Fl .... New York NY 10020-2095
Fax: 212 265-6402
Netherlands: Kingdom of the Netherlands
202 244-5304 *Embassy* 4200 Linnean Ave NW .... Washington DC 20008-3809
Fax: 202 362-3430
212 697-5547 *Mission to the UN* 711 3rd Ave 9th Fl .... New York NY 10017-4014
Fax: 212 370-1954
312 856-0110 *Chicago Consulate General* 303 E Wacker Dr Suite 410 .... Chicago IL 60601-5279
Fax: 312 856-9218
213 380-3440 *Los Angeles Consulate General*
3460 Wilshire Blvd Rm 509 .... Los Angeles CA 90010-2270
Fax: 213 386-6380
212 246-1429 *New York Consulate General* 1 Rockefeller Plaza 11th Fl .... New York NY 10020-2001
Fax: 212 333-3603
215 459-0905 **Neumann College** Convent Rd .... Aston PA 19014-1297
Fax: 215 459-1370
702 687-4322 **Nevada Commission on Tourism** 5151 S Carson St .... Carson City NV 89710-0000
Fax: 702 687-7779
501 887-3115 **Nevada County** County Courthouse .... Prescott AR 71857-0000
916 265-1293 **Nevada County** 201 Church St .... Nevada City CA 95959-2504
Fax: 916 265-4178
702 732-3366 **Nevada Democratic State Party**
9533 W Sahara Ave Suite 236 .... Las Vegas NV 89117-5302
702 789-0190 **Nevada Historical Society** 1650 N Virginia St .... Reno NV 89503-1799
702 786-3030 **Nevada State Chamber of Commerce** PO Box 3499 .... Reno NV 89505-3499
Fax: 702 323-3499
Nevada State Government
702 687-5000 *Information* 406 E 2nd St .... Carson City NV 89710-0001
702 687-4170 *Attorney General* 198 S Carson St .... Carson City NV 89710-0001
Fax: 702 687-5798
702 687-4325 *Commission on Economic Development*
5151 S Carson St 4th Fl .... Carson City NV 89710-0001
Fax: 702 687-4450
702 789-0225 *Council on the Arts* 329 Flint St .... Reno NV 89501-2033
702 789-0180 *Department of Agriculture* PO Box 11100 .... Reno NV 89510-1100
702 885-4250 *Department of Commerce* 1665 Hot Springs Rd .... Carson City NV 89710-0001
Fax: 702 687-4266
702 885-4360 *Department of Conservation & Natural Resources*
123 W Nye Ln Rm 214 .... Carson City NV 89710-0001
702 885-3100 *Department of Education* 400 W King St .... Carson City NV 89710-0001
Fax: 702 687-5660
702 885-5050 *Department of Minerals* 400 W King St Suite 106 .... Carson City NV 89710-0001
Fax: 702 687-3957
702 887-3285 *Department of Prisons* 5500 Snyder Ave Bldg 89 .... Carson City NV 89701-6752
Fax: 702 687-6715
702 885-5040 *Department of Probation & Parole*
1445 Hotsprings Rd Suite 104 .... Carson City NV 89710-0001
Fax: 702 687-5402
702 885-4892 *Department of Taxation* 1340 S Curry St .... Carson City NV 89710-0001
Fax: 702 687-5981
702 885-5440 *Department of Transportation* 1263 S Stewart St .... Carson City NV 89712-0001
Fax: 702 885-4846
702 885-4240 *Division of Emergency Management* 2525 S Carson St .... Carson City NV 89710-0001
Fax: 702 887-7246
702 885-4670 *Division of Environmental Protection*
123 W Nye Ln Rm 108 .... Carson City NV 89710-0000
Fax: 702 885-0868
702 885-5240 *Division of Occupational Safety & Health* 1370 S Curry St Carson City NV 89710-0001
Fax: 702 687-6305
702 885-4380 *Division of Water Resources* 123 W Nye Ln Rm 246 .... Carson City NV 89710-0001
Fax: 702 687-6972
702 885-4635 *Employment Security Dept* 500 E 3rd St .... Carson City NV 89713-0001
Fax: Unlisted
702 885-5670 *Governor* Capitol Bldg Executive Office .... Carson City NV 89710-0001
Fax: 702 667-4486
702 885-4740 *Health Div* 505 E King St .... Carson City NV 89710-0001
702 885-5300 *Highway Patrol* 555 Wright Way .... Carson City NV 89711-0001
702 885-4270 *Insurance Div* 1665 Hot Springs Rd .... Carson City NV 89710-0001
Fax: 702 687-3937
702 885-4850 *Labor Commission* 505 E King St Rm 602 .... Carson City NV 89710-0001
702 687-3034 *Lieutenant Governor* Capitol Complex .... Carson City NV 89710-0001
Fax: Unlisted
702 887-3213 *Northern Nevada Correctional Center* PO Box 7000 .... Carson City NV 89702-7000
702 885-4880 *Public Defender*
308 N Curry St Capitol Complex Suite 200 .... Carson City NV 89710-0001
702 687-6001 *Public Service Commission* 727 Fairview Dr .... Carson City NV 89710-0001
Fax: 702 687-6110
702 885-4870 *Public Works Board* 505 E King St Rm 301 .... Carson City NV 89710-0001
Fax: 702 687-3981
702 885-4094 *Purchasing Div* 505 E King St Rm 400 .... Carson City NV 89701-4761
Fax: 702 687-3688
702 885-4280 *Real Estate Div* 1665 Hot Springs Rd .... Carson City NV 89710-0001
702 885-5203 *Secretary of State* Capitol Complex .... Carson City NV 89710-0001
Fax: 702 687-3471
702 486-4400 *Securities Div* 2501 E Sahara Ave Suite 201 .... Las Vegas NV 89158-0001
Fax: 702 486-4008
702 879-3800 *Southern Desert Correctional Center* PO Box 208 .... Indian Springs NV 89108-0000
702 687-5284 *State Industrial Insurance System* 515 E Musser St .... Carson City NV 89714-0001
Fax: 702 687-3946
702 885-5160 *State Library & Archives* 401 N Carson St .... Carson City NV 89710-0001
Fax: 702 887-2630
702 885-5180 *Supreme Court* 100 N Carson St .... Carson City NV 89710-0001
Fax: 702 687-3155
702 885-5200 *Treasurer* Capitol Complex .... Carson City NV 89710-0001
Fax: 702 687-5532
702 687-4510 *Unemployment Insurance Div* 500 E 3rd St .... Carson City NV 89713-0001
Fax: Unlisted
702 784-4901 *University of Nevada (System)* 2601 Enterprise Rd .... Reno NV 89512-1666
Fax: 702 784-1127
702 885-4480 *Vital Statistics Section* 505 E King St Rm 102 .... Carson City NV 89710-0001
702 687-5130 **Nevada State Library & Archives** 401 N Carson St .... Carson City NV 89710-0001
Fax: 702 887-2630

702 885-4810 **Nevada State Museum** 600 N Carson St .... Carson City NV 89710-0001
414 436-3767 **Neville Public Museum of Brown County** 210 Museum Pl ..... Green Bay WI 54303-2780
508 991-6275 **New Bedford Free Public Library** 613 Pleasant St .... New Bedford MA 02740-6203
Fax: Unlisted
203 229-0257 **New Britain Museum of American Art** 56 Lexington St .... New Britain CT 06052-1412
302 571-4011 **New Castle County** 800 N French St .... Wilmington DE 19801-3542
302 366-7950 **New Castle Dept of Libraries** 187A Old Churchmans Rd ...... New Castle DE 19720-3115
415 626-1694 **New College of California** 50 Fell St .... San Francisco CA 94102-5298
207 799-5979 **New England Baptist Bible College** 879 Sawyer St .... South Portland ME 04106-6533
603 428-2211 **New England College** 23 Bridge St .... Henniker NH 03242-3202
Fax: 603 428-7230
617 266-2030 **New England College of Optometry** 424 Beacon St .... Boston MA 02115-1100
Fax: 617 424-9202
617 262-1120 **New England Conservatory of Music** 290 Huntington Ave .... Boston MA 02115-5000
Fax: 617 262-7894
401 467-7744 **New England Institute of Technology** 2500 Post Rd .... Warwick RI 02886-2244
Fax: 401 738-5122
617 451-0010 **New England School of Law** 154 Stuart St .... Boston MA 02116-5687
Fax: 617 482-6634
603 224-5388 **New Hampshire Business & Industry Assoc**
122 N Main St 3rd Fl .... Concord NH 03301-4033
Fax: 603 224-2872
603 668-2211 **New Hampshire College** 2500 River Rd .... Manchester NH 03104-1394
Fax: 603 645-9603
603 622-9606 **New Hampshire Democratic State Committee**
922 Elm St Suite 210 .... Manchester NH 03101-2010
603 225-3381 **New Hampshire Historical Society** 30 Park St .... Concord NH 03301-6326
603 271-2666 **New Hampshire Office of Vacation Travel** 105 Loudon Rd ...... Concord NH 03301-5601
Fax: 603 271-2629
603 225-9341 **New Hampshire Republican State Headquarters**
134 N Main St .... Concord NH 03301-4917
Fax: 603 225-7498
New Hampshire State Government
603 271-1110 *Information* 107 N Main St .... Concord NH 03301-4951
Fax: Unlisted
603 271-3658 *Attorney General* 25 Capitol St .... Concord NH 03301-6397
Fax: 603 271-2361
603 271-3516 *Bureau of Public Works* PO Box 483 .... Concord NH 03302-0483
Fax: 603 228-0433
603 271-4650 *Bureau of Vital Records & Health Statistics* 6 Hazen Dr .... Concord NH 03301-0000
603 271-3641 *Consumer Protection & Antitrust Bureau* 25 Capitol St .... Concord NH 03301-6332
Fax: 603 271-2361
603 271-2789 *Council on the Arts* 40 N Main St .... Concord NH 03301-4974
603 271-3204 *Department of Administrative Services*
25 Capitol St Rm 120 .... Concord NH 03301-0000
Fax: 603 271-2361
603 271-3551 *Department of Agriculture* 10 Ferry St .... Concord NH 03301-5022
Fax: 603 271-2361
603 271-5600 *Department of Corrections* 105 Pleasant St .... Concord NH 03301-3861
Fax: 603 271-5643
603 271-3144 *Department of Education* 101 Pleasant St .... Concord NH 03301-3860
Fax: 603 271-1953
603 224-3311 *Department of Employment Security* 32 S Main St .... Concord NH 03301-4857
Fax: 603 228-4145
603 271-3503 *Department of Environmental Services* 6 Hazen Dr .... Concord NH 03301-0000
Fax: 603 271-2867
603 271-3176 *Department of Labor* 19 Pillsbury St .... Concord NH 03301-3570
603 271-2191 *Department of Revenue Administration* 61 S Spring St .... Concord NH 03301-2400
603 271-2575 *Department of Safety State Police Div* 10 Hazen Dr .... Concord NH 03305-0001
Fax: 603 271-1153
603 271-3734 *Department of Transportation* Hazen Dr .... Concord NH 03302-0000
Fax: 603 271-3914
603 271-4501 *Division of Public Health Services* 6 Hazen Dr .... Concord NH 03301-6527
Fax: 603 271-3745
603 271-2236 *Division of Records Management & Archives* 71 S Fruit St ... Concord NH 03301-0000
Fax: 603 271-2272
603 271-3406 *Division of Water Resources* PO Box 2008 .... Concord NH 03302-2008
Fax: 603 271-1381
603 271-2231 *Emergency Management* 107 Pleasant St .... Concord NH 03301-3852
Fax: 603 225-7341
603 271-2711 *Energy Office* 2 1/2 Beacon St 2nd Fl .... Concord NH 03301-4498
Fax: 603 271-1728
603 271-2121 *Governor* State House Rm 208 .... Concord NH 03301-3222
Fax: 603 271-2130
603 271-3179 *Inspection Div* 19 Pillsbury St .... Concord NH 03301-3571
603 271-2261 *Insurance Dept* 169 Manchester St .... Concord NH 03301-5127
Fax: 603 271-1406
603 627-4194 *Manchester Community Correctional Center*
126 Lowell St .... Manchester NH 03104-0000
603 271-1800 *New Hampshire State Prison Complex* PO Box 14 .... Concord NH 03302-0014
603 271-1463 *Office of Securities Regulation* 157 Manchester St .... Concord NH 03301-5118
Fax: 603 224-1427
603 271-2155 *Office of State Planning* 2 1/2 Beacon St .... Concord NH 03301-4497
603 271-2555 *Postsecondary Education Commission* 2 Industrial Park Dr .. Concord NH 03301-8512
603 271-2431 *Public Utilities Commission* 8 Old Suncook Rd .... Concord NH 03301-7320
Fax: 603 271-3878
603 271-2201 *Purchasing Div* 25 Capitol St Statehouse Annex Rm 102 ..... Concord NH 03301-0000
Fax: 603 271-2361
603 271-2701 *Real Estate Commission* 107 Pleasant St .... Concord NH 03301-3818
603 271-3727 *Resources & Economic Development Dept* 105 Loudon Rd .. Concord NH 03301-5601
Fax: 603 271-2629
603 271-3351 *Retirement System* 54 Regional Dr .... Concord NH 03301-5183
603 271-1110 *Secretary of State* State House Rm 204 .... Concord NH 03301-0000
603 271-2925 *Solid Waste Compliance Section* 6 Hazen Dr .... Concord NH 03301-0000
Fax: 603 271-2867
603 271-2646 *Supreme Court* Noble Dr Supreme Court Bldg .... Concord NH 03301-0000
603 271-2621 *Treasury Dept* State House Annex 25 Capitol St Rm 121 ...... Concord NH 03301-6312
Fax: 603 271-3922
603 271-2394 **New Hampshire State Library** 20 Park St .... Concord NH 03301-6314
Fax: 603 271-2205
New Hampshire Technical College
603 752-1113 *Berlin Campus* 2020 Riverside Dr .... Berlin NH 03570-3717
Fax: 603 752-6335
603 542-7744 *Claremont Campus* 1 College Dr .... Claremont NH 03743-0000
Fax: 603 543-1844
603 524-3207 *Laconia Campus* Rt 106 Prescott Hill .... Laconia NH 03246-0000
Fax: 603 524-8084
603 668-6706 *Manchester Campus* 1066 Front St .... Manchester NH 03102-8528
Fax: 603 668-5354
603 882-6923 *Nashua Campus* 505 Amherst St .... Nashua NH 03063-1026
Fax: 603 882-8690
603 772-1194 *Stratham Campus* 277R Portsmouth Ave .... Stratham NH 03885-2231
603 225-1800 **New Hampshire Technical Institute** Institute Dr .... Concord NH 03301-7400
919 341-7184 **New Hanover County** 320 Chestnut St Suite 502 .... Wilmington NC 28401-4090
Fax: 919 341-4040
919 341-4390 **New Hanover County Public Library** 201 Chestnut St .... Wilmington NC 28401-3942

203 787-8346 **New Haven County** 200 Orange St New Haven CT 06510-2016
609 392-3367 **New Jersey Democratic State Committee** 150 W State St Trenton NJ 08608-1105
Fax: 609 396-4778
609 292-2470 **New Jersey Div of Travel & Tourism** 20 W State St Trenton NJ 08625-0001
Fax: 609 633-7418
201 596-3000 **New Jersey Institute of Technology**
323 Martin Luther King Jr Blvd Newark NJ 07102-1824
Fax: 201 643-3934 Library
609 989-7300 **New Jersey Republican State Committee** 310 W State St Trenton NJ 08618-5704
Fax: 609 989-8685
201 623-7070 **New Jersey State Chamber of Commerce** 5 Commerce St Newark NJ 07102-3906
Fax: 201 623-8739
New Jersey State Government
609 292-2121 *Information* 3525 Quaker Bridge Rd Trenton NJ 08625-0001
609 530-3200 *Archives & Records Management Div* 2300 Stuyvesant Ave Trenton NJ 08625-0001
Fax: 609 530-6121
609 292-4925 *Attorney General* Hughes Justice Complex CN-080 Trenton NJ 08625-0001
Fax: 609 292-3508
201 648-2026 *Board of Public Utilities* 2 Gateway Ctr Newark NJ 07102-0000
609 292-4256 *Bureau of Parole* Whittlesey Rd CN-864 Trenton NJ 08625-0001
Fax: 609 984-4566
201 648-2040 *Bureau of Securities* 2 Gateway Ctr Newark NJ 07102-5095
609 292-4087 *Bureau of Vital Statistics*
S Warren & Market Sts Health Niagara Culture Bldg Rm 504 Trenton NJ 08625-0001
609 292-6130 *Council on the Arts* 4 N Broad St CN-306 Trenton NJ 08625-0001
Fax: 609 989-1440
609 292-3976 *Department of Agriculture* John Fitch Plaza CN-330 Trenton NJ 08625-0001
Fax: 609 292-3978
609 292-9860 *Department of Corrections* CN-863 Trenton NJ 08625-0001
Fax: 609 777-0445
609 292-4450 *Department of Education* 225 W State St CN-500 Trenton NJ 08625-0001
Fax: 609 292-3830
201 648-3000 *Department of Energy* 101 Commerce St Newark NJ 07102-5102
Fax: 201 642-1119
609 292-2885 *Department of Environmental Protection*
401 W State St CN-402 Trenton NJ 08625-0001
Fax: 609 984-3962
609 292-7837 *Department of Health* John Fitch Plaza CN-360 Trenton NJ 08625-0001
Fax: 609 984-5474
609 292-4310 *Department of Higher Education* 20 W State St Trenton NJ 08625-0001
Fax: 609 984-9300
609 292-5360 *Department of Insurance* 20 W State St CN-325 Trenton NJ 08625-0001
Fax: 609 393-5063
609 292-2323 *Department of Labor* John Fitch Plaza CN-110 Trenton NJ 08625-0001
Fax: 609 393-7375
609 292-7087 *Department of Public Advocate* 25 Market St CN-850 Trenton NJ 08625-0001
Fax: 609 599-9114
609 292-6748 *Department of the Treasury* State House CN-002 Trenton NJ 08625-0001
Fax: 609 292-6145
609 530-3535 *Department of Transportation* 1035 Parkway Ave CN-600 Trenton NJ 08625-0001
Fax: 609 530-3894
201 648-4010 *Division of Consumer Affairs* 1100 Raymond Blvd Newark NJ 07102-5279
Fax: 201 648-3538
609 292-2462 *Division of Economic Development* 20 W State St CN-823 Trenton NJ 08625-0001
Fax: 609 292-9145
609 530-8820 *Division of Housing & Development*
3131 Princeton Pike CN 816 Trenton NJ 08625-0816
Fax: 609 530-8858
609 292-3463 *Division of Pensions* PO Box CN 295 Trenton NJ 08625-0001
Fax: Call company operator
609 882-2000 *Division of State Police* Trooper Dr West Trenton NJ 08628-0068
Fax: 609 882-6523
609 292-5185 *Division of Taxation* 50 Barrack St CN-269 Trenton NJ 08646-0001
Fax: 609 989-0113
609 292-2460 *Division of Unemployment & Disability Insurance*
Labor & Industry Bldg Rm 601 Trenton NJ 08625-0000
Fax: 609 633-2884
609 292-2516 *Division of Worker's Compensation*
Labor & Industry Bldg CN381 Trenton NJ 08625-0001
609 292-6000 *Governor* 125 W State St CN-001 Trenton NJ 08625-0001
Fax: 609 984-6886
609 777-1243 *Management & Policy* 125 W State St CN-001 Trenton NJ 08625-0001
Fax: 609 392-6193
908 499-5010 *New Jersey State Prison* Lock Bag R Rahway NJ 07065-0000
Fax: Call company operator
609 292-9700 *New Jersey State Prison* 3rd & Federal Sts Trenton NJ 08625-0001
Fax: 609 392-3433
609 292-9200 *Office of Financial Management* 1 W State St 3rd Fl Trenton NJ 08625-0001
Fax: 609 292-9439
609 292-7053 *Real Estate Commission* 20 W State St Trenton NJ 08625-0001
Fax: 609 633-3601
609 984-1900 *Secretary of State* 315 W State St CN-300 Trenton NJ 08625-0001
Fax: 609 292-7665
609 984-2090 *State Law Enforcement Planning Agency* 200 Woolverton St Trenton NJ 08625-0001
Fax: 609 633-6075
609 292-4837 *Supreme Court* 25 Market St CN-970 Trenton NJ 08625-0001
Fax: 609 393-0947
609 777-0250 *Workplace Standards Div* Station Plaza 4 CN-386 Trenton NJ 08625-0001
Fax: 609 633-0664
609 292-6200 **New Jersey State Library** 185 W State St CN520 Trenton NJ 08625-0001
Fax: 609 984-7900
609 292-6300 **New Jersey State Museum** 205 W State St Trenton NJ 08625-0001
Fax: 609 599-4098
804 966-9601 **New Kent County** PO Box 98 New Kent VA 23124-0098
314 748-2524 **New Madrid County** PO Box 68 New Madrid MO 63869-0068
505 842-8208 **New Mexico Democratic Party** 315 8th St SW Albuquerque NM 87102-0000
505 425-7511 **New Mexico Highlands University** National Ave Las Vegas NM 87701-0000
Fax: 505 454-0026 Library
505 835-5508 **New Mexico Institute of Mining & Technology** Campus Stn Socorro NM 87801-0000
Fax: 505 835-6329
505 622-6250 **New Mexico Military Institute** 101 W College Blvd Roswell NM 88201-5173
Fax: 505 624-8107
505 841-8837 **New Mexico Museum of Natural History**
1801 Mountain Rd NW Albuquerque NM 87104-1375
Fax: 505 841-8866
505 883-7345 **New Mexico Republican Party**
5500 San Mateo Blvd NE Suite 114 Albuquerque NM 87109-6263
Fax: 505 883-8377
New Mexico State Government
505 827-8110 *Information* 810 W San Mateo Santa Fe NM 87503-0001
Fax: 505 827-8135
505 827-4800 *Administrative Office of the Court*
237 Don Gaspar Ave Rm 25 Santa Fe NM 87503-0001
Fax: 505 827-4946
505 827-0042 *Air Quality Bureau* 1190 St Francis Dr Rm S2100 Santa Fe NM 87503-0001
Fax: 505 827-0045
505 827-6490 *Arts Div* 224 E Palace Ave Santa Fe NM 87501-2013
Fax: 505 827-7308
505 827-6000 *Attorney General* Galisteo St Bataan Memorial Bldg Rm 260 Santa Fe NM 87501-0000
Fax: 505 827-5826
505 865-1622 *Central New Mexico Correctional Facility* PO Box 1328 Los Lunas NM 87031-1328
Fax: Ext 377
505 827-8300 *Commission on Higher Education* 1068 Cerrillos Rd Santa Fe NM 87501-4250
Fax: 505 827-8311
505 827-6060 *Consumer Protection Div*
Galisteo St Bataan Memorial Bldg Room 236 Santa Fe NM 87501-0000
Fax: 505 827-5826
505 827-8645 *Corrections Dept* 1422 Paseo de Peralta Santa Fe NM 87503-0001
Fax: 505 827-8675
505 827-6635 *Department of Education* 300 Don Gaspar Ave Santa Fe NM 87501-2744
Fax: 505 827-6696
505 827-4500 *Department of Insurance*
1120 Paseo De Peralta Perta Bldg 4th Fl Santa Fe NM 87504-0000
Fax: 505 827-4734
505 841-8437 *Department of Labor* PO Box 1928 Albuquerque NM 87103-1928
Fax: 505 841-8491
505 827-2300 *Department of Motor Vehicles* 1100 S St Francis Dr Santa Fe NM 87501-4147
Fax: 505 827-0395
505 827-0274 *Economic Development & Tourism Dept* 1100 St Francis Dr Santa Fe NM 87503-0001
Fax: 505 827-0407
505 827-9236 *Emergency Planning & Coordination Bureau* PO Box 1628 Santa Fe NM 87504-1628
Fax: 505 827-3456
505 827-5900 *Energy Minerals & Natural Resources Div* 2040 S Pacheco Santa Fe NM 87505-0000
Fax: 505 827-5912
505 827-2850 *Environmental Improvement Div* 1190 St Francis Dr Santa Fe NM 87503-0001
Fax: 505 827-2836
505 827-3060 *Finance & Administration Dept*
Bataan Memorial Bldg Rm 180 Santa Fe NM 87503-0001
Fax: 505 827-4948
505 827-3000 *Governor* PERA Bldg 5th Fl Santa Fe NM 87503-0001
Fax: 505 827-3026
505 827-0020 *Health Services Div* 1190 St Francis Dr Santa Fe NM 87503-0001
505 827-6835 *Labor & Industrial Commission*
1596 Pacheco St Aspen Plaza Santa Fe NM 87501-0000
Fax: 505 827-6812
505 827-3050 *Lieutenant Governor* PERA Bldg 5th Fl Santa Fe NM 87503-0001
Fax: 505 827-3026
505 827-5970 *Mining & Minerals Div* 2040 S Pacheco St Santa Fe NM 87505-0000
Fax: 505 827-7195
505 827-5800 *Oil Conservation Div* PO Box 2088 Santa Fe NM 87504-0000
Fax: 505 827-5741
505 827-3591 *Parole Board* 604 W San Mateo St Santa Fe NM 87503-0001
Fax: 505 827-3744
505 471-7300 *Penitentiary of New Mexico* PO Box 1059 Santa Fe NM 87504-1059
505 827-2141 *Property Control Div* 1100 S St Francis Dr Rm 2022 Santa Fe NM 87503-0001
Fax: 505 827-2181
505 827-3900 *Public Defender* 142 Lincoln Ave Suite 500 Santa Fe NM 87501-2006
505 827-6940 *Public Service Commission* 224 E Palace Ave Santa Fe NM 87501-2013
Fax: 505 827-7097
505 827-0472 *Purchasing Div* 1100 St Francis Dr Rm 2016 Santa Fe NM 87503-0001
505 841-6524 *Real Estate Commission* 4125 Carlisle NE Albuquerque NM 87107-4806
505 827-7004 *Regulation & Licensing Dept* 725 St Michaels Dr Santa Fe NM 87504-0000
Fax: 505 827-7107
505 827-3600 *Secretary of State* Lamy Bldg 1st Fl Santa Fe NM 87503-0001
Fax: 505 827-3634
505 827-7140 *Securities Div* 725 St Michael Dr Santa Fe NM 97501-0000
Fax: 505 984-0617
505 827-5100 *State Highways Transportation Dept* PO Box 1149 Santa Fe NM 87504-1149
505 827-9000 *State Police* 4491 Cerrillos Rd Santa Fe NM 87504-0000
Fax: 505 827-3396
505 827-8860 *State Records Center & Archives* 404 Montezuma Ave Santa Fe NM 87503-0001
505 827-4860 *Supreme Court* 237 Don Gasper Ave Rm 104 Santa Fe NM 87503-0000
505 827-0700 *Taxation & Revenue Dept* 1200 St Francis Dr Santa Fe NM 87509-0001
Fax: 505 827-0940 Legal
505 827-6400 *Treasury Dept* PO Box 608 Santa Fe NM 87504-0608
Fax: 505 827-6395
505 841-8431 *Unemployment Insurance Bureau* 401 Broadway NE Albuquerque NM 87102-2330
Fax: 505 841-8421
505 827-2347 *Vital Records & Statistics* 1190 St Francis Dr Santa Fe NM 87503-0001
505 841-8790 *Worker's Compensation Administration* PO Box 27198 Albuquerque NM 87125-7198
Fax: 505 841-9481
505 827-3800 **New Mexico State Library** 325 Don Gaspar Ave Santa Fe NM 87503-0001
Fax: 505 827-3820
505 646-3121 **New Mexico State University** Las Cruces NM 88003-0000
Fax: Unlisted
505 287-7981 *Grants Branch College* 1500 3rd St Grants NM 87020-2025
Fax: 505 287-7992
505 885-8831 **New Mexico State University at Carlsbad** 1500 University Dr Carlsbad NM 88220-3509
Fax: 505 885-4951
505 827-0291 **New Mexico Tourism & Travel Div** 1100 St Francis Dr Santa Fe NM 87503-0001
Fax: 505 887-0396
504 586-4311 **New Orleans City Hall** 1300 Perdido St New Orleans LA 70112-2112
Fax: 504 524-4481
504 282-4455 **New Orleans Baptist Theological Seminary**
3939 Gentilly Blvd New Orleans LA 70126-4858
504 393-6005 **New Orleans Coast Guard Air Station**
New Orleans Naval Air Stn New Orleans LA 70143-0001
Fax: 504 393-6048
504 942-3020 **New Orleans Coast Guard Support Center**
4640 Urquhart St New Orleans LA 70117-0000
Fax: 504 942-3007 Communications
504 488-2631 **New Orleans Museum of Art** PO Box 19123 New Orleans LA 70179-0123
Fax: 504 484-6662
504 596-2550 **New Orleans Public Library** 219 Loyola Ave New Orleans LA 70140-1016
Fax: 504 596-2609
703 674-3600 **New River Community College** PO Box 1127 Dublin VA 24084-1127
Fax: 703 674-3642
212 741-5600 **New School for Social Research** 66 W 12th St New York NY 10011-8693
Fax: 212 691-7172
212 741-8682 *Program in Health Services Administration* 66 5th Ave New York NY 10011-8892
Fax: 212 741-8935
New York City Government
212 406-9800 *Business Development* 17 John St 14th Fl New York NY 10038-4010
Fax: 212 267-2598
212 669-8170 *City Clerk* 265 Municipal Bldg 1 Center St 2nd Fl New York NY 10007-0000
Fax: 212 669-8992
212 566-4446 *City Hall* 1 Center St New York NY 10007-2304
212 312-8000 *Department of Buildings* 60 Hudson St 14th Fl New York NY 10013-3315
Fax: 212 312-8065
212 720-3503 *Department of City Planning* 22 Reade St New York NY 10007-1216
Fax: 212 720-3354

212 566-2525   *Department of Transportation* 40 Worth St .... New York NY 10013-2904
    Fax: 212 385-0539
212 566-5700   *Mayor's Office* 61 Chambers St City Hall .... New York NY 10007-1208
    Fax: Unlisted
212 374-5000   *Police Dept* 1 Police Plaza .... New York NY 10038-1497
    Fax: 212 374-3953
212 806-6700   *Ports & Trade Dept* Battery Maritime Bldg 4th Fl ... New York NY 10004-0000
    Fax: 212 809-7983
212 669-2746   *Treasurer* 1 Center St Rm 727 .... New York NY 10007-2304
    Fax: 212 669-3460
212 374-8742 **New York County** 60 Centre St .... New York NY 10007-1402
    Fax: Unlisted
518 473-0715 **New York Div of Tourism** 1 Commerce Plaza .... Albany NY 12245-0001
    Fax: 518 486-6416
212 873-3400 **New York Historical Society Museum** 170 Central Pk W .... New York NY 10024-5194
    Fax: 212 875-3400
516 686-7907 **New York Institute of Technology** .... Old Westbury NY 11568-0000
    Fax: 516 626-2627
516 348-3000   *Central Islip Campus* 211 Carleton Ave .... Central Islip NY 11722-4501
    Fax: 516 348-6782
212 399-8347   *New York City Campus* 1855 Broadway .... New York NY 10023-7602
914 993-4531 **New York Medical College School of Medicine** Sunshine Bldg .. Valhalla NY 10595-0000
    Fax: Unlisted
718 834-2000 **New York Naval Station** 207 Flushing Ave .... Brooklyn NY 11251-0001
    Fax: 718 834-2330
212 930-0800 **New York Public Library** 5th Ave & 42nd St .... New York NY 10018-0000
    Fax: 212 921-2546
518 462-2601 **New York Republican State Committee** 315 State St .... Albany NY 12210-2001
    Fax: 518 449-7443
212 753-5365 **New York School of Interior Design** 155 E 56th St .... New York NY 10022-2708
    Fax: 212 826-9706
518 462-7407 **New York State Democratic Committee**
  111 Washington Ave Rm 705 .... Albany NY 12210-2207
    Fax: 518 462-5621
New York State Government
518 474-2121   *Information* Empire State Plaza Concourse Level .... Albany NY 12242-0001
518 474-7124   *Attorney General* State Capitol Rm 221 .... Albany NY 12224-0000
    Fax: 518 474-8995
212 341-2222   *Bureau of Investor Protection & Securities*
  120 Broadway 23rd Fl .... New York NY 10271-0002
518 474-3069   *Bureau of Vital Statistics* Corning Tower Rm 321 .... Albany NY 12237-0001
518 492-2511   *Clinton Correctional Facility* PO Box B .... Dannemora NY 12929-9999
    Fax: 518 492-7892
518 474-5105   *Consumer Protection Board* 99 Washington Ave .... Albany NY 12210-2891
    Fax: 518 474-2474
212 614-2900   *Council on the Arts* 915 Broadway .... New York NY 10010-7199
    Fax: 212 614-3983
518 457-4188   *Department of Agriculture & Markets*
  Capitol Plaza 1 Winner Cir .... Albany NY 12235-0001
    Fax: 518 457-3087
518 457-8126   *Department of Correctional Services*
  State Office Campus Bldg 2 .... Albany NY 12226-0001
    Fax: 518 457-7252
518 474-4100   *Department of Economic Development*
  1 Commerce Plaza 9th Fl .... Albany NY 12245-0001
    Fax: 518 474-1512
518 457-3446   *Department of Environmental Conservation*
  50 Wolf Rd Rm 604 .... Albany NY 12233-0001
    Fax: 518 457-6996
518 474-2011   *Department of Health*
  Empire State Plaza Tower Bldg Rm 1408 .... Albany NY 12237-0001
    Fax: 518 474-4471
518 457-9000   *Department of Labor* State Office Campus Bldg 12 Rm 500 .... Albany NY 12240-0001
    Fax: 518 457-0620
518 474-4750   *Department of State* 162 Washington Ave .... Albany NY 12231-0001
    Fax: Unlisted
518 457-2100   *Department of Taxation & Finance*
  Campus Tax & Finance Bldg 9 .... Albany NY 12227-0001
    Fax: 518 457-2486
518 457-5100   *Department of Transportation*
  5 Harriman State Office Campus Bldg 5 .... Albany NY 12232-0001
    Fax: 518 457-5583
518 474-0335   *Design & Construction*
  Empire State Plaza Empire Statza Rm 3508 .... Albany NY 12242-0001
    Fax: 518 473-1406
518 786-4501   *Disaster Preparedness Commission*
  330 Old Niskayuna Rd Rm 414 .... Latham NY 12110-2224
    Fax: 518 786-4509
518 457-7230   *Division of Air Resources* 50 Wolf Rd Rm 128 .... Albany NY 12233-0001
    Fax: 518 457-0794
518 474-5700   *Division of Economic Opportunity* 162 Washington Ave .... Albany NY 12231-0001
    Fax: 518 486-4663
518 474-3454   *Division of Probation & Correctional Alternatives*
  60 S Pearl St .... Albany NY 12207-1595
    Fax: 518 473-2075
518 474-3830   *Division of Professional Licensing Services*
  Cultural Education Ctr .... Albany NY 12230-0001
    Fax: 518 473-0578
518 474-3695   *Division of Purchasing*
  Empire State Plaza Corning Tower 38th Fl .... Albany NY 12242-0001
    Fax: 518 474-2437
518 457-3518   *Division of Safety & Health*
  State Office Campus Bldg 12 Rm 457 .... Albany NY 12240-0000
    Fax: 518 457-0620
518 457-6603   *Division of Solid Waste* 50 Wolf Rd Rm 212 .... Albany NY 12233-0001
    Fax: 518 457-1283
518 474-4250   *Division of the Treasury* PO Box 7002 .... Albany NY 12225-0000
    Fax: 518 473-9163
518 457-1627   *Division of Water* 50 Wolf Rd Rm 308 .... Albany NY 12233-0001
    Fax: 518 457-1088
518 473-4376   *Energy Office* Agency Bldg 2 Empire State Plaza .... Albany NY 12223-0001
    Fax: 518 483-2822
518 457-9337   *Environment Conservation Div of Mineral Resources*
  50 Wolf Rd Rm 202 .... Albany NY 12233-6500
    Fax: 518 457-9298
518 473-4362   *Facilities Development Corp* 44 Holland Ave 5th Fl .... Albany NY 12208-3411
    Fax: 518 473-6631
518 474-8390   *Governor* Executive Chamber State Capitol Bldg .... Albany NY 12224-0000
914 221-2711   *Green Haven Correctional Facility* Rt 216 .... Stormville NY 12582-0000
212 602-0434   *Insurance Dept* 160 W Broadway .... New York NY 10013-3393
    Fax: 212 602-0437
518 474-4623   *Lieutenant Governor* State Capitol Bldg Rm 326 .... Albany NY 12224-0000
    Fax: 518 473-2444
518 474-7736   *New York State Employees Retirement System*
  Swan St Alfred E Smith Office Bldg .... Albany NY 12244-0000

518 474-4688   *Office of Elementary & Secondary Education*
  Education Bldg Annex Rm 875 .... Albany NY 12234-0001
    Fax: 518 473-3072
518 474-5851   *Office of Higher & Continuing Education* Empire State Plaza ... Albany NY 12230-0001
    Fax: 518 486-2175
518 474-4040   *Office of the State Comptroller*
  Swan St Alfred E Smith Office Bldg .... Albany NY 12236-0000
    Fax: 518 473-8940
518 474-4038   *Office of Unclaimed Funds* Swan St Alfred E Smith Office Bldg Albany NY 12236-0000
518 474-2530   *Public Service Commission* Empire State Plaza Bldg 3 .... Albany NY 12223-0001
    Fax: 518 474-7146
518 474-4750   *Secretary of State* 162 Washington Ave .... Albany NY 12231-0001
    Fax: 518 474-4765
518 474-1195   *State Archives*
  Empire State Plaza Cultural Education Ctr Rm 10D45 .... Albany NY 12230-0001
    Fax: 518 474-2718
518 457-6721   *State Police* Public Security Bldg .... Albany NY 12226-0001
    Fax: 518 485-7818
518 445-7714   *Supreme Court* 16 Eagle St Rm 102 .... Albany NY 12207-1077
    Fax: 518 445-7401
518 457-2177   *Unemployment Insurance Div*
  State Office Campus Bldg 12 Rmm 554 .... Albany NY 12240-0001
    Fax: 518 457-0620
718 802-6666   *Workers' Compensation Board* 180 Livingston St .... Brooklyn NY 11248-0001
    Fax: 718 834-3795
518 474-5930 **New York State Library**
  Empire State Plaza Cultural Education Ctr .... Albany NY 12230-0001
    Fax: 518 474-2718
212 998-1212 **New York University** 70 Washington Sq S .... New York NY 10012-1019
    Fax: 212 674-7858 Communications
212 998-9800   *College of Dentistry* 345 E 24th St .... New York NY 10010-4020
    Fax: Unlisted
212 998-3006   *Courant Institute of Mathematical Sciences*
  251 Mercer St Warren Weaver Hall .... New York NY 10012-0000
212 998-7980   *Department of Journalism & Mass Communication*
  10 Washington Pl .... New York NY 10003-6639
212 998-7700   *Department of Physics*
  4 Washington Pl Andre & Bella Meyer Hall of Physics .... New York NY 10003-6603
    Fax: 212 995-4016
212 998-5300   *Division of Nursing* 50 W 4th St Shimkin Hall Rm 429 .... New York NY 10003-0000
    Fax: 212 995-3143
212 998-8200   *Graduate School of Arts & Sciences Department of Chemistry*
  6 Washington Pl .... New York NY 10003-6603
212 998-8200   *Graduate School of Biology*
  1009 Main Bldg Washington Sq E .... New York NY 10003-0000
    Fax: 212 995-4015
212 285-6000   *Graduate School of Business Administration*
  100 Trinity Pl Rm 933 .... New York NY 10006-1594
    Fax: 212 285-6953
212 998-7414   *Graduate School of Public Administration*
  4 Washington Sq N .... New York NY 10003-0000
    Fax: 212 995-3890
212 998-7430   *Program in Urban Planning* 4 Washington Sq N .... New York NY 10003-0000
    Fax: 212 995-3890
212 998-6000   *School of Law* 40 Washington Pl .... New York NY 10003-6638
    Fax: 212 995-3156
212 340-5290   *School of Medicine* 550 1st Ave .... New York NY 10016-6402
New Zealand
202 328-4800   *Embassy* 37 Observatory Cir NW .... Washington DC 20008-3686
    Fax: 202 667-5227
212 826-1960   *Mission to the UN* 1 UN Plaza 25th Fl .... New York NY 10017-0000
    Fax: 212 758-0827
213 477-8241   *Los Angeles Consulate General*
  10960 Wilshire Blvd Suite 1530 .... Los Angeles CA 90024-3701
    Fax: 213 473-5621
201 596-6550 **Newark Museum** 49 Washington St .... Newark NJ 07101-0000
    Fax: 201 642-0459
201 733-7800 **Newark Public Library** 5 Washington St .... Newark NJ 07101-0000
    Fax: 201 733-5648
614 345-8972 **Newark Public Library** 88 W Church St .... Newark OH 43055-5087
    Fax: 614 345-1750
616 689-7235 **Newaygo County** PO Box 293 .... White Cloud MI 49349-0293
    Fax: 616 689-7205
803 276-5010 **Newberry College** 2100 College St .... Newberry SC 29108-2197
    Fax: Ext 336
803 321-2110 **Newberry County** PO Box 278 .... Newberry SC 29108-0278
617 262-9350 **Newbury Junior College** 129 Fisher Ave .... Brookline MA 02146-5796
    Fax: 617 731-9618
401 847-0179 **Newport Art Museum** 76 Bellevue Ave .... Newport RI 02840-7405
401 841-8330 **Newport County** 8 Washington Sq .... Newport RI 02840-7199
401 846-0813 **Newport Historical Society** 82 Touro St .... Newport RI 02840-2978
804 247-8411 **Newport News (Independent City)**
  2400 Washington Ave .... Newport News VA 23607-4300
804 247-8506 **Newport News Public Library System**
  2400 Washington Ave .... Newport News VA 23607-4300
    Fax: 804 247-2632 Admin
501 446-5127 **Newton County** PO Box 435 .... Jasper AR 72641-0435
404 784-2000 **Newton County** 1113 Usher St .... Covington GA 30209-0000
219 474-6081 **Newton County** Courthouse Sq .... Kentland IN 47951-0000
417 451-4540 **Newton County** Main & Wood Sts County Courthouse Sq .... Neosho MO 64850-0000
601 635-2367 **Newton County** PO Box 68 .... Decatur MS 39327-0068
409 379-5341 **Newton County** Courthouse Sq Hwy 190 .... Newton TX 75966-0000
208 799-3090 **Nez Perce County** PO Box 896 .... Lewiston ID 83501-0896
716 439-6100 **Niagara County** PO Box 461 .... Lockport NY 14095-0461
716 731-4101 **Niagara County Community College**
  3111 Saunders Settlement Rd .... Sanborn NY 14132-9460
    Fax: 716 731-4053
716 285-1212 **Niagara University** .... Niagara University NY 14109-9999
    Fax: 716 285-2971 PR
Nicaragua: Republic of Nicaragua
202 939-6531   *Embassy* 1627 New Hampshire Ave NW .... Washington DC 20009-2550
    Fax: 202 939-6574
212 490-7997   *Mission to the UN* 820 2nd Ave .... New York NY 10017-4556
    Fax: 212 286-0815
606 289-5591 **Nicholas County** PO Box 329 .... Carlisle KY 40311-0329
304 872-3630 **Nicholas County** 700 Main St .... Summersville WV 26651-1444
504 446-8111 **Nicholls State University** Hwy 1 & University Stn .... Thibodaux LA 70310-0000
    Fax: 504 448-4921
508 943-1560 **Nichols College** Center Rd .... Dudley MA 01570-0000
    Fax: Ext 102
202 225-3911 **Nichols Dick** (Rep - R - Kansas) 1605 Longworth Bldg ..... Washington DC 20515-0001
    Fax: 202 225-9415
214 205-2503 **Nicholson Memorial Library** 625 Austin St .... Garland TX 75040-6365
    Fax: Unlisted
202 224-5754 **Nickles Don** (Sen - R - Oklahoma) 713 Hart Bldg .... Washington DC 20510-0001
    Fax: 202 224-6008

715 369-4410 **Nicolet Area Technical College** 2951 Hwy G — Rhinelander WI 54501-0000
Fax: 715 369-4445
507 931-6800 **Nicollet County** 501 S Minnesota Ave — Saint Peter MN 56082-2533
Fax: 507 931-9220
Niger: Republic of Niger
202 483-4224 *Embassy* 2204 R St NW — Washington DC 20008-4018
Fax: 202 483-3169
212 421-3260 *Mission to the UN* 417 E 50th St — New York NY 10022-8001
Fax: 212 753-6931
Nigeria: Federal Republic of Nigeria
202 822-1500 *Embassy* 2201 M St NW — Washington DC 20037-1416
Fax: 202 775-1385
212 953-9130 *Mission to the UN* 733 3rd Ave 15th Fl — New York NY 10017-3204
Fax: 212 697-1970
307 334-2211 **Niobrara County** PO Box 420 — Lusk WY 82225-0420
Fax: 307 334-3453
202 377-4190 **NOAA (National Oceanic & Atmospheric Administration)**
14th St & Constitution Ave NW Rm 5805 — Washington DC 20230-0001
Fax: 202 377-8203
219 636-2736 **Noble County** 101 N Orange St — Albion IN 46701-1097
614 732-2969 **Noble County** County Courthouse — Caldwell OH 43724-0000
Fax: Unlisted
405 336-2771 **Noble County** PO Box 409 — Perry OK 73077-0409
Fax: 405 336-3024 Legal
507 372-8263 **Nobles County** 10th St — Worthington MN 56187-0000
Fax: 507 372-4994
816 582-2251 **Nodaway County** PO Box 218 — Maryville MO 64468-0218
915 235-2462 **Nolan County** 102 E 3rd St — Sweetwater TX 79556-4511
615 586-6251 **Nolichucky Regional Library** 315 McCrary Dr — Morristown TN 37814-3196
Fax: Unlisted
512 653-6161 **Non-Commissioned Officers Assn of the USA**
10635 IH-35 N — San Antonio TX 78233-6627
Fax: 512 656-6225
804 441-2471 **Norfolk (Independent City)** 810 Union St — Norfolk VA 23510-2717
804 441-2000 **Norfolk City Hall** 810 Union St — Norfolk VA 23510-2717
Fax: 804 623-5465
617 326-1600 **Norfolk County** 650 High St — Dedham MA 02026-1855
804 444-4791 **Norfolk Naval Air Station** — Norfolk VA 23511-0000
Fax: 804 445-1953
804 396-3000 **Norfolk Naval Shipyard** — Portsmouth VA 23709-0000
Fax: 804 396-9050
804 444-4791 **Norfolk Naval Station** — Norfolk VA 23511-6002
Fax: 804 445-1953
804 441-2887 **Norfolk Public Library** 301 E City Hall Ave — Norfolk VA 23510-1703
Fax: 804 441-1450
804 683-8600 **Norfolk State University** 2401 Corprew Ave — Norfolk VA 23504-3989
Fax: 804 683-8084 Acctg
804 683-8331 *Department of Journalism* 2401 Corprew Ave — Norfolk VA 23504-3989
Fax: 804 683-8084
218 784-2101 **Norman County** 16 3rd Ave E — Ada MN 56510-1362
612 832-6000 **Normandale Community College** 9700 France Ave S — Bloomington MN 55431-4399
Fax: 612 832-6571
413 664-4511 **North Adams State College** 375 Church St — North Adams MA 01247-4100
Fax: Ext 246
212 288-5691 **North American-Chilean Chamber of Commerce**
220 E 81st St — New York NY 10028-2602
Fax: 212 439-6107
501 743-3000 **North Arkansas Community College** 420 Pioneer Dr — Harrison AR 72601-5599
Fax: 501 743-3577
501 741-3665 **North Arkansas Regional Library** 221 W Stephenson Ave — Harrison AR 72601-4225
503 756-9220 **North Bend Coast Guard Air Station** 2000 Connecticut Ave — North Bend OR 97459-2300
Fax: 503 756-9203
919 334-7500 **North Carolina A & T State University** 1601 E Market St — Greensboro NC 27411-0001
Fax: 919 334-7013 Admin
919 560-6100 **North Carolina Central University** 1801 Fayetteville St — Durham NC 27707-3198
Fax: 919 560-6413
919 560-6333 *School of Law* 1801 Fayetteville St — Durham NC 27707-3198
Fax: 919 560-6339
919 828-0758 **North Carolina Citizens for Business & Industry**
225 Hillsborough St Suite 460 — Raleigh NC 27603-0000
Fax: 919 821-4992
919 821-2777 **North Carolina Democratic Party** 220 Hillsborough St — Raleigh NC 27603-1724
Fax: 919 821-2141
919 833-1935 **North Carolina Museum of Art** 2110 Blue Ridge Blvd — Raleigh NC 27607-6494
Fax: Unlisted
919 828-6423 **North Carolina Republican State Committee**
1410 Hillsborough St — Raleigh NC 27605-1829
Fax: 919 834-7464
919 770-3399 **North Carolina School of the Arts** 200 Waughtown St — Winston-Salem NC 27127-2146
Fax: 919 770-3375
North Carolina State Government
919 733-1110 *Information* 116 W Jones St — Raleigh NC 27603-8003
Fax: Unlisted
919 733-3340 *Air Quality Section* 512 N Salisbury St — Raleigh NC 27611-0000
Fax: 919 733-5317
919 733-2821 *Arts Council* 221 E Lane St — Raleigh NC 27601-2812
Fax: 919 733-5679
919 733-3377 *Attorney General* 2 E Morgan St Justice Bldg — Raleigh NC 27601-1447
Fax: 919 733-7491
919 733-7883 *Benefit Claims Administration* 700 Wade Ave — Raleigh NC 27605-1154
919 733-7741 *Consumer Protection & Antitrust Section* PO Box 629 — Raleigh NC 27602-0629
Fax: 919 733-0135
919 733-7125 *Department of Agriculture* 1 W Edenton St — Raleigh NC 27601-1094
Fax: 919 733-0999
919 733-4926 *Department of Corrections* 214 W Jones St — Raleigh NC 27603-1381
Fax: 919 733-4790
919 733-4962 *Department of Economic & Community Development*
430 N Salisbury St Rm 6122 — Raleigh NC 27603-5900
Fax: 919 733-8356
919 733-4984 *Department of Environment Health & Natural Resources*
512 N Salisbury St — Raleigh NC 27611-0000
Fax: 919 733-2622
919 733-7343 *Department of Insurance* 430 N Salisbury St — Raleigh NC 27603-5926
Fax: Unlisted
919 733-7166 *Department of Labor* 4 W Edenton St — Raleigh NC 27601-2805
Fax: 919 733-6197
919 733-3813 *Department of Public Instruction* 116 W Edenton St — Raleigh NC 27603-1799
Fax: 919 733-6499
919 733-7210 *Department of Revenue* Revenue Bldg — Raleigh NC 27640-0001
Fax: 919 733-3149
919 733-2520 *Department of Transportation* 1 S Wilmington St — Raleigh NC 27601-1453
Fax: 919 733-9150
919 733-7305 *Division of Archives & History* 109 E Jones St — Raleigh NC 27601-2807
919 733-2633 *Division of Economic Opportunity* 2413-19 Crabtree Blvd — Raleigh NC 27604-0000
919 733-3867 *Division of Emergency Management* 116 W Jones St — Raleigh NC 27603-1300
Fax: 919 733-7554
919 733-7015 *Division of Environmental Management* 512 N Salisbury St — Raleigh NC 27611-0000
Fax: 919 733-2622
919 733-7384 *Division of Highways* 1 S Wilmington St — Raleigh NC 27611-0000
Fax: 919 733-9150
919 733-3900 *Division of Occupational Safety & Health* 413 N Salisbury St — Raleigh NC 27603-0000
Fax: 919 733-0952
919 733-4131 *Division of Policy & Planning* 116 W Jones St — Raleigh NC 27603-8003
Fax: 919 733-9571
919 733-3581 *Division of Purchase & Contract* 116 W Jones St — Raleigh NC 27603-1300
Fax: 919 733-5037
919 733-7546 *Employment Security Commission* PO Box 25903 — Raleigh NC 27611-5903
Fax: 919 733-9118
919 733-2230 *Energy Div* 430 N Salisbury St — Raleigh NC 27611-0000
Fax: 919 733-2953
919 733-4240 *Governor* State Capitol — Raleigh NC 27603-8001
Fax: 919 733-5166
919 733-7350 *Lieutenant Governor* Capitol Bldg — Raleigh NC 27601-0000
Fax: 919 255-6595
919 733-7428 *Mine & Quarry Div* 4 W Edenton St — Raleigh NC 27601-2805
Fax: 919 733-6197
919 733-0800 *North Carolina Central Prison* 1300 Western Blvd — Raleigh NC 27606-2148
919 733-7061 *Office of State Budget & Management*
116 W Jones St Rm 5111 — Raleigh NC 27603-8005
Fax: 919 733-0640
919 733-3414 *Parole Commission* 831 W Morgan St Randall Bldg — Raleigh NC 27603-1660
Fax: 919 733-8440
704 637-1421 *Piedmont Correctional Center* 977 Camp Rd — Salisbury NC 28145-0000
919 733-9580 *Real Estate Commission* 1313 Navaho Dr — Raleigh NC 27609-7461
Fax: 919 872-0038
919 733-6555 *Retirement System Div* 325 N Salisbury St — Raleigh NC 27603-1388
Fax: 919 733-9586
919 733-4161 *Secretary of State* 300 N Salisbury St — Raleigh NC 27603-1386
Fax: 919 733-5172
919 733-3924 *Securities Div* 300 N Salisbury St Rm 404 — Raleigh NC 27603-5925
Fax: Unlisted
919 733-2178 *Solid & Hazardous Waste Management Branch*
401 Oberlain Rd — Raleigh NC 27605-1350
Fax: 919 733-4810
919 733-7962 *State Construction Div* 300 N Salisbury St Rm 403 — Raleigh NC 27603-5925
919 733-7952 *State Highway Patrol Headquarters* PO Box 27687 — Raleigh NC 27611-7687
Fax: 919 733-6593
919 733-3723 *Supreme Court* Justice Bldg Suite 100 — Raleigh NC 27601-0000
Fax: 919 733-0105
919 733-3951 *Treasurer* 325 N Salisbury St — Raleigh NC 27603-1388
Fax: 919 733-9586
919 962-6981 *University of North Carolina (System)* 910 Raleigh Rd — Chapel Hill NC 27514-3916
Fax: 919 962-0488
919 733-4249 *Utilities Commission* 430 N Salisbury St — Raleigh NC 27603-0000
Fax: 919 733-7300
919 733-3000 *Vital Records Branch* 225 N McDowell St — Raleigh NC 27611-0000
919 733-4064 *Water Resources Div* PO Box 27687 — Raleigh NC 27611-7687
Fax: 919 733-3558
919 733-2570 **North Carolina State Library** 109 E Jones St — Raleigh NC 27601-2806
Fax: 919 733-8748
919 733-7450 **North Carolina State Museum of Natural Science**
102 N Salisbury St — Raleigh NC 27611-0000
Fax: Unlisted
919 737-2011 **North Carolina State University** 2205 Hillsborough St — Raleigh NC 27695-0000
Fax: 919 737-3787
919 737-2311 *College of Engineering* PO Box 7901 — Raleigh NC 27695-0000
Fax: 919 737-2463
919 737-2871 *Graduate School of Agriculture* 104 Peele Hall — Raleigh NC 27695-0001
Fax: Unlisted
919 829-4200 *School of Veterinary Medicine* 4700 Hillsborough St CB 8401 — Raleigh NC 27606-1428
Fax: 919 821-9538
919 733-4171 **North Carolina Travel & Tourism Div** 430 N Salisbury St — Raleigh NC 27603-6651
Fax: 919 733-8582
919 977-7171 **North Carolina Wesleyan College**
3400 N Wesleyan Blvd — Rocky Mount NC 27804-8699
Fax: 919 977-3701
612 332-3491 **North Central Bible College** 910 Elliot Ave — Minneapolis MN 55404-1391
Fax: 612 343-4778
708 420-3400 **North Central College** 30 N Brainard St — Naperville IL 60540-4690
Fax: 708 357-8393
616 347-3973 **North Central Michigan College** 1515 Howard St — Petoskey MI 49770-9271
Fax: 616 347-9871
509 663-1117 **North Central Regional Library** 238 Olds Station Rd — Wenatchee WA 98801-5937
Fax: 509 662-8060
419 755-4800 **North Central Technical College** PO Box 698 — Mansfield OH 44901-0698
Fax: 419 755-4750
518 891-2915 **North Country Community College** 20 Winona Ave — Saranac Lake NY 12983-2046
Fax: Ext 214
315 782-5540 **North Country Library System** Outer W Main St — Watertown NY 13601-1100
Fax: 315 782-8031
701 255-0460 **North Dakota Democratic-NPL** 1902 E Divide Ave — Bismarck ND 58501-2301
Fax: 701 255-7823
701 255-0030 **North Dakota Republican Party** 4007 State St Suite 8 — Bismarck ND 58501-0689
Fax: 701 258-7419
North Dakota State Government
701 224-2000 *Information* State Capitol — Bismarck ND 58505-0000
Fax: 701 224-3000
701 224-5102 *Adjutant General* Fraine Barracks — Bismarck ND 58502-0000
Fax: 701 224-5173
701 224-2210 *Attorney General* 600 E Boulevard Ave 1st Fl — Bismarck ND 58505-0000
Fax: 701 224-2226
701 224-2960 *Board of Higher Education*
600 E Boulevard Ave State Capitol 10th Fl — Bismarck ND 58505-0154
Fax: 701 224-2961
701 224-3404 *Consumer Fraud & Antitrust Dept* 600 E Boulevard Ave — Bismarck ND 58505-0000
Fax: 701 224-2226
701 237-8962 *Council on the Arts* Black Bldg Suite 606 — Fargo ND 58102-4951
701 224-2231 *Department of Agriculture* 600 E Boulevard Ave — Bismarck ND 58505-0000
Fax: 701 224-4756
701 224-2372 *Department of Health & Consolidated Laboratories*
600 E Boulevard Ave 2nd Fl — Bismarck ND 58505-0200
Fax: 701 224-3000
701 224-2660 *Department of Labor*
600 E Boulevard Ave State Capitol Bldg 6th Fl — Bismarck ND 58505-0000
701 224-2260 *Department of Public Instruction* 600 E Boulevard Ave — Bismarck ND 58505-0440
Fax: 701 224-3000
701 224-2360 *Division of Vital Records* 600 E Boulevard Ave State Capitol — Bismarck ND 58505-0001
701 224-2366 *Division of Waste Management* 1200 Missouri Ave Rm 302 — Bismarck ND 58501-0000
Fax: 701 258-0052
701 224-2810 *Economic Development Commission*
604 E Boulevard Ave Liberty Memorial Bldg — Bismarck ND 58505-0000
Fax: 701 223-3081

701 221-6300 *Game & Fish Dept* 100 N Bismarck Expy Bismarck ND 58501-5086
Fax: 701 221-6352
701 224-2200 *Governor* 600 E Boulevard Ave 1st Fl Bismarck ND 58505-0001
Fax: 701 224-2205
701 224-2581 *Highway Dept* 608 E Boulevard Ave Bismarck ND 58505-0663
Fax: 701 224-0426
701 224-2455 *Highway Patrol* 600 E Boulevard Ave State Capitol Bismarck ND 58505-0244
Fax: 701 224-3000
701 224-2471 *Institutions Office* 600 E Boulevard Ave 10th Fl Bismarck ND 58505-0000
Fax: 701 224-3000
701 224-2440 *Insurance Dept* 600 E Boulevard Ave 5th Fl Bismarck ND 58505-0320
Fax: 701 224-4880
701 224-2833 *Job Insurance Div* 1000 E Divide Ave Bismarck ND 58502-0000
Fax: 701 224-4000
701 224-2219 *Licensing Dept* State Capitol 17th Fl Bismarck ND 58505-0001
Fax: 701 224-2226
701 224-2200 *Lieutenant Governor* 600 E Boulevard Ave 1st Fl Bismarck ND 58505-0000
Fax: 701 224-2205
701 221-6100 *North Dakota Penitentiary* 3303 E Main Bismarck ND 58501-0000
701 221-6153 *North Dakota State Farm* PO Box 5521 Bismarck ND 58502-5521
701 224-2348 *Occupational Safety & Health Program* 1200 Missouri Ave Bismarck ND 58502-5520
Fax: 701 258-0052
701 224-2680 *Office of Management & Budget* 600 E Boulevard Ave Bismarck ND 58505-0000
Fax: 701 224-3000
701 224-2969 *Oil & Gas Div* 600 E Boulevard Ave State Capitol Bismarck ND 58505-0849
Fax: 701 224-3000
701 221-6190 *Parole & Probation Dept* PO Box 5521 Bismarck ND 58502-5521
701 224-2400 *Public Service Commission* State Capitol 12th Fl Bismarck ND 58505-0000
Fax: 701 224-2410
701 224-2749 *Real Estate Commission* PO Box 727 Bismarck ND 58502-0727
701 224-2900 *Secretary of State*
600 E Boulevard Ave State Capitol Bldg 1st Fl Bismarck ND 58505-0000
Fax: 701 224-2992
701 224-2910 *Securities Commissioner* State Capitol 5th Fl Bismarck ND 58505-0001
Fax: 701 224-3000
701 224-2668 *State Archives & Historical Research Library*
612 E Boulevard Ave Bismarck ND 58505-0001
Fax: 701 224-3000
701 224-2221 *Supreme Court* 600 E Boulevard Ave Judicial Wing 1st Fl Bismarck ND 58505-0000
Fax: 701 224-3000
701 224-2770 *Tax Commissioner*
600 E Boulevard Ave State Capitol 8th Fl Bismarck ND 58505-0000
Fax: 701 224-3000
701 224-2643 *Treasurer* 600 E Boulevard Ave Bismarck ND 58505-0600
Fax: 701 224-3000
701 224-2750 *Water Commission* 900 E Boulevard Ave Bismarck ND 58505-0859
Fax: 701 224-3696
701 224-2700 *Workmen's Compensation Bureau*
4007 N State St Hwy 83 N Russell Bldg Bismarck ND 58501-0689
Fax: 701 224-3820
701 224-2490 **North Dakota State Library**
604 East Blvd Liberty Memorial Bldg Bismarck ND 58505-0800
Fax: 701 224-2040
701 237-8011 **North Dakota State University** 1301 12th Ave N Fargo ND 58105-0000
Fax: 701 237-7050
701 237-7456 *College of Pharmacy* 13th St & 12th Ave N Fargo ND 58105-0000
Fax: 701 237-7606
701 224-2525 **North Dakota Tourism & Promotion**
604 E Boulevard Ave Liberty Memorial Bldg Bismarck ND 58505-0000
Fax: 701 223-3081
904 973-2288 **North Florida Junior College** 1000 Turner Davis Dr Madison FL 32340-1699
Fax: Ext 104
803 895-1410 **North Greenville College** Tigerville SC 29688-0000
713 443-5400 **North Harris County College** 2700 WW Thorne Dr Houston TX 77073-0000
Fax: 713 443-5402
713 359-1600 *Kingwood Campus* 20000 Kingwood Dr Kingwood TX 77339-3899
Fax: 713 359-1612
208 769-3300 **North Idaho College** 1000 W Garden Ave Coeur d'Alene ID 83814-2199
Fax: 208 765-2761
515 421-4399 **North Iowa Area Community College** 500 College Dr Mason City IA 50401-7213
Fax: 515 424-2011
619 524-0444 **North Island Naval Air Station** San Diego CA 92135-0001
214 659-5220 **North Lake College** 5001 N MacArthur Blvd Irving TX 75038-3899
Fax: Unlisted
717 291-3941 **North Museum Franklin & Marshall College** PO Box 3003 Lancaster PA 17604-3003
312 583-2700 **North Park College & Seminary** 3225 W Foster Ave Chicago IL 60625-4895
Fax: 312 267-2362
206 527-3600 **North Seattle Community College** 9600 College Way N Seattle WA 98103-3599
Fax: 206 527-3606
508 922-6722 **North Shore Community College** 3 Essex St Beverly MA 01915-4560
Fax: 508 922-6134 Admissions
907 852-2611 **North Slope Borough** PO Box 69 Barrow AK 99723-0069
Fax: 907 852-2679
907 452-4761 **North Star Borough** 809 Pioneer Rd Fairbanks AK 99701-2813
Fax: 907 451-6644
817 565-3030 **North Texas State University College of Business Administration**
Business Administration Bldg Denton TX 76203-0000
Fax: 817 565-6540
919 534-2501 **Northampton County** Jefferson St Jackson NC 27845-0000
215 559-3000 **Northampton County** 7th & Washington Sts Easton PA 18042-7411
804 678-5126 **Northampton County** Business Rt 13 Eastville VA 23347-9999
715 675-3331 **Northcentral Technical College** 1000 W Campus Dr Wausau WI 54401-1880
Fax: 715 675-9776
205 228-6001 **Northeast Alabama State Junior College** PO Box 159 Rainsville AL 35986-0159
Fax: 205 228-6558
402 371-2020 **Northeast Community College** PO Box 469 Norfolk NE 68702-0469
Fax: 402 644-0650
Northeast Iowa Community College
319 562-3263 *Calmar Campus* PO Box 400 Calmar IA 52132-0483
Fax: 319 562-3719
319 556-5110 *Peosta Campus* 10250 Sundown Rd Peosta IA 52068-9703
Fax: 319 556-5058
318 342-1000 **Northeast Louisiana University** 700 University Ave Monroe LA 71209-0001
318 342-1600 *College of Pharmacy & Health Sciences* 700 University Ave Monroe LA 71209-0001
Fax: 318 342-3000
601 728-7751 **Northeast Mississippi Community College**
Cunningham Blvd Booneville MS 38829-0000
Fax: 601 728-1165
816 785-4000 **Northeast Missouri State University** E Normal St Kirksville MO 63501-0000
Fax: 816 785-4181
414 498-5400 **Northeast Wisconsin Technical College** 2740 W Mason St Green Bay WI 54307-9042
Fax: 414 498-6260
215 525-6780 **Northeastern Christian Junior College**
1860 Montgomery Ave Villanova PA 19085-1734
Fax: 215 520-9210

312 583-4050 **Northeastern Illinois University** 5500 N St Louis Ave Chicago IL 60625-4625
Fax: 312 794-6243
303 522-6600 **Northeastern Junior College** 100 College Ave Sterling CO 80751-2399
Fax: 303 522-4945
702 738-3418 **Northeastern Nevada Museum** 1515 Idaho St Elko NV 89801-4021
216 325-2511 **Northeastern Ohio University College of Medicine**
4209 SR-44 Rootstown OH 44272-0000
Fax: 216 673-0421
918 456-5511 **Northeastern State University** Tahlequah OK 74464-0000
Fax: 918 458-2193 Mail Rm
617 437-2000 **Northeastern University** 360 Huntington Ave Boston MA 02115-5096
Fax: 617 437-8573
617 437-3321 *College of Pharmacy & Allied Health Professions*
360 Huntington Ave 206 Mugar Bldg Boston MA 02115-5096
Fax: 617 266-6756
617 437-2796 *Graduate School of Public Administration*
360 Huntington Ave Messerve Hall Rm 303 Boston MA 02115-5096
Fax: 617 437-2942
617 437-3236 *School of Journalism* 102 Lake Hall Boston MA 02115-0000
Fax: 617 437-2942
617 437-2395 *School of Law* 400 Huntington Ave Boston MA 02115-5098
Fax: 617 437-8793
602 523-9011 **Northern Arizona University** PO Box 4092 Flagstaff AZ 86011-4092
Fax: 602 523-4230 Admin
508 374-3900 **Northern Essex Community College** Elliott Way Haverhill MA 01830-0000
Fax: Unlisted
815 229-0330 **Northern Illinois Library System** 4034 E State St Rockford IL 61108-2006
Fax: 815 399-3278
815 753-1000 **Northern Illinois University** De Kalb IL 60115-0000
Fax: 815 753-0198
815 753-1067 *College of Law* Swen-Parson Hall De Kalb IL 60115-0000
Fax: Unlisted
815 753-1925 *Department of Journalism* 103 Reavis Hall De Kalb IL 60115-0000
Fax: 815 753-1824
815 753-1231 *School of Nursing* 1240 Normal Rd De Kalb IL 60115-1391
Fax: 815 753-0814
606 572-5100 **Northern Kentucky University** Nunn Dr Highland Heights KY 41076-0000
Fax: 606 572-5566
606 572-5340 *Chase College of Law* Nunn Hall Highland Heights KY 41076-0000
Fax: 606 572-5342
207 769-2461 **Northern Maine Technical College** 33 Edgemont Dr Presque Isle ME 04769-2016
Fax: 207 764-8465
906 227-1000 **Northern Michigan University** Marquette MI 49855-5301
Fax: 906 227-1333
406 265-3700 **Northern Montana College** 300 11th St W Havre MT 59501-4966
Fax: 406 265-3777 Library
702 738-8493 **Northern Nevada Community College** 901 Elm St Elko NV 89801-3348
Fax: 702 738-8771
505 753-7141 **Northern New Mexico Community College** 1002 N Onate St Espanola NM 87532-0000
Fax: 505 753-5237
405 628-2581 **Northern Oklahoma College** 1220 E Grand Tonkawa OK 74653-0000
Fax: 405 628-5260
605 622-3011 **Northern State University** 12th Ave & J St S Aberdeen SD 57401-0000
Fax: 605 622-3022
703 323-3000 **Northern Virginia Community College**
8333 Little River Tpke Annandale VA 22003-3796
Fax: 703 323-3215
715 682-8027 **Northern Waters Library Service** Industrial Park Rd Ashland WI 54806-0000
715 324-5245 **Northland Baptist Bible College** RR 1 Box 31 Dunbar WI 54119-9801
Fax: 715 324-6133
715 682-4531 **Northland College** 1411 Ellis Ave Ashland WI 54806-3999
Fax: 715 682-1308
218 681-2181 **Northland Community College** 1101 US Hwy 1 E Thief River Falls MN 56701-2598
602 524-6111 **Northland Pioneer College** PO Box 610 Holbrook AZ 86025-0610
Fax: 602 524-2772
213 641-3470 **Northrop University** 5800 Arbor Vitae St Los Angeles CA 90045-4704
Fax: 213 645-4120
717 988-4100 **Northumberland County** 2nd & Market Sts Sunbury PA 17801-0000
Fax: 717 988-4445
804 580-3700 **Northumberland County** PO Box 217 Heathsville VA 22473-0217
907 442-2500 **Northwest Arctic Borough** PO Box 1110 Kotzebue AK 99752-1110
Fax: 907 442-2930
503 343-1641 **Northwest Christian College** 828 E 11th Ave Eugene OR 97401-3727
Fax: 503 343-9159
307 754-6111 **Northwest College** 231 W 6th St Powell WY 82435-1898
Fax: 307 754-6010 Library
206 822-8266 **Northwest College of the Assemblies of God**
5520 108th Ave NE Kirkland WA 98033-7523
712 324-5061 **Northwest Iowa Technical College** Hwy 18 W Sheldon IA 51201-0000
Fax: 712 324-4136 Admin
601 562-3200 **Northwest Mississippi Community College** Hwy 51 N Senatobia MS 38668-0000
Fax: 601 562-3911 Admin
816 562-1838 **Northwest Missouri State University** Maryville MO 64468-0000
Fax: 816 562-1900
208 467-8011 **Northwest Nazarene College** 623 Holly St Nampa ID 83686-5897
Fax: 208 467-8360
904 785-3457 **Northwest Regional Library System**
25 W Government St Panama City FL 32401-2719
712 252-5669 **Northwest Regional Library System** 529 Pierce St Sioux City IA 51101-0000
419 267-5511 **Northwest Technical College** RR 1 Box 246-A Archbold OH 43502-9801
Fax: 419 267-3688
712 737-4821 **Northwestern College** 101 7th St SW Orange City IA 51041-1996
Fax: 712 737-8847 Library
612 631-5100 **Northwestern College** 3003 Snelling Ave N Roseville MN 55113-1598
Fax: 612 631-5269
414 261-4352 **Northwestern College** 1300 Western Ave Watertown WI 53094-4899
203 379-8543 **Northwestern Connecticut Community College** Parkplace E Winsted CT 06098-0000
Fax: 203 379-4995 Library
405 327-1700 **Northwestern Oklahoma State University** Oklahoma Blvd Alva OK 73717-0000
Fax: 405 327-1881
415 657-5911 **Northwestern Polytechnic University** 220 Warren Ave Fremont CA 94539-0000
919 835-4894 **Northwestern Regional Library** 111 N Front St Elkin NC 28621-3342
Fax: 919 526-2270
318 357-6361 **Northwestern State University** College Ave Natchitoches LA 71457-0000
Fax: 318 357-3202 Library
708 491-3682 **Northwestern University** 2129 Sheridan Rd Evanston IL 60208-0001
Fax: 708 491-3824
312 908-5950 *Dental School* 240 E Huron St Chicago IL 60611-2972
Fax: 312 908-0810
708 491-5061 *Department of Biochemistry Molecular Biology & Cell Biology*
2153 Sheridan Rd Hogan Hall Evanston IL 60208-0001
Fax: 708 491-5211
708 491-2968 *Department of Chemistry* 2145 Sheridan Rd Tech Bldg Evanston IL 60208-0001
Fax: 708 491-7713

708 491-5410 *Department of Electrical Engineering & Computer Science*
2145 Sheridan Rd ... Evanston IL 60208-0001
Fax: 708 491-4455

708 491-3685 *Department of Physics & Astronomy* 2145 Sheridan Rd ... Evanston IL 60208-0001
Fax: 708 491-9982

708 491-5061 *Graduate School of Biochemistry*
2153 Sheridan Rd Hogan Bldg NWU 2-100 ... Evanston IL 60208-0001
Fax: 708 491-5211

708 491-3238 *Graduate School of Geological Sciences* 1847 Sheridan Rd ... Evanston IL 60208-0001
Fax: 708 491-8060

708 491-3300 *Kellogg Graduate School of Management*
2001 Sheridan Rd Leverone Hall ... Evanston IL 60208-0001
Fax: 708 491-5071

708 491-5665 *Medill School of Journalism* 1845 Sheridan Rd Fisk Hall ... Evanston IL 60208-0001
Fax: 708 491-3956

312 908-8462 *School of Law* 357 E Chicago Ave ... Chicago IL 60611-3069
Fax: 312 908-9230

407 478-5510 **Northwood Institute** 2600 N Military Trail ... West Palm Beach FL 33409-2999
Fax: 407 640-3328

517 631-1600 **Northwood Institute** 3225 Cook Rd ... Midland MI 48640-2398

214 291-1541 **Northwood Institute Texas Campus** 1114 W FM 1382 ... Cedar Hill TX 75104-1204
Fax: 214 291-3824

703 679-1160 **Norton (Independent City)** PO Box 618 ... Norton VA 24273-0618
Fax: 703 679-3510

714 382-1110 **Norton Air Force Base** ... San Bernardino CA 92409-0000

913 877-2363 **Norton County** PO Box 70 ... Norton KS 67654-0070

202 225-8050 **Norton Eleanor Holmes (Rep - D - District of Columbia)**
1631 Longworth Bldg ... Washington DC 20515-0001
Fax: 202 225-3002

407 832-5194 **Norton Gallery & School of Art** 1451 S Olive Ave ... West Palm Beach FL 33401-7198
Fax: 407 659-4689

203 853-2040 **Norwalk Community College** 333 Wilson Ave ... South Norwalk CT 06854-4684
Fax: 203 853-2928

203 855-6600 **Norwalk State Technical College** 181 Richards Ave ... Norwalk CT 06854-1635

Norway: Kingdom of Norway

202 333-6000 *Embassy* 2720 34th St NW ... Washington DC 20008-2714
Fax: 202 337-0870

212 421-0280 *Mission to the UN* 825 3rd Ave 18th Fl ... New York NY 10022-7583
Fax: 212 688-0554

708 956-6969 *Chicago Consulate General* 748 W Algonquin Rd ... Arlington Heights IL 60005-0000
Fax: 708 364-7374

213 933-7717 *Los Angeles Consulate General*
5750 Wilshire Blvd Suite 470 ... Los Angeles CA 90036-0000
Fax: 213 923-8711

212 421-7333 *New York Consulate General* 825 3rd Ave 17th Fl ... New York NY 10022-7519
Fax: 212 754-0583

213 933-7717 **Norwegian-American Chamber of Commerce**
5750 Wilshire Blvd Suite 470 ... Los Angeles CA 90036-0000
Fax: 213 933-8711

415 986-0770 **Norwegian-American Chamber of Commerce**
2 Embarcadero Ctr Suite 2910 ... San Francisco CA 94111-3914
Fax: 415 986-6025

212 421-9210 **Norwegian-American Chamber of Commerce**
800 3rd Ave 23rd Fl ... New York NY 10022-7604
Fax: 212 838-0374

802 485-2000 **Norwich University** 65 S Main St ... Northfield VT 05663-1004
Fax: 802 485-2580

603 669-4298 **Notre Dame College** 2321 Elm St ... Manchester NH 03104-2299
Fax: 603 623-8182

216 381-1680 **Notre Dame College of Ohio** 4545 College Rd ... South Euclid OH 44121-4293
Fax: 216 381-3227

804 645-9043 **Nottoway County** Hwy 625 ... Nottoway VA 23955-9999

602 995-5999 **Nova University** 8601 N Black Canyon Hwy Suite 117 ... Phoenix AZ 85021-4936
Fax: 602 995-7097

305 475-7300 **Nova University** 3301 College Ave ... Fort Lauderdale FL 33314-7796
Fax: 305 476-1999 Admin

305 522-2300 *School of Law* 3100 SW 9th Ave ... Fort Lauderdale FL 33315-3097
Fax: 305 522-9370

202 225-3306 **Nowak Henry J (Rep - D - New York)** 2240 Rayburn Bldg ... Washington DC 20515-0001
Fax: 202 225-3523

918 273-0175 **Nowata County** 229 N Maple St ... Nowata OK 74048-2654

601 726-4243 **Noxubee County** PO Box 147 ... Macon MS 39341-0147

402 225-4361 **Nuckolls County** 150 S Main St ... Nelson NE 68961-0000

301 492-7000 **Nuclear Regulatory Commission** ... Washington DC 20555-0001
Fax: Unlisted

215 337-5000 *Region 1* 475 Allendale Rd ... King of Prussia PA 19406-1415
Fax: 215 337-5324

404 331-4503 *Region 2* 101 Marietta St Suite 2900 ... Atlanta GA 30323-0001
Fax: 404 841-4449

708 790-5500 *Region 3* 799 Roosevelt Rd ... Glen Ellyn IL 60137-5927
Fax: 708 790-5691

817 860-8100 *Region 4* 611 Ryan Plaza Dr ... Arlington TX 76011-8064
Fax: 817 860-8211

415 943-3700 *Region 5* 1450 Maria Ln Suite 210 ... Walnut Creek CA 94596-5368
Fax: 415 943-3804

512 888-0580 **Nueces County** 901 Leopard St ... Corpus Christi TX 78401-3606
Fax: 512 888-0329 Acctg

202 224-3521 **Nunn Sam (Sen - D - Georgia)** 303 Dirksen Bldg ... Washington DC 20510-0001
Fax: 202 224-0072

202 225-2911 **Nussle Jim (Rep - R - Iowa)** 507 Cannon Bldg ... Washington DC 20515-0001
Fax: 202 225-9129

914 358-1710 **Nyack College** ... Nyack NY 10960-0000
Fax: Unlisted

702 482-8127 **Nye County** PO Box 1031 ... Tonopah NV 89049-1031

O

712 757-3255 **O'Brien County** 155 S Hayes ... Primghar IA 51245-0000

615 794-4254 **O'More College of Design** PO Box 908 ... Franklin TN 37065-0908

218 751-8670 **Oak Hills Bible College** 1600 Oak Hills Rd SW ... Bemidji MN 56601-8826

202 225-5871 **Oakar Mary Rose (Rep - D - Ohio)** 2231 Rayburn Bldg ... Washington DC 20515-0001
Fax: 202 225-0663

415 444-2489 **Oakland City Hall** 1 City Hall Plaza ... Oakland CA 94612-1929
Fax: Call company operator

812 749-4781 **Oakland City College** 143 N Lucretia St ... Oakland City IN 47660-1099

313 540-1500 **Oakland Community College (System)**
2480 Opdyke Rd ... Bloomfield Hills MI 48304-2266
Fax: 313 540-1841

Oakland Community College

313 340-6500 *Auburn Hills Campus* 2900 Featherstone Rd ... Auburn Hills MI 48326-2845
Fax: Call company operator

313 360-3000 *Highland Lakes Campus* 7350 Cooley Lake Rd ... Union Lake MI 48387-2400

313 471-7500 *Orchard Ridge Campus* 27055 Orchard Lake Rd ... Farmington Hills MI 48334-4579
Fax: 313 471-7739

313 544-4900 *Royal Oak Campus* 739 S Washington Ave ... Royal Oak MI 48067-3898

313 552-2600 *Southfield Campus* 22322 Rutland Ave ... Southfield MI 48075-4793

313 858-1000 **Oakland County** 1200 N Telegraph Rd ... Pontiac MI 48341-1045
Fax: 313 858-1080

415 273-3402 **Oakland Museum** 1000 Oak St ... Oakland CA 94607-4892
Fax: 415 273-2258

415 273-3281 **Oakland Public Library** 125 14th St ... Oakland CA 94612-4397
Fax: 415 273-2232

313 370-2100 **Oakland University** Walton & Squirrel Sts ... Rochester MI 48309-0000
Fax: 313 370-2286

708 635-1600 **Oakton Community College** 1600 E Golf Rd ... Des Plaines IL 60016-1268
Fax: 708 635-1706

205 726-7000 **Oakwood College** Oakwood Rd ... Huntsville AL 35896-0001
Fax: 205 726-7409

216 775-8121 **Oberlin College** 173 W Lorain St ... Oberlin OH 44074-1023
Fax: 216 775-8886

202 225-6211 **Oberstar James L (Rep - D - Minnesota)**
2209 Rayburn Bldg ... Washington DC 20515-0001
Fax: 202 225-0699

202 225-3365 **Obey David R (Rep - D - Wisconsin)** 2462 Rayburn Bldg ... Washington DC 20515-0001
Fax: Unlisted

901 885-3831 **Obion County** County Courthouse ... Union City TN 38261-0000

202 529-6544 **Oblate College** 391 Michigan Ave NE ... Washington DC 20017-1586

213 259-2500 **Occidental College** 1600 Campus Dr ... Los Angeles CA 90041-3376
Fax: 213 259-2958 Acctg

202 523-8148 **Occupational Safety & Health Administration**
200 Constitution Ave NW Rm N3647 ... Washington DC 20210-0001
Fax: 202 523-7312

617 565-7164 *Region 1* 133 Portland St ... Boston MA 02114-1707
Fax: 617 565-7157

212 337-2378 *Region 2* 201 Varick St Rm 670 ... New York NY 10014-4811
Fax: 212 337-2371

215 596-1201 *Region 3* 3535 Market St Gateway Bldg Suite 2100 ... Philadelphia PA 19104-0000
Fax: 215 596-4872

404 347-3573 *Region 4* 1375 Peachtree St NE Suite 587 ... Atlanta GA 30367-0001
Fax: 404 257-0181

312 353-2220 *Region 5* 230 S Dearborn St Suite 3244 ... Chicago IL 60604-1601
Fax: 312 353-7774

214 767-4731 *Region 6* 525 Griffin St Federal Bldg Rm 602 ... Dallas TX 75202-0000
Fax: 214 767-4137

816 426-5861 *Region 7* 911 Walnut St Rm 406 ... Kansas City MO 64106-2009
Fax: 816 426-2750

303 844-3061 *Region 8* 1961 Stout St Rm 1576 ... Denver CO 80294-0101
Fax: Unlisted

415 744-6670 *Region 9* 71 Stevenson St Suite 420 ... San Francisco CA 94105-2935
Fax: 415 484-7114

206 442-5930 *Region 10* 1111 3rd Ave Rm 715 ... Seattle WA 98101-3207
Fax: 206 442-1663

202 634-7943 **Occupational Safety & Health Review Commission**
1825 K St NW Rm 406 ... Washington DC 20006-1202
Fax: 202 634-4008

404 347-4197 *Atlanta Region* 1365 Peachtree St NE Rm 240 ... Atlanta GA 30309-3119
Fax: 404 347-0113

617 223-9750 *Boston Region* JW McCormack POCH Rm 420 ... Boston MA 02109-0000
Fax: 617 223-4004

214 767-5271 *Dallas Region* 1100 Commerce St Rm 7B11 ... Dallas TX 75242-1003
Fax: 214 767-0350

303 844-2281 *Denver Region* 1244 N Speer Blvd Suite 250 ... Denver CO 80204-3582
Fax: 303 844-3759

908 244-2121 **Ocean County** PO Box CN 2191 ... Toms River NJ 08754-0000

908 255-4000 **Ocean County College** College Dr CN-2001 ... Toms River NJ 08753-0000
Fax: 908 255-0444

616 873-4328 **Oceana County** PO Box 153 ... Hart MI 49420-0000

804 433-3131 **Oceana Naval Air Station** ... Virginia Beach VA 23460-5120
Fax: 804 433-2007

202 647-1561 **Oceans & International Environmental & Scientific Affairs (US Dept of State)**
2201 C St NW Rm 7831 ... Washington DC 20520-0001
Fax: 202 647-0217

806 435-8105 **Ochiltree County** 511 S Main St ... Perryton TX 79070-3154

404 769-5120 **Oconee County** 15 Water St ... Watkinsville GA 30677-2438
Fax: 404 769-0705

803 638-4280 **Oconee County** W Main St ... Walhalla SC 29691-0000

414 834-5322 **Oconto County** 300 Washington St ... Oconto WI 54153-1621
Fax: Unlisted

915 335-6400 **Odessa College** 201 W University Blvd ... Odessa TX 79764-7127
Fax: 915 335-6860

202 456-1414 **Office of Administration** 725 17th St NW Rm 4013 ... Washington DC 20503-0001
Fax: 202 395-5608

202 377-3942 **Office of Business Liaison (US Dept of Commerce)**
14th St & Constitution Ave NW Rm 5898-C ... Washington DC 20230-0001
Fax: 202 377-4054

202 252-5233 **Office of Community Service** 901 D St SW ... Washington DC 20447-0001
Fax: Unlisted

202 634-4140 **Office of Consumer Affairs (US Dept of Health & Human Services)**
1725 I St NW Premier Bldg Rm 1009 ... Washington DC 20006-2403
Fax: 202 634-4135

202 647-9892 **Office of Counterterrorism (US Dept of State)**
2201 C St NW Rm 2507 ... Washington DC 20520-0001
Fax: 202 647-0221

202 447-4164 **Office of Economics (US Dept of Agriculture)**
USDA Administration Bldg Rm 227E ... Washington DC 20250-0001
Fax: 202 475-4915

202 447-5447 *World Agricultural Outlook Board*
14th St & Independence Ave SW Rm 5143 ... Washington DC 20250-0001
Fax: 202 472-5805

202 357-6000 **Office of Educational Research & Improvement (US Dept of Education)**
555 New Jersey Ave NW ... Washington DC 20208-0001
Fax: 202 357-6466

202 208-3891 **Office of Environmental Affairs (US Dept of the Interior)**
1849 C St NW MS-2340 ... Washington DC 20240-0001
Fax: 202 289-7405

505 766-3565 *Albuquerque Region* 421 Gold Ave SW Suite 310 ... Albuquerque NM 87102-3254
Fax: 505 766-1059

907 271-5011 *Anchorage Region* 1689 C St Rm 119 ... Anchorage AK 99501-5126
Fax: 907 271-4102

617 565-6856 *Boston Region* 10 Causeway St Rm 1022 ... Boston MA 02222-1047
Fax:

312 353-6612 *Chicago Region* 230 S Dearborn St Suite 3422 ... Chicago IL 60604-1602

215 597-5378 *Philadelphia Region* 200 Chestnut St Customs House ... Philadelphia PA 19106-0000
Fax: 215 597-0932

503 231-6157 *Portland Region* 1002 NE Holladay St Suite 354 ... Portland OR 97232-4118
Fax: 503 231-2062

202 647-3416 **Office of Foreign Missions (US Dept of State)**
2201 C St NW Rm 2238 ... Washington DC 20520-0001
Fax: 202 647-5764

202 472-7257 **Office of Human Development Services (USDHHS)**
200 Independence Ave SW Suite 348F .... Washington DC 20201-0001
Fax: 202 472-6927
617 565-1101 *Region 1* JFK Federal Bldg Government Ctr Rm 2000 .... Boston MA 02203-0000
Fax: 617 565-1084
212 264-1487 *Region 2* 26 Federal Plaza Rm 4149 .... New York NY 10278-0004
Fax: 212 264-2162
215 596-6776 *Region 3* 3535 Market St .... Philadelphia PA 19104-3309
Fax: 215 596-6455
404 331-2398 *Region 4* 101 Marietta Tower Suite 903 .... Atlanta GA 30323-0001
Fax: 404 242-5490
312 353-8322 *Region 5* 105 W Adams St 21st Fl .... Chicago IL 60603-4102
Fax: 312 353-1194
214 767-4540 *Region 6* 1200 Main Tower Bldg Rm 1050 .... Dallas TX 75202-0000
Fax: 214 767-4537
816 426-3981 *Region 7* 601 E 12th St Rm 384 .... Kansas City MO 64106-2808
Fax: 816 426-2888
303 844-2622 *Region 8* 1961 Stout St Rm 924 .... Denver CO 80294-0101
Fax: Unlisted
415 556-5480 *Region 9* 50 United Nations Plaza .... San Francisco CA 94102-4912
Fax: 415 556-4161
206 442-2430 *Region 10* 2201 6th Ave RX-30 .... Seattle WA 98121-0000
Fax: 206 442-4333
202 653-9309 **Office of International Cooperation & Development (US Dept of Agriculture)**
2121 K St NW Rm 310 .... Washington DC 20250-0001
Fax: 202 653-8715
202 395-3000 **Office of Management & Budget** 725 17th St NW .... Washington DC 20503-0001
Fax: Unlisted
202 586-6450 **Office of Nuclear Energy (US Dept of Energy)**
1000 Independence Ave SW Rm 5A-115 .... Washington DC 20585-0001
Fax: 202 586-8353
202 632-9594 **Office of Personnel Management** 1900 E St NW .... Washington DC 20415-0001
Fax: Unlisted
202 456-6515 **Office of Policy Development** 1600 Pennsylvania Ave NW .. Washington DC 20500-0001
Fax: 202 456-2878
703 875-1101 **Office of Procurement (US Dept of State)**
1100 Wilson Blvd 14th Fl .... Rosslyn VA 22209-2297
Fax: 703 875-1027
202 456-7116 **Office of Science & Technology Policy**
17th St & Pennsylvania Ave .... Washington DC 20506-0001
Fax: 202 395-3261
615 576-1301 **Office of Scientific & Technical Information (US Dept of Energy)**
175 Oak Ridge Tpke .... Oak Ridge TN 37830-7255
Fax: 615 576-2865
202 228-6150 **Office of Technology Assessment**
600 Pennsylvania Ave SE .... Washington DC 20003-4316
Fax: 202 228-6098
202 456-2957 **Office of the First Lady** 1600 Pennsylvania Ave NW 2nd Fl .. Washington DC 20500-0001
Fax: 202 395-4198
202 755-6430 **Office of the Inspector General (US Dept of Housing & Urban Development)**
451 7th St SW Rm 8256 .... Washington DC 20410-0001
Fax: 202 755-0354
202 566-7901 **Office of the Inspector General (US Dept of the Treasury)**
1500 Pennsylvania Ave NW Rm 2412 .... Washington DC 20220-0001
Fax: 202 535-4867
202 233-5394 **Office of the Inspector General Hotline (US Dept of Veterans Affairs)**
810 Vermont Ave NW .... Washington DC 20420-0001
Fax: 202 275-0675
202 208-3100 **Office of the Solicitor (US Dept of the Interior)**
1849 C St NW Rm 6352 .... Washington DC 20240-0001
Fax: 202 343-5584
907 271-4131 *Alaska Region* 222 W 8th Ave Box 34 Rm A-25 .... Anchorage AK 99513-0000
Fax: 907 258-5734
801 524-5677 *Innermountain Region* 125 S State St Rm 6201 .... Salt Lake City UT 84138-1102
Fax: 801 524-5499
617 565-2500 *New England Region* JFK Federal Bldg Rm 1803 .... Boston MA 02203-0000
Fax: 617 565-2142
503 231-2125 *Pacific Northwest Region* 500 NE Multnomah St Suite 607 ... Portland OR 97232-2036
Fax: 503 231-2166
916 978-4821 *Pacific Southwest Region* 2800 Cottage Way Rm E-2753 . Sacramento CA 95825-0000
Fax: 916 978-4715
303 236-8444 *Rocky Mountain Region* PO Box 25007 .... Golden CO 80225-0007
Fax: 303 236-8644
404 658-6618 *Southeast Region* 165 Decatur St 2nd Fl .... Atlanta GA 30335-0001
918 581-7502 *Southwest Region* 333 W 4th St Rm 3068 .... Tulsa OK 74103-3819
Fax: 918 581-7501
202 395-3230 **Office of the US Trade Representative** 600 17th St NW ..... Washington DC 20506-0001
Fax: 202 395-3911
202 456-2326 **Office of the Vice President** Old Executive Office Bldg .... Washington DC 20501-0001
Fax: 202 395-4032
202 653-6060 **Office of Transportation (US Dept of Agriculture)**
PO Box 96575 .... Washington DC 20250-0001
Fax: 202 653-6327
402 294-1110 **Offutt Air Force Base** .... Bellevue NE 68113-5000
Fax: 402 294-5752
517 345-0215 **Ogemaw County** PO Box 8 .... West Branch MI 48661-0008
815 732-3201 **Ogle County** PO Box 357 .... Oregon IL 61061-0357
404 743-5270 **Oglethorpe County** PO Box 261 .... Lexington GA 30648-0261
404 261-1441 **Oglethorpe University** 4484 Peachtree Rd NE .... Atlanta GA 30319-2797
Fax: 404 262-9812
812 438-2062 **Ohio County** Main St .... Rising Sun IN 47040-0000
502 298-3673 **Ohio County** PO Box 85 .... Hartford KY 42347-0085
304 234-3656 **Ohio County** 205 City County Bldg .... Wheeling WV 26003-0000
614 221-6563 **Ohio Democratic State Committee**
88 E Broad St Suite 1920 .... Columbus OH 43215-3506
Fax: 614 221-0721
614 466-8844 **Ohio Div of Travel & Tourism** 77 S High St .... Columbus OH 43266-0001
Fax: 614 466-6744
614 253-2741 **Ohio Dominican College** 1216 Sunbury Rd .... Columbus OH 43219-2099
Fax: 614 252-0776
419 772-2000 **Ohio Northern University** 525 S Main St .... Ada OH 45810-1599
Fax: 419 772-1932
419 772-2211 *Pettit College of Law* .... Ada OH 45810-0000
Fax: 419 772-1932
419 772-2275 *Raade College of Pharmacy* .... Ada OH 45810-0000
Fax: 419 772-1932
614 228-2481 **Ohio Republican State Committee** 172 E State St Suite 400 .. Columbus OH 43215-4300
Fax: 614 228-1093
614 228-4201 **Ohio State Chamber of Commerce** 35 E Gay St .... Columbus OH 43215-3138
Fax: 614 228-6403
Ohio State Government
614 466-2000 *Information* 65 E State St .... Columbus OH 43266-0001
Fax: 614 466-8159
614 466-2613 *Arts Council* 727 E Main St .... Columbus OH 43266-0540
Fax: 614 466-4494
614 466-3376 *Attorney General* 30 E Broad St 17th Fl .... Columbus OH 43266-0001
Fax: 614 644-6135
614 466-6000 *Board of Regents* 30 E Broad St Suite 3600 .... Columbus OH 43266-0001
Fax: Call company operator
614 466-2100 *Bureau of Employment Services* PO Box 1618 .... Columbus OH 43216-1618
Fax: 614 466-5025
614 466-2950 *Bureau of Workers' Compensation* 246 N High St .... Columbus OH 43215-2485
614 773-2616 *Chillicothe Correctional Institute* Rt 104 .... Chillicothe OH 45601-0000
Fax: 614 773-2941
614 466-4986 *Consumer Protection Div* 30 E Broad St 25th Fl .... Columbus OH 43266-0001
Fax: 614 644-6135
614 466-2732 *Department of Agriculture* 65 S Front St .... Columbus OH 43266-0302
Fax: 614 466-6124
614 466-3636 *Department of Commerce* 77 S High St .... Columbus OH 43266-0001
Fax: 614 644-8292
614 466-2480 *Department of Development* 77 S High St .... Columbus OH 43215-6108
Fax: 614 644-5167
614 466-3304 *Department of Education* 65 S Front St Rm 808 .... Columbus OH 43266-0001
Fax: 614 644-5960
614 466-3543 *Department of Health* 246 N High St .... Columbus OH 43266-0001
Fax: 614 644-8526 Personnel
614 466-2550 *Department of Highway Safety* 240 Parsons Ave .... Columbus OH 43215-0000
Fax: 614 466-0433
614 644-2651 *Department of Insurance* 2100 Stella Ct .... Columbus OH 43266-0001
614 265-6722 *Department of Natural Resources Water Div*
1939 Fountain Sq Bldg E-3 .... Columbus OH 43224-0000
Fax: 614 447-9503
614 431-2762 *Department of Rehabilitation & Correction*
1050 Freeway Dr N .... Columbus OH 43229-5411
Fax: 614 466-8852
614 466-2335 *Department of Transportation* 25 S Front St .... Columbus OH 43215-4104
Fax: 614 644-6053
614 466-4130 *Division of Licensing* 77 S High St 23rd Fl .... Columbus OH 43266-0001
Fax: 614 644-8292
614 265-6893 *Division of Oil & Gas* Fountain Sq Bldg A-1 .... Columbus OH 43224-0000
Fax: 614 268-4316
614 431-2776 *Division of Parole & Community Services*
1050 Freeway Dr N .... Columbus OH 43229-5411
Fax: 614 431-6448
614 644-3020 *Division of Pollution Control* 1800 Watermark Dr .... Columbus OH 43266-0001
Fax: 614 644-2329
614 466-4277 *Division of Public Works* 30 E Broad St .... Columbus OH 43215-0000
Fax: 614 644-7982
614 466-4100 *Division of Real Estate* 77 S High St 20th Fl .... Columbus OH 43266-0547
614 466-1276 *Division of Safety & Hygiene* 246 N High St 4th Fl .... Columbus OH 43215-0000
Fax: 614 644-5707
614 466-3440 *Division of Securities* 77 S High St 22nd Fl .... Columbus OH 43266-0548
Fax: 614 466-3316
614 466-2917 *Division of Solid & Hazardous Waste Management*
PO Box 1049 .... Columbus OH 43266-0149
Fax: 614 644-2329
614 866-0578 *Division of Surface Mines* 2242 S Hamilton Rd .... Columbus OH 43232-4304
Fax: 614 469-2506
614 466-2533 *Division of Vital Statistics* 65 S Front St Rm G-20 .... Columbus OH 43266-0003
614 889-7150 *Emergency Management Agency* 2825 W Granville Rd ...... Columbus OH 43235-2712
Fax: 614 889-7183
614 644-3020 *Environmental Protection Agency* 1800 Watermark Dr ...... Columbus OH 43215-1043
Fax: 614 644-2329
614 466-3555 *Governor* 77 S High St 30th Fl .... Columbus OH 43215-6108
Fax: 614 466-9354
614 466-2990 *Highway Patrol* 660 E Main St .... Columbus OH 43205-1713
Fax: 614 644-9749
614 297-2300 *Historical Society* 1982 Velma Ave .... Columbus OH 43211-2497
Fax: 614 297-2411
614 644-2223 *Industrial Relations Dept* 2323 W 5th Ave .... Columbus OH 43216-0000
Fax: 614 644-2618
614 466-3396 *Lieutenant Governor* 77 S High St 30th Fl .... Columbus OH 43215-0000
Fax: 614 466-9354
614 466-4034 *Office of Budget & Management* 30 E Broad St 34th Fl ...... Columbus OH 43215-0000
Fax: 614 466-5400
614 297-2300 *Ohio Historical Center* 1982 Velma Ave .... Columbus OH 43211-2497
419 526-2000 *Ohio State Reformatory* Olivesburg Rd .... Mansfield OH 44903-0000
614 466-5394 *Public Defender* 8 E Long St 11th Fl .... Columbus OH 43215-0000
Fax: 614 644-9972
614 466-3204 *Public Utilities Commission* 180 E Broad St .... Columbus OH 43266-0001
Fax: 614 466-7366
614 466-2655 *Secretary of State* 30 E Broad St 14th Fl .... Columbus OH 43215-3469
Fax: 614 466-2892
614 644-8493 *State Purchasing* 364 S 4th St .... Columbus OH 43266-0001
Fax: 614 644-1785
614 466-3931 *Supreme Court* 30 E Broad St 2nd Fl .... Columbus OH 43266-0001
Fax: 614 644-8854
614 466-2166 *Taxation Dept* 30 E Broad St 22nd Fl .... Columbus OH 43215-3414
Fax: 614 466-7979
614 466-2160 *Treasurer* 30 E Broad St 9 Fl .... Columbus OH 43215-3414
Fax: 614 644-7403
614 466-9755 *Unemployment Compensation Div* 145 S Front St Rm 538 . Columbus OH 43215-0000
Fax: 614 752-9463
614 292-8500 **Ohio State University** 1800 Cannon Dr .... Columbus OH 43210-1249
Fax: 614 292-9180
614 292-6321 *College of Agriculture* 2120 Fyffe Rd .... Columbus OH 43210-1010
Fax: 614 292-7007
614 292-2401 *College of Dentistry* 305 W 12th Ave .... Columbus OH 43210-1241
Fax: 614 292-7619
614 292-2651 *College of Engineering* 2070 Neil Ave 122 Hitchcock Hall ... Columbus OH 43210-0000
Fax: 614 292-9021
614 292-2631 *College of Law* 1659 N High St Rm 112 .... Columbus OH 43210-0000
Fax: 614 292-3202
614 292-7755 *College of Medicine* 370 W 9th Ave Meiling Hall .... Columbus OH 43210-0000
Fax: 614 292-1544
614 292-8900 *College of Nursing* 1585 Neil Ave .... Columbus OH 43210-1216
Fax: 614 292-4948
614 292-2647 *College of Optometry* 338 W-10th Ave .... Columbus OH 43210-1240
Fax: 614 292-7493
614 292-2266 *College of Pharmacy*
500 W 12th Ave Lloyd M Parks Hall Rm 217 .... Columbus OH 43210-0000
Fax: 614 292-2588
614 292-1171 *College of Veterinary Medicine* 1900 Coffey Rd .... Columbus OH 43210-1006
Fax: 614 292-7185
614 292-5567 *Department of Architecture*
190 W 17th Ave Brown Hall Rm 189 .... Columbus OH 43210-0000
Fax: 614 292-7106
614 292-6046 *Department of City & Regional Planning*
190 W 17th Ave Brown Hall Rm 289 .... Columbus OH 43210-0000
Fax: 614 292-7106

614 292-5813 *Department of Computer & Information Science*
2036 Neil Ave .... Columbus OH 43210-1226
Fax: 614 292-9021
614 292-8124 *Department of Geodetic Science & Surveying*
1958 Neil Ave Cockins Hall Rm 404 .... Columbus OH 43210-1247
Fax: 614 292-2957
614 292-8917 *Graduate School of Chemistry* 120 W 18th Ave .... Columbus OH 43210-1106
Fax: 614 292-1685
614 292-5713 *Graduate School of Physics* 174 W 18th Ave Rm 1174 .... Columbus OH 43210-1106
Fax: 614 292-7557
614 292-6175 *Libraries* 1858 Neil Ave .... Columbus OH 43210-0000
419 221-1641 *Lima Campus* 4240 Campus Dr .... Lima OH 45804-3576
Fax: 419 221-0450
419 755-4011 *Mansfield Campus* 1680 University Dr .... Mansfield OH 44906-1547
Fax: 419 755-4327
614 389-2361 *Marion Campus* 1465 Mt Vernon Ave .... Marion OH 43302-5695
614 366-3321 *Newark Campus* University Dr .... Newark OH 43055-1797
Fax: 614 366-5047
614 292-8696 *School of Public Policy & Management*
1775 College Rd 208 Haggerty Hall .... Columbus OH 43210-0000
Fax: 614 292-1651
614 593-1000 **Ohio University** .... Athens OH 45701-0000
Fax: 614 593-4229
614 695-1720 *Belmont Campus* 45425 National Rd W .... Saint Clairsville OH 43950-9724
Fax: Ext 261
614 774-7200 *Chillicothe Campus* 571 W 5th St .... Chillicothe OH 45601-2299
Fax: 614 592-5000
614 593-2590 *EW Scripps School of Journalism* EW Scripps Hall Rm 105B .. Athens OH 45701-0000
Fax: 614 593-2592
614 533-4600 *Ironton Campus* 1804 Liberty Ave .... Ironton OH 45638-0000
Fax: 614 533-4632
614 654-6711 *Lancaster Campus* 1570 Granville Pike .... Lancaster OH 43130-1097
Fax: Ext 284
614 453-0762 *Zanesville Campus* 1425 Newark Rd .... Zanesville OH 43701-2695
Fax: 614 453-0706
304 485-7384 **Ohio Valley College** 4501 College Pkwy .... Parkersburg WV 26101-8100
614 369-4431 **Ohio Wesleyan University** University Hall .... Delaware OH 43015-0000
Fax: 614 368-3498
614 228-2674 **Ohio's Center of Science & Industry** 280 E Broad St .... Columbus OH 43215-3773
Fax: 614 228-6363
415 659-6000 **Ohlone College** 43600 Mission Blvd .... Fremont CA 94539-5884
Fax: 415 651-6758
904 682-2711 **Okaloosa County** Hwy 90 .... Crestview FL 32536-0000
Fax: 904 682-7362
904 678-5111 **Okaloosa-Walton Community College** 100 E College Blvd .... Niceville FL 32578-1294
Fax: 904 729-5215
509 422-3650 **Okanogan County** PO Box 72 .... Okanogan WA 98840-0072
Fax: 509 422-4903
813 763-6441 **Okeechobee County** 304 NW 2nd St .... Okeechobee FL 34972-4146
Fax: 813 769-9529
918 623-0939 **Okfuskee County** PO Box 26 .... Okemah OK 74859-0026
405 275-2850 **Oklahoma Baptist University** 500 W University St .... Shawnee OK 74801-2590
405 425-5000 **Oklahoma Christian University of Science & Art**
2501 W Memorial Rd .... Oklahoma City OK 73134-8002
Fax: 405 425-5316 Library
405 297-2011 **Oklahoma City City Hall** 200 N Walker Ave .... Oklahoma City OK 73102-2232
Fax: 405 231-2406 Mail Rm
405 682-1611 **Oklahoma City Community College** 7777 S May Ave .... Oklahoma City OK 73159-4499
405 521-5000 **Oklahoma City University** 2501 N Blackwelder Ave .... Oklahoma City OK 73106-1498
405 521-5337 *School of Law* 2501 N Blackwelder Ave .... Oklahoma City OK 73106-1498
Fax: 405 521-5172
405 236-2727 **Oklahoma County** 321 Park Ave .... Oklahoma City OK 73102-3603
405 239-2700 **Oklahoma Democratic State Committee**
116 E Sheridan Suite G-100 .... Oklahoma City OK 73104-0000
Fax: 405 236-8588
405 521-2502 **Oklahoma Dept of Libraries** 200 NE 18th St .... Oklahoma City OK 73105-3298
Fax: 405 525-7804
405 658-5446 **Oklahoma Missionary Baptist College** PO Box 71 .... Marlow OK 73055-0071
405 325-4711 **Oklahoma Museum of Natural History** 1335 Asp Ave .... Norman OK 73019-0001
Fax: 405 325-6029
405 349-2611 **Oklahoma Panhandle State University** PO Box 430 .... Goodwell OK 73939-0430
Fax: 405 349-2623
405 528-3501 **Oklahoma Republican Party** 4031 N Lincoln Blvd .... Oklahoma City OK 73105-5232
Fax: 405 528-8513
405 424-4003 **Oklahoma State Chamber of Commerce & Industry**
4020 N Lincoln Blvd .... Oklahoma City OK 73105-5219
Fax: 405 424-3137
Oklahoma State Government
405 521-1601 *Information* PO Box 26980 .... Oklahoma City OK 73126-0980
Fax: 405 841-5199
405 325-3128 *Appellate Public Defender System* 1660 Cross Center Dr .... Norman OK 73019-0001
Fax: 405 325-7567
405 521-3921 *Attorney General* State Capitol Rm 112 .... Oklahoma City OK 73105-0000
Fax: 405 521-6246
405 521-2115 *Central Purchasing Div* State Capitol Rm B-4 .... Oklahoma City OK 73105-0000
Fax: 405 521-3089
405 521-2384 *Conservation Commission*
2800 N Lincoln Blvd Suite 160 .... Oklahoma City OK 73105-4210
Fax: 405 521-6686
405 521-3864 *Department of Agriculture* 2800 N Lincoln Blvd .... Oklahoma City OK 73105-4298
Fax: 405 521-4912
405 521-2481 *Department of Civil Defense* PO Box 53365 .... Oklahoma City OK 73152-3365
Fax: 405 521-4053
405 843-9770 *Department of Commerce* 6601 N Broadway Ext .... Oklahoma City OK 73116-8214
Fax: 405 841-5199
405 521-3653 *Department of Consumer Credit*
4545 N Lincoln Blvd Suite 104 .... Oklahoma City OK 73105-3408
405 425-2500 *Department of Corrections*
3400 N Martin Luther King Ave .... Oklahoma City OK 73111-4298
Fax: 405 425-2064
405 521-3301 *Department of Education* 2500 N Lincoln Blvd .... Oklahoma City OK 73105-4596
Fax: 405 521-6205
405 271-5600 *Department of Health* 1000 NE 10th St .... Oklahoma City OK 73152-0000
Fax: 405 271-7339
405 528-1500 *Department of Labor* 4001 N Lincoln Blvd .... Oklahoma City OK 73105-5212
Fax: 405 528-5751
405 521-2502 *Department of Libraries* 200 NE 18th St .... Oklahoma City OK 73105-3298
Fax: 405 525-7804
405 521-3859 *Department of Mines* 4040 N Lincoln Blvd Suite 107 ... Oklahoma City OK 73105-5282
405 521-2451 *Department of Securities* 2401 N Lincoln Blvd 4th Fl ... Oklahoma City OK 73105-4402
Fax: Unlisted
405 521-2631 *Department of Transportation* 200 NE 21st St .... Oklahoma City OK 73105-3204
Fax: 405 521-2524
405 425-2500 *Division of Programs & Services*
3400 Martin Luther King Ave .... Oklahoma City OK 73111-4219
Fax: 405 425-2064
405 557-7200 *Employment Security Commission*
2401 N Lincoln Blvd .... Oklahoma City OK 73105-4497
Fax: Call company operator
405 521-2342 *Governor* 212 State Capitol .... Oklahoma City OK 73105-4803
Fax: 405 521-3089
405 527-5593 *Harp Joseph Correctional Center* PO Box 548 .... Lexington OK 73051-0548
Fax: 405 527-7040
405 425-2424 *Highway Patrol* 3600 N King Ave .... Oklahoma City OK 73111-0000
Fax: 405 425-2031
405 521-2828 *Insurance Dept* 1901 N Walnut Ave .... Oklahoma City OK 73105-3209
405 527-5676 *Lexington Assessment & Reception Center* PO Box 260 .... Lexington OK 73051-0260
Fax: 405 527-9892
405 521-2161 *Lieutenant Governor* State Capitol Suite 211 .... Oklahoma City OK 73105-0000
Fax: 405 525-2702
405 521-2302 *Oil & Gas Conservation Div*
2101 N Lincoln Blvd 2nd Fl .... Oklahoma City OK 73105-4904
Fax: 405 521-6045
405 521-2121 *Public Affairs Office* State Capitol Rm 104 .... Oklahoma City OK 73105-0000
Fax: 405 521-3089
405 521-3908 *Public Utilities Div* 2101 N Lincoln Blvd 5th Fl .... Oklahoma City OK 73105-4904
Fax: 405 521-6045
405 521-3387 *Real Estate Commission*
4040 N Lincoln Blvd Suite 100 .... Oklahoma City OK 73105-5283
405 528-1500 *Safety Standards Div* 4001 N Lincoln Blvd .... Oklahoma City OK 73105-0000
Fax: 405 528-5751
405 521-3911 *Secretary of State* State Capitol Rm 101 .... Oklahoma City OK 73105-0000
Fax: 405 521-6737
405 521-2931 *State Arts Council* 2101 N Lincoln Blvd Rm 640 .... Oklahoma City OK 73105-4904
Fax: 405 521-6418
405 521-2141 *State Finance Office* State Capitol Rm 122 .... Oklahoma City OK 73105-0000
Fax: 405 521-3089
405 524-9100 *State Regents for Higher Education*
2500 N Lincoln Blvd .... Oklahoma City OK 73105-4503
Fax: 405 524-5130
405 521-2163 *Supreme Court* State Capitol Rm 1 .... Oklahoma City OK 73105-0000
405 521-3114 *Tax Commission* 2501 N Lincoln Blvd .... Oklahoma City OK 73105-4396
Fax: 405 521-3826
405 521-3191 *Treasurer* State Capitol Rm 217 .... Oklahoma City OK 73105-4892
Fax: 405 521-4994
405 271-4040 *Vital Records Div* PO Box 53551 .... Oklahoma City OK 73152-3551
405 271-5338 *Waste Management Service* 1000 NE 10th St .... Oklahoma City OK 73152-0000
Fax: 405 271-7339
405 271-2555 *Water Resources Board* 1000 NE 10th St 12th Fl .... Oklahoma City OK 73152-0000
Fax: 405 271-2740
405 557-7600 *Workers' Compensation Court* 1915 N Stiles .... Oklahoma City OK 73105-4918
Fax: 405 557-7647
405 744-5000 **Oklahoma State University** .... Stillwater OK 74078-0001
405 744-5140 *College of Engineering Architecture & Technology*
Engineering N Bldg Rm 111 .... Stillwater OK 74078-0001
Fax: 405 744-6187
405 744-6648 *College of Veterinary Medicine*
205 Veterinary Medicine Bldg .... Stillwater OK 74078-0001
Fax: 405 744-5275
405 744-6368 *Graduate School* 202 Whitehurst .... Stillwater OK 74078-0001
405 744-6354 *School of Journalism & Broadcasting* 206 Paul Miller Bldg .. Stillwater OK 74078-0001
405 947-4421 *Technical Branch* 900 N Portland Ave .... Oklahoma City OK 73107-6120
Fax: 405 945-3289
405 282-1889 **Oklahoma Territorial Museum** 402 E Oklahoma Ave .... Guthrie OK 73044-3317
405 521-2413 **Oklahoma Tourism & Recreation Dept**
500 Will Rodgers Bldg .... Oklahoma City OK 73105-4402
Fax: 405 521-3089
918 756-3836 **Okmulgee County** 314 W 7th St .... Okmulgee OK 74447-5028
601 323-5834 **Oktibbeha County** 101 E Main St .... Starkville MS 39759-2955
601 636-0741 **Old Courthouse Museum** 1008 Cherry St .... Vicksburg MS 39180-2540
804 683-3000 **Old Dominion University** Hampton Blvd .... Norfolk VA 23529-0001
Fax: 804 683-5155 Admin
501 783-7841 **Old Fort Museum** 320 Rogers Ave .... Fort Smith AR 72901-1937
502 222-9311 **Oldham County** 100 Main St .... La Grange KY 40031-0000
806 267-2667 **Oldham County** PO Box 469 .... Vega TX 79092-0469
202 225-5431 **Olin Jim (Rep - D - Virginia)** 1410 Longworth Bldg .... Washington DC 20515-0001
Fax: 202 225-9623
312 568-3700 **Olive-Harvey College** 10001 S Woodlawn Ave .... Chicago IL 60628-1696
Fax: 312 660-4847
701 794-8748 **Oliver County** PO Box 166 .... Center ND 58530-0166
616 749-7000 **Olivet College** Main St .... Olivet MI 49076-0000
Fax: 616 749-7121 Library
815 939-5011 **Olivet Nazarene University** 240 E Marsile St .... Bourbonnais IL 60914-1996
Fax: 815 939-0153
507 285-8115 **Olmsted County** 515 2nd St SW .... Rochester MN 55902-3124
Fax: 507 285-8106
618 395-4351 **Olney Central College** 305 N West St .... Olney IL 62450-1099
Fax: 618 392-3293 Library
206 478-4506 **Olympic College** 16th & Chester .... Bremerton WA 98310-1699
Fax: 206 478-7161
402 444-7000 **Omaha City Hall** 1704 Harney St .... Omaha NE 68183-0001
402 444-4800 **Omaha Public Library** 215 S 15th St .... Omaha NE 68102-1601
Oman: Sultanate of Oman
202 387-1980 *Embassy* 2342 Massachusetts Ave NW .... Washington DC 20008-2801
Fax: 202 387-2186
212 355-3505 *Mission to the UN* 866 UN Plaza Rm 540 .... New York NY 10017-0000
Fax: 212 644-0070
208 766-4116 **Oneida County** 10 Court St .... Malad City ID 83252-0000
Fax: 208 766-4285
315 798-5700 **Oneida County** 800 Park Ave .... Utica NY 13501-2220
715 369-6144 **Oneida County** PO Box 400 .... Rhinelander WI 54501-0400
Fax: 715 369-6168
315 469-7741 **Onondaga Community College** .... Syracuse NY 13215-0000
Fax: 315 492-9208
315 435-2070 **Onondaga County** 421 Montgomery St .... Syracuse NY 13202-2984
315 448-4636 **Onondaga County Public Library System** 447 S Salina St .... Syracuse NY 13202-2494
919 347-4717 **Onslow County** 521 Mill Ave .... Jacksonville NC 28540-4258
Fax: 919 455-7878
919 455-7350 **Onslow County Public Library** 58 Doris Ave E .... Jacksonville NC 28540-5197
Fax: 919 455-1661
714 988-8481 **Ontario City Library** 215 E 'C' St .... Ontario CA 91764-4198
716 396-4400 **Ontario County** 27 N Main St .... Canandaigua NY 14424-1447
906 884-4255 **Ontonagon County** 725 Greenland Rd .... Ontonagon MI 49953-1492
708 279-9300 **Opportunity International** 360 W Butterfield Rd Suite 225 .... Elmhurst IL 60126-5025
Fax: 708 279-3107
918 495-6161 **Oral Roberts University** 7777 S Lewis Ave .... Tulsa OK 74171-0001
Fax: 918 495-6033
714 432-0202 **Orange Coast College** 2701 Fairview Rd .... Costa Mesa CA 92626-5563
Fax: 714 432-5609
714 834-2200 **Orange County** 700 Civic Center Dr W .... Santa Ana CA 92701-4022
407 236-7300 **Orange County** 201 S Rosalind Ave .... Orlando FL 32801-3547
812 723-2649 **Orange County** Court St .... Paoli IN 47454-0000

919 732-8181 **Orange County** 106 E Margaret Ln ... Hillsborough NC 27278-2546
Fax: 919 732-4743
914 294-5151 **Orange County** 255-275 Main St ... Goshen NY 10924-0000
Fax: 914 294-7486
409 883-7740 **Orange County** PO Box 1536 ... Orange TX 77631-1536
703 672-3313 **Orange County** 109-A W Main St ... Orange VA 22960-1524
Fax: 703 672-1679
802 685-4610 **Orange County** PO Box 95 ... Chelsea VT 05038-0095
914 343-1121 **Orange County Community College** 115 South St ... Middletown NY 10940-6404
Fax: 914 342-8662
407 425-4694 **Orange County Library Systems** 101 E Central Blvd ... Orlando FL 32801-2407
714 834-6841 **Orange County Public Library** 431 City Dr S ... Orange CA 92668-3386
Fax: 714 834-7595
714 532-0391 **Orange Public Library** 101 N Center St ... Orange CA 92666-1501
803 533-1000 **Orangeburg County** 190 Sunnyside St NE ... Orangeburg SC 29115-5463
803 536-0311 **Orangeburg-Calhoun Technical College**
3250 St Matthews Rd NE ... Orangeburg SC 29115-8299
Fax: 803 531-4364
503 226-2811 **Oregon Art Institute** 1219 SW Park Ave ... Portland OR 97205-2486
Fax: Unlisted
417 778-7475 **Oregon County** PO Box 324 ... Alton MO 65606-0324
503 494-8311 **Oregon Health Sciences University**
3181 SW Sam Jackson Park Rd ... Portland OR 97201-3098
Fax: 503 494-5738
503 494-8867 *School of Dentistry* 611 SW Campus Dr ... Portland OR 97201-3001
503 222-1741 **Oregon Historical Society Museum** 1230 SW Park Ave ... Portland OR 97205-2483
Fax: 503 221-2053
503 885-1000 **Oregon Institute of Technology** 3201 Campus Dr ... Klamath Falls OR 97601-8801
Fax: 503 885-1115
503 222-2828 **Oregon Museum of Science & Industry** 4015 SW Canyon Rd ... Portland OR 97221-2705
Fax: 503 274-4566
Oregon State Government
503 378-3131 *Information* 1225 Ferry St SE ... Salem OR 97310-0001
Fax: 503 373-7210
503 378-3272 *Accident Prevention Div* Labor & Industries Bldg Rm 160 ... Salem OR 97310-0001
Fax: 503 378-5729
503 229-5397 *Air Quality Div* 811 SW 6th Ave 11th Fl ... Portland OR 97204-1334
Fax: 503 229-6124
503 378-4241 *Archives Div Secretary of State* 1005 Broadway NE ... Salem OR 97310-0001
503 378-3625 *Arts Commission* 835 Summer St NE ... Salem OR 97301-2595
503 378-6002 *Attorney General* 1162 Court St NE ... Salem OR 97310-0001
Fax: 503 378-4017
503 378-2334 *Board of Parole* 2575 Center St NE ... Salem OR 97310-0001
Fax: 503 378-4908
503 378-3104 *Budget & Management Div* 155 Cottage St NE ... Salem OR 97310-0001
Fax: 503 373-7643
503 229-5737 *Bureau of Labor & Industries* 1400 SW 5th Ave ... Portland OR 97201-5530
Fax: 503 229-6377
503 229-5895 *Center for Health Statistics* 1400 SW 5th Ave ... Portland OR 97201-5530
Fax: 503 229-6702
503 378-4732 *Consumer Affairs Div* 100 Justice Bldg ... Salem OR 97310-0001
Fax: 503 373-7067
503 378-2467 *Corrections Div* 2575 Center St NE ... Salem OR 97310-0001
Fax: 503 373-1173
503 378-4152 *Department of Agriculture* 635 Capitol St NE ... Salem OR 97310-0001
Fax: 503 378-5529
503 373-1205 *Department of Economic Development* 775 Summer St NE ... Salem OR 97310-0001
Fax: 503 581-5115
503 378-3573 *Department of Education* 700 Pringle Pkwy SE ... Salem OR 97310-0001
Fax: 503 373-7968
503 378-4040 *Department of Energy* 625 Marion St NE ... Salem OR 97310-0001
Fax: 503 373-7806
503 229-5696 *Department of Environmental Quality* 811 SW 6th Ave ... Portland OR 97204-1334
Fax: 503 229-6124
503 378-4516 *Department of General Services* 1225 Ferry St SE ... Salem OR 97310-0001
503 229-5580 *Department of Geology & Mineral Industries*
1400 SW 5th Ave Rm 910 ... Portland OR 97201-5528
Fax: 503 229-5639
503 378-4100 *Department of Insurance & Finance*
21 Labor & Industries Bldg ... Salem OR 97310-0001
Fax: 503 378-6828
503 378-3363 *Department of Revenue* 955 Center St NE ... Salem OR 97310-0001
Fax: 503 378-8835
503 378-4329 *Department of the Treasury* 159 State Capitol ... Salem OR 97310-0001
Fax: 503 378-6772
503 378-6388 *Department of Transportation* Transportation Bldg ... Salem OR 97310-0001
Fax: 503 373-7376
503 378-4124 *Emergency Management Div* 603 Chemeketa St NE ... Salem OR 97310-0001
Fax: 503 588-1378
503 378-3211 *Employment Div* 875 Union St NE ... Salem OR 97311-0001
Fax: 503 373-7460
503 378-3121 *Executive Assistant to Governor* State Capitol Rm 254 ... Salem OR 97310-0001
Fax: 503 378-6075
503 378-3111 *Governor* State Capitol Rm 254 ... Salem OR 97310-0001
Fax: 503 378-6075
503 229-5913 *Hazardous & Solid Waste Div* 811 SW 6th Ave ... Portland OR 97204-1334
Fax: 503 229-6124
503 229-5806 *Health Div* 1400 SW 5th Ave ... Portland OR 97201-5530
Fax: 503 274-2524
503 378-6516 *Highway Div* Transportation Bldg Rm 102 ... Salem OR 97310-0001
Fax: 503 373-7770
503 378-4474 *Insurance Div* 21 Labor & Industries Bldg ... Salem OR 97310-0001
Fax: 503 378-4351
503 378-3548 *Natural Resources Dept* State Capitol Rm 160 ... Salem OR 97310-0001
Fax: 503 378-6075
503 373-0105 *Oregon State Correctional Institution* 3405 Deer Park Dr SE ... Salem OR 97310-0001
Fax: 503 378-8919
503 378-3349 *Public Defender* 1655 State St ... Salem OR 97310-0001
503 378-6611 *Public Utility Commission* 351 W Summer St NE ... Salem OR 97310-0001
Fax: 503 373-7752
503 378-4643 *Purchasing Div* 1225 Ferry St SE ... Salem OR 97310-0001
Fax: 503 373-7210
503 378-4170 *Real Estate Agency* 158 12th St NE ... Salem OR 97310-0001
Fax: 503 373-7153
503 378-4139 *Secretary of State* 136 State Capitol ... Salem OR 97310-0001
Fax: 503 373-7414
503 378-4387 *Security Section* 21 Labor & Industries Bldg Rm 130 ... Salem OR 97310-0000
Fax: 503 378-4178
503 378-2445 *State Penitentiary* 2605 State St ... Salem OR 97310-0001
Fax: 503 378-3897
503 378-3720 *State Police* Public Service Bldg Rm 107 ... Salem OR 97310-0001
Fax: 503 363-5475
503 346-5794 *State System of Higher Education* PO Box 3175 ... Eugene OR 97403-0175
Fax: 503 346-5764
503 378-6005 *Supreme Court* 1163 State St ... Salem OR 97310-0001
503 378-2982 *Water Resources Dept* 3850 Portland Rd NE ... Salem OR 97310-0001
Fax: 503 378-8130
503 378-3304 *Workers' Compensation Div*
21 Labor & Industries Bldg Rm 210 ... Salem OR 97310-0001
Fax: 503 378-6828
503 378-4243 **Oregon State Library** State Library Bldg ... Salem OR 97301-2477
Fax: 503 588-7119
503 346-5711 **Oregon State System of Higher Education** PO Box 3175 ... Eugene OR 97403-0175
Fax: 503 686-5764
503 737-0123 **Oregon State University** ... Corvallis OR 97331-0000
Fax: 503 754-2400
503 737-2331 *College of Agricultural Sciences* Strand Ag Hall Rm 126 ... Corvallis OR 97331-0000
Fax: 503 737-3178
503 737-4525 *College of Engineering* Covell Hall Rm 101 ... Corvallis OR 97331-0000
Fax: 503 737-3462
503 737-3725 *College of Pharmacy* Pharmacy Bldg Rm 203 ... Corvallis OR 97331-0000
Fax: 503 737-3999
503 737-4511 *Department of Biochemistry & Biophysics*
Weniger Hall Rm 535 ... Corvallis OR 97331-6503
Fax: 503 737-0481
503 737-4441 *Department of Microbiology* Nash Hall Rm 220 ... Corvallis OR 97331-3804
Fax: 503 737-0496
503 373-1200 **Oregon Tourism Div** 775 Summer St NE ... Salem OR 97310-0001
Fax: 503 581-5115
202 785-6323 **Organization for Economic Cooperation & Development**
2001 L St NW Suite 700 ... Washington DC 20036-4910
Fax: 202 785-0350
202 458-3000 **Organization of American States** 1889 F St NW ... Washington DC 20006-4413
Fax: 202 458-3967
312 702-9520 **Oriental Institute Museum**
1155 E 58th St University of Chicago ... Chicago IL 60637-1570
Fax: 312 702-9853
407 628-5870 **Orlando College** 5500 Diplomat Cir ... Orlando FL 32810-5674
Fax: 407 628-1344
407 896-4231 **Orlando Museum of Art** 2416 N Mills Ave ... Orlando FL 32803-1426
Fax: 407 894-4314
407 646-4111 **Orlando Naval Training Center** ... Orlando FL 32808-8067
407 896-7151 **Orlando Science Center** 810 E Rollins St ... Loch Haven Park FL 32803-1291
Fax: 407 896-3561
716 589-4457 **Orleans County** Courthouse Sq ... Albion NY 14411-0000
802 334-2711 **Orleans County** PO Box 787 ... Newport VT 05855-0787
504 565-6580 **Orleans Parish** 1300 Perdido St ... New Orleans LA 70112-2112
Fax: 504 565-6588
202 225-7742 **Ortiz Solomon P (Rep - D - Texas)** 1524 Longworth Bldg ... Washington DC 20515-0001
Fax: 202 226-1134
202 225-7751 **Orton Bill (Rep - D - Utah)** 1723 Longworth Bldg ... Washington DC 20515-0001
Fax: 202 226-1223
913 828-4812 **Osage County** PO Box 226 ... Lyndon KS 66451-0226
314 897-2139 **Osage County** Main St ... Linn MO 65051-0000
918 287-2615 **Osage County** PO Box 87 ... Pawhuska OK 74056-0087
913 346-2431 **Osborne County** 423 W Main St ... Osborne KS 67473-2302
407 847-1300 **Osceola County** 12 S Vernon Ave ... Kissimmee FL 34741-5188
712 754-3595 **Osceola County** 614 5th Ave ... Sibley IA 51249-1704
616 832-5818 **Osceola County** 301 W Upton Ave ... Reed City MI 49677-1149
517 826-3241 **Oscoda County** 311 Morenci ... Mio MI 48647-0000
Fax: 517 826-3657
202 523-8148 **OSHA (Occupational Safety & Health Administration)**
200 Constitution Ave NW Rm N3647 ... Washington DC 20210-0001
Fax: 202 523-7312
414 236-5150 **Oshkosh Public Museum** 1331 Algoma Blvd ... Oshkosh WI 54901-2799
717 823-0156 **Osterhout Free Library** 71 S Franklin St ... Wilkes-Barre PA 18701-1287
Fax: 717 823-5477
315 349-3400 **Oswego County** 46 E Bridge St ... Oswego NY 13126-2123
719 384-8701 **Otero County** PO Box 511 ... La Junta CO 81050-0000
505 437-7427 **Otero County** PO Box 1749 ... Alamogordo NM 88311-1749
Fax: 505 437-6542
719 384-8721 **Otero Junior College** 18th & Colorado Ave ... La Junta CO 81050-0000
Fax: 719 384-6880
213 251-0505 **Otis Art Institute of Parsons School of Design**
2401 Wilshire Blvd ... Los Angeles CA 90057-3398
Fax: 213 480-0059
402 873-3586 **Otoe County** PO Box 249 ... Nebraska City NE 68410-0249
517 732-6484 **Otsego County** 225 W Main St ... Gaylord MI 49735-1348
607 547-4276 **Otsego County** 197 Main St ... Cooperstown NY 13326-1129
913 392-2279 **Ottawa County** 307 N Concord St ... Minneapolis KS 67467-2140
616 846-8310 **Ottawa County** 414 Washington St ... Grand Haven MI 49417-1473
Fax: 616 846-8115
419 734-6700 **Ottawa County** 315 Madison St Rm 103 ... Port Clinton OH 43452-1936
918 542-9408 **Ottawa County** County Courthouse ... Miami OK 74354-0000
602 371-1188 **Ottawa University** 2340 W Mission Ln ... Phoenix AZ 85021-2818
913 242-5200 **Ottawa University** 10th & Cedar Sts ... Ottawa KS 66067-0000
Fax: 913 242-7429
218 739-2271 **Otter Tail County** Junius Ave County Courthouse ... Fergus Falls MN 56537-0000
614 890-3000 **Otterbein College** 100 W Home St ... Westerville OH 43081-1495
Fax: 614 898-1512
501 246-4531 **Ouachita Baptist University** 410 Ouachita St ... Arkadelphia AR 71923-3200
Fax: Ext 588
501 836-4116 **Ouachita County** 145 Jefferson St ... Camden AR 71701-0000
318 323-5188 **Ouachita Parish** 300 Saint John St ... Monroe LA 71201-7398
318 387-1950 **Ouachita Parish Public Library** 1800 Stubbs Ave ... Monroe LA 71201-5787
504 394-7744 **Our Lady of Holy Cross College** 4123 Woodland Dr ... New Orleans LA 70131-7399
512 434-6711 **Our Lady of the Lake University of San Antonio**
411 SW 24th St ... San Antonio TX 78207-4666
Fax: 512 436-0824
303 325-4961 **Ouray County** 541 4th St ... Ouray CO 81427-0000
414 832-5077 **Outagamie County** 410 S Walnut St ... Appleton WI 54911-5936
203 661-0797 **Outward Bound USA** 384 Field Point Rd ... Greenwich CT 06830-7098
Fax: 203 661-0903
202 234-8701 **Overseas Development Council**
1717 Massachusetts Ave NW Suite 501 ... Washington DC 20036-2061
Fax: 202 745-0067
202 457-7010 **Overseas Private Investment Corp** 1615 M St NW ... Washington DC 20527-0001
Fax: 202 331-4234
605 677-5228 **Overstate WH Museum** 414 E Clark St ... Vermillion SD 57069-2307
615 823-5630 **Overton County** County Courthouse Annex University St ... Livingston TN 38570-0000
812 829-2325 **Owen County** County Courthouse ... Spencer IN 47460-0000
502 484-3405 **Owen County** County Courthouse ... Owenton KY 40359-0000
202 225-6231 **Owens Major R (Rep - D - New York)** 114 Cannon Bldg ... Washington DC 20515-0001
Fax: 202 226-0112
419 666-0580 **Owens Technical College** Oregon Rd ... Toledo OH 43699-0000
Fax: 419 666-4178
202 225-3011 **Owens Wayne (Rep - D - Utah)** 1728 Longworth Bldg ... Washington DC 20515-0001
Fax: 202 225-3524
606 593-5735 **Owsley County** 154 Main St ... Booneville KY 41314-0000
208 495-2421 **Owyhee County** PO Box 128 ... Murphy ID 83650-0128
Fax: 208 495-2806

617 482-1211 **OXFAM-America** 115 Broadway .... Boston MA 02116-5400
Fax: 617 556-8910
207 743-6359 **Oxford County** PO Box 179 .... South Paris ME 04281-0179
202 225-2676 **Oxley Michael G (Rep - R - Ohio)** 2448 Rayburn Bldg .... Washington DC 20515-0001
Fax: Unlisted
805 488-0911 **Oxnard College** 4000 S Rose Ave .... Oxnard CA 93033-6699
Fax: 805 986-5806
805 984-4636 **Oxnard Public Library** 214 S 'C' St .... Oxnard CA 93030-5791
417 451-2057 **Ozark Bible Institute** 906 Summit .... Neosho MO 64850-1034
417 624-2518 **Ozark Christian College** 1111 N Main St .... Joplin MO 64801-1188
417 679-3516 **Ozark County** PO Box 416 .... Gainesville MO 65655-0416
501 442-6253 **Ozarks Regional Library** 217 E Dickson St .... Fayetteville AR 72701-4296
Fax: 501 442-6254
414 377-6400 **Ozaukee County** 121 W Main St .... Port Washington WI 53074-1813

P

212 346-1200 **Pace University** 1 Pace Plaza .... New York NY 10038-1598
Fax: 212 346-1643
212 346-1984 *Graduate School of Business* 1 Pace Plaza .... New York NY 10038-1598
Fax: 212 346-1933
914 773-3200 *Pleasantville-Briarcliff Campus* 861 Bedford Rd .... Pleasantville NY 10570-2799
Fax: 914 773-3541
914 422-4210 *School of Law* 78 N Broadway .... White Plains NY 10603-3796
Fax: 914 422-4139
914 422-4000 *White Plains Campus* 78 N Broadway .... White Plains NY 10603-3796
Fax: 914 422-4028 Admin
818 449-2742 **Pacific Asia Museum** 46 N Los Robles Ave .... Pasadena CA 91101-2071
714 879-3901 **Pacific Christian College** 2500 E Nutwood Ave .... Fullerton CA 92631-3199
Fax: 714 526-0231
714 599-6843 **Pacific Coast Baptist Bible College** 1100 S Valley Ctr .... San Dimas CA 91773-0000
206 875-9300 **Pacific County** PO Box 67 .... South Bend WA 98586-0067
408 372-4212 **Pacific Grove Museum of Natural History**
165 Forest Ave .... Pacific Grove CA 93950-2612
206 531-6900 **Pacific Lutheran University** .... Tacoma WA 98447-0001
Fax: 206 535-8320
503 226-4391 **Pacific Northwest College of Art** 1219 SW Park Ave .... Portland OR 97205-2430
Fax: 503 226-4842
415 848-0528 **Pacific School of Religion** 1798 Scenic Ave .... Berkeley CA 94709-1323
206 443-2001 **Pacific Science Center** 200 2nd Ave N .... Seattle WA 98109-4895
Fax: 206 443-3631
213 551-0304 **Pacific Southern University** 9581 W Pico Blvd .... Los Angeles CA 90035-0000
707 965-6311 **Pacific Union College** Howell Mountain Rd .... Angwin CA 94508-0000
Fax: 707 965-6390
503 357-6151 **Pacific University** 2043 College Way .... Forest Grove OR 97116-1797
Fax: 503 359-2242
503 359-2202 *College of Optometry* 2043 College Way .... Forest Grove OR 97116-1797
Fax: 503 359-2242
213 471-0306 **Pacific Western University** 600 N Sepulveda Blvd .... Los Angeles CA 90049-2108
Fax: 213 471-6456
202 225-3906 **Packard Ron (Rep - R - California)** 434 Cannon Bldg .... Washington DC 20515-0001
Fax: 202 225-0134
202 224-5244 **Packwood Bob (Sen - R - Oregon)** 259 Russell Bldg .... Washington DC 20510-0001
Fax: Unlisted
502 554-9200 **Paducah Community College** PO Box 7380 .... Paducah KY 42002-7380
Fax: 502 554-0330
712 542-3214 **Page County** 112 E Main St .... Clarinda IA 51632-2197
703 743-4142 **Page County** 108 S Court St .... Luray VA 22835-1289
602 645-2231 **Page Public Library** 697 Vista Ave .... Page AZ 86040-0000
Fax: 602 645-2788
203 777-3851 **Paier College of Art Inc** 6 Prospect Ct .... Hamden CT 06517-4025
404 722-4471 **Paine College** 1235 15th St .... Augusta GA 30910-0001
Fax: 404 724-6943
Pakistan: Islamic Republic of Pakistan
202 939-6200 *Embassy* 2315 Massachusetts Ave NW .... Washington DC 20008-2802
Fax: 202 387-0484
212 879-8600 *Mission to the UN* 8 E 65th St .... New York NY 10021-7005
Fax: 212 744-7348
202 225-4671 **Pallone Frank Jr (Rep - D - New Jersey)**
213 Cannon Bldg .... Washington DC 20515-0001
Fax: 202 225-9665
407 650-7700 **Palm Beach Atlantic College** PO Box 3353 .... West Palm Beach FL 33402-3353
Fax: 407 835-8342
407 439-8000 **Palm Beach Community College** 4200 Congress Ave .... Lake Worth FL 33461-4796
Fax: 407 439-8202
407 355-2754 **Palm Beach County** 301 N Olive Ave .... West Palm Beach FL 33401-4705
407 686-0895 **Palm Beach County Public Library System**
3650 Summit Blvd .... West Palm Beach FL 33406-4114
Fax: 407 686-8691
712 852-3603 **Palo Alto County** 11th & Broadway .... Emmetsburg IA 50536-0000
817 659-3651 **Palo Pinto County** PO Box 8 .... Palo Pinto TX 76072-0008
Fax: 817 659-2590
619 922-6168 **Palo Verde Community College** 811 W Chanslor Way .... Blythe CA 92225-1118
619 744-1150 **Palomar Community College** 1140 W Mission Rd .... San Marcos CA 92069-1487
Fax: 619 744-8123
919 249-1851 **Pamlico Community College** Hwy 306 S .... Grantsboro NC 28529-0000
919 745-3133 **Pamlico County** PO Box 776 .... Bayboro NC 28515-0776
Fax: 919 745-5514
202 458-3969 **Pan American Development Foundation**
1889 F St NW Suite 850 .... Washington DC 20006-4413
Fax: 202 458-6316
512 381-2011 **Pan American University** 1201 W University Dr .... Edinburg TX 78539-2999
Fax: 512 381-2150
202 634-6441 **Panama Canal Commission** 2000 L St NW Rm 550 .... Washington DC 20036-4996
Fax: 202 634-6439
212 421-5420 **Panama: Republic of Panama Mission to the UN**
866 UN Plaza Suite 544 .... New York NY 10017-0000
Fax: Unlisted
202 225-2861 **Panetta Leon E (Rep - D - California)** 339 Cannon Bldg .... Washington DC 20515-0001
Fax: Unlisted
806 656-2244 **Panhandle-Plains Historical Museum** 2401 4th Ave .... Canyon TX 79015-4143
Fax: 806 656-2250
903 693-2037 **Panola College** 1109 W Panola St .... Carthage TX 75633-2397
Fax: 903 693-2018
601 563-6205 **Panola County** 151 Public Sq .... Batesville MS 38606-2220
903 693-0302 **Panola County** Sabine & Sycamore Sts Rm 201 .... Carthage TX 75633-0000
Papua New Guinea
202 659-0856 *Embassy* 1330 Connecticut Ave NW Suite 350 .... Washington DC 20036-1711
Fax: 202 466-2412
212 682-6447 *Mission to the UN* 100 E 42nd St Rm 1005 .... New York NY 10017-5613
Fax: 212 682-6454
Paraguay: Republic of Paraguay
202 483-6960 *Embassy* 2400 Massachusetts Ave NW .... Washington DC 20008-2804
Fax: 202 234-4508

212 687-3490 *Mission to the UN* 211 E 43rd St Rm 1202 .... New York NY 10017-4778
Fax: 212 818-1282
301 492-5910 **Pardon Attorney (US Dept of Justice)**
5550 Friendship Blvd Rm 490 .... Chevy Chase MD 20815-7285
Fax: 301 492-5942
213 410-9732 **Parents Anonymous** 6733 S Sepulveda Blvd Suite 270 .... Los Angeles CA 90045-1525
903 785-7661 **Paris Junior College** 2400 Clarksville St .... Paris TX 75460-6298
Fax: 903 784-9370
816 741-2000 **Park College** 8700 NW River Park Dr .... Parkville MO 64152-4358
Fax: 816 741-4911
303 838-7509 **Park County** 501 Main St .... Fairplay CO 80440-0000
Fax: Call company operator
406 222-6120 **Park County** 414 E Callender St .... Livingston MT 59047-2799
Fax: 406 222-6726
307 587-5548 **Park County** 1002 Sheridan Ave .... Cody WY 82414-3590
303 457-2757 **Park's Junior College** 9065 Grant St .... Denver CO 80229-4339
Fax: 303 457-4030
317 569-5132 **Parke County** County Courthouse .... Rockville IN 47872-0000
817 594-7461 **Parker County** PO Box 819 .... Weatherford TX 76086-0819
202 225-5865 **Parker Mike (Rep - D - Mississippi)**
1504 Longworth Bldg .... Washington DC 20515-0001
Fax: 202 225-5886
304 485-6564 **Parkersburg & Wood County Public Library**
3100 Emerson Ave .... Parkersburg WV 26104-0000
217 351-2200 **Parkland College** 2400 W Bradley Ave .... Champaign IL 61821-1899
Fax: 217 351-2592 Admin
618 337-7500 **Parks College of Saint Louis University**
500 Falling Springs Rd .... Cahokia IL 62206-1203
Fax: 618 332-6802
806 481-3691 **Parmer County** 401 3rd St .... Farwell TX 79325-0000
406 657-8257 **Parmly Billings Library** 510 N Broadway .... Billings MT 59101-1126
Fax: 406 657-8293
301 492-5990 **Parole Commission (US Dept of Justice)**
5550 Friendship Blvd 4th Fl .... Chevy Chase MD 20815-7286
Fax: 301 492-6694
816 891-1395 *North Central Region*
10920 NW Ambassador Dr Suite 220 .... Kansas City MO 64153-1269
Fax: 816 891-1352
215 597-6365 *Northeast Region*
2nd & Chestnut Sts US Customs Rm 702 .... Philadelphia PA 19106-0000
Fax: 215 597-6376
214 767-0024 *South Central Region* 525 Griffin St Federal Bldg Suite 820 .... Dallas TX 75202-0000
Fax: 214 767-6259
404 347-4126 *Southeast Region* 1718 Peachtree St NW Suite 250 .... Atlanta GA 30309-2421
Fax: 404 347-7444
415 598-4800 *Western Region* 1301 Shoreway Rd 4th Fl .... Belmont CA 94002-4106
Fax: 415 876-9536
212 741-8900 **Parsons School of Design** 66 W 12th St .... New York NY 10011-8603
Fax: 212 929-2456
202 628-3300 **Partners of the Americas** 1424 K St NW Suite 700 .... Washington DC 20005-2410
Fax: 202 628-3306
818 578-7123 **Pasadena City College** 1570 E Colorado Blvd .... Pasadena CA 91106-2003
Fax: 818 449-2947
818 405-4041 **Pasadena Public Library** 285 E Walnut St .... Pasadena CA 91101-1556
Fax: 818 449-2165
713 477-0276 **Pasadena Public Library** 1201 Minerva St .... Pasadena TX 77506-4895
813 847-8190 **Pasco County** 7530 Little Rd .... New Port Richey FL 34654-5598
904 567-6701 **Pasco-Hernando Community College** 2401 County Rd 41 N .... Dade City FL 33525-7599
Fax: Call company operator
919 335-0865 **Pasquotank County** PO Box 39 .... Elizabeth City NC 27907-0039
201 881-4120 **Passaic County** 77 Hamilton St .... Paterson NJ 07505-2097
Fax: 201 742-7716
201 684-6800 **Passaic County Community College** 1 College Blvd .... Paterson NJ 07509-0000
Fax: 201 684-1925 Admin
202 647-0518 **Passport Services (US Dept of State)** 1425 K St NW .... Washington DC 20524-0001
617 565-6990 *Boston Agency* 10 Causeway St Rm 247 .... Boston MA 02222-1047
312 353-7155 *Chicago Agency* 230 S Dearborn St Suite 380 .... Chicago IL 60604-1503
808 541-1919 *Honolulu Agency*
300 Ala Moana Blvd New Federal Bldg Rm C106 .... Honolulu HI 96850-0001
713 653-3153 *Houston Agency* 1919 Smith St Suite 1100 .... Houston TX 77002-8051
213 209-7075 *Los Angeles Agency*
11000 Wilshire Blvd US Federal Bldg 13th Fl .... Los Angeles CA 90024-0000
305 536-4681 *Miami Agency* 51 SW 1st Ave 16th Fl .... Miami FL 33130-1680
504 589-6161 *New Orleans Agency* 701 Loyola Ave .... New Orleans LA 70113-1931
Fax: 504 589-4996
212 541-7700 *New York Agency* 630 5th Ave Rm 270 .... New York NY 10111-0002
215 597-7480 *Philadelphia Agency* 600 Arch St Suite 4426 .... Philadelphia PA 19106-1685
415 744-4010 *San Francisco Agency* 525 Market St Suite 200 .... San Francisco CA 94105-2773
206 442-7945 *Seattle Agency* 915 2nd Ave Rm 992 .... Seattle WA 98174-1001
203 325-3538 *Stamford Agency* 1 Landmark Sq .... Stamford CT 06901-2601
Fax: 203 967-3741
703 557-5168 **Patent & Trademark Office (US Dept of Commerce)** .... Washington DC 20231-0001
201 881-1060 **Paterson Free Public Library** 250 Broadway .... Paterson NJ 07501-2093
407 494-1110 **Patrick Air Force Base** .... Cocoa Beach FL 32925-0000
703 694-7213 **Patrick County** PO Box 148 .... Stuart VA 24171-0148
703 638-8777 **Patrick Henry Community College** PO Box 5311 .... Martinsville VA 24115-5311
Fax: 703 638-6469
205 575-3156 **Patrick Henry State Junior College** Hwy 21 S .... Monroeville AL 36460-0000
Fax: 205 575-3158 Ext 261
415 533-8300 **Patten College** 2433 Coolidge Ave .... Oakland CA 94601-2699
202 225-6030 **Patterson Elizabeth J (Rep - D - South Carolina)**
1641 Longworth Bldg .... Washington DC 20515-0001
Fax: 202 225-7664
301 863-3000 **Patuxent River Naval Air Station** NATC .... Patuxent River MD 20670-0000
Fax: 301 862-7580
804 562-2171 **Paul D Camp Community College** 100 College Dr N .... Franklin VA 23851-2422
Fax: 804 562-7430
817 753-6415 **Paul Quinn College** 1020 Elm St .... Waco TX 76704-2697
518 327-6211 **Paul Smiths College** Rts 30 & 192 .... Paul Smiths NY 12970-0000
Fax: 518 327-3030
404 445-8871 **Paulding County** 1 Courthouse Sq .... Dallas GA 30132-1401
Fax: 404 445-4627
419 399-8210 **Paulding County** County Courthouse .... Paulding OH 45879-0000
316 285-3721 **Pawnee County** 715 Broadway .... Larned KS 67550-3098
402 852-2962 **Pawnee County** County Courthouse .... Pawnee City NE 68420-0000
918 762-3741 **Pawnee County** County Courthouse .... Pawnee OK 74058-0000
401 725-3714 **Pawtucket Public Library & Regional Library Center**
13 Summer St .... Pawtucket RI 02860-2106
Fax: Unlisted
202 225-5265 **Paxon Bill (Rep - R - New York)** 1314 Longworth Bldg .... Washington DC 20515-0001
Fax: 202 225-5910
208 642-6000 **Payette County** PO Box D .... Payette ID 83661-0277
Fax: 208 642-6011
405 624-9300 **Payne County** 606 S Husband St .... Stillwater OK 74074-4044

202 225-3436 **Payne Donald M (Rep - D - New Jersey)**
417 Cannon Bldg ... Washington DC 20515-0001
Fax: 202 225-4160

202 225-4711 **Payne Lewis F (Rep - D - Virginia)** 1118 Longworth Bldg ... Washington DC 20515-0001
Fax: 202 226-1147

301 659-8100 **Peabody Conservatory of Music Johns Hopkins University**
1 E Mt Vernon Pl ... Baltimore MD 21202-2308
Fax: 301 685-0657

617 495-2248 **Peabody Museum of Archaeology & Ethnology**
11 Divinity Ave Harvard University ... Cambridge MA 02138-2096

203 432-3750 **Peabody Museum of Natural History**
170 Whitney Ave Yale University ... New Haven CT 06511-3748
Fax: 203 432-3134

508 745-1876 **Peabody Museum of Salem** East India Sq ... Salem MA 01970-3783
Fax: 508 744-6776

919 832-2881 **Peace College** 15 E Peace St ... Raleigh NC 27604-1194

202 606-3886 **Peace Corps** 1990 K St NW ... Washington DC 20526-0001
Fax: 202 254-4010

617 565-5555 *Boston Area Office* 10 Causeway St Rm 450 ... Boston MA 02222-1047

312 353-4990 *Chicago Area Office* 50 E Washington St Suite 300 ... Chicago IL 60602-2102

214 767-5435 *Dallas Area Office* PO Box 638 ... Dallas TX 75221-0638

202 254-7970 *DC Area Office* 1990 K St NW ... Washington DC 20526-0001

303 866-1057 *Denver Area Office* 1845 Sherman St Rm 103 ... Denver CO 80203-1166

313 226-7928 *Detroit Area Office* 477 Michigan Ave Rm M-74 ... Detroit MI 48226-0000

913 236-2700 *Kansas City Area Office* 5799 Broadmoor Suite 512 ... Mission KS 66202-2408

213 209-7444 *Los Angeles Area Office*
11000 Wilshire Blvd Suite 8104 ... West Los Angeles CA 90024-3670

305 536-5273 *Miami Area Office* 330 Biscayne Blvd Rm 420 ... Miami FL 33132-2242

612 334-4040 *Minneapolis Area Office* 330 2nd Ave S Rm 420 ... Minneapolis MN 55401-0000

212 264-6981 *New York Area Office* 90 Church St Rm 1317 ... New York NY 10007-2971
Fax: 212 264-6975

215 597-0744 *Philadelphia Area Office* 2nd & Chestnut St Rm 102-A ... Philadelphia PA 19106-2998

415 744-2677 *San Francisco Area Office* 211 Main St Rm 533 ... San Francisco CA 94105-1914
Fax: 415 744-2684

206 442-5490 *Seattle Area Office* 2001 6th Ave Suite 1776 ... Seattle WA 98121-2522

912 825-2535 **Peach County** 205 W Church St ... Fort Valley GA 31030-4155

301 396-1149 **Peale Museum** 225 Holliday St ... Baltimore MD 21202-3693
Fax: 301 962-8757

808 471-0373 **Pearl Harbor Naval Station** ... Pearl Harbor HI 96860-0001

601 795-6801 **Pearl River Community College** Hwys 26 & 11 Stn A ... Poplarville MS 39470-0000
Fax: 601 795-6815 Library

601 795-2237 **Pearl River County** PO Box 431 ... Poplarville MS 39470-0431

603 430-0100 **Pease Air Force Base** ... Portsmouth NH 03803-0000

202 225-3401 **Pease Donald J (Rep - D - Ohio)** 2410 Rayburn Bldg ... Washington DC 20515-0001
Fax: 202 225-0066

915 336-7555 **Pecos County** 103 W Callaghan St ... Fort Stockton TX 79735-7101

215 545-6400 **Peirce Junior College** 1420 Pine St ... Philadelphia PA 19102-4699
Fax: 215 546-5996

202 224-4642 **Pell Claiborne (Sen - D - Rhode Island)** 335 Russell Bldg ... Washington DC 20510-0001
Fax: 202 224-4680

615 694-6400 **Pellissippi State Technical Community College**
Hardin Valley Rd ... Knoxville TN 37933-0000
Fax: 615 694-6435

202 225-4965 **Pelosi Nancy (Rep - D - California)** 109 Cannon Bldg ... Washington DC 20515-0001
Fax: 202 225-8259

701 265-4275 **Pembina County** PO Box 357 ... Cavalier ND 58220-0357

919 521-4214 **Pembroke State University** College Terr ... Pembroke NC 28372-9693
Fax: 919 521-3877

314 333-4203 **Pemiscot County** Ward Ave ... Caruthersville MO 63830-0000
Fax: 314 333-0440

509 447-2435 **Pend Oreille County** PO Box 5000 ... Newport WA 99156-5000

919 259-1200 **Pender County** PO Box 5 ... Burgaw NC 28425-0005
Fax: 919 259-1248

606 654-4321 **Pendleton County** County Courthouse Sq ... Falmouth KY 41040-0000

304 358-2505 **Pendleton County** PO Box 89 ... Franklin WV 26807-0089

206 452-9277 **Peninsula College** 1502 E Lauridsen Blvd ... Port Angeles WA 98362-6698
Fax: 206 457-8100

415 349-5538 **Peninsula Library System** 25 Tower Rd ... Belmont CA 94002-4201
Fax: 415 349-5089

816 932-7600 **Penn Valley Community College** 3201 SW Trafficway ... Kansas City MO 64111-2727
Fax: 816 531-3374

218 681-2407 **Pennington County** PO Box 619 ... Thief River Falls MN 56701-0000

605 394-2575 **Pennington County** PO Box 230 ... Rapid City SD 57709-0230

202 724-9087 **Pennsylvania Avenue Development Corp**
1331 Pennsylvania Ave NW Suite 1220N ... Washington DC 20004-1703
Fax: 202 724-0246

717 787-5453 **Pennsylvania Bureau of Travel Marketing** 453 Forum Bldg ... Harrisburg PA 17120-0001
Fax: 717 234-4560

717 255-3252 **Pennsylvania Chamber of Business & Industry**
222 N 3rd St ... Harrisburg PA 17101-1502
Fax: 717 255-3298

215 276-6000 **Pennsylvania College of Optometry** 1200 W Godfrey Ave ... Philadelphia PA 19141-3323
Fax: 215 276-6082

717 326-3761 **Pennsylvania College of Technology** 1 College Ave ... Williamsport PA 17701-5778
Fax: 717 327-4503

717 238-9381 **Pennsylvania Democratic State Committee** 510 N 3rd St ... Harrisburg PA 17101-1112
Fax: 717 233-3472

215 565-7900 **Pennsylvania Institute of Technology** 800 Manchester Ave ... Media PA 19063-4036
Fax: 215 565-7909 Admin

717 234-4901 **Pennsylvania Republican Party** 112 State St ... Harrisburg PA 17101-1024
Fax: 717 231-3828

Pennsylvania State Government

717 787-2121 *Information* Transportation & Safety Bldg Rm B102 ... Harrisburg PA 17125-0001

717 787-3391 *Attorney General* 4th & Walnut Sts Strawberry Sq 16th Fl ... Harrisburg PA 17120-0001
Fax: 717 787-1190

717 787-5100 *Board of Probation & Parole* 3101 N Front St ... Harrisburg PA 17105-1661
Fax: 717 772-2157

717 787-9702 *Bureau of Air Quality Control*
101 S 2nd St Executive House Rm 116 ... Harrisburg PA 17120-0001
Fax: 717 772-2303

717 787-3051 *Bureau of Archives & History* PO Box 1026 ... Harrisburg PA 17108-1026
Fax: Unlisted

717 787-9707 *Bureau of Consumer Protection*
4th & Walnut Sts Strawberry Sq 14th Fl ... Harrisburg PA 17120-0001
Fax: 717 787-1190

717 787-5103 *Bureau of Mining & Reclamation* 2nd & Chestnut Sts ... Harrisburg PA 17105-2357
Fax: 717 783-4657

717 783-9645 *Bureau of Oil & Gas Management*
2nd & Chestnut Sts Executive House Rm 811 ... Harrisburg PA 17105-2357

717 787-4718 *Bureau of Purchases* Commonwealth Ave & North St ... Harrisburg PA 17125-0001
Fax: 717 783-6241

717 787-2480 *Bureau of Radiation Protection* 200 N 3rd St ... Harrisburg PA 17101-0000
Fax: 717 783-8965

717 787-4394 *Bureau of Real Estate* North Office Bldg Rm 505 ... Harrisburg PA 17125-0001
Fax: 717 787-9138

717 540-5080 *Bureau of Soil & Water Conservation*
1 Ararat Blvd Rm 214 ... Harrisburg PA 17110-9720
Fax: 717 540-5081

717 787-3547 *Bureau of Unemployment* 7th & Forster Sts ... Harrisburg PA 17121-0001
Fax: 717 783-2159

717 787-9870 *Bureau of Waste Management* 200 N 3rd St ... Harrisburg PA 17105-2063
Fax: 717 787-1904

717 783-5421 *Bureau of Workers' Compensation*
1171 S Cameron St Rm 103 ... Harrisburg PA 17104-2501

717 787-3003 *Commerce Dept* 433 Forum Bldg ... Harrisburg PA 17120-0001
Fax: 717 234-4560

717 787-6883 *Council on the Arts* 216 Finance Bldg ... Harrisburg PA 17120-0001
Fax: 717 787-8614

717 787-4737 *Department of Agriculture* 2301 N Cameron St ... Harrisburg PA 17110-9408
Fax: 717 787-2387

717 975-4860 *Department of Corrections* 2520 Lisburn Rd ... Camp Hill PA 17011-8005
Fax: 717 787-1758

717 787-5820 *Department of Education* 333 Market St ... Harrisburg PA 17126-0333
Fax: 717 783-4517

717 787-2814 *Department of Environmental Resources*
3rd & Locust Sts ... Harrisburg PA 17120-0001
Fax: 717 783-2802

717 787-6436 *Department of Health* 7th & Forster St ... Harrisburg PA 17120-0000
Fax: 717 783-3794

717 787-5173 *Department of Insurance* 1326 Strawberry Sq ... Harrisburg PA 17120-0001
Fax: 717 783-1059

717 787-3907 *Department of Labor & Industry*
7th & Forester Sts Rm 1700 ... Harrisburg PA 17120-0001
Fax: 717 787-5785

717 783-3680 *Department of Revenue*
4th & Walnut Sts Strawberry Sq 11th Fl ... Harrisburg PA 17128-0001
Fax: 717 787-3990

717 787-3154 *Department of Transportation*
Commonwealth Ave & Forster St ... Harrisburg PA 17120-0001
Fax: 717 787-5491

717 783-8150 *Emergency Management Agency*
Commonwealth Ave & Forster St Rm B-149 ... Harrisburg PA 17105-0000
Fax: 717 783-7393

717 783-9981 *Energy Office* 116 Pine St 2nd Fl ... Harrisburg PA 17101-1227
Fax: 717 783-2703

717 787-5295 *General Services Dept* North Office Bldg Rm 414 ... Harrisburg PA 17125-0001
Fax: 717 783-6241

717 787-2500 *Governor* Main Capitol Bldg Rm 225 ... Harrisburg PA 17120-0001
Fax: 717 787-7859

717 787-3300 *Lieutenant Governor* Main Capitol Bldg Rm 200 ... Harrisburg PA 17120-0001
Fax: 717 783-0150

717 787-6875 *Office of Highway Administration*
Commonwealth Ave & Forster St Rm 1220 ... Harrisburg PA 17120-0001
Fax: 717 787-5491

717 787-7095 *Office of Public Works* 18th & Herr Sts ... Harrisburg PA 17125-0001

717 787-4095 *Public Utility Commission*
Commonwealth Ave & North St North Office Bldg Rm B-18 Harrisburg PA 17120-0001
Fax: 717 787-0974

717 787-7630 *Secretary of the Commonwealth* N Office Bldg Rm 302 ... Harrisburg PA 17120-0001
Fax: 717 787-1734

717 787-8061 *Securities Commission*
1010 N 7th St Eastgate Office Bldg ... Harrisburg PA 17102-0000
Fax: 717 783-5122

717 737-4531 *State Correctional Institution* PO Box 200 ... Camp Hill PA 17011-0200
Fax: 717 783-7185

215 489-4151 *State Correctional Institution* PO Box 244 ... Graterford PA 19426-0244
Fax: 215 270-1859

717 783-3810 *State Health Data Center* Commonwealth Ave & Forster St Harrisburg PA 17120-0001

717 783-5561 *State Police* 1800 Elmerton Ave ... Harrisburg PA 17110-9758
Fax: 717 783-4384

215 560-6370 *Supreme Court* City Hall Rm 468 ... Philadelphia PA 19107-0000

717 787-2465 *Treasury Dept* Commonwealth Ave & North St Rm 129 ... Harrisburg PA 17120-0000
Fax: 717 783-9760

814 865-4700 **Pennsylvania State University** ... University Park PA 16802-0001

215 285-4811 *Allentown Campus* 6090 Mohr Ln Academic Bldg ... Fogelsville PA 18051-0000
Fax: 215 285-2535

814 949-5000 *Altoona Campus* 3000 Ivyside Park ... Altoona PA 16601-3794
Fax: 814 949-5011

412 773-3500 *Beaver Campus* Brodhead Rd ... Monaca PA 15061-0000
Fax: 412 773-3557

814 898-6000 *Behrend College* Station Rd ... Erie PA 16563-0001
Fax: 814 898-6461

215 320-4800 *Berks Campus* Tulpehocken Rd ... Reading PA 19610-0000
Fax: 215 320-4914

814 865-2541 *College of Agriculture*
201 Agricultural Administration Bldg ... University Park PA 16802-0001
Fax: 814 865-3103

814 863-3064 *College of Engineering* 101 Hammond Bldg ... University Park PA 16802-0001
Fax: 814 863-4749

814 865-1428 *College of Health & Human Development*
201 Henderson Bldg ... University Park PA 16802-0001
Fax: 814 865-3282

814 863-0327 *Commonwealth Educational System* 111 Old Main ... University Park PA 16802-0001
Fax: 814 865-3692

814 865-9505 *Computer Science Dept* 333 Whitmore Lab ... University Park PA 16802-0001
Fax: 814 865-3176

215 565-3300 *Delaware County Campus* 25 Yearsley Mill Rd ... Media PA 19063-5596
Fax: 215 892-0992

814 371-2800 *Du Bois Campus* College Pl ... Du Bois PA 15801-3199
Fax: 814 371-9260

412 430-4100 *Fayette Campus* Rt 119 N ... Uniontown PA 15401-0000
Fax: 412 430-4184 Admin

814 863-4170 *Graduate Dept of Biochemistry* 455 N Frear ... University Park PA 16802-0001

814 865-6553 *Graduate School of Chemistry* 152 Davey Laboratory . University Park PA 16802-0001
Fax: 814 865-3314

814 865-7394 *Graduate School of Geoscience* 303 Deike Bldg ... University Park PA 16802-0001
Fax: 814 865-3191

814 865-2538 *Graduate School of Molecular & Cell Biology*
455 N Frear ... University Park PA 16802-0001

717 948-6000 *Harrisburg Campus* Rt 230 ... Middletown PA 17057-0000
Fax: 717 948-6008

717 450-3000 *Hazleton Campus* Highacres ... Hazleton PA 18201-0000
Fax: 717 450-3182

814 865-6368 *Library* Pattee Library ... University Park PA 16802-0000
Fax: 814 865-3665

412 675-9000 *McKeesport Campus* University Dr ... McKeesport PA 15132-7698
Fax: 412 675-9043

717 531-8521 *Milton S Hershey Medical Center* 500 University Dr ... Hershey PA 17033-2360
Fax: 717 531-6094

717 749-3111 *Mont Alto Campus* ... Mont Alto PA 17237-0000
Fax: 717 749-3933

412 339-5466 *New Kensington Campus* 3550 7th Street Rd .... New Kensington PA 15068-1798
Fax: 412 339-5434
215 886-9400 *Ogontz Campus* 1600 Woodland Rd .... Abington PA 19001-3918
Fax: 215 886-3241
814 865-6597 *School of Communications* James Bldg Rm 302 .... University Park PA 16802-0001
Fax: 814 863-6134
814 863-0245 *School of Nursing*
201 Health & Human Development E .... University Park PA 16802-0001
Fax: 814 865-3779
717 385-6000 *Schuylkill Campus* 200 University Dr .... Schuylkill Haven PA 17972-2208
Fax: 717 385-6232 Library
412 983-5800 *Shenango Valley Campus* 147 Shenango Ave .... Sharon PA 16146-1537
Fax: 412 983-5863
717 675-2171 *Wilkes-Barre Campus* Huntsville Rd .... Lehman PA 18627-9999
Fax: 717 675-8308
717 963-4757 *Worthington-Scranton Campus* 120 Ridge View Dr .... Dunmore PA 18512-0000
Fax: 717 963-4783
717 771-4000 *York Campus* 1031 Edgecombe Ave .... York PA 17403-3326
Fax: 717 771-4062
202 225-2472 **Penny Timothy J (Rep - D - Minnesota)** 436 Cannon Bldg ... Washington DC 20515-0001
Fax: 202 225-0051
207 942-8535 **Penobscot County** 97 Hammond St .... Bangor ME 04401-4922
904 476-1387 **Pensacola Bible Institute** 1171 JoJo Rd .... Pensacola FL 32514-0000
904 433-1559 **Pensacola Historical Museum** 405 S Adams St .... Pensacola FL 32501-6003
904 484-1000 **Pensacola Junior College** 1000 College Blvd .... Pensacola FL 32504-8998
Fax: 904 484-1826
904 432-6247 **Pensacola Museum of Art** 407 S Jefferson St .... Pensacola FL 32501-5997
904 452-2311 **Pensacola Naval Air Station** .... Pensacola FL 32508-0000
Fax: 904 452-3699
202 778-8800 **Pension Benefit Guaranty Corp** 2020 K St NW .... Washington DC 20006-1860
Fax: 202 778-8819
202 467-4999 **People for the American Way** 2000 M St NW Suite 400 ..... Washington DC 20036-3315
Fax: 202 293-2672
719 632-0201 **Peoples Bible College** 2703 W Cucharras .... Colorado Springs CO 80904-0000
309 672-6059 **Peoria County** 324 Main St Rm 101 .... Peoria IL 61602-1319
309 672-8835 **Peoria Public Library** 107 NE Monroe St .... Peoria IL 61602-1070
Fax: 309 674-0116
715 672-8857 **Pepin County** 740 7th Ave W .... Durand WI 54736-1628
213 456-4000 **Pepperdine University** 24255 Pacific Coast Hwy .... Malibu CA 90263-0001
Fax: 213 456-4758
213 456-4211 *School of Communications* 24225 Pacific Coast Hwy .... Malibu CA 90263-0000
Fax: 213 456-4758
213 456-4611 *School of Law* 24255 Pacific Coast Hwy .... Malibu CA 90263-0001
Fax: 213 456-4266
415 466-7200 **Peralta Community College (System)** 333 E 8th St .... Oakland CA 94606-2889
Fax: 415 835-4078
202 225-4935 **Perkins Carl C (Rep - D - Kentucky)** 1004 Longworth Bldg .. Washington DC 20515-0001
Fax: 202 225-1411
308 352-4643 **Perkins County** PO Box 156 .... Grant NE 69140-0156
605 244-5626 **Perkins County** PO Box 27 .... Bison SD 57620-0027
202 225-4121 **Permanent Select Committee on Intelligence (US House of Representatives)**
H-405 US Capitol .... Washington DC 20515-0001
919 426-8484 **Perquimans County** PO Box 45 .... Hertford NC 27944-0045
205 683-6106 **Perry County** PO Box 505 .... Marion AL 36756-0505
501 889-5126 **Perry County** PO Box 358 .... Perryville AR 72126-0358
618 357-5116 **Perry County** Town Sq .... Pinckneyville IL 62274-0000
812 547-3741 **Perry County** 8th St .... Cannelton IN 47520-0000
606 436-4614 **Perry County** PO Box 150 .... Hazard KY 41702-0000
314 547-4242 **Perry County** 15 W Sainte Marie St .... Perryville MO 63775-1399
601 964-8398 **Perry County** PO Box 198 .... New Augusta MS 39462-0198
614 342-2045 **Perry County** 121 W Brown St .... New Lexington OH 43764-1241
Fax: 614 342-1097 Admin
717 582-2131 **Perry County** PO Box 37 .... New Bloomfield PA 17068-0037
Fax: 717 582-8570
615 589-2216 **Perry County** PO Box 16 .... Linden TN 37096-0016
702 273-2208 **Pershing County** PO Box 820 .... Lovelock NV 89419-0820
Fax: 702 273-7635
919 597-7228 **Person County** County Courthouse .... Roxboro NC 27573-0000
402 872-3815 **Peru State College** Park Ave .... Peru NE 68421-0000
Fax: 402 872-2375
Peru: Republic of Peru
202 833-9860 *Embassy* 1700 Massachusetts Ave NW .... Washington DC 20036-1903
Fax: 202 659-3660
212 687-3336 *Mission to the UN* 820 2nd Ave Suite 1600 .... New York NY 10017-4504
Fax: 212 972-6975
213 651-0296 *Los Angeles Consulate General*
6420 Wilshire Blvd Suite 1020 .... Los Angeles CA 90048-6310
Fax: 213 651-1264
804 733-2367 **Petersburg (Independent City)** Courthouse Hill .... Petersburg VA 23803-0000
719 554-7321 **Peterson Air Force Base** .... Colorado Springs CO 80914-0000
202 225-2165 **Peterson Collin C (Rep - D - Minnesota)**
1725 Longworth Bldg .... Washington DC 20515-0001
Fax: 202 225-1593
202 225-5235 **Peterson Pete (Rep - D - Florida)** 1415 Longworth Bldg ..... Washington DC 20515-0001
Fax: 202 225-1586
202 225-2476 **Petri Thomas E (Rep - R - Wisconsin)** 2245 Rayburn Bldg .. Washington DC 20515-0001
Fax: 202 225-2356
406 429-5311 **Petroleum County** 201 E Main .... Winnett MT 59087-0000
816 826-5395 **Pettis County** 415 S Ohio Ave .... Sedalia MO 65301-4496
704 463-7343 **Pfeiffer College** Hwy 52 N .... Misenheimer NC 28109-9999
Fax: Ext 2046
314 364-1891 **Phelps County** 3rd & Rolla Sts .... Rolla MO 65401-0000
308 995-4469 **Phelps County** 715 5th Ave .... Holdrege NE 68949-2256
Philadelphia City Government
215 686-1776 *City Clerk* Broad & Market Sts .... Philadelphia PA 19107-0000
215 686-5665 *City Hall* City Hall Rm 616 .... Philadelphia PA 19107-0000
215 686-3646 *City Representative's Office*
Municipal Services Bldg Rm 1660 .... Philadelphia PA 19102-0000
Fax: 215 686-8304
215 686-3410 *Clerk of Council* City Hall Rm 402 .... Philadelphia PA 19107-0000
215 686-4607 *Department of City Planning* 1515 Market St 17th Fl ...... Philadelphia PA 19107-0000
215 592-5985 *Fire Dept* 3rd & Spring Garden Sts .... Philadelphia PA 19123-0000
Fax: 215 922-3952 Admin
215 686-2250 *Mayor's Office* City Hall Rm 215 .... Philadelphia PA 19107-0000
Fax: 215 686-2555
215 231-3131 *Police Dept* 8th & Race Sts .... Philadelphia PA 19106-0000
215 580-4000 *SEPTA* 841 Chestnut St .... Philadelphia PA 19107-0000
215 686-2300 *Treasurer*
15th & JFK Blvd Municipal Services Bldg Rm 1430 .... Philadelphia PA 19102-0000
Fax: 215 988-0065
215 592-6300 *Water Dept* 101 N Broad St .... Philadelphia PA 19107-0000
Fax: 215 592-6154
215 752-5800 **Philadelphia College of Bible** 200 Manor Ave .... Langhorne PA 19047-2990
215 596-8800 **Philadelphia College of Pharmacy & Science**
43rd St & Woodland Ave .... Philadelphia PA 19104-0000
Fax: 215 895-1100
215 951-2700 **Philadelphia College of Textiles & Science**
4201 Henry Ave .... Philadelphia PA 19144-5409
Fax: 215 951-2615
215 686-1776 **Philadelphia County** Broad & Market Sts .... Philadelphia PA 19107-0000
215 763-8100 **Philadelphia Museum of Art**
26th & Benjamin Franklin Pkwy .... Philadelphia PA 19130-2399
Fax: 215 236-4465
215 897-5000 **Philadelphia Naval Shipyard** S Broad St .... Philadelphia PA 19112-0000
501 375-9845 **Philander Smith College** 812 W 13th St .... Little Rock AR 72202-3799
Fax: 501 372-5278
918 749-7941 **Philbrook Museum of Art** 2727 S Rockford Rd .... Tulsa OK 74114-4104
Fax: 918 743-4230
212 972-9326 **Philippine-American Chamber of Commerce**
711 3rd Ave 17th Fl .... New York NY 10017-4014
Philippines: Republic of the Philippines
202 483-1414 *Embassy* 1617 Massachusetts Ave NW .... Washington DC 20036-2209
Fax: 202 328-7614
212 764-1300 *Mission to the UN* 556 5th Ave 5th Fl .... New York NY 10036-5096
Fax: 212 840-8602
312 332-6458 *Chicago Consulate General* 30 N Michigan Ave Suite 2100 .... Chicago IL 60602-3605
Fax: Unlisted
213 387-5321 *Los Angeles Consulate General*
3660 Wilshire Blvd Suite 1200 .... Los Angeles CA 90010-2205
Fax: Unlisted
212 764-1330 *New York Consulate General* 556 5th Ave Philippine Ctr ..... New York NY 10036-5096
202 387-2151 **Phillips Collection** 1600 21st St NW .... Washington DC 20009-1090
Fax: 202 387-2436
501 338-5505 **Phillips County** 626 Cherry St .... Helena AR 72342-3306
303 854-3131 **Phillips County** 221 S Interocean Ave .... Holyoke CO 80734-1534
913 543-5513 **Phillips County** 3rd & State Sts .... Phillipsburg KS 67661-0000
Fax: 913 543-2244
406 654-2429 **Phillips County** County Courthouse .... Malta MT 59538-0000
501 338-6474 **Phillips County Community College** Campus Dr .... Helena AR 72342-0000
Fax: 501 338-7542
818 895-2220 **Phillips Junior College** 8520 Balboa Blvd .... Northridge CA 91325-3561
405 237-4433 **Phillips University** 102 S University Ave .... Enid OK 73701-6439
Fax: Unlisted
602 257-1222 **Phoenix Art Museum** 1625 N Central Ave .... Phoenix AZ 85004-1686
Phoenix City Government
602 262-6811 *City Clerk* 251 W Washington St Rm 410 .... Phoenix AZ 85003-0000
Fax: 602 495-5847
602 262-7029 *City Council* 251 W Washington St 9th Fl .... Phoenix AZ 85003-0000
Fax: 602 495-2036
602 262-6011 *City Hall* 251 W Washington St .... Phoenix AZ 85003-2201
Fax: 602 256-3325
602 262-6941 *City Manager* 251 W Washington St 9th Fl .... Phoenix AZ 85003-0000
Fax: 602 261-8327
602 495-5252 *Community & Economic Development* 1 N 1st St Suite 700 .. Phoenix AZ 85004-0000
Fax: 602 495-5097
602 262-6297 *Fire Dept* 520 W Van Buren St .... Phoenix AZ 85003-0000
Fax: 602 262-4429
602 262-7111 *Mayor's Office* 251 W Washington St 9th Fl .... Phoenix AZ 85003-0000
Fax: 602 261-8327
602 262-7131 *Planning Dept* 251 W Washington St 3rd Fl .... Phoenix AZ 85004-2342
Fax: 602 495-3793
602 262-6747 *Police Dept* 620 W Washington St .... Phoenix AZ 85003-0000
Fax: 602 495-5620
602 262-7251 *Public Works* 101 S Central Ave .... Phoenix AZ 85004-0000
Fax: 602 495-2095
602 262-6284 *Street Transportation Dept* 125 E Washington St 3rd Fl .... Phoenix AZ 85004-0000
Fax: 602 495-2106
602 262-6216 *Treasurer* 251 W Washington St 3rd Fl .... Phoenix AZ 85003-0000
Fax: 602 495-5605
602 264-2492 **Phoenix College** 1202 W Thomas Rd .... Phoenix AZ 85013-4234
Fax: 602 285-7700
602 262-6451 **Phoenix Public Library** 12 E McDowell Rd .... Phoenix AZ 85004-1684
Fax: 602 495-5841
202 707-5640 **Photoduplication Service (Library of Congress)**
101 Independence Ave SE LA G1009 .... Washington DC 20541-0000
Fax: 202 707-1771
217 762-9487 **Piatt County** 101 W Washington St .... Monticello IL 61856-1650
Fax: 217 762-7563
614 474-6093 **Pickaway County** 207 S Court St .... Circleville OH 43113-1601
205 367-2050 **Pickens County** PO Box 418 .... Carrollton AL 35447-0000
404 692-3556 **Pickens County** 211-1 N Main St .... Jasper GA 30143-0000
803 878-7809 **Pickens County** PO Box 215 .... Pickens SC 29671-0215
803 859-9679 **Pickens County Library** 110 W 1st Ave .... Easley SC 29640-2998
615 864-3879 **Pickett County** County Courthouse .... Byrdstown TN 38549-0000
202 225-4215 **Pickett Owen B (Rep - D - Virginia)** 1204 Longworth Bldg .. Washington DC 20515-0001
Fax: 202 225-4218
202 225-4865 **Pickle JJ (Rep - D - Texas)** 242 Cannon Bldg .... Washington DC 20515-0001
Fax: Unlisted
919 725-8344 **Piedmont Bible College** 716 Franklin St .... Winston-Salem NC 27101-5197
404 778-8033 **Piedmont College** .... Demorest GA 30535-0000
919 599-1181 **Piedmont Community College** PO Box 1197 .... Roxboro NC 27573-1197
Fax: 919 597-3817
803 223-8357 **Piedmont Technical College** PO Box 1467 .... Greenwood SC 29648-1467
Fax: 803 223-1405
804 977-3900 **Piedmont Virginia Community College** RR 6 Box 1-A ..... Charlottesville VA 22901-8714
Fax: 804 296-8395
206 964-6500 **Pierce College** 9401 Farwest Dr SW .... Tacoma WA 98498-1999
Fax: 206 964-6787
912 449-2022 **Pierce County** PO Box 679 .... Blackshear GA 31516-0679
701 776-6161 **Pierce County** 240 2nd St SE .... Rugby ND 58368-1830
402 329-4225 **Pierce County** 111 W Court St .... Pierce NE 68767-1224
206 591-7455 **Pierce County** 930 Tacoma Ave S .... Tacoma WA 98402-2108
Fax: 206 593-2521
715 273-3531 **Pierce County** PO Box 119 .... Ellsworth WI 54011-0119
Fax: 715 273-4047
206 572-6760 **Pierce County Rural Library District** 2356 Tacoma Ave S .... Tacoma WA 98402-1493
Fax: 206 272-6864
212 685-0008 **Pierpont Morgan Library** 29 E 36th St .... New York NY 10016-3490
205 566-6374 **Pike County** 120 W Church St .... Troy AL 36081-1913
501 285-2231 **Pike County** Washington St Courthouse Sq .... Murfreesboro AR 71958-0000
404 567-3406 **Pike County** PO Box 377 .... Zebulon GA 30295-0377
217 285-6812 **Pike County** Rt 36 .... Pittsfield IL 62363-0000
812 354-6025 **Pike County** Main St .... Petersburg IN 47567-0000
606 432-6240 **Pike County** PO Box 631 .... Pikeville KY 41501-0631
Fax: 606 432-6222
314 324-2412 **Pike County** 115 W Main St .... Bowling Green MO 63334-1693
601 783-3362 **Pike County** PO Box 309 .... Magnolia MS 39652-0309
614 947-2715 **Pike County** 100 E 2nd St .... Waverly OH 45690-1399
717 296-7613 **Pike County** 506 Broad St .... Milford PA 18337-1511
Fax: 717 296-6055

719 576-7711 **Pikes Peak Community College**
5675 S Academy Blvd ... Colorado Springs CO 80906-5498
Fax: 719 540-7614
719 473-2080 **Pikes Peak Library District** 20 N Cascade Ave ... Colorado Springs CO 80903-1694
Fax: 719 632-5744
606 432-9200 **Pikeville College** 214 Sycamore St ... Pikeville KY 41501-1194
Fax: 606 432-9372
508 746-1620 **Pilgrim Hall Museum** 75 Court St ... Plymouth MA 02360-3891
601 446-6631 **Pilgrimage Garden Club (Mississippi)** State & Canal Sts ... Natchez MS 39121-0000
507 451-2710 **Pillsbury Baptist Bible College** 315 S Grove ... Owatonna MN 55060-3097
Fax: 507 451-6459
912 743-7403 **Pilot Club International** 244 College St ... Macon GA 31213-0001
Fax: 912 743-2173
602 740-8011 **Pima County** 150 W Congress St ... Tucson AZ 85701-1333
602 884-6965 **Pima County Community College** 2202 W Anklam Rd ... Tucson AZ 85709-0001
Fax: 602 884-6290 Library
602 868-5801 **Pinal County** 100 N Florence ... Florence AZ 85232-9742
Fax: Unlisted
602 868-5801 **Pinal County Free Library** 574 S Central ... Florence AZ 85232-0000
Fax: 602 868-9749
612 629-6781 **Pine County** County Courthouse ... Pine City MN 55063-0000
617 731-7000 **Pine Manor College** 400 Heath St ... Chestnut Hill MA 02167-2332
Fax: 617 731-7199
215 282-4000 **Pinebrook Junior College** 600 S Main St ... Coopersburg PA 18036-2499
813 462-3000 **Pinellas County** 315 Court St ... Clearwater FL 34616-5165
Fax: 813 462-3118
405 321-1481 **Pioneer Library System** 225 N Webster ... Norman OK 73069-7133
Fax: 405 329-7189
612 235-3162 **Pioneerland Library System** 410 W 5th St ... Willmar MN 56201-0000
507 825-4494 **Pipestone County** 408 S Hiawatha Ave ... Pipestone MN 56164-1562
207 564-2161 **Piscataquis County** 51 E Main St ... Dover-Foxcroft ME 04426-1306
303 920-5180 **Pitkin County** 506 E Main St ... Aspen CO 81611-1993
Fax: 303 920-5198
919 355-4200 **Pitt Community College** Hwy 11 S ... Greenville NC 27835-0000
Fax: 919 355-4401
919 830-6302 **Pitt County** 1717 W 5th St ... Greenville NC 27834-1698
Fax: 919 830-6311
918 423-6865 **Pittsburg County** 2nd & Carl Albert ... McAlester OK 74501-0000
316 231-7000 **Pittsburg State University** 1701 S Broadway St ... Pittsburg KS 66762-5880
Fax: 316 232-7515 Admin
412 255-2100 **Pittsburgh City Hall** 414 Grant St ... Pittsburgh PA 15219-2404
Fax: 412 255-2438 Finance
804 432-2041 **Pittsylvania County** 1 S Main St ... Chatham VA 24531-9702
714 621-8129 **Pitzer College** 1050 N Mills Ave ... Claremont CA 91711-6101
Fax: 714 621-0518
801 577-2840 **Piute County** 21 N Main ... Junction UT 84740-0000
916 889-7983 **Placer County** 11960 Heritage Oak Pl Suite 15 ... Auburn CA 95604-5228
214 964-4208 **Plano Public Library System** 5024 Custer Rd ... Plano TX 75023-0000
Fax: 214 964-4210
813 254-1891 **Plant Henry B Museum** 401 W Kennedy Blvd ... Tampa FL 33606-1450
504 333-4343 **Plaquemines Parish** Hwy 39 ... Pointe a la Hache LA 70082-9999
Fax: 504 392-6690 Ext 3210
816 431-2232 **Platte County** PO Box 30CH ... Platte City MO 64079-0000
402 563-4904 **Platte County** 2610 14th St ... Columbus NE 68601-4929
307 322-3555 **Platte County** PO Box 728 ... Wheatland WY 82201-0728
Fax: 307 322-9571
308 632-6933 **Platte Valley Bible College** 305 E 16th St ... Scottsbluff NE 69361-3143
518 565-5000 **Plattsburgh Air Force Base** ... Plattsburgh NY 12903-0000
Fax: 518 565-6442 Personnel
304 684-7542 **Pleasants County** County Courthouse ... Saint Marys WV 26170-0000
916 283-6305 **Plumas County** PO Box 10207 ... Quincy CA 95971-0000
712 546-6100 **Plymouth County** 3rd Ave & 2nd St SE ... Le Mars IA 51031-0000
508 747-1350 **Plymouth County** PO Box 3535 ... Plymouth MA 02361-3535
Fax: 508 830-9280
603 536-5000 **Plymouth State College** 14 Plymouth St ... Plymouth NH 03264-0000
Fax: 603 536-1896 Library
712 335-4208 **Pocahontas County** Court Sq County Courthouse ... Pocahontas IA 50574-0000
304 799-4549 **Pocahontas County** 900C 10th Ave ... Marlinton WV 24954-1310
501 578-5408 **Poinsett County** Courthouse Sq ... Harrisburg AR 72432-0000
619 221-2200 **Point Loma Nazarene College** 3900 Lomaland Dr ... San Diego CA 92106-2810
Fax: 619 221-2579
805 989-1110 **Point Magu Naval Air Station** ... Point Magu CA 93042-0000
412 391-4100 **Point Park College** 201 Wood St ... Pittsburgh PA 15222-1983
504 638-9596 **Pointe Coupee Parish** PO Box 86 ... New Roads LA 70760-0086
Poland: Republic of Poland
202 234-3800 *Embassy* 2640 16th St NW ... Washington DC 20009-4202
Fax: 202 328-6271
212 744-2506 *Mission to the UN* 9 E 66th St ... New York NY 10021-5801
Fax: 212 517-6771
202 466-7820 **Police Executive Research Forum**
2300 M St NW Suite 910 ... Washington DC 20037-1434
Fax: 202 466-7826
202 395-7210 **Policy Coordination** 600 17th St NW Rm 517 ... Washington DC 20506-0001
Fax: 202 395-3911
312 384-3352 **Polish Museum of America** 984 N Milwaukee Ave ... Chicago IL 60622-4101
202 463-5482 **Polish-US Economic Council** 1615 H St NW 6th Fl ... Washington DC 20062-0001
Fax: 202 463-3114
813 294-7771 **Polk Community College** 999 Ave 'H' NE ... Winter Haven FL 33881-4299
Fax: 813 297-1065
501 394-6010 **Polk County** 507 Church Ave ... Mena AR 71953-3297
813 534-4000 **Polk County** 255 N Broadway Ave ... Bartow FL 33830-3912
404 749-2100 **Polk County** PO Box 268 ... Cedartown GA 30125-0268
515 286-3772 **Polk County** 500 Mulberry St ... Des Moines IA 50309-4238
218 281-5408 **Polk County** 612 N Broadway ... Crookston MN 56716-1452
Fax: 218 281-2204
417 326-4031 **Polk County** County Courthouse Rm 12 ... Bolivar MO 65613-0000
704 894-3301 **Polk County** PO Box 308 ... Columbus NC 28722-0308
402 747-5431 **Polk County** County Courthouse ... Osceola NE 68651-0000
503 623-9217 **Polk County** 850 Main St Rm 201 ... Dallas OR 97338-3116
Fax: 503 623-2060
615 338-4524 **Polk County** PO Box 128 ... Benton TN 37307-0158
409 327-8398 **Polk County** 101 W Church St ... Livingston TX 77351-3201
715 485-3161 **Polk County** 914 1st Ave N ... Balsam Lake WI 54810-0000
Fax: 715 485-3453
718 260-3600 **Polytechnic University** 333 Jay St ... Brooklyn NY 11201-2990
Fax: 718 260-3136
718 260-3590 *Dept of Electrical Engineering* 333 Jay St Rm 324 ... Brooklyn NY 11201-2990
Fax: 718 260-3136
718 260-3760 *Management Dept* 333 Jay St 2 Management Dept ... Brooklyn NY 11201-0000
Fax: 718 260-3136
714 621-8134 **Pomona College** 333 N College Way ... Claremont CA 91711-6301
Fax: Unlisted
714 620-2033 **Pomona Public Library** 625 S Garey Ave ... Pomona CA 91766-3322
406 278-7681 **Pondera County** 20 4th Ave SW ... Conrad MT 59425-2340
614 885-5585 **Pontifical College Josephinum** 7625 N High St ... West Worthington OH 43235-1444
Fax: 614 885-2307

601 489-3900 **Pontotoc County** PO Box 209 ... Pontotoc MS 38863-0209
405 332-1425 **Pontotoc County** 13th & Broadway ... Ada OK 74820-0000
816 232-8471 **Pony Express Museum** 914 Penn St ... Saint Joseph MO 64503-2544
919 394-0001 **Pope Air Force Base** ... Fayetteville NC 28308-0000
Fax: 919 486-2125
501 968-7487 **Pope County** 100 W Main St ... Russellville AR 72801-3740
618 683-4466 **Pope County** PO Box 216 ... Golconda IL 62938-0216
612 634-5301 **Pope County** 130 Minnesota Ave E ... Glenwood MN 56334-1628
804 868-7151 **Poquoson (Independent City)** 830 Poquoson Ave ... Poquoson VA 23662-1797
206 457-4401 **Port Angeles Coast Guard Air Station** ... Port Angeles WA 98362-0000
216 297-3644 **Portage County** PO Box 1035 ... Ravenna OH 44266-0000
715 346-1351 **Portage County** 1516 Church St ... Stevens Point WI 54481-3598
Fax: 715 346-1591
216 527-4378 **Portage County District Library** 10482 South St ... Garrettsville OH 44231-1116
Fax: Unlisted
219 465-3400 **Porter County** 16 E Lincolnway ... Valparaiso IN 46383-5698
Fax: 219 462-7558
219 462-0524 **Porter County Public Library System** 103 Jefferson St ... Valparaiso IN 46383-4820
Fax: 219 477-4867
202 225-4835 **Porter John Edward (Rep - R - Illinois)**
1026 Longworth Bldg ... Washington DC 20515-0001
Fax: 202 225-0157
209 781-3130 **Porterville College** 900 S Main St ... Porterville CA 93257-5901
Fax: Ext 375
503 226-3161 **Portland City Hall** 1220 SW 5th Ave ... Portland OR 97204-1913
503 244-6111 **Portland Community College** 12000 SW 49th Ave ... Portland OR 97219-7197
Fax: 503 452-4947
503 228-9411 **Portland Metropolitan Chamber of Commerce**
221 NW 2nd Ave ... Portland OR 97209-3999
Fax: 503 228-5126
207 775-6148 **Portland Museum of Art** 7 Congress Sq ... Portland ME 04101-1119
Fax: 207 773-7324
207 775-3052 **Portland School of Art** 97 Spring St ... Portland ME 04101-3987
503 725-3000 **Portland State University** 724 SW Harrison St ... Portland OR 97201-3295
Fax: 503 725-4882
503 725-4045 *Department of Urban Studies & Planning* PO Box 751 ... Portland OR 97207-0751
Fax: 503 725-4882
804 393-8746 **Portsmouth (Independent City)** PO Box 820 ... Portsmouth VA 23705-0820
804 483-8595 **Portsmouth Coast Guard Support Center**
4000 Coast Guard Blvd ... Portsmouth VA 23703-2135
Fax: 804 483-8623
614 354-5688 **Portsmouth Public Library** 1220 Gallia St ... Portsmouth OH 45662-4185
804 393-8501 **Portsmouth Public Library** 601 Court St ... Portsmouth VA 23704-3607
Fax: 804 393-8973 Admin
Portugal: Republic of Portugal
202 328-8610 *Embassy* 2125 Kalorama Rd NW ... Washington DC 20008-1619
Fax: 202 462-3726
212 759-9444 *Mission to the UN* 777 3rd Ave 27th Fl ... New York NY 10017-1490
Fax: 212 355-1124
617 536-8740 *Boston Consulate General* 899 Boylston St 2nd Fl ... Boston MA 02115-3104
213 277-1491 *Los Angeles Consulate* 1801 Ave of the Stars Suite 400 ... Los Angeles CA 90067-5906
212 246-4580 *New York Consulate General* 630 5th Ave Suite 657 ... New York NY 10111-0100
Fax: 212 459-0190
812 838-1306 **Posey County** County Courthouse ... Mount Vernon IN 47620-0000
202 225-5201 **Poshard Glenn (Rep - D - Illinois)** 314 Cannon Bldg ... Washington DC 20515-0001
Fax: 202 225-1541
202 225-4054 **Post Office & Civil Service Committee (US House of Representatives)**
309 Cannon Bldg ... Washington DC 20515-0001
Fax: 202 225-0895
202 789-6800 **Postal Rate Commission** 1333 H St NW Suite 300 ... Washington DC 20268-0001
Fax: 202 789-6861
202 727-3685 **Postsecondary Education Div (US Dept of Education)**
2100 Martin Luther King Jr Ave SE Rm 400 ... Washington DC 20020-0000
304 788-3011 **Potomac State College** Fort Ave ... Keyser WV 26726-0000
Fax: 304 788-3934
913 457-3314 **Pottawatomie County** PO Box 187 ... Westmoreland KS 66549-0187
405 273-4305 **Pottawatomie County** 325 N Broadway St ... Shawnee OK 74801-6938
712 328-5604 **Pottawattamie County** 227 S 6th St ... Council Bluffs IA 51501-4209
814 274-8290 **Potter County** 227 N Main St ... Coudersport PA 16915-1686
605 765-9472 **Potter County** 201 S Exene St ... Gettysburg SD 57442-1598
806 379-2250 **Potter County** 511 S Taylor St ... Amarillo TX 79101-2432
406 436-2657 **Powder River County** Courthouse Sq ... Broadus MT 59317-0000
606 663-4390 **Powell County** Court St ... Stanton KY 40380-0000
406 846-3680 **Powell County** 409 Missouri Ave ... Deer Lodge MT 59722-1084
208 226-7611 **Power County** 543 Bannock Ave ... American Falls ID 83211-1200
Fax: 208 226-7612
515 623-5644 **Poweshiek County** 302 E Main St ... Montezuma IA 50171-0000
804 598-5600 **Powhatan County** 3834 Old Buckingham Rd ... Powhatan VA 23139-7019
501 256-3741 **Prairie County** PO Box 278 ... Des Arc AR 72040-0278
406 637-5575 **Prairie County** County Courthouse ... Terry MT 59349-0000
708 756-3110 **Prairie State College** 202 S Halsted St ... Chicago Heights IL 60411-1275
Fax: 708 755-2587
409 857-3311 **Prairie View A & M University** US Hwy 290 & FM 1098 ... Prairie View TX 77446-9999
Fax: 409 857-3928
316 672-5641 **Pratt Community College** Hwy 61 ... Pratt KS 67124-0000
Fax: 316 672-5288
316 672-7761 **Pratt County** 300 S Ninnescah St ... Pratt KS 67124-2733
Fax: 316 672-2902
718 636-3600 **Pratt Institute** 200 Willoughby Ave ... Brooklyn NY 11205-3899
Fax: 718 622-6174
718 636-3414 *Graduate Dept of City & Regional Planning*
65 Saint James St Higgins Hall Rm 112 ... Brooklyn NY 11205-3899
Fax: 718 622-6174
513 456-8160 **Preble County** 100 Main St ... Eaton OH 45320-0000
601 728-8151 **Prentiss County** PO Box 477 ... Booneville MS 38829-0477
803 833-2820 **Presbyterian College** 503 S Broad St ... Clinton SC 29325-2998
Fax: 803 833-8481
602 778-2090 **Prescott College** 220 Grove Ave ... Prescott AZ 86301-2990
Fax: 602 776-0724 Library
202 456-1414 **President of the US** 1600 Pennsylvania Ave NW ... Washington DC 20500-0001
Fax: 202 456-2883
202 395-4616 **President's Commission on Executive Exchange**
744 Jackson Pl NW ... Washington DC 20503-0001
Fax: 202 395-6989
202 395-4522 **President's Commission on White House Fellowships**
712 Jackson Pl NW ... Washington DC 20503-0001
Fax: 202 395-6179
202 653-5044 **President's Committee on Employment of People with Disabilities**
1111 20th St NW Rm 636 ... Washington DC 20036-3407
Fax: 202 653-7386
202 272-3421 **President's Council on Physical Fitness & Sports**
450 5th St NW Suite 7103 ... Washington DC 20001-2739
Fax: 202 504-2064
202 456-2100 **Presidential Press Secretary** 1600 Pennsylvania Ave NW ... Washington DC 20500-0001
Fax: 202 456-2883
915 729-4812 **Presidio County** 320 N Highland St ... Marfa TX 79843-0000

517 734-3288 **Presque Isle County** 151 E Huron Ave Rogers City MI 49779-1316
202 224-5842 **Pressler Larry (Sen - R - South Dakota)** 133 Hart Bldg Washington DC 20510-0001
Fax: 202 224-1630
304 329-0070 **Preston County** 101 W Main St Kingwood WV 26537-1121
606 886-3863 **Prestonburg Community College** 1 Burt Combs Dr Prestonburg KY 41653-0000
Fax: 606 886-8693
715 339-3325 **Price County** 100 N Lake Ave Phillips WI 54555-1221
202 225-1784 **Price David E (Rep - D - North Carolina)**
1406 Longworth Bldg Washington DC 20515-0001
Fax: 202 225-6314
804 392-5145 **Prince Edward County** PO Box 304 Farmville VA 23901-0304
804 733-2600 **Prince George County** 6400 Courthouse Rd Prince George VA 23875-2527
301 336-6000 **Prince George's Community College** 301 Largo Rd Largo MD 20772-2199
Fax: 301 808-0960
301 350-9700 **Prince George's County** 7911 Anchor St Landover MD 20785-4804
301 699-3500 **Prince George's County Memorial Library** 6532 Adelphi Rd Hyattsville MD 20782-2008
Fax: Unlisted
703 335-6045 **Prince William County** 9311 Lee Ave Manassas VA 22110-5598
703 361-8211 **Prince William Library** 8601 Mathis Ave Manassas VA 22111-0000
609 258-3000 **Princeton University** Princeton NJ 08544-0001
Fax: Unlisted
609 258-3788 *Art Museum* Princeton NJ 08544-0001
Fax: 609 258-5949
609 258-4116 *Department of Chemistry* Frick Laboratory Rm 121E Princeton NJ 08544-0001
Fax: 609 987-6746
609 258-5030 *Department of Computer Science*
Olden St Computer Science Bldg Princeton NJ 08544-0001
Fax: 609 258-1771
609 258-5807 *Department of Geological & Physical Sciences* Guyot Hall Princeton NJ 08544-0001
Fax: 609 258-1274
609 258-4403 *Graduate School of Physics*
Washington Rd 203 Jadwin Hall Princeton NJ 08544-0001
Fax: 609 258-1124
609 258-3180 *Library* 1 Washington Rd Princeton NJ 08540-0000
Fax: 609 258-4105
609 258-3741 *School of Architecture* Princeton NJ 08544-0001
Fax: 609 258-4740
609 258-4560 *School of Engineering & Applied Science* Engineering Quad Princeton NJ 08544-0001
Fax: 609 258-6744
609 258-4820 *Woodrow Wilson School of Public & International Affairs*
Robertson Hall Princeton NJ 08544-0001
Fax: 609 258-2809
618 374-2131 **Principia College** Elsah IL 62028-0000
Fax: 618 374-5158
212 557-3100 **Private Export Funding Corp** 280 Park Ave 4th Fl W New York NY 10017-1216
Fax: 212 687-9351
202 447-3037 **Procurement Div (US Dept of Agriculture)**
14th St & Independence Ave SW Rm 1575 Washington DC 20250-0001
Fax: 202 447-4529
202 501-8449 **Procurement Information (US Dept of Justice)**
601 David NW Suite 7100 Washington DC 20530-0001
Fax: 202 501-8090
202 377-5555 **Procurement Information Office (US Dept of Commerce)**
14th St & Constitution Ave NW Rm 6517 Washington DC 20230-0001
Fax: 202 377-0546
202 523-6445 **Procurement Information Office (US Dept of Labor)**
200 Constitution Ave NW Rm S5220 Washington DC 20210-0001
Fax: 202 523-6853
202 343-2105 **Procurement Information Office (US Dept of the Interior)**
1849 C St MS-2626 Washington DC 20240-0001
202 566-2586 **Procurement Information Office (US Dept of the Treasury)**
1500 Pennsylvania Ave NW Rm 6101 Washington DC 20220-0001
Fax: 202 786-8455
202 233-3808 **Procurement Office (US Dept of Veterans Affairs)**
810 Vermont Ave NW Rm 760 Washington DC 20420-0001
Fax: 202 233-4801
202 366-4953 **Procurement Operations Div (US Dept of Transportation)**
400 7th St SW Rm 9413 Washington DC 20590-0001
Fax: 202 472-4762
202 586-1370 **Procurement Operations Office (US Dept of Energy)**
1000 Independence Ave SW Rm 1-I 066 Washington DC 20585-0001
Fax: 202 586-3175
202 633-3435 **Professional Responsibility Fraud Hotline (US Dept of Justice)**
10th St & Constitution Ave NW Washington DC 20530-0001
Fax: Unlisted
401 865-1000 **Providence College** River Ave Providence RI 02918-0001
Fax: Unlisted
401 277-3220 **Providence County** 250 Benefit St Providence RI 02903-2700
401 455-8000 **Providence Public Library** 225 Washington St Providence RI 02903-3228
Fax: 401 455-8089
801 224-3636 **Provo/Orem Chamber of Commerce** 777 S State Orem UT 84058-6307
719 336-9001 **Prowers County** 301 S Main St Lamar CO 81052-2857
202 224-2353 **Pryor David (Sen - D - Arkansas)** 267 Russell Bldg Washington DC 20510-0001
Fax: 202 224-8261
202 755-0950 **Public & Indian Housing (US Dept of Housing & Urban Development)**
451 7th St SW Rm 4100 Washington DC 20410-0001
202 872-1790 **Public Affairs Council** 1019 19th St NW Suite 200 Washington DC 20036-5105
Fax: Unlisted
202 732-4576 **Public Affairs Information Branch (US Dept of Education)**
400 Maryland Ave SW Rm 2089 Washington DC 20202-0001
Fax: 202 732-3130
202 447-5197 **Public Affairs Office (US Dept of Agriculture)**
14th St & Independence Ave SW Rm 201-A Washington DC 20250-0001
Fax: 202 382-6191
202 377-4901 **Public Affairs Office (US Dept of Commerce)**
14th St & Constitution Ave NW Rm 5058 Washington DC 20230-0001
Fax: 202 377-2095
202 245-1850 **Public Affairs Office (US Dept of Health & Human Services)**
200 Independence Ave SW Rm 647D Washington DC 20201-0001
Fax: 202 245-2247
202 755-6980 **Public Affairs Office (US Dept of Housing & Urban Development)**
451 7th St SW Rm 10132 Washington DC 20410-0001
Fax: 202 755-0353
202 633-2007 **Public Affairs Office (US Dept of Justice)**
10th St & Constitution Ave NW Rm 1218 Washington DC 20530-0001
Fax: 202 633-5331
202 647-9606 **Public Affairs Office (US Dept of State)**
2201 C St NW Rm 6800 Washington DC 20520-0001
Fax: 202 647-0244
202 343-6416 **Public Affairs Office (US Dept of the Interior)**
1849 C St NW MS-7013 Washington DC 20240-0001
Fax: 202 343-5048
202 566-2041 **Public Affairs Office (US Dept of the Treasury)**
1500 Pennsylvania Ave NW Rm 2315 Washington DC 20220-0001
Fax: 202 786-8433
202 233-2817 **Public Affairs Office (US Dept of Veterans Affairs)**
810 Vermont Ave NW Rm 900 Washington DC 20420-0001
Fax: 202 376-8778
202 293-9142 **Public Citizen** 2000 P St NW Suite 700 Washington DC 20036-5915
Fax: Unlisted
202 697-5737 **Public Communications Office (US Dept of Defense)**
Pentagon Rm 2E-777 Washington DC 20310-0001
202 245-7694 **Public Health Service (US Dept of Health & Human Services)**
200 Independence Ave SW Rm 716G Washington DC 20201-0001
Fax: 202 245-6274
Public Health Service
404 639-3311 *Agency for Toxic Substances & Disease* 1600 Clifton Rd NE Atlanta GA 30333-0000
Fax: 404 639-3030
301 443-3783 *Alcohol Drug Abuse & Mental Health Administration*
5600 Fishers Ln Rm 12C-15 Rockville MD 20857-0001
Fax: 301 443-1719
404 639-3311 *Centers for Disease Control* 1600 Clifton Rd NE Atlanta GA 30329-4018
Fax: 404 639-3030
301 496-4461 *National Institutes of Health* 9000 Rockville Pike Rm 344 Bethesda MD 20892-0001
Fax: 301 496-0017
617 565-1420 *Region 1* JFK Federal Bldg Government Ctr Rm 1400 Boston MA 02203-0000
Fax: 617 565-3044
212 264-2560 *Region 2* 26 Federal Plaza Rm 3337 New York NY 10278-0004
Fax: 212 264-1324
215 596-6637 *Region 3* 3535 Market St Rm 10140 Philadelphia PA 19104-3309
Fax: 215 596-6660
404 331-2316 *Region 4* 101 Marietta Tower Suite 1106 Atlanta GA 30323-0001
Fax: 404 841-2056
312 353-1385 *Region 5* 105 W Adams St 17th Fl Chicago IL 60603-4102
Fax: 312 353-1194
214 767-3879 *Region 6* 1200 Main Tower Bldg Rm 1800 Dallas TX 75202-0000
Fax: 214 767-0404
816 426-3291 *Region 7* 601 E 12th St Rm 501 Kansas City MO 64106-2808
Fax: 816 426-2178
303 844-4461 *Region 8* 1961 Stout St Rm 489 Denver CO 80294-0101
Fax: 303 844-6117
415 556-5810 *Region 9* 50 United Nations Plaza Rm 327 San Francisco CA 94102-4920
Fax: 415 556-3436
206 442-0430 *Region 10* 2201 6th Ave MS RX-20 Seattle WA 98121-0000
Fax: 206 442-0757
517 755-0904 **Public Libraries of Saginaw** 505 Janes St Saginaw MI 48605-0000
Fax: 517 755-1125
301 222-7371 **Public Library of Annapolis & Ann Arundel County**
5 Harry S Truman Pkwy Annapolis MD 21401-0000
Fax: 301 222-7188
205 237-8501 **Public Library of Anniston & Calhoun County** 108 E 10th St Anniston AL 36201-5662
Fax: 205 238-0474
704 336-2725 **Public Library of Charlotte & Mecklenburg County**
310 N Tryon St Charlotte NC 28202-2176
Fax: 704 336-2002
513 369-6000 **Public Library of Cincinnati & Hamilton County** 800 Vine St Cincinnati OH 45202-2009
Fax: Unlisted
515 283-4152 **Public Library of Des Moines** 100 Locust St Des Moines IA 50308-0000
Fax: 515 283-4503
614 282-9782 **Public Library of Steubenville & Jefferson County**
407 S 4th St Steubenville OH 43952-2996
Fax: 614 282-2919
216 744-8636 **Public Library of Youngstown & Mahoning County**
305 Wick Ave Youngstown OH 44503-1079
Fax: Unlisted
616 456-3977 **Public Museum of Grand Rapids** 54 Jefferson St SE Grand Rapids MI 49503-4383
Fax: 616 456-3873
202 626-2400 **Public Technology Inc**
1301 Pennsylvania Ave NW Suite 800 Washington DC 20004-1793
Fax: 202 626-2498
202 225-4472 **Public Works & Transportation Committee (US House of Representatives)**
2165 Rayburn Bldg Washington DC 20515-0001
Fax: 202 226-0921
719 543-3550 **Pueblo County** 215 W 10th St Pueblo CO 81003-2945
602 495-0900 **Pueblo Grande Museum** 4619 E Washington St Phoenix AZ 85034-1909
719 543-9600 **Pueblo Library District** 100 E Abriendo Ave Pueblo CO 81004-4290
Fax: 719 543-9610
206 775-8686 **Puget Sound Christian College** 410 4th Ave N Edmonds WA 98020-3171
206 476-3711 **Puget Sound Naval Shipyard** Bremerton WA 98314-0001
206 526-3444 **Puget Sound Naval Station** Seattle WA 98115-6348
Fax: 206 526-3655
501 372-8305 **Pulaski County** 401 W Markham St Little Rock AR 72201-1417
912 783-4154 **Pulaski County** PO Box 29 Hawkinsville GA 31036-0029
618 748-9360 **Pulaski County** PO Box 218 Mound City IL 62963-0218
219 946-3313 **Pulaski County** 112 E Main St Winamac IN 46996-1344
606 679-2042 **Pulaski County** PO Box 724 Somerset KY 42501-0724
314 774-6609 **Pulaski County** Waynesville Sq Waynesville MO 65583-0000
703 980-8888 **Pulaski County** 45 3rd St NW Pulaski VA 24301-5007
317 494-4600 **Purdue University** West Lafayette IN 47907-0000
Fax: 317 494-0544
219 844-0520 *Calumet Campus* 2233 171st St Hammond IN 46323-2094
Fax: 219 989-2581
317 494-3429 *Communication Dept* 304 Heavilon Hall West Lafayette IN 47907-0001
317 494-4191 *Department of Agriculture* Krannert Bldg West Lafayette IN 47907-1924
Fax: 317 494-4333
317 494-4408 *Department of Biological Sciences*
Lilly Hall of Life Sciences West Lafayette IN 47907-0001
Fax: 317 494-0876
317 494-5200 *Department of Chemistry* Brown Bldg Rm 2100 West Lafayette IN 47907-0001
Fax: 317 494-0239
317 494-3258 *Department of Earth & Atmoshpheric Sciences*
Civil Engineering Bldg Rm 2169 West Lafayette IN 47907-0001
Fax: 317 494-0776
219 785-5200 *North Central Campus* 1401 S US Hwy 421 Westville IN 46391-9528
Fax: 219 785-5355
219 989-2388 *School of Business* Management Dept Hammond IN 46323-0000
Fax: 219 989-2581
317 494-1357 *School of Pharmacy* Pharmacy Bldg West Lafayette IN 47907-0000
Fax: 317 494-7880
317 494-7608 *School of Veterinary Medicine* Lynn Hall West Lafayette IN 47907-1927
Fax: 317 494-0781
317 494-5345 *Schools of Engineering*
Engineering Administration Bldg Suite 101 West Lafayette IN 47907-1914
Fax: 317 494-9321
202 225-4401 **Pursell Carl D (Rep - R - Michigan)** 1414 Longworth Bldg Washington DC 20515-0001
Fax: Unlisted
405 298-2512 **Pushmataha County** 203 SW 3rd St Antlers OK 74523-3899
904 329-0200 **Putnam County** 410 St Johns Ave Palatka FL 32177-4725
Fax: 904 329-0888
404 485-5826 **Putnam County** 108 S Madison Ave Suite 200 Eatonton GA 31024-1094
815 925-7129 **Putnam County** 4th St Hennepin IL 61327-0000

317 653-2648 **Putnam County** PO Box 546 .... Greencastle IN 46135-0546
816 947-2674 **Putnam County** County Courthouse .... Unionville MO 63565-0000
914 225-3641 **Putnam County** 2 County Ctr .... Carmel NY 10512-0000
Fax: 914 225-0294
419 523-3656 **Putnam County** 245 E Main St .... Ottawa OH 45875-1968
615 526-7106 **Putnam County** County Courthouse .... Cookeville TN 38501-0000
304 586-0202 **Putnam County** County Courthouse .... Winfield WV 25213-0000

Q

Qatar: State of Qatar
202 338-0111 *Embassy* 600 New Hampshire Ave NW Suite 1180 .... Washington DC 20037-2403
Fax: 202 337-2989
212 486-9335 *Mission to the UN* 747 3rd Ave 22nd Fl .... New York NY 10017-2803
Fax: 212 758-4952
505 461-2112 **Quay County** 300 S 3rd St .... Tucumcari NM 88401-2870
Fax: 505 461-4498
301 758-0322 **Queen Annes County** 208 N Commerce St .... Centreville MD 21617-1015
Fax: 301 758-1170
213 435-3511 **Queen Mary & Spruce Goose Attractions**
1126 Queens Hwy .... Long Beach CA 90801-0000
Fax: 213 437-4531
415 657-2468 **Queen of the Holy Rosary College** 43326 Mission Blvd .... Fremont CA 94539-5829
704 332-7121 **Queens College** 1900 Selwyn Ave .... Charlotte NC 28274-0001
Fax: 704 337-2503
718 520-3137 **Queens County** 88-11 Sutphin Blvd .... Jamaica NY 11435-3716
Fax: 718 520-4731
718 990-0700 **Queensborough Public Library** 89-11 Merrick Blvd .... Jamaica NY 11432-5242
Fax: 718 291-8936
202 225-6356 **Quillen James H (Rep - R - Tennessee)** 102 Cannon Bldg .. Washington DC 20515-0001
Fax: 202 225-7812
217 222-8020 **Quincy College** 1800 College Ave .... Quincy IL 62301-2670
Fax: 217 228-5354
617 984-1600 **Quincy Junior College** 34 Coddington St .... Quincy MA 02169-4522
Fax: 617 773-7856
217 224-7669 **Quincy Museum of Natural History & Art** 1601 Main St .... Quincy IL 62301-4264
203 774-1130 **Quinebaug Valley Community College** 742 Upper Maple St ... Danielson CT 06239-1440
Fax: 203 774-7768
203 288-5251 **Quinnipiac College** 555 New Rd .... Hamden CT 06518-1908
Fax: 203 248-4703
508 853-2300 **Quinsigamond Community College** 670 W Boylston St .... Worcester MA 01606-2092
Fax: 508 852-6943
912 334-2159 **Quitman County** PO Box 114 .... Georgetown GA 31754-0114
601 326-2661 **Quitman County** PO Box 100 .... Marks MS 38646-0100

R

212 960-5344 **Rabbi Isaac Elchanan Seminary** 2450 Amsterdam Ave .... New York NY 10033-3311
201 267-9404 **Rabbinical College of America** 226 Sussex Ave .... Morristown NJ 07960-3600
216 943-5300 **Rabbinical College of Telshe** 28400 Euclid Ave .... Wickliffe OH 44092-2523
718 268-4700 **Rabbinical Seminary of America** 92-15 69th Ave .... Forest Hills NY 11375-5817
Fax: 718 268-4684
404 782-5271 **Rabun County** PO Box 925 .... Clayton GA 30525-0925
414 636-3121 **Racine County** 730 Wisconsin Ave .... Racine WI 53403-1274
Fax: 414 637-5279
414 636-9241 **Racine Public Library** 75 7th St .... Racine WI 53403-1200
Fax: Unlisted
617 495-8000 **Radcliffe College** 10 Garden St .... Cambridge MA 02138-3600
Fax: 617 495-8422
703 731-3603 **Radford (Independent City)** 619 2nd St .... Radford VA 24141-1431
703 831-5000 **Radford University** Norwood St & Rt 11 .... Radford VA 24142-0000
Fax: 703 831-5946
202 225-3452 **Rahall Nick Joe II (Rep - D - West Virginia)**
2104 Rayburn Bldg .... Washington DC 20515-0001
Fax: 202 225-9061
903 473-2461 **Rains County** PO Box 187 .... Emory TX 75440-0187
218 285-7722 **Rainy River Community College** 1803 Hwy 11-71 ..... International Falls MN 56649-2167
Fax: Ext 209
304 255-9123 **Raleigh County** 215 Main St County Courthouse .... Beckley WV 25801-0000
Fax: 304 255-9166
304 255-0511 **Raleigh County Public Library** PO Box 1876 .... Beckley WV 25802-1876
Fax: Call company operator
314 985-7111 **Ralls County** Main St .... New London MO 63459-0000
914 343-1131 **Ramapo Catskill Library System** 619 North St .... Middletown NY 10940-4395
Fax: 914 342-1205 Admin
201 529-7500 **Ramapo College of New Jersey** 505 Ramapo Valley Rd .... Mahwah NJ 07430-1680
Fax: 201 529-7508
612 298-5980 **Ramsey County** 15 Kellogg Blvd W Rm 286 .... Saint Paul MN 55102-1690
701 662-7069 **Ramsey County** 6th & 4th St .... Devils Lake ND 58301-0000
612 636-6747 **Ramsey County Public Library** 1910 W County Rd B .... Roseville MN 55113-5492
Fax: 612 636-6623
202 225-2871 **Ramstad Jim (Rep - R - Minnesota)** 504 Cannon Bldg .... Washington DC 20515-0001
Fax: Unlisted
714 667-3000 **Rancho Santiago College** 17th & Bristol St .... Santa Ana CA 92706-0000
Fax: 714 667-3434
806 655-7001 **Randall County** 401 15th St .... Canyon TX 79015-3838
Fax: 806 655-7469
512 652-1110 **Randolph Air Force Base** .... Randolph AFB TX 78150-0001
919 629-1471 **Randolph Community College** 629 Industrial Park Ave .... Asheboro NC 27203-7333
Fax: 919 629-4695
205 357-4551 **Randolph County** PO Box 328 .... Wedowee AL 36278-0328
501 892-5264 **Randolph County** 201 Marr St .... Pocahontas AR 72455-0000
912 732-6440 **Randolph County** Court St .... Cuthbert GA 31740-0000
618 826-2510 **Randolph County** 1 Taylor St .... Chester IL 62233-0000
317 584-7070 **Randolph County** County Courthouse 3rd Fl .... Winchester IN 47394-0000
816 277-4717 **Randolph County** S Main St .... Huntsville MO 65259-0000
919 629-2131 **Randolph County** 145 Worth St .... Asheboro NC 27203-5509
304 636-0543 **Randolph County** 2 Randolph Ave .... Elkins WV 26241-4063
804 798-8372 **Randolph-Macon College** Henry St .... Ashland VA 23005-0000
Fax: 804 752-7231
804 846-7392 **Randolph-Macon Woman's College** 2500 Rivermont Ave .... Lynchburg VA 24503-1526
Fax: 804 846-9699
202 225-4365 **Rangel Charles B (Rep - D - New York)**
2252 Rayburn Bldg .... Washington DC 20515-0001
Fax: 202 225-0816
817 647-3234 **Ranger Junior College** 1100 College Cir .... Ranger TX 76470-3298
Fax: 817 647-1656
601 825-2217 **Rankin County** 221 N Timber St .... Brandon MS 39042-3198
605 394-4171 **Rapid City Public Library** 610 Quincy St .... Rapid City SD 57701-3655
318 473-8153 **Rapides Parish** 700 Murray St .... Alexandria LA 71301-8023
318 445-2411 **Rapides Parish Library** 411 Washington St .... Alexandria LA 71301-8338

Rappahannock Community College
804 758-5324 *Glenns Campus* Rt 33 .... Glenns VA 23149-0000
Fax: 804 758-3852
804 333-4024 *Warsaw Campus* PO Box 318 .... Warsaw VA 22572-0318
Fax: 804 333-0106
703 675-3621 **Rappahannock County** PO Box 517 .... Washington VA 22747-0517
908 526-1200 **Raritan Community College** PO Box 3300 .... Somerville NJ 08876-1265
Fax: 908 231-8810
406 363-1900 **Ravalli County** S 2nd & Bedford Sts .... Hamilton MT 59840-0000
202 225-3176 **Ravenel Arthur Jr (Rep - R - South Carolina)**
508 Cannon Bldg .... Washington DC 20515-0001
Fax: 202 225-4340
913 626-3351 **Rawlins County** 607 Main St .... Atwood KS 67730-1896
312 280-3500 **Ray College of Design** 401 N Wabash Ave .... Chicago IL 60611-3532
Fax: 312 280-3157
816 776-3184 **Ray County** PO Box 536 .... Richmond MO 64085-0536
202 225-5901 **Ray Richard (Rep - D - Georgia)** 225 Cannon Bldg .... Washington DC 20515-0001
Fax: Unlisted
513 745-5600 **Raymond Walters College** 9555 Plainfield Rd .... Cincinnati OH 45236-1096
Fax: 513 745-5767
215 372-4721 **Reading Area Community College** 10 S 2nd St .... Reading PA 19602-1029
Fax: 215 375-8255
215 374-4540 **Reading Public Library** 5th & Franklin Sts .... Reading PA 19602-0000
Fax: 215 378-9766
215 371-5850 **Reading Public Museum & Art Gallery** 500 Museum Rd .... Reading PA 19611-1425
915 884-2442 **Reagan County** PO Box 100 .... Big Lake TX 76932-0100
512 232-5202 **Real County** PO Box 656 .... Leakey TX 78873-0656
Fax: 512 232-6629
202 383-1000 **Realtors PAC** 777 14 St NW 9th Fl .... Washington DC 20005-3201
Fax: 202 383-1134
609 452-0606 **Recording for the Blind** 20 Roszel Rd .... Princeton NJ 08540-6294
Fax: 609 987-8116
218 253-2598 **Red Lake County** 100 Langavin St .... Red Lake Falls MN 56750-0000
205 933-4152 **Red Mountain Museum** 1421 22nd St .... Birmingham AL 35205-4109
701 282-2822 **Red River & Northern Plains Regional Museum**
PO Box 719 .... West Fargo ND 58078-0719
903 427-2401 **Red River County** 400 N Walnut St .... Clarksville TX 75426-3041
318 932-5719 **Red River Parish** 615 E Carroll St .... Coushatta LA 71019-8537
303 988-6160 **Red Rocks Community College** 13300 W 6th Ave .... Lakewood CO 80401-5398
Fax: 303 969-8039 Library
308 345-1552 **Red Willow County** 500 Norris Ave .... McCook NE 69001-2006
916 225-4155 **Redding Museum & Art Center** PO Box 427 .... Redding CA 96099-0427
808 262-2341 **Redemption Bible College** 355 N Kainalu Dr .... Kailua HI 96734-2125
507 637-8325 **Redwood County** PO Box 130 .... Redwood Falls MN 56283-0130
Fax: 507 637-2611
503 771-1112 **Reed College** 3203 SE Woodstock Blvd .... Portland OR 97202-8199
Fax: 503 777-7769
202 225-2735 **Reed John F (Rep - D - Rhode Island)**
1229 Longworth Bldg .... Washington DC 20515-0001
Fax: 202 225-9580
901 587-2347 **Reelfoot Regional Library Center** Hwy 45 S .... Martin TN 38237-0000
Fax: Unlisted
806 885-4511 **Reese Air Force Base** .... Lubbock TX 79489-0000
615 929-4392 **Reese B Carroll Museum** PO Box 22300A .... Johnson City TN 37614-1000
915 445-5467 **Reeves County** PO Box 867 .... Pecos TX 79772-0867
616 363-2050 **Reformed Bible College** 3333 East Beltline Ave NE .... Grand Rapids MI 49505-9749
Fax: Unlisted
202 647-5822 **Refugee Programs (US Dept of State)**
2201 C St NW Rm 5824 .... Washington DC 20520-0001
Fax: 202 647-8162
512 526-2233 **Refugio County** PO Box 704 .... Refugio TX 78377-0704
303 458-4100 **Regis College** W 50th Ave & Lowell Blvd .... Denver CO 80221-0000
Fax: 303 458-4921
617 893-1820 **Regis College** 235 Wellesley St .... Weston MA 02193-1571
Fax: 617 899-4725
202 225-3876 **Regula Ralph (Rep - R - Ohio)** 2207 Rayburn Bldg .... Washington DC 20515-0001
Fax: 202 225-3059
202 395-6993 **Regulatory Information Service Center**
725 17th St NW Rm 5216 .... Washington DC 20503-0001
Fax: 202 395-7285
202 732-1282 **Rehabilitation Services Administration (US Dept of Education)**
330 C St SW Rm 3028 .... Washington DC 20202-0001
Fax: 202 732-1372
Rehabilitation Services Administration
617 223-4085 *Region 1* JW McCormack Post Office Bldg Rm 256 .... Boston MA 02109-0000
Fax: 617 223-9324
212 264-4016 *Region 2* 26 Federal Plaza Rm 4104 .... New York NY 10278-0004
Fax: 212 264-4427
215 596-0317 *Region 3* 3535 Market St MS 03-2050 Rm 16120 .... Philadelphia PA 19104-0000
Fax: 215 596-1094
404 331-2352 *Region 4* 101 Marietta Tower Suite 2210 .... Atlanta GA 30301-0000
Fax: 404 331-5382
312 886-5372 *Region 5* 401 S State St Suite 700-E .... Chicago IL 60605-1225
Fax: 312 353-5147
214 767-2961 *Region 6* 1200 Main Tower Bldg Rm 2140 .... Dallas TX 75202-0000
Fax: 214 767-3634
816 891-8015 *Region 7* PO Box 901381 .... Kansas City MO 64153-2312
Fax: 816 374-6442
303 844-2135 *Region 8* 1961 Stout St Rm 398 .... Denver CO 80294-0101
Fax: 303 564-2524
415 556-7333 *Region 9* 50 United Nations Plaza Suite 215 .... San Francisco CA 94102-4917
Fax: 415 556-7242
206 442-5331 *Region 10* 915 2nd Ave Rm 3390 .... Seattle WA 98174-1001
Fax: 206 399-1232
202 224-3542 **Reid Harry (Sen - D - Nevada)** 324 Hart Bldg .... Washington DC 20510-0001
Fax: 202 224-7327
205 578-1313 **Reid State Technical College** PO Box 588 .... Evergreen AL 36401-0588
Fax: 205 578-5355
404 479-1454 **Reinhardt College** PO Box 128 .... Waleska GA 30183-0128
Fax: 404 479-9007
618 437-5321 **Rend Lake College** RR 1 .... Ina IL 62846-9801
Fax: 618 437-5677 Admin
702 323-4145 **Reno Business College** 140 Washington St .... Reno NV 89503-5673
316 665-2931 **Reno County** 206 W 1st Ave .... Hutchinson KS 67501-5245
Fax: 316 665-2944
518 270-2700 **Rensselaer County** 1600 7th Ave .... Troy NY 12180-3409
518 276-6000 **Rensselaer Polytechnic Institute** 110 8th St .... Troy NY 12180-3590
Fax: 518 276-6003
518 276-8393 *Graduate School of Physics* Science Ctr 1st Fl .... Troy NY 12180-0000
Fax: 518 276-6680
518 276-6460 *School of Architecture* 110 8th St .... Troy NY 12180-3590
Fax: 518 276-2999
518 276-6298 *School of Engineering* 110 8th St Johnson Engineering Ctr .... Troy NY 12180-0000
Fax: 518 276-8788
612 523-2080 **Renville County** 500 DePue Ave E .... Olivia MN 56277-1334
Fax: 612 523-2084

701 756-6398 **Renville County** PO Box 68 .... Mohall ND 58761-0068
202 357-2447 **Renwick Gallery (Smithsonian Institution)**
Pennsylvania Ave & 17th St NW .... Washington DC 20560-0001
913 527-5691 **Republic County** County Courthouse .... Belleville KS 66935-0000
202 554-5056 **Republican Congressional Boosters Club** 300 1st St SE .... Washington DC 20003-1801
202 863-8500 **Republican National Committee** 310 1st St SE .... Washington DC 20003-1801
Fax: 202 863-8820
907 276-4467 **Republican Party of Alaska** 750 E Fireweed Ln Suite 102 ..... Anchorage AK 99503-2803
Fax: 907 258-4930
501 372-7301 **Republican Party of Arkansas**
1 Riverfront Pl Suite 550 .... North Little Rock AR 72114-5663
Fax: 501 372-1938
904 222-7920 **Republican Party of Florida** 719 N Calhoun St .... Tallahassee FL 32303-6209
Fax: 904 681-0184
808 526-1755 **Republican Party of Hawaii** 100 N Beretania St Suite 203 ...... Honolulu HI 96817-4712
Fax: 808 545-4039
515 282-8105 **Republican Party of Iowa** 521 E Locust St .... Des Moines IA 50309-1911
Fax: 515 282-9019
502 875-5130 **Republican Party of Kentucky** PO Box 1068 .... Frankfort KY 40602-1068
Fax: 502 223-5625
608 257-4765 **Republican Party of Wisconsin** 121 S Pinckney St .... Madison WI 53703-0000
Fax: 608 257-4141
202 366-4433 **Research & Special Programs Admin (US Dept of Transportation)**
400 7th St SW Rm 8410 .... Washington DC 20590-0001
Fax: 202 366-7431
Research & Special Programs Admin
202 366-9059 *Aviation Information Management*
400 7th St SW Rm 4125 .... Washington DC 20590-0001
Fax: 202 366-3383
202 366-5270 *Emergency Transportation Div* 400 7th St SW Rm 8404 .. Washington DC 20590-0001
Fax: 202 366-3769
202 366-4595 *Office of Pipeline Safety* 400 7th St SW Rm 8417 .... Washington DC 20590-0001
Fax: 202 366-4566
816 426-2654 *Central Region* 911 Walnut St Rm 1811 .... Kansas City MO 64106-2009
Fax: 816 426-2598
202 366-4582 *Eastern Region* 400 7th St SW Rm 8321 .... Washington DC 20590-0001
Fax: 202 472-1032
404 347-2632 *Southern Region* 1720 Peachtree Rd NW Suite 426 .... Atlanta GA 30309-2439
Fax: 404 347-5218
713 750-1746 *Southwest Region* 2320 La Branch St Suite 2116 .... Houston TX 77004-1031
Fax: 713 526-6724
303 236-3424 *Western Region* 555 Zang St 2nd Fl .... Lakewood CO 80228-1010
Fax: 303 986-2779
202 479-2200 **Reserve Officers Assn of the US** 1 Constitution Ave NE ...... Washington DC 20002-5655
Fax: 202 479-0416
202 783-3660 **Responsible Citizens Political League**
815 16th St NW Suite 511 .... Washington DC 20006-4104
Fax: 202 783-0198
303 364-8737 **Retired Enlisted Assn** 14305 E Alamada Ave Suite 300 .... Aurora CO 80012-2505
Fax: 303 364-8774
703 549-2311 **Retired Officers Assn** 201 N Washington St .... Alexandria VA 22314-2539
Fax: 703 838-8173
703 684-0244 **Retired Persons Services Inc** 500 Montgomery St .... Alexandria VA 22314-1563
Fax: 703 684-0246
314 648-2494 **Reynolds County** Courthouse Sq .... Centerville MO 63633-0000
Fax: 314 648-2296
615 775-7808 **Rhea County** 301 N Market St .... Dayton TN 37321-1271
401 456-8000 **Rhode Island College** 600 Mt Pleasant Ave .... Providence RI 02908-1924
Fax: 401 456-8379
401 232-3800 **Rhode Island Democratic State Committee**
1991 Smith St .... North Providence RI 02911-1717
Fax: 401 232-7920
401 277-2726 **Rhode Island Dept of State Library Services**
300 Richmond St .... Providence RI 02903-4222
Fax: 401 351-1311
401 331-8575 **Rhode Island Historical Society Museum**
110 Benevolent St .... Providence RI 02906-3152
401 421-2570 **Rhode Island Republican Party** 400 Smith St Suite 200 ...... Providence RI 02908-3727
Fax: 401 421-3504
401 331-3511 **Rhode Island School of Design** 2 College St .... Providence RI 02903-2707
Fax: 401 831-7106
Rhode Island State Government
401 277-2000 *Information* 1 Capitol Hill .... Providence RI 02908-5803
Fax: Unlisted
401 277-2781 *Agriculture Div* 22 Hayes St Rm 120 .... Providence RI 02908-5025
Fax: 401 277-6047
401 277-2353 *Archives Div* 343-345 Westminster St .... Providence RI 02903-1120
401 789-9391 *Atomic Energy Commission* S Ferry Rd .... Narragansett RI 02882-0000
Fax: 401 792-6160
401 274-4400 *Attorney General* 72 Pine St .... Providence RI 02903-2856
Fax: 401 861-1120
401 277-2764 *Consumer's Council* 365 Broadway .... Providence RI 02909-1498
401 277-3880 *Council on the Arts* 95 Cedar St Suite 103 .... Providence RI 02903-1062
401 277-2280 *Department of Administration* 1 Capitol Hill 4th Fl .... Providence RI 02908-0000
Fax: 401 277-6006
401 277-2246 *Department of Business Regulation* 233 Richmond St ..... Providence RI 02903-4229
Fax: 401 277-6098
401 464-2611 *Department of Corrections* 75 Howard Ave .... Cranston RI 02920-3082
Fax: 401 464-1464
401 277-2031 *Department of Education* 22 Hayes St .... Providence RI 02908-5092
Fax: 401 277-6178
401 277-3648 *Department of Employment & Training* 101 Friendship St . Providence RI 02903-1082
Fax: 401 277-2731
401 277-3434 *Department of Environmental Management* 83 Park St .... Providence RI 02908-0000
Fax: 401 277-2591
401 277-2233 *Department of Health* 3 Capitol Hill .... Providence RI 02908-1006
401 457-1800 *Department of Labor* 220 Elmwood Ave .... Providence RI 02907-0000
401 277-3492 *Department of the Public Defender* 250 Benefit St .... Providence RI 02903-2719
401 277-2481 *Department of Transportation*
2 Capitol Hill State Office Bldg Rm 210 .... Providence RI 02903-0000
Fax: 401 277-6038
401 272-0700 *Department of Workers' Compensation* 610 Manton Ave .. Providence RI 02909-5633
Fax: 401 277-2127
401 277-2797 *Division of Air & Hazardous Materials* 291 Promenade St . Providence RI 02908-5720
Fax: 401 277-2017
401 277-3649 *Division of Benefits* 101 Friendship St .... Providence RI 02903-1029
Fax: 401 277-2731
401 457-1829 *Division of Occupational Safety* 220 Elmwood Ave .... Providence RI 02907-1435
401 277-2656 *Division of Planning* 1 Capitol Hill .... Providence RI 02908-5870
401 277-3496 *Division of Probation & Parole* 1 Dorrance Plaza .... Providence RI 02903-3922
401 277-2827 *Division of Professional Regulation* 3 Capitol Hill .... Providence RI 02908-1006
Fax: 401 277-1272
401 277-3500 *Division of Public Utilities & Carriers* 100 Orange St .... Providence RI 02903-2803
Fax: 401 277-6805
401 277-2317 *Division of Purchases* 1 Capitol Hill .... Providence RI 02908-5810
401 277-3050 *Division of Taxation* 1 Capitol Hill .... Providence RI 02908-5800
Fax: 401 277-6006
401 277-2812 *Division of Vital Statistics* 3 Capitol Hill Rm 101 .... Providence RI 02908-5097
401 277-2601 *Economic Development Dept* 7 Jackson Walkway .... Providence RI 02903-3622
Fax: 401 277-2102
401 421-7333 *Emergency Management Agency*
82 Smith St State House Rm 27 .... Providence RI 02903-0000
Fax: 401 751-0827
401 277-2080 *Governor* 222 State House .... Providence RI 02903-0000
Fax: 401 272-0860
401 464-2125 *High Security Center* PO Box 8200 .... Cranston RI 02920-0200
401 277-2371 *Lieutenant Governor* State House Rm 317 .... Providence RI 02903-0000
Fax: 401 277-2012
401 464-2054 *Maximum Security Facility at Cranston* PO Box 8273 .... Cranston RI 02920-0273
401 277-6920 *Office of Energy Housing & Inter-Governmental Relations*
275 Westminster Mall Rm 143 .... Providence RI 02903-3415
401 277-2685 *Office of Higher Education* 301 Promenade St Rm 217 .... Providence RI 02908-5006
Fax: 401 277-6111
401 277-2357 *Secretary of State* State House Rm 217 .... Providence RI 02903-0000
Fax: 401 277-3295
401 277-3048 *Securities Div* 233 Richmond St Suite 232 .... Providence RI 02903-4232
401 647-3311 *State Police* 311 Danielson Pike .... North Scituate RI 02857-1907
Fax: 401 647-3014
401 277-3272 *Supreme Court* 250 Benefit St .... Providence RI 02903-2794
Fax: 401 277-3865
401 277-2287 *Treasury Dept* 198 Dyer St .... Providence RI 02903-3906
Fax: 401 277-6141
401 277-2443 *Utilities Commission* 100 Orange St .... Providence RI 02903-2803
Fax: 401 277-6805
401 277-2217 *Water Resources Board* 265 Melrose St .... Providence RI 02907-2196
401 277-2601 **Rhode Island Tourism & Promotion Div**
7 Jackson Walkway .... Providence RI 02903-3622
Fax: 401 277-2102
901 726-3000 **Rhodes College** 2000 North Pkwy .... Memphis TN 38112-0000
Fax: 901 726-3718
202 225-2635 **Rhodes John J III (Rep - R - Arizona)** 326 Cannon Bldg ..... Washington DC 20515-0001
Fax: 202 225-0985
316 257-2232 **Rice County** 101 W Commercial St .... Lyons KS 67554-2727
507 334-2281 **Rice County** 218 3rd St NW .... Faribault MN 55021-5146
Fax: Unlisted
713 527-8101 **Rice University** PO Box 1892 .... Houston TX 77251-1892
Fax: 713 523-4117 Library
713 527-4834 *Department of Computer Science*
6100 S Main St Herman Brown Bldg Rm 230 .... Houston TX 77005-0000
Fax: 713 285-5136
713 527-4938 *Department of Physics* 6100 S Main St .... Houston TX 77005-1892
Fax: 713 527-9033
713 527-4009 *George R Brown School of Engineering* PO Box 1892 .... Houston TX 77251-1892
Fax: 713 542-5237
713 527-4037 *Graduate School of Biochemistry* 6100 S Main St .... Houston TX 77005-0000
713 527-4082 *Graduate School of Chemistry* PO Box 1892 .... Houston TX 77251-1892
Fax: 713 285-5155
713 527-4870 *School of Architecture*
6100 S Main St Anderson Hall Rm 110 .... Houston TX 77005-0000
Fax: 713 523-4417 Library
801 793-2415 **Rich County** PO Box 218 .... Randolph UT 84064-0218
804 862-6100 **Richard Bland College** 11301 Johnson Rd .... Petersburg VA 23805-7100
Fax: 804 862-6207 Admin
312 735-3000 **Richard J Daley College** 7500 S Pulaski Rd .... Chicago IL 60652-1299
Fax: 312 838-4876
205 636-9642 **Richard Pearson Hobson State Technical College**
Hwy 43 S .... Thomasville AL 36784-0000
Fax: 205 636-8123
202 225-6190 **Richardson Bill (Rep - D - New Mexico)** 332 Cannon Bldg .. Washington DC 20515-0001
Fax: Unlisted
402 245-2911 **Richardson County** 1701 Stone St .... Falls City NE 68355-2026
214 238-6200 **Richland College** 12800 Abrams Rd .... Dallas TX 75243-2199
Fax: 214 238-6352
217 875-7200 **Richland Community College** 1 College Pk .... Decatur IL 62521-8513
Fax: 217 875-6961
618 392-3111 **Richland County** Main St .... Olney IL 62450-0000
406 482-1706 **Richland County** 201 W Main St .... Sidney MT 59270-4035
Fax: 406 482-3731
701 642-7818 **Richland County** PO Box 966 .... Wahpeton ND 58074-0936
419 755-5501 **Richland County** 50 Park Ave E .... Mansfield OH 44902-1888
803 748-4684 **Richland County** 1701 Main St .... Columbia SC 29201-2833
608 647-2197 **Richland County** Seminary & Central Sts .... Richland Center WI 53581-0000
803 799-9084 **Richland County Public Library** 1400 Sumter St .... Columbia SC 29201-2800
Fax: 803 252-5265
318 728-2061 **Richland Parish** 108 Courthouse Sq .... Rayville LA 71269-2647
804 780-7970 **Richmond (Independent City)** 900 E Broad St .... Richmond VA 23219-6115
Fax: 804 780-7987
919 582-7000 **Richmond Community College** Hwy 74 W .... Hamlet NC 28345-0000
Fax: 919 582-7028
404 821-2300 **Richmond County** 530 Green St .... Augusta GA 30911-0001
Fax: 404 821-2520
718 390-5386 **Richmond County** 18 Richmond Terr .... Staten Island NY 10301-1935
Fax: 718 390-5269
804 333-3781 **Richmond County** 10 Court St .... Warsaw VA 22572-0000
804 780-4256 **Richmond Public Library** 101 E Franklin St .... Richmond VA 23219-2193
Fax: 804 780-4807 Cust Svc
208 356-2011 **Ricks College** .... Rexburg ID 83460-0001
Fax: 208 356-2390
609 896-5041 **Rider College** 2083 Lawrenceville Rd .... Lawrenceville NJ 08648-3099
Fax: 609 895-0448
202 225-5406 **Ridge Thomas J (Rep - R - Pennsylvania)**
1714 Longworth Bldg .... Washington DC 20515-0001
Fax: 202 225-1081
202 224-4822 **Riegle Donald W Jr (Sen - D - Michigan)**
105 Dirksen Bldg .... Washington DC 20510-0001
Fax: 202 224-8834
202 225-3311 **Riggs Frank (Rep - R - California)** 1517 Longworth Bldg .... Washington DC 20515-0001
Fax: 202 225-5577
913 537-0700 **Riley County** 110 Courthouse Plaza .... Manhattan KS 66502-6018
Fax: 913 537-6394
202 225-5361 **Rinaldo Matthew J (Rep - R - New Jersey)**
2469 Rayburn Bldg .... Washington DC 20515-0001
Fax: 202 225-5679
515 464-3234 **Ringgold County** County Courthouse .... Mount Ayr IA 50854-0000
813 355-5101 **Ringling John & Mabel Museum of Art** 5401 Bayshore Rd ..... Sarasota FL 34243-0000
Fax: 813 351-7959
813 351-4614 **Ringling School of Art & Design** 2700 N Tamiami Trail .... Sarasota FL 34234-5895
Fax: 813 951-1452
505 588-7255 **Rio Arriba County** County Courthouse .... Tierra Amarilla NM 87575-0000
303 878-5068 **Rio Blanco County** PO Box 1067 .... Meeker CO 81641-1067
719 657-3334 **Rio Grande County** PO Box 160 .... Del Norte CO 81132-0160

213 692-0921 **Rio Hondo College** 3600 Workman Mill Rd ... Whittier CA 90601-1699
Fax: 213 699-7386
602 223-4000 **Rio Salado Community College** 640 N 1st Ave ... Phoenix AZ 85003-1558
Fax: 602 223-4329
812 689-6115 **Ripley County** PO Box 177 ... Versailles IN 47042-0000
314 996-3215 **Ripley County** County Courthouse ... Doniphan MO 63935-0000
414 748-8106 **Ripon College** PO Box 248 ... Ripon WI 54971-0248
Fax: Unlisted
304 643-2163 **Ritchie County** 115 E Main St ... Harrisville WV 26362-1271
202 225-6411 **Ritter Don (Rep - R - Pennsylvania)** 2202 Rayburn Bldg ... Washington DC 20515-0001
Fax: 202 225-5248
714 782-5201 **Riverside City & County Public Library** 3581 7th St ... Riverside CA 92502-0468
Fax: 714 788-1528
714 684-3240 **Riverside Community College** 4800 Magnolia Ave ... Riverside CA 92506-1293
Fax: 714 784-1160
714 275-1989 **Riverside County** 4050 N Main St ... Riverside CA 92501-3798
603 888-1311 **Rivier College** 420 Main St ... Nashua NH 03060-5086
Fax: 603 888-6447
615 376-5556 **Roane County** PO Box 546 ... Kingston TN 37763-0546
304 927-2860 **Roane County** 200 Main St ... Spencer WV 25276-1497
615 354-3000 **Roane State Community College** Patton Ln ... Harriman TN 37748-0000
Fax: Ext 4462
703 981-2324 **Roanoke (Independent City)** 315 Church Ave SW ... Roanoke VA 24016-5007
Fax: 703 981-2773
919 338-5191 **Roanoke Bible College** 714 1st St ... Elizabeth City NC 27907-0000
703 981-2475 **Roanoke City Public Library System** 706 S Jefferson St ... Roanoke VA 24016-5104
Fax: Unlisted
703 375-2500 **Roanoke College** 221 College Ln ... Salem VA 24153-3794
Fax: 703 375-2261
703 342-5760 **Roanoke Museum of Fine Arts** 1 Market Sq ... Roanoke VA 24011-1417
919 332-5921 **Roanoke-Chowan Community College** RR 2 Box 46-A ... Ahoskie NC 27910-9522
Fax: 919 332-2210
202 224-4024 **Robb Charles S (Sen - D - Virginia)** 493 Russell Bldg ... Washington DC 20510-0001
Fax: 202 224-8689
607 772-0660 **Roberson Center for the Arts & Sciences** 30 Front St ... Binghamton NY 13905-4779
412 262-8200 **Robert Morris College** Narrows Run Rd ... Coraopolis PA 15108-1189
Fax: 412 262-5958
605 698-3395 **Roberts County** 411 2nd Ave E ... Sisseton SD 57262-1495
806 868-2341 **Roberts County** Kiowa & Commercial Sts ... Miami TX 79059-0000
202 225-2715 **Roberts Pat (Rep - R - Kansas)** 1110 Longworth Bldg ... Washington DC 20515-0001
Fax: 202 225-5375
716 594-9471 **Roberts Wesleyan College** 2301 Westside Dr ... Rochester NY 14624-1997
Fax: 716 594-1145
606 724-5212 **Robertson County** PO Box 95 ... Mount Olivet KY 41064-0000
615 384-5895 **Robertson County** County Courthouse Rm 101 ... Springfield TN 37172-0000
409 828-4130 **Robertson County** Center St ... Franklin TX 77856-0000
919 738-7101 **Robeson Community College** PO Box 1420 ... Lumberton NC 28359-1420
919 671-3000 **Robeson County** 500 N Elm St ... Lumberton NC 28358-5595
919 738-4859 **Robeson County Public Library** 101 N Chestnut St ... Lumberton NC 28358-5639
Fax: 919 739-8321
912 926-1110 **Robins Air Force Base** ... Warner Robins GA 31098-0000
605 773-3458 **Robinson State Museum** 900 Governors Dr ... Pierre SD 57501-2200
Fax: 605 773-6041
507 285-7265 **Rochester Community College** 851 30th Ave SE ... Rochester MN 55904-4999
Fax: 507 285-7496
716 475-2411 **Rochester Institute of Technology** 1 Lomb Memorial Dr ... Rochester NY 14623-5640
Fax: 716 475-5476
716 475-2145 *College of Engineering* 1 Lomb Memorial Dr ... Rochester NY 14623-5640
Fax: 716 475-6879
716 475-2992 *Computer Science Dept* Ross Memorial Bldg 10 ... Rochester NY 14623-0000
716 475-2421 *Department of Physics* Bldg 8 ... Rochester NY 14627-0000
Fax: 716 275-8527
716 271-4320 **Rochester Museum & Science Center** 657 East Ave ... Rochester NY 14603-0000
Fax: 716 271-5935
716 428-7300 **Rochester Public Library** 115 South Ave ... Rochester NY 14604-1896
507 283-9501 **Rock County** PO Box 245 ... Luverne MN 56156-0245
Fax: 507 283-9504
402 684-3933 **Rock County** 400 State St ... Bassett NE 68714-0000
608 755-2160 **Rock County** 51 S Main St ... Janesville WI 53545-3978
309 786-4451 **Rock Island County** 1504 3rd Ave ... Rock Island IL 61201-8646
Fax: 309 786-9883
815 654-4250 **Rock Valley College** 3301 N Mulford Rd ... Rockford IL 61111-0000
Fax: 815 654-4459
703 463-2232 **Rockbridge County** 2 S Main St ... Lexington VA 24450-2546
606 256-2831 **Rockcastle County** PO Box 365 ... Mount Vernon KY 40456-0365
404 929-4000 **Rockdale County** 922 Court St NE ... Conyers GA 30207-4540
Fax: Unlisted
202 224-6472 **Rockefeller John D IV (Sen - D - West Virginia)**
724 Hart Bldg ... Washington DC 20510-0001
Fax: 202 224-7665
212 570-8088 **Rockefeller University** 1230 York Ave ... New York NY 10021-6399
Fax: 212 570-7974
212 570-8086 *Graduate School of Biochemistry* 1230 York Ave ... New York NY 10021-6399
Fax: 212 570-7974
212 570-8636 *School of Mathematical Physics* 1230 York Ave ... New York NY 10021-6399
Fax: 212 570-7786
815 226-4000 **Rockford College** 5050 E State St ... Rockford IL 61108-2393
Fax: 815 226-4119
815 965-6731 **Rockford Public Library** 215 N Wyman St ... Rockford IL 61101-1061
Fax: 815 965-0866
816 926-4000 **Rockhurst College** 1100 Rockhurst Rd ... Kansas City MO 64110-2561
Fax: 816 926-4666
919 342-4261 **Rockingham Community College** Hwy 65 ... Wentworth NC 27375-9999
Fax: 919 349-9986
919 342-8700 **Rockingham County** PO Box 26 ... Wentworth NC 27375-0026
603 679-2256 **Rockingham County** North Rd ... Brentwood NH 03042-0000
703 434-4455 **Rockingham County** Circuit Ct ... Harrisonburg VA 22801-0000
Fax: 703 434-7163
703 434-4475 **Rockingham Public Library** 45 Newman Ave ... Harrisonburg VA 22801-4001
914 356-4650 **Rockland Community College** 145 College Rd ... Suffern NY 10901-3699
914 638-5100 **Rockland County** 11 New Hempstead Rd ... New City NY 10956-3636
Fax: 914 638-5675
214 722-5141 **Rockwall County** Hwy 66 & Goliad ... Rockwall TX 75087-0000
Fax: 214 722-0242
412 565-2000 **Rockwell International Corp Good Government Committee**
625 Liberty Ave ... Pittsburgh PA 15222-3123
Fax: 412 565-7389
406 657-1000 **Rocky Mountain College** 1511 Poly Dr ... Billings MT 59102-1796
Fax: 406 259-9751
215 787-5476 **Rodin Museum** 22nd & Benjamin Franklin Pkwy ... Philadelphia PA 19130-0000
Fax: 215 236-4465
202 225-5751 **Roe Robert A (Rep - D - New Jersey)** 2243 Rayburn Bldg ... Washington DC 20515-0001
Fax: 202 225-3071
202 225-3915 **Roemer Timothy J (Rep - D - Indiana)** 415 Cannon Bldg ... Washington DC 20515-0001
Fax: 202 225-6798
405 497-3365 **Roger Mills County** PO Box 708 ... Cheyenne OK 73628-0000
401 253-1040 **Roger Williams College** 1 Old Ferry Rd ... Bristol RI 02809-2921
Fax: 401 254-0490
918 341-0585 **Rogers County** 219 S Missouri Ave ... Claremore OK 74017-7832
Fax: 918 341-0234
202 225-4601 **Rogers Harold (Rep - R - Kentucky)** 343 Cannon Bldg ... Washington DC 20515-0001
Fax: 202 225-0940
601 649-6374 **Rogers Lauren Museum of Art** PO Box 1108 ... Laurel MS 39441-1108
918 341-7510 **Rogers State College** 1720 W Will Rogers Blvd ... Claremore OK 74017-3252
Fax: 918 342-3811
503 479-5541 **Rogue Community College** 3345 Redwood Hwy ... Grants Pass OR 97527-9298
Fax: Ext 286
202 225-2415 **Rohrabacher Dana (Rep - R - California)**
1039 Longworth Bldg ... Washington DC 20515-0001
Fax: 202 225-0145
701 477-3816 **Rolette County** PO Box 460 ... Rolla ND 58367-0460
407 646-2000 **Rollins College** 1000 Holt Ave ... Winter Park FL 32789-4492
Fax: 407 646-2600
407 646-2405 *Crummer Graduate School of Business Administration*
Crummer Bldg ... Winter Park FL 32789-0000
Fax: 407 646-1550
Romania
202 232-4747 *Embassy* 1607 23rd St NW ... Washington DC 20008-2809
Fax: 202 232-4748
212 682-3274 *Mission to the UN* 577 3rd Ave ... New York NY 10016-3109
Fax: 212 682-9746
202 463-5482 **Romanian-US Economic Council** 1615 H St NW 6th Fl ... Washington DC 20062-0001
Fax: 202 463-3114
913 425-6391 **Rooks County** 115 N Walnut St ... Stockton KS 67669-1663
406 653-1590 **Roosevelt County** 400 2nd Ave S ... Wolf Point MT 59201-1600
505 356-8562 **Roosevelt County** County Courthouse ... Portales NM 88130-0000
809 865-2000 **Roosevelt Roads Naval Station** ... Miami FL 35045-0000
312 341-3500 **Roosevelt University** 430 S Michigan Ave ... Chicago IL 60605-1394
Fax: 312 341-3655
202 225-3931 **Ros-Lehtinen Ileana (Rep - R - Florida)** 416 Cannon Bldg ... Washington DC 20515-0001
Fax: 202 225-5620
708 366-2490 **Rosary College** 7900 W Division St ... River Forest IL 60305-1099
Fax: 708 366-5360 Library
517 275-5923 **Roscommon County** PO Box 98 ... Roscommon MI 48653-0098
202 225-2731 **Rose Charles (Rep - D - North Carolina)**
2230 Rayburn Bldg ... Washington DC 20515-0001
Fax: 202 225-2470
405 733-7311 **Rose State College** 6420 SE 15th St ... Midwest City OK 73110-2797
Fax: 405 736-0309
812 877-1511 **Rose-Hulman Institute of Technology** 5500 Wabash Ave ... Terre Haute IN 47803-3999
Fax: 812 877-3198
218 463-2541 **Roseau County** 216 Center St W ... Roseau MN 56751-1498
406 356-2251 **Rosebud County** PO Box 47 ... Forsyth MT 59327-0047
215 527-0200 **Rosemont College** Montgomery & Wendover Aves ... Rosemont PA 19010-1699
614 773-5115 **Ross County** N Paint St ... Chillicothe OH 45601-0000
Fax: 614 774-1602
202 225-4061 **Rostenkowski Dan (Rep - D - Illinois)** 2111 Rayburn Bldg ... Washington DC 20515-0001
Fax: 202 225-4064
505 624-6744 **Roswell Museum & Art Center** 100 W 11th St ... Roswell NM 88201-4998
202 225-5665 **Roth Toby (Rep - R - Wisconsin)** 2352 Rayburn Bldg ... Washington DC 20515-0001
Fax: 202 225-0087
202 224-2441 **Roth William V Jr (Sen - R - Delaware)** 104 Hart Bldg ... Washington DC 20510-0001
Fax: 202 224-2805
202 225-4465 **Roukema Marge (Rep - R - New Jersey)**
2244 Rayburn Bldg ... Washington DC 20515-0001
Fax: 202 225-9048
303 879-0108 **Routt County** PO Box 773598 ... Steamboat Springs CO 80477-3598
606 784-5212 **Rowan County** E Main St 2nd Fl ... Morehead KY 40351-0000
Fax: 606 784-2923
704 636-0361 **Rowan County** 202 N Main St ... Salisbury NC 28144-4346
Fax: 704 638-3092
704 637-0760 **Rowan-Cabarrus Community College**
1333 Jake Alexander Blvd W ... Salisbury NC 28144-6333
Fax: 704 637-6642
202 225-6531 **Rowland J Roy (Rep - D - Georgia)** 423 Cannon Bldg ... Washington DC 20515-0001
Fax: Unlisted
617 427-0060 **Roxbury Community College** 1234 Columbus Ave ... Roxbury MA 02120-3400
202 225-6235 **Roybal Edward R (Rep - D - California)**
2211 Rayburn Bldg ... Washington DC 20515-0001
Fax: 202 226-1251
202 224-3324 **Rudman Warren (Sen - R - New Hampshire)**
530 Hart Bldg ... Washington DC 20510-0001
Fax: Unlisted
916 961-8727 **Rudolf Steiner College** 9200 Fair Oaks Blvd ... Fair Oaks CA 95628-6897
202 546-0023 **Ruff PAC** 501 Capitol Ct NE Suite 100 ... Washington DC 20002-4937
Fax: 202 546-0029
202 224-6352 **Rules & Administration Committee (US Senate)**
305 Russell Bldg ... Washington DC 20510-0001
Fax: Unlisted
202 225-9486 **Rules Committee (US House of Representatives)**
H-312 Capitol Bldg ... Washington DC 20515-0001
Fax: 202 225-5373
915 365-2720 **Runnels County** Hutchings & Broadway ... Ballinger TX 76821-0000
202 382-1255 **Rural Electrification Administration (US Dept of Agriculture)**
USDA Bldg Rm 4042S ... Washington DC 20250-0001
Fax: 202 382-1725
317 932-2086 **Rush County** PO Box 429 ... Rushville IN 46173-0429
913 222-2726 **Rush County** PO Box 220 ... La Crosse KS 67548-0220
312 942-7100 **Rush University** 1743 W Harrison St Rm 119 ... Chicago IL 60612-3823
Fax: 312 942-2219
312 942-6980 *College of Nursing* 1753 W Congress Pkwy ... Chicago IL 60612-3809
Fax: 312 942-2549
903 657-0330 **Rusk County** 115 N Main St ... Henderson TX 75652-3198
715 532-2100 **Rusk County** 311 Miner Ave E ... Ladysmith WI 54848-1862
Fax: 715 532-2175
205 298-0516 **Russell County** PO Box 518 ... Phenix City AL 36867-0000
913 483-4641 **Russell County** PO Box 113 ... Russell KS 67665-0113
502 343-2125 **Russell County** PO Box 579 ... Jamestown KY 42629-0579
703 889-8023 **Russell County** PO Box 435 ... Lebanon VA 24266-0000
518 270-2000 **Russell Sage College** 45 Ferry St ... Troy NY 12180-4115
Fax: 518 271-4545
518 445-1724 *Program in Health Services Administration*
140 New Scotland Ave Administration Bldg ... Albany NY 12208-3491
Fax: Unlisted
518 270-2384 *School of Nursing* 45 Ferry St ... Troy NY 12180-4115
Fax: 518 271-4545
202 225-5736 **Russo Marty (Rep - D - Illinois)** 2233 Rayburn Bldg ... Washington DC 20515-0001
Fax: 202 225-0295
601 252-4661 **Rust College** 150 E Rust Ave ... Holly Springs MS 38635-2328
Fax: 601 252-6107

908 932-1766 **Rutgers University** Van Nest Hall .... New Brunswick NJ 08903-0000
Fax: Unlisted
609 757-1766 *Camden Campus* 311 N 5th St .... Camden NJ 08102-1499
Fax: 609 757-6270
908 932-4452 *College of Engineering* PO Box 909 .... Piscataway NJ 08855-0000
Fax: 908 932-5313
201 648-5018 *College of Nursing* 180 University Ave .... Newark NJ 07102-1803
Fax: 201 648-1277
908 932-2077 *Graduate Program in Biology* Nelson Biological Lab ... New Brunswick NJ 08855-0000
Fax: 908 932-5870
908 932-2816 *Graduate School of Biochemistry*
Allison & Bevier Rds Nelson Labs Rm A-233 .... Piscataway NJ 08854-0000
Fax: 908 932-4213
908 932-7500 *Graduate School of Communication Information & Library Studies*
4 Huntington St .... New Brunswick NJ 08901-1071
Fax: '908 932-6916
908 932-2502 *Graduate School of Physics* Serin Physics Lab .... Piscataway NJ 08855-0000
Fax: 908 932-4343
908 932-7509 *Library* 179 College Ave .... New Brunswick NJ 08901-0000
Fax: 908 932-7637
201 648-1766 *Newark Campus* 249 University Ave .... Newark NJ 07102-1808
Fax: 201 648-5700
908 932-3546 **Rutgers University Bush Department of Computer Science**
Hill Ctr .... New Brunswick NJ 08903-0000
Fax: 908 932-5530
609 757-6375 **Rutgers University Camden School of Law** 5th & Penn Sts .... Camden NJ 08102-0000
Fax: 609 757-6487
908 932-3822 **Rutgers University Kilmer Urban Planning & Policy Development**
Lucy Stone Hall B Wing .... New Brunswick NJ 08903-0000
Fax: 908 932-2253
201 648-5561 **Rutgers University Newark School of Law** 15 Washington St .... Newark NJ 07102-3192
Fax: 201 648-1248
704 286-9136 **Rutherford County** PO Box 630 .... Rutherfordton NC 28139-0630
615 898-7799 **Rutherford County** 26 Public Sq .... Murfreesboro TN 37130-0000
802 775-4394 **Rutland County** 83 Center St .... Rutland VT 05701-4039
Rwanda: Republic of Rwanda
202 232-2882 *Embassy* 1714 New Hampshire Ave NW .... Washington DC 20009-2502
Fax: 202 232-4544
212 696-0644 *Mission to the UN* 124 E 39th St .... New York NY 10016-0906
Fax: Unlisted
213 390-7560 **Ryokan College** 12581 Venice Blvd Suite 202 .... Los Angeles CA 90066-0000

S

409 787-3786 **Sabine County** Oak St .... Hemphill TX 75948-0000
318 256-6223 **Sabine Parish** PO Box 419 .... Many LA 71449-0419
202 225-4755 **Sabo Martin Olav (Rep - D - Minnesota)**
2201 Rayburn Bldg .... Washington DC 20515-0001
Fax: 202 225-4886
712 662-7791 **Sac County** PO Box 368 .... Sac City IA 50583-0368
202 357-4880 **Sackler Arthur M Gallery (Smithsonian Institution)**
1050 Independence Ave SW .... Washington DC 20560-0001
Fax: 202 357-4911
916 449-7441 **Sacramento City College** 3835 Freeport Blvd .... Sacramento CA 95822-1386
Fax: 916 441-4142
916 643-4686 **Sacramento Coast Guard Air Station**
McClellan Air Force Base .... Sacramento CA 95652-6428
916 440-5522 **Sacramento County** 720 9th St .... Sacramento CA 95814-1398
916 440-5926 **Sacramento Public Library** 1010 8th St .... Sacramento CA 95814-3576
Fax: 916 441-3425
313 883-8500 **Sacred Heart Seminary College** 2701 W Chicago Blvd .... Detroit MI 48206-1799
203 371-7999 **Sacred Heart University** 5151 Park Ave .... Fairfield CT 06432-1000
Fax: 203 365-7609
714 582-4500 **Saddleback College** 28000 Marguerite Pkwy .... Mission Viejo CA 92692-3699
Fax: 714 364-2726
207 443-8200 **Sagadahoc County** PO Box 246 .... Bath ME 04530-0246
517 790-5251 **Saginaw County** 111 S Michigan Ave .... Saginaw MI 48602-2086
517 790-4000 **Saginaw Valley State University** 2250 Pierce Rd .... University Center MI 48710-0001
Fax: 517 790-1280
719 655-2231 **Saguache County** PO Box 655 .... Saguache CO 81149-0655
203 668-7393 **Saint Alphonsus College** 1762 Mapleton Ave .... Suffield CT 06078-1491
319 383-8800 **Saint Ambrose University** 518 W Locust St .... Davenport IA 52803-2829
Fax: Unlisted
919 276-3652 **Saint Andrews Presbyterian College**
1700 Dogwood Mile St .... Laurinburg NC 28352-5598
Fax: 919 277-8879
603 669-1030 **Saint Anselm College** 87 St Anselm Dr .... Manchester NH 03102-1310
Fax: 603 641-7116
919 828-4451 **Saint Augustine's College** 1315 Oakwood Ave .... Raleigh NC 27610-2298
Fax: 919 834-6473
203 324-4578 **Saint Basil's College** 195 Glenbrook Road .... Stamford CT 06902-3099
Fax: 203 967-9949
504 277-6371 **Saint Bernard Parish** 8201 W Judge Perez Dr .... Chalmette LA 70043-1696
Fax: 504 271-7343
716 375-2000 **Saint Bonaventure University** .... Saint Bonaventure NY 14778-9999
Fax: 716 375-2005
606 336-9304 **Saint Catharine College** .... Saint Catharine KY 40061-9001
Fax: 606 336-5034
215 667-3394 **Saint Charles Borromeo Seminary** 1000 E Wynnwood Rd .... Overbrook PA 19096-3099
Fax: 215 664-7913 Library
314 441-2300 **Saint Charles City County Library District**
425 Spencer Rd .... Saint Peters MO 63376-2420
Fax: 314 441-3132
314 949-3080 **Saint Charles County** 3rd & Jefferson Sts .... Saint Charles MO 63301-0000
Fax: 314 949-2711
504 783-6246 **Saint Charles Parish** PO Box 302 .... Hahnville LA 70057-0302
Fax: 504 782-2067
205 594-5116 **Saint Clair County** PO Box 397 .... Ashville AL 35953-0397
618 277-6600 **Saint Clair County** 10 Public Sq .... Belleville IL 62220-1698
313 985-2031 **Saint Clair County** 201 McMorran Blvd .... Port Huron MI 48060-4006
Fax: Unlisted
417 646-2315 **Saint Clair County** PO Box 405 .... Osceola MO 64776-0405
313 984-3881 **Saint Clair County Community College** 323 Erie St .... Port Huron MI 48060-3812
Fax: 313 984-4730
313 987-7323 **Saint Clair County Library System** 210 McMorran Blvd .... Port Huron MI 48060-4098
Fax: 313 987-7327
313 771-9021 **Saint Clair Shores Public Library** 22500 11-Mile Rd .. Saint Clair Shores MI 48081-1307
Fax: 313 771-8935
612 255-3822 **Saint Cloud State University** Atwood Ctr .... Saint Cloud MN 56301-0000
Fax: 612 255-4873 Admin
612 255-3293 *Department of Mass Communications* Stewart Hall .... Saint Cloud MN 56301-4498
715 386-4600 **Saint Croix County** 911 4th St .... Hudson WI 54016-1656
Fax: 715 386-9329

512 448-8500 **Saint Edward's University** 3001 S Congress Ave .... Austin TX 78704-6489
Fax: 512 448-8492
219 434-3100 **Saint Francis College** 2701 Spring St .... Fort Wayne IN 46808-3994
718 522-2300 **Saint Francis College** 180 Remsen St .... Brooklyn NY 11201-4398
Fax: 718 522-1274
814 472-7000 **Saint Francis College** College Hts .... Loretto PA 15940-9714
Fax: 814 472-3154 Library
501 633-8640 **Saint Francis County** 313 S Izard St .... Forrest City AR 72335-3856
314 756-5411 **Saint Francis County** County Courthouse Sq .... Farmington MO 63640-0000
405 273-9870 **Saint Gregory's College** 1900 W MacArthur St .... Shawnee OK 74801-2499
504 222-4514 **Saint Helena Parish** Court Sq .... Greensburg LA 70441-0000
907 486-3524 **Saint Herman's Theological Seminary** 414 Mission Rd Suite 1 .. Kodiak AK 99615-7392
413 467-7191 **Saint Hyacinth College & Seminary** 66 School St .... Granby MA 01033-9742
504 562-7431 **Saint James Parish** PO Box 106 .... Convent LA 70723-0063
716 385-8000 **Saint John Fisher College** 3690 East Ave .... Rochester NY 14618-3597
Fax: 716 385-8129
504 652-9569 **Saint John the Baptist Parish** 1801 W Airline Hwy .... La Place LA 70068-3336
Fax: 504 652-4131
305 223-4561 **Saint John Vianney Seminary** 2900 SW 87th Ave .... Miami FL 33165-3244
301 263-2371 **Saint John's College** PO Box 2800 .... Annapolis MD 21404-1671
Fax: 301 263-4828
505 982-3691 **Saint John's College at Santa Fe** 1160 Camino Cruz Blanca .... Santa Fe NM 87501-0000
Fax: 505 989-9269
904 328-1571 **Saint John's River Community College** 5001 St John's Ave ...... Palatka FL 32177-3807
Fax: 904 325-6627 Admin
617 254-2610 **Saint John's Seminary** 127 Lake St .... Brighton MA 02135-3898
805 482-4697 **Saint John's Seminary College** 5118 Seminary Rd .... Camarillo CA 93012-0000
Fax: 805 987-5097
612 363-2011 **Saint John's University** .... Collegeville MN 56321-9999
Fax: 612 363-2504
718 969-8000 **Saint John's University** Grand Central & Utopia Pkwys .... Jamaica NY 11439-0001
Fax: 718 990-6649
718 990-6275 *College of Pharmacy & Allied Health Professions*
Grand Central & Utopia Pkwys .... Jamaica NY 11439-0001
Fax: 718 969-0753
718 990-6600 *School of Law* Grand Central & Utopia Pkwys Fromkes Hall .. Jamaica NY 11439-0001
Fax: 718 990-6649
718 447-4343 *Staten Island Campus* 300 Howard Ave .... Staten Island NY 10301-4496
Fax: 718 442-3612 Library
904 824-8131 **Saint Johns County** 99 Cordova St .... Saint Augustine FL 32084-4415
Fax: 904 829-6145
203 232-4571 **Saint Joseph College** 1678 Asylum Ave .... West Hartford CT 06117-2791
Fax: 203 233-5695
219 284-9534 **Saint Joseph County** 227 W Jefferson Blvd .... South Bend IN 46601-1830
Fax: 219 284-9008
616 467-6361 **Saint Joseph County** PO Box 189 .... Centreville MI 49032-0189
Fax: 616 467-1857
219 282-4625 **Saint Joseph County Public Library** 122 W Wayne St .... South Bend IN 46601-2125
Fax: 219 282-4651
504 892-1800 **Saint Joseph Seminary College** River Rd .... Saint Benedict LA 70457-9999
219 866-6000 **Saint Joseph's College** Hwy 231 S .... Rensselaer IN 47978-0000
Fax: 219 866-4497
207 892-6766 **Saint Joseph's College** .... Windham ME 04062-0000
Fax: 207 892-7746
718 636-6800 **Saint Joseph's College** 245 Clinton Ave .... Brooklyn NY 11205-3688
Fax: 718 398-4836
516 654-3200 *Suffolk Campus* 155 Roe Blvd .... Patchogue NY 11772-2399
Fax: 516 654-1782
215 879-7300 **Saint Joseph's University** 5600 City Ave .... Philadelphia PA 19131-1376
Fax: 215 473-0001
Saint Kitts & Nevis: State of Saint Christopher-Nevis
202 833-3550 *Embassy* 2100 M St NW Suite 608 .... Washington DC 20037-1207
Fax: 202 833-3553
212 535-1234 *Mission to the UN* 414 E 75th St 5th Fl .... New York NY 10021-3403
Fax: 212 879-4789
318 942-5606 **Saint Landry Parish** Court & Landry Sts .... Opelousas LA 70570-0000
315 379-2000 **Saint Lawrence County** 48 Court St .... Canton NY 13617-9987
Fax: 315 379-2333
202 366-0091 **Saint Lawrence Seaway Development Corp**
400 7th St SW Rm 5424 .... Washington DC 20590-0001
Fax: 202 366-7147
202 366-0091 *Trade & Traffic Development* 400 7th St SW Rm 5424 .... Washington DC 20590-0001
Fax: 202 366-7147
315 379-5011 **Saint Lawrence University** 23 Romoda Dr .... Canton NY 13617-0000
Fax: 315 379-5502
904 588-8200 **Saint Leo College** Hwy 52 W .... Saint Leo FL 33574-9999
Fax: 904 588-8350
314 622-4000 **Saint Louis City Hall** 1200 Market St .... Saint Louis MO 63103-2808
314 721-0067 **Saint Louis Art Museum** 1 Fine Arts Dr Forest Pk .... Saint Louis MO 63110-1380
Fax: 314 721-6172
314 837-6777 **Saint Louis Christian College** 1360 Grandview Dr .... Florissant MO 63033-6499
314 425-6803 **Saint Louis Coast Guard Base** Iron St .... Saint Louis MO 63111-0000
314 367-8700 **Saint Louis College of Pharmacy** 4588 Parkview Pl .... Saint Louis MO 63110-1088
Fax: Ext 284
314 539-5000 **Saint Louis Community College** 300 S Broadway .... Saint Louis MO 63102-2800
Fax: 314 539-5170
314 595-4200 *Florissant Valley Campus* 3400 Pershall Rd .... Saint Louis MO 63135-1408
Fax: 314 595-4544
314 644-9100 *Forest Park Campus* 5600 Oakland Ave .... Saint Louis MO 63110-1316
Fax: 314 644-9752
314 966-7500 *Meramec Campus* 11333 Big Bend Blvd .... Kirkwood MO 63122-5799
Fax: 314 966-0649
314 863-3033 **Saint Louis Conservatory of Music** 560 Trinity Ave .... Saint Louis MO 63130-4392
314 421-1023 **Saint Louis Convention & Visitors Commission**
10 S Broadway Suite 300 .... Saint Louis MO 63102-1730
218 726-2380 **Saint Louis County** 100 N 5th Ave W .... Duluth MN 55802-1202
Fax: 218 726-2469
314 889-2016 **Saint Louis County** 41 S Central Ave .... Clayton MO 63105-1719
Fax: 314 889-3727
314 994-3300 **Saint Louis County Library** 1640 S Lindbergh Blvd .... Saint Louis MO 63131-3598
Fax: Unlisted
314 241-2288 **Saint Louis Public Library** 1301 Olive St .... Saint Louis MO 63103-2389
Fax: 314 241-3840 Admin
314 289-4400 **Saint Louis Science Center** 5050 Oakland Ave .... Saint Louis MO 63110-1300
Fax: 314 289-4420
314 658-2222 **Saint Louis University** 221 N Grand Blvd .... Saint Louis MO 63103-2097
Fax: 314 658-3874 Admin
314 577-8124 *Edward A Doisy Dept of Biochemistry & Molecular Biology*
1402 S Grand Blvd .... Saint Louis MO 63104-1028
Fax: 314 772-1307
314 658-2800 *School of Law* 3700 Lindell Blvd .... Saint Louis MO 63108-3412
Fax: 314 658-3966
314 577-8205 *School of Medicine* 1402 S Grand Blvd .... Saint Louis MO 63104-1083
Fax: 314 772-1307 Library
314 577-8907 *School of Nursing* 3525 Caroline St .... Saint Louis MO 63104-1007

Saint Lucia
202 463-7378 *Embassy* 2100 M St NW Suite 309 ... Washington DC 20037-1207
Fax: 202 887-5746
212 697-9360 *Mission to the UN* 820 2nd Ave Suites 907-915 ... New York NY 10017-0000
Fax: 212 808-4975
407 489-6900 **Saint Lucie County** 221 S Indian River Dr ... Fort Pierce FL 34950-4301
407 468-1615 **Saint Lucie County Library System** 124 N Indian River Dr ... Fort Pierce FL 34950-4489
318 394-2210 **Saint Martin Parish** County Courthouse ... Saint Martinville LA 70582-0000
206 491-4700 **Saint Martin's College** 700 College St SE ... Lacey WA 98503-1297
Fax: 206 459-4124
913 682-5151 **Saint Mary College** 4100 S 4th St ... Leavenworth KS 66048-5082
316 225-4171 **Saint Mary of the Plains College** 240 San Jose Dr ... Dodge City KS 67801-2786
Fax: 316 225-6212
318 828-4100 **Saint Mary Parish** 500 Main St Rm 5 ... Franklin LA 70538-6198
612 332-5521 **Saint Mary's Campus of the College of Saint Catherine**
2500 S 6th St ... Minneapolis MN 55454-1401
415 376-4411 **Saint Mary's College** St Marys Rd ... Moraga CA 94575-0000
Fax: 415 376-8497 Admin
219 284-4587 **Saint Mary's College** ... Notre Dame IN 46556-0000
Fax: 219 284-4716
313 682-1885 **Saint Mary's College** Commerce & Orchard Lake Rds ... Orchard Lake MI 48033-0000
Fax: 313 683-0402
507 452-4430 **Saint Mary's College** 700 Terrace Heights ... Winona MN 55987-1399
Fax: 507 457-1633
919 828-2521 **Saint Mary's College** 900 Hillsborough St ... Raleigh NC 27603-1689
Fax: 919 832-4831
301 862-0200 **Saint Mary's College of Maryland** ... Saint Marys City MD 20686-9999
Fax: 301 862-0999
301 323-3200 **Saint Mary's Seminary & University** 5400 Roland Ave ... Baltimore MD 21210-1994
512 436-3011 **Saint Mary's University** 1 Camino Santa Maria St ... San Antonio TX 78228-8500
Fax: 512 436-3500
512 436-3424 *School of Law* 1 Camino Santa Maria St ... San Antonio TX 78228-8500
Fax: 512 436-3515
812 535-5151 **Saint Mary-of-the-Woods College** Rt 150 ... Saint Mary-of-the-Woods IN 47876-0000
301 475-5621 **Saint Marys County** PO Box 653 ... Leonardtown MD 20650-0653
812 357-6611 **Saint Meinrad College** Hwy 545 ... Saint Meinrad IN 47577-0000
Fax: 812 357-6462
802 655-2000 **Saint Michael's College** Winooski Pk ... Colchester VT 05439-0001
Fax: 802 655-3680
414 337-3140 **Saint Norbert College** ... De Pere WI 54115-2099
Fax: 414 337-4088
507 663-2222 **Saint Olaf College** 1500 St Olaf Ave ... Northfield MN 55057-1574
Fax: 507 663-3549
415 325-5621 **Saint Patrick's Seminary** 320 Middlefield Rd ... Menlo Park CA 94025-3509
Fax: 415 322-0997
612 298-4012 **Saint Paul City Hall** 15 Kellogg Blvd W ... Saint Paul MN 55102-1635
Fax: 612 298-4144
612 446-1411 **Saint Paul Bible College** 6425 County Rd 30 ... Saint Bonifacius MN 55375-9001
Fax: 612 446-4149
612 292-6311 **Saint Paul Public Library** 90 W 4th St ... Saint Paul MN 55102-1668
Fax: 612 292-6141
804 848-3111 **Saint Paul's College** 406 Windsor Ave ... Lawrenceville VA 23868-1299
Fax: 804 848-0303
201 333-4400 **Saint Peter's College** 2641 John F Kennedy Blvd ... Jersey City NJ 07306-5997
Fax: Unlisted
813 893-7171 **Saint Petersburg City Hall** 175 5th St N ... Saint Petersburg FL 33701-3713
Fax: 813 892-5262
813 341-3600 **Saint Petersburg Junior College** 8580 66th St N ... Pinellas Park FL 34665-1207
Fax: 813 341-3318 Admin
813 893-7724 **Saint Petersburg Public Library** 3745 9th Ave N ... Saint Petersburg FL 33713-6096
512 531-3200 **Saint Philip's College** 2111 Nevada St ... San Antonio TX 78203-2097
Fax: 512 733-2000
504 898-2430 **Saint Tammany Parish** PO Box 1090 ... Covington LA 70434-1090
Fax: 504 898-2464
504 892-0812 **Saint Tammany Parish Library** 310 W 21st Ave ... Covington LA 70433-3100
914 359-9500 **Saint Thomas Aquinas College** Rt 340 ... Sparkill NY 10976-0000
Fax: Unlisted
305 625-6000 **Saint Thomas University** 16400 NW 32nd Ave ... Miami FL 33054-6492
Fax: 305 628-6510
212 687-4490 **Saint Vincent & the Grenadines Mission to the UN**
801 2nd Ave 21st Fl ... New York NY 10017-4706
Fax: 212 949-5946
412 539-9761 **Saint Vincent College** 701 Fraser Purchase Rd ... Latrobe PA 15650-2690
Fax: 412 537-4554
312 779-3300 **Saint Xavier College** 3700 W 103rd St ... Chicago IL 60655-3198
Fax: 312 779-9061
314 883-5589 **Sainte Genevieve County** 55 S 3rd St ... Sainte Genevieve MO 63670-1601
Fax: 314 883-5315
703 375-3016 **Salem (Independent City)** 114 N Broad St ... Salem VA 24153-3734
919 721-2600 **Salem College** 600 S Church St ... Winston-Salem NC 27108-0000
Fax: 919 724-7102
609 299-2100 **Salem Community College** 460 Hollywood Ave ... Carneys Point NJ 08069-2799
609 935-7510 **Salem County** 92 Market St ... Salem NJ 08079-1913
Fax: 609 935-9012
508 741-6000 **Salem State College** 352 Lafayette St ... Salem MA 01970-5353
304 782-5011 **Salem Teikyo University** Main St ... Salem WV 26426-0000
Fax: 304 782-5395
501 778-2667 **Saline County** 200 N Main St ... Benton AR 72015-3767
618 253-8197 **Saline County** 10 E Poplar St ... Harrisburg IL 62946-1553
913 827-1961 **Saline County** 300 W Ash St ... Salina KS 67401-2396
816 886-3331 **Saline County** County Courthouse ... Marshall MO 65340-0000
402 821-2374 **Saline County** 215 Court St ... Wilber NE 68465-0000
301 543-6000 **Salisbury State College** 1101 Camden Ave ... Salisbury MD 21801-6860
Fax: 301 543-6068
406 675-4800 **Salish Kootenai Community College** PO Box 117 ... Pablo MT 59855-0117
Fax: 406 675-4801
801 363-5733 **Salt Lake City Public Library** 209 E 500 South ... Salt Lake City UT 84111-3280
Fax: 801 524-8272
801 967-4111 **Salt Lake Community College** 4600 S Redwood Rd ... Salt Lake City UT 84130-0000
Fax: 801 965-8008
801 468-3531 **Salt Lake County** 2001 State St Rm S2200 ... Salt Lake City UT 84190-0001
801 943-4636 **Salt Lake County Library System** 2197 E 7000 South ... Salt Lake City UT 84121-3188
Fax: 801 942-6323
803 445-3303 **Saluda County** 101 S 9th St ... Saluda SC 29138-0000
Fax: 803 445-8829
813 823-3767 **Salvador Dali Museum** 1000 3rd St S ... Saint Petersburg FL 33701-4901
Fax: 813 894-6068
201 239-0606 **Salvation Army** 799 Bloomfield Ave ... Verona NJ 07044-1392
Fax: 201 239-8441
401 847-6650 **Salve Regina College** 100 Ochre Point Ave ... Newport RI 02840-4192
Fax: 401 849-6920
409 294-1111 **Sam Houston State University** 1700 Sam Houston Ave ... Huntsville TX 77341-0000
Fax: 409 294-1465 Admin

205 870-2011 **Samford University** 800 Lakeshore Dr ... Birmingham AL 35229-0001
Fax: 205 870-2654
205 870-2701 *Cumberland School of Law* 800 Lakeshore Dr ... Birmingham AL 35229-0001
Fax: 205 870-2673
205 870-2833 *School of Pharmacy* 800 Lakeshore Dr ... Birmingham AL 35229-0001
Fax: 205 870-2654
919 592-8081 **Sampson Community College** Hwy 24 W ... Clinton NC 28328-0000
Fax: 919 592-8048
919 592-6308 **Sampson County** 313 Rowan Rd ... Clinton NC 28328-4700
Fax: 919 592-1945
415 420-6076 **Samuel Merritt College of Nursing** 370 Hawthorne Ave ... Oakland CA 94609-3108
Fax: 415 420-6025
San Antonio City Government
512 299-7253 *City Clerk* 100 Military Plaza ... San Antonio TX 78205-0000
512 299-7011 *City Hall* Military Plaza ... San Antonio TX 78205-2425
512 299-8620 *Finance Dept* 506 Dolorosa St ... San Antonio TX 78205-0000
Fax: 512 270-4072
512 299-8400 *Fire Chief* 115 Auditorium Cir ... San Antonio TX 78205-0000
512 299-7060 *Mayor's Office* 100 Military Plaza ... San Antonio TX 78205-0000
Fax: 512 270-4077
512 299-7360 *Police Chief* 214 W Nueva St ... San Antonio TX 78207-0000
512 299-7235 *Public Information Office* 100 Military Plaza ... San Antonio TX 78205-0000
Fax: Unlisted
512 299-8020 *Public Works* 114 W Commerce ... San Antonio TX 78205-0000
Fax: 512 270-4336
512 733-2000 **San Antonio College** 1300 San Pedro Ave ... San Antonio TX 78212-4201
Fax: 512 733-2204
512 270-8700 **San Antonio Convention & Visitors Bureau**
121 Alamo Plaza ... San Antonio TX 78205-2601
Fax: 512 270-8782
512 226-5544 **San Antonio Museum of Art** PO Box 2601 ... San Antonio TX 78299-2601
Fax: 512 223-9619
512 299-7790 **San Antonio Public Library** 203 S Saint Mary's St ... San Antonio TX 78205-2786
Fax: 512 271-9497
409 275-2452 **San Augustine County** 106 Courthouse ... San Augustine TX 75972-1335
408 637-3786 **San Benito County** 440 5th St ... Hollister CA 95023-3843
714 387-2020 **San Bernardino County** 777 E Rialto Ave ... San Bernardino CA 92415-0001
714 381-8201 **San Bernardino Public Library** 555 W 6th St ... San Bernardino CA 92410-3001
Fax: Unlisted
714 888-6511 **San Bernardino Valley College** 701 S Mt Vernon Ave ... San Bernardino CA 92410-2748
Fax: 714 381-4604
619 286-4362 **San Diego Bible College** 5954 Alta Mesa Way ... San Diego CA 92115-6102
619 230-2400 **San Diego City College** 1313 12th Ave ... San Diego CA 92101-4787
San Diego City Government
619 236-5555 *City Administration* 202 C St ... San Diego CA 92101-4806
Fax: 619 236-6110
619 533-4000 *City Clerk* 202 C St 2nd Fl ... San Diego CA 92101-0000
Fax: 619 231-0897
619 236-6363 *City Manager* 202 C St 9th Fl ... San Diego CA 92101-0000
619 236-6060 *Financial Management* 202 C St ... San Diego CA 92101-0000
Fax: 619 236-6219
619 236-6110 *General Services* 202 C St 9th Fl ... San Diego CA 92101-0000
Fax: 619 236-6219
619 236-6330 *Mayor's Office* 202 C St 11th Fl ... San Diego CA 92101-0000
619 236-6460 *Planning Dept* 202 C St 4th Fl ... San Diego CA 92101-0000
619 531-2000 *Police Dept* 1401 Broadway ... San Diego CA 92101-0000
619 236-6112 *Treasurer* 202 C St 8th Fl ... San Diego CA 92101-0000
Fax: 619 236-6219
619 557-6510 **San Diego Coast Guard Air Station** 2710 N Harbor Dr ... San Diego CA 92101-1028
619 694-3900 **San Diego County** 1600 Pacific Hwy ... San Diego CA 92101-2422
619 694-2414 **San Diego County Library System**
5555 Overland Ave Bldg 15 ... San Diego CA 92123-0000
Fax: 619 495-5981
619 232-6203 **San Diego Historical Society Museum** PO Box 81825 ... San Diego CA 92138-1825
619 560-2600 **San Diego Mesa College** 7250 Mesa College Dr ... San Diego CA 92111-4996
Fax: 619 279-5668
619 693-6800 **San Diego Miramar College** 10440 Black Mountain Rd ... San Diego CA 92126-2999
Fax: 619 693-6837 Library
619 232-7931 **San Diego Museum of Art** PO Box 2107 ... San Diego CA 92112-0000
Fax: 619 232-9367
619 239-2001 **San Diego Museum of Man** 1350 El Prado ... San Diego CA 92101-1681
619 556-1011 **San Diego Naval Station** ... San Diego CA 92136-0001
619 236-5800 **San Diego Public Library** 820 E St ... San Diego CA 92101-6479
Fax: 619 233-0914
619 594-5200 **San Diego State University** College Blvd ... San Diego CA 92182-0001
Fax: 619 594-5642
619 594-6151 *College of Health & Human Services* ... San Diego CA 92182-0001
Fax: 619 594-7103
619 594-6635 *Department of Journalism*
Professional Studies & Fine Arts Bldg ... San Diego CA 92182-0001
Fax: 619 594-6974
619 357-5500 *Imperial Valley Campus* 720 Heber Ave ... Calexico CA 92231-2480
415 554-4000 **San Francisco City Hall** 400 Van Ness Ave ... San Francisco CA 94102-4603
415 771-7020 **San Francisco Art Institute** 800 Chestnut St ... San Francisco CA 94133-2299
415 876-2920 **San Francisco Coast Guard Air Station** ... San Francisco CA 94128-0000
Fax: 415 876-2707
415 564-8086 **San Francisco Conservatory of Music** 1201 Ortega St ... San Francisco CA 94122-4411
Fax: 415 665-4004
415 554-4114 **San Francisco County** 400 Van Ness Ave Rm 317 ... San Francisco CA 94102-4607
415 556-3002 **San Francisco Maritime National Historical Park**
Pope St ... San Francisco CA 94109-0000
Fax: 415 556-6293
415 863-8800 **San Francisco Museum of Modern Art**
401 Van Ness Ave ... San Francisco CA 94102-4522
Fax: 415 863-0603
415 558-4235 **San Francisco Public Library** 200 Larkin St ... San Francisco CA 94102-0000
Fax: 415 864-8351
415 338-1111 **San Francisco State University** 1600 Holloway Ave ... San Francisco CA 94132-1722
Fax: 415 338-2514
San Jacinto College
713 476-1501 *Central Campus* 8060 Spencer Hwy ... Pasadena TX 77505-5998
Fax: 713 476-1892
713 458-4050 *North Campus* 5800 Uvalde Rd ... Houston TX 77049-4599
Fax: 713 459-7132
409 653-2324 **San Jacinto County** Church & Bird Sts ... Coldspring TX 77331-0000
209 468-2355 **San Joaquin County** 222 E Weber Ave Rm 303 ... Stockton CA 95202-2709
209 474-5625 **San Joaquin Delta Community College** 5151 Pacific Ave ... Stockton CA 95207-6370
Fax: 209 474-5649
408 277-4000 **San Jose City Hall** 801 N 1st St ... San Jose CA 95110-1708
Fax: 408 277-3100
408 293-9058 **San Jose Christian College** 790 S 12th St ... San Jose CA 95112-2381
408 298-2181 **San Jose City College** 2100 Moorpark Ave ... San Jose CA 95128-2799
408 287-2290 **San Jose Historical Museum** 635 Phelan Ave ... San Jose CA 95112-2508

84 ALPHABETICAL SECTION
San / Scotts

408 924-2000 **San Jose State University** 1 Washington Sq ... San Jose CA 95192-0001
408 924-3240 *Department of Journalism & Mass Communications*
1 Washington Sq ... San Jose CA 95192-0001
Fax: 408 924-3229
408 924-5882 *Urban & Regional Planning Dept* Bldg DD ... San Jose CA 95192-0001
809 729-6800 **San Juan Coast Guard Base** PO Box 2029 ... San Juan PR 00902-2029
Fax: 809 729-1131
303 387-5671 **San Juan County** PO Box 466 ... Silverton CO 81433-0466
505 334-9471 **San Juan County** PO Box 550 ... Aztec NM 87410-0550
801 587-2231 **San Juan County** PO Box 338 ... Monticello UT 84535-0338
Fax: 801 587-2425
206 378-2163 **San Juan County** PO Box 1249 ... Friday Harbor WA 98250-1249
805 549-5785 **San Luis Obispo City-County Library** 995 Palm St ... San Luis Obispo CA 93401-3218
805 549-5245 **San Luis Obispo County** 1035 Palm St Rm 385 ... San Luis Obispo CA 93408-0001
212 751-1234 **San Marino: Republic of San Marino Mission to the UN**
745 5th Ave Suite 1208 ... New York NY 10151-0105
415 363-4711 **San Mateo County** 401 Marshall St ... Redwood City CA 94063-1636
415 573-2056 **San Mateo County Library** 25 Tower Rd ... San Mateo CA 94402-0000
Fax: 415 573-2982
303 728-3954 **San Miguel County** PO Box 548 ... Telluride CO 81435-0548
Fax: 303 728-6347
505 425-9331 **San Miguel County** County Courthouse ... Las Vegas NM 87701-0000
512 364-2490 **San Patricio County** PO Box 578 ... Sinton TX 78387-0578
915 372-3635 **San Saba County** 518 E Wallace St ... San Saba TX 76877-3611
605 796-4515 **Sanborn County** PO Box 56 ... Woonsocket SD 57385-0056
202 225-4115 **Sanders Bernie (Rep - D - Vermont)** 509 Cannon Bldg ... Washington DC 20515-0001
Fax: 202 225-6790
406 827-4392 **Sanders County** Main St ... Thompson Falls MT 59873-0000
919 692-6185 **Sandhills Community College** 2200 Airport Rd ... Pinehurst NC 28374-9299
Fax: 919 692-2756
505 867-2209 **Sandoval County** PO Box 40 ... Bernalillo NM 87004-0000
Fax: 505 867-6739
419 334-6100 **Sandusky County** 100 N Park Ave ... Fremont OH 43420-2473
508 888-0251 **Sandwich Glass Museum** 129 Main St ... Sandwich MA 02563-2233
202 862-9740 **Sane/Freeze** 1819 H St NW Suite 1000 ... Washington DC 20006-3603
Fax: 202 862-9762
202 224-3154 **Sanford Terry (Sen - D - North Carolina)** 716 Hart Bldg ... Washington DC 20510-0001
Fax: 202 224-7406
217 753-6600 **Sangamon County** 800 E Monroe St ... Springfield IL 62701-1979
217 786-6600 **Sangamon State University** Shepherd Rd ... Springfield IL 62794-0000
Fax: 217 786-7188
202 225-3635 **Sangmeister George E (Rep - D - Illinois)**
1032 Longworth Bldg ... Washington DC 20515-0001
Fax: 202 225-4447
313 648-3212 **Sanilac County** 60 W Sanilac Rd ... Sandusky MI 48471-1094
Fax: 313 648-2900
801 835-2131 **Sanpete County** 160 N Main St ... Manti UT 84642-1266
Fax: 801 835-2143
714 647-5250 **Santa Ana Public Library** 26 Civic Center Plaza ... Santa Ana CA 92701-4078
Fax: 714 647-5356
805 965-0581 **Santa Barbara City College** 721 Cliff Dr ... Santa Barbara CA 93109-2312
Fax: 805 963-7222
805 568-2220 **Santa Barbara County** 1100 Anacapa St ... Santa Barbara CA 93101-2099
805 963-4364 **Santa Barbara Museum of Art** 1130 State St ... Santa Barbara CA 93101-2746
Fax: 805 966-6840
805 682-4711 **Santa Barbara Museum of Natural History**
2559 Puesta del Sol Rd ... Santa Barbara CA 93105-2936
Fax: 805 569-3170
805 962-7653 **Santa Barbara Public Library** 40 E Anapamu St ... Santa Barbara CA 93101-2705
Fax: 805 962-8972
408 299-2424 **Santa Clara County** 70 W Hedding St 11th Fl ... San Jose CA 95110-1768
408 293-2326 **Santa Clara County Free Library** 1095 N 7th St ... San Jose CA 95112-4446
Fax: 408 287-9826
408 554-4764 **Santa Clara University** Alameda ... Santa Clara CA 95053-0001
Fax: 408 554-2700
408 554-4361 *Graduate School of Law* Heafey Law Library Rm 224 ... Santa Clara CA 95053-0001
Fax: 408 554-5318
408 429-3533 **Santa Cruz City-County Public Library System**
224 Church St ... Santa Cruz CA 95060-3873
602 281-2047 **Santa Cruz County** PO Box 1265 ... Nogales AZ 85628-1265
408 425-2790 **Santa Cruz County** 701 Ocean St ... Santa Cruz CA 95060-4027
904 395-5443 **Santa Fe Community College** 3000 NW 83rd St ... Gainesville FL 32602-0000
Fax: 904 395-5581
505 984-5080 **Santa Fe County** PO Box 1985 ... Santa Fe NM 87504-1985
316 285-2054 **Santa Fe Trail Center** RR 3 ... Larned KS 67550-9803
213 450-5150 **Santa Monica College** 1900 Pico Blvd ... Santa Monica CA 90405-1644
Fax: 213 450-2387
904 623-0135 **Santa Rosa County** 801 Caroline St SE ... Milton FL 32570-4978
Fax: 904 623-1684
707 527-4011 **Santa Rosa Junior College** 1501 Mendocino Ave ... Santa Rosa CA 95401-4395
Fax: 707 527-4816
202 225-2135 **Santorum Rick (Rep - R - Pennsylvania)**
1708 Longworth Bldg ... Washington DC 20515-0001
Fax: 202 225-7747
Sao Tome & Principe: Democratic Republic of Sao Tome & Principe
212 697-4211 *Embassy* 801 2nd Ave Suite 1504 ... New York NY 10017-4706
Fax: 212 687-8389
212 697-4211 *Mission to the UN* 801 2nd Ave Suite 1504 ... New York NY 10017-4706
914 337-0700 **Sarah Lawrence College** 1 Meadway ... Bronxville NY 10708-5999
Fax: 914 395-2668
813 365-1000 **Sarasota County** 2000 Main St ... Sarasota FL 34237-6036
518 885-5381 **Saratoga County** 40 McMasters St ... Ballston Spa NY 12020-1999
Fax: Call company operator
202 224-4524 **Sarbanes Paul S (Sen - D - Maryland)** 309 Hart Bldg ... Washington DC 20510-0001
Fax: 202 224-1651
701 724-3355 **Sargent County** PO Box 98 ... Forman ND 58032-0098
202 225-3706 **Sarpalius Bill (Rep - D - Texas)** 126 Cannon Bldg ... Washington DC 20515-0001
Fax: 202 225-6142
402 339-3225 **Sarpy County** 1208 Golden Gate Dr ... Omaha NE 68046-2838
Fax: 402 593-4323
202 224-3344 **Sasser James (Sen - D - Tennessee)** 363 Russell Bldg ... Washington DC 20510-0001
Fax: 202 224-9590
Saudi Arabia: Kingdom of Saudi Arabia
202 342-3800 *Embassy* 601 New Hampshire Ave NW ... Washington DC 20037-2405
Fax: 202 337-3233
212 697-4830 *Mission to the UN* 405 Lexington Ave 56th Fl ... New York NY 10174-0220
Fax: Call company operator
713 785-5577 *Houston Consulate General*
5718 Westheimer Blvd Suite 1500 ... Houston TX 77057-5733
213 208-6566 *Los Angeles Consulate General*
10900 Wilshire Blvd Suite 830 ... Los Angeles CA 90024-6528
Fax: 213 208-5643
212 752-2740 *New York Consulate General*
866 United Nations Plaza Suite 480 ... New York NY 10017-1870
608 356-5581 **Sauk County** 515 Oak St ... Baraboo WI 53913-2416
Fax: 608 355-3292

815 288-5511 **Sauk Valley Community College** 173 Illinois Rt 2 ... Dixon IL 61021-9188
906 635-3217 **Sault Saint Marie Coast Guard Base** 337 Water St ... Sault Sainte Marie MI 49783-9501
Fax: 906 635-3238
402 443-8101 **Saunders County** Chestnut St Courthouse ... Wahoo NE 68066-0000
202 225-0773 **Savage Gus (Rep - D - Illinois)** 2419 Rayburn Bldg ... Washington DC 20515-0001
Fax: 202 886-9402
912 352-6237 **Savannah Coast Guard Air Station** Hunter AAF ... Savannah GA 31409-0001
Fax: 912 352-6556
912 238-2483 **Savannah College of Art & Design** 26 W Harris St ... Savannah GA 31401-4354
Fax: 912 238-2436 Admin
912 356-2186 **Savannah State College** ... Savannah GA 31404-0000
203 226-7271 **Save the Children Federation** 54 Wilton Rd ... Westport CT 06880-3108
Fax: 203 454-3914
202 634-5377 **Savings Bond Div (US Dept of the Treasury)**
1111 20th St NW Rm 305 ... Washington DC 20226-0001
Fax: 202 634-5119
715 634-4866 **Sawyer County** PO Box 273 ... Hayward WI 54843-0273
906 346-6511 **Sawyer KI Air Force Base** ... KI Sawyer AFB MI 49843-0000
202 225-5231 **Sawyer Thomas C (Rep - D - Ohio)** 1518 Longworth Bldg ... Washington DC 20515-0001
Fax: 202 225-5278
202 225-4765 **Saxton Jim (Rep - R - New Jersey)** 324 Cannon Bldg ... Washington DC 20515-0001
Fax: 202 225-0778
202 225-7882 **Schaefer Dan (Rep - R - Colorado)** 1007 Longworth Bldg ... Washington DC 20515-0001
Fax: 202 225-7885
708 885-3373 **Schaumburg Township District Library** 32 W Library Ln ... Schaumburg IL 60194-3497
Fax: 708 885-8271
518 382-3220 **Schenectady County** 620 State St ... Schenectady NY 12305-2113
518 346-6211 **Schenectady County Community College**
78 Washington Ave ... Schenectady NY 12305-2294
Fax: 518 346-0379
518 382-3500 **Schenectady County Public Library System** 99 Clinton St ... Schenectady NY 12305-2083
Fax: Unlisted
518 382-7890 **Schenectady Museum & Planetarium**
Nott Terrace Heights ... Schenectady NY 12308-3198
202 225-5471 **Scheuer James H (Rep - D - New York)**
2221 Rayburn Bldg ... Washington DC 20515-0001
Fax: 202 225-9695
704 866-6900 **Schiele Museum of Natural History & Planetarium**
1500 E Garrison Blvd ... Gastonia NC 28054-5199
202 225-6316 **Schiff Steven (Rep - R - New Mexico)**
1427 Longworth Bldg ... Washington DC 20515-0001
Fax: 202 225-4975
915 853-2833 **Schleicher County** Hwy 277 ... Eldorado TX 76936-0000
912 937-2609 **Schley County** PO Box 352 ... Ellaville GA 31806-0000
716 278-1780 **Schoellkopf Geological Museum**
Prospect Pk Niagara Reservation ... Niagara Falls NY 14303-0000
Fax: 716 278-1744
808 655-4930 **Schofield Barracks** ... Honolulu HI 96857-0001
518 295-8316 **Schoharie County** PO Box 549 ... Schoharie NY 12157-0549
802 257-7751 **School for International Training** Kipling Rd ... Brattleboro VT 05301-0000
Fax: 802 254-6674
802 257-7751 *Graduate School of Public Administration* Kipling Rd ... Brattleboro VT 05301-0000
Fax: 802 257-7526
603 862-1692 **School for Lifelong Learning** Dunlap Ctr ... Durham NH 03824-3545
312 899-5100 **School of the Art Institute of Chicago** 37 S Wabash Ave ... Chicago IL 60603-3199
Fax: 312 263-0141
617 267-6100 **School of the Museum of Fine Arts** 230 Fenway ... Boston MA 02115-5534
Fax: 617 267-0280
417 334-6411 **School of the Ozarks** ... Point Lookout MO 65726-9999
212 679-7350 **School of Visual Arts** 209 E 23rd St ... New York NY 10010-3994
Fax: 212 725-3587
313 591-6400 **Schoolcraft College** 18600 Haggerty Rd ... Livonia MI 48152-2696
Fax: 313 462-4470
906 341-5532 **Schoolcraft County** 300 Walnut St ... Manistique MI 49854-1491
512 896-5411 **Schreiner College** 2100 Memorial Blvd ... Kerrville TX 78028-5697
Fax: 512 896-3232
202 225-4431 **Schroeder Patricia (Rep - D - Colorado)**
2208 Rayburn Bldg ... Washington DC 20515-0001
Fax: 202 225-5842
202 225-5761 **Schulze Richard T (Rep - R - Pennsylvania)**
2369 Rayburn Bldg ... Washington DC 20515-0001
Fax: Unlisted
202 225-6616 **Schumer Charles E (Rep - D - New York)**
2412 Rayburn Bldg ... Washington DC 20515-0001
Fax: 202 225-4183
217 322-4734 **Schuyler County** PO Box 190 ... Rushville IL 62681-0190
816 457-3842 **Schuyler County** PO Box 187 ... Lancaster MO 63548-0187
607 535-2132 **Schuyler County** 105 9th St ... Watkins Glen NY 14891-1496
717 622-5570 **Schuylkill County** N 2nd St & Laurel Blvd ... Pottsville PA 17901-2528
Fax: 717 628-1108 Admin
202 447-5923 **Science & Education Div (US Dept of Agriculture)**
Administration Bldg Rm 217-W ... Washington DC 20250-0001
Fax: 202 755-7842
301 344-2264 *Agricultural Research Service* Bldg 005 BARC-W Rm 307 ... Beltsville MD 20705-0000
Fax: 301 344-1726
202 707-5639 **Science & Technology Div (Library of Congress)**
101 Independence Ave SE LA 5104 ... Washington DC 20540-0000
515 274-4138 **Science Center of Iowa**
4500 Grand Ave Greenwood-Ashword Pk ... Des Moines IA 50312-2402
703 342-5710 **Science Museum of Western Virginia** 1 Market Sq ... Roanoke VA 24011-1417
202 225-6371 **Science Space & Technology Committee (US House of Representatives)**
2321 Rayburn Bldg ... Washington DC 20515-0001
Fax: 202 225-8280
614 353-5111 **Scioto County** 602 7th St ... Portsmouth OH 45662-3948
816 465-7027 **Scotland County** County Courthouse ... Memphis MO 63555-0000
919 277-0470 **Scotland County** 1405 West Blvd ... Laurinburg NC 28352-0000
Fax: 919 277-2411
618 256-1110 **Scott Air Force Base** ... Belleville IL 62225-0000
Fax: Unlisted
501 637-2155 **Scott County** PO Box 1578 ... Waldron AR 72958-1578
319 326-8647 **Scott County** 416 W 4th St ... Davenport IA 52801-1187
217 742-3178 **Scott County** 101 E Market St ... Winchester IL 62694-1258
812 752-4769 **Scott County** 1 E McClain Ave ... Scottsburg IN 47170-1848
316 872-2420 **Scott County** 303 Court St ... Scott City KS 67871-1122
Fax: 316 872-7145
502 863-7875 **Scott County** 101 E Main St ... Georgetown KY 40324-1794
Fax: 502 863-7852
612 445-7750 **Scott County** 428 Holmes St S Rm 212 ... Shakopee MN 55379-1348
Fax: 612 496-8257
314 545-3549 **Scott County** PO Box 188 ... Benton MO 63736-0188
601 469-1922 **Scott County** PO Box 630 ... Forest MS 39074-0630
Fax: 601 469-3514
615 663-2588 **Scott County** PO Box 87 ... Huntsville TN 37756-0087
703 386-7341 **Scott County** 104 E Jackson St ... Gate City VA 24251-3417
308 436-6600 **Scotts Bluff County** 1825 10th St ... Gering NE 69341-2444

For information on alphabetization, see the Alphabetical Section title page.

602 423-6000 **Scottsdale Community College** 9000 E Chaparral Rd .... Scottsdale AZ 85250-2699
Fax: 602 423-6200

602 994-2476 **Scottsdale Public Library System** 3839 Civic Center Blvd ..... Scottsdale AZ 85251-4467
Fax: 602 994-7993

717 348-3000 **Scranton Public Library** Vine St & N Washington Ave .... Scranton PA 18503-0000
Fax: Call company operator

912 564-7535 **Screven County** PO Box 159 .... Sylvania GA 30467-0159

714 621-8282 **Scripps College** 1030 N Columbia Ave .... Claremont CA 91711-3948

915 573-5332 **Scurry County** County Courthouse .... Snyder TX 79549-0000

301 899-0675 **Seafarers' International Union of North America**
5201 Auth Way .... Camp Springs MD 20746-4275
Fax: 301 899-7355

501 448-3554 **Searcy County** PO Box 297 .... Marshall AR 72650-0297

206 386-1234 **Seattle City Hall** 600 4th Ave .... Seattle WA 98104-1876
Fax: 206 684-5360

206 625-8900 **Seattle Art Museum** 1400 E Prospect St .... Seattle WA 98112-3303
Fax: 206 625-8913

206 784-1888 **Seattle Bible College** 2363 NW 80th St .... Seattle WA 98117-4399

206 587-3800 **Seattle Central Community College** 1701 Broadway .... Seattle WA 98122-2400

206 286-9650 **Seattle Coast Guard Support Center** 1519 Alaskan Way S .... Seattle WA 98134-1102

206 587-4155 **Seattle Community College (System)** 1500 Harvard Ave .... Seattle WA 98122-2400
Fax: 206 587-3883

206 281-2000 **Seattle Pacific University** 3307 3rd Ave W .... Seattle WA 98119-1997
Fax: 206 281-2500

206 386-4100 **Seattle Public Library** 1000 4th Ave .... Seattle WA 98104-1193
Fax: 206 386-4119

206 296-6000 **Seattle University** Broadway & Madison .... Seattle WA 98122-0000
Fax: 206 461-5257

501 783-6139 **Sebastian County** 6th & Rogers .... Fort Smith AR 72901-0000

312 263-2303 **Second Harvest** 116 S Michigan Suite 4 .... Chicago IL 60603-6001
Fax: 312 263-5626

202 535-5708 **Secret Service (US Dept of the Treasury)**
1800 G St NW Rm 805 .... Washington DC 20223-0001
Fax: 202 566-2001

202 447-3631 **Secretary of Agriculture (US Dept of Agriculture)**
14th St & Independence Ave SW Rm 200-A .... Washington DC 20250-0001
Fax: 202 447-5043

202 377-2112 **Secretary of Commerce (US Dept of Commerce)**
14th St & Constitution Ave NW Rm 5858 .... Washington DC 20230-0001
Fax: 202 377-5264

202 695-5261 **Secretary of Defense (US Dept of Defense)**
Pentagon Rm 3E-880 .... Washington DC 20301-1000
Fax: 202 697-9080

202 732-3000 **Secretary of Education (US Dept of Education)**
400 Maryland Ave SW Rm 4181 .... Washington DC 20202-0001
Fax: 202 732-2896

202 586-6210 **Secretary of Energy (US Dept of Energy)**
1000 Independence Ave SW Rm 257 .... Washington DC 20585-0001
Fax: Unlisted

202 245-7000 **Secretary of Health & Human Services (US Dept of Health & Human Services)**
200 Independence Ave SW Rm 615F .... Washington DC 20201-0001
Fax: 202 245-7203

202 755-6417 **Secretary of Housing & Urban Development (US Dept of Housing & Urban Development)**
451 7th St SW Rm 10000 .... Washington DC 20410-0001
Fax: 202 755-9476

202 523-8271 **Secretary of Labor (US Dept of Labor)**
200 Constitution Ave NW Rm S-018 .... Washington DC 20210-0001
Fax: 202 523-6161

202 647-5291 **Secretary of State (US Dept of State)** 2201 C St NW 7th Fl .. Washington DC 20520-0001
Fax: 202 647-6434

202 343-7351 **Secretary of the Interior (US Dept of the Interior)**
1849 C St NW MS-6217 .... Washington DC 20240-0001
Fax: 202 343-8950

202 566-2533 **Secretary of the Treasury (US Dept of the Treasury)**
1500 Pennsylvania Ave NW Rm 3330 .... Washington DC 20220-0001
Fax: 202 566-8066

202 366-1111 **Secretary of Transportation (US Dept of Transportation)**
400 7th St SW Rm 10200 .... Washington DC 20590-0001
Fax: 202 426-4508

202 233-3775 **Secretary of Veterans Affairs (US Dept of Veterans Affairs)**
810 Vermont Ave NW Rm 1000S .... Washington DC 20420-0001
Fax: 202 233-4785

202 272-2650 **Securities & Exchange Commission**
450 5th St NW Suite 1012 .... Washington DC 20549-0001
Fax: 202 272-7050

212 264-1636 *Region 1* 75 Park Pl .... New York NY 10007-2146
Fax: 212 264-3044

617 223-9900 *Region 2* JW McCormack POCH Suite 700 .... Boston MA 02109-0000
Fax: 617 223-9901

404 347-4768 *Region 3* 1375 Peachtree St NE Suite 788 .... Atlanta GA 30367-0001
Fax: 404 347-3069

312 353-7390 *Region 4* 219 S Dearborn St Rm 1204 .... Chicago IL 60604-1773
Fax: 312 353-7398

817 334-3821 *Region 5* 411 W 7th St Suite 800 .... Fort Worth TX 76102-3689
Fax: 817 334-2700

303 844-2071 *Region 6* 410 17th St Suite 700 .... Denver CO 80202-4488
Fax: 303 844-2070

213 965-3807 *Region 7* 5757 Wilshire Blvd Suite 500 .... Los Angeles CA 90036-3648
Fax: 213 468-3815

206 442-7990 *Region 8* 915 2nd Ave Rm 3040 .... Seattle WA 98174-1077
Fax: 206 442-0338

215 597-3100 *Region 9* 601 Walnut St Curtis Ctr Suite 1005-E .... Philadelphia PA 19106-0000
Fax: 215 597-5885

202 695-3291 **Security Assistance Agency (US Dept of Defense)**
Pentagon Rm 4E-841 .... Washington DC 20301-0001
Fax: 202 695-0081

202 647-4404 **Security Assistance Science & Technology (US Dept of State)**
2201 C St NW Rm 7208 .... Washington DC 20520-0001
Fax: 202 647-6434

303 474-3346 **Sedgwick County** PO Box 3 .... Julesburg CO 80737-0003

316 383-7166 **Sedgwick County** 525 N Main St .... Wichita KS 67203-3703

813 951-5501 **Selby Public Library** 1001 Blvd of the Arts .... Sarasota FL 34236-4899
Fax: 813 954-3808

202 226-3375 **Select Committee on Aging (US House of Representatives)**
300 New Jersey SE House Annex I Rm 712 .... Washington DC 20515-0001
Fax: Unlisted

202 226-7660 **Select Committee on Children Youth & Families (US House of Representatives)**
2nd & D Sts SW House Annex 2 Rm 385 .... Washington DC 20515-0001
Fax: 202 226-7672

202 224-2981 **Select Committee on Ethics (US Senate)** 220 Hart Bldg ..... Washington DC 20510-0001
Fax: 202 224-7416

202 224-2251 **Select Committee on Indian Affairs (US Senate)**
838 Hart Bldg .... Washington DC 20510-0001
Fax: 202 224-2309

202 224-1700 **Select Committee on Intelligence (US Senate)**
211 Hart Bldg .... Washington DC 20510-0001
Fax: Unlisted

202 226-3040 **Select Committee on Narcotics Abuse & Control (US House of Representatives)**
House Annex II Rm 2234 .... Washington DC 20515-0001
Fax: 202 225-0094

202 724-0419 **Selective Service System** 1023 31st St NW .... Washington DC 20435-0001
Fax: 202 724-1792

205 872-2533 **Selma University** 2501 Lapsley Ave .... Selma AL 36701-0000
Fax: 205 872-7746

407 323-1450 **Seminole Community College** 100 Weldon Blvd .... Sanford FL 32773-6199
Fax: Ext 692

407 323-4482 **Seminole County** 301 N Park Ave .... Sanford FL 32771-1292
Fax: 407 330-7193

912 524-2878 **Seminole County** County Courthouse .... Donalsonville GA 31745-0000

405 257-2450 **Seminole County** PO Box 457 .... Wewoka OK 74884-0457

405 382-9950 **Seminole Junior College** PO Box 351 .... Seminole OK 74868-0000
Fax: 405 382-2998

315 539-5655 **Seneca County** 1 DiPronio Dr .... Waterloo NY 13165-1681
Fax: 315 539-9479

419 447-4550 **Seneca County** 81 Jefferson St .... Tiffin OH 44883-2354
Fax: 419 447-0556

Senegal: Republic of Senegal

202 234-0540 *Embassy* 2112 Wyoming Ave NW .... Washington DC 20008-3906
Fax: 202 332-6315

212 517-9030 *Mission to the UN* 238 E 68th St .... New York NY 10021-6001
Fax: 212 737-7461

202 225-5101 **Sensenbrenner F James Jr (Rep - R - Wisconsin)**
2444 Rayburn Bldg .... Washington DC 20515-0001
Fax: 202 225-3190

615 949-2522 **Sequatchie County** Cherry St .... Dunlap TN 37327-0000

918 775-5539 **Sequoyah County** 120 E Chickasaw Ave Box 8 .... Sallisaw OK 74955-4655

202 225-4361 **Serrano Jose E (Rep - D - New York)**
1107 Longworth Bldg .... Washington DC 20515-0001
Fax: 202 225-6001

816 333-8300 **Sertoma International** 1912 E Meyer Blvd .... Kansas City MO 64132-1174

201 761-9000 **Seton Hall University** 400 S Orange Ave .... South Orange NJ 07079-2697
Fax: 201 761-9600

201 642-8500 *School of Law* 1111 Raymond Blvd .... Newark NJ 07102-5297
Fax: 201 642-8734

412 834-2200 **Seton Hill College** Seton Hill Dr .... Greensburg PA 15601-1599
Fax: Unlisted

501 642-2852 **Sevier County** 115 N 3rd St .... De Queen AR 71832-2852

615 453-5502 **Sevier County** 125 Court Ave .... Sevierville TN 37862-3594

801 896-9262 **Sevier County** 250 N Main St .... Richfield UT 84701-2158
Fax: 801 896-8888

316 624-0211 **Seward County** 415 N Washington Ave .... Liberal KS 67901-3497
Fax: 316 624-4851

402 643-2883 **Seward County** County Courthouse .... Seward NE 68434-0000

316 624-1951 **Seward County Community College** PO Box 1137 .... Liberal KS 67905-1137
Fax: 316 624-0637

Seychelles: Republic of Seychelles

212 687-9766 *Embassy* 820 2nd Ave Suite 900-F .... New York NY 10017-4504
Fax: 212 808-4975

212 687-9766 *Mission to the UN* 820 2nd Ave Suite 900 .... New York NY 10017-4504
Fax: 212 808-4975

919 736-5400 **Seymour Johnson Air Force Base** .... Goldsboro NC 27531-0000
Fax: 919 736-5627 Mail Rm

915 762-2232 **Shackelford County** PO Box 247 .... Albany TX 76430-0247

314 226-3414 **Shannon County** County Courthouse .... Eminence MO 65466-0000

605 745-5131 **Shannon County** 906 N River St .... Hot Springs SD 57747-1387

601 873-2755 **Sharkey County** County Courthouse .... Rolling Fork MS 39159-0000

501 994-7338 **Sharp County** County Courthouse .... Ash Flat AR 72513-0000

202 225-3021 **Sharp Philip R (Rep - D - Indiana)** 2217 Rayburn Bldg ...... Washington DC 20515-0001
Fax: 202 225-8140

916 225-4600 **Shasta College** PO Box 496006 .... Redding CA 96049-6006
Fax: 916 225-4830

916 225-5631 **Shasta County** 1500 Court St .... Redding CA 96001-1694

803 668-8110 **Shaw Air Force Base** .... Sumter SC 29152-0000
Fax: 803 668-2472

202 225-3026 **Shaw E Clay Jr (Rep - R - Florida)** 2338 Rayburn Bldg ...... Washington DC 20515-0001
Fax: 202 225-8398

919 755-4800 **Shaw University** 118 E South St .... Raleigh NC 27601-2399
Fax: 919 755-2965

715 526-9150 **Shawano County** 311 N Main St .... Shawano WI 54166-2198

618 634-2242 **Shawnee Community College** Shawnee College Rd .... Ullin IL 62992-0000
Fax: Unlisted

913 291-4040 **Shawnee County** 200 SE 7th St .... Topeka KS 66603-3922

614 354-3205 **Shawnee State University** 940 2nd St .... Portsmouth OH 45662-9927
Fax: 614 355-2416

202 225-5541 **Shays Christopher (Rep - R - Connecticut)**
1531 Longworth Bldg .... Washington DC 20515-0001
Fax: 202 225-9629

414 459-3003 **Sheboygan County** 615 N 6th St .... Sheboygan WI 53081-4612
Fax: 414 459-4305

802 985-3346 **Shelburne Museum** US Rt 7 .... Shelburne VT 05482-0000

205 669-3760 **Shelby County** Main St .... Columbiana AL 35051-0000

712 755-5543 **Shelby County** PO Box 431 .... Harlan IA 51537-0431

217 774-4421 **Shelby County** 324 E Main St .... Shelbyville IL 62565-1694

317 392-6320 **Shelby County** 315 S Harrison St .... Shelbyville IN 46176-2161

502 633-1220 **Shelby County** 501 Main St .... Shelbyville KY 40065-1133

314 633-2181 **Shelby County** 1 Courthouse Sq .... Shelbyville MO 63469-0000

513 498-7226 **Shelby County** 129 E Court St .... Sidney OH 45365-3095
Fax: 513 498-1293

901 576-4244 **Shelby County** 160 N Mid-America Mall .... Memphis TN 38103-1800

409 598-6361 **Shelby County** Courthouse .... Center TX 75935-3945

202 224-5744 **Shelby Richard (Sen - D - Alabama)** 313 Hart Bldg .... Washington DC 20510-0001
Fax: 202 224-3416

901 528-6700 **Shelby State Community College** 1256 Union Ave .... Memphis TN 38104-3414
Fax: 901 528-8991

907 747-5220 **Sheldon Jackson College** 801 Lincoln St .... Sitka AK 99835-7699
Fax: 907 747-5212

402 472-2461 **Sheldon Memorial Art Gallery**
12th & R Sts University of Nebraska .... Lincoln NE 68588-0300

812 238-1676 **Sheldon Swope Art Museum** 25 S 7th St .... Terre Haute IN 47807-3692

205 759-1541 **Shelton State Community College** 202 Skyland Blvd .... Tuscaloosa AL 35405-4093
Fax: 205 759-2495

907 392-3000 **Shemya Air Force Base** .... Shemya AK 98736-5000
Fax: 907 392-3585

703 459-3791 **Shenandoah County** 112 S Main St .... Woodstock VA 22664-1423

703 665-4500 **Shenandoah University** 1460 College Dr .... Winchester VA 22601-5195
Fax: 703 665-4508

304 876-2511 **Shepherd College** King St .... Shepherdstown WV 25443-0000
Fax: 304 876-3101 Admin

817 676-2511 **Sheppard Air Force Base** .... Wichita Falls TX 76311-5000

612 441-3844 **Sherburne County** 13880 Hwy 10 .... Elk River MN 55330-4601

307 674-6446 **Sheridan College** 3059 Coffeen Ave .... Sheridan WY 82801-9133
Fax: 307 672-6157 Library
913 675-3361 **Sheridan County** PO Box 899 .... Hoxie KS 67740-0899
Fax: 913 675-3050
406 765-2310 **Sheridan County** 100 W Laurel Ave .... Plentywood MT 59254-1699
701 363-2207 **Sheridan County** PO Box 636 .... McClusky ND 58463-0636
308 327-2633 **Sheridan County** 301 E 2nd St .... Rushville NE 69360-0000
Fax: 308 327-2812
307 674-6822 **Sheridan County** 224 S Main St Suite B2 .... Sheridan WY 82801-4855
913 899-7581 **Sherman County** 813 Broadway .... Goodland KS 67735-3056
Fax: 913 899-5563
308 745-1513 **Sherman County** PO Box 456 .... Loup City NE 68853-0456
503 565-3606 **Sherman County** PO Box 365 .... Moro OR 97039-0365
806 396-2371 **Sherman County** 701 N 3rd St .... Stratford TX 79084-0000
517 743-2279 **Shiawassee County** 208 N Shiawassee St .... Corunna MI 48817-1494
415 261-1907 **Shiloh Bible College** 3295 School St .... Oakland CA 94602-3638
708 623-8400 **Shimer College** PO Box A500 .... Waukegan IL 60079-7997
717 532-9121 **Shippensburg University** .... Shippensburg PA 17257-0000
Fax: 717 532-1273
206 546-4101 **Shoreline Community College** 16101 Greenwood Ave N .... Seattle WA 98133-5696
Fax: 206 546-4599
501 374-6305 **Shorter College** 604 N Locust St .... North Little Rock AR 72114-4885
404 291-2121 **Shorter College** 315 Shorter Ave .... Rome GA 30161-4298
Fax: Ext 323
208 752-3331 **Shoshone County** PO Box 1049 .... Wallace ID 83873-1049
Fax: 208 753-0921
318 226-5897 **Shreve Memorial Library** 424 Texas Ave .... Shreveport LA 71120-0000
605 677-5306 **Shrine to Music Museum** 414 E Clark St .... Vermillion SD 57069-0000
202 225-2431 **Shuster Bud (Rep - R - Pennsylvania)** 2268 Rayburn Bldg .. Washington DC 20515-0001
Fax: Unlisted
612 237-2427 **Sibley County** 400 Court St .... Gaylord MN 55334-0000
Fax: 612 237-5142
518 783-2300 **Siena College** .... Loudonville NY 12211-0000
Fax: 518 783-2992
517 263-0731 **Siena Heights College** 1247 E Siena Heights Dr .... Adrian MI 49221-1796
Fax: 517 265-3380
916 624-3333 **Sierra Community College** 5000 Rocklin Rd .... Rocklin CA 95677-3397
Fax: 916 781-0455
916 289-3295 **Sierra County** PO Box D .... Downieville CA 95936-0398
505 894-6215 **Sierra County** 300 Date St .... Truth or Consequences NM 87901-2362
Sierra Leone: Republic of Sierra Leone
202 939-9261 *Embassy* 1701 19th St NW .... Washington DC 20009-1605
212 570-0030 *Mission to the UN* 57 E 64th St .... New York NY 10021-7003
702 831-1314 **Sierra Nevada College** PO Box 4269 .... Incline Village NV 89450-4269
Fax: 702 831-1347
714 545-1133 **Sierra University** 2900 Bristol St Suite D-207 .... Costa Mesa CA 92626-5955
202 225-2271 **Sikorski Gerry (Rep - D - Minnesota)** 403 Cannon Bldg ..... Washington DC 20515-0001
Fax: 202 225-4347
203 574-8222 **Silas Bronson Library** 267 Grand St .... Waterbury CT 06702-1981
406 723-8262 **Silver Bow County** 155 W Granite St .... Butte MT 59701-9215
414 684-6691 **Silver Lake College** 2406 S Alverno Rd .... Manitowoc WI 54220-9319
502 776-1443 **Simmons Bible College** 1811 Dumesnil .... Louisville KY 40210-1401
617 738-2000 **Simmons College** 300 Fenway .... Boston MA 02115-5898
Fax: 617 738-2099
617 738-2225 *Graduate School of Library & Information Science*
300 Fenway .... Boston MA 02115-5898
Fax: 617 738-2099
818 449-6840 **Simon Norton Museum** 411 W Colorado Blvd .... Pasadena CA 91105-1896
Fax: 818 796-4978
202 224-2152 **Simon Paul (Sen - D - Illinois)** 462 Dirksen Bldg .... Washington DC 20510-0001
Fax: Unlisted
413 528-0771 **Simon's Rock of Bard College** 84 Alford Rd .... Great Barrington MA 01230-9702
Fax: Call company operator
202 224-3424 **Simpson Alan K (Sen - R - Wyoming)** 261 Dirksen Bldg ..... Washington DC 20510-0001
Fax: 202 224-1315
916 221-7280 **Simpson College** 2211 College View Dr .... Redding CA 96003-8606
Fax: Unlisted
515 961-6251 **Simpson College** 701 N 'C' St .... Indianola IA 50125-1297
Fax: 515 961-1498
502 586-8161 **Simpson County** PO Box 268 .... Franklin KY 42134-0268
601 847-2626 **Simpson County** 109 W Pine Ave .... Mendenhall MS 39114-3597
Fax: 601 847-1602
513 226-2500 **Sinclair Community College** 444 W 3rd St .... Dayton OH 45402-1453
Fax: Unlisted
Singapore: Republic of Singapore
202 667-7555 *Embassy* 1824 R St NW .... Washington DC 20009-1604
Fax: 202 265-7915
212 826-0840 *Mission to the UN* 2 UN Plaza 25th Fl .... New York NY 10017-0000
Fax: 212 826-2964
605 747-2263 **Sinte Gleska College** Box 490 .... Rosebud SD 57570-0490
Fax: 605 747-2098
712 279-6272 **Sioux City Art Center** 513 Nebraska St .... Sioux City IA 51101-1305
712 252-5669 **Sioux City Public Library** 529 Pierce St .... Sioux City IA 51101-0000
712 279-6174 **Sioux City Public Museum** 2901 Jackson St .... Sioux City IA 51104-3650
712 737-2286 **Sioux County** 210 Central Ave SW .... Orange City IA 51041-1751
701 854-3853 **Sioux County** PO Box L .... Fort Yates ND 58538-0529
308 668-2443 **Sioux County** Main St .... Harrison NE 69346-0000
605 331-5000 **Sioux Falls College** 1501 S Prairie Ave .... Sioux Falls SD 57105-1699
605 339-7081 **Sioux Falls Public Library** 201 N Main Ave .... Sioux Falls SD 57102-0386
Fax: 605 335-4312
605 335-4210 **Siouxland Heritage Museums** 200 W 6th St .... Sioux Falls SD 57102-0302
202 225-6365 **Sisisky Norman (Rep - D - Virginia)** 426 Cannon Bldg ...... Washington DC 20515-0001
Fax: 202 226-1170
916 842-8005 **Siskiyou County** 311 4th St .... Yreka CA 96097-2944
916 938-4462 **Siskiyous Joint Community College District** 800 College Ave ...... Weed CA 96094-2806
Fax: 916 938-5226
907 747-3294 **Sitka Borough** 304 Lake St .... Sitka AK 99835-7563
Fax: 907 747-7403
907 966-5434 **Sitka Coast Guard Air Station** 611 Airport Rd .... Sitka AK 99835-9436
Fax: 907 966-5428
202 225-2161 **Skaggs David E (Rep - D - Colorado)**
1507 Longworth Bldg .... Washington DC 20515-0001
Fax: 202 225-9127
206 336-9440 **Skagit County** PO Box 837 .... Mount Vernon WA 98273-0837
509 427-5141 **Skamania County** PO Box 790 .... Stevenson WA 98648-0790
Fax: 509 427-4165
202 225-2365 **Skeen Joe (Rep - R - New Mexico)** 2447 Rayburn Bldg ..... Washington DC 20515-0001
Fax: 202 225-9599
202 225-2876 **Skelton Ike (Rep - D - Missouri)** 2134 Rayburn Bldg .... Washington DC 20515-0001
Fax: 202 225-2695
518 584-5000 **Skidmore College** N Broadway .... Saratoga Springs NY 12866-0000
Fax: 518 584-3023
415 355-7000 **Skyline College** 3300 College Dr .... San Bruno CA 94066-1698
203 887-2506 **Slater Memorial Museum** 108 Crescent St .... Norwich CT 06360-3556
202 225-6601 **Slattery Jim (Rep - D - Kansas)** 1512 Longworth Bldg .... Washington DC 20515-0001
Fax: 202 225-1445
202 225-6561 **Slaughter D French Jr (Rep - R - Virginia)**
1404 Longworth Bldg .... Washington DC 20515-0001
Fax: Unlisted
202 225-3615 **Slaughter Louise McIntosh (Rep - D - New York)**
1424 Longworth Bldg .... Washington DC 20515-0001
Fax: 202 225-7822
412 738-0512 **Slippery Rock University** .... Slippery Rock PA 16057-0000
Fax: 412 738-2098
701 879-6275 **Slope County** PO Box JJ .... Amidon ND 58620-0449
202 523-9148 **Small & Disadvantaged Business Utilization (US Dept of Labor)**
200 Constitution Ave NW Rm S1004 .... Washington DC 20210-0001
202 208-3493 **Small & Disadvantaged Business Utilization (US Dept of the Interior)**
1849 C St NW MS-2727 .... Washington DC 20240-0001
Fax: 202 343-8950
202 366-1930 **Small & Disadvantaged Business Utilization (US Dept of Transportation)**
400 7th St SW Rm 9414 .... Washington DC 20590-0000
Fax: 202 472-3654
202 653-6823 **Small Business Administration** 1441 L St NW .... Washington DC 20416-0001
Fax: 202 653-2262
617 451-2030 *Region 1* 155 Federal St 9th Fl .... Boston MA 02110-1744
Fax: 617 565-8695
212 264-7772 *Region 2* 26 Federal Plaza Rm 3100 .... New York NY 10278-0112
Fax: 212 264-4963
215 962-3805 *Region 3* 475 Allendale Rd Allendale Sq Suite 201 .... King of Prussia PA 19406-0000
Fax: 215 962-3795
404 347-2441 *Region 4* 1375 Peachtree St NE Suite 500 .... Atlanta GA 30367-0001
Fax: 404 347-2355
312 353-0359 *Region 5* 230 S Dearborn St Suite 510 .... Chicago IL 60604-1593
Fax: 312 353-3426
214 767-7643 *Region 6* 8625 King George Dr Bldg C .... Dallas TX 75235-2201
Fax: 214 767-7870
816 426-2989 *Region 7* 911 Walnut St .... Kansas City MO 64106-2087
Fax: 816 426-5559
303 534-7518 *Region 8* 721 19th St Rm 454 .... Denver CO 80202-2517
415 556-7487 *Region 9* 450 Golden Gate Ave .... San Francisco CA 94102-3476
Fax: 415 556-1840
206 442-5676 *Region 10* 2615 4th Ave Rm 440 .... Seattle WA 98121-1267
Fax: 206 442-4155
202 225-5821 **Small Business Committee (US House of Representatives)**
2361 Rayburn Bldg .... Washington DC 20515-0001
202 224-5175 **Small Business Committee (US Senate)**
428A Russell Bldg .... Washington DC 20510-0001
Fax: Unlisted
202 224-2841 **Smith Bob (Sen - R - New Hampshire)** 825-A Hart Bldg ..... Washington DC 20510-0001
Fax: 202 224-1353
202 225-3765 **Smith Christopher H (Rep - R - New Jersey)**
2440 Rayburn Bldg .... Washington DC 20515-0001
Fax: 202 225-7768
413 584-2700 **Smith College** .... Northampton MA 01063-0001
Fax: 413 585-2075
913 282-6533 **Smith County** 218 S Grant St .... Smith Center KS 66967-2798
601 782-4751 **Smith County** Main St .... Raleigh MS 39153-0000
615 735-9833 **Smith County** 218 Main St .... Carthage TN 37030-1541
903 595-4861 **Smith County** PO Box 1018 .... Tyler TX 75710-1018
413 733-4214 **Smith George Walter Vincent Art Museum** 222 State St ...... Springfield MA 01103-1779
202 225-4236 **Smith Lamar S (Rep - R - Texas)** 422 Cannon Bldg .... Washington DC 20515-0001
Fax: 202 225-8628
202 225-7931 **Smith Lawrence J (Rep - D - Florida)** 113 Cannon Bldg ..... Washington DC 20515-0001
Fax: 202 225-9816
202 225-4426 **Smith Neal (Rep - D - Iowa)** 2373 Rayburn Bldg .... Washington DC 20515-0001
Fax: Unlisted
202 225-6730 **Smith Robert F (Rep - R - Oregon)** 118 Cannon Bldg .... Washington DC 20515-0001
Fax: 202 225-3129
202 357-2700 **Smithsonian Institution** 1000 Jefferson Dr SW .... Washington DC 20560-0001
Fax: Unlisted
516 265-2072 **Smithtown Library** 1 N Country Rd .... Smithtown NY 11787-2102
Fax: 516 265-5945
703 783-7186 **Smyth County** PO Box 1025 .... Marion VA 24354-1025
205 593-5120 **Snead State Junior College** PO Box D .... Boaz AL 35957-0734
Fax: 205 593-7180
219 239-5466 **Snite Museum of Art** University of Notre Dame .... Notre Dame IN 46556-5601
206 659-8447 **Sno-Isle Regional Library** 7312 35th Ave NE .... Marysville WA 98270-9164
206 388-3466 **Snohomish County** 3000 Rockefeller Ave Rm 246 .... Everett WA 98201-4046
206 483-4555 **Snoqualmie Community College** PO Box 1008 .... Bothell WA 98041-0000
801 283-4021 **Snow College** 150 E College Ave .... Ephraim UT 84627-0000
Fax: 801 283-6879
202 225-6306 **Snowe Olympia J (Rep - R - Maine)** 2464 Rayburn Bldg .... Washington DC 20515-0001
Fax: Unlisted
717 837-4207 **Snyder County** 11 W Market St .... Middleburg PA 17842-1018
301 965-2736 **Social Security Administration** 6401 Security Blvd .... Baltimore MD 21235-0001
Fax: 301 625-9956
617 565-2870 *Region 1* JFK Federal Bldg Rm 1100 .... Boston MA 02203-0000
Fax: 617 565-3143
212 264-3915 *Region 2* 26 Federal Plaza Rm 40-102 .... New York NY 10278-0004
Fax: 212 264-6847
215 596-6941 *Region 3* 3535 Market St Rm 8330 .... Philadelphia PA 19104-3309
Fax: 215 382-4586
404 331-2475 *Region 4* 101 Marietta Tower Suite 1904 .... Atlanta GA 30323-0001
312 353-5175 *Region 5* 105 W Adams St 22nd Fl .... Chicago IL 60603-6298
214 767-4210 *Region 6* 1200 Main Tower Bldg Rm 1440 .... Dallas TX 75202-0000
Fax: 903 729-4537
816 426-3701 *Region 7* 601 E 12th St Rm 436 .... Kansas City MO 64106-2868
Fax: 816 426-7853
303 844-2388 *Region 8* 1961 Stout St Rm 1185 .... Denver CO 80294-0101
Fax: 303 564-5568
415 744-4676 *Region 9* 50 United Nations Plaza 7th Fl .... San Francisco CA 94105-3901
Fax: 415 556-8242
206 442-0417 *Region 10* 2201 6th Ave Rm 510 .... Seattle WA 98121-1832
Fax: 206 442-4333
202 282-7206 **Social Security Research (US Dept of Health & Human Services)**
4301 Connecticut Ave NW Rm 205 .... Washington DC 20008-2321
Fax: 202 282-7219
415 494-1532 **Socialist Labor Party** 914 Industrial Ave .... Palo Alto CA 94303-4911
212 675-3820 **Socialist Workers Party** 406 West St .... New York NY 10014-2570
Fax: 212 727-0150
703 549-3800 **Society of American Military Engineers** 607 Prince St .... Alexandria VA 22314-3117
Fax: 703 684-0231
505 835-0589 **Socorro County** 131 Court St .... Socorro NM 87801-4505
202 447-4543 **Soil Conservation Service (US Dept of Agriculture)**
14th St & Independence Ave SW Rm 6110 .... Washington DC 20250-0001
Fax: 202 475-3174
301 276-0306 **Sojourner-Douglas College** 500 N Caroline St .... Baltimore MD 21205-1898
Fax: 301 675-1810
707 864-7000 **Solano Community College** 4000 Suisun Valley Rd .... Suisun City CA 94585-3197
Fax: 707 864-0361
707 429-6218 **Solano County** 580 W Texas St .... Fairfield CA 94533-6321

707 421-6510 **Solano County Library** 1150 Kentucky St .... Fairfield CA 94533-5761
202 225-2361 **Solarz Stephen J (Rep - D - New York)**
1536 Longworth Bldg .... Washington DC 20515-0001
Fax: 202 225-9469
202 225-5614 **Solomon Gerald BH (Rep - R - New York)**
2265 Rayburn Bldg .... Washington DC 20515-0001
Fax: 202 225-1168
212 599-6193 **Solomon Islands Mission to the UN** 820 2nd Ave Suite 800A .. New York NY 10017-4504
Fax: 212 972-3970
212 360-3500 **Solomon R Guggenheim Museum** 1071 5th Ave .... New York NY 10128-0173
Fax: 212 360-3594
Somalia: Somali Democratic Republic
202 342-1575 *Embassy* 600 New Hampshire Ave NW Suite 710 .... Washington DC 20037-2403
Fax: 202 625-0886
212 688-9410 *Mission to the UN* 425 E 61st St Suite 703 .... New York NY 10021-8722
301 651-0320 **Somerset County** 21 Prince William St .... Princess Anne MD 21853-0000
207 474-9861 **Somerset County** County Courthouse .... Skowhegan ME 04976-0000
908 231-7000 **Somerset County** PO Box 3000 .... Somerville NJ 08876-1262
Fax: 908 707-4127
814 445-5154 **Somerset County** 111 E Union St .... Somerset PA 15501-1416
Fax: 814 445-7991
908 526-4016 **Somerset County Library** PO Box 6700 .... Bridgewater NJ 08807-0700
Fax: Unlisted
817 897-4427 **Somervell County** PO Box 1098 .... Glen Rose TX 76043-1098
707 527-2611 **Sonoma County** PO Box 11187 .... Santa Rosa CA 95406-1187
707 545-0831 **Sonoma County Library** 3rd & E Sts .... Santa Rosa CA 95404-0000
Fax: 707 575-0437
707 664-2880 **Sonoma State University** 1801 E Cotati Ave .... Rohnert Park CA 94928-3609
South Africa: Republic of South Africa
202 232-4400 *Embassy* 3051 Massachusetts Ave NW .... Washington DC 20008-3604
Fax: 202 265-1607
212 371-8154 *Mission to the UN* 326 E 48th St .... New York NY 10017-1796
Fax: 212 371-7577
312 939-7929 *Chicago Consulate General* 200 S Michigan Ave 6th Fl .... Chicago IL 60604-2404
Fax: 312 939-7481
213 657-9200 *Los Angeles Consulate General*
50 N La Cienega Suite 300 .... Beverly Hills CA 90211-2227
Fax: Unlisted
212 371-7997 *New York Consulate General* 326 E 48th St .... New York NY 10017-1796
Fax: 212 371-7577
714 530-9650 **South Baylo University** 12012 S Magnolia Ave .... Garden Grove CA 92641-3346
Fax: 714 530-7082
804 572-3621 **South Boston (Independent City)** 455 Ferry St .... South Boston VA 24592-3237
803 799-4601 **South Carolina Chamber of Commerce**
1201 Main St Suite 1810 .... Columbia SC 29201-0000
Fax: 803 779-6043
803 799-7798 **South Carolina Democratic Party** 2730 Devine St .... Columbia SC 29205-2433
Fax: 803 771-7442
803 734-0135 **South Carolina Div of Tourism** 1205 Pendleton St .... Columbia SC 29201-3731
Fax: 803 734-0133
803 798-8999 **South Carolina Republican Party**
720 Gracern Rd Stephenson Ctr Suite 121 .... Columbia SC 29221-0000
Fax: 803 731-9338
803 536-7000 **South Carolina State College** 300 College Ave .... Orangeburg SC 29117-0001
Fax: 803 536-8429
South Carolina State Government
803 734-1000 *Information* 1026 Sumter St .... Columbia SC 29201-3716
Fax: 803 734-1009 Admin
803 734-8696 *Arts Commission* 1800 Gervais St .... Columbia SC 29201-3581
Fax: 803 734-8526
803 734-3970 *Attorney General* 1000 Assembly St .... Columbia SC 29201-3117
Fax: 803 253-6283
803 734-4750 *Bureau of Air Quality Control* 2600 Bull St .... Columbia SC 29201-1708
Fax: 803 734-4556
803 734-4634 *Bureau of Radiological Health* 2600 Bull St .... Columbia SC 29201-1708
Fax: 803 799-6726
803 734-5200 *Bureau of Solid & Hazardous Waste Management*
2600 Bull St .... Columbia SC 29201-1708
Fax: 803 734-5199
803 737-1990 *Central Correctional Institution* 1515 Gist St .... Columbia SC 22911-0000
Fax: 803 737-1804
803 253-6260 *Commission on Higher Education* 1333 Main St Suite 300 .. Columbia SC 29201-3201
Fax: 803 253-6267
803 734-2121 *Comptroller General* Wade Hampton Office Bldg Rm 305 .... Columbia SC 29211-0000
Fax: 803 734-2064
803 734-2210 *Department of Agriculture* 1200 Senate St .... Columbia SC 29201-3734
Fax: 803 734-2192
803 734-8577 *Department of Archives & History* 1430 Senate St .... Columbia SC 29201-0000
Fax: 803 734-8820
803 734-9452 *Department of Consumer Affairs* 2801 Devine St .... Columbia SC 29205-2556
Fax: 803 734-9365
803 737-8500 *Department of Corrections* 4444 Broad River Rd .... Columbia SC 29210-4000
Fax: 803 737-8510
803 734-8492 *Department of Education* 1429 Senate St .... Columbia SC 29201-3799
Fax: 803 734-8624
803 737-1302 *Department of Highways & Public Transportation*
955 Park St .... Columbia SC 29202-0000
Fax: 803 737-6385
803 737-6268 *Department of Insurance* 1612 Marion St .... Columbia SC 29201-2913
803 734-9600 *Department of Labor* 3600 Forest Dr .... Columbia SC 29204-4033
Fax: 803 734-9716
803 734-0662 *Division of Economic Opportunity* 1205 Pendleton St .... Columbia SC 29201-3731
Fax: 803 734-0356
803 734-5360 *Division of Environmental Quality Control* 2600 Bull St ...... Columbia SC 29201-1708
Fax: 803 734-5199
803 734-9100 *Division of Mining & Reclamation*
2221 Devine St Suite 222 .... Columbia SC 29205-2418
Fax: 803 734-9200
803 734-0425 *Division of Public Safety Programs* 1205 Pendleton St .... Columbia SC 29201-3731
Fax: 803 734-0486
803 734-8020 *Emergency Preparedness Div* 1429 Senate St .... Columbia SC 29201-3730
Fax: 803 734-8062
803 737-2400 *Employment Security Commission* 1550 Gadsen St .... Columbia SC 29202-0000
Fax: 803 737-2642
803 656-2267 *Energy Research & Development Center* 386-2 College Ave . Clemson SC 29634-0929
Fax: 803 656-0142
803 734-9818 *Governor* PO Box 11369 .... Columbia SC 29211-1369
Fax: 803 734-1843
803 734-9100 *Land Resources Conservation Commission*
2221 Devine St Suite 222 .... Columbia SC 29205-2474
Fax: 803 734-9200
803 734-2080 *Lieutenant Governor* PO Box 142 .... Columbia SC 29202-0142
Fax: Unlisted
803 734-9643 *Occupational Safety & Health* 3600 Forest Dr .... Columbia SC 29204-0000
Fax: 803 734-9716
803 734-4810 *Office of Vital Records & Public Health Statistics*
2600 Bull St .... Columbia SC 29201-1708
803 737-1752 *Perry Correctional Institution* 430 Oaklawn Rd .... Pelzer SC 29669-9361
Fax: Call company operator
803 734-9244 *Probation Parole & Pardon Services* 2221 Devine St .... Columbia SC 29205-2418
803 737-5143 *Public Service Commission* 111 Doctors Cir .... Columbia SC 29203-6580
Fax: 803 737-5199
803 737-9480 *Real Estate Commission* 1201 Main St Suite 1500 .... Columbia SC 29201-3228
803 734-1660 *Retirement Systems* PO Box 11960 .... Columbia SC 29211-1960
Fax: 803 734-0419
803 734-2170 *Secretary of State* Wade Hampton Office Bldg Rm 109 ...... Columbia SC 29201-0000
803 734-1087 *Securities Div* 1205 Pendleton St Suite 501 .... Columbia SC 29201-3727
803 737-0400 *State Development Board* 1201 Main St 16th Fl .... Columbia SC 29201-3212
Fax: 803 737-0418
803 734-2101 *State Treasurer* Capitol Complex 1st Fl .... Columbia SC 29211-0000
Fax: 803 734-2039
803 734-1080 *Supreme Court* 1231 Gervais St .... Columbia SC 29201-3206
803 737-9830 *Tax Commission* 301 Gervais St .... Columbia SC 29201-3041
Fax: 803 737-9881
803 737-0800 *Water Resources Commission* 1201 Main St Suite 1100 .... Columbia SC 29201-3239
Fax: 803 765-9080
803 737-5697 *Worker's Compensation Commission* 1612 Marion St .... Columbia SC 29201-0000
803 734-8666 **South Carolina State Library** PO Box 11469 .... Columbia SC 29211-1469
Fax: 803 734-8676
803 737-4921 **South Carolina State Museum** 301 Gervais St .... Columbia SC 29202-0000
Fax: 803 737-4969
203 789-7071 **South Central Community College** 60 Sargent Dr .... New Haven CT 06511-5970
605 688-5423 **South Dakota Art Museum** Medary Ave & Harvey Dunn St ..... Brookings SD 57007-0001
605 987-2717 **South Dakota Democratic Party** 1010 S Broadway .... Canton SD 57013-0000
Fax: 605 987-2931
605 224-7347 **South Dakota Republican Party** 401 E Sioux Ave .... Pierre SD 57501-3162
Fax: 605 224-7344
605 394-2511 **South Dakota School of Mines & Technology**
501 E Saint Joseph St .... Rapid City SD 57701-3901
Fax: 605 394-6131
South Dakota State Government
605 773-3011 *Information* 500 E Capitol Ave .... Pierre SD 57501-5070
Fax: 605 773-3686
605 339-6646 *Arts Council* 108 W 11th St .... Sioux Falls SD 57102-0788
605 773-3215 *Attorney General* 500 E Capitol Ave .... Pierre SD 57501-5070
Fax: 605 773-3686
605 339-6780 *Board of Pardons & Paroles* PO Box 911 .... Sioux Falls SD 57117-0911
605 773-3693 *Center for Health Policy & Statistics* 523 E Capitol Ave .... Pierre SD 57501-3182
Fax: 605 773-5683
605 773-4400 *Consumer Affairs Div* 500 E Capitol Ave .... Pierre SD 57501-0000
Fax: 605 773-3686
605 773-3375 *Department of Agriculture* 445 E Capitol Ave Anderson Bldg .... Pierre SD 57501-0000
Fax: 605 773-5926
605 773-3478 *Department of Corrections* 523 E Capitol Ave .... Pierre SD 57501-3182
Fax: 605 773-3686
605 773-3361 *Department of Health* 523 E Capitol Ave .... Pierre SD 57501-3182
Fax: 605 773-4117
605 773-5131 *Department of Revenue* 700 Governors Dr .... Pierre SD 57501-2291
Fax: 605 773-5129
605 773-3265 *Department of Transportation* 700 E Broadway Ave .... Pierre SD 57501-2586
Fax: 605 773-3921
605 773-3151 *Department of Water & Natural Resources* 523 E Capitol Ave ... Pierre SD 57501-3182
Fax: 605 773-6035
605 773-3603 *Division of Alternative Energy* 217 1/2 W Missouri Ave .... Pierre SD 57501-4516
Fax: 605 773-3686
605 773-3243 *Division of Education* 700 Governors Dr .... Pierre SD 57501-2291
Fax: 605 773-4855
605 773-3231 *Division of Emergency & Disaster Services* 500 E Capitol Ave .. Pierre SD 57501-5070
Fax: 605 773-3580
605 773-3563 *Division of Insurance* 910 E Sioux Ave .... Pierre SD 57501-3940
Fax: 605 773-5369
605 773-3178 *Division of Professional & Occupational Licensing*
910 E Sioux Ave .... Pierre SD 57501-3940
Fax: 605 773-5369
605 773-4823 *Division of Securities* 910 E Sioux Ave .... Pierre SD 57501-3940
Fax: 605 773-5369
605 773-3411 *Finance & Management Bureau* 500 E Capitol Ave 2nd Fl .... Pierre SD 57501-0000
Fax: 605 773-4711
605 773-3212 *Governor* 500 E Capitol Ave .... Pierre SD 57501-5070
Fax: 605 773-4711
605 773-4094 *Highway Patrol* 300 N Nicollet Ave .... Pierre SD 57501-5070
Fax: 605 773-5369
605 773-3458 *Historical Archives* 900 Governors Dr .... Pierre SD 57501-2200
Fax: 605 773-6041
605 773-3681 *Labor & Management* 700 Governors Dr .... Pierre SD 57501-2291
Fax: 605 773-4211
605 773-3661 *Lieutenant Governor* 500 E Capitol Ave Suite 215 .... Pierre SD 57501-5070
Fax: 605 773-4711
605 773-4201 *Office of Minerals & Mining* 523 E Capitol Ave .... Pierre SD 57501-3182
Fax: 605 773-6035
605 773-3201 *Public Utilities Commission* 500 E Capitol Ave .... Pierre SD 57501-5070
Fax: 605 773-3686
605 773-3405 *Purchasing & Printing* 523 E Capitol Ave .... Pierre SD 57501-3182
Fax: 605 773-4840
605 773-3600 *Real Estate Commission* 212 E Capitol Ave .... Pierre SD 57501-2518
605 773-3537 *Secretary of State* 500 E Capitol Ave 2nd Fl .... Pierre SD 57501-5070
Fax: 605 773-3686
605 339-6764 *South Dakota Penitentiary* PO Box 911 .... Sioux Falls SD 57117-0911
Fax: 605 335-2924
605 369-2201 *Springfield Correctional Facility* PO Box 322 .... Springfield SD 57062-0322
605 773-3455 *State Board of Regents* 207 E Capitol Ave St Charles Hotel ...... Pierre SD 57501-3159
Fax: 605 773-5320
605 773-3511 *Supreme Court* 500 E Capitol Ave .... Pierre SD 57501-5070
Fax: 605 773-3686
605 773-3378 *Treasurer* 500 E Capitol Ave 2nd Fl Annex .... Pierre SD 57501-0000
Fax: 605 773-3115
605 622-2452 *Unemployment Insurance Div* 420 S Roosevelt St .... Aberdeen SD 57402-4730
605 773-3131 **South Dakota State Library** 800 Governors Dr .... Pierre SD 57501-2294
Fax: 605 773-4950
605 688-4151 **South Dakota State University** .... Brookings SD 57007-0001
Fax: 605 688-5014 Admin
605 688-6197 *College of Pharmacy* PO Box 2202C .... Brookings SD 57007-0001
Fax: 605 688-6232
605 773-3301 **South Dakota Tourism Div** Capitol Lake Plaza .... Pierre SD 57501-3369
Fax: 605 773-3256
813 453-6661 **South Florida Community College** 600 W College Dr .... Avon Park FL 33825-9399
Fax: 813 452-6042
813 746-4132 **South Florida Museum & Bishop Planetarium**
201 10th St W .... Bradenton FL 34205-8604
912 383-4220 **South Georgia College** .... Douglas GA 31533-0000
Fax: 912 383-4322

South Plains College
806 747-0576   *Lubbock Campus* 1302 Main St .... Lubbock TX 79401-3298
     Fax: 806 747-5934
806 894-9611   *Main Campus* 1401 S College Ave .... Levelland TX 79336-6593
     Fax: 806 894-5274
806 885-3048   *Reese Campus* Reese Air Force Base Bldg 920 .... Reese TX 79489-0000
     Fax: 806 885-6376
207 767-0300   **South Portland Coast Guard Base** 259 High St .... South Portland ME 04106-0007
     Fax: 207 767-0328
206 764-5300   **South Seattle Community College** 6000 16th Ave SW .... Seattle WA 98106-1499
     Fax: 206 764-5393
708 596-2000   **South Suburban College** 15800 State St .... South Holland IL 60473-1270
713 659-8040   **South Texas College of Law** 1303 San Jacinto St .... Houston TX 77002-7000
     Fax: 713 659-2217
617 786-2686   **South Weymouth Naval Air Station** .... South Weymouth MA 02190-5000
     Fax: 617 786-2733
804 653-2200   **Southampton County** County Courthouse .... Courtland VA 23837-0000
606 589-2145   **Southeast Community College** 300 College Rd ...... Cumberland KY 40823-1030
     Fax: 606 589-4941
402 471-3333   *Lincoln Campus* 8800 O St .... Lincoln NE 68520-1299
     Fax: 402 471-3134
402 761-2131   *Milford Campus* RR 2 Box D .... Milford NE 68405-9802
     Fax: 402 761-2324
314 651-2000   **Southeast Missouri State University**
     1 University Plaza .... Cape Girardeau MO 63701-4799
     Fax: 314 651-5020
601 426-6346   **Southeastern Baptist College** 4229 Hwy 15 N .... Laurel MS 39441-0000
205 969-0880   **Southeastern Bible College** 3001 Hwy 280 E .... Birmingham AL 35243-4181
813 665-4404   **Southeastern College of the Assemblies of God**
     1000 Longfellow Blvd .... Lakeland FL 33801-6099
319 752-2731   **Southeastern Community College** 1015 S Gear Ave ..... West Burlington IA 52655-1614
     Fax: 319 752-4957
919 642-7141   **Southeastern Community College** Hwy 7476 .... Whiteville NC 28472-0000
     Fax: 919 642-5658
618 252-6376   **Southeastern Illinois College** RR 4 .... Harrisburg IL 62946-9804
205 837-9769   **Southeastern Institute of Technology** 200 Sparkman Dr .... Huntsville AL 35805-0000
504 549-2000   **Southeastern Louisiana University** University Stn .... Hammond LA 70402-0000
     Fax: 504 549-2061
     Southeastern Massachusetts University
508 997-7831   *New Bedford Campus* 1213 Purchase St .... New Bedford MA 02740-6636
508 999-8000   *North Dartmouth Campus* Old Westport Rd .... North Dartmouth MA 02747-0000
     Fax: 508 999-8901
405 924-0121   **Southeastern Oklahoma State University** Stn A .... Durant OK 74701-0000
     Fax: 405 924-8531 Admin
404 283-9911   **Southeastern Power Administration (US Dept of Energy)**
     Samuel Elbert Bldg .... Elberton GA 30635-0000
     Fax: 404 283-9928
918 426-0456   **Southeastern Public Library System** 401 N 2nd St .... McAlester OK 74501-4639
     Fax: 918 423-5731
202 488-8162   **Southeastern University** 501 'I' St SW .... Washington DC 20024-2788
     Fax: 202 488-8093
602 366-5421   **Southern Arizona Bible College** Hwy 92 .... Hereford AZ 85615-0000
501 235-4000   **Southern Arkansas University** Hwy 19 N .... Magnolia AR 71753-0000
     Fax: 501 235-5005
501 862-8131   *El Dorado Branch* 300 Southwest Ave .... El Dorado AR 71730-0000
501 886-6741   **Southern Baptist College** 201 Fulbright Ave .... Walnut Ridge AR 72476-0000
     Fax: 501 886-3924
502 897-4011   **Southern Baptist Theological Seminary** 2825 Lexington Rd ... Louisville KY 40280-0001
     Fax: 502 897-4215
619 287-9342   **Southern California Bible College** 4747 College Ave .... San Diego CA 92115-3906
714 556-3610   **Southern California College** 55 Fair Dr .... Costa Mesa CA 92626-6597
     Fax: 714 957-9317
714 870-7226   **Southern California College of Optometry**
     2575 E Yorba Linda Blvd .... Fullerton CA 92631-1610
     Fax: 714 879-9834
213 829-3482   **Southern California Institute of Architecture**
     1800 Berkeley St .... Santa Monica CA 90404-4198
     Fax: 213 829-7518
901 722-3200   **Southern College of Optometry** 1245 Madison Ave .... Memphis TN 38104-2211
     Fax: Unlisted
615 238-2111   **Southern College of Seventh-Day Adventists**
     4881 Taylor Cir .... Collegedale TN 37315-9999
     Fax: 615 238-3546
404 528-7281   **Southern College of Technology** 1100 S Marietta Pkwy .... Marietta GA 30060-9862
203 397-4000   **Southern Connecticut State University** 501 Crescent St ...... New Haven CT 06515-1355
     Fax: 203 397-4207
618 453-2121   **Southern Illinois University** .... Carbondale IL 62901-0000
     Fax: 618 453-3250 Admissions
618 692-2000   *Edwardsville Campus* .... Edwardsville IL 62026-0001
     Fax: 618 692-3837
618 453-5388   *Museum* Southern Illinois University .... Carbondale IL 62901-4508
     Fax: 618 453-3000
618 463-3864   *School of Dental Medicine* 2800 College Ave Rm 2300 .... Alton IL 62002-4742
     Fax: 618 463-3945
618 536-7711   *School of Law* Lesar Law Bldg .... Carbondale IL 62901-0000
     Fax: 618 453-8768
217 782-3318   *School of Medicine* 801 N Rutledge St .... Springfield IL 62702-4910
     Fax: 217 782-0988
618 536-3361   **Southern Illinois University Carbondale School of Journalism**
     Communications Bldg Rm 1202 .... Carbondale IL 62901-0000
     Fax: 618 453-3000
618 692-2230   **Southern Illinois University Edwardsville Department of Mass Communications**
     CB 1775 .... Edwardsville IL 62026-0001
     Fax: 618 692-2233
205 933-8242   **Southern Institute Junior College** 2015 Highland Ave S ..... Birmingham AL 35205-3898
     Fax: 205 933-0508
207 799-7303   **Southern Maine Vocational College** 2 Fort Rd .... South Portland ME 04106-1698
     Fax: 207 767-2731
214 692-2000   **Southern Methodist University** 6425 Boaz Ln .... Dallas TX 75275-0001
     Fax: 214 692-4138 Admissions
214 692-2618   *School of Law* Story Hall .... Dallas TX 75275-0001
     Fax: 214 692-4330 Library
205 833-8226   **Southern Museum of Flight** 4343 N 73rd St .... Birmingham AL 35206-3642
405 789-6400   **Southern Nazarene University** 6729 NW 39th Expy .... Bethany OK 73008-2694
     Fax: 405 491-6355 Library
503 482-3311   **Southern Oregon State College** 1250 Siskiyou Blvd .... Ashland OR 97520-2268
     Fax: 503 482-6429
703 261-6181   **Southern Seminary College** 201 E 26th St .... Buena Vista VA 24416-2625
     Southern State Community College
513 382-6645   *North Campus* 2698 Old State Rt 73 .... Wilmington OH 45177-9387
     Fax: 513 382-8431
513 695-0307   *South Campus* 12681 US Rt 62 .... Sardinia OH 45171-0000
     Fax: 513 695-0743
205 395-2211   **Southern Union State Junior College** Roberts St .... Wadley AL 36276-0000
     Fax: 205 395-2215

504 771-4680   **Southern University (System)**
     Southern Branch Post Office .... Baton Rouge LA 70813-0000
     Fax: 504 771-2495
     Southern University
504 771-4500   *A & M College* Southern Branch Post Office .... Baton Rouge LA 70813-0000
     Fax: 504 771-2495
504 771-2552   *Law Center* Swan St .... Baton Rouge LA 70813-0000
     Fax: 504 771-2474
504 286-5000   *New Orleans Campus* 6400 Press Dr .... New Orleans LA 70126-0002
     Fax: 504 286-5131
318 674-3300   *Shreveport Campus* 3050 Martin Luther King Jr Dr .... Shreveport LA 71107-4795
     Fax: 318 674-3398
801 586-7700   **Southern Utah State College** 351 W Center St .... Cedar City UT 84720-2498
     Fax: Ext 5475
802 442-5427   **Southern Vermont College** Monument Ave .... Bennington VT 05201-0000
     Fax: 802 442-5529
304 792-4300   **Southern West Virginia Community College** PO Box 2900 .... Logan WV 25601-0000
     Fax: 304 792-4399
804 949-7111   **Southside Virginia Community College** RR 1 Box 60 .... Alberta VA 23821-9801
     Fax: 804 949-7863
501 777-2957   **Southwest Arkansas Regional Library** 5th & Elm Sts .... Hope AR 71801-0000
417 326-5281   **Southwest Baptist University** 1601 S Springfield Ave .... Bolivar MO 65613-2559
207 244-5517   **Southwest Harbor Coast Guard Base** Clark Point Rd .. Southwest Harbor ME 04679-0000
     Fax: Ext 135
601 276-2000   **Southwest Mississippi Community College** College Dr .... Summit MS 39666-0000
     Fax: 601 276-3089
417 836-5000   **Southwest Missouri State University** 901 S National Ave ..... Springfield MO 65804-0087
     Fax: 417 836-4538 Library
213 221-2164   **Southwest Museum** 234 Museum Dr .... Los Angeles CA 90065-5030
     Fax: 213 224-8223
214 428-8351   **Southwest Museum of Science & Technology**
     1st & Martin Luther King Jr Aves .... Dallas TX 75223-0000
602 774-3890   **Southwest School Missions Independent Bible Institute**
     2918 N Aris Ave .... Flagstaff AZ 86001-0000
205 479-7476   **Southwest State Technical College** 925 Dauphin Island Pkwy .... Mobile AL 36605-3299
     Fax: 205 473-2049
507 537-7021   **Southwest State University** N Hwy 23 .... Marshall MN 56258-0000
     Fax: 507 537-7154
512 278-4401   **Southwest Texas Junior College** 2501 Garner Field Rd .... Uvalde TX 78801-6296
     Fax: 512 278-1054
512 245-2111   **Southwest Texas State University** .... San Marcos TX 78666-0000
     Fax: 512 245-3040 Mail Rm
703 964-2555   **Southwest Virginia Community College** PO Box SVCC .... Richlands VA 24641-1510
     Fax: 703 964-5307
608 822-3393   **Southwest Wisconsin Library System** 1775 4th St .... Fennimore WI 53809-1137
     Fax: 608 822-6251
608 822-3262   **Southwest Wisconsin Technical College** Hwy 18 E .... Fennimore WI 53809-0000
     Fax: 608 822-6019
817 645-3921   **Southwestern Adventist College** PO Box 567 .... Keene TX 76059-0000
     Fax: 817 556-4744
214 937-4010   **Southwestern Assemblies of God College**
     1200 Sycamore St .... Waxahachie TX 75165-2342
602 992-6101   **Southwestern Baptist Bible College** 2625 E Cactus Rd .... Phoenix AZ 85032-7097
     Fax: 602 258-4432
214 563-3341   **Southwestern Christian College** 200 Bowser St .... Terrell TX 75160-3402
     Fax: 214 563-7133
619 421-6700   **Southwestern College** 900 Otay Lakes Rd .... Chula Vista CA 92010-7297
     Fax: 619 421-1189
316 221-4150   **Southwestern College** 100 College St .... Winfield KS 67156-2499
     Fax: 316 221-3725
405 789-7661   **Southwestern College of Christian Ministry** PO Box 340 .... Bethany OK 73008-0340
515 782-7081   **Southwestern Community College** 1501 W Townline St .... Creston IA 50801-1042
     Fax: 515 782-3312 Admin
704 586-4091   **Southwestern Community College** 275 Webster Rd .... Sylva NC 28779-9578
     Fax: 704 586-4092 Ext 293
616 782-5113   **Southwestern Michigan College** 58900 Cherry Grove Rd ...... Dowagiac MI 49047-9726
     Fax: 616 782-8414
405 772-6611   **Southwestern Oklahoma State University**
     100 Campus Dr .... Weatherford OK 73096-3001
     Fax: 405 772-5447
405 774-3104   *School of Pharmacy* 100 Campus Dr .... Weatherford OK 73096-3001
     Fax: 405 772-5447
503 888-2525   **Southwestern Oregon Community College**
     1988 Newmark Ave .... Coos Bay OR 97420-2956
     Fax: 503 888-7285
918 581-7474   **Southwestern Power Administration (US Dept of Energy)**
     PO Box 1619 .... Tulsa OK 74101-0000
     Fax: 918 581-7530
512 863-6511   **Southwestern University** E University & Maple Sts .... Georgetown TX 78626-0000
     Fax: 512 863-5788
213 738-6700   *School of Law* 675 S Westmoreland Ave .... Los Angeles CA 90005-3905
     Soviet Union: Union of Soviet Socialist Republics
202 628-7551   *Embassy* 1125 16th St NW .... Washington DC 20036-4801
     Fax: 202 347-5028
212 861-4900   *Mission to the UN* 136 E 67th St .... New York NY 10021-6137
     Fax: 212 628-0252
415 922-6642   *Consulate General* 2790 Green St .... San Francisco CA 94123-4609
505 437-2840   **Space Center** PO Box 533 .... Alamogordo NM 88311-0533
     Fax: 505 437-7722
     Spain
202 265-0190   *Embassy* 2700 15th St NW .... Washington DC 20009-4605
     Fax: 202 328-3212
212 661-1050   *Mission to the UN* 809 UN Plaza 6th Fl .... New York NY 10017-0000
     Fax: 212 949-7247
312 782-4588   *Chicago Consulate General* 180 N Michigan Ave Suite 1500 .. Chicago IL 60601-7401
213 658-6050   *Los Angeles Consulate General*
     6300 Wilshire Blvd Suite 1530 .... Los Angeles CA 90048-5217
     Fax: 213 658-5603
212 355-4080   *New York Consulate General* 150 E 58th St 16th Fl .... New York NY 10155-0035
     Fax: 212 644-3751
212 967-2170   **Spain-US Chamber of Commerce** 350 5th Ave Suite 3514 .... New York NY 10118-0110
     Fax: 212 564-1415
404 228-9900   **Spalding County** 132 E Solomon St .... Griffin GA 30223-3312
502 585-9911   **Spalding University** 851 S 4th St .... Louisville KY 40203-2188
     Fax: 502 581-0108
803 596-2500   **Spartanburg County** 180 Magnolia St .... Spartanburg SC 29301-2392
     Fax: 803 596-2239
803 596-3507   **Spartanburg County Public Library** 333 S Pine St .... Spartanburg SC 29302-2622
     Fax: Unlisted
803 576-3911   **Spartanburg Methodist College** 1200 Textile Rd .... Spartanburg SC 29301-0009
     Fax: 803 574-6919
803 591-3600   **Spartanburg Technical College** PO Box 4386 .... Spartanburg SC 29305-4386
     Fax: 803 591-3642
202 224-5364   **Special Committee on Aging (US Senate)**
     SDG-31 Dirksen Bldg .... Washington DC 20510-0001
     Fax: 202 224-9926

202 732-1265 **Special Education & Rehabilitative Services Div (US Dept of Education)**
330 C St SW Rm 3006 ... Washington DC 20202-0001
Fax: 202 732-1372
202 224-4254 **Specter Arlen (Sen - R - Pennsylvania)** 303 Hart Bldg ... Washington DC 20510-0001
Fax: Unlisted
502 636-2893 **Speed JB Art Museum** 2035 S 3rd St ... Louisville KY 40208-1812
Fax: 502 636-2899
404 681-3643 **Spelman College** 350 Spelman Ln SW ... Atlanta GA 30314-4395
Fax: 404 688-2857
202 225-2452 **Spence Floyd (Rep - R - South Carolina)**
2405 Rayburn Bldg ... Washington DC 20515-0001
Fax: 202 225-2455
812 649-6027 **Spencer County** 541 Main St ... Rockport IN 47635-1478
502 477-8121 **Spencer County** Main St ... Taylorsville KY 40071-0000
913 864-4710 **Spencer Museum of Art**
1301 Mississippi St University of Kansas ... Lawrence KS 66045-0001
Fax: 913 864-3112
605 472-1825 **Spink County** 210 E 7th Ave ... Redfield SD 57469-1299
509 536-7000 **Spokane Community College** N 1810 Greene St ... Spokane WA 99207-0000
Fax: 509 536-7276 Library
509 456-2211 **Spokane County** 1116 W Broadway Ave ... Spokane WA 99260-0001
509 924-4122 **Spokane County Library District** N 2901 Argonne Rd ... Spokane WA 99212-0000
Fax: 509 456-2912
509 459-3500 **Spokane Falls Community College**
W 3410 Fort George Wright Dr ... Spokane WA 99204-0000
Fax: 509 459-3433
509 838-3361 **Spokane Public Library** 906 Main Ave ... Spokane WA 99201-0976
Fax: 509 456-2633
309 647-4645 **Spoon River College** RR 1 ... Canton IL 61520-9801
Fax: 309 647-6498 Library
205 626-3303 **Sports Academy** 1 Academy Dr ... Daphne AL 36526-7055
703 582-7010 **Spotsylvania County** PO Box 99 ... Spotsylvania VA 22553-0099
Fax: 703 582-6304
202 225-5501 **Spratt John M Jr (Rep - D - South Carolina)**
1533 Longworth Bldg ... Washington DC 20515-0001
Fax: 202 225-0464
517 750-1200 **Spring Arbor College** Business Office Stn 8 ... Spring Arbor MI 49283-0000
Fax: 517 750-2108
215 248-7900 **Spring Garden College** 7500 Germantown Ave ... Philadelphia PA 19119-1651
Fax: 215 248-7938
205 460-2011 **Spring Hill College** 4000 Dauphin St ... Mobile AL 36608-1791
Fax: 205 460-2095
417 866-2716 **Springfield Art Museum** 1111 E Brookside Dr ... Springfield MO 65807-1899
413 739-3871 **Springfield City Library** 220 State St ... Springfield MA 01103-1772
Fax: Unlisted
413 788-3000 **Springfield College** 263 Alden St ... Springfield MA 01109-3797
Fax: 413 731-1681
217 525-1420 **Springfield College in Illinois** 1500 N 5th St ... Springfield IL 62702-2694
413 733-1194 **Springfield Science Museum** 236 State St ... Springfield MA 01103-1778
413 781-7822 **Springfield Technical Community College** 1 Armory Sq ... Springfield MA 01105-1296
Fax: Ext 3291
417 869-4621 **Springfield-Greene County Library** 397 E Central ... Springfield MO 65802-3834
Fax: 417 869-0320
801 489-9434 **Springville Museum of Art** PO Box 509 ... Springville UT 84663-0509
Sri Lanka: Democratic Socialist Republic of Sri Lanka
202 483-4025 *Embassy* 2148 Wyoming Ave NW ... Washington DC 20008-3994
Fax: 202 232-7181
212 986-7040 *Mission to the UN* 630 3rd Ave 20th Fl ... New York NY 10017-6759
Fax: 212 986-1838
316 549-3509 **Stafford County** 209 N Broadway St ... Saint John KS 67576-2042
703 659-8603 **Stafford County** PO Box 339 ... Stafford VA 22554-0339
Fax: 703 659-7643
202 225-4331 **Staggers Harley O Jr (Rep - D - West Virginia)**
1323 Longworth Bldg ... Washington DC 20515-0001
Fax: 202 225-2962
202 225-5531 **Stallings Richard H (Rep - D - Idaho)**
1122 Longworth Bldg ... Washington DC 20515-0001
Fax: 202 225-2393
203 322-1646 **Stamford Museum & Nature Center** 39 Scofieldtown Rd ... Stamford CT 06903-4096
202 225-7103 **Standards of Official Conduct Committee (US House of Representatives)**
HT-2 Capitol Bldg ... Washington DC 20515-0001
Fax: Unlisted
415 723-2300 **Stanford University** ... Stanford CA 94305-0000
Fax: 415 723-0010
415 723-2273 *Computer Science Dept* Bldg 460 ... Stanford CA 94305-0000
Fax: 415 725-7411
415 723-6161 *Department of Biochemistry* B-400 Beckman Ctr ... Stanford CA 94305-5307
Fax: 415 723-6783
415 723-2501 *Department of Chemistry* SG Mudd Bldg Rm 121 ... Stanford CA 94305-2240
Fax: 415 725-0259
415 723-1941 *Department of Communications* Bldg 120 Rm 110 ... Stanford CA 94305-0000
Fax: 415 723-3235
415 725-4759 *Department of Microbiology & Immunology*
Sherman Fairchild Bldg D-319 ... Stanford CA 94305-2240
Fax: 415 725-6757
415 723-4344 *Department of Physics* Varian Physics Bldg ... Stanford CA 94305-0000
Fax: 415 725-6544
415 723-2146 *Graduate School of Business* ... Stanford CA 94305-0000
Fax: 415 725-1688
415 723-2538 *Graduate School of Geology* Mitchell Bldg ... Stanford CA 94305-2115
415 723-4985 *Law School* Crown Quadrangle ... Stanford CA 94305-0000
Fax: 415 725-0253
415 723-1811 *Library* Green Library ... Stanford CA 94305-0000
Fax: 415 725-6874
415 723-3935 *School of Engineering* Terman Dr ... Stanford CA 94305-0000
Fax: 415 723-5599
415 725-3900 *School of Medicine* SUMC M-121 ... Stanford CA 94305-0000
Fax: 415 725-7368
209 525-6416 **Stanislaus County** PO Box 1098 ... Modesto CA 95353-1098
704 983-7204 **Stanley County** 201 S 2nd St ... Albemarle NC 28001-5747
605 223-2673 **Stanley County** PO Box 595 ... Fort Pierre SD 57532-0595
704 982-0121 **Stanly Community College** RR 4 Box 55 ... Albemarle NC 28001-9402
Fax: 704 982-0819
316 492-2140 **Stanton County** PO Box 190 ... Johnson KS 67855-0190
Fax: 316 492-2688
402 439-2222 **Stanton County** 804 Ivy St ... Stanton NE 68779-0000
309 286-5911 **Stark County** 130 W Main St ... Toulon IL 61483-0000
701 264-7636 **Stark County** PO Box 130 ... Dickinson ND 58602-0130
216 438-0800 **Stark County** 209 Tuscarawas St W ... Canton OH 44702-2219
216 452-0665 **Stark County District Library** 715 Market Ave N ... Canton OH 44702-1080
Fax: 216 452-0403
202 225-5065 **Stark Fortney H (Rep - D - California)** 239 Cannon Bldg ... Washington DC 20515-0001
Fax: Unlisted
216 494-6170 **Stark Technical College** 6200 Frank Ave NW ... Canton OH 44720-7299
Fax: 216 497-6313 Admin
219 772-9128 **Starke County** Washington St ... Knox IN 46534-0000

512 487-2954 **Starr County** Britton Ave ... Rio Grande City TX 78582-0000
618 583-2500 **State Community College of East Saint Louis**
601 James R Thompson Blvd ... East Saint Louis IL 62201-1100
816 826-7100 **State Fair Community College** 3201 W 16th St ... Sedalia MO 65301-2199
Fax: 816 827-4701
515 281-5111 **State Historical Museum of Iowa** 600 E Locust St ... Des Moines IA 50319-0001
Fax: 515 282-0502
608 262-7700 **State Historical Museum of Wisconsin** 30 N Carroll St ... Madison WI 53703-2707
701 224-2666 **State Historical Society of North Dakota**
612 E Boulevard Ave North Dakota Heritage Ctr ... Bismarck ND 58505-0001
904 487-2651 **State Library of Florida** 500 S Bronough St RA Gray Bldg ... Tallahassee FL 32399-1849
Fax: 904 488-0978
515 281-4118 **State Library of Iowa** E 12th & Grand Aves ... Des Moines IA 50319-0001
Fax: 515 281-3384
517 373-1593 **State Library of Michigan** PO Box 30007 ... Lansing MI 48909-7507
Fax: 517 373-3381
614 644-7061 **State Library of Ohio** 65 S Front St Rm 510 ... Columbus OH 43266-0001
Fax: 614 644-7004
717 787-2646 **State Library of Pennslyvania**
Walnut St & Commonwealth Ave ... Harrisburg PA 17120-0001
Fax: 717 783-2070
402 471-4754 **State Museum of History** 131 N Centennial Mall ... Lincoln NE 68508-3805
405 521-2491 **State Museum of History** 2100 N Lincoln Blvd ... Oklahoma City OK 73105-4915
717 787-4980 **State Museum of Pennsylvania** 3rd & North Sts ... Harrisburg PA 17101-1819
Fax: Unlisted
212 599-0301 **State of Grenada Mission to the UN**
820 2nd Ave Suite 900-D ... New York NY 10017-4504
Fax: 212 808-4975
901 377-4111 **State Technical Institute at Memphis** 5983 Macon Cove ... Memphis TN 38134-7693
Fax: 901 373-2503
718 727-1135 **Staten Island Institute of Arts & Sciences**
75 Stuyvesant Pl ... Staten Island NY 10301-1998
Fax: 718 273-5683
703 885-1251 **Staunton (Independent City)** 113 E Beverley St ... Staunton VA 24401-4390
303 879-6000 **Steamboat Resorts** 2700 Village Dr ... Steamboat Springs CO 80487-9004
Fax: 303 879-8060
202 225-5744 **Stearns Cliff (Rep - R - Florida)** 1123 Longworth Bldg ... Washington DC 20515-0001
Fax: 202 225-3973
612 259-3620 **Stearns County** PO Box 1378 ... Saint Cloud MN 56302-1378
Fax: 612 259-3626
507 451-8040 **Steele County** 111 E Main St ... Owatonna MN 55060-3052
Fax: 507 451-6803
701 524-2790 **Steele County** County Courthouse ... Finley ND 58230-0000
202 225-6605 **Stenholm Charles W (Rep - D - Texas)**
1226 Longworth Bldg ... Washington DC 20515-0001
Fax: 202 225-2234
409 568-2011 **Stephen F Austin State University** PO Box 13050 ... Nacogdoches TX 75962-0001
Fax: 409 568-1117
314 442-2211 **Stephens College** 1200 E Broadway ... Columbia MO 65215-0001
Fax: 314 876-7248
404 886-9491 **Stephens County** PO Box 386 ... Toccoa GA 30577-0000
405 255-4193 **Stephens County** County Courthouse ... Duncan OK 73533-0000
817 559-3700 **Stephens County** County Courthouse ... Breckenridge TX 76024-0000
815 235-8289 **Stephenson County** 15 N Galena Ave ... Freeport IL 61032-4390
413 458-9545 **Sterling & Francine Clark Art Institute** 225 South St ... Williamstown MA 01267-2891
Fax: 413 458-8503
316 278-2173 **Sterling College** ... Sterling KS 67579-0000
Fax: 316 278-2775
915 378-5191 **Sterling County** PO Box 55 ... Sterling City TX 76951-0055
904 822-7000 **Stetson University** 421 N Woodland Blvd ... De Land FL 32720-3799
Fax: Unlisted
813 345-1300 *College of Law* 1401 61st St S ... Saint Petersburg FL 33707-3299
Fax: 813 345-8973
219 665-9364 **Steuben County** SE Public Sq ... Angola IN 46703-1926
607 776-9631 **Steuben County** 3 Pulteney Sq ... Bath NY 14810-1573
Fax: Call company operator
316 544-2541 **Stevens County** 200 E 6th St ... Hugoton KS 67951-2652
612 589-4764 **Stevens County** PO Box 530 ... Morris MN 56267-0530
Fax: 612 589-2036
509 684-3751 **Stevens County** PO Box 191 ... Colville WA 99114-0191
201 420-5100 **Stevens Institute of Technology** Castle Point on the Hudson ... Hoboken NJ 07030-0000
Fax: 201 420-1606
201 420-5234 *Graduate School of Engineering* 1 Castle Point Terr ... Hoboken NJ 07030-5991
Fax: 201 420-1606
202 224-3004 **Stevens Ted (Sen - R - Alaska)** 522 Hart Bldg ... Washington DC 20510-0001
Fax: 202 224-1044
912 838-6769 **Stewart County** PO Box 157 ... Lumpkin GA 31815-0157
615 232-7616 **Stewart County** Main St ... Dover TN 37058-0000
205 349-4240 **Stillman College** 3600 15th St ... Tuscaloosa AL 35401-2602
Fax: 205 758-0821
406 322-4546 **Stillwater County** PO Box 147 ... Columbus MT 59019-0147
Fax: 406 322-4698
609 652-1776 **Stockton State College** Jimmy Leeds Rd ... Pomona NJ 08240-9999
Fax: 609 652-0275
209 944-8415 **Stockton-San Joaquin County Public Library**
605 N El Dorado St ... Stockton CA 95202-1907
314 568-3339 **Stoddard County** PO Box H ... Bloomfield MO 63825-0209
919 593-2811 **Stokes County** Hwy 89 ... Danbury NC 27016-0000
Fax: 919 593-2346
202 225-7032 **Stokes Louis (Rep - D - Ohio)** 2365 Rayburn Bldg ... Washington DC 20515-0001
Fax: 202 225-1339
501 269-3351 **Stone County** PO Box 427 ... Mountain View AR 72560-0427
417 357-6127 **Stone County** PO Box 45 ... Galena MO 65656-0045
601 928-5266 **Stone County** PO Box 7 ... Wiggins MS 39577-0007
508 238-1081 **Stonehill College** 320 Washington St ... North Easton MA 02357-0001
Fax: 508 230-3732
817 989-2272 **Stonewall County** PO Box P ... Aspermont TX 79502-0914
702 847-0968 **Storey County** PO Box D ... Virginia City NV 89440-0139
515 382-6581 **Story County** 900 6th St ... Nevada IA 50201-2004
603 742-3065 **Strafford County** County Farm Rd ... Dover NH 03820-0000
813 576-8929 **Straight Inc** 3001 Gandy Blvd ... Saint Petersburg FL 33702-2043
Fax: 813 576-5635
202 695-8732 **Strategic Defense Initiative Organization (US Dept of Defense)**
Pentagon Rm 1E-1008 ... Washington DC 20301-0001
Fax: 202 697-4027
802 297-2200 **Stratton Mountain Resorts** Stratton Mountain Rd ... Stratton Mountain VT 05155-0000
Fax: 802 297-9395
603 433-1100 **Strawbery Banke Museum** 454 Court St ... Portsmouth NH 03801-4603
Fax: Unlisted
202 728-0048 **Strayer College** 1100 16th St NW ... Washington DC 20036-4802
Fax: Unlisted
703 892-5100 *Arlington Branch* 3045 Columbia Pike ... Arlington VA 22204-0000
202 225-3111 **Studds Gerry E (Rep - D - Massachusetts)**
237 Cannon Bldg ... Washington DC 20515-0001
Fax: 202 225-2212
308 381-5316 **Stuhr Museum of the Prairie Pioneer** 3133 W Hwy 34 ... Grand Island NE 68801-7280

202 225-4576 **Stump Bob (Rep - R - Arizona)** 211 Cannon Bldg ... Washington DC 20515-0001
Fax: 202 225-6328
701 252-9037 **Stutsman County** 511 2nd Ave SE ... Jamestown ND 58401-4210
307 367-4372 **Sublette County** PO Box 250 ... Pinedale WY 82941-0250
Fax: 307 367-6396
Sudan: Republic of the Sudan
202 338-8565 *Embassy* 2210 Massachusetts Ave NW ... Washington DC 20008-2812
212 421-2680 *Mission to the UN* 210 E 49th St ... New York NY 10017-1580
Fax: Unlisted
606 864-2238 **Sue Bennett College** 101 College St ... London KY 40741-1915
804 934-3111 **Suffolk (Independent City)** 441 Market St ... Suffolk VA 23434-5237
Fax: 804 934-3053
516 286-1600 **Suffolk Co-op Library System** 627 N Sunrise Service Rd ... Bellport NY 11713-0000
Fax: 516 286-0093
617 725-8000 **Suffolk County** 55 Pemberton Sq Government Ctr ... Boston MA 02108-1701
516 548-3888 **Suffolk County** County Ctr ... Riverhead NY 11901-0000
Fax: 516 548-4040
Suffolk County Community College
516 434-6700 *Brentwood Campus* Crooked Hill Rd ... Brentwood NY 11717-0000
516 451-4110 *Selden Campus* 533 College Rd ... Selden NY 11784-2899
Fax: 516 451-4715
516 727-2881 **Suffolk County Historical Society** 300 W Main St ... Riverhead NY 11901-2894
617 573-8000 **Suffolk University** 8 Ashburton Pl ... Boston MA 02108-2770
Fax: 617 573-8703 Admissions
617 573-8144 *Law School* 41 Temple St Donahue Bldg ... Boston MA 02114-4280
Fax: 617 573-8706
915 837-8011 **Sul Ross State University** E Hwy 90 ... Alpine TX 79832-0001
Fax: 915 837-8334 Admin
502 456-6504 **Sullivan College** 3101 Bardstown Rd ... Louisville KY 40205-3000
Fax: 502 454-4880
812 268-4657 **Sullivan County** County Courthouse ... Sullivan IN 47882-0000
816 265-3786 **Sullivan County** 2nd St ... Milan MO 63556-0000
603 863-3450 **Sullivan County** PO Box 45 ... Newport NH 03773-0045
914 794-3000 **Sullivan County** 100 North St ... Monticello NY 12701-1160
Fax: 914 794-3459
717 946-5201 **Sullivan County** Main & Muncy ... Laporte PA 18626-0000
615 323-6428 **Sullivan County** PO Box 530 ... Blountville TN 37617-0530
914 434-5750 **Sullivan County Community College** ... Loch Sheldrake NY 12759-0000
Fax: 914 434-4806
615 323-5301 **Sullivan County Public Library** PO Box 510 ... Blountville TN 37617-0510
605 258-2535 **Sully County** Main St ... Onida SD 57564-0000
304 466-3770 **Summers County** Ballengee St ... Hinton WV 25951-0000
219 456-2111 **Summit Christian College** 1025 W Rudisill Blvd ... Fort Wayne IN 46807-2197
303 453-2561 **Summit County** PO Box 68 ... Breckenridge CO 80424-0068
216 379-2512 **Summit County** 175 S Main St ... Akron OH 44308-1306
Fax: 216 379-2507
801 336-4451 **Summit County** PO Box 128 ... Coalville UT 84017-0128
Fax: 801 336-4450
316 326-3395 **Sumner County** 500 N Washington Ave ... Wellington KS 67152-4096
615 452-4063 **Sumner County** County Courthouse Rm 108 ... Gallatin TN 37066-0000
205 652-2291 **Sumter County** Franklin St ... Livingston AL 35470-0000
904 793-0200 **Sumter County** 209 N Florida St ... Bushnell FL 33513-9402
Fax: 904 793-0207
912 924-3090 **Sumter County** PO Box 295 ... Americus GA 31709-0295
803 773-1581 **Sumter County** 141 N Main St ... Sumter SC 29150-4965
Fax: 803 773-1523
803 773-7273 **Sumter County Library** 111 N Harvin St ... Sumter SC 29150-4988
Fax: 803 773-4875
202 225-2811 **Sundquist Don (Rep - R - Tennessee)** 230 Cannon Bldg ... Washington DC 20515-0001
Fax: 202 225-2814
601 887-4703 **Sunflower County** 2nd St ... Indianola MS 38751-0000
305 947-5826 **Sunny Isle Beach Resort Assoc**
3909 Sunny Isles Blvd Suite 307 ... Sunny Isles FL 33160-4126
408 730-7315 **Sunnyvale Public Library** 665 W Olive Ave ... Sunnyvale CA 94086-7622
304 344-8035 **Sunrise Museums** 746 Myrtle Rd ... Charleston WV 25314-1152
518 443-5555 **SUNY (System) State University of New York** 350 Broadway ... Albany NY 12246-0001
Fax: 518 443-5677
SUNY
607 587-4111 *College at Alfred* ... Alfred NY 14802-0000
Fax: 607 587-3298
716 395-2211 *College at Brockport* ... Brockport NY 14420-0000
Fax: 716 395-2246
716 878-4000 *College at Buffalo* 1300 Elmwood Ave ... Buffalo NY 14222-1095
Fax: 716 878-3039
315 386-7011 *College at Canton* 34 Cornell Dr ... Canton NY 13617-1096
Fax: 315 386-7930
607 753-2011 *College at Cortland* PO Box 2000 ... Cortland NY 13045-0000
Fax: Unlisted
607 746-4111 *College at Delhi* Main St ... Delhi NY 13753-0000
Fax: 607 746-4208
716 673-3111 *College at Fredonia* Central Ave ... Fredonia NY 14063-0000
Fax: 716 673-3185 Library
716 245-5211 *College at Geneseo* ... Geneseo NY 14454-0000
315 684-6000 *College at Morrisville* ... Morrisville NY 13408-0000
Fax: 315 684-6116
914 257-2121 *College at New Paltz* ... New Paltz NY 12561-0000
Fax: 914 257-3009
516 876-3000 *College at Old Westbury* PO Box 210 ... Old Westbury NY 11568-0210
Fax: 516 876-3209 Personnel
607 431-3500 *College at Oneonta* Upper West St ... Oneonta NY 13820-0000
Fax: 607 431-2107 Admin
315 341-2500 *College at Oswego* Rt 104 W ... Oswego NY 13126-0000
Fax: 315 341-2260
518 564-2000 *College at Plattsburgh* ... Plattsburgh NY 12901-0000
Fax: 518 564-7827 Mail Rm
315 267-2000 *College at Potsdam* Pierrpont Ave ... Potsdam NY 13676-0000
Fax: 315 267-2170
914 251-6000 *College at Purchase* 735 Anderson Hill Rd ... Purchase NY 10577-1400
518 234-5011 *College of Agriculture & Technology* ... Cobleskill NY 12043-0000
Fax: 518 234-5333
315 470-6600 *College of Environmental Science & Forestry* 1 Forestry Dr ... Syracuse NY 13210-2778
Fax: 315 470-6933
516 420-2000 *College of Technology* Rt 110 ... Farmingdale NY 11735-0000
Fax: 516 420-2753
315 792-7208 *College of Technology* PO Box 3050 ... Utica NY 13504-3050
Fax: 315 792-7222
518 587-2100 *Empire State College* 2 Union Ave ... Saratoga Springs NY 12866-4310
Fax: 518 587-5404
212 760-7675 *Fashion Institute of Technology* 227 W 27th St ... New York NY 10001-5902
Fax: 212 594-9413
212 409-7200 *Maritime College* Fort Schuyler ... Bronx NY 10465-0000
Fax: 212 409-7392
315 464-4570 *Syracuse Health Science Center* 750 E Adams St ... Syracuse NY 13210-2306
Fax: 315 473-4841 Admin

518 442-3300 **SUNY Albany** 1400 Washington Ave ... Albany NY 12222-0001
Fax: 518 442-3567 Library
518 442-4466 *Department of Geological Science* 1400 Washington Ave ... Albany NY 12222-0001
Fax: 518 442-4468
518 442-5254 *Graduate School of Public Affairs*
135th Western Ave Milne Hall ... Albany NY 12222-0001
Fax: 518 442-5298
607 777-2000 **SUNY Binghamton** Vestal Pkwy E ... Binghamton NY 13902-0000
Fax: 607 777-4000
607 777-4964 *Decker School of Nursing*
School of Nursing Bldg Rm 82 ... Binghamton NY 13901-0000
Fax: 607 777-4440
716 831-2000 **SUNY Buffalo** 3435 Main St ... Buffalo NY 14214-3099
Fax: 716 636-2895
716 636-3180 *Computer Science Dept* 226 Bell Hall ... Buffalo NY 14260-0001
Fax: 716 636-3464
716 831-3014 *Department of Chemistry* Main St Campus Acheson Hall ... Buffalo NY 14214-3099
Fax: 716 831-2960
716 636-2141 *Department of Communication*
Millard Fillmore Academic Core Rm 338 ... Buffalo NY 14261-0000
716 831-2176 *Department of Microbiology* 226 Farber Hall ... Buffalo NY 14214-0000
716 636-3204 *School of Business* 206 Jacobs Management Ctr ... Buffalo NY 14260-0001
Fax: 716 688-6603
716 831-2836 *School of Dental Medicine* 325 Squire Hall ... Buffalo NY 14214-0000
Fax: 716 833-3517
716 636-2772 *School of Engineering & Applied Science* 412 Bonner Hall ... Buffalo NY 14260-0001
Fax: 716 636-2495
716 636-2061 *School of Law* 304 O'Brian Hall ... Buffalo NY 14260-0001
Fax: 716 636-2064 Dean
716 831-2775 *School of Medicine & Biomedical Sciences*
174 Cary Farber Sherman Bldg ... Buffalo NY 14214-0000
Fax: 716 831-3395
716 831-2533 *School of Nursing* 3435 Main St Kimball Tower ... Buffalo NY 14214-3099
Fax: 716 831-2021
716 636-2823 *School of Pharmacy* 126 Cooke Hall ... Buffalo NY 14260-0001
Fax: 716 636-3688
716 831-2133 *School of Planning & Design* Hayes Hall Rm 116 ... Buffalo NY 14214-0000
516 689-8333 **SUNY Health Science Center at Stony Brook** Nicolls Rd ... Stony Brook NY 11794-0001
Fax: 516 632-6215
315 464-5540 **SUNY Health Science Center at Syracuse** 750 E Adams St ... Syracuse NY 13210-2399
Fax: 315 464-4663 Acctg
516 689-6000 **SUNY Stony Brook** Nicolls Rd ... Stony Brook NY 11794-0001
Fax: 516 632-6215
516 632-8470 *Computer Science Dept* 1401 Computer Science Bldg ... Stony Brook NY 11794-0001
Fax: 516 632-8334
516 632-8200 *Department of Earth & Space Science* ESF Bldg ... Stony Brook NY 11790-0000
Fax: 516 632-8240
516 632-8497 *Department of Material Science* ... Stony Brook NY 11794-0001
Fax: 516 632-8052
516 632-8080 *Physics Dept* Graduate Physics Bldg ... Stony Brook NY 11794-3800
Fax: 516 632-8176
516 632-8550 *School of Biochemistry* Life Science Bldg Rm 450 ... Stony Brook NY 11794-0001
Fax: 516 632-8575
516 632-7886 *School of Chemistry* Chemistry Bldg ... Stony Brook NY 11794-3400
Fax: 516 632-7960
516 632-8900 *School of Dental Medicine* Rockland Hall ... Stony Brook NY 11794-0001
Fax: 516 632-7130
516 444-2080 *School of Medicine* Health Science Ctr ... Stony Brook NY 11794-0001
Fax: 516 444-2202
906 482-5300 **Suomi College** 601 Quincy St ... Hancock MI 49930-1882
Fax: 906 487-7300
202 479-3000 **Supreme Court of the US** 1 1st St NE ... Washington DC 20543-0001
Fax: Unlisted
202 343-4719 **Surface Mining Reclamation & Enforcement**
1951 Constitution Ave NW ... Washington DC 20240-0001
Fax: 202 842-3771
703 523-4303 *Big Stone Gap Office* PO Box 1216 ... Big Stone Gap VA 24129-0000
205 731-0890 *Birmingham Office* 208 W Valley Rm 302 ... Homewood AL 35209-0000
304 347-7158 *Charleston Office* 603 Morris St ... Charleston WV 25301-1409
Fax: 304 345-4611
412 937-2831 *Eastern Service Center* 10 Parkway Ctr ... Pittsburgh PA 15220-0000
Fax: 412 937-2177
717 782-4036 *Harrisburg Office* 4th & Market Sts Suite 3-C ... Harrisburg PA 17101-0000
317 226-6166 *Indianapolis Office* 575 N Pennsylvania St Suite 301 ... Indianapolis IN 46204-1521
Fax: Unlisted
816 374-6405 *Kansas City Office* 1103 Grand Ave Rm 502 ... Kansas City MO 64106-2419
Fax: 816 374-6777
615 673-4255 *Knoxville Office* 530 N Gay St ... Knoxville TN 37917-7422
Fax: 615 673-4545
217 492-4495 *Springfield Office* 509 W Capitol Ave 2nd Fl ... Springfield IL 62704-0000
303 844-2451 *Western Service Center* 1020 15th St ... Denver CO 80202-2348
Fax: 303 844-4380
305 864-0722 **Surfside Tourist Information** 9301 Collins Ave ... Surfside FL 33154-2693
Suriname: Republic of Suriname
202 244-7488 *Embassy* 4301 Connecticut Ave NW Suite 108 ... Washington DC 20008-2304
Fax: 202 244-5878
212 826-0660 *Mission to the UN* 1 UN Plaza 26th Fl ... New York NY 10017-0000
Fax: 212 980-7029
919 386-8121 **Surry Community College** S Main St ... Dobson NC 27017-0000
Fax: Unlisted
919 386-8131 **Surry County** PO Box 345 ... Dobson NC 27017-0345
804 294-5271 **Surry County** Hwy 10 & School St ... Surry VA 23883-0000
Fax: 804 294-5111
717 278-4600 **Susquehanna County** County Courthouse ... Montrose PA 18801-0000
Fax: Unlisted
717 374-0101 **Susquehanna University** University Ave ... Selinsgrove PA 17870-0000
Fax: 717 372-4310 Library
302 856-5601 **Sussex County** PO Box 609 ... Georgetown DE 19947-0609
201 579-0200 **Sussex County** PO Box 709 ... Newton NJ 07860-0709
Fax: 201 383-1124
804 246-5511 **Sussex County** Rt 735 ... Sussex VA 23884-9999
916 741-7120 **Sutter County** 433 2nd St ... Yuba City CA 95991-5504
915 387-3815 **Sutton County** 300 E Oak St Suite 3 ... Sonora TX 76950-3106
904 362-2827 **Suwannee County** 200 Ohio Ave S ... Live Oak FL 32060-3239
704 488-9273 **Swain County** Mitchell St ... Bryson City NC 28713-0000
Fax: 704 488-2754
215 328-8000 **Swarthmore College** Chester Rd & College Ave ... Swarthmore PA 19081-0000
Fax: 215 328-8673
Swaziland: Kingdom of Swaziland
202 362-6683 *Embassy* 3400 International Dr NW Suite 3M ... Washington DC 20008-3006
Fax: 202 244-8059
212 371-8910 *Mission to the UN* 866 UN Plaza Suite 420 ... New York NY 10017-0000
Fax: 212 754-2755
Sweden: Kingdom of Sweden
202 944-5600 *Embassy* 600 New Hampshire Ave NW Suite 1200 ... Washington DC 20037-2403
Fax: 202 342-1319

212 751-5900 *Mission to the UN* 885 2nd Ave 46th Fl .... New York NY 10017-2201
  Fax: 212 832-0389
312 781-6262 *Chicago Consulate General* 150 N Michigan Ave Suite 1250 .. Chicago IL 60601-7593
  Fax: 312 346-0683
213 470-2555 *Los Angeles Consulate General*
  10880 Wilshire Blvd Suite 505 .... Los Angeles CA 90024-4189
  Fax: 213 475-4683
212 751-5900 *New York Consulate General* 885 2nd Ave 45th Fl .... New York NY 10017-0000
  Fax: 212 755-2732
212 838-5530 **Swedish-American Chamber of Commerce**
  599 Lexington Ave 42nd Fl .... New York NY 10022-7544
  Fax: 212 755-7953
415 781-4188 **Swedish-American Chamber of Commerce of the Western US**
  World Trade Ctr Suite 268 .... San Francisco CA 94111-0000
  Fax: 415 781-4189
804 381-6100 **Sweet Briar College** .... Sweet Briar VA 24595-9999
  Fax: 804 381-6173
406 932-5152 **Sweet Grass County** PO Box 460 .... Big Timber MT 59011-0460
602 978-5511 **Sweetwater Bible College** 14240 N 43rd Ave .... Phoenix AZ 85306-4511
307 875-2611 **Sweetwater County** 50 W Flaming Gorge Way .... Green River WY 82935-4212
  Fax: 307 875-8439
307 875-2611 **Sweetwater County Historical Museum**
  50 W Flaming Gorge Way .... Green River WY 82935-4235
  Fax: 307 875-8439
202 225-5206 **Swett Dick (Rep - D - New Hampshire)** 128 Cannon Bldg ... Washington DC 20515-0001
  Fax: 202 225-0046
202 225-2605 **Swift Al (Rep - D - Washington)** 1502 Longworth Bldg ...... Washington DC 20515-0001
  Fax: 202 225-2608
612 843-2744 **Swift County** PO Box 110 .... Benson MN 56215-0110
  Fax: 612 843-4124 Admin
806 995-3294 **Swisher County** County Courthouse .... Tulia TX 79088-2247
  Fax: 806 995-2214
812 427-3175 **Switzerland County** County Courthouse .... Vevay IN 47043-0000
  Switzerland: Swiss Confederation
202 745-7900 *Embassy* 2900 Cathedral Ave NW .... Washington DC 20008-3405
  Fax: 202 387-2564
212 421-1480 *Mission to the UN* 757 3rd Ave 21st Fl .... New York NY 10017-2013
  Fax: 212 751-2104
312 915-0061 *Chicago Consulate General* 737 N Michigan Ave Suite 2301 .. Chicago IL 60611-2615
  Fax: 312 915-0388
213 388-4127 *Los Angeles Consulate General*
  3440 Wilshire Blvd Suite 817 .... Los Angeles CA 90010-2109
  Fax: 213 385-4514
212 758-2560 *New York Consulate General* 665 5th Ave 8th Fl .... New York NY 10022-5305
  Fax: 212 207-8024
202 224-6142 **Symms Steven D (Sen - R - Idaho)** 509 Hart Bldg .... Washington DC 20510-0001
  Fax: 202 224-5893
202 225-2701 **Synar Mike (Rep - D - Oklahoma)** 2441 Rayburn Bldg .... Washington DC 20515-0001
  Fax: 202 225-2796
315 443-1870 **Syracuse University** .... Syracuse NY 13244-0001
  Fax: 315 443-1954
315 443-2524 *College of Law* .... Syracuse NY 13244-0001
  Fax: 315 443-9568
315 443-2144 *College of Nursing* 426 Ostrom Ave .... Syracuse NY 13210-2938
315 443-5958 *Graduate School of Physics* 201 Physics Bldg .... Syracuse NY 13244-0001
  Fax: 315 443-9103
315 443-2545 *LC Smith College of Engineering* Link Hall Rm 223 .... Syracuse NY 13244-0001
  Fax: 315 443-4936
315 443-2348 *Maxwell School of Citizenship & Public Affairs*
  105 Maxwell Hall .... Syracuse NY 13244-0001
315 443-2301 *Newhouse School of Public Communications*
  215 University Pl .... Syracuse NY 13244-0001
  Fax: 315 443-3946
315 443-2369 *School of Computer & Information Science*
  4-116 Center for Science & Technology .... Syracuse NY 13244-0001
  Fax: 315 443-4954
315 443-2911 *School of Information Studies*
  4-206 Ctr for Science & Technology .... Syracuse NY 13244-0001
  Syria: Syrian Arab Republic
202 232-6313 *Embassy* 2215 Wyoming Ave NW .... Washington DC 20008-3907
  Fax: Unlisted
212 661-1313 *Mission to the UN* 820 2nd Ave 10th Fl .... New York NY 10017-4504
  Fax: 212 983-4439

T

804 420-5476 **Tabernacle Baptist Bible Institute**
  717 N Whitehurst Landing Rd .... Virginia Beach VA 23464-2301
316 947-3121 **Tabor College** 400 S Jefferson St .... Hillsboro KS 67063-1799
  Fax: 316 947-3151
206 272-4258 **Tacoma Art Museum** 1123 Pacific Ave .... Tacoma WA 98402-4399
  Fax: 206 627-1898
206 591-5666 **Tacoma Public Library** 1102 Tacoma Ave S .... Tacoma WA 98402-2098
  Fax: 206 591-5470
805 763-4282 **Taft College** 29 Emmons Park Dr .... Taft CA 93268-2317
  Fax: 805 763-1038
513 241-0343 **Taft Museum** 316 Pike St .... Cincinnati OH 45202-4293
404 665-3220 **Talbot County** Courthouse Sq .... Talbotton GA 31827-0000
301 822-2401 **Talbot County** Washington St .... Easton MD 21601-0000
404 456-2494 **Taliaferro County** Courthouse Sq .... Crawfordville GA 30631-0000
205 362-0206 **Talladega College** 627 Battle St W .... Talladega AL 35160-2399
  Fax: 205 362-2268
205 362-4175 **Talladega County** PO Box 755 .... Talladega AL 35160-0755
  Fax: 205 761-2417
904 488-9200 **Tallahassee Community College** 444 Appleyard Dr .... Tallahassee FL 32304-2895
  Fax: 904 488-2203
601 647-5551 **Tallahatchie County** PO Box H .... Charleston MS 38921-0330
205 825-4268 **Tallapoosa County** 101 N Broadnax St .... Dadeville AL 36853-1395
202 225-3315 **Tallon Robin (Rep - D - South Carolina)** 432 Cannon Bldg ... Washington DC 20515-0001
  Fax: 202 225-2857
716 473-2810 **Talmudical Institution of Upstate New York** 769 Park Ave .... Rochester NY 14607-3098
515 484-3721 **Tama County** County Courthouse .... Toledo IA 52342-0000
813 223-8211 **Tampa City Hall** 306 E Jackson St .... Tampa FL 33602-5223
813 223-8945 **Tampa-Hillsborough County Public Library System**
  900 N Ashley St .... Tampa FL 33602-3704
  Fax: 813 223-8278
417 546-2241 **Taney County** PO Box 156 .... Forsyth MO 65653-0156
504 748-3211 **Tangipahoa Parish** PO Box 215 .... Amite LA 70422-0215
  Fax: 504 748-6503
202 225-4714 **Tanner John S (Rep - D - Tennessee)**
  1232 Longworth Bldg .... Washington DC 20515-0001
  Fax: 202 225-1765
  Tanzania: United Republic of Tanzania
202 939-6125 *Embassy* 2139 R St NW .... Washington DC 20008-1908

212 972-9160 *Mission to the UN* 205 E 42nd St Rm 1300 .... New York NY 10017-5706
  Fax: 212 682-5231
505 758-8836 **Taos County** PO Box 676 .... Taos NM 87571-0676
816 736-4131 **Tarkio College** McNary St .... Tarkio MO 64491-0000
  Fax: 816 736-5268
817 968-9000 **Tarleton State University** 201 Felix St .... Stephenville TX 76401-0000
  Fax: 817 968-9920
817 334-1195 **Tarrant County** 100 W Weatherford .... Fort Worth TX 76196-0001
817 336-7851 **Tarrant County Junior College** 1500 Houston St .... Fort Worth TX 76102-6524
  Fax: 817 877-9295
601 562-5661 **Tate County** 201 S Ward St .... Senatobia MS 38668-2616
912 557-4335 **Tattnall County** Main & Brazell Sts .... Reidsville GA 30453-0000
202 225-4031 **Tauzin Billy (Rep - D - Louisiana)** 2342 Rayburn Bldg .. Washington DC 20515-0001
  Fax: 202 225-0563
202 566-5374 **Tax Analysis Office (US Dept of the Treasury)**
  1500 Pennsylvania Ave NW Rm 4217 .... Washington DC 20220-0001
  Fax: 202 786-8440
202 633-2901 **Tax Div (US Dept of Justice)**
  10th St & Pennsylvania Ave NW Rm 4143 .... Washington DC 20530-0001
  Fax: 202 786-5474
202 225-6401 **Taylor Charles H (Rep - R - North Carolina)**
  516 Cannon Bldg .... Washington DC 20515-0001
  Fax: 202 225-0519
904 584-3531 **Taylor County** PO Box 620 .... Perry FL 32347-0620
  Fax: 904 584-3949
912 862-3336 **Taylor County** PO Box 278 .... Butler GA 31006-0000
712 523-2095 **Taylor County** County Courthouse .... Bedford IA 50833-0000
502 465-6677 **Taylor County** Court & Broadway .... Campbellsville KY 42718-0000
  Fax: 502 465-6678
915 677-1711 **Taylor County** 300 Oak St .... Abilene TX 79602-1521
715 748-3131 **Taylor County** 224 S 2nd St .... Medford WI 54451-1899
  Fax: 715 748-3813
304 265-1401 **Taylor County** 214 W Main St .... Grafton WV 26354-1387
202 225-5772 **Taylor Gene (Rep - D - Mississippi)**
  1429 Longworth Bldg .... Washington DC 20515-0001
  Fax: 202 225-7074
719 634-5581 **Taylor Museum** 30 W Dale St .... Colorado Springs CO 80903-3210
317 998-2751 **Taylor University** 500 W Reade Ave .... Upland IN 46989-1001
  Fax: 317 998-5569
309 477-2264 **Tazewell County** 4th & Court Sts .... Pekin IL 61554-0000
703 988-7541 **Tazewell County** 315 School St .... Tazewell VA 24651-1398
  Fax: 703 988-4246 Admin
803 525-8324 **Technical College of the Low Country** 100 Ribaut Rd ...... Beaufort SC 29902-5428
  Fax: 803 525-8330
202 377-1984 **Technology Administration (US Dept of Commerce)**
  14th St & Constitution Ave NW Rm 4410 .... Washington DC 20230-0001
  Fax: 202 377-4498
916 527-4655 **Tehama County** PO Box 250 .... Red Bluff CA 96080-0250
  Fax: 916 529-0980
203 755-0121 **Teikyo Post University** 800 Country Club Rd .... Waterbury CT 06708-3200
  Fax: 203 756-5810
712 546-7081 **Teikyo-Westmar University** 1002 3rd Ave SE .... Le Mars IA 51031-2699
  Fax: 712 546-4061
202 462-2520 **Telecommunications Research & Action Center**
  PO Box 12038 .... Washington DC 20005-0000
212 393-6288 **Telephone Pioneers of America** 22 Cortlandt St Rm 2565 ..... New York NY 10007-3107
  Fax: 212 393-4777
912 232-1177 **Telfair Academy of Arts & Sciences** 121 Barnard St .... Savannah GA 31401-3612
912 868-5688 **Telfair County** Courthouse Sq .... McRae GA 31055-0000
719 689-2482 **Teller County** PO Box 959 .... Cripple Creek CO 80813-0959
  Fax: 719 689-3268
817 773-9961 **Temple Junior College** 2600 S 1st St .... Temple TX 76504-7435
  Fax: 817 773-7841
215 787-7000 **Temple University** Broad & Montgomery Ave .... Philadelphia PA 19122-0000
215 787-8791 *School of Communication & Theater*
  13th & Norris St Annenberg Hall Rm 321 .... Philadelphia PA 19122-0000
  Fax: 215 787-6641
215 221-2803 *School of Dentistry* 3223 N Broad St .... Philadelphia PA 19140-5096
  Fax: 215 221-2802
215 787-7863 *School of Law* 1719 Broad St Charles Klein Bldg .... Philadelphia PA 19122-0000
  Fax: 215 787-1185
215 221-3656 *School of Medicine*
  Broad & Ontario Sts Faculty-Student Bldg Rm 305 .... Philadelphia PA 19140-0000
215 221-4900 *School of Pharmacy* 3307 N Broad St .... Philadelphia PA 19140-5101
  Fax: Unlisted
615 356-8000 **Tennessee Botanical Gardens & Fine Arts Center**
  Forrest Park Dr .... Nashville TN 37205-0000
615 244-1336 **Tennessee Democratic Party** 431 11th Ave N .... Nashville TN 37203-3315
  Fax: 615 248-6304
615 741-2159 **Tennessee Dept of Tourist Development** 320 6th Ave N .... Nashville TN 37219-5605
  Fax: 615 741-7225
615 321-4521 **Tennessee Republican Party** 2817 West End Ave .... Nashville TN 37203-1453
  Fax: Unlisted
  Tennessee State Government
615 741-3011 *Information* B10 John Sevier Bldg .... Nashville TN 37219-0000
  Fax: 615 741-4996
615 741-3141 *Adult Probation Div Department of Corrections*
  320 6th Ave N 2nd Fl .... Nashville TN 37219-5252
  Fax: 615 741-2696
615 741-3931 *Air Pollution Control Div* 701 Broadway .... Nashville TN 37247-3101
  Fax: 615 741-4666
615 741-1701 *Arts Commission* 320 6th Ave N Suite 100 .... Nashville TN 37219-5605
615 741-3491 *Attorney General* 450 James Robertson Pkwy .... Nashville TN 37219-5025
  Fax: 615 741-2009
615 741-3657 *Bureau of Environment* 150 9th Ave N Terra Bldg 1st Fl ...... Nashville TN 37247-0000
  Fax: 615 741-4608
615 360-0103 *Department of Agriculture* Ellington Agriculture Ctr .... Nashville TN 37204-0000
  Fax: 615 360-0333
615 741-2241 *Department of Commerce & Insurance*
  500 James Robertson Pkwy 5th Fl .... Nashville TN 37243-0000
  Fax: 615 741-4000
615 742-6749 *Department of Conservation* 701 Broadway .... Nashville TN 37243-0000
  Fax: 615 742-6594
615 741-2071 *Department of Corrections* 320 6th Ave N .... Nashville TN 37219-5605
  Fax: 615 741-4605
615 741-1888 *Department of Economic & Community Development*
  320 6th Ave N 8th Fl .... Nashville TN 37219-5605
  Fax: 615 741-7306
615 741-2731 *Department of Education* 100 Cordell Hull Bldg .... Nashville TN 37219-5335
  Fax: 615 741-6236
615 741-2131 *Department of Employment Security*
  500 James Robertson Pkwy 12th Fl .... Nashville TN 37245-0001
  Fax: 615 741-3203
615 741-2140 *Department of Finance & Administration*
  500 Deaderick St Rm 314 .... Nashville TN 37219-5609

Tennessee / Texas

615 741-2461 *Department of Revenue* Andrew Jackson Bldg Suite 1200 ... Nashville TN 37242-0000
Fax: 615 741-0682
615 741-2956 *Department of the Treasury* State Capitol 1st Fl ... Nashville TN 37219-0000
Fax: 615 741-1061
615 741-2848 *Department of Transportation* James K Polk Bldg Suite 700 . Nashville TN 37243-0000
Fax: 615 741-2508
615 741-4737 *Division of Consumer Affairs*
500 James Robertson Pkwy 5th Fl ... Nashville TN 37243-1215
Fax: 615 741-4000
615 742-6691 *Division of Geology* 701 Broadway Suite B-30 ... Nashville TN 37243-0445
Fax: 615 742-6594
615 741-2451 *Division of Library & Archives* 403 7th Ave N ... Nashville TN 37243-0312
Fax: Unlisted
615 562-4914 *Division of Mines* Queener Rd ... Caryville TN 37714-0000
615 741-2793 *Division of Occupational Safety & Health*
501 Union St 3rd Fl ... Nashville TN 37243-0659
Fax: 615 741-5078
615 741-1035 *Division of Purchasing* 503 5th Ave N Rm C2-214 ... Nashville TN 37219-0000
Fax: 615 741-0684
615 741-7063 *Division of Retirement*
500 Deaderick St Andrew Jackson Bldg 10th Fl ... Nashville TN 37219-5609
Fax: 615 741-1061
615 741-2947 *Division of Securities*
500 James Robertson Pkwy Suite 680 ... Nashville TN 37243-0000
Fax: 615 741-4000
615 741-3424 *Division of Solid Waste Management* 701 Broadway ... Nashville TN 37247-5403
Fax: 615 741-4666
615 741-1763 *Division of Vital Records* Cordell Hull Bldg ... Nashville TN 37247-0350
615 252-3311 *Emergency Management Agency* 3041 Sidco Dr ... Nashville TN 37204-4505
Fax: 615 242-9635
615 741-2001 *Governor* State Capitol ... Nashville TN 37219-5601
Fax: 615 741-1416
615 741-3605 *Higher Education Commission*
404 James Robertson Pkwy Parkway Towers Suite 1900 ... Nashville TN 37219-0000
Fax: 615 741-6230
615 741-2368 *Lieutenant Governor* Legislative Plaza Suite 1 ... Nashville TN 37219-0000
Fax: 615 741-7202
615 741-1676 *Planning Office* 500 Charlotte Ave ... Nashville TN 37219-5608
Fax: 615 741-1416
615 741-6888 *Property Services Management*
302 Cordell Hull Bldg Rm C-3 ... Nashville TN 37243-0000
615 741-2904 *Public Service Commission* 460 James Robertson Pkwy ... Nashville TN 37219-5477
Fax: 615 741-2336
615 741-2273 *Real Estate Commission*
500 James Robertson Pkwy Suite 180 ... Nashville TN 37243-0000
Fax: Unlisted
615 741-3449 *Regulatory Boards* 500 James Robertson Pkwy 2nd Fl ... Nashville TN 37243-0572
Fax: 615 741-6470
615 741-2816 *Secretary of State* State Capitol 1st Fl ... Nashville TN 37219-0000
615 881-3251 *Southeastern Tennessee Regional Correctional Facility*
Rt 4 Box 600 ... Pikeville TN 37367-9243
Fax: 615 881-3572
615 741-3181 *State Highway Patrol* 1603 Murfreesboro Rd ... Nashville TN 37217-0000
Fax: 615 741-4975
615 741-2681 *Supreme Court* 401 7th Ave N Supreme Court Bldg Rm 100 Nashville TN 37243-0000
615 741-4611 *Tennessee State Penitentiary* Stn A ... Nashville TN 37219-0000
615 741-7883 *Water Pollution Control* 150 9th Ave N Terra Bldg 1st Fl ... Nashville TN 37247-3420
Fax: 615 741-4608
615 741-2395 *Worker's Compensation Div* 501 Union St ... Nashville TN 37243-0661
Fax: 615 741-5078
615 741-2451 **Tennessee State Library & Archives** 403 7th Ave N ... Nashville TN 37243-0312
Fax: 615 741-6471
615 741-2692 **Tennessee State Museum** 505 Deaderick St ... Nashville TN 37243-1120
Fax: 615 741-7231
615 320-3131 **Tennessee State University** 3500 John A Merritt Blvd ... Nashville TN 37209-1561
Fax: 615 320-3114
615 320-3131 **Tennessee State University & Community College System**
3500 John A Merritt Blvd ... Nashville TN 37209-1561
Fax: 615 320-3114
615 372-3101 **Tennessee Technological University** Dixie Ave ... Cookeville TN 38501-0000
Fax: 615 372-3898
615 493-4100 **Tennessee Temple University** 1815 Union Ave ... Chattanooga TN 37404-3587
Fax: Unlisted
615 745-7504 **Tennessee Wesleyan College** PO Box 40 ... Athens TN 37303-0000
318 766-3921 **Tensas Parish** Courthouse Sq ... Saint Joseph LA 71366-0000
213 514-6400 **Terminal Island Coast Guard Base** Terminal Island Stn ... San Pedro CA 90731-0000
Fax: 213 514-6210
419 334-3886 **Terra Technical College** 2830 Napoleon Rd ... Fremont OH 43420-9600
Fax: 419 334-9414
504 868-5050 **Terrebonne Parish** 301 Goode St ... Houma LA 70360-4513
Fax: 504 873-6880
912 995-4476 **Terrell County** 955 Forrester Dr SE ... Dawson GA 31742-2100
915 345-2391 **Terrell County** PO Box 410 ... Sanderson TX 79848-0410
202 343-4822 **Territorial & International Affairs Office (US Dept of the Interior)**
18th & C Sts NW Rm 4312 ... Washington DC 20240-0001
Fax: 202 343-1390
806 637-8551 **Terry County** 5th & Main ... Brownfield TX 79316-0000
208 354-2905 **Teton County** PO Box 756 ... Driggs ID 83422-0756
406 466-2151 **Teton County** PO Box 610 ... Choteau MT 59422-0000
Fax: 406 466-5782
307 733-4430 **Teton County** PO Box 1727 ... Jackson WY 83001-1727
Fax: 307 733-4451
903 838-4541 **Texarkana College** 2500 N Robison Rd ... Texarkana TX 75501-3099
Fax: 903 832-5030
512 595-2111 **Texas A & I University** Campus Box 105 ... Kingsville TX 78363-0000
Fax: 512 595-3218
409 845-3211 **Texas A & M University** ... College Station TX 77843-0000
Fax: 409 845-9909
409 645-4747 *College of Agriculture* ... College Station TX 77843-0000
Fax: 409 845-9938
409 845-1015 *College of Architecture & Environmental Design* ... College Station TX 77843-0000
Fax: 409 845-4491
409 845-3431 *College of Medicine* Joe H Reynolds Medical Bldg ... College Station TX 77843-0000
Fax: 409 845-7929
409 845-5051 *College of Veterinary Medicine* ... College Station TX 77843-0000
Fax: 409 845-5088
409 845-1046 *Department of Urban & Regional Planning*
College of Architecture & Environmental Design ... College Station TX 77843-0000
Fax: 409 845-4491
409 740-4400 *Galveston Campus* PO Box 1675 ... Galveston TX 77553-1675
Fax: 409 740-4407
409 845-1371 *Geoscience Div* O & M Bldg Rm 204 ... College Station TX 77843-0000
409 845-7200 *Graduate School of Engineering* 204 Zachry Bldg ... College Station TX 77843-0000
Fax: 409 845-6259
817 921-7000 **Texas Christian University** 2800 S University Dr ... Fort Worth TX 76129-0001
Fax: 817 921-7333

903 593-8311 **Texas College** 2404 N Grand Ave ... Tyler TX 75702-1999
Fax: 903 592-2342
417 967-2112 **Texas County** 210 N Grand Ave ... Houston MO 65483-1226
405 338-3233 **Texas County** 319 N Main St ... Guymon OK 73942-4843
512 478-8746 **Texas Democratic Party** 815 Brazos St Suite 200 ... Austin TX 78701-2593
Fax: 512 478-6471
512 379-4161 **Texas Lutheran College** 1000 W Court St ... Seguin TX 78155-5999
Fax: 512 379-3163
512 474-1812 **Texas Medical Assn PAC** 1905 N Lamar Blvd Suite 207 ... Austin TX 78705-4919
Fax: 512 479-6531
512 477-9821 **Texas Republican Party** 211 E 7th St Suite 620 ... Austin TX 78701-3295
Fax: 512 480-0709
713 527-7011 **Texas Southern University** 3100 Cleburne St ... Houston TX 77004-4598
Fax: 713 639-1095 PR
713 527-7164 *College of Pharmacy & Health Sciences* 3100 Cleburne St ... Houston TX 77004-4598
Fax: 713 639-1091
713 527-7112 *Thurgood Marshall School of Law* 3100 Cleburne St ... Houston TX 77004-4598
Fax: 713 639-1049 Dean
512 544-8200 **Texas Southmost College** 80 Fort Brown St ... Brownsville TX 78520-4956
Fax: 512 544-5495 Library
512 472-1594 **Texas State Chamber of Commerce**
900 Congress Ave Suite 501 ... Austin TX 78701-1649
Fax: 512 320-0280
Texas State Government
512 463-4630 *Information* 201 E 14th St ... Austin TX 78701-0000
Fax: 512 463-3445 Purchasing
512 451-5711 *Air Control Board* 6330 Hwy 290 E ... Austin TX 78723-1078
Fax: 512 371-0245
512 463-2100 *Attorney General* PO Box 12548 ... Austin TX 78711-1930
Fax: 512 463-2063 Admin
512 463-2611 *Benefits Dept* 101 E 15th St ... Austin TX 78778-0001
903 928-2217 *Beto 1 Unit* PO Box 128 ... Tennessee Colony TX 75861-0128
Fax: Ext 168
512 459-2700 *Board of Pardons & Paroles* 8610 Shoal Creek Blvd ... Austin TX 78758-6814
Fax: 512 459-2770
512 458-7366 *Bureau of Vital Statistics* 1100 W 49th St ... Austin TX 78756-3101
903 928-2211 *Coffield Unit* Rt 1 Box 150 ... Tennessee Colony TX 75861-9710
Fax: Ext 326
512 463-5535 *Commission on the Arts* PO Box 13406 ... Austin TX 78711-3046
Fax: 512 475-2699
512 463-2070 *Consumer Protection Div* 1500 N Congress Ave ... Austin TX 78701-0000
Fax: 512 473-8301
512 463-7435 *Department of Agriculture* PO Box 12847 ... Austin TX 78711-2847
Fax: 512 463-7643
512 472-5059 *Department of Commerce* 816 Congress Ave Suite 1200 ... Austin TX 78701-2430
Fax: 512 320-9674
512 834-6050 *Department of Community Affairs* 8317 Cross Park Dr ... Austin TX 78711-0000
Fax: 512 834-6245
409 295-6371 *Department of Criminal Justice* 815 11th St ... Huntsville TX 77340-4729
Fax: 409 294-6997
512 458-7375 *Department of Health* 1100 W 49th St ... Austin TX 78756-3197
Fax: 512 458-7477
512 463-8585 *Department of Highways & Public Transportation*
11th & Brazos Sts ... Austin TX 78701-2483
Fax: 512 463-0283
512 463-2906 *Department of Licensing & Regulations* 920 Colorado St ... Austin TX 78701-2325
Fax: 512 475-2854
512 465-2000 *Department of Public Safety* PO Box 4087 ... Austin TX 78773-0001
Fax: 512 225-2872
512 465-2138 *Division of Emergency Management* PO Box 4087 ... Austin TX 78773-0001
Fax: 512 451-2291
512 458-7271 *Division of Solid Waste Management* 1100 W 49th St ... Austin TX 78756-3101
512 463-8985 *Education Agency* 1701 N Congress Ave ... Austin TX 78701-1494
Fax: 512 463-9838
512 464-2222 *Employment Commission* 101 E 15th St ... Austin TX 78778-0001
Fax: 512 475-1133
512 463-2198 *Energy Research & Policy Analysis* 201 E 14th St ... Austin TX 78711-0000
Fax: 512 475-2569
512 463-2012 *Environmental Protection Div* PO Box 12548 ... Austin TX 78711-0000
Fax: 512 440-8002
512 463-3214 *Facilities Construction & Space Management Div*
PO Box 13047 ... Austin TX 78711-3047
Fax: 512 463-3366
512 479-1200 *Finance Commission* 2601 N Lamar Blvd ... Austin TX 78705-4294
Fax: 512 479-1227
512 463-2000 *Governor* PO Box 12428 ... Austin TX 78711-2428
Fax: 512 463-1849
512 462-6400 *Higher Education Coordinating Board* 200 E Riverside Dr ... Austin TX 78704-1205
Fax: 512 462-6453
512 463-0001 *Lieutenant Governor* State Capitol Rm 219 ... Austin TX 78711-0000
Fax: 512 463-0326
512 458-7287 *Occupational Safety & Health Div* 1100 W 49th St ... Austin TX 78756-3101
Fax: 512 458-7407
512 463-6893 *Oil & Gas Div* PO Box 12967 ... Austin TX 78711-2967
Fax: 512 463-7328
512 463-5022 *Petroleum & Minerals Development Div* 1700 N Congress Ave . Austin TX 78701-1436
Fax: 512 463-5233
512 463-1778 *Planning Office* 201 E 14th St ... Austin TX 78711-0000
Fax: 512 468-1849
512 458-0100 *Public Utility Commission* 7800 Shoal Creek Blvd Suite 400 N . Austin TX 78757-1098
Fax: 512 458-8340
512 463-3445 *Purchasing Div* 1711 San Jacinto Blvd ... Austin TX 78701-1416
Fax: Unlisted
512 459-6544 *Real Estate Commission* PO Box 12188 ... Austin TX 78711-2188
512 463-5701 *Secretary of State* PO Box 12697 ... Austin TX 78711-2697
Fax: 512 475-2761
512 474-2233 *Securities Board* PO Box 13167 ... Austin TX 78711-3167
512 463-5480 *State Archives* 1201 Brazos St ... Austin TX 78701-0000
Fax: 512 463-5436
512 463-6464 *State Board of Insurance* 1110 San Jacinto Blvd ... Austin TX 78701-1998
Fax: 512 475-2005
512 463-4865 *State Controllers Office* 111 E 17th St LBJ Bldg ... Austin TX 78711-0000
Fax: 512 463-4902
512 463-1312 *Supreme Court* 200 W 14th St Room AG-11 ... Austin TX 78701-0000
Fax: 512 463-1365
512 463-6000 *Treasury* 111 E 17th St ... Austin TX 78701-1440
Fax: 512 463-6040
512 463-7847 *Water Development Board* PO Box 13231 ... Austin TX 78711-3231
Fax: 512 475-2053
512 463-5460 **Texas State Library** 1201 Brazos St ... Austin TX 78701-0000
Fax: 512 463-5436
Texas State Technical Institute
806 335-2316 *Amarillo Campus* PO Box 11077 ... Amarillo TX 79111-0001
Fax: Ext 523
512 425-4922 *Harlingen Campus* Industrial Air Pk ... Harlingen TX 78550-0000
Fax: 512 825-9796

915 235-7300 *Sweetwater Campus* RR 3 Box 18 ... Sweetwater TX 79556-0000
Fax: 915 235-7359
817 799-3611 *Waco Campus* 3801 Campus Dr ... Waco TX 76705-1695
Fax: 817 867-1700
806 742-2011 **Texas Tech University** Broadway & University Ave ... Lubbock TX 79409-0000
Fax: 806 742-2138 Admin
806 742-2781 *Graduate School* PO Box 4460 ... Lubbock TX 79409-4460
806 742-3791 *School of Law* 1802 Hartford Ave ... Lubbock TX 79409-0000
Fax: 806 742-1629
806 742-3385 *School of Mass Communications* PO Box 4710 ... Lubbock TX 79409-3082
806 743-3000 *School of Medicine* 3601 4th St ... Lubbock TX 79430-0001
Fax: 806 743-2218
512 472-5059 **Texas Tourist Div** 816 Congress Ave Suite 1200 ... Austin TX 78701-2443
Fax: 512 320-9674
817 531-4444 **Texas Wesleyan University** 1201 Wesleyan St ... Fort Worth TX 76105-1536
Fax: 817 531-4814
817 898-3000 **Texas Woman's University** PO Box 22909 ... Denton TX 76204-0909
Fax: 817 898-3198
817 898-2401 *College School of Nursing* 1216 Oakland St Rm 232 ... Denton TX 76201-3169
Fax: 817 898-3196
202 667-0441 **Textile Museum** S St NW ... Washington DC 20008-4088
Thailand: Kingdom of Thailand
202 483-7200 *Embassy* 2300 Kalorama Rd NW ... Washington DC 20008-1623
Fax: 202 234-4498
212 689-1004 *Mission to the UN* 628 2nd Ave ... New York NY 10016-4899
Fax: 212 683-6017
213 937-1894 *Consulate General* 801 N La Brea Ave ... Los Angeles CA 90038-3340
203 886-0177 **Thames Valley State Technical College**
574 New London Tpke ... Norwich CT 06360-6598
Fax: 203 886-4960
402 768-6126 **Thayer County** 235 N 4th St ... Hebron NE 68370-1549
412 588-7700 **Thiel College** 75 College Ave ... Greenville PA 16125-2181
Fax: 412 589-2021
609 984-1150 **Thomas A Edison State College** 101 W State St CN545 ... Trenton NJ 08625-0001
Fax: 609 984-8447
805 525-4417 **Thomas Aquinas College** 10000 N Ojai Rd ... Santa Paula CA 93060-9622
Fax: 805 525-0620
912 226-1621 **Thomas College** 1501 Millpond Rd ... Thomasville GA 31792-7499
207 873-0771 **Thomas College** 180 W River Rd ... Waterville ME 04901-5097
Fax: 207 873-6120
912 225-4100 **Thomas County** PO Box 920 ... Thomasville GA 31799-0920
Fax: 912 228-0441
913 462-2561 **Thomas County** 300 N Court Ave ... Colby KS 67701-2439
Fax: 913 462-8390
308 645-2261 **Thomas County** PO Box 226 ... Thedford NE 69166-0226
202 225-2311 **Thomas Craig (Rep - R - Wyoming)** 1721 Longworth Bldg .. Washington DC 20515-0001
Fax: 202 225-0726
215 955-6000 **Thomas Jefferson University** 111 S 11th St ... Philadelphia PA 19107-0000
Fax: 215 928-5044
517 371-5140 **Thomas M Cooley Law School** 217 S Capitol Ave ... Lansing MI 48933-1586
Fax: 517 334-5714
606 341-5800 **Thomas More College** 333 Thomas More Pkwy ... Crestview Hills KY 41017-3428
Fax: 606 344-3345
804 825-2700 **Thomas Nelson Community College** 99 Thomas Nelson Dr ... Hampton VA 23666-1433
Fax: 804 825-2854
202 225-5831 **Thomas Robert Lindsay (Rep - D - Georgia)**
240 Cannon Bldg ... Washington DC 20515-0001
Fax: 202 225-6922
202 225-2915 **Thomas William M (Rep - R - California)**
2402 Rayburn Bldg ... Washington DC 20515-0001
Fax: 202 225-8798
202 225-2506 **Thornton Ray (Rep - D - Arkansas)** 1705 Longworth Bldg ... Washington DC 20515-0001
Fax: 202 225-9273
314 686-4101 **Three Rivers Community College** Three Rivers Blvd ... Poplar Bluff MO 63901-0000
Fax: Ext 281
817 849-2501 **Throckmorton County** PO Box 309 ... Throckmorton TX 76083-0309
202 224-5972 **Thurmond Strom (Sen - R - South Carolina)**
217 Russell Bldg ... Washington DC 20510-0001
Fax: 202 224-1300
402 385-2343 **Thurston County** 106 S 5th St ... Pender NE 68047-0000
206 754-3800 **Thurston County** 2000 Lakeridge Dr SW ... Olympia WA 98502-6042
804 484-2121 **Tidewater Community College** SR-135 ... Portsmouth VA 23703-0000
Fax: 804 483-9169
419 447-6442 **Tiffin University** 155 Miami St ... Tiffin OH 44883-2161
Fax: 419 447-9605
912 386-7850 **Tift County** 225 N Tift Ave ... Tifton GA 31794-4463
Fax: 912 386-7955
503 842-3402 **Tillamook County** 201 Laurel Ave ... Tillamook OR 97141-2381
Fax: 503 842-2721
503 842-4553 **Tillamook County Pioneer Museum** 2106 2nd St ... Tillamook OR 97141-2399
405 335-3421 **Tillman County** PO Box 992 ... Frederick OK 73542-0992
206 943-5001 **Timberland Regional Library** 415 Airdustrial Way SW ... Olympia WA 98501-5799
Fax: 206 321-6838
815 398-6000 **Time Museum** 7801 E State St ... Rockford IL 61125-0000
Fax: 815 398-0443
405 732-7321 **Tinker Air Force Base** ... Oklahoma City OK 73145-5000
607 687-3133 **Tioga County** 16 Court St ... Owego NY 13827-1515
717 724-1906 **Tioga County** 116-118 Main St ... Wellsboro PA 16901-0000
Fax: 717 724-1363
601 837-7374 **Tippah County** PO Box 99 ... Ripley MS 38663-0099
317 423-9215 **Tippecanoe County** 20 N 3rd St ... Lafayette IN 47901-1222
Fax: 317 423-1922
317 429-0100 **Tippecanoe County Public Library** 627 South St ... Lafayette IN 47901-1470
Fax: 317 429-0150
317 675-2795 **Tipton County** County Courthouse ... Tipton IN 46072-0000
901 476-0207 **Tipton County** PO Box 528 ... Covington TN 38019-0528
601 423-7010 **Tishomingo County** 1008 Hwy 25 S ... Iuka MS 38852-1020
903 572-8891 **Titus County** Courthouse Sq ... Mount Pleasant TX 75455-0000
404 886-6831 **Toccoa Falls College** ... Toccoa Falls GA 30598-0000
Fax: 404 886-0210
502 265-2363 **Todd County** PO Box 157 ... Elkton KY 42220-0157
612 732-4431 **Todd County** 215 1st Ave S ... Long Prairie MN 56347-1351
605 842-2266 **Todd County** 200 E 3rd St ... Winner SD 57580-0000
Togo: Republic of Togo
202 234-4212 *Embassy* 2208 Massachusetts Ave NW ... Washington DC 20008-2812
Fax: 202 232-3190
212 490-3455 *Mission to the UN* 112 E 40th St 1st Fl ... New York NY 10016-1724
419 245-3085 **Toledo City Hall** 1 Government Ctr ... Toledo OH 43604-2279
419 255-8000 **Toledo Museum of Art** 2445 Monroe St ... Toledo OH 43620-1517
Fax: 419 255-5638
419 259-5200 **Toledo-Lucas County Public Library** 325 N Michigan St ... Toledo OH 43624-1628
Fax: 419 259-5313
203 875-6294 **Tolland Judicial District** 69 Brooklyn St ... Rockville CT 06066-3643
915 653-2385 **Tom Green County** 112 W Beauregard Ave ... San Angelo TX 76903-5850
Fax: 915 655-5393

607 844-8211 **Tompkins Cortland Community College** 170 North St ... Dryden NY 13053-9533
Fax: 607 844-9665
607 274-5434 **Tompkins County** 320 N Tioga St ... Ithaca NY 14850-4284
Fax: 607 274-5429
907 225-5600 **Tongass Historical Museum** 629 Dock St ... Ketchikan AK 99901-6529
801 882-5550 **Tooele County** 47 S Main St ... Tooele UT 84074-2194
Fax: 801 882-7317
406 434-5121 **Toole County** 226 1st St S ... Shelby MT 59474-1920
912 526-3311 **Toombs County** Courthouse Sq & Hwy 280 ... Lyons GA 30436-0000
913 233-2040 **Topeka Public Library** 1515 SW 10th St ... Topeka KS 66604-1374
Fax: 913 233-2055
505 384-2221 **Torrance County** 9th & Allen ... Estancia NM 87016-0000
213 618-5950 **Torrance Public Library** 3301 Torrance Blvd ... Torrance CA 90503-5014
Fax: 213 618-5952
202 225-5256 **Torres Esteban Edward (Rep - D - California)**
1740 Longworth Bldg ... Washington DC 20515-0001
Fax: 202 225-9711
202 225-5061 **Torricelli Robert G (Rep - D - New Jersey)**
317 Cannon Bldg ... Washington DC 20515-0001
Fax: 202 225-0843
601 977-7700 **Tougaloo College** ... Tougaloo MS 39174-9999
Fax: 601 977-7866
212 447-0700 **Touro College** 844 Ave of the Americas ... New York NY 10001-4103
Fax: 212 799-2344
516 421-2244 *Jacob D Fuchsberg Law Center* 300 Nassau Rd ... Huntington NY 11743-4342
Fax: 516 421-2675
701 968-3424 **Towner County** PO Box 517 ... Cando ND 58324-0517
404 896-2130 **Towns County** PO Box 178 ... Hiawassee GA 30546-0178
202 225-5936 **Towns Edolphus (Rep - D - New York)**
1726 Longworth Bldg ... Washington DC 20515-0001
Fax: 202 225-1018
301 830-2000 **Towson State University** York Rd ... Towson MD 21204-0000
Fax: 301 296-8782
202 785-4194 **Trade Relations Council of the US**
808 17th St NW Suite 580 ... Washington DC 20006-3910
Fax: 202 785-4188
202 225-5261 **Traficant James A Jr (Rep - D - Ohio)** 312 Cannon Bldg ... Washington DC 20515-0001
Fax: 202 225-3719
701 436-4454 **Traill County** County Courthouse ... Hillsboro ND 58045-0000
216 228-9400 **Transportation Political Education League**
14600 Detroit Ave ... Cleveland OH 44107-4207
Fax: 216 228-5755
704 884-3100 **Transylvania County** 28 E Main St ... Brevard NC 28712-3738
Fax: 704 877-4230 Library
606 233-8300 **Transylvania University** 300 N Broadway St ... Lexington KY 40508-1797
Fax: 606 233-8797
202 377-3811 **Travel & Tourism Administration (US Dept of Commerce)**
14th St & Constitution Ave NW Rm 1524 ... Washington DC 20230-0001
Fax: 202 377-8887
616 922-8214 **Traverse City Coast Guard Air Station** ... Traverse City MI 49684-0000
Fax: 616 922-8213
612 563-4242 **Traverse County** County Courthouse ... Wheaton MN 56296-0000
707 424-5000 **Travis Air Force Base** ... Fairfield CA 94535-0000
512 473-9000 **Travis County** 1000 Guadalupe St ... Austin TX 78701-2336
Fax: 512 473-9185
202 225-2806 **Traxler Bob (Rep - D - Michigan)** 2366 Rayburn Bldg ... Washington DC 20515-0001
Fax: Unlisted
406 342-5547 **Treasure County** PO Box 392 ... Hysham MT 59038-0392
415 395-0111 **Treasure Island Naval Station** ... San Francisco CA 94130-7999
Fax: Unlisted
503 889-6493 **Treasure Valley Community College** 650 College Blvd ... Ontario OR 97914-3423
Fax: Ext 249
202 566-2843 **Treasurer (US Dept of the Treasury)**
1500 Pennsylvania Ave NW Rm 2124 ... Washington DC 20220-0001
Fax: 202 535-4040
913 743-5773 **Trego County** 216 N Main St ... WaKeeney KS 67672-2189
Fax: 913 743-2461
715 538-2311 **Trempealeau County** PO Box 67 ... Whitehall WI 54773-0067
Fax: 715 538-2148
609 771-1855 **Trenton State College** PO Box CN4700 ... Trenton NJ 08650-0000
Fax: 609 771-2836 Personnel
912 529-3664 **Treutlen County** 2nd St ... Soperton GA 30457-0000
615 248-1200 **Trevecca Nazarene College** 333 Murfreesboro Rd ... Nashville TN 37210-2877
704 837-5651 **Tri-County Community College** PO Box 40 ... Murphy NC 28906-0040
803 646-8361 **Tri-County Technical College** Hwy 76 ... Pendleton SC 29670-0000
Fax: 803 646-8256
501 623-3943 **Tri-Lakes Regional Library** 125 B Albert Pike ... Hot Springs AR 71913-0000
901 785-6390 **Tri-State Baptist College** 4655 Apple Cove ... Memphis TN 38109-5701
219 665-4100 **Tri-State University** S Darling St ... Angola IN 46703-0000
Fax: 219 665-4292
803 572-6111 **Trident Technical College** PO Box 10367 ... North Charleston SC 29411-0367
Fax: 803 572-6109
502 522-6661 **Trigg County** PO Box 1310 ... Cadiz KY 42211-0609
502 255-7174 **Trimble County** Main St & Hwy 42 ... Bedford KY 40006-0000
Trinidad & Tobago: Republic of Trinidad & Tobago
202 467-6490 *Embassy* 1708 Massachusetts Ave NW ... Washington DC 20036-1903
Fax: 202 785-3130
212 697-7620 *Mission to the UN* 675 3rd Ave 22nd Fl ... New York NY 10017-5704
Fax: 212 682-3518
719 846-5011 **Trinidad State Junior College** 600 Prospect St ... Trinidad CO 81082-2396
Fax: 719 846-5667
701 349-3621 **Trinity Bible College** 50 S 6th Ave ... Ellendale ND 58436-0000
Fax: 701 349-5443
708 597-3000 **Trinity Christian College** 6601 W College Dr ... Palos Heights IL 60463-0929
Fax: 708 385-5665
203 297-2000 **Trinity College** 300 Summit St ... Hartford CT 06106-3186
Fax: 203 297-2257
202 939-5000 **Trinity College** 125 Michigan Ave NE ... Washington DC 20017-1090
Fax: 202 939-5134
708 948-8980 **Trinity College** 2077 Half Day Rd ... Deerfield IL 60015-1284
Fax: 708 945-6413
802 658-0337 **Trinity College** 208 Colchester Ave ... Burlington VT 05401-1496
Fax: 802 658-5446
916 623-1222 **Trinity County** PO Box 1258 ... Weaverville CA 96093-1258
409 642-1208 **Trinity County** Hwys 94 & 287 ... Groveton TX 75845-0000
916 348-4689 **Trinity Life Bible College** 5225 Hillsdale ... Sacramento CA 95842-3596
512 736-7011 **Trinity University** 715 Stadium Dr ... San Antonio TX 78212-7200
Fax: 512 736-8467
817 478-7672 **Trinity Valley Baptist Seminary** 915 E Mansfield Hwy ... Kennedale TX 76060-3225
605 842-2266 **Tripp County** 200 E 3rd St ... Winner SD 57580-1806
708 456-0300 **Triton College** 2000 N 5th Ave ... River Grove IL 60171-1995
Fax: 708 456-0049
716 826-1200 **Trocaire College** 110 Red Jacket Pkwy ... Buffalo NY 14220-2094
404 883-1600 **Troup County** PO Box 1149 ... La Grange GA 30241-1149
615 374-2906 **Trousdale County** Main St & Court Sq ... Hartsville TN 37074-0000

205 566-8112 **Troy State University** Troy AL 36082-0001
Fax: 205 566-3170
205 983-6556 *Dothan* 3601 US Hwy 231 N Dothan AL 36303-0000
Fax: 205 793-7951
205 834-1400 *Montgomery* 231 Montgomery St Montgomery AL 36104-6003
Fax: 205 241-9505
205 297-1007 *Phenix City* 1 University Pl Phenix City AL 36867-0000
Fax: 205 297-6704
404 865-2135 **Truett-McConnell College** Hwy 115 Cleveland GA 30528-0000
Fax: 404 865-0975
202 395-4831 **Truman Harry S Scholarship Foundation**
712 Jackson Pl NW Washington DC 20006-4901
Fax: 202 395-6995
216 841-0562 **Trumbull County** 160 High St NW Warren OH 44481-1005
304 478-2414 **Tucker County** 1st & Walnut Sts Parsons WV 26287-0000
602 791-4911 **Tucson City Hall** 255 W Alameda St Tucson AZ 85701-1362
602 624-2333 **Tucson Museum of Art** 140 N Main Ave Tucson AZ 85701-8290
602 791-4391 **Tucson Public Library** 101 N Stone Ave Tucson AZ 85701-0000
Fax: 602 791-5341
617 628-5000 **Tufts University** Medford MA 02155-0000
Fax: Unlisted
617 956-6685 *Sackler School of Cellular/Molecular Biology*
136 Harrison Ave Boston MA 02111-1800
Fax: 617 956-0375
617 956-5000 *School of Dental Medicine* 1 Kneeland St Boston MA 02111-1529
617 956-6571 *School of Medicine* 136 Harrison Ave Boston MA 02111-1800
508 839-5302 *School of Veterinary Medicine* 200 Westboro Rd North Grafton MA 01536-1895
Fax: 508 839-5395 Ext 4760
504 865-5000 **Tulane University** 6823 St Charles Ave New Orleans LA 70118-5698
Fax: 504 865-6740
504 865-5930 *School of Law* 6801 Freret St New Orleans LA 70118-5697
Fax: 504 865-6748
504 588-5299 *School of Medicine* 1430 Tulane Ave New Orleans LA 70112-2699
Fax: 504 584-2899
209 733-6266 **Tulare County** 2900 W Burrel Ave Visalia CA 93291-4509
209 733-6954 **Tulare County Library System** 200 W Oak St Visalia CA 93291-4931
918 596-7777 **Tulsa City Hall** 200 Civic Ctr Tulsa OK 74103-3827
Fax: 918 596-1290
918 596-7977 **Tulsa City-County Library** 400 Civic Ctr Tulsa OK 74103-3830
Fax: 918 596-7882
918 596-5000 **Tulsa County** 500 S Denver Ave Tulsa OK 74103-3835
Fax: 918 587-4767
918 587-6561 **Tulsa Junior College** 909 S Boston Ave Tulsa OK 74119-2095
Fax: 918 587-4223 Library
601 363-2451 **Tunica County** PO Box 217 Tunica MS 38676-0217
Tunisia: Republic of Tunisia
202 862-1850 *Embassy* 1515 Massachusetts Ave NW Washington DC 20005-1801
Fax: 202 862-1858
212 557-3344 *Mission to the UN* 405 Lexington Ave 65th Fl New York NY 10174-0089
Fax: 212 697-4090
203 677-7701 **Tunxis Community College** Rts 6 & 177 Farmington CT 06032-0000
Fax: 203 676-8906
209 533-5555 **Tuolumne County** 2 S Green St Sonora CA 95370-4679
Turkey: Republic of Turkey
202 659-8200 *Embassy* 1714 Massachusetts Ave NW Washington DC 20036-1903
Fax: 202 659-0744
212 949-0150 *Mission to the UN* 821 UN Plaza 11th Fl New York NY 10017-0000
Fax: 212 949-0086
912 567-2011 **Turner County** 200 E College Ave Ashburn GA 31714-1275
605 297-3115 **Turner County** PO Box 446 Parker SD 57053-0446
205 349-3870 **Tuscaloosa County** 714 Greensboro Ave Tuscaloosa AL 35401-1895
205 345-5820 **Tuscaloosa Public Library** 1801 River Rd Tuscaloosa AL 35401-1099
Fax: 205 752-8300
216 364-8811 **Tuscarawas County** Public Sq New Philadelphia OH 44663-0000
517 673-5999 **Tuscola County** 440 N State St Caro MI 48723-1555
615 638-1111 **Tusculum College** Tusculum Stn Greeneville TN 37743-0000
Fax: 615 638-7166
205 727-8011 **Tuskegee University** Kresege Ctr Tuskegee AL 36088-0000
Fax: 205 727-8953
212 535-4441 **Twentieth Century Fund** 41 E 70th St New York NY 10021-4972
Fax: 212 879-9197
912 945-3629 **Twiggs County** 101 Magnolia St Jeffersonville GA 31044-0000
208 736-4004 **Twin Falls County** PO Box 126 Twin Falls ID 83303-0126
409 283-2281 **Tyler County** 100 Courthouse Woodville TX 75979-5245
304 758-2102 **Tyler County** PO Box 66 Middlebourne WV 26149-0066
903 531-2200 **Tyler Junior College** 14000 E 5th St Tyler TX 75701-0000
Fax: 903 510-2632
904 283-1113 **Tyndall Air Force Base** Panama City FL 32403-0000
Fax: 904 283-6448
919 796-1371 **Tyrrell County** Water St Columbia NC 27925-0000

U

202 225-4065 **Udall Morris K (Rep - D - Arizona)** 235 Cannon Bldg Washington DC 20515-0001
Fax: Unlisted
Uganda: Republic of Uganda
202 726-7100 *Embassy* 5909 16th St NW Washington DC 20011-2816
Fax: 202 726-1727
212 949-0110 *Mission to the UN* 336 E 45th St New York NY 10017-3401
307 789-2471 **Uinta County** 225 9th St Evanston WY 82930-3415
Fax: 307 789-8953
801 781-0770 **Uintah County** 152 E 100 North Vernal UT 84078-0000
212 535-3418 **Ukrainian Soviet Socialist Republic Mission to the UN**
136 E 67th St 5th Fl New York NY 10021-6137
Fax: 212 288-5361
316 689-3664 **Ulrich Edwin A Museum of Art** PO Box 46 Wichita KS 67208-0000
914 339-5680 **Ulster County** 285 Wall St Kingston NY 12401-3817
Fax: 914 339-6831
914 687-7621 **Ulster County Community College** Stone Ridge NY 12484-0000
Fax: 914 687-4764
503 276-7111 **Umatilla County** 216 SE 4th St Pendleton OR 97801-2590
Fax: 503 276-9204
503 440-4600 **Umpqua Community College** 1140 College Rd Roseburg OR 97470-0000
Fax: 503 440-4637
202 245-7431 **Under Secretary of Health & Human Services (US Dept of Health & Human Services)**
200 Independence Ave SW Rm 614G Washington DC 20201-0001
Fax: 202 472-6928
202 755-7123 **Under Secretary of Housing & Urban Development (US Dept of HUD)**
451 7th St SW Rm 10100 Washington DC 20410-0001
Fax: 202 755-8339
202 343-4863 **Under Secretary of the Interior (US Dept of the Interior)**
1849 C St NW MS-6217 Washington DC 20240-0001
Fax: 202 343-5048
615 743-3381 **Unicoi County Courthouse** PO Box 340 Erwin TN 37650-0340

301 295-3030 **Uniformed Services University of the Health Sciences**
4301 Jones Bridge Rd Bethesda MD 20814-4799
Fax: 301 295-3431
301 295-3030 *School of Medicine* 4301 Jones Bridge Rd Bethesda MD 20814-4799
Fax: 202 295-3431
504 283-1588 **Union Baptist Theological Seminary** 1300 Milton St New Orleans LA 70122-0000
606 546-4151 **Union College** 310 College St Barbourville KY 40906-1499
Fax: 606 546-6913
402 488-2331 **Union College** 3800 S 48th St Lincoln NE 68506-4387
Fax: 402 486-2895
518 370-6000 **Union College** Schenectady NY 12308-0000
501 863-6024 **Union County** Main & Washington Sts El Dorado AR 71730-0000
904 496-3711 **Union County** 55 W Main St Rm 103 Lake Butler FL 32054-1600
404 745-2611 **Union County** RR 8 Box 8005 Blairsville GA 30512-9201
Fax: 404 745-1311
515 782-7315 **Union County** 300 N Pine St Creston IA 50801-2430
618 833-5711 **Union County** 311 W Market St Jonesboro IL 62952-0000
317 458-6121 **Union County** 26 W Union St Rm 105 Liberty IN 47353-1350
502 389-1334 **Union County** PO Box 119 Morganfield KY 42437-0000
601 534-1900 **Union County** 109 Main St New Albany MS 38652-0000
704 283-3500 **Union County** 500 N Main St Monroe NC 28112-4730
Fax: 704 289-4369
908 527-4966 **Union County** 2 Broad St Elizabeth NJ 07201-2204
505 374-9491 **Union County** 200 Court St Clayton NM 88415-3116
513 642-2841 **Union County** 5th & Court St Marysville OH 43040-0000
503 963-1001 **Union County** 1106 K Ave La Grande OR 97850-2131
Fax: 503 963-8580
717 524-4461 **Union County** 103 S 2nd St Lewisburg PA 17837-1996
803 429-1630 **Union County** PO Box G Union SC 29379-0200
Fax: 803 429-1623
605 356-2132 **Union County** PO Box 757 Elk Point SD 57025-0757
615 992-8043 **Union County** PO Box 395 Maynardville TN 37807-0395
908 709-7000 **Union County College** 1033 Springfield Ave Cranford NJ 07016-1528
Fax: 908 709-0527
513 861-6400 **Union Institute** 440 E McMillan St Cincinnati OH 45206-1947
Fax: 513 651-2193
318 368-3055 **Union Parish** Main & Bayou Sts 1st Fl Farmerville LA 71241-0000
901 668-1818 **Union University** 2447 Hwy-45 Bypass N Jackson TN 38305-0000
Fax: 901 668-3886
518 445-5544 *Albany Medical College* 47 New Scotland Ave Albany NY 12208-3412
Fax: 518 445-5029 Admin
518 445-2311 *Law School of Albany* 80 New Scotland Ave Albany NY 12208-3434
Fax: 518 445-2315
United Arab Emirates
202 338-6500 *Embassy* 600 New Hampshire Ave NW Suite 740 Washington DC 20037-2486
Fax: 202 337-7029
212 371-0480 *Mission to the UN* 747 3rd Ave 36th Fl New York NY 10017-2875
Fax: 212 319-5433
313 926-5531 **United Auto Workers Community Action Program**
8000 E Jefferson Ave Detroit MI 48214-2699
Fax: 313 824-5750
212 963-1234 **United Nations** 1st Ave & 46th St New York NY 10017-0000
Fax: 212 963-4879
212 326-7000 **United Nations Children's Fund (UNICEF)** 3 UN Plaza New York NY 10017-0000
Fax: 212 888-7465
212 906-5000 **United Nations Development Program** 1 UN Plaza New York NY 10017-3576
Fax: 212 826-2057
212 963-5995 **United Nations Educational Scientific & Cultural Organization (UNESCO)**
2 UN Plaza Rm 900 New York NY 10017-0000
Fax: 212 355-5627
212 963-8139 **United Nations Environment Program** 2 UN Plaza Rm 803 New York NY 10017-0000
Fax: 212 963-7341
212 963-6882 **United Nations Industrial Development Organization (UNIDO)**
1 UN Plaza Rm DC1-1110 New York NY 10017-3575
Fax: 212 963-4116
212 963-1234 **United Nations Secretariat**
1st Ave & 42nd St UN Headquarters New York NY 10017-0000
Fax: 212 963-4879
212 415-4000 **United States of America Mission to the UN** 799 UN Plaza New York NY 10017-3589
Fax: 212 415-4443
412 562-2400 **United Steelworkers of America PAC** 5 Gateway Ctr Pittsburgh PA 15222-1209
Fax: 412 562-2445
703 836-7100 **United Way of America** 701 N Fairfax St Alexandria VA 22314-2045
Fax: 703 683-7840
207 948-3131 **Unity College** RR 78 Box 1 Unity ME 04988-0000
Fax: 207 948-5626
717 787-0866 **University Center at Harrisburg** 2986 N 2nd St Harrisburg PA 17110-1200
Fax: 717 787-0869
904 392-0201 **University Gallery** 102FAB University of Florida Gainesville FL 32611-0000
216 972-7111 **University of Akron** 302 E Buchtel Ave Akron OH 44325-0001
Fax: 216 972-5101
216 972-7331 *C Blake McDowell Law School*
302 E Buchtel Ave C Blake McDowell Law Ctr Akron OH 44325-0001
Fax: 216 258-2343
216 683-2010 *Wayne College* 10470 Smucker Rd Orrville OH 44667-9757
Fax: 216 683-1517
205 348-5121 **University of Alabama (System)** 401 Queen City Ave Tuscaloosa AL 35401-1551
Fax: 205 348-5206
University of Alabama
205 934-8221 *Birmingham Campus* University Stn Birmingham AL 35294-0001
Fax: 205 934-1221 PR
205 348-5520 *College of Communication* 201 Communication Bldg Tuscaloosa AL 35487-0000
205 934-0621 *Department of Microbiology*
Zeigler Research Bldg Rm 436 Birmingham AL 35294-0001
Fax: 205 934-9256
205 546-2886 *Gadsden Center* PO Box 1280 Gadsden AL 35902-1280
Fax: 205 546-4837
205 895-6120 *Huntsville Campus* 4701 University Dr Huntsville AL 35899-0001
205 348-6047 *Main Library* PO Box 870266 Tuscaloosa AL 35487-0266
205 934-3000 *School of Dentistry* 1919 7th Ave S Birmingham AL 35294-0001
Fax: Unlisted
205 348-5117 *School of Law* PO Box 870382 Tuscaloosa AL 35487-0382
Fax: 205 348-3917
205 934-4964 *School of Medicine* UBA Stn Birmingham AL 35294-0001
Fax: 205 934-8724
205 934-5360 *School of Nursing* 1701 University Blvd UAB Stn Birmingham AL 35294-0001
Fax: Unlisted
205 348-7550 *State Museum of Natural History* Smith Hall Tuscaloosa AL 35487-0000
205 348-6010 *Tuscaloosa Campus* Tuscaloosa AL 35487-0000
205 934-6150 **University of Alabama Birmingham School of Optometry**
1716 University Stn Birmingham AL 35294-0001
Fax: 205 934-2603
University of Alaska
907 786-1800 *Anchorage* 3211 Providence Dr Anchorage AK 99508-4671
Fax: 907 786-4813

907 474-7821 *Fairbanks* ... Fairbanks AK 99775-0001
Fax: 907 474-5379 Admissions
907 786-1848 *Library* 3211 Providence Dr ... Anchorage AK 99508-4675
907 474-7505 *Museum* 907 Yukon Dr ... Fairbanks AK 99775-0001
Fax: 907 474-5469
University of Alaska Southeast
907 789-4458 *Juneau Campus* 11120 Glacier Hwy ... Juneau AK 99801-8699
Fax: 907 789-4549 Library
907 225-6177 *Ketchikan Campus* 7th & Madison ... Ketchikan AK 99901-0000
Fax: 907 225-3624
602 621-2211 **University of Arizona** ... Tucson AZ 85721-0001
Fax: 602 621-4624
602 621-3611 *College of Agriculture* 303 Forbes Bldg ... Tucson AZ 85721-0001
Fax: 602 621-8662
602 621-6032 *College of Engineering & Mines* Geology Bldg Rm 134 ... Tucson AZ 85721-0001
Fax: 602 621-8159
602 621-1373 *College of Law* College of Law Bldg Rm 120 ... Tucson AZ 85721-0001
Fax: 602 621-9140
602 626-6154 *College of Nursing* Mabel & Martin Sts ... Tucson AZ 85721-0001
Fax: 602 626-2211
602 626-1427 *College of Pharmacy* 1703 E Mabel St Rm 344 ... Tucson AZ 85721-0001
Fax: Unlisted
602 621-6613 *Computer Science Dept* Gould-Simpson Bldg Rm 721 ... Tucson AZ 85721-0001
Fax: 602 621-4246
602 621-6343 *Department of Chemistry* Old Chemistry Bldg Rm 227 ... Tucson AZ 85721-0001
Fax: 602 621-8407
602 621-6024 *Department of Geosciences* Gould-Simpson Bldg Rm 208 ... Tucson AZ 85721-0001
Fax: 602 621-2672
602 621-7556 *Department of Journalism* Franklin Bldg Rm 101M ... Tucson AZ 85721-0001
Fax: 602 621-9424 Dean
602 621-6800 *Department of Physics* 1118 E 4th St ... Tucson AZ 85721-0001
Fax: 602 621-4721
602 621-6441 *Library* ... Tucson AZ 85721-0001
Fax: 602 621-4619
602 621-7567 *Museum of Art* Olive & Speedway ... Tucson AZ 85721-0001
Fax: 602 621-3070
602 694-0111 **University of Arizona Medical Center** 1501 N Campbell Ave ... Tucson AZ 85724-0001
Fax: 602 694-4085
501 575-2000 **University of Arkansas** 433 N Garland Ave ... Fayetteville AR 72701-4030
501 575-5346 *Graduate School of Engineering*
Bell Engineering Ctr Rm 4183 ... Fayetteville AR 72701-0000
501 575-4101 *Library* ... Fayetteville AR 72701-0000
Fax: 501 575-6656
501 569-3000 *Little Rock Campus* 2801 S University Ave ... Little Rock AR 72204-1085
Fax: 501 569-3039
501 686-5000 *Medical School* 4301 W Markham St ... Little Rock AR 72205-7101
Fax: 501 686-5905
501 367-6811 *Monticello Campus* PO Box 3598 ... Monticello AR 71655-0000
Fax: 501 460-1922
501 575-3555 *Museum* Museum Bldg University of Arkansas Rm 202 ... Fayetteville AR 72701-0000
501 541-6500 *Pine Bluff Campus* 1200 University Dr ... Pine Bluff AR 71601-2799
Fax: 501 534-2117
University of Arkansas Fayetteville
501 575-3601 *Department of Journalism* Kemple Hall Rm 116 ... Fayetteville AR 72701-0000
Fax: 501 575-2642
501 575-5601 *School of Law* Waterman Hall Rm 107 ... Fayetteville AR 72701-0000
Fax: 501 575-2053
University of Arkansas for Medical Sciences
501 686-5374 *College of Nursing* 4301 W Markham St MS-529 ... Little Rock AR 72205-7101
Fax: 501 686-8350
501 686-5557 *College of Pharmacy* 4301 W Markham St MS-522 ... Little Rock AR 72205-7101
Fax: 501 686-8315
University of Arkansas Little Rock
501 569-3250 *Department of Journalism* 2801 S University Ave ... Little Rock AR 72204-1085
501 371-1071 *School of Law* 400 W Markham St ... Little Rock AR 72201-1408
Fax: 501 371-0167
301 625-3000 **University of Baltimore** 1420 N Charles St ... Baltimore MD 21201-5779
Fax: 301 539-3714 Admin
203 576-4000 **University of Bridgeport** 380 University Ave ... Bridgeport CT 06601-0000
Fax: 203 576-4653
203 576-4041 *School of Law* 303 University Ave Carlson Hall ... Bridgeport CT 06601-0000
Fax: 203 576-4236
415 642-6000 **University of California Berkeley** 120 Sproul Hall ... Berkeley CA 94720-0001
Fax: 415 643-8245
415 642-3345 *Agricultural & Resource Economics Dept* 207 Giannini Hall ... Berkeley CA 94720-0001
Fax: 415 643-8911
415 642-1207 *Art Museum* 2626 Bancroft Way UC Berkeley ... Berkeley CA 94720-0001
Fax: 415 642-4889
415 642-5771 *College of Engineering* 320 McLaughlin Hall ... Berkeley CA 94720-0001
Fax: 415 643-8653
415 642-4942 *Department of Architecture* 232 Wurster Hall ... Berkeley CA 94720-0001
Fax: 415 643-5607
415 642-5882 *Department of Chemistry* Latimar Hall Rm 419 ... Berkeley CA 94720-0001
Fax: 415 642-8369
415 642-3257 *Department of City & Regional Planning* 228 Wurster Hall ... Berkeley CA 94720-0001
Fax: 415 643-9576
415 642-5574 *Department of Geology & Geophysics*
301 Earth Science Bldg ... Berkeley CA 94720-0001
Fax: 415 643-9980
415 642-7166 *Department of Physics* LeConte Bldg Rm 366 ... Berkeley CA 94720-0001
Fax: 415 643-8497
415 642-0253 *Electrical Engineering & Computer Sciences Dept*
231 Cory Hall ... Berkeley CA 94720-0001
Fax: 415 643-8426
415 642-0944 *Graduate School of Biochemistry* 597 Life Sciences Addition Berkeley CA 94720-0000
Fax: 415 643-5035
415 642-3383 *Graduate School of Journalism* 121 North Gate Hall ... Berkeley CA 94720-0001
415 642-1940 *Graduate School of Public Policy* 2607 Hearst Ave ... Berkeley CA 94720-0001
Fax: 415 643-9657
415 643-9999 *Library* ... Berkeley CA 94720-0000
415 642-2274 *School of Law* 220 Boalt Hall ... Berkeley CA 94720-0001
Fax: 415 643-6222
415 642-1464 *School of Library & Information Studies* 102 S Hall ... Berkeley CA 94720-0001
Fax: 415 642-5814
415 642-0944 *School of Molecular & Cell Biology*
597 Life Sciences Addition ... Berkeley CA 94720-0000
Fax: 415 643-5035
415 642-3302 *School of Optometry* 360 Minor Hall ... Berkeley CA 94720-0001
Fax: 415 643-5109
415 642-4093 *Walter A Hahool of Business Administration*
350 Barrows Hall ... Berkeley CA 94720-0001
Fax: 415 643-9428

916 752-1011 **University of California Davis** ... Davis CA 95616-5224
Fax: 916 752-6363
916 752-0107 *College of Agricultural & Environmental Sciences*
228 Mrak Hall ... Davis CA 95616-0000
Fax: 916 752-4789
916 752-0553 *College of Engineering* 2132 Bainer Hall ... Davis CA 95616-0000
Fax: 916 752-8058
916 752-3611 *Department of I of Biochemistry* 149 Briggs Hall ... Davis CA 95616-0000
Fax: 916 752-3085
916 752-0953 *Graduate School of Chemistry* 215 Chemistry Bldg ... Davis CA 95616-0000
916 752-9100 *Graduate School of Geoscience* 174 Physics Bldg ... Davis CA 95616-0000
Fax: 916 752-0951
916 752-0262 *Graduate School of Microbiology* Hutchison Bldg Rm 156 ... Davis CA 95616-0000
Fax: 916 752-9014
916 752-1126 *Library* Shields Library ... Davis CA 95616-0000
916 752-0243 *School of Law* King Hall ... Davis CA 95616-0000
Fax: 916 752-8766 Library
916 752-0331 *School of Medicine* ... Davis CA 95616-5224
Fax: 916 752-3517
916 752-1360 *School of Veterinary Medicine* Harring Hall Rm 1018 ... Davis CA 95616-5224
Fax: 916 752-2801
714 856-5011 **University of California Irvine** ... Irvine CA 92717-0001
Fax: 714 856-6685 Mail Rm
714 856-6119 *College of Medicine* ... Irvine CA 92717-0001
Fax: 714 725-2083
714 856-7403 *Department Computer Science* Computer Science Bldg ... Irvine CA 92717-0001
Fax: 714 856-4056
714 856-5261 *Department of Microbiology & Molecular Genetics*
Medical Sciences Bldg I Rm B240 ... Irvine CA 92717-0001
Fax: 714 856-8598
714 856-5438 *Department of Physics* Physical Sciences Bldg 2 Rm 4129 ... Irvine CA 92717-0001
Fax: 714 725-2174
714 856-7067 *Graduate School of Biochemistry*
Med Science Bldg 1 Rm D240 ... Irvine CA 92717-0001
Fax: 714 725-2688
714 856-4261 *Graduate School of Chemistry* Physical Science Bldg Rm 518 ... Irvine CA 92717-0001
Fax: 714 856-8571
714 856-4841 *Graduate School of Engineering*
Graduate Affairs Office Rockwell Engineering Ctr Rm 314 ... Irvine CA 92717-0001
Fax: 714 856-7966
714 856-6855 *Graduate School of Management*
Student Affairs Office Rm 220 ... Irvine CA 92717-0001
Fax: 714 856-8469
714 856-6836 *Library* PO Box 19557 ... Irvine CA 92713-9557
Fax: 714 856-5740 Research
213 825-4321 **University of California Los Angeles** 405 Hilgard Ave ... Los Angeles CA 90024-1492
Fax: 213 206-8460
213 825-2762 *Deparment of Biological Chemistry*
401 Hilgard Ave Rm 33-257 CHS ... Los Angeles CA 90024-0000
Fax: 213 206-5272
213 825-3150 *Department of Chemistry & Biochemistry*
405 Hilgard Ave ... Los Angeles CA 90024-0000
Fax: 213 206-4038
213 825-1704 *Department of Engineering* 6426 Boelter Hall ... Los Angeles CA 90024-0000
213 825-3791 *Graduate School of Architecture & Urban Planning*
405 Hilgard Ave Perloff Hall Rm 1317 ... Los Angeles CA 90024-1467
Fax: 213 206-5566
213 825-1959 *Graduate School of Biology* Life Sciences Bldg Rm 2316 . Los Angeles CA 90024-0000
Fax: 213 206-3987
213 825-4321 *Graduate School of Cellular/Molecular Biology*
405 Hilgard Ave ... Los Angeles CA 90024-1435
Fax: 213 206-8450
213 825-1704 *Graduate School of Computer Science* 3436 Boelter Hall . Los Angeles CA 90024-0000
Fax: 213 825-2273
213 825-3917 *Graduate School of Geoscience* Geology Bldg Rm 3806 .. Los Angeles CA 90024-0000
Fax: 213 825-2779
213 825-2307 *Graduate School of Physics* Knudsen Hall Rm 3-145G ... Los Angeles CA 90024-0000
Fax: 213 206-5668
213 825-8874 *John E Anderson Graduate School of Management*
405 Hilgard Ave Suite 3371 ... Los Angeles CA 90024-1492
Fax: Unlisted
213 825-1323 *Library* ... Los Angeles CA 90024-0000
213 825-3791 *School of Architecture & Urban Planning*
405 Hilgard Ave Perloff Hall Rm 1317 ... Los Angeles CA 90024-1467
Fax: 213 206-5566
213 825-7354 *School of Dentistry* 10833 Le Conte Ave ... Los Angeles CA 90024-1602
Fax: 213 206-5539
213 825-4841 *School of Law* 405 Hilgard Ave ... Los Angeles CA 90024-1492
Fax: 213 206-3680
213 825-4351 *School of Library & Information Sciences*
120 Powell Library ... Los Angeles CA 90024-0000
Fax: 213 206-4460
213 825-6373 *School of Medicine* 12-138 CHS ... Los Angeles CA 90024-0000
Fax: 213 206-5046
213 825-7181 *School of Nursing* 10833 Le Conte Ave ... Los Angeles CA 90024-1602
Fax: 213 206-7433
714 787-1012 **University of California Riverside** 900 University Ave ... Riverside CA 92521-0001
Fax: 714 787-3800 Admin
714 787-4229 *Graduate School of Biochemistry* Webber Hall E Rm 2478 .. Riverside CA 92521-0001
Fax: 714 787-3590
714 787-3520 *Graduate School of Chemistry* Pierce Hall ... Riverside CA 92521-0001
Fax: 714 787-4713
619 534-2230 **University of California San Diego** ... La Jolla CA 92093-0001
Fax: 619 534-6774
619 534-3293 *Department of Physics Graduate Office* MC B019 ... La Jolla CA 92093-0001
Fax: 619 534-0173
619 534-0558 *Graduate School of Biology*
Humanities & Social Sciences Bldg Rm 2306 ... La Jolla CA 92093-0001
Fax: 619 534-7108
619 534-6870 *Graduate School of Chemistry* B-001 ... La Jolla CA 92093-0001
Fax: 619 534-0058
619 534-3713 *School of Medicine* M002 ... La Jolla CA 92093-0001
Fax: 619 534-6573
415 476-8280 **University of California San Francisco** MU-200 ... San Francisco CA 94143-0001
Fax: 415 476-9690 Admissions
415 476-3941 *Graduate School of Biochemistry*
Box 0448 513 Parnassus Ave ... San Francisco CA 94143-0000
Fax: 415 476-0961
415 565-4727 *Hastings School of Law* 200 McAllister St ... San Francisco CA 94102-4707
Fax: 415 565-4825
415 476-1211 *Joint Group in Bioengineering* Box 0414 Rm S-447 ... San Francisco CA 94143-0000
415 476-1891 *School of Dentistry* 707 Parnassus Ave ... San Francisco CA 94143-0001
415 476-2342 *School of Medicine* 513 Parnassus Ave Bldg S-224 ... San Francisco CA 94143-0001
Fax: 415 476-0689
415 476-1435 *School of Nursing* Office of Student Affairs Rm 319X ... San Francisco CA 94143-0602
Fax: 415 476-9707

415 476-1225 *School of Pharmacy* 513 Parnassus Ave .... San Francisco CA 94143-0000
Fax: 415 476-0688
805 961-8000 **University of California Santa Barbara** .... Santa Barbara CA 93106-0001
Fax: 805 961-8016
805 961-3511 *Department of Cellular/Molecular Biology*
Bldg 478 Rm 1200 .... Santa Barbara CA 93106-0001
Fax: 805 961-4724
805 961-4321 *Department of Computer Science*
Engineering 1 Bldg Rm 2106 .... Santa Barbara CA 93106-0001
Fax: 805 961-8553
805 961-3888 *Department of Physics* 3019 Broida Hall .... Santa Barbara CA 93106-0001
Fax: 805 961-4170
805 961-2931 *Graduate School of Chemistry* Chemistry Bldg .... Santa Barbara CA 93106-0001
Fax: 805 961-4120
805 893-3329 *Graduate School of Geoscience*
Geological Science Bldg .... Santa Barbara CA 93106-0001
Fax: 805 893-2314
408 459-0111 **University of California Santa Cruz** 1156 High St .... Santa Cruz CA 95064-1099
Fax: 408 459-2098 Admin
408 459-4089 *Earth Sciences Board of Studies*
Applied Sciences Bldg Rm 141 .... Santa Cruz CA 95064-0000
Fax: 408 459-3074
501 329-2931 **University of Central Arkansas** .... Conway AR 72032-0000
Fax: 501 327-9938
407 275-2000 **University of Central Florida** 4000 Central Florida Blvd .... Orlando FL 32816-0001
Fax: 407 281-5252
304 357-4800 **University of Charleston** 2300 MacCorkle Ave SE .... Charleston WV 25304-1099
Fax: 304 357-4715
312 702-1234 **University of Chicago** 5801 S Ellis Ave .... Chicago IL 60637-1404
Fax: 312 702-5846 Admissions
312 702-7006 *Department of Physics* 5720 S Ellis Ave .... Chicago IL 60637-1434
Fax: Unlisted
312 702-1330 *Graduate School of Biochemistry* 920 E 58th St .... Chicago IL 60637-1432
Fax: 312 702-0439
312 702-7743 *Graduate School of Business* 1101 E 58th St .... Chicago IL 60637-1511
Fax: 312 702-0458
312 702-7250 *Graduate School of Chemistry* 5735 S Ellis Ave .... Chicago IL 60637-1403
Fax: 312 702-0805
312 702-8101 *Graduate School of Geoscience* 5734 S Ellis Ave .... Chicago IL 60637-1434
Fax: 312 702-9505
312 702-1620 *Graduate School of Molecular Genetics & Cell Biology*
920 E 58th St .... Chicago IL 60637-1432
Fax: 312 702-3172
312 702-9494 *Law School* 1111 E 60th St .... Chicago IL 60637-2786
Fax: 312 702-0730
312 702-1939 *School of Medicine* 5812 S Ellis Box 69 Rm G115-A .... Chicago IL 60637-1435
Fax: 312 702-2598
513 475-8000 **University of Cincinnati** 2624 Clifton Ave .... Cincinnati OH 45221-0001
Fax: 513 556-2042
513 556-4933 *College of Design Architecture Art & Planning*
Mail Location 16 .... Cincinnati OH 45221-0016
Fax: 513 556-3288
513 556-5426 *College of Engineering* 645 Baldwin Hall .... Cincinnati OH 45221-0001
Fax: 513 556-3626
513 556-6805 *College of Law* Mail Location 40 .... Cincinnati OH 45221-0001
Fax: 513 556-6265
513 558-7391 *College of Medicine* 231 Bethesda Ave ML552 .... Cincinnati OH 45267-0000
Fax: 513 558-1165
513 558-5500 *College of Nursing & Health* Mail Location 38 .... Cincinnati OH 45221-0001
Fax: 513 558-7523
513 558-3784 *College of Pharmacy*
Health Professions Bldg Mail Location 4 .... Cincinnati OH 45267-0001
Fax: 513 558-4372
303 492-1411 **University of Colorado** Campus Box 9 .... Boulder CO 80309-0001
Fax: 303 492-3126 PR
719 593-3000 *Colorado Springs Campus* 1420 Austin Bluffs Pkwy Colorado Springs CO 80907-0000
Fax: 719 593-3362
303 556-2400 *Denver Campus* 1200 Larimer St .... Denver CO 80204-5300
Fax: 303 556-3377
303 492-6531 *Department of Chemistry & Biochemistry* Campus Box 215 ... Boulder CO 80309-0001
Fax: 303 492-5894
303 492-8142 *Department of Geological Sciences* CB 250 .... Boulder CO 80309-0001
Fax: 303 492-2606
303 492-7230 *Department of Molecular Cellular & Developmental Biology*
CB 347 .... Boulder CO 80309-0001
Fax: 303 492-7744
303 399-1211 *Health Sciences Center* 4200 E 9th Ave .... Denver CO 80262-0001
303 492-6897 *Libraries* .... Boulder CO 80309-0001
Fax: 303 492-2185
303 492-6165 *Museum* 1550 Broadway .... Boulder CO 80309-0001
303 492-8047 *School of Law* Fleming Law Bldg Campus Box 401 .... Boulder CO 80309-0001
Fax: 303 492-1200
303 270-7565 *School of Medicine* 4200 E 9th Ave .... Denver CO 80262-0001
Fax: 303 270-5969 Communications
University of Colorado Boulder
303 492-5071 *College of Engineering & Applied Science* Campus Box 422 ... Boulder CO 80309-0001
Fax: 303 492-2199
303 492-6954 *Graduate School of Physics* Campus Box 390 .... Boulder CO 80309-0001
Fax: 303 492-3352
303 492-6278 *School of Pharmacy* CB 297 .... Boulder CO 80309-0001
Fax: 303 492-1788
University of Colorado Denver
303 556-2870 *Graduate School of Engineering* 1200 Larimer St .... Denver CO 80204-5300
Fax: 303 556-2368
303 556-3479 *School of Architecture & Planning* PO Box 173364 .... Denver CO 80217-3364
Fax: 303 556-3377
University of Colorado Health Sciences Center
303 270-8017 *School of Dentistry* 4200 E 9th Ave C-284 .... Denver CO 80262-0001
Fax: 303 270-7729
303 270-5592 *School of Nursing* 4200 E 9th Ave Health Science Ctr .... Denver CO 80262-0001
Fax: 303 270-8660 Communications
203 486-2000 **University of Connecticut** Admissions Bldg .... Storrs CT 06269-0000
Fax: 203 486-5744 Computer Ctr
203 486-4467 *Graduate School of Agriculture & Economics* PO Box U21 ...... Storrs CT 06269-0001
Fax: 203 486-4128
203 679-2152 *Health Center School of Medicine*
263 Farmington Ave Rm AG062 .... Farmington CT 06030-0000
Fax: 203 679-2518
203 679-2808 *School of Dental Medicine*
263 Farmington Ave Rm AG009 .... Farmington CT 06030-0000
Fax: 203 679-2518
203 486-2221 *School of Engineering* 191 Auditorium Rd Box U-237 .... Storrs CT 06269-0001
Fax: 203 486-0318
203 241-4638 *School of Law* 55 Elizabeth St Hartranft Hall .... Hartford CT/ 06105-2213
Fax: 203 241-7666
203 486-4729 *School of Nursing* 231 Glenbrook Rd .... Storrs CT 06269-0001
Fax: 203 486-0001
203 486-2129 *School of Pharmacy* 372 Fairfield Rd .... Storrs CT 06269-0001
Fax: 203 486-4998
214 721-5000 **University of Dallas** 1845 E Northgate Dr .... Irving TX 75062-9991
Fax: 214 721-5017 Admissions
513 229-1000 **University of Dayton** 300 College Park Rd .... Dayton OH 45469-0001
Fax: 513 229-4000
513 229-3211 *School of Law* 300 College Park Rd Albert Emanuel Hall .... Dayton OH 45469-1320
Fax: 513 229-4000
302 451-2000 **University of Delaware** Hullian Hall .... Newark DE 19716-0001
Fax: 302 451-8000
302 451-2401 *College of Engineering* 135 Dupont Hall Rm 135 .... Newark DE 19716-0001
Fax: 302 451-6751
302 451-1255 *Graduate School of Nursing* McDowell Hall .... Newark DE 19716-0001
302 451-2432 *Library* .... Newark DE 19717-5267
Fax: 302 451-1046
303 871-2000 **University of Denver** 2199 S University Blvd .... Denver CO 80208-0001
Fax: 303 871-4000
303 871-6000 *College of Law* 7039 E 18th Ave .... Denver CO 80220-1079
303 871-3416 *Graduate School of Business* 2020 S Race St .... Denver CO 80208-0001
Fax: 303 871-2156
313 927-1000 **University of Detroit** 4001 W McNichols Rd .... Detroit MI 48221-3090
Fax: 313 927-1011
313 446-1800 *School of Dentistry* 2985 E Jefferson Ave .... Detroit MI 48207-4279
313 596-0200 *School of Law* 651 E Jefferson Ave .... Detroit MI 48226-4301
Fax: 313 596-0280
313 592-6000 **University of Detroit Mercy** 8200 W Outer Dr .... Detroit MI 48219-3580
Fax: 313 592-6329
319 589-3000 **University of Dubuque** 2000 University Ave .... Dubuque IA 52001-5050
Fax: 319 556-8633
812 479-2000 **University of Evansville** 1800 Lincoln Ave .... Evansville IN 47722-0001
Fax: 812 479-2320
907 443-2201 **University of Fairbanks Northwest Campus** Pouch 400 Front St ... Nome AK 99762-9999
Fax: 907 443-5602
419 422-8313 **University of Findlay** 1000 N Main St .... Findlay OH 45840-3695
Fax: 419 424-4757
904 392-3261 **University of Florida** .... Gainesville FL 32611-0000
Fax: Unlisted
904 392-4836 *College of Architecture* 331 Architecture Bldg .... Gainesville FL 32611-0000
Fax: 904 392-7266
904 392-2946 *College of Dentistry* Miller Health Ctr J-405 .... Gainesville FL 32610-0001
Fax: 904 392-3070
904 392-0941 *College of Engineering* 300 Weil Hall .... Gainesville FL 32611-2083
Fax: 904 392-9673
904 392-0466 *College of Journalism & Communication*
2096 Weimer Hall .... Gainesville FL 32611-0000
Fax: 904 392-3919
904 392-0421 *College of Law* 164 Holland Hall .... Gainesville FL 32611-0000
Fax: 904 392-8727
904 392-5793 *College of Medicine* PO Box J-215 JHMHC .... Gainesville FL 32610-0001
Fax: 904 392-6482
904 392-3751 *College of Nursing* J Hillis Miller Health Ctr J-197 .... Gainesville FL 32610-0001
Fax: 904 392-9395
904 392-2381 *College of Veterinary Medicine* 215 SW 16th Ave .... Gainesville FL 32610-0001
Fax: 904 392-8351
904 392-1906 *Department of Microbiology* 1053 McCarty Hall .... Gainesville FL 32611-0000
904 392-2251 *Graduate School of Agriculture* 1001 McCarty Hall .... Gainesville FL 32611-0000
Fax: 904 392-3165
904 392-9132 *Graduate School of Chemistry*
Chemical Research Bldg Rm 329 .... Gainesville FL 32611-0000
Fax: 904 392-8758
904 392-0997 *Urban & Regional Planning Dept*
431 Architecture Bldg College of Architecture .... Gainesville FL 32611-0000
Fax: 904 392-7266
404 542-3030 **University of Georgia** 114 Academic Bldg .... Athens GA 30602-0000
Fax: 404 542-6578
404 542-7833 *College of Journalism & Mass Communication* Bldg 62 .... Athens GA 30602-0000
Fax: 404 542-9273
404 542-3461 *College of Veterinary Medicine* .... Athens GA 30602-1601
Fax: 404 542-5743
404 542-2059 *Department of Political Science* Baldwin Hall Rm 104 .... Athens GA 30602-0000
Fax: 404 542-4421
404 542-2925 *Graduate School of Agriculture* Boyd Graduate Studies Bldg ... Athens GA 30602-0000
Fax: 404 542-3219
404 542-7140 *Joseph Henry Lumpkin School of Law* Herty Dr .... Athens GA 30602-0000
Fax: 404 542-5556
404 542-1911 *Robert C Wilson College of Pharmacy*
College of Pharmacy Bldg .... Athens GA 30602-1601
Fax: 404 542-5402
203 243-4100 **University of Hartford** 200 Bloomfield Ave .... West Hartford CT 06117-1599
Fax: 203 243-4070
University of Hawaii
808 956-7727 *College of Engineering* 2540 Dole St Holmes Hall Rm 240 ... Honolulu HI 96822-2333
Fax: 808 956-2291
808 956-7530 *Department of Agronomy & Soil Science*
1910 East-West Rd .... Honolulu HI 96822-0000
Fax: 808 956-6539
808 956-7381 *Department of Urban & Regional Planning*
2424 Maile Way Porteus Hall Rm 107 .... Honolulu HI 96822-2223
Fax: 808 956-6870
808 933-3311 *Hilo Campus* .... Hilo HI 96720-4091
Fax: Call company operator
808 956-8287 *John A Burns School of Medicine*
1960 East-West Rd Biomedical Sciences Bldg Rm T101 ...... Honolulu HI 96822-0000
Fax: 808 956-5506
808 956-7214 *Library* 2550 The Mall .... Honolulu HI 96822-2233
Fax: 808 956-5968
808 956-8111 *Manoa Campus* 2444 Dole St .... Honolulu HI 96822-2330
Fax: 808 956-5286
808 956-7225 *School of Architecture* 2560 Campus Rd George Annex 2-3 . Honolulu HI 96822-0000
Fax: 808 956-7778
808 456-5921 *West Oahu Campus* 96-043 Ala Ike .... Pearl City HI 96782-3366
Fax: 808 456-5208
808 956-7966 *William S Richardson School of Law* 2515 Dole St .... Honolulu HI 96822-2328
Fax: 808 956-6402
708 578-3000 **University of Health Sciences Chicago Medical School**
3333 Greenbay Rd .... North Chicago IL 60064-3037
Fax: 708 578-3401
713 749-1011 **University of Houston** 4800 Calhoun Rd University Pk .... Houston TX 77004-8399
Fax: 713 749-4939 Admin
713 488-7170 *Clear Lake Campus* 2700 Bay Area Blvd .... Houston TX 77058-1098
Fax: 713 283-2010 Admin
713 749-1188 *College of Architecture* 4808 Calhoun St .... Houston TX 77204-4431
713 749-2893 *College of Business Administration* 4800 Calhoun Rd .... Houston TX 77204-6283
Fax: Unlisted

713 749-3361 *College of Optometry* 4800 Calhoun Rd Houston TX 77204-0001
Fax: 713 749-1174
713 749-1422 *Law Center* 4800 Calhoun Rd Houston TX 77204-0001
Fax: 713 749-2567
512 576-3151 *Victoria Campus* 2302-C E Red River St Victoria TX 77901-4449
Fax: Ext 239
208 885-6111 **University of Idaho** Administration Bldg Moscow ID 83843-0000
Fax: 208 885-6911
208 885-6422 *College of Law* Albert R Menard Bldg Moscow ID 83843-0000
Fax: 208 885-7609 Library
University of Illinois
217 333-2747 *College of Commerce & Business Administration*
1206 S 6th St Rm 260 Champaign IL 61820-6915
Fax: 217 244-3118
217 333-2151 *College of Engineering*
1308 W Green St Engineering Hall Rm 106 Urbana IL 61801-0000
Fax: 217 244-7705 Admin
217 333-0931 *College of Law* 504 E Pennsylvania Ave Rm 209A Champaign IL 61820-6909
Fax: 217 244-1478
312 996-3500 *College of Medicine* 1853 W Polk St Medical Ctr Chicago IL 60612-4376
Fax: 312 996-9006 Admin
312 996-7800 *College of Nursing* 845 S Damen Ave Chicago IL 60612-0000
Fax: 312 996-8066
217 333-2760 *College of Veterinary Medicine* 2001 S Lincoln Ave Urbana IL 61801-6178
Fax: 217 333-4628
217 333-4428 *Computer Science Dept* 1304 W Springfield Ave Rm 240 DCL Urbana IL 61801-2910
Fax: 217 333-3501
217 333-7149 *Department of Biochemistry*
1209 W California St Roger Adams Lab Rm 415 Urbana IL 61801-0000
Fax: 217 244-8068
217 333-0711 *Department of Chemistry* 505 S Mathews Ave Noyes Lab Urbana IL 61801-0000
Fax: 217 244-8068
217 333-0035 *Graduate College* 801 S Wright St Coble Hall Champaign IL 61820-0000
Fax: 217 333-8019
217 333-3540 *Graduate School of Geology*
1301 W Green St Natural History Bldg Rm 245 Urbana IL 61801-0000
Fax: 217 244-4996
217 333-3280 *Graduate School of Library & Information Sciences*
1407 W Gregory Dr David Kinley Hall Urbana IL 61801-0000
Fax: 217 244-3302
217 333-0460 *School of Architecture* 608 E Lorado Taft Dr Champaign IL 61829-0000
Fax: 217 244-2900
217 333-2290 **University of Illinois at Urbana-Champaign Library**
1408 W Gregory Dr Urbana IL 61801-3607
University of Illinois Chicago
312 996-7520 *College of Dentistry* 801 S Paulina St Rm 102 Chicago IL 60612-4353
Fax: 312 996-1022
312 996-7240 *College of Pharmacy* 833 S Wood St MC-874 Chicago IL 60612-4324
Fax: 312 996-3272
312 996-3000 *East Campus* PO Box 4348 Chicago IL 60680-4348
Fax: 312 996-6896
312 996-7470 *Graduate School of Microbiology* 835 S Wolcott Ave Chicago IL 60612-0000
Fax: 312 996-6415
312 996-8722 *School of Urban Planning & Policy*
1007 W Harrison MC-348 Rm 1180 Chicago IL 60607-0000
Fax: 312 996-9484
University of Illinois Urbana
217 333-3761 *Department of Physics* 1110 W Green St Urbana IL 61801-3003
Fax: 217 333-9819
217 333-3890 *Department of Urban & Regional Planning*
907 1/2 W Nevada St Urbana IL 61801-3810
Fax: 217 244-1717
217 333-1000 **University of Illinois Urbana-Champaign** 506 S Wright St Urbana IL 61801-3620
Fax: 217 333-9758
217 333-3044 *School of Life Sciences*
505 S Goodwin Ave Morrill Hall Rm 393 Urbana IL 61801-0000
Fax: 217 244-1224
317 788-3368 **University of Indianapolis** 1400 E Hanna Ave Indianapolis IN 46227-3630
Fax: 317 788-3275
319 353-2121 **University of Iowa** Iowa City IA 52242-0001
Fax: 319 335-2951
319 335-9650 *College of Dentistry* Iowa City IA 52242-0001
Fax: 319 335-7155
319 335-5766 *College of Engineering* Engineering Bldg Rm 3100 Iowa City IA 52242-0001
319 335-9034 *College of Law* Melrose & Byington Iowa City IA 52242-0001
319 335-8050 *College of Medicine* 240 EMRB Bldg Iowa City IA 52242-0001
Fax: 319 335-8049 Dean
319 335-7018 *College of Nursing* 101 Nursing Bldg Iowa City IA 52242-0001
Fax: 319 335-9990
319 335-8794 *College of Pharmacy* Iowa City IA 52242-0001
Fax: 319 335-9418
319 335-7933 *Department of Biochemistry* 4403 BSB Rm 4 Iowa City IA 52242-0001
Fax: 319 335-9570
319 335-7780 *Department of Microbiology* 3403 BSB Newton Rd Iowa City IA 52242-0001
Fax: 319 335-9006
319 335-2357 *Department of Political Science* Schaeffer Bldg Rm 310 Iowa City IA 52242-0001
Fax: 319 335-2951
319 335-1687 *Department School of Physics & Astronomy*
Van Allen Hall Rm 203 Iowa City IA 52242-0001
Fax: 319 335-1753
319 335-0032 *Graduate Program in Urban & Regional Planning*
347 Jessup Hall Iowa City IA 52242-0001
Fax: 319 335-0008
319 335-5299 *Libraries* Washington & Madison Sts Iowa City IA 52242-0001
319 335-1727 *Museum of Art* 150 N Riverside Dr Iowa City IA 52242-0001
213 476-9777 **University of Judaism** 15600 Mulholland Dr Los Angeles CA 90077-1599
Fax: 213 471-1278
913 864-2700 **University of Kansas** Lawrence KS 66045-0001
Fax: 913 864-0485
913 864-4974 *Department of Geology* 120 Lindley Hall Lawrence KS 66045-0001
913 864-3523 *Department of Political Science* 504 Blake Hall Lawrence KS 66045-0001
Fax: 913 864-3683
913 864-4184 *Graduate Program in Urban Planning* 317 Marvin Hall Lawrence KS 66045-0001
Fax: 913 864-5393
913 864-3881 *School of Engineering* 4010 Learned Hall Lawrence KS 66045-0001
Fax: 913 864-3199
913 864-4550 *School of Law* Green Hall Lawrence KS 66045-0001
Fax: 913 864-3680
913 588-5283 *School of Medicine* 39th St & Rainbow Blvd Rm 107-A Kansas City KS 66103-0000
Fax: 913 588-5259
913 588-1600 *School of Nursing* 39th St & Rainbow Blvd Kansas City KS 66103-3337
Fax: 913 588-1605
913 864-3591 *School of Pharmacy* 2056 Malott Hall Lawrence KS 66045-0001
Fax: 913 864-5265

913 864-4755 *William Allen White School of Journalism & Mass Communications*
200 Stauffer-Flint Lawrence KS 66045-0001
Fax: 913 864-5261
606 257-9000 **University of Kentucky** Lexington KY 40506-0001
Fax: 606 257-4000
606 257-5716 *Art Museum* Rose & Euclid Sts Lexington KY 40506-0001
606 233-5850 *College of Dentistry* 800 Rose St UK Medical Ctr D104 Lexington KY 40536-0001
606 257-1678 *College of Law* Law Bldg Lexington KY 40506-0048
Fax: Unlisted
606 233-6582 *College of Medicine* 800 Rose St Lexington KY 40536-0001
Fax: 606 233-6805
606 233-5406 *College of Nursing*
760 Rose St Nursing Health Sciences Learning Ctr Lexington KY 40536-0232
Fax: 606 258-1057
606 257-2738 *College of Pharmacy* Rose St Pharmacy Bldg Lexington KY 40536-0082
Fax: 606 257-2128
606 257-3592 *Graduate School of Business*
331 Business & Economic Bldg Lexington KY 40506-0001
Fax: 606 257-8938
606 257-3788 *Libraries* King Library S Lexington KY 40506-0000
Fax: 606 257-8379
606 257-1663 *Office of Research & Graduate Studies* Lexington KY 40546-0001
606 257-8608 **University of Kentucky Community College (System)**
Breckenridge Hall Lexington KY 40506-0001
Fax: 606 257-4000
714 593-3511 **University of La Verne** 1950 3rd St La Verne CA 91750-4443
Fax: 714 593-0965
502 588-5555 **University of Louisville** 2301 S 3rd St Louisville KY 40292-0001
Fax: 502 588-7013
502 588-5293 *School of Dentistry* Dental Bldg Louisville KY 40292-0001
Fax: 502 588-7163
502 588-6358 *School of Law* 2301 S 3rd St Louisville KY 40292-0001
Fax: 502 588-0862
502 588-5184 *School of Medicine* 500 S Preston St Louisville KY 40292-0001
Fax: Unlisted
508 934-4000 **University of Lowell** 1 University Ave Lowell MA 01854-2893
Fax: 508 453-6035
207 581-1110 **University of Maine** Chadborne Hall Orono ME 04469-0001
Fax: 207 581-1604
207 622-7131 *Augusta Campus* University Heights Augusta ME 04330-9410
Fax: Ext 239
207 947-0336 *Bangor Campus* 107 Maine Ave Bangor ME 04401-1805
Fax: Ext 293
207 778-3501 *Farmington Campus* 86 Main St Farmington ME 04938-1990
Fax: Ext 537
207 834-3162 *Fort Kent Campus* 25 Pleasant St Fort Kent ME 04743-1292
Fax: 207 834-3144
207 581-3218 *Graduate School of Agriculture* 2 Winslow Hall Orono ME 04469-0001
Fax: 207 581-3232
207 581-1110 *Library* Folger Library Orono ME 04469-0001
Fax: 207 581-1653
207 255-3313 *Machias Campus* 9 O'Brien Ave Machias ME 04654-1321
Fax: 207 255-4864
207 764-0311 *Presque Isle Campus* 181 Main St Presque Isle ME 04769-2888
Fax: Ext 215
207 780-4340 *School of Law* 246 Deering Ave Portland ME 04102-2898
Fax: 207 780-4913
701 255-7500 **University of Mary** 7500 University Dr Bismarck ND 58504-9652
817 939-8642 **University of Mary Hardin-Baylor** College St Belton TX 76513-2599
Fax: 817 939-4535
301 853-3600 **University of Maryland (System)** 3300 Metzerott Rd Adelphi MD 20783-1651
Fax: 301 853-4761
University of Maryland
301 455-1000 *Baltimore Campus* 5401 Wilkins Ave Baltimore MD 21228-0000
Fax: 301 455-1096 Admin
301 328-3100 *Baltimore Professional School* 419 W Redwood St Baltimore MD 21202-0000
301 328-7460 *College of Dental Surgery* 666 W Baltimore St Baltimore MD 21201-1510
Fax: 301 328-3028
301 454-2421 *College of Engineering*
Engineering Classroom Bldg Rm 1131 College Park MD 20742-0001
301 405-1000 *College of Journalism* Journalism Bldg Rm 2109 College Park MD 20742-0001
Fax: 301 454-7912
301 454-5441 *College of Library & Information Services*
4105 Hornbake Library College Park MD 20742-0001
Fax: 301 454-5452
301 454-3311 *College Park Campus* College Park MD 20742-0001
Fax: 301 454-1818 Financial Aid
301 454-0981 *Computer Science Dept* Bldg 115 College Park MD 20742-0001
Fax: 301 454-8346
301 454-3901 *Department Agriculture Engineering*
Shriver Lab Rm 1130 College Park MD 20742-0001
Fax: 301 454-6870
301 454-5231 *Department of Chemistry & Biochemistry*
Chemistry Bldg College Park MD 20742-0001
Fax: 301 454-0556
301 651-2200 *Eastern Shore Campus* Princess Anne MD 21853-0000
Fax: 301 651-2270
301 454-2848 *Graduate School of Microbiology*
Microbiology Bldg Rm 1117 College Park MD 20742-0001
Fax: 301 454-3754
301 454-3514 *Graduate School of Physics* Physics Bldg Rm 1302-D College Park MD 20742-0001
Fax: 301 454-0382
301 454-5704 *Library* McKeldin Library College Park MD 20742-0001
Fax: 301 454-4985
301 454-1823 *Program in Community Planning* Lefrak Hall Rm 1117 College Park MD 20742-0001
Fax: 301 454-8330
301 328-7214 *School of Law* 500 W Baltimore St Baltimore MD 21201-1786
Fax: 301 328-4045
301 328-7410 *School of Medicine* 655 W Baltimore St Baltimore MD 21201-1509
Fax: 301 328-2043
301 328-6740 *School of Nursing* 655 W Lombard St Baltimore MD 21201-1512
Fax: 301 328-8108
301 328-7650 *School of Pharmacy* 20 N Pine St Baltimore MD 21201-1142
Fax: 301 328-7184
413 545-0111 **University of Massachusetts** Goodell Bldg Amherst MA 01003-0001
Fax: 413 545-3203
413 545-0300 *College of Engineering* 125 Marston Hall Amherst MA 01003-0001
Fax: 413 545-0724
413 545-2744 *Department of Computer & Information Science*
Lederle Graduate Research Ctr Amherst MA 01003-0001
Fax: 413 545-1249
413 545-2286 *Department of Geology & Geography*
Morrill Science Ctr Rm 233 Amherst MA 01003-0001
Fax: 413 545-1200
413 545-2490 *Department of Resource Economics* Draper Hall Rm 231 Amherst MA 01003-0001

413 545-2553 *Graduate School of Microbiology* Morril Science Ctr .... Amherst MA 01003-0001
Fax: 413 545-1578
508 856-0011 *Medical School* 55 Lake Ave N .... Worcester MA 01655-0001
Fax: 508 856-5515
617 287-5000 **University of Massachusetts Boston** Harbor Campus .... Boston MA 02125-0000
Fax: 617 265-7173
201 456-4300 **University of Medicine & Dentistry of New Jersey**
150 Bergen St .... Newark NJ 07103-2406
Fax: 201 456-6753
201 456-4300 **University of Medicine & Dentistry of New Jersey Medical School**
150 Bergen St .... Newark NJ 07103-2406
Fax: 201 456-6943
305 284-2211 **University of Miami** .... Coral Gables FL 33124-0000
Fax: 305 284-3768
305 284-2265 *School of Communication*
5202 University Dr Merrick Bldg Rm 120 .... Coral Gables FL 33124-0000
Fax: 305 284-3648
305 284-2392 *School of Law* PO Box 248087 .... Coral Gables FL 33124-8087
Fax: 305 284-2349
305 547-6545 *School of Medicine* 1600 NW 10th Ave .... Miami FL 33136-1015
Fax: 305 526-8341
305 284-3438 *Urban & Regional Planning Program*
1223 Dickinson Dr Rm 48-E .... Coral Gables FL 33124-9178
313 764-1817 **University of Michigan** 503 Thompson Ave .... Ann Arbor MI 48109-0001
Fax: 313 936-7787
313 764-1300 *College of Architecture & Urban Planning*
2000 Bonisteel Blvd .... Ann Arbor MI 48109-0001
Fax: 313 763-2322
313 764-8475 *College of Engineering* 1301 Beal Ave EECS Bldg .... Ann Arbor MI 48109-0001
Fax: 313 763-9487 Admin
313 764-7144 *College of Pharmacy* 428 Church St .... Ann Arbor MI 48109-1065
Fax: 313 763-2022
313 593-5000 *Dearborn Campus* 4901 Evergreen Rd .... Dearborn MI 48128-1491
Fax: 313 593-9967
313 764-8154 *Department of Biochemistry* PO Box 0606 .... Ann Arbor MI 48109-0606
Fax: 313 763-4581
313 764-7278 *Department of Chemistry* Chemistry Bldg Rm 2040 .... Ann Arbor MI 48109-0001
Fax: 313 747-4865
313 764-0420 *Department of Communications* 2020 Frieze Bldg .... Ann Arbor MI 48109-0001
Fax: 313 764-3288
313 764-0478 *Exhibit Museum* 1109 Geddes .... Ann Arbor MI 48109-0001
313 762-3000 *Flint Campus* 303 E Kearsley St .... Flint MI 48502-2186
Fax: Unlisted
313 764-5428 *Graduate School of Cellular & Molecular Biology*
4714 Medical Science II .... Ann Arbor MI 48109-0001
Fax: 313 763-3784
313 764-1435 *Graduate School of Geological Sciences*
CC Little Bldg Rm 1006 .... Ann Arbor MI 48109-1063
Fax: 313 763-4690
313 764-4437 *Graduate School of Physics*
500 E University Randall Lab Rm 1049 .... Ann Arbor MI 48109-0001
Fax: 313 763-9694
313 764-0329 *Institute of Public Policy Studies* 440-B Lorch Hall .... Ann Arbor MI 48109-0001
Fax: 313 764-2769
313 764-1358 *Law School* 625 S State St Hutchins Hall .... Ann Arbor MI 48109-0001
Fax: 313 936-3884
313 764-9373 *Library* Hatcher Graduate Library .... Ann Arbor MI 48109-1205
Fax: 313 763-5080
313 763-9600 *Medical School*
1301 E Katherine St Medical Science Bldg 1 .... Ann Arbor MI 48109-0001
Fax: 313 763-4936
313 764-0395 *Museum of Art* 525 S State .... Ann Arbor MI 48109-0001
313 764-1363 *School of Business Administration* 701 Tappan St .... Ann Arbor MI 48109-1234
Fax: 313 763-5688
313 764-3375 *School of Dentistry* 1011 N University Ave .... Ann Arbor MI 48109-0001
Fax: 313 747-4024
313 764-9376 *School of Information & Library Studies*
550 E University St .... Ann Arbor MI 48109-0001
Fax: 313 764-2475
313 764-7185 *School of Nursing* 400 N Ingalls St .... Ann Arbor MI 48109-0001
Fax: 313 936-3644
313 764-1300 *Urban Planning Program* 2000 Bonisteel Blvd .... Ann Arbor MI 48109-0001
Fax: 313 763-2322
612 625-5000 **University of Minnesota** .... Minneapolis MN 55455-0100
612 624-9876 *Art Museum* 84 Church St SE University of Minnesota .... Minneapolis MN 55455-0000
Fax: 612 624-7843
612 624-3009 *College of Agriculture* 1420 Eckles Ave Coffey Hall Rm 277 Saint Paul MN 55108-0000
Fax: Unlisted
612 624-7866 *College of Architecture & Landscape Architecture*
89 Church St SE Rm 110 .... Minneapolis MN 55455-0109
Fax: 612 624-5743
612 624-1900 *College of Pharmacy*
308 Harvard St SE Health Sciences Unit F Rm 5-130 .... Minneapolis MN 55455-0353
Fax: 612 624-2974
612 624-9227 *College of Veterinary Medicine* 1365 Gortner Ave .... Saint Paul MN 55108-1016
Fax: 612 624-8753
612 625-4002 *Computer Science Dept*
200 Union St EE/CS Bldg Rm 4-196 .... Minneapolis MN 55455-0000
Fax: 612 625-0572
218 281-6510 *Crookston Campus* Selvig Hall .... Crookston MN 56716-0000
Fax: 218 281-5223
612 624-8008 *Department of Chemistry* Smith Hall Rm 141 .... Minneapolis MN 55455-0100
Fax: 612 626-7541
612 624-5947 *Department of Microbiology*
1460 Mayo Bldg Box 196 UMHC .... Minneapolis MN 55455-0000
Fax: 612 626-0623
218 726-8000 *Duluth Campus* 10 University Dr .... Duluth MN 55812-2403
Fax: 218 726-6331
612 625-3394 *Graduate School of Engineering*
101 Pleasant St SE Johnston Hall .... Minneapolis MN 55455-0432
Fax: 612 626-7431
612 624-4344 *Graduate School of Geological Sciences*
310 Pillsbury Dr SE Pillsbury Hall .... Minneapolis MN 55455-0000
Fax: 612 625-3819
612 625-9505 *Graduate School of Public Affairs*
301 19th Ave S Humphrey Ctr Rm 230 .... Minneapolis MN 55455-0000
Fax: 612 625-6351
612 625-1000 *Law School* 229 19th Ave S .... Minneapolis MN 55455-0400
Fax: 612 626-3478
612 624-0303 *Libraries* 309 19th Ave S .... Minneapolis MN 55455-0000
612 589-2211 *Morris Campus* E 4th College Ave .... Morris MN 56267-2134
Fax: 612 589-3811
612 625-9505 *Planning Program*
301 19th Ave S Humphrey Ctr Rm 130 .... Minneapolis MN 55455-0429
Fax: 612 625-6351
612 625-7149 *School of Dentistry*
515 SE Delaware St Moos Tower Rm 15-106 .... Minneapolis MN 55455-0000
Fax: 612 625-7678
612 625-9824 *School of Journalism & Mass Communication*
206 Church St SE Murphy Hall Rm 111 .... Minneapolis MN 55455-0000
Fax: 612 626-7460
612 624-9600 *School of Nursing* 308 Harvard St SE Unit F Rm 6101 .... Minneapolis MN 55455-0353
Fax: 612 624-3174
612 624-6366 *School of Physics & Astronomy* 116 Church St SE .... Minneapolis MN 55455-0149
Fax: 612 624-4578
507 835-1000 *Waseca Campus* 1000 University Dr SW .... Waseca MN 56093-2086
Fax: 507 835-3512
218 726-7571 **University of Minnesota Duluth School of Medicine**
10 University Dr .... Duluth MN 55812-2403
Fax: 218 726-6235
612 626-4949 **University of Minnesota Minneapolis School of Medicine**
420 Delaware St Owre Bldg Box 293 .... Minneapolis MN 55455-0000
Fax: 612 626-5657
601 232-7211 **University of Mississippi** Library Loop .... University MS 38677-9999
Fax: 601 232-5093 PR
601 232-7146 *Department of Journalism* 331 Farley Hall .... University MS 38677-9999
601 232-5820 *School of Business* Conner Hall Rm 218 .... University MS 38677-9999
Fax: 601 232-5917
601 984-6155 *School of Dentistry* 2500 N State St .... Jackson MS 39216-4505
Fax: 601 984-6014
601 232-7361 *School of Law* Law Ctr .... University MS 38677-9999
Fax: 601 232-7731
601 984-1010 *School of Medicine* 2500 N State St .... Jackson MS 39216-4505
Fax: 601 984-0125 Admin
601 232-7265 *School of Pharmacy* Faser Hall Rm 201 .... University MS 38677-9999
Fax: 601 232-5118
601 844-5622 *Tupelo Regional Campus* 655 Eason Blvd .... Tupelo MS 38801-5955
314 882-2121 **University of Missouri** 320 Jesse Hall .... Columbia MO 65211-0001
Fax: 314 882-0973
314 882-8301 *College of Agriculture* 2-64 Agriculture Bldg .... Columbia MO 65211-0001
Fax: 314 882-5127
314 882-2750 *Graduate School of Business* 303-D Middlebush Hall .... Columbia MO 65211-0001
Fax: 314 882-0365
816 276-2080 *Graduate School of Dentistry* 650 E 25th St .... Kansas City MO 64108-2716
Fax: 816 276-2157
314 882-3304 *Graduate School of Public Administration*
315 Middlebush Hall .... Columbia MO 65211-0001
Fax: 314 882-0365
816 276-1000 *Kansas City Campus* 5100 Rockhill Rd .... Kansas City MO 64110-2499
Fax: 816 276-1439
314 882-4701 *Library* Ellis Library .... Columbia MO 65201-0000
Fax: 314 882-8044
314 341-4111 *Rolla Campus* .... Rolla MO 65401-0000
314 553-5000 *Saint Louis Campus* 8001 Natural Bridge Rd .... Saint Louis MO 63121-4499
Fax: Unlisted
314 882-4821 *School of Journalism* PO Box 838 .... Columbia MO 65205-0838
Fax: 314 882-9002
314 882-0292 *School of Nursing* School of Nursing Bldg .... Columbia MO 65211-0001
Fax: 314 884-4544
University of Missouri Columbia
314 882-4375 *College of Engineering* Electrical Engineering Bldg Rm 145 . Columbia MO 65211-0001
Fax: 314 882-7584
314 882-6487 *Law School* Conley & Missouri Sts .... Columbia MO 65211-0001
Fax: 314 882-9676
314 882-1566 *School of Medicine* Health Science Ctr Rm MA-204 .... Columbia MO 65212-0001
Fax: 314 882-5666
University of Missouri Kansas City
816 276-1644 *School of Law* 5100 Rockhill Rd .... Kansas City MO 64110-2499
Fax: 816 444-6560
816 276-1808 *School of Medicine* 2411 Holmes St .... Kansas City MO 64108-2741
Fax: 816 235-5194
816 276-1607 *School of Pharmacy* 5005 Rockhill Rd .... Kansas City MO 64110-2239
Fax: 816 235-5190
314 341-4151 **University of Missouri Rolla School of Engineering**
Engineering Research Lab Rm 1Rm 101-ERL .... Rolla MO 65401-0000
Fax: 314 341-4979 Admin
314 553-5606 **University of Missouri Saint Louis School of Optometry**
8001 Natural Bridge Rd .... Saint Louis MO 63121-4499
Fax: 314 553-5150
406 243-0211 **University of Montana** .... Missoula MT 59812-0001
Fax: 406 243-2797 Admin
406 243-4001 *School of Journalism* Journalism Bldg Rm 209 .... Missoula MT 59812-0001
Fax: 406 243-2060
406 243-4311 *School of Law* Maurice & Eddy Sts Law School Bldg .... Missoula MT 59812-0001
Fax: 406 243-2576
406 243-4621 *School of Pharmacy & Allied Health Sciences*
Pharmacy/Psychology Bldg Rm 119 .... Missoula MT 59812-0001
Fax: 406 243-4353
205 665-6000 **University of Montevallo** Stn 6030 .... Montevallo AL 35115-0000
Fax: 205 665-6062
402 472-2111 **University of Nebraska (System)** 3835 Holdrege St .... Lincoln NE 68583-0001
Fax: 402 472-2038 Admin
University of Nebraska
402 472-3592 *College of Architecture* 210 Architecture Hall .... Lincoln NE 68588-0106
Fax: 402 472-3806
402 472-1344 *College of Dentistry* 40th & Holdrege Sts Rm 107 .... Lincoln NE 68583-0001
Fax: Unlisted
402 554-2460 *College of Engineering & Technology* 116 Engineering Bldg ... Omaha NE 68182-0001
Fax: 402 554-2927
402 472-2161 *College of Law* McCollum Hall Rm 103 .... Lincoln NE 68583-0902
Fax: 402 472-5185
402 559-4204 *College of Medicine* 600 S 42nd St .... Omaha NE 68198-0000
Fax: 402 559-5844
402 472-2848 *Library* .... Lincoln NE 68588-0001
Fax: 402 472-5131
402 472-7211 *Lincoln Campus* 501 N 14th St .... Lincoln NE 68588-0001
Fax: 402 472-2410
402 554-2200 *Omaha Campus* 60th & Dodge Sts .... Omaha NE 68182-0001
Fax: 402 554-2244 Admin
402 472-3779 *State Museum* 14th & U Sts Morrill Hall Rm 307 .... Lincoln NE 68588-0001
University of Nebraska Lincoln
402 472-2201 *College of Agricultural Sciences* 103 Agriculture Hall .... Lincoln NE 68583-0001
Fax: 402 472-7911
402 472-3041 *College of Journalism* 206 Avery Hall .... Lincoln NE 68588-0001
402 472-2338 *Graduate School of Business* College Business Bldg Rm 238 . Lincoln NE 68588-0001
Fax: Unlisted
University of Nebraska Medical Center
402 559-4110 *College of Nursing* 600 42nd St .... Omaha NE 68198-0001
Fax: 402 559-7570
402 559-4333 *College of Pharmacy* 600 S 42nd St .... Omaha NE 68198-6000
Fax: 402 559-5844

University of Nevada
702 739-3011 *Las Vegas Campus* 4505 S Maryland Pkwy .... Las Vegas NV 89154-0001
 Fax: Unlisted
702 784-6508 *Library* .... Reno NV 89557-0044
 Fax: 702 784-1751
702 784-1110 *Reno Campus* 9th Virginia St N .... Reno NV 89557-0001
 Fax: 702 784-1300
702 784-6531 *Reynolds School of Journalism* MSS-7 .... Reno NV 89557-0040
 Fax: 702 784-6656
207 283-0171 **University of New England** 11 Hills Beach Rd .... Biddeford ME 04005-9526
 Fax: 207 282-6379
603 862-1234 **University of New Hampshire** .... Durham NH 03824-3501
 Fax: 603 862-2030 Communications
603 668-0700 **University of New Hampshire at Manchester**
 220 Hackett Hill Rd .... Manchester NH 03102-8503
 Fax: 603 623-2745
203 932-7000 **University of New Haven** 300 Orange Ave .... West Haven CT 06516-1999
 Fax: 203 932-1469
505 277-0111 **University of New Mexico** Scholes Hall Rm 160 .... Albuquerque NM 87131-0001
 Fax: Unlisted
505 277-6413 *Anderson School of Management*
 Robert O Anderson Bldg .... Albuquerque NM 87131-0001
505 277-3241 *College of Pharmacy* Pharmacy Nursing Bldg Rm 184 ... Albuquerque NM 87131-0001
 Fax: 505 277-6749
505 277-5050 *Community & Regional Planning Program*
 2414 Central Ave SE .... Albuquerque NM 87131-0001
505 722-7221 *Gallup Campus* 200 College Rd .... Gallup NM 87301-5603
 Fax: Ext 2132
505 277-5761 *Library* Zimmerman Library .... Albuquerque NM 87131-0001
 Fax: 505 277-6019
505 277-2903 *School of Architecture & Planning* 2414 Central Ave SE .. Albuquerque NM 87131-0001
505 277-2146 *School of Law* 1117 Stanford Dr NE .... Albuquerque NM 87131-1431
 Fax: 505 277-0068
505 277-2321 *School of Medicine*
 University Hill NE Basic Medical Science Bldg .... Albuquerque NM 87131-0001
 Fax: 505 277-7774 Purchasing
504 286-6000 **University of New Orleans** Lake Front .... New Orleans LA 70148-0001
 Fax: 504 286-7393
504 286-6277 *School of Urban & Regional Studies* Math Bldg Rm 308 . New Orleans LA 70148-0001
 Fax: 504 286-6272
205 760-4100 **University of North Alabama** University Stn .... Florence AL 35632-0001
 Fax: 205 760-4644
University of North Carolina
704 251-6600 *Asheville Campus* 1 University Heights .... Asheville NC 28804-3299
 Fax: 704 251-6385
919 962-2211 *Chapel Hill* 910 Raleigh Rd CB-9000 .... Chapel Hill NC 27515-0000
 Fax: 919 962-0794
704 547-2000 *Charlotte Campus* Hwy 49 .... Charlotte NC 28223-0001
 Fax: 704 547-2041
919 962-1700 *Computer Science Dept* CB-3175 Sitterson Hall .... Chapel Hill NC 27599-0001
 Fax: 919 962-1799
919 962-8326 *Department of Biochemistry & Nutrition* CB 7260 .... Chapel Hill NC 27599-0001
 Fax: 919 962-2852
919 962-2172 *Department of Chemistry* Venable Hall CB 3290 .... Chapel Hill NC 27599-3290
 Fax: 919 962-2388
919 962-3983 *Department of City & Regional Planning*
 New East Bldg 3140 .... Chapel Hill NC 27599-3140
 Fax: 919 962-5604
919 962-3236 *Graduate School of Business*
 Carroll Hall Campus Box 3490 .... Chapel Hill NC 27599-0001
 Fax: 919 962-0054
919 966-3026 *Graduate School of Cell Biology & Anatomy*
 Taylor Hall Rm 108 .... Chapel Hill NC 27599-0001
 Fax: 919 966-1856
919 962-2078 *Graduate School of Physics & Astronomy*
 278 Phillips Hall CB-3255 .... Chapel Hill NC 27599-0001
 Fax: 919 962-0480
919 334-5000 *Greensboro Campus* 1000 Spring Gardens St .... Greensboro NC 27412-0001
 Fax: Unlisted
919 962-1356 *Libraries* Davis Library .... Chapel Hill NC 27515-0000
919 966-1161 *School of Dentistry* Brauer Hall Rm 102 .... Chapel Hill NC 27599-0001
 Fax: 919 966-4049
919 962-8366 *School of Information & Library Science*
 100 Manning Hall CB 3360 .... Chapel Hill NC 27599-0001
 Fax: 919 962-8071
919 962-1204 *School of Journalism* 100 Howell Hall CB 3365 .... Chapel Hill NC 27599-0001
 Fax: 919 962-0620
919 962-5106 *School of Law* Campus Box 3380 .... Chapel Hill NC 27599-0001
 Fax: 919 962-1277
919 966-4161 *School of Medicine* CB 7000 .... Chapel Hill NC 27599-0001
 Fax: 919 966-7564
919 966-1121 *School of Pharmacy* 200H Beard Hall Campus Box 7360 ... Chapel Hill NC 27599-0001
 Fax: 919 966-6919
919 966-4152 *School of Public Health* Rosenau Hall CB-7400 .... Chapel Hill NC 27599-0001
 Fax: 919 966-7141
919 395-3000 *Wilmington Campus* 601 S College Rd .... Wilmington NC 28403-3201
 Fax: 919 395-3550
701 777-2011 **University of North Dakota** University Stn .... Grand Forks ND 58202-2020
 Fax: 701 777-3650
701 777-2617 *Library* .... Grand Forks ND 58202-2020
 Fax: 701 777-3319
701 777-2159 *School of Communication* PO Box 8118 .... Grand Forks ND 58202-8118
 Fax: 701 777-3650
701 777-2104 *School of Law* University Stn .... Grand Forks ND 58202-2020
 Fax: 701 777-2217
701 777-2514 *School of Medicine* 501 N Columbia Rd .... Grand Forks ND 58203-2817
 Fax: 701 777-3894
701 774-4200 *Williston* PO Box 1326 .... Williston ND 58802-1326
 Fax: 701 774-4275
904 646-2666 **University of North Florida** 4567 St Johns Bluff Rd S .. Jacksonville FL 32216-6698
 Fax: 904 646-2505
817 565-2000 **University of North Texas** PO Box 13797 .... Denton TX 76203-6797
 Fax: 817 565-2599 Library
817 565-2205 *Department of Journalism* Hickory & Mulberry .... Denton TX 76203-0001
303 351-1890 **University of Northern Colorado** .... Greeley CO 80639-0001
 Fax: 303 351-1837 Admin
303 351-2726 *Department of Journalism & Mass Communications*
 Candelaria Hall Rm 123 .... Greeley CO 80639-0001
 Fax: Call company operator
319 273-2311 **University of Northern Iowa** 23rd & College St .... Cedar Falls IA 50614-0001
 Fax: 319 273-3509
319 273-2188 *Museum* 3219 Hudson Rd University of Northern Iowa .... Cedar Falls IA 50614-0199
219 239-5000 **University of Notre Dame** .... Notre Dame IN 46556-0000
 Fax: 219 239-6772
219 239-5530 *College of Engineering* Fitzpatrick Hall Rm 257 .... Notre Dame IN 46556-0000
 Fax: 219 239-8007

219 239-6627 *Law School* Law Bldg Rm 103 .... Notre Dame IN 46556-0000
 Fax: 219 239-6371
219 239-5206 *School of Business Administration* 133 Hayes-Healy ...... Notre Dame IN 46556-0000
 Fax: 219 239-5255
405 325-0311 **University of Oklahoma** 660 Parrington Oval .... Norman OK 73019-0001
 Fax: 405 325-7605
405 271-6326 *College of Dentistry* 1001 Stanton L Young Blvd .... Oklahoma City OK 73190-0001
405 325-2621 *College of Engineering* 202 W Boyd St Rm 107 .... Norman OK 73019-0001
 Fax: 405 325-7508 Purchasing
405 325-4726 *College of Law* 300 Timberdale Rd .... Norman OK 73019-0001
 Fax: 405 325-6282 Library
405 271-2265 *College of Medicine* 940 Stanton Young Ave Rm 357 . Oklahoma City OK 73104-0000
 Fax: 405 271-3032
405 271-2421 *College of Nursing* PO Box 26901 .... Oklahoma City OK 73190-0001
 Fax: 405 271-3443
405 271-6484 *College of Pharmacy* 1110 N Stonewall Ave .... Oklahoma City OK 73117-1223
 Fax: 405 271-3830
405 325-6591 *Department of City & Regional Planning*
 830 Van Vleet Oval Rm 162 .... Norman OK 73019-0001
 Fax: 405 325-6029
405 325-4321 *Graduate School of Botany & Microbiology*
 770 Van Fleet Oval .... Norman OK 73019-0245
 Fax: 405 325-7619
405 325-6432 *Graduate School of Public Administration*
 455 W Lindsey St Rm 305 .... Norman OK 73019-0001
405 325-2721 *HH Herbert School of Journalism & Mass Communication*
 860 Van Vleet Oval Rm 101 .... Norman OK 73019-0001
405 325-4142 *Library* Bizzell Memorial Library .... Norman OK 73069-0000
 Fax: 405 325-7618
405 325-3272 *Museum of Art* 410 W Boyd St .... Norman OK 73019-0001
405 271-4000 *Oklahoma City Campus* 1100 N Lindsay Ave .... Oklahoma City OK 73190-0001
 Fax: 405 271-2192
503 346-3111 **University of Oregon** 1020 University St .... Eugene OR 97403-0000
 Fax: 503 346-3660
503 346-3300 *College of Business Administration* 268 Gilbert Hall .... Eugene OR 97403-0000
 Fax: 503 346-3341
503 346-4502 *Department of Biology* .... Eugene OR 97403-1210
 Fax: 503 346-2364
503 346-4601 *Department of Chemistry* Klamath Hall .... Eugene OR 97403-0000
 Fax: 503 346-4643
503 346-4751 *Department of Physics* Willamette Hall .... Eugene OR 97403-0000
503 346-3635 *Department of Planning Public Policy & Management*
 119 Hendricks Hall .... Eugene OR 97403-0000
 Fax: 503 686-3127
503 346-4601 *Graduate School of Biochemistry* 91 Klamath Hall .... Eugene OR 97403-0000
 Fax: 503 346-4643
503 346-4573 *Graduate School of Geoscience* Cascade Hall Rm 100 .. Eugene OR 97403-0000
503 346-3053 *Library* Knight Library .... Eugene OR 97403-1299
503 346-3027 *Museum of Art* University of Oregon .... Eugene OR 97403-1205
503 346-3656 *School of Architecture & Allied Arts* Lawrence Hall .... Eugene OR 97403-1206
 Fax: 503 346-3660
503 346-3738 *School of Journalism* Allen Hall Rm 201 .... Eugene OR 97403-0000
503 346-3852 *School of Law* 11th & Kincaid Sts .... Eugene OR 97403-0000
 Fax: 503 346-3985
503 494-8220 *School of Medicine* 3181 SW Sam Jackson Park Rd . Portland OR 97201-3042
 Fax: 503 279-5738
215 898-5000 **University of Pennsylvania**
 3451 Walnut St Franklin Bldg Rm 221 .... Philadelphia PA 19104-6205
 Fax: 215 898-5756
215 898-5728 *Department of Architecture*
 210 S 34th St Meyerson Hall Rm 110 .... Philadelphia PA 19104-6311
 Fax: 215 898-9215
215 898-4829 *Department of Biochemistry*
 38th & Hamilton Walk Anatomy-Chemistry Bldg Rm 414 . Philadelphia PA 19104-6059
215 898-8329 *Department of City & Regional Planning*
 210 S 34th St Myerson Hall Rm 127 .... Philadelphia PA 19104-6311
 Fax: 215 898-9215
215 898-8560 *Department of Computer & Information Science*
 200 S 33rd St Moore Bldg .... Philadelphia PA 19104-0000
 Fax: 215 898-0587
215 898-6861 *Department of Health Care Systems*
 3641 Locust Walk Rm 204 .... Philadelphia PA 19104-6218
 Fax: 215 898-0229
215 898-5720 *Department of Physics* 209 S 33rd St DRL Bldg .... Philadelphia PA 19104-0000
 Fax: 215 898-2010
215 898-9722 *Graduate School of Chemistry*
 231 S 34th St Chemistry Bldg .... Philadelphia PA 19104-6323
 Fax: 215 898-8378
215 898-7483 *Law School* 3400 Chestnut St .... Philadelphia PA 19104-6204
 Fax: 215 898-6619
215 898-4360 *Molecular Biology Graduate Group*
 210 Goddard Laboratory .... Philadelphia PA 19104-0000
215 898-4000 *Museum of Archaeology & Anthropology*
 33rd & Spruce Sts University of Pennsylvania .... Philadelphia PA 19104-6324
 Fax: 215 898-0657
215 898-8961 *School of Dental Medicine* 4001 Spruce St .... Philadelphia PA 19104-6003
 Fax: 215 898-5243
215 898-8241 *School of Engineering & Applied Science*
 220 S 33rd St Towne Bldg Rm 119 .... Philadelphia PA 19104-6391
 Fax: 215 898-1130
215 898-8001 *School of Medicine* Medical Education Bldg Suite 100 .... Philadelphia PA 19104-6382
 Fax: 215 898-0833
215 898-8281 *School of Nursing* 420 Guardian Dr .... Philadelphia PA 19104-0000
 Fax: 215 898-6320
215 898-5438 *School of Veterinary Medicine*
 3800 Spruce Rosenthal Bldg .... Philadelphia PA 19104-0000
 Fax: 215 898-9923
215 898-3030 *Wharton School of Business*
 3620 Locust Walk Suite 1000 .... Philadelphia PA 19104-6302
 Fax: 215 898-2400
602 966-7400 **University of Phoenix** 4615 E Elwood St .... Phoenix AZ 85040-1998
 Fax: 602 829-9030
412 624-4141 **University of Pittsburgh** 4200 5th Ave .... Pittsburgh PA 15260-0001
 Fax: 412 648-5911
814 362-3801 *Bradford Campus* 300 Campus Dr .... Bradford PA 16701-2898
 Fax: 814 362-7684
412 624-8490 *Computer Science Dept* 321 Alumni Hall .... Pittsburgh PA 15260-0001
 Fax: 412 624-8854
412 624-4268 *Graduate School of Biological Sciences*
 Langley Hall Rm A-234 .... Pittsburgh PA 15260-0001
 Fax: 412 624-4759
412 624-9000 *Graduate School of Physics & Astronomy* 100 Allen Hall ... Pittsburgh PA 15260-0001
 Fax: 412 624-9163
412 648-7600 *Graduate School of Public & International Affairs*
 Forbes Quadrangle Rm 3G07 .... Pittsburgh PA 15260-0001
 Fax: 412 648-2605

412 837-7040 *Greensburg Campus* 1150 Mt Pleasant Rd ... Greensburg PA 15601-5898
Fax: 412 836-9901
814 266-9661 *Johnstown Campus* ... Johnstown PA 15904-2990
Fax: Unlisted
412 624-8200 *School of Chemistry*
234 Chevron Science Ctr Parkman & University Dr ... Pittsburgh PA 15260-0001
Fax: 412 624-8552
412 648-8616 *School of Dental Medicine* 3501 Terrace St ... Pittsburgh PA 15261-0001
Fax: 412 648-8219
412 624-9800 *School of Engineering* 253 Benedum Hall ... Pittsburgh PA 15261-0001
Fax: 412 624-1108
412 648-1400 *School of Law* 3900 Forbes Ave ... Pittsburgh PA 15260-0001
Fax: 412 648-1352
412 624-5230 *School of Library & Information Science*
135 N Bellefield Ave LIS Bldg ... Pittsburgh PA 15260-0001
Fax: 412 624-5231
412 648-8975 *School of Medicine* 3550 Terrace St M240 Scaife Hall ... Pittsburgh PA 15261-0001
Fax: 412 648-1236
412 624-2407 *School of Nursing* 3500 Victoria St Victoria Bldg Rm 336 .. Pittsburgh PA 15261-0001
Fax: 412 624-2401
412 648-8650 *School of Pharmacy* 3501 Terrace St Salk Hall Rm 1104 ... Pittsburgh PA 15261-0001
Fax: 412 648-1086
412 648-7630 *School of Public & International Affairs*
Forbes Quadrangle ... Pittsburgh PA 15260-0001
Fax: 412 648-2605
814 827-2702 *Titusville Campus* 504 E Main St ... Titusville PA 16354-2010
Fax: 814 827-4448
503 283-7911 **University of Portland** 5000 N Willamette Blvd ... Portland OR 97203-5798
Fax: 503 283-7399
206 756-3100 **University of Puget Sound** 1500 N Warner St ... Tacoma WA 98416-0001
Fax: 206 756-3500
206 591-6300 *School of Law* 950 Broadway Plaza ... Tacoma WA 98402-4413
Fax: 206 591-6313
714 793-2121 **University of Redlands** 1200 E Colton Ave ... Redlands CA 92373-0999
Fax: 714 793-2029
401 792-1000 **University of Rhode Island** ... Kingston RI 02881-0000
Fax: 401 792-4395 Communications
401 792-2761 *College of Pharmacy* Fogerty Hall ... Kingston RI 02881-0000
Fax: 401 792-2181
401 792-2672 *Library* ... Kingston RI 02881-0000
804 289-8000 **University of Richmond** ... Richmond VA 23173-7301
804 289-8740 *TC Williams School of Law* ... Richmond VA 23173-7301
Fax: 804 289-8683
614 245-5353 **University of Rio Grande** 218 N College Ave ... Rio Grande OH 45674-9999
Fax: 614 245-9220 Library
716 275-2121 **University of Rochester** ... Rochester NY 14627-0000
Fax: 716 275-0359
716 275-4231 *Department of Chemistry* Hutchison Hall Rm 404 ... Rochester NY 14627-0000
Fax: 716 473-6889
716 275-3835 *Graduate School of Biology* Hutchison Hall Rm 402 ... Rochester NY 14627-0000
Fax: 716 473-6889
716 275-4072 *Graduate School of Material Science* 235 Hopeman Bldg ... Rochester NY 14627-0000
Fax: 716 256-2509
716 275-3407 *School of Medicine & Dentistry*
601 Elmwood Ave Medical Ctr ... Rochester NY 14642-0001
Fax: 716 256-1131
716 275-2375 *School of Nursing* 601 Almwood Ave Helenwood Hall ... Rochester NY 14642-0001
Fax: 716 473-1059
716 275-3317 *William E Simon Graduate School of Business Administration*
Dewey Hall ... Rochester NY 14627-1001
Fax: 716 275-0095
612 647-5000 **University of Saint Thomas** 2115 Summit Ave ... Saint Paul MN 55105-1096
Fax: 612 647-5879
713 522-7911 **University of Saint Thomas** 3812 Montrose Blvd ... Houston TX 77006-4694
Fax: 713 522-9920
619 260-4600 **University of San Diego** Alcala Pk ... San Diego CA 92110-2496
Fax: 619 260-4619
415 666-6886 **University of San Francisco** Ignatian Heights ... San Francisco CA 94117-1050
Fax: 415 666-9700
415 666-6254 *College of Professional Studies* Ignagian Heights ... San Francisco CA 94117-0000
Fax: 415 666-2696 Communications
415 666-6544 *School of Law* 2130 Fulton St ... San Francisco CA 94117-1080
Fax: 415 666-6433
405 224-3140 **University of Sciences & Arts of Oklahoma** 2000 S 18th St ... Chickasha OK 73018-0000
Fax: 405 521-6244
717 961-7400 **University of Scranton** Linden & Monroe Aves ... Scranton PA 18510-2192
Fax: 717 961-6369
205 460-6101 **University of South Alabama** 307 University Blvd ... Mobile AL 36688-0001
Fax: 205 460-7205
205 937-3789 *Baldwin Campus* 1900 US Hwy 31 S ... Bay Minette AL 36507-0000
Fax: 205 937-3404
205 460-7174 *College of Medicine* 1005 Medical Sciences Bldg ... Mobile AL 36688-0001
Fax: 205 460-6761
803 777-7000 **University of South Carolina** ... Columbia SC 29208-0001
Fax: 803 777-4760
803 648-6851 *Aiken Campus* 171 University Pkwy ... Aiken SC 29801-6399
Fax: 803 641-3362
803 524-7112 *Beaufort Campus* 800 Carteret St ... Beaufort SC 29902-4602
Fax: Ext 4199
803 347-3161 *Coastal Carolina College* PO Box 1954 ... Conway SC 29526-1954
Fax: 803 349-2990
803 777-4102 *College of Journalism & Mass Communication*
Carolina Coliseum ... Columbia SC 29208-0001
Fax: 803 777-9578
803 777-3861 *College of Nursing* Williams-Bryce Nursing Bldg Rm 202 ... Columbia SC 29208-0001
Fax: 803 777-2027
803 777-2149 *College of Pharmacy* Coker Life Science Bldg Rm 109 ... Columbia SC 29208-0001
Fax: 803 777-7275
803 777-2840 *Computer Science Dept* LeConte Bldg Rm 216 ... Columbia SC 29208-0001
Fax: 803 777-3767
803 777-3869 *Department of Government & International Studies*
Gambrell Hall 3rd Fl ... Columbia SC 29208-0001
803 285-7471 *Lancaster Campus* 909 Hubbard Dr ... Lancaster SC 29720-0000
Fax: 803 285-4348
803 584-3446 *Salkehatchie Campus* Hwy 301 & Spruce St ... Allendale SC 29810-0000
Fax: 803 584-5038
803 777-4535 *School of Geological Sciences* 700 Sumter St Rm 617 ... Columbia SC 29208-0001
Fax: 803 777-6610
803 777-6617 *School of Law* S Main & Green St ... Columbia SC 29208-0001
Fax: 803 777-9405
803 733-3200 *School of Medicine* Administration Bldg Rm 200 ... Columbia SC 29208-0000
Fax: 803 733-3335 Admin
803 599-2000 *Spartanburg Campus* 800 University Way ... Spartanburg SC 29303-9397
Fax: 803 599-2375
803 775-6341 *Sumter Campus* 200 Miller Rd ... Sumter SC 29150-2478
Fax: 803 775-2180

803 427-3681 *Union Campus* 401 E Main St ... Union SC 29379-1902
605 677-5011 **University of South Dakota** 414 E Clark St ... Vermillion SD 57069-2390
Fax: 605 677-5488
605 677-5621 *Lee School of Medicine* 414 E Clark St ... Vermillion SD 57069-2390
Fax: 605 677-5124
605 677-5361 *School of Law* 414 E Clark St ... Vermillion SD 57069-2390
Fax: 605 677-5417
813 974-2011 **University of South Florida** 4202 E Fowler Ave ... Tampa FL 33620-6499
Fax: 813 974-3149
813 974-2591 *Department of Mass Communications*
4202 E Fowler Ave Bldg CPR 107 ... Tampa FL 33620-5550
213 743-2311 **University of Southern California** University Pk ... Los Angeles CA 90089-0001
Fax: 213 747-4176
213 743-2717 *Department of Geological Sciences* University Pk ... Los Angeles CA 90089-0740
213 224-7139 *Department of Microbiology*
2011 Zonal Ave Hoffman Medical Research Bldg Rm 401 . Los Angeles CA 90033-0000
Fax: 213 223-5622
213 224-7151 *Graduate School of Biochemistry*
200 Zonal Ave Hoffman Medical ... Los Angeles CA 90033-0000
213 743-7846 *Graduate School of Business* Bridge Hall Rm 101 ... Los Angeles CA 90089-0001
213 743-2780 *Graduate School of Chemistry*
3620 McClintock Ave SG Mudd Bldg Rm 418 ... Los Angeles CA 90089-1062
Fax: 213 740-2701
213 743-2052 *Graduate School of Urban Planning* University Pk ... Los Angeles CA 90089-0042
Fax: 213 743-7494
213 743-7331 *Law Center* University Pk ... Los Angeles CA 90089-0001
213 743-2540 *Library* Doheny Library ... Los Angeles CA 90089-0001
Fax: 213 749-1221
213 743-0884 *School of Engineering*
200 University Pk Olin Hall of Engineering Suite 200 ... Los Angeles CA 90089-0001
Fax: 213 742-6763
213 743-2391 *School of Journalism* GFS 315 ... Los Angeles CA 90089-1695
Fax: 213 742-6872
213 224-7001 *School of Medicine* 1975 Zonal Ave ... Los Angeles CA 90033-1039
Fax: 213 227-0491
213 224-7501 *School of Pharmacy* 1985 Zonal Ave ... Los Angeles CA 90033-1058
Fax: 213 221-1235 Library
719 549-2100 **University of Southern Colorado** 2200 Bonforte Blvd ... Pueblo CO 81001-4999
Fax: 719 549-2938
812 464-8600 **University of Southern Indiana** 8600 University Blvd ... Evansville IN 47712-3534
Fax: 812 464-1960
207 780-4141 **University of Southern Maine** 96 Falmouth St ... Portland ME 04103-4899
Fax: 207 780-4933
601 266-7011 **University of Southern Mississippi** Hardy St ... Hattiesburg MS 39406-7000
Fax: Unlisted
601 266-4258 *Department of Journalism* Southern Stn Box 5121 ... Hattiesburg MS 39406-0000
601 266-5445 *School of Nursing* PO Box 5095 ... Hattiesburg MS 39406-0000
Fax: 601 266-4410
318 231-6000 **University of Southwestern Louisiana** PO Box 4-400 ... Lafayette LA 70504-0400
813 253-3333 **University of Tampa** 401 W Kennedy Blvd W ... Tampa FL 33606-1490
Fax: 813 254-6215
615 974-1000 **University of Tennessee** Student Service Bldg Rm 305 ... Knoxville TN 37996-0001
Fax: 615 974-8546
615 974-3031 *College of Communications*
Communications Extension Bldg Rm 302 ... Knoxville TN 37996-0001
901 528-6200 *College of Dentistry* 875 Union Ave ... Memphis TN 38163-0001
Fax: 901 528-7104
615 974-5321 *College of Engineering* 124 Perkins Hall ... Knoxville TN 37996-0001
Fax: 615 974-2669
615 974-4241 *College of Law* 1505 W Cumberland Ave ... Knoxville TN 37996-0001
Fax: 615 974-0681
615 974-7231 *Department of Agricultural Economics* 302 Morgan Hall ... Knoxville TN 37996-0001
Fax: 615 974-7447
615 974-5034 *Graduate School of Business* 527 Stokely Management Ctr .. Knoxville TN 37996-0001
615 974-5227 *Graduate School of Planning* 1618 Cumberland Ave ... Knoxville TN 37996-0001
615 974-4171 *Library* 1015 Volunteer Blvd ... Knoxville TN 37996-1000
Fax: 615 974-2708
901 587-7000 *Martin Campus* University St ... Martin TN 38238-0001
901 528-5000 *Memphis Campus* 800 Madison Ave ... Memphis TN 38163-0001
Fax: 901 577-8640
901 528-5539 *Memphis College of Medicine*
800 Madison Blvd Hyman Bldg Suite 400 ... Memphis TN 38163-0000
Fax: 901 577-8640
University of Tennessee Memphis
901 528-6128 *College of Nursing*
877 Madison Ave Lamar Alexander Bldg Suite 620 ... Memphis TN 38163-0001
Fax: 901 577-4121
901 528-6036 *College of Pharmacy* 842 Monroe Faculty Bldg Suite 238 ... Memphis TN 38163-0001
Fax: 901 528-6517
University of Texas
817 273-2011 *Arlington Campus* 800 S Cooper St ... Arlington TX 76019-0001
Fax: 817 273-3392 Library
512 471-3434 *Austin Campus* PO Box T ... Austin TX 78713-8920
Fax: 512 471-5812
512 471-1737 *College of Pharmacy* 200 W 21st St ... Austin TX 78712-0000
Fax: 512 471-8783
214 690-2111 *Dallas Campus* PO Box 830688 ... Richardson TX 75083-0688
Fax: Unlisted
915 747-5000 *El Paso Campus* 500 W University Ave ... El Paso TX 79968-0001
Fax: 915 747-5111
409 761-2769 *Graduate Program of Human Biological Chemistry & Genetics*
Basic Science Bldg Rm 635 ... Galveston TX 77550-0000
Fax: 409 761-5159
512 471-5921 *Graduate School of Business Administration* GSB 2.104 ... Austin TX 78712-1104
Fax: 512 471-3034
512 471-5172 *Graduate School of Geological Sciences* PO Box 7909 ... Austin TX 78713-7909
Fax: 512 471-9425
512 471-3821 *Graduate School of Library & Information Sciences*
Education Bldg Rm 564 ... Austin TX 78712-0000
Fax: 512 471-3071
512 471-1664 *Graduate School of Physics* RLM 5.208 ... Austin TX 78712-1081
Fax: 512 471-9637
713 792-4975 *Health Science Center Houston* PO Box 20036 ... Houston TX 77225-0036
Fax: 713 792-1986
512 567-2621 *Health Science Center San Antonio* 7703 Floyd Curl Dr ... San Antonio TX 78284-0001
Fax: 512 567-6811
713 792-2121 *Houston Campus* 1515 Holcombe Blvd ... Houston TX 77030-3907
Fax: 713 792-7573
512 471-4962 *LBJ School of Public Affairs* PO Box Y University Stn ... Austin TX 78713-8925
Fax: 512 471-1835
512 471-3813 *Libraries* ... Austin TX 78713-7330
Fax: 512 471-1790
214 688-3404 *Medical Center of Dallas* 5323 Harry Hines Blvd ... Dallas TX 75235-7200
Fax: 214 688-8252
512 982-0100 *Pan American* 1614 Ridgely Rd ... Brownsville TX 78520-4991
Fax: 512 982-0115

512 691-4011 *San Antonio Campus* .... San Antonio TX 78285-0001
Fax: 512 691-4571

512 471-1922 *School of Architecture* Goldsmith Hall Rm 2.308 .... Austin TX 78712-0000
Fax: 512 471-0716

512 471-5151 *School of Law* 727 E 26th St .... Austin TX 78705-3299
Fax: 512 471-6988

903 566-7000 *Tyler Campus* 3900 University Blvd .... Tyler TX 75701-6699
Fax: 903 566-2513 Library

University of Texas Arlington

817 273-2067 *City & Regional Planning Div* 601 Campus Dr .... Arlington TX 76010-0000
Fax: 817 794-5008

817 273-2571 *Graduate Dept of Engineering* PO Box 19019 .... Arlington TX 76019-0001
Fax: 817 273-2548

University of Texas Austin

512 471-5775 *College of Commcations* 26th & Whitis Sts Rm CMA 4.130 .... Austin TX 78712-0000
Fax: 512 471-8500

512 471-1166 *College of Engineering* ECJ 10.310 .... Austin TX 78712-0000
Fax: 512 471-3955

512 471-8135 *Community & Regional Planning* School of Architecture .... Austin TX 78712-1104
Fax: 512 471-0716

512 471-7316 *Department of Computer Sciences* Burdin Hall .... Austin TX 78729-0000
Fax: 512 471-0548

512 471-4882 *Division of Biological Sciences* Painter Hall Rm 1.22 .... Austin TX 78712-0000

512 471-7311 *School of Nursing* 1700 Red River St .... Austin TX 78701-1412
Fax: 512 471-4910

214 688-3111 **University of Texas Dallas Southwestern Medical School**
5323 Harry Hines Blvd .... Dallas TX 75235-7200
Fax: 214 688-3277

915 747-5129 **University of Texas El Paso Department of Communications**
202 Cotton Memorial .... El Paso TX 79968-0001
Fax: 915 747-5111

University of Texas Galveston

409 761-6840 *Graduate School of Biomedical Sciences*
Old Red Bldg Rm 2.210 .... Galveston TX 77550-0000

409 761-1011 *Medical Branch* 301 University Blvd .... Galveston TX 77550-2774
Fax: 409 761-4001 Mail Rm

University of Texas Health Science Center

713 792-4750 *Graduate School of Biomedical Sciences* 6901 Bertner .... Houston TX 77030-3901
Fax: 713 794-1601

512 567-7000 *Medical School* 7703 Floyd Curl Dr .... San Antonio TX 78284-0001
Fax: 512 567-2490

University of Texas Houston

713 792-4056 *Dental Branch* 6516 John Freeman Ave Texas Medical Ctr .... Houston TX 77030-3402

713 792-2121 *Medical School* 1515 Holcombe Blvd .... Houston TX 77030-0000
Fax: 713 792-7573

713 792-7800 **University of Texas Houston Health Science Center School of Nursing**
1100 Holcombe Blvd .... Houston TX 77030-3907
Fax: 713 794-1714

915 367-2011 **University of Texas of the Permian Basin**
4901 E University Blvd .... Odessa TX 79762-8192
Fax: 915 367-2115 Library

512 567-3222 **University of Texas San Antonio Dental School**
7703 Floyd Curl Dr .... San Antonio TX 78284-0001
Fax: 512 567-6721 Dean

215 875-2200 **University of the Arts** 250 S Broad St .... Philadelphia PA 19102-5087
Fax: 215 875-1018

202 282-7300 **University of the District of Columbia**
4200 Connecticut Ave NW .... Washington DC 20008-1178
Fax: 202 282-3671

501 754-3839 **University of the Ozarks** 415 N College Ave .... Clarksville AR 72830-2880
Fax: Ext 355

209 946-2011 **University of the Pacific** 3601 Pacific Ave .... Stockton CA 95211-0001
Fax: Ext 2401

916 739-7121 *McGeorge School of Law* 3200 5th Ave .... Sacramento CA 95817-2705
Fax: 916 739-7111

209 946-2561 *School of Pharmacy* 751 Brookside Rd .... Stockton CA 95211-0001
Fax: 209 956-2410

615 598-5931 **University of the South** Administration Bldg .... Sewanee TN 37375-0000
Fax: 615 598-1145

215 875-4800 **University of the Visual Arts** 320 S Broad St .... Philadelphia PA 19102-4994
Fax: 215 875-5467

419 537-2072 **University of Toledo** 2801 W Bancroft St .... Toledo OH 43606-3390
Fax: 419 537-4940

419 537-2882 *College of Law* 2801 W Bancroft St Law Ctr .... Toledo OH 43606-3390
Fax: 419 537-2821

419 537-4235 *College of Pharmacy* 2801 W Bancroft St .... Toledo OH 43606-3390
Fax: 419 537-4940

918 592-6000 **University of Tulsa** 600 S College Ave .... Tulsa OK 74104-3189
Fax: 918 631-3823 Library

918 631-2401 *College of Law* 3120 E 4th Pl John Rogers Hall .... Tulsa OK 74104-2499
Fax: 918 631-3556 Library

801 581-7200 **University of Utah** 1340 E 200 South .... Salt Lake City UT 84112-0000
Fax: 801 581-7880

801 581-6911 *College of Engineering*
Merill Engineering Bldg Rm 2202 .... Salt Lake City UT 84112-0000
Fax: 801 581-8692

801 581-6833 *College of Law* College of Law Bldg .... Salt Lake City UT 84112-0000
Fax: 801 581-6897 Library

801 581-7728 *College of Nursing* 25 S Medical Dr .... Salt Lake City UT 84112-1502

801 581-6731 *College of Pharmacy* 201 Scaggs Hall .... Salt Lake City UT 84112-0000
Fax: 801 581-3716

801 581-2117 *Department of Biochemistry*
211 Medical Education Bldg .... Salt Lake City UT 84132-0001
Fax: 801 581-7959

801 581-6888 *Department of Communications* LeRoy Cowles Bldg .... Salt Lake City UT 84112-0000
Fax: 801 581-7880

801 581-5207 *Graduate School of Cellular/Molecular Biology*
201 S Biology .... Salt Lake City UT 84112-0000
Fax: 801 581-4668

801 581-6681 *Graduate School of Chemistry*
Henry Eyring Bldg Rm 2020 .... Salt Lake City UT 84112-0000
Fax: 801 581-8433

801 581-6553 *Graduate School of Geology & Geophysics*
717 William Browning Bldg .... Salt Lake City UT 84112-0000
Fax: 801 581-5560

801 581-6273 *Libraries* .... Salt Lake City UT 84112-0000
Fax: Call company operator

801 581-7201 *School of Medicine* 50 N Medical Dr .... Salt Lake City UT 84132-0001
Fax: 801 581-3647

802 656-3480 **University of Vermont** 855 Prospect St .... Burlington VT 05405-0001
Fax: 802 656-8429

802 656-2150 *College of Medicine* Given Bldg Rm E-109 .... Burlington VT 05405-0001
Fax: 802 656-8584

802 656-3131 *Library* 855 S Prospect Bailey-Howe Library .... Burlington VT 05405-0001

804 924-0311 **University of Virginia** Miller Hall McCormick Rd .... Charlottesville VA 22906-0000
Fax: 804 924-7890 Personnel

804 924-6317 *Department of Physics* McCormick Rd Physics Bldg .... Charlottesville VA 22903-0000
Fax: 804 924-4576

804 924-3716 *Division of Urban & Environmental Planning*
Campbell Hall .... Charlottesville VA 22903-2443
Fax: 804 982-2678

804 924-7481 *Graduate Business School* PO Box 6550 .... Charlottesville VA 22906-6550
Fax: 804 924-4859

804 924-5139 *Graduate Dept of Biochemistry*
School of Medicine Box 440 .... Charlottesville VA 22908-0001
Fax: 804 924-5069

804 924-5930 *Graduate School of Microbiology* Jordan Hall Box 441 .... Charlottesville VA 22908-0001
Fax: 804 982-1071

804 924-3021 *Library* Alderman Library .... Charlottesville VA 22903-0000
Fax: 804 982-2002

804 924-3715 *School of Architecture* Campbell Hall .... Charlottesville VA 22903-2443
Fax: 804 982-2678

804 924-3073 *School of Engineering & Applied Science*
Thornton Hall .... Charlottesville VA 22903-2448
Fax: 804 924-6270

804 924-7354 *School of Law* Withers Hall 3rd Fl .... Charlottesville VA 22901-0000
Fax: 804 924-7536

804 924-5118 *School of Medicine* Medical Ctr Box 395 .... Charlottesville VA 22908-0001
Fax: 804 982-0874

804 924-2743 *School of Nursing* McLeod Hall .... Charlottesville VA 22903-0000
Fax: 804 982-1809

206 543-2100 **University of Washington** Administrative Offices AH-30 .... Seattle WA 98195-0001
Fax: 206 543-3951

206 543-0340 *College of Engineering* Loew Hall FH-10 .... Seattle WA 98195-0001
Fax: 206 685-0666

206 543-1695 *Computer Science & Engineering Dept*
Sieg Hall Rm 114 FR-35 .... Seattle WA 98195-0001
Fax: 206 543-2969

206 543-4180 *Department of Architecture* JO-20 .... Seattle WA 98195-0001
Fax: 206 543-2463

206 543-4787 *Department of Chemistry* BG-10 .... Seattle WA 98195-0001
Fax: 206 685-8665

206 543-5824 *Department of Microbiology*
Health Sciences Bldg Rm G-311 SC-42 .... Seattle WA 98195-0001
Fax: 206 543-8297

206 543-4190 *Department of Urban Design & Planning*
410 Gould Hall JO-40 .... Seattle WA 98195-0001
Fax: 206 543-2463

206 543-8020 *Graduate School of Geophysics*
Atmospheric Sciences Bldg Rm 202 AK-50 .... Seattle WA 98195-0001

206 543-1794 *Graduate School of Library & Information Science*
133 Suzzallo Library FM-30 .... Seattle WA 98195-0001
Fax: 206 685-8049

206 543-2770 *Graduate School of Physics* FM-15 .... Seattle WA 98195-0001
Fax: 206 685-0635

206 543-0242 *Library* .... Seattle WA 98195-0000

206 543-2660 *School of Communications* Communications Hall DS-40 .... Seattle WA 98195-0001
Fax: 206 543-9285

206 543-5982 *School of Dentistry* Health Sciences Bldg Rm D-322 SC-62 .... Seattle WA 98195-0001
Fax: 206 685-3164

206 543-4550 *School of Law* 1100 NE Campus Pkwy Condon Hall JB-20 .... Seattle WA 98105-0000

206 543-1060 *School of Medicine* 1959 NE Pacific St SC-64 .... Seattle WA 98195-0001
Fax: 206 543-3639

206 543-9175 *School of Nursing* Health Sciences Bldg SC-72 .... Seattle WA 98195-0001
Fax: 206 543-3624

206 543-2030 *School of Pharmacy* SC-69 .... Seattle WA 98195-0001
Fax: 206 543-3835

904 474-2000 **University of West Florida** 11000 University Pkwy .... Pensacola FL 32514-5750
Fax: Unlisted

904 474-2829 *Department of Communication Arts*
11000 University Pkwy Bldg 76 .... Pensacola FL 32514-0000
Fax: 904 474-3130

213 313-1011 **University of West Los Angeles** 12201 Washington Pl .... Los Angeles CA 90066-4998
Fax: 213 313-2124

213 313-1011 *School of Law* 12201 Washington Pl .... Los Angeles CA 90066-4998
Fax: 213 313-2124

608 262-6410 **University of Wisconsin (System)** 1220 Linden Dr .... Madison WI 53706-1557
Fax: 608 263-2046

University of Wisconsin

608 262-1251 *College of Agricultural & Life Sciences* 1450 Linden Dr .... Madison WI 53706-1522
Fax: 608 262-4556 Admin

608 262-3026 *Department of Biochemistry*
420 Henry Mall Biochemistry Bldg Rm 104A .... Madison WI 53706-0001
Fax: 608 262-3453

608 262-1004 *Department of Urban & Regional Planning*
925 Bascom Mall Old Music Hall .... Madison WI 53706-0001
Fax: 608 262-9307

715 836-2637 *Eau Claire Campus* Garfield & Park Aves .... Eau Claire WI 54701-4800
Fax: 715 836-2171

608 262-3203 *Graduate School of Cellular/Molecular Biology*
1525 Lynden Dr Molecular Biology Bldg Rm 413 .... Madison WI 53706-0001
Fax: 608 262-4570

608 262-0806 *Graduate School of Chemistry* 1101 University Ave .... Madison WI 53706-1322
Fax: 608 262-0381

414 465-2000 *Green Bay Campus* 2420 Nicolet Dr .... Green Bay WI 54311-7003
Fax: Unlisted

608 785-8000 *La Crosse Campus* 1725 State St .... La Crosse WI 54601-3767
Fax: 608 785-8809

608 262-2240 *Law School* 975 Bascom Mall .... Madison WI 53706-1317
Fax: 608 262-5485

608 262-3242 *Libraries* 728 State St .... Madison WI 53706-1418

608 262-1234 *Madison Campus* 750 University Ave .... Madison WI 53706-1411

608 263-4910 *Medical School* 1300 University Ave .... Madison WI 53706-1532
Fax: 608 262-2327

414 229-1122 *Milwaukee Campus* Mellencamp Hall .... Milwaukee WI 53201-0000
Fax: Unlisted

414 424-1234 *Oshkosh Campus* 800 Algoma Blvd .... Oshkosh WI 54901-8611
Fax: 414 424-7317

414 553-2345 *Parkside Campus* PO Box 2000 .... Kenosha WI 53141-2000
Fax: 414 553-2630

608 342-1491 *Platteville Campus* 1 University Plaza .... Platteville WI 53818-3024
Fax: 608 348-1501

715 425-3911 *River Falls Campus* 410 S 3rd St .... River Falls WI 54022-0000
Fax: 715 425-4487 Library

414 229-4014 *School of Architecture & Urban Planning*
2033 E Hartford Ave .... Milwaukee WI 53211-3154
Fax: 414 229-6976

608 262-8960 *School of Geology & Geophysics* 1215 W Dayton St .... Madison WI 53706-1612
Fax: 608 262-0693

608 263-2900	*School of Library & Information Science* 600 N Park St	Madison	WI	53706-1403
	Fax: 608 263-3684 Library			
715 346-0123	*Stevens Point Campus* 2100 Main St	Stevens Point	WI	54481-3871
	Fax: 715 346-3955			
715 232-1122	*Stout Campus*	Menomonie	WI	54751-0000
	Fax: 715 232-1432			
715 394-8101	*Superior Campus* 1800 Grand Ave	Superior	WI	54880-2898
	Fax: 715 394-8454 Admin			
414 472-1234	*Whitewater Campus* 800 W Main St	Whitewater	WI	53190-1705
	Fax: 414 472-1518 Admin			
608 262-1783	**University of Wisconsin Centers** 150 E Gilman St	Madison	WI	53708-8680
	Fax: 608 262-7872			
715 234-8176	*Barron County Campus* 1800 College Dr	Rice Lake	WI	54868-2414
	Fax: 715 234-1975			
414 929-3600	*Fond du Lac Campus* 400 Campus Dr	Fond du Lac	WI	54935-2998
	Fax: 414 929-3626 Library			
414 832-2600	*Fox Valley County Campus* 1478 Midway Rd	Menasha	WI	54952-1224
414 683-4700	*Manitowac County Campus* 705 Viebahn St	Manitowoc	WI	54220-6601
715 845-9602	*Marathon County Campus* 518 S 7th Ave	Wausau	WI	54401-5362
	Fax: 715 848-5434			
715 735-7477	*Marinette Campus* 750 W Bay Shore St	Marinette	WI	54143-4299
	Fax: 715 735-0273			
715 387-1147	*Marshfield/Wood County Campus* 2000 W 5th St	Marshfield	WI	54449-3310
	Fax: 715 389-6539			
608 647-6186	*Richland Campus* Hwy 14 W	Richland Center	WI	53581-0000
	Fax: 608 647-6225			
608 755-2811	*Rock County Campus* 2909 Kellogg Ave	Janesville	WI	53546-5606
	Fax: 608 755-3732			
414 459-3700	*Sheboygan County Campus* 1 University Dr	Sheboygan	WI	53081-4789
	Fax: 414 459-4010			
414 335-5200	*Washington County Campus* 400 University Dr	West Bend	WI	53095-3699
	Fax: 414 335-5220			
	University of Wisconsin Madison			
608 262-3481	*College of Engineering* 1513 University Ave	Madison	WI	53706-1512
	Fax: 608 262-6707			
608 262-1204	*Computer Sciences Dept* 1210 W Dayton St	Madison	WI	53706-1613
	Fax: 608 262-9777			
608 262-3077	*Department of Physics* 475 N Charter St 2531 Sterling Hall	Madison	WI	53706-0001
608 263-5155	*School of Nursing*			
	600 Highland Ave Center for Health Sciences	Madison	WI	53792-0001
	Fax: 608 263-5332			
608 262-1414	*School of Pharmacy* 425 N Charter St	Madison	WI	53706-1508
	Fax: 608 262-3397			
	University of Wisconsin Milwaukee			
414 229-4126	*College of Engineering & Applied Science*			
	EMS Bldg Rm E-503	Milwaukee	WI	53201-0000
414 229-5563	*Department of Architecture & Urban Planning*			
	2033 E Hartford Ave	Milwaukee	WI	53211-3154
	Fax: 414 229-6976			
414 229-4801	*School of Nursing* PO Box 413	Milwaukee	WI	53201-0413
	Fax: 414 229-6474			
307 766-1121	**University of Wyoming** PO Box 3434 University Stn	Laramie	WY	82071-3434
	Fax: 307 766-2271			
307 766-4135	*College of Agriculture* University Stn	Laramie	WY	82071-0000
	Fax: 307 766-3379			
307 766-6416	*College of Law* PO Box 3035 University Stn	Laramie	WY	82071-3035
	Fax: 307 766-4044 Library			
307 766-2070	*Libraries*	Laramie	WY	82071-0000
	Fax: 307 766-3062			
307 766-6120	*School of Pharmacy* PO Box 3375	Laramie	WY	82071-3375
	Fax: 307 766-3611			
202 225-3536	**Unsoeld Jolene (Rep - D - Washington)**			
	1508 Longworth Bldg	Washington	DC	20515-0001
	Fax: Unlisted			
614 486-9621	**Upper Arlington Public Library** 2800 Tremont Rd	Upper Arlington	OH	43221-3199
	Fax: 614 486-4530			
319 425-3311	**Upper Iowa University** PO Box 1857	Fayette	IA	52142-1861
	Fax: 319 425-5271			
201 266-7000	**Upsala College** 345 Prospect St	East Orange	NJ	07019-0000
	Fax: 201 678-8837			
903 843-3083	**Upshur County** Hwy 154 & Simpson St	Gilmer	TX	75644-2198
	Fax: 903 843-5492			
304 472-1068	**Upshur County** Main St	Buckhannon	WV	26201-0000
404 647-7012	**Upson County** PO Box 889	Thomaston	GA	30286-0889
	Fax: 404 647-7030			
915 693-2861	**Upton County** PO Box 465	Rankin	TX	79778-0465
	Fax: 915 693-2243			
202 225-3761	**Upton Frederick S (Rep - R - Michigan)**			
	1713 Longworth Bldg	Washington	DC	20515-0001
	Fax: 202 225-4986			
202 833-7200	**Urban Institute** 2100 M St NW	Washington	DC	20037-1297
	Fax: 202 223-3043			
202 624-7000	**Urban Land Institute** 625 Indiana Ave NW Suite 400	Washington	DC	20004-2930
	Fax: 202 624-7140			
202 366-4043	**Urban Mass Transportation Administration (US Dept of Transportation)**			
	400 7th St SW Rm 9314	Washington	DC	20590-0001
	Fax: 202 466-3808			
	Urban Mass Transportation Administration			
202 366-1666	*Private Sector Initiatives* 400 7th St SW Rm 9300	Washington	DC	20590-0001
	Fax: 202 366-7116			
202 366-4980	*Procurement & Third Party Contract Review*			
	400 7th St SW Rm 7405	Washington	DC	20590-0001
	Fax: 202 366-7164			
202 366-4052	*Technical Assistance* 400 7th St SW Rm 6431	Washington	DC	20590-0001
	Fax: 202 366-3765			
617 494-2055	*Region 1* 55 Broadway Rm 921	Cambridge	MA	02142-1003
	Fax: 617 494-2865			
212 264-8162	*Region 2* 26 Federal Plaza 29th Fl	New York	NY	10278-0022
	Fax: 212 264-8973			
215 597-8098	*Region 3* 841 Chestnut St Rm 714	Philadelphia	PA	19107-4414
	Fax: 215 597-2767			
404 347-3948	*Region 4* 1720 Peachtree Rd NW Suite 400	Atlanta	GA	30309-2471
	Fax: 404 347-7849			
312 353-2789	*Region 5* 55 E Monroe St Suite 1415	Chicago	IL	60603-5704
	Fax: 312 886-0351			
817 334-3787	*Region 6* 819 Taylor St Rm 9A32	Fort Worth	TX	76102-6160
	Fax: 817 334-3129			
816 926-5053	*Region 7* 6301 Rockhill Rd Suite 303	Kansas City	MO	64131-1117
	Fax: 816 926-7388			
303 844-3242	*Region 8* 1961 Stout St Rm 520	Denver	CO	80294-0101
	Fax: 303 844-4217			
415 744-3133	*Region 9* 211 Main St Suite 1160	San Francisco	CA	94105-1971
	Fax: Unlisted			
206 442-4210	*Region 10* 915 2nd Ave Rm 3142	Seattle	WA	98174-1012
	Fax: 206 442-4999			
513 652-1301	**Urbana University** 575 College Way	Urbana	OH	43078-2091
215 489-4111	**Ursinus College** Main St	Collegeville	PA	19426-0000
	Fax: 215 489-0627			
216 449-4200	**Ursuline College** 2550 Lander Rd	Cleveland	OH	44124-4399
	Fax: 216 449-3180 Library			
	Uruguay: Oriental Republic of Uruguay			
202 331-1313	*Embassy* 1918 F St NW	Washington	DC	20006-4397
	Fax: 202 331-8142			
212 752-8240	*Mission to the UN* 747 3rd Ave 37th Fl	New York	NY	10017-2828
	Fax: 212 593-0935			
202 485-2457	**US Advisory Commission on Public Diplomacy**			
	301 4th St SW Rm 600	Washington	DC	20547-0001
	Fax: 202 485-2489			
719 472-1818	**US Air Force Academy**	Colorado Springs	CO	80840-5651
	Fax: 719 472-3494			
202 647-8677	**US Arms Control & Disarmament Agency** 320 21st St NW	Washington	DC	20451-0001
	Fax: 202 647-6721			
218 727-2497	**US Army Corp of Engineers Canal Park Marine Museum & Visitors Center**			
	600 Lake Ave S	Duluth	MN	55802-2353
	Fax: 218 720-5270			
202 332-3532	**US Assn of Former Members of Congress**			
	1755 Massachusetts Ave NW Suite 412	Washington	DC	20036-2102
	Fax: Unlisted			
	US Bankruptcy Courts			
205 223-7250	*Alabama Middle* PO Box 1248	Montgomery	AL	36102-1248
	Fax: 205 223-7622			
205 731-1614	*Alabama Northern* 500 22nd St S Rm 101	Birmingham	AL	35233-3115
	Fax: 205 731-0104			
205 690-2391	*Alabama Southern* 201 Saint Louis St	Mobile	AL	36602-2919
	Fax: 205 694-4286			
907 271-2655	*Alaska* 605 W 4th Ave Suite 138	Anchorage	AK	99501-2231
	Fax: 907 271-2645			
602 379-6965	*Arizona* 230 N 1st Ave Rm 5000	Phoenix	AZ	85025-0001
	Fax: Unlisted			
501 378-6357	*Arkansas* 600 W Capitol Ave Rm 101	Little Rock	AR	72201-3320
213 894-4696	*California Central* 312 N Spring St 9th Fl	Los Angeles	CA	90012-4701
	Fax: Unlisted			
916 551-2615	*California Eastern* 650 Capitol Mall Rm 8308	Sacramento	CA	95814-4706
	Fax: Unlisted			
415 556-2250	*California Northern* 450 Golden Gate Ave Rm 15217	San Francisco	CA	94102-3400
	Fax: 415 556-3293			
619 557-5620	*California Southern* 940 Front St Rm 5N26	San Diego	CA	92189-0010
303 844-4045	*Colorado* 1845 Sherman St Suite 400	Denver	CO	80203-1167
203 240-3677	*Connecticut* 450 Main St Suite 717	Hartford	CT	06103-3002
	Fax: 203 244-3211			
302 573-6174	*Delaware* 844 N King St Federal Bldg Rm 6007	Wilmington	DE	19801-0000
202 535-3042	*District of Columbia*			
	3rd St & Constitution Ave NW Rm 2400	Washington	DC	20001-0000
	Fax: 202 535-3513			
813 225-7064	*Florida Middle* 4921 Memorial Hwy Suite 200	Tampa	FL	33634-7506
	Fax: 813 225-7097			
904 681-7500	*Florida Northern* 227 N Bronough St Suite 3120	Tallahassee	FL	32301-1329
	Fax: 904 681-7522			
305 536-5216	*Florida Southern* 51 SW 1st Ave Rm 629	Miami	FL	33130-1625
	Fax: 305 536-4728			
912 752-3506	*Georgia Middle* 475 Mulberry St Rm 126	Macon	GA	31201-7907
	Fax: 912 752-8157			
404 331-6886	*Georgia Northern* 75 Spring St SW Rm 1340	Atlanta	GA	30303-0000
912 944-4100	*Georgia Southern* PO Box 8347	Savannah	GA	31412-8347
808 541-1791	*Hawaii* PO Box 50121	Honolulu	HI	96850-0000
208 334-1074	*Idaho* PO Box 2600	Boise	ID	83701-2600
	Fax: 208 334-9362			
217 492-4551	*Illinois Central* PO Box 2438	Springfield	IL	62705-2438
312 435-5587	*Illinois Northern* 219 S Dearborn St Rm 2268	Chicago	IL	60604-0000
	Fax: Unlisted			
219 236-8247	*Indiana Northern* 204 S Main St Rm 224	South Bend	IN	46601-0000
	Fax: 219 226-8861			
317 226-6710	*Indiana Southern* 46 E Ohio St Rm 123	Indianapolis	IN	46204-1919
	Fax: Unlisted			
319 362-9696	*Iowa Northern* PO Box 74890	Cedar Rapids	IA	52407-4890
	Fax: 319 362-9933			
515 284-6230	*Iowa Southern* 123 E Walnut St Rm 318	Des Moines	IA	50309-2022
	Fax: 515 284-6404			
316 269-6486	*Kansas* 401 N Market St Rm 167	Wichita	KS	67202-2000
606 233-2608	*Kentucky Eastern* Merrill Lynch Bldg Suite 200	Lexington	KY	40507-0000
502 582-5145	*Kentucky Western*			
	601 W Broadway US Courthouse Rm 414	Louisville	KY	40202-0000
	Fax: 502 582-6136			
504 589-6506	*Louisiana Eastern* 500 Camp St Rm 104	New Orleans	LA	70130-3313
	Fax: 504 589-2076			
504 389-0211	*Louisiana Middle* 412 N 4th St Suite 301	Baton Rouge	LA	70802-5523
	Fax: 504 389-0410			
318 226-5267	*Louisiana Western* 500 Fannin St Rm 4A18	Shreveport	LA	71101-3053
207 780-3357	*Maine* 156 Federal St Rm 106	Portland	ME	04101-4152
	Fax: 207 833-3679			
301 962-2688	*Maryland* 101 W Lombard St Rm 919	Baltimore	MD	21201-2611
617 565-6080	*Massachusetts* 10 Causeway St Federal Bldg 11th Fl	Boston	MA	02222-0000
313 226-7064	*Michigan Eastern*			
	231 W Lafayette Blvd US Courthouse Rm 1002	Detroit	MI	48226-2799
616 456-2231	*Michigan Western* 110 Michigan St NW Rm 792	Grand Rapids	MI	49503-2313
612 348-1855	*Minnesota* 330 2nd Ave S Towle Bldg Suite 600	Minneapolis	MN	55401-0000
	Fax: Unlisted			
601 369-2596	*Mississippi Northern* PO Box 867	Aberdeen	MS	39730-0867
601 965-5301	*Mississippi Southern* PO Box 2448	Jackson	MS	39225-2448
	Fax: 601 965-4992			
314 539-2222	*Missouri Eastern* 1114 Market St 7th Fl	Saint Louis	MO	63101-2043
	Fax: 314 539-2063			
406 782-3354	*Montana* 400 N Main St Federal Bldg Rm 273	Butte	MT	59701-0000
402 221-4687	*Nebraska* PO Box 428 Downtown Stn	Omaha	NE	68101-0428
702 388-6257	*Nevada* 300 Las Vegas Blvd S Suite 209	Las Vegas	NV	89101-5814
603 666-7533	*New Hampshire* 275 Chestnut St Rm 715	Manchester	NH	03101-2413
	Fax: 603 666-7408			
609 989-2126	*New Jersey* 402 E State St Rm 234	Trenton	NJ	08608-1507
505 766-2051	*New Mexico* 500 Gold Ave SW 9th Fl	Albuquerque	NM	87102-3152
516 832-8800	*New York Eastern* 1635 Privado Rd	Westbury	NY	11590-5241
315 793-8101	*New York Northern* 10 Broad St US Courthouse Rm 230	Utica	NY	13501-0000
	Fax: 315 793-8128			
212 791-2247	*New York Southern*			
	1 Bowling Green US Customs House Rm 614	New York	NY	10004-0000
	Fax: Unlisted			
716 846-4130	*New York Western* 68 Court St Rm 310	Buffalo	NY	14202-3405
919 237-0440	*North Carolina Eastern* PO Box 2807	Wilson	NC	27894-2807
	Fax: Unlisted			
919 333-5647	*North Carolina Middle* 202 S Elm St	Greensboro	NC	27401-2605
	Fax: Unlisted			
704 371-6103	*North Carolina Western* 401 W Trade St Rm 101	Charlotte	NC	28202-1619

701 239-5377 *North Dakota* PO Box 870 ... Fargo ND 58107-0870
Fax: 701 783-5270

216 522-4373 *Ohio Northern* 201 Superior Ave E US Courthouse Rm 419 . Cleveland OH 44114-0000
Fax: 216 522-2140

614 469-2087 *Ohio Southern* 85 Marconi Blvd Rm 124 ... Columbus OH 43215-2823

918 758-0127 *Oklahoma Eastern* 4th & Grand Sts ... Okmulgee OK 74447-0000
Fax: 918 756-9248

918 581-7181 *Oklahoma Northern* 111 W 5th St ... Tulsa OK 74103-4253

405 231-5143 *Oklahoma Western* 201 Dean A Mcgee Ave ... Oklahoma City OK 73102-3416
Fax: Unlisted

503 326-2231 *Oregon* 1001 SW 5th Ave 9th Fl ... Portland OR 97204-1144
Fax: Unlisted

215 597-1644 *Pennsylvania Eastern* 601 Market St Rm 3726 ... Philadelphia PA 19106-1723

717 826-6450 *Pennsylvania Middle*
197 S Main St Federal Bldg Rm 217 ... Wilkes-Barre PA 18701-0000

412 644-2700 *Pennsylvania Western* 1000 Liberty Ave 16th Fl ... Pittsburgh PA 15222-4002
Fax: 412 722-6512

809 766-5122 *Puerto Rico* Chardon Ave Federal Bldg Rm 459 ... Hato Rey PR 00918-0000

401 528-4477 *Rhode Island* 380 Westminster Mall 6th Fl ... Providence RI 02903-3239
Fax: 401 528-4689

803 765-5211 *South Carolina* PO Box 1448 ... Columbia SC 29202-1448

605 330-4541 *South Dakota* 400 S Phillips Ave ... Sioux Falls SD 57102-0961

615 673-4525 *Tennessee Eastern* Plaza Tower Suite 1501 ... Knoxville TN 37929-0001

615 736-5590 *Tennessee Middle* 701 Broadway Rm 207 ... Nashville TN 37203-3945
Fax: 615 736-2305

901 544-3202 *Tennessee Western* 969 Madison Ave 9th Fl ... Memphis TN 38104-2139
Fax: 901 521-2290

903 592-1212 *Texas Eastern* 211 W Ferguson St 4th Fl ... Tyler TX 75702-7222

214 767-0814 *Texas Northern* 1100 Commerce St Rm 14A7 ... Dallas TX 75242-1003

713 226-4115 *Texas Southern* 515 Rusk St Suite 4603 ... Houston TX 77002-2603

512 229-6720 *Texas Western* 615 E Houston St Rm 115 ... San Antonio TX 78205-2040

801 524-5157 *Utah* 350 S Main St Rm 361 ... Salt Lake City UT 84101-2106

802 773-0219 *Vermont* 67 Merchants Row 2nd Fl ... Rutland VT 05701-5910
Fax: 802 773-0315

809 774-8310 *Virgin Islands* PO Box 720 ... Saint Thomas VI 00804-0720
Fax: 809 774-1293

804 771-2878 *Virginia Eastern* 1100 E Main St Rm 324 ... Richmond VA 23219-3538

703 982-6391 *Virginia Western* 210 Church Ave SW 2nd Fl ... Roanoke VA 24011-1522
Fax: 703 982-4373

509 353-2404 *Washington Eastern* PO Box 2164 ... Spokane WA 99210-2164

206 442-7545 *Washington Western* 1200 6th Ave Parkplace Bldg Suite 315 .. Seattle WA 98101-0000
Fax: Unlisted

304 233-1655 *West Virginia Northern* 12th & Chapline Sts Rm 300 ... Wheeling WV 26003-0000

304 347-5114 *West Virginia Southern*
500 Quarrier St Federal Bldg Rm 2201 ... Charleston WV 25301-0000
Fax: 304 347-5390

414 297-3293 *Wisconsin Eastern* 517 E Wisconsin Ave Rm 216 ... Milwaukee WI 53202-4504
Fax: 414 297-4040

608 264-5178 *Wisconsin Western* 120 N Henry St Rm 340 ... Madison WI 53703-2559
Fax: 608 264-5105

307 772-2191 *Wyoming* 2120 Capitol Ave Rm 6015 ... Cheyenne WY 82001-3647
Fax: 307 772-2778

202 647-9576 **US Bureau of Consular Affairs** 2201 C St NW Rm 6811 ... Washington DC 20520-4818
Fax: 202 647-0341

202 647-6600 **US Bureau of East Asian & Pacific Affairs**
2201 C St NW Rm 6205 ... Washington DC 20520-6310
Fax: 202 647-7350

202 647-9626 **US Bureau of European & Canadian Affairs**
2201 C St NW Rm 6228 ... Washington DC 20520-6211
Fax: 202 647-0967

202 647-9210 **US Bureau of Inter-American Affairs**
2201 C St NW Rm 6263 ... Washington DC 20520-0001
Fax: 202 647-0791

202 633-7257 **US Claims Court** 717 Madison Pl NW ... Washington DC 20005-1004

202 267-2229 **US Coast Guard** 2100 2nd St SW ... Washington DC 20593-0001

212 668-7886 *Atlantic Area* Governors Island Bldg 125 ... New York NY 10004-5000
Fax: 212 668-7766

215 271-4800 *Marine Safety Group* 1 Washington Ave ... Philadelphia PA 19147-4303
Fax: Unlisted

202 267-0972 *Office of Navigation & Waterways Services*
2100 2nd St SW Comandant G-NAB ... Washington DC 20593-0001
Fax: 202 267-4423

415 437-3151 *Pacific Area* Coast Guard Island ... Alameda CA 94501-5100

203 444-8294 *US Coast Guard Academy* 15 Mohegan Ave ... New London CT 06320-4195
Fax: 203 444-8288

202 293-7330 **US Conference of Mayors** 1620 I St NW ... Washington DC 20006-4073
Fax: 202 293-2352

212 354-4480 **US Council for International Business**
1212 Ave of the Americas 21st Fl ... New York NY 10036-1689
Fax: 212 575-0327

212 264-2814 **US Court of International Trade** 1 Federal Plaza ... New York NY 10007-0000
Fax: 212 264-1085

202 272-1448 **US Court of Military Appeals** 450 E St NW ... Washington DC 20442-0001
Fax: Unlisted

US Courts of Appeal

617 223-9057 *Circuit 1* JW McCormack Federal Bldg Rm 1606 ... Boston MA 02109-0000
Fax: 617 223-9056

212 791-0103 *Circuit 2* 40 Foley Sq Rm 1702 ... New York NY 10007-1502
Fax: 212 791-1091

215 597-2995 *Circuit 3* 601 Market St Rm 21400 ... Philadelphia PA 19106-1723
Fax: Unlisted

804 771-2213 *Circuit 4* 10th & Main Sts Rm 202 ... Richmond VA 23219-0000
Fax: 804 771-8017

504 589-6514 *Circuit 5* 600 Camp St Rm 102 ... New Orleans LA 70130-3479
Fax: 504 589-4834

513 684-2953 *Circuit 6* US POCH Bldg Rm 538 ... Cincinnati OH 45202-0000
Fax: Call company operator

312 435-5850 *Circuit 7* 219 S Dearborn St ... Chicago IL 60604-1702
Fax: Call company operator

314 539-3600 *Circuit 8* 1114 Market St Suite 511 ... Saint Louis MO 63101-2036
Fax: Unlisted

415 556-7340 *Circuit 9* PO Box 547 ... San Francisco CA 94101-0547
Fax: Unlisted

303 844-3157 *Circuit 10* 1929 Stout St 4th Fl ... Denver CO 80294-2900
Fax: Unlisted

404 331-6187 *Circuit 11* 56 Forsyth St NW ... Atlanta GA 30303-2205
Fax: 404 331-3785

202 633-6550 *Court of Appeals for the Federal Circuit*
717 Madison Pl NW Rm 401 ... Washington DC 20439-0001
Fax: 202 523-0072

202 535-3308 *District of Columbia Circuit*
333 Constitution Ave NW Rm 5423 ... Washington DC 20001-2801

202 535-3390 *Temporary Emergency Court of Appeals*
3rd St & Constitution Ave NW Rm 1130 ... Washington DC 20001-0000

202 566-5286 **US Customs Service** 1301 Constitution Ave NW Rm 3422 ... Washington DC 20229-0001
Fax: 202 566-9087

212 466-4444 *New York Region* 6 World Trade Ctr Rm 716 ... New York NY 10048-0206
Fax: 212 668-4533

312 353-4733 *North Central Region* 55 E Monroe St Suite 1501 ... Chicago IL 60603-5790
Fax: 312 886-4921

617 565-6300 *Northeast Region* 10 Causeway St Suite 801 ... Boston MA 02222-1047
Fax: 617 835-6277

213 491-7200 *Pacific Region* 1 World Trade Ctr ... Long Beach CA 90831-0002
Fax: 213 491-7341

504 589-6324 *South Central Region* 423 Canal St Rm 337 ... New Orleans LA 70130-2337
Fax: 504 589-2712

305 536-4661 *Southeast Region* 909 SE 1st Ave ... Miami FL 33131-3051
Fax: 305 536-5754

713 953-6843 *Southwest Region* 5850 San Felipe St Suite 500 ... Houston TX 77057-8003
Fax: 713 953-6853

202 447-2791 **US Dept of Agriculture** 14th St & Independence Ave SW ... Washington DC 20250-0001

202 377-2000 **US Dept of Commerce** 14th & Constitution Ave NW ... Washington DC 20230-0001
Fax: 202 377-2592

202 377-5491 **US Dept of Commerce Export Administration Office**
14th St & Constitution Ave NW Rm 3886C ... Washington DC 20230-0001
Fax: 202 377-2387

202 377-2867 **US Dept of Commerce International Trade Administration**
14th St & Constitution Ave NW Rm 3850 ... Washington DC 20230-0001
Fax: 202 377-5933

907 271-5041 *Anchorage* 222 W 7th Ave ... Anchorage AK 99513-7591
Fax: 907 271-5173

404 347-7000 *Atlanta* 1365 Peachtree St NE Suite 504 ... Atlanta GA 30309-3148
Fax: 404 347-0108

512 472-5059 *Austin* 816 Congress Ave Suite 1200 ... Austin TX 78701-2443
Fax: 512 320-9674

301 962-3560 *Baltimore* 40 S Gay St Rm 413 ... Baltimore MD 21202-4022
Fax: 301 962-7813

205 731-1331 *Birmingham* 2015 2nd Ave N Suite 302 ... Birmingham AL 35203-3723
Fax: 205 731-0076

208 334-2470 *Boise* 700 W State St 2nd Fl ... Boise ID 83720-0001
Fax: 208 334-2631

617 565-8563 *Boston* World Trade Ctr Suite 307 ... Boston MA 02210-2083
Fax: 617 565-8530

716 846-4191 *Buffalo* 111 W Huron St Rm 1312 ... Buffalo NY 14202-2386
Fax: 716 846-5290

304 347-5123 *Charleston* 500 Quarrier St ... Charleston WV 25301-2170
Fax: 304 347-5408

312 353-4450 *Chicago* 55 E Monroe St Rm 1406 ... Chicago IL 60603-5797
Fax: 312 886-8025

513 684-2944 *Cincinnati* 550 Main St Rm 9504 ... Cincinnati OH 45202-3251
Fax: 513 684-3200

216 522-4750 *Cleveland* 668 Euclid Ave Suite 600 ... Cleveland OH 44114-3058
Fax: 216 522-2235

803 765-5345 *Columbia* 1835 Assembly St Suite 172 ... Columbia SC 29201-2430
Fax: 803 253-3614

214 767-0542 *Dallas* 1100 Commerce St Rm 7-A5 ... Dallas TX 75242-1001
Fax: 214 767-8240

303 844-3246 *Denver* 1625 Broadway Suite 680 ... Denver CO 80202-4706
Fax: 303 844-5651

515 284-4222 *Des Moines* 210 Walnut St Rm 817 ... Des Moines IA 50309-2105
Fax: 515 284-4021

313 226-3650 *Detroit* 477 Michigan Ave McNamara Bldg Suite 1140 ... Detroit MI 48226-2518
Fax: 313 226-3657

616 456-2411 *Grand Rapids* 300 Monroe NW Rm 406A ... Grand Rapids MI 49503-2206
Fax: 616 456-2695

919 333-5345 *Greensboro* 324 W Market St Rm 203 ... Greensboro NC 27402-0000
Fax: 919 333-5158

203 240-3530 *Hartford* 450 Main St Rm 610-B ... Hartford CT 06103-3093
Fax: 203 240-3473

808 541-1782 *Honolulu* 300 Ala Moana Blvd Rm 4106 ... Honolulu HI 96850-0001
Fax: 808 541-3435

713 229-2578 *Houston* 515 Rusk Ave Rm 2625 ... Houston TX 77002-2652
Fax: 713 229-2203

317 226-6214 *Indianapolis* 1 N Capitol St Suite 520 ... Indianapolis IN 46204-2227
Fax: 317 226-6139

601 965-4388 *Jackson* 300 W Woodrow Wilson Dr Suite 328 ... Jackson MS 39213-7649
Fax: Unlisted

816 426-3142 *Kansas City* 601 E 12th St Rm 635 ... Kansas City MO 64106-2849
Fax: 816 426-3140

501 378-5794 *Little Rock* 320 W Capitol Ave Suite 811 ... Little Rock AR 72201-3526
Fax: 501 378-7380

213 209-7103 *Los Angeles* 11000 Wilshire Blvd Suite 9200 ... Los Angeles CA 90024-0000
Fax: 213 209-6711

502 582-5066 *Louisville* 601 W Broadway Rm 636-B ... Louisville KY 40202-2229
Fax: 502 582-6573

305 536-5267 *Miami* 51 SW 1st Ave Suite 224 ... Miami FL 33130-1617
Fax: 305 536-4765

414 297-3473 *Milwaukee* 517 E Wisconsin Ave Rm 606 ... Milwaukee WI 53202-4507
Fax: 414 297-3470

612 348-1638 *Minneapolis* 110 S 4th St Rm 108 ... Minneapolis MN 55401-2296
Fax: 612 348-1650

504 589-6546 *New Orleans* 2 Canal St Rm 432 ... New Orleans LA 70130-1267
Fax: 504 589-2337

212 264-0634 *New York* 26 Federal Plaza Rm 3718 ... New York NY 10278-0022
Fax: 212 264-1356

405 231-5302 *Oklahoma City* 6601 N Broadway Ext Suite 200 ... Oklahoma City OK 73116-8236
Fax: 405 841-5245

402 221-3665 *Omaha* 11133 'O' St ... Omaha NE 68137-2337
Fax: 402 221-3668

602 280-1371 *Phoenix* 230 N 1st Ave Rm 3412 ... Phoenix AZ 85025-0001
Fax: 602 261-4324

412 644-2850 *Pittsburgh* 1000 Liberty Ave Rm 2002 ... Pittsburgh PA 15222-4004
Fax: 412 644-4875

503 326-3001 *Portland* 121 SW Salmon St 1 World Trade Ctr Suite 242 ... Portland OR 97204-2896
Fax: 503 326-6351

702 784-5203 *Reno* 1755 E Plumb Ln Suite 152 ... Reno NV 89502-3680
Fax: 702 784-5343

804 771-2246 *Richmond* 400 N 8th St Suite 8010 ... Richmond VA 23240-1001
Fax: 804 771-2390

815 987-8123 *Rockford* 515 N Court St ... Rockford IL 61103-6807
Fax: 815 987-8122

314 425-3302 *Saint Louis* 7911 Forsyth Blvd Suite 610 ... Saint Louis MO 63105-3880
Fax: 314 425-3381

801 524-5116 *Salt Lake City* 324 S State St Suite 105 ... Salt Lake City UT 84111-0000
Fax: 801 524-5886

415 556-5860 *San Francisco* 450 Golden Gate Ave ... San Francisco CA 94102-3453
Fax: 415 556-2121

809 766-5555 *San Juan* Federal Bldg Rm G-55 ... Hato Rey PR 00918-0000

714 836-2461 *Santa Ana* 116-A W 4th St Suite 1 ... Santa Ana CA 92701-4626
Fax: 714 836-2332

Phone	Name / Address	City	State	ZIP
505 827-0307	*Santa Fe* 1100 St Francis Dr	Santa Fe	NM	87503-0000
	Fax: 505 827-0263			
206 442-5616	*Seattle* 3131 Elliott Ave Suite 290	Seattle	WA	98121-1047
	Fax: 206 442-7253			
609 989-2100	*Trenton* 3131 Princeton Pike Bldg 6 Suite 100	Trenton	NJ	08648-2207
	Fax: 609 989-2395			
918 581-7650	*Tulsa* 440 S Houston St Rm 505	Tulsa	OK	74127-8913
	Fax: 918 581-2844			
316 269-6160	*Wichita* 727 N Waco River Park Pl Suite 580	Wichita	KS	67203-3956
	Fax: 316 262-5652			
202 545-6700	**US Dept of Defense** Pentagon	Washington	DC	20310-0001
202 401-3000	**US Dept of Education** 400 Maryland Ave SW	Washington	DC	20202-0001
	Fax: 202 732-3130			
617 223-9317	*Region 1* JW McCormack Post Office Bldg Rm 536	Boston	MA	02109-0000
	Fax: 617 223-9324			
212 264-7005	*Region 2* 26 Federal Plaza Rm 36-120	New York	NY	10278-0004
	Fax: 212 264-4427			
215 596-1001	*Region 3* 3535 Market St	Philadelphia	PA	19104-3398
	Fax: 215 596-1094			
404 331-2502	*Region 4* 101 Marietta Tower Suite 2221	Atlanta	GA	30323-0001
	Fax: 404 331-5382			
312 353-5215	*Region 5* 401 S State St Suite 700-A	Chicago	IL	60605-1299
	Fax: 312 353-5147			
214 767-3626	*Region 6* 1200 Main Tower Bldg Rm 2125	Dallas	TX	75202-0000
	Fax: 214 767-3634			
816 891-7972	*Region 7* PO Box 901381	Kansas City	MO	64190-1381
	Fax: 816 374-6442			
303 844-3862	*Region 8* 1961 Stout St Rm 380	Denver	CO	80294-0101
	Fax: 303 844-2524			
415 556-4920	*Region 9* 50 United Nations Plaza Rm 205	San Francisco	CA	94102-4987
	Fax: 415 556-7242			
206 442-0460	*Region 10* 915 2nd Ave Rm 3362	Seattle	WA	98174-1001
	Fax: 206 442-1232			
202 586-5000	**US Dept of Energy** 1000 Independence Ave SW	Washington	DC	20585-0001
202 245-7000	**US Dept of Health & Human Services** 200 Independence Ave SW	Washington	DC	20201-0001
	Fax: 202 245-6277			
617 565-1072	*Region 1* JFK Federal Bldg Suite 1512	Boston	MA	02203-0000
	Fax: 617 565-1084			
212 264-4600	*Region 2* 26 Federal Plaza Rm 3835	New York	NY	10278-0004
	Fax: 212 264-2162			
215 596-6492	*Region 3* 3535 Market St Rm 11480	Philadelphia	PA	19104-3309
	Fax: 215 596-0328			
404 331-6956	*Region 4* 101 Marietta Tower 11th Fl	Atlanta	GA	30323-0001
	Fax: 404 841-5490			
312 353-5160	*Region 5* 105 W Adams St 23rd Fl	Chicago	IL	60603-4102
	Fax: 312 353-1194			
214 767-3301	*Region 6* 1200 Main Tower Bldg Rm 1100	Dallas	TX	75202-0000
	Fax: 903 729-4537			
816 426-2821	*Region 7* 601 E 12th St Rm 210	Kansas City	MO	64106-2808
	Fax: 816 867-5299			
303 844-3373	*Region 8* 1961 Stout St Rm 1185	Denver	CO	80294-0101
	Fax: 303 564-2394			
415 556-6746	*Region 9* 50 United Nations Plaza Rm 431	San Francisco	CA	94102-4923
	Fax: 415 556-4161			
206 442-0420	*Region 10* 2201 6th Ave	Seattle	WA	98121-1832
	Fax: 206 442-4333			
202 708-1112	**US Dept of Housing & Urban Development** 451 7th St SW	Washington	DC	20410-0001
	Fax: 202 755-0525			
617 565-5165	*Region 1* 10 Causeway St 3rd Fl	Boston	MA	02222-1047
	Fax: 617 565-5257			
212 264-8068	*Region 2* 26 Federal Plaza Rm 3541	New York	NY	10278-0004
	Fax: 212 264-0246			
215 597-2560	*Region 3* 105 S 7th St Liberty Square Bldg	Philadelphia	PA	19106-0000
	Fax: 215 597-9627			
404 331-5136	*Region 4* 75 Spring St SW Rm 600	Atlanta	GA	30303-3309
	Fax: 404 331-0845			
312 353-5680	*Region 5* 626 W Jackson Blvd Rm 718	Chicago	IL	60606-5601
	Fax: 312 353-0157			
817 885-5531	*Region 6* 1600 Throckmorton St	Fort Worth	TX	76102-6645
	Fax: 817 728-5629			
816 374-6432	*Region 7* 1103 Grand Ave Rm 1200	Kansas City	MO	64106-2419
	Fax: 816 374-6590			
303 844-4061	*Region 8* 1405 Curtis St	Denver	CO	80202-2349
415 556-4752	*Region 9* 450 Golden Gate Ave	San Francisco	CA	94102-3400
	Fax: 415 556-1319			
206 442-5414	*Region 10* 1321 2nd Ave Arcade Plaza Bldg 10 S	Seattle	WA	98101-0000
	Fax: 206 442-4405			
202 633-2000	**US Dept of Justice** 10th St & Constitution Ave NW	Washington	DC	20530-0001
	Fax: 202 633-4371 Communications			
202 523-7316	**US Dept of Labor** 200 Constitution Ave NW	Washington	DC	20210-0001
	Fax: 202 523-6194			
202 647-4000	**US Dept of State** 2201 C St NW	Washington	DC	20520-0001
	Fax: Unlisted			
202 697-6061	**US Dept of the Air Force** Pentagon Rm 4D-922	Washington	DC	20330-0001
	Fax: 202 695-5853			
719 472-1818	*Air Force Academy*	Colorado Springs	CO	80840-0000
	Fax: 719 472-3494			
202 697-2302	*Manpower Reserve Affairs Installation & Environment* Pentagon Rm 4E-1020	Washington	DC	20330-0001
	Fax: 202 697-1265			
202 697-8675	*Office of Space Systems* Pentagon Rm 4C-1052	Washington	DC	20330-0001
202 697-6061	*Public Affairs* Pentagon Rm 4D-922	Washington	DC	20330-0001
	Fax: 202 695-5853			
202 697-1683	**US Dept of the Army** Pentagon SAPA-CR Rm 2E-631	Washington	DC	20310-0001
	Fax: 202 693-7380 PR			
202 697-8986	*Civil Works* Pentagon Rm 2E-570	Washington	DC	20310-0001
	Fax: 202 697-3366			
202 695-5135	*Public Affairs* Pentagon Rm 2E-636	Washington	DC	20310-0001
	Fax: 202 697-2159			
202 695-6153	*Research Development & Acquisition* Pentagon Rm 2E-672	Washington	DC	20310-0001
	Fax: 202 697-4003			
914 938-4011	*US Military Academy*	West Point	NY	10996-0000
	Fax: 914 938-3828			
202 343-1100	**US Dept of the Interior** 1849 C St NW	Washington	DC	20240-0001
	Fax: 202 343-8950			
202 695-0965	**US Dept of the Navy** Pentagon Rm 2E-335	Washington	DC	20350-0001
	Fax: 202 695-3478			
202 697-7391	*Information* Pentagon Rm 2E-340	Washington	DC	20350-0001
	Fax: 202 695-5318			
301 267-6100	*Naval Academy*	Annapolis	MD	21402-9998
	Fax: 301 281-3734 Mail Rm			
202 695-6315	*Research Engineering & Systems* Pentagon Rm 4E-732	Washington	DC	20350-0001
	Fax: 202 697-0172			

Phone	Name / Address	City	State	ZIP
202 566-2000	**US Dept of the Treasury** 1500 Pennsylvania Ave NW	Washington	DC	20005-1007
	Fax: 202 566-8066			
202 366-4000	**US Dept of Transportation** 400 7th St SW	Washington	DC	20590-0001
202 233-4010	**US Dept of Veterans Affairs** 810 Vermont Ave NW	Washington	DC	20420-0001
	Fax: 202 233-2807			
	US District Courts			
205 223-7308	*Alabama Middle* 15 Lee St Rm 206	Montgomery	AL	36104-4055
	Fax: 205 223-7114			
205 731-1701	*Alabama Northern* 1729 5th Ave N	Birmingham	AL	35203-2000
	Fax: 205 731-0742			
205 690-2371	*Alabama Southern* 113 Saint Joseph St	Mobile	AL	36602-3621
	Fax: Unlisted			
907 271-5568	*Alaska* 222 W 7th Ave Box 4 Rm 261	Anchorage	AK	99513-0000
	Fax: Unlisted			
907 452-3163	*Alaska* 101 12th Ave	Fairbanks	AK	99701-6283
	Fax: Unlisted			
907 586-7458	*Alaska* PO Box 020349	Juneau	AK	99802-0349
	Fax: Unlisted			
907 225-3195	*Alaska* 415 Main St Rm 400	Ketchikan	AK	99901-6399
	Fax: Unlisted			
907 443-5216	*Alaska* PO Box 100	Nome	AK	99762-0100
	Fax: 907 443-2192			
602 379-3341	*Arizona* 230 N 1st Ave US Courthouse Rm 1400	Phoenix	AZ	85025-0001
	Fax: 602 260-3076			
501 972-4610	*Arkansas Eastern* 615 S Main St	Jonesboro	AR	72401-2827
	Fax: 501 972-4612			
501 378-5353	*Arkansas Eastern* 600 W Capitol Ave Rm 402	Little Rock	AR	72201-3325
	Fax: 501 378-6096			
501 536-1190	*Arkansas Eastern* 100 E 8th Ave	Pine Bluff	AR	71601-5037
	Fax: 501 536-6330			
501 862-1202	*Arkansas Western* 101 S Jackson St Rm 205	El Dorado	AR	71731-1566
501 521-6980	*Arkansas Western* 35 E Mountain St Federal Bldg Rm 523	Fayetteville	AR	72701-0000
	Fax: 501 575-0774			
501 783-6833	*Arkansas Western* PO Box 1523	Fort Smith	AR	72902-1523
	Fax: 501 783-6308			
501 623-6411	*Arkansas Western* PO Box I	Hot Springs National Pk	AR	71902-0000
501 773-3381	*Arkansas Western* PO Box 2746	Texarkana	AR	75504-2746
213 894-0289	*California Central* 312 N Spring St	Los Angeles	CA	90012-4701
	Fax: 213 798-6860			
209 487-5757	*California Eastern* 1130 'O' St	Fresno	CA	93721-2201
	Fax: 209 487-5626			
916 551-2615	*California Eastern* 650 Capitol Mall 2nd Fl	Sacramento	CA	95814-4708
	Fax: Unlisted			
415 556-3031	*California Northern* PO Box 36060	San Francisco	CA	94102-0000
	Fax: 415 556-6147			
408 291-7783	*California Northern* 280 S 1st St Rm 4050	San Jose	CA	95113-3011
619 557-5600	*California Southern* 940 Front St Rm 1N20	San Diego	CA	92189-0010
	Fax: 619 895-6684			
303 844-3433	*Colorado* 1929 Stout St Rm C145	Denver	CO	80294-2900
203 579-5861	*Connecticut* 915 Lafayette Blvd	Bridgeport	CT	06604-4706
	Fax: 203 579-5867			
203 240-3200	*Connecticut* 450 Main St	Hartford	CT	06103-3002
	Fax: 203 244-3211			
203 773-2140	*Connecticut* 141 Church St Rm 214	New Haven	CT	06510-2030
	Fax: 203 773-2334			
302 573-6170	*Delaware* 844 N King St Federal Bldg Rm 4209	Wilmington	DE	19801-3519
	Fax: 302 573-6451			
202 535-3594	*District of Columbia* 3rd St & Constitution Ave NW Rm 1834	Washington	DC	20001-0000
	Fax: 202 426-5079			
904 791-2854	*Florida Middle* 311 W Monroe St Suite 110	Jacksonville	FL	32202-4221
	Fax: 904 791-2245			
407 648-6366	*Florida Middle* 80 N Hughey Ave Rm 218	Orlando	FL	32801-2224
	Fax: 407 648-6370			
813 228-2709	*Florida Middle* 611 N Florida Ave	Tampa	FL	33602-4520
	Fax: 813 228-2543			
904 435-8440	*Florida Northern* 100 N Palafox St Rm 129	Pensacola	FL	32501-4858
	Fax: 904 433-5972			
904 681-7165	*Florida Northern* 110 E Park Ave Rm 122	Tallahassee	FL	32301-7726
	Fax: 904 681-7176			
305 527-7075	*Florida Southern* 299 E Broward Blvd	Fort Lauderdale	FL	33301-1901
	Fax: Unlisted			
305 536-4548	*Florida Southern* 301 N Miami Ave Rm 150	Miami	FL	33128-7702
912 430-8432	*Georgia Middle* PO Box 1906	Albany	GA	31702-1906
404 649-7816	*Georgia Middle* 120 12th St	Columbus	GA	31901-2423
912 752-3497	*Georgia Middle* 475 Mulberry St Rm 216	Macon	GA	31202-0000
	Fax: 912 752-3496			
912 242-3616	*Georgia Middle* 401 N Patterson St	Valdosta	GA	31603-0000
404 331-0414	*Georgia Northern* 75 Spring St SW US Courthouse Rm 2211	Atlanta	GA	30335-0001
404 534-5954	*Georgia Northern* 26 Washington St SE Rm 201	Gainesville	GA	30501-0000
404 253-8847	*Georgia Northern* PO Box 939	Newnan	GA	30264-0939
404 291-5629	*Georgia Northern* Federal Bldg Rm 304	Rome	GA	30161-0000
404 722-2074	*Georgia Southern* 500 E Ford St	Augusta	GA	30901-2358
	Fax: Unlisted			
912 265-1758	*Georgia Southern* PO Box 1636	Brunswick	GA	31521-1636
	Fax: 912 265-1594			
912 944-4281	*Georgia Southern* PO Box 8286	Savannah	GA	31412-8286
	Fax: 912 944-4324			
808 541-1300	*Hawaii* PO Box 50129	Honolulu	HI	96850-0001
	Fax: 808 541-1303			
208 334-1361	*Idaho* 550 W Fort St	Boise	ID	83724-0001
	Fax: 208 334-9215			
217 431-4805	*Illinois Central* 201 N Vermilon St	Danville	IL	61832-0000
	Fax: 217 431-4819			
309 671-7117	*Illinois Central* 100 NE Monroe St Rm 174	Peoria	IL	61602-1003
	Fax: Unlisted			
309 793-5778	*Illinois Central* 211 19th St Rm 40	Rock Island	IL	61201-0000
	Fax: 309 793-5878			
217 492-4020	*Illinois Central* 600 E Monroe St Rm 221	Springfield	IL	62701-0000
	Fax: Unlisted			
312 435-5670	*Illinois Northern* 219 S Dearborn St Rm 2050	Chicago	IL	60604-1801
	Fax: Unlisted			
815 987-4354	*Illinois Northern* 211 S Court St	Rockford	IL	61101-1219
	Fax: 815 987-4291			
618 463-6402	*Illinois Southern* 501 Belle St	Alton	IL	62002-6169
	Fax: Unlisted			
618 438-0671	*Illinois Southern* 301 W Main St	Benton	IL	62812-1362
	Fax: Unlisted			
618 482-9371	*Illinois Southern* PO Box 249	East Saint Louis	IL	62202-0249
	Fax: Unlisted			
219 424-7360	*Indiana Northern* 1300 S Harrison St Rm 1108	Fort Wayne	IN	46802-3435
	Fax: 219 422-5474			
219 937-5235	*Indiana Northern* 507 State St	Hammond	IN	46320-1529
	Fax: Unlisted			
317 742-0512	*Indiana Northern* 232 N 4th St	Lafayette	IN	47902-0000
	Fax: 317 742-8471			

219 236-8260 *Indiana Northern* 204 S Main St Rm 102 .... South Bend IN 46601-2119
Fax: 219 236-8861
812 465-6426 *Indiana Southern* 101 NW 7 St Room 304 .... Evansville IN 47708-0000
317 226-6670 *Indiana Southern* 46 E Ohio St Rm 105 .... Indianapolis IN 46204-1919
Fax: 317 226-7902
812 948-5238 *Indiana Southern* 210 Federal Bldg .... New Albany IN 47150-0000
812 232-6236 *Indiana Southern* 30 N 7th St Rm 207 .... Terre Haute IN 47808-0000
319 364-2447 *Iowa Northern* 101 1st St SE Rm 313 .... Cedar Rapids IA 52401-1202
Fax: 319 399-2569
712 233-3203 *Iowa Northern* 320 6th St Rm 301 .... Sioux City IA 51101-1262
712 252-3336 *Iowa Southern* 6th & Broadway .... Council Bluffs IA 51502-0000
319 322-3223 *Iowa Southern* 131 E 4th St .... Davenport IA 52801-1516
Fax: 319 322-2962
515 284-6248 *Iowa Southern* 123 E Walnut St Rm 200 .... Des Moines IA 50309-0000
Fax: 515 284-6210
913 236-3719 *Kansas* 812 N 7th St Rm 151 .... Kansas City KS 66101-3056
913 295-2610 *Kansas* 444 SE Quincy .... Topeka KS 66683-3582
Fax: Unlisted
316 269-6491 *Kansas* 401 N Market St Rm 204 .... Wichita KS 67202-2000
Fax: Unlisted
606 329-2465 *Kentucky Eastern* 1405 Greenup Ave Rm 336 .... Ashland KY 41101-7542
Fax: 606 329-2012
606 292-3167 *Kentucky Eastern*
7th & Scott Sts US Post Office & Courthouse .... Covington KY 41011-0000
Fax: 606 292-8280
502 223-5225 *Kentucky Eastern* 330 W Broadway 3rd Fl .... Frankfort KY 40601-1935
Fax: Unlisted
606 233-2503 *Kentucky Eastern* 206 US Courthouse .... Lexington KY 40586-0000
Fax: 606 223-2470
606 864-5137 *Kentucky Eastern* PO Box 689 .... London KY 40741-0689
Fax: 606 864-6015
606 437-6160 *Kentucky Eastern* 102 Main St Federal Bldg Rm 203 .... Pikeville KY 41501-0000
Fax: Unlisted
502 781-1110 *Kentucky Western* 242 Main St Rm 213 .... Bowling Green KY 42101-0000
Fax: Unlisted
502 582-5156 *Kentucky Western*
601 W Broadway US Courthouse Rm 231 .... Louisville KY 40202-2227
Fax: 502 352-6302
502 683-0221 *Kentucky Western* 423 Frederica St Rm 210 .... Owensboro KY 42302-0000
Fax: 502 685-4601
502 443-1337 *Kentucky Western* 5th & Broadway Federal Bldg Rm 322 ..... Paducah KY 42001-0000
Fax: 502 442-1919
504 589-2946 *Louisiana Eastern* 500 Camp St Rm C151 .... New Orleans LA 70130-3313
504 389-0321 *Louisiana Middle* PO Box 2630 .... Baton Rouge LA 70821-2630
Fax: 504 389-0309
318 473-7415 *Louisiana Western* 515 Murray St Rm 105 .... Alexandria LA 71301-8055
Fax: 318 473-7345
318 264-6613 *Louisiana Western* 705 Jefferson St .... Lafayette LA 70501-0000
Fax: 318 264-6830
318 437-7246 *Louisiana Western* PO Box 393 .... Lake Charles LA 70602-0393
318 322-6740 *Louisiana Western* PO Box 3087 .... Monroe LA 71210-0000
318 226-5273 *Louisiana Western* 500 Fannin St Rm 106 .... Shreveport LA 71101-3022
Fax: 318 226-5234
207 945-0575 *Maine* 202 Harlow St .... Bangor ME 04401-4901
207 780-3357 *Maine* 156 Federal St Rm 106 .... Portland ME 04101-4152
301 962-2600 *Maryland* 101 W Lombard St Rm 409 .... Baltimore MD 21201-2606
Fax: 301 962-7574
617 223-9152 *Massachusetts* POCH Rm 707 .... Boston MA 02109-0000
Fax: 617 223-9096
413 785-0214 *Massachusetts* 1550 Main St .... Springfield MA 01103-1422
Fax: 413 785-0204
508 793-0552 *Massachusetts* 595 Main St Suite 506 .... Worcester MA 01601-2001
Fax: Unlisted
313 668-2380 *Michigan Eastern* 200 E Liberty St .... Ann Arbor MI 48107-0000
Fax: 313 668-2065
517 892-6571 *Michigan Eastern* PO Box X913 .... Bay City MI 48707-0000
Fax: 517 892-6071
313 226-7200 *Michigan Eastern*
231 W Lafayette Blvd US Courthouse Rm 133 .... Detroit MI 48226-0000
Fax: 313 226-6325
313 766-5020 *Michigan Eastern* 600 Church St Rm 140 .... Flint MI 48502-1214
Fax: Unlisted
616 456-2381 *Michigan Western* 110 Michigan St NW Rm 452 .... Grand Rapids MI 49503-2313
Fax: Unlisted
616 349-2922 *Michigan Western* 410 W Michigan Ave Rm B-35 .... Kalamazoo MI 49005-0000
Fax: Unlisted
906 226-2021 *Michigan Western* 229 Federal Bldg .... Marquette MI 49855-0000
Fax: 906 226-6735
218 720-5250 *Minnesota* 515 W 1st St Rm 417 .... Duluth MN 55802-1397
Fax: 218 720-5622
612 348-1821 *Minnesota* 110 S 4th St .... Minneapolis MN 55401-2216
612 290-3212 *Minnesota* 316 Robert St N .... Saint Paul MN 55101-1423
Fax: 612 290-3817
601 369-4952 *Mississippi* 301 W Commerce St Rm 310 .... Aberdeen MS 39730-0000
Fax: 601 369-9569
601 335-1651 *Mississippi* PO Box 190 .... Greenville MS 38702-0190
Fax: 601 332-4292
601 624-6208 *Mississippi Northern* PO Box 190 .... Clarksdale MS 38614-0190
601 234-1971 *Mississippi Northern* PO Box 727 .... Oxford MS 38655-0727
Fax: 601 236-5210
601 432-8623 *Mississippi Southern* PO Box 369 .... Biloxi MS 39533-0369
Fax: 601 436-9632
601 583-2433 *Mississippi Southern* PO Box 511 .... Hattiesburg MS 39401-0000
601 965-4439 *Mississippi Southern* 245 E Capitol St Suite 416 .... Jackson MS 39201-2414
Fax: 601 965-4935
601 693-2883 *Mississippi Southern* 2100 9th St .... Meridian MS 39301-5159
314 335-8538 *Missouri Eastern* 339 Broadway .... Cape Girardeau MO 63701-7344
314 539-6056 *Missouri Eastern* 1114 Market St Rm 302 .... Saint Louis MO 63101-2038
314 636-6124 *Missouri Western* 131 W High St .... Jefferson City MO 65101-1515
Fax: 314 636-3456
816 426-2811 *Missouri Western* 811 Grand Ave Rm 201 .... Kansas City MO 64106-1909
Fax: 816 426-2819
816 279-2428 *Missouri Western* 201 S 8th St Rm 224 .... Saint Joseph MO 64501-2240
Fax: 816 279-0177
417 865-3869 *Missouri Western*
222 N John Q Hammons Pkwy Suite 1400 .... Springfield MO 65806-2515
Fax: 417 865-7719
406 657-6366 *Montana* 316 N 26th St Rm 5405 .... Billings MT 59101-1362
Fax: 406 657-6581
406 782-0432 *Montana* Federal Bldg Rm 273 .... Butte MT 59701-0000
Fax: 406 782-8978
406 727-1922 *Montana* 215 1st Ave N .... Great Falls MT 59401-0000
Fax: 406 727-7648
406 449-5356 *Montana* PO Box 10015 Federal Bldg .... Helena MT 59626-0015
Fax: 406 449-5359

406 329-3598 *Montana* 200 E Broadway Ave Suite 252 .... Missoula MT 59802-0000
Fax: 406 329-3594
402 437-5225 *Nebraska* 100 Centennial Mall N Rm 593 .... Lincoln NE 68508-3892
Fax: 402 437-5226
402 221-4761 *Nebraska* 215 N 17th St Rm 9000 .... Omaha NE 68102-4910
Fax: 402 221-3160
702 388-6351 *Nevada* 300 Las Vegas Blvd S 4th Fl .... Las Vegas NV 89101-5812
Fax: 702 598-6470
702 784-5515 *Nevada* 300 Booth St Rm 5003 .... Reno NV 89509-0000
Fax: 702 470-5814
603 225-1423 *New Hampshire* 55 Pleasant St Rm 514 .... Concord NH 03301-3943
Fax: Unlisted
609 757-5021 *New Jersey*
401 Market St US Post Office & Courthouse Rm 304 .... Camden NJ 08101-0000
Fax: Unlisted
201 645-3730 *New Jersey* PO Box 419 .... Newark NJ 07102-0000
Fax: Unlisted
609 989-2065 *New Jersey* 402 E State St Rm 301 .... Trenton NJ 08605-0000
Fax: 609 989-2080
505 766-6527 *New Mexico* 500 Gold St Suite 10102 .... Albuquerque NM 87102-0000
Fax: 505 766-8448
505 525-2304 *New Mexico* 200 E Griggs Ave .... Las Cruces NM 88001-3523
Fax: 505 525-2267
505 988-6481 *New Mexico* S Federal Pl US Courthouse Bldrthouse Bldg .... Santa Fe NM 87501-0000
Fax: 505 988-6473
718 330-2105 *New York Eastern* 225 Cadman Plaza E .... Brooklyn NY 11201-1818
Fax: 718 330-7162
518 472-5651 *New York Northern* 445 Broadway Rm 442 .... Albany NY 12207-2926
607 773-2893 *New York Northern* 15 Henry St .... Binghamton NY 13901-2723
Fax: Unlisted
315 423-5549 *New York Northern* 100 S Clinton St .... Syracuse NY 13260-0001
Fax: Unlisted
315 793-8151 *New York Northern* 10 Broad St US Courthouse Rm 305 .... Utica NY 13501-1233
Fax: 315 793-8186
212 791-0108 *New York Southern* 40 Foley Sq Rm 18 .... New York NY 10007-1502
Fax: Unlisted
716 846-4211 *New York Western* 68 Court St Rm 304 .... Buffalo NY 14202-3405
Fax: 716 846-4850
716 263-6263 *New York Western* 100 State St Rm 282 .... Rochester NY 14614-1387
Fax: 716 263-3178
919 483-9509 *North Carolina Eastern* PO Box 43 .... Fayetteville NC 28302-0043
Fax: 919 483-4583
919 638-8534 *North Carolina Eastern* PO Box 1336 .... New Bern NC 28563-0000
Fax: 919 638-1529
919 856-4370 *North Carolina Eastern* PO Box 25670 .... Raleigh NC 27611-5670
Fax: 919 856-4160
919 343-4663 *North Carolina Eastern* PO Box 338 .... Wilmington NC 28402-0338
Fax: 919 343-3418
919 333-5347 *North Carolina Middle* PO Box V-1 .... Greensboro NC 27402-0000
Fax: Unlisted
704 259-0648 *North Carolina Western* 100 Otis St Rm 309 .... Asheville NC 28801-2611
704 371-6101 *North Carolina Western* 401 W Trade St Rm 204 .... Charlotte NC 28202-1619
704 873-7112 *North Carolina Western* PO Box 466 .... Statesville NC 28677-0466
701 250-4295 *North Dakota* 220 E Rosser Ave Rm 476 .... Bismarck ND 58501-3869
Fax: 701 250-4259
216 375-5407 *Ohio Northern* 2 S Main St .... Akron OH 44308-1810
Fax: Unlisted
216 522-4359 *Ohio Northern* 201 Superior Ave E Rm 100 .... Cleveland OH 44114-1203
Fax: 216 522-2140
419 259-6411 *Ohio Northern* 1716 Spielbusch Ave US Courthouse .... Toledo OH 43624-0000
Fax: Unlisted
216 746-1726 *Ohio Northern* 9 W Front St Room 329 .... Youngstown OH 44503-1431
Fax: 216 746-2027
513 684-2777 *Ohio Southern* 100 E 5th St Rm 324 .... Cincinnati OH 45202-0000
Fax: 513 684-3440
614 469-5442 *Ohio Southern* 85 Marconi Blvd Rm 260 .... Columbus OH 43215-2823
Fax: 614 943-5953
513 225-2897 *Ohio Southern* 200 W 2nd St Rm 712 .... Dayton OH 45402-1430
Fax: 513 225-2716
918 687-2471 *Oklahoma Eastern* 5th & Okmulgee Sts Rm 210 .... Muskogee OK 74401-0000
918 581-7796 *Oklahoma Northern* 333 W 4th St Rm 411 .... Tulsa OK 74103-3819
405 231-4792 *Oklahoma Western* 200 NW 4th St .... Oklahoma City OK 73102-3020
Fax: 405 231-5307
503 465-6423 *Oregon* 211 E 7th Ave Rm 102 .... Eugene OR 97401-2722
503 326-2202 *Oregon* 620 SW Main St Suite 503 .... Portland OR 97205-3029
Fax: 503 326-7788
215 597-7704 *Pennsylvania Eastern* 601 Market St Rm 2609 .... Philadelphia PA 19106-1723
717 782-4445 *Pennsylvania Middle* 228 Walnut St .... Harrisburg PA 17101-1714
Fax: 717 782-2262
717 347-0205 *Pennsylvania Middle* Washington Ave & Linden St Rm 423 .. Scranton PA 18501-0000
Fax: 717 347-5067
717 323-6380 *Pennsylvania Middle* 240 W 3rd St .... Williamsport PA 17701-6438
814 453-4829 *Pennsylvania Western* State St & S Park Row Rm 227 .... Erie PA 16501-0000
Fax: 814 454-7463
412 644-3528 *Pennsylvania Western* 7th Ave & Grant St Rm 819 .... Pittsburgh PA 15219-0000
Fax: 412 644-5969
809 766-5555 *Puerto Rico* Federal Bldg Rm G55 .... Hato Rey PR 00918-0000
401 528-5100 *Rhode Island* Kennedy Plaza Federal Bldg Rm 119 .... Providence RI 02903-0000
803 724-4688 *South Carolina* PO Box 835 .... Charleston SC 29402-0835
Fax: 803 724-4393
803 253-3470 *South Carolina* 1845 Assembly St 2nd Fl .... Columbia SC 29201-2401
Fax: 803 765-5960
803 662-1223 *South Carolina* 401 W Evans .... Florence SC 29501-3487
803 233-2781 *South Carolina* PO Box 10768 .... Greenville SC 29603-0768
Fax: Unlisted
605 226-7240 *South Dakota* 414 US Post Office & Courthouse .... Aberdeen SD 57401-0000
605 224-5849 *South Dakota* 225 S Pierre St Rm 405 .... Pierre SD 57501-2483
605 342-3066 *South Dakota* 515 9th St Rm 302 .... Rapid City SD 57701-2673
605 338-5566 *South Dakota* 400 S Phillips Ave Rm 220 .... Sioux Falls SD 57102-0959
Fax: 605 330-4312
615 752-5200 *Tennessee Eastern* PO Box 591 .... Chattanooga TN 37401-0591
Fax: Unlisted
615 639-3105 *Tennessee Eastern* 101 Summer St W .... Greeneville TN 37743-4944
Fax: 615 639-7134
615 673-4227 *Tennessee Eastern* PO Box 2348 .... Knoxville TN 37901-2348
Fax: Call company operator
615 736-5728 *Tennessee Middle* 801 Broadway Rm 800 .... Nashville TN 37203-3815
Fax: Unlisted
901 427-6586 *Tennessee Western* 109 S Highland Ave .... Jackson TN 38301-6123
Fax: 901 422-3367
901 544-3317 *Tennessee Western* 167 N Main St Rm 978 .... Memphis TN 38103-1816
Fax: 901 544-3280
409 839-2645 *Texas Eastern* PO Box 3507 .... Beaumont TX 77704-3507
Fax: 409 839-2656
903 935-2912 *Texas Eastern* 100 E Houston St .... Marshall TX 75670-4123
Fax: Unlisted

903 892-2921   *Texas Eastern* 101 E Pecan St .... Sherman TX 75090-5916
    Fax: 903 892-6801
903 794-8561   *Texas Eastern* 500 State Line Ave Rm 301 .... Texarkana TX 75501-0000
903 592-8195   *Texas Eastern* 211 W Ferguson Rm 106 .... Tyler TX 75702-7222
    Fax: 903 592-0815
915 677-6311   *Texas Northern* PO Box 1218 .... Abilene TX 79604-1218
    Fax: Unlisted
806 376-2352   *Texas Northern* 205 E 5th St Rm 210 .... Amarillo TX 79189-0001
    Fax: Unlisted
214 767-9511   *Texas Northern* 1100 Commerce St Rm 14A20 .... Dallas TX 75242-1003
    Fax: 214 767-3366
817 334-4494   *Texas Northern* 10th & Lamar Sts Rm 202 .... Fort Worth TX 76102-0000
    Fax: 817 334-3963
806 743-7624   *Texas Northern* 1205 Texas Ave Rm C-221 .... Lubbock TX 79401-0000
    Fax: Unlisted
915 655-4506   *Texas Northern* 33 E Twohig St Rm 202 .... San Angelo TX 76903-6451
    Fax: 915 658-6826
817 767-1902   *Texas Northern* PO Box 1234 .... Wichita Falls TX 76307-1234
    Fax: 817 767-2526
512 548-2500   *Texas Southern* PO Box 2299 .... Brownsville TX 78520-0000
    Fax: Unlisted
512 888-3142   *Texas Southern* 521 Starr St Rm 101 .... Corpus Christi TX 78401-2349
    Fax: 512 529-3433
409 766-3530   *Texas Southern* 601 Rosenberg St Rm 411 .... Galveston TX 77550-1738
    Fax: 409 766-3549
713 221-9505   *Texas Southern* 515 Rusk St Suite 5300 .... Houston TX 77002-2604
    Fax: Unlisted
512 723-3542   *Texas Southern* 1300 Matamoros St .... Laredo TX 78040-5054
    Fax: 512 726-2289
512 575-3512   *Texas Southern* PO Box 1541 .... Victoria TX 77902-1541
    Fax: Unlisted
512 482-5896   *Texas Western* 200 W 8th St .... Austin TX 78701-2333
    Fax: Unlisted
512 775-2021   *Texas Western* PO Box 1349 .... Del Rio TX 78841-1349
915 534-6725   *Texas Western* 511 E San Antonio St .... El Paso TX 79901-0000
    Fax: 915 534-6722
915 683-2001   *Texas Western* 200 E Wall St Rm 316 .... Midland TX 79701-5248
    Fax: Unlisted
915 445-4228   *Texas Western* 106 W 4th St .... Pecos TX 79772-4002
    Fax: 915 445-9859
512 229-6550   *Texas Western* 655 E Durango Blvd .... San Antonio TX 78206-0001
    Fax: Unlisted
817 756-0307   *Texas Western* PO Box 608 .... Waco TX 76703-0608
801 524-5160   *Utah* 350 S Main St Rm 204 .... Salt Lake City UT 84101-2106
    Fax: 801 524-3473
802 951-6301   *Vermont* PO Box 945 .... Burlington VT 05402-0945
802 773-0245   *Vermont* PO Box 607 .... Rutland VT 05702-0000
809 773-1130   *Virgin Islands* PO Box 3439 .... Christiansted VI 00821-0000
    Fax: 809 773-1563
809 774-0640   *Virgin Islands* PO Box 720 .... Saint Thomas VI 00804-0720
    Fax: 809 774-1293
703 557-5128   *Virginia Eastern* 200 S Washington St .... Alexandria VA 22314-3626
    Fax: 703 557-2830
804 244-0539   *Virginia Eastern* 101 25th St .... Newport News VA 23607-9998
    Fax: Unlisted
804 441-6677   *Virginia Eastern* 600 Granby St 1st Fl .... Norfolk VA 23510-1915
    Fax: 804 441-3803
804 771-2611   *Virginia Eastern* PO Box 2-AD .... Richmond VA 23205-0577
    Fax: 804 771-2057
703 628-5116   *Virginia Western* 180 W Main St .... Abingdon VA 24210-2810
    Fax: 703 628-1028
703 523-3557   *Virginia Western* 322 E Wood Ave .... Big Stone Gap VA 24219-2734
    Fax: 703 523-6214
804 793-7147   *Virginia Western* 700 Main St .... Danville VA 24541-1804
    Fax: 804 793-0284
703 434-3181   *Virginia Western* 116 N Main St .... Harrisonburg VA 22801-3819
    Fax: 703 434-3319
804 847-5722   *Virginia Western* PO Box 744 .... Lynchburg VA 24505-0744
    Fax: 804 847-2002
703 982-6224   *Virginia Western* PO Box 1234 .... Roanoke VA 24006-1234
    Fax: 703 982-4340
509 353-2150   *Washington Eastern* PO Box 1493 .... Spokane WA 99210-1493
    Fax: 509 353-2394
206 442-5598   *Washington Western* 1010 5th Ave Rm 308 .... Seattle WA 98104-1130
    Fax: Unlisted
304 622-8513   *West Virginia Northern* 500 W Pike St Rm 200 .... Clarksburg WV 26301-2664
    Fax: 304 623-4551
304 636-1445   *West Virginia Northern* 300 3rd St .... Elkins WV 26241-3810
    Fax: 304 636-5746
304 232-0011   *West Virginia Northern* 12th & Chapline Sts .... Wheeling WV 26003-0000
    Fax: 304 233-2185
304 253-7481   *West Virginia Southern* Neville St & Woodlawn Ave .... Beckley WV 25801-0000
    Fax: 304 253-3252
304 327-9798   *West Virginia Southern* 601 Federal St Rm 2303 .... Bluefield WV 24701-3033
    Fax: 304 327-6668
304 342-5154   *West Virginia Southern* 500 Quarrier St Rm 5303 .... Charleston WV 25301-2130
    Fax: 304 347-5168
304 529-5588   *West Virginia Southern* 845 5th Ave Rm 101 .... Huntington WV 25701-2014
    Fax: 304 529-5131
414 297-3372   *Wisconsin Eastern* 517 E Wisconsin Ave Rm 362 .... Milwaukee WI 53202-4504
    Fax: 414 362-3203
608 264-5156   *Wisconsin Western* 120 N Henry St Rm 320 .... Madison WI 53703-2559
307 772-2145   *Wyoming* 2120 Capitol Ave Rm 2131 .... Cheyenne WY 82001-3633
202 208-4131 **US Fish & Wildlife Service** 1849 C St NW Rm 3240 .... Washington DC 20240-0001
    Fax: 202 343-4473
505 766-2321   *Albuquerque Office* 500 Gold Ave SW Rm 3018 .... Albuquerque NM 87102-3152
    Fax: 505 766-2289
907 786-3542   *Anchorage Office* 1011 E Tudor Rd .... Anchorage AK 99503-6119
    Fax: 907 562-2297
404 331-3588   *Atlanta Office* 75 Spring St SW Suite 1200 .... Atlanta GA 30303-3308
    Fax: 404 331-6315
303 236-7920   *Denver Office* PO Box 25486DFC .... Denver CO 80225-0000
    Fax: 303 236-8295
617 965-5100   *Newton Corner Office* 1 Gateway Ctr Suite 700 .... Newton Corner MA 02158-2802
    Fax: 617 829-9263
503 231-6118   *Portland Office* 1002 NE Holladay St .... Portland OR 97232-4181
    Fax: 503 231-6116
612 725-3502   *Twin Cities Office* Federal Bldg Fort Snelling 6th Fl .... Twin Cities MN 55111-0000
    Fax: 612 725-3508
202 377-5777 **US Foreign Commercial Service**
  14th St & Constitution Ave NW Rm 3804 .... Washington DC 20230-0001
    Fax: 202 377-5013
202 447-3760 **US Forest Service** 201 14th St SW .... Washington DC 20250-0001
    Fax: 202 447-3610
406 329-3511   *Region 1* 200 E Broadway .... Missoula MT 59807-0000
    Fax: 406 585-3347

303 236-9659   *Region 2* 11177 W 8th Ave .... Lakewood CO 80225-0000
    Fax: 303 236-9587
505 842-3345   *Region 3* 517 Gold Ave SW .... Albuquerque NM 87102-3156
    Fax: 505 842-3800
801 625-5182   *Region 4* 324 25th St .... Ogden UT 84401-2310
    Fax: 801 586-5127
415 705-2880   *Region 5* 630 Sansome St .... San Francisco CA 94111-2206
    Fax: 415 703-2536
503 326-2877   *Region 6* 319 SW Pine St .... Portland OR 97204-2726
    Fax: 503 326-2272
404 347-2384   *Region 8* 1720 Peachtree Rd NW .... Atlanta GA 30367-0001
    Fax: 404 347-3608
414 297-3693   *Region 9* 310 W Wisconsin Ave Rm 500 .... Milwaukee WI 53203-2211
    Fax: 414 297-3808
907 586-8863   *Region 10* PO Box 21628 .... Juneau AK 99802-1628
    Fax: 907 586-8856
202 208-3888 **US Geological Survey** 1849 C St NW Rm 2646 .... Washington DC 20240-0001
    Fax: 202 268-3795
303 236-5438   *Central Region* 6th Ave & Kipling St Bldg 25 .... Denver CO 80225-0000
    Fax: 303 236-5448
703 648-4427   *Eastern Region* 12201 Sunrise Valley Dr MS-109 .... Reston VA 22092-0001
    Fax: 703 648-4466
415 853-8300   *Western Region* 345 Middlefield Rd .... Menlo Park CA 94025-3508
    Fax: 415 329-5110
202 224-3121 **US House of Representatives** Capitol Bldg .... Washington DC 20515-0001
202 377-1780 **US Import Administration Office**
  14th St & Constitution Ave NW Rm 3099-B .... Washington DC 20230-0001
    Fax: 202 377-0947
202 485-2355 **US Information Agency** 301 4th St SW .... Washington DC 20547-0001
    Fax: 202 485-6988
202 663-1449 **US International Development Agency** 320 20th St NE .... Washington DC 20521-0000
    Fax: 202 663-1086
202 377-3022 **US International Economic Policy Dept**
  14th St & Constitution Ave NW Rm 3864 .... Washington DC 20230-0001
    Fax: 202 377-5444
202 252-1000 **US International Trade Commission** 500 E St SW .... Washington DC 20436-0001
    Fax: 202 252-1798
619 271-4300 **US International University** 10455 Pomerado Rd .... San Diego CA 92131-1717
    Fax: 619 693-8562
202 694-2500 **US Marine Corps** Headquarters .... Washington DC 20380-0001
    Fax: 202 695-7366
202 694-8010   *Public Affairs* Arlington Navy Annex Rm 1134 .... Washington DC 20380-0001
    Fax: 202 695-7460
202 307-9600 **US Marshal Service (US Dept of Justice)**
  600 Army-Navy Dr Rm 850 .... Arlington VA 22202-4210
516 773-5000 **US Merchant Marine Academy** Steamboat Rd .... Kings Point NY 11024-0000
    Fax: 516 773-5774
202 653-7175 **US Merit Systems Protection Board**
  1120 Vermont Ave NW .... Washington DC 20419-0001
914 938-4011 **US Military Academy** .... West Point NY 10996-0000
    Fax: 914 938-3828
202 376-0560 **US Mint (US Dept of the Treasury)**
  633 3rd St NW Rm 715 .... Washington DC 20220-0001
    Fax: 202 376-3908
202 272-6999 **US National Central Bureau of Interpol (US Dept of Justice)**
  600 E St NW Suite 600 .... Washington DC 20530-0001
    Fax: 202 272-5941
301 267-6100 **US Naval Academy** .... Annapolis MD 21402-1398
301 268-6110 **US Naval Institute** US Naval Academy .... Annapolis MD 21402-0000
    Fax: 301 269-7940
202 638-1764 **US Pan Asian American Chamber of Commerce**
  1625 K St NW Suite 380 .... Washington DC 20006-1604
    Fax: 202 638-1677
202 268-2000 **US Postal Service** 475 L'Enfant Plaza W SW .... Washington DC 20260-0001
    Fax: Unlisted
312 765-5000   *Central Region* 433 W Van Buren .... Chicago IL 60699-0001
    Fax: 312 765-5596
215 496-6001   *Eastern Region* 1845 Walnut St .... Philadelphia PA 19103-4708
    Fax: 215 496-6314
202 636-2300   *Postal Inspection Service* 900 Brentwood Rd .... Washington DC 20066-6096
    Fax: 202 636-2287
901 722-7373   *Southern Region* 1407 Union Ave .... Memphis TN 38166-0001
    Fax: Unlisted
415 742-4710   *Western Region* 850 Cherry Ave .... San Bruno CA 94099-0001
    Fax: 415 742-4103
312 751-4930 **US Railroad Retirement Board** 844 N Rush St .... Chicago IL 60611-2092
    Fax: 312 751-4923
202 224-3121 **US Senate** Capitol Bldg .... Washington DC 20510-0001
202 722-3000 **US Soldiers' & Airmen's Home** 3700 N Capitol St NW .... Washington DC 20317-0001
    Fax: 202 722-9087 Admin
202 376-2754 **US Tax Court** 400 2nd St NW .... Washington DC 20217-0001
703 875-4357 **US Trade & Development Program** 1621 N Kent St Rm 309 .... Rosslyn VA 22209-2101
    Fax: 703 875-4009
202 377-1461 **US Trade Development Office**
  14th St & Constitution Ave NW Rm 3832 .... Washington DC 20230-0001
    Fax: 202 377-5697
202 331-8010 **US-Arab Chamber of Commerce**
  1825 K St NW Suite 1107 .... Washington DC 20006-3172
    Fax: 202 331-8297
415 398-9200 **US-Arab Chamber of Commerce (Pacific) Inc**
  PO Box 11239 .... San Francisco CA 94101-7239
    Fax: 415 398-7111
212 819-0117 **US-Austrian Chamber of Commerce** 165 W 46th St .... New York NY 10036-2501
202 429-0340 **US-China Business Council** 1818 N St NW Suite 500 .... Washington DC 20036-2406
    Fax: 202 775-2476
202 463-5492 **US-India Business Council** 1615 H St NW 6th Fl .... Washington DC 20062-0001
    Fax: 202 463-3114
202 728-0068 **US-Japan Business Council** 1020 19th St NW Suite 130 .... Washington DC 20036-6101
    Fax: 202 728-0073
202 296-5198 **US-Mexico Chamber of Commerce**
  1900 L St NW Suite 612 .... Washington DC 20036-5002
    Fax: 202 785-4905
212 333-8728 **US-Mexico Chamber of Commerce** 730 5th Ave 9th Fl .... New York NY 10019-0000
815 459-5875 **US-Republic of China Economic Council** 200 S Main St .... Crystal Lake IL 60014-0000
    Fax: 815 459-5011
212 644-4550 **US-USSR Trade & Economic Council** 805 3rd Ave 14th Fl .... New York NY 10022-7513
    Fax: 212 752-0889
202 857-0170 **US-Yugoslav Economic Council Inc** 818 18th St Suite 230 .... Washington DC 20006-3513
    Fax: 202 452-9218
801 373-5510 **Utah County** 51 S University Ave .... Provo UT 84601-4424
801 789-3799 **Utah Field House of Natural History State Park** 235 E Main St .... Vernal UT 84078-2605
801 581-7332 **Utah Museum of Fine Arts**
  101 Art & Architecture Ctr University of Utah .... Salt Lake City UT 84112-0000
801 581-6927 **Utah Museum of Natural History** University of Utah .... Salt Lake City UT 84112-1107
801 533-9777 **Utah Republican Party** 643 E 400 South Suite A .... Salt Lake City UT 84102-2803
    Fax: 801 533-0327

801 484-1200 **Utah State Democratic Committee** 472 Bearcat Dr .... Salt Lake City UT 84115-0000
Fax: 801 487-5191
Utah State Government
801 538-3000 *Information* 1226 State Office Bldg Rm B-69 .... Salt Lake City UT 84114-1201
Fax: Unlisted
801 533-5895 *Arts Council* 617 E South Temple .... Salt Lake City UT 84102-1177
801 538-1015 *Attorney General* State Capitol Rm 236 .... Salt Lake City UT 84114-1191
Fax: 801 538-1760 Admin
801 261-2825 *Board of Pardons* 6100 S 300 East Suite 203 .... Murray UT 84107-7375
Fax: 801 265-5670
801 538-6108 *Bureau of Air Quality* 288 N 1460 West 2nd Fl .... Salt Lake City UT 84116-3100
Fax: 801 538-6016
801 538-6170 *Bureau of Solid & Hazardous Wastes* 288 N 1460 West . Salt Lake City UT 84116-3100
Fax: 801 538-6016
801 538-6186 *Bureau of Vital Records* 288 N 1460 West .... Salt Lake City UT 84116-3100
Fax: 801 538-6694
801 530-6601 *Consumer Protection Div* 160 E 300 South 2nd Fl .... Salt Lake City UT 84111-2316
Fax: 801 530-6438
801 965-4587 *Council for Crime Prevention* 1879 S Main St Suite 180 Salt Lake City UT 84115-0000
Fax: 801 486-8815
801 538-7101 *Department of Agriculture* 350 N Redwood Rd .... Salt Lake City UT 84116-3087
Fax: 801 538-7126
801 530-6628 *Department of Business Regulation Licensing Div*
160 E 300 South 4th Fl .... Salt Lake City UT 84111-2328
Fax: 801 530-6511
801 538-8700 *Department of Community & Economic Development*
324 S State St Suite 200 .... Salt Lake City UT 84111-0000
Fax: 801 538-8899
801 265-5500 *Department of Corrections* 6100 S 300 East .... Murray UT 84107-7378
Fax: 801 265-5670
801 533-2400 *Department of Employment Security*
174 Social Hall Ave .... Salt Lake City UT 84147-0000
Fax: 801 533-2466
801 538-6101 *Department of Health* 288 N 1460 West .... Salt Lake City UT 84116-0000
Fax: 801 538-6694
801 538-7200 *Department of Natural Resources*
1636 W North Temple Suite 316 .... Salt Lake City UT 84116-3193
Fax: 801 538-7315
801 965-4113 *Department of Transportation* 4501 S 2700 West .... Salt Lake City UT 84119-5977
Fax: 801 965-4338
801 584-8370 *Division of Comprehensive Emergency Management*
1543 Sunnyside Ave .... Salt Lake City UT 84105-0000
Fax: 801 584-8377
801 538-3018 *Division of Facilities Construction & Management*
State Office Bldg .... Salt Lake City UT 84114-1201
Fax: 801 538-3267
801 538-3020 *Division of Finance* 6000 State Office Bldg .... Salt Lake City UT 84114-1201
Fax: 801 538-3244
801 538-5340 *Division of Oil Gas & Mining*
355 W North Temple Suite 350 .... Salt Lake City UT 84180-0000
Fax: 801 359-3940
801 538-3026 *Division of Purchasing* State Office Bldg Rm 3150 .... Salt Lake City UT 84114-1201
Fax: 801 538-3882
801 538-5428 *Energy Office* 355 W North Temple Suite 450 .... Salt Lake City UT 84180-1204
Fax: 801 521-0657
801 538-1000 *Governor* 210 State Capitol .... Salt Lake City UT 84114-1202
Fax: Unlisted
801 965-4518 *Highway Patrol Div* 4501 S 2700 West .... Salt Lake City UT 84119-5977
Fax: 801 965-4756
801 530-6922 *Industrial Commission* 160 E 300 South 3rd Fl .... Salt Lake City UT 84111-2316
Fax: 801 530-6804
801 530-6400 *Insurance Dept* 3110 State Office Bldg 3rd Fl .... Salt Lake City UT 84114-0000
Fax: 801 538-3820
801 586-3356 *Iron County Utah State Correctional Facility*
2136 N Main St .... Cedar City UT 84720-9788
Fax: 801 586-7135
801 538-1040 *Lieutenant Governor* 203 State Capitol .... Salt Lake City UT 84114-1202
Fax: 801 538-1528
801 538-7500 *Office of Education* 250 E 500 South .... Salt Lake City UT 84111-3204
Fax: 801 538-7521
801 538-1540 *Office of Planning & Budget* State Capitol Rm 116 .... Salt Lake City UT 84114-1202
Fax: 801 538-1547
801 530-6716 *Public Service Commission* 160 E 300 South .... Salt Lake City UT 84111-2316
Fax: 801 530-6796
801 530-6747 *Real Estate Div* PO Box 45802 .... Salt Lake City UT 84145-0802
Fax: 801 530-6650
801 355-3884 *Retirement System* 540 E 200 South .... Salt Lake City UT 84102-2001
Fax: 801 531-7705
801 530-6600 *Securities Div* 160 E 300 South .... Salt Lake City UT 84111-2316
801 538-3012 *State Archives* Archives Bldg .... Salt Lake City UT 84114-0000
801 538-1044 *Supreme Court* 332 State Capitol .... Salt Lake City UT 84114-1181
Fax: 801 538-1046
801 538-5247 *System of Higher Education*
355 W North Temple Suite 550 .... Salt Lake City UT 84180-1205
Fax: 801 363-7343
801 530-6088 *Tax Commission* 160 E 300 South .... Salt Lake City UT 84134-0001
Fax: 801 530-6911
801 538-3330 *Telecommunication Office* B-69 State Capitol .... Salt Lake City UT 84114-0000
Fax: 801 538-3321
801 533-2201 *Unemployment Insurance Div* 174 Social Hall Ave .... Salt Lake City UT 84111-1504
Fax: 801 533-2466
801 571-2300 *Utah State Prison* PO Box 250 .... Draper UT 84020-0250
Fax: 801 571-0047 Admin
801 530-6800 *Workers' Compensation* 160 E 300 South .... Salt Lake City UT 84111-2316
Fax: 801 530-6804
801 466-5888 **Utah State Library** 2150 S 300 West .... Salt Lake City UT 84115-2579
Fax: 801 533-4657
801 750-1000 **Utah State University** .... Logan UT 84322-0000
Fax: 801 750-2678
801 750-2215 *College of Agriculture* Agricultural Science Bldg .... Logan UT 84322-0000
Fax: 801 750-3321
801 750-2775 *College of Engineering* Engineering Classroom Rm 110 .... Logan UT 84322-0000
Fax: 801 750-3763
801 750-1189 *Department of Biology*
Biology/Natural Resources Bldg Rm 121 .... Logan UT 84322-5305
Fax: 801 750-1575
801 538-1030 **Utah Travel Council** Council Hall Capitol Hill .... Salt Lake City UT 84114-0000
Fax: 801 538-1399
801 226-5000 **Utah Valley Community College** 800 W 1200 South .... Orem UT 84058-5999
Fax: 801 226-5207
315 792-3111 **Utica College of Syracuse University** 1600 Burrstone Rd .... Utica NY 13502-4892
512 278-6614 **Uvalde County** PO Box 284 .... Uvalde TX 78802-0284

V

303 571-1833 **Vail Reservations Inc** 292 E Meadow Dr Suite 101 .... Vail CO 81657-3612
512 774-3611 **Val Verde County** 400 Pecan St .... Del Rio TX 78840-5140
912 333-5800 **Valdosta State College** N Patterson & Oak Sts .... Valdosta GA 31698-0001
Fax: 912 333-7408
407 299-5000 **Valencia Community College** PO Box 3028 .... Orlando FL 32802-3028
505 865-9681 **Valencia County** PO Box 1119 .... Los Lunas NM 87031-1119
Fax: 505 865-8612
804 649-0711 **Valentine Museum** 1015 E Clay St .... Richmond VA 23219-1590
Fax: 804 643-3510
202 225-4531 **Valentine Tim (Rep - D - North Carolina)**
1510 Longworth Bldg .... Washington DC 20515-0001
Fax: 202 225-1539
701 845-7990 **Valley City State University** .... Valley City ND 58072-0000
Fax: 701 845-7245
208 382-4297 **Valley County** PO Box 737 .... Cascade ID 83611-0737
406 228-8221 **Valley County** PO Box 311 .... Glasgow MT 59230-0311
Fax: 406 228-4601
308 728-3700 **Valley County** 125 S 15th St .... Ord NE 68862-0000
215 935-0450 **Valley Forge Christian College** Charlestown Rd .... Phoenixville PA 19460-2399
215 688-1800 **Valley Forge Military Academy & Junior College**
1001 Eagle Rd .... Wayne PA 19087-3613
Fax: 215 688-0829 Library
219 462-2191 **Valparaiso Technical Institute** 1 Center St .... Valparaiso IN 46383-4599
219 464-5000 **Valparaiso University** .... Valparaiso IN 46383-6493
Fax: 219 464-5381
219 465-7829 *School of Law* Weseman Hall Rm 202 .... Valparaiso IN 46383-0000
Fax: 219 465-7872
501 745-4140 **Van Buren County** PO Box 80 .... Clinton AR 72031-0080
319 293-3129 **Van Buren County** PO Box 475 .... Keosauqua IA 52565-0475
616 657-5581 **Van Buren County** 212 Paw Paw St .... Paw Paw MI 49079-1492
Fax: 616 657-7573
615 946-2121 **Van Buren County** Courthouse Sq .... Spencer TN 38585-0000
419 238-6159 **Van Wert County** 121 E Main St 2nd Fl .... Van Wert OH 45891-1795
903 567-6503 **Van Zandt County** PO Box 515 .... Canton TX 75103-0515
Fax: 903 567-2171
405 237-2121 **Vance Air Force Base** .... Enid OK 73705-0001
919 492-2141 **Vance County** 122 Young St .... Henderson NC 27536-4268
919 492-2061 **Vance-Granville Community College** State Rd 1126 .... Henderson NC 27536-0000
Fax: 919 430-0460
805 866-1611 **Vandenberg Air Force Base** .... Vandenberg AFB CA 93437-0000
Fax: 805 866-0107
202 225-3511 **Vander Jagt Guy (Rep - R - Michigan)** 2409 Rayburn Bldg .. Washington DC 20515-0001
Fax: Call company operator
615 322-7311 **Vanderbilt University** West End Ave .... Nashville TN 37232-0001
Fax: 615 343-7286
615 322-3318 *Department of Biochemistry* 607 Light Hall .... Nashville TN 37232-0146
Fax: 615 322-4349
615 322-2087 *Graduate School of Microbiology & Immunology*
A 5321 Medical Ctr N .... Nashville TN 37232-0001
Fax: 615 343-7392
615 322-2615 *Law School* 21st Ave S .... Nashville TN 37240-0001
Fax: 615 322-6631
615 322-2762 *School of Engineering* 1500 21st Ave S 4th Fl .... Nashville TN 37212-3102
615 322-2164 *School of Medicine* 21st & Garland Sts Medical Ctr D-3300 . Nashville TN 37232-0001
Fax: 615 343-7286
615 322-4400 *School of Nursing* 112 Godchaux Hall .... Nashville TN 37240-0001
Fax: 615 343-7711
812 426-5160 **Vanderburgh County** PO Box 3356 .... Evansville IN 47732-3356
Fax: 812 426-5849
312 225-6288 **VanderCook College of Music** 3209 S Michigan Ave .... Chicago IL 60616-3886
212 926-3311 **Vanuatu: Republic of Vanuatu Mission to the UN**
416 Convent Ave .... New York NY 10031-4217
Fax: 212 926-4131
914 437-7000 **Vassar College** 124 Raymond Ave .... Poughkeepsie NY 12601-6198
Fax: 914 437-7187
814 437-6871 **Venango County** Liberty & 12th Sts .... Franklin PA 16323-1295
Fax: 814 432-4741
Venezuela: Republic of Venezuela
202 342-2214 *Embassy* 1099 30th St .... Washington DC 20008-2805
Fax: 202 342-6820
212 557-2055 *Mission to the UN* 335 E 46th St .... New York NY 10017-3096
Fax: 212 557-3528
212 233-7776 **Venezuelan-American Assn of the US**
150 Nassau St Rm 2015 .... New York NY 10038-1516
Fax: 212 233-7779
515 673-8391 **Vennard College** PO Box 29 .... University Park IA 52595-9999
202 225-6631 **Vento Bruce F (Rep - D - Minnesota)** 2304 Rayburn Bldg ... Washington DC 20515-0001
Fax: 202 225-1968
805 642-3211 **Ventura College** 4667 Telegraph Rd .... Ventura CA 93003-3899
Fax: 805 654-6466
805 654-5000 **Ventura County** 800 S Victoria Ave .... Ventura CA 93009-0001
Fax: 805 654-2424
805 642-0161 **Ventura County Community College District** 71 Day Rd .... Ventura CA 93003-2037
Fax: 805 654-6410
218 365-7200 **Vermilion Community College** 1900 E Camp St .... Ely MN 55731-1996
Fax: 218 365-7207
217 431-2555 **Vermilion County** 7 N Vermilion St .... Danville IL 61832-5806
318 898-4310 **Vermilion Parish** PO Box 790 .... Abbeville LA 70511-0790
Fax: 318 898-0404
317 492-3500 **Vermillion County** PO Box 8 .... Newport IN 47966-0008
802 223-3443 **Vermont Chamber of Commerce** PO Box 37 .... Montpelier VT 05601-0000
Fax: 802 229-4581
802 223-8750 **Vermont College of Norwich University** 32 College St .... Montpelier VT 05602-3201
Fax: 802 223-8855
802 229-5986 **Vermont Democratic Party** PO Box 336 .... Montpelier VT 05601-0336
802 828-3261 **Vermont Dept of Libraries** 109 State St .... Montpelier VT 05602-2712
Fax: 802 828-2199
802 828-2291 **Vermont Museum** 109 State St .... Montpelier VT 05602-2710
802 223-3411 **Vermont Republican State Committee** 43 Court St .... Montpelier VT 05602-2947
Fax: 802 229-1864
Vermont State Government
802 828-1110 *Information* State Administration Bldg .... Montpelier VT 05602-0000
Fax: 802 828-2221
802 828-3322 *Agency of Administration*
109 State St Pavilion Office Bldg 5th Fl .... Montpelier VT 05602-0000
Fax: 802 828-3339
802 244-7347 *Agency of Natural Resources* 103 S Main St .... Waterbury VT 05676-1534
Fax: 802 244-1102
802 828-2657 *Agency of Transportation*
133 State St State Administration Bldg .... Montpelier VT 05602-0000
Fax: 802 828-2024

Vermont / Virginia

802 244-8731 *Air Pollution Control Div* 103 S Main St Bldg 3-S ... Waterbury VT 05676-0000
Fax: 802 244-5141
802 828-2308 *Archives Div* 26 Terrace St ... Montpelier VT 05602-0000
802 828-3171 *Attorney General* 109 State St ... Montpelier VT 05602-2716
Fax: 802 828-2154
802 863-7356 *Chittenden Correctional Center* 7 Farrell St ... South Burlington VT 05403-6113
Fax: 802 863-7308
802 828-2393 *Conservation & Renewable Energy Unit* 120 State St ... Montpelier VT 05602-2702
Fax: 802 828-2342
802 828-3291 *Council on the Arts* 136 State St ... Montpelier VT 05602-2707
Fax: 802 828-3233
802 828-3168 *Defender General* 141 Main St State Office Bldg ... Montpelier VT 05602-0000
802 828-2430 *Department of Agriculture* 116 State St State Office Bldg .. Montpelier VT 05602-0000
Fax: 802 828-2361
802 241-2263 *Department of Corrections* 103 S Main St ... Waterbury VT 05676-1534
Fax: 802 244-6207
802 828-3135 *Department of Education* 120 State St ... Montpelier VT 05602-2703
Fax: 802 828-3140
802 244-8755 *Department of Environmental Conservation* 103 S Main St . Waterbury VT 05676-1534
Fax: 802 244-5141
802 828-2309 *Department of Finance & Management* 109 State St ... Montpelier VT 05602-0000
Fax: 802 888-3339
802 863-7280 *Department of Health* PO Box 70 ... Burlington VT 05402-0070
Fax: 802 863-7425
802 828-3301 *Department of Insurance* 120 State St ... Montpelier VT 05602-2702
Fax: 802 828-3306
802 828-2286 *Department of Labor & Industry* State Office Bldg ... Montpelier VT 05602-0000
Fax: 802 828-2195
802 828-2363 *Department of Licensing & Registration*
Pavilion Office Bldg Secretary of State's Office ... Montpelier VT 05602-0000
802 828-2505 *Department of Taxes* 109 State St ... Montpelier VT 05602-2709
802 241-2295 *Division of Probation & Parole* 103 S Main St ... Waterbury VT 05676-1534
Fax: Unlisted
802 828-2211 *Division of Purchasing* 133 State St ... Montpelier VT 05602-2711
Fax: 802 828-2222
802 828-3221 *Economic Development Dept* 109 State St ... Montpelier VT 05602-2712
Fax: 802 828-3258
802 241-2450 *Economic Opportunity Office* 103 S Main St ... Waterbury VT 05676-1534
Fax: 802 244-8103
802 244-8721 *Emergency Management* 103 S Main St ... Waterbury VT 05676-1534
Fax: 802 244-8655
802 828-3333 *Governor* 109 State St Pavilion Office Bldg 5th Fl ... Montpelier VT 05602-2710
Fax: 802 828-3339
802 878-7466 *Higher Education Council* PO Box 47 ... Essex Junction VT 05453-0047
802 828-2226 *Lieutenant Governor* State House ... Montpelier VT 05602-0000
802 524-6771 *Northwest State Correctional Facility* PO Box 279-1 ... Swanton VT 05488-0000
802 828-2886 *Occupational & Radiological Health Div* 10 Baldwin St ... Montpelier VT 05602-2109
Fax: 802 828-2878
802 828-3326 *Office of Policy Research & Coordination*
109 State St Pavilion Office Bldg 5th Fl ... Montpelier VT 05602-2710
Fax: 802 828-3339
802 828-2358 *Public Service Board* City Center Bldg 89 Main St 3rd Fl ... Montpelier VT 05602-0000
Fax: Unlisted
802 828-3228 *Real Estate Commission* 26 Terrace St ... Montpelier VT 05602-2154
802 828-2305 *Retirement Div* 133 State St 2nd Fl ... Montpelier VT 05602-2711
Fax: 802 828-2772
802 828-2363 *Secretary of State* 26 Terrace St ... Montpelier VT 05602-2154
802 244-5164 *State Natural Resources Conservation Council*
103 S Main St ... Waterbury VT 05676-1534
Fax: 802 244-1102
802 244-7345 *State Police* 103 S Main St ... Waterbury VT 05676-1596
Fax: 802 244-1106
802 828-3276 *Supreme Court* 111 State St ... Montpelier VT 05602-2708
802 828-2301 *Treasurer* 133 State St ... Montpelier VT 05602-2711
Fax: 802 828-2772
802 229-0311 *Unemployment Compensation Div* 5 Green Mountain Dr ... Montpelier VT 05601-0000
Fax: 802 223-0850
802 863-7275 *Vital Records Section* 60 Main St ... Burlington VT 05402-0000
802 244-8702 *Waste Management Div* 103 S Main St Bldg 3-W ... Waterbury VT 05676-0000
Fax: 802 244-5141
802 728-3391 **Vermont Technical College** ... Randolph Center VT 05061-0000
Fax: 802 728-9124
802 828-3236 **Vermont Travel Div** 134 State St ... Montpelier VT 05602-2707
Fax: Unlisted
417 667-3157 **Vernon County** 102 W Cherry ... Nevada MO 64772-3368
608 637-3569 **Vernon County** W Decker ... Viroqua WI 54665-0000
318 238-1384 **Vernon Parish** 201 3rd St ... Leesville LA 71496-0000
817 552-6291 **Vernon Regional Junior College** 4400 College Dr ... Vernon TX 76384-4092
Fax: 817 553-3902
202 233-2596 **Veteran's Health Service & Research Administration**
810 Vermont Ave NW Rm 800 ... Washington DC 20420-0001
Fax: 202 233-4725
313 930-5950 *Central Region* PO Box 1407 ... Ann Arbor MI 48106-0000
202 233-2409 *Eastern Region* 9600 N Point Rd ... Fort Howard MD 21052-0000
817 885-7900 *Southern Region* 1901 N Hwy 360 Suite 350 ... Grand Prairie TX 75050-0000
415 744-7506 *Western Region* 211 Main St Suite 1800 ... San Francisco CA 94105-0000
202 225-3527 **Veterans Affairs Committee (US House of Representatives)**
335 Cannon Bldg ... Washington DC 20515-0001
Fax: 202 225-5486
202 224-9126 **Veterans Affairs Committee (US Senate)**
414 Russell Bldg ... Washington DC 20510-0001
Fax: 202 224-9575
619 245-4271 **Victor Valley College** 18422 Bear Valley Rd ... Victorville CA 92392-5849
Fax: 619 245-9744 Admin
512 573-3291 **Victoria College** 2200 E Red River St ... Victoria TX 77901-4494
Fax: 512 572-3850
512 575-4558 **Victoria County** 115 N Bridge St ... Victoria TX 77901-6544
Fax: 512 575-6276
212 679-3779 **Viet Nam: Socialist Republic of Viet Nam Mission to the UN**
20 Waterside Plaza ... New York NY 10010-2612
Fax: 212 686-8534
812 238-8211 **Vigo County** 3rd & Wabash ... Terre Haute IN 47807-0000
812 232-1113 **Vigo County Public Library** 1 Library Sq ... Terre Haute IN 47807-3609
Fax: Unlisted
715 479-3600 **Vilas County** PO Box 369 ... Eagle River WI 54521-0369
301 486-7000 **Villa Julie College** Green Spring Valley Rd ... Stevenson MD 21153-0000
Fax: 301 486-1995
814 838-1966 **Villa Maria College** 2551 W 8th St ... Erie PA 16505-4494
Fax: 814 833-3315
716 896-0700 **Villa Maria College of Buffalo** 240 Pine Ridge Rd ... Buffalo NY 14225-3999
Fax: 716 896-0705
215 645-4500 **Villanova University** Lancaster Ave ... Villanova PA 19085-1699
Fax: 215 645-7599
215 645-7000 *School of Law* Countyline Rd & Springmill Garey Hall ... Villanova PA 19085-0000
Fax: 215 645-7033

812 882-3350 **Vincennes University** 1002 N First St ... Vincennes IN 47591-0000
Fax: 812 885-5868
614 596-4571 **Vinton County** Vinton County Courthouse ... McArthur OH 45651-1296
804 427-4242 **Virginia Beach (Independent City)** Municipal Ctr ... Virginia Beach VA 23456-9099
Fax: 804 427-4135
804 427-4321 **Virginia Beach Dept of Public Libraries**
Courthouse Commons Bldg Suite 110 ... Virginia Beach VA 23456-0000
Fax: 804 427-4220
804 425-7511 **Virginia Beach Tourist Information** 19th & Pacific Ave ... Virginia Beach VA 23451-3362
804 644-1607 **Virginia Chamber of Commerce** 9 S 5th St ... Richmond VA 23219-3823
Fax: 804 783-6112
804 367-1200 **Virginia Commonwealth University** 910 W Franklin St ... Richmond VA 23284-0001
Fax: 804 367-0978
804 367-1134 *Department of Urban Studies & Planning*
812 W Franklin St ... Richmond VA 23284-0001
Fax: 804 367-0102
804 786-9183 *School of Dentistry* 520 N 12th St ... Richmond VA 23298-0001
Fax: 804 786-4913 Admin
804 786-9793 *School of Medicine* 1101 E Marshall St ... Richmond VA 23298-0001
Fax: 804 371-7628
804 786-0724 *School of Nursing* PO Box 567 MCV Stn ... Richmond VA 23298-0001
Fax: 804 371-7743
804 786-8489 *School of Pharmacy* PO Box 581 ... Richmond VA 23298-0001
Fax: 804 786-7436
804 644-1966 **Virginia Democratic Party** 1001 E Broad St Suite LL25 ... Richmond VA 23219-0000
Fax: 804 343-3642
804 786-2051 **Virginia Div of Tourism** 1021 E Cary St 14th Fl ... Richmond VA 23219-4000
Fax: 804 786-1919
703 628-6094 **Virginia Highlands Community College** SR-372 ... Abingdon VA 24210-0000
Fax: 703 628-7576
703 669-6101 **Virginia Intermont College** 1013 Moore St ... Bristol VA 24201-4298
703 464-7000 **Virginia Military Institute** ... Lexington VA 24450-0000
Fax: 703 464-7169
804 367-0844 **Virginia Museum of Fine Arts** 2800 Grove Ave ... Richmond VA 23221-2472
Fax: 804 367-9393
703 961-6000 **Virginia Polytechnic Institute & State University** ... Blacksburg VA 24061-0001
Fax: 703 231-7826
703 231-6336 *College of Agriculture* Hutchinson Hall ... Blacksburg VA 24061-0000
Fax: 703 231-4163
703 231-5383 *College of Architecture* 202 Cowgill Hall ... Blacksburg VA 24061-0001
Fax: 703 231-9938
703 231-6641 *College of Engineering* 333 Norris Hall ... Blacksburg VA 24061-0217
Fax: 703 231-7248
703 231-6522 *Dept Geological Sciences* Derring Hall Rm 4044 ... Blacksburg VA 24061-0001
Fax: 703 231-3386
703 231-5712 *Graduate Dept of Biology* Derring Hall Rm 2123 ... Blacksburg VA 24061-0001
Fax: 703 231-9307
703 231-6691 *School of Public Administration* 100 Sandy Hall ... Blacksburg VA 24061-6801
Fax: 703 231-7060
703 231-5517 *Urban & Regional Planning Program*
Architecture Annex Rm 201H ... Blacksburg VA 24061-0001
Fax: 703 231-3367
804 780-0111 **Virginia Republican Party** 115 E Grace St ... Richmond VA 23219-1741
Fax: 804 343-1060
Virginia State Government
804 786-0000 *Information* 109 Governor St ... Richmond VA 23219-3623
Fax: 804 225-4070
804 786-5597 *Archives & Records Div* 11th St & Capitol Sq ... Richmond VA 23219-0000
Fax: 804 225-4608
804 786-2071 *Attorney General* 101 N 8th St ... Richmond VA 23219-2336
Fax: 804 786-1991
804 786-3741 *Bureau of Insurance* 1220 Bank St Jefferson Bldg ... Richmond VA 23219-0000
Fax: 804 786-3396
804 225-3132 *Commission for the Arts* 101 N 14th St 17th Fl ... Richmond VA 23219-3683
804 786-2042 *Consumer Affairs Office* 1100 Bank St Rm 101 ... Richmond VA 23219-3642
Fax: 804 371-7479
804 225-2600 *Council of Higher Education* 101 N 14th St ... Richmond VA 23219-3681
Fax: 804 225-2604
804 786-4500 *Council on the Environment* 202 N 9th St Suite 900 ... Richmond VA 23219-3402
Fax: 804 225-3933
804 786-3501 *Department of Agriculture & Consumer Services*
1100 Bank St ... Richmond VA 23219-3642
Fax: 804 371-7679
804 786-3248 *Department of Air Pollution Control*
212 N 9th St Suite 900 ... Richmond VA 23219-0000
Fax: 804 225-3933
804 786-2121 *Department of Conservation & Recreation*
203 Governor St Suite 302 ... Richmond VA 23219-2010
Fax: 804 786-6141
804 674-3000 *Department of Corrections* 6900 Atmore Rd ... Richmond VA 23225-5646
Fax: 804 674-3587
804 786-3791 *Department of Economic Development*
1021 E Cary St James Ctr ... Richmond VA 23219-0000
Fax: 804 786-1121
804 225-2023 *Department of Education* 101 N 14th St ... Richmond VA 23219-3663
Fax: 804 225-2819
804 674-2449 *Department of Emergency Services* 310 Turner Rd ... Richmond VA 23225-6400
Fax: 804 674-2431
804 786-3561 *Department of Health* 109 Governor St Suite 400 ... Richmond VA 23219-3623
Fax: 804 786-4616
804 786-2376 *Department of Labor & Industry*
4th St Office Bldg Suite 205 ... Richmond VA 23219-0000
Fax: 804 371-6524
804 367-1310 *Department of Mines-Minerals & Energy* 2201 W Broad St . Richmond VA 23220-2022
Fax: 804 367-6211
804 786-5375 *Department of Planning & Budget* PO Box 1422 ... Richmond VA 23211-1422
Fax: 804 225-3291
804 674-2000 *Department of State Police* 7700 Midlothian Tpke ... Richmond VA 23235-5226
Fax: 804 674-2267
804 367-8000 *Department of Taxation* 2220 W Broad St ... Richmond VA 23220-2008
Fax: 804 367-6020
804 225-2142 *Department of the Treasury* 101 N 14th St ... Richmond VA 23219-3682
Fax: 804 225-3187
804 786-2801 *Department of Transportation* 1401 E Broad St ... Richmond VA 23219-2039
Fax: 804 786-6250
804 786-3611 *Division of Energy Regulation* 1220 Bank St ... Richmond VA 23219-3645
Fax: 804 782-2324
804 786-3263 *Division of Engineering & Buildings* 805 E Broad St ... Richmond VA 23219-1926
Fax: 804 371-7934
703 523-8100 *Division of Mines* 219 Wood Ave ... Big Stone Gap VA 24219-2799
Fax: 703 523-8239
804 786-5873 *Division of Occupational Health & Safety* 205 N 4th St ... Richmond VA 23219-1747
Fax: 804 371-7634
804 786-3845 *Division of Purchases & Supply* 805 E Broad St ... Richmond VA 23219-1992
Fax: 804 225-3707

804 786-7751 Division of Securities & Retail Franchising PO Box 1197 ... Richmond VA 23209-1197
    Fax: 804 649-2036
804 225-2667 Division of Solid & Hazardous Waste Management
    101 N 14th St Monroe Bldg 11th Fl .... Richmond VA 23219-3641
    Fax: 804 225-3753
804 786-6228 Division of Vital Records 109 Governor St .... Richmond VA 23219-3623
804 786-3001 Employment Commission 703 E Main St .... Richmond VA 23219-3307
    Fax: 804 225-3923
804 786-2211 Governor State Capitol Bldg 9th & Grace St .... Richmond VA 23219-3415
    Fax: 804 786-3985
804 786-2078 Lieutenant Governor 101 N 8th St .... Richmond VA 23219-2336
    Fax: 804 786-7514
804 674-3081 Parole Board 6900 Atmore Dr .... Richmond VA 23225-5644
    Fax: 804 674-3284
804 784-3551 Powhatan Correctional Center .... State Farm VA 23160-9999
804 225-3297 Public Defender Commission 701 E Franklin St Suite 910 .. Richmond VA 23219-2502
    Fax: 804 371-8326
804 367-8526 Real Estate Board 3600 W Broad St .... Richmond VA 23230-4915
804 786-2441 Secretary of the Commonwealth 200 N 9th St Suite 114 .... Richmond VA 23219-3402
    Fax: 804 371-0017
804 367-0056 State Water Control Board 2111 N Hamilton St .... Richmond VA 23230-4105
    Fax: 804 367-0067
804 786-2251 Supreme Court 100 N 9th St 4th Fl .... Richmond VA 23219-2334
    Fax: 804 371-8530
804 786-3004 Unemployment Insurance Services Div PO Box 1358 .... Richmond VA 23211-0000
    Fax: 804 786-8492
804 786-2101 Virginia State Penitentiary 500 Spring St .... Richmond VA 23219-6112
    Fax: Call company operator
804 786-8929 **Virginia State Library & Archives** 11th St & Capitol Sq .... Richmond VA 23219-0000
    Fax: 804 225-4035
804 524-5000 **Virginia State University** .... Petersburg VA 23803-2095
804 257-5866 **Virginia Union University** 1500 N Lombardy St .... Richmond VA 23220-1790
    Fax: 804 257-5818
804 455-3200 **Virginia Wesleyan College** 1584 Wesleyan Dr .... Norfolk VA 23502-5599
    Fax: 804 466-8526
703 857-7200 **Virginia Western Community College** PO Box 14045 .... Roanoke VA 24038-4045
703 231-7666 **Virginia-Maryland Regional College of Veterinary Medicine**
    Phase II Duckpond Dr .... Blacksburg VA 24061-0001
    Fax: 703 231-7367
202 225-2461 **Visclosky Peter J (Rep - D - Indiana)** 330 Cannon Bldg ..... Washington DC 20515-0001
    Fax: Unlisted
608 791-0040 **Viterbo College** 815 9th St S .... La Crosse WI 54601-8802
    Fax: 608 791-0367
202 732-2251 **Vocational & Adult Education Div (US Dept of Education)**
    400 Maryland Ave SW Rm 4090 .... Washington DC 20202-0001
    Fax: 202 732-3897
212 777-0700 **Vocational Foundation Inc** 902 Broadway 15th Fl .... New York NY 10010-6002
    Fax: 212 673-8975
202 485-8095 **Voice of America (VOA)** 330 Independence Ave SW .... Washington DC 20547-0001
    Fax: 202 485-8104 Personnel
202 225-2956 **Volkmer Harold L (Rep - D - Missouri)**
    2411 Rayburn Bldg .... Washington DC 20515-0001
    Fax: 202 225-7834
615 452-8600 **Volunteer State Community College** Nashville Pike .... Gallatin TN 37066-0000
    Fax: Ext 502
212 873-2600 **Volunteers of America** 340 W 85th St .... New York NY 10024-3800
    Fax: 212 769-2629
904 736-5902 **Volusia County** 123 W Indiana Ave .... De Land FL 32720-4210
    Fax: 904 822-5711
904 252-8374 **Volusia County Public Library System** City Island .... Daytona Beach FL 32114-3382
    Fax: 904 254-4639
803 793-3351 **Voorhees College** Voorhees Rd .... Denmark SC 29042-0000
    Fax: 803 793-4584
202 822-6640 **Voters for Choice** 2000 P St NW Suite 515 .... Washington DC 20036-5915
    Fax: 202 822-6644
202 225-6155 **Vucanovich Barbara F (Rep - R - Nevada)**
    206 Cannon Bldg .... Washington DC 20515-0001
    Fax: 202 225-2319

W

317 362-1400 **Wabash College** 301 W Wabash Ave .... Crawfordsville IN 47933-2484
    Fax: Unlisted
618 262-4561 **Wabash County** 4th & Market St .... Mount Carmel IL 62863-1582
219 563-0661 **Wabash County** 1 W Hill St .... Wabash IN 46992-3151
618 262-8641 **Wabash Valley College** 2200 College Dr .... Mount Carmel IL 62863-2699
    Fax: Ext 3247 Library
612 565-2648 **Wabasha County** 625 Jefferson Ave .... Wabasha MN 55981-1577
913 765-3414 **Wabaunsee County** PO Box 278 .... Alma KS 66401-0278
817 754-4694 **Waco-McLennan County Library** 1717 Austin Ave .... Waco TX 76701-1741
    Fax: 817 754-0772
218 631-2895 **Wadena County** Jefferson St .... Wadena MN 56482-0000
315 393-4231 **Wadhams Hall Seminary-College** RR 4 Box 80 .... Ogdensburg NY 13669-9308
203 278-2670 **Wadsworth Antheneum** 600 Main St .... Hartford CT 06103-2990
718 390-3411 **Wagner College** 631 Howard Ave .... Staten Island NY 10301-4495
    Fax: 718 390-3467
918 485-2141 **Wagoner County** 307 E Cherokee St .... Wagoner OK 74467-0000
206 795-3558 **Wahkiakum County** PO Box 116 .... Cathlamet WA 98612-0116
919 856-6000 **Wake County** 336 Fayetteville Mall .... Raleigh NC 27602-0000
    Fax: 919 755-6796
919 250-1200 **Wake County Dept of the Public Libraries** 4020 Carya Dr .... Raleigh NC 27610-2913
    Fax: 919 250-1209
919 759-5000 **Wake Forest University** Reynolds Stn .... Winston-Salem NC 27106-5193
    Fax: Unlisted
919 759-5434   *School of Law* PO Box 7206 .... Winston-Salem NC 27109-7206
    Fax: 919 759-6077
919 772-7500 **Wake Technical Community College** 9101 Fayetteville Rd .... Raleigh NC 27603-5696
904 926-3341 **Wakulla County** PO Box 337 .... Crawfordville FL 32327-0337
    Fax: 904 926-8326
207 338-3282 **Waldo County** 73 Church St .... Belfast ME 04915-1705
515 582-2450 **Waldorf College** 106 S 6th St .... Forest City IA 50436-1797
    Fax: 515 582-8111 Library
612 375-7600 **Walker Art Center** Vineland Pl .... Minneapolis MN 55403-1195
    Fax: 612 375-7618
205 384-3404 **Walker County** PO Box 749 .... Jasper AL 35502-0749
404 638-1437 **Walker County** PO Box 445 .... Lafayette GA 30728-0445
409 291-9500 **Walker County** 1100 University Ave .... Huntsville TX 77340-4631
202 225-2411 **Walker Robert S (Rep - R - Pennsylvania)**
    2445 Rayburn Bldg .... Washington DC 20515-0001
    Fax: Unlisted
509 527-2615 **Walla Walla College** 204 S College Ave .... College Place WA 99324-1198
    Fax: 509 527-2253
509 522-2500 **Walla Walla Community College** 500 Tausick Way .... Walla Walla WA 99362-9270
    Fax: 509 527-4480 Library

509 527-3221 **Walla Walla County** PO Box 836 .... Walla Walla WA 99362-0259
913 852-4282 **Wallace County** 313 Main St .... Sharon Springs KS 67758-9998
    Fax: 913 852-4783
409 826-3357 **Waller County** 836 Austin St .... Hempstead TX 77445-4667
    Fax: 409 826-8317
202 224-6441 **Wallop Malcolm (Sen - R - Wyoming)** 237 Russell Bldg .... Washington DC 20510-0001
    Fax: 202 224-3230
503 426-3586 **Wallowa County** 101 S River St Rm 202 .... Enterprise OR 97828-1300
    Fax: 503 426-4095
216 499-7090 **Walsh College** 2020 Easton St NW .... Canton OH 44720-3396
313 689-8282 **Walsh College of Accountancy & Business Administration**
    3838 Livernois Rd .... Troy MI 48083-5066
    Fax: 313 689-9066
701 352-2851 **Walsh County** 600 Cooper Ave .... Grafton ND 58237-1542
    Fax: 701 352-1104
202 225-3701 **Walsh James T (Rep - R - New York)**
    1238 Longworth Bldg .... Washington DC 20515-0001
    Fax: 202 225-4042
301 547-9000 **Walters Art Gallery** 600 N Charles St .... Baltimore MD 21201-5185
    Fax: 301 783-7969
615 587-9722 **Walters State Community College**
    500 S Davy Crockett Pkwy .... Morristown TN 37813-1999
    Fax: Ext 404
601 876-4947 **Walthall County** PO Box 351 .... Tylertown MS 39667-0351
904 892-3137 **Walton County** PO Box 1260 .... De Funiak Springs FL 32433-0000
    Fax: 904 892-9742
404 267-4571 **Walton County** Court St Annex 1 .... Monroe GA 30655-0000
605 649-7878 **Walworth County** PO Box 199 .... Selby SD 57472-0199
414 741-4241 **Walworth County** PO Box 1001 .... Elkhorn WI 53121-1001
    Fax: 414 741-4221
515 683-0060 **Wapello County** 4th & Court Sts .... Ottumwa IA 52501-2599
701 857-6460 **Ward County** 3rd St SE .... Minot ND 58701-6498
915 943-3294 **Ward County** County Courthouse .... Monahans TX 79756-0000
513 328-6903 **Warder Public Library** 201 S Fountain Ave .... Springfield OH 45502-1215
    Fax: Unlisted
912 287-4300 **Ware County** 800 Church St .... Waycross GA 31501-3501
202 224-2023 **Warner John W (Sen - R - Virginia)** 225 Russell Bldg .. Washington DC 20510-0001
    Fax: 202 224-6295
503 775-4366 **Warner Pacific College** 2219 SE 68th Ave .... Portland OR 97215-4099
    Fax: 503 775-8853
813 638-1426 **Warner Southern College** 5301 S Hwy 27 .... Lake Wales FL 33853-8725
404 465-2171 **Warren County** 100 Main St .... Warrenton GA 30828-0000
515 961-1033 **Warren County** PO Box 379 .... Indianola IA 50125-0379
309 734-8592 **Warren County** Public Sq .... Monmouth IL 61462-0000
317 762-3510 **Warren County** N Monroe St .... Williamsport IN 47993-0000
502 843-4146 **Warren County** 429 E 10th St .... Bowling Green KY 42101-2250
314 456-3331 **Warren County** 105 S Market St .... Warrenton MO 63383-1903
601 636-4415 **Warren County** PO Box 351 .... Vicksburg MS 39181-0351
919 257-3261 **Warren County** PO Box 709 .... Warrenton NC 27589-0709
908 475-5361 **Warren County**
    Rt 519 Wayne Dumont Jr Administration Bldg .... Belvidere NJ 07823-0000
    Fax: 908 475-6555 Admin
518 761-6429 **Warren County** Rt 9 .... Lake George NY 12845-0000
    Fax: 518 761-6559
513 932-4040 **Warren County** 320 E Silver St .... Lebanon OH 45036-2361
    Fax: 513 932-7929
814 723-7550 **Warren County** 204 4th Ave .... Warren PA 16365-2399
615 473-2623 **Warren County** PO Box 231 .... McMinnville TN 37110-0231
703 636-9973 **Warren County** 22 S Royal Ave .... Front Royal VA 22630-3202
307 775-1110 **Warren Francis E Air Force Base** .... Cheyenne WY 82005-0001
    Fax: Unlisted
313 264-8720 **Warren Public Libraries** 5951 Beebe St .... Warren MI 48092-1604
704 298-3325 **Warren Wilson College** 701 Warren Wilson Rd .... Swannanoa NC 28778-2099
    Fax: 704 298-2161
216 399-8807 **Warren-Trumbull County Public Library**
    444 Mahoning Ave NW .... Warren OH 44483-4606
    Fax: 216 395-3988
812 897-6120 **Warrick County** County Courthouse .... Boonville IN 47601-1596
319 352-8200 **Wartburg College** 222 9th St NW .... Waverly IA 50677-2215
    Fax: 319 352-8394
401 739-5440 **Warwick Public Library** 600 Sandy Ln .... Warwick RI 02886-3998
801 654-3211 **Wasatch County** 25 N Main St .... Heber City UT 84032-1827
    Fax: 801 654-5116
503 296-2207 **Wasco County** 5th & Washington .... The Dalles OR 97058-0000
    Fax: 503 296-3769
507 835-0617 **Waseca County** 307 N State St .... Waseca MN 56093-2992
    Fax: 507 835-0633
307 347-6491 **Washakie County** 10th St & Big Horn Ave .... Worland WY 82401-0000
    Fax: 307 347-9366
715 468-7808 **Washburn County** 110 W 4th Ave .... Shell Lake WI 54871-0000
913 295-6300 **Washburn University of Topeka** 1700 College Ave .... Topeka KS 66621-0001
913 295-6660   *School of Law* 1700 College Ave .... Topeka KS 66621-0001
    Fax: 913 232-8087
412 222-4400 **Washington & Jefferson College** 45 S Lincoln St .... Washington PA 15301-4801
    Fax: 412 223-5271
703 463-8400 **Washington & Lee University** .... Lexington VA 24450-1799
    Fax: 703 463-8945
703 463-8505   *School of Law* Lewis Hall .... Lexington VA 24450-0000
    Fax: 703 463-8945
301 552-1400 **Washington Bible College Capitol Bible Seminary**
    6511 Princess Garden Pkwy .... Lanham MD 20706-3599
301 778-2800 **Washington College** Washington Ave .... Chestertown MD 21620-0000
    Fax: 301 778-0151
205 847-2208 **Washington County** PO Box 146 .... Chatom AL 36518-0146
501 521-8400 **Washington County** 2 S College Ave .... Fayetteville AR 72701-5393
    Fax: 501 443-9568
303 345-2701 **Washington County** 150 Ash Ave .... Akron CO 80720-1510
904 638-6200 **Washington County** 201 W Cypress Ave Suite B .... Chipley FL 32428-0000
    Fax: 904 638-6106
912 552-2325 **Washington County** PO Box 271 .... Sandersville GA 31082-0271
319 653-7741 **Washington County** PO Box 391 .... Washington IA 52353-0391
208 549-2092 **Washington County** PO Box 670 .... Weiser ID 83672-0670
    Fax: 208 549-3925
618 327-8314 **Washington County** Saint Louis St .... Nashville IL 62263-1599
812 883-5748 **Washington County** County Courthouse .... Salem IN 47167-2086
913 325-2974 **Washington County** 214 C St .... Washington KS 66968-1928
606 336-3471 **Washington County** PO Box 446 .... Springfield KY 40069-0446
301 791-3000 **Washington County** 95 W Washington St .... Hagerstown MD 21740-4831
207 255-3127 **Washington County** PO Box 297 .... Machias ME 04654-0297
612 439-3220 **Washington County** 14900 61st St N .... Stillwater MN 55082-6161
    Fax: 612 779-5498
314 438-4901 **Washington County** 102 N Missouri St .... Potosi MO 63664-1744
601 332-1595 **Washington County** PO Box 309 .... Greenville MS 38702-0309
919 793-5823 **Washington County** 120 Adams St .... Plymouth NC 27962-1308
    Fax: 919 793-9788
402 426-6822 **Washington County** PO Box 466 .... Blair NE 68008-0466

518 747-3374 **Washington County** Upper Broadway .... Fort Edward NY 12828-0000
614 373-6623 **Washington County** 205 Putnam St .... Marietta OH 45750-3017
Fax: 614 373-2025 Admin
918 336-0330 **Washington County** 420 S Johnstone Ave .... Bartlesville OK 74003-6602
503 648-8681 **Washington County** 155 N 1st Ave .... Hillsboro OR 97124-3070
Fax: 503 648-8895
412 228-6700 **Washington County** 100 W Beau St .... Washington PA 15301-4432
Fax: 412 228-6965
401 782-4121 **Washington County** 4800 Tower Hill Rd .... Wakefield RI 02879-2239
615 753-1621 **Washington County** PO Box 218 .... Jonesborough TN 37659-0218
409 836-4300 **Washington County** 105 E Main St .... Brenham TX 77833-0000
801 634-5702 **Washington County** 197 E Tabernacle St .... Saint George UT 84770-3473
Fax: 801 634-5718
703 628-8733 **Washington County** 216 Park St .... Abingdon VA 24210-3312
802 223-2091 **Washington County** PO Box 426 .... Montpelier VT 05602-0426
414 338-4301 **Washington County** 432 E Washington St .... West Bend WI 53095-2500
Fax: 414 338-4490
301 739-3250 **Washington County Free Library** 100 S Potomac St .... Hagerstown MD 21740-5556
301 739-5727 **Washington County Museum of Fine Arts** PO Box 423 .... Hagerstown MD 21741-0423
614 373-1057 **Washington County Public Library** 615 5th St .... Marietta OH 45750-1973
Fax: 614 373-2860
202 225-3816 **Washington Craig (Rep - D - Texas)**
1711 Longworth Bldg .... Washington DC 20515-0001
Fax: 202 225-6186
202 347-7201 **Washington DC Chamber of Commerce**
1411 K St NW 5th Fl .... Washington DC 20005-0000
Fax: 202 347-3538
202 727-1000 **Washington DC City Hall** 300 Indiana Ave NW .... Washington DC 20001-2106
206 583-0664 **Washington Democratic State Committee**
Smith Tower Suite 1701 .... Seattle WA 98104-2322
Fax: 206 583-0301
202 842-0806 **Washington National Monument Assn**
740 Jackson Pl NW .... Washington DC 20503-0001
504 839-4663 **Washington Parish** Washington & Main St .... Franklinton LA 70438-0000
206 753-2580 **Washington State Capital Museum** 211 W 21st Ave .... Olympia WA 98501-0000
Fax: 206 586-8322
Washington State Government
206 753-5000 *Information* 512 12th Ave SE .... Olympia WA 98504-0001
206 459-6256 *Air Programs Div* 4224 6th Ave SE Bldg 4 PV-11 .... Lacey WA 98504-0000
Fax: 206 438-7484
206 753-5485 *Archives & Records Management*
12th Ave & Washington St .... Olympia WA 98504-0001
206 753-3860 *Arts Commission* 110 9th St Columbia Bldg MS GH-11 .... Olympia WA 98504-0001
Fax: 206 586-5351
206 753-2550 *Attorney General* Highways-Licenses Bldg 7th Fl PB-71 .... Olympia WA 98504-0001
Fax: 206 586-8474
206 753-6210 *Consumer & Business Fair Practices Div* N 122 Capitol Way .... Olympia WA 98501-0000
Fax: 206 753-2005
206 753-5050 *Department of Agriculture* 406 General Administration Bldg .... Olympia WA 98504-0001
Fax: 206 586-6402
206 753-2500 *Department of Corrections* 410 W 5th St FN-61 .... Olympia WA 98504-0001
Fax: Unlisted
206 459-6168 *Department of Ecology*
Abbott Raphael Bldg St Martins College Campus PV-11 .... Olympia WA 98504-8711
Fax: 206 459-6007
206 586-6904 *Department of Education*
Legion Way & Washington St Old Capitol Bldg FG-11 .... Olympia WA 98504-0001
Fax: 206 753-6754
206 753-5439 *Department of General Administration* 11th & Columbia Sts .... Olympia WA 98504-0001
Fax: 206 586-5898
206 753-6307 *Department of Labor & Industries*
General Administration Bldg 3rd Fl .... Olympia WA 98504-0001
Fax: 206 586-5240
206 753-6909 *Department of Licensing Agency* 2424 Bristol Ct SW .... Olympia WA 98504-0000
Fax: 206 586-0998
206 753-5327 *Department of Natural Resources* 201 John A Cherberg Bldg Olympia WA 98504-0001
Fax: 206 586-8217
206 753-6909 *Department of Professional Licensing* 2424 Bristol Ct SW .... Olympia WA 98504-0001
Fax: 206 753-0657
206 753-5281 *Department of Retirement Systems* 1025 E Union St .... Olympia WA 98504-0001
Fax: 206 753-3166
206 753-5574 *Department of Revenue* 11th Ave & Columbia St Rm 415 .... Olympia WA 98504-0001
Fax: 206 586-5543
206 753-5630 *Department of Trade & Economic Development*
General Administration Bldg Rm 101-GA .... Olympia WA 98504-0001
Fax: 206 586-1850
206 753-6005 *Department of Transportation* Transportation Bldg .... Olympia WA 98504-0001
Fax: 206 753-6218
206 459-9191 *Division of Emergency Management*
4220 E Martin Way PT-11 .... Olympia WA 98504-0001
Fax: 206 438-7395
206 753-5114 *Employment Security Dept* 212 Maple Pk .... Olympia WA 98504-0001
Fax: 206 753-4851
206 459-6490 *Energy Facility Site Evaluation Council* 4224 6th Ave SE .... Olympia WA 98504-0001
Fax: 206 459-6886
206 586-5000 *Energy Office* 809 Legion Way SE .... Olympia WA 98504-0001
Fax: 206 753-2397
206 753-6780 *Governor* Legislative Bldg AS-13 .... Olympia WA 98504-0001
Fax: 206 753-4110
206 753-3241 *Higher Education Coordinating Board*
917 Lakeridge Way GV-11 .... Olympia WA 98504-0001
Fax: 206 753-1784
206 753-6797 *Indeterminate Sentence Review Board* 410 W 5th Ave 7th Fl .... Olympia WA 98504-0001
Fax: 206 586-7341
206 753-6500 *Industrial Safety & Health Div* 805 Plum St SE HC-402 3rd Fl Olympia WA 98504-0001
Fax: 206 586-5254
206 786-7700 *Lieutenant Governor* Legislative Bldg AS-31 .... Olympia WA 98504-0001
Fax: 206 786-7520
206 753-7301 *Office of the Insurance Commissioner*
Insurance Bldg Rm 200 AQ-21 .... Olympia WA 98504-0001
Fax: 206 586-3535
206 753-6974 *Real Estate Licensing* PO Box 9012 .... Olympia WA 98504-0001
Fax: 206 586-0998
206 753-7121 *Secretary of State* Legislative Bldg AS-22 .... Olympia WA 98504-0001
Fax: 206 586-5629
206 753-6928 *Securities Div* PO Box 648 .... Olympia WA 98504-0000
Fax: 206 438-7400
206 459-6316 *Solid & Hazardous Waste Program*
4224 6th Ave SE Bldg 4 PV-11 .... Olympia WA 98504-0001
Fax: 206 438-7484
206 753-6810 *State Investment Board* 421 S Capitol Way FR-31 .... Olympia WA 98504-0001
Fax: 206 753-7526
206 753-6548 *State Patrol* 11th Ave & Columbia St .... Olympia WA 98504-0001
Fax: 206 753-2492
206 357-2077 *Supreme Court* Temple of Justice AV-11 .... Olympia WA 98504-0001
Fax: 206 357-2104
206 753-7130 *Treasurer* PO Box 1009 .... Olympia WA 98507-1009
Fax: 206 586-6147
206 753-5120 *Unemployment Insurance Div* 212 Maple Pk .... Olympia WA 98504-0001
Fax: 206 586-5659
206 753-6423 *Utilities Transportation Commission*
1300 South Evergreen Park Dr SW .... Olympia WA 98504-0001
Fax: 206 586-1150
206 753-5936 *Vital Records* 1112 S Quince St .... Olympia WA 98504-0001
206 426-4433 *Washington Corrections Center* Airport Dayton Rd .... Shelton WA 98584-0000
Fax: 206 427-8285
509 525-3610 *Washington State Penitentiary* PO Box 520 .... Walla Walla WA 99362-0520
Fax: 509 527-4669
206 459-6056 *Water Resources Program Dept of Ecology*
Baran Hall 3rd Fl PV-11 .... Olympia WA 98504-0001
Fax: 206 438-7537
206 753-6376 *Workers' Benefits* General Administration Bldg .... Olympia WA 98504-0001
Fax: 206 586-5240
206 593-2830 **Washington State Historical Society Museum**
315 N Stadium Way .... Tacoma WA 98403-3226
206 753-5590 **Washington State Library** PO Box AJ-11 .... Olympia WA 98504-0000
Fax: 206 753-3546
206 451-1984 **Washington State Republican Party**
9 Lake Bellevue Dr Suite 203 .... Bellevue WA 98005-2478
Fax: 206 451-9266
509 335-3564 **Washington State University** .... Pullman WA 99164-0001
Fax: 509 335-3421
509 335-4561 *College of Agriculture and Home Economics* 421 Hobart Hall Pullman WA 99164-0001
Fax: 509 335-2863
509 335-4750 *College of Pharmacy* Wegner Hall Rm 105 .... Pullman WA 99164-6510
Fax: 509 335-0162
614 374-8716 **Washington Technical College** RR 2 .... Marietta OH 45750-9802
Fax: 614 373-7496
206 753-5600 **Washington Tourism Development Div**
General Administration Bldg .... Olympia WA 98504-0001
Fax: 206 586-1850
314 889-5000 **Washington University** 1 Brookings Dr .... Saint Louis MO 63130-4899
Fax: 314 889-5799
314 889-5610 *Department of Earth & Planetary Sciences*
1 Brookings Dr CB 1169 .... Saint Louis MO 63130-4899
314 889-6276 *Department of Physics* 1 Brookings Dr Campus Box 1105 Saint Louis MO 63130-4899
Fax: 314 889-6219
314 362-3363 *Division of Biology & Biomedical Sciences*
660 S Euclid Ave Campus Box 8072 .... Saint Louis MO 63110-1093
Fax: 314 362-3369
314 889-6200 *School of Architecture* 1 Brookings Dr .... Saint Louis MO 63130-0000
314 454-0300 *School of Dental Medicine* 4559 Scott Ave .... Saint Louis MO 63110-1087
314 889-6400 *School of Law* CB 1120 .... Saint Louis MO 63130-0000
Fax: 314 889-6493
314 362-5000 *School of Medicine* 1 Barnes Hospital Plaza .... Saint Louis MO 63110-0000
Fax: 314 362-6955
405 832-2284 **Washita County** PO Box 380 .... Cordell OK 73632-0380
702 328-3110 **Washoe County** PO Box 11130 .... Reno NV 89520-0027
Fax: 702 328-3515
702 785-4190 **Washoe County Library** 301 S Center St .... Reno NV 89501-2102
Fax: 702 785-4692
313 973-3300 **Washtenaw Community College** 4800 E Huron River Dr .... Ann Arbor MI 48106-0000
Fax: 313 677-5414
313 994-2400 **Washtenaw County** PO Box 8645 .... Ann Arbor MI 48107-8645
Fax: 313 994-2368
704 264-1300 **Watauga County** 403 W King St .... Boone NC 28607-3531
Fax: 704 262-1282
703 684-2400 **Water Pollution Control Federation** 601 Wythe St .... Alexandria VA 22314-1994
Fax: 703 684-2492
202 225-2201 **Waters Maxine (Rep - D - California)**
1207 Longworth Bldg .... Washington DC 20515-0001
Fax: 202 225-7854
507 375-3341 **Watonwan County** PO Box 518 .... Saint James MN 56081-0518
708 466-4811 **Waubonsee Community College** Rt 47 & Harter Rd .... Sugar Grove IL 60554-0000
Fax: Ext 596
414 548-7010 **Waukesha County** 515 W Moreland Blvd .... Waukesha WI 53188-2428
Fax: 414 548-7043
414 524-3680 **Waukesha Public Library** 321 Wisconsin Ave .... Waukesha WI 53186-4786
715 258-6200 **Waupaca County** 811 Harding St .... Waupaca WI 54981-1588
414 787-4631 **Waushara County** 209 S Saint Marie St .... Wautoma WI 54982-0000
Fax: 414 787-7685
202 225-3976 **Waxman Henry A (Rep - D - California)**
2418 Rayburn Bldg .... Washington DC 20515-0001
Fax: 202 225-4099
912 285-6130 **Waycross College** 2001 Francis St .... Waycross GA 31501-9248
Fax: 912 287-4909
907 248-2122 **Wayland Baptist University** 4240 Wisconsin St .... Anchorage AK 99517-2801
806 296-5521 **Wayland Baptist University** 1900 W 7th St .... Plainview TX 79072-6998
Fax: 806 293-1993
919 735-5151 **Wayne Community College North Campus**
906 US Hwy 70 E .... Goldsboro NC 27533-0000
Fax: 919 736-3204
912 427-5900 **Wayne County** 174 N Brunswick St .... Jesup GA 31545-2808
Fax: 912 427-5906
515 872-2264 **Wayne County** PO Box 424 .... Corydon IA 50060-0424
618 842-5182 **Wayne County** 300 E Main St .... Fairfield IL 62837-2013
317 973-9200 **Wayne County** 401 E Main St .... Richmond IN 47374-4289
606 348-6661 **Wayne County** PO Box 565 .... Monticello KY 42633-0000
313 224-0471 **Wayne County** 600 Randolph St .... Detroit MI 48226-2831
Fax: 313 224-0818
314 224-3221 **Wayne County** County Courthouse .... Greenville MO 63944-0000
601 735-2873 **Wayne County** Azalea Dr .... Waynesboro MS 39367-0000
919 731-1400 **Wayne County** 215 S William St .... Goldsboro NC 27530-4824
402 375-2288 **Wayne County** 510 N Pearl St .... Wayne NE 68787-1939
315 946-5400 **Wayne County** 26 Church St .... Lyons NY 14489-1134
216 263-3124 **Wayne County** 107 W Liberty St .... Wooster OH 44691-4850
717 253-5970 **Wayne County** 925 Court St .... Honesdale PA 18431-1922
Fax: 717 253-2943 Admin
615 722-3653 **Wayne County** PO Box 206 .... Waynesboro TN 38485-0206
801 836-2731 **Wayne County** 18 S Main .... Loa UT 84747-0000
Fax: 801 836-2479
304 272-5101 **Wayne County** Hendricks St .... Wayne WV 25570-0000
313 496-2500 **Wayne County Community College** 801 W Fort St .... Detroit MI 48226-3095
Fax: 313 961-9439
313 326-8910 **Wayne Oakland Library Federation** 33030 Van Born Rd .... Wayne MI 48184-2496
Fax: 313 326-3035
402 375-2200 **Wayne State College** 200 E 10th St .... Wayne NE 68787-1486
Fax: 402 375-7204
313 577-2424 **Wayne State University** 5980 Cass Ave .... Detroit MI 48202-3489
313 577-4082 *College of Nursing* 5557 Cass Ave .... Detroit MI 48202-3615
Fax: 313 577-4571

313 577-0820 *College of Pharmacy & Allied Health Professions* .... Detroit MI 48202-0000
Fax: 313 577-2033
313 577-1591 *Graduate School of Immunology & Microbiology*
540 E Canfield .... Detroit MI 48201-1908
Fax: 313 577-1155
313 577-2627 *Journalism Program* 199 Manoogian .... Detroit MI 48202-0000
313 577-3930 *Law School* 468 W Ferry St .... Detroit MI 48202-3698
Fax: 313 577-5498
313 577-1460 *School of Medicine* 540 E Canfield St .... Detroit MI 48201-1908
Fax: 313 577-8777
703 942-6600 **Waynesboro (Independent City)** 250 S Wayne Ave .... Waynesboro VA 22980-4622
Fax: Unlisted
412 627-8191 **Waynesburg College** 51 W College St .... Waynesburg PA 15370-1258
Fax: Unlisted
202 225-3625 **Ways & Means Committee (US House of Representatives)**
1102 Longworth Bldg .... Washington DC 20515-0001
901 364-2285 **Weakley County** County Courthouse .... Dresden TN 38225-0000
817 594-5471 **Weatherford College** 308 E Park Ave .... Weatherford TX 76086-5699
Fax: 817 594-0627
512 721-2221 **Webb County** 1000 Houston St .... Laredo TX 78040-8023
516 671-2213 **Webb Institute of Naval Architecture** Crescent Beach Rd ...... Glen Cove NY 11542-1398
Fax: 516 674-9838
813 638-1431 **Webber College** PO Box 96 .... Babson Park FL 33827-0096
Fax: 813 638-2823
801 399-8481 **Weber County** 2549 Washington Blvd .... Ogden UT 84401-3111
801 627-6913 **Weber County Library** 2464 Jefferson Ave .... Ogden UT 84401-2488
801 626-6000 **Weber State College** 3750 S Harrison Blvd .... Ogden UT 84408-0001
Fax: 801 626-7930
202 225-2331 **Weber Vin (Rep - R - Minnesota)** 106 Cannon Bldg .... Washington DC 20515-0001
Fax: 202 225-0987
912 828-5775 **Webster County** Washington St & Hwy 280 .... Preston GA 31824-0000
515 576-7115 **Webster County** 701 Central Ave .... Fort Dodge IA 50501-3813
502 639-5042 **Webster County** PO Box 155 .... Dixon KY 42409-0155
417 468-2223 **Webster County** County Courthouse .... Marshfield MO 65706-0000
601 258-4131 **Webster County** Main St .... Walthall MS 39771-9999
402 746-2716 **Webster County** 621 N Cedar St .... Red Cloud NE 68970-2397
304 847-2508 **Webster County** PO Box 32 .... Webster Springs WV 26288-0032
318 371-0366 **Webster Parish** PO Box 370 .... Minden LA 71058-0370
314 968-6900 **Webster University** 470 E Lockwood Ave .... Saint Louis MO 63119-3194
916 637-4111 **Weimer College** 20601 Paoli Ln .... Weimar CA 95736-9999
Fax: 916 637-4408
202 225-5635 **Weiss Ted (Rep - D - New York)** 2467 Rayburn Bldg .... Washington DC 20515-0001
Fax: 202 225-6923
303 356-4000 **Weld County** 915 10th St .... Greeley CO 80631-1123
202 225-2011 **Weldon Curt (Rep - R - Pennsylvania)** 316 Cannon Bldg .... Washington DC 20515-0001
Fax: 202 225-8137
617 235-0320 **Wellesley College** 106 Central St .... Wellesley MA 02181-8201
Fax: 617 235-7361
315 364-3370 **Wells College** .... Aurora NY 13026-1100
Fax: 315 364-3227
219 824-2320 **Wells County** 102 W Market St .... Bluffton IN 46714-2050
701 547-3122 **Wells County** PO Box 596 .... Fessenden ND 58438-0596
202 224-5641 **Wellstone Paul David (Sen - D - Minnesota)**
123 Hart Bldg .... Washington DC 20510-0001
Fax: 202 224-8438
509 662-1651 **Wenatchee Valley College** 1300 5th St .... Wenatchee WA 98801-1799
Fax: 509 664-2538
617 442-9010 **Wentworth Institute of Technology** 550 Huntington Ave .... Boston MA 02115-5998
Fax: 617 427-2852
816 259-2221 **Wentworth Military Academy** 18th & Washington Ave .... Lexington MO 64067-1799
Fax: Unlisted
302 736-2300 **Wesley College** 120 N State St .... Dover DE 19901-3877
601 845-2265 **Wesley College** Hwy 469 .... Florence MS 39073-0000
912 477-1110 **Wesleyan College** 4760 Forsyth Rd .... Macon GA 31297-0001
Fax: 912 477-7572
203 347-9411 **Wesleyan University** High St .... Middletown CT 06457-0000
Fax: 203 344-7957
504 383-4755 **West Baton Rouge Parish** PO Box 757 .... Port Allen LA 70767-0757
Fax: 504 387-0218
615 259-6004 **West Ben Public Library of Nashville & Davidson County**
222 8th Ave N .... Nashville TN 37203-3585
Fax: 615 259-7254
318 428-3390 **West Carroll Parish** PO Box 630 .... Oak Grove LA 71263-0630
215 436-1000 **West Chester University** .... West Chester PA 19383-0001
Fax: 215 436-3540
209 299-7201 **West Coast Christian College** 6901 N Maple Ave .... Fresno CA 93710-4520
Fax: 209 299-0932
213 487-4433 **West Coast University** 440 Shatto Pl .... Los Angeles CA 90020-1765
Fax: 213 380-4362
714 953-2700 *Orange County Center* 550 S Main St .... Orange CA 92668-4593
Fax: Unlisted
504 635-3864 **West Feliciana Parish** Royal & Prosperity .... Saint Francisville LA 70775-0000
904 435-1760 **West Florida Regional Library** 200 W Gregory .... Pensacola FL 32501-4822
404 836-6711 **West Georgia Regional Library** 710 Rome St .... Carrollton GA 30117-3046
209 935-0801 **West Hills College** 300 W Cherry Ln .... Coalinga CA 93210-1399
Fax: 209 935-5655
304 336-5000 **West Liberty State College** Rt 88 .... West Liberty WV 26074-9999
Fax: 304 336-8285
213 836-7110 **West Los Angeles College** 4800 Freshman Dr .... Culver City CA 90230-3500
616 845-6211 **West Shore Community College** 3000 N Stiles Rd .... Scottville MI 49454-9716
Fax: 616 845-0207
708 383-6200 **West Suburban College of Nursing** Erie St & Austin Blvd .... Oak Park IL 60302-2510
Fax: Unlisted
806 656-2000 **West Texas State University**
PO Box 999 West Texas State Stn .... Canyon TX 79016-0001
Fax: 806 656-2071
408 867-2200 **West Valley College** 14000 Fruitvale Ave .... Saratoga CA 95070-5697
Fax: 408 867-1308
304 342-1115 **West Virginia Chamber of Commerce**
300 Capitol St Suite 1000 .... Charleston WV 25301-1794
Fax: 304 342-1130
304 442-3071 **West Virginia Institute of Technology** Rt 61 .... Montgomery WV 25136-0000
Fax: 304 442-3059 Admin
304 348-2041 **West Virginia Library Commission** State Capitol .... Charleston WV 25305-0001
Fax: Unlisted
304 344-3446 **West Virginia Republican State Committee** 101 Dee Dr ...... Charleston WV 25311-1620
304 766-3000 **West Virginia State College** Rt 25 .... Institute WV 25112-9999
Fax: 304 766-9842
304 342-8121 **West Virginia State Democratic Executive Committee**
405 Capitol St Suite 501 .... Charleston WV 25301-1727
Fax: 304 342-8122
West Virginia State Government
304 348-3456 *Information* State Capitol .... Charleston WV 25305-0001
Fax: 304 348-8887
304 348-2300 *Administration Dept* State Capitol Rm E-119 .... Charleston WV 25305-0000
Fax: 304 348-8887
304 348-3286 *Air Pollution Control Commission* 1558 Washington St E .. Charleston WV 25311-0000
Fax: 304 348-8887
304 348-0230 *Archives & History Div* Capitol Complex Cultural Ctr .... Charleston WV 25305-0000
Fax: 304 348-0225
304 348-0240 *Arts & Humanities Div* Capitol Complex Cultural Ctr 2nd Fl Charleston WV 25305-0000
Fax: 304 348-0225
304 348-2021 *Attorney General* State Capitol .... Charleston WV 25305-0000
Fax: 304 348-0140
304 348-2971 *Bureau of Public Health* 1800 Washington St E Suite 206 .. Charleston WV 25305-0001
Fax: 304 348-0045
304 348-0400 *Community & Industrial Development Dept*
State Capitol Complex Bldg 1 Rm M-146 .... Charleston WV 25305-0000
Fax: 304 348-0362
304 348-8986 *Consumer Protection Div* 812 Quarrier St .... Charleston WV 25301-2617
Fax: 304 348-0184
304 348-2201 *Department of Agriculture* State Capitol Complex Rm 28 ... Charleston WV 25305-0000
Fax: 304 348-0451
304 348-2036 *Department of Corrections* 112 California Ave .... Charleston WV 25305-0001
Fax: 304 348-5934
304 348-2681 *Department of Education* 1900 Kanawha Blvd E .... Charleston WV 25305-0001
Fax: 304 348-0048
304 348-2630 *Department of Employment Security* 112 California Ave .... Charleston WV 25305-0001
Fax: 304 348-0301
304 348-8860 *Department of Fuel & Energy* 1204 Kanawha Blvd E .... Charleston WV 25301-2986
Fax: 304 348-0362
304 348-3505 *Department of Highways* 1900 Washington St W Bldg 5 ... Charleston WV 25312-1407
Fax: 304 348-4076
304 348-3394 *Department of Insurance* 2019 Washington St E .... Charleston WV 25311-2214
Fax: 304 348-0412
304 348-7890 *Department of Labor*
1800 Washington St E Bldg 3 Rm 319 .... Charleston WV 25317-0001
304 746-2111 *Department of Public Safety* 725 Jefferson Rd .... South Charleston WV 25309-1698
Fax: 304 746-2230
304 348-2501 *Department of Tax & Revenue*
State Capitol Complex Rm 417 .... Charleston WV 25305-0000
Fax: Unlisted
304 348-8800 *Division of Vital Registration*
State Capitol Complex Bldg 3 Rm 516 .... Charleston WV 25305-0001
304 348-5935 *Division of Waste Management* 1356 Hansford St .... Charleston WV 25301-0000
Fax: 304 348-0256
304 348-2107 *Division of Water Resources* 1201 Greenbrier St .... Charleston WV 25311-1001
Fax: 304 348-5905
304 348-2000 *Governor* State Capitol Complex .... Charleston WV 25305-0000
Fax: 304 342-7025
304 348-2101 *Higher Education Central Office* 1018 Kanawha Blvd E ...... Charleston WV 25301-2887
Fax: 304 348-0259
304 335-2291 *Huttonsville Correctional Center* PO Box 1 .... Huttonsville WV 26273-0010
Fax: Ext 275
304 348-2754 *Natural Resources Dept* 1900 Kanawha Blvd E Rm 669 .... Charleston WV 25305-0660
Fax: 304 348-2768
304 348-8860 *Office of Economic Opportunity* 1204 Kanawha Blvd E ..... Charleston WV 25301-2900
Fax: 304 348-8874
304 348-5380 *Office of Emergency Services*
State Capitol Complex Rm EB-80 .... Charleston WV 25305-0001
Fax: 304 344-4538
304 348-2981 *Office of Environmental Health Services*
1900 Kanawha Blvd E Bldg 3 Rm 550 .... Charleston WV 25305-0000
Fax: 304 348-0045
304 348-3500 *Oil & Gas Conservation Commission*
1615 Washington St E .... Charleston WV 25311-0000
Fax: 304 348-2452
304 348-4010 *Planning Unit* State Capitol Complex Bldg 6 Rm 553 .... Charleston WV 25301-0000
Fax: 304 348-0449
304 348-6366 *Probation & Parole Board* 112 California Ave Rm 304 ...... Charleston WV 25305-0001
304 348-3905 *Public Defender's Services*
1800 Washington St E Rm 330 .... Charleston WV 25305-0001
304 340-0303 *Public Service Commission* 201 Brooks St .... Charleston WV 25301-1827
Fax: 304 340-0325
304 348-2309 *Purchasing Div* State Capitol Complex Rm 110 .... Charleston WV 25305-0001
Fax: 304 348-3970
304 348-3555 *Real Estate Commission* 1033 Quarrier St Suite 400 .... Charleston WV 25301-2315
304 345-4000 *Secretary of State* State Capitol Complex Rm W-157 .... Charleston WV 25305-0000
304 348-2251 *Securities Commissioner*
State Capitol Complex Rm W118 .... Charleston WV 25305-0001
Fax: 304 344-2229
304 348-2601 *Supreme Court* State Capitol Complex Rm 317-E .... Charleston WV 25305-0000
Fax: 304 348-3815
304 343-4000 *Treasury* State Capitol Complex Rm E147 .... Charleston WV 25305-0001
Fax: 304 346-3141
304 348-2624 *Unemployment Compensation* 112 California Ave 6th Fl ... Charleston WV 25305-0001
Fax: 304 348-0301
304 845-2040 *West Virginia Penitentiary* 818 Jefferson Ave .... Moundsville WV 26041-2294
Fax: 304 845-8975
304 348-2580 *Worker's Compensation Fund* 601 Morris St .... Charleston WV 25301-1446
Fax: 304 348-2268
304 348-0230 **West Virginia State Museum** Capitol Complex Cultural Ctr ... Charleston WV 25305-0001
Fax: 304 348-0225
304 348-2200 **West Virginia Tourism & Parks Div** 2101 Washington St E ... Charleston WV 25305-0001
Fax: 304 348-0108
304 293-0111 **West Virginia University** .... Morgantown WV 26506-0001
Fax: 304 293-3080
304 293-5306 *College of Law* University Ave .... Morgantown WV 26506-0001
Fax: 304 293-6891
304 293-3701 *Library* .... Morgantown WV 26506-0001
304 293-3505 *Pearly Isaac Reed School of Journalism* Martin Hall ...... Morgantown WV 26506-0001
304 293-4511 *School of Medicine* 1150 Health Science Ctr N .... Morgantown WV 26506-0001
Fax: 304 293-2901
304 293-5211 *School of Pharmacy* 1136 Health Science Ctr N .... Morgantown WV 26506-0001
Fax: 304 293-2901
304 424-8000 **West Virginia University at Parkersburg** RR 5 Box 167A ... Parkersburg WV 26101-9577
Fax: 304 424-8315 Communications
304 473-8000 **West Virginia Wesleyan College** College Ave .... Buckhannon WV 26201-0000
Fax: 304 472-2571
501 785-7000 **Westark Community College** 5210 Grand Ave .... Fort Smith AR 72903-0000
Fax: 501 785-7003
207 797-7261 **Westbrook College** 716 Stevens Ave .... Portland ME 04103-2693
Fax: 207 797-7225
914 285-6600 **Westchester Community College** 75 Grasslands Rd .... Valhalla NY 10595-1693
Fax: 914 285-6565
914 285-2000 **Westchester County** 110 Grove St .... White Plains NY 10601-2504
401 596-2877 **Westerly Public Library** 38 Broad St .... Westerly RI 02891-1856
303 231-1511 **Western Area Power Administration (US Dept of Energy)**
1627 Cole Blvd Bldg 18 .... Golden CO 80401-0000
Fax: 303 327-1632
503 581-8600 **Western Baptist College** 5000 Deer Park Dr SE .... Salem OR 97301-9392
Fax: 503 585-4316

704 227-7211 **Western Carolina University** Cullowhee NC 28723-0000
Fax: Unlisted
203 797-4347 **Western Connecticut State University** 181 White St Danbury CT 06810-6885
Fax: 203 731-2804
402 444-5071 **Western Heritage Museum** 801 S 10th St Omaha NE 68108-3299
Fax: 402 444-5397
309 343-2380 **Western Illinois Library System** 1518 S Henderson St Galesburg IL 61401-5708
Fax: 309 343-0150
309 295-1414 **Western Illinois University** 900 W Adams St Macomb IL 61455-1396
Fax: 309 298-2400 Admin
602 943-2311 **Western International University** 10202 N 19th Ave Phoenix AZ 85021-1994
Fax: 602 371-8637
712 274-6400 **Western Iowa Tech Community College** 4647 Stone Ave Sioux City IA 51106-1997
Fax: 712 274-6238
502 745-0111 **Western Kentucky University** College Heights Bowling Green KY 42101-3576
Fax: 502 745-5387
301 848-7000 **Western Maryland College** College Hill W Main St Westminster MD 21157-4399
Fax: 301 857-2729
616 387-1000 **Western Michigan University** W Michigan Ave Kalamazoo MI 49008-0000
Fax: Ext 0958
406 683-7011 **Western Montana College** 710 S Atlantic St Dillon MT 59725-3598
Fax: 406 683-7493
308 635-3606 **Western Nebraska Community College** 1601 E 27th St Scottsbluff NE 69361-1815
Fax: 308 635-6100
413 782-3111 **Western New England College** 1215 Wilbraham Rd Springfield MA 01119-2693
Fax: Unlisted
413 782-1231 *School of Business* 1215 Wilbraham Rd Springfield MA 01119-2693
Fax: 413 782-1746
413 782-1406 *School of Law*
1215 Wilbraham Rd S Prestley Blake Law Ctr Springfield MA 01119-2689
Fax: 413 782-1745
505 538-6011 **Western New Mexico University** PO Box 680 Silver City NM 88062-0680
Fax: 505 538-6231
405 477-2000 **Western Oklahoma State College** 2801 N Main St Altus OK 73521-1397
Fax: 405 521-6154
503 838-8000 **Western Oregon State College** 345 Monmouth Ave N Monmouth OR 97361-1394
Fax: 503 838-8474
704 438-6000 **Western Piedmont Community College**
1001 Burkemont Ave Morganton NC 28655-4504
Fax: 704 438-6015
216 721-5722 **Western Reserve Historical Society Museum & Library**
10825 East Blvd Cleveland OH 44106-1788
Western Samoa: Independent State of Western Samoa
212 599-6196 *Embassy* 820 2nd Ave Suite 800D New York NY 10017-4504
Fax: 212 972-3970
212 599-6196 *Mission to the UN* 820 2nd Ave Suite 800D New York NY 10017-4504
Fax: 212 972-3970
303 943-3035 **Western State College of Colorado** College Heights Gunnison CO 81231-0001
Fax: 303 943-7069 Admin
915 573-8511 **Western Texas College** 6200 S College Ave Snyder TX 79549-0000
Fax: Call company operator
206 676-3000 **Western Washington University** 516 High St Bellingham WA 98225-5946
Fax: 206 676-3022
608 785-9200 **Western Wisconsin Technical College** 304 6th St N La Crosse WI 54601-3342
Fax: 608 785-9205 Admin
307 382-1600 **Western Wyoming Community College** 2500 College Dr Rock Springs WY 82901-5802
Fax: 307 382-1624
413 568-3311 **Westfield State College** 577 Western Ave Westfield MA 01086-0000
Fax: 413 562-3613
609 921-7100 **Westminster Choir College** Hamilton Ave & Walnut Ln Princeton NJ 08540-3899
Fax: 609 921-8829
314 642-3361 **Westminster College** 501 Westminster Ave Fulton MO 65251-1299
Fax: Unlisted
412 946-8761 **Westminster College** S Market St New Wilmington PA 16172-0001
Fax: Unlisted
801 484-7651 **Westminster College of Salt Lake City** 1840 S 13th East Salt Lake City UT 84105-3697
Fax: 801 466-6916
805 565-6000 **Westmont College** 955 La Paz Rd Santa Barbara CA 93108-1099
Fax: 805 969-6751 Library
412 830-3000 **Westmoreland County** Main St Greensburg PA 15601-2405
Fax: 412 830-3042
804 493-8911 **Westmoreland County** Polk St Montross VA 22520-0000
412 925-4000 **Westmoreland County Community College** College Stn Youngwood PA 15697-1895
Fax: 412 925-1150
307 746-4744 **Weston County** 1 W Main St Newcastle WY 82701-2106
304 455-1390 **Wetzel County** PO Box 156 New Martinsville WV 26155-0156
Fax: 304 455-4675
616 779-9450 **Wexford County** 437 E Division St Cadillac MI 49601-1905
508 997-0046 **Whaling Museum** 18 Johnny Cake Hill New Bedford MA 02740-6317
409 532-2381 **Wharton County** 101 Milam St Wharton TX 77488-0000
409 532-4560 **Wharton County Junior College** 911 Boling Hwy Wharton TX 77488-3252
Fax: 409 532-2201
206 676-6777 **Whatcom County** PO Box 1144 Bellingham WA 98227-1144
Fax: 206 676-7727
202 225-4535 **Wheat Alan (Rep - D - Missouri)** 1210 Longworth Bldg Washington DC 20515-0001
Fax: 202 225-5990
406 632-4891 **Wheatland County** PO Box C Harlowton MT 59036-0903
708 260-5000 **Wheaton College** 501 E College Ave Wheaton IL 60187-5593
Fax: 708 260-3995
508 285-7722 **Wheaton College** E Main St Norton MA 02766-0000
Fax: 508 285-2908
808 422-0531 **Wheeler Air Force Base** Wahiawa HI 96854-0001
205 353-2993 **Wheeler Basin Regional Library** 504 Cherry St NE Decatur AL 35601-1970
Fax: Unlisted
912 568-7135 **Wheeler County** Pearl St Alamo GA 30411-0000
308 654-3235 **Wheeler County** County Courthouse Bartlett NE 68622-0000
503 763-2400 **Wheeler County** PO Box 327 Fossil OR 97830-0327
806 826-5544 **Wheeler County** PO Box 465 Wheeler TX 79096-0465
304 243-2000 **Wheeling Jesuit College** 316 Washington Ave Wheeling WV 26003-6295
Fax: Unlisted
617 734-5200 **Wheelock College** 200 The Riverway Boston MA 02215-4176
505 982-4636 **Wheelwright Museum of the American Indian** PO Box 5153 Santa Fe NM 87502-5153
206 257-2211 **Whidbey Island Naval Air Station** Oak Harbor WA 98278-0000
501 279-6200 **White County** 300 N Spruce St Searcy AR 72143-7720
404 865-2235 **White County** 1657 S Main St Suite A Cleveland GA 30528-0185
618 382-7211 **White County** Main St Carmi IL 62821-0000
219 583-7032 **White County** PO Box 350 Monticello IN 47960-0350
615 836-3203 **White County** County Courthouse Rm 205 Sparta TN 38583-0000
202 456-1414 **White House** 1600 Pennsylvania Ave NW Washington DC 20500-0001
702 289-8841 **White Pine County** PO Box 1002 Ely NV 89301-1002
603 887-4401 **White Pines College** 40 Chester St Chester NH 03036-4331
816 687-1110 **Whiteman Air Force Base** Knob Noster MO 65305-0000
Fax: 816 687-5104
815 772-7201 **Whiteside County** 200 E Knox St Morrison IL 61270-2819
Fax: 815 772-4299
404 278-8717 **Whitfield County** 300 W Crawford St Dalton GA 30720-4205
Fax: 404 278-2465
904 623-7651 **Whiting Field Naval Air Station** Milton FL 32570-0000
Fax: 904 623-7237
219 248-3102 **Whitley County** 302 S Chauncey St Courthouse Sq Columbia City IN 46725-2402
606 549-6002 **Whitley County** Main St Williamsburg KY 40769-0000
Fax: 606 549-2790
509 527-5111 **Whitman College** 345 Boyer Ave Walla Walla WA 99362-2090
Fax: 509 527-5859 Admin
509 397-4622 **Whitman County** 400 N Main St Colfax WA 99111-2031
212 570-3600 **Whitney Museum of American Art** 945 Madison Ave New York NY 10021-2790
Fax: 212 570-1807
202 225-4306 **Whitten Jamie L (Rep - D - Mississippi)**
2314 Rayburn Bldg Washington DC 20515-0001
Fax: 202 225-4328
213 693-0771 **Whittier College** 7026 Founders Hill Rd Whittier CA 90608-0000
Fax: 213 698-4067
213 938-3621 *School of Law* 5353 W 3rd St Los Angeles CA 90020-4899
Fax: 213 938-3460
509 466-1000 **Whitworth College** Hawthorne Rd Spokane WA 99251-0001
Fax: 509 466-3221 Library
406 795-2410 **Wibaux County** 200 S Wibaux Wibaux MT 59353-0000
316 833-2400 **Wichita Area Vocational Technical School** 301 S Grove St Wichita KS 67211-0000
316 268-4921 **Wichita Art Museum** 619 Stackman Dr Wichita KS 67203-3296
Fax: 316 268-4980
316 375-2731 **Wichita County** PO Box 279 Leoti KS 67861-0279
817 766-8100 **Wichita County** 900 7th St Wichita Falls TX 76301-0000
316 262-0611 **Wichita Public Library** 223 S Main St Wichita KS 67202-3795
Fax: 316 262-2552
316 689-3456 **Wichita State University** 1845 Fairmount St Wichita KS 67208-1586
Fax: 316 689-3795
301 543-6551 **Wicomico County** PO Box 198 Salisbury MD 21803-0198
215 499-4000 **Widener University** 14th & Chestnut St Chester PA 19013-5793
Fax: 215 876-9751
302 478-5280 *School of Law* PO Box 7474 Wilmington DE 19803-0000
Fax: 302 477-2282
213 825-1461 **Wight Art Gallery** 1100 Dickson Art Ctr UCLA Los Angeles CA 90024-0000
Fax: 213 825-1507
817 552-5486 **Wilbarger County** 1700 Wilbarger St Vernon TX 76384-4742
513 376-2911 **Wilberforce University** 1055 N Bickett Rd Wilberforce OH 45384-9999
Fax: 513 376-5793
312 777-7900 **Wilbur Wright College** 3400 N Austin Ave Chicago IL 60634-4276
Fax: 312 794-4982
205 682-4126 **Wilcox County** PO Box 656 Camden AL 36726-0656
912 467-2737 **Wilcox County** Courthouse Sq Abbeville GA 31001-1099
903 938-8341 **Wiley College** 711 Wiley Ave Marshall TX 75670-5199
Fax: 903 938-8100 Admin
919 667-7136 **Wilkes Community College** Collegiate Dr Wilkesboro NC 28697-0000
Fax: 919 651-8749
404 678-2511 **Wilkes County** 23 E Court St Rm 222 Washington GA 30673-1570
919 651-7300 **Wilkes County** 110 North St Wilkesboro NC 28697-0000
Fax: 919 667-5834
717 824-4651 **Wilkes University** PO Box 111 Wilkes-Barre PA 18766-0000
Fax: 717 824-0733
218 643-4972 **Wilkin County** 5th St S Breckenridge MN 56520-0000
Fax: 218 643-5733
912 946-2236 **Wilkinson County** PO Box 161 Irwinton GA 31042-0161
601 888-4381 **Wilkinson County** PO Box 516 Woodville MS 39669-0516
815 740-4615 **Will County** 302 N Chicago St Joliet IL 60431-1059
Fax: 815 740-4699
512 689-2710 **Willacy County** Hidalgo & 3rd St Courthouse Raymondville TX 78580-0000
503 370-6300 **Willamette University** 900 State St Salem OR 97301-3930
Fax: 503 370-6148
503 370-6380 *College of Law* 250 Winter St SE Salem OR 97301-3827
Fax: 503 370-6375
812 425-4309 **Willard Library of Evansville** 21 1st Ave Evansville IN 47710-1294
Fax: 812 421-9742
601 582-5051 **William Carey College** Tuscan Ave Hattiesburg MS 39401-5499
Fax: Unlisted
818 797-1200 **William Carey International University** 1539 E Howard St Pasadena CA 91104-2698
Fax: 818 398-2263 Admin
816 781-3806 **William Jewell College** 500 College Hill Liberty MO 64068-0000
Fax: 816 781-3164
619 298-9040 **William Lyon University** 814 Morena Blvd San Diego CA 92110-2630
Fax: 619 298-9056
201 595-2000 **William Paterson College of New Jersey** 300 Pompton Rd Wayne NJ 07470-2152
Fax: 201 595-2460
515 673-1001 **William Penn College** 201 Trueblood Ave Oskaloosa IA 52577-1799
Fax: 515 673-1098
708 397-3000 **William Rainey Harper College** 1200 W Algonquin Rd Palatine IL 60067-7373
Fax: 708 397-0433
313 553-7200 **William Tyndale College** 35700 W 12-Mile Rd Farmington Hills MI 48331-3147
Fax: 313 553-5963
314 642-2251 **William Woods College** 200 W 12th St Fulton MO 65251-1098
602 988-2611 **Williams Air Force Base** Chandler AZ 85240-0001
Fax: Unlisted
413 597-3131 **Williams College** Hopkins Hall Williamstown MA 01267-0000
Fax: 413 458-4905
701 572-1700 **Williams County** 205 E Broadway Williston ND 58801-6123
419 636-2059 **Williams County** County Courthouse Sq 4th Fl Bryan OH 43506-0000
315 797-0000 **Williams Munson Proctor Institute Museum of Art**
310 Genesee St Utica NY 13502-4764
Fax: 315 797-5608
202 225-3211 **Williams Pat (Rep - D - Montana)** 2457 Rayburn Bldg Washington DC 20515-0001
Fax: 202 225-1257
804 220-6100 **Williamsburg (Independent City)** 401 Lafayette St Williamsburg VA 23185-3617
Fax: 804 220-6109
803 354-6855 **Williamsburg County** 125 W Main St Kingstree SC 29556-3347
803 354-7423 **Williamsburg Technical College** 601 Lane Rd Kingstree SC 29556-4197
Fax: 803 354-7269
618 997-1301 **Williamson County** 200 W Jefferson St Marion IL 62959-2494
615 790-5712 **Williamson County** 1320 W Main St Franklin TN 37064-3700
512 869-4315 **Williamson County** PO Box 18 Georgetown TX 78627-0018
215 443-1776 **Willow Grove Naval Air Station** Willow Grove PA 19090-5001
302 328-9401 **Wilmington College** 320 N Dupont Hwy New Castle DE 19720-6491
513 382-6661 **Wilmington College of Ohio** 251 Ludovic St Wilmington OH 45177-2499
Fax: 513 382-7077
302 571-7400 **Wilmington Institute Library** 10th & Market Sts Wilmington DE 19801-1282
202 225-2401 **Wilson Charles (Rep - D - Texas)** 2256 Rayburn Bldg Washington DC 20515-0001
Fax: 202 225-1764
717 264-4141 **Wilson College** 1015 Philadelphia Ave Chambersburg PA 17201-1285
Fax: 717 264-1578 Library
316 378-2186 **Wilson County** 615 Madison St Fredonia KS 66736-1383
919 237-3913 **Wilson County** PO Box 1728 Wilson NC 27894-1728
Fax: 919 237-4341
615 444-0314 **Wilson County** PO Box 918 Lebanon TN 37088-0918

512 393-2845 **Wilson County** 1420 3rd St .... Floresville TX 78114-2200
202 224-3841 **Wilson Pete (Sen - R - California)** 720 Hart Bldg .... Washington DC 20510-0001
Fax: 202 224-9621
919 291-1195 **Wilson Technical Community College** 902 Herring Ave E .... Wilson NC 27893-3310
Fax: 919 243-7148
703 667-5770 **Winchester (Independent City)** 5 N Kent St .... Winchester VA 22601-5037
802 365-7979 **Windham County** PO Box 207 .... Newfane VT 05345-0207
Fax: 802 365-4360
203 928-7749 **Windham Judicial District** 155 Church St .... Putnam CT 06260-1515
802 457-2121 **Windsor County** 12 The Green .... Woodstock VT 05091-1212
808 235-0077 **Windward Community College** 45-720 Keaahala Rd .... Kaneohe HI 96744-3598
Fax: 808 235-7351
704 233-4061 **Wingate College** Hwy 74 .... Wingate NC 28174-0000
Fax: 704 233-8192
915 586-3401 **Winkler County** 100 E Winkler St .... Kermit TX 79745-4236
318 628-5824 **Winn Parish** PO Box 951 .... Winnfield LA 71483-0951
515 582-4520 **Winnebago County** 126 S Clark St .... Forest City IA 50436-1793
815 987-3050 **Winnebago County** 400 W State St .... Rockford IL 61101-1276
Fax: 815 987-3008
414 235-2500 **Winnebago County** 415 Jackson St .... Oshkosh WI 54901-4751
Fax: 414 236-4799
414 236-5220 **Winnefox Library System** 106 Washington Ave .... Oshkosh WI 54901-4933
Fax: 414 236-5233
319 382-2469 **Winneshiek County** 201 W Main St .... Decorah IA 52101-1775
507 457-6320 **Winona County** 171 W 3rd St .... Winona MN 55987-3192
507 457-5000 **Winona State University** 8th & Johnson Sts .... Winona MN 55987-0000
Fax: 507 457-5586
205 489-5533 **Winston County** PO Box 309 .... Double Springs AL 35553-0309
601 773-3631 **Winston County** 115 S Court Ave .... Louisville MS 39339-2935
919 750-2000 **Winston-Salem State University**
601 S Martin Luther King Jr Dr .... Winston-Salem NC 27110-0001
Fax: 919 750-2953
803 323-2211 **Winthrop College** 701 Oakland Ave .... Rock Hill SC 29733-0001
Fax: 803 328-2855
304 275-4271 **Wirt County** PO Box 53 .... Elizabeth WV 26143-0053
202 224-5852 **Wirth Timothy (Sen - D - Colorado)** 380 Russell Bldg .... Washington DC 20510-0001
Fax: 202 224-0501
608 266-2205 **Wisconsin Library Services Div Dept of Public Instruction**
125 S Webster St .... Madison WI 53702-0001
Fax: 608 267-1052
414 774-8620 **Wisconsin Lutheran College** 8830 W Bluemound Rd .... Milwaukee WI 53226-4699
608 258-3400 **Wisconsin Manufacturers & Commerce** 501 E Washington .... Madison WI 53701-0000
Fax: 608 258-3413
Wisconsin State Government
608 266-2211 *Information* 1301 University Ave .... Madison WI 53715-1054
608 262-9576 *Archives & Records* 816 State St .... Madison WI 53706-1417
608 266-0190 *Arts Board* 131 W Wilson St Suite 301 .... Madison WI 53703-3233
Fax: 608 267-0380
608 266-1221 *Attorney General* 114 E State Capitol .... Madison WI 53702-0001
Fax: 608 267-2779
608 266-0603 *Bureau of Air Management* 101 S Webster St .... Madison WI 53707-0000
Fax: 608 267-0560
608 266-5511 *Bureau of Direct Licensing & Real Estate* PO Box 8935 .... Madison WI 53708-8935
608 266-2605 *Bureau of Procurement* 101 S Webster St 7th Fl .... Madison WI 53702-0001
Fax: 608 266-2164
608 266-1327 *Bureau of Solid Waste Management* 101 S Webster St .... Madison WI 53707-0000
Fax: 608 267-2768
608 266-8030 *Bureau of Water Regulation & Zoning* 101 S Webster St .... Madison WI 53707-0001
Fax: 608 267-3579
608 266-1334 *Center for Health Statistics* 1 W Wilson St .... Madison WI 53702-0001
608 266-3585 *Commissioner of Insurance* 121 E Wilson St 7th Fl .... Madison WI 53702-0001
Fax: 608 266-9935
608 266-7100 *Department of Agriculture Trade & Consumer Protection*
801 W Badger Rd .... Madison WI 53713-2526
Fax: 608 266-1300
608 266-1018 *Department of Development* 123 W Washington Ave .... Madison WI 53702-0001
Fax: 608 267-2829
608 266-7552 *Department of Industry Labor & Human Relations*
201 E Washington Ave .... Madison WI 53702-0001
Fax: 608 267-4592
608 266-2121 *Department of Natural Resources* 101 S Webster St .... Madison WI 53702-0001
Fax: 608 267-3579
608 266-1771 *Department of Public Instruction* 125 S Webster St .... Madison WI 53702-0000
Fax: 608 267-1052
608 266-8609 *Department of Regulation & Licensing*
1400 E Washington Ave .... Madison WI 53702-0000
608 266-1611 *Department of Revenue* 125 N Webster St .... Madison WI 53708-0000
Fax: 608 266-5718
608 266-1113 *Department of Transportation*
4802 Sheboygan Ave Rm 120-B .... Madison WI 53702-0001
Fax: 608 266-9912
608 266-1353 *Division of Budget & Planning* 101 S Webster St .... Madison WI 53702-0001
Fax: 608 266-2164
608 266-2471 *Division of Corrections* 1 W Wilson St Rm 1050 .... Madison WI 53702-0001
Fax: 608 267-0923
608 266-8234 *Division of Energy & Intergovernmental Relations*
101 S Webster St .... Madison WI 53707-0000
Fax: 608 267-0200
608 266-1031 *Division of Facilities Management* 101 S Webster St .... Madison WI 53702-0001
Fax: 608 267-2710
608 266-1511 *Division of Health* 1 W Wilson St .... Madison WI 53702-0001
Fax: 608 267-0352
608 266-3628 *Division of State Finance & Program Management*
101 S Webster St .... Madison WI 53702-0000
Fax: 608 266-2164
608 266-3212 *Division of State Patrol* 4802 Sheboygan Ave .... Madison WI 53702-0001
608 266-1212 *Governor* State Capitol Rm 115 E .... Madison WI 53702-0000
Fax: 608 267-8983
608 266-7884 *Housing & Economic Development Authority*
1 S Pinckney St Suite 500 .... Madison WI 53701-0000
Fax: 608 266-0729
608 266-3516 *Lieutenant Governor* State Capitol Rm 22 E .... Madison WI 53702-0001
Fax: 608 267-8983
608 266-1852 *Office of Consumer Protection & Citizen Advocacy*
PO Box 7856 .... Madison WI 53707-7856
Fax: 608 267-2223
608 266-2050 *Office of Mine Reclamation* 101 S Webster St .... Madison WI 53707-0000
Fax: 608 267-2768
608 266-0087 *Office of the State Public Defender*
131 W Wilson St Rm 100 .... Madison WI 53703-3233
Fax: 608 267-0584
608 266-3834 *Probation & Parole Div* 1 W Wilson St Rm 951 .... Madison WI 53702-0001
Fax: 608 267-0923
608 266-2001 *Public Service Commission* PO Box 7854 .... Madison WI 53707-7854
Fax: Unlisted
608 266-1816 *Safety & Buildings Div* 201 E Washington Ave .... Madison WI 53707-0000
Fax: 608 267-9566
608 266-5594 *Secretary of State* 30 W Mifflin St 10th Fl .... Madison WI 53703-2558
Fax: 608 267-6813
608 266-3431 *Securities Commissioner* 111 W Wilson St .... Madison WI 53703-3235
Fax: 608 256-1259
608 267-2206 *State Higher Education Aids Board* 131 W Wilson Ave .... Madison WI 53703-3233
608 266-1880 *Supreme Court* State Capitol Bldg Rm 231 E .... Madison WI 53702-0001
608 266-1714 *Treasury* PO Box 7871 .... Madison WI 53707-7871
Fax: 608 266-2647
608 266-2284 *Unemployment Compensation Div* PO Box 7905 .... Madison WI 53707-7905
Fax: Unlisted
414 324-5571 *Waupun Correctional Institution* PO Box 351 .... Waupun WI 53963-0351
608 835-5711 *Wisconsin Correctional Center System* PO Box 25 .... Oregon WI 53575-0025
608 266-1340 *Worker's Compensation Div* 201 E Washington Ave .... Madison WI 53702-0001
Fax: 608 267-4592
608 266-2147 **Wisconsin Tourism Development**
123 W Washington Ave 6th Fl .... Madison WI 53702-0001
Fax: 608 266-3403
817 627-3351 **Wise County** PO Box 359 .... Decatur TX 76234-0359
703 328-2321 **Wise County** 108 Main St .... Wise VA 24293-0000
Fax: 703 328-9780
202 225-2711 **Wise Robert E Jr (Rep - D - West Virginia)**
1421 Longworth Bldg .... Washington DC 20515-0001
Fax: 202 225-7856
512 226-5544 **Witte Museum** 3801 Broadway .... San Antonio TX 78209-6396
Fax: 512 824-1400
513 327-6231 **Wittenberg University** PO Box 720 .... Springfield OH 45501-0720
Fax: 513 327-6340
803 585-4821 **Wofford College** 429 N Church St .... Spartanburg SC 29303-3663
Fax: 803 582-1816
202 225-5136 **Wolf Frank R (Rep - R - Virginia)** 104 Cannon Bldg .... Washington DC 20515-0001
Fax: 202 225-0437
606 668-3515 **Wolfe County** PO Box 400 .... Campton KY 41301-0400
202 225-5011 **Wolpe Howard (Rep - D - Michigan)**
1535 Longworth Bldg .... Washington DC 20515-0001
Fax: 202 225-8602
202 523-6611 **Women's Bureau (US Dept of Labor)**
200 Constitution Ave NW Rm S3002 .... Washington DC 20210-0001
Fax: 202 523-7312
617 565-1988 *Region 1* JFK Federal Bldg Rm 1600 .... Boston MA 02203-0000
Fax: 617 565-2023
212 337-2390 *Region 2* 201 Varick St Rm 601 .... New York NY 10014-4811
Fax: 212 337-2304
215 596-1183 *Region 3* 3535 Market St Rm 13280 .... Philadelphia PA 19104-3309
Fax: 215 596-0683
404 347-4461 *Region 4* 1371 Peachtree St NE Suite 323 .... Atlanta GA 30367-0001
Fax: 404 347-4634
312 353-6985 *Region 5* 230 S Dearborn St 10th Fl .... Chicago IL 60604-1502
Fax: 312 353-0127
214 767-6985 *Region 6* 525 Griffin St Federal Bldg Suite 731 .... Dallas TX 75202-0000
816 426-6108 *Region 7* 911 Walnut St Rm 2511 .... Kansas City MO 64106-2009
Fax: 816 426-7157 Admin
303 844-4138 *Region 8* 1961 Stout St Rm 1452 .... Denver CO 80294-0101
Fax: Unlisted
415 744-6679 *Region 9* 71 Stevenson St Suite 927 .... San Francisco CA 94105-2937
Fax: 415 744-6713
206 442-1534 *Region 10* 1111 3rd Ave Rm 885 .... Seattle WA 98101-3207
Fax: 206 442-1663
419 354-9280 **Wood County** 1 Courthouse Sq .... Bowling Green OH 43402-2473
903 763-2711 **Wood County** PO Box 338 .... Quitman TX 75783-0338
715 421-8460 **Wood County** 400 Market St .... Wisconsin Rapids WI 54494-4825
304 424-1850 **Wood County** PO Box 1474 .... Parkersburg WV 26102-1474
212 686-9040 **Wood School** 8 E 40th St .... New York NY 10016-0190
712 279-6616 **Woodbury County** 101 Court St .... Sioux City IA 51101-1909
818 767-0888 **Woodbury University** 7500 N Glenoaks Blvd .... Burbank CA 91504-1099
Fax: 818 501-9320
309 467-2822 **Woodford County** PO Box 38 .... Eureka IL 61530-0038
606 873-3421 **Woodford County** County Courthouse .... Versailles KY 40383-0000
501 347-5206 **Woodruff County** PO Box 356 .... Augusta AR 72006-0356
405 327-2126 **Woods County** PO Box 386 .... Alva OK 73717-0000
316 625-2179 **Woodson County** 105 W Rutledge St .... Yates Center KS 66783-1237
405 256-8097 **Woodward County** 1600 Main St .... Woodward OK 73801-3068
918 336-0307 **Woolaroc Museum** State Hwy 123 .... Bartlesville OK 74003-0000
508 799-4406 **Worcester Art Museum** 55 Salisbury St .... Worcester MA 01609-3123
508 756-2441 **Worcester County** 2 Main St .... Worcester MA 01608-1116
301 632-1194 **Worcester County** 1 W Market St .... Snow Hill MD 21863-1073
Fax: 301 632-2141
508 831-5000 **Worcester Polytechnic Institute** 100 Institute Rd .... Worcester MA 01609-2280
Fax: 508 831-5483
508 793-8000 **Worcester State College** 486 Chandler St .... Worcester MA 01602-2597
Fax: 508 793-8191 Acctg
202 477-1234 **World Bank Group** 1818 H St NW .... Washington DC 20433-0001
Fax: 202 477-6391
707 765-4500 **World College West-International** 101 S San Antonio Rd .... Petaluma CA 94952-9510
Fax: 707 763-7529
219 291-3292 **World Harvest Bible College** 530 E Ireland Rd .... South Bend IN 46614-2660
Fax: 219 299-1106
212 963-3952 **World Health Organization (WHO)**
2 UN Plaza Rm DC2-0973 .... New York NY 10017-0000
Fax: 212 223-2920
217 333-2360 **World Heritage Museum** 702 S Wright St University of Illinois ... Urbana IL 61801-0000
212 963-6813 **World Intellectual Property Organization (WIPO)**
2 UN Plaza Suite 560 .... New York NY 10017-0000
406 723-7211 **World Museum of Mining** PO Box 3333 .... Butte MT 59702-3333
405 946-3333 **World Neighbors** 5116 N Portland Ave .... Oklahoma City OK 73112-2098
Fax: 405 946-9994
805 646-1444 **World University of America** 107 Ventura St N .... Ojai CA 93023-2624
Fax: 805 646-8964
912 776-8200 **Worth County** 201 N Main St .... Sylvester GA 31791-2178
515 324-2840 **Worth County** 1000 Central Ave .... Northwood IA 50459-1523
816 564-2219 **Worth County** County Courthouse .... Grant City MO 64456-0000
507 372-2107 **Worthington Community College** 1450 College Way .... Worthington MN 56187-3024
Fax: 507 372-5801 Admin
515 532-3113 **Wright County** PO Box 306 .... Clarion IA 50525-0306
612 682-3900 **Wright County** 10 2nd St NW .... Buffalo MN 55313-1165
Fax: 612 682-6178 Admin
417 741-6661 **Wright County** PO Box 98 .... Hartville MO 65667-0098
Fax: 417 741-6780
513 873-3333 **Wright State University** 3640 Colonel Glenn Hwy .... Dayton OH 45435-0001
Fax: 513 873-3301
419 586-2365 *Lake Campus* 7600 SR-703 .... Celina OH 45822-0000
Fax: 419 586-9048
513 873-3010 *School of Medicine* PO Box 927 .... Dayton OH 45401-0927
Fax: 513 879-2675

513 257-1110 **Wright-Patterson Air Force Base** .... Dayton OH 45433-0000
Fax: 513 257-2157
517 739-2011 **Wurtsmith Air Force Base** .... Oscoda MI 48753-5000
419 294-1432 **Wyandot County** County Courthouse .... Upper Sandusky OH 43351-0000
913 573-2800 **Wyandotte County** 710 N 7th St .... Kansas City KS 66101-3087
202 225-4811 **Wyden Ron (Rep - D - Oregon)** 2452 Rayburn Bldg .... Washington DC 20515-0001
Fax: Unlisted
202 225-2015 **Wylie Chalmers P (Rep - R - Ohio)** 2310 Rayburn Bldg .... Washington DC 20515-0001
Fax: Unlisted
716 786-8810 **Wyoming County** 143 N Main St .... Warsaw NY 14569-1123
717 836-3200 **Wyoming County** Court House Sq .... Tunkhannock PA 18657-1228
304 732-8000 **Wyoming County** Bank St .... Pineville WV 24874-0000
307 637-8940 **Wyoming Democratic State Party** 419 Randall Ave .... Cheyenne WY 82001-3087
Fax: 307 637-8947
307 234-9166 **Wyoming Republican State Committee** 212 N Wolcott St .... Casper WY 82601-1923
Fax: 307 473-8640
Wyoming State Government
307 777-7220 *Information* 200 W 24th St .... Cheyenne WY 82001-0000
Fax: 307 777-6289
307 777-7391 *Air Quality Div* 122 W 25th St 4th Fl .... Cheyenne WY 82002-0001
Fax: 307 634-0799
307 777-7826 *Archives & Records Management Div* 2301 Central Ave .... Cheyenne WY 82002-0001
Fax: 307 777-6005
307 777-7841 *Attorney General* 123 Capitol Bldg .... Cheyenne WY 82002-0001
Fax: 307 777-6869
307 777-7405 *Board of Charities & Reform*
122 W 25th St Herschler Bldg 1st Fl E .... Cheyenne WY 82002-0001
Fax: 307 777-6869
307 362-5222 *Board of Mines* 1682 Sunset St .... Rock Springs WY 89202-0000
307 777-7763 *Community College Commission*
122 W 25th Herschler Bldg 2 W .... Cheyenne WY 82002-0001
Fax: 307 777-6567
307 777-6286 *Consumer Affairs* 123 Capitol Bldg .... Cheyenne WY 82002-0001
Fax: 307 777-6869
307 777-7742 *Council on the Arts* 2320 Capitol Ave .... Cheyenne WY 82002-0001
Fax: 307 777-6869
307 777-7321 *Department of Agriculture* 2219 Carey Ave .... Cheyenne WY 82002-0001
Fax: 307 777-6593
307 777-7284 *Department of Commerce Div Economic & Community Development*
122 W 25th St 2nd Fl .... Cheyenne WY 82002-0001
Fax: 307 777-5840
307 777-7131 *Department of Economic Development & Stabilization*
Herschler Bldg West Wing 2nd Fl .... Cheyenne WY 82002-0001
Fax: 307 777-5840
307 777-7673 *Department of Education* 2300 Capitol Ave .... Cheyenne WY 82002-0001
Fax: 307 777-6234
307 235-3200 *Department of Employment* 100 W Midwest St .... Casper WY 82601-0000
Fax: 307 235-3293
307 777-7261 *Department of Employment* 122 W 25th St Herschler Bldg . Cheyenne WY 82002-0001
Fax: 307 777-5805
307 777-7656 *Department of Health & Social Services*
Hathaway Bldg Rm 117 .... Cheyenne WY 82002-0000
307 777-7331 *Department of Public Lands* 122 W 25th St Herschler Bldg . Cheyenne WY 82002-0001
Fax: 307 634-0799
307 777-7961 *Department of Revenue & Taxation*
122 W 25th St Herschler Bldg 1st Fl W .... Cheyenne WY 82002-0001
Fax: 307 777-6869
307 777-7253 *Division of Purchasing & Property Control*
2001 Capitol Ave E Rm 323 .... Cheyenne WY 82002-0001
Fax: 307 777-6725
307 777-7566 *Emergency Management Agency* 5500 Bishop Blvd .... Cheyenne WY 82003-0000
Fax: 307 635-6017
307 777-7938 *Environmental Quality Dept*
122 W 25th St Herschler Bldg 4th Fl W .... Cheyenne WY 82002-0001
Fax: 307 634-0799
307 777-7434 *Governor* State Capitol .... Cheyenne WY 82002-0000
Fax: 307 777-6869
307 777-7475 *Highway Dept* 5300 Bishop Blvd .... Cheyenne WY 82002-0001
Fax: 307 777-4163
307 777-7301 *Highway Patrol* 5300 Bishop Blvd .... Cheyenne WY 82002-0001
Fax: 307 777-4163
307 777-7401 *Insurance Dept* 122 W 25th St Herschler Bldg .... Cheyenne WY 82002-0000
Fax: 307 777-5895
307 777-7786 *Occupational Safety & Health*
122 W 25th St Herschler Bldg Rm 2-E .... Cheyenne WY 82002-0001
Fax: 307 777-5805
307 234-7147 *Oil & Gas Commission* 777 W 1st St .... Casper WY 82601-1768
Fax: 307 234-5306
307 777-7208 *Probation & Parole* 5801 Osage Suite B .... Cheyenne WY 82002-0001
307 777-7137 *Public Defender* 1712 Carey 2nd Fl .... Cheyenne WY 82002-0001
307 777-7427 *Public Service Commission* 700 W 21st St .... Cheyenne WY 82002-0001
Fax: 307 777-5700
307 777-7141 *Real Estate Commission* Barrett Bldg 3rd Fl .... Cheyenne WY 82002-0001
307 777-7691 *Retirement System* 122 W 25th St Herschler Bldg .... Cheyenne WY 82002-0001
Fax: 307 777-5995
307 777-7378 *Secretary of State* 200 W 24th St State Capitol .... Cheyenne WY 82002-0001
Fax: 307 777-5339
307 777-7370 *Securities Div* 200 W 24th St State Capitol .... Cheyenne WY 82002-0001
Fax: 307 634-9503
307 777-7752 *Solid Waste Management Program*
122 W 25th St Herschler Bldg .... Cheyenne WY 82002-0001
Fax: 307 634-0799
307 777-7316 *Supreme Court* 2301 Capitol Ave .... Cheyenne WY 82002-0001
Fax: 307 777-6289
307 777-7408 *Treasurer* 200 W 24th St .... Cheyenne WY 82002-0001
Fax: 307 777-5412
307 235-3200 *Unemployment Insurance Div* 100 W Midwest St .... Casper WY 82601-2429
Fax: 307 235-3293
307 777-7591 *Vital Records Services* Hathaway Bldg .... Cheyenne WY 82002-0001
307 777-7441 *Worker's Compensation*
122 W 25th St Herschler Bldg 2nd Fl .... Cheyenne WY 82002-0001
Fax: 307 777-5805
307 347-6144 *Wyoming Boys School* 1550 Hwy 20 S .... Worland WY 82401-0000
307 328-1441 *Wyoming State Penitentiary* PO Box 400 .... Rawlins WY 82301-0400
307 777-7281 **Wyoming State Library** 2301 Capitol Ave .... Cheyenne WY 82002-0001
Fax: 307 777-6289
307 777-7022 **Wyoming State Museum** 2301 Central Ave 1st Fl .... Cheyenne WY 82002-0001
Fax: 307 777-6005
307 777-7777 **Wyoming Tourism & Marketing Div** IH-25 & College Dr .... Cheyenne WY 82002-0001
Fax: 307 777-6904
703 228-6644 **Wythe County** 225 S 4th St .... Wytheville VA 24382-2502
703 228-5541 **Wytheville Community College** 1000 E Main St .... Wytheville VA 24382-3397
Fax: 703 228-6506

X

513 745-3000 **Xavier University** 3800 Victory Pkwy .... Cincinnati OH 45207-1088
Fax: 513 745-1954
504 486-7411 **Xavier University of Louisiana** 7325 Palmetto St .... New Orleans LA 70125-1098
Fax: 504 482-2801
504 483-7419 *College of Pharmacy* 7325 Palmetto St .... New Orleans LA 70125-1098
Fax: 504 488-3108

Y

919 679-4200 **Yadkin County** PO Box 146 .... Yadkinville NC 27055-0146
Fax: 919 679-7982
509 575-4120 **Yakima County** 2nd & B Sts .... Yakima WA 98901-0000
Fax: 509 577-4071
509 575-2350 **Yakima Valley Community College**
S 16th Ave & W Nob Hill Blvd .... Yakima WA 98902-0000
Fax: 509 575-2461
509 452-8541 **Yakima Valley Regional Library** 102 N 3rd St .... Yakima WA 98901-2705
Fax: Unlisted
203 432-4771 **Yale University** PO Box 1604A Yale Stn .... New Haven CT 06520-7430
Fax: Unlisted
203 432-1246 *Computer Science Dept* 51 Prospect St .... New Haven CT 06511-6816
Fax: 203 432-0593
203 432-5598 *Department of Biochemistry* 260 Whitney Ave .... New Haven CT 06511-0000
Fax: 203 432-5175
203 432-4771 *Department of Epidemiology & Public Health*
60 College St .... New Haven CT 06510-3210
Fax: 203 785-7296
203 432-3114 *Department of Geoscience & Geophysics*
Kline Geology Laboratory Rm 203 .... New Haven CT 06511-0000
Fax: 203 432-3134
203 785-4935 *Department of Molecular Biophysics & Biochemistry*
333 Cedar St .... New Haven CT 06510-3219
Fax: 203 785-6404
203 432-3600 *Department of Physics* PO Box 6666 .... New Haven CT 06511-0000
Fax: 203 432-6125
203 432-3916 *Graduate School of Chemistry* PO Box 6666 .... New Haven CT 06511-0000
Fax: 203 423-6144
203 432-5932 *Graduate School of Organization & Management*
135 Prospect St .... New Haven CT 06511-3729
Fax: 203 432-6316
203 432-4992 *Law School* 127 Wall St .... New Haven CT 06511-6636
Fax: 203 432-2592
203 432-1783 *Libraries* 120 High St Rm 152 .... New Haven CT 06520-0000
203 785-4672 *School of Medicine* 333 Cedar St .... New Haven CT 06510-3289
Fax: 203 785-7437
203 432-0600 **Yale University Art Gallery** PO Box 2006 .... New Haven CT 06520-2006
Fax: 203 432-7159
203 432-0822 **Yale University Collection of Musical Instruments**
PO Box 2117 .... New Haven CT 06520-2117
601 473-2091 **Yalobusha County** PO Box 664 .... Water Valley MS 38965-0664
503 472-9371 **Yamhill County** 535 E 5th St .... McMinnville OR 97128-4593
Fax: 503 434-7520
704 682-3971 **Yancey County** County Courthouse .... Burnsville NC 28714-0000
605 668-3438 **Yankton County** 410 Walnut St .... Yankton SD 57078-4313
315 536-4011 **Yates County** 110 Court St Rm 198 .... Penn Yan NY 14527-1130
202 225-2111 **Yates Sidney R (Rep - D - Illinois)** 2234 Rayburn Bldg .... Washington DC 20515-0001
Fax: 202 225-3493
202 225-5546 **Yatron Gus (Rep - D - Pennsylvania)** 2205 Rayburn Bldg ... Washington DC 20515-0001
Fax: 202 225-5548
602 445-7300 **Yavapai College** 1100 E Sheldon St .... Prescott AZ 86301-3297
Fax: 602 776-2193
602 771-3100 **Yavapai County** 255 E Gurley St .... Prescott AZ 86301-3868
601 746-2661 **Yazoo County** PO Box 68 .... Yazoo City MS 39194-0068
501 495-2630 **Yell County** PO Box 219 .... Danville AR 72833-0219
Fax: Call company operator
612 564-3325 **Yellow Medicine County** 415 9th Ave .... Granite Falls MN 56241-1367
406 256-2785 **Yellowstone County** PO Box 35001 .... Billings MT 59107-5001
Fax: 406 256-2736
212 355-1737 **Yemen: People's Democratic Republic of Yemen Mission to the UN**
413 E 51st St .... New York NY 10022-6403
Fax: 212 832-5397
Yemen: Republic of Yemen
202 965-4760 *Embassy* 600 New Hampshire Ave NW Suite 840 .... Washington DC 20037-2403
Fax: 202 337-2017
212 355-1730 *Mission to the UN* 866 UN Plaza Rm 435 .... New York NY 10017-0000
Fax: 212 750-9613
303 629-8200 **Yeshiva Toras Chaim Talmudical Seminary** 1400 Quitman St ... Denver CO 80204-1415
Fax: 303 623-5949
212 960-5400 **Yeshiva University** 500 W 185th St .... New York NY 10033-3299
Fax: 212 960-0055
212 430-2000 *Albert Einstein College of Medicine* 1300 Morris Park Ave .... Bronx NY 10461-1975
Fax: 212 430-2488
212 430-2000 *School of Biochemistry* 1300 Morris Park Ave .... Bronx NY 10461-1988
Fax: 212 430-2488
212 790-0274 *School of Law* 55 5th Ave .... New York NY 10003-4391
Fax: 212 790-0345
213 553-4478 **Yeshiva University of Los Angeles** 9760 W Pico Blvd .... Los Angeles CA 90035-4792
Fax: 213 277-5558
806 456-2721 **Yoakum County** PO Box 309 .... Plains TX 79355-0000
Fax: 806 456-6175
916 666-8195 **Yolo County** 725 Court St .... Woodland CA 95695-3436
Fax: 916 666-8112
914 337-1500 **Yonkers Public Library** 7 Main St .... Yonkers NY 10701-2784
Fax: 914 963-2301
402 362-4441 **York College** 9th & Kiplinger Sts .... York NE 68467-0000
717 846-7788 **York College of Pennsylvania** Country Club Rd .... York PA 17403-0000
Fax: Unlisted
207 324-1571 **York County** Court St .... Alfred ME 04002-0000
402 362-7759 **York County** 510 Lincoln Ave .... York NE 68467-2945
717 771-9675 **York County** 28 E Market St .... York PA 17401-1501
803 684-8532 **York County** 2 Congress St .... York SC 29745-0000
Fax: 803 684-8550
804 898-0200 **York County** PO Box 532 .... Yorktown VA 23690-0532
Fax: 804 898-0256
803 324-3055 **York County Library** PO Box 10032 .... Rock Hill SC 29731-0032
Fax: 803 328-8402
717 757-9685 **York County Library System** 118 Pleasant Acres Rd 2nd Fl .... York PA 17402-9004
Fax: 717 751-0741
803 324-3130 **York Technical College** 452 S Anderson Rd .... Rock Hill SC 29730-7305
Fax: 803 329-8059
817 549-8432 **Young County** PO Box 218 .... Graham TX 76046-0218

202 225-5961 **Young CW (Rep - R - Florida)** 2407 Rayburn Bldg .... Washington DC 20515-0001
Fax: Call company operator
202 225-5765 **Young Don (Rep - R - Alaska)** 2331 Rayburn Bldg .... Washington DC 20515-0001
Fax: Unlisted
404 379-3111 **Young Harris College** 86 College St .... Young Harris GA 30582-0000
Fax: Unlisted
216 742-3000 **Youngstown State University** .... Youngstown OH 44555-0001
Fax: 216 742-1998
916 741-6700 **Yuba Community College** 2088 N Beale Rd .... Marysville CA 95901-7699
Fax: 916 741-3541
916 741-6341 **Yuba County** 215 5th St .... Marysville CA 95901-5794
Yugoslavia: Socialist Federal Republic of Yugoslavia
202 462-6566 *Embassy* 2410 California St NW .... Washington DC 20008-1614
Fax: 202 797-9663
212 879-8700 *Mission to the UN* 854 5th Ave .... New York NY 10021-5890
Fax: 212 879-8705
602 782-4534 **Yuma County** 168 S 2nd Ave .... Yuma AZ 85364-2297
303 332-5809 **Yuma County** PO Box 426 .... Wray CO 80758-0426
602 726-2011 **Yuma Marine Corps Air Station** .... Yuma AZ 85369-0000

Z

Zaire: Republic of Zaire
202 234-7690 *Embassy* 1800 New Hampshire Ave NW .... Washington DC 20009-3206
212 754-1966 *Mission to the UN* 767 3rd Ave 25th Fl .... New York NY 10017-2023
Fax: 212 754-1970
Zambia: Republic of Zambia
202 265-9717 *Embassy* 2419 Massachusetts Ave NW .... Washington DC 20008-2805
212 758-1110 *Mission to the UN* 237 E 52nd St .... New York NY 10022-6301
Fax: 212 758-1319
512 765-9915 **Zapata County** 7th Ave & Hidalgo .... Zapata TX 78076-0000
512 374-2331 **Zavala County** County Courthouse .... Crystal City TX 78839-0000
202 225-5456 **Zeliff Bill (Rep - R - New Hampshire)** 512 Cannon Bldg ..... Washington DC 20515-0001
Fax: 202 225-4370
605 365-5157 **Ziebach County** PO Box 68 .... Dupree SD 57623-0068
Zimbabwe: Republic of Zimbabwe
202 332-7100 *Embassy* 2852 McGill Terr NW .... Washington DC 20008-2748
Fax: 202 483-9326
212 980-5084 *Mission to the UN* 19 E 47th St .... New York NY 10017-1901
Fax: 212 755-4188
202 225-5801 **Zimmer Dick (Rep - R - New Jersey)** 510 Cannon Bldg ...... Washington DC 20515-0001
Fax: 202 225-9181

CLASSIFIED SECTION

WHAT DOES THE CLASSIFIED SECTION CONTAIN?

The classified listings in *Blue Pages USA* represent the nation's largest organizations, educational institutions and government offices in selected categories.

Each listing in the Classified Section consists of a telephone number, formal name, street or mailing address, city, state and zip code. (When available, nine-digit zip codes have been provided. Four zeros have been inserted at the end of a five-digit zip code if the nine-digit zip was unavailable. The four zeros should not be used for mailing.)

HOW DO I FIND WHAT I'M LOOKING FOR?

Listings in both the alphabetical and classified sections of *Blue Pages USA* are alphabetized on a word-by-word basis. A space between two words functions as a "letter" before the letter "a." Therefore, a listing for "San Saba County" will be listed before "Sanborn County." In this example, the space between "San" and "Saba" alphabetizes before the "b" in "Sanborn."

Listings composed of a first name (or initial) and surname—e.g., "Susan Molinari"—are listed last name first: "Molinari Susan." The customary rendering has been retained when "last-name-first" would be awkward or less useful, such as "George Washington University."

The classified section contains several subsections, each representing a specific category. For easy look-up, these category headings are displayed at a glance in the Table of Contents at the front of the book. For further assistance, we've included a mini-table of contents on the title page of each subsection, and footnotes provide information on how listings are organized within each category.

Many of the classified sections are broken down into more specific subsections, with listings organized alphabetically or geographically within these subsections. And, in some subsections, the listing information is organized alphabetically <u>by city and state</u>, allowing you to find the listings you need both categorically and geographically. In these cases, you can easily find the information you seek by scrolling down the state column of the address until you find the correct state, then proceeding to the desired city.

ASSOCIATIONS AND
ORGANIZATIONS

Associations and organizations with annual budgets of $1 million or more are listed by subject category. The listings in this section also appear in the Alphabetical Section.

Business and Professional

CHAMBERS OF COMMERCE

State chambers of commerce appear in state order following the listing for the US Chamber of Commerce. If no statewide chamber of commerce exists, the group serving the state's largest city is listed.

202 659-6000 **US Chamber of Commerce** 1615 H St NW .... Washington DC 20062-0001
205 834-6000 **Business Council of Alabama** 468 S Perry St .... Montgomery AL 36104-4236
907 586-2323 **Alaska State Chamber of Commerce** 217 2nd St Suite 201 .... Juneau AK 99801-1267
602 248-9172 **Arizona Chamber of Commerce** 1221 E Osborn Rd .... Phoenix AZ 85014-5539
501 374-9225 **Arkansas State Chamber of Commerce** 410 Cross St .... Little Rock AR 72201-0000
916 444-6670 **California Chamber of Commerce** 1201 K St 12th Fl .... Sacramento CA 95814-0000
303 831-7411 **Colorado Assn of Commerce & Industry** 1776 Lincoln St Suite 1200 .... Denver CO 80203-0000
203 547-1661 **Connecticut Business & Industry Assn** 370 Asylum St 5th Fl .... Hartford CT 06103-2022
302 655-7221 **Delaware State Chamber of Commerce** 1 Commerce Ctr Suite 200 .... Wilmington DE 19801-5401
202 347-7201 **Washington DC Chamber of Commerce** 1411 K St NW 5th Fl .... Washington DC 20005-0000
904 222-2831 **Florida State Chamber of Commerce** 136 S Bronough St .... Tallahassee FL 32302-0000
404 223-2264 **Business Council of Georgia** 233 Peachtree St Suite 200 .... Atlanta GA 30303-0000
808 522-8800 **Hawaii Chamber of Commerce** 735 Bishop St Suite 220 .... Honolulu HI 96813-4897
208 344-5515 **Boise Area Chamber of Commerce** 300 N 6th St .... Boise ID 83701-0000
312 372-7373 **Illinois State Chamber of Commerce** 20 N Wacker Dr .... Chicago IL 60606-3084
317 634-6407 **Indiana State Chamber of Commerce** 1 N Capitol Suite 200 .... Indianapolis IN 46204-2248
515 281-3251 **Iowa Dept of Economic Development** 200 E Grand Ave .... Des Moines IA 50309-1827
913 357-6321 **Kansas Chamber of Commerce & Industry** 500 Bank IV Tower .... Topeka KS 66603-3406
502 695-4700 **Kentucky Chamber of Commerce** 452 Versailles Rd .... Frankfort KY 40602-0000
504 928-5388 **Louisiana Assn of Business & Industry** 3113 Valley Creek Dr .... Baton Rouge LA 70898-0000
207 623-4568 **Maine Chamber of Commerce & Industry** 126 Sewall St .... Augusta ME 04330-6822
301 269-0642 **Maryland Chamber of Commerce** 275 West St Suite 400 .... Annapolis MD 21401-3400
617 727-3206 **Massachusetts Office of Business Development** 100 Cambridge St 13th Fl .... Boston MA 02202-0000
517 371-2100 **Michigan State Chamber of Commerce** 600 S Walnut St .... Lansing MI 48933-2262
612 292-4650 **Minnesota Chamber of Commerce** 480 Cedar St Suite 500 .... Saint Paul MN 55101-2240
601 969-0022 **Mississippi Economic Council** PO Box 23276 .... Jackson MS 39225-3276
314 634-3511 **Missouri State Chamber of Commerce** 428 E Capitol Ave .... Jefferson City MO 65101-3069
406 442-2405 **Montana Chamber of Commerce** 2030 11th Ave .... Helena MT 59601-0000
402 474-4422 **Nebraska Chamber of Commerce & Industry** 1320 Lincoln Mall .... Lincoln NE 68508-0000
702 786-3030 **Nevada State Chamber of Commerce** PO Box 3499 .... Reno NV 89505-3499
603 224-5388 **New Hampshire Business & Industry Assoc** 122 N Main St 3rd Fl .... Concord NH 03301-4033
201 623-7070 **New Jersey State Chamber of Commerce** 5 Commerce St .... Newark NJ 07102-3906
505 842-0644 **Association of Commerce & Industry of New Mexico** 2309 Renard Pl SE Suite 402 .... Albuquerque NM 87106-4259
919 828-0758 **North Carolina Citizens for Business & Industry** 225 Hillsborough St Suite 460 .... Raleigh NC 27603-0000
701 237-9461 **Greater North Dakota Assn** 808 3rd Ave S .... Fargo ND 58108-0000
614 228-4201 **Ohio State Chamber of Commerce** 35 E Gay St .... Columbus OH 43215-3138
405 424-4003 **Oklahoma State Chamber of Commerce & Industry** 4020 N Lincoln Blvd .... Oklahoma City OK 73105-5219
503 228-9411 **Portland Metropolitan Chamber of Commerce** 221 NW 2nd Ave .... Portland OR 97209-3999
717 255-3252 **Pennsylvania Chamber of Business & Industry** 222 N 3rd St .... Harrisburg PA 17101-1502
401 521-5000 **Greater Providence Chamber of Commerce** 30 Exchange Terr .... Providence RI 02903-1022
803 799-4601 **South Carolina Chamber of Commerce** 1201 Main St Suite 1810 .... Columbia SC 29201-0000
605 224-6161 **Industry & Commerce Assn of South Dakota** 108 N Euclid Ave .... Pierre SD 57501-2521
615 259-4755 **Nashville Area Chamber of Commerce** 161 4th Ave N .... Nashville TN 37219-2411
512 472-1594 **Texas State Chamber of Commerce** 900 Congress Ave Suite 501 .... Austin TX 78701-1649
801 224-3636 **Provo/Orem Chamber of Commerce** 777 S State .... Orem UT 84058-6307
802 223-3443 **Vermont Chamber of Commerce** PO Box 37 .... Montpelier VT 05601-0000
804 644-1607 **Virginia Chamber of Commerce** 9 S 5th St .... Richmond VA 23219-3823
206 389-7200 **Greater Seattle Chamber of Commerce** 600 University St Suite 1200 .... Seattle WA 98101-1129
304 342-1115 **West Virginia Chamber of Commerce** 300 Capitol St Suite 1000 .... Charleston WV 25301-1794
608 258-3400 **Wisconsin Manufacturers & Commerce** 501 E Washington .... Madison WI 53701-0000
307 638-3388 **Greater Cheyenne Chamber of Commerce** 301 W 16th St .... Cheyenne WY 82001-4437

GOVERNMENT AND MILITARY

703 247-5800 **Air Force Assn** 1501 Lee Hwy .... Arlington VA 22209-1198
301 899-3500 **Air Force Sergeants Assn** 5211 Auth Rd .... Suitland MD 20746-4396
703 522-1820 **American Defense Preparedness Assn** 2101 Wilson Blvd Suite 400 .... Arlington VA 22201-9803
305 891-1700 **American Federation of Police** 1100 NE 125th St Suite 100 .... North Miami FL 33161-5083
312 667-2200 **American Public Works Assn** 1313 E 60th St 3rd Fl .... Chicago IL 60637-2882
202 393-7878 **American Society for Public Administration** 1120 G St NW Suite 500 .... Washington DC 20005-3885
703 631-6100 **Armed Forces Communications & Electronics Assn** 4400 Fair Lakes Ct .... Fairfax VA 22033-3899
202 541-0101 **Army Distaff Foundation** 6200 Oregon Ave NW .... Washington DC 20015-1543
703 549-1600 **Association of Old Crows** 1000 N Payne St .... Alexandria VA 22314-1696
703 841-4300 **Association of the US Army** 2425 Wilson Blvd .... Arlington VA 22201-3326
606 252-2291 **Council of State Governments** Iron Works Pike .... Lexington KY 40578-0000
202 624-5386 **Council of State Policy & Planning Agencies** 400 N Capitol St NW Suite 285 .... Washington DC 20001-1511
212 628-3200 **Council of the Americas** 680 Park Ave .... New York NY 10021-5009
312 944-0575 **Defense Research Institute** 750 N Lake Shore Dr Suite 500 .... Chicago IL 60611-4490
202 785-2768 **Fleet Reserve Assn** 1303 New Hampshire Ave NW .... Washington DC 20036-1598
317 545-1000 **Hudson Institute** 5395 Emerson Way .... Indianapolis IN 46226-1415
312 947-2064 **International Assn of Assessing Officers** 1313 E 60th St .... Chicago IL 60637-2830
703 243-6500 **International Assn of Chiefs of Police** 1110 N Glebe Rd Suite 200 .... Arlington VA 22201-5718
202 626-4600 **International City Management Assn** 777 N Capitol St NE Suite 500 .... Washington DC 20002-4239
213 699-0541 **International Conference of Building Officials** 5360 S Workman Mill Rd .... Whittier CA 90601-2299
202 862-1826 **International Organization for Migration** 1750 K St NW Suite 1110 .... Washington DC 23406-0000
508 881-5800 **International Society of Fire Service Instructors** 30 Main St .... Ashland MA 01721-1101
202 547-6223 **National Assn of Conservation Districts** 509 Capitol Court NE .... Washington DC 20002-493
202 393-6226 **National Assn of Counties** 440 1st St NW 8th Fl .... Washington DC 20001-208
202 429-2960 **National Assn of Housing & Redevelopment Officials** 1320 18th St NW .... Washington DC 20036-181
816 842-3600 **National Assn of Insurance Commissioners** 120 W 12th St Suite 1100 .... Kansas City MO 64105-191
202 898-2200 **National Assn of Regulatory Utility Commissioners** 12th & Constitution Ave NW ICC Bldg Rm 1102 .... Washington DC 20423-000
703 648-9300 **National Assn of Rehabilitation Facilities** 1910 Association Dr Suite 200 .... Reston VA 22091-150
303 623-7800 **National Conference of State Legislatures** 1050 17th St Suite 2100 .... Denver CO 80265-210
202 624-7710 **National Council of State Housing Agencies** 444 N Capitol St NW Suite 118 .... Washington DC 20001-151
202 624-5300 **National Governors' Assn** 444 N Capitol St NW Suite 250 .... Washington DC 20001-151
202 626-3000 **National League of Cities** 1301 Pennsylvania Ave NW Suite 600 .... Washington DC 20004-176
202 775-1440 **National Security Industrial Assn** 1025 Connecticut Ave NW Suite 300 .... Washington DC 20036-5405
703 836-7827 **National Sheriffs' Assn** 1450 Duke St .... Alexandria VA 22314-3490
212 310-9000 **National Urban League Inc** 500 E 62nd St .... New York NY 10021-8393
703 528-1775 **Navy League of the US** 2300 Wilson Blvd .... Arlington VA 22201-3308
512 653-6161 **Non-Commissioned Officers Assn of the USA** 10635 IH-35 N .... San Antonio TX 78233-6627
202 466-7820 **Police Executive Research Forum** 2300 M St NW Suite 910 .... Washington DC 20037-1434
202 626-2400 **Public Technology Inc** 1301 Pennsylvania Ave NW Suite 800 .... Washington DC 20004-1793
202 479-2200 **Reserve Officers Assn of the US** 1 Constitution Ave NE .... Washington DC 20002-5655
303 364-8737 **Retired Enlisted Assn** 14305 E Alamada Ave Suite 300 .... Aurora CO 80012-2505
703 549-2311 **Retired Officers Assn** 201 N Washington St .... Alexandria VA 22314-2539
703 549-3800 **Society of American Military Engineers** 607 Prince St .... Alexandria VA 22314-3117
202 624-7000 **Urban Land Institute** 625 Indiana Ave NW Suite 400 .... Washington DC 20004-2930
202 293-7330 **US Conference of Mayors** 1620 I St NW .... Washington DC 20006-4073
301 268-6110 **US Naval Institute** US Naval Academy .... Annapolis MD 21402-0000

Political

MAJOR POLITICAL PARTIES

212 989-4994 **Communist Party USA** 235 W 23rd St 7th Fl .... New York NY 10011-2383
718 921-2158 **Conservative Party** 486 78th St .... Brooklyn NY 11209-3404
202 863-8000 **Democratic National Committee** 430 S Capitol St SE .... Washington DC 20003-4095
202 543-1988 **Libertarian Party** 1528 Pennsylvania Ave SE .... Washington DC 20003-3116
202 546-5611 **Liberty Lobby** 300 Independence Ave SE .... Washington DC 20003-1081
202 863-8500 **Republican National Committee** 310 1st St SE .... Washington DC 20003-1801
415 494-1532 **Socialist Labor Party** 914 Industrial Ave .... Palo Alto CA 94303-4911
212 675-3820 **Socialist Workers Party** 406 West St .... New York NY 10014-2570

POLITICAL ACTION COMMITTEES

PACs with fund-raising receipts greater than $400,000 are included.

202 223-3111 **Active Ballot Club** 1775 K St NW .... Washington DC 20006-1502
202 637-5000 **AFL-CIO Committee on Political Education** 815 16th St NW .... Washington DC 20006-4145
202 797-4033 **Air Line Pilots Assn PAC** 1625 Massachusetts Ave NW .... Washington DC 20036-2283
301 695-2000 **Aircraft Owners & Pilots Assn PAC** 421 Aviation Way .... Frederick MD 21701-4756
202 663-5221 **American Bankers Assn PAC** 1120 Connecticut Ave NW 8th Fl .... Washington DC 20036-3971
202 898-2424 **American Dental PAC** 1111 14th St NW Suite 1100 .... Washington DC 20005-5683
404 323-3431 **American Family Life PAC** 1932 Wynnton Rd .... Columbus GA 31999-0001
202 879-4400 **American Federation of Teachers Committee on Political Education** 555 New Jersey Ave NW .... Washington DC 20001-2079
212 575-6200 **American Institute of Certified Public Accountants Effective Legislation Committee** 1211 Ave of the Americas .... New York NY 10036-8775
202 789-7400 **American Medical Assn PAC** 1101 Vermont Ave NW Suite 1200 .... Washington DC 20005-3583
312 856-6317 **Amoco PAC** 200 E Randolph St .... Chicago IL 60601-7125
202 965-3500 **Association of Trial Lawyers PAC** 1050 31st St NW .... Washington DC 20007-4409
212 272-2000 **Bear Stearns & Co Inc PAC** 245 Park Ave .... New York NY 10167-0024
202 822-0200 **Build PAC of the National Assn of Home Builders** 1201 15th St NW .... Washington DC 20005-2802
202 833-1880 **Business Industry PAC** 1747 Pennsylvania Ave NW Suite 250 .... Washington DC 20006-4604
213 739-8200 **California Real Estate PAC** 525 S Virgil Ave .... Los Angeles CA 90020-1431
202 543-5016 **Campaign America** 511 Capitol Ct NE Suite 100 .... Washington DC 20002-4937
202 546-6206 **Carpenter's Legislative Improvement Committee** 101 Constitution Ave NW .... Washington DC 20001-2133
213 451-8548 **Citizens for the Republic** 233 Wilshire Blvd Suite 275 .... Santa Monica CA 90401-1207
512 340-9100 **Committee for Thorough Agricultural Political Education** 6609 Blanco Rd .... San Antonio TX 78216-6131
202 393-4695 **Committee on Letter Carriers Political Education** 100 Indiana Ave NW .... Washington DC 20001-2144
202 728-2465 **Communications Workers of America COPE Political Contributions Committee** 1925 K St NW Suite 211 .... Washington DC 20006-1153
703 522-2104 **Conservative National Committee** 2030 Clarendon Blvd Suite 305 .... Arlington VA 22201-2915
617 542-2282 **Council for a Livable World** 20 Park Plaza Suite 603 .... Boston MA 02116-4303
703 821-7000 **Dealers Election Action Committee of the National Automobile Dealers Assn** 8400 Westpark Dr 10th Fl .... McLean VA 22102-3522
202 624-8743 **Democratic Republican Independent Voter Education Committee** 25 Louisiana Ave NW .... Washington DC 20001-2130
202 338-9092 **Democrats for the 90s** 3032 N St NW .... Washington DC 20007-3404
202 546-3004 **Free Congress Foundation PAC** 717 2nd St NE .... Washington DC 20002-4368
202 628-4160 **Human Rights Campaign Fund** 1012 14th St NW 6th Fl .... Washington DC 20005-3495
202 628-4321 **Independent Action Inc** 1511 K St NW Suite 619 .... Washington DC 20005-1401
202 783-5880 **International Assn of Sheet Metal Workers Political Action League** 1750 New York Ave NW 6th Fl .... Washington DC 20006-5386
202 833-7000 **International Brotherhood of Electrical Workers Committee on Political Education** 1125 15th St NW .... Washington DC 20005-2707
212 265-7000 **International Ladies Garment Workers Union Campaign Committee** 1710 Broadway .... New York NY 10019-5254
202 628-4546 **International Longshoremen's Assn Committee on Political Education** 815 16th St NW .... Washington DC 20006-4104
202 785-8683 **League of Conservation Voters** 1150 Connecticut Ave NW Suite 201 .... Washington DC 20036-4104
202 857-5295 **Machinists Non-Partisan League** 1300 Connecticut Ave NW Suite 404 .... Washington DC 20036-1703
202 347-8585 **Marine Engineers Beneficial Assn Political Action Fund** 444 N Capitol St NW Suite 800 .... Washington DC 20001-1512
202 347-1444 **National Assn of Life Underwriters PAC** 1922 F St NW .... Washington DC 20006-4305
202 234-0832 **National Assn of Retired Federal Employees PAC** 1533 New Hampshire Ave NW .... Washington DC 20036-1279

Political

202 547-1151 **National Committee for an Effective Congress** 507 Capitol Ct NE — Washington DC 20002-4937
202 822-9459 **National Committee to Preserve Social Security & Medicare** 2000 K St NW Suite 800 — Washington DC 20006-1809
919 850-0399 **National Congressional Club** 4505 Falls of Neuse Rd Suite 600 — Raleigh NC 27609-6265
703 684-1800 **National Conservative PAC** 618 S Alfred St — Alexandria VA 22314-4002
202 879-7710 **National PAC** 555 New Jersey Ave NW Suite 718 — Washington DC 20001-2029
202 828-6000 **National Rifle Assn of America** 1600 Rhode Island Ave NW — Washington DC 20036-3240
202 626-8800 **National Right to Life PAC** 419 7th St NW Suite 500 — Washington DC 20004-2293
718 291-6900 **Nemet Motors International Assn** 153-12 Hillside Ave — Jamaica NY 11432-3322
202 467-4999 **People for the American Way** 2000 M St NW Suite 400 — Washington DC 20036-3315
212 880-5000 **Philip Morris PAC** 120 Park Ave — New York NY 10017-5592
202 383-1000 **Realtors PAC** 777 14 St NW 9th Fl — Washington DC 20005-3201
202 554-5056 **Republican Congressional Boosters Club** 300 1st St SE — Washington DC 20003-1801
202 783-3660 **Responsible Citizens Political League** 815 16th St NW Suite 511 — Washington DC 20006-4104
412 565-2000 **Rockwell International Corp Good Government Committee** 625 Liberty Ave — Pittsburgh PA 15222-3123
202 546-0023 **Ruff PAC** 501 Capitol Ct NE Suite 100 — Washington DC 20002-4937
512 474-1812 **Texas Medical Assn PAC** 1905 N Lamar Blvd Suite 207 — Austin TX 78705-4919
216 228-9400 **Transportation Political Education League** 14600 Detroit Ave — Cleveland OH 44107-4207
313 926-5531 **United Auto Workers Community Action Program** 8000 E Jefferson Ave — Detroit MI 48214-2699
412 562-2400 **United Steelworkers of America PAC** 5 Gateway Ctr — Pittsburgh PA 15222-1209
202 822-6640 **Voters for Choice** 2000 P St NW Suite 515 — Washington DC 20036-5915

STATE COMMITTEES–DEMOCRATIC

Democratic party headquarters are listed in state order.

205 595-9090 **Alabama Democratic State Committee** 4120 3rd Ave S — Birmingham AL 35222-1919
907 258-3050 **Alaska Democratic Party** 1443 W Northern Lights Blvd Suite S — Anchorage AK 99503-2307
602 257-9136 **Arizona Democratic State Party** 1509 N Central Ave Suite 100 — Phoenix AZ 85004-1621
501 374-2361 **Democratic Party of Arkansas** 1300 W Capitol Ave — Little Rock AR 72201-2900
415 896-5503 **California Democratic Party** 329 Bryant St Suite 3-C — San Francisco CA 94107-1406
303 830-8989 **Colorado Democratic State Committee** 1600 Downing St 6th Fl — Denver CO 80218-1532
203 278-6080 **Connecticut Democratic State Central Committee** 634 Asylum Ave — Hartford CT 06105-3836
302 996-9458 **Delaware State Democratic Committee** 609 W Newport Pike Graystone Plaza — Wilmington DE 19804-0000
904 222-3411 **Florida Democratic Party** PO Box 1758 — Tallahassee FL 32302-1758
404 872-1992 **Democratic Party of Georgia** 1100 Spring St Suite 350 — Atlanta GA 30367-0001
808 536-2258 **Democratic Party of Hawaii** 50 S Beretania St KuKui Plaza Suite C101B — Honolulu HI 96813-5105
208 336-1815 **Idaho State Democratic Party** 1020 W Franklin St — Boise ID 83702-5466
312 464-1900 **Illinois Democratic Party** 13126 Merchandise Mart — Chicago IL 60654-0000
317 231-7100 **Indiana Democratic State Committee** 1 N Capitol — Indianapolis IN 46206-0000
515 244-7292 **Iowa Democratic Party** 2116 Grand Ave — Des Moines IA 50312-5304
913 234-0425 **Kansas Democratic State Committee** 700 SW Jackson St Suite 305 — Topeka KS 66603-3738
502 695-4828 **Kentucky Democratic State Committee** PO Box 694 — Frankfort KY 40602-0694
504 927-7895 **Louisiana Democratic Party** 3114 College Dr Suite J — Baton Rouge LA 70808-3119
207 622-6233 **Maine Democratic State Committee** 51 Sewall St — Augusta ME 04330-7313
301 280-2300 **Maryland Democratic State Committee** 224 Main St — Annapolis MD 21401-2009
617 426-4760 **Massachusetts Democratic State Committee** 45 Bromfield St 7th Fl — Boston MA 02108-4116
517 371-5410 **Michigan Democratic State Committee** 606 Townsend St — Lansing MI 48933-2384
612 293-1200 **Democratic Farmer Labor Party of Minnesota** 525 Park St Suite 100 — Saint Paul MN 55103-2106
601 969-2913 **Democratic Party of the State of Mississipi** 832 N Congress St — Jackson MS 39202-2551
314 636-5241 **Missouri Democratic State Committee** PO Box 719 — Jefferson City MO 65102-0719
406 442-9520 **Montana Democratic State Central Committee** 616 Helena Ave — Helena MT 59601-3654
402 475-4584 **Nebraska Democratic State Committee** 715 S 14th St — Lincoln NE 68508-3701
702 732-3366 **Nevada Democratic State Party** 9533 W Sahara Ave Suite 236 — Las Vegas NV 89117-5302
603 622-9606 **New Hampshire Democratic State Committee** 922 Elm St Suite 210 — Manchester NH 03101-2010
609 392-3367 **New Jersey Democratic State Committee** 150 W State St — Trenton NJ 08608-1105
505 842-8208 **New Mexico Democratic Party** 315 8th St SW — Albuquerque NM 87102-0000
518 462-7407 **New York State Democratic Committee** 111 Washington Ave Rm 705 — Albany NY 12210-2207
919 821-2777 **North Carolina Democratic Party** 220 Hillsborough St — Raleigh NC 27603-1724
701 255-0460 **North Dakota Democratic-NPL** 1902 E Divide Ave — Bismarck ND 58501-2301
614 221-6563 **Ohio Democratic State Committee** 88 E Broad St Suite 1920 — Columbus OH 43215-3506
405 239-2700 **Oklahoma Democratic State Committee** 116 E Sheridan Suite G-100 — Oklahoma City OK 73104-0000
503 370-8200 **Democratic Party of Oregon** PO Box 15057 — Salem OR 97309-2057
717 238-9381 **Pennsylvania Democratic State Committee** 510 N 3rd St — Harrisburg PA 17101-1112
401 232-3800 **Rhode Island Democratic State Committee** 1991 Smith St — North Providence RI 02911-1717
803 799-7798 **South Carolina Democratic Party** 2730 Devine St — Columbia SC 29205-2433
605 987-2717 **South Dakota Democratic Party** 1010 S Broadway — Canton SD 57013-0000
615 244-1336 **Tennessee Democratic Party** 431 11th Ave N — Nashville TN 37203-3315
512 478-8746 **Texas Democratic Party** 815 Brazos St Suite 200 — Austin TX 78701-2593
801 484-1200 **Utah State Democratic Committee** 472 Bearcat Dr — Salt Lake City UT 84115-0000
802 229-5986 **Vermont Democratic Party** PO Box 336 — Montpelier VT 05601-0336
804 644-1966 **Virginia Democratic Party** 1001 E Broad St Suite LL25 — Richmond VA 23219-0000
206 583-0664 **Washington Democratic State Committee** Smith Tower Suite 1701 — Seattle WA 98104-2322
304 342-8121 **West Virginia State Democratic Executive Committee** 405 Capitol St Suite 501 — Charleston WV 25301-1727
608 255-5172 **Democratic Party of Wisconsin** 126 S Franklin St — Madison WI 53703-3494
307 637-8940 **Wyoming Democratic State Party** 419 Randall Ave — Cheyenne WY 82001-3087

STATE COMMITTEES–REPUBLICAN

Republican party headquarters are listed in state order.

205 324-1990 **Alabama Republican Party** 2940 Clairmont Ave S — Birmingham AL 35205-1000
907 276-4467 **Republican Party of Alaska** 750 E Fireweed Ln Suite 102 — Anchorage AK 99503-2803
602 957-7770 **Arizona Republican State Committee** 3501 N 24th St — Phoenix AZ 85016-6691
501 372-7301 **Republican Party of Arkansas** 1 Riverfront Pl Suite 550 — North Little Rock AR 72114-5663
818 841-5210 **California Republican Party** 1903 W Magnolia Blvd — Burbank CA 91506-1797
303 893-1776 **Colorado Republican Party** 1275 Tremont Pl — Denver CO 80204-2118
203 547-0589 **Connecticut Republican Party** 78 Oak St — Hartford CT 06106-1514
302 651-0260 **Delaware Republican Party** 2 Mill Rd — Wilmington DE 19806-2114
202 662-1382 **District of Columbia Republican State Committee** 440 1st St NW Suite 300 — Washington DC 20001-2028
904 222-7920 **Republican Party of Florida** 719 N Calhoun St — Tallahassee FL 32303-6209
404 365-7700 **Georgia Republican Party** 3091 Maple Dr Suite 315 — Atlanta GA 30305-2620
808 526-1755 **Republican Party of Hawaii** 100 N Beretania St Suite 203 — Honolulu HI 96817-4712
208 343-6405 **Idaho Republican State Committee** 612 W Hays St — Boise ID 83702-5511
217 525-0011 **Illinois State Central Republican Party** 223 S 3rd St — Springfield IL 62701-1144
317 635-7561 **Indiana Republican Center** 200 S Meridian St Suite 400 — Indianapolis IN 46225-0000
515 282-8105 **Republican Party of Iowa** 521 E Locust St — Des Moines IA 50309-1911
913 234-3416 **Kansas Republican Party** 214 SW 6th Ave — Topeka KS 66603-3719
502 875-5130 **Republican Party of Kentucky** PO Box 1068 — Frankfort KY 40602-1068
504 383-7234 **Louisiana Republican Party** 650 N 6th St — Baton Rouge LA 70802-5319
207 622-6247 **Maine Republican Party** 24 Stone St — Augusta ME 04330-5209
301 269-0113 **Maryland Republican Party** 1623 Forest Dr Suite 400 — Annapolis MD 21403-1020
617 924-8683 **Massachusetts Republican State Committee** 9 Galen St Suite 320 — Watertown MA 02172-4520
517 487-5413 **Michigan Republican State Committee** 2121 E Grand River Ave — Lansing MI 48912-3299
612 854-1446 **Minnesota Independent Republicans** 8030 Cedar Ave Suite 202 — Minneapolis MN 55425-1215
601 948-5191 **Mississippi Republican Party** 555 Tombigbee St — Jackson MS 39201-4806
314 636-3146 **Missouri Republican Party** 204 E Dunklin St — Jefferson City MO 65101-3127
406 442-6469 **Montana Republican State Committee** 1425 Helena Ave — Helena MT 59601-3024
402 475-2122 **Nebraska Republican Party** 421 S 9th St Suite 233 — Lincoln NE 68508-2245
702 737-7031 **Clark County Republican Central Committee** 6116 W Charleston Blvd — Las Vegas NV 89102-0000
603 225-9341 **New Hampshire Republican State Headquarters** 134 N Main St — Concord NH 03301-4917
609 989-7300 **New Jersey Republican State Committee** 310 W State St — Trenton NJ 08618-5704
505 883-7345 **New Mexico Republican Party** 5500 San Mateo Blvd NE Suite 114 — Albuquerque NM 87109-6263
518 462-2601 **New York Republican State Committee** 315 State St — Albany NY 12210-2001
919 828-6423 **North Carolina Republican State Committee** 1410 Hillsborough St — Raleigh NC 27605-1829
701 255-0030 **North Dakota Republican Party** 4007 State St Suite 8 — Bismarck ND 58501-0689
614 228-2481 **Ohio Republican State Committee** 172 E State St Suite 400 — Columbus OH 43215-4300
405 528-3501 **Oklahoma Republican Party** 4031 N Lincoln Blvd — Oklahoma City OK 73105-5232
717 234-4901 **Pennsylvania Republican Party** 112 State St — Harrisburg PA 17101-1024
401 421-2570 **Rhode Island Republican Party** 400 Smith St Suite 200 — Providence RI 02908-3727
803 798-8999 **South Carolina Republican Party** 720 Gracern Rd Stephenson Ctr Suite 121 — Columbia SC 29221-0000
605 224-7347 **South Dakota Republican Party** 401 E Sioux Ave — Pierre SD 57501-3162
615 321-4521 **Tennessee Republican Party** 2817 West End Ave — Nashville TN 37203-1453
512 477-9821 **Texas Republican Party** 211 E 7th St Suite 620 — Austin TX 78701-3295
801 533-9777 **Utah Republican Party** 643 E 400 South Suite A — Salt Lake City UT 84102-2803
802 223-3411 **Vermont Republican State Committee** 43 Court St — Montpelier VT 05602-2947
804 780-0111 **Virginia Republican Party** 115 E Grace St — Richmond VA 23219-1741
206 451-1984 **Washington State Republican Party** 9 Lake Bellevue Dr Suite 203 — Bellevue WA 98005-2478
304 344-3446 **West Virginia Republican State Committee** 101 Dee Dr — Charleston WV 25311-1620
608 257-4765 **Republican Party of Wisconsin** 121 S Pinckney St — Madison WI 53703-0000
307 234-9166 **Wyoming Republican State Committee** 212 N Wolcott St — Casper WY 82601-1923

Special Interest

CONSUMER AFFAIRS AND SOCIAL SERVICES

202 371-6710 **Accuracy in Media Inc** 1275 K St NW Suite 1150 — Washington DC 20005-4090
617 876-6620 **Action for Children's Television** 20 University Rd — Cambridge MA 02138-5756
412 232-3444 **Air & Waste Management Assn** Gateway 3 4 West — Pittsburgh PA 15222-0000
703 823-9800 **American Assn for Counseling & Development** 5999 Stevenson Ave — Alexandria VA 22304-3398
202 429-1825 **American Assn for Marriage & Family Therapy** 1717 K St NW Suite 407 — Washington DC 20006-1504
202 728-4300 **American Assn of Retired Persons** 1909 K St NW — Washington DC 20049-0001
212 944-9800 **American Civil Liberties Union** 132 W 43rd St — New York NY 10036-6599
202 546-6555 **American Conservative Union** 38 Ivy St SE — Washington DC 20003-4097
215 241-7000 **American Friends Service Committee** 1501 Cherry St — Philadelphia PA 19102-1477
303 695-0811 **American Humane Assn** 623 Inverness Dr E — Englewood CO 80112-0000
212 677-4400 **American ORT Federation** 817 Broadway — New York NY 10003-4756
202 682-0100 **American Public Welfare Assn** 810 1st St NE Suite 500 — Washington DC 20002-4227
212 876-7700 **American Society for the Prevention of Cruelty to Animals** 441 E 92nd St — New York NY 10128-6803
415 543-2617 **American Society on Aging** 833 Market St Suite 512 — San Francisco CA 94103-1824
301 925-8811 **American Trauma Society** 1400 Mercantile Ln Suite 188 — Landover MD 20785-5365
202 638-6447 **Americans for Democratic Action** 1511 K St NW Suite 941 — Washington DC 20005-1401
212 807-8400 **Amnesty International of the USA** 322 8th Ave — New York NY 10001-4808
212 490-2525 **Anti-Defamation League** 823 United Nations Plaza — New York NY 10017-3560
202 797-4626 **Arms Control Assn** 11 Dupont Cir NW Suite 250 — Washington DC 20036-1207
301 827-7168 **Aspen Institute** Carmichael Rd — Queenstown MD 21658-0000
212 741-0100 **Association for Children with Retarded Mental Development** 162 5th Ave 11th Fl — New York NY 10010-5902
718 523-2222 **Association for the Advancement of the Blind & Retarded** 164-09 Hillside Ave — Jamaica NY 11432-4140
202 544-5150 **Association to Unite the Democracies** 1506 Pennsylvania Ave SE — Washington DC 20003-3116
617 237-5200 **Automobile Legal Assn** 888 Worcester St — Wellesley MA 02181-3717
202 857-6600 **B'nai B'rith International** 1640 Rhode Island Ave NW — Washington DC 20036-3279
215 567-7000 **Big Brothers/Big Sisters of America** 230 N 13th St — Philadelphia PA 19107-1551
202 269-0200 **Bread for the World** 802 Rhode Island Ave NE — Washington DC 20018-1763
212 686-3110 **CARE** 660 1st Ave — New York NY 10016-3295
202 328-7700 **Center for Auto Safety** 2001 S St NW Suite 410 — Washington DC 20009-1160
202 332-9110 **Center for Science in the Public Interest** 1501 16th St NW — Washington DC 20036-1499
202 638-2952 **Child Welfare League of America** 440 1st St NW Suite 310 — Washington DC 20001-2085
202 544-7190 **Coalition to Stop Gun Violence** 100 Maryland Ave NE — Washington DC 20002-5625
216 736-2161 **Commission for Racial Justice** 700 Prospect Ave E — Cleveland OH 44115-1131
212 688-2063 **Committee for Economic Development** 477 Madison Ave 6th Fl — New York NY 10022-5893
202 833-1200 **Common Cause** 2030 M St NW — Washington DC 20036-3380
703 548-8600 **Community Assns Institute** 1423 Powhatan St Suite 7 — Alexandria VA 22314-1343
719 594-9900 **Compassion International** 3955 Cragwood Dr — Colorado Springs CO 80918-7860
718 434-3580 **Congress of Racial Equality** 1457 Flatbush Ave — Brooklyn NY 11210-2428
202 387-6121 **Consumer Federation of America** 1424 16th St NW Suite 604 — Washington DC 20036-2211
202 785-4835 **Consumers for World Trade** 1726 M St NW Suite 900 — Washington DC 20036-4502
212 870-3000 **Coordination in Development** 475 Riverside Dr Rm 1842 — New York NY 10115-0122
202 466-6512 **Council on Foundations** 1828 L St NW Suite 300 — Washington DC 20036-5168
805 687-3694 **Direct Relief International** 21 N Salsipuedes St — Santa Barbara CA 93103-0000
215 628-2288 **Drug Information Assn** PO Box 3113 — Maple Glen PA 19002-0713
414 359-1040 **Family Service America** 11700 W Lake Park Dr — Milwaukee WI 53224-3099
602 998-3100 **Food for the Hungry Inc** 7729 E Greenway Rd — Scottsdale AZ 85260-1795
202 634-9353 **Foster Grandparents Program** 1100 Vermont Ave NW Rm 6100 — Washington DC 20525-0001
401 826-2500 **Foster Parents Plan International** 804 Quaker Ln — East Greenwich RI 02818-1667

314 882-4856	**Freedom of Information Center** 20 Walter Williams Hall .... Columbia MO 65211-0000
212 247-8077	**Friends of Animals Inc** 1841 Broadway Suite 212 .... New York NY 10023-7999
212 661-5900	**Fund for Peace** 345 E 46th St Suite 712 .... New York NY 10017-3518
301 530-6500	**Goodwill Industries of America Inc** 9200 Wisconsin Ave .... Bethesda MD 20814-3814
202 898-0792	**Handgun Control Inc** 1225 Eye St NW Suite 1100 .... Washington DC 20005-0000
212 807-5800	**Helen Keller International** 15 W 16th St .... New York NY 10011-6301
212 674-6800	**HIAS (Hebrew Immigrant Aid Society)**
	200 Park Ave S 2nd Fl .... New York NY 10003-1503
202 857-1200	**Highway Users Federation for Safety & Mobility**
	1776 Massachusetts Ave NW 5th Fl .... Washington DC 20036-1904
516 747-5400	**Human Resources Center** 201 IU Willetts Rd W .... Albertson NY 11507-1599
202 223-8100	**Independent Sector** 1828 L St NW Suite 1200 .... Washington DC 20036-5107
203 226-6347	**Insurance Crime Prevention Institute** 15 Franklin St .... Westport CT 06880-5985
214 404-9980	**International Airline Passengers Assn** PO Box 870188 .... Dallas TX 75287-0188
213 538-0233	**International Right of Way Assn** 13650 S Gramercy Pl .... Gardena CA 90249-2465
415 921-5225	**Japanese American Citizens League** 1765 Sutter St ...... San Francisco CA 94115-3297
305 446-7608	**Junior Chamber International** 400 University Dr .... Coral Gables FL 33134-7186
202 429-1965	**League of Women Voters of the United States**
	1730 M St NW .... Washington DC 20036-4587
714 727-3227	**Motorcycle Safety Foundation** 2 Jenner St Suite 150 .... Irvine CA 92718-3806
301 358-8900	**NAACP** 4805 Mt Hope Dr .... Baltimore MD 21215-3206
202 408-4600	**National Abortion Rights Action League**
	1101 14th St NW 5th Fl .... Washington DC 20005-5601
703 578-4200	**National Alcoholic Beverage Control Assn** 4216 King St ...... Alexandria VA 22302-1507
703 528-4380	**National Alliance of Senior Citizens** 2525 Wilson Blvd .... Arlington VA 22201-3835
301 263-0991	**National Assn for Senior Living Industries**
	184 Duke of Gloucester St .... Annapolis MD 21401-2515
301 358-8900	**National Assn for the Advancement of Colored People**
	4805 Mt Hope Dr .... Baltimore MD 21215-3206
215 649-7055	**National Assn of Town Watch**
	7 Wynnewood Rd Suite 215 .... Wynnewood PA 19096-1923
708 430-2430	**National Automobile Theft Bureau**
	10330 S Roberts Rd Suite 3A .... Palos Hills IL 60465-1997
202 829-5900	**National Business League** 4324 Georgia Ave NW .... Washington DC 20011-7197
202 637-8400	**National Caucus & Center on Black Aged Inc**
	1424 K St NW Suite 500 .... Washington DC 20005-2410
202 331-1103	**National Center for Neighborhood Enterprise**
	1367 Connecticut Ave NW 3rd Fl .... Washington DC 20036-0000
202 546-9404	**National Congress of American Indians**
	900 Pennsylvania Ave SE .... Washington DC 20003-0000
202 659-0006	**National Council of Negro Women Inc**
	1211 Connecticut Ave NW Suite 702 .... Washington DC 20036-2701
202 347-8800	**National Council of Senior Citizens** 925 15th St NW .... Washington DC 20005-2385
212 697-1278	**National Council of Women of the US** 777 UN Plaza 7th Fl ..... New York NY 10017-0000
415 896-6223	**National Council on Crime & Delinquency**
	685 Market St 4th Fl Suite 620 .... San Francisco CA 94105-0000
202 479-1200	**National Council on the Aging**
	600 Maryland Ave SW Suite 100W .... Washington DC 20024-2571
202 466-6272	**National Crime Prevention Council** 1700 K St NW 2nd Fl ... Washington DC 20006-3817
301 589-5600	**National Foundation for Consumer Credit**
	8701 Georgia Ave Suite 507 .... Silver Spring MD 20910-3713
202 332-6483	**National Gay/Lesbian Task Force** 1517 U St NW .... Washington DC 20009-3911
201 595-9200	**National Industries for the Blind** 524 Hamburg Tpke .... Wayne NJ 07470-2092
301 443-1124	**National Institute of Drug Abuse** 5600 Fishers Ln .... Rockville MD 20857-0001
202 265-7685	**National Planning Assn** 1424 16th St NW Suite 700 .... Washington DC 20036-2211
202 626-8800	**National Right to Life Committee Inc**
	419 7th St NW Suite 500 .... Washington DC 20004-2293
312 527-4800	**National Safety Council** 444 N Michigan Ave .... Chicago IL 60611-3991
708 843-2020	**National Society to Prevent Blindness**
	500 E Remington Rd .... Schaumburg IL 60173-5624
202 543-1300	**National Taxpayers Union** 325 Pennsylvania Ave SE .... Washington DC 20003-1100
608 257-7712	**National Telemedia Council** 120 E Wilson St .... Madison WI 53703-3423
301 495-4999	**National Urban Coalition** 8601 Georgia Ave Suite 500 ...... Silver Spring MD 20910-3439
202 898-1100	**National Women's Political Caucus**
	1275 K St NW Suite 750 .... Washington DC 20005-4051
203 661-0797	**Outward Bound USA** 384 Field Point Rd .... Greenwich CT 06830-7098
617 482-1211	**OXFAM-America** 115 Broadway .... Boston MA 02116-5400
213 410-9732	**Parents Anonymous** 6733 S Sepulveda Blvd Suite 270 ...... Los Angeles CA 90045-1525
912 743-7403	**Pilot Club International** 244 College St .... Macon GA 31213-0001
202 872-1790	**Public Affairs Council** 1019 19th St NW Suite 200 .... Washington DC 20036-5105
202 293-9142	**Public Citizen** 2000 P St NW Suite 700 .... Washington DC 20036-5915
609 452-0606	**Recording for the Blind** 20 Roszel Rd .... Princeton NJ 08540-6294
703 684-0244	**Retired Persons Services Inc** 500 Montgomery St .... Alexandria VA 22314-1563
202 862-9740	**Sane/Freeze** 1819 H St NW Suite 1000 .... Washington DC 20006-3603
203 226-7271	**Save the Children Federation** 54 Wilton Rd .... Westport CT 06880-3108
312 263-2303	**Second Harvest** 116 S Michigan Suite 4 .... Chicago IL 60603-6001
816 333-8300	**Sertoma International** 1912 E Meyer Blvd .... Kansas City MO 64132-1174
813 576-8929	**Straight Inc** 3001 Gandy Blvd .... Saint Petersburg FL 33702-2043
202 462-2520	**Telecommunications Research & Action Center**
	PO Box 12038 .... Washington DC 20005-0000
212 393-6288	**Telephone Pioneers of America** 22 Cortlandt St Rm 2565 ..... New York NY 10007-3107
212 535-4441	**Twentieth Century Fund** 41 E 70th St .... New York NY 10021-4972
703 836-7100	**United Way of America** 701 N Fairfax St .... Alexandria VA 22314-2045
212 777-0700	**Vocational Foundation Inc** 902 Broadway 15th Fl .... New York NY 10010-6002
212 873-2600	**Volunteers of America** 340 W 85th St .... New York NY 10024-3800
703 684-2400	**Water Pollution Control Federation** 601 Wythe St .... Alexandria VA 22314-1994
405 946-3333	**World Neighbors** 5116 N Portland Ave .... Oklahoma City OK 73112-2098

COLLEGES AND

UNIVERSITIES

Four-Year Colleges

Colleges and universities granting bachelors' degrees are listed alphabetically within each state.

ALABAMA

205 851-5000 **Alabama A & M University** .... Normal AL 35762-0000
205 293-4100 **Alabama State University** 915 S Jackson St .... Montgomery AL 36101-0000
205 844-4000 **Auburn University** .... Auburn AL 36849-0000
205 244-3000 *Montgomery Campus* 7300 University Dr .... Montgomery AL 36117-3596
205 226-4600 **Birmingham-Southern College** 900 Arkadelphia Rd .... Birmingham AL 35254-0001
205 272-5820 **Faulkner University** 5345 Atlanta Hwy .... Montgomery AL 36193-4601
205 536-9088 **Forest Institute of Professional Psychology**
2611 Leeman Ferry Rd .... Huntsville AL 35801-5611
205 265-0511 **Huntingdon College** 1500 E Fairview Ave .... Montgomery AL 36194-6201
205 766-6610 **International Bible College** 3625 Pelton Dr .... Florence AL 35630-0000
205 782-5781 **Jacksonville State University** 817 Pelham Rd S .... Jacksonville AL 36265-2796
205 683-6161 **Judson College** Bibb St .... Marion AL 36756-0120
205 652-9661 **Livingston University** College St .... Livingston AL 35470-0000
205 923-2771 **Miles College** 5500 Myron Massey Blvd .... Fairfield AL 35064-2697
205 675-5990 **Mobile College** 5735 College Pkwy .... Mobile AL 36613-2842
205 726-7000 **Oakwood College** Oakwood Rd .... Huntsville AL 35896-0001
205 870-2011 **Samford University** 800 Lakeshore Dr .... Birmingham AL 35229-0001
205 872-2533 **Selma University** 2501 Lapsley Ave .... Selma AL 36701-0000
205 969-0880 **Southeastern Bible College** 3001 Hwy 280 E .... Birmingham AL 35243-4181
205 837-9769 **Southeastern Institute of Technology** 200 Sparkman Dr .... Huntsville AL 35805-0000
205 626-3303 **Sports Academy** 1 Academy Dr .... Daphne AL 36526-7055
205 460-2011 **Spring Hill College** 4000 Dauphin St .... Mobile AL 36608-1791
205 349-4240 **Stillman College** 3600 15th St .... Tuscaloosa AL 35401-2602
205 362-0206 **Talladega College** 627 Battle St W .... Talladega AL 35160-2399
205 566-8112 **Troy State University** .... Troy AL 36082-0001
205 983-6556 *Dothan* 3601 US Hwy 231 N .... Dothan AL 36303-0000
205 834-1400 *Montgomery* 231 Montgomery St .... Montgomery AL 36104-6003
205 297-1007 *Phenix City* 1 University Pl .... Phenix City AL 36867-0000
205 727-8011 **Tuskegee University** Kresege Ctr .... Tuskegee AL 36088-0000
205 348-5121 **University of Alabama (System)** 401 Queen City Ave .... Tuscaloosa AL 35401-1551
University of Alabama
205 934-8221 *Birmingham Campus* University Stn .... Birmingham AL 35294-0001
205 546-2886 *Gadsden Center* PO Box 1280 .... Gadsden AL 35902-1280
205 895-6120 *Huntsville Campus* 4701 University Dr .... Huntsville AL 35899-0001
205 348-6010 *Tuscaloosa Campus* .... Tuscaloosa AL 35487-0000
205 665-6000 **University of Montevallo** Stn 6030 .... Montevallo AL 35115-0000
205 760-4100 **University of North Alabama** University Stn .... Florence AL 35632-0001
205 460-6101 **University of South Alabama** 307 University Blvd .... Mobile AL 36688-0001
205 937-3789 *Baldwin Campus* 1900 US Hwy 31 S .... Bay Minette AL 36507-0000

ALASKA

907 822-3201 **Alaska Bible College** PO Box 289 .... Glennallen AK 99588-0289
907 561-1266 **Alaska Pacific University** 4101 University Dr .... Anchorage AK 99508-4672
907 766-2992 **Covenant Life College** 26th Mile Hanines Hwy .... Haines AK 99827-0000
907 543-4500 **Kuskokwim College** PO Box 368 .... Bethel AK 99559-0368
907 486-3524 **Saint Herman's Theological Seminary** 414 Mission Rd Suite 1 .. Kodiak AK 99615-7392
907 747-5220 **Sheldon Jackson College** 801 Lincoln St .... Sitka AK 99835-7699
University of Alaska
907 786-1800 *Anchorage* 3211 Providence Dr .... Anchorage AK 99508-4671
907 474-7821 *Fairbanks* .... Fairbanks AK 99775-0001
907 789-4458 **University of Alaska Southeast Juneau Campus**
11120 Glacier Hwy .... Juneau AK 99801-8699
907 443-2201 **University of Fairbanks Northwest Campus** Pouch 400 Front St ... Nome AK 99762-9999
907 248-2122 **Wayland Baptist University** 4240 Wisconsin St .... Anchorage AK 99517-2801

ARIZONA

602 944-3335 **American Indian Bible College** 10020 N 15th Ave .... Phoenix AZ 85021-2199
602 995-2670 **Arizona College of the Bible** 2045 W Northern Ave .... Phoenix AZ 85021-5197
602 965-9011 **Arizona State University** .... Tempe AZ 85287-0001
602 870-9222 **DeVry Institute of Technology** 2149 W Dunlap Ave .... Phoenix AZ 85021-2995
602 776-3728 **Embry-Riddle Aeronautical University** 3200 Willow Creek Rd .. Prescott AZ 86301-8662
602 249-3300 **Grand Canyon University** 3300 W Camelback Rd .... Phoenix AZ 85017-3030
602 523-9011 **Northern Arizona University** PO Box 4092 .... Flagstaff AZ 86011-4092
602 995-5999 **Nova University** 8601 N Black Canyon Hwy Suite 117 .... Phoenix AZ 85021-4936
602 371-1188 **Ottawa University** 2340 W Mission Ln .... Phoenix AZ 85021-2818
602 778-2090 **Prescott College** 220 Grove Ave .... Prescott AZ 86301-2990
602 366-5421 **Southern Arizona Bible College** Hwy 92 .... Hereford AZ 85615-0000
602 774-3890 **Southwest School Missions Independent Bible Institute**
2918 N Aris Ave .... Flagstaff AZ 86001-0000
602 992-6101 **Southwestern Baptist Bible College** 2625 E Cactus Rd .... Phoenix AZ 85032-7097
602 978-5511 **Sweetwater Bible College** 14240 N 43rd Ave .... Phoenix AZ 85306-4511
602 621-2211 **University of Arizona** .... Tucson AZ 85721-0001
602 966-7400 **University of Phoenix** 4615 E Elwood St .... Phoenix AZ 85040-1998
602 943-2311 **Western International University** 10202 N 19th Ave .... Phoenix AZ 85021-1994

ARKANSAS

501 374-7856 **Arkansas Baptist College** 1600 Bishop St .... Little Rock AR 72202-6099
501 793-9813 **Arkansas College** 2300 Highland Rd .... Batesville AR 72501-3699
501 972-2100 **Arkansas State University** .... State University AR 72467-9999
501 968-0389 **Arkansas Tech University** .... Russellville AR 72801-0000
501 329-6872 **Central Baptist College** CBC Stn .... Conway AR 72032-6470
501 279-4000 **Harding University** 900 E Center Ave .... Searcy AR 72143-5608
501 246-5511 **Henderson State University** 12th & Henderson .... Arkadelphia AR 71923-4899
501 329-6811 **Hendrix College** 1601 Harkrider St .... Conway AR 72032-0000
501 524-3131 **John Brown University** .... Siloam Springs AR 72761-2121
501 455-4588 **Missionary Baptist Seminary & Institute**
5224 Stagecoach Rd .... Little Rock AR 72204-8599
501 246-4531 **Ouachita Baptist University** 410 Ouachita St .... Arkadelphia AR 71923-3200
501 375-9845 **Philander Smith College** 812 W 13th St .... Little Rock AR 72202-3799
501 235-4000 **Southern Arkansas University** Hwy 19 N .... Magnolia AR 71753-0000
501 886-6741 **Southern Baptist College** 201 Fulbright Ave .... Walnut Ridge AR 72476-0000
501 575-2000 **University of Arkansas** 433 N Garland Ave .... Fayetteville AR 72701-4030
501 569-3000 *Little Rock Campus* 2801 S University Ave .... Little Rock AR 72204-1085
501 367-6811 *Monticello Campus* PO Box 3598 .... Monticello AR 71655-0000
501 541-6500 *Pine Bluff Campus* 1200 University Dr .... Pine Bluff AR 71601-2799
501 329-2931 **University of Central Arkansas** .... Conway AR 72032-0000
501 754-3839 **University of the Ozarks** 415 N College Ave .... Clarksville AR 72830-2880

CALIFORNIA

415 673-4200 **Academy of Art College** 540 Powell St .... San Francisco CA 94108-3893
213 384-1882 **Agape Bible College** 920 S Grandview St .... Los Angeles CA 90006-0000
818 304-6000 **Ambassador College** 300 W Green St .... Pasadena CA 91129-0001
714 593-0432 **American Armenian International College** 1950 3rd St .... La Verne CA 91750-0000
415 841-1905 **American Baptist Seminary of the West** 2606 Dwight Way ..... Berkeley CA 94704-3029
213 470-2000 **American College for the Applied Arts**
1651 Westwood Blvd .... Los Angeles CA 90024-5603
415 848-2500 **Armstrong College** 2222 Harold Way .... Berkeley CA 94704-1489
818 584-5000 **Art Center College of Design** 1700 Lida St .... Pasadena CA 91103-1999
714 497-3309 **Art Institute of Southern California**
2222 Laguna Canyon Rd .... Laguna Beach CA 92651-1136
818 969-3434 **Azusa Pacific University** 921 E Alosta Ave .... Azusa CA 91702-2769
408 438-3800 **Bethany Bible College** 800 Bethany Dr .... Scotts Valley CA 95066-2896
213 944-0351 **Biola University** 13800 Biola Ave .... La Mirada CA 90639-0001
805 966-3888 **Brooks Institute of Photography** 801 Alston Rd .... Santa Barbara CA 93108-2399
714 689-5771 **California Baptist College** 8432 Magnolia Ave .... Riverside CA 92504-3297
209 251-4215 **California Christian College** 4881 E University Ave .... Fresno CA 93703-3533
415 653-8118 **California College of Arts & Crafts** 5212 Broadway .... Oakland CA 94618-1426
818 356-6811 **California Institute of Technology** 1201 E California Blvd .... Pasadena CA 91125-0001
805 255-1050 **California Institute of the Arts** 24700 McBean Pkwy .... Valencia CA 91355-2397
213 381-3719 **California International University** 2706 Wilshire Blvd .... Los Angeles CA 90057-3202
805 492-2411 **California Lutheran University** 60 W Olsen Rd .... Thousand Oaks CA 91360-2787
707 648-4200 **California Maritime Academy** 200 Maritime Academy Dr .... Vallejo CA 94590-8181
213 925-4082 **California Missionary Baptist Institute** 9246 Rosser St .... Bellflower CA 90706-2932
619 695-3292 **California Pacific University** 10650 Treena St Rm 203 .... San Diego CA 92131-2436
805 756-1111 **California Polytech State University** 1 Grand Ave .... San Luis Obispo CA 93407-0001
714 869-7659 **California State Polytechnic University** 3801 W Temple Ave ..... Pomona CA 91768-2557
213 590-5506 **California State University (System)** 400 Golden Shore St .. Long Beach CA 90802-4275
California State University
805 664-2011 *Bakersfield Campus* 9001 Stockdale Hwy .... Bakersfield CA 93311-1022
916 898-6116 *Chico Campus* .... Chico CA 95929-0001
213 516-3300 *Dominguez Hills Campus* 1000 E Victoria St .... Carson CA 90747-0001
209 278-4240 *Fresno Campus* 5241 N Maple .... Fresno CA 93740-0001
714 773-2011 *Fullerton Campus* 800 N State College Blvd .... Fullerton CA 92631-3547
415 881-3000 *Hayward Campus* .... Hayward CA 94542-0000
213 985-4111 *Long Beach Campus* 1250 Bellflower Blvd .... Long Beach CA 90840-0001
213 343-3000 *Los Angeles Campus* 5151 State University Dr .... Los Angeles CA 90032-8000
818 885-1200 *Northridge Campus* 18111 Nordhoff St .... Northridge CA 91330-0001
916 278-6011 *Sacramento Campus* 6000 J St .... Sacramento CA 95819-6000
714 880-5000 *San Bernardino Campus* 5500 University Pkwy .... San Bernardino CA 92407-2393
209 667-3122 *Stanislaus Campus* 801 W Monte Vista Ave .... Turlock CA 95380-0256
619 745-0505 **Cathedral Bible College** 927 Idaho Ave .... Escondido CA 92025-6399
714 997-6815 **Chapman College** 333 N Glassell St .... Orange CA 92666-1099
714 854-8002 **Christ College Irvine** 1530 Concordia Dr .... Irvine CA 92715-3299
619 440-3043 **Christian Heritage College** 2100 Greenfield Dr .... El Cajon CA 92019-1157
408 970-9966 **City University** 3333 Bowers Ave Suite 155 .... Santa Clara CA 95054-2912
213 382-3801 **City University Los Angeles** 3960 Wilshire Blvd Suite 501 .. Los Angeles CA 90010-3306
714 621-8000 **Claremont McKenna College** 500 E 9th St Bauer Ctr .... Claremont CA 91711-0000
714 621-8026 **Claremont University Center (System)** 150 E 10th St .... Claremont CA 91711-6160
408 252-5550 **Cogswell Polytechnical College** 10420 Bubb Rd .... Cupertino CA 95014-4150
619 465-3990 **Coleman College** 7380 Parkway Dr .... La Mesa CA 92042-1500
213 852-1321 **College for Developmental Studies** 563 N Alfred St ..... West Hollywood CA 90048-2512
415 593-1601 **College of Notre Dame** 1500 Ralston Ave .... Belmont CA 94002-1997
213 851-0550 **Columbia College-Hollywood** 925 N La Brea Ave .... Hollywood CA 90038-2392
415 459-1650 **Columbia Pacific University** 1415 3rd St .... San Rafael CA 94901-2860
213 699-9927 **DeVry Institute of Technology**
12801 Crossroads Pkwy S .... City of Industry CA 91746-3595
415 457-4440 **Dominican College of San Rafael** 50 Acacia Ave .... San Rafael CA 94901-2230
415 849-2030 **Dominican School of Philosophy & Theology** 2401 Ridge Rd .. Berkeley CA 94709-1211
213 291-7821 **Eubanks Conservatory of Music & Arts**
4928 S Crenshaw Blvd .... Los Angeles CA 90043-1896
415 848-5232 **Franciscan School of Theology** 1712 Euclid Ave .... Berkeley CA 94709-1294
209 251-7194 **Fresno Pacific College** 1717 S Chestnut Ave .... Fresno CA 93702-4798
818 584-5200 **Fuller Theological Seminary** 135 N Oakland Ave .... Pasadena CA 91182-0001
415 442-7000 **Golden Gate College** 536 Mission St .... San Francisco CA 94105-2968
213 623-6000 **Golden Gate University** 919 S Grand Ave Suite 250 .... Los Angeles CA 90015-0000
714 621-8011 **Harvey Mudd College** 301 E 12th St .... Claremont CA 91711-5990
415 228-9000 **Heald Institute of Technology** 2860 Howe Rd .... Martinez CA 94553-0000
415 436-1000 **Holy Names College** 3500 Mountain Blvd .... Oakland CA 94619-1627
707 826-3011 **Humboldt State University** Plaza Ave .... Arcata CA 95521-0000
209 478-0800 **Humphreys College** 6650 Inglewood Ave .... Stockton CA 95207-3896
213 470-2293 **IHC Center** 10951 W Pico Blvd .... Los Angeles CA 90064-2126
213 939-7179 **International Bible College** 1218 S Fairfax Ave .... Los Angeles CA 90019-0000
818 960-8681 **ITT Technical Institute of West Covina**
1530 W Cameron Ave .... West Covina CA 91790-2711
415 841-8804 **Jesuit School of Theology** 1735 Leroy Ave .... Berkeley CA 94709-1193
818 240-9166 **Kensington University** 124 S Isabel St .... Glendale CA 91205-4911
619 293-3760 **La Jolla University** 5005 Texas St .... San Diego CA 92108-0000
714 599-5433 **Life Bible College** 1100 Covina Blvd .... San Dimas CA 91773-0000
415 221-1212 **Lincoln University** 281 Masonic Ave .... San Francisco CA 94118-4498
714 824-4508 **Loma Linda University** 11139 Anderson St .... Loma Linda CA 92350-0001
415 974-6666 **Louise Salinger Academy of Fashion** 101 Jessie St .... San Francisco CA 94105-3507
213 338-2700 **Loyola Marymount University** 7101 W 80th St .... Los Angeles CA 90045-2699
805 259-3540 **Master's College** 21726 W Placerita Canyon Rd .... Newhall CA 91321-1200
415 323-6141 **Menlo School & College** 1000 El Camino Real .... Atherton CA 94027-4301
415 430-2255 **Mills College** 5000 MacArthur Blvd .... Oakland CA 94613-1301
213 476-2237 **Mount Saint Mary's College** 12001 Chalon Rd .... Los Angeles CA 90049-1597
415 451-0511 **National Hispanic University** 255 E 14th St .... Oakland CA 94606-2235
619 563-7100 **National University** University Pk .... San Diego CA 92108-0000
415 626-1694 **New College of California** 50 Fell St .... San Francisco CA 94102-5298
213 641-3470 **Northrop University** 5800 Arbor Vitae St .... Los Angeles CA 90045-4704
415 657-5911 **Northwestern Polytechnic University** 220 Warren Ave .... Fremont CA 94539-0000
213 259-2500 **Occidental College** 1600 Campus Dr .... Los Angeles CA 90041-3376
213 251-0505 **Otis Art Institute of Parsons School of Design**
2401 Wilshire Blvd .... Los Angeles CA 90057-3398
714 879-3901 **Pacific Christian College** 2500 E Nutwood Ave .... Fullerton CA 92631-3199
714 599-6843 **Pacific Coast Baptist Bible College** 1100 S Valley Ctr .... San Dimas CA 91773-0000
415 848-0528 **Pacific School of Religion** 1798 Scenic Ave .... Berkeley CA 94709-1323
213 551-0304 **Pacific Southern University** 9581 W Pico Blvd .... Los Angeles CA 90035-0000
707 965-6311 **Pacific Union College** Howell Mountain Rd .... Angwin CA 94508-0000
213 471-0306 **Pacific Western University** 600 N Sepulveda Blvd .... Los Angeles CA 90049-2108
415 533-8300 **Patten College** 2433 Coolidge Ave .... Oakland CA 94601-2699
213 456-4000 **Pepperdine University** 24255 Pacific Coast Hwy .... Malibu CA 90263-0001
714 621-8129 **Pitzer College** 1050 N Mills Ave .... Claremont CA 91711-6101
619 221-2200 **Point Loma Nazarene College** 3900 Lomaland Dr .... San Diego CA 92106-2810
714 621-8134 **Pomona College** 333 N College Way .... Claremont CA 91711-6301
213 390-7560 **Ryokan College** 12581 Venice Blvd Suite 202 .... Los Angeles CA 90066-0000
805 482-4697 **Saint John's Seminary College** 5118 Seminary Rd .... Camarillo CA 93012-0000
415 376-4411 **Saint Mary's College** St Marys Rd .... Moraga CA 94575-0000
415 325-5621 **Saint Patrick's Seminary** 320 Middlefield Rd .... Menlo Park CA 94025-3509
415 420-6076 **Samuel Merritt College of Nursing** 370 Hawthorne Ave .... Oakland CA 94609-3108
619 286-4362 **San Diego Bible College** 5954 Alta Mesa Way .... San Diego CA 92115-6102
619 594-5200 **San Diego State University** College Blvd .... San Diego CA 92182-0001
619 357-5500 *Imperial Valley Campus* 720 Heber Ave .... Calexico CA 92231-2480
415 771-7020 **San Francisco Art Institute** 800 Chestnut St .... San Francisco CA 94133-2299
415 564-8086 **San Francisco Conservatory of Music** 1201 Ortega St .... San Francisco CA 94122-4411
415 338-1111 **San Francisco State University** 1600 Holloway Ave .... San Francisco CA 94132-1722
408 293-9058 **San Jose Christian College** 790 S 12th St .... San Jose CA 95112-2381
408 924-2000 **San Jose State University** 1 Washington Sq .... San Jose CA 95192-0001
408 554-4764 **Santa Clara University** Alameda .... Santa Clara CA 95053-0001
714 621-8282 **Scripps College** 1030 N Columbia Ave .... Claremont CA 91711-3948

Four-Year Colleges

415 261-1907 **Shiloh Bible College** 3295 School St — Oakland CA 94602-3638
714 545-1133 **Sierra University** 2900 Bristol St Suite D-207 — Costa Mesa CA 92626-5955
916 221-7280 **Simpson College** 2211 College View Dr — Redding CA 96003-8606
707 664-2880 **Sonoma State University** 1801 E Cotati Ave — Rohnert Park CA 94928-3609
714 530-9650 **South Baylo University** 12012 S Magnolia Ave — Garden Grove CA 92641-3346
619 287-9342 **Southern California Bible College** 4747 College Ave — San Diego CA 92115-3906
714 556-3610 **Southern California College** 55 Fair Dr — Costa Mesa CA 92626-6597
213 829-3482 **Southern California Institute of Architecture** 1800 Berkeley St — Santa Monica CA 90404-4198
415 723-2300 **Stanford University** — Stanford CA 94305-0001
805 525-4417 **Thomas Aquinas College** 10000 N Ojai Rd — Santa Paula CA 93060-9622
916 348-4689 **Trinity Life Bible College** 5225 Hillsdale — Sacramento CA 95842-3596
415 642-6000 **University of California Berkeley** 120 Sproul Hall — Berkeley CA 94720-0001
916 752-1011 **University of California Davis** — Davis CA 95616-5224
714 856-5011 **University of California Irvine** — Irvine CA 92717-0001
213 825-4321 **University of California Los Angeles** 405 Hilgard Ave — Los Angeles CA 90024-1492
714 787-1012 **University of California Riverside** 900 University Ave — Riverside CA 92521-0001
619 534-2230 **University of California San Diego** — La Jolla CA 92093-0001
415 476-8280 **University of California San Francisco** MU-200 — San Francisco CA 94143-0001
805 961-8000 **University of California Santa Barbara** — Santa Barbara CA 93106-0001
408 459-0111 **University of California Santa Cruz** 1156 High St — Santa Cruz CA 95064-1099
213 476-9777 **University of Judaism** 15600 Mulholland Dr — Los Angeles CA 90077-1599
714 593-3511 **University of La Verne** 1950 3rd St — La Verne CA 91750-4443
714 793-2121 **University of Redlands** 1200 E Colton Ave — Redlands CA 92373-0999
619 260-4600 **University of San Diego** Alcala Pk — San Diego CA 92110-2496
415 666-6886 **University of San Francisco** Ignatian Heights — San Francisco CA 94117-1050
213 743-2311 **University of Southern California** University Pk — Los Angeles CA 90089-0001
209 946-2011 **University of the Pacific** 3601 Pacific Ave — Stockton CA 95211-0001
213 313-1011 **University of West Los Angeles** 12201 Washington Pl — Los Angeles CA 90066-4998
619 271-4300 **US International University** 10455 Pomerado Rd — San Diego CA 92131-1717
916 637-4111 **Weimer College** 20601 Paoli Ln — Weimar CA 95736-9999
209 299-7201 **West Coast Christian College** 6901 N Maple Ave — Fresno CA 93710-4520
213 487-4433 **West Coast University** 440 Shatto Pl — Los Angeles CA 90020-1765
714 953-2700 *Orange County Center* 550 S Main St — Orange CA 92668-4593
805 565-6000 **Westmont College** 955 La Paz Rd — Santa Barbara CA 93108-1099
213 693-0771 **Whittier College** 7026 Founders Hill Rd — Whittier CA 90608-0000
818 797-1200 **William Carey International University** 1539 E Howard St — Pasadena CA 91104-2698
619 298-9040 **William Lyon University** 814 Morena Blvd — San Diego CA 92110-2630
818 767-0888 **Woodbury University** 7500 N Glenoaks Blvd — Burbank CA 91504-1099
707 765-4500 **World College West-International** 101 S San Antonio Rd — Petaluma CA 94952-9510
805 646-1444 **World University of America** 107 Ventura St N — Ojai CA 93023-2624
213 553-4478 **Yeshiva University of Los Angeles** 9760 W Pico Blvd — Los Angeles CA 90035-4792

COLORADO

719 589-7121 **Adams State College** — Alamosa CO 81102-0001
303 556-2400 **Auraria Higher Education Center** 1250 7th St — Denver CO 80204-4440
303 427-5461 **Belleview College** 3455 W 83rd Ave — Westminster CO 80030-4098
719 475-5170 **Beth El College of Nursing** 10 N Farragut Ave — Colorado Springs CO 80909-0000
303 238-5386 **Colorado Christian University** 180 S Garrison St — Denver CO 80226-7499
719 473-2233 **Colorado College** 14 E Cache La Poudre St — Colorado Springs CO 80903-3294
303 273-3000 **Colorado School of Mines** 1500 Illinois St — Golden CO 80401-1887
303 491-1101 **Colorado State University** — Fort Collins CO 80523-0001
719 598-0200 **Colorado Technical College** 4435 N Chestnut St — Colorado Springs CO 80907-3895
719 593-7887 **Cornerstone Baptist Bible College** 3615 Vickers Dr — Colorado Springs CO 80918-0000
303 761-2482 **Denver Conservative Baptist Seminary** 3401 S University Blvd — Englewood CO 80110-3198
303 329-3000 **Denver Technical College** 925 S Niagara — Denver CO 80224-1658
303 247-7010 **Fort Lewis College** College Heights — Durango CO 81301-3999
303 248-1020 **Mesa State College** PO Box 2647 — Grand Junction CO 81502-0000
303 556-2400 **Metropolitan State College** PO Box 173362 — Denver CO 80217-3362
303 444-0202 **Naropa Institute** 2130 Arapahoe Ave — Boulder CO 80302-6697
National College
719 471-4205 *Colorado Springs Branch* 2577 N Chelton St — Colorado Springs CO 80909-1345
303 758-6700 *Denver Branch* 1325 S Colorado Blvd Suite 100 — Denver CO 80222-3308
719 545-8763 *Pueblo Branch* 330 Lake Ave — Pueblo CO 81004-2330
303 484-6050 **National Technological University** 700 Centre Ave — Fort Collins CO 80526-0000
719 632-0201 **Peoples Bible College** 2703 W Cucharras — Colorado Springs CO 80904-0000
303 458-4100 **Regis College** W 50th Ave & Lowell Blvd — Denver CO 80221-0000
303 492-1411 **University of Colorado** Campus Box 9 — Boulder CO 80309-0001
719 593-3000 *Colorado Springs Campus* 1420 Austin Bluffs Pkwy — Colorado Springs CO 80907-0000
303 556-2400 *Denver Campus* 1200 Larimer St — Denver CO 80204-5300
303 399-1211 *Health Sciences Center* 4200 E 9th Ave — Denver CO 80262-0001
303 871-2000 **University of Denver** 2199 S University Blvd — Denver CO 80208-0001
303 351-1890 **University of Northern Colorado** — Greeley CO 80639-0001
719 549-2100 **University of Southern Colorado** 2200 Bonforte Blvd — Pueblo CO 81001-4999
719 472-1818 **US Air Force Academy** — Colorado Springs CO 80840-5651
303 943-3035 **Western State College of Colorado** College Heights — Gunnison CO 81231-0001
303 629-8200 **Yeshiva Toras Chaim Talmudical Seminary** 1400 Quitman St — Denver CO 80204-1415

CONNECTICUT

203 773-8550 **Albertus Magnus College** 700 Prospect St — New Haven CT 06511-1189
203 255-2623 **Bridgeport Engineering Institute** 785 Unquowa Rd — Fairfield CT 06430-5002
203 827-7000 **Central Connecticut State University** 1615 Stanley St — New Britain CT 06053-2490
203 447-1911 **Connecticut College** 270 Mohegan Ave — New London CT 06320-4196
203 456-2231 **Eastern Connecticut State University** 83 Windham St — Willimantic CT 06226-2295
203 254-4000 **Fairfield University** 1073 N Benson Rd — Fairfield CT 06430-5195
203 232-4451 **Hartford Seminary** 77 Sherman St — Hartford CT 06105-2260
203 635-5311 **Holy Apostles College & Seminary** 33 Prospect Hill Rd — Cromwell CT 06416-2005
203 777-3851 **Paier College of Art Inc** 6 Prospect Ct — Hamden CT 06517-4025
203 288-5251 **Quinnipiac College** 555 New Rd — Hamden CT 06518-1908
203 371-7999 **Sacred Heart University** 5151 Park Ave — Fairfield CT 06432-1000
203 668-7393 **Saint Alphonsus College** 1762 Mapleton Ave — Suffield CT 06078-1491
203 324-4578 **Saint Basil's College** 195 Glenbrook Road — Stamford CT 06902-3099
203 232-4571 **Saint Joseph College** 1678 Asylum Ave — West Hartford CT 06117-2791
203 397-4000 **Southern Connecticut State University** 501 Crescent St — New Haven CT 06515-1355
203 755-0121 **Teikyo Post University** 800 Country Club Rd — Waterbury CT 06708-3200
203 297-2000 **Trinity College** 300 Summit St — Hartford CT 06106-3186
203 576-4000 **University of Bridgeport** 380 University Ave — Bridgeport CT 06601-0000
203 486-2000 **University of Connecticut** Admissions Bldg — Storrs CT 06269-0000
203 243-4100 **University of Hartford** 200 Bloomfield Ave — West Hartford CT 06117-1599
203 932-7000 **University of New Haven** 300 Orange Ave — West Haven CT 06516-1999
203 444-8294 **US Coast Guard Academy** 15 Mohegan Ave — New London CT 06320-4195
203 347-9411 **Wesleyan University** High St — Middletown CT 06457-0000
203 797-4347 **Western Connecticut State University** 181 White St — Danbury CT 06810-6885
203 432-4771 **Yale University** PO Box 1604A Yale Stn — New Haven CT 06520-7430

DELAWARE

302 736-4917 **Delaware State College** 1200 N Dupont Hwy — Dover DE 19901-2277
302 998-8814 **Goldey Beacom College** 4701 Limestone Rd — Wilmington DE 19808-1999
302 451-2000 **University of Delaware** Hullian Hall — Newark DE 19716-0001
302 736-2300 **Wesley College** 120 N State St — Dover DE 19901-3877
302 328-9401 **Wilmington College** 320 N Dupont Hwy — New Castle DE 19720-6491

DISTRICT OF COLUMBIA

202 686-2000 **American University** 4400 Massachusetts Ave NW — Washington DC 20016-8002
202 319-5000 **Catholic University of America** 620 Michigan Ave NE — Washington DC 20064-0001
202 628-9484 **Corcoran School of Art** 17th St & New York Ave NW — Washington DC 20006-0000
202 651-5000 **Gallaudet University** 800 Florida Ave NE — Washington DC 20002-3660
202 651-5100 *TTY Line* 800 Florida Ave NE — Washington DC 20002-3660
202 994-1000 **George Washington University** 2121 'I' St NW — Washington DC 20052-0001
202 687-1000 **Georgetown University** 37th & 'O' Sts NW — Washington DC 20057-0001
202 636-6100 **Howard University** 2400 6th St NW — Washington DC 20059-0001
202 462-6644 **International Institute of Interior Design** 2225 R St NW — Washington DC 20008-4017
202 331-0400 **Mount Vernon College** 2100 Foxhall Rd NW — Washington DC 20007-1199
202 529-6544 **Oblate College** 391 Michigan Ave NE — Washington DC 20017-1586
202 488-8162 **Southeastern University** 501 'I' St SW — Washington DC 20024-2788
202 728-0048 **Strayer College** 1100 16th St NW — Washington DC 20036-4802
202 939-5000 **Trinity College** 125 Michigan Ave NE — Washington DC 20017-1090
202 282-7300 **University of the District of Columbia** 4200 Connecticut Ave NW — Washington DC 20008-1178

FLORIDA

305 758-3392 **Barry University** 11300 NE 2nd Ave — Miami Shores FL 33161-6690
904 255-1401 **Bethune-Cookman College** 640 2nd Ave — Daytona Beach FL 32114-3099
813 726-1153 **Clearwater Christian College** 3400 Gulf To Bay Blvd — Clearwater FL 34619-4514
407 994-0770 **College of Boca Raton** 3601 N Military Trail — Boca Raton FL 33431-5598
813 867-1166 **Eckerd College** 4200 54th Ave S — Saint Petersburg FL 33711-4744
904 355-3030 **Edward Waters College** 1658 Kings Rd — Jacksonville FL 32209-6199
904 239-6000 **Embry-Riddle Aeronautical University** 600 S Clyde Morris Blvd — Daytona Beach FL 32114-3900
904 829-6481 **Flagler College** 74 King St — Saint Augustine FL 32085-1027
904 599-3000 **Florida A & M University** Martin Luther King Jr Blvd — Tallahassee FL 32307-0001
407 367-3000 **Florida Atlantic University** 500 NW 20th St — Boca Raton FL 33431-6498
904 263-3261 **Florida Baptist Theological College** 1306 College Dr — Graceville FL 32440-1833
813 531-4498 **Florida Beacon Bible College** 6900 142nd Ave N — Largo FL 34641-0000
407 933-4500 **Florida Bible College** 1701 Poinciana Blvd — Kissimmee FL 34758-2096
407 847-8966 **Florida Christian College Inc** 1011 Osceola Blvd — Kissimmee FL 34744-8614
407 768-8000 **Florida Institute of Technology** 150 W University Blvd — Melbourne FL 32901-0000
305 554-2000 **Florida International University** Tamiami Trail — Miami FL 33199-0001
305 625-4141 **Florida Memorial College** 15800 NW 42nd Ave — Opa Locka FL 33054-6198
813 680-4100 **Florida Southern College** 111 Lake Hollingsworth Dr — Lakeland FL 33801-5607
904 644-2525 **Florida State University** College Ave — Tallahassee FL 32306-1096
305 462-3761 **Fort Lauderdale College** 100 E Broward Blvd — Fort Lauderdale FL 33301-3595
407 546-5534 **Hobe Sound Bible College** PO Box 1065 — Hobe Sound FL 33475-1065
813 774-4700 **International College of Naples** 2654 Tamiami Trail E — Naples FL 33962-0000
904 744-3950 **Jacksonville University** 2800 University Blvd N — Jacksonville FL 32211-3396
904 743-1122 **Jones College at Jacksonville** 5353 Arlington Expy — Jacksonville FL 32211-5588
904 453-3451 **Liberty Bible College** 8600 Hwy 98 W — Pensacola FL 32506-0000
904 724-4722 **Luther Rice Seminary** 7565 Beach Blvd — Jacksonville FL 32216-3085
305 953-1122 **Miami Christian College** 2300 NW 135th St — Miami FL 33167-1398
813 238-0455 **National Education Center** 3920 E Hillsborough Ave Tampa Technical Institute Campus — Tampa FL 33610-4595
407 478-5510 **Northwood Institute** 2600 N Military Trail — West Palm Beach FL 33409-2999
305 475-7300 **Nova University** 3301 College Ave — Fort Lauderdale FL 33314-7796
407 628-5870 **Orlando College** 5500 Diplomat Cir — Orlando FL 32810-5674
407 650-7700 **Palm Beach Atlantic College** PO Box 3353 — West Palm Beach FL 33402-3353
904 476-1387 **Pensacola Bible Institute** 1171 JoJo Rd — Pensacola FL 32514-0000
813 351-4614 **Ringling School of Art & Design** 2700 N Tamiami Trail — Sarasota FL 34234-5895
407 646-2000 **Rollins College** 1000 Holt Ave — Winter Park FL 32789-4492
305 223-4561 **Saint John Vianney Seminary** 2900 SW 87th Ave — Miami FL 33165-3244
904 588-8200 **Saint Leo College** Hwy 52 W — Saint Leo FL 33574-9999
305 625-6000 **Saint Thomas University** 16400 NW 32nd Ave — Miami FL 33054-6492
813 665-4404 **Southeastern College of the Assemblies of God** 1000 Longfellow Blvd — Lakeland FL 33801-6099
904 488-4234 **State University System of Florida** 325 W Gaines St — Tallahassee FL 32399-6557
904 822-7000 **Stetson University** 421 N Woodland Blvd — De Land FL 32720-3799
407 275-2000 **University of Central Florida** 4000 Central Florida Blvd — Orlando FL 32816-0001
904 392-3261 **University of Florida** — Gainesville FL 32611-0000
305 284-2211 **University of Miami** — Coral Gables FL 33124-0000
904 646-2666 **University of North Florida** 4567 St Johns Bluff Rd S — Jacksonville FL 32216-6698
813 974-2011 **University of South Florida** 4202 E Fowler Ave — Tampa FL 33620-6499
813 253-3333 **University of Tampa** 401 W Kennedy Blvd W — Tampa FL 33606-1490
904 474-2000 **University of West Florida** 11000 University Pkwy — Pensacola FL 32514-5750
813 638-1426 **Warner Southern College** 5301 S Hwy 27 — Lake Wales FL 33853-8725
813 638-1431 **Webber College** PO Box 96 — Babson Park FL 33827-0096

GEORGIA

404 371-6000 **Agnes Scott College** 141 E College Ave — Decatur GA 30030-3797
912 430-4600 **Albany State College** 504 College Dr — Albany GA 31705-2797
404 231-9000 **American College for the Applied Arts** 3330 Peachtree Rd NE — Atlanta GA 30326-1016
912 927-5275 **Armstrong State College** 11935 Abercorn St — Savannah GA 31419-1988
404 761-8861 **Atlanta Christian College** 2605 Ben Hill Rd — East Point GA 30344-1999
404 898-1164 **Atlanta College of Art** 1280 Peachtree St NE — Atlanta GA 30309-3582
404 737-1400 **Augusta College** 2500 Walton Way — Augusta GA 30910-0001
404 232-5374 **Berry College** 2277 Martha Berry Blvd NE — Rome GA 30149-0000
404 534-6299 **Brenau College** 204 Boulevard St — Gainesville GA 30501-3697
912 583-2241 **Brewton-Parker College** Hwy 280 — Mount Vernon GA 30445-0000
404 527-4520 **Carver Bible Institute & College** 437 Nelson St SW — Atlanta GA 30313-0000
404 880-8000 **Clark-Atlanta University** James P Brawley Dr & Fair St SW — Atlanta GA 30314-4389
404 961-3400 **Clayton State College** 5900 N Lee St — Morrow GA 30260-0000
404 568-2001 **Columbus College** — Columbus GA 31993-0001
404 820-1560 **Covenant College** Scenic Hwy — Lookout Mountain GA 30750-0000
404 292-7900 **DeVry Institute of Technology** 250 N Arcadia Ave — Decatur GA 30030-2198
404 727-6123 **Emory University** — Atlanta GA 30322-1100
912 825-6211 **Fort Valley State College** 1005 State College Dr — Fort Valley GA 31030-3298
404 761-8343 **Georgia Baptist College** 4140 Stacks Rd — College Park GA 30349-2839
912 453-5350 **Georgia College** 231 W Hancock St — Milledgeville GA 31061-0000
404 894-2000 **Georgia Institute of Technology** 225 North Ave NW — Atlanta GA 30332-0001
912 681-5531 **Georgia Southern University** Landrum St — Statesboro GA 30460-0001
912 928-1279 **Georgia Southwestern College** 800 Wheatley St — Americus GA 31709-4635
404 651-2000 **Georgia State University** University Plaza — Atlanta GA 30303-3044
404 423-6000 **Kennesaw State College** 3455 Frey Lake Rd — Kennesaw GA 30144-3031
404 882-2911 **La Grange College** 601 Broad St — La Grange GA 30240-2999
404 721-0211 **Medical College of Georgia** 1120 15th St — Augusta GA 30912-0001
912 752-2700 **Mercer University** 1400 Coleman Ave — Macon GA 31207-0001
404 986-3000 *Atlanta Campus* 3001 Mercer University Dr — Atlanta GA 30341-4155
404 681-2800 **Morehouse College** 830 Westview Dr SW — Atlanta GA 30310-1427
404 525-7831 **Morris Brown College** 643 Martin Luther King Jr Dr NW — Atlanta GA 30314-4140
404 261-1441 **Oglethorpe University** 4484 Peachtree Rd NE — Atlanta GA 30319-2797
404 722-4471 **Paine College** 1235 15th St — Augusta GA 30910-0001
404 778-8033 **Piedmont College** — Demorest GA 30535-0000
912 238-2483 **Savannah College of Art & Design** 26 W Harris St — Savannah GA 31401-4354
912 356-2186 **Savannah State College** — Savannah GA 31404-0000
404 291-2121 **Shorter College** 315 Shorter Ave — Rome GA 30161-4298
404 528-7281 **Southern College of Technology** 1100 S Marietta Pkwy — Marietta GA 30060-9862
404 681-3643 **Spelman College** 350 Spelman Ln SW — Atlanta GA 30314-4395

404 886-6831	**Toccoa Falls College**	Toccoa Falls	GA	30598-0000
404 542-3030	**University of Georgia** 114 Academic Bldg	Athens	GA	30602-0000
912 333-5800	**Valdosta State College** N Patterson & Oak Sts	Valdosta	GA	31698-0001
912 477-1110	**Wesleyan College** 4760 Forsyth Rd	Macon	GA	31297-0001

HAWAII

808 293-3211	**Brigham Young University Hawaii Campus** 55-220 Kulanui St	Laie	HI	96762-1294
808 735-4711	**Chaminade University of Honolulu** 3140 Waialae Ave	Honolulu	HI	96816-1578
808 235-3641	**Hawaii Loa College** 45-045 Kamehameha Hwy	Kaneohe	HI	96744-5297
808 544-0200	**Hawaii Pacific University** 1166 Fort St	Honolulu	HI	96813-2717
808 595-8377	**International College & Graduate School of Theology** 20 Dowsett Ave	Honolulu	HI	96817-1105
808 262-2341	**Redemption Bible College** 355 N Kainalu Dr	Kailua	HI	96734-2125
	University of Hawaii			
808 933-3311	*Hilo Campus*	Hilo	HI	96720-4091
808 956-8111	*Manoa Campus* 2444 Dole St	Honolulu	HI	96822-2330
808 456-5921	*West Oahu Campus* 96-043 Ala Ike	Pearl City	HI	96782-3366

IDAHO

208 376-7731	**Boise Bible College** 8695 Marigold St	Boise	ID	83714-1220
208 385-1011	**Boise State University** 1910 University Dr	Boise	ID	83725-0001
208 459-5011	**College of Idaho** 2112 Cleveland Blvd	Caldwell	ID	83605-4494
208 236-0211	**Idaho State University** 741 S 7th St	Pocatello	ID	83209-0001
208 799-5272	**Lewis-Clark State College** 8th Ave & 6th St	Lewiston	ID	83501-0000
208 467-8011	**Northwest Nazarene College** 623 Holly St	Nampa	ID	83686-5897
208 885-6111	**University of Idaho** Administration Bldg	Moscow	ID	83843-0000

ILLINOIS

312 408-0101	**Aero-Space Institute** 161 W Harrison St	Chicago	IL	60605-1025
312 263-4161	**American Conservatory of Music** 16 N Wabash Ave Suite 1850	Chicago	IL	60602-4792
312 281-4700	**American Islamic College** 640 W Irving Park Rd	Chicago	IL	60613-3106
309 794-7000	**Augustana College** 638 38th St	Rock Island	IL	61201-0000
708 892-6431	**Aurora University** 347 S Gladstone Ave	Aurora	IL	60506-4892
708 234-3000	**Barat College** 700 E Westleigh Rd	Lake Forest	IL	60045-3297
217 854-3231	**Blackburn College** 700 College Ave	Carlinville	IL	62626-1498
309 676-7611	**Bradley University** 1501 W Bradley Ave	Peoria	IL	61625-0001
312 995-2000	**Chicago State University** 9500 S King Dr	Chicago	IL	60628-1502
708 259-1840	**Christian Life College** 400 E Gregory St	Mount Prospect	IL	60056-0000
815 740-3360	**College of Saint Francis** 500 Wilcox St	Joliet	IL	60435-6188
312 663-1600	**Columbia College** 600 S Michigan Ave	Chicago	IL	60605-1996
708 771-8300	**Concordia College** 7400 Augusta St	River Forest	IL	60305-1499
312 362-8000	**DePaul University** 25 E Jackson Blvd	Chicago	IL	60604-2287
312 929-8500	**DeVry Institute of Technology** 3300 N Campbell Ave	Chicago	IL	60618-5994
708 953-1300	**DeVry Institute of Technology** 2000 S Finley Rd	Lombard	IL	60148-4892
312 939-0111	**East-West University** 816 S Michigan Ave	Chicago	IL	60605-2103
217 581-5000	**Eastern Illinois University**	Charleston	IL	61920-0000
708 279-4100	**Elmhurst College** 190 Prospect Ave	Elmhurst	IL	60126-3296
309 467-3721	**Eureka College** 300 E College Ave	Eureka	IL	61530-1562
708 534-5000	**Governors State University** Governors Hwy	University Park	IL	60466-0000
618 664-1840	**Greenville College** 315 E College Ave	Greenville	IL	62246-1199
312 939-4975	**Harrington Institute of Interior Design** 410 S Michigan Ave	Chicago	IL	60605-1496
708 960-1500	**Illinois Benedictine College** 5700 College Rd	Lisle	IL	60532-2851
217 245-3000	**Illinois College** 1101 W College Ave	Jacksonville	IL	62650-2299
312 225-1700	**Illinois College of Optometry** 3241 S Michigan Ave	Chicago	IL	60616-3816
312 567-3000	**Illinois Institute of Technology** 3300 S Federal St	Chicago	IL	60616-3732
312 567-3900	*West Campus* 600 S Lambert Rd	Glen Ellyn	IL	60137-6598
309 745-8927	**Illinois Missionary Baptist Institute** 209 Vohland St	Washington	IL	61571-1933
309 438-2111	**Illinois State University**	Normal	IL	61761-6901
309 556-3131	**Illinois Wesleyan University** PO Box 2900	Bloomington	IL	61702-2900
312 782-6730	**Industrial Engineering College** 316 N Michigan Ave	Chicago	IL	60601-3707
312 820-0422	**International Academy of Merchandising** 350 N Orleans	Chicago	IL	60654-1587
708 695-2500	**Judson College** 1151 N State St	Elgin	IL	60123-1404
708 866-1300	**Kendall College** 2408 Orrington Ave	Evanston	IL	60201-2899
309 343-0112	**Knox College** 2 E South St	Galesburg	IL	61401-4999
708 234-3100	**Lake Forest College** College & Sheridan Rds	Lake Forest	IL	60045-0000
815 838-0500	**Lewis University** Rt 53	Romeoville	IL	60441-0000
217 732-3168	**Lincoln Christian College & Seminary** 100 Campus View Dr	Lincoln	IL	62656-2111
312 915-6000	**Loyola University of Chicago** 820 N Michigan Ave	Chicago	IL	60611-2196
217 245-6151	**MacMurray College** 447 E College Ave	Jacksonville	IL	62650-2590
708 256-1094	**Mallinckrodt College of the North Shore** 1041 Ridge Rd	Wilmette	IL	60091-1591
618 537-4481	**McKendree College** 701 College Rd	Lebanon	IL	62254-1299
217 424-6211	**Millikin University** 1184 W Main St	Decatur	IL	62522-2084
309 457-2311	**Monmouth College** 700 E Broadway Ave	Monmouth	IL	61462-1998
312 329-4000	**Moody Bible Institute** 820 N La Salle St	Chicago	IL	60610-3276
312 262-8100	**Mundelein College** 6363 N Sheridan Rd	Chicago	IL	60660-1793
312 761-5000	**NAES College** 2838 W Peterson Ave	Chicago	IL	60659-3813
708 256-5150	**National-Louis University** 2840 Sheridan Rd	Evanston	IL	60201-1730
312 621-9650	*Urban Campus* 18 S Michigan Ave	Chicago	IL	60603-3301
708 420-3400	**North Central College** 30 N Brainard St	Naperville	IL	60540-4690
312 583-2700	**North Park College & Seminary** 3225 W Foster Ave	Chicago	IL	60625-4895
312 583-4050	**Northeastern Illinois University** 5500 N St Louis Ave	Chicago	IL	60625-4625
815 753-1000	**Northern Illinois University**	De Kalb	IL	60115-0000
708 491-3682	**Northwestern University** 2129 Sheridan Rd	Evanston	IL	60208-0001
815 939-5011	**Olivet Nazarene University** 240 E Marsile St	Bourbonnais	IL	60914-1996
618 337-7500	**Parks College of Saint Louis University** 500 Falling Springs Rd	Cahokia	IL	62206-1203
618 374-2131	**Principia College**	Elsah	IL	62028-0000
217 222-8020	**Quincy College** 1800 College Ave	Quincy	IL	62301-2670
312 280-3500	**Ray College of Design** 401 N Wabash Ave	Chicago	IL	60611-3532
815 226-4000	**Rockford College** 5050 E State St	Rockford	IL	61108-2393
312 341-3500	**Roosevelt University** 430 S Michigan Ave	Chicago	IL	60605-1394
708 366-2490	**Rosary College** 7900 W Division St	River Forest	IL	60305-1099
312 779-3300	**Saint Xavier College** 3700 W 103rd St	Chicago	IL	60655-3198
312 899-5100	**School of the Art Institute of Chicago** 37 S Wabash Ave	Chicago	IL	60603-3199
708 623-8400	**Shimer College** PO Box A500	Waukegan	IL	60079-7997
618 453-2121	**Southern Illinois University**	Carbondale	IL	62901-0000
618 692-2000	*Edwardsville Campus*	Edwardsville	IL	62026-0001
708 597-3000	**Trinity Christian College** 6601 W College Dr	Palos Heights	IL	60463-0929
708 948-8980	**Trinity College** 2077 Half Day Rd	Deerfield	IL	60015-1284
312 702-1234	**University of Chicago** 5801 S Ellis Ave	Chicago	IL	60637-1404
312 996-3000	**University of Illinois Chicago East Campus** PO Box 4348	Chicago	IL	60680-4348
217 333-1000	**University of Illinois Urbana-Champaign** 506 S Wright St	Urbana	IL	61801-3620
312 225-6288	**VanderCook College of Music** 3209 S Michigan Ave	Chicago	IL	60616-3886
708 383-6200	**West Suburban College of Nursing** Erie St & Austin Blvd	Oak Park	IL	60302-2510
309 295-1414	**Western Illinois University** 900 W Adams St	Macomb	IL	61455-1396
708 260-5000	**Wheaton College** 501 E College Ave	Wheaton	IL	60187-5593

INDIANA

317 649-9071	**Anderson University** 1100 E 5th St	Anderson	IN	46012-3495
317 289-1797	**Ball State University**	Muncie	IN	47306-0001
219 259-8511	**Bethel College** 1001 W McKinley Ave	Mishawaka	IN	46545-5591
317 283-8000	**Butler University** 4600 Sunset Ave	Indianapolis	IN	46208-3485
219 473-7770	**Calumet College of Saint Joseph** 2400 New York Ave	Whiting	IN	46394-2195
317 658-4800	**DePauw University** 313 S Locus St	Greencastle	IN	46135-0000
317 983-1200	**Earlham College** 701 National Rd W	Richmond	IN	47374-4000
317 736-8441	**Franklin College of Indiana** 501 E Monroe St	Franklin	IN	46131-2597
219 535-7000	**Goshen College** 1700 S Main St	Goshen	IN	46526-4724
219 372-5100	**Grace College & Seminary** 200 Seminary Dr	Winona Lake	IN	46590-1224
812 866-7000	**Hanover College**	Hanover	IN	47243-0000
219 356-6000	**Huntington College** 2303 College Ave	Huntington	IN	46750-1299
219 422-5561	**Indiana Institute of Technology** 1600 E Washington Blvd	Fort Wayne	IN	46803-1297
812 237-6311	**Indiana State University** 217 N 6th St	Terre Haute	IN	47809-0001
812 332-0211	**Indiana University** 813 E 3rd St	Bloomington	IN	47405-0001
317 966-8261	*East Campus* 2325 Chester Blvd	Richmond	IN	47374-1289
317 453-2000	*Kokomo Campus* 2300 S Washington St	Kokomo	IN	46904-0000
219 980-6500	*Northwest Campus* 3400 Broadway	Gary	IN	46408-1197
219 237-4111	*South Bend Campus* 1700 Mishawaka Ave	South Bend	IN	46634-0000
812 945-2731	*Southeast Campus* 4201 Grant Line Rd	New Albany	IN	47150-6405
219 481-6100	**Indiana University-Purdue University at Fort Wayne** 2101 E Coliseum Blvd	Fort Wayne	IN	46805-1445
317 274-5555	**Indiana University-Purdue University at Indianapolis** 425 University Blvd	Indianapolis	IN	46202-5148
317 674-6901	**Indiana Wesleyan University** 4201 S Washington St	Marion	IN	46953-4999
219 982-2141	**Manchester College** 604 E College Ave	North Manchester	IN	46962-1225
317 929-0123	**Marian College** 3200 Cold Spring Rd	Indianapolis	IN	46222-1997
317 543-3235	**Martin Center College** 2171 Avondale Pl	Indianapolis	IN	46218-3867
812 749-4781	**Oakland City College** 143 N Lucretia St	Oakland City	IN	47660-1099
317 494-4600	**Purdue University**	West Lafayette	IN	47907-0000
219 844-0520	*Calumet Campus* 2233 171st St	Hammond	IN	46323-2094
219 785-5200	*North Central Campus* 1401 S US Hwy 421	Westville	IN	46391-9528
812 877-1511	**Rose-Hulman Institute of Technology** 5500 Wabash Ave	Terre Haute	IN	47803-3999
219 434-3100	**Saint Francis College** 2701 Spring St	Fort Wayne	IN	46808-3994
219 866-6000	**Saint Joseph's College** Hwy 231 S	Rensselaer	IN	47978-0000
219 284-4587	**Saint Mary's College**	Notre Dame	IN	46556-0000
812 535-5151	**Saint Mary-of-the-Woods College** Rt 150	Saint Mary-of-the-Woods	IN	47876-0000
812 357-6611	**Saint Meinrad College** Hwy 545	Saint Meinrad	IN	47577-0000
219 456-2111	**Summit Christian College** 1025 W Rudisill Blvd	Fort Wayne	IN	46807-2197
317 998-2751	**Taylor University** 500 W Reade Ave	Upland	IN	46989-1001
219 665-4100	**Tri-State University** S Darling St	Angola	IN	46703-0000
812 479-2000	**University of Evansville** 1800 Lincoln Ave	Evansville	IN	47722-0001
317 788-3368	**University of Indianapolis** 1400 E Hanna Ave	Indianapolis	IN	46227-3630
219 239-5000	**University of Notre Dame**	Notre Dame	IN	46556-0000
812 464-8600	**University of Southern Indiana** 8600 University Blvd	Evansville	IN	47712-3534
219 462-2191	**Valparaiso Technical Institute** 1 Center St	Valparaiso	IN	46383-4599
219 464-5000	**Valparaiso University**	Valparaiso	IN	46383-6493
317 362-1400	**Wabash College** 301 W Wabash Ave	Crawfordsville	IN	47933-2484
219 291-3292	**World Harvest Bible College** 530 E Ireland Rd	South Bend	IN	46614-2660

IOWA

712 279-5321	**Briar Cliff College** 3303 Rebecca St	Sioux City	IA	51104-2340
712 749-2105	**Buena Vista College** 610 W 4th St	Storm Lake	IA	50588-1798
515 628-4151	**Central University of Iowa** 812 University St	Pella	IA	50219-1902
319 588-6300	**Clarke College** 1550 Clarke Dr	Dubuque	IA	52001-3198
319 399-8000	**Coe College** 1220 1st Ave NE	Cedar Rapids	IA	52402-5092
319 895-4000	**Cornell College** 600 1st St W	Mount Vernon	IA	52314-1098
319 876-3353	**Divine Word College** S Center Ave	Epworth	IA	52045-0000
712 722-3771	**Dordt College** 498 4th Ave NE	Sioux Center	IA	51250-1697
515 271-2011	**Drake University** 25th St & University Ave	Des Moines	IA	50311-0000
319 588-8000	**Emmaus Bible College** 2570 Asbury Rd	Dubuque	IA	52001-3096
515 964-0601	**Faith Baptist Bible College** 1900 NW 4th St	Ankeny	IA	50021-2198
515 784-5000	**Graceland College** 700 College Ave	Lamoni	IA	50140-1611
515 263-2800	**Grand View College** 1200 Grandview Ave	Des Moines	IA	50316-1599
515 269-4000	**Grinnell College** PO Box 805	Grinnell	IA	50112-0810
515 294-4111	**Iowa State University**	Ames	IA	50011-0001
319 385-8021	**Iowa Wesleyan College** 601 N Main St	Mount Pleasant	IA	52641-1398
319 588-7100	**Loras College** 1450 Alta Vista St	Dubuque	IA	52001-4399
319 387-2000	**Luther College** 700 College Dr	Decorah	IA	52101-1043
515 472-5031	**Maharishi International University** 1000 N 4th St	Fairfield	IA	52556-2046
319 326-9512	**Marycrest College** 1607 W 12th St	Davenport	IA	52804-4096
712 274-5000	**Morningside College** 1501 Morningside Ave	Sioux City	IA	51106-1751
319 363-8213	**Mount Mercy College** 1330 Elmhurst Dr NE	Cedar Rapids	IA	52402-4797
319 242-4023	**Mount Saint Clare College** 400 N Bluff Blvd	Clinton	IA	52732-3997
712 737-4821	**Northwestern College** 101 7th St SW	Orange City	IA	51041-1996
319 383-8800	**Saint Ambrose University** 518 W Locust St	Davenport	IA	52803-2829
515 961-6251	**Simpson College** 701 N 'C' St	Indianola	IA	50125-1297
712 546-7081	**Teikyo-Westmar University** 1002 3rd Ave SE	Le Mars	IA	51031-2699
319 589-3000	**University of Dubuque** 2000 University Ave	Dubuque	IA	52001-5050
319 353-2121	**University of Iowa**	Iowa City	IA	52242-0001
319 273-2311	**University of Northern Iowa** 23rd & College St	Cedar Falls	IA	50614-0001
319 425-3311	**Upper Iowa University** PO Box 1857	Fayette	IA	52142-1861
515 673-8391	**Vennard College** PO Box 29	University Park	IA	52595-9999
319 352-8200	**Wartburg College** 222 9th St NW	Waverly	IA	50677-2215
515 673-1001	**William Penn College** 201 Trueblood Ave	Oskaloosa	IA	52577-1799

KANSAS

913 594-6451	**Baker University** 8th & Grove St	Baldwin City	KS	66006-0000
316 862-5252	**Barclay College** 607 N Kingman St	Haviland	KS	67059-0000
913 367-5340	**Benedictine College** 1020 N 2nd St	Atchison	KS	66002-1499
913 227-3311	**Bethany College** 421 N 1st St	Lindsborg	KS	67456-1897
316 283-2500	**Bethel College** 300 E 27th St	North Newton	KS	67117-0000
316 343-1200	**Emporia State University** 12th & Commercial St	Emporia	KS	66801-0000
913 628-4000	**Fort Hays State University** 600 Park St	Hays	KS	67601-4009
316 261-5800	**Friends University** 2100 University St	Wichita	KS	67213-3397
316 942-4291	**Kansas Newman College** 3100 McCormick St	Wichita	KS	67213-2008
913 532-6011	**Kansas State University**	Manhattan	KS	66506-0001
913 827-5541	**Kansas Wesleyan University** 100 E Claflin Ave	Salina	KS	67401-6196
913 539-3571	**Manhattan Christian College** 1415 Anderson Ave	Manhattan	KS	66502-4081
316 241-0731	**McPherson College** 1600 E Euclid St	McPherson	KS	67460-3899
913 782-3750	**MidAmerica Nazarene College** 2030 E Collegeway St	Olathe	KS	66062-1899
816 753-4554	**National College** 600 W 39th St	Kansas City	KS	64111-0000
913 242-5200	**Ottawa University** 10th & Cedar Sts	Ottawa	KS	66067-0000
316 231-7000	**Pittsburg State University** 1701 S Broadway St	Pittsburg	KS	66762-5880
913 682-5151	**Saint Mary College** 4100 S 4th St	Leavenworth	KS	66048-5082
316 225-4171	**Saint Mary of the Plains College** 240 San Jose Dr	Dodge City	KS	67801-2786
316 221-4150	**Southwestern College** 100 College St	Winfield	KS	67156-2499
316 278-2173	**Sterling College**	Sterling	KS	67579-0000
316 947-3121	**Tabor College** 400 S Jefferson St	Hillsboro	KS	67063-1799
913 864-2700	**University of Kansas**	Lawrence	KS	66045-0001
913 295-6300	**Washburn University of Topeka** 1700 College Ave	Topeka	KS	66621-0001
316 689-3456	**Wichita State University** 1845 Fairmount St	Wichita	KS	67208-1586

KENTUCKY

606 368-2101	**Alice Lloyd College** Purpose Rd	Pippa Passes	KY	41844-0000
606 858-3511	**Asbury College** 201 N Lexington Ave	Wilmore	KY	40390-1198

Four-Year Colleges

502 452-8211	**Bellarmine College**	2001 Newburg Rd	Louisville	KY	40205-1877
606 986-9341	**Berea College**	Chestnut St	Berea	KY	40404-0001
502 685-3131	**Brescia College**	717 Frederica St	Owensboro	KY	42301-2298
502 465-8158	**Campbellsville College**	200 W College St	Campbellsville	KY	42718-2799
606 236-5211	**Centre College of Kentucky**	600 W Walnut St	Danville	KY	40422-1394
606 337-3196	**Clear Creek Baptist Bible College**	300 Clear Creek Rd	Pineville	KY	40977-9752
502 451-4144	**College of the Scriptures**	4601 Old Shepherdsville Rd	Louisville	KY	40218-3440
606 549-2200	**Cumberland College**	CC Stn	Williamsburg	KY	40769-0000
606 622-1000	**Eastern Kentucky University**	521 Lancaster Ave	Richmond	KY	40475-3101
502 863-8011	**Georgetown College**	400 E College St	Georgetown	KY	40324-1620
606 474-6613	**Kentucky Christian College**	617 N Carol Malone Blvd	Grayson	KY	41143-1199
502 227-6000	**Kentucky State University**	400 E Main St	Frankfort	KY	40601-2355
502 926-3111	**Kentucky Wesleyan College**	3000 Frederica St	Owensboro	KY	42301-6057
606 252-1130	**Lexington Baptist College**	147 Walton Ave	Lexington	KY	40508-0000
502 384-2126	**Lindsey Wilson College**	210 Lindsey Wilson St	Columbia	KY	42728-1298
502 637-8663	**Louisville Bible College**	PO Box 91046	Louisville	KY	40291-0000
502 247-8521	**Mid-Continent Baptist Bible College**	PO Box 7010	Mayfield	KY	42066-7010
606 846-4421	**Midway College**	512 E Stephens St	Midway	KY	40347-1120
606 783-2221	**Morehead State University**	100 University Blvd	Morehead	KY	40351-1680
502 762-3011	**Murray State University**	University Stn	Murray	KY	42071-0000
606 572-5100	**Northern Kentucky University**	Nunn Dr	Highland Heights	KY	41076-0000
606 432-9200	**Pikeville College**	214 Sycamore St	Pikeville	KY	41501-1194
502 776-1443	**Simmons Bible College**	1811 Dumesnil	Louisville	KY	40210-1401
502 897-4011	**Southern Baptist Theological Seminary**	2825 Lexington Rd	Louisville	KY	40280-0001
502 585-9911	**Spalding University**	851 S 4th St	Louisville	KY	40203-2188
606 341-5800	**Thomas More College**	333 Thomas More Pkwy	Crestview Hills	KY	41017-3428
606 233-8300	**Transylvania University**	300 N Broadway St	Lexington	KY	40508-1797
606 546-4151	**Union College**	310 College St	Barbourville	KY	40906-1499
606 257-9000	**University of Kentucky**		Lexington	KY	40506-0001
502 588-5555	**University of Louisville**	2301 S 3rd St	Louisville	KY	40292-0001
502 745-0111	**Western Kentucky University**	College Heights	Bowling Green	KY	42101-3576

LOUISIANA

318 396-6000	**American Christian Schools of Religion**	3201 N 7th St	West Monroe	LA	71291-2229
318 631-8875	**Baptist Christian College**	3031 Hollywood Ave	Shreveport	LA	71108-0000
318 869-5011	**Centenary College**	2911 Centenary Blvd	Shreveport	LA	71104-3396
504 283-8822	**Dillard University**	2601 Gentilly Blvd	New Orleans	LA	70122-3097
318 274-2435	**Grambling State University**	100 Main St	Grambling	LA	71245-0000
318 487-7776	**Louisiana College**	1140 College Dr	Pineville	LA	71359-0001
504 388-6935	**Louisiana State University (System)** 99 University Lakeshore Dr		Baton Rouge	LA	70803-0001
	Louisiana State University				
504 388-6935	*A & M College*	99 University Lakeshore Dr	Baton Rouge	LA	70803-0001
504 388-3202	*Baton Rouge Campus*	Tower Dr	Baton Rouge	LA	70803-0001
504 568-4808	*Medical Center*	4330 Bolizar St	New Orleans	LA	70112-0000
318 797-5000	*Shreveport Campus*	1 University Pl	Shreveport	LA	71115-2301
318 257-0211	**Louisiana Tech University**	700 W California	Ruston	LA	71272-0001
504 865-2011	**Loyola University**	6363 St Charles Ave	New Orleans	LA	70118-6195
318 475-5000	**McNeese State University**		Lake Charles	LA	70609-0000
504 282-4455	**New Orleans Baptist Theological Seminary** 3939 Gentilly Blvd		New Orleans	LA	70126-4858
504 446-8111	**Nicholls State University**	Hwy 1 & University Stn	Thibodaux	LA	70310-0000
318 342-1000	**Northeast Louisiana University**	700 University Ave	Monroe	LA	71209-0001
318 357-6361	**Northwestern State University**	College Ave	Natchitoches	LA	71457-0000
504 394-7744	**Our Lady of Holy Cross College**	4123 Woodland Dr	New Orleans	LA	70131-7399
504 892-1800	**Saint Joseph Seminary College**	River Rd	Saint Benedict	LA	70457-9999
504 549-2000	**Southeastern Louisiana University**	University Stn	Hammond	LA	70402-0000
504 771-4680	**Southern University (System)** Southern Branch Post Office		Baton Rouge	LA	70813-0000
	Southern University				
504 771-4500	*A & M College*	Southern Branch Post Office	Baton Rouge	LA	70813-0000
504 286-5000	*New Orleans Campus*	6400 Press Dr	New Orleans	LA	70126-0002
504 865-5000	**Tulane University**	6823 St Charles Ave	New Orleans	LA	70118-5698
504 283-1588	**Union Baptist Theological Seminary**	1300 Milton St	New Orleans	LA	70122-0000
504 286-6000	**University of New Orleans**	Lake Front	New Orleans	LA	70148-0001
318 231-6000	**University of Southwestern Louisiana**	PO Box 4-400	Lafayette	LA	70504-0400
504 486-7411	**Xavier University of Louisiana**	7325 Palmetto St	New Orleans	LA	70125-1098

MAINE

207 786-6255	**Bates College**	Andrews Rd Lane Hall	Lewiston	ME	04240-0000
207 725-3000	**Bowdoin College**		Brunswick	ME	04011-0000
207 872-3000	**Colby College**	150 Mayflower Hill Dr	Waterville	ME	04901-4799
207 288-5015	**College of the Atlantic**	105 Eden St	Bar Harbor	ME	04609-1198
207 947-1121	**Husson College**	1 College Cir	Bangor	ME	04401-2999
207 326-4311	**Maine Maritime Academy**	C-3	Castine	ME	04420-0001
207 324-5340	**Nasson College**	7 Bradeen St	Springvale	ME	04083-1901
207 799-5979	**New England Baptist Bible College**	879 Sawyer St	South Portland	ME	04106-6533
207 775-3052	**Portland School of Art**	97 Spring St	Portland	ME	04101-3987
207 892-6766	**Saint Joseph's College**		Windham	ME	04062-0000
207 873-0771	**Thomas College**	180 W River Rd	Waterville	ME	04901-5097
207 948-3131	**Unity College**	RR 78 Box 1	Unity	ME	04988-0000
207 581-1110	**University of Maine**	Chadbourne Hall	Orono	ME	04469-0001
207 622-7131	*Augusta Campus*	University Heights	Augusta	ME	04330-9410
207 947-0336	*Bangor Campus*	107 Maine Ave	Bangor	ME	04401-1805
207 778-3501	*Farmington Campus*	86 Main St	Farmington	ME	04938-1990
207 834-3162	*Fort Kent Campus*	25 Pleasant St	Fort Kent	ME	04743-1292
207 255-3313	*Machias Campus*	9 O'Brien Ave	Machias	ME	04654-1321
207 764-0311	*Presque Isle Campus*	181 Main St	Presque Isle	ME	04769-2888
207 283-0171	**University of New England**	11 Hills Beach Rd	Biddeford	ME	04005-9526
207 780-4141	**University of Southern Maine**	96 Falmouth St	Portland	ME	04103-4899
207 797-7261	**Westbrook College**	716 Stevens Ave	Portland	ME	04103-2693

MARYLAND

301 578-6900	**Baltimore Hebrew University**	5800 Park Heights Ave	Baltimore	MD	21215-3996
301 464-3000	**Bowie State University**	14000 Jericho Park Rd	Bowie	MD	20715-3318
301 953-0060	**Capitol College**	11301 Springfield Rd	Laurel	MD	20708-9758
301 435-0100	**College of Notre Dame of Maryland**	4701 N Charles St	Baltimore	MD	21210-2476
301 270-9200	**Columbia Union College**	7600 Flower Ave	Takoma Park	MD	20912-7796
301 333-5990	**Coppin State College**	2500 W North Ave	Baltimore	MD	21216-3698
301 879-9300	**Eastern Christian College**	PO Box 629	Bel Air	MD	21014-0629
301 689-4000	**Frostburg State University**		Frostburg	MD	21532-0000
301 337-6000	**Goucher College**	Dulaney Valley Rd	Towson	MD	21204-2794
301 663-3131	**Hood College**	Rosemont Ave	Frederick	MD	21701-8599
301 338-8000	**Johns Hopkins University**	3400 N Charles St	Baltimore	MD	21218-2608
301 323-1010	**Loyola College**	4501 N Charles St	Baltimore	MD	21210-2699
301 669-9200	**Maryland Institute College of Art**	1300 W Mt Royal Ave	Baltimore	MD	21217-4191
301 444-3333	**Morgan State University**	Hillen Rd & Cold Spring Ln	Baltimore	MD	21239-0000
301 447-6122	**Mount Saint Mary's College**	16300 Old Emmitsburg Rd	Emmitsburg	MD	21727-7799
301 484-7200	**Ner Israel Rabbinical College**	400 Mt Wilson Ln	Baltimore	MD	21208-1198
301 659-8100	**Peabody Conservatory of Music Johns Hopkins University** 1 E Mt Vernon Pl		Baltimore	MD	21202-2308
301 263-2371	**Saint John's College**	PO Box 2800	Annapolis	MD	21404-1671
301 862-0200	**Saint Mary's College of Maryland**		Saint Marys City	MD	20686-9999
301 323-3200	**Saint Mary's Seminary & University**	5400 Roland Ave	Baltimore	MD	21210-1994
301 543-6000	**Salisbury State College**	1101 Camden Ave	Salisbury	MD	21801-6860
301 276-0306	**Sojourner-Douglas College**	500 N Caroline St	Baltimore	MD	21205-1898
301 830-2000	**Towson State University**	York Rd	Towson	MD	21204-0000
301 625-3000	**University of Baltimore**	1420 N Charles St	Baltimore	MD	21201-5779
301 853-3600	**University of Maryland (System)**	3300 Metzerott Rd	Adelphi	MD	20783-1651
	University of Maryland				
301 455-1000	*Baltimore Campus*	5401 Wilkins Ave	Baltimore	MD	21228-0000
301 328-3100	*Baltimore Professional School*	419 W Redwood St	Baltimore	MD	21202-0000
301 454-3311	*College Park Campus*		College Park	MD	20742-0001
301 651-2200	*Eastern Shore Campus*		Princess Anne	MD	21853-0000
301 267-6100	**US Naval Academy**		Annapolis	MD	21402-1398
301 486-7000	**Villa Julie College**	Green Spring Valley Rd	Stevenson	MD	21153-0000
301 552-1400	**Washington Bible College Capitol Bible Seminary** 6511 Princess Garden Pkwy		Lanham	MD	20706-3599
301 778-2800	**Washington College**	Washington Ave	Chestertown	MD	21620-0000
301 848-7000	**Western Maryland College**	College Hill W Main St	Westminster	MD	21157-4399

MASSACHUSETTS

413 737-7000	**American International College**	1000 State St	Springfield	MA	01109-3189
413 542-2000	**Amherst College**	Stn 2	Amherst	MA	01002-0000
508 757-4586	**Anna Maria College**	50 Sunset Ln	Paxton	MA	01612-1198
508 752-5615	**Assumption College**	500 Salisbury St	Worcester	MA	01609-1296
508 365-4561	**Atlantic Union College**	338 Main St	South Lancaster	MA	01561-0000
617 235-1200	**Babson College**	Babson Pk	Wellesley	MA	02157-0310
413 567-0621	**Bay Path College**	588 Longmeadow St	Longmeadow	MA	01106-2292
617 891-2000	**Bentley College**	175 Forest St	Waltham	MA	02154-4705
617 266-1400	**Berklee College of Music**	1140 Boylston St	Boston	MA	02215-3693
617 552-8000	**Boston College**	140 Commonwealth Ave	Chestnut Hill	MA	02167-9991
617 536-6340	**Boston Conservatory of Music & Dance**	8 Fenway	Boston	MA	02215-4099
617 353-2000	**Boston University**	775 Commonwealth Ave	Boston	MA	02215-9991
508 372-7161	**Bradford College**	320 S Main St	Bradford	MA	01835-7393
617 736-2000	**Brandeis University**	415 South St	Waltham	MA	02154-2700
508 697-1200	**Bridgewater State College**		Bridgewater	MA	02325-0001
508 793-7711	**Clark University**	950 Main St	Worcester	MA	01610-1477
413 594-2761	**College of Our Lady of the Elms**	291 Springfield St	Chicopee	MA	01013-2837
508 793-2011	**College of the Holy Cross**	1 College St	Worcester	MA	01610-2322
508 997-7831	**College of Visual & Performing Arts**	1213 Purchase St	New Bedford	MA	02740-6636
617 333-0500	**Curry College**	1071 Blue Hill Ave	Milton	MA	02186-2395
617 773-6350	**Eastern Nazarene College**	23 E Elm Ave	Quincy	MA	02170-2999
617 578-8500	**Emerson College**	100 Beacon St	Boston	MA	02116-1596
617 277-9340	**Emmanuel College**	400 The Fenway	Boston	MA	02115-5798
508 927-0585	**Endicott College**	376 Hale St	Beverly	MA	01915-2096
508 345-2151	**Fitchburg State College**	160 Pearl St	Fitchburg	MA	01420-2631
508 620-1220	**Framingham State College**	100 State St	Framingham	MA	01701-2460
508 927-2300	**Gordon College**	255 Grapevine Rd	Wenham	MA	01984-1899
413 549-4600	**Hampshire College**	893 West St	Amherst	MA	01002-3328
617 495-1000	**Harvard University**	1350 Massachusetts Ave Holyoke Ctr	Cambridge	MA	02138-3800
617 232-8710	**Hebrew College**	43 Hawes St	Brookline	MA	02146-5495
617 731-3500	**Hellenic College**	50 Goddard Ave	Brookline	MA	02146-7496
617 868-9600	**Lesley College**	29 Everett St	Cambridge	MA	02138-2790
617 232-1555	**Massachusetts College of Art**	621 Huntington Ave	Boston	MA	02115-5882
617 253-1000	**Massachusetts Institute of Technology** 77 Massachusetts Ave		Cambridge	MA	02139-4307
508 759-5761	**Massachusetts Maritime Academy**	Pierless Point	Buzzards Bay	MA	02532-0000
508 683-7111	**Merrimack College**	315 Turnpike St	North Andover	MA	01845-5800
617 253-1000	**MIT**	77 Massachusetts Ave	Cambridge	MA	02139-4307
508 922-8222	**Montserrat College of Art**	PO Box 26	Beverly	MA	01915-0001
413 538-2000	**Mount Holyoke College**	College St	South Hadley	MA	01075-1415
617 262-1120	**New England Conservatory of Music**	290 Huntington Ave	Boston	MA	02115-5000
508 943-1560	**Nichols College**	Center Rd	Dudley	MA	01570-0000
413 664-4511	**North Adams State College**	375 Church St	North Adams	MA	01247-4100
617 437-2000	**Northeastern University**	360 Huntington Ave	Boston	MA	02115-5096
617 731-7000	**Pine Manor College**	400 Heath St	Chestnut Hill	MA	02167-2332
617 495-8000	**Radcliffe College**	10 Garden St	Cambridge	MA	02138-3600
617 893-1820	**Regis College**	235 Wellesley St	Weston	MA	02193-1571
413 467-7191	**Saint Hyacinth College & Seminary**	66 School St	Granby	MA	01033-9742
617 254-2610	**Saint John's Seminary**	127 Lake St	Brighton	MA	02135-3898
508 741-6000	**Salem State College**	352 Lafayette St	Salem	MA	01970-5353
617 267-6100	**School of the Museum of Fine Arts**	230 Fenway	Boston	MA	02115-5534
617 738-2000	**Simmons College**	300 Fenway	Boston	MA	02115-5898
413 528-0771	**Simon's Rock of Bard College**	84 Alford Rd	Great Barrington	MA	01230-9702
413 584-2700	**Smith College**		Northampton	MA	01063-0001
	Southeastern Massachusetts University				
508 997-7831	*New Bedford Campus*	1213 Purchase St	New Bedford	MA	02740-6636
508 999-8000	*North Dartmouth Campus*	Old Westport Rd	North Dartmouth	MA	02747-0000
413 788-3000	**Springfield College**	263 Alden St	Springfield	MA	01109-3797
508 238-1081	**Stonehill College**	320 Washington St	North Easton	MA	02357-0001
617 573-8000	**Suffolk University**	8 Ashburton Pl	Boston	MA	02108-2770
617 628-5000	**Tufts University**		Medford	MA	02155-0000
508 934-4000	**University of Lowell**	1 University Ave	Lowell	MA	01854-2893
413 545-0111	**University of Massachusetts**	Goodell Bldg	Amherst	MA	01003-0001
617 287-5000	**University of Massachusetts Boston**	Harbor Campus	Boston	MA	02125-0000
617 235-0320	**Wellesley College**	106 Central St	Wellesley	MA	02181-8201
617 442-9010	**Wentworth Institute of Technology**	550 Huntington Ave	Boston	MA	02115-5998
413 782-3111	**Western New England College**	1215 Wilbraham Rd	Springfield	MA	01119-2693
413 568-3311	**Westfield State College**	577 Western Ave	Westfield	MA	01086-0000
508 285-7722	**Wheaton College**	E Main St	Norton	MA	02766-0000
617 734-5200	**Wheelock College**	200 The Riverway	Boston	MA	02215-4176
413 597-3131	**Williams College**	Hopkins Hall	Williamstown	MA	01267-0000
508 831-5000	**Worcester Polytechnic Institute**	100 Institute Rd	Worcester	MA	01609-2280
508 793-8000	**Worcester State College**	486 Chandler St	Worcester	MA	01602-2597

MICHIGAN

517 265-5161	**Adrian College**	110 S Madison St	Adrian	MI	49221-2575
517 629-1000	**Albion College**	611 E Porter St	Albion	MI	49224-1899
517 463-7111	**Alma College**	614 W Superior St	Alma	MI	48801-1599
616 471-7771	**Andrews University**	US 31 N	Berrien Springs	MI	49104-0001
616 459-8281	**Aquinas College**	1607 Robinson Rd SE	Grand Rapids	MI	49506-1799
313 767-7600	**Baker College**	G1050 W Bristol Rd	Flint	MI	48507-0000
616 726-4904	**Baker College of Muskegon**	141 Hartford St	Muskegon	MI	49442-3497
616 957-6000	**Calvin College**	3201 Burton St SE	Grand Rapids	MI	49546-4388
313 872-3118	**Center for Creative Studies**	201 E Kirby St	Detroit	MI	48202-4034
517 774-4000	**Central Michigan University**		Mount Pleasant	MI	48859-0001
313 483-4400	**Cleary College**	2170 Washtenaw Ave	Ypsilanti	MI	48197-1788
313 995-7300	**Concordia College**	4090 Geddes Rd	Ann Arbor	MI	48105-2797
313 882-5522	**D'Etre University**	377 Fisher Rd	Grosse Pointe	MI	48230-1602
616 451-3511	**Davenport College**	415 E Fulton St	Grand Rapids	MI	49503-4498
313 581-4400	**Detroit College of Business**	4801 Oakman Blvd	Dearborn	MI	48126-3799
313 239-1443	*Flint Campus*	3115 Lawndale Ave	Flint	MI	48504-2699
313 558-8700	*Warren Campus*	27500 Dequindre Rd	Warren	MI	48092-5209
313 487-1849	**Eastern Michigan University**		Ypsilanti	MI	48197-0000
616 592-2000	**Ferris State University**	901 S State St	Big Rapids	MI	49307-2295
313 762-9500	**GMI Engineering & Management Institute**	1700 W 3rd Ave	Flint	MI	48504-4890

616 538-2330 **Grace Bible College** 1011 Aldon St SW ... Grand Rapids MI 49509-1921
616 949-5300 **Grand Rapids Baptist College & Seminary**
1001 E Beltline Ave NE ... Grand Rapids MI 49505-5803
616 895-6611 **Grand Valley State University** ... Allendale MI 49401-9523
517 321-0242 **Great Lakes Bible College** 6211 W Willow Hwy ... Lansing MI 48917-1231
517 437-7341 **Hillsdale College** 33 E College St ... Hillsdale MI 49242-1298
616 392-5111 **Hope College** 141 E 12th St ... Holland MI 49423-0000
616 696-1180 **Jordan College (System)** 360 W Pine St ... Cedar Springs MI 49319-9686
616 383-8400 **Kalamazoo College** 1200 Academy St ... Kalamazoo MI 49007-3295
616 451-2787 **Kendall College of Art & Design** 111 N Division Ave ... Grand Rapids MI 49503-3102
906 632-6841 **Lake Superior State University** 1000 College Dr ... Sault Sainte Marie MI 49783-0000
313 356-0200 **Lawrence Technological University** 21000 W Ten-Mile Rd ... Southfield MI 48075-1058
313 591-5000 **Madonna College** 36600 Schoolcraft Rd ... Livonia MI 48150-1173
313 862-8000 **Marygrove College** 8425 W McNichols Rd ... Detroit MI 48221-2599
517 355-1855 **Michigan State University** John A Hanna Bldg ... East Lansing MI 48824-0001
906 487-1885 **Michigan Tech University** 1400 Townsend Dr ... Houghton MI 49931-1295
616 349-4200 **Nazareth College** 3333 Gull Rd ... Kalamazoo MI 49001-1282
906 227-1000 **Northern Michigan University** ... Marquette MI 49855-5301
517 631-1600 **Northwood Institute** 3225 Cook Rd ... Midland MI 48640-2398
313 370-2100 **Oakland University** Walton & Squirrel Sts ... Rochester MI 48309-0000
616 749-7000 **Olivet College** Main St ... Olivet MI 49076-0000
616 363-2050 **Reformed Bible College** 3333 East Beltline Ave NE ... Grand Rapids MI 49505-9749
313 883-8500 **Sacred Heart Seminary College** 2701 W Chicago Blvd ... Detroit MI 48206-1799
517 790-4000 **Saginaw Valley State University** 2250 Pierce Rd ... University Center MI 48710-0001
313 682-1885 **Saint Mary's College** Commerce & Orchard Lake Rds ... Orchard Lake MI 48033-0000
517 263-0731 **Siena Heights College** 1247 E Siena Heights Dr ... Adrian MI 49221-1796
517 750-1200 **Spring Arbor College** Business Office Stn 8 ... Spring Arbor MI 49283-0000
313 927-1000 **University of Detroit** 4001 W McNichols Rd ... Detroit MI 48221-3090
313 592-6000 **University of Detroit Mercy** 8200 W Outer Dr ... Detroit MI 48219-3580
313 764-1817 **University of Michigan** 503 Thompson Ave ... Ann Arbor MI 48109-0001
313 593-5000 *Dearborn Campus* 4901 Evergreen Rd ... Dearborn MI 48128-1491
313 762-3000 *Flint Campus* 303 E Kearsley St ... Flint MI 48502-2186
313 689-8282 **Walsh College of Accountancy & Business Administration**
3838 Livernois Rd ... Troy MI 48083-5066
313 577-2424 **Wayne State University** 5980 Cass Ave ... Detroit MI 48202-3489
616 387-1000 **Western Michigan University** W Michigan Ave ... Kalamazoo MI 49008-0000
313 553-7200 **William Tyndale College** 35700 W 12-Mile Rd ... Farmington Hills MI 48331-3147

MINNESOTA

612 739-7686 **Apostolic Bible Institute Inc** 6944 Hudson Blvd N ... Saint Paul MN 55128-0000
612 330-1000 **Augsburg College** 731 21st Ave S ... Minneapolis MN 55454-1398
218 755-2000 **Bemidji State University** 1500 Birchmont Dr NE ... Bemidji MN 56601-2699
612 638-6400 **Bethel College & Seminary** 3900 Bethel Dr ... Saint Paul MN 55112-6999
507 663-4000 **Carleton College** 1 N College St ... Northfield MN 55057-4015
612 363-5011 **College of Saint Benedict** 37 College Ave S ... Saint Joseph MN 56374-2001
612 690-6000 **College of Saint Catherine** 2004 Randolph Ave ... Saint Paul MN 55105-1750
218 723-6000 **College of Saint Scholastica** 1200 Kenwood Ave ... Duluth MN 55811-4199
218 299-4321 **Concordia College at Moorhead** 901 S 8th St ... Moorhead MN 56562-0001
612 641-8278 **Concordia College at Saint Paul** 275 Syndicate St N ... Saint Paul MN 55104-5494
507 931-8000 **Gustavus Adolphus College** College Ave ... Saint Peter MN 56082-0000
612 641-2800 **Hamline University** 1536 Hewitt Ave ... Saint Paul MN 55104-1284
612 696-6000 **Macalester College** 1600 Grand Ave ... Saint Paul MN 55105-1899
507 389-2463 **Mankato State University** Ellis Ave & South Rd ... Mankato MN 56001-0000
507 354-8221 **Martin Luther College** 1884 College Heights ... New Ulm MN 56073-3300
612 296-3875 **Metropolitan State University** 121 Metro Sq ... Saint Paul MN 55101-0000
507 288-4563 **Minnesota Bible College** 920 Mayowood Rd SW ... Rochester MN 55902-2382
612 296-2844 **Minnesota State University (System)** 555 Park St Suite 230 ... Saint Paul MN 55103-2111
218 236-2011 **Moorhead State University** 1104 7th Ave S ... Moorhead MN 56563-0001
612 644-1265 **National College Saint Paul Branch** 1380 Energy Ln ... Saint Paul MN 55108-5271
612 332-3491 **North Central Bible College** 910 Elliot Ave ... Minneapolis MN 55404-1391
612 631-5100 **Northwestern College** 3003 Snelling Ave N ... Roseville MN 55113-1598
218 751-8670 **Oak Hills Bible College** 1600 Oak Hills Rd SW ... Bemidji MN 56601-8826
507 451-2710 **Pillsbury Baptist Bible College** 315 S Grove ... Owatonna MN 55060-3097
612 255-3822 **Saint Cloud State University** Atwood Ctr ... Saint Cloud MN 56301-0000
612 363-2011 **Saint John's University** ... Collegeville MN 56321-9999
507 452-4430 **Saint Mary's College** 700 Terrace Heights ... Winona MN 55987-1399
507 663-2222 **Saint Olaf College** 1500 St Olaf Ave ... Northfield MN 55057-1574
612 446-1411 **Saint Paul Bible College** 6425 County Rd 30 ... Saint Bonifacius MN 55375-9001
507 537-7021 **Southwest State University** N Hwy 23 ... Marshall MN 56258-0000
612 625-5000 **University of Minnesota** ... Minneapolis MN 55455-0100
218 726-8000 *Duluth Campus* 10 University Dr ... Duluth MN 55812-2403
612 589-2211 *Morris Campus* E 4th College Ave ... Morris MN 56267-2134
612 647-5000 **University of Saint Thomas** 2115 Summit Ave ... Saint Paul MN 55105-1096
507 457-5000 **Winona State University** 8th & Johnson Sts ... Winona MN 55987-0000

MISSISSIPPI

601 877-6100 **Alcorn State University** Hwy 552 ... Lorman MS 39096-0000
601 968-5940 **Belhaven College** 1500 Peachtree St ... Jackson MS 39202-1789
601 685-4771 **Blue Mountain College** PO Box 338 ... Blue Mountain MS 38610-0338
601 846-3000 **Delta State University** Hwy 8W ... Cleveland MS 38733-0000
601 981-1611 **Jackson College of Ministries** 1555 Beasley Rd ... Jackson MS 39206-2099
601 968-2121 **Jackson State University** 1400 John R Lynch St ... Jackson MS 39217-0001
601 289-2896 **Magnolia Bible College** 820 S Huntington ... Kosciusko MS 39090-0000
601 354-5201 **Millsaps College** ... Jackson MS 39210-0001
601 925-3000 **Mississippi College** College St ... Clinton MS 39058-0001
601 325-2323 **Mississippi State University** ... Starkville MS 39762-9999
601 329-4750 **Mississippi University for Women** 1224 College St ... Columbus MS 39701-9984
601 254-9041 **Mississippi Valley State University** Hwy 82 W ... Itta Bena MS 38941-0000
601 252-4661 **Rust College** 150 E Rust Ave ... Holly Springs MS 38635-2328
601 426-6346 **Southeastern Baptist College** 4229 Hwy 15 N ... Laurel MS 39441-0000
601 977-7700 **Tougaloo College** ... Tougaloo MS 39174-9999
601 232-7211 **University of Mississippi** Library Loop ... University MS 38677-9999
601 844-5622 *Tupelo Regional Campus* 655 Eason Blvd ... Tupelo MS 38801-5955
601 266-7011 **University of Southern Mississippi** Hardy St ... Hattiesburg MS 39406-7000
601 845-2265 **Wesley College** Hwy 469 ... Florence MS 39073-0000
601 582-5051 **William Carey College** Tuscan Ave ... Hattiesburg MS 39401-5499

MISSOURI

816 942-8400 **Avila College** 11901 Wornall Rd ... Kansas City MO 64145-1698
417 869-9811 **Baptist Bible College** 628 E Kearney St ... Springfield MO 65803-3498
417 862-2781 **Berean College** 1445 Boonville Ave ... Springfield MO 65802-1805
816 322-0110 **Calvary Bible College** 15800 Calvary Rd ... Kansas City MO 64147-1341
417 833-2551 **Central Bible College** 3000 N Grant Ave ... Springfield MO 65803-1096
816 263-3900 **Central Christian College of the Bible** 911 E Urbandale Dr ... Moberly MO 65270-1997
816 248-3391 **Central Methodist College** 411 Central Methodist Sq ... Fayette MO 65248-1129
816 429-4111 **Central Missouri State University** ... Warrensburg MO 64093-5000
314 875-8700 **Columbia College** 10001 Rogers St ... Columbia MO 65216-0001
816 944-2218 **Conception Seminary College** Conception Abbey ... Conception MO 64433-0000
314 288-5221 **Culver-Stockton College** ... Canton MO 63435-0000
314 768-3044 **Deaconess College of Nursing** 6150 Oakland Ave ... Saint Louis MO 63139-3297
816 941-0430 **DeVry Institute of Technology** 11224 Holmes St ... Kansas City MO 64131-3698
417 865-8731 **Drury College** 900 N Benton Ave ... Springfield MO 65802-3791
417 865-2811 **Evangel College** 1111 N Glenstone Ave ... Springfield MO 65802-2191
816 523-6030 **Finlay Engineering College** 7 E 79th Terr ... Kansas City MO 64114-2599
314 862-3456 **Fontbonne College** 6800 Wydown Blvd ... Saint Louis MO 63105-3098
816 833-0524 **Graceland College** 9900 E Winner Rd ... Independence MO 64052-2150
314 221-3675 **Hannibal-LaGrange College** 2800 Palmyra Rd ... Hannibal MO 63401-1999
314 533-3366 **Harris-Stowe State College** 3026 Laclede Ave ... Saint Louis MO 63103-2199
816 561-4852 **Kansas City Art Institute** 4415 Warwick Blvd ... Kansas City MO 64111-1874
314 681-5000 **Lincoln University** 820 Chestnut St ... Jefferson City MO 65101-3500
314 949-2000 **Lindenwood College** 209 S Kingshighway St ... Saint Charles MO 63301-1695
314 576-9300 **Maryville College** 13550 Conway Rd ... Saint Louis MO 63141-7299
314 434-1115 **Missouri Baptist College** 12542 Conway Rd ... Saint Louis MO 63141-8698
417 625-9300 **Missouri Southern State College** 3950 Newman Rd ... Joplin MO 64801-1512
816 886-6924 **Missouri Valley College** 500 E College St ... Marshall MO 65340-3197
816 271-4200 **Missouri Western State College** 4525 Downs Dr ... Saint Joseph MO 64507-2246
816 785-4000 **Northeast Missouri State University** E Normal St ... Kirksville MO 63501-0000
816 562-1838 **Northwest Missouri State University** ... Maryville MO 64468-0000
417 451-2057 **Ozark Bible Institute** 906 Summit ... Neosho MO 64850-1034
417 624-2518 **Ozark Christian College** 1111 N Main St ... Joplin MO 64801-1188
816 741-2000 **Park College** 8700 NW River Park Dr ... Parkville MO 64152-4358
816 926-4000 **Rockhurst College** 1100 Rockhurst Rd ... Kansas City MO 64110-2561
314 837-6777 **Saint Louis Christian College** 1360 Grandview Dr ... Florissant MO 63033-6499
314 367-8700 **Saint Louis College of Pharmacy** 4588 Parkview Pl ... Saint Louis MO 63110-1088
314 863-3033 **Saint Louis Conservatory of Music** 560 Trinity Ave ... Saint Louis MO 63130-4392
314 658-2222 **Saint Louis University** 221 N Grand Blvd ... Saint Louis MO 63103-2097
417 334-6411 **School of the Ozarks** ... Point Lookout MO 65726-9999
314 651-2000 **Southeast Missouri State University**
1 University Plaza ... Cape Girardeau MO 63701-4799
417 326-5281 **Southwest Baptist University** 1601 S Springfield Ave ... Bolivar MO 65613-2559
417 836-5000 **Southwest Missouri State University** 901 S National Ave ... Springfield MO 65804-0087
314 442-2211 **Stephens College** 1200 E Broadway ... Columbia MO 65215-0001
816 736-4131 **Tarkio College** McNary St ... Tarkio MO 64491-0000
314 882-2121 **University of Missouri** 320 Jesse Hall ... Columbia MO 65211-0001
816 276-1000 *Kansas City Campus* 5100 Rockhill Rd ... Kansas City MO 64110-2499
314 341-4111 *Rolla Campus* ... Rolla MO 65401-0000
314 553-5000 *Saint Louis Campus* 8001 Natural Bridge Rd ... Saint Louis MO 63121-4499
314 889-5000 **Washington University** 1 Brookings Dr ... Saint Louis MO 63130-4899
314 968-6900 **Webster University** 470 E Lockwood Ave ... Saint Louis MO 63119-3194
314 642-3361 **Westminster College** 501 Westminster Ave ... Fulton MO 65251-1299
816 781-3806 **William Jewell College** 500 College Hill ... Liberty MO 64068-0000
314 642-2251 **William Woods College** 200 W 12th St ... Fulton MO 65251-1098

MONTANA

406 442-3450 **Carroll College** 1400 N Benton Ave ... Helena MT 59625-0002
406 761-8210 **College of Great Falls** 1301 20th St S ... Great Falls MT 59405-4996
406 657-2011 **Eastern Montana College** 1500 N 30th St ... Billings MT 59101-0298
406 496-4101 **Montana College of Mineral Science & Technology** W Park St ... Butte MT 59701-0000
406 994-0211 **Montana State University** ... Bozeman MT 59717-0001
406 444-6570 **Montana University (System)** 33 S Last Chance Gulch St ... Helena MT 59601-4132
406 761-0308 **Mountain States Baptist College** 824 3rd Ave N ... Great Falls MT 59401-1504
406 265-3700 **Northern Montana College** 300 11th St W ... Havre MT 59501-4966
406 657-1000 **Rocky Mountain College** 1511 Poly Dr ... Billings MT 59102-1796
406 243-0211 **University of Montana** ... Missoula MT 59812-0001
406 683-7011 **Western Montana College** 710 S Atlantic St ... Dillon MT 59725-3598

NEBRASKA

402 291-8100 **Bellevue College** Galvin Rd & Harvell Dr ... Bellevue NE 68005-0000
402 559-3100 **Bishop Clarkson College** 333 S 44th St ... Omaha NE 68131-3703
308 432-4451 **Chadron State College** 10th & Main Sts ... Chadron NE 69337-0000
402 399-2400 **College of Saint Mary** 1901 S 72nd St ... Omaha NE 68124-2377
402 643-3651 **Concordia Teachers College** 800 N Columbia Ave ... Seward NE 68434-1594
402 280-2700 **Creighton University** 2400 California St ... Omaha NE 68178-0001
402 426-4101 **Dana College** 2848 College Dr ... Blair NE 68008-1099
402 826-2161 **Doane College** 1014 Boswell Ave ... Crete NE 68333-2495
402 449-2800 **Grace College of the Bible** 1515 S 10th St ... Omaha NE 68108-3600
402 463-2402 **Hastings College** 7th & Turner Ave ... Hastings NE 68901-7696
308 236-8441 **Kearney State College** 905 W 25th St ... Kearney NE 68849-0001
402 721-5480 **Midland Lutheran College** 900 N Clarkson St ... Fremont NE 68025-4254
402 371-5960 **Nebraska Christian College** 1800 Syracuse ... Norfolk NE 68701-2400
402 466-2371 **Nebraska Wesleyan University** 50th & St Paul Sts ... Lincoln NE 68504-0000
402 872-3815 **Peru State College** Park Ave ... Peru NE 68421-0000
308 632-6933 **Platte Valley Bible College** 305 E 16th St ... Scottsbluff NE 69361-3143
402 488-2331 **Union College** 3800 S 48th St ... Lincoln NE 68506-4387
402 472-2111 **University of Nebraska (System)** 3835 Holdrege St ... Lincoln NE 68583-0001
University of Nebraska
402 472-7211 *Lincoln Campus* 501 N 14th St ... Lincoln NE 68588-0001
402 554-2200 *Omaha Campus* 60th & Dodge Sts ... Omaha NE 68182-0001
402 375-2200 **Wayne State College** 200 E 10th St ... Wayne NE 68787-1486

NEVADA

702 323-4145 **Reno Business College** 140 Washington St ... Reno NV 89503-5673
702 831-1314 **Sierra Nevada College** PO Box 4269 ... Incline Village NV 89450-4269
702 784-4901 **University of Nevada (System)** 2601 Enterprise Rd ... Reno NV 89512-1666
University of Nevada
702 739-3011 *Las Vegas Campus* 4505 S Maryland Pkwy ... Las Vegas NV 89154-0001
702 784-1110 *Reno Campus* 9th Virginia St N ... Reno NV 89557-0001

NEW HAMPSHIRE

603 526-2010 **Colby-Sawyer College** 100 Main St ... New London NH 03257-4648
603 883-3556 **Daniel Webster College** 20 University Dr ... Nashua NH 03063-1300
603 646-1110 **Dartmouth College** ... Hanover NH 03755-0000
Franklin Pierce College
603 749-5587 *Dover Campus* 7 1/2 Summersworth Rd ... Dover NH 03820-2202
603 357-0079 *Keene Campus* 43 Arch St ... Keene NH 03431-2232
603 889-4143 *Nashua Campus* 20 Cotton Rd ... Nashua NH 03063-1204
603 899-5111 *Rindge Campus* College Rd ... Rindge NH 03461-0000
603 898-1263 *Salem Campus* 91 Stiles Rd ... Salem NH 03079-4830
603 352-1909 **Keene State College** 229 Main St ... Keene NH 03431-4183
603 669-7735 **Magdalen College** 270 Daniel Webster Hwy S ... Bedford NH 03102-6170
603 428-2211 **New England College** 23 Bridge St ... Henniker NH 03242-3202
603 668-2211 **New Hampshire College** 2500 River Rd ... Manchester NH 03104-1394
603 669-4298 **Notre Dame College** 2321 Elm St ... Manchester NH 03104-2299
603 536-5000 **Plymouth State College** 14 Plymouth St ... Plymouth NH 03264-0000
603 888-1311 **Rivier College** 420 Main St ... Nashua NH 03060-5086
603 669-1030 **Saint Anselm College** 87 St Anselm Dr ... Manchester NH 03102-1310
603 862-1692 **School for Lifelong Learning** Dunlap Ctr ... Durham NH 03824-3545
603 862-1234 **University of New Hampshire** ... Durham NH 03824-3501

NEW JERSEY

201 748-9000 **Bloomfield College** 467 Franklin St ... Bloomfield NJ 07003-4895
201 228-4424 **Caldwell College** 9 Ryerson Ave ... Caldwell NJ 07006-6195
908 852-1400 **Centenary College** 400 Jefferson St ... Hackettstown NJ 07840-2100
201 292-6300 **College of Saint Elizabeth** 2 Convent Rd ... Convent Station NJ 07960-6989

Four-Year Colleges

Phone	College	City	State	ZIP
201 408-3000	**Drew University** 36 Madison Ave	Madison	NJ	07940-1493
201 460-5000	**Fairleigh Dickinson University** 223 Montross Ave	Rutherford	NJ	07070-1977
201 593-8500	*Florham-Madison Campus* 285 Madison Ave	Madison	NJ	07940-1099
201 692-2000	*Teaneck-Hackensack Campus* 1000 River Rd	Teaneck	NJ	07666-1996
201 778-1190	**Felician College** 260 S Main St	Lodi	NJ	07644-2198
908 364-2200	**Georgian Court College** Lakewood Ave	Lakewood	NJ	08701-0000
609 863-5000	**Glassboro State College**	Glassboro	NJ	08028-0000
201 547-6000	**Jersey City State College** 2039 John F Kennedy Blvd	Jersey City	NJ	07305-1527
908 527-2000	**Kean College of New Jersey** 1000 Morris Ave	Union	NJ	07083-7133
908 222-6600	**Monmouth College** 400 Cedar Ave	West Long Branch	NJ	07764-1890
201 893-4000	**Montclair State College** Normal Ave & Valley Rd	Upper Montclair	NJ	07043-0000
201 596-3000	**New Jersey Institute of Technology** 323 Martin Luther King Jr Blvd	Newark	NJ	07102-1824
609 258-3000	**Princeton University**	Princeton	NJ	08544-0001
201 267-9404	**Rabbinical College of America** 226 Sussex Ave	Morristown	NJ	07960-3600
201 529-7500	**Ramapo College of New Jersey** 505 Ramapo Valley Rd	Mahwah	NJ	07430-1680
609 896-5041	**Rider College** 2083 Lawrenceville Rd	Lawrenceville	NJ	08648-3099
908 932-1766	**Rutgers State University** Van Nest Hall	New Brunswick	NJ	08903-0000
	Rutgers University			
609 757-1766	*Camden Campus* 311 N 5th St	Camden	NJ	08102-1499
201 648-1766	*Newark Campus* 249 University Ave	Newark	NJ	07102-1808
201 333-4400	**Saint Peter's College** 2641 John F Kennedy Blvd	Jersey City	NJ	07306-5997
201 761-9000	**Seton Hall University** 400 S Orange Ave	South Orange	NJ	07079-2697
201 420-5100	**Stevens Institute of Technology** Castle Point on the Hudson	Hoboken	NJ	07030-0000
609 652-1776	**Stockton State College** Jimmy Leeds Rd	Pomona	NJ	08240-9999
609 984-1150	**Thomas A Edison State College** 101 W State St CN545	Trenton	NJ	08625-0001
609 771-1855	**Trenton State College** PO Box CN4700	Trenton	NJ	08650-0000
201 456-4300	**University of Medicine & Dentistry of New Jersey** 150 Bergen St	Newark	NJ	07103-2406
201 266-7000	**Upsala College** 345 Prospect St	East Orange	NJ	07019-0000
609 921-7100	**Westminster Choir College** Hamilton Ave & Walnut Ln	Princeton	NJ	08540-3899
201 595-2000	**William Paterson College of New Jersey** 300 Pompton Rd	Wayne	NJ	07470-2152

NEW MEXICO

Phone	College	City	State	ZIP
505 473-6011	**College of Santa Fe** 1600 St Michaels Dr	Santa Fe	NM	87501-5634
505 392-6561	**College of the Southwest** 6610 N Lovington Hwy	Hobbs	NM	88240-9129
505 562-2121	**Eastern New Mexico University**	Portales	NM	88130-0000
505 265-7517	**National College Albuquerque Branch** 1202 Pennsylvania NE	Albuquerque	NM	87110-0000
505 877-0240	**Nazarene Indian Bible College** 2315 Markham Rd SW	Albuquerque	NM	87105-7028
505 425-7511	**New Mexico Highlands University** National Ave	Las Vegas	NM	87701-0000
505 835-5508	**New Mexico Institute of Mining & Technology** Campus Stn	Socorro	NM	87801-0000
505 646-3121	**New Mexico State University**	Las Cruces	NM	88003-0000
505 982-3691	**Saint John's College at Santa Fe** 1160 Camino Cruz Blanca	Santa Fe	NM	87501-0000
505 277-0111	**University of New Mexico** Scholes Hall Rm 160	Albuquerque	NM	87131-0001
505 722-7221	*Gallup Campus* 200 College Rd	Gallup	NM	87301-5603
505 538-6011	**Western New Mexico University** PO Box 680	Silver City	NM	88062-0680

NEW YORK

Phone	College	City	State	ZIP
516 294-8700	**Adelphi University** 1 South Ave	Garden City	NY	11530-4299
607 871-2111	**Alfred University** 2 Main St	Alfred	NY	14802-0000
914 758-6822	**Bard College**	Annandale-on-Hudson	NY	12504-0000
212 854-5262	**Barnard College** 3009 Broadway	New York	NY	10027-6598
212 694-1000	**Boricua College** 3755 Broadway	New York	NY	10032-1599
716 883-7000	**Canisius College** 2001 Main St	Buffalo	NY	14208-1098
315 655-8283	**Cazenovia College**	Cazenovia	NY	13035-1084
315 268-6400	**Clarkson University** Pierrepontt Ave Snell Hall	Potsdam	NY	13699-0001
315 824-1000	**Colgate University** 13 Oak Dr	Hamilton	NY	13346-1386
212 989-2002	**College for Human Services** 345 Hudson St 14th Fl	New York	NY	10014-4598
718 429-6600	**College of Aeronautics** 86th St & 23rd Ave La Guardia Airport	Flushing	NY	11371-0000
212 962-4111	**College of Insurance** 101 Murray St	New York	NY	10007-2132
212 549-8000	**College of Mount Saint Vincent** Riverdale & 263rd Sts	Riverdale	NY	10471-0000
914 632-5300	**College of New Rochelle** 29 Castle Pl	New Rochelle	NY	10805-2308
518 454-5111	**College of Saint Rose** 432 Western Ave	Albany	NY	12203-1419
212 854-1754	**Columbia University** E 116th St & Broadway	New York	NY	10029-1728
914 337-9300	**Concordia College** 171 White Plains Rd	Bronxville	NY	10708-1998
212 254-6300	**Cooper Union College** E 7th St 41 Cooper Sq	New York	NY	10003-0000
607 255-2000	**Cornell University**	Ithaca	NY	14853-0001
212 794-5555	**CUNY (System) City University of New York** 535 E 80th St	New York	NY	10021-0795
	CUNY			
212 447-3000	*Bernard M Baruch College* 155 E 24th St	New York	NY	10010-3727
718 780-5485	*Brooklyn College* Bedford Ave & Ave H	Brooklyn	NY	11210-0000
212 650-7000	*City College* 138th St & Convent Ave Administration Bldg	New York	NY	10031-0000
718 390-7733	*College of Staten Island* 715 Ocean Terr	Staten Island	NY	10301-4547
212 960-8000	*Herbert H Lehman College* 250 Bedford Park Blvd W	Bronx	NY	10468-1527
212 772-4000	*Hunter College* 695 Park Ave	New York	NY	10021-5085
212 237-8000	*John Jay College of Criminal Justice* 445 W 59th St	New York	NY	10019-1199
718 270-4900	*Medgar Evers College* 1650 Bedford Ave	Brooklyn	NY	11225-2017
718 520-7000	*Queens College* 65-30 Kissena Blvd	Flushing	NY	11367-1597
718 262-2000	*York College* 94-20 Guy R Brewer Blvd	Jamaica	NY	11451-0001
716 881-3200	**D'Youville College** 320 Porter Ave	Buffalo	NY	14201-1084
716 839-3600	**Daemen College** 4380 Main St	Amherst	NY	14226-3591
914 359-7800	**Dominican College** 10 N Western Hwy	Orangeburg	NY	10962-1299
516 589-6100	**Dowling College** 150 Idle Hour Blvd	Oakdale	NY	11769-1999
607 734-3911	**Elmira College** McGrow Bldg	Elmira	NY	14901-0000
212 741-5665	**Eugene Lang College** 65 W 11th St	New York	NY	10011-8601
212 760-7660	**Fashion Institute of Technology** 227 W 27th St	New York	NY	10001-5902
212 579-2000	**Fordham University** 441 E Fordham Rd	Bronx	NY	10458-5149
212 841-5100	*College at Lincoln Center* 113 W 60th St	New York	NY	10023-7484
516 549-5000	**Friends World College** 14 Plover Ln	Huntington	NY	11743-1098
315 859-4011	**Hamilton College** College Hill Rd	Clinton	NY	13323-0000
607 432-4200	**Hartwick College**	Oneonta	NY	13820-0000
212 674-5300	**Hebrew Union College** 1 W 4th St	New York	NY	10012-1186
315 789-5500	**Hobart & William Smith Colleges** 337 Pulteney St	Geneva	NY	14456-0000
516 560-6600	**Hofstra University** 1000 Fulton Ave	Hempstead	NY	11550-1009
716 567-2211	**Houghton College** 1 Willard Ave	Houghton	NY	14744-0000
716 674-6363	*Buffalo Campus* 910 Union Rd	West Seneca	NY	14224-3499
607 274-3011	**Ithaca College** Danby Rd	Ithaca	NY	14850-5815
212 678-8000	**Jewish Theological Seminary of America** 3080 Broadway	New York	NY	10027-4650
212 799-5000	**Juilliard School** 144 W 66th St	New York	NY	10023-6502
315 536-4411	**Keuka College** Keuka Park Rd	Keuka Park	NY	14478-0000
914 941-7200	**King's College** 150 Lodge Rd	Briarcliff Manor	NY	10510-1200
315 445-4100	**Le Moyne College**	Syracuse	NY	13214-1301
516 299-0200	**Long Island University (System)** Northern Blvd	Greenvale	NY	11548-0000
	Long Island University			
516 273-5112	*Brentwood Campus* 100 2nd Ave	Brentwood	NY	11717-5307
718 834-6000	*Brooklyn Campus* 1 University Plaza	Brooklyn	NY	11201-5372
516 299-0200	*CW Post Campus* Northern Blvd	Greenvale	NY	11548-0000
914 359-7200	*Rockland Campus* Rt 340	Orangeburg	NY	10962-2219
516 283-4000	*Southampton Campus* 239 Montauk Hwy	Southampton	NY	11968-0000
718 331-6613	**Machzikei Hadath Rabbinical College** PO Box 799	Brooklyn	NY	11219-0799
212 920-0100	**Manhattan College** 4513 Manhattan College Pkwy	Bronx	NY	10471-4099
212 749-2802	**Manhattan School of Music** 120 Claremont Ave	New York	NY	10027-4698
914 694-2200	**Manhattanville College** 125 Purchase St	Purchase	NY	10577-2400
212 580-0210	**Mannes College of Music** 150 W 85th St	New York	NY	10024-4499
914 471-3240	**Marist College** 290 North Rd	Poughkeepsie	NY	12601-1387
914 631-3200	**Marymount College** 100 Marymount Ave	Tarrytown	NY	10591-3796
212 517-0400	**Marymount Manhattan College** 221 E 71st St	New York	NY	10021-4597
716 884-3281	**Medaille College** 18 Agassiz Cir	Buffalo	NY	14214-2695
914 693-4500	**Mercy College** 555 Broadway	Dobbs Ferry	NY	10522-1189
212 518-7710	*Bronx Branch Campus* 50 Antin Pl	Bronx	NY	10462-3003
914 948-3666	*White Plains Branch Campus* 277 Martine Ave	White Plains	NY	10601-3494
914 245-6100	*Yorktown Heights Branch Campus* 2651 Strang Blvd	Yorktown Heights	NY	10598-2997
516 678-5000	**Molloy College** 1000 Hempstead Ave	Rockville Centre	NY	11570-1199
914 561-0800	**Mount Saint Mary College** 330 Powell Ave	Newburgh	NY	12550-3494
716 586-2525	**Nazareth College of Rochester** 4245 East Ave	Rochester	NY	14618-3790
212 741-5600	**New School for Social Research** 66 W 12th St	New York	NY	10011-8693
516 686-7907	**New York Institute of Technology**	Old Westbury	NY	11568-0000
516 348-3000	*Central Islip Campus* 211 Carleton Ave	Central Islip	NY	11722-4501
212 399-8347	*New York City Campus* 1855 Broadway	New York	NY	10023-7602
212 753-5365	**New York School of Interior Design** 155 E 56th St	New York	NY	10022-2708
212 998-1212	**New York University** 70 Washington Sq S	New York	NY	10012-1019
716 285-1212	**Niagara University**	Niagara University	NY	14109-9999
914 358-1710	**Nyack College**	Nyack	NY	10960-0000
212 346-1200	**Pace University** 1 Pace Plaza	New York	NY	10038-1598
914 773-3200	*Pleasantville-Briarcliff Campus* 861 Bedford Rd	Pleasantville	NY	10570-2799
914 422-4000	*White Plains Campus* 78 N Broadway	White Plains	NY	10603-3796
212 741-8900	**Parsons School of Design** 66 W 12th St	New York	NY	10011-8603
718 260-3600	**Polytechnic University** 333 Jay St	Brooklyn	NY	11201-2990
718 636-3600	**Pratt Institute** 200 Willoughby Ave	Brooklyn	NY	11205-3899
212 960-5344	**Rabbi Isaac Elchanan Seminary** 2450 Amsterdam Ave	New York	NY	10033-3311
718 268-4700	**Rabbinical Seminary of America** 92-15 69th Ave	Forest Hills	NY	11375-5817
518 276-6000	**Rensselaer Polytechnic Institute** 110 8th St	Troy	NY	12180-3590
716 594-9471	**Roberts Wesleyan College** 2301 Westside Dr	Rochester	NY	14624-1997
716 475-2411	**Rochester Institute of Technology** 1 Lomb Memorial Dr	Rochester	NY	14623-5640
518 270-2000	**Russell Sage College** 45 Ferry St	Troy	NY	12180-4115
716 375-2000	**Saint Bonaventure University**	Saint Bonaventure	NY	14778-9999
718 522-2300	**Saint Francis College** 180 Remsen St	Brooklyn	NY	11201-4398
716 385-8000	**Saint John Fisher College** 3690 East Ave	Rochester	NY	14618-3597
718 969-8000	**Saint John's University** Grand Central & Utopia Pkwys	Jamaica	NY	11439-0001
718 447-4343	*Staten Island Campus* 300 Howard Ave	Staten Island	NY	10301-4496
718 636-6800	**Saint Joseph's College** 245 Clinton Ave	Brooklyn	NY	11205-3688
516 654-3200	*Suffolk Campus* 155 Roe Blvd	Patchogue	NY	11772-2399
315 379-5011	**Saint Lawrence University** 23 Romoda Dr	Canton	NY	13617-0000
914 359-9500	**Saint Thomas Aquinas College** Rt 340	Sparkill	NY	10976-0000
914 337-0700	**Sarah Lawrence College** 1 Meadway	Bronxville	NY	10708-5999
212 679-7350	**School of Visual Arts** 209 E 23rd St	New York	NY	10010-3994
518 783-2300	**Siena College**	Loudonville	NY	12211-0000
518 584-5000	**Skidmore College** N Broadway	Saratoga Springs	NY	12866-0000
518 443-5555	**SUNY (System) State University of New York** 350 Broadway	Albany	NY	12246-0001
	SUNY			
518 442-3300	*Albany* 1400 Washington Ave	Albany	NY	12222-0001
607 777-2000	*Binghamton* Vestal Pkwy E	Binghamton	NY	13902-0000
716 831-2000	*Buffalo* 3435 Main St	Buffalo	NY	14214-3099
716 878-4000	*College at Buffalo* 1300 Elmwood Ave	Buffalo	NY	14222-1095
607 753-2011	*College at Cortland* PO Box 2000	Cortland	NY	13045-0000
716 673-3111	*College at Fredonia* Central Ave	Fredonia	NY	14063-0000
716 245-5211	*College at Geneseo*	Geneseo	NY	14454-0000
914 257-2121	*College at New Paltz*	New Paltz	NY	12561-0000
516 876-3000	*College at Old Westbury* PO Box 210	Old Westbury	NY	11568-0210
607 431-3500	*College at Oneonta* Upper West St	Oneonta	NY	13820-0000
315 341-2500	*College at Oswego* Rt 104 W	Oswego	NY	13126-0000
518 564-2000	*College at Plattsburgh*	Plattsburgh	NY	12901-0000
315 267-2000	*College at Potsdam* Pierrpont Ave	Potsdam	NY	13676-0000
914 251-6000	*College at Purchase* 735 Anderson Hill Rd	Purchase	NY	10577-1400
518 234-5011	*College of Agriculture & Technology*	Cobleskill	NY	12043-0000
315 470-6600	*College of Environmental Science & Forestry* 1 Forestry Dr	Syracuse	NY	13210-2778
315 792-7208	*College of Technology* PO Box 3050	Utica	NY	13504-3050
518 587-2100	*Empire State College* 2 Union Ave	Saratoga Springs	NY	12866-4310
212 760-7675	*Fashion Institute of Technology* 227 W 27th St	New York	NY	10001-5902
516 689-8333	*Health Science Center at Stony Brook* Nicolls Rd	Stony Brook	NY	11794-0001
212 409-7200	*Maritime College* Fort Schuyler	Bronx	NY	10465-0000
516 689-6000	*Stony Brook* Nicolls Rd	Stony Brook	NY	11794-0001
315 443-1870	**Syracuse University**	Syracuse	NY	13244-0001
716 473-2810	**Talmudical Institution of Upstate New York** 769 Park Ave	Rochester	NY	14607-3098
212 447-0700	**Touro College** 844 Ave of the Americas	New York	NY	10001-4103
518 370-6000	**Union College**	Schenectady	NY	12308-0000
716 275-2121	**University of Rochester**	Rochester	NY	14627-0000
516 773-5000	**US Merchant Marine Academy** Steamboat Rd	Kings Point	NY	11024-0000
914 938-4011	**US Military Academy**	West Point	NY	10996-0000
315 792-3111	**Utica College of Syracuse University** 1600 Burrstone Rd	Utica	NY	13502-4892
914 437-7000	**Vassar College** 124 Raymond Ave	Poughkeepsie	NY	12601-6198
315 393-4231	**Wadhams Hall Seminary-College** RR 4 Box 80	Ogdensburg	NY	13669-9308
718 390-3411	**Wagner College** 631 Howard Ave	Staten Island	NY	10301-4495
516 671-2213	**Webb Institute of Naval Architecture** Crescent Beach Rd	Glen Cove	NY	11542-1398
315 364-3370	**Wells College**	Aurora	NY	13026-1100
212 960-5400	**Yeshiva University** 500 W 185th St	New York	NY	10033-3299

NORTH CAROLINA

Phone	College	City	State	ZIP
704 262-2000	**Appalachian State University**	Boone	NC	28608-0001
919 237-3161	**Atlantic Christian College** 400 Atlantic Christian College Dr NE ACC Stn	Wilson	NC	27893-2575
704 786-5171	**Barber-Scotia College** 145 Cabarrus Ave W	Concord	NC	28025-5187
704 825-6700	**Belmont Abbey College** 100 Belmont-Mt Holly Rd	Belmont	NC	28012-2795
919 273-4431	**Bennett College** 900 E Washington St	Greensboro	NC	27401-3298
919 893-4111	**Campbell University** PO Box 66	Buies Creek	NC	27506-0066
704 637-4111	**Catawba College** 2300 W Innes St	Salisbury	NC	28144-2488
704 892-2000	**Davidson College** Concord Rd	Davidson	NC	28036-0000
919 684-8111	**Duke University**	Durham	NC	27706-0000
919 757-6131	**East Carolina University** 1000 E 5th St	Greenville	NC	27858-2598
704 394-2307	**East Coast Bible College** 6900 Wilkinson Blvd	Charlotte	NC	28214-3152
919 335-3400	**Elizabeth City State University** 1001 Parkview Dr	Elizabeth City	NC	27909-6426
919 584-9711	**Elon College** 101 W Haggard Ave	Elon College	NC	27244-9344
919 486-1111	**Fayetteville State University** 1200 Murchison Rd	Fayetteville	NC	28301-4298
704 434-2361	**Gardner-Webb College** PO Box 997	Boiling Springs	NC	28017-0997
919 272-7102	**Greensboro College** 815 W Market St	Greensboro	NC	27420-6050
919 292-5511	**Guilford College** 5800 W Friendly Ave	Greensboro	NC	27410-4173
919 892-4268	**Heritage Bible College** PO Box 1628	Dunn	NC	28334-1628
919 841-9000	**High Point College** PO Box HP-2	High Point	NC	27261-1949
704 378-1000	**Johnson C Smith University** 100 Beatties Ford Rd	Charlotte	NC	28216-5398
704 898-5241	**Lees-McRae College** College Dr	Banner Elk	NC	28604-0000
704 328-1741	**Lenoir-Rhyne College** 7th Ave & 8th St NE	Hickory	NC	28603-0000
704 638-5500	**Livingstone College** 701 W Monroe St	Salisbury	NC	28144-5298
704 689-1111	**Mars Hill College**	Mars Hill	NC	28754-0000
919 833-6461	**Meredith College** 3800 Hillsborough St	Raleigh	NC	27607-5298
919 488-7110	**Methodist College** 5400 Ramsey St	Fayetteville	NC	28311-1498
704 669-8011	**Montreat-Anderson College** 310 Gaither Cir	Montreat	NC	28757-9999
919 658-2502	**Mount Olive College** 209 N Breazeale Ave	Mount Olive	NC	28365-1699

Colleges are listed alphabetically within each state. Graduate Schools are listed alphabetically by state, within each area of study.

919 334-7500	**North Carolina A & T State University** 1601 E Market St	Greensboro	NC	27411-0001
919 560-6100	**North Carolina Central University** 1801 Fayetteville St	Durham	NC	27707-3198
919 770-3399	**North Carolina School of the Arts** 200 Waughtown St	Winston-Salem	NC	27127-2146
919 737-2011	**North Carolina State University** 2205 Hillsborough St	Raleigh	NC	27695-0000
919 977-7171	**North Carolina Wesleyan College** 3400 N Wesleyan Blvd	Rocky Mount	NC	27804-8699
919 521-4214	**Pembroke State University** College Terr	Pembroke	NC	28372-9693
704 463-7343	**Pfeiffer College** Hwy 52 N	Misenheimer	NC	28109-9999
919 725-8344	**Piedmont Bible College** 716 Franklin St	Winston-Salem	NC	27101-5197
704 332-7121	**Queens College** 1900 Selwyn Ave	Charlotte	NC	28274-0001
919 338-5191	**Roanoke Bible College** 714 1st St	Elizabeth City	NC	27907-0000
919 276-3652	**Saint Andrews Presbyterian College** 1700 Dogwood Mile St	Laurinburg	NC	28352-5598
919 828-4451	**Saint Augustine's College** 1315 Oakwood Ave	Raleigh	NC	27610-2298
919 721-2600	**Salem College** 600 S Church St	Winston-Salem	NC	27108-0000
919 755-4800	**Shaw University** 118 E South St	Raleigh	NC	27601-2399
919 962-6981	**University of North Carolina (System)** 910 Raleigh Rd	Chapel Hill	NC	27514-3916
	University of North Carolina			
704 251-6600	*Asheville Campus* 1 University Heights	Asheville	NC	28804-3299
919 962-2211	*Chapel Hill* 910 Raleigh Rd CB-9000	Chapel Hill	NC	27515-0000
704 547-2000	*Charlotte Campus* Hwy 49	Charlotte	NC	28223-0001
919 334-5000	*Greensboro Campus* 1000 Spring Gardens St	Greensboro	NC	27412-0001
919 395-3000	*Wilmington Campus* 601 S College Rd	Wilmington	NC	28403-3201
919 759-5000	**Wake Forest University** Reynolds Stn	Winston-Salem	NC	27106-5193
704 298-3325	**Warren Wilson College** 701 Warren Wilson Rd	Swannanoa	NC	28778-2099
704 227-7211	**Western Carolina University**	Cullowhee	NC	28723-0000
704 233-4061	**Wingate College** Hwy 74	Wingate	NC	28174-0000
919 750-2000	**Winston-Salem State University** 601 S Martin Luther King Jr Dr	Winston-Salem	NC	27110-0001

NORTH DAKOTA

701 227-2507	**Dickinson State University** May Hall	Dickinson	ND	58601-0000
701 252-3467	**Jamestown College**	Jamestown	ND	58401-3456
701 786-2301	**Mayville State University** 330 3rd St NE	Mayville	ND	58257-1299
701 857-3000	**Minot State University** 500 University Ave W	Minot	ND	58701-2215
701 237-8011	**North Dakota State University** 1301 12th Ave N	Fargo	ND	58105-0000
701 349-3621	**Trinity Bible College** 50 S 6th Ave	Ellendale	ND	58436-0000
701 255-7500	**University of Mary** 7500 University Dr	Bismarck	ND	58504-9652
701 777-2011	**University of North Dakota** University Stn	Grand Forks	ND	58202-2020
701 845-7990	**Valley City State University**	Valley City	ND	58072-0000

OHIO

216 337-6403	**Allegheny Wesleyan College** 2161 Woodsdale Rd	Salem	OH	44460-9504
513 767-7331	**Antioch College** 795 Livermore St	Yellow Springs	OH	45387-1697
513 721-5205	**Art Academy of Cincinnati** Eden Park Dr	Cincinnati	OH	45202-1597
419 289-4142	**Ashland University** 401 College Ave	Ashland	OH	44805-3702
513 231-2223	**Athenaeum of Ohio** 6616 Beechmont Ave	Cincinnati	OH	45230-2000
216 826-2900	**Baldwin-Wallace College** 275 Eastland Rd	Berea	OH	44017-2088
419 358-8015	**Bluffton College** 280 W College Ave	Bluffton	OH	45817-1198
216 585-5900	**Borromeo College of Ohio** 28700 Euclid Ave	Wickliffe	OH	44092-2585
419 372-2531	**Bowling Green State University**	Bowling Green	OH	43403-0001
614 236-6011	**Capital University** 2199 E Main St	Columbus	OH	43209-2394
216 368-2000	**Case Western Reserve University** 10900 Euclid Ave	Cleveland	OH	44106-1724
513 766-2211	**Cedarville College** 251 S Main St	Cedarville	OH	45314-9725
513 376-6011	**Central State University** 1400 Rush Row Rd	Wilberforce	OH	45384-9999
513 244-8100	**Cincinnati Bible College & Seminary** 2700 Glenway Ave	Cincinnati	OH	45204-1799
614 474-8896	**Circleville Bible College** 1476 Lancaster Pike	Circleville	OH	43113-9487
216 421-4322	**Cleveland Institute of Art** 11141 East Blvd	Cleveland	OH	44106-1700
216 791-5000	**Cleveland Institute of Music** 11021 East Blvd	Cleveland	OH	44106-1705
216 687-2000	**Cleveland State University** 1802 E 25th St	Cleveland	OH	44114-4420
513 244-4200	**College of Mount Saint Joseph on the Ohio** 5701 Delhi Rd	Mount Saint Joseph	OH	45051-0001
216 263-2000	**College of Wooster**	Wooster	OH	44691-0000
614 224-9101	**Columbus College of Art & Design** 107 N 9th St	Columbus	OH	43215-1758
419 784-4010	**Defiance College** 701 N Clinton St	Defiance	OH	43512-1695
614 587-0810	**Denison University** Main St	Granville	OH	43023-0000
614 253-7291	**DeVry Institute of Technology** 1350 Alum Creek Dr	Columbus	OH	43209-2764
216 696-9000	**Dyke College** 112 Prospect Ave E	Cleveland	OH	44115-1096
216 391-9696	**ETI Technical College** 4300 Euclid Ave	Cleveland	OH	44103-3752
614 283-3771	**Franciscan University of Steubenville** Franciscan Way	Steubenville	OH	43952-0000
614 224-6237	**Franklin University** 201 S Grant Ave	Columbus	OH	43215-5301
419 448-2000	**Heidelberg College** 310 E Market St	Tiffin	OH	44883-2434
216 569-3211	**Hiram College**	Hiram	OH	44234-0000
216 397-1886	**John Carroll University** 20700 N Park Blvd	University Heights	OH	44118-4581
216 672-2121	**Kent State University**	Kent	OH	44242-0001
216 964-3322	*Ashtabula Campus* 3325 W 13th St	Ashtabula	OH	44004-2299
614 427-5000	**Kenyon College**	Gambier	OH	43020-0000
216 352-3361	**Lake Erie College** 391 W Washington St	Painesville	OH	44077-3309
216 489-0800	**Malone College** 515 25th St NW	Canton	OH	44709-3897
614 373-4643	**Marietta College**	Marietta	OH	45750-0000
513 529-1809	**Miami University (System)** 500 E High St	Oxford	OH	45056-1618
	Miami University			
513 863-8833	*Hamilton Campus* 1601 Peck Blvd	Hamilton	OH	45011-3399
513 424-4444	*Middletown Campus* 4200 E University Blvd	Middletown	OH	45042-3497
513 529-1809	*Oxford Campus* 500 E High St	Oxford	OH	45056-1618
216 821-5320	**Mount Union College** 1972 Clark Ave	Alliance	OH	44601-3993
614 397-1244	**Mount Vernon Nazarene College** 800 Martinsburg Rd	Mount Vernon	OH	43050-9500
614 826-8211	**Muskingum College** Montgomery	New Concord	OH	43762-0000
216 381-1680	**Notre Dame College of Ohio** 4545 College Rd	South Euclid	OH	44121-4293
216 775-8121	**Oberlin College** 173 W Lorain St	Oberlin	OH	44074-1023
614 253-2741	**Ohio Dominican College** 1216 Sunbury Rd	Columbus	OH	43219-2099
419 772-2000	**Ohio Northern University** 525 S Main St	Ada	OH	45810-1599
614 292-8500	**Ohio State University** 1800 Cannon Dr	Columbus	OH	43210-1249
419 221-1641	*Lima Campus* 4240 Campus Dr	Lima	OH	45804-3576
419 755-4011	*Mansfield Campus* 1680 University Dr	Mansfield	OH	44906-1547
614 389-2361	*Marion Campus* 1465 Mt Vernon Ave	Marion	OH	43302-5695
614 366-3321	*Newark Campus* University Dr	Newark	OH	43055-1797
614 593-1000	**Ohio University**	Athens	OH	45701-0000
614 695-1720	*Belmont Campus* 45425 National Rd W	Saint Clairsville	OH	43950-9724
614 774-7200	*Chillicothe Campus* 571 W 5th St	Chillicothe	OH	45601-2299
614 533-4600	*Ironton Campus* 1804 Liberty Ave	Ironton	OH	45638-0000
614 654-6711	*Lancaster Campus* 1570 Granville Pike	Lancaster	OH	43130-1097
614 453-0762	*Zanesville Campus* 1425 Newark Rd	Zanesville	OH	43701-2695
614 369-4431	**Ohio Wesleyan University** University Hall	Delaware	OH	43015-0000
614 890-3000	**Otterbein College** 100 W Home St	Westerville	OH	43081-1495
614 885-5585	**Pontifical College Josephinum** 7625 N High St	West Worthington	OH	43235-1444
216 943-5300	**Rabbinical College of Telshe** 28400 Euclid Ave	Wickliffe	OH	44092-2523
614 354-3205	**Shawnee State University** 940 2nd St	Portsmouth	OH	45662-9927
419 447-6442	**Tiffin University** 155 Miami St	Tiffin	OH	44883-2161
513 861-6400	**Union Institute** 440 E McMillan St	Cincinnati	OH	45206-1947
216 972-7111	**University of Akron** 302 E Buchtel Ave	Akron	OH	44325-0001
513 475-8000	**University of Cincinnati** 2624 Clifton Ave	Cincinnati	OH	45221-0001
513 229-1000	**University of Dayton** 300 College Park Rd	Dayton	OH	45469-0001
419 422-8313	**University of Findlay** 1000 N Main St	Findlay	OH	45840-3695
614 245-5353	**University of Rio Grande** 218 N College Ave	Rio Grande	OH	45674-9999
419 537-2072	**University of Toledo** 2801 W Bancroft St	Toledo	OH	43606-3390
513 652-1301	**Urbana University** 575 College Way	Urbana	OH	43078-2091
216 449-4200	**Ursuline College** 2550 Lander Rd	Cleveland	OH	44124-4399
216 499-7090	**Walsh College** 2020 Easton St NW	Canton	OH	44720-3396
513 376-2911	**Wilberforce University** 1055 N Bickett Rd	Wilberforce	OH	45384-9999
513 382-6661	**Wilmington College of Ohio** 251 Ludovic St	Wilmington	OH	45177-2499
513 327-6231	**Wittenberg University** PO Box 720	Springfield	OH	45501-0720
513 873-3333	**Wright State University** 3640 Colonel Glenn Hwy	Dayton	OH	45435-0001
513 745-3000	**Xavier University** 3800 Victory Pkwy	Cincinnati	OH	45207-1088
216 742-3000	**Youngstown State University**	Youngstown	OH	44555-0001

OKLAHOMA

918 333-6151	**Bartlesville Wesleyan College** 2201 Silver Lake Rd	Bartlesville	OK	74006-6299
405 581-2255	**Cameron University** 2800 W Gore Blvd	Lawton	OK	73505-6377
405 341-2980	**Central State University** 100 N University Dr	Edmond	OK	73034-5209
405 332-8000	**East Central University**	Ada	OK	74820-0000
405 794-6661	**Hillsdale Free Will Baptist College** PO Box 7208	Moore	OK	73153-1208
405 466-2231	**Langston University**	Langston	OK	73050-9999
405 691-3800	**Mid-America Bible College** 3500 SW 119th St	Oklahoma City	OK	73170-9704
918 456-5511	**Northeastern State University**	Tahlequah	OK	74464-0000
405 327-1700	**Northwestern Oklahoma State University** Oklahoma Blvd	Alva	OK	73717-0000
405 275-2850	**Oklahoma Baptist University** 500 W University St	Shawnee	OK	74801-2590
405 425-5000	**Oklahoma Christian University of Science & Art** 2501 W Memorial Rd	Oklahoma City	OK	73134-8002
405 521-5000	**Oklahoma City University** 2501 N Blackwelder Ave	Oklahoma City	OK	73106-1498
405 658-5446	**Oklahoma Missionary Baptist College** PO Box 71	Marlow	OK	73055-0071
405 349-2611	**Oklahoma Panhandle State University** PO Box 430	Goodwell	OK	73939-0430
405 744-5000	**Oklahoma State University**	Stillwater	OK	74078-0001
918 495-6161	**Oral Roberts University** 7777 S Lewis Ave	Tulsa	OK	74171-0001
405 237-4433	**Phillips University** 102 S University Ave	Enid	OK	73701-6439
405 924-0121	**Southeastern Oklahoma State University** Stn A	Durant	OK	74701-0000
405 789-6400	**Southern Nazarene University** 6729 NW 39th Expy	Bethany	OK	73008-2694
405 789-7661	**Southwestern College of Christian Ministry** PO Box 340	Bethany	OK	73008-0340
405 772-6611	**Southwestern Oklahoma State University** 100 Campus Dr	Weatherford	OK	73096-3001
405 325-0311	**University of Oklahoma** 660 Parrington Oval	Norman	OK	73019-0001
405 271-4000	*Oklahoma City Campus* 1100 N Lindsay Ave	Oklahoma City	OK	73190-0001
405 224-3140	**University of Sciences & Arts of Oklahoma** 2000 S 18th St	Chickasha	OK	73018-0000
918 592-6000	**University of Tulsa** 600 S College Ave	Tulsa	OK	74104-3189

OREGON

503 255-7060	**Columbia Christian College** 9101 E Burnside St	Portland	OR	97216-1599
503 288-9371	**Concordia College** 2811 NE Holman St	Portland	OR	97211-6099
503 963-2171	**Eastern Oregon State College** 1410 L Ave	La Grande	OR	97850-2899
503 485-1780	**Eugene Bible College** 2155 Bailey Hill Rd	Eugene	OR	97405-1194
503 538-8383	**George Fox College** 414 N Meridian St	Newberg	OR	97132-2625
503 244-6161	**Lewis & Clark College** 615 SW Palatine Hill Rd	Portland	OR	97219-7898
503 472-4121	**Linfield College** 900 S Baker St	McMinnville	OR	97128-6894
503 224-5828	**Marylhurst College** US Hwy 43	Marylhurst	OR	97036-9999
503 845-3951	**Mount Angel Seminary**	Saint Benedict	OR	97373-9999
503 255-0332	**Multnomah School of the Bible** 8435 NE Glisan St	Portland	OR	97220-5898
503 343-1641	**Northwest Christian College** 828 E 11th Ave	Eugene	OR	97401-3727
503 494-8311	**Oregon Health Sciences University** 3181 SW Sam Jackson Park Rd	Portland	OR	97201-3098
503 885-1000	**Oregon Institute of Technology** 3201 Campus Dr	Klamath Falls	OR	97601-8801
503 346-5711	**Oregon State System of Higher Education** PO Box 3175	Eugene	OR	97403-0175
503 737-0123	**Oregon State University**	Corvallis	OR	97331-0000
503 226-4391	**Pacific Northwest College of Art** 1219 SW Park Ave	Portland	OR	97205-2430
503 357-6151	**Pacific University** 2043 College Way	Forest Grove	OR	97116-1797
503 725-3000	**Portland State University** 724 SW Harrison St	Portland	OR	97201-3295
503 771-1112	**Reed College** 3203 SE Woodstock Blvd	Portland	OR	97202-8199
503 482-3311	**Southern Oregon State College** 1250 Siskiyou Blvd	Ashland	OR	97520-2268
503 346-3111	**University of Oregon** 1020 University St	Eugene	OR	97403-0000
503 283-7911	**University of Portland** 5000 N Willamette Blvd	Portland	OR	97203-5798
503 775-4366	**Warner Pacific College** 2219 SE 68th Ave	Portland	OR	97215-4099
503 581-8600	**Western Baptist College** 5000 Deer Park Dr SE	Salem	OR	97301-9392
503 838-8000	**Western Oregon State College** 345 Monmouth Ave N	Monmouth	OR	97361-1394
503 370-6300	**Willamette University** 900 State St	Salem	OR	97301-3930

PENNSYLVANIA

215 947-4200	**Academy of the New Church College** 2815 Huntingdon Pike	Bryn Athyn	PA	19009-9999
215 921-2381	**Albright College** 13th & Exeter St	Reading	PA	19612-0000
814 332-3100	**Allegheny College** 520 N Main St	Meadville	PA	16335-3902
215 282-1100	**Allentown College of Saint Francis DeSales** Station Ave	Center Valley	PA	18034-0000
215 777-5411	**Alvernia College** 400 Saint Bernadine St	Reading	PA	19607-1799
717 587-1172	**Baptist Bible College of Pennsylvania** 538 Venard Rd	Clarks Summit	PA	18411-1297
215 572-2900	**Beaver College** Easton & Church Rds	Glenside	PA	19038-0000
717 389-4316	**Bloomsburg University of Pennsylvania**	Bloomsburg	PA	17815-1301
215 526-5000	**Bryn Mawr College**	Bryn Mawr	PA	19010-0000
717 523-1271	**Bucknell University**	Lewisburg	PA	17837-0000
215 971-8100	**Cabrini College** 610 King of Prussia Rd	Radnor	PA	19087-3698
412 938-4000	**California University of Pennsylvania** 3rd St	California	PA	15419-0000
412 578-6000	**Carlow College** 3333 5th Ave	Pittsburgh	PA	15213-3165
412 268-2000	**Carnegie Mellon University** 5000 Forbes Ave	Pittsburgh	PA	15213-3890
215 437-4471	**Cedar Crest College** 100 College Dr	Allentown	PA	18104-6196
412 365-1100	**Chatham College** Woodland Rd	Pittsburgh	PA	15232-2826
215 248-7000	**Chestnut Hill College** Northwestern & Germantown Aves	Philadelphia	PA	19118-0000
215 399-2299	**Cheyney University of Pennsylvania** Cheyney & Creek Rds	Cheyney	PA	19319-0000
814 539-8086	**Christ the Saviour Seminary** 225 Chandler Ave	Johnstown	PA	15906-2103
814 226-2000	**Clarion University of Pennsylvania** 836 Wood St	Clarion	PA	16214-1240
717 675-2181	**College Misericordia** Lake St	Dallas	PA	18612-0000
215 665-0445	**Combs College of Music** 1811 Spring Garden St	Philadelphia	PA	19130-3916
215 893-5252	**Curtis Institute of Music** 1726 Locust St	Philadelphia	PA	19103-6187
215 345-1500	**Delaware Valley College of Science & Agriculture** Route 202	Doylestown	PA	18901-0000
717 245-1231	**Dickinson College** PO Box 1773	Carlisle	PA	17013-2896
215 895-2000	**Drexel University** 32nd & Chestnut Sts	Philadelphia	PA	19104-0000
412 434-6000	**Duquesne University** 600 Forbes Ave	Pittsburgh	PA	15282-0001
717 424-3542	**East Stroudsburg University**	East Stroudsburg	PA	18301-0000
215 341-5800	**Eastern College** 10 Fairview Dr	Saint Davids	PA	19087-3696
814 732-2000	**Edinboro University of Pennsylvania**	Edinboro	PA	16444-0001
717 367-1151	**Elizabethtown College** 1 Alpha Dr	Elizabethtown	PA	17022-2699
717 291-3911	**Franklin & Marshall College** PO Box 3003	Lancaster	PA	17604-3003
814 871-7000	**Gannon University** 109 W 6th St University Sq	Erie	PA	16541-0001
412 846-5100	**Geneva College** 3200 College Ave	Beaver Falls	PA	15010-3599
717 337-6000	**Gettysburg College**	Gettysburg	PA	17325-0000
215 635-7300	**Gratz College** Old York Rd & Melrose Ave	Melrose Park	PA	19126-1297
412 458-2000	**Grove City College**	Grove City	PA	16127-0000
215 646-7300	**Gwynedd Mercy College** Sumneytown Pike	Gwynedd Valley	PA	19437-9999
215 448-7000	**Hahnemann University** Broad & Vine Sts	Philadelphia	PA	19102-1192
215 896-1000	**Haverford College** 370 Lancaster Ave	Haverford	PA	19041-1392

Four-Year Colleges

215 637-7700	**Holy Family College** Grant & Frankford Aves	Philadelphia	PA	19114-2094
215 647-4400	**Immaculata College**	Immaculata	PA	19345-9999
412 357-2230	**Indiana University of Pennsylvania** 216B Pratt Hall	Indiana	PA	15705-0001
814 643-4310	**Juniata College** 1700 Moore St	Huntingdon	PA	16652-2119
717 826-5900	**King's College** 133 Darrow St	Wilkes-Barre	PA	18711-0000
215 683-4000	**Kutztown University**	Kutztown	PA	19530-0000
412 367-9300	**La Roche College** 9000 Babcock Blvd	Pittsburgh	PA	15237-5898
215 951-1000	**La Salle University** 20th & Olney Ave	Philadelphia	PA	19141-0000
215 250-5000	**Lafayette College** High St	Easton	PA	18042-0000
717 569-7071	**Lancaster Bible College** 901 Eden Rd	Lancaster	PA	17601-5036
717 867-6100	**Lebanon Valley College** 101 N College Ave	Annville	PA	17003-1400
215 758-3000	**Lehigh University**	Bethlehem	PA	18015-0000
215 932-8300	**Lincoln University**	Lincoln University	PA	19352-0000
717 893-2002	**Lock Haven University**	Lock Haven	PA	17745-0000
717 321-4000	**Lycoming College** 700 College Pl	Williamsport	PA	17701-5192
215 843-3600	**Manna Bible Institute** 700 E Church Ln	Philadelphia	PA	19144-1496
717 662-4000	**Mansfield University**	Mansfield	PA	16933-0000
717 348-6211	**Marywood College** 2300 Adams Ave	Scranton	PA	18509-1598
814 825-0238	**Mercyhurst College** 501 E 38th St	Erie	PA	16546-0001
717 766-2511	**Messiah College**	Grantham	PA	17027-9999
717 872-3011	**Millersville University of Pennsylvania**	Millersville	PA	17551-0000
215 568-4515	**Moore College of Art & Design** 20th & Race St	Philadelphia	PA	19103-0000
215 861-1300	**Moravian College** 1210 Main St	Bethlehem	PA	18018-6650
215 821-3100	**Muhlenberg College** 2400 W Chew St	Allentown	PA	18104-5586
215 459-0905	**Neumann College** Convent Rd	Aston	PA	19014-1297
814 865-4700	**Pennsylvania State University**	University Park	PA	16802-0001
215 285-4811	*Allentown Campus* 6090 Mohr Ln Academic Bldg	Fogelsville	PA	18051-0000
814 863-0327	*Commonwealth Educational System* 111 Old Main	University Park	PA	16802-0001
717 963-4757	*Worthington-Scranton Campus* 120 Ridge View Dr	Dunmore	PA	18512-0000
215 752-5800	**Philadelphia College of Bible** 200 Manor Ave	Langhorne	PA	19047-2990
215 596-8800	**Philadelphia College of Pharmacy & Science** 43rd St & Woodland Ave	Philadelphia	PA	19104-0000
215 951-2700	**Philadelphia College of Textiles & Science** 4201 Henry Ave	Philadelphia	PA	19144-5409
412 391-4100	**Point Park College** 201 Wood St	Pittsburgh	PA	15222-1983
412 262-8200	**Robert Morris College** Narrows Run Rd	Coraopolis	PA	15108-1189
215 527-0200	**Rosemont College** Montgomery & Wendover Aves	Rosemont	PA	19010-1699
215 667-3394	**Saint Charles Borromeo Seminary** 1000 E Wynnwood Rd	Overbrook	PA	19096-3099
814 472-7000	**Saint Francis College** College Hts	Loretto	PA	15940-9714
215 879-7300	**Saint Joseph's University** 5600 City Ave	Philadelphia	PA	19131-1376
412 539-9761	**Saint Vincent College** 701 Fraser Purchase Rd	Latrobe	PA	15650-2690
412 834-2200	**Seton Hill College** Seton Hill Dr	Greensburg	PA	15601-1599
717 532-9121	**Shippensburg University**	Shippensburg	PA	17257-0000
412 738-0512	**Slippery Rock University**	Slippery Rock	PA	16057-0000
215 248-7900	**Spring Garden College** 7500 Germantown Ave	Philadelphia	PA	19119-1651
717 374-0101	**Susquehanna University** University Ave	Selinsgrove	PA	17870-0000
215 328-8000	**Swarthmore College** Chester Rd & College Ave	Swarthmore	PA	19081-0000
215 787-7000	**Temple University** Broad & Montgomery Ave	Philadelphia	PA	19122-0000
412 588-7700	**Thiel College** 75 College Ave	Greenville	PA	16125-2181
215 955-6000	**Thomas Jefferson University** 111 S 11th St	Philadelphia	PA	19107-0000
717 787-0866	**University Center at Harrisburg** 2986 N 2nd St	Harrisburg	PA	17110-1200
215 898-5000	**University of Pennsylvania** 3451 Walnut St Franklin Bldg Rm 221	Philadelphia	PA	19104-6205
412 624-4141	**University of Pittsburgh** 4200 5th Ave	Pittsburgh	PA	15260-0001
814 362-3801	*Bradford Campus* 300 Campus Dr	Bradford	PA	16701-2898
412 837-7040	*Greensburg Campus* 1150 Mt Pleasant Rd	Greensburg	PA	15601-5898
814 266-9661	*Johnstown Campus*	Johnstown	PA	15904-2990
717 961-7400	**University of Scranton** Linden & Monroe Aves	Scranton	PA	18510-2192
215 875-2200	**University of the Arts** 250 S Broad St	Philadelphia	PA	19102-5087
215 875-4800	**University of the Visual Arts** 320 S Broad St	Philadelphia	PA	19102-4994
215 489-4111	**Ursinus College** Main St	Collegeville	PA	19426-0000
215 935-0450	**Valley Forge Christian College** Charlestown Rd	Phoenixville	PA	19460-2399
814 838-1966	**Villa Maria College** 2551 W 8th St	Erie	PA	16505-4494
215 645-4500	**Villanova University** Lancaster Ave	Villanova	PA	19085-1699
412 222-4400	**Washington & Jefferson College** 45 S Lincoln St	Washington	PA	15301-4801
412 627-8191	**Waynesburg College** 51 W College St	Waynesburg	PA	15370-1258
215 436-1000	**West Chester University**	West Chester	PA	19383-0001
412 946-8761	**Westminster College** S Market St	New Wilmington	PA	16172-0001
215 499-4000	**Widener University** 14th & Chestnut St	Chester	PA	19013-5793
717 824-4651	**Wilkes University** PO Box 111	Wilkes-Barre	PA	18766-0000
717 264-4141	**Wilson College** 1015 Philadelphia Ave	Chambersburg	PA	17201-1285
717 846-7788	**York College of Pennsylvania** Country Club Rd	York	PA	17403-0000

RHODE ISLAND

401 863-1000	**Brown University**	Providence	RI	02912-0001
401 232-6000	**Bryant College** 450 Douglas Pike	Smithfield	RI	02917-1284
401 456-1000	**Johnson & Wales University** 8 Abbott Park Pl	Providence	RI	02903-3775
401 865-1000	**Providence College** River Ave	Providence	RI	02918-0001
401 456-8000	**Rhode Island College** 600 Mt Pleasant Ave	Providence	RI	02908-1924
401 331-3511	**Rhode Island School of Design** 2 College St	Providence	RI	02903-2707
401 253-1040	**Roger Williams College** 1 Old Ferry Rd	Bristol	RI	02809-2921
401 847-6650	**Salve Regina College** 100 Ochre Point Ave	Newport	RI	02840-4192
401 792-1000	**University of Rhode Island**	Kingston	RI	02881-0000

SOUTH CAROLINA

803 254-9735	**Allen University** 1530 Harden St	Columbia	SC	29204-1085
803 797-4011	**Baptist College at Charleston** 9200 University Blvd	Charleston	SC	29418-9121
803 256-4220	**Benedict College** 1600 Harden St	Columbia	SC	29204-1086
803 242-5100	**Bob Jones University** 1700 Wade Hampton Blvd	Greenville	SC	29614-0001
803 639-2453	**Central Wesleyan College** 1 Wesleyan Dr	Central	SC	29630-0000
803 792-5000	**Citadel The** Moultrie St	Charleston	SC	29409-0001
803 534-2710	**Claflin College** 400 College St NE	Orangeburg	SC	29115-4498
803 656-3311	**Clemson University**	Clemson	SC	29634-0001
803 383-8000	**Coker College** 300 E College Ave	Hartsville	SC	29550-3797
803 792-5507	**College of Charleston** 66 George St	Charleston	SC	29424-0001
803 754-4100	**Columbia Bible College & Seminary** PO Box 3122	Columbia	SC	29230-3122
803 786-3012	**Columbia College** 1301 Columbia College Dr	Columbia	SC	29203-5998
803 585-6421	**Converse College** 580 E Main St	Spartanburg	SC	29302-0006
803 379-2131	**Erskine College** PO Box 338	Due West	SC	29639-0338
803 661-1362	**Francis Marion College** 301 N & Marion Hwy	Florence	SC	29501-0000
803 294-2000	**Furman University** Poinsett Hwy	Greenville	SC	29613-0001
803 665-4654	**Gloryland Bible College** PO Box 3966	Florence	SC	29502-3966
803 229-8300	**Lander College** 320 Stanley Ave	Greenwood	SC	29649-2099
803 489-7151	**Limestone College** 1115 College Dr	Gaffney	SC	29340-3798
803 792-2300	**Medical University of South Carolina** 171 Ashley Ave	Charleston	SC	29425-0001
803 775-9371	**Morris College** N Main St	Sumter	SC	29150-0000
803 276-5010	**Newberry College** 2100 College St	Newberry	SC	29108-2197
803 833-2820	**Presbyterian College** 503 S Broad St	Clinton	SC	29325-2998
803 536-7000	**South Carolina State College** 300 College Ave	Orangeburg	SC	29117-0001
803 777-7000	**University of South Carolina**	Columbia	SC	29208-0001
803 648-6851	*Aiken Campus* 171 University Pkwy	Aiken	SC	29801-6399
803 524-7112	*Beaufort Campus* 800 Carteret St	Beaufort	SC	29902-4602
803 347-3161	*Coastal Carolina College* PO Box 1954	Conway	SC	29526-1954
803 599-2000	*Spartanburg Campus* 800 University Way	Spartanburg	SC	29303-9397
803 793-3351	**Voorhees College** Voorhees Rd	Denmark	SC	29042-0000
803 323-2211	**Winthrop College** 701 Oakland Ave	Rock Hill	SC	29733-0001
803 585-4821	**Wofford College** 429 N Church St	Spartanburg	SC	29303-3663

SOUTH DAKOTA

605 336-0770	**Augustana College** 29th & S Summit Ave	Sioux Falls	SD	57197-0001
605 642-6011	**Black Hills State University** 1200 University St	Spearfish	SD	57799-0001
605 256-5139	**Dakota State College** 820 N Washington Ave	Madison	SD	57042-1799
605 995-2600	**Dakota Wesleyan University** 1200 W University Ave	Mitchell	SD	57301-4398
605 352-8721	**Huron University** 333 9th St SW	Huron	SD	57350-2798
605 668-1011	**Mount Marty College** 1105 W 8th St	Yankton	SD	57078-3724
605 394-4800	**National College** 321 Kansas City St	Rapid City	SD	57701-3692
605 334-5430	*Sioux Falls Branch* 3201 S Kiwanis	Sioux Falls	SD	57105-4293
605 622-3011	**Northern State University** 12th Ave & J St S	Aberdeen	SD	57401-0000
605 747-2263	**Sinte Gleska College** Box 490	Rosebud	SD	57570-0490
605 331-5000	**Sioux Falls College** 1501 S Prairie Ave	Sioux Falls	SD	57105-1699
605 394-2511	**South Dakota School of Mines & Technology** 501 E Saint Joseph St	Rapid City	SD	57701-3901
605 688-4151	**South Dakota State University**	Brookings	SD	57007-0001
605 677-5011	**University of South Dakota** 414 E Clark St	Vermillion	SD	57069-2390

TENNESSEE

615 262-3433	**American Baptist College of American Baptist Theology** 1800 White's Creek Pike	Nashville	TN	37207-4994
615 648-7011	**Austin Peay State University** 601 College St	Clarksville	TN	37044-0001
615 383-7001	**Belmont College** 1900 Belmont Blvd	Nashville	TN	37212-3757
901 352-5321	**Bethel College** 212 Cherry St	McKenzie	TN	38201-0000
615 775-2041	**Bryan College** Bryan Hill St Box 7000	Dayton	TN	37321-0000
615 475-9061	**Carson-Newman College** S Russell Ave	Jefferson City	TN	37760-0000
901 722-0200	**Christian Brothers University** 650 East Pkwy S	Memphis	TN	38104-5581
901 367-9800	**Crichton College** PO Box 757830	Memphis	TN	38175-7830
615 444-2562	**Cumberland University** 220 S Greenwood St	Lebanon	TN	37087-3554
615 269-1000	**David Lipscomb University** 3901 Granny White Pike	Nashville	TN	37204-3951
615 929-4112	**East Tennessee State University** Boundry Rd	Johnson City	TN	37614-0000
615 329-8500	**Fisk University** 1000 17th Ave N	Nashville	TN	37208-3045
615 383-1340	**Free Will Baptist Bible College** 3606 West End Ave	Nashville	TN	37205-2498
901 989-6000	**Freed-Hardeman College** 158 E Main St	Henderson	TN	38340-2398
615 968-4201	**Graham Bible College** 2690 Volunteer Pkwy	Bristol	TN	37620-6924
615 573-4517	**Johnson Bible College** 7900 Johnson Dr	Knoxville	TN	37998-0001
615 968-1187	**King College** 1350 King College Rd	Bristol	TN	37620-2632
615 524-6500	**Knoxville College** 901 College St NW	Knoxville	TN	37921-4799
901 425-2500	**Lambuth College** 705 Lambuth Blvd	Jackson	TN	38301-5296
901 424-4600	**Lane College** 545 Lane Ave	Jackson	TN	38301-4598
615 472-2111	**Lee College** 1120 N Ocoee St	Cleveland	TN	37311-4475
901 774-9090	**LeMoyne-Owen College** 807 Walker Ave	Memphis	TN	38126-6595
615 869-3611	**Lincoln Memorial University** Cumberland Pkwy	Harrogate	TN	37752-0000
615 982-6412	**Maryville College**	Maryville	TN	37801-0000
901 726-4085	**Memphis College of Art** 1930 Overton Park Ave	Memphis	TN	38112-5498
901 678-2040	**Memphis State University**	Memphis	TN	38152-0001
615 898-2300	**Middle Tennessee State University**	Murfreesboro	TN	37132-0001
615 929-0116	**Milligan College**	Milligan College	TN	37682-0000
901 726-3000	**Rhodes College** 2000 North Pkwy	Memphis	TN	38112-0000
615 238-2111	**Southern College of Seventh-Day Adventists** 4881 Taylor Cir	Collegedale	TN	37315-9999
615 320-3131	**Tennessee State University** 3500 John A Merritt Blvd	Nashville	TN	37209-1561
615 320-3131	**Tennessee State University & Community College System** 3500 John A Merritt Blvd	Nashville	TN	37209-1561
615 372-3101	**Tennessee Technological University** Dixie Ave	Cookeville	TN	38501-0000
615 493-4100	**Tennessee Temple University** 1815 Union Ave	Chattanooga	TN	37404-3587
615 745-7504	**Tennessee Wesleyan College** PO Box 40	Athens	TN	37303-0000
615 248-1200	**Trevecca Nazarene College** 333 Murfreesboro Rd	Nashville	TN	37210-2877
901 785-6390	**Tri-State Baptist College** 4655 Apple Cove	Memphis	TN	38109-5701
615 638-1111	**Tusculum College** Tusculum Stn	Greeneville	TN	37743-0000
901 668-1818	**Union University** 2447 Hwy-45 Bypass N	Jackson	TN	38305-0000
615 974-1000	**University of Tennessee** Student Service Bldg Rm 305	Knoxville	TN	37996-0001
901 587-7000	*Martin Campus* University St	Martin	TN	38238-0001
901 528-5000	*Memphis Campus* 800 Madison Ave	Memphis	TN	38163-0001
615 598-5931	**University of the South** Administration Bldg	Sewanee	TN	37375-0000
615 322-7311	**Vanderbilt University** West End Ave	Nashville	TN	37232-0001

TEXAS

915 674-2000	**Abilene Christian University** 1600 Campus Ct	Abilene	TX	79699-0001
915 942-2041	**Angelo State University** 2601 West Ave N	San Angelo	TX	76909-0001
817 461-8741	**Arlington Baptist College** 3001 W Division	Arlington	TX	76012-3497
903 813-2000	**Austin College** 900 N Grand Ave	Sherman	TX	75090-4440
817 755-1011	**Baylor University** 500 Speight St	Waco	TX	76798-0001
512 452-7661	**Concordia Lutheran College** 3400 N IH-35	Austin	TX	78705-2799
214 331-8311	**Dallas Baptist University** 7777 W Kiest Blvd	Dallas	TX	75211-9800
214 241-3371	**Dallas Christian College** 2700 Christian Pkwy	Dallas	TX	75234-7299
214 258-6767	**DeVry Institute of Technology** 4250 N Belt Line Rd	Irving	TX	75038-4299
903 935-7963	**East Texas Baptist University** 1209 N Grove St	Marshall	TX	75670-1498
903 886-5014	**East Texas State University** East Texas Stn	Commerce	TX	75428-9998
903 838-6514	*Texarkana Campus* 2600 N Robison Rd	Texarkana	TX	75501-3098
915 670-1000	**Hardin-Simmons University** 2200 Hickory St	Abilene	TX	79698-0001
713 774-7661	**Houston Baptist University** 7502 Fondren Rd	Houston	TX	77074-3298
915 646-2502	**Howard Payne University** 1000 Fisk Ave	Brownwood	TX	76801-2715
512 476-7421	**Huston-Tillotson College** 1820 E 8th St	Austin	TX	78702-2762
512 828-1261	**Incarnate Word College** 4301 Broadway	San Antonio	TX	78209-6398
214 337-3144	**Independent Baptist College** 3940 Blue Ridge	Dallas	TX	78233-0000
512 477-5701	**Institute for Christian Studies** 1909 University Ave	Austin	TX	78705-5610
512 434-5541	**International Bible College** 2369 Benrus Blvd	San Antonio	TX	78228-2353
903 769-2174	**Jarvis Christian College** Hwy 80-E	Hawkins	TX	75765-0000
409 880-7011	**Lamar University** 4400 M L King Pkwy	Beaumont	TX	77710-0000
903 753-0231	**LeTourneau University** 2100 S Mobberly Ave	Longview	TX	75602-3524
806 792-3221	**Lubbock Christian University** 5601 19th St	Lubbock	TX	79407-2099
915 691-6200	**McMurry University** 14th & Sayles St	Abilene	TX	79697-0001
817 692-6611	**Midwestern State University** 3400 Taft Blvd	Wichita Falls	TX	76308-2036
214 291-1541	**Northwood Institute Texas Campus** 1114 W FM 1382	Cedar Hill	TX	75104-1204
512 434-6711	**Our Lady of the Lake University of San Antonio** 411 SW 24th St	San Antonio	TX	78207-4666
512 381-2011	**Pan American University** 1201 W University Dr	Edinburg	TX	78539-2999
817 753-6415	**Paul Quinn College** 1020 Elm St	Waco	TX	76704-2697
409 857-3311	**Prairie View A & M University** US Hwy 290 & FM 1098	Prairie View	TX	77446-9999
713 527-8101	**Rice University** PO Box 1892	Houston	TX	77251-1892
512 448-8500	**Saint Edward's University** 3001 S Congress Ave	Austin	TX	78704-6489
512 436-3011	**Saint Mary's University** 1 Camino Santa Maria St	San Antonio	TX	78228-8500
409 294-1111	**Sam Houston State University** 1700 Sam Houston Ave	Huntsville	TX	77341-0000
512 896-5411	**Schreiner College** 2100 Memorial Blvd	Kerrville	TX	78028-5697
214 692-2000	**Southern Methodist University** 6425 Boaz Ln	Dallas	TX	75275-0001
512 245-2111	**Southwest Texas State University**	San Marcos	TX	78666-0000
817 645-3921	**Southwestern Adventist College** PO Box 567	Keene	TX	76059-0000
512 863-6511	**Southwestern University** E University & Maple Sts	Georgetown	TX	78626-0000
409 568-2011	**Stephen F Austin State University** PO Box 13050	Nacogdoches	TX	75962-0001

Colleges are listed alphabetically within each state. Graduate Schools are listed alphabetically by state, within each area of study.

915 837-8011	**Sul Ross State University** E Hwy 90	Alpine	TX	79832-0001
817 968-9000	**Tarleton State University** 201 Felix St	Stephenville	TX	76401-0000
512 595-2111	**Texas A & I University** Campus Box 105	Kingsville	TX	78363-0000
409 845-3211	**Texas A & M University**	College Station	TX	77843-0000
409 740-4400	*Galveston Campus* PO Box 1675	Galveston	TX	77553-1675
817 921-7000	**Texas Christian University** 2800 S University Dr	Fort Worth	TX	76129-0001
903 593-8311	**Texas College** 2404 N Grand Ave	Tyler	TX	75702-1999
512 379-4161	**Texas Lutheran College** 1000 W Court St	Seguin	TX	78155-5999
713 527-7011	**Texas Southern University** 3100 Cleburne St	Houston	TX	77004-4598
806 742-2011	**Texas Tech University** Broadway & University Ave	Lubbock	TX	79409-0000
817 531-4444	**Texas Wesleyan University** 1201 Wesleyan St	Fort Worth	TX	76105-1536
817 898-3000	**Texas Woman's University** PO Box 22909	Denton	TX	76204-0909
512 736-7011	**Trinity University** 715 Stadium Dr	San Antonio	TX	78212-7200
817 478-7672	**Trinity Valley Baptist Seminary** 915 E Mansfield Hwy	Kennedale	TX	76060-3225
214 721-5000	**University of Dallas** 1845 E Northgate Dr	Irving	TX	75062-9991
713 749-1011	**University of Houston** 4800 Calhoun Rd University Pk	Houston	TX	77004-8399
713 488-7170	*Clear Lake Campus* 2700 Bay Area Blvd	Houston	TX	77058-1098
512 576-3151	*Victoria Campus* 2302-C E Red River St	Victoria	TX	77901-4449
817 939-8642	**University of Mary Hardin-Baylor** College St	Belton	TX	76513-2599
817 565-2000	**University of North Texas** PO Box 13797	Denton	TX	76203-6797
713 522-7911	**University of Saint Thomas** 3812 Montrose Blvd	Houston	TX	77006-4694
	University of Texas			
817 273-2011	*Arlington Campus* 800 S Cooper St	Arlington	TX	76019-0001
512 471-3434	*Austin Campus* PO Box T	Austin	TX	78713-8920
214 690-2111	*Dallas Campus* PO Box 830688	Richardson	TX	75083-0688
915 747-5000	*El Paso Campus* 500 W University Ave	El Paso	TX	79968-0001
713 792-4975	*Health Science Center Houston* PO Box 20036	Houston	TX	77225-0036
512 567-2621	*Health Science Center San Antonio* 7703 Floyd Curl Dr	San Antonio	TX	78284-0001
713 792-2121	*Houston Campus* 1515 Holcombe Blvd	Houston	TX	77030-3907
214 688-3404	*Medical Center of Dallas* 5323 Harry Hines Blvd	Dallas	TX	75235-7200
915 367-2011	**University of Texas of the Permian Basin** 4901 E University Blvd	Odessa	TX	79762-8192
	University of Texas			
512 982-0100	*Pan American* 1614 Ridgely Rd	Brownsville	TX	78520-4991
512 691-4011	*San Antonio Campus*	San Antonio	TX	78285-0001
903 566-7000	*Tyler Campus* 3900 University Blvd	Tyler	TX	75701-6699
806 296-5521	**Wayland Baptist University** 1900 W 7th St	Plainview	TX	79072-6998
806 656-2000	**West Texas State University** PO Box 999 West Texas State Stn	Canyon	TX	79016-0001
903 938-8341	**Wiley College** 711 Wiley Ave	Marshall	TX	75670-5199

UTAH

801 378-1211	**Brigham Young University** Administration Bldg	Provo	UT	84602-0000
801 586-7700	**Southern Utah State College** 351 W Center St	Cedar City	UT	84720-2498
801 581-7200	**University of Utah** 1340 E 200 South	Salt Lake City	UT	84112-0000
801 750-1000	**Utah State University**	Logan	UT	84322-0000
801 626-6000	**Weber State College** 3750 S Harrison Blvd	Ogden	UT	84408-0001
801 484-7651	**Westminster College of Salt Lake City** 1840 S 13th East	Salt Lake City	UT	84105-3697

VERMONT

802 442-5401	**Bennington College** Rt 67 A	Bennington	VT	05201-0000
802 862-9616	**Burlington College** 95 North Ave	Burlington	VT	05401-2998
802 468-5611	**Castleton State College** Seminary St	Castleton	VT	05735-0000
802 773-5900	**College of Saint Joseph in Vermont** 71 Clement Rd	Rutland	VT	05701-3899
802 454-8311	**Goddard College** 2 Pitkin Pl	Plainfield	VT	05667-0000
802 287-9313	**Green Mountain College** College St	Poultney	VT	05764-1199
802 635-2356	**Johnson State College** College Hill	Johnson	VT	05656-0000
802 626-9371	**Lyndon State College** Vail Hill	Lyndonville	VT	05851-0000
802 257-4333	**Marlboro College** College Rd	Marlboro	VT	05344-9999
802 388-3711	**Middlebury College** Old Chapel	Middlebury	VT	05753-0000
802 485-2000	**Norwich University** 65 S Main St	Northfield	VT	05663-1004
802 655-2000	**Saint Michael's College** Winooski Pk	Colchester	VT	05439-0001
802 257-7751	**School for International Training** Kipling Rd	Brattleboro	VT	05301-0000
802 442-5427	**Southern Vermont College** Monument Ave	Bennington	VT	05201-0000
802 658-0337	**Trinity College** 208 Colchester Ave	Burlington	VT	05401-1496
802 656-3480	**University of Vermont** 855 Prospect St	Burlington	VT	05405-0001
802 223-8750	**Vermont College of Norwich University** 32 College St	Montpelier	VT	05602-3201

VIRGINIA

804 791-5600	**Averett College** 420 W Main St	Danville	VA	24541-3692
703 326-3682	**Bluefield College** 3000 College Dr	Bluefield	VA	24605-1799
703 828-2501	**Bridgewater College** 402 E College St	Bridgewater	VA	22812-1599
703 636-2908	**Christendom College** 2101 Shenandoah Shores Rd	Front Royal	VA	22630-5149
804 594-7000	**Christopher Newport College** 50 Shoe Ln	Newport News	VA	23606-2998
703 328-0100	**Clinch Valley College of the University of Virginia** College Ave	Wise	VA	24293-0000
804 221-4000	**College of William & Mary**	Williamsburg	VA	23185-0000
703 433-2771	**Eastern Mennonite College** 1200 Park Rd	Harrisonburg	VA	22801-2462
703 944-3121	**Emory & Henry College** Hillman Hwy	Emory	VA	24327-9999
703 365-2121	**Ferrum College** Rt 40	Ferrum	VA	24088-0000
703 323-2000	**George Mason University** 4400 University Dr	Fairfax	VA	22030-4443
804 223-4381	**Hampden Sydney College** College Rd	Hampden Sydney	VA	23943-0000
804 727-5000	**Hampton University** E Queen St	Hampton	VA	23668-0000
703 362-6000	**Hollins College** 7916 Williamson Rd	Roanoke	VA	24020-4410
703 568-6211	**James Madison University**	Harrisonburg	VA	22807-0001
804 582-2000	**Liberty University** 3765 Candlers Mountain Rd	Lynchburg	VA	24502-2213
703 382-7100	**Life Bible College East** Rt 3 Box 12	Christiansburg	VA	24073-9407
804 395-2000	**Longwood College** 201 High St	Farmville	VA	23901-1899
804 522-8100	**Lynchburg College** 1501 Lakeside Dr	Lynchburg	VA	24501-3199
703 887-7000	**Mary Baldwin College**	Staunton	VA	24401-0000
703 899-4100	**Mary Washington College**	Fredericksburg	VA	22401-0000
703 522-5600	**Marymount University** 2807 N Glebe Rd	Arlington	VA	22207-4299
804 683-8600	**Norfolk State University** 2401 Corprew Ave	Norfolk	VA	23504-3989
804 683-3000	**Old Dominion University** Hampton Blvd	Norfolk	VA	23529-0001
703 831-5000	**Radford University** Norwood St & Rt 11	Radford	VA	24142-0000
804 798-8372	**Randolph-Macon College** Henry St	Ashland	VA	23005-0000
804 846-7392	**Randolph-Macon Woman's College** 2500 Rivermont Ave	Lynchburg	VA	24503-1526
703 375-2500	**Roanoke College** 221 College Ln	Salem	VA	24153-3794
804 848-3111	**Saint Paul's College** 406 Windsor Ave	Lawrenceville	VA	23868-1299
703 665-4500	**Shenandoah University** 1460 College Dr	Winchester	VA	22601-5195
703 892-5100	**Strayer College Arlington Branch** 3045 Columbia Pike	Arlington	VA	22204-0000
804 381-6100	**Sweet Briar College**	Sweet Briar	VA	24595-9999
804 420-5476	**Tabernacle Baptist Bible Institute** 717 N Whitehurst Landing Rd	Virginia Beach	VA	23464-2301
804 289-8000	**University of Richmond**	Richmond	VA	23173-7301
804 924-0311	**University of Virginia** Miller Hall McCormick Rd	Charlottesville	VA	22906-0000
804 367-1200	**Virginia Commonwealth University** 910 W Franklin St	Richmond	VA	23284-0001
703 669-6101	**Virginia Intermont College** 1013 Moore St	Bristol	VA	24201-4298
703 464-7000	**Virginia Military Institute**	Lexington	VA	24450-0000
703 961-6000	**Virginia Polytechnic Institute & State University**	Blacksburg	VA	24061-0001
804 524-5000	**Virginia State University**	Petersburg	VA	23803-2095
804 257-5866	**Virginia Union University** 1500 N Lombardy St	Richmond	VA	23220-1790
804 455-3200	**Virginia Wesleyan College** 1584 Wesleyan Dr	Norfolk	VA	23502-5599
703 463-8400	**Washington & Lee University**	Lexington	VA	24450-1799

WASHINGTON

206 441-5352	**Antioch University** 2607 2nd Ave	Seattle	WA	98121-1211
509 963-1111	**Central Washington University**	Ellensburg	WA	98926-0000
206 624-1688	**City University** 16661 Northrup Way	Bellevue	WA	98008-0000
206 822-3137	**Cogswell College North** 10626 NE 37th Cir	Kirkland	WA	98033-7921
206 323-1400	**Cornish College of the Arts** 710 E Roy St	Seattle	WA	98102-4696
509 359-6200	**Eastern Washington University**	Cheney	WA	99004-0000
206 866-6000	**Evergreen State College** 2700 Evergreen Pkwy NW	Olympia	WA	98505-0001
509 328-4220	**Gonzaga University** E 502 Boone Ave	Spokane	WA	99258-0001
206 728-6800	**Griffin College** 2025 2nd Ave	Seattle	WA	98121-2205
509 865-2244	**Heritage College** 3540 Fort Rd	Toppenish	WA	98948-0000
206 392-0400	**Lutheran Bible Institute of Seattle** 4221 228th Ave SE Suite 7	Issaquah	WA	98027-9299
206 822-8266	**Northwest College of the Assemblies of God** 5520 108th Ave NE	Kirkland	WA	98033-7523
206 531-6900	**Pacific Lutheran University**	Tacoma	WA	98447-0001
206 775-8686	**Puget Sound Christian College** 410 4th Ave N	Edmonds	WA	98020-3171
206 491-4700	**Saint Martin's College** 700 College St SE	Lacey	WA	98503-1297
206 784-1888	**Seattle Bible College** 2363 NW 80th St	Seattle	WA	98117-4399
206 281-2000	**Seattle Pacific University** 3307 3rd Ave W	Seattle	WA	98119-1997
206 296-6000	**Seattle University** Broadway & Madison	Seattle	WA	98122-0000
206 756-3100	**University of Puget Sound** 1500 N Warner St	Tacoma	WA	98416-0001
206 543-2100	**University of Washington** Administrative Offices AH-30	Seattle	WA	98195-0001
509 527-2615	**Walla Walla College** 204 S College Ave	College Place	WA	99324-1198
509 335-3564	**Washington State University**	Pullman	WA	99164-0001
206 676-3000	**Western Washington University** 516 High St	Bellingham	WA	98225-5946
509 527-5111	**Whitman College** 345 Boyer Ave	Walla Walla	WA	99362-2090
509 466-1000	**Whitworth College** Hawthorne Rd	Spokane	WA	99251-0001

WEST VIRGINIA

304 457-1700	**Alderson-Broaddus College** College Hill	Philippi	WV	26416-1051
304 877-6428	**Appalachian Bible College** PO Box ABC	Bradley	WV	25818-1353
304 829-7000	**Bethany College** Main St	Bethany	WV	26032-0000
304 327-4065	**Bluefield State College** 219 Rock St	Bluefield	WV	24701-2198
304 384-3115	**Concord College** Vermillion St	Athens	WV	24712-0000
304 636-1900	**Davis & Elkins College** 100 Sycamore St	Elkins	WV	26241-3996
304 367-4000	**Fairmont State College** 1201 Locust Ave	Fairmont	WV	26554-2491
304 462-7361	**Glenville State College** 200 High St	Glenville	WV	26351-1200
304 696-3170	**Marshall University** 400 Hal Greer Blvd	Huntington	WV	25755-0001
304 782-5011	**Salem Teikyo University** Main St	Salem	WV	26426-0000
304 876-2511	**Shepherd College** King St	Shepherdstown	WV	25443-0000
304 357-4800	**University of Charleston** 2300 MacCorkle Ave SE	Charleston	WV	25304-1099
304 336-5000	**West Liberty State College** Rt 88	West Liberty	WV	26074-9999
304 442-3071	**West Virginia Institute of Technology** Rt 61	Montgomery	WV	25136-0000
304 766-3000	**West Virginia State College** Rt 25	Institute	WV	25112-9999
304 293-0111	**West Virginia University**	Morgantown	WV	26506-0001
304 473-8000	**West Virginia Wesleyan College** College Ave	Buckhannon	WV	26201-0000
304 243-2000	**Wheeling Jesuit College** 316 Washington Ave	Wheeling	WV	26003-6295

WISCONSIN

414 382-6000	**Alverno College** 3401 S 39th St	Milwaukee	WI	53215-4093
414 433-3560	**Bellin College of Nursing** 929 Cass St	Green Bay	WI	54301-3510
608 365-3391	**Beloit College** 700 College St	Beloit	WI	53511-5595
414 352-5400	**Cardinal Stritch College** 6801 N Yates Rd	Milwaukee	WI	53217-3985
414 547-1211	**Carroll College** 100 N East Ave	Waukesha	WI	53186-5593
414 551-8500	**Carthage College** 2001 Alford Dr	Kenosha	WI	53140-1994
414 961-4202	**Columbia College** 2121 E Newport Ave	Milwaukee	WI	53211-2952
414 243-5700	**Concordia College** 12800 N Lake Shore Dr	Mequon	WI	53092-7699
608 257-4861	**Edgewood College** 855 Woodrow St	Madison	WI	53711-1997
715 834-3301	**Immanuel Lutheran College** 501 Grover Rd	Eau Claire	WI	54701-7199
414 565-2111	**Lakeland College** RR 4	Plymouth	WI	53073-9804
414 832-7000	**Lawrence University** 115 S Drew St	Appleton	WI	54911-5798
414 261-9300	**Maranatha Baptist Bible College Inc** 745 W Main St	Watertown	WI	53094-7638
414 923-7600	**Marian College of Fond du Lac** 45 S National Ave	Fond du Lac	WI	54935-4699
414 224-7700	**Marquette University** 1217 W Wisconsin Ave	Milwaukee	WI	53233-2290
414 276-7889	**Milwaukee Institute of Art & Design** 342 N Water St	Milwaukee	WI	53202-5700
414 277-7300	**Milwaukee School of Engineering** 1025 N Milwaukee St	Milwaukee	WI	53202-3182
414 258-4810	**Mount Mary College** 2900 N Menomonee River Pkwy	Milwaukee	WI	53222-4597
715 532-5511	**Mount Senario College** 1500 College Ave W	Ladysmith	WI	54848-2196
715 324-5245	**Northland Baptist Bible College** RR 1 Box 31	Dunbar	WI	54119-9801
715 682-4531	**Northland College** 1411 Ellis Ave	Ashland	WI	54806-3999
414 261-4352	**Northwestern College** 1300 Western Ave	Watertown	WI	53094-4899
414 748-8106	**Ripon College** PO Box 248	Ripon	WI	54971-0248
414 337-3140	**Saint Norbert College**	De Pere	WI	54115-2099
414 684-6691	**Silver Lake College** 2406 S Alverno Rd	Manitowoc	WI	54220-9319
608 262-6410	**University of Wisconsin (System)** 1220 Linden Dr	Madison	WI	53706-1557
	University of Wisconsin			
715 836-2637	*Eau Claire Campus* Garfield & Park Aves	Eau Claire	WI	54701-4800
414 465-2000	*Green Bay Campus* 2420 Nicolet Dr	Green Bay	WI	54311-7003
608 785-8000	*La Crosse Campus* 1725 State St	La Crosse	WI	54601-3767
608 262-1234	*Madison Campus* 750 University Ave	Madison	WI	53706-1411
414 229-1122	*Milwaukee Campus* Mellencamp Hall	Milwaukee	WI	53201-0000
414 424-1234	*Oshkosh Campus* 800 Algoma Blvd	Oshkosh	WI	54901-8611
414 553-2345	*Parkside Campus* PO Box 2000	Kenosha	WI	53141-2000
608 342-1491	*Platteville Campus* 1 University Plaza	Platteville	WI	53818-3024
715 425-3911	*River Falls Campus* 410 S 3rd St	River Falls	WI	54022-0000
715 346-0123	*Stevens Point Campus* 2100 Main St	Stevens Point	WI	54481-3871
715 232-1122	*Stout Campus*	Menomonie	WI	54751-0000
715 394-8101	*Superior Campus* 1800 Grand Ave	Superior	WI	54880-2898
414 472-1234	*Whitewater Campus* 800 W Main St	Whitewater	WI	53190-1705
608 791-0040	**Viterbo College** 815 9th St S	La Crosse	WI	54601-8802
414 774-8620	**Wisconsin Lutheran College** 8830 W Bluemound Rd	Milwaukee	WI	53226-4699

WYOMING

307 766-1121	**University of Wyoming** PO Box 3434 University Stn	Laramie	WY	82071-3434

Graduate and Professional Schools

Leading graduate programs offering advanced and professional degrees in selected disciplines are listed alphabetically by state within each area of study.

AGRICULTURE

205 844-2345	**Auburn University** Comer Hall Rm 107	Auburn	AL	36849-0000
602 621-3611	**University of Arizona** 303 Forbes Bldg	Tucson	AZ	85721-0001
415 642-3345	**University of California Berkeley** 207 Giannini Hall	Berkeley	CA	94720-0001
916 752-0107	**University of California Davis** 228 Mrak Hall	Davis	CA	95616-0000
303 491-6273	**Colorado State University** Shepardson Bldg Rm 121	Fort Collins	CO	80523-0001
203 486-4467	**University of Connecticut** PO Box U21	Storrs	CT	06269-0001
904 392-2251	**University of Florida** 1001 McCarty Hall	Gainesville	FL	32611-0000
404 542-2925	**University of Georgia** Boyd Graduate Studies Bldg	Athens	GA	30602-0000

808 956-7530	**University of Hawaii**	1910 East-West Rd	Honolulu	HI	96822-0000
217 333-0035	**University of Illinois**	801 S Wright St Coble Hall	Champaign	IL	61820-0000
317 494-4191	**Purdue University**	Krannert Bldg	West Lafayette	IN	47907-1924
515 294-4531	**Iowa State University**	207 Beardshear	Ames	IA	50011-0001
913 532-6147	**Kansas State University**	Waters Hall Rm 117	Manhattan	KS	66506-0001
606 257-1663	**University of Kentucky**		Lexington	KY	40546-0001
504 388-2311	**Louisiana State University**	124 Agriculture Administration Bldg	Baton Rouge	LA	70803-0001
207 581-3218	**University of Maine**	2 Winslow Hall	Orono	ME	04469-0001
301 454-3901	**University of Maryland**	Shriver Lab Rm 1130	College Park	MD	20742-0001
413 545-2490	**University of Massachusetts**	Draper Hall Rm 231	Amherst	MA	01003-0001
517 355-0234	**Michigan State University**	121 Agriculture Hall	East Lansing	MI	48824-0001
612 624-3009	**University of Minnesota**	1420 Eckles Ave Coffey Hall Rm 277	Saint Paul	MN	55108-0000
601 325-2110	**Mississippi State University**	130 Lloyd Ricks Bldg	Mississippi State	MS	39762-9999
314 882-8301	**University of Missouri**	2-64 Agriculture Bldg	Columbia	MO	65211-0001
402 472-2201	**University of Nebraska Lincoln**	103 Agriculture Hall	Lincoln	NE	68583-0001
607 255-2241	**Cornell University**	Roberts Hall Rm 260	Ithaca	NY	14853-0001
919 737-2871	**North Carolina State University**	104 Peele Hall	Raleigh	NC	27695-0001
614 292-6321	**Ohio State University**	2120 Fyffe Rd	Columbus	OH	43210-1010
405 744-6368	**Oklahoma State University**	202 Whitehurst	Stillwater	OK	74078-0001
503 737-2331	**Oregon State University**	Strand Ag Hall Rm 126	Corvallis	OR	97331-0000
814 865-2541	**Pennsylvania State University**	201 Agricultural Administration Bldg	University Park	PA	16802-0001
803 656-3013	**Clemson University**	102 Barr Hall Rm 102	Clemson	SC	29634-0001
615 974-7231	**University of Tennessee**	302 Morgan Hall	Knoxville	TN	37996-0001
409 645-4747	**Texas A & M University**		College Station	TX	77843-0000
806 742-2781	**Texas Tech University**	PO Box 4460	Lubbock	TX	79409-4460
801 750-2215	**Utah State University**	Agricultural Science Bldg	Logan	UT	84322-0000
703 231-6336	**Virginia Polytechnic Institute & State University**	Hutchinson Hall	Blacksburg	VA	24061-0000
509 335-4561	**Washington State University**	421 Hobart Hall	Pullman	WA	99164-0001
608 262-1251	**University of Wisconsin**	1450 Linden Dr	Madison	WI	53706-1522
307 766-4135	**University of Wyoming**	University Stn	Laramie	WY	82071-0000

ARCHITECTURE

602 965-3536	**Arizona State University**	University St & Forrest St	Tempe	AZ	85287-0001
415 642-4942	**University of California Berkeley**	232 Wurster Hall	Berkeley	CA	94720-0001
213 825-3791	**University of California Los Angeles**	405 Hilgard Ave Perloff Hall Rm 1317	Los Angeles	CA	90024-1467
904 392-4836	**University of Florida**	331 Architecture Bldg	Gainesville	FL	32611-0000
404 894-3880	**Georgia Institute of Technology**	247 4th St	Atlanta	GA	30332-0155
808 956-7225	**University of Hawaii**	2560 Campus Rd George Annex 2-3	Honolulu	HI	96822-0000
217 333-0460	**University of Illinois**	608 E Lorado Taft Dr	Champaign	IL	61829-0000
617 495-2591	**Harvard University**	48 Quincy St Gund Hall	Cambridge	MA	02138-0000
617 253-7791	**Massachusetts Institute of Technology**	77 Massachusetts Ave Rm 7-303	Cambridge	MA	02139-4307
313 764-1300	**University of Michigan**	2000 Bonisteel Blvd	Ann Arbor	MI	48109-0001
612 624-7866	**University of Minnesota**	89 Church St SE Rm 110	Minneapolis	MN	55455-0109
314 889-6200	**Washington University**	1 Brookings Dr	Saint Louis	MO	63130-0000
609 258-3741	**Princeton University**		Princeton	NJ	08544-0001
505 277-2903	**University of New Mexico**	2414 Central Ave SE	Albuquerque	NM	87131-0001
212 854-3414	**Columbia University**	Broadway & W 116th St Avery Hall Rm 400	New York	NY	10027-0000
518 276-6460	**Rensselaer Polytechnic Institute**	110 8th St	Troy	NY	12180-3590
614 292-5567	**Ohio State University**	190 W 17th Ave Brown Hall Rm 189	Columbus	OH	43210-0000
503 346-3656	**University of Oregon**	Lawrence Hall	Eugene	OR	97403-1206
412 268-2355	**Carnegie Mellon University**	Schenley Pk CFA 201	Pittsburgh	PA	15213-0000
215 898-5728	**University of Pennsylvania**	210 S 34th St Meyerson Hall Rm 110	Philadelphia	PA	19104-6311
713 527-4870	**Rice University**	6100 S Main St Anderson Hall Rm 110	Houston	TX	77005-0000
409 845-1015	**Texas A & M University**		College Station	TX	77843-0000
713 749-1188	**University of Houston**	4808 Calhoun St	Houston	TX	77204-4431
512 471-1922	**University of Texas**	Goldsmith Hall Rm 2.308	Austin	TX	78712-0000
804 924-3715	**University of Virginia**	Campbell Hall	Charlottesville	VA	22903-2443
703 231-5383	**Virginia Polytechnic Institute & State University**	202 Cowgill Hall	Blacksburg	VA	24061-0001
206 543-4180	**University of Washington**	JO-20	Seattle	WA	98195-0001
414 229-4014	**University of Wisconsin**	2033 E Hartford Ave	Milwaukee	WI	53211-3154

BIOCHEMISTRY

415 723-6161	**Stanford University**	B-400 Beckman Ctr	Stanford	CA	94305-5307
415 642-0944	**University of California Berkeley**	597 Life Sciences Addition	Berkeley	CA	94720-0000
916 752-3611	**University of California Davis**	149 Briggs Hall	Davis	CA	95616-0000
714 856-7067	**University of California Irvine**	Med Science Bldg 1 Rm D240	Irvine	CA	92717-0001
213 825-2762	**University of California Los Angeles**	401 Hilgard Ave Rm 33-257 CHS	Los Angeles	CA	90024-0000
714 787-4229	**University of California Riverside**	Webber Hall E Rm 2478	Riverside	CA	92521-0001
415 476-3941	**University of California San Francisco**	Box 0448 513 Parnassus Ave	San Francisco	CA	94143-0000
213 224-7151	**University of Southern California**	200 Zonal Ave Hoffman Medical	Los Angeles	CA	90033-0000
303 492-8978	**University of Colorado**	Campus Box 215	Boulder	CO	80309-0001
203 432-5598	**Yale University**	260 Whitney Ave	New Haven	CT	06511-0000
708 491-5061	**Northwestern University**	2153 Sheridan Rd Hogan Bldg NWU 2-100	Evanston	IL	60208-0001
312 702-1330	**University of Chicago**	920 E 58th St	Chicago	IL	60637-1432
217 333-7149	**University of Illinois**	1209 W California St Roger Adams Lab Rm 415	Urbana	IL	61801-0000
515 294-5836	**Iowa State University**	Gilman Hall Rm 397	Ames	IA	50011-0001
319 335-7933	**University of Iowa**	4403 BSB Rm 4	Iowa City	IA	52242-0001
301 955-3671	**Johns Hopkins University**	615 N Wolfe St	Baltimore	MD	21205-2103
617 736-2300	**Brandeis University**	415 South St	Waltham	MA	02254-2700
617 495-4106	**Harvard University**	7 Divinity Ave	Cambridge	MA	02138-2019
617 253-4791	**Massachusetts Institute of Technology**	77 Massachusetts Ave	Cambridge	MA	02139-0000
517 355-1600	**Michigan State University**	Biochemistry Bldg Rm 212	East Lansing	MI	48824-0001
313 764-8154	**University of Michigan**	PO Box 0606	Ann Arbor	MI	48109-0606
314 577-8124	**Saint Louis University**	1402 S Grand Blvd	Saint Louis	MO	63104-1028
908 932-2816	**Rutgers University**	Allison & Bevier Rds Nelson Labs Rm A-233	Piscataway	NJ	08854-0000
212 305-3882	**Columbia University**	630 W 168th St	New York	NY	10032-3702
607 255-2376	**Cornell University**	Biotechnology Bldg Rm 169	Ithaca	NY	14853-0001
212 570-8086	**Rockefeller University**	1230 York Ave	New York	NY	10021-6399
516 632-8550	**SUNY Stony Brook*School of Biochemistry**	Life Science Bldg Rm 450	Stony Brook	NY	11794-0001
212 430-2000	**Yeshiva University**	1300 Morris Park Ave	Bronx	NY	10461-1988
919 684-3913	**Duke University**	321 Nanaline Duke Box 3711	Durham	NC	27706-0000
919 962-8326	**University of North Carolina**	CB 7260	Chapel Hill	NC	27599-0001
216 368-3344	**Case Western Reserve University**	2119 Abington Rd	Cleveland	OH	44106-2333
503 737-4511	**Oregon State University**	Weniger Hall Rm 535	Corvallis	OR	97331-6503
503 346-4601	**University of Oregon**	91 Klamath Hall	Eugene	OR	97403-0000
814 863-4170	**Pennsylvania State University**	455 N Frear	University Park	PA	16802-0001
215 898-4829	**University of Pennsylvania**	38th & Hamilton Walk Anatomy-Chemistry Bldg Rm 414	Philadelphia	PA	19104-6059
615 322-3318	**Vanderbilt University**	607 Light Hall	Nashville	TN	37232-0146
713 527-4037	**Rice University**	6100 S Main St	Houston	TX	77005-0000
409 761-2769	**University of Texas**	Basic Science Bldg Rm 635	Galveston	TX	77550-0000
801 581-2117	**University of Utah**	211 Medical Education Bldg	Salt Lake City	UT	84132-0001
804 924-5139	**University of Virginia**	School of Medicine Box 440	Charlottesville	VA	22908-0001
608 262-3026	**University of Wisconsin**	420 Henry Mall Biochemistry Bldg Rm 104A	Madison	WI	53706-0001

BIOLOGICAL SCIENCES

205 934-0621	**University of Alabama**	Zeigler Research Bldg Rm 436	Birmingham	AL	35294-0001
818 356-6444	**California Institute of Technology**	1201 E California Blvd MS 147-75	Pasadena	CA	91125-0000
415 725-4759	**Stanford University**	Sherman Fairchild Bldg D-319	Stanford	CA	94305-2240
415 642-0944	**University of California Berkeley**	597 Life Sciences Addition	Berkeley	CA	94720-0000
916 752-0262	**University of California Davis**	Hutchison Bldg Rm 156	Davis	CA	95616-0000
714 856-5261	**University of California Irvine**	Medical Sciences Bldg I Rm B240	Irvine	CA	92717-0001
213 825-1959	**University of California Los Angeles**	Life Sciences Bldg Rm 2316	Los Angeles	CA	90024-0000
213 825-4321	**University of California Los Angeles**	405 Hilgard Ave	Los Angeles	CA	90024-1435
619 534-0558	**University of California San Diego**	Humanities & Social Sciences Bldg Rm 2306	La Jolla	CA	92093-0001
805 961-3511	**University of California Santa Barbara**	Bldg 478 Rm 1200	Santa Barbara	CA	93106-0001
213 224-7139	**University of Southern California**	2011 Zonal Ave Hoffman Medical Research Bldg Rm 401	Los Angeles	CA	90033-0000
303 492-7230	**University of Colorado**	CB 347	Boulder	CO	80309-0001
203 785-4935	**Yale University**	333 Cedar St	New Haven	CT	06510-3219
904 644-3023	**Florida State University**	204 Conradi Bldg	Tallahassee	FL	32306-2043
904 392-1906	**University of Florida**	1053 McCarty Hall	Gainesville	FL	32611-0000
708 491-5061	**Northwestern University**	2153 Sheridan Rd Hogan Hall	Evanston	IL	60208-0001
312 702-1620	**University of Chicago**	920 E 58th St	Chicago	IL	60637-1432
312 996-7470	**University of Illinois Chicago**	835 S Wolcott Ave	Chicago	IL	60612-0000
217 333-3044	**University of Illinois Urbana-Champaign**	505 S Goodwin Ave Morrill Hall Rm 393	Urbana	IL	61801-0000
812 855-9343	**Indiana University**	Jordan Hall Rm 127	Bloomington	IN	47405-0001
812 855-7323	**Indiana University**	Jordan Hall Rm 142	Bloomington	IN	47405-0001
317 494-4408	**Purdue University**	Lilly Hall of Life Sciences	West Lafayette	IN	47907-0001
319 335-7780	**University of Iowa**	3403 BSB Newton Rd	Iowa City	IA	52242-0001
301 955-3204	**Johns Hopkins University**	725 N Wolfe St	Baltimore	MD	21205-2105
301 454-2848	**University of Maryland**	Microbiology Bldg Rm 1117	College Park	MD	20742-0001
617 736-3100	**Brandeis University**	415 South St Bassine Bldg Rm 235	Waltham	MA	02254-0000
617 253-4738	**Massachusetts Institute of Technology**	77 Massachusetts Ave Bldg 56-524	Cambridge	MA	02139-4307
617 956-6685	**Tufts University**	136 Harrison Ave	Boston	MA	02111-1800
413 545-2553	**University of Massachusetts**	Morril Science Ctr	Amherst	MA	01003-0001
517 355-6498	**Michigan State University**	Giltner Hall Rm 152	East Lansing	MI	48824-0001
313 764-5428	**University of Michigan**	4714 Medical Science II	Ann Arbor	MI	48109-0001
313 577-1591	**Wayne State University**	540 E Canfield	Detroit	MI	48201-1908
612 624-5947	**University of Minnesota**	1460 Mayo Bldg Box 196 UMHC	Minneapolis	MN	55455-0000
314 362-3363	**Washington University**	660 S Euclid Ave Campus Box 8072	Saint Louis	MO	63110-1093
908 932-2077	**Rutgers University**	Nelson Biological Lab	New Brunswick	NJ	08855-0000
212 305-3451	**Columbia University**	630 W 168th St	New York	NY	10032-3702
607 255-2203	**Cornell University**	Biotechnology Bldg	Ithaca	NY	14853-0001
212 998-8200	**New York University**	1009 Main Bldg Washington Sq E	New York	NY	10003-0000
212 570-8088	**Rockefeller University**	1230 York Ave	New York	NY	10021-6399
716 831-2176	**SUNY Buffalo**	226 Farber Hall	Buffalo	NY	14214-0000
716 275-3835	**University of Rochester**	Hutchison Hall Rm 402	Rochester	NY	14627-0000
919 684-5138	**Duke University**	PO Box 3020	Durham	NC	27710-0001
919 966-3026	**University of North Carolina**	Taylor Hall Rm 108	Chapel Hill	NC	27599-0001
503 737-4441	**Oregon State University**	Nash Hall Rm 220	Corvallis	OR	97331-3804
503 346-4502	**University of Oregon**		Eugene	OR	97403-1210
814 865-2538	**Pennsylvania State University**	455 N Frear	University Park	PA	16802-0001
215 898-4360	**University of Pennsylvania**	210 Goddard Laboratory	Philadelphia	PA	19104-0000
412 624-4268	**University of Pittsburgh**	Langley Hall Rm A-234	Pittsburgh	PA	15260-0001
401 863-1661	**Brown University**	PO Box G	Providence	RI	02912-0000
615 322-2087	**Vanderbilt University**	A 5321 Medical Ctr N	Nashville	TN	37232-0001
817 755-2911	**Baylor University**	BU Box 7388	Waco	TX	76798-0001
512 471-4882	**University of Texas Austin**	Painter Hall Rm 1.22	Austin	TX	78712-0000
409 761-6840	**University of Texas Galveston**	Old Red Bldg Rm 2.210	Galveston	TX	77550-0000
713 792-4750	**University of Texas Health Science Center**	6901 Bertner	Houston	TX	77030-3901
801 581-5207	**University of Utah**	201 S Biology	Salt Lake City	UT	84112-0000
801 750-1189	**Utah State University**	Biology/Natural Resources Bldg Rm 121	Logan	UT	84322-5305
804 924-5930	**University of Virginia**	Jordan Hall Box 441	Charlottesville	VA	22908-0001
703 231-5712	**Virginia Polytechnic Institute & State University**	Derring Hall Rm 2123	Blacksburg	VA	24061-0001
206 543-5824	**University of Washington**	Health Sciences Bldg Rm G-311 SC-42	Seattle	WA	98195-0001
608 262-3203	**University of Wisconsin**	1525 Lynden Dr Molecular Biology Bldg Rm 413	Madison	WI	53706-0001

BUSINESS ADMINISTRATION

415 442-7225	**Golden Gate University**	536 Mission St	San Francisco	CA	94105-2967
415 723-2146	**Stanford University**		Stanford	CA	94305-0000
415 642-4093	**University of California Berkeley**	350 Barrows Hall	Berkeley	CA	94720-0001
714 856-6855	**University of California Irvine**	Student Affairs Office Rm 220	Irvine	CA	92717-0001
213 825-8874	**University of California Los Angeles**	405 Hilgard Ave Suite 3371	Los Angeles	CA	90024-1492
213 743-7846	**University of Southern California**	Bridge Hall Rm 101	Los Angeles	CA	90089-0001
303 871-3416	**University of Denver**	2020 S Race St	Denver	CO	80208-0001
203 432-5932	**Yale University**	135 Prospect St	New Haven	CT	06511-3729
202 994-6584	**George Washington University**	710 21st St NW Government Hall Rm 208	Washington	DC	20052-0001
407 646-2405	**Rollins College**	Crummer Bldg	Winter Park	FL	32789-0001
708 491-3300	**Northwestern University**	2001 Sheridan Rd Leverone Hall	Evanston	IL	60208-0001
312 702-7743	**University of Chicago**	1101 E 58th St	Chicago	IL	60637-1511
217 333-2747	**University of Illinois**	1206 S 6th St Rm 260	Champaign	IL	61820-6915
812 855-8006	**Indiana University**	10th & Feelane St	Bloomington	IN	47405-0000
219 989-2388	**Purdue University**	Management Dept	Hammond	IN	46323-0000
219 239-5206	**University of Notre Dame**	133 Hayes-Healy	Notre Dame	IN	46556-0000
606 257-3592	**University of Kentucky**	331 Business & Economic Bldg	Lexington	KY	40506-0001
617 495-6550	**Harvard University**	Soldiers Field	Boston	MA	02163-0000
617 253-3730	**Massachusetts Institute of Technology**	50 Memorial Dr Rm E52-112	Cambridge	MA	02139-0000
313 764-1363	**University of Michigan**	701 Tappan St	Ann Arbor	MI	48109-1234
601 232-5820	**University of Mississippi**	Conner Hall Rm 218	University	MS	38677-9999
314 882-2750	**University of Missouri**	303-D Middlebush Hall	Columbia	MO	65211-0001
402 472-2338	**University of Nebraska Lincoln**	College Business Bldg Rm 238	Lincoln	NE	68588-0001
603 646-2460	**Dartmouth College**		Hanover	NH	03755-0000
505 277-6413	**University of New Mexico**	Robert O Anderson Bldg	Albuquerque	NM	87131-0001
516 663-1177	**Adelphi University**	South Ave Rm 107	Garden City	NY	11530-4299

Colleges are listed alphabetically within each state. Graduate Schools are listed alphabetically by state, within each area of study.

212 854-2747	**Columbia University** Broadway & W 116th St Uris Hall Rm 810	New York	NY	10027-0000
607 255-5036	**Cornell University** Malott Hall	Ithaca	NY	14853-0001
212 285-6000	**New York University** 100 Trinity Pl Rm 933	New York	NY	10006-1594
212 346-1984	**Pace University** 1 Pace Plaza	New York	NY	10038-1598
718 260-3760	**Polytechnic University** 333 Jay St 2 Management Dept	Brooklyn	NY	11201-0000
716 636-3204	**SUNY Buffalo** 206 Jacobs Management Ctr	Buffalo	NY	14260-0001
716 275-3317	**University of Rochester** Dewey Hall	Rochester	NY	14627-1001
919 684-2495	**Duke University** Towerview Dr	Durham	NC	27706-0000
919 962-3236	**University of North Carolina** Carroll Hall Campus Box 3490	Chapel Hill	NC	27599-0001
503 346-3300	**University of Oregon** 268 Gilbert Hall	Eugene	OR	97403-0000
412 268-2265	**Carnegie Mellon University** Frew & Tech Sts	Pittsburgh	PA	15213-0000
215 898-3030	**University of Pennsylvania** 3620 Locust Walk Suite 1000	Philadelphia	PA	19104-6302
401 232-6231	**Bryant College** 1150 Douglas Pike	Smithfield	RI	02917-0000
901 678-2431	**Memphis State University**	Memphis	TN	38152-0001
615 974-5034	**University of Tennessee** 527 Stokely Management Ctr	Knoxville	TN	37996-0001
817 565-3030	**North Texas State University** Business Administration Bldg	Denton	TX	76203-0000
512 471-5921	**University of Texas** GSB 2.104	Austin	TX	78712-1104
804 924-7481	**University of Virginia** PO Box 6550	Charlottesville	VA	22906-6550

CHEMISTRY

602 621-6343	**University of Arizona** Old Chemistry Bldg Rm 227	Tucson	AZ	85721-0001
818 356-6110	**California Institute of Technology** 1201 E California Blvd Jorgensen Bldg MS 164-30	Pasadena	CA	91125-0001
415 723-2501	**Stanford University** SG Mudd Bldg Rm 121	Stanford	CA	94305-2240
415 642-5882	**University of California Berkeley** Latimar Hall Rm 419	Berkeley	CA	94720-0001
916 752-0953	**University of California Davis** 215 Chemistry Bldg	Davis	CA	95616-0000
714 856-4261	**University of California Irvine** Physical Science Bldg Rm 518	Irvine	CA	92717-0001
213 825-3150	**University of California Los Angeles** 405 Hilgard Ave	Los Angeles	CA	90024-0000
714 787-3520	**University of California Riverside** Pierce Hall	Riverside	CA	92521-0001
619 534-6870	**University of California San Diego** B-001	La Jolla	CA	92093-0001
805 961-2931	**University of California Santa Barbara** Chemistry Bldg	Santa Barbara	CA	93106-0001
213 743-2780	**University of Southern California** 3620 McClintock Ave SG Mudd Bldg Rm 418	Los Angeles	CA	90089-1062
303 491-6381	**Colorado State University** Chemistry Bldg Rm B101	Fort Collins	CO	80523-0001
303 492-6531	**University of Colorado** Campus Box 215	Boulder	CO	80309-0001
203 432-3916	**Yale University** PO Box 6666	New Haven	CT	06511-0000
904 644-3810	**Florida State University** Hoffman Teaching Laboratory	Tallahassee	FL	32306-1096
904 392-9132	**University of Florida** Chemical Research Bldg Rm 329	Gainesville	FL	32611-0000
404 894-8227	**Georgia Institute of Technology** Boggs Bldg Rm 156	Atlanta	GA	30332-0001
708 491-2968	**Northwestern University** 2145 Sheridan Rd Tech Bldg	Evanston	IL	60208-0001
312 702-7250	**University of Chicago** 5735 S Ellis Ave	Chicago	IL	60637-1403
217 333-0711	**University of Illinois** 505 S Mathews Ave Noyes Lab	Urbana	IL	61801-0000
812 855-2068	**Indiana University** Department of Chemistry Chemistry Bldg	Bloomington	IN	47405-0001
317 494-5200	**Purdue University** Brown Bldg Rm 2100	West Lafayette	IN	47907-0001
515 294-7810	**Iowa State University** Gilman Hall Rm A111F	Ames	IA	50011-0001
301 338-7429	**Johns Hopkins University** 3400 N Charles St Remsen Hall	Baltimore	MD	21218-0000
301 454-5231	**University of Maryland** Chemistry Bldg	College Park	MD	20742-0001
617 736-3410	**Brandeis University** 415 South St	Waltham	MA	02254-0000
617 495-4076	**Harvard University** 12 Oxford St	Cambridge	MA	02138-2902
617 253-1845	**Massachusetts Institute of Technology** Dreyfus Bldg Rm 18392	Cambridge	MA	02139-0000
517 355-9717	**Michigan State University** 320 W Shaw Ln	East Lansing	MI	48824-0001
313 764-7278	**University of Michigan** Chemistry Bldg Rm 2040	Ann Arbor	MI	48109-0001
612 624-8008	**University of Minnesota** Smith Hall Rm 141	Minneapolis	MN	55455-0100
609 258-4116	**Princeton University** Frick Laboratory Rm 121E	Princeton	NJ	08544-0001
212 854-2433	**Columbia University** Havemeyer Hall Rm 344	New York	NY	10027-0000
607 255-4139	**Cornell University** Baker Laboratory	Ithaca	NY	14853-0001
212 998-8200	**New York University** 6 Washington Pl	New York	NY	10003-6603
716 831-3014	**SUNY Buffalo** Main St Campus Acheson Hall	Buffalo	NY	14214-3099
516 632-7886	**SUNY Stony Brook*School of Chemistry** Chemistry Bldg	Stony Brook	NY	11794-3400
716 275-4231	**University of Rochester** Hutchison Hall Rm 404	Rochester	NY	14627-0001
919 684-6204	**Duke University** Towerview Dr Gross Chemistry Lab Rm 328	Durham	NC	27706-0000
919 962-2172	**University of North Carolina** Venable Hall CB 3290	Chapel Hill	NC	27599-3290
614 292-8917	**Ohio State University** 120 W 18th Ave	Columbus	OH	43210-1106
503 346-4601	**University of Oregon** Klamath Hall	Eugene	OR	97403-0000
412 268-3125	**Carnegie Mellon University** 4400 5th Ave Mellon Institute	Pittsburgh	PA	15213-0000
814 865-6553	**Pennsylvania State University** 152 Davey Laboratory	University Park	PA	16802-0001
215 898-9722	**University of Pennsylvania** 231 S 34th St Chemistry Bldg	Philadelphia	PA	19104-6323
412 624-8200	**University of Pittsburgh** 234 Chevron Science Ctr Parkman & University Dr	Pittsburgh	PA	15260-0001
401 863-2256	**Brown University** 324 Brook St	Providence	RI	02912-0001
713 527-4082	**Rice University** PO Box 1892	Houston	TX	77251-1892
801 581-6681	**University of Utah** Henry Eyring Bldg Rm 2020	Salt Lake City	UT	84112-0000
206 543-4787	**University of Washington** BG-10	Seattle	WA	98195-0001
608 262-0806	**University of Wisconsin** 1101 University Ave	Madison	WI	53706-1322

COMMUNICATIONS

205 348-5520	**University of Alabama** 201 Communication Bldg	Tuscaloosa	AL	35487-0000
602 965-5011	**Arizona State University** Forrest Mall Stauffer Hall	Tempe	AZ	85287-0001
602 621-7556	**University of Arizona** Franklin Bldg Rm 101M	Tucson	AZ	85721-0001
501 972-2468	**Arkansas State University** PO Box 540	State University	AR	72467-0024
501 575-3601	**University of Arkansas Fayetteville** Kemple Hall Rm 116	Fayetteville	AR	72701-0000
501 569-3250	**University of Arkansas Little Rock** 2801 S University Ave	Little Rock	AR	72204-1085
209 278-2087	**California State University Fresno** Cedar & Shaw Aves	Fresno	CA	93740-0001
714 773-3517	**California State University Fullerton** 800 N State College Blvd	Fullerton	CA	92631-3547
818 885-3135	**California State University Northridge** 18111 Nordhoff St	Northridge	CA	91330-0001
213 456-4211	**Pepperdine University** 24225 Pacific Coast Hwy	Malibu	CA	90263-0000
619 594-6635	**San Diego State University** Professional Studies & Fine Arts Bldg	San Diego	CA	92182-0001
408 924-3240	**San Jose State University** 1 Washington Sq	San Jose	CA	95192-0001
415 723-1941	**Stanford University** Bldg 120 Rm 110	Stanford	CA	94305-0000
415 642-3383	**University of California Berkeley** 121 North Gate Hall	Berkeley	CA	94720-0001
213 743-2391	**University of Southern California** GFS 315	Los Angeles	CA	90089-1695
303 351-2726	**University of Northern Colorado** Candelaria Hall Rm 123	Greeley	CO	80639-0001
202 885-2060	**American University** 4400 Massachusetts Ave NW	Washington	DC	20016-8099
904 392-0466	**University of Florida** 2096 Weimer Hall	Gainesville	FL	32611-0000
305 284-2265	**University of Miami** 5202 University Dr Merrick Bldg Rm 120	Coral Gables	FL	33124-0000
813 974-2591	**University of South Florida** 4202 E Fowler Ave Bldg CPR 107	Tampa	FL	33620-5550
904 474-2829	**University of West Florida** 11000 University Pkwy Bldg 76	Pensacola	FL	32514-0000
404 542-7833	**University of Georgia** Bldg 62	Athens	GA	30602-0000
815 753-1925	**Northern Illinois University** 103 Reavis Hall	De Kalb	IL	60115-0000
708 491-5665	**Northwestern University** 1845 Sheridan Rd Fisk Hall	Evanston	IL	60208-0001
618 536-3361	**Southern Illinois University Carbondale** Communications Bldg Rm 1202	Carbondale	IL	62901-0000
618 692-2230	**Southern Illinois University Edwardsville** CB 1775	Edwardsville	IL	62026-0001
317 285-8200	**Ball State University** W Quad 308	Muncie	IN	47306-0001
812 855-9247	**Indiana University** Ernie Pyle Hall Rm 200	Bloomington	IN	47405-0001
317 494-3429	**Purdue University** 304 Heavilon Hall	West Lafayette	IN	47907-0001
515 271-3194	**Drake University** Meredith Hall Rm 118	Des Moines	IA	50311-0000
515 294-4340	**Iowa State University** Hamilton Hall Rm 114	Ames	IA	50011-1180
913 532-6890	**Kansas State University** Kedzie Hall Rm 104	Manhattan	KS	66506-0001
913 864-4755	**University of Kansas** 200 Stauffer-Flint	Lawrence	KS	66045-0001
502 762-2387	**Murray State University** University Stn	Murray	KY	42071-3311
504 388-2336	**Louisiana State University** Journalism Bldg Rm 222	Baton Rouge	LA	70803-0001
301 405-1000	**University of Maryland** Journalism Bldg Rm 2109	College Park	MD	20742-0001
617 437-3236	**Northeastern University** 102 Lake Hall	Boston	MA	02115-0000
517 353-6430	**Michigan State University** 305 Communication Art Bldg	East Lansing	MI	48824-0001
313 764-0420	**University of Michigan** 2020 Frieze Bldg	Ann Arbor	MI	48109-0001
313 577-2627	**Wayne State University** 199 Manoogian	Detroit	MI	48202-0000
612 255-3293	**Saint Cloud State University** Stewart Hall	Saint Cloud	MN	56301-4498
612 625-9824	**University of Minnesota** 206 Church St SE Murphy Hall Rm 111	Minneapolis	MN	55455-0000
601 232-7146	**University of Mississippi** 331 Farley Hall	University	MS	38677-9999
601 266-4258	**University of Southern Mississippi** Southern Stn Box 5121	Hattiesburg	MS	39406-0000
816 429-4840	**Central Missouri State University** Martin Bldg	Warrensburg	MO	64093-0000
314 882-4821	**University of Missouri** PO Box 838	Columbia	MO	65205-0838
406 243-4001	**University of Montana** Journalism Bldg Rm 209	Missoula	MT	59812-0001
402 472-3041	**University of Nebraska Lincoln** 206 Avery Hall	Lincoln	NE	68588-0001
702 784-6531	**University of Nevada** MSS-7	Reno	NV	89557-0040
212 854-4150	**Columbia University** Broadway & W 116th St 7th Fl	New York	NY	10027-0000
212 998-7980	**New York University** 10 Washington Pl	New York	NY	10003-6639
716 636-2141	**SUNY Buffalo** Millard Fillmore Academic Core Rm 338	Buffalo	NY	14261-0000
315 443-2301	**Syracuse University** 215 University Pl	Syracuse	NY	13244-0001
919 962-1204	**University of North Carolina** 100 Howell Hall CB 3365	Chapel Hill	NC	27599-0001
701 777-2159	**University of North Dakota** PO Box 8118	Grand Forks	ND	58202-8118
419 372-2076	**Bowling Green State University** 319 West Hall	Bowling Green	OH	43403-0001
216 672-2572	**Kent State University** 130 Taylor Hall	Kent	OH	44242-0001
614 593-2590	**Ohio University** EW Scripps Hall Rm 105B	Athens	OH	45701-0000
405 744-6354	**Oklahoma State University** 206 Paul Miller Bldg	Stillwater	OK	74078-0001
405 325-2721	**University of Oklahoma** 860 Van Vleet Oval Rm 101	Norman	OK	73019-0001
503 346-3738	**University of Oregon** Allen Hall Rm 201	Eugene	OR	97403-0000
814 865-6597	**Pennsylvania State University** James Bldg Rm 302	University Park	PA	16802-0001
215 787-8791	**Temple University** 13th & Norris St Annenberg Hall Rm 321	Philadelphia	PA	19122-0000
803 777-4102	**University of South Carolina** Carolina Coliseum	Columbia	SC	29208-0001
901 678-2401	**Memphis State University** 3711 Veterans St Meeman Journalism Bldg Rm 300	Memphis	TN	38152-0001
615 974-3031	**University of Tennessee** Communications Extension Bldg Rm 302	Knoxville	TN	37996-0001
915 674-2296	**Abilene Christian University** ACU Stn	Abilene	TX	79699-0001
817 755-3261	**Baylor University** Castellaw Bldg BU-Box 7353	Waco	TX	76798-0001
903 886-5239	**East Texas State University** University Dr	Commerce	TX	75428-0000
806 742-3385	**Texas Tech University** PO Box 4710	Lubbock	TX	79409-3082
817 565-2205	**University of North Texas** Hickory & Mulberry	Denton	TX	76203-0001
512 471-5775	**University of Texas Austin** 26th & Whitis Sts RM CMA 4.130	Austin	TX	78712-0000
915 747-5129	**University of Texas El Paso** 202 Cotton Memorial	El Paso	TX	79968-0001
801 378-2077	**Brigham Young University** E-509 Harris Fine Arts Ctr	Provo	UT	84602-0000
801 581-6888	**University of Utah** LeRoy Cowles Bldg	Salt Lake City	UT	84112-0000
804 683-8331	**Norfolk State University** 2401 Corprew Ave	Norfolk	VA	23504-3989
206 543-2660	**University of Washington** Communications Hall DS-40	Seattle	WA	98195-0001
304 696-2360	**Marshall University** Smith Hall Rm 321	Huntington	WV	25701-0000
304 293-3505	**West Virginia University** Martin Hall	Morgantown	WV	26506-0001
414 288-7132	**Marquette University** 1131 W Wisconsin Ave	Milwaukee	WI	53233-2382

COMPUTER SCIENCE

602 621-6613	**University of Arizona** Gould-Simpson Bldg Rm 721	Tucson	AZ	85721-0001
818 356-6842	**California Institute of Technology** 1201 E California Blvd Jorgensen Bldg MS 256-80	Pasadena	CA	91125-0001
415 723-2273	**Stanford University** Bldg 460	Stanford	CA	94305-0000
415 642-0253	**University of California Berkeley** 231 Cory Hall	Berkeley	CA	94720-0001
714 856-7403	**University of California Irvine** Computer Science Bldg	Irvine	CA	92717-0001
213 825-1704	**University of California Los Angeles** 3436 Boelter Hall	Los Angeles	CA	90024-0000
805 961-4321	**University of California Santa Barbara** Engineering 1 Bldg Rm 2106	Santa Barbara	CA	93106-0001
203 432-1246	**Yale University** 51 Prospect St	New Haven	CT	06511-6816
404 894-3152	**Georgia Institute of Technology** 801 Atlantic Dr	Atlanta	GA	30332-0280
708 491-5410	**Northwestern University** 2145 Sheridan Rd	Evanston	IL	60208-0001
217 333-4428	**University of Illinois** 1304 W Springfield Ave Rm 240 DCL	Urbana	IL	61801-2910
301 454-0981	**University of Maryland** Bldg 115	College Park	MD	20742-0001
617 253-4603	**Massachusetts Institute of Technology** 50 Vassar St Bldg 38 Rm 444	Cambridge	MA	02139-4309
413 545-2744	**University of Massachusetts** Lederle Graduate Research Ctr	Amherst	MA	01003-0001
612 625-4002	**University of Minnesota** 200 Union St EE/CS Bldg Rm 4-196	Minneapolis	MN	55455-0000
609 258-5030	**Princeton University** Olden St Computer Science Bldg	Princeton	NJ	08544-0001
908 932-3546	**Rutgers University Bush Campus** Hill Ctr	New Brunswick	NJ	08903-0000
212 854-2931	**Columbia University** 500 W 120th St Mudd Bldg Rm 530	New York	NY	10027-0000
607 255-8593	**Cornell University** Upson Hall Rm 4126	Ithaca	NY	14853-0001
212 998-3006	**New York University** 251 Mercer St Warren Weaver Hall	New York	NY	10012-0000
716 475-2992	**Rochester Institute of Technology** Ross Memorial Bldg 10	Rochester	NY	14623-0000
716 636-3180	**SUNY Buffalo** 226 Bell Hall	Buffalo	NY	14260-0001
516 632-8470	**SUNY Stony Brook Computer Science Dept** 1401 Computer Science Bldg	Stony Brook	NY	11794-0001
315 443-2369	**Syracuse University** 4-116 Center for Science & Technology	Syracuse	NY	13244-0001
919 684-3048	**Duke University** 202 North Bldg	Durham	NC	27706-0000
919 962-1700	**University of North Carolina** CB-3175 Sitterson Hall	Chapel Hill	NC	27599-0001
614 292-5813	**Ohio State University** 2036 Neil Ave	Columbus	OH	43210-1226
412 268-2592	**Carnegie Mellon University** Wean Hall	Pittsburgh	PA	15213-0000
814 865-9505	**Pennsylvania State University** 333 Whitmore Lab	University Park	PA	16802-0001
215 898-8560	**University of Pennsylvania** 200 S 33rd St Moore Bldg	Philadelphia	PA	19104-0000
412 624-8490	**University of Pittsburgh** 321 Alumni Hall	Pittsburgh	PA	15260-0001
401 863-7600	**Brown University** 115 Waterman St	Providence	RI	02906-1101
803 777-2840	**University of South Carolina** LeConte Bldg Rm 216	Columbia	SC	29208-0001
713 527-4834	**Rice University** 6100 S Main St Herman Brown Bldg Rm 230	Houston	TX	77005-0000
512 471-7316	**University of Texas Austin** Burdin Hall	Austin	TX	78729-0000
206 543-1695	**University of Washington** Sieg Hall Rm 114 FR-35	Seattle	WA	98195-0001
608 262-1204	**University of Wisconsin Madison** 1210 W Dayton St	Madison	WI	53706-1613

DENTISTRY

205 934-3000	**University of Alabama** 1919 7th Ave S	Birmingham	AL	35294-0001
714 796-0141	**Loma Linda University** 24777 University Ave	Loma Linda	CA	92350-0001
213 825-7354	**University of California Los Angeles** 10833 Le Conte Ave	Los Angeles	CA	90024-1602
415 476-1891	**University of California San Francisco** 707 Parnassus Ave	San Francisco	CA	94143-0001
303 270-8017	**University of Colorado Health Sciences Center** 4200 E 9th Ave C-284	Denver	CO	80262-0001
203 679-2808	**University of Connecticut** 263 Farmington Ave Rm AG009	Farmington	CT	06030-0000
202 806-0100	**Howard University** 600 W St NW	Washington	DC	20059-0001
904 392-2946	**University of Florida** Miller Health Ctr J-405	Gainesville	FL	32610-0001
404 721-2117	**Medical College of Georgia** 15th St & Laney-Walker Blvd Rm AD109	Augusta	GA	30912-0001
708 216-4200	**Loyola University** 2160 S 1st Ave	Maywood	IL	60153-5589
312 908-5950	**Northwestern University** 240 E Huron St	Chicago	IL	60611-2972

Graduate and Professional Schools

618 463-3864 **Southern Illinois University** 2800 College Ave Rm 2300 ... Alton IL 62002-4742
312 996-7520 **University of Illinois Chicago** 801 S Paulina St Rm 102 ... Chicago IL 60612-4353
317 274-8191 **Indiana University** 1121 W Michigan St ... Indianapolis IN 46202-5211
319 335-9650 **University of Iowa** ... Iowa City IA 52242-0001
606 233-5850 **University of Kentucky** 800 Rose St UK Medical Ctr D104 ... Lexington KY 40536-0001
502 588-5293 **University of Louisville** Dental Bldg ... Louisville KY 40292-0001
504 947-9961 **Louisiana State University** 1100 Florida Ave Rm 2103 ... New Orleans LA 70119-2714
301 328-7460 **University of Maryland** 666 W Baltimore St ... Baltimore MD 21201-1510
617 638-4700 **Boston University** 100 E Newton St ... Boston MA 02118-2392
617 432-1000 **Harvard University** 188 Longwood Ave ... Boston MA 02115-5888
617 956-5000 **Tufts University** 1 Kneeland St ... Boston MA 02111-1529
313 446-1800 **University of Detroit** 2985 E Jefferson Ave ... Detroit MI 48207-4279
313 764-3375 **University of Michigan** 1011 N University Ave ... Ann Arbor MI 48109-0001
612 625-7149 **University of Minnesota** 515 SE Delaware St Moos Tower Rm 15-106 ... Minneapolis MN 55455-0000
601 984-6155 **University of Mississippi** 2500 N State St ... Jackson MS 39216-4505
816 276-2080 **University of Missouri** 650 E 25th St ... Kansas City MO 64108-2716
314 454-0300 **Washington University** 4559 Scott Ave ... Saint Louis MO 63110-1087
402 280-5060 **Creighton University** 2500 California St ... Omaha NE 68178-0001
402 472-1344 **University of Nebraska** 40th & Holdrege Sts Rm 107 ... Lincoln NE 68583-0001
212 305-3478 **Columbia University** 630 W 168th St ... New York NY 10032-3702
212 998-9800 **New York University** 345 E 24th St ... New York NY 10010-4020
716 831-2836 **SUNY Buffalo** 325 Squire Hall ... Buffalo NY 14214-0000
516 632-8900 **SUNY Stony Brook*School of Dental Medicine** Rockland Hall ... Stony Brook NY 11794-0001
919 966-1161 **University of North Carolina** Brauer Hall Rm 102 ... Chapel Hill NC 27599-0001
216 368-3200 **Case Western Reserve University** 2123 Abington Rd ... Cleveland OH 44106-2333
614 292-2401 **Ohio State University** 305 W 12th Ave ... Columbus OH 43210-1241
405 271-6326 **University of Oklahoma** 1001 Stanton L Young Blvd ... Oklahoma City OK 73190-0001
503 494-8867 **Oregon Health Sciences University** 611 SW Campus Dr ... Portland OR 97201-3001
215 221-2803 **Temple University** 3223 N Broad St ... Philadelphia PA 19140-5096
215 898-8961 **University of Pennsylvania** 4001 Spruce St ... Philadelphia PA 19104-6003
412 648-8616 **University of Pittsburgh** 3501 Terrace St ... Pittsburgh PA 15261-0001
615 327-6207 **Meharry Medical College** 1005 Dr DB Todd Jr Blvd ... Nashville TN 37208-3599
901 528-6200 **University of Tennessee** 875 Union Ave ... Memphis TN 38163-0001
214 828-8100 **Baylor University** 3302 Gaston Ave ... Dallas TX 75246-2098
713 792-4056 **University of Texas Houston** 6516 John Freeman Ave Texas Medical Ctr ... Houston TX 77030-3402
512 567-3222 **University of Texas San Antonio** 7703 Floyd Curl Dr ... San Antonio TX 78284-0001
804 786-9183 **Virginia Commonwealth University** 520 N 12th St ... Richmond VA 23298-0001
206 543-5982 **University of Washington** Health Sciences Bldg Rm D-322 SC-62 ... Seattle WA 98195-0001
414 288-3532 **Marquette University** 604 N 16th St Rm 304 ... Milwaukee WI 53233-2188

ENGINEERING

205 844-4326 **Auburn University** Ramsay Hall Rm 108 ... Auburn AL 36849-0000
602 621-6032 **University of Arizona** Geology Bldg Rm 134 ... Tucson AZ 85721-0001
501 575-5346 **University of Arkansas** Bell Engineering Ctr Rm 4183 ... Fayetteville AR 72701-0000
818 356-6367 **California Institute of Technology** 1201 E California Blvd ... Pasadena CA 91125-0001
805 756-2132 **California Polytech State University** ... San Luis Obispo CA 93407-0001
415 723-3935 **Stanford University** Terman Dr ... Stanford CA 94305-0000
415 642-5771 **University of California Berkeley** 320 McLaughlin Hall ... Berkeley CA 94720-0001
916 752-0553 **University of California Davis** 2132 Bainer Hall ... Davis CA 95616-0000
714 856-4841 **University of California Irvine** Graduate Affairs Office Rockwell Engineering Ctr Rm 314 ... Irvine CA 92717-0001
213 825-1704 **University of California Los Angeles** 6426 Boelter Hall ... Los Angeles CA 90024-0000
415 476-1211 **University of California San Francisco** Box 0414 Rm S-447 ... San Francisco CA 94143-0000
213 743-0884 **University of Southern California** 200 University Pk Olin Hall of Engineering Suite 200 ... Los Angeles CA 90089-0001
303 491-6603 **Colorado State University** Engineering Bldg Rm 111 ... Fort Collins CO 80523-0001
303 492-5071 **University of Colorado Boulder** Campus Box 422 ... Boulder CO 80309-0001
303 556-2870 **University of Colorado Denver** 1200 Larimer St ... Denver CO 80204-5300
203 486-2221 **University of Connecticut** 191 Auditorium Rd Box U-237 ... Storrs CT 06269-0001
302 451-2401 **University of Delaware** 135 Dupont Hall Rm 135 ... Newark DE 19716-0001
904 392-0941 **University of Florida** 300 Weil Hall ... Gainesville FL 32611-2083
404 894-3350 **Georgia Institute of Technology** 225 North Ave ... Atlanta GA 30332-0001
808 956-7727 **University of Hawaii** 2540 Dole St Holmes Hall Rm 240 ... Honolulu HI 96822-2333
708 491-5220 **McCormick School of Engineering** 2145 Sheridan Rd Rm 2390 ... Evanston IL 60208-0001
217 333-2151 **University of Illinois** 1308 W Green St Engineering Hall Rm 106 ... Urbana IL 61801-0000
317 494-5345 **Purdue University** Engineering Administration Bldg Suite 101 ... West Lafayette IN 47907-1914
219 239-5530 **University of Notre Dame** Fitzpatrick Hall Rm 257 ... Notre Dame IN 46556-0000
515 294-5933 **Iowa State University** 104 Marston Hall ... Ames IA 50011-0001
319 335-5766 **University of Iowa** Engineering Bldg Rm 3100 ... Iowa City IA 52242-0001
913 864-3881 **University of Kansas** 4010 Learned Hall ... Lawrence KS 66045-0001
318 257-4647 **Louisiana Tech University** Arizona Ave Bogart Hall ... Ruston LA 71272-0001
301 338-8350 **Johns Hopkins University** 3400 N Charles St New Engineering Bldg Rm 120 ... Baltimore MD 21218-0000
301 454-2421 **University of Maryland** Engineering Classroom Bldg Rm 1131 ... College Park MD 20742-0001
617 353-9760 **Boston University** 705 Commonwealth Ave Rm 112 ... Boston MA 02215-1401
617 253-3291 **Massachusetts Institute of Technology** 77 Massachusetts Ave ... Cambridge MA 02139-4307
413 545-0300 **University of Massachusetts** 125 Marston Hall ... Amherst MA 01003-0001
313 764-8475 **University of Michigan** 1301 Beal Ave EECS Bldg ... Ann Arbor MI 48109-0001
612 625-3394 **University of Minnesota** 101 Pleasant St SE Johnston Hall .. Minneapolis MN 55455-0432
314 882-4375 **University of Missouri Columbia** Electrical Engineering Bldg Rm 145 ... Columbia MO 65211-0001
314 341-4151 **University of Missouri Rolla** Engineering Research Lab Rm 1Rm 101-ERL ... Rolla MO 65401-0001
402 554-2460 **University of Nebraska** 116 Engineering Bldg ... Omaha NE 68182-0001
609 258-4560 **Princeton University** Engineering Quad ... Princeton NJ 08544-0001
908 932-4452 **Rutgers University** PO Box 909 ... Picataway NJ 08855-0001
201 420-5234 **Stevens Institute of Technology** 1 Castle Point Terr ... Hoboken NJ 07030-5991
607 871-2141 **Alfred University** PO Box 1155 ... Alfred NY 14802-0155
315 268-6446 **Clarkson University** 126 Old Main St ... Potsdam NY 13699-0001
212 854-2993 **Columbia University** 500 W 120th St Mudd Bldg Rm 510 ... New York NY 10027-0000
607 255-4326 **Cornell University** 242 Carpenter Hall ... Ithaca NY 14853-0001
212 690-5439 **CUNY City College** Convent Ave & W 140th St Steinman Hall .. New York NY 10031-0000
718 260-3590 **Polytechnic University** 333 Jay St Rm 324 ... Brooklyn NY 11201-2990
518 276-6298 **Rensselaer Polytechnic Institute** 110 8th St Johnson Engineering Ctr ... Troy NY 12180-0000
716 475-2145 **Rochester Institute of Technology** 1 Lomb Memorial Dr ... Rochester NY 14623-5640
716 636-2772 **SUNY Buffalo** 412 Bonner Hall ... Buffalo NY 14260-0001
516 632-8497 **SUNY Stony Brook*Department of Material Science** ... Stony Brook NY 11794-0001
315 443-2545 **Syracuse University** Link Hall Rm 223 ... Syracuse NY 13244-0001
716 275-4072 **University of Rochester** 235 Hopeman Bldg ... Rochester NY 14627-0000
919 737-2311 **North Carolina State University** PO Box 7901 ... Raleigh NC 27695-0000
614 292-2651 **Ohio State University** 2070 Neil Ave 122 Hitchcock Hall ... Columbus OH 43210-0000
513 556-5426 **University of Cincinnati** 645 Baldwin Hall ... Cincinnati OH 45221-0001
405 744-5140 **Oklahoma State University** Engineering N Bldg Rm 111 ... Stillwater OK 74078-0001
405 325-2621 **University of Oklahoma** 202 W Boyd St Rm 107 ... Norman OK 73019-0001
503 737-4525 **Oregon State University** Covell Hall Rm 101 ... Corvallis OR 97331-0000
412 268-2477 **Carnegie Mellon University** 101 Scaife Hall ... Pittsburgh PA 15261-2001
215 758-4025 **Lehigh University** 308 Packard Laboratory ... Bethlehem PA 18015-0000
814 863-3064 **Pennsylvania State University** 101 Hammond Bldg ... University Park PA 16802-0001
215 898-8241 **University of Pennsylvania** 220 S 33rd St Towne Bldg Rm 119 ... Philadelphia PA 19104-6391
412 624-9800 **University of Pittsburgh** 253 Benedum Hall ... Pittsburgh PA 15261-0001
803 656-3201 **Clemson University** Riggs Hall Rm 109 ... Clemson SC 29634-0001
615 974-5321 **University of Tennessee** 124 Perkins Hall ... Knoxville TN 37996-0001
615 322-2762 **Vanderbilt University** 1500 21st Ave S 4th Fl ... Nashville TN 37212-3102
713 527-4009 **Rice University** PO Box 1892 ... Houston TX 77251-1892
409 845-7200 **Texas A & M University** 204 Zachry Bldg ... College Station TX 77843-0000
817 273-2571 **University of Texas Arlington** PO Box 19019 ... Arlington TX 76019-0001
512 471-1166 **University of Texas Austin** ECJ 10.310 ... Austin TX 78712-0000
801 581-6911 **University of Utah** Merill Engineering Bldg Rm 2202 ... Salt Lake City UT 84112-0000
801 750-2775 **Utah State University** Engineering Classroom Rm 110 ... Logan UT 84322-0000
804 924-3073 **University of Virginia** Thornton Hall ... Charlottesville VA 22903-2448
703 231-6641 **Virginia Polytechnic Institute & State University** 333 Norris Hall ... Blacksburg VA 24061-0217
206 543-0340 **University of Washington** Loew Hall FH-10 ... Seattle WA 98195-0001
608 262-3481 **University of Wisconsin Madison** 1513 University Ave ... Madison WI 53706-1512
414 229-4126 **University of Wisconsin Milwaukee** EMS Bldg Rm E-503 ... Milwaukee WI 53201-0000

GEOSCIENCE

602 965-5081 **Arizona State University** Physical Science Bldg ... Tempe AZ 85287-0001
602 621-6024 **University of Arizona** Gould-Simpson Bldg Rm 208 ... Tucson AZ 85721-0001
818 356-6346 **California Institute of Technology** 1201 E California Blvd ... Pasadena CA 91125-0001
415 723-2538 **Stanford University** Mitchell Bldg ... Stanford CA 94305-2115
415 642-5574 **University of California Berkeley** 301 Earth Science Bldg ... Berkeley CA 94720-0001
916 752-9100 **University of California Davis** 174 Physics Bldg ... Davis CA 95616-0000
213 825-3917 **University of California Los Angeles** Geology Bldg Rm 3806 ... Los Angeles CA 90024-0000
805 893-3329 **University of California Santa Barbara** Geological Science Bldg ... Santa Barbara CA 93106-0001
408 459-4089 **University of California Santa Cruz** Applied Sciences Bldg Rm 141 ... Santa Cruz CA 95064-0000
213 743-2717 **University of Southern California** University Pk ... Los Angeles CA 90089-0740
303 492-8142 **University of Colorado** CB 250 ... Boulder CO 80309-0001
203 432-3114 **Yale University** Kline Geology Laboratory Rm 203 ... New Haven CT 06511-0000
708 491-3238 **Northwestern University** 1847 Sheridan Rd ... Evanston IL 60208-0001
312 702-8101 **University of Chicago** 5734 S Ellis Ave ... Chicago IL 60637-1434
217 333-3540 **University of Illinois** 1301 W Green St Natural History Bldg Rm 245 ... Urbana IL 61801-0000
812 855-5582 **Indiana University Bloomington** 1005 E 10th St Rm 129 ... Bloomington IN 47405-0001
317 494-3258 **Purdue University** Civil Engineering Bldg Rm 2169 ... West Lafayette IN 47907-0001
913 864-4974 **University of Kansas** 120 Lindley Hall ... Lawrence KS 66045-0001
301 338-7034 **Johns Hopkins University** 3400 N Charles St Olin Hall ... Baltimore MD 21218-0000
617 495-2351 **Harvard University** 20 Oxford St Hoffman Laboratory ... Cambridge MA 02138-2902
617 253-3381 **Massachusetts Institute of Technology** 77 Massachusetts Ave Bldg 54 Rm 913 ... Cambridge MA 02139-4307
413 545-2286 **University of Massachusetts** Morrill Science Ctr Rm 233 ... Amherst MA 01003-0001
313 764-1435 **University of Michigan** CC Little Bldg Rm 1006 ... Ann Arbor MI 48109-1063
612 624-4344 **University of Minnesota** 310 Pillsbury Dr SE Pillsbury Hall .. Minneapolis MN 55455-0000
314 889-5610 **Washington University** 1 Brookings Dr CB 1169 ... Saint Louis MO 63130-4899
609 258-5807 **Princeton University** Guyot Hall ... Princeton NJ 08544-0001
212 854-4737 **Columbia University** 107 Low Memorial Library ... New York NY 10027-0000
607 255-5267 **Cornell University** Snee Hall Rm 4122 ... Ithaca NY 14853-0001
518 442-4466 **SUNY Albany** 1400 Washington Ave ... Albany NY 12222-0001
516 632-8200 **SUNY Stony Brook*Department of Earth & Space Science** ESF Bldg ... Stony Brook NY 11790-0000
614 292-8124 **Ohio State University** 1958 Neil Ave Cockins Hall Rm 404 ... Columbus OH 43210-1247
503 346-4573 **University of Oregon** Cascade Hall Rm 100 ... Eugene OR 97403-0000
814 865-7394 **Pennsylvania State University** 303 Deike Bldg ... University Park PA 16802-0001
401 863-3357 **Brown University** PO Box 1846 ... Providence RI 02912-0001
803 777-4535 **University of South Carolina** 700 Sumter St Rm 617 ... Columbia SC 29208-0001
409 845-1371 **Texas A & M University** O & M Bldg Rm 204 ... College Station TX 77843-0000
512 471-5172 **University of Texas** PO Box 7909 ... Austin TX 78713-7909
801 581-6553 **University of Utah** 717 William Browning Bldg ... Salt Lake City UT 84112-0000
703 231-6522 **Virginia Polytechnic Institute & State University** Derring Hall Rm 4044 ... Blacksburg VA 24061-0001
206 543-8020 **University of Washington** Atmospheric Sciences Bldg Rm 202 AK-50 ... Seattle WA 98195-0001
608 262-8960 **University of Wisconsin** 1215 W Dayton St ... Madison WI 53706-1612

LAW

205 870-2701 **Samford University** 800 Lakeshore Dr ... Birmingham AL 35229-0001
205 348-5117 **University of Alabama** PO Box 870382 ... Tuscaloosa AL 35487-0382
602 965-6181 **Arizona State University** Armstrong Hall ... Tempe AZ 85287-0001
602 621-1373 **University of Arizona** College of Law Bldg Rm 120 ... Tucson AZ 85721-0001
501 575-5601 **University of Arkansas Fayetteville** Waterman Hall Rm 107 ... Fayetteville AR 72701-0000
501 371-1071 **University of Arkansas Little Rock** 400 W Markham St ... Little Rock AR 72201-1408
619 239-0391 **California Western School of Law** 350 Cedar St ... San Diego CA 92101-3196
415 442-7250 **Golden Gate University** 536 Mission St ... San Francisco CA 94105-2967
213 736-1000 **Loyola University** 1441 W Olympic Blvd ... Los Angeles CA 90015-3980
213 456-4611 **Pepperdine University** 24255 Pacific Coast Hwy ... Malibu CA 90263-0001
408 554-4361 **Santa Clara University** Heafey Law Library Rm 224 ... Santa Clara CA 95053-0001
213 738-6700 **Southwestern University** 675 S Westmoreland Ave ... Los Angeles CA 90005-3905
415 723-4985 **Stanford University** Crown Quadrangle ... Stanford CA 94305-0000
415 642-2274 **University of California Berkeley** 220 Boalt Hall ... Berkeley CA 94720-0001
916 752-0243 **University of California Davis** King Hall ... Davis CA 95616-0000
213 825-4841 **University of California Los Angeles** 405 Hilgard Ave ... Los Angeles CA 90024-1492
415 565-4727 **University of California San Francisco** 200 McAllister St ... San Francisco CA 94102-4707
415 666-6544 **University of San Francisco** 2130 Fulton St ... San Francisco CA 94117-1080
213 743-7331 **University of Southern California** University Pk ... Los Angeles CA 90089-0001
916 739-7121 **University of the Pacific** 3200 5th Ave ... Sacramento CA 95817-2705
213 313-1011 **University of West Los Angeles** 12201 Washington Pl ... Los Angeles CA 90066-4998
213 938-3621 **Whittier College** 5353 W 3rd St ... Los Angeles CA 90020-4899
303 492-8047 **University of Colorado** Fleming Law Bldg Campus Box 401 ... Boulder CO 80309-0001
303 871-6000 **University of Denver** 7039 E 18th Ave ... Denver CO 80220-1079
203 576-4041 **University of Bridgeport** 303 University Ave Carlson Hall ... Bridgeport CT 06601-0000
203 241-4638 **University of Connecticut** 55 Elizabeth St Hartranft Hall ... Hartford CT 06105-2213
203 432-4992 **Yale University** 127 Wall St ... New Haven CT 06511-6636
302 478-5280 **Widener University** PO Box 7474 ... Wilmington DE 19803-0000
202 885-2605 **American University** 4400 Massachusetts Ave NW ... Washington DC 20016-8002
202 319-5144 **Catholic University of America** 620 Michigan Ave NE ... Washington DC 20064-0001
202 727-5225 **District of Columbia School of Law** 719 13th St NW ... Washington DC 20005-3997
202 994-6260 **George Washington University** 720 20th St NW ... Washington DC 20052-0001
202 662-9000 **Georgetown University** 600 New Jersey Ave NW ... Washington DC 20001-2075
202 806-8000 **Howard University** 2900 Van Ness St NW Houston Hall Rm 106 ... Washington DC 20008-1196
904 644-3400 **Florida State University** 425 W Jefferson St Rm 210 ... Tallahassee FL 32306-0001
305 522-2300 **Nova University** 3100 SW 9th Ave ... Fort Lauderdale FL 33315-3097

Colleges are listed alphabetically within each state. Graduate Schools are listed alphabetically by state, within each area of study.

813 345-1300 **Stetson University** 1401 61st St S ... Saint Petersburg FL 33707-3299
904 392-0421 **University of Florida** 164 Holland Hall ... Gainesville FL 32611-0000
305 284-2392 **University of Miami** PO Box 248087 ... Coral Gables FL 33124-8087
404 727-6802 **Emory University** Gambrell Hall ... Atlanta GA 30322-0000
404 651-2048 **Georgia State University** PO Box 4037 ... Atlanta GA 30302-4037
912 752-2601 **Mercer University** 1021 Georgia Ave ... Macon GA 31207-0001
404 542-7140 **University of Georgia** Herty Dr ... Athens GA 30602-0000
808 956-7966 **University of Hawaii** 2515 Dole St ... Honolulu HI 96822-2328
208 885-6422 **University of Idaho** Albert R Menard Bldg ... Moscow ID 83843-0000
312 341-8701 **DePaul University** 25 E Jackson Blvd ... Chicago IL 60604-2287
312 427-2737 **John Marshall Law School** 315 S Plymouth Ct ... Chicago IL 60604-3968
312 915-7120 **Loyola University of Chicago** 1 E Pearson St ... Chicago IL 60611-2001
815 753-1067 **Northern Illinois University** Swen-Parson Hall ... De Kalb IL 60115-0000
312 908-8462 **Northwestern University** 357 E Chicago Ave ... Chicago IL 60611-3069
618 536-7711 **Southern Illinois University** Lesar Law Bldg ... Carbondale IL 62901-0000
312 702-9494 **University of Chicago** 1111 E 60th St ... Chicago IL 60637-2786
217 333-0931 **University of Illinois** 504 E Pennsylvania Ave Rm 209A ... Champaign IL 61820-6909
812 855-7995 **Indiana University Bloomington** 3rd St & Indiana Ave ... Bloomington IN 47405-0000
317 274-8523 **Indiana University Indianapolis** 735 W New York St ... Indianapolis IN 46202-5222
219 239-6627 **University of Notre Dame** Law Bldg Rm 103 ... Notre Dame IN 46556-0000
219 465-7829 **Valparaiso University** Weseman Hall Rm 202 ... Valparaiso IN 46383-0000
515 271-2824 **Drake University** 27th St & Carpenter ... Des Moines IA 50311-0000
319 335-9034 **University of Iowa** Melrose & Byington ... Iowa City IA 52242-0001
913 864-4550 **University of Kansas** Green Hall ... Lawrence KS 66045-0001
913 295-6660 **Washburn University of Topeka** 1700 College Ave ... Topeka KS 66621-0001
606 572-5340 **Northern Kentucky University** Nunn Hall ... Highland Heights KY 41076-0000
606 257-1678 **University of Kentucky** Law Bldg ... Lexington KY 40506-0048
502 588-6358 **University of Louisville** 2301 S 3rd St ... Louisville KY 40292-0001
504 388-8491 **Louisiana State University**
Paul M Hebert Law Ctr Rm 210 ... Baton Rouge LA 70803-0001
504 861-5575 **Loyola University** 7214 St Charles Ave ... New Orleans LA 70118-3538
504 771-2552 **Southern University** Swan St ... Baton Rouge LA 70813-0000
504 865-5930 **Tulane University** 6801 Freret St ... New Orleans LA 70118-5697
207 780-4340 **University of Maine** 246 Deering Ave ... Portland ME 04102-2898
301 328-7214 **University of Maryland** 500 W Baltimore St ... Baltimore MD 21201-1786
617 552-8550 **Boston College** 885 Centre St ... Newton MA 02159-1100
617 353-3112 **Boston University** 765 Commonwealth Ave ... Boston MA 02215-1401
617 495-3100 **Harvard University** Griswold Hall ... Cambridge MA 02138-3800
617 451-0010 **New England School of Law** 154 Stuart St ... Boston MA 02116-5687
617 437-2395 **Northeastern University** 400 Huntington Ave ... Boston MA 02115-5098
617 573-8144 **Suffolk University** 41 Temple St Donahue Bldg ... Boston MA 02114-4280
413 782-1406 **Western New England College**
1215 Wilbraham Rd S Prestley Blake Law Ctr ... Springfield MA 01119-2689
313 965-0150 **Detroit College of Law** 130 E Elizabeth St ... Detroit MI 48201-3454
517 371-5140 **Thomas M Cooley Law School** 217 S Capitol Ave ... Lansing MI 48933-1586
313 596-0200 **University of Detroit** 651 E Jefferson Ave ... Detroit MI 48226-4301
313 764-1358 **University of Michigan** 625 S State St Hutchins Hall ... Ann Arbor MI 48109-0001
313 577-3930 **Wayne State University** 468 W Ferry St ... Detroit MI 48202-3698
612 641-2400 **Hamline University** 1536 Hewitt Ave ... Saint Paul MN 55104-1284
612 227-9171 **Mitchell William College of Law** 875 Summit Ave ... Saint Paul MN 55105-3076
612 625-1000 **University of Minnesota** 229 19th Ave S ... Minneapolis MN 55455-0400
601 944-1950 **Mississippi College** 151 E Griffith St ... Jackson MS 39201-1302
601 232-7361 **University of Mississippi** Law Ctr ... University MS 38677-9999
314 658-2800 **Saint Louis University** 3700 Lindell Blvd ... Saint Louis MO 63108-3412
314 882-6487 **University of Missouri Columbia** Conley & Missouri Sts ... Columbia MO 65211-0001
816 276-1644 **University of Missouri Kansas City** 5100 Rockhill Rd ... Kansas City MO 64110-2499
314 889-6400 **Washington University** CB 1120 ... Saint Louis MO 63130-0000
406 243-4311 **University of Montana** Maurice & Eddy Sts Law School Bldg ... Missoula MT 59812-0001
402 280-2875 **Creighton University** 2133 California St ... Omaha NE 68178-0001
402 472-2161 **University of Nebraska** McCollum Hall Rm 103 ... Lincoln NE 68583-0902
603 228-1541 **Franklin Pierce Law Center** 2 White St ... Concord NH 03301-4197
609 757-6375 **Rutgers University Camden** 5th & Penn Sts ... Camden NJ 08102-0000
201 648-5561 **Rutgers University Newark** 15 Washington St ... Newark NJ 07102-3192
201 642-8500 **Seton Hall University** 1111 Raymond Blvd ... Newark NJ 07102-5297
505 277-2146 **University of New Mexico** 1117 Stanford Dr NE ... Albuquerque NM 87131-1431
718 625-2200 **Brooklyn Law School** 250 Joralemon St ... Brooklyn NY 11201-3798
212 854-2640 **Columbia University** 435 W 116th St ... New York NY 10027-7201
607 255-3626 **Cornell University** Myron Taylor Hall ... Ithaca NY 14853-0001
516 560-5916 **Hofstra University** California Ave ... Hempstead NY 11550-0000
212 998-6000 **New York University** 40 Washington Pl ... New York NY 10003-6638
914 422-4210 **Pace University** 78 N Broadway ... White Plains NY 10603-3796
718 990-6600 **Saint John's University**
Grand Central & Utopia Pkwys Fromkes Hall ... Jamaica NY 11439-0001
716 636-2061 **SUNY Buffalo** 304 O'Brian Hall ... Buffalo NY 14260-0001
315 443-2524 **Syracuse University** ... Syracuse NY 13244-0001
516 421-2244 **Touro College** 300 Nassau Rd ... Huntington NY 11743-4342
518 445-2311 **Union University** 80 New Scotland Ave ... Albany NY 12208-3434
212 790-0274 **Yeshiva University** 55 5th Ave ... New York NY 10003-4391
919 893-2773 **Campbell University** Kivett Hall ... Buies Creek NC 27506-0000
919 684-2834 **Duke University** Towerview Dr & Science Dr ... Durham NC 27706-0000
919 560-6333 **North Carolina Central University** 1801 Fayetteville St ... Durham NC 27707-3198
919 962-5106 **University of North Carolina** Campus Box 3380 ... Chapel Hill NC 27599-0001
919 759-5434 **Wake Forest University** PO Box 7206 ... Winston-Salem NC 27109-7206
701 777-2104 **University of North Dakota** University Stn ... Grand Forks ND 58202-2020
614 445-8836 **Capital University** 665 S High St ... Columbus OH 43215-5683
216 368-3280 **Case Western Reserve University** 11075 E Blvd ... Cleveland OH 44106-0000
216 687-2344 **Cleveland State University** 1801 Euclid Ave ... Cleveland OH 44115-2223
419 772-2211 **Ohio Northern University** ... Ada OH 45810-0000
614 292-2631 **Ohio State University** 1659 N High St Rm 112 ... Columbus OH 43210-0000
216 972-7331 **University of Akron**
302 E Buchtel Ave C Blake McDowell Law Ctr ... Akron OH 44325-0001
513 556-6805 **University of Cincinnati** Mail Location 40 ... Cincinnati OH 45221-0001
513 229-3211 **University of Dayton** 300 College Park Rd Albert Emanuel Hall ... Dayton OH 45469-1320
419 537-2882 **University of Toledo** 2801 W Bancroft St Law Ctr ... Toledo OH 43606-3390
405 521-5337 **Oklahoma City University** 2501 N Blackwelder Ave ... Oklahoma City OK 73106-1498
405 325-4726 **University of Oklahoma** 300 Timberdale Rd ... Norman OK 73019-0001
918 631-2401 **University of Tulsa** 3120 E 4th Pl John Rogers Hall ... Tulsa OK 74104-2499
503 244-1181 **Lewis & Clark College** 10015 SW Terwilliger Blvd ... Portland OR 97219-7768
503 346-3852 **University of Oregon** 11th & Kincaid Sts ... Eugene OR 97403-0000
503 370-6380 **Willamette University** 250 Winter St SE ... Salem OR 97301-3827
717 243-4611 **Dickinson School of Law** 150 S College St ... Carlisle PA 17013-2877
412 434-6300 **Duquesne University** 900 Locust St ... Pittsburgh PA 15282-0001
215 787-7863 **Temple University** 1719 Broad St Charles Klein Bldg ... Philadelphia PA 19122-0000
215 898-7483 **University of Pennsylvania** 3400 Chestnut St ... Philadelphia PA 19104-6204
412 648-1400 **University of Pittsburgh** 3900 Forbes Ave ... Pittsburgh PA 15260-0001
215 645-7000 **Villanova University** Countyline Rd & Springmill Garey Hall ... Villanova PA 19085-0000
803 777-6617 **University of South Carolina** S Main & Green St ... Columbia SC 29208-0001
605 677-5361 **University of South Dakota** 414 E Clark St ... Vermillion SD 57069-2390
901 678-2421 **Memphis State University** Central Ave Rm 207 ... Memphis TN 38152-0001
615 974-4241 **University of Tennessee** 1505 W Cumberland Ave ... Knoxville TN 37996-0001
615 322-2615 **Vanderbilt University** 21st Ave S ... Nashville TN 37240-0001
817 755-1911 **Baylor University** BU Box 7288 ... Waco TX 76798-0001
512 436-3424 **Saint Mary's University** 1 Camino Santa Maria St ... San Antonio TX 78228-8500
713 659-8040 **South Texas College of Law** 1303 San Jacinto St ... Houston TX 77002-7000
214 692-2618 **Southern Methodist University** Story Hall ... Dallas TX 75275-0001
713 527-7112 **Texas Southern University** 3100 Cleburne St ... Houston TX 77004-4598
806 742-3791 **Texas Tech University** 1802 Hartford Ave ... Lubbock TX 79409-0000
713 749-1422 **University of Houston** 4800 Calhoun Rd ... Houston TX 77204-0001
512 471-5151 **University of Texas** 727 E 26th St ... Austin TX 78705-3299
801 378-4274 **Brigham Young University** 348 J Reuben Clark Bldg ... Provo UT 84602-0000
801 581-6833 **University of Utah** College of Law Bldg ... Salt Lake City UT 84112-0000
804 221-3800 **College of William & Mary** S Henry St ... Williamsburg VA 23185-0000
703 841-2600 **George Mason University** 3401 N Fairfax Dr ... Arlington VA 22201-4411
804 289-8740 **University of Richmond** ... Richmond VA 23173-7301
804 924-7354 **University of Virginia** Withers Hall 3rd Fl ... Charlottesville VA 22901-0000
703 463-8505 **Washington & Lee University** Lewis Hall ... Lexington VA 24450-0000
509 484-6481 **Gonzaga University** E 601 Sharp ... Spokane WA 99220-0000
206 591-6300 **University of Puget Sound** 950 Broadway Plaza ... Tacoma WA 98402-4413
206 543-4550 **University of Washington**
1100 NE Campus Pkwy Condon Hall JB-20 ... Seattle WA 98105-0000
304 293-5306 **West Virginia University** University Ave ... Morgantown WV 26506-0001
414 288-7090 **Marquette University** 1103 W Wisconsin Ave ... Milwaukee WI 53233-2381
608 262-2240 **University of Wisconsin** 975 Bascom Mall ... Madison WI 53706-1317
307 766-6416 **University of Wyoming** PO Box 3035 University Stn ... Laramie WY 82071-3035

LIBRARY SCIENCE

415 642-1464 **University of California Berkeley** 102 S Hall ... Berkeley CA 94720-0001
213 825-4351 **University of California Los Angeles** 120 Powell Library ... Los Angeles CA 90024-0000
904 644-5775 **Florida State University** 101 Lewis Schores Bldg ... Tallahassee FL 32306-2048
217 333-3280 **University of Illinois** 1407 W Gregory Dr David Kinley Hall ... Urbana IL 61801-0000
301 454-5441 **University of Maryland** 4105 Hornbake Library ... College Park MD 20742-0001
617 738-2225 **Simmons College** 300 Fenway ... Boston MA 02115-5898
313 764-9376 **University of Michigan** 550 E University St ... Ann Arbor MI 48109-0001
908 932-7500 **Rutgers University** 4 Huntington St ... New Brunswick NJ 08901-1071
212 854-2294 **Columbia University** 516 Butler Library ... New York NY 10027-0000
315 443-2911 **Syracuse University** 4-206 Ctr for Science & Technology ... Syracuse NY 13244-0001
919 962-8366 **University of North Carolina** 100 Manning Hall CB 3360 ... Chapel Hill NC 27599-0001
215 895-2474 **Drexel University** Rush Bldg Rm 306 ... Philadelphia PA 19104-0000
412 624-5230 **University of Pittsburgh** 135 N Bellefield Ave LIS Bldg ... Pittsburgh PA 15260-0001
512 471-3821 **University of Texas** Education Bldg Rm 564 ... Austin TX 78712-0000
206 543-1794 **University of Washington** 133 Suzzallo Library FM-30 ... Seattle WA 98195-0001
608 263-2900 **University of Wisconsin** 600 N Park St ... Madison WI 53706-1403

MEDICINE

205 934-4964 **University of Alabama** UBA Stn ... Birmingham AL 35294-0001
205 460-7174 **University of South Alabama** 1005 Medical Sciences Bldg ... Mobile AL 36688-0001
501 686-5000 **University of Arkansas** 4301 W Markham St ... Little Rock AR 72205-7101
714 824-4463 **Loma Linda University** 11234 Anderson St ... Loma Linda CA 92350-0001
415 725-3900 **Stanford University** SUMC M-121 ... Stanford CA 94305-0000
916 752-0331 **University of California Davis** ... Davis CA 95616-5224
714 856-6119 **University of California Irvine** ... Irvine CA 92717-0001
213 825-6373 **University of California Los Angeles** 12-138 CHS ... Los Angeles CA 90024-0000
619 534-3713 **University of California San Diego** M002 ... La Jolla CA 92093-0001
415 476-2342 **University of California San Francisco**
513 Parnassus Ave Bldg S-224 ... San Francisco CA 94143-0001
213 224-7001 **University of Southern California** 1975 Zonal Ave ... Los Angeles CA 90033-1039
303 270-7565 **University of Colorado** 4200 E 9th Ave ... Denver CO 80262-0001
203 679-2152 **University of Connecticut** 263 Farmington Ave Rm AG062 ... Farmington CT 06030-0000
203 785-4672 **Yale University** 333 Cedar St ... New Haven CT 06510-3289
202 994-3506 **George Washington University**
2300 'I' St NW Ross Hall Rm 615 ... Washington DC 20037-0000
202 687-1164 **Georgetown University** 3900 Reservoir Rd NW ... Washington DC 20007-2187
202 806-6270 **Howard University** 520 W St NW ... Washington DC 20059-0001
904 392-5793 **University of Florida** PO Box J-215 JHMHC ... Gainesville FL 32610-0001
305 547-6545 **University of Miami** 1600 NW 10th Ave ... Miami FL 33136-1015
404 727-5660 **Emory University** 1440 Clifton Rd NE ... Atlanta GA 30307-1053
404 721-2231 **Medical College of Georgia** 1459 Laney-Walker Blvd ... Augusta GA 30912-0001
912 752-2524 **Mercer University** 1550 College St ... Macon GA 31207-0001
404 752-1500 **Morehouse School of Medicine** 720 Westview Dr SW ... Atlanta GA 30310-1495
808 956-8287 **University of Hawaii**
1960 East-West Rd Biomedical Sciences Bldg Rm T101 ... Honolulu HI 96822-0000
708 531-3000 **Loyola University** 2160 S 1st Ave ... Maywood IL 60153-5589
217 782-3318 **Southern Illinois University** 801 N Rutledge St ... Springfield IL 62702-4910
312 702-1939 **University of Chicago** 5812 S Ellis Box 69 Rm G115-A ... Chicago IL 60637-1435
708 578-3000 **University of Health Sciences** 3333 Greenbay Rd ... North Chicago IL 60064-3037
312 996-3500 **University of Illinois** 1853 W Polk St Medical Ctr ... Chicago IL 60612-4376
317 274-8157 **Indiana University** 1120 South Dr ... Indianapolis IN 46202-5135
319 335-8050 **University of Iowa** 240 EMRB Bldg ... Iowa City IA 52242-0001
913 588-5283 **University of Kansas** 39th St & Rainbow Blvd Rm 107-A ... Kansas City KS 66103-0000
606 233-6582 **University of Kentucky** 800 Rose St ... Lexington KY 40536-0001
502 588-5184 **University of Louisville** 500 S Preston St ... Louisville KY 40292-0001
504 568-4006 **Louisiana State University** 1542 Tulane Ave ... New Orleans LA 70112-2865
318 674-5000 **Louisiana State University Shreveport** 1501 Kings Hwy ... Shreveport LA 71103-4228
504 588-5299 **Tulane University** 1430 Tulane Ave ... New Orleans LA 70112-2699
301 955-5000 **Johns Hopkins Medical Institutions** 720 Rutland Ave ... Baltimore MD 21205-2109
301 295-3030 **Uniformed Services University of the Health Sciences**
4301 Jones Bridge Rd ... Bethesda MD 20814-4799
301 328-7410 **University of Maryland** 655 W Baltimore St ... Baltimore MD 21201-1509
617 638-4630 **Boston University** 80 E Concord St ... Boston MA 02118-2394
617 432-1580 **Harvard University** 25 Shattuck St ... Boston MA 02115-6092
617 956-6571 **Tufts University** 136 Harrison Ave ... Boston MA 02111-1800
508 856-0011 **University of Massachusetts** 55 Lake Ave N ... Worcester MA 01655-0001
517 353-1730 **Michigan State University** E Fee Hall Rm A-118 ... East Lansing MI 48824-0001
313 763-9600 **University of Michigan**
1301 E Katherine St Medical Science Bldg 1 ... Ann Arbor MI 48109-0001
313 577-1460 **Wayne State University** 540 E Canfield St ... Detroit MI 48201-1908
507 284-3671 **Mayo Medical School** 200 1st St SW ... Rochester MN 55905-0001
218 726-7571 **University of Minnesota Duluth** 10 University Dr ... Duluth MN 55812-2403
612 626-4949 **University of Minnesota Minneapolis**
420 Delaware St Owre Bldg Box 293 ... Minneapolis MN 55455-0000
601 984-1010 **University of Mississippi** 2500 N State St ... Jackson MS 39216-4505
314 577-8205 **Saint Louis University** 1402 S Grand Blvd ... Saint Louis MO 63104-1083
314 882-1566 **University of Missouri Columbia**
Health Science Ctr Rm MA-204 ... Columbia MO 65212-0001
816 276-1808 **University of Missouri Kansas City** 2411 Holmes St ... Kansas City MO 64108-2741
314 362-5000 **Washington University** 1 Barnes Hospital Plaza ... Saint Louis MO 63110-0000
402 280-2900 **Creighton University** 24th & California Sts ... Omaha NE 68178-0001
402 559-4204 **University of Nebraska** 600 S 42nd St ... Omaha NE 68198-0000
603 646-7480 **Dartmouth College** Remsen Bldg Rm 300 ... Hanover NH 03756-0000
201 456-4300 **University of Medicine & Dentistry of New Jersey Medical School**
150 Bergen St ... Newark NJ 07103-2406
505 277-2321 **University of New Mexico**
University Hill NE Basic Medical Science Bldg ... Albuquerque NM 87131-0001
212 305-3592 **Columbia University** 630 W 168th St ... New York NY 10032-3702
212 746-5454 **Cornell University** 1300 York Ave ... New York NY 10021-4896
212 241-7335 **CUNY** 1 Gustave L Levy Pl ... New York NY 10029-6504
914 993-4531 **New York Medical College** Sunshine Bldg ... Valhalla NY 10595-0000
212 340-5290 **New York University** 550 1st Ave ... New York NY 10016-6402
716 831-2775 **SUNY Buffalo** 174 Cary Farber Sherman Bldg ... Buffalo NY 14214-0000
315 464-5540 **SUNY** 750 E Adams St ... Syracuse NY 13210-2399

Graduate and Professional Schools

516 444-2080 **SUNY Stony Brook** Health Science Ctr — Stony Brook NY 11794-0001
315 464-4570 **SUNY Syracuse** 750 E Adams St — Syracuse NY 13210-2306
518 445-5544 **Union University** 47 New Scotland Ave — Albany NY 12208-3412
716 275-3407 **University of Rochester** 601 Elmwood Ave Medical Ctr — Rochester NY 14642-0001
212 430-2000 **Yeshiva University** 1300 Morris Park Ave — Bronx NY 10461-1975
919 684-2498 **Duke University** PO Box 3005 — Durham NC 27710-0000
919 551-2201 **East Carolina University** Brody Medical Sciences Bldg Rm 1N-12 — Greenville NC 27858-0000
919 966-4161 **University of North Carolina** CB 7000 — Chapel Hill NC 27599-0001
701 777-2514 **University of North Dakota** 501 N Columbia Rd — Grand Forks ND 58203-2817
216 368-2820 **Case Western Reserve University** 2107 Adelbert Rd Rm T-106 — Cleveland OH 44106-2624
419 381-4107 **Medical College of Ohio** PO Box 10008 — Toledo OH 43699-0008
216 325-2511 **Northeastern Ohio University** 4209 SR-44 — Rootstown OH 44272-0000
614 292-7755 **Ohio State University** 370 W 9th Ave Meiling Hall — Columbus OH 43210-0000
513 558-7391 **University of Cincinnati** 231 Bethesda Ave ML552 — Cincinnati OH 45267-0000
513 873-3010 **Wright State University** PO Box 927 — Dayton OH 45401-0927
405 271-2265 **University of Oklahoma** 940 Stanton Young Ave Rm 357 — Oklahoma City OK 73104-0000
503 494-8220 **University of Oregon** 3181 SW Sam Jackson Park Rd — Portland OR 97201-3042
215 448-7604 **Hahnemann University** Broad & Vine Sts MS-440 — Philadelphia PA 19102-1192
215 842-4166 **Medical College of Pennsylvania** 3200 Henry Ave — Philadelphia PA 19129-1137
717 531-8521 **Pennsylvania State University** 500 University Dr — Hershey PA 17033-2360
215 221-3656 **Temple University** Broad & Ontario Sts Faculty-Student Bldg Rm 305 — Philadelphia PA 19140-0000
215 898-8001 **University of Pennsylvania** Medical Education Bldg Suite 100 — Philadelphia PA 19104-6382
412 648-8975 **University of Pittsburgh** 3550 Terrace St M240 Scaife Hall — Pittsburgh PA 15261-0001
401 863-2149 **Brown University** 97 Waterman St G-A212 — Providence RI 02912-0001
803 733-3200 **University of South Carolina** Administration Bldg Rm 200 — Columbia SC 29208-0000
605 677-5621 **University of South Dakota** 414 E Clark St — Vermillion SD 57069-2390
615 929-6219 **East Tennessee State University** PO Box 19900A — Johnson City TN 37614-1000
615 327-6000 **Meharry Medical College** 1005 Dr DB Todd Jr Blvd — Nashville TN 37208-3599
901 528-5539 **University of Tennessee** 800 Madison Blvd Hyman Bldg Suite 400 — Memphis TN 38163-0000
615 322-2164 **Vanderbilt University** 21st & Garland Sts Medical Ctr D-3300 — Nashville TN 37232-0001
713 798-4841 **Baylor College of Medicine** 1 Baylor Plaza — Houston TX 77030-3498
409 845-3431 **Texas A & M University** Joe H Reynolds Medical Bldg — College Station TX 77843-0000
806 743-3000 **Texas Tech University** 3601 4th St — Lubbock TX 79430-0001
214 688-3111 **University of Texas Dallas** 5323 Harry Hines Blvd — Dallas TX 75235-7200
409 761-1011 **University of Texas Galveston** 301 University Blvd — Galveston TX 77550-2774
512 567-7000 **University of Texas Health Science Center** 7703 Floyd Curl Dr — San Antonio TX 78284-0001
713 792-2121 **University of Texas Houston** 1515 Holcombe Blvd — Houston TX 77030-0000
801 581-7201 **University of Utah** 50 N Medical Dr — Salt Lake City UT 84132-0001
802 656-2150 **University of Vermont** Given Bldg Rm E-109 — Burlington VT 05405-0001
804 446-5600 **Medical College of Hampton Roads** PO Box 1980 — Norfolk VA 23501-1980
804 924-5118 **University of Virginia** Medical Ctr Box 395 — Charlottesville VA 22908-0001
804 786-9793 **Virginia Commonwealth University** 1101 E Marshall St — Richmond VA 23298-0001
206 543-1060 **University of Washington** 1959 NE Pacific St SC-64 — Seattle WA 98195-0001
304 696-7000 **Marshall University** 1801 6th Ave — Huntington WV 25755-0001
304 293-4511 **West Virginia University** 1150 Health Science Ctr N — Morgantown WV 26506-0001
608 263-4910 **University of Wisconsin** 1300 University Ave — Madison WI 53706-1532

NURSING

205 934-5360 **University of Alabama** 1701 University Blvd UAB Stn — Birmingham AL 35294-0001
602 965-3244 **Arizona State University** — Tempe AZ 85287-0001
602 626-6154 **University of Arizona** Mabel & Martin Sts — Tucson AZ 85721-0001
501 686-5374 **University of Arkansas for Medical Sciences** 4301 W Markham St MS-529 — Little Rock AR 72205-7101
209 278-2041 **California State University Fresno** MS-25 — Fresno CA 93740-0001
213 343-4730 **California State University Los Angeles** 5151 State University Dr — Los Angeles CA 90032-8000
213 825-7181 **University of California Los Angeles** 10833 Le Conte Ave — Los Angeles CA 90024-1602
415 476-1435 **University of California San Francisco** Office of Student Affairs Rm 319X — San Francisco CA 94143-0602
303 270-5592 **University of Colorado Health Science Center** 4200 E 9th Ave Health Science Ctr — Denver CO 80262-0001
203 486-4729 **University of Connecticut** 231 Glenbrook Rd — Storrs CT 06269-0001
302 451-1255 **University of Delaware** McDowell Hall — Newark DE 19716-0001
202 319-5400 **Catholic University of America** 620 Michigan Ave NE Gowan Hall — Washington DC 20064-0001
904 392-3751 **University of Florida** J Hillis Miller Health Ctr J-197 — Gainesville FL 32610-0001
404 721-3771 **Medical College of Georgia** 1446 Harper St — Augusta GA 30912-0001
312 362-8150 **DePaul University** 2323 N Seminary Ave — Chicago IL 60614-3298
312 508-3249 **Loyola University of Chicago** 6525 N Sheridan Rd — Chicago IL 60626-5385
815 753-1231 **Northern Illinois University** 1240 Normal Rd — De Kalb IL 60115-1391
312 942-6980 **Rush University** 1753 W Congress Pkwy — Chicago IL 60612-3809
312 996-7800 **University of Illinois** 845 S Damen Ave — Chicago IL 60612-0000
319 335-7018 **University of Iowa** 101 Nursing Bldg — Iowa City IA 52242-0001
913 588-1600 **University of Kansas** 39th St & Rainbow Blvd — Kansas City KS 66103-3337
606 233-5406 **University of Kentucky** 760 Rose St Nursing Health Sciences Learning Ctr — Lexington KY 40536-0232
504 568-4101 **Louisiana State University Medical Center** 1900 Gravier St — New Orleans LA 70112-2262
301 328-6740 **University of Maryland** 655 W Lombard St — Baltimore MD 21201-1512
617 552-4250 **Boston College** 140 Commonwealth Ave — Chestnut Hill MA 02167-9991
313 764-7185 **University of Michigan** 400 N Ingalls St — Ann Arbor MI 48109-0001
313 577-4082 **Wayne State University** 5557 Cass Ave — Detroit MI 48202-3615
612 624-9600 **University of Minnesota** 308 Harvard St SE Unit F Rm 6101 — Minneapolis MN 55455-0353
601 266-5445 **University of Southern Mississippi** PO Box 5095 — Hattiesburg MS 39406-0000
314 577-8907 **Saint Louis University** 3525 Caroline St — Saint Louis MO 63104-1007
314 882-0292 **University of Missouri** School of Nursing Bldg — Columbia MO 65211-0001
402 559-4110 **University of Nebraska Medical Center** 600 42nd St — Omaha NE 68198-0001
201 648-5018 **Rutgers University** 180 University Ave — Newark NJ 07102-1803
212 305-5756 **Columbia University** 617 W 168th St — New York NY 10032-3703
212 481-4312 **CUNY Hunter-Bellevue College** 425 E 25th St — New York NY 10010-2547
212 998-5300 **New York University** 50 W 4th St Shimkin Hall Rm 429 — New York NY 10003-0000
518 270-2384 **Russell Sage College** 45 Ferry St — Troy NY 12180-4115
607 777-4964 **SUNY Binghamton** School of Nursing Bldg Rm 82 — Binghamton NY 13901-0000
716 831-2533 **SUNY Buffalo** 3435 Main St Kimball Tower — Buffalo NY 14214-3099
315 443-2144 **Syracuse University** 426 Ostrom Ave — Syracuse NY 13210-2938
716 275-2375 **University of Rochester** 601 Almwood Ave Helenwood Hall — Rochester NY 14642-0001
216 368-2540 **Case Western Reserve University** 2121 Abington Rd — Cleveland OH 44106-2333
614 292-8900 **Ohio State University** 1585 Neil Ave — Columbus OH 43210-1216
513 558-5500 **University of Cincinnati** Mail Location 38 — Cincinnati OH 45221-0001
405 271-2421 **University of Oklahoma** PO Box 26901 — Oklahoma City OK 73190-0001
814 863-0245 **Pennsylvania State University** 201 Health & Human Development E — University Park PA 16802-0001
215 898-8281 **University of Pennsylvania** 420 Guardian Dr — Philadelphia PA 19104-0000
412 624-2407 **University of Pittsburgh** 3500 Victoria St Victoria Bldg Rm 336 — Pittsburgh PA 15261-0001
803 777-3861 **University of South Carolina** Williams Brice Nursing Bldg Rm 202 — Columbia SC 29208-0001

901 528-6128 **University of Tennessee Memphis** 877 Madison Ave Lamar Alexander Bldg Suite 620 — Memphis TN 38163-0001
615 322-4400 **Vanderbilt University** 112 Godchaux Hall — Nashville TN 37240-0001
817 898-2401 **Texas Woman's University** 1216 Oakland St Rm 232 — Denton TX 76201-3169
512 471-7311 **University of Texas Austin** 1700 Red River St — Austin TX 78701-1412
713 792-7800 **University of Texas Houston** 1100 Holcombe Blvd — Houston TX 77030-3907
801 378-4144 **Brigham Young University** Spencer W Kimball Tower Suite 500 — Provo UT 84602-0000
801 581-7728 **University of Utah** 25 S Medical Dr — Salt Lake City UT 84112-1502
804 924-2743 **University of Virginia** McLeod Hall — Charlottesville VA 22903-0000
804 786-0724 **Virginia Commonwealth University** PO Box 567 MCV Stn — Richmond VA 23298-0001
206 543-9175 **University of Washington** Health Sciences Bldg SC-72 — Seattle WA 98195-0001
414 288-3811 **Marquette University** 530 N 16th St Emory T Clark Hall Rm 265 — Milwaukee WI 53233-0000
608 263-5155 **University of Wisconsin Madison** 600 Highland Ave Center for Health Sciences — Madison WI 53792-0001
414 229-4801 **University of Wisconsin Milwaukee** PO Box 413 — Milwaukee WI 53201-0413

OPTOMETRY

205 934-6150 **University of Alabama Birmingham** 1716 University Stn — Birmingham AL 35294-0001
714 870-7226 **Southern California College of Optometry** 2575 E Yorba Linda Blvd — Fullerton CA 92631-1610
415 642-3302 **University of California Berkeley** 360 Minor Hall — Berkeley CA 94720-0001
312 225-1700 **Illinois College of Optometry** 3241 S Michigan Ave — Chicago IL 60616-3816
812 855-4447 **Indiana University** 800 E Atwater Ave — Bloomington IN 47405-3680
617 266-2030 **New England College of Optometry** 424 Beacon St — Boston MA 02115-1100
616 592-3700 **Ferris State University** 901 S State St — Big Rapids MI 49307-2295
314 553-5606 **University of Missouri Saint Louis** 8001 Natural Bridge Rd — Saint Louis MO 63121-4499
614 292-2647 **Ohio State University** 338 W 10th Ave — Columbus OH 43210-1240
503 359-2202 **Pacific University** 2043 College Way — Forest Grove OR 97116-1797
215 276-6000 **Pennsylvania College of Optometry** 1200 W Godfrey Ave — Philadelphia PA 19141-3323
901 722-3200 **Southern College of Optometry** 1245 Madison Ave — Memphis TN 38104-2211
713 749-3361 **University of Houston** 4800 Calhoun Rd — Houston TX 77204-0001

PHARMACY

205 844-4740 **Auburn University** Pharmacy Bldg — Auburn AL 36849-0000
205 870-2833 **Samford University** 800 Lakeshore Dr — Birmingham AL 35229-0001
602 626-1427 **University of Arizona** 1703 E Mabel St Rm 344 — Tucson AZ 85721-0001
501 686-5557 **University of Arkansas for Medical Sciences** 4301 W Markham St MS-522 — Little Rock AR 72205-7101
415 476-1225 **University of California San Francisco** 513 Parnassus Ave — San Francisco CA 94143-0000
213 224-7501 **University of Southern California** 1985 Zonal Ave — Los Angeles CA 90033-1058
209 946-2561 **University of the Pacific** 751 Brookside Rd — Stockton CA 95211-0001
303 492-6278 **University of Colorado Boulder** CB 297 — Boulder CO 80309-0001
203 486-2129 **University of Connecticut** 372 Fairfield Rd — Storrs CT 06269-0001
202 806-6530 **Howard University** 2300 4th St NW — Washington DC 20059-0001
904 599-3593 **Florida A & M University** Pharmacy Bldg Rm 201 — Tallahassee FL 32307-0001
404 653-8800 **Mercer University** 345 Boulevard NE — Atlanta GA 30312-1252
404 542-1911 **University of Georgia** College of Pharmacy Bldg — Athens GA 30602-1601
208 236-2175 **Idaho State University** Campus Box 8288 — Pocatello ID 83209-0001
312 996-7240 **University of Illinois Chicago** 833 S Wood St MC-874 — Chicago IL 60612-4324
317 283-9322 **Butler University** 4600 Sunset Ave — Indianapolis IN 46208-3485
317 494-1357 **Purdue University** Pharmacy Bldg — West Lafayette IN 47907-0000
515 271-2172 **Drake University** Fitch Hall — Des Moines IA 50311-0000
319 335-8794 **University of Iowa** — Iowa City IA 52242-0001
913 864-3591 **University of Kansas** 2056 Malott Hall — Lawrence KS 66045-0001
606 257-2738 **University of Kentucky** Rose St Pharmacy Bldg — Lexington KY 40536-0082
318 342-1600 **Northeast Louisiana University** 700 University Ave — Monroe LA 71209-0001
504 483-7419 **Xavier University of Louisiana** 7325 Palmetto St — New Orleans LA 70125-1098
301 328-7650 **University of Maryland** 20 N Pine St — Baltimore MD 21201-1142
617 437-3321 **Northeastern University** 360 Huntington Ave 206 Mugar Bldg — Boston MA 02115-5096
616 592-3780 **Ferris State University** 901 S State St — Big Rapids MI 49307-2295
313 764-7144 **University of Michigan** 428 Church St — Ann Arbor MI 48109-1065
313 577-0820 **Wayne State University** — Detroit MI 48202-0000
612 624-1900 **University of Minnesota** 308 Harvard St SE Health Sciences Unit F Rm 5-130 — Minneapolis MN 55455-0353
601 232-7265 **University of Mississippi** Faser Hall Rm 201 — University MS 38677-9999
816 276-1607 **University of Missouri Kansas City** 5005 Rockhill Rd — Kansas City MO 64110-2239
406 243-4621 **University of Montana** Pharmacy/Psychology Bldg Rm 119 — Missoula MT 59812-0001
402 280-2950 **Creighton University** 24th & California Sts — Omaha NE 68178-0001
402 559-4333 **University of Nebraska Medical Center** 600 S 42nd St — Omaha NE 68198-6000
505 277-3241 **University of New Mexico** Pharmacy Nursing Bldg Rm 184 — Albuquerque NM 87131-0001
718 403-1060 **Long Island University** 75 Dekalb Ave — Brooklyn NY 11201-5423
718 990-6275 **Saint John's University** Grand Central & Utopia Pkwys — Jamaica NY 11439-0001
716 636-2823 **SUNY Buffalo** 126 Cooke Hall — Buffalo NY 14260-0001
919 893-4111 **Campbell University** PO Box 1090 — Buies Creek NC 27506-1090
919 966-1121 **University of North Carolina** 200H Beard Hall Campus Box 7360 — Chapel Hill NC 27599-0001
701 237-7456 **North Dakota State University** 13th St & 12th Ave N — Fargo ND 58105-0000
419 772-2275 **Ohio Northern University** — Ada OH 45810-0000
614 292-2266 **Ohio State University** 500 W 12th Ave Lloyd M Parks Hall Rm 217 — Columbus OH 43210-0000
513 558-3784 **University of Cincinnati** Health Professions Bldg Mail Location 4 — Cincinnati OH 45267-0001
419 537-4235 **University of Toledo** 2801 W Bancroft St — Toledo OH 43606-3390
405 774-3104 **Southwestern Oklahoma State University** 100 Campus Dr — Weatherford OK 73096-3001
405 271-6484 **University of Oklahoma** 1110 N Stonewall Ave — Oklahoma City OK 73117-1223
503 737-3725 **Oregon State University** Pharmacy Bldg Rm 203 — Corvallis OR 97331-0000
412 434-6380 **Duquesne University** 410 Mellon Hall — Pittsburgh PA 15282-0001
215 221-4900 **Temple University** 3307 N Broad St — Philadelphia PA 19140-5101
412 648-8650 **University of Pittsburgh** 3501 Terrace St Salk Hall Rm 1104 — Pittsburgh PA 15261-0001
401 792-2761 **University of Rhode Island** Fogerty Hall — Kingston RI 02881-0000
803 792-3116 **Medical University of South Carolina** 171 Ashley Ave — Charleston SC 29425-0001
803 777-2149 **University of South Carolina** Coker Life Science Bldg Rm 109 — Columbia SC 29208-0001
605 688-6197 **South Dakota State University** PO Box 2202C — Brookings SD 57007-0001
901 528-6036 **University of Tennessee Memphis** 842 Monroe Suite 238 — Memphis TN 38163-0001
713 527-7164 **Texas Southern University** 3100 Cleburne St — Houston TX 77004-4598
512 471-1737 **University of Texas** 200 W 21st St — Austin TX 78712-0000
801 581-6731 **University of Utah** 201 Scaggs Hall — Salt Lake City UT 84112-0000
804 786-8489 **Virginia Commonwealth University** PO Box 581 — Richmond VA 23298-0001
206 543-2030 **University of Washington** SC-69 — Seattle WA 98195-0001
509 335-4750 **Washington State University** Wegner Hall Rm 105 — Pullman WA 99164-6510
304 293-5211 **West Virginia University** 1136 Health Science Ctr N — Morgantown WV 26506-0001
608 262-1414 **University of Wisconsin Madison** 425 N Charter St — Madison WI 53706-1508
307 766-6120 **University of Wyoming** PO Box 3375 — Laramie WY 82071-3375

PHYSICS

602 621-6800 **University of Arizona** 1118 E 4th St — Tucson AZ 85721-0001
818 356-4585 **California Institute of Technology** 1201 E California Blvd Jorgensen Bldg MS 103-33 — Pasadena CA 91125-0001

415 723-4344 **Stanford University** Varian Physics Bldg ... Stanford CA 94305-0000
415 642-7166 **University of California Berkeley** LeConte Bldg Rm 366 ... Berkeley CA 94720-0001
714 856-5438 **University of California Irvine**
Physical Sciences Bldg 2 Rm 4129 ... Irvine CA 92717-0001
213 825-2307 **University of California Los Angeles**
Knudsen Hall Rm 3-145G ... Los Angeles CA 90024-0000
619 534-3293 **University of California San Diego** MC B019 ... La Jolla CA 92093-0001
805 961-3888 **University of California Santa Barbara** 3019 Broida Hall .. Santa Barbara CA 93106-0001
303 492-6954 **University of Colorado Boulder** Campus Box 390 ... Boulder CO 80309-0001
203 432-3600 **Yale University** PO Box 6666 ... New Haven CT 06511-0000
904 644-4473 **Florida State University** 307 Keen Bldg ... Tallahassee FL 22306-0000
708 491-3685 **Northwestern University** 2145 Sheridan Rd ... Evanston IL 60208-0001
312 702-7006 **University of Chicago** 5720 S Ellis Ave ... Chicago IL 60637-1434
217 333-3761 **University of Illinois Urbana** 1110 W Green St ... Urbana IL 61801-3003
812 855-3973 **Indiana University** Swain W Rm 132 ... Bloomington IN 47405-0001
515 294-5440 **Iowa State University** Physics Bldg Rm 12 ... Ames IA 50011-0001
319 335-1687 **University of Iowa** Van Allen Hall Rm 203 ... Iowa City IA 52242-0001
301 338-7347 **Johns Hopkins University**
3400 N Charles St Bloomberg Ctr Rm 366-K ... Baltimore MD 21218-0000
301 454-3514 **University of Maryland** Physics Bldg Rm 1302-D ... College Park MD 20742-0001
617 736-2803 **Brandeis University** 415 South St Bass Bldg Rm 210 ... Waltham MA 02254-9110
617 495-2872 **Harvard University** Jefferson Physical Laboratory ... Cambridge MA 02138-0000
617 253-4851 **Massachusetts Institute of Technology**
77 Massachusetts Ave Bldg 6-107 ... Cambridge MA 02139-4307
517 355-9666 **Michigan State University**
Physics-Astronomy Bldg Rm 106 ... East Lansing MI 48824-0001
313 764-4437 **University of Michigan**
500 E University Randall Lab Rm 1049 ... Ann Arbor MI 48109-0001
612 624-6366 **University of Minnesota** 116 Church St SE ... Minneapolis MN 55455-0149
314 889-6276 **Washington University** 1 Brookings Dr Campus Box 1105 ... Saint Louis MO 63130-4899
603 646-2359 **Dartmouth College** Wilder Hall ... Hanover NH 03755-1477
609 258-4403 **Princeton University** Washington Rd 203 Jadwin Hall ... Princeton NJ 08544-0001
908 932-2502 **Rutgers University** Serin Physics Lab ... Piscataway NJ 08855-0000
212 854-3366 **Columbia University** 538 W 120th St ... New York NY 10027-6601
607 255-4884 **Cornell University** 117 Clark Hall ... Ithaca NY 14853-0001
718 390-7994 **CUNY College of Staten Island** 50 Bay St ... Staten Island NY 10301-2511
212 998-7700 **New York University**
4 Washington Pl Andre & Bella Meyer Hall of Physics ... New York NY 10003-6603
518 276-8393 **Rensselaer Polytechnic Institute** Science Ctr 1st Fl ... Troy NY 12180-0000
716 475-2421 **Rochester Institute of Technology** Bldg 8 ... Rochester NY 14627-0000
212 570-8636 **Rockefeller University** 1230 York Ave ... New York NY 10021-6399
516 632-8080 **SUNY Stony Brook*Physics Department**
Graduate Physics Bldg ... Stony Brook NY 11794-3800
315 443-5958 **Syracuse University** 201 Physics Bldg ... Syracuse NY 13244-0001
919 684-8140 **Duke University** Physics Bldg Rm 107 ... Durham NC 27706-0000
919 962-2078 **University of North Carolina** 278 Phillips Hall CB-3255 ... Chapel Hill NC 27599-0001
614 292-5713 **Ohio State University** 174 W 18th Ave Rm 1174 ... Columbus OH 43210-1106
503 346-4751 **University of Oregon** Willamette Hall ... Eugene OR 97403-0000
412 268-2734 **Carnegie Mellon University** Wean Hall Rm 7325 ... Pittsburgh PA 15213-0000
215 898-5720 **University of Pennsylvania** 209 S 33rd St DRL Bldg ... Philadelphia PA 19104-0000
412 624-9000 **University of Pittsburgh** 100 Allen Hall ... Pittsburgh PA 15260-0001
401 863-2378 **Brown University** 42 Charlesfield St ... Providence RI 02912-0001
713 527-4938 **Rice University** 6100 S Main St ... Houston TX 77005-1892
512 471-1664 **University of Texas** RLM 5.208 ... Austin TX 78712-1081
804 924-6317 **University of Virginia** McCormick Rd Physics Bldg ... Charlottesville VA 22903-0000
206 543-2770 **University of Washington** FM-15 ... Seattle WA 98195-0001
608 262-3077 **University of Wisconsin Madison**
475 N Charter St 2531 Sterling Hall ... Madison WI 53706-0001

PUBLIC AFFAIRS AND ADMINISTRATION

602 965-3926 **Arizona State University** Wilson Hall ... Tempe AZ 85287-0001
415 442-7870 **Golden Gate University** 536 Mission St ... San Francisco CA 94105-2967
415 642-1940 **University of California** 2607 Hearst Ave ... Berkeley CA 94720-0001
415 666-6254 **University of San Francisco** Ignagian Heights ... San Francisco CA 94117-0000
202 885-2944 **American University**
4400 Massachusetts Ave NW Ward Circle Bldg Rm 104 ... Washington DC 20016-8002
202 994-6295 **George Washington University**
2115 G St NW Monroe Hall Rm 302 ... Washington DC 20052-0001
904 644-3525 **Florida State University** Bellamy Bldg Rm 614 ... Tallahassee FL 32306-0001
404 542-2059 **University of Georgia** Baldwin Hall Rm 104 ... Athens GA 30602-0000
319 335-2357 **University of Iowa** Schaeffer Bldg Rm 310 ... Iowa City IA 52242-0001
913 864-3523 **University of Kansas** 504 Blake Hall ... Lawrence KS 66045-0001
508 757-4586 **Anna Maria College** Trinity Hall ... Paxton MA 01612-1198
617 495-1105 **Harvard University** 79 John F Kennedy St ... Cambridge MA 02138-5801
617 868-9600 **Lesley College** 29 Everett St ... Cambridge MA 02138-2790
617 437-2796 **Northeastern University**
360 Huntington Ave Messerve Hall Rm 303 ... Boston MA 02115-5096
313 764-0329 **University of Michigan** 440-B Lorch Hall ... Ann Arbor MI 48109-0001
612 625-9505 **University of Minnesota**
301 19th Ave S Humphrey Ctr Rm 230 ... Minneapolis MN 55455-0000
314 882-3304 **University of Missouri** 315 Middlebush Hall ... Columbia MO 65211-0001
609 258-4820 **Princeton University** Robertson Hall ... Princeton NJ 08544-0001
516 299-2716 **Long Island University CW Post Campus** Roth Hall Rm 302 ... Brookville NY 11548-0000
212 998-7414 **New York University** 4 Washington Sq N ... New York NY 10003-0000
518 442-5254 **SUNY Albany** 135th Western Ave Milne Hall ... Albany NY 12222-0001
315 443-2348 **Syracuse University** 105 Maxwell Hall ... Syracuse NY 13244-0001
614 292-8696 **Ohio State University** 1775 College Rd 208 Haggerty Hall ... Columbus OH 43210-0000
405 325-6432 **University of Oklahoma** 455 W Lindsey St Rm 305 ... Norman OK 73019-0001
412 268-2159 **Carnegie Mellon University** Hamburg Hall Rm 1104 ... Pittsburgh PA 15213-0000
412 648-7600 **University of Pittsburgh** Forbes Quadrangle Rm 3G07 ... Pittsburgh PA 15260-0001
803 777-3869 **University of South Carolina** Gambrell Hall 3rd Fl ... Columbia SC 29208-0001
512 471-4962 **University of Texas** PO Box Y University Stn ... Austin TX 78713-8925
802 257-7751 **School for International Training** Kipling Rd ... Brattleboro VT 05301-0000
703 231-6691 **Virginia Polytechnic Institute & State University**
100 Sandy Hall ... Blacksburg VA 24061-6801

PUBLIC HEALTH

415 442-7216 **Golden Gate University** 536 Mission St ... San Francisco CA 94105-2967
619 594-6151 **San Diego State University** ... San Diego CA 92182-0001
203 432-4771 **Yale University** 60 College St ... New Haven CT 06510-3210
305 940-5895 **Florida International University**
North Miami Campus Bldg AC1 Rm 225 ... North Miami FL 33181-0000
815 740-3478 **College of Saint Francis** 500 Wilcox St ... Joliet IL 60435-6188
317 274-4656 **Indiana University** 801 W Michigan BS-3027 ... Indianapolis IN 46202-5152
301 955-3543 **Johns Hopkins University** 615 N Wolfe St ... Baltimore MD 21205-2103
617 638-5052 **Boston University** 80 E Concord St Bldg A 4th Fl ... Boston MA 02118-2394
617 432-1035 **Harvard University** 677 Huntington Ave ... Boston MA 02115-0000
413 782-1231 **Western New England College** 1215 Wilbraham Rd ... Springfield MA 01119-2693
314 576-9317 **Maryville College** 13550 Conway Rd ... Saint Louis MO 63141-7299
212 305-4122 **Columbia University** 600 W 168th St ... New York NY 10032-3702
718 403-1105 **Long Island University** 75 DeKalb Ave ... Brooklyn NY 11201-5423
516 299-2771 **Long Island University CW Post Campus** Roth Hall Rm 100 ... Brookville NY 11548-0000
212 741-8682 **New School for Social Research** 66 5th Ave ... New York NY 10011-8892

518 445-1724 **Russell Sage College**
140 New Scotland Ave Administration Bldg ... Albany NY 12208-3491
919 966-4152 **University of North Carolina** Rosenau Hall CB-7400 ... Chapel Hill NC 27599-0001
814 865-1428 **Pennsylvania State University** 201 Henderson Bldg ... University Park PA 16802-0001
215 898-6861 **University of Pennsylvania** 3641 Locust Walk Rm 204 ... Philadelphia PA 19104-6218
512 221-6443 **Baylor University** Stanley Rd ... Fort Sam Houston TX 78234-0000
713 749-2893 **University of Houston** 4800 Calhoun Rd ... Houston TX 77204-6283

URBAN PLANNING

205 851-5425 **Alabama A & M University** Carver Complex S Rm 218 ... Normal AL 35762-0000
714 869-2688 **California State Polytechnic University** 3801 W Temple Ave ... Pomona CA 91768-2557
408 924-5882 **San Jose State University** Bldg DD ... San Jose CA 95192-0001
415 642-3257 **University of California Berkeley** 228 Wurster Hall ... Berkeley CA 94720-0001
213 825-3791 **University of California Los Angeles**
405 Hilgard Ave Perloff Hall Rm 1317 ... Los Angeles CA 90024-1467
213 743-2052 **University of Southern California** University Pk ... Los Angeles CA 90089-0042
303 556-3479 **University of Colorado Denver** PO Box 173364 ... Denver CO 80217-3364
904 644-4510 **Florida State University** Bellamy Bldg Rm 355 ... Tallahassee FL 32306-0001
904 392-0997 **University of Florida**
431 Architecture Bldg College of Architecture ... Gainesville FL 32611-0000
305 284-3438 **University of Miami** 1223 Dickinson Dr Rm 48-E ... Coral Gables FL 33124-9178
404 894-2351 **Georgia Institute of Technology** Old Architecture Bldg Rm 217 ... Atlanta GA 30332-0155
808 956-7381 **University of Hawaii** 2424 Maile Way Porteus Hall Rm 107 ... Honolulu HI 96822-2223
312 996-8722 **University of Illinois Chicago**
1007 W Harrison MC-348 Rm 1180 ... Chicago IL 60607-0000
217 333-3890 **University of Illinois Urbana** 907 1/2 W Nevada St ... Urbana IL 61801-3810
515 294-8958 **Iowa State University** College of Design Rm 126 ... Ames IA 50011-0001
319 335-0032 **University of Iowa** 347 Jessup Hall ... Iowa City IA 52242-0001
913 532-5958 **Kansas State University** Seaton Hall Rm 302 ... Manhattan KS 66506-0001
913 864-4184 **University of Kansas** 317 Marvin Hall ... Lawrence KS 66045-0001
504 286-6277 **University of New Orleans** Math Bldg Rm 308 ... New Orleans LA 70148-0001
301 444-3225 **Morgan State University** Cold Spring Ln & Hillen Rd ... Baltimore MD 21239-4098
301 454-1823 **University of Maryland** Lefrak Hall Rm 1117 ... College Park MD 20742-0001
617 253-2022 **Massachusetts Institute of Technology**
77 Massachusetts Ave Bldg 7 Rm 338 ... Cambridge MA 02139-4307
517 353-9055 **Michigan State University**
Urban Planning & Landscape Architecture Bldg Rm 201 ... East Lansing MI 48824-0001
313 764-1300 **University of Michigan** 2000 Bonisteel Blvd ... Ann Arbor MI 48109-0001
612 625-9505 **University of Minnesota**
301 19th Ave S Humphrey Ctr Rm 130 ... Minneapolis MN 55455-0429
908 932-3822 **Rutgers University Kilmer** Lucy Stone Hall B Wing ... New Brunswick NJ 08903-0000
505 277-5050 **University of New Mexico** 2414 Central Ave SE ... Albuquerque NM 87131-0001
212 854-3513 **Columbia University**
Broadway & W 116th St Avery Hall Rm 400 ... New York NY 10027-0000
607 255-6848 **Cornell University** W Sibley Hall ... Ithaca NY 14853-0001
212 772-5517 **CUNY Hunter College** 695 Park Ave ... New York NY 10021-5085
212 998-7430 **New York University** 4 Washington Sq N ... New York NY 10003-0000
718 636-3414 **Pratt Institute** 65 Saint James St Higgins Hall Rm 112 ... Brooklyn NY 11205-3899
716 831-2133 **SUNY Buffalo** Hayes Hall Rm 116 ... Buffalo NY 14214-0000
919 962-3983 **University of North Carolina** New East Bldg 3140 ... Chapel Hill NC 27599-3140
614 292-6046 **Ohio State University** 190 W 17th Ave Brown Hall Rm 289 ... Columbus OH 43210-0000
513 556-4933 **University of Cincinnati** Mail Location 16 ... Cincinnati OH 45221-0016
405 325-6591 **University of Oklahoma** 830 Van Vleet Oval Rm 162 ... Norman OK 73019-0001
503 725-4045 **Portland State University** PO Box 751 ... Portland OR 97207-0751
503 346-3635 **University of Oregon** 119 Hendricks Hall ... Eugene OR 97403-0000
215 898-8329 **University of Pennsylvania**
210 S 34th St Myerson Hall Rm 127 ... Philadelphia PA 19104-6311
412 648-7630 **University of Pittsburgh** Forbes Quadrangle ... Pittsburgh PA 15260-0001
803 656-3926 **Clemson University** Lee Hall Rm 125 ... Clemson SC 29634-0001
901 678-2161 **Memphis State University** 226 Johnson Hall ... Memphis TN 38152-0001
615 974-5227 **University of Tennessee** 1618 Cumberland Ave ... Knoxville TN 37996-0001
409 845-1046 **Texas A & M University**
College of Architecture & Environmental Design ... College Station TX 77843-0000
817 273-2067 **University of Texas Arlington** 601 Campus Dr ... Arlington TX 76010-0000
512 471-8135 **University of Texas Austin** School of Architecture ... Austin TX 78712-1104
804 924-3716 **University of Virginia** Campbell Hall ... Charlottesville VA 22903-2443
804 367-1134 **Virginia Commonwealth University** 812 W Franklin St ... Richmond VA 23284-0001
703 231-5517 **Virginia Polytechnic Institute & State University**
Architecture Annex Rm 201H ... Blacksburg VA 24061-0001
509 359-2288 **Eastern Washington University** 201 Isle Hall ... Cheney WA 99004-0000
206 543-4190 **University of Washington** 410 Gould Hall JO-40 ... Seattle WA 98195-0001
608 262-1004 **University of Wisconsin** 925 Bascom Mall Old Music Hall ... Madison WI 53706-0001
414 229-5563 **University of Wisconsin Milwaukee** 2033 E Hartford Ave ... Milwaukee WI 53211-3154

VETERINARY MEDICINE

916 752-1360 **University of California** Harring Hall Rm 1018 ... Davis CA 95616-5224
303 491-7051 **Colorado State University** Anatomy Bldg Rm W-102 ... Fort Collins CO 80523-0001
904 392-2381 **University of Florida** 215 SW 16th Ave ... Gainesville FL 32610-0001
404 542-3461 **University of Georgia** ... Athens GA 30602-1601
217 333-2760 **University of Illinois** 2001 S Lincoln Ave ... Urbana IL 61801-6178
317 494-7608 **Purdue University** Lynn Hall ... West Lafayette IN 47907-1927
515 294-1242 **Iowa State University** ... Ames IA 50011-0001
913 532-5660 **Kansas State University** Trotter Hall Rm 101 ... Manhattan KS 66506-0001
504 346-3100 **Louisiana State University** S Stadium Dr ... Baton Rouge LA 70803-0001
508 839-5302 **Tufts University** 200 Westboro Rd ... North Grafton MA 01536-1895
517 355-6509 **Michigan State University** A-133 E Fee Hall ... East Lansing MI 48824-0001
612 624-9227 **University of Minnesota** 1365 Gortner Ave ... Saint Paul MN 55108-1016
607 253-3000 **Cornell University** Tower Rd ... Ithaca NY 14853-0001
919 829-4200 **North Carolina State University** 4700 Hillsborough St CB 8401 .. Raleigh NC 27606-1428
614 292-1171 **Ohio State University** 1900 Coffey Rd ... Columbus OH 43210-1006
405 744-6648 **Oklahoma State University** 205 Veterinary Medicine Bldg ... Stillwater OK 74078-0001
215 898-5438 **University of Pennsylvania** 3800 Spruce Rosenthal Bldg ... Philadelphia PA 19104-0000
409 845-5051 **Texas A & M University** ... College Station TX 77843-0000
703 231-7666 **Virginia-Maryland Regional College of Veterinary Medicine**
Phase II Duckpond Dr ... Blacksburg VA 24061-0001

Two-Year Colleges

Selected junior and community colleges are listed alphabetically within each state.

ALABAMA

205 774-5113 **Alabama Aviation & Technical College** PO Box 1209 ... Ozark AL 36361-1209
205 233-8100 **Athens State College** 300 N Beaty St ... Athens AL 35611-1999
205 428-6391 **Bessemer State Technical College** PO Box 308 ... Bessemer AL 35021-0308
205 690-6412 **Bishop State Community College** 351 N Broad St ... Mobile AL 36603-5898
205 932-3221 **Brewer State Junior College** 2631 Temple Ave N ... Fayette AL 35555-1198
205 234-6346 **Central Alabama Community College** PO Box 699 ... Alexander City AL 35010-0699
205 378-5576 **Central Alabama Community College** PO Box 389 ... Childersburg AL 35044-0389
205 291-4900 **Chattahoochee Valley Community College**
2602 College Dr ... Phenix City AL 36867-0000
205 293-7064 **Community College of the Air Force** CCAF-RR Bldg 836 ... Maxwell AFB AL 36112-0000
205 874-5700 **Concordia College** 1804 Green St ... Selma AL 36701-3323

Two-Year Colleges

Phone	College	Address	City	State	ZIP
205 493-3573	**Douglas MacArthur State Technical College**	PO Box 649	Opp	AL	36467-0649
205 347-2623	**Enterprise State Junior College**	600 Plaza Dr	Enterprise	AL	36330-0000
205 546-0484	**Gadsden State Community College**	1001 George Wallace Dr	Gadsden	AL	35903-2269
	George C Wallace State Community College				
205 983-3521	*Dothan Campus*		Dothan	AL	36303-0000
205 352-6403	*Hanceville Campus*	801 Main St NW	Hanceville	AL	35077-0000
205 875-2634	*Selma Campus*	3000 Rangeline Rd	Selma	AL	36701-0000
205 831-4540	**Harry M Ayers State Technical College**	1801 Coleman Rd	Anniston	AL	36201-6858
205 937-9581	**James H Faulkner State Junior College**	1900 US Hwy 31 S	Bay Minette	AL	36507-0000
205 867-4832	**Jefferson Davis State Junior College**	Alco Dr	Brewton	AL	36426-0000
205 853-1200	**Jefferson State Community College**	2601 Carson Rd	Birmingham	AL	35215-3007
205 539-8161	**JF Drake State Technical College**	3421 Meridian St N	Huntsville	AL	35811-1544
205 353-3102	**John C Calhoun State Community College**	Hwy 31 N	Decatur	AL	35609-0000
205 288-1080	**John M Patterson State Technical College**	3920 Troy Hwy	Montgomery	AL	36116-2612
205 925-2515	**Lawson State Community College**	3060 Wilson Rd SW	Birmingham	AL	35221-1717
205 222-6591	**Lurleen B Wallace State Junior College**	PO Box 1418	Andalusia	AL	36420-1418
205 683-6172	**Marion Military Institute**	PO Box 420	Marion	AL	36756-0420
205 228-6001	**Northeast Alabama State Junior College**	PO Box 159	Rainsville	AL	35986-0159
205 575-3156	**Patrick Henry State Junior College**	Hwy 21 S	Monroeville	AL	36460-0000
205 578-1313	**Reid State Technical College**	PO Box 588	Evergreen	AL	36401-0588
205 636-9642	**Richard Pearson Hobson State Technical College**	Hwy 43 S	Thomasville	AL	36784-0000
205 759-1541	**Shelton State Community College**	202 Skyland Blvd	Tuscaloosa	AL	35405-4093
205 593-5120	**Snead State Junior College**	PO Box D	Boaz	AL	35957-0734
205 933-8242	**Southern Institute Junior College**	2015 Highland Ave S	Birmingham	AL	35205-3898
205 395-2211	**Southern Union State Junior College**	Roberts St	Wadley	AL	36276-0000
205 479-7476	**Southwest State Technical College**	925 Dauphin Island Pkwy	Mobile	AL	36605-3299

ALASKA

Phone	College	Address	City	State	ZIP
907 262-5801	**Kenai Peninsula College**	34820 College Dr	Soldotna	AK	99669-9732
907 486-4161	**Kodiak College**	117 Benny Benson Dr	Kodiak	AK	99615-6998
907 745-4255	**Matanuska-Susitna College**	Mile 2 Trunk Rd	Palmer	AK	99645-0000
907 225-6177	**University of Alaska Southeast Ketchikan Campus**	7th & Madison	Ketchikan	AK	99901-0000

ARIZONA

Phone	College	Address	City	State	ZIP
602 726-1000	**Arizona Western College**	Hwy 95 & Araby Rd	Yuma	AZ	85366-0000
602 723-4141	**Central Arizona College**	8470 N Overfield Rd	Coolidge	AZ	85228-9030
602 364-7943	**Cochise College**	RR 1 Box 100	Douglas	AZ	85607-9724
602 428-1133	**Eastern Arizona College**	600 Church St	Thatcher	AZ	85552-0000
602 275-8500	**Gateway Community College**	108 N 40th St	Phoenix	AZ	85034-1795
602 435-3000	**Glendale Community College**	6000 W Olive Ave	Glendale	AZ	85302-3006
602 461-7000	**Mesa Community College**	1833 W Southern Ave	Mesa	AZ	85202-4866
602 757-4331	**Mohave Community College**	1971 Jagerson Ave	Kingman	AZ	86401-1299
602 724-3311	**Navajo Community College**		Tsaile	AZ	86556-0000
602 524-6111	**Northland Pioneer College**	PO Box 610	Holbrook	AZ	86025-0610
602 264-2492	**Phoenix College**	1202 W Thomas Rd	Phoenix	AZ	85013-4234
602 884-6965	**Pima County Community College**	2202 W Anklam Rd	Tucson	AZ	85709-0001
602 223-4000	**Rio Salado Community College**	640 N 1st Ave	Phoenix	AZ	85003-1558
602 423-6000	**Scottsdale Community College**	9000 E Chaparral Rd	Scottsdale	AZ	85250-2699
602 445-7300	**Yavapai College**	1100 E Sheldon St	Prescott	AZ	86301-3297

ARKANSAS

Phone	College	Address	City	State	ZIP
501 882-6452	**Arkansas State University**	N Palm & Iowa Sts	Beebe	AR	72012-0000
501 633-4480	**East Arkansas Community College**	Newcastle Rd	Forrest City	AR	72335-0000
501 767-9371	**Garland County Community College**	1 College Dr	Hot Springs	AR	71913-9120
501 762-1020	**Mississippi County Community College**	S Hwy 61	Blytheville	AR	72316-0000
501 743-3000	**North Arkansas Community College**	420 Pioneer Dr	Harrison	AR	72601-5599
501 338-6474	**Phillips County Community College**	Campus Dr	Helena	AR	72342-0000
501 374-6305	**Shorter College**	604 N Locust St	North Little Rock	AR	72114-4885
501 862-8131	**Southern Arkansas University El Dorado Branch**	300 Southwest Ave	El Dorado	AR	71730-0000
501 785-7000	**Westark Community College**	5210 Grand Ave	Fort Smith	AR	72903-0000

CALIFORNIA

Phone	College	Address	City	State	ZIP
805 922-6966	**Allan Hancock College**	800 S College Dr	Santa Maria	CA	93454-6368
818 798-0777	**American Academy of Dramatic Arts**	2550 Paloma St	Pasadena	CA	91107-2697
213 856-7628	**American Film Institute**	2021 N Western Ave	Los Angeles	CA	90027-1625
916 484-8011	**American River College**	4700 College Oak Dr	Sacramento	CA	95841-4286
805 943-3241	**Antelope Valley College**	3041 W Ave 'K'	Lancaster	CA	93536-5426
805 395-4011	**Bakersfield College**	1801 Panorama Dr	Bakersfield	CA	93305-1299
619 252-2411	**Barstow College**	2700 Barstow Rd	Barstow	CA	92311-6699
916 895-2361	**Butte College**	3536 Butte Campus Dr	Oroville	CA	95965-8399
408 479-6100	**Cabrillo College**	6500 Soquel Dr	Aptos	CA	95003-3198
714 639-3961	**California Christian Institute**	1744 W Katella Suite 26	Orange	CA	92667-3432
415 364-1212	**Canada College**	4200 Farm Hill Blvd	Redwood City	CA	94061-1099
213 860-2451	**Cerritos Community College**	11110 Alondra Blvd	Norwalk	CA	90650-6296
619 375-5001	**Cerro Coso Community College**	3000 College Heights Blvd	Ridgecrest	CA	93555-9571
415 786-6600	**Chabot College**	25555 Hesperian Blvd	Hayward	CA	94545-2447
714 987-1737	**Chaffey Community College**	5885 S Haven Ave	Alta Loma	CA	91701-3002
818 963-0323	**Citrus Community College**	1000 W Foothill Blvd	Glendora	CA	91740-1899
415 239-3000	**City College of San Francisco**	50 Phelan Ave	San Francisco	CA	94112-1821
714 432-5898	**Coast Community College (System)**	1370 Adams Ave	Costa Mesa	CA	92626-5429
714 546-7600	**Coastline Community College**	11460 Warner Ave	Fountain Valley	CA	92708-2597
415 522-7221	**College of Alameda**	555 Atlantic Ave	Alameda	CA	94501-2109
415 457-8811	**College of Marin**	835 College Ave	Kentfield	CA	94904-2590
415 883-2211	*Indian Valley Campus*	1800 Ignacio Blvd	Novato	CA	94949-4912
415 574-6161	**College of San Mateo**	1700 W Hillsdale Blvd	San Mateo	CA	94402-3784
805 259-7800	**College of the Canyons**	26455 N Rockwell Canyon Rd	Valencia	CA	91355-1899
619 346-8041	**College of the Desert**	43500 Monterey Ave	Palm Desert	CA	92260-2499
707 445-6700	**College of the Redwoods**	7351 Tompkins Hill Rd	Eureka	CA	95501-9300
209 733-2050	**College of the Sequoias**	915 S Mooney Blvd	Visalia	CA	93277-2234
209 533-5100	**Columbia College**	PO Box 1849	Columbia	CA	95310-1849
213 637-2660	**Compton Community College**	1111 E Artesia Blvd	Compton	CA	90221-5393
415 229-1000	**Contra Costa Community College (System)**	500 Court St	Martinez	CA	94553-1278
415 235-7800	**Contra Costa Community College San Pablo Campus**	2600 Mission Bell Dr	San Pablo	CA	94806-3195
714 794-2161	**Crafton Hills College**	11711 Sand Canyon Rd	Yucaipa	CA	92399-1799
805 546-3100	**Cuesta Community College**	Hwy 1	San Luis Obispo	CA	93401-0000
619 670-1980	**Cuyamaca College**	2950 Jamacha Rd	El Cajon	CA	92019-4304
714 826-2220	**Cypress College**	9200 Valley View St	Cypress	CA	90630-5897
916 758-0470	**D-Q University**	PO Box 409	Davis	CA	95617-0409
415 685-1230	**Diablo Valley College**	321 Golf Club Rd	Pleasant Hill	CA	94523-1576
818 280-0451	**Don Bosco Technical Institute**	1151 San Gabriel Blvd	Rosemead	CA	91770-4299
213 265-8650	**East Los Angeles College**	1301 W Brooklyn Ave	Monterey Park	CA	91754-6099
213 532-3670	**El Camino College**	16007 S Crenshaw Blvd	Torrance	CA	90506-0001
408 274-7900	**Evergreen Valley College**	3095 Yerba Buena Rd	San Jose	CA	95135-1598
213 624-1200	**Fashion Institute of Design & Merchandising**	919 S Grand Ave	Los Angeles	CA	90015-1426
916 283-0202	**Feather River College**	PO Box 11110	Quincy	CA	95971-0000
415 949-7777	**Foothill College**	12345 El Monte Rd	Los Altos Hills	CA	94022-4599
209 442-4600	**Fresno City College**	1101 E University Ave	Fresno	CA	93741-0001
714 992-7000	**Fullerton Community College**	321 E Chapman Ave	Fullerton	CA	92632-2095
408 847-1400	**Gavilan College**	5055 Santa Teresa Blvd	Gilroy	CA	95020-9599
818 240-1000	**Glendale Community College**	1500 N Verdugo Rd	Glendale	CA	91208-2809
714 892-7711	**Golden West College**	15744 Golden West St	Huntington Beach	CA	92647-0000
619 465-1700	**Grossmont College**	8800 Grossmont College Dr	El Cajon	CA	92020-1765
408 755-6700	**Hartnell College**	156 Homestead Ave	Salinas	CA	93901-1698
415 441-5555	**Heald Institute of Technology**	150 4th St	San Francisco	CA	94103-3048
213 749-3424	**Hebrew Union College California Branch**	3077 University Ave	Los Angeles	CA	90007-3796
619 352-8320	**Imperial Valley College**	PO Box 158	Imperial	CA	92251-0158
714 559-9300	**Irvine Valley College**	5500 Irvine Center Dr	Irvine	CA	92720-4399
209 638-3641	**Kings River Community College**	995 N Reed Ave	Reedley	CA	93654-2099
916 541-4660	**Lake Tahoe Community College**	PO Box 14445	South Lake Tahoe	CA	95702-4445
415 834-5740	**Laney College**	900 Fallon St	Oakland	CA	94607-4893
916 257-6181	**Lassen College**	PO Box 3000	Susanville	CA	96130-3000
213 420-4111	**Long Beach Community College**	4901 E Carson St	Long Beach	CA	90808-1780
213 669-4000	**Los Angeles City College**	855 N Vermont Ave	Los Angeles	CA	90029-3588
213 891-2000	**Los Angeles Community College (System)**	617 W 7th St	Los Angeles	CA	90017-3895
213 518-1000	**Los Angeles Harbor College**	1111 Figueroa Pl	Wilmington	CA	90744-2311
818 365-8271	**Los Angeles Mission College**	1320 San Fernando Rd	San Fernando	CA	91340-3214
818 347-0551	**Los Angeles Pierce College**	6201 Winnetka Ave	Woodland Hills	CA	91371-0000
213 777-2225	**Los Angeles Southwest College**	1600 W Imperial Hwy	Los Angeles	CA	90047-4899
213 744-9500	**Los Angeles Trade-Technical College**	400 W Washington Blvd	Los Angeles	CA	90015-4180
818 781-1200	**Los Angeles Valley College**	5800 Fulton Ave	Van Nuys	CA	91401-4062
415 439-2181	**Los Medanos College**	2700 E Leland Rd	Pittsburg	CA	94565-5197
213 377-5501	**Marymount College Palos Verdes**	30800 Palos Verdes Dr E	Rancho Palos Verdes	CA	90274-6299
209 384-6000	**Merced College**	3600 M St	Merced	CA	95348-2898
415 531-4911	**Merritt College**	12500 Campus Dr	Oakland	CA	94619-3196
619 757-2121	**Mira Costa College**	1 Barnard Dr	Oceanside	CA	92056-3899
408 988-2200	**Mission College**	3000 Mission College Blvd	Santa Clara	CA	95054-1897
209 575-6498	**Modesto Junior College**	435 College Ave	Modesto	CA	95350-5800
408 646-4000	**Monterey Peninsula College**	980 Fremont St	Monterey	CA	93940-4799
805 529-2321	**Moorpark College**	7075 Campus Rd	Moorpark	CA	93021-1695
213 746-0450	**Mount Saint Mary's College Doheny Campus**	10 Chester Pl	Los Angeles	CA	90007-2598
714 594-5611	**Mount San Antonio College**	1100 N Grand Ave	Walnut	CA	91789-1399
714 654-8011	**Mount San Jacinto College**	1499 N State St	San Jacinto	CA	92383-2399
707 253-3000	**Napa Valley College**		Napa	CA	94558-6236
415 659-6000	**Ohlone College**	43600 Mission Blvd	Fremont	CA	94539-5884
714 432-0202	**Orange Coast College**	2701 Fairview Rd	Costa Mesa	CA	92626-5563
805 488-0911	**Oxnard College**	4000 S Rose Ave	Oxnard	CA	93033-6699
619 922-6168	**Palo Verde Community College**	811 W Chanslor Way	Blythe	CA	92225-1118
619 744-1150	**Palomar Community College**	1140 W Mission Rd	San Marcos	CA	92069-1487
818 578-7123	**Pasadena City College**	1570 E Colorado Blvd	Pasadena	CA	91106-2003
415 466-7200	**Peralta Community College (System)**	333 E 8th St	Oakland	CA	94606-2889
818 895-2220	**Phillips Junior College**	8520 Balboa Blvd	Northridge	CA	91325-3561
209 781-3130	**Porterville College**	900 S Main St	Porterville	CA	93257-5901
415 657-2468	**Queen of the Holy Rosary College**	43326 Mission Blvd	Fremont	CA	94539-5829
714 667-3000	**Rancho Santiago College**	17th & Bristol St	Santa Ana	CA	92706-0000
213 692-0921	**Rio Hondo College**	3600 Workman Mill Rd	Whittier	CA	90601-1699
714 684-3240	**Riverside Community College**	4800 Magnolia Ave	Riverside	CA	92506-1293
916 961-8727	**Rudolf Steiner College**	9200 Fair Oaks Blvd	Fair Oaks	CA	95628-6897
916 449-7441	**Sacramento City College**	3835 Freeport Blvd	Sacramento	CA	95822-1386
714 582-4500	**Saddleback College**	28000 Marguerite Pkwy	Mission Viejo	CA	92692-3699
714 888-6511	**San Bernardino Valley College**	701 S Mt Vernon Ave	San Bernardino	CA	92410-2748
619 230-2400	**San Diego City College**	1313 12th Ave	San Diego	CA	92101-4787
619 560-2600	**San Diego Mesa College**	7250 Mesa College Dr	San Diego	CA	92111-4996
619 693-6800	**San Diego Miramar College**	10440 Black Mountain Rd	San Diego	CA	92126-2999
209 474-5625	**San Joaquin Delta Community College**	5151 Pacific Ave	Stockton	CA	95207-6370
408 298-2181	**San Jose City College**	2100 Moorpark Ave	San Jose	CA	95128-2799
805 965-0581	**Santa Barbara City College**	721 Cliff Dr	Santa Barbara	CA	93109-2312
213 450-5150	**Santa Monica College**	1900 Pico Blvd	Santa Monica	CA	90405-1644
707 527-4011	**Santa Rosa Junior College**	1501 Mendocino Ave	Santa Rosa	CA	95401-4395
916 225-4600	**Shasta College**	PO Box 496006	Redding	CA	96049-6006
916 624-3333	**Sierra Community College**	5000 Rocklin Rd	Rocklin	CA	95677-3397
916 938-4462	**Siskiyous Joint Community College District**	800 College Ave	Weed	CA	96094-2806
415 355-7000	**Skyline College**	3300 College Dr	San Bruno	CA	94066-1698
707 864-7000	**Solano Community College**	4000 Suisun Valley Rd	Suisun City	CA	94585-3197
619 421-6700	**Southwestern College**	900 Otay Lakes Rd	Chula Vista	CA	92010-7297
805 763-4282	**Taft College**	29 Emmons Park Dr	Taft	CA	93268-2317
805 642-3211	**Ventura College**	4667 Telegraph Rd	Ventura	CA	93003-3899
805 642-0161	**Ventura County Community College District**	71 Day Rd	Ventura	CA	93003-2037
619 245-4271	**Victor Valley College**	18422 Bear Valley Rd	Victorville	CA	92392-5849
209 935-0801	**West Hills College**	300 W Cherry Ln	Coalinga	CA	93210-1399
213 836-7110	**West Los Angeles College**	4800 Freshman Dr	Culver City	CA	90230-3500
408 867-2200	**West Valley College**	14000 Fruitvale Ave	Saratoga	CA	95070-5697
916 741-6700	**Yuba Community College**	2088 N Beale Rd	Marysville	CA	95901-7699

COLORADO

Phone	College	Address	City	State	ZIP
303 330-8008	**Aims Community College**	5401 W 20th St	Greeley	CO	80634-3000
303 794-1550	**Arapahoe Community College**	2500 W College Dr	Littleton	CO	80120-1955
303 945-8691	**Colorado Mountain College (System)**	215 9th St	Glenwood Springs	CO	81601-3307
	Colorado Mountain College				
303 945-7481	*Spring Valley Campus*	3000 County Rd 114	Glenwood Springs	CO	81601-9394
719 486-2015	*Timberline Campus*		Leadville	CO	80461-0000
303 675-2261	**Colorado Northwestern Community College**	500 Kennedy Dr	Rangely	CO	81648-3502
303 556-2600	**Community College of Denver**	PO Box 173363	Denver	CO	80217-3363
303 466-8811	**Front Range Community College**	3645 W 112th Ave	Westminster	CO	80030-2199
719 336-2248	**Lamar Community College**	2401 S Main St	Lamar	CO	81052-3999
303 867-3081	**Morgan Community College**	17800 County Rd 20	Fort Morgan	CO	80701-4399
303 522-6600	**Northeastern Junior College**	100 College Ave	Sterling	CO	80751-2399
719 384-8721	**Otero Junior College**	18th & Colorado Ave	La Junta	CO	81050-0000
303 457-2757	**Park's Junior College**	9065 Grant St	Denver	CO	80229-4339
719 576-7711	**Pikes Peak Community College**	5675 S Academy Blvd	Colorado Springs	CO	80906-5498
303 988-6160	**Red Rocks Community College**	13300 W 6th Ave	Lakewood	CO	80401-5398
719 846-5011	**Trinidad State Junior College**	600 Prospect St	Trinidad	CO	81082-2396

CONNECTICUT

Phone	College	Address	City	State	ZIP
203 745-1603	**Asnuntuck Community College**	170 Elm St	Enfield	CT	06082-3800
203 520-7800	**Greater Hartford Community College**	61 Woodland St	Hartford	CT	06105-2354
203 236-1215	**Hartford College for Women**	1265 Asylum Ave	Hartford	CT	06105-2299
203 527-4111	**Hartford State Technical College**	401 Flatbush Ave	Hartford	CT	06106-3757
203 579-6400	**Housatonic Community College**	510 Barnum Ave	Bridgeport	CT	06608-2408
203 646-4900	**Manchester Community College**	60 Bidwell St	Manchester	CT	06040-6497
203 575-0328	**Mattatuck Community College**	750 Chase Pkwy	Waterbury	CT	06708-3000
203 344-3011	**Middlesex Community College**	100 Training Hill Rd	Middletown	CT	06457-4889
203 443-2811	**Mitchell College**	437 Pequot Ave	New London	CT	06320-4498
203 886-1931	**Mohegan Community College**	21 Mahan Dr	Norwich	CT	06360-2497
203 379-8543	**Northwestern Connecticut Community College**	Parkplace E	Winsted	CT	06098-0000

203 853-2040 **Norwalk Community College** 333 Wilson Ave ... South Norwalk CT 06854-4684
203 855-6600 **Norwalk State Technical College** 181 Richards Ave ... Norwalk CT 06854-1635
203 774-1130 **Quinebaug Valley Community College** 742 Upper Maple St ... Danielson CT 06239-1440
203 789-7071 **South Central Community College** 60 Sargent Dr ... New Haven CT 06511-5970
203 886-0177 **Thames Valley State Technical College**
574 New London Tpke ... Norwich CT 06360-6598
203 677-7701 **Tunxis Community College** Rts 6 & 177 ... Farmington CT 06032-0000

DELAWARE

302 478-3000 **Brandywine College** 4601 Concord Pike ... Wilmington DE 19803-1435
Delaware Technical & Community College
302 856-5400 *Southern Campus* Rt 18 ... Georgetown DE 19947-0000
302 454-3900 *Stanton Campus* 400 Stanton-Christiana Rd ... Newark DE 19713-2111
302 736-5414 *Terry Campus* 1832 N Dupont Hwy ... Dover DE 19901-2221

FLORIDA

305 491-7171 **Bauder Fashion College** 4801 N Dixie Hwy ... Fort Lauderdale FL 33334-3971
407 632-1111 **Brevard Community College** 1519 Clearlake Rd ... Cocoa FL 32922-6597
305 475-6500 **Broward Community College** 225 E Las Olas Blvd ... Fort Lauderdale FL 33301-2298
904 237-2111 **Central Florida Community College** 3001 SW College Rd ... Ocala FL 32674-4478
904 526-2761 **Chipola Junior College** 1200 College St ... Marianna FL 32446-2000
904 255-8131 **Daytona Beach Community College** 1200 Volusia Ave ... Daytona Beach FL 32114-2817
813 489-9300 **Edison Community College** 8099 College Pkwy SW ... Fort Myers FL 33919-5598
813 988-5131 **Florida College** 119 N Glen Arven Ave ... Temple Terrace FL 33617-5527
904 632-3000 **Florida Community College of Jacksonville**
501 W State St ... Jacksonville FL 32202-4097
305 296-9081 **Florida Keys Community College** 5901 W Junior College Rd .. Key West FL 33040-4397
904 769-1551 **Gulf Coast Community College** 5230 W Hwy 98 ... Panama City FL 32401-1041
813 253-7000 **Hillsborough Community College** PO Box 31127 ... Tampa FL 33631-3127
407 468-4700 **Indian River Community College** 3209 Virginia Ave ... Fort Pierce FL 34981-5599
305 373-4684 **International Fine Arts College** 1737 N Bayshore Dr ... Miami FL 33132-1121
904 752-1822 **Lake City Community College** RR 3 Box 7 ... Lake City FL 32055-8703
904 787-3747 **Lake-Sumter Community College** 9501 S US Hwy 441 ... Leesburg FL 34788-8751
813 755-1511 **Manatee Community College** 5840 26th St W ... Bradenton FL 34207-3596
Miami-Dade Community College
305 347-1000 *North Campus* 11380 NW 27th Ave ... Miami FL 33167-3495
305 347-2000 *South Campus* 11011 SW 104th St ... Miami FL 33176-3393
904 973-2288 **North Florida Junior College** 1000 Turner Davis Dr ... Madison FL 32340-1699
904 678-5111 **Okaloosa-Walton Community College** 100 E College Blvd ... Niceville FL 32578-1294
407 439-8000 **Palm Beach Community College** 4200 Congress Ave ... Lake Worth FL 33461-4796
904 567-6701 **Pasco-Hernando Community College** 2401 County Rd 41 N ... Dade City FL 33525-7599
904 484-1000 **Pensacola Junior College** 1000 College Blvd ... Pensacola FL 32504-8998
813 294-7771 **Polk Community College** 999 Ave 'H' NE ... Winter Haven FL 33881-4299
904 328-1571 **Saint John's River Community College** 5001 St John's Ave ... Palatka FL 32177-3807
813 341-3600 **Saint Petersburg Junior College** 8580 66th St N ... Pinellas Park FL 34665-1207
904 395-5443 **Santa Fe Community College** 3000 NW 83rd St ... Gainesville FL 32602-0000
407 323-1450 **Seminole Community College** 100 Weldon Blvd ... Sanford FL 32773-6199
813 453-6661 **South Florida Community College** 600 W College Dr ... Avon Park FL 33825-9399
904 488-9200 **Tallahassee Community College** 444 Appleyard Dr ... Tallahassee FL 32304-2895
407 299-5000 **Valencia Community College** PO Box 3028 ... Orlando FL 32802-3028

GEORGIA

912 386-3236 **Abraham Baldwin Agricultural College** PO Box 3 ABAC Stn ... Tifton GA 31793-0003
912 732-2171 **Andrew College** 413 College St ... Cuthbert GA 31740-1395
404 756-4358 **Atlanta Metropolitan College** 1630 Stewart Ave SW ... Atlanta GA 30310-4498
912 248-2500 **Bainbridge College** US Hwy 84-E ... Bainbridge GA 31717-0000
912 264-7253 **Brunswick College** Altama & 4th St ... Brunswick GA 31523-0001
404 278-3113 **Dalton College** 213 N College Dr ... Dalton GA 30720-3797
912 237-7831 **East Georgia College** 237 Thigpen Dr ... Swainsboro GA 30401-2699
404 245-7226 **Emmanuel College** 212 Spring St ... Franklin Springs GA 30639-9999
404 295-6339 **Floyd College** PO Box 1864 ... Rome GA 30162-1864
404 535-6239 **Gainesville College** 3820 Mundy Mill Rd ... Gainesville GA 30501-8299
912 453-3481 **Georgia Military College** 201 Green St ... Milledgeville GA 31061-3398
404 358-5000 **Gordon College** 103 College Dr ... Barnesville GA 30204-1799
912 471-2700 **Macon College** College Station Dr ... Macon GA 31297-0001
912 934-6221 **Middle Georgia College** Sarah St ... Cochran GA 31014-0000
404 479-1454 **Reinhardt College** PO Box 128 ... Waleska GA 30183-0128
912 383-4220 **South Georgia College** ... Douglas GA 31533-0000
912 226-1621 **Thomas College** 1501 Millpond Rd ... Thomasville GA 31792-7499
404 865-2135 **Truett-McConnell College** Hwy 115 ... Cleveland GA 30528-0000
912 285-6130 **Waycross College** 2001 Francis St ... Waycross GA 31501-9248
404 379-3111 **Young Harris College** 86 College St ... Young Harris GA 30582-0000

HAWAII

808 734-9111 **Kapiolani Community College** 4303 Diamond Head Rd ... Honolulu HI 96816-4416
808 245-8311 **Kauai Community College** 3-1901 Kaumualii Hwy ... Lihue HI 96766-9591
808 455-0217 **Leeward Community College** 96-045 Ala Ike St ... Pearl City HI 96782-3393
808 235-0077 **Windward Community College** 45-720 Keaahala Rd ... Kaneohe HI 96744-3598

IDAHO

208 733-9554 **College of Southern Idaho** 315 Falls Ave ... Twin Falls ID 83301-3367
208 769-3300 **North Idaho College** 1000 W Garden Ave ... Coeur d'Alene ID 83814-2199
208 356-2011 **Ricks College** ... Rexburg ID 83460-0001

ILLINOIS

618 235-2700 **Belleville Area College** 2500 Carlyle Rd ... Belleville IL 62221-5899
Black Hawk College
309 852-5671 *East Campus* PO Box 489 ... Kewanee IL 61443-0489
309 796-1311 *Quad Cities Campus* 6600 34th Ave ... Moline IL 61265-5899
309 344-2518 **Carl Sandburg College** 2232 S Lake Storey Rd ... Galesburg IL 61401-9576
312 641-2595 **Chicago Citywide College** 226 W Jackson Blvd ... Chicago IL 60606-6997
708 858-2800 **College of DuPage** 22nd St & Lambert Rd ... Glen Ellyn IL 60137-6599
708 223-6601 **College of Lake County** 19351 W Washington St ... Grayslake IL 60030-1198
217 443-1811 **Danville Area Community College** 2000 E Main St ... Danville IL 61832-5199
708 697-1000 **Elgin Community College** 1700 Spartan Dr ... Elgin IL 60123-7193
618 842-3711 **Frontier Community College** Frontier Dr Lot 2 ... Fairfield IL 62837-9801
312 878-1700 **Harry S Truman College** 1145 W Wilson Ave ... Chicago IL 60640-5691
312 267-9800 **Hebrew Theological College** 7135 N Carpenter Rd ... Skokie IL 60077-3263
815 235-6121 **Highland Community College** 2998 W Pearl City Rd ... Freeport IL 61032-9341
309 694-5011 **Illinois Central College East Campus** 1 College Dr ... Peoria IL 61635-0001
618 393-2982 **Illinois Eastern Community College (System)** 233 E Chestnut St .. Olney IL 62450-2227
815 224-2720 **Illinois Valley Community College** 2578 E 350th Rd ... Oglesby IL 61348-1074
618 985-3741 **John A Logan College** ... Carterville IL 62918-0000
217 224-6500 **John Wood Community College** 150 S 48th St ... Quincy IL 62301-9147
815 729-9020 **Joliet Junior College** 1216 Houbolt Ave ... Joliet IL 60436-9352
815 933-0345 **Kankakee Community College** River Rd ... Kankakee IL 60901-0000
618 532-1981 **Kaskaskia College** Shattuc Rd ... Centralia IL 62801-0000
312 962-3200 **Kennedy-King College** 6800 S Wentworth Ave ... Chicago IL 60621-3798
815 825-2086 **Kishwaukee College** Malta Rd & Hwy 38 ... Malta IL 60150-0000
217 235-3131 **Lake Land College** SR-45 ... Mattoon IL 61938-0000
618 466-3411 **Lewis & Clark Community College** 5800 Godfrey Rd ... Godfrey IL 62035-2466
217 732-3155 **Lincoln Junior College** 300 Keokuk St ... Lincoln IL 62656-1699
217 786-2200 **Lincoln Land Community College** Shepherd Rd ... Springfield IL 62792-0000
618 544-8657 **Lincoln Trail College** RR 3 ... Robinson IL 62454-9803
312 922-1884 **MacCormac Junior College** 327 S La Salle St ... Chicago IL 60604-3395
312 942-3000 **Malcolm X College** 1900 W Van Buren St ... Chicago IL 60612-3197
815 455-3700 **McHenry County College** RR 14 & Lucas Rd ... Crystal Lake IL 60012-0000
309 673-6365 **Midstate College** 244 SW Jefferson Ave ... Peoria IL 61602-1489
312 539-1919 **Montay College** 3750 W Peterson Ave ... Chicago IL 60659-3115
708 974-4300 **Moraine Valley Community College** 10900 S 88th Ave ... Palos Hills IL 60465-0937
708 656-8000 **Morton College** 3801 S Central Ave ... Cicero IL 60650-4398
708 635-1600 **Oakton Community College** 1600 E Golf Rd ... Des Plaines IL 60016-1268
312 568-3700 **Olive-Harvey College** 10001 S Woodlawn Ave ... Chicago IL 60628-1696
618 395-4351 **Olney Central College** 305 N West St ... Olney IL 62450-1099
217 351-2200 **Parkland College** 2400 W Bradley Ave ... Champaign IL 61821-1899
708 756-3110 **Prairie State College** 202 S Halsted St ... Chicago Heights IL 60411-1275
618 437-5321 **Rend Lake College** RR 1 ... Ina IL 62846-9801
312 735-3000 **Richard J Daley College** 7500 S Pulaski Rd ... Chicago IL 60652-1299
217 875-7200 **Richland Community College** 1 College Pk ... Decatur IL 62521-8513
815 654-4250 **Rock Valley College** 3301 N Mulford Rd ... Rockford IL 61111-0000
312 942-7100 **Rush University** 1743 W Harrison St Rm 119 ... Chicago IL 60612-3823
217 786-6600 **Sangamon State University** Shepherd Rd ... Springfield IL 62794-0000
815 288-5511 **Sauk Valley Community College** 173 Illinois Rt 2 ... Dixon IL 61021-9188
618 634-2242 **Shawnee Community College** Shawnee College Rd ... Ullin IL 62992-0000
708 596-2000 **South Suburban College** 15800 State St ... South Holland IL 60473-1270
618 252-6376 **Southeastern Illinois College** RR 4 ... Harrisburg IL 62946-9804
309 647-4645 **Spoon River College** RR 1 ... Canton IL 61520-9801
217 525-1420 **Springfield College in Illinois** 1500 N 5th St ... Springfield IL 62702-2694
618 583-2500 **State Community College of East Saint Louis**
601 James R Thompson Blvd ... East Saint Louis IL 62201-1100
708 456-0300 **Triton College** 2000 N 5th Ave ... River Grove IL 60171-1995
618 262-8641 **Wabash Valley College** 2200 College Dr ... Mount Carmel IL 62863-2699
708 466-4811 **Waubonsee Community College** Rt 47 & Harter Rd ... Sugar Grove IL 60554-0000
312 777-7900 **Wilbur Wright College** 3400 N Austin Ave ... Chicago IL 60634-4276
708 397-3000 **William Rainey Harper College** 1200 W Algonquin Rd ... Palatine IL 60067-7373

INDIANA

219 936-8898 **Ancilla College** Union Rd ... Donaldson IN 46513-9999
Indiana Vocational Technical College
317 921-4882 *Central Indiana Campus* 1 W 26th St ... Indianapolis IN 46208-4777
812 372-9925 *Columbus Campus* 4475 Central Ave ... Columbus IN 47203-1868
317 289-2291 *East Central Campus* 4301 S Cowan Rd ... Muncie IN 47302-9448
317 459-0561 *Kokomo Campus* 1815 E Morgan St ... Kokomo IN 46901-2548
317 477-7401 *Lafayette Campus* 3208 Ross Rd ... Lafayette IN 47905-5217
219 289-7001 *North Central Campus* 1534 W Sample St ... South Bend IN 46619-3837
219 482-9171 *Northeast Campus* 3800 N Anthony Blvd ... Fort Wayne IN 46805-1489
219 981-1111 *Northwest Campus* 1440 E 35th Ave ... Gary IN 46409-1499
812 246-3301 *South Central Campus* 8204 Hwy 311 ... Sellersburg IN 47172-1829
812 265-2579 *Southeast Campus* Ivy Tech Dr & Hwy 62 ... Madison IN 47250-0000
812 426-2865 *Southwest Campus* 3501 N 1st Ave ... Evansville IN 47710-3319
812 299-1121 *Wabash Valley Campus* 7377 S Dixie Bee Rd ... Terre Haute IN 47802-4845
317 966-2656 *Whitewater Campus* 2325 Chester Blvd ... Richmond IN 47374-1289
812 882-3350 **Vincennes University** 1002 N First St ... Vincennes IN 47591-0000

IOWA

515 576-4881 **Buena Vista College** 330 Ave M Library Bldg Rm 104 ... Fort Dodge IA 50501-0000
319 242-6841 **Clinton Community College** 1000 Lincoln Blvd ... Clinton IA 52732-6299
515 964-6200 **Des Moines Area Community College** 2006 S Ankeny Blvd ... Ankeny IA 50021-3993
319 322-5015 **Eastern Iowa Community College District (System)**
306 W River Dr ... Davenport IA 52801-1221
515 648-4611 **Ellsworth Community College** 1100 College Ave ... Iowa Falls IA 50126-1199
319 296-2320 **Hawkeye Institute of Technology** 1501 E Orange Rd ... Waterloo IA 50701-9298
515 856-2143 **Indian Hills Community College** 721 N 1st St ... Centerville IA 52544-0000
712 362-2604 **Iowa Lakes Community College** 300 S 18th St ... Estherville IA 51334-2721
Iowa Western Community College
712 542-5117 *Clarinda Campus* 923 E Washington St ... Clarinda IA 51632-1958
712 325-3200 *Council Bluffs Campus* 2700 College Rd ... Council Bluffs IA 51503-0567
319 398-5411 **Kirkwood Community College** 6301 Kirkwood Blvd SW ... Cedar Rapids IA 52404-5260
515 752-7106 **Marshalltown Community College** 3700 S Center St ... Marshalltown IA 50158-4760
319 263-8250 **Muscatine Community College** 152 Colorado St ... Muscatine IA 52761-5396
515 421-4399 **North Iowa Area Community College** 500 College Dr ... Mason City IA 50401-7213
Northeast Iowa Community College
319 562-3263 *Calmar Campus* PO Box 400 ... Calmar IA 52132-0483
319 556-5110 *Peosta Campus* 10250 Sundown Rd ... Peosta IA 52068-9703
712 324-5061 **Northwest Iowa Technical College** Hwy 18 W ... Sheldon IA 51201-0000
319 752-2731 **Southeastern Community College** 1015 S Gear Ave ... West Burlington IA 52655-1614
515 782-7081 **Southwestern Community College** 1501 W Townline St ... Creston IA 50801-1042
515 582-2450 **Waldorf College** 106 S 6th St ... Forest City IA 50436-1797
712 274-6400 **Western Iowa Tech Community College** 4647 Stone Ave ... Sioux City IA 51106-1997

KANSAS

316 365-5116 **Allen County Community College** 1801 N Cottonwood St ... Iola KS 66749-1698
316 321-5083 **Butler County Community College** 901 S Haverhill Rd ... El Dorado KS 67042-3280
316 241-0723 **Central College** 1200 S Main St ... McPherson KS 67460-5799
913 243-1435 **Cloud County Community College** 2221 Campus Dr ... Concordia KS 66901-5305
316 251-7700 **Coffeyville Community College** 11th & Willow ... Coffeyville KS 67337-5064
913 462-3984 **Colby Community College** 1255 S Range Ave ... Colby KS 67701-4099
316 442-0430 **Cowley County Community College** 125 S 2nd St ... Arkansas City KS 67005-2662
316 225-1321 **Dodge City Community College** 2501 N 14th Ave ... Dodge City KS 67801-2399
913 621-6070 **Donnelly College** 608 N 18th St ... Kansas City KS 66102-4298
316 223-2700 **Fort Scott Community College** 2108 Horton St ... Fort Scott KS 66701-3199
316 276-7611 **Garden City Community College** 801 Campus Dr ... Garden City KS 67846-6399
316 327-4221 **Hesston College** PO Box 3000 ... Hesston KS 67062-9989
913 442-3238 **Highland Community College** Hwy 36 W ... Highland KS 66035-0000
316 665-3500 **Hutchinson Community College** 1300 N Plum St ... Hutchinson KS 67501-5894
316 331-4100 **Independence Community College**
Brookside Dr & College Ave ... Independence KS 67301-3791
913 469-8500 **Johnson County Community College**
12345 College & Quivira ... Overland Park KS 66210-0000
913 334-1100 **Kansas City Kansas Community College** 7250 State Ave ... Kansas City KS 66112-3003
913 825-0275 **Kansas College of Technology** 2409 Scanlan Ave ... Salina KS 67401-8196
316 421-6700 **Labette Community College** 200 S 14th St ... Parsons KS 67357-4299
316 431-2820 **Neosho County Community College** 1000 S Allen Ave ... Chanute KS 66720-2699
316 672-5641 **Pratt Community College** Hwy 61 ... Pratt KS 67124-0000
316 624-1951 **Seward County Community College** PO Box 1137 ... Liberal KS 67905-1137
316 833-2400 **Wichita Area Vocational Technical School** 301 S Grove St ... Wichita KS 67211-0000

KENTUCKY

606 329-2999 **Ashland Community College** 1400 College Dr ... Ashland KY 41101-3683
502 769-2371 **Elizabethtown Community College** College Street Rd ... Elizabethtown KY 42701-0000
606 436-5721 **Hazard Community College** 1 Community College Dr ... Hazard KY 41701-2403
502 827-1867 **Henderson Community College** 2660 S Green St ... Henderson KY 42420-4623

Two-Year Colleges

502 886-3921 **Hopkinsville Community College** PO Box 2100 — Hopkinsville KY 42241-0000
502 584-0181 **Jefferson Community College** 109 E Broadway — Louisville KY 40202-2000
606 666-7521 **Lees College** 601 Jefferson Ave — Jackson KY 41339-1196
606 257-4871 **Lexington Community College** Cooper Dr Oswald Bldg — Lexington KY 40506-0001
502 821-2250 **Madisonville Community College** 2000 College Dr — Madisonville KY 42431-9185
606 759-7141 **Maysville Community College** RR 2 — Maysville KY 41056-9807
502 554-9200 **Paducah Community College** PO Box 7380 — Paducah KY 42002-7380
606 886-3863 **Prestonburg Community College** 1 Burt Combs Dr — Prestonburg KY 41653-0000
606 336-9304 **Saint Catharine College** — Saint Catharine KY 40061-9001
606 589-2145 **Southeast Community College** 300 College Rd — Cumberland KY 40823-1030
606 864-2238 **Sue Bennett College** 101 College St — London KY 40741-1915
502 456-6504 **Sullivan College** 3101 Bardstown Rd — Louisville KY 40205-3000
606 257-8608 **University of Kentucky Community College (System)**
Breckenridge Hall — Lexington KY 40506-0001

LOUISIANA

504 483-4114 **Delgado Community College** 501 City Park Ave — New Orleans LA 70119-4324
Louisiana State University
318 445-3672 *Alexandria Campus* 8100 US Hwy 71 S — Alexandria LA 71302-9119
318 457-7311 *Eunice Campus* PO Box 1129 — Eunice LA 70535-1129
318 674-3300 **Southern University Shreveport Campus**
3050 Martin Luther King Jr Dr — Shreveport LA 71107-4795

MAINE

207 947-4591 **Beal College** 629 Main St — Bangor ME 04401-6896
207 795-2840 **Central Maine Medical Center School of Nursing**
300 Main St — Lewiston ME 04240-0305
207 784-2385 **Central Maine Vocational College** 1250 Turner St — Auburn ME 04210-6436
207 941-4600 **Eastern Maine Vocational College** 354 Hogan Rd — Bangor ME 04401-4206
207 769-2461 **Northern Maine Technical College** 33 Edgemont Dr — Presque Isle ME 04769-2016
207 799-7303 **Southern Maine Vocational College** 2 Fort Rd — South Portland ME 04106-1698

MARYLAND

301 724-7700 **Allegany Community College** Willow Brook Rd — Cumberland MD 21502-0000
301 647-7100 **Anne Arundel Community College** 101 College Pkwy — Arnold MD 21012-1895
301 455-6050 **Catonsville Community College** 800 S Rolling Rd — Catonsville MD 21228-5384
301 287-6060 **Cecil Community College** 1000 N East Rd — North East MD 21901-1999
301 934-2251 **Charles County Community College** Mitchell Rd — La Plata MD 20646-0000
301 758-1537 **Chesapeake College** PO Box 8 — Wye Mills MD 21679-0008
301 396-0203 **Community College of Baltimore** 2901 Liberty Heights Ave — Baltimore MD 21215-7807
301 282-6700 **Dundalk Community College** 7200 Sollers Point Rd — Baltimore MD 21222-4694
301 682-6000 **Essex Community College** 7201 Rossville Blvd — Baltimore MD 21237-3898
301 694-5240 **Frederick Community College** 7932 Opossumtown Pike — Frederick MD 21702-0000
301 387-6666 **Garrett Community College** Mosser Rd — McHenry MD 21541-0000
301 790-2800 **Hagerstown Junior College** 751 Robinwood Dr — Hagerstown MD 21740-6590
301 879-8920 **Harford Community College** 401 Thomas Run Rd — Bel Air MD 21014-1698
301 992-4800 **Howard Community College** 10901 Little Patuxent Pkwy — Columbia MD 21044-3197
Montgomery College
301 353-7700 *Germantown Campus* 20200 Observation Dr — Germantown MD 20876-4098
301 279-5000 *Rockville Campus* 51 Mannakee St — Rockville MD 20850-1195
301 336-6000 **Prince George's Community College** 301 Largo Rd — Largo MD 20772-2199

MASSACHUSETTS

617 696-3100 **Aquinas College at Milton** 303 Adams St — Milton MA 02186-4296
508 791-9241 **Becker Junior College** 61 Sever St — Worcester MA 01609-2195
413 499-4660 **Berkshire Community College** 1350 West St — Pittsfield MA 01201-5786
508 678-2811 **Bristol Community College** 777 Elsbree St — Fall River MA 02720-7395
617 241-8600 **Bunker Hill Community College** New Rutherford Ave — Boston MA 02129-0000
508 362-2131 **Cape Cod Community College** 2240 Rt 132 — West Barnstable MA 02668-1599
508 528-9100 **Dean Junior College** 99 Main St — Franklin MA 02038-1994
508 774-0050 **Essex Agricultural & Technical Institute** 562 Maple St — Hathorne MA 01937-9999
617 262-3240 **Fisher Junior College** 118 Beacon St — Boston MA 02116-1500
617 423-4630 **Franklin Institute of Boston** 41 Berkeley St — Boston MA 02116-6296
413 774-3131 **Greenfield Community College** 1 College Dr — Greenfield MA 01301-9700
413 538-7000 **Holyoke Community College** 303 Homestead Ave — Holyoke MA 01040-1091
617 296-8300 **Laboure College** 2120 Dorchester Ave — Boston MA 02124-5698
617 243-2000 **Lasell Junior College** 1844 Commonwealth Ave — Auburndale MA 02166-2716
617 237-1100 **Massachusetts Bay Community College** 50 Oakland St — Wellesley Hills MA 02181-5359
508 588-9100 **Massasoit Community College** 1 Massasoit Blvd — Brockton MA 02402-3996
617 275-8910 **Middlesex Community College** 202 Springs Rd — Bedford MA 01730-1197
617 969-7000 **Mount Ida College** 777 Dedham St — Newton Center MA 02159-3310
508 632-6600 **Mount Wachusett Community College** 444 Green St — Gardner MA 01440-1337
617 262-9350 **Newbury Junior College** 129 Fisher Ave — Brookline MA 02146-5796
508 922-6722 **North Shore Community College** 3 Essex St — Beverly MA 01915-4560
508 374-3900 **Northern Essex Community College** Elliott Way — Haverhill MA 01830-0000
617 984-1600 **Quincy Junior College** 34 Coddington St — Quincy MA 02169-4522
508 853-2300 **Quinsigamond Community College** 670 W Boylston St — Worcester MA 01606-2092
617 427-0060 **Roxbury Community College** 1234 Columbus Ave — Roxbury MA 02120-3400
413 781-7822 **Springfield Technical Community College** 1 Armory Sq — Springfield MA 01105-1296

MICHIGAN

517 356-9021 **Alpena Community College** 666 Johnson St — Alpena MI 49707-1495
517 723-5251 **Baker Junior College** 1020 S Washington St — Owosso MI 48867-4400
906 786-5802 **Bay de Noc Community College** 2001 N Lincoln Rd — Escanaba MI 49829-2511
313 762-0200 **Charles Stewart Mott Community College** 1401 E Court St — Flint MI 48503-6208
517 686-9000 **Delta College** — University Center MI 48710-0001
616 467-9945 **Glen Oaks Community College** 62249 Shimmel Rd — Centreville MI 49032-9719
906 932-4231 **Gogebic Community College** E 4946 Jackson Rd — Ironwood MI 49938-0000
616 456-4899 **Grand Rapids Junior College** 143 Bostwick Ave NE — Grand Rapids MI 49503-3295
313 271-2750 **Henry Ford Community College** 5101 Evergreen Rd — Dearborn MI 48128-1495
313 252-0475 **Highland Park Community College** Glendale & 3rd Sts — Highland Park MI 48203-3190
517 787-0800 **Jackson Community College** 2111 Emmons Rd — Jackson MI 49201-8399
616 372-5000 **Kalamazoo Valley Community College** 6767 W 'O' Ave — Kalamazoo MI 49009-9606
616 965-3931 **Kellogg Community College** 450 North Ave — Battle Creek MI 49017-3397
517 275-5121 **Kirtland Community College** 10775 N St Helen Rd — Roscommon MI 48653-9699
616 927-3571 **Lake Michigan College** 2755 E Napier Ave — Benton Harbor MI 49022-1899
517 483-1957 **Lansing Community College** 422 Washington Sq N — Lansing MI 48901-0000
313 862-6300 **Lewis College of Business** 17370 Meyers Rd — Detroit MI 48235-1498
313 286-2000 **Macomb Community College** 44575 Garfield Rd — Mount Clemens MI 48044-1498
313 445-7000 *South Campus* 14500 E 12-Mile Rd — Warren MI 48093-0000
313 651-5800 **Michigan Christian College** 800 W Avon Rd — Rochester Hills MI 48307-2764
517 386-7792 **Mid Michigan Community College** 1375 S Clare Ave — Harrison MI 48625-9447
313 242-7300 **Monroe County Community College** 1555 S Raisinville Rd — Monroe MI 48161-9746
517 328-2111 **Montcalm Community College** 2800 College Dr — Sidney MI 48885-9746
616 773-9131 **Muskegon Community College** 221 S Quarterline Rd — Muskegon MI 49442-1493
616 347-3973 **North Central Michigan College** 1515 Howard St — Petoskey MI 49770-9271
313 540-1500 **Oakland Community College (System)**
2480 Opdyke Rd — Bloomfield Hills MI 48304-2266
Oakland Community College
313 340-6500 *Auburn Hills Campus* 2900 Featherstone Rd — Auburn Hills MI 48326-2845
313 360-3000 *Highland Lakes Campus* 7350 Cooley Lake Rd — Union Lake MI 48387-2400
313 471-7500 *Orchard Ridge Campus* 27055 Orchard Lake Rd — Farmington Hills MI 48334-4579
313 544-4900 *Royal Oak Campus* 739 S Washington Ave — Royal Oak MI 48067-3898
313 552-2600 *Southfield Campus* 22322 Rutland Ave — Southfield MI 48075-4793
313 984-3881 **Saint Clair County Community College** 323 Erie St — Port Huron MI 48060-3812
313 591-6400 **Schoolcraft College** 18600 Haggerty Rd — Livonia MI 48152-2696
616 782-5113 **Southwestern Michigan College** 58900 Cherry Grove Rd — Dowagiac MI 49047-9726
906 482-5300 **Suomi College** 601 Quincy St — Hancock MI 49930-1882
313 973-3300 **Washtenaw Community College** 4800 E Huron River Dr — Ann Arbor MI 48106-0000
313 496-2500 **Wayne County Community College** 801 W Fort St — Detroit MI 48226-3095
616 845-6211 **West Shore Community College** 3000 N Stiles Rd — Scottville MI 49454-9716

MINNESOTA

612 762-0221 **Alexandria Technical College** 1601 Jefferson St — Alexandria MN 56308-3799
612 427-2600 **Anoka-Ramsey Community College**
11200 Mississippi Blvd NW — Coon Rapids MN 55433-3499
507 433-0505 **Austin Community College** 1600 8th Ave NW — Austin MN 55912-1400
507 625-2977 **Bethany Lutheran College** 734 Marsh St — Mankato MN 56001-4490
218 828-2525 **Brainerd Community College** 501 W College Dr — Brainerd MN 56401-3900
218 739-7500 **Fergus Falls Community College** 1414 College Way — Fergus Falls MN 56537-1009
218 262-6700 **Hibbing Community College** 1515 E 25th St — Hibbing MN 55746-3354
612 450-8501 **Inver Hills Community College**
8445 College Trail E — Inver Grove Heights MN 55076-0000
218 327-4461 **Itasca Community College** 1851 E Hwy 169 — Grand Rapids MN 55744-3361
218 749-7700 **Mesabi Community College** 9th Ave & W Chestnut St — Virginia MN 55792-0000
612 341-7000 **Minneapolis Community College** 1501 Hennepin Ave — Minneapolis MN 55403-1710
612 296-3990 **Minnesota Community College (System)**
550 Cedar St 2nd Fl — Saint Paul MN 55101-2233
612 832-6000 **Normandale Community College** 9700 France Ave S — Bloomington MN 55431-4399
218 681-2181 **Northland Community College** 1101 US Hwy 1 E — Thief River Falls MN 56701-2598
218 285-7722 **Rainy River Community College** 1803 Hwy 11-71 — International Falls MN 56649-2167
507 285-7265 **Rochester Community College** 851 30th Ave SE — Rochester MN 55904-4999
612 332-5521 **Saint Mary's Campus of the College of Saint Catherine**
2500 S 6th St — Minneapolis MN 55454-1401
University of Minnesota
218 281-6510 *Crookston Campus* Selvig Hall — Crookston MN 56716-0000
507 835-1000 *Waseca Campus* 1000 University Dr SW — Waseca MN 56093-2086
218 365-7200 **Vermilion Community College** 1900 E Camp St — Ely MN 55731-1996
507 372-2107 **Worthington Community College** 1450 College Way — Worthington MN 56187-3024

MISSISSIPPI

601 683-2061 **Clarke College** College St — Newton MS 39345-0000
601 643-5101 **Copiah-Lincoln Community College** PO Box 457 — Wesson MS 39191-0457
601 635-2126 **East Central Community College** Broad St — Decatur MS 39327-0000
601 476-8442 **East Mississippi Community College** Kemper St — Scooba MS 39358-0000
601 857-5261 **Hinds Community College** Main St — Raymond MS 39154-9778
601 354-2327 *Utica Campus* Hwy 18 W — Utica MS 39175-0000
601 472-2312 **Holmes Community College** PO Box 369 — Goodman MS 39079-0369
601 862-3101 **Itawamba Community College** 602 W Hill St — Fulton MS 38843-1099
601 477-9311 **Jones County Junior College** College Dr — Ellisville MS 39437-3901
601 494-6820 **Mary Holmes College** Hwy 50 W — West Point MS 39773-0000
601 483-8241 **Meridian Community College** 910 Hwy 19 N — Meridian MS 39307-5890
601 246-5631 **Mississippi Delta Community College** PO Box 668 — Moorhead MS 38761-0668
601 928-5211 **Mississippi Gulf Coast Community College** Hwy 49 S — Perkinston MS 39573-0000
601 728-7751 **Northeast Mississippi Community College**
Cunningham Blvd — Booneville MS 38829-0000
601 562-3200 **Northwest Mississippi Community College** Hwy 51 N — Senatobia MS 38668-0000
601 795-6801 **Pearl River Community College** Hwys 26 & 11 Stn A — Poplarville MS 39470-0000
601 276-2000 **Southwest Mississippi Community College** College Dr — Summit MS 39666-0000

MISSOURI

417 667-8181 **Cottey College** 1000 W Austin St — Nevada MO 64772-2700
417 451-3223 **Crowder College** 601 Laclede Ave — Neosho MO 64850-9160
314 583-5193 **East Central College** PO Box 529 — Union MO 63084-0529
314 789-3951 **Jefferson College** Hwy 21 — Hillsboro MO 63050-0000
816 882-5623 **Kemper Military School & College** 701 3rd St — Boonville MO 65233-1670
816 763-7777 **Longview Community College** 500 SW Longview Rd — Lees Summit MO 64081-2100
816 436-6500 **Maple Woods Community College** 2601 NE Barry Rd — Kansas City MO 64156-1254
314 431-4593 **Mineral Area College** — Flat River MO 63601-0000
816 263-4110 **Moberly Area Junior College** College & Rollins Sts — Moberly MO 65270-0000
816 932-7600 **Penn Valley Community College** 3201 SW Trafficway — Kansas City MO 64111-2727
314 539-5000 **Saint Louis Community College** 300 S Broadway — Saint Louis MO 63102-2800
314 595-4200 *Florissant Valley Campus* 3400 Pershall Rd — Saint Louis MO 63135-1408
314 644-9100 *Forest Park Campus* 5600 Oakland Ave — Saint Louis MO 63110-1316
314 966-7500 *Meramec Campus* 11333 Big Bend Blvd — Kirkwood MO 63122-5799
816 826-7100 **State Fair Community College** 3201 W 16th St — Sedalia MO 65301-2199
314 686-4101 **Three Rivers Community College** Three Rivers Blvd — Poplar Bluff MO 63901-0000
816 259-2221 **Wentworth Military Academy** 18th & Washington Ave — Lexington MO 64067-1799

MONTANA

406 338-5441 **Blackfeet Community College** PO Box 819 — Browning MT 59417-0819
406 365-3396 **Dawson Community College** 300 College Dr — Glendive MT 59330-1405
406 752-5222 **Flathead Valley Community College** 1 1st St E — Kalispell MT 59901-4599
406 232-3031 **Miles Community College** 2715 Dickinson St — Miles City MT 59301-4799
406 542-6811 **Missoula Vocational Technical Center** 909 South Ave W — Missoula MT 59801-7910
406 675-4800 **Salish Kootenai Community College** PO Box 117 — Pablo MT 59855-0117

NEBRASKA

402 463-9811 **Central Community College** E Hwy 6 — Hastings NE 68901-0000
402 564-7132 *Platte Campus* 4500 63rd St — Columbus NE 68601-8031
308 345-6303 **McCook Community College** 1205 E 3rd St — McCook NE 69001-2631
402 449-8400 **Metropolitan Technical Community College** PO Box 3777 — Omaha NE 68103-0777
308 532-8740 **Mid Plains Community College Voc-Tech Campus**
RR 4 Box 1 — North Platte NE 69101-9499
308 367-4124 **Nebraska College of Technical Agriculture** 404 E 7th St — Curtis NE 69025-0000
402 371-2020 **Northeast Community College** PO Box 469 — Norfolk NE 68702-0469
Southeast Community College
402 471-3333 *Lincoln Campus* 8800 O St — Lincoln NE 68520-1299
402 761-2131 *Milford Campus* RR 2 Box D — Milford NE 68405-9802
308 635-3606 **Western Nebraska Community College** 1601 E 27th St — Scottsbluff NE 69361-1815
402 362-4441 **York College** 9th & Kiplinger Sts — York NE 68467-0000

NEVADA

702 643-6060 **Clark County Community College**
3200 E Cheyenne Ave — North Las Vegas NV 89030-4228
702 738-8493 **Northern Nevada Community College** 901 Elm St — Elko NV 89801-3348

NEW HAMPSHIRE

New Hampshire Technical College
603 752-1113 *Berlin Campus* 2020 Riverside Dr ... Berlin NH 03570-3717
603 542-7744 *Claremont Campus* 1 College Dr ... Claremont NH 03743-0000
603 524-3207 *Laconia Campus* Rt 106 Prescott Hill ... Laconia NH 03246-0000
603 668-6706 *Manchester Campus* 1066 Front St ... Manchester NH 03102-8528
603 882-6923 *Nashua Campus* 505 Amherst St ... Nashua NH 03063-1026
603 772-1194 *Stratham Campus* 277R Portsmouth Ave ... Stratham NH 03885-2231
603 225-1800 **New Hampshire Technical Institute** Institute Dr ... Concord NH 03301-7400
603 668-0700 **University of New Hampshire at Manchester**
220 Hackett Hill Rd ... Manchester NH 03102-8503
603 887-4401 **White Pines College** 40 Chester St ... Chester NH 03036-4331

NEW JERSEY

201 543-6528 **Assumption College for Sisters**
Mallinckrodt Convent Hilltop Rd ... Mendham NJ 07945-0000
609 625-1111 **Atlantic Community College** Black Horse Pike ... Mays Landing NJ 08330-9115
201 447-7200 **Bergen Community College** 400 Paramus Rd ... Paramus NJ 07652-1595
908 842-1900 **Brookdale Community College** 765 Newman Springs Rd ... Lincroft NJ 07738-1597
609 894-9311 **Burlington County College** Rt 530 ... Pemberton NJ 08068-0000
609 227-7200 **Camden County College** Little Gloucester Rd ... Blackwood NJ 08012-3398
201 361-5000 **County College of Morris** Rt 10 & Center Grove Rd ... Randolph NJ 07869-0000
609 691-8600 **Cumberland County College** Orchard & Sherman Ave ... Vineland NJ 08360-0000
201 692-2675 **Edward Williams College** 150 Kotte Pl ... Hackensack NJ 07601-6199
201 877-3000 **Essex County College** 303 University Ave ... Newark NJ 07102-1798
609 468-5000 **Gloucester County College** Tanyard Rd ... Sewell NJ 08080-9191
201 656-2020 **Hudson County Community College** 168 Sip Ave ... Jersey City NJ 07306-3009
609 586-4800 **Mercer County Community College** PO Box B ... Trenton NJ 08690-0182
908 548-6000 **Middlesex County College** 155 Mill Rd Box 3050 ... Edison NJ 08837-3675
908 255-4000 **Ocean County College** College Dr CN-2001 ... Toms River NJ 08753-0000
201 684-6800 **Passaic County Community College** 1 College Blvd ... Paterson NJ 07509-0000
908 526-1200 **Raritan Community College** PO Box 3300 ... Somerville NJ 08876-1265
609 299-2100 **Salem Community College** 460 Hollywood Ave ... Carneys Point NJ 08069-2799
908 709-7000 **Union County College** 1033 Springfield Ave ... Cranford NJ 07016-1528

NEW MEXICO

505 988-6493 **Institute of American Indian Arts** St Michaels Dr ... Santa Fe NM 87501-0000
505 622-6250 **New Mexico Military Institute** 101 W College Blvd ... Roswell NM 88201-5173
505 885-8831 **New Mexico State University at Carlsbad** 1500 University Dr .. Carlsbad NM 88220-3509
505 287-7981 **New Mexico State University Grants Branch** 1500 3rd St ... Grants NM 87020-2025
505 753-7141 **Northern New Mexico Community College** 1002 N Onate St ... Espanola NM 87532-0000

NEW YORK

518 793-4491 **Adirondack Community College** 440 Bay Rd ... Queensbury NY 12804-5816
212 686-9244 **American Academy of Dramatic Arts** 120 Madison Ave ... New York NY 10016-7089
607 771-5000 **Broome Community College** PO Box 1017 ... Binghamton NY 13902-1017
315 255-1743 **Cayuga County Community College** 197 Franklin St ... Auburn NY 13021-3099
518 561-6650 **Clinton Community College** Rt 9 S ... Plattsburgh NY 12901-0000
518 828-4181 **Columbia-Greene Community College** Rt 23 ... Hudson NY 12534-0000
716 394-3500 **Community College of the Finger Lakes** Lincoln Hill Rd ... Canandaigua NY 14424-0000
607 962-9011 **Corning Community College** Spencer Hill Rd ... Corning NY 14830-0000
914 452-9600 **Culinary Institute of America** 433 Albany Post Rd ... Hyde Park NY 12538-1499
CUNY
212 618-1000 *Borough of Manhattan Community College*
199 Chambers St ... New York NY 10007-1006
212 220-6450 *Bronx Community College* W 181st & University Ave ... Bronx NY 10453-2805
212 960-1114 *Hostos Community College* 475 Grand Concourse ... Bronx NY 10451-5307
718 368-5000 *Kingsborough Community College* 2001 Oriental Blvd ... Brooklyn NY 11235-2336
718 482-5000 *La Guardia Community College* 31-10 Thomson Ave . Long Island City NY 11101-3071
718 643-4900 *New York City Technical College* 300 Jay St ... Brooklyn NY 11201-2902
718 631-6262 *Queensborough Community College* 222-05 56th Ave ... Bayside NY 11364-1432
914 471-4500 **Dutchess Community College** 53 Pendell Rd ... Poughkeepsie NY 12601-1595
Erie Community College
716 842-2770 *City Campus* 121 Ellicott St ... Buffalo NY 14203-2698
716 634-0800 *North Campus* Main St & Youngs Rd ... Williamsville NY 14221-7095
716 648-5400 *South Campus* 4140 Southwestern Blvd ... Orchard Park NY 14127-2199
518 762-4651 **Fulton-Montgomery Community College** Rt 67 ... Johnstown NY 12095-0000
716 343-0055 **Genesee Community College** 1 College Rd ... Batavia NY 14020-0000
315 866-0300 **Herkimer County Community College** Reservoir Rd ... Herkimer NY 13350-0000
716 649-7900 **Hilbert College** 5200 S Park Ave ... Hamburg NY 14075-1597
518 283-1100 **Hudson Valley Community College** 80 Vandenburgh Ave ... Troy NY 12180-6096
914 633-2000 **Iona College** 715 North Ave ... New Rochelle NY 10801-1890
914 969-4000 **Iona College Elizabeth Seton School** 1061 N Broadway ... Yonkers NY 10701-1105
716 665-5220 **Jamestown Community College** 525 Falconer St ... Jamestown NY 14701-0000
315 782-5250 **Jefferson Community College** Outer Coffeen St ... Watertown NY 13601-1899
212 752-1530 **Laboratory Institute of Merchandising** 12 E 53rd St ... New York NY 10022-5208
518 438-3111 **Maria College** 700 New Scotland Ave ... Albany NY 12208-1798
315 393-5930 **Mater Dei College** Riverside Dr ... Ogdensburg NY 13669-0000
315 792-5400 **Mohawk Valley Community College** 1101 Sherman Dr ... Utica NY 13501-5308
716 424-5200 **Monroe Community College** 1000 E Henrietta Rd ... Rochester NY 14623-5780
516 222-7355 **Nassau Community College** Stewart Ave ... Garden City NY 11530-2200
716 731-4101 **Niagara County Community College**
3111 Saunders Settlement Rd ... Sanborn NY 14132-9460
518 891-2915 **North Country Community College** 20 Winona Ave ... Saranac Lake NY 12983-2046
315 469-7741 **Onondaga Community College** ... Syracuse NY 13215-0000
914 343-1121 **Orange County Community College** 115 South St ... Middletown NY 10940-6404
518 327-6211 **Paul Smiths College** Rts 30 & 192 ... Paul Smiths NY 12970-0000
914 356-4650 **Rockland Community College** 145 College Rd ... Suffern NY 10901-3699
518 346-6211 **Schenectady County Community College**
78 Washington Ave ... Schenectady NY 12305-2294
Suffolk County Community College
516 434-6700 *Brentwood Campus* Crooked Hill Rd ... Brentwood NY 11717-0000
516 451-4110 *Selden Campus* 533 College Rd ... Selden NY 11784-2899
914 434-5750 **Sullivan County Community College** ... Loch Sheldrake NY 12759-0000
SUNY
607 587-4111 *College at Alfred* ... Alfred NY 14802-0000
716 395-2211 *College at Brockport* ... Brockport NY 14420-0000
315 386-7011 *College at Canton* 34 Cornell Dr ... Canton NY 13617-1096
607 746-4111 *College at Delhi* Main St ... Delhi NY 13753-0000
315 684-6000 *College at Morrisville* ... Morrisville NY 13408-0000
516 420-2000 *College of Technology* Rt 110 ... Farmingdale NY 11735-0000
607 844-8211 **Tompkins Cortland Community College** 170 North St ... Dryden NY 13053-9533
716 826-1200 **Trocaire College** 110 Red Jacket Pkwy ... Buffalo NY 14220-2094
914 687-7621 **Ulster County Community College** ... Stone Ridge NY 12484-0000
716 896-0700 **Villa Maria College of Buffalo** 240 Pine Ridge Rd ... Buffalo NY 14225-3999
914 285-6600 **Westchester Community College** 75 Grasslands Rd ... Valhalla NY 10595-1693
212 686-9040 **Wood School** 8 E 40th St ... New York NY 10016-0190

NORTH CAROLINA

919 578-2002 **Alamance Community College** Jimmy Kerr Rd & I-85 ... Haw River NC 27258-0000
704 826-8333 **Anson Community College** Hwy 52 ... Ansonville NC 28007-9999
704 254-1921 **Asheville-Buncombe Technical Community College**
340 Victoria Rd ... Asheville NC 28801-4816
919 946-6194 **Beaufort County Community College** Hwy 264 E ... Washington NC 27889-0000
704 692-3572 **Blue Ridge Community College** RR 2 Box 133-A ... Flat Rock NC 28731-9802
704 883-8292 **Brevard College** 400 N Broad St ... Brevard NC 28712-9904
704 726-2200 **Caldwell Community College & Technical Institute**
1000 Hickory Blvd ... Hudson NC 28638-2397
919 343-0481 **Cape Fear Community College** 411 N Front St ... Wilmington NC 28401-3993
704 327-9124 **Catawba Valley Community College** RR 3 Box 283 ... Hickory NC 28602-9803
919 775-5401 **Central Carolina Community College** 1105 Kelly Dr ... Sanford NC 27330-9000
704 342-6633 **Central Piedmont Community College** PO Box 35009 ... Charlotte NC 28235-6099
919 398-4101 **Chowan College** 200 Jones Dr ... Murfreesboro NC 27855-1844
704 484-4000 **Cleveland Community College** 137 S Post Rd ... Shelby NC 28150-6296
919 455-1221 **Coastal Carolina Community College** 444 Western Blvd ... Jacksonville NC 28546-6899
919 335-0821 **College of the Albemarle** Hwy 17 N ... Elizabeth City NC 27909-0000
919 638-4131 **Craven Community College** 800 College Ct ... New Bern NC 28562-5184
704 249-8186 **Davidson County Community College** PO Box 1287 ... Lexington NC 27293-1287
919 598-9222 **Durham Technical Institute** 1637 E Lawson St ... Durham NC 27703-5023
919 823-5166 **Edgecombe Community College** 20009 W Wilson St ... Tarboro NC 27886-0000
919 323-1961 **Fayetteville Technical Community College** 2201 Hull Rd ... Fayetteville NC 28303-4761
919 723-0371 **Forsyth Technical Community College**
2100 Silas Creek Pkwy ... Winston-Salem NC 27103-5150
704 922-6200 **Gaston Community College** 201 Hwy 321-S ... Dallas NC 28034-1499
919 334-4822 **Guilford Technical Community College** High Point Rd ... Jamestown NC 27282-0000
919 536-2551 **Halifax Community College** Hwy 158 W ... Weldon NC 27890-0000
704 627-2821 **Haywood Community College** 1 Freedlander Dr ... Clyde NC 28721-9454
704 286-3636 **Isothermal Community College** PO Box 804 ... Spindale NC 28160-0804
919 296-1341 **James Sprunt Technical College** Hwy 11 S ... Kenansville NC 28349-0000
919 934-3051 **Johnston Technical Institute** Hwy 70 E ... Smithfield NC 27577-0000
919 527-6223 **Lenoir Community College** Hwy 70 E ... Kinston NC 28502-0000
919 496-2521 **Louisburg College** 501 N Main St ... Louisburg NC 27549-2399
919 792-1521 **Martin Community College** Kehukee Park Rd ... Williamston NC 27892-0000
704 765-7351 **Mayland Community College** Hwy 19 E ... Spruce Pine NC 28777-0000
704 652-6021 **McDowell Technical Community College** RR 1 Box 170 ... Marion NC 28752-9725
704 878-3200 **Mitchell Community College** 500 W Broad St ... Statesville NC 28677-5293
919 572-3691 **Montgomery Community College** Old Biscoe Rd ... Troy NC 27371-0000
919 443-4011 **Nash Community College** Old Carriage Rd ... Rocky Mount NC 27804-0000
919 249-1851 **Pamlico Community College** Hwy 306 S ... Grantsboro NC 28529-0000
919 832-2881 **Peace College** 15 E Peace St ... Raleigh NC 27604-1194
919 599-1181 **Piedmont Community College** PO Box 1197 ... Roxboro NC 27573-1197
919 355-4200 **Pitt Community College** Hwy 11 S ... Greenville NC 27835-0000
919 629-1471 **Randolph Community College** 629 Industrial Park Ave ... Asheboro NC 27203-7333
919 582-7000 **Richmond Community College** Hwy 74 W ... Hamlet NC 28345-0000
919 332-5921 **Roanoke-Chowan Community College** RR 2 Box 46-A ... Ahoskie NC 27910-9522
919 738-7101 **Robeson Community College** PO Box 1420 ... Lumberton NC 28359-1420
919 342-4261 **Rockingham Community College** Hwy 65 ... Wentworth NC 27375-9999
704 637-0760 **Rowan-Cabarrus Community College**
1333 Jake Alexander Blvd W ... Salisbury NC 28144-6333
919 828-2521 **Saint Mary's College** 900 Hillsborough St ... Raleigh NC 27603-1689
919 592-8081 **Sampson Community College** Hwy 24 W ... Clinton NC 28328-0000
919 692-6185 **Sandhills Community College** 2200 Airport Rd ... Pinehurst NC 28374-9299
919 642-7141 **Southeastern Community College** Hwy 7476 ... Whiteville NC 28472-0000
704 586-4091 **Southwestern Community College** 275 Webster Rd ... Sylva NC 28779-9578
704 982-0121 **Stanly Community College** RR 4 Box 55 ... Albemarle NC 28001-9402
919 386-8121 **Surry Community College** S Main St ... Dobson NC 27017-0000
704 837-5651 **Tri-County Community College** PO Box 40 ... Murphy NC 28906-0040
919 492-2061 **Vance-Granville Community College** State Rd 1126 ... Henderson NC 27536-0000
919 772-7500 **Wake Technical Community College** 9101 Fayetteville Rd ... Raleigh NC 27603-5696
919 735-5151 **Wayne Community College North Campus**
906 US Hwy 70 E ... Goldsboro NC 27533-0000
704 438-6000 **Western Piedmont Community College**
1001 Burkemont Ave ... Morganton NC 28655-4504
919 667-7136 **Wilkes Community College** Collegiate Dr ... Wilkesboro NC 28697-0000
919 291-1195 **Wilson Technical Community College** 902 Herring Ave E ... Wilson NC 27893-3310

NORTH DAKOTA

701 774-4200 **University of North Dakota Williston** PO Box 1326 ... Williston ND 58802-1326

OHIO

216 264-3911 **Agriculture Technical Institution** 1328 Dover Rd ... Wooster OH 44691-8905
614 695-9500 **Belmont Technical College** 120 Fox Shannon Pl ... Saint Clairsville OH 43950-9766
419 433-5560 **Bowling Green State University Firelands College**
901 Rye Beach Rd ... Huron OH 44839-9791
614 366-1351 **Central Ohio Technical College** University Dr ... Newark OH 43055-0000
513 875-3344 **Chatfield College** 20918 SR-251 ... Saint Martin OH 45118-0000
513 569-1500 **Cincinnati Technical College** 3520 Central Pkwy ... Cincinnati OH 45223-2612
513 325-0691 **Clark Technical College** 570 E Leffel Ln ... Springfield OH 45505-4795
614 227-2400 **Columbus State Community College** 550 E Spring St ... Columbus OH 43215-1786
216 987-4000 **Cuyahoga Community College** 700 Carnegie Ave ... Cleveland OH 44115-2878
513 778-8600 **Edison State Community College** 1973 Edison Dr ... Piqua OH 45356-9253
614 753-3591 **Hocking Technical College** 3301 Hocking Pkwy ... Nelsonville OH 45764-9588
614 264-5591 **Jefferson Technical College** 4000 Sunset Blvd ... Steubenville OH 43952-3512
Kent State University
216 385-3805 *East Liverpool Campus* 400 E 4th St ... East Liverpool OH 43920-3497
216 332-0361 *Salem Campus* 2491 SR-45 S ... Salem OH 44460-9412
216 499-9600 *Stark Campus* 6000 Frank Ave NW ... Canton OH 44720-7599
216 847-0571 *Trumbull Campus* 4314 Mahoning Ave NW ... Warren OH 44483-1998
216 339-3391 *Tuscarawas Campus* University Dr NE ... New Philadelphia OH 44663-9422
513 296-7201 **Kettering College of Medical Arts** 3737 Southern Blvd ... Kettering OH 45429-1299
216 953-7000 **Lakeland Community College** SR-306 & I-90 ... Mentor OH 44060-0000
419 222-8324 **Lima Technical College** 4240 Campus Dr ... Lima OH 45804-3597
216 365-4191 **Lorain County Community College** 1005 N Abbe Rd ... Elyria OH 44035-1691
419 885-3211 **Lourdes College** 6832 Convent Blvd ... Sylvania OH 43560-2898
614 389-4636 **Marion Technical College** 1465 Mt Vernon Ave ... Marion OH 43302-5628
614 454-2501 **Muskingum Area Technical College** 1555 Newark Rd ... Zanesville OH 43701-2694
419 755-4800 **North Central Technical College** PO Box 698 ... Mansfield OH 44901-0698
419 267-5511 **Northwest Technical College** RR 1 Box 246-A ... Archbold OH 43502-9801
419 666-0580 **Owens Technical College** Oregon Rd ... Toledo OH 43699-0000
513 745-5600 **Raymond Walters College** 9555 Plainfield Rd ... Cincinnati OH 45236-1096
513 226-2500 **Sinclair Community College** 444 W 3rd St ... Dayton OH 45402-1453
Southern State Community College
513 382-6645 *North Campus* 2698 Old State Rt 73 ... Wilmington OH 45177-9387
513 695-0307 *South Campus* 12681 US Rt 62 ... Sardinia OH 45171-0000
216 494-6170 **Stark Technical College** 6200 Frank Ave NW ... Canton OH 44720-7299
419 334-3886 **Terra Technical College** 2830 Napoleon Rd ... Fremont OH 43420-9600
216 683-2010 **University of Akron Wayne College** 10470 Smucker Rd ... Orrville OH 44667-9757
614 374-8716 **Washington Technical College** RR 2 ... Marietta OH 45750-9802
419 586-2365 **Wright State University Lake Campus** 7600 SR-703 ... Celina OH 45822-0000

OKLAHOMA

918 683-4581 **Bacone College** 99 Bacone Rd ... Muskogee OK 74403-1597
918 463-2931 **Connors State College** RR 1 Box 1000 ... Warner OK 74469-9700
918 465-2361 **Eastern Oklahoma State College** 1301 W Main St ... Wilburton OK 74578-4999

Two-Year Colleges

405 262-2552 **El Reno Junior College** PO Box 370 .... El Reno OK 73036-0370
405 371-2371 **Murray State College** Byrd St .... Tishomingo OK 73460-0000
405 628-2581 **Northern Oklahoma College** 1220 E Grand .... Tonkawa OK 74653-0000
405 682-1611 **Oklahoma City Community College** 7777 S May Ave .... Oklahoma City OK 73159-4499
405 947-4421 **Oklahoma State University Technical Branch**
900 N Portland Ave .... Oklahoma City OK 73107-6120
918 341-7510 **Rogers State College** 1720 W Will Rogers Blvd .... Claremore OK 74017-3252
405 733-7311 **Rose State College** 6420 SE 15th St .... Midwest City OK 73110-2797
405 273-9870 **Saint Gregory's College** 1900 W MacArthur St .... Shawnee OK 74801-2499
405 382-9950 **Seminole Junior College** PO Box 351 .... Seminole OK 74868-0000
918 587-6561 **Tulsa Junior College** 909 S Boston Ave .... Tulsa OK 74119-2095
405 477-2000 **Western Oklahoma State College** 2801 N Main St .... Altus OK 73521-1397

OREGON

503 228-6528 **Bassist College** 2000 SW 5th Ave .... Portland OR 97201-4907
503 276-1260 **Blue Mountain Community College** 2411 NW Carden Ave .... Pendleton OR 97801-1166
503 382-6112 **Central Oregon Community College** 2600 NW College Way .... Bend OR 97701-5998
503 399-5006 **Chemeketa Community College** 4000 Lancaster Dr NE .... Salem OR 97305-1453
503 657-8400 **Clackamas Community College** 19600 S Molalla Ave .... Oregon City OR 97045-9049
503 325-0910 **Clatsop Community College** 1653 Jerome Ave .... Astoria OR 97103-3698
503 747-4501 **Lane Community College** 4000 E 30th Ave .... Eugene OR 97405-0640
503 928-2361 **Linn-Benton Community College** 6500 Pacific Blvd SW .... Albany OR 97321-3774
503 667-6422 **Mount Hood Community College** 26000 SE Stark St .... Gresham OR 97030-3300
503 244-6111 **Portland Community College** 12000 SW 49th Ave .... Portland OR 97219-7197
503 479-5541 **Rogue Community College** 3345 Redwood Hwy .... Grants Pass OR 97527-9298
503 888-2525 **Southwestern Oregon Community College**
1988 Newmark Ave .... Coos Bay OR 97420-2956
503 889-6493 **Treasure Valley Community College** 650 College Blvd .... Ontario OR 97914-3423
503 440-4600 **Umpqua Community College** 1140 College Rd .... Roseburg OR 97470-0000

PENNSYLVANIA

412 287-8711 **Butler County Community College** PO Box 1203 .... Butler PA 16003-1203
717 732-0702 **Central Pennsylvania Business School** College Hill Rd .... Summerdale PA 17093-9999
814 676-6591 **Clarion University of Pennsylvania Venango Campus**
1801 W 1st St .... Oil City PA 16301-3254
Community College of Allegheny County
412 237-2525 *Allegheny Campus* 808 Ridge Ave .... Pittsburgh PA 15212-6097
412 371-8651 *Boyce Campus* 595 Beatty Rd .... Monroeville PA 15146-1348
412 366-7000 *North Campus* 1130 Perry Hwy .... Pittsburgh PA 15237-2174
412 469-1100 *South Campus* 1750 Carton Rd .... West Mifflin PA 15122-0000
412 775-8561 **Community College of Beaver County** 1 Campus Dr .... Monaca PA 15061-2588
215 751-8000 **Community College of Philadelphia**
1700 Spring Garden St .... Philadelphia PA 19130-3991
215 359-5000 **Delaware County Community College** Rt 252 & Medialine Rd .... Media PA 19063-0000
215 525-4100 **Harcum Junior College** Morris & Montgomery Aves .... Bryn Mawr PA 19010-3505
717 780-2300 **Harrisburg Area Community College** 3300 Cameron St .... Harrisburg PA 17110-2902
717 342-7701 **International Correspondence School Center for Degree Studies**
925 Oak St .... Scranton PA 18515-0001
717 945-5141 **Keystone Junior College** PO Box 50 .... La Plume PA 18440-0200
717 961-7810 **Lackawanna Junior College** 901 Prospect Ave .... Scranton PA 18505-1870
215 799-2121 **Lehigh County Community College** 2370 Main St .... Schnecksville PA 18078-9329
717 829-7300 **Luzerne County Community College**
S Prospect St & Middle Rd .... Nanticoke PA 18634-3814
215 885-2360 **Manor Junior College** Fox Chase Rd & Forest Ave .... Jenkintown PA 19046-0000
215 641-6300 **Montgomery County Community College** 340 DeKalb Pike .... Blue Bell PA 19422-1400
814 886-4131 **Mount Aloysius Junior College** William Penn Hwy .... Cresson PA 16630-0000
215 525-6780 **Northeastern Christian Junior College**
1860 Montgomery Ave .... Villanova PA 19085-1734
215 545-6400 **Peirce Junior College** 1420 Pine St .... Philadelphia PA 19102-4699
717 326-3761 **Pennsylvania College of Technology** 1 College Ave .... Williamsport PA 17701-5778
215 565-7900 **Pennsylvania Institute of Technology** 800 Manchester Ave .... Media PA 19063-4036
Pennsylvania State University
814 949-5000 *Altoona Campus* 3000 Ivyside Park .... Altoona PA 16601-3794
412 773-3500 *Beaver Campus* Brodhead Rd .... Monaca PA 15061-0000
814 898-6000 *Behrend College* Station Rd .... Erie PA 16563-0001
215 320-4800 *Berks Campus* Tulpehocken Rd .... Reading PA 19610-0000
215 565-3300 *Delaware County Campus* 25 Yearsley Mill Rd .... Media PA 19063-5596
814 371-2800 *Du Bois Campus* College Pl .... Du Bois PA 15801-3199
412 430-4100 *Fayette Campus* Rt 119 N .... Uniontown PA 15401-0000
717 948-6000 *Harrisburg Campus* Rt 230 .... Middletown PA 17057-0000
717 450-3000 *Hazleton Campus* Highacres .... Hazleton PA 18201-0000
412 675-9000 *McKeesport Campus* University Dr .... McKeesport PA 15132-7698
717 749-3111 *Mont Alto Campus* .... Mont Alto PA 17237-0000
412 339-5466 *New Kensington Campus* 3550 7th Street Rd .... New Kensington PA 15068-1798
215 886-9400 *Ogontz Campus* 1600 Woodland Rd .... Abington PA 19001-3918
717 385-6000 *Schuylkill Campus* 200 University Dr .... Schuylkill Haven PA 17972-2208
412 983-5800 *Shenango Valley Campus* 147 Shenango Ave .... Sharon PA 16146-1537
717 675-2171 *Wilkes-Barre Campus* Huntsville Rd .... Lehman PA 18627-9999
717 771-4000 *York Campus* 1031 Edgecombe Ave .... York PA 17403-3326
215 282-4000 **Pinebrook Junior College** 600 S Main St .... Coopersburg PA 18036-2499
215 372-4721 **Reading Area Community College** 10 S 2nd St .... Reading PA 19602-1029
814 827-2702 **University of Pittsburgh Titusville Campus** 504 E Main St .... Titusville PA 16354-2010
215 688-1800 **Valley Forge Military Academy & Junior College**
1001 Eagle Rd .... Wayne PA 19087-3613
412 925-4000 **Westmoreland County Community College** College Stn .... Youngwood PA 15697-1895

RHODE ISLAND

Community College of Rhode Island
401 333-7000 *Flanagan Campus* 1762 Louisquissett Pike .... Lincoln RI 02865-4585
401 825-1000 *Knight Campus* 400 East Ave .... Warwick RI 02886-1807
401 467-7744 **New England Institute of Technology** 2500 Post Rd .... Warwick RI 02886-2244

SOUTH CAROLINA

803 593-9231 **Aiken Technical College** PO Box 696 .... Graniteville SC 29802-0600
803 537-5286 **Chesterfield-Marlboro Technical College** PO Box 1007 .... Cheraw SC 29520-1007
803 793-3301 **Denmark Technical College** PO Box 327 .... Denmark SC 29042-0327
803 661-8324 **Florence-Darlington Technical College** PO Box F8000 .... Florence SC 29501-0057
803 250-8000 **Greenville Technical College** PO Box 5616 .... Greenville SC 29606-5616
803 347-3186 **Horry-Georgetown Technical College** PO Box 1966 .... Conway SC 29526-1966
803 738-1400 **Midlands Technical College** 316 S Beltline Blvd .... Columbia SC 29205-4204
803 895-1410 **North Greenville College** .... Tigerville SC 29688-0000
803 536-0311 **Orangeburg-Calhoun Technical College**
3250 St Matthews Rd NE .... Orangeburg SC 29115-8299
803 223-8357 **Piedmont Technical College** PO Box 1467 .... Greenwood SC 29648-1467
803 576-3911 **Spartanburg Methodist College** 1200 Textile Rd .... Spartanburg SC 29301-0009
803 591-3600 **Spartanburg Technical College** PO Box 4386 .... Spartanburg SC 29305-4386
803 525-8324 **Technical College of the Low Country** 100 Ribaut Rd .... Beaufort SC 29902-5428
803 646-8361 **Tri-County Technical College** Hwy 76 .... Pendleton SC 29670-0000
803 572-6111 **Trident Technical College** PO Box 10367 .... North Charleston SC 29411-0367
University of South Carolina
803 285-7471 *Lancaster Campus* 909 Hubbard Dr .... Lancaster SC 29720-0000
803 584-3446 *Salkehatchie Campus* Hwy 301 & Spruce St .... Allendale SC 29810-0000
803 775-6341 *Sumter Campus* 200 Miller Rd .... Sumter SC 29150-2478
803 427-3681 *Union Campus* 401 E Main St .... Union SC 29379-1902
803 354-7423 **Williamsburg Technical College** 601 Lane Rd .... Kingstree SC 29556-4197
803 324-3130 **York Technical College** 452 S Anderson Rd .... Rock Hill SC 29730-7305

TENNESSEE

615 297-7545 **Aquinas Junior College** 4210 Harding Rd .... Nashville TN 37205-2086
615 697-4400 **Chattanooga State Technical Community College**
4501 Amnicola Hwy .... Chattanooga TN 37406-1018
615 472-7141 **Cleveland State Community College** 3570 Adkisson Dr NW .... Cleveland TN 37312-2858
615 388-0120 **Columbia State Community College** Hwy 99 W .... Columbia TN 38402-0000
615 282-3320 **Draughon Junior College** 2220 College Rd .... Johnson City TN 37601-1744
901 286-3200 **Dyersburg State Community College** 1510 Nichols Ave .... Dyersburg TN 38024-2450
615 442-2001 **Hiwassee College** Hiwassee Rd .... Madisonville TN 37354-0000
901 424-3520 **Jackson State Community College** 2046 North Pkwy .... Jackson TN 38301-3797
615 327-3927 **John A Gupton College** 2507 West End Ave .... Nashville TN 37203-1494
615 586-5262 **Knoxville College Morristown Branch** 417 N James St .... Morristown TN 37814-4470
615 363-7456 **Martin Methodist College** 433 W Madison St .... Pulaski TN 38478-2799
615 455-8511 **Motlow State Community College** Lynchburg Hwy .... Tullahoma TN 37388-0000
615 353-3333 **Nashville State Technical Institute** 120 White Bridge Rd .... Nashville TN 37209-4515
615 794-4254 **O'More College of Design** PO Box 908 .... Franklin TN 37065-0908
615 694-6400 **Pellissippi State Technical Community College**
Hardin Valley Rd .... Knoxville TN 37933-0000
615 354-3000 **Roane State Community College** Patton Ln .... Harriman TN 37748-0000
901 528-6700 **Shelby State Community College** 1256 Union Ave .... Memphis TN 38104-3414
901 377-4111 **State Technical Institute at Memphis** 5983 Macon Cove .... Memphis TN 38134-7693
615 452-8600 **Volunteer State Community College** Nashville Pike .... Gallatin TN 37066-0000
615 587-9722 **Walters State Community College**
500 S Davy Crockett Pkwy .... Morristown TN 37813-1999

TEXAS

713 331-6111 **Alvin Community College** 3110 Mustang Rd .... Alvin TX 77511-4895
806 371-5000 **Amarillo College** 2201 S Washington St .... Amarillo TX 79178-0001
409 639-1301 **Angelina Community College** PO Box 1768 .... Lufkin TX 75901-0000
512 483-7000 **Austin Community College** PO Box 140526 .... Austin TX 78714-0526
512 358-3130 **Bee County College** 3800 Charco Rd .... Beeville TX 78102-2197
409 830-4150 **Blinn College** 902 College Ave .... Brenham TX 77833-4049
409 265-6131 **Brazosport College** 500 College Dr .... Lake Jackson TX 77566-3199
214 620-4803 **Brookhaven Community College** 3939 Valley View Ln .... Farmers Branch TX 75244-4997
817 526-1211 **Central Texas College** American Educational Complex Hwy 190 .... Killeen TX 76540-0000
817 442-2567 **Cisco Junior College** RR 3 Box 3 .... Cisco TX 76437-9321
806 874-3571 **Clarendon College** PO Box 968 .... Clarendon TX 79226-0968
409 938-1211 **College of the Mainland** 1200 N Amburn Rd .... Texas City TX 77591-2499
817 668-7731 **Cooke County College** 1525 W California St .... Gainesville TX 76240-4699
512 991-6810 **Corpus Christi State University** 6300 Ocean Dr .... Corpus Christi TX 78412-5599
214 746-2125 **Dallas County Community College (System)** 701 Elm St .... Dallas TX 75202-3299
512 886-1200 **Del Mar College** 101 Baldwin Blvd .... Corpus Christi TX 78404-3894
214 324-7694 **Eastfield College** 3737 Motley Dr .... Mesquite TX 75150-2099
214 746-2200 **El Centro College** Main & Lamar .... Dallas TX 75204-0000
915 594-2000 **El Paso Community College** PO Box 20500 .... El Paso TX 79998-0500
806 274-5311 **Frank Phillips College** 1301 Roosevelt St .... Borger TX 79007-4427
409 763-6551 **Galveston College** 4015 Ave Q .... Galveston TX 77550-7496
903 465-6030 **Grayson County College** 6101 Grayson Dr .... Denison TX 75020-8238
713 869-5021 **Houston Community College** PO Box 7849 .... Houston TX 77270-7849
915 264-5000 **Howard County Junior College District** 1001 Birdwell Ln .... Big Spring TX 79720-3702
903 586-2518 **Jacksonville College** 500 W Pine St .... Jacksonville TX 75766-4746
903 984-8531 **Kilgore College** 1100 Broadway .... Kilgore TX 75662-0000
512 722-0521 **Laredo Junior College** Washington St .... Laredo TX 78040-4396
512 722-8001 **Laredo State University** Washington St .... Laredo TX 78040-4398
713 427-5611 **Lee College** 511 S Whiting St .... Baytown TX 77520-4796
903 586-2471 **Lon Morris College** 800 College Ave .... Jacksonville TX 75766-2900
817 756-6551 **McLennan Community College** 1400 College Dr .... Waco TX 76708-1498
214 333-8600 **Mountain View College** 4849 W Illinois Ave .... Dallas TX 75211-6599
903 874-6501 **Navarro College** 3200 W Hwy 31 .... Corsicana TX 75110-9796
713 443-5400 **North Harris County College** 2700 WW Thorne Dr .... Houston TX 77073-0000
713 359-1600 *Kingwood Campus* 20000 Kingwood Dr .... Kingwood TX 77339-3899
214 659-5220 **North Lake College** 5001 N MacArthur Blvd .... Irving TX 75038-3899
915 335-6400 **Odessa College** 201 W University Blvd .... Odessa TX 79764-7127
903 693-2037 **Panola College** 1109 W Panola St .... Carthage TX 75633-2397
903 785-7661 **Paris Junior College** 2400 Clarksville St .... Paris TX 75460-6298
817 647-3234 **Ranger Junior College** 1100 College Cir .... Ranger TX 76470-3298
214 238-6200 **Richland College** 12800 Abrams Rd .... Dallas TX 75243-2199
512 531-3200 **Saint Philip's College** 2111 Nevada St .... San Antonio TX 78203-2097
512 733-2000 **San Antonio College** 1300 San Pedro Ave .... San Antonio TX 78212-4201
San Jacinto College
713 476-1501 *Central Campus* 8060 Spencer Hwy .... Pasadena TX 77505-5998
713 458-4050 *North Campus* 5800 Uvalde Rd .... Houston TX 77049-4599
South Plains College
806 747-0576 *Lubbock Campus* 1302 Main St .... Lubbock TX 79401-3298
806 894-9611 *Main Campus* 1401 S College Ave .... Levelland TX 79336-6593
806 885-3048 *Reese Campus* Reese Air Force Base Bldg 920 .... Reese TX 79489-0000
512 278-4401 **Southwest Texas Junior College** 2501 Garner Field Rd .... Uvalde TX 78801-6296
214 937-4010 **Southwestern Assemblies of God College**
1200 Sycamore St .... Waxahachie TX 75165-2342
214 563-3341 **Southwestern Christian College** 200 Bowser St .... Terrell TX 75160-3402
817 336-7851 **Tarrant County Junior College** 1500 Houston St .... Fort Worth TX 76102-6524
817 773-9961 **Temple Junior College** 2600 S 1st St .... Temple TX 76504-7435
903 838-4541 **Texarkana College** 2500 N Robison Rd .... Texarkana TX 75501-3099
512 544-8200 **Texas Southmost College** 80 Fort Brown St .... Brownsville TX 78520-4956
Texas State Technical Institute
806 335-2316 *Amarillo Campus* PO Box 11077 .... Amarillo TX 79111-0001
512 425-4922 *Harlingen Campus* Industrial Air Pk .... Harlingen TX 78550-0000
915 235-7300 *Sweetwater Campus* RR 3 Box 18 .... Sweetwater TX 79556-0000
817 799-3611 *Waco Campus* 3801 Campus Dr .... Waco TX 76705-1695
903 531-2200 **Tyler Junior College** 14000 E 5th St .... Tyler TX 75701-0000
817 552-6291 **Vernon Regional Junior College** 4400 College Dr .... Vernon TX 76384-4092
512 573-3291 **Victoria College** 2200 E Red River St .... Victoria TX 77901-4494
817 594-5471 **Weatherford College** 308 E Park Ave .... Weatherford TX 76086-5699
915 573-8511 **Western Texas College** 6200 S College Ave .... Snyder TX 79549-0000
409 532-4560 **Wharton County Junior College** 911 Boling Hwy .... Wharton TX 77488-3252

UTAH

801 637-2120 **College of Eastern Utah** 451 E 400 North .... Price UT 84501-2699
801 673-4811 **Dixie College** 225 S 700 East .... Saint George UT 84770-3876
801 363-2765 **Latter Day Saints Business College** 411 E South Temple .... Salt Lake City UT 84111-1302
801 967-4111 **Salt Lake Community College** 4600 S Redwood Rd .... Salt Lake City UT 84130-0000
801 283-4021 **Snow College** 150 E College Ave .... Ephraim UT 84627-0000
801 226-5000 **Utah Valley Community College** 800 W 1200 South .... Orem UT 84058-5999

... listed alphabetically within each state. Graduate Schools are listed alphabetically by state, within each area of study.

VERMONT

802 658-0800	Champlain College 163 S Willard St	Burlington VT	05401-3950
802 241-3535	Community College of Vermont PO Box 120	Waterbury VT	05676-0120
802 728-3391	Vermont Technical College	Randolph Center VT	05061-0000

VIRGINIA

703 234-9261	Blue Ridge Community College PO Box 80	Weyers Cave VA	24486-0080
804 386-4500	Central Virginia Commmunity College 3506 Wards Rd	Lynchburg VA	24502-2498
703 862-4246	Dabney S Lancaster Community College PO Box 1000	Clifton Forge VA	24422-1000
804 797-3553	Danville Community College 1008 S Main St	Danville VA	24541-4004
804 787-5900	Eastern Shore Community College RR 1 Box 6	Melfa VA	23410-9755
703 399-1333	Germanna Community College PO Box 339	Locust Grove VA	22508-0339
804 371-3000	J Sargeant Reynolds Community College PO Box C-32040	Richmond VA	23261-2040
804 796-4000	John Tyler Community College 13101 Jefferson Davis Hwy	Chester VA	23831-5316
703 869-1120	Lord Fairfax Community College Rt 11	Middletown VA	22645-0000
703 523-2400	Mountain Empire Community College PO Box 700	Big Stone Gap VA	24219-0700
703 674-3600	New River Community College PO Box 1127	Dublin VA	24084-1127
703 323-3000	Northern Virginia Community College		
	8333 Little River Tpke	Annandale VA	22003-3796
703 638-8777	Patrick Henry Community College PO Box 5311	Martinsville VA	24115-5311
804 562-2171	Paul D Camp Community College 100 College Dr N	Franklin VA	23851-2422
804 977-3900	Piedmont Virginia Community College RR 6 Box 1-A	Charlottesville VA	22901-8714
	Rappahannock Community College		
804 758-5324	*Glenns Campus* Rt 33	Glenns VA	23149-0000
804 333-4024	*Warsaw Campus* PO Box 318	Warsaw VA	22572-0318
804 862-6100	Richard Bland College 11301 Johnson Rd	Petersburg VA	23805-7100
703 261-6181	Southern Seminary College 201 E 26th St	Buena Vista VA	24416-2625
804 949-7111	Southside Virginia Community College RR 1 Box 60	Alberta VA	23821-9801
703 964-2555	Southwest Virginia Community College PO Box SVCC	Richlands VA	24641-1510
804 825-2700	Thomas Nelson Community College 99 Thomas Nelson Dr	Hampton VA	23666-1433
804 484-2121	Tidewater Community College SR-135	Portsmouth VA	23703-0000
703 628-6094	Virginia Highlands Community College SR-372	Abingdon VA	24210-0000
703 857-7200	Virginia Western Community College PO Box 14045	Roanoke VA	24038-4045
703 228-5541	Wytheville Community College 1000 E Main St	Wytheville VA	24382-3397

WASHINGTON

206 641-0111	Bellevue Community College 3000 Landerholm Cir SE	Bellevue WA	98007-0000
509 762-5351	Big Bend Community College 28th Ave & Chanute St	Moses Lake WA	98837-0000
206 694-6521	Clark College 1800 E McLoughlin Blvd	Vancouver WA	98663-3598
509 547-0511	Columbia Basin College 2600 N 20th Ave	Pasco WA	99301-3397
206 771-1545	Edmonds Community College 20000 68th Ave W	Lynnwood WA	98036-5999
206 259-7151	Everett Community College 801 Wetmore Ave	Everett WA	98201-1390
206 833-9111	Green River Community College 12401 SE 320th St	Auburn WA	98002-3699
206 878-3710	Highline Community College PO Box 98000	Des Moines WA	98198-9800
206 527-3600	North Seattle Community College 9600 College Way N	Seattle WA	98103-3599
206 478-4506	Olympic College 16th & Chester	Bremerton WA	98310-1699
206 452-9277	Peninsula College 1502 E Lauridsen Blvd	Port Angeles WA	98362-6698
206 964-6500	Pierce College 9401 Farwest Dr SW	Tacoma WA	98498-1999
206 587-3800	Seattle Central Community College 1701 Broadway	Seattle WA	98122-2400
206 587-4155	Seattle Community College (System) 1500 Harvard Ave	Seattle WA	98122-2400
206 546-4101	Shoreline Community College 16101 Greenwood Ave N	Seattle WA	98133-5696
206 483-4555	Snoqualmie Community College PO Box 1008	Bothell WA	98041-0000
206 764-5300	South Seattle Community College 6000 16th Ave SW	Seattle WA	98106-1499
509 536-7000	Spokane Community College N 1810 Greene St	Spokane WA	99207-0000
509 459-3500	Spokane Falls Community College		
	W 3410 Fort George Wright Dr	Spokane WA	99204-0000
509 522-2500	Walla Walla Community College 500 Tausick Way	Walla Walla WA	99362-9270
509 662-1651	Wenatchee Valley College 1300 5th St	Wenatchee WA	98801-1799
509 575-2350	Yakima Valley Community College		
	S 16th Ave & W Nob Hill Blvd	Yakima WA	98902-0000

WEST VIRGINIA

304 253-7351	Beckley College 609 S Kanawha St	Beckley WV	25801-5624
304 485-7384	Ohio Valley College 4501 College Pkwy	Parkersburg WV	26101-8100
304 788-3011	Potomac State College Fort Ave	Keyser WV	26726-0000
304 792-4300	Southern West Virginia Community College PO Box 2900	Logan WV	25601-0000
304 424-8000	West Virginia University at Parkersburg RR 5 Box 167A	Parkersburg WV	26101-9577

WISCONSIN

608 756-4121	Blackhawk Technical College 6004 Prairie Rd	Janesville WI	53546-9528
715 833-6200	Chippewa Valley Technical College 620 W Clairemont Ave	Eau Claire WI	54701-6162
414 735-5600	Fox Valley Technical College 1825 N Bluemound Dr	Appleton WI	54913-0000
414 656-6900	Gateway Technical College 3520 30th Ave	Kenosha WI	53144-0000
414 458-4183	Lakeshore Technical College 1290 North Ave	Cleveland WI	53015-0000
414 278-6600	Milwaukee Area Technical College 700 W State St	Milwaukee WI	53233-1419
414 922-8611	Moraine Park Technical College 235 N National Ave	Fond du Lac WI	54935-2897
715 369-4410	Nicolet Area Technical College 2951 Hwy G	Rhinelander WI	54501-0000
715 675-3331	Northcentral Technical College 1000 W Campus Dr	Wausau WI	54401-1880
414 498-5400	Northeast Wisconsin Technical College 2740 W Mason St	Green Bay WI	54307-9042
608 822-3262	Southwest Wisconsin Technical College Hwy 18 E	Fennimore WI	53809-0000
608 262-1783	University of Wisconsin Centers 150 E Gilman St	Madison WI	53708-8680
715 234-8176	*Barron County Campus* 1800 College Dr	Rice Lake WI	54868-2414
414 929-3600	*Fond du Lac Campus* 400 Campus Dr	Fond du Lac WI	54935-2998
414 832-2600	*Fox Valley County Campus* 1478 Midway Rd	Menasha WI	54952-1224
414 683-4700	*Manitowoc County Campus* 705 Viebahn St	Manitowoc WI	54220-6601
715 845-9602	*Marathon County Campus* 518 S 7th Ave	Wausau WI	54401-5362
715 735-7477	*Marinette Campus* 750 W Bay Shore St	Marinette WI	54143-4299
715 387-1147	*Marshfield/Wood County Campus* 2000 W 5th St	Marshfield WI	54449-3310
608 647-6186	*Richland Campus* Hwy 14 W	Richland Center WI	53581-0000
608 755-2811	*Rock County Campus* 2909 Kellogg Ave	Janesville WI	53546-5606
414 459-3700	*Sheboygan County Campus* 1 University Dr	Sheboygan WI	53081-4789
414 335-5200	*Washington County Campus* 400 University Dr	West Bend WI	53095-3699
608 785-9200	Western Wisconsin Technical College 304 6th St N	La Crosse WI	54601-3342

WYOMING

307 268-2110	Casper College 125 College Dr	Casper WY	82601-4699
307 856-9291	Central Wyoming College 2660 Peck St	Riverton WY	82501-2273
307 532-7111	Eastern Wyoming College 3200 W 'C' St	Torrington WY	82240-1699
307 634-5853	Laramie County Community College 1400 E College Dr	Cheyenne WY	82007-3204
307 754-6111	Northwest College 231 W 6th St	Powell WY	82435-1898
307 674-6446	Sheridan College 3059 Coffeen Ave	Sheridan WY	82801-9133
307 382-1600	Western Wyoming Community College 2500 College Dr	Rock Springs WY	82901-5802

GOVERNMENT

Federal Government–Federal Information Centers

Local toll-free phone numbers for federal government information are listed alphabetically by the name of the city or state each phone number serves.

City	Phone	City	Phone
Akron	800 347-1997	Minneapolis	800 366-2998
Albany	800 347-1997	Missouri	800 735-8004
Albuquerque	800 359-3997	Mobile	800 366-2998
Anchorage	800 729-8003	Nashville	800 366-2998
Atlanta	800 347-1997	Nebraska	800 735-8004
Austin	800 366-2998	New Haven	800 347-1997
Baltimore	800 347-1997	New Orleans	800 366-2998
Birmingham	800 366-2998	New York	800 347-1997
Boston	800 347-1997	Newark	800 347-1997
Buffalo	800 347-1997	Norfolk	800 347-1997
Charlotte	800 347-1997	Oklahoma City	800 366-2998
Chattanooga	800 347-1997	Omaha	800 366-2998
Chicago	800 366-2998	Orlando	800 347-1997
Cincinnati	800 347-1997	Philadelphia	800 347-1997
Cleveland	800 347-1997	Phoenix	800 359-3997
Colorado Springs	800 359-3997	Pittsburgh	800 347-1997
Columbus	800 347-1997	Portland	800 726-4995
Dallas	800 366-2998	Providence	800 347-1997
Dayton	800 347-1997	Pueblo	800 359-3997
Denver	800 359-3997	Richmond	800 347-1997
Detroit	800 347-1997	Roanoke	800 347-1997
Fort Lauderdale	800 347-1997	Rochester	800 347-1997
Fort Worth	800 366-2998	Sacramento	916 978-4010
Gary	800 366-2998	Saint Louis	800 366-2998
Grand Rapids	800 347-1997	Saint Petersburg	800 347-1997
Hartford	800 347-1997	Salt Lake City	800 359-3997
Honolulu	800 733-5996	San Antonio	800 366-2998
Houston	800 366-2998	San Diego	800 726-4995
Indianapolis	800 347-1997	San Francisco	800 726-4995
Iowa	800 753-8004	Santa Ana	800 726-4995
Jacksonville	800 347-1997	Seattle	800 726-4995
Kansas	800 735-8004	Syracuse	800 347-1997
Little Rock	800 366-2998	Tacoma	800 726-4995
Los Angeles	800 726-4995	Tampa	800 347-1997
Louisville	800 347-1997	Toledo	800 347-1997
Memphis	800 366-2998	Trenton	800 347-1997
Miami	800 347-1997	Tulsa	800 366-2998
Milwaukee	800 366-2998	West Palm Beach	800 347-1997

Federal Government–Executive Branch

Listings for the President, Vice President, Presidential Secretary and Office of the First Lady are followed by an alphabetical listing of selected important Executive Branch offices reporting directly to the President.

Phone	Office	City	State	ZIP
202 456-1414	**President of the US** 1600 Pennsylvania Ave NW	Washington	DC	20500-0001
202 456-1414	**White House** 1600 Pennsylvania Ave NW	Washington	DC	20500-0001
202 456-2326	**Office of the Vice President** Old Executive Office Bldg	Washington	DC	20501-0001
202 456-2957	**Office of the First Lady** 1600 Pennsylvania Ave NW 2nd Fl	Washington	DC	20500-0001
202 456-2100	**Presidential Press Secretary** 1600 Pennsylvania Ave NW	Washington	DC	20500-0001
202 482-1100	**Central Intelligence Agency**	Washington	DC	20505-0001
202 395-5108	**Council of Economic Advisers** 17th St & Pennsylvania Ave	Washington	DC	20500-0001
202 395-5750	**Council on Environmental Quality** 722 Jackson Pl NW	Washington	DC	20503-0001
202 395-4974	**National Security Council** 17th & Pennsylvania Ave	Washington	DC	20500-0001
202 456-1414	**Office of Administration** 725 17th St NW Rm 4013	Washington	DC	20503-0001
202 395-3000	**Office of Management & Budget** 725 17th St NW	Washington	DC	20503-0001
202 456-6515	**Office of Policy Development** 1600 Pennsylvania Ave NW	Washington	DC	20500-0001
202 456-7116	**Office of Science & Technology Policy** 17th St & Pennsylvania Ave	Washington	DC	20506-0001
202 395-3230	**Office of the US Trade Representative** 600 17th St NW	Washington	DC	20506-0001
202 395-6993	**Regulatory Information Service Center** 725 17th St NW Rm 5216	Washington	DC	20503-0001

DEPARTMENT OF AGRICULTURE

Selected offices of each cabinet-level department are listed alphabetically. The main listing for the department and listings for the Secretary and Deputy Secretary or Under Secretary appear first.

Phone	Office	City	State	ZIP
202 447-2791	**Department of Agriculture** 14th St & Independence Ave SW	Washington	DC	20250-0001
202 447-3631	**Secretary of Agriculture** 14th St & Independence Ave SW Rm 200-A	Washington	DC	20250-0001
202 447-6158	**Deputy Secretary of Agriculture** 14th St & Independence Ave SW Rm 200-A	Washington	DC	20250-0001
202 447-5115	**Agricultural Marketing Service** 14th St & Independence Ave SW Rm 3071	Washington	DC	20250-0001
202 447-2511	**Animal & Plant Health Inspection Service** 14th St & Independence Ave SW	Washington	DC	20250-0001
202 447-4785	**Commodity Credit Corp** 14th St & Independence Ave SW Rm 5714-S	Washington	DC	20250-0001
202 447-7095	**Congressional Relations** 14th St & Independence Ave SW Administration Bldg Rm 205-E	Washington	DC	20250-0001
202 447-6795	**Federal Crop Insurance Corp** 14th St & Independence Ave SW Rm 4096	Washington	DC	20250-0001
314 875-2909	*Claims Office* Parkade Ctr Rm 128	Columbia	MO	65203-0000
605 353-1882	*Claims Office* 200 4th St SW Rm 317	Huron	SD	57350-2476
509 353-2319	*AK ID OR UT WA* W 601 1st Ave Suite 507	Spokane	WA	99204-0000
601 965-4328	*AL LA MS* 100 W Capitol St Suite 1201	Jackson	MS	39269-0001
916 551-1717	*AZ HI CA NV* 1303 J St Suite 470	Sacramento	CA	95814-2941
913 537-4980	*CO KS* 2601 Anderson Ave	Manhattan	KS	66502-2898
717 782-4803	*CT DE ME MD MA NH NJ NY PA RI VT* 1 Credit Union Pl Suite 310	Harrisburg	PA	17110-2995
803 765-5766	*FL GA SC* 1835 Assembly St Rm 1222	Columbia	SC	29201-2430
515 284-4316	*IA MO* 210 Walnut St Federal Bldg Rm 509	Des Moines	IA	50309-2174
217 492-4280	*IL* 2305 W Monroe St Suite 2	Springfield	IL	62704-1401
317 290-3050	*IN MI OH* 5969 Lakeside Blvd Suite B	Indianapolis	IN	46278-1996
615 736-5591	*KY TN AR* 8th & Broad Sts US Courthouse Rm 301	Nashville	TN	37203-0000
612 290-3871	*MN WI* 375 Jackson St Rm 300	Saint Paul	MN	55101-1810
406 657-6196	*MT WY* 2110 Overland Ave Suite 108	Billings	MT	59102-7496
919 856-4470	*NC VA WV* 4407 Bland Rd Suite 280	Raleigh	NC	27609-6296
701 250-4271	*ND* 309 N Mandan St	Bismarck	ND	58501-3859
402 437-5531	*NE SD* 100 Centennial Mall N Rm 259	Lincoln	NE	68508-3886

Federal Government–Executive Branch

Phone	Office	City	State	ZIP
409 260-9391	*NM OK TX* 7607 E Mark Dr Suite 240	College Station	TX	77840-0000
703 756-3276	**Food & Nutrition Service** 3101 Park Center Dr	Alexandria	VA	22302-1509
202 447-7943	**Food Safety & Inspection Service** 14th St & Independence Ave SW	Washington	DC	20250-0001
202 447-7115	**Foreign Agricultural Service Information** 14th St & Independence Ave SW Rm 5074	Washington	DC	20250-0001
202 447-3760	**Forest Service** 201 14th St SW	Washington	DC	20250-0001
406 329-3511	*Region 1* 200 E Broadway	Missoula	MT	59807-0000
303 236-9659	*Region 2* 11177 W 8th Ave	Lakewood	CO	80225-0000
505 842-3345	*Region 3* 517 Gold Ave SW	Albuquerque	NM	87102-3156
801 625-5182	*Region 4* 324 25th St	Ogden	UT	84401-2310
415 705-2880	*Region 5* 630 Sansome St	San Francisco	CA	94111-2206
503 326-2877	*Region 6* 319 SW Pine St	Portland	OR	97204-2726
404 347-2384	*Region 8* 1720 Peachtree Rd NW	Atlanta	GA	30367-0001
414 297-3693	*Region 9* 310 W Wisconsin Ave Rm 500	Milwaukee	WI	53203-2211
907 586-8863	*Region 10* PO Box 21628	Juneau	AK	99802-1628
202 472-1388	**Fraud Hotline** PO Box 23399	Washington	DC	20026-3399
202 447-8164	**Freedom of Information Office** 14th St & Independence Ave SW Rm 536A	Washington	DC	20250-0001
301 344-3778	**National Agricultural Library** 10301 Baltimore Blvd	Beltsville	MD	20705-2351
202 447-3638	**National Agricultural Statistics Service State Statistical Div** 14th St & Independence Ave SW 4143 South Bldg	Washington	DC	20250-0001
202 447-4164	**Office of Economics** USDA Administration Bldg Rm 227E	Washington	DC	20250-0001
202 447-5447	*World Agricultural Outlook Board* 14th St & Independence Ave SW Rm 5143	Washington	DC	20250-0001
202 653-9309	**Office of International Cooperation & Development** 2121 K St NW Rm 310	Washington	DC	20250-0001
202 653-6060	**Office of Transportation** PO Box 96575	Washington	DC	20250-0001
202 447-3037	**Procurement Div** 14th St & Independence Ave SW Rm 1575	Washington	DC	20250-0001
202 447-5197	**Public Affairs** 14th St & Independence Ave SW Rm 201-A	Washington	DC	20250-0001
202 382-1255	**Rural Electrification Administration** USDA Bldg Rm 4042S	Washington	DC	20250-0001
202 447-5923	**Science & Education** Administration Bldg Rm 217-W	Washington	DC	20250-0001
301 344-2264	*Agricultural Research Service* Bldg 005 BARC-W Rm 307	Beltsville	MD	20705-0000
202 447-4543	**Soil Conservation Service** 14th St & Independence Ave SW Rm 6110	Washington	DC	20250-0001

DEPARTMENT OF COMMERCE

Phone	Office	City	State	ZIP
202 377-2000	**Department of Commerce** 14th & Constitution Ave NW	Washington	DC	20230-0001
202 377-2112	**Secretary of Commerce** 14th St & Constitution Ave NW Rm 5858	Washington	DC	20230-0001
202 377-4625	**Deputy Secretary of Commerce** 14th St & Constitution Ave NW Rm 5838	Washington	DC	20230-0001
202 523-0693	**Bureau of Economic Analysis** 1401 K St NW Tower Bldg Rm 705	Washington	DC	20230-0001
202 377-5491	**Bureau of Export Administration** 14th St & Constitution Ave NW Rm 3886C	Washington	DC	20230-0001
301 763-4040	**Bureau of the Census** 8903 Presidential Pkwy Bldg 3	Suitland	MD	20746-0000
404 347-2274	*Atlanta Region* 1365 Peachtree St NE	Atlanta	GA	30309-3147
617 565-7200	*Boston Region* 10 Causeway St Rm 553	Boston	MA	02222-1047
704 371-6142	*Charlotte Region* 222 S Church St Suite 505	Charlotte	NC	28202-3213
312 353-6251	*Chicago Region* 175 W Jackson Blvd Suite 557	Chicago	IL	60604-2689
214 767-0621	*Dallas Region* 1100 Commerce St Rm 3C54	Dallas	TX	75242-1003
303 969-6750	*Denver Region* 7655 W Mississippi Ave	Denver	CO	80226-4332
313 226-7742	*Detroit Region* 231 W Lafayette Blvd Rm 565	Detroit	MI	48226-2769
913 236-3728	*Kansas City Region* 4th & State Sts 1 Gateway Ctr Suite 500	Kansas City	KS	66101-0000
213 253-1200	*Los Angeles Region* 262 Los Angeles St 3rd Fl	Los Angeles	CA	90012-0000
212 264-3860	*New York Region* Jacob Javitz Bldg 26 Federal Plaza Rm 37-130	New York	NY	10278-0000
215 597-4920	*Philadelphia Region* 105 S 7th St 1st Fl	Philadelphia	PA	19106-3395
206 728-5500	*Seattle Region* 101 Stewart St Rm 500	Seattle	WA	98101-1048
301 763-4040	*Data Requests/Information* 8903 Presidential Pkwy Bldg 3	Suitland	MD	20772-2656
202 377-3271	**Central Reference & Records Inspection Facility** 14th St & Constitution Ave NW Rm 6622	Washington	DC	20230-0001
202 377-2235	**Economic Affairs** 14th St & Constitution Ave NW Rm 4855	Washington	DC	20230-0001
800 424-5197	**Fraud Hotline** Office of Inspector General	Washington	DC	20044-0000
202 377-3271	**Freedom of Information Office** 14th St & Constitution Ave NW Rm 6622	Washington	DC	20230-0001
202 377-5087	**International Trade Administration** 14th St & Constitution Ave NW Rm 3414	Washington	DC	20230-0001
505 766-2070	*Albuquerque Office* 625 Silver SW Rm 320	Albuquerque	NM	87102-3123
907 271-5041	*Anchorage Office* 222 W 7th Ave Box 32	Anchorage	AK	99513-7504
404 347-4872	*Atlanta Office* 1365 Peachtree St NE Suite 504	Atlanta	GA	30309-3120
301 962-3560	*Baltimore Office* 40 S Gay St Rm 413	Baltimore	MD	21202-4022
205 731-1331	*Birmingham Office* 2015 2nd Ave N Suite 302	Birmingham	AL	35203-3711
617 565-8576	*Boston Office* World Trade Ctr Suite 307	Boston	MA	02210-1595
716 846-4191	*Buffalo Office* 111 W Huron St Rm 1312	Buffalo	NY	14202-2301
304 347-5123	*Charleston Office* 500 Quarrier St Rm 3402	Charleston	WV	25301-2130
312 353-4450	*Chicago Office* 55 E Monroe St Rm 1406	Chicago	IL	60603-5704
513 684-2944	*Cincinnati Office* 550 Main St Rm 9504	Cincinnati	OH	45202-3222
216 522-4750	*Cleveland Office* 668 Euclid Ave Suite 600	Cleveland	OH	44114-3002
803 765-5345	*Columbia Office* 1835 Assembly St Suite 172	Columbia	SC	29201-2430
214 767-0542	*Dallas Office* 1100 Commerce St Suite 7A5	Dallas	TX	75242-1001
303 844-3246	*Denver Office* 1625 Broadway Suite 680	Denver	CO	80202-4706
515 284-4222	*Des Moines Office* 210 Walnut St Rm 817	Des Moines	IA	50309-2105
313 226-3650	*Detroit Office* 477 Michigan Ave McNamara Bldg Suite 1140	Detroit	MI	48226-2518
202 377-3181	*District of Columbia Office* 14th St & Constitution Ave NW Rm 1066	Washington	DC	20230-0001
203 240-3530	*Hartford Office* 450 Main St Rm 610-B	Hartford	CT	06103-3002
808 541-1782	*Honolulu Office* 300 Ala Moana Blvd Rm 4106	Honolulu	HI	96850-0001
713 229-2578	*Houston Office* 515 Rusk Ave Rm 2625	Houston	TX	77002-2603
317 226-6214	*Indianapolis Office* 1 N Capitol St Suite 520	Indianapolis	IN	46204-2227
601 965-4388	*Jackson Office* 300 W Woodrow Wilson Dr Suite 328	Jackson	MS	39213-7649
816 426-3141	*Kansas City Office* 601 E 12th St Rm 635	Kansas City	MO	64106-2855
501 378-5794	*Little Rock Office* 320 W Capitol Ave Suite 811	Little Rock	AR	72201-3520
502 582-5066	*Louisville Office* 601 W Broadway Rm 636-B	Louisville	KY	40202-0000
901 521-4137	*Memphis Office* 22 N Front St Suite 200	Memphis	TN	38103-2109
305 536-5267	*Miami Office* 51 SW 1st Ave Suite 224	Miami	FL	33130-1623
414 297-3473	*Milwaukee Office* 517 E Wisconsin Ave Rm 606	Milwaukee	WI	53202-4507
612 348-1638	*Minneapolis Office* 110 S 4th St Rm 108	Minneapolis	MN	55401-2227
615 736-5161	*Nashville Office* 404 James Robertson Pkwy Suite 1114	Nashville	TN	37219-1505
504 589-6546	*New Orleans Office* 2 Canal St World Trade Ctr Suite 432	New Orleans	LA	70130-1408
212 264-0634	*New York Office* 26 Federal Plaza Rm 3718	New York	NY	10278-0022
405 231-5302	*Oklahoma City Office* 6601 N Broadway Ext Suite 200	Oklahoma City	OK	73116-8214
402 221-3665	*Omaha Office* 11133 'O' St	Omaha	NE	68137-2337
602 379-3285	*Phoenix Office* 230 N 1st Ave Rm 3412	Phoenix	AZ	85025-0001
412 644-2850	*Pittsburgh Office* 1000 Liberty Ave Rm 2002	Pittsburgh	PA	15222-4004
503 326-3001	*Portland Office* 121 SW Salmon St Suite 242	Portland	OR	97204-0000
809 766-5555	*Puerto Rico Office* Federal Bldg Rm G55	Hato Rey	PR	00918-0000
702 784-5203	*Reno Office* 1755 E Plumb Ln Suite 152	Reno	NV	89502-3600
804 771-2246	*Richmond Office* 400 N 8th St Suite 8010	Richmond	VA	23240-1001

Federal Government–Executive Branch

314 425-3302 *Saint Louis Office* 7911 Forsyth Blvd Suite 610 .... Saint Louis MO 63105-3860
801 524-5116 *Salt Lake City Office* 324 S State St Suite 105 .... Salt Lake City UT 84101-2106
619 557-5395 *San Diego Office* 6363 Greenwich Dr .... San Diego CA 92122-3939
415 556-5860 *San Francisco Office* 450 Golden Gate Ave .... San Francisco CA 94102-3400
714 836-2461 *Santa Ana Office* 116-A W 4th St Suite 1 .... Santa Ana CA 92701-0000
912 944-4204 *Savannah Office* 120 Barnard St Rm A-107 .... Savannah GA 31401-3641
206 442-5615 *Seattle Office* 3131 Elliott Ave Suite 290 .... Seattle WA 98121-1047
202 377-1461 *Trade Development Office* 14th St & Constitution Ave NW Rm 3832 .... Washington DC 20230-0001
609 989-2100 *Trenton Office* 3131 Princeton Pike Bldg 6 Suite 100 .... Trenton NJ 08648-2207
202 377-1780 *Import Administration* 14th St & Constitution Ave NW Rm 3099B .... Washington DC 20230-0001
202 377-3022 *International Economic Policy* 14th St & Constitution Ave NW Rm 3864 .... Washington DC 20230-0001
202 377-2414 **Minority Business Development Agency** 14th St & Constitution Ave NW Rm 5099 .... Washington DC 20230-0001
404 347-4091 *Atlanta Region* 1371 Peachtree St NE Suite 505 .... Atlanta GA 30367-7101
312 353-0182 *Chicago Region* 55 E Monroe St Suite 1440 .... Chicago IL 60603-5760
214 767-8001 *Dallas Region* 1100 Commerce St Suite 7B-23 .... Dallas TX 75242-0790
212 264-3262 *New York Region* 26 Federal Plaza Rm 3720 .... New York NY 10278-0004
415 744-3001 *San Francisco Region* 221 Main St Suite 1280 .... San Francisco CA 94105-1929
202 377-8275 *Washington DC Region* 14th St & Constitution Ave NW Rm 6723 .... Washington DC 20230-0001
301 975-3058 **National Institute of Standards & Technology** Quince Orchard Rd .... Gaithersburg MD 20899-0001
301 427-2239 **National Marine Fisheries Service** 1335 East-West Hwy ... Silver Spring MD 20910-0000
907 586-7221 *Alaska Region* PO Box 21668 .... Juneau AK 99802-1668
508 281-9300 *Northeastern Region* 1 Blackburn Dr .... Gloucester MA 01930-2298
206 526-6150 *Northwestern Region* 7600 Sand Point Way NE .... Seattle WA 98115-6349
813 893-3141 *Southeastern Region* 9450 Koger Blvd N .... Saint Petersburg FL 33702-2496
213 514-6196 *Southwestern Region* 300 Ferry St Suite 2005 .... Terminal Island CA 90731-7495
202 377-4190 **National Oceanic & Atmospheric Administration** 14th St & Constitution Ave NW Rm 5805 .... Washington DC 20230-0001
202 763-7190 *Environmental Satellite Data Service* Federal Bldg 4 .... Washington DC 20233-0001
301 443-8910 *Oceanic & Atmospheric Research* 6010 Executive Blvd ...... Rockville MD 20852-3809
202 377-1840 **National Telecommunication Information Administration** 14th St & Constitution Ave NW Rm 4898 .... Washington DC 20230-0001
301 427-7689 **National Weather Service** 1325 East-West Hwy .... Silver Spring MD 20912-0000
907 271-5136 *Alaska Region* 222 W 7th Ave .... Anchorage AK 99513-7575
816 426-5400 *Central Region* 601 E 12th St Rm 1835 .... Kansas City MO 64106-2808
516 244-0100 *Eastern Region* 630 Johnson Ave .... Bohemia NY 11716-2640
808 541-1641 *Pacific Region* PO Box 50027 .... Honolulu HI 96850-0001
817 334-2668 *Southern Region* 819 Taylor St Rm 10-A26 .... Fort Worth TX 76102-6114
801 524-5122 *Western Region* 125 S State St Rm 1215 .... Salt Lake City UT 84138-1102
202 377-4190 **NOAA** 14th St & Constitution Ave NW Rm 5805 .... Washington DC 20230-0001
202 377-3942 **Office of Business Liaison** 14th St & Constitution Ave NW Rm 5898-C .... Washington DC 20230-0001
703 557-5168 **Patent & Trademark Office** .... Washington DC 20231-0001
202 377-5555 **Procurement Information** 14th St & Constitution Ave NW Rm 6517 .... Washington DC 20230-0001
202 377-4901 **Public Affairs** 14th St & Constitution Ave NW Rm 5058 ...... Washington DC 20230-0001
202 377-1984 **Technology Administration** 14th St & Constitution Ave NW Rm 4410 .... Washington DC 20230-0001
202 377-3811 **Travel & Tourism Administration** 14th St & Constitution Ave NW Rm 1524 .... Washington DC 20230-0001

DEPARTMENT OF DEFENSE

202 545-6700 **Department of Defense** Pentagon .... Washington DC 20310-0001
202 695-5261 **Secretary of Defense** Pentagon Rm 3E-880 .... Washington DC 20301-1000
202 695-6352 **Deputy Secretary of Defense** Pentagon Rm 3E-944 .... Washington DC 20301-1000
703 274-4839 **American Forces Information Service** 601 N Fairfax St Suite 311 .... Alexandria VA 22314-2060
804 444-5231 **Armed Forces Staff College** 7800 Hampton Blvd .... Norfolk VA 23511-1739
703 756-8500 **Armed Services Board of Contract Appeals** 5109 Leesburg Pike Skyline 6 7th Fl .... Falls Church VA 22041-0000
202 697-9108 **Audit Service** 400 Army-Navy Dr Rm 808 .... Arlington VA 22202-2885
703 694-3007 **Defense Advanced Research Projects Agency** 1400 Wilson Blvd .... Arlington VA 22209-2300
703 692-0018 **Defense Communications Agency** 8th & S Courthouse Rd ...... Arlington VA 22204-0000
703 274-6785 **Defense Contract Audit Agency** Cameron Stn Rm 4C-346 ..... Alexandria VA 22304-0000
703 693-5080 **Defense Hotline** Pentagon .... Washington DC 20301-1900
202 697-5128 **Defense Intelligence Agency** Pentagon Rm 3E-258 .... Washington DC 20340-0001
703 285-9144 **Defense Mapping Agency** 8613 Lee Hwy .... Fairfax VA 22031-2137
703 325-7328 **Defense Nuclear Agency** 6801 Telegraph Rd .... Alexandria VA 22310-3398
202 697-6061 **Department of the Air Force** Pentagon Rm 4D-922 .... Washington DC 20330-0001
719 472-1818 *Air Force Academy* .... Colorado Springs CO 80840-0000
202 697-2302 *Manpower Reserve Affairs Installation & Environment* Pentagon Rm 4E-1020 .... Washington DC 20330-0001
202 697-8675 *Office of Space Systems* Pentagon Rm 4C-1052 .... Washington DC 20330-0001
202 697-6061 *Public Affairs* Pentagon Rm 4D-922 .... Washington DC 20330-0001
202 697-1683 **Department of the Army** Pentagon SAPA-CR Rm 2E-631 .... Washington DC 20310-0001
202 697-8986 *Civil Works* Pentagon Rm 2E-570 .... Washington DC 20310-0001
202 695-5135 *Public Affairs* Pentagon Rm 2E-636 .... Washington DC 20310-0001
202 695-6153 *Research Development & Acquisition* Pentagon Rm 2E-672 .... Washington DC 20310-0001
914 938-4011 *US Military Academy* .... West Point NY 10996-0000
202 695-0965 **Department of the Navy** Pentagon Rm 2E-335 .... Washington DC 20350-0001
202 697-7391 *Information* Pentagon Rm 2E-340 .... Washington DC 20350-0001
301 267-6100 *Naval Academy* .... Annapolis MD 21402-9998
202 695-6315 *Research Engineering & Systems* Pentagon Rm 4E-732 .. Washington DC 20350-0001
202 697-1180 **Freedom of Information Office** Pentagon Rm 2C-757 .... Washington DC 20301-0001
202 475-1716 **Industrial College of the Armed Forces** 4th & P Sts SW Fort McNair .... Washington DC 20319-0001
703 693-0044 **Investigative Service** 400 Army-Navy Dr Rm 901-E .... Arlington VA 22202-2885
202 697-4272 **Joint Chiefs of Staff (Chairman)** Pentagon Rm 2E-857 ...... Washington DC 20318-0001
202 697-9225 *Air Force Chief of Staff* Pentagon Rm 4E-924 .... Washington DC 20330-0001
202 695-2077 *Army Chief of Staff* Pentagon Rm 3E-668 .... Washington DC 20310-0001
202 695-6007 *Chief of Naval Operations* Pentagon Rm 4E-658 .... Washington DC 20350-0001
202 694-2500 *Office of the Commandant of the Marine Corps* Headquarters US Marine Corps .... Washington DC 20380-0001
703 274-6135 **Logistics Agency** Cameron Stn .... Alexandria VA 22304-0000
202 475-1966 **National Defense University** 4th & P Sts SW Fort McNair Bldg 59 .... Washington DC 20319-0001
301 688-6524 **National Security Agency** 9800 Savage Rd .... Fort Meade MD 20755-0000
202 475-1776 **National War College** 4th & P Sts SW Fort McNair Bldg 61 .... Washington DC 20319-0001
202 697-5737 **Public Communications** Pentagon Rm 2E-777 .... Washington DC 20310-0001
202 695-3291 **Security Assistance Agency** Pentagon Rm 4E-841 .... Washington DC 20301-0001
202 695-8732 **Strategic Defense Initiative Organization** Pentagon Rm 1E-1008 .... Washington DC 20301-0001
301 295-3030 **Uniformed Services University of the Health Sciences** 4301 Jones Bridge Rd .... Bethesda MD 20814-4799
202 694-2500 **US Marine Corps** Headquarters .... Washington DC 20380-0001
202 694-8010 *Public Affairs* Arlington Navy Annex Rm 1134 .... Washington DC 20380-0001

DEPARTMENT OF EDUCATION

202 401-3000 **Department of Education** 400 Maryland Ave SW .... Washington DC 20202-0001
617 223-9317 *Region 1* JW McCormack Post Office Bldg Rm 536 .... Boston MA 02109-0000
212 264-7005 *Region 2* 26 Federal Plaza Rm 36-120 .... New York NY 10278-0004
215 596-1001 *Region 3* 3535 Market St .... Philadelphia PA 19104-3398
404 331-2502 *Region 4* 101 Marietta Tower Suite 2221 .... Atlanta GA 30323-0001
312 353-5215 *Region 5* 401 S State St Suite 700-A .... Chicago IL 60605-1299
214 767-3626 *Region 6* 1200 Main Tower Bldg Rm 2125 .... Dallas TX 75202-0000
816 891-7972 *Region 7* PO Box 901381 .... Kansas City MO 64190-1381
303 844-3862 *Region 8* 1961 Stout St Rm 380 .... Denver CO 80294-0101
415 556-4920 *Region 9* 50 United Nations Plaza Rm 205 .... San Francisco CA 94102-4987
206 442-0460 *Region 10* 915 2nd Ave Rm 3362 .... Seattle WA 98174-1001
202 732-3000 **Secretary of Education** 400 Maryland Ave SW Rm 4181 ..... Washington DC 20202-0001
202 732-5404 **Deputy Under Secretary of Education** 400 Maryland Ave SW Rm 3073 .... Washington DC 20202-0001
202 732-2270 **Adult Education** 400 Maryland Ave SW Rm 4428 .... Washington DC 20202-0001
202 732-5113 **Elementary & Secondary Education** 400 Maryland Ave SW Rm 2189 .... Washington DC 20202-0001
202 732-4568 **Freedom of Information Office** 400 Maryland Ave SW Rm 2089 .... Washington DC 20202-0001
716 475-6400 **National Technical Institute for the Deaf** 1 Lomb Memorial Dr .... Rochester NY 14623-5603
202 357-6000 **Office of Educational Research & Improvement** 555 New Jersey Ave NW .... Washington DC 20208-0001
202 727-3685 **Postsecondary Education** 2100 Martin Luther King Jr Ave SE Rm 400 .... Washington DC 20020-0000
202 732-4576 **Public Affairs Information Branch** 400 Maryland Ave SW Rm 2089 .... Washington DC 20202-0001
202 732-1282 **Rehabilitation Services Administration** 330 C St SW Rm 3028 .... Washington DC 20202-0001
617 223-4085 *Region 1* JW McCormack Post Office Bldg Rm 256 .... Boston MA 02109-0000
212 264-4016 *Region 2* 26 Federal Plaza Rm 4104 .... New York NY 10278-0004
215 596-0317 *Region 3* 3535 Market St MS 03-2050 Rm 16120 .... Philadelphia PA 19104-0000
404 331-2352 *Region 4* 101 Marietta Tower Suite 2210 .... Atlanta GA 30301-0000
312 886-5372 *Region 5* 401 S State St Suite 700-E .... Chicago IL 60605-1225
214 767-2961 *Region 6* 1200 Main Tower Bldg Rm 2140 .... Dallas TX 75202-0000
816 891-8015 *Region 7* PO Box 901381 .... Kansas City MO 64153-2312
303 844-2135 *Region 8* 1961 Stout St Rm 398 .... Denver CO 80294-0101
415 556-7333 *Region 9* 50 United Nations Plaza Suite 215 .... San Francisco CA 94102-4917
206 442-5331 *Region 10* 915 2nd Ave Rm 3390 .... Seattle WA 98174-1001
202 732-1265 **Special Education & Rehabilitative Services** 330 C St SW Rm 3006 .... Washington DC 20202-0001
202 732-2251 **Vocational & Adult Education** 400 Maryland Ave SW Rm 4090 .... Washington DC 20202-0001

DEPARTMENT OF ENERGY

202 586-5000 **Department of Energy** 1000 Independence Ave SW .... Washington DC 20585-0001
202 586-6210 **Secretary of Energy** 1000 Independence Ave SW Rm 257 ... Washington DC 20585-0001
202 586-5500 **Deputy Secretary of Energy** 1000 Independence Ave SW Rm 7B-252 .... Washington DC 20585-0001
907 586-7405 **Alaska Power Administration** PO Box 020050 .... Juneau AK 99802-0050
503 230-5101 **Bonneville Power Administration** 905 NE 11th Ave .... Portland OR 97232-4170
202 586-6850 **Civilian Radioactive Waste Management** 1000 Independence Ave SW Rm 5A-085 .... Washington DC 20585-0001
202 586-5450 **Congressional & Intergovernmental Affairs** 1000 Independence Ave SW Rm 7B-138 .... Washington DC 20585-0001
800 523-2929 **Conservation & Renewal Energy Hotline** 200 N 15th St S Suite 407 .... Arlington VA 22202-3304
202 586-6781 **Economic Regulatory Administration** 1000 Independence Ave SW Rm 5B-148 .... Washington DC 20585-0001
214 655-6900 *Dallas Office* Frito-Lay Tower Suite 225-B .... Dallas TX 75235-0000
713 653-3089 *Houston Office* 1919 Smith St Suite 450 .... Houston TX 77002-8050
202 208-0000 **Energy Regulatory Commission** 825 N Capitol St NE 2nd Fl .... Washington DC 20426-0000
404 347-4134 *Atlanta Region* 730 Peachtree St NE Rm 800 .... Atlanta GA 30308-1212
312 353-6173 *Chicago Region* 230 S Dearborn St Rm 3130 .... Chicago IL 60604-1670
212 337-2609 *New York Region* 201 Varick St Rm 664 .... New York NY 10014-4811
503 326-5840 *Portland Region* 1120 SW 5th Ave Suite 1340 .... Portland OR 97204-1933
415 744-3075 *San Francisco Region* 901 Market St Suite 350 .... San Francisco CA 94103-1778
202 586-5430 **Energy Research** 1000 Independence Ave SW Rm 7B-058 .. Washington DC 20585-0001
202 586-6151 **Environment Safety & Health** 1000 Independence Ave SW Rm 7A-097 .... Washington DC 20585-0001
202 586-4695 **Fossil Energy** 1000 Independence Ave SW Rm 4G-084 ...... Washington DC 20585-0001
800 424-9098 **Fraud Hotline** Pentagon .... Washington DC 20301-1900
202 586-5955 **Freedom of Information Office** 1000 Independence Ave SW Rm 1G-051 .... Washington DC 20585-0001
202 586-5800 **International Affairs & Energy Emergencies** 1000 Independence Ave SW Rm 7C-016 .... Washington DC 20585-0001
202 586-8800 **National Energy Information Center** 1000 Independence Ave SW Rm 1F-048 .... Washington DC 20585-0001
202 586-6450 **Office of Nuclear Energy** 1000 Independence Ave SW Rm 5A-115 .... Washington DC 20585-0001
615 576-1301 **Office of Scientific & Technical Information** 175 Oak Ridge Tpke .... Oak Ridge TN 37830-7255
202 586-1370 **Procurement Operations** 1000 Independence Ave SW Rm 1-I 066 .... Washington DC 20585-0001
404 283-9911 **Southeastern Power Administration** Samuel Elbert Bldg .... Elberton GA 30635-0000
918 581-7474 **Southwestern Power Administration** PO Box 1619 .... Tulsa OK 74101-0000
303 231-1511 **Western Area Power Administration** 1627 Cole Blvd Bldg 18 ..... Golden CO 80401-0000

DEPARTMENT OF HEALTH AND HUMAN SERVICES

202 245-7000 **Department of Health & Human Services** 200 Independence Ave SW .... Washington DC 20201-0001
617 565-1072 *Region 1* JFK Federal Bldg Suite 1512 .... Boston MA 02203-0000
212 264-4600 *Region 2* 26 Federal Plaza Rm 3835 .... New York NY 10278-0004
215 596-6492 *Region 3* 3535 Market St Rm 11480 .... Philadelphia PA 19104-3309
404 331-6956 *Region 4* 101 Marietta Tower 11th Fl .... Atlanta GA 30323-0001
312 353-5160 *Region 5* 105 W Adams St 23rd Fl .... Chicago IL 60603-4102
214 767-3301 *Region 6* 1200 Main Tower Bldg Rm 1100 .... Dallas TX 75202-0000
816 426-2821 *Region 7* 601 E 12th St Rm 210 .... Kansas City MO 64106-2808
303 844-3373 *Region 8* 1961 Stout St Rm 1185 .... Denver CO 80294-0101
415 556-6746 *Region 9* 50 United Nations Plaza Rm 431 .... San Francisco CA 94102-4923
206 442-0420 *Region 10* 2201 6th Ave .... Seattle WA 98121-1832
202 245-7000 **Secretary of Health & Human Services** 200 Independence Ave SW Rm 615F .... Washington DC 20201-0001
202 245-7431 **Under Secretary of Health & Human Services** 200 Independence Ave SW Rm 614G .... Washington DC 20201-0001
202 252-4500 **Family Support Administration** 370 L'Enfant Promenade SW 6th Fl .... Washington DC 20447-0001
301 443-2410 **Food & Drug Administration** 5600 Fishers Ln Rm 14-71 .... Rockville MD 20852-0000
404 347-7355 *Atlanta Office* 60 8th St NE .... Atlanta GA 30309-3959
301 962-3731 *Baltimore Office* 900 Madison Ave .... Baltimore MD 21201-2199
617 565-4701 *Boston Office* 1 Montvale Ave 4th Fl .... Stoneham MA 02180-3500

716 846-4483 *Buffalo Office* 599 Delaware Ave ... Buffalo NY 14202-1291
312 353-7126 *Chicago Office* 433 W Van Buren Rm 1222 ... Chicago IL 60607-3926
513 684-3501 *Cincinnati Office* 1141 Central Pkwy ... Cincinnati OH 45202-1097
214 655-5315 *Dallas Office* 1200 Main Tower Bldg Rm 2100 ... Dallas TX 75202-0000
303 236-3000 *Denver Office*
6th & Kipling Sts Denver Federal Center Bldg 20 ... Denver CO 80225-0087
313 226-6274 *Detroit Office* 1560 E Jefferson Ave ... Detroit MI 48207-3179
713 220-2322 *Houston Office* 1445 North Loop W Suite 420 ... Houston TX 77008-0000
317 226-6500 *Indianapolis Office* 101 W Ohio St Suite 1300 ... Indianapolis IN 46204-1586
816 374-6371 *Kansas City Office* 1009 Cherry St ... Kansas City MO 64106-2694
213 252-7597 *Los Angeles Office* 1521 W Pico Blvd ... Los Angeles CA 90015-2486
612 334-4100 *Minneapolis Office* 240 Hennepin Ave ... Minneapolis MN 55401-1999
615 736-2088 *Nashville Office* 297 Plus Park Blvd ... Nashville TN 37217-1088
504 589-2420 *New Orleans Office* 4298 Elysian Fields Ave ... New Orleans LA 70122-3896
718 965-5043 *New York Office* 850 3rd Ave 7th Fl ... Brooklyn NY 11232-1593
402 331-8536 *Omaha Office* 11061 "I" St ... Omaha NE 68137-0000
407 855-0900 *Orlando Office* 7200 Lake Ellenor Dr Suite 120 ... Orlando FL 32809-5797
215 597-4390 *Philadelphia Office*
2nd & Chestnut Sts US Custom House Rm 900 ... Philadelphia PA 19106-2973
809 729-6852 *Puerto Rico Office* PO Box 5719 ... San Juan PR 00906-5719
314 425-5021 *Saint Louis Office* 808 N Collins Alley ... Saint Louis MO 63102-2140
512 229-6737 *San Antonio Office* 727 E Durango Rm B-406 ... San Antonio TX 78206-0001
415 556-1457 *San Francisco Office* 50 United Nations Plaza Rm 526 .. San Francisco CA 94102-4980
206 483-4999 *Seattle Office* 22201 23rd Dr SE ... Bothell WA 98021-4421
201 645-3265 *West Orange Office* 61 Main St ... West Orange NJ 07052-5390
301 443-3170 *Consumer Affairs* 5600 Fishers Ln Rm 16-63 ... Rockville MD 20857-0001
301 966-3000 **Health Care Financing Administration**
6325 Security Blvd Rm 700 ... Baltimore MD 21207-5161
617 565-1232 *Region 1* JFK Federal Bldg Government Ctr Suite 1301 ... Boston MA 02203-0000
212 264-4488 *Region 2* 26 Federal Plaza Rm 3811 ... New York NY 10278-0022
215 596-1351 *Region 3* 3535 Market St Rm 3100 ... Philadelphia PA 19104-3309
404 331-2329 *Region 4* 101 Marietta Tower Suite 701 ... Atlanta GA 30323-0001
312 353-7180 *Region 5* 105 W Adams St 15th Fl ... Chicago IL 60603-6201
214 767-6427 *Region 6* 1200 Main Tower Bldg Rm 2000 ... Dallas TX 75202-0000
816 426-5233 *Region 7* 601 E 12th St Rm 235 ... Kansas City MO 64106-2808
303 844-2111 *Region 8* 1961 Stout St Rm 1185 ... Denver CO 80294-0101
415 744-3501 *Region 9* 50 United Nations Plaza 4th Fl ... San Francisco CA 94105-3901
206 442-0425 *Region 10* 2201 6th Ave ... Seattle WA 98121-1832
301 436-8500 **National Center for Health Statistics**
6525 Belcrest Rd Rm 1100 ... Hyattsville MD 20782-0000
301 565-4167 **National Health Information Center**
1010 Wayne Ave Suite 300 ... Silver Spring MD 20910-5600
301 496-6308 **National Library of Medicine** 8600 Rockville Pike Rm 2F-10 ... Bethesda MD 20894-0001
202 634-4140 **Office of Consumer Affairs**
1725 I St NW Premier Bldg Rm 1009 ... Washington DC 20006-2403
202 472-7257 **Office of Human Development Services**
200 Independence Ave SW Suite 348F ... Washington DC 20201-0001
617 565-1101 *Region 1* JFK Federal Bldg Government Ctr Rm 2000 ... Boston MA 02203-0000
212 264-1487 *Region 2* 26 Federal Plaza Rm 4149 ... New York NY 10278-0004
215 596-6776 *Region 3* 3535 Market St ... Philadelphia PA 19104-3309
404 331-2398 *Region 4* 101 Marietta Tower Suite 903 ... Atlanta GA 30323-0001
312 353-8322 *Region 5* 105 W Adams St 21st Fl ... Chicago IL 60603-4102
214 767-4540 *Region 6* 1200 Main Tower Bldg Rm 1050 ... Dallas TX 75202-0000
816 426-3981 *Region 7* 601 E 12th St Rm 384 ... Kansas City MO 64106-2808
303 844-2622 *Region 8* 1961 Stout St Rm 924 ... Denver CO 80294-0101
415 556-5480 *Region 9* 50 United Nations Plaza ... San Francisco CA 94102-4912
206 442-2430 *Region 10* 2201 6th Ave RX-30 ... Seattle WA 98121-0000
202 245-1850 **Public Affairs** 200 Independence Ave SW Rm 647D ... Washington DC 20201-0001
202 245-7694 **Public Health Service**
200 Independence Ave SW Rm 716G ... Washington DC 20201-0001
617 565-1420 *Region 1* JFK Federal Bldg Government Ctr Rm 1400 ... Boston MA 02203-0000
212 264-2560 *Region 2* 26 Federal Plaza Rm 3337 ... New York NY 10278-0004
215 596-6637 *Region 3* 3535 Market St Rm 10140 ... Philadelphia PA 19104-3309
404 331-2316 *Region 4* 101 Marietta Tower Suite 1106 ... Atlanta GA 30323-0001
312 353-1385 *Region 5* 105 W Adams St 17th Fl ... Chicago IL 60603-4102
214 767-3879 *Region 6* 1200 Main Tower Bldg Rm 1800 ... Dallas TX 75202-0000
816 426-3291 *Region 7* 601 E 12th St Rm 501 ... Kansas City MO 64106-2808
303 844-4461 *Region 8* 1961 Stout St Rm 489 ... Denver CO 80294-0101
415 556-5810 *Region 9* 50 United Nations Plaza Rm 327 ... San Francisco CA 94102-4920
206 442-0430 *Region 10* 2201 6th Ave MS RX-20 ... Seattle WA 98121-0000
404 639-3311 *Agency for Toxic Substances & Disease* 1600 Clifton Rd NE ... Atlanta GA 30333-0000
301 443-3783 *Alcohol Drug Abuse & Mental Health Administration*
5600 Fishers Ln Rm 12C-15 ... Rockville MD 20857-0001
404 639-3311 *Centers for Disease Control* 1600 Clifton Rd NE ... Atlanta GA 30329-4018
301 496-4461 *National Institutes of Health* 9000 Rockville Pike Rm 344 ... Bethesda MD 20892-0001
301 965-2736 **Social Security Administration** 6401 Security Blvd ... Baltimore MD 21235-0001
617 565-2870 *Region 1* JFK Federal Bldg Rm 1100 ... Boston MA 02203-0000
212 264-3915 *Region 2* 26 Federal Plaza Rm 40-102 ... New York NY 10278-0004
215 596-6941 *Region 3* 3535 Market St Rm 8330 ... Philadelphia PA 19104-3309
404 331-2475 *Region 4* 101 Marietta Tower Suite 1904 ... Atlanta GA 30323-0001
312 353-5175 *Region 5* 105 W Adams St 22nd Fl ... Chicago IL 60603-6298
214 767-4210 *Region 6* 1200 Main Tower Bldg Rm 1440 ... Dallas TX 75202-0000
816 426-3701 *Region 7* 601 E 12th St Rm 436 ... Kansas City MO 64106-2868
303 844-2388 *Region 8* 1961 Stout St Rm 1185 ... Denver CO 80294-0101
415 744-4676 *Region 9* 50 United Nations Plaza 7th Fl ... San Francisco CA 94105-3901
206 442-0417 *Region 10* 2201 6th Ave Rm 510 ... Seattle WA 98121-1832
202 282-7206 **Social Security Research**
4301 Connecticut Ave NW Rm 205 ... Washington DC 20008-2321

DEPARTMENT OF HOUSING AND URBAN DEVELOPMENT

202 708-1112 **Department of Housing & Urban Development**
451 7th St SW ... Washington DC 20410-0001
617 565-5165 *Region 1* 10 Causeway St 3rd Fl ... Boston MA 02222-1047
212 264-8068 *Region 2* 26 Federal Plaza Rm 3541 ... New York NY 10278-0004
215 597-2560 *Region 3* 105 S 7th St Liberty Square Bldg ... Philadelphia PA 19106-0000
404 331-5136 *Region 4* 75 Spring St SW Rm 600 ... Atlanta GA 30303-3309
312 353-5680 *Region 5* 626 W Jackson Blvd Rm 718 ... Chicago IL 60606-5601
817 885-5531 *Region 6* 1600 Throckmorton St ... Fort Worth TX 76102-6645
816 374-6432 *Region 7* 1103 Grand Ave Rm 1200 ... Kansas City MO 64106-2419
303 844-4061 *Region 8* 1405 Curtis St ... Denver CO 80202-2349
415 556-4752 *Region 9* 450 Golden Gate Ave ... San Francisco CA 94102-3400
206 442-5414 *Region 10* 1321 2nd Ave Arcade Plaza Bldg 10 S ... Seattle WA 98101-0000
202 755-6417 **Secretary of Housing & Urban Development**
451 7th St SW Rm 10000 ... Washington DC 20410-0001
202 755-7123 **Under Secretary of Housing & Urban Development**
451 7th St SW Rm 10100 ... Washington DC 20410-0001
202 755-6270 **Community Planning & Development**
451 7th St SW Rm 7100 ... Washington DC 20410-0001
202 426-3500 **Discrimination Complaint Hotline** 451 7th St SW ... Washington DC 20410-0001
202 755-7252 **Fair Housing & Equal Opportunity**
451 7th St SW Rm 5100 ... Washington DC 20410-0001
202 755-6600 **Federal Housing Commissioner** 451 7th St SW Rm 9100 ... Washington DC 20410-0001
202 752-7000 **Federal National Mortgage Assn** 3900 Wisconsin Ave NW .. Washington DC 20016-2896
312 641-0740 *Midwestern Region* 1 S Wacker Dr Suite 3100 ... Chicago IL 60606-4667
215 574-1400 *Northeastern Region* 510 Walnut St 16th Fl ... Philadelphia PA 19106-3696
404 365-6000 *Southeastern Region* 950 E Paces Ferry Rd NE Suite 1800 ... Atlanta GA 30326-1161
214 991-7771 *Southwestern Region*
13455 Noel Rd 2 Galleria Tower Suite 600 ... Dallas TX 75240-0000
818 568-5000 *Western Region* 135 N Los Robles Ave Suite 300 ... Pasadena CA 91101-1758
202 755-6420 **Freedom of Information Office** 451 7th St SW Rm 8141 ... Washington DC 20410-0001
202 755-5926 **Government National Mortgage Assn**
451 7th St SW Suite 6100 ... Washington DC 20410-0001
202 755-6420 **Library & Information Services** 451 7th St SW Rm 8141 ... Washington DC 20410-0001
202 755-6430 **Office of the Inspector General** 451 7th St SW Rm 8256 ... Washington DC 20410-0001
202 755-0950 **Public & Indian Housing** 451 7th St SW Rm 4100 ... Washington DC 20410-0001
202 755-6980 **Public Affairs** 451 7th St SW Rm 10132 ... Washington DC 20410-0001

DEPARTMENT OF THE INTERIOR

202 343-1100 **Department of the Interior** 1849 C St NW ... Washington DC 20240-0001
202 343-7351 **Secretary of the Interior** 1849 C St NW MS-6217 ... Washington DC 20240-0001
202 343-4863 **Under Secretary of the Interior** 1849 C St NW MS-6217 ... Washington DC 20240-0001
202 343-5951 **Black Colleges & Job Corps** 1849 C St NW Rm 2759 ... Washington DC 20240-0001
202 208-5116 **Bureau of Indian Affairs** 1849 C St NW ... Washington DC 20245-0001
605 226-7343 *Aberdeen Area* 115 4th Ave SE ... Aberdeen SD 57401-4382
505 766-3170 *Albuquerque Area* 615 1st St NW ... Albuquerque NM 87102-2305
405 247-6673 *Anadarko Area* PO Box 368 ... Anadarko OK 73005-0000
406 657-6315 *Billings Area* 316 N 26th St Rm 4430 ... Billings MT 59101-1397
703 235-2571 *Eastern Area* 3701 N Fairfax Dr ... Arlington VA 22203-0000
907 586-7177 *Juneau Area* PO Box 3-8000 ... Juneau AK 99802-1219
612 349-3631 *Minneapolis Area* 15 S 5th St ... Minneapolis MN 55402-1020
918 687-2295 *Muskogee Area* 5th & W Okmulgee ... Muskogee OK 74401-0000
602 871-5151 *Navajo Area* PO Box M ... Window Rock AZ 86515-0714
602 379-6600 *Phoenix Area* PO Box 10 ... Phoenix AZ 85001-0010
503 231-6702 *Portland Area* 1002 NE Holladay St ... Portland OR 97232-4182
916 978-4691 *Sacramento Area* 2800 Cottage Way ... Sacramento CA 95825-1884
202 208-3801 **Bureau of Land Management** 1849 C St NW Rm 5600 ... Washington DC 20240-0001
907 271-5076 *Anchorage Office* 222 W 7th Ave Box 13 ... Anchorage AK 99513-7504
208 334-1401 *Boise Office* 3380 Americana Terr ... Boise ID 83706-2544
307 772-2326 *Cheyenne Office* 2515 Warren Ave ... Cheyenne WY 82001-3198
303 236-2100 *Denver Office* 2850 Youngfield St ... Lakewood CO 80215-7093
703 461-1400 *Eastern States Office* 350 S Pickett St ... Alexandria VA 22304-4714
406 255-2904 *Montana Office* 222 N 32nd St ... Billings MT 59101-1911
602 640-5547 *Phoenix Office* PO Box 16563 ... Phoenix AZ 85011-6563
503 280-7026 *Portland Office* 825 NE Multnomah St ... Portland OR 97232-2162
702 328-6202 *Reno Office* 850 Harvard Way ... Reno NV 89502-2055
916 978-4743 *Sacramento Office* 2800 Cottage Way Rm E-2841 ... Sacramento CA 95825-0000
801 539-4010 *Salt Lake City Office* 324 S State St Suite 301 ... Salt Lake City UT 84111-2397
505 988-6030 *Santa Fe Office* 120 S Federal Pl Suite 304 ... Santa Fe NM 87501-1902
202 634-1001 **Bureau of Mines** 2401 E St NW MS-1040 ... Washington DC 20241-0001
202 208-4157 **Bureau of Reclamation** 1849 C St NW Rm 7644 ... Washington DC 20240-0001
406 657-6214 *Great Plains Region* PO Box 36900 ... Billings MT 59107-6900
702 293-8000 *Lower Colorado Region* PO Box 427 ... Boulder City NV 89005-0427
916 978-5135 *Mid-Pacific Region* 2800 Cottage Way Rm 1105 ... Sacramento CA 95825-1897
208 334-1908 *Pacific Northwest Region* 550 W Fort St ... Boise ID 83724-0001
801 524-5566 *Upper Colorado Region* 125 S State St Rm 6224 ... Salt Lake City UT 84138-1102
202 343-7693 **Congressional & Legislative Affairs**
1849 C St NW MS-6246 ... Washington DC 20240-0001
Environmental Project Review
404 331-4524 *Atlanta Region* 75 Spring St SW Suite 1320 ... Atlanta GA 30303-3308
303 236-6900 *Denver Region* PO Box 25007 ... Denver CO 80225-0007
415 556-8200 *San Francisco Region*
450 Golden Gate Ave Box 36098 Rm 14448 ... San Francisco CA 94102-3506
202 208-4131 **Fish & Wildlife Service** 1849 C St NW Rm 3240 ... Washington DC 20240-0001
505 766-2321 *Albuquerque Office* 500 Gold Ave SW Rm 3018 ... Albuquerque NM 87102-3152
907 786-3542 *Anchorage Office* 1011 E Tudor Rd ... Anchorage AK 99503-6119
404 331-3588 *Atlanta Office* 75 Spring St SW Suite 1200 ... Atlanta GA 30303-3308
303 236-7920 *Denver Office* PO Box 25486DFC ... Denver CO 80225-0000
617 965-5100 *Newton Corner Office* 1 Gateway Ctr Suite 700 ... Newton Corner MA 02158-2802
503 231-6118 *Portland Office* 1002 NE Holladay St ... Portland OR 97232-4181
612 725-3502 *Twin Cities Office* Federal Bldg Fort Snelling 6th Fl ... Twin Cities MN 55111-0000
800 424-5081 **Fraud Hotline** ... Washington DC 20240-0001
202 785-3704 **Freedom of Information Clearinghouse**
2000 P St NW Suite 700 ... Washington DC 20036-5915
202 208-3888 **Geological Survey** 1849 C St NW Rm 2646 ... Washington DC 20240-0001
303 236-5438 *Central Region* 6th Ave & Kipling St Bldg 25 ... Denver CO 80225-0000
703 648-4427 *Eastern Region* 12201 Sunrise Valley Dr MS-109 ... Reston VA 22092-0001
415 853-8300 *Western Region* 345 Middlefield Rd ... Menlo Park CA 94025-3508
202 343-3983 **Minerals Management Service** 1849 C St Rm 4245 ... Washington DC 20240-0001
202 343-7394 **National Park Service** 1849 C St NW Rm 3424 ... Washington DC 20240-0001
907 271-2737 *Alaska Region* 2525 Gambell St ... Anchorage AK 99503-2892
215 597-7018 *Mid-Atlantic Region* 143 S 3rd St ... Philadelphia PA 19106-2878
402 221-3431 *Midwest Region* 1709 Jackson St ... Omaha NE 68102-2571
202 426-6612 *National Capitol Region* 1100 Ohio Dr SW Rm 336 ... Washington DC 20242-0001
617 223-5200 *North Atlantic Region* 15 State St ... Boston MA 02109-3572
206 442-5565 *Pacific Northwest Region* 83 S King St Suite 212 ... Seattle WA 98104-2887
303 969-2000 *Rocky Mountain Region* 12795 W Alameda Pkwy ... Denver CO 80228-2849
404 331-5187 *Southeast Region* 75 Spring St SW ... Atlanta GA 30303-3378
505 988-6388 *Southwest Region* PO Box 728 ... Santa Fe NM 87504-0728
415 556-4196 *Western Region* 450 Golden Gate Ave ... San Francisco CA 94102-3491
202 426-6650 *US Park Police* 1100 Ohio Dr SW ... Washington DC 20242-0001
202 208-3891 **Office of Environmental Affairs** 1849 C St NW MS-2340 ... Washington DC 20240-0001
505 766-3565 *Albuquerque Region* 421 Gold Ave SW Suite 310 ... Albuquerque NM 87102-3254
907 271-5011 *Anchorage Region* 1689 C St Rm 119 ... Anchorage AK 99501-5126
617 565-6856 *Boston Region* 10 Causeway St Rm 1022 ... Boston MA 02222-1047
312 353-6612 *Chicago Region* 230 S Dearborn St Suite 3422 ... Chicago IL 60604-1602
215 597-5378 *Philadelphia Region* 200 Chestnut St Customs House ... Philadelphia PA 19106-0000
503 231-6157 *Portland Region* 1002 NE Holladay St Suite 354 ... Portland OR 97232-4118
202 208-3100 **Office of the Solicitor** 1849 C St NW Rm 6352 ... Washington DC 20240-0001
907 271-4131 *Alaska Region* 222 W 8th Ave Box 34 Rm A-25 ... Anchorage AK 99513-0000
801 524-5677 *Innermountain Region* 125 S State St Rm 6201 ... Salt Lake City UT 84138-1102
617 565-2500 *New England Region* JFK Federal Bldg Rm 1803 ... Boston MA 02203-0000
503 231-2125 *Pacific Northwest Region* 500 NE Multnomah St Suite 607 ... Portland OR 97232-2036
916 978-4821 *Pacific Southwest Region* 2800 Cottage Way Rm E-2753 . Sacramento CA 95825-0000
303 236-8444 *Rocky Mountain Region* PO Box 25007 ... Golden CO 80225-0007
404 658-6618 *Southeast Region* 165 Decatur St 2nd Fl ... Atlanta GA 30335-0001
918 581-7502 *Southwest Region* 333 W 4th St Rm 3068 ... Tulsa OK 74103-3819
202 343-2105 **Procurement Information** 1849 C St MS-2626 ... Washington DC 20240-0001
202 343-6416 **Public Affairs** 1849 C St NW MS-7013 ... Washington DC 20240-0001
202 208-3493 **Small & Disadvantaged Business Utilization**
1849 C St NW MS-2727 ... Washington DC 20240-0001
202 343-4719 **Surface Mining Reclamation & Enforcement**
1951 Constitution Ave NW ... Washington DC 20240-0001
703 523-4303 *Big Stone Gap Office* PO Box 1216 ... Big Stone Gap VA 24129-0000
205 731-0890 *Birmingham Office* 208 W Valley Rm 302 ... Homewood AL 35209-0000
304 347-7158 *Charleston Office* 603 Morris St ... Charleston WV 25301-1409
717 782-4036 *Harrisburg Office* 4th & Market Sts Suite 3-C ... Harrisburg PA 17101-0000
317 226-6166 *Indianapolis Office* 575 N Pennsylvania St Suite 301 ... Indianapolis IN 46204-1521
816 374-6405 *Kansas City Office* 1103 Grand Ave Rm 502 ... Kansas City MO 64106-2419
615 673-4255 *Knoxville Office* 530 N Gay St ... Knoxville TN 37917-7422
217 492-4495 *Springfield Office* 509 W Capitol Ave 2nd Fl ... Springfield IL 62704-0000

Federal Government–Executive Branch

412 937-2831 *Eastern Service Center* 10 Parkway Ctr — Pittsburgh PA 15220-0000
303 844-2451 *Western Service Center* 1020 15th St — Denver CO 80202-2348
202 343-4822 **Territorial & International Affairs** 18th & C Sts NW Rm 4312 — Washington DC 20240-0001

DEPARTMENT OF JUSTICE

202 633-2000 **Department of Justice** 10th St & Constitution Ave NW — Washington DC 20530-0001
202 633-2001 **Attorney General** 10th St & Constitution Ave NW Rm 5111 — Washington DC 20530-0001
202 633-2101 **Deputy Attorney General** 10th St & Constitution Ave NW Rm 4111 — Washington DC 20530-0001
202 633-2401 **Antitrust Div** 10th St & Constitution Ave NW Rm 3107 — Washington DC 20530-0001
404 331-7100 *Atlanta Office* 75 Spring St SW Suite 1394 — Atlanta GA 30303-3308
312 353-7530 *Chicago Office* 230 S Dearborn St Suite 3820 — Chicago IL 60604-1662
216 522-4070 *Cleveland Office* 1240 E 9th St Rm 995 — Cleveland OH 44199-2063
214 767-8051 *Dallas Office* 1100 Commerce St Rm 8C6 — Dallas TX 75242-1003
212 264-0390 *New York Office* 26 Federal Plaza Rm 3630 — New York NY 10278-0004
215 597-7405 *Philadelphia Office* 7th & Walnut Sts Curtis Ctr Suite 650 W — Philadelphia PA 19106-0000
415 556-6300 *San Francisco Office* 450 Golden Gate Ave — San Francisco CA 94102-3478
703 756-6121 **Audit Div** 5113 Leesburg Pike Suite 701 — Falls Church VA 22041-3204
404 331-5928 *Atlanta Office* 101 Marietta Tower Suite 2322 — Atlanta GA 30323-0001
307 261-5776 *Casper Office* 100 E 'B' St — Casper WY 82601-0000
312 353-1203 *Chicago Office* 175 W Jackson Blvd Rm A-1335 — Chicago IL 60604-0000
214 939-6625 *Dallas Office* 207 S Houston St Rm 334 — Dallas TX 75202-0000
303 844-3638 *Denver Office* 1244 Steer Blvd Suite 640 — Denver CO 80204-0000
703 756-6121 *District of Columbia Office* 5113 Leesburg Pike Suite 701 — Falls Church VA 22041-3204
415 744-6567 *San Francisco Office* 525 Market St Suite 3522 — San Francisco CA 94105-2743
918 581-6430 *Tulsa Office* 5100 E Skelly Dr — Tulsa OK 74135-0000
202 307-3198 **Bureau of Prisons** 320 1st St NW Suite 640 — Washington DC 20534-0001
301 317-7000 *Mid-Atlantic Region* 10010 Junction Dr Junction Business Park Suite 100-N Annapolis JunctionMD20701-0000
816 891-7007 *North Central Region* 10920 NW Ambassador Dr Suite 200 — Kansas City MO 64153-1270
215 597-6317 *Northeastern Region* 2nd & Chestnut Sts US Customs House 7th Fl — Philadelphia PA 19106-0000
214 767-9700 *South Central Region* 4211 Cedar Springs Rd Suite 300 — Dallas TX 75219-2690
404 624-5202 *Southeastern Region* 523 McDonough Blvd SE — Atlanta GA 30315-4215
415 595-8160 *Western Region* 1301 Shoreway Rd 4th Fl — Belmont CA 94002-4106
913 682-8700 *US Penitentiary–Leavenworth* 1300 Metropolitan — Leavenworth KS 66048-1254
717 523-1251 *US Penitentiary–Lewisburg* — Lewisburg PA 17837-0000
805 735-2771 *US Penitentiary–Lompoc* 3901 Klein Blvd — Lompoc CA 93436-2706
618 964-1441 *US Penitentiary–Marion* PO Box 2000 — Marion IL 62959-0901
202 633-3301 **Civil Div** 10th St & Constitution Ave NW Rm 3143 — Washington DC 20530-0001
202 633-2151 **Civil Rights Div** 10th St & Constitution Ave NW Rm 5643 — Washington DC 20530-0001
301 492-5929 **Community Relations Service** 5550 Friendship Blvd Rm 330 — Chevy Chase MD 20815-7287
617 565-6830 *Region 1* 10 Causeway St Rm 1192 — Boston MA 02222-1047
212 264-0700 *Region 2* 26 Federal Plaza Suite 3402 — New York NY 10278-0140
215 597-2344 *Region 3* 2nd & Chestnut Sts Rm 309 — Philadelphia PA 19106-0000
404 331-6883 *Region 4* 75 Piedmont Ave NE Suite 900 — Atlanta GA 30303-2588
312 353-4391 *Region 5* 175 W Jackson Blvd Suite 1113 — Chicago IL 60604-2701
214 767-0824 *Region 6* 1100 Commerce St Suite 13B37 — Dallas TX 75242-1003
816 426-2022 *Region 7* 911 Walnut St Suite 2411 — Kansas City MO 64106-2009
303 844-2973 *Region 8* 1244 N Speer Blvd Suite 650 — Denver CO 80204-3584
415 744-6565 *Region 9* 211 Main St Suite 1040 — San Francisco CA 94105-1924
206 442-4465 *Region 10* 915 2nd Ave Rm 1898 — Seattle WA 98174-1001
202 633-2601 **Criminal Div** 10th St & Constitution Ave NW Rm 2107 — Washington DC 20530-0001
202 307-1000 **Drug Enforcement Administration** 700 Army Navy Dr — Arlington VA 20537-0001
404 331-7308 *Atlanta Office* 75 Spring St SW Rm 740 — Atlanta GA 30303-3307
617 565-2800 *Boston Office* 50 Staniford St Suite 200 — Boston MA 02114-2503
312 353-7875 *Chicago Office* 219 S Dearborn St Rm 500 — Chicago IL 60604-1792
214 767-7151 *Dallas Office* 1880 Regal Row — Dallas TX 75235-2392
303 844-3951 *Denver Office* PO Box 1860 — Denver CO 80201-1860
313 226-7290 *Detroit Office* 231 W Lafayette St Federal Bldg Rm 357 — Detroit MI 48226-2793
713 681-1771 *Houston Office* 333 West Loop N Suite 300 — Houston TX 77024-7794
213 894-2650 *Los Angeles Office* 350 S Figueroa St — Los Angeles CA 90071-1101
305 591-4870 *Miami Office* 8400 NW 53rd St — Miami FL 33166-4580
504 589-3894 *New Orleans Office* 1661 Canal St Suite 2200 — New Orleans LA 70112-2888
212 399-5151 *New York Office* 555 W 57th St Suite 1900 — New York NY 10019-2925
201 645-6060 *Newark Office* 970 Broad St Rm 806 — Newark NJ 07102-2580
215 597-9530 *Philadelphia Office* 600 Arch St Suite 10224 — Philadelphia PA 19106-1650
602 640-5700 *Phoenix Office* 3010 N 2nd Street Suite 301 — Phoenix AZ 85012-0000
314 425-3241 *Saint Louis Office* 7911 Forsyth Suite 500 — Saint Louis MO 63105-3860
619 585-4200 *San Diego Office* 402 W 35th St — National City CA 92050-7963
415 556-6771 *San Francisco Office* 450 Golden Gate Ave — San Francisco CA 94102-3584
206 442-5443 *Seattle Office* 220 W Mercer St — Seattle WA 98119-3964
202 724-7834 *Washington Office* 400 6th St SW Rm 2558 — Washington DC 20024-2780
202 633-2121 **Executive Office for US Attorneys** 10th St & Constitution Ave NW Rm 1619 — Washington DC 20530-0001
202 724-8391 **Executive Office of US Trustees** 320 1st St NW Rm 812 — Washington DC 23530-0001
202 324-3000 **Federal Bureau of Investigation** 9th St & Pennsylvania Ave NW — Washington DC 20535-0001
202 653-5883 **Foreign Claims Settlement Commission** 1111 20th St NW Rm 400 — Washington DC 20579-0001
202 633-3642 **Freedom of Information Office** 10th St & Constitution Ave NW Rm 7238 — Washington DC 20530-0001
202 514-4316 **Immigration & Naturalization Service** 425 I St NW Rm 7016 — Washington DC 20536-0001
802 951-6223 *Eastern Region* Elmwood Ave Federal Bldg — Burlington VT 05401-0000
612 725-3850 *Northern Region* Fort Snelling Federal Bldg — Twin Cities MN 55111-0000
214 767-7010 *Southern Region* 311 N Stemmons Fwy — Dallas TX 75207-4324
714 643-4775 *Western Region* 24000 Avila Rd — Laguna Niguel CA 92607-0000
202 633-1689 *US Border Patrol* 425 I St NW Rm 6023 — Washington DC 20536-0001
202 633-2701 **Land & Natural Resources Div** 10th St & Constitution Ave NW Room 2143 — Washington DC 20530-0001
301 492-5910 **Pardon Attorney** 5550 Friendship Blvd Rm 490 — Chevy Chase MD 20815-7285
301 492-5990 **Parole Commission** 5550 Friendship Blvd 4th Fl — Chevy Chase MD 20815-7286
816 891-1395 *North Central Region* 10920 NW Ambassador Dr Suite 220 — Kansas City MO 64153-1269
215 597-6365 *Northeast Region* 2nd & Chestnut Sts US Customs Rm 702 — Philadelphia PA 19106-0000
214 767-0024 *South Central Region* 525 Griffin St Federal Bldg Suite 820 — Dallas TX 75202-0000
404 347-4126 *Southeast Region* 1718 Peachtree St NW Suite 250 — Atlanta GA 30309-2421
415 598-4800 *Western Region* 1301 Shoreway Rd 4th Fl — Belmont CA 94002-4106
202 501-8449 **Procurement Information** 601 David NW Suite 7100 — Washington DC 20530-0001
202 633-3435 **Professional Responsibility Fraud Hotline** 10th St & Constitution Ave NW — Washington DC 20530-0001
202 633-2007 **Public Affairs** 10th St & Constitution Ave NW Rm 1218 — Washington DC 20530-0001
202 633-2901 **Tax Div** 10th St & Pennsylvania Ave NW Rm 4143 — Washington DC 20530-0001
202 307-9600 **US Marshal Service** 600 Army-Navy Dr Rm 850 — Arlington VA 22202-4210
202 272-6999 **US National Central Bureau of Interpol** 600 E St NW Suite 600 — Washington DC 20530-0001

DEPARTMENT OF LABOR

202 523-7316 **Department of Labor** 200 Constitution Ave NW — Washington DC 20210-0001
202 523-8271 **Secretary of Labor** 200 Constitution Ave NW Rm S-018 — Washington DC 20210-0001
202 523-6151 **Deputy Secretary of Labor** 200 Constitution Ave NW Rm S-2018 — Washington DC 20210-0001
202 523-6043 **Bureau of International Labor Affairs** 200 Constitution Ave NW Rm S2235 — Washington DC 20210-0001
202 523-1913 **Bureau of Labor Statistics** 441 G St NW — Washington DC 20212-0001
404 347-4418 *Atlanta Office* 1371 Peachtree St NE Suite 540 — Atlanta GA 30367-0001
617 565-2327 *Boston Office* JFK Federal Bldg Government Ctr Rm 1603 — Boston MA 02203-0000
312 353-7226 *Chicago Office* 230 S Dearborn St 9th Fl — Chicago IL 60604-1502
214 767-6953 *Dallas Office* 525 Griffin St Federal Bldg Rm 221 — Dallas TX 75202-0000
816 426-2378 *Kansas City Office* 911 Walnut St Rm 1604 — Kansas City MO 64106-2009
212 337-2400 *New York Office* 201 Varick St Rm 808 — New York NY 10014-4800
215 596-1154 *Philadelphia Office* PO Box 13309 — Philadelphia PA 19101-3309
415 744-6600 *San Francisco Office* 71 Stevenson St — San Francisco CA 94105-2934
202 523-1180 *Employment & Unemployment Statistics* 441 G St NW Rm 2919 — Washington DC 20212-0001
202 523-1382 *Office of Compensation & Working Conditions* 441 G St NW Rm 2021 — Washington DC 20212-0001
202 272-5381 *Office of Employment Projections* 600 E St NW Rm 9216 Washington DC 20212-0001
202 523-6871 **Employment & Training Administration** 200 Constitution Ave NW Rm S2307 — Washington DC 20210-0001
617 565-2240 *Region 1* JFK Federal Bldg Rm 1703 — Boston MA 02203-0000
212 337-2139 *Region 2* 201 Varick St Rm 755 — New York NY 10014-4800
215 596-6336 *Region 3* 3535 Market St Gateway Bldg Rm 13300 — Philadelphia PA 19104-0000
404 347-4411 *Region 4* 1371 Peachtree St NE Rm 400 — Atlanta GA 30367-0001
312 353-0313 *Region 5* 230 S Dearborn St 6th Fl — Chicago IL 60604-1591
214 767-2154 *Region 6* 525 Griffin St Federal Bldg Rm 317 — Dallas TX 75202-0000
816 426-3796 *Region 7* 911 Walnut St Rm 700 — Kansas City MO 64106-2009
303 844-4477 *Region 8* 1961 Stout St 16th Fl — Denver CO 80294-0101
415 744-6650 *Region 9* 71 Stevenson St — San Francisco CA 94105-2934
206 442-7700 *Region 10* 1111 3rd Ave Suite 900 — Seattle WA 98101-3207
202 523-8743 **Employment Standards Administration** 200 Constitution Ave NW Rm C4331 — Washington DC 20210-0001
617 565-2066 *Region 1* JFK Federal Bldg Rm 1612-C — Boston MA 02203-0000
212 337-2000 *Region 2* 201 Varick St Rm 750 — New York NY 10014-4800
215 596-1185 *Region 3* 3535 Market St Rm 15230 — Philadelphia PA 19104-3309
404 347-2818 *Region 4* 1375 Peachtree St NE Rm 664 — Atlanta GA 30367-0001
312 353-7280 *Region 5* 230 S Dearborn St Rm 820 — Chicago IL 60604-1503
214 767-6894 *Region 6* 525 S Griffin St Federal Bldg Suite 800 — Dallas TX 75202-0000
816 426-5381 *Region 7* 911 Walnut St Rm 2000 — Kansas City MO 64106-2009
303 844-5903 *Region 8* 1961 Stout St Rm 1490 — Denver CO 80294-0101
415 744-6620 *Region 9* 211 Main St Rm 341 — San Francisco CA 94105-1910
206 442-1536 *Region 10* 1111 3rd Ave Suite 600 — Seattle WA 98101-3207
202 523-8088 **Freedom of Information Office** 200 Constitution Ave NW Rm N2428 — Washington DC 20210-0001
202 523-9711 **Information & Public Affairs** 200 Constitution Ave NW Rm S1032 — Washington DC 20210-0001
202 357-0227 **Inspector General Fraud Hotline** 200 Constitution Ave NW Rm S5512 — Washington DC 20210-0001
202 523-9674 **Labor Management Standards** 200 Constitution Ave NW Rm S2203 — Washington DC 20210-0001
404 347-4237 *Atlanta Office* 1371 Peachtree St NE Suite 300 — Atlanta GA 30367-0001
205 731-0239 *Birmingham Office* 1800 5th Ave N Rm 420 — Birmingham AL 35203-2114
617 223-9990 *Boston Office* JW McCormack POCH Rm 801 — Boston MA 02109-0000
312 353-7264 *Chicago Office* 230 S Dearborn St Rm 774 — Chicago IL 60604-1503
216 522-3855 *Cleveland Office* 1240 E 9th St Rm 831 — Cleveland OH 44199-2002
214 767-6834 *Dallas Office* 525 Griffin St Federal Bldg Rm 300 — Dallas TX 75202-0000
313 226-6200 *Detroit Office* 231 W Lafayette Rm 630 — Detroit MI 48226-2799
616 456-2335 *Grand Rapids Office* 148 Federal Bldg — Grand Rapids MI 49503-0000
808 541-2705 *Honolulu Office* 300 Ala Moana Blvd Rm 5115 — Honolulu HI 96850-0001
816 426-2547 *Kansas City Office* 911 Walnut St Suite 1606 — Kansas City MO 64106-2009
213 252-7508 *Los Angeles Office* 3660 Wilshire Blvd Suite 708 — Los Angeles CA 90010-2713
212 337-2580 *New York Office* 201 Varick St Rm 878 — New York NY 10014-4811
215 597-4960 *Philadelphia Office* 600 Arch St Rm 9452 — Philadelphia PA 19106-1611
412 644-2925 *Pittsburgh Office* 1000 Liberty Ave Rm 804 — Pittsburgh PA 15222-4004
619 557-6153 *San Diego Office* 880 Front St Rm 5N-37A — San Diego CA 92188-1003
415 974-0544 *San Francisco Office* 71 Stevenson St Suite 725 — San Francisco CA 94105-2936
202 254-6510 *Washington DC Office* 1730 K St NW Riddell Bldg Suite 558 — Washington DC 20006-0000
703 235-1452 **Mine Safety & Health Administration** 4015 Wilson Blvd — Arlington VA 22203-1984
304 547-0400 *Approval & Certification Center* Industrial Park Rd — Triadelphia WV 26059-0000
703 235-1140 *Coal Mine Safety & Health* 4015 Wilson Blvd — Arlington VA 22203-1984
703 235-8480 *Metal & Non-Metal Mine Safety & Health* 4015 Wilson Blvd — Arlington VA 22203-1984
303 231-5449 *Mining Information Systems* PO Box 25367 — Denver CO 80225-0367
304 255-0451 *National Mine Health & Safety Academy* PO Box 1166 — Beckley WV 25802-1166
202 523-8148 **Occupational Safety & Health Administration** 200 Constitution Ave NW Rm N3647 — Washington DC 20210-0001
617 565-7164 *Region 1* 133 Portland St — Boston MA 02114-1707
212 337-2378 *Region 2* 201 Varick St Rm 670 — New York NY 10014-4811
215 596-1201 *Region 3* 3535 Market St Gateway Bldg Suite 2100 — Philadelphia PA 19104-0000
404 347-3573 *Region 4* 1375 Peachtree St NE Suite 587 — Atlanta GA 30367-0001
312 353-2220 *Region 5* 230 S Dearborn St Suite 3244 — Chicago IL 60604-1601
214 767-4731 *Region 6* 525 Griffin St Federal Bldg Rm 602 — Dallas TX 75202-0000
816 426-5861 *Region 7* 911 Walnut St Rm 406 — Kansas City MO 64106-2009
303 844-3061 *Region 8* 1961 Stout St Rm 1576 — Denver CO 80294-0101
415 744-6670 *Region 9* 71 Stevenson St Suite 420 — San Francisco CA 94105-2935
206 442-5930 *Region 10* 1111 3rd Ave Rm 715 — Seattle WA 98101-3207
202 523-8148 **OSHA** 200 Constitution Ave NW Rm N3647 — Washington DC 20210-0001
202 523-6445 **Procurement Information** 200 Constitution Ave NW Rm S5220 — Washington DC 20210-0001
202 523-9148 **Small & Disadvantaged Business Utilization** 200 Constitution Ave NW Rm S1004 — Washington DC 20210-0001
202 523-6611 **Women's Bureau** 200 Constitution Ave NW Rm S3002 — Washington DC 20210-0001
617 565-1988 *Region 1* JFK Federal Bldg Rm 1600 — Boston MA 02203-0000
212 337-2390 *Region 2* 201 Varick St Rm 601 — New York NY 10014-4811
215 596-1183 *Region 3* 3535 Market St Rm 13280 — Philadelphia PA 19104-3309
404 347-4461 *Region 4* 1371 Peachtree St NE Suite 323 — Atlanta GA 30367-0001
312 353-6985 *Region 5* 230 S Dearborn St 10th Fl — Chicago IL 60604-1502
214 767-6985 *Region 6* 525 Griffin St Federal Bldg Suite 731 — Dallas TX 75202-0000
816 426-6108 *Region 7* 911 Walnut St Rm 2511 — Kansas City MO 64106-2009
303 844-4138 *Region 8* 1961 Stout St Rm 1452 — Denver CO 80294-0101
415 744-6679 *Region 9* 71 Stevenson St Suite 927 — San Francisco CA 94105-2937
206 442-1534 *Region 10* 1111 3rd Ave Rm 885 — Seattle WA 98101-3207

DEPARTMENT OF STATE

202 647-4000 **Department of State** 2201 C St NW — Washington DC 20520-0001
202 647-5291 **Secretary of State** 2201 C St NW 7th Fl — Washington DC 20520-0001
202 647-9640 **Deputy Secretary of State** 2201 C St NW Rm D-7220 — Washington DC 20520-7512
202 647-7371 **African Affairs** 2201 C St NW Rm 3509 — Washington DC 20520-0001

202 647-1488	**Consular Affairs** 2201 C St NW Rm 5807 CA-PA	Washington	DC	20520-0001
202 647-4835	**East Asian & Pacific Affairs** 2201 C St NW Rm 6205	Washington	DC	20520-0001
202 647-1942	**Economic & Business Affairs** 2201 C St NW Rm 6822	Washington	DC	20520-0001
202 647-9626	**European & Canadian Affairs** 2201 C St NW Rm 6228	Washington	DC	20520-0001
703 875-5370	**Foreign Service Institute** 1400 Key Blvd	Arlington	VA	22209-1518
202 647-7740	**Freedom of Information Office** 2201 C St NW Rm 1239	Washington	DC	20520-0001
202 647-9567	**Inspector General** 2201 C St NW Rm 6817	Washington	DC	20520-0001
202 647-9673	**Intelligence & Research** 2201 C St NW 8th Fl	Washington	DC	20520-0001
202 647-9210	**Inter-American Affairs** 2201 C St NW Rm 6263	Washington	DC	20520-0001
202 647-5727	**International Communications & Information Policy** 2201 C St NW Rm 6317	Washington	DC	20520-0001
202 647-7399	**International Narcotics Matters** 2201 C St NW Rm 7333	Washington	DC	20520-0001
202 647-9600	**International Organization Affairs** 2201 C St NW Rm 6323	Washington	DC	20520-0001
202 647-7207	**Near Eastern & South Asian Affairs** 2201 C St NW Rm 6242	Washington	DC	20520-0001
202 647-1561	**Oceans & International Environmental & Scientific Affairs** 2201 C St NW Rm 7831	Washington	DC	20520-0001
202 647-9892	**Office of Counterterrorism** 2201 C St NW Rm 2507	Washington	DC	20520-0001
202 647-3416	**Office of Foreign Missions** 2201 C St NW Rm 2238	Washington	DC	20520-0001
703 875-1101	**Office of Procurement** 1100 Wilson Blvd 14th Fl	Rosslyn	VA	22209-2297
202 647-0518	**Passport Services** 1425 K St NW	Washington	DC	20524-0001
617 565-6990	*Boston Agency* 10 Causeway St Rm 247	Boston	MA	02222-1047
312 353-7155	*Chicago Agency* 230 S Dearborn St Suite 380	Chicago	IL	60604-1503
808 541-1919	*Honolulu Agency* 300 Ala Moana Blvd New Federal Bldg Rm C106	Honolulu	HI	96850-0001
713 653-3153	*Houston Agency* 1919 Smith St Suite 1100	Houston	TX	77002-8051
213 209-7075	*Los Angeles Agency* 11000 Wilshire Blvd US Federal Bldg 13th Fl	Los Angeles	CA	90024-0000
305 536-4681	*Miami Agency* 51 SW 1st Ave 16th Fl	Miami	FL	33130-1680
504 589-6161	*New Orleans Agency* 701 Loyola Ave	New Orleans	LA	70113-1931
212 541-7700	*New York Agency* 630 5th Ave Rm 270	New York	NY	10111-0002
215 597-7480	*Philadelphia Agency* 600 Arch St Suite 4426	Philadelphia	PA	19106-1685
415 744-4010	*San Francisco Agency* 525 Market St Suite 200	San Francisco	CA	94105-2773
206 442-7945	*Seattle Agency* 915 2nd Ave Rm 992	Seattle	WA	98174-1001
203 325-3538	*Stamford Agency* 1 Landmark Sq	Stamford	CT	06901-2601
202 647-9606	**Public Affairs** 2201 C St NW Rm 6800	Washington	DC	20520-0001
202 647-5822	**Refugee Programs** 2201 C St NW Rm 5824	Washington	DC	20520-0001
202 647-4404	**Security Assistance Science & Technology** 2201 C St NW Rm 7208	Washington	DC	20520-0001

DEPARTMENT OF TRANSPORTATION

202 366-4000	**Department of Transportation** 400 7th St SW	Washington	DC	20590-0001
202 366-1111	**Secretary of Transportation** 400 7th St SW Rm 10200	Washington	DC	20590-0001
202 366-2222	**Deputy Secretary of Transportation** 400 7th St SW Rm 10200	Washington	DC	20590-0001
202 366-4305	**Board of Contract Appeals** 400 7th St SW Rm 5101	Washington	DC	20590-0000
202 366-2937	**Commercial Space Transportation** 400 7th St SW Rm 10401	Washington	DC	20590-0000
202 267-3484	**Federal Aviation Administration** 800 Independence Ave SW Rm 600E	Washington	DC	20591-0001
907 271-5645	*Alaska Region* 222 W 7th Ave	Anchorage	AK	99513-7540
816 426-5626	*Central Region* 601 E 12th St Rm 1501B	Kansas City	MO	64106-2808
718 917-1005	*Eastern Region* Fitzgerald Bldg JFK International Airport	Jamaica	NY	11430-0000
312 694-7294	*Great Lakes Region* 2300 E Devon Ave Rm 401	Des Plaines	IL	60018-4686
617 273-7244	*New England Region* 12 New England Executive Pk	Burlington	MA	01803-5299
206 431-2001	*Northwestern Region* PO Box C68966	Seattle	WA	98168-0000
404 763-7527	*Southern Region* 3400 Norman Berry Dr	East Point	GA	30344-5198
817 624-5000	*Southwestern Region* 4400 Blue Mound Rd	Fort Worth	TX	76193-0001
213 297-1427	*Western Pacific Region* PO Box 92007 World Way Postal Ctr	Los Angeles	CA	90009-2007
202 267-9613	*Aviation Safety Office* 800 Independence Ave SW Rm 1000E	Washington	DC	20591-0000
202 267-8781	*Air Traffic Evaluations & Analysis* 800 Independence Ave SW Rm 400E	Washington	DC	20591-0000
202 267-3053	*Airport Standards* 800 Independence Ave SW Rm 600E	Washington	DC	20591-0001
405 680-3011	*Aviation Standards* 6500 S MacArthur Blvd Rm 116	Oklahoma City	OK	73169-6969
202 267-8237	*Flight Standards* 800 Independence Ave SW Rm 302	Washington	DC	20591-0000
202 267-3213	*International Aviation* 800 Independence Ave SW Rm 1027	Washington	DC	20591-0000
405 680-3011	*Monroney Aeronautical Center* 6500 S MacArthur Blvd	Oklahoma City	OK	73169-6969
202 267-3557	*Research & Development* 800 Independence Ave SW Rm 508	Washington	DC	20591-0000
202 366-0660	**Federal Highway Administration** 400 7th St SW Rm 4210	Washington	DC	20590-0001
518 472-6476	*Regions 1 & 2* Clinton Ave & N Pearl St Leo O'Brien Federal Bldg Rm 719	Albany	NY	12207-0000
301 962-2773	*Region 3* 31 Hopkins Plaza Rm 1621	Baltimore	MD	21201-2822
404 347-4078	*Region 4* 1720 Peachtree Rd NW Suite 200	Atlanta	GA	30367-0001
708 799-6300	*Region 5* 18209 Dixie Hwy	Homewood	IL	60430-2294
817 334-3232	*Region 6* 819 Taylor St Rm 8A00	Fort Worth	TX	76102-6114
816 926-7563	*Region 7* 6301 Rockhill Rd 2nd Fl	Kansas City	MO	64131-1117
303 969-6704	*Region 8* 555 Zang St Rm 400	Lakewood	CO	80228-1097
415 744-3100	*Region 9* 211 Main St Rm 1100	San Francisco	CA	94105-1926
503 326-2053	*Region 10* 708 SW 3rd Ave Rm 312	Portland	OR	97204-2489
703 285-0000	*Eastern District* 21400 Ridgetop Cir	Sterling	VA	22170-6511
202 366-2045	*Environmental Policy* 400 7th St SW Rm 3232	Washington	DC	20590-0000
202 366-1153	*Highway Safety* 400 7th St SW Rm 3401	Washington	DC	20590-0000
703 285-2770	*National Highway Institute* 6300 Georgetown Pike	McLean	VA	22101-0000
202 366-0342	*Office of Right-Of-Way* 400 7th St SW Rm 3221	Washington	DC	20590-0000
202 366-0881	**Federal Railroad Administration** 400 7th St SW	Washington	DC	20590-0001
312 353-6203	*Central Region* 165 N Canal St Rm 1400SA	Chicago	IL	60606-1510
215 597-0750	*Eastern Region* 841 Chestnut St Rm 712	Philadelphia	PA	19107-4433
816 426-2497	*Midwest Region* 911 Walnut St Rm 1806	Kansas City	MO	64106-2095
617 494-2302	*Northeastern Region* 55 Broadway 10th Fl	Cambridge	MA	02142-1003
503 326-3011	*Northwest Region* 1500 SW 1st Ave Suite 250	Portland	OR	97201-5871
404 347-2751	*Southern Region* 1720 Peachtree Rd NW Suite 440-N	Atlanta	GA	30309-2469
817 334-3601	*Southwest Region* 819 Taylor St Rm 7A35	Fort Worth	TX	76102-6114
415 744-3092	*Western Region* 211 Main St Rm 1085	San Francisco	CA	94105-1924
202 366-9657	*Freight Services* 400 7th St SW Rm 8128	Washington	DC	20590-0000
202 366-9332	*Passenger Services* 400 7th St SW Rm 5407	Washington	DC	20590-0000
202 366-9252	*Safety Enforcement* 400 7th St SW Rm 8326	Washington	DC	20590-0000
202 366-4542	**Freedom of Information Office** 400 7th St SW Suite 5432	Washington	DC	20590-0001
202 366-5807	**Maritime Administration** 400 7th St SW Rm 7219	Washington	DC	20590-0001
504 589-6556	*Central Region* 365 Canal St Suite 2590	New Orleans	LA	70130-1137
708 298-4535	*Great Lakes Region* 2300 E Devon Ave Suite 366	Des Plaines	IL	60018-4608
212 264-1300	*North Atlantic Region* 26 Federal Plaza Rm 3737	New York	NY	10278-0004
804 441-6393	*South Atlantic Region* 7737 Hampton Blvd Bldg 4D Rm 211	Norfolk	VA	23505-0000
415 744-3125	*Western Region* 211 Main St Rm 1112	San Francisco	CA	94105-1926
202 366-5123	*Domestic Shipping* 400 7th St SW Rm 7301	Washington	DC	20590-0001
202 366-5773	*International Activities* 400 7th St SW Rm 7119	Washington	DC	20590-0001
202 366-5517	*Market Development* 400 7th St SW Rm 7209	Washington	DC	20590-0001
202 366-2323	*Ship Operating Assistance* 400 7th St SW Rm 8114	Washington	DC	20590-0001
202 366-1875	*Ship Operations* 400 7th St SW Rm 2122	Washington	DC	20590-0001
516 773-5000	*US Merchant Marine Academy* Steamboat Rd	Kings Point	NY	11024-0000
202 366-9550	**National Highway Traffic Safety Administration** 400 7th St SW Rm 5232	Washington	DC	20590-0001
617 494-3427	*Region 1* 55 Broadway	Cambridge	MA	02142-1003
914 683-9690	*Region 2* 222 Mamaroneck Ave Suite 204	White Plains	NY	10605-1316
301 768-7111	*Region 3* 7526 Connelley Dr Suite L	Hanover	MD	21076-1600
404 347-4537	*Region 4* 1720 Peachtree Rd NW Suite 501	Atlanta	GA	30309-2486
708 799-6067	*Region 5* 18209 Dixie Hwy Suite A	Homewood	IL	60430-2205
817 334-3653	*Region 6* 819 Taylor St Rm 8A38	Fort Worth	TX	76102-6114
816 926-7887	*Region 7* 6301 Rockhill Rd Rm 106	Kansas City	MO	64131-1117
303 969-6917	*Region 8* 555 Zang St 4th Fl	Denver	CO	80228-1000
415 744-3089	*Region 9* 211 Main St Suite 1000	San Francisco	CA	94105-1924
206 442-5934	*Region 10* 915 2nd Ave Rm 3140	Seattle	WA	98174-1001
202 366-9588	*Alcohol & State Programs* 400 7th St SW Rm 5130	Washington	DC	20590-0000
202 366-1503	*Center for Statistics & Analysis* 400 7th St SW Rm 6125	Washington	DC	20590-0000
202 366-2850	*Defects Investigation* 400 7th St SW Rm 5326	Washington	DC	20590-0001
513 666-4511	*Vehicle Research & Test Center* Hwy 33	East Liberty	OH	43319-0000
202 366-2832	*Vehicle Safety Compliance* 400 7th St SW Rm 6111	Washington	DC	20590-0001
202 366-0842	*Vehicle Safety Standards* 400 7th St SW Rm 5320	Washington	DC	20590-0000
202 366-4953	**Procurement Operations Div** 400 7th St SW Rm 9413	Washington	DC	20590-0001
202 366-4433	**Research & Special Programs Admin** 400 7th St SW Rm 8410	Washington	DC	20590-0001
202 366-9059	*Aviation Information Management* 400 7th St SW Rm 4125	Washington	DC	20590-0001
202 366-5270	*Emergency Transportation Div* 400 7th St SW Rm 8404	Washington	DC	20590-0001
202 366-4595	*Office of Pipeline Safety* 400 7th St SW Rm 8417	Washington	DC	20590-0001
816 426-2654	*Central Region* 911 Walnut St Rm 1811	Kansas City	MO	64106-2009
202 366-4582	*Eastern Region* 400 7th St SW Rm 8321	Washington	DC	20590-0001
713 750-1746	*Southwest Region* 2320 La Branch St Suite 2116	Houston	TX	77004-1031
404 347-2632	*Southern Region* 1720 Peachtree Rd NW Suite 426	Atlanta	GA	30309-2439
303 236-3424	*Western Region* 555 Zang St 2nd Fl	Lakewood	CO	80228-1010
202 366-0091	**Saint Lawrence Seaway Development Corp** 400 7th St SW Rm 5424	Washington	DC	20590-0001
202 366-0091	*Trade & Traffic Development* 400 7th St SW Rm 5424	Washington	DC	20590-0001
202 366-4043	**Urban Mass Transportation Administration** 400 7th St SW Rm 9314	Washington	DC	20590-0001
617 494-2055	*Region 1* 55 Broadway Rm 921	Cambridge	MA	02142-1003
212 264-8162	*Region 2* 26 Federal Plaza 29th Fl	New York	NY	10278-0022
215 597-8098	*Region 3* 841 Chestnut St Rm 714	Philadelphia	PA	19107-4414
404 347-3948	*Region 4* 1720 Peachtree Rd NW Suite 400	Atlanta	GA	30309-2471
312 353-2789	*Region 5* 55 E Monroe St Suite 1415	Chicago	IL	60603-5704
817 334-3787	*Region 6* 819 Taylor St Rm 9A32	Fort Worth	TX	76102-6160
816 926-5053	*Region 7* 6301 Rockhill Rd Suite 303	Kansas City	MO	64131-1117
303 844-3242	*Region 8* 1961 Stout St Rm 520	Denver	CO	80294-0101
415 744-3133	*Region 9* 211 Main St Suite 1160	San Francisco	CA	94105-1971
206 442-4210	*Region 10* 915 2nd Ave Rm 3142	Seattle	WA	98174-1012
202 366-1666	*Private Sector Initiatives* 400 7th St SW Rm 9300	Washington	DC	20590-0001
202 366-4980	*Procurement & Third Party Contract Review* 400 7th St SW Rm 7405	Washington	DC	20590-0001
202 366-4052	*Technical Assistance* 400 7th St SW Rm 6431	Washington	DC	20590-0001
202 267-2229	**US Coast Guard** 2100 2nd St SW	Washington	DC	20593-0001
212 668-7886	*Atlantic Area* Governors Island Bldg 125	New York	NY	10004-5000
202 267-0972	*Office of Navigation & Waterways Services* 2100 2nd St SW Comandant G-NAB	Washington	DC	20593-0001
415 437-3151	*Pacific Area* Coast Guard Island	Alameda	CA	94501-5100
203 444-8294	*US Coast Guard Academy* 15 Mohegan Ave	New London	CT	06320-4195

DEPARTMENT OF THE TREASURY

202 566-2000	**Department of the Treasury** 1500 Pennsylvania Ave NW	Washington	DC	20005-1007
202 566-2533	**Secretary of the Treasury** 1500 Pennsylvania Ave NW Rm 3330	Washington	DC	20220-0001
202 566-2801	**Deputy Secretary of the Treasury** 1500 Pennsylvania Ave NW Rm 3326	Washington	DC	20220-0001
202 566-7135	**Bureau of Alcohol Tobacco & Firearms** 1200 Pennsylvania Ave NW Rm 4402	Washington	DC	20226-0001
312 353-3778	*Midwest Region* 230 S Dearborn St 15th Fl	Chicago	IL	60604-1502
212 264-2328	*North Atlantic Region* 6 World Trade Ctr Rm 620	New York	NY	10048-0206
404 986-6040	*Southeast Region* 3835 Presidential Pkwy	Atlanta	GA	30340-3792
214 767-2277	*Southwest Region* 1114 Commerce St	Dallas	TX	75242-1001
415 744-7013	*Western Region* 221 Main St 11th Fl	San Francisco	CA	94105-1906
202 447-0917	**Bureau of Engraving & Printing** 14th & C Sts SW	Washington	DC	20228-0001
202 287-4113	**Bureau of the Public Debt** 1300 C St SW	Washington	DC	20239-0001
202 447-1750	**Comptroller of the Currency** 490 L'Enfant Plaza SW	Washington	DC	20219-0001
312 663-8000	*Central District* 440 S La Salle St	Chicago	IL	60605-1073
816 556-1800	*Midwestern District* 2345 Grand Ave Suite 700	Kansas City	MO	64108-2600
212 819-9860	*Northeastern District* 1114 Ave of the Americas Suite 3900	New York	NY	10036-7703
404 659-8855	*Southeastern District* 245 Peachtree Center Ave NE 1 Marquis Tower Suite 600	Atlanta	GA	30303-1246
214 720-0656	*Southwestern District* 500 N Akard St Suite 1600	Dallas	TX	75201-3342
415 545-5900	*Western District* 50 Fremont St Suite 3900	San Francisco	CA	94105-2240
202 566-5286	**Customs Service** 1301 Constitution Ave NW Rm 3422	Washington	DC	20229-0001
212 466-4444	*New York Region* 6 World Trade Ctr Rm 716	New York	NY	10048-0206
312 353-4733	*North Central Region* 55 E Monroe St Suite 1501	Chicago	IL	60603-5790
617 565-6300	*Northeast Region* 10 Causeway St Suite 801	Boston	MA	02222-1047
213 491-7200	*Pacific Region* 1 World Trade Ctr	Long Beach	CA	90831-0002
504 589-6324	*South Central Region* 423 Canal St Rm 337	New Orleans	LA	70130-2337
305 536-4661	*Southeast Region* 909 SE 1st Ave	Miami	FL	33131-3051
713 953-6843	*Southwest Region* 5850 San Felipe St Suite 500	Houston	TX	77057-8003
202 566-2103	**Domestic Finance Office** 1500 Pennsylvania Ave NW Rm 2326	Washington	DC	20220-0001
912 267-2100	**Federal Law Enforcement Training Center** Hwy 303	Brunswick	GA	31524-0001
202 566-2789	**Freedom of Information Office** 1500 Pennsylvania Ave NW Rm 1054	Washington	DC	20220-0000
202 623-1000	**Inter-American Development Bank** 1300 New York Ave NW	Washington	DC	20577-0001
202 566-4743	**Internal Revenue Service** 1111 Constitution Ave NW	Washington	DC	20224-0001
513 684-3613	*Central Region* 550 Main St Rm 7112	Cincinnati	OH	45202-3212
215 597-2040	*Mid-Atlantic Region* 841 Chestnut St	Philadelphia	PA	19107-4414
312 886-5600	*Midwest Region* 1 N Wacker Dr	Chicago	IL	60606-3303
212 264-7061	*North Atlantic Region* 90 Church St Rm 1128	New York	NY	10007-2919
404 522-0050	*Southeast Region* 401 W Peachtree St	Atlanta	GA	30365-0000
214 308-7000	*Southwest Region* 4050 Alpha Rd	Dallas	TX	75244-4203
415 556-3009	*Western Region* 1650 Mission St	San Francisco	CA	94103-0000
202 233-1580	*Corporation Statistics* 1201 East St NW Rm 406	Washington	DC	20224-0001
313 226-3562	*Detroit Computing Center* 1300 John C Lodge Dr	Detroit	MI	48226-2414
202 233-1658	*Individual Statistics Branch* 500 N Capitol St NW 5th Fl	Washington	DC	20001-0000
304 267-2911	*National Computer Center* Rt 9 & Needy Rd	Martinsburg	WV	25401-9809
202 233-1741	*Statistics & Income Div* 500 N Capitol St NW 5th Fl	Washington	DC	20224-0001
202 566-2269	**International Affairs** 1500 Pennsylvania Ave NW Rm 3430	Washington	DC	20220-0001
202 566-2773	*Foreign Exchange* 1500 Pennsylvania Ave NW Rm 5037	Washington	DC	20220-0001
202 566-5628	*International Banking & Portfolio Investment* 1500 Pennsylvania Ave NW Rm 5323	Washington	DC	20220-0001
202 566-5081	*International Monetary Policy* 1500 Pennsylvania Ave NW Rm 5050	Washington	DC	20220-0001
202 623-7000	**International Monetary Fund (IMF)** 700 19th St NW	Washington	DC	20431-0001

Federal Government–Executive Branch

202 566-2748	**International Trade & Investment Policy** 1500 Pennsylvania Ave NW Rm 3208	Washington	DC	20220-0001
202 566-4743	**IRS** 1111 Constitution Ave NW	Washington	DC	20224-0001
202 566-7901	**Office of the Inspector General** 1500 Pennsylvania Ave NW Rm 2412	Washington	DC	20220-0001
202 566-2586	**Procurement Information** 1500 Pennsylvania Ave NW Rm 6101	Washington	DC	20220-0001
202 566-2041	**Public Affairs** 1500 Pennsylvania Ave NW Rm 2315	Washington	DC	20220-0001
202 634-5377	**Savings Bond Div** 1111 20th St NW Rm 305	Washington	DC	20226-0001
202 535-5708	**Secret Service** 1800 G St NW Rm 805	Washington	DC	20223-0001
202 566-5374	**Tax Analysis** 1500 Pennsylvania Ave NW Rm 4217	Washington	DC	20220-0001
202 566-2843	**Treasurer** 1500 Pennsylvania Ave NW Rm 2124	Washington	DC	20220-0001
202 376-0560	**US Mint** 633 3rd St NW Rm 715	Washington	DC	20220-0001

DEPARTMENT OF VETERANS AFFAIRS

202 233-4010	**Department of Veterans Affairs** 810 Vermont Ave NW	Washington	DC	20420-0001
202 233-3775	**Secretary of Veterans Affairs** 810 Vermont Ave NW Rm 1000S	Washington	DC	20420-0001
202 233-5515	**Deputy Secretary** 810 Vermont Ave NW Rm 1001	Washington	DC	20420-0001
202 233-5394	**Fraud Hotline**	Washington	DC	20420-0001
202 233-5394	**Office of the Inspector General Hotline** 810 Vermont Ave NW	Washington	DC	20420-0001
202 233-3808	**Procurement** 810 Vermont Ave NW Rm 760	Washington	DC	20420-0001
202 233-2817	**Public Affairs** 810 Vermont Ave NW Rm 900	Washington	DC	20420-0001
202 233-2596	**Veteran's Health Service & Research Administration** 810 Vermont Ave NW Rm 800	Washington	DC	20420-0001
313 930-5950	*Central Region* PO Box 1407	Ann Arbor	MI	48106-0000
202 233-2409	*Eastern Region* 9600 N Point Rd	Fort Howard	MD	21052-0000
817 885-7900	*Southern Region* 1901 N Hwy 360 Suite 350	Grand Prairie	TX	75050-0000
415 744-7506	*Western Region* 211 Main St Suite 1800	San Francisco	CA	94105-0000

Federal Government–Legislative Branch

Selected offices with responsibility to the Congress are listed alphabetically following the entries for the Senate and the House of Representatives.

202 224-3121	**US Senate** Capitol Bldg	Washington	DC	20510-0001
202 224-3121	**US House of Representatives** Capitol Bldg	Washington	DC	20515-0001
202 226-2621	**Congressional Budget Office** 2nd & D Sts SW	Washington	DC	20515-0001
202 479-0700	**Copyright Office** 101 Independence Ave SE	Washington	DC	20559-0001
202 653-5175	**Copyright Royalty Tribunal** 1111 20th St NW Suite 450	Washington	DC	20036-3477
202 275-5067	**General Accounting Office** 441 G St NW	Washington	DC	20548-0001
202 272-5557	*Fraud Hotline* 600 E St NW Rm 1000	Washington	DC	20548-0001
202 275-2091	**Government Printing Office** 710 N Capitol St NW	Washington	DC	20042-0001
205 731-1056	*Birmingham Bookstore* 2021 3rd Ave N	Birmingham	AL	35203-3301
617 565-6680	*Boston Bookstore* 10 Causeway St Rm 179	Boston	MA	02222-0000
312 353-5133	*Chicago Bookstore* 219 S Dearborn St Rm 1365	Chicago	IL	60604-1705
216 522-4922	*Cleveland Bookstore* 1240 E 9th St Rm 1653	Cleveland	OH	44199-2002
614 469-6956	*Columbus Bookstore* 200 N High St	Columbus	OH	43215-2493
214 767-0076	*Dallas Bookstore* 1100 Commerce St Rm 1C46	Dallas	TX	75242-1001
303 844-3964	*Denver Bookstore* 1961 Stout St	Denver	CO	80294-0101
313 226-7816	*Detroit Bookstore* 477 Michigan Ave Rm 160	Detroit	MI	48226-2518
713 653-3100	*Houston Bookstore* 801 Travis Suite 120	Houston	TX	77002-5727
904 791-3801	*Jacksonville Bookstore* PO Box 35089	Jacksonville	FL	32202-0089
816 765-2256	*Kansas City Bookstore* 5600 E Bannister Rd 120 Bannister Mall	Kansas City	MO	64137-0000
301 953-7974	*Laurel Bookstore* 8660 Cherry Ln	Laurel	MD	20707-4989
213 239-9844	*Los Angeles Bookstore* 505 S Flower St Level C	Los Angeles	CA	90071-0000
414 297-1304	*Milwaukee Bookstore* 517 E Wisconsin Ave Rm 190	Milwaukee	WI	53202-4504
212 264-3825	*New York Bookstore* 26 Federal Plaza Rm 110	New York	NY	10278-0022
215 597-0677	*Philadelphia Bookstore* 100 N 17th St 1st Fl	Philadelphia	PA	19103-2737
412 644-2721	*Pittsburgh Bookstore* 1000 Liberty Ave Rm 118	Pittsburgh	PA	15222-4004
719 544-3142	*Pueblo Bookstore* 720 N Main St	Pueblo	CO	81003-3020
415 556-0643	*San Francisco Bookstore* 450 Golden Gate Ave	San Francisco	CA	94102-3400
206 442-4270	*Seattle Bookstore* 915 2nd Ave Rm 194	Seattle	WA	98174-1009
202 228-6150	**Office of Technology Assessment** 600 Pennsylvania Ave SE	Washington	DC	20003-4316

US SENATORS AND REPRESENTATIVES

Members of the 102nd Congress are listed alphabetically by state with Senators listed first.

Alabama

202 224-4124	**Heflin Howell (D)** 728 Hart Bldg	Washington	DC	20510-0001
202 224-5744	**Shelby Richard (D)** 313 Hart Bldg	Washington	DC	20510-0001
202 225-4876	**Bevill Tom (D)** 2302 Rayburn Bldg	Washington	DC	20515-0001
202 225-3261	**Browder Glenn (D)** 1221 Longworth Bldg	Washington	DC	20515-0000
202 225-4931	**Callahan Sonny (R)** 1330 Longworth Bldg	Washington	DC	20515-0001
202 225-4801	**Cramer Bud (D)** 1431 Longworth Bldg	Washington	DC	20515-0001
202 225-2901	**Dickinson William L (R)** 2406 Rayburn Bldg	Washington	DC	20515-0001
202 225-4921	**Erdreich Ben (D)** 439 Cannon Bldg	Washington	DC	20515-0001
202 225-2665	**Harris Claude (D)** 1009 Longworth Bldg	Washington	DC	20515-0001

Alaska

202 224-6665	**Murkowski Frank H (R)** 709 Hart Bldg	Washington	DC	20510-0001
202 224-3004	**Stevens Ted (R)** 522 Hart Bldg	Washington	DC	20510-0001
202 225-5765	**Young Don (R)** 2331 Rayburn Bldg	Washington	DC	20515-0001

American Samoa

202 225-8577	**Faleomavaega Eni (D)** 413 Cannon Bldg	Washington	DC	20515-0001

Arizona

202 224-4521	**DeConcini Dennis (D)** 328 Hart Bldg	Washington	DC	20510-0001
202 224-2235	**McCain John (R)** 111 Russell Bldg	Washington	DC	20510-0001
202 225-2542	**Kolbe Jim (R)** 410 Cannon Bldg	Washington	DC	20515-0001
202 225-3361	**Kyl Jon L (R)** 336 Cannon Bldg	Washington	DC	20515-0001
202 225-2635	**Rhodes John J III (R)** 326 Cannon Bldg	Washington	DC	20515-0001
202 225-4576	**Stump Bob (R)** 211 Cannon Bldg	Washington	DC	20515-0001
202 225-4065	**Udall Morris K (D)** 235 Cannon Bldg	Washington	DC	20515-0001

Arkansas

202 224-4843	**Bumpers Dale (D)** 229 Dirksen Bldg	Washington	DC	20510-0001
202 224-2353	**Pryor David (D)** 267 Russell Bldg	Washington	DC	20510-0001
202 225-4076	**Alexander Bill (D)** 233 Cannon Bldg	Washington	DC	20515-0001
202 225-3772	**Anthony Beryl Jr (D)** 1212 Longworth Bldg	Washington	DC	20515-0001
202 225-4301	**Hammerschmidt John Paul (R)** 2110 Rayburn Bldg	Washington	DC	20515-0000
202 225-2506	**Thornton Ray (D)** 1705 Longworth Bldg	Washington	DC	20515-0001

California

202 224-3553	**Cranston Alan (D)** 112 Hart Bldg	Washington	DC	20510-0001
202 224-3841	**Wilson Pete (R)** 720 Hart Bldg	Washington	DC	20510-0001
202 225-6676	**Anderson Glenn M (D)** 2329 Rayburn Bldg	Washington	DC	20515-0001
202 225-5911	**Beilenson Anthony C (D)** 1025 Longworth Bldg	Washington	DC	20515-0001
202 225-4695	**Berman Howard L (D)** 137 Cannon Bldg	Washington	DC	20515-0001
202 225-5161	**Boxer Barbara (D)** 307 Cannon Bldg	Washington	DC	20515-0001
202 225-6161	**Brown George E (D)** 2188 Rayburn Bldg	Washington	DC	20515-0001
202 225-5411	**Campbell Tom (R)** 313 Cannon Bldg	Washington	DC	20515-0001
202 225-6131	**Condit Gary (D)** 1529 Longworth Bldg	Washington	DC	20515-0001
202 225-5611	**Cox Christopher (R)** 412 Cannon Bldg	Washington	DC	20515-0001
202 225-5452	**Cunningham Randy (R)** 1017 Longworth Bldg	Washington	DC	20515-0001
202 225-4111	**Dannemeyer William E (R)** 2351 Rayburn Bldg	Washington	DC	20515-0001
202 225-2661	**Dellums Ronald V (D)** 2136 Rayburn Bldg	Washington	DC	20515-0001
202 225-7084	**Dixon Julian C (D)** 2400 Rayburn Bldg	Washington	DC	20515-0001
202 225-3341	**Dooley Calvin (D)** 1022 Longworth Bldg	Washington	DC	20515-0001
202 225-2511	**Doolittle John T (R)** 1223 Longworth Bldg	Washington	DC	20515-0001
202 225-2965	**Dornan Robert K (R)** 301 Cannon Bldg	Washington	DC	20515-0001
202 225-2305	**Dreier David (R)** 411 Cannon Bldg	Washington	DC	20515-0001
202 225-5425	**Dymally Mervyn M (D)** 1717 Longworth Bldg	Washington	DC	20515-0001
202 225-3072	**Edwards Don (D)** 2307 Rayburn Bldg	Washington	DC	20515-0001
302 225-5716	**Fazio Vic (D)** 2113 Rayburn Bldg	Washington	DC	20515-0001
202 225-5811	**Gallegly Elton (R)** 107 Cannon Bldg	Washington	DC	20515-0000
202 225-3076	**Herger Wally (R)** 1108 Longworth Bldg	Washington	DC	20515-0000
202 225-5672	**Hunter Duncan (R)** 133 Cannon Bldg	Washington	DC	20515-0000
202 225-3601	**Lagomarsino Robert J (R)** 2332 Rayburn Bldg	Washington	DC	20515-0001
202 225-3531	**Lantos Tom (D)** 1526 Longworth Bldg	Washington	DC	20515-0001
202 225-4540	**Lehman Richard H (D)** 1319 Longworth Bldg	Washington	DC	20515-0001
202 225-6451	**Levine Mel (D)** 2443 Rayburn Bldg	Washington	DC	20515-0001
202 225-5861	**Lewis Jerry (R)** 2312 Rayburn Bldg	Washington	DC	20515-0001
202 225-3201	**Lowery Bill (R)** 2433 Rayburn Bldg	Washington	DC	20515-0001
202 225-5464	**Martinez Matthew G (D)** 2446 Rayburn Bldg	Washington	DC	20515-0001
202 225-7163	**Matsui Robert T (D)** 2353 Rayburn Bldg	Washington	DC	20515-0001
202 225-5330	**McCandless Alfred A (R)** 2422 Rayburn Bldg	Washington	DC	20515-0001
202 225-2095	**Miller George (D)** 2228 Rayburn Bldg	Washington	DC	20515-0001
202 225-2631	**Mineta Norman Y (D)** 2350 Rayburn Bldg	Washington	DC	20515-0001
202 225-4176	**Moorhead Carlos J (R)** 2346 Rayburn Bldg	Washington	DC	20515-0001
202 225-3906	**Packard Ron (R)** 434 Cannon Bldg	Washington	DC	20515-0001
202 225-2861	**Panetta Leon E (D)** 339 Cannon Bldg	Washington	DC	20515-0001
202 225-4965	**Pelosi Nancy (D)** 109 Cannon Bldg	Washington	DC	20515-0001
202 225-3311	**Riggs Frank (R)** 1517 Longworth Bldg	Washington	DC	20515-0001
202 225-2415	**Rohrabacher Dana (R)** 1039 Longworth Bldg	Washington	DC	20515-0001
202 225-6235	**Roybal Edward R (D)** 2211 Rayburn Bldg	Washington	DC	20515-0001
202 225-5065	**Stark Fortney H (D)** 239 Cannon Bldg	Washington	DC	20515-0001
202 225-2915	**Thomas William M (R)** 2402 Rayburn Bldg	Washington	DC	20515-0001
202 225-5256	**Torres Esteban Edward (D)** 1740 Longworth Bldg	Washington	DC	20515-0001
202 225-2201	**Waters Maxine (D)** 1207 Longworth Bldg	Washington	DC	20515-0001
202 225-3976	**Waxman Henry A (D)** 2418 Rayburn Bldg	Washington	DC	20515-0001

Colorado

202 224-5941	**Brown Hank (R)** 902-B Hart Bldg	Washington	DC	20510-0001
202 224-5852	**Wirth Timothy (D)** 380 Russell Bldg	Washington	DC	20510-0001
202 225-4676	**Allard Wayne (R)** 513 Cannon Bldg	Washington	DC	20515-0001
202 225-4761	**Campbell Ben Nighthorse (D)** 1530 Longworth Bldg	Washington	DC	20515-0001
202 225-4422	**Hefley Joel (R)** 222 Cannon Bldg	Washington	DC	20515-0001
202 225-7882	**Schaefer Dan (R)** 1007 Longworth Bldg	Washington	DC	20515-0001
202 225-4431	**Schroeder Patricia (D)** 2208 Rayburn Bldg	Washington	DC	20515-0001
202 225-2161	**Skaggs David E (D)** 1507 Longworth Bldg	Washington	DC	20515-0001

Connecticut

202 224-2823	**Dodd Christopher J (D)** 444 Russell Bldg	Washington	DC	20510-0001
202 224-4041	**Lieberman Joseph (D)** 502 Hart Bldg	Washington	DC	20510-0001
202 225-3661	**DeLauro Rosa L (D)** 327 Cannon Bldg	Washington	DC	20515-0001
202 225-3822	**Franks Gary A (R)** 1609 Longworth Bldg	Washington	DC	20515-0001
202 225-2076	**Gejdenson Sam (D)** 2416 Rayburn Bldg	Washington	DC	20515-0001
202 225-4476	**Johnson Nancy L (R)** 227 Cannon Bldg	Washington	DC	20515-0001
202 225-2265	**Kennelly Barbara B (D)** 204 Cannon Bldg	Washington	DC	20515-0001
202 225-5541	**Shays Christopher (R)** 1531 Longworth Bldg	Washington	DC	20515-0001

Delaware

202 224-5042	**Biden Joseph R Jr (D)** 221 Russell Bldg	Washington	DC	20510-0001
202 224-2441	**Roth William V Jr (R)** 104 Hart Bldg	Washington	DC	20510-0001
202 225-4165	**Carper Thomas R (D)** 131 Cannon Bldg	Washington	DC	20515-0001

District of Columbia

202 225-8050	**Norton Eleanor Holmes (D)** 1631 Longworth Bldg	Washington	DC	20515-0001

Florida

202 224-3041	**Graham Bob (D)** 241 Dirksen Bldg	Washington	DC	20510-0001
202 224-5274	**Mack Connie (R)** 517 Hart Bldg	Washington	DC	20510-0001
202 225-3671	**Bacchus Jim (D)** 431 Cannon Bldg	Washington	DC	20515-0001
202 225-2501	**Bennett Charles E (D)** 2107 Rayburn Bldg	Washington	DC	20515-0001
202 225-5755	**Bilirakis Michael (R)** 2432 Rayburn Bldg	Washington	DC	20515-0001
202 225-4506	**Fascell Dante B (D)** 2354 Rayburn Bldg	Washington	DC	20515-0001
202 225-3376	**Gibbons Sam (D)** 2204 Rayburn Bldg	Washington	DC	20515-0001
202 225-2536	**Goss Porter J (R)** 224 Cannon Bldg	Washington	DC	20515-0001
202 225-4136	**Hutto Earl (D)** 2435 Rayburn Bldg	Washington	DC	20515-0001
202 225-5015	**Ireland Andy (R)** 2466 Rayburn Bldg	Washington	DC	20515-0001
202 225-4035	**James Craig T (R)** 1408 Longworth Bldg	Washington	DC	20515-0001
202 225-3001	**Johnston Harry A (D)** 1028 Longworth Bldg	Washington	DC	20515-0001
202 225-4211	**Lehman William (D)** 2347 Rayburn Bldg	Washington	DC	20515-0001
202 225-5792	**Lewis Tom (R)** 1216 Longworth Bldg	Washington	DC	20515-0001
202 225-2176	**McCollum Bill (R)** 2453 Rayburn Bldg	Washington	DC	20515-0001
202 225-5235	**Peterson Pete (D)** 1415 Longworth Bldg	Washington	DC	20515-0001
202 225-3931	**Ros-Lehtinen Ileana (R)** 416 Cannon Bldg	Washington	DC	20515-0001
202 225-3026	**Shaw E Clay Jr (R)** 2338 Rayburn Bldg	Washington	DC	20515-0001
202 225-7931	**Smith Lawrence J (D)** 113 Cannon Bldg	Washington	DC	20515-0001
202 225-5744	**Stearns Cliff (R)** 1123 Longworth Bldg	Washington	DC	20515-0001
202 225-5961	**Young CW (R)** 2407 Rayburn Bldg	Washington	DC	20515-0001

Georgia

202 224-3643	**Fowler Wyche Jr (D)**	204 Russell Bldg	Washington DC	20510-0001
202 224-3521	**Nunn Sam (D)**	303 Dirksen Bldg	Washington DC	20510-0001
202 225-4101	**Barnard Doug Jr (D)**	2227 Rayburn Bldg	Washington DC	20515-0001
202 225-2931	**Darden George (D)**	228 Cannon Bldg	Washington DC	20515-0001
202 225-4501	**Gingrich Newt (R)**	2438 Rayburn Bldg	Washington DC	20515-0001
202 225-3631	**Hatcher Charles (D)**	2434 Rayburn Bldg	Washington DC	20515-0001
202 225-5211	**Jenkins Ed (D)**	2427 Rayburn Bldg	Washington DC	20515-0001
202 225-4272	**Jones Ben (D)**	514 Cannon Bldg	Washington DC	20515-0001
202 225-3801	**Lewis John (D)**	329 Cannon Bldg	Washington DC	20515-0001
202 225-5901	**Ray Richard (D)**	225 Cannon Bldg	Washington DC	20515-0001
202 225-6531	**Rowland J Roy (D)**	423 Cannon Bldg	Washington DC	20515-0001
202 225-5831	**Thomas Robert Lindsay (D)**	240 Cannon Bldg	Washington DC	20515-0001

Guam

202 225-1188	**Blaz Ben (R)**	1130 Longworth Bldg	Washington DC	20515-0001

Hawaii

202 224-6361	**Akaka Daniel K (D)**	109 Hart Bldg	Washington DC	20510-0001
202 224-3934	**Inouye Daniel K (D)**	722 Hart Bldg	Washington DC	20510-0001
202 225-2726	**Abercrombie Neil (D)**	1440 Longworth Bldg	Washington DC	20515-0001
202 225-4906	**Mink Patsy (D)**	2135 Rayburn Bldg	Washington DC	20515-0001

Idaho

202 224-2752	**Craig Larry E (R)**	708 Hart Bldg	Washington DC	20510-0001
202 224-6142	**Symms Steven D (R)**	509 Hart Bldg	Washington DC	20510-0001
202 225-6611	**LaRocco Larry (D)**	1117 Longworth Bldg	Washington DC	20515-0001
202 225-5531	**Stallings Richard H (D)**	1122 Longworth Bldg	Washington DC	20515-0001

Illinois

202 224-2854	**Dixon Alan J (D)**	331 Hart Bldg	Washington DC	20510-0001
202 224-2152	**Simon Paul (D)**	462 Dirksen Bldg	Washington DC	20510-0001
202 225-6661	**Annunzio Frank (D)**	2303 Rayburn Bldg	Washington DC	20515-0001
202 225-5001	**Bruce Terry L (D)**	419 Cannon Bldg	Washington DC	20515-0001
202 225-5006	**Collins Cardiss (D)**	2264 Rayburn Bldg	Washington DC	20515-0001
202 225-5661	**Costello Jerry (D)**	119 Cannon Bldg	Washington DC	20515-0001
202 225-5676	**Cox John W Jr (D)**	501 Cannon Bldg	Washington DC	20515-0001
202 225-3711	**Crane Philip M (R)**	1035 Longworth Bldg	Washington DC	20515-0001
202 225-5271	**Durbin Richard J (D)**	129 Cannon Bldg	Washington DC	20515-0001
202 225-5905	**Evans Lane (D)**	1121 Longworth Bldg	Washington DC	20515-0001
202 225-3515	**Fawell Harris W (R)**	435 Cannon Bldg	Washington DC	20515-0001
202 225-2976	**Hastert J Dennis (R)**	515 Cannon Bldg	Washington DC	20515-0001
202 225-4372	**Hayes Charles A (D)**	1131 Longworth Bldg	Washington DC	20515-0001
202 225-4561	**Hyde Henry J (R)**	2262 Rayburn Bldg	Washington DC	20515-0001
202 225-5701	**Lipinski William O (D)**	1501 Longworth Bldg	Washington DC	20515-0001
202 225-2371	**Madigan Edward R (R)**	2109 Rayburn Bldg	Washington DC	20515-0001
202 225-6201	**Michel Robert H (R)**	2112 Rayburn Bldg	Washington DC	20515-0001
202 225-4835	**Porter John Edward (R)**	1026 Longworth Bldg	Washington DC	20515-0001
202 225-5201	**Poshard Glenn (D)**	314 Cannon Bldg	Washington DC	20515-0001
202 225-4061	**Rostenkowski Dan (D)**	2111 Rayburn Bldg	Washington DC	20515-0001
202 225-5736	**Russo Marty (D)**	2233 Rayburn Bldg	Washington DC	20515-0001
202 225-3635	**Sangmeister George E (D)**	1032 Longworth Bldg	Washington DC	20515-0001
202 225-0773	**Savage Gus (D)**	2419 Rayburn Bldg	Washington DC	20515-0001
202 225-2111	**Yates Sidney R (D)**	2234 Rayburn Bldg	Washington DC	20515-0001

Indiana

202 224-5623	**Coats Dan (R)**	407 Russell Bldg	Washington DC	20510-1403
202 224-4814	**Lugar Richard G (R)**	306 Hart Bldg	Washington DC	20510-0001
202 225-2276	**Burton Dan (R)**	120 Cannon Bldg	Washington DC	20515-0001
202 225-5315	**Hamilton Lee H (D)**	2187 Rayburn Bldg	Washington DC	20515-0001
202 225-4011	**Jacobs Andrew Jr (D)**	2313 Rayburn Bldg	Washington DC	20515-0001
202 225-5037	**Jontz James (D)**	1317 Longworth Bldg	Washington DC	20515-0001
202 225-4436	**Long Jill L (D)**	1513 Longworth Bldg	Washington DC	20515-0001
202 225-4636	**McCloskey Frank (D)**	127 Cannon Bldg	Washington DC	20515-0000
202 225-5805	**Myers John T (R)**	2372 Rayburn Bldg	Washington DC	20515-0001
202 225-3915	**Roemer Timothy J (D)**	415 Cannon Bldg	Washington DC	20515-0001
202 225-3021	**Sharp Philip R (D)**	2217 Rayburn Bldg	Washington DC	20515-0001
202 225-2461	**Visclosky Peter J (D)**	330 Cannon Bldg	Washington DC	20515-0001

Iowa

202 224-3744	**Grassley Charles E (R)**	135 Hart Bldg	Washington DC	20510-0001
202 224-3254	**Harkin Tom (D)**	316 Hart Bldg	Washington DC	20510-0001
202 225-5476	**Grandy Fred (R)**	418 Cannon Bldg	Washington DC	20515-0001
202 225-6576	**Leach Jim (R)**	1514 Longworth Bldg	Washington DC	20515-0001
202 225-3806	**Lightfoot Jim (R)**	1222 Longworth Bldg	Washington DC	20515-0001
202 225-3301	**Nagle David R (D)**	214 Cannon Bldg	Washington DC	20515-0001
202 225-2911	**Nussle Jim (R)**	507 Cannon Bldg	Washington DC	20515-0001
202 225-4426	**Smith Neal (D)**	2373 Rayburn Bldg	Washington DC	20515-0001

Kansas

202 224-6521	**Dole Robert (R)**	141 Hart Bldg	Washington DC	20510-0001
202 224-4774	**Kassebaum Nancy Landon (R)**	302 Russell Bldg	Washington DC	20510-0001
202 225-6216	**Glickman Dan (D)**	2311 Rayburn Bldg	Washington DC	20515-0001
202 225-2865	**Meyers Jan (R)**	1230 Longworth Bldg	Washington DC	20515-0001
202 225-3911	**Nichols Dick (R)**	1605 Longworth Bldg	Washington DC	20515-0001
202 225-2715	**Roberts Pat (R)**	1110 Longworth Bldg	Washington DC	20515-0001
202 225-6601	**Slattery Jim (D)**	1512 Longworth Bldg	Washington DC	20515-0001

Kentucky

202 224-4343	**Ford Wendell H (D)**	173-A Russell Bldg	Washington DC	20510-0001
202 224-2541	**McConnell Mitch (R)**	120 Russell Bldg	Washington DC	20510-0001
202 225-3465	**Bunning Jim (R)**	116 Cannon Bldg	Washington DC	20515-0001
202 225-4706	**Hopkins Larry J (R)**	2437 Rayburn Bldg	Washington DC	20515-0001
202 225-3115	**Hubbard Carroll Jr (D)**	2267 Rayburn Bldg	Washington DC	20515-0001
202 225-5401	**Mazzoli Romano L (D)**	2246 Rayburn Bldg	Washington DC	20515-0001
202 225-3501	**Natcher William H (D)**	2333 Rayburn Bldg	Washington DC	20515-0001
202 225-4935	**Perkins Carl C (D)**	1004 Longworth Bldg	Washington DC	20515-0001
202 225-4601	**Rogers Harold (R)**	343 Cannon Bldg	Washington DC	20515-0001

Louisiana

202 224-4623	**Breaux John B (D)**	516 Hart Bldg	Washington DC	20510-0001
202 224-5824	**Johnston J Bennett (D)**	136 Hart Bldg	Washington DC	20510-0001
202 225-3901	**Baker Richard H (R)**	404 Cannon Bldg	Washington DC	20515-0001
202 225-2031	**Hayes James A (D)**	503 Cannon Bldg	Washington DC	20515-0001
202 225-4926	**Holloway Clyde C (R)**	1206 Longworth Bldg	Washington DC	20515-0001
202 225-2376	**Huckaby Jerry (D)**	2182 Rayburn Bldg	Washington DC	20515-0001
202 225-6636	**Jefferson William J (D)**	506 Cannon Bldg	Washington DC	20515-0001
202 225-3015	**Livingston Bob (R)**	2368 Rayburn Bldg	Washington DC	20515-0001
202 225-2777	**McCrery Jim (R)**	429 Cannon Bldg	Washington DC	20515-0001
202 225-4031	**Tauzin Billy (D)**	2342 Rayburn Bldg	Washington DC	20515-0001

Maine

202 224-2523	**Cohen William S (R)**	322 Hart Bldg	Washington DC	20510-0001
202 224-5344	**Mitchell George J (D)**	176 Russell Bldg	Washington DC	20510-0001
202 225-6116	**Andrews Thomas H (D)**	1724 Longworth Bldg	Washington DC	20515-0001
202 225-6306	**Snowe Olympia J (R)**	2464 Rayburn Bldg	Washington DC	20515-0001

Maryland

202 224-4654	**Mikulski Barbara A (D)**	320 Hart Bldg	Washington DC	20510-0001
202 224-4524	**Sarbanes Paul S (D)**	309 Hart Bldg	Washington DC	20510-0001
202 225-3061	**Bentley Helen Delich (R)**	1610 Longworth Bldg	Washington DC	20515-0001
202 225-2721	**Byron Beverly B (D)**	2430 Rayburn Bldg	Washington DC	20515-0001
202 225-4016	**Cardin Benjamin L (D)**	117 Cannon Bldg	Washington DC	20515-0001
202 225-5311	**Gilchrest Wayne T (D)**	502 Cannon Bldg	Washington DC	20515-0001
202 225-4131	**Hoyer Steny H (D)**	1214 Longworth Bldg	Washington DC	20515-0001
202 225-8090	**McMillen C Thomas (D)**	420 Cannon Bldg	Washington DC	20515-0001
202 225-4741	**Mfume Kweisi (D)**	217 Cannon Bldg	Washington DC	20515-0001
202 225-5341	**Morella Constance A (R)**	1024 Longworth Bldg	Washington DC	20515-0001

Massachusetts

202 224-4543	**Kennedy Edward M (D)**	315 Russell Bldg	Washington DC	20510-0001
202 224-2742	**Kerry John F (D)**	421 Russell Bldg	Washington DC	20510-0001
202 225-3411	**Atkins Chester G (D)**	123 Cannon Bldg	Washington DC	20515-0001
202 225-5335	**Conte Silvio O (R)**	2300 Rayburn Bldg	Washington DC	20515-0001
202 225-3215	**Donnelly Brian J (D)**	2229 Rayburn Bldg	Washington DC	20515-0001
202 225-6101	**Early Joseph D (D)**	2349 Rayburn Bldg	Washington DC	20515-0001
202 225-5931	**Frank Barney (D)**	2404 Rayburn Bldg	Washington DC	20515-0001
202 225-5111	**Kennedy Joseph P II (D)**	1208 Longworth Bldg	Washington DC	20515-0001
202 225-2836	**Markey Edward J (D)**	2133 Rayburn Bldg	Washington DC	20515-0001
202 225-8020	**Mavroules Nicholas (D)**	2334 Rayburn Bldg	Washington DC	20515-0001
202 225-8273	**Moakley Joe (D)**	221 Cannon Bldg	Washington DC	20515-0001
202 225-5601	**Neal Richard E (D)**	437 Cannon Bldg	Washington DC	20515-0001
202 225-3111	**Studds Gerry E (D)**	237 Cannon Bldg	Washington DC	20515-0001

Michigan

202 224-6221	**Levin Carl (D)**	459 Russell Bldg	Washington DC	20510-0001
202 224-4822	**Riegle Donald W Jr (D)**	105 Dirksen Bldg	Washington DC	20510-0001
202 225-2106	**Bonior David E (D)**	2242 Rayburn Bldg	Washington DC	20515-0001
202 225-6135	**Broomfield William S (R)**	2306 Rayburn Bldg	Washington DC	20515-0001
202 225-3561	**Camp Dave (D)**	511 Cannon Bldg	Washington DC	20515-0001
202 225-4872	**Carr Bob (D)**	2439 Rayburn Bldg	Washington DC	20515-0001
202 225-2261	**Collins Barbara-Rose (D)**	1541 Longworth Bldg	Washington DC	20515-0001
202 225-5126	**Conyers John Jr (D)**	2426 Rayburn Bldg	Washington DC	20515-0001
202 225-4735	**Davis Robert W (R)**	2417 Rayburn Bldg	Washington DC	20515-0001
202 225-4071	**Dingell John D (D)**	2328 Rayburn Bldg	Washington DC	20515-0001
202 225-6261	**Ford William D (D)**	2371 Rayburn Bldg	Washington DC	20515-0001
202 225-3831	**Henry Paul B (R)**	215 Cannon Bldg	Washington DC	20515-0001
202 225-6276	**Hertel Dennis M (D)**	2442 Rayburn Bldg	Washington DC	20515-0001
202 225-3611	**Kildee Dale E (D)**	2239 Rayburn Bldg	Washington DC	20515-0001
202 225-4961	**Levin Sander M (D)**	323 Cannon Bldg	Washington DC	20515-0001
202 225-4401	**Pursell Carl D (R)**	1414 Longworth Bldg	Washington DC	20515-0001
202 225-2806	**Traxler Bob (D)**	2366 Rayburn Bldg	Washington DC	20515-0001
202 225-3761	**Upton Frederick S (R)**	1713 Longworth Bldg	Washington DC	20515-0001
202 225-3511	**Vander Jagt Guy (R)**	2409 Rayburn Bldg	Washington DC	20515-0001
202 225-5011	**Wolpe Howard (D)**	1535 Longworth Bldg	Washington DC	20515-0001

Minnesota

202 224-3244	**Durenberger Dave (R)**	154 Russell Bldg	Washington DC	20510-0001
202 224-5641	**Wellstone Paul David (D)**	123 Hart Bldg	Washington DC	20510-0001
202 225-6211	**Oberstar James L (D)**	2209 Rayburn Bldg	Washington DC	20515-0001
202 225-2472	**Penny Timothy J (D)**	436 Cannon Bldg	Washington DC	20515-0001
202 225-2165	**Peterson Collin C (D)**	1725 Longworth Bldg	Washington DC	20515-0001
202 225-2871	**Ramstad Jim (R)**	504 Cannon Bldg	Washington DC	20515-0001
202 225-4755	**Sabo Martin Olav (D)**	2201 Rayburn Bldg	Washington DC	20515-0001
202 225-2271	**Sikorski Gerry (D)**	403 Cannon Bldg	Washington DC	20515-0001
202 225-6631	**Vento Bruce F (D)**	2304 Rayburn Bldg	Washington DC	20515-0001
202 225-2331	**Weber Vin (R)**	106 Cannon Bldg	Washington DC	20515-0001

Mississippi

202 224-5054	**Cochran Thad (R)**	326 Russell Bldg	Washington DC	20510-0001
202 224-6253	**Lott Trent (R)**	487 Russell Bldg	Washington DC	20510-0001
202 225-5876	**Espy Mike (D)**	216 Cannon Bldg	Washington DC	20515-0001
202 225-5031	**Montgomery GV (D)**	2184 Rayburn Bldg	Washington DC	20515-0001
202 225-5865	**Parker Mike (D)**	1504 Longworth Bldg	Washington DC	20515-0001
202 225-5772	**Taylor Gene (D)**	1429 Longworth Bldg	Washington DC	20515-0001
202 225-4306	**Whitten Jamie L (D)**	2314 Rayburn Bldg	Washington DC	20515-0001

Missouri

202 224-5721	**Bond Christopher (R)**	293 Russell Bldg	Washington DC	20510-0001
202 224-6154	**Danforth John C (R)**	249 Russell Bldg	Washington DC	20510-0001
202 225-2406	**Clay William (D)**	2470 Rayburn Bldg	Washington DC	20515-0001
202 225-7041	**Coleman E Thomas (R)**	2468 Rayburn Bldg	Washington DC	20515-0001
202 225-4404	**Emerson Bill (R)**	438 Cannon Bldg	Washington DC	20515-0001
202 225-2671	**Gephardt Richard A (D)**	1432 Longworth Bldg	Washington DC	20515-0001
202 225-6536	**Hancock Melton D (R)**	318 Cannon Bldg	Washington DC	20515-0001
202 225-2561	**Horn Joan Kelly (D)**	1008 Longworth Bldg	Washington DC	20515-0001
202 225-2876	**Skelton Ike (D)**	2134 Rayburn Bldg	Washington DC	20515-0001
202 225-2956	**Volkmer Harold L (D)**	2411 Rayburn Bldg	Washington DC	20515-0001
202 225-4535	**Wheat Alan (D)**	1210 Longworth Bldg	Washington DC	20515-0001

Federal Government–Legislative Branch

Montana

202 224-2651 **Baucus Max (D)** 706 Hart Bldg .... Washington DC 20510-0001
202 224-2644 **Burns Conrad (R)** 183 Dirksen Bldg .... Washington DC 20510-0001

202 225-1555 **Marlenee Ron (R)** 2465 Rayburn Bldg .... Washington DC 20515-0001
202 225-3211 **Williams Pat (D)** 2457 Rayburn Bldg .... Washington DC 20515-0001

Nebraska

202 224-4224 **Exon J James (D)** 330 Hart Bldg .... Washington DC 20510-0001
202 224-6551 **Kerrey Bob (D)** 302 Hart Bldg .... Washington DC 20510-0001

202 225-6435 **Barrett Bill (R)** 1607 Longworth Bldg .... Washington DC 20515-0001
202 225-4806 **Bereuter Doug (R)** 2348 Rayburn Bldg .... Washington DC 20515-0001
202 225-4155 **Hoagland Peter (D)** 1709 Longworth Bldg .... Washington DC 20515-0001

Nevada

202 224-6244 **Bryan Richard H (D)** 364 Russell Bldg .... Washington DC 20510-0001
202 224-3542 **Reid Harry (D)** 324 Hart Bldg .... Washington DC 20510-0001

202 225-5965 **Bilbray James H (D)** 319 Cannon Bldg .... Washington DC 20515-0001
202 225-6155 **Vucanovich Barbara F (R)** 206 Cannon Bldg .... Washington DC 20515-0001

New Hampshire

202 224-3324 **Rudman Warren (R)** 530 Hart Bldg .... Washington DC 20510-0001
202 224-2841 **Smith Bob (R)** 825-A Hart Bldg .... Washington DC 20510-0001

202 225-5206 **Swett Dick (D)** 128 Cannon Bldg .... Washington DC 20515-0001
202 225-5456 **Zeliff Bill (R)** 512 Cannon Bldg .... Washington DC 20515-0001

New Jersey

202 224-3224 **Bradley Bill (D)** 731 Hart Bldg .... Washington DC 20510-0001
202 224-4744 **Lautenberg Frank R (D)** 717 Hart Bldg .... Washington DC 20510-0001

202 225-6501 **Andrews Robert E (D)** 1005 Longworth Bldg .... Washington DC 20515-0001
202 225-6301 **Dwyer Bernard J (D)** 2428 Rayburn Bldg .... Washington DC 20515-0001
202 225-5034 **Gallo Dean A (R)** 1318 Longworth Bldg .... Washington DC 20515-0001
202 225-2765 **Guarini Frank J (D)** 2458 Rayburn Bldg .... Washington DC 20515-0001
202 225-6572 **Hughes William J (D)** 341 Cannon Bldg .... Washington DC 20515-0001
202 225-4671 **Pallone Frank Jr (D)** 213 Cannon Bldg .... Washington DC 20515-0001
202 225-3436 **Payne Donald M (D)** 417 Cannon Bldg .... Washington DC 20515-0001
202 225-5361 **Rinaldo Matthew J (R)** 2469 Rayburn Bldg .... Washington DC 20515-0001
202 225-5751 **Roe Robert A (D)** 2243 Rayburn Bldg .... Washington DC 20515-0001
202 225-4465 **Roukema Marge (R)** 2244 Rayburn Bldg .... Washington DC 20515-0001
202 225-4765 **Saxton Jim (R)** 324 Cannon Bldg .... Washington DC 20515-0001
202 225-3765 **Smith Christopher H (R)** 2440 Rayburn Bldg .... Washington DC 20515-0001
202 225-5061 **Torricelli Robert G (D)** 317 Cannon Bldg .... Washington DC 20515-0001
202 225-5801 **Zimmer Dick (R)** 510 Cannon Bldg .... Washington DC 20515-0001

New Mexico

202 224-5521 **Bingaman Jeff (D)** 524 Hart Bldg .... Washington DC 20510-0001
202 224-6621 **Domenici Pete V (R)** 434 Dirksen Bldg .... Washington DC 20510-0001

202 225-6190 **Richardson Bill (D)** 332 Cannon Bldg .... Washington DC 20515-0001
202 225-6316 **Schiff Steven (R)** 1427 Longworth Bldg .... Washington DC 20515-0001
202 225-2365 **Skeen Joe (R)** 2447 Rayburn Bldg .... Washington DC 20515-0001

New York

202 224-6542 **D'Amato Alfonse M (R)** 520 Hart Bldg .... Washington DC 20510-0001
202 224-4451 **Moynihan Daniel Patrick (D)** 464 Russell Bldg .... Washington DC 20510-0001

202 225-2601 **Ackerman Gary L (D)** 238 Cannon Bldg .... Washington DC 20515-0001
202 225-3665 **Boehlert Sherwood L (R)** 1127 Longworth Bldg .... Washington DC 20515-0001
202 225-3335 **Downey Thomas J (D)** 2232 Rayburn Bldg .... Washington DC 20515-0001
202 225-2464 **Engel Eliot L (D)** 1213 Longworth Bldg .... Washington DC 20515-0001
202 225-5441 **Fish Hamilton Jr (R)** 2269 Rayburn Bldg .... Washington DC 20515-0001
202 225-3461 **Flake Floyd H (D)** 1034 Longworth Bldg .... Washington DC 20515-0001
202 225-3776 **Gilman Benjamin A (R)** 2185 Rayburn Bldg .... Washington DC 20515-0001
202 225-2436 **Green Bill (R)** 2301 Rayburn Bldg .... Washington DC 20515-0001
202 225-3826 **Hochbrueckner George J (D)** 124 Cannon Bldg .... Washington DC 20515-0001
202 225-4916 **Horton Frank (R)** 2108 Rayburn Bldg .... Washington DC 20515-0001
202 225-3161 **Houghton Amo (R)** 1217 Longworth Bldg .... Washington DC 20515-0001
202 225-3231 **LaFalce John J (D)** 2367 Rayburn Bldg .... Washington DC 20515-0001
202 225-7896 **Lent Norman (R)** 2408 Rayburn Bldg .... Washington DC 20515-0001
202 225-6506 **Lowey Nita M (D)** 1313 Longworth Bldg .... Washington DC 20515-0001
202 225-3965 **Manton Thomas J (D)** 331 Cannon Bldg .... Washington DC 20515-0001
202 225-4611 **Martin David (R)** 442 Cannon Bldg .... Washington DC 20515-0001
202 225-5516 **McGrath Raymond J (R)** 205 Cannon Bldg .... Washington DC 20515-0001
202 225-6335 **McHugh Matthew F (D)** 2335 Rayburn Bldg .... Washington DC 20515-0001
202 225-5076 **McNulty Michael R (D)** 414 Cannon Bldg .... Washington DC 20515-0001
202 225-3371 **Molinari Susan (R)** 315 Cannon Bldg .... Washington DC 20515-0001
202 225-5956 **Mrazek Robert J (D)** 306 Cannon Bldg .... Washington DC 20515-0001
202 225-3306 **Nowak Henry J (D)** 2240 Rayburn Bldg .... Washington DC 20515-0001
202 225-6231 **Owens Major R (D)** 114 Cannon Bldg .... Washington DC 20515-0001
202 225-5265 **Paxon Bill (R)** 1314 Longworth Bldg .... Washington DC 20515-0001
202 225-4365 **Rangel Charles B (D)** 2252 Rayburn Bldg .... Washington DC 20515-0001
202 225-5471 **Scheuer James H (D)** 2221 Rayburn Bldg .... Washington DC 20515-0001
202 225-6616 **Schumer Charles E (D)** 2412 Rayburn Bldg .... Washington DC 20515-0001
202 225-4361 **Serrano Jose E (D)** 1107 Longworth Bldg .... Washington DC 20515-0001
202 225-3615 **Slaughter Louise McIntosh (D)** 1424 Longworth Bldg .... Washington DC 20515-0001
202 225-2361 **Solarz Stephen J (D)** 1536 Longworth Bldg .... Washington DC 20515-0001
202 225-5614 **Solomon Gerald BH (R)** 2265 Rayburn Bldg .... Washington DC 20515-0001
202 225-5936 **Towns Edolphus (D)** 1726 Longworth Bldg .... Washington DC 20515-0001
202 225-3701 **Walsh James T (R)** 1238 Longworth Bldg .... Washington DC 20515-0001
202 225-5635 **Weiss Ted (D)** 2467 Rayburn Bldg .... Washington DC 20515-0001

North Carolina

202 224-6342 **Helms Jesse (R)** 403 Dirksen Bldg .... Washington DC 20510-0001
202 224-3154 **Sanford Terry (D)** 716 Hart Bldg .... Washington DC 20510-0001

202 225-2576 **Ballenger Cass (R)** 328 Cannon Bldg .... Washington DC 20515-0001
202 225-3065 **Coble Howard (R)** 430 Cannon Bldg .... Washington DC 20515-0001
202 225-3715 **Hefner WG (D)** 2161 Rayburn Bldg .... Washington DC 20515-0001
202 225-3101 **Jones Walter B (D)** 241 Cannon Bldg .... Washington DC 20515-0001
202 225-3415 **Lancaster H Martin (D)** 1417 Longworth Bldg .... Washington DC 20515-0001
202 225-1976 **McMillan J Alex (R)** 401 Cannon Bldg .... Washington DC 20515-0001
202 225-2071 **Neal Stephen L (D)** 2463 Rayburn Bldg .... Washington DC 20515-0001
202 225-1784 **Price David E (D)** 1406 Longworth Bldg .... Washington DC 20515-0001
202 225-2731 **Rose Charles (D)** 2230 Rayburn Bldg .... Washington DC 20515-0001

202 225-6401 **Taylor Charles H (R)** 516 Cannon Bldg .... Washington DC 20515-0001
202 225-4531 **Valentine Tim (D)** 1510 Longworth Bldg .... Washington DC 20515-0001

North Dakota

202 224-2551 **Burdick Quentin N (D)** 511 Hart Bldg .... Washington DC 20510-0001
202 224-2043 **Conrad Kent (D)** 361 Dirksen Bldg .... Washington DC 20510-0001

202 225-2611 **Dorgan Byron L (D)** 203 Cannon Bldg .... Washington DC 20515-0001

Ohio

202 224-3353 **Glenn John (D)** 503 Hart Bldg .... Washington DC 20510-0001
202 224-2315 **Metzenbaum Howard M (D)** 140 Russell Bldg .... Washington DC 20510-0001

202 225-6265 **Applegate Douglas (D)** 2183 Rayburn Bldg .... Washington DC 20515-0001
202 225-6205 **Boehner John A (R)** 1020 Longworth Bldg .... Washington DC 20515-0001
202 225-6331 **Eckart Dennis E (D)** 1111 Longworth Bldg .... Washington DC 20515-0001
202 225-5731 **Feighan Edward F (D)** 1124 Longworth Bldg .... Washington DC 20515-0001
202 225-6405 **Gillmor Paul E (R)** 1203 Longworth Bldg .... Washington DC 20515-0001
202 225-3164 **Gradison Willis D Jr (R)** 1125 Rayburn Bldg .... Washington DC 20515-0001
202 225-6465 **Hall Tony P (D)** 2162 Rayburn Bldg .... Washington DC 20515-0001
202 225-4324 **Hobson David L (R)** 1338 Longworth Bldg .... Washington DC 20515-0001
202 225-4146 **Kaptur Marcy (D)** 1228 Longworth Bldg .... Washington DC 20515-0001
202 225-5355 **Kasich John R (R)** 1133 Longworth Bldg .... Washington DC 20515-0001
202 225-2216 **Luken Charles (D)** 1632 Longworth Bldg .... Washington DC 20515-0001
202 225-5705 **McEwen Bob (R)** 2431 Rayburn Bldg .... Washington DC 20515-0001
202 225-5131 **Miller Clarence E (R)** 2308 Rayburn Bldg .... Washington DC 20515-0001
202 225-5871 **Oakar Mary Rose (D)** 2231 Rayburn Bldg .... Washington DC 20515-0001
202 225-2676 **Oxley Michael G (R)** 2448 Rayburn Bldg .... Washington DC 20515-0001
202 225-3401 **Pease Donald J (D)** 2410 Rayburn Bldg .... Washington DC 20515-0001
202 225-3876 **Regula Ralph (R)** 2207 Rayburn Bldg .... Washington DC 20515-0001
202 225-5231 **Sawyer Thomas C (D)** 1518 Longworth Bldg .... Washington DC 20515-0001
202 225-7032 **Stokes Louis (D)** 2365 Rayburn Bldg .... Washington DC 20515-0001
202 225-5261 **Traficant James A Jr (D)** 312 Cannon Bldg .... Washington DC 20515-0001
202 225-2015 **Wylie Chalmers P (R)** 2310 Rayburn Bldg .... Washington DC 20515-0001

Oklahoma

202 224-4721 **Boren David L (D)** 453 Russell Bldg .... Washington DC 20510-0001
202 224-5754 **Nickles Don (R)** 713 Hart Bldg .... Washington DC 20510-0001

202 225-4565 **Brewster Bill (D)** 1407 Longworth Bldg .... Washington DC 20515-0001
202 225-2132 **Edwards Mickey (R)** 2330 Rayburn Bldg .... Washington DC 20515-0001
202 225-5565 **English Glenn (D)** 2206 Rayburn Bldg .... Washington DC 20515-0001
202 225-2211 **Inhofe James M (R)** 408 Cannon Bldg .... Washington DC 20515-0001
202 225-6165 **McCurdy Dave (D)** 2344 Rayburn Bldg .... Washington DC 20515-0001
202 225-2701 **Synar Mike (D)** 2441 Rayburn Bldg .... Washington DC 20515-0001

Oregon

202 224-3753 **Hatfield Mark O (R)** 711 Hart Bldg .... Washington DC 20510-0001
202 224-5244 **Packwood Bob (R)** 259 Russell Bldg .... Washington DC 20510-0001

202 225-0855 **AuCoin Les (D)** 2159 Rayburn Bldg .... Washington DC 20515-0001
202 225-6416 **DeFazio Peter A (D)** 1233 Longworth Bldg .... Washington DC 20515-0001
202 225-5711 **Kopetski Mike (D)** 1520 Longworth Bldg .... Washington DC 20515-0001
202 225-6730 **Smith Robert F (R)** 118 Cannon Bldg .... Washington DC 20515-0001
202 225-4811 **Wyden Ron (D)** 2452 Rayburn Bldg .... Washington DC 20515-0001

Pennsylvania

202 224-6324 **Heinz John (R)** 277 Russell Bldg .... Washington DC 20510-0001
202 224-4254 **Specter Arlen (R)** 303 Hart Bldg .... Washington DC 20510-0001

202 225-8251 **Borski Robert A (D)** 407 Cannon Bldg .... Washington DC 20515-0001
202 225-5121 **Clinger William F Jr (R)** 2160 Rayburn Bldg .... Washington DC 20515-0001
202 225-6111 **Coughlin Lawrence (R)** 2309 Rayburn Bldg .... Washington DC 20515-0001
202 225-2301 **Coyne William J (D)** 2455 Rayburn Bldg .... Washington DC 20515-0001
202 225-4731 **Foglietta Thomas M (D)** 231 Cannon Bldg .... Washington DC 20515-0001
202 225-4631 **Gaydos Joseph M (D)** 2186 Rayburn Bldg .... Washington DC 20515-0001
202 225-4315 **Gekas George W (R)** 1519 Longworth Bldg .... Washington DC 20515-0001
202 225-5836 **Goodling William F (R)** 2263 Rayburn Bldg .... Washington DC 20515-0001
202 225-4001 **Gray William H III (D)** 2454 Rayburn Bldg .... Washington DC 20515-0001
202 225-6511 **Kanjorski Paul E (D)** 424 Cannon Bldg .... Washington DC 20515-0001
202 225-2565 **Kolter Joe (D)** 212 Cannon Bldg .... Washington DC 20515-0001
202 225-4276 **Kostmayer Peter H (D)** 2436 Rayburn Bldg .... Washington DC 20515-0001
202 225-3731 **McDade Joseph M (R)** 2370 Rayburn Bldg .... Washington DC 20515-0001
202 225-4665 **Murphy Austin J (D)** 2210 Rayburn Bldg .... Washington DC 20515-0001
202 225-2065 **Murtha John P (D)** 2423 Rayburn Bldg .... Washington DC 20515-0001
202 225-5406 **Ridge Thomas J (R)** 1714 Longworth Bldg .... Washington DC 20515-0001
202 225-6411 **Ritter Don (R)** 2202 Rayburn Bldg .... Washington DC 20515-0001
202 225-2135 **Santorum Rick (R)** 1708 Longworth Bldg .... Washington DC 20515-0001
202 225-5761 **Schulze Richard T (R)** 2369 Rayburn Bldg .... Washington DC 20515-0001
202 225-2431 **Shuster Bud (R)** 2268 Rayburn Bldg .... Washington DC 20515-0001
202 225-2411 **Walker Robert S (R)** 2445 Rayburn Bldg .... Washington DC 20515-0001
202 225-2011 **Weldon Curt (R)** 316 Cannon Bldg .... Washington DC 20515-0001
202 225-5546 **Yatron Gus (D)** 2205 Rayburn Bldg .... Washington DC 20515-0001

Puerto Rico

202 225-2615 **Fuster Jaime B (D)** 427 Cannon Bldg .... Washington DC 20515-0001

Rhode Island

202 224-2921 **Chafee John H (R)** 567 Dirksen Bldg .... Washington DC 20510-0001
202 224-4642 **Pell Claiborne (D)** 335 Russell Bldg .... Washington DC 20510-0001

202 225-4911 **Machtley Ronald K (R)** 132 Cannon Bldg .... Washington DC 20515-0001
202 225-2735 **Reed John F (D)** 1229 Longworth Bldg .... Washington DC 20515-0001

South Carolina

202 224-6121 **Hollings Ernest F (D)** 125 Russell Bldg .... Washington DC 20510-0001
202 224-5972 **Thurmond Strom (R)** 217 Russell Bldg .... Washington DC 20510-0001

202 225-5301 **Derrick Butler Jr (D)** 201 Cannon Bldg .... Washington DC 20515-0001
202 225-6030 **Patterson Elizabeth J (D)** 1641 Longworth Bldg .... Washington DC 20515-0001
202 225-3176 **Ravenel Arthur Jr (R)** 508 Cannon Bldg .... Washington DC 20515-0001
202 225-2452 **Spence Floyd (R)** 2405 Rayburn Bldg .... Washington DC 20515-0001
202 225-5501 **Spratt John M Jr (D)** 1533 Longworth Bldg .... Washington DC 20515-0001
202 225-3315 **Tallon Robin (D)** 432 Cannon Bldg .... Washington DC 20515-0001

South Dakota

202 224-2321 **Daschle Thomas A (D)** 317 Hart Bldg .... Washington DC 20510-0001

The text at the beginning of each category provides information on how government offices are listed. Refer to the front page of the section for a list of the categories included.

202 224-5842	**Pressler Larry (R)**	133 Hart Bldg	Washington	DC	20510-0001
202 225-2801	**Johnson Tim (D)**	428 Cannon Bldg	Washington	DC	20515-0001

Tennessee

202 224-4944	**Gore Albert Jr (D)**	393 Russell Bldg	Washington	DC	20510-0001
202 224-3344	**Sasser James (D)**	363 Russell Bldg	Washington	DC	20510-0001
202 225-4311	**Clement Bob (D)**	325 Cannon Bldg	Washington	DC	20515-0001
202 225-6831	**Cooper Jim (D)**	125 Cannon Bldg	Washington	DC	20515-0001
202 225-5435	**Duncan John J (R)**	115 Cannon Bldg	Washington	DC	20515-0001
202 225-3265	**Ford Harold E (D)**	2305 Rayburn Bldg	Washington	DC	20515-0001
202 225-4231	**Gordon Bart (D)**	103 Cannon Bldg	Washington	DC	20515-0001
202 225-3271	**Lloyd Marilyn (D)**	2266 Rayburn Bldg	Washington	DC	20515-0001
202 225-6356	**Quillen James H (R)**	102 Cannon Bldg	Washington	DC	20515-0001
202 225-2811	**Sundquist Don (R)**	230 Cannon Bldg	Washington	DC	20515-0001
202 225-4714	**Tanner John S (D)**	1232 Longworth Bldg	Washington	DC	20515-0001

Texas

202 224-5922	**Bentsen Lloyd (D)**	703 Hart Bldg	Washington	DC	20510-0001
202 224-2934	**Gramm Phil (R)**	370 Russell Bldg	Washington	DC	20510-0001
202 225-7508	**Andrews Michael A (D)**	303 Cannon Bldg	Washington	DC	20515-0001
202 225-2571	**Archer Bill (R)**	1236 Longworth Bldg	Washington	DC	20515-0001
202 225-7772	**Armey Richard K (R)**	130 Cannon Bldg	Washington	DC	20515-0001
202 225-4201	**Bartlett Steve (R)**	1113 Longworth Bldg	Washington	DC	20515-0001
202 225-2002	**Barton Joe (R)**	1225 Longworth Bldg	Washington	DC	20515-0001
202 225-6565	**Brooks Jack (D)**	2449 Rayburn Bldg	Washington	DC	20515-0001
202 225-2231	**Bryant John (D)**	208 Cannon Bldg	Washington	DC	20515-0001
202 225-4511	**Bustamante Albert G (D)**	1116 Longworth Bldg	Washington	DC	20515-0001
202 225-3035	**Chapman Jim (D)**	236 Cannon Bldg	Washington	DC	20515-0001
202 225-4831	**Coleman Ronald D (D)**	440 Cannon Bldg	Washington	DC	20515-0001
202 225-4005	**Combest Larry (R)**	1527 Longworth Bldg	Washington	DC	20515-0001
202 225-2531	**De la Garza E (D)**	1401 Longworth Bldg	Washington	DC	20515-0001
202 225-5951	**DeLay Tom (R)**	308 Cannon Bldg	Washington	DC	20515-0001
202 225-6105	**Edwards Chet (D)**	425 Cannon Bldg	Washington	DC	20515-0001
202 225-4901	**Fields Jack (R)**	108 Cannon Bldg	Washington	DC	20515-0001
202 225-3605	**Frost Martin (D)**	2459 Rayburn Bldg	Washington	DC	20515-0001
202 225-5071	**Geren Pete (D)**	1730 Longworth Bldg	Washington	DC	20515-0001
202 225-3236	**Gonzalez Henry B (D)**	2413 Rayburn Bldg	Washington	DC	20515-0001
202 225-6673	**Hall Ralph M (D)**	2236 Rayburn Bldg	Washington	DC	20515-0001
202 225-2831	**Laughlin Greg (D)**	218 Cannon Bldg	Washington	DC	20515-0001
202 225-7742	**Ortiz Solomon P (D)**	1524 Longworth Bldg	Washington	DC	20515-0001
202 225-4865	**Pickle JJ (D)**	242 Cannon Bldg	Washington	DC	20515-0001
202 225-3706	**Sarpalius Bill (D)**	126 Cannon Bldg	Washington	DC	20515-0001
202 225-4236	**Smith Lamar S (R)**	422 Cannon Bldg	Washington	DC	20515-0001
202 225-6605	**Stenholm Charles W (D)**	1226 Longworth Bldg	Washington	DC	20515-0001
202 225-3816	**Washington Craig (D)**	1711 Longworth Bldg	Washington	DC	20515-0001
202 225-2401	**Wilson Charles (D)**	2256 Rayburn Bldg	Washington	DC	20515-0001

Utah

202 224-5444	**Garn Jake (R)**	505 Dirksen Bldg	Washington	DC	20510-0001
202 224-5251	**Hatch Orrin G (R)**	135 Russell Bldg	Washington	DC	20510-0001
202 225-0453	**Hansen James V (R)**	2421 Rayburn Bldg	Washington	DC	20515-0001
202 225-7751	**Orton Bill (D)**	1723 Longworth Bldg	Washington	DC	20515-0001
202 225-3011	**Owens Wayne (D)**	1728 Longworth Bldg	Washington	DC	20515-0001

Vermont

202 224-5141	**Jeffords James M (R)**	530 Dirksen Bldg	Washington	DC	20510-0001
202 224-4242	**Leahy Patrick J (D)**	433 Russell Bldg	Washington	DC	20510-0001
202 225-4115	**Sanders Bernie (D)**	509 Cannon Bldg	Washington	DC	20515-0001

Virgin Islands

202 225-1790	**De Lugo Ron (D)**	2238 Rayburn Bldg	Washington	DC	20515-0001

Virginia

202 224-4024	**Robb Charles S (D)**	493 Russell Bldg	Washington	DC	20510-0001
202 224-2023	**Warner John W (R)**	225 Russell Bldg	Washington	DC	20510-0001
202 225-4261	**Bateman Herbert H (R)**	1030 Longworth Bldg	Washington	DC	20515-0001
202 225-2815	**Bliley Thomas J Jr (R)**	2241 Rayburn Bldg	Washington	DC	20515-0001
202 225-3861	**Boucher Rick (D)**	405 Cannon Bldg	Washington	DC	20515-0001
202 225-4376	**Moran James P Jr (D)**	1523 Longworth Bldg	Washington	DC	20515-0001
202 225-5431	**Olin Jim (D)**	1410 Longworth Bldg	Washington	DC	20515-0001
202 225-4711	**Payne Lewis F (D)**	1118 Longworth Bldg	Washington	DC	20515-0001
202 225-4215	**Pickett Owen B (D)**	1204 Longworth Bldg	Washington	DC	20515-0001
202 225-6365	**Sisisky Norman (D)**	426 Cannon Bldg	Washington	DC	20515-0001
202 225-6561	**Slaughter D French Jr (R)**	1404 Longworth Bldg	Washington	DC	20515-0001
202 225-5136	**Wolf Frank R (R)**	104 Cannon Bldg	Washington	DC	20515-0001

Washington

202 224-2621	**Adams Brock (D)**	513 Hart Bldg	Washington	DC	20510-0001
202 224-3441	**Gorton Slade (R)**	730 Hart Bldg	Washington	DC	20510-0001
202 225-7761	**Chandler Rod (R)**	223 Cannon Bldg	Washington	DC	20515-0001
202 225-5916	**Dicks Norman D (D)**	2429 Rayburn Bldg	Washington	DC	20515-0001
202 225-2006	**Foley Thomas S (D)**	1201 Longworth Bldg	Washington	DC	20515-0001
202 225-3106	**McDermott James A (D)**	1707 Longworth Bldg	Washington	DC	20515-0001
202 225-6311	**Miller John R (R)**	322 Cannon Bldg	Washington	DC	20515-0001
202 225-5816	**Morrison Sid (R)**	1434 Longworth Bldg	Washington	DC	20515-0001
202 225-2605	**Swift Al (D)**	1502 Longworth Bldg	Washington	DC	20515-0001
202 225-3536	**Unsoeld Jolene (D)**	1508 Longworth Bldg	Washington	DC	20515-0001

West Virginia

202 224-3954	**Byrd Robert C (D)**	311 Hart Bldg	Washington	DC	20510-0001
202 224-6472	**Rockefeller John D IV (D)**	724 Hart Bldg	Washington	DC	20510-0001
202 225-4172	**Mollohan Alan B (D)**	229 Cannon Bldg	Washington	DC	20515-0001
202 225-3452	**Rahall Nick Joe II (D)**	2104 Rayburn Bldg	Washington	DC	20515-0001
202 225-4331	**Staggers Harley O Jr (D)**	1323 Longworth Bldg	Washington	DC	20515-0001
202 225-2711	**Wise Robert E Jr (D)**	1421 Longworth Bldg	Washington	DC	20515-0001

Wisconsin

202 224-5323	**Kasten Robert W Jr (R)**	110 Hart Bldg	Washington	DC	20510-0001
202 224-5653	**Kohl Herbert H (D)**	702 Hart Bldg	Washington	DC	20510-0001
202 225-3031	**Aspin Les (D)**	2336 Rayburn Bldg	Washington	DC	20515-0001
202 225-5506	**Gunderson Steve (R)**	2235 Rayburn Bldg	Washington	DC	20515-0001
202 225-4572	**Kleczka Gerald D (D)**	226 Cannon Bldg	Washington	DC	20515-0001
202 225-2906	**Klug Scott L (R)**	1224 Longworth Bldg	Washington	DC	20515-0001
202 225-3571	**Moody Jim (D)**	1019 Longworth Bldg	Washington	DC	20515-0001
202 225-3365	**Obey David R (D)**	2462 Rayburn Bldg	Washington	DC	20515-0001
202 225-2476	**Petri Thomas E (R)**	2245 Rayburn Bldg	Washington	DC	20515-0001
202 225-5665	**Roth Toby (R)**	2352 Rayburn Bldg	Washington	DC	20515-0001
202 225-5101	**Sensenbrenner F James Jr (R)**	2444 Rayburn Bldg	Washington	DC	20515-0001

Wyoming

202 224-3424	**Simpson Alan K (R)**	261 Dirksen Bldg	Washington	DC	20510-0001
202 224-6441	**Wallop Malcolm (R)**	237 Russell Bldg	Washington	DC	20510-0001
202 225-2311	**Thomas Craig (R)**	1721 Longworth Bldg	Washington	DC	20515-0001

CONGRESSIONAL COMMITTEES

Selected Congressional Committees are listed alphabetically.

Senate Committees

202 224-2035	**Agriculture Nutrition & Forestry**	328-A Russell Bldg	Washington	DC	20510-0001
202 224-3471	**Appropriations**	Capitol Bldg Rm S-128	Washington	DC	20510-0001
202 224-3871	**Armed Services**	228 Russell Bldg	Washington	DC	20510-0001
202 224-7391	**Banking Housing & Urban Affairs**	534 Dirksen Bldg Suite 235	Washington	DC	20510-0001
202 224-0642	**Budget**	621 Dirksen Bldg	Washington	DC	20510-0001
202 224-5115	**Commerce Science & Transportation**	508 Dirksen Bldg	Washington	DC	20510-0001
202 224-4971	**Energy & Natural Resources**	364 Dirksen Bldg	Washington	DC	20510-0001
202 224-6176	**Environment & Public Works**	458 Dirksen Bldg	Washington	DC	20510-0001
202 224-4515	**Finance**	205 Dirksen Bldg	Washington	DC	20510-0001
202 224-4651	**Foreign Relations**	423 Dirksen Bldg	Washington	DC	20510-0001
202 224-4751	**Governmental Affairs**	340 Dirksen Bldg	Washington	DC	20510-0001
202 224-5225	**Judiciary**	224 Dirksen Bldg	Washington	DC	20510-0001
202 224-5375	**Labor & Human Resources**	428 Dirksen Bldg	Washington	DC	20510-0001
202 224-6352	**Rules & Administration**	305 Russell Bldg	Washington	DC	20510-0001
202 224-2981	**Select Committee on Ethics**	220 Hart Bldg	Washington	DC	20510-0001
202 224-2251	**Select Committee on Indian Affairs**	838 Hart Bldg	Washington	DC	20510-0001
202 224-1700	**Select Committee on Intelligence**	211 Hart Bldg	Washington	DC	20510-0001
202 224-5175	**Small Business**	428A Russell Bldg	Washington	DC	20510-0001
202 224-5364	**Special Committee on Aging**	SDG-31 Dirksen Bldg	Washington	DC	20510-0001
202 224-9126	**Veterans Affairs**	414 Russell Bldg	Washington	DC	20510-0001

House Committees

202 225-2171	**Agriculture**	1301 Longworth Bldg	Washington	DC	20515-0001
202 225-2771	**Appropriations**	Capitol Bldg Suite H-218	Washington	DC	20515-0001
202 225-4151	**Armed Services**	2120 Rayburn Bldg	Washington	DC	20515-0001
202 225-4247	**Banking Finance & Urban Affairs**	2129 Rayburn Bldg	Washington	DC	20515-0001
202 226-7200	**Budget**	House Annex 1 Rm 214	Washington	DC	20515-0001
202 225-4457	**District of Columbia**	1310 Longworth Bldg	Washington	DC	20515-0001
202 225-4527	**Education & Labor**	2181 Rayburn Bldg	Washington	DC	20515-0001
202 225-2927	**Energy & Commerce**	2125 Rayburn Bldg	Washington	DC	20515-0001
202 225-5021	**Foreign Affairs**	2170 Rayburn Bldg	Washington	DC	20515-0001
202 225-5051	**Government Operations**	2157 Rayburn Bldg	Washington	DC	20515-0001
202 225-2061	**House Administration**	Capitol Bldg Rm H-326	Washington	DC	20515-0001
202 225-2761	**Interior & Insular Affairs**	1324 Longworth Bldg	Washington	DC	20515-0001
202 225-3951	**Judiciary**	2138 Rayburn Bldg	Washington	DC	20515-0001
202 225-4047	**Merchant Marine & Fisheries**	1334 Longworth Bldg	Washington	DC	20515-0001
202 225-4121	**Permanent Select Committee on Intelligence**	H-405 US Capitol	Washington	DC	20515-0001
202 225-4054	**Post Office & Civil Service**	309 Cannon Bldg	Washington	DC	20515-0001
202 225-4472	**Public Works & Transportation**	2165 Rayburn Bldg	Washington	DC	20515-0001
202 225-9486	**Rules**	H-312 Capitol Bldg	Washington	DC	20515-0001
202 225-6371	**Science Space & Technology**	2321 Rayburn Bldg	Washington	DC	20515-0001
202 226-3375	**Select Committee on Aging**	300 New Jersey SE House Annex I Rm 712	Washington	DC	20515-0001
202 226-7660	**Select Committee on Children Youth & Families**	2nd & D Sts SW House Annex 2 Rm 385	Washington	DC	20515-0001
202 226-3040	**Select Committee on Narcotics Abuse & Control**	H-2234 House Annex II	Washington	DC	20515-0001
202 225-5821	**Small Business**	2361 Rayburn Bldg	Washington	DC	20515-0001
202 225-7103	**Standards of Official Conduct**	HT-2 Capitol Bldg	Washington	DC	20515-0001
202 225-3527	**Veterans Affairs**	335 Cannon Bldg	Washington	DC	20515-0001
202 225-3625	**Ways & Means**	1102 Longworth Bldg	Washington	DC	20515-0001

Joint Committees

202 224-5241	**Joint Committee on Printing**	818 Hart Bldg	Washington	DC	20510-0001
202 225-3621	**Joint Committee on Taxation**	1015 Longworth Bldg	Washington	DC	20515-0001
202 226-7633	**Joint Committee on the Library**	House Annex 1 Rm 103	Washington	DC	20510-0001
202 224-5171	**Joint Economic Committee**	G-01 Dirksen Bldg	Washington	DC	20510-0001

LIBRARY OF CONGRESS

202 707-5000	**Library of Congress**	101 Independence Ave SE	Washington	DC	20540-0001
202 707-2905	**Library of Congress Public Affairs Office**	101 Independence Ave SE LM 105	Washington	DC	20540-0000
202 707-6100	**Cataloging Distribution Service**	101 Independence Ave SE JA 3014W	Washington	DC	20541-0000
202 707-5700	**Congressional Research Service**	101 Independence Ave SE LM 213	Washington	DC	20540-0000
202 707-5522	**General Reading Rooms Div**	101 Independence Ave SE	Washington	DC	20540-0000
202 707-5100	**National Library Service for the Blind & Physically Handicapped**	1291 Taylor St NW	Washington	DC	20542-0000
202 707-5640	**Photoduplication Service**	101 Independence Ave SE LA G1009	Washington	DC	20541-0000
202 707-5639	**Science & Technology Div**	101 Independence Ave SE LA 5104	Washington	DC	20540-0000

Federal Government–Judicial Branch

Federal judicial bodies are listed alphabetically following the entry for the Supreme Court.

202 479-3000	**Supreme Court of the US**	1 1st St NE	Washington	DC	20543-0001
202 633-6097	**Administrative Office of the US Courts**	811 Vermont Ave NW Rm 655	Washington	DC	20544-0001
202 633-6550	**Federal Circuit Court**	717 Madison Pl NW Rm 401	Washington	DC	20439-0001
202 633-6347	**Federal Judicial Center**	1520 H St NW	Washington	DC	20005-1081
202 633-7257	**US Claims Court**	717 Madison Pl NW	Washington	DC	20005-1004
212 264-2814	**US Court of International Trade**	1 Federal Plaza	New York	NY	10007-0000
202 272-1448	**US Court of Military Appeals**	450 E St NW	Washington	DC	20442-0001
202 376-2754	**US Tax Court**	400 2nd St NW	Washington	DC	20217-0001

Federal Government–Judicial Branch

US APPEALS COURTS

617 223-9057	**Circuit 1**	JW McCormack Federal Bldg Rm 1606	Boston	MA	02109-0000
212 791-0103	**Circuit 2**	40 Foley Sq Rm 1702	New York	NY	10007-1502
215 597-2995	**Circuit 3**	601 Market St Rm 21400	Philadelphia	PA	19106-1723
804 771-2213	**Circuit 4**	10th & Main Sts Rm 202	Richmond	VA	23219-0000
504 589-6514	**Circuit 5**	600 Camp St Rm 102	New Orleans	LA	70130-3479
513 684-2953	**Circuit 6**	US POCH Bldg Rm 538	Cincinnati	OH	45202-0000
312 435-5850	**Circuit 7**	219 S Dearborn St	Chicago	IL	60604-1702
314 539-3600	**Circuit 8**	1114 Market St Suite 511	Saint Louis	MO	63101-2036
415 556-7340	**Circuit 9**	PO Box 547	San Francisco	CA	94101-0547
303 844-3157	**Circuit 10**	1929 Stout St 4th Fl	Denver	CO	80294-2900
404 331-6187	**Circuit 11**	56 Forsyth St NW	Atlanta	GA	30303-2205
202 633-6550	**Court of Appeals for the Federal Circuit**	717 Madison Pl NW Rm 401	Washington	DC	20439-0001
202 535-3308	**District of Columbia Circuit**	333 Constitution Ave NW Rm 5423	Washington	DC	20001-2801
202 535-3390	**Temporary Emergency Court of Appeals**	3rd St & Constitution Ave NW Rm 1130	Washington	DC	20001-0000

US BANKRUPTCY COURTS

205 223-7250	**Alabama Middle**	PO Box 1248	Montgomery	AL	36102-1248
205 731-1614	**Alabama Northern**	500 22nd St S Rm 101	Birmingham	AL	35233-3115
205 690-2391	**Alabama Southern**	201 Saint Louis St	Mobile	AL	36602-2919
907 271-2655	**Alaska**	605 W 4th Ave Suite 138	Anchorage	AK	99501-2231
602 379-6965	**Arizona**	230 N 1st Ave Rm 5000	Phoenix	AZ	85025-0001
501 378-6357	**Arkansas**	600 W Capitol Ave Rm 101	Little Rock	AR	72201-3320
213 894-4696	**California Central**	312 N Spring St 9th Fl	Los Angeles	CA	90012-4701
916 551-2615	**California Eastern**	650 Capitol Mall Rm 8308	Sacramento	CA	95814-4706
415 556-2250	**California Northern**	450 Golden Gate Ave Rm 15217	San Francisco	CA	94102-3400
619 557-5620	**California Southern**	940 Front St Rm 5N26	San Diego	CA	92189-0010
303 844-4045	**Colorado**	1845 Sherman St Suite 400	Denver	CO	80203-1167
203 240-3677	**Connecticut**	450 Main St Suite 717	Hartford	CT	06103-3002
302 573-6174	**Delaware**	844 N King St Federal Bldg Rm 6007	Wilmington	DE	19801-0000
202 535-3042	**District of Columbia**	3rd St & Constitution Ave NW Rm 2400	Washington	DC	20001-0000
813 225-7064	**Florida Middle**	4921 Memorial Hwy Suite 200	Tampa	FL	33634-7506
904 681-7500	**Florida Northern**	227 N Bronough St Suite 3120	Tallahassee	FL	32301-1329
305 536-5216	**Florida Southern**	51 SW 1st Ave Rm 629	Miami	FL	33130-1625
912 752-3506	**Georgia Middle**	475 Mulberry St Rm 126	Macon	GA	31201-7907
404 331-6886	**Georgia Northern**	75 Spring St SW Rm 1340	Atlanta	GA	30303-0000
912 944-4100	**Georgia Southern**	PO Box 8347	Savannah	GA	31412-8347
808 541-1791	**Hawaii**	PO Box 50121	Honolulu	HI	96850-0000
208 334-1074	**Idaho**	PO Box 2600	Boise	ID	83701-2600
217 492-4551	**Illinois Central**	PO Box 2438	Springfield	IL	62705-2438
312 435-5587	**Illinois Northern**	219 S Dearborn St Rm 2268	Chicago	IL	60604-0000
219 236-8247	**Indiana Northern**	204 S Main St Rm 224	South Bend	IN	46601-0000
317 226-6710	**Indiana Southern**	46 E Ohio St Rm 123	Indianapolis	IN	46204-1919
319 362-9696	**Iowa Northern**	PO Box 74890	Cedar Rapids	IA	52407-4890
515 284-6230	**Iowa Southern**	123 E Walnut St Rm 318	Des Moines	IA	50309-2022
316 269-6486	**Kansas**	401 N Market St Rm 167	Wichita	KS	67202-2000
606 233-2608	**Kentucky Eastern**	Merrill Lynch Bldg Suite 200	Lexington	KY	40507-0000
502 582-5145	**Kentucky Western**	601 W Broadway US Courthouse Rm 414	Louisville	KY	40202-0000
504 589-6506	**Louisiana Eastern**	500 Camp St Rm 104	New Orleans	LA	70130-3313
504 389-0211	**Louisiana Middle**	412 N 4th St Suite 301	Baton Rouge	LA	70802-5523
318 226-5267	**Louisiana Western**	500 Fannin St Rm 4A18	Shreveport	LA	71101-3053
207 780-3357	**Maine**	156 Federal St Rm 106	Portland	ME	04101-4152
301 962-2688	**Maryland**	101 W Lombard St Rm 919	Baltimore	MD	21201-2611
617 565-6080	**Massachusetts**	10 Causeway St Federal Bldg 11th Fl	Boston	MA	02222-0000
313 226-7064	**Michigan Eastern**	231 W Lafayette Blvd US Courthouse Rm 1002	Detroit	MI	48226-2799
616 456-2231	**Michigan Western**	110 Michigan St NW Rm 792	Grand Rapids	MI	49503-2313
612 348-1855	**Minnesota**	330 2nd Ave S Towle Bldg Suite 600	Minneapolis	MN	55401-0000
601 369-2596	**Mississippi Northern**	PO Box 867	Aberdeen	MS	39730-0867
601 965-5301	**Mississippi Southern**	PO Box 2448	Jackson	MS	39225-2448
314 539-2222	**Missouri Eastern District**	1114 Market St 7th Fl	Saint Louis	MO	63101-2043
406 782-3354	**Montana**	400 N Main St Federal Bldg Rm 273	Butte	MT	59701-0000
402 221-4687	**Nebraska**	PO Box 428 Downtown Stn	Omaha	NE	68101-0428
702 388-6257	**Nevada**	300 Las Vegas Blvd S Suite 209	Las Vegas	NV	89101-5814
603 666-7533	**New Hampshire**	275 Chestnut St Rm 715	Manchester	NH	03101-2413
609 989-2126	**New Jersey**	402 E State St Rm 234	Trenton	NJ	08608-1507
505 766-2051	**New Mexico**	500 Gold Ave SW 9th Fl	Albuquerque	NM	87102-3152
516 832-8800	**New York Eastern**	1635 Privado Rd	Westbury	NY	11590-5241
315 793-8101	**New York Northern**	10 Broad St US Courthouse Rm 230	Utica	NY	13501-0000
212 791-2247	**New York Southern**	1 Bowling Green US Customs House Rm 614	New York	NY	10004-0000
716 846-4130	**New York Western**	68 Court St Rm 310	Buffalo	NY	14202-3405
919 237-0440	**North Carolina Eastern**	PO Box 2807	Wilson	NC	27894-2807
919 333-5647	**North Carolina Middle**	202 S Elm St	Greensboro	NC	27401-2605
704 371-6103	**North Carolina Western**	401 W Trade St Rm 101	Charlotte	NC	28202-1619
701 239-5377	**North Dakota**	PO Box 870	Fargo	ND	58107-0870
216 522-4373	**Ohio Northern**	201 Superior Ave E US Courthouse Rm 419	Cleveland	OH	44114-0000
614 469-2087	**Ohio Southern**	85 Marconi Blvd Rm 124	Columbus	OH	43215-2823
918 758-0127	**Oklahoma Eastern**	4th & Grand Sts	Okmulgee	OK	74447-0000
918 581-7181	**Oklahoma Northern**	111 W 5th St	Tulsa	OK	74103-4253
405 231-5143	**Oklahoma Western**	201 Dean A Mcgee Ave	Oklahoma City	OK	73102-3416
503 326-2231	**Oregon**	1001 SW 5th Ave 9th Fl	Portland	OR	97204-1144
215 597-1644	**Pennsylvania Eastern**	601 Market St Rm 3726	Philadelphia	PA	19106-1723
717 826-6450	**Pennsylvania Middle**	197 S Main St Federal Bldg Rm 217	Wilkes-Barre	PA	18701-0000
412 644-2700	**Pennsylvania Western**	1000 Liberty Ave 16th Fl	Pittsburgh	PA	15222-4002
809 766-5122	**Puerto Rico**	Chardon Ave Federal Bldg Rm 459	Hato Rey	PR	00918-0000
401 528-4477	**Rhode Island**	380 Westminster Mall 6th Fl	Providence	RI	02903-3239
803 765-5211	**South Carolina**	PO Box 1448	Columbia	SC	29202-1448
605 330-4541	**South Dakota**	400 S Phillips Ave	Sioux Falls	SD	57102-0961
615 673-4525	**Tennessee Eastern**	Plaza Tower Suite 1501	Knoxville	TN	37929-0001
615 736-5590	**Tennessee Middle**	701 Broadway Rm 207	Nashville	TN	37203-3945
901 544-3202	**Tennessee Western**	969 Madison Ave 9th Fl	Memphis	TN	38104-2139
903 592-1212	**Texas Eastern**	211 W Ferguson St 4th Fl	Tyler	TX	75702-7222
214 767-0814	**Texas Northern**	1100 Commerce St Rm 14A7	Dallas	TX	75242-1003
713 226-4115	**Texas Southern**	515 Rusk St Suite 4603	Houston	TX	77002-2603
512 229-6720	**Texas Western**	615 E Houston St Rm 115	San Antonio	TX	78205-2040
801 524-5157	**Utah**	350 S Main St Rm 361	Salt Lake City	UT	84101-2106
802 773-0219	**Vermont**	67 Merchants Row 2nd Fl	Rutland	VT	05701-5910
809 774-8310	**Virgin Islands**	PO Box 720	Saint Thomas	VI	00804-0720
804 771-2878	**Virginia Eastern**	1100 E Main St Rm 324	Richmond	VA	23219-3538
703 982-6391	**Virginia Western**	210 Church Ave SW 2nd Fl	Roanoke	VA	24011-1522
509 353-2404	**Washington Eastern**	PO Box 2164	Spokane	WA	99210-2164
206 442-7545	**Washington Western**	1200 6th Ave Parkplace Bldg Suite 315	Seattle	WA	98101-0000
304 233-1655	**West Virginia Northern**	12th & Chapline Sts Rm 300	Wheeling	WV	26003-0000
304 347-5114	**West Virginia Southern**	500 Quarrier St Federal Bldg Rm 2201	Charleston	WV	25301-0000
414 297-3293	**Wisconsin Eastern**	517 E Wisconsin Ave Rm 216	Milwaukee	WI	53202-4504
608 264-5178	**Wisconsin Western**	120 N Henry St Rm 340	Madison	WI	53703-2559
307 772-2191	**Wyoming**	2120 Capitol Ave Rm 6015	Cheyenne	WY	82001-3647

US DISTRICT COURTS

205 223-7308	**Alabama Middle**	15 Lee St Rm 206	Montgomery	AL	36104-4055
205 731-1701	**Alabama Northern**	1729 5th Ave N	Birmingham	AL	35203-2000
205 690-2371	**Alabama Southern**	113 Saint Joseph St	Mobile	AL	36602-3621
907 271-5568	**Alaska**	222 W 7th Ave Box 4 Rm 261	Anchorage	AK	99513-0000
907 452-3163	**Alaska**	101 12th Ave	Fairbanks	AK	99701-6283
907 586-7458	**Alaska**	PO Box 020349	Juneau	AK	99802-0349
907 225-3195	**Alaska**	415 Main St Rm 400	Ketchikan	AK	99901-6399
907 443-5216	**Alaska**	PO Box 100	Nome	AK	99762-0100
602 379-3341	**Arizona**	230 N 1st Ave US Courthouse Rm 1400	Phoenix	AZ	85025-0001
501 972-4610	**Arkansas Eastern**	615 S Main St	Jonesboro	AR	72401-2827
501 378-5353	**Arkansas Eastern**	600 W Capitol Ave Rm 402	Little Rock	AR	72201-3325
501 536-1190	**Arkansas Eastern**	100 E 8th Ave	Pine Bluff	AR	71601-5037
501 862-1202	**Arkansas Western**	101 S Jackson St Rm 205	El Dorado	AR	71731-1566
501 521-6980	**Arkansas Western**	35 E Mountain St Federal Bldg Rm 523	Fayetteville	AR	72701-0000
501 783-6833	**Arkansas Western**	PO Box 1523	Fort Smith	AR	72902-1523
501 623-6411	**Arkansas Western**	PO Box I	Hot Springs National Pk	AR	71902-0000
501 773-3381	**Arkansas Western**	PO Box 2746	Texarkana	AR	75504-2746
213 894-0289	**California Central**	312 N Spring St	Los Angeles	CA	90012-4701
209 487-5757	**California Eastern**	1130 'O' St	Fresno	CA	93721-2201
916 551-2615	**California Eastern**	650 Capitol Mall 2nd Fl	Sacramento	CA	95814-4708
415 556-3031	**California Northern**	PO Box 36060	San Francisco	CA	94102-0000
408 291-7783	**California Northern**	280 S 1st St Rm 4050	San Jose	CA	95113-3011
619 557-5600	**California Southern**	940 Front St Rm 1N20	San Diego	CA	92189-0010
303 844-3433	**Colorado**	1929 Stout St Rm C145	Denver	CO	80294-2900
203 579-5861	**Connecticut**	915 Lafayette Blvd	Bridgeport	CT	06604-4706
203 240-3200	**Connecticut**	450 Main St	Hartford	CT	06103-3002
203 773-2140	**Connecticut**	141 Church St Rm 214	New Haven	CT	06510-2030
302 573-6170	**Delaware**	844 N King St Federal Bldg Rm 4209	Wilmington	DE	19801-3519
202 535-3594	**District of Columbia**	3rd St & Constitution Ave NW Rm 1834	Washington	DC	20001-0000
904 791-2854	**Florida Middle**	311 W Monroe St Suite 110	Jacksonville	FL	32202-4221
407 648-6366	**Florida Middle**	80 N Hughey Ave Rm 218	Orlando	FL	32801-2224
813 228-2709	**Florida Middle**	611 N Florida Ave	Tampa	FL	33602-4520
904 435-8440	**Florida Northern**	100 N Palafox St Rm 129	Pensacola	FL	32501-4858
904 681-7165	**Florida Northern**	110 E Park Ave Rm 122	Tallahassee	FL	32301-7726
305 527-7075	**Florida Southern**	299 E Broward Blvd	Fort Lauderdale	FL	33301-1901
305 536-4548	**Florida Southern**	301 N Miami Ave Rm 150	Miami	FL	33128-7702
912 430-8432	**Georgia Middle**	PO Box 1906	Albany	GA	31702-1906
404 649-7816	**Georgia Middle**	120 12th St	Columbus	GA	31901-2423
912 752-3497	**Georgia Middle**	475 Mulberry St Rm 216	Macon	GA	31202-0000
912 242-3616	**Georgia Middle**	401 N Patterson St	Valdosta	GA	31603-0000
404 331-0414	**Georgia Northern**	75 Spring St SW US Courthouse Rm 2211	Atlanta	GA	30335-0001
404 534-5954	**Georgia Northern**	26 Washington St SE Rm 201	Gainesville	GA	30501-0000
404 253-8847	**Georgia Northern**	PO Box 939	Newnan	GA	30264-0939
404 291-5629	**Georgia Northern**	Federal Bldg Rm 304	Rome	GA	30161-0000
404 722-2074	**Georgia Southern**	500 E Ford St	Augusta	GA	30901-2358
912 265-1758	**Georgia Southern**	PO Box 1636	Brunswick	GA	31521-1636
912 944-4281	**Georgia Southern**	PO Box 8286	Savannah	GA	31412-8286
808 541-1300	**Hawaii**	PO Box 50129	Honolulu	HI	96850-0001
208 334-1361	**Idaho**	550 W Fort St	Boise	ID	83724-0001
217 431-4805	**Illinois Central**	201 N Vermilon St	Danville	IL	61832-0000
309 671-7117	**Illinois Central**	100 NE Monroe St Rm 174	Peoria	IL	61602-1003
309 793-5778	**Illinois Central**	211 19th St Rm 40	Rock Island	IL	61201-0000
217 492-4020	**Illinois Central**	600 E Monroe St Rm 221	Springfield	IL	62701-0000
312 435-5670	**Illinois Northern**	219 S Dearborn St Rm 2050	Chicago	IL	60604-1801
815 987-4354	**Illinois Northern**	211 S Court St	Rockford	IL	61101-1219
618 463-6402	**Illinois Southern**	501 Belle St	Alton	IL	62002-6169
618 438-0671	**Illinois Southern**	301 W Main St	Benton	IL	62812-1362
618 482-9371	**Illinois Southern**	PO Box 249	East Saint Louis	IL	62202-0249
219 424-7360	**Indiana Northern**	1300 S Harrison St Rm 1108	Fort Wayne	IN	46802-3435
219 937-5235	**Indiana Northern**	507 State St	Hammond	IN	46320-1529
317 742-0512	**Indiana Northern**	232 N 4th St	Lafayette	IN	47902-0000
219 236-8260	**Indiana Northern**	204 S Main St Rm 102	South Bend	IN	46601-2119
812 465-6426	**Indiana Southern**	101 NW 7 St Room 304	Evansville	IN	47708-0000
317 226-6670	**Indiana Southern**	46 E Ohio St Rm 105	Indianapolis	IN	46204-1919
812 948-5238	**Indiana Southern**	210 Federal Bldg	New Albany	IN	47150-0000
812 232-6236	**Indiana Southern**	30 N 7th St Rm 207	Terre Haute	IN	47808-0000
319 364-2447	**Iowa Northern**	101 1st St SE Rm 313	Cedar Rapids	IA	52401-1202
712 233-3203	**Iowa Northern**	320 6th St Rm 301	Sioux City	IA	51101-1262
712 252-3336	**Iowa Southern**	6th & Broadway	Council Bluffs	IA	51502-0000
319 322-3223	**Iowa Southern**	131 E 4th St	Davenport	IA	52801-1516
515 284-6248	**Iowa Southern**	123 E Walnut St Rm 200	Des Moines	IA	50309-0000
913 236-3719	**Kansas**	812 N 7th St Rm 151	Kansas City	KS	66101-3056
913 295-2610	**Kansas**	444 SE Quincy	Topeka	KS	66683-3582
316 269-6491	**Kansas**	401 N Market St Rm 204	Wichita	KS	67202-2000
606 329-2465	**Kentucky Eastern**	1405 Greenup Ave Rm 336	Ashland	KY	41101-7542
606 292-3167	**Kentucky Eastern**	7th & Scott Sts US Post Office & Courthouse	Covington	KY	41011-0000
502 223-5225	**Kentucky Eastern**	330 W Broadway 3rd Fl	Frankfort	KY	40601-1935
606 233-2503	**Kentucky Eastern**	206 US Courthouse	Lexington	KY	40586-0000
606 864-5137	**Kentucky Eastern**	PO Box 689	London	KY	40741-0689
606 437-6160	**Kentucky Eastern**	102 Main St Federal Bldg Rm 203	Pikeville	KY	41501-0000
502 781-1110	**Kentucky Western**	242 Main St Rm 213	Bowling Green	KY	42101-0000
502 582-5156	**Kentucky Western**	601 W Broadway US Courthouse Rm 231	Louisville	KY	40202-2227
502 683-0221	**Kentucky Western**	423 Frederica St Rm 210	Owensboro	KY	42302-0000
502 443-1337	**Kentucky Western**	5th & Broadway Federal Bldg Rm 322	Paducah	KY	42001-0000
504 589-2946	**Louisiana Eastern**	500 Camp St Rm C151	New Orleans	LA	70130-3313
504 389-0321	**Louisiana Middle**	PO Box 2630	Baton Rouge	LA	70821-2630
318 473-7415	**Louisiana Western**	515 Murray St Rm 105	Alexandria	LA	71301-8055
318 264-6613	**Louisiana Western**	705 Jefferson St	Lafayette	LA	70501-0000
318 437-7246	**Louisiana Western**	PO Box 393	Lake Charles	LA	70602-0393
318 322-6740	**Louisiana Western**	PO Box 3087	Monroe	LA	71210-0000
318 226-5273	**Louisiana Western**	500 Fannin St Rm 106	Shreveport	LA	71101-3022
207 945-0575	**Maine**	202 Harlow St	Bangor	ME	04401-4901
207 780-3357	**Maine**	156 Federal St Rm 106	Portland	ME	04101-4152
301 962-2600	**Maryland**	101 W Lombard St Rm 409	Baltimore	MD	21201-2606
617 223-9152	**Massachusetts**	POCH Rm 707	Boston	MA	02109-0000
413 785-0214	**Massachusetts**	1550 Main St	Springfield	MA	01103-1422
508 793-0552	**Massachusetts**	595 Main St Suite 506	Worcester	MA	01601-2001
313 668-2380	**Michigan Eastern**	200 E Liberty St	Ann Arbor	MI	48107-0000
517 892-6571	**Michigan Eastern**	PO Box X913	Bay City	MI	48707-0000
313 226-7200	**Michigan Eastern**	231 W Lafayette Blvd US Courthouse Rm 133	Detroit	MI	48226-0000
313 766-5020	**Michigan Eastern**	600 Church St Rm 140	Flint	MI	48502-1214
616 456-2381	**Michigan Western**	110 Michigan St NW Rm 452	Grand Rapids	MI	49503-2313
616 349-2922	**Michigan Western**	410 W Michigan Ave Rm B-35	Kalamazoo	MI	49005-0000
906 226-2021	**Michigan Western**	229 Federal Bldg	Marquette	MI	49855-0000
218 720-5250	**Minnesota**	515 W 1st St Rm 417	Duluth	MN	55802-1397
612 348-1821	**Minnesota**	110 S 4th St	Minneapolis	MN	55401-2216
612 290-3212	**Minnesota**	316 Robert St N	Saint Paul	MN	55101-1423
601 369-4952	**Mississippi**	301 W Commerce St Rm 310	Aberdeen	MS	39730-0000
601 335-1651	**Mississippi**	PO Box 190	Greenville	MS	38702-0190
601 624-6208	**Mississippi Northern**	PO Box 190	Clarksdale	MS	38614-0190
601 234-1971	**Mississippi Northern**	PO Box 727	Oxford	MS	38655-0727

601 432-8623	**Mississippi Southern** PO Box 369	Biloxi	MS	39533-0369
601 583-2433	**Mississippi Southern** PO Box 511	Hattiesburg	MS	39401-0000
601 965-4439	**Mississippi Southern** 245 E Capitol St Suite 416	Jackson	MS	39201-2414
601 693-2883	**Mississippi Southern** 2100 9th St	Meridian	MS	39301-5159
314 335-8538	**Missouri Eastern** 339 Broadway	Cape Girardeau	MO	63701-7344
314 539-6056	**Missouri Eastern** 1114 Market St Rm 302	Saint Louis	MO	63101-2038
314 636-6124	**Missouri Western** 131 W High St	Jefferson City	MO	65101-1515
816 426-2811	**Missouri Western** 811 Grand Ave Rm 201	Kansas City	MO	64106-1909
816 279-2428	**Missouri Western** 201 S 8th St Rm 224	Saint Joseph	MO	64501-2240
417 865-3869	**Missouri Western** 222 N John Q Hammons Pkwy Suite 1400	Springfield	MO	65806-2515
406 657-6366	**Montana** 316 N 26th St Rm 5405	Billings	MT	59101-1362
406 782-0432	**Montana** Federal Bldg Rm 273	Butte	MT	59701-0000
406 727-1922	**Montana** 215 1st Ave N	Great Falls	MT	59401-0000
406 449-5356	**Montana** PO Box 10015 Federal Bldg	Helena	MT	59626-0015
406 329-3598	**Montana** 200 E Broadway Ave Suite 252	Missoula	MT	59802-0000
402 437-5225	**Nebraska** 100 Centennial Mall N Rm 593	Lincoln	NE	68508-3892
402 221-4761	**Nebraska** 215 N 17th St Rm 9000	Omaha	NE	68102-4910
702 388-6351	**Nevada** 300 Las Vegas Blvd S 4th Fl	Las Vegas	NV	89101-5812
702 784-5515	**Nevada** 300 Booth St Rm 5003	Reno	NV	89509-0000
603 225-1423	**New Hampshire** 55 Pleasant St Rm 514	Concord	NH	03301-3943
609 757-5021	**New Jersey** 401 Market St US Post Office & Courthouse Rm 304	Camden	NJ	08101-0000
201 645-3730	**New Jersey** PO Box 419	Newark	NJ	07102-0000
609 989-2065	**New Jersey** 402 E State St Rm 301	Trenton	NJ	08605-0000
505 766-6527	**New Mexico** 500 Gold St Suite 10102	Albuquerque	NM	87102-0000
505 525-2304	**New Mexico** 200 E Griggs Ave	Las Cruces	NM	88001-3523
505 988-6481	**New Mexico** S Federal Pl US Courthouse Bldrthouse Bldg	Santa Fe	NM	87501-0000
718 330-2105	**New York Eastern** 225 Cadman Plaza E	Brooklyn	NY	11201-1818
518 472-5651	**New York Northern** 445 Broadway Rm 442	Albany	NY	12207-2926
607 773-2893	**New York Northern** 15 Henry St	Binghamton	NY	13901-2723
315 423-5549	**New York Northern** 100 S Clinton St	Syracuse	NY	13260-0001
315 793-8151	**New York Northern** 10 Broad St US Courthouse Rm 305	Utica	NY	13501-1233
212 791-0108	**New York Southern** 40 Foley Sq Rm 18	New York	NY	10007-1502
716 846-4211	**New York Western** 68 Court St Rm 304	Buffalo	NY	14202-3405
716 263-6263	**New York Western** 100 State St Rm 282	Rochester	NY	14614-1387
919 483-9509	**North Carolina Eastern** PO Box 43	Fayetteville	NC	28302-0043
919 638-8534	**North Carolina Eastern** PO Box 1336	New Bern	NC	28563-0000
919 856-4370	**North Carolina Eastern** PO Box 25670	Raleigh	NC	27611-5670
919 343-4663	**North Carolina Eastern** PO Box 338	Wilmington	NC	28402-0338
919 333-5347	**North Carolina Middle** PO Box V-1	Greensboro	NC	27402-0000
704 259-0648	**North Carolina Western** 100 Otis St Rm 309	Asheville	NC	28801-2611
704 371-6101	**North Carolina Western** 401 W Trade St Rm 204	Charlotte	NC	28202-1619
704 873-7112	**North Carolina Western** PO Box 466	Statesville	NC	28677-0466
701 250-4295	**North Dakota** 220 E Rosser Ave Rm 476	Bismarck	ND	58501-3869
216 375-5407	**Ohio Northern** 2 S Main St	Akron	OH	44308-1810
216 522-4359	**Ohio Northern** 201 Superior Ave E Rm 100	Cleveland	OH	44114-1203
419 259-6411	**Ohio Northern** 1716 Spielbusch Ave US Courthouse	Toledo	OH	43624-0000
216 746-1726	**Ohio Northern** 9 W Front St Room 329	Youngstown	OH	44503-1431
513 684-2777	**Ohio Southern** 100 E 5th St Rm 324	Cincinnati	OH	45202-0000
614 469-5442	**Ohio Southern** 85 Marconi Blvd Rm 260	Columbus	OH	43215-2823
513 225-2897	**Ohio Southern** 200 W 2nd St Rm 712	Dayton	OH	45402-1430
918 687-2471	**Oklahoma Eastern** 5th & Okmulgee Sts Rm 210	Muskogee	OK	74401-0000
918 581-7796	**Oklahoma Northern** 333 W 4th St Rm 411	Tulsa	OK	74103-3819
405 231-4792	**Oklahoma Western** 200 NW 4th St	Oklahoma City	OK	73102-3020
503 465-6423	**Oregon** 211 E 7th Ave Rm 102	Eugene	OR	97401-2722
503 326-2202	**Oregon** 620 SW Main St Suite 503	Portland	OR	97205-3029
215 597-7704	**Pennsylvania Eastern** 601 Market St Rm 2609	Philadelphia	PA	19106-1723
717 782-4445	**Pennsylvania Middle** 228 Walnut St	Harrisburg	PA	17101-1714
717 347-0205	**Pennsylvania Middle** Washington Ave & Linden St Rm 423	Scranton	PA	18501-0000
717 323-6380	**Pennsylvania Middle** 240 W 3rd St	Williamsport	PA	17701-6438
814 453-4829	**Pennsylvania Western** State St & S Park Row Rm 227	Erie	PA	16501-0000
412 644-3528	**Pennsylvania Western** 7th Ave & Grant St Rm 819	Pittsburgh	PA	15219-0000
809 766-5555	**Puerto Rico** Federal Bldg Rm G55	Hato Rey	PR	00918-0000
401 528-5100	**Rhode Island** Kennedy Plaza Federal Bldg Rm 119	Providence	RI	02903-0000
803 724-4688	**South Carolina** PO Box 835	Charleston	SC	29402-0835
803 253-3470	**South Carolina** 1845 Assembly St 2nd Fl	Columbia	SC	29201-2401
803 662-1223	**South Carolina** 401 W Evans	Florence	SC	29501-3487
803 233-2781	**South Carolina** PO Box 10768	Greenville	SC	29603-0768
605 226-7240	**South Dakota** 414 US Post Office & Courthouse	Aberdeen	SD	57401-0000
605 224-5849	**South Dakota** 225 S Pierre St Rm 405	Pierre	SD	57501-2483
605 342-3066	**South Dakota** 515 9th St Rm 302	Rapid City	SD	57701-2673
605 338-5566	**South Dakota** 400 S Phillips Ave Rm 220	Sioux Falls	SD	57102-0959
615 752-5200	**Tennessee Eastern** PO Box 591	Chattanooga	TN	37401-0591
615 639-3105	**Tennessee Eastern** 101 Summer St W	Greeneville	TN	37743-4944
615 673-4227	**Tennessee Eastern** PO Box 2348	Knoxville	TN	37901-2348
615 736-5728	**Tennessee Middle** 801 Broadway Rm 800	Nashville	TN	37203-3815
901 427-6586	**Tennessee Western** 109 S Highland Ave	Jackson	TN	38301-6123
901 544-3317	**Tennessee Western** 167 N Main St Rm 978	Memphis	TN	38103-1816
409 839-2645	**Texas Eastern** PO Box 3507	Beaumont	TX	77704-3507
903 935-2912	**Texas Eastern** 100 E Houston St	Marshall	TX	75670-4123
903 892-2921	**Texas Eastern** 101 E Pecan St	Sherman	TX	75090-5916
903 794-8561	**Texas Eastern** 500 State Line Ave Rm 301	Texarkana	TX	75501-0000
903 592-8195	**Texas Eastern** 211 W Ferguson Rm 106	Tyler	TX	75702-7222
915 677-6311	**Texas Northern** PO Box 1218	Abilene	TX	79604-1218
806 376-2352	**Texas Northern** 205 E 5th St Rm 210	Amarillo	TX	79189-0001
214 767-9511	**Texas Northern** 1100 Commerce St Rm 14A20	Dallas	TX	75242-1003
817 334-4494	**Texas Northern** 10th & Lamar Sts Rm 202	Fort Worth	TX	76102-0000
806 743-7624	**Texas Northern** 1205 Texas Ave Rm C-221	Lubbock	TX	79401-0000
915 655-4506	**Texas Northern** 33 E Twohig St Rm 202	San Angelo	TX	76903-6451
817 767-1902	**Texas Northern** PO Box 1234	Wichita Falls	TX	76307-1234
512 548-2500	**Texas Southern** PO Box 2299	Brownsville	TX	78520-0000
512 888-3142	**Texas Southern** 521 Starr St Rm 101	Corpus Christi	TX	78401-2349
409 766-3530	**Texas Southern** 601 Rosenberg St Rm 411	Galveston	TX	77550-1738
713 221-9505	**Texas Southern** 515 Rusk St Suite 5300	Houston	TX	77002-2604
512 723-3542	**Texas Southern** 1300 Matamoros St	Laredo	TX	78040-5054
512 575-3512	**Texas Southern** PO Box 1541	Victoria	TX	77902-1541
512 482-5896	**Texas Western** 200 W 8th St	Austin	TX	78701-2333
512 775-2021	**Texas Western** PO Box 1349	Del Rio	TX	78841-1349
915 534-6725	**Texas Western** 511 E San Antonio St	El Paso	TX	79901-0000
915 683-2001	**Texas Western** 200 E Wall St Rm 316	Midland	TX	79701-5248
915 445-4228	**Texas Western** 106 W 4th St	Pecos	TX	79772-4002
512 229-6550	**Texas Western** 655 E Durango Blvd	San Antonio	TX	78206-0001
817 756-0307	**Texas Western** PO Box 608	Waco	TX	76703-0608
801 524-5160	**Utah** 350 S Main St Rm 204	Salt Lake City	UT	84101-2106
802 951-6301	**Vermont** PO Box 945	Burlington	VT	05402-0945
802 773-0245	**Vermont** PO Box 607	Rutland	VT	05702-0000
809 773-1130	**Virgin Islands** PO Box 3439	Christiansted	VI	00821-0000
809 774-0640	**Virgin Islands** PO Box 720	Saint Thomas	VI	00804-0720
703 557-5128	**Virginia Eastern** 200 S Washington St	Alexandria	VA	22314-3626
804 244-0539	**Virginia Eastern** 101 25th St	Newport News	VA	23607-9998
804 441-6677	**Virginia Eastern** 600 Granby St 1st Fl	Norfolk	VA	23510-1915
804 771-2611	**Virginia Eastern** PO Box 2-AD	Richmond	VA	23205-0577
703 628-5116	**Virginia Western** 180 W Main St	Abingdon	VA	24210-2810
703 523-3557	**Virginia Western** 322 E Wood Ave	Big Stone Gap	VA	24219-2734
804 793-7147	**Virginia Western** 700 Main St	Danville	VA	24541-1804
703 434-3181	**Virginia Western** 116 N Main St	Harrisonburg	VA	22801-3819
804 847-5722	**Virginia Western** PO Box 744	Lynchburg	VA	24505-0744
703 982-6224	**Virginia Western** PO Box 1234	Roanoke	VA	24006-1234
509 353-2150	**Washington Eastern** PO Box 1493	Spokane	WA	99210-1493
206 442-5598	**Washington Western** 1010 5th Ave Rm 308	Seattle	WA	98104-1130
304 622-8513	**West Virginia Northern** 500 W Pike St Rm 200	Clarksburg	WV	26301-2664
304 636-1445	**West Virginia Northern** 300 3rd St	Elkins	WV	26241-3810
304 232-0011	**West Virginia Northern** 12th & Chapline Sts	Wheeling	WV	26003-0000
304 253-7481	**West Virginia Southern** Neville St & Woodlawn Ave	Beckley	WV	25801-0000
304 327-9798	**West Virginia Southern** 601 Federal St Rm 2303	Bluefield	WV	24701-3033
304 342-5154	**West Virginia Southern** 500 Quarrier St Rm 5303	Charleston	WV	25301-2130
304 529-5588	**West Virginia Southern** 845 5th Ave Rm 101	Huntington	WV	25701-2014
414 297-3372	**Wisconsin Eastern** 517 E Wisconsin Ave Rm 362	Milwaukee	WI	53202-4504
608 264-5156	**Wisconsin Western** 120 N Henry St Rm 320	Madison	WI	53703-2559
307 772-2145	**Wyoming** 2120 Capitol Ave Rm 2131	Cheyenne	WY	82001-3633

Federal Government–Independent Agencies and Commissions

Selected agencies are listed alphabetically.

202 634-9282	**Action** 1100 Vermont Ave NW	Washington	DC	20525-0001
617 565-7000	*Region 1* 10 Causeway St Rm 473	Boston	MA	02222-1039
212 466-3481	*Region 2* 6 World Trade Ctr Rm 758	New York	NY	10048-0084
215 597-9972	*Region 3* 2nd & Chestnut Sts Rm 108	Philadelphia	PA	19106-0000
404 331-2859	*Region 4* 101 Marietta St NW Suite 1003	Atlanta	GA	30323-0001
312 353-5107	*Region 5* 10 W Jackson Blvd 6th Fl	Chicago	IL	60604-3909
214 767-9494	*Region 6* 1100 Commerce St Rm 6B11	Dallas	TX	75242-1001
303 844-2671	*Region 8* 1405 Curtis St Suite 2930	Denver	CO	80202-2358
415 744-3013	*Region 9* 211 Main St Rm 530	San Francisco	CA	94105-1974
206 442-1558	*Region 10* 909 1st Ave Suite 3039	Seattle	WA	98174-1101
202 254-7020	**Administrative Conference of the US** 2120 L St NW Suite 500	Washington	DC	20037-1568
202 653-5640	**Advisory Commission on Intergovernmental Relations** 1111 20th St NW Suite 2000	Washington	DC	20575-0001
202 786-0503	**Advisory Council on Historic Preservation** 1100 Pennsylvania Ave NW Rm 809	Washington	DC	20004-2501
202 663-1451	**Agency for International Development** 2401 E St NW	Washington	DC	20523-0001
202 906-3000	**Amtrak** 60 Massachusetts Ave NE	Washington	DC	20002-4225
202 673-7968	**Appalachian Regional Commission** 1666 Connecticut Ave NW	Washington	DC	20235-0001
202 647-8715	**Arms Control & Disarmament Agency** 320 21st St NW Rm 5843	Washington	DC	20451-0001
202 254-8040	**Board for International Broadcasting** 1201 Connecticut Ave NW Suite 400	Washington	DC	20036-2605
202 659-6000	**Chamber of Commerce of the US** 1615 H St NW	Washington	DC	20062-0001
202 504-2200	**Commission of Fine Arts** 401 F St NW Tension Bldg Suite 312	Washington	DC	20001-0000
202 376-8364	**Commission on Civil Rights** 1121 Vermont Ave NW	Washington	DC	20425-0001
816 426-5253	*Central Region* 911 Walnut St	Kansas City	MO	64106-2009
202 523-5264	*Eastern Region* 1121 Vermont Ave NW	Washington	DC	20425-0001
213 894-3437	*Western Region* 3660 Wilshire Blvd Suite 810	Los Angeles	CA	90010-2714
703 557-1145	**Committee for Purchase from the Blind & Other Severely Handicapped** 1755 Jefferson Davis Hwy Suite 1107	Arlington	VA	22202-3509
202 254-8630	**Commodity Futures Trading Commission** 2033 K St NW	Washington	DC	20581-0001
312 353-6642	*Central Region* 233 S Wacker Dr Suite 4600	Chicago	IL	60606-6397
212 466-2071	*Eastern Region* 1 World Trade Ctr Suite 4747	New York	NY	10048-0471
816 374-6602	*Southwestern Region* 4900 Main St Suite 721	Kansas City	MO	64112-2644
213 209-6783	*Western Region* 10880 Wilshire Blvd Suite 1005	Los Angeles	CA	90024-4111
202 332-1155	**Congressional Club** 2001 New Hampshire Ave NW	Washington	DC	20009-3484
301 492-6800	**Consumer Product Safety Commission** 5401 Westbard Ave	Bethesda	MD	20816-0000
404 347-2231	*Atlanta Region* 730 Peachtree St NE Suite 871	Atlanta	GA	30365-0001
312 353-8260	*Chicago Region* 230 S Dearborn St Rm 2944	Chicago	IL	60604-1671
212 264-1125	*New York Region* 6 World Trade Ctr Suite 301	New York	NY	10048-0950
415 705-1816	*San Francisco Region* 555 Battery St Suite 415	San Francisco	CA	94111-2390
202 879-9600	**Corporation for Public Broadcasting** 901 E St NW	Washington	DC	20004-0000
202 382-2090	**Environmental Protection Agency** 401 M St SW	Washington	DC	20460-0001
617 565-3715	*Region 1* JFK Federal Bldg Rm 2203	Boston	MA	02203-0000
212 264-2525	*Region 2* 26 Federal Plaza Rm 906	New York	NY	10278-0012
215 597-9800	*Region 3* 841 Chestnut St	Philadelphia	PA	19107-4431
404 347-4727	*Region 4* 345 Courtland St NE	Atlanta	GA	30365-0001
312 353-2000	*Region 5* 230 S Dearborn St	Chicago	IL	60604-1586
214 655-2100	*Region 6* 1445 Ross Ave Suite 1200	Dallas	TX	75202-2733
913 551-7006	*Region 7* 726 Minnesota Ave	Kansas City	KS	66101-2798
303 293-1603	*Region 8* 999 18th St Suite 500	Denver	CO	80202-2405
415 556-6322	*Region 9* 215 Fremont St	San Francisco	CA	94105-2350
206 442-1200	*Region 10* 1200 6th Ave	Seattle	WA	98101-1128
202 663-4264	**Equal Employment Opportunity Commission** 1801 L St NW	Washington	DC	20507-0001
404 331-6531	*Atlanta District* 75 Piedmont Ave Suite 1150	Atlanta	GA	30335-0001
301 962-3932	*Baltimore District* 111 Market Pl Suite 4000	Baltimore	MD	21202-4012
205 731-1166	*Birmingham District* 1900 3rd Ave N	Birmingham	AL	35203-3502
704 563-2501	*Charlotte District* 5500 Central Ave	Charlotte	NC	28212-2708
312 353-8550	*Chicago District* 536 S Clark St Suite 900	Chicago	IL	60605-1526
216 522-2001	*Cleveland District* 1375 Euclid Ave Rm 600	Cleveland	OH	44115-1808
214 767-7015	*Dallas District* 8303 Elmbrook Dr	Dallas	TX	75247-4014
303 866-1300	*Denver District* 1845 Sherman St Rm 201	Denver	CO	80203-1166
313 226-7639	*Detroit District* 477 Michigan Ave Rm 1540	Detroit	MI	48226-2519
713 653-3320	*Houston District* 1919 Smith St 6th Fl	Houston	TX	77002-8049
317 226-7210	*Indianapolis District* 46 E Ohio St	Indianapolis	IN	46204-1903
213 251-7278	*Los Angeles District* 3660 Wilshire Blvd Suite 500	Los Angeles	CA	90010-2782
901 722-2540	*Memphis District* 1407 Union Ave Suite 621	Memphis	TN	38104-3629
305 536-4491	*Miami District* 1 NE 1st St Metro Mall 6th Fl	Miami	FL	33132-0000
414 297-1111	*Milwaukee District* 310 W Wisconsin Ave Suite 800	Milwaukee	WI	53203-2292
504 589-3842	*New Orleans District* 701 Loyola Ave Suite 600	New Orleans	LA	70113-1931
212 264-3332	*New York District* 90 Church St Rm 1501	New York	NY	10007-2967
215 597-7784	*Philadelphia District* 1421 Cherry St 10th Fl	Philadelphia	PA	19102-1428
602 640-5000	*Phoenix District* 4520 N Central Ave Suite 300	Phoenix	AZ	85012-1833
314 425-6585	*Saint Louis District* 625 N Euclid Ave 5th Fl	Saint Louis	MO	63108-1660
512 229-4810	*San Antonio District* 5410 Fredrickburg Rd Suite 200	San Antonio	TX	78229-3550
415 744-6500	*San Francisco District* 901 Market St Suite 500	San Francisco	CA	94103-1735
206 442-0968	*Seattle District* 2815 2nd Ave Suite 500	Seattle	WA	98121-1261
202 566-8990	**Export-Import Bank of the US** 811 Vermont Ave NW	Washington	DC	20571-0001
703 883-4000	**Farm Credit Administration** 1501 Farm Credit Dr	McLean	VA	22102-5090
314 966-5070	*Central Region* 13537 Barrett Parkway Dr Suite 300	Ballwin	MO	63021-5866
703 883-4251	*Eastern Region* 1501 Farm Credit Dr	McLean	VA	22102-0000
303 696-9737	*Western Region* 3131 S Vaughn Way Suite 227	Aurora	CO	80014-0000
202 632-7000	**Federal Communications Commission** 1919 M St NW	Washington	DC	20554-0001
404 347-2631	*Atlanta Region* 1365 Peachtree St NE Rm 440	Atlanta	GA	30309-3152
617 770-4023	*Boston Region* 1 Batterymarch Pk	Quincy	MA	02169-7495
708 298-5171	*Chicago Region* 1550 Northwest Hwy Rm 306	Park Ridge	IL	60068-0000
816 926-5179	*Kansas City Region* 8800 E 63rd St Rm 320	Kansas City	MO	64133-4895
415 744-2722	*San Francisco Region* 211 Main St Rm 537	San Francisco	CA	94105-1914
206 764-3324	*Seattle Region* 3605 132nd Ave SE Rm 414	Bellevue	WA	98006-1333

Federal Government–Independent Agencies and Commissions

202 619-2451 **Federal Council on the Aging**
330 Independence Ave SW Rm 4280 .... Washington DC 20201-0001
202 393-8400 **Federal Deposit Insurance Corp** 550 17th St NW .... Washington DC 20429-0001
404 525-0308 *Atlanta Region* 245 Peachtree Center Ave NE Suite 1200 .... Atlanta GA 30303-1225
617 449-9080 *Boston Region* 160 Gould St .... Needham MA 02194-2300
312 207-0210 *Chicago Region* 30 S Wacker Dr Suite 3100 .... Chicago IL 60606-7406
214 220-3342 *Dallas Region* 1910 Pacific Ave Suite 1700 .... Dallas TX 75201-4522
816 234-8000 *Kansas City Region* 2345 Grand Ave Suite 1500 .... Kansas City MO 64108-2679
901 685-1603 *Memphis Region* 5100 Poplar Ave Suite 1900 .... Memphis TN 38137-1901
212 704-1200 *New York Region* 452 5th Ave .... New York NY 10018-2796
415 546-0160 *San Francisco Region* 25 Ecker Pl .... San Francisco CA 94105-2780
202 376-5140 **Federal Election Commission** 999 E St NW .... Washington DC 20463-0001
202 646-2500 **Federal Emergency Management Agency** 500 C St SW .... Washington DC 20472-0001
617 223-9540 *Region 1* JW McCormack POCH Rm 442 .... Boston MA 02109-0000
212 238-8200 *Region 2* 26 Federal Plaza .... New York NY 10278-0183
215 931-5500 *Region 3* 105 S 7th St .... Philadelphia PA 19106-3324
404 853-4200 *Region 4* 1371 Peachtree St NE Suite 700 .... Atlanta GA 30309-3166
312 408-5500 *Region 5* 175 W Jackson Blvd 4th Fl .... Chicago IL 60604-2607
817 898-9399 *Region 6* 800 N Loop 288 .... Denton TX 76201-0000
816 283-7063 *Region 7* 911 Walnut St Rm 200 .... Kansas City MO 64106-2009
303 235-4800 *Region 8* PO Box 25267 .... Denver CO 80225-0267
415 923-7120 *Region 9* 940 Presidio Ave Bldg 105 .... San Francisco CA 94129-0000
206 481-8800 *Region 10* 130 228th St SW .... Bothell WA 98021-8627
202 566-2468 **Federal Financing Bank**
1500 Pennsylvania Ave NW Rm 3054-MT .... Washington DC 20220-0001
202 906-6000 **Federal Home Loan Bank Board** 1700 G St NW .... Washington DC 20552-0001
617 542-0150 *Region 1* 1 Financial Ctr 20th Fl .... Boston MA 02111-2664
212 912-4600 *Region 2* 1 World Trade Ctr 103rd Fl .... New York NY 10048-0610
412 288-3400 *Region 3* 20 Stanwix St .... Pittsburgh PA 15222-4893
404 888-8000 *Region 4* 1475 Peachtree St NE .... Atlanta GA 30309-3037
513 852-7500 *Region 5* 221 E 4th St 2000 Atrium II .... Cincinnati OH 45202-0000
317 465-0200 *Region 6* 8250 Woodfield Crossing Ln .... Indianapolis IN 46240-2480
312 565-5700 *Region 7* 111 E Wacker Dr Suite 800 .... Chicago IL 60601-4360
515 243-4211 *Region 8* 907 Walnut St .... Des Moines IA 50309-3500
214 541-8500 *Region 9* 500 E John W Carpenter Fwy .... Irving TX 75062-3997
913 233-0507 *Region 10* 200 E 6th St 2 Townsite Plaza .... Topeka KS 66603-0000
415 393-1000 *Region 11* PO Box 7948 .... San Francisco CA 94120-7948
206 340-2300 *Region 12* 1501 4th Ave 19th Fl .... Seattle WA 98101-1693
202 759-8000 **Federal Home Loan Mortgage Corp** 1776 G St NW .... Washington DC 20006-4705
202 382-0711 **Federal Labor Relations Authority** 500 C St SW .... Washington DC 20424-0001
617 565-7280 *Region 1* 10 Causeway St Rm 1017 .... Boston MA 02222-1046
212 264-4934 *Region 2* 26 Federal Plaza Rm 3700 .... New York NY 10278-0179
202 653-8500 *Region 3* PO Box 33758 .... Washington DC 20033-0758
404 347-2324 *Region 4* 1371 Peachtree St NE Suite 736 .... Atlanta GA 30367-0001
312 353-6306 *Region 5* 175 W Jackson Blvd Suite A-1359 .... Chicago IL 60604-0000
214 767-4996 *Region 6* 525 Griffin St Suite 926 LB 107 .... Dallas TX 75202-0000
303 844-5224 *Region 7* 535 16th St Suite 310 .... Denver CO 80202-4238
213 894-3805 *Region 8* 350 S Figueroa St Suite 370 .... Los Angeles CA 90071-1395
415 744-4000 *Region 9* 901 Market St Suite 220 .... San Francisco CA 94103-1791
202 523-5725 **Federal Maritime Commission** 1100 L St NW .... Washington DC 20573-0001
213 514-6127 *Los Angeles Office* PO Box 3184 .... Terminal Island CA 90731-0000
305 536-6963 *Miami Office* 1001 North American Way .... Miami FL 33132-2060
504 589-6662 *New Orleans Office*
2 Canal St World Trade Ctr Suite 440 .... New Orleans LA 70130-0000
212 264-1430 *New York Office* 6 World Trade Ctr Suite 614 .... New York NY 10048-0949
809 766-5581 *Puerto Rico Office* Federal Office Bldg Rm 762 .... Hato Rey PR 00918-0000
415 744-7016 *San Francisco Office* 525 Market St Rm 3510 .... San Francisco CA 94105-2743
202 523-5860 *Bureau of Investigations* 1100 L St NW .... Washington DC 20573-0001
708 887-4750 **Federal Mediation & Conciliation District Hinsdale District**
908 N Elm St Elm Plaza Suite 203 .... Hinsdale IL 60521-0000
202 653-5290 **Federal Mediation & Conciliation Service** 2100 K St NW .... Washington DC 20427-0001
404 347-2473 *Atlanta District* 1720 Peachtree St NW .... Atlanta GA 30309-0000
213 965-3814 *Los Angeles District* 4221 Wilshire Blvd Suite 210 .... Los Angeles CA 90010-0000
612 670-3300 *Minneapolis District* 1300 Godward St Suite 3950 .... Minneapolis MN 55413-0000
212 399-5038 *New York District* 1633 Broadway 2nd Fl .... New York NY 10019-0000
215 597-7690 *Philadelphia District* 600 Arch St Federal Bldg Rm 3456 .... Philadelphia PA 19106-0000
314 576-3922 *Saint Louis District* 12140 Woodcrest Executive Dr .... Saint Louis MO 63141-0000
206 442-5800 *Seattle District* 2001 6th Ave Westin Bldg Rm 310 .... Seattle WA 98121-0000
202 653-5390 *Washington District* 2100 K St NW .... Washington DC 20427-0000
216 522-4800 **Federal Mediation & Conciliaton Service Broadview Heights District**
3505 East Royalton Rd Suite 200 .... Broadview Heights OH 44147-0000
202 653-5633 **Federal Mine Safety & Health Review Commission**
1730 K St NW Suite 600 .... Washington DC 20006-3868
202 452-3000 **Federal Reserve System** 20th & C Sts NW .... Washington DC 20551-0001
202 326-2000 **Federal Trade Commission**
Pennsylvania Ave & 6th St NW .... Washington DC 20580-0001
404 347-4836 *Atlanta Region* 1718 Peachtree St NW Rm 1000 .... Atlanta GA 30367-0001
617 565-7240 *Boston Region* 10 Causeway St Rm 1184 .... Boston MA 02222-1073
312 353-4423 *Chicago Region* 55 E Monroe St Suite 1437 .... Chicago IL 60603-5793
216 522-4207 *Cleveland Region* 668 Euclid Ave Suite 520-A .... Cleveland OH 44114-3006
214 767-5501 *Dallas Region* 100 N Central Expy Suite 500 .... Dallas TX 75201-4329
303 844-2271 *Denver Region* 5353 16th St Suite 310 .... Denver CO 80202-0000
213 209-7575 *Los Angeles Region* 11000 Wilshire Blvd Suite 13209 .... Los Angeles CA 90024-3679
212 264-1207 *New York Region* 150 William St 13th Fl .... New York NY 10038-2688
415 744-7920 *San Francisco Region* 901 Market St Suite 570 .... San Francisco CA 94103-1768
206 442-4655 *Seattle Region* 915 2nd Ave Federal Bldg Rm 2806 .... Seattle WA 98174-0000
202 377-2862 **Foreign-Trade Zones Board**
14th St & Constitution Ave NW Rm 2835 .... Washington DC 20230-0001
202 501-1231 **General Services Administration**
18th & F Sts NW Rm 6010 .... Washington DC 20405-0001
202 472-1100 *National Capitol Region* 7th & D Sts SW .... Washington DC 20407-0001
617 565-8121 *Region 1* 10 Causeway St .... Boston MA 02222-1047
212 264-2600 *Region 2* 26 Federal Plaza .... New York NY 10278-0022
215 597-1237 *Region 3* 9th & Market Sts .... Philadelphia PA 19107-4278
404 331-6891 *Region 4* 75 Spring St SW .... Atlanta GA 30303-3309
312 353-5395 *Region 5* 230 S Dearborn St .... Chicago IL 60604-1505
816 926-7201 *Region 6* 1500 E Bannister Rd .... Kansas City MO 64131-3009
817 334-3284 *Region 7* 819 Taylor St .... Fort Worth TX 76102-6181
303 236-7329 *Region 8* PO Box 25006 .... Denver CO 80225-0006
415 724-5246 *Region 9* 525 Market St .... San Francisco CA 94102-3464
206 931-7000 *Region 10* 15th & C Sts SW .... Auburn WA 98001-6599
202 501-1780 *Fraud Hotline* 18th & F Sts NW .... Washington DC 20405-0001
202 472-1804 **GSA Business Service Center** 7th & D Sts SW Rm 1050 .... Washington DC 20407-0001
617 565-8100 *Region 1* 10 Causeway St Rm 290 .... Boston MA 02222-1047
212 264-1234 *Region 2* 26 Federal Plaza Rm 112 .... New York NY 10278-0022
215 597-9613 *Region 3* 9th & Market Sts Rm 5151 .... Philadelphia PA 19107-0000
404 331-5103 *Region 4* 75 Spring St SW .... Atlanta GA 30303-3309
312 353-5383 *Region 5* 230 S Dearborn St Rm 3714 .... Chicago IL 60604-1602
816 926-7203 *Region 6* 1500 E Bannister Rd .... Kansas City MO 64131-3009
817 334-3284 *Region 7* 819 Taylor St Rm 11A05 .... Fort Worth TX 76102-6114
303 236-7408 *Region 8* Denver Federal Ctr Bldg 41 Rm 145 .... Denver CO 80225-0006
415 744-5050 *Region 9* 525 Market St .... San Francisco CA 94105-2799
206 931-7956 *Region 10* 15th & C Sts SW Rm 2413 .... Auburn WA 98001-0000
202 566-5305 **International Trade Office** 15th St & Pennsylvania Ave .... Washington DC 20220-0001

202 275-7252 **Interstate Commerce Commission**
12th St & Constitution Ave NW .... Washington DC 20423-0001
312 353-6204 *Central Region* 219 S Dearborn St Rm 1304 .... Chicago IL 60604-1705
215 596-4040 *Eastern Region* 3535 Market St Rm 16400 .... Philadelphia PA 19104-3309
415 744-6527 *Western Region* 211 Main St Suite 500 .... San Francisco CA 94105-1914
202 632-4950 **Labor Relations Board** 1717 Pennsylvania Ave NW .... Washington DC 20570-0001
202 863-1820 **Legal Services Corp** 400 Virginia Ave SW .... Washington DC 20024-2730
202 453-1000 **NASA** 600 Independence Ave SW .... Washington DC 20546-0001
202 566-5227 **National Advisory Council on International Monetary & Financial Policies**
15th St & Pennsylvania Ave NW .... Washington DC 20220-0001
202 453-1000 **National Aeronautics & Space Administration**
600 Independence Ave SW .... Washington DC 20546-0001
202 523-3616 **National Archives & Records Administration**
8th St & Pennsylvania Ave NW .... Washington DC 20408-0001
202 724-0174 **National Capital Planning Commission**
1325 G St NW 10th Fl .... Washington DC 20576-0001
202 254-3100 **National Commission on Libraries & Information Science**
1111 18th St NW Suite 310 .... Washington DC 20036-3810
202 682-9600 **National Credit Union Administration**
1776 G St NW 6th Fl .... Washington DC 20456-0001
518 472-4554 *Region 1* 9 Washington Sq Washington Ave Ext .... Albany NY 12205-5576
202 682-1900 *Region 2* 1776 G St NW Suite 800 .... Washington DC 20006-4791
404 396-4042 *Region 3* 7000 Central Pkwy NE Suite 1600 .... Atlanta GA 30328-4598
708 250-6000 *Region 4* 300 Park Blvd Suite 155 .... Itasca IL 60143-2652
512 482-4500 *Region 5* 4807 Spicewood Springs Rd Suite 5200 .... Austin TX 78759-8490
415 825-6125 *Region 6* 2300 Clayton Rd Suite 1350 .... Concord CA 94520-2407
202 682-5400 **National Endowment for the Arts**
1100 Pennsylvania Ave NW Rm 803 .... Washington DC 20506-0001
202 786-0438 **National Endowment for the Humanities**
1100 Pennsylvania Ave NW Rm 406 .... Washington DC 20506-0001
202 254-9200 **National Labor Relations Board**
1717 Pennsylvania Ave NW .... Washington DC 20570-0001
617 565-6700 *Region 1* 10 Causeway St Rm 601 .... Boston MA 02222-1072
212 264-0330 *Region 2* 26 Federal Plaza Rm 3614 .... New York NY 10278-0179
716 846-4931 *Region 3* 111 W Huron St Rm 901 .... Buffalo NY 14202-2387
215 597-7608 *Region 4* 1 Independence Mall 7th Fl .... Philadelphia PA 19106-0000
301 962-2737 *Region 5* 109 Market Pl 4th Fl .... Baltimore MD 21202-4035
412 644-2977 *Region 6* 1000 Liberty Ave Rm 1501 .... Pittsburgh PA 15222-4173
313 226-3210 *Region 7* 477 Michigan Ave Rm 300 .... Detroit MI 48226-2569
216 522-3715 *Region 8* 1240 E 9th St Suite 1695 .... Cleveland OH 44199-2086
513 684-3686 *Region 9* 550 Main St Rm 3003 .... Cincinnati OH 45202-3271
404 331-2896 *Region 10* 101 Marietta St NW Marietta Tower Suite 2400 .... Atlanta GA 30323-0001
919 631-5201 *Region 11* 251 N Main St Federal Bldg Rm 447 .... Winston-Salem NC 27101-0000
813 228-2641 *Region 12* 700 Twiggs St Suite 511 .... Tampa FL 33602-4018
312 353-7574 *Region 13* 200 W Adams St Suite 800 .... Chicago IL 60606-5208
314 425-4142 *Region 14* 210 N Tucker Blvd .... Saint Louis MO 63101-1947
504 589-6361 *Region 15* 1515 Poydras St Suite 610 .... New Orleans LA 70112-3723
817 334-2938 *Region 16* 819 Taylor St Rm 8A24 .... Fort Worth TX 76102-6114
913 236-2777 *Region 17* 5799 Broadmoor St Suite 500 .... Mission KS 66202-2408
612 348-1757 *Region 18* 110 S 4th St Rm 316 .... Minneapolis MN 55401-2291
206 442-4532 *Region 19* 915 2nd Ave Rm 2948 .... Seattle WA 98174-1078
415 744-6810 *Region 20* 901 Market St Suite 400 .... San Francisco CA 94103-1797
213 894-5254 *Region 21* 615 S Flower St 11th Fl .... Los Angeles CA 90017-2803
201 645-2100 *Region 22* 970 Broad St Rm 1600 .... Newark NJ 07102-2570
809 766-5225 *Region 24* Federal Office Bldg Rm 591 .... Hato Rey PR 00918-0000
317 226-7401 *Region 25* 575 N Pennsylvania St Suite 238 .... Indianapolis IN 46204-1577
901 722-2707 *Region 26* 1407 Union Ave Suite 800 .... Memphis TN 38104-3642
303 844-3551 *Region 27* 600 17th St Suite 300S .... Denver CO 80202-5459
602 379-3361 *Region 28* 234 N Central Ave Suite 440 .... Phoenix AZ 85004-2212
718 330-7713 *Region 29* 75 Clinton St 8th Fl .... Brooklyn NY 11201-4201
414 297-3870 *Region 30* 310 W Wisconsin Ave Suite 700 .... Milwaukee WI 53203-2283
213 209-7371 *Region 31* 11000 Wilshire Blvd 12th Fl .... Los Angeles CA 90024-3602
415 273-4285 *Region 32* PO Box 12983 .... Oakland CA 94604-2983
309 671-7080 *Region 33* 411 Hamilton Blvd 16th Fl .... Peoria IL 61602-1104
202 523-5920 **National Mediation Board** 1425 K St NW Suite 910 .... Washington DC 20572-0001
202 785-4500 **National Park Foundation** 1850 K St NW Suite 210 .... Washington DC 20006-2213
202 382-6735 **National Transportation Safety Board**
800 Independence Ave SW .... Washington DC 20594-0001
703 524-1544 **National Water Resources Assn** 3800 N Fairfax Dr Suite 4 .... Arlington VA 22203-0000
301 492-7000 **Nuclear Regulatory Commission** .... Washington DC 20555-0001
215 337-5000 *Region 1* 475 Allendale Rd .... King of Prussia PA 19406-1415
404 331-4503 *Region 2* 101 Marietta St Suite 2900 .... Atlanta GA 30323-0001
708 790-5500 *Region 3* 799 Roosevelt Rd .... Glen Ellyn IL 60137-5927
817 860-8100 *Region 4* 611 Ryan Plaza Dr .... Arlington TX 76011-8064
415 943-3700 *Region 5* 1450 Maria Ln Suite 210 .... Walnut Creek CA 94596-5368
202 634-7943 **Occupational Safety & Health Review Commission**
1825 K St NW Rm 406 .... Washington DC 20006-1202
404 347-4197 *Atlanta Region* 1365 Peachtree St NE Rm 240 .... Atlanta GA 30309-3119
617 223-9750 *Boston Region* JW McCormack POCH Rm 420 .... Boston MA 02109-0000
214 767-5271 *Dallas Region* 1100 Commerce St Rm 7B11 .... Dallas TX 75242-1003
303 844-2281 *Denver Region* 1244 N Speer Blvd Suite 250 .... Denver CO 80204-3582
202 252-5233 **Office of Community Service** 901 D St SW .... Washington DC 20447-0001
202 632-9594 **Office of Personnel Management** 1900 E St NW .... Washington DC 20415-0001
202 634-6441 **Panama Canal Commission** 2000 L St NW Rm 550 .... Washington DC 20036-4996
202 606-3886 **Peace Corps** 1990 K St NW .... Washington DC 20526-0001
617 565-5555 *Boston Area Office* 10 Causeway St Rm 450 .... Boston MA 02222-1047
312 353-4990 *Chicago Area Office* 50 E Washington St Suite 300 .... Chicago IL 60602-2102
214 767-5435 *Dallas Area Office* PO Box 638 .... Dallas TX 75221-0638
202 254-7970 *DC Area Office* 1990 K St NW .... Washington DC 20526-0001
303 866-1057 *Denver Area Office* 1845 Sherman St Rm 103 .... Denver CO 80203-1166
313 226-7928 *Detroit Area Office* 477 Michigan Ave Rm M-74 .... Detroit MI 48226-0000
913 236-2700 *Kansas City Area Office* 5799 Broadmoor Suite 512 .... Mission KS 66202-2408
213 209-7444 *Los Angeles Area Office*
11000 Wilshire Blvd Suite 8104 .... West Los Angeles CA 90024-3670
305 536-5273 *Miami Area Office* 330 Biscayne Blvd Rm 420 .... Miami FL 33132-2242
612 334-4040 *Minneapolis Area Office* 330 2nd Ave S Rm 420 .... Minneapolis MN 55401-0000
212 264-6981 *New York Area Office* 90 Church St Rm 1317 .... New York NY 10007-2971
215 597-0744 *Philadelphia Area Office* 2nd & Chestnut St Rm 102-A .... Philadelphia PA 19106-2998
415 744-2677 *San Francisco Area Office* 211 Main St Rm 533 .... San Francisco CA 94105-1914
206 442-5490 *Seattle Area Office* 2001 6th Ave Suite 1776 .... Seattle WA 98121-2522
202 724-9087 **Pennsylvania Avenue Development Corp**
1331 Pennsylvania Ave NW Suite 1220N .... Washington DC 20004-1703
202 778-8800 **Pension Benefit Guaranty Corp** 2020 K St NW .... Washington DC 20006-1860
202 395-7210 **Policy Coordination** 600 17th St NW Rm 517 .... Washington DC 20506-0001
202 789-6800 **Postal Rate Commission** 1333 H St NW Suite 300 .... Washington DC 20268-0001
202 395-4616 **President's Commission on Executive Exchange**
744 Jackson Pl NW .... Washington DC 20503-0001
202 395-4522 **President's Commission on White House Fellowships**
712 Jackson Pl NW .... Washington DC 20503-0001
202 653-5044 **President's Committee on Employment of People with Disabilities**
1111 20th St NW Rm 636 .... Washington DC 20036-3407
202 272-3421 **President's Council on Physical Fitness & Sports**
450 5th St NW Suite 7103 .... Washington DC 20001-2739
202 272-2650 **Securities & Exchange Commission**
450 5th St NW Suite 1012 .... Washington DC 20549-0001
212 264-1636 *Region 1* 75 Park Pl .... New York NY 10007-2146

617 223-9900	*Region 2* JW McCormack POCH Suite 700	Boston	MA	02109-0000
404 347-4768	*Region 3* 1375 Peachtree St NE Suite 788	Atlanta	GA	30367-0001
312 353-7390	*Region 4* 219 S Dearborn St Rm 1204	Chicago	IL	60604-1773
817 334-3821	*Region 5* 411 W 7th St Suite 800	Fort Worth	TX	76102-3689
303 844-2071	*Region 6* 410 17th St Suite 700	Denver	CO	80202-4488
213 965-3807	*Region 7* 5757 Wilshire Blvd Suite 500	Los Angeles	CA	90036-3648
206 442-7990	*Region 8* 915 2nd Ave Rm 3040	Seattle	WA	98174-1077
215 597-3100	*Region 9* 601 Walnut St Curtis Ctr Suite 1005-E	Philadelphia	PA	19106-0000
202 724-0419	**Selective Service System** 1023 31st St NW	Washington	DC	20435-0001
202 653-6823	**Small Business Administration** 1441 L St NW	Washington	DC	20416-0001
617 451-2030	*Region 1* 155 Federal St 9th Fl	Boston	MA	02110-1744
212 264-7772	*Region 2* 26 Federal Plaza Rm 3100	New York	NY	10278-0112
215 962-3805	*Region 3* 475 Allendale Rd Allendale Sq Suite 201	King of Prussia	PA	19406-0000
404 347-2441	*Region 4* 1375 Peachtree St NE Suite 500	Atlanta	GA	30367-0001
312 353-0359	*Region 5* 230 S Dearborn St Suite 510	Chicago	IL	60604-1593
214 767-7643	*Region 6* 8625 King George Dr Bldg C	Dallas	TX	75235-2201
816 426-2989	*Region 7* 911 Walnut St	Kansas City	MO	64106-2087
303 534-7518	*Region 8* 721 19th St Rm 454	Denver	CO	80202-2517
415 556-7487	*Region 9* 450 Golden Gate Ave	San Francisco	CA	94102-3476
206 442-5676	*Region 10* 2615 4th Ave Rm 440	Seattle	WA	98121-1267
202 357-2700	**Smithsonian Institution** 1000 Jefferson Dr SW	Washington	DC	20560-0001
202 395-4831	**Truman Harry S Scholarship Foundation** 712 Jackson Pl NW	Washington	DC	20006-4901
202 485-2457	**US Advisory Commission on Public Diplomacy** 301 4th St SW Rm 600	Washington	DC	20547-0001
202 647-8677	**US Arms Control & Disarmament Agency** 320 21st St NW	Washington	DC	20451-0001
202 332-3532	**US Assn of Former Members of Congress** 1755 Massachusetts Ave NW Suite 412	Washington	DC	20036-2102
202 485-2355	**US Information Agency** 301 4th St SW	Washington	DC	20547-0001
202 663-1449	**US International Development Agency** 320 20th St NE	Washington	DC	20521-0000
202 653-7175	**US Merit Systems Protection Board** 1120 Vermont Ave NW	Washington	DC	20419-0001
202 268-2000	**US Postal Service** 475 L'Enfant Plaza W SW	Washington	DC	20260-0001
312 765-5000	*Central Region* 433 W Van Buren	Chicago	IL	60699-0001
215 496-6001	*Eastern Region* 1845 Walnut St	Philadelphia	PA	19103-4708
901 722-7373	*Southern Region* 1407 Union Ave	Memphis	TN	38166-0001
415 742-4710	*Western Region* 850 Cherry Ave	San Bruno	CA	94099-0001
202 636-2300	*Postal Inspection Service* 900 Brentwood Rd	Washington	DC	20066-6096
312 751-4930	**US Railroad Retirement Board** 844 N Rush St	Chicago	IL	60611-2092
202 722-3000	**US Soldiers' & Airmen's Home** 3700 N Capitol St NW	Washington	DC	20317-0001
202 485-8095	**Voice of America (VOA)** 330 Independence Ave SW	Washington	DC	20547-0001
202 842-0806	**Washington National Monument Assn** 740 Jackson Pl NW	Washington	DC	20503-0001

Federal Government–Military Bases

Military installations are listed alphabetically followed by the city and state in which the facility is located.

AIR FORCE BASES

405 482-8100	**Altus Air Force Base**	Altus	OK	73523-0000
301 981-4511	**Andrews Air Force Base**	Camp Springs	MD	20331-0001
318 456-2252	**Barksdale Air Force Base**	Bossier City	LA	71110-5000
916 634-3000	**Beale Air Force Base**	Marysville	CA	95903-0000
512 479-4100	**Bergstrom Air Force Base**	Austin	TX	78743-0001
202 545-6700	**Bolling Air Force Base**	Washington	DC	20332-0001
512 536-1110	**Brooks Air Force Base**	San Antonio	TX	78235-0000
505 784-3311	**Cannon Air Force Base**	Clovis	NM	88103-0000
817 782-5000	**Carswell Air Force Base**	Fort Worth	TX	76127-0000
209 726-2011	**Castle Air Force Base**	Merced	CA	95342-0001
217 495-1110	**Chanute Air Force Base**	Rantoul	IL	61868-0000
803 554-0230	**Charleston Air Force Base**	Charleston	SC	29404-0000
601 434-7322	**Columbus Air Force Base**	Columbus	MS	39701-0000
602 750-3900	**Davis-Monthan Air Force Base**	Tucson	AZ	85707-5000
302 677-3000	**Dover Air Force Base**	Dover	DE	19902-0000
915 696-0212	**Dyess Air Force Base**	Abilene	TX	79607-0000
501 762-7000	**Eaker Air Force Base**	Blytheville	AR	72315-0000
805 277-1110	**Edwards Air Force Base**	Edwards AFB	CA	93523-0000
904 882-1110	**Eglin Air Force Base**	Eglin AFB	FL	32542-7000
907 377-1178	**Eielson Air Force Base**	Eielson AFB	AK	99702-0000
605 385-1000	**Ellsworth Air Force Base**	Rapid City	SD	57706-0000
907 552-1110	**Elmendorf Air Force Base**	Anchorage	AK	99506-0000
318 448-2100	**England Air Force Base**	Alexandria	LA	71311-0001
509 247-1212	**Fairchild Air Force Base**	Fairchild AFB	WA	99011-0000
619 269-1110	**George Air Force Base**	Adelanto	CA	92394-0000
915 654-3231	**Goodfellow Air Force Base**	San Angelo	TX	76908-0001
701 747-3000	**Grand Forks Air Force Base**	Grand Forks	ND	58205-0000
315 330-1110	**Griffiss Air Force Base**	Rome	NY	13441-0000
317 688-5211	**Grissom Air Force Base**	Bunker Hill	IN	46971-0000
617 377-4441	**Hanscom Air Force Base**	Bedford	MA	01731-0001
808 449-2490	**Hickam Air Force Base**	Honolulu	HI	96853-0001
801 777-7221	**Hill Air Force Base**	Ogden	UT	84056-0000
505 479-7510	**Holloman Air Force Base**	Alamogordo	NM	88330-5000
305 257-7113	**Homestead Air Force Base**	Homestead	FL	33039-5000
919 736-5400	**Johnson Seymour Air Force Base**	Goldsboro	NC	27531-0000
601 377-1110	**Keesler Air Force Base**	Biloxi	MS	39534-0000
512 925-1110	**Kelly Air Force Base**	San Antonio	TX	78241-5000
505 844-0011	**Kirtland Air Force Base**	Albuquerque	NM	87117-0001
512 671-1110	**Lackland Air Force Base**	San Antonio	TX	78236-5000
804 764-9990	**Langley Air Force Base**	Hampton	VA	23665-0000
512 298-3511	**Laughlin Air Force Base**	Del Rio	TX	78843-0001
501 988-3131	**Little Rock Air Force Base**	Jacksonville	AR	72099-0001
207 999-1110	**Loring Air Force Base**	Limestone	ME	04751-5000
303 370-1110	**Lowry Air Force Base**	Denver	CO	80230-0000
602 856-7411	**Luke Air Force Base**	Litchfield Park	AZ	85309-0000
813 830-1110	**MacDill Air Force Base**	Tampa	FL	33608-0000
406 731-1110	**Malmstrom Air Force Base**	Great Falls	MT	59402-0000
714 655-1110	**March Air Force Base**	Riverside	CA	92518-0000
916 364-1110	**Mather Air Force Base**	Mather	CA	95655-0000
205 293-1110	**Maxwell Air Force Base**	Montgomery	AL	36112-9799
206 984-2521	**McChord Air Force Base**	Tacoma	WA	98438-0001
916 643-2111	**McClellan Air Force Base**	Sacramento	CA	95652-0000
316 652-6100	**McConnell Air Force Base**	Wichita	KS	67221-0000
609 724-1100	**McGuire Air Force Base**	Wrightstown	NJ	08641-7999
701 723-1110	**Minot Air Force Base**	Minot	ND	58705-0001
912 333-4211	**Moody Air Force Base** Bemis Rd	Valdosta	GA	31699-0001
208 828-2111	**Mountain Home Air Force Base**	Mountain Home	ID	83648-0000
803 238-7211	**Myrtle Beach Air Force Base**	Myrtle Beach	SC	29579-0001
702 652-1110	**Nellis Air Force Base**	Las Vegas	NV	89191-5000
714 382-1110	**Norton Air Force Base**	San Bernardino	CA	92409-0000
402 294-1110	**Offutt Air Force Base**	Bellevue	NE	68113-5000
407 494-1110	**Patrick Air Force Base**	Cocoa Beach	FL	32925-0000
603 430-0100	**Pease Air Force Base**	Portsmouth	NH	03803-0000
719 554-7321	**Peterson Air Force Base**	Colorado Springs	CO	80914-0000
518 565-5000	**Plattsburgh Air Force Base**	Plattsburgh	NY	12903-0000

919 394-0001	**Pope Air Force Base**	Fayetteville	NC	28308-0000
512 652-1110	**Randolph Air Force Base**	Randolph AFB	TX	78150-0001
806 885-4511	**Reese Air Force Base**	Lubbock	TX	79489-0000
912 926-1110	**Robins Air Force Base**	Warner Robins	GA	31098-0000
906 346-6511	**Sawyer KI Air Force Base**	KI Sawyer AFB	MI	49843-0000
618 256-1110	**Scott Air Force Base**	Belleville	IL	62225-0000
803 668-8110	**Shaw Air Force Base**	Sumter	SC	29152-0000
907 392-3000	**Shemya Air Force Base**	Shemya	AK	98736-5000
817 676-2511	**Sheppard Air Force Base**	Wichita Falls	TX	76311-5000
405 732-7321	**Tinker Air Force Base**	Oklahoma City	OK	73145-5000
707 424-5000	**Travis Air Force Base**	Fairfield	CA	94535-0000
904 283-1113	**Tyndall Air Force Base**	Panama City	FL	32403-0000
405 237-2121	**Vance Air Force Base**	Enid	OK	73705-0001
805 866-1611	**Vandenberg Air Force Base**	Vandenberg AFB	CA	93437-0000
307 775-1110	**Warren Francis E Air Force Base**	Cheyenne	WY	82005-0001
808 422-0531	**Wheeler Air Force Base**	Wahiawa	HI	96854-0001
816 687-1110	**Whiteman Air Force Base**	Knob Noster	MO	65305-0000
602 988-2611	**Williams Air Force Base**	Chandler	AZ	85240-0001
513 257-1110	**Wright-Patterson Air Force Base**	Dayton	OH	45433-0000
517 739-2011	**Wurtsmith Air Force Base**	Oscoda	MI	48753-5000

ARMY BASES

703 664-6071	**Fort Belvoir**	Fort Belvoir	VA	22060-0000
317 546-9211	**Fort Benjamin Harrison**	Fort Benjamin Harrison	IN	46216-0000
404 544-1011	**Fort Benning**	Fort Benning	GA	31905-0000
915 568-2121	**Fort Bliss**	El Paso	TX	79916-0001
919 396-0011	**Fort Bragg**	Fort Bragg	NC	28307-5000
809 793-0370	**Fort Buchanan**	Fort Buchanan	PR	00934-0000
502 798-2151	**Fort Campbell**	Fort Campbell	KY	42223-5000
719 579-5811	**Fort Carson**	Fort Carson	CO	80913-2505
501 484-2141	**Fort Chaffee**	Fort Chaffee	AR	72905-5000
808 438-1834	**Fort DeRussy**	Honolulu	HI	96815-0000
301 663-8000	**Fort Detrick**	Fort Detrick	MD	21701-0000
508 796-3911	**Fort Devens**	Fort Devens	MA	01433-1241
609 562-1011	**Fort Dix**	Fort Dix	NJ	08640-0000
801 524-4155	**Fort Douglas**	Fort Douglas	UT	84113-5007
315 772-6900	**Fort Drum**	Fort Drum	NY	13602-0001
804 878-5251	**Fort Eustis**	Fort Eustis	VA	23604-0000
404 363-5000	**Fort Gillem**	Forest Park	GA	30050-0000
404 791-0110	**Fort Gordon**	Fort Gordon	GA	30905-0000
907 873-1121	**Fort Greely**	Fort Greely	AK	98733-5000
718 630-4101	**Fort Hamilton**	Fort Hamilton	NY	11252-0001
804 633-5041	**Fort Hill AP**	Bowling Green	VA	22427-0000
817 287-1110	**Fort Hood**	Fort Hood	TX	76544-0000
512 221-1211	**Fort Houston Sam**	San Antonio	TX	78234-5000
602 538-7111	**Fort Huachuca**	Fort Huachuca	AZ	85613-0000
717 865-5444	**Fort Indiantown Gap**	Annville	PA	17003-0000
619 386-1111	**Fort Irwin**	Fort Irwin	CA	92310-0000
803 751-7601	**Fort Jackson**	Fort Jackson	SC	29207-0000
502 624-1181	**Fort Knox**	Fort Knox	KY	40121-0000
913 684-4021	**Fort Leavenworth**	Fort Leavenworth	KS	66027-0000
804 734-1011	**Fort Lee** Bldg 8045	Fort Lee	VA	23801-0000
206 967-3158	**Fort Lewis**	Fort Lewis	WA	98433-9998
205 848-4611	**Fort McClellan**	Fort McClellan	AL	36205-0000
608 388-2222	**Fort McCoy**	Fort McCoy	WI	54656-5000
202 545-6700	**Fort McNair Leslie J**	Fort McNair	DC	20319-0001
404 752-3113	**Fort McPherson** Bldg 65	Fort McPherson	GA	30330-5000
301 677-6261	**Fort Meade George G** Bldg 4215-A	Fort Meade	MD	20755-0000
908 532-9000	**Fort Monmouth**	Fort Monmouth	NJ	07703-0000
804 727-2111	**Fort Monroe**	Fort Monroe	VA	23651-9998
202 696-3189	**Fort Myer**	Fort Myer	VA	22211-5000
408 242-2211	**Fort Ord**	Fort Ord	CA	93941-5000
804 292-8621	**Fort Pickett**	Blackstone	VA	23824-5000
318 535-2911	**Fort Polk**	Fort Polk	LA	71459-0000
907 864-0113	**Fort Richardson**	Fort Richardson	AK	99505-0000
913 239-3911	**Fort Riley**	Fort Riley	KS	66442-0000
301 733-7100	**Fort Ritchie**	Fort Ritchie	MD	21719-0000
205 255-6181	**Fort Rucker**	Fort Rucker	AL	36362-0000
808 438-1175	**Fort Shafter**	Fort Shafter	HI	96858-0001
708 926-4111	**Fort Sheridan**	Fort Sheridan	IL	60037-0000
405 351-8111	**Fort Sill**	Fort Sill	OK	73503-0000
912 767-1110	**Fort Stewart**	Fort Stewart	GA	31314-0000
804 422-7102	**Fort Story**	Fort Story	VA	23459-5066
907 353-6113	**Fort Wainwright**	Fort Wainwright	AK	99703-0000
314 596-0131	**Fort Wood Leonard**	Fort Wood	MO	65473-0000
808 655-4930	**Schofield Barracks**	Honolulu	HI	96857-0001

COAST GUARD INSTALLATIONS

415 437-3171	**Alameda Coast Guard Support Center** Coast Guard Island	Alameda	CA	94501-5100
503 861-0105	**Astoria Coast Guard Air Station** 2185 SE Airport Rd	Warrenton	OR	97146-9694
808 682-2614	**Barbers Point Coast Guard Air Station**	Barbers Point	HI	96862-0001
809 882-3513	**Borinquen Coast Guard Air Station**	Aguadilla	PR	00604-0000
617 223-3257	**Boston Coast Guard Support Center** 427 Commercial St	Boston	MA	02109-1096
718 615-2420	**Brooklyn Coast Guard Air Station** Floyd Bennett Field	Brooklyn	NY	11234-7097
508 968-5300	**Cape Cod Coast Guard Air Station** Otis Air National Guard Base	Buzzards Bay	MA	02542-0000
609 884-3491	**Cape May Coast Guard Air Station**	Cape May	NJ	08204-0000
803 724-7600	**Charleston Coast Guard Base** 196 Tradd St	Charleston	SC	29401-1899
708 657-2145	**Chicago Coast Guard Air Station**	Glenview	IL	60026-0000
813 535-1437	**Clearwater Coast Guard Air Station**	Clearwater	FL	34622-2990
716 846-4184	**Coast Guard Group at Buffalo** 1 Fuhrmann Blvd	Buffalo	NY	14203-0000
305 292-8800	**Coast Guard Group at Key West**	Key West	FL	33040-0005
408 647-7300	**Coast Guard Group at Monterey** 100 Lighthouse Ave	Monterey	CA	93940-1497
813 893-3454	**Coast Guard Group at Saint Petersburg** 600 8th Ave SE	Saint Petersburg	FL	33701-5030
512 939-2070	**Corpus Christi Coast Guard Air Station** US Coast Guard Group Hangar 41	Corpus Christi	TX	78419-5500
313 466-4745	**Detroit Coast Guard Air Station** Selfridge Air National Guard Base Bldg 1401	Mount Clemens	MI	48045-0000
313 331-3110	**Detroit Coast Guard Base** Bell Isle	Detroit	MI	48207-4345
919 335-6360	**Elizabeth City Coast Guard Air Station**	Elizabeth City	NC	27909-0000
919 247-4598	**Fort Macon Coast Guard Base** Fort Macon Road	Atlantic Beach	NC	28512-9999
409 766-5601	**Galveston Coast Guard Base** PO Box 1912	Galveston	TX	77553-0000
212 668-7354	**Governor's Island Coast Guard Support Center** Governor's Island Bldg 110	New York	NY	10004-0000
808 541-2481	**Honolulu Coast Guard Base** Sand Island Access Rd	Honolulu	HI	96819-0000
713 481-0025	**Houston Coast Guard Air Station** 1178 Ellington Field	Houston	TX	77209-0001
707 839-6115	**Humboldt Bay Coast Guard Air Station**	McKenleyville	CA	95521-9309
907 228-0220	**Ketchikan Coast Guard Base**	Ketchikan	AK	99901-0000
907 487-5733	**Kodiak Coast Guard Air Station** PO Box 33	Kodiak	AK	99619-0001
907 487-5920	**Kodiak Coast Guard Support Center** PO Box 14	Kodiak	AK	99619-5000
213 215-2204	**Los Angeles Coast Guard Air Station** 7159 World Way W	Los Angeles	CA	90045-5824
904 247-7301	**Mayport Coast Guard Base** 4200 Ocean St	Mayport	FL	32267-0385
305 953-2100	**Miami Coast Guard Air Station** Opa Locka Airport	Opa Locka	FL	33054-2397

Federal Government–Military Bases

305 535-4300	**Miami Coast Guard Base** 100 MacArthur Cswy	Miami Beach	FL	33139-5101
414 747-7170	**Milwaukee Coast Guard Base** 2420 S Lincoln Memorial Dr	Milwaukee	WI	53207-1902
205 690-2217	**Mobile Coast Guard Base** S Broad St	Mobile	AL	36615-1390
504 393-6005	**New Orleans Coast Guard Air Station** New Orleans Naval Air Stn	New Orleans	LA	70143-0001
504 942-3020	**New Orleans Coast Guard Support Center** 4640 Urquhart St	New Orleans	LA	70117-0000
503 756-9220	**North Bend Coast Guard Air Station** 2000 Connecticut Ave	North Bend	OR	97459-2300
206 457-4401	**Port Angeles Coast Guard Air Station**	Port Angeles	WA	98362-0000
804 483-8595	**Portsmouth Coast Guard Support Center** 4000 Coast Guard Blvd	Portsmouth	VA	23703-2135
916 643-4686	**Sacramento Coast Guard Air Station** McClellan Air Force Base	Sacramento	CA	95652-6428
314 425-6803	**Saint Louis Coast Guard Base** Iron St	Saint Louis	MO	63111-0000
619 557-6510	**San Diego Coast Guard Air Station** 2710 N Harbor Dr	San Diego	CA	92101-1028
415 876-2920	**San Francisco Coast Guard Air Station**	San Francisco	CA	94128-0000
809 729-6800	**San Juan Coast Guard Base** PO Box 2029	San Juan	PR	00902-2029
906 635-3217	**Sault Saint Marie Coast Guard Base** 337 Water St	Sault Sainte Marie	MI	49783-9501
912 352-6237	**Savannah Coast Guard Air Station** Hunter AAF	Savannah	GA	31409-0001
206 286-9650	**Seattle Coast Guard Support Center** 1519 Alaskan Way S	Seattle	WA	98134-1102
907 966-5434	**Sitka Coast Guard Air Station** 611 Airport Rd	Sitka	AK	99835-9436
207 767-0300	**South Portland Coast Guard Base** 259 High St	South Portland	ME	04106-0007
207 244-5517	**Southwest Harbor Coast Guard Base** Clark Point Rd	Southwest Harbor	ME	04679-0000
213 514-6400	**Terminal Island Coast Guard Base** Terminal Island Stn	San Pedro	CA	90731-0000
616 922-8214	**Traverse City Coast Guard Air Station**	Traverse City	MI	49684-0000
215 271-4800	**US Coast Guard Marine Safety Group** 1 Washington Ave	Philadelphia	PA	19147-4303

MARINE CORPS BASES

803 522-7100	**Beaufort Marine Corps Air Station**	Beaufort	SC	29902-0000
919 451-1113	**Camp Lejeune Marine Corps Base**	Camp Lejeune	NC	28542-0000
619 725-4111	**Camp Pendleton Marine Corps Base**	Camp Pendleton	CA	92055-9998
808 477-5052	**Camp Smith HM Marine Corps Base**	Oahu	HI	96861-0001
919 466-2811	**Cherry Point Marine Corps Air Station**	Cherry Point	NC	28533-5000
714 726-2100	**El Toro Marine Corps Air Station** Trabuco Rd	Santa Ana	CA	92709-0000
808 257-2170	**Kaneohe Bay Marine Corps Air Station**	Kaneohe Bay	HI	96863-0001
602 726-2011	**Yuma Marine Corps Air Station**	Yuma	AZ	85369-0000

NAVAL INSTALLATIONS

907 592-8251	**Adak Naval Air Station**	Adak	AK	98111-0002
671 344-8103	**Agana Naval Air Station**	Agana	GU	96637-1250
415 263-3079	**Alameda Naval Air Station**	Alameda	CA	94501-5000
808 684-3176	**Barbers Point Naval Air Station**	Ewa Beach	HI	96862-0001
504 393-3011	**Belle Chasse Naval Air Station**	New Orleans	LA	70143-0001
305 292-2107	**Boca Chica Naval Air Station**	Key West	FL	33040-0000
207 921-1110	**Brunswick Naval Air Station**	Brunswick	ME	04011-2494
904 778-6052	**Cecil Field Naval Air Station**	Cecil Field	FL	32215-9998
803 743-4111	**Charleston Naval Base**	Charleston	SC	29408-0000
512 354-5119	**Chase Field Naval Air Station**	Beeville	TX	78103-0001
512 939-2674	**Corpus Christi Naval Air Station**	Corpus Christi	TX	78418-0000
214 266-6111	**Dallas Naval Air Station**	Dallas	TX	75211-0000
702 426-2880	**Fallon Naval Air Station**	Fallon	NV	89406-5099
708 657-2107	**Glenview Naval Air Station**	Glenview	IL	60026-0000
708 688-3300	**Great Lakes Naval Training Center**	Great Lakes	IL	60088-0000
904 772-2345	**Jacksonville Naval Air Station**	Jacksonville	FL	32212-0000
512 595-6146	**Kingsville Naval Air Station**	Kingsville	TX	78363-5000
209 998-2211	**LeMoore Naval Air Station**	LeMoore	CA	93246-5001
213 547-6721	**Long Beach Naval Station**	Long Beach	CA	90822-0000
904 246-5226	**Mayport Naval Station**	Mayport	FL	32228-0000
901 873-5111	**Memphis Naval Air Station**	Millington	TN	38054-0000
601 679-2318	**Meridian Naval Air Station**	Meridian	MS	39309-0001
619 537-1011	**Miramar Naval Air Station**	San Diego	CA	92145-0001
415 966-5976	**Moffett Field Naval Air Station**	Moffett Field	CA	94035-5000
718 834-2000	**New York Naval Station** 207 Flushing Ave	Brooklyn	NY	11251-0001
804 444-4791	**Norfolk Naval Air Station**	Norfolk	VA	23511-0000
804 396-3000	**Norfolk Naval Shipyard**	Portsmouth	VA	23709-0000
804 444-4791	**Norfolk Naval Station**	Norfolk	VA	23511-6002
619 524-0444	**North Island Naval Air Station**	San Diego	CA	92135-0001
804 433-3131	**Oceana Naval Air Station**	Virginia Beach	VA	23460-5120
407 646-4111	**Orlando Naval Training Center**	Orlando	FL	32808-8067
301 863-3000	**Patuxent River Naval Air Station** NATC	Patuxent River	MD	20670-0000
808 471-0373	**Pearl Harbor Naval Station**	Pearl Harbor	HI	96860-0001
904 452-2311	**Pensacola Naval Air Station**	Pensacola	FL	32508-0000
215 897-5000	**Philadelphia Naval Shipyard** S Broad St	Philadelphia	PA	19112-0000
805 989-1110	**Point Magu Naval Air Station**	Point Magu	CA	93042-0000
206 476-3711	**Puget Sound Naval Shipyard**	Bremerton	WA	98314-0001
206 526-3444	**Puget Sound Naval Station**	Seattle	WA	98115-6348
809 865-2000	**Roosevelt Roads Naval Station**	Miami	FL	35045-0000
619 556-1011	**San Diego Naval Station**	San Diego	CA	92136-0001
617 786-2686	**South Weymouth Naval Air Station**	South Weymouth	MA	02190-5000
415 395-0111	**Treasure Island Naval Station**	San Francisco	CA	94130-7999
206 257-2211	**Whidbey Island Naval Air Station**	Oak Harbor	WA	98278-0000
904 623-7651	**Whiting Field Naval Air Station**	Milton	FL	32570-0000
215 443-1776	**Willow Grove Naval Air Station**	Willow Grove	PA	19090-5001

Local Government–City

Central city government numbers for the largest US cities, selected on the basis of population, are listed alphabetically. Major departments are also listed for the ten largest cities.

505 768-2000	**Albuquerque City Hall** 400 Marquette Ave	Albuquerque	NM	87103-0000
404 330-6000	**Atlanta City Hall** 55 Trinity Ave SW	Atlanta	GA	30335-0001
512 499-2000	**Austin City Hall** 124 W 8th St	Austin	TX	78701-2300
301 396-3100	**Baltimore City Hall** 100 N Holliday St	Baltimore	MD	21202-3417
504 389-3000	**Baton Rouge City Hall** 222 Saint Louis St	Baton Rouge	LA	70802-5817
	Boston			
617 725-4600	*City Clerk* 1 City Hall Plaza Rm 601	Boston	MA	02201-0000
617 725-4000	*City Hall* 1 City Hall Plaza	Boston	MA	02201-0001
617 725-4488	*Department of Transportation* 1 City Hall Plaza Rm 721	Boston	MA	02201-0000
617 725-3550	*Fire Dept* 115 Southampton St	Boston	MA	02118-0000
617 725-3562	*Human Rights Commission* 1 City Hall Plaza Rm 716	Boston	MA	02201-0000
617 725-4500	*Mayor's Office* 1 City Hall Plaza 5th Fl	Boston	MA	02201-0000
617 247-4500	*Police Dept* 154 Berkeley St	Boston	MA	12116-0000
617 725-4352	*Public Facilities* 26 Court St	Boston	MA	02108-0000
617 725-4900	*Public Works* 1 City Hall Plaza Rm 714	Boston	MA	02201-0000
617 722-4300	*Redevelopment Authority* 1 City Hall Sq 9th Fl	Boston	MA	02201-0000
617 725-4138	*Treasurer* 1 City Hall Plaza Rm M-5	Boston	MA	02201-0000
716 851-4200	**Buffalo City Hall** 65 Niagara Sq	Buffalo	NY	14202-3331
704 336-2040	**Charlotte City Hall** 600 E 4th St	Charlotte	NC	28202-2870
	Chicago			
312 744-6878	*City Clerk* 121 N La Salle St Rm 107	Chicago	IL	60601-0000
312 408-7485	*Department of Economic Development* 24 E Congress Pkwy	Chicago	IL	60605-1226
312 744-3400	*Department of Inspectional Services* 121 N La Salle St Suite 900	Chicago	IL	60602-1202
312 646-4400	*Illinois International Port* 3600 E 95th St	Chicago	IL	60617-0000
312 744-5000	*Mayor's Office* 121 N La Salle St Rm 507	Chicago	IL	60602-1207
312 744-5000	*Mayor's Office of Inquiry & Information* 121 N La Salle St	Chicago	IL	60602-1201
312 744-4471	*Planning Dept* 121 N La Salle St 10th Fl	Chicago	IL	60602-1202
312 744-6230	*Police Dept* 1121 S State St	Chicago	IL	60605-2398
312 744-3674	*Public Works* 121 N La Salle St	Chicago	IL	60602-1202
312 744-3360	*Treasurer* 121 N La Salle St Rm 204	Chicago	IL	60602-1204
513 352-3000	**Cincinnati City Hall** 801 Plum St	Cincinnati	OH	45202-1927
216 664-2000	**Cleveland City Hall** 601 Lakeside Ave E	Cleveland	OH	44114-1078
614 645-8100	**Columbus City Hall** 90 W Broad St	Columbus	OH	43215-4144
	Dallas			
214 670-3536	*City Controller* 1500 Marilla St	Dallas	TX	75201-0000
214 670-4050	*City Council* 1500 Marilla St	Dallas	TX	75201-0000
214 670-3011	*City Hall* 1500 Marilla St	Dallas	TX	75201-6320
214 670-3302	*City Manager* 1500 Marilla St Rm 4E-N	Dallas	TX	75201-0000
214 670-3738	*City Secretary* 1500 Marilla St	Dallas	TX	75201-0000
214 670-4026	*Department of Transportation* 1500 Marilla St	Dallas	TX	75201-0000
214 670-4048	*Mayor's Office* 1500 Marilla St Rm 5E-N	Dallas	TX	75201-0000
214 670-4127	*Planning Dept* 1500 Marilla St	Dallas	TX	75201-0000
214 670-4403	*Police Dept* 2014 Main St Rm 504	Dallas	TX	75201-0000
214 948-4200	*Public Works* 320 E Jefferson St	Dallas	TX	75203-0000
303 575-5555	**Denver City Hall** 14th & Bannock	Denver	CO	80202-0000
	Detroit			
313 224-3260	*City Clerk* 2 Woodward St Rm 1304	Detroit	MI	48226-0000
313 224-3270	*City Hall* 2 Woodward St	Detroit	MI	48226-3400
313 224-3252	*Department of Buildings & Safety* 2 Woodward St Rm 401	Detroit	MI	48226-0000
313 833-7670	*Department of Transportation* 1301 E Warren Ave	Detroit	MI	48207-0000
313 596-2900	*Fire Dept* 250 W Larned St	Detroit	MI	48226-0000
313 224-3400	*Mayor's Office* 2 Woodward St Rm 1126	Detroit	MI	48226-0000
313 224-6380	*Planning Dept* 2300 Cadillac Tower	Detroit	MI	48226-0000
313 596-2200	*Police Dept* 1300 Beaubien St	Detroit	MI	48226-0000
313 224-3901	*Public Works* 2 Woodward St City County Bldg Rm 513	Detroit	MI	48226-0000
313 224-3540	*Treasurer* 2 Woodward St Rm 650	Detroit	MI	48226-0000
313 224-4800	*Water Dept* 735 Randolph St	Detroit	MI	48226-0000
915 541-4000	**El Paso City Hall** 2 Civic Center Plaza	El Paso	TX	79901-1124
817 870-6000	**Fort Worth City Hall** 1000 Throckmorton St	Fort Worth	TX	76102-6311
808 523-4385	**Honolulu City Hall** 530 S King St	Honolulu	HI	96813-3014
	Houston			
713 247-1000	*City Hall* 901 Bagby St	Houston	TX	77002-2526
713 247-1840	*City Secretary* PO Box 1562	Houston	TX	77251-0000
713 247-2087	*Department of Finance & Administration* 901 Bagby St	Houston	TX	77002-0000
713 658-4340	*Department of Traffic & Transportation* 500 Jefferson Suite 1600	Houston	TX	77002-0000
713 247-2200	*Mayor's Office* 901 Bagby St	Houston	TX	77002-0000
713 247-5420	*Police Dept* 61 Riesner St	Houston	TX	77002-0000
713 247-2033	*Public Works Dept* 901 Bagby St	Houston	TX	77002-0000
317 236-3200	**Indianapolis City Hall** 200 E Washington St	Indianapolis	IN	46204-3307
904 630-1919	**Jacksonville City Hall** 220 E Bay St	Jacksonville	FL	32202-3418
816 274-2000	**Kansas City City Hall** 414 E 12th St	Kansas City	MO	64106-2705
702 386-6011	**Las Vegas City Hall** 400 E Stewart Ave	Las Vegas	NV	89101-2986
213 590-6101	**Long Beach City Hall** 333 W Ocean Blvd	Long Beach	CA	90802-4604
	Los Angeles			
213 485-5705	*City Clerk* 200 N Spring St Rm 395	Los Angeles	CA	90012-4801
213 485-2121	*City Hall* 200 N Spring St	Los Angeles	CA	90012-4800
213 485-7826	*City Planning Dept* 200 N Spring St Rm 460	Los Angeles	CA	90012-4806
213 519-3400	*Harbor Dept* 425 S Palos Verdes St	San Pedro	CA	90731-3309
213 485-3311	*Mayor's Office* 200 N Spring St Rm 305	Los Angeles	CA	90012-4805
213 626-5273	*Police Dept* 150 N Los Angeles St	Los Angeles	CA	90012-3392
213 485-3719	*Public Works Dept* 200 N Spring St Rm 373	Los Angeles	CA	90012-4805
213 485-2496	*Treasurer* 200 N Spring St Rm 295	Los Angeles	CA	90012-4804
502 625-3131	**Louisville City Hall** 601 E Jefferson St	Louisville	KY	40202-1184
901 576-6500	**Memphis City Hall** 125 N Main St	Memphis	TN	38103-2017
305 579-6065	**Miami City Hall** 3500 Pan American Dr	Miami	FL	33133-5504
414 278-3200	**Milwaukee City Hall** 200 E Wells St	Milwaukee	WI	53202-3515
612 673-3000	**Minneapolis City Hall** 350 S 5th St	Minneapolis	MN	55415-1318
615 259-5620	**Nashville City Hall** 110 Public Sq	Nashville	TN	37201-0000
504 586-4311	**New Orleans City Hall** 1300 Perdido St	New Orleans	LA	70112-2112
	New York			
212 406-9800	*Business Development* 17 John St 14th Fl	New York	NY	10038-4010
212 669-8170	*City Clerk* 265 Municipal Bldg 1 Center St 2nd Fl	New York	NY	10007-0000
212 566-4446	*City Hall* 1 Center St	New York	NY	10007-2304
212 312-8000	*Department of Buildings* 60 Hudson St 14th Fl	New York	NY	10013-3315
212 720-3503	*Department of City Planning* 22 Reade St	New York	NY	10007-1216
212 566-2525	*Department of Transportation* 40 Worth St	New York	NY	10013-2904
212 566-5700	*Mayor's Office* 61 Chambers St City Hall	New York	NY	10007-1208
212 374-5000	*Police Dept* 1 Police Plaza	New York	NY	10038-1497
212 806-6700	*Ports & Trade Dept* Battery Maritime Bldg 4th Fl	New York	NY	10004-0000
212 669-2746	*Treasurer* 1 Center St Rm 727	New York	NY	10007-2304
804 441-2000	**Norfolk City Hall** 810 Union St	Norfolk	VA	23510-2717
415 444-2489	**Oakland City Hall** 1 City Hall Plaza	Oakland	CA	94612-1929
405 297-2011	**Oklahoma City City Hall** 200 N Walker Ave	Oklahoma City	OK	73102-2232
402 444-7000	**Omaha City Hall** 1704 Harney St	Omaha	NE	68183-0001
	Philadelphia			
215 686-1776	*City Clerk* Broad & Market Sts	Philadelphia	PA	19107-0000
215 686-5665	*City Hall* City Hall Rm 616	Philadelphia	PA	19107-0000
215 686-3646	*City Representative's Office* Municipal Services Bldg Rm 1660	Philadelphia	PA	19102-0000
215 686-3410	*Clerk of Council* City Hall Rm 402	Philadelphia	PA	19107-0000
215 686-4607	*Department of City Planning* 1515 Market St 17th Fl	Philadelphia	PA	19107-0000
215 592-5985	*Fire Dept* 3rd & Spring Garden Sts	Philadelphia	PA	19123-0000
215 686-2250	*Mayor's Office* City Hall Rm 215	Philadelphia	PA	19107-0000
215 231-3131	*Police Dept* 8th & Race Sts	Philadelphia	PA	19106-0000
215 580-4000	*SEPTA* 841 Chestnut St	Philadelphia	PA	19107-0000
215 686-2300	*Treasurer* 15th & JFK Blvd Municipal Services Bldg Rm 1430	Philadelphia	PA	19102-0000
215 592-6300	*Water Dept* 101 N Broad St	Philadelphia	PA	19107-0000
	Phoenix			
602 262-6811	*City Clerk* 251 W Washington St Rm 410	Phoenix	AZ	85003-0000
602 262-7029	*City Council* 251 W Washington St 9th Fl	Phoenix	AZ	85003-0000
602 262-6011	*City Hall* 251 W Washington St	Phoenix	AZ	85003-2201
602 262-6941	*City Manager* 251 W Washington St 9th Fl	Phoenix	AZ	85003-0000
602 495-5252	*Community & Economic Development* 1 N 1st St Suite 700	Phoenix	AZ	85004-0000
602 262-6297	*Fire Dept* 520 W Van Buren St	Phoenix	AZ	85003-0000
602 262-7111	*Mayor's Office* 251 W Washington St 9th Fl	Phoenix	AZ	85003-0000
602 262-7131	*Planning Dept* 251 W Washington St 3rd Fl	Phoenix	AZ	85004-2342
602 262-6747	*Police Dept* 620 W Washington St	Phoenix	AZ	85003-0000
602 262-7251	*Public Works* 101 S Central Ave	Phoenix	AZ	85004-0000
602 262-6284	*Street Transportation Dept* 125 E Washington St 3rd Fl	Phoenix	AZ	85004-0000
602 262-6216	*Treasurer* 251 W Washington St 3rd Fl	Phoenix	AZ	85003-0000
412 255-2100	**Pittsburgh City Hall** 414 Grant St	Pittsburgh	PA	15219-2404
503 226-3161	**Portland City Hall** 1220 SW 5th Ave	Portland	OR	97204-1913
314 622-4000	**Saint Louis City Hall** 1200 Market St	Saint Louis	MO	63103-2808
612 298-4012	**Saint Paul City Hall** 15 Kellogg Blvd W	Saint Paul	MN	55102-1635
813 893-7171	**Saint Petersburg City Hall** 175 5th St N	Saint Petersburg	FL	33701-3713
	San Antonio			
512 299-7253	*City Clerk* 100 Military Plaza	San Antonio	TX	78205-0000

The text at the beginning of each category provides information on how government offices are listed. Refer to the front page of the section for a list of the categories included.

512 299-7011	*City Hall*	Military Plaza	San Antonio	TX	78205-2425
512 299-8620	*Finance Dept*	506 Dolorosa St	San Antonio	TX	78205-0000
512 299-8400	*Fire Chief*	115 Auditorium Cir	San Antonio	TX	78205-0000
512 299-7060	*Mayor's Office*	100 Military Plaza	San Antonio	TX	78205-0000
512 299-7360	*Police Chief*	214 W Nueva St	San Antonio	TX	78205-0000
512 299-7235	*Public Information Office*	100 Military Plaza	San Antonio	TX	78207-0000
512 299-8020	*Public Works*	114 W Commerce	San Antonio	TX	78205-0000
	San Diego				
619 236-5555	*City Administration*	202 C St	San Diego	CA	92101-4806
619 533-4000	*City Clerk*	202 C St 2nd Fl	San Diego	CA	92101-0000
619 236-6363	*City Manager*	202 C St 9th Fl	San Diego	CA	92101-0000
619 236-6060	*Financial Management*	202 C St	San Diego	CA	92101-0000
619 236-6110	*General Services*	202 C St 9th Fl	San Diego	CA	92101-0000
619 236-6330	*Mayor's Office*	202 C St 11th Fl	San Diego	CA	92101-0000
619 236-6460	*Planning Dept*	202 C St 4th Fl	San Diego	CA	92101-0000
619 531-2000	*Police Dept*	1401 Broadway	San Diego	CA	92101-0000
619 236-6112	*Treasurer*	202 C St 8th Fl	San Diego	CA	92101-0000
415 554-4000	**San Francisco City Hall**	400 Van Ness Ave	San Francisco	CA	94102-4603
408 277-4000	**San Jose City Hall**	801 N 1st St	San Jose	CA	95110-1708
206 386-1234	**Seattle City Hall**	600 4th Ave	Seattle	WA	98104-1876
813 223-8211	**Tampa City Hall**	306 E Jackson St	Tampa	FL	33602-5223
419 245-3085	**Toledo City Hall**	1 Government Ctr	Toledo	OH	43604-2279
602 791-4911	**Tucson City Hall**	255 W Alameda St	Tucson	AZ	85701-1362
918 596-7777	**Tulsa City Hall**	200 Civic Ctr	Tulsa	OK	74103-3827
202 727-1000	**Washington DC City Hall**	300 Indiana Ave NW	Washington	DC	20001-2106

Local Government–County

US county seats are listed alphabetically within each state.

ALABAMA

205 365-2281	**Autauga County**	4th & Court Sts	Prattville	AL	36067-0000
205 937-0347	**Baldwin County**	PO Box 639	Bay Minette	AL	36507-0639
205 775-3203	**Barbour County**	PO Box 398	Clayton	AL	36016-0398
205 926-4745	**Bibb County**	Court Sq	Centreville	AL	35042-1244
205 274-9111	**Blount County**	220 2nd Ave E	Oneonta	AL	35121-1716
205 738-2280	**Bullock County**	PO Box 230	Union Springs	AL	36089-0230
205 382-3612	**Butler County**	PO Box 756	Greenville	AL	36037-0756
205 236-3521	**Calhoun County**	1702 Noble St Suite 103	Anniston	AL	36201-3889
205 864-8823	**Chambers County**	County Courthouse	Lafayette	AL	36862-0000
205 927-3079	**Cherokee County**	Courthouse Annex Rm 303	Centre	AL	35960-0000
205 755-1551	**Chilton County**	PO Box 557	Clanton	AL	35045-0557
205 459-2155	**Choctaw County**	117 S Mulberry Ave	Butler	AL	36904-2557
205 275-3507	**Clarke County**	117 Court St	Grove Hill	AL	36451-0000
205 463-2651	**Cleburne County**	Vickery St	Heflin	AL	36264-0000
205 897-2954	**Coffee County**	PO Box 402	Elba	AL	36323-0402
205 386-8500	**Colbert County**	201 N Main St	Tuscumbia	AL	35674-2060
205 578-2095	**Conecuh County**	PO Box 347	Evergreen	AL	36401-0347
205 377-2420	**Coosa County**	PO Box 218	Rockford	AL	35136-0218
205 222-4313	**Covington County**	County Courthouse	Andalusia	AL	36420-0000
205 335-6568	**Crenshaw County**	PO Box 227	Luverne	AL	36049-0227
205 739-3530	**Cullman County**	500 2nd Ave SW	Cullman	AL	35055-4155
205 774-6025	**Dale County**	PO Box 246	Ozark	AL	36361-0246
205 875-4401	**Dallas County**	PO Box 997	Selma	AL	36702-0997
205 845-0404	**Dekalb County**	300 Grand Ave SW	Fort Payne	AL	35967-1863
205 567-2571	**Elmore County**	PO Box 338	Wetumpka	AL	36092-0338
205 867-6261	**Escambia County**	PO Box 848	Brewton	AL	36427-0848
205 549-5313	**Etowah County**	800 Forrest Ave	Gadsden	AL	35901-3641
205 932-4510	**Fayette County**	PO Box 819	Fayette	AL	35555-0819
205 332-1210	**Franklin County**	410 N Jackson St	Russellville	AL	35653-0000
205 684-2275	**Geneva County**	PO Box 430	Geneva	AL	36340-0430
205 372-3349	**Greene County**	PO Box 656	Eutaw	AL	35462-0656
205 624-4257	**Hale County**	1001 Main St	Greensboro	AL	36744-1510
205 585-2753	**Henry County**	Court Sq	Abbeville	AL	36310-2135
205 677-4800	**Houston County**	PO Box 6406	Dothan	AL	36302-6406
205 574-9320	**Jackson County**	PO Box 397	Scottsboro	AL	35768-0397
205 325-5300	**Jefferson County**	716 N 21st St	Birmingham	AL	35263-0001
205 695-7333	**Lamar County**	Pond St	Vernon	AL	35592-0000
205 760-5700	**Lauderdale County**	PO Box 1059	Florence	AL	35631-1059
205 974-0663	**Lawrence County**	750 Main St	Moulton	AL	35650-1553
205 745-9767	**Lee County**	215 S 9th St	Opelika	AL	36801-4919
205 233-6400	**Limestone County**	310 W Washington St	Athens	AL	35611-2597
205 548-2331	**Lowndes County**	PO Box 65	Hayneville	AL	36040-0065
205 727-5120	**Macon County**	210 N Elm St	Tuskegee	AL	36083-1757
205 532-3300	**Madison County**	100 Courthouse Sq SE	Huntsville	AL	35801-4820
205 295-2200	**Marengo County**	101 E Coats Ave	Linden	AL	36748-1546
205 921-7451	**Marion County**	PO Box 1595	Hamilton	AL	35570-1595
205 571-7701	**Marshall County**	540 Ringo St	Guntersville	AL	35976-0000
205 690-8615	**Mobile County**	109 Government St	Mobile	AL	36602-3108
205 743-3782	**Monroe County**	S Mount Plaza Ave	Monroeville	AL	36461-0000
205 832-4950	**Montgomery County**	PO Box 1667	Montgomery	AL	36192-0000
205 351-4600	**Morgan County**	302 Lee St NE	Decatur	AL	35601-1999
205 683-6106	**Perry County**	PO Box 505	Marion	AL	36756-0505
205 367-2050	**Pickens County**	PO Box 418	Carrollton	AL	35447-0000
205 566-6374	**Pike County**	120 W Church St	Troy	AL	36081-1913
205 357-4551	**Randolph County**	PO Box 328	Wedowee	AL	36278-0328
205 298-0516	**Russell County**	PO Box 518	Phenix City	AL	36867-0000
205 594-5116	**Saint Clair County**	PO Box 397	Ashville	AL	35953-0397
205 669-3760	**Shelby County**	Main St	Columbiana	AL	35051-0000
205 652-2291	**Sumter County**	Franklin St	Livingston	AL	35470-0000
205 362-4175	**Talladega County**	PO Box 755	Talladega	AL	35160-0755
205 825-4268	**Tallapoosa County**	101 N Broadnax St	Dadeville	AL	36853-1395
205 349-3870	**Tuscaloosa County**	714 Greensboro Ave	Tuscaloosa	AL	35401-1895
205 384-3404	**Walker County**	PO Box 749	Jasper	AL	35502-0749
205 847-2208	**Washington County**	PO Box 146	Chatom	AL	36518-0146
205 682-4126	**Wilcox County**	PO Box 656	Camden	AL	36726-0656
205 489-5533	**Winston County**	PO Box 309	Double Springs	AL	35553-0309

ALASKA

907 246-4224	**Bristol Bay Borough**	PO Box 189	Naknek	AK	99633-0189
907 766-2711	**Haines Borough**	PO Box 1209	Haines	AK	99827-1209
907 586-3300	**Juneau Borough**	155 S Seward St	Juneau	AK	99801-1332
907 262-4441	**Kenai Peninsula Borough**	144 N Binkley	Soldotna	AK	99669-7520
907 225-6151	**Ketchikan Borough**	344 Front St	Ketchikan	AK	99901-6494
907 486-5736	**Kodiak Borough**	710 Mill Bay Rd	Kodiak	AK	99615-6398
907 745-4801	**Matanuska-Susitna Borough**	PO Box 1608	Palmer	AK	99645-1608
907 343-4311	**Municipality of Anchorage**	PO Box 196650	Anchorage	AK	99519-6650
907 852-2611	**North Slope Borough**	PO Box 69	Barrow	AK	99723-0069
907 452-4761	**North Star Borough**	809 Pioneer Rd	Fairbanks	AK	99701-2813
907 442-2500	**Northwest Arctic Borough**	PO Box 1110	Kotzebue	AK	99752-1110
907 747-3294	**Sitka Borough**	304 Lake St	Sitka	AK	99835-7563

ARIZONA

602 337-4364	**Apache County**	PO Box 428	Saint Johns	AZ	85936-0428
602 432-5471	**Cochise County**	PO Box CK	Bisbee	AZ	85603-0000
602 779-6806	**Coconino County**	100 E Birch Ave Flagstaff Justice Ct	Flagstaff	AZ	86001-4696
602 425-3231	**Gila County**	1400 E Ash St	Globe	AZ	85501-1414
602 428-3250	**Graham County**	800 Main St	Safford	AZ	85546-2829
602 865-4242	**Greenlee County**	PO Box 1027	Clifton	AZ	85533-1027
602 669-6131	**La Paz County**	1713 Kofa Suite C	Parker	AZ	85344-6477
602 262-3011	**Maricopa County**	111 S 3rd Ave	Phoenix	AZ	85003-2225
602 753-9141	**Mohave County**	401 E Spring St	Kingman	AZ	86401-5878
602 524-6161	**Navajo County**	PO Box 668	Holbrook	AZ	86025-0668
602 740-8011	**Pima County**	150 W Congress St	Tucson	AZ	85701-1333
602 868-5801	**Pinal County**	100 N Florence	Florence	AZ	85232-9742
602 281-2047	**Santa Cruz County**	PO Box 1265	Nogales	AZ	85628-1265
602 771-3100	**Yavapai County**	255 E Gurley St	Prescott	AZ	86301-3868
602 782-4534	**Yuma County**	168 S 2nd Ave	Yuma	AZ	85364-2297

ARKANSAS

501 673-7311	**Arkansas County**	PO Box 719	Stuttgart	AR	72160-0719
501 853-5144	**Ashley County**	215 E Jefferson Ave	Hamburg	AR	71646-3007
501 425-3475	**Baxter County**	County Courthouse	Mountain Home	AR	72653-0000
501 271-1015	**Benton County**	PO Box 699	Bentonville	AR	72712-0699
501 741-8428	**Boone County**	PO Box 846	Harrison	AR	72602-0846
501 226-3853	**Bradley County**	County Courthouse	Warren	AR	71671-0000
501 798-2517	**Calhoun County**	Main St	Hampton	AR	71744-0000
501 423-2022	**Carroll County**	210 W Church Ave	Berryville	AR	72616-4233
501 265-2208	**Chicot County**	County Courthouse	Lake Village	AR	71653-0000
501 246-4491	**Clark County**	County Courthouse Sq	Arkadelphia	AR	71923-0000
501 598-2813	**Clay County**	2nd St	Piggott	AR	72454-0000
501 362-8141	**Cleburne County**	301 W Main St	Heber Springs	AR	72543-3016
501 325-6521	**Cleveland County**	Main & Magnolia Sts	Rison	AR	71665-0000
501 234-2542	**Columbia County**	1 Court Sq	Magnolia	AR	71753-3527
501 354-9621	**Conway County**	Moose & Church Sts	Morrilton	AR	72110-0000
501 933-4500	**Craighead County**	511 S Main St	Jonesboro	AR	72401-2849
501 474-1511	**Crawford County**	3rd & Main Sts	Van Buren	AR	72956-0000
501 739-4434	**Crittenden County**	County Courthouse	Marion	AR	72364-0000
501 238-3373	**Cross County**	705 E Union Ave	Wynne	AR	72396-3039
501 352-3371	**Dallas County**	3rd & Oak Sts	Fordyce	AR	71742-0000
501 877-2426	**Desha County**	PO Box 188	Arkansas City	AR	71630-0188
501 367-3574	**Drew County**	210 S Main St	Monticello	AR	71655-4796
501 450-4900	**Faulkner County**	801 Locust St	Conway	AR	72032-5360
501 667-3607	**Franklin County**	Commercial St	Ozark	AR	72949-0000
501 895-3341	**Fulton County**	PO Box 278	Salem	AR	72576-0278
501 321-2819	**Garland County**	501 Ouachita Ave	Hot Springs	AR	71901-5154
501 942-2631	**Grant County**	Main & Center Sts	Sheridan	AR	72150-0000
501 239-4097	**Greene County**	PO Box 364	Paragould	AR	72451-0364
501 777-6164	**Hempstead County**	PO Box 1420	Hope	AR	71801-1420
501 332-2261	**Hot Spring County**	3rd & Locust St	Malvern	AR	72104-0000
501 845-5916	**Howard County**	421 N Main St	Nashville	AR	71852-2008
501 793-8800	**Independence County**	192 E Main St	Batesville	AR	72501-5510
501 368-4316	**Izard County**	PO Box 95	Melbourne	AR	72556-0095
501 523-6152	**Jackson County**	Main St	Newport	AR	72112-0000
501 541-5322	**Jefferson County**	PO Box 6317	Pine Bluff	AR	71611-6317
501 754-2175	**Johnson County**	PO Box 278	Clarksville	AR	72830-0278
501 921-4858	**Lafayette County**	PO Box 754	Lewisville	AR	71845-0754
501 886-2167	**Lawrence County**	PO Box 553	Walnut Ridge	AR	72476-0553
501 295-2339	**Lee County**	15 E Chestnut St	Marianna	AR	72360-2330
501 628-4147	**Lincoln County**	Drew & Wiley Sts	Star City	AR	71667-0000
501 898-5021	**Little River County**	351 N 2nd St	Ashdown	AR	71822-2753
501 675-2951	**Logan County**	Broadway St	Booneville	AR	72927-0000
501 676-6403	**Lonoke County**	PO Box 431	Lonoke	AR	72086-0431
501 738-6721	**Madison County**	PO Box 37	Huntsville	AR	72740-0037
501 449-6231	**Marion County**	Courthouse Sq	Yellville	AR	72687-0000
501 774-1500	**Miller County**	4 Laurel St	Texarkana	AR	75502-0000
501 763-3212	**Mississippi County**	Walnut & 2nd Sts	Blytheville	AR	72315-0000
501 747-3921	**Monroe County**	123 Madison St	Clarendon	AR	72029-2794
501 867-3114	**Montgomery County**	PO Box 717	Mount Ida	AR	71957-0717
501 887-3115	**Nevada County**	County Courthouse	Prescott	AR	71857-0000
501 446-5127	**Newton County**	PO Box 435	Jasper	AR	72641-0435
501 836-4116	**Ouachita County**	145 Jefferson St	Camden	AR	71701-0000
501 889-5126	**Perry County**	PO Box 358	Perryville	AR	72126-0358
501 338-5505	**Phillips County**	626 Cherry St	Helena	AR	72342-3306
501 285-2231	**Pike County**	Washington St Courthouse Sq	Murfreesboro	AR	71958-0000
501 578-5408	**Poinsett County**	Courthouse Sq	Harrisburg	AR	72432-0000
501 394-6010	**Polk County**	507 Church Ave	Mena	AR	71953-3297
501 968-7487	**Pope County**	100 W Main St	Russellville	AR	72801-3740
501 256-3741	**Prairie County**	PO Box 278	Des Arc	AR	72040-0278
501 372-8305	**Pulaski County**	401 W Markham St	Little Rock	AR	72201-1417
501 892-5264	**Randolph County**	201 Marr St	Pocahontas	AR	72455-0000
501 633-8640	**Saint Francis County**	313 S Izard St	Forrest City	AR	72335-3856
501 778-2667	**Saline County**	200 N Main St	Benton	AR	72015-3767
501 637-2155	**Scott County**	PO Box 1578	Waldron	AR	72958-1578
501 448-3554	**Searcy County**	PO Box 297	Marshall	AR	72650-0297
501 783-6139	**Sebastian County**	6th & Rogers	Fort Smith	AR	72901-0000
501 642-2852	**Sevier County**	115 N 3rd St	De Queen	AR	71832-2852
501 994-7338	**Sharp County**	County Courthouse	Ash Flat	AR	72513-0000
501 269-3351	**Stone County**	PO Box 427	Mountain View	AR	72560-0427
501 863-6024	**Union County**	Main & Washington Sts	El Dorado	AR	71730-0000
501 745-4140	**Van Buren County**	PO Box 80	Clinton	AR	72031-0080
501 521-8400	**Washington County**	2 S College Ave	Fayetteville	AR	72701-5393
501 279-6200	**White County**	300 N Spruce St	Searcy	AR	72143-7720
501 347-5206	**Woodruff County**	PO Box 356	Augusta	AR	72006-0356
501 495-2630	**Yell County**	PO Box 219	Danville	AR	72833-0219

CALIFORNIA

415 272-6790	**Alameda County**	1225 Fallon St	Oakland	CA	94612-4218
916 694-2281	**Alpine County**	PO Box 158	Markleeville	CA	96120-0158
209 223-6463	**Amador County**	108 Court St	Jackson	CA	95642-2379
916 538-7551	**Butte County**	25 County Center Dr	Oroville	CA	95965-3316
209 754-6310	**Calaveras County**	891 Mountain Ranch Rd	San Andreas	CA	95249-9713
916 458-5146	**Colusa County**	546 Jay St	Colusa	CA	95932-2443
415 646-2950	**Contra Costa County**	725 Court St	Martinez	CA	94553-1233
707 464-7205	**Del Norte County**	625 6th St	Crescent City	CA	95531-0000
916 621-6426	**El Dorado County**	495 Main St	Placerville	CA	95667-5699
209 488-3531	**Fresno County**	2281 Tulare St Rm 300	Fresno	CA	93721-2105
916 934-3834	**Glenn County**	526 W Sycamore	Willows	CA	95988-2746
707 445-7258	**Humboldt County**	825 5th St	Eureka	CA	95501-1153
619 339-4256	**Imperial County**	852 Broadway	El Centro	CA	92243-2312
619 878-2411	**Inyo County**	168 N Edwards St	Independence	CA	93526-0000
805 861-2111	**Kern County**	1415 Truxtun Ave	Bakersfield	CA	93301-5222
209 582-3211	**Kings County**	1400 W Lacey Blvd	Hanford	CA	93230-5925
707 263-2372	**Lake County**	255 N Forbes St	Lakeport	CA	95453-4747
916 257-8311	**Lassen County**	220 S Lassen St	Susanville	CA	96130-4324

Local Government–County

213 974-5401 **Los Angeles County** 111 N Hill St .... Los Angeles CA 90012-3117
209 675-7721 **Madera County** 209 W Yosemite Ave .... Madera CA 93637-3534
415 499-6407 **Marin County** 1501 Civic Center Dr .... San Rafael CA 94903-0000
209 966-2005 **Mariposa County** PO Box 247 .... Mariposa CA 95338-0247
707 463-4379 **Mendocino County** State & Perkins .... Ukiah CA 95482-0000
209 385-7434 **Merced County** 2222 M St .... Merced CA 95340-3780
916 233-3939 **Modoc County** PO Box 131 .... Alturas CA 96101-0131
619 932-7911 **Mono County** PO Box 537 .... Bridgeport CA 93517-0537
408 755-5030 **Monterey County** PO Box 1819 .... Salinas CA 93902-1819
707 253-4481 **Napa County** PO Box 880 .... Napa CA 94559-0880
916 265-1293 **Nevada County** 201 Church St .... Nevada City CA 95959-2504
714 834-2200 **Orange County** 700 Civic Center Dr W .... Santa Ana CA 92701-4022
916 889-7983 **Placer County** 11960 Heritage Oak Pl Suite 15 .... Auburn CA 95604-5228
916 283-6305 **Plumas County** PO Box 10207 .... Quincy CA 95971-0000
714 275-1989 **Riverside County** 4050 N Main St .... Riverside CA 92501-3798
916 440-5522 **Sacramento County** 720 9th St .... Sacramento CA 95814-1398
408 637-3786 **San Benito County** 440 5th St .... Hollister CA 95023-3843
714 387-2020 **San Bernardino County** 777 E Rialto Ave .... San Bernardino CA 92415-0001
619 694-3900 **San Diego County** 1600 Pacific Hwy .... San Diego CA 92101-2422
415 554-4114 **San Francisco County** 400 Van Ness Ave Rm 317 .... San Francisco CA 94102-4607
209 468-2355 **San Joaquin County** 222 E Weber Ave Rm 303 .... Stockton CA 95202-2709
805 549-5245 **San Luis Obispo County** 1035 Palm St Rm 385 .... San Luis Obispo CA 93408-0001
415 363-4711 **San Mateo County** 401 Marshall St .... Redwood City CA 94063-1636
805 568-2220 **Santa Barbara County** 1100 Anacapa St .... Santa Barbara CA 93101-2099
408 299-2424 **Santa Clara County** 70 W Hedding St 11th Fl .... San Jose CA 95110-1768
408 425-2790 **Santa Cruz County** 701 Ocean St .... Santa Cruz CA 95060-4027
916 225-5631 **Shasta County** 1500 Court St .... Redding CA 96001-1694
916 289-3295 **Sierra County** PO Box D .... Downieville CA 95936-0398
916 842-8005 **Siskiyou County** 311 4th St .... Yreka CA 96097-2944
707 429-6218 **Solano County** 580 W Texas St .... Fairfield CA 94533-6321
707 527-2611 **Sonoma County** PO Box 11187 .... Santa Rosa CA 95406-1187
209 525-6416 **Stanislaus County** PO Box 1098 .... Modesto CA 95353-1098
916 741-7120 **Sutter County** 433 2nd St .... Yuba City CA 95991-5504
916 527-4655 **Tehama County** PO Box 250 .... Red Bluff CA 96080-0250
916 623-1222 **Trinity County** PO Box 1258 .... Weaverville CA 96093-1258
209 733-6266 **Tulare County** 2900 W Burrel Ave .... Visalia CA 93291-4509
209 533-5555 **Tuolumne County** 2 S Green St .... Sonora CA 95370-4679
805 654-5000 **Ventura County** 800 S Victoria Ave .... Ventura CA 93009-0001
916 666-8195 **Yolo County** 725 Court St .... Woodland CA 95695-3436
916 741-6341 **Yuba County** 215 5th St .... Marysville CA 95901-5794

COLORADO

303 659-2120 **Adams County** 450 S 4th Ave .... Brighton CO 80601-3196
719 589-5887 **Alamosa County** 402 Edison Ave .... Alamosa CO 81101-2560
303 795-4630 **Arapahoe County** 5334 S Prince St .... Littleton CO 80166-0001
303 264-2536 **Archuleta County** PO Box 1507 .... Pagosa Springs CO 81147-1507
719 523-4372 **Baca County** 741 Main St .... Springfield CO 81073-1548
719 456-2009 **Bent County** PO Box 350 .... Las Animas CO 81054-0350
303 441-3131 **Boulder County** PO Box 471 .... Boulder CO 80306-0471
719 539-4004 **Chaffee County** 132 Crestone Ave .... Salida CO 81201-1566
719 767-5685 **Cheyenne County** PO Box 67 .... Cheyenne Wells CO 80810-0067
303 534-5777 **Clear Creek County** PO Box 2000 .... Georgetown CO 80444-2000
719 376-5772 **Conejos County** PO Box 157 .... Conejos CO 81129-0157
719 672-3962 **Costilla County** PO Box 100 .... San Luis CO 81152-0100
719 267-4643 **Crowley County** 6th & Main St .... Ordway CO 81063-0000
719 783-2441 **Custer County** 205 S 6th St .... Westcliffe CO 81252-9504
303 874-7595 **Delta County** 501 Palmer St .... Delta CO 81416-1753
303 575-2721 **Denver County** City-County Bldg Rm 350 .... Denver CO 80202-0000
303 677-2383 **Dolores County** 4th & Main Sts .... Dove Creek CO 81324-0000
303 688-6260 **Douglas County** 301 Wilcox St .... Castle Rock CO 80104-2454
303 328-7311 **Eagle County** PO Box 850 .... Eagle CO 81631-0850
719 630-2800 **El Paso County** 20 E Vermijo Ave .... Colorado Springs CO 80903-2214
303 621-2080 **Elbert County** PO Box 37 .... Kiowa CO 80117-0037
719 275-7521 **Fremont County** 615 Macon Rm 100 .... Canon City CO 81212-0000
303 945-2377 **Garfield County** 109 8th St Suite 200 .... Glenwood Springs CO 81601-3362
303 572-0567 **Gilpin County** PO Box 366 .... Central City CO 80427-0366
303 725-3347 **Grand County** 308 Byers Ave .... Hot Sulphur Springs CO 80451-9999
303 641-0248 **Gunnison County** 200 E Virginia Ave .... Gunnison CO 81230-2297
303 944-2225 **Hinsdale County** PO Box 277 .... Lake City CO 81235-0277
719 738-2370 **Huerfano County** 400 Main St .... Walsenburg CO 81089-2034
303 723-4334 **Jackson County** PO Box 337 .... Walden CO 80480-0337
303 279-6511 **Jefferson County** 1700 Arapahoe St .... Golden CO 80419-0001
719 438-5421 **Kiowa County** 1305 Goff St .... Eads CO 81036-0000
719 346-8638 **Kit Carson County** PO Box 249 .... Burlington CO 80807-0249
303 259-4000 **La Plata County** 1060 E 2nd Ave .... Durango CO 81301-5157
719 486-1410 **Lake County** PO Box 917 .... Leadville CO 80461-0917
303 221-7000 **Larimer County** PO Box 1190 .... Fort Collins CO 80522-1190
719 846-3481 **Las Animas County** 1st & Maple Sts .... Trinidad CO 81082-0000
719 743-2444 **Lincoln County** 718 3rd Ave .... Hugo CO 80821-0000
303 522-0888 **Logan County** 315 Main St .... Sterling CO 80751-4349
303 244-1670 **Mesa County** PO Box 20000 .... Grand Junction CO 81502-0000
719 658-2440 **Mineral County** Creede Ave .... Creede CO 81130-0000
303 824-5517 **Moffat County** 221 W Victory Way .... Craig CO 81625-2716
303 565-8317 **Montezuma County** 109 W Main St Suite 302 .... Cortez CO 81321-3154
303 249-7755 **Montrose County** PO Box 1289 .... Montrose CO 81402-1289
303 867-8202 **Morgan County** 231 Ensign St .... Fort Morgan CO 80701-2307
719 384-8701 **Otero County** PO Box 511 .... La Junta CO 81050-0000
303 325-4961 **Ouray County** 541 4th St .... Ouray CO 81427-0000
303 838-7509 **Park County** 501 Main St .... Fairplay CO 80440-0000
303 854-3131 **Phillips County** 221 S Interocean Ave .... Holyoke CO 80734-1534
303 920-5180 **Pitkin County** 506 E Main St .... Aspen CO 81611-1993
719 336-9001 **Prowers County** 301 S Main St .... Lamar CO 81052-2857
719 543-3550 **Pueblo County** 215 W 10th St .... Pueblo CO 81003-2945
303 878-5068 **Rio Blanco County** PO Box 1067 .... Meeker CO 81641-1067
719 657-3334 **Rio Grande County** PO Box 160 .... Del Norte CO 81132-0160
303 879-0108 **Routt County** PO Box 773598 .... Steamboat Springs CO 80477-3598
719 655-2231 **Saguache County** PO Box 655 .... Saguache CO 81149-0655
303 387-5671 **San Juan County** PO Box 466 .... Silverton CO 81433-0466
303 728-3954 **San Miguel County** PO Box 548 .... Telluride CO 81435-0548
303 474-3346 **Sedgwick County** PO Box 3 .... Julesburg CO 80737-0003
303 453-2561 **Summit County** PO Box 68 .... Breckenridge CO 80424-0068
719 689-2482 **Teller County** PO Box 959 .... Cripple Creek CO 80813-0959
303 345-2701 **Washington County** 150 Ash Ave .... Akron CO 80720-1510
303 356-4000 **Weld County** 915 10th St .... Greeley CO 80631-1123
303 332-5809 **Yuma County** PO Box 426 .... Wray CO 80758-0426

CONNECTICUT

203 579-6527 **Fairfield Judicial District** 1061 Main St .... Bridgeport CT 06601-0000
203 566-3170 **Hartford Judicial District** 95 Washington St .... Hartford CT 06106-4406
203 567-0885 **Litchfield Judicial District** 20 West St .... Litchfield CT 06759-3500
203 344-2966 **Middlesex Judicial District** 265 DeKoven Dr .... Middletown CT 06457-3460
203 787-8346 **New Haven County** 200 Orange St .... New Haven CT 06510-2016
203 875-6294 **Tolland Judicial District** 69 Brooklyn St .... Rockville CT 06066-3643
203 928-7749 **Windham Judicial District** 155 Church St .... Putnam CT 06260-1515

DELAWARE

302 736-2040 **Kent County** 414 Federal St .... Dover DE 19901-3615
302 571-4011 **New Castle County** 800 N French St .... Wilmington DE 19801-3542
302 856-5601 **Sussex County** PO Box 609 .... Georgetown DE 19947-0609

DISTRICT OF COLUMBIA

202 879-1010 **District of Columbia** 500 Indiana Ave NW .... Washington DC 20001-2131

FLORIDA

904 374-5210 **Alachua County** 21 E University Ave .... Gainesville FL 32601-5348
904 259-3613 **Baker County** 55 N 3rd St .... Macclenny FL 32063-2100
904 763-9061 **Bay County** 300 E 4th St .... Panama City FL 32401-3073
904 964-6280 **Bradford County** PO Box B .... Starke FL 32091-1286
407 269-8011 **Brevard County** 700 S Park Ave .... Titusville FL 32780-4001
305 357-7283 **Broward County** PO Box 14668 .... Fort Lauderdale FL 33302-0000
904 674-4545 **Calhoun County** 425 E Central Ave .... Blountstown FL 32424-2242
813 637-2279 **Charlotte County** 116 W Olympia Ave .... Punta Gorda FL 33950-4431
904 726-2881 **Citrus County** 110 N Apopka Ave .... Inverness FL 32650-4245
904 284-6300 **Clay County** PO Box 698 .... Green Cove Springs FL 32043-0698
813 774-8999 **Collier County** 3301 Tamiami Trail E .... Naples FL 33962-4902
904 755-4100 **Columbia County** 35 N Hernando St .... Lake City FL 32055-4008
305 375-5124 **Dade County** 111 NW 1st Ave Suite 220 .... Miami FL 33128-1895
813 494-3773 **De Soto County** 201 E Oak St .... Arcadia FL 33821-4425
904 498-7021 **Dixie County** PO Box 1206 .... Cross City FL 32628-1206
904 630-2028 **Duval County** 330 E Bay St .... Jacksonville FL 32202-2997
904 436-5783 **Escambia County** 223 S Palafox Pl .... Pensacola FL 32501-5845
904 437-2218 **Flagler County** 200 E Moody Blvd .... Bunnell FL 32110-0000
904 653-8861 **Franklin County** Market St .... Apalachicola FL 32320-0000
904 875-4700 **Gadsden County** 10 E Jefferson St .... Quincy FL 32351-2406
904 463-2345 **Gilchrist County** 112 S Main St .... Trenton FL 32693-0000
813 946-0949 **Glades County** PO Box 10 .... Moore Haven FL 33471-0010
904 229-6113 **Gulf County** 1000 5th St .... Port Saint Joe FL 32456-1648
904 792-1288 **Hamilton County** 207 NE 1st St .... Jasper FL 32052-0000
813 773-6952 **Hardee County** 412 W Orange St .... Wauchula FL 33873-2831
813 675-5217 **Hendry County** Hwys 80 & 29 .... La Belle FL 33935-1760
904 754-4000 **Hernando County** 20 N Main St .... Brooksville FL 34601-0000
813 385-2581 **Highlands County** 430 S Commerce Ave .... Sebring FL 33870-3705
813 272-5000 **Hillsborough County** 419 N Pierce St .... Tampa FL 33602-4022
904 547-2835 **Holmes County** 201 N Oklahoma St .... Bonifay FL 32425-2243
407 567-8000 **Indian River County** 1840 25th St .... Vero Beach FL 32960-3416
904 482-9552 **Jackson County** PO Box 510 .... Marianna FL 32446-0510
904 997-3596 **Jefferson County** US Hwys 90 & 19 County Courthouse .... Monticello FL 32344-1498
904 294-1600 **Lafayette County** Main St .... Mayo FL 32066-0000
904 343-9850 **Lake County** 315 W Main St .... Tavares FL 32778-3878
813 335-2259 **Lee County** 2115 2nd St .... Fort Myers FL 33901-3053
904 488-4710 **Leon County** 301 S Monroe St .... Tallahassee FL 32301-1856
904 486-4311 **Levy County** PO Box 610 .... Bronson FL 32621-0610
904 643-5404 **Liberty County** Hwy 20 .... Bristol FL 32321-0000
904 973-4176 **Madison County** PO Box 237 .... Madison FL 32340-0237
813 749-1800 **Manatee County** PO Box 1000 .... Bradenton FL 34206-1000
904 622-0305 **Marion County** 601 SE 25th Ave .... Ocala FL 32671-2690
407 288-5400 **Martin County** 2401 SE Monterey Rd .... Stuart FL 34996-3397
305 294-4641 **Monroe County** 500 Whitehead St .... Key West FL 33040-6581
904 261-6127 **Nassau County** 416 Centre St .... Fernandina Beach FL 32034-4243
904 682-2711 **Okaloosa County** Hwy 90 .... Crestview FL 32536-0000
813 763-6441 **Okeechobee County** 304 NW 2nd St .... Okeechobee FL 34972-4146
407 236-7300 **Orange County** 201 S Rosalind Ave .... Orlando FL 32801-3547
407 847-1300 **Osceola County** 12 S Vernon Ave .... Kissimmee FL 34741-5188
407 355-2754 **Palm Beach County** 301 N Olive Ave .... West Palm Beach FL 33401-4705
813 847-8190 **Pasco County** 7530 Little Rd .... New Port Richey FL 34654-5598
813 462-3000 **Pinellas County** 315 Court St .... Clearwater FL 34616-5165
813 534-4000 **Polk County** 255 N Broadway Ave .... Bartow FL 33830-3912
904 329-0200 **Putnam County** 410 St Johns Ave .... Palatka FL 32177-4725
904 824-8131 **Saint Johns County** 99 Cordova St .... Saint Augustine FL 32084-4415
407 489-6900 **Saint Lucie County** 221 S Indian River Dr .... Fort Pierce FL 34950-4301
904 623-0135 **Santa Rosa County** 801 Caroline St SE .... Milton FL 32570-4978
813 365-1000 **Sarasota County** 2000 Main St .... Sarasota FL 34237-6036
407 323-4482 **Seminole County** 301 N Park Ave .... Sanford FL 32771-1292
904 793-0200 **Sumter County** 209 N Florida St .... Bushnell FL 33513-9402
904 362-2827 **Suwannee County** 200 Ohio Ave S .... Live Oak FL 32060-3239
904 584-3531 **Taylor County** PO Box 620 .... Perry FL 32347-0620
904 496-3711 **Union County** 55 W Main St Rm 103 .... Lake Butler FL 32054-1600
904 736-5902 **Volusia County** 123 W Indiana Ave .... De Land FL 32720-4210
904 926-3341 **Wakulla County** PO Box 337 .... Crawfordville FL 32327-0337
904 892-3137 **Walton County** PO Box 1260 .... De Funiak Springs FL 32433-0000
904 638-6200 **Washington County** 201 W Cypress Ave Suite B .... Chipley FL 32428-0000

GEORGIA

912 367-8100 **Appling County** 100 N Oak St .... Baxley GA 31513-2097
912 422-3391 **Atkinson County** PO Box 518 .... Pearson GA 31642-0518
912 632-5214 **Bacon County** 502 W 12th St .... Alma GA 31510-1957
912 734-3004 **Baker County** Courthouse Way .... Newton GA 31770-0000
912 453-4007 **Baldwin County** 201 W Hancock St .... Milledgeville GA 31061-3346
404 677-2320 **Banks County** PO Box 130 .... Homer GA 30547-0130
404 867-7581 **Barrow County** 310 S Broad St .... Winder GA 30680-1973
404 382-4766 **Bartow County** PO Box 543 .... Cartersville GA 30120-0543
912 423-2455 **Ben Hill County** 401 E Central Ave .... Fitzgerald GA 31750-2596
912 686-5421 **Berrien County** 105 E Washington Ave .... Nashville GA 31639-2256
912 749-6527 **Bibb County** 601 Mulberry St .... Macon GA 31201-2672
912 934-3200 **Bleckley County** 306 2nd St SE .... Cochran GA 31014-1633
912 462-5256 **Brantley County** PO Box 398 .... Nahunta GA 31553-0398
912 263-5561 **Brooks County** Hwy 76 & Hwy 33 .... Quitman GA 31643-0000
912 653-4912 **Bryan County** 401 S College St .... Pembroke GA 31321-0000
912 764-9009 **Bulloch County** N Main St .... Statesboro GA 30458-0000
404 554-2324 **Burke County** 6th & Liberty St .... Waynesboro GA 30830-0000
404 775-8215 **Butts County** PO Box 320 .... Jackson GA 30233-0320
912 849-4835 **Calhoun County** Courthouse Sq .... Morgan GA 31766-0000
912 576-5601 **Camden County** 4th St .... Woodbine GA 31569-0000
912 685-2835 **Candler County** Courthouse Sq .... Metter GA 30439-0000
404 834-0064 **Carroll County** 311 Newnan St .... Carrollton GA 30117-3124
404 935-2500 **Catoosa County** 206 E Nashville St .... Ringgold GA 30736-1799
912 496-2549 **Charlton County** 100 3rd St .... Folkston GA 31537-0000
912 944-4984 **Chatham County** 133 Montgomery St .... Savannah GA 31401-3230
404 989-3602 **Chattahoochee County** PO Box 299 .... Cusseta GA 31805-0000
404 857-4796 **Chattooga County** PO Box 211 .... Summerville GA 30747-0211
404 479-1953 **Cherokee County** 100 North St .... Canton GA 30114-2794
404 354-2660 **Clarke County** 325 E Washington St .... Athens GA 30601-2750
912 768-2631 **Clay County** PO Box 550 .... Fort Gaines GA 31751-0550
404 478-9911 **Clayton County** 121 S McDonough St .... Jonesboro GA 30236-3694
912 487-2667 **Clinch County** 100 Court Sq .... Homerville GA 31634-1400
404 429-3210 **Cobb County** 10 E Park Sq .... Marietta GA 30090-0001
912 384-4799 **Coffee County** 210 S Coffee Ave .... Douglas GA 31533-3815

Local Government–County

912 985-1324	**Colquitt County**	Main St	Moultrie	GA	31776-0000
404 541-1139	**Columbia County**	PO Box 100	Appling	GA	30802-0100
912 896-2266	**Cook County**	212 N Hutchinson Ave	Adel	GA	31620-2400
404 254-2600	**Coweta County**	PO Box 945	Newnan	GA	30264-0945
912 836-3782	**Crawford County**	PO Box 389	Knoxville	GA	31050-0389
912 276-2672	**Crisp County**	210 7th St S	Cordele	GA	31015-4295
404 657-4778	**Dade County**	PO Box 417	Trenton	GA	30752-0000
404 265-3164	**Dawson County**	PO Box 192	Dawsonville	GA	30534-0192
912 248-3031	**Decatur County**	122 W Water St	Bainbridge	GA	31717-3664
404 371-2000	**DeKalb County**	556 N McDonough St	Decatur	GA	30030-3356
912 374-4361	**Dodge County**	PO Box 818	Eastman	GA	31023-0818
912 268-4228	**Dooly County**	PO Box 322	Vienna	GA	31092-0322
912 431-2198	**Dougherty County**	PO Box 1827	Albany	GA	31703-5301
404 949-2000	**Douglas County**	6754 Broad St	Douglasville	GA	30134-4501
912 723-3033	**Early County**	105 Courthouse Sq	Blakely	GA	31723-1890
912 559-6538	**Echols County**	PO Box 190	Statenville	GA	31648-0190
912 754-6071	**Effingham County**	901 N Pine St	Springfield	GA	31329-0000
404 283-4702	**Elbert County**	14 N Oliver St	Elberton	GA	30635-1498
912 237-3881	**Emanuel County**	101 N Main St	Swainsboro	GA	30401-2042
912 739-1141	**Evans County**	3 Freeman St	Claxton	GA	30417-0000
404 632-2203	**Fannin County**	PO Box 487	Blue Ridge	GA	30513-0487
404 461-6041	**Fayette County**	200 Courthouse Sq	Fayetteville	GA	30214-2198
404 291-5110	**Floyd County**	PO Box 946	Rome	GA	30162-0946
404 781-2100	**Forsyth County**	PO Box 128	Cumming	GA	30130-0128
404 384-2514	**Franklin County**	Courthouse Sq	Carnesville	GA	30521-0000
404 730-4000	**Fulton County**	160 Pryor St Rm 208	Atlanta	GA	30303-3405
404 635-4361	**Gilmer County**	1 Westside Sq	Ellijay	GA	30540-0000
404 598-2084	**Glascock County**	PO Box 231	Gibson	GA	30810-0231
912 267-5600	**Glynn County**	701 G St	Brunswick	GA	31520-6750
404 629-3795	**Gordon County**	100 S Wall St Annex 1	Calhoun	GA	30701-2244
912 377-1512	**Grady County**	250 N Broad St	Cairo	GA	31728-4101
404 453-7716	**Greene County**	201 N Main St	Greensboro	GA	30642-1109
404 822-8000	**Gwinnett County**	75 Langley Dr	Lawrenceville	GA	30245-6935
404 754-6264	**Habersham County**	PO Box 227	Clarkesville	GA	30523-0227
404 531-7000	**Hall County**	116 Spring St E	Gainesville	GA	30501-3765
404 444-5746	**Hancock County**	Courthouse Sq	Sparta	GA	31087-0000
404 646-2002	**Haralson County**	PO Box 488	Buchanan	GA	30113-0488
404 628-4944	**Harris County**	PO Box 528	Hamilton	GA	31811-0528
404 376-2024	**Hart County**	PO Box 279	Hartwell	GA	30643-0279
404 675-3821	**Heard County**	PO Box 40	Franklin	GA	30217-0040
404 954-2400	**Henry County**	345 Phillips Dr	McDonough	GA	30253-3425
912 922-4471	**Houston County**	200 Carl Vinson Pkwy	Warner Robins	GA	31088-5808
912 468-9441	**Irwin County**	S Irwin Ave	Ocilla	GA	31774-1098
404 367-1199	**Jackson County**	PO Box 68	Jefferson	GA	30549-0068
404 468-2812	**Jasper County**	County Courthouse	Monticello	GA	31064-0000
912 375-6611	**Jeff Davis County**	Jeff Davis St	Hazlehurst	GA	31539-0000
912 625-3332	**Jefferson County**	202 E Broad St	Louisville	GA	30434-1622
912 982-2563	**Jenkins County**	PO Box 797	Millen	GA	30442-0797
912 864-3388	**Johnson County**	PO Box 269	Wrightsville	GA	31096-0269
912 986-6405	**Jones County**	PO Box 1359	Gray	GA	31032-1359
404 358-0150	**Lamar County**	327 Thomaston St	Barnesville	GA	30204-1616
912 482-2088	**Lanier County**	100 W Main St	Lakeland	GA	31635-1191
912 272-4755	**Laurens County**	101 N Jefferson St	Dublin	GA	31021-6198
912 759-6000	**Lee County**	PO Box 56	Leesburg	GA	31763-0056
912 876-2164	**Liberty County**	Courthouse Sq	Hinesville	GA	31313-3240
404 359-4444	**Lincoln County**	Humphrey St	Lincolnton	GA	30817-0000
912 545-2143	**Long County**	McDonald St	Ludowici	GA	31316-0000
912 333-5117	**Lowndes County**	PO Box 1349	Valdosta	GA	31603-0000
404 864-3742	**Lumpkin County**	280 Courthouse Cir NE	Dahlonega	GA	30533-1167
912 472-7021	**Macon County**	Sumter St	Oglethorpe	GA	31068-0000
404 795-3351	**Madison County**	PO Box 147	Danielsville	GA	30633-0147
912 649-2603	**Marion County**	Courthouse Sq	Buena Vista	GA	31803-0000
404 595-3982	**McDuffie County**	PO Box 28	Thomson	GA	30824-0028
912 437-6671	**McIntosh County**	PO Box 584	Darien	GA	31305-0584
404 672-1314	**Meriwether County**	PO Box 428	Greenville	GA	30222-0428
912 758-4104	**Miller County**	155 S 1st St Suite 2	Colquitt	GA	31737-1284
912 336-2000	**Mitchell County**	12 Broad St	Camilla	GA	31730-0000
912 994-7000	**Monroe County**	PO Box 189	Forsyth	GA	31029-0189
912 583-2363	**Montgomery County**	Railroad Ave	Mount Vernon	GA	30445-0000
404 342-0725	**Morgan County**	PO Box 168	Madison	GA	30650-0168
404 695-2932	**Murray County**	3rd Ave	Chatsworth	GA	30705-0000
404 571-4860	**Muscogee County**	100 10th St	Columbus	GA	31901-2736
404 784-2000	**Newton County**	1113 Usher St	Covington	GA	30209-0000
404 769-5120	**Oconee County**	15 Water St	Watkinsville	GA	30677-2438
404 743-5270	**Oglethorpe County**	PO Box 261	Lexington	GA	30648-0261
404 445-8871	**Paulding County**	1 Courthouse Sq	Dallas	GA	30132-1401
912 825-2535	**Peach County**	205 W Church St	Fort Valley	GA	31030-4155
404 692-3556	**Pickens County**	211-1 N Main St	Jasper	GA	30143-0000
912 449-2022	**Pierce County**	PO Box 679	Blackshear	GA	31516-0679
404 567-3406	**Pike County**	PO Box 377	Zebulon	GA	30295-0377
404 749-2100	**Polk County**	PO Box 268	Cedartown	GA	30125-0268
912 783-4154	**Pulaski County**	PO Box 29	Hawkinsville	GA	31036-0029
404 485-5826	**Putnam County**	108 S Madison Ave Suite 200	Eatonton	GA	31024-1094
912 334-2159	**Quitman County**	PO Box 114	Georgetown	GA	31754-0114
404 782-5271	**Rabun County**	PO Box 925	Clayton	GA	30525-0925
912 732-6440	**Randolph County**	Court St	Cuthbert	GA	31740-0000
404 821-2300	**Richmond County**	530 Green St	Augusta	GA	30911-0001
404 929-4000	**Rockdale County**	922 Court St NE	Conyers	GA	30207-4540
912 937-2609	**Schley County**	PO Box 352	Ellaville	GA	31806-0000
912 564-7535	**Screven County**	PO Box 159	Sylvania	GA	30467-0159
912 524-2878	**Seminole County**	County Courthouse	Donalsonville	GA	31745-0000
404 228-9900	**Spalding County**	132 E Solomon St	Griffin	GA	30223-3312
404 886-9491	**Stephens County**	PO Box 386	Toccoa	GA	30577-0000
912 838-6769	**Stewart County**	PO Box 157	Lumpkin	GA	31815-0157
912 924-3090	**Sumter County**	PO Box 295	Americus	GA	31709-0295
404 665-3220	**Talbot County**	Courthouse Sq	Talbotton	GA	31827-0000
404 456-2494	**Taliaferro County**	Courthouse Sq	Crawfordville	GA	30631-0000
912 557-4335	**Tattnall County**	Main & Brazell Sts	Reidsville	GA	30453-0000
912 862-3336	**Taylor County**	PO Box 278	Butler	GA	31006-0000
912 868-5688	**Telfair County**	Courthouse Sq	McRae	GA	31055-0000
912 995-4476	**Terrell County**	955 Forrester Dr SE	Dawson	GA	31742-2100
912 225-4100	**Thomas County**	PO Box 920	Thomasville	GA	31799-0920
912 386-7850	**Tift County**	225 N Tift Ave	Tifton	GA	31794-4463
912 526-3311	**Toombs County**	Courthouse Sq & Hwy 280	Lyons	GA	30436-0000
404 896-2130	**Towns County**	PO Box 178	Hiawassee	GA	30546-0178
912 529-3664	**Treutlen County**	2nd St	Soperton	GA	30457-0000
404 883-1600	**Troup County**	PO Box 1149	La Grange	GA	30241-1149
912 567-2011	**Turner County**	200 E College Ave	Ashburn	GA	31714-1275
912 945-3629	**Twiggs County**	101 Magnolia St	Jeffersonville	GA	31044-0000
404 745-2611	**Union County**	RR 8 Box 8005	Blairsville	GA	30512-9201
404 647-7012	**Upson County**	PO Box 889	Thomaston	GA	30286-0889
404 638-1437	**Walker County**	PO Box 445	Lafayette	GA	30728-0445
404 267-4571	**Walton County**	Court St Annex 1	Monroe	GA	30655-0000
912 287-4300	**Ware County**	800 Church St	Waycross	GA	31501-3501
404 465-2171	**Warren County**	100 Main St	Warrenton	GA	30828-0000
912 552-2325	**Washington County**	PO Box 271	Sandersville	GA	31082-0271
912 427-5900	**Wayne County**	174 N Brunswick St	Jesup	GA	31545-2808
912 828-5775	**Webster County**	Washington St & Hwy 280	Preston	GA	31824-0000
912 568-7135	**Wheeler County**	Pearl St	Alamo	GA	30411-0000
404 865-2235	**White County**	1657 S Main St Suite A	Cleveland	GA	30528-0185
404 278-8717	**Whitfield County**	300 W Crawford St	Dalton	GA	30720-4205
912 467-2737	**Wilcox County**	Courthouse Sq	Abbeville	GA	31001-1099
404 678-2511	**Wilkes County**	23 E Court St Rm 222	Washington	GA	30673-1570
912 946-2236	**Wilkinson County**	PO Box 161	Irwinton	GA	31042-0161
912 776-8200	**Worth County**	201 N Main St	Sylvester	GA	31791-2178

HAWAII

808 961-8255	**Hawaii County**	25 Aupuni St	Hilo	HI	96720-4252
808 523-4141	**Honolulu County**	530 S King St	Honolulu	HI	96813-3014
808 245-4785	**Kauai County**	4396 Rice St	Lihue	HI	96766-1337
808 243-7825	**Maui County**	200 S High St	Wailuku	HI	96793-2134

IDAHO

208 383-4417	**Ada County**	650 Main St	Boise	ID	83702-5986
208 253-4561	**Adams County**	PO Box 48	Council	ID	83612-0048
208 236-7210	**Bannock County**	624 E Center St	Pocatello	ID	83201-6274
208 945-2212	**Bear Lake County**	7 E Center St	Paris	ID	83261-0000
208 245-2234	**Benewah County**	7th & College Aves	Saint Maries	ID	83861-0000
208 785-5005	**Bingham County**	501 N Maple St	Blackfoot	ID	83221-1700
208 788-4290	**Blaine County**	PO Box 400	Hailey	ID	83333-0400
208 392-4431	**Boise County**	PO Box 157	Idaho City	ID	83631-0157
208 263-6841	**Bonner County**	215 S 1st Ave	Sandpoint	ID	83864-1392
208 529-1350	**Bonneville County**	605 N Capital Ave	Idaho Falls	ID	83402-3582
208 267-2242	**Boundary County**	315 Kootnai St	Bonners Ferry	ID	83805-0000
208 527-3021	**Butte County**	PO Box 737	Arco	ID	83213-0737
208 764-2242	**Camas County**	PO Box 430	Fairfield	ID	83327-0430
208 454-7300	**Canyon County**	1115 Albany St	Caldwell	ID	83605-3542
208 547-4324	**Caribou County**	PO Box 775	Soda Springs	ID	83276-0775
208 678-7302	**Cassia County**	County Courthouse	Burley	ID	83318-0000
208 374-5304	**Clark County**	PO Box 205	Dubois	ID	83423-0205
208 476-3615	**Clearwater County**	PO Box 586	Orofino	ID	83544-0586
208 879-2325	**Custer County**	PO Box 597	Challis	ID	83226-0000
208 587-2129	**Elmore County**	150 S 4th East St	Mountain Home	ID	83647-3028
208 852-1091	**Franklin County**	39 W Oneida St	Preston	ID	83263-1234
208 624-7332	**Fremont County**	151 W 1st North	Saint Anthony	ID	83445-1403
208 365-4561	**Gem County**	415 E Main St	Emmett	ID	83617-3049
208 934-4221	**Gooding County**	PO Box 417	Gooding	ID	83330-0417
208 983-2751	**Idaho County**	320 W Main St	Grangeville	ID	83530-1948
208 745-9222	**Jefferson County**	134 N Clark St	Rigby	ID	83442-1437
208 324-8811	**Jerome County**	300 N Lincoln Ave	Jerome	ID	83338-2344
208 769-4400	**Kootenai County**	501 N Government Way	Coeur d'Alene	ID	83814-2990
208 882-8580	**Latah County**	522 S Adams St	Moscow	ID	83843-2963
208 756-2815	**Lemhi County**	206 Courthouse Dr	Salmon	ID	83467-3992
208 937-2661	**Lewis County**	510 Oak St	Nezperce	ID	83543-0000
208 886-7641	**Lincoln County**	111 W 'B' St	Shoshone	ID	83352-0000
208 356-3662	**Madison County**	PO Box 389	Rexburg	ID	83440-0389
208 436-9511	**Minidoka County**	715 G St	Rupert	ID	83350-0000
208 799-3090	**Nez Perce County**	PO Box 896	Lewiston	ID	83501-0896
208 766-4116	**Oneida County**	10 Court St	Malad City	ID	83252-0000
208 495-2421	**Owyhee County**	PO Box 128	Murphy	ID	83650-0128
208 642-6000	**Payette County**	PO Box D	Payette	ID	83661-0277
208 226-7611	**Power County**	543 Bannock Ave	American Falls	ID	83211-1200
208 752-3331	**Shoshone County**	PO Box 1049	Wallace	ID	83873-1049
208 354-2905	**Teton County**	PO Box 756	Driggs	ID	83422-0756
208 736-4004	**Twin Falls County**	PO Box 126	Twin Falls	ID	83303-0126
208 382-4297	**Valley County**	PO Box 737	Cascade	ID	83611-0737
208 549-2092	**Washington County**	PO Box 670	Weiser	ID	83672-0670

ILLINOIS

217 223-6300	**Adams County**	521 Vermont St	Quincy	IL	62301-2934
618 734-3947	**Alexander County**	2000 Washington Ave	Cairo	IL	62914-1717
618 664-0449	**Bond County**	PO Box 407	Greenville	IL	62246-0407
815 544-3103	**Boone County**	601 N Main St	Belvidere	IL	61008-2600
217 773-3421	**Brown County**	21 W Court St	Mount Sterling	IL	62353-1241
815 875-2014	**Bureau County**	County Courthouse	Princeton	IL	61356-0000
618 576-2351	**Calhoun County**	County Rd	Hardin	IL	62047-0000
815 244-9171	**Carroll County**	Rt 78 & Rapp Rd	Mount Carroll	IL	61053-0000
217 452-7217	**Cass County**	County Courthouse	Virginia	IL	62691-0000
217 384-3720	**Champaign County**	204 E Elm St	Urbana	IL	61801-3324
217 824-4969	**Christian County**	600 N Main St	Taylorville	IL	62568-1599
217 826-8311	**Clark County**	501 Archer Ave	Marshall	IL	62441-1275
618 665-3626	**Clay County**	County Courthouse	Louisville	IL	62858-0000
618 594-2464	**Clinton County**	850 Fairfax County Courthouse	Carlyle	IL	62231-0000
217 348-0501	**Coles County**	PO Box 207	Charleston	IL	61920-0207
312 443-6398	**Cook County**	118 N Clark St Suite 567	Chicago	IL	60602-1311
618 546-1212	**Crawford County**	Douglas St	Robinson	IL	62454-2146
217 849-2631	**Cumberland County**	Courthouse Sq	Toledo	IL	62468-0000
217 935-2119	**De Witt County**	201 W Washington St	Clinton	IL	61727-1639
815 895-9161	**DeKalb County**	110 E Sycamore St	Sycamore	IL	60178-1497
217 253-2411	**Douglas County**	401 S Center St	Tuscola	IL	61953-1603
708 682-7035	**Du Page County**	421 N County Farm Rd	Wheaton	IL	60187-3978
217 465-4151	**Edgar County**	County Courthouse	Paris	IL	61944-0000
618 445-2115	**Edwards County**	50 E Main St	Albion	IL	62806-1262
217 342-6535	**Effingham County**	PO Box 628	Effingham	IL	62401-0628
618 283-5000	**Fayette County**	221 S 7th St	Vandalia	IL	62471-2755
217 379-2721	**Ford County**	200 W State St Rm 101	Paxton	IL	60957-1145
618 438-3221	**Franklin County**	Public Sq	Benton	IL	62812-2264
309 547-3041	**Fulton County**	100 N Main St	Lewistown	IL	61542-1445
618 269-3025	**Gallatin County**	PO Box K	Shawneetown	IL	62984-0550
217 942-5443	**Greene County**	519 N Main St	Carrollton	IL	62016-1033
815 942-9024	**Grundy County**	111 E Washington St	Morris	IL	60450-2268
618 643-2721	**Hamilton County**	Public Sq	McLeansboro	IL	62859-1489
217 357-3911	**Hancock County**	Courthouse Sq	Carthage	IL	62321-1359
618 287-2251	**Hardin County**	Main St	Elizabethtown	IL	62931-0000
309 867-2911	**Henderson County**	PO Box 308	Oquawka	IL	61469-0308
309 937-2426	**Henry County**	100 S Main	Cambridge	IL	61238-0000
815 432-6960	**Iroquois County**	550 S 10th	Watseka	IL	60970-1810
618 684-2151	**Jackson County**	1001 Walnut St	Murphysboro	IL	62966-2177
618 783-3124	**Jasper County**	100 W Jourdan St	Newton	IL	62448-1973
618 244-8020	**Jefferson County**	County Courthouse Rm 105	Mount Vernon	IL	62864-4086
618 498-5571	**Jersey County**	201 W Pearl St	Jerseyville	IL	62052-1675
815 777-0161	**Jo Daviess County**	330 N Bench St	Galena	IL	61036-1828
618 658-3611	**Johnson County**	PO Box 96	Vienna	IL	62995-0096
708 232-3400	**Kane County**	100 S 3rd St	Geneva	IL	60134-2722
815 937-2990	**Kankakee County**	450 E Court St	Kankakee	IL	60901-3997
708 553-4104	**Kendall County**	110 W Ridge St	Yorkville	IL	60560-1432
309 343-3121	**Knox County**	200 S Cherry St	Galesburg	IL	61401-4991
708 360-6600	**Lake County**	18 N County St	Waukegan	IL	60085-4339
815 434-8202	**LaSalle County**	707 E Etna Rd	Ottawa	IL	61350-1033

Local Government–County

618 943-2346	**Lawrence County**	County Courthouse	Lawrenceville	IL	62439-0000
815 288-3309	**Lee County**	Galena & 3rd Sts	Dixon	IL	61021-0000
815 844-5166	**Livingston County**	112 W Madison St	Pontiac	IL	61764-1871
217 732-4148	**Logan County**	601 Broadway St	Lincoln	IL	62656-2732
217 424-1305	**Macon County**	253 E Wood St Rm 52	Decatur	IL	62523-1488
217 854-3214	**Macoupin County**	County Courthouse	Carlinville	IL	62626-0000
618 692-6290	**Madison County**	155 N Main St	Edwardsville	IL	62025-1999
618 548-3400	**Marion County**	Broadway & Main St	Salem	IL	62881-0000
309 246-6325	**Marshall County**	122 N Prairie St	Lacon	IL	61540-1216
309 543-6661	**Mason County**	County Courthouse	Havana	IL	62644-0000
618 524-5213	**Massac County**	PO Box 429	Metropolis	IL	62960-0429
309 833-2474	**McDonough County**	County Courthouse	Macomb	IL	61455-0000
815 338-2040	**McHenry County**	2200 N Seminary Ave	Woodstock	IL	60098-2621
309 888-5001	**McLean County**	104 W Front St	Bloomington	IL	61701-5091
217 632-2415	**Menard County**	PO Box 456	Petersburg	IL	62675-0456
309 582-7021	**Mercer County**	College Ave & SW 3rd St	Aledo	IL	61231-0000
618 939-8681	**Monroe County**	100 S Main St	Waterloo	IL	62298-1399
217 532-9530	**Montgomery County**	1 Courthouse Sq	Hillsboro	IL	62049-1137
217 245-4619	**Morgan County**	300 W State St	Jacksonville	IL	62650-2063
217 728-4389	**Moultrie County**	Courthouse	Sullivan	IL	61951-0000
815 732-3201	**Ogle County**	PO Box 357	Oregon	IL	61061-0357
309 672-6059	**Peoria County**	324 Main St Rm 101	Peoria	IL	61602-1319
618 357-5116	**Perry County**	Town Sq	Pinckneyville	IL	62274-0000
217 762-9487	**Piatt County**	101 W Washington St	Monticello	IL	61856-1650
217 285-6812	**Pike County**	Rt 36	Pittsfield	IL	62363-0000
618 683-4466	**Pope County**	PO Box 216	Golconda	IL	62938-0216
618 748-9360	**Pulaski County**	PO Box 218	Mound City	IL	62963-0218
815 925-7129	**Putnam County**	4th St	Hennepin	IL	61327-0000
618 826-2510	**Randolph County**	1 Taylor St	Chester	IL	62233-0000
618 392-3111	**Richland County**	Main St	Olney	IL	62450-0000
309 786-4451	**Rock Island County**	1504 3rd Ave	Rock Island	IL	61201-8646
618 277-6600	**Saint Clair County**	10 Public Sq	Belleville	IL	62220-1698
618 253-8197	**Saline County**	10 E Poplar St	Harrisburg	IL	62946-1553
217 753-6600	**Sangamon County**	800 E Monroe St	Springfield	IL	62701-1979
217 322-4734	**Schuyler County**	PO Box 190	Rushville	IL	62681-0190
217 742-3178	**Scott County**	101 E Market St	Winchester	IL	62694-1258
217 774-4421	**Shelby County**	324 E Main St	Shelbyville	IL	62565-1694
309 286-5911	**Stark County**	130 W Main St	Toulon	IL	61483-0000
815 235-8289	**Stephenson County**	15 N Galena Ave	Freeport	IL	61032-4390
309 477-2264	**Tazewell County**	4th & Court Sts	Pekin	IL	61554-0000
618 833-5711	**Union County**	311 W Market St	Jonesboro	IL	62952-0000
217 431-2555	**Vermilion County**	7 N Vermilion St	Danville	IL	61832-5806
618 262-4561	**Wabash County**	4th & Market St	Mount Carmel	IL	62863-1582
309 734-8592	**Warren County**	Public Sq	Monmouth	IL	61462-0000
618 327-8314	**Washington County**	Saint Louis St	Nashville	IL	62263-1599
618 842-5182	**Wayne County**	300 E Main St	Fairfield	IL	62837-2013
618 382-7211	**White County**	Main St	Carmi	IL	62821-0000
815 772-7201	**Whiteside County**	200 E Knox St	Morrison	IL	61270-2819
815 740-4615	**Will County**	302 N Chicago St	Joliet	IL	60431-1059
618 997-1301	**Williamson County**	200 W Jefferson St	Marion	IL	62959-2494
815 987-3050	**Winnebago County**	400 W State St	Rockford	IL	61101-1276
309 467-2822	**Woodford County**	PO Box 38	Eureka	IL	61530-0038

INDIANA

219 724-2600	**Adams County**	112 S 2nd St	Decatur	IN	46733-1694
219 428-7124	**Allen County**	1 E Main St	Fort Wayne	IN	46802-1887
812 379-1600	**Bartholomew County**	PO Box 924	Columbus	IN	47202-0924
317 884-0930	**Benton County**	700 E 5th St	Fowler	IN	47944-1556
317 348-3213	**Blackford County**	110 W Washington St	Hartford City	IN	47348-2251
317 482-3510	**Boone County**	1 Courthouse Sq Rm 212	Lebanon	IN	46052-2150
812 988-4796	**Brown County**	Van Buren & Main Sts	Nashville	IN	47448-0000
317 564-4485	**Carroll County**	County Courthouse	Delphi	IN	46923-0000
219 753-7700	**Cass County**	200 Court Pk	Logansport	IN	46947-3114
812 285-6200	**Clark County**	City Court Bldg 501 E Court Ave	Jeffersonville	IN	47130-0000
812 448-8727	**Clay County**	1206 E National Ave	Brazil	IN	47834-2797
317 659-1891	**Clinton County**	50 N Jackson St	Frankfort	IN	46041-1993
812 338-2565	**Crawford County**	PO Box 375	English	IN	47118-0375
812 254-1090	**Daviess County**	County Courthouse	Washington	IN	47501-0000
219 925-2362	**De Kalb County**	100 Main St	Auburn	IN	46706-0000
812 537-1040	**Dearborn County**	215-B W High St	Lawrenceburg	IN	47025-1909
812 663-2546	**Decatur County**	150 Courthouse Sq Suite 5	Greensburg	IN	47240-2091
317 747-7726	**Delaware County**	PO Box 1089	Muncie	IN	47308-1089
812 482-1633	**Dubois County**	Main St	Jasper	IN	47546-0000
219 534-3541	**Elkhart County**	117 N 2nd St	Goshen	IN	46526-3297
317 825-1813	**Fayette County**	401 N Central Ave	Connersville	IN	47331-1997
812 948-5411	**Floyd County**	211 W 1st St	New Albany	IN	47150-3501
317 793-2192	**Fountain County**	County Courthouse	Covington	IN	47932-1293
317 647-5111	**Franklin County**	459 Main St	Brookville	IN	47012-1405
219 223-2911	**Fulton County**	815 Main St	Rochester	IN	46975-1546
812 385-8260	**Gibson County**	Courthouse Sq	Princeton	IN	47670-1542
317 668-8121	**Grant County**	County Courthouse	Marion	IN	46952-0000
812 384-8532	**Greene County**	Main & Washington Sts	Bloomfield	IN	47424-0000
317 773-6110	**Hamilton County**	Public Sq	Noblesville	IN	46060-1697
317 462-1106	**Hancock County**	9 E Main St	Greenfield	IN	46140-2320
812 738-8241	**Harrison County**	300 N Capitol Ave	Corydon	IN	47112-1139
317 745-9207	**Hendricks County**	County Courthouse	Danville	IN	46122-1993
317 529-4705	**Henry County**	Broad St	New Castle	IN	47362-0000
317 456-2204	**Howard County**	Main & Sycamore	Kokomo	IN	46901-4543
219 356-3122	**Huntington County**	N Jefferson St	Huntington	IN	46750-0000
812 358-6116	**Jackson County**	PO Box 122	Brownstown	IN	47220-0122
219 866-4933	**Jasper County**	Courthouse Sq	Rensselaer	IN	47978-0000
219 726-4951	**Jay County**	Court St	Portland	IN	47371-0000
812 265-8900	**Jefferson County**	300 E Main St	Madison	IN	47250-3537
812 346-5977	**Jennings County**	County Courthouse	Vernon	IN	47282-0000
317 736-5000	**Johnson County**	5 E Jefferson St	Franklin	IN	46131-0000
812 885-2521	**Knox County**	7th & Broadway	Vincennes	IN	47591-0000
219 267-4444	**Kosciusko County**	100 W Center St	Warsaw	IN	46580-2846
219 326-6808	**La Porte County**	Courthouse Sq	La Porte	IN	46350-0000
219 463-2183	**Lagrange County**	114 W Michigan St	Lagrange	IN	46761-1853
219 755-3440	**Lake County**	2293 N Main St	Crown Point	IN	46307-1896
812 275-7543	**Lawrence County**	Bedford Sq	Bedford	IN	47421-0000
317 641-9480	**Madison County**	16 E 9th St	Anderson	IN	46016-1576
317 236-3200	**Marion County**	200 E Washington St	Indianapolis	IN	46204-3353
219 936-8922	**Marshall County**	211 W Madison St	Plymouth	IN	46563-1762
812 247-3651	**Martin County**	PO Box 170	Shoals	IN	47581-0170
317 472-3901	**Miami County**	21 Court St	Peru	IN	46970-2266
812 333-3600	**Monroe County**	PO Box 547	Bloomington	IN	47402-0547
317 364-6400	**Montgomery County**	100 E Main St	Crawfordsville	IN	47933-1715
317 342-1025	**Morgan County**	PO Box 1556	Martinsville	IN	46151-0556
219 474-6081	**Newton County**	Courthouse Sq	Kentland	IN	47951-0000
219 636-2736	**Noble County**	101 N Orange St	Albion	IN	46701-1097
812 438-2062	**Ohio County**	Main St	Rising Sun	IN	47040-0000
812 723-2649	**Orange County**	Court St	Paoli	IN	47454-0000
812 829-2325	**Owen County**	County Courthouse	Spencer	IN	47460-0000
317 569-5132	**Parke County**	County Courthouse	Rockville	IN	47872-0000
812 547-3741	**Perry County**	8th St	Cannelton	IN	47520-0000
812 354-6025	**Pike County**	Main St	Petersburg	IN	47567-0000
219 465-3400	**Porter County**	16 E Lincolnway	Valparaiso	IN	46383-5698
812 838-1306	**Posey County**	County Courthouse	Mount Vernon	IN	47620-0000
219 946-3313	**Pulaski County**	112 E Main St	Winamac	IN	46996-1344
317 653-2648	**Putnam County**	PO Box 546	Greencastle	IN	46135-0546
317 584-7070	**Randolph County**	County Courthouse 3rd Fl	Winchester	IN	47394-0000
812 689-6115	**Ripley County**	PO Box 177	Versailles	IN	47042-0000
317 932-2086	**Rush County**	PO Box 429	Rushville	IN	46173-0429
219 284-9534	**Saint Joseph County**	227 W Jefferson Blvd	South Bend	IN	46601-1830
812 752-4769	**Scott County**	1 E McClain Ave	Scottsburg	IN	47170-1848
317 392-6320	**Shelby County**	315 S Harrison St	Shelbyville	IN	46176-2161
812 649-6027	**Spencer County**	541 Main St	Rockport	IN	47635-1478
219 772-9128	**Starke County**	Washington St	Knox	IN	46534-0000
219 665-9364	**Steuben County**	SE Public Sq	Angola	IN	46703-1926
812 268-4657	**Sullivan County**	County Courthouse	Sullivan	IN	47882-0000
812 427-3175	**Switzerland County**	County Courthouse	Vevay	IN	47043-0000
317 423-9215	**Tippecanoe County**	20 N 3rd St	Lafayette	IN	47901-1222
317 675-2795	**Tipton County**	County Courthouse	Tipton	IN	46072-0000
317 458-6121	**Union County**	26 W Union St Rm 105	Liberty	IN	47353-1350
812 426-5160	**Vanderburgh County**	PO Box 3356	Evansville	IN	47732-3356
317 492-3500	**Vermillion County**	PO Box 8	Newport	IN	47966-0008
812 238-8211	**Vigo County**	3rd & Wabash	Terre Haute	IN	47807-0000
219 563-0661	**Wabash County**	1 W Hill St	Wabash	IN	46992-3151
317 762-3510	**Warren County**	N Monroe St	Williamsport	IN	47993-0000
812 897-6120	**Warrick County**	County Courthouse	Boonville	IN	47601-1596
812 883-5748	**Washington County**	County Courthouse	Salem	IN	47167-2086
317 973-9200	**Wayne County**	401 E Main St	Richmond	IN	47374-4289
219 824-2320	**Wells County**	102 W Market St	Bluffton	IN	46714-2050
219 583-7032	**White County**	PO Box 350	Monticello	IN	47960-0350
219 248-3102	**Whitley County**	302 S Chauncey St Courthouse Sq	Columbia City	IN	46725-2402

IOWA

515 743-2445	**Adair County**	PO Box L	Greenfield	IA	50849-1290
515 322-4711	**Adams County**	Davis & 9th	Corning	IA	50841-0000
319 568-3318	**Allamakee County**	PO Box 248	Waukon	IA	52172-0248
515 856-6101	**Appanoose County**	County Courthouse	Centerville	IA	52544-0000
712 563-4275	**Audubon County**	County Courthouse	Audubon	IA	50025-0000
319 472-2766	**Benton County**	100 E 4th St	Vinton	IA	52349-1771
319 291-2500	**Black Hawk County**	316 E 5th St	Waterloo	IA	50703-4712
515 432-6291	**Boone County**	County Courthouse	Boone	IA	50036-0000
319 352-5040	**Bremer County**	415 E Bremer Ave	Waverly	IA	50677-3536
319 334-2196	**Buchanan County**	210 5th Ave NE	Independence	IA	50644-1959
712 749-2546	**Buena Vista County**	PO Box 1186	Storm Lake	IA	50588-1186
319 267-2487	**Butler County**	PO Box 325	Allison	IA	50602-0307
712 297-8122	**Calhoun County**	PO Box 273	Rockwell City	IA	50579-0273
712 792-4327	**Carroll County**	PO Box 867	Carroll	IA	51401-0867
712 243-2105	**Cass County**	7th St Courthouse	Atlantic	IA	50022-0000
319 886-2101	**Cedar County**	400 Cedar St	Tipton	IA	52772-1752
515 421-3074	**Cerro Gordo County**	220 N Washington Ave	Mason City	IA	50401-3254
712 225-2706	**Cherokee County**	PO Box F	Cherokee	IA	51012-0000
515 394-2106	**Chickasaw County**	Prospect St	New Hampton	IA	50659-0000
515 342-2213	**Clarke County**	117 1/2 S Main St	Osceola	IA	50213-1299
712 262-4335	**Clay County**	215 W 4th St	Spencer	IA	51301-3822
319 245-2204	**Clayton County**	111 High St	Elkader	IA	52043-0000
319 243-6210	**Clinton County**	PO Box 157	Clinton	IA	52732-0157
712 263-2242	**Crawford County**	PO Box 546	Denison	IA	51442-0546
515 993-4789	**Dallas County**	801 Court St	Adel	IA	50003-1478
515 664-2011	**Davis County**	Courthouse Sq	Bloomfield	IA	52537-1600
515 446-4331	**Decatur County**	207 N Main St	Leon	IA	50144-1647
319 927-4942	**Delaware County**	PO Box 527	Manchester	IA	52057-0527
319 753-8272	**Des Moines County**	PO Box 158	Burlington	IA	52601-0158
712 336-1138	**Dickinson County**	18th & Hill County Courthouse	Spirit Lake	IA	51360-0000
319 589-4418	**Dubuque County**	720 Central Ave	Dubuque	IA	52001-7079
712 362-3325	**Emmet County**	609 1st Ave N	Estherville	IA	51334-0000
319 422-6061	**Fayette County**	Vine St	West Union	IA	52175-0000
515 228-7111	**Floyd County**	101 S Main St	Charles City	IA	50616-2756
515 456-5626	**Franklin County**	12 1st Ave NW	Hampton	IA	50441-0000
712 374-2232	**Fremont County**	Courthouse Sq	Sidney	IA	51652-0549
515 386-2516	**Greene County**	County Courthouse	Jefferson	IA	50129-2294
319 824-5229	**Grundy County**	700 G Ave	Grundy Center	IA	50638-1440
515 747-3415	**Guthrie County**	200 N 5th St	Guthrie Center	IA	50115-1331
515 832-1771	**Hamilton County**	County Courthouse	Webster City	IA	50595-3158
515 923-2532	**Hancock County**	855 State St	Garner	IA	50438-1645
515 858-3461	**Hardin County**	Edgington Ave	Eldora	IA	50627-1741
712 644-2665	**Harrison County**	113 N 2nd Ave	Logan	IA	51546-1331
319 385-8480	**Henry County**	100 E Washington St	Mount Pleasant	IA	52641-1931
319 547-2661	**Howard County**	218 N Elm St	Cresco	IA	52136-1522
515 332-1806	**Humboldt County**	County Courthouse	Dakota City	IA	50529-9999
712 364-2628	**Ida County**	401 Moorehead St	Ida Grove	IA	51445-1429
319 642-3914	**Iowa County**	Court Ave	Marengo	IA	52301-0000
319 652-4946	**Jackson County**	201 W Platt St	Maquoketa	IA	52060-2243
515 792-3255	**Jasper County**	100 1st St	Newton	IA	50208-0000
515 472-3454	**Jefferson County**	PO Box 984	Fairfield	IA	52556-0984
319 356-6060	**Johnson County**	417 S Clinton St	Iowa City	IA	52240-4108
319 462-4341	**Jones County**	High St	Anamosa	IA	52205-0000
515 622-2210	**Keokuk County**	Courthouse Sq	Sigourney	IA	52591-1499
515 295-3240	**Kossuth County**	114 W State St	Algona	IA	50511-2613
319 372-3523	**Lee County**	PO Box 1443	Fort Madison	IA	52627-1443
319 398-3411	**Linn County**	50 3rd Ave Bridge	Cedar Rapids	IA	52401-1704
319 523-4541	**Louisa County**	117 S Main St	Wapello	IA	52653-1547
515 774-4421	**Lucas County**	County Courthouse	Chariton	IA	50049-0000
712 472-2623	**Lyon County**	206 S 2nd Ave	Rock Rapids	IA	51246-1597
515 462-4451	**Madison County**	PO Box 152	Winterset	IA	50273-0152
515 673-7786	**Mahaska County**	PO Box 30	Oskaloosa	IA	52577-0030
515 828-2207	**Marion County**	PO Box 497	Knoxville	IA	50138-0497
515 754-6373	**Marshall County**	17 E Main St	Marshalltown	IA	50158-4906
712 527-4880	**Mills County**	418 Sharp St	Glenwood	IA	51534-1756
515 732-3726	**Mitchell County**	County Courthouse	Osage	IA	50461-0000
712 423-2491	**Monona County**	610 Iowa Ave	Onawa	IA	51040-1699
515 932-5212	**Monroe County**	County Courthouse	Albia	IA	52531-0000
712 623-4986	**Montgomery County**	105 Coolbaugh St	Red Oak	IA	51566-0000
319 263-6511	**Muscatine County**	PO Box 327	Muscatine	IA	52761-0327
712 757-3255	**O'Brien County**	155 S Hayes	Primghar	IA	51245-0000
712 754-3595	**Osceola County**	614 5th Ave	Sibley	IA	51249-1704
712 542-3214	**Page County**	112 E Main St	Clarinda	IA	51632-2197
712 852-3603	**Palo Alto County**	11th & Broadway	Emmetsburg	IA	50536-0000
712 546-6100	**Plymouth County**	3rd Ave & 2nd St SE	Le Mars	IA	51031-0000
712 335-4208	**Pocahontas County**	Court Sq County Courthouse	Pocahontas	IA	50574-0000
515 286-3772	**Polk County**	500 Mulberry St	Des Moines	IA	50309-4238
712 328-5604	**Pottawattamie County**	227 S 6th St	Council Bluffs	IA	51501-4209
515 623-5644	**Poweshiek County**	302 E Main St	Montezuma	IA	50171-0000
515 464-3234	**Ringgold County**	County Courthouse	Mount Ayr	IA	50854-0000
712 662-7791	**Sac County**	PO Box 368	Sac City	IA	50583-0368
319 326-8647	**Scott County**	416 W 4th St	Davenport	IA	52801-1187

712 755-5543	**Shelby County**	PO Box 431	Harlan	IA	51537-0431
712 737-2286	**Sioux County**	210 Central Ave SW	Orange City	IA	51041-1751
515 382-6581	**Story County**	900 6th St	Nevada	IA	50201-2004
515 484-3721	**Tama County**	County Courthouse	Toledo	IA	52342-0000
712 523-2095	**Taylor County**	County Courthouse	Bedford	IA	50833-0000
515 782-7315	**Union County**	300 N Pine St	Creston	IA	50801-2430
319 293-3129	**Van Buren County**	PO Box 475	Keosauqua	IA	52565-0475
515 683-0060	**Wapello County**	4th & Court Sts	Ottumwa	IA	52501-2599
515 961-1033	**Warren County**	PO Box 379	Indianola	IA	50125-0379
319 653-7741	**Washington County**	PO Box 391	Washington	IA	52353-0391
515 872-2264	**Wayne County**	PO Box 424	Corydon	IA	50060-0424
515 576-7115	**Webster County**	701 Central Ave	Fort Dodge	IA	50501-3813
515 582-4520	**Winnebago County**	126 S Clark St	Forest City	IA	50436-1793
319 382-2469	**Winneshiek County**	201 W Main St	Decorah	IA	52101-1775
712 279-6616	**Woodbury County**	101 Court St	Sioux City	IA	51101-1909
515 324-2840	**Worth County**	1000 Central Ave	Northwood	IA	50459-1523
515 532-3113	**Wright County**	PO Box 306	Clarion	IA	50525-0306

KANSAS

316 365-7491	**Allen County**	1 N Washington St	Iola	KS	66749-2841
913 448-6841	**Anderson County**	100 E 4th Ave	Garnett	KS	66032-1595
913 367-1653	**Atchison County**	5th & Parallel	Atchison	KS	66002-0000
316 886-3961	**Barber County**	120 E Washington Ave	Medicine Lodge	KS	67104-1421
316 792-7391	**Barton County**	PO Box 1089	Great Bend	KS	67530-1089
316 223-3800	**Bourbon County**	210 S National Ave	Fort Scott	KS	66701-1328
913 742-2581	**Brown County**	Courthouse Sq	Hiawatha	KS	66434-0000
316 321-1960	**Butler County**	200 W Central Ave	El Dorado	KS	67042-2101
316 273-6423	**Chase County**	PO Box 547	Cottonwood Falls	KS	66845-0547
316 725-3370	**Chautauqua County**	215 N Chautauqua St	Sedan	KS	67361-1397
316 429-2042	**Cherokee County**	PO Box 14	Columbus	KS	66725-0014
913 332-2401	**Cheyenne County**	PO Box 985	Saint Francis	KS	67756-0985
316 635-2813	**Clark County**	PO Box 886	Ashland	KS	67831-0886
913 632-2552	**Clay County**	PO Box 98	Clay Center	KS	67432-0098
913 243-4319	**Cloud County**	811 Washington St	Concordia	KS	66901-3415
316 364-2191	**Coffey County**	6th & Neosho	Burlington	KS	66839-0000
316 582-2361	**Comanche County**	PO Box 397	Coldwater	KS	67029-0397
316 221-4066	**Cowley County**	311 E 9th Ave	Winfield	KS	67156-2864
316 724-6115	**Crawford County**	County Courthouse	Girard	KS	66743-0000
913 475-2132	**Decatur County**	194 S Penn Ave	Oberlin	KS	67749-2243
913 263-3774	**Dickinson County**	PO Box 248	Abilene	KS	67410-0248
913 985-3513	**Doniphan County**	Main St	Troy	KS	66087-0000
913 841-7700	**Douglas County**	111 E 11th St	Lawrence	KS	66044-2990
316 659-3121	**Edwards County**	312 Massachusetts Ave	Kinsley	KS	67547-1099
316 374-2490	**Elk County**	PO Box 606	Howard	KS	67349-0606
913 625-6558	**Ellis County**	1204 Fort St	Hays	KS	67601-3899
913 472-4161	**Ellsworth County**	PO Box 396	Ellsworth	KS	67439-0396
316 276-3051	**Finney County**	PO Box M	Garden City	KS	67846-0450
316 227-3184	**Ford County**	Central & Spruce Sts	Dodge City	KS	67801-4482
913 242-1471	**Franklin County**	3rd & Main Sts	Ottawa	KS	66067-0000
913 238-3912	**Geary County**	8th & Franklin	Junction City	KS	66441-0000
913 938-2300	**Gove County**	PO Box 128	Gove	KS	67736-0128
913 674-3453	**Graham County**	410 N Pomeroy St	Hill City	KS	67642-1645
316 356-1335	**Grant County**	108 S Glenn St	Ulysses	KS	67880-2551
316 855-3618	**Gray County**	PO Box 487	Cimarron	KS	67835-0487
316 376-4256	**Greeley County**	PO Box 277	Tribune	KS	67879-0277
316 583-7421	**Greenwood County**	311 N Main St	Eureka	KS	67045-1321
316 384-5629	**Hamilton County**	N Main St	Syracuse	KS	67878-0000
316 842-5555	**Harper County**	County Courthouse	Anthony	KS	67003-2799
316 283-6900	**Harvey County**	PO Box 687	Newton	KS	67114-0687
316 675-2263	**Haskell County**	PO Box 518	Sublette	KS	67877-0518
316 357-6421	**Hodgeman County**	PO Box 247	Jetmore	KS	67854-0247
913 364-2891	**Jackson County**	Courthouse Sq	Holton	KS	66436-1791
913 863-2272	**Jefferson County**	PO Box 321	Oskaloosa	KS	66066-0321
913 378-3121	**Jewell County**	307 N Commercial St	Mankato	KS	66956-2025
913 782-5000	**Johnson County**	Santa Fe & Kansas Aves	Olathe	KS	66061-3195
316 355-6422	**Kearny County**	305 N Main St	Lakin	KS	67860-0000
316 532-2521	**Kingman County**	130 N Spruce St	Kingman	KS	67068-1647
316 723-3366	**Kiowa County**	211 E Florida Ave	Greensburg	KS	67054-2294
316 795-2138	**Labette County**	PO Box 387	Oswego	KS	67356-0387
316 397-5356	**Lane County**	144 South Ln	Dighton	KS	67839-0000
913 682-7611	**Leavenworth County**	S 4th & Walnut St	Leavenworth	KS	66048-2781
913 524-4757	**Lincoln County**	216 E Lincoln Ave	Lincoln	KS	67455-2097
913 795-2660	**Linn County**	PO Box B	Mound City	KS	66056-0601
913 672-4244	**Logan County**	710 W 2nd St	Oakley	KS	67748-1233
316 342-4950	**Lyon County**	402 Commercial St	Emporia	KS	66801-4000
316 382-2185	**Marion County**	S 3rd St Courthouse Sq	Marion	KS	66861-0000
913 562-5361	**Marshall County**	1201 Broadway	Marysville	KS	66508-1844
316 241-3656	**McPherson County**	Kansas & Maple Sts	McPherson	KS	67460-0000
316 873-2581	**Meade County**	200 N Fowler St	Meade	KS	67864-0000
913 294-3976	**Miami County**	120 S Pearl St	Paola	KS	66071-1774
913 738-3652	**Mitchell County**	PO Box 190	Beloit	KS	67420-0190
316 331-4840	**Montgomery County**	PO Box 446	Independence	KS	67301-0446
316 767-5518	**Morris County**	501 W Main St	Council Grove	KS	66846-1701
316 697-2157	**Morton County**	PO Box 1116	Elkhart	KS	67950-1116
913 336-2146	**Nemaha County**	607 Nemaha St	Seneca	KS	66538-1761
316 244-3293	**Neosho County**	PO Box 138	Erie	KS	66733-0237
913 798-2401	**Ness County**	202 W Sycamore St	Ness City	KS	67560-1558
913 877-2363	**Norton County**	PO Box 70	Norton	KS	67654-0070
913 828-4812	**Osage County**	PO Box 226	Lyndon	KS	66451-0226
913 346-2431	**Osborne County**	423 W Main St	Osborne	KS	67473-2302
913 392-2279	**Ottawa County**	307 N Concord St	Minneapolis	KS	67467-2140
316 285-3721	**Pawnee County**	715 Broadway	Larned	KS	67550-3098
913 543-5513	**Phillips County**	3rd & State Sts	Phillipsburg	KS	67661-0000
913 457-3314	**Pottawatomie County**	PO Box 187	Westmoreland	KS	66549-0187
316 672-7761	**Pratt County**	300 S Ninnescah St	Pratt	KS	67124-2733
913 626-3351	**Rawlins County**	607 Main St	Atwood	KS	67730-1896
316 665-2931	**Reno County**	206 W 1st Ave	Hutchinson	KS	67501-5245
913 527-5691	**Republic County**	County Courthouse	Belleville	KS	66935-0000
316 257-2232	**Rice County**	101 W Commercial St	Lyons	KS	67554-2727
913 537-0700	**Riley County**	110 Courthouse Plaza	Manhattan	KS	66502-6018
913 425-6391	**Rooks County**	115 N Walnut St	Stockton	KS	67669-1663
913 222-2726	**Rush County**	PO Box 220	La Crosse	KS	67548-0220
913 483-4641	**Russell County**	PO Box 113	Russell	KS	67665-0113
913 827-1961	**Saline County**	300 W Ash St	Salina	KS	67401-2396
316 872-2420	**Scott County**	303 Court St	Scott City	KS	67871-1122
316 383-7166	**Sedgwick County**	525 N Main St	Wichita	KS	67203-3703
316 624-0211	**Seward County**	415 N Washington Ave	Liberal	KS	67901-3497
913 291-4040	**Shawnee County**	200 SE 7th St	Topeka	KS	66603-3922
913 675-3361	**Sheridan County**	PO Box 899	Hoxie	KS	67740-0899
913 899-7581	**Sherman County**	813 Broadway	Goodland	KS	67735-3056
913 282-6533	**Smith County**	218 S Grant St	Smith Center	KS	66967-2798
316 549-3509	**Stafford County**	209 N Broadway St	Saint John	KS	67576-2042
316 492-2140	**Stanton County**	PO Box 190	Johnson	KS	67855-0190
316 544-2541	**Stevens County**	200 E 6th St	Hugoton	KS	67951-2652
316 326-3395	**Sumner County**	500 N Washington Ave	Wellington	KS	67152-4096
913 462-2561	**Thomas County**	300 N Court Ave	Colby	KS	67701-2439
913 743-5773	**Trego County**	216 N Main St	WaKeeney	KS	67672-2189
913 765-3414	**Wabaunsee County**	PO Box 278	Alma	KS	66401-0278
913 852-4282	**Wallace County**	313 Main St	Sharon Springs	KS	67758-9998
913 325-2974	**Washington County**	214 C St	Washington	KS	66968-1928
316 375-2731	**Wichita County**	PO Box 279	Leoti	KS	67861-0279
316 378-2186	**Wilson County**	615 Madison St	Fredonia	KS	66736-1383
316 625-2179	**Woodson County**	105 W Rutledge St	Yates Center	KS	66783-1237
913 573-2800	**Wyandotte County**	710 N 7th St	Kansas City	KS	66101-3087

KENTUCKY

502 384-2801	**Adair County**	500 Public Sq	Columbia	KY	42728-1451
502 237-3706	**Allen County**	PO Box 336	Scottsville	KY	42164-0336
502 839-3041	**Anderson County**	151 S Main St	Lawrenceburg	KY	40342-1192
502 335-5168	**Ballard County**	PO Box 145	Wickliffe	KY	42087-0145
502 651-3783	**Barren County**	County Courthouse 1st Fl	Glasgow	KY	42141-2812
606 674-2613	**Bath County**	Main St	Owingsville	KY	40360-0000
606 337-6143	**Bell County**	County Courthouse	Pineville	KY	40977-0000
606 334-2108	**Boone County**	2950 E Washington Sq	Burlington	KY	41005-0000
606 987-2430	**Bourbon County**	Main St	Paris	KY	40361-0000
606 739-5116	**Boyd County**	2800 Louisa St	Catlettsburg	KY	41129-1610
606 238-1100	**Boyle County**	Main St	Danville	KY	40422-0000
606 735-2952	**Bracken County**	Locus St	Brooksville	KY	41004-0000
606 666-3810	**Breathitt County**	1127 Main St	Jackson	KY	41339-1194
502 756-2269	**Breckinridge County**	PO Box 227	Hardinsburg	KY	40143-0227
502 543-2262	**Bullitt County**	Buckman St	Shepherdsville	KY	40165-0000
502 526-5676	**Butler County**	PO Box 448	Morgantown	KY	42261-0448
502 365-6754	**Caldwell County**	100 E Market St Rm 3	Princeton	KY	42445-1675
502 753-2920	**Calloway County**	101 S 5th St	Murray	KY	42071-2583
606 292-3838	**Campbell County**	PO Box 340	Newport	KY	41071-0000
502 628-5451	**Carlisle County**	Court St	Bardwell	KY	42023-0000
502 732-2446	**Carroll County**	Court St County Courthouse	Carrollton	KY	41008-0000
606 474-5188	**Carter County**	Courthouse Rm 232	Grayson	KY	41143-0000
606 787-6471	**Casey County**	PO Box 310	Liberty	KY	42539-0310
502 887-4105	**Christian County**	511 S Main St	Hopkinsville	KY	42240-2300
606 745-0200	**Clark County**	34 S Main St Rm 103	Winchester	KY	40391-2600
606 598-3663	**Clay County**	PO Box 463	Manchester	KY	40962-0463
606 387-5234	**Clinton County**	County Courthouse	Albany	KY	42602-0000
502 965-5251	**Crittenden County**	107 S Main St	Marion	KY	42064-1500
502 864-3726	**Cumberland County**	PO Box 275	Burkesville	KY	42717-0275
502 685-8434	**Daviess County**	PO Box 389	Owensboro	KY	42302-0389
502 597-2819	**Edmonson County**	Main & Cross St	Brownsville	KY	42210-0000
606 738-5421	**Elliott County**	PO Box 225	Sandy Hook	KY	41171-0225
606 723-5156	**Estill County**	130 Main St	Irvine	KY	40336-1098
606 253-3344	**Fayette County**	162 E Main St	Lexington	KY	40507-1363
606 845-7571	**Fleming County**	Court Sq	Flemingsburg	KY	41041-1399
606 886-9193	**Floyd County**	3rd Ave	Prestonsburg	KY	41653-0000
502 875-8702	**Franklin County**	PO Box 338	Frankfort	KY	40602-0338
502 236-2727	**Fulton County**	Moulton & Wellington Sts	Hickman	KY	42050-0000
606 567-5411	**Gallatin County**	PO Box 616	Warsaw	KY	41095-0616
606 792-3531	**Garrard County**	Public Sq	Lancaster	KY	40444-0000
606 824-3321	**Grant County**	PO Box 469	Williamstown	KY	41097-0469
502 247-3626	**Graves County**	Courthouse	Mayfield	KY	42066-0000
502 259-3201	**Grayson County**	100 Court Sq	Leitchfield	KY	42754-0000
502 932-4024	**Green County**	203 W Court St	Greensburg	KY	42743-1522
606 473-7455	**Greenup County**	301 Main St	Greenup	KY	41144-1055
502 927-6117	**Hancock County**	County Administration Bldg	Hawesville	KY	42348-0000
502 765-2171	**Hardin County**	14 Public Sq	Elizabethtown	KY	42701-1437
606 573-2600	**Harlan County**	PO Box 956	Harlan	KY	40831-0956
606 234-2232	**Harrison County**	190 W Pike St	Cynthiana	KY	41031-1426
502 524-2751	**Hart County**	PO Box 277	Munfordville	KY	42765-0000
502 827-5671	**Henderson County**	232 1st St	Henderson	KY	42420-3146
502 845-2891	**Henry County**	PO Box 202	New Castle	KY	40050-0202
502 653-4369	**Hickman County**	Courthouse Sq	Clinton	KY	42031-1295
502 821-8294	**Hopkins County**	Main & Center	Madisonville	KY	42431-2064
606 287-7800	**Jackson County**	PO Box 700	McKee	KY	40447-0000
502 625-5000	**Jefferson County**	527 W Jefferson St	Louisville	KY	40202-2814
606 885-4161	**Jessamine County**	PO Box 38	Nicholasville	KY	40356-0036
606 789-2550	**Johnson County**	Court St	Paintsville	KY	41240-0000
606 491-0702	**Kenton County**	3rd & Court St 1st Fl	Covington	KY	41012-0000
606 785-5651	**Knott County**	PO Box 446	Hindman	KY	41822-0446
606 546-3568	**Knox County**	PO Box 105	Barbourville	KY	40906-0105
502 358-3544	**Larue County**	County Courthouse	Hodgenville	KY	42748-0000
606 864-5158	**Laurel County**	County Courthouse	London	KY	40741-0000
606 638-4108	**Lawrence County**	122 S Main Cross St	Louisa	KY	41230-1393
606 464-2596	**Lee County**	PO Box 551	Beattyville	KY	41311-0000
606 672-2193	**Leslie County**	PO Box 916	Hyden	KY	41749-0000
606 633-2432	**Letcher County**	PO Box 58	Whitesburg	KY	41858-0058
606 796-3062	**Lewis County**	2nd St	Vanceburg	KY	41179-0000
606 365-2601	**Lincoln County**	County Courthouse	Stanford	KY	40484-0000
502 928-2162	**Livingston County**	PO Box 400	Smithland	KY	42081-0400
502 726-6061	**Logan County**	426 E 4th St	Russellville	KY	42276-1897
502 388-2331	**Lyon County**	PO Box 350	Eddyville	KY	42038-0350
606 624-4703	**Madison County**	101 W Main St	Richmond	KY	40475-1415
606 349-2216	**Magoffin County**	Court St	Salyersville	KY	41465-0000
502 692-2651	**Marion County**	Main St	Lebanon	KY	40033-0000
502 527-3323	**Marshall County**	1101 Main St	Benton	KY	42025-1498
606 298-2810	**Martin County**	Main St	Inez	KY	41224-0000
606 564-3341	**Mason County**	PO Box 234	Maysville	KY	41056-0234
502 444-4700	**McCracken County**	Washington & 7th Sts	Paducah	KY	42003-0000
606 376-2411	**McCreary County**	Main St	Whitley City	KY	42653-0000
502 273-3082	**McLean County**	PO Box 57	Calhoun	KY	42327-0057
502 422-2152	**Meade County**	PO Box 614	Brandenburg	KY	40108-0614
606 768-3512	**Menifee County**	County Courthouse	Frenchburg	KY	40322-0000
606 734-6310	**Mercer County**	224 S Main St	Harrodsburg	KY	40330-1696
502 432-4821	**Metcalfe County**	PO Box 850	Edmonton	KY	42129-0000
502 487-5471	**Monroe County**	PO Box 335	Tompkinsville	KY	42167-0335
606 498-8700	**Montgomery County**	Court St	Mount Sterling	KY	40353-0000
606 743-3897	**Morgan County**	505 Prestonsburg St	West Liberty	KY	41472-1162
502 338-1441	**Muhlenberg County**	PO Box 272	Greenville	KY	42345-0272
502 348-1800	**Nelson County**	113 E Stephen Foster Ave	Bardstown	KY	40004-1546
606 289-5591	**Nicholas County**	PO Box 329	Carlisle	KY	40311-0329
502 298-3673	**Ohio County**	PO Box 85	Hartford	KY	42347-0085
502 222-9311	**Oldham County**	100 Main St	La Grange	KY	40031-0000
502 484-3405	**Owen County**	County Courthouse	Owenton	KY	40359-0000
606 593-5735	**Owsley County**	154 Main St	Booneville	KY	41314-0000
606 654-4321	**Pendleton County**	County Courthouse Sq	Falmouth	KY	41040-0000
606 436-4614	**Perry County**	PO Box 150	Hazard	KY	41702-0000
606 432-6240	**Pike County**	PO Box 631	Pikeville	KY	41501-0631
606 663-4390	**Powell County**	Court St	Stanton	KY	40380-0000
606 679-2042	**Pulaski County**	PO Box 724	Somerset	KY	42501-0724
606 724-5212	**Robertson County**	PO Box 95	Mount Olivet	KY	41064-0000
606 256-2831	**Rockcastle County**	PO Box 365	Mount Vernon	KY	40456-0365
606 784-5212	**Rowan County**	E Main St 2nd Fl	Morehead	KY	40351-0000
502 343-2125	**Russell County**	PO Box 579	Jamestown	KY	42629-0579

Local Government–County

502 863-7875	**Scott County** 101 E Main St	Georgetown	KY	40324-1794
502 633-1220	**Shelby County** 501 Main St	Shelbyville	KY	40065-1133
502 586-8161	**Simpson County** PO Box 268	Franklin	KY	42134-0268
502 477-8121	**Spencer County** Main St	Taylorsville	KY	40071-0000
502 465-6677	**Taylor County** Court & Broadway	Campbellsville	KY	42718-0000
502 265-2363	**Todd County** PO Box 157	Elkton	KY	42220-0157
502 522-6661	**Trigg County** PO Box 1310	Cadiz	KY	42211-0609
502 255-7174	**Trimble County** Main St & Hwy 42	Bedford	KY	40006-0000
502 389-1334	**Union County** PO Box 119	Morganfield	KY	42437-0000
502 843-4146	**Warren County** 429 E 10th St	Bowling Green	KY	42101-2250
606 336-3471	**Washington County** PO Box 446	Springfield	KY	40069-0446
606 348-6661	**Wayne County** PO Box 565	Monticello	KY	42633-0000
502 639-5042	**Webster County** PO Box 155	Dixon	KY	42409-0155
606 549-6002	**Whitley County** Main St	Williamsburg	KY	40769-0000
606 668-3515	**Wolfe County** PO Box 400	Campton	KY	41301-0400
606 873-3421	**Woodford County** County Courthouse	Versailles	KY	40383-0000

LOUISIANA

318 788-8881	**Acadia Parish** PO Box 922	Crowley	LA	70527-0922
318 639-4396	**Allen Parish** PO Box G	Oberlin	LA	70655-2007
504 473-9866	**Ascension Parish** Houmas St	Donaldsonville	LA	70346-0000
504 369-7435	**Assumption Parish** Martin Luther King Dr & Hwy 1	Napoleonville	LA	70390-0000
318 253-7523	**Avoyelles Parish** 301 N Main St	Marksville	LA	71351-2493
318 463-7019	**Beauregard Parish** PO Box 310	De Ridder	LA	70634-0310
318 263-2123	**Bienville Parish** 300 Courthouse Sq	Arcadia	LA	71001-0000
318 965-2336	**Bossier Parish** PO Box 369	Benton	LA	71006-0369
318 226-6911	**Caddo Parish** 501 Texas St	Shreveport	LA	71101-5476
318 437-3550	**Calcasieu Parish** PO Box 1030	Lake Charles	LA	70602-1030
318 649-2681	**Caldwell Parish** Main St	Columbia	LA	71418-0000
318 775-5316	**Cameron Parish** PO Box 549	Cameron	LA	70631-0549
318 744-5497	**Catahoula Parish** PO Box 198	Harrisonburg	LA	71340-0198
318 927-9601	**Claiborne Parish** Courthouse Sq	Homer	LA	71040-0000
318 336-4204	**Concordia Parish** PO Box 790	Vidalia	LA	71373-0790
318 872-0738	**DeSoto Parish** Parish Courthouse	Mansfield	LA	71052-0000
504 389-3000	**East Baton Rouge Parish** 222 Saint Louis St	Baton Rouge	LA	70802-5817
318 559-2256	**East Carroll Parish** 400 1st St	Lake Providence	LA	71254-2616
504 683-5145	**East Feliciana Parish** PO Box 595	Clinton	LA	70722-0595
318 363-5651	**Evangeline Parish** Court St 2nd Fl	Ville Platte	LA	70586-0000
318 435-9429	**Franklin Parish** 210 Main St	Winnsboro	LA	71295-2750
318 627-3157	**Grant Parish** Main St	Colfax	LA	71417-0000
318 365-8246	**Iberia Parish** 300 Iberia St Suite 400	New Iberia	LA	70560-4543
504 687-5160	**Iberville Parish** PO Box 423	Plaquemine	LA	70765-0423
318 259-2424	**Jackson Parish** PO Box 737	Jonesboro	LA	71251-0737
318 824-4792	**Jefferson Davis Parish** PO Box 1409	Jennings	LA	70546-1409
504 364-2800	**Jefferson Parish** 2nd & Derbigny	Gretna	LA	70053-3299
318 233-6220	**Lafayette Parish** PO Box 4508	Lafayette	LA	70502-4508
504 446-8427	**Lafourche Parish** 209 Green St	Thibodaux	LA	70301-3021
318 992-2101	**LaSalle Parish** PO Box 57	Jena	LA	71342-0057
318 255-3663	**Lincoln Parish** 100 W Texas Ave	Ruston	LA	71270-4463
504 686-2266	**Livingston Parish** PO Box 427	Livingston	LA	70754-0427
318 574-0655	**Madison Parish** 100 N Cedar St	Tallulah	LA	71282-3840
318 281-4132	**Morehouse Parish** 125 E Madison St	Bastrop	LA	71221-0000
318 352-2714	**Natchitoches Parish** PO Box 799	Natchitoches	LA	71458-0799
504 565-6580	**Orleans Parish** 1300 Perdido St	New Orleans	LA	70112-2112
318 323-5188	**Ouachita Parish** 300 Saint John St	Monroe	LA	71201-7398
504 333-4343	**Plaquemines Parish** Hwy 39	Pointe a la Hache	LA	70082-9999
504 638-9596	**Pointe Coupee Parish** PO Box 86	New Roads	LA	70760-0086
318 473-8153	**Rapides Parish** 700 Murray St	Alexandria	LA	71301-8023
318 932-5719	**Red River Parish** 615 E Carroll St	Coushatta	LA	71019-8537
318 728-2061	**Richland Parish** 108 Courthouse Sq	Rayville	LA	71269-2647
318 256-6223	**Sabine Parish** PO Box 419	Many	LA	71449-0419
504 277-6371	**Saint Bernard Parish** 8201 W Judge Perez Dr	Chalmette	LA	70043-1696
504 783-6246	**Saint Charles Parish** PO Box 302	Hahnville	LA	70057-0302
504 222-4514	**Saint Helena Parish** Court Sq	Greensburg	LA	70441-0000
504 562-7431	**Saint James Parish** PO Box 106	Convent	LA	70723-0063
504 652-9569	**Saint John the Baptist Parish** 1801 W Airline Hwy	La Place	LA	70068-3336
318 942-5606	**Saint Landry Parish** Court & Landry Sts	Opelousas	LA	70570-0000
318 394-2210	**Saint Martin Parish** County Courthouse	Saint Martinville	LA	70582-0000
318 828-4100	**Saint Mary Parish** 500 Main St Rm 5	Franklin	LA	70538-6198
504 898-2430	**Saint Tammany Parish** PO Box 1090	Covington	LA	70434-1090
504 748-3211	**Tangipahoa Parish** PO Box 215	Amite	LA	70422-0215
318 766-3921	**Tensas Parish** Courthouse Sq	Saint Joseph	LA	71366-0000
504 868-5050	**Terrebonne Parish** 301 Goode St	Houma	LA	70360-4513
318 368-3055	**Union Parish** Main & Bayou Sts 1st Fl	Farmerville	LA	71241-0000
318 898-4310	**Vermilion Parish** PO Box 790	Abbeville	LA	70511-0790
318 238-1384	**Vernon Parish** 201 3rd St	Leesville	LA	71496-0000
504 839-4663	**Washington Parish** Washington & Main St	Franklinton	LA	70438-0000
318 371-0366	**Webster Parish** PO Box 370	Minden	LA	71058-0370
504 383-4755	**West Baton Rouge Parish** PO Box 757	Port Allen	LA	70767-0757
318 428-3390	**West Carroll Parish** PO Box 630	Oak Grove	LA	71263-0630
504 635-3864	**West Feliciana Parish** Royal & Prosperity	Saint Francisville	LA	70775-0000
318 628-5824	**Winn Parish** PO Box 951	Winnfield	LA	71483-0951

MAINE

207 784-8390	**Androscoggin County** 2 Turner St	Auburn	ME	04210-5978
207 532-7317	**Aroostook County** PO Box 803	Houlton	ME	04730-0787
207 871-8380	**Cumberland County** 142 Federal St	Portland	ME	04101-4151
207 778-6614	**Franklin County** 38 Main St	Farmington	ME	04938-1818
207 667-9542	**Hancock County** 60 State St	Ellsworth	ME	04605-1926
207 622-0971	**Kennebec County** 95 State St	Augusta	ME	04330-5611
207 594-0420	**Knox County** PO Box 885	Rockland	ME	04841-0885
207 882-6311	**Lincoln County** High St County Courthouse	Wiscasset	ME	04578-0000
207 743-6359	**Oxford County** PO Box 179	South Paris	ME	04281-0179
207 942-8535	**Penobscot County** 97 Hammond St	Bangor	ME	04401-4922
207 564-2161	**Piscataquis County** 51 E Main St	Dover-Foxcroft	ME	04426-1306
207 443-8200	**Sagadahoc County** PO Box 246	Bath	ME	04530-0246
207 474-9861	**Somerset County** County Courthouse	Skowhegan	ME	04976-0000
207 338-3282	**Waldo County** 73 Church St	Belfast	ME	04915-1705
207 255-3127	**Washington County** PO Box 297	Machias	ME	04654-0297
207 324-1571	**York County** Court St	Alfred	ME	04002-0000

MARYLAND

301 777-5911	**Allegany County** 3 Pershing St	Cumberland	MD	21502-3043
301 222-1821	**Anne Arundel County** 44 Calvert St	Annapolis	MD	21401-1986
301 396-3100	**Baltimore City (Independent City)** 100 N Holliday St	Baltimore	MD	21202-3417
301 887-3196	**Baltimore County** 400 Washington Ave	Towson	MD	21204-4606
301 535-1600	**Calvert County** 175 Main St	Prince Frederick	MD	20678-9302
301 479-0660	**Caroline County** PO Box 207	Denton	MD	21629-0207
301 876-2085	**Carroll County** 225 N Center St	Westminster	MD	21157-5194
301 398-0200	**Cecil County** E Main St	Elkton	MD	21921-0000
301 645-0550	**Charles County** PO Box B	La Plata	MD	20646-0167
301 228-1700	**Dorchester County** PO Box 26	Cambridge	MD	21613-0026
301 694-1100	**Frederick County** 12 E Church St	Frederick	MD	21701-5402
301 334-8970	**Garrett County** 203 S 4th St	Oakland	MD	21550-1535
301 838-6000	**Harford County** 220 S Main St	Bel Air	MD	21014-3833
301 992-2025	**Howard County** 3430 Courthouse Dr	Ellicott City	MD	21043-4300
301 778-4600	**Kent County** 230 N Cross St	Chestertown	MD	21620-1512
301 217-1000	**Montgomery County** 100 Maryland Ave Courthouse 2nd Fl	Rockville	MD	20850-0000
301 350-9700	**Prince George's County** 7911 Anchor St	Landover	MD	20785-4804
301 758-0322	**Queen Annes County** 208 N Commerce St	Centreville	MD	21617-1015
301 475-5621	**Saint Marys County** PO Box 653	Leonardtown	MD	20650-0653
301 651-0320	**Somerset County** 21 Prince William St	Princess Anne	MD	21853-0000
301 822-2401	**Talbot County** Washington St	Easton	MD	21601-0000
301 791-3000	**Washington County** 95 W Washington St	Hagerstown	MD	21740-4831
301 543-6551	**Wicomico County** PO Box 198	Salisbury	MD	21803-0198
301 632-1194	**Worcester County** 1 W Market St	Snow Hill	MD	21863-1073

MASSACHUSETTS

508 362-2511	**Barnstable County** Rt 6-A	Barnstable	MA	02630-0000
413 448-8424	**Berkshire County** 76 East St	Pittsfield	MA	01201-5304
508 823-6588	**Bristol County** 9 Court St	Taunton	MA	02780-3223
508 627-5535	**Dukes County** PO Box 190	Edgartown	MA	02539-0000
508 741-0200	**Essex County** 36 Federal St	Salem	MA	01970-3437
413 774-4015	**Franklin County** 425 Main St	Greenfield	MA	01301-3313
413 781-8100	**Hampden County** 50 State St	Springfield	MA	01103-2002
413 584-0557	**Hampshire County** 99 Main St	Northampton	MA	01060-3119
617 494-4003	**Middlesex County** 40 Thorndike St	East Cambridge	MA	02141-1755
508 228-7229	**Nantucket County** Town & County Bldg	Nantucket	MA	02554-0000
617 326-1600	**Norfolk County** 650 High St	Dedham	MA	02026-1855
508 747-1350	**Plymouth County** PO Box 3535	Plymouth	MA	02361-3535
617 725-8000	**Suffolk County** 55 Pemberton Sq Government Ctr	Boston	MA	02108-1701
508 756-2441	**Worcester County** 2 Main St	Worcester	MA	01608-1116

MICHIGAN

517 724-5374	**Alcona County** 106 5th St	Harrisville	MI	48740-0000
906 387-2076	**Alger County** 101 Court St	Munising	MI	49862-1196
616 673-8471	**Allegan County** 113 Chestnut St	Allegan	MI	49010-1362
517 356-0115	**Alpena County** 720 W Chisholm St	Alpena	MI	49707-2453
616 533-8607	**Antrim County** PO Box 520	Bellaire	MI	49615-0520
517 846-4626	**Arenac County** PO Box 747	Standish	MI	48658-0747
906 524-6183	**Baraga County** 12 S 3rd St	L'Anse	MI	49946-1090
616 948-4810	**Barry County** 220 W State St	Hastings	MI	49058-1849
517 892-3528	**Bay County** 515 Center Ave	Bay City	MI	48708-5941
616 882-9671	**Benzie County** 224 Court Pl	Beulah	MI	49617-0000
616 983-7111	**Berrien County** 811 Port St	Saint Joseph	MI	49085-1114
517 279-8411	**Branch County** 31 Division St	Coldwater	MI	49036-1904
616 781-0700	**Calhoun County** 315 W Green St	Marshall	MI	49068-1585
616 445-8621	**Cass County** 120 N Broadway St	Cassopolis	MI	49031-1302
616 547-7200	**Charlevoix County** 301 State St County Bldg	Charlevoix	MI	49720-0000
616 627-8808	**Cheboygan County** 870 S Main St	Cheboygan	MI	49721-2220
906 635-6300	**Chippewa County** 319 Court St	Sault Sainte Marie	MI	49783-2183
517 539-7131	**Clare County** PO Box 438	Harrison	MI	48625-0438
517 224-5100	**Clinton County** 100 E State St	Saint Johns	MI	48879-1571
517 348-2841	**Crawford County** 200 W Michigan Ave	Grayling	MI	49738-1745
906 786-1763	**Delta County** 310 Ludington St	Escanaba	MI	49829-4057
906 774-0988	**Dickinson County** PO Box 609	Iron Mountain	MI	49801-0609
517 543-7500	**Eaton County** 1045 Independence Dr	Charlotte	MI	48813-1095
616 348-1744	**Emmet County** 200 Division St	Petoskey	MI	49770-2444
313 257-3283	**Genesee County** 900 S Saginaw St Rm 202	Flint	MI	48502-0000
517 426-7351	**Gladwin County** 401 W Cedar Ave	Gladwin	MI	48624-2023
906 663-4518	**Gogebic County** 200 N Moore St	Bessemer	MI	49911-1052
616 922-4700	**Grand Traverse County** 400 Boardman Ave	Traverse City	MI	49684-2577
517 875-5215	**Gratiot County** 214 E Center St	Ithaca	MI	48847-1446
517 437-3391	**Hillsdale County** 29 N Howell St County Courthouse	Hillsdale	MI	49242-1865
906 482-1150	**Houghton County** 401 E Houghton Ave	Houghton	MI	49931-2016
517 269-9942	**Huron County** 250 E Huron Ave	Bad Axe	MI	48413-1317
517 676-0240	**Ingham County** PO Box 179	Mason	MI	48854-0179
616 527-5322	**Ionia County** Main St	Ionia	MI	48846-0000
517 362-3497	**Iosco County** PO Box 838	Tawas City	MI	48764-0838
906 875-3221	**Iron County** 2 S 6th St	Crystal Falls	MI	49920-1413
517 772-0911	**Isabella County** 200 N Main St	Mount Pleasant	MI	48858-2321
517 788-4265	**Jackson County** 120 W Michigan Ave	Jackson	MI	49201-1315
616 383-8840	**Kalamazoo County** 201 W Kalamazoo Ave	Kalamazoo	MI	49007-0000
616 258-3300	**Kalkaska County** 605 N Birch St	Kalkaska	MI	49646-0000
616 774-3548	**Kent County** 300 Monroe Ave NW	Grand Rapids	MI	49503-0000
906 337-2229	**Keweenaw County** 4th St County Courthouse	Eagle River	MI	49924-9999
616 745-4641	**Lake County** 800 10th St	Baldwin	MI	49304-0000
313 667-0356	**Lapeer County** 255 Clay St	Lapeer	MI	48446-2298
616 256-9824	**Leelanau County** PO Box 467	Leland	MI	49654-0467
517 263-8831	**Lenawee County** 425 N Main St	Adrian	MI	49221-2198
517 546-0500	**Livingston County** 200 E Grand River Ave	Howell	MI	48843-2267
906 293-5521	**Luce County** E Court St	Newberry	MI	49868-0000
906 643-7300	**Mackinac County** 100 Marley St	Saint Ignace	MI	49781-0000
313 469-5100	**Macomb County** 40 N Gratiot Ave	Mount Clemens	MI	48043-5688
616 723-3331	**Manistee County** 415 3rd St	Manistee	MI	49660-1606
906 228-1501	**Marquette County** 234 W Baraga Ave	Marquette	MI	49855-4751
616 843-8202	**Mason County** 300 E Ludington Ave	Ludington	MI	49431-2121
616 592-0783	**Mecosta County** 400 Elm St	Big Rapids	MI	49307-1849
906 863-9968	**Menominee County** 839 10th Ave	Menominee	MI	49858-3000
517 832-6739	**Midland County** 220 W Ellsworth St	Midland	MI	48640-5180
616 839-4967	**Missaukee County** PO Box J	Lake City	MI	49651-0000
313 243-7081	**Monroe County** 106 E 1st St	Monroe	MI	48161-2143
517 831-5226	**Montcalm County** 211 W Main St	Stanton	MI	48888-0000
517 785-4794	**Montmorency County** County Courthouse	Atlanta	MI	49709-0000
616 724-6221	**Muskegon County** 990 Terrace St	Muskegon	MI	49442-3398
616 689-7235	**Newaygo County** PO Box 293	White Cloud	MI	49349-0293
313 858-1000	**Oakland County** 1200 N Telegraph Rd	Pontiac	MI	48341-1045
616 873-4328	**Oceana County** PO Box 153	Hart	MI	49420-0000
517 345-0215	**Ogemaw County** PO Box 8	West Branch	MI	48661-0008
906 884-4255	**Ontonagon County** 725 Greenland Rd	Ontonagon	MI	49953-1492
616 832-5818	**Osceola County** 301 W Upton Ave	Reed City	MI	49677-1149
517 826-3241	**Oscoda County** 311 Morenci	Mio	MI	48647-0000
517 732-6484	**Otsego County** 225 W Main St	Gaylord	MI	49735-1348
616 846-8310	**Ottawa County** 414 Washington St	Grand Haven	MI	49417-1473
517 734-3288	**Presque Isle County** 151 E Huron Ave	Rogers City	MI	49779-1316
517 275-5923	**Roscommon County** PO Box 98	Roscommon	MI	48653-0098
517 790-5251	**Saginaw County** 111 S Michigan Ave	Saginaw	MI	48602-2086
313 985-2031	**Saint Clair County** 201 McMorran Blvd	Port Huron	MI	48060-4006
616 467-6361	**Saint Joseph County** PO Box 189	Centreville	MI	49032-0189
313 648-3212	**Sanilac County** 60 W Sanilac Rd	Sandusky	MI	48471-1094
906 341-5532	**Schoolcraft County** 300 Walnut St	Manistique	MI	49854-1491
517 743-2279	**Shiawassee County** 208 N Shiawassee St	Corunna	MI	48817-1494
517 673-5999	**Tuscola County** 440 N State St	Caro	MI	48723-1555
616 657-5581	**Van Buren County** 212 Paw Paw St	Paw Paw	MI	49079-1492
313 994-2400	**Washtenaw County** PO Box 8645	Ann Arbor	MI	48107-8645
313 224-0471	**Wayne County** 600 Randolph St	Detroit	MI	48226-2831
616 779-9450	**Wexford County** 437 E Division St	Cadillac	MI	49601-1905

MINNESOTA

218 927-2102	**Aitkin County**	209 2nd St NW	Aitkin	MN	56431-1297
612 421-4760	**Anoka County**	325 E Main St	Anoka	MN	55303-2479
218 847-7659	**Becker County**	PO Box 787	Detroit Lakes	MN	56501-0787
218 759-4109	**Beltrami County**	619 Beltrami Ave NW	Bemidji	MN	56601-3041
612 968-6254	**Benton County**	531 Dewey St	Foley	MN	56329-0000
612 839-2537	**Big Stone County**	20 2nd St SE	Ortonville	MN	56278-1544
507 625-3031	**Blue Earth County**	204 S 5th St	Mankato	MN	56001-4585
507 359-7900	**Brown County**	Center & State Sts	New Ulm	MN	56073-0000
218 384-4281	**Carlton County**	30 Maple St	Carlton	MN	55718-0000
612 448-3435	**Carver County**	600 E 4th St	Chaska	MN	55318-2183
218 547-3300	**Cass County**	Hwy 371	Walker	MN	56484-0000
612 269-7774	**Chippewa County**	11th St & Hwy 7	Montevideo	MN	56265-0000
612 257-1300	**Chisago County**	County Courthouse	Center City	MN	55012-0000
218 299-5002	**Clay County**	807 11th St N	Moorhead	MN	56560-1500
218 694-6520	**Clearwater County**	213 N Main Ave	Bagley	MN	56621-0000
218 387-2524	**Cook County**	PO Box 1048	Grand Marais	MN	55604-0117
507 831-1905	**Cottonwood County**	900 3rd Ave	Windom	MN	56101-1699
218 828-3970	**Crow Wing County**	326 Laurel St	Brainerd	MN	56401-3523
612 438-4295	**Dakota County**	1560 Hwy 55 W	Hastings	MN	55033-2392
507 635-6230	**Dodge County**	PO Box 38	Mantorville	MN	55955-0038
612 762-2381	**Douglas County**	305 8th Ave W	Alexandria	MN	56308-1758
507 526-5145	**Faribault County**	N Main St	Blue Earth	MN	56013-0000
507 765-2144	**Fillmore County**	Fillmore St	Preston	MN	55965-0000
507 377-5153	**Freeborn County**	411 S Broadway Ave	Albert Lea	MN	56007-4506
612 388-8261	**Goodhue County**	509 5th St W Rm 310	Red Wing	MN	55066-2525
218 685-4520	**Grant County**	County Courthouse	Elbow Lake	MN	56531-0000
612 348-7574	**Hennepin County**	300 S 6th St	Minneapolis	MN	55487-0001
507 724-5211	**Houston County**	304 S Marshall St	Caledonia	MN	55921-1324
218 732-3196	**Hubbard County**	301 Court St	Park Rapids	MN	56470-1421
612 689-3859	**Isanti County**	237 2nd Ave SW	Cambridge	MN	55008-1536
218 327-2941	**Itasca County**	Courthouse	Grand Rapids	MN	55744-2600
507 847-4400	**Jackson County**	413 4th St	Jackson	MN	56143-1529
612 679-1022	**Kanabec County**	18 Vine St N	Mora	MN	55051-1351
612 231-6202	**Kandiyohi County**	515 Becker Ave SW	Willmar	MN	56201-3281
218 843-3632	**Kittson County**	410 S 5th St	Hallock	MN	56728-0000
218 283-6261	**Koochiching County**	4th St & 6th Ave	International Falls	MN	56649-0000
612 598-3536	**Lac qui Parle County**	600 6th St	Madison	MN	56256-1233
218 834-8300	**Lake County**	601 3rd Ave	Two Harbors	MN	55616-0000
218 634-2836	**Lake of the Woods County**	206 SE 8th Ave	Baudette	MN	56623-0000
612 357-2251	**Le Sueur County**	88 South Pk	Le Center	MN	56057-0000
507 694-1529	**Lincoln County**	N Rebecca	Ivanhoe	MN	56142-0000
507 537-6727	**Lyon County**	607 Main St W	Marshall	MN	56258-3021
218 935-5669	**Mahnomen County**	PO Box 379	Mahnomen	MN	56557-0379
218 745-4851	**Marshall County**	208 E Colbin Ave	Warren	MN	56762-0000
507 238-3214	**Martin County**	201 Lake Ave	Fairmont	MN	56031-1845
612 864-5551	**McLeod County**	830 11th St E	Glencoe	MN	55336-2216
612 693-2458	**Meeker County**	325 N Sibley Ave	Litchfield	MN	55355-2155
612 983-2561	**Mille Lacs County**	635 2nd St SE	Milaca	MN	56353-1305
612 632-2941	**Morrison County**	County Courthouse	Little Falls	MN	56345-0000
507 437-9535	**Mower County**	201 1st St NE	Austin	MN	55912-3475
507 836-6148	**Murray County**	2500 28th St	Slayton	MN	56172-0000
507 931-6800	**Nicollet County**	501 S Minnesota Ave	Saint Peter	MN	56082-2533
507 372-8263	**Nobles County**	10th St	Worthington	MN	56187-0000
218 784-2101	**Norman County**	16 3rd Ave E	Ada	MN	56510-1362
507 285-8115	**Olmsted County**	515 2nd St SW	Rochester	MN	55902-3124
218 739-2271	**Otter Tail County**	Junius Ave County Courthouse	Fergus Falls	MN	56537-0000
218 681-2407	**Pennington County**	PO Box 619	Thief River Falls	MN	56701-0000
612 629-6781	**Pine County**	County Courthouse	Pine City	MN	55063-0000
507 825-4494	**Pipestone County**	408 S Hiawatha Ave	Pipestone	MN	56164-1562
218 281-5408	**Polk County**	612 N Broadway	Crookston	MN	56716-1452
612 634-5301	**Pope County**	130 Minnesota Ave E	Glenwood	MN	56334-1628
612 298-5980	**Ramsey County**	15 Kellogg Blvd W Rm 286	Saint Paul	MN	55102-1690
218 253-2598	**Red Lake County**	100 Langavin St	Red Lake Falls	MN	56750-0000
507 637-8325	**Redwood County**	PO Box 130	Redwood Falls	MN	56283-0130
612 523-2080	**Renville County**	500 DePue Ave E	Olivia	MN	56277-1334
507 334-2281	**Rice County**	218 3rd St NW	Faribault	MN	55021-5146
507 283-9501	**Rock County**	PO Box 245	Luverne	MN	56156-0245
218 463-2541	**Roseau County**	216 Center St W	Roseau	MN	56751-1498
218 726-2380	**Saint Louis County**	100 N 5th Ave W	Duluth	MN	55802-1202
612 445-7750	**Scott County**	428 Holmes St S Rm 212	Shakopee	MN	55379-1348
612 441-3844	**Sherburne County**	13880 Hwy 10	Elk River	MN	55330-4601
612 237-2427	**Sibley County**	400 Court St	Gaylord	MN	55334-0000
612 259-3620	**Stearns County**	PO Box 1378	Saint Cloud	MN	56302-1378
507 451-8040	**Steele County**	111 E Main St	Owatonna	MN	55060-3052
612 589-4764	**Stevens County**	PO Box 530	Morris	MN	56267-0530
612 843-2744	**Swift County**	PO Box 110	Benson	MN	56215-0110
612 732-4431	**Todd County**	215 1st Ave S	Long Prairie	MN	56347-1351
612 563-4242	**Traverse County**	County Courthouse	Wheaton	MN	56296-0000
612 565-2648	**Wabasha County**	625 Jefferson Ave	Wabasha	MN	55981-1577
218 631-2895	**Wadena County**	Jefferson St	Wadena	MN	56482-0000
507 835-0617	**Waseca County**	307 N State St	Waseca	MN	56093-2992
612 439-3220	**Washington County**	14900 61st St N	Stillwater	MN	55082-6161
507 375-3341	**Watonwan County**	PO Box 518	Saint James	MN	56081-0518
218 643-4972	**Wilkin County**	5th St S	Breckenridge	MN	56520-0000
507 457-6320	**Winona County**	171 W 3rd St	Winona	MN	55987-3192
612 682-3900	**Wright County**	10 2nd St NW	Buffalo	MN	55313-1165
612 564-3325	**Yellow Medicine County**	415 9th Ave	Granite Falls	MN	56241-1367

MISSISSIPPI

601 446-6684	**Adams County**	1 Court St	Natchez	MS	39120-2011
601 286-7700	**Alcorn County**	PO Box 112	Corinth	MS	38834-0112
601 657-8022	**Amite County**	PO Box 680	Liberty	MS	39645-0000
601 289-2921	**Attala County**	W Washington St	Kosciusko	MS	39090-0000
601 224-6611	**Benton County**	Main St	Ashland	MS	38603-0000
601 843-2071	**Bolivar County**	401 S Court St	Cleveland	MS	38732-2696
601 983-3117	**Calhoun County**	PO Box 8	Pittsboro	MS	38951-0008
601 237-9283	**Carroll County**	PO Box 291	Carrollton	MS	38917-0291
601 456-2513	**Chickasaw County**	County Courthouse	Houston	MS	38851-0000
601 285-6329	**Choctaw County**	112 Quinn St	Ackerman	MS	39735-0000
601 437-5841	**Claiborne County**	PO Box 449	Port Gibson	MS	39150-0449
601 776-2126	**Clarke County**	PO Box M	Quitman	MS	39355-1013
601 494-3124	**Clay County**	PO Box 815	West Point	MS	39773-0815
601 624-3001	**Coahoma County**	115 1st St	Clarksdale	MS	38614-4227
601 894-3021	**Copiah County**	PO Box 507	Hazlehurst	MS	39083-0507
601 765-4242	**Covington County**	PO Box 1679	Collins	MS	39428-1679
601 429-5011	**De Soto County**	2535 Hwy 51 S Courthouse Sq	Hernando	MS	38632-2134
601 582-3213	**Forrest County**	629 Main St	Hattiesburg	MS	39401-3453
601 384-2330	**Franklin County**	PO Box 297	Meadville	MS	39653-0297
601 947-7506	**George County**	Courthouse Sq	Lucedale	MS	39452-0000
601 394-2377	**Greene County**	PO Box 610	Leakesville	MS	39451-0610
601 226-1821	**Grenada County**	PO Box 1208	Grenada	MS	38901-1208
601 467-5404	**Hancock County**	242 Main St	Bay Saint Louis	MS	39520-3595
601 865-4001	**Harrison County**	1801 23rd Ave	Gulfport	MS	39501-2983
601 968-6501	**Hinds County**	PO Box 686	Jackson	MS	39205-0686
601 834-2508	**Holmes County**	PO Box 239	Lexington	MS	39095-0239
601 247-1740	**Humphreys County**	PO Box 547	Belzoni	MS	39038-0547
601 873-2761	**Issaquena County**	PO Box 27	Mayersville	MS	39113-0027
601 862-3421	**Itawamba County**	201 W Main St	Fulton	MS	38843-1153
601 769-3131	**Jackson County**	3109 Canty St	Pascagoula	MS	39567-4209
601 764-3368	**Jasper County**	Court St	Bay Springs	MS	39422-0000
601 786-3021	**Jefferson County**	307 Main St	Fayette	MS	39069-0000
601 792-4204	**Jefferson Davis County**	PO Box 1137	Prentiss	MS	39474-1137
601 428-0527	**Jones County**	PO Box 1468	Laurel	MS	39441-1468
601 743-2460	**Kemper County**	PO Box 188	De Kalb	MS	39328-0188
601 234-7563	**Lafayette County**	PO Box 1240	Oxford	MS	38655-1240
601 794-8504	**Lamar County**	PO Box 247	Purvis	MS	39475-0247
601 482-9714	**Lauderdale County**	500 Constitution Ave	Meridian	MS	39301-5160
601 587-7162	**Lawrence County**	PO Box 40	Monticello	MS	39654-0040
601 267-7372	**Leake County**	Court Sq	Carthage	MS	39051-0000
601 841-9100	**Lee County**	300 W Main St	Tupelo	MS	38801-3920
601 453-1041	**Leflore County**	315 W Market St	Greenwood	MS	38930-4330
601 835-3411	**Lincoln County**	300 S 1st St	Brookhaven	MS	39601-3321
601 329-5880	**Lowndes County**	PO Box 1364	Columbus	MS	39703-1364
601 859-1177	**Madison County**	PO Box 404	Canton	MS	39046-0404
601 736-2691	**Marion County**	502 Broad St Suite 2	Columbia	MS	39429-3037
601 252-4431	**Marshall County**	PO Box 219	Holly Springs	MS	38635-0219
601 369-8143	**Monroe County**	PO Box 578	Aberdeen	MS	39730-0578
601 283-2333	**Montgomery County**	PO Box 71	Winona	MS	38967-0071
601 656-3581	**Neshoba County**	PO Box 67	Philadelphia	MS	39350-0067
601 635-2367	**Newton County**	PO Box 68	Decatur	MS	39327-0068
601 726-4243	**Noxubee County**	PO Box 147	Macon	MS	39341-0147
601 323-5834	**Oktibbeha County**	101 E Main St	Starkville	MS	39759-2955
601 563-6205	**Panola County**	151 Public Sq	Batesville	MS	38606-2220
601 795-2237	**Pearl River County**	PO Box 431	Poplarville	MS	39470-0431
601 964-8398	**Perry County**	PO Box 198	New Augusta	MS	39462-0198
601 783-3362	**Pike County**	PO Box 309	Magnolia	MS	39652-0309
601 489-3900	**Pontotoc County**	PO Box 209	Pontotoc	MS	38863-0209
601 728-8151	**Prentiss County**	PO Box 477	Booneville	MS	38829-0477
601 326-2661	**Quitman County**	PO Box 100	Marks	MS	38646-0100
601 825-2217	**Rankin County**	221 N Timber St	Brandon	MS	39042-3198
601 469-1922	**Scott County**	PO Box 630	Forest	MS	39074-0630
601 873-2755	**Sharkey County**	County Courthouse	Rolling Fork	MS	39159-0000
601 847-2626	**Simpson County**	109 W Pine Ave	Mendenhall	MS	39114-3597
601 782-4751	**Smith County**	Main St	Raleigh	MS	39153-0000
601 928-5266	**Stone County**	PO Box 7	Wiggins	MS	39577-0007
601 887-4703	**Sunflower County**	2nd St	Indianola	MS	38751-0000
601 647-5551	**Tallahatchie County**	PO Box H	Charleston	MS	38921-0330
601 562-5661	**Tate County**	201 S Ward St	Senatobia	MS	38668-2616
601 837-7374	**Tippah County**	PO Box 99	Ripley	MS	38663-0099
601 423-7010	**Tishomingo County**	1008 Hwy 25 S	Iuka	MS	38852-1020
601 363-2451	**Tunica County**	PO Box 217	Tunica	MS	38676-0217
601 534-1900	**Union County**	109 Main St	New Albany	MS	38652-0000
601 876-4947	**Walthall County**	PO Box 351	Tylertown	MS	39667-0351
601 636-4415	**Warren County**	PO Box 351	Vicksburg	MS	39181-0351
601 332-1595	**Washington County**	PO Box 309	Greenville	MS	38702-0309
601 735-2873	**Wayne County**	Azalea Dr	Waynesboro	MS	39367-0000
601 258-4131	**Webster County**	Main St	Walthall	MS	39771-9999
601 888-4381	**Wilkinson County**	PO Box 516	Woodville	MS	39669-0516
601 773-3631	**Winston County**	115 S Court Ave	Louisville	MS	39339-2935
601 473-2091	**Yalobusha County**	PO Box 664	Water Valley	MS	38965-0664
601 746-2661	**Yazoo County**	PO Box 68	Yazoo City	MS	39194-0068

MISSOURI

816 665-3350	**Adair County**	County Courthouse	Kirksville	MO	63501-0000
816 324-3624	**Andrew County**	PO Box 206	Savannah	MO	64485-0206
816 744-2707	**Atchison County**	PO Box J	Rock Port	MO	64482-0410
314 581-8211	**Audrain County**	County Courthouse	Mexico	MO	65265-0000
417 847-2561	**Barry County**	County Courthouse	Cassville	MO	65625-0000
417 682-3529	**Barton County**	County Courthouse	Lamar	MO	64759-0000
816 679-3371	**Bates County**	County Courthouse	Butler	MO	64730-0000
816 438-7326	**Benton County**	PO Box 1238	Warsaw	MO	65355-1238
314 238-2126	**Bollinger County**	PO Box 46	Marble Hill	MO	63764-0046
314 874-7574	**Boone County**	8th & Walnut	Columbia	MO	65201-0000
816 271-1411	**Buchanan County**	5th & Jules Sts	Saint Joseph	MO	64501-0000
314 785-8201	**Butler County**	County Courthouse	Poplar Bluff	MO	63901-0000
816 586-2571	**Caldwell County**	PO Box 67	Kingston	MO	64650-0067
314 642-0730	**Callaway County**	5 E 5th St	Fulton	MO	65251-1700
314 346-4440	**Camden County**	1 Court Cir	Camdenton	MO	65020-0000
314 243-3547	**Cape Girardeau County**	1 Barton Sq	Jackson	MO	63755-1866
816 542-0615	**Carroll County**	County Courthouse	Carrollton	MO	64633-0000
314 323-4527	**Carter County**	PO Box 517	Van Buren	MO	63965-0517
816 884-5100	**Cass County**	County Courthouse	Harrisonville	MO	64701-0000
417 276-3514	**Cedar County**	PO Box 126	Stockton	MO	65785-0126
816 288-3273	**Chariton County**	County Courthouse	Keytesville	MO	65261-0000
417 485-6360	**Christian County**	PO Box 549	Ozark	MO	65721-0549
816 727-3283	**Clark County**	111 E Court St	Kahoka	MO	63445-1268
816 792-7733	**Clay County**	Administration Bldg Courthouse Sq	Liberty	MO	64068-0000
816 539-3713	**Clinton County**	PO Box 245	Plattsburg	MO	64477-0245
314 634-9110	**Cole County**	301 E High St	Jefferson City	MO	65101-3212
816 882-2114	**Cooper County**	PO Box 123	Boonville	MO	65233-0123
314 775-2376	**Crawford County**	201 Main St	Steelville	MO	65565-0000
417 637-2724	**Dade County**	County Courthouse	Greenfield	MO	65661-0000
417 345-2632	**Dallas County**	PO Box 436	Buffalo	MO	65622-0436
816 663-2641	**Daviess County**	County Courthouse	Gallatin	MO	64640-0000
816 449-5402	**De Kalb County**	PO Box 248	Maysville	MO	64469-0248
314 729-4144	**Dent County**	County Courthouse	Salem	MO	65560-0000
417 683-4714	**Douglas County**	203 SE 2nd Ave	Ava	MO	65608-0000
314 888-2796	**Dunklin County**	PO Box 188	Kennett	MO	63857-0188
314 583-6355	**Franklin County**	PO Box 311	Union	MO	63084-0311
314 486-5427	**Gasconade County**	PO Box 295	Hermann	MO	65041-0295
816 726-3618	**Gentry County**	County Courthouse	Albany	MO	64402-1499
417 868-4055	**Greene County**	940 Boonville Ave	Springfield	MO	65802-0000
816 359-6305	**Grundy County**	700 Main St	Trenton	MO	64683-2063
816 425-6424	**Harrison County**	PO Box 27	Bethany	MO	64424-0027
816 885-6963	**Henry County**	Main & Franklin Sts	Clinton	MO	64735-2199
417 745-6450	**Hickory County**	Main & Polk Sts	Hermitage	MO	65668-0000
816 446-3303	**Holt County**	102 Nodaway St	Oregon	MO	64473-9643
816 248-2284	**Howard County**	PO Box 551	Fayette	MO	65248-0551
417 256-2591	**Howell County**	County Courthouse Sq	West Plains	MO	65775-0000
314 546-2912	**Iron County**	250 S Main St	Ironton	MO	63650-1308
816 881-3333	**Jackson County**	415 E 12th St	Kansas City	MO	64106-2706
417 358-0416	**Jasper County**	County Courthouse	Carthage	MO	64836-1696
314 789-3911	**Jefferson County**	PO Box 100	Hillsboro	MO	63050-0100
816 747-6161	**Johnson County**	County Courthouse	Warrensburg	MO	64093-1794
816 397-2184	**Knox County**	305 E Lafayette St	Edina	MO	63537-0000
417 532-5471	**Laclede County**	2nd & Adam Sts	Lebanon	MO	65536-0000
816 259-4315	**Lafayette County**	Main St	Lexington	MO	64067-0000
417 466-2638	**Lawrence County**	PO Box 309	Mount Vernon	MO	65712-0309

Local Government–County

314 767-5205	**Lewis County**	100 E Lafayette St	Monticello	MO	63457-0000
314 528-4415	**Lincoln County**	201 Main St	Troy	MO	63379-1194
816 895-5417	**Linn County**	County Courthouse	Linneus	MO	64653-0000
816 646-2293	**Livingston County**	County Courthouse	Chillicothe	MO	64601-0000
816 385-2913	**Macon County**	PO Box 96	Macon	MO	63552-0096
314 783-2176	**Madison County**	1 Courthouse Sq	Fredericktown	MO	63645-1137
314 422-3388	**Maries County**	PO Box 167	Vienna	MO	65582-0167
314 769-2549	**Marion County**	County Courthouse	Palmyra	MO	63461-0000
417 223-4717	**McDonald County**	PO Box 665	Pineville	MO	64856-0665
816 748-3425	**Mercer County**	County Courthouse	Princeton	MO	64673-0000
314 369-2731	**Miller County**	Courthouse Sq	Tuscumbia	MO	65082-0000
314 683-2146	**Mississippi County**	PO Box 304	Charleston	MO	63834-0304
314 796-4661	**Moniteau County**	200 E Main St	California	MO	65018-1675
816 327-5817	**Monroe County**	300 N Main St	Paris	MO	65275-1399
314 564-3357	**Montgomery County**	211 E 3rd St	Montgomery City	MO	63361-1956
314 378-5436	**Morgan County**	100 E Newton St	Versailles	MO	65084-1298
314 748-2524	**New Madrid County**	PO Box 68	New Madrid	MO	63869-0068
417 451-4540	**Newton County**	Main & Wood Sts County Courthouse Sq	Neosho	MO	64850-0000
816 582-2251	**Nodaway County**	PO Box 218	Maryville	MO	64468-0218
417 778-7475	**Oregon County**	PO Box 324	Alton	MO	65606-0324
314 897-2139	**Osage County**	Main St	Linn	MO	65051-0000
417 679-3516	**Ozark County**	PO Box 416	Gainesville	MO	65655-0416
314 333-4203	**Pemiscot County**	Ward Ave	Caruthersville	MO	63830-0000
314 547-4242	**Perry County**	15 W Sainte Marie St	Perryville	MO	63775-1399
816 826-5395	**Pettis County**	415 S Ohio Ave	Sedalia	MO	65301-4496
314 364-1891	**Phelps County**	3rd & Rolla Sts	Rolla	MO	65401-0000
314 324-2412	**Pike County**	115 W Main St	Bowling Green	MO	63334-1693
816 431-2232	**Platte County**	PO Box 30CH	Platte City	MO	64079-0000
417 326-4031	**Polk County**	County Courthouse Rm 12	Bolivar	MO	65613-0000
314 774-6609	**Pulaski County**	Waynesville Sq	Waynesville	MO	65583-0000
816 947-2674	**Putnam County**	County Courthouse	Unionville	MO	63565-0000
314 985-7111	**Ralls County**	Main St	New London	MO	63459-0000
816 277-4717	**Randolph County**	S Main St	Huntsville	MO	65259-0000
816 776-3184	**Ray County**	PO Box 536	Richmond	MO	64085-0536
314 648-2494	**Reynolds County**	Courthouse Sq	Centerville	MO	63633-0000
314 996-3215	**Ripley County**	County Courthouse	Doniphan	MO	63935-0000
314 949-3080	**Saint Charles County**	3rd & Jefferson Sts	Saint Charles	MO	63301-0000
417 646-2315	**Saint Clair County**	PO Box 405	Osceola	MO	64776-0405
314 756-5411	**Saint Francis County**	County Courthouse Sq	Farmington	MO	63640-0000
314 889-2016	**Saint Louis County**	41 S Central Ave	Clayton	MO	63105-1719
314 883-5589	**Sainte Genevieve County**	55 S 3rd St	Sainte Genevieve	MO	63670-1601
816 886-3331	**Saline County**	County Courthouse	Marshall	MO	65340-0000
816 457-3842	**Schuyler County**	PO Box 187	Lancaster	MO	63548-0187
816 465-7027	**Scotland County**	County Courthouse	Memphis	MO	63555-0000
314 545-3549	**Scott County**	PO Box 188	Benton	MO	63736-0188
314 226-3414	**Shannon County**	County Courthouse	Eminence	MO	65466-0000
314 633-2181	**Shelby County**	1 Courthouse Sq	Shelbyville	MO	63469-0000
314 568-3339	**Stoddard County**	PO Box H	Bloomfield	MO	63825-0209
417 357-6127	**Stone County**	PO Box 45	Galena	MO	65656-0045
816 265-3786	**Sullivan County**	2nd St	Milan	MO	63556-0000
417 546-2241	**Taney County**	PO Box 156	Forsyth	MO	65653-0156
417 967-2112	**Texas County**	210 N Grand Ave	Houston	MO	65483-1226
417 667-3157	**Vernon County**	102 W Cherry	Nevada	MO	64772-3368
314 456-3331	**Warren County**	105 S Market St	Warrenton	MO	63383-1903
314 438-4901	**Washington County**	102 N Missouri St	Potosi	MO	63664-1744
314 224-3221	**Wayne County**	County Courthouse	Greenville	MO	63944-0000
417 468-2223	**Webster County**	County Courthouse	Marshfield	MO	65706-0000
816 564-2219	**Worth County**	County Courthouse	Grant City	MO	64456-0000
417 741-6661	**Wright County**	PO Box 98	Hartville	MO	65667-0098

MONTANA

406 683-5245	**Beaverhead County**	2 S Pacific Cluster 3	Dillon	MT	59725-0000
406 665-3520	**Big Horn County**	121 3rd St W	Hardin	MT	59034-1905
406 357-3250	**Blaine County**	PO Box 278	Chinook	MT	59523-0278
406 266-3443	**Broadwater County**	PO Box 489	Townsend	MT	59644-0489
406 446-1595	**Carbon County**	PO Box 887	Red Lodge	MT	59068-0887
406 775-8749	**Carter County**	Courthouse Park St	Ekalaka	MT	59324-0000
406 761-6700	**Cascade County**	415 2nd Ave N	Great Falls	MT	59401-2536
406 622-5151	**Chouteau County**	1308 Franklin	Fort Benton	MT	59442-0000
406 232-7800	**Custer County**	1010 Main St	Miles City	MT	59301-3419
406 487-5561	**Daniels County**	PO Box 247	Scobey	MT	59263-0247
406 365-3562	**Dawson County**	207 W Bell St	Glendive	MT	59330-1694
406 563-8421	**Deer Lodge County**	800 S Main St	Anaconda	MT	59711-2999
406 778-2883	**Fallon County**	10 W Fallon Ave	Baker	MT	59313-0000
406 538-5119	**Fergus County**	712 W Main St	Lewistown	MT	59457-2562
406 752-5300	**Flathead County**	800 S Main St	Kalispell	MT	59901-5400
406 585-1430	**Gallatin County**	311 W Main St Rm 204	Bozeman	MT	59715-4576
406 557-2760	**Garfield County**	PO Box 7	Jordan	MT	59337-0007
406 873-5063	**Glacier County**	502 E Main St	Cut Bank	MT	59427-3025
406 568-2231	**Golden Valley County**	PO Box 10	Ryegate	MT	59074-0010
406 859-3771	**Granite County**	Sampson & Kearney Sts	Philipsburg	MT	59858-0000
406 265-5481	**Hill County**	315 4th St County Courthouse	Havre	MT	59501-3999
406 225-4251	**Jefferson County**	PO Box H	Boulder	MT	59632-0249
406 566-2250	**Judith Basin County**	Courthouse	Stanford	MT	59479-0000
406 883-6211	**Lake County**	106 4th Ave E	Polson	MT	59860-2125
406 443-1010	**Lewis & Clark County**	316 N Park Ave	Helena	MT	59624-0000
406 759-5365	**Liberty County**	101 1st St E	Chester	MT	59522-0000
406 293-7781	**Lincoln County**	512 California Ave	Libby	MT	59923-0000
406 843-5392	**Madison County**	110 W Wallace St	Virginia City	MT	59755-0000
406 485-3505	**McCone County**	206 2nd Ave	Circle	MT	59215-0000
406 547-3612	**Meagher County**	15 W Main St	White Sulphur Springs	MT	59645-0000
406 822-4541	**Mineral County**	300 River St	Superior	MT	59872-0000
406 721-5700	**Missoula County**	200 W Broadway St	Missoula	MT	59802-4292
406 323-1104	**Musselshell County**	506 Main St	Roundup	MT	59072-2498
406 222-6120	**Park County**	414 E Callender St	Livingston	MT	59047-2799
406 429-5311	**Petroleum County**	201 E Main	Winnett	MT	59087-0000
406 654-2429	**Phillips County**	County Courthouse	Malta	MT	59538-0000
406 278-7681	**Pondera County**	20 4th Ave SW	Conrad	MT	59425-2340
406 436-2657	**Powder River County**	Courthouse Sq	Broadus	MT	59317-0000
406 846-3680	**Powell County**	409 Missouri Ave	Deer Lodge	MT	59722-1084
406 637-5575	**Prairie County**	County Courthouse	Terry	MT	59349-0000
406 363-1900	**Ravalli County**	S 2nd & Bedford Sts	Hamilton	MT	59840-0000
406 482-1706	**Richland County**	201 W Main St	Sidney	MT	59270-4035
406 653-1590	**Roosevelt County**	400 2nd Ave S	Wolf Point	MT	59201-1600
406 356-2251	**Rosebud County**	PO Box 47	Forsyth	MT	59327-0047
406 827-4392	**Sanders County**	Main St	Thompson Falls	MT	59873-0000
406 765-2310	**Sheridan County**	100 W Laurel Ave	Plentywood	MT	59254-1699
406 723-8262	**Silver Bow County**	155 W Granite St	Butte	MT	59701-9215
406 322-4546	**Stillwater County**	PO Box 147	Columbus	MT	59019-0147
406 932-5152	**Sweet Grass County**	PO Box 460	Big Timber	MT	59011-0460
406 466-2151	**Teton County**	PO Box 610	Choteau	MT	59422-0000
406 434-5121	**Toole County**	226 1st St S	Shelby	MT	59474-1920
406 342-5547	**Treasure County**	PO Box 392	Hysham	MT	59038-0392
406 228-8221	**Valley County**	PO Box 311	Glasgow	MT	59230-0311
406 632-4891	**Wheatland County**	PO Box C	Harlowton	MT	59036-0903
406 795-2410	**Wibaux County**	200 S Wibaux	Wibaux	MT	59353-0000
406 256-2785	**Yellowstone County**	PO Box 35001	Billings	MT	59107-5001

NEBRASKA

402 461-7107	**Adams County**	4th & Denver Sts	Hastings	NE	68901-0000
402 887-4410	**Antelope County**	501 Main St	Neligh	NE	68756-1424
308 764-2203	**Arthur County**	Main St	Arthur	NE	69121-0000
308 436-5265	**Banner County**	State St	Harrisburg	NE	69345-0000
308 547-2222	**Blaine County**	Lincoln Ave	Brewster	NE	68821-0000
402 395-2055	**Boone County**	222 S 4th St	Albion	NE	68620-1247
308 762-6565	**Box Butte County**	5th & Box Butte Sts	Alliance	NE	69301-0000
402 775-2391	**Boyd County**	County Courthouse	Butte	NE	68722-0000
402 387-2705	**Brown County**	148 W 4th St	Ainsworth	NE	69210-1696
308 236-1226	**Buffalo County**	16th & Central Ave	Kearney	NE	68848-0000
402 374-1955	**Burt County**	111 N 13th St	Tekamah	NE	68061-1043
402 367-3091	**Butler County**	451 5th St	David City	NE	68632-0000
402 296-2164	**Cass County**	4th & Main Sts	Plattsmouth	NE	68048-0000
402 254-7411	**Cedar County**	101 S Broadway Ave	Hartington	NE	68739-0000
308 882-5266	**Chase County**	921 Broadway	Imperial	NE	69033-0000
402 376-2771	**Cherry County**	PO Box 120	Valentine	NE	69201-0120
308 254-2141	**Cheyenne County**	1000 10th Ave	Sidney	NE	69162-1612
402 762-3463	**Clay County**	111 W Fairfield St	Clay Center	NE	68933-1436
402 352-3434	**Colfax County**	411 E 11th St	Schuyler	NE	68661-1940
402 372-2144	**Cuming County**	PO Box 290	West Point	NE	68788-0290
308 872-5701	**Custer County**	431 S 10th Ave	Broken Bow	NE	68822-2099
402 987-2126	**Dakota County**	PO Box 38	Dakota City	NE	68731-0038
308 432-2863	**Dawes County**	451 Main St	Chadron	NE	69337-2649
308 324-2127	**Dawson County**	7th & Washington Sts	Lexington	NE	68850-0000
308 874-3308	**Deuel County**	3rd & Vincent	Chappell	NE	69129-0000
402 755-2881	**Dixon County**	302 3rd St	Ponca	NE	68770-0000
402 727-2765	**Dodge County**	435 N Park Ave	Fremont	NE	68025-4967
402 444-7000	**Douglas County**	1819 Farnam St	Omaha	NE	68183-0001
308 423-2058	**Dundy County**	Chief St	Benkelman	NE	69021-0000
402 759-4931	**Fillmore County**	900 G St	Geneva	NE	68361-2005
308 425-6202	**Franklin County**	405 15th Ave	Franklin	NE	68939-1309
308 367-8641	**Frontier County**	1 Wellington St	Stockville	NE	69042-0040
308 268-4145	**Furnas County**	PO Box 387	Beaver City	NE	68926-0387
402 228-3355	**Gage County**	PO Box 429	Beatrice	NE	68310-0429
308 772-3924	**Garden County**	Main St	Oshkosh	NE	69154-0000
308 346-4161	**Garfield County**	PO Box 218	Burwell	NE	68823-0218
308 785-2611	**Gosper County**	PO Box 136	Elwood	NE	68937-0136
308 458-2488	**Grant County**	PO Box 139	Hyannis	NE	69350-0139
308 428-3625	**Greeley County**	28th & Kildare Sts	Greeley	NE	68842-0000
308 381-5080	**Hall County**	121 S Pine St	Grand Island	NE	68801-0000
402 694-3443	**Hamilton County**	County Courthouse	Aurora	NE	68818-2097
308 928-2173	**Harlan County**	PO Box 379	Alma	NE	68920-0379
308 286-3413	**Hayes County**	Troth St	Hayes Center	NE	69032-0000
308 334-5646	**Hitchcock County**	229 E 'D' St	Trenton	NE	69044-0000
402 336-1762	**Holt County**	PO Box 329	O'Neill	NE	68763-0329
308 546-2244	**Hooker County**	PO Box 184	Mullen	NE	69152-0184
308 754-4343	**Howard County**	612 Indian St	Saint Paul	NE	68873-1642
402 729-2323	**Jefferson County**	411 4th St	Fairbury	NE	68352-2536
402 335-3246	**Johnson County**	PO Box 416	Tecumseh	NE	68450-0416
308 832-1155	**Kearney County**	PO Box 339	Minden	NE	68959-0339
308 284-4726	**Keith County**	PO Box 149	Ogallala	NE	69153-0149
402 497-3791	**Keya Paha County**	PO Box 349	Springview	NE	68778-0349
308 235-2241	**Kimball County**	114 E 3rd St	Kimball	NE	69145-1456
402 288-4282	**Knox County**	Main St	Center	NE	68724-0000
402 471-7481	**Lancaster County**	555 S 10th St	Lincoln	NE	68508-2803
308 534-4350	**Lincoln County**	County Sq	North Platte	NE	69101-0000
308 636-2311	**Logan County**	PO Box 8	Stapleton	NE	69163-0008
308 942-3135	**Loup County**	4th St	Taylor	NE	68879-0000
402 454-3311	**Madison County**	PO Box 290	Madison	NE	68748-0290
308 587-2363	**McPherson County**	PO Box 122	Tryon	NE	69167-0122
308 946-2881	**Merrick County**	PO Box 27	Central City	NE	68826-0027
308 262-0860	**Morrill County**	PO Box 610	Bridgeport	NE	69336-0610
308 536-2331	**Nance County**	PO Box 338	Fullerton	NE	68638-0338
402 274-4213	**Nemaha County**	1824 N St	Auburn	NE	68305-2341
402 225-4361	**Nuckolls County**	150 S Main St	Nelson	NE	68961-0000
402 873-3586	**Otoe County**	PO Box 249	Nebraska City	NE	68410-0249
402 852-2962	**Pawnee County**	County Courthouse	Pawnee City	NE	68420-0000
308 352-4643	**Perkins County**	PO Box 156	Grant	NE	69140-0156
308 995-4469	**Phelps County**	715 5th Ave	Holdrege	NE	68949-2256
402 329-4225	**Pierce County**	111 W Court St	Pierce	NE	68767-1224
402 563-4904	**Platte County**	2610 14th St	Columbus	NE	68601-4929
402 747-5431	**Polk County**	County Courthouse	Osceola	NE	68651-0000
308 345-1552	**Red Willow County**	500 Norris Ave	McCook	NE	69001-2006
402 245-2911	**Richardson County**	1701 Stone St	Falls City	NE	68355-2026
402 684-3933	**Rock County**	400 State St	Bassett	NE	68714-0000
402 821-2374	**Saline County**	215 Court St	Wilber	NE	68465-0000
402 339-3225	**Sarpy County**	1208 Golden Gate Dr	Omaha	NE	68046-2838
402 443-8101	**Saunders County**	Chestnut St Courthouse	Wahoo	NE	68066-0000
308 436-6600	**Scotts Bluff County**	1825 10th St	Gering	NE	69341-2444
402 643-2883	**Seward County**	County Courthouse	Seward	NE	68434-0000
308 327-2633	**Sheridan County**	301 E 2nd St	Rushville	NE	69360-0000
308 745-1513	**Sherman County**	PO Box 456	Loup City	NE	68853-0456
308 668-2443	**Sioux County**	Main St	Harrison	NE	69346-0000
402 439-2222	**Stanton County**	804 Ivy St	Stanton	NE	68779-0000
402 768-6126	**Thayer County**	235 N 4th St	Hebron	NE	68370-1549
308 645-2261	**Thomas County**	PO Box 226	Thedford	NE	69166-0226
402 385-2343	**Thurston County**	106 S 5th St	Pender	NE	68047-0000
308 728-3700	**Valley County**	125 S 15th St	Ord	NE	68862-0000
402 426-6822	**Washington County**	PO Box 466	Blair	NE	68008-0466
402 375-2288	**Wayne County**	510 N Pearl St	Wayne	NE	68787-1939
402 746-2716	**Webster County**	621 N Cedar St	Red Cloud	NE	68970-2397
308 654-3235	**Wheeler County**	County Courthouse	Bartlett	NE	68622-0000
402 362-7759	**York County**	510 Lincoln Ave	York	NE	68467-2945

NEVADA

702 887-2100	**Carson City (Independent City)**	2621 Northgate Ln	Carson City	NV	89706-1619
702 423-6028	**Churchill County**	10 W Williams Ave	Fallon	NV	89406-2940
702 455-3156	**Clark County**	200 S 3rd St	Las Vegas	NV	89155-0001
702 782-9821	**Douglas County**	PO Box 218	Minden	NV	89423-0218
702 738-5398	**Elko County**	571 Idaho St	Elko	NV	89801-3787
702 485-6367	**Esmeralda County**	PO Box 547	Goldfield	NV	89013-0547
702 237-5262	**Eureka County**	PO Box 677	Eureka	NV	89316-0677
702 623-6343	**Humboldt County**	Bridge & 5th Sts	Winnemucca	NV	89445-3199
702 635-5738	**Lander County**	315 S Humboldt	Battle Mountain	NV	89820-1982
702 962-5390	**Lincoln County**	1 Main St	Pioche	NV	89043-0000
702 463-3341	**Lyon County**	31 S Main St	Yerington	NV	89447-2532
702 945-2446	**Mineral County**	PO Box 1450	Hawthorne	NV	89415-1450
702 482-8127	**Nye County**	PO Box 1031	Tonopah	NV	89049-1031
702 273-2208	**Pershing County**	PO Box 820	Lovelock	NV	89419-0820
702 847-0968	**Storey County**	PO Box D	Virginia City	NV	89440-0139

The text at the beginning of each category provides information on how government offices are listed. Refer to the front page of the section for a list of the categories included.

702 328-3110	**Washoe County** PO Box 11130	Reno	NV	89520-0027
702 289-8841	**White Pine County** PO Box 1002	Ely	NV	89301-1002

NEW HAMPSHIRE

603 524-3570	**Belknap County** 64 Court St	Laconia	NH	03246-3679
603 539-7751	**Carroll County** Rt 171	Ossipee	NH	03864-0000
603 352-0056	**Cheshire County** 33 West St	Keene	NH	03431-3355
603 788-4900	**Coos County** PO Box 309	Lancaster	NH	03584-0309
603 787-6941	**Grafton County** PO Box 108	Woodsville	NH	03785-0108
603 882-9471	**Hillsborough County** 19 Temple St	Nashua	NH	03060-3472
603 228-0331	**Merrimack County** 163 N Main St	Concord	NH	03301-5001
603 679-2256	**Rockingham County** North Rd	Brentwood	NH	03042-0000
603 742-3065	**Strafford County** County Farm Rd	Dover	NH	03820-0000
603 863-3450	**Sullivan County** PO Box 45	Newport	NH	03773-0045

NEW JERSEY

609 625-4011	**Atlantic County** 2 Main St W	Mays Landing	NJ	08330-1800
201 646-2500	**Bergen County** 21 Main St	Hackensack	NJ	07601-7000
609 265-5000	**Burlington County** 49 Rancocas Rd	Mount Holly	NJ	08060-1384
609 757-8457	**Camden County** 5th & Mickle Blvd	Camden	NJ	08103-4000
609 465-7111	**Cape May County** 7 N Main St	Cape May Court House	NJ	08210-2117
609 451-8000	**Cumberland County** Broad & Fayette St	Bridgeton	NJ	08302-2552
201 621-4916	**Essex County** 469 King Blvd	Newark	NJ	07102-0000
609 853-3237	**Gloucester County** 1 N Broad St	Woodbury	NJ	08096-4611
201 795-6000	**Hudson County** 595 Newark Ave	Jersey City	NJ	07306-2301
908 782-4300	**Hunterdon County** 71 Main St	Flemington	NJ	08822-1412
609 989-6517	**Mercer County** PO Box 8068	Trenton	NJ	08650-0068
908 745-3000	**Middlesex County** 1 John F Kennedy Sq	New Brunswick	NJ	08901-2149
908 431-7387	**Monmouth County** Main St Hall of Records	Freehold	NJ	07728-0000
201 285-6040	**Morris County** PO Box 900	Morristown	NJ	07963-0900
908 244-2121	**Ocean County** PO Box CN 2191	Toms River	NJ	08754-0000
201 881-4120	**Passaic County** 77 Hamilton St	Paterson	NJ	07505-2097
609 935-7510	**Salem County** 92 Market St	Salem	NJ	08079-1913
908 231-7000	**Somerset County** PO Box 3000	Somerville	NJ	08876-1262
201 579-0200	**Sussex County** PO Box 709	Newton	NJ	07860-0709
908 527-4966	**Union County** 2 Broad St	Elizabeth	NJ	07201-2204
908 475-5361	**Warren County** Rt 519 Wayne Dumont Jr Administration Bldg	Belvidere	NJ	07823-0000

NEW MEXICO

505 768-4000	**Bernalillo County** 1 Civic Plaza 10th Fl	Albuquerque	NM	87102-0000
505 533-6423	**Catron County** PO Box 507	Reserve	NM	87830-0507
505 624-6614	**Chaves County** 401 N Main St	Roswell	NM	88201-4726
505 287-9431	**Cibola County** 515 W High Ave	Grants	NM	87020-2526
505 445-9661	**Colfax County** PO Box 1498	Raton	NM	87740-1498
505 763-5591	**Curry County** 700 N Main St	Clovis	NM	88101-6664
505 355-2601	**De Baca County** PO Box 347	Fort Sumner	NM	88119-0347
505 525-6659	**Dona Ana County** 251 W Amador Ave	Las Cruces	NM	88005-2800
505 887-9511	**Eddy County** PO Box 1139	Carlsbad	NM	88221-1139
505 538-9581	**Grant County** PO Box 898	Silver City	NM	88062-0898
505 472-3791	**Guadalupe County** 420 Park Ave	Santa Rosa	NM	88435-0000
505 673-2301	**Harding County** PO Box 1002	Mosquero	NM	87733-1002
505 542-9213	**Hidalgo County** 300 S Shakespeare St	Lordsburg	NM	88045-1939
505 396-8521	**Lea County** PO Box 4C	Lovington	NM	88260-0000
505 648-2331	**Lincoln County** 300 Central Ave	Carrizozo	NM	88301-0000
505 662-8010	**Los Alamos County** 2300 Trinity Dr	Los Alamos	NM	87544-3051
505 546-6501	**Luna County** 700 S Silver Ave	Deming	NM	88030-4173
505 722-3869	**McKinley County** 200 W Hill Ave	Gallup	NM	87301-6309
505 387-5279	**Mora County** Hwy 518	Mora	NM	87732-0000
505 437-7427	**Otero County** PO Box 1749	Alamogordo	NM	88311-1749
505 461-2112	**Quay County** 300 S 3rd St	Tucumcari	NM	88401-2870
505 588-7255	**Rio Arriba County** County Courthouse	Tierra Amarilla	NM	87575-0000
505 356-8562	**Roosevelt County** County Courthouse	Portales	NM	88130-0000
505 334-9471	**San Juan County** PO Box 550	Aztec	NM	87410-0550
505 425-9331	**San Miguel County** County Courthouse	Las Vegas	NM	87701-0000
505 867-2209	**Sandoval County** PO Box 40	Bernalillo	NM	87004-0000
505 984-5080	**Santa Fe County** PO Box 1985	Santa Fe	NM	87504-1985
505 894-6215	**Sierra County** 300 Date St	Truth or Consequences	NM	87901-2362
505 835-0589	**Socorro County** 131 Court St	Socorro	NM	87801-4505
505 758-8836	**Taos County** PO Box 676	Taos	NM	87571-0676
505 384-2221	**Torrance County** 9th & Allen	Estancia	NM	87016-0000
505 374-9491	**Union County** 200 Court St	Clayton	NM	88415-3116
505 865-9681	**Valencia County** PO Box 1119	Los Lunas	NM	87031-1119

NEW YORK

518 445-7644	**Albany County** 16 Eagle St	Albany	NY	12207-1019
716 268-7612	**Allegany County** Court St	Belmont	NY	14813-0000
212 590-3644	**Bronx County** 851 Grand Concourse Rm 118	Bronx	NY	10451-2937
607 778-2451	**Broome County** 44 Hawley St	Binghamton	NY	13901-3722
716 938-9111	**Cattaraugus County** 303 Court St	Little Valley	NY	14755-1028
315 253-1011	**Cayuga County** 160 Genesee St	Auburn	NY	13021-3421
716 753-4211	**Chautauqua County** Gerace Office Bldg	Mayville	NY	14757-0000
607 737-2811	**Chemung County** 425 Pennsylvania Ave	Elmira	NY	14904-1762
607 335-4500	**Chenango County** 5 Court St	Norwich	NY	13815-1676
518 565-4700	**Clinton County** 137 Margaret St	Plattsburgh	NY	12901-2933
518 828-3339	**Columbia County** Allen & Union Sts	Hudson	NY	12534-0000
607 753-5052	**Cortland County** 60 Central Ave	Cortland	NY	13045-2718
607 746-2123	**Delaware County** 4 Court St	Delhi	NY	13753-1081
914 431-2020	**Dutchess County** 22 Market St	Poughkeepsie	NY	12601-3233
716 858-6392	**Erie County** 95 Franklin St	Buffalo	NY	14202-3968
518 873-6301	**Essex County** Court St	Elizabethtown	NY	12932-0000
518 483-6767	**Franklin County** 63 W Main St	Malone	NY	12953-1817
518 762-0540	**Fulton County** 223 W Main St	Johnstown	NY	12095-2309
716 344-2550	**Genesee County** Main & Court Sts	Batavia	NY	14020-3199
518 943-2050	**Greene County** Main St	Catskill	NY	12414-1396
518 548-7111	**Hamilton County** Rt 8	Lake Pleasant	NY	12108-0000
315 867-1002	**Herkimer County** 109 Mary St	Herkimer	NY	13350-1921
315 785-3090	**Jefferson County** 175 Arsenal St	Watertown	NY	13601-2522
718 643-5771	**Kings County** 360 Adams St	Brooklyn	NY	11201-3712
315 376-5333	**Lewis County** 7660 N State St	Lowville	NY	13367-1328
716 243-2500	**Livingston County** 2 Court St	Geneseo	NY	14454-0000
315 366-2011	**Madison County** N Court St	Wampsville	NY	13163-9999
716 428-5151	**Monroe County** 39 W Main St	Rochester	NY	14614-1408
518 853-3431	**Montgomery County** Broadway	Fonda	NY	12068-0000
516 535-2663	**Nassau County** 240 Old Country Rd	Mineola	NY	11501-4248
212 374-8742	**New York County** 60 Centre St	New York	NY	10007-1402
716 439-6100	**Niagara County** PO Box 461	Lockport	NY	14095-0461
315 798-5700	**Oneida County** 800 Park Ave	Utica	NY	13501-2220
315 435-2070	**Onondaga County** 421 Montgomery St	Syracuse	NY	13202-2984
716 396-4400	**Ontario County** 27 N Main St	Canandaigua	NY	14424-1447
914 294-5151	**Orange County** 255-275 Main St	Goshen	NY	10924-0000
716 589-4457	**Orleans County** Courthouse Sq	Albion	NY	14411-0000
315 349-3400	**Oswego County** 46 E Bridge St	Oswego	NY	13126-2123
607 547-4276	**Otsego County** 197 Main St	Cooperstown	NY	13326-1129
914 225-3641	**Putnam County** 2 County Ctr	Carmel	NY	10512-0000
718 520-3137	**Queens County** 88-11 Sutphin Blvd	Jamaica	NY	11435-3716
518 270-2700	**Rensselaer County** 1600 7th Ave	Troy	NY	12180-3409
718 390-5386	**Richmond County** 18 Richmond Terr	Staten Island	NY	10301-1935
914 638-5100	**Rockland County** 11 New Hempstead Rd	New City	NY	10956-3636
315 379-2000	**Saint Lawrence County** 48 Court St	Canton	NY	13617-9987
518 885-5381	**Saratoga County** 40 McMasters St	Ballston Spa	NY	12020-1999
518 382-3220	**Schenectady County** 620 State St	Schenectady	NY	12305-2113
518 295-8316	**Schoharie County** PO Box 549	Schoharie	NY	12157-0549
607 535-2132	**Schuyler County** 105 9th St	Watkins Glen	NY	14891-1496
315 539-5655	**Seneca County** 1 DiPronio Dr	Waterloo	NY	13165-1681
607 776-9631	**Steuben County** 3 Pulteney Sq	Bath	NY	14810-1573
516 548-3888	**Suffolk County** County Ctr	Riverhead	NY	11901-0000
914 794-3000	**Sullivan County** 100 North St	Monticello	NY	12701-1160
607 687-3133	**Tioga County** 16 Court St	Owego	NY	13827-1515
607 274-5434	**Tompkins County** 320 N Tioga St	Ithaca	NY	14850-4284
914 339-5680	**Ulster County** 285 Wall St	Kingston	NY	12401-3817
518 761-6429	**Warren County** Rt 9	Lake George	NY	12845-0000
518 747-3374	**Washington County** Upper Broadway	Fort Edward	NY	12828-0000
315 946-5400	**Wayne County** 26 Church St	Lyons	NY	14489-1134
914 285-2000	**Westchester County** 110 Grove St	White Plains	NY	10601-2504
716 786-8810	**Wyoming County** 143 N Main St	Warsaw	NY	14569-1123
315 536-4011	**Yates County** 110 Court St Rm 198	Penn Yan	NY	14527-1130

NORTH CAROLINA

919 228-1312	**Alamance County** 124 W Elm St	Graham	NC	27253-2802
704 632-2215	**Alexander County** 100 1st St SW	Taylorsville	NC	28681-2592
919 372-8949	**Alleghany County** Main St	Sparta	NC	28675-0000
704 694-2796	**Anson County** N Green St	Wadesboro	NC	28170-0000
919 246-8841	**Ashe County** Court St	Jefferson	NC	28640-0000
704 733-5186	**Avery County** Main St	Newland	NC	28657-0000
919 946-7721	**Beaufort County** 112 W 2nd St	Washington	NC	27889-4940
919 794-5300	**Bertie County** 106 W Dundee St	Windsor	NC	27983-1208
919 862-3438	**Bladen County** Courthouse Dr	Elizabethtown	NC	28337-0000
919 253-4331	**Brunswick County** PO Box 249	Bolivia	NC	28422-0249
704 251-6007	**Buncombe County** 60 Courthouse Plaza	Asheville	NC	28801-3519
704 438-5540	**Burke County** PO Box 796	Morganton	NC	28655-0000
704 786-4137	**Cabarrus County** PO Box 70	Concord	NC	28026-0070
704 758-0161	**Caldwell County** PO Box 1376	Lenoir	NC	28645-0000
919 338-0066	**Camden County** Hwy 343	Camden	NC	27921-0000
919 728-8500	**Carteret County** Courthouse Sq	Beaufort	NC	28516-0000
919 694-4193	**Caswell County** E Church St & North Ave	Yanceyville	NC	27379-0000
704 464-7880	**Catawba County** PO Box 389	Newton	NC	28658-0389
919 542-3240	**Chatham County** Courthouse Sq	Pittsboro	NC	27312-0000
704 837-5527	**Cherokee County** 201 Peachtree St	Murphy	NC	28906-2994
919 482-2323	**Chowan County** S Broad St	Edenton	NC	27932-0000
704 389-6301	**Clay County** PO Box 118	Hayesville	NC	28904-0118
704 484-4800	**Cleveland County** PO Box 1210	Shelby	NC	28150-0000
919 642-5700	**Columbus County** 111 Washington St	Whiteville	NC	28472-3323
919 633-3126	**Craven County** 302 Broad St	New Bern	NC	28560-4903
919 486-1351	**Cumberland County** 113 Dick St	Fayetteville	NC	28301-5725
919 232-2075	**Currituck County** PO Box 39	Currituck	NC	27929-0039
919 473-1101	**Dare County** Budleigh St	Manteo	NC	27954-0000
704 249-7011	**Davidson County** PO Box 1067	Lexington	NC	27292-0000
704 634-5513	**Davie County** 123 S Main St	Mocksville	NC	27028-2424
919 296-1240	**Duplin County** Courthouse Plaza	Kenansville	NC	28349-0000
919 560-0025	**Durham County** 201 E Main St	Durham	NC	27701-3641
919 823-6161	**Edgecombe County** 301 Saint Andrews St	Tarboro	NC	27886-5111
919 727-2071	**Forsyth County** Hall of Justice Rm 700	Winston-Salem	NC	27101-0000
919 496-5994	**Franklin County** 215 E Nash St	Louisburg	NC	27549-2545
704 868-5800	**Gaston County** 151 South St	Gastonia	NC	28052-4128
919 357-1240	**Gates County** PO Box 141	Gatesville	NC	27938-0141
704 479-3361	**Graham County** PO Box 575	Robbinsville	NC	28771-0575
919 693-5240	**Granville County** 141 Williamsboro St	Oxford	NC	27565-3318
919 747-3505	**Greene County** 2nd & Greene	Snow Hill	NC	28580-0675
919 373-3778	**Guilford County** 301 Market St	Greensboro	NC	27402-0000
919 583-1131	**Halifax County** King St	Halifax	NC	27839-0000
919 893-7500	**Harnett County** 729 S Main St	Lillington	NC	27546-0000
704 452-6625	**Haywood County** County Courthouse Annex	Waynesville	NC	28786-0000
704 697-4808	**Henderson County** 100 N King St	Hendersonville	NC	28792-5053
919 358-7845	**Hertford County** King St	Winton	NC	27986-0000
919 875-8751	**Hoke County** 227 N Main St	Raeford	NC	28376-0266
919 926-5711	**Hyde County** 264 Business Hwy	Swan Quarter	NC	27885-0000
704 878-3000	**Iredell County** PO Box 788	Statesville	NC	28677-0788
704 586-4312	**Jackson County** 50 Keener St Suite 102	Sylva	NC	28779-0000
919 989-5100	**Johnston County** 207 E Johnston St	Smithfield	NC	27577-4515
919 448-7571	**Jones County** PO Box 266	Trenton	NC	28585-0266
919 774-8403	**Lee County** PO Box 1968	Sanford	NC	27331-1968
919 523-2417	**Lenoir County** PO Box 3289	Kinston	NC	28502-3289
704 732-3361	**Lincoln County** 115 W Main St	Lincolnton	NC	28092-2643
704 524-6421	**Macon County** 5 W Main St	Franklin	NC	28734-3005
704 649-2531	**Madison County** PO Box 684	Marshall	NC	28753-0684
919 792-1901	**Martin County** PO Box 668	Williamston	NC	27892-0668
704 652-7121	**McDowell County** 10 E Court St	Marion	NC	28752-4041
704 336-2040	**Mecklenburg County** 600 E 4th St	Charlotte	NC	28202-2835
704 688-2434	**Mitchell County** Crimson Laurel Way Administration Bldg	Bakersville	NC	28705-0000
919 572-2575	**Montgomery County** PO Box 637	Troy	NC	27371-0637
919 947-2396	**Moore County** PO Box 936	Carthage	NC	28327-0936
919 341-7184	**New Hanover County** 320 Chestnut St Suite 502	Wilmington	NC	28401-4090
919 534-2501	**Northampton County** Jefferson St	Jackson	NC	27845-0000
919 347-4717	**Onslow County** 521 Mill Ave	Jacksonville	NC	28540-4258
919 732-8181	**Orange County** 106 E Margaret Ln	Hillsborough	NC	27278-2546
919 745-3133	**Pamlico County** PO Box 776	Bayboro	NC	28515-0776
919 335-0865	**Pasquotank County** PO Box 39	Elizabeth City	NC	27907-0039
919 259-1200	**Pender County** PO Box 5	Burgaw	NC	28425-0005
919 426-8484	**Perquimans County** PO Box 45	Hertford	NC	27944-0045
919 597-7228	**Person County** County Courthouse	Roxboro	NC	27573-0000
919 830-6302	**Pitt County** 1717 W 5th St	Greenville	NC	27834-1698
704 894-3301	**Polk County** PO Box 308	Columbus	NC	28722-0308
919 629-2131	**Randolph County** 145 Worth St	Asheboro	NC	27203-5509
919 671-3000	**Robeson County** 500 N Elm St	Lumberton	NC	28358-5595
919 342-8700	**Rockingham County** PO Box 26	Wentworth	NC	27375-0026
704 636-0361	**Rowan County** 202 N Main St	Salisbury	NC	28144-4346
704 286-9136	**Rutherford County** PO Box 630	Rutherfordton	NC	28139-0630
919 592-6308	**Sampson County** 313 Rowan Rd	Clinton	NC	28328-4700
919 277-0470	**Scotland County** 1405 West Blvd	Laurinburg	NC	28352-0000
704 983-7204	**Stanley County** 201 S 2nd St	Albemarle	NC	28001-5747
919 593-2811	**Stokes County** Hwy 89	Danbury	NC	27016-0000
919 386-8131	**Surry County** PO Box 345	Dobson	NC	27017-0345
704 488-9273	**Swain County** Mitchell St	Bryson City	NC	28713-0000
704 884-3100	**Transylvania County** 28 E Main St	Brevard	NC	28712-3738
919 796-1371	**Tyrrell County** Water St	Columbia	NC	27925-0000
704 283-3500	**Union County** 500 N Main St	Monroe	NC	28112-4730

Local Government–County

919 492-2141	**Vance County** 122 Young St	Henderson	NC	27536-4268
919 856-6000	**Wake County** 336 Fayetteville Mall	Raleigh	NC	27602-0000
919 257-3261	**Warren County** PO Box 709	Warrenton	NC	27589-0709
919 793-5823	**Washington County** 120 Adams St	Plymouth	NC	27962-1308
704 264-1300	**Watauga County** 403 W King St	Boone	NC	28607-3531
919 731-1400	**Wayne County** 215 S William St	Goldsboro	NC	27530-4824
919 651-7300	**Wilkes County** 110 North St	Wilkesboro	NC	28697-0000
919 237-3913	**Wilson County** PO Box 1728	Wilson	NC	27894-1728
919 679-4200	**Yadkin County** PO Box 146	Yadkinville	NC	27055-0146
704 682-3971	**Yancey County** County Courthouse	Burnsville	NC	28714-0000
	NORTH DAKOTA			
701 567-2460	**Adams County** County Courthouse	Hettinger	ND	58639-0000
701 845-8512	**Barnes County** PO Box 774	Valley City	ND	58072-0774
701 473-5340	**Benson County** 311 B Ave S	Minnewaukan	ND	58351-0000
701 623-4491	**Billings County** PO Box 138	Medora	ND	58645-0138
701 228-3983	**Bottineau County** 315 W 5th St	Bottineau	ND	58318-1214
701 523-3450	**Bowman County** 104 W 1st	Bowman	ND	58623-0000
701 377-2718	**Burke County** PO Box 219	Bowbells	ND	58721-0219
701 222-6702	**Burleigh County** 514 E Thayer Ave	Bismarck	ND	58501-4413
701 241-5660	**Cass County** 207 9th St S	Fargo	ND	58103-1833
701 256-2124	**Cavalier County** 901 3rd St	Langdon	ND	58249-2457
701 349-3560	**Dickey County** 309 N 2nd St	Ellendale	ND	58436-0000
701 965-6351	**Divide County** 300 N Main St	Crosby	ND	58730-0000
701 573-4447	**Dunn County** County Courthouse	Manning	ND	58642-0000
701 947-2434	**Eddy County** 524 Central Ave	New Rockford	ND	58356-1698
701 254-4701	**Emmons County** PO Box 87	Linton	ND	58552-0087
701 652-2491	**Foster County** 1000 5th St N	Carrington	ND	58421-1113
701 872-4352	**Golden Valley County** PO Box 596	Beach	ND	58621-0596
701 780-8238	**Grand Forks County** PO Box 1477	Grand Forks	ND	58206-1477
701 622-3615	**Grant County** County Courthouse	Carson	ND	58529-0000
701 797-2772	**Griggs County** PO Box 326	Cooperstown	ND	58425-0326
701 824-2545	**Hettinger County** 336 Pacific Ave	Mott	ND	58646-0000
701 475-2672	**Kidder County** PO Box 110	Steele	ND	58482-0110
701 883-5193	**La Moure County** 202 4th Ave NE	La Moure	ND	58458-0000
701 754-2504	**Logan County** 301 Main St	Napoleon	ND	58561-0000
701 537-5729	**McHenry County** 407 Main St S	Towner	ND	58788-0000
701 288-3450	**McIntosh County** 112 NE 1st St	Ashley	ND	58413-0000
701 842-3451	**McKenzie County** PO Box 523	Watford City	ND	58854-0523
701 462-8541	**McLean County** 712 5th Ave	Washburn	ND	58577-0000
701 745-3262	**Mercer County** PO Box 39	Stanton	ND	58571-0039
701 667-3355	**Morton County** 210 2nd Ave NW	Mandan	ND	58554-3158
701 628-2915	**Mountrail County** PO Box 69	Stanley	ND	58784-0069
701 247-2462	**Nelson County** PO Box 565	Lakota	ND	58344-0565
701 794-8748	**Oliver County** PO Box 166	Center	ND	58530-0166
701 265-4275	**Pembina County** PO Box 357	Cavalier	ND	58220-0357
701 776-6161	**Pierce County** 240 2nd St SE	Rugby	ND	58368-1830
701 662-7069	**Ramsey County** 6th & 4th St	Devils Lake	ND	58301-0000
701 756-6398	**Renville County** PO Box 68	Mohall	ND	58761-0068
701 642-7818	**Richland County** PO Box 966	Wahpeton	ND	58074-0936
701 477-3816	**Rolette County** PO Box 460	Rolla	ND	58367-0460
701 724-3355	**Sargent County** PO Box 98	Forman	ND	58032-0098
701 363-2207	**Sheridan County** PO Box 636	McClusky	ND	58463-0636
701 854-3853	**Sioux County** PO Box L	Fort Yates	ND	58538-0529
701 879-6275	**Slope County** PO Box JJ	Amidon	ND	58620-0449
701 264-7636	**Stark County** PO Box 130	Dickinson	ND	58602-0130
701 524-2790	**Steele County** County Courthouse	Finley	ND	58230-0000
701 252-9037	**Stutsman County** 511 2nd Ave SE	Jamestown	ND	58401-4210
701 968-3424	**Towner County** PO Box 517	Cando	ND	58324-0517
701 436-4454	**Traill County** County Courthouse	Hillsboro	ND	58045-0000
701 352-2851	**Walsh County** 600 Cooper Ave	Grafton	ND	58237-1542
701 857-6460	**Ward County** 3rd St SE	Minot	ND	58701-6498
701 547-3122	**Wells County** PO Box 596	Fessenden	ND	58438-0596
701 572-1700	**Williams County** 205 E Broadway	Williston	ND	58801-6123
	OHIO			
513 544-2344	**Adams County** 110 W Main St	West Union	OH	45693-1347
419 228-3700	**Allen County** 301 N Main St	Lima	OH	45801-4456
419 289-0000	**Ashland County** 110 W 2nd St	Ashland	OH	44805-2101
216 576-9090	**Ashtabula County** 25 W Jefferson St	Jefferson	OH	44047-1092
614 592-3242	**Athens County** Court & Washington Sts	Athens	OH	45701-0000
419 738-7896	**Auglaize County** 36 E Auglaize St	Wapakoneta	OH	45895-1505
614 695-2121	**Belmont County** 100 W Main St	Saint Clairsville	OH	43950-1225
513 378-3100	**Brown County** Danny L Pride Courthouse	Georgetown	OH	45121-0000
513 887-3000	**Butler County** 130 High St	Hamilton	OH	45011-2756
216 627-2250	**Carroll County** 119 Public Sq	Carrollton	OH	44615-1448
513 653-5896	**Champaign County** Main & Court St	Urbana	OH	43078-0000
513 328-2458	**Clark County** 101 N Limestone St	Springfield	OH	45502-1123
513 732-7300	**Clermont County** 76 S Riverside Dr	Batavia	OH	45103-2635
513 382-2103	**Clinton County** 46 S South St	Wilmington	OH	45177-2214
216 424-9511	**Columbiana County** 105 S Market St	Lisbon	OH	44432-1255
614 622-1753	**Coshocton County** 349 1/2 Main St	Coshocton	OH	43812-1510
419 562-5876	**Crawford County** 112 E Mansfield St	Bucyrus	OH	44820-2389
216 443-7950	**Cuyahoga County** 1200 Ontario St	Cleveland	OH	44113-1604
513 547-7370	**Darke County** 4th & Broadway	Greenville	OH	45331-0000
419 782-4761	**Defiance County** 500 Court St	Defiance	OH	43512-2157
614 369-8761	**Delaware County** 91 N Sandusky St	Delaware	OH	43015-1797
419 627-7705	**Erie County** 323 Columbus Ave	Sandusky	OH	44870-2695
614 687-7030	**Fairfield County** 224 E Main St	Lancaster	OH	43130-3842
614 335-0720	**Fayette County** 110 E Court St	Washington Court House	OH	43160-1355
614 462-3322	**Franklin County** 410 S High St	Columbus	OH	43215-0000
419 337-9255	**Fulton County** 210 S Fulton St Rm B-10	Wauseon	OH	43567-1355
614 446-4374	**Gallia County** 18 Locust St	Gallipolis	OH	45631-1251
216 285-2222	**Geauga County** 231 Main St	Chardon	OH	44024-1243
513 376-5000	**Greene County** 45 N Detroit St	Xenia	OH	45385-3199
614 432-2505	**Guernsey County** 836 Steubenville Ave	Cambridge	OH	43725-2335
513 632-6500	**Hamilton County** 1000 Main St	Cincinnati	OH	45202-1217
419 424-7037	**Hancock County** 300 S Main St	Findlay	OH	45840-3345
419 674-2205	**Hardin County** Public Sq	Kenton	OH	43326-9700
614 942-8861	**Harrison County** 100 W Market St	Cadiz	OH	43907-1132
419 592-4876	**Henry County** PO Box 546	Napoleon	OH	43545-0546
513 393-1911	**Highland County** 114 Governor Foraker Pl	Hillsboro	OH	45133-1055
614 385-5195	**Hocking County** 1 E Main St	Logan	OH	43138-1207
216 674-0286	**Holmes County** E Jackson St	Millersburg	OH	44654-1349
419 668-3092	**Huron County** 2 E Main St	Norwalk	OH	44857-0000
614 286-3301	**Jackson County** 226 Main St	Jackson	OH	45640-0000
614 283-4111	**Jefferson County** 301 Market St	Steubenville	OH	43952-2149
614 397-2727	**Knox County** 106 E High St	Mount Vernon	OH	43050-3453
216 357-2500	**Lake County** 105 Main St	Painesville	OH	44077-3414
614 533-4355	**Lawrence County** 5th & Park Ave	Ironton	OH	45638-0000
614 349-6000	**Licking County** 20 S 2nd St	Newark	OH	43055-5663
513 599-7275	**Logan County** Main & E Columbus 2nd Fl	Bellefontaine	OH	43311-0000
216 329-5536	**Lorain County** PO Box 749	Elyria	OH	44036-0749
419 245-4000	**Lucus County** 1 Government Ctr Suite 800	Toledo	OH	43604-2202
614 852-2972	**Madison County** County Courthouse	London	OH	43140-0000
216 740-2104	**Mahoning County** 120 Market St	Youngstown	OH	44503-1710
614 387-5871	**Marion County** 114 N Main St	Marion	OH	43302-3030
216 723-3641	**Medina County** 93 Public Sq	Medina	OH	44256-2292
614 992-2895	**Meigs County** 2nd St	Pomeroy	OH	45769-0000
419 586-3178	**Mercer County** 101 N Main St	Celina	OH	45822-1794
513 332-6800	**Miami County** 201 W Main St	Troy	OH	45373-3263
614 472-5181	**Monroe County** PO Box 574	Woodsfield	OH	43793-0574
513 225-4000	**Montgomery County** 451 W 3rd St	Dayton	OH	45422-0002
614 962-4752	**Morgan County** 19 E Main St	McConnelsville	OH	43756-1198
419 947-2085	**Morrow County** 48 E High St	Mount Gilead	OH	43338-1430
614 455-7104	**Muskingum County** PO Box 268	Zanesville	OH	43702-0268
614 732-2969	**Noble County** County Courthouse	Caldwell	OH	43724-0000
419 734-6700	**Ottawa County** 315 Madison St Rm 103	Port Clinton	OH	43452-1936
419 399-8210	**Paulding County** County Courthouse	Paulding	OH	45879-0000
614 342-2045	**Perry County** 121 W Brown St	New Lexington	OH	43764-1241
614 474-6093	**Pickaway County** 207 S Court St	Circleville	OH	43113-1601
614 947-2715	**Pike County** 100 E 2nd St	Waverly	OH	45690-1399
216 297-3644	**Portage County** PO Box 1035	Ravenna	OH	44266-0000
513 456-8160	**Preble County** 100 Main St	Eaton	OH	45320-0000
419 523-3656	**Putnam County** 245 E Main St	Ottawa	OH	45875-1968
419 755-5501	**Richland County** 50 Park Ave E	Mansfield	OH	44902-1888
614 773-5115	**Ross County** N Paint St	Chillicothe	OH	45601-0000
419 334-6100	**Sandusky County** 100 N Park Ave	Fremont	OH	43420-2473
614 353-5111	**Scioto County** 602 7th St	Portsmouth	OH	45662-3948
419 447-4550	**Seneca County** 81 Jefferson St	Tiffin	OH	44883-2354
513 498-7226	**Shelby County** 129 E Court St	Sidney	OH	45365-3095
216 438-0800	**Stark County** 209 Tuscarawas St W	Canton	OH	44702-2219
216 379-2512	**Summit County** 175 S Main St	Akron	OH	44308-1306
216 841-0562	**Trumbull County** 160 High St NW	Warren	OH	44481-1005
216 364-8811	**Tuscarawas County** Public Sq	New Philadelphia	OH	44663-0000
513 642-2841	**Union County** 5th & Court St	Marysville	OH	43040-0000
419 238-6159	**Van Wert County** 121 E Main St 2nd Fl	Van Wert	OH	45891-1795
614 596-4571	**Vinton County** Vinton County Courthouse	McArthur	OH	45651-1296
513 932-4040	**Warren County** 320 E Silver St	Lebanon	OH	45036-2361
614 373-6623	**Washington County** 205 Putnam St	Marietta	OH	45750-3017
216 263-3124	**Wayne County** 107 W Liberty St	Wooster	OH	44691-4850
419 636-2059	**Williams County** County Courthouse Sq 4th Fl	Bryan	OH	43506-0000
419 354-9280	**Wood County** 1 Courthouse Sq	Bowling Green	OH	43402-2473
419 294-1432	**Wyandot County** County Courthouse	Upper Sandusky	OH	43351-0000
	OKLAHOMA			
918 696-7198	**Adair County** PO Box 169	Stilwell	OK	74960-0169
405 596-2392	**Alfalfa County** 300 S Grand Ave County Courthouse	Cherokee	OK	73728-0000
405 889-2643	**Atoka County** 201 E Court St	Atoka	OK	74525-2056
405 625-3151	**Beaver County** 111 W 2nd St	Beaver	OK	73932-0000
405 928-2457	**Beckham County** PO Box 67	Sayre	OK	73662-0067
405 623-5890	**Blaine County** 212 N Weigle Ave	Watonga	OK	73772-3893
405 924-2201	**Bryan County** 402 W Evergreen St	Durant	OK	74701-4703
405 247-3105	**Caddo County** PO Box 1427	Anadarko	OK	73005-1427
405 262-1070	**Canadian County** 301 N Choctaw Ave	El Reno	OK	73036-2407
405 223-8162	**Carter County** 1st & B St SW	Ardmore	OK	73401-0000
918 456-3171	**Cherokee County** 213 W Delaware St	Tahlequah	OK	74464-3639
405 326-5331	**Choctaw County** County Courthouse	Hugo	OK	74743-0000
405 544-2251	**Cimarron County** PO Box 145	Boise City	OK	73933-0145
405 366-0201	**Cleveland County** 201 S Jones Ave	Norman	OK	73069-6046
405 927-3122	**Coal County** 3 N Main St	Coalgate	OK	74538-2832
405 353-3717	**Comanche County** PO Box 9026	Lawton	OK	73501-0000
405 875-3026	**Cotton County** 301 N Broadway St	Walters	OK	73572-1271
918 256-2507	**Craig County** 301 W Canadian Ave	Vinita	OK	74301-3640
918 224-0278	**Creek County** PO Box 129	Sapulpa	OK	74067-0129
405 323-4420	**Custer County** 675 W 'B' St	Arapaho	OK	73620-0000
918 253-4432	**Delaware County** Krouse St	Jay	OK	74346-0000
405 328-5390	**Dewey County** PO Box 368	Taloga	OK	73667-0368
405 885-7301	**Ellis County** 100 S Washington Courthouse Sq	Arnett	OK	73832-0000
405 237-0227	**Garfield County** County Courthouse Rm 101	Enid	OK	73701-0000
405 238-2685	**Garvin County** Walnut & Grant	Pauls Valley	OK	73075-3290
405 224-5211	**Grady County** PO Box 459	Chickasha	OK	73023-0459
405 395-2214	**Grant County** County Courthouse Rm 104	Medford	OK	73759-1244
405 782-2329	**Greer County** Courthouse Sq	Mangum	OK	73554-4260
405 688-3658	**Harmon County** 114 W Hollis County Courthouse	Hollis	OK	73550-0000
405 735-2012	**Harper County** 311 SE 1st	Buffalo	OK	73834-0000
918 967-4352	**Haskell County** 202 E Main St	Stigler	OK	74462-2439
405 379-2746	**Hughes County** PO Box 914	Holdenville	OK	74848-0914
405 482-4420	**Jackson County** 101 W Broadway	Altus	OK	73521-3898
405 228-2241	**Jefferson County** 220 N Main St Rm 101	Waurika	OK	73573-2235
405 371-3058	**Johnston County** PO Box 338	Tishomingo	OK	73460-0338
405 362-3116	**Kay County** PO Box 450	Newkirk	OK	74647-0450
405 375-3808	**Kingfisher County** PO Box 118	Kingfisher	OK	73750-0118
405 726-5125	**Kiowa County** County Courthouse	Hobart	OK	73651-0000
918 465-2021	**Latimer County** 109 N Central St	Wilburton	OK	74578-2440
918 647-2527	**Le Flore County** PO Box 607	Poteau	OK	74953-0607
405 258-1264	**Lincoln County** PO Box 126	Chandler	OK	74834-0126
405 282-2124	**Logan County** 301 E Harrison Ave	Guthrie	OK	73044-4939
405 276-3059	**Love County** 405 W Main St	Marietta	OK	73448-2837
405 227-4732	**Major County** PO Box 379	Fairview	OK	73737-0379
405 795-3165	**Marshall County** County Courthouse	Madill	OK	73446-2261
918 825-0639	**Mayes County** PO Box 95	Pryor	OK	74362-0095
405 527-3117	**McClain County** PO Box 629	Purcell	OK	73080-0629
405 286-7428	**McCurtain County** 108 N Central Ave	Idabel	OK	74745-3835
918 689-2362	**McIntosh County** 110 N 1st St	Eufaula	OK	74432-2449
405 622-3777	**Murray County** PO Box 240	Sulphur	OK	73086-0240
918 682-9601	**Muskogee County** PO Box 2307	Muskogee	OK	74402-2307
405 336-2771	**Noble County** PO Box 409	Perry	OK	73077-0409
918 273-0175	**Nowata County** 229 N Maple St	Nowata	OK	74048-2654
918 623-0939	**Okfuskee County** PO Box 26	Okemah	OK	74859-0026
405 236-2727	**Oklahoma County** 321 Park Ave	Oklahoma City	OK	73102-3603
918 756-3836	**Okmulgee County** 314 W 7th St	Okmulgee	OK	74447-5028
918 287-2615	**Osage County** PO Box 87	Pawhuska	OK	74056-0087
918 542-9408	**Ottawa County** County Courthouse	Miami	OK	74354-0000
918 762-3741	**Pawnee County** County Courthouse	Pawnee	OK	74058-0000
405 624-9300	**Payne County** 606 S Husband St	Stillwater	OK	74074-4044
918 423-6865	**Pittsburg County** 2nd & Carl Albert	McAlester	OK	74501-0000
405 332-1425	**Pontotoc County** 13th & Broadway	Ada	OK	74820-0000
405 273-4305	**Pottawatomie County** 325 N Broadway St	Shawnee	OK	74801-6938
405 298-2512	**Pushmataha County** 203 SW 3rd St	Antlers	OK	74523-3899
405 497-3365	**Roger Mills County** PO Box 708	Cheyenne	OK	73628-0000
918 341-0585	**Rogers County** 219 S Missouri Ave	Claremore	OK	74017-7832
405 257-2450	**Seminole County** PO Box 457	Wewoka	OK	74884-0457
918 775-5539	**Sequoyah County** 120 E Chickasaw Ave Box 8	Sallisaw	OK	74955-4655
405 255-4193	**Stephens County** County Courthouse	Duncan	OK	73533-0000
405 338-3233	**Texas County** 319 N Main St	Guymon	OK	73942-4843
405 335-3421	**Tillman County** PO Box 992	Frederick	OK	73542-0992
918 596-5000	**Tulsa County** 500 S Denver Ave	Tulsa	OK	74103-3835
918 485-2141	**Wagoner County** 307 E Cherokee St	Wagoner	OK	74467-0000

918 336-0330	**Washington County**	420 S Johnstone Ave	Bartlesville	OK	74003-6602
405 832-2284	**Washita County**	PO Box 380	Cordell	OK	73632-0380
405 327-2126	**Woods County**	PO Box 386	Alva	OK	73717-0000
405 256-8097	**Woodward County**	1600 Main St	Woodward	OK	73801-3068

OREGON

503 523-6414	**Baker County**	1995 3rd St	Baker	OR	97814-3399
503 757-6800	**Benton County**	180 NW 5th St	Corvallis	OR	97330-4777
503 655-8581	**Clackamas County**	906 Main St	Oregon City	OR	97045-1881
503 325-1000	**Clatsop County**	PO Box 179	Astoria	OR	97103-0179
503 397-4322	**Columbia County**	County Courthouse	Saint Helens	OR	97051-0000
503 396-3121	**Coos County**	250 N Baxter St	Coquille	OR	97423-1894
503 447-6555	**Crook County**	300 E 3rd St	Prineville	OR	97754-1949
503 247-7011	**Curry County**	PO Box 746	Gold Beach	OR	97444-0746
503 388-6570	**Deschutes County**	1130 NW Harriman St	Bend	OR	97701-1947
503 672-3311	**Douglas County**	1036 SE Douglas Ave	Roseburg	OR	97470-3396
503 384-2311	**Gilliam County**	221 S Oregon St	Condon	OR	97823-0000
503 575-0059	**Grant County**	200 S Canyon Blvd	Canyon City	OR	97820-0000
503 573-6641	**Harney County**	450 N Buena Vista St	Burns	OR	97720-1565
503 386-3970	**Hood River County**	309 State St	Hood River	OR	97031-2037
503 776-7231	**Jackson County**	10 S Oakdale	Medford	OR	97501-2952
503 475-2449	**Jefferson County**	657 C St	Madras	OR	97741-1709
503 474-5221	**Josephine County**	County Courthouse	Grants Pass	OR	97526-0000
503 883-5134	**Klamath County**	316 Main St	Klamath Falls	OR	97601-6385
503 947-6006	**Lake County**	513 Center St	Lakeview	OR	97630-1579
503 687-4203	**Lane County**	125 E 8th Ave	Eugene	OR	97401-2926
503 265-6611	**Lincoln County**	225 W Olive St	Newport	OR	97365-3811
503 967-3825	**Linn County**	PO Box 100	Albany	OR	97321-0031
503 473-5151	**Malheur County**	PO Box 4	Vale	OR	97918-0004
503 588-5212	**Marion County**	100 High St NE	Salem	OR	97301-3665
503 676-9061	**Morrow County**	PO Box 338	Heppner	OR	97836-0338
503 248-3511	**Multnomah County**	1021 SW 4th Ave	Portland	OR	97204-1123
503 623-9217	**Polk County**	850 Main St Rm 201	Dallas	OR	97338-3116
503 565-3606	**Sherman County**	PO Box 365	Moro	OR	97039-0365
503 842-3402	**Tillamook County**	201 Laurel Ave	Tillamook	OR	97141-2381
503 276-7111	**Umatilla County**	216 SE 4th St	Pendleton	OR	97801-2590
503 963-1001	**Union County**	1106 K Ave	La Grande	OR	97850-2131
503 426-3586	**Wallowa County**	101 S River St Rm 202	Enterprise	OR	97828-1300
503 296-2207	**Wasco County**	5th & Washington	The Dalles	OR	97058-0000
503 648-8681	**Washington County**	155 N 1st Ave	Hillsboro	OR	97124-3070
503 763-2400	**Wheeler County**	PO Box 327	Fossil	OR	97830-0327
503 472-9371	**Yamhill County**	535 E 5th St	McMinnville	OR	97128-4593

PENNSYLVANIA

717 334-6781	**Adams County**	111 Baltimore St	Gettysburg	PA	17325-2312
412 355-5313	**Allegheny County**	436 Grant St	Pittsburgh	PA	15219-2403
412 543-2500	**Armstrong County**	Market St	Kittanning	PA	16201-0000
412 728-5700	**Beaver County**	3rd & Turnpike St	Beaver	PA	15009-0000
814 623-4836	**Bedford County**	230 S Juliana St	Bedford	PA	15522-1716
215 378-8000	**Berks County**	33 N 6th St	Reading	PA	19601-3540
814 695-5541	**Blair County**	423 Allegheny St	Hollidaysburg	PA	16648-2022
717 265-5700	**Bradford County**	301 Main St	Towanda	PA	18848-1884
215 348-6000	**Bucks County**	Main & Court Sts	Doylestown	PA	18901-0000
412 285-4731	**Butler County**	Main St	Butler	PA	16001-0000
814 472-5440	**Cambria County**	200 S Center St	Ebensburg	PA	15931-1936
814 486-2315	**Cameron County**	20 E 5th St	Emporium	PA	15834-1469
717 325-3611	**Carbon County**	Broadway Lock Box 129	Jim Thorpe	PA	18229-0129
814 355-6700	**Centre County**	County Courthouse	Bellefonte	PA	16823-3005
215 344-6000	**Chester County**	Market & High Sts	West Chester	PA	19380-0000
814 226-4000	**Clarion County**	421 Main St	Clarion	PA	16214-1028
814 765-2641	**Clearfield County**	N 2nd & Market Sts	Clearfield	PA	16830-0000
717 893-4000	**Clinton County**	County Courthouse	Lock Haven	PA	17745-0000
717 784-1991	**Columbia County**	PO Box 380	Bloomsburg	PA	17815-0380
814 336-1151	**Crawford County**	360 Center St	Meadville	PA	16335-0000
717 240-6100	**Cumberland County**	Hanover & High Sts	Carlisle	PA	17013-0000
717 255-2741	**Dauphin County**	Front & Market Sts	Harrisburg	PA	17101-2012
215 891-4000	**Delaware County**	W Front St	Media	PA	19063-0000
814 776-1161	**Elk County**	Main St	Ridgway	PA	15853-0000
814 451-6000	**Erie County**	140 W 6th St	Erie	PA	16501-1002
412 430-1201	**Fayette County**	61 E Main St	Uniontown	PA	15401-3514
814 755-3537	**Forest County**	526 Elm St	Tionesta	PA	16353-0000
717 264-4125	**Franklin County**	157 Lincoln Way E	Chambersburg	PA	17201-2211
717 485-4212	**Fulton County**	N 2nd St	McConnellsburg	PA	17233-0000
412 852-1171	**Greene County**	93 E High St County Office Bldg	Waynesburg	PA	15370-1888
814 643-3091	**Huntingdon County**	223 Penn St	Huntingdon	PA	16652-1443
412 465-3800	**Indiana County**	825 Philadelphia St	Indiana	PA	15701-3934
814 849-8031	**Jefferson County**	200 Main St	Brookville	PA	15825-1236
717 436-8991	**Juniata County**	PO Box 68	Mifflintown	PA	17059-0068
717 963-6723	**Lackawanna County**	PO Box 133	Scranton	PA	18503-0000
717 299-8300	**Lancaster County**	50 N Duke St	Lancaster	PA	17602-2805
412 658-2541	**Lawrence County**	433 Court St	New Castle	PA	16101-3599
717 274-2801	**Lebanon County**	400 S 8th St	Lebanon	PA	17042-6794
215 820-3000	**Lehigh County**	455 Hamilton St	Allentown	PA	18101-1614
717 825-1500	**Luzerne County**	211 N River St	Wilkes-Barre	PA	18704-5038
717 327-2200	**Lycoming County**	48 W 3rd St	Williamsport	PA	17701-6536
814 887-5571	**McKean County**	500 W Main St	Smethport	PA	16749-1144
412 662-3800	**Mercer County**	138 S Diamond St	Mercer	PA	16137-1284
717 248-6733	**Mifflin County**	20 N Wayne St	Lewistown	PA	17044-1770
717 424-5100	**Monroe County**	County Courthouse Sq	Stroudsburg	PA	18360-0000
215 278-3000	**Montgomery County**	Swede & Airy Sts	Norristown	PA	19404-0000
717 271-3012	**Montour County**	29 Mill St	Danville	PA	17821-1945
215 559-3000	**Northampton County**	7th & Washington Sts	Easton	PA	18042-7411
717 988-4100	**Northumberland County**	2nd & Market Sts	Sunbury	PA	17801-0000
717 582-2131	**Perry County**	PO Box 37	New Bloomfield	PA	17068-0037
215 686-1776	**Philadelphia County**	Broad & Market Sts	Philadelphia	PA	19107-0000
717 296-7613	**Pike County**	506 Broad St	Milford	PA	18337-1511
814 274-8290	**Potter County**	227 N Main St	Coudersport	PA	16915-1686
717 622-5570	**Schuylkill County**	N 2nd St & Laurel Blvd	Pottsville	PA	17901-2528
717 837-4207	**Snyder County**	11 W Market St	Middleburg	PA	17842-1018
814 445-5154	**Somerset County**	111 E Union St	Somerset	PA	15501-1416
717 946-5201	**Sullivan County**	Main & Muncy	Laporte	PA	18626-0000
717 278-4600	**Susquehanna County**	County Courthouse	Montrose	PA	18801-0000
717 724-1906	**Tioga County**	116-118 Main St	Wellsboro	PA	16901-0000
717 524-4461	**Union County**	103 S 2nd St	Lewisburg	PA	17837-1996
814 437-6871	**Venango County**	Liberty & 12th Sts	Franklin	PA	16323-1295
814 723-7550	**Warren County**	204 4th Ave	Warren	PA	16365-2399
412 228-6700	**Washington County**	100 W Beau St	Washington	PA	15301-4432
717 253-5970	**Wayne County**	925 Court St	Honesdale	PA	18431-1922
412 830-3000	**Westmoreland County**	Main St	Greensburg	PA	15601-2405
717 836-3200	**Wyoming County**	Court House Sq	Tunkhannock	PA	18657-1228
717 771-9675	**York County**	28 E Market St	York	PA	17401-1501

RHODE ISLAND

401 245-7977	**Bristol County**	516 Main St	Warren	RI	02885-4369
401 822-1311	**Kent County**	222 Quaker Ln	West Warwick	RI	02893-2144
401 841-8330	**Newport County**	8 Washington Sq	Newport	RI	02840-7199
401 277-3220	**Providence County**	250 Benefit St	Providence	RI	02903-2700
401 782-4121	**Washington County**	4800 Tower Hill Rd	Wakefield	RI	02879-2239

SOUTH CAROLINA

803 459-5074	**Abbeville County**	PO Box 99	Abbeville	SC	29620-0099
803 642-2013	**Aiken County**	828 Richland Ave W	Aiken	SC	29801-3834
803 584-2737	**Allendale County**	PO Box 126	Allendale	SC	29810-0126
803 260-4053	**Anderson County**	PO Box 1656	Anderson	SC	29622-1656
803 245-3025	**Bamberg County**	PO Box 150	Bamberg	SC	29003-0150
803 259-3485	**Barnwell County**	PO Box 723	Barnwell	SC	29812-0723
803 525-7307	**Beaufort County**	PO Box 1128	Beaufort	SC	29901-1228
803 761-8210	**Berkeley County**	223 N Live Oak Dr	Moncks Corner	SC	29461-3707
803 874-3524	**Calhoun County**	302 S Railroad Ave	Saint Matthews	SC	29135-1452
803 723-6724	**Charleston County**	PO Box 70219	North Charleston	SC	29415-0000
803 487-2562	**Cherokee County**	PO Box 866	Gaffney	SC	29342-0866
803 385-2605	**Chester County**	Main St	Chester	SC	29706-0000
803 623-2574	**Chesterfield County**	200 W Main St	Chesterfield	SC	29709-1527
803 435-4444	**Clarendon County**	PO Box E	Manning	SC	29102-0136
803 549-5791	**Colleton County**	PO Box 620	Walterboro	SC	29488-0620
803 393-3836	**Darlington County**	Courthouse Public Sq	Darlington	SC	29532-0000
803 774-1400	**Dillon County**	PO Box 449	Dillon	SC	29536-0449
803 563-2331	**Dorchester County**	PO Box 613	Saint George	SC	29477-0000
803 637-5781	**Edgefield County**	PO Box 663	Edgefield	SC	29824-0663
803 635-1415	**Fairfield County**	115 S Congress St Drawer 60	Winnsboro	SC	29180-0060
803 665-3031	**Florence County**	180 N Irby St	Florence	SC	29501-3456
803 546-5011	**Georgetown County**	715 Prince St	Georgetown	SC	29440-3631
803 240-7105	**Greenville County**	301 University Ridge Suite 100	Greenville	SC	29601-3665
803 229-6622	**Greenwood County**	528 Monument St	Greenwood	SC	29646-0000
803 943-3668	**Hampton County**	PO Box 7	Hampton	SC	29924-0007
803 248-1200	**Horry County**	PO Box 677	Conway	SC	29526-0677
803 726-8832	**Jasper County**	PO Box 248	Ridgeland	SC	29936-0248
803 425-1527	**Kershaw County**	1121 Broad St	Camden	SC	29020-3638
803 285-1581	**Lancaster County**	PO Box 1809	Lancaster	SC	29720-1411
803 984-5214	**Laurens County**	PO Box 445	Laurens	SC	29360-0445
803 484-5341	**Lee County**	PO Box 309	Bishopville	SC	29010-0000
803 359-8212	**Lexington County**	139 E Main St	Lexington	SC	29072-3456
803 423-3904	**Marion County**	PO Box 183	Marion	SC	29571-0183
803 479-5613	**Marlboro County**	PO Box 996	Bennettsville	SC	29512-0996
803 465-2195	**McCormick County**	PO Box 86	McCormick	SC	29835-0086
803 321-2110	**Newberry County**	PO Box 278	Newberry	SC	29108-0278
803 638-4280	**Oconee County**	W Main St	Walhalla	SC	29691-0000
803 533-1000	**Orangeburg County**	190 Sunnyside St NE	Orangeburg	SC	29115-5463
803 878-7809	**Pickens County**	PO Box 215	Pickens	SC	29671-0215
803 748-4684	**Richland County**	1701 Main St	Columbia	SC	29201-2833
803 445-3303	**Saluda County**	101 S 9th St	Saluda	SC	29138-0000
803 596-2500	**Spartanburg County**	180 Magnolia St	Spartanburg	SC	29301-2392
803 773-1581	**Sumter County**	141 N Main St	Sumter	SC	29150-4965
803 429-1630	**Union County**	PO Box G	Union	SC	29379-0200
803 354-6855	**Williamsburg County**	125 W Main St	Kingstree	SC	29556-3347
803 684-8532	**York County**	2 Congress St	York	SC	29745-0000

SOUTH DAKOTA

605 942-7165	**Aurora County**	PO Box 366	Plankinton	SD	57368-0366
605 353-7165	**Beadle County**	450 3rd St SW	Huron	SD	57350-1814
605 685-6969	**Bennett County**	PO Box 281	Martin	SD	57551-0281
605 589-3382	**Bon Homme County**	PO Box 6	Tyndall	SD	57066-0006
605 688-4208	**Brookings County**	314 6th Ave	Brookings	SD	57006-2041
605 622-2451	**Brown County**	101 1st Ave SE	Aberdeen	SD	57401-4203
605 734-5443	**Brule County**	300 S Courtland St	Chamberlain	SD	57325-1599
605 293-3234	**Buffalo County**	PO Box 148	Gann Valley	SD	57341-0148
605 892-4485	**Butte County**	839 5th Ave	Belle Fourche	SD	57717-1799
605 955-3366	**Campbell County**	PO Box 37	Mound City	SD	57646-0000
605 487-7131	**Charles Mix County**	PO Box 640	Lake Andes	SD	57356-0640
605 532-5851	**Clark County**	PO Box 294	Clark	SD	57225-0000
605 624-2281	**Clay County**	211 W Main St	Vermillion	SD	57069-2097
605 886-8497	**Codington County**	14 1st Ave SE	Watertown	SD	57201-3611
605 273-4201	**Corson County**	PO Box 175	McIntosh	SD	57641-0175
605 673-4816	**Custer County**	420 Mt Rushmore Rd	Custer	SD	57730-1998
605 996-7727	**Davison County**	200 E 4th Ave	Mitchell	SD	57301-2692
605 345-3771	**Day County**	710 W 1st St	Webster	SD	57274-1391
605 874-2120	**Deuel County**	PO Box 125	Clear Lake	SD	57226-0000
605 865-3672	**Dewey County**	County Courthouse	Timber Lake	SD	57656-0000
605 724-2585	**Douglas County**	PO Box 36	Armour	SD	57313-0000
605 426-6671	**Edmunds County**	2nd St	Ipswich	SD	57451-0000
605 745-5132	**Fall River County**	906 N River St	Hot Springs	SD	57747-1387
605 598-6224	**Faulk County**	PO Box 309	Faulkton	SD	57438-0309
605 432-6711	**Grant County**	210 E 5th Ave	Milbank	SD	57252-2433
605 775-2665	**Gregory County**	PO Box 430	Burke	SD	57523-0430
605 859-2627	**Haakon County**	PO Box 70	Philip	SD	57567-0070
605 783-3751	**Hamlin County**	PO Box 256	Hayti	SD	57241-0256
605 853-3337	**Hand County**	415 W 1st Ave	Miller	SD	57362-1346
605 239-4446	**Hanson County**	PO Box 127	Alexandria	SD	57311-0127
605 375-3351	**Harding County**	901 Ramsland St	Buffalo	SD	57720-0000
605 773-3713	**Hughes County**	104 E Capitol Ave	Pierre	SD	57501-2563
605 387-5335	**Hutchinson County**	PO Box 7	Olivet	SD	57052-0007
605 852-2512	**Hyde County**	PO Box 306	Highmore	SD	57345-0306
605 837-2121	**Jackson County**	1 Main St	Kadoka	SD	57543-0000
605 539-1202	**Jerauld County**	PO Box 435	Wessington Springs	SD	57382-0435
605 669-2361	**Jones County**	PO Box 448	Murdo	SD	57559-0448
605 854-3811	**Kingsbury County**	101 2nd St SE	De Smet	SD	57231-0000
605 256-5644	**Lake County**	200 E Center County Courthouse	Madison	SD	57042-0000
605 578-1941	**Lawrence County**		Deadwood	SD	57732-0000
605 987-2581	**Lincoln County**	100 E 5th St	Canton	SD	57013-1732
605 869-2247	**Lyman County**	County Courthouse	Kennebec	SD	57544-0000
605 448-5213	**Marshall County**	County Courthouse	Britton	SD	57430-0000
605 425-2781	**McCook County**	130 W Essex Ave	Salem	SD	57058-8901
605 439-3316	**McPherson County**	County Courthouse	Leola	SD	57456-0000
605 347-4411	**Meade County**	PO Box 939	Sturgis	SD	57785-0939
605 259-3230	**Mellette County**	S 1st St	White River	SD	57579-0000
605 772-4612	**Miner County**	N Main St	Howard	SD	57349-0000
605 339-6418	**Minnehaha County**	415 N Dakota Ave	Sioux Falls	SD	57102-0136
605 997-3181	**Moody County**	101 E Pipestone Ave	Flandreau	SD	57028-1730
605 394-2575	**Pennington County**	PO Box 230	Rapid City	SD	57709-0230
605 244-5626	**Perkins County**	PO Box 27	Bison	SD	57620-0027
605 765-9472	**Potter County**	201 S Exene St	Gettysburg	SD	57442-1598
605 698-3395	**Roberts County**	411 2nd Ave E	Sisseton	SD	57262-1495
605 796-4515	**Sanborn County**	PO Box 56	Woonsocket	SD	57385-0056
605 745-5131	**Shannon County**	906 N River St	Hot Springs	SD	57747-1387
605 472-1825	**Spink County**	210 E 7th Ave	Redfield	SD	57469-1299

Local Government–County

605 223-2673	**Stanley County**	PO Box 595	Fort Pierre	SD	57532-0595
605 258-2535	**Sully County**	Main St	Onida	SD	57564-0000
605 842-2266	**Todd County**	200 E 3rd St	Winner	SD	57580-0000
605 842-2266	**Tripp County**	200 E 3rd St	Winner	SD	57580-1806
605 297-3115	**Turner County**	PO Box 446	Parker	SD	57053-0446
605 356-2132	**Union County**	PO Box 757	Elk Point	SD	57025-0757
605 649-7878	**Walworth County**	PO Box 199	Selby	SD	57472-0199
605 668-3438	**Yankton County**	410 Walnut St	Yankton	SD	57078-4313
605 365-5157	**Ziebach County**	PO Box 68	Dupree	SD	57623-0068

TENNESSEE

615 457-5400	**Anderson County**	100 N Main St	Clinton	TN	37716-3615
615 684-1921	**Bedford County**	1 Public Sq	Shelbyville	TN	37160-3953
901 584-6053	**Benton County**	Court Sq	Camden	TN	38320-0000
615 447-2137	**Bledsoe County**	PO Box 212	Pikeville	TN	37367-0212
615 982-4391	**Blount County**	301 Court St	Maryville	TN	37801-4997
615 479-9654	**Bradley County**	PO Box 46	Cleveland	TN	37364-0046
615 562-4985	**Campbell County**	PO Box 13	Jacksboro	TN	37757-0013
615 563-4278	**Cannon County**	County Courthouse	Woodbury	TN	37190-0000
901 986-8237	**Carroll County**	PO Box 110	Huntingdon	TN	38344-0000
615 542-1814	**Carter County**	Main St County Courthouse	Elizabethton	TN	37643-0000
615 792-5179	**Cheatham County**	100 Public Sq	Ashland City	TN	37015-1711
901 989-2233	**Chester County**	PO Box 205	Henderson	TN	38340-0205
615 626-3283	**Claiborne County**	PO Box 173	Tazewell	TN	37879-0173
615 243-2249	**Clay County**	PO Box 218	Celina	TN	38551-0218
615 623-6176	**Cocke County**	Court Ave	Newport	TN	37821-0000
615 728-3024	**Coffee County**	300 Hillsboro Blvd Box 8	Manchester	TN	37355-2702
901 696-5452	**Crockett County**	County Courthouse	Alamo	TN	38001-0000
615 484-8212	**Cumberland County**	Main St	Crossville	TN	38555-0000
615 244-1000	**Davidson County**	700 2nd Ave S	Nashville	TN	37210-2006
901 852-3417	**Decatur County**	PO Box 488	Decaturville	TN	38329-0488
615 597-5177	**DeKalb County**	County Courthouse Rm 205	Smithville	TN	37166-0000
615 789-4171	**Dickson County**	Court Sq	Charlotte	TN	37036-4935
901 286-7814	**Dyer County**	PO Box 1360	Dyersburg	TN	38025-1360
901 465-5213	**Fayette County**	Court Sq County Courthouse	Somerville	TN	38068-0000
615 879-8014	**Fentress County**	PO Box C	Jamestown	TN	38556-0200
615 967-2541	**Franklin County**	Public Sq	Winchester	TN	37398-0000
901 855-7642	**Gibson County**	County Courthouse	Trenton	TN	38382-0000
615 363-1509	**Giles County**	PO Box 678	Pulaski	TN	38478-0678
615 828-3511	**Grainger County**	County Courthouse	Rutledge	TN	37861-0000
615 639-5321	**Greene County**	101 S Main St	Greeneville	TN	37743-4932
615 692-3622	**Grundy County**	PO Box 215	Altamont	TN	37301-0215
615 586-1993	**Hamblen County**	511 W 2nd North St	Morristown	TN	37814-3964
615 757-2185	**Hamilton County**	County Courthouse	Chattanooga	TN	37402-0000
615 733-4341	**Hancock County**	Main St	Sneedville	TN	37869-9501
901 658-3541	**Hardeman County**	100 N Main St	Bolivar	TN	38008-2322
901 925-3921	**Hardin County**	601 Main St	Savannah	TN	38372-2061
615 272-7002	**Hawkins County**	Main St	Rogersville	TN	37857-3390
901 772-2362	**Haywood County**	1 N Washington St	Brownsville	TN	38012-2561
901 968-2856	**Henderson County**	Church & Main Sts	Lexington	TN	38351-0000
901 642-2412	**Henry County**	County Courthouse	Paris	TN	38242-0024
615 729-2621	**Hickman County**	Public Sq Rm 8	Centerville	TN	37033-0000
615 289-3141	**Houston County**	PO Box 388	Erin	TN	37061-0388
615 296-7671	**Humphreys County**	102 Thompson St	Waverly	TN	37185-0000
615 268-9212	**Jackson County**	PO Box 346	Gainesboro	TN	38562-0346
615 397-2935	**Jefferson County**	PO Box 710	Dandridge	TN	37725-0710
615 727-9633	**Johnson County**	222 Main St	Mountain City	TN	37683-0000
615 521-2385	**Knox County**	300 W Main Ave	Knoxville	TN	37902-1805
901 253-7582	**Lake County**	229 Church St	Tiptonville	TN	38079-1162
901 635-2561	**Lauderdale County**	County Courthouse	Ripley	TN	38063-0000
615 762-7700	**Lawrence County**	PO Box NBU 2	Lawrenceburg	TN	38464-0000
615 796-3378	**Lewis County**	County Courthouse	Hohenwald	TN	38462-0000
615 433-2454	**Lincoln County**	PO Box 577	Fayetteville	TN	37334-0577
615 458-3314	**Loudon County**	Grove St	Loudon	TN	37774-0000
615 666-2333	**Macon County**	Public Sq Courthouse	Lafayette	TN	37083-0000
901 423-6022	**Madison County**	County Courthouse Rm 105	Jackson	TN	38301-0000
615 942-2515	**Marion County**	County Courthouse Sq	Jasper	TN	37347-0000
615 359-1072	**Marshall County**	Public Sq	Lewisburg	TN	37091-0000
615 381-3690	**Maury County**	PO Box 1615	Columbia	TN	38402-1615
615 745-1281	**McMinn County**	6 E Madison Ave	Athens	TN	37303-3659
901 645-3511	**McNairy County**	County Courthouse	Selmer	TN	38375-0000
615 334-5747	**Meigs County**	Main St	Decatur	TN	37322-0000
615 442-3981	**Monroe County**	105 College St	Madisonville	TN	37354-1451
615 648-5711	**Montgomery County**	PO Box 687	Clarksville	TN	37041-0687
615 759-7346	**Moore County**	County Courthouse	Lynchburg	TN	37352-0000
615 346-3480	**Morgan County**	Main St	Wartburg	TN	37887-0000
901 885-3831	**Obion County**	County Courthouse	Union City	TN	38261-0000
615 823-5630	**Overton County**	County Courthouse Annex University St	Livingston	TN	38570-0000
615 589-2216	**Perry County**	PO Box 16	Linden	TN	37096-0016
615 864-3879	**Pickett County**	County Courthouse	Byrdstown	TN	38549-0000
615 338-4524	**Polk County**	PO Box 128	Benton	TN	37307-0158
615 526-7106	**Putnam County**	County Courthouse	Cookeville	TN	38501-0000
615 775-7808	**Rhea County**	301 N Market St	Dayton	TN	37321-1271
615 376-5556	**Roane County**	PO Box 546	Kingston	TN	37763-0546
615 384-5895	**Robertson County**	County Courthouse Rm 101	Springfield	TN	37172-0000
615 898-7799	**Rutherford County**	26 Public Sq	Murfreesboro	TN	37130-0000
615 663-2588	**Scott County**	PO Box 87	Huntsville	TN	37756-0087
615 949-2522	**Sequatchie County**	Cherry St	Dunlap	TN	37327-0000
615 453-5502	**Sevier County**	125 Court Ave	Sevierville	TN	37862-3594
901 576-4244	**Shelby County**	160 N Mid-America Mall	Memphis	TN	38103-1800
615 735-9833	**Smith County**	218 Main St	Carthage	TN	37030-1541
615 232-7616	**Stewart County**	Main St	Dover	TN	37058-0000
615 323-6428	**Sullivan County**	PO Box 530	Blountville	TN	37617-0530
615 452-4063	**Sumner County**	County Courthouse Rm 108	Gallatin	TN	37066-0000
901 476-0207	**Tipton County**	PO Box 528	Covington	TN	38019-0528
615 374-2906	**Trousdale County**	Main St & Court Sq	Hartsville	TN	37074-0000
615 743-3381	**Unicoi County Courthouse**	PO Box 340	Erwin	TN	37650-0340
615 992-8043	**Union County**	PO Box 395	Maynardville	TN	37807-0395
615 946-2121	**Van Buren County**	Courthouse Sq	Spencer	TN	38585-0000
615 473-2623	**Warren County**	PO Box 231	McMinnville	TN	37110-0231
615 753-1621	**Washington County**	PO Box 218	Jonesborough	TN	37659-0218
615 722-3653	**Wayne County**	PO Box 206	Waynesboro	TN	38485-0206
901 364-2285	**Weakley County**	County Courthouse	Dresden	TN	38225-0000
615 836-3203	**White County**	County Courthouse Rm 205	Sparta	TN	38583-0000
615 790-5712	**Williamson County**	1320 W Main St	Franklin	TN	37064-3700
615 444-0314	**Wilson County**	PO Box 918	Lebanon	TN	37088-0918

TEXAS

903 723-7432	**Anderson County**	500 N Church St	Palestine	TX	75801-3024
915 524-1426	**Andrews County**	PO Box 727	Andrews	TX	79714-0727
409 634-8339	**Angelina County**	215 E Lufkin Ave	Lufkin	TX	75901-3047
512 729-7430	**Aransas County**	301 N Liveoak St	Rockport	TX	78382-2744
817 574-4615	**Archer County**	PO Box 815	Archer City	TX	76351-0815
806 226-2081	**Armstrong County**	PO Box 189	Claude	TX	79019-0000
512 769-2511	**Atascosa County**	Circle Dr	Jourdanton	TX	78026-0000
409 865-5911	**Austin County**	1 E Main St	Bellville	TX	77418-1598
806 272-3044	**Bailey County**	300 S 1st St	Muleshoe	TX	79347-3621
512 796-3332	**Bandera County**	500 Main St	Bandera	TX	78003-0000
512 321-4443	**Bastrop County**	803 Pine St	Bastrop	TX	78602-3841
817 888-3322	**Baylor County**	PO Box 689	Seymour	TX	76380-0689
512 358-3664	**Bee County**	105 W Corpus Christi St	Beeville	TX	78102-5684
817 939-3521	**Bell County**	Main & Central Sts	Belton	TX	76513-0000
512 220-2011	**Bexar County**	100 Dolorosa St Rm 1120-A	San Antonio	TX	78205-3002
512 868-7357	**Blanco County**	PO Box 65	Johnson City	TX	78636-0117
915 856-4312	**Borden County**	101 Main St	Gail	TX	79738-0000
817 435-2201	**Bosque County**	Morgan & Main Sts	Meridian	TX	76665-0000
903 628-2571	**Bowie County**	PO Box 248	New Boston	TX	75570-0248
409 849-5711	**Brazoria County**	111 E Locust St	Angleton	TX	77515-4622
409 775-7400	**Brazos County**	300 E 26th St	Bryan	TX	77803-5359
915 837-3366	**Brewster County**	201 W Ave	Alpine	TX	79830-0000
806 823-2131	**Briscoe County**	415 Main St	Silverton	TX	79257-0000
512 325-5604	**Brooks County**	County Courthouse	Falfurrias	TX	78355-0000
915 643-2594	**Brown County**	200 S Broadway St	Brownwood	TX	76801-3136
409 567-4326	**Burleson County**	205 W Buck St	Caldwell	TX	77836-1798
512 756-5420	**Burnet County**	220 S Pierce St	Burnet	TX	78611-3136
512 398-2428	**Caldwell County**	Main St	Lockhart	TX	78644-0000
512 553-4411	**Calhoun County**	211 S Ann St	Port Lavaca	TX	77979-4249
915 854-1217	**Callahan County**	400 Market St	Baird	TX	79504-5305
512 544-0815	**Cameron County**	964 E Harrison St	Brownsville	TX	78520-7123
903 856-2731	**Camp County**	126 Church St	Pittsburg	TX	75686-0000
806 537-3873	**Carson County**	501 Main St	Panhandle	TX	79068-0000
903 756-5071	**Cass County**	PO Box 468	Linden	TX	75563-0468
806 647-3338	**Castro County**	100 E Bedford St	Dimmitt	TX	79027-2643
409 267-3471	**Chambers County**	404 Washington	Anahuac	TX	77514-0000
903 683-2350	**Cherokee County**	6th St	Rusk	TX	75785-0000
817 937-6143	**Childress County**	100 Ave 'E' NW	Childress	TX	79201-3755
817 538-4631	**Clay County**	100 N Bridge St	Henrietta	TX	76365-2858
806 266-5450	**Cochran County**	100 N Main St	Morton	TX	79346-2558
915 453-2631	**Coke County**	13 E 7th St	Robert Lee	TX	76945-0000
915 625-2889	**Coleman County**	PO Box 591	Coleman	TX	76834-0591
214 548-4100	**Collin County**	210 S McDonald St	McKinney	TX	75069-5655
806 447-2408	**Collingsworth County**	County Courthouse	Wellington	TX	79095-0000
409 732-2155	**Colorado County**	400 Spring St	Columbus	TX	78934-2456
512 620-5501	**Comal County**	100 Main Plaza	New Braunfels	TX	78130-5140
915 356-2655	**Comanche County**	County Courthouse	Comanche	TX	76442-0000
915 732-4322	**Concho County**	PO Box 98	Paint Rock	TX	76866-0098
817 668-5420	**Cooke County**	Dixon St County Courthouse	Gainesville	TX	76240-0000
817 865-5016	**Coryell County**	PO Box 237	Gatesville	TX	76528-0237
806 492-3823	**Cottle County**	PO Box 717	Paducah	TX	79248-0717
915 558-3581	**Crane County**	PO Box 578	Crane	TX	79731-0578
915 392-2022	**Crockett County**	907 Ave D	Ozona	TX	76943-0000
806 675-2334	**Crosby County**	PO Box 218	Crosbyton	TX	79322-0218
915 283-2058	**Culberson County**	PO Box 158	Van Horn	TX	79855-0158
806 249-4751	**Dallam County**	101 E 5th St	Dalhart	TX	79022-2728
214 653-7131	**Dallas County**	500 Main St	Dallas	TX	75202-3513
806 872-3778	**Dawson County**	N 1st & Main Sts	Lamesa	TX	79331-0000
806 364-1746	**Deaf Smith County**	243 E 3rd County Courthouse	Hereford	TX	79045-0000
903 395-4110	**Delta County**	PO Box 455	Cooper	TX	75432-0455
817 565-8500	**Denton County**	401 W Hickory St	Denton	TX	76201-9030
512 275-3724	**DeWitt County**	307 N Gonzales St	Cuero	TX	77954-2970
806 623-5531	**Dickens County**	PO Box 120	Dickens	TX	79229-0120
512 876-3569	**Dimmit County**	103 N 5th St	Carrizo Springs	TX	78834-3198
806 874-3436	**Donley County**	PO Box U	Clarendon	TX	79226-2020
512 279-3322	**Duval County**	400 E Gravis St	San Diego	TX	78384-1816
817 629-8622	**Eastland County**	PO Box 110	Eastland	TX	76448-0110
915 335-3045	**Ector County**	300 N Grant Ave	Odessa	TX	79761-5162
512 683-2235	**Edwards County**	PO Box 184	Rocksprings	TX	78880-0184
915 546-2071	**El Paso County**	500 E San Antonio Ave	El Paso	TX	79901-2421
214 937-8620	**Ellis County**	PO Box 250	Waxahachie	TX	75165-0250
817 965-1482	**Erath County**	County Courthouse Sq	Stephenville	TX	76401-4219
817 883-2061	**Falls County**	PO Box 458	Marlin	TX	76661-0458
903 583-7486	**Fannin County**	County Courthouse	Bonham	TX	75418-0000
409 968-3251	**Fayette County**	151 N Washington St	La Grange	TX	78945-2657
915 776-2401	**Fisher County**	PO Box 368	Roby	TX	79543-0368
806 983-3236	**Floyd County**	100 Main St	Floydada	TX	79235-0000
817 684-1365	**Foard County**	PO Box 539	Crowell	TX	79227-0539
713 342-3411	**Fort Bend County**	PO Box 520	Richmond	TX	77469-0000
903 537-4252	**Franklin County**	Dallas & Kaufman Sts	Mount Vernon	TX	75457-0000
903 389-2635	**Freestone County**	Main & Mount Sts	Fairfield	TX	75840-1594
512 334-2214	**Frio County**	PO Box X	Pearsall	TX	78061-1423
915 758-3521	**Gaines County**	100 S Main St	Seminole	TX	79360-4342
409 766-2210	**Galveston County**	722 Moody Ave	Galveston	TX	77550-2317
806 495-3535	**Garza County**	County Courthouse	Post	TX	79356-3241
512 997-6515	**Gillespie County**	PO Box 351	Fredericksburg	TX	78624-0000
915 354-2371	**Glasscock County**	PO Box 190	Garden City	TX	79739-0190
512 645-3294	**Goliad County**	PO Box 5	Goliad	TX	77963-0005
512 672-2801	**Gonzales County**	414 Saint Joseph St	Gonzales	TX	78629-4069
806 669-8004	**Gray County**	205 N Russell St	Pampa	TX	79065-6441
903 868-9515	**Grayson County**	Houston & Lamar Sts	Sherman	TX	75090-0000
903 758-6181	**Gregg County**	PO Box 3049	Longview	TX	75606-3049
409 873-2662	**Grimes County**	Main St	Anderson	TX	77830-0000
512 379-4188	**Guadalupe County**	101 E Court St	Seguin	TX	78155-5700
806 293-8481	**Hale County**	500 Broadway	Plainview	TX	79072-0000
806 259-2511	**Hall County**	County Courthouse	Memphis	TX	79245-3343
817 386-3518	**Hamilton County**	County Courthouse	Hamilton	TX	76531-1859
806 659-2666	**Hansford County**	1 NW Court	Spearman	TX	79081-3499
817 663-2901	**Hardeman County**	PO Box 30	Quanah	TX	79252-0030
409 246-5185	**Hardin County**	Hwy 326 & Courthouse Sq	Kountze	TX	77625-0000
713 221-5000	**Harris County**	1001 Preston St	Houston	TX	77002-1816
903 935-4858	**Harrison County**	Houston & Wellington Sts	Marshall	TX	75670-0000
806 235-3582	**Hartley County**	PO Box T	Channing	TX	79018-0400
817 864-2451	**Haskell County**	PO Box 725	Haskell	TX	79521-0725
512 396-2601	**Hays County**	County Courthouse	San Marcos	TX	78666-0000
806 323-6212	**Hemphill County**	PO Box 867	Canadian	TX	79014-0867
903 675-6140	**Henderson County**	Courthouse Sq	Athens	TX	75751-0000
512 383-2751	**Hidalgo County**	100 N Closner St	Edinburg	TX	78539-3563
817 582-2161	**Hill County**	PO Box 398	Hillsboro	TX	76645-0398
806 894-3185	**Hockley County**	800 Houston St Courthouse Box 13	Levelland	TX	79336-0000
817 579-3222	**Hood County**	101 Pearl St	Granbury	TX	76048-2498
903 885-3929	**Hopkins County**	PO Box 288	Sulphur Springs	TX	75482-0288
409 544-3256	**Houston County**	PO Box 370	Crockett	TX	75835-0370
915 263-7247	**Howard County**	300 Main St	Big Spring	TX	79720-2521
915 369-2301	**Hudspeth County**	PO Box A	Sierra Blanca	TX	79851-0058
903 455-6460	**Hunt County**	2500 Lee St	Greenville	TX	75401-4246
806 878-2829	**Hutchinson County**	PO Box F	Stinnett	TX	79083-0526
915 835-2421	**Irion County**	County Courthouse	Mertzon	TX	76941-0000
817 567-2111	**Jack County**	100 N Main St	Jacksboro	TX	76056-1746
512 782-3563	**Jackson County**	115 W Main St	Edna	TX	77957-2733
409 384-2632	**Jasper County**	Main & Lamar St	Jasper	TX	75951-0000
915 426-3251	**Jeff Davis County**	PO Box 398	Fort Davis	TX	79734-0398

Phone	County	Address	City	State	ZIP
409 835-8475	**Jefferson County**	1149 Pearl St	Beaumont	TX	77701-3619
512 527-4031	**Jim Hogg County**	PO Box 729	Hebbronville	TX	78361-0729
512 668-5702	**Jim Wells County**	PO Box 1459	Alice	TX	78333-1459
817 641-4421	**Johnson County**	PO Box 662	Cleburne	TX	76033-0662
915 823-3762	**Jones County**	PO Box 552	Anson	TX	79501-0552
512 780-3938	**Karnes County**	101 N Panna Maria St	Karnes City	TX	78118-2959
214 932-4331	**Kaufman County**	Washington St	Kaufman	TX	75142-0000
512 249-9343	**Kendall County**	204 E San Antonio St	Boerne	TX	78006-2050
512 294-5220	**Kenedy County**	PO Box 7	Sarita	TX	78385-0007
806 237-3881	**Kent County**	Main St	Jayton	TX	79528-0000
512 257-6181	**Kerr County**	700 Main St	Kerrville	TX	78028-5323
915 446-3353	**Kimble County**	501 Main St	Junction	TX	76849-4763
806 596-4412	**King County**	County Courthouse	Guthrie	TX	79236-9999
512 563-2521	**Kinney County**	Ann & James Sts	Brackettville	TX	78832-0000
512 592-6448	**Kleberg County**	PO Box 1327	Kingsville	TX	78364-1327
817 454-2441	**Knox County**	PO Box 196	Benjamin	TX	79505-0196
903 737-2420	**Lamar County**	119 N Main St	Paris	TX	75460-4265
806 385-5173	**Lamb County**	100 6th St	Littlefield	TX	79339-3367
512 556-8271	**Lampasas County**	PO Box 231	Lampasas	TX	76550-0231
512 879-2421	**LaSalle County**	PO Box 340	Cotulla	TX	78014-0340
512 798-3612	**Lavaca County**	PO Box 326	Hallettsville	TX	77964-0326
409 542-3684	**Lee County**	Main & Hempstead Sts	Giddings	TX	78942-0000
903 536-2352	**Leon County**	PO Box 98	Centerville	TX	75833-0098
409 336-8071	**Liberty County**	1923 Sam Houston St	Liberty	TX	77575-4899
817 729-5504	**Limestone County**	PO Box 350	Groesbeck	TX	76642-0350
806 862-3091	**Lipscomb County**	PO Box 175	Lipscomb	TX	79056-0175
512 449-2733	**Live Oak County**	PO Box 280	George West	TX	78022-0280
915 247-4455	**Llano County**	801 Ford St	Llano	TX	78643-1997
915 377-2441	**Loving County**	Hwy 302	Mentone	TX	79754-9999
806 741-8089	**Lubbock County**	904 Broadway St	Lubbock	TX	79401-3420
806 998-4750	**Lynn County**	PO Box 937	Tahoka	TX	79373-0937
409 348-2639	**Madison County**	101 W Main St	Madisonville	TX	77864-1901
903 665-3971	**Marion County**	PO Box F	Jefferson	TX	75657-0420
915 756-3412	**Martin County**	PO Box 906	Stanton	TX	79782-0906
915 347-5253	**Mason County**	Westmoreland St & Post Hill	Mason	TX	76856-0000
409 244-7680	**Matagorda County**	1700 7th St	Bay City	TX	77414-5034
512 773-2829	**Maverick County**	PO Box 4050	Eagle Pass	TX	78853-4050
915 597-2355	**McCulloch County**	County Courthouse	Brady	TX	76825-0000
817 757-5000	**McLennan County**	5th & Washington New Records Bldg	Waco	TX	76701-0000
512 274-3215	**McMullen County**	River & Elm Sts	Tilden	TX	78072-0000
512 426-5381	**Medina County**	County Courthouse	Hondo	TX	78861-0000
915 396-4682	**Menard County**	PO Box 1028	Menard	TX	76859-1028
915 688-1000	**Midland County**	200 W Wall St	Midland	TX	79701-4512
817 697-6596	**Milam County**	100 S Fannin Ave	Cameron	TX	76520-4216
915 648-2711	**Mills County**	PO Box 646	Goldthwaite	TX	76844-0646
915 728-3481	**Mitchell County**	301 Oak St	Colorado City	TX	79512-6225
817 894-2461	**Montague County**	PO Box 77	Montague	TX	76251-0077
409 539-7885	**Montgomery County**	300 N Main St	Conroe	TX	77301-2898
806 935-6164	**Moore County**	PO Box 396	Dumas	TX	79029-0396
903 645-3911	**Morris County**	500 Broadnax St	Daingerfield	TX	75638-1315
806 347-2621	**Motley County**	Main St	Matador	TX	79244-0000
409 560-7733	**Nacogdoches County**	101 W Main St	Nacogdoches	TX	75961-5119
903 654-3035	**Navarro County**	300 W 3rd Ave	Corsicana	TX	75110-4694
409 379-5341	**Newton County**	Courthouse Sq Hwy 190	Newton	TX	75966-0000
915 235-2462	**Nolan County**	102 E 3rd St	Sweetwater	TX	79556-4511
512 888-0580	**Nueces County**	901 Leopard St	Corpus Christi	TX	78401-3606
806 435-8105	**Ochiltree County**	511 S Main St	Perryton	TX	79070-3154
806 267-2667	**Oldham County**	PO Box 469	Vega	TX	79092-0469
409 883-7740	**Orange County**	PO Box 1536	Orange	TX	77631-1536
817 659-3651	**Palo Pinto County**	PO Box 8	Palo Pinto	TX	76072-0008
903 693-0302	**Panola County**	Sabine & Sycamore Sts Rm 201	Carthage	TX	75633-0000
817 594-7461	**Parker County**	PO Box 819	Weatherford	TX	76086-0819
806 481-3691	**Parmer County**	401 3rd St	Farwell	TX	79325-0000
915 336-7555	**Pecos County**	103 W Callaghan St	Fort Stockton	TX	79735-7101
409 327-8398	**Polk County**	101 W Church St	Livingston	TX	77351-3201
806 379-2250	**Potter County**	511 S Taylor St	Amarillo	TX	79101-2432
915 729-4812	**Presidio County**	320 N Highland St	Marfa	TX	79843-0000
903 473-2461	**Rains County**	PO Box 187	Emory	TX	75440-0187
806 655-7001	**Randall County**	401 15th St	Canyon	TX	79015-3838
915 884-2442	**Reagan County**	PO Box 100	Big Lake	TX	76932-0100
512 232-5202	**Real County**	PO Box 656	Leakey	TX	78873-0656
903 427-2401	**Red River County**	400 N Walnut St	Clarksville	TX	75426-3041
915 445-5467	**Reeves County**	PO Box 867	Pecos	TX	79772-0867
512 526-2233	**Refugio County**	PO Box 704	Refugio	TX	78377-0704
806 868-2341	**Roberts County**	Kiowa & Commercial Sts	Miami	TX	79059-0000
409 828-4130	**Robertson County**	Center St	Franklin	TX	77856-0000
214 722-5141	**Rockwall County**	Hwy 66 & Goliad	Rockwall	TX	75087-0000
915 365-2720	**Runnels County**	Hutchings & Broadway	Ballinger	TX	76821-0000
903 657-0330	**Rusk County**	115 N Main St	Henderson	TX	75652-3198
409 787-3786	**Sabine County**	Oak St	Hemphill	TX	75948-0000
409 275-2452	**San Augustine County**	106 Courthouse	San Augustine	TX	75972-1335
409 653-2324	**San Jacinto County**	Church & Bird Sts	Coldspring	TX	77331-0000
512 364-2490	**San Patricio County**	PO Box 578	Sinton	TX	78387-0578
915 372-3635	**San Saba County**	518 E Wallace St	San Saba	TX	76877-3611
915 853-2833	**Schleicher County**	Hwy 277	Eldorado	TX	76936-0000
915 573-5332	**Scurry County**	County Courthouse	Snyder	TX	79549-0000
915 762-2232	**Shackelford County**	PO Box 247	Albany	TX	76430-0247
409 598-6361	**Shelby County**	Courthouse	Center	TX	75935-3945
806 396-2371	**Sherman County**	701 N 3rd St	Stratford	TX	79084-0000
903 595-4861	**Smith County**	PO Box 1018	Tyler	TX	75710-1018
817 897-4427	**Somervell County**	PO Box 1098	Glen Rose	TX	76043-1098
512 487-2954	**Starr County**	Britton Ave	Rio Grande City	TX	78582-0000
817 559-3700	**Stephens County**	County Courthouse	Breckenridge	TX	76024-0000
915 378-5191	**Sterling County**	PO Box 55	Sterling City	TX	76951-0055
817 989-2272	**Stonewall County**	PO Box P	Aspermont	TX	79502-0914
915 387-3815	**Sutton County**	300 E Oak St Suite 3	Sonora	TX	76950-3106
806 995-3294	**Swisher County**	County Courthouse	Tulia	TX	79088-2247
817 334-1195	**Tarrant County**	100 W Weatherford	Fort Worth	TX	76196-0001
915 677-1711	**Taylor County**	300 Oak St	Abilene	TX	79602-1521
915 345-2391	**Terrell County**	PO Box 410	Sanderson	TX	79848-0410
806 637-8551	**Terry County**	5th & Main	Brownfield	TX	79316-0000
817 849-2501	**Throckmorton County**	PO Box 309	Throckmorton	TX	76083-0309
903 572-8891	**Titus County**	Courthouse Sq	Mount Pleasant	TX	75455-0000
915 653-2385	**Tom Green County**	112 W Beauregard Ave	San Angelo	TX	76903-5850
512 473-9000	**Travis County**	1000 Guadalupe St	Austin	TX	78701-2336
409 642-1208	**Trinity County**	Hwys 94 & 287	Groveton	TX	75845-0000
409 283-2281	**Tyler County**	100 Courthouse	Woodville	TX	75979-5245
903 843-3083	**Upshur County**	Hwy 154 & Simpson St	Gilmer	TX	75644-2198
915 693-2861	**Upton County**	PO Box 465	Rankin	TX	79778-0465
512 278-6614	**Uvalde County**	PO Box 284	Uvalde	TX	78802-0284
512 774-3611	**Val Verde County**	400 Pecan St	Del Rio	TX	78840-5140
903 567-6503	**Van Zandt County**	PO Box 515	Canton	TX	75103-0515
512 575-4558	**Victoria County**	115 N Bridge St	Victoria	TX	77901-6544
409 291-9500	**Walker County**	1100 University Ave	Huntsville	TX	77340-4631
409 826-3357	**Waller County**	836 Austin St	Hempstead	TX	77445-4667
915 943-3294	**Ward County**	County Courthouse	Monahans	TX	79756-0000
409 836-4300	**Washington County**	105 E Main St	Brenham	TX	77833-0000
512 721-2221	**Webb County**	1000 Houston St	Laredo	TX	78040-8023
409 532-2381	**Wharton County**	101 Milam St	Wharton	TX	77488-0000
806 826-5544	**Wheeler County**	PO Box 465	Wheeler	TX	79096-0465
817 766-8100	**Wichita County**	900 7th St	Wichita Falls	TX	76301-0000
817 552-5486	**Wilbarger County**	1700 Wilbarger St	Vernon	TX	76384-4742
512 689-2710	**Willacy County**	Hidalgo & 3rd St Courthouse	Raymondville	TX	78580-0000
512 869-4315	**Williamson County**	PO Box 18	Georgetown	TX	78627-0018
512 393-2845	**Wilson County**	1420 3rd St	Floresville	TX	78114-2200
915 586-3401	**Winkler County**	100 E Winkler St	Kermit	TX	79745-4236
817 627-3351	**Wise County**	PO Box 359	Decatur	TX	76234-0359
903 763-2711	**Wood County**	PO Box 338	Quitman	TX	75783-0338
806 456-2721	**Yoakum County**	PO Box 309	Plains	TX	79355-0000
817 549-8432	**Young County**	PO Box 218	Graham	TX	76046-0218
512 765-9915	**Zapata County**	7th Ave & Hidalgo	Zapata	TX	78076-0000
512 374-2331	**Zavala County**	County Courthouse	Crystal City	TX	78839-0000

UTAH

Phone	County	Address	City	State	ZIP
801 438-2352	**Beaver County**	PO Box 392	Beaver	UT	84713-0392
801 734-2031	**Box Elder County**	1 S Main St	Brigham City	UT	84302-2599
801 752-3542	**Cache County**	170 N Main St	Logan	UT	84321-4541
801 637-4700	**Carbon County**	120 E Main St	Price	UT	84501-3057
801 784-3154	**Daggett County**	PO Box 218	Manila	UT	84046-0218
801 451-3214	**Davis County**	PO Box 618	Farmington	UT	84025-0618
801 738-2435	**Duchesne County**	PO Box 270	Duchesne	UT	84021-0270
801 381-2465	**Emery County**	PO Box 907	Castle Dale	UT	84513-0907
801 676-8826	**Garfield County**	PO Box 77	Panguitch	UT	84759-0077
801 259-5645	**Grand County**	125 E Center St	Moab	UT	84532-2449
801 477-3375	**Iron County**	PO Box 429	Parowan	UT	84761-0429
801 623-0271	**Juab County**	160 N Main St	Nephi	UT	84648-1412
801 644-2551	**Kane County**	76 N Main St	Kanab	UT	84741-3219
801 743-6223	**Millard County**	PO Box 226	Fillmore	UT	84631-0226
801 829-6811	**Morgan County**	48th W Young St	Morgan	UT	84050-0000
801 577-2840	**Piute County**	21 N Main	Junction	UT	84740-0000
801 793-2415	**Rich County**	PO Box 218	Randolph	UT	84064-0218
801 468-3531	**Salt Lake County**	2001 State St Rm S2200	Salt Lake City	UT	84190-0001
801 587-2231	**San Juan County**	PO Box 338	Monticello	UT	84535-0338
801 835-2131	**Sanpete County**	160 N Main St	Manti	UT	84642-1266
801 896-9262	**Sevier County**	250 N Main St	Richfield	UT	84701-2158
801 336-4451	**Summit County**	PO Box 128	Coalville	UT	84017-0128
801 882-5550	**Tooele County**	47 S Main St	Tooele	UT	84074-2194
801 781-0770	**Uintah County**	152 E 100 North	Vernal	UT	84078-0000
801 373-5510	**Utah County**	51 S University Ave	Provo	UT	84601-4424
801 654-3211	**Wasatch County**	25 N Main St	Heber City	UT	84032-1827
801 634-5702	**Washington County**	197 E Tabernacle St	Saint George	UT	84770-3473
801 836-2731	**Wayne County**	18 S Main	Loa	UT	84747-0000
801 399-8481	**Weber County**	2549 Washington Blvd	Ogden	UT	84401-3111

VERMONT

Phone	County	Address	City	State	ZIP
802 388-4237	**Addison County**	5 Court St	Middlebury	VT	05753-1405
802 447-2700	**Bennington County**	207 South St	Bennington	VT	05201-2247
802 748-6600	**Caledonia County**	PO Box 404	Saint Johnsbury	VT	05819-0404
802 863-3467	**Chittenden County**	175 Main St	Burlington	VT	05401-8310
802 676-3910	**Essex County**	PO Box 75	Guildhall	VT	05905-0075
802 524-3863	**Franklin County**	PO Box 808	Saint Albans	VT	05478-0808
802 372-8350	**Grand Isle County**	Rt 2	North Hero	VT	05474-0000
802 888-2207	**Lamoille County**	PO Box 303	Hyde Park	VT	05655-0303
802 685-4610	**Orange County**	PO Box 95	Chelsea	VT	05038-0095
802 334-2711	**Orleans County**	PO Box 787	Newport	VT	05855-0787
802 775-4394	**Rutland County**	83 Center St	Rutland	VT	05701-4039
802 223-2091	**Washington County**	PO Box 426	Montpelier	VT	05602-0426
802 365-7979	**Windham County**	PO Box 207	Newfane	VT	05345-0207
802 457-2121	**Windsor County**	12 The Green	Woodstock	VT	05091-1212

VIRGINIA

Phone	County	Address	City	State	ZIP
804 787-5776	**Accomack County**	County Courthouse	Accomac	VA	23301-0000
804 296-5841	**Albemarle County**	401 McIntire Rd	Charlottesville	VA	22901-4579
703 838-4550	**Alexandria (Independent City)**	301 King St	Alexandria	VA	22314-3211
703 962-3906	**Alleghany County**	266 W Main St	Covington	VA	24426-1550
804 561-3039	**Amelia County**	PO Box A	Amelia Court House	VA	23002-0066
804 929-9321	**Amherst County**	100 E Court St	Amherst	VA	24521-2702
804 352-5275	**Appomattox County**	PO Box 672	Appomattox	VA	24522-0000
703 358-3000	**Arlington County**	2100 Clarendon Blvd	Arlington	VA	22201-5445
703 885-8931	**Augusta County**	6 E Johnson St	Staunton	VA	24401-4303
703 839-2361	**Bath County**	PO Box 180	Warm Springs	VA	24484-0180
703 586-7102	**Bedford (Independent City)**	215 E Main St	Bedford	VA	24523-2012
703 586-7601	**Bedford County**	129 E Main St	Bedford	VA	24523-2034
703 688-4562	**Bland County**	PO Box 295	Bland	VA	24315-0295
703 473-8220	**Botetourt County**	1 W Main St Box 1	Fincastle	VA	24090-3006
703 466-2221	**Bristol (Independent City)**	497 Cumberland St	Bristol	VA	24201-4394
804 848-3107	**Brunswick County**	102 Tobacco St	Lawrenceville	VA	23868-1824
703 935-6500	**Buchanan County**	PO Box 950	Grundy	VA	24614-0950
804 969-4242	**Buckingham County**	PO Box 252	Buckingham	VA	23921-0252
703 261-6121	**Buena Vista (Independent City)**	2039 Sycamore Ave	Buena Vista	VA	24416-3133
804 332-5161	**Campbell County**	PO Box 7	Rustburg	VA	24588-0007
804 633-5800	**Caroline County**	PO Box 309	Bowling Green	VA	22427-0309
703 728-3331	**Carroll County**	PO Box 515	Hillsville	VA	24343-0515
804 829-2401	**Charles City County**	PO Box 128	Charles City	VA	23030-0128
804 542-5147	**Charlotte County**	PO Box 38	Charlotte Court House	VA	23923-0038
804 971-3101	**Charlottesville (Independent City)**	605 E Main St	Charlottesville	VA	22901-5397
804 547-6166	**Chesapeake (Independent City)**	306 Cedar Rd	Chesapeake	VA	23320-5514
804 748-1200	**Chesterfield County**	9901 Lori Rd	Chesterfield	VA	23832-6626
703 955-1309	**Clarke County**	102 N Church St	Berryville	VA	22611-1110
703 863-5091	**Clifton Forge (Independent City)**	PO Box 631	Clifton Forge	VA	24422-0631
804 520-9265	**Colonial Heights (Independent City)**	1507 Boulevard	Colonial Heights	VA	23834-3049
703 965-6300	**Covington (Independent City)**	158 N Court Ave	Covington	VA	24426-1534
703 864-6141	**Craig County**	PO Box 185	New Castle	VA	24127-0185
703 825-3035	**Culpeper County**	135 W Cameron St	Culpeper	VA	22701-0000
804 492-4280	**Cumberland County**	County Courthouse	Cumberland	VA	23040-0000
804 799-5171	**Danville (Independent City)**	212 Lynn St	Danville	VA	24541-1208
703 926-1616	**Dickenson County**	PO Box 190	Clintwood	VA	24228-0190
804 469-4533	**Dinwiddie County**	PO Box 280	Dinwiddie	VA	23841-0280
804 634-3332	**Emporia (Independent City)**	201 N Main St	Emporia	VA	23847-1605
804 443-3541	**Essex County**	PO Box 445	Tappahannock	VA	22560-0000
703 385-7855	**Fairfax (Independent City)**	10455 Armstrong St	Fairfax	VA	22030-3630
703 246-2000	**Fairfax County**	4110 Chain Bridge Rd	Fairfax	VA	22030-4041
703 241-5014	**Falls Church (Independent City)**	300 Park Ave	Falls Church	VA	22046-3332
703 347-8600	**Fauquier County**	40 Culpeper St	Warrenton	VA	22186-3298
703 745-4158	**Floyd County**	100 E Main St Rm 200	Floyd	VA	24091-2100
804 589-3138	**Fluvanna County**	PO Box 299	Palmyra	VA	22963-0000
804 562-8500	**Franklin (Independent City)**	207 2nd Ave W	Franklin	VA	23851-1713
703 483-3065	**Franklin County**	Main St	Rocky Mount	VA	24151-1392
703 665-5666	**Frederick County**	9 Court Sq	Winchester	VA	22601-4736

Local Government–County

703 372-1010	**Fredericksburg (Independent City)** PO Box 7447	Fredericksburg	VA	22404-7447
703 236-3441	**Galax (Independent City)** 123 Main St N	Galax	VA	24333-2907
703 921-1722	**Giles County** PO Box 502	Pearisburg	VA	24134-0502
804 693-4042	**Gloucester County** PO Box 329	Gloucester	VA	23061-0329
804 556-5300	**Goochland County** 2938 River Rd W	Goochland	VA	23063-3229
703 773-2231	**Grayson County** 129 Davis St	Independence	VA	24348-0000
804 985-5299	**Greene County** Court Sq	Stanardsville	VA	22973-0000
804 348-4215	**Greensville County** 337 S Main St	Emporia	VA	23847-2027
804 476-2141	**Halifax County** Main St Courthouse Sq	Halifax	VA	24558-0786
804 727-6000	**Hampton (Independent City)** 22 Lincoln St	Hampton	VA	23669-0000
804 537-6000	**Hanover County** PO Box 470	Hanover	VA	23069-0470
703 434-6776	**Harrisonburg (Independent City)** 345 S Main St	Harrisonburg	VA	22801-3638
804 672-4000	**Henrico County** 4301 E Parham Rd	Richmond	VA	23229-0000
703 638-3961	**Henry County** PO Box 1049	Martinsville	VA	24114-1049
703 468-2447	**Highland County** Main St	Monterey	VA	24465-0000
804 541-2243	**Hopewell (Independent City)** 300 N Main St	Hopewell	VA	23860-2740
804 357-3191	**Isle of Wight County** Hwy 258 County Courthouse	Isle of Wight	VA	23397-9999
804 229-2552	**James City County** 321-45 Court St W	Williamsburg	VA	23185-0000
804 785-2460	**King & Queen County** County Courthouse	King & Queen Courthouse	VA	23085-0000
703 775-3322	**King George County** PO Box 105	King George	VA	22485-0105
804 769-4927	**King William County** PO Box 215	King William	VA	23086-0215
804 462-5611	**Lancaster County** PO Box 125	Lancaster	VA	22503-0125
703 346-7763	**Lee County** PO Box 326	Jonesville	VA	24263-0326
703 463-7133	**Lexington (Independent City)** PO Box 922	Lexington	VA	24450-0922
703 777-0200	**Loudoun County** 18 N King St	Leesburg	VA	22075-2818
703 967-0401	**Louisa County** PO Box 160	Louisa	VA	23093-0160
804 696-2230	**Lunenburg County** County Courthouse	Lunenburg	VA	23952-0000
804 847-1443	**Lynchburg (Independent City)** 900 Church St	Lynchburg	VA	24504-1620
703 948-6102	**Madison County** PO Box 220	Madison	VA	22727-0220
703 335-8800	**Manassas Park (Independent City)** 1 Park Center Pl	Manassas Park	VA	22111-1800
703 638-3971	**Martinsville (Independent City)** PO Box 1112	Martinsville	VA	24114-1112
804 725-2550	**Mathews County** PO Box 463	Mathews	VA	23109-0463
804 738-6191	**Mecklenburg County** Washington St	Boydton	VA	23917-0000
804 758-5317	**Middlesex County** Rts 17 & 33	Saluda	VA	23149-0000
703 382-5700	**Montgomery County** 1 E Main St	Christiansburg	VA	24073-3027
804 263-4245	**Nelson County** PO Box 55	Lovingston	VA	22949-0055
804 966-9601	**New Kent County** PO Box 98	New Kent	VA	23124-0098
804 247-8411	**Newport News (Independent City)** 2400 Washington Ave	Newport News	VA	23607-4300
804 441-2471	**Norfolk (Independent City)** 810 Union St	Norfolk	VA	23510-2717
804 678-5126	**Northampton County** Business Rt 13	Eastville	VA	23347-9999
804 580-3700	**Northumberland County** PO Box 217	Heathsville	VA	22473-0217
703 679-1160	**Norton (Independent City)** PO Box 618	Norton	VA	24273-0618
804 645-9043	**Nottoway County** Hwy 625	Nottoway	VA	23955-9999
703 672-3313	**Orange County** 109-A W Main St	Orange	VA	22960-1524
703 743-4142	**Page County** 108 S Court St	Luray	VA	22835-1289
703 694-7213	**Patrick County** PO Box 148	Stuart	VA	24171-0148
804 733-2367	**Petersburg (Independent City)** Courthouse Hill	Petersburg	VA	23803-0000
804 432-2041	**Pittsylvania County** 1 S Main St	Chatham	VA	24531-9702
804 868-7151	**Poquoson (Independent City)** 830 Poquoson Ave	Poquoson	VA	23662-1797
804 393-8746	**Portsmouth (Independent City)** PO Box 820	Portsmouth	VA	23705-0820
804 598-5600	**Powhatan County** 3834 Old Buckingham Rd	Powhatan	VA	23139-7019
804 392-5145	**Prince Edward County** PO Box 304	Farmville	VA	23901-0304
804 733-2600	**Prince George County** 6400 Courthouse Rd	Prince George	VA	23875-2527
703 335-6045	**Prince William County** 9311 Lee Ave	Manassas	VA	22110-5598
703 980-8888	**Pulaski County** 45 3rd St NW	Pulaski	VA	24301-5007
703 731-3603	**Radford (Independent City)** 619 2nd St	Radford	VA	24141-1431
703 675-3621	**Rappahannock County** PO Box 517	Washington	VA	22747-0517
804 780-7970	**Richmond (Independent City)** 900 E Broad St	Richmond	VA	23219-6115
804 333-3781	**Richmond County** 10 Court St	Warsaw	VA	22572-0000
703 981-2324	**Roanoke (Independent City)** 315 Church Ave SW	Roanoke	VA	24016-5007
703 463-2232	**Rockbridge County** 2 S Main St	Lexington	VA	24450-2546
703 434-4455	**Rockingham County** Circuit Ct	Harrisonburg	VA	22801-0000
703 889-8023	**Russell County** PO Box 435	Lebanon	VA	24266-0000
703 375-3016	**Salem (Independent City)** 114 N Broad St	Salem	VA	24153-3734
703 386-7341	**Scott County** 104 E Jackson St	Gate City	VA	24251-3417
703 459-3791	**Shenandoah County** 112 S Main St	Woodstock	VA	22664-1423
703 783-7186	**Smyth County** PO Box 1025	Marion	VA	24354-1025
804 572-3621	**South Boston (Independent City)** 455 Ferry St	South Boston	VA	24592-3237
804 653-2200	**Southampton County** County Courthouse	Courtland	VA	23837-0000
703 582-7010	**Spotsylvania County** PO Box 99	Spotsylvania	VA	22553-0099
703 659-8603	**Stafford County** PO Box 339	Stafford	VA	22554-0339
703 885-1251	**Staunton (Independent City)** 113 E Beverley St	Staunton	VA	24401-4390
804 934-3111	**Suffolk (Independent City)** 441 Market St	Suffolk	VA	23434-5237
804 294-5271	**Surry County** Hwy 10 & School St	Surry	VA	23883-0000
804 246-5511	**Sussex County** Rt 735	Sussex	VA	23884-9999
703 988-7541	**Tazewell County** 315 School St	Tazewell	VA	24651-1398
804 427-4242	**Virginia Beach (Independent City)** Municipal Ctr	Virginia Beach	VA	23456-9099
703 636-9973	**Warren County** 22 S Royal Ave	Front Royal	VA	22630-3202
703 628-8733	**Washington County** 216 Park St	Abingdon	VA	24210-3312
703 942-6600	**Waynesboro (Independent City)** 250 S Wayne Ave	Waynesboro	VA	22980-4622
804 493-8911	**Westmoreland County** Polk St	Montross	VA	22520-0000
804 220-6100	**Williamsburg (Independent City)** 401 Lafayette St	Williamsburg	VA	23185-3617
703 667-5770	**Winchester (Independent City)** 5 N Kent St	Winchester	VA	22601-5037
703 328-2321	**Wise County** 108 Main St	Wise	VA	24293-0000
703 228-6644	**Wythe County** 225 S 4th St	Wytheville	VA	24382-2502
804 898-0200	**York County** PO Box 532	Yorktown	VA	23690-0532

WASHINGTON

509 659-0090	**Adams County** 210 W Broadway Ave	Ritzville	WA	99169-1860
509 243-4181	**Asotin County** PO Box 159	Asotin	WA	99402-0159
509 786-5600	**Benton County** PO Box 190	Prosser	WA	99350-0190
509 664-5380	**Chelan County** PO Box 3025	Wenatchee	WA	98807-3025
206 452-7831	**Clallam County** 223 E 4th St	Port Angeles	WA	98362-3025
206 699-2292	**Clark County** PO Box 5000	Vancouver	WA	98668-0000
509 382-4542	**Columbia County** 341 E Main St	Dayton	WA	99328-1361
206 577-3016	**Cowlitz County** 312 SW 1st Ave	Kelso	WA	98626-1798
509 745-8529	**Douglas County** PO Box 516	Waterville	WA	98858-0516
509 775-3161	**Ferry County** PO Box 302	Republic	WA	99166-0302
509 545-3525	**Franklin County** 1016 N 4th Ave	Pasco	WA	99301-3706
509 843-3731	**Garfield County** PO Box 915	Pomeroy	WA	99347-0915
509 754-2011	**Grant County** PO Box 37	Ephrata	WA	98823-0037
206 249-3842	**Grays Harbor County** PO Box 711	Montesano	WA	98563-0590
206 679-7359	**Island County** PO Box 5000	Coupeville	WA	98239-5000
206 385-9125	**Jefferson County** PO Box 1220	Port Townsend	WA	98368-0920
206 344-4040	**King County** 516 3rd Ave	Seattle	WA	98104-0000
206 876-7164	**Kitsap County** 614 Division St	Port Orchard	WA	98366-4676
509 962-7531	**Kittitas County** 205 W 5th Ave	Ellensburg	WA	98926-2887
509 773-5744	**Klickitat County** 205 S Columbus Ave Rm 204	Goldendale	WA	98620-9294
206 748-9121	**Lewis County** 351 NW North St	Chehalis	WA	98532-1926
509 725-1401	**Lincoln County** PO Box 369	Davenport	WA	99122-0369
206 427-9670	**Mason County** PO Box 186	Shelton	WA	98584-0186
509 422-3650	**Okanogan County** PO Box 72	Okanogan	WA	98840-0072
206 875-9300	**Pacific County** PO Box 67	South Bend	WA	98586-0067
509 447-2435	**Pend Oreille County** PO Box 5000	Newport	WA	99156-5000
206 591-7455	**Pierce County** 930 Tacoma Ave S	Tacoma	WA	98402-2108
206 378-2163	**San Juan County** PO Box 1249	Friday Harbor	WA	98250-1249
206 336-9440	**Skagit County** PO Box 837	Mount Vernon	WA	98273-0837
509 427-5141	**Skamania County** PO Box 790	Stevenson	WA	98648-0790
206 388-3466	**Snohomish County** 3000 Rockefeller Ave Rm 246	Everett	WA	98201-4046
509 456-2211	**Spokane County** 1116 W Broadway Ave	Spokane	WA	99260-0001
509 684-3751	**Stevens County** PO Box 191	Colville	WA	99114-0191
206 754-3800	**Thurston County** 2000 Lakeridge Dr SW	Olympia	WA	98502-6042
206 795-3558	**Wahkiakum County** PO Box 116	Cathlamet	WA	98612-0116
509 527-3221	**Walla Walla County** PO Box 836	Walla Walla	WA	99362-0259
206 676-6777	**Whatcom County** PO Box 1144	Bellingham	WA	98227-1144
509 397-4622	**Whitman County** 400 N Main St	Colfax	WA	99111-2031
509 575-4120	**Yakima County** 2nd & B Sts	Yakima	WA	98901-0000

WEST VIRGINIA

304 457-2232	**Barbour County** PO Box 310	Philippi	WV	26416-0310
304 267-3000	**Berkeley County** 119 W King St	Martinsburg	WV	25401-3209
304 369-3925	**Boone County** 200 State St	Madison	WV	25130-1152
304 765-2833	**Braxton County** PO Box 486	Sutton	WV	26601-0486
304 737-3661	**Brooke County** Main & 7th Sts	Wellsburg	WV	26070-0000
304 526-8625	**Cabell County** 8th St & 4th Ave	Huntington	WV	25701-0000
304 354-6725	**Calhoun County** Main St	Grantsville	WV	26147-0000
304 587-4259	**Clay County** Main St	Clay	WV	25043-0000
304 873-2631	**Doddridge County** 118 E Court St	West Union	WV	26456-1262
304 574-1200	**Fayette County** Court St	Fayetteville	WV	25840-1298
304 462-7641	**Gilmer County** 10 Howard St	Glenville	WV	26351-1246
304 257-4422	**Grant County** 5 Highland Ave	Petersburg	WV	26847-1705
304 645-2373	**Greenbrier County** PO Box 506	Lewisburg	WV	24901-0506
304 822-5112	**Hampshire County** Main St	Romney	WV	26757-1696
304 564-3311	**Hancock County** PO Box 367	New Cumberland	WV	26047-0367
304 538-2929	**Hardy County** Washington St	Moorefield	WV	26836-0000
304 624-8611	**Harrison County** 301 W Main St	Clarksburg	WV	26301-2909
304 372-2011	**Jackson County** Court St	Ripley	WV	25271-0000
304 725-9761	**Jefferson County** George & Washington Sts	Charles Town	WV	25414-0000
304 357-0101	**Kanawha County** PO Box 3627	Charleston	WV	25336-0000
304 269-8215	**Lewis County** 110 Center Ave	Weston	WV	26452-0000
304 824-3336	**Lincoln County** 8000 Court Ave	Hamlin	WV	25523-1419
304 752-2000	**Logan County** Main & Stratton Sts	Logan	WV	25601-0000
304 367-5440	**Marion County** 211 Adams St	Fairmont	WV	26554-2876
304 845-1220	**Marshall County** 7th St	Moundsville	WV	26041-0000
304 675-1997	**Mason County** 6th & Main St	Point Pleasant	WV	25550-0000
304 436-6587	**McDowell County** PO Box 447	Welch	WV	24801-0447
304 425-9571	**Mercer County** County Courthouse Sq	Princeton	WV	24740-0000
304 788-3924	**Mineral County** 150 Armstrong St	Keyser	WV	26726-3505
304 235-1638	**Mingo County** PO Box 1197	Williamson	WV	25661-1197
304 291-7230	**Monongalia County** 243 High St	Morgantown	WV	26505-5434
304 772-3096	**Monroe County** Main St	Union	WV	24983-0000
304 258-2774	**Morgan County** 202 Fairfax St	Berkeley Springs	WV	25411-1501
304 872-3630	**Nicholas County** 700 Main St	Summersville	WV	26651-1444
304 234-3656	**Ohio County** 205 City County Bldg	Wheeling	WV	26003-0000
304 358-2505	**Pendleton County** PO Box 89	Franklin	WV	26807-0089
304 684-7542	**Pleasants County** County Courthouse	Saint Marys	WV	26170-0000
304 799-4549	**Pocahontas County** 900C 10th Ave	Marlinton	WV	24954-1310
304 329-0070	**Preston County** 101 W Main St	Kingwood	WV	26537-1121
304 586-0202	**Putnam County** County Courthouse	Winfield	WV	25213-0000
304 255-9123	**Raleigh County** 215 Main St County Courthouse	Beckley	WV	25801-0000
304 636-0543	**Randolph County** 2 Randolph Ave	Elkins	WV	26241-4063
304 643-2163	**Ritchie County** 115 E Main St	Harrisville	WV	26362-1271
304 927-2860	**Roane County** 200 Main St	Spencer	WV	25276-1497
304 466-3770	**Summers County** Ballengee St	Hinton	WV	25951-0000
304 265-1401	**Taylor County** 214 W Main St	Grafton	WV	26354-1387
304 478-2414	**Tucker County** 1st & Walnut Sts	Parsons	WV	26287-0000
304 758-2102	**Tyler County** PO Box 66	Middlebourne	WV	26149-0066
304 472-1068	**Upshur County** Main St	Buckhannon	WV	26201-0000
304 272-5101	**Wayne County** Hendricks St	Wayne	WV	25570-0000
304 847-2508	**Webster County** PO Box 32	Webster Springs	WV	26288-0032
304 455-1390	**Wetzel County** PO Box 156	New Martinsville	WV	26155-0156
304 275-4271	**Wirt County** PO Box 53	Elizabeth	WV	26143-0053
304 424-1850	**Wood County** PO Box 1474	Parkersburg	WV	26102-1474
304 732-8000	**Wyoming County** Bank St	Pineville	WV	24874-0000

WISCONSIN

608 339-4200	**Adams County** PO Box 278	Friendship	WI	53934-0278
715 682-7000	**Ashland County** 201 2nd St W	Ashland	WI	54806-1652
715 537-6200	**Barron County** 330 E La Salle Ave	Barron	WI	54812-1591
715 373-6100	**Bayfield County** 117 E 5th St	Washburn	WI	54891-9464
414 436-3250	**Brown County** PO Box 1600	Green Bay	WI	54305-5600
608 685-4940	**Buffalo County** 407 N 2nd St	Alma	WI	54610-9673
715 349-2147	**Burnett County** 7410 County Rd K Box 115	Siren	WI	54872-9043
414 849-2361	**Calumet County** 206 Court St	Chilton	WI	53014-1198
715 723-1831	**Chippewa County** 711 N Bridge St	Chippewa Falls	WI	54729-1876
715 743-3241	**Clark County** 517 Court St	Neillsville	WI	54456-1992
608 742-2191	**Columbia County** PO Box 177	Portage	WI	53901-0177
608 326-0200	**Crawford County** 220 N Beaumont Rd	Prairie du Chien	WI	53821-1405
608 266-4121	**Dane County** 210 Martin Luther King Jr Blvd Rm 12	Madison	WI	53709-0001
414 386-4411	**Dodge County** County Courthouse	Juneau	WI	53039-0000
414 743-5511	**Door County** 138 S 4th Ave	Sturgeon Bay	WI	54235-2204
715 394-0341	**Douglas County** 1313 Belknap St	Superior	WI	54880-2769
715 232-1677	**Dunn County** 800 Wilson Ave	Menomonie	WI	54751-2785
715 839-5106	**Eau Claire County** 721 Oxford Ave	Eau Claire	WI	54703-5481
715 528-3201	**Florence County** PO Box 410	Florence	WI	54121-0410
414 929-3000	**Fond du Lac County** 160 S Macy St	Fond du Lac	WI	54935-4241
715 478-2422	**Forest County** County Courthouse	Crandon	WI	54520-0000
608 723-2675	**Grant County** 130 W Maple St	Lancaster	WI	53813-1625
608 328-9430	**Green County** County Courthouse	Monroe	WI	53566-2098
414 294-4060	**Green Lake County** 570 South St	Green Lake	WI	54941-9720
608 935-5445	**Iowa County** 222 N Iowa St	Dodgeville	WI	53533-1557
715 561-3375	**Iron County** 300 Taconite St	Hurley	WI	54534-1546
715 284-0208	**Jackson County** 307 Main St	Black River Falls	WI	54615-1756
414 674-2500	**Jefferson County** 320 S Main St	Jefferson	WI	53549-1718
608 847-9300	**Juneau County** 220 E State St	Mauston	WI	53948-1345
414 656-6400	**Kenosha County** 912 56th St	Kenosha	WI	53140-3747
414 388-4410	**Kewaunee County** 613 Dodge St	Kewaunee	WI	54216-0000
608 785-9581	**La Crosse County** 400 4th St N	La Crosse	WI	54601-3200
608 776-4850	**Lafayette County** 626 Main St	Darlington	WI	53530-1396
715 627-6200	**Langlade County** 800 Clermont St	Antigo	WI	54409-1985
715 536-0312	**Lincoln County** 1110 E Main St	Merrill	WI	54452-2554
414 683-4000	**Manitowoc County** 1010 S 8th St	Manitowoc	WI	54220-5392
715 847-5500	**Marathon County** 500 Forest St	Wausau	WI	54401-5568
715 735-3371	**Marinette County** 1926 Hall Ave	Marinette	WI	54143-1728
608 297-9114	**Marquette County** 77 W Park St	Montello	WI	53949-0000
715 799-3311	**Menominee County** County Courthouse	Keshena	WI	54135-0000
414 278-4067	**Milwaukee County** 901 N 9th St	Milwaukee	WI	53233-1417
608 269-8705	**Monroe County** 112 S Court St	Sparta	WI	54656-1764

414 834-5322 **Oconto County** 300 Washington St ... Oconto WI 54153-1621
715 369-6144 **Oneida County** PO Box 400 ... Rhinelander WI 54501-0400
414 832-5077 **Outagamie County** 410 S Walnut St ... Appleton WI 54911-5936
414 377-6400 **Ozaukee County** 121 W Main St ... Port Washington WI 53074-1813
715 672-8857 **Pepin County** 740 7th Ave W ... Durand WI 54736-1628
715 273-3531 **Pierce County** PO Box 119 ... Ellsworth WI 54011-0119
715 485-3161 **Polk County** 914 1st Ave N ... Balsam Lake WI 54810-0000
715 346-1351 **Portage County** 1516 Church St ... Stevens Point WI 54481-3598
715 339-3325 **Price County** 100 N Lake Ave ... Phillips WI 54555-1221
414 636-3121 **Racine County** 730 Wisconsin Ave ... Racine WI 53403-1274
608 647-2197 **Richland County** Seminary & Central Sts ... Richland Center WI 53581-0000
608 755-2160 **Rock County** 51 S Main St ... Janesville WI 53545-3978
715 532-2100 **Rusk County** 311 Miner Ave E ... Ladysmith WI 54848-1862
715 386-4600 **Saint Croix County** 911 4th St ... Hudson WI 54016-1656
608 356-5581 **Sauk County** 515 Oak St ... Baraboo WI 53913-2416
715 634-4866 **Sawyer County** PO Box 273 ... Hayward WI 54843-0273
715 526-9150 **Shawano County** 311 N Main St ... Shawano WI 54166-2198
414 459-3003 **Sheboygan County** 615 N 6th St ... Sheboygan WI 53081-4612
715 748-3131 **Taylor County** 224 S 2nd St ... Medford WI 54451-1899
715 538-2311 **Trempealeau County** PO Box 67 ... Whitehall WI 54773-0067
608 637-3569 **Vernon County** W Decker ... Viroqua WI 54665-0000
715 479-3600 **Vilas County** PO Box 369 ... Eagle River WI 54521-0369
414 741-4241 **Walworth County** PO Box 1001 ... Elkhorn WI 53121-1001
715 468-7808 **Washburn County** 110 W 4th Ave ... Shell Lake WI 54871-0000
414 338-4301 **Washington County** 432 E Washington St ... West Bend WI 53095-2500
414 548-7010 **Waukesha County** 515 W Moreland Blvd ... Waukesha WI 53188-2428
715 258-6200 **Waupaca County** 811 Harding St ... Waupaca WI 54981-1588
414 787-4631 **Waushara County** 209 S Saint Marie St ... Wautoma WI 54982-0000
414 235-2500 **Winnebago County** 415 Jackson St ... Oshkosh WI 54901-4751
715 421-8460 **Wood County** 400 Market St ... Wisconsin Rapids WI 54494-4825

WYOMING

307 721-2541 **Albany County** County Courthouse ... Laramie WY 82070-0000
307 568-2357 **Big Horn County** PO Box 31 ... Basin WY 82410-0031
307 682-7285 **Campbell County** 500 S Gillette Ave Suite 220 ... Gillette WY 82716-4208
307 328-2668 **Carbon County** PO Box 6 ... Rawlins WY 82301-0006
307 358-2061 **Converse County** PO Box 990 ... Douglas WY 82633-0990
307 283-1323 **Crook County** PO Box 37 ... Sundance WY 82729-0037
307 332-2405 **Fremont County** PO Box CC ... Lander WY 82520-0900
307 532-4051 **Goshen County** PO Box 160 ... Torrington WY 82240-0160
307 864-3515 **Hot Springs County** Arapahoe St ... Thermopolis WY 82443-2299
307 684-7272 **Johnson County** 76 N Main St ... Buffalo WY 82834-1847
307 638-4296 **Laramie County** 19th St & Cary Ave ... Cheyenne WY 82001-0000
307 877-9056 **Lincoln County** PO Box 670 ... Kemmerer WY 83101-0670
307 235-9206 **Natrona County** 200 N Center St Rm 157 ... Casper WY 82601-1991
307 334-2211 **Niobrara County** PO Box 420 ... Lusk WY 82225-0420
307 587-5548 **Park County** 1002 Sheridan Ave ... Cody WY 82414-3590
307 322-3555 **Platte County** PO Box 728 ... Wheatland WY 82201-0728
307 674-6822 **Sheridan County** 224 S Main St Suite B2 ... Sheridan WY 82801-4855
307 367-4372 **Sublette County** PO Box 250 ... Pinedale WY 82941-0250
307 875-2611 **Sweetwater County** 50 W Flaming Gorge Way ... Green River WY 82935-4212
307 733-4430 **Teton County** PO Box 1727 ... Jackson WY 83001-1727
307 789-2471 **Uinta County** 225 9th St ... Evanston WY 82930-3415
307 347-6491 **Washakie County** 10th St & Big Horn Ave ... Worland WY 82401-0000
307 746-4744 **Weston County** 1 W Main St ... Newcastle WY 82701-2106

State Government

State agencies and departments, selected for their usefulness, are listed alphabetically following a general information number for each state.

ALABAMA

205 261-2500 **State Government Information** 501 Dexter Ave ... Montgomery AL 36130-0001
205 261-7305 **Attorney General** 11 S Union St ... Montgomery AL 36130-0001
205 242-8700 **Board of Pardons & Paroles**
50 North Ripley St Gordon Persons Bldg Plaza Level ... Montgomery AL 36130-0001
205 261-5033 **Bureau of Vital Statistics** 434 Monroe St Rm 215 ... Montgomery AL 36130-0001
205 269-2700 **Commission on Higher Education** 1 Court Sq Suite 221 ... Montgomery AL 36197-0000
205 261-2650 **Department of Agriculture & Industries** PO Box 3336 ... Montgomery AL 36193-0000
205 261-3486 **Department of Conservation & Natural Resources**
64 N Union St Rm 702 ... Montgomery AL 36130-0001
205 242-9400 **Department of Corrections**
50 Ripley St Gordon Persons Bldg 3rd Fl ... Montgomery AL 36130-0001
205 242-8672 **Department of Economics & Community Affairs**
3465 Norman Bridge Rd ... Montgomery AL 36105-2310
205 242-9700 **Department of Education** 50 N Ripley St ... Montgomery AL 36130-0001
205 271-7700 **Department of Environmental Management**
1751 Congressman WL Dickinson Dr ... Montgomery AL 36130-0001
205 261-7160 **Department of Finance** 11 S Union St Rm 207 ... Montgomery AL 36130-0001
205 261-3460 **Department of Labor** 64 N Union St Rm 651 ... Montgomery AL 36130-0001
205 261-5052 **Department of Public Health** 434 Monroe St ... Montgomery AL 36130-0001
205 242-4371 **Department of Public Safety** PO Box 1511 ... Montgomery AL 36102-1511
205 242-1175 **Department of Revenue** 50 N Ripley St ... Montgomery AL 36132-0001
205 242-7334 **Division of Consumer Protection** 11 S Union St Rm 429 ... Montgomery AL 36130-0001
205 261-7250 **Division of Purchasing** 11 S Union St Rm 200 ... Montgomery AL 36130-0001
205 254-1275 **Division of Safety & Inspection** PO Box 10444 ... Birmingham AL 35202-0444
205 567-2221 **Draper Correctional Center** PO Box 1107 ... Elmore AL 36025-0000
205 261-3318 **Emergency Management Agency** 520 S Court St ... Montgomery AL 36130-0001
205 349-2852 **Geological Survey** 420 Hackberry Ln ... Tuscaloosa AL 35486-0000
205 261-7100 **Governor** 11 S Union St Rm 217 ... Montgomery AL 36130-0001
205 261-6311 **Highway Dept** 1409 Coliseum Blvd ... Montgomery AL 36130-0001
205 261-4361 **History & Archives** 624 Washington Ave ... Montgomery AL 36130-0001
205 269-3550 **Insurance Dept** 135 S Union St ... Montgomery AL 36130-0001
205 242-5891 **Law Enforcement Planning Agency**
3465 Norman Bridge Rd ... Montgomery AL 36105-2310
205 261-7900 **Lieutenant Governor** 11 S Union St Rm 725 ... Montgomery AL 36130-0001
205 261-5218 **Public Service Commission** PO Box 991 ... Montgomery AL 36101-0991
205 261-5544 **Real Estate Commission** 4121 Carmichael Rd Suite 401 ... Montgomery AL 36106-0000
205 832-4140 **Retirement Systems** 135 S Union St ... Montgomery AL 36130-0001
205 467-6112 **Saint Clair Correctional Facilities** 1000 St Clair Rd ... Springville AL 35146-9790
205 284-8952 **Science Technology & Energy Div**
3465 Norman Bridge Rd ... Montgomery AL 36105-2399
205 261-7200 **Secretary of State** 11 S Union St Rm 208 ... Montgomery AL 36130-0001
205 261-2984 **Securities Commission** 166 Commerce St 2nd Fl ... Montgomery AL 36130-0001
205 261-4076 **State Council on the Arts** 1 Dexter Ave ... Montgomery AL 36130-0001
205 261-4609 **Supreme Court** 445 Dexter Ave ... Montgomery AL 36130-0001
205 261-7500 **Treasury Dept** 11 S Union St Rm 240 ... Montgomery AL 36130-0001
205 242-8025 **Unemployment Compensation Div** 649 Monroe St ... Montgomery AL 36130-0001
205 261-2868 **Workmen's Compensation Div** Industrial Relations Bldg ... Montgomery AL 36130-0001

ALASKA

907 465-2111 **State Government Information** 333 Willoughby Ave 8th Fl ... Juneau AK 99811-0001
907 561-7877 **Alaska Energy Authority** PO Box 190869 ... Anchorage AK 99519-0869
907 465-3384 **Alaska State Board of Parole** PO Box T ... Juneau AK 99811-2000
907 465-2270 **Archives & Records Management** 141 Willoughby Ave ... Juneau AK 99801-1720
907 465-3600 **Attorney General** PO Box K ... Juneau AK 99811-0000
907 465-3393 **Bureau of Vital Records** PO Box H ... Juneau AK 99822-0675
907 465-2500 **Commerce & Economic Development**
333 Willoughby Ave 9th Fl ... Juneau AK 99801-0000
907 465-2854 **Commission of Postsecondary Education**
400 Willoughby Ave 1st Fl ... Juneau AK 99811-0001
907 465-3376 **Department of Corrections** PO Box T ... Juneau AK 99811-0000
907 465-2800 **Department of Education** PO Box F ... Juneau AK 99811-0001
907 465-2600 **Department of Environmental Conservation** PO Box O ... Juneau AK 99811-0001
907 465-2700 **Department of Labor** 1111 W 8th St ... Juneau AK 99801-1894
907 465-2400 **Department of Natural Resources** 400 Willoughby Ave ... Juneau AK 99801-1796
907 465-4322 **Department of Public Safety** PO Box N ... Juneau AK 99811-0001
907 465-2300 **Department of Revenue** 333 Willoughby Ave ... Juneau AK 99811-0001
907 465-3900 **Department of Transportation & Public Facilities** PO Box Z ... Juneau AK 99811-0001
907 745-7200 **Division of Agriculture** 915 S Bailey St ... Palmer AK 99645-6923
907 465-2521 **Division of Banking Securities & Corps**
333 Willoughby Ave 9th Fl ... Juneau AK 99801-0000
907 376-3061 **Division of Emergency Services** 3501 E Bogard Rd ... Wasilla AK 99687-8998
907 465-3082 **Division of Finance** PO Box H-02 ... Juneau AK 99811-0000
907 465-2250 **Division of General Services & Supply**
333 Willoughby Ave 7th Fl ... Juneau AK 99811-0001
907 465-2515 **Division of Insurance** 333 Willoughby Ave ... Juneau AK 99801-0000
907 762-2518 **Division of Mining** PO Box 107016 ... Anchorage AK 99510-7016
907 465-2534 **Division of Occupational Licensing** 333 Willoughby Ave ... Juneau AK 99801-0001
907 465-3573 **Division of Policy** 4th & Main Sts Diamond Court Bldg 4th Fl ... Juneau AK 99811-0000
907 465-3090 **Division of Public Health** 350 Main St Rm 503 ... Juneau AK 99801-0000
907 465-4460 **Division of Retirement & Benefits** PO Box CR-0203 ... Juneau AK 99811-0001
907 269-5641 **Division of State Troopers** 5700 E Tudor Rd ... Anchorage AK 99507-1225
907 465-2790 **Division of Workers' Compensation** 1111 W 8th St ... Juneau AK 99801-1802
907 465-2712 **Employment Security Div** 1111 W 8th St ... Juneau AK 99801-1802
907 452-3125 **Fairbanks Correctional Center** PO Box 70317 ... Fairbanks AK 99707-0317
907 465-3500 **Governor** PO Box A ... Juneau AK 99811-0001
907 694-9511 **Highland Mountain Correctional Center** PO Box 600 ... Eagle River AK 99577-0600
907 465-3520 **Lieutenant Governor** PO Box AA ... Juneau AK 99811-0001
907 465-4855 **Occupational Safety & Health Section** 1111 W 8th St ... Juneau AK 99801-1802
907 279-7541 **Public Defender Agency** 900 W 5th St Suite 200 ... Anchorage AK 99501-2090
907 276-6222 **Public Utilities Commission** 1016 W 6th Ave Suite 400 ... Anchorage AK 99501-1963
907 563-2169 **Real Estate Commission** 3601 C St Suite 722 ... Anchorage AK 99503-5934
907 279-1558 **State Council on the Arts** 619 Warehouse Ave Suite 220 ... Anchorage AK 99501-1665
907 264-0607 **Supreme Court** 303 K St ... Anchorage AK 99501-2013
907 465-2712 **Unemployment Insurance** 1111 W 8th St ... Juneau AK 99801-1802

ARIZONA

602 542-4900 **State Government Information** 1700 W Washington St ... Phoenix AZ 85007-2812
602 868-4011 **Arizona State Prison** E Butte ... Florence AZ 85232-0000
602 574-0024 **Arizona State Prison–Tucson** 10000 S Wilmot Rd ... Tucson AZ 85777-0001
602 542-5025 **Attorney General** 1275 W Washington St ... Phoenix AZ 85007-2926
602 542-5656 **Board of Pardons & Paroles** 1645 W Jefferson St Suite 326 ... Phoenix AZ 85007-3009
602 255-3109 **Commission for Postsecondary Education**
3030 N Central Ave Suite 1407 ... Phoenix AZ 85012-2720
602 542-4373 **Commission of Agriculture & Horticulture**
1688 W Adams St Rm 421 ... Phoenix AZ 85007-2621
602 255-5882 **Commission on the Arts** 417 W Roosevelt St ... Phoenix AZ 85003-1326
602 255-2114 **Consumer Affairs** 3030 N 3rd St Suite 1100 ... Phoenix AZ 85012-3049
602 280-1300 **Department of Commerce** 3800 N Central Ave Suite 1400 ... Phoenix AZ 85012-1908
602 542-5536 **Department of Corrections** 1601 W Jefferson St ... Phoenix AZ 85007-3056
602 542-4791 **Department of Economic Security** 1717 W Jefferson St ... Phoenix AZ 85007-3295
602 542-4271 **Department of Education** 1535 W Jefferson St ... Phoenix AZ 85007-3280
602 542-1024 **Department of Health Services** 1740 W Adams St Rm 407 ... Phoenix AZ 85007-0000
602 542-4035 **Department of Library Archives & Public Record**
1700 W Washington St Rm 200 ... Phoenix AZ 85007-2877
602 255-3791 **Department of Mines & Mineral Resources**
State Fairgrounds Mineral Bldg ... Phoenix AZ 85007-0000
602 223-2000 **Department of Public Safety** 2102 W Encanto Blvd ... Phoenix AZ 85009-0000
602 255-4345 **Department of Real Estate** 202 E Earll Dr Suite 400 ... Phoenix AZ 85012-2633
602 255-3381 **Department of Revenue** 1600 W Monroe St ... Phoenix AZ 85007-2650
602 255-7226 **Department of Transportation** 206 S 17th Ave ... Phoenix AZ 85007-3213
602 542-1554 **Department of Water Resources** 15 S 15th Ave ... Phoenix AZ 85007-3226
602 244-0504 **Division of Emergency Services** 5636 E McDowell Rd ... Phoenix AZ 85008-0000
602 542-4886 **Division of Finance** 1700 W Washington St Rm 210 ... Phoenix AZ 85007-2803
602 255-7437 **Division of Highways** 206 S 17th Ave Room 102-A ... Phoenix AZ 85007-3213
602 542-5795 **Division of Occupational Safety & Health**
800 W Washington St Rm 202 ... Phoenix AZ 85007-2934
602 542-4331 **Division of Planning & Policy Development**
1700 W Washington St ... Phoenix AZ 85007-2810
602 280-1300 **Energy Commission** 3800 N Central Ave Suite 1400 ... Phoenix AZ 85012-0000
602 542-4331 **Governor** 1700 W Washington St ... Phoenix AZ 85007-2883
602 255-5400 **Insurance Dept** 3030 N 3rd St Suite 1100 ... Phoenix AZ 85012-3039
602 542-4515 **Labor Dept** 800 W Washington St Rm 102 ... Phoenix AZ 85007-2934
602 542-4625 **Natural Resources Div** 1616 W Adams St ... Phoenix AZ 85007-2606
602 257-2277 **Office of Air Quality** 2005 N Central Ave Suite 603 ... Phoenix AZ 85004-1546
602 542-1084 **Office of Vital Records** PO Box 3887 ... Phoenix AZ 85030-0000
602 255-5161 **Oil & Gas Conservation Commission**
5150 N 16th St Suite B-141 ... Phoenix AZ 85016-0000
602 542-4285 **Secretary of State** 1700 W Washington St 7th Fl ... Phoenix AZ 85007-2888
602 542-4242 **Securities Div** 1200 W Washington St ... Phoenix AZ 85007-2927
602 631-2000 **State Compensation Fund** 3031 N 2nd St ... Phoenix AZ 85012-3009
602 542-5482 **State Personnel Dept of Administration** 1831 W Jefferson St ... Phoenix AZ 85007-3293
602 542-1463 **State Treasurer** 1700 W Washington St ... Phoenix AZ 85007-2867
602 542-4536 **Supreme Court** State Capitol Bldg 201 W Wing ... Phoenix AZ 85007-0000
602 542-3667 **Unemployment Insurance Administration**
1300 W Washington ... Phoenix AZ 85007-2929
602 542-4251 **Utilities Div** 1200 W Washington St ... Phoenix AZ 85007-2927

ARKANSAS

501 682-3000 **State Government Information** 1 State Capitol Mall ... Little Rock AR 72201-1090
501 371-2539 **Arts Council** 225 E Markham St Suite 200 ... Little Rock AR 72201-1647
501 682-2007 **Attorney General** 323 Center St Tower Bldg Suite 200 ... Little Rock AR 72201-0000
501 682-5193 **Community Assistance Div** 1 State Capitol Mall Rm 4B-210 ... Little Rock AR 72201-1012
501 682-2341 **Consumer Advocacy Div**
323 Center St Tower Bldg Suite 200 ... Little Rock AR 72201-0000
501 247-1800 **Department of Corrections** RR 8 Box 65 ... Pine Bluff AR 71602-9401
501 682-4475 **Department of Education** 4 State Capitol Mall ... Little Rock AR 72201-1011
501 682-2242 **Department of Finance & Administration**
1509 W 7th St Rm 401 ... Little Rock AR 72201-3933
501 371-1441 **Department of Higher Education** 1220 W 3rd St ... Little Rock AR 72201-1933
501 682-4500 **Department of Labor** 10421 W Markham St ... Little Rock AR 72205-2193
501 562-7444 **Department of Pollution Control & Ecology**
8001 National Dr ... Little Rock AR 72209-4800
501 247-1800 **Division of Parole Services** Rt 8 Box 65 ... Pine Bluff AR 71602-9401
501 682-7000 **Division of Revenues** PO Box 1272 ... Little Rock AR 72203-1272

State Government

Phone	Office / Address	City	State	ZIP
501 661-2134	**Division of Vital Records** 4815 W Markham St	Little Rock	AR	72205-3866
501 682-2121	**Employment Security Div** 2 State Capitol Mall	Little Rock	AR	72201-1011
501 682-1370	**Energy Office** 1 State Capitol Mall Rm 4B-215	Little Rock	AR	72201-1012
501 682-2345	**Governor** 250 State Capitol	Little Rock	AR	72201-1091
501 661-2509	**Health Services Agency** 4815 W Markham St	Little Rock	AR	72205-3866
501 682-6900	**History Commission** 1 State Capitol Mall	Little Rock	AR	72201-1014
501 682-1121	**Industrial Development Commission** 1 State Capitol Mall	Little Rock	AR	72201-1012
501 371-1325	**Insurance Dept** 400 University Tower Bldg	Little Rock	AR	72204-0000
501 682-2144	**Lieutenant Governor** 270 State Capitol Bldg	Little Rock	AR	72201-0000
501 783-2103	**Mine Inspection Div** 616 Garrison Ave Rm 205	Fort Smith	AR	72901-2521
501 329-5601	**Office of Emergency Services** PO Box 758	Conway	AR	72032-0758
501 371-2336	**Office of State Purchasing** PO Box 2940	Little Rock	AR	72203-2940
501 862-4965	**Oil & Gas Commission** PO Box 1472	El Dorado	AR	71731-1472
501 682-1453	**Public Service Commission** 1000 Center St	Little Rock	AR	72202-3800
501 371-1247	**Real Estate Commission** 1 Riverfront Pl Suite 660	North Little Rock	AR	72114-5646
501 569-2235	**Safety Div** 10324 I-30	Little Rock	AR	72203-0000
501 682-1010	**Secretary of State** 256 State Capitol Bldg	Little Rock	AR	72201-0000
501 371-1011	**Securities Dept** 201 E Markham St Suite 300	Little Rock	AR	72201-1692
501 682-1611	**Soil & Water Conservation Commission** 1 Capitol Mall Suite 2D	Little Rock	AR	72201-1012
501 562-7444	**Solid Waste Div** 8001 National Dr	Little Rock	AR	72209-4800
501 569-2000	**State Hwy & Transportation Dept** 10324 I-30	Little Rock	AR	72209-0000
501 224-4111	**State Police** PO Box 5901	Little Rock	AR	72215-5901
501 682-6849	**Supreme Court** 625 Marshall St	Little Rock	AR	72201-1079
501 682-5888	**Treasurer** State Capitol Bldg Rm 220	Little Rock	AR	72201-0000
501 842-2519	**Tucker Unit Correctional Facility** Star Rt Box 228	Tucker	AR	72168-9999
501 372-3930	**Worker's Compensation Commission** 625 Marshall St Justice Bldg	Little Rock	AR	72201-0000

CALIFORNIA

Phone	Office / Address	City	State	ZIP
916 322-9900	**State Government Information (Northern)** 601 Sequoia Pacific Blvd	Sacramento	CA	95814-0000
213 620-3030	**State Government Information (Southern)**	Sacramento	CA	95814-0000
916 445-4383	**Air Resources Board** 1102 Q St	Sacramento	CA	95814-6511
916 322-8911	**Arts Council** 1901 Broadway Suite A	Sacramento	CA	95818-2492
916 445-9555	**Attorney General** 1515 K St Suite 511	Sacramento	CA	95814-4030
916 445-3956	**Board of Equalization** 1020 N St	Sacramento	CA	95814-5691
916 322-3330	**California Integrated Waste Management Board** 1020 9th St Suite 300	Sacramento	CA	95814-3515
707 448-6841	**California Medical Facility** 1600 California Dr	Vacaville	CA	95696-0000
805 543-2700	**California Men's Colony** Hwy 1	San Luis Obispo	CA	93409-0001
916 985-2561	**California State Prison–Old Folsom** PO Box W	Represa	CA	95671-7100
415 454-1460	**California State Prison–San Quentin** 100 Main St	San Quentin	CA	94974-0000
916 445-3028	**Controller's Office** PO Box 942850	Sacramento	CA	94250-0001
916 322-3241	**Department of Commerce** 1121 L St Suite 600	Sacramento	CA	95814-3981
916 445-4465	**Department of Consumer Affairs** 1020 N St	Sacramento	CA	95814-5624
916 445-7688	**Department of Corrections** 1515 S St Rm 351-N	Sacramento	CA	95814-7243
916 322-2940	**Department of Economic Opportunity** 700 N Pent	Sacramento	CA	95814-6422
916 445-2700	**Department of Education** 721 Capitol Mall Rm 524	Sacramento	CA	95814-4785
916 445-4141	**Department of Finance** State Capitol Rm 1145	Sacramento	CA	95814-4998
916 445-7126	**Department of Food & Agriculture** 1220 N St	Sacramento	CA	95814-5621
916 445-1248	**Department of Health Services** 714 P St	Sacramento	CA	95814-6414
415 557-3356	**Department of Industrial Relations** 525 Golden Gate Ave	San Francisco	CA	94102-3284
213 736-2551	**Department of Insurance** 3450 Wilshire Blvd	Los Angeles	CA	90010-2208
916 739-3600	**Department of Real Estate** PO Box 187000	Sacramento	CA	95818-7000
916 445-2201	**Department of Transportation** 1120 N St	Sacramento	CA	95814-5620
916 445-9248	**Department of Water Resources** 1416 9th St	Sacramento	CA	95814-5511
415 737-2618	**Division of Industrial Accidents** 395 Oyster Point Blvd 5th Fl Wing B	South San Francisco	CA	94080-0000
916 445-1825	**Division of Mines & Geology** 1416 9th St Rm 1341	Sacramento	CA	95814-5511
916 324-3331	**Energy Commission** 1516 9th St	Sacramento	CA	95814-5504
916 322-4203	**Environmental Affairs Agency** 1102 Q St	Sacramento	CA	95814-6511
916 445-2841	**Governor** State Capitol 1st Fl	Sacramento	CA	95814-4991
916 445-1719	**Health Data & Statistics Branch** 410 N St	Sacramento	CA	95814-4381
916 445-8994	**Lieutenant Governor** State Capitol Rm 1114	Sacramento	CA	95814-4905
916 322-3640	**Oaccupational Safety & Health Standards Board** 1006 4th St 3rd Fl	Sacramento	CA	95814-3314
916 324-9100	**Office of Criminal Justice Planning** 1130 K St Suite 300	Sacramento	CA	95814-3927
916 427-4201	**Office of Emergency Services** 2800 Meadowview Rd	Sacramento	CA	95832-1441
916 322-8515	**Office of Planning & Research** 1400 10th St Rm 108	Sacramento	CA	95814-5502
916 445-6942	**Office of Procurement** 1823 14th St	Sacramento	CA	95814-7131
916 322-5639	**Office of Tourism** 1121 L St Suite 103	Sacramento	CA	95814-0000
916 445-6200	**Parole & Community Services Div** 1615 S St Rm 212N	Sacramento	CA	95814-0000
916 445-1000	**Postsecondary Education Commission** 1020 12th St 3rd Fl	Sacramento	CA	95814-3985
415 557-1600	**Public Defender** 1390 Market St Suite 425	San Francisco	CA	94102-5470
415 557-1487	**Public Utilities Commission** 505 Van Ness Ave	San Francisco	CA	94102-3214
916 445-5656	**Resources Agency** 1416 9th St Rm 1311	Sacramento	CA	95814-5569
916 445-6371	**Secretary of State** 1230 J St	Sacramento	CA	95814-2974
916 445-4293	**State Archives** 1020 'O' St Rm 130	Sacramento	CA	95814-5777
916 445-1150	**State Police** 815 S St	Sacramento	CA	95814-7040
415 557-0587	**Supreme Court** 455 Golden Gate Ave	San Francisco	CA	94102-3674
916 445-6562	**Treasurer** 915 Capitol Mall Rm 110	Sacramento	CA	95814-4810

COLORADO

Phone	Office / Address	City	State	ZIP
303 866-5000	**State Government Information** 1525 Sherman St	Denver	CO	80203-1712
303 866-3281	**Accounts & Control Div** 1525 Sherman St 7th Fl	Denver	CO	80203-1712
303 331-8500	**Air Quality Commission** 4210 E 11th Ave	Denver	CO	80220-3700
719 267-3520	**Arkansas Valley Correctional Facility** 12750 Ln 13	Crowley	CO	81034-0001
303 866-3611	**Attorney General** 1525 Sherman St 3rd Fl	Denver	CO	80203-1760
719 395-2404	**Buena Vista Correctional Facility** PO Box 2017	Buena Vista	CO	81211-2017
303 866-2723	**Commission on Higher Education** 1300 Broadway 2nd Fl	Denver	CO	80203-2104
303 866-5167	**Consumer Protection Unit** 1525 Sherman St Rm 215	Denver	CO	80203-1717
303 894-2617	**Council on the Arts & Humanities** 750 Pennsylvania St	Denver	CO	80203-3699
303 866-2811	**Department of Agriculture** 1525 Sherman St 4th Fl	Denver	CO	80203-1712
719 579-9580	**Department of Corrections** 2862 S Circle Dr Suite 400	Colorado Springs	CO	80906-4195
303 866-6806	**Department of Education** 201 E Colfax Ave	Denver	CO	80203-1799
303 320-8333	**Department of Health** 4210 E 11th Ave	Denver	CO	80220-3783
303 866-3311	**Department of Natural Resources** 1313 Sherman St Rm 718	Denver	CO	80203-2239
303 866-3304	**Department of Regulatory Agencies** 1525 Sherman St Rm 110	Denver	CO	80203-1749
303 534-1208	**Department of Revenue** 1375 Sherman St	Denver	CO	80261-0001
303 866-2442	**Department of the Treasury** 200 E Colfax Ave Rm 140	Denver	CO	80203-1716
303 892-3840	**Division of Commerce & Development** 1625 Broadway Suite 1710	Denver	CO	80202-4729
303 239-4442	**Division of Criminal Justice** 700 Kipling St Suite 3000	Denver	CO	80215-5865
303 273-1624	**Division of Disaster Emergency Services** Camp George W	Golden	CO	80401-0000
303 764-2913	**Division of Labor** 1120 Lincoln Chancery Bldg 14th Fl	Denver	CO	80203-0000
303 866-3401	**Division of Mines** 1313 Sherman St Rm 215	Denver	CO	80203-2243
303 620-4441	**Division of Purchasing** 303 W Colfax Ave Suite 600	Denver	CO	80204-2623
303 894-2320	**Division of Securities** 1580 Lincoln St Suite 420	Denver	CO	80203-0000
303 866-2055	**Division of State Archives & Public Records** 1313 Sherman St Rm 1B-20	Denver	CO	80203-2236
303 866-3581	**Division of Water Resources** 1313 Sherman St Rm 818	Denver	CO	80203-2238
303 866-2471	**Governor** 136 State Capitol	Denver	CO	80203-0000
303 331-4902	**Health & Statistics Div** 4210 E 11th Ave	Denver	CO	80220-3700
303 757-9011	**Highways Dept** 4201 E Arkansas Ave	Denver	CO	80222-3406
303 620-4300	**Insurance Div** 303 W Colfax Ave Suite 500	Denver	CO	80204-2623
303 866-2087	**Lieutenant Governor** 130 State Capitol	Denver	CO	80203-0000
303 894-2144	**Office of Energy Conservation** 112 E 14th Ave	Denver	CO	80203-2129
303 866-3386	**Office of State Planning & Budgeting** 111 State Capitol	Denver	CO	80203-0000
303 894-2100	**Oil & Gas Conservation Commission** 1580 Logan St Suite 380	Denver	CO	80203-1940
303 620-4888	**Public Defender** 110 16th St Suite 800	Denver	CO	80202-5210
303 894-2001	**Public Utilities Commission** 1580 Logan St 2nd Fl	Denver	CO	80203-1939
303 894-2166	**Real Estate Commission** 1776 Logan St 4th Fl	Denver	CO	80203-1248
303 894-2200	**Secretary of State** 1560 Broadway Suite 200	Denver	CO	80202-5169
303 866-5700	**Social Services Dept** 1575 Sherman St	Denver	CO	80203-1714
303 894-2465	**State Board of Parole** 1580 Lincoln St Suite 920	Denver	CO	80203-1511
303 620-4451	**State Buildings Div** 303 W Colfax Ave Suite 1450	Denver	CO	80204-2600
303 239-4403	**State Patrol** 700 Kipling St Suite 3000	Denver	CO	80215-5885
303 861-1111	**Supreme Court** 1301 Pennsylvania Ave	Denver	CO	80203-2116
303 866-6357	**Unemployment Insurance Section** 251 E 12th Ave	Denver	CO	80203-2272
303 331-4830	**Waste Management Div** 4210 E 11th Ave	Denver	CO	80220-3700

CONNECTICUT

Phone	Office / Address	City	State	ZIP
203 566-2750	**State Government Information** 165 Capitol Ave	Hartford	CT	06106-1630
203 566-4667	**Agriculture Dept** 165 Capitol Ave	Hartford	CT	06106-1630
203 566-3690	**Archives Dept** 231 Capitol Ave	Hartford	CT	06106-1537
203 566-7098	**Attorney General** 55 Elm St 4th Fl	Hartford	CT	06106-1774
203 566-4030	**Bureau of Air Management** 165 Capitol Ave Rm 144	Hartford	CT	06106-1630
203 566-3854	**Bureau of Highways** 24 Wolcott Hill Rd	Wethersfield	CT	06109-1154
203 566-7177	**Bureau of Licensing & Regulation** 165 Capitol Ave	Hartford	CT	06106-1630
203 566-3360	**Bureau of Public Works** 165 Capitol Ave	Hartford	CT	06106-1630
203 638-3267	**Bureau of Purchases** 460 Silver St	Middletown	CT	06457-0000
203 566-5328	**Chief Public Defender Services Commission** 1 Hartford Sq W Suite 201	Hartford	CT	06106-5114
203 566-4770	**Commission on the Arts** 227 Lawrence St	Hartford	CT	06106-1430
203 566-4298	**Comprehensive Planning Div Office of Policy & Management** 80 Washington St	Hartford	CT	06106-4417
203 749-8391	**Connecticut Correctional Institution** PO Box 100	Somers	CT	06071-0100
203 566-7528	**Department of Administrative Services** 165 Capitol Ave	Hartford	CT	06106-1630
203 566-4999	**Department of Consumer Protection** 165 Capitol Ave	Hartford	CT	06106-1630
203 566-4457	**Department of Corrections** 340 Capitol Ave	Hartford	CT	06106-1494
203 258-4244	**Department of Economic Development** 865 Brook St	Rocky Hill	CT	06067-3405
203 566-5061	**Department of Education** 165 Capitol Ave	Hartford	CT	06106-1630
203 566-2110	**Department of Environmental Protection** 165 Capitol Ave	Hartford	CT	06106-1600
203 566-2038	**Department of Health Services** 150 Washington St	Hartford	CT	06106-4476
203 566-3913	**Department of Higher Education** 61 Woodland St	Hartford	CT	06105-2326
203 566-4384	**Department of Labor** 200 Folly Brook Blvd	Wethersfield	CT	06109-1109
203 827-1553	**Department of Public Utility Control** 1 Central Park Plaza	New Britain	CT	06051-2291
203 566-8520	**Department of Revenue Services** 92 Farmington Ave	Hartford	CT	06105-3712
203 566-3477	**Department of Transportation** 24 Wolcott Hill Rd	Wethersfield	CT	06109-1100
203 566-4550	**Division of Occupational Safety & Health** 200 Folly Brook Blvd	Wethersfield	CT	06109-1109
203 566-4560	**Division of Securities & Business Investments** 44 Capitol Ave	Hartford	CT	06106-1706
203 566-3200	**Division of State Police** 100 Washington St	Hartford	CT	06106-4419
203 240-3256	**Economic Development Branch of Commerce** 450 Main St Rm 519	Hartford	CT	06106-0000
203 566-4280	**Employment Security Div** 200 Folly Brook Blvd	Wethersfield	CT	06109-1113
203 566-2800	**Energy Div** 80 Washington St	Hartford	CT	06106-4417
203 566-4840	**Governor** 210 Capitol Ave	Hartford	CT	06106-1568
203 297-3800	**Insurance Dept** 165 Capitol Ave	Hartford	CT	06106-1630
203 566-2614	**Lieutenant Governor** 210 Capitol Ave	Hartford	CT	06106-1501
203 566-3020	**Management & Justice Planning Div** 80 Washington St	Hartford	CT	06106-4417
203 566-8350	**Office of Adult Probation** 643 Maple Ave	Hartford	CT	06114-1888
203 566-3180	**Office of Emergency Management** 360 Broad St	Hartford	CT	06105-3713
203 566-8070	**Office of Policy & Management** 80 Washington St	Hartford	CT	06106-4458
203 566-5131	**Real Estate Commission** 165 Capitol Ave	Hartford	CT	06106-1630
203 566-2668	**Secretary of State** State Capitol Bldg Rm 104	Hartford	CT	06106-0000
203 566-3672	**Solid Waste Management Unit** 1820 Trinity St	Hartford	CT	06106-0000
203 566-8160	**Supreme Court** PO Box Z Stn A	Hartford	CT	06106-0977
203 566-5050	**Treasurer** 55 Elm St	Hartford	CT	06106-1773
203 566-5790	**Unemployment Compensation Div** 90 Washington St	Hartford	CT	06103-1085
203 566-1188	**Vital Records & Statistics** 150 Washington St	Hartford	CT	06106-4405
203 566-7220	**Water Resources Unit** 165 Capitol Ave	Hartford	CT	06106-1630
203 789-7783	**Worker's Compensation Commission** 1890 Dixwell Ave	Hamden	CT	06514-3182

DELAWARE

Phone	Office / Address	City	State	ZIP
302 736-4000	**State Government Information** 604 Otis Dr	Dover	DE	19901-0000
302 571-3838	**Attorney General** 820 N French St 8th Fl	Wilmington	DE	19801-3509
302 571-3452	**Board of Parole** 820 N French St	Wilmington	DE	19801-3509
302 736-5318	**Bureau of Archives & Records Management** Hall of Records	Dover	DE	19901-0000
302 571-4169	**Commerce Dept** 800 N French St 9th Fl	Wilmington	DE	19801-3590
302 571-3250	**Consumer Affairs** 820 N French St 4th Fl	Wilmington	DE	19801-3509
302 571-3430	**Criminal Justice Council** 820 N French St	Wilmington	DE	19801-3509
302 653-9261	**Delaware Correctional Center** PO Box 500	Smyrna	DE	19977-0000
302 736-3611	**Department of Administrative Services** Federal St Townsend Bldg 3rd Fl	Dover	DE	19901-0000
302 736-4811	**Department of Agriculture** 2320 S DuPont Hwy	Dover	DE	19901-5501
302 736-5601	**Department of Corrections** 80 Monrovia Ave	Smyrna	DE	19977-1597
302 736-4201	**Department of Finance** 540 S DuPont Hwy	Dover	DE	19901-4516
302 571-2710	**Department of Labor** 820 N French St 6th Fl	Wilmington	DE	19801-3534
302 736-4629	**Department of Public Instruction** Lockerman & Federal Sts	Dover	DE	19901-7421
302 739-4306	**Department of Transportation** Rt 113	Dover	DE	19901-0000
302 736-4271	**Development Uffice** 99 Kings Hwy	Dover	DE	19901-3816
302 834-4531	**Division of Emergency Planning & Operations** PO Box 527	Delaware City	DE	19706-0527
302 739-4301	**Division of Highways** Rt 113	Dover	DE	19903-0000
302 736-4522	**Division of Professional Regulation** Federal St	Dover	DE	19901-0000
302 736-4701	**Division of Public Health** PO Box 637	Dover	DE	19903-0637
302 834-7081	**Division of Purchasing** PO Box 299	Delaware City	DE	19706-0299
302 571-3302	**Division of Revenue** 820 N French St	Wilmington	DE	19801-3530
302 571-2515	**Division of Securities** 820 N French St 8th Fl	Wilmington	DE	19801-3530
302 736-4411	**Division of Soil & Water Conservation** 89 Kings Hwy 2nd Fl	Dover	DE	19903-0000
302 736-5911	**Division of State Police** PO Box 430	Dover	DE	19903-0430
302 571-3540	**Division of the Arts/State Arts Council** 820 N French St	Wilmington	DE	19801-3530
302 368-6730	**Division of Unemployment Insurance** Rt 273 & Chapman Rd	Newark	DE	19714-0000
302 736-4101	**Governor** Legislative Ave Legislative Hall	Dover	DE	19901-0000
302 571-3594	**Industrial Accident Board** 820 N French St	Wilmington	DE	19801-3533
302 736-4251	**Insurance Dept** 841 Silver Lake Blvd	Dover	DE	19901-2407
302 736-4151	**Lieutenant Governor** 820 N French St 11th Fl	Wilmington	DE	19801-3509
302 736-4403	**Natural Resources & Environmental Control Dept** 89 Kings Hwy	Dover	DE	19901-3816
302 571-3908	**Occupational Safety & Health** 820 N French St	Wilmington	DE	19801-3509
302 736-4208	**Office of Pensions** 540 S DuPont Hwy	Dover	DE	19901-4516

302 736-4721 **Office of Vital Statistics**
Federal & Water Sts Jessie Cooper Bldg .... Dover DE 19901-0000
302 571-3240 **Postsecondary Education Commission**
820 N French St 4th Fl .... Wilmington DE 19801-3561
302 571-3230 **Public Defender's Office** 820 N French St 5th Fl .... Wilmington DE 19801-3509
302 736-4247 **Public Service Commission** 1560 S DuPont Hwy .... Dover DE 19901-4906
302 736-4186 **Real Estate Commission** Federal St O'Neil Bldg Box 1401 .... Dover DE 19903-0000
302 736-4111 **Secretary of State** Federal & Duke of York Sts Townsend Bldg .... Dover DE 19903-0000
302 736-5361 **Solid Waste Authority** PO Box 455 .... Dover DE 19903-0455
302 571-2427 **Supreme Court** 820 N French St .... Wilmington DE 19801-3509
302 856-5548 **Sussex Correctional Institution** Rt 1 Box 500 .... Georgetown DE 19947-9780
302 736-3382 **Treasurer** PO Box 1401 .... Dover DE 19903-1401

FLORIDA

904 488-1234 **State Government Information**
Koger Executive Ctr 2737 Center Knight Bldg Suite 110 .... Tallahassee FL 32399-0950
904 487-1963 **Attorney General** Capitol Bldg .... Tallahassee FL 32399-0000
904 488-0090 **Bureau of Public Safety Management** 2740 Centerview Dr .... Tallahassee FL 32399-6558
904 488-6971 **Department of Agriculture & Consumer Services**
407 S Calhoun St .... Tallahassee FL 32399-0800
904 488-0520 **Department of Banking & Finance** State Capitol .... Tallahassee FL 32399-0350
904 488-3104 **Department of Commerce**
107 W Gaines St Collins Bldg Suite 510-C .... Tallahassee FL 32399-0000
904 488-5021 **Department of Corrections** 1311 Winewood Blvd .... Tallahassee FL 32399-2500
904 487-1785 **Department of Education**
325 W Gaines St Florida Education Center Suite 101 .... Tallahassee FL 32399-0400
904 488-4805 **Department of Environmental Regulation**
2600 Blair Stone Rd Twin Towers Office Bldg .... Tallahassee FL 32399-2400
904 488-2786 **Department of General Services**
2737 Centerview Dr Knight Bldg Suite 307 .... Tallahassee FL 32399-0000
904 488-4115 **Department of Health & Rehabilitative Services**
1323 Winewood Blvd Bldg 1 Rm 115 .... Tallahassee FL 32399-0700
904 488-3440 **Department of Insurance** 200 E Gaines St .... Tallahassee FL 32399-0300
904 488-8771 **Department of Law Enforcement** 208 W Carolina St .... Tallahassee FL 32301-1128
904 488-1554 **Department of Natural Resources**
3900 Commonwealth Blvd .... Tallahassee FL 32399-3000
904 487-2252 **Department of Professional Regulation**
1940 N Monroe St .... Tallahassee FL 32399-0750
904 488-5050 **Department of Revenue** 501 S Calhoun St Rm 104 .... Tallahassee FL 32399-0100
904 488-6721 **Department of Transportation** 605 Suwannee Burns Bldg .... Tallahassee FL 32399-0000
904 488-1344 **Division of Air Resources Management**
2600 Blair Stone Rd .... Tallahassee FL 32399-6564
904 488-2774 **Division of Building Construction**
2737 Centerview Dr Knight Bldg Suite 300 .... Tallahassee FL 32399-0950
904 488-2226 **Division of Consumer Services** 508 Mayo Bldg .... Tallahassee FL 32399-0000
904 488-1083 **Division of Cultural Affairs** State Capitol .... Tallahassee FL 32399-0000
904 488-6300 **Division of Economic Development**
107 W Gaines St Collins Bldg Suite 501-B .... Tallahassee FL 32399-2000
904 487-4918 **Division of Emergency Management** 2740 Centerview Dr .... Tallahassee FL 32399-6558
904 488-7228 **Division of Labor Employment & Training**
1320 Executive Center Dr Suite 300 .... Tallahassee FL 32399-6511
904 487-2651 **Division of Library & Information Services**
500 S Bronough St RA Gray Bldg .... Tallahassee FL 32399-6519
904 488-1194 **Division of Purchasing**
2737 Centerview Dr Night Bldg Suite 110 .... Tallahassee FL 32399-0950
407 423-6053 **Division of Real Estate** 400 W Robinson St .... Orlando FL 32801-1736
904 488-5541 **Division of Retirement** 2639 N Monroe St .... Tallahassee FL 32399-1560
904 488-6093 **Division of Unemployment Compensation**
107 E Madison St .... Tallahassee FL 32399-6545
904 488-2514 **Division of Worker's Compensation** 2728 Centerview Dr .... Tallahassee FL 32399-0680
904 488-6764 **Energy Office** 214 S Bronough St .... Tallahassee FL 32301-1705
904 964-8125 **Florida State Prison** PO Box 747 .... Starke FL 32091-0747
904 488-4441 **Governor** Capitol Bldg .... Tallahassee FL 32399-0001
904 488-4711 **Lieutenant Governor** Capitol Bldg Plaza Level 5 .... Tallahassee FL 32399-0000
407 597-3705 **Martin Correctional Institution** 1150 SW Allapattah Rd .... Indiantown FL 34956-4397
904 488-7810 **Office of Planning & Budgeting** Carlton Bldg Rm 415 .... Tallahassee FL 32399-0001
904 359-6971 **Office of Vital Statistics** 1217 Pearl St .... Jacksonville FL 32202-3926
904 488-1653 **Parole Commission** 1309 Winewood Blvd .... Tallahassee FL 32399-6568
904 488-7181 **Public Service Commission** 101 E Gaines St .... Tallahassee FL 32399-0850
904 488-3680 **Secretary of State** State Capitol Plaza Level Rm 2 .... Tallahassee FL 32399-0000
904 488-0125 **Supreme Court** 500 S Duval St .... Tallahassee FL 32399-1900

GEORGIA

404 656-2000 **State Government Information** 330 Capitol Ave SW .... Atlanta GA 30334-9002
404 656-6900 **Air Protection Branch** 205 Butler St SE East Tower Rm 1162 .... Atlanta GA 30334-0000
404 656-4586 **Attorney General** 132 State Judicial Bldg .... Atlanta GA 30334-0000
404 656-5651 **Board of Pardons & Paroles** 2 Martin Luther King Jr Dr SE .... Atlanta GA 30334-9008
404 656-2202 **Board of Regents** 244 Washington St SW .... Atlanta GA 30334-5809
404 656-3250 **Building Authority** 1 Martin Luther King Jr Dr SW .... Atlanta GA 30334-9004
404 656-2190 **Business Services & Regulation**
2 Martin Luther King Jr Dr West Tower Suite 315 .... Atlanta GA 30334-9008
404 656-2056 **Commissioner of Insurance**
2 Martin Luther King Jr Dr SW 716 West Tower .... Atlanta GA 30334-9008
404 656-3790 **Consumer Affairs** 2 Martin Luther King Jr Dr SW Suite 356 .... Atlanta GA 30334-9008
404 493-5780 **Council for the Arts** 2082 E Exchange Pl Suite 100 .... Tucker GA 30084-5334
404 656-1721 **Criminal Justice Coordinating Council**
10 Park Place S Suite 200 .... Atlanta GA 30303-0000
404 656-3608 **Department of Agriculture** 19 Martin Luther King Jr Dr SW .... Atlanta GA 30334-9900
404 656-2358 **Department of Archives & History** 330 Capitol Ave SE .... Atlanta GA 30334-0000
404 986-1633 **Department of Banking & Finance**
2990 Brandywine Rd Suite 200 .... Atlanta GA 30341-0000
404 656-4605 **Department of Corrections**
2 Martin Luther King Jr Dr SW East Tower 7th Fl .... Atlanta GA 30334-9008
404 624-7000 **Department of Defense** 935 E Confederate Ave SE .... Atlanta GA 30316-2531
404 656-2534 **Department of Education** 205 Butler St SE .... Atlanta GA 30334-4909
404 656-5542 **Department of Human Resources** 47 Trinity Ave .... Atlanta GA 30334-0000
404 656-3545 **Department of Industry & Trade**
285 Peachtree Center Ave NE Suite 1100 .... Atlanta GA 30303-1232
404 656-3011 **Department of Labor** 148 International Blvd NE .... Atlanta GA 30303-1752
404 894-7505 **Division of Public Health** 878 Peachtree St NE Suite 201 .... Atlanta GA 30309-3917
404 656-3240 **Division of Purchasing & Surplus Property**
200 Piedmont Ave NE Suite 1302 .... Atlanta GA 30303-1702
404 656-4713 **Environmental Protection Div**
205 Butler St East Tower Suite 1152 .... Atlanta GA 30334-9001
404 656-3900 **Examining Boards Div** 166 Pryor St SW .... Atlanta GA 30303-3422
404 775-3161 **Georgia Diagnostic & Classification Center** PO Box 3877 .... Jackson GA 30233-0877
404 778-2273 **Georgia Industrial Institute** PO Box 709 .... Alto GA 30510-0709
404 656-1776 **Governor** 203 State Capitol .... Atlanta GA 30334-0000
404 656-5030 **Lieutenant Governor** 240 State Capitol SW .... Atlanta GA 30334-1600
404 656-3530 **Natural Resources Dept** 205 Butler St SE .... Atlanta GA 30334-4100
404 656-5176 **Office of Energy Resources** 270 Washington St SW Suite 615 .... Atlanta GA 30334-9009
404 656-3820 **Office of Planning & Budget** 270 Washington St SW Rm 611 .... Atlanta GA 30334-9009
404 656-4501 **Public Service Commission** 244 Washington St SW .... Atlanta GA 30334-5700
404 656-3916 **Real Estate Commission** 148 International Blvd NE Suite 500 .... Atlanta GA 30303-1734
404 656-4015 **Revenue Dept** 410 Trinity Washington Bldg .... Atlanta GA 30334-0000
404 656-2881 **Secretary of State** 214 State Capitol SW .... Atlanta GA 30334-1600
404 624-6077 **State Patrol** 959 E Confederate Ave SE .... Atlanta GA 30371-0001
404 656-3470 **Supreme Court** 244 Washington St SW .... Atlanta GA 30334-9007
404 656-5206 **Transportation Dept** 2 Capitol Sq SW .... Atlanta GA 30334-9003
404 656-2168 **Treasurer** PO Box 38918 .... Atlanta GA 30334-0000
404 656-3050 **Unemployment Insurance Div**
148 International Blvd Sussex Bldg .... Atlanta GA 30303-0000
404 656-4750 **Vital Records Service** 47 Trinity Ave SW Rm 217-H .... Atlanta GA 30334-9006
404 656-2034 **Worker's Compensation Board** 1 CNN Ctr S Tower Suite 1000 .... Atlanta GA 30303-2788

HAWAII

808 548-2211 **State Government Information** 415 S Beretania St .... Honolulu HI 96813-2407
808 548-4511 **Accounting & General Services Dept** 1151 Punchbowl St .... Honolulu HI 96813-3007
808 548-2355 **Archives Div** Iolani Palace Grounds .... Honolulu HI 96813-0000
808 548-4740 **Attorney General** 415 S Beretania St Rm 405 .... Honolulu HI 96813-2407
808 956-8213 **Board of Regents** University of Hawaii Bachman Hall Rm 209 .... Honolulu HI 96822-2394
808 548-2560 **Consumer Protection Office** 828 Fort Street Mall Suite 600-B .... Honolulu HI 96813-4321
808 847-4491 **Corrections Div** 2199 Kam Hwy .... Honolulu HI 96819-0000
808 548-7101 **Department of Agriculture** 1428 S King St .... Honolulu HI 96814-2512
808 548-2325 **Department of Budget & Finance** 415 S Beretania St .... Honolulu HI 96813-2407
808 548-7505 **Department of Commerce & Consumer Affairs**
1010 Richards St 2nd Fl .... Honolulu HI 96813-2920
808 734-2195 **Department of Defense** 3949 Diamond Head Rd .... Honolulu HI 96816-4413
808 586-3310 **Department of Education** 1390 Miller St .... Honolulu HI 96813-2418
808 548-6505 **Department of Health** PO Box 3378 .... Honolulu HI 96801-3378
808 548-3150 **Department of Labor & Industrial Relations**
830 Punchbowl St Rm 321 .... Honolulu HI 96813-5045
808 548-3205 **Department of Transportation** 869 Punchbowl St .... Honolulu HI 96813-5036
808 548-5414 **Disability Compensation Div** 830 Punchbowl St .... Honolulu HI 96813-5045
808 548-6590 **Division of Consumer Advocacy** PO Box 541 .... Honolulu HI 96809-0541
808 548-7510 **Division of Occupational Safety & Health** 830 Punchbowl St .... Honolulu HI 96813-5045
808 548-4560 **Division of Public Works** 1151 Punchbowl St .... Honolulu HI 96813-3024
808 548-4080 **Energy Div** 335 Merchant St Rm 110 .... Honolulu HI 96813-2921
808 548-4145 **Foundation on Culture & Art** 335 Merchant St Rm 202 .... Honolulu HI 96813-2921
808 548-5420 **Governor** State Capitol Bldg 5th Fl .... Honolulu HI 96813-0000
808 486-2600 **Halawa Correctional Facility** 99-902 Moanalua Hwy .... Aiea HI 96701-3252
808 548-5710 **Highways Div** 869 Punchbowl St .... Honolulu HI 96813-5036
808 548-6522 **Insurance Div** 250 S King St 5th Fl .... Honolulu HI 96813-2920
808 548-6550 **Land & Natural Resources Dept** 1151 Punchbowl St Rm 130 .... Honolulu HI 96813-3007
808 548-2544 **Lieutenant Governor** 415 S Beretania St .... Honolulu HI 96813-2407
808 847-4491 **Oahu Community Correctional Center** 2199 Kam Hwy .... Honolulu HI 96819-2307
808 548-6915 **Office of Environmental Quality Control**
465 S King St Rm 104 .... Honolulu HI 96813-2910
808 548-6454 **Office of Health Status Monitoring** 1250 Punchbowl St .... Honolulu HI 96813-2428
808 548-2530 **Paroling Authority** 250 S King St Rm 400 .... Honolulu HI 96813-4521
808 548-6520 **Professional & Vocational Licensing Div** 1010 Richards St .... Honolulu HI 96813-2920
808 548-6273 **Public Defender** 1130 N Nimitz Hwy Suite A135 .... Honolulu HI 96817-4580
808 548-3990 **Public Utility Commission** 465 S King St Rm 103 .... Honolulu HI 96813-2910
808 548-4057 **Purchasing & Supply Div** 1151 Punchbowl St .... Honolulu HI 96813-3024
808 548-7464 **Real Estate Commission** PO Box 3469 .... Honolulu HI 96801-3469
808 548-3800 **Resource Coordination Div** 425 Queen St Rm 221 .... Honolulu HI 96813-2904
808 548-3120 **Sheriff's Dept** 111 Alakea St .... Honolulu HI 96813-0000
808 548-7431 **Supreme Court** 417 S King St .... Honolulu HI 96813-2912
808 548-7650 **Taxation Dept** 830 Punchbowl St .... Honolulu HI 96813-5045
808 548-6951 **Unemployment Insurance Div** 830 Punchbowl St Rm 325 .... Honolulu HI 96813-5045

IDAHO

208 334-2411 **State Government Information** 650 W State St Rm 100 .... Boise ID 83720-0001
208 334-3356 **Archives & Records** 610 N Julia Davis Dr .... Boise ID 83702-7646
208 334-2400 **Attorney General** State Capitol Rm 210 .... Boise ID 83720-0001
208 334-5898 **Bureau of Air Quality** 1410 N Hilton .... Boise ID 83706-0000
208 334-3460 **Bureau of Disaster Services** 650 W State St .... Boise ID 83720-0000
208 334-3233 **Bureau of Occupational Licenses** 2417 Bank Dr Rm 312 .... Boise ID 83705-2578
208 334-5976 **Bureau of Vital Statistics Standards & Local Health Services**
450 W State St .... Boise ID 83720-0001
208 334-2318 **Commission for Pardons & Paroles**
1075 Park Blvd State House Mail .... Boise ID 83720-0001
208 334-2119 **Commission on the Arts** 304 W State St .... Boise ID 83720-0001
208 334-2424 **Consumer Protection Unit** State Capitol Bldg Rm 210 .... Boise ID 83720-0001
208 334-3240 **Department of Agriculture** 2270 Old Penitentiary Rd .... Boise ID 83712-8298
208 334-2470 **Department of Commerce** 700 W State St 2nd Fl .... Boise ID 83720-0001
208 334-2318 **Department of Corrections** 1075 Park Blvd .... Boise ID 83720-0001
208 334-3301 **Department of Education** 650 W State St .... Boise ID 83720-0001
208 334-6200 **Department of Employment** 317 Main St .... Boise ID 83735-0000
208 334-3313 **Department of Finance** 700 W State St .... Boise ID 83720-0001
208 334-5500 **Department of Health & Welfare** 450 W State St .... Boise ID 83720-0000
208 334-2250 **Department of Insurance** 500 S 10th St .... Boise ID 83720-0001
208 334-2327 **Department of Labor & Industrial Services** 277 N 6th St .... Boise ID 83720-0001
208 334-3284 **Department of Lands** State Capitol Bldg Rm 121 .... Boise ID 83720-0001
208 334-3560 **Department of Revenue & Taxation** 700 W State St .... Boise ID 83702-5822
208 327-7900 **Department of Water Resources** 1301 N Orchard .... Boise ID 83720-0000
208 334-5839 **Division of Environmental Quality** 1410 N Hilton St .... Boise ID 83706-1255
208 334-8300 **Division of Highways** PO Box 8028 .... Boise ID 83707-2028
208 334-3453 **Division of Public Works** 502 N 4th St .... Boise ID 83720-0001
208 334-2465 **Division of Purchasing** 801 Reserve St .... Boise ID 83720-0001
208 334-2100 **Governor** 700 W Jefferson State House .... Boise ID 83720-0001
208 336-0740 **Idaho State Correctional Institution** PO Box 14 .... Boise ID 83707-0014
208 334-6000 **Industrial Commission** 317 Main St .... Boise ID 83720-0001
208 334-2200 **Lieutenant Governor** Jefferson & Capitol Blvd State House .... Boise ID 83720-0001
208 334-0300 **Public Utilities Commission** 472 W Washington St .... Boise ID 83702-5983
208 334-3285 **Real Estate Commission** 633 N 4th St .... Boise ID 83702-4500
208 334-2300 **Secretary of State** State House Rm 203 .... Boise ID 83720-0001
208 334-3684 **Securities Bureau** 700 W State St .... Boise ID 83720-0001
208 334-2270 **State Board of Education** 650 W State St Rm 307 .... Boise ID 83720-0001
208 334-5731 **State Economic Opportunity Office** 450 W State St .... Boise ID 83720-0001
208 334-2503 **State Police** PO Box 55 .... Boise ID 83707-0055
208 334-2210 **Supreme Court** 451 W State St .... Boise ID 83720-0001
208 334-8000 **Transportation Dept** 3311 W State St .... Boise ID 83703-5881
208 334-3200 **Treasurer** State Capitol Bldg Rm 102 .... Boise ID 83720-0001

ILLINOIS

217 782-2000 **State Government Information** 501 S 2nd St Rm 176 .... Springfield IL 62706-0001
217 782-2172 **Agriculture Dept** 8th & Sangamon St State Fairgrounds .... Springfield IL 62794-0000
312 814-6750 **Arts Council** 100 W Randolph St Suite 10-500 .... Chicago IL 60601-3220
217 782-1090 **Attorney General** 500 S 2nd St .... Springfield IL 62706-0001
217 782-2551 **Board of Higher Education** 4 W Old State Capitol Plaza .... Springfield IL 62701-1214
217 782-8725 **Capital Development Board**
401 S Spring St William G Stratton Bldg 3rd Fl .... Springfield IL 62706-0001
217 782-9011 **Consumer Protection Div** 500 S 2nd St .... Springfield IL 62706-0001
312 793-8550 **Criminal Justice Authority** 120 S Riverside Plaza Suite 1016 .... Chicago IL 60606-3910
217 782-2141 **Department of Central Management Services**
715 William G Stratton Bldg 7th Fl .... Springfield IL 62706-0001

State Government

217 782-7500	**Department of Commerce & Community Affairs** 620 E Adams St	Springfield	IL	62701-1615
217 522-2666	**Department of Corrections** 1301 Concordia Ct	Springfield	IL	62702-5699
312 793-5700	**Department of Employment Security** 401 S State St	Chicago	IL	60605-0000
217 785-2800	**Department of Energy & Natural Resources** 325 W Adams St 3rd Fl	Springfield	IL	62704-0000
217 782-4515	**Department of Insurance** 320 W Washington St	Springfield	IL	62767-0001
217 782-6206	**Department of Labor** 1 W Old State Capitol Plaza 3rd Fl	Springfield	IL	62701-1217
217 782-6791	**Department of Mines & Minerals** 300 W Jefferson St Suite 300	Springfield	IL	62791-0000
217 785-9900	**Department of Nuclear Safety** 1035 Outer Park Dr	Springfield	IL	62704-0000
217 785-0800	**Department of Professional Regulation** 320 W Washington St 3rd Fl	Springfield	IL	62786-0001
217 782-4977	**Department of Public Health** 535 W Jefferson St	Springfield	IL	62761-0000
217 785-2602	**Department of Revenue** 101 W Jefferson St	Springfield	IL	62702-5145
217 785-4941	**Department of Securities** 900 S Spring St	Springfield	IL	62704-2725
217 782-2841	**Department of State Police** 103 Armory Bldg	Springfield	IL	62706-0001
217 782-5597	**Department of Transportation** 2300 S Dirksen Pkwy	Springfield	IL	62764-0001
217 782-7326	**Division of Air Pollution Control** 1340 N 9th St	Springfield	IL	62702-0000
217 782-2151	**Division of Highways** 2300 S Dirksen Pkwy	Springfield	IL	62764-0001
217 782-7756	**Division of Oil & Gas** 300 W Jefferson St Suite 300	Springfield	IL	62791-0000
312 793-4240	**Division of Unemployment Insurance** 401 S State St	Chicago	IL	60605-1225
217 782-6553	**Division of Vital Records** 605 W Jefferson St	Springfield	IL	62702-5035
217 782-2152	**Division of Water Resources** 2300 S Dirksen Pkwy	Springfield	IL	62764-0001
217 782-7860	**Emergency Services & Disaster Agency** 110 E Adams St	Springfield	IL	62706-0001
217 782-3397	**Environmental Protection Agency** 2200 Churchill Rd	Springfield	IL	62702-3406
217 782-6830	**Governor** 207 State House	Springfield	IL	62706-0001
312 814-6500	**Industrial Commission** 100 W Randolph St	Chicago	IL	60601-3275
217 782-7884	**Lieutenant Governor** 214 State House	Springfield	IL	62706-0001
618 826-5071	**Menard Correctional Center** Kaskaskia St	Menard	IL	62259-9999
217 782-2654	**Office of Planning** 107 Stratton Bldg	Springfield	IL	62706-0001
217 782-7273	**Prisoner Review Board** 319 E Madison St Suite A	Springfield	IL	62701-1096
217 782-4705	**Procurement Services Div** 801 Stratton Office Bldg	Springfield	IL	62706-0001
217 782-7892	**Public Utility Div** 527 E Capitol Ave 3rd Fl	Springfield	IL	62701-1827
217 785-0800	**Real Estate Commission** 320 W Washington St	Springfield	IL	62786-0001
217 782-2201	**Secretary of State** 213 State House Capitol Bldg Rm 213	Springfield	IL	62756-0001
217 782-7203	**State Appellate Defender's Office** PO Box 5780	Springfield	IL	62705-0000
217 782-4682	**State Archives** Archives Bldg	Springfield	IL	62756-0001
217 782-2221	**State Board of Education** 100 N 1st St	Springfield	IL	62777-0001
815 727-3607	**Stateville Correctional Center** PO Box 112	Joliet	IL	60434-0112
217 782-2035	**Supreme Court** Supreme Court Bldg	Springfield	IL	62706-0001
217 782-2211	**Treasurer** State Capitol Rm 219	Springfield	IL	62706-0001

INDIANA

317 232-1000	**State Government Information** 100 N Senate Ave	Indianapolis	IN	46204-2208
317 232-8770	**Agriculture Div** 1 N Capitol Ave Suite 600	Indianapolis	IN	46204-2026
317 232-3661	**Archives Div Commission on Public Records** 100 N Senate Ave Indiana State Library Bldg Rm 117	Indianapolis	IN	46204-0000
317 232-1286	**Arts Commission** 47 S Pennsylvania St 6th Fl	Indianapolis	IN	46204-3663
317 232-6201	**Attorney General** 219 State House	Indianapolis	IN	46204-0000
317 232-5610	**Budget Agency** 100 N Senate St State House Rm 212	Indianapolis	IN	46204-0000
812 254-1040	**Bureau of Mines & Mining Safety** 6 NE 21st St	Washington	IN	47501-3134
317 232-1900	**Commission for Higher Education** 101 W Ohio St Suite 550	Indianapolis	IN	46204-1971
317 232-6201	**Consumer Protection Div** 219 State House	Indianapolis	IN	46204-0000
317 232-3114	**Department of Administration** 100 N Senate Ave Rm 508	Indianapolis	IN	46204-2215
317 232-8801	**Department of Commerce** 1 N Capitol Ave Suite 700	Indianapolis	IN	46204-2026
317 232-5766	**Department of Corrections** 100 N Senate Ave State Office Bldg Suite 804	Indianapolis	IN	46204-0000
317 232-6610	**Department of Education** 229 State House	Indianapolis	IN	46204-2798
317 232-7670	**Department of Employment & Training Services** 100 N Senate Ave	Indianapolis	IN	46204-2201
317 232-3210	**Department of Environmental Management** 105 S Meridian St	Indianapolis	IN	46225-0000
317 232-2385	**Department of Insurance** 311 W Washington St Suite 300	Indianapolis	IN	46204-2720
317 232-2663	**Department of Labor** 100 N Senate Ave State Office Bldg Rm 1013	Indianapolis	IN	46204-0000
317 232-4020	**Department of Natural Resources** State Office Bldg Rm 608	Indianapolis	IN	46204-0000
317 232-2101	**Department of Revenue** 100 N Senate Ave	Indianapolis	IN	46204-2253
317 232-5115	**Department of Transportation** 100 N Senate Ave	Indianapolis	IN	46204-2208
317 232-8940	**Division of Energy Policy** 1 N Capitol St	Indianapolis	IN	46204-2026
317 633-0147	**Division of Industrial Hygiene & Radiological Health** 1330 W Michigan St	Indianapolis	IN	46206-0000
317 232-4055	**Division of Oil & Gas** 309 W Washington St Old Trails Bldg Suite 601	Indianapolis	IN	46204-2721
317 232-4161	**Division of Water** 2475 Directors Row	Indianapolis	IN	46241-4938
317 232-3830	**Emergency Management Agency** 100 N Senate Ave Rm 90B	Indianapolis	IN	46204-2252
317 232-4567	**Governor** 206 State House	Indianapolis	IN	46204-0000
219 874-7258	**Indiana State Prison** PO Box 41	Michigan City	IN	46360-0440
317 232-4545	**Lieutenant Governor** 333 State House	Indianapolis	IN	46201-0000
317 232-8222	**Office of Air Management** 105 S Meridian St Rm 201	Indianapolis	IN	46225-1016
317 232-4454	**Office of Solid & Hazardous Waste Management** 105 S Meridian St	Indianapolis	IN	46225-0000
317 232-5726	**Parole Services Section** 100 N Senate Ave State Office Bldg Suite 804	Indianapolis	IN	46204-2218
317 232-3032	**Procurement Div** 100 N Senate Ave	Indianapolis	IN	46204-2208
317 232-2980	**Professional Licensing Agency** 100 N Senate Ave	Indianapolis	IN	46204-2208
317 232-2490	**Public Defender Council** 309 W Washington St Suite 401	Indianapolis	IN	46204-2700
317 633-8512	**Public Health Statistics** 1330 W Michigan St Rm 332	Indianapolis	IN	46206-0000
317 232-3000	**Public Works Div** 100 N Senate Ave Rm 510	Indianapolis	IN	46204-2215
317 232-6531	**Secretary of State** 201 State House	Indianapolis	IN	46204-0000
317 232-6681	**Securities Div** 1 N Capitol St Suite 560	Indianapolis	IN	46204-2227
317 633-8400	**State Board of Health** 1330 W Michigan St	Indianapolis	IN	46202-2874
317 232-8241	**State Police** 100 N Senate Ave Rm 301	Indianapolis	IN	46204-2259
317 232-1930	**Supreme Court** 217 State House	Indianapolis	IN	46204-0000
317 232-6386	**Treasurer** 242 State House	Indianapolis	IN	46204-0000
317 232-8087	**Unemployment Insurance** 10 N Senate Ave	Indianapolis	IN	46204-2277
317 232-2700	**Utility Regulatory Commission** 913 State Office Bldg	Indianapolis	IN	46204-0000
219 785-2511	**Westville Correctional Center** 1100 W County Rd	Westville	IN	46391-0000

IOWA

515 281-5011	**State Government Information** E 10th & Grand Ave	Des Moines	IA	50319-0001
515 281-4451	**Arts Council** 1223 E Court Ave State Capitol Complex	Des Moines	IA	50319-0001
515 281-5164	**Attorney General** 1300 E Walnut St	Des Moines	IA	50319-0001
515 281-4817	**Board of Parole** 523 E 12th St Capitol Annex Basement	Des Moines	IA	50319-0001
515 281-5526	**Bureau of Job Insurance** 1000 E Grand Ave	Des Moines	IA	50319-0001
515 281-3007	**Bureau of Library/Archives** 600 E Locust St	Des Moines	IA	50319-0001
515 281-5926	**Consumer Protection Div** 1300 E Walnut St	Des Moines	IA	50319-0001
515 281-5321	**Department of Agriculture & Land Stewardship** E 9th & Grand Ave	Des Moines	IA	50319-0001
515 281-7400	**Department of Commerce** 1918 SE Hulsizer Ave	Ankeny	IA	50021-3941
515 281-4811	**Department of Corrections** 523 E 12th St Capitol Annex	Des Moines	IA	50319-0001
515 281-7636	**Department of Economic Development** 200 E Grand Ave	Des Moines	IA	50309-0000
515 281-5294	**Department of Education** Grimes State Office Bldg	Des Moines	IA	50319-0001
515 281-5361	**Department of Employment Services** 1000 E Grand Ave	Des Moines	IA	50319-0000
515 281-3322	**Department of Management** 1070 E Grand Ave State Capitol Bldg Rm 12	Des Moines	IA	50319-0001
515 281-5145	**Department of Natural Resources** 900 E Grand Ave	Des Moines	IA	50319-0001
515 281-8852	*Air Quality & Solid Waste Protection Bureau* 900 E Grand Ave	Des Moines	IA	50319-0001
515 281-8681	*Energy Bureau* 900 E Grand Ave Wallis State Office Bldg	Des Moines	IA	50319-0001
515 281-5605	**Department of Public Health** 321 E 12th St	Des Moines	IA	50319-0001
515 281-3112	**Department of Revenue & Finance** 1300 E Walnut St	Des Moines	IA	50319-0001
515 239-1101	**Department of Transportation** 800 Lincoln Way	Ames	IA	50010-6915
515 281-3231	**Disaster Services Div** 1300 E Walnut St	Des Moines	IA	50319-0001
515 281-5934	**Division of Industrial Services** 1000 E Grand Ave	Des Moines	IA	50319-0001
515 281-3606	**Division of Labor** 1000 E Grand Ave	Des Moines	IA	50319-0001
515 281-4159	**Employment Appeal Board** Lucas State Office Bldg 2nd Fl	Des Moines	IA	50319-0001
515 281-6284	**Environmental Protection Div** 900 E Grand Ave	Des Moines	IA	50319-0001
515 281-5856	**General Services Dept** 1305 E Walnut St Hoover Bldg	Des Moines	IA	50319-0001
515 281-5211	**Governor** State Capitol	Des Moines	IA	50319-0001
515 239-1124	**Highway Div** 800 Lincoln Way	Ames	IA	50010-6915
515 281-5705	**Insurance Div** E 12th & Walnut Sts 6th Fl	Des Moines	IA	50319-0001
319 372-5432	**Iowa State Penitentiary** PO Box 316	Fort Madison	IA	52627-0316
515 281-3421	**Lieutenant Governor** State Capitol	Des Moines	IA	50319-0001
319 462-3504	**Men's Reformatory** PO Box B	Anamosa	IA	52205-0010
515 281-4126	**Professional Licensing & Regulation** 1918 SE Hulsizer Ave	Ankeny	IA	50021-0000
515 281-5981	**Purchasing Div** 1305 E Walnut St Hoover Bldg Level A	Des Moines	IA	50319-0001
515 281-3183	**Real Estate Commission** 1918 SE Hulsizer Ave	Ankeny	IA	50021-0000
515 281-5864	**Secretary of State** State House	Des Moines	IA	50319-0001
515 281-4441	**Securities Bureau** Lucas State Office Bldg 2nd Fl	Des Moines	IA	50319-0001
515 281-3934	**State Board of Regents** E 12th & Grand Sts Old Historical Bldg	Des Moines	IA	50319-0001
515 281-5824	**State Patrol** E 9th & Grand Ave	Des Moines	IA	50319-0001
515 281-5911	**Supreme Court** State Capitol Ground Fl	Des Moines	IA	50319-0001
515 281-5366	**Treasurer** Hoover State Office Bldg 1st Fl	Des Moines	IA	50319-0001
515 281-5256	**Utilities Board** E 12th & Walnut Sts Lucas Bldg 5th Fl	Des Moines	IA	50319-0001
515 281-4944	**Vital Records Section** 321 E 12th St	Des Moines	IA	50319-0001

KANSAS

913 296-0111	**State Government Information** 915 SW Harrison St	Topeka	KS	66612-1505
913 296-3251	**Archives & Records** 120 W 10th St	Topeka	KS	66612-0000
913 296-3335	**Arts Commission** 700 SW Jackson St Suite 1004	Topeka	KS	66603-3742
913 296-2215	**Attorney General** 301 W 10th St 2nd Fl	Topeka	KS	66612-0000
913 296-3558	**Board of Agriculture** 109 SW 9th St	Topeka	KS	66612-1215
913 296-3421	**Board of Regents** 400 SW 8th St	Topeka	KS	66603-3958
913 296-1540	**Bureau of Air Quality & Radiation Control** Forbes Field Bldg 740	Topeka	KS	66620-0001
913 296-1593	**Bureau of Waste Management** Forbes Field Bldg 740	Topeka	KS	66620-0001
913 296-3751	**Consumer Protection Div** 301 W 10th St	Topeka	KS	66612-0000
913 296-3011	**Department of Administration** 9th & Jackson Sts State Capitol Rm 263-E	Topeka	KS	66612-0000
913 296-3317	**Department of Corrections** 900 SW Jackson St Landon State Office Bldg 4th Fl	Topeka	KS	66612-1284
913 296-3201	**Department of Education** 120 E 10th St	Topeka	KS	66612-0000
913 296-5076	**Department of Human Resources** 401 Topeka Blvd	Topeka	KS	66603-0000
913 296-3041	**Department of Revenue** State Office Bldg 2nd Fl	Topeka	KS	66612-0000
913 296-3461	**Department of Transportation** Docking State Office Bldg 7th Fl	Topeka	KS	66612-0000
913 266-1000	**Division of Emergency Preparedness** 2800 Topeka Ave	Topeka	KS	66601-0000
913 296-1535	**Division of Environment** Forbes Field Bldg 740	Topeka	KS	66620-0001
913 296-7475	**Division of Labor-Management Relations & Employment Standards** 1430 SW Topeka Blvd	Topeka	KS	66612-1853
913 296-2376	**Division of Purchasing** 900 SW Jackson St Rm 102 N	Topeka	KS	66612-1220
913 296-3441	**Division of Worker's Compensation** 800 S W Jackson St Merchants Bank Tower Suite 600	Topeka	KS	66612-1227
913 271-3170	**Energy Programs Div Kansas Corporation Commission** 1500 SW Arrowhead Rd	Topeka	KS	66604-0000
913 296-3232	**Governor** 9th & Jackson Sts State Capitol 2nd Fl	Topeka	KS	66612-1590
913 296-6800	**Highway Patrol** 122 SW 7th St	Topeka	KS	66603-3847
913 296-4505	**Indigents' Defense Services** 900 SW Jackson St Rm 506 N	Topeka	KS	66612-1255
913 296-3483	**Industrial Development Div Kansas Dept of Commerce** 400 SW 8th St Suite 500	Topeka	KS	66603-0000
913 296-4386	**Indusfrial Safety & Health Section** 512 W 6th St	Topeka	KS	66603-0000
913 296-3071	**Insurance Dept** 420 SW 9th St	Topeka	KS	66612-1678
316 662-2321	**Kansas State Industrial Reformatory** PO Box 1568	Hutchinson	KS	67504-1568
913 727-3235	**Kansas State Penitentiary** Kansas Ave	Lansing	KS	66043-0002
913 296-2213	**Lieutenant Governor** State Capitol Rm 222-S	Topeka	KS	66612-0000
913 296-1400	**Office of Vital Statistics** 900 SW Jackson St	Topeka	KS	66612-1290
913 296-3469	**Parole Board** 900 SW Jackson St 4th Fl	Topeka	KS	66612-1236
913 296-3411	**Real Estate Commission** 900 SW Jackson St Rm 501	Topeka	KS	66612-1226
913 296-2236	**Secretary of State** State Capitol 2nd Fl	Topeka	KS	66612-0000
913 296-3307	**Securities Commissioner** 618 S Kansas Ave 2nd Fl	Topeka	KS	66603-3804
913 296-3289	**State Historical Society** 120 W 10th St	Topeka	KS	66612-1291
913 296-3229	**Supreme Court** 301 SW 10th St	Topeka	KS	66612-1599
913 296-3171	**Treasurer** 900 Jackson St Suite 201	Topeka	KS	66612-1235
913 296-1796	**Unemployment Insurance Program** 1431 Topeka Ave	Topeka	KS	66612-0000
913 296-4191	**Utilities Div** Docking State Office Bldg 4th Fl	Topeka	KS	66612-0000
913 296-3185	**Water Office** 109 SW 9th St Suite 200	Topeka	KS	66612-1249

KENTUCKY

502 564-2500	**State Government Information** State Capitol Annex Rm 52	Frankfort	KY	40601-3410
502 564-7600	**Attorney General** Capitol Ave Rm 116	Frankfort	KY	40601-0000
502 564-4726	**Corrections Cabinet** Holmes & High Sts State Office Bldg 5th Fl	Frankfort	KY	40601-0000
502 564-3553	**Council on Higher Education** 1050 US Hwy 127 S	Frankfort	KY	40601-4326
502 564-5331	**Department for Employment Services** 275 E Main St	Frankfort	KY	40621-0001
502 564-3970	**Department for Health Services** 275 E Main St	Frankfort	KY	40621-0001
502 875-7000	**Department for Libraries & Archives** 300 Coffee Tree Rd	Frankfort	KY	40601-0000
502 564-4696	**Department of Agriculture** 500 Capitol Plaza Towers 7th Fl	Frankfort	KY	40601-1970
502 564-4770	**Department of Education** Capitol Plaza Tower 1st Fl	Frankfort	KY	40601-1972
502 564-2150	**Department of Environmental Protection** 18 Reilly Rd	Frankfort	KY	40601-1139
502 564-4890	**Department of Highways** Clinton & High Sts	Frankfort	KY	40622-0001
502 564-3630	**Department of Insurance** 229 W Main St	Frankfort	KY	40601-0000
606 254-0367	**Department of Mines & Minerals** 3572 Iron Works Pike	Lexington	KY	40511-0000
502 564-5213	**Department of Public Advocacy** 1264 Louisville Rd Perimeter Pk W	Frankfort	KY	40601-0000
502 695-6300	**Department of State Police** 919 Versailles Rd	Frankfort	KY	40601-4740
502 564-8076	**Department of the Arts** Berry Hill Mansion	Frankfort	KY	40601-0000
502 564-5550	**Department of Workers' Claims** 1270 Louisville Rd Bldg C	Frankfort	KY	40601-0000
502 564-3382	**Division of Air Pollution Control** 316 St Clair Mall	Frankfort	KY	40601-1189
502 564-2200	**Division of Consumer Protection** 209 Saint Clair St	Frankfort	KY	40601-1855
502 564-8682	**Division of Disaster & Emergency Services** Boone National Guard Ctr	Frankfort	KY	40601-1189
502 564-2980	**Division of Engineering** State Capitol Annex Rm 128	Frankfort	KY	40601-0000
502 564-3296	**Division of Occupational & Professional Licensing** PO Box 456	Frankfort	KY	40602-0456

502 564-4510 **Division of Purchases** State Capitol Annex Rm 348 ... Frankfort KY 40601-0000
502 564-2180 **Division of Securities** 911 Leawood Dr ... Frankfort KY 40601-3319
502 564-2900 **Division of Unemployment Insurance** 275 E Main St 2nd Fl E .. Frankfort KY 40621-0001
502 564-6716 **Division of Waste Management** 18 Reilly Rd ... Frankfort KY 40601-1189
502 564-3410 **Division of Water** 18 Reilly Rd ... Frankfort KY 40601-1189
502 564-4240 **Finance & Administration Cabinet**
State Capitol Annex Rm 301 ... Frankfort KY 40601-0000
502 564-2611 **Governor** State Capitol Rm 100 ... Frankfort KY 40601-3492
502 564-7300 **Governors Office for Policy & Management**
State Capitol Annex Rm 209 ... Frankfort KY 40601-0000
502 388-2211 **Kentucky State Penitentiary** Rt 2 & Old Eddyville Rd ... Eddyville KY 42038-9802
502 222-9441 **Kentucky State Reformatory** 3001 W Hwy 146 ... La Grange KY 40032-0001
502 564-3070 **Labor Cabinet** 1049 US Hwy 127 S ... Frankfort KY 40601-0000
502 564-7562 **Lieutenant Governor** State Capitol Rm 142 ... Frankfort KY 40601-0000
502 564-6892 **Occupational Safety & Health Review Commission**
Rt 3 & Millville Rd Mill Creek Pk Suite 4 ... Frankfort KY 40601-9803
606 252-5535 **Office for Coal & Energy Policy** PO Box 11888 ... Lexington KY 40578-1916
502 564-4212 **Office of Vital Statistics** 275 E Main St 1st Fl ... Frankfort KY 40621-0001
606 254-0367 **Oil & Gas Div Dept of Mines & Minerals**
3572 Iron Works Pike ... Lexington KY 40511-8410
502 564-4221 **Probation & Parole Div**
Holmes & High Sts State Office Bldg Rm 514 ... Frankfort KY 40601-0000
502 564-3940 **Public Services Commission** 730 Schenkel Ln ... Frankfort KY 40601-1402
502 425-4273 **Real Estate Commission** 10200 Linn Station Rd Suite 201 ... Louisville KY 40223-0000
502 564-4646 **Retirement Systems** 1260 Louisville Rd ... Frankfort KY 40601-6157
502 564-3226 **Revenue Cabinet** State Capitol Annex Rm 401 ... Frankfort KY 40601-0000
502 564-3490 **Secretary of State** State Capitol Rm 150 ... Frankfort KY 40601-0000
502 564-4720 **Supreme Court** State Capitol Rm 209 ... Frankfort KY 40601-0000
502 564-4890 **Transportation Cabinet** Clinton & High Sts 10th Fl ... Frankfort KY 40622-0001
502 564-4722 **Treasury Dept** State Capitol Annex Rm 129 ... Frankfort KY 40601-0000

LOUISIANA

504 342-6600 **State Government Information** 150 Riverside Mall ... Baton Rouge LA 70801-1303
504 922-1200 **Administrative Offices of Archives Records Management & History**
3851 Essen Ln ... Baton Rouge LA 70809-2137
504 342-1206 **Air Quality Div** PO Box 44096 ... Baton Rouge LA 70804-4096
504 342-7013 **Attorney General** PO Box 94005 ... Baton Rouge LA 70804-9005
504 342-4253 **Board of Regents** 150 Riverside Mall ... Baton Rouge LA 70801-1303
504 342-7071 **Budget Office** State Capitol Annex ... Baton Rouge LA 70804-0401
504 342-7013 **Consumer Protection Section** State Capitol ... Baton Rouge LA 70804-0401
504 922-1234 **Department of Agriculture & Forestry** 5825 Florida Blvd ... Baton Rouge LA 70806-4248
504 342-3602 **Department of Education** 626 N 4th St ... Baton Rouge LA 70802-5321
504 295-8900 **Department of Environmental Quality** 11720 Airline Hwy .. Baton Rouge LA 70817-4401
504 342-9500 **Department of Health & Hospitals**
1201 Capitol Access Rd ... Baton Rouge LA 70802-4438
504 342-5900 **Department of Insurance** 950 N 5th St ... Baton Rouge LA 70802-5213
504 342-3111 **Department of Labor** 1001 N 23rd St ... Baton Rouge LA 70802-3338
504 342-4503 **Department of Natural Resources** 625 N 4th St ... Baton Rouge LA 70802-5364
504 342-6740 **Department of Public Safety & Corrections**
504 Mayflower St ... Baton Rouge LA 70802-6419
504 925-7680 **Department of Revenue & Taxation**
330 N Ardenwood Dr ... Baton Rouge LA 70806-2650
504 379-1200 **Department of Transportation & Development**
1201 Capitol Access Rd ... Baton Rouge LA 70802-4438
504 342-7410 **Division of Administration** PO Box 94095 ... Baton Rouge LA 70804-9095
504 342-6448 **Division of Health Standards**
1201 Capital Access Rd 6th Fl ... Baton Rouge LA 70801-1807
504 342-6609 **Division of Probation & Parole** 504 Mayflower St ... Baton Rouge LA 70802-6419
504 342-8180 **Division of the Arts** 900 Riverside St N Rm 420 ... Baton Rouge LA 70802-5236
504 342-1399 **Energy Div** 625 N 4th St ... Baton Rouge LA 70802-5364
504 379-1220 **Flood Control & Water Management Div**
1201 Capitol Access Rd Rm 211 ... Baton Rouge LA 70802-4438
504 342-7015 **Governor** State Capitol Bldg 4th Fl ... Baton Rouge LA 70804-0402
504 642-3306 **Hunt Correctional Center** PO Box 174 ... Saint Gabriel LA 70776-0174
504 342-7009 **Lieutenant Governor** State Capitol ... Baton Rouge LA 70804-0401
504 655-4411 **Louisiana State Penitentiary** General Delivery ... Angola LA 70712-9999
504 925-4518 **Nuclear Energy Div** 8955 Whitehall Dr ... Baton Rouge LA 70808-3225
504 342-3126 **Occupational Safety & Health Survey** 1001 N 23rd St ... Baton Rouge LA 70805-0000
504 342-5470 **Office of Emergency Preparedness** 625 N 4th St ... Baton Rouge LA 70802-5364
504 342-3124 **Office of Employment Security** 1001 N 23rd St ... Baton Rouge LA 70802-3338
504 379-1208 **Office of Highways** 1201 Capitol Access Rd ... Baton Rouge LA 70804-0000
504 342-4615 **Office of Mineral Resources** 625 N 4th St ... Baton Rouge LA 70802-0000
504 342-1216 **Office of Solid & Hazardous Waste Management**
438 Main ... Baton Rouge LA 70802-0000
504 342-6363 **Office of Water Resources** PO Box 44091 ... Baton Rouge LA 70804-4091
504 342-4404 **Public Service Dept** PO Box 91154 ... Baton Rouge LA 70821-9154
504 342-8010 **Purchasing Section** 950 N 5th St ... Baton Rouge LA 70802-5213
504 925-4800 **Real Estate Commission** 9071 Interline Ave ... Baton Rouge LA 70809-1904
504 342-4479 **Secretary of State** 900 Riverside St N 20th Fl ... Baton Rouge LA 70802-5236
504 925-6117 **State Police** PO Box 66614 ... Baton Rouge LA 70896-6614
504 568-5707 **Supreme Court** 301 Loyola Ave ... New Orleans LA 70112-1841
504 342-0010 **Treasurer** PO Box 44154 ... Baton Rouge LA 70804-4154
504 342-3017 **Unemployment Insurance Services** 1001 N 23rd St ... Baton Rouge LA 70802-3338
504 568-8353 **Vital Records Section** 325 Loyola Ave ... New Orleans LA 70112-1829
504 342-7558 **Worker's Compensation Administration** 1001 N 23rd St ... Baton Rouge LA 70802-0000

MAINE

207 289-1110 **State Government Information** State St ... Augusta ME 04333-0001
207 289-2724 **Arts Commission** 55 Capitol St Stn 25 ... Augusta ME 04333-0001
207 289-3661 **Attorney General** State House Stn 6 ... Augusta ME 04333-0001
207 289-2437 **Bureau of Air Quality Control** Hospital St ... Augusta ME 04333-0001
207 582-8718 **Bureau of Consumer Credit Protection** State House Stn 35 ... Augusta ME 04333-0001
207 289-3201 **Bureau of Health** 151 Capitol St ... Augusta ME 04333-0001
207 582-8707 **Bureau of Insurance** 124 Northern Ave ... Gardiner ME 04344-2809
207 289-3881 **Bureau of Public Improvements**
State Office Bldg Stn 77 Rm 211 ... Augusta ME 04333-0001
207 289-3521 **Bureau of Purchases** Capitol St State House Stn 9 ... Augusta ME 04333-0001
207 289-2950 **Bureau of State Police** 36 Hospital St ... Augusta ME 04333-0001
207 289-2076 **Bureau of Taxation** Capitol St State House Stn 24 ... Augusta ME 04330-0000
207 289-3871 **Department of Agriculture** Blossom Ln State House Stn 28 ... Augusta ME 04333-0001
207 289-2711 **Department of Corrections** State House Stn 111 Rm 400 ... Augusta ME 04333-0001
207 289-2183 **Department of Educational & Cultural Services**
State House Stn 119 ... Augusta ME 04333-0001
207 289-7688 **Department of Environmental Protection** State House Stn 17 ... Augusta ME 04333-0001
207 289-3446 **Department of Finance** State Office Bldg Rm 317 ... Augusta ME 04333-0000
207 289-3788 **Department of Labor** 20 Union St State House Stn 54 ... Augusta ME 04333-0001
207 289-2316 *Bureau of Employment Security* 20 Union St ... Augusta ME 04330-0000
207 289-2551 **Department of Transportation** Child St State House Stn 16 ... Augusta ME 04333-0001
207 582-8723 **Division of Licensing & Enforcement Professional & Financial Regulation**
State House Stn 35 ... Augusta ME 04333-0001
207 289-6460 **Division of Safety** State House Stn 82 ... Augusta ME 04333-0000
207 289-4080 **Emergency Management Agency** State Office Bldg Stn 72 ... Augusta ME 04333-0000
207 289-6000 **Energy Divison Department of Economic & Community Development**
State House Stn 53 ... Augusta ME 04333-0001

207 289-3531 **Governor** State House Stn 1 ... Augusta ME 04333-000
207 892-6716 **Maine Correctional Center** 17 Mallison Falls Rd ... Windham ME 04062-413
207 354-2535 **Maine State Prison** PO Box A ... Thomaston ME 04861-050
207 289-3001 **Office of Data Research & Vital Statistics**
32 Winthrop St State House Stn 11 ... Augusta ME 04333-001
207 289-3261 **Planning Office** 184 State St State House Stn 38 ... Augusta ME 04333-000
207 289-3831 **Public Utilities Commission** 242 State St State House Stn 18 ... Augusta ME 04333-000
207 582-8727 **Real Estate Commission** State House Stn 35 ... Augusta ME 04333-000
207 289-1090 **Secretary of State** State House Stn 148 ... Augusta ME 04333-000
207 289-5790 **State Archives** State House Stn 84 ... Augusta ME 04333-0001
207 879-4765 **Supreme Judicial Court** 142 Federal St ... Portland ME 04101-4161
207 289-2771 **Treasury Dept** State Office Bldg Rm 318 ... Augusta ME 04333-0001
207 289-3831 **Water & Gas Div** 242 State St State House Stn 18 ... Augusta ME 04333-0001
207 289-3751 **Worker's Compensation Commission**
Deering Bldg AMHI Grounds Stn 27 ... Augusta ME 04333-0001

MARYLAND

301 974-3431 **State Government Information** 80 Calvert St Rm 105 ... Annapolis MD 21401-1931
301 631-3255 **Air Management Administration** 2500 Broening Hwy ... Baltimore MD 21224-6612
301 333-8232 **Arts Council** 15 W Mulberry St ... Baltimore MD 21201-4479
301 576-6300 **Attorney General** 200 St Paul Pl 2nd Fl ... Baltimore MD 21202-2004
301 974-3443 **Board of Public Works** Goldstein Treasury Bldg Rm 213 ... Annapolis MD 21404-0000
301 689-4136 **Bureau of Mines** 69 Hill St ... Frostburg MD 21532-2299
301 528-8662 **Consumer Protection Div** 200 St Paul Pl ... Baltimore MD 21202-2022
301 841-5880 **Department of Agriculture** 50 Harry S Truman Pkwy ... Annapolis MD 21401-7080
301 333-2000 **Department of Education** 200 W Baltimore St ... Baltimore MD 21201-2595
301 225-6500 **Department of Health & Mental Hygiene** 201 W Preston St ... Baltimore MD 21201-2323
301 974-2700 **Department of Housing & Community Development/Office of Management Services**
45 Calvert St ... Annapolis MD 21401-1940
301 974-3041 **Department of Natural Resources** 580 Taylor Ave ... Annapolis MD 21401-0000
301 859-7397 **Department of Transportation** BWI Airport ... Baltimore MD 21201-0000
301 764-4100 **Division of Corrections** 6776 Reisterstown Rd Suite 309 ... Baltimore MD 21215-2311
301 333-4195 **Division of Labor & Industry** 501 St Paul Pl 3rd Fl ... Baltimore MD 21202-2235
301 764-4276 **Division of Parole & Probation**
6776 Reisterstown Rd Suite 305 ... Baltimore MD 21215-2311
301 576-6360 **Division of Securities** 200 St Paul Pl 20th Fl ... Baltimore MD 21202-1958
301 764-3034 **Division of Vital Records** 4201 Patterson Ave ... Baltimore MD 21215-0000
301 651-9000 **Eastern Correctional Institution** RR 1 Box 500 ... Westover MD 21871-9799
301 261-8596 **Environmental Service** 2020 Industrial Dr ... Annapolis MD 21401-2995
301 554-5500 **Geological Survey** 2300 Saint Paul St ... Baltimore MD 21218-5210
301 974-3901 **Governor** State House ... Annapolis MD 21401-0000
301 321-3521 **Governor's Office of Justice Assistants**
300 E Joppa Rd Suite 1105 ... Towson MD 21204-3016
301 333-1111 **Highway Administration** 707 N Calvert St ... Baltimore MD 21202-3615
301 974-3441 **Income Tax Div** 110 Carroll St ... Annapolis MD 21411-0001
301 333-6300 **Insurance Div** 501 St Paul Pl 7th Fl ... Baltimore MD 21202-2235
301 974-2804 **Lieutenant Governor** State House 2nd Fl ... Annapolis MD 21401-0000
301 791-7200 **Maryland Correctional Training Center**
18800 Rocksbury Rd ... Hagerstown MD 21744-0000
301 225-4500 **Office of Planning** 301 W Preston St Rm 1101 ... Baltimore MD 21201-2305
301 974-2261 **Power Plant & Environmental Review Div** 580 Taylor Ave ... Annapolis MD 21401-0000
301 333-4826 **Public Defender System** 201 Saint Paul Pl ... Baltimore MD 21202-2001
301 333-6000 **Public Service Commission** 231 E Baltimore St 14th Fl ... Baltimore MD 21202-3486
301 225-4620 **Purchasing Bureau** 301 W Preston St Rm M2 ... Baltimore MD 21201-2367
301 333-6230 **Real Estate Commission** 501 St Paul Pl ... Baltimore MD 21202-2269
301 974-5521 **Secretary of State** 16 Francis St ... Annapolis MD 21401-1733
301 974-3915 **State Archives** 350 Rowe Blvd ... Annapolis MD 21401-1685
301 974-2971 **State Board for Higher Education** 16 Francis St ... Annapolis MD 21401-1781
301 974-3341 **State Court of Appeals** 361 Rowe Blvd 4th Fl ... Annapolis MD 21401-1698
301 653-4219 **State Police** 1201 Reisterstown Rd ... Pikesville MD 21208-3898
301 974-3533 **Treasurer** 80 Calvert St Rm 109 ... Annapolis MD 21401-1931
301 333-5309 **Unemployment Insurance Div** 1100 N Eutaw St Rm 501 ... Baltimore MD 21201-2206
301 974-3846 **Water Resources Administration** 580 Taylor Ave ... Annapolis MD 21401-2397
301 333-4775 **Workers' Compensation Commission** 6 N Liberty St 9th Fl ... Baltimore MD 21201-3785

MASSACHUSETTS

617 727-7030 **State Government Information** 1 Ashburton Pl ... Boston MA 02108-1518
617 727-2816 **Archives Div** 220 Morrissey Blvd ... Boston MA 02125-0000
617 727-2200 **Attorney General** 1 Ashburton Pl ... Boston MA 02108-1698
617 727-8872 **Board of Regents of Higher Education**
1 Ashburton Pl Rm 1401 ... Boston MA 02108-1518
617 727-7376 **Board of Registration of Real Estate**
100 Cambridge St Rm 1518 ... Boston MA 02202-0001
508 820-2000 **Civil Defense Agency** 400 Worcester Rd ... Framingham MA 01701-0000
617 482-6212 **Committee for Public Counsel Services**
80 Boylston St Suite 600 ... Boston MA 02116-4802
617 727-6300 **Committee on Criminal Justice** 100 Cambridge St ... Boston MA 02202-0001
617 727-8400 **Consumer Protection Div** 131 Tremont St ... Boston MA 02111-1317
617 727-3301 **Department of Corrections** 100 Cambridge St ... Boston MA 02202-0001
617 770-7300 **Department of Education** 1385 Hancock St ... Quincy MA 02169-5183
617 727-6600 **Department of Employment & Training** 19 Staniford St ... Boston MA 02114-2526
617 727-3159 **Department of Environmental Management** 100 Cambridge St .. Boston MA 02202-0001
617 292-5961 **Department of Environmental Protection** 1 Winter St 4th Fl ... Boston MA 02108-4703
617 727-3000 **Department of Food & Agriculture** 100 Cambridge St ... Boston MA 02202-0001
617 727-3454 **Department of Labor & Industries** 100 Cambridge St 11th Fl ... Boston MA 02202-0001
617 727-2882 **Department of Procurement & General Services**
1 Ashburton Pl Rm 1017 ... Boston MA 02108-1518
617 727-0201 **Department of Public Health** 150 Tremont St ... Boston MA 02111-1197
617 566-4500 **Department of Public Safety** 1010 Commonwealth Ave ... Boston MA 02215-1200
617 727-3500 **Department of Public Utilities** 100 Cambridge St 12th Fl ... Boston MA 02202-0001
617 973-7800 **Department of Public Works** 10 Park Plaza ... Boston MA 02116-3973
617 727-4201 **Department of Revenue** 100 Cambridge St ... Boston MA 02204-0000
617 292-5593 **Division of Air Quality Control** 1 Winter St 8th Fl ... Boston MA 02108-4703
617 727-3333 **Division of Insurance** 280 Friend St ... Boston MA 02114-1808
617 727-3246 **Division of Neighborhoods & Economic Opportunity**
100 Cambridge St Rm 1103 ... Boston MA 02202-0001
617 727-3074 **Division of Registration** 100 Cambridge St Rm 1520 ... Boston MA 02202-0001
617 727-3267 **Division of Water Resources** 100 Cambridge St Rm 1304 ... Boston MA 02202-0001
617 727-1136 **Energy Facilities Siting Council** 100 Cambridge St Suite 2109 ... Boston MA 02202-0001
617 727-2040 **Executive Office for Administration & Finance**
State House Rm 373 ... Boston MA 02133-0000
617 727-4732 **Executive Office of Energy Resources**
100 Cambridge St Rm 1500 ... Boston MA 02202-0001
617 727-9800 **Executive Office of Environmental Affairs**
100 Cambridge St 20th Fl ... Boston MA 02202-0001
617 727-3600 **Governor** State House Executive Office ... Boston MA 02133-0000
617 727-4900 **Industrial Accident Board** 600 Washington St 7th Fl ... Boston MA 02111-1704
617 727-7200 **Lieutenant Governor** State House Rm 259 ... Boston MA 02133-0000
617 727-1480 **Massachusetts Correctional Institution** 2 Clark St ... Norfolk MA 02056-0000
617 727-3668 **Massachusetts Cultural Council** 80 Boylston St 10th Fl ... Boston MA 02116-4802
617 727-1686 **Massachusetts State Prison** 2405 N Main St ... South Walpole MA 02071-0000
617 727-3281 **Parole Board** 27-43 Wormwood St 3rd Fl ... Boston MA 02210-0000
617 727-5300 **Probation Office of the Commissioner** 1 Ashburton Pl Rm 405 .. Boston MA 02108-1518
617 727-0036 **Registry of Vital Records & Statistics** 150 Tremont St ... Boston MA 02111-1126

State Government

617 727-7030	**Secretary of State** State House Rm 337	Boston	MA	02133-1003
617 727-3548	**Securities Div** 1 Ashburton Pl Rm 1701	Boston	MA	02108-1552
617 367-7770	**State Board of Retirement** 1 Ashburton Pl Rm 1219	Boston	MA	02108-1506
617 725-8055	**Supreme Court** 1412 Pemberton Sq	Boston	MA	02108-0000
617 973-7031	**Transportation Dept** 10 Park Plaza	Boston	MA	02116-3933
617 367-6900	**Treasurer** State House Rm 227	Boston	MA	02133-0000

MICHIGAN

517 373-1837	**State Government Information** PO Box 30026	Lansing	MI	48909-7526
517 373-7023	**Air Quality Div Dept of Natural Resources** PO Box 30028	Lansing	MI	48909-7528
517 373-1110	**Attorney General** 525 W Ottawa St	Lansing	MI	48913-0001
517 335-9218	**Bureau of Environmental & Occupational Health** 3423 N Logan St	Lansing	MI	48906-0000
517 373-0510	**Bureau of History** 717 W Allegan Ave	Lansing	MI	48918-0001
517 322-6215	**Bureau of Retirement Systems** PO Box 30171	Lansing	MI	48909-7671
517 373-3196	**Bureau of Revenue** Allegan St Treasury Bldg 1st Fl	Lansing	MI	48922-0001
313 876-5465	**Bureau of Unemployment Insurance** 7310 Woodward Ave Rm 506	Detroit	MI	48202-3152
517 373-3490	**Bureau of Workers' Disability Compensation** 201 N Washington St 2nd Fl	Lansing	MI	48933-0000
517 335-8676	**Center for Health Statistics** 3423 N Logan St	Lansing	MI	48906-2934
517 373-0947	**Consumers Council** 106 W Allegan St	Lansing	MI	48933-1793
517 334-6206	**Corporation & Securities Bureau** 6546 Mercantile Way	Lansing	MI	48909-0000
313 475-1358	**Corrections Camp Program** 6000 Maute Rd	Grass Lake	MI	49240-9225
313 256-3735	**Council for the Arts** 1200 6th St 11th Fl	Detroit	MI	48226-2418
517 373-1050	**Department of Agriculture** PO Box 30017	Lansing	MI	48909-7517
517 373-7230	**Department of Commerce** 525 W Ottawa St 4th Fl	Lansing	MI	48933-1067
517 373-0720	**Department of Corrections** PO Box 30003	Lansing	MI	48909-7503
517 373-3354	**Department of Education** 608 W Allegan St	Lansing	MI	48909-0000
517 373-9600	**Department of Labor** Victor Bldg 201 N Washington 5th Floor	Lansing	MI	48933-0000
517 373-1870	**Department of Licensing & Regulation** 611 W Ottawa St	Lansing	MI	48909-0000
517 373-1220	**Department of Natural Resources** PO Box 30028	Lansing	MI	48909-7528
517 373-3200	**Department of the Treasury** 430 W Allegan St Treasury Building	Lansing	MI	48922-0001
517 373-2090	**Department of Transportation** 425 W Ottawa St 4th Fl	Lansing	MI	48933-1532
517 335-4933	**Division of Postsecondary Education** 608 W Allegan St	Lansing	MI	48933-0000
517 373-6271	**Emergency Management Div** 300 S Washington Sq Suite 300	Lansing	MI	48913-0001
313 876-5500	**Employment Security Commission** 7310 Woodward Ave	Detroit	MI	48202-3152
517 334-6951	**Geological Survey Div** PO Box 30028	Lansing	MI	48909-0000
517 373-3400	**Governor** State Capitol Bldg 2nd Fl	Lansing	MI	48913-0001
517 373-9273	**Insurance Bureau** PO Box 30220	Lansing	MI	48909-7720
517 373-6800	**Lieutenant Governor** State Capitol Bldg Rm 128	Lansing	MI	48913-0001
517 373-6655	**Office of Criminal Justice** 320 S Walnut St	Lansing	MI	48933-2014
517 373-0330	**Office of Purchasing** PO Box 30026	Lansing	MI	48909-7526
517 373-0270	**Parole Board** Grandview Plaza 2nd Fl	Lansing	MI	48909-0000
517 335-8000	**Public Health** 3500 N Logan	Lansing	MI	48906-2933
517 334-6424	**Public Service Commission** 6545 Mercantile Way	Lansing	MI	48909-0000
517 373-2510	**Secretary of State** Treasury Bldg 1st Fl	Lansing	MI	48918-0001
517 332-2521	**State Police** 714 S Harrison Rd	East Lansing	MI	48823-5196
517 788-7560	**State Prison of Southern Michigan** 4000 Cooper St	Jackson	MI	49201-9503
517 373-0120	**Supreme Court** PO Box 30052	Lansing	MI	48909-7552
517 373-1949	**Surface Water Quality Div** PO Box 30028	Lansing	MI	48909-7528

MINNESOTA

612 296-6013	**State Government Information** 50 Sherburne Ave Rm G18B	Saint Paul	MN	55155-0001
612 297-2603	**Arts Board** 432 Summit Ave	Saint Paul	MN	55102-2624
612 296-6196	**Attorney General** 102 State Capitol Bldg	Saint Paul	MN	55155-0001
612 296-4645	**Building Construction Div** 50 Sherburne Ave Rm G10	Saint Paul	MN	55155-0001
612 296-3353	**Consumer Div** 117 University Ave Ford Bldg Rm 124	Saint Paul	MN	55155-0001
612 297-3219	**Department of Agriculture** 90 Plato Blvd W	Saint Paul	MN	55107-2094
612 296-4026	**Department of Commerce** 133 E 7th St	Saint Paul	MN	55101-0000
612 642-0282	**Department of Corrections** 450 Syndicate St N Suite 300	Saint Paul	MN	55104-4107
612 297-2436	**Department of Criminal Justice** 658 Cedar St Centennial Bldg Suite 300	Saint Paul	MN	55155-0001
612 296-2358	**Department of Education** 550 Cedar St	Saint Paul	MN	55101-2270
612 296-2438	**Department of Finance** 658 Cedar St 400 Centennial Bldg	Saint Paul	MN	55155-0001
612 296-6107	**Department of Labor & Industry** 443 Lafayette Rd	Saint Paul	MN	55155-0001
612 296-2549	**Department of Natural Resources** 500 Lafayette Rd	Saint Paul	MN	55155-0001
612 296-7107	**Department of Public Service** 150 Kellogg Blvd E	Saint Paul	MN	55101-1421
612 296-3401	**Department of Revenue** 10 River Park Plaza	Saint Paul	MN	55146-0001
612 297-1291	**Department of Trade & Economic Development** 150 E Kellog Blvd 900 American Center Bldg	Saint Paul	MN	55101-1495
612 296-7331	**Division of Air Quality** 520 Lafayette Rd	Saint Paul	MN	55155-0001
612 296-2233	**Division of Emergency Management** Aurora Ave & Park St State Capitol Rm B-5	Saint Paul	MN	55155-0000
612 296-4807	**Division of Minerals** 500 Lafayette Rd	Saint Paul	MN	55155-0001
612 643-3403	**Division of Solid & Hazardous Waste** 520 Lafayette Rd	Saint Paul	MN	55155-0001
612 296-4810	**Division of Water** 500 Lafayette Rd	Saint Paul	MN	55155-0001
612 296-4657	**Economic Opportunity Office** 150 E Kellogg Blvd Rm 670	Saint Paul	MN	55101-1421
612 297-4685	**Energy Div Dept of Public Service** 150 Kellogg Blvd E Suite 900	Saint Paul	MN	55101-1421
612 296-2603	**Environmental Quality Board** 658 Cedar St Centennial Bldg Suite 300	Saint Paul	MN	55155-0001
612 296-3391	**Governor** 130 State Capitol Bldg	Saint Paul	MN	55155-0001
612 623-5000	**Health Dept** 717 Delaware St SE	Minneapolis	MN	55440-0000
612 296-9665	**Higher Education Coordinating Board** 550 Cedar St Capitol Square Bldg Rm 400	Saint Paul	MN	55101-2233
612 296-2374	**Lieutenant Governor** State Capitol Bldg Rm 121	Saint Paul	MN	55155-0001
612 296-6152	**Materials Management Div** 50 Sherburne Ave Rm 112	Saint Paul	MN	55155-0001
612 255-5000	**Minnesota Correctional Facility Saint Cloud** PO Box B	Saint Cloud	MN	56302-1000
612 779-2700	**Minnesota Correctional Facility Stillwater** 5500 Pickett Ave N	Stillwater	MN	55082-0000
612 642-0270	**Office of Adult & Juvenile Release** 450 Syndicate St N Bigelow Bldg Rm 300	Saint Paul	MN	55104-0000
612 297-2325	**Planning Agency** 658 Cedar St Centennial Bldg Suite 300	Saint Paul	MN	55155-0001
612 296-2878	**Power Plant Siting Section** 658 Cedar St Centennial Office Bldg Suite 300	Saint Paul	MN	55155-0001
612 625-5008	**Public Defender** University of Minnesota 95 Law Ctr	Minneapolis	MN	55455-0000
612 296-3266	**Secretary of State** 180 State Office Bldg	Saint Paul	MN	55155-0001
612 296-4520	**Securities Registration Unit** 133 E 7th St	Saint Paul	MN	55101-0000
612 296-6980	**State Archives** 1500 Mississippi St	Saint Paul	MN	55101-3101
612 296-3080	**State Patrol Div** Transportation Bldg Rm 107	Saint Paul	MN	55155-0001
612 296-2581	**Supreme Court** 230 State Capitol Bldg	Saint Paul	MN	55155-0001
612 296-7091	**Treasurer** 50 Sherburne Ave Rm 303	Saint Paul	MN	55155-0001
612 623-5121	**Vital Records & Statistics** PO Box 9441	Minneapolis	MN	55440-9441
612 296-6490	**Worker's Compensation Div** 443 Lafayette Rd	Saint Paul	MN	55155-0000

MISSISSIPPI

601 359-1000	**State Government Information** 239 N Lamar St	Jackson	MS	39201-1311
601 359-6030	**Arts Commission** 239 N Lamar St Suite 207	Jackson	MS	39201-1393
601 359-3680	**Attorney General** 450 High St Gartin Bldg	Jackson	MS	39201-1081
601 961-5171	**Bureau of Pollution Control** 2380 Hwy 80 W	Jackson	MS	39204-2312
601 359-3409	**Bureau of Purchasing** 1504 Walter Sillers Bldg	Jackson	MS	39201-1113
601 354-6018	**Consumer Protection Div** 802 N State St	Jackson	MS	39202-2605
601 359-6850	**Department of Archives & History** 100 S State St	Jackson	MS	39201-2812
601 354-6454	**Department of Corrections** 723 N President St	Jackson	MS	39202-3097
601 359-3449	**Department of Economic Development** 550 High St Suite 1400	Jackson	MS	39201-1113
601 961-4733	**Department of Economics & Community Development Energy & Transportation Div** 510 George St Suite 101	Jackson	MS	39202-0000
601 359-3513	**Department of Education** PO Box 771	Jackson	MS	39205-0771
601 961-5000	**Department of Enviromental Quality** PO Box 20305	Jackson	MS	39289-1305
601 359-3402	**Department of Finance & Administration** 550 High St Suite 906	Jackson	MS	39201-1113
601 960-7635	**Department of Health** 2423 N State St	Jackson	MS	39216-0000
601 359-3569	**Department of Insurance** 550 High St Walter Sillers Bldg Suite 1804	Jackson	MS	39205-0000
601 961-5062	**Division of Hazardous Waste Management** 2380 Hwy 80 W	Jackson	MS	39204-2312
601 949-2225	**Division of Public Safety Planning** 301 W Pearl St	Jackson	MS	39203-3039
601 352-9100	**Emergency Management Agency** 1410 Riverside Dr	Jackson	MS	39202-1237
601 354-8711	**Employment Security Commission** 1520 W Capitol St	Jackson	MS	39203-1601
601 359-3150	**Governor** PO Box 139	Jackson	MS	39205-0139
601 359-1209	**Highway Dept** 500 N West St 1004 Woolfolk Bldg	Jackson	MS	39201-0000
601 987-1212	**Highway Safety Patrol** 1900 E Woodrow Wilson Dr	Jackson	MS	39216-5118
601 982-6611	**Institutions of Higher Learning** 3825 Ridgewood Rd	Jackson	MS	39211-6463
601 359-3200	**Lieutenant Governor** PO Box 1018	Jackson	MS	39215-1018
601 354-6228	**Mining & Reclamation Div** 2525 N West St	Jackson	MS	39216-3840
601 745-6611	**Mississippi State Penitentiary**	Parchman	MS	38738-0000
601 987-3981	**Occupational Safety & Health Branch** 305 W Lorenz Blvd	Jackson	MS	39213-7034
601 359-3621	**Office of Building Ground & Real Property Management** Walter Sillers Bldg 15th Fl	Jackson	MS	39201-0000
601 960-7960	**Office of Public Health Statistics** 2423 N State St Rm 110	Jackson	MS	39216-4504
601 359-3598	**Office of Research Planning Policy & Development State Dept of Education** Walter Sillers Bldg Rm 306	Jackson	MS	39201-0000
601 354-7142	**Oil & Gas Board** 500 Greymont Ave Suite E	Jackson	MS	39202-3446
601 354-6454	**Parole Board** 723 N President St	Jackson	MS	39202-3029
601 961-5400	**Public Service Commission** 550 High St Walter Sillers Bldg	Jackson	MS	39201-1182
601 932-2880	**Rankin County Correctional Facility** PO Box 88550	Pearl	MS	39288-8550
601 987-3969	**Real Estate Commission** 1920 Dunbarton Dr	Jackson	MS	39216-5087
601 359-1350	**Secretary of State** 401 Mississippi St	Jackson	MS	39201-1012
601 359-1350	**Security Div** 401 Mississippi St	Jackson	MS	39201-1012
601 359-3694	**Supreme Court** 450 High St Gartin Bldg 3rd Fl	Jackson	MS	39201-0000
601 359-1098	**Tax Commission** PO Box 1033	Jackson	MS	39215-1033
601 359-3531	**Treasury Dept** 550 High St Rm 404	Jackson	MS	39201-1192
601 961-7700	**Unemployment Insurance Div** 1520 W Capitol St	Jackson	MS	39203-1601
601 987-4200	**Workers' Compensation Commission** 1428 Lakeland Dr	Jackson	MS	39216-4788

MISSOURI

314 751-2000	**State Government Information** 301 W High St	Jefferson City	MO	65101-1580
314 751-4817	**Air Pollution Control Program** 205 Jefferson St	Jefferson City	MO	65101-2982
314 751-3321	**Attorney General** Supreme Court Bldg 1st Fl	Jefferson City	MO	65101-0000
314 751-2389	**Board of Probation & Parole** PO Box 267	Jefferson City	MO	65102-0267
314 751-6383	**Bureau of Vital Records** 1730 E Elm St	Jefferson City	MO	65101-4130
314 751-3359	**Department of Agriculture** 1616 Missouri Blvd	Jefferson City	MO	65109-1764
314 751-2389	**Department of Corrections** 2729 Plaza Dr	Jefferson City	MO	65109-4406
314 751-4241	**Department of Economic Development** 301 W High St	Jefferson City	MO	65101-1580
314 751-3503	**Department of Elementary & Secondary Education** PO Box 480	Jefferson City	MO	65102-0480
314 751-6001	**Department of Health** 1730 E Elm St	Jefferson City	MO	65101-4130
314 751-2361	**Department of Higher Education** 101 Adams St	Jefferson City	MO	65101-3000
314 751-4091	**Department of Labor & Industrial Relations** PO Box 504	Jefferson City	MO	65102-3138
314 751-4422	**Department of Natural Resources** 205 Jefferson St	Jefferson City	MO	65101-2981
314 751-4905	**Department of Public Safety** 301 W High St Truman Bldg	Jefferson City	MO	65101-1580
314 751-4450	**Department of Revenue** 301 W High St Truman Bldg	Jefferson City	MO	65101-0000
314 751-2345	**Division of Budget & Planning** PO Box 809	Jefferson City	MO	65102-0809
314 751-3339	**Division of Design & Construction** 301 W High St Truman Bldg Rm 730	Jefferson City	MO	65102-0000
314 751-3215	**Division of Employment Security** 421 E Dunklin St	Jefferson City	MO	65104-0001
314 751-4000	**Division of Energy** 205 Jefferson St	Jefferson City	MO	65102-0000
314 751-4810	**Division of Environmental Quality** PO Box 176	Jefferson City	MO	65102-0176
314 751-3242	**Division of Finance** Truman State Office Bldg Rm 630	Jefferson City	MO	65102-0000
314 751-4126	**Division of Insurance** 301 W High St Truman Bldg	Jefferson City	MO	65101-1580
314 751-0293	**Division of Professional Registration** 3523 N Ten-Mile Dr	Jefferson City	MO	65109-0000
314 751-2387	**Division of Purchasing** 301 W High St Truman Bldg Rm 580	Jefferson City	MO	65101-1580
314 751-4231	**Division of Worker's Compensation** 3315 W Truman Blvd	Jefferson City	MO	65109-5711
314 751-9571	**Emergency Management Agency** 1717 Industrial Dr	Jefferson City	MO	65109-1403
314 751-3222	**Governor** 216 State Capitol	Jefferson City	MO	65101-1556
314 751-2551	**Highway Dept** Capitol Ave & Jefferson St	Jefferson City	MO	65101-2983
314 751-3313	**Highway Patrol** 1510 E Elm St	Jefferson City	MO	65101-4118
314 751-3000	**Lieutenant Governor** PO Box 563	Jefferson City	MO	65102-0563
314 751-3224	**Missouri State Penitentiary for Men** 631 State St	Jefferson City	MO	65101-3026
816 263-3778	**Missouri Training Center for Men** PO Box 7	Moberly	MO	65270-0007
417 887-9800	**Public Defender Commission** Plaza Towers Suite 811	Springfield	MO	65804-1686
314 751-3234	**Public Service Commission** 301 W High St Suite 530	Jefferson City	MO	65101-1580
314 751-2628	**Real Estate Commission** 3523 N Ten-Mile Dr	Jefferson City	MO	65101-0000
314 751-4717	**Records Management & Archives** 1001 Industrial Dr	Jefferson City	MO	65109-1459
314 751-3318	**Secretary of State** 301 W High St Truman Bldg Rm 208	Jefferson City	MO	65101-0000
314 751-4136	**Security Div** 301 W High St Truman Bldg Rm 830	Jefferson City	MO	65102-0000
314 751-4932	**Soil & Water Conservation Program** 205 Jefferson St	Jefferson City	MO	65101-2982
314 444-6845	**State Council on the Arts** 111 N 7th St Suite 105	Saint Louis	MO	63101-2134
314 751-4144	**Supreme Court** PO Box 150	Jefferson City	MO	65102-0150
314 751-5333	**Trade Offense Div** Supreme Court Bldg	Jefferson City	MO	65101-0000
314 751-4123	**Treasurer** PO Box 210	Jefferson City	MO	65102-0210
314 751-3643	**Unemployment Insurance Operations** 421 E Dunklin St	Jefferson City	MO	65101-0000
314 751-3176	**Waste Management Program** 205 Jefferson St	Jefferson City	MO	65101-2982

MONTANA

406 444-2511	**State Government Information** Mitchell Bldg Rm 219	Helena	MT	59620-0000
406 444-3454	**Air Quality Bureau** 1400 Broadway Cogswell Bldg	Helena	MT	59620-0000
406 444-3104	**Architecture & Engineering Div** 1520 E 6th Ave	Helena	MT	59620-0103
406 444-2681	**Archives & Library Div** 225 N Roberts St	Helena	MT	59620-0000
406 444-6430	**Arts Council** 48 N Last Chance Gulch St	Helena	MT	59601-4122
406 444-2026	**Attorney General** 215 N Sanders St Justice Bldg 3rd Fl	Helena	MT	59620-0000
406 444-2961	**Board of Realty Regulation** 1424 9th Ave	Helena	MT	59620-0000
406 496-4180	**Bureau of Mines & Geology** W Park St	Butte	MT	59701-0000
406 444-4912	**Community Corrections Bureau (Probation & Parole)** 1539 11th Ave	Helena	MT	59620-0000
406 444-4312	**Consumer Affairs Unit** 1424 9th Ave	Helena	MT	59601-4503
406 444-3604	**Crime Control Div** 303 N Roberts St 4th Fl	Helena	MT	59620-0000
406 444-3144	**Department of Agriculture** Agriculture/Livestock Bldg Capitol Stn	Helena	MT	59620-0000
406 444-3494	**Department of Commerce** 1424 9th Ave	Helena	MT	59601-4503

The text at the beginning of each category provides information on how government offices are listed. Refer to the front page of the section for a list of the categories included.

406 444-2544 **Department of Health & Environmental Sciences**
1400 Broadway Cogswell Bldg Rm C108 ... Helena MT 59620-0000
406 444-6201 **Department of Highways** 2701 Prospect Ave ... Helena MT 59620-0000
406 444-5671 **Department of Institutions** 1539 11th Ave ... Helena MT 59601-4599
406 444-3555 **Department of Labor & Industry** PO Box 1728 ... Helena MT 59624-1728
406 444-6699 **Department of Natural Resources & Conservation**
1520 E 6th Ave ... Helena MT 59601-4541
406 444-2460 **Department of Revenue**
205 Roberts Sam W Mitchell Bldg Rm 455 ... Helena MT 59620-0000
406 444-6911 **Disaster & Emergency Services Div** 1100 N Main St ... Helena MT 59601-0000
406 444-6754 **Energy Div** 1520 E 6th Ave ... Helena MT 59620-0000
406 444-3948 **Environmental Sciences Div**
Lockey Ave & Roberts St Cogswell Bldg ... Helena MT 59620-0000
406 444-3111 **Governor** State Capitol ... Helena MT 59620-0001
406 444-3780 **Highway Patrol** 303 N Roberts ... Helena MT 59620-0000
406 444-3111 **Lieutenant Governor** State Capitol ... Helena MT 59620-1901
406 846-1320 **Montana State Prison** 400 Conley Lake Rd ... Deer Lodge MT 59722-9755
406 444-3671 **Occupational Health Bureau**
1400 Broadway Cogswell Bldg Rm A113 ... Helena MT 59620-0000
406 444-3616 **Office of Budget & Program Planning** State Capitol Rm 220 ... Helena MT 59620-0000
406 444-3095 **Office of Public Instruction** Capitol Stn ... Helena MT 59620-0000
406 444-6675 **Oil & Gas Conservation Div** 1520 E 6th Ave ... Helena MT 59620-0000
406 444-3737 **Professional & Occupational Licensing Business Regulation Div**
1424 9th Ave ... Helena MT 59620-0000
406 444-6199 **Public Service Commission** 2701 Prospect Ave ... Helena MT 59601-9726
406 444-2575 **Purchasing Div** 205 Robert St Mitchell Bldg Rm 165 ... Helena MT 59620-0000
406 444-2034 **Secretary of State** State Capitol Rm 225 ... Helena MT 59620-0000
406 444-2821 **Solid & Hazardous Waste Bureau** Cogswell Bldg ... Helena MT 59620-0000
406 444-2040 **State Auditor Office Insurance Dept**
126 N Sanders St Mitchell Bldg Rm 270 ... Helena MT 59620-0000
406 444-6518 **State Compensation Mutual Insurance** 5 S Last Chance Gulch ... Helena MT 59601-4132
406 444-3858 **Supreme Court** 215 N Sanders St Justice Bldg Rm 323 ... Helena MT 59620-0000
406 444-6190 **Transportation Div** 2701 Prospect Ave ... Helena MT 59601-9726
406 444-2032 **Treasurer** 205 Robert St Rm 175 ... Helena MT 59620-0000
406 444-2723 **Unemployment Insurance Div** PO Box 1728 ... Helena MT 59624-1728
406 444-2614 **Vital Records & Statistics Bureau**
1400 Broadway Cogswell Bldg Rm C118 ... Helena MT 59620-0000
406 444-6601 **Water Resources Div** 1520 E 6th Ave ... Helena MT 59620-2301

NEBRASKA

402 471-2311 **State Government Information** 301 Centennial Mall ... Lincoln NE 68509-0000
402 471-2189 **Air Quality Div** PO Box 98922 ... Lincoln NE 68509-8922
402 595-2122 **Arts Council** 1313 Farnam on the Mall ... Omaha NE 68102-1873
402 471-2682 **Attorney General** PO Box 98920 ... Lincoln NE 68509-8920
402 471-3445 **Bureau of Securities** 301 Centennial Mall S ... Lincoln NE 68508-2529
402 471-2871 **Bureau of Vital Statistics** 301 Centennial Mall S ... Lincoln NE 68509-0000
402 473-1430 **Civil Defense Agency** 1300 Military Rd ... Lincoln NE 68508-1051
402 471-2194 **Commission on Law Enforcement & Criminal Justice**
PO Box 94946 ... Lincoln NE 68509-4946
402 471-4723 **Consumer Fraud Div** 2115 State Capitol ... Lincoln NE 68509-0000
402 471-2847 **Coordinating Commission for Postsecondary Education**
PO Box 95005 ... Lincoln NE 68509-5005
402 471-2526 **Department of Administrative Services Budget Dept**
1445 K St Rm 1322 ... Lincoln NE 68508-2731
402 471-2341 **Department of Agriculture** 301 Centennial Mall S ... Lincoln NE 68508-2529
402 471-2654 **Department of Corrections** 801 W Van Dorn St Bldg 15 ... Lincoln NE 68522-1970
402 471-3111 **Department of Economic Development** 301 Centennial Mall S ... Lincoln NE 68508-2529
402 471-2465 **Department of Education** 301 Centennial Mall S ... Lincoln NE 68509-0000
402 471-2186 **Department of Environmental Control** PO Box 98922 ... Lincoln NE 68509-8922
402 471-2133 **Department of Health** 301 Centennial Mall S ... Lincoln NE 68508-2529
402 471-2201 **Department of Insurance** 941 'O' St Suite 400 ... Lincoln NE 68508-3626
402 475-8451 **Department of Labor** 550 S 16th St ... Lincoln NE 68508-1829
402 471-2971 **Department of Revenue** 301 Centennial Mall S ... Lincoln NE 68508-2529
402 471-4567 **Department of Roads** 1500 SR-2 ... Lincoln NE 68502-0000
402 471-2363 **Department of Water Resources** 301 Centennial Mall S ... Lincoln NE 68508-2529
402 471-4771 **Division of Archives/Library** 1500 R St ... Lincoln NE 68508-1651
402 471-2239 **Division of Safety** PO Box 95024 ... Lincoln NE 68509-5024
402 471-2867 **Energy Office** 1445 K St ... Lincoln NE 68509-0000
402 471-2244 **Governor** 2316 State Capitol ... Lincoln NE 68509-0000
402 471-2256 **Lieutenant Governor** State Capitol Rm 2315 ... Lincoln NE 68509-0000
402 471-2861 **Lincoln Correctional Center** PO Box 2800 ... Lincoln NE 68502-0800
402 471-2081 **Natural Resources Commission** 301 Centennial Mall S ... Lincoln NE 68508-2529
402 471-3161 **Nebraska State Penitentiary** 14th & Pioneer Blvd ... Lincoln NE 68502-0000
308 254-4595 **Oil & Gas Conservation Commission** PO Box 399 ... Sidney NE 69162-0399
402 471-2654 **Parole Administration** 801 W Van Dorn St ... Lincoln NE 68509-0000
402 471-3101 **Public Service Commission** 1200 N St Suite 300 ... Lincoln NE 68508-2006
402 471-2401 **Purchasing Div** 301 Centennial Mall S 1st Fl ... Lincoln NE 68508-2529
402 471-2004 **Real Estate Commission** 301 Centennial Mall S ... Lincoln NE 68508-2529
402 471-2554 **Secretary of State** 2300 State Capitol ... Lincoln NE 68509-0000
402 471-3191 **State Building Div** 1445 K St ... Lincoln NE 68509-0000
402 471-4545 **State Patrol** PO Box 94907 ... Lincoln NE 68509-4907
402 471-3731 **Supreme Court** 2413 State Capitol ... Lincoln NE 68509-0000
402 471-2455 **Treasurer** PO Box 94788 ... Lincoln NE 68509-4788
402 475-8451 **Unemployment Insurance Div** 550 S 16th St ... Lincoln NE 68509-0000
402 471-2568 **Worker's Compensation Court** 1445 K St ... Lincoln NE 68508-2731

NEVADA

702 687-5000 **State Government Information** 406 E 2nd St ... Carson City NV 89710-0001
702 687-4170 **Attorney General** 198 S Carson St ... Carson City NV 89710-0001
702 687-4325 **Commission on Economic Development**
5151 S Carson St 4th Fl ... Carson City NV 89710-0001
702 789-0225 **Council on the Arts** 329 Flint St ... Reno NV 89501-2033
702 789-0180 **Department of Agriculture** PO Box 11100 ... Reno NV 89510-1100
702 885-4250 **Department of Commerce** 1665 Hot Springs Rd ... Carson City NV 89710-0001
702 885-4360 **Department of Conservation & Natural Resources**
123 W Nye Ln Rm 214 ... Carson City NV 89710-0001
702 885-3100 **Department of Education** 400 W King St ... Carson City NV 89710-0001
702 885-5050 **Department of Minerals** 400 W King St Suite 106 ... Carson City NV 89710-0001
702 887-3285 **Department of Prisons** 5500 Snyder Ave Bldg 89 ... Carson City NV 89701-6752
702 885-5040 **Department of Probation & Parole**
1445 Hotsprings Rd Suite 104 ... Carson City NV 89710-0001
702 885-4892 **Department of Taxation** 1340 S Curry St ... Carson City NV 89710-0001
702 885-5440 **Department of Transportation** 1263 S Stewart St ... Carson City NV 89712-0001
702 885-4240 **Division of Emergency Management** 2525 S Carson St ... Carson City NV 89710-0001
702 885-4670 **Division of Environmental Protection**
123 W Nye Ln Rm 108 ... Carson City NV 89710-0000
702 885-5240 **Division of Occupational Safety & Health** 1370 S Curry St ... Carson City NV 89710-0001
702 885-4380 **Division of Water Resources** 123 W Nye Ln Rm 246 ... Carson City NV 89710-0001
702 885-4635 **Employment Security Dept** 500 E 3rd St ... Carson City NV 89713-0001
702 885-5670 **Governor** Capitol Bldg Executive Office ... Carson City NV 89710-0001
702 885-4740 **Health Div** 505 E King St ... Carson City NV 89710-0001
702 885-5300 **Highway Patrol** 555 Wright Way ... Carson City NV 89711-0001
702 885-4270 **Insurance Div** 1665 Hot Springs Rd ... Carson City NV 89710-0001
702 885-4850 **Labor Commission** 505 E King St Rm 602 ... Carson City NV 89710-0001
702 687-3034 **Lieutenant Governor** Capitol Complex ... Carson City NV 89710-0001
702 887-3213 **Northern Nevada Correctional Center** PO Box 7000 ... Carson City NV 89702-7000
702 885-4880 **Public Defender** 308 N Curry St Capitol Complex Suite 200 ... Carson City NV 89710-0001
702 687-6001 **Public Service Commission** 727 Fairview Dr ... Carson City NV 89710-0001
702 885-4870 **Public Works Board** 505 E King St Rm 301 ... Carson City NV 89710-0001
702 885-4094 **Purchasing Div** 505 E King St Rm 400 ... Carson City NV 89701-4761
702 885-4280 **Real Estate Div** 1665 Hot Springs Rd ... Carson City NV 89710-0001
702 885-5203 **Secretary of State** Capitol Complex ... Carson City NV 89710-0001
702 486-4400 **Securities Div** 2501 E Sahara Ave Suite 201 ... Las Vegas NV 89158-0001
702 879-3800 **Southern Desert Correctional Center** PO Box 208 ... Indian Springs NV 89108-0000
702 687-5284 **State Industrial Insurance System** 515 E Musser St ... Carson City NV 89714-0001
702 885-5160 **State Library & Archives** 401 N Carson St ... Carson City NV 89710-0001
702 885-5180 **Supreme Court** 100 N Carson St ... Carson City NV 89710-0001
702 885-5200 **Treasurer** Capitol Complex ... Carson City NV 89710-0001
702 687-4510 **Unemployment Insurance Div** 500 E 3rd St ... Carson City NV 89713-0001
702 885-4480 **Vital Statistics Section** 505 E King St Rm 102 ... Carson City NV 89710-0001

NEW HAMPSHIRE

603 271-1110 **State Government Information** 107 N Main St ... Concord NH 03301-4951
603 271-3658 **Attorney General** 25 Capitol St ... Concord NH 03301-6397
603 271-3516 **Bureau of Public Works** PO Box 483 ... Concord NH 03302-0483
603 271-4650 **Bureau of Vital Records & Health Statistics** 6 Hazen Dr ... Concord NH 03301-0000
603 271-3641 **Consumer Protection & Antitrust Bureau** 25 Capitol St ... Concord NH 03301-6332
603 271-2789 **Council on the Arts** 40 N Main St ... Concord NH 03301-4974
603 271-3204 **Department of Administrative Services** 25 Capitol St Rm 120 ... Concord NH 03301-0000
603 271-3551 **Department of Agriculture** 10 Ferry St ... Concord NH 03301-5022
603 271-5600 **Department of Corrections** 105 Pleasant St ... Concord NH 03301-3861
603 271-3144 **Department of Education** 101 Pleasant St ... Concord NH 03301-3860
603 224-3311 **Department of Employment Security** 32 S Main St ... Concord NH 03301-4857
603 271-3503 **Department of Environmental Services** 6 Hazen Dr ... Concord NH 03301-0000
603 271-3176 **Department of Labor** 19 Pillsbury St ... Concord NH 03301-3570
603 271-2191 **Department of Revenue Administration** 61 S Spring St ... Concord NH 03301-2400
603 271-2575 **Department of Safety State Police Div** 10 Hazen Dr ... Concord NH 03305-0001
603 271-3734 **Department of Transportation** Hazen Dr ... Concord NH 03302-0000
603 271-4501 **Division of Public Health Services** 6 Hazen Dr ... Concord NH 03301-6527
603 271-2236 **Division of Records Management & Archives** 71 S Fruit St ... Concord NH 03301-0000
603 271-3406 **Division of Water Resources** PO Box 2008 ... Concord NH 03302-2008
603 271-2231 **Emergency Management** 107 Pleasant St ... Concord NH 03301-3852
603 271-2711 **Energy Office** 2 1/2 Beacon St 2nd Fl ... Concord NH 03301-4498
603 271-2121 **Governor** State House Rm 208 ... Concord NH 03301-3222
603 271-3179 **Inspection Div** 19 Pillsbury St ... Concord NH 03301-3571
603 271-2261 **Insurance Dept** 169 Manchester St ... Concord NH 03301-5127
603 627-4194 **Manchester Community Correctional Center**
126 Lowell St ... Manchester NH 03104-0000
603 271-1800 **New Hampshire State Prison Complex** PO Box 14 ... Concord NH 03302-0014
603 271-1463 **Office of Securities Regulation** 157 Manchester St ... Concord NH 03301-5118
603 271-2155 **Office of State Planning** 2 1/2 Beacon St ... Concord NH 03301-4497
603 271-2555 **Postsecondary Education Commission** 2 Industrial Park Dr ... Concord NH 03301-8512
603 271-2431 **Public Utilities Commission** 8 Old Suncook Rd ... Concord NH 03301-7320
603 271-2201 **Purchasing Div** 25 Capitol St Statehouse Annex Rm 102 ... Concord NH 03301-0000
603 271-2701 **Real Estate Commission** 107 Pleasant St ... Concord NH 03301-3818
603 271-3727 **Resources & Economic Development Dept** 105 Loudon Rd ... Concord NH 03301-5601
603 271-3351 **Retirement System** 54 Regional Dr ... Concord NH 03301-5183
603 271-1110 **Secretary of State** State House Rm 204 ... Concord NH 03301-0000
603 271-2925 **Solid Waste Compliance Section** 6 Hazen Dr ... Concord NH 03301-0000
603 271-2646 **Supreme Court** Noble Dr Supreme Court Bldg ... Concord NH 03301-0000
603 271-2621 **Treasury Dept** State House Annex 25 Capitol St Rm 121 ... Concord NH 03301-6312

NEW JERSEY

609 292-2121 **State Government Information** 3525 Quaker Bridge Rd ... Trenton NJ 08625-0001
609 530-3200 **Archives & Records Management Div** 2300 Stuyvesant Ave ... Trenton NJ 08625-0001
609 292-4925 **Attorney General** Hughes Justice Complex CN-080 ... Trenton NJ 08625-0001
201 648-2026 **Board of Public Utilities** 2 Gateway Ctr ... Newark NJ 07102-0000
609 292-4256 **Bureau of Parole** Whittlesey Rd CN-864 ... Trenton NJ 08625-0001
201 648-2040 **Bureau of Securities** 2 Gateway Ctr ... Newark NJ 07102-5095
609 292-4087 **Bureau of Vital Statistics**
S Warren & Market Sts Health Niagara Culture Bldg Rm 504 ... Trenton NJ 08625-0001
609 292-6130 **Council on the Arts** 4 N Broad St CN-306 ... Trenton NJ 08625-0001
609 292-3976 **Department of Agriculture** John Fitch Plaza CN-330 ... Trenton NJ 08625-0001
609 292-9860 **Department of Corrections** CN-863 ... Trenton NJ 08625-0001
609 292-4450 **Department of Education** 225 W State St CN-500 ... Trenton NJ 08625-0001
201 648-3000 **Department of Energy** 101 Commerce St ... Newark NJ 07102-5102
609 292-2885 **Department of Environmental Protection**
401 W State St CN-402 ... Trenton NJ 08625-0001
609 292-7837 **Department of Health** John Fitch Plaza CN-360 ... Trenton NJ 08625-0001
609 292-4310 **Department of Higher Education** 20 W State St ... Trenton NJ 08625-0001
609 292-5360 **Department of Insurance** 20 W State St CN-325 ... Trenton NJ 08625-0001
609 292-2323 **Department of Labor** John Fitch Plaza CN-110 ... Trenton NJ 08625-0001
609 292-7087 **Department of Public Advocate** 25 Market St CN-850 ... Trenton NJ 08625-0001
609 292-6748 **Department of the Treasury** State House CN-002 ... Trenton NJ 08625-0001
609 530-3535 **Department of Transportation** 1035 Parkway Ave CN-600 ... Trenton NJ 08625-0001
201 648-4010 **Division of Consumer Affairs** 1100 Raymond Blvd ... Newark NJ 07102-5279
609 292-2462 **Division of Economic Development** 20 W State St CN-823 ... Trenton NJ 08625-0001
609 530-8820 **Division of Housing & Development**
3131 Princeton Pike CN 816 ... Trenton NJ 08625-0816
609 292-3463 **Division of Pensions** PO Box CN 295 ... Trenton NJ 08625-0001
609 882-2000 **Division of State Police** Trooper Dr ... West Trenton NJ 08628-0068
609 292-5185 **Division of Taxation** 50 Barrack St CN-269 ... Trenton NJ 08646-0001
609 292-2460 **Division of Unemployment & Disability Insurance**
Labor & Industry Bldg Rm 601 ... Trenton NJ 08625-0000
609 292-2516 **Division of Worker's Compensation**
Labor & Industry Bldg CN381 ... Trenton NJ 08625-0001
609 292-6000 **Governor** 125 W State St CN-001 ... Trenton NJ 08625-0001
609 777-1243 **Management & Policy** 125 W State St CN-001 ... Trenton NJ 08625-0001
609 292-9700 **New Jersey State Prison** 3rd & Federal Sts ... Trenton NJ 08625-0001
908 499-5010 **New Jersey State Prison** Lock Bag R ... Rahway NJ 07065-0000
609 292-9200 **Office of Financial Management** 1 W State St 3rd Fl ... Trenton NJ 08625-0001
609 292-7053 **Real Estate Commission** 20 W State St ... Trenton NJ 08625-0001
609 984-1900 **Secretary of State** 315 W State St CN-300 ... Trenton NJ 08625-0001
609 984-2090 **State Law Enforcement Planning Agency** 200 Woolverton St ... Trenton NJ 08625-0001
609 292-4837 **Supreme Court** 25 Market St CN-970 ... Trenton NJ 08625-0001
609 777-0250 **Workplace Standards Div** Station Plaza 4 CN-386 ... Trenton NJ 08625-0001

NEW MEXICO

505 827-8110 **State Government Information** 810 W San Mateo ... Santa Fe NM 87503-0001
505 827-4800 **Administrative Office of the Court**
237 Don Gaspar Ave Rm 25 ... Santa Fe NM 87503-0001
505 827-0042 **Air Quality Bureau** 1190 St Francis Dr Rm S2100 ... Santa Fe NM 87503-0001
505 827-6490 **Arts Div** 224 E Palace Ave ... Santa Fe NM 87501-2013
505 827-6000 **Attorney General** Galisteo St Bataan Memorial Bldg Rm 260 ... Santa Fe NM 87501-0000
505 865-1622 **Central New Mexico Correctional Facility** PO Box 1328 ... Los Lunas NM 87031-1328
505 827-8300 **Commission on Higher Education** 1068 Cerrillos Rd ... Santa Fe NM 87501-4250

State Government

505 827-6060 **Consumer Protection Div**
Galisteo St Bataan Memorial Bldg Room 236 .... Santa Fe NM 87501-0000
505 827-8645 **Corrections Dept** 1422 Paseo de Peralta .... Santa Fe NM 87503-0001
505 646-3007 **Department of Agriculture** PO Box 30005 Dept 3189
505 827-6635 **Department of Education** 300 Don Gaspar Ave .... Santa Fe NM 87501-2744
505 827-4500 **Department of Insurance**
1120 Paseo De Peralta Perta Bldg 4th Fl .... Santa Fe NM 87504-0000
505 841-8437 **Department of Labor** PO Box 1928 .... Albuquerque NM 87103-1928
505 827-2300 **Department of Motor Vehicles** 1100 S St Francis Dr .... Santa Fe NM 87501-4147
505 827-0274 **Economic Development & Tourism Dept** 1100 St Francis Dr .. Santa Fe NM 87503-0001
505 827-9236 **Emergency Planning & Coordination Bureau** PO Box 1628 ..... Santa Fe NM 87504-1628
505 827-5900 **Energy Minerals & Natural Resources Conservation & Management Div**
2040 S Pacheco .... Santa Fe NM 87505-0000
505 827-2850 **Environmental Improvement Div** 1190 St Francis Dr .... Santa Fe NM 87503-0001
505 827-3060 **Finance & Administration Dept**
Bataan Memorial Bldg Rm 180 .... Santa Fe NM 87503-0001
505 827-3000 **Governor** PERA Bldg 5th Fl .... Santa Fe NM 87503-0001
505 827-0020 **Health Services Div** 1190 St Francis Dr .... Santa Fe NM 87503-0001
505 827-6835 **Labor & Industrial Commission**
1596 Pacheco St Aspen Plaza .... Santa Fe NM 87501-0000
505 827-3050 **Lieutenant Governor** PERA Bldg 5th Fl .... Santa Fe NM 87503-0001
505 827-5970 **Mining & Minerals Div** 2040 S Pacheco St .... Santa Fe NM 87505-0000
505 827-5800 **Oil Conservation Div** PO Box 2088 .... Santa Fe NM 87504-0000
505 827-3591 **Parole Board** 604 W San Mateo St .... Santa Fe NM 87503-0001
505 471-7300 **Penitentiary of New Mexico** PO Box 1059 .... Santa Fe NM 87504-1059
505 827-2141 **Property Control Div** 1100 S St Francis Dr Rm 2022 .... Santa Fe NM 87503-0001
505 827-3900 **Public Defender** 142 Lincoln Ave Suite 500 .... Santa Fe NM 87501-2006
505 827-6940 **Public Service Commission** 224 E Palace Ave .... Santa Fe NM 87501-2013
505 827-0472 **Purchasing Div** 1100 St Francis Dr Rm 2016 .... Santa Fe NM 87503-0001
505 841-8431 **Real Estate Commission** 4125 Carlisle NE .... Albuquerque NM 87107-4806
505 827-7004 **Regulation & Licensing Dept** 725 St Michaels Dr .... Santa Fe NM 87504-0000
505 827-3600 **Secretary of State** Lamy Bldg 1st Fl .... Santa Fe NM 87503-0001
505 827-7140 **Securities Div** 725 St Michael Dr .... Santa Fe NM 97501-0000
505 827-5100 **State Highways Transportation Dept** PO Box 1149 .... Santa Fe NM 87504-1149
505 827-9000 **State Police** 4491 Cerrillos Rd .... Santa Fe NM 87504-0000
505 827-8860 **State Records Center & Archives** 404 Montezuma Ave .... Santa Fe NM 87503-0001
505 827-4860 **Supreme Court** 237 Don Gasper Ave Rm 104 .... Santa Fe NM 87503-0001
505 827-0700 **Taxation & Revenue Dept** 1200 St Francis Dr .... Santa Fe NM 87509-0001
505 827-6400 **Treasury Dept** PO Box 608 .... Santa Fe NM 87503-0001
505 841-8431 **Unemployment Insurance Bureau** 401 Broadway NE .... Albuquerque NM 87102-2330
505 827-2347 **Vital Records & Statistics** 1190 St Francis Dr .... Santa Fe NM 87503-0001
505 841-8790 **Worker's Compensation Administration** PO Box 27198 .... Albuquerque NM 87125-7198

NEW YORK

518 474-2121 **State Government Information**
Empire State Plaza Concourse Level .... Albany NY 12242-0001
518 474-7124 **Attorney General** State Capitol Rm 221 .... Albany NY 12224-0000
212 341-2222 **Bureau of Investor Protection & Securities**
120 Broadway 23rd Fl .... New York NY 10271-0002
518 474-3069 **Bureau of Vital Statistics** Corning Tower Rm 321 .... Albany NY 12237-0001
518 492-2511 **Clinton Correctional Facility** PO Box B .... Dannemora NY 12929-9999
518 474-5105 **Consumer Protection Board** 99 Washington Ave .... Albany NY 12210-2891
212 614-2900 **Council on the Arts** 915 Broadway .... New York NY 10010-7199
518 457-4188 **Department of Agriculture & Markets**
Capitol Plaza 1 Winner Cir .... Albany NY 12235-0001
518 457-8126 **Department of Correctional Services**
State Office Campus Bldg 2 .... Albany NY 12226-0001
518 474-4100 **Department of Economic Development**
1 Commerce Plaza 9th Fl .... Albany NY 12245-0001
518 457-3446 **Department of Environmental Conservation**
50 Wolf Rd Rm 604 .... Albany NY 12233-0001
518 474-2011 **Department of Health** Empire State Plaza Tower Bldg Rm 1408 .. Albany NY 12237-0001
518 457-9000 **Department of Labor** State Office Campus Bldg 12 Rm 500 ..... Albany NY 12240-0001
518 474-4750 **Department of State** 162 Washington Ave .... Albany NY 12231-0001
518 457-2100 **Department of Taxation & Finance**
Campus Tax & Finance Bldg 9 .... Albany NY 12227-0001
518 457-5100 **Department of Transportation**
5 Harriman State Office Campus Bldg 5 .... Albany NY 12232-0001
518 474-0335 **Design & Construction**
Empire State Plaza Empire Statza Rm 3508 .... Albany NY 12242-0001
518 786-4501 **Disaster Preparedness Commission**
330 Old Niskayuna Rd Rm 414 .... Latham NY 12110-2224
518 457-7230 **Division of Air Resources** 50 Wolf Rd Rm 128 .... Albany NY 12233-0001
518 474-5700 **Division of Economic Opportunity** 162 Washington Ave ...... Albany NY 12231-0001
518 474-3454 **Division of Probation & Correctional Alternatives**
60 S Pearl St .... Albany NY 12207-1595
518 474-3830 **Division of Professional Licensing Services**
Cultural Education Ctr .... Albany NY 12230-0001
518 474-3695 **Division of Purchasing**
Empire State Plaza Corning Tower 38th Fl .... Albany NY 12242-0001
518 457-3518 **Division of Safety & Health**
State Office Campus Bldg 12 Rm 457 .... Albany NY 12240-0000
518 457-6603 **Division of Solid Waste** 50 Wolf Rd Rm 212 .... Albany NY 12233-0001
518 474-4250 **Division of the Treasury** PO Box 7002 .... Albany NY 12225-0000
518 457-1627 **Division of Water** 50 Wolf Rd Rm 308 .... Albany NY 12233-0001
518 473-4376 **Energy Office** Agency Bldg 2 Empire State Plaza .... Albany NY 12223-0001
518 457-9337 **Environment Conservation Div of Mineral Resources**
50 Wolf Rd Rm 202 .... Albany NY 12233-6500
518 473-4362 **Facilities Development Corp** 44 Holland Ave 5th Fl .... Albany NY 12208-3411
518 474-8390 **Governor** Executive Chamber State Capitol Bldg .... Albany NY 12224-0000
914 221-2711 **Green Haven Correctional Facility** Rt 216 .... Stormville NY 12582-0000
212 602-0434 **Insurance Dept** 160 W Broadway .... New York NY 10013-3393
518 474-4623 **Lieutenant Governor** State Capitol Bldg Rm 326 .... Albany NY 12224-0000
518 474-7736 **New York State Employees Retirement System**
Swan St Alfred E Smith Office Bldg .... Albany NY 12244-0000
518 474-4688 **Office of Elementary & Secondary Education**
Education Bldg Annex Rm 875 .... Albany NY 12234-0001
518 474-5851 **Office of Higher & Continuing Education** Empire State Plaza ...... Albany NY 12230-0001
518 474-4040 **Office of the State Comptroller**
Swan St Alfred E Smith-Office Bldg .... Albany NY 12236-0000
518 474-4038 **Office of Unclaimed Funds** Swan St Alfred E Smith Office Bldg ... Albany NY 12236-0000
518 474-2530 **Public Service Commission** Empire State Plaza Bldg 3 .... Albany NY 12223-0001
518 474-4750 **Secretary of State** 162 Washington Ave .... Albany NY 12231-0001
518 474-1195 **State Archives**
Empire State Plaza Cultural Education Ctr Rm 10D45 .... Albany NY 12230-0001
518 457-6721 **State Police** Public Security Bldg .... Albany NY 12226-0001
518 445-7714 **Supreme Court** 16 Eagle St Rm 102 .... Albany NY 12207-1077
518 457-2177 **Unemployment Insurance Div**
State Office Campus Bldg 12 Rmm 554 .... Albany NY 12240-0001
718 802-6666 **Workers' Compensation Board** 180 Livingston St .... Brooklyn NY 11248-0001

NORTH CAROLINA

919 733-1110 **State Government Information** 116 W Jones St .... Raleigh NC 27603-8003
919 733-3340 **Air Quality Section** 512 N Salisbury St .... Raleigh NC 27611-0000

919 733-2821 **Arts Council** 221 E Lane St .... Raleigh NC 27601-2812
919 733-3377 **Attorney General** 2 E Morgan St Justice Bldg .... Raleigh NC 27601-1447
919 733-7883 **Benefit Claims Administration** 700 Wade Ave .... Raleigh NC 27605-1154
919 733-7741 **Consumer Protection & Antitrust Section** PO Box 629 ...... Raleigh NC 27602-0629
919 733-7125 **Department of Agriculture** 1 W Edenton St .... Raleigh NC 27601-1094
919 733-4926 **Department of Corrections** 214 W Jones St .... Raleigh NC 27603-1381
919 733-4962 **Department of Economic & Community Development**
430 N Salisbury St Rm 6122 .... Raleigh NC 27603-5900
919 733-4984 **Department of Environment Health & Natural Resources**
512 N Salisbury St .... Raleigh NC 27611-0000
919 733-7343 **Department of Insurance** 430 N Salisbury St .... Raleigh NC 27603-5926
919 733-7166 **Department of Labor** 4 W Edenton St .... Raleigh NC 27601-2805
919 733-3813 **Department of Public Instruction** 116 W Edenton St .... Raleigh NC 27603-1799
919 733-7210 **Department of Revenue** Revenue Bldg .... Raleigh NC 27640-0001
919 733-2520 **Department of Transportation** 1 S Wilmington St .... Raleigh NC 27601-1453
919 733-7305 **Division of Archives & History** 109 E Jones St .... Raleigh NC 27601-2807
919 733-2633 **Division of Economic Opportunity** 2413-19 Crabtree Blvd ... Raleigh NC 27604-0000
919 733-3867 **Division of Emergency Management** 116 W Jones St .... Raleigh NC 27603-1300
919 733-7015 **Division of Environmental Management** 512 N Salisbury St .. Raleigh NC 27611-0000
919 733-7384 **Division of Highways** 1 S Wilmington St .... Raleigh NC 27611-0000
919 733-3900 **Division of Occupational Safety & Health** 413 N Salisbury St .. Raleigh NC 27603-0000
919 733-4131 **Division of Policy & Planning** 116 W Jones St .... Raleigh NC 27603-8003
919 733-3581 **Division of Purchase & Contract** 116 W Jones St .... Raleigh NC 27603-1300
919 733-7546 **Employment Security Commission** PO Box 25903 .... Raleigh NC 27611-5903
919 733-2230 **Energy Div** 430 N Salisbury St .... Raleigh NC 27611-0000
919 733-4240 **Governor** State Capitol .... Raleigh NC 27603-8001
919 733-7350 **Lieutenant Governor** Capitol Bldg .... Raleigh NC 27601-0001
919 733-7428 **Mine & Quarry Div** 4 W Edenton St .... Raleigh NC 27601-2805
919 733-0800 **North Carolina Central Prison** 1300 Western Blvd .... Raleigh NC 27606-2148
919 733-7061 **Office of State Budget & Management**
116 W Jones St Rm 5111 .... Raleigh NC 27603-8005
919 733-3414 **Parole Commission** 831 W Morgan St Randall Bldg .... Raleigh NC 27603-1660
704 637-1421 **Piedmont Correctional Center** 977 Camp Rd .... Salisbury NC 28145-0000
919 733-9580 **Real Estate Commission** 1313 Navaho Dr .... Raleigh NC 27609-7461
919 733-6555 **Retirement System Div** 325 N Salisbury St .... Raleigh NC 27603-1388
919 733-4161 **Secretary of State** 300 N Salisbury St .... Raleigh NC 27603-1386
919 733-3924 **Securities Div** 300 N Salisbury St Rm 404 .... Raleigh NC 27603-5925
919 733-2178 **Solid & Hazardous Waste Management Branch**
401 Oberlain Rd .... Raleigh NC 27605-1350
919 733-7962 **State Construction Div** 300 N Salisbury St Rm 403 .... Raleigh NC 27603-5925
919 733-7952 **State Highway Patrol Headquarters** PO Box 27687 .... Raleigh NC 27611-7687
919 733-3723 **Supreme Court** Justice Bldg Suite 100 .... Raleigh NC 27601-0000
919 733-3951 **Treasurer** 325 N Salisbury St .... Raleigh NC 27603-1388
919 733-4249 **Utilities Commission** 430 N Salisbury St .... Raleigh NC 27603-0000
919 733-3000 **Vital Records Branch** 225 N McDowell St .... Raleigh NC 27611-0000
919 733-4064 **Water Resources Div** PO Box 27687 .... Raleigh NC 27611-7687

NORTH DAKOTA

701 224-2000 **State Government Information** State Capitol .... Bismarck ND 58505-0000
701 224-5102 **Adjutant General** Fraine Barracks .... Bismarck ND 58502-0000
701 224-2210 **Attorney General** 600 E Boulevard Ave 1st Fl .... Bismarck ND 58505-0000
701 224-2960 **Board of Higher Education**
600 E Boulevard Ave State Capitol 10th Fl .... Bismarck ND 58505-0154
701 224-3404 **Consumer Fraud & Antitrust Dept** 600 E Boulevard Ave ...... Bismarck ND 58505-0000
701 237-8962 **Council on the Arts** Black Bldg Suite 606 .... Fargo ND 58102-4951
701 224-2231 **Department of Agriculture** 600 E Boulevard Ave .... Bismarck ND 58505-0000
701 224-2372 **Department of Health & Consolidated Laboratories**
600 E Boulevard Ave State Capitol 2nd Fl .... Bismarck ND 58505-0200
701 224-2660 **Department of Labor**
600 E Boulevard Ave State Capitol Bldg 6th Fl .... Bismarck ND 58505-0000
701 224-2260 **Department of Public Instruction** 600 E Boulevard Ave ...... Bismarck ND 58505-0440
701 224-2360 **Division of Vital Records** 600 E Boulevard Ave State Capitol ... Bismarck ND 58505-0001
701 224-2366 **Division of Waste Management** 1200 Missouri Ave Rm 302 ... Bismarck ND 58501-0000
701 224-2810 **Economic Development Commission**
604 E Boulevard Ave Liberty Memorial Bldg .... Bismarck ND 58505-0000
701 221-6300 **Game & Fish Dept** 100 N Bismarck Expy .... Bismarck ND 58501-5086
701 224-2200 **Governor** 600 E Boulevard Ave 1st Fl .... Bismarck ND 58505-0001
701 224-2581 **Highway Dept** 608 E Boulevard Ave .... Bismarck ND 58505-0663
701 224-2455 **Highway Patrol** 600 E Boulevard Ave State Capitol .... Bismarck ND 58505-0244
701 224-2471 **Institutions Office** 600 E Boulevard Ave 10th Fl .... Bismarck ND 58505-0000
701 224-2440 **Insurance Dept** 600 E Boulevard Ave 5th Fl .... Bismarck ND 58505-0320
701 224-2833 **Job Insurance Div** 1000 E Divide Ave .... Bismarck ND 58502-0000
701 224-2219 **Licensing Dept** State Capitol 17th Fl .... Bismarck ND 58505-0001
701 224-2200 **Lieutenant Governor** 600 E Boulevard Ave 1st Fl .... Bismarck ND 58505-0000
701 221-6100 **North Dakota Penitentiary** 3303 E Main .... Bismarck ND 58501-0000
701 221-6153 **North Dakota State Farm** PO Box 5521 .... Bismarck ND 58502-5521
701 224-2348 **Occupational Safety & Health Program** 1200 Missouri Ave .... Bismarck ND 58502-5520
701 224-2680 **Office of Management & Budget** 600 E Boulevard Ave .... Bismarck ND 58505-0000
701 224-2969 **Oil & Gas Div** 600 E Boulevard Ave State Capitol .... Bismarck ND 58505-0849
701 221-6190 **Parole & Probation Dept** PO Box 5521 .... Bismarck ND 58502-5521
701 224-2400 **Public Service Commission** State Capitol 12th Fl .... Bismarck ND 58505-0000
701 224-2749 **Real Estate Commission** PO Box 727 .... Bismarck ND 58502-0727
701 224-2900 **Secretary of State**
600 E Boulevard Ave State Capitol Bldg 1st Fl .... Bismarck ND 58505-0000
701 224-2910 **Securities Commissioner** State Capitol 5th Fl .... Bismarck ND 58505-0001
701 224-2668 **State Archives & Historical Research Library**
612 E Boulevard Ave North Dakota Heritage Ctr .... Bismarck ND 58505-0000
701 224-2221 **Supreme Court** 600 E Boulevard Ave Judicial Wing 1st Fl ...... Bismarck ND 58505-0000
701 224-2770 **Tax Commissioner** 600 E Boulevard Ave State Capitol 8th Fl ... Bismarck ND 58505-0000
701 224-2643 **Treasurer** 600 E Boulevard Ave .... Bismarck ND 58505-0600
701 224-2750 **Water Commission** 900 E Boulevard Ave .... Bismarck ND 58505-0859
701 224-2700 **Workmen's Compensation Bureau**
4007 N State St Hwy 83 N Russell Bldg .... Bismarck ND 58501-0689

OHIO

614 466-2000 **State Government Information** 65 E State St .... Columbus OH 43266-0001
614 466-2613 **Arts Council** 727 E Main St .... Columbus OH 43266-0540
614 466-3376 **Attorney General** 30 E Broad St 17th Fl .... Columbus OH 43266-0001
614 466-6000 **Board of Regents** 30 E Broad St Suite 3600 .... Columbus OH 43266-0001
614 466-2100 **Bureau of Employment Services** PO Box 1618 .... Columbus OH 43216-1618
614 466-2950 **Bureau of Workers' Compensation** 246 N High St .... Columbus OH 43215-2485
614 773-2616 **Chillicothe Correctional Institute** Rt 104 .... Chillicothe OH 45601-0000
614 466-4986 **Consumer Protection Div** 30 E Broad St 25th Fl .... Columbus OH 43266-0001
614 466-2732 **Department of Agriculture** 65 S Front St .... Columbus OH 43266-0302
614 466-3636 **Department of Commerce** 77 S High St .... Columbus OH 43266-0001
614 466-2480 **Department of Development** 77 S High St .... Columbus OH 43215-6108
614 466-3304 **Department of Education** 65 S Front St Rm 808 .... Columbus OH 43266-0001
614 466-3543 **Department of Health** 246 N High St .... Columbus OH 43266-0001
614 466-2550 **Department of Highway Safety** 240 Parsons Ave .... Columbus OH 43215-0000
614 644-2651 **Department of Insurance** 2100 Stella Ct .... Columbus OH 43266-0001
614 265-6722 **Department of Natural Resources Water Div**
1939 Fountain Sq Bldg E-3 .... Columbus OH 43224-0000
614 431-2762 **Department of Rehabilitation & Correction**
1050 Freeway Dr N .... Columbus OH 43229-5411

614 466-2335	**Department of Transportation** 25 S Front St	Columbus	OH	43215-4104
614 466-4130	**Division of Licensing** 77 S High St 23rd Fl	Columbus	OH	43266-0001
614 265-6893	**Division of Oil & Gas** Fountain Sq Bldg A-1	Columbus	OH	43224-0000
614 431-2776	**Division of Parole & Community Services** 1050 Freeway Dr N	Columbus	OH	43229-5411
614 644-3020	**Division of Pollution Control** 1800 Watermark Dr	Columbus	OH	43266-0001
614 466-4277	**Division of Public Works** 30 E Broad St	Columbus	OH	43215-0000
614 466-4100	**Division of Real Estate** 77 S High St 20th Fl	Columbus	OH	43266-0547
614 466-1276	**Division of Safety & Hygiene** 246 N High St 4th Fl	Columbus	OH	43215-0000
614 466-3440	**Division of Securities** 77 S High St 22nd Fl	Columbus	OH	43266-0548
614 466-2917	**Division of Solid & Hazardous Waste Management** PO Box 1049	Columbus	OH	43266-0149
614 866-0578	**Division of Surface Mines** 2242 S Hamilton Rd	Columbus	OH	43232-4304
614 466-2533	**Division of Vital Statistics** 65 S Front St Rm G-20	Columbus	OH	43266-0003
614 889-7150	**Emergency Management Agency** 2825 W Granville Rd	Columbus	OH	43235-2712
614 644-3020	**Environmental Protection Agency** 1800 Watermark Dr	Columbus	OH	43215-1043
614 466-3555	**Governor** 77 S High St 30th Fl	Columbus	OH	43215-6108
614 466-2990	**Highway Patrol** 660 E Main St	Columbus	OH	43205-1713
614 297-2300	**Historical Society** 1982 Velma Ave	Columbus	OH	43211-2497
614 644-2223	**Industrial Relations Dept** 2323 W 5th Ave	Columbus	OH	43216-0000
614 466-3396	**Lieutenant Governor** 77 S High St 30th Fl	Columbus	OH	43215-0000
614 466-4034	**Office of Budget & Management** 30 E Broad St 34th Fl	Columbus	OH	43215-0000
614 297-2300	**Ohio Historical Center** 1982 Velma Ave	Columbus	OH	43211-2497
419 526-2000	**Ohio State Reformatory** Olivesburg Rd	Mansfield	OH	44903-0000
614 466-5394	**Public Defender** 8 E Long St 11th Fl	Columbus	OH	43215-0000
614 466-3204	**Public Utilities Commission** 180 E Broad St	Columbus	OH	43266-0001
614 466-2655	**Secretary of State** 30 E Broad St 14th Fl	Columbus	OH	43215-3469
614 644-8493	**State Purchasing** 364 S 4th St	Columbus	OH	43266-0001
614 466-3931	**Supreme Court** 30 E Broad St 2nd Fl	Columbus	OH	43266-0001
614 466-2166	**Taxation Dept** 30 E Broad St 22nd Fl	Columbus	OH	43215-3414
614 466-2160	**Treasurer** 30 E Broad St 9 Fl	Columbus	OH	43215-3414
614 466-9755	**Unemployment Compensation Div** 145 S Front St Rm 538	Columbus	OH	43215-0000

OKLAHOMA

405 521-1601	**State Government Information** PO Box 26980	Oklahoma City	OK	73126-0980
405 325-3128	**Appellate Public Defender System** 1660 Cross Center Dr	Norman	OK	73019-0001
405 521-3921	**Attorney General** State Capitol Rm 112	Oklahoma City	OK	73105-0000
405 521-2115	**Central Purchasing Div** State Capitol Rm B-4	Oklahoma City	OK	73105-0000
405 521-2384	**Conservation Commission** 2800 N Lincoln Blvd Suite 160	Oklahoma City	OK	73105-4210
405 521-3864	**Department of Agriculture** 2800 N Lincoln Blvd	Oklahoma City	OK	73105-4298
405 521-2481	**Department of Civil Defense** PO Box 53365	Oklahoma City	OK	73152-3365
405 843-9770	**Department of Commerce** 6601 N Broadway Ext	Oklahoma City	OK	73116-8214
405 521-3653	**Department of Consumer Credit** 4545 N Lincoln Blvd Suite 104	Oklahoma City	OK	73105-3408
405 425-2500	**Department of Corrections** 3400 N Martin Luther King Ave	Oklahoma City	OK	73111-4298
405 521-3301	**Department of Education** 2500 N Lincoln Blvd	Oklahoma City	OK	73105-4596
405 271-5600	**Department of Health** 1000 NE 10th St	Oklahoma City	OK	73152-0000
405 528-1500	**Department of Labor** 4001 N Lincoln Blvd	Oklahoma City	OK	73105-5212
405 521-2502	**Department of Libraries** 200 NE 18th St	Oklahoma City	OK	73105-3298
405 521-3859	**Department of Mines** 4040 N Lincoln Blvd Suite 107	Oklahoma City	OK	73105-5282
405 521-2451	**Department of Securities** 2401 N Lincoln Blvd 4th Fl	Oklahoma City	OK	73105-4402
405 521-2631	**Department of Transportation** 200 NE 21st St	Oklahoma City	OK	73105-3204
405 425-2500	**Division of Programs & Services** 3400 Martin Luther King Ave	Oklahoma City	OK	73111-4219
405 557-7200	**Employment Security Commission** 2401 N Lincoln Blvd	Oklahoma City	OK	73105-4497
405 521-2342	**Governor** 212 State Capitol	Oklahoma City	OK	73105-4803
405 527-5593	**Harp Joseph Correctional Center** PO Box 548	Lexington	OK	73051-0548
405 425-2424	**Highway Patrol** 3600 N King Ave	Oklahoma City	OK	73111-0000
405 521-2828	**Insurance Dept** 1901 N Walnut Ave	Oklahoma City	OK	73105-3209
405 527-5676	**Lexington Assessment & Reception Center** PO Box 260	Lexington	OK	73051-0260
405 521-2161	**Lieutenant Governor** State Capitol Suite 211	Oklahoma City	OK	73105-0000
405 521-2302	**Oil & Gas Conservation Div** 2101 N Lincoln Blvd 2nd Fl	Oklahoma City	OK	73105-4904
405 521-2121	**Public Affairs Office** State Capitol Rm 104	Oklahoma City	OK	73105-0000
405 521-3908	**Public Utilities Div** 2101 N Lincoln Blvd 5th Fl	Oklahoma City	OK	73105-4904
405 521-3387	**Real Estate Commission** 4040 N Lincoln Blvd Suite 100	Oklahoma City	OK	73105-5283
405 528-1500	**Safety Standards Div** 4001 N Lincoln Blvd	Oklahoma City	OK	73105-0000
405 521-3911	**Secretary of State** State Capitol Rm 101	Oklahoma City	OK	73105-0000
405 521-2931	**State Arts Council** 2101 N Lincoln Blvd Rm 640	Oklahoma City	OK	73105-4904
405 521-2141	**State Finance Office** State Capitol Rm 122	Oklahoma City	OK	73105-0000
405 524-9100	**State Regents for Higher Education** 2500 N Lincoln Blvd	Oklahoma City	OK	73105-4503
405 521-2163	**Supreme Court** State Capitol Rm 1	Oklahoma City	OK	73105-0000
405 521-3114	**Tax Commission** 2501 N Lincoln Blvd	Oklahoma City	OK	73105-4396
405 521-3191	**Treasurer** State Capitol Rm 217	Oklahoma City	OK	73105-4892
405 271-4040	**Vital Records Div** PO Box 53551	Oklahoma City	OK	73152-3551
405 271-5338	**Waste Management Service** 1000 NE 10th St	Oklahoma City	OK	73152-0000
405 271-2555	**Water Resources Board** 1000 NE 10th St 12th Fl	Oklahoma City	OK	73152-0000
405 557-7600	**Workers' Compensation Court** 1915 N Stiles	Oklahoma City	OK	73105-4918

OREGON

503 378-3131	**State Government Information** 1225 Ferry St SE	Salem	OR	97310-0001
503 378-3272	**Accident Prevention Div** Labor & Industries Bldg Rm 160	Salem	OR	97310-0001
503 229-5397	**Air Quality Div** 811 SW 6th Ave 11th Fl	Portland	OR	97204-1334
503 378-4241	**Archives Div Secretary of State** 1005 Broadway NE	Salem	OR	97310-0001
503 378-3625	**Arts Commission** 835 Summer St NE	Salem	OR	97301-2595
503 378-6002	**Attorney General** 1162 Court St NE	Salem	OR	97310-0001
503 378-2334	**Board of Parole** 2575 Center St NE	Salem	OR	97310-0001
503 378-3104	**Budget & Management Div** 155 Cottage St NE	Salem	OR	97310-0001
503 229-5737	**Bureau of Labor & Industries** 1400 SW 5th Ave	Portland	OR	97201-5530
503 229-5895	**Center for Health Statistics** 1400 SW 5th Ave	Portland	OR	97201-5530
503 378-4732	**Consumer Affairs Div** 100 Justice Bldg	Salem	OR	97310-0001
503 378-2467	**Corrections Div** 2575 Center St NE	Salem	OR	97310-0001
503 378-4152	**Department of Agriculture** 635 Capitol St NE	Salem	OR	97310-0001
503 373-1205	**Department of Economic Development** 775 Summer St NE	Salem	OR	97310-0001
503 378-3573	**Department of Education** 700 Pringle Pkwy SE	Salem	OR	97310-0001
503 378-4040	**Department of Energy** 625 Marion St NE	Salem	OR	97310-0001
503 229-5696	**Department of Environmental Quality** 811 SW 6th Ave	Portland	OR	97204-1334
503 378-4516	**Department of General Services** 1225 Ferry St SE	Salem	OR	97310-0001
503 229-5580	**Department of Geology & Mineral Industries** 1400 SW 5th Ave Rm 910	Portland	OR	97201-5528
503 378-4100	**Department of Insurance & Finance** 21 Labor & Industries Bldg	Salem	OR	97310-0001
503 378-3363	**Department of Revenue** 955 Center St NE	Salem	OR	97310-0001
503 378-4329	**Department of the Treasury** 159 State Capitol	Salem	OR	97310-0001
503 378-6388	**Department of Transportation** Transportation Bldg	Salem	OR	97310-0001
503 378-4124	**Emergency Management Div** 603 Chemeketa St NE	Salem	OR	97310-0001
503 378-3211	**Employment Div** 875 Union St NE	Salem	OR	97311-0001
503 378-3121	**Executive Assistant to Governor** State Capitol Rm 254	Salem	OR	97310-0001
503 378-3111	**Governor** State Capitol Rm 254	Salem	OR	97310-0001
503 229-5913	**Hazardous & Solid Waste Div** 811 SW 6th Ave	Portland	OR	97204-1334
503 229-5806	**Health Div** 1400 SW 5th Ave	Portland	OR	97201-5530
503 378-6516	**Highway Div** Transportation Bldg Rm 102	Salem	OR	97310-0001
503 378-4474	**Insurance Div** 21 Labor & Industries Bldg	Salem	OR	97310-0001
503 378-3548	**Natural Resources Dept** State Capitol Rm 160	Salem	OR	97310-0001
503 373-0105	**Oregon State Correctional Institution** 3405 Deer Park Dr SE	Salem	OR	97310-0001
503 378-3349	**Public Defender** 1655 State St	Salem	OR	97310-0001
503 378-6611	**Public Utility Commission** 351 W Summer St NE	Salem	OR	97310-0001
503 378-4643	**Purchasing Div** 1225 Ferry St SE	Salem	OR	97310-0001
503 378-4170	**Real Estate Agency** 158 12th St NE	Salem	OR	97310-0001
503 378-4139	**Secretary of State** 136 State Capitol	Salem	OR	97310-0001
503 378-4387	**Security Section** 21 Labor & Industries Bldg Rm 130	Salem	OR	97310-0000
503 378-2445	**State Penitentiary** 2605 State St	Salem	OR	97310-0001
503 378-3720	**State Police** Public Service Bldg Rm 107	Salem	OR	97310-0001
503 346-5794	**State System of Higher Education** PO Box 3175	Eugene	OR	97403-0175
503 378-6005	**Supreme Court** 1163 State St	Salem	OR	97310-0001
503 378-2982	**Water Resources Dept** 3850 Portland Rd NE	Salem	OR	97310-0001
503 378-3304	**Workers' Compensation Div** 21 Labor & Industries Bldg Rm 210	Salem	OR	97310-0001

PENNSYLVANIA

717 787-2121	**State Government Information** Transportation & Safety Bldg Rm B102	Harrisburg	PA	17125-0001
717 787-3391	**Attorney General** 4th & Walnut Sts Strawberry Sq 16th Fl	Harrisburg	PA	17120-0001
717 787-5100	**Board of Probation & Parole** 3101 N Front St	Harrisburg	PA	17105-1661
717 787-9702	**Bureau of Air Quality Control** 101 S 2nd St Executive House Rm 116	Harrisburg	PA	17120-0001
717 787-3051	**Bureau of Archives & History** PO Box 1026	Harrisburg	PA	17108-1026
717 787-9707	**Bureau of Consumer Protection** 4th & Walnut Sts Strawberry Sq 14th Fl	Harrisburg	PA	17120-0001
717 787-5103	**Bureau of Mining & Reclamation** 2nd & Chestnut Sts	Harrisburg	PA	17105-2357
717 783-9645	**Bureau of Oil & Gas Management** 2nd & Chestnut Sts Executive House Rm 811	Harrisburg	PA	17105-2357
717 787-4718	**Bureau of Purchases** Commonwealth Ave & North St	Harrisburg	PA	17125-0001
717 787-2480	**Bureau of Radiation Protection** 200 N 3rd St	Harrisburg	PA	17101-0000
717 787-4394	**Bureau of Real Estate** North Office Bldg Rm 505	Harrisburg	PA	17125-0001
717 540-5080	**Bureau of Soil & Water Conservation** 1 Ararat Blvd Rm 214	Harrisburg	PA	17110-9720
717 787-3547	**Bureau of Unemployment** 7th & Forster Sts	Harrisburg	PA	17121-0001
717 787-9870	**Bureau of Waste Management** 200 N 3rd St	Harrisburg	PA	17105-2063
717 783-5421	**Bureau of Workers' Compensation** 1171 S Cameron St Rm 103	Harrisburg	PA	17104-2501
717 787-3003	**Commerce Dept** 433 Forum Bldg	Harrisburg	PA	17120-0001
717 787-6883	**Council on the Arts** 216 Finance Bldg	Harrisburg	PA	17120-0001
717 787-4737	**Department of Agriculture** 2301 N Cameron St	Harrisburg	PA	17110-9408
717 975-4860	**Department of Corrections** 2520 Lisburn Rd	Camp Hill	PA	17011-8005
717 787-5820	**Department of Education** 333 Market St	Harrisburg	PA	17126-0333
717 787-2814	**Department of Environmental Resources** 3rd & Locust Sts	Harrisburg	PA	17120-0001
717 787-6436	**Department of Health** 7th & Forster St	Harrisburg	PA	17120-0000
717 787-5173	**Department of Insurance** 1326 Strawberry Sq	Harrisburg	PA	17120-0001
717 787-3907	**Department of Labor & Industry** 7th & Forester Sts Rm 1700	Harrisburg	PA	17120-0001
717 783-3680	**Department of Revenue** 4th & Walnut Sts Strawberry Sq 11th Fl	Harrisburg	PA	17128-0001
717 787-3154	**Department of Transportation** Commonwealth Ave & Forster St Transportation & Safety Bldg	Harrisburg	PA	17120-0001
717 783-8150	**Emergency Management Agency** Commonwealth Ave & Forster St Rm B-149	Harrisburg	PA	17105-0000
717 783-9981	**Energy Office** 116 Pine St 2nd Fl	Harrisburg	PA	17101-1227
717 787-5295	**General Services Dept** North Office Bldg Rm 414	Harrisburg	PA	17125-0001
717 787-2500	**Governor** Main Capitol Bldg Rm 225	Harrisburg	PA	17120-0001
717 787-3300	**Lieutenant Governor** Main Capitol Bldg Rm 200	Harrisburg	PA	17120-0001
717 787-6875	**Office of Highway Administration** Commonwealth Ave & Forster St Rm 1220	Harrisburg	PA	17120-0001
717 787-7095	**Office of Public Works** 18th & Herr Sts	Harrisburg	PA	17125-0001
717 787-4095	**Public Utility Commission** Commonwealth Ave & North St North Office Bldg Rm B-18	Harrisburg	PA	17120-0001
717 787-7630	**Secretary of the Commonwealth** N Office Bldg Rm 302	Harrisburg	PA	17120-0001
717 787-8061	**Securities Commission** 1010 N 7th St Eastgate Office Bldg	Harrisburg	PA	17102-0000
717 737-4531	**State Correctional Institution** PO Box 200	Camp Hill	PA	17011-0200
215 489-4151	**State Correctional Institution** PO Box 244	Graterford	PA	19426-0244
717 783-3810	**State Health Data Center** Commonwealth Ave & Forster St	Harrisburg	PA	17120-0001
717 783-5561	**State Police** 1800 Elmerton Ave	Harrisburg	PA	17110-9758
215 560-6370	**Supreme Court** City Hall Rm 468	Philadelphia	PA	19107-0000
717 787-2465	**Treasury Dept** Commonwealth Ave & North St Rm 129	Harrisburg	PA	17120-0000

RHODE ISLAND

401 277-2000	**State Government Information** 1 Capitol Hill	Providence	RI	02908-5803
401 277-2781	**Agriculture Div** 22 Hayes St Rm 120	Providence	RI	02908-5025
401 277-2353	**Archives Div** 343-345 Westminster St	Providence	RI	02903-1120
401 789-9391	**Atomic Energy Commission** S Ferry Rd	Narragansett	RI	02882-0000
401 274-4400	**Attorney General** 72 Pine St	Providence	RI	02903-2856
401 277-2764	**Consumer's Council** 365 Broadway	Providence	RI	02909-1498
401 277-3880	**Council on the Arts** 95 Cedar St Suite 103	Providence	RI	02903-1062
401 277-2280	**Department of Administration** 1 Capitol Hill 4th Fl	Providence	RI	02908-0000
401 277-2246	**Department of Business Regulation** 233 Richmond St	Providence	RI	02903-4229
401 464-2611	**Department of Corrections** 75 Howard Ave	Cranston	RI	02920-3082
401 277-2031	**Department of Education** 22 Hayes St	Providence	RI	02908-5092
401 277-3648	**Department of Employment & Training** 101 Friendship St	Providence	RI	02903-1082
401 277-3434	**Department of Environmental Management** 83 Park St	Providence	RI	02908-0000
401 277-2233	**Department of Health** 3 Capitol Hill	Providence	RI	02908-1006
401 457-1800	**Department of Labor** 220 Elmwood Ave	Providence	RI	02907-0000
401 277-3492	**Department of the Public Defender** 250 Benefit St	Providence	RI	02903-2719
401 277-2481	**Department of Transportation** 2 Capitol Hill State Office Bldg Rm 210	Providence	RI	02903-0000
401 272-0700	**Department of Workers' Compensation** 610 Manton Ave	Providence	RI	02909-5633
401 277-2797	**Division of Air & Hazardous Materials** 291 Promenade St	Providence	RI	02908-5720
401 277-3649	**Division of Benefits** 101 Friendship St	Providence	RI	02903-1029
401 457-1829	**Division of Occupational Safety** 220 Elmwood Ave	Providence	RI	02907-1435
401 277-2656	**Division of Planning** 1 Capitol Hill	Providence	RI	02908-5870
401 277-3496	**Division of Probation & Parole** 1 Dorrance Plaza	Providence	RI	02903-3922
401 277-2827	**Division of Professional Regulation** 3 Capitol Hill	Providence	RI	02908-1006
401 277-3500	**Division of Public Utilities & Carriers** 100 Orange St	Providence	RI	02903-2803
401 277-2317	**Division of Purchases** 1 Capitol Hill	Providence	RI	02908-5810
401 277-3050	**Division of Taxation** 1 Capitol Hill	Providence	RI	02908-5800
401 277-2812	**Division of Vital Statistics** 3 Capitol Hill Rm 101	Providence	RI	02908-5097
401 277-2601	**Economic Development Dept** 7 Jackson Walkway	Providence	RI	02903-3622
401 421-7333	**Emergency Management Agency** 82 Smith St State House Rm 27	Providence	RI	02903-0000
401 277-2080	**Governor** 222 State House	Providence	RI	02903-0000
401 277-6920	**Governor's Office of Energy-Housing & Inter Governmental Relations** 275 Westminster Mall Rm 143	Providence	RI	02903-3415
401 464-2125	**High Security Center** PO Box 8200	Cranston	RI	02920-0200
401 277-2371	**Lieutenant Governor** State House Rm 317	Providence	RI	02903-0000
401 464-2054	**Maximum Security Facility at Cranston** PO Box 8273	Cranston	RI	02920-0273
401 277-2685	**Office of Higher Education** 301 Promenade St Rm 217	Providence	RI	02908-5006
401 277-2357	**Secretary of State** State House Rm 217	Providence	RI	02903-0000

State Government

401 277-3048	**Securities Div** 233 Richmond St Suite 232	Providence	RI	02903-4232
401 647-3311	**State Police** 311 Danielson Pike	North Scituate	RI	02857-1907
401 277-3272	**Supreme Court** 250 Benefit St	Providence	RI	02903-2794
401 277-2287	**Treasury Dept** 198 Dyer St	Providence	RI	02903-3906
401 277-2443	**Utilities Commission** 100 Orange St	Providence	RI	02903-2803
401 277-2217	**Water Resources Board** 265 Melrose St	Providence	RI	02907-2196

SOUTH CAROLINA

803 734-1000	**State Government Information** 1026 Sumter St	Columbia	SC	29201-3716
803 734-8696	**Arts Commission** 1800 Gervais St	Columbia	SC	29201-3581
803 734-3970	**Attorney General** 1000 Assembly St	Columbia	SC	29201-3117
803 734-4750	**Bureau of Air Quality Control** 2600 Bull St	Columbia	SC	29201-1708
803 734-4634	**Bureau of Radiological Health** 2600 Bull St	Columbia	SC	29201-1708
803 734-5200	**Bureau of Solid & Hazardous Waste Management** 2600 Bull St	Columbia	SC	29201-1708
803 737-1990	**Central Correctional Institution** 1515 Gist St	Columbia	SC	22911-0000
803 253-6260	**Commission on Higher Education** 1333 Main St Suite 300	Columbia	SC	29201-3201
803 734-2121	**Comptroller General** Wade Hampton Office Bldg Rm 305	Columbia	SC	29211-0000
803 734-2210	**Department of Agriculture** 1200 Senate St	Columbia	SC	29201-3734
803 734-8577	**Department of Archives & History** 1430 Senate St	Columbia	SC	29201-0000
803 734-9452	**Department of Consumer Affairs** 2801 Devine St	Columbia	SC	29205-2556
803 737-8500	**Department of Corrections** 4444 Broad River Rd	Columbia	SC	29210-4000
803 734-8492	**Department of Education** 1429 Senate St	Columbia	SC	29201-3799
803 737-1302	**Department of Highways & Public Transportation** 955 Park St	Columbia	SC	29202-0000
803 737-6268	**Department of Insurance** 1612 Marion St	Columbia	SC	29201-2913
803 734-9600	**Department of Labor** 3600 Forest Dr	Columbia	SC	29204-4033
803 734-0662	**Division of Economic Opportunity** 1205 Pendleton St	Columbia	SC	29201-3731
803 734-5360	**Division of Environmental Quality Control** 2600 Bull St	Columbia	SC	29201-1708
803 734-9100	**Division of Mining & Reclamation** 2221 Devine St Suite 222	Columbia	SC	29205-2418
803 734-0425	**Division of Public Safety Programs** 1205 Pendleton St	Columbia	SC	29201-3731
803 734-8020	**Emergency Preparedness Div** 1429 Senate St	Columbia	SC	29201-3730
803 737-2400	**Employment Security Commission** 1550 Gadsen St	Columbia	SC	29202-0000
803 656-2267	**Energy Research & Development Center** 386-2 College Ave	Clemson	SC	29634-0929
803 734-9818	**Governor** PO Box 11369	Columbia	SC	29211-1369
803 734-9100	**Land Resources Conservation Commission** 2221 Devine St Suite 222	Columbia	SC	29205-2474
803 734-2080	**Lieutenant Governor** PO Box 142	Columbia	SC	29202-0142
803 734-9643	**Occupational Safety & Health** 3600 Forest Dr	Columbia	SC	29204-0000
803 734-4810	**Office of Vital Records & Public Health Statistics** 2600 Bull St	Columbia	SC	29201-1708
803 737-1752	**Perry Correctional Institution** 430 Oaklawn Rd	Pelzer	SC	29669-9361
803 734-9244	**Probation Parole & Pardon Services** 2221 Devine St	Columbia	SC	29205-2418
803 737-5143	**Public Service Commission** 111 Doctors Cir	Columbia	SC	29203-6580
803 737-9480	**Real Estate Commission** 1201 Main St Suite 1500	Columbia	SC	29201-3228
803 734-1660	**Retirement Systems** PO Box 11960	Columbia	SC	29211-1960
803 734-2170	**Secretary of State** Wade Hampton Office Bldg Rm 109	Columbia	SC	29201-0000
803 734-1087	**Securities Div** 1205 Pendleton St Suite 501	Columbia	SC	29201-3727
803 737-0400	**State Development Board** 1201 Main St 16th Fl	Columbia	SC	29201-3212
803 734-2101	**State Treasurer** Capitol Complex 1st Fl	Columbia	SC	29211-0000
803 734-1080	**Supreme Court** 1231 Gervais St	Columbia	SC	29201-3206
803 737-9830	**Tax Commission** 301 Gervais St	Columbia	SC	29201-3041
803 737-0800	**Water Resources Commission** 1201 Main St Suite 1100	Columbia	SC	29201-3239
803 737-5697	**Worker's Compensation Commission** 1612 Marion St	Columbia	SC	29201-0000

SOUTH DAKOTA

605 773-3011	**State Government Information** 500 E Capitol Ave	Pierre	SD	57501-5070
605 339-6646	**Arts Council** 108 W 11th St	Sioux Falls	SD	57102-0788
605 773-3215	**Attorney General** 500 E Capitol Ave	Pierre	SD	57501-5070
605 339-6780	**Board of Pardons & Paroles** PO Box 911	Sioux Falls	SD	57117-0911
605 773-3693	**Center for Health Policy & Statistics** 523 E Capitol Ave	Pierre	SD	57501-3182
605 773-4400	**Consumer Affairs Div** 500 E Capitol Ave	Pierre	SD	57501-0000
605 773-3375	**Department of Agriculture** 445 E Capitol Ave Anderson Bldg	Pierre	SD	57501-0000
605 773-3478	**Department of Corrections** 523 E Capitol Ave	Pierre	SD	57501-3182
605 773-3361	**Department of Health** 523 E Capitol Ave	Pierre	SD	57501-3182
605 773-5131	**Department of Revenue** 700 Governors Dr	Pierre	SD	57501-2291
605 773-3265	**Department of Transportation** 700 E Broadway Ave	Pierre	SD	57501-2586
605 773-3151	**Department of Water & Natural Resources** 523 E Capitol Ave	Pierre	SD	57501-3182
605 773-3603	**Division of Alternative Energy** 217 1/2 W Missouri Ave	Pierre	SD	57501-4516
605 773-3243	**Division of Education** 700 Governors Dr	Pierre	SD	57501-2291
605 773-3231	**Division of Emergency & Disaster Services** 500 E Capitol Ave	Pierre	SD	57501-5070
605 773-3563	**Division of Insurance** 910 E Sioux Ave	Pierre	SD	57501-3940
605 773-3178	**Division of Professional & Occupational Licensing** 910 E Sioux Ave	Pierre	SD	57501-3940
605 773-4823	**Division of Securities** 910 E Sioux Ave	Pierre	SD	57501-3940
605 773-3411	**Finance & Management Bureau** 500 E Capitol Ave 2nd Fl	Pierre	SD	57501-0000
605 773-3212	**Governor** 500 E Capitol Ave	Pierre	SD	57501-5070
605 773-4094	**Highway Patrol** 300 N Nicollet Ave	Pierre	SD	57501-5070
605 773-3458	**Historical Archives** 900 Governors Dr	Pierre	SD	57501-2200
605 773-3681	**Labor & Management** 700 Governors Dr	Pierre	SD	57501-2291
605 773-3661	**Lieutenant Governor** 500 E Capitol Ave Suite 215	Pierre	SD	57501-5070
605 773-4201	**Office of Minerals & Mining** 523 E Capitol Ave	Pierre	SD	57501-3182
605 773-3201	**Public Utilities Commission** 500 E Capitol Ave	Pierre	SD	57501-5070
605 773-3405	**Purchasing & Printing** 523 E Capitol Ave	Pierre	SD	57501-3182
605 773-3600	**Real Estate Commission** 212 E Capitol Ave	Pierre	SD	57501-2518
605 773-3537	**Secretary of State** 500 E Capitol Ave 2nd Fl	Pierre	SD	57501-5070
605 339-6764	**South Dakota Penitentiary** PO Box 911	Sioux Falls	SD	57117-0911
605 369-2201	**Springfield Correctional Facility** PO Box 322	Springfield	SD	57062-0322
605 773-3455	**State Board of Regents** 207 E Capitol Ave St Charles Hotel	Pierre	SD	57501-3159
605 773-3511	**Supreme Court** 500 E Capitol Ave	Pierre	SD	57501-5070
605 773-3378	**Treasurer** 500 E Capitol Ave 2nd Fl Annex	Pierre	SD	57501-0000
605 622-2452	**Unemployment Insurance Div** 420 S Roosevelt St	Aberdeen	SD	57402-4730

TENNESSEE

615 741-3011	**State Government Information** B10 John Sevier Bldg	Nashville	TN	37219-0000
615 741-3141	**Adult Probation Div Department of Corrections** 320 6th Ave N 2nd Fl	Nashville	TN	37219-5252
615 741-3931	**Air Pollution Control Div** 701 Broadway	Nashville	TN	37247-3101
615 741-1701	**Arts Commission** 320 6th Ave N Suite 100	Nashville	TN	37219-5605
615 741-3491	**Attorney General** 450 James Robertson Pkwy	Nashville	TN	37219-5025
615 741-3657	**Bureau of Environment** 150 9th Ave N Terra Bldg 1st Fl	Nashville	TN	37247-0000
615 360-0103	**Department of Agriculture** Ellington Agriculture Ctr	Nashville	TN	37204-0000
615 741-2241	**Department of Commerce & Insurance** 500 James Robertson Pkwy 5th Fl	Nashville	TN	37243-0000
615 742-6749	**Department of Conservation** 701 Broadway	Nashville	TN	37243-0000
615 741-2071	**Department of Corrections** 320 6th Ave N	Nashville	TN	37219-5605
615 741-1888	**Department of Economic & Community Development** 320 6th Ave N 8th Fl	Nashville	TN	37219-5605
615 741-2731	**Department of Education** 100 Cordell Hull Bldg	Nashville	TN	37219-5335
615 741-2131	**Department of Employment Security** 500 James Robertson Pkwy 12th Fl	Nashville	TN	37245-0001
615 741-2140	**Department of Finance & Administration** 500 Deaderick St Rm 314	Nashville	TN	37219-5609
615 741-2461	**Department of Revenue** Andrew Jackson Bldg Suite 1200	Nashville	TN	37242-0000
615 741-2956	**Department of the Treasury** State Capitol 1st Fl	Nashville	TN	37219-0000
615 741-2848	**Department of Transportation** James K Polk Bldg Suite 700	Nashville	TN	37243-0000
615 741-4737	**Division of Consumer Affairs** 500 James Robertson Pkwy 5th Fl	Nashville	TN	37243-1215
615 742-6691	**Division of Geology** 701 Broadway Suite B-30	Nashville	TN	37243-0445
615 741-2451	**Division of Library & Archives** 403 7th Ave N	Nashville	TN	37243-0312
615 562-4914	**Division of Mines** Queener Rd	Caryville	TN	37714-0000
615 741-2793	**Division of Occupational Safety & Health** 501 Union St 3rd Fl	Nashville	TN	37243-0659
615 741-1035	**Division of Purchasing** 503 5th Ave N Rm C2-214	Nashville	TN	37219-0000
615 741-7063	**Division of Retirement** 500 Deaderick St Andrew Jackson Bldg 10th Fl	Nashville	TN	37219-5609
615 741-2947	**Division of Securities** 500 James Robertson Pkwy Suite 680	Nashville	TN	37243-0000
615 741-3424	**Division of Solid Waste Management** 701 Broadway	Nashville	TN	37247-5403
615 741-1763	**Division of Vital Records** Cordell Hull Bldg	Nashville	TN	37247-0350
615 252-3311	**Emergency Management Agency** 3041 Sidco Dr	Nashville	TN	37204-4505
615 741-2001	**Governor** State Capitol	Nashville	TN	37219-5601
615 741-3605	**Higher Education Commission** 404 James Robertson Pkwy Parkway Towers Suite 1900	Nashville	TN	37219-0000
615 741-2368	**Lieutenant Governor** Legislative Plaza Suite 1	Nashville	TN	37219-0000
615 741-1676	**Planning Office** 500 Charlotte Ave	Nashville	TN	37219-5608
615 741-6888	**Property Services Management** 302 Cordell Hull Bldg Rm C-3	Nashville	TN	37243-0000
615 741-2904	**Public Service Commission** 460 James Robertson Pkwy	Nashville	TN	37219-5477
615 741-2273	**Real Estate Commission** 500 James Robertson Pkwy Suite 180	Nashville	TN	37243-0000
615 741-3449	**Regulatory Boards** 500 James Robertson Pkwy 2nd Fl	Nashville	TN	37243-0572
615 741-2816	**Secretary of State** State Capitol 1st Fl	Nashville	TN	37219-0000
615 881-3251	**Southeastern Tennessee State Regional Correctional Facility** Rt 4 Box 600	Pikeville	TN	37367-9243
615 741-3181	**State Highway Patrol** 1603 Murfreesboro Rd	Nashville	TN	37217-0000
615 741-2681	**Supreme Court** 401 7th Ave N Supreme Court Bldg Rm 100	Nashville	TN	37243-0000
615 741-4611	**Tennessee State Penitentiary** Stn A	Nashville	TN	37219-0000
615 741-7883	**Water Pollution Control** 150 9th Ave N Terra Bldg 1st Fl	Nashville	TN	37247-3420
615 741-2395	**Worker's Compensation Div** 501 Union St	Nashville	TN	37243-0661

TEXAS

512 463-4630	**State Government Information** 201 E 14th St	Austin	TX	78701-0000
512 451-5711	**Air Control Board** 6330 Hwy 290 E	Austin	TX	78723-1078
512 463-2100	**Attorney General** PO Box 12548	Austin	TX	78711-1930
512 463-2611	**Benefits Dept** 101 E 15th St	Austin	TX	78778-0001
903 928-2217	**Beto 1 Unit** PO Box 128	Tennessee Colony	TX	75861-0128
512 459-2700	**Board of Pardons & Paroles** 8610 Shoal Creek Blvd	Austin	TX	78758-6814
512 458-7366	**Bureau of Vital Statistics** 1100 W 49th St	Austin	TX	78756-3101
903 928-2211	**Coffield Unit** Rt 1 Box 150	Tennessee Colony	TX	75861-9710
512 463-5535	**Commission on the Arts** PO Box 13406	Austin	TX	78711-3046
512 463-2070	**Consumer Protection Div** 1500 N Congress Ave	Austin	TX	78701-0000
512 463-7435	**Department of Agriculture** PO Box 12847	Austin	TX	78711-2847
512 472-5059	**Department of Commerce** 816 Congress Ave Suite 1200	Austin	TX	78701-2430
512 834-6050	**Department of Community Affairs** 8317 Cross Park Dr	Austin	TX	78711-0000
409 295-6371	**Department of Criminal Justice** 815 11th St	Huntsville	TX	77340-4729
512 458-7375	**Department of Health** 1100 W 49th St	Austin	TX	78756-3197
512 463-8585	**Department of Highways & Public Transportation** 11th & Brazos Sts	Austin	TX	78701-2483
512 463-2906	**Department of Licensing & Regulations** 920 Colorado St	Austin	TX	78701-2325
512 465-2000	**Department of Public Safety** PO Box 4087	Austin	TX	78773-0001
512 465-2138	**Division of Emergency Management** PO Box 4087	Austin	TX	78773-0001
512 458-7271	**Division of Solid Waste Management** 1100 W 49th St	Austin	TX	78756-3101
512 463-8985	**Education Agency** 1701 N Congress Ave	Austin	TX	78701-1494
512 464-2222	**Employment Commission** 101 E 15th St	Austin	TX	78778-0001
512 463-2198	**Energy Research & Policy Analysis** 201 E 14th St	Austin	TX	78711-0000
512 463-2012	**Environmental Protection Div** PO Box 12548	Austin	TX	78711-0000
512 463-3214	**Facilities Construction & Space Management Div** PO Box 13047	Austin	TX	78711-3047
512 479-1200	**Finance Commission** 2601 N Lamar Blvd	Austin	TX	78705-4294
512 463-2000	**Governor** PO Box 12428	Austin	TX	78711-2428
512 462-6400	**Higher Education Coordinating Board** 200 E Riverside Dr	Austin	TX	78704-1205
512 463-0001	**Lieutenant Governor** State Capitol Rm 219	Austin	TX	78711-0000
512 458-7287	**Occupational Safety & Health Div** 1100 W 49th St	Austin	TX	78756-3101
512 463-6893	**Oil & Gas Div** PO Box 12967	Austin	TX	78711-2967
512 463-5022	**Petroleum & Minerals Development Div** 1700 N Congress Ave	Austin	TX	78701-1436
512 463-1778	**Planning Office** 201 E 14th St	Austin	TX	78711-0000
512 458-0100	**Public Utility Commission** 7800 Shoal Creek Blvd Suite 400 N	Austin	TX	78757-1098
512 463-3445	**Purchasing Div** 1711 San Jacinto Blvd	Austin	TX	78701-1416
512 459-6544	**Real Estate Commission** PO Box 12188	Austin	TX	78711-2188
512 463-5701	**Secretary of State** PO Box 12697	Austin	TX	78711-2697
512 474-2233	**Securities Board** PO Box 13167	Austin	TX	78711-3167
512 463-5480	**State Archives** 1201 Brazos St	Austin	TX	78701-0000
512 463-6464	**State Board of Insurance** 1110 San Jacinto Blvd	Austin	TX	78701-1998
512 463-4865	**State Controllers Office** 111 E 17th St LBJ Bldg	Austin	TX	78711-0000
512 463-1312	**Supreme Court** 200 W 14th St Room AG-11	Austin	TX	78701-0000
512 463-6000	**Treasury** 111 E 17th St	Austin	TX	78701-1440
512 463-7847	**Water Development Board** PO Box 13231	Austin	TX	78711-3231

UTAH

801 538-3000	**State Government Information** 1226 State Office Bldg Rm B-69	Salt Lake City	UT	84114-1201
801 533-5895	**Arts Council** 617 E South Temple	Salt Lake City	UT	84102-1177
801 538-1015	**Attorney General** State Capitol Rm 236	Salt Lake City	UT	84114-1191
801 261-2825	**Board of Pardons** 6100 S 300 East Suite 203	Murray	UT	84107-7375
801 538-6108	**Bureau of Air Quality** 288 N 1460 West 2nd Fl	Salt Lake City	UT	84116-3100
801 538-6170	**Bureau of Solid & Hazardous Wastes** 288 N 1460 West	Salt Lake City	UT	84116-3100
801 538-6186	**Bureau of Vital Records** 288 N 1460 West	Salt Lake City	UT	84116-3100
801 530-6601	**Consumer Protection Div** 160 E 300 South 2nd Fl	Salt Lake City	UT	84111-2316
801 965-4587	**Council for Crime Prevention** 1879 S Main St Suite 180	Salt Lake City	UT	84115-0000
801 538-7101	**Department of Agriculture** 350 N Redwood Rd	Salt Lake City	UT	84116-3087
801 530-6628	**Department of Business Regulation Div Occupational & Professional Licensing** 160 E 300 South 4th Fl	Salt Lake City	UT	84111-2328
801 538-8700	**Department of Community & Economic Development** 324 S State St Suite 200	Salt Lake City	UT	84111-0000
801 265-5500	**Department of Corrections** 6100 S 300 East	Murray	UT	84107-7378
801 533-2400	**Department of Employment Security** 174 Social Hall Ave	Salt Lake City	UT	84147-0000
801 538-6101	**Department of Health** 288 N 1460 West	Salt Lake City	UT	84116-0000
801 538-7200	**Department of Natural Resources** 1636 W North Temple Suite 316	Salt Lake City	UT	84116-3193
801 965-4113	**Department of Transportation** 4501 S 2700 West	Salt Lake City	UT	84119-5977
801 584-8370	**Division of Comprehensive Emergency Management** 1543 Sunnyside Ave	Salt Lake City	UT	84105-0000
801 538-3018	**Division of Facilities Construction & Management** State Office Bldg	Salt Lake City	UT	84114-1201
801 538-3020	**Division of Finance** 6000 State Office Bldg	Salt Lake City	UT	84114-1201

801 538-5340 **Division of Oil Gas & Mining**
355 W North Temple Suite 350 ... Salt Lake City UT 84180-0000
801 538-3026 **Division of Purchasing** State Office Bldg Rm 3150 ... Salt Lake City UT 84114-1201
801 538-5428 **Energy Office** 355 W North Temple Suite 450 ... Salt Lake City UT 84180-1204
801 538-1000 **Governor** 210 State Capitol ... Salt Lake City UT 84114-1202
801 965-4518 **Highway Patrol Div** 4501 S 2700 West ... Salt Lake City UT 84119-5977
801 530-6922 **Industrial Commission** 160 E 300 South 3rd Fl ... Salt Lake City UT 84111-2316
801 530-6400 **Insurance Dept** 3110 State Office Bldg 3rd Fl ... Salt Lake City UT 84114-0000
801 586-3356 **Iron County Utah State Correctional Facility**
2136 N Main St ... Cedar City UT 84720-9788
801 538-1040 **Lieutenant Governor** 203 State Capitol ... Salt Lake City UT 84114-1202
801 538-7500 **Office of Education** 250 E 500 South ... Salt Lake City UT 84111-3204
801 538-1540 **Office of Planning & Budget** State Capitol Rm 116 ... Salt Lake City UT 84114-1202
801 530-6716 **Public Service Commission** 160 E 300 South ... Salt Lake City UT 84111-2316
801 530-6747 **Real Estate Div** PO Box 45802 ... Salt Lake City UT 84145-0802
801 355-3884 **Retirement System** 540 E 200 South ... Salt Lake City UT 84102-2001
801 530-6600 **Securities Div** 160 E 300 South ... Salt Lake City UT 84111-2316
801 538-3012 **State Archives** Archives Bldg ... Salt Lake City UT 84114-0000
801 538-1044 **Supreme Court** 332 State Capitol ... Salt Lake City UT 84114-1181
801 538-5247 **System of Higher Education**
355 W North Temple Suite 550 ... Salt Lake City UT 84180-1205
801 530-6088 **Tax Commission** 160 E 300 South ... Salt Lake City UT 84134-0001
801 538-3330 **Telecommunication Office** B-69 State Capitol ... Salt Lake City UT 84114-0000
801 533-2201 **Unemployment Insurance Div** 174 Social Hall Ave ... Salt Lake City UT 84111-1504
801 571-2300 **Utah State Prison** PO Box 250 ... Draper UT 84020-0250
801 530-6800 **Workers' Compensation** 160 E 300 South ... Salt Lake City UT 84111-2316

VERMONT

802 828-1110 **State Government Information** State Administration Bldg ... Montpelier VT 05602-0000
802 828-3322 **Agency of Administration**
109 State St Pavilion Office Bldg 5th Fl ... Montpelier VT 05602-0000
802 244-7347 **Agency of Natural Resources** 103 S Main St ... Waterbury VT 05676-1534
802 828-2657 **Agency of Transportation**
133 State St State Administration Bldg ... Montpelier VT 05602-0000
802 244-8731 **Air Pollution Control Div** 103 S Main St Bldg 3-S ... Waterbury VT 05676-0000
802 828-2308 **Archives Div** 26 Terrace St ... Montpelier VT 05602-0000
802 828-3171 **Attorney General** 109 State St ... Montpelier VT 05602-2716
802 863-7356 **Chittenden Correctional Center** 7 Farrell St ... South Burlington VT 05403-6113
802 828-2393 **Conservation & Renewable Energy Unit** 120 State St ... Montpelier VT 05602-2702
802 828-3291 **Council on the Arts** 136 State St ... Montpelier VT 05602-2707
802 828-3168 **Defender General** 141 Main St State Office Bldg ... Montpelier VT 05602-0000
802 828-2430 **Department of Agriculture** 116 State St State Office Bldg ... Montpelier VT 05602-0000
802 241-2263 **Department of Corrections** 103 S Main St ... Waterbury VT 05676-1534
802 828-3135 **Department of Education** 120 State St ... Montpelier VT 05602-2703
802 244-8755 **Department of Environmental Conservation** 103 S Main St ... Waterbury VT 05676-1534
802 828-2309 **Department of Finance & Management** 109 State St ... Montpelier VT 05602-0000
802 863-7280 **Department of Health** PO Box 70 ... Burlington VT 05402-0070
802 828-3301 **Department of Insurance** 120 State St ... Montpelier VT 05602-2702
802 828-2286 **Department of Labor & Industry** State Office Bldg ... Montpelier VT 05602-0000
802 828-2363 **Department of Licensing & Registration**
Pavilion Office Bldg Secretary of State's Office ... Montpelier VT 05602-0000
802 828-2505 **Department of Taxes** 109 State St ... Montpelier VT 05602-2709
802 241-2295 **Division of Probation & Parole** 103 S Main St ... Waterbury VT 05676-1534
802 828-2211 **Division of Purchasing** 133 State St ... Montpelier VT 05602-2711
802 828-3221 **Economic Development Dept** 109 State St ... Montpelier VT 05602-2712
802 241-2450 **Economic Opportunity Office** 103 S Main St ... Waterbury VT 05676-1534
802 244-8721 **Emergency Management** 103 S Main St ... Waterbury VT 05676-1534
802 828-3333 **Governor** 109 State St Pavilion Office Bldg 5th Fl ... Montpelier VT 05602-2710
802 878-7466 **Higher Education Council** PO Box 47 ... Essex Junction VT 05453-0047
802 828-2226 **Lieutenant Governor** State House ... Montpelier VT 05602-0000
802 524-6771 **Northwest State Correctional Facility** PO Box 279-1 ... Swanton VT 05488-0000
802 828-2886 **Occupational & Radiological Health Div** 10 Baldwin St ... Montpelier VT 05602-2109
802 828-3326 **Office of Policy Research & Coordination**
109 State St Pavilion Office Bldg 5th Fl ... Montpelier VT 05602-2710
802 828-2358 **Public Service Board** City Center Bldg 89 Main St 3rd Fl ... Montpelier VT 05602-0000
802 828-3228 **Real Estate Commission** 26 Terrace St ... Montpelier VT 05602-2154
802 828-2305 **Retirement Div** 133 State St 2nd Fl ... Montpelier VT 05602-2711
802 828-2363 **Secretary of State** 26 Terrace St ... Montpelier VT 05602-2154
802 244-5164 **State Natural Resources Conservation Council**
103 S Main St ... Waterbury VT 05676-1534
802 244-7345 **State Police** 103 S Main St ... Waterbury VT 05676-1596
802 828-3276 **Supreme Court** 111 State St ... Montpelier VT 05602-2708
802 828-2301 **Treasurer** 133 State St ... Montpelier VT 05602-2711
802 229-0311 **Unemployment Compensation Div** 5 Green Mountain Dr ... Montpelier VT 05601-0000
802 863-7275 **Vital Records Section** 60 Main St ... Burlington VT 05402-0000
802 244-8702 **Waste Management Div** 103 S Main St Bldg 3-W ... Waterbury VT 05676-0000

VIRGINIA

804 786-0000 **State Government Information** 109 Governor St ... Richmond VA 23219-3623
804 786-5597 **Archives & Records Div** 11th St & Capitol Sq ... Richmond VA 23219-0000
804 786-2071 **Attorney General** 101 N 8th St ... Richmond VA 23219-2336
804 786-3741 **Bureau of Insurance** 1220 Bank St Jefferson Bldg ... Richmond VA 23219-0000
804 225-3132 **Commission for the Arts** 101 N 14th St 17th Fl ... Richmond VA 23219-3683
804 786-2042 **Consumer Affairs Office** 1100 Bank St Rm 101 ... Richmond VA 23219-3642
804 225-2600 **Council of Higher Education** 101 N 14th St ... Richmond VA 23219-3681
804 786-4500 **Council on the Environment** 202 N 9th St Suite 900 ... Richmond VA 23219-3402
804 786-3501 **Department of Agriculture & Consumer Services**
1100 Bank St ... Richmond VA 23219-3642
804 786-3248 **Department of Air Pollution Control** 212 N 9th St Suite 900 .. Richmond VA 23219-0000
804 786-2121 **Department of Conservation & Recreation**
203 Governor St Suite 302 ... Richmond VA 23219-2010
804 674-3000 **Department of Corrections** 6900 Atmore Rd ... Richmond VA 23225-5646
804 786-3791 **Department of Economic Development**
1021 E Cary St James Ctr ... Richmond VA 23219-0000
804 225-2023 **Department of Education** 101 N 14th St ... Richmond VA 23219-3663
804 674-2449 **Department of Emergency Services** 310 Turner Rd ... Richmond VA 23225-6400
804 786-3561 **Department of Health** 109 Governor St Suite 400 ... Richmond VA 23219-3623
804 786-2376 **Department of Labor & Industry**
4th St Office Bldg Suite 205 ... Richmond VA 23219-0000
804 367-1310 **Department of Mines-Minerals & Energy** 2201 W Broad St ... Richmond VA 23220-2022
804 786-5375 **Department of Planning & Budget** PO Box 1422 ... Richmond VA 23211-1422
804 674-2000 **Department of State Police** 7700 Midlothian Tpke ... Richmond VA 23235-5226
804 367-8000 **Department of Taxation** 2220 W Broad St ... Richmond VA 23220-2008
804 225-2142 **Department of the Treasury** 101 N 14th St ... Richmond VA 23219-3682
804 786-2801 **Department of Transportation** 1401 E Broad St ... Richmond VA 23219-2039
804 786-3611 **Division of Energy Regulation** 1220 Bank St ... Richmond VA 23219-3645
804 786-3263 **Division of Engineering & Buildings** 805 E Broad St ... Richmond VA 23219-1926
703 523-8100 **Division of Mines** 219 Wood Ave ... Big Stone Gap VA 24219-2799
804 786-5873 **Division of Occupational Health & Safety** 205 N 4th St ... Richmond VA 23219-1747
804 786-3845 **Division of Purchases & Supply** 805 E Broad St ... Richmond VA 23219-1992
804 786-7751 **Division of Securities & Retail Franchising** PO Box 1197 ... Richmond VA 23209-1197
804 225-2667 **Division of Solid & Hazardous Waste Management**
101 N 14th St Monroe Bldg 11th Fl ... Richmond VA 23219-3641
804 786-6228 **Division of Vital Records** 109 Governor St ... Richmond VA 23219-3623
804 786-3001 **Employment Commission** 703 E Main St ... Richmond VA 23219-3307
804 786-2211 **Governor** State Capitol Bldg 9th & Grace St ... Richmond VA 23219-3415
804 786-2078 **Lieutenant Governor** 101 N 8th St ... Richmond VA 23219-2336
804 674-3081 **Parole Board** 6900 Atmore Dr ... Richmond VA 23225-5644
804 784-3551 **Powhatan Correctional Center** ... State Farm VA 23160-9999
804 225-3297 **Public Defender Commission** 701 E Franklin St Suite 910 ... Richmond VA 23219-2502
804 367-8526 **Real Estate Board** 3600 W Broad St ... Richmond VA 23230-4915
804 786-2441 **Secretary of the Commonwealth** 200 N 9th St Suite 114 ... Richmond VA 23219-3402
804 367-0056 **State Water Control Board** 2111 N Hamilton St ... Richmond VA 23230-4105
804 786-2251 **Supreme Court** 100 N 9th St 4th Fl ... Richmond VA 23219-2334
804 786-3004 **Unemployment Insurance Services Div** PO Box 1358 ... Richmond VA 23211-0000
804 786-2101 **Virginia State Penitentiary** 500 Spring St ... Richmond VA 23219-6112

WASHINGTON

206 753-5000 **State Government Information** 512 12th Ave SE ... Olympia WA 98504-0001
206 459-6256 **Air Programs Div** 4224 6th Ave SE Bldg 4 PV-11 ... Lacey WA 98504-0000
206 753-5485 **Archives & Records Management** 12th Ave & Washington St ... Olympia WA 98504-0001
206 753-3860 **Arts Commission** 110 9th St Columbia Bldg MS GH-11 ... Olympia WA 98504-0001
206 753-2550 **Attorney General** Highways-Licenses Bldg 7th Fl PB-71 ... Olympia WA 98504-0001
206 753-6210 **Consumer & Business Fair Practices Div** N 122 Capitol Way ... Olympia WA 98501-0000
206 753-5050 **Department of Agriculture** 406 General Administration Bldg ... Olympia WA 98504-0001
206 753-2500 **Department of Corrections** 410 W 5th St FN-61 ... Olympia WA 98504-0001
206 459-6168 **Department of Ecology**
Abbott Raphael Bldg St Martins College Campus PV-11 ... Olympia WA 98504-8711
206 586-6904 **Department of Education**
Legion Way & Washington St Old Capitol Bldg FG-11 ... Olympia WA 98504-0001
206 753-5439 **Department of General Administration** 11th & Columbia Sts ... Olympia WA 98504-0001
206 753-6307 **Department of Labor & Industries**
General Administration Bldg 3rd Fl ... Olympia WA 98504-0001
206 753-6909 **Department of Licensing Agency** 2424 Bristol Ct SW ... Olympia WA 98504-0000
206 753-5327 **Department of Natural Resources** 201 John A Cherberg Bldg ... Olympia WA 98504-0001
206 753-6909 **Department of Professional Licensing** 2424 Bristol Ct SW ... Olympia WA 98504-0001
206 753-5281 **Department of Retirement Systems** 1025 E Union St ... Olympia WA 98504-0001
206 753-5574 **Department of Revenue** 11th Ave & Columbia St Rm 415 ... Olympia WA 98504-0001
206 753-5630 **Department of Trade & Economic Development**
General Administration Bldg Rm 101-GA ... Olympia WA 98504-0001
206 753-6005 **Department of Transportation** Transportation Bldg ... Olympia WA 98504-0001
206 459-9191 **Division of Emergency Management**
4220 E Martin Way PT-11 ... Olympia WA 98504-0001
206 753-5114 **Employment Security Dept** 212 Maple Pk ... Olympia WA 98504-0001
206 459-6490 **Energy Facility Site Evaluation Council** 4224 6th Ave SE ... Olympia WA 98504-0001
206 586-5000 **Energy Office** 809 Legion Way SE ... Olympia WA 98504-0001
206 753-6780 **Governor** Legislative Bldg AS-13 ... Olympia WA 98504-0001
206 753-3241 **Higher Education Coordinating Board**
917 Lakeridge Way GV-11 ... Olympia WA 98504-0001
206 753-6797 **Indeterminate Sentence Review Board** 410 W 5th Ave 7th Fl ... Olympia WA 98504-0001
206 753-6500 **Industrial Safety & Health Div** 805 Plum St SE HC-402 3rd Fl ... Olympia WA 98504-0001
206 786-7700 **Lieutenant Governor** Legislative Bldg AS-31 ... Olympia WA 98504-0001
206 753-7301 **Office of the Insurance Commissioner**
Insurance Bldg Rm 200 AQ-21 ... Olympia WA 98504-0001
206 753-6974 **Real Estate Licensing** PO Box 9012 ... Olympia WA 98504-0001
206 753-7121 **Secretary of State** Legislative Bldg AS-22 ... Olympia WA 98504-0001
206 753-6928 **Securities Div** PO Box 648 ... Olympia WA 98504-0000
206 459-6316 **Solid & Hazardous Waste Program**
4224 6th Ave SE Bldg 4 PV-11 ... Olympia WA 98504-0001
206 753-6810 **State Investment Board** 421 S Capitol Way FR-31 ... Olympia WA 98504-0001
206 753-6548 **State Patrol** 11th Ave & Columbia St ... Olympia WA 98504-0001
206 357-2077 **Supreme Court** Temple of Justice AV-11 ... Olympia WA 98504-0001
206 753-7130 **Treasurer** PO Box 1009 ... Olympia WA 98507-1009
206 753-5120 **Unemployment Insurance Div** 212 Maple Pk ... Olympia WA 98504-0001
206 753-6423 **Utilities Transportation Commission**
1300 South Evergreen Park Dr SW ... Olympia WA 98504-0001
206 753-5936 **Vital Records** 1112 S Quince St ... Olympia WA 98504-0001
206 426-4433 **Washington Corrections Center** Airport Dayton Rd ... Shelton WA 98584-0000
509 525-3610 **Washington State Penitentiary** PO Box 520 ... Walla Walla WA 99362-0520
206 459-6056 **Water Resources Program Dept of Ecology**
Baran Hall 3rd Fl PV-11 ... Olympia WA 98504-0001
206 753-6376 **Workers' Benefits** General Administration Bldg ... Olympia WA 98504-0001

WEST VIRGINIA

304 348-3456 **State Government Information** State Capitol ... Charleston WV 25305-0001
304 348-2300 **Administration Dept** State Capitol Rm E-119 ... Charleston WV 25305-0000
304 348-3286 **Air Pollution Control Commission** 1558 Washington St E ... Charleston WV 25311-0000
304 348-0230 **Archives & History Div** Capitol Complex Cultural Ctr ... Charleston WV 25305-0000
304 348-0240 **Arts & Humanities Div** Capitol Complex Cultural Ctr 2nd Fl ... Charleston WV 25305-0000
304 348-2021 **Attorney General** State Capitol ... Charleston WV 25305-0000
304 348-2971 **Bureau of Public Health** 1800 Washington St E Suite 206 ... Charleston WV 25305-0001
304 348-0400 **Community & Industrial Development Dept**
State Capitol Complex Bldg 1 Rm M-146
304 348-8986 **Consumer Protection Div** 812 Quarrier St ... Charleston WV 25305-0000
304 348-2201 **Department of Agriculture** State Capitol Complex Rm 28 ... Charleston WV 25301-2617
304 348-2036 **Department of Corrections** 112 California Ave ... Charleston WV 25305-0000
304 348-2681 **Department of Education** 1900 Kanawha Blvd E ... Charleston WV 25305-0001
304 348-2630 **Department of Employment Security** 112 California Ave ... Charleston WV 25305-0001
304 348-8860 **Department of Fuel & Energy** 1204 Kanawha Blvd E ... Charleston WV 25301-2986
304 348-3505 **Department of Highways** 1900 Washington St W Bldg 5 ... Charleston WV 25312-1407
304 348-3394 **Department of Insurance** 2019 Washington St E ... Charleston WV 25311-2214
304 348-7890 **Department of Labor** 1800 Washington St E Bldg 3 Rm 319 .. Charleston WV 25317-0001
304 746-2111 **Department of Public Safety** 725 Jefferson Rd ... South Charleston WV 25309-1698
304 348-2501 **Department of Tax & Revenue**
State Capitol Complex Rm 417 ... Charleston WV 25305-0000
304 348-8800 **Division of Vital Registration**
State Capitol Complex Bldg 3 Rm 516 ... Charleston WV 25305-0001
304 348-5935 **Division of Waste Management** 1356 Hansford St ... Charleston WV 25301-0000
304 348-2107 **Division of Water Resources** 1201 Greenbrier St ... Charleston WV 25311-1001
304 348-2000 **Governor** State Capitol Complex ... Charleston WV 25305-0000
304 348-2101 **Higher Education Central Office** 1018 Kanawha Blvd E ... Charleston WV 25301-2887
304 335-2291 **Huttonsville Correctional Center** PO Box 1 ... Huttonsville WV 26273-0010
304 348-2754 **Natural Resources Dept** 1900 Kanawha Blvd E Rm 669 ... Charleston WV 25305-0660
304 348-8860 **Office of Economic Opportunity** 1204 Kanawha Blvd E ... Charleston WV 25301-2900
304 348-5380 **Office of Emergency Services**
State Capitol Complex Rm EB-80 ... Charleston WV 25305-0001
304 348-2981 **Office of Environmental Health Services**
1900 Kanawha Blvd E State Capitol Complex Bldg 3 Rm 550 .. Charleston WV 25305-0000
304 348-3500 **Oil & Gas Conservation Commission**
1615 Washington St E ... Charleston WV 25311-0000
304 348-4010 **Planning Unit** State Capitol Complex Bldg 6 Rm 553 ... Charleston WV 25305-0000
304 348-6366 **Probation & Parole Board** 112 California Ave Rm 304 ... Charleston WV 25301-0000
304 348-3905 **Public Defender's Services** 1800 Washington St E Rm 330 .. Charleston WV 25305-0001
304 340-0303 **Public Service Commission** 201 Brooks St ... Charleston WV 25301-1827
304 348-2309 **Purchasing Div** State Capitol Complex Rm 110 ... Charleston WV 25305-0001
304 348-3555 **Real Estate Commission** 1033 Quarrier St Suite 400 ... Charleston WV 25301-2315
304 345-4000 **Secretary of State** State Capitol Complex Rm W-157 ... Charleston WV 25305-0000
304 348-2251 **Securities Commissioner** State Capitol Complex Rm W118 .. Charleston WV 25305-0001

State Government

304 348-2601	**Supreme Court** State Capitol Complex Rm 317-E	Charleston	WV 25305-0000
304 343-4000	**Treasury** State Capitol Complex Rm E147	Charleston	WV 25305-0001
304 348-2624	**Unemployment Compensation** 112 California Ave 6th Fl	Charleston	WV 25305-0001
304 845-2040	**West Virginia Penitentiary** 818 Jefferson Ave	Moundsville	WV 26041-2294
304 348-2580	**Worker's Compensation Fund** 601 Morris St	Charleston	WV 25301-1446

WISCONSIN

608 266-2211	**State Government Information** 1301 University Ave	Madison	WI 53715-1054
608 262-9576	**Archives & Records** 816 State St	Madison	WI 53706-1417
608 266-0190	**Arts Board** 131 W Wilson St Suite 301	Madison	WI 53703-3233
608 266-1221	**Attorney General** 114 E State Capitol	Madison	WI 53702-0001
608 266-0603	**Bureau of Air Management** 101 S Webster St	Madison	WI 53707-0000
608 266-5511	**Bureau of Direct Licensing & Real Estate** PO Box 8935	Madison	WI 53708-8935
608 266-2605	**Bureau of Procurement** 101 S Webster St 7th Fl	Madison	WI 53702-0001
608 266-1327	**Bureau of Solid Waste Management** 101 S Webster St	Madison	WI 53707-0000
608 266-8030	**Bureau of Water Regulation & Zoning** 101 S Webster St	Madison	WI 53707-0001
608 266-1334	**Center for Health Statistics** 1 W Wilson St	Madison	WI 53702-0001
608 266-3585	**Commissioner of Insurance** 121 E Wilson St 7th Fl	Madison	WI 53702-0001
608 266-7100	**Department of Agriculture Trade & Consumer Protection** 801 W Badger Rd	Madison	WI 53713-2526
608 266-1018	**Department of Development** 123 W Washington Ave	Madison	WI 53702-0001
608 266-7552	**Department of Industry Labor & Human Relations** 201 E Washington Ave	Madison	WI 53702-0001
608 266-2121	**Department of Natural Resources** 101 S Webster St	Madison	WI 53702-0001
608 266-1771	**Department of Public Instruction** 125 S Webster St	Madison	WI 53702-0000
608 266-8609	**Department of Regulation & Licensing** 1400 E Washington Ave	Madison	WI 53702-0000
608 266-1611	**Department of Revenue** 125 N Webster St	Madison	WI 53708-0000
608 266-1113	**Department of Transportation** 4802 Sheboygan Ave Rm 120-B	Madison	WI 53702-0001
608 266-1353	**Division of Budget & Planning** 101 S Webster St	Madison	WI 53702-0001
608 266-2471	**Division of Corrections** 1 W Wilson St Rm 1050	Madison	WI 53702-0001
608 266-8234	**Division of Energy & Intergovernmental Relations** 101 S Webster St	Madison	WI 53707-0000
608 266-1031	**Division of Facilities Management** 101 S Webster St	Madison	WI 53702-0001
608 266-1511	**Division of Health** 1 W Wilson St	Madison	WI 53702-0001
608 266-3628	**Division of State Finance & Program Management** 101 S Webster St	Madison	WI 53702-0000
608 266-3212	**Division of State Patrol** 4802 Sheboygan Ave	Madison	WI 53702-0001
608 266-1212	**Governor** State Capitol Rm 115 E	Madison	WI 53702-0000
608 266-7884	**Housing & Economic Development Authority** 1 S Pinckney St Suite 500	Madison	WI 53701-0000
608 266-3516	**Lieutenant Governor** State Capitol Rm 22 E	Madison	WI 53702-0001
608 266-1852	**Office of Consumer Protection & Citizen Advocacy** PO Box 7856	Madison	WI 53707-7856
608 266-2050	**Office of Mine Reclamation** 101 S Webster St	Madison	WI 53707-0000
608 266-0087	**Office of the State Public Defender** 131 W Wilson St Rm 100 ..	Madison	WI 53703-3233
608 266-3834	**Probation & Parole Div** 1 W Wilson St Rm 951	Madison	WI 53702-0001
608 266-2001	**Public Service Commission** PO Box 7854	Madison	WI 53707-7854
608 266-1816	**Safety & Buildings Div** 201 E Washington Ave	Madison	WI 53707-0000
608 266-5594	**Secretary of State** 30 W Mifflin St 10th Fl	Madison	WI 53703-2558
608 266-3431	**Securities Commissioner** 111 W Wilson St	Madison	WI 53703-3235
608 267-2206	**State Higher Education Aids Board** 131 W Wilson Ave	Madison	WI 53703-3233
608 266-1880	**Supreme Court** State Capitol Bldg Rm 231 E	Madison	WI 53702-0001
608 266-1714	**Treasury** PO Box 7871	Madison	WI 53707-7871
608 266-2284	**Unemployment Compensation Div** PO Box 7905	Madison	WI 53707-7905
414 324-5571	**Waupun Correctional Institution** PO Box 351	Waupun	WI 53963-0351
608 835-5711	**Wisconsin Correctional Center System** PO Box 25	Oregon	WI 53575-0025
608 266-1340	**Worker's Compensation Div** 201 E Washington Ave	Madison	WI 53702-0001

WYOMING

307 777-7220	**State Government Information** 200 W 24th St	Cheyenne	WY 82001-0000
307 777-7391	**Air Quality Div** 122 W 25th St 4th Fl	Cheyenne	WY 82002-0001
307 777-7826	**Archives & Records Management Div** 2301 Central Ave	Cheyenne	WY 82002-0001
307 777-7841	**Attorney General** 123 Capitol Bldg	Cheyenne	WY 82002-0001
307 777-7405	**Board of Charities & Reform** 122 W 25th St Herschler Bldg 1st Fl E	Cheyenne	WY 82002-0001
307 362-5222	**Board of Mines** 1682 Sunset St	Rock Springs	WY 89202-0000
307 777-7763	**Community College Commission** 122 W 25th Herschler Bldg 2 W	Cheyenne	WY 82002-0001
307 777-6286	**Consumer Affairs** 123 Capitol Bldg	Cheyenne	WY 82002-0001
307 777-7742	**Council on the Arts** 2320 Capitol Ave	Cheyenne	WY 82002-0001
307 777-7321	**Department of Agriculture** 2219 Carey Ave	Cheyenne	WY 82002-0001
307 777-7284	**Department of Commerce Div Economic & Community Development** 122 W 25th St Herschler Bldg 2nd Fl	Cheyenne	WY 82002-0001
307 777-7673	**Department of Education** 2300 Capitol Ave	Cheyenne	WY 82002-0001
307 777-7261	**Department of Employment** 122 W 25th St Herschler Bldg	Cheyenne	WY 82002-0001
307 235-3200	**Department of Employment** 100 W Midwest St	Casper	WY 82601-0000
307 777-7656	**Department of Health & Social Services** Hathaway Bldg Rm 117	Cheyenne	WY 82002-0000
307 777-7331	**Department of Public Lands** 122 W 25th St Herschler Bldg	Cheyenne	WY 82002-0001
307 777-7961	**Department of Revenue & Taxation** 122 W 25th St Herschler Bldg 1st Fl W	Cheyenne	WY 82002-0001
307 777-7253	**Division of Purchasing & Property Control** 2001 Capitol Ave E Rm 323	Cheyenne	WY 82002-0001
307 777-7131	**Economic Development & Stabilization Department Energy Conservation Div** Herschler Bldg West Wing 2nd Fl	Cheyenne	WY 82002-0001
307 777-7566	**Emergency Management Agency** 5500 Bishop Blvd	Cheyenne	WY 82003-0000
307 777-7938	**Environmental Quality Dept** 122 W 25th St Herschler Bldg 4th Fl W	Cheyenne	WY 82002-0001
307 777-7434	**Governor** State Capitol	Cheyenne	WY 82002-0000
307 777-7475	**Highway Dept** 5300 Bishop Blvd	Cheyenne	WY 82002-0001
307 777-7301	**Highway Patrol** 5300 Bishop Blvd	Cheyenne	WY 82002-0001
307 777-7401	**Insurance Dept** 122 W 25th St Herschler Bldg	Cheyenne	WY 82002-0001
307 777-7786	**Occupational Safety & Health** 122 W 25th St Herschler Bldg Rm 2-E	Cheyenne	WY 82002-0001
307 234-7147	**Oil & Gas Commission** 777 W 1st St	Casper	WY 82601-1768
307 777-7208	**Probation & Parole** 5801 Osage Suite B	Cheyenne	WY 82002-0001
307 777-7137	**Public Defender** 1712 Carey 2nd Fl	Cheyenne	WY 82002-0001
307 777-7427	**Public Service Commission** 700 W 21st St	Cheyenne	WY 82002-0001
307 777-7141	**Real Estate Commission** Barrett Bldg 3rd Fl	Cheyenne	WY 82002-0001
307 777-7691	**Retirement System** 122 W 25th St Herschler Bldg	Cheyenne	WY 82002-0001
307 777-7378	**Secretary of State** 200 W 24th St State Capitol	Cheyenne	WY 82002-0001
307 777-7370	**Securities Div** 200 W 24th St State Capitol	Cheyenne	WY 82002-0001
307 777-7752	**Solid Waste Management Program** 122 W 25th St Herschler Bldg	Cheyenne	WY 82002-0001
307 777-7316	**Supreme Court** 2301 Capitol Ave	Cheyenne	WY 82002-0001
307 777-7408	**Treasurer** 200 W 24th St	Cheyenne	WY 82002-0001
307 235-3200	**Unemployment Insurance Div** 100 W Midwest St	Casper	WY 82601-2429
307 777-7591	**Vital Records Services** Hathaway Bldg	Cheyenne	WY 82002-0001
307 777-7441	**Worker's Compensation** 122 W 25th St Herschler Bldg 2nd Fl	Cheyenne	WY 82002-0001
307 347-6144	**Wyoming Boys School** 1550 Hwy 20 S	Worland	WY 82401-0000
307 328-1441	**Wyoming State Penitentiary** PO Box 400	Rawlins	WY 82301-0400

INTERNATIONAL

Foreign Chambers of Commerce in the US

Groups are listed alphabetically. If a familiar country name or region does not appear at the beginning of the name, the group is listed by the familiar name of the country or region, followed by the official name of the group, e.g., Greece: Hellenic-American Chamber of Commerce.

212 564-3855 **Argentine-American Chamber of Commerce**
50 W 34th St 6th Fl Suite C2 .... New York NY 10001-0000

202 638-1764 **Asia: US Pan Asian American Chamber of Commerce**
1625 K St NW Suite 380 .... Washington DC 20006-1604
Fax: 202 638-1677

212 819-0117 **Austria: US-Austrian Chamber of Commerce** 165 W 46th St .. New York NY 10036-2501

212 967-9898 **Belgian-American Chamber of Commerce in US**
350 5th Ave Suite 703 .... New York NY 10118-0110
Fax: 212 629-0349

212 575-9030 **Brazilian-American Chamber of Commerce**
22 W 48th St Rm 404 .... New York NY 10036-1803
Fax: 212 921-1078

212 288-5691 **Chile: North American-Chilean Chamber of Commerce**
220 E 81st St .... New York NY 10028-2602
Fax: 212 439-6107

415 982-3000 **Chinese Chamber of Commerce of San Francisco**
730 Sacramento St .... San Francisco CA 94108-2571
Fax: 415 982-4720

212 233-7776 **Colombian-American Assn** 150 Nassau St Rm 2015 .... New York NY 10038-1516
Fax: 212 233-7779

212 432-9498 **Dominican Republic Export Promotion Center**
1 World Trade Ctr Rm 2441 .... New York NY 10048-0577
Fax: 212 432-9376

212 233-7776 **Ecuadorean-American Assn** 150 Nassau St Rm 2015 .... New York NY 10038-1516
Fax: 212 233-7779

212 832-2588 **Finland: Finnish-American Chamber of Commerce**
380 Madison Ave 24th Fl .... New York NY 10017-0000
Fax: 212 370-2863

312 670-4700 **Finland: Finnish-American Chamber of Commerce of the Midwest**
321 N Clark St Suite 2880 .... Chicago IL 60610-4717
Fax: 312 670-4777

212 371-4466 **France: French-American Chamber of Commerce in the US**
509 Madison Ave Suite 1900 .... New York NY 10022-5599
Fax: 212 371-5623

212 974-8830 **German-American Chamber of Commerce Inc**
666 5th Ave 21st Fl .... New York NY 10103-0166
Fax: 212 974-8867

312 782-8557 **German-American Chamber of Commerce of Chicago**
104 S Michigan St Suite 600 .... Chicago IL 60603-5978
Fax: 312 782-3892

213 381-2236 **German-American Chamber of Commerce of Los Angeles**
3250 Wilshire Blvd Suite 1612 .... Los Angeles CA 90010-1676
Fax: 213 381-3449

415 392-2262 **German-American Chamber of Commerce of the Pacific Coast**
465 California St Suite 910 .... San Francisco CA 94104-1822
Fax: 415 392-1314

212 889-0680 **Great Britain: British-American Chamber of Commerce**
275 Madison Ave Suite 1714 .... New York NY 10016-1101
Fax: 212 683-0621

212 629-6380 **Greece: Hellenic-American Chamber of Commerce**
960 Ave of the Americas Suite 1204 .... New York NY 10001-2112

312 621-1200 **India: Indo-American Chamber of Commerce**
19 S La Salle St Suite 200 .... Chicago IL 60603-1402
Fax: 312 621-0740

212 687-4505 **Indonesia: American-Indonesian Chamber of Commerce**
711 3rd Ave 17th Fl .... New York NY 10017-4014
Fax: 212 867-9882

212 751-2660 **Ireland-US Council** 460 Park Ave 22nd Fl .... New York NY 10022-1906
Fax: 212 751-8951

312 641-2937 **Israel: American-Israel Chamber of Commerce & Industry**
180 N Michigan Ave Suite 911 .... Chicago IL 60601-7453
Fax: 312 641-2941

212 971-0310 **Israel: American-Israel Chamber of Commerce & Industry**
350 5th Ave Suite 1919 .... New York NY 10118-0110
Fax: 212 971-0331

216 267-1200 **Israel: American-Israel Chamber of Commerce & Industry**
10800 Brookpark Rd .... Cleveland OH 44130-1119
Fax: 216 267-3925

312 661-1336 **Italian-American Chamber of Commerce of Chicago**
126 W Grand Ave .... Chicago IL 60610-4206

212 279-5520 **Italy-America Chamber of Commerce**
350 5th Ave Suite 3015 .... New York NY 10118-0110
Fax: 212 279-5839

213 485-0160 **Japan Business Assn of Southern California**
345 S Figueroa St Suite 206 .... Los Angeles CA 90071-1002
Fax: 213 626-5526

808 949-5531 **Japan: Honolulu-Japanese Chamber of Commerce**
2454 S Beretania St .... Honolulu HI 96826-1502
Fax: 808 949-3020

212 935-0303 **Japanese Chamber of Commerce** 115 E 57th St 6th Fl .... New York NY 10022-2049
Fax: 212 935-0908

312 332-6199 **Japanese Chamber of Commerce & Industry of Chicago**
401 N Michigan Ave Suite 602 .... Chicago IL 60611-4205
Fax: 312 822-9773

415 543-8522 **Japanese Chamber of Commerce of Northern California**
685 Market St Suite 820 .... San Francisco CA 94105-4212
Fax: 415 543-8799

213 626-3067 **Japanese Chamber of Commerce of Southern California**
244 S San Pedro St Suite 504 .... Los Angeles CA 90012-3888
Fax: 213 626-3070

213 688-7330 **Mexican Chamber of Commerce of the County of Los Angeles**
125 Paseo de la Plaza Rm 404 .... Los Angeles CA 90012-2922
Fax: 213 688-7562

602 252-6448 **Mexico: Arizona-Mexico Chamber of Commerce** PO Box 626 .. Phoenix AZ 85001-0000

202 296-5198 **Mexico: US-Mexico Chamber of Commerce**
1900 L St NW Suite 612 .... Washington DC 20036-5002
Fax: 202 785-4905

212 333-8728 **Mexico: US-Mexico Chamber of Commerce**
730 5th Ave 9th Fl .... New York NY 10019-0000

312 782-4654 **Middle East: MidAmerica-Arab Chamber of Commerce**
135 S La Salle St Suite 1020 .... Chicago IL 60603-4202
Fax: 312 782-4871

202 331-8010 **Middle East: US-Arab Chamber of Commerce**
1825 K St NW Suite 1107 .... Washington DC 20006-3172
Fax: 202 331-8297

415 398-9200 **Middle East: US-Arab Chamber of Commerce (Pacific) Inc**
PO Box 11239 .... San Francisco CA 94101-7239
Fax: 415 398-7111

212 986-7229 **Middle East: American-Mideast Business Association**
80 Park Ave Suite 17N .... New York NY 10016-2540
Fax: Unlisted

212 265-6460 **Netherlands Chamber of Commerce in the US**
1 Rockefeller Plaza 11th Fl .... New York NY 10020-2095
Fax: 212 265-6402

213 933-7717 **Norway: Norwegian-American Chamber of Commerce**
5750 Wilshire Blvd Suite 470 .... Los Angeles CA 90036-0000
Fax: 213 933-8711

415 986-0770 **Norway: Norwegian-American Chamber of Commerce**
2 Embarcadero Ctr Suite 2910 .... San Francisco CA 94111-3914
Fax: 415 986-6025

212 421-9210 **Norway: Norwegian-American Chamber of Commerce**
800 3rd Ave 23rd Fl .... New York NY 10022-7604
Fax: 212 838-0374

212 972-9326 **Philippine-American Chamber of Commerce**
711 3rd Ave 17th Fl .... New York NY 10017-4014

212 967-2170 **Spain-US Chamber of Commerce** 350 5th Ave Suite 3514 ..... New York NY 10118-0110
Fax: 212 564-1415

212 838-5530 **Swedish-American Chamber of Commerce**
599 Lexington Ave 42nd Fl .... New York NY 10022-7544
Fax: 212 755-7953

415 781-4188 **Swedish-American Chamber of Commerce of the Western US**
World Trade Ctr Suite 268 .... San Francisco CA 94111-0000
Fax: 415 781-4189

212 233-7776 **Venezuelan-American Assn of the US**
150 Nassau St Rm 2015 .... New York NY 10038-1516
Fax: 212 233-7779

Foreign Embassies and Consulates in the US

CONSULATES

Selected consular offices in major cities are listed alphabetically by the country's familiar name.

Argentina

312 263-7435 *Chicago Consulate* 20 N Clark St Suite 602 .... Chicago IL 60602-4183
Fax: 312 263-0674

213 739-5959 *Los Angeles Consulate* 3550 Wilshire Blvd Suite 1450 .... Los Angeles CA 90010-2415
Fax: 213 487-1491

212 603-0400 *New York Consulate General* 12 W 56th St .... New York NY 10019-3890
Fax: 212 397-3523

Australia

312 645-9440 *Chicago Consulate General* 321 N Clark Suite 2930 .... Chicago IL 60610-4794
Fax: 312 645-1940

213 469-4300 *Los Angeles Consulate General* 611 N Larchmount Blvd .... Hollywood CA 90004-1321
Fax: 213 469-9176

212 245-4000 *New York Consulate General*
636 5th Ave Rockefeller Ctr 4th Fl .... New York NY 10111-0000
Fax: 212 265-1917

415 362-6160 *San Francisco Consulate General* 360 Post St .... San Francisco CA 94108-4979
Fax: 415 986-5440

Austria

312 222-1515 *Chicago Consulate General* 400 N Michigan Ave Suite 707 .... Chicago IL 60611-4102
Fax: 312 222-4113

213 444-9310 *Los Angeles Consulate General*
11859 Wilshire Blvd Suite 501 .... Los Angeles CA 90025-6601
Fax: 213 477-9897

212 737-6400 *New York Consulate General* 31 E 69th St .... New York NY 10021-4976
Fax: 212 772-8926

Bahamas

305 373-6295 *Miami Consulate General* 25 SE 2nd Ave .... Miami FL 33131-1506
Fax: 305 373-6312

212 421-6420 *New York Consulate General* 767 3rd Ave .... New York NY 10017-2023
Fax: 212 759-2135

Barbados

213 380-2198 *Los Angeles Consulate* 3440 Wilshire Blvd Suite 1215 .... Los Angeles CA 90010-2113
Fax: 213 384-2763

212 867-8435 *New York Consulate General* 800 2nd Ave 18th Fl .... New York NY 10017-4709
Fax: 212 986-1030

Belgium

312 263-6624 *Chicago Consulate General* 333 N Michigan Ave .... Chicago IL 60601-4186
Fax: 312 263-4805

213 857-1244 *Los Angeles Consulate General*
6100 Wilshire Blvd Suite 1200 .... Los Angeles CA 90048-5119
Fax: 213 936-2564

212 586-5110 *New York Consulate General*
50 Rockefeller Plaza Rm 1120 .... New York NY 10020-1605
Fax: 212 582-9657

Brazil

312 372-2177 *Chicago Consulate General* 20 N Wacker Dr Suite 1010 .... Chicago IL 60606-2901
Fax: 312 372-1806

213 382-3133 *Los Angeles Consulate General*
3810 Wilshire Blvd Suite 1500 .... Los Angeles CA 90010-4014
Fax: 213 487-4341

212 757-3080 *New York Consulate General* 630 5th Ave Suite 2720 .... New York NY 10111-0252

Canada

312 427-1031 *Chicago Consulate General* 310 S Michigan Ave Suite 1200 .. Chicago IL 60604-4295
Fax: 312 922-0637

213 687-7432 *Los Angeles Consulate General* 300 S Grand Ave 10th Fl . Los Angeles CA 90071-3100
Fax: 213 620-8827

212 768-2400 *New York Consulate General* 1251 Ave of the Americas ..... New York NY 10020-1194
Fax: 212 768-2440

415 495-6021 *San Francisco Consulate General*
50 Fremont St Suite 2100 .... San Francisco CA 94105-2277
Fax: 415 541-7708

206 443-1777 *Seattle Consulate General*
6th & Stewart Sts Plaza 600 Rm 412 .... Seattle WA 98101-0000
Fax: 206 443-1782

China

312 346-0287 *Chicago Consulate General* 104 S Michigan Ave Suite 500 .... Chicago IL 60603-5907
Fax: 312 580-2570

212 868-7752 *New York Consulate General* 520 12th Ave .... New York NY 10036-1007
Fax: 212 629-2698

415 563-4885 *San Francisco Consulate General* 1450 Laguna St .... San Francisco CA 94115-3717
Fax: 415 563-0494

Denmark

312 787-8780 *Chicago Consulate General*
875 N Michigan Ave John Hancock Ctr Suite 3430 .... Chicago IL 60611-0000
Fax: 312 787-8740

213 387-4277 *Los Angeles Consulate General*
3440 Wilshire Blvd Suite 904 .... Los Angeles CA 90010-2110
Fax: 213 387-9456

212 223-4545 *New York Consulate General* 825 3rd Ave 32nd Fl .... New York NY 10022-7519
Fax: 212 754-1904

Foreign Embassies and Consulates in the US

Egypt
312 443-1190 *Chicago Consulate General* 30 S Michigan Ave 7th Fl .... Chicago IL 60603-3201
Fax: 312 443-1463
212 759-7120 *NY Consulate General* 1110 2nd Ave Rm 201 .... New York NY 10022-2021
Fax: 212 308-7643
415 346-9700 *San Francisco Consulate General* 3001 Pacific Ave ...... San Francisco CA 94115-1013
Fax: 415 346-9480

Finland
312 670-4700 *Chicago Consulate General* 321 N Clark St Suite 2880 .... Chicago IL 60610-4717
Fax: 312 670-4777
213 203-9903 *Los Angeles Consulate General*
1900 Ave of the Stars Suite 1025 .... Los Angeles CA 90067-4401
Fax: 213 203-0301
212 573-6007 *New York Consulate General* 380 Madison Ave 24th Fl ...... New York NY 10017-0000
Fax: 212 573-6310

France
312 787-5359 *Chicago Consulate General* 737 N Michigan Ave Suite 2020 .. Chicago IL 60611-2694
Fax: 312 664-4196
213 653-3120 *Los Angeles Consulate General* 8350 Wilshire Blvd .... Beverly Hills CA 90211-2327
212 606-3600 *New York Consulate General* 934 5th Ave .... New York NY 10021-2697
Fax: 212 606-3688 Admin
415 397-4330 *San Francisco Consulate General* 540 Bush St .... San Francisco CA 94108-3604
Fax: 415 433-8357

Germany
312 263-0850 *Chicago Consulate General* 104 S Michigan Ave .... Chicago IL 60603-5902
Fax: 312 853-1940
213 930-2703 *Los Angeles Consulate General*
6222 Wilshire Blvd Suite 500 .... Los Angeles CA 90048-5123
Fax: Unlisted
212 308-8700 *New York Consulate General* 460 Park Ave .... New York NY 10022-1906
Fax: 212 308-3422

Great Britain
617 248-9555 *Boston Consulate General*
600 Atlantic Ave Federal Reserve Plaza 25th Fl .... Boston MA 02210-0000
Fax: 617 248-9578
312 346-1810 *Chicago Consulate General* 33 N Dearborn St .... Chicago IL 60602-3102
Fax: 312 346-7021
713 659-6270 *Houston Consulate General* 601 Jefferson Suite 2250 .... Houston TX 77002-7910
Fax: 713 659-7094
213 385-7381 *Los Angeles Consulate General*
3701 Wilshire Blvd Suite 312 .... Los Angeles CA 90010-2810
Fax: 213 381-5450
212 752-8400 *New York Consulate General* 845 3rd Ave .... New York NY 10022-6601
Fax: 212 754-3062
415 981-3030 *San Francisco Consulate General*
1 Sansome St Suite 850 .... San Francisco CA 94104-4429
Fax: 415 434-2018

Greece
312 372-5356 *Chicago Consulate General* 168 N Michigan Ave .... Chicago IL 60601-7509
Fax: 312 372-6272
212 988-5500 *New York Consulate General* 69 E 79th St .... New York NY 10021-0291
Fax: 212 734-8492
415 775-2102 *San Francisco Consulate General* 2441 Gough St .... San Francisco CA 94123-5010
Fax: 415 776-6815

India
312 781-6280 *Chicago Consulate General* 150 N Michigan Ave Suite 1100 .. Chicago IL 60601-7524
Fax: 312 781-6269
212 879-7800 *New York Consulate General* 3 E 64th St .... New York NY 10021-7097
Fax: 212 988-6423
415 668-0662 *San Francisco Consulate General* 540 Arguello Blvd .... San Francisco CA 94118-3203
Fax: 415 668-2073

Ireland
617 267-9330 *Boston Consulate General* 535 Boylston St .... Boston MA 02116-3720
Fax: 617 267-6375
312 337-1868 *Chicago Consulate General* 400 N Michigan Ave Rm 911 ...... Chicago IL 60611-4102
Fax: Unlisted
212 319-2555 *New York Consulate General* 515 Madison Ave .... New York NY 10022-5403
Fax: 212 980-9475
415 392-4214 *San Francisco Consulate General*
655 Montgomery St 9th Fl .... San Francisco CA 94111-2635
Fax: Unlisted

Israel
312 565-3300 *Chicago Consulate General* 111 E Wacker Dr Suite 1308 ...... Chicago IL 60601-4402
Fax: 312 565-2063
213 651-5700 *Los Angeles Consulate General*
6380 Wilshire Blvd Suite 1700 .... Los Angeles CA 90048-5019
Fax: 213 651-3123
305 358-8111 *Miami Consulate General* 330 Biscayne Blvd Suite 510 .... Miami FL 33132-2229
Fax: 305 371-5034
212 351-5200 *New York Consulate General* 800 2nd Ave .... New York NY 10017-4755
Fax: Unlisted
415 398-8885 *San Francisco Consulate General*
220 Bush St Suite 550 .... San Francisco CA 94104-3507
Fax: 415 398-8589

Italy
312 467-1550 *Chicago Consulate General* 500 N Michigan Ave .... Chicago IL 60611-3771
213 820-0622 *Los Angeles Consulate General*
12400 Wilshire Blvd Suite 300 .... Los Angeles CA 90025-1022
212-737-9100 *New York Consulate General* 690 Park Ave .... New York NY 10022-6815
Fax: 212 832-5914

Jamaica
305 374-8431 *Miami Consulate General* 25 SE 2nd Ave Suite 842 .... Miami FL 33131-1680
Fax: 305 577-4970
212 935-9000 *New York Consulate General* 866 2nd Ave .... New York NY 10017-2993
Fax: 212 832-0411

Japan
213 624-8305 *Los Angeles Consulate General* 250 E 1st St Suite 1507 .. Los Angeles CA 90012-3831
Fax: 213 625-2231
212 371-8222 *New York Consulate General* 299 Park Ave .... New York NY 10171-0102
Fax: 212 319-6357
415 777-3533 *San Francisco Consulate General*
50 Fremont St 23rd Fl .... San Francisco CA 94105-2230
Fax: 415 974-3660

Korea
312 822-9485 *Chicago Consulate General* 500 N Michigan Ave Suite 900 .... Chicago IL 60611-3701
213 385-9300 *Los Angeles Consulate General*
3243 Wilshire Blvd 2nd Fl .... Los Angeles CA 90010-1303
Fax: 213 385-1849
212 752-1700 *New York Consulate General* 460 Park Ave .... New York NY 10022-1906
Fax: 212 348-1756

415 788-0816 **Luxembourg Consulate General**
1 Sansome St Suite 830 .... San Francisco CA 94104-4429
Fax: 415 788-0985

Mexico
512 478-2866 *Austin Consulate* 200 E 6th St Suite 200 .... Austin TX 78701-3648
Fax: 512 478-8008
312 855-1380 *Chicago Consulate General* 300 N Michigan Ave 2nd Fl .... Chicago IL 60601-3702
214 630-7341 *Dallas Consulate General* 1349 Empire Central Suite 100 .... Dallas TX 75247-4029
Fax: 214 630-3511
602 242-7398 *Phoenix Consulate* 1990 W Camelback .... Phoenix AZ 85015-0000
415 392-5554 *San Francisco Consulate General*
870 Market St Suite 528 .... San Francisco CA 94102-3012
Fax: 415 392-3233
206 448-3526 *Seattle Consulate* 2132 3rd Ave .... Seattle WA 98121-0000

Netherlands
312 856-0110 *Chicago Consulate General* 303 E Wacker Dr Suite 410 .... Chicago IL 60601-5279
Fax: 312 856-9218
213 380-3440 *Los Angeles Consulate General*
3460 Wilshire Blvd Rm 509 .... Los Angeles CA 90010-2270
Fax: 213 386-6380
212 246-1429 *New York Consulate General* 1 Rockefeller Plaza 11th Fl .... New York NY 10020-2001
Fax: 212 333-3603

213 477-8241 **New Zealand Los Angeles Consulate General**
10960 Wilshire Blvd Suite 1530 .... Los Angeles CA 90024-3701
Fax: 213 473-5621

Norway
708 956-6969 *Chicago Consulate General* 748 W Algonquin Rd .... Arlington Heights IL 60005-0000
Fax: 708 364-7374
213 933-7717 *Los Angeles Consulate General*
5750 Wilshire Blvd Suite 470 .... Los Angeles CA 90036-0000
Fax: 213 923-8711
212 421-7333 *New York Consulate General* 825 3rd Ave 17th Fl .... New York NY 10022-7519
Fax: 212 754-0583

213 651-0296 **Peru Los Angeles Consulate General**
6420 Wilshire Blvd Suite 1020 .... Los Angeles CA 90048-6310
Fax: 213 651-1264

Philippines
312 332-6458 *Chicago Consulate General* 30 N Michigan Ave Suite 2100 .... Chicago IL 60602-3605
Fax: Unlisted
213 387-5321 *Los Angeles Consulate General*
3660 Wilshire Blvd Suite 1200 .... Los Angeles CA 90010-2205
Fax: Unlisted
212 764-1330 *New York Consulate General* 556 5th Ave Philippine Ctr ..... New York NY 10036-5096

Portugal
617 536-8740 *Boston Consulate General* 899 Boylston St 2nd Fl .... Boston MA 02115-3104
213 277-1491 *Los Angeles Consulate* 1801 Ave of the Stars Suite 400 .. Los Angeles CA 90067-5906
212 246-4580 *New York Consulate General* 630 5th Ave Suite 657 .... New York NY 10111-0100
Fax: 212 459-0190

Saudi Arabia
713 785-5577 *Houston Consulate General*
5718 Westheimer Blvd Suite 1500 .... Houston TX 77057-5733
213 208-6566 *Los Angeles Consulate General*
10900 Wilshire Blvd Suite 830 .... Los Angeles CA 90024-6528
Fax: 213 208-5643
212 752-2740 *New York Consulate General*
866 United Nations Plaza Suite 480 .... New York NY 10017-1870

South Africa
312 939-7929 *Chicago Consulate General* 200 S Michigan Ave 6th Fl .... Chicago IL 60604-2404
Fax: 312 939-7481
213 657-9200 *Los Angeles Consulate General*
50 N La Cienega Suite 300 .... Beverly Hills CA 90211-2227
Fax: Unlisted
212 371-7997 *New York Consulate General* 326 E 48th St .... New York NY 10017-1796
Fax: 212 371-7577

415 922-6642 **Soviet Union Consulate General** 2790 Green St .... San Francisco CA 94123-4609

Spain
312 782-4588 *Chicago Consulate General* 180 N Michigan Ave Suite 1500 .. Chicago IL 60601-7401
213 658-6050 *Los Angeles Consulate General*
6300 Wilshire Blvd Suite 1530 .... Los Angeles CA 90048-5217
Fax: 213 658-5603
212 355-4080 *New York Consulate General* 150 E 58th St 16th Fl .... New York NY 10155-0035
Fax: 212 644-3751

Sweden
312 781-6262 *Chicago Consulate General* 150 N Michigan Ave Suite 1250 .. Chicago IL 60601-7593
Fax: 312 346-0683
213 470-2555 *Los Angeles Consulate General*
10880 Wilshire Blvd Suite 505 .... Los Angeles CA 90024-4189
Fax: 213 475-4683
212 751-5900 *New York Consulate General* 885 2nd Ave 45th Fl .... New York NY 10017-0000
Fax: 212 755-2732

Switzerland
312 915-0061 *Chicago Consulate General* 737 N Michigan Ave Suite 2301 .. Chicago IL 60611-2615
Fax: 312 915-0388
213 388-4127 *Los Angeles Consulate General*
3440 Wilshire Blvd Suite 817 .... Los Angeles CA 90010-2109
Fax: 213 385-4514
212 758-2560 *New York Consulate General* 665 5th Ave 8th Fl .... New York NY 10022-5305
Fax: 212 207-8024

213 937-1894 **Thailand Consulate General** 801 N La Brea Ave .... Los Angeles CA 90038-3340

EMBASSIES

Every foreign embassy in the United States is listed alphabetically by the country's familiar name followed by the country's official name, e.g., Egypt: Arab Republic of Egypt.

202 234-3770 **Afghanistan: Republic of Afghanistan**
2341 Wyoming Ave NW .... Washington DC 20008-1642
Fax: 202 328-3516
202 265-2800 **Algeria: Democratic & Popular Republic of Algeria**
2137 Wyoming Ave NW .... Washington DC 20008-3905
202 362-5122 **Antigua & Barbuda** 3400 International Dr NW Suite 4-M ..... Washington DC 20008-3006
Fax: 202 362-5225
202 939-6400 **Argentina: Argentine Republic**
1600 New Hampshire Ave NW .... Washington DC 20009-2512
Fax: 202 332-3171
202 797-3000 **Australia: Commonwealth of Australia**
1601 Massachusetts Ave NW .... Washington DC 20036-2209
Fax: 202 797-3168
202 483-4474 **Austria: Republic of Austria**
2343 Massachusetts Ave NW .... Washington DC 20008-2803
Fax: 202 483-2743
202 944-3390 **Bahamas: Commonwealth of the Bahamas**
600 New Hampshire Ave NW Suite 865 .... Washington DC 20037-2403
Fax: 202 333-7487
202 342-0741 **Bahrain: State of Bahrain** 3502 International Dr NW .... Washington DC 20008-3035
Fax: 202 362-2192
202 342-8372 **Bangladesh: People's Republic of Bangladesh**
2201 Wisconsin Ave NW Suite 300 .... Washington DC 20007-4105
Fax: 202 333-4971
202 939-9200 **Barbados** 2144 Wyoming Ave NW .... Washington DC 20008-3995
Fax: 202 332-7467

Foreign Embassies and Consulates in the US

202 333-6900 **Belgium: Kingdom of Belgium** 3330 Garfield St NW .... Washington DC 20008-3515
Fax: 202 333-3079

202 363-4505 **Belize** 3400 International Dr NW Suite 2J .... Washington DC 20008-3006
Fax: 202 362-7468

202 232-6656 **Benin: People's Republic of Benin**
2737 Cathedral Ave NW .... Washington DC 20008-4119

202 483-4410 **Bolivia: Republic of Bolivia** 3014 Massachusetts Ave NW .. Washington DC 20008-3603
Fax: 202 328-3712

202 244-4990 **Botswana: Republic of Botswana**
8400 International Dr NW Intelfat Bldg Suite 7-M .... Washington DC 20008-0000
Fax: 202 244-4164

202 745-2700 **Brazil: Federative Republic of Brazil**
3006 Massachusetts Ave NW .... Washington DC 20008-3603
Fax: 202 745-2827

202 342-0159 **Brunei: Sultanate of Brunei Darussalam**
2600 Virginia Ave NW Suite 300 .... Washington DC 20037-1905
Fax: 202 342-0158

202 387-7969 **Bulgaria: Republic of Bulgaria** 1621 22nd St NW ... Washington DC 20008-1921
Fax: 202 234-7973

202 332-5577 **Burkina Faso** 2340 Massachusetts Ave NW .... Washington DC 20008-2801
202 342-2574 **Burundi: Republic of Burundi**
2233 Wisconsin Ave NW Suite 212 .... Washington DC 20007-4104
Fax: 202 342-2578

202 265-8790 **Cameroon: Republic of Cameroon**
2349 Massachusetts Ave NW .... Washington DC 20008-2803
Fax: 202 387-3826

202 682-1740 **Canada** 501 Pennsylvania Ave NW .... Washington DC 20001-2111
Fax: 202 682-7726

202 965-6820 **Cape Verde: Republic of Cape Verde**
3415 Massachusetts Ave NW .... Washington DC 20007-1446
Fax: 202 965-1207

202 483-7800 **Central African Republic** 1618 22nd St NW .... Washington DC 20008-1920
202 462-4009 **Chad: Republic of Chad** 2002 R St NW .... Washington DC 20009-1012
202 785-1746 **Chile: Republic of Chile** 1732 Massachusetts Ave NW ... Washington DC 20036-1903
Fax: 202 887-5579

202 328-2500 **China: People's Republic of China**
2300 Connecticut Ave NW .... Washington DC 20008-1724
Fax: 202 234-4055

202 387-8338 **Colombia: Republic of Colombia** 2118 Leroy Pl NW .... Washington DC 20008-1847
Fax: 202 232-8643

202 726-5500 **Congo: People's Republic of the Congo**
4891 Colorado Ave NW .... Washington DC 20011-3731

202 234-2945 **Costa Rica: Republic of Costa Rica**
1825 Connecticut Ave NW Suite 211 .... Washington DC 20009-5708
Fax: 202 234-8653

202 462-5772 **Cyprus: Republic of Cyprus** 2211 R St NW .... Washington DC 20008-4017
Fax: 202 483-6710

202 363-6315 **Czechoslovakia: Czechoslovak Federal Republic**
3900 Linnean Ave NW .... Washington DC 20008-3803
Fax: 202 966-8540

202 234-4300 **Denmark: Kingdom of Denmark**
3200 White Haven St NW .... Washington DC 20008-0000
Fax: 202 328-1470

202 331-0270 **Djibouti: Republic of Djibouti** 1156 15th St NW Suite 515 .. Washington DC 20005-1704
Fax: 202 331-0302

202 332-6280 **Dominican Republic** 1715 22nd St NW .... Washington DC 20008-1902
Fax: 202 265-8057

202 234-7200 **Ecuador: Republic of Ecuador** 2535 15th St NW ..... Washington DC 20009-4102
Fax: 202 667-3482

202 232-5400 **Egypt: Arab Republic of Egypt** 2310 Decatur Pl NW .... Washington DC 20008-4010
Fax: 202 332-7894

202 331-4032 **El Salvador: Republic of El Salvador**
2308 California St NW .... Washington DC 20008-1637
Fax: 202 332-5103

212 247-1450 **Estonia** 9 Rockefeller Plaza Suite 1421 .... New York NY 10020-2081
202 234-2281 **Ethiopia: People's Democratic Republic of Ethiopia**
2134 Kalorama Rd NW .... Washington DC 20008-1618
Fax: 202 328-7950

202 862-9500 **European Economic Community:**
Delegation of the Commission of European Communities
2100 M St NW Suite 707 .... Washington DC 20037-1292
Fax: 202 429-1766

202 337-8320 **Fiji** 2233 Wisconsin Ave NW Suite 240 .... Washington DC 20007-4104
Fax: 202 337-1996

202 363-2430 **Finland** 3216 New Mexico Ave NW .... Washington DC 20016-2745
Fax: 202 363-8233

202 944-6000 **France: French Republic** 4101 Reservoir Rd .... Washington DC 20007-2186
Fax: 202 944-6116

202 797-1000 **Gabon: Gabonese Republic** 2034 20th St NW .... Washington DC 20009-5001
Fax: 202 332-0668

202 842-1356 **Gambia: Republic of Gambia** 1030 15th St Suite 720 ... Washington DC 20005-1503
Fax: 202 842-2073

202 298-4000 **Germany: Federal Republic of Germany**
4645 Reservoir Rd NW .... Washington DC 20007-1918
Fax: 202 298-4249

202 686-4520 **Ghana: Republic of Ghana** 3512 International Dr NW .... Washington DC 20008-3035
Fax: 202 686-4527

202 462-1340 **Great Britain: United Kingdom of Great Britain & Northern Ireland**
3100 Massachusetts Ave NW .... Washington DC 20008-3605
Fax: 202 898-4255

202 667-3168 **Greece: Hellenic Republic** 2221 Massachusetts Ave NW ... Washington DC 20008-2813
Fax: 202 939-5824

202 265-2561 **Grenada** 1701 New Hampshire Ave NW .... Washington DC 20009-2501
Fax: 202 265-2468

202 745-4952 **Guatemala: Republic of Guatemala** 2220 R St NW .... Washington DC 20008-4018
Fax: 202 745-1908

212 661-3977 **Guinea-Bissau: Republic of Guinea-Bissau**
211 E 43rd St Suite 604 .... New York NY 10017-4793
Fax: 212 983-2794

202 483-9420 **Guinea: Republic of Guinea** 2112 Leroy Pl NW ...... Washington DC 20008-1847
202 265-6900 **Guyana: Cooperative Republic of Guyana**
2490 Tracy Pl NW .... Washington DC 20008-1627
Fax: 202 232-1297

202 332-4090 **Haiti: Republic of Haiti** 2311 Massachusetts Ave NW .... Washington DC 20008-2802
Fax: 202 745-7215

202 333-7121 **Holy See: State of the Vatican City**
3339 Massachusetts Ave NW .... Washington DC 20008-3610
Fax: 202 337-4036

202 966-7702 **Honduras: Republic of Honduras**
3007 Tilden St NW Pod 4M .... Washington DC 20008-0000
Fax: 202 966-9751

202 362-6730 **Hungary: Republic of Hungary** 3910 Shoemaker St NW .... Washington DC 20008-3811
Fax: 202 966-8135

202 265-6653 **Iceland: Republic of Iceland** 2022 Connecticut Ave NW .... Washington DC 20008-6131
Fax: 202 265-6656

202 939-7000 **India: Republic of India** 2107 Massachusetts Ave NW ...... Washington DC 20008-2811
Fax: 202 939-7027

202 775-5200 **Indonesia: Republic of Indonesia**
2020 Massachusetts Ave NW .... Washington DC 20036-1083
Fax: 202 775-5365

202 483-7500 **Iraq: Republic of Iraq** 1801 P St NW .... Washington DC 20236-0000
Fax: 202 462-5066

202 462-3939 **Ireland: Republic of Ireland**
2234 Massachusetts Ave NW .... Washington DC 20008-2812
Fax: 202 232-5993

202 364-5500 **Israel: State of Israel** 3514 International Dr NW .... Washington DC 20008-3035
Fax: 202 363-4156

202 328-5500 **Italy: Italian Republic** 1601 Fuller St NW .... Washington DC 20009-5601
Fax: 202 238-5542

202 483-2400 **Ivory Coast: Republic of the Ivory Coast**
2424 Massachusetts Ave NW .... Washington DC 20008-2804
Fax: 202 483-8482

202 452-0660 **Jamaica** 1850 K St NW International Sq Bldg Suite 355 ... Washington DC 20006-0000
Fax: 202 452-0081

202 234-2266 **Japan** 2520 Massachusetts Ave NW .... Washington DC 20008-2822
Fax: 202 328-2187

202 966-2664 **Jordan: Hashemite Kingdom of Jordan**
3504 International Dr NW .... Washington DC 20008-3035
Fax: 202 966-3110

202 387-6101 **Kenya: Republic of Kenya** 2249 R St NW .... Washington DC 20008-4017
Fax: 202 462-3829

202 939-5600 **Korea: Republic of Korea** 2370 Massachusetts Ave NW .... Washington DC 20008-2801
Fax: 202 797-0595

202 966-0702 **Kuwait: State of Kuwait** 2940 Tilden St NW .... Washington DC 20008-1193
Fax: 202 966-0517

202 332-6416 **Laos: Lao People's Democratic Republic** 2222 S St NW ... Washington DC 20008-4014
202 726-8213 **Latvia** 4325 17th St NW .... Washington DC 20011-4203
Fax: Unlisted

202 939-6300 **Lebanon: Republic of Lebanon** 2560 28th St NW ..... Washington DC 20008-2744
Fax: Unlisted

202 797-5533 **Lesotho: Kingdom of Lesotho**
2511 Massachusetts Ave NW .... Washington DC 20008-2823
Fax: 202 234-6815

202 723-0437 **Liberia: Republic of Liberia** 5201 16th St NW .... Washington DC 20011-3615
202 234-5860 **Lithuania** 2622 16th St NW .... Washington DC 20009-4292
Fax: Unlisted

202 265-4171 **Luxembourg: Grand Duchy of Luxembourg**
2200 Massachusetts Ave NW .... Washington DC 20008-2812
Fax: 202 328-8270

202 265-5525 **Madagascar: Democratic Republic of Madagascar**
2374 Massachusetts Ave NW .... Washington DC 20008-2801
Fax: 202 483-7603

202 328-2700 **Malaysia** 2401 Massachusetts Ave NW .... Washington DC 20008-2805
Fax: 202 483-7661

202 332-2249 **Mali: Republic of Mali** 2130 R St NW .... Washington DC 20008-1907
202 462-3611 **Malta: Republic of Malta** 2017 Connecticut Ave NW .... Washington DC 20008-6132
Fax: 202 387-5470

202 232-5700 **Mauritania: Islamic Republic of Mauritania**
2129 Leroy Pl NW .... Washington DC 20008-1848

202 244-1491 **Mauritius** 4301 Connecticut Ave NW Suite 134 .... Washington DC 20008-2304
Fax: 202 966-0983

202 293-1710 **Mexico: United Mexican States** 1019 19th St NW ...... Washington DC 20036-5105
Fax: 202 775-4552

202 462-7979 **Morocco: Kingdom of Morocco** 1601 21st St NW ...... Washington DC 20009-1002
Fax: 202 265-0161

202 293-7146 **Mozambique: People's Republic of Mozambique**
1990 M St NW Suite 570 .... Washington DC 20036-3404
Fax: 202 835-0245

202 332-9044 **Myanmar: Union of Myanmar** 2300 S St NW .... Washington DC 20008-4016
Fax: 202 332-9046

202 667-4550 **Nepal: Kingdom of Nepal** 2131 Leroy Pl NW .... Washington DC 20008-1848
Fax: 202 667-5534

202 244-5304 **Netherlands: Kingdom of the Netherlands**
4200 Linnean Ave NW .... Washington DC 20008-3809
Fax: 202 362-3430

202 328-4800 **New Zealand** 37 Observatory Cir NW .... Washington DC 20008-3686
Fax: 202 667-5227

202 939-6531 **Nicaragua: Republic of Nicaragua**
1627 New Hampshire Ave NW .... Washington DC 20009-2550
Fax: 202 939-6574

202 483-4224 **Niger: Republic of Niger** 2204 R St NW .... Washington DC 20008-4018
Fax: 202 483-3169

202 822-1500 **Nigeria: Federal Republic of Nigeria** 2201 M St NW ... Washington DC 20037-1416
Fax: 202 775-1385

202 333-6000 **Norway: Kingdom of Norway** 2720 34th St NW ...... Washington DC 20008-2714
Fax: 202 337-0870

202 387-1980 **Oman: Sultanate of Oman** 2342 Massachusetts Ave NW .. Washington DC 20008-2801
Fax: 202 387-2186

202 939-6200 **Pakistan: Islamic Republic of Pakistan**
2315 Massachusetts Ave NW .... Washington DC 20008-2802
Fax: 202 387-0484

202 659-0856 **Papua New Guinea** 1330 Connecticut Ave NW Suite 350 .... Washington DC 20036-1711
Fax: 202 466-2412

202 483-6960 **Paraguay: Republic of Paraguay**
2400 Massachusetts Ave NW .... Washington DC 20008-2804
Fax: 202 234-4508

202 833-9860 **Peru: Republic of Peru** 1700 Massachusetts Ave NW ... Washington DC 20036-1903
Fax: 202 659-3660

202 483-1414 **Philippines: Republic of the Philippines**
1617 Massachusetts Ave NW .... Washington DC 20036-2209
Fax: 202 328-7614

202 234-3800 **Poland: Republic of Poland** 2640 16th St NW .... Washington DC 20009-4202
Fax: 202 328-6271

202 328-8610 **Portugal: Republic of Portugal** 2125 Kalorama Rd NW ...... Washington DC 20008-1619
Fax: 202 462-3726

202 338-0111 **Qatar: State of Qatar**
600 New Hampshire Ave NW Suite 1180 .... Washington DC 20037-2403
Fax: 202 337-2989

202 232-4747 **Romania** 1607 23rd St NW .... Washington DC 20008-2809
Fax: 202 232-4748

202 232-2882 **Rwanda: Republic of Rwanda**
1714 New Hampshire Ave NW .... Washington DC 20009-2502
Fax: 202 232-4544

202 833-3550 **Saint Kitts & Nevis: State of Saint Christopher-Nevis**
2100 M St NW Suite 608 .... Washington DC 20037-1207
Fax: 202 833-3553

202 463-7378 **Saint Lucia** 2100 M St NW Suite 309 .... Washington DC 20037-1207
Fax: 202 887-5746

212 697-4211 **Sao Tome & Principe: Democratic Republic of Sao Tome & Principe**
801 2nd Ave Suite 1504 .... New York NY 10017-4706
Fax: 212 687-8389

Foreign Embassies and Consulates in the US

202 342-3800 **Saudi Arabia: Kingdom of Saudi Arabia**
601 New Hampshire Ave NW .... Washington DC 20037-2405
Fax: 202 337-3233

202 234-0540 **Senegal: Republic of Senegal** 2112 Wyoming Ave NW ..... Washington DC 20008-3906
Fax: 202 332-6315

212 687-9766 **Seychelles: Republic of Seychelles**
820 2nd Ave Suite 900-F .... New York NY 10017-4504
Fax: 212 808-4975

202 939-9261 **Sierra Leone: Republic of Sierra Leone** 1701 19th St NW ..Washington DC 20009-1605
202 667-7555 **Singapore: Republic of Singapore** 1824 R St NW .... Washington DC 20009-1604
Fax: 202 265-7915

202 342-1575 **Somalia: Somali Democratic Republic**
600 New Hampshire Ave NW Suite 710 .... Washington DC 20037-2403
Fax: 202 625-0886

202 232-4400 **South Africa: Republic of South Africa**
3051 Massachusetts Ave NW .... Washington DC 20008-3604
Fax: 202 265-1607

202 628-7551 **Soviet Union: Union of Soviet Socialist Republics**
1125 16th St NW .... Washington DC 20036-4801
Fax: 202 347-5028

202 265-0190 **Spain** 2700 15th St NW .... Washington DC 20009-4605
Fax: 202 328-3212

202 483-4025 **Sri Lanka: Democratic Socialist Republic of Sri Lanka**
2148 Wyoming Ave NW .... Washington DC 20008-3994
Fax: 202 232-7181

202 338-8565 **Sudan: Republic of the Sudan**
2210 Massachusetts Ave NW .... Washington DC 20008-2812

202 244-7488 **Suriname: Republic of Suriname**
4301 Connecticut Ave NW Suite 108 .... Washington DC 20008-2304
Fax: 202 244-5878

202 362-6683 **Swaziland: Kingdom of Swaziland**
3400 International Dr NW Suite 3M .... Washington DC 20008-3006
Fax: 202 244-8059

202 944-5600 **Sweden: Kingdom of Sweden**
600 New Hampshire Ave NW Suite 1200 .... Washington DC 20037-2403
Fax: 202 342-1319

202 745-7900 **Switzerland: Swiss Confederation**
2900 Cathedral Ave NW .... Washington DC 20008-3405
Fax: 202 387-2564

202 232-6313 **Syria: Syrian Arab Republic** 2215 Wyoming Ave NW ....Washington DC 20008-3907
Fax: Unlisted

202 939-6125 **Tanzania: United Republic of Tanzania** 2139 R St NW ..... Washington DC 20008-1908
202 483-7200 **Thailand: Kingdom of Thailand** 2300 Kalorama Rd NW ..... Washington DC 20008-1623
Fax: 202 234-4498

202 234-4212 **Togo: Republic of Togo** 2208 Massachusetts Ave NW .... Washington DC 20008-2812
Fax: 202 232-3190

202 467-6490 **Trinidad & Tobago: Republic of Trinidad & Tobago**
1708 Massachusetts Ave NW .... Washington DC 20036-1903
Fax: 202 785-3130

202 862-1850 **Tunisia: Republic of Tunisia**
1515 Massachusetts Ave NW .... Washington DC 20005-1801
Fax: 202 862-1858

202 659-8200 **Turkey: Republic of Turkey** 1714 Massachusetts Ave NW .. Washington DC 20036-1903
Fax: 202 659-0744

202 726-7100 **Uganda: Republic of Uganda** 5909 16th St NW .... Washington DC 20011-2816
Fax: 202 726-1727

202 338-6500 **United Arab Emirates**
600 New Hampshire Ave NW Suite 740 .... Washington DC 20037-2486
Fax: 202 337-7029

202 331-1313 **Uruguay: Oriental Republic of Uruguay** 1918 F St NW ..... Washington DC 20006-4397
Fax: 202 331-8142

202 342-2214 **Venezuela: Republic of Venezuela** 1099 30th St .... Washington DC 20008-2805
Fax: 202 342-6820

212 599-6196 **Western Samoa: Independent State of Western Samoa**
820 2nd Ave Suite 800D .... New York NY 10017-4504
Fax: 212 972-3970

202 965-4760 **Yemen: Republic of Yemen**
600 New Hampshire Ave NW Suite 840 .... Washington DC 20037-2403
Fax: 202 337-2017

202 462-6566 **Yugoslavia: Socialist Federal Republic of Yugoslavia**
2410 California St NW .... Washington DC 20008-1614
Fax: 202 797-9663

202 234-7690 **Zaire: Republic of Zaire** 1800 New Hampshire Ave NW ..... Washington DC 20009-3206
202 265-9717 **Zambia: Republic of Zambia**
2419 Massachusetts Ave NW .... Washington DC 20008-2805
202 332-7100 **Zimbabwe: Republic of Zimbabwe** 2852 McGill Terr NW ... Washington DC 20008-2748
Fax: 202 483-9326

United Nations

212 963-1234 **United Nations General Information** 1st Ave & 46th St .... New York NY 10017-0000
Fax: 212 963-4879

212 963-1234 **United Nations Secretariat**
1st Ave & 42nd St UN Headquarters .... New York NY 10017-0000
Fax: 212 963-4879

AGENCIES OF THE UN

Selected agencies are listed alphabetically.

212 963-6011 **International Atomic Energy Agency**
1 UN Plaza Rm DC1-1155 .... New York NY 10017-0000
Fax: 212 751-4117

212 697-0150 **International Labor Organization (ILO)** 820 2nd Ave 18th Fl ... New York NY 10017-0000
Fax: 212 883-0844

212 326-7000 **UN Children's Fund (UNICEF)** 3 UN Plaza .... New York NY 10017-0000
Fax: 212 888-7465

212 906-5000 **UN Development Program** 1 UN Plaza .... New York NY 10017-3576
Fax: 212 826-2057

212 963-5995 **UN Educational Scientific & Cultural Organization (UNESCO)**
2 UN Plaza Rm 900 .... New York NY 10017-0000
Fax: 212 355-5627

212 963-8139 **UN Environment Program** 2 UN Plaza Rm 803 .... New York NY 10017-0000
Fax: 212 963-7341

212 963-6882 **UN Industrial Development Organization (UNIDO)**
1 UN Plaza Rm DC1-1110 .... New York NY 10017-3575
Fax: 212 963-4116

212 963-3952 **World Health Organization (WHO)**
2 UN Plaza Rm DC2-0973 .... New York NY 10017-0000
Fax: 212 223-2920

212 963-6813 **World Intellectual Property Organization (WIPO)**
2 UN Plaza Suite 560 .... New York NY 10017-0000

PERMANENT MISSIONS TO THE UN

Missions are listed alphabetically by the country's familiar name, followed by the country's official name, e.g., Egypt: Arab Republic of Egypt.

212 754-1191 **Afghanistan: Democratic Republic of Afghanistan**
866 UN Plaza Rm 520 .... New York NY 10017-1890

212 249-2059 **Albania: People's Socialist Republic of Albania**
320 E 79th St .... New York NY 10021-0904

212 750-1960 **Algeria: Democratic & Popular Republic of Algeria**
15 E 47th St .... New York NY 10017-1982

212 861-5656 **Angola: People's Republic of Angola** 135 E 73rd St .... New York NY 10021-0000
Fax: 212 832-8191

212 541-4117 **Antigua & Barbuda** 610 5th Ave Suite 311 .... New York NY 10020-2403
Fax: 212 757-1607

212 688-6300 **Argentina: Argentine Republic** 1 UN Plaza 25th Fl .... New York NY 10017-0000
Fax: 212 980-8395

212 421-6910 **Australia: Commonwealth of Australia** 885 2nd Ave 16th Fl ... New York NY 10017-2201
Fax: 212 371-5843

212 949-1840 **Austria: Republic of Austria** 809 UN Plaza 7th Fl .... New York NY 10017-0000
Fax: 212 953-1302

212 421-6925 **Bahamas: Commonwealth of the Bahamas**
767 3rd Ave 9th Fl .... New York NY 10017-2076
Fax: 212 759-2135

212 223-6200 **Bahrain: State of Bahrain** 2 UN Plaza 25th Fl .... New York NY 10017-0000
Fax: 212 319-0687

212 867-3434 **Bangladesh: People's Republic of Bangladesh**
821 UN Plaza 8th Fl .... New York NY 10017-0000
Fax: 212 972-4038

212 867-8431 **Barbados** 800 2nd Ave 18th Fl .... New York NY 10017-4790
Fax: 212 682-5496

212 599-5250 **Belgium: Kingdom of Belgium** 809 UN Plaza 2nd Fl ...... New York NY 10017-0000
Fax: 212 599-6843

212 599-0233 **Belize** 820 2nd Ave Suite 922 .... New York NY 10017-4504
Fax: 212 599-3391

212 249-6014 **Benin: People's Republic of Benin** 4 E 73rd St .... New York NY 10021-4135
Fax: 212 734-4735

212 826-1919 **Bhutan: Kingdom of Bhutan** 2 UN Plaza 27th Fl .... New York NY 10017-0000
Fax: 212 826-2998

212 682-8132 **Bolivia: Republic of Bolivia** 211 E 43rd St Rm 802 .... New York NY 10017-4707
Fax: 212 687-4642

212 889-2277 **Botswana: Republic of Botswana** 103 E 37th St .... New York NY 10016-3002
Fax: 212 725-5061

212 832-6868 **Brazil: Federative Republic of Brazil** 747 3rd Ave 9th Fl ... New York NY 10017-2803
Fax: 212 371-5716

212 838-1600 **Brunei: Sultanate of Brunei Darussalam**
866 United Nations Plaza Rm 248 .... New York NY 10017-1811

212 737-4790 **Bulgaria: People's Republic of Bulgaria** 11 E 84th St .... New York NY 10028-0407
212 288-7515 **Burkina Faso** 115 E 73rd St .... New York NY 10021-3575
212 687-1180 **Burundi: Republic of Burundi** 201 E 42nd St 28th Fl ...... New York NY 10017-5704
Fax: Unlisted

212 535-3420 **Byelorussian Soviet Socialist Republic** 136 E 67th St .... New York NY 10021-6137
Fax: 212 734-4810

212 888-6646 **Cambodia** 747 3rd Ave 8th Fl .... New York NY 10017-2803
212 794-2295 **Cameroon: Republic of Cameroon** 22 E 73rd St .... New York NY 10021-4138
212 751-5600 **Canada** 866 UN Plaza Suite 250 .... New York NY 10017-0000
Fax: 212 486-1295

212 472-0333 **Cape Verde: Republic of Cape Verde** 27 E 69th St .... New York NY 10021-4917
Fax: 212 794-1398

212 689-6195 **Central African Republic** 386 Park Ave S Suite 1614 ...... New York NY 10016-8851
212 490-2072 **Chad: Republic of Chad** 211 E 43rd St Rm 1703 .... New York NY 10017-4707
212 687-7547 **Chile: Republic of Chile** 809 UN Plaza 4th Fl .... New York NY 10017-0000
Fax: 212 972-9875

212 787-3838 **China: People's Republic of China** 155 W 66th St .... New York NY 10023-6501
Fax: 212 787-1173

212 355-7776 **Colombia: Republic of Colombia** 140 E 57th St 5th Fl .... New York NY 10022-2706
Fax: 212 371-2813

212 972-8010 **Comoros: Islamic Federal Republic of the Comoros**
336 E 45th St 2nd Fl .... New York NY 10017-3401
212 744-7840 **Congo: People's Republic of the Congo** 14 E 65th St .... New York NY 10021-7005
212 986-6373 **Costa Rica: Republic of Costa Rica** 211 E 43rd St Suite 903 .. New York NY 10017-4707
Fax: 212 986-6842

212 689-7215 **Cuba: Republic of Cuba** 315 Lexington Ave .... New York NY 10016-2606
212 481-6023 **Cyprus: Republic of Cyprus** 13 E 40th St .... New York NY 10016-0110
Fax: 212 685-7316

212 535-8814 **Czechoslovakia: Czechoslovak Federal Republic**
1109-11 Madison Ave .... New York NY 10028-0000
Fax: 212 772-0586

212 308-7009 **Denmark: Kingdom of Denmark** 2 UN Plaza 26th Fl .... New York NY 10017-0000
Fax: 212 308-3384

212 753-3163 **Djibouti: Republic of Djibouti** 866 UN Plaza Suite 4011 .... New York NY 10017-1811
212 867-0833 **Dominican Republic** 144 E 44th St 4th Fl .... New York NY 10017-4053
212 935-1680 **Ecuador: Republic of Ecuador**
5th Ave & 48th St 866 UN Plaza Suite 516 .... New York NY 10017-0000
Fax: 212 935-1835

212 879-6300 **Egypt: Arab Republic of Egypt** 36 E 67th St .... New York NY 10021-6120
Fax: Call company operator

212 679-1616 **El Salvador: Republic of El Salvador** 46 Park Ave 3rd Fl ... New York NY 10016-3407
Fax: 212 725-7831

212 421-1830 **Ethiopia: People's Democratic Republic of Ethiopia**
866 UN Plaza Rm 560 .... New York NY 10017-0000
Fax: 212 754-0360

212 355-7316 **Fiji** 1 UN Plaza 26th Fl .... New York NY 10017-0000
Fax: 212 319-1896

212 355-2100 **Finland: Republic of Finland** 866 UN Plaza Rm 222 .... New York NY 10017-0000
Fax: 212 759-6156

212 308-5700 **France: French Republic** 245 E 47th St .... New York NY 10017-2201
Fax: 212 355-2763

212 686-9720 **Gabon: Gabonese Republic** 18 E 41st St 6th Fl .... New York NY 10017-6222
212 949-6640 **Gambia: Republic of Gambia** 820 2nd Ave Suite 900-C .... New York NY 10017-4504
Fax: 212 808-4975

212 949-9200 **Germany: Federal Republic of Germany** 600 3rd Ave 41st Fl .. New York NY 10016-1902
Fax: 212 490-0857

212 832-1300 **Ghana: Republic of Ghana** 19 E 47th St .... New York NY 10017-1984
Fax: 212 751-6743

212 752-8400 **Great Britain: United Kingdom of Great Britain & Northern Ireland**
845 3rd Ave 10th Fl .... New York NY 10022-6601
Fax: 212 306-0316

212 490-6060 **Greece: Hellenic Republic** 733 3rd Ave 23rd Fl .... New York NY 10017-3296
Fax: 212 490-5894

212 679-4760 **Guatemala: Republic of Guatemala** 57 Park Ave 2nd Fl ...... New York NY 10016-3006
Fax: 212 685-8741

212 661-3977 **Guinea-Bissau: Republic of Guinea-Bissau** 211 E 43rd St ...... New York NY 10017-4793
212 687-8115 **Guinea: Republic of Guinea** 140 E 39th St 29th Fl .... New York NY 10016-0000

212 527-3232 **Guyana: Cooperative Republic of Guyana**
866 UN Plaza Suite 555 .... New York NY 10017-0000
Fax: 212 935-7548

212 370-4840 **Haiti: Republic of Haiti** 801 2nd Ave Rm 300 .... New York NY 10017-4706
Fax: 212 661-8698

212 752-3370 **Honduras: Republic of Honduras** 866 UN Plaza Suite 417 .... New York NY 10017-0000
Fax: 212 223-0498

212 535-8660 **Hungary: Republic of Hungary** 10 E 75th St .... New York NY 10021-2687
Fax: 212 734-6036

212 686-4100 **Iceland: Republic of Iceland** 370 Lexington Ave Suite 505 .... New York NY 10017-6503
Fax: 212 532-4138

212 751-0900 **India: Republic of India** 866 UN Plaza Suite 505 .... New York NY 10017-0000
Fax: 212 751-1393

212 972-8333 **Indonesia: Republic of Indonesia** 325 E 38th St .... New York NY 10016-2745
Fax: 212 972-9780

212 687-2020 **Iran: Islamic Republic of Iran** 622 3rd Ave 34th Fl .... New York NY 10017-6707
Fax: 212 867-7086

212 737-4433 **Iraq: Republic of Iraq** 14 E 79th St .... New York NY 10021-0106

212 421-6934 **Ireland: Republic of Ireland** 885 2nd Ave 19th Fl .... New York NY 10017-2201
Fax: 212 223-0926

212 351-5200 **Israel: State of Israel** 800 2nd Ave .... New York NY 10017-4755
Fax: 212 953-0317

212 486-9191 **Italy: Italian Republic** 2 UN Plaza 24th Fl .... New York NY 10017-0000
Fax: 212 486-1036

212 371-7036 **Ivory Coast: Republic of the Ivory Coast**
866 UN Plaza Rm 580 .... New York NY 10017-0000
Fax: 212 935-5347

212 688-7040 **Jamaica** 866 2nd Ave 15th Fl .... New York NY 10017-2998
Fax: 212 308-3730

212 223-4300 **Japan** 866 UN Plaza Suite 230 .... New York NY 10017-0000
Fax: 212 751-1966

212 752-0135 **Jordan: Hashemite Kingdom of Jordan**
866 UN Plaza Rm 552 .... New York NY 10017-0000

212 421-4740 **Kenya: Republic of Kenya** 866 UN Plaza Rm 486 .... New York NY 10017-0000

212 973-4300 **Kuwait: State of Kuwait** 321 E 44th St .... New York NY 10017-4401
Fax: 212 370-1733

212 986-0227 **Laos: Lao People's Democratic Republic**
820 2nd Ave Suite 1200 .... New York NY 10017-0000

212 355-5460 **Lebanon: Republic of Lebanon** 866 UN Plaza Rm 531 .... New York NY 10017-0000
Fax: 212 838-2819

212 661-1690 **Lesotho: Kingdom of Lesotho** 204 E 39th St .... New York NY 10016-0911
Fax: 212 682-4388

212 687-1033 **Liberia: Republic of Liberia** 300 E 44th St 4th Fl .... New York NY 10017-4403

212 752-5775 **Libya: Socialist People's Libyan Arab Jamahiriya**
309 E 48th St .... New York NY 10017-1746
Fax: 212 593-4787

212 370-9850 **Luxembourg: Grand Duchy of Luxembourg**
801 2nd Ave 13th Fl .... New York NY 10017-0000
Fax: 212 697-5529

212 986-9491 **Madagascar: Democratic Republic of Madagascar**
801 2nd Ave Rm 404 .... New York NY 10017-4759
Fax: 212 986-6271

212 949-0180 **Malawi: Republic of Malawi** 600 3rd Ave 30th Fl .... New York NY 10016-0000
Fax: 212 599-5021

212 986-6310 **Malaysia** 140 E 45th St 43rd Fl .... New York NY 10017-3144
Fax: 212 490-8576

212 599-6195 **Maldives: Republic of Maldives** 820 2nd Ave Suite 800C .... New York NY 10017-0000
Fax: 212 972-3970

212 737-4150 **Mali: Republic of Mali** 111 E 69th St .... New York NY 10021-5004
Fax: 212 472-3778

212 725-2345 **Malta: Republic of Malta** 249 E 35th St .... New York NY 10016-4259
Fax: 212 779-7097

212 737-7780 **Mauritania: Islamic Republic of Mauritania** 9 E 77th St .... New York NY 10021-1703
Fax: 212 472-3314

212 949-0190 **Mauritius** 211 E 43rd St 15th Fl .... New York NY 10017-4707
Fax: 212 697-3829

212 752-0220 **Mexico: United Mexican States** 2 UN Plaza 28th Fl .... New York NY 10017-0000
Fax: 212 688-8862

212 861-9460 **Mongolia: Mongolian People's Republic** 6 E 77th St .... New York NY 10021-1791
Fax: 212 861-9464

212 421-1580 **Morocco: Kingdom of Morocco** 767 3rd Ave 30th Fl .... New York NY 10017-2023

212 517-4550 **Mozambique: People's Republic of Mozambique**
70 E 79th St .... New York NY 10021-0299

212 535-1310 **Myanmar: Union of Myanmar** 10 E 77th St .... New York NY 10021-1704
Fax: 212 737-2421

212 370-4188 **Nepal: Kingdom of Nepal** 820 2nd Ave Rm 202 .... New York NY 10017-4504
Fax: 212 953-2038

212 697-5547 **Netherlands: Kingdom of the Netherlands**
711 3rd Ave 9th Fl .... New York NY 10017-4014
Fax: 212 370-1954

212 826-1960 **New Zealand** 1 UN Plaza 25th Fl .... New York NY 10017-0000
Fax: 212 758-0827

212 490-7997 **Nicaragua: Republic of Nicaragua** 820 2nd Ave .... New York NY 10017-4556
Fax: 212 286-0815

212 421-3260 **Niger: Republic of Niger** 417 E 50th St .... New York NY 10022-8001
Fax: 212 753-6931

212 953-9130 **Nigeria: Federal Republic of Nigeria** 733 3rd Ave 15th Fl .... New York NY 10017-3204
Fax: 212 697-1970

212 421-0280 **Norway: Kingdom of Norway** 825 3rd Ave 18th Fl .... New York NY 10022-7583
Fax: 212 688-0554

212 355-3505 **Oman: Sultanate of Oman** 866 UN Plaza Rm 540 .... New York NY 10017-0000
Fax: 212 644-0070

212 879-8600 **Pakistan: Islamic Republic of Pakistan** 8 E 65th St .... New York NY 10021-7005
Fax: 212 744-7348

212 421-5420 **Panama: Republic of Panama** 866 UN Plaza Suite 544 .... New York NY 10017-0000

212 682-6447 **Papua New Guinea** 100 E 42nd St Rm 1005 .... New York NY 10017-5613
Fax: 212 682-6454

212 687-3490 **Paraguay: Republic of Paraguay** 211 E 43rd St Rm 1202 .... New York NY 10017-4778
Fax: 212 818-1282

212 687-3336 **Peru: Republic of Peru** 820 2nd Ave Suite 1600 .... New York NY 10017-4504
Fax: 212 972-6975

212 764-1300 **Philippines: Republic of the Philippines** 556 5th Ave 5th Fl .... New York NY 10036-5096
Fax: 212 840-8602

212 744-2506 **Poland: Republic of Poland** 9 E 66th St .... New York NY 10021-5801
Fax: 212 517-6771

212 759-9444 **Portugal: Republic of Portugal** 777 3rd Ave 27th Fl .... New York NY 10017-1490
Fax: 212 355-1124

212 486-9335 **Qatar: State of Qatar** 747 3rd Ave 22nd Fl .... New York NY 10017-2803
Fax: 212 758-4952

212 682-3274 **Romania** 577 3rd Ave .... New York NY 10016-3109
Fax: 212 682-9746

212 696-0644 **Rwanda: Republic of Rwanda** 124 E 39th St .... New York NY 10016-0906

212 535-1234 **Saint Kitts & Nevis: State of Saint Christopher-Nevis**
414 E 75th St 5th Fl .... New York NY 10021-3403
Fax: 212 879-4789

212 697-9360 **Saint Lucia** 820 2nd Ave Suites 907-915 .... New York NY 10017-0000
Fax: 212 808-4975

212 687-4490 **Saint Vincent & the Grenadines** 801 2nd Ave 21st Fl .... New York NY 10017-4706
Fax: 212 949-5946

212 697-4211 **Sao Tome & Principe: Democratic Republic of Sao Tome & Principe**
801 2nd Ave Suite 1504 .... New York NY 10017-4706

212 697-4830 **Saudi Arabia: Kingdom of Saudi Arabia**
405 Lexington Ave 56th Fl .... New York NY 10174-0220
Fax: Call company operator

212 517-9030 **Senegal: Republic of Senegal** 238 E 68th St .... New York NY 10021-6001
Fax: 212 737-7461

212 687-9766 **Seychelles: Republic of Seychelles** 820 2nd Ave Suite 900 .... New York NY 10017-4504
Fax: 212 808-4975

212 570-0030 **Sierra Leone: Republic of Sierra Leone** 57 E 64th St .... New York NY 10021-7003

212 826-0840 **Singapore: Republic of Singapore** 2 UN Plaza 25th Fl .... New York NY 10017-0000
Fax: 212 826-2964

212 599-6193 **Solomon Islands** 820 2nd Ave Suite 800A .... New York NY 10017-4504
Fax: 212 972-3970

212 688-9410 **Somalia: Somali Democratic Republic**
425 E 61st St Suite 703 .... New York NY 10021-8722

212 371-8154 **South Africa: Republic of South Africa** 326 E 48th St .... New York NY 10017-1796
Fax: 212 371-7577

212 861-4900 **Soviet Union: Union of Soviet Socialist Republics**
136 E 67th St .... New York NY 10021-6137
Fax: 212 628-0252

212 661-1050 **Spain** 809 UN Plaza 6th Fl .... New York NY 10017-0000
Fax: 212 949-7247

212 986-7040 **Sri Lanka: Democratic Socialist Republic of Sri Lanka**
630 3rd Ave 20th Fl .... New York NY 10017-6759
Fax: 212 986-1838

212 599-0301 **State of Grenada** 820 2nd Ave Suite 900-D .... New York NY 10017-4504
Fax: 212 808-4975

212 421-2680 **Sudan: Republic of the Sudan** 210 E 49th St .... New York NY 10017-1580
Fax: Unlisted

212 826-0660 **Suriname: Republic of Suriname** 1 UN Plaza 26th Fl .... New York NY 10017-0000
Fax: 212 980-7029

212 371-8910 **Swaziland: Kingdom of Swaziland** 866 UN Plaza Suite 420 .... New York NY 10017-0000
Fax: 212 754-2755

212 751-5900 **Sweden: Kingdom of Sweden** 885 2nd Ave 46th Fl .... New York NY 10017-2201
Fax: 212 832-0389

212 661-1313 **Syria: Syrian Arab Republic** 820 2nd Ave 10th Fl .... New York NY 10017-4504
Fax: 212 983-4439

212 972-9160 **Tanzania: United Republic of Tanzania**
205 E 42nd St Rm 1300 .... New York NY 10017-5706
Fax: 212 682-5231

212 689-1004 **Thailand: Kingdom of Thailand** 628 2nd Ave .... New York NY 10016-4899
Fax: 212 683-6017

212 490-3455 **Togo: Republic of Togo** 112 E 40th St 1st Fl .... New York NY 10016-1724

212 697-7620 **Trinidad & Tobago: Republic of Trinidad & Tobago**
675 3rd Ave 22nd Fl .... New York NY 10017-5704
Fax: 212 682-3518

212 557-3344 **Tunisia: Republic of Tunisia** 405 Lexington Ave 65th Fl .... New York NY 10174-0089
Fax: 212 697-4090

212 949-0150 **Turkey: Republic of Turkey** 821 UN Plaza 11th Fl .... New York NY 10017-0000
Fax: 212 949-0086

212 949-0110 **Uganda: Republic of Uganda** 336 E 45th St .... New York NY 10017-3401

212 535-3418 **Ukrainian Soviet Socialist Republic** 136 E 67th St 5th Fl .... New York NY 10021-6137
Fax: 212 288-5361

212 371-0480 **United Arab Emirates** 747 3rd Ave 36th Fl .... New York NY 10017-2875
Fax: 212 319-5433

212 415-4000 **United States of America** 799 UN Plaza .... New York NY 10017-3589
Fax: 212 415-4443

212 752-8240 **Uruguay: Oriental Republic of Uruguay** 747 3rd Ave 37th Fl .... New York NY 10017-2828
Fax: 212 593-0935

212 926-3311 **Vanuatu: Republic of Vanuatu** 416 Convent Ave .... New York NY 10031-4217
Fax: 212 926-4131

212 557-2055 **Venezuela: Republic of Venezuela** 335 E 46th St .... New York NY 10017-3096
Fax: 212 557-3528

212 679-3779 **Viet Nam: Socialist Republic of Viet Nam**
20 Waterside Plaza .... New York NY 10010-2612
Fax: 212 686-8534

212 599-6196 **Western Samoa: Independent State of Western Samoa**
820 2nd Ave Suite 800D .... New York NY 10017-4504
Fax: 212 972-3970

212 355-1737 **Yemen: People's Democratic Republic of Yemen**
413 E 51st St .... New York NY 10022-6403
Fax: 212 832-5397

212 355-1730 **Yemen: Republic of Yemen** 866 UN Plaza Rm 435 .... New York NY 10017-0000
Fax: 212 750-9613

212 879-8700 **Yugoslavia: Socialist Federal Republic of Yugoslavia**
854 5th Ave .... New York NY 10021-5890
Fax: 212 879-8705

212 754-1966 **Zaire: Republic of Zaire** 767 3rd Ave 25th Fl .... New York NY 10017-2023
Fax: 212 754-1970

212 758-1110 **Zambia: Republic of Zambia** 237 E 52nd St .... New York NY 10022-6301
Fax: 212 758-1319

212 980-5084 **Zimbabwe: Republic of Zimbabwe** 19 E 47th St .... New York NY 10017-1901
Fax: 212 755-4188

PERMANENT OBSERVER MISSIONS TO THE UN

212 734-2900 **Holy See: State of the Vatican City** 20 E 72nd St .... New York NY 10021-4106
Fax: 212 988-3633

212 371-1280 **Korea: Republic of Korea**
866 United Nations Plaza Suite 300 .... New York NY 10017-1811

212 759-5227 **Monaco: Principality of Monaco** 845 3rd Ave 19th Fl .... New York NY 10022-6601
Fax: 212 754-9320

212 751-1234 **San Marino: Republic of San Marino**
745 5th Ave Suite 1208 .... New York NY 10151-0105

212 421-1480 **Switzerland: Swiss Confederation** 757 3rd Ave 21st Fl .... New York NY 10017-2013
Fax: 212 751-2104

US Agencies That Foster Trade

Selected US agencies that encourage overseas trade or provide counsel on foreign trade policy are listed alphabetically. See also the Government section and the Associations and Organizations section.

202 647-9620 **Agency for International Development**
320 21st St NW Rm 6226 .... Washington DC 20523-0001
Fax: 202 647-8511

215 540-2295 **American Society of International Executives**
18 Sentry Pkwy Suite 1 .... Blue Bell PA 19422-2339
Fax: 215 540-2290

US Agencies That Foster Trade

202 463-5485 **Association of American Chambers of Commerce in Latin America**
1615 H St NW 6th Fl .... Washington DC 20062-0001
Fax: 202 463-3114

202 463-5485 **Brazil-US Business Council** 1615 H St NW 6th Fl ..... Washington DC 20062-0001
Fax: 202 463-3114

202 647-4440 **Bureau of African Affairs Dept of State**
2201 C St NW Rm 6234-A .... Washington DC 20520-3430
Fax: 202 647-6301

202 647-7971 **Bureau of Economic & Business Affairs Dept of State**
2201 C St NW Rm 6828 .... Washington DC 20520-0001
Fax: 202 647-5713

202 647-7209 **Bureau of Near Eastern & South Asian Affairs Dept of State**
2201 C St NW Rm 6242 .... Washington DC 20520-0001
Fax: 202 647-7720

202 466-7464 **Caribbean Central American Action**
1211 Connecticut Ave NW Suite 510 .... Washington DC 20036-2701
Fax: 202 822-0075

202 463-5482 **Central & Eastern Europe Trade & Technical Assistance Center**
1615 H St NW 6th Fl .... Washington DC 20062-0001
Fax: 202 463-3114

202 296-6107 **Coalition for Employment Through Exports Inc**
1801 K St NW 8th Fl .... Washington DC 20006-1301
Fax: 202 463-3114

202 463-5482 **Czechoslovak-US Economic Council** 1615 H St NW 6th Fl .. Washington DC 20062-0001
Fax: 202 463-3114

202 659-5147 **Emergency Committee for American Trade**
1211 Connecticut Ave Suite 801 .... Washington DC 20036-2701
Fax: 202 659-1347

202 566-8990 **Export-Import Bank of the US** 811 Vermont Ave NW ... Washington DC 20571-0001
Fax: 202 566-7524

212 947-5368 **Foreign Credit Interchange Bureau National Assn of Credit Management**
520 8th Ave .... New York NY 10018-0000
Fax: 212 465-8360

212 758-3007 **Fund for Multinational Management Education**
40 E 49th St Suite 501 .... New York NY 10017-1110
Fax: 212 371-7420

202 463-5482 **Hungarian-US Business Council** 1615 H St NW 6th Fl .... Washington DC 20062-0001
Fax: 202 463-3114

703 841-3800 **Inter-American Foundation** 1515 Wilson Blvd .... Rosslyn VA 22209-2402
Fax: 703 841-0973

202 477-1234 **International Bank for Reconstruction & Development**
1818 H St NW .... Washington DC 20433-0001
Fax: 202 477-6391

202 477-1234 **International Development Assn** 1818 H St NW .... Washington DC 20433-0001
Fax: 202 477-6391

203 967-6000 **International Executives Service Corps** 8 Stamford Forum ..... Stamford CT 06904-2005
Fax: 203 324-2531

202 477-1234 **International Finance Corp** 1818 H St NW .... Washington DC 20433-0001
Fax: 202 477-6391

202 624-5411 **National Assn of State Development Agencies**
444 N Capitol NW Suite 611 .... Washington DC 20001-1512
Fax: 202 624-5417

212 697-5895 **National Export Traffic League** 234 5th Ave Rm 301 ..... New York NY 10001-7607
Fax: 212 213-6737

212 925-1400 **NCITD-International Trade Facilitation Council**
350 Broadway Suite 205 .... New York NY 10013-3982
Fax: 212 941-0371

708 279-9300 **Opportunity International** 360 W Butterfield Rd Suite 225 ...... Elmhurst IL 60126-5025
Fax: 708 279-3107

202 785-6323 **Organization for Economic Cooperation & Development**
2001 L St NW Suite 700 .... Washington DC 20036-4910
Fax: 202 785-0350

202 458-3000 **Organization of American States** 1889 F St NW ..... Washington DC 20006-4413
Fax: 202 458-3967

202 457-7010 **Overseas Private Investment Corp** 1615 M St NW ..... Washington DC 20527-0001
Fax: 202 331-4234

202 458-3969 **Pan American Development Foundation**
1889 F St NW Suite 850 .... Washington DC 20006-4413
Fax: 202 458-6316

202 628-3300 **Partners of the Americas** 1424 K St NW Suite 700 .... Washington DC 20005-2410
Fax: 202 628-3306

202 463-5482 **Polish-US Economic Council** 1615 H St NW 6th Fl .... Washington DC 20062-0001
Fax: 202 463-3114

202 463-5482 **Romanian-US Economic Council** 1615 H St NW 6th Fl .... Washington DC 20062-0001
Fax: 202 463-3114

202 785-4194 **Trade Relations Council of the US**
808 17th St NW Suite 580 .... Washington DC 20006-3910
Fax: 202 785-4188

202 647-9576 **US Bureau of Consular Affairs** 2201 C St NW Rm 6811 ...... Washington DC 20520-4818
Fax: 202 647-0341

202 647-6600 **US Bureau of East Asian & Pacific Affairs**
2201 C St NW Rm 6205 .... Washington DC 20520-6310
Fax: 202 647-7350

202 647-9626 **US Bureau of European & Canadian Affairs**
2201 C St NW Rm 6228 .... Washington DC 20520-6211
Fax: 202 647-0967

202 647-9210 **US Bureau of Inter-American Affairs**
2201 C St NW Rm 6263 .... Washington DC 20520-0001
Fax: 202 647-0791

202 377-5491 **US Dept of Commerce Export Administration Office**
14th St & Constitution Ave NW Rm 3886C .... Washington DC 20230-0001
Fax: 202 377-2387

202 377-2867 **US Dept of Commerce International Trade Administration**
14th St & Constitution Ave NW Rm 3850 .... Washington DC 20230-0001
Fax: 202 377-5933

907 271-5041 *Anchorage* 222 W 7th Ave .... Anchorage AK 99513-7591
Fax: 907 271-5173

404 347-7000 *Atlanta* 1365 Peachtree St NE Suite 504 .... Atlanta GA 30309-3148
Fax: 404 347-0108

512 472-5059 *Austin* 816 Congress Ave Suite 1200 .... Austin TX 78701-2443
Fax: 512 320-9674

301 962-3560 *Baltimore* 40 S Gay St Rm 413 .... Baltimore MD 21202-4022
Fax: 301 962-7813

205 731-1331 *Birmingham* 2015 2nd Ave N Suite 302 .... Birmingham AL 35203-3723
Fax: 205 731-0076

208 334-2470 *Boise* 700 W State St 2nd Fl .... Boise ID 83720-0001
Fax: 208 334-2631

617 565-8563 *Boston* World Trade Ctr Suite 307 .... Boston MA 02210-2083
Fax: 617 565-8530

716 846-4191 *Buffalo* 111 W Huron St Rm 1312 .... Buffalo NY 14202-2386
Fax: 716 846-5290

304 347-5123 *Charleston* 500 Quarrier St .... Charleston WV 25301-2170
Fax: 304 347-5408

312 353-4450 *Chicago* 55 E Monroe St Rm 1406 .... Chicago IL 60603-5797
Fax: 312 886-8025

513 684-2944 *Cincinnati* 550 Main St Rm 9504 .... Cincinnati OH 45202-3251
Fax: 513 684-3200

216 522-4750 *Cleveland* 668 Euclid Ave Suite 600 .... Cleveland OH 44114-3058
Fax: 216 522-2235

803 765-5345 *Columbia* 1835 Assembly St Suite 172 .... Columbia SC 29201-2430
Fax: 803 253-3614

214 767-0542 *Dallas* 1100 Commerce St Rm 7-A5 .... Dallas TX 75242-1001
Fax: 214 767-8240

303 844-3246 *Denver* 1625 Broadway Suite 680 .... Denver CO 80202-4706
Fax: 303 844-5651

515 284-4222 *Des Moines* 210 Walnut St Rm 817 .... Des Moines IA 50309-2105
Fax: 515 284-4021

313 226-3650 *Detroit* 477 Michigan Ave McNamara Bldg Suite 1140 .... Detroit MI 48226-2518
Fax: 313 226-3657

616 456-2411 *Grand Rapids* 300 Monroe NW Rm 406A .... Grand Rapids MI 49503-2206
Fax: 616 456-2695

919 333-5345 *Greensboro* 324 W Market St Rm 203 .... Greensboro NC 27402-0000
Fax: 919 333-5158

203 240-3530 *Hartford* 450 Main St Rm 610-B .... Hartford CT 06103-3093
Fax: 203 240-3473

808 541-1782 *Honolulu* 300 Ala Moana Blvd Rm 4106 .... Honolulu HI 96850-0001
Fax: 808 541-3435

713 229-2578 *Houston* 515 Rusk Ave Rm 2625 .... Houston TX 77002-2652
Fax: 713 229-2203

317 226-6214 *Indianapolis* 1 N Capitol St Suite 520 .... Indianapolis IN 46204-2227
Fax: 317 226-6139

601 965-4388 *Jackson* 300 W Woodrow Wilson Dr Suite 328 .... Jackson MS 39213-7649
Fax: Unlisted

816 426-3142 *Kansas City* 601 E 12th St Rm 635 .... Kansas City MO 64106-2849
Fax: 816 426-3140

501 378-5794 *Little Rock* 320 W Capitol Ave Suite 811 .... Little Rock AR 72201-3526
Fax: 501 378-7380

213 209-7103 *Los Angeles* 11000 Wilshire Blvd Suite 9200 .... Los Angeles CA 90024-0000
Fax: 213 209-6711

502 582-5066 *Louisville* 601 W Broadway Rm 636-B .... Louisville KY 40202-2229
Fax: 502 582-6573

305 536-5267 *Miami* 51 SW 1st Ave Suite 224 .... Miami FL 33130-1617
Fax: 305 536-4765

414 297-3473 *Milwaukee* 517 E Wisconsin Ave Rm 606 .... Milwaukee WI 53202-4507
Fax: 414 297-3470

612 348-1638 *Minneapolis* 110 S 4th St Rm 108 .... Minneapolis MN 55401-2296
Fax: 612 348-1650

504 589-6546 *New Orleans* 2 Canal St Rm 432 .... New Orleans LA 70130-1267
Fax: 504 589-2337

212 264-0634 *New York* 26 Federal Plaza Rm 3718 .... New York NY 10278-0022
Fax: 212 264-1356

405 231-5302 *Oklahoma City* 6601 N Broadway Ext Suite 200 ... Oklahoma City OK 73116-8236
Fax: 405 841-5245

402 221-3665 *Omaha* 11133 'O' St .... Omaha NE 68137-2337
Fax: 402 221-3668

602 280-1371 *Phoenix* 230 N 1st Ave Rm 3412 .... Phoenix AZ 85025-0001
Fax: 602 261-4324

412 644-2850 *Pittsburgh* 1000 Liberty Ave Rm 2002 .... Pittsburgh PA 15222-4004
Fax: 412 644-4875

503 326-3001 *Portland* 121 SW Salmon St 1 World Trade Ctr Suite 242 ..... Portland OR 97204-2896
Fax: 503 326-6351

702 784-5203 *Reno* 1755 E Plumb Ln Suite 152 .... Reno NV 89502-3680
Fax: 702 784-5343

804 771-2246 *Richmond* 400 N 8th St Suite 8010 .... Richmond VA 23240-1001
Fax: 804 771-2390

815 987-8123 *Rockford* 515 N Court St .... Rockford IL 61103-6807
Fax: 815 987-8122

314 425-3302 *Saint Louis* 7911 Forsyth Blvd Suite 610 .... Saint Louis MO 63105-3880
Fax: 314 425-3381

801 524-5116 *Salt Lake City* 324 S State St Suite 105 .... Salt Lake City UT 84111-0000
Fax: 801 524-5886

415 556-5860 *San Francisco* 450 Golden Gate Ave .... San Francisco CA 94102-3453
Fax: 415 556-2121

809 766-5555 *San Juan* Federal Bldg Rm G-55 .... Hato Rey PR 00918-0000
714 836-2461 *Santa Ana* 116-A W 4th St Suite 1 .... Santa Ana CA 92701-4626
Fax: 714 836-2332

505 827-0307 *Santa Fe* 1100 St Francis Dr .... Santa Fe NM 87503-0000
Fax: 505 827-0263

206 442-5616 *Seattle* 3131 Elliott Ave Suite 290 .... Seattle WA 98121-1047
Fax: 206 442-7253

609 989-2100 *Trenton* 3131 Princeton Pike Bldg 6 Suite 100 .... Trenton NJ 08648-2207
Fax: 609 989-2395

918 581-7650 *Tulsa* 440 S Houston St Rm 505 .... Tulsa OK 74127-8913
Fax: 918 581-2844

316 269-6160 *Wichita* 727 N Waco River Park Pl Suite 580 .... Wichita KS 67203-3956
Fax: 316 262-5652

202 377-5777 **US Foreign Commercial Service**
14th St & Constitution Ave NW Rm 3804 .... Washington DC 20230-0001
Fax: 202 377-5013

202 377-1780 **US Import Administration Office**
14th St & Constitution Ave NW Rm 3099-B .... Washington DC 20230-0001
Fax: 202 377-0947

202 377-3022 **US International Economic Policy Dept**
14th St & Constitution Ave NW Rm 3864 .... Washington DC 20230-0001
Fax: 202 377-5444

202 252-1000 **US International Trade Commission** 500 E St SW .... Washington DC 20436-0001
Fax: 202 252-1798

703 875-4357 **US Trade & Development Program** 1621 N Kent St Rm 309 ..... Rosslyn VA 22209-2101
Fax: 703 875-4009

202 377-1461 **US Trade Development Office**
14th St & Constitution Ave NW Rm 3832 .... Washington DC 20230-0001
Fax: 202 377-5697

202 429-0340 **US-China Business Council** 1818 N St NW Suite 500 .... Washington DC 20036-2406
Fax: 202 775-2476

202 463-5492 **US-India Business Council** 1615 H St NW 6th Fl .... Washington DC 20062-0001
Fax: 202 463-3114

202 728-0068 **US-Japan Business Council** 1020 19th St NW Suite 130 .. Washington DC 20036-6101
Fax: 202 728-0073

815 459-5875 **US-Republic of China Economic Council** 200 S Main St .. Crystal Lake IL 60014-0000
Fax: 815 459-5011

212 644-4550 **US-USSR Trade & Economic Council** 805 3rd Ave 14th Fl ..... New York NY 10022-7513
Fax: 212 752-0889

202 857-0170 **US-Yugoslav Economic Council Inc** 818 18th St Suite 230 .. Washington DC 20006-3513
Fax: 202 452-9218

202 477-1234 **World Bank Group** 1818 H St NW .... Washington DC 20433-0001
Fax: 202 477-6391

LIBRARIES AND MUSEUMS

Libraries - Public

Major public libraries and library systems, selected on the basis of number of volumes and annual acquisition expenditures, are listed alphabetically by city within each state.

ALABAMA

205 237-8501 **Public Library of Anniston & Calhoun County** 108 E 10th St — Anniston AL 36201-5662
205 226-3600 **Birmingham Public & Jefferson County Free Library** 2100 Park Pl — Birmingham AL 35203-2744
205 825-9232 **Horseshoe Bend Regional Library** 203 West St — Dadeville AL 36853-1301
205 353-2993 **Wheeler Basin Regional Library** 504 Cherry St NE — Decatur AL 35601-1970
205 764-6563 **Muscle Shoals Regional Library System** 218 N Wood Ave — Florence AL 35630-4793
205 549-4699 **Gadsden-Etowah County Library** 254 College St — Gadsden AL 35999-0000
205 463-7125 **Cheaha Regional Library** 111 W Coleman St — Heflin AL 36264-0000
205 532-5940 **Huntsville-Madison County Public Library** 915 Monroe St — Huntsville AL 35801-5007
205 221-2568 **Elliott Carl Regional Library** 20 E 18th St — Jasper AL 35501-5402
205 434-7073 **Mobile Public Library** 701 Government St — Mobile AL 36602-1499
205 284-7920 **Montgomery City-County Public Library** 135 Norman Dale Arcade — Montgomery AL 36111-0000
205 493-9526 **Cross Trails Regional Library Service** PO Box 717 — Opp AL 36467-0717
205 774-3112 **Choctawhatchee Regional Library System** 320 James St — Ozark AL 36360-2015
205 345-5820 **Tuscaloosa Public Library** 1801 River Rd — Tuscaloosa AL 35401-1099

ALASKA

907 261-2975 **Anchorage Municipal Libraries** 3600 Denali St — Anchorage AK 99503-6055
907 452-5177 **Fairbanks North Star Borough Public Library & Regional Center** 1215 Cowles St — Fairbanks AK 99701-4313

ARIZONA

602 432-2950 **Cochise County Library System** Old Bisbee High School — Bisbee AZ 85603-0000
602 634-7559 **Cottonwood Public Library** 401 E Mingus Ave — Cottonwood AZ 86326-0000
602 779-7670 **Flagstaff City-Coconino County Public Library System** 300 W Aspen Ave — Flagstaff AZ 86001-5304
602 868-5801 **Pinal County Free Library** 574 S Central — Florence AZ 85232-0000
602 435-4953 **Glendale Public Library** 5959 W Brown St — Glendale AZ 85302-1248
602 644-2702 **Mesa Public Library** 64 E 1st St — Mesa AZ 85201-6768
602 645-2231 **Page Public Library** 697 Vista Ave — Page AZ 86040-0000
602 269-2535 **Maricopa County Library District** 3375 W Durango — Phoenix AZ 85009-6298
602 262-6451 **Phoenix Public Library** 12 E McDowell Rd — Phoenix AZ 85004-1684
602 994-2476 **Scottsdale Public Library System** 3839 Civic Center Blvd — Scottsdale AZ 85251-4467
602 791-4391 **Tucson Public Library** 101 N Stone Ave — Tucson AZ 85701-0000

ARKANSAS

501 229-4418 **Arkansas River Valley Regional Library** 501 N Front St — Dardanelle AR 72834-0000
501 442-6253 **Ozarks Regional Library** 217 E Dickson St — Fayetteville AR 72701-4296
501 783-0229 **Fort Smith Public Library** 61 S 8th St — Fort Smith AR 72901-2415
501 741-3665 **North Arkansas Regional Library** 221 W Stephenson Ave — Harrison AR 72601-4225
501 777-2957 **Southwest Arkansas Regional Library** 5th & Elm Sts — Hope AR 71801-0000
501 623-3943 **Tri-Lakes Regional Library** 125 B Albert Pike — Hot Springs AR 71913-0000
501 935-5133 **Crowley Ridge Regional Library** 315 W Oak St — Jonesboro AR 72401-3594
501 370-5954 **Central Arkansas Library System** 700 Louisiana St — Little Rock AR 72201-4698

CALIFORNIA

714 999-1880 **Anaheim Public Library** 500 W Broadway — Anaheim CA 92805-3699
805 861-2130 **Kern County Library** 701 Truxten Ave — Bakersfield CA 93301-4800
415 349-5538 **Peninsula Library System** 25 Tower Rd — Belmont CA 94002-4201
415 644-6095 **Berkeley Public Library** 2090 Kittredge St — Berkeley CA 94704-1491
619 691-5168 **Chula Vista Public Library** 365 F St — Chula Vista CA 92010-2697
213 940-8462 **Los Angeles County Public Library Headquarters** 7400 E Imperial Hwy — Downey CA 90242-3375
707 445-7284 **Humboldt County Library** 636 F St — Eureka CA 95501-1012
707 421-6510 **Solano County Library** 1150 Kentucky St — Fairfield CA 94533-5761
415 745-1500 **Alameda County Libraries** 2450 Stevenson Blvd — Fremont CA 94538-0000
209 488-3191 **Fresno County Free Library** 2420 Mariposa St — Fresno CA 93721-2204
714 738-6380 **Fullerton Public Library** 353 W Commonwealth Ave — Fullerton CA 92632-1796
818 956-2020 **Glendale Public Library** 222 E Harvard St — Glendale CA 91205-1075
415 784-8688 **Hayward Public Library** 835 C St — Hayward CA 94541-5120
714 842-4481 **Huntington Beach Library** 7111 Talbert Ave — Huntington Beach CA 92648-1296
213 412-5397 **City of Inglewood Public Library** 101 W Manchester Blvd — Inglewood CA 90301-1753
213 437-2949 **Long Beach Public Library & Information Center** 101 Pacific Ave — Long Beach CA 90802-0000
213 660-3880 **Braille Institute of America Library** 4205 Melrose Ave — Los Angeles CA 90029-3508
213 612-3200 **Los Angeles Public Library System** 630 W 5th St — Los Angeles CA 90071-2097
209 385-7484 **Merced County Library** 2100 'O' St — Merced CA 95340-3637
707 253-4241 **Napa City-County Library** 1150 Division St — Napa CA 94559-3334
415 273-3281 **Oakland Public Library** 125 14th St — Oakland CA 94612-4397
714 988-8481 **Ontario City Library** 215 E 'C' St — Ontario CA 91764-4198
714 834-6841 **Orange County Public Library** 431 City Dr S — Orange CA 92668-3386
714 532-0391 **Orange Public Library** 101 N Center St — Orange CA 92666-1501
916 538-7642 **Butte County Library** 1820 Mitchell Ave — Oroville CA 95966-5387
805 984-4636 **Oxnard Public Library** 214 S 'C' St — Oxnard CA 93030-5791
818 405-4041 **Pasadena Public Library** 285 E Walnut St — Pasadena CA 91101-1556
415 646-6423 **Contra Costa County Library** 1750 Oak Park Blvd — Pleasant Hill CA 94523-4412
714 620-2033 **Pomona Public Library** 625 S Garey Ave — Pomona CA 91766-3322
714 782-5201 **Riverside City & County Public Library** 3581 7th St — Riverside CA 92502-0468
916 440-5926 **Sacramento Public Library** 1010 8th St — Sacramento CA 95814-3576
408 424-3244 **Monterey County Free Library** 26 Central Ave — Salinas CA 93901-2628
714 381-8201 **San Bernardino Public Library** 555 W 6th St — San Bernardino CA 92410-3001
619 694-2414 **San Diego County Library System** 5555 Overland Ave Bldg 15 — San Diego CA 92123-0000
619 236-5800 **San Diego Public Library** 820 E St — San Diego CA 92101-6479
415 558-4235 **San Francisco Public Library** 200 Larkin St — San Francisco CA 94102-0000
408 277-4822 **Martin Luther King Jr Library** 180 W San Carlos St — San Jose CA 95113-2096
408 293-2326 **Santa Clara County Free Library** 1095 N 7th St — San Jose CA 95112-4446
805 549-5785 **San Luis Obispo City-County Library** 995 Palm St — San Luis Obispo CA 93401-3218
415 573-2056 **San Mateo County Library** 25 Tower Rd — San Mateo CA 94402-0000
415 499-6051 **Civic Center Library** Administration Bldg — San Rafael CA 94903-9992
714 647-5250 **Santa Ana Public Library** 26 Civic Center Plaza — Santa Ana CA 92701-4078
805 962-7653 **Santa Barbara Public Library** 40 E Anapamu St — Santa Barbara CA 93101-2705
408 429-3533 **Santa Cruz City-County Public Library System** 224 Church St — Santa Cruz CA 95060-3873
707 545-0831 **Sonoma County Library** 3rd & E Sts — Santa Rosa CA 95404-0000
209 944-8415 **Stockton-San Joaquin County Public Library** 605 N El Dorado St — Stockton CA 95202-1907
408 730-7315 **Sunnyvale Public Library** 665 W Olive Ave — Sunnyvale CA 94086-7622
213 618-5950 **Torrance Public Library** 3301 Torrance Blvd — Torrance CA 90503-5014
805 648-2715 **EP Foster Library** 651 E Main St — Ventura CA 93001-2814
209 733-6954 **Tulare County Library System** 200 W Oak St — Visalia CA 93291-4931

COLORADO

303 340-2240 **Aurora Public Library** 14949 E Alameda Dr — Aurora CO 80012-1500
303 441-3100 **Boulder Public Library** 1000 Canyon Blvd — Boulder CO 80302-5120
719 473-2080 **Pikes Peak Library District** 20 N Cascade Ave — Colorado Springs CO 80903-1694
303 571-2000 **Denver Public Library** 1357 Broadway — Denver CO 80203-2165
303 356-4357 **High Plains Regional Library Service System** 800 8th Ave Suite 341 — Greeley CO 80631-1100
303 232-7114 **Jefferson County Public Library** 10200 W 20th Ave — Lakewood CO 80215-1402
303 798-2444 **Arapahoe Library District** 2305 E Arapahoe Rd — Littleton CO 80122-1522
719 543-9600 **Pueblo Library District** 100 E Abriendo Ave — Pueblo CO 81004-4290
303 288-2001 **Adams County Public Library** 8992 N Washington St — Thornton CO 80229-4537

CONNECTICUT

203 576-7777 **Bridgeport Public Library** 925 Broad St — Bridgeport CT 06604-4871
203 293-6000 **Hartford Public Library** 500 Main St — Hartford CT 06103-3075
203 964-1000 **Ferguson Library** 1 Public Library Plaza — Stamford CT 06904-0000
203 574-8222 **Silas Bronson Library** 267 Grand St — Waterbury CT 06702-1981

DELAWARE

302 366-7950 **New Castle Dept of Libraries** 187A Old Churchmans Rd — New Castle DE 19720-3115
302 571-7400 **Wilmington Institute Library** 10th & Market Sts — Wilmington DE 19801-1282

DISTRICT OF COLUMBIA

202 727-1101 **District of Columbia Public Library** 901 G St NW — Washington DC 20001-4531
202 707-5000 **Library of Congress** 101 Independence Ave SE — Washington DC 20540-0001

FLORIDA

813 748-5555 **Manatee County Public Library System** 1301 Barcarrota Blvd W — Bradenton FL 34205-7599
904 252-8374 **Volusia County Public Library System** City Island — Daytona Beach FL 32114-3382
305 357-7444 **Broward County Library System** 100 S Andrews Ave — Fort Lauderdale FL 33301-1830
813 334-3221 **Lee County Library System** 2050 Lee St — Fort Myers FL 33901-3989
407 468-1615 **Saint Lucie County Library System** 124 N Indian River Dr — Fort Pierce FL 34950-4489
904 371-2665 **Alachua Library District** 222 E University Ave — Gainesville FL 32601-5456
305 821-2700 **Kennedy John F Library** 190 W 49th St — Hialeah FL 33012-3712
904 630-1994 **Jacksonville Public Library System** 122 N Ocean St — Jacksonville FL 32202-3314
305 375-2665 **Miami-Dade Public Library System** 101 W Flagler St — Miami FL 33130-1504
813 262-4130 **Collier County Public Library** 650 Central Ave — Naples FL 33940-6087
904 629-8551 **Central Florida Regional Library** 15 SE Osceola Ave — Ocala FL 32671-2150
407 425-4694 **Orange County Library Systems** 101 E Central Blvd — Orlando FL 32801-2407
904 785-3457 **Northwest Regional Library System** 25 W Government St — Panama City FL 32401-2719
904 435-1760 **West Florida Regional Library** 200 W Gregory — Pensacola FL 32501-4822
813 893-7724 **Saint Petersburg Public Library** 3745 9th Ave N — Saint Petersburg FL 33713-6096
813 951-5501 **Selby Public Library** 1001 Blvd of the Arts — Sarasota FL 34236-4899
904 487-2665 **Leon County Public Library System** 1940 N Monroe St Suite 26 — Tallahassee FL 32303-4797
813 223-8945 **Tampa-Hillsborough County Public Library System** 900 N Ashley St — Tampa FL 33602-3704
407 686-0895 **Palm Beach County Public Library System** 3650 Summit Blvd — West Palm Beach FL 33406-4114

GEORGIA

912 431-2900 **Dougherty County Public Library** 300 Pine Ave — Albany GA 31701-2533
404 354-2620 **Athens Regional Library** 120 W Dougherty St — Athens GA 30601-2653
404 730-1700 **Atlanta-Fulton Public Library** 1 Margaret Mitchell Sq NW — Atlanta GA 30303-1089
404 821-2600 **East Central Georgia Regional Library** 902 Greene St — Augusta GA 30901-2232
912 267-1212 **Brunswick-Glynn County Regional Library** 208 Gloucester St — Brunswick GA 31523-0901
404 836-6711 **West Georgia Regional Library** 710 Rome St — Carrollton GA 30117-3046
404 327-0211 **Chattahoochee Valley Regional Library** 1120 Bradley Dr — Columbus GA 31906-0000
404 278-4507 **Dalton Regional Library** 310 Cappes St — Dalton GA 30720-4123
404 294-6641 **De Kalb County Public Library** 3560 Kensington Rd — Decatur GA 30032-1328
404 227-2756 **Flint River Regional Library** 800 Memorial Dr — Griffin GA 30223-4443
912 744-0800 **Middle Georgia Regional Library** 1180 Washington Ave — Macon GA 31201-1762
404 528-2320 **Cobb County Public Library System** 266 Roswell St — Marietta GA 30060-1975
404 236-4600 **Hightower Sara Regional Library** 205 Riverside Pkwy — Rome GA 30161-2913
912 234-5127 **Chatham-Effingham-Liberty Regional Library** 2002 Bull St — Savannah GA 31499-0001

IDAHO

208 384-4466 **Boise Public Library & Information Center** 715 S Capitol Blvd — Boise ID 83702-7195

ILLINOIS

708 759-2102 **Fountaindale Public Library** 300 W Briarcliffe Rd — Bolingbrook IL 60440-0000
217 352-0047 **Lincoln Trail Libraries System** 1704 W Interstate Dr — Champaign IL 61821-1088
312 269-2800 **Chicago Public Library** 400 N Franklin St — Chicago IL 60610-4481
309 343-2380 **Western Illinois Library System** 1518 S Henderson St — Galesburg IL 61401-5708
708 232-8457 **DuPage Library System** PO Box 268 — Geneva IL 60134-0268
309 452-4485 **Corn Belt Library System** 1809 Hovey Ave — Normal IL 61761-4395
309 672-8835 **Peoria Public Library** 107 NE Monroe St — Peoria IL 61602-1070
815 229-0330 **Northern Illinois Library System** 4034 E State St — Rockford IL 61108-2006
815 965-6731 **Rockford Public Library** 215 N Wyman St — Rockford IL 61101-1061
708 885-3373 **Schaumburg Township District Library** 32 W Library Ln — Schaumburg IL 60194-3497
217 753-4900 **Lincoln Library** 326 S 7th St — Springfield IL 62701-1691

INDIANA

812 339-2271 **Monroe County Public Library** 303 E Kirkwood Ave — Bloomington IN 47408-3592
812 428-8200 **Evansville-Vanderburgh County Public Library** 22 SE 5th St — Evansville IN 47708-1604
812 425-4309 **Willard Library of Evansville** 21 1st Ave — Evansville IN 47710-1294
219 424-7241 **Allen County Public Library** 900 Webster St — Fort Wayne IN 46802-3699
219 886-2484 **Gary Public Library** 220 W 5th Ave — Gary IN 46402-1270
317 269-1700 **Indianapolis-Marion County Public Library** PO Box 211 — Indianapolis IN 46206-0211
317 429-0100 **Tippecanoe County Public Library** 627 South St — Lafayette IN 47901-1470
219 769-3541 **Lake County Public Library** 1919 W 81st Ave — Merrillville IN 46410-5382
219 282-4625 **Saint Joseph County Public Library** 122 W Wayne St — South Bend IN 46601-2125
812 232-1113 **Vigo County Public Library** 1 Library Sq — Terre Haute IN 47807-3609
219 462-0524 **Porter County Public Library System** 103 Jefferson St — Valparaiso IN 46383-4820

IOWA

319 398-5123 **Cedar Rapids Public Library** 500 1st St SE — Cedar Rapids IA 52401-2002
319 365-0521 **East Central Regional Library** 625 Guarantee Bldg — Cedar Rapids IA 52401-0000
319 326-7832 **Davenport Public Library** 321 Main St — Davenport IA 52801-1490
515 277-0220 **Central Iowa Regional Library System** 4715 Grand Ave — Des Moines IA 50312-2001
515 283-4152 **Public Library of Des Moines** 100 Locust St — Des Moines IA 50308-0000
712 252-5669 **Northwest Regional Library System** 529 Pierce St — Sioux City IA 51101-0000
712 252-5669 **Sioux City Public Library** 529 Pierce St — Sioux City IA 51101-0000

Libraries

KANSAS

913 621-3073	**Kansas City Kansas Public Library System** 625 Minnesota Ave	Kansas City	KS	66101-2899
913 831-1550	**Johnson County Library** 8700 W 63rd St	Shawnee Mission	KS	66202-2892
913 233-2040	**Topeka Public Library** 1515 SW 10th St	Topeka	KS	66604-1374
316 262-0611	**Wichita Public Library** 223 S Main St	Wichita	KS	67202-3795

KENTUCKY

606 491-7610	**Kenton County Public Library** 502 Scott St	Covington	KY	41011-1590
606 231-5504	**Lexington Public Library** 140 E Main St	Lexington	KY	40507-1376
502 561-8600	**Louisville Free Public Library** 301 York St	Louisville	KY	40203-2257

LOUISIANA

318 445-2411	**Rapides Parish Library** 411 Washington St	Alexandria	LA	71301-8338
504 389-3360	**East Baton Rouge Parish Library** 7711 Goodwood Blvd	Baton Rouge	LA	70806-7625
504 892-0812	**Saint Tammany Parish Library** 310 W 21st Ave	Covington	LA	70433-3100
318 261-5775	**Lafayette Parish Public Library** 301 W Congress St	Lafayette	LA	70502-0000
318 437-3485	**Calcasieu Parish Public Library System** 411 Pujo St	Lake Charles	LA	70601-4254
504 834-5850	**Jefferson Parish Library Dept** 3420 N Causeway Blvd	Metairie	LA	70002-3509
318 387-1950	**Ouachita Parish Public Library** 1800 Stubbs Ave	Monroe	LA	71201-5787
504 596-2550	**New Orleans Public Library** 219 Loyola Ave	New Orleans	LA	70140-1016
318 226-5897	**Shreve Memorial Library** 424 Texas Ave	Shreveport	LA	71120-0000

MARYLAND

301 222-7371	**Public Library of Annapolis & Ann Arundel County** 5 Harry S Truman Pkwy	Annapolis	MD	21401-0000
301 396-5430	**Enoch Pratt Free Library** 400 Cathedral St	Baltimore	MD	21201-4484
301 838-7484	**Harford County Library** 100 Pennslyvania Ave	Bel Air	MD	21014-3799
301 997-8000	**Howard County Central Library** 10375 Little Patuxent Pkwy	Columbia	MD	21044-3499
301 694-1613	**Frederick County Public Library** 110 E Patrick St	Frederick	MD	21701-5630
301 739-3250	**Washington County Free Library** 100 S Potomac St	Hagerstown	MD	21740-5556
301 699-3500	**Prince George's County Memorial Library** 6532 Adelphi Rd	Hyattsville	MD	20782-2008
301 217-3850	**Montgomery County Dept of Public Libraries** 99 Maryland Ave	Rockville	MD	20850-2372
301 887-6100	**Baltimore County Public Library** 320 York Rd	Towson	MD	21204-5179

MASSACHUSETTS

617 536-5400	**Boston Public Library** 666 Boylston St	Boston	MA	02117-0000
617 498-9080	**Cambridge Public Library** 449 Broadway	Cambridge	MA	02138-4191
508 991-6275	**New Bedford Free Public Library** 613 Pleasant St	New Bedford	MA	02740-6203
413 739-3871	**Springfield City Library** 220 State St	Springfield	MA	01103-1772
508 799-1654	**Central Massachusetts Regional Library System** Salem Sq	Worcester	MA	01608-2015

MICHIGAN

313 994-2333	**Ann Arbor Public Library** 343 S 5th Ave	Ann Arbor	MI	48104-2293
517 894-2837	**Bay County Library System** 307 Lafayette Ave	Bay City	MI	48708-7796
313 943-2330	**Dearborn Department of Libraries** 16301 Michigan Ave	Dearborn	MI	48126-2792
313 833-1000	**Detroit Public Library** 5201 Woodward Ave	Detroit	MI	48202-4093
313 232-7111	**Flint Public Library** 1026 E Kearsley St	Flint	MI	48502-0000
313 732-0110	**Genesee District Library** G-4195 W Pasadena Ave	Flint	MI	48504-0000
616 456-3600	**Grand Rapids Public Library** 60 Library Plaza NE	Grand Rapids	MI	49503-3093
616 774-3250	**Kent County Library System** 775 Ball Ave NE	Grand Rapids	MI	49503-1397
517 788-4087	**Jackson District Library** 244 W Michigan Ave	Jackson	MI	49201-2275
616 342-9837	**Kalamazoo Public Library** 315 S Rose St	Kalamazoo	MI	49007-5270
517 374-4600	**Lansing Public Library** 401 S Capitol Ave	Lansing	MI	48933-2003
313 421-6600	**Lavonia Public Library** 32901 Plymouth Rd	Livonia	MI	48150-1717
517 676-8440	**Ingham County Library** 407 N Cedar St	Mason	MI	48854-1012
313 241-5277	**Monroe County Library System** 3700 S Custer Rd	Monroe	MI	48161-9732
313 286-6660	**Macomb County Library** 16480 Hall Rd	Mount Clemens	MI	48044-3198
616 724-6248	**Muskegon County Library System** 635 Ottawa St	Muskegon	MI	49442-1094
313 987-7323	**Saint Clair County Library System** 210 McMorran Blvd	Port Huron	MI	48060-4098
517 755-0904	**Public Libraries of Saginaw** 505 Janes St	Saginaw	MI	48605-0000
313 771-9021	**Saint Clair Shores Public Library** 22500 11-Mile Rd	Saint Clair Shores	MI	48081-1307
313 264-8720	**Warren Public Libraries** 5951 Beebe St	Warren	MI	48092-1604
313 326-8910	**Wayne Oakland Library Federation** 33030 Van Born Rd	Wayne	MI	48184-2496

MINNESOTA

612 780-1463	**Anoka County Library** 707 Hwy 10 NE	Blaine	MN	55434-2398
612 689-1901	**East Central Regional Library** 244 S Birch St	Cambridge	MN	55008-1588
218 723-3800	**Duluth Public Library** 520 W Superior St	Duluth	MN	55802-1578
612 452-9600	**Dakota County Library System** 1340 Wescott Rd	Eagan	MN	55123-1099
612 372-6500	**Minneapolis Public Library** 300 Nicollet Mall	Minneapolis	MN	55401-1992
612 541-8530	**Hennepin County Library** 12601 Ridgedale Dr	Minnetonka	MN	55343-5638
218 233-3757	**Lake Agassiz Regional Library** 118 S 5th St	Moorhead	MN	56560-2713
612 636-6747	**Ramsey County Public Library** 1910 W County Rd B	Roseville	MN	55113-5492
612 251-7282	**Great River Regional Library** 405 St Germain	Saint Cloud	MN	56301-3667
612 292-6311	**Saint Paul Public Library** 90 W 4th St	Saint Paul	MN	55102-1668
612 235-3162	**Pioneerland Library System** 410 W 5th St	Willmar	MN	56201-0000

MISSISSIPPI

601 868-1383	**Harrison County Library System** 14th St & 21st Ave	Gulfport	MS	39501-2092
601 429-4439	**First Regional Library** 370 W Commerce St	Hernando	MS	38632-2130
601 968-5811	**Jackson/Hinds Library System** 300 N State St	Jackson	MS	39201-1799
601 769-3060	**Jackson-George Regional Library System** 3214 Pascagoula St	Pascagoula	MS	39567-4217

MISSOURI

314 443-3161	**Daniel Boone Regional Library** 100 W Broadway St	Columbia	MO	65203-3302
816 836-5200	**Mid-Continent Public Library** 15616 E 24 Hwy	Independence	MO	64050-0000
816 221-2685	**Kansas City Public Library** 311 E 12th St	Kansas City	MO	64106-2412
314 994-3300	**Saint Louis County Library** 1640 S Lindbergh Blvd	Saint Louis	MO	63131-3598
314 241-2288	**Saint Louis Public Library** 1301 Olive St	Saint Louis	MO	63103-2389
314 441-2300	**Saint Charles City County Library District** 425 Spencer Rd	Saint Peters	MO	63376-2420
417 869-4621	**Springfield-Greene County Library** 397 E Central	Springfield	MO	65802-3834

MONTANA

406 657-8257	**Parmly Billings Library** 510 N Broadway	Billings	MT	59101-1126
406 453-0349	**Great Falls Public Library** 301 2nd Ave N	Great Falls	MT	59401-2593
406 721-2665	**Missoula Public Library** 301 E Main	Missoula	MT	59802-4799

NEBRASKA

402 471-8500	**Lincoln City Libraries** 136 S 14th St	Lincoln	NE	68508-1899
402 444-4800	**Omaha Public Library** 215 S 15th St	Omaha	NE	68102-1601

NEVADA

702 733-7810	**Las Vegas-Clark County Library District** 1401 E Flamingo Rd	Las Vegas	NV	89119-5256
702 785-4190	**Washoe County Library** 301 S Center St	Reno	NV	89501-2102

NEW HAMPSHIRE

603 624-6550	**Manchester City Library** 405 Pine St	Manchester	NH	03104-6199
603 883-4141	**Nashua Public Library** 2 Court St	Nashua	NH	03060-3475

NEW JERSEY

609 453-2210	**Cumberland County Library** 800 E Commerce St	Bridgeton	NJ	08302-2295
908 526-4016	**Somerset County Library** PO Box 6700	Bridgewater	NJ	08807-0700
908 354-6060	**Elizabeth Public Library** 11 S Broad St	Elizabeth	NJ	07202-3486
201 547-4500	**Jersey City Public Library** 472 Jersey Ave	Jersey City	NJ	07302-3499
609 989-6916	**Mercer County Library** 2751 Brunswick Pike	Lawrenceville	NJ	08648-4132
609 646-8699	**Atlantic County Library-Mays Landing** 2 S Farragut Ave	Mays Landing	NJ	08330-1750
609 267-9660	**Burlington County Library** W Woodlane Rd	Mount Holly	NJ	08060-0000
201 733-7800	**Newark Public Library** 5 Washington St	Newark	NJ	07101-0000
201 881-1060	**Paterson Free Public Library** 250 Broadway	Paterson	NJ	07501-2093
609 589-2000	**Gloucester County Library** 200 Holly Dell Dr	Sewell	NJ	08080-9191
609 392-7188	**Free Public Library of the City of Trenton** 120 Academy St	Trenton	NJ	08608-1302
609 772-1636	**Camden County Free Library** Laurel Rd Echelon Urban Ctr	Voorhees	NJ	08043-2378
201 285-6930	**Morris County Free Library** 30 E Hanover Ave	Whippany	NJ	07981-1853
908 634-4450	**Free Public Library of Woodbridge** George Frederick Plaza	Woodbridge	NJ	07095-0000

NEW MEXICO

505 768-5140	**Albuquerque Public Library** 501 Copper Ave NW	Albuquerque	NM	87102-3129
505 526-1047	**Branigan Thomas Memorial Library** 200 E Picacho Ave	Las Cruces	NM	88001-3499

NEW YORK

518 449-3380	**Albany Public Library** 161 Washington Ave	Albany	NY	12210-2398
516 286-1600	**Suffolk Co-op Library System** 627 N Sunrise Service Rd	Bellport	NY	11713-0000
607 723-6457	**Broome County Public Library** 78 Exchange St	Binghamton	NY	13901-3489
607 723-8236	**Four County Library System** 304 Clubhouse Rd	Binghamton	NY	13903-1296
516 273-7883	**Brentwood Public Library** 2nd Ave & 4th St	Brentwood	NY	11717-4676
718 780-7700	**Brooklyn Public Library** Grand Army Plaza	Brooklyn	NY	11238-5698
716 858-8900	**Buffalo & Erie County Public Library** Lafayette Sq	Buffalo	NY	14203-0000
716 892-8089	**Cheektowaga Public Library** 2580 Harlem Rd	Cheektowaga	NY	14225-4026
607 733-9173	**Chemung-Southern Tier Library System/Steele Memorial Library** 1 Library Plaza	Elmira	NY	14901-2739
607 273-4074	**Finger Lakes Library System** 314 N Cayuga St	Ithaca	NY	14850-4279
718 990-0700	**Queensborough Public Library** 89-11 Merrick Blvd	Jamaica	NY	11432-5242
716 484-7135	**Chautauqua-Cattaraugus Library System** PO Box 730	Jamestown	NY	14702-0730
914 343-1131	**Ramapo Catskill Library System** 619 North St	Middletown	NY	10940-4395
212 930-0800	**New York Public Library** 5th Ave & 42nd St	New York	NY	10018-0000
518 563-5190	**Clinton-Essex-Franklin Library System** 17 Oak St	Plattsburgh	NY	12901-2810
914 471-6060	**Mid-Hudson Library System** 103 Market St	Poughkeepsie	NY	12601-4098
716 428-7300	**Rochester Public Library** 115 South Ave	Rochester	NY	14604-1896
518 382-3500	**Schenectady County Public Library System** 99 Clinton St	Schenectady	NY	12305-2083
516 265-2072	**Smithtown Library** 1 N Country Rd	Smithtown	NY	11787-2102
315 448-4636	**Onondaga County Public Library System** 447 S Salina St	Syracuse	NY	13202-2494
516 292-8920	**Nassau Library System** 900 Jerusalem Ave	Uniondale	NY	11553-3097
315 735-8328	**Mid-York Library System** 1600 Lincoln Ave	Utica	NY	13502-5395
315 782-5540	**North Country Library System** Outer W Main St	Watertown	NY	13601-1100
914 337-1500	**Yonkers Public Library** 7 Main St	Yonkers	NY	10701-2784

NORTH CAROLINA

704 255-5203	**Asheville-Buncombe Library System** 67 Haywood St	Asheville	NC	28801-2834
919 227-2096	**Central North Carolina Regional Library** 342 S Spring St	Burlington	NC	27215-5863
704 336-2725	**Public Library of Charlotte & Mecklenburg County** 310 N Tryon St	Charlotte	NC	28202-2176
919 560-0220	**Durham County Library** 300 N Roxboro St	Durham	NC	27701-3414
919 835-4894	**Northwestern Regional Library** 111 N Front St	Elkin	NC	28621-3342
919 483-1580	**Cumberland County Public Library** 300 Maiden Ln	Fayetteville	NC	28301-5000
704 868-2164	**Gaston County Public Library** 1555 E Garrison Blvd	Gastonia	NC	28054-4556
919 373-2474	**Greensboro Public Library** 201 N Greene St	Greensboro	NC	27401-2410
919 455-7350	**Onslow County Public Library** 58 Doris Ave E	Jacksonville	NC	28540-5197
919 738-4859	**Robeson County Public Library** 101 N Chestnut St	Lumberton	NC	28358-5639
919 638-2127	**Craven-Pamlico-Carteret Regional Library** 400 Johnson St	New Bern	NC	28560-4048
704 464-2421	**Catawba County Library** 115 W 'C' St	Newton	NC	28658-3397
919 838-2818	**Appalachian Regional Library** 913 C St	North Wilkesboro	NC	28659-4119
919 250-1200	**Wake County Dept of the Public Libraries** 4020 Carya Dr	Raleigh	NC	27610-2913
919 341-4390	**New Hanover County Public Library** 201 Chestnut St	Wilmington	NC	28401-3942
919 727-2556	**Forsyth County Public Library** 660 W 5th St	Winston-Salem	NC	27101-2705
919 694-6241	**Gunn Memorial Public Library** 317 E Main St	Yanceyville	NC	27379-0000

NORTH DAKOTA

701 241-1490	**Fargo Public Library** 102 N 3rd St	Fargo	ND	58102-4899

OHIO

216 762-7621	**Akron-Summit County Public Library** 55 S Main St	Akron	OH	44326-0001
513 732-2736	**Clermont County Public Library** 326 Broadway St	Batavia	OH	45103-2806
216 452-0665	**Stark County District Library** 715 Market Ave N	Canton	OH	44702-1080
513 369-6000	**Public Library of Cincinnati & Hamilton County** 800 Vine St	Cincinnati	OH	45202-2009
216 623-2800	**Cleveland Public Library** 325 Superior Ave	Cleveland	OH	44114-1271
216 398-1800	**Cuyahoga County Public Library** 4510 Memphis Ave	Cleveland	OH	44144-1999
216 932-3600	**Cleveland Heights-University Heights Public Library** 2345 Lee Rd	Cleveland Heights	OH	44118-3434
614 231-2793	**Bexley Public Library** 2411 E Main St	Columbus	OH	43209-2498
614 645-2800	**Columbus Metropolitan Library** 28 S Hamilton Rd	Columbus	OH	43213-2013
513 227-9500	**Dayton & Montgomery County Public Library** 215 E 3rd St	Dayton	OH	45402-2135
216 527-4378	**Portage County District Library** 10482 South St	Garrettsville	OH	44231-1116
513 894-7156	**Lane Public Library** 300 N 3rd & Buckeye St	Hamilton	OH	45011-1692
614 653-2745	**Fairfield County District Library** 219 N Broad St	Lancaster	OH	43130-3098
419 228-5113	**Lima Public Library** 650 W Market St	Lima	OH	45801-4678
216 244-1192	**Lorain Public Library** 351 6th St	Lorain	OH	44052-1770
419 524-1041	**Mansfield-Richland County Public Library** 43 W 3rd	Mansfield	OH	44902-1295
614 373-1057	**Washington County Public Library** 615 5th St	Marietta	OH	45750-1973
216 725-0588	**Medina County District Library** 210 S Broadway	Medina	OH	44256-2602
513 424-1251	**Middletown Public Library** 125 S Broad St	Middletown	OH	45044-4004
614 345-8972	**Newark Public Library** 88 W Church St	Newark	OH	43055-5087
614 354-5688	**Portsmouth Public Library** 1220 Gallia St	Portsmouth	OH	45662-4185
513 328-6903	**Warder Public Library** 201 S Fountain Ave	Springfield	OH	45502-1215
614 282-9782	**Public Library of Steubenville & Jefferson County** 407 S 4th St	Steubenville	OH	43952-2996
419 259-5200	**Toledo-Lucas County Public Library** 325 N Michigan St	Toledo	OH	43624-1628
614 486-9621	**Upper Arlington Public Library** 2800 Tremont Rd	Upper Arlington	OH	43221-3199

216 399-8807 **Warren-Trumbull County Public Library** 444 Mahoning Ave NW — Warren OH 44483-4606
513 376-2995 **Greene County District Library** 76 E Market St — Xenia OH 45385-3100
216 744-8636 **Public Library of Youngstown & Mahoning County** 305 Wick Ave — Youngstown OH 44503-1079
614 453-0391 **Muskingum County Library System** 220 N 5th St — Zanesville OH 43701-3508

OKLAHOMA

405 581-3450 **Lawton Public Library** 110 SW 4th St — Lawton OK 73501-4034
918 426-0456 **Southeastern Public Library System** 401 N 2nd St — McAlester OK 74501-4639
918 683-2846 **Eastern Oklahoma District Library System** 801 W Okmulgee Ave — Muskogee OK 74401-6840
405 321-1481 **Pioneer Library System** 225 N Webster — Norman OK 73069-7133
405 235-0571 **Metropolitan Library System of Oklahoma County** 131 Dean A McGee Ave — Oklahoma City OK 73102-6499
918 596-7977 **Tulsa City-County Library** 400 Civic Ctr — Tulsa OK 74103-3830

OREGON

503 687-5450 **Eugene Public Library** 100 W 13th Ave — Eugene OR 97401-3484
503 776-7281 **Jackson County Library System** 413 W Main St — Medford OR 97501-2730
503 655-8543 **Clackamas County Library** 16201 SE McLoughlin Blvd — Oak Grove OR 97267-4653
503 223-7201 **Multnomah County Library** 801 SW 10th Ave — Portland OR 97205-2597

PENNSYLVANIA

215 820-2400 **Allentown Public Library** 1210 Hamilton St — Allentown PA 18102-4371
814 946-0417 **Altoona Area Public Library** 1600 5th Ave — Altoona PA 16602-3621
215 867-3761 **Bethlehem Area Public Library** 11 W Church St — Bethlehem PA 18018-5804
814 226-6340 **Clarion District Library Assn** 663 Main St — Clarion PA 16214-1292
215 348-0332 **Bucks County Free Library** 150 S Pine St — Doylestown PA 18901-4626
814 451-6900 **Erie County Library System** 3 S Perry Sq — Erie PA 16501-1102
215 363-0884 **Chester County Library** 400 Exton Square Pkwy — Exton PA 19341-2496
717 234-4961 **Dauphin County Library System** 101 Walnut St — Harrisburg PA 17101-1696
814 536-5131 **Cambria County Library System** 248 Main St — Johnstown PA 15901-1677
717 394-2651 **Lancaster County Library** 125 N Duke St — Lancaster PA 17602-2883
717 273-7624 **Lebanon Community Library** 125 N 7th St — Lebanon PA 17042-5000
412 684-4750 **Monessen Public Library & District Center** 326 Donner Ave — Monessen PA 15062-1182
215 278-5100 **Montgomery County-Norristown Public Library** Swede & Elm Sts — Norristown PA 19401-0000
215 686-5322 **Free Library of Philadelphia** Logan Sq — Philadelphia PA 19103-0000
412 622-3100 **Carnegie Library of Pittsburgh** 4400 Forbes Ave — Pittsburgh PA 15213-4080
215 374-4540 **Reading Public Library** 5th & Franklin Sts — Reading PA 19602-0000
717 348-3000 **Scranton Public Library** Vine St & N Washington Ave — Scranton PA 18503-0000
717 823-0156 **Osterhout Free Library** 71 S Franklin St — Wilkes-Barre PA 18701-1287
717 326-0536 **James V Brown Library of Williamsport & Lycoming County** 19 E 4th St — Williamsport PA 17701-6390
717 846-5300 **Martin Memorial Library** 159 E Market St — York PA 17401-1269
717 757-9685 **York County Library System** 118 Pleasant Acres Rd 2nd Fl — York PA 17402-9004

RHODE ISLAND

401 822-9100 **Coventry Public Library** 1672 Flat River Rd — Coventry RI 02816-0000
401 725-3714 **Pawtucket Public Library & Regional Library Center** 13 Summer St — Pawtucket RI 02860-2106
401 455-8000 **Providence Public Library** 225 Washington St — Providence RI 02903-3228
401 739-5440 **Warwick Public Library** 600 Sandy Ln — Warwick RI 02886-3998
401 596-2877 **Westerly Public Library** 38 Broad St — Westerly RI 02891-1856

SOUTH CAROLINA

803 642-7575 **Aiken-Bamberg-Barnwell-Edgefield Regional Library System** 314 Chesterfield St SW — Aiken SC 29801-3850
803 260-4500 **Anderson County Library** 202 E Greenville St — Anderson SC 29621-5595
803 532-9223 **Lexington County Circulating Library** 203 Armory St — Batesburg SC 29006-0000
803 723-1645 **Charleston County Library** 404 King St — Charleston SC 29403-6466
803 799-9084 **Richland County Public Library** 1400 Sumter St — Columbia SC 29201-2800
803 248-4898 **Horry County Memorial Library** 1008 5th Ave — Conway SC 29526-5196
803 859-9679 **Pickens County Library** 110 W 1st Ave — Easley SC 29640-2998
803 662-8424 **Florence County Library** 319 S Irby St — Florence SC 29501-4795
803 242-5000 **Greenville County Library** 300 College St — Greenville SC 29601-2086
803 223-4515 **Greenwood-Abbeville Regional Library** 106 N Main St — Greenwood SC 29646-2240
803 761-8082 **Berkeley County Library** 100 Library St — Moncks Corner SC 29461-2355
803 324-3055 **York County Library** PO Box 10032 — Rock Hill SC 29731-0032
803 596-3507 **Spartanburg County Public Library** 333 S Pine St — Spartanburg SC 29302-2622
803 773-7273 **Sumter County Library** 111 N Harvin St — Sumter SC 29150-4988

SOUTH DAKOTA

605 394-4171 **Rapid City Public Library** 610 Quincy St — Rapid City SD 57701-3655
605 339-7081 **Sioux Falls Public Library** 201 N Main Ave — Sioux Falls SD 57102-0386

TENNESSEE

615 323-5301 **Sullivan County Public Library** PO Box 510 — Blountville TN 37617-0510
615 757-5310 **Chattanooga-Hamilton County Bicentennial Library** 1001 Broad St — Chattanooga TN 37402-2620
615 388-9282 **Blue Grass Regional Library** 104 E 6th St — Columbia TN 38401-3359
615 544-5750 **Knox County Public Library System** 500 W Church Ave — Knoxville TN 37902-2505
901 587-2347 **Reelfoot Regional Library Center** Hwy 45 S — Martin TN 38237-0000
901 725-8855 **Memphis/Shelby County Public Library & Information Center** 1850 Peabody Ave — Memphis TN 38104-4025
615 586-6251 **Nolichucky Regional Library** 315 McCrary Dr — Morristown TN 37814-3196
615 893-3380 **Highland Rim Regional Library Center** 2102 Mercury Blvd — Murfreesboro TN 37130-4098
615 259-6004 **West Ben Public Library of Nashville & Davidson County** 222 8th Ave N — Nashville TN 37203-3585

TEXAS

915 677-2474 **Abilene Public Library** 202 Cedar St — Abilene TX 79601-5793
806 378-3054 **Amarillo Public Library** 413 E 4th St — Amarillo TX 79101-1523
409 849-5711 **Brazoria County Library System** 401 E Cedar St — Angleton TX 77515-0000
817 459-6900 **Arlington Public Library** 101 E Abram — Arlington TX 76010-1183
512 499-7300 **Austin Public Library** 800 Guadalupe St — Austin TX 78701-2314
409 838-6606 **Beaumont Public Library System** 801 Pearl St — Beaumont TX 77704-0000
409 779-1736 **Bryan Public Library** 201 E 26th St — Bryan TX 77803-5389
512 880-7000 **Corpus Christi Public Libraries** 805 Comanche St — Corpus Christi TX 78401-2715
214 670-1400 **Johnson J Eric Public Library** 1515 Young St — Dallas TX 75201-5499
915 543-5433 **El Paso Public Library** 501 N Oregon St — El Paso TX 79901-1195
817 870-7700 **Fort Worth Public Library** 3rd & Taylor St — Fort Worth TX 76102-7333
214 205-2503 **Nicholson Memorial Library** 625 Austin St — Garland TX 75040-6365
713 221-5350 **Harris County Public Library System** 49 San Jacinto Suite 200 — Houston TX 77002-1214
713 236-1313 **Houston Public Library** 500 McKinney Ave — Houston TX 77002-2534
214 721-2639 **Irving Public Library System** 801 W Irving Blvd — Irving TX 75060-2845
806 762-6411 **Lubbock City-County Library** 1306 9th St — Lubbock TX 79401-2708
915 683-2708 **Midland County Public Library** 301 W Missouri St — Midland TX 79701-5108
713 477-0276 **Pasadena Public Library** 1201 Minerva St — Pasadena TX 77506-4895
214 964-4208 **Plano Public Library System** 5024 Custer Rd — Plano TX 75023-0000
713 342-4455 **Fort Bend County Library System** 1001 Golfview St — Richmond TX 77469-5141
512 299-7790 **San Antonio Public Library** 203 S Saint Mary's St — San Antonio TX 78205-2786
817 754-4694 **Waco-McLennan County Library** 1717 Austin Ave — Waco TX 76701-1741

UTAH

801 451-2322 **Davis County Library** 38 S 100 East — Farmington UT 84025-0000
801 627-6913 **Weber County Library** 2464 Jefferson Ave — Ogden UT 84401-2488
801 363-5733 **Salt Lake City Public Library** 209 E 500 South — Salt Lake City UT 84111-3280
801 943-4636 **Salt Lake County Library System** 2197 E 7000 South — Salt Lake City UT 84121-3188

VIRGINIA

703 838-4555 **Alexandria Library** 717 Queen St — Alexandria VA 22314-2471
703 358-5990 **Arlington Public Library** 1015 N Quincy St — Arlington VA 22201-4603
804 979-7151 **Jefferson-Madison Regional Library** 201 E Market St — Charlottesville VA 22901-5287
804 547-6579 **Chesapeake Public Library** 298 Cedar Rd — Chesapeake VA 23320-5514
804 748-1601 **Chesterfield County Public Library** 9501 Lori Rd — Chesterfield VA 23832-6631
703 222-3155 **Fairfax County Public Library** 13135 Lee Jackson Memorial Hwy Suite 301 — Fairfax VA 22033-0000
804 727-1154 **Hampton Public Library** 4207 Victoria Blvd — Hampton VA 23669-4243
703 434-4475 **Rockingham Public Library** 45 Newman Ave — Harrisonburg VA 22801-4001
703 361-8211 **Prince William Library** 8601 Mathis Ave — Manassas VA 22111-0000
804 247-8506 **Newport News Public Library System** 2400 Washington Ave — Newport News VA 23607-4300
804 441-2887 **Norfolk Public Library** 301 E City Hall Ave — Norfolk VA 23510-1703
804 393-8501 **Portsmouth Public Library** 601 Court St — Portsmouth VA 23704-3607
804 222-1643 **County of Henrico Public Library** 1001 N Laburnum Ave — Richmond VA 23223-2705
804 780-4256 **Richmond Public Library** 101 E Franklin St — Richmond VA 23219-2193
703 981-2475 **Roanoke City Public Library System** 706 S Jefferson St — Roanoke VA 24016-5104
804 427-4321 **Virginia Beach Dept of Public Libraries** Courthouse Commons Bldg Suite 110 — Virginia Beach VA 23456-0000
703 328-8061 **Lonesome Pine Regional Library** PO Box 1379 — Wise VA 24293-1379

WASHINGTON

206 377-7601 **Kitsap Regional Library** 1301 Sylvan Way — Bremerton WA 98310-3498
206 659-8447 **Sno-Isle Regional Library** 7312 35th Ave NE — Marysville WA 98270-9164
206 943-5001 **Timberland Regional Library** 415 Airdustrial Way SW — Olympia WA 98501-5799
206 684-6600 **King County Library System** 300 8th Ave N — Seattle WA 98109-5191
206 386-4100 **Seattle Public Library** 1000 4th Ave — Seattle WA 98104-1193
509 924-4122 **Spokane County Library District** N 2901 Argonne Rd — Spokane WA 99212-0000
509 838-3361 **Spokane Public Library** 906 Main Ave — Spokane WA 99201-0976
206 572-6760 **Pierce County Rural Library District** 2356 Tacoma Ave S — Tacoma WA 98402-1493
206 591-5666 **Tacoma Public Library** 1102 Tacoma Ave S — Tacoma WA 98402-2098
206 695-1561 **Fort Vancouver Regional Library** 1007 E Mill Plain Blvd — Vancouver WA 98663-3504
509 663-1117 **North Central Regional Library** 238 Olds Station Rd — Wenatchee WA 98801-5937
509 452-8541 **Yakima Valley Regional Library** 102 N 3rd St — Yakima WA 98901-2705

WEST VIRGINIA

304 255-0511 **Raleigh County Public Library** PO Box 1876 — Beckley WV 25802-1876
304 325-3943 **Craft Memorial Library** 600 Commerce St — Bluefield WV 24701-3107
304 343-4646 **Kanawha County Public Library** 123 Capitol St — Charleston WV 25301-2686
304 523-9451 **Cabell County Public Library** 455 9th Street Plaza — Huntington WV 25701-1482
304 291-7425 **Morgantown Public Library** 373 Spruce St — Morgantown WV 26505-5564
304 845-6911 **Miracle Valley Regional Library System** 700 5th St — Moundsville WV 26041-1906
304 485-6564 **Parkersburg & Wood County Public Library** 3100 Emerson Ave — Parkersburg WV 26104-0000

WISCONSIN

715 682-8027 **Northern Waters Library Service** Industrial Park Rd — Ashland WI 54806-0000
715 839-5082 **Indianhead Federated Library System** 3301 Golf Rd — Eau Claire WI 54701-8017
608 822-3393 **Southwest Wisconsin Library System** 1775 4th St — Fennimore WI 53809-1137
414 921-3670 **Mid-Wisconsin Federated Library System** 32 Sheboygan St — Fond du Lac WI 54935-4220
414 497-3452 **Brown County Library** 515 Pine St — Green Bay WI 54301-5194
608 755-2490 **Arrowhead Library System** 20 E Milwaukee Suite 204 — Janesville WI 53545-0000
608 755-2800 **Janesville Public Library** 316 S Main St — Janesville WI 53545-3912
608 266-6300 **Madison Public Library** 201 W Mifflin St — Madison WI 53703-2597
414 683-4863 **Manitowoc-Calumet Library System** 808 Hamilton St — Manitowoc WI 54220-5390
414 278-3000 **Milwaukee Public Library** 814 W Wisconsin Ave — Milwaukee WI 53233-2385
414 236-5220 **Winnefox Library System** 106 Washington Ave — Oshkosh WI 54901-4933
414 636-9211 **Lakeshores Library System** 730 Wisconsin Ave — Racine WI 53403-1238
414 636-9241 **Racine Public Library** 75 7th St — Racine WI 53403-1200
414 459-3400 **Mead Public Library** 710 Plaza 8 — Sheboygan WI 53081-0000
414 524-3680 **Waukesha Public Library** 321 Wisconsin Ave — Waukesha WI 53186-4786
715 847-5400 **Marathon County Public Library** 400 1st St — Wausau WI 54401-5445

Libraries - State

The libraries or archives of each state are listed alphabetically in state order.

205 277-7330 **Alabama Public Library Service** 6030 Monticello Dr — Montgomery AL 36130-0001
907 465-2910 **Alaska State Library** PO Box G — Juneau AK 99811-0000
602 542-4035 **Library of Archives & Public Records** 1700 W Washington St Rm 200 — Phoenix AZ 85007-2877
501 682-1527 **Arkansas State Library** 1 Capitol Mall — Little Rock AR 72201-1081
916 445-2585 **California State Library** 914 Capitol Mall — Sacramento CA 95814-4877
303 866-6900 **Colorado State Library** 201 E Colfax Ave — Denver CO 80203-1704
203 566-4301 **Connecticut State Library** 231 Capitol Ave — Hartford CT 06106-1537
302 739-4748 **Delaware Div of Libraries** 43 S Dupont Hwy — Dover DE 19901-7430
904 487-2651 **State Library of Florida** 500 S Bronough St RA Gray Bldg — Tallahassee FL 32399-1849
404 656-2461 **Georgia State Public Library Services Div Dept of Education** 156 Trinity Ave SW 1st Fl — Atlanta GA 30303-3600
808 548-5596 **Hawaii State Public Library System** 465 S King St Rm B-1 — Honolulu HI 96813-0000
208 334-2150 **Idaho State Library** 325 W State St — Boise ID 83702-6055
217 782-2994 **Illinois State Library** 300 S 2nd St — Springfield IL 62701-0000
317 232-3675 **Indiana State Library** 140 N Senate Ave — Indianapolis IN 46204-2207
515 281-4118 **State Library of Iowa** E 12th & Grand Aves — Des Moines IA 50319-0001
913 296-3296 **Kansas State Library** State Capitol 3rd Fl — Topeka KS 66612-0000
502 875-7000 **Kentucky Department for Libraries & Archives** 300 Coffee Tree Rd — Frankfort KY 40601-0000
504 342-4922 **Louisiana State Library** 760 Riverside St N — Baton Rouge LA 70802-5232
207 289-5600 **Maine State Library** LMA Bldg State House Stn 64 — Augusta ME 04333-0001
301 333-2113 **Maryland Library Development & Services Div Dept of Education** 200 W Baltimore St — Baltimore MD 21201-2500
617 267-9400 **Massachusetts Board of Library Commissioners** 648 Beacon St — Boston MA 02215-2002

Libraries

517 373-1593 **State Library of Michigan** PO Box 30007 Lansing MI 48909-7507
612 296-2821 **Minnesota State Library Agency** 550 Cedar St Rm 440 Saint Paul MN 55101-2233
601 359-1036 **Mississippi Library Commission** 1221 Ellis Ave Jackson MS 39289-0700
314 751-3615 **Missouri State Library** PO Box 387 Jefferson City MO 65102-0387
406 444-3115 **Montana State Library** 1515 E 6th Ave Helena MT 59620-0000
402 471-3189 **Nebraska State Library** State Capitol 3rd Fl S Lincoln NE 68509-0000
702 687-5130 **Nevada State Library & Archives** 401 N Carson St Carson City NV 89710-0001
603 271-2394 **New Hampshire State Library** 20 Park St Concord NH 03301-6314
609 292-6200 **New Jersey State Library** 185 W State St CN520 Trenton NJ 08625-0001
505 827-3800 **New Mexico State Library** 325 Don Gaspar Ave Santa Fe NM 87503-0001
518 474-5930 **New York State Library** Empire State Plaza Cultural Education Ctr Albany NY 12230-0001
919 733-2570 **North Carolina State Library** 109 E Jones St Raleigh NC 27601-2806
701 224-2490 **North Dakota State Library** 604 East Blvd Liberty Memorial Bldg Bismarck ND 58505-0800
614 644-7061 **State Library of Ohio** 65 S Front St Rm 510 Columbus OH 43266-0001
405 521-2502 **Oklahoma Dept of Libraries** 200 NE 18th St Oklahoma City OK 73105-3298
503 378-4243 **Oregon State Library** State Library Bldg Salem OR 97301-2477
717 787-2646 **State Library of Pennsylvania** Walnut St & Commonwealth Ave Harrisburg PA 17120-0001
401 277-2726 **Rhode Island Dept of State Library Services** 300 Richmond St Providence RI 02903-4222
803 734-8666 **South Carolina State Library** PO Box 11469 Columbia SC 29211-1469
605 773-3131 **South Dakota State Library** 800 Governors Dr Pierre SD 57501-2294
615 741-2451 **Tennessee State Library & Archives** 403 7th Ave N Nashville TN 37243-0312
512 463-5460 **Texas State Library** 1201 Brazos St Austin TX 78701-0000
801 466-5888 **Utah State Library** 2150 S 300 West Salt Lake City UT 84115-2579
802 828-3261 **Vermont Dept of Libraries** 109 State St Montpelier VT 05602-2712
804 786-8929 **Virginia State Library & Archives** 11th St & Capitol Sq Richmond VA 23219-0000
206 753-5590 **Washington State Library** PO Box AJ-11 Olympia WA 98504-0000
304 348-2041 **West Virginia Library Commission** State Capitol Charleston WV 25305-0001
608 266-2205 **Wisconsin Library Services Div Dept of Public Instruction** 125 S Webster St Madison WI 53702-0001
307 777-7281 **Wyoming State Library** 2301 Capitol Ave Cheyenne WY 82002-0001

Libraries - University

The top university libraries, selected on the basis of annual acquisition budget, are listed alphabetically by state.

205 348-6047 **University of Alabama Main Library** PO Box 870266 Tuscaloosa AL 35487-0266
907 786-1848 **University of Alaska Library** 3211 Providence Dr Anchorage AK 99508-4675
602 965-6164 **Arizona State University Library** Hayden Library Tempe AZ 85287-0000
602 621-6441 **University of Arizona Library** Tucson AZ 85721-0001
501 575-4101 **University of Arkansas Library** Fayetteville AR 72701-0000
415 723-1811 **Stanford University Library** Green Library Stanford CA 94305-0000
415 643-9999 **University of California Berkeley Library** Berkeley CA 94720-0000
916 752-1126 **University of California Davis Library** Shields Library Davis CA 95616-0000
714 856-6836 **University of California Irvine Library** PO Box 19557 Irvine CA 92713-9557
213 825-1323 **University of California Los Angeles Library** Los Angeles CA 90024-0000
213 743-2540 **University of Southern California Library** Doheny Library Los Angeles CA 90089-0001
303 492-6897 **University of Colorado Libraries** Boulder CO 80309-0001
203 432-1783 **Yale University Libraries** 120 High St Rm 152 New Haven CT 06520-0000
302 451-2432 **University of Delaware Library** Newark DE 19717-5267
202 687-7452 **Georgetown University Library** 37th & N St Washington DC 20057-0001
808 956-7214 **University of Hawaii Library** 2550 The Mall Honolulu HI 96822-2233
208 385-3301 **Boise State University Library** 1910 University Dr Boise ID 83725-0001
217 333-2290 **University of Illinois at Urbana-Champaign Library** 1408 W Gregory Dr Urbana IL 61801-3607
812 855-8028 **Indiana University Libraries** 10th & Jordan Sts Bloomington IN 47405-0000
319 335-5299 **University of Iowa Libraries** Washington & Madison Sts Iowa City IA 52242-0001
606 257-3788 **University of Kentucky Libraries** King Library S Lexington KY 40506-0000
504 388-8875 **Louisiana State University Library** Baton Rouge LA 70803-0001
207 581-1110 **University of Maine Library** Folger Library Orono ME 04469-0001
301 454-5704 **University of Maryland Library** McKeldin Library College Park MD 20742-0001
617 495-2411 **Harvard University Library** Wadsworth House Cambridge MA 02138-0000
313 764-9373 **University of Michigan Library** Hatcher Graduate Library Ann Arbor MI 48109-1205
612 624-0303 **University of Minnesota Libraries** 309 19th Ave S Minneapolis MN 55455-0000
601 325-7667 **Mississippi State University Library** Hardy Rd Starkville MS 39762-9999
314 882-4701 **University of Missouri Library** Ellis Library Columbia MO 65201-0000
406 994-3171 **Montana State University Library** Renne Library Bozeman MT 59717-0001
402 472-2848 **University of Nebraska Library** Lincoln NE 68588-0001
702 784-6508 **University of Nevada Library** Reno NV 89557-0044
609 258-3180 **Princeton University Library** 1 Washington Rd Princeton NJ 08540-0000
908 932-7509 **Rutgers University Library** 179 College Ave New Brunswick NJ 08901-0000
505 277-5761 **University of New Mexico Library** Zimmerman Library Albuquerque NM 87131-0001
212 854-2241 **Columbia University Library** Butler Library New York NY 10027-0000
607 255-4144 **Cornell University Library** Olin Library Ithaca NY 14850-0000
919 962-1356 **University of North Carolina Libraries** Davis Library Chapel Hill NC 27515-0000
701 777-2617 **University of North Dakota Library** Grand Forks ND 58202-2020
614 292-6175 **Ohio State University Libraries** 1858 Neil Ave Columbus OH 43210-0000
405 325-4142 **University of Oklahoma Library** Bizzell Memorial Library Norman OK 73069-0000
503 346-3053 **University of Oregon Library** Knight Library Eugene OR 97403-1299
814 865-6368 **Pennsylvania State University Library** Pattee Library University Park PA 16802-0000
401 792-2672 **University of Rhode Island Library** Kingston RI 02881-0000
615 974-4171 **University of Tennessee Library** 1015 Volunteer Blvd Knoxville TN 37996-1000
512 471-3813 **University of Texas Libraries** Austin TX 78713-7330
801 581-6273 **University of Utah Libraries** Salt Lake City UT 84112-0000
802 656-3131 **University of Vermont Library** 855 S Prospect Bailey-Howe Library Burlington VT 05405-0001
804 924-3021 **University of Virginia Library** Alderman Library Charlottesville VA 22903-0000
206 543-0242 **University of Washington Library** Seattle WA 98195-0000
304 293-3701 **West Virginia University Library** Morgantown WV 26506-0001
608 262-3242 **University of Wisconsin Libraries** 728 State St Madison WI 53706-1418
307 766-2070 **University of Wyoming Libraries** Laramie WY 82071-0000

Museums

Prestigious museums are listed alphabetically by city within each state.

ALABAMA

205 237-6766 **Anniston Museum of Natural History** PO Box 1587 Anniston AL 36202-1587
205 254-2565 **Birmingham Museum of Art** 2000 8th Ave N Birmingham AL 35203-2278
205 933-4152 **Red Mountain Museum** 1421 22nd St Birmingham AL 35205-4109
205 833-8226 **Southern Museum of Flight** 4343 N 73rd St Birmingham AL 35206-3642
205 837-3400 **Alabama Space & Rocket Center** 1 Tranquility Base Huntsville AL 35807-0000
205 536-2882 **Burritt Museum & Park** 3101 Burritt Dr Huntsville AL 35801-1142
205 535-4350 **Huntsville Museum of Art** 700 Monroe St SW Huntsville AL 35801-5523
205 343-2667 **Fine Arts Museum of the South at Mobile** 4850 Museum Dr Langan Pk Mobile AL 36608-0000
205 434-7620 **Museums of the City of Mobile** 355 Government St Mobile AL 36602-2315
205 348-7550 **University of Alabama State Museum of Natural History** Smith Hall Tuscaloosa AL 35487-0000

ALASKA

907 343-4326 **Anchorage Museum of History & Art** 121 W 7th Ave Anchorage AK 99501-3611
907 474-7505 **University of Alaska Museum** 907 Yukon Dr Fairbanks AK 99775-0001
907 465-2901 **Alaska State Museum** 395 Whittier St Juneau AK 99801-1718
907 586-3572 **Juneau Douglas City Museum** 115 S Seward St Juneau AK 99801-1332
907 225-5600 **Tongass Historical Museum** 629 Dock St Ketchikan AK 99901-6529
907 486-5920 **Baranov Museum** 101 Marine Way Erskine House Kodiak AK 99615-0000
907 747-8981 **Jackson Sheldon Museum** 104 College Dr Sitka AK 99835-7657

ARIZONA

602 774-5211 **Museum of Northern Arizona** RR 4 Box 720 Fort Valley Rd Flagstaff AZ 86001-9302
602 638-7769 **Grand Canyon National Park Museum** Grand Canyon Village South Rim Grand Canyon AZ 86023-9999
602 255-4470 **Arizona Historical Society** 1242 N Central Ave Phoenix AZ 85004-1887
602 255-3791 **Arizona Mineral Museum** State Fairgrounds Mineral Bldg Phoenix AZ 85007-0000
602 253-2734 **Arizona Museum** PO Box 926 Phoenix AZ 85001-0926
602 542-4581 **Arizona State Capitol Museum** 1700 W Washington Ave Phoenix AZ 85007-2810
602 252-8840 **Heard Museum** 22 E Montevista Rd Phoenix AZ 85004-1480
602 257-1222 **Phoenix Art Museum** 1625 N Central Ave Phoenix AZ 85004-1686
602 495-0900 **Pueblo Grande Museum** 4619 E Washington St Phoenix AZ 85034-1909
602 621-6281 **Arizona State Museum** University of Arizona Bldg 26 Tucson AZ 85721-0001
602 883-1380 **Arizona-Sonora Desert Museum** 2021 N Kinney Rd Tucson AZ 85743-9719
602 299-9191 **DeGrazia Art & Cultural Foundation** 6300 N Swan Rd Tucson AZ 85718-3697
602 624-2333 **Tucson Museum of Art** 140 N Main Ave Tucson AZ 85701-8290
602 621-7567 **University of Arizona Museum of Art** Olive & Speedway Tucson AZ 85721-0001

ARKANSAS

501 253-8961 **Miles Musical Museum** PO Box 488 Eureka Springs AR 72632-0488
501 575-3555 **University Museum** Museum Bldg University of Arkansas Rm 202 Fayetteville AR 72701-0000
501 783-7841 **Old Fort Museum** 320 Rogers Ave Fort Smith AR 72901-1937
501 972-2074 **Arkansas State University Museum** PO Box 490 Jonesboro AR 72403-0490
501 371-3521 **Arkansas Museum of Science & History** MacArthur Pk Little Rock AR 72202-0000

CALIFORNIA

805 861-2132 **Kern County Museum** 3801 Chester Ave Bakersfield CA 93301-1345
415 642-3681 **Lowie Museum of Anthropology** University of California 103 Kroeber Hall Berkeley CA 94720-0001
415 849-2710 **Magnes Judah L Memorial Museum** 2911 Russell St Berkeley CA 94705-2333
415 642-1207 **University Art Museum** 2626 Bancroft Way UC Berkeley Berkeley CA 94720-0001
619 786-2331 **Death Valley Museum** Death Valley National Monument Death Valley CA 92328-0000
707 443-1947 **Clarke Memorial Museum** 240 E St Eureka CA 95501-0433
209 485-4810 **Fresno Arts Museum** 2233 N 1st St Fresno CA 93703-2364
213 435-3511 **Queen Mary & Spruce Goose Attractions** 1126 Queens Hwy Long Beach CA 90801-0000
213 985-5761 **University Art Museum** 1250 Bellflower Blvd CSULB Long Beach CA 90840-0001
213 744-2160 **California Museum of Science & Industry** 700 State Dr Exposition Pk Los Angeles CA 90037-1210
213 743-2799 **Fisher Gallery** University of Southern California Los Angeles CA 90089-0292
213 825-4361 **Fowler Museum of Cultural History** Haines Hall UCLA Los Angeles CA 90024-0000
213 857-6111 **Los Angeles County Museum of Art** 5905 Wilshire Blvd Los Angeles CA 90036-4504
213 621-2766 **Museum of Contemporary Art** 250 S Grand Ave Los Angeles CA 90012-3007
213 617-0274 **Museum of Neon Art** 704 Traction Ave Los Angeles CA 90013-1814
213 744-3414 **Natural History Museum of Los Angeles County** 900 Exposition Blvd Los Angeles CA 90007-4057
213 221-2164 **Southwest Museum** 234 Museum Dr Los Angeles CA 90065-5030
213 825-1461 **Wight Art Gallery** 1100 Dickson Art Ctr UCLA Los Angeles CA 90024-0000
213 459-7611 **Getty J Paul Museum** 17985 Pacific Coast Hwy Malibu CA 90265-5799
408 372-7591 **Monterey Peninsula Museum of Art** 559 Pacific St Monterey CA 93940-2880
415 273-3402 **Oakland Museum** 1000 Oak St Oakland CA 94607-4892
408 372-4212 **Pacific Grove Museum of Natural History** 165 Forest Ave Pacific Grove CA 93950-2612
818 449-2742 **Pacific Asia Museum** 46 N Los Robles Ave Pasadena CA 91101-2071
818 449-6840 **Simon Norton Museum** 411 W Colorado Blvd Pasadena CA 91105-1896
916 225-4155 **Redding Museum & Art Center** PO Box 427 Redding CA 96099-0427
916 449-5423 **Crocker Art Museum** 216 'O' St Sacramento CA 95814-5399
619 297-3258 **Junipero Serra Museum** PO Box 81825 San Diego CA 92138-1825
619 232-3821 **Natural History Museum** 1788 El Prado San Diego CA 92112-0000
619 232-6203 **San Diego Historical Society Museum** PO Box 81825 San Diego CA 92138-1825
619 232-7931 **San Diego Museum of Art** PO Box 2107 San Diego CA 92112-0000
619 239-2001 **San Diego Museum of Man** 1350 El Prado San Diego CA 92101-1681
415 668-8922 **Asian Art Museum of San Francisco** Golden Gate Pk San Francisco CA 94118-4598
415 221-5100 **California Academy of Sciences** Golden Gate Pk San Francisco CA 94118-4599
415 750-3600 **Fine Arts Museums of San Francisco** Golden Gate Pk San Francisco CA 94118-0000
415 556-3002 **San Francisco Maritime National Historical Park** Pope St San Francisco CA 94109-0000
415 863-8800 **San Francisco Museum of Modern Art** 401 Van Ness Ave San Francisco CA 94102-4522
408 287-2290 **San Jose Historical Museum** 635 Phelan Ave San Jose CA 95112-2508
805 963-4364 **Santa Barbara Museum of Art** 1130 State St Santa Barbara CA 93101-2746
805 682-4711 **Santa Barbara Museum of Natural History** 2559 Puesta del Sol Rd Santa Barbara CA 93105-2936

COLORADO

303 492-6165 **University of Colorado Museum** 1550 Broadway Boulder CO 80309-0001
719 634-5581 **Taylor Museum** 30 W Dale St Colorado Springs CO 80903-3210
303 866-3682 **Colorado History Museum** 1300 Broadway Denver CO 80203-2104
303 575-2295 **Denver Art Museum** 100 W 14th Ave Pkwy Denver CO 80204-2788
303 370-6347 **Denver Museum of Natural History** 2001 Colorado Blvd Denver CO 80205-5798
303 296-1880 **Museum of Western Art** 1727 Tremont Pl Denver CO 80202-4028

CONNECTICUT

203 372-3521 **Museum of Art Science & Industry Inc** 4450 Park Ave Bridgeport CT 06604-1098
203 583-6070 **American Clock & Watch Museum** 100 Maple St Bristol CT 06010-5034
203 677-4787 **Hill-Stead Museum** 35 Mountain Rd Farmington CT 06032-2304
203 869-0376 **Bruce Museum** 1 Museum Dr Greenwich CT 06830-7100
203 236-5621 **Connecticut Historical Society Museum** 1 Elizabeth St Hartford CT 06105-2292
203 278-2670 **Wadsworth Antheneum** 600 Main St Hartford CT 06103-2990
203 572-0711 **Mystic Seaport Museum** 50 Greenmanville Ave Mystic CT 06355-1935
203 229-0257 **New Britain Museum of American Art** 56 Lexington St New Britain CT 06052-1412
203 432-3750 **Peabody Museum of Natural History** 170 Whitney Ave Yale University New Haven CT 06511-3748
203 432-0600 **Yale University Art Gallery** PO Box 2006 New Haven CT 06520-2006
203 432-0822 **Yale University Collection of Musical Instruments** PO Box 2117 New Haven CT 06520-2117
203 443-2545 **Lyman Allyn Art Museum** 625 Williams St New London CT 06320-4199
203 887-2506 **Slater Memorial Museum** 108 Crescent St Norwich CT 06360-3556
203 322-1646 **Stamford Museum & Nature Center** 39 Scofieldtown Rd Stamford CT 06903-4096
203 486-4460 **Connecticut State Museum of Natural History** 75 N Eagleville Rd University of Connecticut U-23 Storrs CT 06269-0001

203 868-0518 **American Indian Archaeological Institute**
38 Curtis Rd ... Washington Green CT 06793-1701
203 753-0381 **Mattatuck Museum** 144 W Main St ... Waterbury CT 06702-1298

DELAWARE

302 739-3260 **Delaware State Museum Meeting House Gallery**
316 S Governor's Ave ... Dover DE 19901-6706
302 645-0458 **Lewes Historical Society** 119 W 3rd St ... Lewes DE 19958-1315
302 571-9590 **Delaware Art Museum** 2301 Kentmere Pkwy ... Wilmington DE 19806-2096
302 658-9111 **Delaware Museum of Natural History** PO Box 3937 ... Wilmington DE 19807-0937
302 658-2400 **Hagley Museum & Library** 298 Buck Rd E ... Wilmington DE 19807-0000
302 888-4600 **Du Pont Henry Francis Winterthur Museum & Garden** ... Winterthur DE 19735-0001

DISTRICT OF COLUMBIA

202 287-3306 **Anacostia Museum (Smithsonian Institution)**
1901 Fort Pl SE ... Washington DC 20020-3298
202 857-6583 **B'nai B'rith Klutznick Museum**
1640 Rhode Island Ave NW ... Washington DC 20036-3287
202 638-3211 **Corcoran Gallery of Art** 17th St & New York Ave NW ... Washington DC 20006-0000
202 342-3200 **Dumbarton Oaks Collection** 1703 32nd NW ... Washington DC 20007-2961
202 357-3091 **Hirshhorn Museum & Sculpture Garden (Smithsonian Institution)**
Independence Ave & 8th St SW ... Washington DC 20560-0001
202 357-1400 **National Air & Space Museum (Smithsonian Institution)**
Independence Ave & 6th St SW ... Washington DC 20560-0001
202 737-4215 **National Gallery of Art** 4th St & Constitution Ave NW ... Washington DC 20565-0001
202 357-4600 **National Museum of African Art (Smithsonian Institution)**
950 Independence Ave SW ... Washington DC 20560-0001
202 357-1959 **National Museum of American Art (Smithsonian Institution)**
8th & G Sts NW ... Washington DC 20560-0001
202 357-1300 **National Museum of American History (Smithsonian Institution)**
12th St & Constitution Ave NW ... Washington DC 20560-0001
202 357-2664 **National Museum of Natural History (Smithsonian Institution)**
10th St & Constitution Ave NW ... Washington DC 20560-0001
202 357-1300 **National Portrait Gallery (Smithsonian Institution)**
F St & 8th NW ... Washington DC 20560-0001
202 387-2151 **Phillips Collection** 1600 21st St NW ... Washington DC 20009-1090
202 357-2447 **Renwick Gallery (Smithsonian Institution)**
Pennsylvania Ave & 17th St NW ... Washington DC 20560-0001
202 357-4880 **Sackler Arthur M Gallery (Smithsonian Institution)**
1050 Independence Ave SW ... Washington DC 20560-0001
202 667-0441 **Textile Museum** S St NW ... Washington DC 20008-4088

FLORIDA

813 746-4132 **South Florida Museum & Bishop Planetarium**
201 10th St W ... Bradenton FL 34205-8604
305 284-3536 **Lowe Art Museum** 1301 Stanford Dr University of Miami ... Coral Gables FL 33124-6310
904 255-0285 **Museum of Arts & Sciences** 1040 Museum Blvd ... Daytona Beach FL 32114-4597
305 525-5500 **Museum of Art** 1 E Los Olas Blvd ... Fort Lauderdale FL 33301-1845
904 243-6521 **Indian Temple Mound Museum**
139 Miraclestrip Pkwy SE ... Fort Walton Beach FL 32548-5817
904 392-1721 **Florida Museum of Natural History**
Museum Rd University of Florida ... Gainesville FL 32611-2035
904 392-0201 **University Gallery** 102FAB University of Florida ... Gainesville FL 32611-0000
904 356-6857 **Cummer Gallery of Art** 829 Riverside Ave ... Jacksonville FL 32204-3386
904 398-8336 **Jacksonville Art Museum** 4160 Boulevard Center Dr ... Jacksonville FL 32207-2805
904 396-7062 **Museum of Science & History** 1025 Gulf Life Dr ... Jacksonville FL 32207-9053
407 896-7151 **Orlando Science Center** 810 E Rollins St ... Loch Haven Park FL 32803-1291
305 375-1492 **Historical Museum of Southern Florida** 101 W Flagler St ... Miami FL 33130-1538
305 854-4247 **Museum of Science** 3280 S Miami Ave ... Miami FL 33129-2899
305 673-7530 **Bass Museum of Art** 2121 Park Ave ... Miami Beach FL 33139-1756
407 896-4231 **Orlando Museum of Art** 2416 N Mills Ave ... Orlando FL 32803-1426
407 655-2833 **Flagler Henry M Museum** PO Box 969 ... Palm Beach FL 33480-0969
904 433-1559 **Pensacola Historical Museum** 405 S Adams St ... Pensacola FL 32501-6003
904 432-6247 **Pensacola Museum of Art** 407 S Jefferson St ... Pensacola FL 32501-5997
813 823-3767 **Salvador Dali Museum** 1000 3rd St S ... Saint Petersburg FL 33701-4901
813 355-5101 **Ringling John & Mabel Museum of Art** 5401 Bayshore Rd ... Sarasota FL 34243-0000
904 488-1484 **Museum of Florida History** 500 S Bronough St ... Tallahassee FL 32399-6519
813 985-5531 **Museum of Science & Industry** 4801 E Fowler Ave ... Tampa FL 33617-2099
813 254-1891 **Plant Henry B Museum** 401 W Kennedy Blvd ... Tampa FL 33606-1450
407 832-5194 **Norton Gallery & School of Art** 1451 S Olive Ave ... West Palm Beach FL 33401-7198
407 644-3686 **Morse Charles Hosmer Museum of American Art**
131 E Welbourne Ave ... Winter Park FL 32789-4337

GEORGIA

404 542-3255 **Georgia Museum of Art** Jackson St North Campus ... Athens GA 30602-0000
404 872-8233 **Atlanta Museum** 537-39 Peachtree St NE ... Atlanta GA 30308-0000
404 727-4282 **Emory University Museum of Art & Archaeology**
571 S Kilgo Cir Carlos Hall ... Atlanta GA 30322-0000
404 378-4311 **Fernbank Science Center** 156 Heaton Park Dr NE ... Atlanta GA 30307-1398
404 656-2846 **Georgia State Museum of Science & Industry**
State Capitol Bldg Rm 432 ... Atlanta GA 30334-0000
404 892-3600 **High Museum of Art** 1280 Peachtree St NE ... Atlanta GA 30309-3549
404 722-8454 **Augusta Richmond County Museum** 540 Telfair St ... Augusta GA 30901-2396
404 322-0400 **Columbus Museum** 1251 Wynnton Rd ... Columbus GA 31906-2810
912 477-3232 **Museum of Arts & Sciences** 4182 Forsyth Rd ... Macon GA 31210-4806
912 232-1177 **Telfair Academy of Arts & Sciences** 121 Barnard St ... Savannah GA 31401-3612

HAWAII

808 935-5021 **Lyman House Memorial Museum** 276 Haili St ... Hilo HI 96720-2978
808 847-3511 **Bishop Museum** 1525 Bernice St ... Honolulu HI 96817-2704
808 538-3693 **Honolulu Academy of Arts** 900 S Beretania St ... Honolulu HI 96814-1495
808 531-0481 **Mission Houses Museum** 553 S King St ... Honolulu HI 96813-3002

IDAHO

208 334-2120 **Idaho State Historical Museum** 610 N Julia Davis Dr ... Boise ID 83702-7695
208 664-3448 **Museum of North Idaho** PO Box 812 ... Coeur d'Alene ID 83814-0812
208 743-2535 **Luna House Museum** 3rd & C Sts ... Lewiston ID 83501-0000
208 236-3168 **Idaho Museum of Natural History** Idaho State University ... Pocatello ID 83209-0001
208 733-9554 **Herrett Museum** 315 Falls Ave College of Southern Idaho ... Twin Falls ID 83303-1238

ILLINOIS

618 453-5388 **University Museum** Southern Illinois University ... Carbondale IL 62901-4508
217 333-1860 **Krannert Art Museum**
500 E Peabody Dr University of Illinios ... Champaign IL 61820-6986
312 322-0304 **Adler Planetarium** 1300 S Lake Shore Dr ... Chicago IL 60605-2489
312 443-3600 **Art Institute of Chicago** Michigan Ave & Adams St ... Chicago IL 60603-6494
312 642-4600 **Chicago Historical Society Museum** Clark St & North Ave ... Chicago IL 60614-6099
312 922-9410 **Field Museum of Natural History**
Roosevelt Rd & Lake Shore Dr ... Chicago IL 60605-0000
312 280-2660 **Museum of Contemporary Art** 237 E Ontario St ... Chicago IL 60611-3236
312 663-5554 **Museum of Contemporary Photography**
600 S Michigan Ave Columbia College ... Chicago IL 60605-1996
312 684-1414 **Museum of Science & Industry** 57th St & Lake Shore Dr ... Chicago IL 60637-0000
312 549-0607 **Museum of the Chicago Academy of Sciences**
2001 N Clark St ... Chicago IL 60614-4712
312 702-9520 **Oriental Institute Museum**
1155 E 58th St University of Chicago ... Chicago IL 60637-1570
312 384-3352 **Polish Museum of America** 984 N Milwaukee Ave ... Chicago IL 60622-4101
309 438-8800 **University Museum** Illinois State University ... Normal IL 61761-6901
309 686-7000 **Lakeview Museum of Arts & Sciences** 1125 W Lake Ave ... Peoria IL 61614-5985
217 224-7669 **Quincy Museum of Natural History & Art** 1601 Main St ... Quincy IL 62301-4264
815 398-6000 **Time Museum** 7801 E State St ... Rockford IL 61125-0000
217 782-7386 **Illinois State Museum** Spring & Edwards Sts ... Springfield IL 62706-0001
217 333-2360 **World Heritage Museum** 702 S Wright St University of Illinois ... Urbana IL 61801-0000

INDIANA

812 855-5445 **Indiana University Art Museum** 7th St Fine Arts Plaza ... Bloomington IN 47405-0001
812 855-6873 **Mathers Museum** 601 E 8th St Indiana University ... Bloomington IN 47405-0001
812 425-2406 **Evansville Museum of Arts & Sciences** 441 SE Riverside Dr .. Evansville IN 47713-1098
219 422-6467 **Fort Wayne Museum of Art** 311 E Main St ... Fort Wayne IN 46802-1997
219 427-3864 **Lincoln Museum** PO Box 1110 ... Fort Wayne IN 46801-1110
317 924-5431 **Children's Museum** 3000 N Meridian St ... Indianapolis IN 46208-4716
317 232-1637 **Indiana State Museum** 202 N Alabama St ... Indianapolis IN 46204-2185
317 923-1331 **Indianapolis Museum of Art** 1200 W 38th St ... Indianapolis IN 46208-4196
317 776-6000 **Conner Prairie Museum** 13400 Allisonville Rd ... Noblesville IN 46060-4499
219 239-5466 **Snite Museum of Art** University of Notre Dame ... Notre Dame IN 46556-5601
812 238-1676 **Sheldon Swope Art Museum** 25 S 7th St ... Terre Haute IN 47807-3692

IOWA

319 273-2188 **University Museum**
3219 Hudson Rd University of Northern Iowa ... Cedar Falls IA 50614-0199
319 366-7503 **Cedar Rapids Museum of Art** 410 3rd Ave SE ... Cedar Rapids IA 52401-1606
319 326-7804 **Davenport Museum of Art** 1737 W 12th St ... Davenport IA 52804-3596
515 277-4405 **Des Moines Art Center** 4700 Grand Ave ... Des Moines IA 50312-2099
515 274-4138 **Science Center of Iowa**
4500 Grand Ave Greenwood-Ashword Pk ... Des Moines IA 50312-2402
515 281-5111 **State Historical Museum of Iowa** 600 E Locust St ... Des Moines IA 50319-0001
319 335-1727 **University of Iowa Museum of Art** 150 N Riverside Dr ... Iowa City IA 52242-0001
712 279-6272 **Sioux City Art Center** 513 Nebraska St ... Sioux City IA 51101-1305
712 279-6174 **Sioux City Public Museum** 2901 Jackson St ... Sioux City IA 51104-3650

KANSAS

316 227-8188 **Boot Hill Museum** Front St ... Dodge City KS 67801-0000
316 285-2054 **Santa Fe Trail Center** RR 3 ... Larned KS 67550-9803
913 864-4710 **Spencer Museum of Art**
1301 Mississippi St University of Kansas ... Lawrence KS 66045-0001
913 272-8681 **Kansas Museum of History** 6425 SW 6th St ... Topeka KS 66615-1099
316 292-5594 **Fellow-Reeve Museum of History & Science**
2100 University St ... Wichita KS 67213-3379
316 689-3664 **Ulrich Edwin A Museum of Art** PO Box 46 ... Wichita KS 67208-0000
316 268-4921 **Wichita Art Museum** 619 Stackman Dr ... Wichita KS 67203-3296

KENTUCKY

606 986-9341 **Appalachian Museum** PO Box CPO2298 ... Berea KY 40404-0001
502 745-2592 **Kentucky Museum**
Western Kentucky University College Heights ... Bowling Green KY 42101-3576
502 827-1893 **Audubon John James Museum** PO Box 576 ... Henderson KY 42420-0576
606 255-6653 **Headley-Whitney Museum** 4435 Old Frankfort Pike ... Lexington KY 40510-9623
606 257-5716 **University of Kentucky Art Museum** Rose & Euclid Sts ... Lexington KY 40506-0001
502 561-6103 **Museum of History & Science** 727 W Main St ... Louisville KY 40202-2681
502 636-2893 **Speed JB Art Museum** 2035 S 3rd St ... Louisville KY 40208-1812

LOUISIANA

504 344-9463 **Louisiana Arts & Science Center** 100 S River Rd ... Baton Rouge LA 70801-0000
504 388-2934 **Louisiana State University Museum of Geoscience**
109 Howe-Russell Geoscience Bldg ... Baton Rouge LA 70803-0001
504 388-2855 **Museum of Natural Science**
119 Foster Hall Louisiana State University ... Baton Rouge LA 70803-0001
318 234-2208 **Lafayette Museum** 1122 Lafayette St ... Lafayette LA 70501-6838
318 268-5544 **Lafayette Natural History Museum & Planetarium**
637 Girard Park Dr ... Lafayette LA 70503-2803
318 439-3797 **Imperial Calcasieu Museum** 204 W Sallier St ... Lake Charles LA 70601-5844
504 523-6722 **Gallier House Museum** 1118-32 Royal St ... New Orleans LA 70116-0000
504 523-4662 **Historic New Orleans Collection** 533 Royal St ... New Orleans LA 70130-2179
504 568-6968 **Louisiana State Museum** 751 Chartres St ... New Orleans LA 70116-3289
504 488-2631 **New Orleans Museum of Art** PO Box 19123 ... New Orleans LA 70179-0123
318 632-2020 **Louisiana State Museum-Shreveport** 3015 Greenwood Rd .. Shreveport LA 71109-4640
318 869-5169 **Meadows Museum of Art of Centenary College**
2911 Centenary Blvd ... Shreveport LA 71104-3335

MAINE

207 289-2301 **Maine State Museum** State House Complex ... Augusta ME 04333-0001
207 288-3519 **Abbe Museum** PO Box 286 ... Bar Harbor ME 04609-0286
207 443-1316 **Maine Maritime Museum** 243 Washington St ... Bath ME 04530-1638
207 725-3275 **Bowdoin College Museum of Art** Walker Art Bldg ... Brunswick ME 04011-2599
207 985-4802 **Brick Store Museum** PO Box 177 ... Kennebunk ME 04043-0177
207 775-6148 **Portland Museum of Art** 7 Congress Sq ... Portland ME 04101-1119
207 596-6457 **Farnsworth William A Library & Art Museum** PO Box 466 ... Rockland ME 04841-0466
207 872-3228 **Colby College Museum of Art** Mayflower Hill ... Waterville ME 04901-4799

MARYLAND

301 283-2113 **National Colonial Farm of Accokeek Foundation**
3400 Bryan Point Rd ... Accokeek MD 20607-9654
301 396-7100 **Baltimore Museum of Art** 10 Art Museum Dr ... Baltimore MD 21218-3801
301 396-0180 **Cylburn Arboretum** 4915 Greenspring Ave ... Baltimore MD 21209-4698
301 685-2370 **Maryland Academy of Sciences** 601 Light St ... Baltimore MD 21230-3812
301 396-1149 **Peale Museum** 225 Holliday St ... Baltimore MD 21202-3693
301 547-9000 **Walters Art Gallery** 600 N Charles St ... Baltimore MD 21201-5185
301 739-5727 **Washington County Museum of Fine Arts** PO Box 423 ... Hagerstown MD 21741-0423
301 745-2916 **Chesapeake Bay Maritime Museum** PO Box 636 ... Saint Michaels MD 21663-0636
301 326-2042 **Calvert Marine Museum** 14130 Solomons Island Rd ... Solomons MD 20688-0000

MASSACHUSETTS

508 475-7515 **Addison Gallery of American Art** Main St ... Andover MA 01810-0000
617 267-9300 **Boston Museum of Fine Arts** 465 Huntington Ave ... Boston MA 02115-5519
617 426-6500 **Children's Museum** 300 Congress St Museum Wharf ... Boston MA 02210-1034
617 426-2800 **Computer Museum** 300 Congress St ... Boston MA 02210-0000

Museums

617 566-1401 **Gardner Isabella Stewart Museum** 280 The Fenway — Boston MA 02115-5809
617 589-0100 **Museum of Science** Science Pk — Boston MA 02114-1099
508 588-6000 **Fuller Museum of Art** 455 Oak St — Brockton MA 02401-1340
617 495-2317 **Busch-Reisinger Museum** 32 Quincy St Harvard University — Cambridge MA 02138-3804
617 495-9400 **Fogg Art Museum** 32 Quincy St Harvard University — Cambridge MA 02138-3883
617 253-4444 **Massachusetts Institute of Technology Museum** 265 Massachusetts Ave — Cambridge MA 02139-4109
617 495-2463 **Museum of Comparative Zoology** 26 Oxford St — Cambridge MA 02138-2902
617 495-2248 **Peabody Museum of Archaeology & Ethnology** 11 Divinity Ave Harvard University — Cambridge MA 02138-2096
617 861-6559 **Museum of Our National Heritage** 33 Marrett Rd — Lexington MA 02173-5703
508 997-0046 **Whaling Museum** 18 Johnny Cake Hill — New Bedford MA 02740-6317
413 442-1793 **Berkshire County Historical Society** 780 Holmes Rd — Pittsfield MA 01201-7199
508 746-1620 **Pilgrim Hall Museum** 75 Court St — Plymouth MA 02360-3891
508 745-1876 **Peabody Museum of Salem** East India Sq — Salem MA 01970-3783
508 888-0251 **Sandwich Glass Museum** 129 Main St — Sandwich MA 02563-2233
617 784-5642 **Kendall Whaling Museum** 27 Everett St — Sharon MA 02067-1018
413 732-3080 **Connecticut Valley Historical Museum** 194 State St — Springfield MA 01103-1715
413 732-6092 **Museum of Fine Arts** 49 Chestnut St — Springfield MA 01103-1788
413 733-4214 **Smith George Walter Vincent Art Museum** 222 State St — Springfield MA 01103-1779
413 733-1194 **Springfield Science Museum** 236 State St — Springfield MA 01103-1778
413 458-9545 **Sterling & Francine Clark Art Institute** 225 South St — Williamstown MA 01267-2891
508 799-4406 **Worcester Art Museum** 55 Salisbury St — Worcester MA 01609-3123

MICHIGAN

313 763-3559 **Kelsey Museum of Ancient & Medieval Archaeology** 434 S State St University of Michigan — Ann Arbor MI 48109-1390
313 764-0478 **University of Michigan Exhibit Museum** 1109 Geddes — Ann Arbor MI 48109-0001
313 764-0395 **University of Michigan Museum of Art** 525 S State — Ann Arbor MI 48109-0001
616 965-5117 **Kingman Museum of Natural History** W Michigan Ave & 20th St — Battle Creek MI 49017-0000
313 645-3323 **Cranbrook Academy of Art Museum** 500 Lone Pine Rd — Bloomfield Hills MI 48013-0000
313 645-3230 **Cranbrook Institute of Science** PO Box 801 — Bloomfield Hills MI 48304-0000
313 494-1210 **Children's Museum** 67 E Kirby St — Detroit MI 48202-4001
313 833-1805 **Detroit Historical Museum** 5401 Woodward Ave — Detroit MI 48202-4097
313 833-7900 **Detroit Institute of Arts** 5200 Woodward Ave — Detroit MI 48202-4094
313 577-8400 **Detroit Science Center** 5020 John R St — Detroit MI 48202-4045
517 355-2370 **Michigan State University Museum** W Circle Dr — East Lansing MI 48824-0001
616 459-4677 **Grand Rapids Art Museum** 155 Division N — Grand Rapids MI 49503-3154
616 456-3977 **Public Museum of Grand Rapids** 54 Jefferson St SE — Grand Rapids MI 49503-4383
616 723-5531 **Manistee County Historical Museum** 425 River St — Manistee MI 49660-1522
313 243-7137 **Monroe County Historical Museum** 126 S Monroe St — Monroe MI 48161-2275

MINNESOTA

218 727-0687 **Lake Superior Museum of Transportation** 506 W Michigan St — Duluth MN 55802-1505
218 727-2497 **US Army Corp of Engineers Canal Park Marine Museum & Visitors Center** 600 Lake Ave S — Duluth MN 55802-2353
612 624-9876 **University Art Museum** 84 Church St SE University of Minnesota — Minneapolis MN 55455-0000
612 375-7600 **Walker Art Center** Vineland Pl — Minneapolis MN 55403-1195
612 292-4355 **Minnesota Museum of Art** 5th & Market — Saint Paul MN 55102-0000

MISSISSIPPI

601 354-7303 **Mississippi Museum of Natural Science** 111 N Jefferson St — Jackson MS 30202-2897
601 359-6920 **Mississippi State Historical Museum** PO Box 571 — Jackson MS 39205-0571
601 649-6374 **Rogers Lauren Museum of Art** PO Box 1108 — Laurel MS 39441-1108
601 636-0741 **Old Courthouse Museum** 1008 Cherry St — Vicksburg MS 39180-2540

MISSOURI

314 882-3764 **Museum of Anthropology** 104 Swallow Hall University of Missouri — Columbia MO 65211-0001
314 882-3591 **Museum of Art & Archaeology** Pickard Hall University of Missouri — Columbia MO 65211-0001
816 483-8300 **Kansas City Museum** 3218 Gladstone Blvd — Kansas City MO 64123-1199
816 561-4000 **Nelson-Atkins Museum of Art** 4525 Oak St — Kansas City MO 64111-1818
816 232-8471 **Pony Express Museum** 914 Penn St — Saint Joseph MO 64503-2544
314 361-1424 **History Museum** Jefferson Memorial Bldg Forest Pk — Saint Louis MO 63112-1099
314 965-6885 **National Museum of Transport** 3015 Barrett Station Rd — Saint Louis MO 63122-3303
314 721-0067 **Saint Louis Art Museum** 1 Fine Arts Dr Forest Pk — Saint Louis MO 63110-1380
314 289-4400 **Saint Louis Science Center** 5050 Oakland Ave — Saint Louis MO 63110-1300
417 866-2716 **Springfield Art Museum** 1111 E Brookside Dr — Springfield MO 65807-1899

MONTANA

406 994-2251 **Museum of the Rockies** Montana State University — Bozeman MT 59717-0001
406 338-2230 **Museum of the Plains Indians & Crafts Center** PO Box 400 — Browning MT 59417-0400
406 723-7211 **World Museum of Mining** PO Box 3333 — Butte MT 59702-3333
406 727-8787 **CM Russell Museum** 400 13th St N — Great Falls MT 59401-1498

NEBRASKA

308 381-5316 **Stuhr Museum of the Prairie Pioneer** 3133 W Hwy 34 — Grand Island NE 68801-7280
402 461-2399 **Hastings Museum** 1330 N Burlington — Hastings NE 68901-3099
402 472-2461 **Sheldon Memorial Art Gallery** 12th & R Sts — Lincoln NE 68588-0300
402 471-4754 **State Museum of History** 131 N Centennial Mall — Lincoln NE 68508-3805
402 472-3779 **University of Nebraska State Museum** 14th & U Sts Morrill Hall Rm 307 — Lincoln NE 68588-0001
402 342-3300 **Joslyn Art Museum** 2200 Dodge St — Omaha NE 68102-1294
402 444-5071 **Western Heritage Museum** 801 S 10th St — Omaha NE 68108-3299

NEVADA

702 885-4810 **Nevada State Museum** 600 N Carson St — Carson City NV 89710-0001
702 738-3418 **Northeastern Nevada Museum** 1515 Idaho St — Elko NV 89801-4021
702 423-3677 **Churchill County Museum & Archives** 1050 S Maine St — Fallon NV 89406-8925
702 455-7955 **Clark County Heritage Museum** 1830 S Boulder Hwy — Henderson NV 89015-8502
702 739-3381 **Barrick Marjorie Museum of Natural History** 4505 S Maryland Pkwy UNLV — Las Vegas NV 89154-0001
702 397-2193 **Lost City Museum** 721 S Hwy 169 — Overton NV 89040-0000
702 784-6988 **Mackay School of Mines Museum** University of Nevada — Reno NV 89557-0001
702 789-0190 **Nevada Historical Society** 1650 N Virginia St — Reno NV 89503-1799

NEW HAMPSHIRE

603 225-3381 **New Hampshire Historical Society** 30 Park St — Concord NH 03301-6326
603 646-2808 **Hood Museum of Art** Dartmouth College Wheelock St — Hanover NH 03755-1812
603 669-6144 **Currier Gallery of Art** 192 Orange St — Manchester NH 03104-4393
603 433-1100 **Strawbery Banke Museum** 454 Court St — Portsmouth NH 03801-4603

NEW JERSEY

201 538-0454 **Morris Museum** 6 Normandy Heights Rd — Morristown NJ 07960-4627
201 596-6550 **Newark Museum** 49 Washington St — Newark NJ 07101-0000
609 258-3788 **Princeton University Art Museum** — Princeton NJ 08544-0001
609 292-6300 **New Jersey State Museum** 205 W State St — Trenton NJ 08625-0001

NEW MEXICO

505 437-2840 **Space Center** PO Box 533 — Alamogordo NM 88311-0533
505 243-7255 **Albuquerque Museum** 2000 Mountain Rd NW — Albuquerque NM 87104-1459
505 277-4404 **Maxwell Museum of Anthropology** University of New Mexico — Albuquerque NM 87131-0001
505 845-6670 **National Atomic Museum** Kirtland Air Force Base Bldg 20358 — Albuquerque NM 87115-0000
505 841-8837 **New Mexico Museum of Natural History** 1801 Mountain Rd NW — Albuquerque NM 87104-1375
505 667-4444 **Bradbury Science Museum** Diamond Dr MS-M897 — Los Alamos NM 87545-0001
505 662-6272 **Los Alamos Historical Museum** 1921 Juniper St 3rd Fl — Los Alamos NM 87544-3026
505 624-6744 **Roswell Museum & Art Center** 100 W 11th St — Roswell NM 88201-4998
505 827-8350 **Museum of International Folk Art** PO Box 2087 — Santa Fe NM 87504-2087
505 827-6450 **Museum of New Mexico** PO Box 2087 — Santa Fe NM 87504-2087
505 982-4636 **Wheelwright Museum of the American Indian** PO Box 5153 — Santa Fe NM 87502-5153

NEW YORK

607 772-0660 **Roberson Center for the Arts & Sciences** 30 Front St — Binghamton NY 13905-4779
718 638-5000 **Brooklyn Museum** 200 Eastern Pkwy — Brooklyn NY 11238-6052
716 882-8700 **Albright-Knox Art Gallery** 1285 Elmwood Ave — Buffalo NY 14222-1096
716 873-9644 **Buffalo & Erie County Historical Society** 25 Nottingham Ct — Buffalo NY 14216-3119
716 896-5200 **Buffalo Museum of Science** 1020 Humboldt Pkwy — Buffalo NY 14211-1208
607 937-5371 **Corning Museum of Glass** 1 Museum Way — Corning NY 14830-2253
518 792-1761 **Hyde Collection** 161 Warren St — Glens Falls NY 12801-4520
607 255-6464 **Johnson Herbert F Museum of Art** Cornell University — Ithaca NY 14853-0001
212 956-3535 **American Craft Museum** 40 W 53rd St — New York NY 10019-6112
212 769-5000 **American Museum of Natural History** Central Pk W & 79th St — New York NY 10024-5192
212 234-3130 **American Numismatic Society Museum** Broadway & 155th St — New York NY 10032-7598
212 860-6868 **Cooper-Hewitt Museum (Smithsonian Institution)** 2 E 91st St — New York NY 10128-0669
212 288-0700 **Frick Collection** 1 E 70th St — New York NY 10021-4907
212 860-1889 **Jewish Museum** 1109 5th Ave — New York NY 10128-0118
212 879-5500 **Metropolitan Museum of Art** 1000 5th Ave — New York NY 10028-0198
212 708-9400 **Museum of Modern Art** 11 W 53rd St — New York NY 10019-5498
212 534-1672 **Museum of the City of New York** 5th Ave & 103rd St — New York NY 10029-0000
212 283-2420 **National Museum of the American Indian** Broadway & 155th St — New York NY 10032-0000
212 873-3400 **New York Historical Society Museum** 170 Central Pk W — New York NY 10024-5194
212 685-0008 **Pierpont Morgan Library** 29 E 36th St — New York NY 10016-3490
212 360-3500 **Solomon R Guggenheim Museum** 1071 5th Ave — New York NY 10128-0173
212 570-3600 **Whitney Museum of American Art** 945 Madison Ave — New York NY 10021-2790
716 278-1780 **Schoellkopf Geological Museum** Prospect Pk Niagara Reservation — Niagara Falls NY 14303-0000
607 432-4200 **Museums at Hartwick** Hartwick College — Oneonta NY 13820-1764
516 727-2881 **Suffolk County Historical Society** 300 W Main St — Riverhead NY 11901-2894
716 473-7720 **Memorial Art Gallery** 500 University Ave University of Rochester — Rochester NY 14607-1415
716 271-4320 **Rochester Museum & Science Center** 657 East Ave — Rochester NY 14603-0000
518 382-7890 **Schenectady Museum & Planetarium** Nott Terrace Heights — Schenectady NY 12308-3198
718 727-1135 **Staten Island Institute of Arts & Sciences** 75 Stuyvesant Pl — Staten Island NY 10301-1998
516 751-0066 **Museums at Stony Brook** 1208 Rt 25A — Stony Brook NY 11790-1992
315 474-6064 **Everson Museum of Art** 401 Harrison St — Syracuse NY 13202-3091
315 797-0000 **Williams Munson Proctor Institute Museum of Art** 310 Genesee St — Utica NY 13502-4764
315 782-3491 **Jefferson County Historical Society** 228 Washington St — Watertown NY 13601-3379

NORTH CAROLINA

704 253-3227 **Asheville Art Museum** Asheville Civic Ctr — Asheville NC 28801-4556
704 254-7162 **Coburn Memorial Mineral Museum** Asheville Civic Ctr — Asheville NC 28801-0000
704 298-7928 **Folk Art Center** PO Box 9545 — Asheville NC 28815-0545
704 337-2000 **Mint Museum of Art** 2730 Randolph Rd — Charlotte NC 28207-2031
704 372-6261 **Nature Museum** 1658 Sterling Rd — Charlotte NC 28209-1599
704 497-3481 **Museum of the Cherokee Indian** PO Box 1599 — Cherokee NC 28719-0000
919 684-5135 **Duke University Museum of Art** College Stn — Durham NC 27708-0000
704 866-6900 **Schiele Museum of Natural History & Planetarium** 1500 E Garrison Blvd — Gastonia NC 28054-5199
919 373-2043 **Greensboro Historical Museum** 130 Summit Ave — Greensboro NC 27401-3016
919 758-1946 **Greenville Museum of Art** 802 S Evans St — Greenville NC 27834-3268
919 833-1935 **North Carolina Museum of Art** 2110 Blue Ridge Blvd — Raleigh NC 27607-6494
919 733-7450 **North Carolina State Museum of Natural Science** 102 N Salisbury St — Raleigh NC 27611-0000
919 759-5282 **Museum of Anthropology** Wake Forest University — Winston-Salem NC 27109-0000
919 767-6730 **Nature Science Center** Museum Dr — Winston-Salem NC 27105-0000

NORTH DAKOTA

701 224-2666 **State Historical Society of North Dakota** 612 E Boulevard Ave North Dakota Heritage Ctr — Bismarck ND 58505-0001
701 282-2822 **Red River & Northern Plains Regional Museum** PO Box 719 — West Fargo ND 58078-0719

OHIO

216 376-9185 **Akron Art Museum** 70 E Market St — Akron OH 44308-2084
513 721-5204 **Cincinnati Art Museum** 958 Eden Park Dr — Cincinnati OH 45202-0000
513 287-7000 **Cincinnati Museum of Natural History** 1301 Western Ave Museum Ctr — Cincinnati OH 45203-0000
513 241-0343 **Taft Museum** 316 Pike St — Cincinnati OH 45202-4293
216 231-5010 **Cleveland Health Education Museum** 8911 Euclid Ave — Cleveland OH 44106-2039
216 421-7340 **Cleveland Museum of Art** 11150 East Blvd — Cleveland OH 44106-1797
216 231-4600 **Cleveland Museum of Natural History** Wade Oval University Cir — Cleveland OH 44106-1797
216 368-3648 **Dittrick Museum of Medical History** 11000 Euclid Ave — Cleveland OH 44106-1714
216 721-5722 **Western Reserve Historical Society Museum & Library** 10825 East Blvd — Cleveland OH 44106-1788
614 221-6801 **Columbus Museum of Art** 480 E Broad St — Columbus OH 43215-3886
614 228-2674 **Ohio's Center of Science & Industry** 280 E Broad St — Columbus OH 43215-3773
513 223-5277 **Dayton Art Institute** Forest & Riverview Aves — Dayton OH 45405-0000
513 275-7431 **Dayton Museum of Natural History** 2629 Ridge Ave — Dayton OH 45414-5499
419 255-8000 **Toledo Museum of Art** 2445 Monroe St — Toledo OH 43620-1517
216 743-1711 **Butler Institute of American Art** 524 Wick Ave — Youngstown OH 44502-1213

OKLAHOMA

918 336-0307 **Woolaroc Museum** State Hwy 123 — Bartlesville OK 74003-0000

405 258-2425 **Lincoln County Historical Society Museum of Pioneer History**
PO Box 458 .... Chandler OK 74834-0458
405 282-1889 **Oklahoma Territorial Museum** 402 E Oklahoma Ave .... Guthrie OK 73044-3317
918 683-1701 **Five Civilized Tribes Museum** Honor Heights Dr .... Muskogee OK 74401-0000
405 325-4711 **Oklahoma Museum of Natural History** 1335 Asp Ave .... Norman OK 73019-0001
405 325-3272 **University of Oklahoma Museum of Art** 410 W Boyd St .... Norman OK 73019-0001
405 427-5461 **Kirkpatrick Center Museum Complex** 2100 NE 52nd St .. Oklahoma City OK 73111-7107
405 521-2491 **State Museum of History** 2100 N Lincoln Blvd .... Oklahoma City OK 73105-4915
918 582-3122 **Gilcrease Thomas Institute of American History & Art**
1400 Gilcrease Museum Rd .... Tulsa OK 74127-2100
918 749-7941 **Philbrook Museum of Art** 2727 S Rockford Rd .... Tulsa OK 74114-4104

OREGON

503 325-2323 **Columbia River Maritime Museum** 1792 Marine Dr .... Astoria OR 97103-3525
503 346-3027 **University of Oregon Museum of Art** University of Oregon .... Eugene OR 97403-1205
503 883-4208 **Klamath County Museum** 1451 Main St .... Klamath Falls OR 97601-5989
503 226-2811 **Oregon Art Institute** 1219 SW Park Ave .... Portland OR 97205-2486
503 222-1741 **Oregon Historical Society Museum** 1230 SW Park Ave .... Portland OR 97205-2483
503 222-2828 **Oregon Museum of Science & Industry** 4015 SW Canyon Rd ... Portland OR 97221-2705
503 842-4553 **Tillamook County Pioneer Museum** 2106 2nd St .... Tillamook OR 97141-2399

PENNSYLVANIA

717 787-4980 **State Museum of Pennsylvania** 3rd & North Sts .... Harrisburg PA 17101-1819
717 291-3941 **North Museum Franklin & Marshall College** PO Box 3003 ... Lancaster PA 17604-3003
215 299-1000 **Academy of Natural Sciences Museum**
19th & Ben Franklin Pkwy .... Philadelphia PA 19103-0000
215 922-3031 **Atwater Kent Museum-History Museum of Philadelphia**
15 S 7th St .... Philadelphia PA 19106-2313
215 448-1200 **Franklin Institute Science Museum & Planetarium**
20th St & Benjamin Franklin Pkwy .... Philadelphia PA 19103-0000
215 895-2424 **Museum at Drexel University** 32nd & Chestnut Sts .... Philadelphia PA 19104-2884
215 763-8100 **Philadelphia Museum of Art**
26th & Benjamin Franklin Pkwy .... Philadelphia PA 19130-2399
215 787-5476 **Rodin Museum** 22nd & Benjamin Franklin Pkwy .... Philadelphia PA 19130-0000
215 898-4000 **University Museum of Archaeology & Anthropology**
33rd & Spruce Sts University of Pennsylvania .... Philadelphia PA 19104-6324
412 622-3200 **Carnegie Museum of Art** 4400 Forbes Ave .... Pittsburgh PA 15213-4080
412 622-3243 **Carnegie Museum of Natural History** 4400 Forbes Ave .... Pittsburgh PA 15213-4080
412 281-9284 **Fort Pitt Museum** 101 Commonwealth Pl .... Pittsburgh PA 15222-0000
412 371-0600 **Frick Art Museum** 7227 Reynolds St .... Pittsburgh PA 15208-2923
215 371-5850 **Reading Public Museum & Art Gallery** 500 Museum Rd .... Reading PA 19611-1425

RHODE ISLAND

401 253-8388 **Haffenreffer Museum of Anthropology**
Mt Hope Grant Brown University .... Bristol RI 02809-0000
401 847-0179 **Newport Art Museum** 76 Bellevue Ave .... Newport RI 02840-7405
401 846-0813 **Newport Historical Society** 82 Touro St .... Newport RI 02840-2978
401 331-3511 **Museum of Art-Rhode Island School of Design**
224 Benefit St .... Providence RI 02903-2711
401 331-8575 **Rhode Island Historical Society Museum**
110 Benevolent St .... Providence RI 02906-3152

SOUTH CAROLINA

803 722-2996 **Charleston Museum** 360 Meeting St .... Charleston SC 29403-6297
803 722-2706 **Gibbes Museum of Art** 135 Meeting St .... Charleston SC 29401-2217
803 799-2810 **Columbia Museum of Art** 1112 Bull St .... Columbia SC 29201-3703
803 777-7251 **McKissick Museum** University of South Carolina .... Columbia SC 29208-0001
803 737-4921 **South Carolina State Museum** 301 Gervais St .... Columbia SC 29202-0000
803 242-5100 **Bob Jones University Collection of Sacred Art**
1700 Wade Hampton .... Greenville SC 29614-0001
803 271-7570 **Greenville County Museum of Art** 420 College St .... Greenville SC 29601-2017

SOUTH DAKOTA

605 688-5423 **South Dakota Art Museum** Medary Ave & Harvey Dunn St ..... Brookings SD 57007-0001
605 773-3458 **Robinson State Museum** 900 Governors Dr .... Pierre SD 57501-2200
605 394-2467 **Museum of Geology**
501 E Saint Joseph St South Dakota School of Mines .... Rapid City SD 57701-3901
605 335-4210 **Siouxland Heritage Museums** 200 W 6th St .... Sioux Falls SD 57102-0302
605 677-5228 **Overstate WH Museum** 414 E Clark St .... Vermillion SD 57069-2307
605 677-5306 **Shrine to Music Museum** 414 E Clark St .... Vermillion SD 57069-0000

TENNESSEE

615 267-0968 **Hunter Museum of Art** 10 Bluff View .... Chattanooga TN 37403-1197
615 929-4392 **Reese B Carroll Museum** PO Box 22300A .... Johnson City TN 37614-1000
615 974-2144 **McClung Frank H Museum**
1327 Circle Park Dr University of Tennessee .... Knoxville TN 37996-0001
901 722-3525 **Memphis Brooks Museum of Art** Overton Pk .... Memphis TN 38112-5497
901 320-6320 **Memphis Pink Palace Museum & Planetarium**
3050 Central Ave .... Memphis TN 38111-3399
615 356-8000 **Tennessee Botanical Gardens & Fine Arts Center**
Forrest Park Dr .... Nashville TN 37205-0000
615 741-2692 **Tennessee State Museum** 505 Deaderick St .... Nashville TN 37243-1120
615 576-3200 **American Museum of Science & Energy** 300 S Tulane Ave ... Oak Ridge TN 37830-6726

TEXAS

512 471-7324 **Huntington Archer M Art Gallery**
23rd & San Jacinto Sts University of Texas .... Austin TX 78712-0000
806 656-2244 **Panhandle-Plains Historical Museum** 2401 4th Ave .... Canyon TX 79015-4143
512 884-3844 **Art Museum of South Texas** 1902 N Shoreline Rd .... Corpus Christi TX 78401-1164
214 922-1200 **Dallas Museum of Art** 1717 N Harwood St .... Dallas TX 75201-2398
214 670-8460 **Dallas Museum of Natural History** PO Box 26193 .... Dallas TX 75226-0193
214 692-2516 **Meadows Museum**
Owen Fine Arts Ctr Southern Methodist University .... Dallas TX 75275-0001
214 428-8351 **Southwest Museum of Science & Technology**
1st & Martin Luther King Jr Aves .... Dallas TX 75223-0000
915 541-4040 **El Paso Museum of Art** 1211 Montana Ave .... El Paso TX 79902-5588
817 738-1933 **Carter Amon Museum** 3501 Camp Bowie Blvd .... Fort Worth TX 76107-2695
817 732-1631 **Fort Worth Museum of Science & History**
1501 Montgomery St .... Fort Worth TX 76107-3017
817 332-8451 **Kimball Art Museum** 3333 Camp Bowie Blvd .... Fort Worth TX 76107-2792
817 738-9215 **Modern Art Museum of Fort Worth** 1309 Montgomery St ... Fort Worth TX 76107-3080
713 526-0773 **Contemporary Arts Museum** 5216 Montrose Blvd .... Houston TX 77006-6598
713 639-4600 **Houston Museum of Natural Science** 1 Hermann Circle Dr ... Houston TX 77030-1799
713 526-1361 **Museum of Fine Arts** 1001 Bissonnet St .... Houston TX 77005-1896
713 483-4241 **NASA Lyndon B Johnson Space Center** 2101 NASA Rd 1 ... Houston TX 77058-0000
512 824-5368 **McNay Marion Koogler Art Museum**
6000 N New Braunfels .... San Antonio TX 78209-4618
512 226-5544 **San Antonio Museum of Art** PO Box 2601 .... San Antonio TX 78299-2601
512 226-5544 **Witte Museum** 3801 Broadway .... San Antonio TX 78209-6396

UTAH

801 581-7332 **Utah Museum of Fine Arts**
101 Art & Architecture Ctr University of Utah .... Salt Lake City UT 84112-0000
801 581-6927 **Utah Museum of Natural History** University of Utah ...... Salt Lake City UT 84112-1107
801 489-9434 **Springville Museum of Art** PO Box 509 .... Springville UT 84663-0509
801 789-3799 **Utah Field House of Natural History State Park** 235 E Main St ... Vernal UT 84078-2605

VERMONT

802 447-1571 **Bennington Museum** W Main St .... Bennington VT 05201-2194
802 656-0750 **Fleming Robert Hull Museum**
Colchester Ave University of Vermont .... Burlington VT 05405-0001
802 828-2291 **Vermont Museum** 109 State St .... Montpelier VT 05602-2710
802 748-2372 **Fairbanks Museum of Natural Science & Planetarium**
Main St .... Saint Johnsbury VT 05819-2295
802 985-3346 **Shelburne Museum** US Rt 7 .... Shelburne VT 05482-0000

VIRGINIA

804 595-0368 **Mariners' Museum** 100 Museum Dr .... Newport News VA 23606-3757
804 622-1211 **Chrysler Museum** Olney Rd & Mowbray Arch .... Norfolk VA 23510-1587
804 367-1522 **Anderson Gallery**
907 1/2 W Franklin St Virginia Commonwealth University ...... Richmond VA 23284-0001
804 649-1861 **Museum of the Confederacy** 1201 E Clay St .... Richmond VA 23219-1615
804 649-0711 **Valentine Museum** 1015 E Clay St .... Richmond VA 23219-1590
804 367-0844 **Virginia Museum of Fine Arts** 2800 Grove Ave .... Richmond VA 23221-2472
703 342-5760 **Roanoke Museum of Fine Arts** 1 Market Sq .... Roanoke VA 24011-1417
703 342-5710 **Science Museum of Western Virginia** 1 Market Sq .... Roanoke VA 24011-1417
804 220-7671 **Abbey Rockefeller Folk Art Center** 307 S England St .... Williamsburg VA 23185-0000
804 229-1000 **Colonial Williamsburg Foundation** PO Box C .... Williamsburg VA 23187-3707
804 221-2700 **Muscarelle Museum of Art** College of William & Mary ...... Williamsburg VA 23185-0000

WASHINGTON

206 753-2580 **Washington State Capital Museum** 211 W 21st Ave .... Olympia WA 98501-0000
206 543-5590 **Burke Thomas Memorial Museum**
University of Washington DB-10 .... Seattle WA 98195-0001
206 622-9250 **Frye Charles & Emma Art Museum** PO Box 3005 .... Seattle WA 98114-3005
206 543-2280 **Henry Art Gallery** University of Washington DE-15 .... Seattle WA 98195-0001
206 324-1125 **Museum of History & Industry** 2700 24th Ave E .... Seattle WA 98112-2099
206 443-2001 **Pacific Science Center** 200 2nd Ave N .... Seattle WA 98109-4895
206 625-8900 **Seattle Art Museum** 1400 E Prospect St .... Seattle WA 98112-3303
509 456-3931 **Cowles Cheney Museum** W 2316 1st Ave .... Spokane WA 99204-1099
206 272-4258 **Tacoma Art Museum** 1123 Pacific Ave .... Tacoma WA 98402-4399
206 593-2830 **Washington State Historical Society Museum**
315 N Stadium Way .... Tacoma WA 98403-3226

WEST VIRGINIA

304 344-8035 **Sunrise Museums** 746 Myrtle Rd .... Charleston WV 25314-1152
304 348-0230 **West Virginia State Museum** Capitol Complex Cultural Ctr ... Charleston WV 25305-0001
304 529-2701 **Huntington Museum of Art** 2033 McCoy Rd .... Huntington WV 25701-4999

WISCONSIN

608 356-8341 **Circus World Museum** 426 Water St .... Baraboo WI 53913-2597
414 436-3767 **Neville Public Museum of Brown County** 210 Museum Pl ..... Green Bay WI 54303-2780
414 656-8026 **Kenosha Public Museum** 5608 10th Ave .... Kenosha WI 53140-4091
608 263-2246 **Elvehjem Museum of Art**
800 University Ave University of Wisconsin .... Madison WI 53706-0001
608 262-7700 **State Historical Museum of Wisconsin** 30 N Carroll St .... Madison WI 53703-2707
414 765-9966 **Discovery World Museum of Science Economics & Technology**
818 W Wisconsin Ave .... Milwaukee WI 53233-2309
414 271-9508 **Milwaukee Art Museum** 750 N Lincoln Memorial Dr .... Milwaukee WI 53202-4077
414 273-8288 **Milwaukee County Historical Society Museum**
910 N Old World 3rd St .... Milwaukee WI 53203-1501
414 278-2702 **Milwaukee Public Museum** 800 W Wells St .... Milwaukee WI 53233-1478
414 426-4800 **Experimental Aircraft Assn Air Adventure Museum**
3000 Poberezny Rd .... Oshkosh WI 54903-0000
414 236-5150 **Oshkosh Public Museum** 1331 Algoma Blvd .... Oshkosh WI 54901-2799

WYOMING

307 777-7022 **Wyoming State Museum** 2301 Central Ave 1st Fl .... Cheyenne WY 82002-0001
307 587-4771 **Buffalo Bill Historical Center** 720 Sheridan Ave .... Cody WY 82414-3428
307 875-2611 **Sweetwater County Historical Museum**
50 W Flaming Gorge Way .... Green River WY 82935-4235
307 332-4137 **Fremont County Pioneer Museum** 630 Lincoln St .... Lander WY 82520-2732
307 766-4218 **Geological Museum** University of Wyoming .... Laramie WY 82070-3404
307 742-4448 **Laramie Plains Museum** 603 Ivinson St .... Laramie WY 82070-3243

TOLL-FREE NUMBERS

Government and Social Services

Services are listed alphabetically. Most toll-free numbers can be dialed nationwide. If not, a toll number is also listed.

Abortion Alternative	800 848-5683
Alzheimers Assn	800 621-0379
Within IL	800 572-6037
America the Beautiful Fund	800 522-3557
Within DC	202 638-1649
American Assn on Mental Retardation	800 424-3688
Within DC	202 387-1968
American Council of the Blind	800 424-8666
Within DC	202 467-5081
American Kidney Fund	800 638-8299
Within MD	800 492-8361
American Speech-Language-Hearing Assn	800 638-8255
Within MD	301 897-8682
American Trauma Society	800 556-7890
Amtrak	800 872-7245
APA Spinal Cord Injuries Hotline	800 526-3456
Assn for Advanced Training in Behavioral Science	800 472-1931
Within CA	800 472-1932
Associated Media Production Services	800 334-4373
Auto Safety Hotline	800 424-9393
Aviation Safety Institute	800 848-7386
Within OH	614 885-4242
Bethany Christian Services	800 238-4269
Better Hearing Institute	800 424-8576
Within VA	703 642-0580
Chemical Referral Center	800 262-8200
Within DC	202 887-1318
Childfind	800 426-5678
Childhelp's National Child Abuse Hotline	800 422-4453
Collins Kevin Foundation for Missing Children	800 272-0012
Combat Support Branch US Army Reserve	800 325-4095
Within MO	314 263-7425
Commission on Civil Rights	
Complaints	800 552-6843
Conservation & Renewal Energy Hotline	800 523-2929
Consumer Product Safety Commission	800 638-2772
Cuban Haitian Entrant Program US Justice Dept	800 424-9304
Within MD	301 492-5818
Defense Hotline	800 424-9098
Within DC	800 693-5080
Defense Personnel Support Center	800 523-0705
Department of Agriculture Fraud Hotline	800 424-9121
Within DC	202 472-1388
Department of Agriculture Meat & Poultry Hotline	800 535-4555
Within DC	202 447-3333
Department of Commerce	
Inspector General	800 424-5197
Within DC	202 377-4661
Department of Defense Fraud Hotline	800 424-9098
Department of Defense Nuclear Agency	800 462-3683
Department of Education Student Loan Collections	800 227-3237
Within CA	800 652-1780
Department of Housing & Urban Development	800 424-8590
Director of Officer Personnel Management	800 325-4740
Discrimination Complaint Hotline	800 424-8590
Within DC	202 426-3500
Edna Gladney Center	
Maternity	800 433-2922
Within TX	800 772-2740
Enlisted Combat Arms Div	800 325-1878
Within MO	314 263-7585
Environmental Protection Agency	800 424-4000
Within DC & VA	703 557-1938
Personnel	800 382-3305
Fair Oaks Hospital	800 672-1907
Cocaine Help Line	800 262-2463
Federal Election Commission	800 424-9530
Fraud Hotline	800 424-9121
Within DC	202 472-1388
Friends of Animals Inc	800 631-2212
General Accounting Office Fraud Hotline	800 424-5454
General Health Inc	800 424-2775
General Services Administration Fraud Hotline	800 424-5210
Inspector General Fraud Hotline	800 424-5409
Within DC	202 357-0227
Interface Action For Economic Justice	800 424-7290
Within DC	202 543-2800
International Service Agencies	800 638-8079
Within MD	301 881-2468
International SOS Assistance Inc	800 523-8930
Juvenile Diabetes Foundation International	800 223-1138
Within NY	212 889-7575
Life-Cycle Learning Inc	800 526-2287
Lifeline Systems Inc	800 451-0525
Living Bank	800 528-2971
Maryland Port Administration	800 638-7519
Within MD	301 333-4450
Minnesota Dept of Trade & Economic Development	800 652-9747
Missing Children Help Center	800 872-5437
Within FL	813 623-5437
National Abortion Federation Hotline	800 772-9100
Within DC	202 667-5881
National Academy of Medical Hypnosis	800 241-1472
National Center for Missing & Exploited Children	800 843-5678
National Civic League	800 223-6004
Within CO	303 832-5615
National Committee for Citizens in Education	800 638-9675
Within MD	301 997-9300
National Downs Syndrome Congress	800 232-6372
National Downs Syndrome Society	800 221-4602
National Flood Insurance Program	800 638-6620
National Futures Assn	
Info	800 621-3570
Within IL	800 572-9400
National Health Information Center	800 336-4797
Within MD	301 565-4167
National Health Service Scholarship Program	800 638-0824
Within MD	301 443-3744
National Hearing Aid Society	800 521-5247

National Highway Traffic Safety Administration	
Auto Safety Hotline	800 424-9393
Within DC	202 366-0123
National Literacy Hotline	800 228-8813
National Response Center	800 424-8802
Within DC	202 267-2675
National Reye's Syndrome Foundation	800 233-7393
Within OH	800 231-7393
National Technical Information Service	
Orders	800 336-4700
NEAR (Nationwide Emergency Ambulance Return)	800 654-6700
Nevada Commission on Economic Development	800 336-1600
Within NV	702 687-4325
Office of Refugee Resettlement	800 327-3463
Within FL	800 432-0908
Office of the Inspector General Hotline	800 424-5081
Orton Dyslexia Society	800 222-3123
Within MD	301 296-0232
Outward Bound USA	800 243-8520
Within CT	203 661-0797
Parkinson's Educational Program	800 344-7872
Peace Corps DC Area Office	800 424-8580
PMS Access	800 222-4767
Retinitis Pigmentosa Foundation	800 638-2300
Runaway Hotline	800 231-6946
Within TX	800 392-3352
Sales Education Institute	800 647-9166
Within TN	901 767-5700
Second Opinion Surgery Hotline	800 638-6833
Within MD	800 492-6603
Social Security Administration Region 4	
Cust Svc	800 234-5772
Social Security Administration Region 5	800 234-5772
Social Studies School Service	800 421-4246
Society of American Military Engineers	800 336-3097
Within VA	703 549-3800
UN Children's Fund (UNICEF)	
Orders	800 553-1200
United Scleroderma Foundation Inc	800 722-4673
Within CA	408 728-2202
United Student Aid Funds Inc	
Cust Svc	800 824-7044
US Air Force Fraud Waste & Abuse Hotline	800 538-8429
Within VA	800 468-6661
US Air Force Voluntary Reserve Officer Recall	800 531-5809
Within TX	800 292-5355
US Army Office of Inspector General	800 446-9000
US Army Personnel Management	800 325-4895
Within MO	314 263-7872
Armor	800 325-4953
Within MO	314 263-7874
Artillery	800 325-4950
Within MO	314 263-7871
Aviation	800 325-4382
Within MO	800 325-4950
Civil Affairs	800 562-3349
Within MO	314 263-7817
Colonels	800 325-4387
Within MO	314 263-7431
Infantry	800 325-4882
Within MO	314 263-7812
Lieutenants	800 325-4389
Within MO	314 263-7288
Medical Service Corp	800 325-4973
Within MO	314 263-7885
Military Police	800 325-4986
Within MO	314 263-7826
Overseas	800 325-1868
Warrant Officers	800 325-4361
Within MO	314 263-7763
US Army Reserve Personnel Center	800 325-4985
Adjutant General	800 325-4981
Armor Branch	800 325-4953
Within MO	314 263-7883
Chaplain Branch	800 325-4914
Within MO	314 263-7500
Judge Advocate General	800 325-4916
Nurse Branch	800 325-4912
OCONUS Branch	800 325-1868
Within MO	314 263-7602
Quartermaster	800 325-4957
Within MO	314 263-7844
Transportation	800 325-4980
Within MO	314 623-7846
US Army Retired Activities CFSC-FSR	800 336-4909
US Coast Guard	
Boating Safety	800 368-5647
Within DC	202 267-0780
Recruiting	800 424-8883
US Dept of Veterans Affairs	202 233-4010
Within AK	800 478-2500
Within AL	800 392-8054
Within AR	800 482-5434
Within AZ	800 352-0451
Within CA Northern	800 652-1240
Within CA Southern	800 532-3811
Within CO	800 332-6742
Within CT	800 842-4315
Within DE	800 292-7855
Within FL	800 282-8821
Within GA	800 282-0232
Within HI	800 232-2535
Within IA	800 362-2222
Within ID	800 632-2003
Within IL	800 972-5327
Within IN	800 382-4540
Within KS	800 362-2444
Within KY	800 292-4562
Within LA	800 462-9510
Within MA	800 392-6015
Within MD	800 492-9503
Within ME	800 452-1935
Within MI	800 827-1996
Within MN	800 692-2121
Within MO	800 392-3761
Within MS	800 682-5270

Government and Social Services

Within MT	800 332-6125
Within NC	800 642-0841
Within ND	800 342-4790
Within NE	800 742-7554
Within NH	800 562-5260
Within NJ	800 242-5867
Within NM	800 432-6853
Within NV	800 992-5740
Within NY Southern	800 442-5882
Within NY Western	800 462-1130
Within OH	800 827-8272
Within OK	800 482-2800
Within OR	800 452-7276
Within PA Eastern	800 822-3920
Within PA Western	800 242-0233
Within RI	800 322-0230
Within SC	800 922-1000
Within SD	800 952-3550
Within TN	800 342-8330
Within TX Northern	800 392-2200
Within TX Southern	800 792-3271
Within UT	800 662-9163
Within VA	800 542-5826
Within VT	800 622-4134
Within WA	800 552-7480
Within WI	800 242-9025
Within WV	800 642-3520
Within WY	800 442-2761
US General Svcs Administration Inspector General	800 424-5210
Within DC	202 501-0450
US Government Student Loans Collection	800 621-3115
Within IL	800 972-3189
US Marine Corps Reserve Support Center	800 255-5082
US Navy Recruiting District	
Enlisted Programs	800 228-4022
Officer Programs	800 228-4036
Vanished Children's Alliance	800 826-4743
Women's Community Health Center	800 666-7247
Within ME	207 773-7247
World Vision	800 423-4200

TRAVEL

Tourist and Travel Information

Agencies offering information on popular travel destinations are listed alphabetically.

212 949-4242 **AFS International Intercultural Programs** 313 E 43rd St ...... New York NY 10017-4809
205 242-4169 **Alabama Bureau of Tourism & Travel** 532 S Perry St .... Montgomery AL 36104-4616
Resv: 800 252-2262
907 465-2010 **Alaska Div of Tourism** 333 Willoughby Ave .... Juneau AK 99811-0001
213 641-0030 **American Tourist Bureau** 6045 W Century Blvd Suite 720 ...Los Angeles CA 90045-5309
Resv: 800 569-8785
602 542-3618 **Arizona Office of Tourism** 1100 W Washington St .... Phoenix AZ 85007-2939
501 682-7777 **Arkansas Div of Parks & Tourism** 1 Capitol Mall .... Little Rock AR 72201-1087
303 925-4000 **Aspen Reservations Inc** 517 E Hopkins Ave Suite 203 .... Aspen CO 81611-2951
Resv: 800 872-7547
303 925-9500 **Aspen Ski Tours** 300 S Spring St .... Aspen CO 81611-2085
Resv: 800 525-8149
212 687-6300 **Australian Tourist Commission** 489 5th Ave .... New York NY 10017-6182
212 944-6880 **Austrian National Tourist Office** 500 5th Ave .... New York NY 10110-0199
212 286-9600 **Brazil Tourism** 551 5th Ave Suite 915 .... New York NY 10176-0000
212 581-4708 **British Tourist Authority** 40 W 57th St Suite 320 .... New York NY 10019-4096
916 322-2881 **California Office of Tourism** 1121 L St Suite 103 .... Sacramento CA 95814-3926
Resv: 800 862-2543
202 452-1270 **Capitol Reservations**
1730 Rhode Island Ave NW Suite 302 .... Washington DC 20036-3101
Resv: 800 847-4832
708 699-7570 **Caribbean Information Office** 3166 S River Rd Suite 33 ...... Des Plaines IL 60018-4204
Resv: 800 621-1270
804 253-2277 **Colonial Williamsburg Reservation Center**
102 Visitors Center Dr .... Williamsburg VA 23187-0000
Resv: 800 447-8679
303 592-5410 **Colorado Tourism Board** 1625 Broadway Suite 1700 .... Denver CO 80202-4734
Resv: 800 433-2656
203 258-4286 **Connecticut Tourism Div** 865 Brook St .... Rocky Hill CT 06067-3405
302 739-4271 **Delaware Tourism Office** 99 Kings Hwy .... Dover DE 19901-3816
Resv: 800 441-8846
904 487-0162 **Florida Div of Tourism** 107 W Gaines St Rm 505 .... Tallahassee FL 32399-2000
212 757-1125 **French Government Tourist Office** 610 5th Ave .... New York NY 10020-2493
305 923-2808 **Fun in the Sun Yacht Charters** 320 N Federal Hwy .... Dania FL 33004-2808
Resv: 800 327-0228
404 656-3553 **Georgia Dept of Industry Trade & Tourism**
285 Peachtree Ctr Ave NE Marquis Tower II Suite 1000 ...... Atlanta GA 30303-1505
212 308-3300 **German National Tourist Office** 747 3rd Ave ....New York NY 10017-2852
808 548-7700 **Hawaii Dept of Business Economic Development & Tourism**
737 Bishop St Grosvenor Center Mauka Tower Suite 1900 .... Honolulu HI 96813-0000
803 785-9050 **Hilton Head Central Reservations** 3 Towne Ctr ....Hilton Head Island SC 29928-0000
Resv: 800 845-7018
501 321-2277 **Hot Springs Tourist Information** 134 Convention Blvd .... Hot Springs AR 71901-4135
Resv: 800 543-2284
713 523-5050 **Houston Convention & Visitors Bureau** 3300 Main St .... Houston TX 77002-9319
Resv: 800 231-7799
208 334-2017 **Idaho Tourism Div** 700 W State St 2nd Fl .... Boise ID 83720-0001
Resv: 800 635-7820
312 793-2094 **Illinois Tourist Informational Center** 310 S Michigan .... Chicago IL 60604-4287
Resv: 800 223-0121
317 232-8860 **Indiana Dept of Commerce Tourism & Film Development Div**
1 N Capitol Ave Suite 700 .... Indianapolis IN 46204-2026
515 281-3100 **Iowa Div of Tourism** 200 E Grand Ave .... Des Moines IA 50309-1827
Resv: 800 345-4692
212 418-0800 **Irish Tourist Board** 757 3rd Ave .... New York NY 10017-2082
Resv: 800 223-6470
212 245-4822 **Italian Government Travel Office** 630 5th Ave 15th Fl ...... New York NY 10111-0100
305 667-1774 **Jamaica Reservation Service Inc** 1320 S Dixie Hwy Suite 1102 .. Miami FL 33146-2903
Resv: 800 526-2422
212 757-5640 **Japanese National Tourist Organization**
630 5th Ave Suite 2101 .... New York NY 10111-0007
913 296-2009 **Kansas Div of Travel & Tourism** 400 SW 8th St 5th Fl .... Topeka KS 66603-0000
Resv: 800 252-6727
502 564-4930 **Kentucky Dept of Travel Development**
Capital Plaza Tower 22nd Fl .... Frankfort KY 40601-0000
Resv: 800 225-8747
407 847-5000 **Kissimmee Convention & Visitors Bureau** 1925 E 192 Hwy ..Kissimmee FL 34744-0000
Resv: 800 327-9159
518 523-2445 **Lake Placid Commerce & Visitor's Bureau** Olympic Ctr ......Lake Placid NY 12946-0000
Resv: 800 447-5224
916 544-5050 **Lake Tahoe Visitors Authority** PO Box 16299 .... South Lake Tahoe CA 95706-0299
Resv: 800 288-2463
504 342-8119 **Louisiana Office of Tourism** 900 Riverside St N .... Baton Rouge LA 70802-5236
Resv: 800 334-8620
207 289-5710 **Maine Div of Tourism** 189 State St .... Augusta ME 04333-0001
207 288-3395 **Marine Atlantic** 121 Eden St .... Bar Harbor ME 04609-1137
Resv: 800 341-7981
301 333-6611 **Maryland Office of Tourist Development**
217 E Redwood St 9th Fl .... Baltimore MD 21202-3316
617 727-3205 **Massachusetts Office of Travel & Tourism**
100 Cambridge St 13th Fl .... Boston MA 02202-0001
Resv: 800 447-6277
517 373-0670 **Michigan Travel Bureau** 333 S Capitol Ave Suite F .... Lansing MI 48933-2022
Resv: 800 543-2937
612 296-5029 **Minnesota Office of Tourism** 375 Jackson St Suite 250 .... Saint Paul MN 55101-1810
Resv: 800 657-3700
601 359-3297 **Mississippi Tourism Div** 550 High St Suite 1200 .... Jackson MS 39201-1113
Resv: 800 647-2290
314 751-4133 **Missouri Div of Tourism** 301 W High St .... Jefferson City MO 65102-0000
Resv: 800 877-1234
406 444-2654 **Montana Promotion Div** 1424 9th Ave .... Helena MT 59601-4503
Resv: 800 541-1447
402 471-3794 **Nebraska Travel & Tourism Div Department Economic Development**
301 Centennial Mall S .... Lincoln NE 68508-2529
212 370-7367 **Netherlands Board of Tourism** 355 Lexington Ave 21st Fl ...... New York NY 10017-6603
702 687-4322 **Nevada Commission on Tourism** 5151 S Carson St .... Carson City NV 89710-0000
Resv: 800 237-0774
603 271-2666 **New Hampshire Office of Vacation Travel** 105 Loudon Rd ...... Concord NH 03301-5601
609 292-2470 **New Jersey Div of Travel & Tourism** 20 W State St .... Trenton NJ 08625-0001
Resv: 800 537-7397
505 827-0291 **New Mexico Tourism & Travel Div** 1100 St Francis Dr .... Santa Fe NM 87503-0001
Resv: 800 545-2040
518 473-0715 **New York Div of Tourism** 1 Commerce Plaza .... Albany NY 12245-0001
Resv: 800 225-5697
919 733-4171 **North Carolina Travel & Tourism Div** 430 N Salisbury St .... Raleigh NC 27603-6651
701 224-2525 **North Dakota Tourism & Promotion**
604 E Boulevard Ave Liberty Memorial Bldg .... Bismarck ND 58505-0000
708 574-6000 **Official Airline Guides** 2000 Clearwater Dr .... Oak Brook IL 60521-8806
Resv: 800 323-3537
614 466-8844 **Ohio Div of Travel & Tourism** 77 S High St .... Columbus OH 43266-0001
Resv: 800 282-5393

405 521-2413 **Oklahoma Tourism & Recreation Dept**
500 Will Rodgers Bldg .... Oklahoma City OK 73105-440
Resv: 800 652-6552
503 373-1200 **Oregon Tourism Div** 775 Summer St NE .... Salem OR 97310-000
Resv: 800 233-3306
717 787-5453 **Pennsylvania Bureau of Travel Marketing** 453 Forum Bldg .. Harrisburg PA 17120-000
Resv: 800 237-4363
601 446-6631 **Pilgrimage Garden Club (Mississippi)** State & Canal Sts .... Natchez MS 39121-000
Resv: 800 647-6742
401 277-2601 **Rhode Island Tourism & Promotion Div**
7 Jackson Walkway .... Providence RI 02903-362
314 421-1023 **Saint Louis Convention & Visitors Commission**
10 S Broadway Suite 300 .... Saint Louis MO 63102-173
Resv: 800 247-9791
512 270-8700 **San Antonio Convention & Visitors Bureau**
121 Alamo Plaza .... San Antonio TX 78205-260
Resv: 800 447-4557
803 734-0135 **South Carolina Div of Tourism** 1205 Pendleton St .... Columbia SC 29201-3731
605 773-3301 **South Dakota Tourism Div** Capitol Lake Plaza .... Pierre SD 57501-3369
Resv: 800 952-3625
303 879-6000 **Steamboat Resorts** 2700 Village Dr .... Steamboat Springs CO 80487-9004
Resv: 800 332-9595
802 297-2200 **Stratton Mountain Resorts** Stratton Mountain Rd ..... Stratton Mountain VT 05155-0000
Resv: 800 843-6867
305 947-5826 **Sunny Isle Beach Resort Assoc**
3909 Sunny Isles Blvd Suite 307 .... Sunny Isles FL 33160-4126
Resv: 800 327-6366
305 864-0722 **Surfside Tourist Information** 9301 Collins Ave .... Surfside FL 33154-2693
Resv: 800 327-4557
615 741-2159 **Tennessee Dept of Tourist Development** 320 6th Ave N ...... Nashville TN 37219-5605
512 472-5059 **Texas Tourist Div** 816 Congress Ave Suite 1200 .... Austin TX 78701-2443
Resv: 800 888-8839
801 538-1030 **Utah Travel Council** Council Hall Capitol Hill .... Salt Lake City UT 84114-0000
303 571-1833 **Vail Reservations Inc** 292 E Meadow Dr Suite 101 .... Vail CO 81657-3612
Resv: 800 525-8930
802 828-3236 **Vermont Travel Div** 134 State St .... Montpelier VT 05602-2707
804 425-7511 **Virginia Beach Tourist Information** 19th & Pacific Ave ....Virginia Beach VA 23451-3362
Resv: 800 446-8038
804 786-2051 **Virginia Div of Tourism** 1021 E Cary St 14th Fl .... Richmond VA 23219-4000
206 753-5600 **Washington Tourism Development Div**
General Administration Bldg .... Olympia WA 98504-0001
304 348-2200 **West Virginia Tourism & Parks Div** 2101 Washington St E ... Charleston WV 25305-0001
Resv: 800 225-5982
608 266-2147 **Wisconsin Tourism Development**
123 W Washington Ave 6th Fl .... Madison WI 53702-0001
Resv: 800 432-8747
307 777-7777 **Wyoming Tourism & Marketing Div** IH-25 & College Dr .... Cheyenne WY 82002-0001
Resv: 800 225-5996

AREA CODE AND ZIP CODE GUIDE

AREA AND ZIP CODE GUIDE

Cities, selected on the basis of population, are listed alphabetically with corresponding area and zip codes. An "*" denotes that the zip codes listed do not represent a complete list of zip codes for the city indicated. In those cases, the zip codes listed do include the main post office or the main zip code range. ZIP PLUS FOUR: When available, nine-digit zips are shown for listings throughout *The National Directory*. For listings where a nine-digit zip was unavailable, four zeros have been added to the end of the five-digit zip. The zeros should not be used when mailing.

A

205	Abbeville, AL	36310
912	Abbeville, GA	31001
318	Abbeville, LA	70510, 70511
803	Abbeville, SC	29620
316	Abbyville, KS	67510
208	Aberdeen, ID	83210
301	Aberdeen, MD	21001
601	Aberdeen, MS	39730
919	Aberdeen, NC	28315
201	Aberdeen, NJ	07747
605	Aberdeen, SD	57401, 57474
206	Aberdeen, WA	98520
913	Abilene, KS	67410
915	Abilene, TX	79600–79608, 79697–79699
703	Abingdon, VA	24210
617	Abington, MA	02351
215	Abington, PA	19001, 19111
301	Accokeek, MD	20607
804	Accomac, VA	23301
617	Accord, MA	02018
601	Ackerman, MS	39735
508	Acton, MA	01718–01720
616	Ada, MI	49301, 49355
218	Ada, MN	56510
419	Ada, OH	45810
405	Ada, OK	74820, 74821
515	Adair, IA	50002
413	Adams, MA	01220
315	Adams, NY	13605
608	Adams, WI	53910
301	Adamstown, MD	21710
215	Adamstown, PA	19501
708	Addison, IL	60101
517	Addison, MI	49220
214	Addison, TX	75001
912	Adel, GA	31620
515	Adel, IA	50003
301	Adelphi, MD	20783, 20787
201	Adelphia, NJ	07710
517	Adrian, MI	49221
314	Advance, MO	63730
918	Afton, OK	74331
615	Afton, TN	37616
307	Afton, WY	83110, 83112
413	Agawam, MA	01001
818	Agoura, CA	91301
818	Agoura Hills, CA	91301, 91376
809	Aguadilla, PR	00603–00605
919	Ahoskie, NC	27910
808	Aiea, HI	96701, 96861
803	Aiken, SC	29801, 29802
912	Ailey, GA	30410
402	Ainsworth, NE	69210
218	Aitkin, MN	56431
303	Akron, CO	80720
219	Akron, IN	46910
716	Akron, NY	14001
216	Akron, OH	44300–44372, 44397
717	Akron, PA	17501
205	Alabaster, AL	35007
904	Alachua, FL	32615, 32616
415	Alameda, CA	94501
912	Alamo, GA	30411
901	Alamo, TN	38001
512	Alamo, TX	78516
505	Alamogordo, NM	88310, 88311
719	Alamosa, CO	81101, 81102
415	Albany, CA	94706
912	Albany, GA	31700–31708
606	Albany, KY	42602
816	Albany, MO	64402
518	Albany, NY	12200–12211, 12222–12246 *
503	Albany, OR	97321
915	Albany, TX	76430
704	Albemarle, NC	28001, 28002
712	Albert City, IA	50510
507	Albert Lea, MN	56007, 56064
205	Alberta, AL	36720
804	Alberta, VA	23821
516	Albertson, NY	11507
205	Albertville, AL	35950
515	Albia, IA	52531
618	Albion, IL	62806
219	Albion, IN	46701
517	Albion, MI	49224
402	Albion, NE	68620
716	Albion, NY	14411
304	Albright, WV	26519
505	Albuquerque, NM	87100–87199
615	Alcoa, TN	37701
518	Alcove, NY	12007
215	Aldan, PA	19018
515	Alden, IA	50006, 50043
716	Alden, NY	14004
309	Aledo, IL	61231
515	Alexander, IA	50420
205	Alexander City, AL	35010
318	Alexandria, LA	71301–71315
612	Alexandria, MN	56308
814	Alexandria, PA	16611

605	Alexandria, SD	57311
703	Alexandria, VA	22300–22320
315	Alexandria Bay, NY	13607
207	Alfred, ME	04002
607	Alfred, NY	14802
419	Alger, OH	45812
414	Algoma, WI	54201, 54231
515	Algona, IA	50511
206	Algona, WA	98002
313	Algonac, MI	48001, 48052
708	Algonquin, IL	60102
818	Alhambra, CA	91800–91899
512	Alice, TX	78332, 78342
205	Aliceville, AL	35442
713	Alief, TX	77411
412	Aliquippa, PA	15001
616	Allegan, MI	49010
515	Alleman, IA	50007
606	Allen, KY	41601
214	Allen, TX	75002
313	Allen Park, MI	48101
616	Allendale, MI	49401
201	Allendale, NJ	07401
803	Allendale, SC	29810
414	Allenton, WI	53002
215	Allentown, PA	18100–18195
908	Allenwood, NJ	08720
217	Allerton, IL	61810
308	Alliance, NE	69301
216	Alliance, OH	44601
319	Allison, IA	50602
412	Allison Park, PA	15101
617	Allston, MA	02134
912	Alma, GA	31510
913	Alma, KS	66401
517	Alma, MI	48801, 48802
308	Alma, NE	68920
608	Alma, WI	54610
303	Almont, CO	81210
313	Almont, MI	48003
503	Aloha, OR	97005–97007
517	Alpena, MI	49707
908	Alpha, NJ	08865
404	Alpharetta, GA	30201, 30202, 30239
205	Alpine, AL	35014
915	Alpine, TX	79830–79832
708	Alsip, IL	60658
712	Alta, IA	51002
714	Alta Loma, CA	91701
818	Altadena, CA	91001–91003
618	Altamont, IL	62411
615	Altamont, TN	37301
407	Altamonte Springs, FL	32701, 32714–32716
804	Altavista, VA	24517
505	Alto, NM	88312
712	Alton, IA	51003
618	Alton, IL	62002
417	Alton, MO	65606
309	Altona, IL	61414
515	Altoona, IA	50009
814	Altoona, PA	16601–16603
916	Alturas, CA	96101
405	Altus, OK	73521–73523
405	Alva, OK	73717
713	Alvin, TX	77511, 77512
516	Amagansett, NY	11930
505	Amalia, NM	87512
319	Amana, IA	52203, 52204
614	Amanda, OH	43102
806	Amarillo, TX	79100–79124, 79177, 79187 *
215	Ambler, PA	19002
815	Amboy, IL	61310
412	Ambridge, PA	15003
504	Amelia, LA	70340
513	Amelia, OH	45102
208	American Falls, ID	83211
801	American Fork, UT	84003, 84004
912	Americus, GA	31709, 31710
515	Ames, IA	50010–50013
508	Amesbury, MA	01913
303	Amherst, CO	80721
413	Amherst, MA	01002–01059
603	Amherst, NH	03031
716	Amherst, NY	14051, 14226, 14228
216	Amherst, OH	44001
605	Amherst, SD	57421
715	Amherst Junction, WI	54407
701	Amidon, ND	58620
504	Amite, LA	70422
516	Amityville, NY	11701
601	Amlin, OH	43002
601	Amory, MS	38821
518	Amsterdam, NY	12010
406	Anaconda, MT	59711
405	Anadarko, OK	73005, 73094
714	Anaheim, CA	92800–92816, 92825, 92850
714	Anaheim Hills, CA	92807, 92817
717	Analomink, PA	18320
319	Anamosa, IA	52205
907	Anchorage, AK	99501–99540, 99695
205	Andalusia, AL	36420
215	Andalusia, PA	19020
916	Anderson, CA	96007
317	Anderson, IN	46011–46018, 47630
803	Anderson, SC	29621–29625
409	Anderson, TX	77830, 77875
508	Andover, MA	01810
207	Andover, ME	04216
607	Andover, NY	14806
704	Andrews, NC	28901
803	Andrews, SC	29510
915	Andrews, TX	79714
409	Angleton, TX	77515, 77516
219	Angola, IN	46703
716	Angola, NY	14006
707	Angwin, CA	94508, 94576

515	Ankeny, IA	50015, 50021
313	Ann Arbor, MI	48103–48109
618	Anna, IL	62906
612	Annandale, MN	55302
703	Annandale, VA	22003
301	Annapolis, MD	21400–21404, 21411, 21412
205	Anniston, AL	36201–36203, 36206
717	Annville, PA	17003
612	Anoka, MN	55303, 55304
915	Anson, TX	79501
203	Ansonia, CT	06401
513	Ansonia, OH	45303
704	Ansonville, NC	28007
316	Anthony, KS	67003
715	Antigo, WI	54409
415	Antioch, CA	94509, 94531
708	Antioch, IL	60002
701	Antler, ND	58711
405	Antlers, OK	74523
603	Antrim, NH	03440
405	Apache, OK	73006
904	Apalachicola, FL	32320
607	Apalachin, NY	13732
412	Apollo, PA	15613
407	Apopka, FL	32703, 32712
612	Apple Valley, MN	55124
612	Appleton, MN	56208
414	Appleton, WI	54911–54915, 54919
804	Appomattox, VA	24522
408	Aptos, CA	95001–95003
516	Aquebogue, NY	11931
205	Arab, AL	35016
504	Arabi, LA	70032
512	Aransas Pass, TX	78336
405	Arapaho, OK	73620
916	Arcade, CA	95821
716	Arcade, NY	14009
818	Arcadia, CA	91006, 91007, 91077
813	Arcadia, FL	33821
712	Arcadia, IA	51430
318	Arcadia, LA	71001
814	Arcadia, PA	15712, 17563
803	Arcadia, SC	29320
608	Arcadia, WI	54612
707	Arcata, CA	95521
717	Archbald, PA	18403
419	Archbold, OH	43502
712	Archer, IA	51231
817	Archer City, TX	76351
208	Arco, ID	83213
217	Arcola, IL	61910
916	Arden, CA	95825, 95864
704	Arden, NC	28704
612	Arden Hills, MN	55112
405	Ardmore, OK	73401, 73402
215	Ardmore, PA	19003
914	Ardsley, NY	10502
515	Aredale, IA	50605
708	Argo, IL	60501
218	Argyle, MN	56713
518	Argyle, NY	12809
602	Arizona City, AZ	85223
501	Arkadelphia, AR	71923
501	Arkansas City, AR	71630
316	Arkansas City, KS	67005
912	Arlington, GA	31713
319	Arlington, IA	50606
502	Arlington, KY	42021
617	Arlington, MA	02174
612	Arlington, MN	55307
817	Arlington, TX	76003–76007, 76010–76019
703	Arlington, VA	22200–22216, 22227, 22229
802	Arlington, VT	05250
708	Arlington Heights, IL	60004–60006
914	Armonk, NY	10504
605	Armour, SD	57313
712	Armstrong, IA	50514
405	Arnett, OK	73550, 73832
301	Arnold, MD	21012
314	Arnold, MO	63010
805	Arroyo Grande, CA	93420
213	Artesia, CA	90701–90703
505	Artesia, NM	88210, 88211
217	Arthur, IL	61911
701	Arthur, ND	58006
308	Arthur, NE	69121
916	Artois, CA	95913
303	Arvada, CO	80001–80005
805	Arvin, CA	93203
908	Asbury, NJ	08802
908	Asbury Park, NJ	07712
501	Ash Flat, AR	72513
401	Ashaway, RI	02804
912	Ashburn, GA	31714
501	Ashdown, AR	71822
919	Asheboro, NC	27203, 27204
704	Asheville, NC	28800–28812
205	Ashford, AL	36312
414	Ashippun, WI	53003
815	Ashkum, IL	60911
217	Ashland, IL	62612
316	Ashland, KS	67831
606	Ashland, KY	41101, 41102
508	Ashland, MA	01721
207	Ashland, ME	04732–04759
314	Ashland, MO	65010
601	Ashland, MS	38603
603	Ashland, NH	03217
419	Ashland, OH	44805
503	Ashland, OR	97520
717	Ashland, PA	17921
804	Ashland, VA	23005
715	Ashland, WI	54806
615	Ashland City, TN	37015
701	Ashley, ND	58413
217	Ashmore, IL	61912

Area	Location	ZIP
216	Ashtabula, OH	44004
815	Ashton, IL	61006
401	Ashton, RI	02864
205	Ashville, AL	35953
509	Asotin, WA	99402
303	Aspen, CO	81611, 81612
301	Aspen Hill, MD	20906
817	Aspermont, TX	79502
217	Assumption, IL	62510
215	Aston, PA	19014
503	Astoria, OR	97103
805	Atascadero, CA	93422, 93423
913	Atchison, KS	66002
609	Atco, NJ	08004
215	Atglen, PA	19310
205	Athens, AL	35611
404	Athens, GA	30601–30613
217	Athens, IL	62613
614	Athens, OH	45701
615	Athens, TN	37303
903	Athens, TX	75751
304	Athens, WV	24712
415	Atherton, CA	94025, 94027
508	Athol, MA	01331–01368
501	Atkins, AR	72822, 72823
703	Atkins, VA	24311
309	Atkinson, IL	61235
402	Atkinson, NE	68713
404	Atlanta, GA	30301–30378, 30380–30383
517	Atlanta, MI	49709
903	Atlanta, TX	75551
712	Atlantic, IA	50022
609	Atlantic City, NJ	08400–08406
205	Atmore, AL	36502–36504
405	Atoka, OK	74525, 74542
205	Attalla, AL	35954
317	Attica, IN	47918
716	Attica, NY	14011
508	Attleboro, MA	02703
508	Attleboro Falls, MA	02763
209	Atwater, CA	95301
913	Atwood, KS	67730
517	Au Gres, MI	48703
205	Auburn, AL	36830–36849
916	Auburn, CA	95603
217	Auburn, IL	62441, 62615
219	Auburn, IN	46706
502	Auburn, KY	42206
508	Auburn, MA	01501
207	Auburn, ME	04210–04212
517	Auburn, MI	48611
402	Auburn, NE	68305
315	Auburn, NY	13021, 13022
206	Auburn, WA	98001–98003, 98071
313	Auburn Heights, MI	48057
313	Auburn Hills, MI	48057, 48321, 48326
813	Auburndale, FL	33823
712	Audubon, IA	50025
609	Audubon, NJ	08106
501	Augusta, AR	72006
404	Augusta, GA	30900–30919
207	Augusta, ME	04330–04338
616	Augusta, MI	49012
715	Augusta, WI	54722
503	Aumsville, OR	97325
712	Aurelia, IA	51005
303	Aurora, CO	80010–80019, 80040–80045
708	Aurora, IL	60504–60507
812	Aurora, IN	47001
417	Aurora, MO	65605
402	Aurora, NE	68818
315	Aurora, NY	13026
216	Aurora, OH	44202
404	Austell, GA	30001
812	Austin, IN	47102
507	Austin, MN	55912
814	Austin, PA	16720
512	Austin, TX	78700–78769, 78778
216	Austintown, OH	44515
417	Ava, MO	65608
609	Avalon, NJ	08202
908	Avenel, NJ	07001
618	Aviston, IL	62216
303	Avon, CO	81620
203	Avon, CT	06001
508	Avon, MA	02322
612	Avon, MN	56310
716	Avon, NY	14414
216	Avon, OH	44011
216	Avon Lake, OH	44012
813	Avon Park, FL	33825
412	Avonmore, PA	15618
508	Ayer, MA	01432, 01433
817	Azle, TX	76020
505	Aztec, NM	87410
818	Azusa, CA	91702

B

Area	Location	ZIP
813	Babson Park, FL	33827
617	Babson Park, MA	02157
516	Babylon, NY	11702–11704
517	Bad Axe, MI	48413
412	Baden, PA	15005
218	Bagley, MN	56621
703	Baileys Crossroads, VA	22041
414	Baileys Harbor, WI	54202
815	Baileyville, IL	61007
912	Bainbridge, GA	31717
607	Bainbridge, NY	13733
206	Bainbridge Island, WA	98110
915	Baird, TX	79504
406	Baker, MT	59313
503	Baker, OR	97814
805	Bakersfield, CA	93300–93389
412	Bakerstown, PA	15007
704	Bakersville, NC	28705
305	Bal Harbour, FL	33154
215	Bala-Cynwyd, PA	19004
616	Baldwin, MI	49304
516	Baldwin, NY	11510
913	Baldwin City, KS	66006
818	Baldwin Park, CA	91706
315	Baldwinsville, NY	13027
508	Baldwinville, MA	01436
601	Baldwyn, MS	38824
617	Ballardvale, MA	01810
915	Ballinger, TX	76821
518	Ballston Lake, NY	12019
518	Ballston Spa, NY	12020
314	Ballwin, MO	63011, 63021, 63022
215	Bally, PA	19503
315	Balmat, NY	13609
715	Balsam Lake, WI	54024, 54810
203	Baltic, CT	06330
301	Baltimore, MD	21200–21240, 21278
803	Bamberg, SC	29003
512	Bandera, TX	78003
503	Bandon, OR	97411
207	Bangor, ME	04401
616	Bangor, MI	49013
215	Bangor, PA	18010–18013
704	Banner Elk, NC	28604, 28691
614	Bannock, OH	43972
708	Bannockburn, IL	60015
203	Bantam, CT	06750
207	Bar Harbor, ME	04609
608	Baraboo, WI	53913
906	Baraga, MI	49908, 49944
216	Barberton, OH	44203
606	Barbourville, KY	40906–40911
809	Barceloneta, PR	00617
301	Barclay, MD	21607
502	Bardstown, KY	40004
502	Bardwell, KY	42023
515	Barnes City, IA	50027
404	Barnesville, GA	30204
218	Barnesville, MN	56514
614	Barnesville, OH	43713
314	Barnhart, MO	63012
918	Barnsdall, OK	74002
508	Barnstable, MA	02630
803	Barnwell, SC	29812–29814
508	Barre, MA	01005
802	Barre, VT	05641
901	Barretville, TN	38053
708	Barrington, IL	60010, 60011
609	Barrington, NJ	08007
401	Barrington, RI	02806
715	Barron, WI	54812
907	Barrow, AK	99723, 99791
612	Barry, MN	55037, 56210
619	Barstow, CA	92310–92312
918	Bartlesville, OK	74003–74006
708	Bartlett, IL	60103
316	Bartlett, KS	67332
308	Bartlett, NE	68622
813	Bartow, FL	33830
913	Basehor, KS	66007
307	Basin, WY	82410
908	Basking Ridge, NJ	07920
402	Bassett, NE	68714, 68772
703	Bassett, VA	24055
318	Bastrop, LA	71220, 71221
512	Bastrop, TX	78602
703	Basye, VA	22810
708	Batavia, IL	60510, 60539
716	Batavia, NY	14020, 14021
513	Batavia, OH	45103
501	Batesville, AR	72501, 72522
812	Batesville, IN	47006
601	Batesville, MS	38606
207	Bath, ME	04530
607	Bath, NY	14810
215	Bath, PA	18014
504	Baton Rouge, LA	70800–70898
616	Battle Creek, MI	49015–49017
402	Battle Creek, NE	68715
206	Battle Ground, WA	98604
702	Battle Mountain, NV	89820
919	Battleboro, NC	27809
218	Baudette, MN	56623
912	Baxley, GA	31513
606	Baxter, KY	40806
316	Baxter Springs, KS	66713
517	Bay City, MI	48706–48708, 48710
409	Bay City, TX	77404, 77414
305	Bay Harbor Islands, FL	33154
205	Bay Minette, AL	36507
813	Bay Pines, FL	33504
601	Bay Saint Louis, MS	39520–39529
516	Bay Shore, NY	11706
601	Bay Springs, MS	39422
809	Bayamon, PR	00619, 00620
712	Bayard, IA	50029
919	Bayboro, NC	28515
201	Bayonne, NJ	07002
205	Bayou La Batre, AL	36509
612	Bayport, MN	55003
516	Bayport, NY	11705
718	Bayside, NY	11360, 11361
414	Bayside, WI	53217
713	Baytown, TX	77520–77522
908	Bayville, NJ	08721
701	Beach, ND	58621
609	Beach Haven, NJ	08008
201	Beachwood, NJ	08722
216	Beachwood, OH	44122
914	Beacon, NY	12508
203	Beacon Falls, CT	06403
515	Beaman, IA	50609
615	Bean Station, TN	37708
616	Bear Lake, MI	49614
501	Bearden, AR	71720
612	Beardsley, MN	56211
402	Beatrice, NE	68310, 68458
913	Beattie, KS	66406
606	Beattyville, KY	41311
919	Beaufort, NC	28516
803	Beaufort, SC	29901–29903
409	Beaumont, TX	77700–77726
405	Beaver, OK	73932, 73935
412	Beaver, PA	15009, 17985
308	Beaver City, NE	68926, 68946
414	Beaver Dam, WI	53916
315	Beaver Falls, NY	13305
412	Beaver Falls, PA	15010
717	Beaver Meadows, PA	18216
513	Beavercreek, OH	45385, 45440
517	Beaverton, MI	48612
503	Beaverton, OR	97005–97007, 97076, 97077
304	Beckley, WV	25801, 25802
712	Bedford, IA	50833
812	Bedford, IN	47421
502	Bedford, KY	40006
617	Bedford, MA	01730
603	Bedford, NH	03102
216	Bedford, OH	44146
814	Bedford, PA	15522
703	Bedford, VA	22824, 24523
216	Bedford Heights, OH	44128, 44146
914	Bedford Hills, NY	10507
708	Bedford Park, IL	60499, 60638
501	Beebe, AR	72012
717	Beech Creek, PA	16822, 16864
317	Beech Grove, IN	46107
618	Beecher City, IL	62414, 62444
802	Beecher Falls, VT	05902
512	Beeville, TX	78102–78104
301	Bel Air, MD	21014, 21502
301	Belcamp, MD	21017
701	Belcourt, ND	58316
616	Belding, MI	48809, 48887
505	Belen, NM	87002
207	Belfast, ME	04915
414	Belgium, WI	53004
406	Belgrade, MT	59714
919	Belhaven, NC	27810
213	Bell, CA	90201, 90270
213	Bell Gardens, CA	90201
616	Bellaire, MI	49615
713	Bellaire, TX	77401, 77402
304	Belle, WV	25015
504	Belle Chasse, LA	70037
605	Belle Fourche, SD	57717, 57742
407	Belle Glade, FL	33430
804	Belle Haven, VA	23306
908	Belle Mead, NJ	08502
319	Belle Plaine, IA	52208
612	Belle Plaine, MN	56011
504	Belle Rose, LA	70341
412	Belle Vernon, PA	15012
813	Belleair, FL	34616
813	Belleair Bluffs, FL	34640
513	Bellefontaine, OH	43311
814	Bellefonte, PA	16823, 16880
718	Bellerose, NY	11426
618	Belleville, IL	62220–62225
913	Belleville, KS	66935
313	Belleville, MI	48111
201	Belleville, NJ	07109, 07110
717	Belleville, PA	17004
608	Belleville, WI	53508
402	Bellevue, NE	68005, 68147
419	Bellevue, OH	44811
206	Bellevue, WA	98004–98009
213	Bellflower, CA	90706, 90707
508	Bellingham, MA	02019
206	Bellingham, WA	98225–98227
609	Bellmawr, NJ	08031
516	Bellmore, NY	11710
802	Bellows Falls, VT	05101
901	Bells, TN	38006
419	Bellville, OH	44813
409	Bellville, TX	77418
708	Bellwood, IL	60104
402	Bellwood, NE	68624
814	Bellwood, PA	16617
908	Belmar, NJ	07719
415	Belmont, CA	94002
617	Belmont, MA	02178
601	Belmont, MS	38827
704	Belmont, NC	28012
716	Belmont, NY	14813
304	Belmont, WV	26134
913	Beloit, KS	67420
608	Beloit, WI	53511
816	Belton, MO	64012
803	Belton, SC	29627
817	Belton, TX	76513
301	Beltsville, MD	20705
815	Belvidere, IL	61008
908	Belvidere, NJ	07823
601	Belzoni, MS	39038
217	Bement, IL	61813
218	Bemidji, MN	56601–56619
408	Ben Lomond, CA	95005
503	Bend, OR	97701–97709
402	Benedict, NE	68316
707	Benicia, CA	94510
817	Benjamin, TX	79505
308	Benkelman, NE	69021
803	Bennettsville, SC	29512
603	Bennington, NH	03442
802	Bennington, VT	05201
215	Bensalem, PA	19020

Area	City	Zip
708	Bensenville, IL	60106
602	Benson, AZ	85602
309	Benson, IL	61516
612	Benson, MN	56215
501	Benton, AR	72015
618	Benton, IL	62812
502	Benton, KY	42025
318	Benton, LA	71006
314	Benton, MO	63736
615	Benton, TN	37307
616	Benton Harbor, MI	49022
501	Bentonville, AR	72712–72716
606	Berea, KY	40403, 40404
216	Berea, OH	
201	Bergenfield, NJ	07621
415	Berkeley, CA	94701–94710, 94702
314	Berkeley, MO	63134, 63140
908	Berkeley Heights, NJ	07922
304	Berkeley Springs, WV	25411
313	Berkley, MI	48072
203	Berlin, CT	06037
301	Berlin, MD	21811
603	Berlin, NH	03570
609	Berlin, NJ	08009, 08091
216	Berlin, OH	44401, 44610
814	Berlin, PA	15530
414	Berlin, WI	54923
505	Bernalillo, NM	87001, 87004
908	Bernardsville, NJ	07924
219	Berne, IN	46711, 46769
314	Bernie, MO	63822
616	Berrien Springs, MI	49103, 49104
404	Berryton, GA	30747
501	Berryville, AR	72616
703	Berryville, VA	22611
701	Berthold, ND	58718, 58738
308	Bertrand, NE	68927
504	Berwick, LA	70342
207	Berwick, ME	03901
717	Berwick, PA	18603
708	Berwyn, IL	60402
215	Berwyn, PA	19312
205	Bessemer, AL	35020–35023
906	Bessemer, MI	
704	Bessemer City, NC	28016
203	Bethany, CT	06525
217	Bethany, IL	61914
816	Bethany, MO	64424
405	Bethany, OK	73008
304	Bethany, WV	26032
907	Bethel, AK	99559, 99679, 99680
203	Bethel, CT	06801
207	Bethel, ME	04217
802	Bethel, VT	05032
415	Bethel Island, CA	94511
412	Bethel Park, PA	15102
301	Bethesda, MD	20814–20817, 20892, 20894
404	Bethlehem, GA	30620
215	Bethlehem, PA	18015–18018
516	Bethpage, NY	11714
319	Bettendorf, IA	52722
616	Beulah, MI	49617
508	Beverly, MA	01915
609	Beverly, NJ	08010
617	Beverly Farms, MA	01915
213	Beverly Hills, CA	90209–90213
313	Beverly Hills, MI	48009, 48010
614	Bexley, OH	43209
612	Bible College, MN	55375
207	Biddeford, ME	04005, 04007
916	Bieber, CA	96009
714	Big Bear Lake, CA	92315
404	Big Canoe, GA	30143
915	Big Lake, TX	76932
616	Big Rapids, MI	49307
406	Big Sky, MT	59716
915	Big Spring, TX	79720, 79721
605	Big Stone City, SD	57216
703	Big Stone Gap, VA	24219
406	Big Timber, MT	59011
507	Bigelow, MN	56117
406	Bigfork, MT	59911
814	Bigler, PA	16825
717	Biglerville, PA	17307
508	Billerica, MA	01821–01862
406	Billings, MT	59002, 59100–59107
601	Biloxi, MS	39530–39535
509	Bingen, WA	98605
405	Binger, OK	73009
607	Binghamton, NY	13900–13905
913	Bird City, KS	67731
215	Birdsboro, PA	19508
205	Birmingham, AL	35200–35263, 35291–35298 *
313	Birmingham, MI	48009, 48010, 48025
609	Birmingham, NJ	08011
602	Bisbee, AZ	85603
701	Bisbee, ND	
919	Biscoe, NC	27209
803	Bishopville, SC	29010
701	Bismarck, ND	58501–58505, 58553
701	Bismark, ND	58501, 58504
605	Bison, SD	57620, 57650
918	Bixby, OK	74008
414	Black Creek, WI	
715	Black River Falls, WI	54615
208	Blackfoot, ID	83221
614	Blacklick, OH	43004
803	Blacksburg, SC	29702
703	Blacksburg, VA	24060–24063, 24416
912	Blackshear, GA	31516
804	Blackstone, VA	23824
405	Blackwell, OK	74631
609	Blackwood, NJ	08012
301	Bladensburg, MD	20710
612	Blaine, MN	55014, 55432–55434
206	Blaine, WA	98230
402	Blair, NE	68008
515	Blairsburg, IA	50034
404	Blairsville, GA	30512
412	Blairsville, PA	15717
912	Blakely, GA	31723
717	Blakeslee, PA	18610
303	Blanca, CO	81123
513	Blanchester, OH	45107
512	Blanco, TX	78606
703	Bland, VA	24315
215	Blandon, PA	19510
914	Blauvelt, NY	10913
517	Blissfield, MI	49228
401	Block Island, RI	02807
203	Bloomfield, CT	06002
515	Bloomfield, IA	52537
812	Bloomfield, IN	47424
314	Bloomfield, MO	63825
201	Bloomfield, NJ	07003
313	Bloomfield Hills, MI	48013, 48302, 48304
507	Blooming Prairie, MN	55917
708	Bloomingdale, IL	60108
714	Bloomington, CA	92316
309	Bloomington, IL	61701–61704, 61710
812	Bloomington, IN	47401–47408
612	Bloomington, MN	55420–55425, 55431–55438
717	Bloomsburg, PA	17815
908	Bloomsbury, NJ	08804
717	Blossburg, PA	16912
904	Blountstown, FL	32424
615	Blountville, TN	37617
704	Blowing Rock, NC	28605
717	Blue Ball, PA	17506
215	Blue Bell, PA	19422, 19424
304	Blue Creek, WV	25026
507	Blue Earth, MN	56013
708	Blue Island, IL	60406
217	Blue Mound, IL	62513
205	Blue Mountain, AL	36201, 36204
601	Blue Mountain, MS	38610
404	Blue Ridge, GA	30513
816	Blue Springs, MO	64013–64015
703	Bluefield, VA	24605
304	Bluefield, WV	24701
217	Bluff Springs, IL	62622
217	Bluffs, IL	62621
219	Bluffton, IN	46714
419	Bluffton, OH	45817
817	Blum, TX	76627
619	Blythe, CA	92225, 92280
501	Blytheville, AR	72315–72319
216	Boardman, OH	44512, 44513
503	Boardman, OR	97818
205	Boaz, AL	35957
407	Boca Raton, FL	33427–33434, 33486–33498
515	Bode, IA	50519
512	Boerne, TX	78004, 78006
504	Bogalusa, LA	70427
201	Bogota, NJ	07603
601	Bogue Chitto, MS	39629
516	Bohemia, NY	11716
704	Boiling Springs, NC	28017
208	Boise, ID	83702–83714, 83720–83729 *
405	Boise City, OK	73933
708	Bolingbrook, IL	60439, 60440
417	Bolivar, MO	65613, 65727
216	Bolivar, OH	44612
901	Bolivar, TN	38008, 38074
919	Bolivia, NC	28422
203	Bolton, CT	06040, 06043
508	Bolton, MA	01740
802	Bolton, VT	05676
518	Bolton Landing, NY	12814
205	Bon Secour, AL	36511
515	Bondurant, IA	50035
612	Bongards, MN	55368
903	Bonham, TX	75418
904	Bonifay, FL	32425
919	Bonlee, NC	27213
314	Bonne Terre, MO	63628
913	Bonner Springs, KS	66012
208	Bonners Ferry, ID	83805
515	Boone, IA	50036
704	Boone, NC	28607, 28608
501	Booneville, AR	72927
606	Booneville, KY	41314
601	Booneville, MS	38829
201	Boonton, NJ	07005
812	Boonville, IN	47601
816	Boonville, MO	65233
315	Boonville, NY	13309
207	Boothbay Harbor, ME	04536–04570
812	Borden, IN	47106
609	Bordentown, NJ	08505
806	Borger, TX	79007, 79008
619	Borrego Springs, CA	92004
603	Boscawen, NH	03303
314	Boss, MO	65440
318	Bossier City, LA	71111–71113
617	Boston, MA	02100–02222
716	Boston, NY	14025
814	Boswell, PA	15531, 15546
206	Bothell, WA	98011, 98012, 98041
513	Botkins, OH	45306
203	Botsford, CT	06404
701	Bottineau, ND	58318
303	Boulder, CO	80301–80309
406	Boulder, MT	59632
702	Boulder City, NV	89005, 89006
908	Bound Brook, NJ	08805
801	Bountiful, UT	84010, 84087
219	Bourbon, IN	46504
314	Bourbon, MO	65441
815	Bourbonnais, IL	60914
603	Bow, NH	03304
701	Bowbells, ND	58721, 58728
404	Bowdon, GA	30108
614	Bowerston, OH	44695
301	Bowie, MD	20715, 20716
817	Bowie, TX	76230
502	Bowling Green, KY	42101–42104
314	Bowling Green, MO	63334
419	Bowling Green, OH	43332, 43402, 43403
804	Bowling Green, VA	22427
404	Bowman, GA	30624
701	Bowman, ND	58623
215	Bowmanstown, PA	18030
716	Bowmansville, NY	14026
215	Bowmansville, PA	17507
617	Boxborough, MA	01719
712	Boyden, IA	51234
804	Boydton, VA	23917
215	Boyertown, PA	19512
616	Boyne City, MI	49712
616	Boyne Falls, MI	49713
407	Boynton Beach, FL	33424–33426, 33435–33437
406	Bozeman, MT	59715, 59717, 59772
412	Brackenridge, PA	15014
512	Brackettville, TX	78832
412	Braddock, PA	15104
813	Bradenton, FL	34201–34210
814	Bradford, PA	16701
401	Bradford, RI	02808
802	Bradford, VT	05033
304	Bradley, WV	25818
915	Brady, TX	75935, 76825
612	Braham, MN	55006
402	Brainard, NE	68626
218	Brainerd, MN	56401, 56456
617	Braintree, MA	02184
504	Braithwaite, LA	70040
414	Branch, WI	54203
201	Branchville, NJ	07826, 07827, 07890
502	Brandenburg, KY	40108
813	Brandon, FL	33509–33511
601	Brandon, MS	39042, 39047
301	Brandywine, MD	20613
203	Branford, CT	06405
417	Branson, MO	65616
717	Brass, PA	17849
802	Brattleboro, VT	05301–05351
619	Brawley, CA	92227
812	Brazil, IN	47834
714	Brea, CA	92621, 92622
318	Breaux Bridge, LA	70517
303	Breckenridge, CO	80424
517	Breckenridge, MI	48615
218	Breckenridge, MN	56520
817	Breckenridge, TX	76024
216	Brecksville, OH	44141
618	Breese, IL	62230
814	Breezewood, PA	15533
404	Bremen, GA	30110
219	Bremen, IN	46506
614	Bremen, OH	43107
206	Bremerton, WA	98310–98315
409	Brenham, TX	77833
205	Brent, AL	35034
213	Brentwood, CA	94513
301	Brentwood, MD	20722
314	Brentwood, MO	63144
516	Brentwood, NY	11717
615	Brentwood, TN	37024, 37027
603	Bretton Woods, NH	03575
704	Brevard, NC	28712
207	Brewer, ME	04412
913	Brewster, KS	67732
308	Brewster, NE	68821
914	Brewster, NY	10509
509	Brewster, WA	98812
205	Brewton, AL	36426, 36427
914	Briarcliff Manor, NY	10510
908	Brick, NJ	08723, 08724
619	Bridgeport, CA	93517, 95338
203	Bridgeport, CT	06497–06650
517	Bridgeport, MI	48722
308	Bridgeport, NE	69336
609	Bridgeport, NJ	08014
315	Bridgeport, NY	13030
614	Bridgeport, OH	43912
215	Bridgeport, PA	17040, 19405
304	Bridgeport, WV	26330
314	Bridgeton, MO	63044, 63045
609	Bridgeton, NJ	08302
708	Bridgeview, IL	60455
302	Bridgeville, DE	19933
412	Bridgeville, PA	15017
508	Bridgewater, MA	02324, 02325
908	Bridgewater, NJ	08807
703	Bridgewater, VA	22812
616	Bridgman, MI	49106
801	Brigham City, UT	84302, 84309
303	Brighton, CO	80601
617	Brighton, MA	02135
313	Brighton, MI	48116
716	Brighton, NY	13439, 14610
614	Brilliant, OH	43913
414	Brillion, WI	54110
309	Brimfield, IL	61517, 61518
413	Brimfield, MA	01010
415	Brisbane, CA	94005
203	Bristol, CT	06010
904	Bristol, FL	32321
219	Bristol, IN	46507
603	Bristol, NH	03222
215	Bristol, PA	19007
401	Bristol, RI	02809
615	Bristol, TN	37620–37625
703	Bristol, VA	24201–24209
802	Bristol, VT	05443
414	Bristol, WI	53104
918	Bristow, OK	74010

515	Britt, IA	50423
605	Britton, SD	57430
518	Broadalbin, NY	12025
406	Broadus, MT	59317, 59348
708	Broadview, IL	60153
216	Broadview Heights, OH	44147
703	Broadway, VA	22815
716	Brockport, NY	14420
508	Brockton, MA	02400–02403
406	Brockway, MT	59214
814	Brockway, PA	15824
716	Brocton, NY	14716
916	Broderick, CA	95605
608	Brodhead, WI	53520
918	Broken Arrow, OK	74011–74014
308	Broken Bow, NE	68822
405	Broken Bow, OK	74728
904	Bronson, FL	32621
517	Bronson, MI	49028
212	Bronx, NY	10400–10475
914	Bronxville, NY	10708
216	Brook Park, OH	44142
203	Brookfield, CT	06804
708	Brookfield, IL	60513
508	Brookfield, MA	01506
216	Brookfield, OH	43732, 44403
414	Brookfield, WI	53005, 53008, 53045
601	Brookhaven, MS	39601
215	Brookhaven, PA	19015
503	Brookings, OR	97415
605	Brookings, SD	57006, 57007
617	Brookline, MA	02146
517	Brooklyn, MI	49230
718	Brooklyn, NY	11200–11256
216	Brooklyn, OH	44144
612	Brooklyn Center, MN	55428–55430, 55443–55445
216	Brooklyn Heights, OH	44131
612	Brooklyn Park, MN	55428, 55443–55445
904	Brooksville, FL	34601–34614
606	Brooksville, KY	41004
317	Brookville, IN	47012
513	Brookville, OH	45309
814	Brookville, PA	15825
215	Broomall, PA	19008
303	Broomfield, CO	80020, 80021, 80038
318	Broussard, LA	70518
313	Brown City, MI	48416
414	Brown Deer, WI	53209, 53223
806	Brownfield, TX	79316
406	Browning, MT	59417
507	Brownsdale, MN	55918
812	Brownstown, IN	47118, 47220
502	Brownsville, KY	42210
412	Brownsville, PA	15417, 19565
901	Brownsville, TN	38012
512	Brownsville, TX	78520–78526
414	Brownsville, WI	53006
608	Browntown, WI	53522
915	Brownwood, TX	76801–76804
601	Bruce, MS	38913, 38915
715	Bruce, WI	54819
912	Brunswick, GA	31520–31524
207	Brunswick, ME	04011, 04053
216	Brunswick, OH	44212
303	Brush, CO	80723
419	Bryan, OH	43506
409	Bryan, TX	77801–77806
215	Bryn Athyn, PA	19009
215	Bryn Mawr, PA	19010
704	Bryson City, NC	28713
404	Buchanan, GA	30113
616	Buchanan, MI	49107
914	Buchanan, NY	10511
901	Buchanan, TN	38222
703	Buchanan, VA	24066
717	Buck Hill Falls, PA	18323
602	Buckeye, AZ	85326
304	Buckhannon, WV	26201
319	Buckingham, IA	50612
215	Buckingham, PA	18912
804	Buckingham, VA	23921
502	Buckner, KY	40010
816	Buckner, MO	64016
207	Bucksport, ME	04416
419	Bucyrus, OH	44820
609	Buena, NJ	08310
714	Buena Park, CA	90620–90624
912	Buena Vista, GA	31803
703	Buena Vista, VA	24416
612	Buffalo, MN	55313
417	Buffalo, MO	65622
716	Buffalo, NY	14200–14228, 14240, 14261 *
405	Buffalo, OK	73834
605	Buffalo, SD	57720
903	Buffalo, TX	75831
307	Buffalo, WY	82834, 82840
708	Buffalo Grove, IL	60089
612	Buffalo Lake, MN	55314
404	Buford, GA	30518
208	Buhl, ID	83316
919	Buies Creek, NC	27506
602	Bullhead City, AZ	86430, 86442
318	Bunkie, LA	71322
904	Bunnell, FL	32110
818	Burbank, CA	91500–91510, 91520–91523
708	Burbank, IL	60459
919	Burgaw, NC	28425
412	Burgettstown, PA	15021
605	Burke, SD	57523
703	Burke, VA	22015
502	Burkesville, KY	42717
609	Burleigh, NJ	08210
208	Burley, ID	83318
415	Burlingame, CA	94010, 94011
913	Burlingame, KS	66413
719	Burlington, CO	80807
319	Burlington, IA	52601
316	Burlington, KS	66839
606	Burlington, KY	41005
617	Burlington, MA	01803, 01805
919	Burlington, NC	27215–27217, 27220
609	Burlington, NJ	08016
405	Burlington, OK	73722
802	Burlington, VT	05401–05404
206	Burlington, WA	98233
414	Burlington, WI	53105
901	Burlison, TN	38015
512	Burnet, TX	78611
717	Burnham, PA	17009
503	Burns, OR	97710–97722
612	Burnsville, MN	55337
704	Burnsville, NC	28135, 28714
708	Burr Ridge, IL	60521, 60525
515	Burt, IA	50522
313	Burton, MI	48509–48529
216	Burton, OH	44021
308	Burwell, NE	68823, 68837
717	Bushkill, PA	18324, 18371
904	Bushnell, FL	33513
309	Bushnell, IL	61422
205	Butler, AL	36904
912	Butler, GA	31006
219	Butler, IN	46721
301	Butler, MD	21023
816	Butler, MO	64730
201	Butler, NJ	07405
412	Butler, PA	16001–16003
414	Butler, WI	53007
919	Butner, NC	27509
406	Butte, MT	59701–59703, 59707, 59750
402	Butte, NE	68722
805	Buttonwillow, CA	93206
508	Buzzards Bay, MA	02532, 02542
817	Byers, TX	76357
614	Byesville, OH	43723
601	Byhalia, MS	38611
919	Bynum, NC	27228
203	Byram, CT	06830
615	Byrdstown, TN	38549
815	Byron, IL	61010
507	Byron, MN	55920, 56072
616	Byron Center, MI	49315

C

715	Cable, WI	54821
802	Cabot, VT	05647
616	Cadillac, MI	49601
502	Cadiz, KY	42211
614	Cadiz, OH	43907
618	Cahokia, IL	62206
912	Cairo, GA	31728
618	Cairo, IL	62914
308	Cairo, NE	68824
818	Calabasas, CA	91302
208	Caldwell, ID	83605, 83606
316	Caldwell, KS	67022, 67032
908	Caldwell, NJ	07006
614	Caldwell, OH	43724
409	Caldwell, TX	77836
507	Caledonia, MN	55921
716	Caledonia, NY	14423
404	Calhoun, GA	30701
502	Calhoun, KY	42327
615	Calhoun, TN	37309
908	Califon, NJ	07830
314	California, MO	65018
412	California, PA	15419, 17777
412	Callery, PA	16024
319	Calmar, IA	52132
906	Calumet, MI	49913
708	Calumet City, IL	60409
502	Calvert City, KY	42029
919	Calypso, NC	28325
319	Camanche, IA	52730
805	Camarillo, CA	93010–93012
206	Camas, WA	98607
309	Cambridge, IL	61238
617	Cambridge, MA	02138–02163
301	Cambridge, MD	21613
612	Cambridge, MN	55008
614	Cambridge, OH	43725
317	Cambridge City, IN	47327
814	Cambridge Springs, PA	16403
205	Camden, AL	36726
501	Camden, AR	71701
219	Camden, IN	46917
207	Camden, ME	04843, 04847
919	Camden, NC	27921
609	Camden, NJ	08100–08110
315	Camden, NY	13316
803	Camden, SC	29020
901	Camden, TN	38320
314	Camdenton, MO	65020
318	Cameron, LA	70631
816	Cameron, MO	64429
817	Cameron, TX	76520
912	Camilla, GA	31730
315	Camillus, NY	13031
916	Camino, CA	95709
717	Camp Hill, PA	17001, 17011, 17089
919	Camp Lejeune, NC	28542
217	Camp Point, IL	62320
408	Campbell, CA	95008–95011
502	Campbellsville, KY	42718, 42719
717	Campbelltown, PA	17010
606	Campton, KY	41301
203	Canaan, CT	06018, 06031
806	Canadian, TX	79014
518	Canajoharie, NY	13317
614	Canal Winchester, OH	43110
716	Canandaigua, NY	14424, 14425
315	Canastota, NY	13032
503	Canby, OR	97013
404	Candler-McAfee, GA	30032
701	Cando, ND	58324
216	Canfield, OH	44406
812	Cannelton, IN	47520
507	Cannon Falls, MN	55009
818	Canoga Park, CA	91303–91307
719	Canon City, CO	81212, 81246
412	Canonsburg, PA	15317
809	Canovanas, PR	00629
404	Canton, GA	30114
309	Canton, IL	61520
617	Canton, MA	02021
313	Canton, MI	48187, 48188
314	Canton, MO	63435
601	Canton, MS	39046
704	Canton, NC	28716
315	Canton, NY	13617
216	Canton, OH	44700–44735, 44750
717	Canton, PA	17724, 17743
605	Canton, SD	57013
903	Canton, TX	75103
203	Canton Center, CT	06020
806	Canyon, TX	79015, 79016
503	Canyon City, OR	97820
313	Capac, MI	48014
809	Caparra Heights, PR	00921
804	Cape Charles, VA	23310
813	Cape Coral, FL	33904, 33990
314	Cape Girardeau, MO	63701, 63702
609	Cape May, NJ	08204
714	Capistrano Beach, CA	92624
301	Capitol Heights, MD	20743, 20791
813	Captiva Island, FL	33924
303	Carbondale, CO	81623
618	Carbondale, IL	62901–62903
717	Carbondale, PA	18407
619	Cardiff by the Sea, CA	92007
314	Cardwell, MO	63829
602	Carefree, AZ	85377
419	Carey, OH	43316
207	Caribou, ME	04736
516	Carle Place, NY	11514
402	Carleton, NE	68326
217	Carlinville, IL	62626
606	Carlisle, KY	40311
717	Carlisle, PA	17013
619	Carlsbad, CA	92008, 92009, 92018
505	Carlsbad, NM	88220, 88221
201	Carlstadt, NJ	07072
218	Carlton, MN	55718
503	Carlton, OR	97111
618	Carlyle, IL	62231
408	Carmel, CA	93922, 93923
317	Carmel, IN	46032
914	Carmel, NY	10512
408	Carmel Valley, CA	93924
618	Carmi, IL	62821
916	Carmichael, CA	95608, 95609
409	Carmine, TX	78932
405	Carnegie, OK	73015
412	Carnegie, PA	15106
404	Carnesville, GA	30521
517	Caro, MI	48723
305	Carol City, FL	33055, 33056
708	Carol Stream, IL	60188
809	Carolina, PR	00628, 00630
708	Carpentersville, IL	60110
805	Carpinteria, CA	93013
701	Carrington, ND	58421
512	Carrizo Springs, TX	78834
505	Carrizozo, NM	88301
712	Carroll, IA	51401
614	Carroll, OH	43112, 43449
205	Carrollton, AL	35447
404	Carrollton, GA	30117, 30119
217	Carrollton, IL	62016
502	Carrollton, KY	41008, 41045
816	Carrollton, MO	64633
601	Carrollton, MS	38917
216	Carrollton, OH	44615
214	Carrollton, TX	75006–75008, 75011
213	Carson, CA	90745–90747, 90810
701	Carson, ND	58529
804	Carson, VA	23830
517	Carson City, MI	48811
702	Carson City, NV	89701–89721
908	Carteret, NJ	07008
404	Cartersville, GA	30120
618	Carterville, IL	62918
217	Carthage, IL	62321
417	Carthage, MO	64836
601	Carthage, MS	39051
919	Carthage, NC	28327
315	Carthage, NY	13619
615	Carthage, TN	37030
903	Carthage, TX	75633
314	Caruthersville, MO	63830
708	Cary, IL	60013
919	Cary, NC	27511–27513, 27519
602	Casa Grande, AZ	85222, 85223
303	Cascade, CO	80809
208	Cascade, ID	83611
503	Cascade Locks, OR	97014
217	Casey, IL	62420
704	Cashiers, NC	28717
509	Cashmere, WA	98815
307	Casper, WY	82601–82615, 82646
906	Caspian, MI	49915
517	Cass City, MI	48726
407	Casselberry, FL	32707, 32730
616	Cassopolis, MI	49031
417	Cassville, MO	65623, 65625

Area	City	Zip
608	Cassville, WI	53806
716	Castile, NY	14427
207	Castine, ME	04420
801	Castle Dale, UT	84513
303	Castle Rock, CO	80104
802	Castleton, VT	05735
518	Castleton on Hudson, NY	12033
318	Castor, LA	71016
315	Castorland, NY	13620
415	Castro Valley, CA	94546, 94552
408	Castroville, CA	95012
809	Catano, PR	00632
215	Catasauqua, PA	18032
508	Cataumet, MA	02534
803	Catawba, SC	29704
717	Catawissa, PA	17820
206	Cathlamet, WA	98612
606	Catlettsburg, KY	41129
315	Cato, NY	13033
301	Catonsville, MD	21228
918	Catoosa, OK	74015
518	Catskill, NY	12414
716	Cattaraugus, NY	14719
701	Cavalier, ND	58220
502	Cave City, KY	42127
803	Cayce, SC	29033
315	Cayuga, NY	13034
315	Cazenovia, NY	13035
318	Cecilia, LA	70521
616	Cedar, MI	49621
612	Cedar, MN	55011, 56176
801	Cedar City, UT	84720–84722, 84783
319	Cedar Falls, IA	50613, 50614
201	Cedar Grove, NJ	07009
214	Cedar Hill, TX	75104
201	Cedar Knolls, NJ	07927
319	Cedar Rapids, IA	52400–52409, 52498, 52499
912	Cedar Springs, GA	31732
616	Cedar Springs, MI	49319
414	Cedarburg, WI	53012
516	Cedarhurst, NY	11516
404	Cedartown, GA	30125
513	Cedarville, OH	45314
419	Celina, OH	45822
615	Celina, TN	38551
214	Celina, TX	75009
518	Cementon, NY	12415
701	Center, ND	58530
402	Center, NE	68724, 68949
409	Center, TX	75935, 76642
603	Center Barnstead, NH	03225
612	Center City, MN	55002, 55012
603	Center Harbor, NH	03226
313	Center Line, MI	48015
215	Center Square, PA	19422
215	Center Valley, PA	18034
401	Centerdale, RI	02911
516	Centereach, NY	11720
515	Centerville, IA	50036, 52544
617	Centerville, MA	02632–02636
314	Centerville, MO	63633
615	Centerville, TN	37033
903	Centerville, TX	75833
801	Centerville, UT	84014
803	Central, SC	29630
303	Central City, CO	80427
502	Central City, KY	42330
308	Central City, NE	68826
401	Central Falls, RI	02863
516	Central Islip, NY	11722
503	Central Point, OR	97502
618	Centralia, IL	62801
206	Centralia, WA	98531
205	Centre, AL	35960
205	Centreville, AL	35042
301	Centreville, MD	21617
616	Centreville, MI	49032
601	Centreville, MS	39631
213	Century City, CA	90067
304	Ceredo, WV	25507
209	Ceres, CA	95307
402	Ceresco, NE	68017
213	Cerritos, CA	90701, 90703
217	Cerro Gordo, IL	61818
308	Chadron, NE	69337
315	Chadwicks, NY	13319
216	Chagrin Falls, OH	44022
215	Chalfont, PA	18914
208	Challis, ID	83226
504	Chalmette, LA	70043, 70044
605	Chamberlain, SD	57325
717	Chambersburg, PA	17201
404	Chamblee, GA	30341
217	Champaign, IL	61820–61826
412	Champion, PA	15622
518	Champlain, NY	12919
602	Chandler, AZ	85224–85227, 85244–85249
405	Chandler, OK	74834
713	Channelview, TX	77530
806	Channing, TX	79018, 79058
703	Chantilly, VA	22021
316	Chanute, KS	66720
919	Chapel Hill, NC	27514–27516, 27599
803	Chapin, SC	29036
914	Chappaqua, NY	10514
308	Chappell, NE	69129
216	Chardon, OH	44024
515	Chariton, IA	50049
412	Charleroi, PA	15022
515	Charles City, IA	50616, 50620
804	Charles City, VA	23030
304	Charles Town, WV	25414
217	Charleston, IL	61920
314	Charleston, MO	63834
601	Charleston, MS	38921
803	Charleston, SC	29401–29409, 29412–29425
304	Charleston, WV	25300–25375, 25389
803	Charleston Heights, SC	29415
617	Charlestown, MA	02129
304	Charlestown, WV	25414
616	Charlevoix, MI	49711, 49720
517	Charlotte, MI	48813
704	Charlotte, NC	28200–28284, 28286–28288
615	Charlotte, TN	37036
804	Charlottesville, VA	22900–22906, 22908
508	Charlton City, MA	01508
508	Chartley, MA	02712
804	Chase City, VA	23924
701	Chaseley, ND	58423
612	Chaska, MN	55318
501	Chatfield, AR	72323
508	Chatham, MA	02633
201	Chatham, NJ	07928
518	Chatham, NY	12037
804	Chatham, VA	24531
205	Chatom, AL	36518
818	Chatsworth, CA	91311–91313
404	Chatsworth, GA	30705
904	Chattahoochee, FL	32324
615	Chattanooga, TN	37400–37422, 37450
616	Cheboygan, MI	49721
918	Checotah, OK	74426
716	Cheektowaga, NY	14206, 14227
206	Chehalis, WA	98532
509	Chelan, WA	98816
508	Chelmsford, MA	01824
617	Chelsea, MA	02150
313	Chelsea, MI	48118
802	Chelsea, VT	05038
215	Cheltenham, PA	19012, 19126
607	Chenango Bridge, NY	13745
509	Cheney, WA	99004
815	Chenoa, IL	61726
803	Cheraw, SC	29520
712	Cherokee, IA	51012
405	Cherokee, OK	73728
303	Cherry Creek, CO	80206
609	Cherry Hill, NJ	08002–08034, 08358
815	Cherry Valley, IL	61016
704	Cherryville, NC	28021
517	Chesaning, MI	48616
804	Chesapeake, VA	23320–23325
203	Cheshire, CT	06410
916	Chester, CA	96020
618	Chester, IL	62233
406	Chester, MT	59522
603	Chester, NH	03036
908	Chester, NJ	07930
914	Chester, NY	10918
215	Chester, PA	19013–19015
803	Chester, SC	29706
804	Chester, VA	23831
304	Chester, WV	26034
215	Chester Springs, PA	19425
314	Chesterfield, MO	63005, 63017
803	Chesterfield, SC	29709
804	Chesterfield, VA	23832
219	Chesterton, IN	46304
301	Chestertown, MD	21620
217	Chestnut, IL	62518
617	Chestnut Hill, MA	02167
215	Chestnut Hill, PA	19118
404	Chestnut Mountain, GA	30502
412	Cheswick, PA	15024
301	Cheverly, MD	20784, 20785
301	Chevy Chase, MD	20813, 20815
405	Cheyenne, OK	73628
307	Cheyenne, WY	82001–82009
719	Cheyenne Wells, CO	80810
215	Cheyney, PA	19319
312	Chicago, IL	60600–60697, 60699
708	Chicago Heights, IL	60411
708	Chicago Ridge, IL	60415
603	Chichester, NH	03258
205	Chickasaw, AL	36611
405	Chickasha, OK	73018, 73023
916	Chico, CA	95926–95929
413	Chicopee, MA	01013–01022
904	Chiefland, FL	32626
205	Childersburg, AL	35044
817	Childress, TX	79201
309	Chillicothe, IL	61523
816	Chillicothe, MO	64601, 64621
614	Chillicothe, OH	45601
301	Chillum, MD	20783
503	Chiloquin, OR	97604, 97639
414	Chilton, WI	53014
704	China Grove, NC	28023
804	Chincoteague, VA	23336, 23337
602	Chinle, AZ	86503, 86556
714	Chino, CA	91708–91710
406	Chinook, MT	59523
904	Chipley, FL	32428
715	Chippewa Falls, WI	54729, 54774
216	Chippewa Lake, OH	44215
315	Chittenango, NY	13037
603	Chocorua, NH	03817
406	Choteau, MT	59422
812	Chrisney, IN	47611
215	Christiana, PA	17509
703	Christiansburg, VA	24068, 24073
915	Christoval, TX	76935
816	Chula, MO	64635
619	Chula Vista, CA	92010–92013
318	Church Point, LA	70525
708	Cicero, IL	60650
315	Cicero, NY	13039
809	Cidra, PR	00639
316	Cimarron, KS	67835
513	Cincinnati, OH	45200–45275
609	Cinnaminson, NJ	08077
406	Circle, MT	59215
612	Circle Pines, MN	55014
614	Circleville, OH	43113
217	Cisco, IL	61830
817	Cisco, TX	76437
815	Cissna Park, IL	60924
916	Citrus Heights, CA	95610, 95621
213	City of Commerce, CA	90040
818	City of Industry, CA	91744–91746, 91899
503	Clackamas, OR	97015
412	Clairton, PA	15025
205	Clanton, AL	35045
612	Clara City, MN	56222
515	Clare, IA	50524
517	Clare, MI	48617
714	Claremont, CA	91711
704	Claremont, NC	28610
603	Claremont, NH	03743
918	Claremore, OK	74017, 74018
319	Clarence, IA	52216
716	Clarence, NY	14031
501	Clarendon, AR	72029
814	Clarendon, PA	16313
806	Clarendon, TX	79226
708	Clarendon Hills, IL	60514
712	Clarinda, IA	51632
515	Clarion, IA	50525
814	Clarion, PA	16214
908	Clark, NJ	07066
605	Clark, SD	57225
404	Clarkesville, GA	30523
612	Clarkfield, MN	56223
308	Clarks, NE	68628
717	Clarks Summit, PA	18411
301	Clarksburg, MD	20871
304	Clarksburg, WV	26301, 26302
601	Clarksdale, MS	38614, 38758
404	Clarkston, GA	30021
313	Clarkston, MI	48016, 48346
509	Clarkston, WA	99403
501	Clarksville, AR	72830
812	Clarksville, IN	47129, 47130
615	Clarksville, TN	37040–37044
903	Clarksville, TX	75426, 78704
806	Claude, TX	79019
313	Clawson, MI	48017
912	Claxton, GA	30414, 30417, 30438
315	Clay, NY	13041
304	Clay, WV	25043
913	Clay Center, KS	67432
402	Clay Center, NE	68933
812	Clay City, IN	47550, 47841
302	Claymont, DE	19703
814	Claysburg, PA	16625
205	Clayton, AL	36016
404	Clayton, GA	30525
314	Clayton, MO	63105, 63124
609	Clayton, NJ	08312
505	Clayton, NM	88415
315	Clayton, NY	13624
515	Clear Lake, IA	50428
605	Clear Lake, SD	57226
715	Clear Lake, WI	54005
814	Clearfield, PA	16830
801	Clearfield, UT	84015, 84016, 84056
813	Clearwater, FL	34615–34630
316	Clearwater, KS	67026
813	Clearwater Beach, FL	34630
817	Cleburne, TX	76031–76033
919	Clemmons, NC	27012
803	Clemson, SC	29631–29634
404	Cleveland, GA	30528
601	Cleveland, MS	38732, 38733
216	Cleveland, OH	44100–44199
918	Cleveland, OK	74020
615	Cleveland, TN	37311, 37312, 37364
713	Cleveland, TX	77327, 77328
414	Cleveland, WI	53015
216	Cleveland Heights, OH	44106, 44121
813	Clewiston, FL	33440
704	Cliffside, NC	28024
908	Cliffwood, NJ	07721
602	Clifton, AZ	85533
815	Clifton, IL	60927
201	Clifton, NJ	07011–07015
817	Clifton, TX	76634
703	Clifton Forge, VA	24422
215	Clifton Heights, PA	19018
518	Clifton Park, NY	12065
315	Clifton Springs, NY	14432
218	Climax, MN	56523
501	Clinton, AR	72031
203	Clinton, CT	06413
319	Clinton, IA	52732
217	Clinton, IL	61727
317	Clinton, IN	47842
502	Clinton, KY	42031
504	Clinton, LA	70722
508	Clinton, MA	01510
301	Clinton, MD	20735
207	Clinton, ME	04927
517	Clinton, MI	49236
816	Clinton, MO	64735
601	Clinton, MS	39056, 39058, 39060
919	Clinton, NC	28328
908	Clinton, NJ	08801, 08809
315	Clinton, NY	12514, 13323
405	Clinton, OK	73601
412	Clinton, PA	15026, 17752
803	Clinton, SC	29325
615	Clinton, TN	37716, 37717
715	Clintonville, WI	54929
703	Clintwood, VA	24228
313	Clio, MI	48420
515	Clive, IA	50053
218	Cloquet, MN	55720
201	Closter, NJ	07624

Clover / Dallastown

Area	City, State	ZIP Code(s)
803	Clover, SC	29710
209	Clovis, CA	93612, 93613
505	Clovis, NM	88101–88103
409	Clute, TX	77531
704	Clyde, NC	28721
716	Clymer, NY	14724
619	Coachella, CA	92236
405	Coalgate, OK	74538
209	Coalinga, CA	93210
801	Coalville, UT	84017
317	Coatesville, IN	46121
215	Coatesville, PA	19320
707	Cobb, CA	95426
518	Cobleskill, NY	12043
617	Cochituate, MA	01778
912	Cochran, GA	31014, 31026
301	Cockeysville, MD	21030, 21031
407	Cocoa, FL	32922–32927
305	Coconut Grove, FL	33133, 33233
307	Cody, WY	82414
703	Coeburn, VA	24230
208	Coeur d' Alene, ID	83814
518	Coeymans, NY	12045
316	Coffeyville, KS	67331, 67337
617	Cohasset, MA	02025
518	Cohoes, NY	12047
612	Cokato, MN	55321
913	Colby, KS	67701
802	Colchester, VT	05439, 05446
612	Cold Spring, MN	56320
914	Cold Spring, NY	10516
606	Cold Springs, KY	41076
409	Coldspring, TX	77331
316	Coldwater, KS	67029
517	Coldwater, MI	49036
419	Coldwater, OH	45828
603	Colebrook, NH	03576
517	Coleman, MI	48618
915	Coleman, TX	76834
414	Coleman, WI	54112
515	Colfax, IA	50054
318	Colfax, LA	71417
509	Colfax, WA	99111
513	College Corner, OH	45003
404	College Park, GA	30337, 30349
301	College Park, MD	20740, 20742
509	College Place, WA	99324
718	College Point, NY	11356
409	College Station, TX	77840–77845
615	Collegedale, TN	37315
612	Collegeville, MN	56321
215	Collegeville, PA	19426, 19473
304	Colliers, WV	26035
901	Collierville, TN	38017, 38027
215	Collingdale, PA	19023
609	Collingswood, NJ	08108
601	Collins, MS	39428
618	Collinsville, IL	62234
918	Collinsville, OK	74021
615	Collinwood, TN	38450
605	Colman, SD	57017
215	Colmar, PA	18915
515	Colo, IA	50056
908	Colonia, NJ	07067
804	Colonial Beach, VA	22443
804	Colonial Heights, VA	23834
518	Colonie, NY	12205, 12212
915	Colorado City, TX	79512
719	Colorado Springs, CO	80840, 80903–80935, 80962
912	Colquitt, GA	31737
714	Colton, CA	92324
908	Colts Neck, NJ	07722
205	Columbia, AL	36319
209	Columbia, CA	95310
618	Columbia, IL	62236
502	Columbia, KY	42728
318	Columbia, LA	71418
301	Columbia, MD	21044–21046
314	Columbia, MO	65201–65205, 65211–65218
601	Columbia, MS	39429
919	Columbia, NC	27925
717	Columbia, PA	17512
803	Columbia, SC	29200–29292
615	Columbia, TN	38401, 38402
219	Columbia City, IN	46725
406	Columbia Falls, MT	59912, 59928
205	Columbiana, AL	35051
216	Columbiana, OH	44408
404	Columbus, GA	31900–31909, 31993–31999 *
812	Columbus, IN	47201–47203
316	Columbus, KS	66725
601	Columbus, MS	39701–39705
406	Columbus, MT	59019
704	Columbus, NC	28722
402	Columbus, NE	68601, 68602
614	Columbus, OH	43085, 43200–43236, 43251 *
409	Columbus, TX	78934, 78935
414	Columbus, WI	53912, 53925
916	Colusa, CA	95932
217	Colusa, IL	62329
509	Colville, WA	99114
316	Colwich, KS	67030
915	Comanche, TX	76442
414	Combined Locks, WI	54113
516	Commack, NY	11725
213	Commerce, CA	90040, 90091
404	Commerce, GA	30529
918	Commerce, OK	74339
903	Commerce, TX	75428, 75429
303	Commerce City, CO	80022, 80037
213	Compton, CA	90220–90224
815	Compton, IL	61318
616	Comstock Park, MI	49321
816	Conception, MO	64433
415	Concord, CA	94518–94524, 94527
508	Concord, MA	01742
704	Concord, NC	28018, 28025–28027
603	Concord, NH	03300–03306
615	Concord, TN	37922
913	Concordia, KS	66901
816	Concordia, MO	64020
215	Concordville, PA	19331
503	Condon, OR	97823
719	Conejos, CO	81129
717	Conestoga, PA	17516
914	Congers, NY	10920
607	Conklin, NY	13748
404	Conley, GA	30027
216	Conneaut, OH	44030
814	Conneautville, PA	16406
412	Connellsville, PA	15425
317	Connersville, IN	47331
704	Conover, NC	28613
515	Conrad, IA	50621
406	Conrad, MT	59425
409	Conroe, TX	77301–77305, 77385
319	Conroy, IA	52220
215	Conshohocken, PA	19428
616	Constantine, MI	49042
603	Contoocook, NH	03229
504	Convent, LA	70723
201	Convent Station, NJ	07961
419	Convoy, OH	45832
501	Conway, AR	72032
603	Conway, NH	03818, 03866
803	Conway, SC	29526, 29527
316	Conway Springs, KS	67031
404	Conyers, GA	30207, 30208
615	Cookeville, TN	38501–38503, 38505
602	Coolidge, AZ	85228
712	Coon Rapids, IA	50058
612	Coon Rapids, MN	55433
903	Cooper, TX	75432
215	Coopersburg, PA	18036
701	Cooperstown, ND	58425
607	Cooperstown, NY	13326
503	Coos Bay, OR	97420
516	Copiague, NY	11726
215	Coplay, PA	18037
216	Copley, OH	44321
214	Coppell, TX	75019
503	Coquille, OR	97423
305	Coral Gables, FL	33133, 33134, 33156
305	Coral Springs, FL	33065, 33071–33076
305	Coral Way Village, FL	33155, 33165
319	Coralville, IA	52241
516	Coram, NY	11727
412	Coraopolis, PA	15108
606	Corbin, KY	40701, 40702
209	Corcoran, CA	93212, 93282
912	Cordele, GA	31015
405	Cordell, OK	73632
205	Cordova, AL	35550
901	Cordova, TN	38018
716	Corfu, NY	14036
207	Corinna, ME	04928
601	Corinth, MS	38834
518	Corinth, NY	12822
404	Cornelia, GA	30531
916	Corning, CA	96021, 96029
515	Corning, IA	50841
607	Corning, NY	14830, 14831
402	Cornlea, NE	68630
914	Cornwall, NY	12518
215	Cornwells Heights, PA	19020
714	Corona, CA	91718–91720
718	Corona, NY	11368
714	Corona del Mar, CA	92625
714	Coronado, CA	92118
809	Corozal, PR	00643
512	Corpus Christi, TX	78400–78427, 78460–78482
814	Corry, PA	16407
903	Corsicana, TX	75110, 75151
415	Corte Madera, CA	94925
303	Cortez, CO	81321
607	Cortland, NY	13045
216	Cortland, OH	44410
517	Corunna, MI	48817
503	Corvallis, OR	97330, 97331, 97339
515	Corydon, IA	50060
812	Corydon, IN	47112
203	Cos Cob, CT	06807
614	Coshocton, OH	43812
714	Costa Mesa, CA	92626–92628
707	Cotati, CA	94927–94931
612	Cottage Grove, MN	55016
503	Cottage Grove, OR	97424, 97472
608	Cottage Grove, WI	53527
904	Cottondale, FL	32431
316	Cottonwood Falls, KS	66845
512	Cotulla, TX	78001, 78014
814	Coudersport, PA	16915
901	Counce, TN	38326
208	Council, ID	83612
712	Council Bluffs, IA	51501–51503, 51593
316	Council Grove, KS	66846
708	Country Club Hills, IL	60478
708	Countryside, IL	60525
206	Coupeville, WA	98239
318	Coushatta, LA	71019
401	Coventry, RI	02816, 02817, 02827
818	Covina, CA	91722–91724
404	Covington, GA	30209
317	Covington, IN	47932
606	Covington, KY	41011–41018
504	Covington, LA	70433, 70434
513	Covington, OH	45318
901	Covington, TN	38019
703	Covington, VA	24426
803	Cowpens, SC	29330
308	Cozad, NE	69130
303	Craig, CO	81625, 81626
609	Cranbury, NJ	08512, 08570
715	Crandon, WI	54520
417	Crane, MO	65633
915	Crane, TX	79731
218	Crane Lake, MN	55725
908	Cranford, NJ	07016
401	Cranston, RI	02905–02921
317	Crawfordsville, IN	47933
904	Crawfordville, FL	32327
404	Crawfordville, GA	30631
719	Creede, CO	81130
412	Creighton, PA	15030
707	Crescent City, CA	95531, 95538
916	Crescent Mills, CA	95934
319	Cresco, IA	52136
717	Cresco, PA	18326
201	Cresskill, NJ	07626
814	Cresson, PA	16630
717	Cressona, PA	17929
515	Creston, IA	50801
904	Crestview, FL	32536
606	Crestview Hills, KY	41017
708	Crestwood, IL	60445
919	Creswell, NC	27928
503	Creswell, OR	97426
708	Crete, IL	60417
402	Crete, NE	68333
309	Creve Coeur, IL	61611
314	Creve Coeur, MO	63141
804	Crewe, VA	23930
719	Cripple Creek, CO	80813
301	Crisfield, MD	21817
409	Crockett, TX	75835
203	Cromwell, CT	06416
218	Crookston, MN	56716
614	Crooksville, OH	43731
218	Crosby, MN	55037, 56441
701	Crosby, ND	58730
806	Crosbyton, TX	79322
904	Cross City, FL	32628
501	Crossett, AR	71635
618	Crossville, IL	62827
615	Crossville, TN	38555, 38557
914	Croton Falls, NY	10519
817	Crowell, TX	79227, 79260
318	Crowley, LA	70526, 70527
817	Crowley, TX	76036
219	Crown Point, IN	46307
504	Crown Point, LA	70072
301	Crownsville, MD	21032
215	Croydon, PA	19020, 19021
804	Crozet, VA	22932
304	Crumpler, WV	24825
612	Crystal, MN	55422, 55428
702	Crystal Bay, NV	89402, 89451
314	Crystal City, MO	63019
512	Crystal City, TX	78839
906	Crystal Falls, MI	49920
815	Crystal Lake, IL	60012, 60014
716	Cuba, NY	14727
714	Cucamonga, CA	91730
414	Cudahy, WI	53110
512	Cuero, TX	77954
205	Cullman, AL	35055, 35056
304	Culloden, WV	25510
815	Cullom, IL	60929
704	Cullowhee, NC	28723
703	Culpeper, VA	22701
219	Culver, IN	46511
213	Culver City, CA	90230–90233
606	Cumberland, KY	40823
301	Cumberland, MD	21501–21505
614	Cumberland, OH	43732
401	Cumberland, RI	02864
804	Cumberland, VA	23040
404	Cumming, GA	30130
408	Cupertino, CA	95014–95016
712	Curlew, IA	50527
919	Currituck, NC	27929
308	Curtis, NE	69025
814	Curwensville, PA	16833
918	Cushing, OK	74023
404	Cusseta, GA	31805
605	Custer, SD	57730
405	Custer City, OK	73639
406	Cut Bank, MT	59427, 59473
912	Cuthbert, GA	31740
209	Cutler, CA	93615
216	Cuyahoga Falls, OH	44221–44224
712	Cylinder, IA	50528
606	Cynthiana, KY	41031
714	Cypress, CA	90623, 90630
813	Cypress Gardens, FL	33884

D

Area	City, State	ZIP Code(s)
405	Dacoma, OK	73731
904	Dade City, FL	33525, 33526
205	Dadeville, AL	36853
404	Dahlonega, GA	30533
903	Daingerfield, TX	75638
515	Dakota City, IA	50529
402	Dakota City, NE	68731
812	Dale, IN	47523
703	Dale City, VA	22192, 22193
205	Daleville, AL	36322, 36362
806	Dalhart, TX	79022
404	Dallas, GA	30132
704	Dallas, NC	28034
503	Dallas, OR	97338
717	Dallas, PA	18612, 18690
214	Dallas, TX	75200–75398
515	Dallas Center, IA	50063
717	Dallastown, PA	17313

Area	City	ZIP
404	Dalton, GA	30720–30722
413	Dalton, MA	01226, 01227
717	Dalton, PA	18414
415	Daly City, CA	94014–94017
301	Damascus, MD	20872
515	Dana, IA	50064
203	Danbury, CT	06810–06813, 06816, 06817
919	Danbury, NC	27016
615	Dandridge, TN	37725
409	Danevang, TX	77432
305	Dania, FL	33004
304	Daniels, WV	25832
203	Danielson, CT	06239
404	Danielsville, GA	30633
215	Danielsville, PA	18038
716	Dansville, NY	14437
508	Danvers, MA	01923
501	Danville, AR	72833
415	Danville, CA	94506, 94526
319	Danville, IA	52623
217	Danville, IL	61832–61834
317	Danville, IN	46122
316	Danville, KS	67036
606	Danville, KY	40422
717	Danville, PA	17821, 17822
804	Danville, VA	24540–24543
215	Darby, PA	19023
203	Darien, CT	06820
912	Darien, GA	31305
716	Darien Center, NY	14040
412	Darlington, PA	16115, 19063
803	Darlington, SC	29532, 29540
608	Darlington, WI	53530
612	Dassel, MN	55325
408	Davenport, CA	95017
813	Davenport, FL	33837
319	Davenport, IA	52800–52809
509	Davenport, WA	99122
402	David City, NE	68632
704	Davidson, NC	28036
405	Davidson, OK	73530
305	Davie, FL	33312–33317, 33324–33332
916	Davis, CA	95616–95618
304	Davis, WV	26260
313	Davison, MI	48423
912	Dawson, GA	31042, 31742
612	Dawson, MN	56232
404	Dawsonville, GA	30534
515	Dayton, IA	50530
908	Dayton, NJ	08810
513	Dayton, OH	45390–45490
615	Dayton, TN	37321
409	Dayton, TX	77535
703	Dayton, VA	22821
509	Dayton, WA	99328
904	Daytona Beach, FL	32114, 32117–32129
203	Dayville, CT	06241
605	Deadwood, SD	57732
313	Dearborn, MI	48120–48126, 48128
313	Dearborn Heights, MI	48125, 48127
205	Decatur, AL	35601–35609
501	Decatur, AR	72722
404	Decatur, GA	30030–30038
217	Decatur, IL	62521–62526
219	Decatur, IN	46733
601	Decatur, MS	39327
615	Decatur, TN	37322
817	Decatur, TX	76234
901	Decaturville, TN	38329
615	Decherd, TN	37324
406	Decker, MT	59025
313	Deckerville, MI	48427
319	Decorah, IA	52101, 52131
712	Dedham, IA	51440
617	Dedham, MA	02026
203	Deep River, CT	06417
406	Deer Lodge, MT	59722, 59733
516	Deer Park, NY	11729
713	Deer Park, TX	77536
708	Deerfield, IL	60015
305	Deerfield Beach, FL	33064, 33441–33443
218	Deerwood, MN	56444
315	Deferiet, NY	13628
419	Defiance, OH	43512
608	DeForest, WI	53532
904	DeFuniak Springs, FL	32433
815	DeKalb, IL	60115
601	DeKalb, MS	39328
405	Del City, OK	73115, 73135
619	Del Mar, CA	92014
719	Del Norte, CO	81132
209	Del Rey, CA	93616
512	Del Rio, TX	78835, 78840–78843
609	Delair, NJ	08110
609	Delanco, NJ	08075
904	DeLand, FL	32720–32724
217	DeLand, IL	61839
805	Delano, CA	93215, 93216
612	Delano, MN	55328
717	Delano, PA	18220
309	Delavan, IL	61734
507	Delavan, MN	56023
414	Delavan, WI	53115
614	Delaware, OH	43015, 43556
302	Delaware City, DE	19706
717	Delaware Water Gap, PA	18327
318	Delhi, LA	71232
607	Delhi, NY	13753
513	Delhi Hills, OH	45238
216	Dellroy, OH	44620
518	Delmar, NY	12054
412	Delmont, PA	15626
317	Delphi, IN	46923
419	Delphos, OH	45833
609	Delran, NJ	08075
407	Delray Beach, FL	33444–33447, 33483, 33484
303	Delta, CO	81416
318	Delta, LA	71233
419	Delta, OH	43515
505	Deming, NM	88030, 88031
205	Demopolis, AL	36732
404	Demorest, GA	30535, 30544
219	Demotte, IN	46310
504	Denham Springs, LA	70726, 70727
712	Denison, IA	51442
903	Denison, TX	75020, 75021
803	Denmark, SC	29042
301	Denton, MD	21629
817	Denton, TX	76201–76206
303	Denver, CO	80014, 80201–80295
812	Denver, IN	46926
704	Denver, NC	28037
215	Denver, PA	17517
201	Denville, NJ	07834
414	DePere, WI	54115
716	Depew, NY	14043
609	Deptford, NJ	08096
501	DeQueen, AR	71832
203	Derby, CT	06418
316	Derby, KS	67037
716	Derby, NY	14047
802	Derby Line, VT	05830
318	DeRidder, LA	70634
603	Derry, NH	03038
412	Derry, PA	15627, 17821
501	Des Arc, AR	72040
515	Des Moines, IA	50309–50325, 50392–50397 *
206	Des Moines, WA	98188, 98198
314	Des Peres, MO	63102, 63131
708	Des Plaines, IL	60016–60019
402	Deshler, NE	68340
605	DeSmet, SD	57231
912	DeSoto, GA	31743
214	DeSoto, TX	75115
904	Destin, FL	32541
207	Detroit, ME	04929
313	Detroit, MI	48200–48277, 48288
218	Detroit Lakes, MN	56501, 56578
215	Devault, PA	19432
701	Devils Lake, ND	58301
215	Devon, PA	19333
217	Dewey, IL	61840
501	DeWitt, AR	72042
319	DeWitt, IA	52742
402	DeWitt, NE	68341
315	DeWitt, NY	13214
207	Dexter, ME	04930
313	Dexter, MI	48130
314	Dexter, MO	63841
805	Di Giorgio, CA	93217
714	Diamond Bar, CA	91765
518	Diamond Point, NY	12824
409	Diboll, TX	75941
806	Dickens, TX	79229
701	Dickinson, ND	58601, 58643
615	Dickson, TN	37055
316	Dighton, KS	67839
508	Dighton, MA	02715, 02764
319	Dike, IA	50624
303	Dillon, CO	80435
406	Dillon, MT	59724, 59725, 59746
803	Dillon, SC	29536
614	Dillonvale, OH	43917, 45236
804	Dillwyn, VA	23911, 23936
218	Dilworth, MN	56529
806	Dimmitt, TX	79027
209	Dinuba, CA	93618
814	Distant, PA	16223
516	Dix Hills, NY	11746
207	Dixfield, ME	04224
916	Dixon, CA	95620
815	Dixon, IL	61021
502	Dixon, KY	42409
412	Dixonville, PA	15734
603	Dixville Notch, NH	03576
914	Dobbs Ferry, NY	10522
919	Dobson, NC	27017
507	Dodge Center, MN	55927
316	Dodge City, KS	67801
608	Dodgeville, WI	53533, 53595
501	Dogpatch, AR	72648
708	Dolton, IL	60419
219	Donaldson, IN	46513
218	Donaldson, MN	56720
504	Donaldsonville, LA	70346
912	Donalsonville, GA	31745
314	Doniphan, MO	63935
512	Donna, TX	78537
412	Donora, PA	15033
809	Dorado, PR	00646
404	Doraville, GA	30340
617	Dorchester, MA	02121–02125
301	Dorsey, MD	21076, 21227
209	Dos Palos, CA	93620
804	Doswell, VA	23047
205	Dothan, AL	36301–36303
205	Double Springs, AL	35553
602	Douglas, AZ	85607, 85655
912	Douglas, GA	31533
307	Douglas, WY	82633
215	Douglassville, PA	19518
718	Douglaston, NY	11363
404	Douglasville, GA	30133–30135
303	Dove Creek, CO	81324
302	Dover, DE	19901, 19964
813	Dover, FL	33527
603	Dover, NH	03820
201	Dover, NJ	07801–08753
216	Dover, OH	43567, 44622, 45761
615	Dover, TN	37058
914	Dover Plains, NY	12522
207	Dover-Foxcroft, ME	04426
616	Dowagiac, MI	49047
708	Downers Grove, IL	60515–60517
213	Downey, CA	90240–90242
916	Downieville, CA	95936
215	Downingtown, PA	19335, 19372
215	Doylestown, PA	18901, 18933
508	Dracut, MA	01826
503	Drain, OR	97435
412	Dravosburg, PA	15034
313	Drayton Plains, MI	48020
901	Dresden, TN	38225
215	Dresher, PA	19025
704	Drexel, NC	28619
215	Drexel Hill, PA	19026
208	Driggs, ID	83422
606	Dry Ridge, KY	41035
313	Dryden, MI	48428
607	Dryden, NY	13053
818	Duarte, CA	91009, 91010
415	Dublin, CA	94568
912	Dublin, GA	31021, 31040
919	Dublin, NC	28332
603	Dublin, NH	03444
614	Dublin, OH	43017
215	Dublin, PA	17223, 18917
703	Dublin, VA	24084
208	Dubois, ID	83423, 83446
814	DuBois, PA	15801
319	Dubuque, IA	52001–52004
801	Duchesne, UT	84021, 84073
912	Dudley, GA	31022
508	Dudley, MA	01570
919	Dudley, NC	28333
803	Due West, SC	29639
405	Duke, OK	73532
504	Dulac, LA	70353
404	Duluth, GA	30136, 30199
218	Duluth, MN	55728, 55800–55816
501	Dumas, AR	71639
806	Dumas, TX	79029
703	Dumfries, VA	22026
602	Duna, AZ	86041
412	Dunbar, PA	15431
304	Dunbar, WV	25064
405	Duncan, OK	73533, 73536, 73575
803	Duncan, SC	29334
717	Duncannon, PA	17020
814	Duncansville, PA	16635
214	Duncanville, TX	75116, 75137, 75138
301	Dundalk, MD	21222
708	Dundee, IL	60118
313	Dundee, MI	48131
607	Dundee, NY	14837
813	Dunedin, FL	34697, 34698
908	Dunellen, NJ	08812
319	Dunkerton, IA	50626
317	Dunkirk, IN	47336
301	Dunkirk, MD	20754
716	Dunkirk, NY	14048, 14166
309	Dunlap, IL	61525
615	Dunlap, TN	37327
717	Dunmore, PA	18512
919	Dunn, NC	28334
308	Dunning, NE	68833
404	Dunwoody, GA	30338, 30350
605	Dupree, SD	57623, 57628
618	DuQuoin, IL	62832
517	Durand, MI	48429
715	Durand, WI	54736
303	Durango, CO	81301, 81302
601	Durant, MS	39063
405	Durant, OK	74701, 74702
203	Durham, CT	06422
919	Durham, NC	27700–27722
603	Durham, NH	03824
717	Duryea, PA	18642
617	Duxbury, MA	02332
901	Dyer, TN	38330
901	Dyersburg, TN	38024, 38025
319	Dyersville, IA	52040
319	Dysart, IA	52224

E

Area	City	ZIP
719	Eads, CO	81026
612	Eagan, MN	55120–55123
303	Eagle, CO	81631
515	Eagle Grove, IA	50533
409	Eagle Lake, TX	77434
512	Eagle Pass, TX	78852, 78853
906	Eagle River, MI	49924
715	Eagle River, WI	54521
319	Earlville, IA	52041
314	Earth City, MO	63045
803	Easley, SC	29640, 29641
618	East Alton, IL	62024
802	East Arlington, VT	05252
716	East Aurora, NY	14052
203	East Berlin, CT	06023
717	East Berlin, PA	17316
606	East Bernstadt, KY	40729
617	East Boston, MA	02128
508	East Bridgewater, MA	02333
508	East Brookfield, MA	01515
908	East Brunswick, NJ	08816
412	East Butler, PA	16029
501	East Camden, AR	71701
219	East Chicago, IN	46312
216	East Cleveland, OH	44112, 44118
313	East Detroit, MI	48021
508	East Douglas, MA	01516
815	East Dubuque, IL	61025
518	East Durham, NY	12423
717	East Earl, PA	17519

Area	City	ZIP
718	East Elmhurst, NY	11369
702	East Ely, NV	89301
508	East Falmouth, MA	02536
516	East Farmingdale, NY	11735
508	East Freetown, MA	02717
205	East Gadsden, AL	35903
406	East Glacier Park, MT	59434
203	East Granby, CT	06026
218	East Grand Forks, MN	56721
215	East Greenville, PA	18041
401	East Greenwich, RI	02818
203	East Hampton, CT	06424, 06447
516	East Hampton, NY	11937
201	East Hanover, NJ	07936
203	East Hartford, CT	06108, 06118
203	East Haven, CT	06512, 06513
603	East Hebron, NH	03232
406	East Helena, MT	59635
516	East Islip, NY	11730
616	East Jordan, MI	49727
517	East Lansing, MI	48823–48826
513	East Liberty, OH	43074, 43319
412	East Liberty, PA	15206
216	East Liverpool, OH	43920
413	East Longmeadow, MA	01028
213	East Los Angeles, CA	90022
203	East Lyme, CT	06333
412	East McKeesport, PA	15035
516	East Meadow, NY	11554
309	East Moline, IL	61244
201	East Newark, NJ	07029
516	East Northport, NY	11731
203	East Norwalk, CT	06855
201	East Orange, NJ	07017–07019
216	East Palestine, OH	44413
309	East Peoria, IL	61611
617	East Pepperell, MA	01463
717	East Petersburg, PA	17520
404	East Point, GA	30344
401	East Providence, RI	02914–02916
716	East Rochester, NY	14445
216	East Rochester, OH	44625
201	East Rutherford, NJ	07073
618	East St Louis, IL	62201, 62202
717	East Stroudsburg, PA	18301
315	East Syracuse, NY	13057
508	East Taunton, MA	02718
215	East Texas, PA	18046
414	East Troy, WI	53120
802	East Wallingford, VT	05742
508	East Walpole, MA	02032
617	East Weymouth, MA	02189
203	East Windsor, CT	06016, 06088
609	East Windsor, NJ	08512, 08520
607	East Worcester, NY	12064
914	Eastchester, NY	10709
413	Easthampton, MA	01027
216	Eastlake, OH	44095
817	Eastland, TX	76448
912	Eastman, GA	31023
203	Easton, CT	06612
309	Easton, IL	62633
508	Easton, MA	02334
301	Easton, MD	21601
207	Easton, ME	04740
215	Easton, PA	18042–18044
207	Eastport, ME	04631
516	Eastport, NY	11941
804	Eastville, VA	23347
303	Eaton, CO	80615
513	Eaton, OH	45320
813	Eaton Park, FL	33840
517	Eaton Rapids, MI	48827
404	Eatonton, GA	31024
908	Eatontown, NJ	07724
715	Eau Claire, WI	54701–54703
814	Ebensburg, PA	15931
313	Ecorse, MI	48229
512	Edcouch, TX	78538
215	Eddington, PA	19020
215	Eddystone, PA	19013
502	Eddyville, KY	42038
919	Eden, NC	27288
802	Eden, VT	05652, 05653
612	Eden Prairie, MN	55344, 55346, 55347
919	Edenton, NC	27932
508	Edgartown, MA	02539
803	Edgefield, SC	29824
507	Edgerton, MN	56128
608	Edgerton, WI	53534
201	Edgewater, NJ	07020
612	Edina, MN	55410, 55424, 55436, 55439
816	Edina, MO	63537
814	Edinboro, PA	16412, 16444
412	Edinburg, PA	16116
512	Edinburg, TX	78539, 78540
703	Edinburg, VA	22824
812	Edinburgh, IN	46124
805	Edison, CA	93220
308	Edison, NE	68936
908	Edison, NJ	08817–08837
419	Edison, OH	43320
803	Edisto Island, SC	29438
405	Edmond, OK	73013, 73034, 73083
206	Edmonds, WA	98020, 98026
806	Edmonson, TX	79032
502	Edmonton, KY	42129
517	Edmore, MI	48829
512	Edna, TX	77957
616	Edwardsburg, MI	49112, 49130
618	Edwardsville, IL	62025, 62026
217	Effingham, IL	62401
609	Egg Harbor City, NJ	08215
406	Ekalaka, MT	59324
619	El Cajon, CA	92019–92022
409	El Campo, TX	77437
619	El Centro, CA	92243, 92244
415	El Cerrito, CA	91720, 94530
501	El Dorado, AR	71730, 71731
316	El Dorado, KS	67042
417	El Dorado Springs, MO	64744
818	El Monte, CA	91731–91734
309	El Paso, IL	61738
915	El Paso, TX	79900–79955, 79982–79999 *
405	El Reno, OK	73036
213	El Segundo, CA	90245
415	El Sobrante, CA	94803
714	El Toro, CA	92630
205	Elba, AL	36323
812	Elberfeld, IN	47613
404	Elberton, GA	30635
218	Elbow Lake, MN	56531
315	Elbridge, NY	13060
708	Elburn, IL	60119
314	Eldon, MO	65026, 65072
515	Eldora, IA	50627
618	Eldorado, IL	61411, 62930
915	Eldorado, TX	76936
814	Eldred, PA	16731, 17964
707	Eldridge, CA	95431
808	Eleele, HI	96705
815	Elferoy, IL	61027
708	Elgin, IL	60120–60123
402	Elgin, NE	68636
419	Elgin, OH	45838
803	Elgin, SC	29045
908	Elizabeth, NJ	07200–07208
412	Elizabeth, PA	15037, 17543
304	Elizabeth, WV	26143
919	Elizabeth City, NC	27906–27909
615	Elizabethton, TN	37643, 37644
618	Elizabethtown, IL	62931
502	Elizabethtown, KY	42701, 42702
919	Elizabethtown, NC	28337
518	Elizabethtown, NY	12932
717	Elizabethtown, PA	17022
717	Elizabethville, PA	17023
405	Elk City, OK	73644, 73648
916	Elk Grove, CA	95624, 95759
708	Elk Grove Village, IL	60007, 60009
605	Elk Point, SD	57025
616	Elk Rapids, MI	49629
612	Elk River, MN	55330
319	Elkader, IA	52043
217	Elkhart, IL	62634
219	Elkhart, IN	46514–46517
316	Elkhart, KS	67950
414	Elkhorn, WI	53121
919	Elkin, NC	28621
304	Elkins, WV	26241
215	Elkins Park, PA	19012, 19117
814	Elkland, PA	16920
702	Elko, NV	89801, 89828
301	Elkridge, MD	21227
502	Elkton, KY	42220
301	Elkton, MD	21921
517	Elkton, MI	48731
912	Ellaville, GA	31806
701	Ellendale, ND	58436
509	Ellensburg, WA	98926
914	Ellenville, NY	12428
404	Ellenwood, GA	30049
301	Ellicott City, MD	21043 ,
716	Ellicottville, NY	14731
404	Ellijay, GA	30540
203	Ellington, CT	06029
217	Elliott, IL	60933
913	Ellis, KS	67637
314	Ellisville, MO	63011, 63021
601	Ellisville, MS	39437
913	Ellsworth, KS	67439
207	Ellsworth, ME	04605
715	Ellsworth, WI	54003, 54011
412	Ellwood City, PA	16117
414	Elm Grove, WI	53122
501	Elm Springs, AR	72728
515	Elma, IA	50628
716	Elma, NY	14059
708	Elmhurst, IL	60126
718	Elmhurst, NY	11373
607	Elmira, NY	14900–14905
607	Elmira Heights, NY	14903
516	Elmont, NY	11003
914	Elmsford, NY	10523
708	Elmwood Park, IL	60635
201	Elmwood Park, NJ	07407
919	Elon College, NC	27244
512	Elsa, TX	78543
618	Elsah, IL	62028
215	Elverson, PA	19520
815	Elwood, IL	60421
317	Elwood, IN	46036
913	Elwood, KS	66024
308	Elwood, NE	68937, 68976
215	Elwyn, PA	19063
319	Ely, IA	52227
218	Ely, MN	55731
216	Elyria, OH	44035–44039
717	Elysburg, PA	17824
201	Emerson, NJ	07630
415	Emeryville, CA	94608
717	Emigsville, PA	17318
314	Eminence, MO	65466
816	Emma, MO	65327
215	Emmaus, PA	18049, 18098
712	Emmetsburg, IA	50536
208	Emmett, ID	83617, 83670
301	Emmitsburg, MD	21727
903	Emory, TX	75440
703	Emory, VA	24327
316	Emporia, KS	66801
804	Emporia, VA	23847
814	Emporium, PA	15834
619	Encinitas, CA	92023, 92024
818	Encino, CA	91316, 91436
607	Endicott, NY	13760
607	Endwell, NY	13760
203	Enfield, CT	06082
919	Enfield, NC	27823
919	Engelhard, NC	27824
303	Englewood, CO	80110–80112, 80150–80156
813	Englewood, FL	34223, 34295
201	Englewood, NJ	07631, 07632
513	Englewood, OH	45315, 45322
201	Englewood Cliffs, NJ	07632
812	English, IN	47118
908	Englishtown, NJ	07726
405	Enid, OK	73701–73703, 73705
704	Enka, NC	28728
214	Ennis, TX	75119, 75120
802	Enosburg Falls, VT	05450
316	Ensign, KS	67841
205	Ensley, AL	35208, 35218
205	Enterprise, AL	36330, 36331
601	Enterprise, MS	39330, 39645
503	Enteprise, OR	97828
206	Enumclaw, WA	98022
801	Ephraim, UT	84627
717	Ephrata, PA	17522, 17549
509	Ephrata, WA	98823
603	Epsom, NH	03234
215	Erdenheim, PA	19118
309	Erie, IL	61250
316	Erie, KS	66733
313	Erie, MI	48133
814	Erie, PA	16500–16566
615	Erin, TN	37061
606	Erlanger, KY	41018
508	Erving, MA	01344
615	Erwin, TN	37650
209	Escalon, CA	95320
906	Escanaba, MI	49829
619	Escondido, CA	92025–92027, 92029, 92030
401	Esmond, RI	02917
505	Espanola, NM	87532, 87578
203	Essex, CT	06426
301	Essex, MD	21221
201	Essex Fells, NJ	07021
802	Essex Junction, VT	05452, 05453
215	Essington, PA	19029
505	Estancia, NM	87016, 87057
303	Estes Park, CO	80511, 80517
712	Estherville, IA	51334
318	Estherwood, LA	70534
803	Estill, SC	29918
714	Etiwanda, CA	91739
404	Eton, GA	30724
615	Etowah, TN	37331
216	Euclid, OH	44117–44123, 44143
205	Eufaula, AL	36027, 36072
918	Eufaula, OK	74432
503	Eugene, OR	97401–97405, 97455
817	Euless, TX	76039, 76040
318	Eunice, LA	70535
601	Eupora, MS	39744
707	Eureka, CA	95501, 95534
309	Eureka, IL	61530
316	Eureka, KS	67045
314	Eureka, MO	63025
702	Eureka, NV	89316
501	Eureka Springs, AR	72632
904	Eustis, FL	32726, 32727
205	Eutaw, AL	35462
412	Evans City, PA	16033
708	Evanston, IL	60201–60204, 60208
307	Evanston, WY	82930, 82931
812	Evansville, IN	47700–47741, 47744–47750
215	Evansville, PA	19522
608	Evansville, WI	53536
307	Evansville, WY	82636
616	Evart, MI	49631
218	Eveleth, MN	55734
617	Everett, MA	02149
814	Everett, PA	15537
206	Everett, WA	98200–98208
205	Evergreen, AL	36401, 36469
303	Evergreen, CO	80439
708	Evergreen Park, IL	60642
712	Everly, IA	51338
808	Ewa Beach, HI	96706, 96707, 96862
609	Ewing, NJ	08618
612	Excelsior, MN	55331
816	Excelsior Springs, MO	64024
209	Exeter, CA	93221
603	Exeter, NH	03833
717	Exeter, PA	18643
401	Exeter, RI	02822
804	Exmore, VA	23350
412	Export, PA	15632
215	Exton, PA	19341, 19353
717	Eynon, PA	18403

F

Area	City	ZIP
915	Fabens, TX	79838
313	Fair Haven, MI	48023
201	Fair Lawn, NJ	07410
907	Fairbanks, AK	99701–99714, 99775, 99790
513	Fairborn, OH	45324
404	Fairburn, GA	30213
815	Fairbury, IL	61739
402	Fairbury, NE	68352
507	Fairfax, MN	55332
703	Fairfax, VA	22021, 22030–22039
205	Fairfield, AL	35064, 36420
707	Fairfield, CA	94533–94535

203	Fairfield, CT	06430–06432
515	Fairfield, IA	52556
208	Fairfield, ID	83322, 83327
618	Fairfield, IL	61283, 62837
201	Fairfield, NJ	07004, 07006
513	Fairfield, OH	44408, 45014, 45724
717	Fairfield, PA	17320, 17754
903	Fairfield, TX	75840
501	Fairfield Bay, AR	72088, 72153
508	Fairhaven, MA	02719
205	Fairhope, AL	36532, 36533
216	Fairlawn, OH	44313, 44333
215	Fairless Hills, PA	19030
507	Fairmont, MN	56031
304	Fairmont, WV	26554, 26555
217	Fairmount, IL	61841, 62960
303	Fairplay, CO	80432, 80440
716	Fairport, NY	14450
201	Fairview, NJ	07022–08104
405	Fairview, OK	73737
503	Fairview, OR	97024, 97423
814	Fairview, PA	16415, 17872
615	Fairview, TN	37062
618	Fairview Heights, IL	62208, 62232
913	Fairway, KS	66205
919	Faison, NC	28341
716	Falconer, NY	14733
512	Falfurrias, TX	78355
508	Fall River, MA	02720–02726
414	Fall River, WI	53932
619	Fallbrook, CA	92028
702	Fallon, NV	89406
215	Falls, PA	18615, 19054
703	Falls Church, VA	22040–22047
402	Falls City, NE	68355
814	Falls Creek, PA	15840
215	Fallsington, PA	19054
606	Falmouth, KY	41040
508	Falmouth, MA	02540–02543
908	Far Hills, NJ	07931
701	Fargo, ND	58102–58109, 58121–58126
507	Faribault, MN	55021
618	Farina, IL	62838
309	Farmer City, IL	61842
214	Farmers Branch, TX	75234, 75244
209	Farmersville, CA	93223
318	Farmerville, LA	71241
207	Farmingdale, ME	04345
908	Farmingdale, NJ	07727
516	Farmingdale, NY	11735
203	Farmington, CT	06030, 06032, 06034
207	Farmington, ME	04938
313	Farmington, MI	48018, 48332, 48334–48336
314	Farmington, MO	63640
505	Farmington, NM	87401, 87402, 87499
801	Farmington, UT	84025
313	Farmington Hills, MI	48018, 48333–48336
919	Farmville, NC	27828
804	Farmville, VA	23901
712	Farnhamville, IA	50538
412	Farrell, PA	16121
806	Farwell, TX	79325
605	Faulkton, SD	57438
205	Fayette, AL	35555
319	Fayette, IA	52142
816	Fayette, MO	65248
601	Fayette, MS	39069
419	Fayette, OH	43521, 45680
412	Fayette City, PA	15438
501	Fayetteville, AR	72701–72703
404	Fayetteville, GA	30214, 30269
919	Fayetteville, NC	28301–28314
315	Fayetteville, NY	13066
615	Fayetteville, TN	37334
304	Fayetteville, WV	25840
617	Fayville, MA	01745
215	Feasterville, PA	19047
206	Federal Way, WA	98003, 98063
301	Federalsburg, MD	21632
717	Felton, PA	17322
608	Fennimore, WI	53809
515	Fenton, IA	50539
313	Fenton, MI	48430
314	Fenton, MO	63026, 63099
812	Ferdinand, IN	47532
218	Fergus Falls, MN	56533–56538
314	Ferguson, MO	63135, 63145
407	Fern Park, FL	32730
904	Fernandina Beach, FL	32034
707	Fernbridge, CA	95540
313	Ferndale, MI	48220
814	Ferndale, PA	15905, 18921
702	Fernley, NV	89408
601	Fernwood, MS	39635
318	Ferriday, LA	71334
214	Ferris, TX	75125
703	Ferrum, VA	24088
616	Ferrysburg, MI	49409
518	Feura Bush, NY	12067
703	Fieldale, VA	24089
616	Filer City, MI	49634
801	Fillmore, UT	84631, 84656
703	Fincastle, VA	24090
419	Findlay, OH	45839, 45840
701	Finley, ND	58230
209	Firebaugh, CA	93622
208	Firth, ID	83236
703	Fishersville, VA	22939
401	Fiskeville, RI	02823
508	Fitchburg, MA	01420
912	Fitzgerald, GA	31750
602	Flagstaff, AZ	86001–86004, 86038
201	Flanders, NJ	07836
605	Flandreau, SD	57028
314	Flat River, MO	63601, 63653
313	Flat Rock, MI	48134

704	Flat Rock, NC	27043, 28731
512	Flatonia, TX	78941
215	Fleetwood, PA	19522
606	Flemingsburg, KY	41041
908	Flemington, NJ	08822
313	Flint, MI	48500–48532, 48550–48556
618	Flora, IL	62839
219	Flora, IN	46929
516	Floral Park, NY	11001–11005
205	Florala, AL	36442
205	Florence, AL	35630–35633
602	Florence, AZ	85232, 85279
213	Florence, CA	90001
606	Florence, KY	41022, 41042
413	Florence, MA	01060
601	Florence, MS	39073
908	Florence, NJ	08518, 08554
803	Florence, SC	29501–29504, 29506
802	Florence, VT	05744
715	Florence, WI	54121
512	Floresville, TX	78114
201	Florham Park, NJ	07932
914	Florida, NY	10921
305	Florida City, FL	33034
318	Florien, LA	71429
314	Florissant, MO	63031–63034
215	Flourtown, PA	19031
703	Floyd, VA	24091
806	Floydada, TX	79235
313	Flushing, MI	48433
718	Flushing, NY	11300–11386
215	Fogelsville, PA	18051
215	Folcroft, PA	19032
205	Foley, AL	36535, 36536
612	Foley, MN	56329, 56357
912	Folkston, GA	31537
916	Folsom, CA	95630
609	Folsom, NJ	08037
414	Fond du Lac, WI	54935, 54936
518	Fonda, NY	12068
714	Fontana, CA	92334–92336
414	Fontana, WI	53125
704	Fontana Dam, NC	28733
515	Fontanelle, IA	50846
316	Ford, KS	67842
412	Ford City, PA	16226
908	Fords, NJ	08863
501	Fordyce, AR	71742
601	Forest, MS	39074
804	Forest, VA	24551
515	Forest City, IA	50436
309	Forest City, IL	61532
816	Forest City, MO	64451
704	Forest City, NC	28043
503	Forest Grove, OR	97116, 97117
301	Forest Hill, MD	21050
718	Forest Hills, NY	11375
412	Forest Hills, PA	15221
404	Forest Park, GA	30050, 30051
708	Forest Park, IL	60130
203	Forestville, CT	06010
301	Forestville, MD	20747
609	Forked River, NJ	08731
206	Forks, WA	98331
701	Forman, ND	58032
501	Forrest City, AR	72335
912	Forsyth, GA	31029
417	Forsyth, MO	65653
406	Forsyth, MT	59327
414	Fort Atkinson, WI	53538
703	Fort Belvoir, VA	22060
406	Fort Benton, MT	59442
919	Fort Bragg, NC	28307
812	Fort Branch, IN	47648
402	Fort Calhoun, NE	68023
303	Fort Collins, CO	80521–80526
915	Fort Davis, TX	79734
602	Fort Defiance, AZ	86504, 86549
205	Fort Deposit, AL	36032
515	Fort Dodge, IA	50501
518	Fort Edward, NY	12828
904	Fort George Island, FL	32226
404	Fort Gordon, GA	30905
817	Fort Hood, TX	76544
207	Fort Kent, ME	04743
502	Fort Knox, KY	40121
305	Fort Lauderdale, FL	33301–33351, 33394
201	Fort Lee, NJ	07024
513	Fort Loramie, OH	45845
303	Fort Lupton, CO	80621
319	Fort Madison, IA	52627
301	Fort Meade, MD	20755
803	Fort Mill, SC	29715
606	Fort Mitchell, KY	41017
804	Fort Monroe, VA	23651
303	Fort Morgan, CO	80701
813	Fort Myers, FL	33901–33919, 33990, 33991
813	Fort Myers Beach, FL	33931, 33932
404	Fort Oglethorpe, GA	30742
205	Fort Payne, AL	35967
407	Fort Pierce, FL	34945–34954, 34981–34988
605	Fort Pierre, SD	57532
419	Fort Recovery, OH	45846
316	Fort Scott, KS	66701
501	Fort Smith, AR	72901–72923
915	Fort Stockton, TX	79735
505	Fort Sumner, NM	88119
405	Fort Supply, OK	73841
701	Fort Totten, ND	58335
912	Fort Valley, GA	31030
904	Fort Walton Beach, FL	32547–32549
301	Fort Washington, MD	20744
215	Fort Washington, PA	19025, 19034
219	Fort Wayne, IN	46800–46899
817	Fort Worth, TX	76100–76185, 76193, 76196
606	Fort Wright, KY	41011

701	Fort Yates, ND	58528, 58538
717	Forty Fort, PA	18704
503	Fossil, OR	97830
415	Foster City, CA	94404
419	Fostoria, OH	44830
602	Fountain Hills, AZ	85268, 85269
803	Fountain Inn, SC	29644
714	Fountain Valley, CA	92708
209	Fowler, CA	93625
317	Fowler, IN	47944
316	Fowler, KS	67844
517	Fowlerville, MI	48836
508	Foxboro, MA	02035
717	Frackville, PA	17931
508	Framingham, MA	01701
603	Franconia, NH	03580
215	Franconia, PA	18924
517	Frankenmuth, MI	48734, 48787
815	Frankfort, IL	60423, 62896
317	Frankfort, IN	46041
502	Frankfort, KY	40601–40604, 40621, 40622
616	Frankfort, MI	49635
315	Frankfort, NY	13340
404	Franklin, GA	30217
317	Franklin, IN	46131, 47431
502	Franklin, KY	42134, 42135
318	Franklin, LA	70538
508	Franklin, MA	02038
704	Franklin, NC	28734
308	Franklin, NE	68939
603	Franklin, NH	03235
201	Franklin, NJ	07416–08873
513	Franklin, OH	43055, 45005
814	Franklin, PA	15909, 16323, 17846
615	Franklin, TN	37064, 37065
409	Franklin, TX	77856
804	Franklin, VA	23851
304	Franklin, WV	26807
201	Franklin Lakes, NJ	07417
708	Franklin Park, IL	60131
404	Franklin Springs, GA	30639
516	Franklin Square, NY	11010
504	Franklinton, LA	70438
414	Franksville, WI	53126
313	Fraser, MI	48026
218	Frazee, MN	56544
215	Frazer, PA	19355
301	Frederick, MD	21701, 21702
405	Frederick, OK	73542
319	Fredericksburg, IA	50630
717	Fredericksburg, PA	17026
512	Fredericksburg, TX	78624
703	Fredericksburg, VA	22401–22405
314	Fredericktown, MO	63645
614	Fredericktown, OH	43019
316	Fredonia, KS	66736
716	Fredonia, NY	14063
618	Freeburg, IL	62243
908	Freehold, NJ	07728
518	Freehold, NY	12431
717	Freeland, PA	18224
815	Freeport, IL	61032
207	Freeport, ME	04032, 04033
516	Freeport, NY	11520
412	Freeport, PA	16226
409	Freeport, TX	77541
415	Fremont, CA	94536–94539, 94555
219	Fremont, IN	46737
616	Fremont, MI	49412, 49413
919	Fremont, NC	27830
402	Fremont, NE	68025
419	Fremont, OH	43420
414	Fremont, WI	54940
812	French Lick, IN	47432
606	Frenchburg, KY	40322
908	Frenchtown, NJ	08825
718	Fresh Meadows, NY	11365
209	Fresno, CA	93650, 93700–93794
716	Frewsburg, NY	14738
206	Friday Harbor, WA	98250
612	Fridley, MN	54421, 54432, 55421, 55432
716	Friendship, NY	14739
608	Friendship, WI	53927, 53934
703	Fries, VA	24330
806	Friona, TX	79035
803	Fripp Island, SC	29920
303	Frisco, CO	80443
205	Frisco City, AL	36445
803	Frogmore, SC	29920
703	Front Royal, VA	22630, 22651
307	Frontier, WY	83121
301	Frostburg, MD	21532
813	Frostproof, FL	33843
208	Fruitland, ID	83619
616	Fruitport, MI	49415
207	Fryeburg, ME	04037
714	Fullerton, CA	92631–92635
308	Fullerton, NE	68638
205	Fulton, AL	36436, 36446
815	Fulton, IL	61252
502	Fulton, KY	42041
314	Fulton, MO	65251
601	Fulton, MS	38843
315	Fulton, NY	13069
518	Fultonville, NY	12016, 12072
308	Funk, NE	68940
919	Fuquay-Varina, NC	27526
215	Furlong, PA	18925

G

205	Gadsden, AL	35901–35905, 35999
803	Gaffney, SC	29340–29342
915	Gail, TX	79738

Area	Place	ZIP
615	Gainesboro, TN	38562
904	Gainesville, FL	32600–32614
404	Gainesville, GA	30501–30507
417	Gainesville, MO	65655, 65758
817	Gainesville, TX	76240
703	Gainesville, VA	22065
301	Gaithersburg, MD	20877–20886, 20899
703	Galax, VA	24333
815	Galena, IL	61036
417	Galena, MO	65656
713	Galena Park, TX	77547
203	Gales Ferry, CT	06335, 06339
309	Galesburg, IL	61401, 61402
616	Galesburg, MI	49053
814	Galeton, PA	16922
419	Galion, OH	44833
816	Gallatin, MO	64640
615	Gallatin, TN	37066
901	Gallaway, TN	38036
504	Galliano, LA	70354
614	Gallipolis, OH	45631
505	Gallup, NM	87301–87375
309	Galva, IL	61434
409	Galveston, TX	77550–77554
614	Gambier, OH	43022
602	Ganado, AZ	86505, 86540
605	Gann Valley, SD	57341
912	Garden City, GA	31408, 31418
316	Garden City, KS	67846
313	Garden City, MI	48135
516	Garden City, NY	11530, 11599
605	Garden City, SD	57236
915	Garden City, TX	77088, 79739
801	Garden City, UT	84028
516	Garden City Park, NY	11040
714	Garden Grove, CA	92640–92645
316	Garden Plain, KS	67050
213	Gardena, CA	90247–90249
716	Gardenville, NY	14224
207	Gardiner, ME	04344, 04345
914	Gardiner, NY	12525
815	Gardner, IL	60424
913	Gardner, KS	66030, 66031
508	Gardner, MA	01440, 01441
717	Gardners, PA	17324
702	Gardnerville, NV	89410
719	Garfield, CO	81227
201	Garfield, NJ	07026
216	Garfield Heights, OH	44105, 44125, 44128
214	Garland, TX	75040–75048, 75559
515	Garner, IA	50438
913	Garnett, KS	66032
605	Garretson, SD	57030
219	Garrett, IN	46738
301	Garrison, MD	21055
701	Garrison, ND	58540
409	Garrison, TX	75946
801	Garrison, UT	84728
908	Garwood, NJ	07027
409	Garwood, TX	77442
219	Gary, IN	46400–46410
716	Gasport, NY	14067
317	Gaston, IN	47342
503	Gaston, OR	97119
803	Gaston, SC	29053
704	Gastonia, NC	28052–28056
703	Gate City, VA	24251
919	Gatesville, NC	27938
817	Gatesville, TX	76528, 76576
615	Gatlinburg, TN	37738
601	Gautier, MS	39553
517	Gaylord, MI	49735
612	Gaylord, MN	55334
503	Gearhart, OR	97138
504	Geismar, LA	70734
414	Genesee Depot, WI	53127
309	Geneseo, IL	61254
716	Geneseo, NY	14454
205	Geneva, AL	36340
708	Geneva, IL	60134
402	Geneva, NE	68361
315	Geneva, NY	14456
216	Geneva, OH	43107, 44041
815	Genoa, IL	60135
712	George, IA	51237
512	George West, TX	78022
303	Georgetown, CO	80444
203	Georgetown, CT	06829
302	Georgetown, DE	19947
912	Georgetown, GA	31754
217	Georgetown, IL	61846
502	Georgetown, KY	40324
508	Georgetown, MA	01833
513	Georgetown, OH	43907, 45121
803	Georgetown, SC	29440–29442
512	Georgetown, TX	78626–78628
401	Georgiaville, RI	02917
308	Gering, NE	69341
301	Germantown, MD	20874, 20876
513	Germantown, OH	45325, 45327, 45745
414	Germantown, WI	53022
513	Gettysburg, OH	45328
717	Gettysburg, PA	17325
605	Gettysburg, SD	57442
609	Gibbstown, NJ	08027
215	Gibraltar, PA	19508
404	Gibson, GA	30810
217	Gibson City, IL	60936
419	Gibsonburg, OH	43431
412	Gibsonia, PA	15044
409	Giddings, TX	78942
314	Gideon, MO	63848
206	Gig Harbor, WA	98332, 98335
602	Gilbert, AZ	85234
215	Gilbert, PA	18331
708	Gilberts, IL	60136
502	Gilbertsville, KY	42044
307	Gillette, WY	82716, 82732
515	Gilman, IA	50106
815	Gilman, IL	60938
802	Gilman, VT	05904
903	Gilmer, TX	75644
408	Gilroy, CA	95020, 95021
217	Girard, IL	62640
316	Girard, KS	66743
216	Girard, OH	44420
814	Girard, PA	16417
907	Girdwood, AK	99587, 99693
515	Gladbrook, IA	50635
903	Gladewater, TX	75647
816	Gladstone, MO	64118
517	Gladwin, MI	48624
502	Glasgow, KY	42141, 42142
406	Glasgow, MT	59230
814	Glasgow, PA	16644
609	Glassboro, NJ	08028
203	Glastonbury, CT	06033
616	Glen Arbor, MI	49636
301	Glen Arm, MD	21057
301	Glen Burnie, MD	21060, 21061
516	Glen Cove, NY	11542
708	Glen Ellyn, IL	60137, 60138
516	Glen Head, NY	11545
919	Glen Raven, NC	27215
201	Glen Ridge, NJ	07028
201	Glen Rock, NJ	07450, 07452
717	Glen Rock, PA	17327
817	Glen Rose, TX	76043
304	Glen White, WV	25849
414	Glenbeulah, WI	53023
203	Glenbrook, CT	06906
612	Glencoe, MN	55336
602	Glendale, AZ	85301–85312
818	Glendale, CA	91200–91214, 91221–91226
718	Glendale, NY	11385, 13343
503	Glendale, OR	97442
708	Glendale Heights, IL	60139
406	Glendive, MT	59330
818	Glendora, CA	91740
609	Glendora, NJ	08029
503	Gleneden Beach, OR	97388
518	Glenmont, NY	12077
804	Glenns, VA	23149
518	Glens Falls, NY	12801–12804
412	Glenshaw, PA	15116
215	Glenside, PA	19038
708	Glenview, IL	60025, 60026
304	Glenville, WV	26351
412	Glenwillard, PA	15046
712	Glenwood, IA	51534
708	Glenwood, IL	60425
612	Glenwood, MN	56334
303	Glenwood Springs, CO	81601, 81628
712	Glidden, IA	51443
602	Globe, AZ	85501, 85502
508	Gloucester, MA	01930, 01931
804	Gloucester, VA	23061, 23943
609	Gloucester City, NJ	08030
804	Gloucester Point, VA	23062
518	Gloversville, NY	12078
912	Glynco, GA	31520
618	Godfrey, IL	62002, 62035
817	Godley, TX	76044
618	Golconda, IL	62938
503	Gold Beach, OR	97444
303	Golden, CO	80401–80403, 80419
504	Golden Meadow, LA	70357
612	Golden Valley, MN	55416, 55422, 55427
509	Goldendale, WA	98620
515	Goldfield, IA	50542
702	Goldfield, NV	89013
919	Goldsboro, NC	27530–27534
919	Goldston, NC	27252
915	Goldthwaite, TX	76844
805	Goleta, CA	93111, 93117
512	Goliad, TX	77963
603	Gonic, NH	03867
504	Gonzales, LA	70707, 70737, 70738
512	Gonzales, TX	78629
804	Goochland, VA	23014, 23063
309	Goodfield, IL	61742
208	Gooding, ID	83330
219	Goodland, IN	47948
913	Goodland, KS	67735
615	Goodlettsville, TN	37072
601	Goodman, MS	39079
313	Goodrich, MI	48438
215	Goodville, PA	17094, 17528
205	Goodwater, AL	35072
405	Goodwell, OK	73939
602	Goodyear, AZ	85323, 85338
918	Gore, OK	74435
913	Gorham, KS	67640
207	Gorham, ME	04038
603	Gorham, NH	03581
219	Goshen, IN	46526, 47170
914	Goshen, NY	10924
703	Goshen, VA	24439
308	Gothenburg, NE	69138
501	Gould, AR	71643
315	Gouverneur, NY	13642
913	Gove, KS	67736
716	Gowanda, NY	14070
515	Gowrie, IA	50543
219	Grabill, IN	46741
904	Graceville, FL	32440
712	Graettinger, IA	51342
515	Grafton, IA	50440
508	Grafton, MA	01519
701	Grafton, ND	58237
216	Grafton, OH	44044
802	Grafton, VT	05146
414	Grafton, WI	53024
304	Grafton, WV	26354
919	Graham, NC	27253
817	Graham, TX	76046
206	Graham, WA	98338
816	Grain Valley, MO	64029
318	Grambling, LA	71245
803	Gramling, SC	29348
814	Grampian, PA	16838
817	Granbury, TX	76048, 76049
303	Granby, CO	80446
313	Grand Blanc, MI	48439
701	Grand Forks, ND	58201–58213
616	Grand Haven, MI	49417
308	Grand Island, NE	68801–68803
716	Grand Island, NY	14072
303	Grand Junction, CO	81501–81523
218	Grand Marais, MN	55604
507	Grand Meadow, MN	55936
218	Grand Portage, MN	55605
214	Grand Prairie, TX	75050–75053
616	Grand Rapids, MI	49500–49523, 49548, 49588 *
218	Grand Rapids, MN	55744
502	Grand Rivers, KY	42045
715	Grand View, WI	54839
816	Grandview, MO	64030
817	Grandview, TX	75501, 76050
509	Grandview, WA	98930
616	Grandville, MI	49418, 49468
208	Grangeville, ID	83530, 83531
618	Granite City, IL	62040
612	Granite Falls, MN	56241
704	Granite Falls, NC	28630
206	Granite Falls, WA	98252
803	Graniteville, SC	29829
501	Grannis, AR	71944
308	Grant, NE	68812, 69140
816	Grant City, MO	63801, 64458
603	Grantham, NH	03753
717	Grantham, PA	17027
505	Grants, NM	87020, 87034
503	Grants Pass, OR	97526–97543
919	Grantsboro, NC	28529
715	Grantsburg, WI	54840
304	Grantsville, WV	26147
717	Grantville, PA	17028
815	Granville, IL	61326
518	Granville, NY	12832
614	Granville, OH	43023
304	Granville, WV	26534
412	Grapeville, PA	15634
817	Grapevine, TX	76051, 76092
916	Grass Valley, CA	95945, 95949
314	Gravois Mills, MO	65037
616	Grawn, MI	49637
912	Gray, GA	31032
615	Gray, TN	37615
517	Grayling, MI	49738
815	Graymont, IL	61743
708	Grayslake, IL	60030
606	Grayson, KY	41143
205	Graysville, AL	35073
618	Grayville, IL	62844
413	Great Barrington, MA	01230
316	Great Bend, KS	67530
406	Great Falls, MT	59401–59414, 59476
516	Great Neck, NY	11020–11027
303	Greeley, CO	80631–80634, 80639
913	Greeley, KS	66033
308	Greeley, NE	68842
414	Green Bay, WI	54300–54324
908	Green Brook, NJ	08812
614	Green Camp, OH	43322
904	Green Cove Springs, FL	32043
518	Green Island, NY	12183
414	Green Lake, WI	54941
205	Green Pond, AL	35074
307	Green River, WY	82935, 82938
419	Green Springs, OH	44836
602	Green Valley, AZ	85614, 85622
309	Green Valley, IL	61534
615	Greenback, TN	37742
301	Greenbelt, MD	20770
317	Greencastle, IN	46135
717	Greencastle, PA	17225
414	Greendale, WI	53129
515	Greene, IA	50636
607	Greene, NY	13778
615	Greeneville, TN	37743, 37744
515	Greenfield, IA	50849
317	Greenfield, IN	46140, 47118
413	Greenfield, MA	01301, 01302
417	Greenfield, MO	65661
513	Greenfield, OH	45123, 45658
414	Greenfield, WI	53220, 53228
516	Greenlawn, NY	11740
516	Greenport, NY	11944, 12534
205	Greensboro, AL	36744
404	Greensboro, GA	30642
919	Greensboro, NC	27400–27495
812	Greensburg, IN	47240
316	Greensburg, KS	67054
502	Greensburg, KY	42743
504	Greensburg, LA	70441
412	Greensburg, PA	15601
317	Greentown, IN	46936
606	Greenup, KY	41144
516	Greenvale, NY	11548
205	Greenville, AL	36037
404	Greenville, GA	30222, 31548
618	Greenville, IL	62246
502	Greenville, KY	42345
616	Greenville, MI	48838
314	Greenville, MO	63944
601	Greenville, MS	38701–38704, 38782
919	Greenville, NC	27834–27836, 27858

Area	City	ZIP
603	Greenville, NH	03048
518	Greenville, NY	10583, 12083
513	Greenville, OH	45331
412	Greenville, PA	16125
803	Greenville, SC	29601–29615
903	Greenville, TX	75401
203	Greenwich, CT	06830–06836
518	Greenwich, NY	12834
302	Greenwood, DE	19950
904	Greenwood, FL	32443
317	Greenwood, IN	46142, 46143
601	Greenwood, MS	38912, 38930
402	Greenwood, NE	68366
803	Greenwood, SC	29646–29649
715	Greenwood, WI	54437
803	Greer, SC	29650–29652
601	Grenada, MS	38901, 38926
609	Grenloch, NJ	08032
503	Gresham, OR	97030, 97080, 97230–97236
504	Gretna, LA	70053, 70056
201	Greystone Park, NJ	07950
916	Gridley, CA	95948
404	Griffin, GA	30223, 30224
219	Griffith, IN	46319
804	Grimstead, VA	23064
515	Grinnell, IA	50112
913	Grinnell, KS	67738
413	Griswoldville, MA	01340
817	Groesbeck, TX	76642
313	Grosse Ile, MI	48138
313	Grosse Pointe, MI	48225, 48230, 48236
313	Grosse Pointe Farms, MI	48236
914	Grossinger, NY	12734
203	Groton, CT	06340–06349
508	Groton, MA	01450, 01471
607	Groton, NY	13073
802	Groton, VT	05046
614	Grove City, OH	43123
412	Grove City, PA	16127
205	Grove Hill, AL	36419, 36451
904	Groveland, FL	34736
508	Groveland, MA	01834
614	Groveport, OH	43125
704	Grover, NC	28073, 28074
409	Groves, TX	77619
603	Groveton, NH	03582
409	Groveton, TX	75845
404	Grovetown, GA	30813
703	Grundy, VA	24614
319	Grundy Center, IA	50638
714	Guasti, CA	91743
809	Guayama, PR	00654, 00655
809	Guaynabo, PR	00657
318	Gueydan, LA	70542
603	Guild, NH	03754
518	Guilderland, NY	12084
518	Guilderland Center, NY	12085
802	Guildhall, VT	05905
203	Guilford, CT	06437
207	Guilford, ME	04443, 04482
205	Gulf Shores, AL	36542, 36547
813	Gulfport, FL	33707, 33737
601	Gulfport, MS	39501–39507
906	Gulliver, MI	49840
303	Gunnison, CO	81230, 81231, 81247
205	Guntersville, AL	35976
501	Gurdon, AR	71743
708	Gurnee, IL	60031
405	Guthrie, OK	73044
806	Guthrie, TX	79236
515	Guthrie Center, IA	50115
319	Guttenberg, IA	52052
201	Guttenberg, NJ	07093
405	Guymon, OK	73942
215	Gwynedd Valley, PA	19437

H

Area	City	ZIP
818	Hacienda Heights, CA	91745
201	Hackensack, NJ	07601–07608
908	Hackettstown, NJ	07840
203	Haddam, CT	06438
609	Haddon Heights, NJ	08035
609	Haddonfield, NJ	08033
301	Hagerstown, MD	21740, 21746
912	Hahira, GA	31632
504	Hahnville, LA	70057
208	Hailey, ID	83333
907	Haines, AK	99827
813	Haines City, FL	33844, 33845
518	Haines Falls, NY	12436
609	Hainesport, NJ	08036
712	Halbur, IA	51444
201	Haledon, NJ	07508
414	Hales Corners, WI	53130–53132
205	Haleyville, AL	35565
919	Halifax, NC	27839
804	Halifax, VA	24558
305	Hallandale, FL	33008, 33009
512	Hallettsville, TX	77964
218	Hallock, MN	56728
717	Hallstead, PA	18822
804	Hallwood, VA	23359
218	Halstad, MN	56548
316	Halstead, KS	67056
817	Haltom City, TX	76117
501	Hamburg, AR	71646
313	Hamburg, MI	48139
201	Hamburg, NJ	07419
716	Hamburg, NY	14075
215	Hamburg, PA	19526
203	Hamden, CT	06514, 06517, 06518
618	Hamel, IL	62046
612	Hamel, MN	55340
205	Hamilton, AL	35570
404	Hamilton, GA	31811
217	Hamilton, IL	62341
616	Hamilton, MI	49419
406	Hamilton, MT	59840, 59841
315	Hamilton, NY	13346
513	Hamilton, OH	45011–45015, 45020, 45656 *
817	Hamilton, TX	76531
609	Hamilton Square, NJ	08690
919	Hamlet, NC	28345
304	Hamlin, WV	25523
217	Hammond, IL	61929
219	Hammond, IN	46320–46327
504	Hammond, LA	70401–70404
607	Hammondsport, NY	14840
609	Hammonton, NJ	08037
804	Hampden Sydney, VA	23943
301	Hampstead, MD	21074
501	Hampton, AR	71744
404	Hampton, GA	30228
515	Hampton, IA	50441
402	Hampton, NE	68843
603	Hampton, NH	03842
803	Hampton, SC	29913, 29924
804	Hampton, VA	23651–23670
919	Hamptonville, NC	27020
313	Hamtramck, MI	48212
205	Hanceville, AL	35077
712	Hancock, IA	51536
207	Hancock, ME	04640
906	Hancock, MI	49930
607	Hancock, NY	13783
802	Hancock, VT	05748
209	Hanford, CA	93230–93232
314	Hannibal, MO	63401
614	Hannibal, OH	43931
812	Hanover, IN	47243
617	Hanover, MA	02339
301	Hanover, MD	21076
603	Hanover, NH	03755, 03756
717	Hanover, PA	17331
804	Hanover, VA	23069
708	Hanover Park, IL	60103
507	Hanska, MN	56041
404	Hapeville, GA	30354
504	Harahan, LA	70123
517	Harbor Beach, MI	48441
213	Harbor City, CA	90710
616	Harbor Springs, MI	49737, 49740
618	Hardin, IL	62047
406	Hardin, MT	59034
502	Hardinsburg, KY	40143
515	Hardy, IA	50545
712	Harlan, IA	51537
606	Harlan, KY	40831–40840
404	Harlem, GA	30814
215	Harleysville, PA	19438, 19451
512	Harlingen, TX	78550–78552
406	Harlowton, MT	59036
703	Harman, VA	24618
815	Harmon, IL	61042
412	Harmony, PA	16037
401	Harmony, RI	02829
606	Harold, KY	41635
515	Harper, IA	52231
304	Harpers Ferry, WV	25410, 25425
914	Harriman, NY	10926
615	Harriman, TN	37748
509	Harrington, WA	99134
201	Harrington Park, NJ	07640
501	Harrisburg, AR	72432
618	Harrisburg, IL	62946
704	Harrisburg, NC	28075
308	Harrisburg, NE	69345
717	Harrisburg, PA	17100–17113, 17120–17128
501	Harrison, AR	72601, 72602
517	Harrison, MI	48625
308	Harrison, NE	68852, 69346
201	Harrison, NJ	07029
914	Harrison, NY	10528
513	Harrison, OH	43103, 45030
318	Harrisonburg, LA	71340
703	Harrisonburg, VA	22801, 22807
816	Harrisonville, MO	64701
517	Harrisville, MI	48740
304	Harrisville, WV	26362
606	Harrodsburg, KY	40330
615	Harrogate, TN	37752
616	Hart, MI	49420
205	Hartford, AL	36344
203	Hartford, CT	06100–06199
502	Hartford, KY	42347
616	Hartford, MI	49057
414	Hartford, WI	53027
317	Hartford City, IN	47348
402	Hartington, NE	68739
207	Hartland, ME	04943
806	Hartley, TX	79044
914	Hartsdale, NY	10530
205	Hartselle, AL	35640
918	Hartshorne, OK	74547
803	Hartsville, SC	29550
615	Hartsville, TN	37074
417	Hartville, MO	65667
216	Hartville, OH	44632
404	Hartwell, GA	30643
815	Harvard, IL	60001, 60033
708	Harvey, IL	60426
504	Harvey, LA	70058, 70059
508	Harwich Port, MA	02646
708	Harwood Heights, IL	60656
201	Hasbrouck Heights, NJ	07604
201	Haskell, NJ	07420
817	Haskell, TX	79521
517	Haslett, MI	48840
616	Hastings, MI	49058
612	Hastings, MN	55033
402	Hastings, NE	68901, 68902
914	Hastings-on-Hudson, NY	10706
215	Hatboro, PA	19040
215	Hatfield, PA	19440
508	Hathorne, MA	01937
809	Hato Rey, PR	00917–00936
601	Hattiesburg, MS	39401–39407
516	Hauppauge, NY	11788
309	Havana, IL	62644
919	Havelock, NC	28532, 28533
316	Haven, KS	67543
215	Haverford, PA	19041
508	Haverhill, MA	01830–01835
914	Haverstraw, NY	10927
215	Havertown, PA	19083
316	Haviland, KS	67059
406	Havre, MT	59501
301	Havre de Grace, MD	21078
919	Haw River, NC	27258
213	Hawaiian Gardens, CA	90716
712	Hawarden, IA	51011, 51023
502	Hawesville, KY	42348
319	Hawkeye, IA	52147
903	Hawkins, TX	75765
715	Hawkins, WI	54530
912	Hawkinsville, GA	31036
717	Hawley, PA	18428, 18438
814	Hawthorn, PA	16230
213	Hawthorne, CA	90250, 90251
201	Hawthorne, NJ	07506
702	Hawthorne, NV	89415, 89416
914	Hawthorne, NY	10532
303	Haxtun, CO	80731
208	Hayden Lake, ID	83835
308	Hayes Center, NE	69032
704	Hayesville, NC	28904
419	Hayesville, OH	44838
205	Hayneville, AL	36040
913	Hays, KS	67601
605	Hayti, SD	57241
415	Hayward, CA	94540–94546, 94557
715	Hayward, WI	54843
606	Hazard, KY	41701, 41702
708	Hazel Crest, IL	60429
313	Hazel Park, MI	48030
316	Hazelton, KS	67061
314	Hazelwood, MO	63042–63045
503	Hazelwood, OR	97230
912	Hazlehurst, GA	31539
601	Hazlehurst, MS	39083
908	Hazlet, NJ	07730
717	Hazleton, PA	18201
205	Headland, AL	36345
707	Healdsburg, CA	95448
405	Healdton, OK	73438
907	Healy, AK	99743
804	Heathsville, VA	22473
512	Hebbronville, TX	78361
619	Heber, CA	92249
801	Heber City, UT	84032
501	Heber Springs, AR	72543
815	Hebron, IL	60034
606	Hebron, KY	41048
301	Hebron, MD	21830
402	Hebron, NE	68362, 68370
614	Hebron, OH	43025
612	Hector, MN	55342
205	Heflin, AL	36264
717	Hegins, PA	17938
412	Heidelberg, PA	15106
205	Helena, AL	35080
501	Helena, AR	72342
406	Helena, MT	59601–59626
717	Hellam, PA	17406
716	Helmuth, NY	14079
714	Hemet, CA	92343, 92344
517	Hemlock, MI	48626
409	Hemphill, TX	75948
516	Hempstead, NY	11550–11554
409	Hempstead, TX	77445
205	Henagar, AL	35978
303	Henderson, CO	80640
502	Henderson, KY	42420
919	Henderson, NC	27536
702	Henderson, NV	89009, 89015, 89044
901	Henderson, TN	38340
903	Henderson, TX	75652, 75653
704	Hendersonville, NC	28739, 28792, 28793
615	Hendersonville, TN	37075, 37077
815	Hennepin, IL	61327
405	Hennessey, OK	73742
603	Henniker, NH	03242
716	Henrietta, NY	14467
817	Henrietta, TX	76365
309	Henry, IL	61537
901	Henry, TN	38231
703	Henry, VA	24102
503	Heppner, OR	97836, 97839
806	Hereford, TX	79045
315	Herkimer, NY	13350
314	Hermann, MO	65041, 65056
503	Hermiston, OR	97838
417	Hermitage, MO	65668
412	Hermitage, PA	16148
213	Hermosa Beach, CA	90254
601	Hernando, MS	38632
703	Herndon, VA	22070, 22071, 22090–22096
618	Herrin, IL	62948
308	Hershey, NE	69143
717	Hershey, PA	17033
919	Hertford, NC	27930, 27944
619	Hesperia, CA	92345
316	Hesston, KS	67062
701	Hettinger, ND	58639
315	Heuvelton, NY	13654

Area	City	ZIP
817	Hewitt, TX	76643
516	Hewlett, NY	11557
305	Hialeah, FL	33010, 33012–33016, 33054
305	Hialeah Gardens, FL	33010, 33016
404	Hiawassee, GA	30546
913	Hiawatha, KS	66434
218	Hibbing, MN	55746, 55747
502	Hickman, KY	42050
704	Hickory, NC	28601–28603
708	Hickory Hills, IL	60457
501	Hickory Ridge, AR	72347
516	Hicksville, NY	11801–11804
419	Hicksville, OH	43526
203	Higganum, CT	06441
914	High Falls, NY	12440
919	High Point, NC	27260–27265
314	High Ridge, MO	63049
904	High Springs, FL	32643
802	Highgate Springs, VT	05460
714	Highland, CA	92346
618	Highland, IL	62249
219	Highland, IN	46322, 47854
913	Highland, KS	66035
313	Highland, MI	48031, 48357
914	Highland, NY	12528
407	Highland Beach, FL	33487
606	Highland Heights, KY	41076
708	Highland Park, IL	60035, 62930
313	Highland Park, MI	48203
908	Highland Park, NJ	08904
713	Highlands, TX	77562
605	Highmore, SD	57345
609	Hightstown, NJ	08520
602	Higley, AZ	85236
913	Hill City, KS	67642
218	Hill City, MN	55748, 55785
914	Hillburn, NY	10931
301	Hillcrest Heights, MD	20748
614	Hilliard, OH	43026
319	Hills, IA	52235
217	Hillsboro, IL	62049
316	Hillsboro, KS	67063
314	Hillsboro, MO	63050
701	Hillsboro, ND	58009, 58045
603	Hillsboro, NH	03244
513	Hillsboro, OH	45133
503	Hillsboro, OR	97123, 97124
817	Hillsboro, TX	76645
415	Hillsborough, CA	94010
919	Hillsborough, NC	27278
517	Hillsdale, MI	49242
201	Hillsdale, NJ	07642
708	Hillside, IL	60162, 60163
908	Hillside, NJ	07205
703	Hillsville, VA	24343
808	Hilo, HI	96720, 96721
716	Hilton, NY	14468
803	Hilton Head Island, SC	29925, 29926, 29938
606	Hindman, KY	41822
708	Hines, IL	60141
802	Hinesburg, VT	05301, 05461
912	Hinesville, GA	31313, 31314
617	Hingham, MA	02018, 02043
708	Hinsdale, IL	60521, 60522
603	Hinsdale, NH	03451
405	Hinton, OK	73047
703	Hinton, VA	22831
304	Hinton, WV	25951
216	Hiram, OH	44234
615	Hixson, TN	37343
219	Hobart, IN	46342
405	Hobart, OK	73651
505	Hobbs, NM	88240, 88241
919	Hobbsville, NC	27946
407	Hobe Sound, FL	33455, 33475
908	Hoboken, NJ	07030
502	Hodgenville, KY	42748
708	Hoffman Estates, IL	60192, 60194–60196
615	Hohenwald, TN	38462
201	Hohokus, NJ	07423
602	Holbrook, AZ	85942, 86025
617	Holbrook, MA	02343
516	Holbrook, NY	11741
716	Holcomb, NY	14469
508	Holden, MA	01520
405	Holdenville, OK	74848
309	Holder, IL	61736
308	Holdrege, NE	68949, 68969
812	Holland, IN	47541
616	Holland, MI	49422–49424
419	Holland, OH	43528
507	Hollandale, MN	56045
601	Hollandale, MS	38748
716	Holley, NY	14470
814	Hollidaysburg, PA	16648
703	Hollins College, VA	24020
405	Hollis, OK	73550
408	Hollister, CA	95023, 95024
508	Holliston, MA	01746
719	Holly, CO	81047
803	Holly Hill, SC	29059
919	Holly Ridge, NC	28445
601	Holly Springs, MS	38635, 38649
213	Hollywood, CA	90028, 90068
305	Hollywood, FL	33019–33021, 33023–33029
803	Hollywood, SC	29138, 29449
908	Holmdel, NJ	07733
215	Holmes, PA	19043
712	Holstein, IA	51025
205	Holt, AL	35404
517	Holt, MI	48842
913	Holton, KS	66436
619	Holtville, CA	92250
303	Holyoke, CO	80734
413	Holyoke, MA	01040, 01041
907	Homer, AK	99603
404	Homer, GA	30547
318	Homer, LA	71040
607	Homer, NY	13077
412	Homer City, PA	15748
912	Homerville, GA	31634
305	Homestead, FL	33030–33035, 33090
412	Homestead, PA	15120
708	Homewood, IL	60430
512	Hondo, TX	78861
716	Honeoye, NY	14471
716	Honeoye Falls, NY	14472
717	Honesdale, PA	18431
808	Honokaa, HI	96727
808	Honolulu, HI	96800–96898
503	Hood River, OR	97031
405	Hooker, OK	73945
603	Hooksett, NH	03106
402	Hooper, NE	68031
701	Hoople, ND	58243
518	Hoosick Falls, NY	12090
501	Hope, AR	71801
205	Hope Hull, AL	36043
201	Hopelawn, NJ	08861
609	Hopewell, NJ	08525, 08560
804	Hopewell, VA	23860
612	Hopkins, MN	55343–55347
502	Hopkinsville, KY	42240, 42241
319	Hopkinton, IA	52237
508	Hopkinton, MA	01748
603	Hopkinton, NH	03229
206	Hoquiam, WA	98550
414	Horicon, WI	53032
601	Horn Lake, MS	38637
607	Hornell, NY	14843
712	Hornick, IA	51015, 51026
502	Horse Cave, KY	42749
607	Horseheads, NY	14844, 14845
512	Horseshoe Bay, TX	78654
501	Horseshoe Bend, AR	72512
215	Horsham, PA	19044
414	Hortonville, WI	54944
712	Hospers, IA	51238
605	Hot Springs, SD	57747
703	Hot Springs, VA	24445
501	Hot Springs National Park, AR	71901–71914, 71951
303	Hot Sulphur Springs, CO	80451
319	Houghton, IA	52631
906	Houghton, MI	49921, 49931
716	Houghton, NY	14744
207	Houlton, ME	04730
504	Houma, LA	70360–70364
413	Housatonic, MA	01236
507	Houston, MN	55943
417	Houston, MO	65483
601	Houston, MS	38851
713	Houston, TX	77000–77293
316	Howard, KS	67349
605	Howard, SD	57349
517	Howell, MI	48843, 48863
904	Howey in the Hills, FL	34737
501	Hoxie, AR	72433
913	Hoxie, KS	67740
515	Hubbard, IA	50122
216	Hubbard, OH	44425
508	Hubbardston, MA	01452
513	Huber Heights, OH	45424
813	Hudson, FL	34667, 34669
319	Hudson, IA	50643
508	Hudson, MA	01749
517	Hudson, MI	49247
704	Hudson, NC	28638
603	Hudson, NH	03051
518	Hudson, NY	12534
216	Hudson, OH	44236
715	Hudson, WI	54016
518	Hudson Falls, NY	12839
616	Hudsonville, MI	49426
501	Hughes, AR	72348
301	Hughesville, MD	20637
719	Hugo, CO	80806, 80821
612	Hugo, MN	55038
405	Hugo, OK	74743
316	Hugoton, KS	67951
809	Humacao, PR	00661
713	Humble, TX	77325, 77338, 77339, 77396
515	Humboldt, IA	50548
316	Humboldt, KS	66748
402	Humboldt, NE	68376
901	Humboldt, TN	38343
515	Humeston, IA	50123
717	Hummels Wharf, PA	17831
717	Hummelstown, PA	17036
301	Hunt Valley, MD	21031
701	Hunter, ND	58048
704	Huntersville, NC	28078
812	Huntingburg, IN	47542
814	Huntingdon, PA	16652
901	Huntingdon, TN	38344
215	Huntingdon Valley, PA	19006
714	Huntington, CA	92646
219	Huntington, IN	46750
516	Huntington, NY	11743
801	Huntington, UT	84528
304	Huntington, WV	25700–25779
714	Huntington Beach, CA	92605, 92646–92649
213	Huntington Park, CA	90255
516	Huntington Station, NY	11746, 11747
708	Huntley, IL	60142
205	Huntsville, AL	35800–35824, 35896, 35899
501	Huntsville, AR	72740
816	Huntsville, MO	65259
615	Huntsville, TN	37756
409	Huntsville, TX	77340–77342
715	Hurley, WI	54534
419	Huron, OH	44839
605	Huron, SD	57350
801	Hurricane, UT	84737, 84779
304	Hurricane, WV	25526
817	Hurst, TX	76053, 76054
316	Hutchinson, KS	67501–67505, 67558
612	Hutchinson, MN	55350
508	Hyannis, MA	02601
308	Hyannis, NE	69350
301	Hyattsville, MD	20780–20788
814	Hyde, PA	16843
617	Hyde Park, MA	02136
914	Hyde Park, NY	12538
412	Hyde Park, PA	15641
802	Hyde Park, VT	05655
606	Hyden, KY	41749, 41762
405	Hydro, OK	73048
801	Hyrum, UT	84319
406	Hysham, MT	59038

I

Area	City	ZIP
313	Ida, MI	48140
712	Ida Grove, IA	51445
405	Idabel, OK	74745
208	Idaho City, ID	83631, 83666
208	Idaho Falls, ID	83401–83406, 83415
315	Ilion, NY	13357
313	Imlay City, MI	48444
215	Immaculata, PA	19345
707	Imola, CA	94558
619	Imperial, CA	92251
314	Imperial, MO	63052
308	Imperial, NE	69033
412	Imperial, PA	15126
618	Ina, IL	62846
702	Incline Village, NV	89451
619	Independence, CA	93526
319	Independence, IA	50644
316	Independence, KS	67301
606	Independence, KY	41051
816	Independence, MO	64050–64058
216	Independence, OH	43512, 44131
703	Independence, VA	24348
413	Indian Orchard, MA	01151
412	Indiana, PA	15701, 15705
317	Indianapolis, IN	46107, 46200–46290
515	Indianola, IA	50125
601	Indianola, MS	38749–38751
619	Indio, CA	92201, 92202
913	Industrial Airport, KS	66031
606	Inez, KY	41224
316	Ingalls, KS	67853
512	Ingleside, TX	78362
213	Inglewood, CA	90300–90312
208	Inkom, ID	83245
313	Inkster, MI	48141
315	Inlet, NY	13360
803	Inman, SC	29349
304	Institute, WV	25112
717	Intercourse, PA	17534
218	International Falls, MN	56649
603	Intervale, NH	03845
612	Inver Grove Heights, MN	55076, 55077
904	Inverness, FL	32650–32652
708	Inverness, IL	60067
516	Inwood, NY	10034, 11696
316	Iola, KS	66749
209	Ione, CA	95640
616	Ionia, MI	48846
319	Iowa City, IA	52240–52246
515	Iowa Falls, IA	50126
508	Ipswich, MA	01938
605	Ipswich, SD	57451
906	Iron Mountain, MI	49801
205	Irondale, AL	35210
716	Irondequoit, NY	14617
314	Ironton, MO	63650
614	Ironton, OH	45638
906	Ironwood, MI	49938
503	Irrigon, OR	97844
714	Irvine, CA	92650, 92709–92720, 92730
606	Irvine, KY	40336, 40472
814	Irvine, PA	16329
214	Irving, TX	75015, 75038, 75060–75063 *
618	Irvington, IL	62848
201	Irvington, NJ	07111
914	Irvington, NY	10533
804	Irvington, VA	22480
412	Irwin, PA	15642
818	Irwindale, CA	91706
912	Irwinton, GA	31042
908	Iselin, NJ	08830
906	Ishpeming, MI	49849
305	Islamorada, FL	33036
207	Island Falls, ME	04747
516	Island Park, NY	11558
803	Isle of Palms, SC	29451
804	Isle of Wight, VA	23397
206	Issaquah, WA	98027
708	Itasca, IL	60143
817	Itasca, TX	76055
517	Ithaca, MI	48847
607	Ithaca, NY	14850–14853, 14882
601	Itta Bena, MS	38941
601	Iuka, MS	38852
803	Iva, SC	29655
507	Ivanhoe, MN	56142
217	Ivesdale, IL	61851
203	Ivoryton, CT	06442
215	Ivyland, PA	18974
414	Ixonia, WI	53036

J

Area	City	ZIP
207	Jackman, ME	04945
615	Jacksboro, TN	37757
817	Jacksboro, TX	76056
205	Jackson, AL	36501, 36545
209	Jackson, CA	95642
404	Jackson, GA	30233
606	Jackson, KY	41339
504	Jackson, LA	70748
517	Jackson, MI	49201–49204
507	Jackson, MN	55379, 56143
314	Jackson, MO	63755
601	Jackson, MS	39200–39298
919	Jackson, NC	27845
908	Jackson, NJ	07305, 08527
614	Jackson, OH	43113, 45730
901	Jackson, TN	38301–38314
414	Jackson, WI	53037
307	Jackson, WY	83001, 83025
513	Jackson Center, OH	45334
718	Jackson Heights, NY	11372
205	Jacksonville, AL	36265
501	Jacksonville, AR	72076, 72099
904	Jacksonville, FL	32099, 32200–32276
217	Jacksonville, IL	62650, 62651
919	Jacksonville, NC	28540–28546
903	Jacksonville, TX	75766
904	Jacksonville Beach, FL	32227, 32250
717	Jacobus, PA	17407
603	Jaffrey, NH	03452
718	Jamaica, NY	11400–11460
617	Jamaica Plain, MA	02130
908	Jamesburg, NJ	08831
502	Jamestown, KY	42629
919	Jamestown, NC	27282
701	Jamestown, ND	58401, 58473
716	Jamestown, NY	14701, 14702
803	Jamestown, SC	29453
615	Jamestown, TN	38556
304	Jane Lew, WV	26378
608	Janesville, WI	53542–53547
205	Jasper, AL	35501, 35502
501	Jasper, AR	72641
904	Jasper, FL	32052
404	Jasper, GA	30143
812	Jasper, IN	47546, 47547, 47549
507	Jasper, MN	56144
503	Jasper, OR	97438
615	Jasper, TN	37347
409	Jasper, TX	75951
207	Jay, ME	04239, 04262
518	Jay, NY	12941
918	Jay, OK	74346
806	Jayton, TX	79528
318	Jeanerette, LA	70544
412	Jeannette, PA	15644
507	Jeffers, MN	56145
404	Jefferson, GA	30549
515	Jefferson, IA	50129
504	Jefferson, LA	70121
919	Jefferson, NC	28640
603	Jefferson, NH	03583
216	Jefferson, OH	43112, 45684
412	Jefferson, PA	15344, 19506
903	Jefferson, TX	75657
414	Jefferson, WI	53549
314	Jefferson City, MO	65101–65110
615	Jefferson City, TN	37760
914	Jefferson Valley, NY	10535
912	Jeffersonville, GA	31044
812	Jeffersonville, IN	47130, 47131
802	Jeffersonville, VT	05464
912	Jekyll Island, GA	31520
318	Jena, LA	71342
215	Jenkintown, PA	19046
318	Jennings, LA	70546
314	Jennings, MO	63136
407	Jensen Beach, FL	34957, 34958
516	Jericho, NY	11753, 12910
717	Jermyn, PA	18433
208	Jerome, ID	83338
201	Jersey City, NJ	07097–07311
717	Jersey Shore, PA	11723, 17740
618	Jerseyville, IL	62052
304	Jesse, WV	24849
301	Jessup, MD	20794
912	Jesup, GA	31545
319	Jesup, IA	50648
316	Jetmore, KS	67854
515	Jewell, IA	50130
419	Jewell, OH	43530
903	Jewett, TX	75846
203	Jewett City, CT	06351
715	Jim Falls, WI	54748
717	Jim Thorpe, PA	18229
316	Johnson, KS	67855
802	Johnson, VT	05656
607	Johnson City, NY	13790
615	Johnson City, TN	37601–37615
512	Johnson City, TX	78636
414	Johnson Creek, WI	53038
908	Johnsonburg, NJ	07846
814	Johnsonburg, PA	15845
803	Johnsonville, SC	29555
401	Johnston, RI	02919
518	Johnstown, NY	12095
614	Johnstown, OH	43031
814	Johnstown, PA	15901–15906
515	Joice, IA	50446
815	Joliet, IL	60431–60436
501	Jonesboro, AR	72401–72403
404	Jonesboro, GA	30236, 30237
618	Jonesboro, IL	62952
318	Jonesboro, LA	71251
615	Jonesboro, TN	37659
717	Jonestown, PA	17038, 17901
517	Jonesville, MI	49250
703	Jonesville, VA	24263
417	Joplin, MO	64801–64804
618	Joppa, IL	62953
301	Joppa, MD	21085
612	Jordan, MN	55352
406	Jordan, MT	59337
315	Jordan, NY	13080
512	Jourdanton, TX	78026
318	Joyce, LA	71440
608	Juda, WI	53550
303	Julesburg, CO	80737
915	Junction, TX	76849
801	Junction, UT	84712, 84743
404	Junction City, GA	31812
913	Junction City, KS	66441, 66442
503	Junction City, OR	97448
907	Juneau, AK	99801–99803, 99811, 99850
414	Juneau, WI	53039
402	Juniata, NE	68955
407	Jupiter, FL	33458, 33477, 33478

K

Area	City	ZIP
808	Kaanapali, HI	96761
605	Kadoka, SD	57543
816	Kahoka, MO	63445
808	Kahuku, HI	96731
808	Kahului, HI	96732, 96733
808	Kailua, HI	96734, 96863
616	Kalamazoo, MI	49001–49009
419	Kalida, OH	45853
406	Kalispell, MT	59901–59903
616	Kalkaska, MI	49646
319	Kalona, IA	52247
808	Kamuela, HI	96743
801	Kanab, UT	84741, 84784
515	Kanawha, IA	50447
814	Kane, PA	16735
808	Kaneohe, HI	96744
815	Kankakee, IL	60901
704	Kannapolis, NC	28081–28083
913	Kansas City, KS	66100–66119
816	Kansas City, MO	61095–64179, 64190–64199
808	Kapaa, HI	96746
808	Kapalua, HI	96761
318	Kaplan, LA	70548
512	Karnes City, TX	78118
914	Katonah, NY	10536
713	Katy, TX	77449, 77450, 77491–77494
214	Kaufman, TX	75142
414	Kaukauna, WI	54130, 54131
801	Kaysville, UT	84037
808	Keaau, HI	96749
816	Kearney, MO	64060
308	Kearney, NE	68847–68849
801	Kearns, UT	84118
201	Kearny, NJ	07032, 07099
908	Keasbey, NJ	08832
805	Keene, CA	93531
603	Keene, NH	03431
817	Keene, TX	76059
218	Keewatin, MN	55753
808	Kekaha, HI	96752
817	Keller, TX	76248
515	Kellogg, IA	50135
208	Kellogg, ID	83837
707	Kelseyville, CA	95451
206	Kelso, WA	98626
713	Kemah, TX	77565
307	Kemmerer, WY	83101
907	Kenai, AK	99611, 99635
919	Kenansville, NC	28349
804	Kenbridge, VA	23944
305	Kendale Lakes, FL	33183
305	Kendall, FL	33156, 33256
219	Kendallville, IN	46720, 46755
208	Kendrick, ID	83537
708	Kenilworth, IL	60043
908	Kenilworth, NJ	07033
919	Kenly, NC	27542
716	Kenmore, NY	14200, 14217, 14223
206	Kenmore, WA	98028
605	Kennebec, SD	57544
207	Kennebunk, ME	04043
207	Kennebunkport, ME	04014, 04046
817	Kennedale, TX	76060
301	Kennedyville, MD	21645
504	Kenner, LA	70062–70065
814	Kennerdell, PA	16374
314	Kennett, MO	63857
215	Kennett Square, PA	19348
509	Kennewick, WA	99336, 99337
414	Kenosha, WI	53140–53144
304	Kenova, WV	25530
203	Kensington, CT	06037
301	Kensington, MD	20895
216	Kent, OH	44211, 44240, 44242
206	Kent, WA	98031–98035, 98064
415	Kentfield, CA	94904, 94914
219	Kentland, IN	47951
419	Kenton, OH	43326
504	Kentwood, LA	70444
616	Kentwood, MI	49506–49518, 49548
201	Kenvil, NJ	07847
507	Kenyon, MN	55946
401	Kenyon, RI	02836
319	Keokuk, IA	52632
319	Keosauqua, IA	52565
209	Kerman, CA	93630
915	Kermit, TX	79745
919	Kernersville, NC	27284, 27285
512	Kerrville, TX	78028, 78029
715	Keshena, WI	54135
907	Ketchikan, AK	99901–99950
208	Ketchum, ID	83340
513	Kettering, OH	45409, 45459
315	Keuka Park, NY	14478
309	Kewanee, IL	61443
414	Kewaskum, WI	53040
414	Kewaunee, WI	54216
305	Key Biscayne, FL	33149
305	Key Largo, FL	33037, 33070
305	Key West, FL	33040, 33045
908	Keyport, NJ	07735
304	Keyser, WV	26726
904	Keystone Heights, FL	32656
804	Keysville, VA	23947
816	Keytesville, MO	65261
216	Kidron, OH	44636
507	Kiester, MN	56051
808	Kihei, HI	96753
903	Kilgore, TX	75662, 75663
919	Kill Devil Hills, NC	27948
216	Killbuck, OH	44637
817	Killeen, TX	76540–76547
802	Killington, VT	05751
308	Kimball, NE	69145
417	Kimberling City, MO	65686
414	Kimberly, WI	54136
215	Kimberton, PA	19442
517	Kinde, MI	48445
701	Kindred, ND	58051
408	King City, CA	93930
703	King George, VA	22485
215	King of Prussia, PA	19406, 19485
804	King William, VA	23086
207	Kingfield, ME	04947
405	Kingfisher, OK	73750
602	Kingman, AZ	86401, 86441–86445
316	Kingman, KS	67014, 67068
513	Kings Island, OH	45034
704	Kings Mountain, NC	28086
516	Kings Park, NY	11754
516	Kings Point, NY	11024
209	Kingsburg, CA	93631
906	Kingsford, MI	49801
915	Kingsland, TX	78639
712	Kingsley, IA	51028
615	Kingsport, TN	37660–37665
508	Kingston, MA	02364
816	Kingston, MO	64650
603	Kingston, NH	03848
609	Kingston, NJ	08528
914	Kingston, NY	12401
614	Kingston, OH	45644
405	Kingston, OK	73439
717	Kingston, PA	18704
401	Kingston, RI	02881
615	Kingston, TN	37763
615	Kingston Springs, TN	37082
803	Kingstree, SC	29556
816	Kingsville, MO	64061
512	Kingsville, TX	78363, 78364
713	Kingwood, TX	77325, 77345
304	Kingwood, WV	26519, 26537
316	Kinsley, KS	67547
919	Kinston, NC	28501, 28502
303	Kiowa, CO	80117
409	Kirbyville, TX	75956
206	Kirkland, WA	98033, 98034, 98083
816	Kirksville, MO	63501
315	Kirkville, NY	13082
314	Kirkwood, MO	63122
407	Kissimmee, FL	32741, 34741–34759
412	Kittanning, PA	16201
207	Kittery, ME	03904
207	Kittery Point, ME	03905
503	Klamath Falls, OR	97601–97603, 97625
515	Klemme, IA	50449
218	Klunder, MN	56217
712	Knierim, IA	50552
916	Knights Landing, CA	95645
317	Knightstown, IN	46148
219	Knox, IN	46534
814	Knox, PA	16232
912	Knoxville, GA	31050
515	Knoxville, IA	50138
615	Knoxville, TN	37900–37998
907	Kodiak, AK	99615, 99619, 99697
414	Kohler, WI	53044
317	Kokomo, IN	46901–46904
808	Koloa, HI	96756
405	Konawa, OK	74849
601	Kosciusko, MS	39090
409	Kountze, TX	77625
219	Kouts, IN	46347
717	Kreamer, PA	17833
405	Kremlin, OK	73753
609	Kresson, NJ	08053
318	Krotz Springs, LA	70750
215	Kulpsville, PA	19443
215	Kunkletown, PA	18058
215	Kutztown, PA	17067, 19530
605	Kyle, SD	57752
512	Kyle, TX	78640

L

Area	City	ZIP
906	L'Anse, MI	49946
813	La Belle, FL	33935
818	La Canada, CA	91011, 91023
818	La Crescenta, CA	91214, 91224
219	La Crosse, IN	46348
913	La Crosse, KS	67548
509	La Crosse, WA	99143

Area	City	ZIP
608	La Crosse, WI	54601–54603
913	La Cygne, KS	66040
404	La Fayette, GA	30728
615	La Follette, TN	37729, 37766
803	La France, SC	29656
503	La Grande, OR	97850, 97876
404	La Grange, GA	30240, 30261
708	La Grange, IL	60525
502	La Grange, KY	40031, 40032
919	La Grange, NC	28551
409	La Grange, TX	78945
708	La Grange Park, IL	60525
213	La Habra, CA	90631–90633
619	La Jolla, CA	92037–92039, 92093, 92670
719	La Junta, CO	81050
409	La Marque, TX	77568
619	La Mesa, CA	92041–92044
714	La Mirada, CA	90637–90639
701	La Moure, ND	58415, 58458
714	La Palma, CA	90623
217	La Place, IL	61936
301	La Plata, MD	20646
717	La Plume, PA	18440
219	La Porte, IN	46350
713	La Porte, TX	77571, 77572
319	La Porte City, IA	50651
818	La Puente, CA	91744–91749
619	La Quinta, CA	92253
815	La Salle, IL	61301
301	La Vale, MD	21502
608	La Valle, WI	53941
615	La Vergne, TN	37086
714	La Verne, CA	91750
402	La Vista, NE	68128
715	Lac du Flambeau, WI	54538
206	Lacey, WA	98503
717	Laceyville, PA	18623
716	Lackawanna, NY	14200, 14218
309	Lacon, IL	61540
515	Lacona, IA	50139
315	Lacona, NY	13083
603	Laconia, NH	03246, 03247
715	Ladysmith, WI	54848
315	Lafargeville, NY	13656
205	Lafayette, AL	36862
415	Lafayette, CA	94549
303	Lafayette, CO	80026
317	Lafayette, IN	47119, 47901–47907
318	Lafayette, LA	70501–70509, 70598
507	Lafayette, MN	56054
615	Lafayette, TN	37083
215	Lafayette Hill, PA	19444
219	Lagrange, IN	46761
714	Laguna Beach, CA	92651–92653, 92656, 92677
714	Laguna Hills, CA	92653–92656
714	Laguna Niguel, CA	92651, 92656, 92677
808	Lahaina, HI	96761, 96767
808	Laie, HI	96762
813	Lake Alfred, FL	33850
605	Lake Andes, SD	57356
708	Lake Bluff, IL	60044
407	Lake Buena Vista, FL	32830
904	Lake Butler, FL	32054, 32061
318	Lake Charles, LA	70601–70616, 70629
303	Lake City, CO	81235
904	Lake City, FL	32055, 32056
616	Lake City, MI	49651
612	Lake City, MN	55041
814	Lake City, PA	16423
615	Lake City, TN	37769
507	Lake Crystal, MN	56055
608	Lake Delton, WI	53940
714	Lake Forest, CA	92630
708	Lake Forest, IL	60045
414	Lake Geneva, WI	53147
518	Lake George, NY	12845
813	Lake Hamilton, FL	33851
602	Lake Havasu City, AZ	86403
409	Lake Jackson, TX	77566
612	Lake Lillian, MN	56253
518	Lake Luzerne, NY	12846
407	Lake Mary, FL	32746, 32795
414	Lake Mills, WI	53551
616	Lake Odessa, MI	48849
503	Lake Oswego, OR	97034, 97035
314	Lake Ozark, MO	65049
407	Lake Park, FL	33403
712	Lake Park, IA	51347
813	Lake Placid, FL	33852
518	Lake Placid, NY	12946
518	Lake Pleasant, NY	12108
318	Lake Providence, LA	71254
516	Lake Ronkonkoma, NY	11779
516	Lake Success, NY	11040, 11042
501	Lake Village, AR	71653
813	Lake Wales, FL	33853–33859
407	Lake Worth, FL	33460–33464, 33467
708	Lake Zurich, IL	60047, 60049
813	Lakeland, FL	33801–33813
912	Lakeland, GA	31635
901	Lakeland, TN	38002
707	Lakeport, CA	95453
602	Lakeside, AZ	85929
619	Lakeside, CA	92040
419	Lakeside, OH	43331, 43440
219	Laketon, IN	46943
501	Lakeview, AR	72642
517	Lakeview, MI	48850
503	Lakeview, OR	97630
203	Lakeville, CT	06039
219	Lakeville, IN	46536
612	Lakeville, MN	55044
717	Lakeville, PA	18438
512	Lakeway, TX	78734, 78738
213	Lakewood, CA	90711–90716
303	Lakewood, CO	80214, 80215, 80226, 80228 *
908	Lakewood, NJ	08701
716	Lakewood, NY	14750
216	Lakewood, OH	44107
206	Lakewood Center, WA	98439, 98499
316	Lakin, KS	67860
701	Lakota, ND	58344
719	Lamar, CO	81052
417	Lamar, MO	64759
609	Lambertville, NJ	08530
406	Lame Deer, MT	59043
806	Lamesa, TX	79331
515	Lamoni, IA	50140
805	Lamont, CA	93241
512	Lampasas, TX	76550
815	Lanark, IL	61046
805	Lancaster, CA	93534–93536, 93584
606	Lancaster, KY	40444
617	Lancaster, MA	01523
816	Lancaster, MO	63548
603	Lancaster, NH	03584
716	Lancaster, NY	14086
614	Lancaster, OH	43130
717	Lancaster, PA	17600–17605
803	Lancaster, SC	29720
214	Lancaster, TX	75134, 75146
804	Lancaster, VA	22503
608	Lancaster, WI	53813
307	Lander, WY	82520
704	Landis, NC	28088
609	Landisville, NJ	08326
717	Landisville, PA	17538
803	Lando, SC	29724
301	Landover, MD	20785
301	Landover Hills, MD	20784
803	Landrum, SC	29356
701	Langdon, ND	58249, 58255
412	Langeloth, PA	15054
215	Langhorne, PA	19047, 19049, 19053
405	Langston, OK	73050
301	Lanham, MD	20706
215	Lansdale, PA	19446
215	Lansdowne, PA	19050
717	Lansford, PA	18232
319	Lansing, IA	52151
708	Lansing, IL	60438
517	Lansing, MI	48900–48933
407	Lantana, FL	33462, 33465
313	Lapeer, MI	48446
504	Laplace, LA	70068
307	Laramie, WY	82057–82070
914	Larchmont, NY	10538
512	Laredo, TX	78040–78044
412	Large, PA	15025
813	Largo, FL	34640–34649
701	Larimore, ND	58251
415	Larkspur, CA	94939
316	Larned, KS	67550
504	Larose, LA	70373
719	Las Animas, CO	81054
505	Las Cruces, NM	88001–88008
505	Las Vegas, NM	87701, 87745
702	Las Vegas, NV	89101–89122, 89150–89158 *
217	Latham, IL	62543
518	Latham, NY	12110
313	Lathrup Village, MI	48076
412	Latrobe, PA	15650
305	Lauderdale Lakes, FL	33311, 33319
305	Lauderhill, FL	33311–33319, 33351
302	Laurel, DE	19956
301	Laurel, MD	20707, 20708, 20723, 20724
601	Laurel, MS	39440–39442
919	Laurel Hill, NC	28351
908	Laurence Harbor, NJ	08879
712	Laurens, IA	50554
803	Laurens, SC	29360
919	Laurinburg, NC	28352
602	Laveen, AZ	85339
213	Lawndale, CA	90260, 90261, 95452
704	Lawndale, NC	28090
317	Lawrence, IN	46216, 46226
913	Lawrence, KS	66044–66046, 66049
508	Lawrence, MA	01840–01845
516	Lawrence, NY	11559
412	Lawrence, PA	15055
812	Lawrenceburg, IN	47025
502	Lawrenceburg, KY	40342
615	Lawrenceburg, TN	38464
404	Lawrenceville, GA	30243–30246
618	Lawrenceville, IL	62439
609	Lawrenceville, NJ	08648
804	Lawrenceville, VA	23868
405	Lawton, OK	73501, 73505, 73507, 73558
801	Layton, UT	84040, 84041, 84075
612	Le Center, MN	56057
712	Le Mars, IA	51017, 51031, 51057
507	Le Roy, MN	55951
716	Le Roy, NY	14482
719	Leadville, CO	80429, 80461
713	League City, TX	77573, 77574
601	Leakesville, MS	39451
512	Leakey, TX	78873
912	Leary, GA	31762
913	Leavenworth, KS	66027, 66048
913	Leawood, KS	66206, 66224
618	Lebanon, IL	62254
317	Lebanon, IN	46052
502	Lebanon, KY	40033
417	Lebanon, MO	65536
603	Lebanon, NH	03766, 03784
201	Lebanon, NJ	08833
513	Lebanon, OH	45036, 45770
503	Lebanon, OR	97355
717	Lebanon, PA	17042
615	Lebanon, TN	37087, 37088
703	Lebanon, VA	24266
904	Lee, FL	32059, 32160
413	Lee, MA	01238, 01264
603	Lee, NH	03820–03857
412	Leechburg, PA	15656
205	Leeds, AL	35094
413	Leeds, MA	01053
816	Lees Summit, MO	64063, 64082
205	Leesburg, AL	35983
904	Leesburg, FL	34748, 34789
912	Leesburg, GA	31763
703	Leesburg, VA	22075
215	Leesport, PA	19517, 19533
318	Leesville, LA	71446, 71496
803	Leesville, SC	29070
412	Leetsdale, PA	15056
801	Lehi, UT	84043
813	Lehigh Acres, FL	33936, 33971
215	Lehigh Valley, PA	18001
215	Lehighton, PA	18235
717	Lehman, PA	18627
508	Leicester, MA	01524
716	Leicester, NY	14481
502	Leitchfield, KY	42754, 42755
616	Leland, MI	49654
601	Leland, MS	38756, 38779
919	Leland, NC	28451
314	Lemay, MO	63125
619	Lemon Grove, CA	92045
708	Lemont, IL	60439
717	Lemoyne, PA	17043
414	Lena, WI	54139
913	Lenexa, KS	66210, 66215, 66227
215	Lenni, PA	19052
605	Lennox, SD	57039
704	Lenoir, NC	28633, 28645
615	Lenoir City, TN	37771
413	Lenox, MA	01240
717	Leola, PA	17540
605	Leola, SD	57456
508	Leominster, MA	01453
515	Leon, IA	50144
301	Leonardtown, MD	20650
201	Leonia, NJ	07605
316	Leoti, KS	67861
304	LeSage, WV	25537
215	Lester, PA	19029, 19113
612	Lester Prairie, MN	55354
314	Lesterville, MO	63654
806	Levelland, TX	79336–79338
516	Levittown, NY	11756
215	Levittown, PA	19053–19059
316	Lewis, KS	67552
717	Lewisburg, PA	17837
615	Lewisburg, TN	37091
304	Lewisburg, WV	24901, 24902
208	Lewiston, ID	83501
207	Lewiston, ME	04240–04243
919	Lewiston, NC	27849
309	Lewistown, IL	61542
406	Lewistown, MT	59445, 59457
717	Lewistown, PA	17044
501	Lewisville, AR	71845
208	Lewisville, ID	83431
214	Lewisville, TX	75028, 75057, 75067
404	Lexington, GA	30648
309	Lexington, IL	61753
606	Lexington, KY	40500–40596
617	Lexington, MA	02173
313	Lexington, MI	48450
816	Lexington, MO	64067
601	Lexington, MS	39095
704	Lexington, NC	27292, 27293
308	Lexington, NE	68850
419	Lexington, OH	44904
503	Lexington, OR	97839
803	Lexington, SC	29072
901	Lexington, TN	38351
703	Lexington, VA	24450
301	Lexington Park, MD	20653
406	Libby, MT	59923
316	Liberal, KS	67901–67905
317	Liberty, IN	46766, 47383
606	Liberty, KY	42220, 42539
816	Liberty, MO	64068
601	Liberty, MS	39645
919	Liberty, NC	27298, 28071
914	Liberty, NY	12754
409	Liberty, TX	75652, 77575
908	Liberty Corner, NJ	07938
708	Libertyville, IL	60048
314	Licking, MO	65542
804	Lightfoot, VA	23090
305	Lighthouse Point, FL	33064
219	Ligonier, IN	46767
808	Lihue, HI	96715, 96766
704	Lilesville, NC	28091
919	Lillington, NC	27546
716	Lima, NY	14485
419	Lima, OH	45801–45809, 45854
319	Lime Springs, IA	52155
215	Limerick, PA	19468
615	Limestone, TN	37681
207	Limington, ME	04049
217	Lincoln, IL	62656
913	Lincoln, KS	67455
617	Lincoln, MA	01773
207	Lincoln, ME	04457
402	Lincoln, NE	68500–68532, 68588, 68959 *
603	Lincoln, NH	03251
401	Lincoln, RI	02838–02865
207	Lincoln Center, ME	04458
503	Lincoln City, OR	97367, 97388
313	Lincoln Park, MI	48146
201	Lincoln Park, NJ	07035
215	Lincoln University, PA	19352
708	Lincolnshire, IL	60069
404	Lincolnton, GA	30817

Area	City	ZIP
704	Lincolnton, NC	28092, 28093
708	Lincolnwood, IL	60645, 60646
908	Lincroft, NJ	07738
509	Lind, WA	99341
903	Lindale, TX	75771
205	Linden, AL	36748
209	Linden, CA	95236
317	Linden, IN	47955
313	Linden, MI	48451
908	Linden, NJ	07036
615	Linden, TN	37096
903	Linden, TX	75563
516	Lindenhurst, NY	11757
609	Lindenwold, NJ	08021
209	Lindsay, CA	93247
402	Lindsay, NE	68644
405	Lindsay, OK	73052
503	Lindsay, OR	97508
913	Lindsborg, KS	67456
612	Lindstrom, MN	55045
215	Line Lexington, PA	18932
814	Linesville, PA	16424
205	Lineville, AL	36266
307	Lingle, WY	82223
314	Linn, MO	65051
816	Linneus, MO	64653
301	Linthicum Heights, MD	21090
812	Linton, IN	47441, 47802
701	Linton, ND	58552
704	Linville, NC	28646
609	Linwood, NJ	08221
215	Lionville, PA	19353
806	Lipscomb, TX	79056
603	Lisbon, NH	03585
216	Lisbon, OH	44432
207	Lisbon Falls, ME	04252
708	Lisle, IL	60532, 60572
203	Litchfield, CT	06750, 06759
217	Litchfield, IL	62056
612	Litchfield, MN	55355
602	Litchfield Park, AZ	85340
813	Lithia, FL	33547
404	Lithia Springs, GA	30057
404	Lithonia, GA	30038, 30058
717	Lititz, PA	17543
414	Little Chute, WI	54140
612	Little Falls, MN	56345
201	Little Falls, NJ	07424
315	Little Falls, NY	13365
201	Little Ferry, NJ	07643
718	Little Neck, NY	11362
501	Little Rock, AR	72200–72297
908	Little Silver, NJ	07739
716	Little Valley, NY	14755
806	Littlefield, TX	79339
717	Littlestown, PA	17340
303	Littleton, CO	80120–80127, 80160–80166
508	Littleton, MA	01460
603	Littleton, NH	03561
916	Live Oak, CA	95062, 95953
904	Live Oak, FL	32060
415	Livermore, CA	94550, 94551
315	Liverpool, NY	13088–13090
717	Liverpool, PA	17045
205	Livingston, AL	35470
209	Livingston, CA	95334
504	Livingston, LA	70754
406	Livingston, MT	59047
201	Livingston, NJ	07039
615	Livingston, TN	38570
409	Livingston, TX	77351
313	Livonia, MI	48150–48154
915	Llano, TX	78643
801	Loa, UT	84747
914	Loch Sheldrake, NY	12759
301	Lochearn, MD	21207
717	Lock Haven, PA	17745
614	Lockbourne, OH	43137
207	Locke Mills, ME	04255
209	Lockeford, CA	95237
803	Lockhart, SC	29364
512	Lockhart, TX	78644
513	Lockland, OH	45215
815	Lockport, IL	60441
504	Lockport, LA	70374
716	Lockport, NY	14094, 14095
704	Locust, NC	28097
703	Locust Grove, VA	22508
217	Loda, IL	60948
209	Lodi, CA	95240–95242
201	Lodi, NJ	07644
712	Logan, IA	51546
614	Logan, OH	43138
801	Logan, UT	84321, 84322
304	Logan, WV	25601
219	Logansport, IN	46947
404	Loganville, GA	30249
608	Loganville, WI	53943
406	Lolo, MT	59847
714	Loma Linda, CA	92350, 92354, 92357
708	Lombard, IL	60148
414	Lomira, WI	53048
213	Lomita, CA	90717
805	Lompoc, CA	93436, 93437
606	London, KY	40741
614	London, OH	43140
903	Lone Star, TX	75558, 75668
213	Long Beach, CA	90745–90749, 90800–90853
516	Long Beach, NY	11561
908	Long Branch, NJ	07740
708	Long Grove, IL	60047, 60069
718	Long Island City, NY	11100–11106
612	Long Lake, MN	55356, 56401
612	Long Prairie, MN	56346, 56347
908	Long Valley, NJ	07853
813	Longboat Key, FL	34228

Area	City	ZIP
413	Longmeadow, MA	01106
303	Longmont, CO	80501–80504
903	Longview, TX	75601–75615
206	Longview, WA	98632
407	Longwood, FL	32750, 32791
501	Lonoke, AR	72086
615	Lookout Mountain, TN	37350
308	Loomis, NE	68958
216	Lorain, OH	44052–44055
505	Lordsburg, NM	88009, 88045, 88055
814	Loretto, PA	15940
601	Lorman, MS	39096
703	Lorton, VA	22079
213	Los Alamitos, CA	90720, 90721
505	Los Alamos, NM	87544, 87545
415	Los Altos, CA	94022–94024
415	Los Altos Hills, CA	94022
213	Los Angeles, CA	90000–90101
209	Los Banos, CA	93635
408	Los Gatos, CA	95030–95032
505	Los Lunas, NM	87031
213	Los Nietos, CA	90606, 90610
319	Lost Nation, IA	52254
304	Lost River, WV	26811
615	Loudon, TN	37774
518	Loudonville, NY	12211
606	Louisa, KY	41201, 41230
703	Louisa, VA	23093
919	Louisburg, NC	27549
601	Louise, MS	39097
314	Louisiana, MO	63353
303	Louisville, CO	80027, 80028
912	Louisville, GA	30434
618	Louisville, IL	62858
502	Louisville, KY	40200–40299
601	Louisville, MS	39339
402	Louisville, NE	68037
216	Louisville, OH	44641
615	Louisville, TN	37777
308	Loup City, NE	68853
303	Loveland, CO	80537–80539
513	Loveland, OH	45111, 45140
702	Lovelock, NV	89419
815	Loves Park, IL	61111
804	Lovingston, VA	22949
505	Lovington, NM	88260
501	Lowell, AR	72745
904	Lowell, FL	32663
219	Lowell, IN	46356, 46399
508	Lowell, MA	01850–01854
616	Lowell, MI	49331
704	Lowell, NC	28098
216	Lowellville, OH	44436
412	Lower Burrell, PA	15068
215	Lower Merion, PA	19003
315	Lowville, NY	13367
318	Lu, LA	71244
806	Lubbock, TX	79400–79499
601	Lucedale, MS	39452
303	Lucerne, CO	80646
616	Ludington, MI	49431
606	Ludlow, KY	41016
413	Ludlow, MA	01056
802	Ludlow, VT	05149
912	Ludowici, GA	31316
409	Lufkin, TX	75901–75915
803	Lugoff, SC	29078
504	Luling, LA	70070
919	Lumber Bridge, NC	28357
912	Lumber City, GA	31549
919	Lumberton, NC	28358, 28359
609	Lumberton, NJ	08048
215	Lumberville, PA	18933
912	Lumpkin, GA	31815
702	Lund, NV	89317
508	Lunenburg, MA	01462
802	Lunenburg, VT	05906
703	Luray, VA	22835
307	Lusk, WY	82225
504	Lutcher, LA	70071
301	Lutherville, MD	21093
301	Lutherville-Timonium, MD	21093
218	Lutsen, MN	55612
615	Luttrell, TN	37779
205	Luverne, AL	36049
507	Luverne, MN	56156
414	Luxemburg, WI	54217
717	Luzerne, PA	18709
717	Lykens, PA	17048, 17978
803	Lyman, SC	29365
516	Lynbrook, NY	11563, 11564
615	Lynchburg, TN	37352
804	Lynchburg, VA	24501–24506
201	Lyndhurst, NJ	07071
913	Lyndon, KS	66451
716	Lyndonville, NY	14098
802	Lyndonville, VT	05851
317	Lynn, IN	47355
617	Lynn, MA	01901–01908, 01910
515	Lynnville, IA	50153
812	Lynnville, IN	47619
206	Lynnwood, WA	98036, 98037, 98046
213	Lynwood, CA	90262
215	Lyon Station, PA	19536
912	Lyons, GA	30436
708	Lyons, IL	60534
316	Lyons, KS	67554
908	Lyons, NJ	07939
315	Lyons, NY	14489
503	Lyons, OR	97358, 97384
315	Lyons Falls, NY	13368
512	Lytle, TX	78052

M

Area	City	ZIP
601	Maben, MS	39750
404	Mableton, GA	30059
304	Mabscott, WV	25871
904	Macclenny, FL	32063
315	Macedon, NY	14502
216	Macedonia, OH	44056
207	Machias, ME	04654, 04686
906	Mackinac Island, MI	49757
309	Mackinaw, IL	61755
616	Mackinaw City, MI	49701
316	Macksville, KS	67557
309	Macomb, IL	61455
912	Macon, GA	31200–31295, 31297, 31298
816	Macon, MO	63552
601	Macon, MS	39341
215	Macungie, PA	18062
207	Madawaska, ME	04756
701	Maddock, ND	58348
813	Madeira Beach, FL	33708, 33738
209	Madera, CA	93637–93639
814	Madera, PA	16661
405	Madill, OK	73446
203	Madison, CT	06443
904	Madison, FL	32340
404	Madison, GA	30650
618	Madison, IL	62060, 62450
812	Madison, IN	47108, 47250, 47567
207	Madison, ME	04950
612	Madison, MN	56256
601	Madison, MS	39110, 39130
919	Madison, NC	27025
402	Madison, NE	68748
201	Madison, NJ	07940, 08857
216	Madison, OH	43160, 45656
605	Madison, SD	57042
615	Madison, TN	37115, 37116
703	Madison, VA	22719–22727
608	Madison, WI	53562, 53700–53719, 53783 *
304	Madison, WV	25130
313	Madison Heights, MI	48071
804	Madison Heights, VA	24572
502	Madisonville, KY	42431
615	Madisonville, TN	37354
409	Madisonville, TX	77864
503	Madras, OR	97741
601	Magee, MS	39111
704	Maggie Valley, NC	28751
501	Magnolia, AR	71753
507	Magnolia, MN	56158
601	Magnolia, MS	39652
717	Mahanoy City, PA	17948
218	Mahnomen, MN	56557
201	Mahwah, NJ	07430, 07495–07498
704	Maiden, NC	28650
407	Maitland, FL	32751, 32794
808	Makaweli, HI	96769
208	Malad City, ID	83243, 83280
515	Malcom, IA	50157
617	Malden, MA	02148
314	Malden, MO	63863
213	Malibu, CA	90263–90265
518	Malone, NY	12953
815	Malta, IL	60150
406	Malta, MT	59538
501	Malvern, AR	72104
712	Malvern, IA	51551
215	Malvern, PA	19355
914	Mamaroneck, NY	10543
502	Mammoth Cave, KY	42259
619	Mammoth Lakes, CA	93546
609	Manahawkin, NJ	08050
908	Manasquan, NJ	08736
703	Manassas, VA	22110, 22111
703	Manassas Park, VA	22110, 22111
809	Manati, PR	00701
414	Manawa, WI	54949
508	Manchaug, MA	01526
203	Manchester, CT	06040–06043
404	Manchester, GA	31816
319	Manchester, IA	52057
606	Manchester, KY	40962
301	Manchester, MD	21088, 21102
313	Manchester, MI	48158
314	Manchester, MO	63021
603	Manchester, NH	03100–03108
716	Manchester, NY	14504
405	Manchester, OK	73758
615	Manchester, TN	37355
802	Manchester, VT	05254, 05255
802	Manchester Center, VT	05255
701	Mandan, ND	58554
504	Mandeville, LA	70448, 70470
813	Mango, FL	33550
405	Mangum, OK	73554
516	Manhasset, NY	11030
913	Manhattan, KS	66502, 66506
213	Manhattan Beach, CA	90266
717	Manheim, PA	17545
801	Manila, UT	84046
616	Manistee, MI	49660
906	Manistique, MI	49854
719	Manitou Springs, CO	80829
715	Manitowish Waters, WI	54545
414	Manitowoc, WI	54220, 54221
913	Mankato, KS	66956
507	Mankato, MN	56001, 56002
315	Manlius, NY	13104
712	Manning, IA	51432, 51455
701	Manning, ND	58642
803	Manning, SC	29102
512	Manor, TX	78653
318	Mansfield, LA	71052
508	Mansfield, MA	02048

Mansfield / Midland

Area	City	ZIP
417	Mansfield, MO	65704
419	Mansfield, OH	44900–44907
717	Mansfield, PA	16933
817	Mansfield, TX	76063
712	Manson, IA	50563
509	Manson, WA	98831
318	Mansura, LA	71350
209	Manteca, CA	95336
815	Manteno, IL	60950
919	Manteo, NC	27954
801	Manti, UT	84642, 84665
507	Mantorville, MN	55955
318	Many, LA	71449
612	Maple Grove, MN	55369, 56450
216	Maple Heights, OH	43724, 44137
612	Maple Lake, MN	55358
612	Maple Plain, MN	55359
609	Maple Shade, NJ	08052
712	Mapleton, IA	51034
503	Mapleton, OR	97453
612	Maplewood, MN	55109, 55119
314	Maplewood, MO	63143
201	Maplewood, NJ	07040
319	Maquoketa, IA	52060
213	Mar Vista, CA	90066
918	Maramec, OK	74045
305	Marathon, FL	33050, 33051
512	Marble Falls, TX	78654
314	Marble Hill, MO	63764
617	Marblehead, MA	01945
816	Marceline, MO	64658
813	Marco Island, FL	33937
712	Marcus, IA	51035
215	Marcus Hook, PA	19061
315	Marcy, NY	13403
319	Marengo, IA	52301
815	Marengo, IL	60152
915	Marfa, TX	79843
305	Margate, FL	33063, 33073
609	Margate City, NJ	08402
501	Marianna, AR	72360
904	Marianna, FL	32446
805	Maricopa, CA	93252
814	Marienville, PA	16239
404	Marietta, GA	30007, 30060–30068, 30090
601	Marietta, MS	38856
614	Marietta, OH	45750
405	Marietta, OK	73448
717	Marietta, PA	17547
213	Marina del Rey, CA	90291, 90292
715	Marinette, WI	54143
205	Marion, AL	36756
501	Marion, AR	72364
319	Marion, IA	52302, 52328
618	Marion, IL	62959
317	Marion, IN	46952, 46953, 47590
316	Marion, KS	66861
502	Marion, KY	42064
318	Marion, LA	71260
508	Marion, MA	02738
704	Marion, NC	28752
315	Marion, NY	14505
614	Marion, OH	43138, 43524
803	Marion, SC	29571
703	Marion, VA	24354
715	Marion, WI	54950
417	Marionville, MO	65705
209	Mariposa, CA	95338
708	Markham, IL	60426
219	Markle, IN	46770
916	Markleeville, CA	96120
601	Marks, MS	38646
318	Marksville, LA	71351
508	Marlboro, MA	01752
908	Marlboro, NJ	07746
802	Marlboro, VT	05344
508	Marlborough, MA	01752
517	Marlette, MI	48453
817	Marlin, TX	76661
304	Marlinton, WV	24954
301	Marlow Heights, MD	20748
609	Marlton, NJ	08053
609	Marmora, NJ	08223
906	Marquette, MI	49855
504	Marrero, LA	70072, 70073
412	Mars, PA	16046
704	Mars Hill, NC	28754
501	Marshall, AR	72617, 72650
217	Marshall, IL	62441
616	Marshall, MI	49068
507	Marshall, MN	55953, 56258
816	Marshall, MO	65340
704	Marshall, NC	28753
903	Marshall, TX	75670, 75671
703	Marshall, VA	22115
515	Marshalltown, IA	50158
912	Marshallville, GA	31057
617	Marshfield, MA	02050
417	Marshfield, MO	65706
715	Marshfield, WI	54404, 54449
704	Marshville, NC	28103
605	Martin, SD	57551
901	Martin, TN	38237, 38238
415	Martinez, CA	94553
404	Martinez, GA	30907
614	Martins Ferry, OH	43935
304	Martinsburg, WV	25401
406	Martinsdale, MT	59053
317	Martinsville, IN	46116, 46151
201	Martinsville, NJ	08836
703	Martinsville, VA	24112–24115
815	Martinton, IL	60951
501	Marvell, AR	72366
314	Maryland Heights, MO	63043, 63146
503	Maryhurst, OR	97036
916	Marysville, CA	95901–95903
913	Marysville, KS	66433, 66508
313	Marysville, MI	48040
513	Marysville, OH	43040, 43041
206	Marysville, WA	98270
816	Maryville, MO	64468
615	Maryville, TN	37801–37804, 37878
517	Mason, MI	48854
513	Mason, OH	45040
915	Mason, TX	76856
515	Mason City, IA	50401, 50467
217	Mason City, IL	62664
412	Masontown, PA	15461
718	Maspeth, NY	11378
516	Massapequa, NY	11758
315	Massena, NY	13662
216	Massillon, OH	44646–44648
806	Matador, TX	79244
717	Matamoras, PA	17032, 18336
908	Matawan, NJ	07747
804	Mathews, VA	23109
601	Mathiston, MS	39752
207	Mattawamkeag, ME	04459
616	Mattawan, MI	49071
708	Matteson, IL	60443
704	Matthews, NC	28105, 28106
516	Mattituck, NY	11952
217	Mattoon, IL	61938
301	Maugansville, MD	21767
803	Mauldin, SC	29662
419	Maumee, OH	43537
808	Maunaloa, HI	96770
901	Maury City, TN	38050
608	Mauston, WI	53948
919	Maxton, NC	28364
916	Maxwell, CA	95955
317	Maxwell, IN	46154
809	Mayaguez, PR	00708–00746
914	Maybrook, NY	12543
601	Mayersville, MS	39113
502	Mayfield, KY	42066
216	Mayfield, OH	44124
319	Maynard, IA	50655
508	Maynard, MA	01754
612	Maynard, MN	56260
615	Maynardville, TN	37807
904	Mayo, FL	32066
609	Mays Landing, NJ	08330
606	Maysville, KY	41056
816	Maysville, MO	64447, 64469
919	Maysville, NC	28555
701	Mayville, ND	58219, 58257
716	Mayville, NY	14757
414	Mayville, WI	53050
708	Maywood, IL	60153, 60154
201	Maywood, NJ	07607
608	Mazomanie, WI	53560
815	Mazon, IL	60444
704	McAdenville, NC	28101
717	McAdoo, PA	18237
201	McAfee, NJ	07428
918	McAlester, OK	74501
512	McAllen, TX	78501, 78503, 78504
614	McArthur, OH	45651
208	McCall, ID	83638
515	McCallsburg, IA	50154
412	McCandless, PA	15237
419	McClure, OH	43534
701	McClusky, ND	58463
601	McComb, MS	39648
419	McComb, OH	45858
717	McConnellsburg, PA	17233
315	McConnellsville, NY	13401
614	McConnelsville, OH	43756
308	McCook, NE	69001
317	McCordsville, IN	46055
803	McCormick, SC	29835
404	McDonough, GA	30253
703	McGaheysville, VA	22840
708	McGaw Park, IL	60085
815	McHenry, IL	60050
301	McHenry, MD	21541
605	McIntosh, SD	57641
606	McKee, KY	40447
412	McKees Rocks, PA	15136
412	McKeesport, PA	15130
901	McKenzie, TN	38201, 38257
214	McKinney, TX	75069
605	McLaughlin, SD	57642
309	McLean, IL	61754
703	McLean, VA	22101–22103
618	McLeansboro, IL	62859
503	McMinnville, OR	97128
615	McMinnville, TN	37110
412	McMurray, PA	15317
316	McPherson, KS	67460
912	McRae, GA	31055
205	McShan, AL	35471
402	Mead, NE	68041
316	Meade, KS	67864
412	Meadow Lands, PA	15347
601	Meadville, MS	39653
814	Meadville, PA	16335
919	Mebane, NC	27302
207	Mechanic Falls, ME	04256
217	Mechanicsburg, IL	62545
717	Mechanicsburg, PA	17055
804	Mechanicsville, VA	23111
518	Mechanicville, NY	12118
508	Medfield, MA	02052
617	Medford, MA	02155
609	Medford, NJ	08055
516	Medford, NY	11763
405	Medford, OK	73759
503	Medford, OR	97501–97504
715	Medford, WI	54451
609	Medford Lakes, NJ	08055
215	Media, PA	19063, 19064, 19086, 19091
316	Medicine Lodge, KS	67104
716	Medina, NY	14103
216	Medina, OH	44256–44259
305	Medley, FL	33166, 33178
701	Medora, ND	58645
508	Medway, MA	02053
303	Meeker, CO	81641
717	Mehoopany, PA	18629
501	Melbourne, AR	72556
407	Melbourne, FL	32901–32909, 32934–32951 *
804	Melfa, VA	23410
617	Melrose, MA	02176, 02177
708	Melrose Park, IL	60160–60165
215	Melrose Park, PA	19012, 19126
516	Melville, NY	11747
217	Melvin, IL	60952
313	Melvindale, MI	48122
313	Memphis, MI	48041
816	Memphis, MO	63555
315	Memphis, NY	13112
901	Memphis, TN	38100–38187, 38193–38197
806	Memphis, TX	79245
501	Mena, AR	71953
518	Menands, NY	12204
915	Menard, TX	76859
414	Menasha, WI	54952
601	Mendenhall, MS	39114
201	Mendham, NJ	07945
616	Mendon, MI	49072
209	Mendota, CA	93640
815	Mendota, IL	61342
612	Mendota Heights, MN	55118, 55120
415	Menlo Park, CA	94025–94028
906	Menominee, MI	49858
715	Menomonie, WI	54751
414	Menomonee Falls, WI	53051
915	Mentone, TX	79754
216	Mentor, OH	44060, 44061
414	Mequon, WI	53092
504	Meraux, LA	70075
209	Merced, CA	95339–95348
512	Mercedes, TX	78570
412	Mercer, PA	16137
206	Mercer Island, WA	98040
717	Mercersburg, PA	17236
609	Mercerville, NJ	08619
609	Merchantville, NJ	08109
603	Meredith, NH	03253
203	Meriden, CT	06450
208	Meridian, ID	83642
601	Meridian, MS	39301–39307, 39309
817	Meridian, TX	76665
913	Merriam, KS	66202–66204
516	Merrick, NY	11566
715	Merrill, WI	54452
219	Merrillville, IN	46410, 46411
603	Merrimack, NH	03054
407	Merritt Island, FL	32952–32954
915	Mertzon, TX	76941
215	Mertztown, PA	19539
602	Mesa, AZ	85201–85216, 85275
505	Mescalero, NM	88340
505	Mesquite, NM	88048
214	Mesquite, TX	75149, 75150, 75180–75187
504	Metairie, LA	70001–70011, 70055
216	Metals Park, OH	44073
309	Metamora, IL	61548
313	Metamora, MI	48455
419	Metamora, OH	43540
508	Methuen, MA	01844
618	Metropolis, IL	62960
912	Metter, GA	30439
908	Metuchen, NJ	08840
817	Mexia, TX	76667
314	Mexico, MO	65265
305	Miami, FL	33010–33269, 34001–34099
918	Miami, OK	74354, 74355
806	Miami, TX	79059
305	Miami Beach, FL	33109, 33139–33160
305	Miami Lakes, FL	33014–33016
305	Miami Shores, FL	33138, 33153
513	Miamisburg, OH	45342, 45343
219	Michigan City, IN	46360
317	Michigantown, IN	46057
609	Mickleton, NJ	08056
301	Middle River, MD	21220
718	Middle Village, NY	11379
508	Middleboro, MA	02346, 02347, 02349
304	Middlebourne, WV	26149
717	Middleburg, PA	17842
703	Middleburg, VA	22117
216	Middleburg Heights, OH	44130
203	Middlebury, CT	06762
219	Middlebury, IN	46540
802	Middlebury, VT	05753–05766
203	Middlefield, CT	06455
216	Middlefield, OH	44062
716	Middleport, NY	13346, 14105
606	Middlesboro, KY	40965
908	Middlesex, NJ	08846
508	Middleton, MA	01949
608	Middleton, WI	53562
203	Middletown, CT	06457
302	Middletown, DE	19709
502	Middletown, KY	40243, 42629
908	Middletown, NJ	07748
914	Middletown, NY	10940
513	Middletown, OH	43009, 45042–45044
717	Middletown, PA	17057, 19056
401	Middletown, RI	02840
703	Middletown, VA	22645, 22649
616	Middleville, MI	49333
517	Midland, MI	48640, 48641, 48670, 48674 *
412	Midland, PA	15059
915	Midland, TX	79701–79712

Code	Place	ZIP
703	Midland, VA	22728
201	Midland Park, NJ	07432
708	Midlothian, IL	60445
214	Midlothian, TX	76065
804	Midlothian, VA	23112, 23113
614	Midvale, OH	44653
801	Midvale, UT	84047
606	Midway, KY	40142, 40347, 42064
206	Midway, WA	98032
405	Midwest City, OK	73110, 73150
717	Mifflinburg, PA	17844
717	Mifflintown, PA	17059
612	Milaca, MN	56353
309	Milan, IL	61264
816	Milan, MO	63556
419	Milan, OH	44846
605	Milbank, SD	57252, 57253
207	Milbridge, ME	04658
406	Miles City, MT	59301, 59345
203	Milford, CT	06460
302	Milford, DE	19963
815	Milford, IL	60953
219	Milford, IN	46542, 47240
508	Milford, MA	01757
313	Milford, MI	48042, 48381
402	Milford, NE	68405
603	Milford, NH	03055
908	Milford, NJ	08848
513	Milford, OH	43526, 45150
717	Milford, PA	17059, 18337
503	Mill City, OR	97346, 97360
717	Mill Hall, PA	17751
415	Mill Valley, CA	94941, 94942
415	Millbrae, CA	94030
201	Millburn, NJ	07041
508	Millbury, MA	01527, 01586
912	Milledgeville, GA	31061, 31062
912	Millen, GA	30442
605	Miller, SD	57362
413	Millers Falls, MA	01349
606	Millersburg, KY	40348
216	Millersburg, OH	44654
717	Millersburg, PA	17061
301	Millersville, MD	21108
717	Millersville, PA	17551
615	Milligan College, TN	37682
201	Millington, NJ	07946
901	Millington, TN	38053, 38083
207	Millinocket, ME	04462
508	Millis, MA	02054
205	Millport, AL	35576
307	Mills, WY	82644
302	Millsboro, DE	19966
618	Millstadt, IL	62260
908	Milltown, NJ	08850
609	Millville, NJ	08332
717	Millville, PA	17846
914	Millwood, NY	10546
408	Milpitas, CA	95035
717	Milroy, PA	17063
904	Milton, FL	32570-32572
617	Milton, MA	02186
914	Milton, NY	10380, 12547
717	Milton, PA	17847
608	Milton, WI	53563
304	Milton, WV	25541
414	Milwaukee, WI	53200-53295
503	Milwaukie, OR	97222, 97267
515	Minburn, IA	50167
318	Minden, LA	71055-71058
308	Minden, NE	68959
702	Minden, NV	89423
516	Mineola, NY	11501
903	Mineola, TX	75773
501	Mineral Springs, AR	71851
704	Mineral Springs, NC	28108
817	Mineral Wells, TX	76067
304	Mineralwells, WV	26150
801	Minersville, UT	84752
216	Minerva, OH	44657
309	Minier, IL	61759
913	Minneapolis, KS	67467
612	Minneapolis, MN	55400-55480, 55487, 55488
507	Minnesota City, MN	55959
507	Minnesota Lake, MN	56068
612	Minnetonka, MN	55343, 55345
701	Minnewaukan, ND	58320, 58351
715	Minocqua, WI	54548
815	Minooka, IL	60447
701	Minot, ND	58701-58705
419	Minster, OH	45865
517	Mio, MI	48647
215	Miquon, PA	19452
305	Miramar, FL	33023, 33029
603	Mirror Lake, NH	03853
704	Misenheimer, NC	28109
219	Mishawaka, IN	46544, 46545
414	Mishicot, WI	54228
913	Mission, KS	66202, 66205
512	Mission, TX	78572
714	Mission Viejo, CA	92675, 92692
913	Mission Woods, KS	66205
601	Mississippi State, MS	39762
406	Missoula, MT	59801-59807, 59812
713	Missouri City, TX	77459, 77489
712	Missouri Valley, IA	51555
812	Mitchell, IN	47446
605	Mitchell, SD	57301
801	Moab, UT	84515, 84532, 84540
816	Moberly, MO	65270
205	Mobile, AL	36600-36695
704	Mocksville, NC	27028
209	Modesto, CA	95350-95356
216	Mogadore, OH	44260
701	Mohall, ND	58761
315	Mohawk, NY	12068, 13407
215	Mohnton, PA	19540
708	Mokena, IL	60448
503	Molalla, OR	97038
309	Moline, IL	61265
412	Monaca, PA	15061
915	Monahans, TX	79756
803	Moncks Corner, SC	29430, 29461
712	Mondamin, IA	51557
715	Mondovi, WI	54755
412	Monessen, PA	15062
417	Monett, MO	65708
715	Monico, WI	54549
309	Monmouth, IL	61462
503	Monmouth, OR	97361
908	Monmouth Junction, NJ	08852
412	Monongahela, PA	15063
203	Monroe, CT	06468
404	Monroe, GA	30655
219	Monroe, IN	46772, 47584
318	Monroe, LA	71201-71213
313	Monroe, MI	48133, 48157-48166
704	Monroe, NC	28110, 28112
609	Monroe, NJ	07871, 08520
914	Monroe, NY	10950
513	Monroe, OH	43140, 45050
206	Monroe, WA	98272
608	Monroe, WI	53566
314	Monroe City, MO	63456
205	Monroeville, AL	36460, 36461
412	Monroeville, PA	15146
818	Monrovia, CA	91016, 91017
914	Monsey, NY	10952
413	Monson, MA	01057
717	Mont Alto, PA	17237
616	Montague, MI	49437
817	Montague, TX	76251
516	Montauk, NY	11954
302	Montchanin, DE	19710
714	Montclair, CA	91763
201	Montclair, NJ	07042-07044
213	Montebello, CA	90640
805	Montecito, CA	93108
608	Montello, WI	53949
408	Monterey, CA	93940-93944
703	Monterey, VA	24465
213	Monterey Park, CA	91754
206	Montesano, WA	98563
205	Montevallo, AL	35115
612	Montevideo, MN	56265
912	Montezuma, GA	31063
515	Montezuma, IA	50171, 50172
316	Montezuma, KS	67867
205	Montgomery, AL	36100-36199
708	Montgomery, IL	60538, 62427
612	Montgomery, MN	56069
717	Montgomery, PA	17236, 17752
304	Montgomery, WV	25136
314	Montgomery City, MO	63361
215	Montgomeryville, PA	18936
501	Monticello, AR	71655
904	Monticello, FL	32344
404	Monticello, GA	31064
319	Monticello, IA	52252, 52310
217	Monticello, IL	61856
219	Monticello, IN	47960
606	Monticello, KY	42633
314	Monticello, MO	63457
601	Monticello, MS	39654
914	Monticello, NY	12701, 12777
801	Monticello, UT	84535
607	Montour Falls, NY	14865
717	Montoursville, PA	17754
419	Montpelier, OH	43543
802	Montpelier, VT	05601, 05602, 05604
704	Montreat, NC	28757
205	Montrose, AL	36559
818	Montrose, CA	91020, 91021
303	Montrose, CO	81401, 81402
319	Montrose, IA	52639
313	Montrose, MI	48457
914	Montrose, NY	10548
717	Montrose, PA	18801
804	Montrose, VA	23231
804	Montross, VA	22520
201	Montvale, NJ	07645
203	Montville, CT	06353
201	Montville, NJ	07045
719	Monument, CO	80132
203	Moodus, CT	06469
412	Moon Run, PA	15136
201	Moonachie, NJ	07074
405	Moore, OK	73139, 73160-73170
813	Moore Haven, FL	33471
304	Moorefield, WV	26836
609	Moorestown, NJ	08057
317	Mooresville, IN	46158
704	Mooresville, NC	28115
701	Mooreton, ND	58061
218	Moorhead, MN	56560, 56562, 56563
601	Moorhead, MS	38761
805	Moorpark, CA	93020, 93021
218	Moose Lake, MN	55767
708	Mooseheart, IL	60539
717	Moosic, PA	18507
203	Moosup, CT	06354
612	Mora, MN	55051
505	Mora, NM	87732
415	Moraga, CA	94556
307	Moran, WY	83013
606	Morehead, KY	40351
919	Morehead City, NC	28557
912	Morgan, GA	31766
507	Morgan, MN	56266
801	Morgan, UT	84018, 84050
504	Morgan City, LA	70380, 70381
408	Morgan Hill, CA	95037, 95038
704	Morganton, NC	28655
502	Morgantown, KY	42261
704	Morgantown, NC	27215
215	Morgantown, PA	19543
304	Morgantown, WV	26505-26507
908	Morganville, NJ	07751
503	Moro, OR	97039
801	Moroni, UT	84623, 84646, 84667
308	Morrill, NE	69358
501	Morrilton, AR	72110
815	Morris, IL	60450
612	Morris, MN	56267
908	Morris Plains, NJ	07950
303	Morrison, CO	80465
815	Morrison, IL	61270
217	Morrisonville, IL	62546
317	Morristown, IN	46161
908	Morristown, NJ	07960-07963
614	Morristown, OH	43759
615	Morristown, TN	37813-37816
315	Morrisville, NY	13408
215	Morrisville, PA	19067
802	Morrisville, VT	05661
404	Morrow, GA	30260, 30287
309	Morton, IL	61550
215	Morton, PA	19070
806	Morton, TX	75640, 79346
206	Morton, WA	98356
708	Morton Grove, IL	60053
208	Moscow, ID	83843
901	Moscow, TN	38057
509	Moses Lake, WA	98837
715	Mosinee, WI	54455
505	Mosquero, NM	87733
701	Mott, ND	58646
205	Moulton, AL	35650
912	Moultrie, GA	31768, 31776
612	Mound, MN	55364, 56156
618	Mound City, IL	62963
913	Mound City, KS	66056
816	Mound City, MO	64470
605	Mound City, SD	57646
316	Moundridge, KS	67107
304	Moundsville, WV	26041
919	Mount Airy, NC	27030, 27031
503	Mount Angel, OR	97362
515	Mount Ayr, IA	50854
404	Mount Berry, GA	30149
717	Mount Bethel, PA	18343
412	Mount Braddock, PA	15465
618	Mount Carmel, IL	62863
717	Mount Carmel, PA	17851
815	Mount Carroll, IL	61053
313	Mount Clemens, MI	48043-48046
904	Mount Dora, FL	32745, 32757
919	Mount Gilead, NC	27306
419	Mount Gilead, OH	43338
704	Mount Holly, NC	28120
609	Mount Holly, NJ	08060
717	Mount Holly Springs, PA	17065
304	Mount Hope, WV	25686, 25880, 26160
501	Mount Ida, AR	71957
703	Mount Jackson, VA	22842
717	Mount Joy, PA	17022, 17552
914	Mount Kisco, NY	10549
609	Mount Laurel, NJ	08054
412	Mount Lebanon, PA	15228
914	Mount Marion, NY	12456
815	Mount Morris, IL	61054
716	Mount Morris, NY	14510
601	Mount Olive, MS	39119, 39664
919	Mount Olive, NC	28365
606	Mount Olivet, KY	41064
319	Mount Pleasant, IA	52641
517	Mount Pleasant, MI	48804, 48858, 48859
704	Mount Pleasant, NC	27011, 28657
412	Mount Pleasant, PA	15666, 19506
803	Mount Pleasant, SC	29464
615	Mount Pleasant, TN	38474
903	Mount Pleasant, TX	75455
717	Mount Pocono, PA	18344
708	Mount Prospect, IL	60056
217	Mount Pulaski, IL	62548
802	Mount Snow, VT	05356
217	Mount Sterling, IL	62353
606	Mount Sterling, KY	40353
314	Mount Sterling, MO	65062
614	Mount Sterling, OH	43143
317	Mount Summit, IN	47361
319	Mount Union, IA	52644
814	Mount Union, PA	17066
205	Mount Vernon, AL	36560
912	Mount Vernon, GA	30445
319	Mount Vernon, IA	52314
618	Mount Vernon, IL	62864
812	Mount Vernon, IN	47620
606	Mount Vernon, KY	40456
417	Mount Vernon, MO	65712
914	Mount Vernon, NY	10550-10553
614	Mount Vernon, OH	43050, 43203
903	Mount Vernon, TX	75457
206	Mount Vernon, WA	98273
717	Mount Wolf, PA	17347
615	Mountain City, TN	37680, 37683
417	Mountain Grove, MO	65711
501	Mountain Home, AR	72121, 72653
208	Mountain Home, ID	83647, 83648
704	Mountain Home, NC	28758
615	Mountain Home, TN	37684
717	Mountain Top, PA	18707
501	Mountain View, AR	72533, 72657
415	Mountain View, CA	93307, 94039-94043
417	Mountain View, MO	65548
908	Mountainside, NJ	07092
914	Mountainville, NY	10953
206	Mountlake Terrace, WA	98043

Area	Place	ZIP
717	Mountville, PA	17554
217	Moweaqua, IL	62550
414	Mukwonago, WI	53149
813	Mulberry, FL	33860
806	Muleshoe, TX	79347
205	Mulga, AL	35118
308	Mullen, NE	69152
304	Mullens, WV	25882
803	Mullins, SC	29574
317	Muncie, IN	47302–47308
717	Muncy, PA	17756
708	Mundelein, IL	60060
502	Munfordville, KY	42765
412	Munhall, PA	15120
906	Munising, MI	49862
216	Munroe Falls, OH	44262
219	Munster, IN	46321
605	Murdo, SD	57559
501	Murfreesboro, AR	71958
919	Murfreesboro, NC	27855
615	Murfreesboro, TN	37129–37133
208	Murphy, ID	83650
704	Murphy, NC	28906
618	Murphysboro, IL	62966
502	Murray, KY	42046, 42071
801	Murray, UT	84107, 84123
908	Murray Hill, NJ	07974
404	Murrayville, GA	30564
412	Murrysville, PA	15668
319	Muscatine, IA	52761
205	Muscle Shoals, AL	35660, 35661
414	Muskego, WI	53150
616	Muskegon, MI	49440–49445
616	Muskegon Heights, MI	49444
918	Muskogee, OK	74401–74403
717	Myerstown, PA	17067, 17324
803	Myrtle Beach, SC	29572, 29578, 29579
203	Mystic, CT	06355

N

Area	Place	ZIP
409	Nacogdoches, TX	75961–75963
919	Nags Head, NC	27959
809	Naguabo, PR	00718
912	Nahunta, GA	31553
907	Naknek, AK	99633
208	Nampa, ID	83651–83653, 83686, 83687
301	Nanticoke, MD	21840
717	Nanticoke, PA	18634
508	Nantucket, MA	02554–02584
914	Nanuet, NY	10954
707	Napa, CA	94558, 94559, 94581
708	Naperville, IL	60540, 60563–60567
813	Naples, FL	33939–33942, 33961–33964
716	Naples, NY	14512
701	Napoleon, ND	58561
419	Napoleon, OH	43545
504	Napoleonville, LA	70390
219	Nappanee, IN	46550
215	Narberth, PA	19072
401	Narragansett, RI	02882
914	Narrowsburg, NY	12764
414	Nashotah, WI	53058
515	Nashua, IA	50658
603	Nashua, NH	03060–03063
501	Nashville, AR	71852
912	Nashville, GA	31639
618	Nashville, IL	62263
812	Nashville, IN	47448
919	Nashville, NC	27856
615	Nashville, TN	37200–37237, 37239–37250
218	Nashwauk, MN	55769
401	Nasonville, RI	02895
601	Natchez, MS	39120–39122
318	Natchitoches, LA	71457, 71458
508	Natick, MA	01760
619	National City, CA	92047, 92050
517	National City, MI	48748
517	National Mine, MI	49865
412	Natrona Heights, PA	15065
203	Naugatuck, CT	06770
217	Nauvoo, IL	62354
505	Navajo, NM	87328
216	Navarre, OH	44662
409	Navasota, TX	77868
616	Nazareth, MI	49074
215	Nazareth, PA	18064
402	Nebraska City, NE	68410
608	Necedah, WI	54646
409	Nederland, TX	77627
617	Needham, MA	02192, 02194
617	Needham Heights, MA	02194
619	Needles, CA	92363
414	Neenah, WI	54956, 54957
402	Nehawka, NE	68413
715	Neillsville, WI	54456
715	Nekoosa, WI	54457
402	Neligh, NE	68756
402	Nelson, NE	68961
614	Nelsonville, OH	45717, 45764
316	Neodesha, KS	66757
715	Neopit, WI	54150
417	Neosho, MO	64850
801	Nephi, UT	84648
908	Neptune, NJ	07753, 07754
717	Nescopeck, PA	18635
201	Neshanic, NJ	08853
717	Nesquehoning, PA	18240
913	Ness City, KS	67560
201	Netcong, NJ	07857
515	Nevada, IA	50201
417	Nevada, MO	64772
916	Nevada City, CA	95959
412	Neville Island, PA	15225
812	New Albany, IN	47150
601	New Albany, MS	38652
717	New Albany, PA	18833
412	New Alexandria, PA	15670
618	New Athens, IL	62264
601	New Augusta, MS	39462
419	New Bavaria, OH	43548
508	New Bedford, MA	02740–02747
607	New Berlin, NY	13411
717	New Berlin, PA	17855
414	New Berlin, WI	53146, 53151
919	New Bern, NC	28560–28562
814	New Bethlehem, PA	16242
717	New Bloomfield, PA	17068
512	New Braunfels, TX	78130–78133
419	New Bremen, OH	45869
612	New Brighton, MN	55112
412	New Brighton, PA	15066
203	New Britain, CT	06050–06053
215	New Britain, PA	18901
908	New Brunswick, NJ	08901–08906, 08933
616	New Buffalo, MI	49117
203	New Canaan, CT	06840
301	New Carrollton, MD	20784
302	New Castle, DE	19720, 19721
317	New Castle, IN	47362
502	New Castle, KY	40050
412	New Castle, PA	16101–16108, 17970
703	New Castle, VA	24127
914	New City, NY	10956
717	New Columbia, PA	17856
614	New Concord, OH	43762
717	New Cumberland, PA	17070
304	New Cumberland, WV	26047
618	New Douglas, IL	62074
814	New Enterprise, PA	16664
717	New Freedom, PA	17349
609	New Gretna, NJ	08224
515	New Hampton, IA	50659
203	New Hartford, CT	06057
315	New Hartford, NY	13413
203	New Haven, CT	06500–06536
219	New Haven, IN	46774
313	New Haven, MI	48048
304	New Haven, WV	25265
217	New Holland, IL	62671
717	New Holland, PA	17557
414	New Holstein, WI	53061, 53062
612	New Hope, MN	55427, 55428
215	New Hope, PA	18938
516	New Hyde Park, NY	11040–11043, 11099
318	New Iberia, LA	70560–70562
603	New Ipswich, NH	03071
412	New Kensington, PA	15068
804	New Kent, VA	23124
419	New Knoxville, OH	45871
518	New Lebanon Center, NY	12125
815	New Lenox, IL	60451
614	New Lexington, OH	43764, 45381
317	New Lisbon, IN	47366, 47390
608	New Lisbon, WI	53950
203	New London, CT	06320
314	New London, MO	63459
603	New London, NH	03257
419	New London, OH	44851
414	New London, WI	54961
314	New Madrid, MO	63869
317	New Market, IN	47965
703	New Market, VA	22844
304	New Martinsville, WV	26155
203	New Milford, CT	06776
201	New Milford, NJ	07646
504	New Orleans, LA	70100–70190
717	New Oxford, PA	17350
914	New Paltz, NY	12561
513	New Paris, OH	45347
216	New Philadelphia, OH	44663
717	New Philadelphia, PA	17959
813	New Port Richey, FL	34652–34656
612	New Prague, MN	56071
203	New Preston, CT	06777
515	New Providence, IA	50206
317	New Richmond, IN	47967
513	New Richmond, OH	45157
715	New Richmond, WI	54017
504	New Roads, LA	70760
914	New Rochelle, NY	10800–10805
701	New Rockford, ND	58319, 58356
812	New Salisbury, IN	47161
515	New Sharon, IA	50207
904	New Smyrna Beach, FL	32168–32170
914	New Square, NY	10977
412	New Stanton, PA	15672
507	New Ulm, MN	56030, 56084
513	New Vienna, OH	45159
412	New Wilmington, PA	16142, 16172
914	New Windsor, NY	12553
212	New York, NY	09001–10286, 10292
315	New York Mills, NY	13417
415	Newark, CA	94560
302	Newark, DE	19702, 19711, 19713–19717
201	Newark, NJ	07100–07175
315	Newark, NY	14513
614	Newark, OH	43055, 43056
616	Newaygo, MI	49337
503	Newberg, OR	97132
901	Newbern, TN	38059
906	Newberry, MI	49868
803	Newberry, SC	29108
812	Newburgh, IN	47629, 47630
914	Newburgh, NY	12550, 12553
216	Newbury, OH	44022, 44065
805	Newbury Park, CA	91319, 91320
508	Newburyport, MA	01950–01952
916	Newcastle, CA	95658
307	Newcastle, WY	82701, 82715
205	Newell, AL	36270
802	Newfane, VT	05345
609	Newfield, NJ	08344
603	Newfields, NH	03856
805	Newhall, CA	91321, 91382
601	Newhebron, MS	39140
203	Newington, CT	06111
603	Newington, NH	03801
405	Newkirk, OK	74647
704	Newland, NC	28657
209	Newman, CA	95360
603	Newmarket, NH	03857
404	Newnan, GA	30254, 30263–30265
501	Newport, AR	72112
714	Newport, CA	92660
317	Newport, IN	47966
606	Newport, KY	41071–41076
207	Newport, ME	04953
612	Newport, MN	55055
919	Newport, NC	28570
603	Newport, NH	03773
503	Newport, OR	97365, 97369
717	Newport, PA	17074
401	Newport, RI	02840
615	Newport, TN	37821
802	Newport, VT	05855–05857
509	Newport, WA	98004, 99156
714	Newport Beach, CA	92658–92663
802	Newport Center, VT	05857
804	Newport News, VA	23600–23612
912	Newton, GA	31770
515	Newton, IA	50208
618	Newton, IL	61250, 62448
316	Newton, KS	67114
617	Newton, MA	02158–02258
601	Newton, MS	39345
704	Newton, NC	28658
201	Newton, NJ	07860
409	Newton, TX	75966
617	Newton Center, MA	02159
617	Newton Centre, MA	02159
315	Newton Falls, NY	13666
216	Newton Falls, OH	44444
919	Newton Grove, NC	28366
617	Newton Highlands, MA	02161
617	Newton Lower Falls, MA	02162
617	Newton Upper Falls, MA	02164
617	Newtonville, MA	02158–02165
203	Newtown, CT	06470
816	Newtown, MO	64645, 64667
215	Newtown, PA	17512, 18940
717	Newville, PA	17241
208	Nezperce, ID	83543
716	Niagara, NY	14300
715	Niagara, WI	54151
716	Niagara Falls, NY	14300–14305
716	Niagara University, NY	14109
203	Niantic, CT	06357
904	Niceville, FL	32578
606	Nicholasville, KY	40356
316	Nickerson, KS	67561
708	Niles, IL	60648
616	Niles, MI	49120
216	Niles, OH	44446
803	Ninety Six, SC	29666
615	Niota, TN	37826
615	Niota, TN	25143
304	Nitro, WV	08817
201	Nixon, NJ	78140
512	Nixon, TX	73068
405	Noble, OK	46038, 46060
317	Noblesville, IN	76255
817	Nocona, TX	64854
417	Noel, MO	85621, 85628
602	Nogales, AZ	62075
217	Nokomis, IL	99762
907	Nome, AK	70079
504	Norco, LA	30071–30093
404	Norcross, GA	68701, 68738
402	Norfolk, NE	23500–23523, 23529, 23530 *
804	Norfolk, VA	33169, 33269
305	Norland, FL	08347
609	Norma, NJ	35762
205	Normal, AL	61761
309	Normal, IL	73019, 73069–73072
405	Norman, OK	60634, 60656
708	Norridge, IL	19401–19409, 19485
215	Norristown, PA	60201
708	North [illegible], IL	02351
617	North Abington, MA	01247
413	North Adams, MA	01845
508	North Andover, MA	04958
207	North Anson, ME	07032
201	North Arlington, NJ	30319
404	North Atlanta, GA	02760–02763
508	North Attleboro, MA	29841, 29842
803	North Augusta, SC	60542
708	North Aurora, IL	11703
516	North Babylon, NY	45872
419	North Baltimore, OH	11706
516	North Bay Shore, NY	33141
305	North Bay Village, FL	11710
516	North Bellmore, NY	05257
802	North Bennington, VT	07047
201	North Bergen, NJ	03906
207	North Berwick, ME	01821, 01862
508	North Billerica, MA	08876
908	North Branch, NJ	06471
203	North Branford, CT	01535
508	North Brookfield, MA	08902
908	North Brunswick, NJ	07006
201	North Caldwell, NJ	06059
203	North Canton, CT	44720, 44721
216	North Canton, OH	29404–29406, 29418–29420
803	North Charleston, SC	60064, 60088
708	North Chicago, IL	14514
716	North Chili, NY	

Area	City	Zip
603	North Conway, NH	03860
518	North Creek, NY	12853
508	North Dartmouth, MA	02747
508	North Dighton, MA	02754, 02764
301	North East, MD	21901
814	North East, PA	16428
508	North Easton, MA	02356, 02357
508	North Falmouth, MA	02556, 02565
203	North Franklin, CT	06254
508	North Grafton, MA	01536
203	North Grosvenordale, CT	06255
201	North Hackensack, NJ	07661
203	North Haven, CT	06473
516	North Haven, NY	11963
802	North Hero, VT	05474
916	North Highlands, CA	95660
516	North Hills, NY	11040, 11507
818	North Hollywood, CA	91600–91609, 91615–91617
412	North Huntingdon, PA	15642
216	North Jackson, OH	44451
816	North Kansas City, MO	64116
401	North Kingstown, RI	02852–02854
216	North Kingsville, OH	44068
702	North Las Vegas, NV	89030, 89031
219	North Liberty, IN	46554
216	North Lima, OH	44452
516	North Lindenhurst, NY	11757
501	North Little Rock, AR	72100, 72114–72120
213	North Long Beach, CA	90805
219	North Manchester, IN	46962
507	North Mankato, MN	56001
516	North Merrick, NY	11566
305	North Miami, FL	33161, 33181
305	North Miami Beach, FL	33160–33169, 33179–33181
207	North Monmouth, ME	04265
803	North Myrtle Beach, SC	29582, 29598
316	North Newton, KS	67117
216	North Olmsted, OH	44070
508	North Oxford, MA	01537
407	North Palm Beach, FL	33408
503	North Plains, OR	97133
308	North Platte, NE	69101, 69132
802	North Pownal, VT	05260
401	North Providence, RI	02904, 02911
216	North Randall, OH	44128
617	North Randolph, MA	02368
508	North Reading, MA	01864
817	North Richland Hills, TX	76118, 76180–76182
216	North Ridgeville, OH	44039
708	North Riverside, IL	60546
801	North Salt Lake, UT	84054
401	North Smithfield, RI	02876, 02895
802	North Springfield, VT	05150
203	North Stonington, CT	06359
315	North Syracuse, NY	13212
914	North Tarrytown, NY	10591
703	North Tazewell, VA	24630
716	North Tonawanda, NY	14120
508	North Uxbridge, MA	01538
812	North Vernon, IN	47265
412	North Versailles, PA	15137
215	North Wales, PA	19436, 19454, 19477
603	North Walpole, NH	03609
914	North White Plains, NY	10603
919	North Wilkesboro, NC	28659
207	North Windham, ME	04062
413	Northampton, MA	01060, 01061, 01063
215	Northampton, PA	18067
508	Northborough, MA	01532
508	Northbridge, MA	01534
708	Northbrook, IL	60022, 60062, 60065
207	Northeast Harbor, ME	04662
708	Northfield, IL	60093
413	Northfield, MA	01354, 01360
507	Northfield, MN	55057
609	Northfield, NJ	08225
216	Northfield, OH	44056, 44067
802	Northfield, VT	05663
203	Northford, CT	06472
303	Northglenn, CO	80233, 80234, 80241
708	Northlake, IL	60164
516	Northport, NY	11768
818	Northridge, CA	91324–91330
717	Northumberland, PA	17857
201	Northvale, NJ	07647
313	Northville, MI	48167
515	Northwood, IA	50459
419	Northwood, OH	43619
913	Norton, KS	67654
508	Norton, MA	02766
216	Norton, OH	43356, 44203
703	Norton, VA	24273
714	Norton Air Force Base, CA	92409
213	Norwalk, CA	90650–90652
203	Norwalk, CT	06850–06857, 06859
515	Norwalk, IA	50211
419	Norwalk, OH	44857
319	Norway, IA	52318
207	Norway, ME	04268
906	Norway, MI	49870
617	Norwell, MA	02061
203	Norwich, CT	06360
607	Norwich, NY	13815
203	Norwichtown, CT	06360
617	Norwood, MA	02062
704	Norwood, NC	28128
201	Norwood, NJ	07648
513	Norwood, OH	45212, 45237
503	Noti, OR	97461
219	Notre Dame, IN	46556
215	Nottingham, PA	19362
804	Nottoway, VA	23955
415	Novato, CA	94945–94949, 94998
313	Novi, MI	48050, 48374, 48375, 48377
918	Nowata, OK	74048
512	Nursery, TX	77976
707	Nut Tree, CA	95688
201	Nutley, NJ	07110
508	Nutting Lake, MA	01865
914	Nyack, NY	10960

O

Area	City	Zip
314	O'Fallon, MO	63366
402	O'Neill, NE	68763
708	Oak Brook, IL	60521
414	Oak Creek, WI	53154
708	Oak Forest, IL	60452
708	Oak Grove, IL	61264
318	Oak Grove, LA	71263, 71423
503	Oak Grove, OR	97222, 97267
804	Oak Grove, VA	22443
419	Oak Harbor, OH	43449
206	Oak Harbor, WA	98277, 98278
518	Oak Hill, NY	12422, 12460
304	Oak Hill, WV	25901
708	Oak Lawn, IL	60453–60459
708	Oak Park, IL	60301–60304
313	Oak Park, MI	48237
615	Oak Ridge, TN	37830, 37831
704	Oakboro, NC	28129
708	Oakbrook Terrace, IL	60181
209	Oakdale, CA	95361
516	Oakdale, NY	11769, 13790
412	Oakdale, PA	15071
608	Oakdale, WI	54649
716	Oakfield, NY	14125
908	Oakhurst, NJ	07755
415	Oakland, CA	94601–94627, 94660, 94662 *
407	Oakland, FL	34760
712	Oakland, IA	51560
301	Oakland, MD	21550
207	Oakland, ME	04963
402	Oakland, NE	68045
201	Oakland, NJ	07436
812	Oakland City, IN	47660
913	Oakley, KS	67748
412	Oakmont, PA	15139
215	Oaks, PA	19456
703	Oakton, VA	22124
812	Oaktown, IN	47561
707	Oakville, CA	94562
203	Oakville, CT	06779, 06795
319	Oakville, IA	52646
317	Oakville, IN	47367
206	Oakville, WA	98568
404	Oakwood, GA	30566
419	Oakwood, OH	45409, 45873
913	Oberlin, KS	67749
318	Oberlin, LA	70655
216	Oberlin, OH	44074
618	Oblong, IL	62449
904	Ocala, FL	32670–32678
908	Ocean, NJ	07712–08758
301	Ocean City, MD	21842
609	Ocean City, NJ	08226
601	Ocean Springs, MS	39564, 39565
908	Oceanport, NJ	07757
619	Oceanside, CA	92051–92058
516	Oceanside, NY	11572
712	Ocheyedan, IA	51330, 51354
912	Ocilla, GA	31774
414	Oconomowoc, WI	53066
414	Oconto, WI	54153
414	Oconto Falls, WI	54154
712	Odebolt, IA	51458
503	Odell, OR	97044
301	Odenton, MD	21113, 21114
816	Odessa, MO	64076
607	Odessa, NY	14869
915	Odessa, TX	79760–79768
509	Odessa, WA	99144, 99159
319	Oelwein, IA	50662
316	Offerle, KS	67563
308	Ogallala, NE	69153
501	Ogden, AR	71853
217	Ogden, IL	61859
801	Ogden, UT	84400–84414
315	Ogdensburg, NY	13669
815	Oglesby, IL	61348
912	Oglethorpe, GA	31068
207	Ogunquit, ME	03907
318	Oil City, LA	71061
814	Oil City, PA	16301
805	Ojai, CA	93023
509	Okanogan, WA	98840
405	Okarche, OK	73762
813	Okeechobee, FL	34972–34974
918	Okemah, OK	74859
517	Okemos, MI	48805, 48864
405	Oklahoma City, OK	73100–73180, 73190
218	Oklee, MN	56742
918	Okmulgee, OK	74447
712	Okoboji, IA	51355
601	Okolona, MS	38860
913	Olathe, KS	66061, 66062
516	Old Bethpage, NY	11804
908	Old Bridge, NJ	08857
717	Old Forge, PA	18518
704	Old Fort, NC	28762
203	Old Greenwich, CT	06870
203	Old Lyme, CT	06371
203	Old Saybrook, CT	06475
207	Old Town, ME	04468
516	Old Westbury, NY	11568
813	Oldsmar, FL	34677
908	Oldwick, NJ	08858
716	Olean, NY	14760
601	Olive Branch, MS	38654
606	Olive Hill, KY	41164
616	Olivet, MI	49076
605	Olivet, SD	57052
612	Olivia, MN	56277
512	Olmito, TX	78575
216	Olmsted Falls, OH	44138
618	Olney, IL	62450
406	Olney, MT	59927
817	Olney, TX	76374
206	Olympia, WA	98501–98507
708	Olympia Fields, IL	60461
305	Olympia Heights, FL	33165, 33265
717	Olyphant, PA	18447
402	Omaha, NE	51510, 68100–68172
608	Onalaska, WI	54650
612	Onamia, MN	56359
712	Onawa, IA	51040
517	Onaway, MI	49765
813	Oneco, FL	34264
315	Oneida, NY	13421
615	Oneida, TN	37841
205	Oneonta, AL	35121
607	Oneonta, NY	13820, 13861
402	Ong, NE	68452
605	Onida, SD	57564
517	Onsted, MI	49265
714	Ontario, CA	91761, 91762, 91764
315	Ontario, NY	14519
503	Ontario, OR	97903–97914
315	Ontario Center, NY	14520
906	Ontonagon, MI	49953
305	Opa Locka, FL	33014, 33054–33056
205	Opelika, AL	36801–36803
318	Opelousas, LA	70570, 70571
205	Opp, AL	36467
309	Oquawka, IL	61469
201	Oradell, NJ	07649
714	Orange, CA	92613, 92664–92669
203	Orange, CT	06477
508	Orange, MA	01355, 01364
201	Orange, NJ	07050–07052
409	Orange, TX	77630–77632
703	Orange, VA	22960
712	Orange City, IA	51041
904	Orange Park, FL	32065, 32073
914	Orangeburg, NY	10962
803	Orangeburg, SC	29115–29117
206	Orcas, WA	98280
313	Orchard Lake Village, MI	48033
716	Orchard Park, NY	14127
308	Ord, NE	68862
916	Ordbend, CA	95943
719	Ordway, CO	81063
815	Oregon, IL	61061
816	Oregon, MO	64473
608	Oregon, WI	53575
503	Oregon City, OR	97045
215	Oreland, PA	19075
801	Orem, UT	84057–84059
415	Orinda, CA	94563
309	Orion, IL	61273
315	Oriskany, NY	13424
315	Oriskany Falls, NY	13425
916	Orland, CA	95963
708	Orland Park, IL	60462
407	Orlando, FL	32799–32872, 32887
812	Orleans, IN	47452
508	Orleans, MA	02653
802	Orleans, VT	05860
904	Ormond Beach, FL	32174–32176
208	Orofino, ID	83544
207	Orono, ME	04469, 04473
916	Oroville, CA	95915, 95966
216	Orrville, OH	44667
612	Ortonville, MN	56278
216	Orwell, OH	44076
717	Orwigsburg, PA	17961
515	Osage, IA	50454, 50461
314	Osage Beach, MO	65065
913	Osawatomie, KS	66064
913	Osborne, KS	67473
501	Osceola, AR	72370
515	Osceola, IA	50213
417	Osceola, MO	64776
402	Osceola, NE	68651
715	Osceola, WI	54020
812	Osgood, IN	47037
308	Oshkosh, NE	69154
414	Oshkosh, WI	54901–54904, 54906
616	Oshtemo, MI	49077
515	Oskaloosa, IA	52577
913	Oskaloosa, KS	66066
813	Osprey, FL	34229
612	Osseo, MN	55369
319	Ossian, IA	52161
914	Ossining, NY	10562
603	Ossipee, NH	03864
316	Oswego, KS	67356
315	Oswego, NY	13126
509	Othello, WA	99327, 99344
913	Otis, KS	67565
914	Otisville, NY	10963, 12970
616	Otsego, MI	49078
815	Ottawa, IL	61350
913	Ottawa, KS	66067
419	Ottawa, OH	45875
313	Ottawa Lake, MI	49267
503	Otter Crest, OR	97365
515	Ottumwa, IA	52501
303	Ouray, CO	81427
913	Overbrook, KS	66524
913	Overland Park, KS	66202–66215, 66221–66224
407	Oviedo, FL	32765, 32766
918	Owasso, OK	74055
507	Owatonna, MN	55060
607	Owego, NY	13827
715	Owen, WI	54460

Area	Location	ZIP
502	Owensboro, KY	42301–42303
314	Owensville, MO	65066
502	Owenton, KY	40359
903	Owentown, TX	75708, 75792
301	Owings Mills, MD	21117
606	Owingsville, KY	40360
517	Owosso, MI	48867
205	Oxford, AL	36201, 36203
203	Oxford, CT	06483
508	Oxford, MA	01540
207	Oxford, ME	04270
601	Oxford, MS	38655, 39638
919	Oxford, NC	27565
908	Oxford, NJ	07863
513	Oxford, OH	43773, 45056
215	Oxford, PA	19363
805	Oxnard, CA	93030–93035
301	Oxon Hill, MD	20745
516	Oyster Bay, NY	11771
205	Ozark, AL	36360, 36361
501	Ozark, AR	72949
417	Ozark, MO	65721
915	Ozona, TX	76943
718	Ozone Park, NY	11416, 11417

P

Area	Location	ZIP
808	Paauilo, HI	96776
406	Pablo, MT	59855
415	Pacheco, CA	94553
206	Pacific Beach, WA	98571
408	Pacific Grove, CA	93950
213	Pacific Palisades, CA	90272
415	Pacifica, CA	94044
818	Pacoima, CA	91331–91334
502	Paducah, KY	42001–42003
806	Paducah, TX	79248
602	Page, AZ	86036, 86040
803	Pageland, SC	29728
303	Pagosa Springs, CO	81147, 81157
407	Pahokee, FL	33476
504	Paincourtville, LA	70391
216	Painesville, OH	44077
915	Paint Rock, TX	76866
607	Painted Post, NY	14870
606	Paintsville, KY	41240
708	Palatine, IL	60067, 60074, 60078
518	Palatine Bridge, NY	13428
904	Palatka, FL	32177, 32178
903	Palestine, TX	75801, 75802
303	Palisade, CO	81526
201	Palisades Park, NJ	07650
407	Palm Bay, FL	32905–32910
407	Palm Beach, FL	33480
407	Palm Beach Gardens, FL	33410, 33418, 34410
407	Palm City, FL	34990
904	Palm Coast, FL	32135–32142
619	Palm Desert, CA	92210, 92261
813	Palm Harbor, FL	34682–34685
619	Palm Springs, CA	92262–92264
907	Palmer, AK	99645
712	Palmer, IA	50571
217	Palmer, IL	62556
413	Palmer, MA	01069
215	Palmerton, PA	18071
813	Palmetto, FL	34220, 34221
404	Palmetto, GA	30268
812	Palmyra, IN	47164
314	Palmyra, MO	63461
609	Palmyra, NJ	08065
315	Palmyra, NY	14522
717	Palmyra, PA	17078
415	Palo Alto, CA	94300–94309
817	Palo Pinto, TX	76072
217	Paloma, IL	62359
708	Palos Heights, IL	60463
708	Palos Hills, IL	60465
213	Palos Verdes Estates, CA	90274
213	Palos Verdes Peninsula, CA	90274
806	Pampa, TX	79065, 79066
217	Pana, IL	62557
904	Panama City, FL	32401–32413
904	Panama City Beach, FL	32407
419	Pandora, OH	45877
801	Panguitch, UT	84717, 84764
806	Panhandle, TX	75560, 79068
515	Panora, IA	50216
818	Panorama City, CA	91402
919	Pantego, NC	27860
913	Paola, KS	66071
812	Paoli, IN	47454
215	Paoli, PA	19301
402	Papillion, NE	68046, 68157
702	Paradise, NV	89109
717	Paradise, PA	17562, 17963
501	Paragould, AR	72439–72451
213	Paramount, CA	90723
201	Paramus, NJ	07652, 07653
208	Paris, ID	83261, 83287
217	Paris, IL	61944
606	Paris, KY	40361
816	Paris, MO	65275
901	Paris, TN	38242
903	Paris, TX	75460, 75461
502	Park City, KY	42160
801	Park City, UT	84060, 84068
715	Park Falls, WI	54552
708	Park Forest, IL	60466
918	Park Hill, OK	74451
218	Park Rapids, MN	56470
708	Park Ridge, IL	60068
201	Park Ridge, NJ	07656
412	Parker, PA	16049
605	Parker, SD	57053
218	Parkers Prairie, MN	56361
319	Parkersburg, IA	50665
618	Parkersburg, IL	62452
304	Parkersburg, WV	26101–26105
215	Parkesburg, PA	19365
605	Parkston, SD	57366
301	Parkton, MD	21120
301	Parkville, MD	21234, 21236
816	Parkville, MO	64152
916	Parkway, CA	95823
908	Parlin, NJ	08859
216	Parma, OH	44129, 44134
801	Parowan, UT	84719, 84772
201	Parsippany, NJ	07054
316	Parsons, KS	67357
901	Parsons, TN	38363
304	Parsons, WV	26287
316	Partridge, KS	67566
818	Pasadena, CA	91100–91117, 91124–91129 *
301	Pasadena, MD	21122
713	Pasadena, TX	77501–77508
601	Pascagoula, MS	39563, 39567, 39568, 39581
509	Pasco, WA	99301, 99302
805	Paso Robles, CA	93446, 93447
201	Passaic, NJ	07055–07057
516	Patchogue, NY	11728, 11772
201	Paterson, NJ	07501–07544
209	Patterson, CA	95363
504	Patterson, LA	70392
704	Patterson, NC	28661
914	Patterson, NY	12563
714	Patton, CA	92369
518	Paul Smiths, NY	12970
419	Paulding, OH	45879
712	Paullina, IA	51046
405	Pauls Valley, OK	73075
609	Paulsboro, NJ	08066
704	Paw Creek, NC	28130
616	Paw Paw, MI	49079
304	Paw Paw, WV	25431, 25434
203	Pawcatuck, CT	06379
918	Pawhuska, OK	74009, 74056
914	Pawling, NY	12564
402	Pawnee City, NE	68420
401	Pawtucket, RI	02860–02865
717	Paxinos, PA	17860
217	Paxton, IL	60957
508	Paxton, MA	01612
208	Payette, ID	83661
508	Peabody, MA	01960, 01961
401	Peace Dale, RI	02883
717	Peach Glen, PA	17306
404	Peachtree City, GA	30269
908	Peapack, NJ	07977
703	Pearisburg, VA	24134
808	Pearl City, HI	96782
914	Pearl River, NY	10965
713	Pearland, TX	77581, 77584, 77588
512	Pearsall, TX	78061
912	Pearson, GA	31642
408	Pebble Beach, CA	93953
313	Peck, MI	48466
717	Peckville, PA	18452
915	Pecos, TX	79772
609	Pedricktown, NJ	08067
914	Peekskill, NY	10566
309	Pekin, IL	61554, 61555, 61558
205	Pelham, AL	35124
912	Pelham, GA	31779
603	Pelham, NH	03076
914	Pelham, NY	10803
914	Pelham Manor, NY	10803
218	Pelican Rapids, MN	56572
205	Pell City, AL	35125
515	Pella, IA	50219
609	Pemberton, NJ	08068
912	Pembroke, GA	31321
617	Pembroke, MA	02359
919	Pembroke, NC	28372
305	Pembroke Pines, FL	33019–33029, 33084
215	Pen Argyl, PA	18072
603	Penacook, NH	03303
402	Pender, NE	68047
503	Pendleton, OR	97801, 97859
803	Pendleton, SC	29670
814	Penfield, PA	15849
412	Penn, PA	15675, 19506
412	Penn Hills, PA	15235
315	Penn Yan, NY	14527
215	Penndel, PA	19047
609	Pennington, NJ	08534
717	Penns Creek, PA	17862
609	Penns Grove, NJ	08069
609	Pennsauken, NJ	08105–08110
215	Pennsburg, PA	18073
913	Penokee, KS	67659
904	Pensacola, FL	32501–32534, 32573–32598
904	Pensacola Beach, FL	32561
309	Peoria, IL	61600–61656
319	Peosta, IA	52068
708	Peotone, IL	60468
216	Pepper Pike, OH	44122, 44124
201	Pequannock, NJ	07440
218	Perham, MN	56573
215	Perkasie, PA	18944
601	Perkinston, MS	39573
512	Perrin, TX	76075
714	Perris, CA	92370
904	Perry, FL	32347
912	Perry, GA	31069
716	Perry, NY	14530
216	Perry, OH	43055, 44081, 45658
405	Perry, OK	73077
301	Perry Point, MD	21902
419	Perrysburg, OH	43551
419	Perrysville, OH	43988, 44864
806	Perryton, TX	79070
501	Perryville, AR	72126
314	Perryville, MO	63747, 63775, 63783
908	Perth Amboy, NJ	08861–08863
815	Peru, IL	61354
317	Peru, IN	46970, 46971
402	Peru, NE	68421
509	Peshastin, WA	98847
715	Peshtigo, WI	54157
707	Petaluma, CA	94952–94954, 94999
603	Peterborough, NH	03458, 03460
205	Peterman, AL	36471
907	Petersburg, AK	99833
217	Petersburg, IL	62659, 62675
812	Petersburg, IN	47567
814	Petersburg, PA	16669
804	Petersburg, VA	23801–23805
304	Petersburg, WV	26847
616	Petoskey, MI	49770
412	Petrolia, PA	16050
419	Pettisville, OH	43553
414	Pewaukee, WI	53072
205	Phenix City, AL	36867, 36868
601	Philadelphia, MS	39350
215	Philadelphia, PA	19099–19160, 19172, 19181 *
605	Philip, SD	57567
304	Philippi, WV	26416
406	Philipsburg, MT	59858
814	Philipsburg, PA	16866
715	Phillips, WI	54555
913	Phillipsburg, KS	67661
908	Phillipsburg, NJ	08865
518	Philmont, NY	12565
503	Philomath, OR	97370
602	Phoenix, AZ	85000–85082
215	Phoenixville, PA	19453, 19460
601	Picayune, MS	39466
803	Pickens, SC	29671
614	Pickerington, OH	43147
213	Pico Rivera, CA	90660, 90661
415	Piedmont, CA	94611, 94620
605	Piedmont, SD	57769
402	Pierce, NE	68767
219	Pierceton, IN	46562
605	Pierre, SD	57501, 57537
712	Pierson, IA	51048
517	Pigeon, MI	48755
615	Pigeon Forge, TN	37863, 37868
501	Piggott, AR	72454
301	Pikesville, MD	21208
614	Piketon, OH	45661
606	Pikeville, KY	41501–41503
615	Pikeville, TN	37367
319	Pilot Grove, IA	52648
919	Pilot Mountain, NC	27041
602	Pima, AZ	85535, 85543
603	Pinardville, NH	03102
618	Pinckneyville, IL	62274
517	Pinconning, MI	48650
303	Pine, CO	80425, 80470
501	Pine Bluff, AR	71601–71613
201	Pine Brook, NJ	07058
612	Pine City, MN	55063
717	Pine Grove, PA	17047, 17963
305	Pine Hills, FL	32808, 32818
404	Pine Mountain, GA	31822
307	Pinedale, WY	82941
919	Pinehurst, NC	28374
813	Pinellas Park, FL	34664–34666
606	Pineville, KY	40977
318	Pineville, LA	71359–71361
417	Pineville, MO	64856
704	Pineville, NC	28134
304	Pineville, WV	24859, 24874
615	Piney Flats, TN	37686
702	Pioche, NV	89043
507	Pipestone, MN	56164
606	Pippa Passes, KY	41844, 41861
513	Piqua, OH	45356
908	Piscataway, NJ	08854, 08855
609	Pitman, NJ	08071
601	Pittsboro, MS	38951
919	Pittsboro, NC	27228, 27312
415	Pittsburg, CA	94565
316	Pittsburg, KS	66762
903	Pittsburg, TX	75686
412	Pittsburgh, PA	15201–15243, 15258–15266 *
217	Pittsfield, IL	62332, 62363
413	Pittsfield, MA	01201–01203
207	Pittsfield, ME	04967
603	Pittsfield, NH	03263
814	Pittsfield, PA	16340
716	Pittsford, NY	14534
717	Pittston, PA	18640–18644
715	Pittsville, WI	54466
714	Placentia, CA	92670
916	Placerville, CA	95643, 95667
813	Placida, FL	33946, 33947
608	Plain, WI	53577
614	Plain City, OH	43064
203	Plainfield, CT	06374
815	Plainfield, IL	60544
317	Plainfield, IN	46168
908	Plainfield, NJ	07060–07063
802	Plainfield, VT	05667
316	Plains, KS	67869
717	Plains, PA	18705
806	Plains, TX	79355
516	Plainview, NY	11803
806	Plainview, TX	79072, 79073
203	Plainville, CT	06062
508	Plainville, MA	02762
616	Plainwell, MI	49080
603	Plaistow, NH	03865
605	Plankinton, SD	57368
708	Plano, IL	60545

Area	City	Zip
214	Plano, TX	75023–75026, 75074–75094
813	Plant City, FL	33564–33567
305	Plantation, FL	33311–33318, 33322–33327
203	Plantsville, CT	06479
504	Plaquemine, LA	70764, 70765
816	Platte City, MO	64079
608	Platteville, WI	53818
816	Plattsburg, MO	64477
518	Plattsburgh, NY	12901–12903
402	Plattsmouth, NE	68048
919	Pleasant Garden, NC	27313
801	Pleasant Grove, UT	84042, 84062
415	Pleasant Hill, CA	94523
217	Pleasant Plains, IL	62677
914	Pleasant Valley, NY	12569, 13480
415	Pleasanton, CA	94566, 94588
609	Pleasantville, NJ	08232
914	Pleasantville, NY	10570
502	Pleasure Ridge Park, KY	40258
406	Plentywood, MT	59254
715	Plover, WI	54467
412	Plum, PA	15239
208	Plummer, ID	83851
215	Plumsteadville, PA	18949
203	Plymouth, CT	06782
407	Plymouth, FL	32768
309	Plymouth, IL	62367
219	Plymouth, IN	46563
508	Plymouth, MA	02360–02364
313	Plymouth, MI	48170
612	Plymouth, MN	55441, 55442, 55447
919	Plymouth, NC	27962
402	Plymouth, NE	68424
603	Plymouth, NH	03264
419	Plymouth, OH	44004, 44865
717	Plymouth, PA	18651
801	Plymouth, UT	84330
414	Plymouth, WI	53073
215	Plymouth Meeting, PA	19462
501	Pocahontas, AR	72455, 72478
712	Pocahontas, IA	50574
508	Pocasset, MA	02559
208	Pocatello, ID	83201–83206, 83209
717	Pocono Manor, PA	18349
205	Point Clear, AL	36564
417	Point Lookout, MO	65726
412	Point Marion, PA	15474
301	Point of Rocks, MD	21777
908	Point Pleasant, NJ	08742
304	Point Pleasant, WV	25550
908	Point Pleasant Beach, NJ	08742
504	Pointe A La Hache, LA	70082
216	Poland, OH	44514
704	Polkton, NC	28135
919	Pollocksville, NC	28573
815	Polo, IL	61064
406	Polson, MT	59860
712	Pomeroy, IA	50575
614	Pomeroy, OH	45769
215	Pomeroy, PA	19367
509	Pomeroy, WA	99347
203	Pomfret, CT	06258
203	Pomfret Center, CT	06259
714	Pomona, CA	91765–91769
609	Pomona, NJ	08240
914	Pomona, NY	10970
305	Pompano Beach, FL	33060–33069, 33071–33076
201	Pompton Lakes, NJ	07442
201	Pompton Plains, NJ	07444
402	Ponca, NE	68770
405	Ponca City, OK	74601–74604
809	Ponce, PR	00731–00734
405	Pond Creek, OK	73766
904	Ponte Vedra Beach, FL	32004, 32082
815	Pontiac, IL	61764
313	Pontiac, MI	48033, 48056, 48340–48342 *
601	Pontotoc, MS	38863
314	Poplar Bluff, MO	63901
601	Poplarville, MS	39470
804	Poquoson, VA	23662
814	Port Allegany, PA	16743
504	Port Allen, LA	70767
206	Port Angeles, WA	98362
409	Port Arthur, TX	77640–77643
318	Port Barre, LA	70577
309	Port Byron, IL	61275
315	Port Byron, NY	13140
717	Port Carbon, PA	17965
813	Port Charlotte, FL	33948–33954, 33981
914	Port Chester, NY	10573
419	Port Clinton, OH	43452
415	Port Costa, CA	94569
301	Port Deposit, MD	21904
715	Port Edwards, WI	54469
914	Port Ewen, NY	12466
601	Port Gibson, MS	39150
313	Port Huron, MI	48060, 48301
516	Port Jefferson, NY	11777
914	Port Jervis, NY	12771, 12785
512	Port Lavaca, TX	77972, 77979
206	Port Ludlow, WA	98365
201	Port Monmouth, NJ	07758
409	Port Neches, TX	77651
206	Port Orchard, WA	98366
904	Port Saint Joe, FL	32453, 32456
407	Port Saint Lucie, FL	34952, 34983–34988
206	Port Townsend, WA	98368
717	Port Trevorton, PA	17864
516	Port Washington, NY	11050
414	Port Washington, WI	53074
219	Portage, IN	46368
616	Portage, MI	49001, 49081
814	Portage, PA	15946
608	Portage, WI	53901
505	Portales, NM	88123, 88130
209	Porterville, CA	93257, 93258
501	Portland, AR	71663
203	Portland, CT	06480
219	Portland, IN	47371, 47381
207	Portland, ME	04100–04112, 04122
517	Portland, MI	48875
503	Portland, OR	97200–97269
615	Portland, TN	37148
603	Portsmouth, NH	03801–03804
614	Portsmouth, OH	45662
401	Portsmouth, RI	02871
804	Portsmouth, VA	23700–23709
716	Portville, NY	14770
806	Post, TX	79356
319	Postville, IA	52162
918	Poteau, OK	74953
301	Potomac, MD	20854
314	Potosi, MO	63663, 63664
315	Potsdam, NY	13676, 13699
215	Pottstown, PA	19464
501	Pottsville, AR	72858
717	Pottsville, PA	17901, 17974
914	Poughkeepsie, NY	12600–12603
802	Poultney, VT	05741, 05764
703	Pound, VA	24279
414	Pound, WI	54161
619	Poway, CA	92064, 92074
615	Powell, TN	37849
307	Powell, WY	82435
804	Powhatan, VA	23139
802	Pownal, VT	05261
608	Prairie du Chien, WI	53821
708	Prairie View, IL	60069
409	Prairie View, TX	77446
913	Prairie Village, KS	66202, 66206–66208
316	Pratt, KS	67124
205	Prattville, AL	36067
601	Prentiss, MS	39474
501	Prescott, AR	71857
602	Prescott, AZ	86301–86330
715	Prescott, WI	54021
207	Presque Isle, ME	04769
912	Preston, GA	31824
208	Preston, ID	83263
316	Preston, KS	67124, 67569
301	Preston, MD	21655
507	Preston, MN	55965
606	Prestonsburg, KY	41653
801	Price, UT	84501, 84527
205	Prichard, AL	36610
208	Priest River, ID	83822, 83856
712	Primghar, IA	51245
215	Primos, PA	19018
301	Prince Frederick, MD	20678
804	Prince George, VA	23875
301	Princess Anne, MD	21853
208	Princeton, ID	83857
815	Princeton, IL	61356
812	Princeton, IN	47670, 47671
502	Princeton, KY	42445
318	Princeton, LA	71067
816	Princeton, MO	64673
908	Princeton, NJ	08540–08544
414	Princeton, WI	54968
304	Princeton, WV	24739, 24740
609	Princeton Junction, NJ	08550
808	Princeville, HI	96722
309	Princeville, IL	61559
503	Prineville, OR	97754
612	Prinsburg, MN	56281
802	Proctor, VT	05765
512	Progreso, TX	78579
815	Prophetstown, IL	61277
502	Prospect, KY	40059
207	Prospect Harbor, ME	04669
708	Prospect Heights, IL	60070
215	Prospect Park, PA	19076
509	Prosser, WA	99350
319	Protivin, IA	52163
207	Prouts Neck, ME	04074
502	Providence, KY	40011, 42450
401	Providence, RI	02900–02940
508	Provincetown, MA	02657
801	Provo, UT	84601–84606
918	Pryor, OK	74361, 74362
719	Pueblo, CO	81001–81019
315	Pulaski, NY	13142
615	Pulaski, TN	38478
703	Pulaski, VA	24301
414	Pulaski, WI	54162
616	Pullman, MI	49450
509	Pullman, WA	99163–99165
813	Punta Gorda, FL	33927, 33948–33983
814	Punxsutawney, PA	15730, 15763–15776
405	Purcell, OK	73080
703	Purcellville, VA	22078, 22132
914	Purchase, NY	10577
601	Purvis, MS	39475
203	Putnam, CT	06260
802	Putney, VT	05346
206	Puyallup, WA	98371–98374

Area	City	Zip
215	Quakertown, PA	18951
817	Quanah, TX	79252
918	Quapaw, OK	74363
717	Quarryville, PA	17566
809	Quebradillas, PR	00742
602	Queen Creek, AZ	85242
718	Queens Village, NY	11427–11429
301	Queenstown, MD	21658
712	Quimby, IA	51049
206	Quinault, WA	98575
916	Quincy, CA	95952, 95971
904	Quincy, FL	32351, 32352
217	Quincy, IL	62301, 62328
617	Quincy, MA	02169–02269
517	Quincy, MI	49082
717	Quincy, PA	17247
913	Quinter, KS	67752
912	Quitman, GA	31643
601	Quitman, MS	39355
903	Quitman, TX	75783

Area	City	Zip
504	Raceland, LA	70394
414	Racine, WI	53400–53408
703	Radford, VA	24141–24143
215	Radnor, PA	19087
919	Raeford, NC	28361, 28376
908	Rahway, NJ	07065–07067
304	Rainelle, WV	25962
205	Rainsville, AL	35986
515	Rake, IA	50465
601	Raleigh, MS	39153
919	Raleigh, NC	27600–27661, 27695
712	Ralston, IA	51459
402	Ralston, NE	68117, 68127
717	Ralston, PA	17763
205	Ramer, AL	36069
619	Ramona, CA	92065
919	Ramseur, NC	27316
201	Ramsey, NJ	07446
619	Rancho Bernardo, CA	92128
916	Rancho Cordova, CA	95670, 95742
714	Rancho Cucamonga, CA	91701, 91739
213	Rancho Dominguez, CA	90220, 90221
213	Rancho Palos Verdes, CA	90274, 90732
619	Rancho Santa Fe, CA	92067
609	Rancocas, NJ	08073
515	Randall, IA	50231
301	Randallstown, MD	21133
206	Randle, WA	98377
919	Randleman, NC	27317
617	Randolph, MA	02368
201	Randolph, NJ	07869
716	Randolph, NY	14772
801	Randolph, UT	84064
802	Randolph, VT	05060
802	Randolph Center, VT	05061
303	Rangely, CO	81648
817	Ranger, TX	76470
412	Rankin, PA	15104
915	Rankin, TX	79778
815	Ransom, IL	60470
717	Ransom, PA	18653
716	Ransomville, NY	14131
304	Ranson, WV	25438
217	Rantoul, IL	61866–61868
605	Rapid City, SD	57701–57709
908	Raritan, NJ	08822, 08869
505	Raton, NM	87740
518	Ravena, NY	12143
308	Ravenna, NE	68869
216	Ravenna, OH	44266
307	Rawlins, WY	82301–82310
701	Ray, ND	58849
207	Raymond, ME	04071
601	Raymond, MS	39154
512	Raymondville, TX	78580, 78598
816	Raymore, MO	64083
318	Rayne, LA	70578
508	Raynham, MA	02767
816	Raytown, MO	64133, 64138
318	Rayville, LA	71269
409	Raywood, TX	77582
617	Reading, MA	01867
517	Reading, MI	49274
513	Reading, OH	43783, 45215
215	Reading, PA	19600–19612, 19640
215	Reamstown, PA	17567
501	Rector, AR	72461
908	Red Bank, NJ	07701–07704
205	Red Bay, AL	35582
916	Red Bluff, CA	96075, 96080
402	Red Cloud, NE	68970
215	Red Hill, PA	18073, 18076
218	Red Lake Falls, MN	56750
717	Red Lion, PA	17356
406	Red Lodge, MT	59051, 59068
712	Red Oak, IA	51566
919	Red Springs, NC	28377
612	Red Wing, MN	55066
916	Redding, CA	96001–96003, 96099
605	Redfield, SD	57469
313	Redford, MI	48239, 48240
714	Redlands, CA	92373–92375
503	Redmond, OR	97756
206	Redmond, WA	98052, 98053, 98073
213	Redondo Beach, CA	90254, 90277, 90278
315	Redwood, NY	11963, 13679
415	Redwood City, CA	94061–94065
507	Redwood Falls, MN	56283
616	Reed City, MI	49677
209	Reedley, CA	93654
608	Reedsburg, WI	53959
717	Reedsville, PA	17084
517	Reese, MI	48757
512	Refugio, TX	78377
718	Rego Park, NY	11374
302	Rehoboth Beach, DE	19971
912	Reidsville, GA	30453
919	Reidsville, NC	27320–27323
319	Reinbeck, IA	50669
219	Remington, IN	47977
712	Remsen, IA	51050
304	Renick, WV	24966

702	Reno, NV	89500–89570, 89595
219	Rensselaer, IN	47978
518	Rensselaer, NY	12144
206	Renton, WA	98055–98058
612	Renville, MN	56284
515	Renwick, IA	50577
417	Republic, MO	65738
509	Republic, WA	99166
919	Research Triangle Park, NC	27709, 27713
818	Reseda, CA	91335
504	Reserve, LA	70076, 70084
505	Reserve, NM	87830
703	Reston, VA	22070, 22090, 22094
716	Retsof, NY	14539
617	Revere, MA	02151
208	Rexburg, ID	83440, 83441, 83460
912	Reynolds, GA	31076
614	Reynoldsburg, OH	43068
717	Rheems, PA	17570
914	Rhinebeck, NY	12572
715	Rhinelander, WI	54501, 54549
714	Rialto, CA	92376, 92377
715	Rice Lake, WI	54868
912	Riceboro, GA	31323
919	Rich Square, NC	27869
214	Richardson, TX	75080–75085
612	Richfield, MN	55423
704	Richfield, NC	28137
216	Richfield, OH	43504, 44286
801	Richfield, UT	84657, 84701, 84744
414	Richfield, WI	53076
802	Richford, VT	05476
616	Richland, MI	49083
717	Richland, PA	15904, 17087
509	Richland, WA	99352
608	Richland Center, WI	53581
703	Richlands, VA	24641
415	Richmond, CA	94801–94808
815	Richmond, IL	60071
317	Richmond, IN	47374, 47375
913	Richmond, KS	66080
606	Richmond, KY	40475
313	Richmond, MI	48062
816	Richmond, MO	64085
713	Richmond, TX	77469
804	Richmond, VA	23200–23261, 23279, 23293 *
912	Richmond Hill, GA	31324
718	Richmond Hill, NY	11418
304	Richwood, WV	26261
503	Rickreall, OR	97371
503	Riddle, OR	97469
301	Riderwood, MD	21139, 21204
619	Ridgecrest, CA	93555, 93556
203	Ridgefield, CT	06877
201	Ridgefield, NJ	07657
201	Ridgefield Park, NJ	07660
803	Ridgeland, SC	29912, 29936
317	Ridgeville, IN	47380
703	Ridgeway, VA	24148, 24597
201	Ridgewood, NJ	07450–07452
718	Ridgewood, NY	11385
814	Ridgway, PA	15853
215	Ridley, PA	19033
215	Ridley Park, PA	19078
919	Riegelwood, NC	28456
208	Rigby, ID	83442
814	Rimersburg, PA	16248
603	Rindge, NH	03461
404	Ringgold, GA	30736
406	Ringling, MT	59642
717	Ringtown, PA	17967, 19539
201	Ringwood, NJ	07456
414	Rio, WI	53960
614	Rio Grande, OH	45674
512	Rio Grande City, TX	78582
512	Rio Hondo, TX	78583
809	Rio Piedras, PR	00921–00928
505	Rio Rancho, NM	87124
707	Rio Vista, CA	94571
817	Rio Vista, TX	76093
601	Ripley, MS	38663
716	Ripley, NY	14775
901	Ripley, TN	38063
304	Ripley, WV	25271
209	Ripon, CA	95366
414	Ripon, WI	54971
515	Rippey, IA	50235
208	Ririe, ID	83443
812	Rising Sun, IN	47040
301	Rising Sun, MD	21911
419	Rising Sun, OH	43457
501	Rison, AR	71665
509	Ritzville, WA	99169
715	River Falls, WI	54022
708	River Forest, IL	60305
708	River Grove, IL	60171, 60199
404	Riverdale, GA	30274, 30296
708	Riverdale, IL	60627
301	Riverdale, MD	20737, 21146
201	Riverdale, NJ	07457
516	Riverhead, NY	11901
714	Riverside, CA	92500–92519, 92521, 92523
203	Riverside, CT	06878
708	Riverside, IL	60546
816	Riverside, MO	63829, 64150
609	Riverside, NJ	08075
203	Riverton, CT	06065
609	Riverton, NJ	08077
801	Riverton, UT	84065
703	Riverton, VA	22651
307	Riverton, WY	82501–82510
407	Riviera Beach, FL	33404
205	Roanoke, AL	36274
703	Roanoke, VA	24001–24038, 24042
919	Roanoke Rapids, NC	27870
814	Roaring Spring, PA	16673
612	Robbinsdale, MN	55422
704	Robbinsville, NC	28771
609	Robbinsville, NJ	08691
915	Robert Lee, TX	76945
217	Roberts, IL	60962
215	Robesonia, PA	19551
618	Robinson, IL	62454
913	Robinson, KS	66532
915	Roby, TX	79543
508	Rochdale, MA	01542
815	Rochelle, IL	61045, 61068
201	Rochelle Park, NJ	07662
219	Rochester, IN	46975
313	Rochester, MI	48063, 48306, 48307, 48309
507	Rochester, MN	55901–55906, 55938
603	Rochester, NH	03867
716	Rochester, NY	14600–14692, 14694
412	Rochester, PA	15074
414	Rochester, WI	53167
313	Rochester Hills, MI	48063, 48307, 48309
815	Rock Falls, IL	61058, 61071
803	Rock Hill, SC	29730–29733
309	Rock Island, IL	61201–61206, 61299
701	Rock Lake, ND	58365
816	Rock Port, MO	64482, 64496
712	Rock Rapids, IA	51246
307	Rock Springs, WY	82901, 82942
201	Rockaway, NJ	07866
718	Rockaway Beach, NY	11693
203	Rockfall, CT	06481
205	Rockford, AL	35136
815	Rockford, IL	61100–61132
616	Rockford, MI	49341, 49351
615	Rockford, TN	37853
509	Rockford, WA	99030
919	Rockingham, NC	28379
617	Rockland, MA	02370
207	Rockland, ME	04841
201	Rockleigh, NJ	07647
916	Rocklin, CA	95677
812	Rockport, IN	47635
508	Rockport, MA	01966
207	Rockport, ME	04856
512	Rockport, TX	78382
512	Rocksprings, TX	78880
815	Rockton, IL	61072
203	Rockville, CT	06066
317	Rockville, IN	47872
301	Rockville, MD	20849–20859
516	Rockville, NY	10940
516	Rockville Centre, NY	11570–11572
214	Rockwall, TX	75087
515	Rockwell, IA	50469
712	Rockwell City, IA	50579
814	Rockwood, PA	15557
615	Rockwood, TN	37854
405	Rocky, OK	73661
719	Rocky Ford, CO	81067
203	Rocky Hill, CT	06067
609	Rocky Hill, NJ	08553
919	Rocky Mount, NC	27801–27804
703	Rocky Mount, VA	24151
919	Rocky Point, NC	28457
516	Rocky Point, NY	11778
216	Rocky River, OH	44116
609	Roebling, NJ	08554
803	Roebuck, SC	29376
913	Roeland Park, KS	66202, 66205
501	Rogers, AR	72756, 72757
203	Rogers, CT	06263
517	Rogers City, MI	49779
205	Rogersville, AL	35652
615	Rogersville, TN	37857
707	Rohnert Park, CA	94927, 94928
515	Roland, IA	50236
314	Rolla, MO	65401
701	Rolla, ND	58367
601	Rolling Fork, MS	39070, 39159
213	Rolling Hills Estates, CA	90274
708	Rolling Meadows, IL	60008
404	Rome, GA	30149–30164
315	Rome, NY	13440, 13441
815	Romeoville, IL	60441
304	Romney, WV	26757
313	Romulus, MI	48174
516	Ronkonkoma, NY	11779
516	Roosevelt, NY	11575
801	Roosevelt, UT	84066
509	Rosalia, WA	99028, 99170
815	Roscoe, IL	61073
607	Roscoe, NY	12776
412	Roscoe, PA	15477
517	Roscommon, MI	48653
919	Rose Hill, NC	28458
218	Roseau, MN	56751
503	Roseburg, OR	97470
601	Rosedale, MS	38769
201	Roseland, NJ	07068
708	Roselle, IL	60172, 60192–60196
908	Roselle, NJ	07203
908	Roselle Park, NJ	07204
818	Rosemead, CA	91770
708	Rosemont, IL	60018, 60019
215	Rosemont, PA	19010
612	Rosemount, MN	55068
713	Rosenberg, TX	77471
916	Roseville, CA	95661, 95678, 95746
313	Roseville, MI	48066, 48305
612	Roseville, MN	55112, 55113
614	Roseville, OH	43777
605	Rosholt, SD	57260
617	Roslindale, MA	02131
516	Roslyn, NY	11576
215	Roslyn, PA	19001
516	Roslyn Heights, NY	11577
412	Ross, PA	15237
703	Rosslyn, VA	22209
404	Rossville, GA	30741, 30742
404	Roswell, GA	30075–30077
505	Roswell, NM	88201, 88202
616	Rothbury, MI	49452
715	Rothschild, WI	54474
708	Round Lake, IL	60073
507	Round Lake, MN	56167
512	Round Rock, TX	78664, 78681
406	Roundup, MT	59072, 59073
518	Rouses Point, NY	12979
814	Rouseville, PA	16344
818	Rowland Heights, CA	91748
508	Rowley, MA	01969
919	Roxboro, NC	27573
617	Roxbury, MA	02118–02120
801	Roy, UT	84067
206	Roy, WA	98580
217	Royal, IL	61871
313	Royal Oak, MI	48067–48073
215	Royersford, PA	19468
701	Rugby, ND	58315, 58368
505	Ruidoso, NM	88345
601	Ruleville, MS	38771
207	Rumford, ME	04276
401	Rumford, RI	02916
201	Rumson, NJ	07760
609	Runnemede, NJ	08078
714	Running Springs, CA	92341
208	Rupert, ID	83343, 83350
304	Rupert, WV	25984
612	Rush City, MN	55067, 55069
507	Rushford, MN	55971
217	Rushville, IL	62681
317	Rushville, IN	46173
308	Rushville, NE	69360
903	Rusk, TX	75785
813	Ruskin, FL	33570–33573
913	Russell, KS	67665
606	Russell, KY	41169
413	Russell, MA	01071
205	Russellville, AL	35653
501	Russellville, AR	72801
502	Russellville, KY	42276
317	Russiaville, IN	46979
804	Rustburg, VA	24588
318	Ruston, LA	71270–71273
517	Ruth, MI	48470
201	Rutherford, NJ	07070–07075
704	Rutherfordton, NC	28139
712	Ruthven, IA	51358
802	Rutland, VT	05701, 05702
615	Rutledge, TN	37861
301	Ruxton, MD	21204
215	Rydal, PA	19046
914	Rye, NY	10580
406	Ryegate, MT	59074

S

513	Sabina, OH	45169
712	Sac City, IA	50583
207	Saco, ME	04072
916	Sacramento, CA	94203–94299, 95814–95838 *
612	Sacred Heart, MN	56285
201	Saddle Brook, NJ	07662
201	Saddle River, NJ	07458
217	Sadorus, IL	61872
814	Saegertown, PA	16433
602	Safford, AZ	85546, 85548
516	Sag Harbor, NY	11963
412	Sagamore, PA	16250
517	Saginaw, MI	48601–48608
719	Saguache, CO	81149
602	Sahuarita, AZ	85629
718	Saint Albans, NY	11412
802	Saint Albans, VT	05478
304	Saint Albans, WV	25177
314	Saint Ann, MO	63074
208	Saint Anthony, ID	83445
904	Saint Augustine, FL	32084–32086, 32092, 32095
503	Saint Benedict, OR	97373
504	Saint Bernard, LA	70085
716	Saint Bonaventure, NY	14778
606	Saint Catharine, KY	40061
708	Saint Charles, IL	60174, 60175
517	Saint Charles, MI	48655
314	Saint Charles, MO	63301–63303
313	Saint Clair, MI	48079
314	Saint Clair, MO	63077
313	Saint Clair Shores, MI	48080–48082
614	Saint Clairsville, OH	43950
612	Saint Cloud, MN	56301–56304, 56487
812	Saint Croix, IN	47576
215	Saint Davids, PA	19087
913	Saint Francis, KS	67756
504	Saint Francisville, LA	70775
803	Saint George, SC	29477
801	Saint George, UT	84746, 84770
707	Saint Helena, CA	94574
503	Saint Helens, OR	97051–97054
906	Saint Ignace, MI	49781
504	Saint James, LA	70086
507	Saint James, MN	56081
516	Saint James, NY	11780
316	Saint John, KS	67576
509	Saint John, WA	99127, 99171
602	Saint Johns, AZ	85936
517	Saint Johns, MI	48879
802	Saint Johnsbury, VT	05819
318	Saint Joseph, LA	71366
616	Saint Joseph, MI	49085
612	Saint Joseph, MN	56374, 56375
816	Saint Joseph, MO	64500–64508

904	Saint Leo, FL	33574
618	Saint Libory, IL	62282
314	Saint Louis, MO	63100–63188
314	Saint Louis County, MO	63100
612	Saint Louis Park, MN	55416, 55426
208	Saint Maries, ID	83861
318	Saint Martinville, LA	70582
812	Saint Mary-of-the-Woods, IN	47876
419	Saint Marys, OH	45885
814	Saint Marys, PA	15857
301	Saint Marys City, MD	20686
803	Saint Matthews, SC	29135
812	Saint Meinrad, IN	47577
414	Saint Nazianz, WI	54232
513	Saint Paris, OH	43072
612	Saint Paul, MN	55100–55189
308	Saint Paul, NE	68873
612	Saint Paul Park, MN	55071
507	Saint Peter, MN	56082
314	Saint Peters, MO	63376
813	Saint Petersburg, FL	33700–33716, 33730–33743
813	Saint Petersburg Beach, FL	33706, 33736
504	Saint Rose, LA	70087
912	Saint Simons Island, GA	31522
314	Sainte Genevieve, MO	63670
817	Salado, TX	76571
716	Salamanca, NY	14779
501	Salem, AR	71943, 72576
618	Salem, IL	62881
812	Salem, IN	47167, 47353, 47633
508	Salem, MA	01970, 01971
314	Salem, MO	65560
603	Salem, NH	03079
609	Salem, NJ	08079
216	Salem, OH	43449, 45745
503	Salem, OR	97301–97312
605	Salem, SD	57058
703	Salem, VA	22701, 24153, 24156
304	Salem, WV	26426
719	Salida, CO	81201, 81251
913	Salina, KS	67401, 67402
801	Salina, UT	84654
408	Salinas, CA	93901–93915
313	Saline, MI	48176
508	Salisbury, MA	01950, 01952
301	Salisbury, MD	21801, 21875
704	Salisbury, NC	28144–28146
803	Salley, SC	29137
918	Sallisaw, OK	74955
208	Salmon, ID	83467
801	Salt Lake City, UT	84100–84180, 84190
412	Saltsburg, PA	15681
803	Saluda, SC	29138
804	Saluda, VA	23031, 23149
606	Salyersville, KY	41465
707	Samoa, CA	95564
209	San Andreas, CA	95249, 95250
915	San Angelo, TX	76901–76906, 76908, 76909
512	San Antonio, TX	78163–78299
409	San Augustine, TX	75972
512	San Benito, TX	78586
714	San Bernardino, CA	92400–92427
415	San Bruno, CA	94066, 94099
805	San Buenaventura, CA	93001
415	San Carlos, CA	94070
714	San Clemente, CA	92624, 92672
619	San Diego, CA	92073, 92100–92199
512	San Diego, TX	78384
714	San Dimas, CA	91773
818	San Fernando, CA	91340–91346, 91393–91395
415	San Francisco, CA	94100–94188, 96202–96699
818	San Gabriel, CA	91775–91778
809	San German, PR	00753
714	San Jacinto, CA	92383
408	San Jose, CA	95100–95172, 95190–95196 *
809	San Juan, PR	00619–00950
714	San Juan Capistrano, CA	92675, 92688–92693
415	San Leandro, CA	94577–94579
415	San Lorenzo, CA	94580
719	San Luis, CO	81134, 81152
805	San Luis Obispo, CA	93401–93412
619	San Marcos, CA	92069, 92079
512	San Marcos, TX	78666, 78667
818	San Marino, CA	91108, 91118
415	San Mateo, CA	94400–94404
415	San Pablo, CA	94806
213	San Pedro, CA	90731–90734
415	San Rafael, CA	94901–94915
415	San Ramon, CA	94583
915	San Saba, TX	76877
712	Sanborn, IA	51248
507	Sanborn, MN	56083
716	Sanborn, NY	14132
918	Sand Springs, OK	74063
904	Sanderson, FL	32072, 32087
915	Sanderson, TX	79848
912	Sandersville, GA	31082
208	Sandpoint, ID	83809, 83862–83865
804	Sandston, VA	23150
313	Sandusky, MI	48471
419	Sandusky, OH	44870, 44871
815	Sandwich, IL	60548
503	Sandy, OR	97055
801	Sandy, UT	84070, 84090–84094
203	Sandy Hook, CT	06482
606	Sandy Hook, KY	41171
301	Sandy Spring, MD	20860
404	Sandy Springs, GA	30328
407	Sanford, FL	32771–32773
207	Sanford, ME	04073
919	Sanford, NC	27237, 27330, 27331
209	Sanger, CA	93657
817	Sanger, TX	76266
315	Sangerfield, NY	13455
813	Sanibel Island, FL	33957
714	Santa Ana, CA	92701–92712, 92799
805	Santa Barbara, CA	93101–93160
408	Santa Clara, CA	95050–95055
408	Santa Cruz, CA	95060–95066
505	Santa Fe, NM	87501–87506, 87509, 87540
213	Santa Fe Springs, CA	90670, 90671
805	Santa Maria, CA	93454–93456
213	Santa Monica, CA	90400–90406
805	Santa Paula, CA	93060
707	Santa Rosa, CA	95401–95409
505	Santa Rosa, NM	88432, 88435
512	Santa Rosa, TX	78593
619	Santee, CA	92071, 92072
803	Santee, SC	29142
809	Santurce, PR	00907–00940
704	Sapphire, NC	28774
918	Sapulpa, OK	74066, 74067
205	Saraland, AL	36571
518	Saranac Lake, NY	12982, 12983
813	Sarasota, FL	34230–34243, 34278
408	Saratoga, CA	95070, 95071
518	Saratoga Springs, NY	12866
513	Sardinia, OH	45171
308	Sargent, NE	68874
512	Sarita, TX	78385
412	Sarver, PA	16055
316	Satanta, KS	67870
805	Saticoy, CA	93004
914	Saugerties, NY	12477
618	Sauget, IL	62201
805	Saugus, CA	91310, 91350, 91380–91386
617	Saugus, MA	01906
608	Sauk City, WI	53583
612	Sauk Rapids, MN	56379
414	Saukville, WI	53080
906	Sault Sainte Marie, MI	49783, 49788
415	Sausalito, CA	94965, 94966
301	Savage, MD	20763
612	Savage, MN	55337, 55378
912	Savannah, GA	31400–31420, 31498, 31499
816	Savannah, MO	64485
901	Savannah, TN	38372
217	Savoy, IL	61874
412	Saxonburg, PA	16056
814	Saxton, PA	16678
715	Sayner, WI	54560
405	Sayre, OK	73662
717	Sayre, PA	18840
908	Sayreville, NJ	08871, 08872
516	Sayville, NY	11782
913	Scandia, KS	66966
207	Scarborough, ME	04074
914	Scarsdale, NY	10583
717	Schaefferstown, PA	17088
708	Schaumburg, IL	60159, 60173, 60193–60196
518	Schenectady, NY	12300–12325, 12345
219	Schererville, IN	46375
708	Schiller Park, IL	60176
215	Schnecksville, PA	18078
715	Schofield, WI	54476
518	Schoharie, NY	12157
616	Schoolcraft, MI	49087
402	Schuyler, NE	68661
717	Schuylkill, PA	19146
717	Schuylkill Haven, PA	17972
614	Scio, OH	43988
406	Scobey, MT	59224, 59263
908	Scobeyville, NJ	07724
601	Scooba, MS	39358
908	Scotch Plains, NJ	07076, 07090
518	Scotia, NY	12302
919	Scotland Neck, NC	27874
717	Scotrun, PA	18355
601	Scott, MS	38772
316	Scott City, KS	67871
404	Scottdale, GA	30079
412	Scottdale, PA	15683
408	Scotts Valley, CA	95060, 95066
308	Scottsbluff, NE	69353, 69361, 69363
205	Scottsboro, AL	35768
812	Scottsburg, IN	47170, 47177
602	Scottsdale, AZ	85250–85271
502	Scottsville, KY	42164
716	Scottsville, NY	14546
616	Scottville, MI	49454
701	Scranton, ND	58653
717	Scranton, PA	18500–18519
803	Scranton, SC	29591
201	Sea Girt, NJ	08750
912	Sea Island, GA	31561
301	Seabrook, MD	20706
603	Seabrook, NH	03874
609	Seabrook, NJ	08302
713	Seabrook, TX	77586
302	Seaford, DE	19973
516	Seaford, NY	11783
214	Seagoville, TX	75159
213	Seal Beach, CA	90740
713	Sealy, TX	77474
501	Searcy, AR	72143
207	Searsmont, ME	04915, 04973
408	Seaside, CA	93955
206	Seattle, WA	98028–98199, 98704–98799
207	Sebasco Estates, ME	04565
407	Sebastian, FL	32958, 32978
707	Sebastopol, CA	95472, 95473
517	Sebewaing, MI	48759
813	Sebring, FL	33870–33872
216	Sebring, OH	44672
201	Secaucus, NJ	07094, 07096
303	Sedalia, CO	80135
816	Sedalia, MO	65301
316	Sedan, KS	67361
602	Sedona, AZ	86336
206	Sedro Woolley, WA	98284
508	Seekonk, MA	02771
406	Seeley Lake, MT	59868
813	Seffner, FL	33584
512	Seguin, TX	78155, 78156
509	Selah, WA	98942
605	Selby, SD	57472
302	Selbyville, DE	19944, 19975
516	Selden, NY	11784
717	Selinsgrove, PA	17870
518	Selkirk, NY	12158
812	Sellersburg, IN	47172
215	Sellersville, PA	18960
205	Selma, AL	36701, 36702
209	Selma, CA	93662
919	Selma, NC	27576
901	Selmer, TN	38375
813	Seminole, FL	34642, 34643
405	Seminole, OK	74818, 74868
915	Seminole, TX	79360
601	Senatobia, MS	38668
913	Seneca, KS	66538
315	Seneca Falls, NY	13148
818	Sepulveda, CA	91343, 91393
206	Sequim, WA	98334, 98382
717	Seven Valleys, PA	17360
919	Severn, NC	27877
301	Severna Park, MD	21146
615	Sevierville, TN	37862–37868
615	Sewanee, TN	37375
402	Seward, NE	68434
609	Sewell, NJ	08080
412	Sewickley, PA	15143
203	Seymour, CT	06483
812	Seymour, IN	47274
817	Seymour, TX	76380
717	Shady Grove, PA	17256
802	Shaftsbury, VT	05262
216	Shaker Heights, OH	44118, 44122
612	Shakopee, MN	55379
412	Shaler, PA	15116
904	Shalimar, FL	32579
919	Shallotte, NC	28459, 28467–28470
717	Shamokin, PA	17866, 17872
617	Sharon, MA	02067
412	Sharon, PA	16146–16148
901	Sharon, TN	38255
215	Sharon Hill, PA	19079
913	Sharon Springs, KS	67758
412	Sharpsville, PA	16150
601	Shaw, MS	38773
715	Shawano, WI	54166
913	Shawnee, KS	66203, 66226
405	Shawnee, OK	74801, 74838
913	Shawnee Mission, KS	66200–66227, 66262
618	Shawneetown, IL	62984
414	Sheboygan, WI	53081–53083
414	Sheboygan Falls, WI	53085
205	Sheffield, AL	35660–35662
515	Sheffield, IA	50475
815	Sheffield, IL	61361
413	Sheffield, MA	01257
814	Sheffield, PA	16347
802	Shelburne, VT	05482
219	Shelby, IN	46377
601	Shelby, MS	38774
406	Shelby, MT	59474
704	Shelby, NC	28150, 28151
402	Shelby, NE	68662
419	Shelby, OH	44875
217	Shelbyville, IL	62565
317	Shelbyville, IN	46176
502	Shelbyville, KY	40065, 40066
314	Shelbyville, MO	63469
615	Shelbyville, TN	37160
712	Sheldon, IA	51201, 51244
802	Sheldon Springs, VT	05485
715	Shell Lake, WI	54871
208	Shelley, ID	83274
912	Shellman, GA	31786
516	Shelter Island Heights, NY	11965
203	Shelton, CT	06484
206	Shelton, WA	98584
712	Shenandoah, IA	51601, 51603, 51693
717	Shenandoah, PA	17976
703	Shenandoah, VA	22849
304	Shepherdstown, WV	25443
502	Shepherdsville, KY	40165
717	Sheppton, PA	18248
607	Sherburne, NY	13460
501	Sheridan, AR	72150
317	Sheridan, IN	46069
517	Sheridan, MI	48884
307	Sheridan, WY	82801
903	Sherman, TX	75090, 75091
818	Sherman Oaks, CA	91403, 91423
207	Sherman Station, ME	04777
503	Sherwood, OR	97140
215	Shillington, PA	19607
512	Shiner, TX	77984
304	Shinnston, WV	26431
618	Shipman, IL	62685
717	Shippensburg, PA	17257
814	Shippenville, PA	16254
219	Shipshewana, IN	46565
717	Shiremanstown, PA	17011
317	Shirley, IN	47384
508	Shirley, MA	01464
516	Shirley, NY	11967
812	Shoals, IN	47581
802	Shoreham, VT	05770
612	Shorewood, MN	55331, 55364
414	Shorewood, WI	53211
201	Short Hills, NJ	07078
208	Shoshone, ID	83324, 83352
301	Showell, MD	21862
318	Shreveport, LA	71100–71149, 71161–71172
508	Shrewsbury, MA	01545
908	Shrewsbury, NJ	07701, 07702

Shullsburg / Stillwater

Area	City	ZIP
608	Shullsburg, WI	53586
712	Sibley, IA	51249
712	Sidney, IA	51652
517	Sidney, MI	48885
406	Sidney, MT	59270
308	Sidney, NE	69160, 69162
607	Sidney, NY	13838
513	Sidney, OH	45365
915	Sierra Blanca, TX	79851
818	Sierra Madre, CA	91024, 91025
602	Sierra Vista, AZ	85613, 85635, 85636
213	Signal Hill, CA	90804, 90806, 90807
515	Sigourney, IA	52591
314	Sikeston, MO	63801
919	Siler City, NC	27344
501	Siloam Springs, AR	72761
409	Silsbee, TX	77656
218	Silver Bay, MN	55607, 55614
406	Silver Bow, MT	59750
505	Silver City, NM	88036, 88062
301	Silver Hill, MD	20746
219	Silver Lake, IN	46982
503	Silver Lake, OR	97638, 97641
301	Silver Spring, MD	20900–20912
904	Silver Springs, FL	32688
716	Silver Springs, NY	14550
206	Silverdale, WA	98315, 98383
303	Silverthcrne, CO	80498
303	Silverton, CO	81433
503	Silverton, OR	97381
806	Silverton, TX	79257
309	Silvis, IL	61282
805	Simi Valley, CA	93062–93065
717	Simpson, PA	18407
803	Simpsonville, SC	29681
203	Simsbury, CT	06070–06092
307	Sinclair, WY	82334
215	Sinking Spring, PA	19608
512	Sinton, TX	78387
712	Sioux Center, IA	51250
712	Sioux City, IA	51100–51111
605	Sioux Falls, SD	57100–57118, 57192, 57193 *
605	Sisseton, SD	57262
304	Sistersville, WV	26175
907	Sitka, AK	99835, 99836
907	Skagway, AK	99840
315	Skaneateles Falls, NY	13153
708	Skokie, IL	60076, 60077
207	Skowhegan, ME	04976
717	Skytop, PA	18357
401	Slatersville, RI	02876
215	Slatington, PA	18080
507	Slayton, MN	56172
507	Sleepy Eye, MN	56085
504	Slidell, LA	70458–70469
414	Slinger, WI	53086
412	Slippery Rock, PA	16057
712	Sloan, IA	51055
814	Smethport, PA	16749
913	Smith Center, KS	66967
919	Smithfield, NC	27577
401	Smithfield, RI	02828, 02917
801	Smithfield, UT	84335
804	Smithfield, VA	23430
502	Smithland, KY	42081
309	Smithshire, IL	61478
516	Smithtown, NY	11787, 11788
609	Smithville, NJ	08201
216	Smithville, OH	43351, 44677
615	Smithville, TN	37166
717	Smoketown, PA	17201, 17576
302	Smyrna, DE	19977
404	Smyrna, GA	30080–30082
615	Smyrna, TN	37167, 38318
615	Sneedville, TN	37765, 37869
206	Snohomish, WA	98290
313	Snover, MI	48472
301	Snow Hill, MD	21863
919	Snow Hill, NC	28580
814	Snow Shoe, PA	16874
801	Snowbird, UT	84092
602	Snowflake, AZ	85937
303	Snowmass Village, CO	81615
304	Snowshoe, WV	26209
402	Snyder, NE	68664
915	Snyder, TX	79549
404	Social Circle, GA	30279
505	Socorro, NM	87801
208	Soda Springs, ID	83230, 83276, 83285
315	Sodus, NY	14551
619	Solana Beach, CA	92075
907	Soldotna, AK	99669
207	Solon, ME	04979
216	Solon, OH	44139
805	Solvang, CA	93463
609	Somerdale, NJ	08083
914	Somers, NY	10589
609	Somers Point, NJ	08244
606	Somerset, KY	42501, 42564
508	Somerset, MA	02725, 02726
908	Somerset, NJ	08873–08875
814	Somerset, PA	15501, 15502
603	Somersworth, NH	03878
602	Somerton, AZ	85350
617	Somerville, MA	02143–02145
908	Somerville, NJ	08807, 08876, 08877
901	Somerville, TN	38068
707	Sonoma, CA	95476
209	Sonora, CA	95370
915	Sonora, TX	76950
912	Soperton, GA	30457
215	Souderton, PA	18924, 18964
409	Sour Lake, TX	77659
617	South Acton, MA	01720
908	South Amboy, NJ	08878, 08879
508	South Attleboro, MA	02703
404	South Augusta, GA	30901
407	South Bay, FL	33493
815	South Beloit, IL	61080
219	South Bend, IN	46600–46680, 46699
206	South Bend, WA	98586
207	South Berwick, ME	03908
518	South Bethlehem, NY	12161
617	South Boston, MA	02127
804	South Boston, VA	24592
908	South Bound Brook, NJ	08880
802	South Burlington, VT	05401–05407
518	South Cairo, NY	12482
207	South Casco, ME	04077
304	South Charleston, WV	25303
904	South Daytona, FL	32121
413	South Deerfield, MA	01373
508	South Dennis, MA	02660
508	South Easton, MA	02375
818	South El Monte, CA	91733
708	South Elgin, IL	60177
216	South Euclid, OH	44118, 44121
914	South Fallsburg, NY	12779
207	South Freeport, ME	04013, 04078
207	South Gardiner, ME	04359
213	South Gate, CA	90280
203	South Glastonbury, CT	06073
518	South Glens Falls, NY	12803
508	South Grafton, MA	01560
201	South Hackensack, NJ	07606
413	South Hadley, MA	01075
508	South Hamilton, MA	01982
616	South Haven, MI	49090
516	South Hempstead, NY	11550
804	South Hill, VA	23970
708	South Holland, IL	60473
713	South Houston, TX	77587
316	South Hutchinson, KS	67505
201	South Kearny, NJ	07032
714	South Laguna, CA	92677
916	South Lake Tahoe, CA	95702, 95761
508	South Lancaster, MA	01561
413	South Lee, MA	01260
802	South Londonderry, VT	05155
313	South Lyon, MI	48178
305	South Miami, FL	33143, 33243
414	South Milwaukee, WI	53172
717	South Montrose, PA	18843
508	South Natick, MA	01760
203	South Norwalk, CT	06854
201	South Orange, NJ	07079
315	South Otselic, NY	13155
718	South Ozone Park, NY	11420, 11436
512	South Padre Island, TX	78578, 78597
207	South Paris, ME	04281
818	South Pasadena, CA	91030, 91031
615	South Pittsburg, TN	37380
908	South Plainfield, NJ	07080
614	South Point, OH	45680
207	South Portland, ME	04106
908	South River, NJ	08882
313	South Rockwood, MI	48179
802	South Royalton, VT	05068
612	South Saint Paul, MN	55075–55077
415	South San Francisco, CA	94080–94083
402	South Sioux City, NE	68776
508	South Walpole, MA	02071
617	South Weymouth, MA	02190
219	South Whitley, IN	46787
213	South Whittier, CA	90605
717	South Williamsport, PA	17701
203	South Windham, CT	06266
207	South Windham, ME	04082
203	South Windsor, CT	06074
508	South Yarmouth, MA	02664
614	South Zanesville, OH	43701
413	Southampton, MA	01073
516	Southampton, NY	11968, 11969
215	Southampton, PA	17244, 18966
405	Southard, OK	73770
508	Southboro, MA	01772
508	Southborough, MA	01745, 01772
508	Southbridge, MA	01550
203	Southbury, CT	06488
919	Southern Pines, NC	28387
313	Southfield, MI	48034, 48075–48086
313	Southgate, MI	48195
303	Southglenn, CO	80121–80126, 80161
203	Southington, CT	06489
516	Southold, NY	11971
203	Southport, CT	06490
207	Southport, ME	04576
801	Spanish Fork, UT	84660
914	Sparkill, NY	10976
301	Sparks, MD	21152
702	Sparks, NV	89431–89436
404	Sparta, GA	31087
618	Sparta, IL	62286
616	Sparta, MI	49345
919	Sparta, NC	28675
201	Sparta, NJ	07871
615	Sparta, TN	38583
608	Sparta, WI	54656
803	Spartanburg, SC	29301–29318
605	Spearfish, SD	57783, 57799
806	Spearman, TX	79081
712	Spencer, IA	51301, 51343
812	Spencer, IN	47115, 47460
508	Spencer, MA	01562
216	Spencer, OH	44275
615	Spencer, TN	38585
304	Spencer, WV	25276
716	Spencerport, NY	14559
419	Spencerville, OH	45887
704	Spindale, NC	28160
712	Spirit Lake, IA	51360
509	Spokane, WA	99201–99212, 99251–99260 *
908	Spotswood, NJ	08884
703	Spotsylvania, VA	22553
609	Spray Beach, NJ	08008
713	Spring, TX	77373, 77388, 77389, 77391
517	Spring Arbor, MI	49283
215	Spring City, PA	19475
914	Spring Glen, NY	12483
815	Spring Grove, IL	60081
507	Spring Grove, MN	55974
717	Spring Grove, PA	17346, 17362
215	Spring House, PA	19477
616	Spring Lake, MI	49456
908	Spring Lake, NJ	07762
612	Spring Lake Park, MN	55432
612	Spring Park, MN	55384
619	Spring Valley, CA	92077, 92078
815	Spring Valley, IL	61362
914	Spring Valley, NY	10977
501	Springdale, AR	72764, 72765
513	Springdale, OH	45246
412	Springdale, PA	15144
719	Springfield, CO	81073
912	Springfield, GA	31329
217	Springfield, IL	62700–62794
606	Springfield, KY	40069
413	Springfield, MA	01101–01152, 01199
507	Springfield, MN	56087, 56101
417	Springfield, MO	65800–65810, 65890–65899
908	Springfield, NJ	07081
513	Springfield, OH	45501–45506
503	Springfield, OR	97477, 97478, 97482
215	Springfield, PA	16914, 19118
605	Springfield, SD	57062
615	Springfield, TN	37172
703	Springfield, VA	22015, 22150–22161, 22835
802	Springfield, VT	05156
718	Springfield Gardens, NY	11413
517	Springport, MI	49284
207	Springvale, ME	04083
402	Springview, NE	68778
205	Springville, AL	35146
716	Springville, NY	11946, 14141
801	Springville, UT	84663, 84664
704	Spruce Pine, NC	28777
612	Stacy, MN	55079
515	Stacyville, IA	50476
316	Stafford, KS	67578
713	Stafford, TX	77477, 77497
703	Stafford, VA	22554
203	Stafford Springs, CT	06076
203	Stamford, CT	06900–06912, 06921–06927
501	Stamps, AR	71860
804	Stanardsville, VA	22973
207	Standish, ME	04084
517	Standish, MI	48658
415	Stanford, CA	94305
309	Stanford, IL	61774, 62824
606	Stanford, KY	40484
406	Stanford, MT	59479
201	Stanhope, NJ	07874
913	Stanley, KS	66221, 66224
704	Stanley, NC	28164
701	Stanley, ND	58784
703	Stanleytown, VA	24168
714	Stanton, CA	90680
302	Stanton, DE	19804
606	Stanton, KY	40380
517	Stanton, MI	48888
701	Stanton, ND	58571
402	Stanton, NE	68779
915	Stanton, TX	79782
206	Stanwood, WA	98292
308	Stapleton, NE	69163
718	Stapleton, NY	10304
919	Star, NC	27356
501	Star City, AR	71667
612	Starbuck, MN	56381
904	Starke, FL	32091
601	Starkville, MS	39759
814	State College, PA	16801–16805
501	State University, AR	72467
702	Stateline, NV	89019
718	Staten Island, NY	10300–10314
912	Statenville, GA	31648
912	Statesboro, GA	30458, 30460
704	Statesville, NC	28677
703	Staunton, VA	24401
503	Stayton, OR	97383, 97384
303	Steamboat Springs, CO	80477, 80487, 80488
701	Steele, ND	58482
717	Steelton, PA	17113
314	Steelville, MO	65565, 65566
206	Steilacoom, WA	98388
218	Stephen, MN	56757
501	Stephens, AR	71764
703	Stephens City, VA	22655
817	Stephenville, TX	76401
303	Sterling, CO	80751
815	Sterling, IL	61017, 61081
316	Sterling, KS	67579
703	Sterling, VA	22170
915	Sterling City, TX	76951
313	Sterling Heights, MI	48077, 48310, 48312–48314
614	Steubenville, OH	43952
215	Stevens, PA	17578
715	Stevens Point, WI	54481
203	Stevenson, CT	06491
301	Stevenson, MD	21153
509	Stevenson, WA	98648
616	Stevensville, MI	49127
507	Stewartville, MN	55976
708	Stickney, IL	60402
918	Stigler, OK	74462
207	Stillwater, ME	04489
612	Stillwater, MN	55082, 55083
614	Stillwater, OH	44679

Area	City	ZIP
405	Stillwater, OK	74074–74076, 74078
918	Stilwell, OK	74960
806	Stinnett, TX	79083
908	Stirling, NJ	07980
413	Stockbridge, MA	01262
517	Stockbridge, MI	49285
215	Stockertown, PA	18083
209	Stockton, CA	95201–95219, 95269, 95290
319	Stockton, IA	52769
913	Stockton, KS	67669
417	Stockton, MO	65785
308	Stockville, NE	69042
216	Stone Creek, OH	43840
715	Stone Lake, WI	54876
404	Stone Mountain, GA	30083, 30086–30088
914	Stone Ridge, NY	12484
617	Stoneham, MA	02180
601	Stonewall, MS	39363
203	Stonington, CT	06378
516	Stony Brook, NY	11790, 11794
804	Stony Creek, VA	23882
914	Stony Point, NY	10980
507	Storden, MN	56174
712	Storm Lake, IA	50588
914	Stormville, NY	12582
203	Storrs, CT	06268
515	Story City, IA	50248
518	Stottville, NY	12172
617	Stoughton, MA	02072
608	Stoughton, WI	53589
216	Stow, OH	44224
215	Stowe, PA	19464
802	Stowe, VT	05672
215	Strafford, PA	19087
217	Strasburg, IL	62465
717	Strasburg, PA	17579
703	Strasburg, VA	22641, 22657
209	Stratford, CA	93266
203	Stratford, CT	06497
515	Stratford, IA	50249
806	Stratford, TX	79084
715	Stratford, WI	54484
603	Stratham, NH	03885
719	Stratton, CO	80836
802	Stratton Mountain, VT	05155
215	Strausstown, PA	19559
319	Strawberry Point, IA	52076
815	Streator, IL	61311, 61364
402	Stromsburg, NE	68666
207	Strong, ME	04983
216	Strongsville, OH	44136
717	Stroudsburg, PA	18360
407	Stuart, FL	34994–34997
703	Stuart, VA	24171
818	Studio City, CA	91604, 91614
913	Studley, KS	67759
508	Sturbridge, MA	01566
414	Sturgeon Bay, WI	54235
616	Sturgis, MI	49091
605	Sturgis, SD	57785
414	Sturtevant, WI	53177
501	Stuttgart, AR	72160
316	Sublette, KS	67877
201	Succasunna, NJ	07876
806	Sudan, TX	79371
508	Sudbury, MA	01776
914	Suffern, NY	10901
203	Suffield, CT	06078, 06093
804	Suffolk, VA	23432–23438
208	Sugar City, ID	83448
708	Sugar Grove, IL	60554, 61231
713	Sugar Land, TX	77478–77487
707	Suisun City, CA	94585
301	Suitland, MD	20746
205	Sulligent, AL	35586
217	Sullivan, IL	61951
812	Sullivan, IN	47864, 47882
414	Sullivan, WI	53178
515	Sully, IA	50251
318	Sulphur, LA	70663, 70664
405	Sulphur, OK	73086
903	Sulphur Springs, TX	75482
205	Summerdale, AL	36580
717	Summerdale, PA	17093
806	Summerfield, TX	79085
814	Summerhill, PA	15958
304	Summersville, WV	26651
404	Summerville, GA	30747
814	Summerville, PA	15864
803	Summerville, SC	29483–29485
601	Summit, MS	39666
908	Summit, NJ	07901–07999
216	Summitville, OH	43962
206	Sumner, WA	98390
803	Sumter, SC	29150–29154
904	Sumterville, FL	33585
602	Sun City, AZ	85351, 85372–85375
608	Sun Prairie, WI	53590, 53596
818	Sun Valley, CA	91352, 91353
208	Sun Valley, ID	83353, 83354
603	Sunapee, NH	03782
717	Sunbury, PA	17801, 17877
603	Suncook, NH	03275
307	Sundance, WY	82710, 82729
413	Sunderland, MA	01375
517	Sunfield, MI	48890
818	Sunland, CA	91040, 91041
505	Sunland Park, NM	88063
714	Sunnymead, CA	92388
408	Sunnyvale, CA	94086–94089
305	Sunrise, FL	33304, 33322, 33323, 33351
702	Sunrise Manor, NV	89110
712	Superior, IA	51363
406	Superior, MT	59872
715	Superior, WI	54836, 54880
615	Surgoinsville, TN	37873
414	Suring, WI	54174
518	Surprise, NY	12176
804	Surry, VA	23883
916	Susanville, CA	96130
804	Sussex, VA	23884
412	Sutersville, PA	15083
712	Sutherland, IA	51058
503	Sutherlin, OR	97479
916	Sutter, CA	95982
508	Sutton, MA	01590
402	Sutton, NE	68975, 68979
304	Sutton, WV	26601
404	Suwanee, GA	30174
912	Swainsboro, GA	30401, 30466
617	Swampscott, MA	01907
914	Swan Lake, NY	12783
704	Swannanoa, NC	28778
919	Swanquarter, NC	27885
508	Swansea, MA	02777
419	Swanton, OH	43558
802	Swanton, VT	05488
215	Swarthmore, PA	19081
318	Swartz, LA	71281
609	Swedesboro, NJ	08085
804	Sweet Briar, VA	24595
501	Sweet Home, AR	72164
503	Sweet Home, OR	97386
615	Sweetwater, TN	37874
915	Sweetwater, TX	79556
412	Swissvale, PA	15218
812	Switz City, IN	47465
717	Swoyerville, PA	18704
205	Sycamore, AL	35149
815	Sycamore, IL	60178
301	Sykesville, MD	21784
814	Sykesville, PA	15865
205	Sylacauga, AL	35150
818	Sylmar, CA	91342, 91392
704	Sylva, NC	28779
912	Sylvania, GA	30467
419	Sylvania, OH	43560
912	Sylvester, GA	31791
516	Syosset, NY	11791
219	Syracuse, IN	46567
316	Syracuse, KS	67878
315	Syracuse, NY	13200–13261

T

Area	City	ZIP
206	Tacoma, WA	98303, 98397–98499
805	Taft, CA	93268
203	Taftville, CT	06380
518	Tahawus, NY	12879
918	Tahlequah, OK	74464, 74465
916	Tahoe City, CA	95730
806	Tahoka, TX	79373
301	Takoma Park, MD	20912
404	Talbotton, GA	31827
205	Talladega, AL	35160
904	Tallahassee, FL	32301–32317, 32399
404	Tallapoosa, GA	30176
205	Tallassee, AL	36023, 36078
813	Tallevast, FL	34270
216	Tallmadge, OH	44278
318	Tallulah, LA	71282–71284
717	Talmage, PA	17580
405	Taloga, OK	73667
515	Tama, IA	52339
717	Tamaqua, PA	18252
305	Tamarac, FL	33309, 33321, 33351
717	Tamiment, PA	18371
813	Tampa, FL	33600–33651, 33672–33697
815	Tampico, IL	61283
301	Taneytown, MD	21787
503	Tangent, OR	97389
205	Tanner, AL	35671
717	Tannersville, PA	18372
505	Taos, NM	87525, 87571
804	Tappahannock, VA	22560
914	Tappan, NY	10983
919	Tarboro, NC	27886
412	Tarentum, PA	15084
816	Tarkio, MO	64491
813	Tarpon Springs, FL	34688–34691
412	Tarrs, PA	15688
914	Tarrytown, NY	10591
818	Tarzana, CA	91356, 91357
508	Taunton, MA	02779, 02780
904	Tavares, FL	32778
305	Tavernier, FL	33070
517	Tawas City, MI	48763, 48764
318	Taylor, LA	71080
313	Taylor, MI	48180
308	Taylor, NE	68879
717	Taylor, PA	18517
512	Taylor, TX	76574
309	Taylor Ridge, IL	61284
803	Taylors, SC	29687
502	Taylorsville, KY	40071
601	Taylorsville, MS	39168
704	Taylorsville, NC	28681
217	Taylorville, IL	62568
615	Tazewell, TN	37879
703	Tazewell, VA	24608, 24651
201	Teaneck, NJ	07666
517	Tecumseh, MI	49286
402	Tecumseh, NE	68450
402	Tekamah, NE	68061
215	Telford, PA	18969
812	Tell City, IN	47586
303	Telluride, CO	81435
714	Temecula, CA	92390
602	Tempe, AZ	85280–85285, 85287
405	Temple, OK	73568
215	Temple, PA	19560
817	Temple, TX	76501–76505, 76508
818	Temple City, CA	91780
813	Temple Terrace, FL	33617, 33637, 33687
508	Templeton, MA	01468
201	Tenafly, NJ	07670
409	Tenaha, TX	75974
201	Tennent, NJ	07763
213	Terminal Island, CA	90731
304	Terra Alta, WV	26764
209	Terra Bella, CA	93270
812	Terre Haute, IN	47801–47809
215	Terre Hill, PA	17581
214	Terrell, TX	75160
406	Terry, MT	59349
203	Terryville, CT	06786
201	Teterboro, NJ	07608
307	Teton Village, WY	83025
217	Teutopolis, IL	62467, 62476
508	Tewksbury, MA	01876
501	Texarkana, AR	75502
903	Texarkana, TX	75501, 75503
409	Texas City, TX	77590–77592
405	Texhoma, OK	73949
602	Thatcher, AZ	85552
217	Thawville, IL	60968
503	The Dalles, OR	97058
713	The Woodlands, TX	77380, 77387
308	Thedford, NE	69166
205	Theodore, AL	36582, 36590
619	Thermal, CA	92274
307	Thermopolis, WY	82443
504	Thibodaux, LA	70301, 70302
218	Thief River Falls, MN	56701
414	Thiensville, WI	53092
203	Thomaston, CT	06778, 06787
404	Thomaston, GA	30286
205	Thomasville, AL	36784
912	Thomasville, GA	31792, 31799
919	Thomasville, NC	27360, 27361
717	Thomasville, PA	17364
515	Thompson, IA	50478
701	Thompson, ND	58278
406	Thompson Falls, MT	59873
404	Thomson, GA	30824
215	Thorndale, PA	19372
413	Thorndike, MA	01079
303	Thornton, CO	80221, 80229, 80241
515	Thornton, IA	50479
708	Thornton, IL	60476
215	Thornton, PA	19373
614	Thornville, OH	43076
609	Thorofare, NJ	08086
805	Thousand Oaks, CA	91319, 91320, 91358–91362
715	Three Lakes, WI	54562
616	Three Rivers, MI	49093
512	Three Rivers, TX	78060, 78071
817	Throckmorton, TX	76083
301	Thurmont, MD	21788
415	Tiburon, CA	94920
518	Ticonderoga, NY	12858, 12883
505	Tierra Amarilla, NM	87575
419	Tiffin, OH	44883
912	Tifton, GA	31793, 31794
503	Tigard, OR	97223, 97224, 97281
803	Tigerville, SC	29688
512	Tilden, TX	78072
503	Tillamook, OR	97107, 97141, 97143
603	Tilton, NH	03276
605	Timber Lake, SD	57656
703	Timberville, VA	22853
803	Timmonsville, SC	29161
301	Timonium, MD	21093
708	Tinley Park, IL	60477, 60478
908	Tinton Falls, NJ	07724
814	Tionesta, PA	16353
513	Tipp City, OH	45371
319	Tipton, IA	52772
317	Tipton, IN	46072
913	Tipton, KS	67485
816	Tipton, MO	65081
814	Tipton, PA	16684
901	Tiptonville, TN	38079
601	Tishomingo, MS	38873
405	Tishomingo, OK	73460
407	Titusville, FL	32780–32783, 32796
814	Titusville, PA	16354
404	Toccoa, GA	30577, 30598
404	Toccoa Falls, GA	30598
207	Togus, ME	04330
515	Toledo, IA	52342
217	Toledo, IL	62468
419	Toledo, OH	43601–43624, 43652–43666 *
203	Tolland, CT	06084
815	Toluca, IL	61369
608	Tomah, WI	54660
715	Tomahawk, WI	54487
713	Tomball, TX	77337, 77375
502	Tompkinsville, KY	42167
908	Toms River, NJ	08753–08757
716	Tonawanda, NY	14150, 14223
405	Tonkawa, OK	74653
702	Tonopah, NV	89049
801	Tooele, UT	84074
901	Toone, TN	38381
219	Topeka, IN	46571
913	Topeka, KS	66600–66686
508	Topsfield, MA	01983
215	Topton, PA	19562
614	Toronto, OH	43964
213	Torrance, CA	90500–90510
412	Torrance, PA	15779
203	Torrington, CT	06790, 06791
307	Torrington, WY	82240
201	Totowa, NJ	07511, 07512
601	Tougaloo, MS	39174

Toulon / Walpole

Area	City	Zip
309	Toulon, IL	61483
217	Tovey, IL	62570
201	Towaco, NJ	07082
309	Towanda, IL	61776
717	Towanda, PA	18848
701	Towner, ND	58788
508	Townsend, MA	01469, 01474
406	Townsend, MT	59644
814	Townville, PA	16360
301	Towson, MD	21204
412	Trafford, PA	15085
215	Trainer, PA	19013
215	Trainer, PA	29690
803	Travelers Rest, SC	29690
616	Traverse City, MI	49684, 49685
904	Trenton, FL	32693
404	Trenton, GA	30752
618	Trenton, IL	62293
313	Trenton, MI	48183
816	Trenton, MO	64665, 64683
919	Trenton, NC	28585
308	Trenton, NE	69044
609	Trenton, NJ	08600–08691
513	Trenton, OH	45067
901	Trenton, TN	38382
215	Trevose, PA	19047
215	Trexlertown, PA	18087
304	Triadelphia, WV	26059
316	Tribune, KS	67879
719	Trinidad, CO	81074, 81082
404	Trion, GA	30753
503	Troutdale, OR	97060
704	Troutman, NC	28166
205	Troy, AL	36081, 36082
515	Troy, IA	52537
913	Troy, KS	66087
313	Troy, MI	48007, 48083, 48084, 48099
314	Troy, MO	63379
919	Troy, NC	27371
603	Troy, NH	03465
518	Troy, NY	12180–12183
513	Troy, OH	43443, 45373, 45374
513	Troy, OH	16947
717	Troy, PA	76579
817	Troy, TX	07054
201	Troy Hills, NJ	95734
916	Truckee, CA	18708
717	Trucksville, PA	56088
507	Truman, MN	72472
501	Trumann, AR	18970
215	Trumbauersville, PA	06611
203	Trumbull, CT	35173
205	Trussville, AL	87901
505	Truth or Consequences, NM	28782
704	Tryon, NC	69167
308	Tryon, NE	86556
602	Tsaile, AZ	97062
503	Tualatin, OR	10707, 11968
914	Tuckahoe, NY	23229
804	Tuckahoe, VA	30084, 30085
404	Tucker, GA	08087
609	Tuckerton, NJ	85700–85751, 85777
602	Tucson, AZ	88401, 88441
505	Tucumcari, NM	98108, 98188
206	Tukwila, WA	93274, 93275
209	Tulare, CA	79088
806	Tulia, TX	37388, 37389
615	Tullahoma, TN	13159
315	Tully, NY	19007
215	Tullytown, PA	74100–74171, 74182, 74186
918	Tulsa, OK	98501, 98502
206	Tumwater, WA	38676
601	Tunica, MS	18657
717	Tunkhannock, PA	38801–38803
601	Tupelo, MS	29162
803	Turbeville, SC	95380, 95381
209	Turlock, CA	04282, 04283
207	Turner, ME	01349, 01376
413	Turners Falls, MA	54004, 54889
715	Turtle Lake, WI	35401–35406, 35485–35487
205	Tuscaloosa, AL	61953
217	Tuscola, IL	35674
205	Tuscumbia, AL	65082
314	Tuscumbia, MO	36083
205	Tuskegee, AL	36088
205	Tuskegee Institute, AL	92680, 92681
714	Tustin, CA	38963
601	Tutwiler, MS	10987
914	Tuxedo Park, NY	55111
612	Twin Cities, MN	83301–83303, 83348
208	Twin Falls, ID	44087
216	Twinsburg, OH	55616
218	Two Harbors, MN	54241
414	Two Rivers, WI	79563
915	Tye, TX	75701–75713
903	Tyler, TX	39667
601	Tylertown, MS	78391
512	Tynan, TX	57066
605	Tyndall, SD	01879
508	Tyngsboro, MA	16686, 17040
814	Tyrone, PA	

U

Area	City	Zip
614	Uhrichsville, OH	44683
707	Ukiah, CA	95418, 95482
217	Ullin, IL	62992
803	Ulmer, SC	29849
316	Ulysses, KS	67880
904	Umatilla, FL	32784
607	Unadilla, NY	13849
203	Uncasville, CT	06382
815	Union, IL	60180, 62424–62635
616	Union, MI	49130
314	Union, MO	63084
601	Union, MS	38862, 39365, 39437

Area	City	Zip
603	Union, NH	03887
908	Union, NJ	07083
803	Union, SC	29379
206	Union, WA	98592
304	Union, WV	24983
201	Union Beach, NJ	07735
415	Union City, CA	94587
404	Union City, GA	30291
201	Union City, NJ	07087
814	Union City, PA	16438
901	Union City, TN	38261
414	Union Grove, WI	53182
313	Union Lake, MI	48085, 48386, 48387
404	Union Point, GA	30669–30671
205	Union Springs, AL	36089
315	Union Springs, NY	13160
516	Uniondale, NY	11553, 11555, 11556
412	Uniontown, PA	15401
203	Unionville, CT	06013, 06085–06087
816	Unionville, MO	63565
914	Unionville, NY	10988, 13676
207	Unity, ME	04988
818	Universal City, CA	91608
601	University, MS	38677
314	University City, MO	63124, 63130
216	University Heights, OH	44118
515	University Park, IA	52595
708	University Park, IL	60466
714	Upland, CA	91785, 91786
317	Upland, IN	46989
614	Upper Arlington, OH	43221
215	Upper Darby, PA	19082, 19083
301	Upper Marlboro, MD	20772–20775
215	Upper Merion, PA	19406
201	Upper Montclair, NJ	07043
215	Upper Moreland, PA	19090
201	Upper Saddle River, NJ	07458
419	Upper Sandusky, OH	43351
217	Urbana, IL	61801
219	Urbana, IN	46990
513	Urbana, OH	43078
804	Urbanna, VA	23175
217	Ursa, IL	62376
815	Utica, IL	61373
313	Utica, MI	48077–48087, 48310–48312 *
601	Utica, MS	39175
402	Utica, NE	68456
315	Utica, NY	13500–13505
614	Utica, OH	43080
605	Utica, SD	57067
512	Uvalde, TX	78801, 78802
508	Uxbridge, MA	01569

V

Area	City	Zip
707	Vacaville, CA	95687, 95688, 95696
303	Vail, CO	81657, 81658
704	Valdese, NC	28690
912	Valdosta, GA	31601–31604, 31698, 31699
503	Vale, OR	97918
805	Valencia, CA	91354, 91355, 91385
412	Valencia, PA	16059
402	Valentine, NE	69201, 69220
914	Valhalla, NY	10595
818	Valinda, CA	91744
707	Vallejo, CA	94589–94592
402	Valley, NE	68035, 68064, 68840
619	Valley Center, CA	92082
701	Valley City, ND	58072
216	Valley City, OH	44280
914	Valley Cottage, NY	10989
215	Valley Forge, PA	19481, 19482
314	Valley Park, MO	63088
516	Valley Stream, NY	11580–11582
216	Valley View, OH	43910, 44131
904	Valparaiso, FL	32580
219	Valparaiso, IN	46383, 46384
402	Valparaiso, NE	68065
214	Van, TX	75790
501	Van Buren, AR	72956
314	Van Buren, MO	63965
915	Van Horn, TX	79855
818	Van Nuys, CA	91316, 91401–91411, 91436
419	Van Wert, OH	45891
606	Vanceburg, KY	41179
206	Vancouver, WA	98660–98668, 98682–98686
618	Vandalia, IL	62471
513	Vandalia, OH	45377
412	Vandergrift, PA	15690
414	Vandyne, WI	54979
703	Vansant, VA	24656
206	Vashon, WA	98013, 98070
517	Vassar, MI	48768, 48769
908	Vauxhall, NJ	07088
806	Vega, TX	79092
809	Vega Baja, PR	00763, 00764
308	Venango, NE	69168
213	Venice, CA	90291–90296
813	Venice, FL	34284–34293
805	Ventura, CA	93001–93006, 93009
515	Ventura, IA	50482
509	Veradale, WA	99037
702	Verdi, NV	89439
802	Vergennes, VT	05491
216	Vermilion, OH	44089
605	Vermillion, SD	57069
309	Vermont, IL	61484
801	Vernal, UT	84008, 84078, 84079
205	Vernon, AL	35592
213	Vernon, CA	90058
203	Vernon, CT	06066
812	Vernon, IN	47108, 47242
517	Vernon, MI	48476
201	Vernon, NJ	07462

Area	City	Zip
315	Vernon, NY	13476
817	Vernon, TX	76384
407	Vero Beach, FL	32960–32968
601	Verona, MS	38879
201	Verona, NJ	07044
412	Verona, PA	15147
703	Verona, VA	24482
203	Versailles, CT	06383
812	Versailles, IN	47042
606	Versailles, KY	40383
314	Versailles, MO	65084
513	Versailles, OH	45380
607	Vestal, NY	13850, 13851
205	Vestavia Hills, AL	35216
812	Vevay, IN	47043
601	Vicksburg, MS	39180–39182
406	Victor, MT	59875
716	Victor, NY	14564
612	Victoria, MN	55386
512	Victoria, TX	77901–77905
619	Victorville, CA	92392–92394
912	Vidalia, GA	30474
318	Vidalia, LA	71373
912	Vienna, GA	31092
618	Vienna, IL	62995
216	Vienna, OH	44473
703	Vienna, VA	22027, 22180–22184
304	Vienna, WV	26105
708	Villa Park, IL	60181
215	Villanova, PA	19085
318	Ville Platte, LA	70586
712	Villisca, IA	50864
812	Vincennes, IN	47591
515	Vincent, IA	50594
609	Vineland, NJ	08360
918	Vinita, OK	74301
319	Vinton, IA	52349
217	Virden, IL	62690
606	Virgie, KY	41572
217	Virginia, IL	62691
218	Virginia, MN	55777, 55792
804	Virginia Beach, VA	23450–23464
406	Virginia City, MT	59755
702	Virginia City, NV	89440
815	Viroqua, WI	54665
608	Viroqua, WI	54665
209	Visalia, CA	93277–93279, 93291, 93292
619	Vista, CA	92083–92085
815	Volo, IL	60073
609	Voorhees, NJ	08043
518	Voorheesville, NY	12186

W

Area	City	Zip
219	Wabash, IN	46992, 47860
612	Wabasha, MN	55981
407	Wabasso, FL	32970
507	Wabasso, MN	56293
817	Waco, TX	76700–76716, 76797, 76798
612	Waconia, MN	55387
218	Wadena, MN	56482
919	Wadesboro, NC	28170
205	Wadley, AL	36276
216	Wadsworth, OH	44281
918	Wagoner, OK	74467, 74477
808	Wahiawa, HI	96786, 96854–96857
402	Wahoo, NE	68066
701	Wahpeton, ND	58039, 58075
808	Waianae, HI	96792
808	Wailea, HI	96746
808	Wailua, HI	96793
808	Wailuku, HI	96793
516	Wainscott, NY	11975
808	Waipahu, HI	96797
612	Waite Park, MN	56387
509	Waitsburg, WA	99361
802	Waitsfield, VT	05673
219	Wakarusa, IN	46573
919	Wake Forest, NC	27587
913	WaKeeney, KS	67672
617	Wakefield, MA	01880
402	Wakefield, NE	68784
401	Wakefield, RI	02879–02883
419	Walbridge, OH	43465
319	Walcott, IA	52773
303	Walden, CO	80430, 80480
914	Walden, NY	12586
614	Waldo, OH	43356
207	Waldoboro, ME	04572
301	Waldorf, MD	20601–20604
501	Waldron, AR	72924, 72958
201	Waldwick, NJ	07463
404	Waleska, GA	30183
803	Walhalla, SC	29691
218	Walker, MN	56484
301	Walkersville, MD	21793
919	Walkertown, NC	27051
908	Wall, NJ	07719
509	Walla Walla, WA	99362
208	Wallace, ID	83873, 83874
919	Wallace, NC	28466
814	Wallaceton, PA	16876
313	Walled Lake, MI	48088, 48390
203	Wallingford, CT	06492
215	Wallingford, PA	19086
201	Wallington, NJ	07057
409	Wallisville, TX	77597
914	Wallkill, NY	10919, 12589
914	Wallkill, NY	07881
201	Wallpack Center, NJ	07881
714	Walnut, CA	91788, 91789
415	Walnut Creek, CA	94595–94598
916	Walnut Grove, CA	95690
501	Walnut Ridge, AR	72476
215	Walnutport, PA	18088
508	Walpole, MA	02081
603	Walpole, NH	03604–03609

719	Walsenburg, CO	81066, 81089
303	Walsh, CO	81090
919	Walstonburg, NC	27888
803	Walterboro, SC	29488
405	Walters, OK	73572
601	Walthall, MS	39771
617	Waltham, MA	02154, 02254
219	Walton, IN	46994
607	Walton, NY	13856
414	Walworth, WI	53184
913	Wamego, KS	66547
315	Wampsville, NY	13163
419	Wapakoneta, OH	45895
509	Wapato, WA	98951
319	Wapello, IA	52653
914	Wappingers Falls, NY	12590
413	Ware, MA	01082
803	Ware Shoals, SC	29692
508	Wareham, MA	02571
203	Warehouse Point, CT	06088
503	Warm Springs, OR	97761
703	Warm Springs, VA	24484
215	Warminster, PA	18974
406	Warmsprings, MT	59756
918	Warner, OK	74469
912	Warner Robins, GA	31028, 31088, 31093–31099
501	Warren, AR	71671
413	Warren, MA	01083, 01092
207	Warren, ME	04864
313	Warren, MI	48089–48093
218	Warren, MN	56762
908	Warren, NJ	07059, 07060
216	Warren, OH	44481–44486
814	Warren, PA	16365, 16366
401	Warren, RI	02885
802	Warren, VT	05674
412	Warrendale, PA	15086, 15095, 15096
816	Warrensburg, MO	64093
216	Warrensville Heights, OH	44122, 44128
404	Warrenton, GA	30828
314	Warrenton, MO	63383
919	Warrenton, NC	27589
503	Warrenton, OR	97146
703	Warrenton, VA	22186
215	Warrington, PA	18976
218	Warroad, MN	56763
219	Warsaw, IN	46580
606	Warsaw, KY	41095
816	Warsaw, MO	65355
919	Warsaw, NC	28398
716	Warsaw, NY	14569
804	Warsaw, VA	22572
615	Wartburg, TN	37887
914	Warwick, NY	10990
401	Warwick, RI	02886–02889
503	Wasco, OR	97065
507	Waseca, MN	56093
701	Washburn, ND	58577
202	Washington, DC	20000–20380, 20402–20472 *
404	Washington, GA	30673
319	Washington, IA	52353
309	Washington, IL	61571
812	Washington, IN	46725, 47859
913	Washington, KS	66968
313	Washington, MI	48094
314	Washington, MO	63090
919	Washington, NC	27889
908	Washington, NJ	07675, 07882
405	Washington, OK	73093
412	Washington, PA	15301, 19512
703	Washington, VA	22747
304	Washington, WV	26181
614	Washington Court House, OH	43160
215	Washington Crossing, PA	18977
907	Wasilla, AK	99652, 99687, 99694
214	Waskom, TX	75692
908	Watchung, NJ	07060
601	Water Valley, MS	38965
203	Waterbury, CT	06702–06726, 06749
802	Waterbury, VT	05676
203	Waterford, CT	06385, 06386
313	Waterford, MI	48095, 48329
518	Waterford, NY	12188
814	Waterford, PA	16441
414	Waterford, WI	53185
319	Waterloo, IA	50700–50707
618	Waterloo, IL	62298
219	Waterloo, IN	46793, 47331
402	Waterloo, NE	68069
315	Waterloo, NY	13165
414	Waterloo, WI	53594
203	Watertown, CT	06779, 06795
617	Watertown, MA	02172, 02272–02277
315	Watertown, NY	13601–13603
605	Watertown, SD	57201, 57246
414	Watertown, WI	53094
913	Waterville, KS	66548
207	Waterville, ME	04901
315	Waterville, NY	13480
509	Waterville, WA	98858
603	Waterville Valley, NH	03215, 03223
616	Watervliet, MI	49098
518	Watervliet, NY	12189
701	Watford City, ND	58854
913	Wathena, KS	66090
612	Watkins, MN	55389
607	Watkins Glen, NY	14891
404	Watkinsville, GA	30677
405	Watonga, OK	73772
815	Watseka, IL	60970
717	Watsontown, PA	17777
408	Watsonville, CA	95076, 95077
813	Wauchula, FL	33873
708	Waukegan, IL	60079, 60085, 60087
414	Waukesha, WI	53146, 53186–53188
319	Waukon, IA	52172
308	Wauneta, NE	69045
715	Waupaca, WI	54981
414	Waupun, WI	53963
203	Wauregan, CT	06387
405	Waurika, OK	73573
715	Wausau, WI	54401, 54402
419	Wauseon, OH	43567
414	Wautoma, WI	54982
414	Wauwatosa, WI	53210, 53213, 53226
601	Waveland, MS	39576
813	Waverly, FL	33877
319	Waverly, IA	50677
402	Waverly, NE	68462
607	Waverly, NY	14892
614	Waverly, OH	45690
615	Waverly, TN	37185
804	Waverly, VA	23890
214	Waxahachie, TX	75165
912	Waycross, GA	31501, 31502
508	Wayland, MA	01778
816	Wayland, MO	63472
716	Wayland, NY	14572
717	Waymart, PA	18472
313	Wayne, MI	48184–48188
402	Wayne, NE	68787, 68860
201	Wayne, NJ	07470–07477
215	Wayne, PA	17032, 19087–19089
304	Wayne, WV	25570
404	Waynesboro, GA	30830
601	Waynesboro, MS	39367
717	Waynesboro, PA	17268
615	Waynesboro, TN	38485
703	Waynesboro, VA	22980
216	Waynesburg, OH	44688
412	Waynesburg, PA	15370
314	Waynesville, MO	65583
704	Waynesville, NC	28786
612	Wayzata, MN	55361, 55391, 55392
405	Weatherford, OK	73096
817	Weatherford, TX	76086, 76087
717	Weatherly, PA	18255
916	Weaverville, CA	96093
704	Weaverville, NC	28787
417	Webb City, MO	64870
508	Webster, MA	01570
716	Webster, NY	14580
605	Webster, SD	57274
713	Webster, TX	77598
515	Webster City, IA	50595
314	Webster Groves, MO	63119
304	Webster Springs, WV	26288
205	Wedowee, AL	36278
916	Weed, CA	96094
201	Weehawken, NJ	07087
409	Weimar, TX	78962
501	Weiner, AR	72479
304	Weirton, WV	26062
208	Weiser, ID	83672
304	Welch, WV	24801
503	Welches, OR	97067
919	Weldon, NC	27890
617	Wellesley, MA	02181
617	Wellesley Hills, MA	02181
803	Wellford, SC	29385
316	Wellington, KS	67152
216	Wellington, OH	44090
806	Wellington, TX	79095
207	Wells, ME	04090
507	Wells, MN	55021, 56097
717	Wellsboro, PA	16901
304	Wellsburg, WV	26070
614	Wellston, OH	45692
314	Wellsville, MO	63384
716	Wellsville, NY	14895
216	Wellsville, OH	43968
318	Welsh, LA	70591
509	Wenatchee, WA	98801–98807
801	Wendover, UT	84034, 84083
508	Wenham, MA	01984
919	Wentworth, NC	27375
215	Wernersville, PA	19565
215	Wescosville, PA	18106
512	Weslaco, TX	78596
813	Wesley Chapel, FL	33543, 34249
605	Wessington Springs, SD	57382
601	Wesson, MS	39191
513	West Alexandria, OH	45381
412	West Aliquippa, PA	15001
414	West Allis, WI	53214, 53227
617	West Andover, MA	01810
516	West Babylon, NY	11704, 11707
508	West Barnstable, MA	02668
515	West Bend, IA	50597
414	West Bend, WI	53095
313	West Bloomfield, MI	48033, 48322
508	West Boylston, MA	01583
517	West Branch, MI	48661
516	West Brentwood, NY	11717
508	West Bridgewater, MA	02379
412	West Bridgewater, PA	15009
508	West Brookfield, MA	01585
319	West Burlington, IA	52655
201	West Caldwell, NJ	07006, 07007
513	West Carrollton, OH	45439, 45449
508	West Chelmsford, MA	01863
513	West Chester, OH	44699, 45069
215	West Chester, PA	19380–19383
708	West Chicago, IL	60185
803	West Columbia, SC	29033, 29169, 29171
508	West Concord, MA	01742
507	West Concord, MN	55985
215	West Conshohocken, PA	19428
203	West Cornwall, CT	06796
818	West Covina, CA	91790–91793
515	West Des Moines, IA	50265
412	West Elizabeth, PA	15088
701	West Fargo, ND	58078
215	West Grove, PA	19390
617	West Hanover, MA	02339
203	West Hartford, CT	06107–06119
203	West Haven, CT	06516
914	West Haverstraw, NY	10993
717	West Hazleton, PA	18201
501	West Helena, AR	72390
516	West Hempstead, NY	11552
213	West Hollywood, CA	90048, 90069
305	West Hollywood, FL	33023, 33083
412	West Homestead, PA	15120
914	West Hurley, NY	12491
516	West Islip, NY	11795
919	West Jefferson, NC	28694
801	West Jordan, UT	84084, 84088
401	West Kingston, RI	02892
317	West Lafayette, IN	47906, 47907
614	West Lafayette, OH	43845
603	West Lebanon, NH	03784
319	West Liberty, IA	52776
606	West Liberty, KY	41472
304	West Liberty, WV	26074
908	West Long Branch, NJ	07764
213	West Los Angeles, CA	90025
617	West Lynn, MA	01905
617	West Mansfield, MA	02048
513	West Mansfield, OH	43358
501	West Memphis, AR	72301
412	West Middlesex, PA	16159
412	West Mifflin, PA	15122, 15123
201	West Milford, NJ	07480
318	West Monroe, LA	71291–71294
201	West New York, NJ	07093
617	West Newton, MA	02165
914	West Nyack, NY	10994
201	West Orange, NJ	07052
407	West Palm Beach, FL	33401–33420
201	West Paterson, NJ	07424
412	West Pittsburg, PA	16160
717	West Pittston, PA	18643
417	West Plains, MO	65775, 65776
404	West Point, GA	31833
601	West Point, MS	39773
402	West Point, NE	68788
914	West Point, NY	10996, 10997
215	West Point, PA	19486
804	West Point, VA	23037, 23181
606	West Prestonsburg, KY	41668
215	West Reading, PA	19602, 19611
617	West Roxbury, MA	02132
916	West Sacramento, CA	95605, 95691
618	West Salem, IL	62476
216	West Salem, OH	44287
518	West Sand Lake, NY	12196
516	West Sayville, NY	11796
716	West Seneca, NY	14200, 14219–14224
413	West Springfield, MA	01089, 01090
703	West Springfield, VA	22152, 22153
603	West Swanzey, NH	03469
609	West Trenton, NJ	08628
319	West Union, IA	52175
217	West Union, IL	62477
513	West Union, OH	45693
803	West Union, SC	29696
304	West Union, WV	26456
419	West Unity, OH	43570, 45693
716	West Valley, NY	14171
801	West Valley, UT	84119, 84120
413	West Warren, MA	01092
401	West Warwick, RI	02893
406	West Yellowstone, MT	59758
508	Westboro, MA	01581
508	Westborough, MA	01580–01582
203	Westbrook, CT	06498
207	Westbrook, ME	04092
507	Westbrook, MN	56183
516	Westbury, NY	11568, 11590
608	Westby, WI	54667
305	Westchester, FL	33165
708	Westchester, IL	60154
719	Westcliffe, CO	81252
518	Westerlo, NY	12055, 12193
401	Westerly, RI	02891, 06379
901	Western Institute, TN	38074
708	Western Springs, IL	60558
614	Westerville, OH	43081
413	Westfield, MA	01085, 01086
908	Westfield, NJ	07090–07092
716	Westfield, NY	14787
216	Westfield Center, OH	44251
508	Westford, MA	01886
516	Westhampton, NY	11977
516	Westhampton Beach, NY	11978
318	Westlake, LA	70669
216	Westlake, OH	44145
818	Westlake Village, CA	91359, 91361, 91362
313	Westland, MI	48185
714	Westminster, CA	92683, 92684
303	Westminster, CO	80003, 80234
508	Westminster, MA	01473
301	Westminster, MD	21157
803	Westminster, SC	29693
213	Westmont, CA	90047
708	Westmont, IL	60559
609	Westmont, NJ	08108
913	Westmoreland, KS	66426, 66549
203	Weston, CT	06883
617	Weston, MA	02193
816	Weston, MO	64098
304	Weston, WV	26452
203	Westport, CT	06880–06883
508	Westport, MA	02790
219	Westville, IN	46391
609	Westville, NJ	08093
504	Westwego, LA	70094

Westwood / Yuma

Area	City	ZIP
213	Westwood, CA	96137
913	Westwood, KS	66205
617	Westwood, MA	02090
201	Westwood, NJ	07675
203	Wethersfield, CT	06109
205	Wetumpka, AL	36092
405	Wewoka, OK	74884
412	Wexford, PA	15090
703	Weyers Cave, VA	24486
617	Weymouth, MA	02188–02191
201	Wharton, NJ	07885
409	Wharton, TX	77488
303	Wheat Ridge, CO	80033
319	Wheatland, IA	52777
412	Wheatland, PA	16161
307	Wheatland, WY	82201
516	Wheatley Heights, NY	11798
708	Wheaton, IL	60187–60189
301	Wheaton, MD	20902
612	Wheaton, MN	56296
806	Wheeler, TX	79096
708	Wheeling, IL	60089, 60090
304	Wheeling, WV	26003
201	Whippany, NJ	07981
612	White Bear Lake, MN	55110, 55127
504	White Castle, LA	70788
503	White City, OR	97503
616	White Cloud, MI	49349
717	White Haven, PA	18661
301	White Marsh, MD	21162
616	White Pigeon, MI	49099
914	White Plains, NY	10600–10607, 10625, 10650
605	White River, SD	57579
802	White River Junction, VT	05001
406	White Sulphur Springs, MT	59645
304	White Sulphur Springs, WV	24961, 24986
603	Whitefield, NH	03598
406	Whitefish, MT	59937
414	Whitefish Bay, WI	53211, 53217
215	Whitehall, PA	15227, 18052
715	Whitehall, WI	54773
908	Whitehouse, NJ	08888
419	Whitehouse, OH	43571
908	Whitehouse Station, NJ	08889
315	Whitesboro, NY	13492
606	Whitesburg, KY	41858
718	Whitestone, NY	11357
919	Whiteville, NC	28472
414	Whitewater, WI	53190
605	Whitewood, SD	57793
601	Whitfield, MS	39193, 39464
219	Whiting, IN	46394
908	Whiting, NJ	08759
508	Whitinsville, MA	01588
606	Whitley City, KY	42653
617	Whitman, MA	02382
313	Whitmore Lake, MI	48189
607	Whitney Point, NY	13862
512	Whitsett, TX	78075
515	Whittemore, IA	50598
213	Whittier, CA	90601–90610
406	Wibaux, MT	59353
316	Wichita, KS	67055, 67202–67226, 67278 *
817	Wichita Falls, TX	76301–76311
602	Wickenburg, AZ	85358, 85390
502	Wickliffe, KY	42087
216	Wickliffe, OH	44092, 44515
717	Wiconisco, PA	17097
601	Wiggins, MS	39577
402	Wilber, NE	68465
513	Wilberforce, OH	45384
413	Wilbraham, MA	01095
918	Wilburton, OK	74578
814	Wilcox, PA	15870
606	Wilder, KY	41071
802	Wilder, VT	05088
609	Wildwood, NJ	08260
609	Wildwood Crest, NJ	08260
717	Wilkes-Barre, PA	18602, 18700–18774
919	Wilkesboro, NC	28697
607	Willard, NY	14588
419	Willard, OH	44890
602	Willcox, AZ	85643, 85644
503	Williams, OR	97544
319	Williamsburg, IA	52361
606	Williamsburg, KY	40769
513	Williamsburg, OH	45176
814	Williamsburg, PA	16693
804	Williamsburg, VA	23081, 23185, 23187, 23188
309	Williamsfield, IL	61489
315	Williamson, NY	14589
304	Williamson, WV	25661
317	Williamsport, IN	47993
301	Williamsport, MD	21795
717	Williamsport, PA	17701–17705
517	Williamston, MI	48895
919	Williamston, NC	27892
606	Williamstown, KY	41097
413	Williamstown, MA	01267
609	Williamstown, NJ	08094
315	Williamstown, NY	13493
717	Williamstown, PA	17098
304	Williamstown, WV	26187
217	Williamsville, IL	62693
716	Williamsville, NY	14200, 14221, 14231
203	Willimantic, CT	06226
609	Willingboro, NJ	08046
701	Williston, ND	58801, 58802
802	Williston, VT	05495
516	Williston Park, NY	11596
707	Willits, CA	95429, 95490
612	Willmar, MN	56201
216	Willoughby, OH	44094, 44095
213	Willow Brook, CA	90222
215	Willow Grove, PA	19090
618	Willow Hill, IL	62480
417	Willow Springs, MO	65793
708	Willowbrook, IL	60514, 60521
916	Willows, CA	95988
214	Wills Point, TX	75169
518	Willsboro, NY	12996
214	Wilmer, TX	75172
412	Wilmerding, PA	15148
708	Wilmette, IL	60091
213	Wilmington, CA	90744, 90748
302	Wilmington, DE	19801–19810, 19890–19899 *
508	Wilmington, MA	01887
919	Wilmington, NC	28401–28412
513	Wilmington, OH	45177
606	Wilmore, KY	40390
501	Wilson, AR	72395, 72823
919	Wilson, NC	27893–27895
503	Wilsonville, OR	97070
203	Wilton, CT	06897
319	Wilton, IA	52778
207	Wilton, ME	04294
603	Wilton, NH	03086
512	Wimberley, TX	78676
219	Winamac, IN	46996
217	Winchester, IL	62694
317	Winchester, IN	47394
606	Winchester, KY	40391, 40470
617	Winchester, MA	01890
603	Winchester, NH	03470
615	Winchester, TN	37398
703	Winchester, VA	22601, 22638
215	Wind Gap, PA	18091
814	Windber, PA	15963
404	Winder, GA	30680
317	Windfall, IN	46076
804	Windmill Point, VA	22578
507	Windom, MN	56101, 56165
602	Window Rock, AZ	86515
203	Windsor, CT	06006, 06095
919	Windsor, NC	27983
607	Windsor, NY	13865
216	Windsor, OH	43787, 44903
802	Windsor, VT	05089
608	Windsor, WI	53598
304	Windsor Heights, WV	26075
203	Windsor Locks, CT	06096
817	Windthorst, TX	76389
205	Winfield, AL	35594
708	Winfield, IL	60190
316	Winfield, KS	67156
717	Winfield, PA	17889
304	Winfield, WV	25213, 26554
704	Wingate, NC	28174
814	Wingate, PA	16880
914	Wingdale, NY	12594
206	Winlock, WA	98596
207	Winn, ME	04495
517	Winn, MI	48896
702	Winnemucca, NV	89445
605	Winner, SD	57580
708	Winnetka, IL	60093
406	Winnett, MT	59017, 59087
318	Winnfield, LA	71483
409	Winnie, TX	77665
603	Winnisquam, NH	03289
318	Winnsboro, LA	71295
803	Winnsboro, SC	29180
903	Winnsboro, TX	75494
507	Winona, MN	55942, 55987, 55988
601	Winona, MS	38967
219	Winona Lake, IN	46590
802	Winooski, VT	05404
207	Winslow, ME	04901
609	Winslow, NJ	08095
203	Winsted, CT	06094, 06098
612	Winsted, MN	55395
919	Winston-Salem, NC	27100–27127
407	Winter Garden, FL	32787, 34787
813	Winter Haven, FL	33880–33884
303	Winter Park, CO	80482
407	Winter Park, FL	32789, 32793
804	Wintergreen, VA	22958
915	Winters, TX	79567
515	Winterset, IA	50273
614	Wintersville, OH	43952
919	Winterville, NC	28590
319	Winthrop, IA	50682
617	Winthrop, MA	02152
207	Winthrop, ME	04364
919	Winton, NC	27986
207	Wiscasset, ME	04578
608	Wisconsin Dells, WI	53965
715	Wisconsin Rapids, WI	54494, 54495
703	Wise, VA	24293
804	Withams, VA	23488
313	Wixom, MI	48096, 48393
617	Woburn, MA	01801, 01888
315	Wolcott, NY	14590
406	Wolf Point, MT	59201
903	Wolfe City, TX	75496
215	Womelsdorf, PA	19567
708	Wood Dale, IL	60191
618	Wood River, IL	62095
308	Wood River, NE	68860, 68883
401	Wood River Junction, RI	02894
912	Woodbine, GA	31569
203	Woodbridge, CT	06525
908	Woodbridge, NJ	07095
703	Woodbridge, VA	22191–22194
219	Woodburn, IN	46797
503	Woodburn, OR	97071
612	Woodbury, MN	55125
609	Woodbury, NJ	08096, 08097
516	Woodbury, NY	10930, 11797
615	Woodbury, TN	37190
201	Woodcliff Lake, NJ	07675
309	Woodhull, IL	61490
206	Woodinville, WA	98072
916	Woodland, CA	95695
207	Woodland, ME	04694, 04736
814	Woodland, PA	16881, 17084
206	Woodland, WA	98674
818	Woodland Hills, CA	91302, 91364–91372, 91399
719	Woodland Park, CO	80863, 80866
516	Woodmere, NY	11598
708	Woodridge, IL	60517
914	Woodridge, NY	12789
803	Woodruff, SC	29388
801	Woods Cross, UT	84087
508	Woods Hole, MA	02543
614	Woodsfield, OH	43793
415	Woodside, CA	94062
718	Woodside, NY	11377
217	Woodson, IL	62695
203	Woodstock, CT	06281
404	Woodstock, GA	30188
815	Woodstock, IL	60098
914	Woodstock, NY	12498
703	Woodstock, VA	22664
802	Woodstock, VT	05091
609	Woodstown, NJ	08098
603	Woodsville, NH	03785
601	Woodville, MS	39669
419	Woodville, OH	43469
401	Woodville, RI	02832, 02911
409	Woodville, TX	75979
515	Woodward, IA	50276
405	Woodward, OK	73801–73803
717	Woolrich, PA	17779
515	Woolstock, IA	50599
401	Woonsocket, RI	02895
605	Woonsocket, SD	57358, 57385
216	Wooster, OH	44691
508	Worcester, MA	01600–01615, 01655
215	Worcester, PA	19490
307	Worland, WY	82401, 82430
708	Worth, IL	60482, 61548
507	Worthington, MN	56187
614	Worthington, OH	43085
412	Worthington, PA	16262
303	Wray, CO	80739, 80758
508	Wrentham, MA	02093
316	Wright, KS	67882
912	Wrightsville, GA	31096
717	Wrightsville, PA	17368
717	Wyalusing, PA	18853
516	Wyandanch, NY	11798
313	Wyandotte, MI	48192–48195
201	Wyckoff, NJ	07481
304	Wyco, WV	25943
301	Wye Mills, MD	21679
215	Wyncote, PA	19095
215	Wyndmoor, PA	19118
501	Wynne, AR	72396, 72397
215	Wynnewood, PA	19096
616	Wyoming, MI	49508, 49509, 49548
716	Wyoming, NY	14591
717	Wyoming, PA	18644
215	Wyomissing, PA	19610
703	Wytheville, VA	24382

X

Area	City	ZIP
513	Xenia, OH	45385

Y

Area	City	ZIP
809	Yabucoa, PR	00767
919	Yadkinville, NC	27055
509	Yakima, WA	98901–98909
919	Yanceyville, NC	27379
605	Yankton, SD	57078
203	Yantic, CT	06389
516	Yaphank, NY	11980
215	Yardley, PA	19067
609	Yardville, NJ	08620
207	Yarmouth, ME	04096
508	Yarmouth Port, MA	02675
316	Yates Center, KS	66783
601	Yazoo City, MS	39194
513	Yellow Springs, OH	45387
501	Yellville, AR	72687
803	Yemassee, SC	29945
702	Yerington, NV	89447
512	Yoakum, TX	77995
914	Yonkers, NY	10700–10710
714	Yorba Linda, CA	92686, 92687
402	York, NE	68467
717	York, PA	17315, 17400–17407
803	York, SC	29745
207	York Harbor, ME	03911
302	Yorklyn, DE	19736
804	Yorktown, VA	23690–23692
914	Yorktown Heights, NY	10598
708	Yorkville, IL	60560
315	Yorkville, NY	10128, 13495
209	Yosemite, CA	95389
404	Young Harris, GA	30582
216	Youngstown, OH	44500–44515, 44555
412	Youngwood, PA	15697
707	Yountville, CA	94599
313	Ypsilanti, MI	48197, 48198
916	Yreka, CA	96097
916	Yuba City, CA	95991–95993
714	Yucaipa, CA	92399
619	Yucca Valley, CA	92284–92286
405	Yukon, OK	73085, 73099
602	Yuma, AZ	85364–85369
303	Yuma, CO	80759

	Z	
614	Zanesville, OH	43701, 43702
512	Zapata, TX	78076
404	Zebulon, GA	30295
919	Zebulon, NC	27597
616	Zeeland, MI	49464
412	Zelienople, PA	16063
407	Zellwood, FL	32798
702	Zephyr Cove, NV	89449
813	Zephyrhills, FL	33539–33544
708	Zion, IL	60099

INDEX